ProQuest Statistical Abstract of the United States 2013

ProQuest Statistical Abstract of United States Staff Listing:

Advisory Board for ProQuest Statistical Abstract:

Acknowledgements:

All of the people listed above contributed immensely to the quality and success of the work that follows. ProQuest would especially like to thank former Chief of the Census Bureau Statistical Compendia Branch Lars Johanson, who both advised ProQuest staff in understanding how the book was put together and actually updated some of the most difficult tables in the collection.

Another important contributor, not listed above, who was essential to the success of the project was John Hoffman of SDL (www.sdl.com). His role in advising and guiding us on the data conversion and print composition was invaluable.

Finally, the ProQuest staff would like to dedicate this book to the Census Bureau branch chiefs, statisticians, editors and others who conceived and created such a tremendously valuable resource and who made it look so easy.

ProQuest Statistical Abstract of the United States 2013

Issued December 2012

ProQuest®

Start here.

Published in the United States of America by ◀ **Bernan**, a wholly owned subsidiary of **The Rowman & Littlefield** Publishing Group
4501 Forbes Boulevard, Suite 200 Lanham, Maryland 20706

Bernan Press
800-865-3457
www.bernan.com

ISBN 13: 978-1-59888-591-0

Suggested Citation:
ProQuest LLC. *ProQuest Statistical Abstract of the United States, 2013*. (1st ed.) Bethesda, MD, 2012

Preface

The *Statistical Abstract of the United States,* published since 1878, is the best-known statistical reference publication in the country. As a comprehensive collection of statistics on the social, political, and economic conditions of the United States, it is a snapshot of America and its people. In the spring of 2011, the Census Bureau announced that the edition published that year would be the last one produced at government expense. ProQuest has now taken on responsibility for updating and releasing this publication, the most used statistical reference tool in U.S. libraries.

The editors at ProQuest have endeavored to continue the tradition established by the Census Bureau Statistical Compendia Branch. Like its predecessors, the *ProQuest Statistical Abstract of the United States* is designed to serve as a convenient volume for statistical reference and as a guide to other statistical publications and sources. The latter function is served by the introductory text to each section, the source note appearing below each table, and Appendix I, which is comprised of the *Guide to Sources of Statistics,* the *Guide to State Statistical Abstracts,* and the *Guide to Foreign Statistical Abstracts.*

This volume includes a selection of data from many statistical sources, both government and private. Publications cited as sources usually contain additional statistical detail and more comprehensive discussions of definitions and concepts. Data not available in publications issued by the contributing agency, but obtained from the Internet or unpublished records are identified in the source notes. More information on the subjects covered in the tables may generally be obtained from the source.

Except as indicated, figures are for the United States as presently constituted. Although emphasis in the *ProQuest Statistical Abstract* is primarily given to national data, many tables present data for regions and individual states and a smaller number for metropolitan areas and cities. "Appendix II, Metropolitan and Micropolitan Statistical Areas: Concepts, Components, and Population," presents explanatory text, a complete current listing, and population data for metropolitan and micropolitan areas defined as of November 2009. Statistics for the Commonwealth of Puerto Rico and for island areas of the United States are included in many state tables and are supplemented by information in Section 29.

Statistics in this edition are generally for the most recent year or period available, as of early August 2012. Each year over 1,400 tables are reviewed and evaluated, new tables of current interest are added, continuing series are updated, and less timely data are condensed or eliminated. Text notes and appendices are revised as appropriate.

Changes in this edition—This year ProQuest has introduced 39 new tables covering a wide range of subject areas and replacing content lost due to licensing issues not previously faced by the Census Bureau. We are presenting new material on a wide variety of topics, including same-sex couple households, student loan debt, mortgage loan applications and denials, negative equity mortgages, electronic device ownership, childhood obesity, and employment in the "green" sector. For a complete list of new tables, see "New Tables," p. xii.

ProQuest Statistical Abstract is also available in an online edition. This dynamic edition features table-specific capabilities for narrowing results by source, data date, subject, and type of data breakdown. Additionally, the online edition will be updated with new statistical content on a monthly basis, enabling users to regularly access new and revised data. The online product will function as a repository for additional back year's data that cannot fit into the print publication. Users will find spreadsheets that correspond to each table in the book. In many cases, these spreadsheets present expanded coverage of the data shown in print. It is available as a stand-alone or fully integrated part of *ProQuest Statistical Insight.*

Limitations of the data—The contents of this volume were taken from many sources. All data from censuses, surveys, and administrative records are subject to error arising from a number of factors including the following: sampling variability (for statistics based on samples), reporting errors in the data for individual units, incomplete coverage, nonresponse, and imputation and processing errors. (See also Appendix III). ProQuest cannot accept responsibility for the accuracy or limitations of the data presented here. However, selection of the material and its proper presentation is the responsibility of ProQuest.

For additional information on data presented—Please consult the source publications available in local libraries and on the Internet, or contact the agency indicated in the source notes.

Suggestions and comments—ProQuest welcomes feedback on the *Statistical Abstract,* so we can continue to provide our users with content deemed timely and important and presented in the most useful manner. Users are encouraged to make their data needs known for consideration in planning future editions. Suggestions and comments for improving coverage and presentation of data should be made via email to the Statistical Abstract team at **statab@proquest.com.**

Contents

[Numbers following subject are page numbers]

A Brief History of the Statistical Abstract

Although many users of the *Statistical Abstract of the United States* automatically associate that publication with the U.S. Census Bureau, its history predates even the existence of the Census Bureau as a permanent government agency. The Bureau of Statistics in the Treasury Department issued the first edition in 1879 and continued to do so until 1902. Beginning in 1903 the *Abstract* was published by various bureaus within the Department of Commerce and its predecessor. In 1938 the Census Bureau took over responsibility for the *Abstract*. It remained there until 2011 when the 131st edition was released. At that time Census Bureau management decided to terminate the Statistical Compendia program in order to use funds from that program for programs it considered a higher priority.

The decision was a controversial one. The petitions and letters of protest from librarians and other data users did not succeed in reversing that decision but did demonstrate that the research community still regards the *Statistical Abstract* as an essential 21st century research tool.

The early editions of the *Statistical Abstract* strongly reflected the interest and responsibilities of the Treasury Department. The dominant subjects were thus imports and exports, public finance, shipping, and banking. The data on population occupied little more than one page. However, within 20 years, the population data expanded to 24 pages of coverage. It is also interesting that two pages of various data for "principal countries of the world" appeared for the first time in the 1902 Abstract. During subsequent decades various new topics started to appear as various government agencies published new data series.

For example, in the 1930s and 1940s the Bureau of Economic Analysis introduced a set of national economic accounts and annual estimates of gross national product. In the 1940s, the Current Population Survey began collecting a variety of labor force, income, and other social and demographic statistics. The introduction of various government programs such as Social Security in the 1930s and Medicare in the 1960s also led to the availability of more statistical data. As each of these new data series became available, they were included in the *Statistical Abstract*.

As Federal statistical programs increased in number and scope, the coverage of the *Statistical Abstract* expanded along with them. In the 1950s, a typical volume contained 1,200 tables selected from roughly 140 sources and arranged in 34 sections. Since the 1990s a typical volume has contained 1,350-1,400 tables from more than 250 sources and arranged in 30 sections.

However, the value of the *Statistical Abstract* was not solely dependent on its statistical tables. The subject index, bibliography (Guide to Sources of Statistics), and the source citations below each table served as reference aids for those who needed more data. Among those who needed more were librarians, who were identified as the largest bloc of users in the very first user survey in 1943.

This focus on the needs of *Abstract* users was always the primary determinant in the selection of data and complemented an effort to portray in numbers the state of the nation. In the latter half of the 20th century it led to the introduction of more new subjects such as drug usage, day care arrangements, and various poverty measures. By the end of the century new means of data dissemination, compact disks and the Internet, provided further opportunities to release the *Statistical Abstract* in faster and more user-friendly ways.

Two examples will provide some insight into how the *Abstract* has been useful. Many users start looking for data by using popular ambiguous terms such as "binge drinking" or "dropouts." In those instances an *Abstract* table will help sharpen a user's thinking by providing a definition for such a term and leading the user to meaningful statistics. Also the *Abstract* has been useful just for idle browsing. For example, a user inquired about how much popcorn is eaten in movie theaters. Although no such data existed, the user was happy to start exploring about movie attendance, number of teenagers, and total popcorn production.

Such curiosity about the social and economic conditions of the United States has led many people the world over to the *Statistical Abstract* and will continue to guide the further development of this unique statistical resource.

--Lars Johanson

ProQuest consulting editor

Census Bureau statistician, 1975 to 2009

New and Deleted Tables in 2013 Edition

New Tables, 2013

Tables Deleted From the 2012 Edition of the Statistical Abstract

[Many tables have been replaced with tables illustrating similar content. Where applicable, please see reference to new table number]

2012 Number	Section/Table Title	Replaced By...
	Section 2: Births, Deaths, Marriages, and Divorces	
Table 127..........	Suicide Deaths And Death Rates By Age And Method: 2007 *	Table 133
	Section 3: Health and Nutrition	
Table 201..........	Injuries Associated With Selected Consumer Products: 2009*	Table 219
Table 202..........	Costs Of Unintentional Injuries: 2009*	
	Section 4: Education	
Table 262..........	Public Elementary And Secondary Estimated Finances: 1980 To 2009, And By State, 2009*	Table 275
	Section 8: State and Local Government Finances and Employment	
Table 445..........	Bond Ratings for State Government by State: 2010	
Table 446..........	Bond Ratings for City Governments by Largest Cities: 2010	
	Section 12: Labor Force, Employment, and Earnings	
Table 657..........	Workers Killed Or Disabled On The Job: 1970 To 2009*	Table 673
Table 658..........	Worker Deaths, Injuries, And Production Time Lost: 2000 To 2009*	Table 674
	Section 14: Prices	
Table 738..........	Producer Price Indexes For The Net Output Of Selected Industries: 2005 To 2010	
	Section 16: Science and Technology	
Table 818..........	Employment And Earnings In Science And Engineering (S & E) Occupations By Industry: 2006	Table 832
	Section 20: Construction and Housing	
Table 962..........	Construction Materials--Producer Price Indexes: 1990 To 2010	
	Section 21: Manufactures	
Table 1025.......	Cotton, Wool, and Man-Made Fibers--Consumption by End Use: 2005 to 2009*	
Table 1029.......	Iron and Steel Industry--Summary: 1990 to 2010*	
Table 1033.......	U.S. Consumer Electronics Sales and Forecasts by Product Category, 2007 to 2010, and Projection, 2011*	
	Section 22: Wholesale and Retail Trade	
Table 1059.......	Retail Trade And Food Services-Sales By Type Of Store And State: 2009*	
Table 1061........	Shopping Centers--Number And Gross Leasable Area: 1990 To 2010*	
	Section 23: Transportation	
Table 1077.......	Worldwide Airline Fatalities: 1990 To 2008	Table 1089
Table 1103........	Motor Vehicle Accidents--Number And Deaths: 1990 To 2009*	Table 1119
Table 1114........	Licensed Drivers And Number In Accidents By Age: 2009*	Table 1120
	Section 25: Banking, Finance, and Insurance	
Table 1197........	Money Market Interest Rates And Mortgage Rates: 1990 To 2010*	
	Section 28: Foreign Commerce and Aid	
Table 1304........	Export And Import Unit Value Indexes--Selected Countries: 2006 To 2010*	Table 1327
	Section 30: International Statistics	
Table 1341.......	People Infected With HIV And AIDS-Related Deaths By Region: 2001 And 2008	
Table 1356.......	Annual Percent Changes In Consumer Prices By Country: 2000 To 2010*	Table 1379
Table 1375.......	Fisheries--Commercial Catch By Country: 1990 To 2008	
Table 1391.......	Key Global Telecom Indicators For The World Telecommunication Service Sector: 2005 To 2010*	Table 1407
Table 1399.......	Reserve Assets And International Transaction Balances By Country: 2000 To 2010*	Table 1419
Table 1400........	International Tourism Arrivals, Expenditures, and Receipts--Leading Countries: 2000-2009*	Table 1418

* Unable to reach agreement with source in order to continue covering content.

Guide to Tabular Presentation

Example of Table Structure

Table 1269. Top 20 U.S. Gateways for Nonstop International Air Travel: 2009 and 2010

[151,324 represents 151,324,000. International passengers are residents of any country traveling nonstop to and from the United States on U.S. and foreign carriers. The data cover all passengers arriving and departing from U.S. airports on nonstop commercial international flights with 60 seats or more]

Gateway airport	2009 [1]	2010	Percent change 2009– 2010	Gateway airport	2009 [1]	2010	Percent change 2009– 2010
Total.................................	**151,324**	**160,018**	5.7	Washington (Dulles), DC........	5,986	6,170	3.1
Total, top 20.....................	**136,317**	**144,724**	6.2	Dallas-Ft. Worth, TX............	4,667	5,050	8.2
Top 20, percentage of total...	**90.1**	**90.4**	0.4	Philadelphia, PA..................	3,738	3,799	1.6
				Boston, MA........................	3,472	3,647	5.0
New York (JFK), NY...............	21,487	22,783	6.0	Honolulu, HI.......................	3,276	3,609	10.2
Miami, FL............................	15,836	16,734	5.7	Fort Lauderdale, FL..............	2,932	3,328	13.5
Los Angeles, CA...................	14,833	15,518	4.6	Orlando, FL........................	2,815	3,078	9.3
Newark, NJ..........................	10,676	11,376	6.6	Detroit, MI..........................	2,738	2,884	5.3
Chicago (O'Hare), IL..............	10,184	10,444	2.5	Guam Island, GU.................	2,333	2,732	17.1
Atlanta, GA.........................	8,764	9,124	4.1	Charlotte, NC......................	2,344	2,690	14.8
San Francisco, CA.................	7,889	8,479	7.5	Seattle-Tacoma, WA.............	2,528	2,672	5.7
Houston (G. Bush), TX...........	7,605	8,323	9.4	Minneapolis-St. Paul, MN......	2,213	2,283	3.1

[1] Data have been revised.

Source: U.S. Department of Transportation, Research and Innovative Technology Administration, Bureau of Transportation Statistics, Office of Airline Information, T-100 International Segment data, September 2011 <http://www.transtats.bts.gov/>.

Headnotes immediately below table titles provide information important for correct interpretation or evaluation of the table as a whole or for a major segment of it.

Footnotes below the bottom rule of tables give information relating to specific items or figures within the table.

Unit indicators show the *specified quantities* in which data items are presented. They are used for two primary reasons. Sometimes data are not available in absolute form and are estimates (as in the case of many surveys). In other cases we round the numbers in order to save space to show more data, as in the case above.

When a table presents data with more than one unit indicator, they are found in the headnotes and column headings (Tables 2 and 26), spanner (Table 37), stub (Table 21), or unit column (Table 162). When the data in a table are shown in the same unit indicator, it is shown as the first part of the headnote (Table 2). If no unit indicator is shown, data presented are in absolute form (Table 1).

Vertical rules are used to separate independent sections of a table (Table 1), or in tables where the stub is continued into one or more additional columns (Table 2).

Averages—An average is a single number or value that is often used to represent the "typical value" of a group of numbers. It is regarded as a measure of "location" or "central tendency" of a number.

The *arithmetic mean* is the type of average used most frequently. It is derived by summing the individual item values of a particular group and dividing the total by the number of items. The arithmetic mean is often referred to as simply the "mean" or "average."

The *median* of a group of numbers is the middle number or value when each item in the group is arranged according to size (lowest to highest or vice versa); it generally has the same number of items above it as well as below it. If there is an even number of items in the group, the median is taken to be the average of the two middle numbers.

Per capita (or per person) quantities—a per capita figure represents an average computed for every person in a specified group (or population). It is derived by taking the total for an item (such as income, taxes, or retail sales) and dividing it by the number of persons in the specified population.

Index numbers—An index number is the measure of difference or change, usually expressed as a percent, relating one quantity (the variable) of a specified kind to another quantity of the same kind. Index numbers are widely used to express changes in prices over periods of time, but may also be used to express differences between related subjects for a single point in time.

To compute a price index, a base year or period is selected. The base year price (of the commodity or service) is then designated as the base or reference price to which the prices for other years or periods are related. Many price indexes use the year 1982 as the base year; in tables this is shown as "1982 = 100." A method expressing the price relationship is: The price of a set of one or more items for a related year (e.g. 1990) divided by the price of the same set of items for the base year (e.g. 1982). The result multiplied by 100 provides the index number. When 100 is subtracted from the index number, the result equals the percent change in price from the base year.

Average annual percent change—Unless otherwise stated in the *Abstract* (as in Section 1, Population), average annual percent change is computed by use of a *compound interest formula*. This formula assumes that the rate of change is constant throughout a specified compounding period (1 year for average annual rates of change). The formula is similar to that used to compute the balance of a savings account that receives compound interest. According to this formula, at the end of a compounding period the amount of accrued change (e.g., school enrollment or bank interest) is added to the amount that existed at the beginning of the period. As a result, over time (e.g., with each year or quarter), the same rate of change is applied to a larger and larger figure.

The *exponential formula,* which is based on continuous compounding, is often used to measure population change. It is preferred by population experts, because they view population and population-related subjects as changing without interruption, ever ongoing. Both exponential and compound interest formulas assume a constant rate of change. The former, however, applies the amount of change continuously to the base rather than at the end of each compounding period. When the average annual rates are small (e.g., less than 5 percent) both formulas give virtually the same results. For an explanation of these two formulas as they relate to population, see U.S. Census Bureau, *The Methods and Materials of Demography,* Vol. 2, 3rd printing (rev.), 1975, pp. 372 to 381.

Current and constant dollars—Statistics in some tables in a number of sections are expressed in both current and constant dollars (see, e.g., Table 656 in Section 13, Income, Expenditures, Poverty, and Wealth). Current dollar figures reflect actual prices or costs prevailing during the specified year(s). Constant dollar figures are estimates representing an effort to remove the effects of price changes from statistical series reported in dollar terms. In general, constant dollar series are derived by dividing current dollar estimates by the appropriate price index for the appropriate period (e.g., the Consumer Price Index).

The result is a series as it would presumably exist if prices were the same throughout, as in the base year—in other words, as if the dollar had constant purchasing power. Any changes in this constant dollar series would reflect only changes in real volume of output, income, expenditures, or other measure.

Explanation of Symbols

The following symbols, used in the tables throughout this book, are explained in condensed form in footnotes to the tables where they appear:

— Represents zero or rounds to less than half the unit of measurement shown.

B Base figure too small to meet statistical standards for reliability of a derived figure.

D Figure withheld to avoid disclosure pertaining to a specific organization or individual.

NA Data not enumerated, tabulated, or otherwise available separately.

P Data are preliminary.

S Figure does not meet publication standards for reasons other than that covered by symbol B, above.

X Figure not applicable because column heading and stub line make entry impossible, absurd, or meaningless.

Z Entry would amount to less than half the unit of measurement shown.

In many tables, details will not add to the totals shown because of rounding.

Section 1
Population

This section presents statistics on the growth, distribution, and characteristics of the U.S. population. The principal source of these data is the U.S. Census Bureau, which conducts a decennial census of population, a monthly population survey, a program of population estimates and projections, and a number of other periodic surveys.

Decennial censuses—The U.S. Constitution provides for a census of the population every 10 years, primarily to establish a basis for apportionment of members of the House of Representatives among the states. For over a century after the first census in 1790, the census organization was a temporary one, created only for each decennial census. In 1902, the Census Bureau was established as a permanent federal agency, responsible for enumerating the population and also for compiling statistics on other population and housing characteristics.

Historically, the enumeration of the population has been a complete (100 percent) count. That is, an attempt is made to account for every person, for each person's residence, and for other characteristics (sex, age, family relationships, etc.). Since the 1940 census, in addition to the complete count information, some data have been obtained from representative samples of the population. In the 1990 and 2000 censuses, variable sampling rates were employed. For most of the country, 1 in every 6 households (about 17 percent) received the long form or sample questionnaire; in governmental units estimated to have fewer than 2,500 inhabitants, every other household (50 percent) received the sample questionnaire to enhance the reliability of sample data for small areas. Exact agreement is not to be expected between sample data and the 100-percent count. For Census 2010, only the short form questionnaire was used. Sample data may be used with confidence where large numbers are involved and assumed to indicate trends and relationships where small numbers are involved.

Current Population Survey (CPS)—This is a monthly nationwide survey of a scientifically selected sample representing the noninstitutionalized civilian population. The sample is located in 824 areas with coverage in every state and the District of Columbia and is subject to sampling error. At the present time, about 60,000 occupied households are eligible for interview every month; of these, about 8 percent are, for various reasons, unavailable for interview.

While the primary purpose of the CPS is to obtain monthly statistics on the labor force, it also serves as a vehicle for inquiries on other subjects. Using CPS data, the Census Bureau issues a series of publications under the general title of *Current Population Reports*.

Estimates of population characteristics based on the CPS will not agree with the counts from the census because the CPS and the census use different procedures for collecting and processing the data for racial groups, the Hispanic population, and other topics. Caution should also be used when comparing estimates for various years because of the periodic introduction of changes into the CPS. Beginning in January 1994, a number of changes were introduced into the CPS that affect all data comparisons with prior years. These changes included the results of a major redesign of the survey questionnaire and collection methodology and the introduction of 1990 census population controls, adjusted for the estimated undercount. Beginning with the 2001 CPS Annual Demographic Supplement, the independent estimates used as control totals for the CPS are based on civilian population benchmarks consistent with Census 2000. In March 2002, the sample size of the Annual Demographic Supplement was increased to approximately 78,000. In 2003 the name of the March supplement was changed to Annual Social and Economic Supplement. These changes in population controls had relatively little impact on derived measures such as means, medians, and percent distribution, but did have a significant impact on levels.

American Community Survey (ACS)—This is a nationwide survey to obtain data about demographic, social, economic, and housing information of people, households, and housing units. The survey collects the same type of information that has been collected from the long-form questionnaire of Census 2000, which the American Community Survey has replaced. Beginning 2006, the estimates include the household population and the population living in institutions, college dormitories, and other group quarters.

Population estimates and projections—Estimates of the United States population are derived by updating the resident population enumerated in Census 2010 with information on the components of population change: births, deaths, and net international migration. The population estimates base reflects changes to the decennial census population due to the Count Question Resolution (CQR) program and geographic program revisions. The 2010 base population and subsequent estimates do not reflect any CQR changes because no CQR revisions had been determined as of the release of 2011 population estimates.

Registered births and deaths are estimated from data supplied by the National Center for Health Statistics. The net international migration component consists of four parts: (1) the net international migration of the foreign born, (2) the net migration of natives to and from the United States, (3) the net migration between the United States and Puerto Rico, and (4) the net overseas movement of the Armed Forces population. Data from the ACS are used to estimate the annual net migration of the foreign-born population. Estimates of the net migration of natives and net migration between Puerto Rico and the United States prior to 2005 are derived from the Demographic Analysis and Population Estimates (DAPE) project (see Population Division Working Paper Series, No. 63 and No. 64). Estimates for net migration between Puerto Rico and the U.S. for 2005 and later years are derived from the ACS and the Puerto Rico Community Survey. Estimates of the net overseas movement of the Armed Forces are derived from data collected by the Defense Manpower Data Center.

Estimates for state and county areas are based on the same components of change data and sources as the national estimates with the addition of net internal migration. Estimates of net internal migration are derived from federal income tax returns from the Internal Revenue Service, group quarters data from the Federal-State Cooperative Program, and Medicare data from the Centers for Medicare and Medicaid Services.

The population by age for April 1, 1990, reflects modifications to the 1990 census data counts. The review of detailed 1990 information indicated that respondents tended to report age as of the date of completion of the questionnaire, not as of April 1, 1990. In addition, there may have been a tendency for respondents to round up their age if they were close to having a birthday. A detailed explanation of the age modification procedure appears in 1990 Census of Population and Housing, Data Paper Listing CPH-L74.

Population estimates and projections are available on the Census Bureau Web site, see <http://www.census.gov>. These estimates and projections are consistent with official decennial census figures with no adjustment for estimated net census coverage. However, the categories for these estimates and projections by race have been modified and are not comparable to the census race categories (see section below under "Race"). For details on methodology, see the sources cited below the individual tables.

Immigration—Immigration (migration to a country) is one component of international migration; the other component is emigration (migration *from* a country). In its simplest form, international migration is defined as any movement across a national border. In the United States, federal statistics on international migration are produced primarily by the U.S. Census Bureau and the Office of Immigration Statistics of the U.S. Department of Homeland Security (DHS).

The Census Bureau collects data used to estimate international migration through its decennial censuses and numerous surveys of the U.S. population.

The Office of Immigration Statistics publishes immigration data in annual flow reports and the *Yearbook of Immigration Statistics*. Data for these publications are collected from several administrative data sources including the DS-230 Application for Immigrant Visa and Alien Registration (U.S. Department of State) for applicants living abroad, and the I-485 Application to Register Permanent Residence or Adjust Status (U.S. Citizenship and Immigration Services—USCIS) for applicants living in the United States.

An immigrant, or legal permanent resident, is a foreign national who has been granted lawful permanent residence in the United States. New arrivals are foreign nationals living abroad who apply for an immigrant visa at a consular office of the Department of State, while individuals adjusting status are already living in the United States and file an application for adjustment of status to lawful permanent residence with USCIS. Individuals adjusting status include refugees, asylees, and various classes of nonimmigrants. A refugee is an alien outside the United States who is unable or unwilling to return to his or her country of nationality because of persecution or a well-founded fear of persecution. Asylees must meet the same criteria as refugees, but are located in the United States or at a port of entry. After 1 year of residence, refugees and asylees are required by statute to apply for legal permanent

resident status. Nonimmigrants are foreign nationals granted temporary entry into the United States. The major activities for which nonimmigrant admission is authorized include temporary visits for business or pleasure, academic or vocational study, temporary employment, and to act as a representative of a foreign government or international organization. DHS collects information on the characteristics of a proportion of nonimmigrant admissions, those recorded on the I-94 Arrival/Departure Record.

U.S. immigration law gives preferential immigration status to persons with a close family relationship with a U.S. citizen or legal permanent resident, persons with needed job skills, persons who qualify as refugees or asylees, and persons who are from countries with relatively low levels of immigration to the United States. Immigration to the United States can be divided into two general categories: (1) classes of admission subject to the annual worldwide limitation and (2) classes of admission exempt from worldwide limitations. Numerical limits are imposed on visas issued and not on admissions. In 2011, the annual limit for preference visas subject to limitation was 366,000, which included a family-sponsored preference limit of 226,000 and an employment-based preference limit of 140,000. Classes of admission exempt from the worldwide limitation include immediate relatives of U.S. citizens, refugees and asylees adjusting to permanent residence, and other various classes of special immigrants.

Metropolitan and micropolitan areas—The U.S. Office of Management and Budget (OMB) defines metropolitan and micropolitan statistical areas according to published standards that are applied to Census Bureau data. The general concept of a metropolitan or micropolitan statistical area is that of a core area containing a substantial population nucleus, together with adjacent communities having a high degree of economic and social integration with that core. Currently defined metropolitan and micropolitan statistical areas are based on application of 2000 standards to 2000 decennial census data as updated by application of those standards to more recent Census Bureau population estimates. The term "metropolitan area" (MA) was adopted in 1990 and referred collectively to metropolitan statistical areas (MSAs), consolidated metropolitan statistical areas (CMSAs), and primary metropolitan statistical areas (PMSAs). The term "core-based statistical area" (CBSA) became effective in 2003 and refers collectively to metropolitan and micropolitan statistical areas. For descriptive details and a list of titles and components of metropolitan and micropolitan statistical areas, see Appendix II.

Urban and rural—For Census 2000 and 2010, the Census Bureau classified as urban all territory, population, and housing units located within urbanized areas (UAs) and urban clusters (UCs). A UA consists of densely settled territory that contains 50,000 or more people, while a UC consists of densely settled territory with at least 2,500 people but fewer than 50,000 people. From the 1950 census through the 1990 census, the urban population consisted of all people living in UAs and most places outside of UAs with a census population of 2,500 or more.

UAs and UCs encompass territory that generally consists of:

1 A cluster of one or more block groups or census blocks each of which has a population density of at least 1,000 people per square mile at the time.

2 Surrounding block groups and census blocks each of which has a population density of at least 500 people per square mile at the time.

3 Less densely settled blocks that form enclaves or indentations, or are used to connect discontiguous areas with qualifying densities.

They also may include an airport located adjacent to qualifying densely settled area if it has an annual enplanement (aircraft boarding) of at least 10,000 people. "Rural" for Census 2010 consists of all territory, population, and housing units located outside of UAs and UCs. Prior to Census 2000, rural consisted of all territory, population, and housing outside of UAs and outside of other places designated as "urban." For Census 2010, many more geographic entities, including metropolitan areas, counties, and places, contain both urban and rural territory, population, and housing units.

Residence—In determining residence, the Census Bureau counts each person as an inhabitant of a usual place of residence (i.e., the place where one lives and sleeps most of the time). While this place is not necessarily a person's legal residence or voting residence, the use of these different bases of classification would produce the same results in the vast majority of cases.

Race—For the 1990 census, the Census Bureau collected and published racial statistics as outlined in Statistical Policy Directive No. 15 issued by the OMB. This directive provided standards on ethnic and racial categories for statistical reporting to be used by all federal agencies. According to the directive, the basic racial categories were American Indian or Alaska Native, Asian or Pacific Islander, Black, and White. (The directive identified Hispanic origin as an ethnicity.) The question on race for Census 2000 was different from the one for the 1990 census in several ways. Most significantly, respondents were given the option of selecting one or more race categories to indicate their racial identities. Because of these changes, the Census 2000 data on race are not directly comparable with data from the 1990 census or earlier censuses. Caution must be used when interpreting changes in the racial composition of the United States population over time. Census 2010 adheres to the federal standards for collecting and presenting data on race and ethnicity as established by the OMB in October 1997. Starting with Census 2000, the OMB requires federal agencies to use a minimum of five race categories: White, Black or African American, American Indian or Alaska Native, Asian, and Native Hawaiian or Other Pacific Islander. Additionally, to collect data on individuals of mixed race parentage, respondents were allowed to select one or more races. For respondents unable to identify with any of these five race categories, the OMB approved and included a sixth category—"Some other race" on the Census 2000 and 2010 questionnaire. The Census 2000 and 2010 question on race included 15 separate response categories and three areas where respondents could write in a more specific race group. The response categories and write-in answers can be combined to create the five minimum OMB race categories plus "Some other race." People who responded to the question on race by indicating only one race are referred to as the *race alone* population, or the group that reported only one race category. Six categories make up this population: White alone, Black or African American alone, American Indian and Alaska Native alone, Asian alone, Native Hawaiian and Other Pacific Islander alone, and Some other race alone. Individuals who chose more than one of the six race categories are referred to as the *Two or More Races* population, or as the group that reported more than one race. Additionally, respondents who reported one race together with those who reported the same race plus one or more other races are combined to create the race alone or in *combination* categories. For example, the *White alone or in combination group* consists of those respondents who reported only White or who reported White combined with one or more other race groups, such as "White and Black or African American," or "White and Asian and American Indian and Alaska Native." Another way to think of the group who reported White alone or in combination is as the total number of people who identified entirely or partially as White. This group is also described as people who reported White, whether or not they reported any other race.

The *alone or in combination* categories are tallies of *responses* rather than *respondents*. That is, the alone or in combination categories are not mutually exclusive. Individuals who reported two races were counted in two separate and distinct alone or in combination race categories, while those who reported three races were counted in three categories, and so on. Consequently, the sum of all alone or in combination categories equals the number of races reported, which exceeds the total population.

The concept of race, as used by the Census Bureau, reflects self-identification by people according to the race or races with which they most closely identify. These categories are sociopolitical constructs and should not be interpreted as being scientific or anthropological in nature. Furthermore, the race categories include both racial and national-origin groups. Additionally, data are available for the American Indian and Alaska Native tribes. A detailed explanation of race can be found at <http://www.census.gov/prod/cen2010/doc/sf1.pdf>.

Data for the population by race for April 1, 2000 and 2010, (shown in Tables 6 and 10) are modified counts and are not comparable to Census 2000 and 2010 race categories. These numbers were computed using Census 2000 and 2010 data by race and had been modified to be consistent with the 1997 OMB's "Revisions to the Standards for the Classification of Federal Data on Race and Ethnicity," (Federal Register Notice, Vol. 62, No 210, October 1997). A detailed explanation of the race modification procedure appears at <http://www.census.gov/popest/data/historical/files/MRSF-01-US1.pdf>.

In the CPS and other household sample surveys in which data are obtained through personal interview, respondents are asked to classify their race as: (1) White; (2) Black, African American, or Negro; (3) American Indian or Alaska Native; (4) Asian; or (5) Native Hawaiian or Other Pacific Islander. Beginning January 2003, respondents were allowed to report more than one race to indicate their mixed racial heritage.

Hispanic population—The Census Bureau collected data on the Hispanic-origin population in the 2000 and 2010 censuses by using a self-identification question. Persons of Spanish/Hispanic/Latino origin are those who classified themselves in one of the specific Hispanic origin categories listed on the questionnaire—Mexican, Puerto Rican, Cuban, as well as those who indicated that they were of Other

Spanish/ Hispanic/Latino origin (persons whose origins are from Spain, the Spanish-speaking countries of Central or South America, or the Dominican Republic).

In the CPS, information on Hispanic persons is gathered by using a self-identification question. The respondents are first asked whether they are of Hispanic, Spanish, or Latino origin and based on their response are further classified into the following categories: Mexican or Mexican American or Chicano; Puerto Rican; Cuban; Central or South American; or Other Hispanic, Spanish, or Latino origin group.

Traditional and current data collection and classification treat race and Hispanic origin as two separate and distinct concepts in accordance with guidelines from the OMB. Race and Hispanic origin are two separate concepts in the federal statistical system. People who are Hispanic may be any race and people in each race group may be either Hispanic or Not Hispanic. Also, each person has two attributes, their race (or races) and whether or not they are Hispanic. The overlap of race and Hispanic origin is the main comparability issue. For example, Black Hispanics (Hispanic Blacks) are included in both the number of Blacks and in the number of Hispanics. For further information, see <http://www.census.gov/population/www/socdemo/compraceho.html>.

Foreign-born and native populations—The Census Bureau separates the U.S. resident population into two groups based on whether a person was a U.S. citizen or U.S. national at the time of birth. Anyone born in the United States, Puerto Rico, or a U.S. Island Area (such as Guam), or born abroad to a U.S. citizen parent is a U.S. citizen at the time of birth and consequently included in the *native population*. The term *foreign-born population* refers to anyone who is not a U.S. citizen or a U.S. national at birth. This includes naturalized U.S. citizens, legal permanent resident aliens (immigrants), temporary migrants (such as foreign students), humanitarian migrants (such as refugees), and people illegally present in the United States. The Census Bureau provides a variety of demographic, social, economic, geographic, and housing information on the foreign-born population in the United States at <http://www.census.gov/population/foreign/>.

Mobility status—The U.S. population is classified according to mobility status on the basis of a comparison between the place of residence of each individual at the time of the survey or census and the place of residence at a specified earlier date. Nonmovers are all persons who were living in the same house or apartment at the end of the period as at the beginning of the period. Movers are all persons who were living in a different house or apartment at the end of the period than at the beginning of the period. Movers are further classified as to whether they were living in the same or different county, state, region, or were movers from abroad. Movers from abroad include all persons whose place of residence was outside the United States (including Puerto Rico, other U.S. Island Area, or a foreign country) at the beginning of the period.

Living arrangements—Living arrangements refer to residency in households or in group quarters. A "household" comprises all persons who occupy a "housing unit," that is, a house, an apartment or other group of rooms, or a single room that constitutes "separate living quarters." A household includes the related family members and all the unrelated persons, if any, such as lodgers, foster children, or employees who share the housing unit. A person living alone or a group of unrelated persons sharing the same housing unit is also counted as a household. See text, Section 20, Construction and Housing, for definition of housing unit.

All persons not living in housing units are classified as living in group quarters. These individuals may be institutionalized, e.g., under care or custody in juvenile facilities, jails, correctional centers, hospitals, or nursing homes; or they may be residents in noninstitutional group quarters such as college dormitories, group homes, or military barracks.

Householder—The householder is the person in whose name the home is owned or rented. If a home is owned or rented jointly by a married couple, either the husband or the wife may be listed first.

Family—The term family refers to a group of two or more persons related by birth, marriage, or adoption and residing together in a household. A family includes among its members the householder.

Subfamily—A subfamily consists of a married couple and their children, if any, or one parent with one or more never-married children under 18 years old living in a household. Subfamilies are divided into "related" and "unrelated" subfamilies. A related subfamily is related to, but does not include, the householder or the spouse of the householder. Members of a related subfamily are also members of the family with whom they live. The number of related subfamilies, therefore, is not included in the count of families. An unrelated subfamily may include persons such as guests, lodgers, or resident employees and their spouses and/or children; none of whom is related to the householder.

Married couple—A married couple is defined as a husband and wife living together in the same household, with or without children and other relatives.

Statistical reliability—For a discussion of statistical collection and estimation, sampling procedures, and measures of statistical reliability applicable to Census Bureau data, see Appendix III.

Figure 1.1
Percent Change in Population for States: April 1, 2000 to April 1, 2010

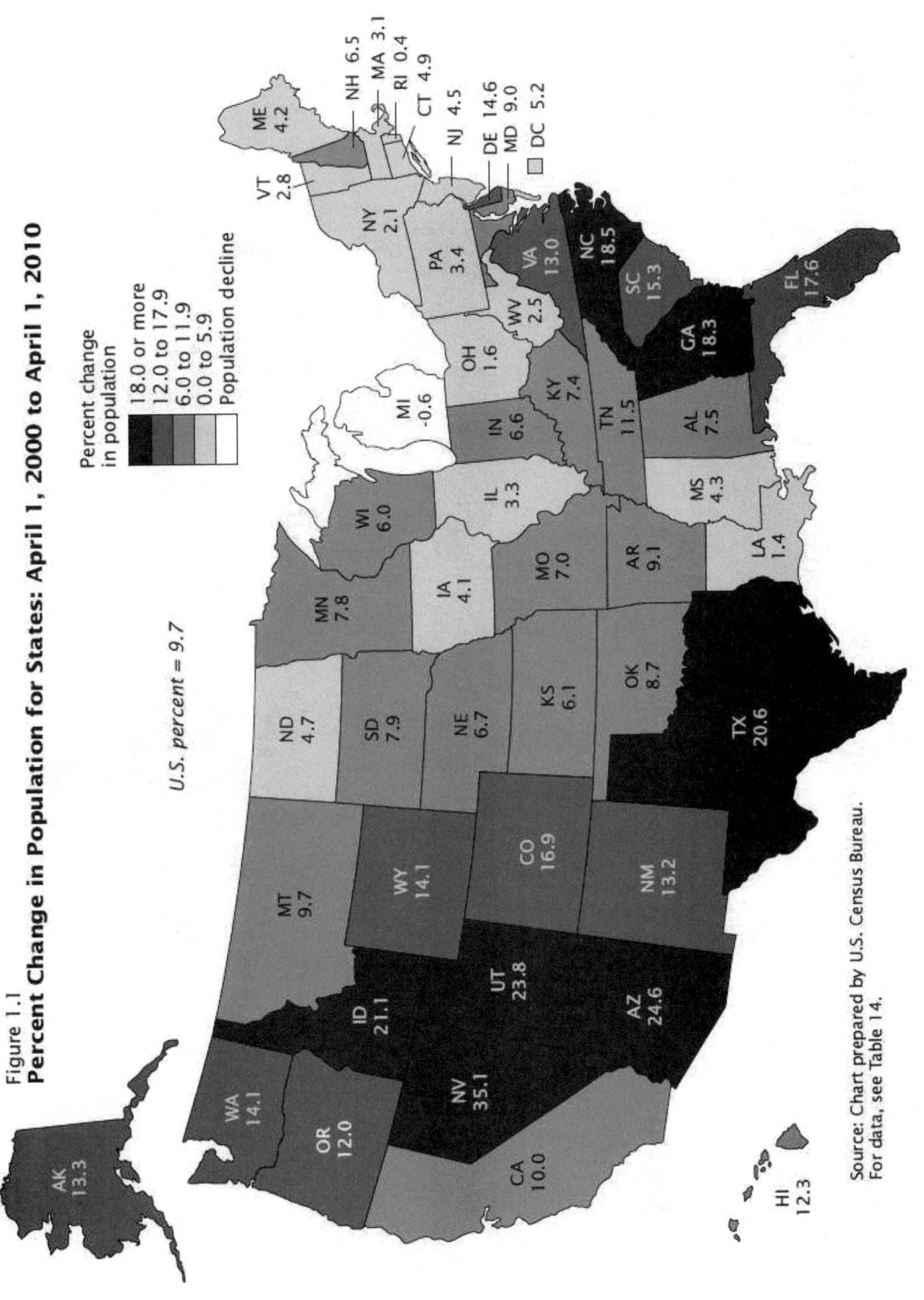

Percent change
in population

18.0 or more
12.0 to 17.9
6.0 to 11.9
0.0 to 5.9
Population decline

U.S. percent = 9.7

Source: Chart prepared by U.S. Census Bureau.
For data, see Table 14.

NH 6.5
MA 3.1
RI 0.4
CT 4.9
NJ 4.5
DE 14.6
MD 9.0
DC 5.2

ME 4.2
VT 2.8
NY 2.1
PA 3.4
VA 13.0
NC 18.5
SC 15.3
GA 18.3
FL 17.6

WV 2.5
OH 1.6
KY 7.4
TN 11.5
AL 7.5
MS 4.3
LA 1.4

MI -0.6
IN 6.6
IL 3.3
WI 6.0
IA 4.1
MO 7.0
AR 9.1

MN 7.8
ND 4.7
SD 7.9
NE 6.7
KS 6.1
OK 8.7
TX 20.6

MT 9.7
WY 14.1
CO 16.9
NM 13.2

ID 21.1
UT 23.8
AZ 24.6

WA 14.1
OR 12.0
NV 35.1
CA 10.0

AK 13.3
HI 12.3

Percent Change in Population for States and Puerto Rico: April 1, 2010 to July 1, 2011

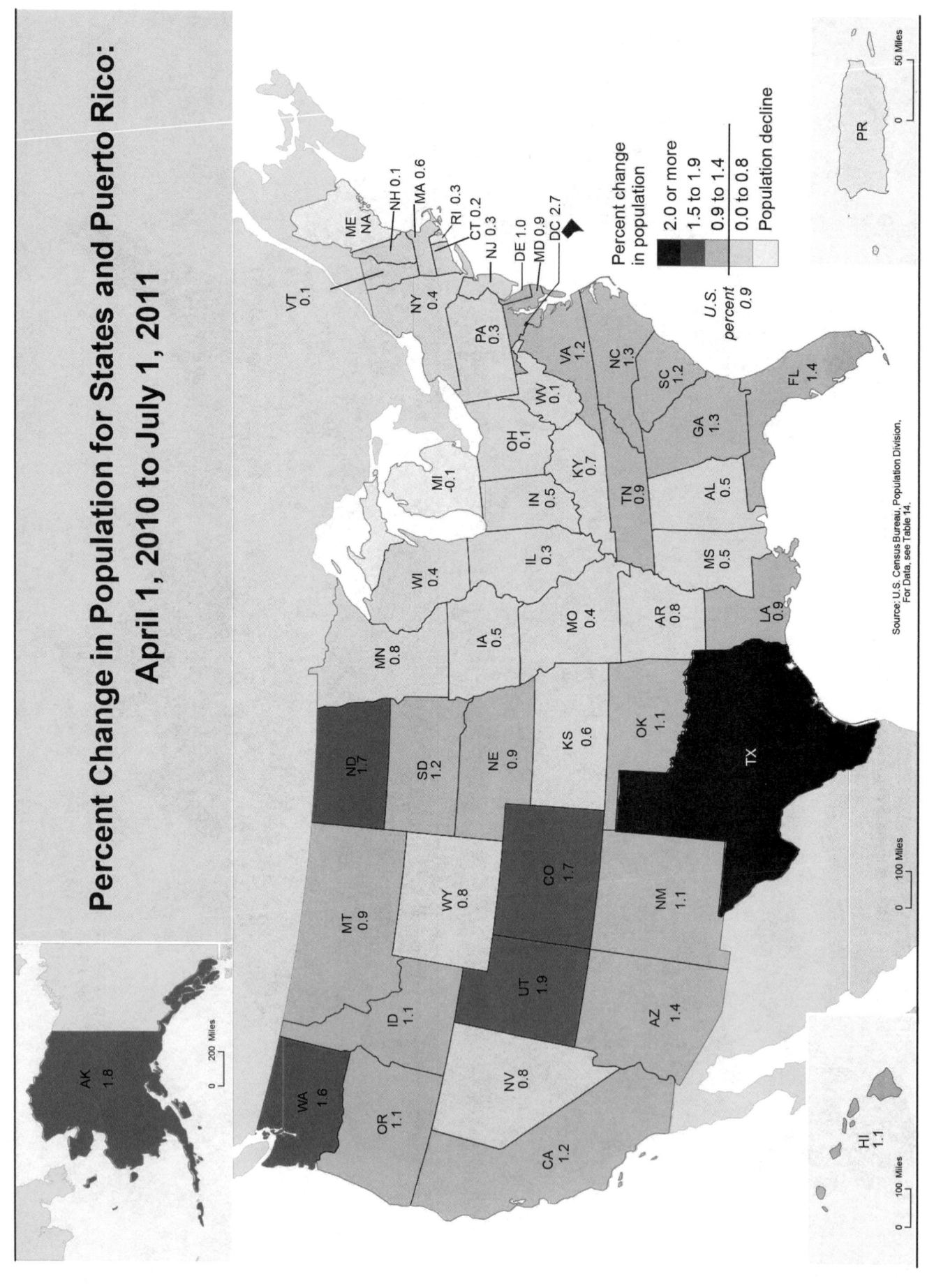

Percent change in population

- 2.0 or more
- 1.5 to 1.9
- 0.9 to 1.4
- 0.0 to 0.8
- Population decline

U.S. percent 0.9

Source: U.S. Census Bureau, Population Division, For Data, see Table 14.

State	Value
AK	1.8
WA	1.6
OR	1.1
CA	1.2
NV	0.8
ID	1.1
MT	0.9
WY	0.8
UT	1.9
AZ	1.4
CO	1.7
NM	1.1
ND	1.7
SD	1.2
NE	0.9
KS	0.6
OK	1.1
TX	
MN	0.8
IA	0.5
MO	0.4
AR	0.8
LA	0.9
WI	0.4
IL	0.3
IN	0.5
MI	-0.1
OH	0.1
KY	0.7
TN	0.9
MS	0.5
AL	0.5
GA	1.3
FL	1.4
SC	1.2
NC	1.3
VA	1.2
WV	0.1
PA	0.3
NY	0.4
VT	0.1
ME	NA
NH	0.1
MA	0.6
RI	0.3
CT	0.2
NJ	0.3
DE	1.0
MD	0.9
DC	2.7
HI	1.1

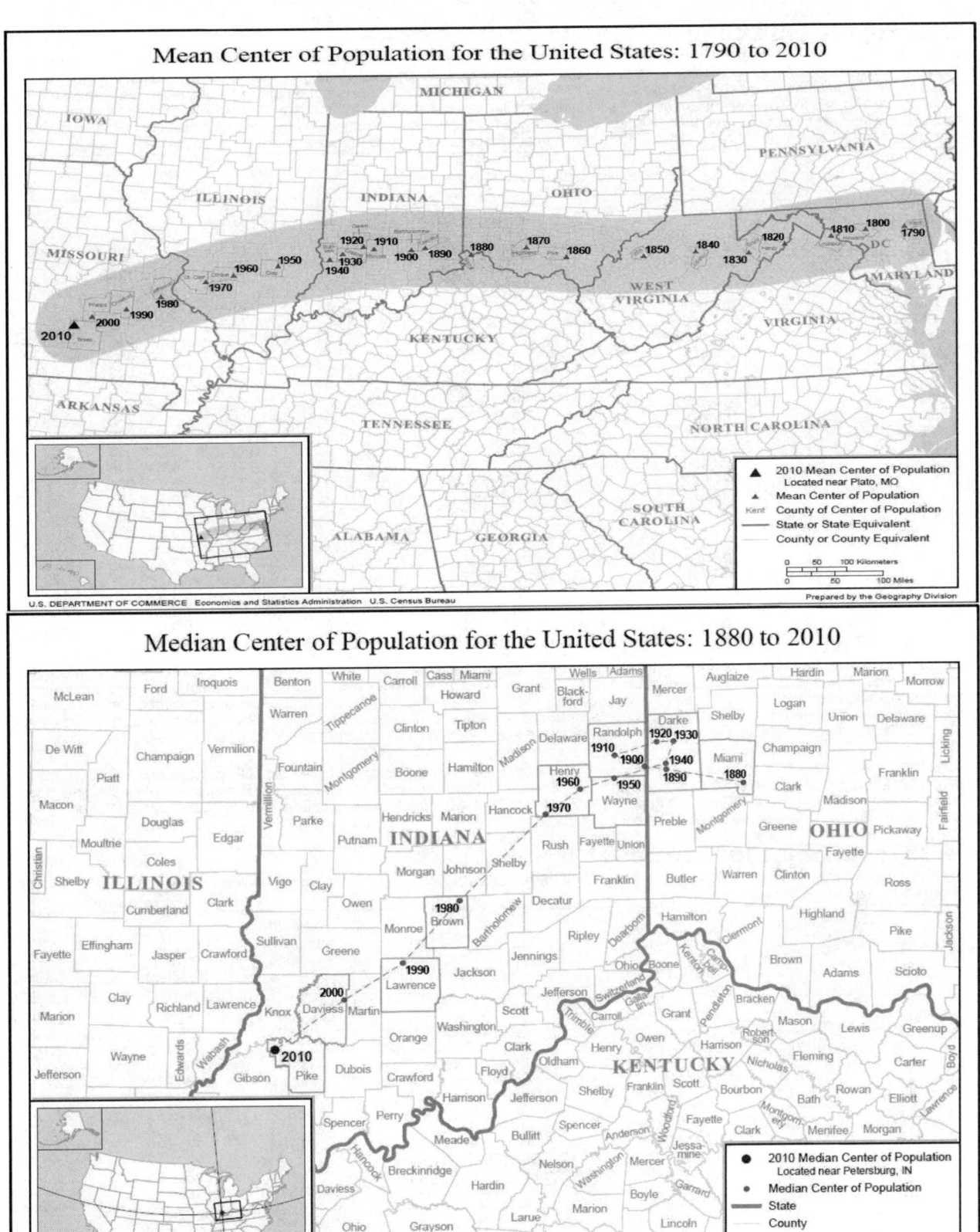

Mean Center of Population for the United States: 1790 to 2010

2010 Mean Center of Population
Located near Plato, MO
▲ Mean Center of Population
Kent County of Center of Population
— State or State Equivalent
County or County Equivalent

U.S. DEPARTMENT OF COMMERCE Economics and Statistics Administration U.S. Census Bureau

Prepared by the Geography Division

Median Center of Population for the United States: 1880 to 2010

● 2010 Median Center of Population
Located near Petersburg, IN
● Median Center of Population
State
County

U.S. DEPARTMENT OF COMMERCE Economics and Statistics Administration U.S. Census Bureau

Prepared by the Geography Division

Table 1. Population and Area: 1790 to 2010

[Area figures represent area on indicated date including in some cases considerable areas not then organized or settled, and not covered by the census. Area data include Alaska beginning in 1870 and Hawaii beginning in 1900. Total area figures for 1790 to 1970 have been recalculated on the basis of the remeasurement of states and counties for the 1980 census, but not on the basis of subsequent censuses. The land and water area figures for past censuses have not been adjusted and are not strictly comparable with the total area data for comparable dates because the land areas were derived from different base data, and these values are known to have changed with the construction of reservoirs, draining of lakes, etc. Density figures are based on land area measurements as reported in earlier censuses]

| Census date | Resident population | | | | Area (square miles) | | |
| | Number | Per square mile of land area | Increase over preceding census | | Total | Land | Water [1] |
			Number	Percent			
1790 (Aug. 2)..............	3,929,214	4.5	(X)	(X)	891,364	864,746	24,065
1800 (Aug. 4)..............	5,308,483	6.1	1,379,269	35.1	891,364	864,746	24,065
1810 (Aug. 6)..............	7,239,881	4.3	1,931,398	36.4	1,722,685	1,681,828	34,175
1820 (Aug. 7)..............	9,638,453	5.5	2,398,572	33.1	1,792,552	1,749,462	38,544
1830 (June 1)..............	12,866,020	7.4	3,227,567	33.5	1,792,552	1,749,462	38,544
1840 (June 1)..............	17,069,453	9.8	4,203,433	32.7	1,792,552	1,749,462	38,544
1850 (June 1)..............	23,191,876	7.9	6,122,423	35.9	2,991,655	2,940,042	52,705
1860 (June 1)..............	31,443,321	10.6	8,251,445	35.6	3,021,295	2,969,640	52,747
1870 (June 1)..............	[2] 39,818,449	[2] 11.2	8,375,128	26.6	3,612,299	3,540,705	68,082
1880 (June 1)..............	50,189,209	14.2	10,370,760	26.0	3,612,299	3,540,705	68,082
1890 (June 1)..............	62,979,766	17.8	12,790,557	25.5	3,612,299	3,540,705	68,082
1900 (June 1)..............	76,212,168	21.5	13,232,402	21.0	3,618,770	3,547,314	67,901
1910 (Apr. 15)..............	92,228,496	26.0	16,016,328	21.0	3,618,770	3,547,045	68,170
1920 (Jan. 1)..............	106,021,537	29.9	13,793,041	15.0	3,618,770	3,546,931	68,284
1930 (Apr. 1)..............	123,202,624	34.7	17,181,087	16.2	3,618,770	3,554,608	60,607
1940 (Apr. 1)..............	132,164,569	37.2	8,961,945	7.3	3,618,770	3,554,608	60,607
1950 (Apr. 1)..............	151,325,798	42.6	19,161,229	14.5	3,618,770	3,552,206	63,005
1960 (Apr. 1)..............	179,323,175	50.6	27,997,377	18.5	3,618,770	3,540,911	74,212
1970 (Apr. 1)..............	203,302,031	57.5	23,978,856	13.4	3,618,770	3,536,855	78,444
1980 (Apr. 1)..............	[3] 226,542,199	64.0	23,240,168	11.4	3,618,770	3,539,289	79,481
1990 (Apr. 1)..............	[4] 248,718,302	70.3	22,176,103	9.8	[5] 3,717,796	3,536,278	[5] 181,518
2000 (Apr. 1)..............	[6] 281,424,603	79.6	32,706,301	13.1	3,794,083	3,537,438	256,645
2010 (Apr. 1)..............	308,745,538	87.4	27,320,935	9.7	3,796,742	3,531,905	264,837

X Not applicable. [1] Data for 1790 to 1980 cover inland water only. Data for 1990 comprise Great Lakes, inland, and coastal water. Data for 2000 and 2010 comprise Great Lakes, inland, territorial, and coastal water. [2] Revised to include adjustments for underenumeration in southern states; unrevised number is 38,558,371 (10.9 per square mile). [3] Total population count has been revised since the 1980 census publications. Numbers by age, race, Hispanic origin, and sex have not been corrected. [4] The April 1, 1990, census count includes count question resolution corrections processed through December 1997, and does not include adjustments for census coverage errors. [5] Data reflect corrections made after publication of the results. [6] Reflects modifications to the Census 2000 population as documented in the Count Question Resolution program.

Source: U.S. Census Bureau, 2010 Census, National Summary File of Redistricting Data; 2000 Census of Population and Housing, *Population and Housing Counts*, Series PHC-3-1, United States Summary; *Notes and Errata, 2000* SF/01-ER, <http://www.census.gov/prod/cen2000/notes/errata.pdf>; *Areas of the United States: 1940*; Area data for 1990: unpublished data from TIGER ®; and Davis, Warren, personal correspondence, U.S. Census Bureau, June 23, 2006.

Table 2. Population: 1970 to 2011

[In thousands, except as indicated (205,052 represents 205,052,000). Estimates as of July 1. Civilian population excludes Armed Forces. For basis of estimates, see text, this section]

Year	Resident population, including Armed Forces overseas	Resident population	Civilian population	Year	Resident population, including Armed Forces overseas	Resident population	Civilian population
1970........	205,052	203,984	201,895	1991........	253,493	252,981	251,370
1971........	207,661	206,827	204,866	1992........	256,894	256,514	254,929
1972........	209,896	209,284	207,511	1993........	260,255	259,919	258,446
1973........	211,909	211,357	209,600	1994........	263,436	263,126	261,714
1974........	213,854	213,342	211,636	1995........	266,557	266,278	264,927
1975........	215,973	215,465	213,789	1996........	269,667	269,394	268,108
1976........	218,035	217,563	215,894	1997........	272,912	272,647	271,394
1977........	220,239	219,760	218,106	1998........	276,115	275,854	274,633
1978........	222,585	222,095	220,467	1999........	279,295	279,040	277,841
1979........	225,055	224,567	222,969	2000........	(NA)	282,162	(NA)
1980........	227,726	227,225	225,621	2001........	(NA)	284,969	(NA)
1981........	229,966	229,466	227,818	2002........	(NA)	287,625	(NA)
1982........	232,188	231,664	229,995	2003........	(NA)	290,108	(NA)
1983........	234,307	233,792	232,097	2004........	(NA)	292,805	(NA)
1984........	236,348	235,825	234,110	2005........	(NA)	295,517	(NA)
1985........	238,466	237,924	236,219	2006........	(NA)	298,380	(NA)
1986........	240,651	240,133	238,412	2007........	(NA)	301,231	(NA)
1987........	242,804	242,289	240,550	2008........	(NA)	304,094	(NA)
1988........	245,021	244,499	242,817	2009........	(NA)	306,772	(NA)
1989........	247,342	246,819	245,131	2010........	309,750	309,330	308,095
1990........	250,132	249,623	247,983	2011........	312,009	311,592	310,374

NA Not available.

Source: U.S. Census Bureau, Population Division, 1970 to 1979: Current Population Reports P25-917; 1980 to 1989: "Monthly Estimates of the United States Population: April 1, 1980 to July 1, 1999, with Short-Term Projections to November 1, 2000," January 2001, <http://www.census.gov/popest/archives/1990s/nat-total.txt>; 1990 to 1999: "National Intercensal Estimates (1990–2000)," August 2004, <http://www.census.gov/popest/archives/EST90INTERCENSAL/US-EST90INT-datasets.html>; 2000 to 2009: "Monthly Intercensal Resident Population Estimates for the United States: April 1, 2000 to July 1, 2010," September 2011 <http://www.census.gov/popest/data/intercensal/national/nat2010.html>; 2010 and 2011: "Monthly Population Estimates for the United States: April 1, 2010 to June 1, 2012 (NA-EST2011-01)," July 2012, <http://www.census.gov/popest/data/state/totals/2011/tables/NA-EST2011-01.xls>.

Table 3. Resident Population Projections: 2012 to 2050

[In thousands, except as indicated (316,266 represents 316,266,000). As of July 1. Projections are based on assumptions about future births, deaths, and net international migration. Data do not reflect results of 2010 Census. More information on methodology and assumptions is available at <http://www.census.gov/population/www/projections/methodstatement.html>]

Year	Population	Percent change [1]	Year	Population	Percent change [1]	Year	Population	Percent change [1]
2012..........	316,266	1.0	2025..........	357,452	0.9	2038.........	399,184	0.8
2013..........	319,330	1.0	2026..........	360,667	0.9	2039.........	402,415	0.8
2014..........	322,423	1.0	2027..........	363,880	0.9	2040.........	405,655	0.8
2015..........	325,540	1.0	2028..........	367,090	0.9	2041.........	408,906	0.8
2016..........	328,678	1.0	2029..........	370,298	0.9	2042.........	412,170	0.8
2017..........	331,833	1.0	2030..........	373,504	0.9	2043.........	415,448	0.8
2018..........	335,005	1.0	2031..........	376,708	0.9	2044.........	418,743	0.8
2019..........	338,190	1.0	2032..........	379,912	0.9	2045.........	422,059	0.8
2020..........	341,387	0.9	2033..........	383,117	0.8	2046.........	425,395	0.8
2021..........	344,592	0.9	2034..........	386,323	0.8	2047.........	428,756	0.8
2022..........	347,803	0.9	2035..........	389,531	0.8	2048.........	432,143	0.8
2023..........	351,018	0.9	2036..........	392,743	0.8	2049.........	435,560	0.8
2024..........	354,235	0.9	2037..........	395,961	0.8	2050.........	439,010	0.8

[1] Percent change from immediate preceding year. 2012, change from 2011.

Source: U.S. Census Bureau, Population Division, "2008 National Population Projections," August 2008, <http://www.census.gov/population/www/projections/2008projections.html>.

Table 4. Components of Population Change: 2010 to 2011

[In thousands, except as indicated (308,746 represents 308,746,000). Resident population]

Period	Population as of beginning of period	Net increase [1]		Births	Deaths	Net international migration [3]	Population as of end of period
		Total	Percent [2]				
April 1, 2010 to July 1, 2011 [4].................	308,746	2,846	0.9	4,998	3,046	894	311,592
July 1, 2010 to July 1, 2011...................	309,330	2,262	0.7	4,008	2,450	704	311,592

[1] Net increase includes a residual. This residual represents the change in population that cannot be attributed to any specific demographic component. [2] Percent of population at beginning of period. [3] Net international migration includes the international migration of both native and foreign-born populations. Specifically, it includes: (a) the net international migration of the foreign born, (b) the net migration between the United States and Puerto Rico, (c) the net migration of natives to and from the United States, and (d) the net movement of the Armed Forces population between the United States and overseas. [4] The April 1, 2010, population estimates base reflects geographic program revisions but not changes from the Count Question Resolution program.

Source: U.S. Census Bureau, Population Estimates, "National Totals: Vintage 2011," <http://www.census.gov/popest/data/national/totals/2011/index.html>.

Table 5. Components of Population Change by Race and Hispanic Origin: 2010 to 2011

[In thousands (2,846 represents 2,846,000). Resident population. Covers period April 1, 2010, to July 1, 2011. The April 1, 2010 population estimates base reflects changes to the Census 2010 population from geographic program revisions but does not reflect changes from the Count Question Resolution program. Responses of "Some Other Race" from the 2010 Census are modified. This results in differences between the population for specific race categories shown for the 2010 Census population in this table versus those in the original 2010 Census data]

Race and Hispanic origin	April 1, 2010 to July 1, 2011				
	Net increase [1]	Natural increase	Births	Deaths	Net international migration [2]
Total...........................	**2,846**	**1,952**	**4,998**	**3,046**	**894**
One race...............	2,545	1,663	4,684	3,021	882
White................	1,533	1,004	3,592	2,588	529
Black or African American....................	500	410	764	354	90
American Indian and Alaska Native....................	75	66	83	17	10
Asian..................	419	170	231	60	248
Native Hawaiian and Other Pacific Islander.....................	17	13	15	2	4
Two or more races................	301	289	314	25	12
Race alone or in combination: [3]					
White..................	1,812	1,271	3,881	2,610	541
Black or African American..................	671	575	937	362	96
American Indian and Alaska Native..................	128	114	145	32	14
Asian..................	529	277	343	66	252
Native Hawaiian and Other Pacific Islander.....................	39	34	37	3	5
Hispanic [4].................	1,568	1,125	1,307	182	443
White alone, not Hispanic.................	192	72	2,483	2,411	120

[1] See footnote 1, Table 4. [2] See footnote 3, Table 4. [3] In combination with one or more other races. The sum of the five race groups adds to more than the total population because individuals may report more than one race. [4] Hispanic origin is considered an ethnicity, not a race. Hispanics may be of any race.

Source: U.S. Census Bureau, Population Division, "Table 4. Cumulative Estimates of the Components of Resident Population Change by Race and Hispanic Origin for the United States: April 1, 2010 to July 1, 2011 (NC-EST2011-04)," May 2012; <http://www.census.gov/popest/data/national/asrh/2011/index.html>.

Table 6. Resident Population by Sex, Race, and Hispanic-Origin Status: 2000 to 2011

[281,425 represents 281,425,000. Data shown are modified race counts; see text, this section]

Characteristic	Number (1,000)				Percent change	
	2000 [1] (April)	2005 (July)	2010 [1] (April)	2011 (July)	2000 to 2010	2010 to 2011
BOTH SEXES						
Total	**281,425**	**295,517**	**308,746**	**311,592**	**9.7**	**0.9**
One race	277,527	290,178	301,761	304,306	8.7	0.8
White	228,106	235,492	241,937	243,470	6.1	0.6
Black or African American	35,705	37,962	40,251	40,751	12.7	1.2
American Indian and Alaska Native	2,664	3,148	3,740	3,815	40.4	2.0
Asian	10,589	13,008	15,160	15,578	43.2	2.8
Native Hawaiian and Other Pacific Islander	463	569	675	692	45.9	2.6
Two or more races	3,898	5,339	6,984	7,285	79.2	4.3
Race alone or in combination: [2]						
White	(NA)	(NA)	248,068	249,880	(NA)	0.7
Black or African American	(NA)	(NA)	43,213	43,884	(NA)	1.6
American Indian and Alaska Native	(NA)	(NA)	6,138	6,266	(NA)	2.1
Asian	(NA)	(NA)	17,677	18,206	(NA)	3.0
Native Hawaiian and Other Pacific Islander	(NA)	(NA)	1,332	1,372	(NA)	2.9
Not Hispanic	246,118	252,493	258,268	259,547	4.9	0.5
One race	242,712	248,046	252,663	253,712	4.1	0.4
White	195,577	196,621	197,319	197,511	0.9	0.1
Black or African American	34,314	36,147	37,923	38,337	10.5	1.1
American Indian and Alaska Native	2,097	2,186	2,263	2,291	7.9	1.2
Asian	10,357	12,658	14,662	15,064	41.6	2.7
Native Hawaiian and Other Pacific Islander	367	434	497	509	35.4	2.4
Two or more races	3,406	4,447	5,604	5,835	64.5	4.1
Race alone or in combination: [2]						
White	(NA)	(NA)	202,230	202,636	(NA)	0.2
Black or African American	(NA)	(NA)	40,283	40,832	(NA)	1.4
American Indian and Alaska Native	(NA)	(NA)	4,042	4,097	(NA)	1.4
Asian	(NA)	(NA)	16,795	17,287	(NA)	2.9
Native Hawaiian and Other Pacific Islander	(NA)	(NA)	1,020	1,047	(NA)	2.6
Hispanic [3]	35,306	43,024	50,478	52,045	43.0	3.1
One race	34,815	42,131	49,098	50,595	41.0	3.0
White	32,530	38,871	44,618	45,960	37.2	3.0
Black or African American	1,391	1,814	2,328	2,414	67.4	3.7
American Indian and Alaska Native	566	962	1,476	1,524	160.6	3.2
Asian	232	350	498	515	114.2	3.4
Native Hawaiian and Other Pacific Islander	95	135	177	183	85.9	3.1
Two or more races	491	893	1,380	1,451	180.8	5.1
Race alone or in combination: [2]						
White	(NA)	(NA)	45,838	47,244	(NA)	3.1
Black or African American	(NA)	(NA)	2,930	3,052	(NA)	4.2
American Indian and Alaska Native	(NA)	(NA)	2,097	2,169	(NA)	3.5
Asian	(NA)	(NA)	881	919	(NA)	4.2
Native Hawaiian and Other Pacific Islander	(NA)	(NA)	312	324	(NA)	3.9
MALE						
Total	**138,056**	**145,197**	**151,781**	**153,291**	**9.9**	**1.0**
One race	136,146	142,578	148,355	149,710	9.0	0.9
White	112,478	116,388	119,699	120,547	6.4	0.7
Black or African American	16,972	18,080	19,205	19,463	13.2	1.3
American Indian and Alaska Native	1,333	1,579	1,890	1,929	41.8	2.1
Asian	5,128	6,241	7,218	7,420	40.8	2.8
Native Hawaiian and Other Pacific Islander	235	289	343	352	45.8	2.6
Two or more races	1,910	2,619	3,426	3,580	79.4	4.5
Race alone or in combination: [2]						
White	(NA)	(NA)	122,716	123,707	(NA)	0.8
Black or African American	(NA)	(NA)	20,633	20,978	(NA)	1.7
American Indian and Alaska Native	(NA)	(NA)	3,055	3,121	(NA)	2.2
Asian	(NA)	(NA)	8,468	8,726	(NA)	3.0
Native Hawaiian and Other Pacific Islander	(NA)	(NA)	668	688	(NA)	3.0
Not Hispanic	119,894	123,209	126,163	126,848	5.2	0.5
Hispanic [3]	18,162	21,988	25,619	26,443	41.1	3.2
FEMALE						
Total	**143,368**	**150,320**	**156,964**	**158,301**	**9.5**	**0.9**
One race	141,381	147,600	153,406	154,596	8.5	0.8
White	115,628	119,103	122,238	122,924	5.7	0.6
Black or African American	18,733	19,882	21,046	21,288	12.3	1.1
American Indian and Alaska Native	1,331	1,568	1,850	1,886	39.0	2.0
Asian	5,461	6,767	7,941	8,159	45.4	2.7
Native Hawaiian and Other Pacific Islander	227	280	332	340	45.9	2.6
Two or more races	1,987	2,720	3,558	3,705	79.0	4.1
Race alone or in combination: [2]						
White	(NA)	(NA)	125,351	126,173	(NA)	0.7
Black or African American	(NA)	(NA)	22,580	22,906	(NA)	1.4
American Indian and Alaska Native	(NA)	(NA)	3,084	3,145	(NA)	2.0
Asian	(NA)	(NA)	9,208	9,480	(NA)	3.0
Native Hawaiian and Other Pacific Islander	(NA)	(NA)	665	684	(NA)	2.9
Not Hispanic	126,224	129,284	132,105	132,699	4.7	0.4
Hispanic [3]	17,144	21,036	24,859	25,602	45.0	3.0

NA Not available. [1] See footnote 4, Table 4. [2] In combination with one or more other races. The sum of the five race groups adds to more than the total population because individuals may report more than one race. [3] See footnote 4, Table 5.

Source: U.S. Census Bureau, Population Division, "Intercensal Estimates of the Resident Population by Sex, Race, and Hispanic Origin for the United States: April 1, 2000 to July 1, 2010 (US-EST00INT-02)," September 2011, <http://www.census.gov/popest/data/intercensal/national /nat2010.html>; and "Annual Estimates of the Resident Population by Sex, Race, and Hispanic Origin for the United States: April 1, 2010 to July 1, 2011 (NC-EST2011-03)," May 2012, <http://www.census.gov/popest/data/national/asrh/2011/index.html>.

Table 7. Resident Population by Sex and Age: 1990 to 2011

[In thousands, except as indicated (248,791 represents 248,791,000). As of April 1, except 2011 as of July 1. Excludes Armed Forces overseas. For definition of median, see Guide to Tabular Presentation]

Age	1990 [1]			2000 [2]			2010 [3]			2011		
	Total	Male	Female	Total	Male	Female	Total	Male	Female	Total	Male	Female
Total..................	248,791	121,284	127,507	281,425	138,056	143,368	308,746	151,781	156,964	311,592	153,291	158,301
Under 5 years.........	18,765	9,603	9,162	19,176	9,811	9,365	20,201	10,319	9,882	20,162	10,300	9,863
5 to 9 years............	18,042	9,236	8,806	20,550	10,523	10,026	20,349	10,390	9,959	20,334	10,384	9,950
10 to 14 years.........	17,067	8,742	8,325	20,528	10,520	10,008	20,677	10,580	10,097	20,705	10,587	10,118
15 to 19 years.........	17,893	9,178	8,714	20,219	10,391	9,828	22,040	11,304	10,737	21,644	11,119	10,525
20 to 24 years.........	19,143	9,749	9,394	18,963	9,688	9,275	21,586	11,014	10,572	22,154	11,313	10,841
25 to 29 years.........	21,336	10,708	10,629	19,382	9,799	9,583	21,102	10,636	10,466	21,280	10,762	10,518
30 to 34 years.........	21,838	10,866	10,973	20,511	10,322	10,189	19,962	9,997	9,966	20,511	10,283	10,228
35 to 39 years.........	19,851	9,837	10,014	22,707	11,319	11,388	20,180	10,042	10,138	19,594	9,761	9,833
40 to 44 years.........	17,593	8,679	8,914	22,442	11,130	11,313	20,891	10,394	10,497	21,034	10,462	10,571
45 to 49 years.........	13,747	6,741	7,006	20,093	9,890	10,203	22,709	11,209	11,500	22,158	10,953	11,205
50 to 54 years.........	11,315	5,494	5,821	17,586	8,608	8,978	22,298	10,933	11,365	22,560	11,067	11,494
55 to 59 years.........	10,489	5,009	5,480	13,469	6,509	6,961	19,665	9,524	10,141	20,256	9,816	10,439
60 to 64 years.........	10,627	4,947	5,679	10,806	5,137	5,669	16,818	8,078	8,740	17,807	8,542	9,264
65 to 74 years.........	18,048	7,908	10,140	18,391	8,303	10,088	21,713	10,097	11,617	22,482	10,476	12,005
75 to 84 years.........	10,014	3,745	6,268	12,361	4,879	7,482	13,061	5,477	7,584	13,175	5,573	7,602
85 years and over..................	3,022	841	2,181	4,240	1,227	3,013	5,493	1,790	3,704	5,737	1,894	3,843
5 to 13 years.........	31,839	16,301	15,538	37,026	18,964	18,062	36,860	18,834	18,026	36,910	18,861	18,049
14 to 17 years.........	13,345	6,860	6,485	16,093	8,285	7,808	17,120	8,792	8,328	16,862	8,645	8,218
18 to 24 years.........	26,961	13,744	13,217	27,141	13,873	13,268	30,672	15,662	15,010	31,065	15,897	15,167
18 years and over....	184,841	88,519	96,322	209,130	100,996	108,133	234,564	113,836	120,728	237,658	115,486	122,172
55 years and over....	52,200	22,450	29,748	59,267	26,055	33,212	76,751	34,964	41,787	79,456	36,302	43,155
65 years and over....	31,084	12,494	18,589	34,992	14,410	20,582	40,268	17,363	22,905	41,394	17,943	23,451
75 years and over....	13,036	4,586	8,449	16,601	6,106	10,495	18,555	7,266	11,288	18,912	7,467	11,445
Median age (years)................	32.8	31.6	34.0	35.3	34.0	36.5	37.2	35.8	38.5	37.3	36.0	38.7

[1] The data shown have been modified from the official 1990 census counts. See text, this section, for explanation. The April 1, 1990, estimates base (248,790,925) includes count question resolution corrections processed through August 1997. It generally does not include adjustments for census coverage errors. However, it includes adjustments estimated for the 1995 Test Census in various localities in California, New Jersey, and Louisiana, and the 1998 census dress rehearsals in localities in California and Wisconsin. These adjustments amounted to a total of 81,052 persons. [2] The April 1, 2000 population estimates base reflects changes to the Census 2000 population from the Count Question Resolution program. [3] The April 1, 2010 population estimates base reflects changes to the Census 2010 population from geographic program revisions. It does not reflect changes from the Count Question Resolution program.

Source: U.S. Census Bureau, "Table US-EST90INT-04—Intercensal Estimates of the United States Resident Population by Age Groups and Sex, 1990–2000: Selected Months," September 2002; "Table 1. Annual Estimates of the Resident Population by Sex and Five-Year Age Group for the United States: April 1, 2010 to July 1, 2011 (NC-EST2011-01);" and "Table 2. Annual Estimates of the Resident Population for Selected Age Groups by Sex for the United States: April 1, 2010 to July 1, 2011 (NC-EST2011-02)," May 2012, <http://www.census.gov/popest/data/national/asrh/2011/index.html>.

Table 8. Intercensal Resident Population by Age: 2001 to 2009

[In thousands, except as indicated (284,969 represents 284,969,000). As of July 1. Excludes Armed Forces overseas. For definition of median, see Guide to Tabular Presentation]

Age	2001	2002	2003	2004	2005	2006	2007	2008	2009
Total....................	284,969	287,625	290,108	292,805	295,517	298,380	301,231	304,094	306,772
Under 5 years...........	19,298	19,429	19,592	19,786	19,917	19,939	20,126	20,271	20,245
5 to 9 years.............	20,173	19,872	19,621	19,454	19,389	19,545	19,715	19,930	20,182
10 to 14 years..........	20,979	21,261	21,415	21,412	21,213	21,033	20,841	20,707	20,661
15 to 19 years..........	20,456	20,610	20,797	21,103	21,486	21,808	22,068	22,211	22,193
20 to 24 years..........	19,757	20,244	20,592	20,846	20,960	21,036	21,078	21,181	21,384
25 to 29 years..........	18,819	18,691	18,772	19,107	19,535	20,110	20,543	20,903	21,078
30 to 34 years..........	20,652	20,658	20,472	20,160	19,724	19,285	19,171	19,305	19,645
35 to 39 years..........	22,236	21,751	21,264	20,875	20,799	20,941	20,964	20,817	20,508
40 to 44 years..........	22,816	22,889	22,890	22,926	22,707	22,303	21,832	21,375	20,980
45 to 49 years..........	20,699	21,252	21,723	22,065	22,417	22,715	22,800	22,821	22,862
50 to 54 years..........	18,687	18,740	19,097	19,565	20,079	20,571	21,140	21,639	22,005
55 to 59 years..........	13,969	15,143	15,815	16,607	17,503	18,397	18,455	18,815	19,281
60 to 64 years..........	11,136	11,560	12,194	12,698	13,138	13,533	14,674	15,342	16,125
65 to 74 years..........	18,384	18,389	18,501	18,668	18,882	19,203	19,699	20,506	21,233
75 to 84 years..........	12,594	12,765	12,896	12,990	13,075	13,095	13,087	13,076	13,023
85 years and over.......	4,312	4,369	4,466	4,546	4,693	4,866	5,040	5,196	5,367
5 to 13 years............	37,093	37,001	36,814	36,458	36,248	36,269	36,296	36,438	36,657
14 to 17 years..........	16,280	16,506	16,694	17,054	17,358	17,549	17,597	17,395	17,232
18 to 24 years..........	27,993	28,481	28,917	29,302	29,442	29,603	29,808	30,194	30,530
18 years and over.......	212,298	214,689	217,007	219,508	221,993	224,622	227,212	229,989	232,637
55 years and over.......	60,396	62,226	63,872	65,509	67,291	69,094	70,954	72,935	75,029
65 years and over.......	35,290	35,522	35,864	36,203	36,650	37,164	37,826	38,778	39,623
75 years and over.......	16,906	17,134	17,363	17,536	17,768	17,961	18,127	18,272	18,390
Median age (years).....	35.6	35.8	35.9	36.1	36.3	36.5	36.7	36.9	37.1

Source: U.S. Census Bureau, "Table 1. Intercensal Estimates of the Resident Population by Sex and Age for the United States: April 1, 2000 to July 1, 2010 (US-EST00INT-01)," September 2011, <http://www.census.gov/popest/data/intercensal/national/nat2010.html>.

Table 9. Resident Population Projections by Sex and Age: 2015 to 2050

[In thousands, except as indicated (325,540 represents 325,540,000). As of July 1. Projections are based on assumptions about future births, deaths, and net international migration. Data do not reflect results of the 2010 Census. More information on methodology and assumptions is available at <http://www.census.gov/population/www/projections/methodstatement.html>]

Age	2015 Total	2015 Male	2015 Female	2020	2025	2030	2035	2040	2045	2050	Pct. dist. 2015	Pct. dist. 2020	Pct. dist. 2025	Pct. dist. 2050
Total	325,540	160,424	165,116	341,387	357,452	373,504	389,531	405,655	422,059	439,010	100.0	100.0	100.0	100.0
Under 5 years	22,076	11,278	10,798	22,846	23,484	24,161	25,056	26,117	27,171	28,148	6.8	6.7	6.6	6.4
5 to 9 years	21,707	11,074	10,633	22,732	23,548	24,232	24,953	25,893	26,998	28,096	6.7	6.7	6.6	6.4
10 to 14 years	21,658	11,049	10,609	22,571	23,677	24,567	25,319	26,105	27,108	28,274	6.7	6.6	6.6	6.4
15 to 19 years	21,209	10,844	10,365	22,554	23,545	24,723	25,682	26,501	27,354	28,422	6.5	6.6	6.5	6.5
20 to 24 years	22,342	11,378	10,963	21,799	23,168	24,191	24,855	26,102	27,272	28,171	6.9	6.4	6.5	6.4
25 to 29 years	22,400	11,353	11,048	22,949	22,417	23,804	25,408	26,408	27,138	28,039	6.9	6.7	6.3	6.4
30 to 34 years	22,099	11,182	10,917	23,112	23,699	23,216	24,647	25,745	27,040	28,126	6.8	6.8	6.6	6.4
35 to 39 years	20,841	10,506	10,335	22,586	23,645	24,279	23,848	25,321	26,462	27,799	6.4	6.6	6.6	6.3
40 to 44 years	20,460	10,247	10,214	21,078	22,851	23,944	24,612	24,759	25,726	26,897	6.3	6.2	6.4	6.1
45 to 49 years	21,001	10,447	10,553	20,502	21,154	22,943	24,061	24,025	24,411	25,933	6.5	6.0	5.9	5.9
50 to 54 years	22,367	10,977	11,390	20,852	20,404	21,087	22,884	24,621	24,750	24,445	6.9	6.1	5.7	5.6
55 to 59 years	21,682	10,524	11,158	21,994	20,575	20,186	20,903	23,867	23,867	24,621	6.7	6.4	5.8	5.6
60 to 64 years	18,861	9,023	9,838	21,009	21,377	20,080	19,760	22,703	22,305	23,490	5.8	6.2	6.0	5.4
65 to 69 years	15,812	7,449	8,364	17,861	19,957	20,381	19,230	20,513	19,776	21,543	4.9	5.2	5.6	4.9
70 to 74 years	11,155	5,109	6,046	14,452	16,399	18,404	18,879	18,989	17,754	18,570	3.4	4.2	4.6	4.2
75 to 79 years	7,901	3,480	4,421	9,656	12,598	14,390	16,249	17,906	16,016	15,964	2.4	2.8	3.5	3.6
80 to 84 years	5,676	2,342	3,334	6,239	7,715	10,173	11,735	16,771	13,925	13,429	1.7	1.8	2.2	3.1
85 to 89 years	3,786	1,409	2,376	3,817	4,278	5,383	7,215	13,375	9,767	10,303	1.2	1.1	1.2	2.3
90 to 94 years	1,856	591	1,265	1,976	2,047	2,360	3,044	8,450	5,007	5,909	0.6	0.6	0.6	1.3
95 to 99 years	546	142	404	669	739	795	952	4,180	1,803	2,229	0.2	0.2	0.2	0.5
100 years and over	105	21	84	135	175	208	239	298	409	601	(Z)	(Z)	(Z)	0.1
5 to 13 years	39,011	19,900	19,111	40,792	42,490	43,858	45,170	46,743	48,664	50,697	12.0	11.9	11.9	11.5
14 to 17 years	17,019	8,699	8,320	18,048	18,892	19,796	20,496	21,126	21,834	22,728	5.2	5.3	5.3	5.2
18 to 24 years	30,885	15,746	15,139	30,817	32,555	34,059	35,695	37,038	38,234	39,538	9.5	9.0	9.1	9.0
16 years and over	255,864	124,858	131,006	268,722	282,014	295,595	309,084	322,265	335,328	348,811	78.6	78.7	78.9	79.5
18 years and over	247,434	120,547	126,887	259,702	272,585	285,688	298,809	311,669	324,389	337,437	76.0	76.1	76.3	76.9
16 to 64 years	209,027	104,316	104,711	213,917	218,107	223,503	231,540	241,027	250,872	260,264	64.2	62.7	61.0	59.3
55 years and over	87,381	40,090	47,291	97,807	105,860	112,358	118,206	124,455	130,628	136,658	26.8	28.6	29.6	31.1
65 years and over	46,837	20,542	26,295	54,804	63,907	72,092	77,543	81,238	84,456	88,547	14.4	16.1	17.9	20.2
75 years and over	19,870	7,985	11,885	22,492	27,551	33,308	39,435	44,343	46,926	48,434	6.1	6.6	7.7	11.0
85 years and over	6,292	2,163	4,130	6,597	7,239	8,745	11,450	14,198	16,985	19,041	1.9	1.9	2.0	4.3
Median age (years) [1]	37.1	35.9	38.4	37.7	38.2	38.7	39.0	38.9	38.9	39.0	(X)	(X)	(X)	(X)

X Not applicable. Z Less than 0.05 percent. [1] For definition of median, see Guide to Tabular Presentation.

Source: U.S. Census Bureau, "2008 National Population Projections," August 2008, <http://www.census.gov/population/www/projections/2008projections.html>.

Table 10. Resident Population by Race, Hispanic Origin, and Age: 2010 and 2011

[In thousands, except as indicated (308,746 represents 308,746,000). 2010, as of April 1, and 2011, as of July 1]

Age	Total 2010[1]	Total 2011	White alone 2010[1]	White alone 2011	Black or African American alone 2010[1]	Black or African American alone 2011	American Indian, Alaska Native alone 2010[1]	American Indian, Alaska Native alone 2011	Asian alone 2010[1]	Asian alone 2011	Native Hawaiian, Other Pacific Islander alone 2010[1]	Native Hawaiian, Other Pacific Islander alone 2011	Two or more races 2010[1]	Two or more races 2011	Hispanic origin[2] 2010[1]	Hispanic origin[2] 2011	Not Hispanic White alone 2010[1]	Not Hispanic White alone 2011
Total	308,746	311,592	241,937	243,470	40,251	40,751	3,740	3,815	15,160	15,578	675	692	6,984	7,285	50,478	52,045	197,319	197,511
Under 5 years	20,201	20,162	14,691	14,576	3,055	3,065	330	331	948	962	59	60	1,119	1,169	5,114	5,192	10,307	10,141
5 to 9 years	20,349	20,334	15,044	14,988	3,013	2,997	321	324	972	986	56	57	944	983	4,791	4,910	10,885	10,734
10 to 14 years	20,677	20,705	15,399	15,375	3,154	3,151	318	320	922	945	54	55	829	860	4,525	4,628	11,449	11,339
15 to 19 years	22,040	21,644	16,346	16,076	3,573	3,451	340	333	999	977	60	58	723	749	4,532	4,582	12,387	12,065
20 to 24 years	21,586	22,154	16,246	16,552	3,240	3,423	319	330	1,149	1,172	66	67	566	609	4,322	4,478	12,467	12,640
25 to 29 years	21,102	21,280	16,061	16,162	2,911	2,948	300	304	1,279	1,299	64	65	488	501	4,310	4,368	12,268	12,321
30 to 34 years	19,962	20,511	15,184	15,588	2,743	2,826	275	284	1,284	1,312	56	59	420	442	4,124	4,237	11,534	11,844
35 to 39 years	20,180	19,594	15,473	14,940	2,706	2,639	261	260	1,334	1,342	49	50	357	363	3,856	3,933	12,018	11,423
40 to 44 years	20,891	21,034	16,341	16,398	2,752	2,757	251	255	1,188	1,248	45	47	314	329	3,442	3,575	13,250	13,189
45 to 49 years	22,709	22,158	18,103	17,557	2,901	2,870	255	254	1,105	1,130	43	44	302	302	3,022	3,137	15,387	14,739
50 to 54 years	22,298	22,560	18,008	18,184	2,753	2,799	228	236	1,004	1,025	37	39	268	278	2,441	2,579	15,813	15,866
55 to 59 years	19,665	20,256	16,143	16,564	2,246	2,344	177	189	863	907	28	30	207	221	1,841	1,975	14,476	14,781
60 to 64 years	16,818	17,807	14,089	14,852	1,715	1,859	134	146	703	758	21	23	156	169	1,372	1,483	12,839	13,505
65 to 69 years	12,435	12,874	10,564	10,907	1,181	1,227	89	95	483	518	14	15	105	112	949	1,019	9,693	9,975
70 to 74 years	9,278	9,608	7,910	8,171	865	900	60	65	361	384	9	10	72	77	700	736	7,265	7,494
75 to 79 years	7,318	7,389	6,341	6,360	625	655	39	43	255	272	6	7	51	53	511	535	5,867	5,865
80 to 84 years	5,743	5,787	5,079	5,097	430	439	25	27	171	184	4	4	35	36	351	375	4,748	4,748
85 to 89 years	3,620	3,706	3,244	3,307	248	258	13	14	94	104	2	2	20	21	185	205	3,071	3,117
90 to 94 years	1,448	1,571	1,300	1,410	101	106	5	5	35	41	1	1	7	8	65	75	1,240	1,341
95 to 99 years	371	398	328	353	31	30	1	1	9	11	0	0	2	2	18	20	312	335
100 years and over	53	62	45	52	7	7	0	0	1	1	0	0	0	1	2	4	42	49
5 to 13 years	36,860	36,910	27,331	27,286	5,530	5,518	576	581	1,707	1,743	99	101	1,617	1,681	8,426	8,639	20,002	19,782
14 to 17 years	17,120	16,862	12,724	12,552	2,732	2,624	263	257	756	761	45	44	601	623	3,591	3,619	9,581	9,386
18 to 24 years	30,672	31,065	22,980	23,152	4,718	4,879	459	469	1,579	1,576	92	91	844	897	6,154	6,340	17,605	17,609
16 years and over	243,276	246,234	193,648	195,429	30,358	30,906	2,706	2,777	12,130	12,495	495	510	3,939	4,117	35,153	36,419	162,303	162,978
18 years and over	234,564	237,658	187,192	189,056	28,934	29,543	2,571	2,646	11,749	12,112	471	487	3,647	3,813	33,347	34,595	157,429	158,202
16 to 64 years	203,008	204,840	158,838	159,770	26,870	27,285	2,474	2,527	10,720	10,979	459	471	3,646	3,808	32,372	33,450	130,062	130,052
55 years and over	76,751	79,456	65,042	67,075	7,449	7,825	543	584	2,976	3,180	85	92	656	700	5,995	6,427	59,556	61,211
65 years and over	40,268	41,394	34,810	35,658	3,487	3,622	232	250	1,410	1,515	36	39	293	310	2,782	2,969	32,241	32,926
75 years and over	18,555	18,912	16,335	16,580	1,442	1,494	83	91	566	613	13	14	116	121	1,133	1,213	15,282	15,456
85 years and over	5,493	5,737	4,916	5,123	386	400	19	21	140	157	3	3	30	32	271	304	4,664	4,843
Median age (years)[3]	37.2	37.3	(NA)	39.2	(NA)	32.3	(NA)	29.4	(NA)	35.5	(NA)	28.8	(NA)	19.2	(NA)	27.6	(NA)	42.3

NA Not available. [1] The April 1, 2010 population estimates base reflects changes to the Census 2010 population from geographic program revisions. It does not reflect changes from the Count Question Resolution program. [2] Hispanic origin is considered an ethnicity, not a race. Hispanics may be of any race. [3] For definition of median, see Guide to Tabular Presentation.

Source: U.S. Census Bureau, Population Division, "2011 Monthly National Population Estimates," May 2012, <http://www.census.gov/popest/data/national/asrh/2011/2011-nat-detail.html>.

Table 11. Resident Population by Race, Hispanic Origin, and Single Years of Age: 2011

[In thousands, except as indicated (311,592 represents 311,592,000). As of July 1. For derivation of estimates, see text, this section]

Age	Total	Race						Hispanic origin [1]	Non-Hispanic White alone
		White alone	Black or African American alone	American Indian, Alaska Native alone	Asian alone	Native Hawaiian and Other Pacific Islander alone	Two or more races		
Total.....................	311,592	243,470	40,751	3,815	15,578	692	7,285	52,045	197,511
Under 5 years old........	20,162	14,576	3,065	331	962	60	1,169	5,192	10,141
Under 1 year old........	3,997	2,872	608	66	188	12	251	1,050	1,981
1 year old...............	3,969	2,858	605	65	191	12	238	1,034	1,978
2 years old..............	3,972	2,874	604	64	189	12	228	1,015	2,007
3 years old..............	4,102	2,972	624	67	198	12	229	1,047	2,074
4 years old..............	4,122	3,000	624	68	197	12	222	1,047	2,101
5 to 9 years old..........	20,334	14,988	2,997	324	986	57	983	4,910	10,734
5 years old..............	4,088	2,993	608	67	196	12	212	1,024	2,110
6 years old..............	4,075	2,993	599	66	200	12	204	1,001	2,129
7 years old..............	4,083	3,014	595	65	200	11	197	979	2,166
8 years old..............	4,053	2,999	592	64	199	11	188	960	2,165
9 years old..............	4,035	2,988	602	63	190	11	181	946	2,165
10 to 14 years old........	20,705	15,375	3,151	320	945	55	860	4,628	11,339
10 years old.............	4,134	3,059	623	64	196	11	181	952	2,230
11 years old.............	4,196	3,107	642	65	192	11	178	951	2,278
12 years old.............	4,124	3,068	626	64	183	11	172	919	2,267
13 years old.............	4,122	3,065	630	64	186	11	167	906	2,274
14 years old.............	4,129	3,076	630	63	188	11	161	899	2,291
15 to 19 years old.......	21,644	16,076	3,451	333	977	58	749	4,582	12,065
15 years old.............	4,157	3,104	631	63	190	11	157	896	2,320
16 years old.............	4,245	3,161	665	65	190	11	154	907	2,367
17 years old.............	4,331	3,211	698	66	193	11	151	916	2,408
18 years old.............	4,396	3,255	720	68	196	12	145	922	2,447
19 years old.............	4,515	3,345	736	71	207	12	143	940	2,522
20 to 24 years old.......	22,154	16,552	3,423	330	1,172	67	609	4,478	12,640
20 years old.............	4,596	3,404	745	70	225	13	138	933	2,591
21 years old.............	4,592	3,411	734	69	235	14	130	924	2,605
22 years old.............	4,411	3,287	686	65	239	13	120	879	2,520
23 years old.............	4,312	3,243	642	64	237	13	113	875	2,476
24 years old.............	4,243	3,207	616	62	237	13	108	866	2,447
25 to 29 years old.......	21,280	16,162	2,948	304	1,299	65	501	4,368	12,321
25 years old.............	4,268	3,238	605	62	245	13	104	874	2,471
26 years old.............	4,311	3,276	602	62	256	13	102	882	2,501
27 years old.............	4,181	3,175	576	60	260	13	98	857	2,421
28 years old.............	4,256	3,233	583	61	267	13	99	875	2,464
29 years old.............	4,264	3,240	583	60	272	13	97	879	2,465
30 to 34 years old.......	20,511	15,588	2,826	284	1,312	59	442	4,237	11,844
30 years old.............	4,225	3,215	579	59	265	12	95	869	2,449
31 years old.............	4,317	3,272	604	60	273	13	95	896	2,481
32 years old.............	4,053	3,074	563	56	261	12	87	828	2,343
33 years old.............	3,976	3,028	543	55	255	11	84	825	2,297
34 years old.............	3,940	2,999	537	54	258	11	81	819	2,273
35 to 39 years old.......	19,594	14,940	2,639	260	1,342	50	363	3,933	11,423
35 years old.............	3,828	2,911	516	52	261	10	77	805	2,195
36 years old.............	3,953	3,012	531	53	272	10	74	813	2,285
37 years old.............	3,833	2,921	513	51	268	10	71	780	2,222
38 years old.............	3,899	2,967	529	51	271	10	70	770	2,277
39 years old.............	4,082	3,130	549	52	271	10	70	764	2,445
40 to 44 years old.......	21,034	16,398	2,757	255	1,248	47	329	3,575	13,189
40 years old.............	4,324	3,348	574	53	266	10	72	760	2,667
41 years old.............	4,384	3,407	575	53	268	10	71	757	2,728
42 years old.............	4,160	3,249	534	50	252	9	65	706	2,615
43 years old.............	4,078	3,181	538	49	240	9	62	689	2,562
44 years old.............	4,088	3,212	537	49	222	9	60	662	2,617
45 to 49 years old.......	22,158	17,557	2,870	254	1,130	44	302	3,137	14,739
45 years old.............	4,171	3,270	558	50	225	9	59	655	2,682
46 years old.............	4,429	3,490	586	52	230	9	61	661	2,897
47 years old.............	4,518	3,581	583	52	232	9	61	634	3,011
48 years old.............	4,521	3,595	575	51	231	9	61	605	3,051
49 years old.............	4,519	3,621	569	50	211	9	60	582	3,098
50 to 54 years old.......	22,560	18,184	2,799	236	1,025	39	278	2,579	15,866
50 years old.............	4,582	3,687	572	49	207	8	59	559	3,184
51 years old.............	4,626	3,706	586	50	217	8	59	560	3,203
52 years old.............	4,478	3,607	560	47	202	8	55	511	3,148
53 years old.............	4,458	3,606	543	45	203	7	54	483	3,172
54 years old.............	4,416	3,578	538	44	196	7	52	466	3,159
55 to 59 years old.......	20,256	16,564	2,344	189	907	30	221	1,975	14,781
55 years old.............	4,264	3,456	515	42	195	7	50	444	3,056
56 years old.............	4,233	3,443	502	41	194	6	48	430	3,054
57 years old.............	4,066	3,327	470	38	181	6	44	394	2,971
58 years old.............	3,919	3,223	440	35	173	6	42	367	2,891
59 years old.............	3,774	3,116	417	33	164	5	38	340	2,808

See footnotes at end of table.

Table 11. Resident Population by Race, Hispanic Origin, and Single Years of Age: 2011-Continued.

See headnote on page 14.

Age	Total	Race						Hispanic origin [1]	Non-Hispanic White alone
		White alone	Black or African American alone	American Indian, Alaska Native alone	Asian alone	Native Hawaiian and Other Pacific Islander alone	Two or more races		
60 to 64 years old........	17,807	14,852	1,859	146	758	23	169	1,483	13,505
60 years old............	3,665	3,022	411	32	158	5	37	329	2,724
61 years old............	3,584	2,948	399	31	166	5	35	317	2,661
62 years old............	3,487	2,898	370	29	153	5	33	292	2,633
63 years old............	3,459	2,902	350	27	145	4	32	280	2,647
64 years old............	3,611	3,083	330	27	135	4	32	266	2,840
65 to 69 years old........	12,874	10,907	1,227	95	518	15	112	1,019	9,975
65 years old............	2,673	2,244	265	21	115	4	25	231	2,033
66 years old............	2,643	2,222	262	20	111	3	24	220	2,021
67 years old............	2,585	2,192	245	19	103	3	22	202	2,007
68 years old............	2,652	2,274	240	18	96	3	22	193	2,098
69 years old............	2,321	1,975	215	16	92	2	19	174	1,816
70 to 74 years old........	9,608	8,171	900	65	384	10	77	736	7,494
70 years old............	2,130	1,807	202	15	86	2	18	163	1,657
71 years old............	2,022	1,709	196	14	84	2	17	158	1,564
72 years old............	1,912	1,629	177	13	76	2	15	147	1,494
73 years old............	1,839	1,570	169	12	72	2	14	139	1,442
74 years old............	1,705	1,456	156	11	67	2	13	129	1,337
75 to 79 years old........	7,389	6,360	655	43	272	7	53	535	5,865
75 years old............	1,638	1,400	151	10	63	2	12	123	1,287
76 years old............	1,581	1,357	143	10	59	1	12	118	1,248
77 years old............	1,431	1,229	128	8	53	1	10	104	1,133
78 years old............	1,395	1,204	121	8	51	1	10	97	1,113
79 years old............	1,344	1,170	111	7	46	1	9	93	1,084
80 to 84 years old........	5,787	5,097	439	27	184	4	36	375	4,748
80 years old............	1,293	1,133	101	6	43	1	8	88	1,051
81 years old............	1,253	1,098	98	6	42	1	8	85	1,019
82 years old............	1,145	1,009	87	5	36	1	7	74	940
83 years old............	1,087	962	80	5	33	1	7	68	899
84 years old............	1,008	894	73	4	30	1	6	60	838
85 to 89 years old........	3,706	3,307	258	14	104	2	21	205	3,117
90 to 94 years old........	1,571	1,410	106	5	41	1	8	75	1,341
95 to 99 years old........	398	353	30	1	11	–	2	20	335
100 years old and over...	62	52	7	–	2	–	1	4	49
Median age (years) [2]....	37.3	39.2	32.3	29.4	35.5	28.8	19.2	27.6	42.3

[1] Hispanic origin is considered an ethnicity, not a race. Hispanics may be of any race. [2] For definition of median, see Guide to Tabular Presentation.

Source: U.S. Census Bureau, Population Division, "National Population Estimates for the 2010s, Monthly Postcensal Resident Population by Single Year of Age, Sex, Race, and Hispanic Origin," May 2012, <http://www.census.gov/popest/data/national/asrh/2011/2011-nat-res. html>. and "Table 6 Median Age of the Resident Population by Race and Hispanic Origin for the United States and States: July 1, 2011 (SC-EST2011-06)," May 2012, <http://www.census.gov/popest/data/state/asrh/2011/index.html>.

Table 12. Resident Population Projections by Race, Hispanic-Origin Status, and Age: 2015

[In thousands, except as indicated (325,540 represents 325,540,000). As of July 1. Projections are based on assumptions about future births, deaths, and net international migration. Data do not reflect results of the 2010 Census. More information on methodology and assumptions is available at <http://www.census.gov/population/www/projections/methodstatement08.html>]

Age group	Total	White alone	Black or African American alone	American Indian /Alaska Native alone	Asian alone	Native Hawaiian /Other Pacific Islander alone	Two or more races	Hispanic origin [1]	Not Hispanic White alone
Total	325,540	256,306	42,137	3,472	16,527	662	6,435	57,711	203,208
Under 5 years	22,076	16,563	3,191	311	1,004	56	951	5,622	11,487
5 to 9 years	21,707	16,412	3,084	292	1,018	55	845	5,452	11,465
10 to 14 years	21,658	16,467	3,080	271	1,034	52	754	5,401	11,540
15 to 19 years	21,209	16,143	3,096	252	1,030	48	639	5,040	11,524
20 to 24 years	22,342	16,976	3,449	273	1,047	50	546	4,873	12,499
25 to 29 years	22,400	17,125	3,374	279	1,106	49	467	4,311	13,160
30 to 34 years	22,099	16,915	3,158	264	1,305	52	405	4,166	13,068
35 to 39 years	20,841	15,946	2,872	230	1,413	54	325	4,236	12,023
40 to 44 years	20,460	15,763	2,690	211	1,476	48	272	3,979	12,062
45 to 49 years	21,001	16,561	2,679	204	1,272	43	242	3,491	13,316
50 to 54 years	22,367	17,998	2,765	214	1,115	40	234	3,036	15,177
55 to 59 years	21,682	17,691	2,545	196	1,001	34	216	2,450	15,417
60 to 64 years	18,861	15,582	2,042	160	875	27	176	1,867	13,849
65 to 69 years	15,812	13,285	1,528	123	717	21	138	1,387	11,994
70 to 74 years	11,155	9,511	990	80	469	14	91	920	8,650
75 to 79 years	7,901	6,780	690	53	310	9	60	637	6,183
80 to 84 years	5,676	4,957	458	32	186	5	38	424	4,558
85 to 89 years	3,786	3,374	271	17	99	3	22	257	3,131
90 to 94 years	1,856	1,674	125	7	39	1	10	117	1,564
95 to 99 years	546	492	40	2	9	–	3	35	459
100 years and over	105	92	10	–	1	–	1	9	83
5 to 13 years	39,011	29,577	5,529	511	1,844	97	1,454	9,786	20,678
14 to 17 years	17,019	12,937	2,478	204	818	39	543	4,112	9,175
18 to 24 years	30,885	23,483	4,703	374	1,468	70	787	6,869	17,173
16 years and over	255,864	203,643	32,171	2,547	13,267	489	3,747	40,202	166,441
18 years and over	247,434	197,229	30,940	2,446	12,861	470	3,487	38,192	161,868
16 to 64 years	209,027	163,478	28,059	2,232	11,437	436	3,384	36,416	129,819
55 years and over	87,381	73,437	8,698	671	3,706	114	755	8,104	55,888
65 years and over	46,837	40,164	4,111	314	1,831	53	363	3,786	36,623
75 years and over	19,870	17,368	1,594	111	645	18	133	1,479	15,978
85 years and over	6,292	5,632	445	26	149	4	36	418	5,238
Median age (years) [2]	37.1	38.6	32.8	31.1	37.5	32.0	20.2	27.8	42.1

– Represents or rounds to zero. [1] Hispanic origin is considered an ethnicity, not a race. Hispanics may be of any race. [2] For definition of median, see Guide to Tabular Presentation.

Source: U.S. Census Bureau, Population Division, "2008 National Population Projections," August 2008, <http://www.census.gov/population/www/projections/2008projections.html>.

Table 13. Resident Population—States: 1990 to 2011

[In thousands (248,791 represents 248,791,000). 1990, 2000, and 2010 data as of April 1, data for other years of July 1. Insofar as possible, population shown for all years is that of present area of state. See Appendix III]

State	1990, estimates base [1]	2000, estimates base [2]	2005	2006	2007	2008	2009	2010, estimates base [3]	2011
United States..........	**248,791**	**281,425**	**295,517**	**298,380**	**301,231**	**304,094**	**306,772**	**308,746**	**311,592**
Alabama..................	4,040	4,447	4,570	4,629	4,673	4,718	4,758	4,780	4,803
Alaska....................	550	627	667	675	680	687	699	710	723
Arizona...................	3,665	5,130	5,839	6,029	6,168	6,280	6,343	6,392	6,483
Arkansas.................	2,351	2,673	2,781	2,822	2,849	2,875	2,897	2,916	2,938
California................	29,811	33,872	35,828	36,021	36,250	36,604	36,961	37,254	37,692
Colorado.................	3,294	4,302	4,632	4,720	4,804	4,890	4,972	5,029	5,117
Connecticut.............	3,287	3,406	3,507	3,517	3,527	3,546	3,562	3,574	3,581
Delaware.................	666	784	845	859	872	884	892	898	907
District of Columbia.....	607	572	567	571	574	580	592	602	618
Florida...................	12,938	15,983	17,842	18,167	18,368	18,527	18,653	18,801	19,058
Georgia..................	6,478	8,187	8,926	9,156	9,350	9,505	9,621	9,688	9,815
Hawaii...................	1,108	1,211	1,293	1,310	1,316	1,332	1,347	1,360	1,375
Idaho....................	1,007	1,294	1,428	1,469	1,505	1,534	1,554	1,568	1,585
Illinois...................	11,431	12,420	12,610	12,644	12,696	12,747	12,797	12,831	12,869
Indiana..................	5,544	6,081	6,279	6,333	6,380	6,425	6,459	6,484	6,517
Iowa.....................	2,777	2,927	2,964	2,983	2,999	3,017	3,033	3,046	3,062
Kansas...................	2,478	2,689	2,745	2,763	2,784	2,808	2,833	2,853	2,871
Kentucky.................	3,687	4,042	4,183	4,219	4,257	4,290	4,317	4,339	4,369
Louisiana................	4,222	4,469	4,577	4,303	4,376	4,436	4,492	4,533	4,575
Maine....................	1,228	1,275	1,319	1,324	1,327	1,331	1,330	1,328	1,328
Maryland.................	4,781	5,297	5,592	5,627	5,653	5,685	5,730	5,774	5,828
Massachusetts...........	6,016	6,349	6,403	6,410	6,432	6,469	6,518	6,548	6,588
Michigan.................	9,295	9,939	10,051	10,036	10,001	9,947	9,902	9,884	9,876
Minnesota...............	4,376	4,920	5,120	5,164	5,207	5,247	5,281	5,304	5,345
Mississippi..............	2,575	2,845	2,906	2,905	2,928	2,948	2,959	2,967	2,979
Missouri.................	5,117	5,597	5,790	5,843	5,888	5,924	5,961	5,989	6,011
Montana.................	799	902	940	953	965	976	984	989	998
Nebraska................	1,578	1,711	1,761	1,773	1,783	1,796	1,813	1,826	1,843
Nevada..................	1,202	1,998	2,432	2,523	2,601	2,654	2,685	2,701	2,723
New Hampshire..........	1,109	1,236	1,298	1,308	1,313	1,316	1,316	1,316	1,318
New Jersey..............	7,748	8,415	8,652	8,662	8,678	8,711	8,756	8,792	8,821
New Mexico..............	1,515	1,819	1,932	1,962	1,990	2,011	2,037	2,059	2,082
New York................	17,991	18,977	19,133	19,105	19,132	19,212	19,307	19,378	19,465
North Carolina...........	6,632	8,046	8,705	8,917	9,118	9,309	9,450	9,535	9,656
North Dakota............	639	642	646	649	653	658	665	673	684
Ohio.....................	10,847	11,353	11,463	11,481	11,500	11,515	11,529	11,537	11,545
Oklahoma................	3,146	3,450	3,549	3,594	3,634	3,669	3,718	3,751	3,792
Oregon..................	2,842	3,422	3,613	3,671	3,722	3,769	3,809	3,831	3,872
Pennsylvania............	11,883	12,281	12,450	12,511	12,564	12,612	12,667	12,702	12,743
Rhode Island............	1,003	1,048	1,068	1,063	1,057	1,055	1,054	1,053	1,051
South Carolina..........	3,486	4,012	4,270	4,358	4,444	4,529	4,590	4,625	4,679
South Dakota...........	696	755	775	783	792	799	807	814	824
Tennessee...............	4,877	5,689	5,991	6,089	6,176	6,247	6,306	6,346	6,403
Texas...................	16,986	20,851	22,778	23,360	23,832	24,309	24,802	25,146	25,675
Utah....................	1,723	2,233	2,458	2,526	2,598	2,663	2,723	2,764	2,817
Vermont.................	563	609	621	623	623	624	625	626	626
Virginia..................	6,189	7,079	7,577	7,674	7,751	7,833	7,926	8,001	8,097
Washington..............	4,867	5,894	6,257	6,371	6,462	6,562	6,667	6,725	6,830
West Virginia............	1,793	1,808	1,820	1,828	1,834	1,840	1,848	1,853	1,855
Wisconsin...............	4,892	5,364	5,546	5,578	5,611	5,641	5,669	5,687	5,712
Wyoming................	454	494	514	523	535	546	560	564	568

[1] The April 1, 1990, census counts include corrections processed through August 1997, results of special censuses and test censuses, and do not include adjustments for census coverage errors. [2] The April 1, 2000 population estimates base reflects changes to the Census 2000 population from the Count Question Resolution program, legal boundary updates, and other geographic program revisions. [3] The April 1, 2010 population estimates base reflects changes to the Census 2010 population from geographic program revisions. It does not reflect changes from the Count Question Resolution program.

Source: U.S. Census Bureau,"Table CO-EST2001-12-00 - Time Series of Intercensal State Population Estimates: April 1, 1990 to April 1, 2000," April 2002, <http://www.census.gov/popest/data/intercensal/st-co/files/CO-EST2001-12-00.pdf>; "Table 1. Intercensal Estimates of the Resident Population for the United States, Regions, States, and Puerto Rico: April 1, 2000 to July 1, 2010 (ST-EST00INT-01)," September 2011, <http://www.census.gov/popest/data/intercensal/state/state2010.html> and "Table 1. Annual Estimates of the Population for the United States, Regions, States, and Puerto Rico: April 1, 2010 to July 1, 2011 (NST-EST2011-01)," December 2011, <http://www.census.gov/popest/data/state/totals/2011/index.html>.

Table 14. State Population—Rank, Percent Change, and Population Density: 1990 to 2011

[As of April 1, except 2011 as of July 1. Insofar as possible, population shown for all years is that of present area of state. For area figures of states, see Table 365. Minus sign (–) indicates decrease. See Appendix III]

State	Rank				Percent change			Population per square mile of land area [1]		
	1990	2000	2010	2011	1990–2000	2000–2010	2010–2011	2000	2010	2011
United States............	(X)	(X)	(X)	(X)	**13.1**	**9.7**	**0.9**	**79.7**	**87.4**	**88.2**
Alabama.....................	22	23	23	23	10.1	7.5	0.5	87.8	94.4	94.8
Alaska......................	49	48	47	47	14.0	13.3	1.8	1.1	1.2	1.3
Arizona.....................	24	20	16	16	40.0	24.6	1.4	45.2	56.3	57.1
Arkansas...................	33	33	32	32	13.7	9.1	0.8	51.4	56.0	56.5
California..................	1	1	1	1	13.8	10.0	1.2	217.4	239.1	242.0
Colorado...................	26	24	22	22	30.6	16.9	1.7	41.5	48.5	49.4
Connecticut................	27	29	29	29	3.6	4.9	0.2	703.3	738.1	739.5
Delaware...................	46	45	45	45	17.6	14.6	1.0	402.1	460.8	465.5
District of Columbia........	(X)	(X)	(X)	(X)	-5.7	5.2	2.7	9,370.6	9,856.5	10,122.8
Florida.....................	4	4	4	4	23.5	17.6	1.4	298.0	350.6	355.4
Georgia....................	11	10	9	9	26.4	18.3	1.3	142.3	168.4	170.7
Hawaii.....................	41	42	40	40	9.3	12.3	1.1	188.6	211.8	214.1
Idaho......................	42	39	39	39	28.5	21.1	1.1	15.7	19.0	19.2
Illinois....................	6	5	5	5	8.6	3.3	0.3	223.7	231.1	231.8
Indiana....................	14	14	15	15	9.7	6.6	0.5	169.7	181.0	181.9
Iowa.......................	30	30	30	30	5.4	4.1	0.5	52.4	54.5	54.8
Kansas.....................	32	32	33	33	8.5	6.1	0.6	32.9	34.9	35.1
Kentucky...................	23	25	26	26	9.6	7.4	0.7	102.4	109.9	110.7
Louisiana..................	21	22	25	25	5.9	1.4	0.9	103.4	104.9	105.9
Maine......................	38	40	41	41	3.8	4.2	(Z)	41.3	43.1	43.1
Maryland...................	19	19	19	19	10.8	9.0	0.9	545.6	594.8	600.4
Massachusetts.............	13	13	14	14	5.5	3.1	0.6	814.0	839.4	844.5
Michigan...................	8	8	8	8	6.9	-0.6	-0.1	175.8	174.8	174.7
Minnesota..................	20	21	21	21	12.4	7.8	0.8	61.8	66.6	67.1
Mississippi.................	31	31	31	31	10.5	4.3	0.4	60.6	63.2	63.5
Missouri...................	15	17	18	18	9.3	7.0	0.4	81.4	87.1	87.4
Montana...................	44	44	44	44	12.9	9.7	0.9	6.2	6.8	6.9
Nebraska..................	36	38	38	38	8.4	6.7	0.9	22.3	23.8	24.0
Nevada....................	39	35	35	35	66.3	35.1	0.8	18.2	24.6	24.8
New Hampshire.............	40	41	42	42	11.4	6.5	0.1	138.0	147.0	147.2
New Jersey.................	9	9	11	11	8.9	4.5	0.3	1,144.2	1,195.5	1,199.5
New Mexico................	37	36	36	36	20.1	13.2	1.1	15.0	17.0	17.2
New York..................	2	3	3	3	5.5	2.1	0.4	402.7	411.2	413.0
North Carolina.............	10	11	10	10	21.4	18.5	1.3	165.6	196.1	198.6
North Dakota...............	47	47	48	48	0.5	4.7	1.7	9.3	9.7	9.9
Ohio.......................	7	7	7	7	4.7	1.6	0.1	277.8	282.3	282.5
Oklahoma..................	28	27	28	28	9.7	8.7	1.1	50.3	54.7	55.3
Oregon....................	29	28	27	27	20.4	12.0	1.1	35.6	39.9	40.3
Pennsylvania...............	5	6	6	6	3.4	3.4	0.3	274.5	283.9	284.8
Rhode Island...............	43	43	43	43	4.5	0.4	-0.1	1,014.0	1,018.1	1,016.9
South Carolina.............	25	26	24	24	15.1	15.3	1.2	133.5	153.9	155.7
South Dakota..............	45	46	46	46	8.5	7.9	1.2	10.0	10.7	10.9
Tennessee.................	17	16	17	17	16.7	11.5	0.9	138.0	153.9	155.3
Texas.....................	3	2	2	2	22.8	20.6	2.1	79.8	96.3	98.3
Utah.......................	35	34	34	34	29.6	23.8	1.9	27.2	33.6	34.3
Vermont...................	48	49	49	49	8.2	2.8	0.1	66.1	67.9	68.0
Virginia....................	12	12	12	12	14.4	13.0	1.2	179.2	202.6	205.0
Washington................	18	15	13	13	21.1	14.1	1.6	88.7	101.2	102.8
West Virginia..............	34	37	37	37	0.8	2.5	0.1	75.2	77.1	77.2
Wisconsin..................	16	18	20	20	9.6	6.0	0.4	99.0	105.0	105.5
Wyoming..................	50	50	50	50	8.9	14.1	0.8	5.1	5.8	5.9

X Not applicable. [1] Persons per square mile were calculated on the basis of land area data from the 2010 census.

Source: U.S. Census Bureau, United States Summary: 2000 (PHC-3-1), <http://www.census.gov/prod/cen2000/phc3-us-pt1.pdf> and "Table 2. Cumulative Estimates of Resident Population Change for the United States, Regions, States, and Puerto Rico and Region and State Rankings April 1, 2010 to July 1, 2011 (NST-EST2011-02)," December 2011, <http://www.census.gov/popest/data/state/totals/2011/index.html>.

Table 15. State Resident Population—Components of Change: 2010 to 2011

[Covers period April 1, 2010 to July 1, 2011. Minus sign (–) indicates net decrease or net outflow]

State	Numeric population change [1]	Births	Deaths	Natural increase (births minus deaths)	Net migration Total	Net migration Inter-national [2]	Net migration Domestic
United States.............	2,846,379	4,998,000	3,045,912	1,952,088	894,291	894,291	(X)
Alabama...................	23,005	74,348	59,330	15,018	7,922	5,948	1,974
Alaska.....................	12,487	14,027	3,985	10,042	2,383	1,643	740
Arizona...................	90,492	108,787	57,063	51,724	38,891	25,741	13,150
Arkansas..................	22,058	47,374	35,237	12,137	9,853	4,129	5,724
California.................	437,956	631,242	291,912	339,330	98,740	164,445	-65,705
Colorado..................	87,600	82,666	38,473	44,193	42,899	11,704	31,195
Connecticut................	6,612	46,560	35,099	11,461	-4,634	12,214	-16,848
Delaware..................	9,201	13,946	9,531	4,415	4,802	2,455	2,347
District of Columbia........	16,273	11,235	5,871	5,364	10,794	2,460	8,334
Florida.....................	256,231	264,829	213,354	51,475	205,193	86,437	118,756
Georgia...................	127,550	166,852	87,328	79,524	47,182	29,456	17,726
Hawaii....................	14,509	23,101	11,971	11,130	3,496	5,816	-2,320
Idaho.....................	17,403	28,743	13,820	14,923	2,429	2,685	-256
Illinois....................	38,625	209,060	125,135	83,925	-45,403	34,055	-79,458
Indiana...................	33,122	106,018	70,621	35,397	-2,226	9,186	-11,412
Iowa......................	15,959	47,724	34,328	13,396	2,638	3,999	-1,361
Kansas....................	18,120	49,977	29,497	20,480	-2,365	5,563	-7,928
Kentucky..................	29,994	70,438	52,431	18,007	12,064	6,303	5,761
Louisiana.................	41,464	79,540	50,551	28,989	12,179	5,094	7,085
Maine.....................	-173	16,054	15,978	76	-181	819	-1,000
Maryland..................	54,737	91,097	54,169	36,928	17,934	20,928	-2,994
Massachusetts.............	39,907	91,957	65,313	26,644	13,684	24,570	-10,886
Michigan..................	-7,448	142,826	108,447	34,379	-42,018	15,216	-57,234
Minnesota.................	40,936	85,067	47,762	37,305	3,807	11,880	-8,073
Mississippi................	11,215	49,979	35,353	14,626	-3,513	3,159	-6,672
Missouri..................	21,761	94,510	67,711	26,799	-4,874	6,957	-11,831
Montana..................	8,784	14,884	10,469	4,415	4,403	515	3,888
Nebraska..................	16,300	32,307	18,240	14,067	2,299	3,276	-977
Nevada...................	22,771	45,934	24,116	21,818	948	12,061	-11,113
New Hampshire............	1,722	15,986	12,128	3,858	-2,081	1,564	-3,645
New Jersey................	29,261	129,618	85,256	44,362	-14,936	39,162	-54,098
New Mexico...............	23,044	35,620	19,396	16,224	6,761	4,559	2,202
New York..................	87,093	304,098	182,998	121,100	-33,232	80,525	-113,757
North Carolina.............	120,926	151,908	97,404	54,504	66,062	25,029	41,033
North Dakota..............	11,341	11,240	7,141	4,099	7,156	788	6,368
Ohio......................	8,449	176,295	134,426	41,869	-33,149	11,719	-44,868
Oklahoma.................	40,154	67,093	42,458	24,635	15,405	6,472	8,933
Oregon...................	40,785	57,969	39,153	18,816	22,134	8,498	13,636
Pennsylvania..............	40,507	179,565	155,957	23,608	17,746	18,867	-1,121
Rhode Island..............	-1,265	13,773	11,436	2,337	-3,586	2,687	-6,273
South Carolina.............	53,866	74,303	51,245	23,058	30,686	8,673	22,013
South Dakota..............	9,902	14,731	8,101	6,630	3,300	690	2,610
Tennessee................	57,243	100,612	73,507	27,105	30,203	9,875	20,328
Texas.....................	529,120	493,650	205,171	288,479	238,956	93,641	145,315
Utah......................	53,337	65,156	17,734	47,422	5,912	6,738	-826
Vermont..................	690	7,485	6,407	1,078	-339	502	-841
Virginia...................	95,574	127,114	72,880	54,234	41,156	25,618	15,538
Washington...............	105,498	108,600	60,198	48,402	57,054	21,888	35,166
West Virginia..............	2,368	25,769	27,020	-1,251	3,728	914	2,814
Wisconsin.................	24,781	86,923	57,446	29,477	-4,432	6,558	-10,990
Wyoming.................	4,532	9,410	5,355	4,055	461	610	-149

X Not applicable. [1] Total population change includes a residual. This residual represents the change in population that cannot be attributed to any specific demographic component. [2] Net international migration includes the international migration of both native and foreign-born populations. Specifically, it includes: (a) the net international migration of the foreign born, (b) the net migration between the United States and Puerto Rico, (c) the net migration of natives to and from the United States, and (d) the net movement of the Armed Forces population between the United States and overseas.

Source: U.S. Census Bureau, Population Division, "Table 4. Cumulative Estimates of the Components of Resident Population Change for the United States, Regions, States, and Puerto Rico: April 1, 2010 to July 1, 2011 (NST-EST2011-04)," December 2011, <http://www.census.gov/popest/data/state/totals/2011/index.html>.

Table 16. Resident Population by Age and State: 2011

[In thousands, except percent (311,592 represents 311,592,000). As of July 1]

State	Total	Under 5 years	5 to 14 years	15 to 24 years	25 to 34 years	35 to 44 years	45 to 54 years	55 to 64 years	65 to 74 years	75 to 84 years	85 years and over	Percent 65 years old and over
U.S......	311,592	20,162	41,039	43,798	41,790	40,628	44,718	38,062	22,482	13,175	5,737	13.3
AL........	4,803	304	627	681	615	608	685	610	380	215	78	14.0
AK........	723	55	103	108	107	92	110	91	38	15	5	8.1
AZ........	6,483	450	905	914	871	822	842	756	522	290	110	14.2
AR........	2,938	196	397	403	382	364	404	364	240	136	53	14.6
CA........	37,692	2,539	5,091	5,617	5,412	5,164	5,250	4,220	2,377	1,388	634	11.7
CO........	5,117	342	689	700	746	701	734	629	328	174	74	11.3
CT........	3,581	197	457	480	428	469	572	462	263	165	87	14.4
DE........	907	56	113	127	114	113	133	116	75	42	16	14.7
DC........	618	36	53	101	133	82	76	67	38	21	11	11.4
FL........	19,058	1,075	2,211	2,480	2,344	2,405	2,749	2,434	1,778	1,114	467	17.6
GA........	9,815	683	1,393	1,408	1,359	1,383	1,395	1,116	637	321	119	11.0
HI........	1,375	89	166	183	192	174	189	180	105	64	33	14.7
ID........	1,585	119	240	226	211	192	206	189	115	61	26	12.8
IL........	12,869	828	1,725	1,795	1,788	1,704	1,851	1,537	873	525	243	12.7
IN........	6,517	430	894	932	835	830	935	803	465	274	120	13.2
IA........	3,062	199	402	433	388	360	432	389	228	153	77	14.9
KS........	2,871	204	401	412	383	343	399	346	195	126	61	13.3
KY........	4,369	281	568	591	569	570	638	560	335	186	71	13.5
LA........	4,575	317	616	662	642	559	646	560	322	182	69	12.5
ME........	1,328	68	151	166	146	166	215	200	117	70	30	16.3
MD........	5,828	366	745	798	783	780	901	726	402	225	102	12.5
MA........	6,588	366	784	935	868	866	1,010	838	473	298	150	14.0
MI........	9,876	584	1,291	1,414	1,170	1,242	1,482	1,304	746	444	199	14.1
MN........	5,345	352	709	721	730	670	800	661	367	224	111	13.1
MS........	2,979	209	414	436	390	370	411	360	219	123	45	13.0
MO........	6,011	384	786	834	788	735	875	754	461	276	118	14.2
MT........	998	62	122	136	125	112	145	145	84	47	21	15.2
NE........	1,843	131	254	260	249	220	254	224	126	84	41	13.6
NV........	2,723	186	367	361	389	378	375	326	207	100	33	12.5
NH........	1,318	68	159	178	147	172	223	186	101	57	26	14.0
NJ........	8,821	536	1,143	1,138	1,123	1,212	1,374	1,087	631	392	186	13.7
NM........	2,082	146	288	293	274	247	286	266	160	88	34	13.6
NY........	19,465	1,164	2,351	2,757	2,714	2,561	2,865	2,389	1,397	863	405	13.7
NC........	9,656	630	1,280	1,332	1,263	1,316	1,370	1,187	727	398	154	13.2
ND........	684	45	81	109	94	75	95	86	48	34	17	14.4
OH........	11,545	710	1,507	1,579	1,426	1,448	1,711	1,516	869	540	239	14.3
OK........	3,792	266	519	539	516	460	517	458	287	166	64	13.7
OR........	3,872	237	480	512	531	501	530	529	305	167	81	14.3
PA........	12,743	724	1,533	1,771	1,547	1,576	1,916	1,695	1,000	665	316	15.6
RI........	1,051	56	123	162	129	132	160	136	76	50	28	14.7
SC........	4,679	303	598	661	601	593	658	607	387	198	74	14.1
SD........	824	60	110	116	108	93	115	103	59	40	20	14.4
TN........	6,403	405	833	868	835	844	921	817	503	272	104	13.7
TX........	25,675	1,960	3,874	3,757	3,695	3,492	3,456	2,735	1,539	845	323	10.5
UT........	2,817	262	488	458	447	344	306	254	144	82	33	9.2
VT........	626	31	71	90	71	76	100	94	52	29	13	15.0
VA........	8,097	510	1,029	1,128	1,120	1,094	1,209	995	573	310	128	12.5
WA........	6,830	444	871	933	962	907	976	872	484	258	123	12.7
WV........	1,855	103	214	239	221	234	270	273	167	98	37	16.2
WI........	5,712	355	741	786	731	709	864	733	412	259	122	13.9
WY........	568	40	74	79	79	67	81	77	41	22	9	12.7

Source: U.S. Census Bureau, "Table 1. Estimates of the Resident Population by Selected Age Groups for the United States, States, and Puerto Rico: July 1, 2011 (SC-EST2011-01)," May 2012, <http://www.census.gov/popest/data/state/asrh/2011/index.html>, and "Annual Estimates of the Resident Population by Sex and Age for States and for Puerto Rico: April 1, 2010 to July 1, 2011," May 2012, <http://www.census.gov/popest/data/state/asrh/2011/SC-EST2011-02.html>.

Table 17. Age Dependency Ratios by State: 2000 to 2011

[As of April, except 2011 as of July]

State	Age dependency ratio [1]			Child dependency ratio [2]			Old-age dependency ratio [3]		
	2000	2010	2011	2000	2010	2011	2000	2010	2011
United States........	**61.6**	**58.9**	**58.8**	**41.5**	**38.2**	**37.7**	**20.1**	**20.7**	**21.1**
Alabama...............	62.1	59.9	59.9	40.9	37.9	37.5	21.1	22.0	22.4
Alaska................	56.5	51.8	51.8	47.6	40.0	39.6	8.9	11.7	12.2
Arizona...............	65.7	64.7	64.7	44.2	42.0	41.3	21.6	22.7	23.4
Arkansas..............	65.1	63.4	63.4	42.0	39.9	39.5	23.1	23.5	23.9
California.............	61.1	57.1	56.9	44.0	39.2	38.6	17.1	17.9	18.3
Colorado..............	54.5	54.6	54.5	39.5	37.7	37.2	14.9	16.9	17.4
Connecticut...........	62.7	58.8	58.3	40.2	36.3	35.5	22.5	22.5	22.8
Delaware..............	60.8	59.5	59.4	39.9	36.6	36.0	20.9	23.0	23.5
District of Columbia....	47.8	39.3	39.7	29.7	23.3	23.8	18.1	15.9	15.9
Florida................	67.7	62.9	62.8	38.3	34.7	34.1	29.5	28.2	28.7
Georgia...............	56.5	57.2	57.1	41.5	40.4	39.9	15.0	16.7	17.2
Hawaii................	60.4	57.9	58.4	39.2	35.3	35.1	21.3	22.7	23.3
Idaho.................	66.1	66.1	66.1	47.4	45.5	44.9	18.7	20.6	21.2
Illinois...............	61.8	58.6	58.3	42.3	38.7	38.1	19.5	19.9	20.2
Indiana...............	62.0	60.7	60.5	41.9	39.9	39.3	20.1	20.8	21.1
Iowa..................	66.6	63.3	62.9	41.8	39.0	38.5	24.8	24.3	24.3
Kansas................	66.0	63.0	62.7	44.0	41.5	41.0	22.0	21.5	21.7
Kentucky..............	59.0	58.5	58.5	39.1	37.4	37.0	19.9	21.1	21.5
Louisiana.............	63.6	58.6	58.6	44.6	39.1	38.8	18.9	19.5	19.8
Maine.................	61.3	57.6	57.6	38.1	32.6	31.9	23.2	25.0	25.7
Maryland..............	58.5	55.5	55.3	40.6	36.4	35.9	17.9	19.1	19.4
Massachusetts.........	59.2	54.9	54.6	37.6	33.6	33.0	21.6	21.4	21.6
Michigan..............	62.3	60.0	59.5	42.4	37.9	37.1	19.9	22.0	22.4
Minnesota.............	61.9	59.0	58.8	42.4	38.5	38.0	19.6	20.5	20.9
Mississippi............	64.8	62.0	61.9	44.9	41.3	40.8	19.9	20.8	21.1
Missouri...............	64.0	60.8	60.5	41.8	38.3	37.7	22.1	22.5	22.8
Montana...............	63.7	59.8	59.9	41.7	36.1	35.6	21.9	23.7	24.3
Nebraska..............	66.3	63.0	62.7	43.8	41.0	40.6	22.6	22.0	22.1
Nevada................	57.6	57.8	58.3	40.4	38.9	38.6	17.3	19.0	19.7
New Hampshire........	58.8	54.7	54.4	39.8	33.8	32.8	19.0	20.9	21.6
New Jersey............	61.4	58.7	58.4	40.0	37.3	36.7	21.4	21.4	21.7
New Mexico............	65.6	62.4	62.6	46.3	40.9	40.6	19.3	21.5	22.1
New York..............	60.3	55.8	55.5	39.6	34.8	34.2	20.7	21.1	21.3
North Carolina.........	57.3	58.4	58.6	38.4	37.9	37.6	19.0	20.5	21.0
North Dakota..........	66.0	58.2	57.5	41.6	35.2	34.8	24.4	22.9	22.7
Ohio..................	63.2	60.6	60.3	41.5	38.0	37.4	21.7	22.6	22.9
Oklahoma.............	64.1	62.0	62.2	42.4	40.2	40.0	21.7	21.9	22.1
Oregon...............	60.1	57.6	57.7	39.6	35.6	35.2	20.5	21.9	22.5
Pennsylvania..........	65.1	59.8	59.3	39.3	35.1	34.5	25.8	24.6	24.8
Rhode Island..........	61.8	55.5	55.1	38.2	33.1	32.4	23.5	22.4	22.7
South Carolina.........	59.4	58.8	59.2	40.1	37.1	36.8	19.3	21.7	22.4
South Dakota..........	70.0	64.5	64.1	45.6	41.0	40.4	24.4	23.6	23.6
Tennessee.............	58.6	58.8	58.8	39.0	37.4	37.0	19.6	21.4	21.8
Texas.................	61.7	60.4	60.4	45.7	43.8	43.5	16.1	16.6	16.9
Utah..................	68.6	68.2	67.9	54.3	53.0	52.5	14.4	15.2	15.5
Vermont...............	58.6	54.3	54.2	38.4	31.9	31.0	20.2	22.5	23.2
Virginia...............	55.6	54.7	54.8	38.2	35.9	35.4	17.4	18.9	19.3
Washington............	58.5	55.8	55.8	40.7	36.6	36.1	17.8	19.2	19.7
West Virginia..........	60.2	58.6	58.6	35.6	33.2	32.9	24.5	25.5	25.7
Wisconsin.............	62.9	59.3	59.0	41.6	37.5	36.9	21.3	21.8	22.1
Wyoming..............	60.7	57.4	57.4	41.9	37.8	37.4	18.8	19.6	20.0

[1] The age dependency ratio is derived by dividing the combined under 18 and 65-and-over populations by the 18-to-64 population and multiplying by 100. [2] The child dependency ratio is derived by dividing the population under 18 by the 18-to-64 population and multiplying by 100. [3] The old-age dependency ratio is derived by dividing the population 65 and over by the 18-to-64 population and multiplying by 100.

Source: U.S. Census Bureau, Census 2010 Briefs, "Age and Sex Composition: 2010," May 2011; "Table 1. Estimates of the Resident Population by Selected Age Groups for the United States, States, and Puerto Rico: July 1, 2011 (SC-EST2011-01)," May 2012, <http://www.census.gov/popest/data/state/asrh/2011/index.html>, and "Annual Estimates of the Resident Population by Sex and Age for States and for Puerto Rico: April 1, 2010 to July 1, 2011," May 2012, <http://www.census.gov/popest/data/state/asrh/2011/SC-EST2011-02.html>.

Table 18. Resident Population by Hispanic Origin and State: 2011

[In thousands, except as indicated (311,592 represents 311,592,000). As of July 1. Hispanic origin is considered an ethnicity, not a race. Persons of Hispanic origin may be of any race]

State	Number (1,000)				Percent distribution		
	Total population	Hispanic or Latino	Total Non-Hispanic	Non-Hispanic White alone	Hispanic or Latino	Total Non-Hispanic	Non-Hispanic White alone
U.S.	**311,592**	**52,045**	**259,547**	**197,511**	**16.7**	**83.3**	**63.4**
AL	4,803	194	4,609	3,207	4.0	96.0	66.8
AK	723	42	681	461	5.8	94.2	63.7
AZ	6,483	1,949	4,533	3,720	30.1	69.9	57.4
AR	2,938	195	2,743	2,180	6.6	93.4	74.2
CA	37,692	14,360	23,332	14,977	38.1	61.9	39.7
CO	5,117	1,071	4,046	3,568	20.9	79.1	69.7
CT	3,581	494	3,086	2,540	13.8	86.2	70.9
DE	907	76	831	590	8.4	91.6	65.1
DC	618	59	559	218	9.5	90.5	35.3
FL	19,058	4,356	14,702	10,962	22.9	77.1	57.5
GA	9,815	892	8,923	5,450	9.1	90.9	55.5
HI	1,375	126	1,248	316	9.2	90.8	22.9
ID	1,585	182	1,403	1,325	11.5	88.5	83.6
IL	12,869	2,080	10,790	8,147	16.2	83.8	63.3
IN	6,517	404	6,113	5,299	6.2	93.8	81.3
IA	3,062	158	2,904	2,706	5.2	94.8	88.4
KS	2,871	310	2,561	2,234	10.8	89.2	77.8
KY	4,369	139	4,231	3,763	3.2	96.8	86.1
LA	4,575	202	4,373	2,749	4.4	95.6	60.1
ME	1,328	18	1,310	1,253	1.4	98.6	94.3
MD	5,828	491	5,338	3,170	8.4	91.6	54.4
MA	6,588	651	5,937	5,033	9.9	90.1	76.4
MI	9,876	448	9,428	7,546	4.5	95.5	76.4
MN	5,345	259	5,086	4,425	4.9	95.1	82.8
MS	2,979	86	2,893	1,719	2.9	97.1	57.7
MO	6,011	221	5,790	4,859	3.7	96.3	80.8
MT	998	31	968	873	3.1	96.9	87.5
NE	1,843	175	1,668	1,507	9.5	90.5	81.8
NV	2,723	737	1,986	1,459	27.1	72.9	53.6
NH	1,318	39	1,280	1,215	2.9	97.1	92.2
NJ	8,821	1,601	7,220	5,194	18.1	81.9	58.9
NM	2,082	973	1,109	837	46.7	53.3	40.2
NY	19,465	3,495	15,970	11,294	18.0	82.0	58.0
NC	9,656	832	8,824	6,277	8.6	91.4	65.0
ND	684	15	669	606	2.2	97.8	88.6
OH	11,545	367	11,178	9,352	3.2	96.8	81.0
OK	3,792	348	3,444	2,587	9.2	90.8	68.2
OR	3,872	466	3,406	3,025	12.0	88.0	78.1
PA	12,743	750	11,992	10,092	5.9	94.1	79.2
RI	1,051	135	917	804	12.8	87.2	76.5
SC	4,679	246	4,434	2,994	5.3	94.7	64.0
SD	824	24	800	695	2.9	97.1	84.4
TN	6,403	303	6,100	4,830	4.7	95.3	75.4
TX	25,675	9,792	15,883	11,508	38.1	61.9	44.8
UT	2,817	373	2,444	2,255	13.2	86.8	80.1
VT	626	10	617	590	1.6	98.4	94.2
VA	8,097	661	7,436	5,222	8.2	91.8	64.5
WA	6,830	789	6,041	4,924	11.6	88.4	72.1
WV	1,855	24	1,831	1,725	1.3	98.7	93.0
WI	5,712	348	5,363	4,744	6.1	93.9	83.1
WY	568	52	516	486	9.1	90.9	85.5

Source: U.S. Census Bureau, "Table 4. Estimates of the Resident Population by Race and Hispanic Origin for the United States and States: July 1, 2011 (SC-EST2011-04)," May 2012, <http://www.census.gov/popest/data/state/asrh/2011/index.html>.

Table 19. Resident Population by Race and State: 2011

[In thousands, except as indicated (311,592 represents 311,592,000), As of July 1]

State	Total population	Number (1,000) — One race						Percent distribution — One race					
		White alone	Black or African American alone	American Indian, Alaska Native alone	Asian alone	Native Hawaiian and Other Pacific Islander alone	Two or more races	White alone	Black or African American alone	American Indian, Alaska Native alone	Asian alone	Native Hawaiian and Other Pacific Islander alone	Two or more races
U.S.	311,592	243,470	40,751	3,815	15,578	692	7,285	78.1	13.1	1.2	5.0	0.2	2.3
AL	4,803	3,368	1,272	33	57	5	67	70.1	26.5	0.7	1.2	0.1	1.4
AK	723	490	26	107	40	8	51	67.9	3.6	14.9	5.6	1.1	7.0
AZ	6,483	5,481	290	340	195	17	160	84.6	4.5	5.2	3.0	0.3	2.5
AR	2,938	2,354	458	28	40	7	52	80.1	15.6	0.9	1.3	0.2	1.8
CA	37,692	27,883	2,505	637	5,142	185	1,339	74.0	6.6	1.7	13.6	0.5	3.6
CO	5,117	4,516	222	81	150	9	140	88.3	4.3	1.6	2.9	0.2	2.7
CT	3,581	2,947	396	17	144	4	73	82.3	11.1	0.5	4.0	0.1	2.0
DE	907	651	199	6	30	1	21	71.7	21.9	0.7	3.4	0.1	2.3
DC	618	262	313	3	23	1	15	42.4	50.7	0.6	3.7	0.1	2.5
FL	19,058	14,959	3,142	93	494	20	350	78.5	16.5	0.5	2.6	0.1	1.8
GA	9,815	6,198	3,045	50	335	11	176	63.2	31.0	0.5	3.4	0.1	1.8
HI	1,375	358	27	6	530	138	315	26.0	2.0	0.4	38.5	10.1	22.9
ID	1,585	1,488	12	26	21	3	34	93.9	0.8	1.7	1.3	0.2	2.1
IL	12,869	10,042	1,906	75	619	8	220	78.0	14.8	0.6	4.8	0.1	1.7
IN	6,517	5,656	611	25	110	4	112	86.8	9.4	0.4	1.7	0.1	1.7
IA	3,062	2,848	94	14	57	3	47	93.0	3.1	0.5	1.9	0.1	1.5
KS	2,871	2,510	176	34	72	3	76	87.4	6.1	1.2	2.5	0.1	2.7
KY	4,369	3,882	350	13	52	3	69	88.9	8.0	0.3	1.2	0.1	1.6
LA	4,575	2,918	1,482	34	75	3	64	63.8	32.4	0.7	1.6	0.1	1.4
ME	1,328	1,268	17	9	14	(Z)	20	95.4	1.3	0.7	1.1	(Z)	1.5
MD	5,828	3,561	1,749	31	338	6	143	61.1	30.0	0.5	5.8	0.1	2.5
MA	6,588	5,539	512	30	371	6	129	84.1	7.8	0.5	5.6	0.1	2.0
MI	9,876	7,925	1,417	69	251	4	210	80.2	14.3	0.7	2.5	(Z)	2.1
MN	5,345	4,646	286	68	225	3	116	86.9	5.4	1.3	4.2	0.1	2.2
MS	2,979	1,788	1,112	17	28	2	32	60.0	37.3	0.6	0.9	0.1	1.1
MO	6,011	5,048	704	31	103	7	117	84.0	11.7	0.5	1.7	0.1	1.9
MT	998	897	5	64	7	1	24	89.9	0.5	6.4	0.7	0.1	2.4
NE	1,843	1,661	87	24	35	2	34	90.1	4.7	1.3	1.9	0.1	1.8
NV	2,723	2,116	234	44	209	20	101	77.7	8.6	1.6	7.7	0.7	3.7
NH	1,318	1,247	17	4	30	1	20	94.6	1.3	0.3	2.3	(Z)	1.5
NJ	8,821	6,540	1,289	51	766	8	167	74.1	14.6	0.6	8.7	0.1	1.9
NM	2,082	1,736	52	210	32	3	49	83.4	2.5	10.1	1.6	0.2	2.3
NY	19,465	13,910	3,401	185	1,518	25	427	71.5	17.5	1.0	7.8	0.1	2.2
NC	9,656	6,966	2,121	150	226	11	183	72.1	22.0	1.5	2.3	0.1	1.9
ND	684	618	9	38	7	(Z)	12	90.4	1.3	5.5	1.1	(Z)	1.7
OH	11,545	9,654	1,433	30	202	6	220	83.6	12.4	0.3	1.7	(Z)	1.9
OK	3,792	2,873	290	338	70	6	215	75.8	7.7	8.9	1.8	0.1	5.7
OR	3,872	3,429	76	68	150	15	133	88.6	2.0	1.8	3.9	0.4	3.4
PA	12,743	10,673	1,444	40	369	7	210	83.8	11.3	0.3	2.9	0.1	1.6
RI	1,051	907	76	9	32	2	25	86.3	7.2	0.9	3.1	0.2	2.4
SC	4,679	3,199	1,315	25	64	4	72	68.4	28.1	0.5	1.4	0.1	1.5
SD	824	714	12	73	8	1	17	86.6	1.4	8.9	1.0	0.1	2.0
TN	6,403	5,090	1,083	27	97	6	100	79.5	16.9	0.4	1.5	0.1	1.6
TX	25,675	20,769	3,139	263	1,039	33	431	80.9	12.2	1.0	4.0	0.1	1.7
UT	2,817	2,589	36	42	61	27	62	91.9	1.3	1.5	2.2	1.0	2.2

See footnotes at end of table.

Table 19. Resident Population by Race and State: 2011-Continued.

See headnote on page 23.

| State | Number (1,000) | | | | | | | Percent distribution | | | | | |
| | Total population | One race | | | | | Two or more races | One race | | | | | Two or more races |
		White alone	Black or African American alone	American Indian, Alaska Native alone	Asian alone	Native Hawaiian and Other Pacific Islander alone		White alone	Black or African American alone	American Indian, Alaska Native alone	Asian alone	Native Hawaiian and Other Pacific Islander alone	
VT......	626	598	7	2	8	(Z)	10	95.5	1.1	0.4	1.4	(Z)	1.7
VA......	8,097	5,773	1,600	43	466	9	206	71.3	19.8	0.5	5.8	0.1	2.5
WA......	6,830	5,598	262	125	509	44	291	82.0	3.8	1.8	7.5	0.7	4.3
WV......	1,855	1,745	66	4	13	1	26	94.1	3.5	0.2	0.7	(Z)	1.4
WI......	5,712	5,049	370	61	137	3	93	88.4	6.5	1.1	2.4	(Z)	1.6
WY......	568	531	6	15	5	1	10	93.5	1.1	2.6	0.9	0.1	1.8

Z Less than 500 or 0.05 percent.

Source: U.S. Census Bureau, "Table 4. Estimates of the Resident Population by Race and Hispanic Origin for the United States and States: July 1, 2011 (SC-EST2011-04)," May 2012, <http://www.census.gov/popest/data/state/asrh/2011/index.html>.

Table 20. Large Metropolitan Statistical Areas—Population: 2000 to 2011

[As of April 1, except 2011 as of July 1. In thousands, except as indicated (695 represents 695,000). Covers metropolitan statistical areas with 250,000 and over population in 2011, as defined by the U.S. Office of Management and Budget as of December 2009. All geographic boundaries for 2010 and 2011 population are defined as of January 1, 2011. For definitions and components of all metropolitan and micropolitan areas, see Appendix II. Minus sign (–) indicates decrease]

Metropolitan statistical area	2000	2010, estimates base[1]	2011	Change 2000–2010[2]		Change 2010–2011		Rank, 2011
				Number	Percent	Number	Percent	
Akron, OH...........................	695	703	701	8	1.2	-2	-0.2	75
Albany-Schenectady-Troy, NY................	826	871	871	45	5.4	1	0.1	59
Albuquerque, NM........................	730	887	899	157	21.6	12	1.3	57
Allentown-Bethlehem-Easton, PA-NJ..........	740	821	825	81	10.9	4	0.5	64
Amarillo, TX............................	226	250	254	23	10.3	4	1.6	184
Anchorage, AK..........................	320	381	388	61	19.2	7	1.8	133
Ann Arbor, MI..........................	323	345	348	22	6.8	3	0.9	146
Asheville, NC...........................	369	425	429	56	15.1	4	1.0	116
Atlanta-Sandy Springs-Marietta, GA.........	4,248	5,269	5,359	1,021	24.0	90	1.7	9
Atlantic City-Hammonton, NJ...............	253	275	274	22	8.7	(Z)	-0.1	169
Augusta-Richmond County, GA-SC...........	500	557	562	57	11.4	5	0.9	92
Austin-Round Rock-San Marcos, TX.........	1,250	1,716	1,784	467	37.3	67	3.9	34
Bakersfield-Delano, CA...................	662	840	852	178	26.9	12	1.4	61
Baltimore-Towson, MD....................	2,553	2,710	2,729	157	6.2	19	0.7	20
Baton Rouge, LA........................	706	802	808	97	13.7	6	0.7	66
Beaumont-Port Arthur, TX.................	385	389	391	4	0.9	2	0.5	132
Binghamton, NY.........................	252	252	250	-1	-0.2	-2	-0.7	186
Birmingham-Hoover, AL..................	1,052	1,128	1,132	76	7.2	4	0.4	50
Boise City-Nampa, ID....................	465	617	628	152	32.6	11	1.8	85
Boston-Cambridge-Quincy, MA-NH..........	4,391	4,552	4,591	161	3.7	39	0.9	10
Boulder, CO[3].........................	270	295	299	25	9.2	5	1.6	159
Boulder, CO[3].........................	232	251	255	19	8.3	4	1.4	182
Bridgeport-Stamford-Norwalk, CT...........	883	917	926	34	3.9	9	1.0	56
Brownsville-Harlingen, TX.................	335	406	414	71	21.2	8	1.9	124
Buffalo-Niagara Falls, NY.................	1,170	1,136	1,134	-35	-3.0	-1	-0.1	49
Canton-Massillon, OH....................	407	404	404	-3	-0.6	-1	-0.1	128
Cape Coral-Fort Myers, FL.................	441	619	631	178	40.3	13	2.0	84
Cedar Rapids, IA........................	237	258	261	21	8.7	3	1.0	177
Charleston, WV.........................	310	304	304	-5	-1.7	-1	-0.2	156
Charleston-North Charleston-Summerville, SC. ...	549	665	682	116	21.1	18	2.6	78
Charlotte-Gastonia-Rock Hill, NC-SC.........	1,330	1,758	1,795	428	32.1	37	2.1	33
Chattanooga, TN-GA.....................	477	528	533	52	10.8	5	1.0	98
Chicago-Joliet-Naperville, IL-IN-WI..........	9,098	9,461	9,505	363	4.0	44	0.5	3
Cincinnati-Middletown, OH-KY-IN............	2,010	2,130	2,138	121	6.0	8	0.4	27
Clarksville, TN-KY.......................	232	274	278	42	18.1	4	1.4	166
Cleveland-Elyria-Mentor, OH...............	2,148	2,077	2,068	-71	-3.3	-9	-0.4	28
Colorado Springs, CO....................	537	646	660	108	20.1	15	2.3	81
Columbia, SC..........................	647	768	777	120	18.6	10	1.2	70
Columbus, GA-AL.......................	282	295	301	13	4.6	7	2.2	157
Columbus, OH.........................	1,613	1,837	1,858	224	13.9	22	1.2	32
Corpus Christi, TX......................	403	428	431	25	6.2	3	0.7	114
Dallas-Fort Worth-Arlington, TX............	5,162	6,372	6,527	1,210	23.4	155	2.4	4
Davenport-Moline-Rock Island, IA-IL.........	376	380	381	4	1.0	2	0.4	134
Dayton, OH............................	848	842	845	-7	-0.8	4	0.5	62
Deltona-Daytona Beach-Ormond Beach, FL......	443	495	495	51	11.6	(Z)	(Z)	103
Denver-Aurora-Broomfield, CO[3]...........	2,179	2,543	2,600	364	16.7	56	2.2	21
Des Moines-West Des Moines, IA...........	481	570	580	88	18.3	11	1.9	88
Detroit-Warren-Livonia, MI................	4,453	4,296	4,286	-156	-3.5	-10	-0.2	13
Duluth, MN-WI..........................	275	280	280	4	1.6	(Z)	(Z)	165
Durham-Chapel Hill, NC..................	426	504	513	78	18.3	9	1.7	102
El Paso, TX............................	680	801	821	121	17.8	20	2.5	65
Erie, PA...............................	281	281	281	(-Z)	-0.1	(Z)	0.1	164
Eugene-Springfield, OR..................	323	352	353	29	8.9	2	0.5	144
Evansville, IN-KY.......................	343	359	360	16	4.6	1	0.3	142
Fayetteville, NC........................	337	366	374	30	8.8	8	2.1	137
Fayetteville-Springdale-Rogers, AR-MO........	347	463	474	116	33.5	11	2.3	107
Flint, MI..............................	436	426	422	-10	-2.4	-4	-0.9	120
Fort Collins-Loveland, CO................	251	300	306	48	19.1	6	2.0	155
Fort Smith, AR-OK......................	273	299	300	25	9.3	1	0.5	158
Fort Wayne, IN.........................	390	416	419	26	6.7	3	0.8	122
Fresno, CA............................	799	930	943	131	16.4	12	1.3	55
Gainesville, FL.........................	232	264	266	32	13.7	2	0.8	173
Grand Rapids-Wyoming, MI................	740	774	780	34	4.5	5	0.7	69
Greeley, CO[3].........................	181	253	259	72	39.7	6	2.3	179
Green Bay, WI.........................	283	306	309	24	8.4	3	1.1	152
Greensboro-High Point, NC...............	643	724	731	80	12.5	7	1.0	71
Greenville-Mauldin-Easley, SC.............	560	637	647	77	13.8	10	1.6	83
Gulfport-Biloxi, MS.....................	246	249	254	3	1.1	5	1.9	185
Hagerstown-Martinsburg, MD-WV...........	223	269	271	46	20.8	2	0.9	172
Harrisburg-Carlisle, PA..................	509	549	553	40	7.9	3	0.6	94
Hartford-West Hartford-East Hartford, CT......	1,149	1,212	1,213	64	5.6	1	0.1	45
Hickory-Lenoir-Morganton, NC.............	342	365	365	24	6.9	-1	-0.3	141
Holland-Grand Haven, MI.................	238	264	266	25	10.7	2	0.9	174
Honolulu, HI...........................	876	953	964	77	8.8	10	1.1	53
Houston-Sugar Land-Baytown, TX...........	4,715	5,947	6,087	1,231	26.1	140	2.3	5
Huntington-Ashland, WV-KY-OH............	289	288	288	-1	-0.3	(-Z)	(-Z)	162
Huntsville, AL.........................	342	418	425	75	22.0	8	1.9	119
Indianapolis-Carmel, IN..................	1,525	1,756	1,779	231	15.2	22	1.3	35
Jackson, MS...........................	497	539	545	42	8.4	6	1.2	95
Jacksonville, FL........................	1,123	1,346	1,360	223	19.8	15	1.1	40
Kalamazoo-Portage, MI..................	315	327	328	12	3.7	2	0.5	148
Kansas City, MO-KS.....................	1,836	2,035	2,053	199	10.9	17	0.9	29

See footnotes at end of table.

Table 20. Large Metropolitan Statistical Areas—Population: 2000 to 2011-Continued.

See headnote on page 25.

Metropolitan statistical area	2000	2010, estimates base [1]	2011	Change 2000–2010 [2] Number	Change 2000–2010 [2] Percent	Change 2010–2011 Number	Change 2010–2011 Percent	Rank, 2011
Kennewick-Pasco-Richland, WA.	192	253	264	62	32.1	11	4.3	176
Killeen-Temple-Fort Hood, TX.	331	405	412	75	22.6	6	1.6	127
Kingsport-Bristol-Bristol, TN-VA.	298	310	310	11	3.7	(Z)	0.1	151
Knoxville, TN.	616	698	705	82	13.3	6	0.9	74
Lafayette, LA.	239	274	277	35	14.5	4	1.3	167
Lakeland-Winter Haven, FL.	484	602	609	118	24.4	7	1.2	87
Lancaster, PA.	471	519	524	49	10.4	4	0.8	99
Lansing-East Lansing, MI.	448	464	465	16	3.6	1	0.2	109
Laredo, TX.	193	250	256	57	29.6	6	2.5	181
Las Vegas-Paradise, NV.	1,376	1,951	1,970	576	41.8	19	1.0	30
Lexington-Fayette, KY.	408	472	479	64	15.6	7	1.5	106
Lincoln, NE.	267	302	307	35	13.3	4	1.4	154
Little Rock-North Little Rock-Conway, AR.	611	700	710	89	14.6	10	1.4	72
Los Angeles-Long Beach-Santa Ana, CA.	12,366	12,829	12,945	463	3.7	116	0.9	2
Louisville/Jefferson County, KY-IN.	1,162	1,284	1,295	122	10.5	11	0.9	42
Lubbock, TX.	250	285	290	35	14.1	5	1.8	161
Lynchburg, VA.	229	253	254	24	10.5	2	0.6	183
Madison, WI.	502	569	576	67	13.3	8	1.4	89
Manchester-Nashua, NH.	381	401	402	20	5.2	1	0.2	130
McAllen-Edinburg-Mission, TX.	569	775	798	205	36.1	23	3.0	68
Memphis, TN-MS-AR.	1,205	1,316	1,326	111	9.2	10	0.7	41
Merced, CA.	211	256	260	45	21.5	4	1.6	178
Miami-Fort Lauderdale-Pompano Beach, FL.	5,008	5,565	5,670	557	11.1	105	1.9	8
Milwaukee-Waukesha-West Allis, WI.	1,501	1,556	1,562	55	3.7	6	0.4	39
Minneapolis-St. Paul-Bloomington, MN-WI.	2,969	3,280	3,318	311	10.5	39	1.2	16
Mobile, AL.	400	413	413	13	3.3	(-Z)	-0.1	126
Modesto, CA.	447	514	519	67	15.1	4	0.8	100
Montgomery, AL.	347	375	379	28	8.1	4	1.1	136
Myrtle Beach-North Myrtle Beach-Conway, SC.	197	269	276	73	37.0	7	2.6	168
Naples-Marco Island, FL.	251	322	328	70	27.9	7	2.1	149
Nashville-Davidson--Murfreesboro--Franklin, TN.	1,312	1,590	1,617	278	21.2	27	1.7	37
New Haven-Milford, CT.	824	862	861	38	4.7	-1	-0.2	60
New Orleans-Metairie-Kenner, LA.	1,317	1,168	1,191	-149	-11.3	23	2.0	46
New York-Northern New Jersey-Long Island, NY-NJ-PA.	18,323	18,897	19,016	574	3.1	119	0.6	1
North Port-Bradenton-Sarasota, FL.	590	702	709	112	19.0	7	1.0	73
Norwich-New London, CT.	259	274	274	15	5.8	-1	-0.2	170
Ocala, FL.	259	331	333	72	28.0	1	0.4	147
Ogden-Clearfield, UT.	443	547	556	105	23.6	9	1.6	93
Oklahoma City, OK.	1,095	1,253	1,278	158	14.4	25	2.0	43
Olympia, WA.	207	252	257	45	21.7	4	1.7	180
Omaha-Council Bluffs, NE-IA.	767	865	877	98	12.8	12	1.4	58
Orlando-Kissimmee-Sanford, FL.	1,645	2,134	2,171	490	29.8	37	1.7	26
Oxnard-Thousand Oaks-Ventura, CA.	753	823	832	70	9.3	8	1.0	63
Palm Bay-Melbourne-Titusville, FL.	476	543	544	67	14.1	(Z)	(Z)	96
Pensacola-Ferry Pass-Brent, FL.	412	449	453	37	8.9	4	0.9	110
Peoria, IL.	367	379	380	12	3.3	(Z)	0.1	135
Philadelphia-Camden-Wilmington, PA-NJ-DE-MD.	5,687	5,965	5,992	278	4.9	27	0.5	6
Phoenix-Mesa-Glendale, AZ.	3,252	4,193	4,263	941	28.9	70	1.7	14
Pittsburgh, PA.	2,431	2,356	2,360	-75	-3.1	3	0.1	22
Portland-South Portland-Biddeford, ME.	488	514	516	27	5.4	2	0.3	101
Portland-Vancouver-Hillsboro, OR-WA.	1,928	2,226	2,263	298	15.5	37	1.6	23
Port St. Lucie, FL.	319	424	428	105	32.8	4	0.9	117
Poughkeepsie-Newburgh-Middletown, NY.	622	670	673	49	7.8	3	0.4	79
Providence-New Bedford-Fall River, RI-MA.	1,583	1,601	1,600	18	1.1	-1	(Z)	38
Provo-Orem, UT.	377	527	541	150	39.8	14	2.7	97
Raleigh-Cary, NC.	797	1,130	1,164	333	41.8	33	2.9	47
Reading, PA.	374	411	413	38	10.1	1	0.3	125
Reno-Sparks, NV.	343	425	430	83	24.1	4	1.0	115
Richmond, VA.	1,097	1,258	1,269	161	14.7	11	0.9	44
Riverside-San Bernardino-Ontario, CA.	3,255	4,225	4,305	970	29.8	80	1.9	12
Roanoke, VA.	288	309	309	20	7.1	(Z)	(Z)	153
Rochester, NY.	1,038	1,054	1,055	16	1.6	1	0.1	51
Rockford, IL.	320	349	348	29	9.1	-1	-0.3	145
Sacramento--Arden-Arcade--Roseville, CA.	1,797	2,149	2,176	352	19.6	27	1.3	25
St. Louis, MO-IL [4]	2,699	2,813	2,817	114	4.2	4	0.2	19
Salem, OR.	347	391	395	44	12.5	4	1.1	131
Salinas, CA.	402	415	422	13	3.3	7	1.6	121
Salt Lake City, UT.	969	1,124	1,146	155	16.0	22	1.9	48
San Antonio-New Braunfels, TX.	1,712	2,143	2,195	431	25.2	52	2.4	24
San Diego-Carlsbad-San Marcos, CA.	2,814	3,095	3,140	281	10.0	45	1.4	17
San Francisco-Oakland-Fremont, CA.	4,124	4,335	4,391	212	5.1	56	1.3	11
San Jose-Sunnyvale-Santa Clara, CA.	1,736	1,837	1,865	101	5.8	29	1.6	31
San Luis Obispo-Paso Robles, CA.	247	270	272	23	9.3	2	0.9	171
Santa Barbara-Santa Maria-Goleta, CA.	399	424	427	25	6.1	3	0.7	118
Santa Cruz-Watsonville, CA.	256	262	264	7	2.7	2	0.7	175
Santa Rosa-Petaluma, CA.	459	484	488	25	5.5	4	0.9	104
Savannah, GA.	293	348	356	55	18.6	8	2.3	143
Scranton--Wilkes-Barre, PA.	561	564	563	3	0.5	(-Z)	-0.1	90
Seattle-Tacoma-Bellevue, WA.	3,044	3,440	3,500	396	13.0	60	1.8	15
Shreveport-Bossier City, LA.	376	399	404	23	6.0	5	1.3	129
South Bend-Mishawaka, IN-MI.	317	319	319	3	0.8	-1	-0.2	150
Spartanburg, SC.	254	284	287	31	12.0	3	0.9	163
Spokane, WA.	418	471	474	53	12.7	3	0.5	108

See footnotes at end of table.

Table 20. Large Metropolitan Statistical Areas—Population: 2000 to 2011-Continued.

See headnote on page 25.

Metropolitan statistical area	2000	2010, estimates base [1]	2011	Change				Rank, 2011
				2000–2010 [2]		2010–2011		
				Number	Percent	Number	Percent	
Springfield, MA..........................	680	693	693	13	1.9	(Z)	(Z)	77
Springfield, MO..........................	368	437	440	68	18.6	3	0.8	112
Stockton, CA............................	564	685	696	122	21.6	11	1.6	76
Syracuse, NY...........................	650	663	663	12	1.9	(-Z)	(-Z)	80
Tallahassee, FL.........................	320	367	370	47	14.7	2	0.6	138
Tampa-St. Petersburg-Clearwater, FL..............	2,396	2,783	2,825	387	16.2	41	1.5	18
Toledo, OH.............................	659	651	650	-8	-1.2	-1	-0.2	82
Trenton-Ewing, NJ.......................	351	367	367	16	4.5	1	0.2	140
Tucson, AZ.............................	844	980	990	137	16.2	9	0.9	52
Tulsa, OK..............................	860	937	947	78	9.1	9	1.0	54
Utica-Rome, NY.........................	300	299	298	(-Z)	-0.2	-1	-0.3	160
Vallejo-Fairfield, CA.....................	395	413	416	19	4.8	3	0.8	123
Virginia Beach-Norfolk-Newport News, VA-NC.....	1,576	1,672	1,680	95	6.0	8	0.5	36
Visalia-Porterville, CA...................	368	442	449	74	20.2	7	1.6	111
Washington-Arlington-Alexandria, DC-VA-MD-WV.........................	4,796	5,582	5,704	786	16.4	122	2.2	7
Wichita, KS.............................	571	623	626	52	9.1	2	0.4	86
Wilmington, NC.........................	275	362	370	88	32.0	7	2.0	139
Winston-Salem, NC......................	422	478	482	56	13.2	4	0.9	105
Worcester, MA..........................	751	799	801	48	6.3	3	0.3	67
York-Hanover, PA........................	382	435	437	53	13.9	2	0.4	113
Youngstown-Warren-Boardman, OH-PA...........	603	566	563	-37	-6.2	-3	-0.5	91

Z Less than 500 or .05 percent. [1] The April 1, 2010 population estimates base reflects changes to the Census 2010 population from geographic program revisions and does not reflect changes from the Count Question Resolution program. [2] Based on census data. [3] Broomfield County, CO, was formed from parts of Adams, Boulder, Jefferson, and Weld Counties, CO, on November 15, 2001, and is coextensive with Broomfield city. For purposes of defining and presenting data for metropolitan statistical areas, Broomfield city is treated as if it were a county at the time of the 2000 census. [4] The portion of Sullivan city in Crawford County, Missouri, is legally part of the St. Louis, MO-IL MSA. Data shown here do not include this area.

Source: U.S. Census Bureau, Census 2000, <http://www.census.gov/prod/www/abs/decennial/>; and "Table 1. Annual Estimates of the Population of Metropolitan and Micropolitan Statistical Areas: April 1, 2010 to July 1, 2011 (CBSA-EST2011-01)," April 2012, <http://www.census.gov/popest/data/metro/totals/2011/index.html>.

Table 21. Population in Coastal Counties: 1980 to 2011

[1980 to 2010 as of April 1, 2011 as of July 1 (3,537 represents 3,537,000). Areas as defined by U.S. National Oceanic and Atmospheric Administration, 1992. Covers 675 counties and equivalent areas with at least 15 percent of their land area either in a coastal watershed (drainage area) or in a coastal cataloging unit (a coastal area between watersheds). See Appendix III]

Year	Total	Counties in coastal regions					Balance of United States
		Total	Atlantic	Gulf of Mexico	Great Lakes	Pacific	
Land area, 2010 (1,000 sq. mi.)......	3,537	886	147	114	115	510	2,649
POPULATION							
1980 (mil.).............................	226.5	119.8	53.7	13.1	26.0	27.0	106.7
1990 (mil.).............................	248.7	133.4	59.0	15.2	25.9	33.2	115.3
2000 (mil.).............................	281.4	148.3	65.2	18.0	27.3	37.8	133.1
2010 (mil.).............................	308.7	159.6	70.2	20.8	27.2	41.4	149.1
2011 (mil.).............................	311.6	161.0	70.8	21.1	27.2	41.9	150.6
1980 (percent)..........................	100	53	24	6	11	12	47
1990 (percent)..........................	100	54	24	6	10	13	46
2000 (percent)..........................	100	53	23	6	10	13	47
2010 (percent)..........................	100	52	23	7	9	13	48
2011 (percent)..........................	100	52	23	7	9	13	48

Source: U.S. Census Bureau, U.S. Summary, 1980 Census of Population, Vol. 1, Chapter A (PC80-1-A-1); 1990 Census of Population and Housing (CPH1); GCT-PH1 Population, Housing Units, Area, and Density: 2010 - United States -- County by State; and for Puerto Rico 2010 Census Summary File 1, American FactFinder, accessed 13 July 2012; "Population, population change and estimated components of population change: April 1, 2010 to July 1, 2011 (CO-EST2011-alldata)," April 2012, <http://www.census.gov/popest/data/counties/totals/2011/index.html>.

Table 22. Metropolitan Statistical Areas With More Than 750,000 Persons in 2010—Population by Age: 2010

[In thousands (871 represents 871,000). As of April 1. Covers metropolitan statistical areas as defined by the U.S. Office of Management and Budget as of December 2009. All geographic boundaries are defined as of January 1, 2010. For definitions and components of all metropolitan and micropolitan areas, see Appendix II]

Metropolitan statistical area	Number (1,000)						Percent under 18 years	Percent 65 years and over
	Total	Under 18 years	18 to 44 years	45 to 64 years	65 to 74 years	75 years and over		
Albany-Schenectady-Troy, NY	871	186	313	249	62	60	21.4	14.0
Albuquerque, NM	887	218	323	237	61	48	24.6	12.3
Allentown-Bethlehem-Easton, PA-NJ	821	187	275	234	62	63	22.8	15.2
Atlanta-Sandy Springs-Marietta, GA	5,269	1,396	2,076	1,325	283	189	26.5	9.0
Austin-Round Rock-San Marcos, TX	1,716	435	750	392	81	58	25.3	8.1
Bakersfield-Delano, CA	840	254	324	186	44	32	30.3	9.0
Baltimore-Towson, MD	2,710	623	992	753	183	159	23.0	12.6
Baton Rouge, LA	802	198	313	205	50	37	24.7	10.7
Birmingham-Hoover, AL	1,128	270	409	304	80	66	23.9	13.0
Boston-Cambridge-Quincy, MA-NH	4,552	983	1,721	1,252	306	290	21.6	13.1
Bridgeport-Stamford-Norwalk, CT	917	227	309	256	62	62	24.8	13.5
Buffalo-Niagara Falls, NY	1,136	245	388	323	87	92	21.6	15.7
Charlotte-Gastonia-Rock Hill, NC-SC	1,758	456	688	437	102	76	25.9	10.1
Chicago-Joliet-Naperville, IL-IN-WI	9,461	2,378	3,574	2,429	579	501	25.1	11.4
Cincinnati-Middletown, OH-KY-IN	2,130	531	761	578	140	120	24.9	12.2
Cleveland-Elyria-Mentor, OH	2,077	481	682	598	159	157	23.2	15.2
Columbia, SC	768	180	299	201	50	37	23.5	11.4
Columbus, OH	1,837	455	720	468	108	86	24.8	10.6
Dallas-Fort Worth-Arlington, TX	6,372	1,774	2,506	1,532	328	233	27.8	8.8
Dayton, OH	842	193	290	233	66	60	23.0	14.9
Denver-Aurora-Broomfield, CO [1]	2,543	634	987	666	144	112	24.9	10.0
Detroit-Warren-Livonia, MI	4,296	1,044	1,471	1,215	296	271	24.3	13.2
El Paso, TX	801	241	301	177	44	38	30.1	10.3
Fresno, CA	930	278	356	204	49	44	29.8	10.0
Grand Rapids-Wyoming, MI	774	200	281	202	48	43	25.9	11.7
Hartford-West Hartford-East Hartford, CT	1,212	270	420	348	87	87	22.3	14.3
Honolulu, HI	953	211	358	246	69	70	22.1	14.5
Houston-Sugar Land-Baytown, TX	5,947	1,662	2,329	1,444	303	208	28.0	8.6
Indianapolis-Carmel, IN	1,756	460	653	453	105	86	26.2	10.9
Jacksonville, FL	1,346	321	493	369	93	70	23.8	12.1
Kansas City, MO-KS	2,035	522	730	540	130	113	25.6	12.0
Las Vegas-Paradise, NV	1,951	489	762	480	135	86	25.0	11.3
Los Angeles-Long Beach-Santa Ana, CA	12,829	3,139	5,126	3,148	756	659	24.5	11.0
Louisville/Jefferson County, KY-IN	1,284	308	455	356	90	75	24.0	12.8
McAllen-Edinburg-Mission, TX	775	268	294	140	40	33	34.7	9.3
Memphis, TN-MS-AR	1,316	350	487	340	79	60	26.6	10.5
Miami-Fort Lauderdale-Pompano Beach, FL	5,565	1,206	2,001	1,471	443	444	21.7	15.9
Milwaukee-Waukesha-West Allis, WI	1,556	383	560	417	97	99	24.6	12.6
Minneapolis-St. Paul-Bloomington, MN-WI	3,280	820	1,232	879	188	162	25.0	10.7
Nashville-Davidson—Murfreesboro—Franklin, TN	1,590	388	619	413	98	72	24.4	10.7
New Haven-Milford, CT	862	193	308	238	61	63	22.4	14.4
New Orleans-Metairie-Kenner, LA	1,168	273	431	322	79	63	23.4	12.2
New York-Northern New Jersey-Long Island, NY-NJ-PA	18,897	4,312	7,132	4,980	1,288	1,185	22.8	13.1
Oklahoma City, OK	1,253	313	477	315	82	66	25.0	11.8
Omaha-Council Bluffs, NE-IA	865	227	323	219	51	45	26.3	11.1
Orlando-Kissimmee-Sanford, FL	2,134	499	830	542	146	117	23.4	12.3
Oxnard-Thousand Oaks-Ventura, CA	823	212	298	217	51	45	25.7	11.7
Philadelphia-Camden-Wilmington, PA-NJ-DE-MD	5,965	1,391	2,160	1,622	405	388	23.3	13.3
Phoenix-Mesa-Glendale, AZ	4,193	1,108	1,581	989	289	226	26.4	12.3
Pittsburgh, PA	2,356	475	778	696	195	212	20.2	17.3
Portland-Vancouver-Hillsboro, OR-WA	2,226	527	854	593	138	114	23.7	11.3
Providence-New Bedford-Fall River, RI-MA	1,601	346	578	447	113	117	21.6	14.4
Raleigh-Cary, NC	1,130	296	453	280	60	42	26.2	9.0
Richmond, VA	1,258	294	462	350	85	68	23.3	12.1
Riverside-San Bernardino-Ontario, CA	4,225	1,215	1,589	981	244	196	28.8	10.4
Rochester, NY	1,054	238	370	298	76	72	22.6	14.1
Sacramento—Arden-Arcade—Roseville, CA	2,149	535	797	559	138	120	24.9	12.0
St. Louis, MO-IL [2]	2,813	671	990	777	196	179	23.8	13.3
Salt Lake City, UT	1,124	331	455	241	54	43	29.4	8.6
San Antonio-New Braunfels, TX	2,143	576	808	524	131	104	26.9	11.0
San Diego-Carlsbad-San Marcos, CA	3,095	724	1,259	760	181	171	23.4	11.4
San Francisco-Oakland-Fremont, CA	4,335	921	1,689	1,179	289	258	21.2	12.6
San Jose-Sunnyvale-Santa Clara, CA	1,837	446	726	463	109	93	24.3	11.0
Seattle-Tacoma-Bellevue, WA	3,440	786	1,353	929	203	169	22.8	10.8
Tampa-St. Petersburg-Clearwater, FL	2,783	590	943	770	249	231	21.2	17.2
Tucson, AZ	980	225	350	254	82	70	23.0	15.4
Tulsa, OK	937	239	333	245	67	54	25.5	12.8
Virginia Beach-Norfolk-Newport News, VA-NC	1,672	394	648	436	107	86	23.6	11.6
Washington-Arlington-Alexandria, DC-VA-MD-WV	5,582	1,332	2,212	1,480	320	238	23.9	10.0
Worcester, MA	799	187	282	227	51	51	23.4	12.8

[1] See footnote 1, Table 20. [2] The portion of Sullivan city in Crawford County, Missouri, is legally part of the St. Louis, MO-IL MSA. Data shown here do not include this area.

Source: U.S. Census Bureau, USA Counties, <http://censtats.census.gov/usa/usa.shtml>, accessed June 2011.

Table 23. Metropolitan Statistical Areas With More Than 750,000 Persons in 2010—Population by Race and Hispanic or Latino Origin: 2010

[In thousands (871 represents 871,000). As of April 1. Covers metropolitan statistical areas as defined by the U.S. Office of Management and Budget as of December 2009. All geographic boundaries are defined as of January 1, 2010. For definitions and components of all metropolitan and micropolitan areas, see Appendix II]

Metropolitan statistical area	Total	White alone	Black or African American alone	American Indian and Alaska Native alone	Asian alone	Native Hawaiian and Other Pacific Islander alone	Two or more races	Hispanic or Latino origin [1]
Albany-Schenectady-Troy, NY	871	739	67	2	27	(Z)	21	36
Albuquerque, NM	887	618	24	52	18	1	38	414
Allentown-Bethlehem-Easton, PA-NJ	821	694	41	2	20	(Z)	19	107
Atlanta-Sandy Springs-Marietta, GA	5,269	2,920	1,708	18	254	3	126	547
Austin-Round Rock-San Marcos, TX	1,716	1,250	127	13	82	1	55	538
Bakersfield-Delano, CA	840	500	49	13	35	1	38	413
Baltimore-Towson, MD	2,710	1,684	779	9	123	1	68	124
Baton Rouge, LA	802	480	286	2	14	(Z)	10	27
Birmingham-Hoover, AL	1,128	753	318	3	14	1	13	49
Boston-Cambridge-Quincy, MA-NH	4,552	3,588	331	11	295	1	118	411
Bridgeport-Stamford-Norwalk, CT	917	686	99	2	42	(Z)	24	155
Buffalo-Niagara Falls, NY	1,136	927	139	8	26	(Z)	21	46
Charlotte-Gastonia-Rock Hill, NC-SC	1,758	1,145	421	9	55	1	39	173
Chicago-Joliet-Naperville, IL-IN-WI	9,461	6,184	1,646	37	533	3	230	1,957
Cincinnati-Middletown, OH-KY-IN	2,130	1,766	256	4	40	1	39	55
Cleveland-Elyria-Mentor, OH	2,077	1,538	417	4	41	(Z)	42	98
Columbia, SC	768	464	255	3	13	1	15	39
Columbus, OH	1,837	1,424	274	4	57	1	46	66
Dallas-Fort Worth-Arlington, TX	6,372	4,161	962	43	342	6	180	1,752
Dayton, OH	842	673	126	2	15	(Z)	19	17
Denver-Aurora-Broomfield, CO [2]	2,543	1,983	143	25	94	3	91	571
Detroit-Warren-Livonia, MI	4,296	3,011	980	15	141	1	95	168
El Paso, TX	801	657	25	6	8	1	20	658
Fresno, CA	930	515	50	16	89	1	42	468
Grand Rapids-Wyoming, MI	774	643	62	4	15	(Z)	21	65
Hartford-West Hartford-East Hartford, CT	1,212	932	132	3	47	(Z)	30	151
Honolulu, HI	953	199	19	2	418	91	213	77
Houston-Sugar Land-Baytown, TX	5,947	3,581	1,026	38	389	4	180	2,099
Indianapolis-Carmel, IN	1,756	1,353	263	5	40	1	38	108
Jacksonville, FL	1,346	940	293	5	46	1	35	93
Kansas City, MO-KS	2,035	1,597	255	10	46	3	56	167
Las Vegas-Paradise, NV	1,951	1,188	204	14	169	14	99	569
Los Angeles-Long Beach-Santa Ana, CA	12,829	6,767	908	91	1,885	35	567	5,701
Louisville/Jefferson County, KY-IN	1,284	1,037	176	3	20	1	26	50
McAllen-Edinburg-Mission, TX	775	682	5	3	7	(Z)	10	702
Memphis, TN-MS-AR	1,316	631	601	3	24	1	18	65
Miami-Fort Lauderdale-Pompano Beach, FL	5,565	3,914	1,169	16	126	2	140	2,313
Milwaukee-Waukesha-West Allis, WI	1,556	1,147	261	8	46	1	36	148
Minneapolis-St. Paul-Bloomington, MN-WI	3,280	2,657	243	23	188	1	91	176
Nashville-Davidson–Murfreesboro–Franklin, TN	1,590	1,222	242	5	36	1	33	105
New Haven-Milford, CT	862	645	110	2	30	(Z)	23	130
New Orleans-Metairie-Kenner, LA	1,168	680	397	5	32	1	23	92
New York-Northern New Jersey-Long Island, NY-NJ-PA	18,897	11,178	3,363	93	1,878	9	613	4,328
Oklahoma City, OK	1,253	901	131	51	35	1	65	142
Omaha-Council Bluffs, NE-IA	865	714	68	5	18	1	22	78
Orlando-Kissimmee-Sanford, FL	2,134	1,494	345	9	85	2	69	539
Oxnard-Thousand Oaks-Ventura, CA	823	566	15	8	55	2	37	332
Philadelphia-Camden-Wilmington, PA-NJ-DE-MD	5,965	4,068	1,242	16	296	2	139	468
Phoenix-Mesa-Glendale, AZ	4,193	3,059	208	99	139	9	146	1,236
Pittsburgh, PA	2,356	2,069	197	3	41	(Z)	37	30
Portland-Vancouver-Hillsboro, OR-WA	2,226	1,804	64	21	127	10	91	242
Providence-New Bedford-Fall River, RI-MA	1,601	1,342	78	8	41	1	49	164
Raleigh-Cary, NC	1,130	763	228	6	50	(Z)	27	115
Richmond, VA	1,258	780	375	5	39	1	29	63
Riverside-San Bernardino-Ontario, CA	4,225	2,488	322	46	259	14	207	1,996
Rochester, NY	1,054	855	123	3	27	(Z)	24	65
Sacramento–Arden-Arcade–Roseville, CA	2,149	1,390	158	22	256	16	127	434
St. Louis, MO-IL [3]	2,813	2,153	516	7	60	1	51	72
Salt Lake City, UT	1,124	922	17	10	35	16	35	187
San Antonio-New Braunfels, TX	2,143	1,617	141	17	45	3	70	1,158
San Diego-Carlsbad-San Marcos, CA	3,095	1,981	158	26	336	15	158	991
San Francisco-Oakland-Fremont, CA	4,335	2,240	364	25	1,006	32	240	939
San Jose-Sunnyvale-Santa Clara, CA	1,837	872	47	14	572	7	90	510
Seattle-Tacoma-Bellevue, WA	3,440	2,475	192	37	393	28	184	309
Tampa-St. Petersburg-Clearwater, FL	2,783	2,193	329	10	81	2	73	452
Tucson, AZ	980	729	35	33	26	2	36	339
Tulsa, OK	937	665	79	77	17	1	60	78
Virginia Beach-Norfolk-Newport News, VA-NC	1,672	997	522	7	58	2	57	90
Washington-Arlington-Alexandria, DC-VA-MD-WV	5,582	3,059	1,438	23	517	4	206	771
Worcester, MA	799	683	33	2	32	(Z)	19	75

Z Less than 500. [1] Persons of Hispanic origin may be any race. [2] See footnote 1, Table 20. [3] The portion of Sullivan city in Crawford County, Missouri, is legally part of the St. Louis, MO-IL MSA. Data shown here do not include this area.

Source: U.S. Census Bureau, USA Counties, <http://censtats.census.gov/usa/usa.shtml>, accessed June 2011.

Table 24. Population by Core Based Statistical Area (CBSA) Status and State: 2011

[As of July 1. (311,592 represents 311,592,000). Covers core-based statistical areas (metropolitan and micropolitan statistical areas) as defined by the U.S. Office of Management and Budget as of December 2009. All geographic boundaries for 2010 and 2011 population estimates are defined as of January 1, 2011. For definitions and components of all metropolitan and micropolitan areas, see Appendix II. Minus sign (–) indicates decrease]

State	Total population, 2011 (1,000)	Inside Core-Based Statistical Area (metropolitan or micropolitan statistical area), 2011				Outside CBSA, 2011		Percent change, 2010–2011		
		Total		Metro-politan (1,000)	Micro-politan (1,000)	Number (1,000)	Percent	Metro-politan	Micro-politan	Outside CBSAs
		Number (1,000)	Percent							
U.S........	311,592	292,139	93.8	261,104	31,035	19,453	6.2	1.1	0.3	-0.2
AL.........	4,803	4,318	89.9	3,439	879	485	10.1	0.7	0.4	-0.8
AK.........	723	546	75.6	487	60	176	24.4	1.7	2.2	1.7
AZ.........	6,483	6,390	98.6	6,002	387	93	1.4	1.5	0.5	0.9
AR.........	2,938	2,357	80.2	1,781	576	581	19.8	1.3	0.1	-0.3
CA.........	37,692	37,435	99.3	36,850	585	257	0.7	1.2	-0.3	-0.6
CO.........	5,117	4,709	92.0	4,431	278	407	8.0	2.1	0.2	-0.5
CT.........	3,581	3,581	100.0	3,274	307	0	0.0	0.2	-0.5	0.0
DE.........	907	907	100.0	707	200	0	0.0	0.9	1.6	0.0
DC.........	618	618	100.0	618	0	0	0.0	2.7	0.0	0.0
FL.........	19,058	18,637	97.8	17,943	694	421	2.2	1.4	0.5	-0.1
GA.........	9,815	8,945	91.1	7,972	973	870	8.9	1.6	0.4	(-Z)
HI.........	1,375	1,375	100.0	964	411	(Z)	(Z)	1.1	1.0	0.0
ID.........	1,585	1,383	87.2	1,045	338	202	12.8	1.6	0.5	-0.4
IL.........	12,869	12,264	95.3	11,203	1,061	605	4.7	0.4	-0.2	-0.5
IN.........	6,517	6,149	94.4	5,113	1,037	368	5.6	0.7	0.0	-0.1
IA.........	3,062	2,258	73.7	1,741	517	804	26.3	1.1	-0.2	-0.3
KS.........	2,871	2,460	85.7	1,967	493	411	14.3	0.9	0.3	-0.4
KY.........	4,369	3,359	76.9	2,549	810	1,010	23.1	1.0	0.6	(Z)
LA.........	4,575	4,270	93.3	3,422	849	304	6.7	1.2	0.2	-0.4
ME.........	1,328	939	70.7	777	162	390	29.3	0.2	-0.2	-0.3
MD.........	5,828	5,745	98.6	5,515	230	83	1.4	1.0	1.2	-0.1
MA.........	6,588	6,561	99.6	6,561	0	27	0.4	0.6	0.0	0.8
MI.........	9,876	9,109	92.2	8,028	1,081	767	7.8	-0.1	0.1	-0.5
MN.........	5,345	4,691	87.8	4,013	678	654	12.2	1.1	0.1	-0.3
MS.........	2,979	2,346	78.8	1,347	999	633	21.2	1.2	-0.1	-0.6
MO.........	6,011	5,204	86.6	4,485	719	807	13.4	0.5	0.5	-0.4
MT.........	998	661	66.2	352	309	337	33.8	1.0	1.2	0.5
NE.........	1,843	1,493	81.0	1,087	406	350	19.0	1.5	0.4	-0.3
NV.........	2,723	2,673	98.2	2,455	218	50	1.8	0.9	-0.2	0.2
NH.........	1,318	1,271	96.4	822	449	48	3.6	0.3	-0.2	-0.4
NJ.........	8,821	8,821	100.0	8,821	0	0	0.0	0.3	0.0	0.0
NM.........	2,082	2,005	96.3	1,386	619	78	3.7	1.1	1.3	-0.7
NY.........	19,465	19,036	97.8	17,906	1,130	429	2.2	0.5	-0.2	-0.5
NC.........	9,656	8,900	92.2	6,817	2,082	757	7.8	1.7	0.5	-0.3
ND.........	684	490	71.6	330	160	194	28.4	1.4	3.5	0.8
OH.........	11,545	11,032	95.6	9,311	1,721	513	4.4	0.1	-0.1	-0.1
OK.........	3,792	3,248	85.7	2,444	804	543	14.3	1.5	0.6	-0.2
OR.........	3,872	3,728	96.3	3,017	711	144	3.7	1.3	0.3	-0.1
PA.........	12,743	12,355	97.0	10,727	1,628	388	3.0	0.4	(-Z)	-0.1
RI.........	1,051	1,051	100.0	1,051	0	0	0.0	-0.1	0.0	0.0
SC.........	4,679	4,408	94.2	3,590	818	272	5.8	1.5	0.3	-0.9
SD.........	824	604	73.3	375	228	220	26.7	1.7	0.9	0.7
TN.........	6,403	5,766	90.0	4,713	1,052	638	10.0	1.2	0.4	-0.1
TX.........	25,675	24,299	94.6	22,599	1,700	1,375	5.4	2.3	0.6	0.3
UT.........	2,817	2,675	94.9	2,499	176	142	5.1	2.0	1.3	0.7
VT.........	626	462	73.8	213	250	164	26.2	0.6	-0.1	-0.1
VA.........	8,097	7,263	89.7	6,985	278	834	10.3	1.4	(-Z)	-0.2
WA.........	6,830	6,597	96.6	5,999	598	233	3.4	1.7	0.9	0.4
WV.........	1,855	1,402	75.6	1,036	366	453	24.4	0.3	0.2	-0.4
WI.........	5,712	4,936	86.4	4,166	770	776	13.6	0.6	0.1	(Z)
WY.........	568	409	72.0	169	240	159	28.0	1.1	0.9	0.3

Z Less than 500 or .05 percent.

Source: U.S. Census Bureau, "Combined statistical area population and estimated components of change: April 1, 2010 to July 1, 2011 (CSA-EST2011-alldata);" April 2012, <http://www.census.gov/popest/data/metro/totals/2011/>.

Table 25. The 50 Largest Metropolitan Statistical Areas in 2011— Components of Population Change: 2010 to 2011

[Covers period April 1, 2010 to July 1, 2011 (90 represents 90,000). Covers metropolitan statistical areas as defined by the U.S. Office of Management and Budget as of December 2009. All geographic boundaries for 2010 to 2011 population estimates are defined as of January 1, 2011. For definitions and components of all metropolitan and micropolitan areas, see Appendix II. Minus sign (–) indicates decrease or outmigration]

| Metropolitan statistical area | Number (1,000) | | | | | | | |
| | Total change [1] | Natural increase | | | Net migration | | | Percent change |
		Total	Births	Deaths	Total	International	Domestic migration	
Atlanta-Sandy Springs-Marietta, GA	90	53	92	39	37	22	15	1.7
Austin-Round Rock, TX	67	23	32	10	44	8	36	3.9
Baltimore-Towson, MD	19	14	42	28	5	7	-2	0.7
Birmingham-Hoover, AL	4	5	19	14	-1	2	-3	0.4
Boston-Cambridge-Quincy, MA-NH	39	23	65	42	16	19	-3	0.9
Buffalo-Niagara Falls, NY	-1	(Z)	15	15	-2	1	-3	-0.1
Charlotte-Gastonia-Concord, NC-SC	37	16	31	14	21	6	15	2.1
Chicago-Naperville-Joliet, IL-IN-WI	44	78	160	83	-34	30	-65	0.5
Cincinnati-Middletown, OH-KY-IN	8	13	36	22	-6	3	-8	0.4
Cleveland-Elyria-Mentor, OH	-9	4	29	25	-13	2	-16	-0.4
Columbus, OH	22	16	32	17	6	4	2	1.2
Dallas-Fort Worth-Arlington, TX	155	79	125	45	75	29	46	2.4
Denver-Aurora-Broomfield, CO	56	25	44	19	31	7	24	2.2
Detroit-Warren-Livonia, MI	-10	15	63	48	-26	9	-35	-0.2
Hartford-West Hartford-East Hartford, CT	1	3	15	12	-2	4	-6	0.1
Houston-Sugar Land-Baytown, TX	140	80	122	42	59	30	29	2.3
Indianapolis-Carmel, IN	22	16	32	16	6	4	2	1.3
Jacksonville, FL	15	8	22	14	6	3	4	1.1
Kansas City, MO-KS	17	16	35	19	1	4	-2	0.9
Las Vegas-Paradise, NV	19	18	34	16	1	10	-9	1.0
Los Angeles-Long Beach-Santa Ana, CA	116	119	213	94	-3	68	-71	0.9
Louisville/Jefferson County, KY-IN	11	7	21	14	5	2	2	0.9
Memphis, TN-MS-AR	10	11	24	13	-1	2	-4	0.7
Miami-Fort Lauderdale-Pompano Beach, FL	105	25	82	57	80	44	37	1.9
Milwaukee-Waukesha-West Allis, WI	6	11	26	16	-4	2	-7	0.4
Minneapolis-St. Paul-Bloomington, MN-WI	39	30	55	24	8	10	-2	1.2
Nashville-Davidson-Murfreesboro-Franklin, TN	27	12	27	15	15	4	11	1.7
New Orleans-Metairie-Kenner, LA	23	7	19	12	16	2	14	2.0
New York-Northern New Jersey-Long Island, NY-NJ-PA	119	140	306	166	-21	104	-125	0.6
Oklahoma City, OK	25	11	23	12	14	3	11	2.0
Orlando-Kissimmee, FL	37	14	32	18	23	12	10	1.7
Philadelphia-Camden-Wilmington, PA-NJ-DE-MD	27	29	93	64	-1	15	-16	0.5
Phoenix-Mesa-Scottsdale, AZ	70	41	74	33	30	20	10	1.7
Pittsburgh, PA	3	-4	30	34	8	2	6	0.1
Portland-Vancouver-Hillsboro, OR-WA	37	17	36	19	19	6	13	1.6
Providence-New Bedford-Fall River, RI-MA	-1	4	21	18	-4	3	-8	(-Z)
Raleigh-Cary, NC	33	12	19	7	21	4	17	2.9
Richmond, VA	11	7	19	12	4	3	2	0.9
Riverside-San Bernardino-Ontario, CA	80	44	77	32	36	11	25	1.9
Sacramento-Arden-Arcade-Roseville, CA	27	16	34	19	11	8	4	1.3
St. Louis, MO-IL [2]	4	13	43	31	-8	4	-12	0.2
Salt Lake City, UT	22	17	25	7	5	4	1	1.9
San Antonio, TX	52	22	40	18	30	5	25	2.4
San Diego-Carlsbad-San Marcos, CA	45	31	55	24	14	13	1	1.4
San Francisco-Oakland-Fremont, CA	56	30	64	35	26	22	4	1.3
San Jose-Sunnyvale-Santa Clara, CA	29	19	31	12	10	14	-4	1.6
Seattle-Tacoma-Bellevue, WA	60	28	56	28	32	15	17	1.8
Tampa-St. Petersburg-Clearwater, FL	41	3	38	36	39	9	30	1.5
Virginia Beach-Norfolk-Newport News, VA-NC	8	12	28	16	-4	4	-8	0.5
Washington-Arlington-Alexandria, DC-VA-MD-WV	122	61	98	38	61	32	29	2.2

Z Less than 500 or .05 percent. [1] Total population change includes residual. This residual represents the change in population that cannot be attributed to any specific demographic component of change. [2] The portion of Sullivan city in Crawford County, Missouri, is legally part of the St. Louis, MO-IL MSA. Data shown here do not include this area.

Source: U.S. Census Bureau, "Table 11. Cumulative Estimates of the Components of Population Change for Metropolitan and Micropolitan Statistical Areas: April 1, 2010 to July 1, 2011 (CBSA-EST2011-11);" April 2012; <http://www.census.gov/popest/data/metro/totals/2011/index.html>.

Table 26. States With Coastal Counties—Population and Housing Units, Establishments, and Employees by Coastal Region and State: 2009 to 2011

[308,746 represents 308,746,000. 2010 as of April 1, 2011 as of July 1. 2010 data reflect population estimates base. See headnote, Table 21. Minus sign (–) indicates decrease]

Coastal region and state	Population					Housing units			Private nonfarm [2]	
		2011		Percent change, 2010– 2011	Per square mile, 2011 [1]	Number		Percent change, 2010– 2011	Establish- ments, 2009 (1,000)	Employees, 2009 (1,000)
	2010 (1,000)	Number (1,000)	Percent of state, total			2010 (1,000)	2011 (1,000)			
United States, total......	**308,746**	**311,592**	**(X)**	**0.9**	**88**	**131,705**	**132,312**	**0.5**	**7,433**	**114,510**
Interior U.S..............	149,148	150,574	(X)	1.0	57	64,704	65,060	0.6	3,481	55,294
Coastal counties, total..	**159,597**	**161,018**	**(X)**	**0.9**	**182**	**67,001**	**67,252**	**0.4**	**3,953**	**59,216**
Atlantic......................	70,217	70,802	(X)	0.8	481	29,908	30,029	0.4	1,840	27,037
Maine..................	1,239	1,239	93.3	(Z)	61	667	671	0.5	38	461
New Hampshire............	1,073	1,076	81.6	0.3	256	485	487	0.4	31	439
Massachusetts.............	6,318	6,358	96.5	0.6	967	2,712	2,722	0.4	165	2,863
Rhode Island...............	1,053	1,051	100.0	-0.1	1,017	463	465	0.3	29	414
Connecticut................	3,574	3,581	100.0	0.2	739	1,488	1,494	0.4	90	1,468
New York..................	13,952	14,044	72.1	0.7	1,818	5,601	5,606	0.1	395	5,365
New Jersey................	8,683	8,713	98.8	0.3	1,245	3,509	3,518	0.3	228	3,365
Pennsylvania..............	6,108	6,140	48.2	0.5	894	2,512	2,521	0.3	143	2,515
Delaware..................	898	907	100.0	1.0	466	406	410	1.0	25	371
Maryland..................	5,288	5,339	91.6	1.0	710	2,176	2,187	0.5	123	1,935
District of Columbia........	602	618	100.0	2.7	10,123	297	299	0.7	21	467
Virginia...................	5,426	5,505	68.0	1.5	397	2,216	2,231	0.7	133	2,161
North Carolina............	2,233	2,252	23.3	0.9	115	1,069	1,078	0.8	47	614
South Carolina.............	1,932	1,959	41.9	1.4	129	953	963	1.1	46	591
Georgia...................	945	962	9.8	1.7	81	414	419	1.1	20	267
Florida...................	10,894	11,058	58.0	1.5	594	4,940	4,959	0.4	306	3,742
Gulf of Mexico...............	20,761	21,067	(X)	1.5	185	9,229	9,303	0.8	455	6,797
Florida...................	7,435	7,526	39.5	1.2	241	3,832	3,849	0.5	178	2,180
Georgia...................	98	98	1.0	0.1	61	43	43	-0.4	2	28
Alabama..................	765	768	16.0	0.4	88	363	365	0.6	17	244
Mississippi................	629	635	21.3	1.0	94	280	286	2.2	12	185
Louisiana.................	3,548	3,585	78.4	1.0	141	1,533	1,546	0.8	82	1,299
Texas....................	8,288	8,456	32.9	2.0	211	3,178	3,215	1.1	163	2,862
Great Lakes.................	27,190	27,208	(X)	0.1	236	12,128	12,128	(-Z)	638	10,468
New York..................	3,635	3,634	18.7	(-Z)	170	1,647	1,650	0.2	82	1,335
Pennsylvania..............	281	281	2.2	0.1	352	119	119	0.2	7	114
Ohio.....................	4,326	4,312	37.3	-0.3	409	1,967	1,968	(Z)	103	1,735
Michigan..................	8,797	8,793	89.0	(-Z)	173	4,050	4,045	-0.1	200	3,015
Indiana...................	1,433	1,434	22.0	0.1	353	607	607	(Z)	32	525
Illinois...................	5,898	5,923	46.0	0.4	4,264	2,441	2,437	-0.1	147	2,565
Wisconsin.................	2,569	2,580	45.2	0.4	168	1,165	1,169	0.4	60	1,084
Minnesota.................	252	252	4.7	(Z)	24	132	133	0.4	7	95
Pacific.....................	41,429	41,940	(X)	1.2	82	15,737	15,792	0.4	1,020	14,914
Washington...............	5,229	5,311	77.8	1.6	216	2,264	2,279	0.7	142	1,944
Oregon...................	1,982	2,001	51.7	1.0	95	895	900	0.5	59	756
California.................	32,259	32,644	86.6	1.2	420	11,803	11,833	0.3	769	11,507
Alaska...................	598	609	84.2	1.8	2	255	259	1.2	17	219
Hawaii...................	1,360	1,375	100.0	1.1	214	520	522	0.5	32	488

X Not applicable. Z Less than .05 percent. [1] Calculated on the basis of land area data from the 2010 census. [2] Covers establishments with payroll. Excludes most government employees, railroad employees, and self-employed persons. Employees are for the week including March 12.

Source: U.S. Census Bureau, "GCT-PH1 Population, Housing Units, Area, and Density: 2010 - United States -- County by State; and for Puerto Rico," 2010 Census Summary File 1, American FactFinder, accessed 13 July 2012; "Population, population change and estimated components of population change: April 1, 2010 to July 1, 2011 (CO-EST2011-alldata)," April 2012, <http://www.census.gov/popest/data/counties/totals/2011/index.html>; "County-Level Housing Unit Estimates County Housing Unit Estimates by State: April 1, 2010 to July 1, 2011," June 2012, <http://www.census.gov/popest/data/housing/totals/2011/HU-EST2011-CO.html>; and "County Business Patterns," <http://www.census.gov/econ/cbp/index.html>.

Table 27. Incorporated Places With 175,000 or More Inhabitants in 2011—Population: 1980 to 2011

[In thousands, except as indicated (237 represents 237,000). As of April 1, except 2011 as of July 1. Data for 2010 and percent change, 2010 to 2011 are based on 2010 estimates base. For 2010 and 2011 geographic boundaries are defined as of January 1, 2011. For 1990 and 2000, the counts relate to places as defined on January 1, 2000. Data for 1980 refer to boundaries in effect for that census. For 1980, the counts relate to places as defined at that census. Minus sign (–) indicates decrease. See Appendix III]

City	Number (1,000)					Percent change		Rank, 2011
	1980	1990	2000 [1]	2010	2011	2000 to 2010 [1]	2010 to 2011	
Akron, OH	237	223	217	199	198	-8.3	-0.4	113
Albuquerque, NM	332	385	449	546	553	21.7	1.3	32
Amarillo, TX	149	158	174	191	194	9.8	1.6	120
Anaheim, CA	219	267	328	336	341	2.5	1.5	54
Anchorage, AK	174	226	260	292	296	12.1	1.3	65
Arlington, TX	160	262	333	365	374	9.8	2.3	50
Atlanta, GA	425	394	416	420	432	0.8	3.0	40
Augusta–Richmond County, GA [2]	[3] 48	186	200	196	196	-2.0	0.3	116
Aurora, CO	159	222	276	325	332	17.6	2.2	56
Aurora, IL	81	100	143	198	200	38.4	0.9	111
Austin, TX	346	466	657	790	821	20.4	3.8	13
Bakersfield, CA	106	175	247	347	352	40.6	1.4	52
Baltimore, MD	787	736	651	621	619	-4.6	-0.2	24
Baton Rouge, LA	220	223	228	229	230	0.7	0.3	88
Birmingham, AL	284	265	243	212	212	-12.6	0.1	98
Boise City, ID	102	126	186	206	210	10.7	2.2	101
Boston, MA	563	575	589	618	625	4.8	1.2	21
Brownsville, TX	85	114	140	175	178	25.3	1.9	131
Buffalo, NY	358	328	293	261	261	-10.7	-0.1	72
Chandler, AZ	30	90	177	236	240	33.7	1.7	81
Charlotte, NC	315	428	541	731	751	35.2	2.7	17
Chesapeake, VA	114	152	199	222	225	11.6	1.3	91
Chicago, IL	3,005	2,783	2,896	2,696	2,707	-6.9	0.4	3
Chula Vista, CA	84	135	174	244	248	40.5	1.5	76
Cincinnati, OH	385	364	331	297	296	-10.4	-0.2	64
Cleveland, OH	574	506	478	397	394	-17.1	-0.8	47
Colorado Springs, CO	215	280	361	416	426	15.4	2.4	41
Columbus, GA	[2] 169	[2] 179	[2] 186	190	194	1.9	2.2	119
Columbus, OH	565	633	711	787	797	10.6	1.3	15
Corpus Christi, TX	232	258	277	305	308	10.0	0.9	60
Dallas, TX	905	1,008	1,189	1,198	1,223	0.8	2.1	9
Denver, CO	493	468	555	600	620	8.2	3.3	23
Des Moines, IA	191	193	199	203	207	2.4	1.6	104
Detroit, MI	1,203	1,028	951	714	707	-25.0	-1.0	18
Durham, NC	101	137	187	228	233	22.1	2.2	84
El Paso, TX	425	515	564	649	666	15.2	2.5	19
Fayetteville, NC	60	76	121	201	204	65.7	1.7	106
Fontana, CA	37	88	129	196	199	52.1	1.5	112
Fort Wayne, IN	172	173	206	254	256	23.3	0.8	74
Fort Worth, TX	385	448	535	742	759	38.6	2.3	16
Fremont, CA	132	173	203	214	217	5.2	1.3	95
Fresno, CA	217	354	428	495	501	15.7	1.3	34
Garland, TX	139	181	216	227	232	5.1	2.0	86
Gilbert, AZ	6	29	110	208	212	90.0	1.7	99
Glendale, AZ	97	148	219	227	230	3.6	1.7	87
Glendale, CA	139	180	195	192	193	-1.7	0.7	121
Grand Prairie, TX	71	100	127	175	179	37.6	2.1	130
Grand Rapids, MI	182	189	198	188	190	-4.9	0.9	124
Greensboro, NC	156	184	224	270	273	20.4	1.4	69
Henderson, NV	24	65	175	258	260	47.0	1.0	73
Hialeah, FL	145	188	226	225	230	-0.8	2.4	89
Houston, TX	1,595	1,631	1,954	2,099	2,145	7.5	2.2	4
Huntington Beach, CA	171	182	190	190	193	0.2	1.5	122
Huntsville, AL	143	160	158	180	183	13.8	1.6	126
Indianapolis, IN [2]	701	731	792	820	828	3.6	0.9	12
Irvine, CA	62	110	143	212	216	48.4	1.5	96
Irving, TX	110	155	192	216	221	12.9	2.0	93
Jackson, MS	203	197	184	174	176	-5.8	1.2	135
Jacksonville, FL	541	635	736	822	828	11.7	0.7	11
Jersey City, NJ	224	229	240	248	250	3.1	1.1	75
Kansas City, MO	448	435	442	460	463	4.1	0.7	37
Knoxville, TN	175	165	174	179	181	2.9	1.1	128
Laredo, TX	91	123	177	236	242	33.7	2.5	80
Las Vegas, NV	165	258	478	584	589	22.0	1.0	31
Lexington–Fayette, KY	204	225	261	296	302	13.5	1.9	62
Lincoln, NE	172	192	226	258	262	14.5	1.5	71
Little Rock, AR	159	176	183	194	195	5.7	0.9	117
Long Beach, CA	361	429	462	462	466	0.2	0.7	36
Los Angeles, CA	2,969	3,486	3,695	3,793	3,820	2.6	0.7	2
Louisville/Jefferson County, KY [2]	[4] 299	[4] 270	[4] 256	597	602	(X)	0.8	27
Lubbock, TX	174	186	200	230	234	15.0	1.8	83
Madison, WI	171	191	208	233	237	12.1	1.6	82
Memphis, TN	646	610	650	647	652	-0.5	0.8	20
Mesa, AZ	152	288	396	439	447	10.8	1.7	38
Miami, FL	347	359	362	399	409	10.2	2.3	44
Milwaukee, WI	636	628	597	595	598	-0.4	0.5	28
Minneapolis, MN	371	368	383	383	388	(Z)	1.4	48
Mobile, AL	200	196	199	195	195	-1.9	-0.1	118
Modesto, CA	107	165	189	201	203	6.5	0.8	107
Montgomery, AL	178	188	202	206	208	2.1	1.2	103
Moreno Valley, CA	([5])	119	142	193	198	35.8	2.3	114

See footnotes at end of table.

Table 27. Incorporated Places With 175,000 or More Inhabitants in 2011—Population: 1980 to 2011-Continued.

See headnote on page 33.

City	Number (1,000)					Percent change		Rank, 2011
	1980	1990	2000 [1]	2010	2011	2000 to 2010 [1]	2010 to 2011	
Nashville–Davidson, TN [2]	456	488	570	601	610	5.5	1.4	26
New Orleans, LA	558	497	485	344	361	-29.1	4.9	51
New York, NY	7,072	7,323	8,008	8,175	8,245	2.1	0.9	1
Newark, NJ	329	275	274	277	278	1.3	0.1	68
Newport News, VA	145	171	180	181	180	0.3	-0.6	129
Norfolk, VA	267	261	234	243	243	3.6	-0.1	79
North Las Vegas, NV	43	48	115	217	219	87.9	1.0	94
Oakland, CA	339	372	399	391	396	-2.2	1.3	46
Oklahoma City, OK	404	445	506	580	592	14.6	2.1	30
Omaha, NE	314	336	390	409	415	4.9	1.5	43
Orlando, FL	128	165	186	238	243	28.2	2.1	78
Overland Park, KS	82	112	149	173	176	16.3	1.6	134
Oxnard, CA	108	143	170	198	200	16.2	1.0	110
Philadelphia, PA	1,688	1,586	1,518	1,526	1,536	0.6	0.7	5
Phoenix, AZ	790	983	1,321	1,446	1,469	9.4	1.6	6
Pittsburgh, PA	424	370	335	306	307	-8.6	0.6	61
Plano, TX	72	128	222	260	270	17.0	3.8	70
Portland, OR	368	439	529	584	594	10.3	1.7	29
Providence, RI	157	161	174	178	178	2.5	(Z)	132
Raleigh, NC	150	212	276	404	416	46.3	3.1	42
Reno, NV	101	134	180	225	228	24.8	1.0	90
Richmond, VA	219	203	198	204	206	3.2	0.6	105
Riverside, CA	171	227	255	304	311	19.1	2.2	59
Rochester, NY	242	230	220	211	211	-4.2	0.1	100
Sacramento, CA	276	369	407	466	472	14.6	1.2	35
Salt Lake City, UT	163	160	182	186	190	2.6	1.9	123
San Antonio, TX	786	935	1,145	1,328	1,360	16.0	2.4	7
San Bernardino, CA	119	165	185	210	213	13.2	1.5	97
San Diego, CA	876	1,111	1,223	1,307	1,326	6.9	1.4	8
San Francisco, CA	679	724	777	805	813	3.7	0.9	14
San Jose, CA	629	782	895	953	967	5.7	1.6	10
Santa Ana, CA	204	294	338	325	329	-4.0	1.5	57
Santa Clarita, CA	([5])	111	151	176	178	16.7	0.7	133
Scottsdale, AZ	89	130	203	217	221	7.2	1.7	92
Seattle, WA	494	516	563	609	621	8.0	2.0	22
Shreveport, LA	206	199	200	199	201	-0.4	0.8	108
Spokane, WA	171	177	196	209	210	6.8	0.6	102
St. Louis, MO	453	397	348	319	318	-8.3	-0.4	58
St. Paul, MN	270	272	287	285	288	-0.7	1.2	66
St. Petersburg, FL	239	240	248	245	245	-1.4	0.1	77
Stockton, CA	150	211	244	292	296	19.7	1.6	63
Tacoma, WA	159	177	194	198	201	2.5	1.1	109
Tallahassee, FL	82	125	151	181	183	20.4	0.9	125
Tampa, FL	272	280	303	336	346	10.6	3.1	53
Toledo, OH	355	333	314	287	286	-8.4	-0.4	67
Tucson, AZ	331	405	487	520	526	6.9	1.1	33
Tulsa, OK	361	367	393	392	396	-0.3	1.2	45
Urban Honolulu CDP, HI [6]	(NA)	(NA)	(NA)	337	341	(NA)	1.1	55
Virginia Beach, VA	262	393	425	438	443	3.0	1.1	39
Washington, DC	638	607	572	602	618	5.2	2.7	25
Wichita, KS	280	304	344	382	384	11.1	0.5	49
Winston–Salem, NC	132	143	186	230	232	23.6	1.2	85
Worcester, MA	162	170	173	181	182	4.9	0.3	127
Yonkers, NY	195	188	196	196	197	-0.1	0.7	115

NA Not available. Z Less than .05 percent. [1] Based on 2000 Census numbers as tabulated. [2] Represents the portion of a consolidated city that is not within one or more separately incorporated places. [3] Data are for the incorporated places of Athens city and Augusta city before consolidation of the city and county governments. [4] Data are for the incorporated place of Louisville city before consolidation of the city and county governments. [5] Not incorporated. [6] CDP=Census Designated Place.

Source: U.S. Census Bureau, 1980 data: U.S. Census Bureau, *1980 Census of Population, Vol. 1, Characteristics of the Population, PC80-1*. 1990 data: U.S. Census Bureau, *1990 Census CP-1-1, General Population Characteristics*, and *1990 CPH-L-157 Corrected Counts*. 2000 Census data: 2000 Census of Population and Housing, *Population and Housing Unit Counts PHC-3*. 2010 Census data: *2010 Census Redistricting Data (Public Law 94-171) Summary File*, Table P1; beginning 2010: *Annual Estimates of the Resident Population for Incorporated Places over 50,000, Ranked by July 1, 2011 Population: April 1, 2010 to July 1, 2011 (SUB-EST2011-01)*, June 2012, <http://www.census.gov/popest/data/cities/totals/2011/index.html>.

Table 28. Incorporated Places by Population Size: 1990 to 2011

[153.1 represents 153,100,000. See Appendix III]

Population size	Number of incorporated places				Population (mil.)				Percent of total			
	1990	2000	2010	2011	1990	2000	2010	2011	1990	2000	2010	2011
Total.....................	19,262	19,452	19,540	19,516	153.1	173.5	192.0	194.4	100.0	100.0	100.0	100.0
1,000,000 or more.........	8	9	9	9	20.0	22.9	23.6	23.8	13.1	13.2	12.3	12.3
500,000 to 999,999.........	15	20	24	25	10.1	12.9	16.1	16.9	6.6	7.4	8.4	8.7
250,000 to 499,999.........	41	37	40	41	14.2	13.3	14.0	14.2	9.3	7.7	7.3	7.3
100,000 to 249,999.........	131	172	200	210	19.1	25.5	30.2	31.4	12.5	14.7	15.7	16.2
50,000 to 99,999............	309	363	432	430	21.2	24.9	30.1	29.8	13.8	14.4	15.7	15.4
25,000 to 49,999............	567	644	723	719	20.0	22.6	25.2	25.1	13.1	13.0	13.1	12.9
10,000 to 24,999............	1,290	1,435	1,542	1,544	20.3	22.6	24.2	24.3	13.3	13.0	12.6	12.5
Under 10,000................	16,901	16,772	16,570	16,538	28.2	28.7	28.7	28.8	18.4	16.5	14.9	14.8

Source: U.S. Census Bureau, *1990 Census of Population and Housing, Population and Housing Unit Counts (CPH-2-1)*; Census 2000 PHC-3, *Population and Housing Unit Counts; 2010 Census Redistricting Data (Public Law 94-171) Summary File*; "Annual Estimates of Incorporated Places: April 1, 2010 to July 1, 2011," <http://www.census.gov/popest/data/cities/totals/2011/index.html>.

Table 29. Urban and Rural Population by State: 1990 and 2000

[222,361 represents 222,361,000. As of April 1. Resident population. For urban definitions, see text, this section]

State	Urban population				Rural popula-tion, 2000 (1,000)	State	Urban population				Rural popula-tion, 2000 (1,000)
	1990		2000, current definition				1990		2000, current definition		
	Former definition (percent)	Current definition (percent)	Number (1,000)	Percent			Former definition (percent)	Current definition (percent)	Number (1,000)	Percent	
U.S. total....	75.2	78.0	222,361	79.0	59,061						
						MO.........	68.7	69.6	3,883	69.4	1,712
AL.........	60.4	56.8	2,466	55.4	1,981	MT.........	52.5	56.4	488	54.1	414
AK.........	67.5	61.0	411	65.6	216	NE.........	66.1	67.2	1,194	69.8	518
AZ.........	87.5	86.5	4,524	88.2	607	NV.........	88.3	87.4	1,829	91.5	170
AR.........	53.5	52.0	1,404	52.5	1,269	NH.........	51.0	57.2	732	59.3	503
CA.........	92.6	93.7	31,990	94.4	1,882	NJ.........	89.4	93.5	7,939	94.4	475
CO.........	82.4	83.8	3,633	84.5	668	NM.........	73.0	75.0	1,364	75.0	456
CT.........	79.1	87.0	2,988	87.7	418	NY.........	84.3	87.4	16,603	87.5	2,374
DE.........	73.0	79.2	628	80.1	156	NC.........	50.4	57.8	4,849	60.2	3,200
DC.........	100.0	100.0	572	100.0	–	ND.........	53.3	53.4	359	55.9	283
FL.........	84.8	88.0	14,270	89.3	1,712						
						OH.........	74.1	77.5	8,782	77.4	2,571
GA.........	63.2	68.7	5,864	71.6	2,322	OK.........	67.7	65.2	2,255	65.3	1,196
HI.........	89.0	90.5	1,108	91.5	103	OR.........	70.5	74.9	2,694	78.7	727
ID.........	57.4	62.2	859	66.4	434	PA.........	68.9	76.8	9,464	77.1	2,817
IL.........	84.6	86.4	10,910	87.8	1,510	RI.........	86.0	89.9	953	90.9	95
IN.........	64.9	69.1	4,304	70.8	1,776	SC.........	54.6	61.5	2,427	60.5	1,585
IA.........	60.6	59.4	1,787	61.1	1,139	SD.........	50.0	50.3	391	51.9	363
KS.........	69.1	69.5	1,921	71.4	768	TN.........	60.9	62.7	3,620	63.6	2,069
KY.........	51.8	55.9	2,254	55.8	1,788	TX.........	80.3	81.2	17,204	82.5	3,648
LA.........	68.1	72.9	3,246	72.6	1,223	UT.........	87.0	86.8	1,970	88.2	263
ME.........	44.6	42.6	513	40.2	762						
						VT.........	32.2	40.2	232	38.2	376
MD.........	81.3	85.0	4,559	86.1	738	VA.........	69.4	71.5	5,170	73.0	1,909
MA.........	84.3	90.5	5,801	91.4	548	WA.........	76.4	79.9	4,831	82.0	1,063
MI.........	70.5	75.2	7,419	74.7	2,519	WV.........	36.1	46.9	833	46.1	976
MN.........	69.9	69.0	3,490	70.9	1,429	WI.........	65.7	67.3	3,664	68.3	1,700
MS.........	47.1	49.1	1,387	48.8	1,457	WY.........	65.0	67.1	321	65.1	172

– Represents zero.

Source: U.S. Census Bureau, 2000 Census of Population and Housing, *Population and Housing Unit Counts PHC-3*. See also <http://www.census.gov/prod/cen2000/index.html>.

Table 30. Mobility Status of the Population by Selected Characteristics: 1981 to 2011

[As of March (221,641 represents 221,641,000). For persons 1 year old and over. Based on comparison of place of residence in immediate prior year and year shown. Excludes members of the Armed Forces except those living off post or with their families on post. Based on Current Population Survey, Annual Social and Economic Supplement. See text, this section and Appendix III. For composition of regions, see map, inside front cover]

Mobility period and characteristic	Total (1,000)	Non–movers	Movers (different house in United States)		Different county			Movers from abroad
			Total	Same county	Total	Same state	Different state	
1981	221,641	83	17	10	6	3	3	1
1991	244,884	83	16	10	6	3	3	1
2001	275,611	86	14	8	6	3	3	1
2011, total	**302,005**	**88**	**11**	**8**	**4**	**2**	**2**	**-**
1 to 4 years old	17,160	82	18	12	5	3	2	-
5 to 9 years old	20,870	86	14	10	4	2	2	-
10 to 14 years old	20,020	89	11	8	3	2	1	-
15 to 19 years old	20,886	89	11	8	3	2	1	-
20 to 24 years old	21,525	76	23	16	7	4	3	1
25 to 29 years old	21,382	76	23	15	8	4	3	1
30 to 44 years old	60,044	87	13	9	4	2	2	-
45 to 64 years old	80,939	94	6	4	2	1	1	-
65 to 74 years old	21,414	97	3	2	1	1	1	-
75 to 84 years old	12,807	97	3	2	1	1	1	-
85 years old and over	4,957	97	3	3	1	-	-	-
Northeast	54,179	92	8	5	2	1	1	-
Midwest	65,257	89	11	7	4	2	1	-
South	111,651	88	12	8	4	2	2	-
West	70,918	86	13	10	3	2	2	-
Persons 16 years old and over	239,917	89	11	7	3	2	2	-
Civilian labor force	152,868	88	12	8	4	2	2	-
Employed	138,410	88	11	8	4	2	1	-
Unemployed	14,458	82	18	12	5	3	3	1
Armed Forces	919	66	30	14	16	3	12	4
Not in labor force	86,131	91	8	6	3	1	1	-
Employed civilians, 16 years old and over	138,410	88	11	8	4	2	1	-
Management, business, and financial	21,427	91	9	6	4	2	2	-
Professional	31,277	89	11	6	4	2	2	-
Service	24,287	85	14	10	4	3	1	1
Sales	15,057	87	12	8	4	3	2	-
Office and administrative support	17,941	90	10	7	3	2	1	-
Farming, fishing, and forestry	841	87	13	8	5	3	2	-
Construction and extraction	6,907	87	12	10	3	2	1	-
Installation, maintenance, and repair	4,690	90	10	8	3	1	1	-
Production	8,038	89	11	9	3	2	1	-
Transportation and material moving	7,945	89	11	8	3	2	1	-
Tenure:								
Owner occupied units	205,122	95	5	3	2	1	1	-
Renter occupied units	93,383	74	26	18	7	4	3	1
No cash renter occupied units	3,500	83	17	9	8	4	4	1

– Represents or rounds to zero.

Source: U.S. Census Bureau, "Geographical Mobility: 2010 to 2011," November 2011, <http://www.census.gov/hhes/migration/data/cps/cps2011.html> and previous reports.

Table 31. Movers by Type of Move and Reason for Moving: 2011

[As of March (35,075 represents 35,075,000). For persons 1 year old and over. Based on comparison of place of residence in 2010 and 2011. Excludes members of the Armed Forces except those living off post or with their families on post. Based on Current Population Survey, Annual Social and Economic Supplement. See text, this section and Appendix III]

Reason for move	All movers	Intra-county	Inter-county	From abroad	Reason for move	All movers	Intra-county	Inter-county	From abroad
Total (1,000)	35,075	23,325	10,691	1,058	Housing–related reasons	44.9	55.7	24.6	11.2
					Wanted to own home/not rent	4.4	5.2	2.9	-
PERCENT DISTRIBUTION					New/better house/apartment	16.2	21.4	6.1	1.8
Total	100.0	100.0	100.0	100.0	Better neighborhood/less crime	3.9	4.4	2.9	2.5
Family–related reasons	27.9	27.7	27.6	35.4	Cheaper housing	10.5	12.5	7.0	2.5
Change in marital status	5.6	5.5	5.5	7.0	Other housing	10.0	12.2	5.7	4.4
To establish own household	9.5	11.3	6.0	6.5					
Other family reasons	12.8	10.9	16.1	21.9	Other reasons	8.8	6.8	11.6	24.0
Work–related reasons	18.5	9.8	36.3	29.4	Attend/leave college	2.5	1.3	4.5	9.4
New job/job transfer	8.1	2.0	20.4	16.4	Change of climate	0.4	0.2	1.0	0.1
To look for work/lost job	2.6	1.2	5.2	7.3	Health reasons	1.6	1.6	1.6	0.8
Closer to work/easier commute	5.9	5.6	7.3	0.5	Natural disaster	0.1	0.1	0.1	-
Retired	0.3	0.2	0.6	0.9	Other reason	4.1	3.5	4.4	13.8
Other job–related reason	1.5	0.8	2.9	4.3					

– Represents or rounds to zero.

Source: U.S. Census Bureau, "Geographical Mobility: 2010 to 2011," November 2011, <http://www.census.gov/hhes/migration/data/cps/cps2011.html>.

Table 32. Mobility Status of Households by Household Income: 2011

[As of March (118,702 represents 118,702,000). Covers householders 15 years old and over. Based on comparison of place of residence in 2010 and 2011. Excludes members of the Armed Forces except those living off post or with their families on post. Based on Current Population Survey, Annual Social and Economic Supplement. See text, this section and Appendix III]

Household income in 2010	Total (1,000)	Non–movers	Percent distribution						Movers from abroad
			Movers (different house in United States)						
			Total	Same county	Different county				
					Total	Same state	Different state	
Householders, 15 years and over......	118,702	89	11	7	3	2	2	-
Under $5,000 or loss.........................	4,183	78	21	15	6	4	2	2
$5,000 to $9,999............................	5,055	82	18	13	4	3	2	-
$10,000 to $14,999.........................	7,061	85	14	10	4	2	2	-
$15,000 to $24,999.........................	14,197	87	13	9	4	2	2	-
$25,000 to $34,999.........................	12,881	87	12	9	4	2	2	-
$35,000 to $49,999.........................	16,466	88	12	8	4	2	2	-
$50,000 to $69,999.........................	17,284	90	10	7	3	2	1	-
$70,000 to $99,999.........................	17,337	91	8	5	3	1	2	-
$100,000 and over..........................	24,237	93	7	4	3	1	1	-

– Represents or rounds to zero.

Source: U.S. Census Bureau, "Geographical Mobility: 2010 to 2011," November 2011, <http://www.census.gov/hhes/migration/data/cps/cps2011.html>.

Table 33. Mobility Status of Resident Population by State: 2010

[In percent, except as indicated (305,629 represents 305,629,000). Based on comparison of place of residence in 2009 and 2010. The American Community Survey universe includes the household population and the population living in institutions, college dormitories, and other group quarters. Based on a sample and subject to sampling variability. See text, this section and Appendix III]

State	Population 1 year old and over [1] (1,000)	Same house in 2009	Different house in United States in 2009		State	Population 1 year old and over [1] (1,000)	Same house in 2009	Different house in United States in 2009	
			Same county	Different county				Same county	Different county
U.S...	305,629	84.6	9.4	5.4	MO.......	5,921	83.9	9.1	6.6
AL.......	4,730	84.3	9.6	5.8	MT........	979	84.0	8.7	7.0
AK.......	703	80.4	10.9	8.0	NE........	1,803	83.0	10.1	6.4
AZ.......	6,333	80.0	13.9	5.5	NV........	2,667	76.1	18.4	4.9
AR.......	2,888	82.7	10.1	6.9	NH........	1,304	85.8	8.4	5.4
CA.......	36,908	83.4	11.7	4.2	NJ........	8,710	90.0	5.7	3.6
CO.......	4,988	81.0	9.8	8.5	NM......	2,040	85.1	8.5	6.0
CT.......	3,541	87.6	7.7	4.2	NY........	19,172	88.5	6.8	3.8
DE.......	890	85.9	9.3	4.3	NC........	9,443	84.5	8.7	6.2
DC.......	597	79.5	10.7	8.6	ND........	666	83.6	8.5	7.4
FL.......	18,648	83.4	10.3	5.5	OH........	11,405	85.4	9.5	4.7
GA.......	9,587	83.6	8.7	7.3	OK........	3,716	82.5	10.4	6.7
HI........	1,346	84.7	9.2	4.8	OR........	3,794	82.0	11.0	6.5
ID........	1,551	82.5	10.1	7.0	PA........	12,578	87.9	7.3	4.5
IL........	12,680	86.8	8.6	4.1	RI........	1,042	86.4	8.1	4.5
IN........	6,415	84.7	9.4	5.5	SC........	4,577	84.6	8.4	6.6
IA........	3,013	84.7	8.9	5.9	SD........	806	84.5	7.9	7.3
KS.......	2,821	83.0	9.7	6.9	TN........	6,283	84.4	9.8	5.5
KY.......	4,297	84.7	8.7	6.2	TX.......	24,899	82.3	10.9	6.1
LA.......	4,484	85.3	8.9	5.5	UT........	2,724	82.3	11.3	5.8
ME......	1,314	86.5	8.3	5.0	VT........	619	86.4	7.6	5.6
MD......	5,717	86.0	7.6	5.5	VA........	7,931	85.1	6.2	8.0
MA......	6,489	86.0	8.2	4.8	WA.......	6,661	82.0	11.2	5.9
MI.......	9,762	85.1	9.5	4.9	WV.......	1,834	88.6	6.6	4.7
MN......	5,244	85.4	8.1	6.0	WI........	5,623	85.8	9.2	4.7
MS.......	2,931	85.7	8.0	6.1	WY.......	557	79.8	11.9	7.9

[1] Includes persons moving from abroad, not shown separately.

Source: U.S. Census Bureau, 2010 American Community Survey, B07003, "Residence 1 Year Ago by Sex," <http://factfinder2.census.gov/>, accessed July 2012.

Table 34. Persons 65 Years Old and Over—Characteristics by Sex: 2000 to 2011

[As of March, except as noted (32.6 represents 32,600,000). Covers civilian noninstitutional population. Excludes members of Armed Forces except those living off post or with their families on post. Data for 2000 data based on 1990 census population controls; beginning 2005, data based on 2000 census population controls and an expanded sample of households. Based on Current Population Survey. See text, this section and Appendix III]

Characteristic	Total				Male				Female			
	2000	2005	2010	2011	2000	2005	2010	2011	2000	2005	2010	2011
Total (million)	**32.6**	**35.2**	**38.6**	**39.2**	**13.9**	**15.1**	**16.8**	**17.1**	**18.7**	**20.0**	**21.8**	**22.1**
PERCENT DISTRIBUTION												
Marital status:												
Never married	3.9	4.1	4.3	4.4	4.2	4.4	4.1	4.4	3.6	3.9	4.5	4.3
Married	57.2	57.7	57.6	57.8	75.2	74.9	74.5	73.3	43.8	44.7	44.5	45.8
Spouse present	54.6	54.8	55.2	55.4	72.6	71.7	71.7	70.5	41.3	42.0	42.4	43.7
Spouse absent [1]	2.6	2.9	2.4	2.4	2.6	3.2	2.8	2.8	2.5	2.7	2.1	2.1
Widowed	32.1	30.3	28.1	27.3	14.4	13.7	12.7	12.6	45.3	42.9	39.9	38.6
Divorced	6.7	7.9	10.0	10.6	6.1	7.0	8.7	9.6	7.2	8.5	11.1	11.4
Educational attainment:												
Less than ninth grade	16.7	13.4	10.2	9.8	17.8	13.2	10.2	10.2	15.9	13.5	10.1	9.5
Completed 9th to 12th grade, but no high school diploma	13.8	12.7	10.3	9.6	12.7	11.9	9.7	8.6	14.7	13.3	10.8	10.3
High school graduate	35.9	36.3	36.4	36.3	30.4	31.6	32.0	31.8	39.9	39.9	39.8	39.8
Some college or associate's degree	18.0	18.7	20.6	21.1	17.8	18.4	19.7	20.5	18.2	19.0	21.2	21.6
Bachelor's or advanced degree	15.6	18.9	22.5	23.2	21.4	24.9	28.4	28.9	11.4	14.3	18.0	18.8
Labor force participation: [2]												
Employed	12.4	14.5	16.2	16.7	16.9	19.1	20.5	21.3	9.1	11.1	12.9	13.1
Unemployed	0.4	0.5	1.2	1.2	0.6	0.7	1.6	1.6	0.3	0.4	0.9	0.9
Not in labor force	87.2	84.9	82.6	82.1	82.5	80.2	77.9	77.2	90.6	88.5	86.2	86.0
Percent below poverty level [3]	9.7	9.8	8.9	9.0	6.9	7.0	6.6	6.7	11.8	11.9	10.7	10.7

[1] Includes separated. [2] Annual averages of monthly figures. Source: U.S. Bureau of Labor Statistics,"Labor Force Characteristics," <http://www.bls.gov/cps/lfcharacteristics.htm#laborforce>. See footnote 2, Table 596. [3] Poverty status based on income in preceding year.

Source: Except as noted, U.S. Census Bureau, Current Population Reports, "The Older Population in the United States: March 2000," <http://www.census.gov/population/age/data/2000.html>; "Educational Attainment," <http://www.census.gov/population/www/socdemo/educ-attn.html>; "Families and Living Arrangements," <http://www.census.gov/population/www/socdemo/hh-fam.html>; and "Detailed Poverty Tabulations from the CPS," <http://www.census.gov/hhes/www/cpstables/032010/pov/toc.htm>.

Table 35. Persons 65 Years and Over—Living Arrangements and Disability Status: 2010

[In thousands (40,434 represents 40,434,000), except as indicated. Based on the American Community Survey (ACS). Disability data limited to civilian noninstitutionalized population. Based on a sample and subject to sampling variability; see text, this section and Appendix III]

Relationship by household type	Number	Percent distribution	Type of disability	Total	65 to 74 years old	75 years old and over
Total	**40,434**	**100.0**	**Persons with any disability**	**14,352**	**5,498**	**8,854**
In households	38,869	96.1				
In family households	26,809	66.3	With a hearing difficulty	5,904	1,931	3,973
Householder	13,379	33.1	With a vision difficulty	2,688	899	1,789
Spouse	9,563	23.7	With a cognitive difficulty	3,712	1,175	2,537
Parent	2,208	5.5	With an ambulatory difficulty	9,315	3,465	5,850
Other relatives	1,468	3.6	With a self-care difficulty	3,428	991	2,437
Nonrelatives	191	0.5	With an independent living difficulty	6,338	1,753	4,584
In nonfamily households	12,060	29.8				
Householder	11,495	28.4				
Living alone	10,908	27.0				
Not living alone	587	1.5				
Nonrelatives	565	1.4				
In group quarters	1,565	3.9				

Source: U.S. Census Bureau, 2010 American Community Survey, B09017, "Relationship by Household Type (Including Living Alone) for the Population 65 Years and Over;" B18101, "Sex by Age by Disability Status;" B18102, "Sex by Age by Hearing Difficulty;" B18103, "Sex by Age by Vision Difficulty;" B18104, "Sex by Age by Cognitive Difficulty;" B18105, "Sex by Age by Ambulatory Difficulty;" B18106, "Sex by Age by Self-Care Difficulty;" B18107, "Sex by Age by Independent Living Difficulty," <http://factfinder.census.gov/>, accessed March 2012.

Table 36. Selected Characteristics of Racial Groups and Hispanic or Latino Population: 2010

[In thousands (204,289 represents 204,289,000), except as indicated. The American Community Survey universe includes the household population and the population living in institutions, college dormitories, and other group quarters. Based on a sample and subject to sampling variability; see text, this section and Appendix III]

Characteristic	Total population	White alone	Black or African American alone	American Indian, Alaska Native alone	Asian alone	Native Hawaiian and Other Pacific Islander alone	Some other race alone	Two or more races	Hispanic or Latino origin [1]	White alone, not Hispanic or Latino
EDUCATIONAL ATTAINMENT										
Persons 25 years old and over, total	**204,289**	**157,437**	**23,531**	**1,504**	**9,964**	**287**	**8,150**	**3,416**	**27,314**	**139,695**
Less than 9th grade	12,453	7,805	1,244	134	861	11	2,154	244	6,149	4,055
9th to 12th grade, no diploma	17,010	11,493	3,010	207	589	26	1,380	304	4,172	8,894
High school graduate (includes equivalency)	58,226	45,587	7,459	462	1,594	105	2,189	830	7,225	40,927
Some college, no degree	43,469	33,715	5,852	385	1,302	79	1,278	859	4,709	30,603
Associate's degree	15,553	12,349	1,753	115	649	24	370	294	1,498	11,325
Bachelor's degree	36,244	29,269	2,748	134	2,945	33	551	566	2,431	27,519
Graduate degree	21,334	17,219	1,465	68	2,024	10	229	318	1,130	16,372
Percent high school graduate or higher	85.6	87.7	81.9	77.3	85.4	87.4	56.6	83.9	62.2	90.7
Percent bachelor's degree or higher	28.2	29.5	17.9	13.4	49.9	14.9	9.6	25.9	13.0	31.4
OCCUPATION										
Employed civilian population, 16 years old and over, total	**139,034**	**106,817**	**14,927**	**925**	**7,131**	**216**	**6,395**	**2,623**	**20,756**	**93,545**
Management, business, science, and arts occupations	49,976	40,197	4,234	243	3,431	55	969	847	3,953	37,443
Management, business, and financial occupations	19,971	16,454	1,545	96	1,124	26	405	321	1,640	15,311
Computer, engineering, and science occupations	7,161	5,436	434	27	1,022	7	110	125	456	5,109
Education, legal, community service, arts, and media occupations	15,210	12,365	1,509	84	623	16	333	281	1,346	11,441
Healthcare practitioners and technical occupations	7,634	5,942	746	35	662	6	120	120	511	5,582
Service occupations	25,059	17,321	3,801	232	1,226	51	1,857	571	5,519	13,954
Sales and office occupations	34,711	26,995	3,872	219	1,556	59	1,316	694	4,628	23,953
Natural resources, construction, and maintenance occupations	12,697	10,234	806	109	230	20	1,078	220	3,219	8,226
Farming, fishing, and forestry occupations	1,047	775	49	11	15	1	180	16	536	437
Construction and extraction occupations	7,070	5,677	406	67	93	10	691	126	1,981	4,468
Installation, maintenance, and repair occupations	4,581	3,782	351	30	123	8	207	79	703	3,321
Production, transportation, and material moving occupations	16,590	12,071	2,214	122	687	31	1,175	290	3,437	9,968
Production occupations	8,221	6,032	914	58	455	11	617	135	1,754	4,969
Transportation occupations	4,877	3,614	748	33	136	11	253	83	780	3,125
Material moving occupations	3,493	2,425	552	32	97	9	306	72	903	1,874
FAMILY INCOME IN THE PAST 12 MONTHS										
Total families	**76,089**	**58,982**	**8,733**	**557**	**3,396**	**103**	**3,068**	**1,251**	**10,345**	**52,234**
Less than $10,000	3,824	2,229	1,014	62	130	6	283	100	837	1,732
$10,000 to $19,999	5,803	3,756	1,183	74	208	8	440	134	1,378	2,895
$20,000 to $29,999	7,196	5,107	1,170	75	241	10	457	135	1,482	4,155
$30,000 to $39,999	7,376	5,500	1,008	70	249	10	415	124	1,325	4,653
$40,000 to $49,999	6,967	5,390	813	57	243	10	336	117	1,094	4,688
$50,000 to $59,999	6,443	5,082	698	47	241	9	262	105	881	4,508
$60,000 to $74,999	8,548	6,909	806	52	345	12	292	131	1,015	6,232
$75,000 to $99,999	10,639	8,780	878	55	473	14	285	153	1,036	8,080
$100,000 to $124,999	7,097	5,932	510	29	377	10	146	94	574	5,532
$125,000 to $149,999	4,164	3,492	273	15	256	6	69	53	296	3,281
$150,000 to $199,999	4,131	3,445	236	13	322	4	53	57	255	3,256
$200,000 or more	3,901	3,359	145	9	310	4	29	46	173	3,222
Median family income in the past 12 months (dol.) [2]	60,609	64,818	39,900	39,664	76,736	58,083	38,157	51,115	41,102	67,892
POVERTY STATUS IN THE PAST 12 MONTHS [3]										
Persons below poverty level	46,216	27,952	10,100	701	1,801	93	3,931	1,638	12,307	20,438
Percent below poverty level	15.3	12.5	27.1	28.4	12.5	18.8	27.0	20.1	24.8	10.6
Families below poverty level	8,580	5,113	2,031	132	309	17	763	216	2,301	3,707
Percent below poverty level	11.3	8.7	23.3	23.7	9.1	16.1	24.9	17.3	22.2	7.1

See footnotes at end of table.

Table 36. Selected Characteristics of Racial Groups and Hispanic or Latino Population: 2010-Continued.

See headnote on page 39.

Characteristic	Total population	White alone	Black or African American alone	American Indian, Alaska Native alone	Asian alone	Native Hawaiian and Other Pacific Islander alone	Some other race alone	Two or more races	Hispanic or Latino origin [1]	White alone, not Hispanic or Latino
HOUSING TENURE										
Total households..............	**114,567**	**89,549**	**13,738**	**813**	**4,583**	**131**	**3,831**	**1,922**	**13,269**	**80,857**
Owner-occupied................	74,873	63,129	6,071	441	2,675	58	1,522	978	6,255	58,684
Renter-occupied...............	39,694	26,420	7,668	372	1,908	73	2,309	944	7,014	22,173

[1] Persons of Hispanic origin may be of any race. [2] For definition of median, see Guide to Tabular Presentation. [3] For explanation of poverty level, see text, Section 13.

Source: U.S. Census Bureau, 2010 American Community Survey, B15002, "Sex by Educational Attainment for the Population 25 Years and Over"; B24010, "Sex by Occupation for the Employed Civilian Population 16 Years and Over," B19101, "Family Income in the Past 12 Months (In 2010 Inflation-Adjusted Dollars);" B19113, "Median Family Income in the Past 12 Months (In 2010 Inflation-Adjusted Dollars);" B19101, "Family Incomes in the Past 12 Months by Sex by Age;" B17010, "Poverty Status in the Past 12 Months by Sex by Age;" B17001, "Poverty Status in the Past 12 Months by Family Type by Presence of Related Children Under 18 Years by Age of Related Children;" B25003, "Tenure," <http://factfinder2.census.gov/>; accessed July 2012.

Table 37. Social and Economic Characteristics of the Hispanic Population: 2010

[As of March, except labor force status, annual average (48,901 represents 48,901,000). Excludes members of the Armed Forces except those living off post or with their families on post. Based on Current Population Survey; see text, this section and Appendix III]

Characteristic	Number (1,000)					Percent distribution				
	His-panic, total [1]	Mexi-can	Puerto Rican	Cuban	Central, South Ameri-can	His-panic, total [1]	Mexi-can	Puerto Rican	Cuban	Central, South Ameri-can
Total persons.....................	**48,901**	**32,071**	**4,406**	**1,826**	**6,697**	**100.0**	**100.0**	**100.0**	**100.0**	**100.0**
Under 5 years old.....................	5,559	3,972	497	95	599	11.4	12.4	11.3	5.2	8.9
5 to 14 years old.....................	9,054	6,392	796	224	955	18.5	19.9	18.1	12.3	14.3
15 to 44 years old.....................	23,069	15,263	1,928	706	3,466	47.2	47.6	43.8	38.7	51.8
45 to 64 years old.....................	8,405	4,972	854	455	1,314	17.2	15.5	19.4	25.0	19.6
65 years old and over.................	2,815	1,472	329	346	363	5.8	4.6	7.4	18.9	5.4
EDUCATIONAL ATTAINMENT										
Persons 25 years old and over.....	**26,375**	**16,421**	**2,395**	**1,285**	**4,143**	**100.0**	**100.0**	**100.0**	**100.0**	**100.0**
High school graduate or more..........	16,580	9,419	1,791	1,046	2,717	62.9	57.4	74.8	81.4	65.6
Bachelor's degree or more.............	3,665	1,743	420	336	785	13.9	10.6	17.5	26.2	18.9
LABOR FORCE STATUS [2]										
Civilians 16 years old and over.....	**33,713**	**21,267**	**3,110**	**1,549**	**(NA)**	**100.0**	**100.0**	**100.0**	**100.0**	**(NA)**
Civilian labor force.....................	22,748	14,403	1,906	970	(NA)	67.5	67.7	61.3	62.6	(NA)
Employed.....................	19,906	12,622	1,612	850	(NA)	59.0	59.4	51.8	54.9	(NA)
Unemployed.....................	2,843	1,781	293	120	(NA)	8.4	8.4	9.4	7.7	(NA)
Unemployment rate [3]............	12.5	12.4	15.4	12.4	(NA)	(X)	(X)	(X)	(X)	(NA)
Male.....................	12.7	12.3	17.3	12.9	(NA)	(X)	(X)	(X)	(X)	(NA)
Female.....................	12.3	12.4	13.3	11.7	(NA)	(X)	(X)	(X)	(X)	(NA)
Not in labor force.....................	10,964	6,864	1,204	579	(NA)	32.5	32.3	38.7	37.4	(NA)
HOUSEHOLDS [4]										
Total.....................	**13,298**	**8,070**	**1,430**	**702**	**1,863**	**100.0**	**100.0**	**100.0**	**100.0**	**100.0**
Family households.....................	10,412	6,564	1,009	473	1,458	78.3	81.3	70.6	67.4	78.3
Married-couple families.................	6,589	4,308	532	317	906	49.5	53.4	37.2	45.2	48.6
Male householder, no spouse present.....................	1,079	682	98	44	174	8.1	8.4	6.9	6.3	9.3
Female householder, no spouse present.....................	2,745	1,574	379	111	377	20.6	19.5	26.5	15.9	20.2
Nonfamily households.....................	2,885	1,507	421	229	405	21.7	18.7	29.4	32.6	21.7
Male householder.....................	1,625	927	197	104	233	12.2	11.5	13.8	14.8	12.5
Female householder.....................	1,260	580	224	125	171	9.5	7.2	15.6	17.9	9.2
Size:										
One person.....................	2,054	1,015	333	178	277	15.4	12.6	23.3	25.3	14.9
Two people.....................	3,039	1,653	390	223	418	22.9	20.5	27.3	31.7	22.4
Three people.....................	2,531	1,448	300	130	409	19.0	17.9	21.0	18.6	22.0
Four people.....................	2,632	1,732	212	113	380	19.8	21.5	14.8	16.1	20.4
Five or more people.....................	3,041	2,222	195	58	379	22.9	27.5	13.7	8.3	20.3
FAMILY INCOME IN 2009										
Total families.....................	**10,412**	**6,564**	**1,009**	**473**	**1,458**	**100.0**	**100.0**	**100.0**	**100.0**	**100.0**
Less than $5,000.....................	341	228	40	9	28	3.3	3.5	3.9	1.9	1.9
$5,000 to $14,999.....................	1,006	672	106	40	101	9.7	10.3	10.5	8.5	6.9
$15,000 to $24,999.....................	1,510	1,027	117	52	194	14.5	15.7	11.5	10.9	13.3
$25,000 to $34,999.....................	1,507	976	135	76	197	14.5	14.9	13.3	16.1	13.5
$35,000 to $49,999.....................	1,667	1,092	140	58	228	16.0	16.6	13.9	12.3	15.6
$50,000 to $74,999.....................	1,958	1,192	197	85	310	18.8	18.2	19.6	17.9	21.3
$75,000 to $99,999.....................	1,067	651	104	56	170	10.2	9.9	10.4	11.8	11.7
$100,000 and over.....................	1,356	727	170	97	229	13.0	11.1	16.9	20.6	15.7
POVERTY STATUS IN 2009										
Persons below poverty level [5]..........	12,350	8,862	985	313	1,315	25.3	27.7	22.4	17.1	19.7
HOUSEHOLD TENURE										
Total occupied units.................	**13,298**	**8,070**	**1,430**	**702**	**1,863**	**100.0**	**100.0**	**100.0**	**100.0**	**100.0**
Owner occupied.....................	6,325	4,008	556	395	787	47.6	49.7	38.9	56.4	42.2
Renter occupied [6].....................	6,973	4,062	874	306	1,076	52.4	50.3	61.1	43.6	57.8

NA Not available. X Not applicable. [1] Includes other Hispanic groups not shown separately. [2] Source: U.S. Bureau of Labor Statistics, "Employment and Earnings Online," January 2011, <http://stats.bls.gov/opub/ee/home.htm>. [3] Total unemployment as percent of civilian labor force. [4] Household type is shown by the Hispanic origin of the householder. [5] For explanation of poverty level; see text, Section 13. [6] Includes no cash rent.

Source: Except as noted, U.S. Census Bureau, "Educational Attainment," <http://www.census.gov/population/www/socdemo/educ-attn.html>; "Families and Living Arrangements," <http://www.census.gov/population/www/socdemo/hh-fam.html>; "Detailed Income Tabulations from the CPS," <http://www.census.gov/hhes/www/income/dinctabs.html>; "Detailed Poverty Tabulations from the CPS," <http://www.census.gov/hhes/www/cpstables/032009/pov/toc.htm>; and unpublished data.

Table 38. Native and Foreign-Born Population by State: 2010

[269,394 represents 269,394,000. The American Community Survey universe includes the household population and the population living in institutions, college dormitories, and other group quarters. Based on a sample and subject to sampling variability; see text, this section and Appendix III. See headnote, Table 42]

State	Native population (1,000)	Foreign-born population Number (1,000)	Percent of total population	Percent entered 2000 or later	State	Native population (1,000)	Foreign-born population Number (1,000)	Percent of total population	Percent entered 2000 or later
U.S........	269,394	39,956	12.9	34.7	MO.........	5,764	233	3.9	44.9
AL..........	4,617	169	3.5	56.5	MT.........	971	20	2.0	32.0
AK..........	665	49	6.9	35.1	NE.........	1,718	112	6.1	38.5
AZ..........	5,557	857	13.4	31.7	NV.........	2,196	508	18.8	31.9
AR..........	2,790	132	4.5	47.5	NH.........	1,247	70	5.3	33.2
CA..........	27,199	10,150	27.2	27.8	NJ.........	6,957	1,845	21.0	34.1
CO.........	4,552	497	9.8	40.1	NM.........	1,861	205	9.9	35.0
CT..........	3,090	487	13.6	37.4	NY.........	15,095	4,298	22.2	31.2
DE..........	828	72	8.0	43.0	NC.........	8,842	719	7.5	45.7
DC..........	523	82	13.5	45.1	ND.........	658	17	2.5	48.8
FL..........	15,185	3,658	19.4	35.3	OH.........	11,066	470	4.1	41.8
GA.........	8,770	943	9.7	43.3	OK.........	3,555	206	5.5	44.7
HI..........	1,115	248	18.2	31.4	OR.........	3,463	376	9.8	34.1
ID..........	1,484	87	5.5	35.8	PA.........	11,971	739	5.8	40.4
IL..........	11,083	1,760	13.7	32.5	RI.........	919	134	12.8	35.8
IN..........	6,190	301	4.6	48.0	SC.........	4,418	218	4.7	50.7
IA..........	2,910	139	4.6	46.1	SD.........	794	22	2.7	48.1
KS..........	2,672	187	6.5	40.2	TN.........	6,068	289	4.5	51.6
KY..........	4,206	141	3.2	51.1	TX.........	21,115	4,142	16.4	36.4
LA..........	4,371	173	3.8	45.2	UT.........	2,554	223	8.0	37.7
ME..........	1,282	46	3.4	31.7	VT.........	598	28	4.4	36.1
MD.........	4,982	804	13.9	41.7	VA.........	7,113	911	11.4	41.6
MA.........	5,574	984	15.0	38.1	WA.........	5,858	886	13.1	37.5
MI..........	9,290	588	6.0	37.2	WV.........	1,831	23	1.2	41.3
MN.........	4,932	378	7.1	43.8	WI.........	5,436	255	4.5	40.4
MS.........	2,909	61	2.1	49.0	WY.........	549	16	2.8	49.6

Source: U.S. Census Bureau, 2010 American Community Survey, C05002, "Place of Birth by Nativity" and C05005, "Year of Entry by Nativity in the United States," <http://factfinder2.census.gov>, accessed July 2012.

Table 39. Nativity and Place of Birth of Resident Population— 25 Largest Cities: 2010

[796 represents 796,000. The American Community Survey universe includes the household population and the population living in institutions, college dormitories, and other group quarters. Based on a sample and subject to sampling variability; see text, this section and Appendix III. See headnote, Table 42]

City	Total population (1,000)	Native population Total (1,000)	Born in United States (1,000)	Born outside United States (1,000)	Foreign born Total Number (1,000)	Percent of total population	Entered 2000 or later Number (1,000)	Percent of foreign-born population
Austin, TX..............	796	647	637	11	148	18.7	76	51.3
Baltimore, MD.............	621	577	571	5	44	7.1	23	51.3
Boston, MA..............	621	454	433	21	167	26.9	66	39.4
Charlotte, NC............	734	628	620	8	106	14.4	54	50.7
Chicago, IL..............	2,699	2,141	2,093	48	558	20.7	179	32.1
Columbus, OH............	790	703	695	8	87	11.0	50	57.8
Dallas, TX...............	1,203	898	889	9	305	25.3	128	41.9
Denver, CO..............	604	506	497	9	98	16.3	43	44.2
Detroit, MI..............	712	678	674	4	34	4.8	15	44.9
El Paso, TX..............	652	492	480	12	160	24.6	38	23.8
Fort Worth, TX...........	744	618	608	11	126	16.9	43	34.5
Houston, TX.............	2,107	1,502	1,484	18	605	28.7	270	44.5
Indianapolis, IN [1]........	824	750	745	4	74	9.0	47	62.8
Jacksonville, FL.........	823	746	728	18	77	9.4	30	38.4
Los Angeles, CA.........	3,797	2,311	2,278	33	1,486	39.1	424	28.5
Memphis, TN............	648	607	604	3	40	6.2	22	55.0
New York, NY............	8,185	5,143	4,833	310	3,042	37.2	963	31.7
Philadelphia, PA.........	1,528	1,351	1,297	54	177	11.6	79	44.3
Phoenix, AZ.............	1,449	1,160	1,147	13	289	20.0	105	36.1
San Antonio, TX.........	1,334	1,142	1,117	25	193	14.4	66	34.2
San Diego, CA...........	1,312	969	945	24	343	26.1	110	32.2
San Francisco, CA.......	805	519	502	18	286	35.5	86	30.1
San Jose, CA............	949	583	572	11	366	38.6	112	30.6
Seattle, WA.............	611	505	493	13	105	17.2	40	38.3
Washington, DC.........	604	523	512	11	82	13.5	37	45.1

[1] Represents the portion of a consolidated city that is not within one or more separately incorporated places.

Source: U.S. Census Bureau, 2010 American Community Survey, C05002, "Place of Birth by Nativity" and C05005, "Year of Entry by Nativity in the United States," <http://factfinder2.census.gov>, accessed July 2012.

Table 40. Native and Foreign-Born Populations by Selected Characteristics: 2010

[In thousands (304,280 represents 304,280,000). As of March. The foreign-born population includes anyone who is not a U.S. citizen at birth. This includes legal permanent residents (immigrants), temporary migrants (such as students), humanitarian migrants (such as refugees), and persons illegally present in the United States. Based on Current Population Survey, Annual Social and Economic Supplement which includes the civilian noninstitutional population plus Armed Forces living off post or with their families on post; see text, this section, and Appendix III]

Characteristic	Total population	Native population	Foreign-born population			
			Total	Natural-ized citizen	Not U.S. citizen	Year of entry: 2000 to March 2010
Total...........	**304,280**	**266,674**	**37,606**	**16,024**	**21,581**	**13,085**
Under 5 years old.........	21,434	21,162	272	53	219	272
5 to 14 years old.........	40,678	39,028	1,651	314	1,337	1,415
15 to 24 years old.........	42,240	38,433	3,807	878	2,929	2,345
25 to 34 years old.........	41,085	33,507	7,577	1,974	5,603	4,106
35 to 44 years old.........	40,447	31,905	8,542	3,323	5,219	2,570
45 to 54 years old.........	44,387	37,611	6,776	3,546	3,230	1,303
55 to 64 years old.........	35,395	31,003	4,391	2,747	1,643	624
65 to 74 years old.........	20,956	18,294	2,663	1,795	868	263
75 to 84 years old.........	12,964	11,499	1,466	1,048	419	151
85 years old and over.........	4,693	4,233	460	347	114	35
Median age (years) [1].........	36.7	35.4	41.3	48.9	36.2	31.0
Male.........	149,485	130,728	18,758	7,470	11,288	6,690
Female.........	154,795	135,946	18,849	8,555	10,294	6,395
MARITAL STATUS						
Persons 15 years old and over.........	**242,168**	**206,485**	**35,683**	**15,658**	**20,025**	**11,398**
Married.........	124,219	102,435	21,784	10,300	11,484	6,316
Widowed.........	14,356	12,605	1,751	1,078	673	267
Divorced.........	23,758	21,374	2,384	1,322	1,062	409
Separated.........	5,541	4,348	1,193	455	738	355
Never married.........	74,294	65,723	8,570	2,503	6,067	4,052
EDUCATIONAL ATTAINMENT						
Persons 25 years old and over.........	**199,928**	**168,052**	**31,876**	**14,780**	**17,096**	**9,052**
Not high school graduate.........	25,711	16,212	9,499	2,802	6,697	2,799
High school graduate/some college.........	114,376	101,203	13,174	6,785	6,389	3,359
Bachelor's degree.........	38,784	33,016	5,769	3,296	2,473	1,831
Advanced degree.........	21,056	17,620	3,434	1,897	1,537	1,062
EARNINGS IN 2009 [2]						
Persons 15 years old and over with earnings.......	**99,270**	**83,790**	**15,480**	**7,459**	**8,020**	**4,524**
Under $15,000.........	5,685	4,290	1,394	426	969	525
$15,000 to $24,999.........	14,845	11,294	3,551	1,075	2,475	1,422
$25,000 to $34,999.........	17,553	14,528	3,025	1,415	1,610	845
$35,000 to $49,999.........	21,591	18,931	2,660	1,522	1,138	586
$50,000 to $74,999.........	21,131	18,706	2,425	1,461	964	561
$75,000 and over.........	18,465	16,040	2,425	1,561	864	584
Median earnings (dollars) [1].........	41,480	42,283	32,932	41,339	27,170	27,198
HOUSEHOLD SIZE [3]						
Total households.........	**117,538**	**102,039**	**15,499**	**7,834**	**7,665**	**3,978**
One person.........	31,399	28,615	2,784	1,626	1,158	578
Two persons.........	39,487	35,720	3,767	2,172	1,595	931
Three persons.........	18,638	15,736	2,902	1,346	1,556	885
Four persons.........	16,122	13,121	3,001	1,383	1,618	833
Five persons.........	7,367	5,709	1,658	776	882	412
Six persons.........	2,784	2,010	774	312	463	179
Seven persons or more.........	1,740	1,128	612	218	394	160
INCOME IN 2009 [3]						
Total family households.........	**78,833**	**66,840**	**11,993**	**5,952**	**6,041**	**3,066**
Under $15,000.........	6,030	4,769	1,261	410	851	431
$15,000 to $24,999.........	6,968	5,500	1,469	520	949	418
$25,000 to $34,999.........	7,795	6,274	1,522	613	908	439
$35,000 to $49,999.........	10,881	9,187	1,694	819	875	451
$50,000 to $74,999.........	15,633	13,387	2,246	1,194	1,052	534
$75,000 and over.........	31,525	27,724	3,801	2,395	1,406	794
Median income (dollars) [1].........	61,265	63,231	50,341	61,333	39,542	41,507
POVERTY STATUS IN 2009 [4]						
Persons below poverty level.........	43,569	36,407	7,162	1,736	5,425	3,350
Persons at or above poverty level.........	260,251	229,815	30,435	14,288	16,147	9,727
HOUSEHOLD TENURE [3]						
Total households.........	**117,539**	**102,039**	**15,500**	**7,834**	**7,666**	**3,978**
Owner occupied unit.........	78,780	70,687	8,092	5,261	2,831	1,121
Renter occupied unit [5].........	38,759	31,352	7,408	2,573	4,835	2,857

[1] For definition of median, see Guide to Tabular Presentation. [2] Covers only year-round, full-time workers. [3] Based on citizenship of householder. [4] Persons for whom poverty status is determined. Excludes unrelated individuals under 15 years old. [5] Includes occupiers who paid no cash rent.

Source: U.S. Census Bureau, "Current Population Survey - March 2010 Detailed Tables, Characteristics of the Foreign-Born Population by Nativity and U.S. Citizenship Status," <http://www.census.gov/population/foreign/data/cps2010.html>.

Table 41. Foreign-Born Population—Selected Characteristics by Region of Origin: 2010

[In thousands (37,606 represents 37,606,000). As of March. The term foreign-born refers to anyone who is not a U.S. citizen at birth. This includes naturalized U.S. citizens, legal permanent residents (immigrants), temporary migrants (such as foreign students), humanitarian migrants (such as refugees), and persons illegally present in the United States. Based on Current Population Survey, Annual Social and Economic Supplement; see text, this section and Appendix III]

Characteristic	Total foreign-born	Europe	Asia	Latin America Total	Carib-bean	Central America [1]	South America	Other areas
Total............................	**37,606**	**4,509**	**10,126**	**20,419**	**3,649**	**14,400**	**2,370**	**2,553**
Under 5 years old.........................	272	35	100	83	4	76	2	54
5 to 14 years old........................	1,651	151	466	892	152	667	73	142
15 to 24 years old.......................	3,807	296	848	2,390	351	1,822	217	273
25 to 34 years old.......................	7,577	544	1,868	4,620	536	3,648	436	545
35 to 44 years old.......................	8,542	778	2,190	5,005	637	3,805	563	569
45 to 54 years old.......................	6,776	742	1,927	3,661	805	2,329	527	446
55 to 64 years old.......................	4,391	695	1,405	2,036	523	1,244	268	255
65 to 74 years old.......................	2,663	683	753	1,071	352	534	184	156
75 to 84 years old.......................	1,466	412	457	515	233	205	77	82
85 years old and over....................	460	171	111	147	55	69	23	31
EDUCATIONAL ATTAINMENT								
Persons 25 years old and over..............	**31,876**	**4,026**	**8,712**	**17,054**	**3,142**	**11,834**	**2,078**	**2,083**
Less than ninth grade....................	5,906	302	618	4,844	394	4,273	177	142
9th to 12th grade (no diploma)............	3,593	154	438	2,909	331	2,405	173	92
High school graduate.....................	8,138	1,102	1,836	4,725	967	3,055	703	475
Some college or associate's degree...........	5,035	814	1,259	2,436	748	1,245	443	526
Bachelor's degree........................	5,769	996	2,753	1,554	500	682	372	466
Advanced degree........................	3,434	659	1,807	586	202	176	209	382
High school graduate or more..................	22,377	3,570	7,655	9,301	2,417	5,157	1,728	1,851
Bachelor's degree or more.....................	9,204	1,654	4,561	2,141	702	857	582	848
INCOME IN 2009								
Total family households...................	**11,993**	**1,444**	**3,365**	**6,362**	**1,218**	**4,439**	**705**	**821**
Under $15,000...........................	1,261	87	241	834	167	614	53	100
$15,000 to $24,999.......................	1,469	128	249	1,035	171	798	66	57
$25,000 to $34,999.......................	1,522	152	276	995	169	753	74	99
$35,000 to $49,999.......................	1,694	165	373	1,050	190	768	92	107
$50,000 to $74,999.......................	2,246	292	633	1,191	200	806	185	130
$75,000 and over.........................	3,801	621	1,595	1,257	322	700	235	328
Median income (dol.) [2]....................	50,341	64,340	70,856	38,785	41,972	35,789	56,963	55,758
POVERTY STATUS IN 2009 [3]								
Persons below poverty level................	7,162	442	1,325	4,957	689	3,984	285	438
Persons at or above poverty level............	30,435	4,067	8,801	15,455	2,960	10,409	2,085	2,112

[1] Includes Mexico. [2] For definition of median, see Guide to Tabular Presentation. [3] Persons for whom poverty status is determined. Excludes unrelated individuals under 15 years old.

Source: U.S. Census Bureau, "Current Population Survey - March 2010 Detailed Tables, Characteristics of the Foreign-Born Population by Nativity and U.S. Citizenship Status," <http://www.census.gov/population/foreign/data/cps2010.html>.

Table 42. Foreign-Born Population by Citizenship Status and Place of Birth: 2010

[The term foreign-born refers to anyone who is not a U.S. citizen at birth. This includes naturalized U.S. citizens, legal permanent residents (immigrants), temporary migrants (such as foreign students), humanitarian migrants (such as refugees), and persons illegally present in the United States. The American Community Survey universe includes the household population and the population living in institutions, college dormitories, and other group quarters. Based on a sample and subject to sampling variability; see text, this section and Appendix III]

Region	Foreign-born population, total	Naturalized citizen	Not U.S. citizen Number	Not U.S. citizen Percent of foreign-born
Total [1].................................	**39,955,854**	**17,476,082**	**22,479,772**	**56.3**
Latin America............................	21,224,087	6,813,369	14,410,718	67.9
Caribbean............................	3,730,644	2,019,954	1,710,690	45.9
Central America........................	14,763,612	3,582,087	11,181,525	75.7
Mexico............................	11,711,103	2,679,152	9,031,951	77.1
Other Central America................	3,052,509	902,935	2,149,574	70.4
South America........................	2,729,831	1,211,328	1,518,503	55.6
Asia....................................	11,283,574	6,509,558	4,774,016	42.3
Europe..................................	4,817,437	2,975,218	1,842,219	38.2
Africa...................................	1,606,914	(NA)	(NA)	(NA)
Northern America.........................	806,925	(NA)	(NA)	(NA)
Oceania.................................	216,736	(NA)	(NA)	(NA)

NA Not available. [1] Includes persons born at sea.

Source: U.S. Census Bureau, 2010 American Community Survey, B05002, "Place of Birth by Citizenship Status;" C05006, "Place of Birth for the Foreign-Born Population;" and B05007, "Place of Birth by Year of Entry by Citizenship Status for the Foreign-Born Population," <http://factfinder2.census.gov>, accessed July 2012.

Table 43. Persons Obtaining Legal Permanent Resident Status: 1901 to 2011

[8,795 represents 8,795,000. For fiscal years ending in year shown; see text, Section 8. Rates based on Census Bureau estimates as of July 1 for resident population through 1929 and for total population thereafter (excluding Alaska and Hawaii prior to 1959)]

Period	Number (1,000)	Rate [1]	Year	Number (1,000)	Rate [1]
1901 to 1910	8,795	10.4	1990	1,536	6.1
1911 to 1920	5,736	5.7	1995	720	2.7
1921 to 1930	4,107	3.5	2000	841	3.0
1931 to 1940	528	0.4	2004	958	3.3
1941 to 1950	1,035	0.7	2005	1,122	3.8
1951 to 1960	2,515	1.5	2006	1,266	4.2
1961 to 1970	3,322	1.7	2007	1,052	3.5
1971 to 1980	4,399	2.0	2008	1,107	3.6
1981 to 1990	7,256	3.0	2009	1,131	3.7
1991 to 2000	9,081	3.4	2010	1,043	3.4
2001 to 2010	10,501	3.5	2011	1,062	3.4

[1] Annual rate per 1,000 U.S. population. Rate computed by dividing sum of annual immigration totals by sum of annual U.S. population totals for same number of years.

Source: U.S. Department of Homeland Security, Office of Immigration Statistics, *2011 Yearbook of Immigration Statistics.* See also <http://www.dhs.gov/files/statistics/publications/yearbook.shtm>.

Table 44. Refugee Arrivals and Individuals Granted Asylum by Country of Nationality: 2005 to 2011

[For year ending September 30. Data shown provide information on the number of persons admitted to the United States as refugees or granted asylum in the United States in the year shown. In cases with no country of nationality, refers to country of last residence. For definitions of refugee and asylee, see text, this section. Based on data from the Bureau of Population, Refugees, and Migration of the U.S. Department of State and the Executive Office for Immigration Review of the U.S. Department of Justice]

Country of nationality	Refugee arrivals			Country of nationality	Asylees		
	2005	2010	2011		2005	2010	2011
Total	**53,738**	**73,293**	**56,384**	**Total**	**25,228**	**21,056**	**24,988**
Burma	1,447	16,693	16,972	China	5,247	6,678	8,601
Bhutan	0	12,363	14,999	Venezuela	1,105	648	1,107
Iraq	198	18,016	9,388	Ethiopia	730	1,086	1,076
Somalia	10,405	4,884	3,161	Egypt	336	531	1,028
Cuba	6,360	4,818	2,920	Haiti	2,935	833	878
Iran	1,856	3,543	2,032	Nepal	313	638	749
Eritrea	327	2,570	2,032	Russia	487	548	663
Congo (Kinshasa)	424	3,174	977	Eritrea	(NA)	358	640
Ethiopia	1,663	668	560	Colombia	3,362	592	538
Afghanistan	(NA)	515	428	Guatemala	389	464	484
Other countries [1]	31,058	6,049	2,915	Other countries [1]	10,324	8,680	9,224

NA Not available. [1] Includes unknown.

Source: U.S. Department of Homeland Security, Office of Immigration Statistics, *Annual Flow Report, Refugees and Asylees: 2011.* See also <http://www.dhs.gov/xlibrary/assets/statistics/publications/ois_rfa_fr_2011.pdf>.

Table 45. Estimated Unauthorized Immigrants by Selected States and Countries of Birth: 2000 and 2011

[In thousands (8,460 represents 8,460,000). As of January. The unauthorized resident immigrant population is defined as all foreign-born non-citizens who are not legal residents. Most unauthorized residents either entered the United States without inspection or were admitted temporarily and stayed past the date they were required to leave. Unauthorized aliens who have applied for but have not yet received approval to lawfully remain in the United States are considered to be unauthorized. These estimates were calculated using a "residual method," whereby estimates of the legally resident foreign born population were subtracted from the total foreign-born population in order to derive the unauthorized immigrant population. All of these component populations were resident in the United States on January 1, 2011, and entered during the 1980–2010 period. Persons who entered the United States prior to 1980 were assumed to be legally resident. Estimates of the legally resident foreign-born population were based primarily on administrative data of the Department of Homeland Security, while estimates of the total foreign-born population were obtained from the American Community Survey of the U.S. Census Bureau. Estimates for 2000 are based on the same methodology, assumptions, and definitions with the exception that data from Census 2000 were used to estimate the foreign-born population in 2000 that entered the United States from January 1, 1980 through December 31, 1999]

State of residence	2000	2011	Country of birth	2000	2011
United States, total	**8,460**	**11,510**	**Total**	**8,460**	**11,510**
California	2,510	2,830	Mexico	4,680	6,800
Texas	1,090	1,790	El Salvador	430	660
Florida	800	740	Guatemala	290	520
New York	540	630	Honduras	160	380
Illinois	440	550	China	190	280
Georgia	220	440	Philippines	200	270
New Jersey	350	420	India	120	240
North Carolina	260	400	Korea	180	230
Arizona	330	360	Ecuador	110	210
Washington	170	260	Vietnam	160	170
Other states	1,750	3,100	Other countries	1,940	1,750

Source: U.S. Department of Homeland Security, Office of Immigration Statistics, "Estimates of the Unauthorized Immigrant Population Residing in the United States: January 2011." See also <http://www.dhs.gov/xlibrary/assets/statistics/publications/ois_ill_pe_2011.pdf>.

Table 46. Immigrant Orphans Adopted by U.S. Citizens by Sex, Age, Region, and Country of Birth: 2011

[For years ending September 30]

Region and country of birth	Total	Male	Female	Under 1 year old	1 to 4 years old	5 years old and over
REGION						
Total	**9,504**	**4,209**	**5,295**	**1,394**	**5,276**	**2,834**
Africa	2,575	1,325	1,250	565	1,283	727
Asia	4,322	1,628	2,694	702	2,818	802
Europe	1,845	939	906	64	969	812
North America	428	187	241	4	121	303
Oceania	29	11	18	19	(D)	(D)
South America	303	118	185	40	(D)	(D)
Unknown	2	1	1	-	-	2
COUNTRY						
Total [1]	**9,504**	**4,209**	**5,295**	**1,394**	**5,276**	**2,834**
Armenia	22	4	18	6	10	6
Bulgaria	76	37	39	-	30	46
Cameroon	25	12	13	-	5	20
China [2]	2,607	706	1,901	288	1,840	479
Colombia	218	83	135	39	67	112
Congo (Brazzaville)	46	26	20	17	20	9
Congo (Kinshasa)	83	44	39	25	46	12
Ethiopia	1,734	883	851	444	882	408
Ghana	113	50	63	(D)	(D)	63
Guatemala	31	12	19	-	20	11
Guyana	47	21	26	-	7	40
Haiti	155	71	84	-	55	100
India	226	86	140	6	148	72
Jamaica	100	36	64	(D)	(D)	86
Japan	26	10	16	(D)	(D)	-
Kazakhstan	86	38	48	24	51	11
Korea, South	741	480	261	244	483	14
Latvia	56	25	31	-	(D)	(D)
Liberia	36	21	15	-	7	29
Lithuania	20	9	11	-	(D)	(D)
Mexico	30	16	14	-	5	25
Morocco	46	31	15	24	18	4
Nepal	64	18	46	-	64	-
Nicaragua	32	18	14	-	5	27
Nigeria	152	79	73	16	69	67
Pakistan	25	10	15	17	4	4
Philippines	224	103	121	-	85	139
Poland	55	28	27	(D)	(D)	30
Russia	964	507	457	56	734	174
Rwanda	57	32	25	13	39	5
Taiwan [2]	205	121	84	82	76	47
Thailand	46	25	21	-	34	12
Uganda	200	110	90	21	118	61
Ukraine	631	312	319	6	151	474

– Represents zero. D Data withheld to limit disclosure. [1] Includes unknown and other countries not shown separately. [2] See footnote 4, Table 1348.

Source: U.S. Department of Homeland Security, Office of Immigration Statistics, *2011 Yearbook of Immigration Statistics*. See also <http://www.dhs.gov/files/statistics/publications/yearbook.shtm>.

Table 47. Petitions for Naturalization Filed, Persons Naturalized, and Petitions Denied: 1990 to 2011

[For fiscal years ending in year shown; see text, Section 8. Naturalizations refer to persons 18 and over who become citizens of the United States]

Year	Petitions filed	Persons naturalized				Petitions denied
		Total	Civilian	Military	Not reported	
1990	233,843	267,586	245,410	1,618	20,558	6,516
1995	959,963	485,720	472,518	3,855	9,347	46,067
1997	1,412,712	596,010	532,871	531	62,608	130,676
1998	932,957	461,169	437,689	961	22,519	137,395
1999	765,346	837,418	740,718	711	95,989	379,993
2000	460,916	886,026	812,579	836	72,611	399,670
2001	501,643	606,259	575,030	758	30,471	218,326
2002	700,649	572,646	550,835	1,053	20,758	139,779
2003	523,370	462,435	449,123	3,865	9,447	91,599
2004	662,796	537,151	520,771	4,668	11,712	103,339
2005	602,972	604,280	589,269	4,614	10,397	108,247
2006	730,642	702,589	684,484	6,259	11,846	120,722
2007	1,382,993	660,477	648,005	3,808	8,664	89,683
2008	525,786	1,046,539	1,032,281	4,342	9,916	121,283
2009	570,442	743,715	726,043	7,100	10,572	109,832
2010	710,544	619,913	604,410	9,122	6,381	56,994
2011	756,008	694,193	677,385	8,373	8,435	57,065

Source: U.S. Department of Homeland Security, Office of Immigration Statistics, *2011 Yearbook of Immigration Statistics*. See also <http://www.dhs.gov/files/statistics/publications/yearbook.shtm>.

Table 48. Persons Obtaining Legal Permanent Resident Status by Class of Admission: 2000 to 2011

[For years ending September 30. For definition of immigrants, see text, this section]

Class of admission	2000	2005	2008	2009	2010	2011
Total	841,002	1,122,257	1,107,126	1,130,818	1,042,625	1,062,040
New arrivals	407,279	383,955	466,558	463,042	476,049	481,948
Adjustments	433,723	738,302	640,568	667,776	566,576	580,092
Family-sponsored preferences	235,092	212,970	227,761	211,859	214,589	234,931
Unmarried sons/daughters of U.S. citizens and their children	27,635	24,729	26,173	23,965	26,998	27,299
Spouses, unmarried sons/daughters of alien residents and their children	124,540	100,139	103,456	98,567	92,088	108,618
Married sons/daughters of U.S. citizens [1]	22,804	22,953	29,273	25,930	32,817	27,704
Brothers or sisters of U.S. citizens [1]	60,113	65,149	68,859	63,397	62,686	71,310
Employment-based preferences	106,642	246,865	164,741	140,903	148,343	139,339
Priority workers [1]	27,566	64,731	36,678	40,924	41,055	25,251
Professionals with advanced degrees or aliens of exceptional ability [1]	20,255	42,597	70,046	45,552	53,946	66,831
Skilled workers, professionals, unskilled workers [1]	49,589	129,070	48,903	40,398	39,762	37,216
Special immigrants [1]	9,014	10,121	7,754	10,341	11,100	6,701
Employment creation (investors) [1]	218	346	1,360	3,688	2,480	3,340
Immediate relatives of U.S. citizens	346,350	436,115	488,483	535,554	476,414	453,158
Spouses	196,405	259,144	265,671	317,129	271,909	258,320
Children [2]	82,638	94,858	101,342	98,270	88,297	80,311
Parents	67,307	82,113	121,470	120,155	116,208	114,527
Refugees	56,091	112,676	90,030	118,836	92,741	113,045
Asylees	6,837	30,286	76,362	58,532	43,550	55,415
Diversity [3]	50,920	46,234	41,761	47,879	49,763	50,103
Cancellation of removal	12,154	20,785	11,128	8,156	8,180	7,430
Parolees	3,162	7,715	1,172	2,385	1,592	1,147
Nicaraguan Adjustment and Central American Relief Act (NACARA)	20,364	1,155	296	296	248	158
Children born abroad to alien residents	(NA)	571	637	587	716	633
Haitian Refugee Immigration Fairness Act (HRIFA)	435	2,820	1,580	552	386	154
Other	2,955	4,065	3,175	5,279	6,103	6,527

NA Not available. [1] Includes spouses and children. [2] Includes orphans. [3] Includes categories of immigrants admitted under three laws intended to diversify immigration: P.L. 99-603, P.L. 100-658, and P.L. 101-649.

Source: U.S. Department of Homeland Security, Office of Immigration Statistics, *2011 Yearbook of Immigration Statistics*. See also <http://www.dhs.gov/files/statistics/publications/yearbook.shtm>.

Table 49. Persons Obtaining Legal Permanent Resident Status by Selected Country of Birth and Selected Characteristics: 2011

[For year ending September 30]

Age, marital status, class of admission	All countries [1]	Mexico	China	India	Philip-pines	Dominican Republic	Cuba	Vietnam	Korea, South
Total	1,062,040	143,446	87,016	69,013	57,011	46,109	36,452	34,157	22,824
Under 18 years old	212,394	27,610	15,667	7,670	11,932	16,281	6,437	6,805	4,598
18 to 24 years old	148,221	24,530	11,398	4,812	7,041	7,167	4,556	6,003	2,225
25 to 34 years old	252,917	30,705	15,631	24,864	10,314	7,457	6,254	6,111	4,172
35 to 44 years old	197,377	27,972	20,001	15,824	9,558	6,474	7,453	5,382	6,169
45 to 54 years old	120,797	15,865	12,232	5,900	7,441	4,418	5,153	5,525	3,825
55 to 64 years old	77,198	9,156	6,890	5,504	6,809	2,583	3,198	3,075	1,172
65 years old and over	53,126	7,607	5,197	4,438	3,916	1,726	3,401	1,256	663
Unknown	10	1	–	1	–	3	–	–	–
Single	405,164	48,468	29,854	13,934	23,423	27,964	15,564	13,243	7,638
Married	599,122	87,680	53,256	51,944	30,443	16,336	15,478	19,066	14,428
Other	53,017	6,543	3,636	2,931	3,051	1,694	5,239	1,814	689
Unknown	4,737	755	270	204	94	115	171	34	69
Family-sponsored preferences	234,931	43,631	17,840	13,527	20,191	24,539	680	19,491	2,503
Employment-based preferences	139,339	9,164	17,544	33,587	7,398	333	8	333	12,593
Immediate relatives of U.S. citizens	453,158	84,280	24,374	20,472	29,279	21,063	2,404	12,551	7,637
Diversity programs	50,103	12	25	51	5	10	208	4	10
Refugees and asylees	168,460	605	27,097	1,217	46	85	33,129	1,703	10
Other	16,049	5,754	136	159	92	79	23	75	71

– Represents zero. [1] Includes other countries not shown separately.

Source: U.S. Department of Homeland Security, Office of Immigration Statistics, <http://www.dhs.gov/files/statistics/data/DSLPR11c.shtm>.

Table 50. Persons Obtaining Legal Permanent Resident Status by Country of Birth: 1981 to 2011

[In thousands (7,256.0 represents 7,256,000). For years ending Sept. 30. Persons by country prior to 1996 are unrevised]

Region and Country of birth	1981–1990, total	1991–2000, total	2001-2010, total	2011
All countries [1]	7,256.0	9,080.5	10,501.1	1,062.0
Europe [1]	705.6	1,226.0	1,263.9	83.9
Albania	(NA)	26.2	50.5	3.6
Belarus	(X)	[2] 28.9	25.7	2.0
Bosnia and Herzegovina	(X)	[2] 38.8	89.0	0.9
Bulgaria	(NA)	23.1	39.2	2.7
France	23.1	27.4	39.6	3.7
Germany	70.1	67.6	77.7	6.1
Ireland	32.8	58.9	15.5	1.4
Italy	32.9	22.5	26.5	2.4
Poland	97.4	169.5	116.8	6.9
Romania	38.9	57.5	53.6	3.9
Russia	(X)	[2] 127.8	139.7	7.9
Serbia and Montenegro [3,4]	19.2	25.8	46.2	1.4
Soviet Union [3]	84.0	103.8	37.5	3.7
Ukraine	(X)	[2] 141.0	149.3	8.3
United Kingdom	142.1	135.6	153.5	11.6
Asia	2,817.4	2,973.2	3,784.6	451.6
Armenia	(X)	[2] 26.6	29.9	3.0
Bangladesh	15.2	66.0	106.7	16.7
Burma	9.2	11.0	45.0	16.5
Cambodia	116.6	18.5	35.6	2.7
China [5]	[6] 388.8	424.4	662.7	87.0
Hong Kong	63.0	74.0	40.8	2.3
India	261.9	383.0	662.5	69.0
Iran	154.8	112.5	125.9	14.8
Iraq	19.6	40.7	65.0	21.1
Israel	36.3	31.9	46.6	3.8
Japan	43.2	61.4	76.1	6.2
Jordan [7]	32.6	39.7	38.7	3.9
Korea, South [8]	338.8	171.1	221.5	22.8
Laos	145.6	43.5	16.5	1.0
Lebanon	41.6	43.4	39.5	3.3
Pakistan	61.3	124.5	157.0	15.5
Philippines	495.3	505.3	587.2	57.0
Taiwan [5]	([6])	106.3	87.9	6.2
Thailand	64.4	48.4	68.3	10.0
Turkey	20.9	26.3	41.1	4.4
Uzbekistan	(X)	[2] 22.9	36.0	5.1
Vietnam	401.4	420.8	306.1	34.2
Africa	192.3	382.5	860.4	100.4
Egypt	31.4	46.7	73.1	7.8
Ethiopia	27.2	49.3	109.7	13.8
Ghana	14.9	35.6	65.3	8.8
Kenya	7.9	14.0	59.7	7.8
Morocco	6.7	20.0	44.4	4.4
Nigeria	35.3	67.2	111.2	11.8
Somalia	(NA)	20.1	64.2	4.5
Oceania	(NA)	47.9	58.1	5.0
North America	3,125.0	3,910.1	3,605.1	333.9
Canada	119.2	137.2	168.2	12.8
Mexico	1,653.3	2,250.5	1,693.2	143.4
Cuba	159.2	178.7	318.4	36.5
Dominican Republic	251.8	340.8	329.1	46.1
Haiti	140.2	181.7	213.8	22.1
Jamaica	213.8	173.4	180.7	19.7
Trinidad and Tobago	39.5	63.2	61.8	5.0
El Salvador	214.6	217.3	252.8	18.7
Guatemala	87.9	103.0	160.7	11.1
Honduras	49.5	66.7	65.4	6.1
Nicaragua	44.1	94.6	60.9	3.4
South America	455.9	539.3	906.0	86.1
Argentina	25.7	24.3	50.5	4.5
Brazil	23.7	52.2	123.8	11.8
Colombia	124.4	130.8	251.3	22.6
Ecuador	56.0	76.3	112.5	11.1
Guyana	95.4	73.8	76.2	6.6
Peru	64.4	105.6	145.7	14.1
Venezuela	17.9	29.9	84.4	9.2

NA Not available. X Not applicable. [1] Includes countries not shown separately. [2] Covers years 1992–2000. [3] Prior to 1992, data include independent republics; beginning in 1992, data are for unknown republic only. [4] Yugoslavia (unknown republic) prior to February 7, 2003. [5] See footnote 4, Table 1348. [6] Data for Taiwan included with China. [7] Prior to 2003, includes Palestine; beginning in 2003, Palestine included in Unknown. [8] Prior to 2009, includes a small number of cases from North Korea.

Source: U.S. Department of Homeland Security, Office of Immigration Statistics, *2011 Yearbook of Immigration Statistics*. See also <http://www.dhs.gov/files/statistics/publications/yearbook.shtm>.

Table 51. Refugees and Asylees Obtaining Legal Permanent Resident Status by Country of Birth: 1991 to 2011

[For years ending September 30]

Country of birth	1991–2000, total	2001–2010, total	2011
Total [1]	1,016,820	1,325,365	168,460
Europe [1]	425,047	296,794	4,760
Albania	3,250	10,905	415
Belarus	[2] 21,592	9,310	356
Bosnia and Herzegovina	[2] 37,251	82,485	251
Croatia	1,786	9,498	20
Moldova	[2] 10,150	10,813	601
Romania	15,682	1,423	59
Russia	[2] 54,488	32,819	892
Serbia and Montenegro [3,4]	[2] 6,242	25,422	226
Soviet Union [3]	117,783	6,794	395
Ukraine	[2] 96,974	57,186	833
Asia [1]	[2] 350,702	389,469	97,031
Afghanistan	9,711	13,533	501
Armenia	1,794	12,408	767
Azerbaijan	[2] 10,566	6,045	133
Bhutan	(D)	6,762	10,119
Burma	721	32,904	14,833
China [5]	7,577	111,632	27,097
India	2,538	24,010	1,217
Iran	24,251	45,515	5,386
Iraq	22,488	40,789	19,104
Laos	37,203	6,538	107
Nepal	32	6,000	5,299
Pakistan	1,649	8,339	512
Thailand	22,716	22,405	5,247
Uzbekistan	[2] 17,991	14,047	472
Vietnam	206,530	36,990	1,703
Africa [1]	51,469	242,839	23,523
Ethiopia [6]	17,829	31,900	3,352
Kenya	1,438	15,351	1,961
Liberia	3,836	28,808	1,615
Sierra Leone	272	10,369	364
Somalia	16,737	59,069	3,622
Sudan	5,174	23,580	1,428
Oceania	291	1,453	49
North America [1]	183,251	326,846	38,022
Cuba	142,571	276,331	33,129
Guatemala	2,029	7,399	794
Haiti	9,354	29,824	2,388
Nicaragua	22,468	2,060	141
South America [1]	5,840	65,912	4,868
Colombia	1,129	40,321	1,920
Peru	2,500	7,258	509
Venezuela	1,390	10,726	1,348

D Data withheld to avoid disclosure. [1] Includes other countries and unknown not shown separately. [2] Covers years 1992–2000. [3] Prior to 1992, data include independent republics; beginning in 1992, data are for unknown republic only. [4] Yugoslavia (unknown republic) prior to February 7, 2003. [5] See footnote 4, Table 1348. [6] Prior to 1993, data include Eritrea.

Source: U.S. Department of Homeland Security, Office of Immigration Statistics, *2011 Yearbook of Immigration Statistics*. See also <http://www.dhs.gov/files/statistics/publications/yearbook.shtm>.

Table 52. Population by Selected Ancestry Group and Region: 2010

[In thousands (309,350 represents 309,350,000), except percent. Covers single and multiple ancestries. Ancestry refers to a person's ethnic origin or descent, "roots," or heritage; or the place of birth of the person, the person's parents, or ancestors before their arrival in the United States. The American Community Survey universe includes the household population and the population living in institutions, college dormitories, and other group quarters. Based on a sample and subject to sampling variability; see text, this section, and Appendix III. For composition of regions of the United States, see map, inside front cover]

Ancestry group	Total, (1,000)	Percent distribution by region				Ancestry group	Total, (1,000)	Percent distribution by region			
		North-east	Mid-west	South	West			North-east	Mid-west	South	West
Total population [1]	**309,350**	**18**	**22**	**37**	**23**	Irish	34,670	26	24	32	18
						Israeli	129	41	9	27	24
Afghan	80	23	6	19	52	Italian	17,236	45	17	22	17
Albanian	194	55	24	16	5	Latvian	85	27	29	23	22
American	19,976	11	21	55	13	Lithuanian	660	39	28	18	15
Arab [1]	1,646	25	24	27	24	Macedonian	61	34	48	10	8
Egyptian	190	38	12	26	25	Northern European	283	14	21	20	46
Iraqi	106	9	38	20	34	Norwegian	4,470	6	49	12	33
Jordanian	62	17	23	28	31	Pennsylvania					
Lebanese	502	25	25	31	19	German	332	57	24	12	6
Moroccan	82	36	11	32	21	Polish	9,569	33	37	18	12
Palestinian	93	14	31	25	29	Portuguese	1,406	46	4	13	37
Syrian	148	35	19	23	23	Romanian	447	25	26	24	25
Arab	291	23	31	25	22	Russian	2,972	36	17	21	26
Armenian	475	22	9	9	61	Scandinavian	571	8	31	19	42
Assyrian/						Scotch-Irish	3,257	12	17	51	20
Chaldean/Syriac	106	4	51	3	43	Scottish	5,461	17	20	37	26
Australian	93	19	14	26	41	Serbian	188	20	42	18	20
Austrian	722	30	24	22	24	Slavic	137	32	24	22	22
Belgian	361	11	55	17	18	Slovak	762	44	33	14	8
Brazilian	362	47	6	33	14	Slovene	172	16	55	14	14
British	1,181	16	16	39	29	Sub-Saharan					
Bulgarian	96	20	31	20	29	African [1]	2,789	22	19	43	16
Cajun	103	3	4	85	8	Cape Verdean	95	88	0	8	3
Canadian	717	28	16	26	30	Ethiopian	202	10	17	44	29
Croatian	411	24	40	14	23	Ghanian	91	48	10	32	9
Czech	1,525	11	45	27	17	Nigerian	259	23	15	50	12
Czechoslovakian	304	23	32	24	21	Somalian	120	11	48	15	26
Danish	1,376	8	32	14	46	African	1,676	18	18	48	16
Dutch	4,645	16	35	27	23	Swedish	4,089	14	38	16	32
Eastern European	490	45	14	21	21	Swiss	961	16	35	19	31
English	25,926	17	21	38	24	Turkish	195	31	13	33	23
European	3,617	13	20	33	34	Ukrainian	940	39	20	18	23
Finnish	648	12	47	14	27	Welsh	1,793	20	22	31	27
French						West Indian [1,2]	2,624	47	3	45	4
(except Basque)	8,761	25	23	33	20	British					
French						West Indian	88	67	3	25	4
Canadian	2,043	41	20	24	15	Haitian	881	41	2	55	1
German	47,902	16	39	26	19	Jamaican	965	49	4	42	5
Greek	1,316	34	21	25	20	Trinidadian and					
Guyanese	214	75	2	21	1	Tobagonian	198	61	2	33	4
Hungarian	1,502	32	30	21	17	West Indian	299	58	3	34	5
Iranian	464	12	8	26	54	Yugoslavian	327	19	32	23	26

[1] Includes other groups, not shown separately. [2] Excludes Hispanic-origin groups.

Source: U.S. Census Bureau, 2010 American Community Survey, B04006, "People Reporting Ancestry," <http://factfinder2.census.gov/>, accessed July 2012.

Table 53. Language Spoken at Home: 2010

[The American Community Survey universe includes the household population and the population living in institutions, college dormitories, and other group quarters. Based on a sample and subject to sampling variability; see text, this section, and Appendix III]

Language	Number	Language	Number
Total population 5 years old and over	**289,215,746**	Urdu	388,909
Speak only English	229,673,150	Other Indic languages	741,339
Spanish or Spanish Creole	36,995,602	Other Indo-European languages	435,615
French (including Patois, Cajun)	1,322,650	Chinese	2,808,692
French Creole	746,702	Japanese	443,497
Italian	725,223	Korean	1,137,325
Portuguese or Portuguese Creole	688,326	Mon-Khmer, Cambodian	220,900
German	1,067,651	Hmong	211,500
Yiddish	154,763	Thai	150,885
Other West Germanic languages	299,028	Laotian	158,847
Scandinavian languages	130,992	Vietnamese	1,381,488
Greek	307,178	Other Asian languages	839,294
Russian	854,955	Tagalog	1,573,720
Polish	608,333	Other Pacific Island languages	414,435
Serbo-Croatian	284,077	Navajo	172,873
Other Slavic languages	323,431	Other Native North American languages	197,480
Armenian	240,402	Hungarian	90,453
Persian	381,408	Arabic	864,961
Gujarathi	356,394	Hebrew	204,593
Hindi	609,395	African languages	862,441
		Other and unspecified languages	146,839

Source: U.S. Census Bureau, 2010 American Community Survey, B16001, "Language Spoken at Home by Ability to Speak English for the Population 5 Years and Over," <http://factfinder2.census.gov/>, accessed July 2012.

Table 54. Language Spoken at Home by State: 2010

[In thousands (289,216 represents 289,216,000), except percent. The American Community Survey universe includes the household population and the population living in institutions, college dormitories, and other group quarters. Based on a sample and subject to sampling variability; see text, this section, and Appendix III]

State	Population 5 years and over (1,000)	English only (1,000)	Language other than English		State	Population 5 years and over (1,000)	English only (1,000)	Language other than English	
			Number (1,000)	Percent of population 5 years and over				Number (1,000)	Percent of population 5 years and over
U.S.......	289,216	229,673	59,543	20.6	MO.........	5,609	5,267	342	6.1
AL.........	4,477	4,247	231	5.2	MT.........	929	886	43	4.6
AK.........	660	551	109	16.5	NE.........	1,699	1,523	176	10.4
AZ.........	5,958	4,365	1,593	26.7	NV.........	2,518	1,799	719	28.6
AR.........	2,727	2,539	188	6.9	NH.........	1,248	1,151	97	7.8
CA.........	34,820	19,588	15,232	43.7	NJ.........	8,263	5,811	2,452	29.7
CO.........	4,707	3,902	805	17.1	NM.........	1,922	1,220	702	36.5
CT.........	3,375	2,658	718	21.3	NY.........	18,241	12,777	5,464	30.0
DE.........	844	742	102	12.0	NC.........	8,930	7,959	970	10.9
DC.........	572	489	83	14.5	ND.........	630	598	32	5.1
FL.........	17,775	12,907	4,868	27.4	OH.........	10,820	10,101	720	6.7
GA.........	9,030	7,848	1,182	13.1	OK.........	3,498	3,178	320	9.1
HI.........	1,277	946	331	25.9	OR.........	3,603	3,085	518	14.4
ID.........	1,451	1,298	152	10.5	PA.........	11,983	10,772	1,211	10.1
IL.........	12,010	9,366	2,644	22.0	RI.........	996	787	208	20.9
IN.........	6,057	5,570	487	8.0	SC.........	4,335	4,040	295	6.8
IA.........	2,850	2,640	210	7.4	SD.........	759	702	57	7.5
KS.........	2,654	2,362	292	11.0	TN.........	5,950	5,568	382	6.4
KY.........	4,067	3,871	195	4.8	TX.........	23,328	15,208	8,120	34.8
LA.........	4,230	3,854	377	8.9	UT.........	2,513	2,155	358	14.2
ME.........	1,259	1,175	84	6.7	VT.........	594	561	33	5.6
MD.........	5,421	4,525	896	16.5	VA.........	7,517	6,404	1,113	14.8
MA.........	6,191	4,850	1,341	21.7	WA.........	6,306	5,152	1,154	18.3
MI.........	9,285	8,486	799	8.6	WV.........	1,752	1,713	39	2.2
MN.........	4,954	4,433	521	10.5	WI.........	5,336	4,890	446	8.3
MS.........	2,761	2,661	100	3.6	WY.........	523	490	33	6.4

Source: U.S. Census Bureau, 2010 American Community Survey, C16005, "Nativity by Language Spoken at Home by Ability to Speak English for the Population 5 Years and Over," <http://factfinder2.census.gov/>, accessed July 2012.

Table 55. Language Spoken at Home—25 Largest Cities: 2010

[736 represents 736,000. The American Community Survey universe includes the household population and the population living in institutions, college dormitories, and other group quarters. Based on a sample and subject to sampling variability; see text, this section, and Appendix III]

City	Popula-tion 5 years and over (1,000)	English only (1,000)	Language other than English, total [1]			Spanish (1,000)	Other Indo-European languages (1,000)	Asian and Pacific Island lan-guages (1,000)
			Number (1,000)	Percent of population 5 years and over	Speak English less than "very well" (1,000)			
Austin, TX.................	736	494	242	32.9	109	191	19	29
Baltimore, MD..............	580	527	52	9.0	21	21	16	8
Boston, MA................	590	380	209	35.5	101	88	70	41
Charlotte, NC..............	678	545	133	19.6	64	78	23	25
Chicago, IL................	2,511	1,628	883	35.2	410	603	155	90
Columbus, OH.............	729	629	100	13.7	44	33	21	23
Dallas, TX.................	1,100	631	469	42.6	246	412	20	21
Denver, CO................	561	404	157	28.0	71	118	16	14
Detroit, MI.................	661	607	54	8.2	23	35	9	3
El Paso, TX................	602	167	435	72.3	171	422	6	5
Fort Worth, TX.............	676	460	216	31.9	101	182	12	19
Houston, TX...............	1,936	1,038	898	46.4	461	722	66	80
Indianapolis, IN [2]..........	762	665	96	12.7	50	65	14	10
Jacksonville, FL............	767	663	104	13.5	36	45	31	21
Los Angeles, CA...........	3,544	1,409	2,135	60.2	1,061	1,541	228	309
Memphis, TN..............	600	547	54	8.9	28	34	6	7
New York, NY..............	7,668	3,898	3,770	49.2	1,798	1,904	1,011	668
Philadelphia, PA...........	1,427	1,127	300	21.0	140	140	73	68
Phoenix, AZ...............	1,337	860	477	35.7	196	397	31	26
San Antonio, TX...........	1,236	655	582	47.1	169	539	20	19
San Diego, CA.............	1,229	732	497	40.5	202	286	50	141
San Francisco, CA.........	770	424	347	45.0	186	89	50	202
San Jose, CA..............	881	394	487	55.3	233	206	53	215
Seattle, WA...............	579	449	130	22.5	54	26	23	67
Washington, DC............	572	489	83	14.5	24	39	23	10

[1] Includes other language groups, not shown separately. [2] Represents the portion of a consolidated city that is not within one or more separately incorporated places.

Source: U.S. Census Bureau, 2010 American Community Survey, C16005, "Nativity by Language Spoken at Home by Ability to Speak English for the Population 5 Years and Over," <http://factfinder2.census.gov/>, accessed July 2012.

Table 56. Marital Status of the Population by Sex, Race, and Hispanic Origin: 2000 to 2011

[In millions, except percent (201.8 represents 201,800,000). As of March. Persons 18 years old and over. Excludes members of Armed Forces except those living off post or with their families on post. Beginning 2005, population controls based on Census 2000 and an expanded sample of households. Based on Current Population Survey, see text, this section and Appendix III]

Marital status, race and Hispanic origin	Total				Male				Female			
	2000	2005	2010	2011	2000	2005	2010	2011	2000	2005	2010	2011
Total [1]	**201.8**	**217.2**	**229.1**	**231.1**	**96.9**	**104.8**	**111.1**	**112.3**	**104.9**	**112.3**	**118.0**	**118.8**
Never married	48.2	53.9	61.5	63.3	26.1	29.6	33.7	34.4	22.1	24.3	27.8	28.9
Married [2]	120.1	127.4	129.5	129.2	59.6	63.3	64.4	64.3	60.4	64.0	65.1	64.9
Widowed	13.7	13.8	14.3	14.2	2.6	2.7	3.0	2.9	11.1	11.1	11.4	11.3
Divorced	19.8	22.1	23.7	24.4	8.5	9.2	10.0	10.7	11.3	12.9	13.7	13.8
Percent of total	100.0	100.0	100.0	100.0	100.0	100.0	100.0	100.0	100.0	100.0	100.0	100.0
Never married	23.9	24.8	26.9	27.4	27.0	28.2	30.4	30.6	21.1	21.6	23.6	24.3
Married [2]	59.5	58.6	56.4	55.9	61.5	60.4	57.9	57.3	57.6	56.9	55.1	54.5
Widowed	6.8	6.4	6.3	6.2	2.7	2.6	2.7	2.6	10.5	9.9	9.6	9.5
Divorced	9.8	10.2	10.4	10.6	8.8	8.8	9.0	9.5	10.8	11.5	11.7	11.6
White, total [3]	**168.1**	**177.5**	**185.7**	**186.7**	**81.6**	**86.6**	**91.2**	**91.8**	**86.6**	**90.9**	**94.5**	**94.9**
Never married	36.0	39.7	45.1	46.2	20.3	22.6	25.7	26.0	15.7	17.0	19.4	20.2
Married [2]	104.1	108.3	109.4	108.9	51.8	54.0	54.7	54.4	52.2	54.2	54.7	54.5
Widowed	11.5	11.5	11.8	11.7	2.2	2.3	2.5	2.4	9.3	9.2	9.3	9.3
Divorced	16.5	18.1	19.4	19.9	7.2	7.6	8.3	8.9	9.3	10.4	11.1	11.0
Percent of total	100.0	100.0	100.0	100.0	100.0	100.0	100.0	100.0	100.0	100.0	100.0	100.0
Never married	21.4	22.3	24.3	24.7	24.9	26.1	28.2	28.3	18.1	18.7	20.6	21.2
Married [2]	62.0	61.0	58.9	58.3	63.5	62.4	60.0	59.4	60.3	59.7	57.9	57.4
Widowed	6.8	6.5	6.3	6.3	2.7	2.6	2.7	2.7	10.8	10.2	9.8	9.8
Divorced	9.8	10.2	10.4	10.7	8.8	8.8	9.1	9.7	10.7	11.5	11.7	11.6
Black, total [3]	**24.0**	**25.2**	**27.3**	**27.8**	**10.7**	**11.2**	**12.3**	**12.6**	**13.3**	**13.9**	**15.0**	**15.3**
Never married	9.5	10.2	11.7	12.2	4.3	4.7	5.5	5.7	5.1	5.5	6.2	6.5
Married [2]	10.1	10.3	10.6	10.6	5.0	5.0	5.2	5.2	5.1	5.2	5.3	5.4
Widowed	1.7	1.7	1.8	1.7	0.3	0.3	0.4	0.3	1.4	1.4	1.5	1.4
Divorced	2.8	2.9	3.2	3.3	1.1	1.1	1.2	1.3	1.7	1.8	2.0	2.0
Percent of total	100.0	100.0	100.0	100.0	100.0	100.0	100.0	100.0	100.0	100.0	100.0	100.0
Never married	39.4	40.6	42.8	43.8	40.2	42.0	44.5	45.3	38.3	39.5	41.4	42.6
Married [2]	42.1	41.0	38.8	38.1	46.7	45.5	42.7	41.7	38.3	37.4	35.6	35.1
Widowed	7.0	6.6	6.7	6.1	2.8	2.7	2.9	2.6	10.5	10.0	9.8	9.0
Divorced	11.5	11.7	11.7	12.0	10.3	9.8	9.9	10.3	12.8	13.3	13.2	13.3
Asian, total [3]	**(NA)**	**9.4**	**10.7**	**11.0**	**(NA)**	**4.5**	**5.1**	**5.2**	**(NA)**	**4.9**	**5.6**	**5.8**
Never married	(NA)	2.3	2.7	2.9	(NA)	1.3	1.5	1.6	(NA)	1.0	1.2	1.3
Married [2]	(NA)	6.2	7.0	7.1	(NA)	2.9	3.3	3.3	(NA)	3.3	3.7	3.8
Widowed	(NA)	0.4	0.5	0.5	(NA)	0.1	0.1	0.1	(NA)	0.3	0.5	0.5
Divorced	(NA)	0.5	0.5	0.5	(NA)	0.2	0.2	0.2	(NA)	0.3	0.3	0.3
Percent of total	100.0	100.0	100.0	100.0	100.0	100.0	100.0	100.0	100.0	100.0	100.0	100.0
Never married	(NA)	24.8	25.1	26.1	(NA)	29.7	29.8	30.5	(NA)	20.3	20.8	22.1
Married [2]	(NA)	65.6	65.5	64.4	(NA)	64.7	65.5	64.4	(NA)	66.5	65.7	64.4
Widowed	(NA)	4.3	4.9	4.8	(NA)	1.3	1.3	1.6	(NA)	6.7	8.1	7.7
Divorced	(NA)	5.3	4.5	4.7	(NA)	4.1	3.4	3.5	(NA)	6.4	5.4	5.7
Hispanic, total [4]	**21.1**	**27.5**	**31.8**	**32.4**	**10.4**	**14.1**	**16.4**	**16.7**	**10.7**	**13.4**	**15.4**	**15.7**
Never married	5.9	8.6	10.9	11.4	3.4	5.2	6.5	6.8	2.5	3.4	4.4	4.7
Married [2]	12.7	15.6	17.1	17.1	6.2	7.8	8.6	8.6	6.5	7.8	8.5	8.6
Widowed	0.9	1.0	1.2	1.2	0.2	0.2	0.3	0.3	0.7	0.8	0.9	0.9
Divorced	1.6	2.2	2.6	2.6	0.7	0.9	1.1	1.1	1.0	1.3	1.5	1.5
Percent of total	100.0	100.0	100.0	100.0	100.0	100.0	100.0	100.0	100.0	100.0	100.0	100.0
Never married	28.0	31.3	34.2	35.3	32.3	36.7	39.3	40.4	23.4	25.6	28.7	29.9
Married [2]	60.2	57.0	53.8	52.9	59.7	55.6	52.2	51.2	60.7	58.7	55.6	54.6
Widowed	4.2	3.7	3.8	3.8	1.6	1.5	1.8	1.8	6.5	6.1	5.8	6.0
Divorced	7.6	7.9	8.2	8.0	6.4	6.3	6.7	6.5	9.3	9.7	9.9	9.5
Non-Hispanic White, total [3]	**(NA)**	**151.9**	**156.2**	**156.6**	**(NA)**	**73.4**	**75.9**	**76.2**	**(NA)**	**78.5**	**80.3**	**80.4**
Never married	(NA)	31.8	35.2	35.7	(NA)	17.8	19.8	19.8	(NA)	13.9	15.5	15.9
Married [2]	(NA)	93.5	93.3	92.8	(NA)	46.6	46.6	46.4	(NA)	47.0	46.7	46.5
Widowed	(NA)	10.6	10.6	10.5	(NA)	2.1	2.2	2.2	(NA)	8.5	8.4	8.4
Divorced	(NA)	16.0	17.0	17.6	(NA)	6.8	7.3	7.9	(NA)	9.2	9.7	9.7
Percent of total	100.0	100.0	100.0	100.0	100.0	100.0	100.0	100.0	100.0	100.0	100.0	100.0
Never married	(NA)	20.9	22.6	22.8	(NA)	24.3	26.0	26.0	(NA)	17.7	19.3	19.8
Married [2]	(NA)	61.5	59.7	59.3	(NA)	63.5	61.4	60.8	(NA)	59.7	58.1	57.7
Widowed	(NA)	6.9	6.8	6.7	(NA)	2.8	2.9	2.8	(NA)	10.8	10.5	10.4
Divorced	(NA)	10.6	10.9	11.2	(NA)	9.3	9.7	10.4	(NA)	11.7	12.1	12.0

NA Not available. [1] Includes persons of other races not shown separately. [2] Includes persons who are married with spouse present, married with spouse absent, and separated. [3] Beginning 2005, data represent persons who selected this race group only and exclude persons reporting more than one race. The CPS in 2000 only allowed respondents to report one race group. See also comments on race in the text for this section. [4] Hispanic persons may be of any race.

Source: U.S. Census Bureau, Current Population Reports, P20-537, 2001; and "America's Families and Living Arrangements," <http://www.census.gov/population/www/socdemo/hh-fam.html>.

Table 57. Marital Status of the Population by Sex and Age: 2011

[As of March (112,258 represents 112,258,000). Excludes members of Armed Forces except those living off post or with their families on post. Population controls based on Census 2000. Based on Current Population Survey, see text, this section, and Appendix III]

Sex and age	Number of persons (1,000)					Percent distribution				
	Total	Never married	Married [1]	Widowed	Divorced	Total	Never married	Married [1]	Widowed	Divorced
Male	**112,258**	**34,390**	**64,286**	**2,929**	**10,652**	**100.0**	**30.6**	**57.3**	**2.6**	**9.5**
18 to 19 years old	4,120	4,016	100	–	4	100.0	97.5	2.4	–	0.1
20 to 24 years old	10,953	9,763	1,096	3	92	100.0	89.1	10.0	–	0.8
25 to 29 years old	10,913	6,980	3,622	12	300	100.0	64.0	33.2	0.1	2.8
30 to 34 years old	10,065	3,896	5,506	21	641	100.0	38.7	54.7	0.2	6.4
35 to 39 years old	9,540	2,293	6,381	46	821	100.0	24.0	66.9	0.5	8.6
40 to 44 years old	10,169	1,973	6,944	49	1,202	100.0	19.4	68.2	0.5	11.8
45 to 54 years old	21,486	3,105	15,005	227	3,150	100.0	14.5	69.8	1.1	14.7
55 to 64 years old	17,937	1,605	13,106	422	2,804	100.0	8.9	73.1	2.4	15.6
65 to 74 years old	9,837	494	7,525	627	1,191	100.0	5.0	76.5	6.4	12.1
75 years old and over	7,239	266	5,005	1,522	446	100.0	3.7	69.1	21.0	6.2
Female	**118,841**	**28,892**	**64,894**	**11,301**	**13,754**	**100.0**	**24.3**	**54.5**	**9.5**	**11.6**
18 to 19 years old	4,004	3,818	171	–	14	100.0	95.4	4.2	–	0.4
20 to 24 years old	10,564	8,526	1,852	17	169	100.0	80.7	17.5	0.2	1.6
25 to 29 years old	10,460	5,243	4,733	43	440	100.0	50.1	45.2	0.4	4.2
30 to 34 years old	10,134	2,862	6,393	44	835	100.0	28.2	63.1	0.4	8.2
35 to 39 years old	9,708	1,824	6,604	83	1,197	100.0	18.8	68.0	0.9	12.3
40 to 44 years old	10,414	1,532	7,281	129	1,472	100.0	14.7	69.9	1.2	14.1
45 to 54 years old	22,450	2,594	15,309	815	3,733	100.0	11.6	68.2	3.6	16.6
55 to 64 years old	19,032	1,544	12,459	1,645	3,384	100.0	8.1	65.5	8.6	17.8
65 to 74 years old	11,559	587	6,597	2,637	1,738	100.0	5.1	57.1	22.8	15.0
75 years old and over	10,516	361	3,498	5,889	770	100.0	3.4	33.3	56.0	7.3

– Represents or rounds to zero. [1] Includes persons who are married with spouse present, married with spouse absent, and separated.

Source: U.S. Census Bureau, "America's Families and Living Arrangements: 2011, Table 1A. Marital Status of People 15 Years and Over, by Age, Sex, Personal Earnings, Race, and Hispanic Origin: 2011," <http://www.census.gov/hhes/families/data/cps2011.html>.

Table 58. Living Arrangements of Persons 15 Years Old and Over by Age and Sex: 2011

[As of March (243,858 represents 243,858,000). See headnote, Table 57]

Living arrangement	Total	15 to 19 years old	20 to 24 years old	25 to 34 years old	35 to 44 years old	45 to 54 years old	55 to 64 years old	65 to 74 years old	75 years old and over
NUMBER (1,000)									
Total	**243,858**	**20,884**	**21,517**	**41,571**	**39,830**	**43,937**	**36,968**	**21,396**	**17,755**
Alone	32,723	110	1,336	4,157	3,552	5,572	6,693	4,805	6,499
With spouse	120,310	151	2,453	18,368	25,152	28,258	24,236	13,570	8,122
With other persons	90,825	20,624	17,728	19,047	11,127	10,106	6,039	3,021	3,136
Male	118,828	10,690	10,953	20,978	19,709	21,486	17,937	9,837	7,239
Alone	14,539	48	686	2,318	2,162	3,034	3,081	1,598	1,611
With spouse	60,155	50	875	8,300	12,341	14,070	12,476	7,223	4,821
With other persons	44,134	10,592	9,392	10,360	5,206	4,382	2,380	1,016	807
Female	125,030	10,194	10,564	20,594	20,122	22,450	19,032	11,559	10,516
Alone	18,184	61	650	1,839	1,390	2,538	3,613	3,207	4,886
With spouse	60,155	101	1,578	10,068	12,811	14,188	11,760	6,347	3,301
With other persons	46,691	10,032	8,336	8,687	5,921	5,724	3,659	2,005	2,329
PERCENT DISTRIBUTION									
Total	100.0	100.0	100.0	100.0	100.0	100.0	100.0	100.0	100.0
Alone	13.4	0.5	6.2	10.0	8.9	12.7	18.1	22.5	36.6
With spouse	49.3	0.7	11.4	44.2	63.1	64.3	65.6	63.4	45.7
With other persons	37.2	98.8	82.4	45.8	27.9	23.0	16.3	14.1	17.7
Male	100.0	100.0	100.0	100.0	100.0	100.0	100.0	100.0	100.0
Alone	12.2	0.4	6.3	11.0	11.0	14.1	17.2	16.2	22.3
With spouse	50.6	0.5	8.0	39.6	62.6	65.5	69.6	73.4	66.6
With other persons	37.1	99.1	85.7	49.4	26.4	20.4	13.3	10.3	11.1
Female	100.0	100.0	100.0	100.0	100.0	100.0	100.0	100.0	100.0
Alone	14.5	0.6	6.2	8.9	6.9	11.3	19.0	27.7	46.5
With spouse	48.1	1.0	14.9	48.9	63.7	63.2	61.8	54.9	31.4
With other persons	37.3	98.4	78.9	42.2	29.4	25.5	19.2	17.3	22.1

Source: U.S. Census Bureau, "America's Families and Living Arrangements: 2011, Table A2. Family Status and Household Relationship of People 15 Years and Over, by Marital Status, Age, and Sex: 2011," <http://www.census.gov/hhes/families/data/cps2011.html>.

Table 59. Households, Families, Subfamilies, and Married Couples: 1980 to 2011

[In thousands, except as indicated (80,776 represents 80,776,000). As of March. Excludes members of Armed Forces except those living off post or with their families on post. Beginning 2005, population controls based on Census 2000 and an expanded sample of households. Based on Current Population Survey, see text, this section and Appendix III. Minus sign (–) indicates decrease]

Type of unit	1980	1990	2000	2005	2010	2011	Percent change 1980 to 1990	1990 to 2000	2000 to 2010	2010 to 2011
Households.................	**80,776**	**93,347**	**104,705**	**113,343**	**117,538**	**118,682**	**16**	**12**	**12**	**1**
Persons per household.....	2.76	2.63	2.62	2.57	2.59	2.58	(X)	(X)	(X)	(X)
White [1].......................	70,766	80,163	87,671	92,880	95,489	96,144	13	9	9	1
Black [1]......................	8,586	10,486	12,849	13,809	14,730	15,065	22	23	15	2
Hispanic [2]..................	3,684	5,933	9,319	12,178	13,298	13,665	61	57	43	3
Family households...........	59,550	66,090	72,025	76,858	78,833	78,613	11	9	9	0
Married couple..............	49,112	52,317	55,311	57,975	58,410	58,036	7	6	6	-1
Male householder [3].......	1,733	2,884	4,028	4,901	5,580	5,559	66	40	39	0
Female householder [3]......	8,705	10,890	12,687	13,981	14,843	15,019	25	17	17	1
Nonfamily households.......	21,226	27,257	32,680	36,485	38,705	40,069	28	20	18	4
Male householder...........	8,807	11,606	14,641	16,543	18,263	18,835	32	26	25	3
Female householder........	12,419	15,651	18,039	19,942	20,442	21,234	26	15	13	4
One person..................	18,296	22,999	26,724	30,137	31,399	32,723	26	16	17	4
Families......................	**59,550**	**66,090**	**72,025**	**76,858**	**78,833**	**78,613**	**11**	**9**	**9**	**0**
Persons per family..........	3.29	3.17	3.17	3.13	3.16	3.18	(X)	(X)	(X)	(X)
With own children [4].........	31,022	32,289	34,605	36,211	35,218	34,760	4	7	2	-1
Without own children [4].......	28,528	33,801	37,420	40,647	43,615	43,853	18	11	17	1
Married couple..............	49,112	52,317	55,311	57,975	58,410	58,036	7	6	6	-1
With own children [4]......	24,961	24,537	25,248	25,919	24,575	23,938	-2	3	-3	-3
Without own children [4]......	24,151	27,780	30,062	32,056	33,835	34,098	15	8	13	1
Male householder [3]..........	1,733	2,884	4,028	4,901	5,580	5,559	66	40	39	0
With own children [4]......	616	1,153	1,786	2,021	2,224	2,225	87	55	25	0
Without own children [4]......	1,117	1,731	2,242	2,880	3,356	3,334	55	30	50	-1
Female householder [3].......	8,705	10,890	12,687	13,981	14,843	15,019	25	17	17	1
With own children [4]......	5,445	6,599	7,571	8,270	8,419	8,597	21	15	11	2
Without own children [4]......	3,261	4,290	5,116	5,711	6,424	6,422	32	19	26	0
Unrelated subfamilies.........	360	534	571	515	484	565	48	7	-15	17
Married couple..............	20	68	37	62	93	88	(B)	(B)	(B)	-5
Male reference persons [3]....	36	45	57	61	44	76	(B)	(B)	(B)	(B)
Female reference persons [3].....................	304	421	477	392	347	401	38	13	-27	16
Related subfamilies............	1,150	2,403	2,984	3,427	4,300	4,345	109	24	44	1
Married couple..............	582	871	1,149	1,336	1,881	2,030	50	32	64	8
Father-child [3]...............	54	153	201	387	313	283	(B)	31	56	-10
Mother-child [3]...............	512	1,378	1,634	1,704	2,106	2,032	169	19	29	-4
Married couples..............	**49,714**	**53,256**	**56,497**	**59,373**	**60,384**	**60,155**	**7**	**6**	**7**	**0**
With own household..........	49,112	52,317	55,311	57,975	58,410	58,036	7	6	6	-1
Without own household......	602	939	1,186	1,398	1,974	2,119	56	26	66	7
Percent without..............	1.2	1.8	2.1	2.4	3.2	3.5	(X)	(X)	(X)	(X)

B Base less than 75,000. X Not applicable. [1] Beginning with the 2003 Current Population Survey (CPS), respondents could choose more than one race. Beginning 2005, data shown represent persons who selected this race group only and exclude persons reporting more than one race. The CPS prior to 2003 only allowed respondents to report one race group. See also comments on race in the text for this section. [2] Persons of Hispanic origin may be any race. [3] No spouse present. [4] Under 18 years old.

Source: U.S. Census Bureau, "America's Families and Living Arrangements," <http://www.census.gov/hhes/families/data/cps.html>.

Table 60. Interracially Married Couples by Race and Hispanic Origin of Spouses: 1980 to 2011

[In thousands (49,714 represents 49,714,000). As of March. Persons 15 years old and over. Persons of Hispanic origin may be of any race. Based on Current Population Survey; see headnote, Table 59 and Appendix III]

Race and origin of spouses	1980	1990	2000	2009	2010	2011
Married couples, total [1]..	**49,714**	**53,256**	**56,497**	**60,844**	**60,384**	**60,155**
Interracial married couples, total................................	651	964	1,464	2,437	2,413	2,393
White [2]/Black [2]..	167	211	363	550	558	515
Black husband/White wife......................................	122	150	268	354	390	356
White husband/Black wife......................................	45	61	95	196	168	159
White [2]/other race [3]...	450	720	1,051	1,759	1,723	1,748
Black [2]/other race [3]...	34	33	50	128	132	130
HISPANIC ORIGIN						
Hispanic/Hispanic...	1,906	3,085	4,739	6,317	6,166	6,255
Hispanic/other origin (not Hispanic)............................	891	1,193	1,743	2,421	2,289	2,363
All other couples (not of Hispanic origin)......................	46,917	48,979	50,015	52,107	51,928	51,536

[1] Includes other married couples not shown separately. [2] See footnote 1, Table 59. [3] "Other race," is any race other than White or Black, such as American Indian, Japanese, Chinese, etc. This total excludes combinations of other races by other races.

Source: U.S. Census Bureau, "Families and Living Arrangements, Table MS-3. Interracial Married Couples: 1980 to 2002," and "America's Families and Living Arrangements, Table FG3. Married Couple Family Groups, By Presence Of Own Children Under 18, And Age, Earnings, Education, And Race And Hispanic Origin Of Both Spouses," <http://www.census.gov/hhes/families/data/cps.html>.

Table 61. Households and Persons Per Household by Type of Household: 2000 to 2011

[As of March (104,705 represents 104,705,000). See headnote, Table 59]

Type of household	Households						Persons per household		
	Number (1,000)			Percent distribution					
	2000	2010	2011	2000	2010	2011	2000	2010	2011
Total households...............	**104,705**	**117,538**	**118,682**	**100**	**100**	**100**	**2.62**	**2.59**	**2.58**
Family households........................	72,025	78,833	78,613	69	67	66	3.24	3.24	3.25
Married couple family..................	55,311	58,410	58,036	53	50	49	3.26	3.24	3.25
Male householder, no spouse present.........	4,028	5,580	5,559	4	5	5	3.16	3.24	3.28
Female householder, no spouse present.....	12,687	14,843	15,019	12	13	13	3.17	3.23	3.27
Nonfamily households....................	32,680	38,705	40,069	31	33	34	1.25	1.26	1.25
Living alone............................	26,724	31,399	32,723	26	27	28	1.00	1.00	1.00
Male householder........................	14,641	18,263	18,835	14	16	16	1.34	1.35	1.33
Living alone............................	11,181	13,971	14,539	11	12	12	1.00	1.00	1.00
Female householder......................	18,039	20,442	21,234	17	17	18	1.17	1.18	1.19
Living alone............................	15,543	17,428	18,184	15	15	15	1.00	1.00	1.00

Source: U.S. Census Bureau, Current Population Reports, P20-537, 2001; and "America's Families and Living Arrangements," <http://www.census.gov/hhes/families/data/cps.html>.

Table 62. Households by Age of Householder and Size of Household: 1990 to 2011

[In millions (93.3 represents 93,300,000). As of March. Based on Current Population Survey; see headnote, Table 59]

Age of householder and size of household	1990	2000	2010	2011					
				Total [1]	White [2]	Black [2]	Asian [2]	Hispanic [3]	Non-Hispanic White [2]
Total........................	**93.3**	**104.7**	**117.5**	**118.7**	**96.1**	**15.1**	**4.7**	**13.7**	**83.5**
15 to 24 years old............	5.1	5.9	6.2	6.1	4.5	1.1	0.3	1.1	3.5
25 to 29 years old............	9.4	8.5	9.4	9.3	7.2	1.4	0.4	1.5	5.8
30 to 34 years old............	11.0	10.1	9.8	10.2	7.9	1.5	0.5	1.7	6.3
35 to 44 years old............	20.6	24.0	21.5	21.3	16.7	2.9	1.1	3.4	13.6
45 to 54 years old............	14.5	20.9	24.9	24.5	19.8	3.2	1.0	2.7	17.2
55 to 64 years old............	12.5	13.6	20.4	21.8	18.1	2.6	0.7	1.7	16.4
65 to 74 years old............	11.7	11.3	13.2	13.3	11.3	1.4	0.4	0.9	10.5
75 years old and over.......	8.4	10.4	12.1	12.0	10.6	1.0	0.3	0.6	10.1
One person...................	23.0	26.7	31.4	32.7	26.2	5.0	0.9	2.2	24.1
Male.......................	9.0	11.2	14.0	14.5	11.7	2.1	0.4	1.1	10.7
Female.....................	14.0	15.5	17.4	18.2	14.5	2.8	0.5	1.1	13.5
Two persons.................	30.1	34.7	39.5	39.7	33.5	4.2	1.3	3.2	30.5
Three persons...............	16.1	17.2	18.6	18.5	14.6	2.5	0.9	2.5	12.3
Four persons................	14.5	15.3	16.1	15.9	12.7	1.9	0.9	2.6	10.3
Five persons................	6.2	7.0	7.4	7.3	5.8	0.9	0.4	1.7	4.2
Six persons.................	2.1	2.4	2.8	2.8	2.1	0.4	0.2	0.8	1.4
Seven persons or more.....	1.3	1.4	1.7	1.7	1.2	0.2	0.1	0.6	0.6

[1] Includes other races, not shown separately. [2] Represents persons who selected this race group only and excludes persons reporting more than one race. See also comments on race in the text for this section. [3] Hispanic persons may be of any race.

Source: U.S. Census Bureau, Current Population Reports, P20-537, and earlier reports; "Table HINC-01. Selected Characteristics of Households, by Total Money Income in 2010," <http://www.census.gov/hhes/www/cpstables/032011/hhinc/new01_000.htm> and "Table HINC-02. Age of Householder--Households, by Total Money Income in 2010, Type of Household, Race and Hispanic Origin of Householder," <http://www.census.gov/hhes/www/cpstables/032011/hhinc/new02_000.htm>, and earlier releases.

Table 63. Unmarried-Partner Households by Region and Sex of Partners: 2010

[The American Community Survey universe includes the household population and the population living in institutions, college dormitories, and other group quarters. For composition of regions, see inside front cover. Based on a sample and subject to sampling variability; see text, this section and Appendix III]

Item	Total	Northeast	Midwest	South	West
Total households..........................	**114,567,419**	**20,904,171**	**25,920,925**	**42,389,513**	**25,352,810**
Unmarried-partner households.................	6,768,083	1,287,629	1,549,633	2,260,798	1,670,023
Male householder and male partner...........	287,687	60,270	50,845	95,163	81,409
Male householder and female partner.........	3,070,784	561,422	718,642	1,034,188	756,532
Female householder and female partner.......	305,637	65,273	56,171	98,567	85,626
Female householder and male partner.........	3,103,975	600,664	723,975	1,032,880	746,456
All other households........................	107,799,336	19,616,542	24,371,292	40,128,715	23,682,787

Source: U.S. Census Bureau, 2010 American Community Survey, B11009, "Unmarried-Partner Households by Sex of Partner," <http://factfinder2.census.gov/>, accessed July 2012.

Table 64. Family Households by Number of Own Children Under 18 Years of Age: 2000 to 2011

[As of March (72,025 represents 72,025,000). Based on Current Population Survey; see headnote, Table 67]

Race, Hispanic origin, and year	Number of families (1,000)					Percent distribution				
	Total	No children	One child	Two children	Three or more children	Total	No children	One child	Two children	Three or more children
ALL FAMILIES [1]										
2000	72,025	37,420	14,311	13,215	7,080	100	52	20	18	10
2010	78,833	43,615	15,149	12,947	7,122	100	55	19	16	9
2011, total	**78,613**	**43,853**	**15,012**	**12,835**	**6,913**	**100**	**56**	**19**	**16**	**9**
Married couple	58,036	34,098	9,300	9,527	5,111	100	59	16	16	9
Male householder [2]	5,559	3,334	1,337	627	262	100	60	24	11	5
Female householder [2]	15,019	6,422	4,375	2,681	1,541	100	43	29	18	10
WHITE FAMILIES [3]										
2000	60,251	32,144	11,496	10,918	5,693	100	53	19	18	9
2010	64,120	36,464	11,856	10,275	5,525	100	57	18	16	9
2011, total	**63,818**	**36,472**	**11,690**	**10,256**	**5,400**	**100**	**57**	**18**	**16**	**8**
Married couple	49,888	29,775	7,767	8,018	4,328	100	60	16	16	9
Male householder [2]	4,172	2,454	1,032	489	197	100	59	25	12	5
Female householder [2]	9,758	4,243	2,892	1,749	874	100	43	30	18	9
BLACK FAMILIES [3]										
2000	8,664	3,882	2,101	1,624	1,058	100	45	24	19	12
2010	9,358	4,502	2,142	1,608	1,106	100	48	23	17	12
2011, total	**9,418**	**4,670**	**2,197**	**1,520**	**1,031**	**100**	**50**	**23**	**16**	**11**
Married couple	4,179	2,386	748	641	404	100	57	18	15	10
Male householder [2]	899	544	200	102	52	100	61	22	11	6
Female householder [2]	4,340	1,741	1,250	777	573	100	40	29	18	13
ASIAN FAMILIES [3]										
2010	3,592	1,794	777	754	267	100	50	22	21	7
2011, total	**3,537**	**1,854**	**694**	**749**	**239**	**100**	**52**	**20**	**21**	**7**
Married couple	2,820	1,361	567	677	215	100	48	20	24	8
Male householder [2]	272	233	31	6	2	100	86	11	2	1
Female householder [2]	445	260	96	66	24	100	58	22	15	5
HISPANIC FAMILIES [4]										
2000	7,561	2,747	1,791	1,693	1,330	100	36	24	22	18
2010	10,412	4,173	2,344	2,269	1,626	100	40	23	22	16
2011, total	**10,659**	**4,285**	**2,403**	**2,319**	**1,651**	**100**	**40**	**23**	**22**	**15**
Married couple	6,725	2,619	1,350	1,601	1,155	100	39	20	24	17
Male householder [2]	1,180	715	245	140	79	100	61	21	12	7
Female householder [2]	2,754	952	808	578	416	100	35	29	21	15
NON-HISPANIC WHITE FAMILIES [3]										
2010	54,445	32,569	9,691	8,173	4,012	100	60	18	15	7
2011, total	**53,909**	**32,452**	**9,488**	**8,106**	**3,863**	**100**	**60**	**18**	**15**	**7**
Married couple	43,554	27,286	6,504	6,524	3,240	100	63	15	15	7
Male householder [2]	3,078	1,791	809	356	122	100	58	26	12	4
Female householder [2]	7,277	3,375	2,175	1,226	501	100	46	30	17	7

[1] Includes other races and non-Hispanic groups, not shown separately. [2] No spouse present. [3] Beginning with the 2003 Current Population Survey (CPS), respondents could choose more than one race. Beginning 2010 data represent persons who selected this race group only and exclude persons reporting more than one race. The CPS prior to 2003 only allowed respondents to report one race group. See also comments on race in the text for this section. [4] Hispanic persons may be of any race.

Source: U.S. Census Bureau, Current Population Reports, P20-537; and "America's Families and Living Arrangements," <http://www.census.gov/hhes/families/data/cps.html>.

Table 65. Family Households With Own Children Under Age 18 by Type of Family, 2000 to 2011, and by Age of Householder, 2011

[As of March (34,605 represents 34,605,000). See headnote, Table 67]

Age of householder	Family households with children		Married couple households with children		Male householder with children [1]		Female householder with children [1]	
	Number (1,000)	Percent of all family households	Number (1,000)	Percent of all married couple households	Number (1,000)	Percent of all male householder families [1]	Number (1,000)	Percent of all female householder families [1]
2000, total	34,605	48	25,248	46	1,786	44	7,571	60
2010, total	35,218	45	24,575	42	2,224	40	8,419	57
2011, total	**34,760**	**44**	**23,938**	**41**	**2,225**	**40**	**8,597**	**57**
15 to 24 years old	1,737	52	579	54	197	24	963	68
25 to 34 years old	9,853	75	6,276	73	669	54	2,905	89
35 to 44 years old	13,401	80	9,712	80	763	67	2,926	84
45 to 54 years old	8,207	46	6,154	46	471	41	1,584	51
55 to 64 years old	1,371	10	1,086	9	108	16	176	10
65 years old and over	189	1	129	1	18	3	42	2

[1] No spouse present.

Source: Current Population Reports, P20-537, 2001 and earlier reports; and "America's Families and Living Arrangements," <http://www.census.gov/hhes/families/data/cps.html>.

Table 66. Families by Type, Race, and Hispanic Origin: 2011

[In thousands (78,613 represents 78,613,000). As of March. Excludes members of Armed Forces except those living off post or with their families on post. Population controls based on Census 2000 and an expanded sample of households. Based on Current Population Survey; see text, this section and Appendix III]

Characteristic	All families	Married couple families						Female family householder[4]						Male family householder,[4] all races
		All races[1]	White[2]	Black[2]	Asian[2]	His-panic[3]	Non-Hispanic White[2]	All races[1]	White[2]	Black[2]	Asian[2]	His-panic[3]	Non-Hispanic White[2]	
All families	**78,613**	**58,036**	**49,888**	**4,179**	**2,820**	**6,725**	**43,554**	**15,019**	**9,758**	**4,340**	**445**	**2,754**	**7,277**	**5,559**
Age of householder:														
Under 25 years old	3,315	1,077	944	81	26	269	694	1,414	873	439	44	335	574	825
25 to 34 years old	13,066	8,551	7,261	591	472	1,526	5,847	3,281	1,921	1,138	97	720	1,270	1,233
35 to 44 years old	16,708	12,087	10,090	933	762	1,919	8,269	3,480	2,266	1,016	91	710	1,641	1,141
45 to 54 years old	17,790	13,506	11,484	1,064	716	1,520	10,049	3,134	2,111	835	97	516	1,653	1,150
55 to 64 years old	14,269	11,851	10,301	870	486	878	9,467	1,745	1,169	469	61	266	917	672
65 to 74 years old	8,147	6,871	6,062	443	250	416	5,672	976	684	234	32	135	556	300
75 years old and over	5,317	4,092	3,746	196	109	196	3,557	988	735	210	24	73	665	237
Without own children under 18	43,853	34,098	29,775	2,386	1,361	2,619	27,286	6,422	4,243	1,741	260	952	3,375	3,334
With own children under 18	34,760	23,938	20,113	1,793	1,459	4,106	16,268	8,597	5,515	2,600	186	1,802	3,902	2,225
One own child under 18	15,012	9,300	7,767	748	567	1,350	6,504	4,375	2,892	1,250	96	808	2,175	1,337
Two own children under 18	12,835	9,527	8,018	641	677	1,601	6,524	2,681	1,749	777	66	578	1,226	627
Three or more own children under 18	6,913	5,111	4,328	404	215	1,155	3,240	1,541	874	573	24	416	501	262
Age of own children:														
Of any age	47,150	30,928	25,831	2,452	1,924	5,034	21,110	12,794	8,392	3,676	308	2,345	6,292	3,428
Under 25 years old	41,108	28,129	23,617	2,135	1,719	4,654	19,254	10,196	6,534	3,078	234	2,045	4,720	2,783
Under 12 years old	25,392	17,778	14,850	1,333	1,145	3,215	11,836	6,005	3,752	1,901	128	1,312	2,579	1,609
Under 6 years old	15,314	10,887	9,120	789	690	2,062	7,194	3,427	2,089	1,142	68	773	1,398	1,000
Under 3 years old	8,674	6,323	5,364	447	376	1,143	4,286	1,772	1,102	566	38	418	731	579
Under 1 year old	2,942	2,135	1,823	143	130	322	1,526	596	375	186	16	156	236	211
Members 65 and older:														
Without members 65 and older	61,513	44,676	38,169	3,324	2,260	5,809	32,699	12,316	7,846	3,715	344	2,390	5,706	4,520
With members 65 and older	17,100	13,360	11,720	855	560	916	10,854	2,702	1,911	625	101	365	1,572	1,038
Marital status of householder:														
Married, spouse present	58,036	58,036	49,888	4,179	2,820	6,725	43,554	(X)	(X)	(X)	(X)	(X)	(X)	(X)
Married, spouse absent	2,771	(X)	(X)	(X)	(X)	(X)	(X)	2,094	1,352	600	83	550	(NA)	677
Separated	1,912	(X)	(X)	(X)	(X)	(X)	(X)	1,487	965	439	38	392	(NA)	425
Other	859	(X)	(X)	(X)	(X)	(X)	(X)	607	387	161	45	158	(NA)	252
Widowed	2,895	(X)	(X)	(X)	(X)	(X)	(X)	2,368	1,769	461	82	299	(NA)	527
Divorced	6,506	(X)	(X)	(X)	(X)	(X)	(X)	4,856	3,647	942	111	678	(NA)	1,650
Never married	8,405	(X)	(X)	(X)	(X)	(X)	(X)	5,700	2,997	2,338	169	1,233	(NA)	2,705

NA Not available. X Not applicable. [1] Includes other races and non-Hispanic groups, not shown separately. [2] Beginning with the 2003 Current Population Survey (CPS), respondents could choose more than one race. Data represent persons who selected this race group only and exclude persons reporting more than one race. See also comments on race in the text for this section. [3] Persons of Hispanic origin may be of any race. [4] No spouse present. Data by race, Hispanic origin and marital status based on tabulations from CPS Table Creator. While tabulations may be conceptually the same as published estimates, in many cases they will not exactly match published estimates because the Table Creator uses the CPS public use file.

Source: U.S. Census Bureau, "America's Families and Living Arrangements: 2011," <http://www.census.gov/hhes/families/data/cps2011.html> and tabulations from CPS Table Creator, <http://www.census.gov/cps/data/cpstablecreator.html>, accessed July 2012.

Table 67. Family Groups With Children Under 18 Years Old by Race and Hispanic Origin: 2000 to 2011

[In thousands. As of March (37,496 represents 37,496,000). Family groups comprise family households, related subfamilies, and unrelated subfamilies. Excludes members of Armed Forces except those living off post or with their families on post. Beginning 2005, population controls based on Census 2000 and an expanded sample of households. Based on Current Population Survey, see text, this section and Appendix III]

Race and Hispanic origin of householder or reference person	Number (1,000)				Percent distribution			
	2000	2005	2010	2011	2000	2005	2010	2011
All races, total [1]	**37,496**	**39,317**	**38,768**	**38,350**	**100**	**100**	**100**	**100**
Two-parent family groups [2]	25,771	26,482	27,082	26,590	69	67	70	69
One-parent family groups	11,725	12,835	11,686	11,760	31	32	30	31
Maintained by mother	9,681	10,366	9,924	10,025	26	26	26	26
Maintained by father	2,044	2,469	1,762	1,735	5	6	5	5
White, total [3]	**30,079**	**30,960**	**30,186**	**29,921**	**100**	**100**	**100**	**100**
Two-parent family groups [2]	22,241	22,319	22,457	22,126	74	72	74	74
One-parent family groups	7,838	8,641	7,729	7,795	26	28	26	26
Maintained by mother	6,216	6,747	6,396	6,460	21	22	21	22
Maintained by father	1,622	1,894	1,333	1,335	5	6	4	4
Black, total [3]	**5,530**	**5,495**	**5,555**	**5,424**	**100**	**100**	**100**	**100**
Two-parent family groups [2]	2,135	2,065	2,275	2,159	39	38	41	40
One-parent family groups	3,396	3,430	3,280	3,265	61	62	59	60
Maintained by mother	3,060	3,037	2,977	2,991	55	55	54	55
Maintained by father	335	393	303	274	6	7	5	5
Asian, total [3]	**1,469**	**1,757**	**1,986**	**1,858**	**100**	**100**	**100**	**100**
Two-parent family groups [2]	1,184	1,472	1,694	1,594	81	84	85	86
One-parent family groups	285	285	292	264	19	16	15	14
Maintained by mother	236	222	235	220	16	13	12	12
Maintained by father	49	63	57	44	3	4	3	2
Hispanic, total [4]	**5,503**	**6,752**	**7,355**	**7,437**	**100**	**100**	**100**	**100**
Two-parent family groups [2]	3,625	4,346	4,856	4,977	66	64	66	67
One-parent family groups	1,877	2,406	2,499	2,460	34	36	34	33
Maintained by mother	1,565	1,964	2,186	2,177	28	29	30	29
Maintained by father	313	442	313	283	6	7	4	4
Non-Hispanic White, total [3]	**24,847**	**24,730**	**23,368**	**23,061**	**100**	**100**	**100**	**100**
Two-parent family groups [2]	18,750	18,253	17,911	17,488	75	74	77	76
One-parent family groups	6,096	6,476	5,457	5,573	25	26	23	24
Maintained by mother	4,766	4,984	4,404	4,497	19	20	19	20
Maintained by father	1,331	1,492	1,053	1,076	5	6	5	5

[1] Includes other races and non-Hispanic groups, not shown separately. [2] Beginning 2007, includes children living both with married and unmarried parents. [3] Beginning with the 2003 Current Population Survey (CPS), respondents could choose more than one race. Beginning 2005, data represent persons who selected this race group only and exclude persons reporting more than one race. The CPS prior to 2003 allowed respondents to report only one race group. See also comments on race in the text for this section. [4] Hispanic persons may be of any race.

Source: U.S. Census Bureau, *Families and Living Arrangements,* Current Population Reports, P20-537, 2001; and "America's Families and Living Arrangements," <http://www.census.gov/hhes/families/data/cps.html>.

Table 68. Parents and Children in Stay-At-Home Parent Family Groups: 1995 to 2011

[In thousands (22,973 represents 22,973,000). Family groups with children include those families that maintain their own household (family households with own children); those that live in the home of a relative (related subfamilies); and those that live in the home of a nonrelative (unrelated subfamilies). Stay-at-home family groups are married-couple family groups with children under 15 where one parent is in the labor force all of the previous year and their spouse is out of the labor force for the entire year with the reason 'taking care of home and family.' Only married couples with children under 15 are included. Based on Current Population Survey; see Appendix III]

Year	Married-couple family groups with children under 15 years old			Children under 15 years old in married-couple family groups		
	Total	With stay-at-home mothers	With stay-at-home fathers	Total	With stay-at-home mothers	With stay-at-home fathers
1995	22,973	4,440	64	41,008	9,106	125
1996	22,808	4,633	49	40,739	9,693	115
1997	22,779	4,617	71	40,798	9,788	140
1998	22,881	4,555	90	41,038	9,432	196
1999	22,754	4,731	71	41,003	9,796	143
2000	22,953	4,785	93	41,860	10,087	180
2001	22,922	4,934	81	41,862	10,194	148
2002	23,339	5,206	106	41,802	10,573	189
2003	23,209	5,388	98	41,654	11,028	175
2004	23,160	5,571	147	41,409	11,205	268
2005	23,305	5,584	142	41,111	11,224	247
2006	23,232	5,646	159	41,259	11,372	283
2007	23,507	5,563	165	41,559	11,193	303
2008	22,445	5,327	140	41,037	11,132	234
2009	22,523	5,095	158	41,208	10,934	290
2010	22,138	5,020	154	41,026	10,833	287
2011	21,689	4,976	176	40,592	10,763	343

Source: U.S. Census Bureau, "Families and Living Arrangements, Table SHP-1. Parents and Children in Stay-At-Home Parent Family Groups: 1994 to Present," <http://www.census.gov/population/www/socdemo/hh-fam.html>.

Table 69. Children Under 18 Years Old by Presence of Parents: 2000 to 2011

[As of March (72,012 represents 72,012,000). Excludes persons under 18 years old who maintained households or family groups. Based on Current Population Survey; see headnote, Table 67]

Race, Hispanic origin, and year	Number (1,000)	Both parents [1]	Percent living with—					Father only	Neither parent
			Mother only						
			Total	Divorced	Married, spouse absent	Never married	Widowed		
ALL RACES [2]									
2000	72,012	69.1	22.4	7.9	4.5	9.2	1.0	4.2	4.2
2005	73,494	67.3	23.4	7.9	4.6	10.1	0.8	4.8	4.5
2009	74,230	69.8	22.8	7.0	4.9	10.0	0.8	3.4	4.0
2010	74,718	69.4	23.1	7.1	5.1	10.1	0.8	3.4	4.1
2011	74,630	68.9	23.6	7.2	4.7	10.8	0.9	3.5	3.9
WHITE [3]									
2000	56,455	75.3	17.3	(NA)	(NA)	(NA)	(NA)	4.3	3.1
2005	56,234	73.5	18.4	7.9	4.0	5.8	0.7	4.7	3.4
2009	56,254	75.8	17.7	7.0	4.2	5.8	0.7	3.4	3.1
2010	56,416	74.9	18.3	6.9	4.5	6.1	0.8	3.5	3.4
2011	56,319	74.6	18.7	7.1	4.1	6.6	0.9	3.6	3.2
BLACK [3]									
2000	11,412	37.6	49.0	(NA)	(NA)	(NA)	(NA)	4.2	9.2
2005	11,293	35.0	50.2	8.7	8.1	32.0	1.3	5.0	9.8
2009	11,235	38.1	50.2	7.9	8.7	32.4	1.3	3.5	8.3
2010	11,272	39.2	49.7	8.6	8.4	31.5	1.2	3.6	7.5
2011	11,155	37.7	51.3	8.6	8.2	33.5	1.0	3.5	7.6
ASIAN [3]									
2005	2,843	83.6	10.2	4.0	2.3	2.7	1.3	3.6	2.5
2009	3,035	85.2	10.2	2.8	4.5	2.0	1.0	2.5	2.0
2010	3,300	85.5	10.1	3.8	3.7	2.1	0.6	2.2	2.1
2011	3,297	87.4	9.1	3.5	2.8	2.1	0.6	1.3	2.3
HISPANIC [4]									
2000	11,613	65.1	25.1	(NA)	(NA)	(NA)	(NA)	4.4	5.4
2005	14,241	64.7	25.4	6.1	7.1	11.4	0.8	4.8	5.2
2009	16,360	68.7	24.9	5.2	7.2	11.7	0.8	2.5	3.9
2010	16,941	67.0	26.3	5.8	8.1	11.7	0.7	2.7	4.0
2011	17,418	66.9	26.5	6.2	6.7	12.8	0.7	2.8	3.9
NON-HISPANIC WHITE [3]									
2005	43,106	75.9	16.4	8.5	3.1	4.2	0.7	4.8	2.9
2009	41,418	78.1	15.3	7.6	3.1	3.9	0.7	3.8	2.8
2010	41,809	77.5	15.5	7.5	3.1	4.2	0.8	3.8	3.1
2011	40,616	77.2	15.9	7.6	3.1	4.3	0.9	4.0	3.0

NA Not available. [1] Beginning in 2007, includes children living both with married and unmarried parents. [2] Includes other races and non-Hispanic groups, not shown separately. [3] Beginning with the 2003 Current Population Survey (CPS), respondents could choose more than one race. Beginning 2005, data represent persons who selected this race group only and exclude persons reporting more than one race. The CPS prior to 2003 allowed respondents to report only one race group. See also comments on race in the text for this section. [4] Hispanic persons may be of any race.

Source: U.S. Census Bureau, "America's Families and Living Arrangements," <http://www.census.gov/hhes/families/data/cps.html>.

Table 70. Grandparents Living With Grandchildren by Race and Sex: 2010

[In thousands (7,010 represents 7,010,000) except percent. Covers both grandparents living in own home with grandchildren present and grandparents living in grandchildren's home. The American Community Survey universe includes the household population and the population living in institutions, college dormitories, and other group quarters. Based on a sample and subject to sampling variability; see text, this section, and Appendix III]

Race, Hispanic origin, and sex	Grandparents living with own grandchildren, total	Grandparents responsible for grandchildren		
		Total	30 to 59 years old	60 years old and over
Grandparents living with own grandchildren under 18 years old (1,000)	**7,010**	**2,738**	**1,823**	**915**
PERCENT DISTRIBUTION				
Total	100.0	100.0	100.0	100.0
White alone	62.2	64.2	63.5	65.4
Black or African American alone	18.6	22.7	23.3	21.6
American Indian and Alaska Native alone	1.4	1.8	1.9	1.6
Asian alone	7.5	3.0	2.1	4.9
Native Hawaiian and Other Pacific Islander alone	0.3	0.3	0.3	0.4
Some other race alone	8.1	6.2	7.2	4.2
Two or more races	1.9	1.8	1.8	1.8
Hispanic origin [1]	25.3	20.3	22.9	15.2
White alone, not Hispanic	46.1	51.1	49.0	55.1
Male	35.9	37.0	34.5	42.0
Female	64.1	63.0	65.5	58.0

[1] Persons of Hispanic origin may be of any race.

Source: U.S. Census Bureau, American Community Survey 2010, Subject Table S1002, "Grandparents," <http://factfinder2.census.gov/>, accessed July 2012.

Table 71. Nonfamily Households by Sex and Age of Householder: 2011

[In thousands (18,835 represents 18,835,000). As of March. See headnote, Table 73]

Item	Male householder					Female householder				
	Total	15 to 24 yrs. old	25 to 44 yrs. old	45 to 64 yrs. old	65 yrs. old and over	Total	15 to 24 yrs. old	25 to 44 yrs. old	45 to 64 yrs. old	65 yrs. old and over
Total.............	**18,835**	**1,468**	**6,673**	**7,185**	**3,508**	**21,234**	**1,355**	**4,375**	**7,114**	**8,389**
One person (living alone).....	14,539	734	4,480	6,115	3,209	18,184	711	3,229	6,151	8,093
Nonrelatives present..........	4,296	734	2,193	1,070	299	3,050	644	1,146	963	296
Never married..................	9,357	1,395	4,856	2,591	516	7,204	1,273	3,308	2,018	604
Married [1].......................	1,676	46	566	770	296	1,245	44	337	612	254
Widowed.......................	1,881	0	53	341	1,487	7,002	4	73	1,146	5,780
Divorced.......................	5,919	28	1,199	3,484	1,210	5,784	35	656	3,339	1,753

[1] No spouse present, includes separated.

Source: U.S. Census Bureau, "America's Families and Living Arrangements, Table A2. Family Status and Household Relationship of People 15 Years and Over, by Marital Status, Age, and Sex," <http://www.census.gov/hhes/families/data/cps2011.html>.

Table 72. Group Quarters Population by Type of Group Quarter and Selected Characteristics: 2010

[In percent, except as indicated (7,987 represents 7,987,000). The American Community Survey universe includes the household population and the population living in institutions, college dormitories, and other group quarters. Based on a sample and subject to sampling variability; see text, this section, and Appendix III]

Characteristic	Total group quarters population [1]	Adult correctional facilities	Nursing facilities/ skilled nursing facilities	College/ university housing	Characteristic	Total group quarters population [1]	Adult correctional facilities	Nursing facilities/ skilled nursing facilities	College/ university housing
Total population (1,000)..............	**7,987**	**2,268**	**1,502**	**2,520**	One race (1,000).......	7,755	2,187	1,492	2,432
					Two or more races (1,000)..................	232	81	10	88
PERCENT DISTRIBUTION					**PERCENT DISTRIBUTION**				
Male..................	60.9	90.7	33.6	47.0	One race...............	100.0	100.0	100.0	100.0
Female................	39.1	9.3	66.4	53.0	White.................	69.0	50.8	83.2	77.2
					Black..................	22.6	40.1	13.4	12.8
Under 15 years old.....	0.8	(X)	(X)	(X)	American Indian and				
15 to 17 years old......	2.0	0.4	(X)	1.3	Alaska Native.........	1.2	2.0	0.5	0.4
18 to 24 years old......	41.0	18.0	0.4	96.3	Asian.................	3.5	0.9	1.5	7.7
25 to 34 years old......	12.7	32.8	0.8	1.7	Native Hawaiian/				
35 to 44 years old......	9.7	24.9	1.5	0.2	Pacific Islander.......	0.2	0.2	0.1	0.1
45 to 54 years old......	8.7	17.3	4.3	0.2	Some other race......	3.5	6.0	1.3	1.8
55 to 64 years old......	5.5	5.3	9.3	0.2	Hispanic origin [2]........	11.6	19.8	4.9	7.1
65 to 74 years old......	4.0	1.1	13.9	0.0	Not Hispanic...........	88.4	80.2	95.1	92.9
75 to 84 years old......	6.5	0.2	28.2	(X)	White alone,				
85 years old and over..	9.1	0.0	41.6	(X)	Not Hispanic.........	60.0	37.0	79.2	70.1

X Not applicable. [1] Includes other types of group quarters, not shown separately. [2] Persons of Hispanic origin may be any race.

Source: U.S. Census Bureau, 2010 American Community Survey, S2601A, "Characteristics of the Group Quarters Population;" S2601B, "Characteristics of the Group Quarters Population by Group Quarters Type," <http://factfinder2.census.gov/>, accessed July 2012.

Table 73. Persons Living Alone by Sex and Age: 2000 to 2011

[As of March (26,724 represents 26,724,000). Excludes members of Armed Forces except those living off post or with their families on post. Beginning 2005, population controls based on Census 2000 and an expanded sample of households. Based on Current Population Survey, see text, this section and Appendix III]

Sex and age	Number of persons (1,000)						Percent distribution				
				2011					2011		
	2000	2005	2010	Total	Male	Female	2000	2010	Total	Male	Female
Total........................	**26,724**	**30,137**	**31,399**	**32,723**	**14,539**	**18,184**	**100**	**100**	**100**	**100**	**100**
15 to 24 years old..........	1,144	1,521	1,367	1,446	734	711	4	4	4	5	4
25 to 34 years old..........	3,848	3,836	3,917	4,157	2,318	1,839	14	12	13	16	10
35 to 44 years old..........	4,109	3,988	3,453	3,552	2,162	1,390	15	11	11	15	8
45 to 64 years old..........	7,842	10,180	11,345	12,265	6,115	6,151	29	36	37	42	34
65 to 74 years old..........	4,091	4,222	4,709	4,805	1,598	3,207	15	15	15	11	18
75 years old and over.......	5,692	6,391	6,608	6,499	1,611	4,886	21	21	20	11	27

Source: U.S. Census Bureau, Current Population Reports, P20-537, 2001, and "America's Families and Living Arrangements," <http://www.census.gov/hhes/families/data/cps.html>.

Table 74. Population in Group Quarters by State: 2000 to 2011

[In thousands (7,780 represents 7,780,000). As of April, except 2011 as of July. For definition of group quarters, see text, this section]

State	2000 [1]	2010 [2]	2011	State	2000 [1]	2010 [2]	2011	State	2000 [1]	2010 [2]	2011
U.S.	**7,780**	**7,987**	**8,006**	KS	82	79	79	NC	254	257	257
AL	115	116	116	KY	115	126	126	ND	24	25	25
AK	19	26	26	LA	136	127	127	OH	299	306	306
AZ	110	139	144	ME	35	36	36	OK	112	112	110
AR	74	79	79	MD	134	138	138	OR	77	87	87
CA	820	820	820	MA	221	239	238	PA	433	426	433
CO	103	116	115	MI	250	229	229	RI	39	43	43
CT	108	118	118	MN	136	135	135	SC	135	139	139
DE	25	24	24	MS	95	92	92	SD	28	34	34
DC	36	40	40	MO	164	174	174	TN	148	153	153
FL	389	422	422	MT	25	29	29	TX	561	581	581
GA	234	253	256	NE	51	51	51	UT	40	46	46
HI	36	43	43	NV	34	36	36	VT	21	25	25
ID	31	29	29	NH	36	40	40	VA	231	240	240
IL	322	302	302	NJ	195	187	186	WA	136	139	145
IN	178	187	187	NM	36	43	43	WV	43	49	49
IA	104	98	98	NY	581	586	586	WI	156	150	151
								WY	14	14	14

[1] The April 1, 2000, Population Estimates base reflects changes to the Census 2000 population from the Count Question Resolution program and geographic program revisions. [2] The April 1, 2010 population estimates base reflects changes to the Census 2010 population from geographic program revisions. It does not reflect changes from the Count Question Resolution program.

Source: U.S. Census Bureau, "Annual Resident Population Estimates, Estimated Components of Resident Population Change, and Rates of the Components of Resident Population Change for States and Counties: April 1, 2000 to July 1, 2009," <http://www.census.gov/popest/data/counties/totals/2009/files/CO-EST2009-ALLDATA.csv> and "Population, population change and estimated components of population change: April 1, 2010 to July 1, 2011 (CO-EST2011-alldata)," <http://www.census.gov/popest/data/counties/totals/2011/index.html>.

Table 75. Same-Sex Couple Households by Legal Recognition of Same-Sex Couple Marriages and Unions: 2010

[Data are based on a sample and are subject to sampling variability. For information on confidentiality protection, sampling and nonsampling errors, and definitions, see <http://www.census.gov/acs/www/ >]

Legal recognition	Total	Percent reported as spouse	Percent reported as unmarried partner
Total same-sex couple households	**593,324**	**25.7**	**74.3**
States performing same-sex marriages [1]	42,195	42.4	57.6
Domestic partnership/civil unions [2]	169,205	28.2	71.8
California [3]	90,023	32.1	67.9
All other states	381,924	22.7	77.3

[1] Includes Connecticut, Iowa, Massachusetts, New Hampshire, Vermont, and the District of Columbia. [2] Includes California, Colorado, Delaware, Hawaii, Maine, Nevada, New Jersey, Oregon, Washington, and Wisconsin. [3] California performed same-sex marriages from June to November 2008.

Source: U.S. Census Bureau, American Community Survey Briefs: *Same-Sex Couple Households*, ACSBR/10-03, September 2011. See also <http://www.census.gov/hhes/samesex/>.

Table 76. Same-Sex Couple Households by Sex, Partner Status and Presence of Children—States: 2010

[As of April. These preferred figures revise earlier estimates of same-sex unmarried partners released from the 2010 Census Summary File 1 because Census Bureau staff discovered an inconsistency in the responses in the 2010 Census summary file statistics that artificially inflated the number of same-sex couples. Statistics on same-sex couple households are derived from two questions on the census: relationship to householder and the sex of each person. When data were captured for these two questions on the 2010 Census door-to-door form, the wrong box may have been checked for the sex of a small percentage of opposite-sex spouses and unmarried partners. Because the population of opposite-sex married couples is large and the population of same-sex married couples in particular is small, an error of this type artificially inflates the number of same-sex married partners. After discovering the inconsistency, Census Bureau staff developed another set of estimates to provide a more accurate way to measure same-sex couple households. The revised figures were developed by using an index of names to re-estimate the number of same-sex married and unmarried partners by the sex commonly associated with the person's first name]

State	Same-sex households			Male householder			Female householder		
	Total	With own children under 18 years [1]	Without own children under 18 years	Total	Same-sex unmarried partner	Reported same-sex spouse	Total	Same-sex unmarried partner	Reported same-sex spouse
United States	**646,464**	**111,033**	**535,431**	**313,577**	**249,354**	**64,223**	**332,887**	**265,381**	**67,506**
Alabama	6,582	1,341	5,241	2,985	2,190	795	3,597	2,688	909
Alaska	1,228	284	944	466	331	135	762	619	143
Arizona	15,817	2,608	13,209	7,521	6,315	1,206	8,296	7,237	1,059
Arkansas	4,226	898	3,328	1,914	1,371	543	2,312	1,815	497
California	98,153	15,698	82,455	52,490	38,093	14,397	45,663	31,748	13,915
Colorado	12,424	1,975	10,449	5,366	4,567	799	7,058	6,239	819
Connecticut	7,852	1,338	6,514	3,473	2,329	1,144	4,379	2,819	1,560
Delaware	2,646	412	2,234	1,250	1,069	181	1,396	1,197	199
District of Columbia	4,822	419	4,403	3,583	3,086	497	1,239	991	248
Florida	48,496	6,453	42,043	26,625	23,040	3,585	21,871	18,672	3,199
Georgia	21,318	4,179	17,139	10,703	8,882	1,821	10,615	8,775	1,840
Hawaii	3,239	513	2,726	1,715	1,417	298	1,524	1,242	282
Idaho	2,042	455	1,587	801	592	209	1,241	1,004	237
Illinois	23,049	3,831	19,218	12,068	10,253	1,815	10,981	9,189	1,792
Indiana	11,074	2,090	8,984	4,838	4,050	788	6,236	5,421	815
Iowa	4,093	761	3,332	1,730	1,179	551	2,363	1,541	822
Kansas	4,009	873	3,136	1,694	1,272	422	2,315	1,904	411
Kentucky	7,195	1,328	5,867	3,230	2,570	660	3,965	3,297	668
Louisiana	8,076	1,611	6,465	3,659	2,847	812	4,417	3,498	919
Maine	3,958	547	3,411	1,497	1,309	188	2,461	2,242	219
Maryland	12,538	2,544	9,994	5,320	4,260	1,060	7,218	5,957	1,261
Massachusetts	20,256	3,459	16,797	8,683	5,332	3,351	11,573	6,061	5,512
Michigan	14,598	2,650	11,948	6,314	5,262	1,052	8,284	7,134	1,150
Minnesota	10,207	1,681	8,526	4,658	4,031	627	5,549	4,846	703
Mississippi	3,484	895	2,589	1,459	992	467	2,025	1,442	583
Missouri	10,557	1,828	8,729	4,953	4,127	826	5,604	4,838	766
Montana	1,348	297	1,051	525	373	152	823	689	134
Nebraska	2,356	462	1,894	1,040	801	239	1,316	1,045	271
Nevada	7,140	1,217	5,923	3,768	3,087	681	3,372	2,801	571
New Hampshire	3,260	538	2,722	1,186	818	368	2,074	1,426	648
New Jersey	16,875	3,323	13,552	8,097	5,962	2,135	8,778	6,466	2,312
New Mexico	5,825	1,038	4,787	2,222	1,844	378	3,603	3,123	480
New York	48,932	8,025	40,907	26,681	21,572	5,109	22,251	17,235	5,016
North Carolina	18,309	3,380	14,929	8,037	6,461	1,576	10,272	8,624	1,648
North Dakota	559	121	438	247	169	78	312	244	68
Ohio	19,684	3,480	16,204	8,987	7,643	1,344	10,697	9,380	1,317
Oklahoma	6,134	1,280	4,854	2,778	2,092	686	3,356	2,707	649
Oregon	11,773	1,920	9,853	4,622	3,746	876	7,151	6,025	1,126
Pennsylvania	22,336	3,543	18,793	10,519	8,989	1,530	11,817	10,119	1,698
Rhode Island	2,785	432	2,353	1,215	961	254	1,570	1,232	338
South Carolina	7,214	1,360	5,854	3,160	2,400	760	4,054	3,218	836
South Dakota	714	151	563	313	219	94	401	320	81
Tennessee	10,898	1,968	8,930	5,054	4,099	955	5,844	4,840	1,004
Texas	46,401	9,191	37,210	22,412	18,137	4,275	23,989	19,867	4,122
Utah	3,909	786	3,123	1,841	1,405	436	2,068	1,695	373
Vermont	2,143	399	1,744	718	463	255	1,425	925	500
Virginia	14,243	2,279	11,964	6,990	5,731	1,259	7,253	6,038	1,215
Washington	19,003	2,998	16,005	8,636	7,139	1,497	10,367	8,792	1,575
West Virginia	2,848	507	2,341	1,330	974	356	1,518	1,194	324
Wisconsin	9,179	1,505	7,674	3,936	3,334	602	5,243	4,651	592
Wyoming	657	162	495	268	169	99	389	309	80

[1] The "own children" category includes any child under 18 years who is a son or daughter by birth, a stepchild, or an adopted child of the householder.

Source: U.S. Census Bureau, "Same-sex Couple Household Statistics from the 2010 Census," September 2011, <http://www.census.gov/hhes/samesex/>.

Table 77. Self-Described Religious Identification of Adult Population: 1990, 2001, and 2008

[In thousands (175,440 represents 175,440,000). The methodology of the American Religious Identification Survey (ARIS) 2008 replicated that used in previous surveys. The three surveys are based on random-digit-dialing telephone surveys of residential households in the continental U.S. (48 states): 54,461 interviews in 2008, 50,281 in 2001, and 113,723 in 1990. Respondents were asked to describe themselves in terms of religion with an open-ended question. Interviewers did not prompt or offer a suggested list of potential answers. Moreover, the self-description of respondents was not based on whether established religious bodies, institutions, churches, mosques or synagogues considered them to be members. Instead, the surveys sought to determine whether the respondents regarded themselves as adherents of a religious community. Subjective rather than objective standards of religious identification were tapped by the surveys]

Religious group	1990	2001	2008	Religious group	1990	2001	2008
Adult population, total [1]	**175,440**	**207,983**	**228,182**	Christian Reform	40	79	381
Christian, total [2]	151,225	159,514	173,402	Christian Science	214	194	339
Catholic	46,004	50,873	57,199	Church of the Brethren	206	358	231
Baptist	33,964	33,820	36,148	Mormon/Latter-Day Saints	2,487	2,697	3,158
Methodist	14,174	14,039	11,366	Other Christian [4]	105	254	206
Lutheran	9,110	9,580	8,674				
Presbyterian	4,985	5,596	4,723	Other religions, total [2]	5,853	7,740	8,796
Episcopalian/Anglican	3,043	3,451	2,405	Jewish	3,137	2,837	2,680
Orthodox (Eastern)	502	645	824	Buddhist	404	1,082	1,189
United Church of Christ	438	1,378	736	Hindu	227	766	582
Disciples of Christ	144	492	263	Sikh	13	57	78
Reformed/Dutch Reform	161	289	206	Muslim	527	1,104	1,349
Quaker	67	217	130	Unitarian/Universalist	502	629	586
Christian unspecified	8,073	14,190	16,834	Spiritualist	(NA)	116	426
Nondenominational Christian [3]	194	2,489	8,032	Wiccan	8	134	342
Protestant unspecified	17,214	4,647	5,187	Pagan	(NA)	140	340
Evangelical/Born Again [3]	546	1,088	2,154	Native American	47	103	186
Independent Christian Church	25	71	86	Other unclassified [4]	991	774	1,030
Pentecostal unspecified	3,116	4,407	5,416				
Assemblies of God	617	1,105	810	No religion specified, total [2]	14,331	29,481	34,169
Church of God	590	943	663	Agnostic	[5]1,186	991	1,985
Holiness/Holy	610	569	352	Atheist	(5)	902	1,621
Church of the Nazarene	549	544	358	Humanist	29	49	90
Foursquare Gospel	28	70	116	No Religion [4]	13,116	27,486	30,427
Churches of Christ	1,769	2,593	1,921	Other No Religion [4]	(NA)	57	45
Jehovah's Witness	1,381	1,331	1,914				
Apostolic/New Apostolic	117	254	970	Refused to reply to question	4,031	11,246	11,815
Seventh-Day Adventist	668	724	938				
Mennonite	235	346	438				

NA Not available. [1] Refers to the total number of adults in all fifty states. All other figures are based on projections from surveys conducted in the continental United States (48 states). [2] Includes other groups, not shown separately. [3] Because of the subjective nature of replies to open-ended questions, these categories are the most unstable as they do not refer to clearly identifiable denominations as much as underlying feelings about religion. Thus they may be the most subject to fluctuation over time. [4] Estimates for subpopulations smaller than 75,000 adults are aggregated to minimize sampling errors. [5] Atheist included in Agnostic.

Source: 1990 data, Barry A. Kosmin and Seymour P. Lachman, "One Nation Under God: Religion in Contemporary American Society, 1993;" 2001 data, Barry A. Kosmin and Ariela Keysar, Religion in A Free Market: Religious and Non-Religious Americans. Who, What, Why, Where, 2006; and 2008 data, Barry A. Kosmin & Ariela Keysar, American Religious Identification Survey (ARIS 2008) Summary Report, 2009, Institute for the Study of Secularism in Society and Culture, Trinity College, Hartford, CT <http://www.trincoll.edu/Academics/centers/ISSSC/Pages/ARIS-Data-Archive.aspx> and <www.AmericanReligionSurvey-ARIS.org> (copyright).

Table 78. Religious Adherents, 2010, and Jewish Population, 2011—States

[137,450 represents 137,450,000. Adherents were defined as "all members, including full members, their children and others who regularly attend services." The Jewish population includes Jews who define themselves as Jewish by religion as well as those who define themselves as Jewish in cultural or ethnic terms. Data on Jewish population are based on scientific studies and informant estimates provided by local Jewish communities]

State	Number (1,000)			Percent of population [3]		
	Christian adherents [1], 2010	Other religious adherents [2], 2010	Jewish population, 2011	Christian adherents [1], 2010	Other religious adherents [2], 2010	Jewish population, 2011
United States..............................	137,450	10,890	6,588	44.5	3.5	2.1
Alabama.............................	2,948	52	9	61.7	1.1	0.2
Alaska..............................	200	40	6	28.1	5.7	0.9
Arizona.............................	1,894	466	106	29.6	7.3	1.7
Arkansas............................	1,573	40	2	53.9	1.4	0.1
California...........................	15,021	1,530	1,220	40.3	4.1	3.3
Colorado............................	1,684	199	91	33.5	4.0	1.8
Connecticut.........................	1,735	48	116	48.6	1.3	3.2
Delaware............................	349	22	15	38.9	2.5	1.7
District of Columbia.................	298	16	28	49.6	2.7	4.7
Florida..............................	6,829	400	639	36.3	2.1	3.4
Georgia.............................	4,702	186	128	48.5	1.9	1.3
Hawaii..............................	421	140	7	31.0	10.3	0.5
Idaho...............................	384	417	2	24.5	26.6	0.1
Illinois.............................	6,529	486	298	50.9	3.8	2.3
Indiana.............................	2,793	69	17	43.1	1.1	0.3
Iowa................................	1,592	46	6	52.3	1.5	0.2
Kansas..............................	1,375	61	18	48.2	2.1	0.6
Kentucky............................	2,182	49	11	50.3	1.1	0.3
Louisiana...........................	2,688	50	11	59.3	1.1	0.2
Maine...............................	345	19	14	26.0	1.4	1.0
Maryland............................	2,214	118	238	38.3	2.0	4.1
Massachusetts.......................	3,546	122	278	54.2	1.9	4.2
Michigan............................	3,910	211	82	39.6	2.1	0.8
Minnesota...........................	2,894	69	46	54.6	1.3	0.9
Mississippi..........................	1,709	33	2	57.6	1.1	0.1
Missouri............................	2,806	123	59	46.9	2.0	1.0
Montana............................	326	50	1	33.0	5.0	0.1
Nebraska............................	974	38	6	53.3	2.1	0.3
Nevada.............................	725	196	74	26.8	7.3	2.8
New Hampshire......................	444	14	10	33.7	1.1	0.8
New Jersey..........................	4,321	272	504	49.1	3.1	5.7
New Mexico.........................	940	87	12	45.6	4.2	0.6
New York............................	8,529	611	1,635	44.0	3.2	8.4
North Carolina......................	4,372	140	31	45.9	1.5	0.3
North Dakota........................	443	8	(Z)	65.9	1.2	0.1
Ohio................................	4,861	146	148	42.1	1.3	1.3
Oklahoma...........................	2,148	75	5	57.3	2.0	0.1
Oregon..............................	998	187	41	26.1	4.9	1.1
Pennsylvania........................	6,530	206	295	51.4	1.6	2.3
Rhode Island........................	558	10	19	53.1	0.9	1.8
South Carolina......................	2,337	70	13	50.5	1.5	0.3
South Dakota........................	464	13	(Z)	57.0	1.6	0.0
Tennessee..........................	3,425	82	20	54.0	1.3	0.3
Texas...............................	13,062	872	140	51.9	3.5	0.6
Utah................................	256	1,929	6	9.3	69.8	0.2
Vermont.............................	199	9	5	31.8	1.4	0.9
Virginia.............................	3,206	351	97	40.1	4.4	1.2
Washington..........................	1,945	364	46	28.9	5.4	0.7
West Virginia........................	635	22	2	34.3	1.2	0.1
Wisconsin...........................	2,973	62	28	52.3	1.1	0.5
Wyoming............................	158	65	1	28.0	11.5	0.2

Z Fewer than 500. [1] Comprises evangelical Protestants, Black Protestants, mainline Protestants, Orthodox and Catholic groups. [2] Includes counts of Jain, Shinto, Sikh, Tao, National Spiritualist Association, Church of Jesus Christ of Latter Day Saints, Unitarian Universalist, Jehovah's Witnesses, Church of Christ. Scientist, Bahá'í, three Buddhist groupings, four Hindu grouping Jehovah's Witnesses, Church of Christ. Scientist, Bahá'í, three Buddhist groupings, four Hindu groupings, Muslims, and Zoroastrians. Excludes four Judaism groups. [3] Based on U.S. Census Bureau data for resident population enumerated as of April 1, 2010 and estimated as of July 2011.

Source: Religious adherents: Clifford Grammich, Kirk Hadaway, Richard Houseal, Dale E. Jones, Alexei Krindatch, Richie Stanley, and Richard H. Taylor, *2010 U.S. Religion Census: Religious Congregations & Membership Study*, 2012, (copyright), Association of Statisticians of American Religious Bodies, see also <http://www.asarb.org>. Jewish population: Ira M. Sheskin and Arnold Dashefsky, University of Miami and University of Connecticut, "Jewish Population of the United States, 2011," published by the Mandell L. Berman North American Jewish Data Bank in cooperation with the Association for the Social Scientific Study of Jewry and the Jewish Federations of North America, see also <http://www.jewishdatabank.org>.

Table 79. Religious Bodies—Selected Data, 1988-2010

[Includes the self-reported membership of religious bodies with 750,000 or more as reported to the Yearbook of American and Canadian Churches. Groups may be excluded if they do not supply information. The data are not standardized so comparisons between groups are difficult. The definition of "church member" is determined by the religious body]

Religious body	Year reported	Churches reported	Membership
African Methodist Episcopal Church	2009	4,100	2,500,000
African Methodist Episcopal Zion Church	2010	(NA)	1,400,000
American Baptist Churches in the USA	2010	5,366	1,308,054
Assemblies of God	2010	12,457	3,030,944
Catholic Church	2010	18,199	68,202,492
Christian Churches and Churches of Christ	1988	5,579	1,071,616
Christian Methodist Episcopal Church	2006	3,500	850,000
Church of God in Christ	1991	15,300	5,499,875
Church of God (Cleveland, Tennessee)	2010	6,481	1,074,047
Church of Jesus Christ of Latter-day Saints	2010	13,601	6,157,238
Churches of Christ	2006	13,000	1,639,495
Episcopal Church	2010	6,794	1,951,907
Evangelical Lutheran Church in America	2010	9,995	4,274,855
Greek Orthodox Archdiocese of America	2006	560	1,500,000
Jehovah's Witnesses	2010	13,021	1,184,249
Lutheran Church—Missouri Synod	2010	6,158	2,278,586
National Baptist Convention of America Inc	2000	(NA)	3,500,000
National Baptist Convention, U.S.A., Inc.	2010	10,358	5,197,512
National Missionary Baptist Convention of America	1992	(NA)	2,500,000
Pentecostal Assemblies of the World, Inc.	2010	2,550	1,800,000
Presbyterian Church (U.S.A.)	2010	10,560	2,675,873
Progressive National Baptist Convention, Inc.	2009	1,500	1,010,000
Seventh Day Adventist Church	2010	4,916	1,060,386
Southern Baptist Convention	2010	45,727	16,136,044
United Church of Christ	2010	5,227	1,058,423
United Methodist Church	2009	33,583	7,679,850

NA Not available.

Source: National Council of Churches USA, New York, NY, *2012 Yearbook of American & Canadian Churches,* annual (copyright). See also <http://www.ncccusa.org>, or call 888-870-3325.

Table 80. Religious Adherents by Metropolitan Area Status and Religious Groups: 2010

[Groups shown have 500,000 adherents or more. Adherents were defined as all members, including full members, their children and the estimated number of other participants who are not considered members. Based on a study of 236 religious bodies sponsored by the Association of Statisticians of American Religious Bodies. Participants included 217 Christian denominations, associations, or communions (including Latter-day Saints, Messianic Jews, and Unitarian/Universalist groups); counts of Jain, Shinto, Sikh, Tao, and National Spiritualist Association congregations, and counts of congregations and individuals for Bahá'í, three Buddhist groupings, four Hindu groupings, four Jewish groupings, Muslims, and Zoroastrians. For definition of metropolitan and micropolitan areas, see Appendix II]

Religious group	Total adherents (1,000)	Percent		
		In metropolitan area	In micropolitan area	Outside metro/micro area
U.S. population, total	308,746	83.7	10.0	6.3
Total adherents	**150,686**	**83.5**	**10.0**	**6.5**
Catholic	58,929	90.5	6.2	3.3
Southern Baptist Convention	19,897	69.3	17.2	13.5
Non-denominational Christian Churches	12,241	88.7	7.8	3.5
United Methodist Church	9,948	73.6	15.3	11.1
Church of Jesus Christ of Latter-day Saints	6,145	82.8	11.6	5.6
Evangelical Lutheran Church in America	4,181	70.4	16.0	13.6
Assemblies of God	2,945	82.7	11.0	6.3
Muslim Estimate	2,600	97.4	2.0	0.6
Presbyterian Church (U.S.A.)	2,452	82.5	11.4	6.1
Lutheran Church—Missouri Synod	2,271	72.7	13.7	13.6
Episcopal	1,952	88.2	8.1	3.7
National Baptist Convention, USA, Inc	1,881	90.3	7	2.7
Churches of Christ	1,584	69.8	17.1	13.1
American Baptist Churches in the USA	1,561	83.8	9.8	6.4
Christian Churches and Churches of Christ	1,453	72.6	15.9	11.5
United Church of Christ	1,284	79.3	13.5	7.2
Seventh-day Adventist Church	1,195	87.7	8.2	4.1
Church of God (Cleveland, Tennessee)	1,110	72.2	17.5	10.3
African Methodist Episcopal Church	1,010	77.7	12.3	10.0
Orthodox Judaism	947	99.6	0.0	0.4
Church of the Nazarene	894	76.2	15.6	8.2
Christian Church (Disciples of Christ)	786	70.3	17.7	12.0
Reform Judaism	766	98.3	1.3	0.4
Mahayana Buddhism	733	92.8	6.8	0.4
Church of God in Christ	624	87.8	7.3	4.9
Conservative Judaism	502	99.5	0.4	0.1

Source: Clifford Grammich, Kirk Hadaway, Richard Houseal, Dale E. Jones, Alexei Krindatch, Richie Stanley, and Richard H. Taylor. *2010 U.S. Religion Census: Religious Congregations & Membership Study,* 2012 (copyright). Association of Statisticians of American Religious Bodies.

Births, Deaths, Marriages, and Divorces

This section presents vital statistics data on natality, mortality, marriages, and divorces, as well as factors that help explain fertility, such as, use of contraception, sexual activity, and prevalence of abortions and fetal deaths. Vital statistics are collected and disseminated for the nation through the National Vital Statistics System by the National Center for Health Statistics (NCHS) and published annually in *Vital Statistics of the United States, National Vital Statistics Reports (NVSR)*, and other selected publications. Reports are also issued by various state bureaus participating in the National Vital Statistics System. Factors influencing fertility are collected in NCHS's National Survey of Family Growth and the U.S. Census Bureau's Current Population Survey and American Community Survey published in *Fertility of American Women*. Data on abortions are published by the Alan Guttmacher Institute in selected issues of *Perspectives on Sexual and Reproductive Health*.

Registration of vital events—The registration of births, deaths, fetal deaths, and other vital events in the United States is primarily a state and local function. There are 57 vital registration jurisdictions in the United States: the 50 states, five territories (Puerto Rico, etc.), District of Columbia, and New York City. Each of the 57 jurisdictions has a direct statistical reporting relationship with NCHS. Vital events occurring to U.S. residents outside the United States are not included in the data.

Births and deaths—The live-birth, death, and fetal-death statistics prepared by NCHS are based on vital records filed in the registration offices of all states, New York City, and the District of Columbia. The annual collection of death statistics on a national basis began in 1900 with a national death-registration area of ten states and the District of Columbia; a similar annual collection of birth statistics for a national birth-registration area began in 1915, also with ten reporting states and the District of Columbia. Since 1933, the birth- and death-registration areas have comprised the entire United States, including Alaska (beginning 1959) and Hawaii (beginning 1960). National statistics on fetal deaths were first compiled for 1918 and annually since 1922. Prior to 1951, birth statistics came from a complete count of records received in the Public Health Service (now received in NCHS). From 1951 through 1971, they were based on a 50-percent sample of all registered births (except for a complete count in 1955 and a 20- to 50-percent sample in 1967). Beginning in 1972, they have been based on a complete count for states participating in the Vital Statistics Cooperative Program (VSCP) (for details, see the technical appendix in *Vital Statistics of the United States*) and on a 50-percent sample of all other areas. Beginning in 1986, all reporting areas participated in the VSCP. Mortality data have been based on a complete count of records for each area (except for a 50-percent sample in 1972). Beginning in 1970, births to and deaths of nonresident aliens of the United States and U.S. citizens outside the United States have been excluded from the data. Fetal deaths and deaths among Armed Forces abroad are excluded. Data based on samples are subject to sampling error; for details, see annual issues of *Vital Statistics of the United States.*

Mortality statistics by cause of death are compiled in accordance with World Health Organization regulations according to the *International Classification of Diseases* (ICD). The ICD is revised approximately every 10 years. The tenth revision of the ICD was employed beginning in 1999. Deaths for prior years were classified according to the revision of the ICD in use at the time. Each revision of the ICD introduces a number of discontinuities in mortality statistics; for a discussion of those between the ninth and tenth revisions of the ICD, see *National Vital Statistics Reports*, Vol. 60, No. 3. Preliminary mortality data are based on a percentage of death records weighted up to the total number of deaths reported for the given year; for a discussion of preliminary data, see *National Vital Statistics Reports*, Vol. 60, No. 4. Information on tests of statistical significance, differences between death rates, and standard errors can also be found in the reports mentioned above. Some of the tables present age-adjusted death rates in addition to crude death rates. Age-adjusted death rates shown in this section were prepared using the direct method, in which age-specific death rates for a population of interest are applied to a standard population distributed by age. Age adjustment eliminates the differences in observed rates between points in time or among compared population groups that result from age differences in population composition.

Fertility and life expectancy—The total fertility rate, defined as the number of births that 1,000 women would have in their lifetime if, at each year of age, they experienced the birth rates occurring in the specified year, is compiled and published by NCHS. See Births: Final Data for 2009, *National Vital Statistics Reports*, Vol. 60, No. 1. Data on life expectancy, the average remaining lifetime in years for persons who attain a given age, are computed and published by NCHS. For details, see Deaths: Final Data for 2009, *National Vital Statistics Reports*, Vol. 60, No. 3 and <http://www.cdc.gov/nchs/deaths.htm>.

Marriage and divorce—In 1957 and 1958 respectively, the National Office of Vital Statistics established marriage- and divorce-registration areas. Beginning in 1957, the marriage-registration area comprised 30 states, plus Alaska, Hawaii, Puerto Rico, and the Virgin Islands; it currently includes 42 states and the District of Columbia. The divorce-registration area, starting in 1958 with 14 states, Alaska, Hawaii, and the Virgin Islands, currently includes a total of 31 states and the Virgin Islands. Procedures for estimating the number of marriages and divorces in the registration states are discussed in *Vital Statistics of the United States, Vol. III—Marriage and Divorce*. Total counts of events for registration and nonregistration states are gathered by collecting already summarized data on marriages and divorces reported by state offices of vital statistics and by county offices of registration. The collection and publication of detailed marriage and divorce statistics was suspended beginning in January 1996. For additional information, contact the National Center for Health Statistics online at <http://www.cdc.gov/nchs/mardiv.htm>.

Vital statistics rates—Except as noted, vital statistics rates computed by NCHS are based on decennial census population figures as of April 1 for 1960, 1970, 1980, 1990, and 2000; and on midyear population figures for other years, as estimated by the Census Bureau (see text, Section 1).

Race—Data by race for births, deaths, marriages, and divorces from NCHS are based on information contained in the certificates of registration. The Census Bureau's Current Population Survey obtains information on race by asking respondents to classify their race as (1) White, (2) Black, (3) American Indian or Alaska Native, (4) Native Hawaiian or Other Pacific Islander, and (5) Asian. Beginning with the 1989 data year, NCHS is tabulating its birth data primarily by race of the mother. In 1988 and prior years, births were tabulated by race of the child, which was determined from the race of the parents as entered on the birth certificate. Trend data by race shown in this section are by race of mother beginning with the 1980 data. Hispanic origin of the mother is reported and tabulated independently of race. Thus, persons of Hispanic origin may be any race. The majority of women of Hispanic origin are reported as White.

Statistical reliability—For a discussion of statistical collection, estimation, and sampling procedures and measures of reliability applicable to data from NCHS and the Census Bureau, see Appendix III.

Table 81. Live Births, Deaths, Marriages, and Divorces: 1960 to 2009

[4,258 represents 4,258,000. Beginning 1970, excludes births to, and deaths of nonresidents of the United States. See Appendix III]

Year	Number					Rate per 1,000 population				
		Deaths					Deaths			
	Births (1,000)	Total (1,000)	Infant [1] (1,000)	Marriages [2] (1,000)	Divorces [3] (1,000)	Births	Total	Infant [1]	Mar-riages [2]	Divorces [3]
1960	4,258	1,712	111	1,523	393	23.7	9.5	26.0	8.5	2.2
1970	3,731	1,921	75	2,159	708	18.4	9.5	20.0	10.6	3.5
1971	3,556	1,928	68	2,190	773	17.2	9.3	19.1	10.6	3.7
1972	3,258	1,964	60	2,282	845	15.6	9.4	18.5	10.9	4.0
1973	3,137	1,973	56	2,284	915	14.8	9.3	17.7	10.8	4.3
1974	3,160	1,934	53	2,230	977	14.8	9.1	16.7	10.5	4.6
1975	3,144	1,893	51	2,153	1,036	14.6	8.8	16.1	10.0	4.8
1976	3,168	1,909	48	2,155	1,083	14.6	8.8	15.2	9.9	5.0
1977	3,327	1,900	47	2,178	1,091	15.1	8.6	14.1	9.9	5.0
1978	3,333	1,928	46	2,282	1,130	15.0	8.7	13.8	10.3	5.1
1979	3,494	1,914	46	2,331	1,181	15.6	8.5	13.1	10.4	5.3
1980	3,612	1,990	46	2,390	1,189	15.9	8.8	12.6	10.6	5.2
1981	3,629	1,978	43	2,422	1,213	15.8	8.6	11.9	10.6	5.3
1982	3,681	1,975	42	2,456	1,170	15.9	8.5	11.5	10.6	5.1
1983	3,639	2,019	41	2,446	1,158	15.6	8.6	11.2	10.5	5.0
1984	3,669	2,039	40	2,477	1,169	15.6	8.6	10.8	10.5	5.0
1985	3,761	2,086	40	2,413	1,190	15.8	8.8	10.6	10.1	5.0
1986	3,757	2,105	39	2,407	1,178	15.6	8.8	10.4	10.0	4.9
1987	3,809	2,123	38	2,403	1,166	15.7	8.8	10.1	9.9	4.8
1988	3,910	2,168	39	2,396	1,167	16.0	8.9	10.0	9.8	4.8
1989	4,041	2,150	40	2,403	1,157	16.4	8.7	9.8	9.7	4.7
1990	4,158	2,148	38	2,443	1,182	16.7	8.6	9.2	9.8	4.7
1991	4,111	2,170	37	2,371	1,187	16.2	8.6	8.9	9.4	4.7
1992	4,065	2,176	35	2,362	1,215	15.8	8.5	8.5	9.3	4.8
1993	4,000	2,269	33	2,334	1,187	15.4	8.8	8.4	9.0	4.6
1994	3,953	2,279	31	2,362	1,191	15.0	8.8	8.0	9.1	4.6
1995	3,900	2,312	30	2,336	1,169	14.6	8.7	7.6	8.9	4.4
1996	3,891	2,315	28	2,344	1,150	14.4	8.6	7.3	8.8	4.3
1997	3,881	2,314	28	2,384	1,163	14.2	8.5	7.2	8.9	4.3
1998	3,942	2,337	28	2,244	[4] 1,135	14.3	8.5	7.2	8.4	[4] 4.2
1999	3,959	2,391	28	2,358	(NA)	14.2	8.6	7.1	8.6	[4] 4.1
2000	4,059	2,403	28	2,315	[4] 944	14.4	8.5	6.9	8.3	[4] 4.1
2001	4,026	2,416	28	2,326	[4] 940	14.1	8.5	6.8	8.2	[4] 4.0
2002	4,022	2,443	28	2,290	[5] 955	13.9	8.5	7.0	7.8	[5] 3.9
2003	4,090	2,448	28	2,245	[6] 927	14.1	8.4	6.9	7.7	[6] 3.8
2004	4,112	2,398	28	2,279	[7] 879	14.0	8.2	6.8	7.8	[7] 3.7
2005	4,138	2,448	28	2,249	[8] 847	14.0	8.3	6.9	7.6	[8] 3.6
2006	4,266	2,426	29	[9] 2,193	[8] 872	14.2	8.1	6.7	[9] 7.4	[8] 3.7
2007	4,316	2,424	29	2,197	[8] 856	14.3	8.0	6.8	7.3	[8] 3.6
2008	4,248	2,472	28	2,157	[8] 844	14.0	8.1	6.6	7.1	[8] 3.5
2009	4,131	2,437	26	2,080	[8] 840	13.5	7.9	6.4	6.8	[8] 3.5

NA Not available. [1] Infant mortality rate; infants under 1 year, excluding fetal deaths. [2] Marriages and marriage rates are by place of occurrence. Beginning 1991 data are provisional. Includes estimates for some States through 1965 and also for 1976 and 1977 and marriage licenses for some states for all years except 1973 and 1975. Beginning 1978, includes nonlicensed marriages in California. [3] Divorces and divorce rates are by place of occurrence. Includes reported annulments and some estimated state figures for all years. Beginning 1991 data are provisional. [4] Excludes data for California, Colorado, Indiana, and Louisiana. [5] Excludes data for California, Indiana, and Oklahoma. [6] Excludes data for California, Hawaii, Indiana, and Oklahoma [7] Excludes data for California, Georgia, Hawaii, Indiana, and Louisiana. [8] Excludes data for California, Georgia, Hawaii, Indiana, Louisiana, and Minnesota. [9] Excludes Louisiana.

Source: U.S. National Center for Health Statistics, Vital Statistics of the United States, and National Vital Statistics Reports (NVSR), <http://www.cdc.gov/nchs/nvss.htm>.

Table 82. Live Births, Birth Rates, and Fertility Rates by Hispanic Origin: 2000 to 2009

[4,059 represents 4,059,000. Represents registered births. Excludes births to nonresidents of the United States. Data are based on Hispanic origin and race of mother. Persons of Hispanic origin may be of any race. See Appendix III]

Hispanic-origin status and race of mother	Number of births (1,000)				Birth rate per 1,000 population				Fertility rate [1]			
	2000	2005	2008	2009	2000	2005	2008	2009	2000	2005	2008	2009
Total [2]	4,059	4,138	4,248	4,131	14.4	14.0	14.0	13.5	65.9	66.7	68.6	66.7
Hispanic	816	986	1,041	1,000	23.1	23.1	22.2	20.6	95.9	99.4	98.8	93.3
Mexican	582	693	685	645	25.0	24.7	22.1	20.1	105.1	107.7	98.9	91.4
Puerto Rico	58	63	69	68	18.1	17.2	16.7	15.8	73.5	72.1	71.5	68.7
Cuban	13	16	17	17	9.7	10.2	10.2	9.6	49.3	50.4	53.3	49.5
Central and South American [3]	113	151	156	149	21.8	22.8	26.6	26.0	85.1	93.2	116.1	115.7
Other and unknown Hispanic	49	62	115	120	(3)	(3)	(3)	(3)	(3)	(3)	(3)	(3)
Non-Hispanic [4]	3,200	3,123	3,174	3,101	13.2	12.4	12.5	12.1	61.1	60.4	62.4	61.1
White	2,363	2,280	2,268	2,213	12.2	11.5	11.3	11.0	58.5	58.3	59.4	58.4
Black	604	584	623	610	17.3	15.7	16.4	15.8	71.4	67.2	71.1	68.9

[1] Live births per 1,000 women aged 15 to 44 years in specified group. [2] Includes all races and Hispanic origin status not stated. [3] Rates for the Central and South American population include other and unknown Hispanic. [4] Includes other races not shown separately.

Source: U.S. National Center for Health Statistics, National Vital Statistics Reports (NVSR), *Births: Final Data for 2009*, Vol. 60, No. 1, November 2011, <http://www.cdc.gov/nchs/births.htm>.

Table 83. Births, Birth Rates, and Fertility Rates by Race, Sex, and Age: 1980 to 2009

[Births in thousands (3,612 represents 3,612,000). Except as indicated, births by race of mother. Excludes births to nonresidents of the United States. For population bases used to derive these data; see text, this section and Appendix III]

Item	1980	1990	2000	2002	2003	2004	2005	2006	2007	2008	2009
Live births [1]	**3,612**	**4,158**	**4,059**	**4,022**	**4,090**	**4,112**	**4,138**	**4,266**	**4,316**	**4,248**	**4,131**
White	2,936	3,290	3,194	3,175	3,226	3,223	3,229	3,310	3,337	3,274	3,173
Black	568	684	623	594	600	616	633	666	676	671	658
American Indian or Alaska Native	29	39	42	42	43	44	45	47	49	50	49
Asian or Pacific Islander	74	142	201	211	221	229	231	241	254	253	251
Male	1,853	2,129	2,077	2,058	2,094	2,105	2,119	2,184	2,208	2,173	2,114
Female	1,760	2,029	1,982	1,964	1,996	2,007	2,019	2,081	2,108	2,074	2,017
Males per 100 females (sex ratio)	105	105	105	105	105	105	105	105	105	105	105
Age of mother:											
Under 20 years	562	533	478	433	421	422	421	442	451	441	415
20 to 24 years	1,226	1,094	1,018	1,022	1,032	1,034	1,040	1,081	1,082	1,052	1,006
25 to 29 years	1,108	1,277	1,088	1,060	1,086	1,104	1,132	1,182	1,208	1,196	1,167
30 to 34 years	550	886	929	951	976	966	951	950	962	957	955
35 to 39 years	141	318	452	454	468	476	483	499	500	489	474
40 to 44 years	(NA)	(NA)	90	96	101	104	105	106	105	106	106
45 to 54 years	(NA)	(NA)	4	5	6	6	6	7	7	7	8
Mean age of mother at first birth (years)	22.7	24.2	24.9	25.1	25.2	25.2	25.2	25.0	25.0	25.1	25.2
Birth rate per 1,000 population	**15.9**	**16.7**	**14.4**	**13.9**	**14.1**	**14.0**	**14.0**	**14.2**	**14.3**	**14.0**	**13.5**
White	15.1	15.8	13.9	13.5	13.6	13.5	13.4	13.7	13.7	13.4	12.8
Black	21.3	22.4	17.0	15.7	15.7	16.0	16.2	16.8	16.9	16.6	16.0
American Indian or Alaska Native	20.7	18.9	14.0	13.8	13.8	14.0	14.2	14.9	15.3	14.5	13.9
Asian or Pacific Islander	19.9	19.0	17.1	16.5	16.8	16.8	16.5	16.6	17.2	16.8	16.2
Age of mother:											
10 to 14 years	1.1	1.4	0.9	0.7	0.6	0.7	0.7	0.6	0.6	0.6	0.5
15 to 19 years	53.0	59.9	47.7	43.0	41.6	41.1	40.4	41.9	42.5	41.5	39.1
20 to 24 years	115.1	116.5	109.7	103.6	102.6	101.7	102.2	105.9	106.3	103.0	96.3
25 to 29 years	112.9	120.2	113.5	113.6	115.6	115.5	115.5	116.7	117.5	115.1	110.5
30 to 34 years	61.9	80.8	91.2	91.5	95.1	95.3	95.8	97.7	99.9	99.3	97.7
35 to 39 years	19.8	31.7	39.7	41.4	43.8	45.4	46.3	47.3	47.5	46.9	46.5
40 to 44 years	3.9	5.5	8.0	8.3	8.7	8.9	9.1	9.4	9.5	9.8	10.1
45 to 54 years [2]	0.2	0.2	0.5	0.5	0.5	0.5	0.6	0.6	0.6	0.7	0.7
Fertility rate per 1,000 women [3]	**68.4**	**70.9**	**65.9**	**64.8**	**66.1**	**66.3**	**66.7**	**68.5**	**69.5**	**68.6**	**66.7**
White [3]	65.6	68.3	65.3	64.8	66.1	66.1	66.3	68.0	68.8	67.8	66.0
Black [3]	84.9	84.8	70.0	65.8	66.3	67.6	69.0	72.1	72.7	71.9	69.9
American Indian or Alaska Native [3]	82.7	76.2	58.7	58.0	58.4	58.9	59.9	63.1	64.9	64.6	62.8
Asian or Pacific Islander [3]	73.2	69.6	65.8	64.1	66.3	67.1	66.6	67.5	71.3	71.3	68.7

NA Not available. [1] Includes other races not shown separately. [2] The number of births shown is the total for women aged 45–54 years. The rate is computed by relating the births to women aged 45–54 years to women aged 45–49 years. [3] Number of live births per 1,000 women, 15 to 44 years old in specified group.

Source: U.S. National Center for Health Statistics, National Vital Statistics Reports (NVSR), *Births: Final Data for 2009*, Vol. 60, No. 1, November 2011, <http://www.cdc.gov/nchs/births.htm>.

Table 84. Births and Multiple Births by Race and Hispanic Origin of Mother: 1990 to 2009

[Represents registered births. Excludes births to nonresidents of the United States. Data are based on Hispanic origin and race of mother. Persons of Hispanic origin may be of any race. See Appendix III]

Birth order	1990 [1]	2000	2005	2007	2008	2009
All births, total number [2]	**4,158,212**	**4,058,814**	**4,138,349**	**4,316,233**	**4,247,694**	**4,130,665**
Twin births	93,865	118,916	133,122	138,961	138,660	137,217
Triplet and higher order multiple births	3,028	7,325	6,694	6,427	6,268	6,340
Multiple birth rate [3]	23.3	31.1	33.8	33.7	34.1	34.8
Twin birth rate [4]	22.6	29.3	32.2	32.2	32.6	33.2
Triplet and higher order multiple birth rate [5]	72.8	180.5	161.8	148.9	147.6	153.5
Non-Hispanic White births, total number	**2,626,500**	**2,362,968**	**2,279,768**	**2,310,333**	**2,267,817**	**2,212,552**
Twin births	60,210	76,018	82,223	83,632	82,903	81,954
Triplet and higher order multiple births	2,358	5,821	4,966	4,559	4,493	4,457
Multiple birth rate [3]	23.8	34.6	38.2	38.2	38.5	39.1
Twin birth rate [4]	22.9	32.2	36.1	36.2	36.6	37.0
Non-Hispanic Black births, total number	**661,701**	**604,346**	**583,759**	**627,191**	**623,029**	**609,584**
Twin births	17,646	20,173	21,254	23,101	22,924	23,159
Triplet and higher order multiple births	306	506	616	612	569	644
Multiple birth rate [3]	27.1	34.2	33.8	37.8	37.7	39.0
Twin birth rate [4]	26.7	33.4	32.2	36.8	36.8	38.0
Hispanic births, total number	**595,073**	**815,868**	**985,505**	**1,062,799**	**1,041,239**	**999,548**
Twin births	10,713	16,470	21,723	23,405	23,266	22,481
Triplet and higher order multiple births	235	659	761	857	834	835
Multiple birth rate [3]	18.4	21.0	22.8	22.8	23.1	23.3
Twin birth rate [4]	18.0	20.2	22.0	22.0	22.3	22.5

[1] Data by Hispanic-origin status exclude data for New Hampshire and Oklahoma, which did not report Hispanic origin. [2] Includes other races not shown separately. [3] Number of live births in all multiple deliveries per 1,000 live births. [4] Number of live births in twin deliveries per 1,000 live births. [5] Births in greater than twin deliveries per 100,000 live births.

Source: U.S. National Center for Health Statistics, National Vital Statistics Report (NVSR), *Births: Final Data for 2009*, Vol. 60, No. 1, November 2011, <http://www.cdc.gov/nchs/births.htm>.

Table 85. Births—Number and Rate by State and Island Areas: Preliminary 2010

[Number of births, except rates. Registered births by place of residence. Excludes births to nonresidents of the United States. Based on race and Hispanic origin of mother. Preliminary data are based on 100 percent of registered vital records occurring in calendar year 2010. See Appendix III]

State	All races [1]	Non-Hispanic White	Non-Hispanic Black	American Indian or Alaska Native	Asian or Pacific Islander	Hispanic [2]	Birth rate [3]	Fertility rate [4]
United States...........	4,000,279	2,161,669	589,139	46,760	246,915	946,000	13.0	64.1
Alabama..........	60,053	35,823	18,200	205	978	4,840	12.6	62.5
Alaska..........	11,466	6,261	409	2,899	1,053	660	16.1	80.1
Arizona..........	88,905	39,442	4,081	6,135	3,359	36,113	13.9	70.4
Arkansas..........	38,539	26,112	7,354	285	636	4,047	13.2	67.7
California..........	509,968	145,835	30,327	3,609	68,915	257,511	13.7	64.7
Colorado..........	66,344	40,155	3,201	713	2,575	19,457	13.2	64.7
Connecticut..........	39,441	23,239	4,856	298	2,478	8,522	11.0	57.1
Delaware..........	39,441	23,239	4,856	298	2,478	8,522	11.0	57.1
District of Columbia..........	9,167	2,491	4,874	18	513	1,359	15.2	56.5
Florida..........	214,552	97,950	49,486	380	7,080	59,596	11.4	60.3
Georgia..........	133,915	59,682	44,819	335	5,780	21,215	13.8	64.6
Hawaii..........	18,985	4,756	508	71	12,439	2,967	14.0	72.4
Idaho..........	23,194	18,612	159	466	444	3,638	14.8	75.7
Illinois..........	165,194	89,158	28,264	258	9,652	37,359	12.9	62.8
Indiana..........	83,939	64,303	9,953	127	1,960	7,568	12.9	65.2
Iowa..........	38,715	32,510	1,840	274	1,118	3,091	12.7	67.1
Kansas..........	40,640	29,545	3,044	359	1,329	6,428	14.2	73.3
Kentucky..........	55,790	46,615	5,232	102	1,041	2,858	12.9	65.3
Louisiana..........	62,383	32,901	24,162	490	1,288	3,586	13.8	67.2
Maine..........	12,967	12,024	377	112	226	210	9.8	53.6
Maryland..........	73,776	33,559	24,422	199	5,586	10,260	12.8	61.8
Massachusetts..........	72,757	48,843	7,048	142	5,950	10,602	11.1	53.9
Michigan..........	114,523	79,977	22,131	845	3,861	7,807	11.6	59.7
Minnesota..........	68,605	50,091	6,521	1,583	5,131	5,139	12.9	65.6
Mississippi..........	40,033	20,342	17,509	269	452	1,426	13.5	66.3
Missouri..........	76,756	58,467	11,381	407	1,970	4,334	12.8	65.2
Montana..........	12,060	9,952	64	1,430	139	433	12.2	67.1
Nebraska..........	25,916	19,203	1,723	553	753	3,943	14.2	73.0
Nevada..........	35,862	15,703	3,536	436	2,948	13,387	13.3	65.2
New Hampshire..........	12,867	11,506	224	23	531	528	9.8	51.4
New Jersey..........	109,249	52,137	16,568	242	11,897	28,218	12.4	62.8
New Mexico..........	27,769	7,846	486	3,614	540	15,476	13.5	69.7
New York..........	241,711	116,253	39,115	784	23,136	58,192	12.5	59.7
North Carolina..........	122,267	68,654	28,982	1,821	4,401	18,716	12.8	62.7
North Dakota..........	9,100	7,437	193	967	175	304	13.5	70.5
Ohio..........	139,137	105,366	22,957	285	3,593	6,324	12.1	62.2
Oklahoma..........	53,234	34,100	4,803	6,332	1,311	6,931	14.2	72.3
Oregon..........	45,535	31,674	1,141	895	2,744	9,257	11.9	60.4
Pennsylvania..........	142,325	100,405	20,900	410	6,213	13,669	11.2	58.3
Rhode Island..........	11,149	6,982	952	164	554	2,433	10.6	51.9
South Carolina..........	58,293	33,155	18,665	207	1,198	4,945	12.6	62.8
South Dakota..........	11,809	9,003	260	1,935	152	509	14.5	77.5
Tennessee..........	79,485	53,912	16,628	218	1,845	7,139	12.5	62.4
Texas..........	386,096	134,906	44,559	1,179	16,818	189,120	15.4	72.5
Utah..........	52,232	41,464	585	707	1,634	8,051	18.9	86.7
Vermont..........	6,223	5,896	112	18	110	77	9.9	52.6
Virginia..........	102,972	59,705	21,700	173	7,639	12,415	12.9	62.3
Washington..........	86,530	55,077	4,087	2,217	9,079	16,219	12.9	63.8
West Virginia..........	20,471	19,234	745	21	189	210	11.0	59.9
Wisconsin..........	68,483	51,034	6,862	1,238	2,892	6,545	12.0	62.4
Wyoming..........	7,555	6,047	86	296	88	939	13.4	70.9
Puerto Rico..........	42,159	1,142	143	(NA)	(NA)	40,846	11.3	54.3
Virgin Islands..........	(NA)	(NA)	(NA)	(NA)	(NA)	(NA)	(NA)	(NA)
Guam..........	3,416	208	35	10	3,122	47	18.9	87.1
American Samoa..........	1,234	(NA)	(NA)	(NA)	1,233	(NA)	18.6	81.8
Northern Marianas..........	(NA)	(NA)	(NA)	(NA)	(NA)	(NA)	(NA)	(NA)

NA Not available. [1] Includes persons of other groups, not shown separately. [2] Persons of Hispanic origin may be any race. [3] Per 1,000 estimated population. [4] Number of births per 1,000 women aged 15 to 44 years.

Source: U.S. National Center for Health Statistics, National Vital Statistics Reports (NVSR), *Births: Preliminary Data for 2010*, Vol.60, No. 2, November 2011, <http://www.cdc.gov/nchs/births.htm>.

Table 86. Total Fertility Rate by Race and Hispanic Origin: 1980 to 2009

[Based on race of mother. Excludes births to nonresidents of United States. The *total fertility rate* is the number of births that 1,000 women would have in their lifetime if, at each year of age, they experienced the birth rates occurring in the specified year. A total fertility rate of 2,100 represents "replacement level" fertility for the total population under current mortality conditions (assuming no net immigration). See Appendix III]

Race and Hispanic origin	1980	1990	2000	2005	2006	2007	2008	2009
Total [1]	**1,840**	**2,081**	**2,056**	**2,054**	**2,101**	**2,122**	**2,085**	**2,007**
White	1,773	2,003	2,051	2,056	2,096	2,112	2,067	1,992
Black	2,177	2,480	2,129	2,071	2,155	2,168	2,132	2,056
American Indian, Eskimo, Aleut	2,165	2,185	1,773	1,750	1,829	1,867	1,844	1,780
Asian or Pacific Islander	1,954	2,003	1,892	1,889	1,919	2,039	2,055	1,957
Hispanic [2]	(NA)	2,960	2,730	2,885	2,960	2,995	2,912	2,733

NA Not available. [1] For 1970 to 1991 includes births to races not shown separately. Beginning 1992 unknown race of mother is imputed. [2] Persons of Hispanic origin may be any race.

Source: U.S. National Center for Health Statistics, National Vital Statistics Report (NVSR), *Births: Final Data for 2009*, Vol. 60, No. 1, November 2011, <http://www.cdc.gov/nchs/births.htm>.

Table 87. Teenagers—Births and Birth Rates by Age, Race, and Hispanic Origin: 1990 to 2009

[Birth rates per 1,000 women in specified group. Based on race and Hispanic origin of mother. See text this section]

Item	Number of births					Birth rate				
	1990	2000	2005	2008	2009 [1]	1990	2000	2005	2008	2009 [1]
All races, 15 to 19 years	[2] **521,826**	**468,990**	**414,593**	**434,758**	**409,802**	**59.9**	**47.7**	**40.5**	**41.5**	**39.1**
15 to 17 years	183,327	157,209	133,191	135,664	124,247	37.5	26.9	21.4	21.7	20.1
18 to 19 years	338,499	311,781	281,402	299,094	285,555	88.6	78.1	69.9	70.6	66.2
White	354,482	333,013	295,265	306,402	288,709	50.8	43.2	37.0	37.8	35.7
Black	151,613	118,954	103,905	112,004	105,725	112.8	77.4	62.0	63.4	59.5
American Indian or Alaska Native	(NA)	8,055	7,807	8,815	8,315	81.1	58.3	52.7	58.4	55.5
Asian or Pacific Islander	(NA)	8,968	7,616	7,537	7,053	26.4	20.5	17.0	16.2	14.7
Hispanic [3]	(NA)	129,469	136,906	144,914	136,263	100.3	87.3	81.7	77.5	70.1
Non-Hispanic White	(NA)	204,056	165,005	168,684	159,579	42.5	32.6	25.9	26.7	25.6
Non-Hispanic Black	(NA)	116,019	96,813	104,559	98,448	116.2	79.2	60.9	62.8	59.0

NA Not available. [1] Data have been revised. [2] Includes races other than White and Black, not shown separately. [3] Persons of Hispanic origin may be any race.

Source: U.S. National Center for Health Statistics, National Vital Statistics Reports (NVSR), *Births: Final Data for 2009*, Vol. 60, No. 1, November 2011, and earlier reports. See also: <http://www.cdc.gov/nchs/births.htm>.

Table 88. Births to Unmarried Women by Race, Hispanic Origin, and Age of Mother: 1990 to 2009

[1,165 represents 1,165,000. Excludes births to nonresidents of the United States. Persons of Hispanic origin may be any race. Marital status is inferred from a comparison of the child's and parents' surnames on the birth certificate for those states that do not report on marital status. No estimates included for misstatements on birth records or failure to register births. Based on race and Hispanic origin of mother. See also Appendix III]

Race and age of mother	Number (1,000)				Percent distribution				Birth rate [1]			
	1990	2000	2005	2009	1990	2000	2005	2009	1990	2000	2005	2009
Total live births [2]	**1,165**	**1,347**	**1,527**	**1,694**	**100.0**	**100.0**	**100.0**	**100.0**	**43.8**	**44.1**	**47.5**	**50.5**
White	670	866	1,023	1,143	57.5	64.3	67.0	67.5	32.9	38.2	43.0	46.3
Black	455	427	439	476	39.1	31.7	28.7	28.1	90.5	70.5	67.8	69.9
American Indian or Alaska Native	(NA)	(NA)	28	32	(NA)	(NA)	1.9	1.9	(NA)	(NA)	(NA)	(NA)
Asian or Pacific Islander	(NA)	(NA)	37	43	(NA)	(NA)	2.4	2.6	(NA)	20.9	24.9	27.4
Hispanic	[3] 219	348	473	531	[3] 18.8	25.8	31.0	31.4	[3] 89.6	87.2	100.3	96.8
Non-Hispanic White	[3] 443	522	578	641	[3] 38.0	38.7	37.8	37.9	[3] 24.4	28.0	30.1	33.0
Non-Hispanic Black	(NA)	415	408	444	(NA)	30.8	26.7	26.2	(NA)	(NA)	(NA)	(NA)
Under 15 years	11	8	7	5	0.9	0.6	0.4	0.3	(NA)	(NA)	(NA)	(NA)
15 to 19 years	350	369	345	357	30.0	27.4	22.6	21.1	42.5	39.0	34.5	35.0
20 to 24 years	404	504	585	624	34.7	37.4	38.3	36.9	65.1	72.2	74.9	74.6
25 to 29 years	230	255	332	395	19.7	18.9	21.7	23.3	56.0	58.5	71.1	72.7
30 to 34 years	118	130	162	198	10.1	9.7	10.6	11.7	37.6	39.3	50.0	57.5
35 to 39 years	44	65	76	90	3.8	4.8	5.0	5.3	17.3	19.7	24.5	30.2
40 years and over	9	16	21	24	0.7	1.2	1.4	1.4	3.6	5.0	[4] 6.2	[4] 7.9

NA Not available. [1] Rate per 1,000 unmarried women (never-married, widowed, and divorced) estimated as of July 1. Total rate and rates by race cover women 15 to 44 years old. [2] Includes races other than White and Black, not shown separately. [3] Excludes data for New Hampshire and Oklahoma, which did not report Hispanic origin. [4] Birth rates computed by relating births to unmarried mothers aged 40 years and over to unmarried women aged 40–44 years.

Source: U.S. National Center for Health Statistics, National Vital Statistics Reports (NVSR), *Births: Final Data for 2009*, Vol. 60, No. 1, November 2011; and earlier reports, <http://www.cdc.gov/nchs/births.htm>.

Table 89. Percent of Births to Teens, Unmarried Mothers, and Births With Low Birth Weight: 1990 to 2009

[Represents registered births. Excludes births to nonresidents of the United States. Data are based on race and Hispanic origin of mother. See Appendix III]

Characteristics	1990	1995	2000	2005	2007	2008	2009
Percent of births to teenage mothers [1]	**12.8**	**13.1**	**11.8**	**10.2**	**10.5**	**10.4**	**10.0**
White	10.9	11.5	10.6	9.3	9.5	9.5	9.2
Black	23.1	23.1	19.7	16.9	17.2	17.0	16.4
American Indian or Alaska Native	19.5	21.4	19.7	17.7	18.4	18.0	17.3
Asian or Pacific Islander	5.7	5.6	4.5	3.3	3.1	3.0	2.8
Hispanic origin [2]	16.8	17.9	16.2	14.1	14.2	14.1	13.8
Mexican	17.7	18.8	17.0	14.9	14.9	14.8	14.5
Puerto Rican	21.7	23.5	20.0	17.4	17.2	17.3	16.5
Cuban	7.7	7.7	7.5	7.7	8.2	7.8	7.0
Central and South American	9.0	10.6	9.9	8.6	9.0	8.4	7.8
Other and unknown Hispanic	(NA)	20.1	18.8	17.1	17.2	17.1	17.3
Non-Hispanic	(NA)	(NA)	10.7	8.9	9.2	9.1	8.8
White	(NA)	(NA)	8.7	7.3	7.5	7.5	7.3
Black	(NA)	(NA)	19.8	17.0	17.3	17.1	16.4
Percent of births to unmarried mothers	**26.6**	**32.2**	**33.2**	**36.9**	**39.7**	**40.6**	**41.1**
White	16.9	25.3	27.1	31.7	34.8	35.7	36.0
Black	66.7	69.9	68.5	69.3	71.2	71.8	72.3
American Indian or Alaska Native	53.6	57.2	58.4	63.5	65.3	65.8	65.4
Asian or Pacific Islander	13.2	16.3	14.8	16.2	16.6	16.9	17.2
Hispanic origin [2]	36.7	40.8	42.7	48.0	51.3	52.6	53.2
Mexican	33.3	38.1	40.7	46.7	50.1	51.3	51.8
Puerto Rican	55.9	60.0	59.6	61.7	63.4	64.6	65.2
Cuban	18.2	23.8	27.3	36.4	41.8	44.2	46.0
Central and South American	41.2	44.1	44.7	49.2	52.7	52.3	52.4
Other and unknown Hispanic	(NA)	44.0	46.2	48.6	51.3	54.4	55.8
Non-Hispanic	(NA)	(NA)	30.8	33.4	35.9	36.7	37.1
White	(NA)	(NA)	22.1	25.3	27.8	28.7	29.0
Black	(NA)	(NA)	68.7	69.9	71.6	72.3	72.8
Percent of births with low birth weight [3]	**7.0**	**7.3**	**7.6**	**8.2**	**8.2**	**8.2**	**8.2**
White	5.7	6.2	6.5	7.2	7.2	7.1	7.1
Black	13.3	13.1	13.0	13.6	13.6	13.4	13.3
American Indian or Alaska Native	6.1	6.6	6.8	7.4	7.5	7.4	7.3
Asian or Pacific Islander	(NA)	6.9	7.3	8.0	8.1	8.2	8.3
Hispanic origin [2]	6.1	6.3	6.4	6.9	6.9	7.0	6.9
Mexican	5.5	5.8	6.0	6.5	6.5	6.5	6.5
Puerto Rican	9.0	9.4	9.3	9.9	9.8	9.9	9.6
Cuban	5.7	6.5	6.5	7.6	7.7	7.8	7.5
Central and South American	5.8	6.2	6.3	6.8	6.7	6.7	6.6
Other and unknown Hispanic	(NA)	7.5	7.8	8.3	8.6	8.2	8.3
Non-Hispanic	(NA)	(NA)	7.9	8.6	8.6	8.6	8.5
White	(NA)	(NA)	6.6	7.3	7.3	7.2	7.2
Black	(NA)	(NA)	13.1	14.0	13.9	13.7	13.6

NA Not available. [1] Mothers under 20 years. [2] Hispanic persons may be any race. [3] Births less than 2,500 grams (5 pounds–8 ounces).

Source: U.S. National Center for Health Statistics, National Vital Statistics Reports (NVSR), *Births: Final Data for 2009*, Vol. 60, No. 1, November 2011, <http://www.cdc.gov/nchs/births.htm>.

Table 90. Births by Race, Hispanic Origin, and Method of Delivery: 1990 to 2009

[In thousands (4,111 represents 4,111,000), except rate. Persons of Hispanic origin may be any race. See Appendix III]

Method of delivery	1990 [1]	2000	2005	2009 Total [2]	2009 Hispanic	2009 Non-Hispanic White	2009 Non-Hispanic Black
Births, total	**4,111**	**4,059**	**4,138**	**4,131**	**1,000**	**2,213**	**610**
Vaginal	3,111	3,108	2,874	2,764	683	1,482	393
Cesarean deliveries	914	924	1,249	1,354	315	724	215
Not stated	85	27	16	13	2	7	2
Cesarean delivery rate [3]	22.7	22.9	30.3	32.9	31.6	32.8	35.4

[1] 1990 excludes data for Oklahoma, which did not report method of delivery on the birth certificate. [2] Includes other races, not shown separately. [3] Percent of all live births by cesarean delivery.

Source: U.S. National Center for Health Statistics, National Vital Statistics Reports (NVSR), *Births: Final Data for 2009*, Vol. 60, No. 1, November 2011, and earlier reports, <http://www.cdc.gov/nchs/births.htm>.

Table 91. Induction of Labor by Gestational Age: 1990 to 2010

[In percent. Data are for singleton births]

Gestational age	1990 [1]	1995	2000	2003	2004	2005	2006	2007	2008	2009	2010
All gestations	**9.2**	**15.9**	**19.7**	**20.5**	**21.2**	**22.2**	**22.5**	**22.7**	**22.9**	**23.1**	**23.3**
Under 20 weeks	8.2	11.3	13.9	11.9	12.0	12.0	11.2	11.8	10.0	10.2	12.5
20-27 weeks	4.1	5.7	6.5	5.4	5.7	5.5	5.4	5.3	5.6	5.7	5.7
28-31 weeks	4.6	7.8	9.0	8.2	8.3	8.7	8.6	8.7	8.8	8.8	9.0
32-35 weeks	6.4	11.1	13.8	13.1	13.5	13.9	13.9	13.8	13.8	13.8	14.0
36 weeks	7.5	12.8	16.3	16.2	16.7	17.3	17.3	16.9	17.0	16.6	16.7
37-39 weeks	7.6	14.2	18.7	19.7	20.5	21.6	21.8	21.8	22.0	21.8	21.9
40 weeks	8.6	16.1	20.6	22.7	23.2	24.9	25.5	26.0	26.1	27.1	27.3
41 weeks	13.0	22.4	26.9	28.7	29.4	30.7	31.4	31.8	32.2	32.9	33.6
42 weeks and over	14.4	21.1	24.1	24.2	25.2	26.0	26.6	26.7	27.2	27.8	28.2

[1] Oklahoma did not report induction of labor.

Source: U.S. National Center for Health Statistics, "VitalStats," accessed September 2012, <http://www.cdc.gov/nchs/vitalstats.htm>.

Table 92. Percent of Births to Teenage Mothers, Unmarried Women, and Births with Low Birth Weight by State and Island Areas: 2000 to 2010

[In percent. By place of residence. Excludes nonresidents of the United States]

State and Island Area	Births to teenage mothers [1]		Births to unmarried women		Births with low birth weight [2]		State and Island Area	Births to teenage mothers [1]		Births to unmarried women		Births with low birth weight [2]	
	2000	2010 [3]	2000	2010 [3]	2000	2010 [3]		2000	2010 [3]	2000	2010 [3]	2000	2010 [3]
U.S. [4]	**11.8**	**9.3**	**33.2**	**40.8**	**7.8**	**8.1**	NE	10.2	7.6	27.2	33.6	7.2	7.1
AL	15.7	12.4	34.3	41.9	9.9	10.3	NV	12.7	9.7	36.4	44.3	7.5	8.3
AK	11.8	8.4	33.0	37.6	5.8	5.7	NH	6.8	5.6	24.7	33.2	6.3	6.8
AZ	14.3	10.8	39.3	44.9	6.8	7.1	NJ	7.1	5.4	28.9	35.0	8.0	8.3
AR	17.3	13.8	35.7	45.3	8.6	8.8	NM	17.4	14.1	45.6	52.3	8.0	8.7
CA	10.6	8.5	32.7	40.5	6.4	6.8	NY	8.2	6.3	36.6	42.0	7.9	8.2
CO	11.7	8.3	25.0	23.9	8.9	8.8	NC	13.0	10.2	33.3	42.0	9.0	9.1
CT	7.8	5.9	29.3	36.5	7.8	8.0	ND	9.2	7.3	28.3	32.7	6.3	6.7
DE	12.3	8.7	37.9	47.6	9.9	8.9	OH	12.1	10.0	34.6	43.8	8.3	8.6
DC	14.2	10.5	60.3	54.8	11.6	10.2	OK	15.9	12.4	34.3	41.8	8.0	8.4
FL	12.6	9.0	38.2	47.5	8.4	8.7	OR	11.3	7.7	30.1	35.7	5.8	6.3
GA	13.9	10.9	37.0	45.8	8.9	9.7	PA	9.9	8.5	32.7	41.7	8.2	8.3
HI	10.3	7.1	32.2	37.8	8.3	8.4	RI	10.2	8.0	35.5	45.0	7.9	7.7
ID	11.6	8.1	21.6	26.5	6.1	6.8	SC	15.3	11.9	39.8	47.5	10.0	9.9
IL	11.4	9.1	34.5	40.5	8.2	8.3	SD	11.6	8.3	33.5	37.6	7.2	6.8
IN	12.5	10.4	34.7	43.0	7.6	8.0	TN	14.7	11.8	34.5	44.1	9.2	9.0
IA	10.0	7.9	28.0	34.2	6.6	7.0	TX	15.3	12.6	30.5	42.4	7.7	8.4
KS	12.0	9.6	29.0	37.8	7.0	7.1	UT	8.9	5.9	17.3	19.2	6.4	7.0
KY	14.1	12.1	31.0	41.2	8.6	9.0	VT	8.0	6.5	28.1	39.2	6.4	6.1
LA	17.0	12.5	45.6	53.3	10.4	10.7	VA	9.9	7.2	29.9	35.5	7.9	8.2
ME	9.4	7.1	31.0	41.2	6.3	6.3	WA	10.2	7.0	28.2	33.0	5.9	6.3
MD	9.9	7.4	34.6	41.9	9.0	8.8	WV	15.9	12.9	31.7	44.0	9.0	9.2
MA	6.6	5.4	26.5	34.7	7.5	7.7	WI	10.2	7.5	29.3	36.7	6.6	7.0
MI	10.5	9.6	33.3	41.8	8.0	8.4	WY	13.5	9.6	28.8	34.0	8.4	9.0
MN	8.3	5.9	25.8	33.2	6.3	6.4	PR	(NA)	17.2	49.7	65.4	11.5	12.6
MS	18.8	15.5	46.0	54.8	11.2	12.1	VI	(NA)	(NA)	66.7	(NA)	11.8	(NA)
MO	13.1	10.1	34.6	40.2	8.0	8.2	GU	(NA)	12.3	54.8	59.7	8.0	8.6
MT	11.6	9.5	30.8	36.4	6.8	7.5	AS	(NA)	9.8	35.5	35.4	3.9	3.7
							MP	(NA)	(NA)	(NA)	(NA)	6.9	(NA)

NA Not available. [1] Defined as mothers who are 20 years of age or younger. [2] Less than 2,500 grams (5 pounds–8 ounces). [3] Data are preliminary. [4] Excludes data for the territories.

Source: U.S. National Center for Health Statistics, National Vital Statistics Reports (NVSR), *Births: Preliminary Data for 2010*, Vol. 60, No. 2, November 2011, <http://www.cdc.gov/nchs/births.htm>.

Table 93. Women Who had a Child in the Last Year by Living Arrangement, Age, and Educational Attainment: 2010

[In percent except total. (480 represents 480,000). As of June. Based on Current Population Survey. See headnote Table 94]

Living arrangement	Less than high school		High school graduate		Some college		Bachelor's degree or more	
	15 to 29 years old	30 to 44 years old	15 to 29 years old	30 to 44 years old	15 to 29 years old	30 to 44 years old	15 to 29 years old	30 to 44 years old
Total (1,000)	**480**	**141**	**723**	**281**	**681**	**336**	**347**	**697**
PERCENT								
Total	**100.0**	**100.0**	**100.0**	**100.0**	**100.0**	**100.0**	**100.0**	**100.0**
Married spouse present	29.7	71.1	40.7	68.2	46.7	81.2	85.0	91.3
Cohabiting	17.8	9.7	19.7	7.2	16.9	6.2	8.0	3.7
Not living with spouse or partner	52.5	19.2	39.6	24.5	36.4	12.7	6.9	5.0

Source: U.S Census Bureau, Current Population Survey, "Fertility of American Women," <http://www.census.gov/hhes/fertility/>.

Table 94. Women Who Had a Child in the Last Year by Selected Characteristics: 1990 to 2010

[58,381 represents 58,381,000. As of June. Covers civilian noninstitutional population. Since the number of women who had a birth during the 12-month period was tabulated and not the actual numbers of births, some small underestimation of fertility for this period may exist due to the omission of: (1) Multiple births, (2) Two or more live births spaced within the 12-month period (the woman is counted only once), (3) Women who had births in the period and who did not survive to the survey date, (4) Women who were in institutions and therefore not in the survey universe. These losses may be somewhat offset by the inclusion in the Current Population Survey (CPS) of births to immigrants who did not have their children born in the United States and births to nonresident women. These births would not have been recorded in the vital registration system. Based on June supplement, Current Population Survey. The 2003 Current Population Survey allowed respondents to choose more than one race. Beginning 2003 data represent persons who selected this race group only and exclude persons reporting more than one race. The Current Population Survey in prior years allowed respondents to report only one race group. See also comments on race in Section 1]

| Characteristic | Total women (1,000) | Percent childless | Women who had a child in the last year | | | |
| | | | Total births | | First births | |
			Number (1,000)	Per 1,000 women	Number (1,000)	Per 1,000 women
1990	58,381	41.6	3,913	67.0	1,540	26.4
2000	60,873	42.8	3,934	64.6	1,626	26.7
2010, total [1]	**61,481**	**47.1**	**3,686**	**60.0**	**1,467**	**23.9**
Age:						
15 to 19 years old	10,273	94.6	301	29.3	229	22.3
20 to 24 years old	10,493	70.5	916	87.3	462	44.0
25 to 29 years old	10,501	47.6	1,014	96.6	405	38.6
30 to 34 years old	9,923	29.7	820	82.7	225	22.7
35 to 39 years old	9,917	19.7	503	50.7	126	12.7
40 to 44 years old	10,374	18.8	131	12.6	20	1.9
Race and Hispanic origin:						
White alone	47,186	47.6	2,763	58.6	1,135	24.1
White alone, non-Hispanic	37,271	49.9	2,069	55.5	868	23.3
Black alone	9,035	43.3	574	63.5	186	20.6
Asian alone	3,353	48.8	237	70.6	93	27.6
Hispanic [2]	10,845	39.0	756	69.7	296	27.3
Marital status:						
Married, husband present	25,018	18.6	2,250	89.9	765	30.6
Married, husband absent [3]	2,298	25.4	124	54.1	29	12.4
Widowed or divorced	4,518	21.3	152	33.6	48	10.6
Never married	29,648	76.8	1,160	39.1	625	21.1
Educational attainment:						
Not a high school graduate	12,380	64.1	621	50.2	230	18.6
High school, 4 years	14,763	35.9	1,004	68.0	398	27.0
Some college, no degree	12,463	50.3	667	53.6	291	23.4
Associate's degree	5,498	33.5	349	63.5	139	25.3
Bachelor's degree	11,527	48.0	688	59.7	254	22.0
Graduate or professional degree	4,851	42.7	356	73.3	154	31.7
Labor force status:						
In labor force	41,467	45.8	2,026	48.9	851	20.5
Employed	36,983	45.5	1,771	47.9	748	20.2
Unemployed	4,484	48.7	256	57.0	103	22.9
Not in labor force	20,014	49.7	1,660	82.9	616	30.8
Family income:						
Under $10,000	3,810	40.4	374	98.3	127	33.3
$10,000 to $19,999	5,327	40.3	398	74.7	156	29.3
$20,000 to $24,999	2,879	43.2	179	62.1	50	17.5
$25,000 to $29,999	3,039	45.5	202	66.4	82	26.8
$30,000 to $34,999	3,066	41.8	208	67.9	87	28.5
$35,000 to $49,999	7,336	47.9	403	55.0	171	23.3
$50,000 to $74,999	9,893	49.7	549	55.5	220	22.2
$75,000 and over	15,714	51.1	862	54.8	340	21.6

[1] Includes women of other races and women with family income not reported, not shown separately. [2] Persons of Hispanic origin may be any race. [3] Includes separated women.

Source: U.S. Census Bureau, Current Population Reports, "Fertility of American Women, Detailed Tables" and unpublished data.

Table 95. Women Who Had a Child in the Last Year by Age: 1990 to 2010

[3,913 represents 3,913,000. As of June. Based on Current Population Survey. See headnote Table 94]

| Age of mother | Women who had a child in last year (1,000) | | | Total births per 1,000 women | | | First births per 1,000 women | | |
	1990	2000	2010	1990	2000	2010	1990	2000	2010
Total	**3,913**	**3,934**	**3,686**	**67.0**	**64.6**	**60.0**	**26.4**	**26.7**	**23.9**
15 to 29 years old	2,568	2,432	2,231	90.8	85.9	71.4	43.2	43.1	35.1
15 to 19 years old	338	586	301	39.8	59.7	29.3	30.1	38.7	22.3
20 to 24 years old	1,038	850	916	113.4	91.8	87.3	51.8	47.1	44.0
25 to 29 years old	1,192	996	1,014	112.1	107.9	96.6	46.2	43.7	38.6
30 to 44 years old	1,346	1,502	1,454	44.7	46.1	48.1	10.6	12.5	12.3
30 to 34 years old	892	871	820	80.4	87.9	82.7	21.9	27.5	22.7
35 to 39 years old	377	506	503	37.3	45.1	50.7	6.5	9.6	12.7
40 to 44 years old	77	125	131	8.6	10.9	12.6	1.2	2.3	1.9

Source: U.S. Census Bureau, Current Population Reports, "Fertility of American Women" and earlier reports, and unpublished data. See also <http://www.census.gov/hhes/fertility/>.

Table 96. Women With Births in the Past 12 Months by Citizenship Status, Educational Attainment, and Poverty Status, by State: 2010

[In percent, except for total. For women 15 to 50 years old. Based on 2010 American Community Survey (ACS). The ACS universe includes the household population and the population living in institutions, college dormitories, and other group quarters. Based on a sample and subject to sampling variability; See Appendix III]

State	Total (number)	Citizenship status		Educational attainment					Below poverty [2]
		Native born	Foreign born [1]	Less than high school graduate	High school graduate (includes equivalency)	Some college or associate's degree	Bachelor's degree	Graduate or professional degree	
United States	**4,168,720**	**78.9**	**21.1**	**17.0**	**24.4**	**31.0**	**17.8**	**9.7**	**27.7**
Alabama	66,243	91.7	8.3	18.7	28.3	32.4	11.9	8.6	34.2
Alaska	12,494	88.7	11.3	18.0	29.0	32.6	14.8	5.7	26.9
Arizona	86,210	78.5	21.5	20.4	25.4	36.3	12.9	5.0	33.0
Arkansas	37,344	92.4	7.6	15.4	31.3	35.8	12.6	4.9	35.7
California	508,113	60.9	39.1	22.5	22.3	29.3	16.7	9.2	27.0
Colorado	68,838	78.2	21.8	16.7	21.9	29.1	21.0	11.3	24.4
Connecticut	42,002	78.5	21.5	13.3	23.4	26.7	18.9	17.8	21.4
Delaware	9,902	83.8	16.2	15.0	19.1	37.7	15.2	13.0	27.4
District of Columbia	9,098	77.4	22.6	12.8	18.3	21.3	24.0	23.7	24.5
Florida	211,737	71.8	28.2	16.1	28.5	32.1	15.8	7.6	29.4
Georgia	145,715	82.1	17.9	19.3	25.0	30.3	16.9	8.6	30.4
Hawaii	19,939	74.5	25.5	7.8	29.9	34.5	20.5	7.4	21.2
Idaho	23,489	90.8	9.2	10.1	26.4	40.5	17.5	5.6	22.5
Illinois	179,328	76.7	23.3	14.0	21.6	29.3	21.8	13.3	23.2
Indiana	82,273	91.2	8.8	18.3	24.9	31.9	17.5	7.3	28.7
Iowa	41,387	89.3	10.7	14.2	20.3	37.2	20.6	7.7	28.3
Kansas	40,095	83.3	16.7	13.6	21.6	30.7	26.0	8.0	24.2
Kentucky	57,337	93.0	7.0	18.1	24.8	35.8	14.0	7.3	32.8
Louisiana	67,832	94.5	5.5	19.5	28.7	30.9	14.4	6.6	36.5
Maine	14,244	95.3	4.7	8.9	21.6	35.6	20.3	13.5	28.1
Maryland	79,000	76.7	23.3	12.4	22.8	30.7	18.1	16.0	19.6
Massachusetts	79,068	71.4	28.6	11.0	18.6	25.9	23.8	20.7	19.8
Michigan	128,835	90.4	9.6	15.3	22.7	34.7	18.1	9.2	33.4
Minnesota	73,251	82.7	17.3	12.1	17.0	35.4	26.2	9.4	21.6
Mississippi	45,919	95.1	4.9	20.7	26.8	37.8	9.9	4.9	39.8
Missouri	82,335	91.4	8.6	14.5	24.6	33.8	18.6	8.5	29.1
Montana	14,037	98.8	1.2	14.7	24.0	29.0	25.6	6.8	28.0
Nebraska	28,509	87.2	12.8	12.8	15.6	38.5	24.1	9.0	25.2
Nevada	41,465	69.2	30.8	21.8	31.2	26.9	14.4	5.7	23.8
New Hampshire	16,194	91.5	8.5	10.5	30.4	27.8	23.4	7.9	22.5
New Jersey	110,473	68.6	31.4	9.6	24.7	24.1	25.9	15.7	17.3
New Mexico	28,502	83.9	16.1	20.5	25.3	35.3	14.7	4.3	35.1
New York	247,003	68.2	31.8	17.5	23.8	26.0	17.1	15.7	26.9
North Carolina	130,058	83.1	16.9	17.8	23.9	32.4	17.6	8.3	31.7
North Dakota	8,895	94.2	5.8	4.3	14.5	44.2	29.5	7.4	18.8
Ohio	145,431	92.0	8.0	14.3	25.7	33.8	17.1	9.2	30.9
Oklahoma	49,557	86.4	13.6	16.2	31.2	30.9	16.1	5.5	30.7
Oregon	48,873	78.3	21.7	16.8	22.0	33.3	17.4	10.5	25.7
Pennsylvania	144,791	89.5	10.5	14.7	25.3	27.7	20.9	11.4	25.3
Rhode Island	12,732	82.2	17.8	14.7	27.5	31.4	16.5	10.0	26.8
South Carolina	63,648	94.2	5.8	20.4	24.3	34.2	14.6	6.4	35.8
South Dakota	10,804	93.9	6.1	15.2	21.1	35.9	19.5	8.3	29.9
Tennessee	96,604	87.8	12.2	16.2	30.0	33.2	13.9	6.7	31.0
Texas	395,185	73.8	26.2	22.0	26.0	29.7	15.6	6.7	31.0
Utah	54,635	88.6	11.4	9.9	21.9	36.0	25.6	6.5	17.1
Vermont	6,885	94.3	5.7	4.7	26.2	31.2	20.8	17.1	23.1
Virginia	105,477	76.5	23.5	13.2	22.3	32.1	19.1	13.3	19.8
Washington	94,636	74.2	25.8	15.1	23.5	31.7	18.1	11.6	26.0
West Virginia	20,260	97.8	2.2	17.7	31.0	29.8	13.8	7.7	37.6
Wisconsin	73,724	88.3	11.7	13.2	25.4	30.3	19.5	11.6	23.0
Wyoming	8,314	94.8	5.2	18.4	16.2	36.5	21.0	7.9	23.0

[1] Foreign born excludes people born outside the United States to a parent who is a U.S. citizen. [2] The population universe used when determining poverty status excludes institutionalized people, people in military group quarters, people in college dormitories, and unrelated individuals under 15 years old.

Source: U.S. Census Bureau, 2010 American Community Survey, B13008, "Women 15 to 50 Years Who Had a Birth in the Past 12 Months by Marital Status and Citizenship;" B13010 "Women 15 to 50 Years Who Had a Birth in the Past 12 Months by Marital Status and Poverty Status in the past 12 Months;" and B13014, "Women 15 to 50 Years Who Had a Birth in the Past 12 Months by Marital Status and Educational Attainment," <http://factfinder.census.gov>.

Table 97. Women Who Had a Child in the Last Year by Age and Labor Force Status: 1980 to 2010

[3,913 represents 3,913,000. As of June. Based on Current Population Survey. See headnote, Table 94]

Year	Total, 15 to 44 years old — Number (1,000)	Total — In the labor force Number (1,000)	Total — In the labor force Percent	15 to 29 years old — Number (1,000)	15 to 29 — In the labor force Number (1,000)	15 to 29 — In the labor force Percent	30 to 44 years old — Number (1,000)	30 to 44 — In the labor force Number (1,000)	30 to 44 — In the labor force Percent
1990...........	3,913	2,068	53	2,568	1,275	50	1,346	793	59
1995...........	3,696	2,034	55	2,252	1,150	51	1,444	884	61
2000...........	3,934	2,170	55	2,432	1,304	54	1,502	866	58
2006...........	3,974	2,221	56	2,399	1,273	53	1,576	948	60
2008...........	3,960	2,261	57	2,372	1,299	55	1,587	962	61
2010...........	3,686	2,026	55	2,231	1,114	50	1,454	912	63

Source: U.S. Bureau of the Census, Current Population Reports, "Fertility of American Women," and earlier reports, and unpublished data. See also <http://www.census.gov/hhes/fertility/>.

Table 98. Persons Who Have Ever Had Sexual Contact by Selected Characteristics: 2006 to 2008

[In percent except as indicated (62,199 represents 62,199,000). Based on the National Survey of Family Growth conducted from July 2006 through December 2008. See Appendix III]

Characteristic	Number (1,000)	Any [1]	One	Two	3 to 6	7 to 14	15 or more	Median number [2]	Any same-sex sexual contact [3]
Males, 15 to 44 years old [4].............	**62,199**	**88.8**	**15.0**	**7.6**	**26.5**	**18.1**	**21.4**	**5.1**	**5.2**
15 to 19 years old...........................	10,777	58.0	21.2	9.4	17.6	5.4	3.1	1.8	2.5
20 to 24 years old...........................	10,404	85.7	19.1	8.0	26.1	18.1	14.2	4.1	5.6
25 to 44 years old...........................	41,019	97.7	12.3	7.0	28.9	21.5	27.9	6.1	5.8
25 to 29 years old...........................	10,431	96.2	11.8	8.9	29.5	22.9	23.1	5.7	5.2
30 to 34 years old...........................	9,575	96.9	14.2	6.1	26.6	21.7	28.3	6.4	4.0
35 to 39 years old...........................	10,318	98.7	13.3	5.6	29.7	19.6	30.6	6.2	5.7
40 to 44 years old...........................	10,695	98.8	10.3	7.2	29.7	21.6	30.0	6.4	8.1
Hispanic.....................................	11,724	92.0	12.5	10.2	32.6	17.8	19.1	4.6	3.8
Non-Hispanic White..........................	37,374	88.5	16.1	7.3	25.7	18.4	20.9	5.1	6.0
Non-Hispanic Black..........................	7,186	90.7	8.3	5.0	25.6	21.6	30.0	6.9	2.4
Currently married...........................	24,763	100.0	19.1	7.5	30.7	20.7	22.1	4.9	3.5
Currently cohabiting.........................	7,301	100.0	10.3	7.6	24.4	25.9	31.8	7.3	3.2
Never married, not cohabiting...............	27,012	74.2	14.1	8.2	23.6	12.9	14.9	4.1	7.2
Formerly married, not cohabiting............	3,123	100.0	1.4	2.2	23.9	25.1	47.4	11.9	6.4
Females, 15 to 44 years old [4]............	**61,865**	**89.0**	**22.2**	**10.7**	**31.6**	**16.0**	**8.3**	**3.2**	**12.5**
15 to 19 years old...........................	10,431	53.0	22.7	8.2	15.7	4.1	1.1	1.4	11.0
20 to 24 years old...........................	10,140	87.7	24.5	12.5	31.6	11.7	7.2	2.6	15.8
25 to 44 years old...........................	41,294	98.4	21.4	10.9	35.6	20.1	10.4	3.6	12.0
25 to 29 years old...........................	10,250	96.6	20.0	12.4	31.0	20.4	12.8	3.6	15.0
30 to 34 years old...........................	9,587	98.1	20.9	10.6	31.9	21.3	13.4	4.2	14.2
35 to 39 years old...........................	10,475	99.1	22.2	9.9	38.3	20.8	7.9	3.5	11.5
40 to 44 years old...........................	10,982	99.7	22.4	10.8	40.5	18.0	8.0	3.4	7.9
Hispanic.....................................	10,377	89.5	35.0	16.7	26.6	6.6	4.4	1.6	6.3
Non-Hispanic White..........................	37,660	88.4	19.2	9.7	31.4	18.9	8.9	3.7	14.6
Non-Hispanic Black..........................	8,452	90.2	12.3	8.3	40.9	16.7	11.3	4.4	11.3
Currently married...........................	27,006	100.0	32.2	12.3	34.4	15.0	6.1	2.5	8.3
Currently cohabiting.........................	6,821	100.0	12.8	11.6	37.0	24.9	13.7	4.6	20.5
Never married, not cohabiting...............	22,847	70.1	16.4	9.1	25.2	11.9	6.9	3.2	13.4
Formerly married, not cohabiting............	5,190	100.0	6.8	8.7	37.7	28.0	18.8	5.3	19.6

[1] Includes vaginal, oral, or anal sex. [2] Excludes those who have never had sexual intercourse with a person of the opposite sex. For definition of median, see Guide to Tabular Presentation. [3] For females includes oral sex or any sexual experience. For males includes oral or anal sex with male partners. [4] Includes persons of other or multiple race and origin groups, not shown separately.

Source: U.S. National Center for Health Statistics, National Health Statistics Report, No.36, "Sexual Behavior, Sexual Attraction, and Sexual Identity in the United States: Data From the 2006–2008 National Survey of Family Growth," March 2011. See also <http://www.cdc.gov/nchs/nsfg.htm>.

Table 99. Number and Type of Sexual Partners in the Past 12 Months: 2006 to 2008

[In percent except as indicated (62,199 represents 62,199,000). Based on the National Survey of Family Growth conducted from July 2006 through December 2008. See Appendix III]

Sex and age	Number (1,000)	Sexual partners in last 12 months [1]				
		No partner in last month	Any same-sex partners	One opposite-sex partner, but no same-sex partners	Two or more opposite-sex partners, but no same sex-sex partners	Did not report
Males 15 to 44 years old....................	**62,199**	**16.0**	**4.3**	**60.2**	**17.6**	**2.0**
15 to 19 years old............................	10,777	48.9	1.5	25.1	21.2	3.3
20 to 24 years old............................	10,404	18.3	4.6	48.0	27.2	1.9
25 to 44 years old............................	41,019	6.8	4.9	72.4	14.2	1.7
25 to 29 years old............................	10,431	7.6	4.8	65.7	20.3	1.6
30 to 34 years old............................	9,575	6.6	3.6	75.3	13.0	1.4
35 to 39 years old............................	10,318	5.1	5.0	73.7	14.2	2.0
40 to 44 years old............................	10,695	7.7	6.2	75.2	9.3	1.6
Females 15 to 44 years old.................	**61,865**	**15.9**	**11.7**	**61.3**	**9.4**	**1.7**
15 to 19 years old............................	10,431	51.3	9.5	24.2	13.5	1.6
20 to 24 years old............................	10,140	15.8	15.2	49.5	17.7	1.8
25 to 44 years old............................	41,294	7.0	11.4	73.6	6.3	1.8
25 to 29 years old............................	10,250	7.6	14.3	65.1	10.6	2.4
30 to 34 years old............................	9,587	5.2	13.6	73.8	6.0	1.5
35 to 39 years old............................	10,475	6.8	10.8	76.2	4.2	2.0
40 to 44 years old............................	10,982	8.3	7.1	79.0	4.5	1.1

[1] Includes vaginal, oral, or anal sex.

Source: U.S. National Center for Health Statistics, National Health Statistics Report, No.36, "Sexual Behavior, Sexual Attraction, and Sexual Identity in the United States: Data From the 2006–2008 National Survey of Family Growth," March 2011. See also <http://www.cdc.gov/nchs/nsfg.htm>.

Table 100. Sexual Identity Among Men and Women: 2006 to 2008

[In percent except as indicated (55,556 represents 55,556,000). For men and women 18 to 44 years of age. Based on the National Survey of Family Growth conducted from July 2006 through December 2008. See Appendix III]

Characteristic	Number (1,000)	Sexual identity				Did not report
		Heterosexual or straight	Homosexual or gay	Bisexual	Something else	
Males, 18 to 44 years old [1]...............	**55,556**	**95.7**	**1.7**	**1.1**	**0.2**	**1.3**
18 to 19 years old............................	4,134	96.6	1.6	1.1	(S)	0.6
20 to 24 years old............................	10,404	95.1	1.2	2.0	0.4	1.3
25 to 29 years old............................	10,431	96.3	1.7	0.8	0.5	0.8
30 to 34 years old............................	9,575	96.2	1.5	0.6	(S)	1.8
35 to 44 years old............................	21,013	95.2	2.1	1.0	0.2	1.5
Hispanic..	10,618	93.4	1.2	0.9	0.6	3.9
Non-Hispanic White........................	33,573	96.6	1.8	1.1	0.1	0.4
Non-Hispanic Black........................	6,208	97.8	1.2	(S)	(S)	0.4
Females, 18 to 44 years old [1]............	**56,032**	**93.7**	**1.1**	**3.5**	**0.6**	**1.1**
18 to 19 years old............................	4,598	90.1	1.9	5.8	(S)	(S)
20 to 24 years old............................	10,140	90.4	1.3	6.3	0.9	1.2
25 to 29 years old............................	10,250	91.9	1.2	5.4	0.6	0.9
30 to 34 years old............................	9,587	94.4	1.1	2.9	0.8	1.0
35 to 44 years old............................	21,457	96.6	0.7	1.1	0.2	1.3
Hispanic..	9,272	92.1	0.9	2.2	0.7	4.1
Non-Hispanic White........................	34,410	94.2	0.9	4.1	0.5	0.4
Non-Hispanic Black........................	7,520	93.3	1.6	3.0	1.5	0.7

S Figure does not meet publication standards. [1] Includes person of other or multiple race and origin groups, not shown separately.

Source: U.S. National Center for Health Statistics, National Health Statistics Report, No. 36, "Sexual Behavior, Sexual Attraction, and Sexual Identity in the United States: Data From the 2006–2008 National Survey of Family Growth," March 2011. See also <http://www.cdc.gov/nchs/nsfg.htm>.

Table 101. Outcomes of Assisted Reproductive Technology (ART) by Procedures: 2000 to 2006

[In 1996, Centers for Disease Control (CDC) initiated data collection regarding Assisted Reproductive Technology (ART) procedures performed in the United States, as mandated by the Fertility Clinic Success Rate and Certification Act. ARTs include those infertility treatments in which both eggs and sperm are handled in the laboratory for the purpose of establishing a pregnancy (i.e., in vitro fertilization and related procedures)]

Year	Procedures started [1]	Number of pregnancies	Live birth deliveries [2]	Live born infants
2000........................	99,629	30,557	25,228	35,025
2001........................	107,587	35,726	29,344	40,687
2002........................	115,392	40,046	33,141	45,751
2003........................	122,872	43,503	35,785	48,756
2004........................	127,977	44,774	36,760	49,458
2005........................	134,260	47,651	38,910	52,041
2006........................	138,198	50,571	41,343	54,656

[1] Excludes procedures for which new treatments were being evaluated. [2] A live-birth delivery is defined as the delivery of one or more live born infants.

Source: U.S. Centers for Disease Control and Prevention, Morbidity and Mortality Weekly Report (MMWR) Surveillance Summary Reports, *Assisted Reproductive Technology Surveillance—United States, 2006*, Vol. 58, No. SS-5, June 2009. See also <http://www.cdc.gov/mmwr/mmwr_ss/ss_pvol.html>.

Table 102. Infants Who Were Ever Breastfed by Maternal Age and Race-Ethnicity: 1999 to 2006

[In percent. Covers period from 1999 through 2006. Breastfeeding was defined as ever having been breastfed or received breast milk. Based on data from National Health and Nutrition Examination Surveys (NHANES)]

Race and ethnicity	Under 20 years old	20 to 29 years old	30 years old and older
Total..................................	**43**	**65**	**75**
Non-Hispanic White................	40	65	77
Non-Hispanic Black................	30	44	56
Mexican American.................	66	75	76

Source: U.S. National Center for Health Statistics, *Breastfeeding in the United States Findings from the National Health and Nutrition Examination Surveys: 1999–2006*, NCHS Data Brief, No. 5, April 2008. See also <http://www.cdc.gov/nchs/products/databriefs.htm>.

Table 103. Current Contraceptive Use by Women by Race, Hispanic Origin, Marital, and Cohabitation Status: 2006 to 2008

[61,864 represents 61,864,000. Based on the National Survey of Family Growth conducted from July 2006 through December 2008. Contraceptive use reported by women 15–44 years of age during heterosexual vaginal intercourse. Women using more than one method of contraception are classified by most effective method reported]

Contraceptive status and method	Unit	All wo-men [1]	Race/ethnicity			Marital and cohabitation status			
			White only, Non-His-panic	Black only, Non-His-panic	His-panic [2]	Never mar-ried, not cohab-iting	Cur-rently mar-ried	For-merly mar-ried, not cohab-iting	Cur-rently cohab-iting
All women.........................	**(1,000)**	**61,864**	**37,660**	**8,452**	**10,377**	**22,847**	**27,006**	**5,190**	**6,821**
PERCENT DISTRIBUTION									
Using contraception (contraceptors) [3]............	Percent	61.8	64.7	54.5	58.5	39.3	78.6	60.6	71.2
Female sterilization................................	Percent	16.7	14.9	21.8	19.6	4.5	23.6	35.3	16.3
Male sterilization...................................	Percent	6.1	8.3	1.1	3.4	0.3	12.7	2.3	2.2
Pill..	Percent	17.3	21.2	11.4	11.4	18.1	16.3	11.4	23.2
Implant, Lunelle™..................................	Percent	0.7	0.5	0.6	1.5	0.6	0.7	(S)	1.0
3-month injectable (Depo-Provera™)...........	Percent	2.0	1.4	4.1	2.6	2.2	1.4	2.6	3.1
Intrauterine device (IUD).........................	Percent	1.5	1.6	1.7	1.2	1.5	1.0	0.8	3.7
Diaphragm..	Percent	3.4	3.3	2.8	4.8	1.1	5.3	2.1	4.7
Condom..	Percent	10.0	9.5	8.8	9.4	9.1	11.7	4.1	10.2
Periodic abstinence-calendar rhythm...........	Percent	0.5	0.5	(S)	0.6	0.2	1.0	(S)	0.4
Periodic abstinence-natural family planning....	Percent	0.1	(S)	(S)	(S)	(S)	0.2	(S)	(S)
Withdrawal..	Percent	3.2	3.3	2.1	3.0	1.5	4.5	1.4	5.3
Other methods [3].................................	Percent	0.3	0.3	(S)	0.5	0.2	0.3	(S)	(S)
Not using contraception...........................	Percent	38.2	35.3	45.5	41.5	60.7	21.4	39.4	28.8
Surgically sterile-female (noncontraceptive)...	Percent	0.4	0.2	0.4	0.7	0.4	0.3	1.0	(S)
Nonsurgically sterile-female or male [4]........	Percent	1.7	1.6	1.8	1.8	2.1	1.0	2.7	2.2
Pregnant or postpartum...........................	Percent	5.4	4.9	5.7	8.3	2.6	7.2	2.6	10.5
Seeking pregnancy.................................	Percent	4.1	3.5	4.4	6.2	1.3	6.4	0.8	7.1
Other nonuse:									
Never had intercourse or no intercourse in 3 months before interview......................	Percent	19.2	18.3	22.6	18.8	45.6	0.9	21.1	1.8
Had intercourse in 3 months before interview..	Percent	7.3	6.7	10.6	5.8	8.7	5.5	11.3	6.9

S Figure does not meet publication standards. [1] Includes other races not shown separately. [2] Persons of Hispanic origin may be any race. [3] Includes diaphragm, emergency contraception, female condom or vaginal pouch, foam, cervical cap, Today™ sponge, suppository or insert, jelly or cream, and other methods. [4] Persons sterile from illness, accident, or congenital conditions.

Source: U.S. National Center for Health Statistics, *National Survey of Family Growth*, "Use of Contraception in the United States: 1982–2008," Series 23, No. 29, May 2010. See also <http://www.cdc.gov/nchs/nsfg.htm>.

Table 104. Abortions—Number and Rate by Race: 1990 to 2008

[58,700 represents 58,700,000. Data for 2000-07 have been revised based on Census Bureau intercensal population estimates, as of July 2011]

	All races			White			Black			Other		
Year	Women 15 to 44 years old (1,000)	Abortions		Women 15 to 44 years old (1,000)	Abortions		Women 15 to 44 years old (1,000)	Abortions		Women 15 to 44 years old (1,000)	Abortions	
		Number (1,000)	Rate per 1,000 women [1]		Number (1,000)	Rate per 1,000 women [1]		Number (1,000)	Rate per 1,000 women [1]		Number (1,000)	Rate per 1,000 women [1]
1990 [2]	58,700	1,609	27.4	48,224	1,039	21.5	7,905	505	63.9	2,571	65	25.1
1991	59,305	1,557	26.2	48,560	982	20.2	8,053	507	62.9	2,692	68	26.2
1992	59,417	1,529	25.7	48,435	943	19.5	8,170	517	63.3	2,812	69	24.4
1993 [2]	59,712	1,495	25.0	48,497	908	18.7	8,282	517	62.4	2,933	70	23.9
1994 [2]	60,020	1,423	23.7	48,592	856	17.6	8,390	492	58.6	3,039	76	23.7
1995	60,368	1,359	22.5	48,719	817	16.8	8,496	462	54.4	3,153	80	25.3
1996	60,704	1,360	22.4	48,837	797	16.3	8,592	483	56.2	3,275	81	24.6
1997 [2]	61,041	1,335	21.9	48,942	777	15.9	8,694	479	55.1	3,405	79	23.1
1998 [2]	61,326	1,319	21.5	49,012	762	15.5	8,785	476	54.2	3,528	81	23.1
1999	61,475	1,315	21.4	48,974	743	15.2	8,851	485	54.8	3,650	87	24.0
2000	61,642	1,313	21.3	48,939	733	15.0	8,911	488	54.8	3,792	92	24.3
2001 [2]	61,795	1,291	20.9	48,877	717	14.7	8,977	476	53.0	3,941	99	25.1
2002 [2]	61,856	1,269	20.5	48,735	706	14.5	9,034	468	51.8	4,088	96	23.4
2003 [2]	61,888	1,250	20.2	48,570	695	14.3	9,092	458	50.4	4,227	97	23.0
2004	61,969	1,222	19.7	48,438	674	13.9	9,168	453	49.4	4,364	95	21.8
2005	62,071	1,206	19.4	48,321	662	13.7	9,246	452	48.9	4,504	92	20.5
2006 [2]	62,190	1,242	20.0	48,205	681	14.1	9,335	464	49.7	4,649	97	20.8
2007	62,292	1,210	19.4	48,082	668	13.9	9,421	448	47.6	4,789	93	19.5
2008	62,360	1,212	19.4	47,943	664	13.8	9,499	458	48.2	4,918	90	18.4

[1] Aged 15–44. [2] Total numbers of abortions have been estimated by interpolation.

Source: R.K. Jones and K. Kooistra, *Abortion Incidence and Access to Services in the United States, 2008, Perspectives on Sexual and Reproductive Health, 2011*, 43(1):41-50; and unpublished data from the Guttmacher Institute (copyright).

Table 105. Abortions by Selected Characteristics: 1990 to 2008

[1,609 represents 1,609,000. Number of abortions from surveys conducted by source; characteristics from the U.S. Centers for Disease Control's (CDC) annual abortion surveillance summaries, with adjustments for changes in states reporting data to the Centers for Disease Control each year. Data for 2000 have been revised based on Census Bureau intercensal population estimates, as of July 2011]

Characteristic	Number (1,000)			Percent distribution			Abortion rate per 1,000 women		
	1990	2000	2008	1990	2000	2008	1990	2000	2008
Total abortions	**1,609**	**1,313**	**1,212**	**100.0**	**100.0**	**100.0**	**27.4**	**21.3**	**19.4**
Age of woman:									
Less than 15 years [1]	13	9	6	0.8	0.7	0.5	7.9	4.3	2.9
15 to 19 years	351	235	192	21.8	17.9	15.9	40.6	23.9	17.8
20 to 24 years	532	430	397	33.1	32.7	32.7	56.7	45.9	38.4
25 to 29 years	360	303	298	22.4	23.0	24.6	34.0	31.7	28.6
30 to 34 years	216	190	177	13.4	14.5	14.6	19.7	18.6	18.4
35 to 39 years	108	110	106	6.7	8.4	8.7	10.7	9.7	10.2
40 years and over [2]	29	37	37	1.8	2.8	3.0	3.2	3.2	3.4
Hispanic	195	261	267	12.1	19.8	22.0	35.1	30.3	23.8
Non-Hispanic White	852	479	411	52.9	36.5	33.9	19.7	11.7	10.9
Marital status of woman: [3]									
Married	341	246	188	21.0	19.0	12.0	10.6	7.9	6.5
Unmarried	1,268	1,067	1,024	79.0	81.0	88.0	47.7	35.0	30.6
Number of prior live births:									
None	780	533	487	49.0	41.0	40.2	32.0	20.2	16.6
One	396	361	331	25.0	28.0	27.2	36.9	32.5	31.3
Two	280	260	232	17.0	20.0	19.1	20.5	18.9	18.2
Three	102	104	104	6.0	8.0	8.6	15.6	14.8	16.0
Four or more	50	56	59	3.0	4.0	4.9	14.7	16.5	18.4
Number of prior induced abortions:									
None	891	699	646	55.0	53.0	53.3	(NA)	(NA)	(NA)
One	443	355	322	28.0	27.0	26.5	(NA)	(NA)	(NA)
Two or more	275	259	245	17.0	20.0	20.2	(NA)	(NA)	(NA)
Weeks of gestation:									
Less than 9 weeks	825	749	747	51.3	57.1	61.6	(NA)	(NA)	(NA)
9 to 10 weeks	416	269	207	25.8	20.5	17.1	(NA)	(NA)	(NA)
11 to 12 weeks	195	138	119	12.1	10.5	9.8	(NA)	(NA)	(NA)
13 weeks or more	173	156	139	10.8	11.9	11.5	(NA)	(NA)	(NA)

NA Not available. [1] Denominator of rate is women aged 14. [2] Denominator of rate is women aged 40–44. [3] Separated women are included with married.

Source: R.K. Jones and K. Kooistra, Abortion Incidence and Access to Services in the United States, 2008, *Perspectives on Sexual and Reproductive Health, 2011,* 430(1):41-50; S.K. Henshaw and K. Kost, *Trends in the Characteristics of Women Obtaining Abortions, 1974–2004*, New York: Guttmacher Institute, 2008; and unpublished data from the Guttmacher Institute (copyright).

Table 106. Abortions—Number and Rate by State of Occurrence: 2000 to 2008

[Number of abortions by state of occurrence from surveys of hospitals, clinics, and physicians identified as providers of abortion services conducted by the Guttmacher Institute]

State	State of occurrence Number 2000	2005	2008	Rate [1] 2000	2005	2008	State	State of occurrence Number 2000	2005	2008	Rate [1] 2000	2005	2008
U.S.....	1,312,990	1,206,200	1,211,500	21.3	19.4	19.6	MO......	7,920	8,400	7,440	6.6	7.0	6.3
AL.......	13,830	11,340	11,270	14.2	12.1	12.0	MT.......	2,510	2,150	2,230	13.5	11.9	12.3
AK.......	1,660	1,880	1,700	11.7	13.2	12.0	NE......	4,250	3,220	2,840	11.6	9.1	8.1
AZ.......	17,940	19,480	19,500	16.5	16.1	15.2	NV......	13,740	13,530	13,450	32.4	27.7	25.9
AR.......	5,540	4,710	4,890	9.8	8.4	8.7	NH......	3,010	3,170	3,200	11.2	11.8	12.3
CA......	236,060	208,430	214,190	31.2	26.9	27.6	NJ......	65,780	61,150	54,160	36.3	34.5	31.3
CO......	15,530	16,120	15,960	16.0	16.2	15.7	NM.....	5,760	6,220	6,150	14.7	15.7	15.5
CT......	15,240	16,780	17,030	21.1	23.8	24.6	NY......	164,630	155,960	153,110	39.1	37.7	37.6
DE......	5,440	5,150	7,070	31.3	29.2	40.0	NC......	37,610	34,500	33,140	21.1	18.9	17.5
DC......	9,800	7,230	4,450	68.2	50.0	29.9	ND......	1,340	1,230	1,400	9.9	9.6	11.2
FL.......	103,050	92,300	94,360	32.0	26.7	27.2	OH......	40,230	35,060	33,550	16.5	14.9	14.7
GA......	32,140	33,180	39,820	16.9	16.6	19.2	OK......	7,390	6,950	7,160	10.1	9.7	9.9
HI.......	5,630	5,350	5,630	22.2	21.3	22.6	OR......	17,010	13,200	12,920	23.6	18.1	17.3
ID.......	1,950	1,810	1,800	7.0	6.2	6.0	PA......	36,570	34,150	41,000	14.3	13.9	17.0
IL.......	63,690	50,970	54,920	23.2	18.9	20.5	RI.......	5,600	5,290	5,000	24.1	23.3	22.9
IN.......	12,490	11,150	10,680	9.4	8.6	8.3	SC.......	8,210	7,080	7,300	9.3	8.0	8.1
IA.......	5,970	6,370	6,560	9.8	10.9	11.3	SD.......	870	790	850	5.5	5.1	5.6
KS......	12,270	10,700	10,620	21.4	19.2	19.2	TN......	19,010	18,140	19,550	15.2	14.5	15.5
KY......	4,700	3,870	4,430	5.3	4.5	5.1	TX......	89,160	85,760	84,610	18.8	17.4	16.5
LA......	13,100	11,400	14,860	13.0	11.8	16.1	UT.......	3,510	3,630	4,000	6.7	6.4	6.7
ME......	2,650	2,770	2,800	9.9	10.7	11.2	VT.......	1,660	1,490	1,510	12.7	11.9	12.5
MD.....	34,560	37,590	34,290	29.0	31.3	29.0	VA......	28,780	26,520	28,520	18.1	16.4	17.6
MA.....	30,410	27,270	24,900	21.4	19.8	18.3	WA......	26,200	23,260	24,320	20.3	17.8	18.3
MI......	46,470	40,600	36,790	21.6	19.5	18.4	WV......	2,540	2,360	2,280	6.8	6.7	6.6
MN.....	14,610	13,910	13,060	13.5	13.1	12.5	WI......	11,130	9,800	8,230	9.6	8.6	7.4
MS......	3,780	3,090	2,770	6.0	5.0	4.6	WY.....	100	70	90	1.0	0.7	0.9

[1] Rate per 1,000 women, 15 to 44 years old on July 1 of specified year.

Source: R.K. Jones et al., *Abortion in the United States: Incidence and Access to Services, 2005, Perspectives on Sexual and Reproductive Health 40:6, 2008*; R.K. Jones and K. Kooistra, *Abortion Incidence and Access to Services in the United States, 2008, Perspectives on Sexual and Reproductive Health 43:1, 2011*; and unpublished data from the Guttmacher Institute (copyright). See also <http://www.guttmacher.org/>.

Table 107. Life Expectancy by Sex, Age, and Race: 2009

[Average number of years of life remaining. Excludes deaths of nonresidents of the United States. Data are preliminary]

Age	Total [1] Total	Male	Female	White Total	Male	Female	Black Total	Male	Female
0......................	78.5	76.0	80.9	78.8	76.4	81.2	74.5	71.1	77.6
1......................	78.0	75.5	80.4	78.3	75.9	80.6	74.5	71.1	77.5
5......................	74.1	71.6	76.4	74.3	71.9	76.7	70.6	67.2	73.6
10....................	69.2	66.6	71.5	69.4	67.0	71.7	65.6	62.3	68.7
15....................	64.2	61.7	66.5	64.4	62.0	66.7	60.7	57.3	63.7
20....................	59.4	56.9	61.6	59.6	57.2	61.8	55.9	52.6	58.8
25....................	54.6	52.3	56.8	54.8	52.6	57.0	51.2	48.1	54.0
30....................	49.9	47.6	51.9	50.0	47.9	52.1	46.6	43.5	49.2
35....................	45.1	42.9	47.1	45.3	43.2	47.3	42.0	39.0	44.5
40....................	40.4	38.3	42.3	40.6	38.5	42.5	37.4	34.5	39.8
45....................	35.8	33.7	37.7	36.0	34.0	37.8	33.0	30.2	35.3
50....................	31.4	29.4	33.1	31.5	29.6	33.2	28.7	26.0	31.0
55....................	27.1	25.3	28.7	27.2	25.4	28.8	24.8	22.3	26.9
60....................	23.1	21.3	24.4	23.1	21.5	24.5	21.2	18.9	23.0
65....................	19.2	17.6	20.3	19.1	17.7	20.4	17.8	15.8	19.3
70....................	15.5	14.2	16.5	15.5	14.2	16.5	14.6	13.0	15.8
75....................	12.2	11.0	12.9	12.1	11.0	12.9	11.7	10.3	12.6
80....................	9.2	8.2	9.7	9.1	8.2	9.7	9.1	7.9	9.7
85....................	6.7	5.9	7.0	6.6	5.8	7.0	6.8	5.9	7.2
90....................	4.7	4.1	4.9	4.6	4.1	4.8	5.1	4.4	5.3
95....................	3.3	2.9	3.4	3.2	2.8	3.3	3.8	3.3	3.9
100..................	2.4	2.1	2.4	2.3	2.1	2.3	2.9	2.5	2.9

[1] Includes races other than White and Black.

Source: U.S. National Center for Health Statistics, National Vital Statistics Reports (NVSR), *Deaths: Final Data for 2009*, Vol. 60, No. 3, June 2012, <http://www.cdc.gov/nchs/deaths.htm>.

Table 108. Expectation of Life at Birth, 1970 to 2010, and Projections, 2015 to 2020

[In years. Excludes deaths of nonresidents of the United States. See Appendix III]

Year	Total			White			Black		
	Total	Male	Female	Total	Male	Female	Total	Male	Female
1970	70.8	67.1	74.7	71.7	68.0	75.6	64.1	60.0	68.3
1980	73.7	70.0	77.4	74.4	70.7	78.1	68.1	63.8	72.5
1983	74.6	71.0	78.1	75.2	71.6	78.7	69.4	65.2	73.5
1984	74.7	71.1	78.2	75.3	71.8	78.7	69.5	65.3	73.6
1985	74.7	71.1	78.2	75.3	71.8	78.7	69.3	65.0	73.4
1986	74.7	71.2	78.2	75.4	71.9	78.8	69.1	64.8	73.4
1987	74.9	71.4	78.3	75.6	72.1	78.9	69.1	64.7	73.4
1988	74.9	71.4	78.3	75.6	72.2	78.9	68.9	64.4	73.2
1989	75.1	71.7	78.5	75.9	72.5	79.2	68.8	64.3	73.3
1990	75.4	71.8	78.8	76.1	72.7	79.4	69.1	64.5	73.6
1991	75.5	72.0	78.9	76.3	72.9	79.6	69.3	64.6	73.8
1992	75.8	72.3	79.1	76.5	73.2	79.8	69.6	65.0	73.9
1993	75.5	72.2	78.8	76.3	73.1	79.5	69.2	64.6	73.7
1994	75.7	72.4	79.0	76.5	73.3	79.6	69.5	64.9	73.9
1995	75.8	72.5	78.9	76.5	73.4	79.6	69.6	65.2	73.9
1996	76.1	73.1	79.1	76.8	73.9	79.7	70.2	66.1	74.2
1997	76.5	73.6	79.4	77.2	74.3	79.9	71.1	67.2	74.7
1998	76.7	73.8	79.5	77.3	74.5	80.0	71.3	67.6	74.8
1999	76.7	73.9	79.4	77.3	74.6	79.9	71.4	67.8	74.7
2000 [1]	76.8	74.1	79.3	77.3	74.7	79.9	71.8	68.2	75.1
2001 [1]	76.9	74.2	79.4	77.4	74.8	79.9	72.0	68.4	75.2
2002 [1]	76.9	74.3	79.5	77.4	74.9	79.9	72.1	68.6	75.4
2003 [1,2]	77.1	74.5	79.6	77.6	75.0	80.0	72.3	68.8	75.6
2004 [1,2]	77.5	74.9	79.9	77.9	75.4	80.4	72.8	69.3	76.0
2005 [1,2]	77.4	74.9	79.9	77.9	75.4	80.4	72.8	69.3	76.1
2006 [1,2]	77.7	75.1	80.2	78.2	75.7	80.6	73.2	69.7	76.5
2007 [1,2]	77.9	75.4	80.4	78.4	75.9	80.8	73.6	70.0	76.8
2008 [1,2]	78.1	75.6	80.6	78.5	76.1	80.9	74.0	70.6	77.2
2009 [1,2]	78.5	76.0	80.9	78.8	76.4	81.2	74.5	71.1	77.6
2010 [1,2,3]	78.7	76.2	81.1	79.0	76.5	81.3	75.1	71.8	78.0
Projections: [4]									
2015	78.9	76.4	81.4	79.5	77.1	81.8	75.0	71.4	78.2
2020	79.5	77.1	81.9	80.0	77.7	82.4	76.1	72.6	79.2

[1] Life expectancies for 2000–2010 were calculated using a revised methodology and may differ from those previously published. [2] Multiple-race data were bridged to the single-race categories of the 1977 OMB standards for comparability with other reporting areas. [3] Data are preliminary. [4] Based on middle mortality assumptions; for details, see source: U.S. Census Bureau, "2008 National Population Projections," released August, 2008, <http://www.census.gov/population/www/projections/2008projections.html>.

Source: Except as noted. U.S. National Center for Health Statistics, National Vital Statistics Reports (NVSR), *Deaths: Final Data for 2009*, Vol. 60, No. 3, June 2012, and earlier reports, <http://www.cdc.gov/nchs/products/nvsr.htm>.

Table 109. Selected Life Table Values: 1959 to 2008

[Decennial life tables are based on population data from a decennial census and reported deaths of the 3-year period surrounding the census year; the census year is the middle year. The annual tables are based on deaths in a single year, and except for census years, on postcensal population estimates. Beginning in 1970, data excludes deaths of nonresidents of the United States. See Appendix III]

Age and sex	All races 1959–1961	1969–1971	1979–1981	1989–1991	1999–2001	2008	White 1959–1961	1969–1971	1979–1981	1989–1991	1999–2001	2008	Black [1] 1959–1961	1969–1971	1979–1981	1989–1991	1999–2001	2008
EXPECTATION OF LIFE IN YEARS																		
At birth: Male	66.8	67.0	70.1	71.8	74.1	75.5	67.6	67.9	70.8	72.7	74.7	75.9	61.5	60.0	64.1	64.5	68.1	70.9
At birth: Female	73.2	74.6	77.6	78.8	79.5	80.5	74.2	75.5	78.2	79.5	80.0	80.8	66.5	68.3	72.9	73.7	75.1	77.4
Age 20: Male	49.8	49.5	51.9	53.3	55.2	56.5	50.3	50.2	52.5	54.0	55.7	56.8	45.8	43.5	46.5	46.7	49.8	52.6
Age 20: Female	55.6	56.6	59.0	59.9	60.3	61.2	56.3	57.2	59.4	60.4	60.7	61.4	50.8	51.2	54.9	55.5	56.5	58.7
Age 40: Male	31.4	31.5	33.6	35.1	36.6	37.9	31.7	31.9	34.0	35.6	37.0	38.1	28.7	27.6	29.5	30.1	32.1	34.5
Age 40: Female	36.6	37.6	39.8	40.7	41.0	41.9	37.1	38.1	40.2	41.0	41.3	42.1	32.2	33.3	36.3	37.0	37.7	39.6
Age 50: Male	23.0	23.1	25.0	26.4	27.8	29.0	23.2	23.3	25.3	26.7	28.1	29.2	21.3	20.7	22.0	22.5	24.1	26.0
Age 50: Female	27.7	28.8	30.7	31.4	31.7	32.7	28.1	29.1	31.0	31.7	32.0	32.8	24.3	25.5	27.8	28.4	29.0	30.8
Age 65: Male	13.0	13.0	14.2	15.1	16.1	17.2	13.0	13.0	14.3	15.2	16.2	17.3	12.8	12.5	13.3	13.3	14.1	15.5
Age 65: Female	15.8	16.8	18.4	19.0	19.1	19.9	15.9	16.9	18.6	19.1	19.2	19.9	15.1	15.7	17.1	17.4	17.7	18.9
NUMBER OF SURVIVORS OUT OF 1,000 BORN ALIVE [2]																		
At birth: Male	1,000	1,000	1,000	1,000	1,000	1,000	1,000	1,000	1,000	1,000	1,000	1,000	1,000	1,000	1,000	1,000	1,000	1,000
At birth: Female	1,000	1,000	1,000	1,000	1,000	1,000	1,000	1,000	1,000	1,000	1,000	1,000	1,000	1,000	1,000	1,000	1,000	1,000
Age 20: Male	955	961	973	979	984	986	959	965	975	981	986	987	931	941	961	963	973	980
Age 20: Female	968	973	982	986	989	990	971	976	984	988	990	991	947	957	972	976	981	976
Age 40: Male	916	915	933	938	954	957	924	926	940	946	959	960	857	834	885	879	919	948
Age 40: Female	946	951	965	970	975	977	953	958	969	975	978	979	897	908	941	944	956	933
Age 50: Male	862	861	890	899	918	925	874	877	901	911	926	929	772	733	801	800	856	910
Age 50: Female	913	919	941	949	954	956	925	929	947	956	960	959	830	842	896	903	917	887
Age 65: Male	642	643	706	740	781	800	658	663	724	760	795	809	514	475	551	568	646	762
Age 65: Female	785	797	835	851	864	876	807	816	848	863	874	883	608	647	733	750	778	703
PERCENT SURVIVING OUT OF 1,000 BORN ALIVE																		
At birth: Male	100.0	100.0	100.0	100.0	100.0	100.0	100.0	100.0	100.0	100.0	100.0	100.0	100.0	100.0	100.0	100.0	100.0	100.0
At birth: Female	100.0	100.0	100.0	100.0	100.0	100.0	100.0	100.0	100.0	100.0	100.0	100.0	100.0	100.0	100.0	100.0	100.0	100.0
Age 20: Male	95.5	96.1	97.3	97.9	98.4	98.6	95.9	96.5	97.5	98.1	98.6	98.7	93.1	94.1	96.1	96.3	97.3	98.0
Age 20: Female	96.8	97.3	98.2	98.6	98.9	99.0	97.1	97.6	98.4	98.8	99.0	99.1	94.7	95.7	97.2	97.6	98.1	97.6
Age 40: Male	91.6	91.5	93.3	93.8	95.4	95.7	92.4	92.6	94.0	94.6	95.9	96.0	85.7	83.4	88.5	87.9	91.9	94.8
Age 40: Female	94.6	95.1	96.5	97.0	97.5	97.7	95.3	95.8	96.9	97.5	97.8	97.9	89.7	90.8	94.1	94.4	95.6	93.3
Age 50: Male	86.2	86.1	89.0	89.9	91.8	92.5	87.4	87.7	90.1	91.1	92.6	92.9	77.2	73.3	80.1	80.0	85.6	91.0
Age 50: Female	91.3	91.9	94.1	94.9	95.4	95.6	92.5	92.9	94.7	95.6	96.0	95.9	83.0	84.2	89.6	90.3	91.7	88.7
Age 65: Male	64.2	64.3	70.6	74.0	78.1	80.0	65.8	66.3	72.4	76.0	79.5	80.9	51.4	47.5	55.1	56.8	64.6	76.2
Age 65: Female	78.5	79.7	83.5	85.1	86.4	87.6	80.7	81.6	84.8	86.3	87.4	88.3	60.8	64.7	73.3	75.0	77.8	70.3

[1] Prior to 1970, data for the Black population are not available. Data shown for 1959–1970 are for the Non-White population. [2] The number of persons from the original synthetic cohort of 1,000 live births, who survive the beginning of each age interval.

Source: U.S. National Center for Health Statistics, National Vital Statistics Reports (NVSR), *U.S. Decennial Life Tables for 1999–2001, United States Life Tables, Vol. 57, No. 1, August 2008; United States Life Tables, 2006, Vol. 58, No. 21, June 2010;* and unpublished data, <http://www.cdc.gov/nchs/products/life_tables.htm>.

Births, Deaths, Marriages, and Divorces

Table 110. Expectation of Life and Expected Deaths by Race, Sex, and Age: 2008

[Life expectancies were calculated using a revised methodology and may differ from those previously published. The methodology uses vital statistics death rates for ages under 66 and modeled probabilities of death for ages 66 to 100 based on blended vital statistics and Medicare probabilities of dying]

Age (years)	Expectation of life in years					Expected deaths per 1,000 alive at specified age [1]				
		White		Black			White		Black	
	Total [2]	Male	Female	Male	Female	Total [1]	Male	Female	Male	Female
At birth...........	78.0	75.9	80.8	70.9	77.4	6.81	6.29	5.22	14.42	11.92
1.................	77.6	75.4	80.2	71.0	77.4	0.45	0.46	0.39	0.74	0.52
2.................	76.6	74.4	79.2	70.0	76.4	0.28	0.30	0.22	0.43	0.33
3.................	75.6	73.5	78.2	69.1	75.4	0.22	0.23	0.16	0.33	0.31
4.................	74.6	72.5	77.2	68.1	74.5	0.17	0.17	0.14	0.30	0.19
5.................	73.7	71.5	76.3	67.1	73.5	0.15	0.16	0.13	0.26	0.17
6.................	72.7	70.5	75.3	66.1	72.5	0.14	0.14	0.11	0.24	0.14
7.................	71.7	69.5	74.3	65.1	71.5	0.12	0.12	0.11	0.22	0.13
8.................	70.7	68.5	73.3	64.1	70.5	0.11	0.10	0.10	0.18	0.12
9.................	69.7	67.5	72.3	63.2	69.5	0.09	0.08	0.09	0.13	0.11
10................	68.7	66.5	71.3	62.2	68.5	0.08	0.07	0.08	0.09	0.12
11................	67.7	65.5	70.3	61.2	67.5	0.09	0.07	0.09	0.08	0.13
12................	66.7	64.5	69.3	60.2	66.5	0.12	0.12	0.11	0.15	0.16
13................	65.7	63.5	68.3	59.2	65.6	0.19	0.22	0.14	0.31	0.19
14................	64.7	62.6	67.3	58.2	64.6	0.29	0.35	0.19	0.53	0.23
15................	63.8	61.6	66.3	57.2	63.6	0.39	0.49	0.24	0.76	0.28
16................	62.8	60.6	65.4	56.3	62.6	0.48	0.61	0.29	0.96	0.32
17................	61.8	59.6	64.4	55.3	61.6	0.57	0.74	0.33	1.15	0.36
18................	60.8	58.7	63.4	54.4	60.6	0.65	0.87	0.35	1.32	0.40
19................	59.9	57.7	62.4	53.5	59.7	0.73	1.00	0.37	1.48	0.44
20................	58.9	56.8	61.4	52.6	58.7	0.82	1.13	0.39	1.67	0.49
21................	58.0	55.9	60.5	51.6	57.7	0.90	1.26	0.41	1.85	0.54
22................	57.0	54.9	59.5	50.7	56.8	0.95	1.34	0.43	1.98	0.59
23................	56.1	54.0	58.5	49.8	55.8	0.97	1.36	0.45	2.03	0.63
24................	55.1	53.1	57.5	48.9	54.8	0.96	1.33	0.46	2.01	0.66
25................	54.2	52.2	56.6	48.0	53.9	0.95	1.29	0.48	1.97	0.69
26................	53.2	51.2	55.6	47.1	52.9	0.94	1.26	0.49	1.94	0.72
27................	52.3	50.3	54.6	46.2	51.9	0.94	1.24	0.51	1.92	0.75
28................	51.3	49.4	53.7	45.3	51.0	0.95	1.24	0.52	1.95	0.80
29................	50.4	48.4	52.7	44.4	50.0	0.96	1.26	0.54	2.00	0.85
30................	49.4	47.5	51.7	43.5	49.1	0.99	1.28	0.57	2.07	0.91
31................	48.5	46.5	50.7	42.6	48.1	1.02	1.30	0.60	2.14	0.98
32................	47.5	45.6	49.8	41.7	47.2	1.05	1.33	0.64	2.24	1.06
33................	46.6	44.7	48.8	40.8	46.2	1.10	1.38	0.69	2.26	1.13
34................	45.6	43.7	47.8	39.9	45.3	1.14	1.42	0.74	2.30	1.21
35................	44.7	42.8	46.9	39.0	44.3	1.20	1.48	0.79	2.35	1.29
36................	43.8	41.9	45.9	38.1	43.4	1.27	1.56	0.85	2.43	1.38
37................	42.8	40.9	44.9	37.2	42.4	1.35	1.64	0.93	2.53	1.50
38................	41.9	40.0	44.0	36.3	41.5	1.45	1.75	1.01	2.67	1.65
39................	40.9	39.1	43.0	35.4	40.6	1.57	1.88	1.11	2.86	1.83
40................	40.0	38.1	42.1	34.5	39.6	1.70	2.02	1.22	3.06	2.03
41................	39.1	37.2	41.1	33.6	38.7	1.85	2.18	1.34	3.30	2.23
42................	38.1	36.3	40.2	32.7	37.8	2.03	2.38	1.48	3.57	2.46
43................	37.2	35.4	39.3	31.8	36.9	2.24	2.63	1.64	3.87	2.72
44................	36.3	34.5	38.3	31.0	36.0	2.46	2.90	1.81	4.21	2.99
45................	35.4	33.6	37.4	30.1	35.1	2.69	3.17	1.99	4.54	3.27
46................	34.5	32.7	36.5	29.3	34.2	2.92	3.44	2.16	4.91	3.55
47................	33.6	31.8	35.5	28.4	33.4	3.17	3.74	2.33	5.36	3.84
48................	32.7	30.9	34.6	27.6	32.5	3.44	4.06	2.51	5.93	4.16
49................	31.8	30.1	33.7	26.8	31.7	3.73	4.42	2.69	6.60	4.50
50................	31.0	29.2	32.8	26.0	30.8	4.05	4.80	2.90	7.33	4.87
51................	30.1	28.4	31.9	25.2	30.0	4.37	5.19	3.12	8.06	5.24
52................	29.2	27.5	31.0	24.4	29.1	4.70	5.58	3.34	8.80	5.61
53................	28.4	26.7	30.1	23.6	28.3	5.02	5.97	3.56	9.53	5.94
54................	27.5	25.9	29.2	22.9	27.5	5.35	6.36	3.79	10.26	6.25
55................	26.7	25.0	28.3	22.2	26.7	5.69	6.76	4.03	11.04	6.58
56................	25.8	24.2	27.5	21.5	25.9	6.06	7.21	4.31	11.84	6.93
57................	25.0	23.4	26.6	20.8	25.1	6.48	7.69	4.65	12.56	7.33
58................	24.2	22.6	25.7	20.1	24.3	6.94	8.21	5.06	13.16	7.78
59................	23.4	21.8	24.9	19.4	23.5	7.44	8.78	5.55	13.67	8.29
60................	22.6	21.0	24.0	18.7	22.7	8.00	9.38	6.09	14.18	8.88
61................	21.8	20.3	23.2	18.1	21.9	8.58	10.02	6.66	14.76	9.53
62................	21.0	19.5	22.3	17.4	21.2	9.20	10.69	7.25	15.44	10.21
63................	20.2	18.7	21.5	16.8	20.4	9.84	11.39	7.85	16.24	10.87
64................	19.4	18.0	20.7	16.1	19.7	10.53	12.15	8.48	17.12	11.51
65................	18.7	17.3	19.9	15.5	18.9	11.31	13.01	9.20	18.05	12.17
70................	15.0	13.7	16.0	12.6	15.4	15.71	17.98	13.41	21.52	16.03
75................	11.7	10.6	12.4	10.0	12.2	22.88	25.49	20.76	26.01	22.27
80................	8.8	7.9	9.3	7.8	9.5	30.58	32.38	29.96	27.35	28.25
85................	6.5	5.7	6.8	6.0	7.1	34.98	34.17	37.38	24.52	31.42
90................	4.6	4.1	4.8	4.6	5.3	31.07	26.79	36.44	17.49	28.56
95................	3.2	2.9	3.3	3.5	3.8	18.50	13.21	23.65	9.05	19.11
100.............	2.3	2.0	2.2	2.6	2.8	18.45	8.92	24.78	10.40	30.63

[1] Based on the proportion of the cohort who are alive at the beginning of the indicated age who will die before reaching the age shown plus 1. For example, out of every 1,000 people alive and exactly 50 years old at the beginning of the period, 4 (4.05) people will die before reaching their 51st birthdays. [2] Includes other races, not shown separately.

Source: U.S. National Center for Health Statistics, unpublished data. See also, <http://www.cdc.gov/nchs/products/life_tables.htm>.

Table 111. Life Expectancy by Sex, Race, and State: 1979 to 1991

[Average number of years of life remaining. Excludes deaths of nonresidents of the United States. Decennial life tables are based on population data from a decennial census and reported deaths of the 3-year period surrounding the census year; the census year is the middle year. The annual tables are based on deaths in a single year, and except for census years, on postcensal population estimates]

State	Total, 1979–1981	1989–1991						
		Total	Male			Female		
			Total	White	Black	Total	White	Black
United States.............	**73.88**	**75.37**	**71.83**	**72.72**	**64.47**	**78.81**	**79.4.5**	**73.73**
Alabama........................	72.53	73.64	69.59	71.12	64.37	77.61	78.85	73.76
Alaska...........................	72.24	74.83	71.60	72.82	(B)	78.60	79.40	(B)
Arizona.........................	74.30	76.10	72.66	73.04	67.20	79.58	79.84	74.90
Arkansas.......................	73.72	74.33	70.54	71.54	64.03	78.13	78.89	73.58
California.......................	74.57	75.86	72.53	72.61	65.43	79.19	79.26	74.07
Colorado.......................	75.30	76.96	73.79	73.88	68.96	80.01	80.13	75.89
Connecticut...................	75.12	76.91	73.62	74.25	66.04	79.97	80.37	75.44
Delaware.......................	73.21	74.76	71.63	72.75	65.51	77.74	78.62	72.91
District of Columbia..........	69.20	67.99	61.97	71.36	57.53	74.23	81.06	71.61
Florida..........................	74.00	75.84	72.10	73.19	64.26	79.60	80.46	73.28
Georgia........................	72.22	73.61	69.65	71.46	63.98	77.46	78.94	73.34
Hawaii..........................	77.02	78.21	75.37	75.12	(B)	81.26	81.09	(B)
Idaho...........................	75.19	76.88	73.88	73.90	(B)	79.93	79.93	(B)
Illinois..........................	73.37	74.90	71.34	72.83	62.41	78.31	79.33	72.39
Indiana.........................	73.84	75.39	71.99	72.44	65.87	78.62	79.03	73.56
Iowa............................	75.81	77.29	73.89	73.98	(B)	80.54	80.62	(B)
Kansas.........................	75.31	76.76	73.40	73.72	67.48	79.99	80.25	75.04
Kentucky.......................	73.06	74.37	70.72	71.01	66.06	77.97	78.24	74.13
Louisiana......................	71.74	73.05	69.10	71.15	63.84	76.93	78.54	73.16
Maine..........................	74.59	76.35	72.98	72.98	(B)	79.61	79.61	(B)
Maryland.......................	73.32	74.79	71.31	73.20	64.99	78.13	79.23	74.31
Massachusetts................	75.01	76.72	73.32	73.54	68.17	79.80	79.95	76.50
Michigan.......................	73.67	75.04	71.71	73.06	63.68	78.24	79.14	73.18
Minnesota.....................	76.15	77.76	74.53	74.78	(B)	80.85	81.02	(B)
Mississippi....................	71.98	73.03	68.90	70.74	64.66	77.10	78.82	73.82
Missouri........................	73.84	75.25	71.54	72.43	63.87	78.82	79.48	73.52
Montana........................	73.93	76.23	73.05	73.59	(B)	79.49	79.92	(B)
Nebraska.......................	75.49	76.92	73.57	73.87	(B)	80.17	80.44	(B)
Nevada.........................	72.64	74.18	70.96	71.26	(B)	77.76	77.99	(B)
New Hampshire................	74.98	76.72	73.52	73.48	(B)	79.77	79.74	(B)
New Jersey.....................	74.00	75.42	72.16	73.37	63.87	78.49	79.34	72.88
New Mexico....................	74.01	75.74	72.20	72.66	(B)	79.33	79.53	(B)
New York.......................	73.70	74.68	70.86	72.01	63.86	78.32	79.03	74.35
North Carolina.................	72.96	74.48	70.58	72.21	64.38	78.27	79.44	74.24
North Dakota..................	75.71	77.62	74.35	74.74	(B)	80.99	81.32	(B)
Ohio............................	73.49	75.32	71.99	72.70	65.80	78.45	78.95	74.29
Oklahoma......................	73.67	75.10	71.63	71.76	67.10	78.49	78.59	74.48
Oregon.........................	74.99	76.44	73.21	73.28	(B)	79.67	79.73	(B)
Pennsylvania..................	73.58	75.38	71.91	72.81	63.33	78.66	79.28	73.02
Rhode Island..................	74.76	76.54	73.00	73.31	(B)	79.77	79.97	(B)
South Carolina................	71.85	73.51	69.59	71.62	64.07	77.34	78.97	73.35
South Dakota.................	74.97	76.91	73.17	74.30	(B)	80.77	81.59	(B)
Tennessee.....................	73.30	74.32	70.38	71.38	64.41	78.18	79.10	73.24
Texas..........................	73.64	75.14	71.41	72.08	65.36	78.87	79.42	74.23
Utah............................	75.76	77.70	74.93	75.00	(B)	80.38	80.44	(B)
Vermont........................	74.79	76.54	73.29	73.25	(B)	79.68	79.65	(B)
Virginia.........................	73.43	75.22	71.77	73.04	65.75	78.56	79.48	74.37
Washington....................	75.13	76.82	73.84	73.97	67.91	79.74	79.81	75.58
West Virginia..................	72.84	74.26	70.53	70.66	65.00	77.93	78.02	74.36
Wisconsin.....................	75.35	76.87	73.61	73.99	66.42	80.03	80.27	75.27
Wyoming.......................	73.85	76.21	73.16	73.27	(B)	79.29	79.46	(B)

B Base figure too small to meet statistical standards for reliability.

Source: U.S. National Center for Health Statistics, National Vital Statistics Reports (NVSR), *U.S. Decennial Life Tables for 1989–91*, Vol. 1, No. 3., and *Trends and Comparisons of United States Life Table Data: 1900–1991*. See also <http://www.cdc.gov/nchs/products/life_tables.htm>.

Table 112. Deaths and Death Rates by Sex, Race, and Hispanic Origin: 1970 to 2009

[1,921 represents 1,921,000. Rates are per 1,000 population for specified groups. Excludes deaths of nonresidents of the United States and fetal deaths. For explanation of age adjustment, see text, this section. Data for Hispanic origin and specified races other than White and Black should be interpreted with caution because of inconsistencies between reporting Hispanic origin and race on death certificates and censuses and surveys]

Sex and race	1970	1980	1990	2000	2003	2004	2005	2006	2007	2008	2009
Deaths [1] (1,000)	**1,921**	**1,990**	**2,148**	**2,403**	**2,448**	**2,398**	**2,448**	**2,426**	**2,424**	**2,472**	**2,437**
Male [1] (1,000)	1,078	1,075	1,113	1,178	1,202	1,182	1,208	1,202	1,204	1,226	1,217
Female [1] (1,000)	843	915	1,035	1,226	1,246	1,216	1,240	1,224	1,220	1,246	1,220
White (1,000)	1,682	1,739	1,853	2,071	2,104	2,057	2,098	2,078	2,074	2,120	2,086
Male (1,000)	942	934	951	1,007	1,026	1,007	1,028	1,022	1,024	1,046	1,037
Female (1,000)	740	805	902	1,064	1,078	1,049	1,070	1,055	1,050	1,074	1,049
Black (1,000)	226	233	265	286	291	287	293	290	290	289	287
Male (1,000)	128	130	145	145	148	146	149	149	148	147	146
Female (1,000)	98	103	120	141	143	141	144	141	141	142	140
Asian or Pacific Islander (1,000)	(NA)	11	21	35	40	41	43	45	46	48	49
Male (1,000)	(NA)	7	12	19	21	21	23	23	24	25	26
Female (1,000)	(NA)	4	9	16	19	19	20	21	22	23	24
American Indian or Alaska Native (1,000)	6	7	8	11	13	13	14	14	14	15	15
Male (1,000)	3	4	5	6	7	7	8	8	8	8	8
Female (1,000)	2	3	3	5	6	6	6	6	6	7	7
Hispanic origin [2]	(NA)	(NA)	(NA)	107	122	122	131	133	136	139	142
Male (1,000)	(NA)	(NA)	(NA)	60	68	69	74	74	76	77	78
Female (1,000)	(NA)	(NA)	(NA)	47	54	54	57	59	60	62	63
Non-Hispanic, White (1,000)	(NA)	(NA)	(NA)	1,960	1,979	1,933	1,967	1,945	1,940	1,981	1,945
Male (1,000)	(NA)	(NA)	(NA)	945	956	938	954	948	949	969	959
Female (1,000)	(NA)	(NA)	(NA)	1,015	1,023	995	1,013	997	991	1,012	986
Death rates [1]	**9.5**	**8.8**	**8.6**	**8.5**	**8.4**	**8.2**	**8.3**	**8.1**	**8.0**	**8.1**	**7.9**
Male [1]	10.9	9.8	9.2	8.5	8.4	8.2	8.3	8.1	8.1	8.2	8.0
Female [1]	8.1	7.9	8.1	8.6	8.4	8.2	8.2	8.1	8.0	8.1	7.8
White	9.5	8.9	8.9	9.0	8.9	8.6	8.7	8.6	8.5	8.6	8.4
Male	10.9	9.8	9.3	8.9	8.8	8.5	8.6	8.5	8.5	8.6	8.5
Female	8.1	8.1	8.5	9.1	9.0	8.7	8.8	8.6	8.5	8.7	8.4
Black	10.0	8.8	8.7	7.8	7.6	7.4	7.5	7.3	7.2	7.2	7.0
Male	11.9	10.3	10.1	8.3	8.1	7.9	8.0	7.9	7.8	7.6	7.5
Female	8.3	7.3	7.5	7.3	7.2	7.0	7.0	6.8	6.8	6.7	6.6
Asian or Pacific Islander	(NA)	3.0	2.8	3.0	3.0	3.0	3.1	3.1	3.1	3.2	3.2
Male	(NA)	3.8	3.3	3.3	3.3	3.2	3.3	3.3	3.3	3.4	3.4
Female	(NA)	2.2	2.3	2.6	2.8	2.7	2.8	2.9	2.9	3.0	3.0
American Indian or Alaska Native	(NA)	4.9	4.0	3.8	4.2	4.2	4.4	4.4	4.4	4.3	4.3
Male	(NA)	6.0	4.8	4.2	4.6	4.5	4.8	4.8	4.9	4.8	4.6
Female	(NA)	3.8	3.3	3.5	3.9	3.8	4.0	4.0	4.0	3.9	3.9
Hispanic origin [2]	(NA)	(NA)	(NA)	3.0	3.1	3.0	3.1	3.0	3.0	3.0	2.9
Male	(NA)	(NA)	4.1	3.3	3.3	3.2	3.3	3.2	3.2	3.2	3.1
Female	(NA)	(NA)	2.9	2.7	2.8	2.7	2.8	2.7	2.7	2.7	2.7
Non-Hispanic, White	(NA)	(NA)	(NA)	9.9	9.9	9.7	9.8	9.7	9.6	9.8	9.6
Male	(NA)	(NA)	9.9	9.8	9.8	9.6	9.7	9.6	9.6	9.8	9.7
Female	(NA)	(NA)	9.0	10.1	10.1	9.8	9.9	9.7	9.7	9.9	9.6
Age-adjusted death rates [1, 3]	**12.2**	**10.4**	**9.4**	**8.7**	**8.3**	**8.0**	**8.0**	**7.8**	**7.6**	**7.6**	**7.4**
Male [1]	15.4	13.5	12.0	10.5	9.9	9.6	9.5	9.2	9.1	9.0	8.9
Female [1]	9.7	8.2	7.5	7.3	7.1	6.8	6.8	6.6	6.4	6.4	6.3
White	11.9	10.1	9.1	8.5	8.2	7.9	7.9	7.6	7.5	7.5	7.3
Male	15.1	13.2	11.7	10.3	9.7	9.4	9.3	9.1	8.9	8.9	8.8
Female	9.4	8.0	7.3	7.2	6.9	6.7	6.5	6.5	6.3	6.4	6.2
Black	15.2	13.1	12.5	11.2	10.7	10.3	10.2	9.8	9.6	9.3	9.2
Male	18.7	17.0	16.4	14.0	13.2	12.7	12.5	12.2	11.8	11.5	11.5
Female	12.3	10.3	9.8	9.3	8.9	8.6	8.5	8.1	7.9	7.8	7.7
Asian or Pacific Islander	(NA)	5.9	5.8	5.1	4.7	4.4	4.4	4.3	4.2	4.1	4.1
Male	(NA)	7.9	7.2	6.2	5.6	5.3	5.3	5.2	5.0	4.9	4.9
Female	(NA)	4.3	4.7	4.2	3.9	3.8	3.7	3.6	3.5	3.5	3.5
American Indian or Alaska Native	(NA)	8.7	7.2	7.1	6.9	6.5	6.6	6.4	6.3	6.1	6.0
Male	(NA)	11.1	9.2	8.4	8.0	7.6	7.8	7.4	7.4	7.2	7.0
Female	(NA)	6.6	5.6	6.0	5.9	5.6	5.7	5.6	5.3	5.2	5.2
Hispanic origin [2]	(NA)	(NA)	(NA)	6.7	6.2	5.9	5.9	5.6	5.5	5.3	5.2
Male	(NA)	(NA)	8.9	8.2	7.5	7.1	7.2	6.8	6.5	6.3	6.2
Female	(NA)	(NA)	5.4	5.5	5.2	4.9	4.9	4.7	4.5	4.5	4.4
Non-Hispanic, White	(NA)	(NA)	(NA)	8.6	8.3	8.0	8.0	7.8	7.6	7.7	7.5
Male	(NA)	(NA)	11.7	10.4	9.8	9.5	9.5	9.2	9.1	9.1	9.0
Female	(NA)	(NA)	7.3	7.2	7.0	6.8	6.8	6.6	6.5	6.5	6.3

NA Not available. [1] Includes other races not shown separately. [2] Persons of Hispanic origin may be any race. [3] Age-adjusted death rates are better indicators than crude death rates for showing changes in the risk of death over time when the age distribution of the population is changing, and for comparing the mortality of population subgroups that have different age compositions. All age-adjusted death rates are standardized to the year 2000 population.

Source: U.S. National Center for Health Statistics, National Vital Statistics Reports (NVSR), *Deaths: Final Data for 2009*, Vol. 60, No. 3, December 2011, <http://www.cdc.gov/nchs/deaths.htm/>.

Table 113. Death Rates by Age, Sex, and Race: 1950 to 2008
[Rates per 100,000 population]

Characteristic	All ages[1]	Under 1 year	1 to 4 years	5 to 14 years	15 to 24 years	25 to 34 years	35 to 44 years	45 to 54 years	55 to 64 years	65 to 74 years	75 to 84 years	85 years and over
MALE												
1950	1,106	3,728	152	71	168	217	429	1,067	2,395	4,931	10,426	21,636
1960	1,105	3,059	120	56	152	188	373	992	2,310	4,914	10,178	21,186
1970	1,090	2,410	93	51	189	215	403	959	2,283	4,874	10,010	17,822
1980	977	1,429	73	37	172	196	299	767	1,815	4,105	8,817	18,801
1990	918	1,083	52	29	147	204	310	610	1,553	3,492	7,889	18,057
2000	853	807	36	21	115	139	255	543	1,231	2,980	6,973	17,501
2005	827	762	33	19	118	143	243	548	1,131	2,612	6,350	14,889
2008	818	710	32	16	110	142	224	526	1,105	2,433	6,032	14,017
White:												
1990	931	896	46	26	131	176	268	549	1,467	3,398	7,845	18,268
2000	888	668	33	20	106	124	234	497	1,163	2,906	6,933	17,716
2005	865	640	31	17	110	131	229	509	1,068	2,553	6,343	15,157
2006	852	633	28	16	112	135	224	505	1,051	2,456	6,182	14,577
2007	848	628	28	16	108	134	218	498	1,043	2,397	6,049	14,286
2008	860	600	29	15	103	133	214	501	1,052	2,377	6,052	14,354
Black:												
1990	1,008	2,112	86	41	252	431	700	1,261	2,618	4,946	9,130	16,955
2000	834	1,568	55	28	181	261	453	1,018	2,080	4,254	8,486	16,791
2005	799	1,437	47	27	172	254	396	949	1,954	3,747	7,667	13,810
2006	787	1,407	47	25	171	254	392	922	1,892	3,669	7,393	13,206
2007	776	1,363	45	25	168	240	379	877	1,871	3,605	7,169	12,965
2008	763	1,299	47	24	159	225	348	828	1,826	3,538	7,102	12,528
Asian or Pacific Islander:[2]												
1990	334	605	45	21	76	80	131	287	789	2,041	5,009	12,446
2000	333	529	23	13	55	55	105	250	642	1,661	4,328	12,125
2005	334	465	21	14	57	56	94	242	545	1,404	3,759	9,839
2006	331	470	18	11	62	54	89	233	551	1,329	3,606	9,525
2007	331	484	25	12	61	50	89	229	523	1,305	3,538	8,918
2008	338	464	17	12	50	55	87	223	529	1,313	3,497	8,725
American Indian, or Alaska Native:[2]												
1990	476	1,057	77	33	220	256	365	620	1,211	2,462	5,389	11,244
2000	416	700	45	20	136	179	295	520	1,090	2,478	5,351	10,726
2005	482	882	72	23	145	206	337	589	1,124	2,254	4,373	8,419
2006	477	1,058	58	17	156	194	339	592	1,030	2,147	4,198	7,540
2007	488	1,010	64	23	144	198	333	573	1,037	2,132	4,193	7,639
2008	478	660	38	19	151	198	316	618	1,038	2,170	4,150	6,514
FEMALE												
1950	824	2,855	127	49	89	143	290	642	1,405	3,333	8,400	19,195
1960	809	2,321	98	37	61	107	229	527	1,196	2,872	7,633	19,008
1970	808	1,864	75	32	68	102	231	517	1,099	2,580	6,678	15,518
1980	785	1,142	55	24	58	76	159	413	934	2,145	5,440	14,747
1990	812	856	41	19	49	74	138	343	879	1,991	4,883	14,274
2000	855	663	29	15	43	64	143	313	772	1,921	4,815	14,719
2007	797	618	26	13	42	64	137	315	670	1,633	4,304	12,442
2008	808	589	25	12	40	63	135	318	669	1,623	4,314	12,531
White:												
1990	847	690	36	18	46	62	117	309	823	1,924	4,839	14,401
2000	912	551	26	14	41	55	126	281	731	1,868	4,785	14,891
2005	883	515	23	13	42	58	130	291	664	1,700	4,519	13,498
2006	864	517	24	12	42	59	129	292	655	1,646	4,395	12,966
2007	855	517	23	12	41	60	126	291	638	1,600	4,318	12,647
2008	869	497	23	11	38	58	126	295	639	1,595	4,342	12,765
Black:												
1990	748	1,736	68	28	69	160	299	639	1,453	2,866	5,688	13,310
2000	733	1,280	45	20	58	122	272	588	1,227	2,690	5,697	13,941
2005	704	1,180	37	19	51	110	250	568	1,104	2,342	5,264	12,790
2006	684	1,195	39	17	51	107	245	548	1,076	2,240	5,029	12,197
2007	676	1,132	39	17	49	102	229	537	1,047	2,210	4,903	11,997
2008	674	1,086	36	16	51	97	222	525	1,029	2,155	4,816	11,864
Asian or Pacific Islander:[2]												
1990	234	518	32	13	29	38	70	183	483	1,089	3,128	10,254
2000	262	434	20	12	22	28	66	156	391	996	2,882	9,052
2005	283	395	18	12	26	29	58	143	353	906	2,530	7,793
2006	286	357	21	10	25	29	57	145	333	898	2,526	7,560
2007	287	398	18	10	24	28	55	136	329	833	2,471	7,334
2008	301	377	20	9	23	35	49	136	328	867	2,437	7,479
American Indian, or Alaska Native:[2]												
1990	330	689	38	26	69	102	156	381	806	1,679	3,073	8,201
2000	346	492	40	18	59	85	172	285	772	1,900	3,850	9,118
2005	399	753	46	17	68	91	194	366	699	1,781	3,603	7,065
2006	400	690	51	17	64	92	205	342	687	1,657	3,746	6,634
2007	400	830	46	13	61	91	196	346	694	1,612	3,437	6,248
2008	386	495	40	17	58	99	218	342	668	1,562	3,261	5,997

[1] Figures for age not stated are included in "All ages" but not distributed among age groups. [2] The death rates for specified races other than white and black should be interpreted with caution because of inconsistencies between reporting race on death certificates and censuses and surveys.

Source: U.S. National Center for Health Statistics, *Health, United States, 2011*. See also <http://cdc.gov/nchs/hus.htm>.

Table 114. Age-Adjusted Death Rates by Sex, Race, and Hispanic Origin: 1970 to 2009

[Age-adjusted rates per 100,000 population. Age-adjusted death rates are better indicators than crude death rates for showing changes in the risk of death over time when the age distribution of the population is changing, and for comparing the mortality of population subgroups that have different age compositions. Populations enumerated as of April 1 for census years and estimated as of July 1 for all other years. Excludes deaths of nonresidents of the United States. Data for Hispanic-origin and specified races other than White and Black should be interpreted with caution because of inconsistencies reporting race on death certificates and on censuses and surveys. See text this section and Appendix III]

Sex, race, and Hispanic origin	1970	1980	1990	2000	2004	2005	2006	2007	2008	2009
ALL RACES [1]										
Total	**1,223**	**1,039**	**939**	**869**	**801**	**799**	**777**	**760**	**758**	**741**
Male	1,542	1,348	1,203	1,054	956	951	925	906	901	888
Female	971	818	751	731	679	678	658	643	643	626
WHITE										
Total	**1,193**	**1,013**	**910**	**850**	**786**	**785**	**764**	**749**	**750**	**733**
Male	1,514	1,318	1,166	1,029	937	933	908	891	889	876
Female	944	796	729	715	667	667	648	635	637	619
BLACK										
Total	**1,518**	**1,315**	**1,250**	**1,121**	**1,027**	**1,017**	**982**	**958**	**935**	**923**
Male	1,874	1,698	1,645	1,404	1,269	1,253	1,216	1,184	1,150	1,147
Female	1,229	1,033	975	928	855	846	813	794	778	767
ASIAN OR PACIFIC ISLANDER										
Total	**(NA)**	**590**	**582**	**506**	**444**	**440**	**429**	**415**	**414**	**411**
Male	(NA)	787	716	624	535	534	516	499	493	495
Female	(NA)	426	469	417	376	369	363	351	353	346
AMERICAN INDIAN OR ALASKA NATIVE										
Total	**(NA)**	**867**	**716**	**709**	**650**	**663**	**642**	**627**	**610**	**604**
Male	(NA)	1,112	916	842	758	775	740	737	717	698
Female	(NA)	662	562	605	558	568	556	533	515	522
HISPANIC ORIGIN [2]										
Total	**(NA)**	**(NA)**	**(NA)**	**666**	**587**	**591**	**564**	**546**	**532**	**523**
Male	(NA)	(NA)	886	818	707	717	676	655	631	624
Female	(NA)	(NA)	537	546	486	485	469	453	446	437
NON-HISPANIC, WHITE										
Total	**(NA)**	**(NA)**	**(NA)**	**856**	**797**	**797**	**777**	**763**	**766**	**748**
Male	(NA)	(NA)	1,171	1,035	949	945	923	907	909	896
Female	(NA)	(NA)	735	722	678	678	660	648	651	632

NA Not available. [1] For 1970 to 1990 includes deaths among races not shown separately. [2] Persons of Hispanic origin may be any race.

Source: U.S. National Center for Health Statistics, National Vital Statistics Reports (NVSR), *Deaths: Final Data for 2009*, Vol.60, No. 3, December 2011.

Table 115. Death Rates by Hispanic-Origin Status, Sex, and Age: 2000 to 2009

[Rates per 100,000 U.S. standard population. Rates are based on populations enumerated as of April 1 for census years and estimated as of July 1 for all other years. Excludes deaths of nonresidents of the United States. Data for Hispanic-origin should be interpreted with caution because of inconsistencies between reporting Hispanic origin and race on death certificates and censuses and surveys]

Age	Hispanic male			Hispanic female			Non-Hispanic White male			Non-Hispanic White female		
	2000	2005	2009	2000	2005	2009	2000	2005	2009	2000	2005	2009
Age adjusted [1]	818	717	624	546	485	437	1,035	945	896	722	678	632
Crude [2]	331	334	312	275	278	272	979	971	966	1,007	993	958
Under 1 year	637	670	530	554	555	450	659	626	565	531	497	461
1 to 4 years	32	33	24	28	25	22	32	30	27	24	22	21
5 to 14 years	18	15	14	13	12	12	20	17	14	14	13	10
15 to 24 years	108	120	96	32	37	32	104	106	92	43	42	38
25 to 34 years	120	116	104	43	41	46	123	134	137	57	62	65
35 to 44 years	211	182	154	101	91	86	234	236	226	128	137	136
45 to 54 years	439	417	376	224	216	209	498	517	514	285	299	312
55 to 64 years	966	876	823	548	494	474	1,171	1,080	1,058	742	677	646
65 to 74 years	2,288	2,029	1,783	1,423	1,292	1,136	2,931	2,585	2,333	1,891	1,730	1,568
75 to 84 years	5,395	4,857	4,110	3,625	3,366	3,071	6,978	6,420	5,858	4,819	4,580	4,217
85 years and over	13,086	10,141	8,769	11,203	9,068	7,805	17,853	15,401	15,361	14,972	13,683	12,609

[1] Age-adjusted death rates are better indicators than crude death rates for showing changes in the risk of death over time when the age distribution of the population is changing, and for comparing the mortality of population subgroups that have different age compositions. All age-adjusted death rates are standardized to the year 2000 population. [2] The total number of deaths in a given time period divided by the total resident population as of July 1.

Source: U.S. National Center for Health Statistics, National Vital Statistics Reports (NVSR), *Deaths: Final Data for 2009*, Vol. 60, No. 3, December 2011, and earlier reports.

Table 116. Deaths and Death Rates by State and Island Areas: 1990 to 2009

[2,148 represents 2,148,000. By state of residence. Except as noted, excludes deaths of nonresidents of the United States. Caution should be used in comparing death rates by state; rates are affected by the population composition of the area. See also Appendix III]

State	Number of deaths (1,000)						Death rate per 1,000 population [1]						Age-adjusted rate 2009 [1,2]
	1990	1995	2000	2005	2008	2009	1990	1995	2000	2005	2008	2009	
United States	**2,148**	**2,312**	**2,403**	**2,448**	**2,472**	**2,437**	**8.6**	**8.7**	**8.5**	**8.3**	**8.1**	**7.9**	**7.4**
Alabama	39	42	45	47	48	47	9.7	10.0	10.1	10.3	10.2	10.1	9.2
Alaska	2	3	3	3	3	4	4.0	4.2	4.6	4.8	5.1	5.2	7.6
Arizona	29	35	41	46	46	46	7.9	8.4	7.9	7.7	7.0	6.9	6.5
Arkansas	25	27	28	28	29	29	10.5	10.8	10.6	10.1	10.3	9.9	8.7
California	214	224	230	237	235	233	7.2	7.1	6.8	6.6	6.4	6.3	6.5
Colorado	22	25	27	30	31	31	6.6	6.7	6.3	6.4	6.3	6.2	6.9
Connecticut	28	29	30	29	29	29	8.4	9.0	8.8	8.4	8.2	8.1	6.8
Delaware	6	6	7	7	8	8	8.7	8.8	8.8	8.9	8.7	8.5	7.5
District of Columbia	7	7	6	5	5	5	12.0	12.4	10.5	10.0	8.7	8.1	8.1
Florida	134	153	164	171	171	170	10.4	10.8	10.3	9.6	9.3	9.2	6.7
Georgia	52	58	64	67	70	70	8.0	8.1	7.8	7.4	7.2	7.1	8.2
Hawaii	7	8	8	9	10	10	6.1	6.4	6.8	7.2	7.4	7.7	6.2
Idaho	7	9	10	11	11	11	7.4	7.3	7.4	7.4	7.2	7.2	7.2
Illinois	103	108	107	104	103	100	9.0	9.2	8.6	8.1	8.0	7.8	7.4
Indiana	50	53	55	56	57	56	8.9	9.2	9.1	8.9	8.9	8.7	8.2
Iowa	27	28	28	28	29	28	9.7	9.9	9.6	9.4	9.5	9.2	7.2
Kansas	22	24	25	25	25	24	9.0	9.3	9.2	9.0	8.9	8.5	7.6
Kentucky	35	37	40	40	41	41	9.5	9.6	9.8	9.6	9.7	9.6	9.0
Louisiana	38	40	41	44	41	40	8.9	9.1	9.2	9.8	9.3	9.0	8.9
Maine	11	12	12	13	13	13	9.0	9.5	9.7	9.7	9.5	9.6	7.6
Maryland	38	42	44	44	44	44	8.0	8.3	8.3	7.8	7.8	7.7	7.6
Massachusetts	53	55	57	54	54	52	8.8	9.1	8.9	8.4	8.2	7.9	6.8
Michigan	79	84	87	87	88	86	8.5	8.8	8.7	8.6	8.8	8.7	7.9
Minnesota	35	38	38	38	38	38	7.9	8.1	7.7	7.3	7.4	7.2	6.5
Mississippi	25	27	29	29	29	28	9.8	10.0	10.1	10.0	9.9	9.6	9.3
Missouri	50	54	55	55	57	54	9.8	10.2	9.8	9.4	9.6	9.1	8.0
Montana	7	8	8	9	9	9	8.6	8.8	9.0	9.1	9.2	9.0	7.6
Nebraska	15	15	15	15	15	15	9.4	9.3	8.8	8.5	8.7	8.2	7.2
Nevada	9	13	15	19	19	19	7.8	8.2	7.6	7.9	7.4	7.3	7.8
New Hampshire	8	9	10	10	10	10	7.7	8.0	7.8	7.8	7.8	7.6	6.8
New Jersey	70	74	75	72	70	68	9.1	9.3	8.9	8.3	8.1	7.8	6.9
New Mexico	11	13	13	15	16	16	7.0	7.4	7.4	7.8	8.1	7.8	7.4
New York	169	168	158	152	149	146	9.4	9.3	8.3	7.9	7.6	7.5	6.7
North Carolina	57	65	72	75	77	77	8.6	9.0	8.9	8.6	8.4	8.2	8.0
North Dakota	6	6	6	6	6	6	8.9	9.3	9.1	9.0	9.2	9.1	7.2
Ohio	99	106	108	109	110	107	9.1	9.5	9.5	9.5	9.6	9.3	8.1
Oklahoma	30	33	35	36	37	36	9.7	10.0	10.2	10.2	10.2	9.7	8.9
Oregon	25	28	30	31	32	32	8.8	9.0	8.6	8.5	8.4	8.3	7.3
Pennsylvania	122	128	131	130	127	125	10.3	10.6	10.7	10.4	10.2	9.9	7.7
Rhode Island	10	10	10	10	10	9	9.5	9.8	9.6	9.3	9.3	8.9	7.2
South Carolina	30	34	37	39	40	40	8.5	9.1	9.2	9.1	9.0	8.9	8.2
South Dakota	6	7	7	7	7	7	9.1	9.5	9.3	9.1	8.8	8.5	6.9
Tennessee	46	51	55	57	59	58	9.5	9.8	9.7	9.6	9.5	9.3	8.7
Texas	125	138	150	156	165	163	7.4	7.4	7.2	6.8	6.8	6.6	7.5
Utah	9	11	12	13	14	14	5.3	5.6	5.5	5.4	5.1	5.1	6.6
Vermont	5	5	5	5	5	5	8.2	8.5	8.4	8.1	8.4	8.1	6.8
Virginia	48	53	56	58	59	59	7.8	8.0	8.0	7.6	7.6	7.4	7.5
Washington	37	41	44	46	49	48	7.6	7.5	7.5	7.3	7.4	7.2	7.1
West Virginia	19	20	21	21	22	21	10.8	11.1	11.7	11.4	11.9	11.8	9.5
Wisconsin	43	45	46	47	47	46	8.7	8.8	8.7	8.4	8.3	8.1	7.1
Wyoming	3	4	4	4	4	4	7.1	7.7	7.9	8.0	7.9	7.9	7.8
Puerto Rico	26	30	28	30	29	29	7.3	8.1	7.2	7.5	7.3	7.3	6.9
Virgin Islands	(Z)	1	1	1	1	1	4.6	5.8	5.3	6.1	6.8	6.1	6.3
Guam	1	1	1	1	1	1	3.9	4.1	4.2	4.0	4.4	4.7	6.9
American Samoa	(NA)	(NA)	(Z)	(Z)	(Z)	(Z)	(NA)	(NA)	3.3	4.4	3.7	4.7	12.2
Northern Marianas	(NA)	(NA)	(Z)	(Z)	(Z)	(Z)	(NA)	(NA)	1.9	2.3	3.2	3.9	9.4

NA Not available. Z Less than 500. [1] Rates based on enumerated resident population as of April 1 for 1990 and 2000; estimated resident population as of July 1 for all other years. [2] Age-adjusted death rates are better indicators than crude death rates for showing changes in the risk of death over time when the age distribution of the population is changing, and for comparing the mortality of population subgroups that have different age compositions. See text this section.

Source: U.S. National Center for Health Statistics, National Vital Statistics Reports (NVSR), *Deaths: Final Data for 2009*, Vol. 60, No. 3, December 2011, and earlier reports.

Table 117. Fetal and Infant Deaths: 1990 to 2006

[The term "fetal death" defined on an all inclusive basis to end confusion arising from the use of such terms as stillbirth, spontaneous abortion, and miscarriage have been adopted by the National Center for Health Statistics (NCHS) as the nationally recommended standard. Fetal deaths do not include induced terminations of pregnancy. See also Appendix III]

Year	Fetal deaths [1]			Infant deaths		Fetal mortality rate [2]			Perinatal mortality rate	
	Total [1]	20 to 27 weeks [3]	28 weeks or more [3]	Less than 7 days	Less than 28 days	Total [1]	20–27 weeks [3]	28 weeks or more [3]	Defi-nition I [4]	Defi-nition II [5]
1990.....	31,386	13,427	17,959	19,439	23,591	7.49	3.22	4.30	8.95	13.12
1995.....	27,294	13,043	14,251	15,483	19,186	6.95	3.33	3.64	7.60	11.84
1996.....	27,069	12,990	14,079	14,947	18,556	6.91	3.33	3.60	7.43	11.64
1997.....	26,486	12,800	13,686	14,827	18,507	6.78	3.29	3.51	7.32	11.51
1998.....	26,702	13,229	13,473	15,061	18,915	6.73	3.35	3.41	7.21	11.50
1999.....	26,884	13,457	13,427	14,874	18,700	6.74	3.39	3.38	7.12	11.44
2000.....	27,003	13,497	13,506	14,893	18,733	6.61	3.31	3.32	6.97	11.19
2001.....	26,373	13,122	13,251	14,622	18,275	6.51	3.25	3.28	6.90	11.02
2002.....	25,943	13,072	12,871	15,020	18,791	6.41	3.24	3.19	6.91	11.05
2003.....	26,004	13,348	12,656	15,152	18,935	6.32	3.25	3.08	6.78	10.92
2004.....	26,001	13,068	12,933	14,836	18,602	6.28	3.17	3.14	6.73	10.78
2005.....	25,894	13,327	12,567	15,013	18,782	6.22	3.21	3.03	6.64	10.73
2006.....	25,972	13,270	12,702	15,148	19,041	6.05	3.10	2.97	6.51	10.49

[1] Fetal deaths with stated or presumed gestation of 20 weeks or more. [2] Rate per 1,000 live births and fetal deaths in specified group. [3] Not stated gestational age proportionally distributed. [4] Infant deaths of less than 7 days and fetal deaths with stated or presumed period of gestation of 28 weeks or more, per 1,000 live births and fetal deaths. [5] Infant deaths of less than 28 days and fetal deaths with stated or presumed period of gestation of 20 weeks or more per 1,000 live births and fetal deaths.

Source: U.S. National Center for Health Statistics, National Vital Statistics Reports (NVSR), *Fetal and Perinatal Mortality, U.S., 2006*, Vol. 60. No. 8, August 2012. See also <http://www.cdc.gov/nchs/fetal_death.htm>.

Table 118. Infant, Neonatal, and Maternal Mortality Rates by Race: 1980 to 2008

[Deaths per 1,000 live births, except as noted. Data based on death certificates, fetal death records, and birth certificates. Excludes deaths of nonresidents of the United States. See also Appendix III]

Race and year	Infant [1]	Neonatal [1]		Post-neonatal [1]	Fetal mortality rate [2]	Late fetal mortality rate [3]	Perinatal mortality rate [4]	Maternal mortality rate [5]
		Under 28 days	Under 7 days					
ALL RACES								
1980........................	12.6	8.5	7.1	4.1	9.1	6.2	13.2	9.2
1990........................	9.2	5.8	4.8	3.4	7.5	4.3	9.1	8.2
1995........................	7.6	4.9	4.0	2.7	7.0	3.6	7.6	7.1
2000........................	6.9	4.6	3.7	2.3	6.6	3.3	7.0	9.8
2003........................	6.9	4.6	3.7	2.2	6.3	3.1	6.8	[6] 12.1
2004........................	6.8	4.5	3.6	2.3	6.3	3.1	6.7	[6] 13.1
2005........................	6.9	4.5	3.6	2.3	6.2	3.0	6.6	[6] 15.1
2006........................	6.7	4.5	3.5	2.2	(NA)	(NA)	(NA)	13.3
2007........................	6.8	4.4	3.5	2.3	(NA)	(NA)	(NA)	12.7
2008........................	6.6	4.3	3.4	2.3	(NA)	(NA)	(NA)	(NA)
WHITE [7]								
1980........................	10.9	7.4	6.1	3.5	8.1	5.7	11.8	6.7
1990........................	7.6	4.8	3.9	2.8	6.4	3.8	7.7	5.4
1995........................	6.3	4.1	3.3	2.2	5.9	3.3	6.5	4.2
2000........................	5.7	3.8	3.0	1.9	5.6	2.9	5.9	7.5
2003........................	5.7	3.9	3.1	1.8	5.2	2.7	5.8	[6] 8.7
2004........................	5.7	3.8	3.0	1.9	5.4	2.8	5.8	[6] 9.3
2005........................	5.7	3.8	3.0	1.9	5.3	2.7	5.7	[6] 11.1
2006........................	5.6	3.7	2.9	1.8	(NA)	(NA)	(NA)	9.5
2007........................	5.6	3.7	2.9	1.9	(NA)	(NA)	(NA)	10.0
2008........................	5.5	3.6	2.9	1.9	(NA)	(NA)	(NA)	(NA)
BLACK [7]								
1980........................	22.2	14.6	12.3	7.6	14.7	9.1	21.3	21.5
1990........................	18.0	11.6	9.7	6.4	13.3	6.7	16.4	22.4
1995........................	15.1	9.8	8.2	5.3	12.7	5.7	13.8	22.1
2000........................	14.1	9.4	7.6	4.7	12.4	5.4	13.0	22.0
2003........................	14.0	9.4	7.5	4.6	12.1	5.1	12.5	[6] 30.5
2004........................	13.8	9.1	7.3	4.7	11.6	5.0	12.2	[6] 34.7
2005........................	13.7	9.1	7.3	4.7	11.4	4.9	12.1	[6] 36.5
2006........................	13.3	8.8	7.0	4.5	(NA)	(NA)	(NA)	32.7
2007........................	13.2	8.6	6.9	4.6	(NA)	(NA)	(NA)	26.5
2008........................	12.7	8.2	6.6	4.5	(NA)	(NA)	(NA)	(NA)

NA Not available. [1] Infant (under 1 year of age), neonatal (under 28 days), early neonatal (under 7 days), and postneonatal (28 days–11 months). [2] Number of fetal deaths of 20 weeks or more gestation per 1,000 live births plus fetal deaths. [3] Number of fetal deaths of 28 weeks or more gestation (late fetal deaths) per 1,000 live births plus late fetal deaths. [4] Number of late fetal deaths plus infant deaths within 7 days of birth per 1,000 live births plus late fetal deaths. [5] Per 100,000 live births from deliveries and complications of pregnancy, childbirth, and the puerperium. Beginning 2000, deaths are classified according to the tenth revision of the International Classification of Diseases; earlier years classified according to the revision in use at the time; see text, this section. [6] Increase partially reflects the use of a separate item on the death certificate on pregnancy status by an increasing number of states. [7] Infant deaths are tabulated by race of decedent; fetal deaths and live births are tabulated by race of mother.

Source: U.S. National Center for Health Statistics, *Health, United States, 2011*. See also <http://cdc.gov/nchs/hus.htm>.

Table 119. Infant Mortality Rates by Race, States, and Island Areas: 1980 to 2008

[Deaths per 1,000 live births, by place of residence. Represents deaths of infants under 1 year old, exclusive of fetal deaths. Excludes deaths of nonresidents of the United States. See headnote, Table 115 and Appendix III]

State	Total [1]				White				Black			
	1980	1990	2000	2008	1980	1990	2000	2008	1980	1990	2000	2008
United States....	**12.6**	**9.2**	**6.9**	**6.6**	**10.9**	**7.6**	**5.7**	**5.5**	**22.2**	**18.0**	**14.1**	**12.74**
Alabama...........	15.1	10.8	9.4	9.5	11.6	8.1	6.6	7.6	21.6	16.0	15.4	13.98
Alaska..............	12.3	10.5	6.8	5.9	9.4	7.6	5.8	3.4	19.5	(B)	(B)	(B)
Arizona............	12.4	8.8	6.7	6.4	11.8	7.8	6.2	5.6	18.4	20.6	17.6	17.14
Arkansas..........	12.7	9.2	8.4	7.4	10.3	8.4	7.0	6.0	20.0	13.9	13.7	13.22
California..........	11.1	7.9	5.4	5.1	10.6	7.0	5.1	4.8	18.0	16.8	12.9	12.06
Colorado...........	10.1	8.8	6.2	6.2	9.8	7.8	5.6	5.8	19.1	19.4	19.5	14.93
Connecticut........	11.2	7.9	6.6	6.0	10.2	6.3	5.6	4.8	19.1	17.6	14.4	12.4
Delaware..........	13.9	10.1	9.2	8.4	9.8	9.7	7.9	6.1	27.9	20.1	14.8	15.5
District of Columbia........	25.0	20.7	12.0	10.8	17.8	(B)	(B)	(B)	26.7	24.6	16.1	15.6
Florida..............	14.6	9.6	7.0	7.2	11.8	6.7	5.4	5.8	22.8	16.8	12.6	11.94
Georgia............	14.5	12.4	8.5	8.1	10.8	7.4	5.9	5.6	21.0	18.3	13.9	12.64
Hawaii..............	10.3	6.7	8.1	5.5	11.6	6.1	6.5	4.3	(B)	(B)	(B)	(B)
Idaho...............	10.7	8.7	7.5	5.9	10.7	8.6	7.5	6.0	(NA)	(B)	(B)	(B)
Illinois..............	14.8	10.7	8.5	7.1	11.7	7.9	6.6	5.7	26.3	22.4	17.1	14.08
Indiana.............	11.9	9.6	7.8	6.9	10.5	7.9	6.9	5.9	23.4	17.4	15.8	14.7
Iowa...............	11.8	8.1	6.5	5.7	11.5	7.9	6.0	5.3	27.2	21.9	21.1	14.16
Kansas.............	10.4	8.4	6.8	7.3	9.5	8.0	6.4	6.6	20.6	17.7	12.2	13.73
Kentucky...........	12.9	8.5	7.2	6.9	12.0	8.2	6.7	6.5	22.0	14.3	12.7	10.91
Louisiana..........	14.3	11.1	9.0	9.1	10.5	8.1	5.9	6.7	20.6	16.7	13.3	12.85
Maine..............	9.2	6.2	4.9	5.5	9.4	6.7	4.8	5.4	(B)	(B)	(B)	(B)
Maryland...........	14.0	9.5	7.6	8.0	11.6	6.8	4.8	5.4	20.4	17.1	13.2	13.17
Massachusetts.....	10.5	7.0	4.6	5.1	10.1	6.1	4.0	4.6	16.8	11.9	9.9	9.43
Michigan...........	12.8	10.7	8.2	7.4	10.6	7.4	6.0	5.8	24.2	21.6	18.2	14.51
Minnesota.........	10.0	7.3	5.6	6.0	9.6	6.7	4.8	5.1	20.0	23.7	14.6	11.59
Mississippi.........	17.0	12.1	10.7	10.0	11.1	7.4	6.8	7.5	23.7	16.2	15.3	13.15
Missouri............	12.4	9.4	7.2	7.2	11.1	7.9	5.9	6.0	20.7	18.2	14.7	15.01
Montana............	12.4	9.0	6.1	6.8	11.8	6.0	5.5	6.6	(NA)	(B)	(B)	(B)
Nebraska...........	11.5	8.3	7.3	5.4	10.7	6.9	6.4	4.8	25.2	18.9	20.3	14.55
Nevada............	10.7	8.4	6.5	5.3	10.0	8.2	6.0	4.9	20.6	14.2	12.7	12.65
New Hampshire....	9.9	7.1	5.7	4.0	9.9	6.0	5.5	4.1	22.5	(B)	(B)	(B)
New Jersey........	12.5	9.0	6.3	5.6	10.3	6.4	5.0	4.5	21.9	18.4	13.6	11.98
New Mexico........	11.5	9.0	6.6	5.6	11.3	7.6	6.3	5.8	23.1	(B)	(B)	(B)
New York..........	12.5	9.6	6.4	5.5	10.8	7.4	5.4	4.5	20.0	18.1	10.9	10.5
North Carolina......	14.5	10.6	8.6	8.2	12.1	8.0	6.3	6.1	20.0	16.5	15.7	14.71
North Dakota.......	12.1	8.0	8.1	5.8	11.7	7.2	7.5	5.0	27.5	(B)	(B)	(B)
Ohio................	12.8	9.8	7.6	7.7	11.2	7.8	6.3	6.0	23.0	19.5	15.4	16.29
Oklahoma..........	12.7	9.2	8.5	7.3	12.1	9.1	7.9	6.4	21.8	14.3	16.9	14.95
Oregon.............	12.2	8.3	5.6	5.2	12.2	7.0	5.5	4.8	15.9	(B)	(B)	(B)
Pennsylvania.......	13.2	9.6	7.1	7.4	11.9	7.4	5.8	6.5	23.1	20.5	15.7	12.25
Rhode Island.......	11.0	8.1	6.3	5.9	10.9	7.0	5.9	5.3	(B)	(B)	(B)	(B)
South Carolina.....	15.6	11.7	8.7	8.0	10.8	8.1	5.4	6.4	22.9	17.3	14.8	11.39
South Dakota.......	10.9	10.1	5.5	8.4	9.0	8.0	4.3	6.6	(NA)	(B)	(B)	(B)
Tennessee..........	13.5	10.3	9.1	8.1	11.9	7.3	6.8	6.4	19.3	17.9	18.0	14.71
Texas..............	12.2	8.1	5.7	6.2	11.2	6.7	5.1	5.8	18.8	14.7	11.4	9.77
Utah................	10.4	7.5	5.2	4.8	10.5	6.0	5.1	4.6	27.3	(B)	(B)	(B)
Vermont............	10.7	6.4	6.0	4.6	10.7	5.9	6.1	4.4	(B)	(B)	(B)	(B)
Virginia............	13.6	10.2	6.9	6.9	11.9	7.4	5.4	5.5	19.8	19.5	12.4	12.17
Washington.........	11.8	7.8	5.2	5.4	11.5	7.3	4.9	5.1	16.4	20.6	9.4	10.29
West Virginia.......	11.8	9.9	7.6	7.7	11.4	8.1	7.4	7.2	21.5	(B)	(B)	(B)
Wisconsin..........	10.3	8.2	6.6	7.0	9.7	7.7	5.5	5.9	18.5	19.0	17.2	15.77
Wyoming...........	9.8	8.6	6.7	7.0	9.3	7.5	6.5	6.2	25.9	(B)	(B)	(B)
Puerto Rico.......	(NA)	(NA)	9.7	8.5	(NA)	(NA)	10.2	9.2	(NA)	(NA)	(B)	(B)
Virgin Islands.....	(NA)	(NA)	13.4	(B)	(NA)	(NA)	(B)	(B)	(B)	(B)	(B)	(B)
Guam..............	(NA)	(NA)	5.8	8.7	(NA)	(NA)	(B)	(B)	(B)	(B)	(B)	(B)
American Samoa...........	(NA)	(NA)	(B)	(B)	(B)	(B)	(B)	(B)	(B)	(B)	(B)	(B)
Northern Marianas.........	(NA)	(NA)	(B)	(B)	(B)	(B)	(B)	(B)	(B)	(B)	(B)	(B)

B Base figure too small to meet statistical standards for reliability. NA Not available. [1] Includes other races, not shown separately.

Source: U.S. National Center for Health Statistics, National Vital Statistics Reports (NVSR), *Deaths: Final Data for 2008*, Vol. 59, No. 10, December 2011, and earlier reports. See also <http://www.cdc.gov/nchs/nvss.htm>.

Table 120. Age-Adjusted Death Rates by Major Causes: 1960 to 2010

[Age-adjusted rates per 100,000 population. Age adjusted death rates were prepared using the direct method, in which age specific death rates for a population of interest are applied to a standard population distributed by age. Age adjustment eliminates the differences in observed rates between points in time or among compared population groups that result from age differences in population composition. Beginning 1999 deaths classified according to tenth revision of International Classification of Diseases; for earlier years, causes of death were classified according to the revisions then in use. Changes in classification of causes of death due to these revisions may result in discontinuities in cause-of-death trends. See Appendix III]

Year	Dis-eases of the heart	Malignant neo-plasms (cancer)	Cerebro-vascular diseases	Chronic lower res-piratory diseases	Acci-dents [1]	Alz-heimer's disease	Dia-betes mellitus	Influenza and pneu-monia	Nephritis, nephrotic syndrome and nephrosis	Inten-tional self-harm (suicide)
1960......	559.0	193.9	177.9	12.5	63.1	(NA)	22.5	53.7	10.6	12.5
1961......	545.3	193.4	173.1	12.6	60.6	(NA)	22.1	43.4	10.0	12.2
1962......	556.9	193.3	174.0	14.2	62.9	(NA)	22.6	47.1	9.6	12.8
1963......	563.4	194.7	173.9	16.5	64.0	(NA)	23.1	55.6	9.2	13.0
1964......	543.3	193.6	167.0	16.3	64.1	(NA)	22.5	45.4	8.9	12.7
1965......	542.5	195.6	166.4	18.3	65.8	(NA)	22.9	46.8	8.3	13.0
1966......	541.2	196.5	165.8	19.2	67.6	(NA)	23.6	47.9	7.9	12.7
1967......	524.7	197.3	159.3	19.2	66.2	(NA)	23.4	42.2	7.3	12.5
1968......	531.0	198.8	162.5	20.7	65.5	(NA)	25.3	52.8	6.1	12.4
1969......	516.8	198.5	155.4	20.9	64.9	(NA)	25.1	47.9	6.0	12.7
1970......	492.7	198.6	147.7	21.3	62.2	(NA)	24.3	41.7	5.5	13.1
1971......	492.9	199.3	147.6	21.8	60.3	(NA)	23.9	38.4	5.2	13.1
1972......	490.2	200.3	147.3	22.8	60.2	(NA)	23.7	41.3	5.2	13.3
1973......	482.0	200.0	145.2	23.6	59.3	(NA)	23.0	41.2	5.0	13.1
1974......	458.8	201.5	136.8	23.2	52.7	(NA)	22.1	35.5	4.7	13.2
1975......	431.2	200.1	123.5	23.7	50.8	(NA)	20.3	34.9	4.7	13.6
1976......	426.9	202.5	117.4	24.9	48.7	(NA)	19.5	38.8	4.9	13.2
1977......	413.7	203.5	110.4	24.7	48.8	(NA)	18.2	31.0	4.8	13.7
1978......	409.9	204.9	103.7	26.3	48.9	(NA)	18.3	34.5	4.8	12.9
1979......	401.6	204.0	97.1	25.5	46.5	(NA)	17.5	26.1	8.6	12.6
1980......	412.1	207.9	96.4	28.3	46.4	(NA)	18.1	31.4	9.1	12.2
1981......	397.0	206.4	89.5	29.0	43.4	0.9	17.6	30.0	9.1	12.3
1982......	389.0	208.3	84.2	29.1	40.1	1.3	17.2	26.5	9.4	12.5
1983......	388.9	209.1	81.2	31.6	39.1	2.2	17.6	29.8	9.6	12.4
1984......	378.8	210.8	78.7	32.4	38.8	3.1	17.2	30.6	10.0	12.6
1985......	375.0	211.3	76.6	34.5	38.5	4.1	17.4	34.5	10.4	12.5
1986......	365.1	211.5	73.1	34.8	38.6	4.6	17.2	34.8	10.4	13.0
1987......	355.9	211.7	71.6	35.0	38.2	5.5	17.4	33.8	10.4	12.8
1988......	352.5	212.5	70.6	36.5	38.9	5.8	18.0	37.3	10.4	12.5
1989......	332.0	214.2	66.9	36.6	37.7	6.1	20.5	35.9	9.6	12.3
1990......	321.8	216.0	65.3	37.2	36.3	6.3	20.7	36.8	9.3	12.5
1991......	312.5	215.2	62.9	37.9	34.7	6.3	20.7	34.7	9.3	12.3
1992......	304.0	213.5	61.5	37.7	33.2	6.3	20.7	32.8	9.4	12.0
1993......	308.1	213.5	62.7	40.7	34.2	7.1	21.9	35.0	9.7	12.1
1994......	297.5	211.7	62.6	40.3	34.2	7.7	22.6	33.6	9.4	11.9
1995......	293.4	209.9	63.1	40.1	34.4	8.4	23.2	33.4	9.5	11.8
1996......	285.7	206.7	62.5	40.6	34.5	8.5	23.8	32.9	9.6	11.5
1997......	277.7	203.4	61.1	41.1	34.2	8.7	23.7	33.3	9.8	11.2
1998......	267.4	202.1	62.8	43.8	35.6	8.6	24.2	24.2	9.8	11.1
1999......	266.5	200.8	61.6	45.4	35.3	16.5	25.0	23.5	13.0	10.5
2000......	257.6	199.6	60.9	44.2	34.9	18.1	25.0	23.7	13.5	10.4
2001......	247.8	196.0	57.9	43.7	35.7	19.1	25.3	22.0	14.0	10.7
2002......	240.8	193.5	56.2	43.5	36.9	20.2	25.4	22.6	14.2	10.9
2003......	232.3	190.1	53.5	43.3	37.3	21.4	25.3	22.0	14.4	10.8
2004......	217.0	185.8	50.0	41.1	37.7	21.8	24.5	19.8	14.2	10.9
2005......	211.1	183.8	46.6	43.2	39.1	22.9	24.6	20.3	14.3	10.9
2006......	200.2	180.7	43.6	40.5	39.8	22.6	23.3	17.8	14.5	10.9
2007......	190.9	178.4	42.2	40.8	40.0	22.7	22.5	16.2	14.5	11.3
2008......	186.5	175.3	40.7	44.0	38.8	24.4	21.8	16.9	14.8	11.6
2009......	182.8	173.5	39.6	42.7	37.5	24.2	21.0	16.5	15.1	11.8
2010 [2].....	178.5	172.5	39.0	42.1	37.1	25.0	20.8	15.1	15.3	11.9

NA Not available. [1] Unintentional injuries. [2] Preliminary data.

Source: U.S. National Center for Health Statistics, National Vital Statistics Reports (NVSR), *Deaths: Final Data for 2008*, Vol. 59, No. 10, December 2011 and *Deaths: Preliminary Data for 2010*, Vol. 60, No. 4, January 2012. See also <http://www.cdc.gov/nchs/products/nvsr.htm>.

Table 121. Leading Causes of Deaths by Race: 2008

[Cause of death based on International Classification of Diseases (ICD), tenth edition]

Cause of death	White			Black			American Indian/ Alaskan Native			Asian/ Pacific Islander		
	Rank [1]	Deaths	Percent	Rank	Deaths	Percent	Rank	Deaths	Percent	Rank	Deaths	Percent
All causes	(X)	**2,120,233**	**100.0**	(X)	**289,072**	**100.0**	(X)	**14,776**	**100.0**	(X)	**47,903**	**100.0**
Diseases of heart	1	532,304	25.1	1	70,731	24.5	2	2,657	18.0	2	11,136	23.2
Malignant neoplasms	2	485,893	22.9	2	63,954	22.1	1	2,727	18.5	1	12,895	26.9
Chronic lower respiratory diseases	3	130,221	6.1	6	8,766	3.0	6	619	4.2	7	1,484	3.1
Cerebrovascular diseases	4	113,244	5.3	3	16,710	5.8	7	517	3.5	3	3,677	7.7
Accidents (unintentional injuries)	5	105,715	5.0	4	12,447	4.3	3	1,682	11.4	4	2,058	4.3
Alzheimer's disease	6	76,263	3.6	12	5,075	1.8	13	204	1.4	9	893	1.9
Diabetes mellitus	7	55,893	2.6	5	12,064	4.2	4	779	5.3	5	1,817	3.8
Influenza and pneumonia	8	48,941	2.3	11	5,456	1.9	9	379	2.6	6	1,508	3.1
Nephritis, nephrotic syndrome and nephrosis	9	38,352	1.8	7	8,619	3.0	10	338	2.3	8	928	1.9
Intentional self harm (suicide)	10	32,644	1.5	16	2,106	0.7	8	409	2.8	10	876	1.8
Septicemia	11	28,697	1.4	9	6,426	2.2	12	244	1.7	12	560	1.2
Chronic liver disease and cirrhosis	12	26,275	1.2	15	2,506	0.9	5	742	5.0	14	440	0.9
Assault (homicide)	18	8,893	0.4	8	8,335	2.9	11	255	1.7	15	343	0.7
Human immunodeficiency virus (HIV)	24	4,339	0.2	10	5,780	2.0	20	66	0.4	23	100	0.2

X Not applicable. [1] Rank based on number of deaths.

Source: U.S. National Center for Health Statistics, National Vital Statistics Reports (NVSR), *Deaths: Leading Causes for 2008*, Vol. 60, No. 6, June 2012. See also <http://www.cdc.gov/nchs/deaths.htm>.

Table 122. Leading Causes of Deaths by Hispanic Origin: 2008

[Race and Hispanic origin are reported separately on death certificate. Persons of Hispanic origin may be any race. Cause of death based on International Classification of Diseases (ICD), tenth edition]

Cause of death	Hispanic			Non-Hispanic			Non-Hispanic White			Non-Hispanic Black		
	Rank	Deaths	Percent	Rank	Deaths	Percent	Rank	Deaths	Percent	Rank	Deaths	Percent
All causes	(X)	**139,241**	**100.0**	(X)	**2,327,636**	**100.0**	(X)	**1,981,034**	**100.0**	(X)	**285,522**	**100.0**
Diseases of heart	1	28,951	20.8	1	586,514	25.2	1	503,096	25.4	1	69,918	24.5
Malignant neoplasms	2	28,851	20.7	2	535,675	23.0	2	457,084	23.1	2	63,279	22.2
Accidents (unintentional injuries)	3	11,080	8.0	5	110,476	4.7	5	94,722	4.8	4	12,215	4.3
Cerebrovascular diseases	4	7,121	5.1	4	126,777	5.4	4	106,134	5.4	3	16,527	5.8
Diabetes mellitus	5	6,544	4.7	7	63,848	2.7	7	49,388	2.5	5	11,934	4.2
Chronic liver disease and cirrhosis	6	4,091	2.9	12	25,813	1.1	12	22,210	1.1	15	2,464	0.9
Chronic lower respiratory diseases	7	3,949	2.8	3	136,895	5.9	3	126,146	6.4	6	8,679	3.0
Assault (homicide)	8	3,331	2.4	16	14,427	0.6	22	5,656	0.3	8	8,206	2.9
Influenza and pneumonia	9	3,176	2.3	8	53,024	2.3	8	45,780	2.3	11	5,396	1.9
Alzheimer's disease	10	3,005	2.2	6	79,323	3.4	6	73,219	3.7	13	5,024	1.8
Nephritis, nephrotic syndrome and nephrosis	11	2,903	2.1	9	45,245	1.9	9	35,439	1.8	7	8,564	3.0
Intentional self harm (suicide)	13	2,345	1.7	11	33,589	1.4	10	30,281	1.5	16	2,063	0.7
Septicemia	15	2,004	1.4	10	33,839	1.5	11	26,692	1.3	9	6,359	2.2
Human immunodeficiency virus (HIV)	17	1,365	1.0	20	8,846	0.4	25	3,003	0.2	10	5,686	2.0

X Not applicable.

Source: U.S. National Center for Health Statistics, National Vital Statistics Reports (NVSR), *Deaths: Leading Causes for 2008*, Vol. 60, No.6, June 2012. See also http://www.cdc.gov/nchs/deaths.htm>.

Table 123. Deaths and Death Rates by Selected Causes: 2007 and 2008

[Rates per 100,000 population. Figures are weighted data rounded to the nearest individual, so categories may not add to total or subtotal. Excludes deaths of nonresidents of the United States. Deaths classified according to tenth revision of International Classification of Diseases (ICD). See also Appendix III]

Cause of death	2007			2008		
	Number	Rate	Age-adjusted rate [1]	Number	Rate	Age-adjusted rate [1]
All causes [2]	2,423,712	803.6	760.2	2,471,984	813.0	758.3
Major cardiovascular diseases [2]	806,156	267.3	249.9	804,483	264.6	243.5
Diseases of heart	616,067	204.3	190.9	616,828	202.9	186.5
Acute rheumatic fever and chronic rheumatic heart disease	3,201	1.1	1.0	3,141	1.0	1.0
Hypertensive heart disease	30,780	10.2	9.5	32,391	10.7	9.8
Hypertensive heart and renal disease	2,987	1.0	0.9	2,872	0.9	0.9
Ischemic heart disease	406,351	134.7	126.0	405,309	133.3	122.7
Acute myocardial infarction	132,968	44.1	41.4	133,958	44.1	40.7
Other heart diseases	172,748	57.3	53.4	173,115	56.9	52.3
Heart failure	56,565	18.8	17.3	56,830	18.7	16.9
Essential (primary) hypertension and hypertensive renal disease	23,965	7.9	7.4	25,742	8.5	7.7
Cerebrovascular diseases	135,952	45.1	42.2	134,148	44.1	40.7
Atherosclerosis	8,232	2.7	2.5	7,836	2.6	2.3
Malignant neoplasms [2]	562,875	186.6	178.4	565,469	186.0	175.3
Malignant neoplasms of lip, oral cavity, and pharynx	8,067	2.7	2.5	8,019	2.6	2.4
Malignant neoplasms of esophagus	13,592	4.5	4.3	13,714	4.5	4.2
Malignant neoplasms of stomach	11,388	3.8	36.0	11,352	3.7	3.5
Malignant neoplasms of colon, rectum and anus	53,586	17.8	16.9	53,321	17.5	16.4
Malignant neoplasms of liver and intrahepatic bile ducts	17,146	5.7	5.4	18,213	6.0	5.6
Malignant neoplasms of pancreas	34,117	11.3	10.8	35,236	11.6	10.9
Malignant neoplasms of trachea, bronchus and lung	158,760	52.6	50.6	158,656	52.2	49.5
Malignant melanoma of skin	8,461	2.8	2.7	8,623	2.8	2.7
Malignant neoplasm of breast	40,970	13.6	12.9	41,026	13.5	12.6
Malignant neoplasm of ovary	14,621	4.8	4.6	14,362	4.7	4.4
Malignant neoplasm of prostate	29,093	9.6	9.2	28,475	9.4	8.8
Malignant neoplasms of kidney and renal pelvis	12,703	4.2	4.0	12,895	4.2	4.0
Malignant neoplasms of bladder	13,843	4.6	4.4	14,036	4.6	4.3
Malignant neoplasms of meninges, brain and other parts of central nervous system	13,234	4.4	4.2	13,724	4.5	4.3
Malignant neoplasms of lymphoid, hematopoietic and related tissue [2]	54,991	18.2	17.6	54,954	18.1	17.2
Non-Hodgkins' lymphoma	20,528	6.8	6.5	20,369	6.7	6.3
Leukemia	21,825	7.2	7.0	22,335	7.3	7.0
Accidents (unintentional injuries)	123,706	41.0	40.0	121,902	40.1	38.8
Transport accidents [2]	46,844	15.5	15.3	42,709	14.0	13.8
Motor vehicle accidents	43,945	14.6	14.4	39,790	13.1	12.9
Nontransport accidents [2]	76,862	25.5	24.6	79,193	26.0	25.0
Falls	22,631	7.5	7.0	24,013	7.9	7.3
Accidental drowning and submersion	3,443	1.1	1.1	3,548	1.2	1.2
Accidental exposure to smoke, fire and flames	3,286	1.1	1.1	2,912	1.0	0.9
Accidental poisoning and exposure to noxious substances	29,846	9.9	9.8	31,116	10.2	10.2
Chronic lower respiratory diseases [2]	127,924	42.4	40.8	141,090	46.4	44.0
Emphysema	12,790	4.2	4.1	12,448	4.1	3.9
Asthma	3,447	1.1	1.1	3,397	1.1	1.0
Influenza and pneumonia [2]	52,717	17.5	16.2	56,284	18.5	16.9
Pneumonia	52,306	17.3	16.1	54,562	17.9	16.4
Septicemia (blood poisoning)	34,828	11.5	11.0	35,927	11.8	11.1
Viral hepatitis	7,407	2.5	2.3	7,629	2.5	2.3
Human immunodeficiency virus (HIV) disease	11,295	3.7	3.7	10,285	3.4	3.3
Anemias	4,829	1.6	1.5	5,018	1.7	1.5
Diabetes mellitus	71,382	23.7	22.5	70,553	23.2	21.8
Nutritional deficiencies	2,852	0.9	0.9	2,976	1.0	0.9
Malnutrition	2,644	0.9	0.8	2,760	0.9	0.8
Parkinson's disease	20,058	6.7	6.4	20,483	6.7	6.4
Alzheimer's disease	74,632	24.7	22.7	82,435	27.1	24.4
Chronic liver disease and cirrhosis	29,165	9.7	9.1	29,963	9.9	9.2
Alcoholic liver disease	14,406	4.8	4.5	14,864	4.9	4.5
Nephritis, nephrotic syndrome, and nephrosis [2]	46,448	15.4	14.5	48,237	15.9	14.8
Renal failure	43,263	14.3	13.6	43,935	14.4	13.5
Intentional self-harm (suicide)	34,598	11.5	11.3	36,035	11.9	11.6
Intentional self-harm (suicide) by discharge of firearms	17,352	5.8	5.6	18,223	6.0	5.8
Assault (homicide)	18,361	6.1	6.1	17,826	5.9	5.9
Assault (homicide) by discharge of firearms	12,632	4.2	4.2	12,179	4.0	4.0
Events of undetermined intent	5,381	1.8	1.8	5,051	1.7	1.6
Drug-induced deaths [3]	38,371	12.7	12.6	38,649	12.7	12.6
Alcohol-induced deaths [3]	23,199	7.7	7.3	24,189	8.0	7.4

[1] See text, this section. [2] Includes other causes, not shown separately. [3] Included in selected categories.

Source: U.S. National Center for Health Statistics, National Vital Statistics Reports (NVSR), *Deaths: Final Data for 2008*, Vol. 59, No. 10, December 2011. See also: <http://www.cdc.gov/nchs/deaths.htm>.

Table 124. Deaths by Age and Selected Causes: 2008

[Deaths are classified according to the tenth revision of the International Classification of Diseases. See Appendix III]

Cause of death	All ages [1]	Under 1 year	1 to 4 years	5 to 14 years	15 to 24 years	25 to 34 years	35 to 44 years	45 to 54 years	55 to 64 years	65 to 74 years	75 to 84 years	85 years and over
All causes [2]	2,471,984	28,059	4,730	5,651	32,198	42,275	76,370	186,542	296,182	401,579	653,560	744,691
Septicemia	35,927	289	93	61	139	359	892	2,514	4,552	6,448	10,717	9,863
Human immunodeficiency virus (HIV) disease	10,285	–	2	1	168	975	2,838	3,730	1,908	516	116	31
Malignant neoplasms [2]	565,469	70	394	890	1,663	3,521	12,699	50,403	104,091	141,159	160,960	89,610
Malignant neoplasm of esophagus	13,714	–	–	3	3	29	236	1,441	3,304	3,838	3,443	1,417
Malignant neoplasms of colon, rectum, and anus	53,321	1	–	3	52	314	1,419	4,802	9,076	11,770	14,936	10,948
Malignant neoplasms of liver and intrahepatic bile ducts	18,213	1	20	17	38	81	335	2,480	4,737	4,105	4,465	1,934
Malignant neoplasms of pancreas	35,236	1	–	1	7	53	506	2,840	6,681	9,115	10,414	5,616
Malignant neoplasms of trachea, bronchus, and lung	158,656	4	3	5	29	145	1,604	12,532	30,796	48,293	47,948	17,297
Malignant neoplasm of breast	41,026	–	–	–	13	331	2,148	5,962	8,797	8,441	8,820	6,514
Malignant neoplasm of ovary	14,362	–	–	3	12	94	379	1,539	2,921	3,609	3,783	2,022
Malignant neoplasm of prostate	28,472	–	–	–	–	–	23	458	2,385	5,645	10,721	9,237
Malignant neoplasm of bladder	14,036	1	–	–	3	14	95	592	1,600	2,952	4,932	3,847
Malignant neoplasms of lymphoid, hematopoietic and related tissue [2]	54,954	28	127	287	594	813	1,320	3,555	7,859	12,329	17,591	10,449
Non-Hodgkins lymphoma	20,369	1	4	34	127	221	469	1,290	2,910	4,413	6,791	4,108
Leukemia	22,335	27	123	252	410	490	621	1,436	2,956	4,798	6,840	4,381
Diabetes mellitus	70,553	4	5	36	204	574	1,854	5,622	11,370	15,315	20,037	15,531
Parkinson's disease	20,483	–	–	–	4	4	13	68	398	2,512	9,304	8,179
Alzheimer's disease	82,435	–	–	–	–	1	8	107	745	4,326	25,172	52,075
Major cardiovascular diseases [2]	804,483	571	256	337	1,333	4,058	14,226	46,432	82,009	116,296	222,494	316,436
Diseases of heart	616,828	396	186	229	1,065	3,254	11,336	37,892	66,711	90,520	166,286	238,924
Hypertensive heart disease	32,391	1	4	–	53	353	1,390	3,895	4,837	4,251	6,416	11,189
Ischemic heart diseases	405,309	12	2	21	144	1,045	5,952	24,359	46,665	63,623	112,397	151,064
Acute myocardial infarction	133,958	4	8	5	57	416	2,250	9,511	18,164	23,410	37,190	42,945
Heart failure	56,830	23	8	10	36	99	294	1,166	2,765	5,627	15,396	31,406
Essential (primary) hypertension and hypertensive renal disease	25,742	7	3	1	22	126	438	1,322	2,464	3,387	6,783	11,189
Cerebrovascular diseases	134,148	141	63	97	189	539	2,035	6,112	10,459	17,897	40,963	55,648
Influenza and pneumonia	56,284	226	142	89	206	372	880	2,253	3,734	6,252	15,512	26,618
Pneumonia	54,562	210	118	57	186	343	836	2,176	3,612	6,123	15,099	25,802
Chronic lower respiratory diseases [2]	141,090	32	54	119	163	254	812	4,392	14,042	31,975	51,700	37,548
Emphysema	12,448	–	–	–	–	4	69	502	1,485	3,260	4,585	2,541
Pneumonitis due to solids and liquids	16,608	11	10	5	41	81	158	467	923	1,683	5,031	8,198
Chronic liver disease and cirrhosis	29,963	10	–	1	24	423	2,562	8,220	8,526	5,395	3,664	1,137
Nephritis, nephrotic syndrome, and nephrosis [2]	48,237	143	12	17	80	258	780	2,220	4,803	8,182	14,819	16,920
Renal failure	43,935	139	8	16	69	236	736	2,074	4,474	7,619	13,574	14,988
Accidents (unintentional injuries) [2]	121,902	1,315	1,469	1,859	14,089	14,588	16,065	20,354	12,782	8,994	13,827	16,538
Transport accidents	42,709	104	489	1,090	9,297	6,930	6,164	6,766	4,840	3,110	2,655	1,258
Motor vehicle accidents	39,790	103	463	1,027	8,946	6,570	5,672	6,101	4,356	2,826	2,515	1,208
Nontransport accidents	79,193	1,211	980	769	4,792	7,658	9,901	13,588	7,942	5,884	11,172	15,280
Falls	24,013	13	38	40	233	297	540	1,300	1,809	2,745	7,007	9,990
Accidental poisoning and exposure to noxious substances	31,116	11	35	48	3,188	5,946	7,545	9,496	3,547	725	375	196
Intentional self-harm (suicide)	36,035	(NA)	(NA)	222	4,298	5,300	6,703	8,287	5,465	2,796	2,108	851
Assault (homicide)	17,826	340	421	320	5,275	4,610	2,906	2,137	987	466	235	122
Assault (homicide) by discharge of firearms	12,179	9	56	187	4,394	3,612	1,966	1,146	489	196	88	34
Enterocolitis due to clostridium difficile	7,476	3	1	–	3	12	35	128	411	968	2,673	3,241

– Represents zero. NA Not available. [1] Includes persons with age not stated, not shown separately. [2] Includes other causes, not shown separately.

Source: U.S. National Center for Health Statistics, National Vital Statistics Reports, *Deaths: Final Data for 2008*, Vol. 59, No. 10, December 2011. See also: <http://www.cdc.gov/nchs/deaths.htm>.

Table 125. Deaths and Death Rates by Leading Causes of Death and Age: 2008

[Rates per 100,000 population in specified group. Data are based on the tenth revision of the International Classification of Diseases (ICD). See Appendix III]

Age and cause of death	Number	Rate
ALL AGES [1]		
All causes	**2,471,984**	**813.0**
Diseases of heart	616,828	202.9
Malignant neoplasms	565,469	186.0
Chronic lower respiratory diseases	141,090	46.4
Cerebrovascular diseases	134,148	44.1
Accidents (unintentional injuries)	121,902	40.1
Alzheimer's disease	82,435	27.1
Diabetes mellitus	70,553	23.2
Influenza and pneumonia	56,284	18.5
Nephritis, nephrotic syndrome and nephrosis	48,237	15.9
Intentional self-harm (suicide)	36,035	11.9
1 TO 4 YEARS		
All causes	**4,730**	**28.3**
Accidents (unintentional injuries)	1,469	8.8
Congenital malformations, deformations and chromosomal abnormalities	521	3.1
Assault (homicide)	421	2.5
Malignant neoplasms	394	2.4
Diseases of heart	186	1.1
Influenza and pneumonia	142	0.9
Septicemia	93	0.6
Cerebrovascular diseases	63	0.4
Chronic lower respiratory diseases	54	0.3
Certain conditions originating in the perinatal period	51	0.3
5 TO 9 YEARS		
All causes	**2,502**	**12.5**
Accidents (unintentional injuries)	835	4.2
Malignant neoplasms	457	2.3
Congenital malformations, deformations and chromosomal abnormalities	170	0.8
Assault (homicide)	113	0.6
Diseases of heart	97	0.5
In situ neoplasms, benign neoplasms and neoplasms of uncertain or unknown behavior	59	0.3
Chronic lower respiratory diseases	55	0.3
Cerebrovascular disease	41	0.2
Influenza and pneumonia	40	0.2
Septicemia	25	0.1
10 TO 14 YEARS		
All causes	**3,149**	**15.7**
Accidents (unintentional injuries)	1,024	5.1
Malignant neoplasms	433	2.2
Intentional self-harm (suicide)	215	1.1
Assault (homicide)	207	1.0
Congenital malformations, deformations and chromosomal abnormalities	161	0.8
Diseases of heart	132	0.7
Chronic lower respiratory diseases	64	0.3
Cerebrovascular diseases	56	0.3
Influenza and pneumonia	49	0.2
Septicemia	36	0.2
15 TO 19 YEARS		
All causes	**12,407**	**57.7**
Accidents (unintentional injuries)	5,541	25.8
Assault (homicide)	2,095	9.7
Intentional self-harm (suicide)	1,604	7.5
Malignant neoplasms	685	3.2
Diseases of heart	363	1.7
Congenital malformations, deformations and chromosomal abnormalities	230	1.1
Cerebrovascular diseases	72	0.3
Chronic lower respiratory diseases	71	0.3
Influenza and pneumonia	64	0.3
Septicemia	54	0.3
20 TO 24 YEARS		
All causes	**19,791**	**94.0**
Accidents (unintentional injuries)	8,548	40.6
Assault (homicide)	3,180	15.1

Age and cause of death	Number	Rate
Intentional self-harm (suicide)	2,694	12.8
Malignant neoplasms	978	4.6
Diseases of heart	702	3.3
Congenital malformations, deformations and chromosomal abnormalities	237	1.1
Diabetes mellitus	152	0.7
Influenza and pneumonia	142	0.7
Human immunodeficiency virus (HIV)	140	0.7
Pregnancy, childbirth and the puerperium	128	0.6
25 TO 34 YEARS		
All causes	**42,275**	**103.3**
Accidents (unintentional injuries)	14,588	35.6
Intentional self-harm (suicide)	5,300	12.9
Assault (homicide)	4,610	11.3
Malignant neoplasms	3,521	8.6
Diseases of heart	3,254	7.9
Human immunodeficiency virus (HIV)	975	2.4
Diabetes mellitus	574	1.4
Cerebrovascular diseases	539	1.3
Chronic liver disease and cirrhosis	423	1.0
Congenital malformations, deformations and chromosomal abnormalities	379	0.9
35 TO 44 YEARS		
All causes	**76,370**	**179.7**
Accidents	16,065	37.8
Malignant neoplasms	12,699	29.9
Diseases of heart	11,336	26.7
Intentional self-harm (suicide)	6,703	15.8
Assault (homicide)	2,906	6.8
Human immunodeficiency virus (HIV)	2,838	6.7
Chronic liver disease and cirrhosis	2,562	6.0
Cerebrovascular diseases	2,035	4.8
Diabetes mellitus	1,854	4.4
Septicemia	892	2.1
45 TO 54 YEARS		
All causes	**186,542**	**420.4**
Malignant neoplasms	50,403	113.6
Diseases of heart	37,892	85.4
Accidents	20,354	45.9
Intentional self-harm (suicide)	8,287	18.7
Chronic liver disease and cirrhosis	8,220	18.5
Cerebrovascular diseases	6,112	13.8
Diabetes mellitus	5,622	12.7
Chronic lower respiratory diseases	4,392	9.9
Human immunodeficiency virus (HIV)	3,730	8.4
Viral hepatitis	2,732	6.2
55 TO 64 YEARS		
All causes	**296,182**	**879.2**
Malignant neoplasms	104,091	309.0
Diseases of heart	66,711	198.0
Chronic lower respiratory diseases	14,042	41.7
Accidents (unintentional injuries)	12,782	37.9
Diabetes mellitus	11,370	33.8
Cerebrovascular diseases	10,459	31.0
Chronic liver disease and cirrhosis	8,526	25.3
Intentional self-harm (suicide)	5,465	16.2
Nephritis, nephrotic syndrome and nephrosis	4,803	14.3
Septicemia	4,552	13.5
65 YEARS AND OLDER		
All causes	**1,799,830**	**4,630.4**
Diseases of heart	495,730	1,275.4
Malignant neoplasms	391,729	1,007.8
Chronic lower respiratory diseases	121,223	311.9
Cerebrovascular diseases	114,508	294.6
Alzheimer's disease	81,573	209.9
Diabetes mellitus	50,883	130.9
Influenza and pneumonia	48,382	124.5
Nephritis, nephrotic syndrome and nephrosis	39,921	102.7
Accidents (unintentional injuries)	39,359	101.3
Septicemia	27,028	69.5

[1] Includes deaths under 1 year of age.

Source: U.S. National Center for Health Statistics, National Vital Statistics Reports (NVSR), *Deaths: Leading Causes for 2008*, Vol. 60, No. 6, June 2012. See also: <http://www.cdc.gov/nchs/deaths.htm>.

Table 126. Age-Adjusted Death Rates for Major Causes of Death—States and Island Areas: 2009

[Age adjusted rates per 100,000 resident population estimated as of July 1. By place of residence. Excludes nonresidents of the United States. Causes of death classified according to the tenth revision of International Classification of Diseases. See text this section and Appendix III. In 2009, death records pending investigation were not updated by several states for a greater number of records than usual; therefore, caution should be used in interpreting trends by cause of death and state]

State and Island Areas	All causes of death	Diseases of heart	Malig-nant neo-plasms	Cerebro-vascular diseases	Chronic lower respira-tory disease	Accidents Total	Motor vehicle acci-dents	Alz-heimer's disease	Diabetes mellitus	Influ-enza and pneu-monia	Inten-tional self-harm (suicide)
U.S.	741.1	180.1	173.2	38.9	42.3	37.3	11.7	23.5	20.9	16.2	11.8
AL.	921.3	231.5	195.6	51.9	53.2	49.0	19.5	29.6	24.2	18.5	13.9
AK.	755.0	156.9	182.8	40.8	48.9	53.1	11.9	20.6	17.9	12.2	19.8
AZ.	652.2	144.6	147.1	29.2	40.4	43.1	12.2	28.8	15.6	15.1	16.2
AR.	874.6	218.8	197.3	50.8	55.2	49.8	22.2	25.9	27.1	21.1	14.5
CA.	652.0	165.6	159.1	38.1	37.3	29.4	8.8	27.5	19.8	17.9	10.3
CO.	688.1	136.5	151.3	35.2	47.7	44.2	11.1	31.4	17.2	14.8	18.6
CT.	684.1	164.8	167.6	34.0	34.8	33.7	7.4	17.3	15.0	16.1	8.6
DE.	753.5	177.8	177.9	41.2	42.4	36.7	12.1	16.2	20.5	13.1	11.8
DC.	812.7	219.1	191.0	33.8	23.7	24.0	6.1	15.9	21.7	12.3	4.4
FL.	673.7	154.4	165.7	31.3	38.8	42.9	13.8	15.6	19.7	9.3	14.6
GA.	818.4	192.5	172.8	45.4	45.6	41.1	14.0	24.6	18.3	18.4	11.7
HI.	619.7	145.0	144.3	40.2	19.0	31.0	9.2	13.7	19.8	17.3	13.1
ID.	721.3	154.6	159.4	41.1	48.1	44.0	15.9	24.2	24.2	13.5	20.4
IL.	743.5	183.2	181.5	38.8	40.2	30.2	8.3	20.8	20.5	17.7	9.0
IN.	815.8	195.0	190.8	43.5	55.3	39.3	11.1	26.8	24.0	17.1	12.8
IA.	724.7	175.9	172.3	41.0	49.1	37.1	12.6	29.5	18.9	16.5	11.9
KS.	760.2	163.1	173.8	43.1	51.0	43.0	14.6	23.8	20.4	17.9	13.7
KY.	898.7	210.2	204.3	45.2	61.6	54.6	18.9	29.9	29.1	22.2	13.4
LA.	888.3	223.8	197.0	46.0	41.7	47.8	19.0	30.4	27.4	19.9	10.9
ME.	757.7	157.4	187.0	38.2	49.0	41.1	12.1	27.0	20.9	14.6	14.1
MD.	762.6	195.0	178.3	40.4	36.8	24.6	10.6	16.9	20.8	17.3	9.4
MA.	680.3	156.3	174.9	32.6	33.8	29.0	5.8	20.7	13.2	17.0	7.7
MI.	785.9	207.0	182.6	40.1	45.3	35.5	9.5	23.2	24.5	14.6	11.4
MN.	651.8	121.9	169.1	34.3	34.9	36.2	9.2	22.1	17.7	10.2	10.8
MS.	926.1	244.9	198.8	47.0	51.3	56.0	25.3	29.6	29.2	19.0	13.2
MO.	804.6	202.5	185.6	44.0	51.6	47.0	15.5	24.7	19.7	19.2	14.2
MT.	758.0	154.0	164.7	39.2	51.8	60.5	23.3	21.2	19.4	14.8	21.3
NE.	716.1	153.9	167.7	40.3	48.9	35.8	14.1	25.5	22.0	12.3	9.4
NV.	784.8	191.8	176.4	36.0	52.5	39.5	9.7	14.5	15.4	22.7	19.1
NH.	677.3	150.1	170.4	33.3	44.5	34.3	8.0	24.3	18.3	12.8	11.7
NJ.	694.8	180.4	170.0	32.9	32.0	20.2	6.4	18.1	20.1	13.1	6.2
NM.	739.4	149.5	150.0	33.9	46.3	63.6	17.7	17.3	28.3	16.2	18.5
NY.	667.1	211.0	162.3	26.8	31.1	23.6	6.3	10.4	17.1	20.3	6.9
NC.	800.7	178.4	178.0	46.6	45.2	43.7	14.8	28.4	21.6	18.4	12.4
ND.	719.4	166.2	160.4	38.0	42.2	45.2	19.3	38.1	25.7	15.6	14.3
OH.	813.4	189.7	190.9	41.8	50.4	32.9	8.7	28.3	25.7	15.4	9.9
OK.	890.5	226.9	190.0	48.6	64.7	61.3	20.0	24.3	28.6	21.9	15.5
OR.	733.1	142.6	173.6	43.9	45.6	39.3	10.0	27.6	25.0	11.8	16.1
PA.	770.8	192.1	182.7	40.3	39.4	39.4	10.6	19.6	20.2	15.5	12.2
RI.	717.6	176.3	175.8	31.8	40.2	36.2	7.8	22.2	16.7	16.3	10.7
SC.	818.2	182.1	179.5	48.8	46.5	47.8	19.7	30.6	22.5	15.6	13.1
SD.	689.3	168.2	156.2	38.8	43.9	40.1	16.7	35.3	20.6	12.5	16.2
TN.	867.2	210.9	195.9	47.2	52.0	50.1	16.5	33.6	25.8	20.9	14.6
TX.	754.3	178.6	163.8	43.6	41.7	39.9	14.4	24.9	22.5	15.9	11.7
UT.	658.7	135.9	120.6	35.9	28.4	37.0	9.9	18.5	21.8	15.6	17.5
VT.	681.6	156.0	168.8	29.6	49.1	43.5	11.7	25.4	19.2	6.9	13.0
VA.	749.3	171.7	176.5	42.3	39.4	33.3	10.3	23.3	19.6	16.2	11.9
WA.	709.8	154.4	174.9	38.7	44.3	39.5	8.4	44.8	22.8	10.7	13.4
WV.	949.7	218.1	208.2	46.2	64.4	48.5	20.1	24.0	32.4	19.5	13.3
WI.	708.9	164.7	171.0	38.0	38.9	40.1	10.1	23.6	17.3	14.8	12.5
WY.	776.4	173.0	168.3	42.5	57.6	54.7	19.4	25.1	18.3	26.6	21.0
PR [1]	686.9	122.0	117.3	34.5	27.3	24.5	9.4	38.7	64.5	24.2	8.2
VI [1]	629.8	160.3	96.5	40.3	(S)	37.6	(S)	(S)	43.7	(S)	(S)
GU [1]	685.5	230.5	115.4	55.0	26.2	16.6	(S)	(S)	40.8	16.8	15.2
AS [1]	1,216.9	227.0	192.4	120.8	(S)	112.1	(S)	(S)	108.9	(S)	(S)
MP [1]	938.7	226.9	132.6	103.3	(S)	(S)	(S)	(S)	(S)	(S)	(S)

S Figure does not meet standards of reliability or precision. [1] Age-adjusted death rates for Puerto Rico, Virgin Islands, American Samoa, and Northern Marianas are calculated using different age groups in the weighting procedure. See source "Technical Notes."

Source: U.S. National Center for Health Statistics, National Vital Statistics Reports, (NVSR), *Deaths: Final Data for 2009*, Vol. 60, No. 3, December 2011. See also <http://www.cdc.gov/nchs/deaths.htm>.

Table 127. Death Rates From Heart Disease by Selected Characteristics: 1980 to 2008

[Rates per 100,000 population. See headnotes, Tables 110 and 118. See Appendix III]

Characteristics	1980	1990	2000	2003	2004	2005	2006	2007	2008
All ages, age adjusted [1]	**412.1**	**321.8**	**257.6**	**232.3**	**217.0**	**211.1**	**200.2**	**190.9**	**186.5**
All ages, crude rate [2]	**336.0**	**289.5**	**252.6**	**235.6**	**222.2**	**220.0**	**211.0**	**204.3**	**202.9**
Under 1 year	22.8	20.1	13.0	11.0	10.3	8.7	8.4	10.0	9.2
1 to 4 years	2.6	1.9	1.2	1.2	1.2	0.9	1.0	1.1	1.1
5 to 14 years	0.9	0.9	0.7	0.6	0.6	0.6	0.6	0.6	0.6
15 to 24 years	2.9	2.5	2.6	2.7	2.5	2.7	2.5	2.6	2.5
25 to 34 years	8.3	7.6	7.4	8.2	7.9	8.1	8.2	7.9	7.9
35 to 44 years	44.6	31.4	29.2	30.7	29.3	28.9	28.3	27.4	26.7
45 to 54 years	180.2	120.5	94.2	92.5	90.2	89.7	88.0	85.3	85.4
55 to 64 years	494.1	367.3	261.2	233.2	218.8	214.8	207.3	200.3	198.0
65 to 74 years	1,218.6	894.3	665.6	585.0	541.6	518.9	490.3	462.9	449.8
75 to 84 years	2,993.1	2,295.7	1,780.3	1,611.1	1,506.3	1,460.8	1,383.1	1,315.0	1,276.7
85 years and over	7,777.1	6,739.9	5,926.1	5,278.4	4,895.9	4,778.4	4,480.8	4,267.7	4,175.7
Male, age adjusted [1]	**538.9**	**412.4**	**320.0**	**286.6**	**267.9**	**260.9**	**248.5**	**237.7**	**232.3**
White	539.6	409.2	316.7	282.9	264.6	258.0	245.2	234.8	229.9
Black	561.4	485.4	392.5	364.3	342.1	329.8	320.6	305.9	295.6
American Indian, Alaska Native	320.5	264.1	222.2	203.2	182.7	173.2	170.2	159.8	149.1
Asian, Pacific Islander	286.9	220.7	185.5	158.3	146.5	141.1	136.3	126.0	124.7
Hispanic origin [3]	(NA)	270.0	238.2	206.8	193.9	192.4	175.2	165.0	151.9
Non-Hispanic, White [3]	(NA)	413.6	319.9	286.9	268.7	262.2	250.0	239.8	235.9
Male, crude rate [2]	**368.6**	**297.6**	**249.8**	**235.0**	**222.8**	**221.1**	**214.0**	**208.4**	**207.6**
Under 1 year	25.5	21.9	13.3	12.1	10.9	9.4	8.8	10.9	9.8
1 to 14 years	2.8	1.9	1.4	1.1	1.1	1.0	1.1	1.0	1.1
5 to 14 years	1.0	0.9	0.8	0.7	0.6	0.6	0.7	0.6	0.6
15 to 24 years	3.7	3.1	3.2	3.4	3.2	3.6	3.3	3.2	3.4
25 to 34 years	11.4	10.3	9.6	10.5	10.5	10.8	11.2	10.5	10.4
35 to 44 years	68.7	48.1	41.4	42.8	40.9	40.7	39.5	38.6	36.8
45 to 54 years	282.6	183.0	140.2	136.2	132.3	131.5	128.9	124.6	123.0
55 to 64 years	746.8	537.3	371.7	331.7	312.8	306.9	296.8	288.8	284.7
65 to 74 years	1,728.0	1,250.0	898.3	785.3	723.8	692.3	660.5	624.9	609.2
75 to 84 years	3,834.3	2,968.2	2,248.1	2,030.3	1,893.6	1,829.4	1,743.5	1,656.5	1,609.1
85 years and over	8,752.7	7,418.4	6,430.0	5,621.5	5,239.3	5,143.4	4,819.9	4,621.8	4,535.9
Female, age adjusted [1]	**320.8**	**257.0**	**210.9**	**190.3**	**177.3**	**172.3**	**162.2**	**154.0**	**150.4**
White	315.9	250.9	205.6	185.4	172.9	168.2	158.6	150.5	147.2
Black	378.6	327.5	277.6	253.8	236.5	228.3	212.5	204.5	197.5
American Indian, Alaska Native	175.4	153.1	143.6	127.5	119.9	115.9	113.2	99.8	94.3
Asian, Pacific Islander	132.3	149.2	115.7	104.2	96.1	91.9	87.3	82.0	81.7
Hispanic origin [3]	(NA)	177.2	163.7	145.8	130.0	129.1	118.9	111.8	104.6
Non-Hispanic, White [3]	(NA)	252.6	206.8	187.1	175.1	170.3	160.9	153.0	150.0
Female, crude rate [2]	**305.1**	**281.8**	**255.3**	**236.2**	**221.6**	**218.9**	**208.0**	**200.2**	**198.3**
Under 1 year	20.0	18.3	12.5	9.8	9.7	8.0	7.9	9.0	8.5
1 to 14 years	2.5	1.9	1.0	1.3	1.2	0.9	0.9	1.1	1.1
5 to 14 years	0.9	0.8	0.5	0.5	0.6	0.6	0.6	0.6	0.5
15 to 24 years	2.1	1.8	2.1	2.1	1.7	1.7	1.8	1.9	1.6
25 to 34 years	5.3	5.0	5.2	5.7	5.2	5.3	5.1	5.3	5.4
35 to 44 years	21.4	15.1	17.2	18.6	17.7	17.1	17.0	16.2	16.4
45 to 54 years	84.5	61.0	49.8	50.2	49.6	49.2	48.5	47.2	48.9
55 to 64 years	272.1	215.7	159.3	141.9	131.5	129.1	124.1	117.9	117.2
65 to 74 years	828.6	616.8	474.0	417.9	388.6	372.7	346.3	325.4	313.9
75 to 84 years	2,497.0	1,893.8	1,475.1	1,331.1	1,245.6	1,210.5	1,136.7	1,079.7	1,046.0
85 years and over	7,350.5	6,478.1	5,720.9	5,126.7	4,741.5	4,610.8	4,322.1	4,099.3	4,001.7

NA Not available. [1] Age-adjusted death rates were prepared using the direct method, in which age-specific death rates for a population of interest are applied to a standard population distributed by age. Age adjustment eliminates the differences in observed rates between points in time or among compared population groups that result from age differences in population composition. [2] The total number of deaths in a given time period divided by the total resident population as of July 1. [3] Persons of Hispanic origin may be any race. Prior to 1997 excludes data from States lacking an Hispanic-origin item on their death certificates. See text, this section.

Source: U.S. National Center for Health Statistics, *Health, United States, 2011*. See also <http://cdc.gov/nchs/hus.htm>.

Table 128. Death Rates From Cerebrovascular Diseases by Sex and Age: 1990 to 2008

[Rates per 100,000 population. See headnote, Tables 110 and 118. See Appendix III]

Characteristics	Total				Male				Female			
	1990	2000	2005	2008	1990	2000	2005	2008	1990	2000	2005	2008
All ages, age adjusted [1]	**65.3**	**60.9**	**46.6**	**40.7**	**68.5**	**62.4**	**46.9**	**40.9**	**62.6**	**59.1**	**45.6**	**39.9**
All ages, crude rate [2]	**57.8**	**59.6**	**48.4**	**44.1**	**46.7**	**46.9**	**38.8**	**35.7**	**68.4**	**71.8**	**57.8**	**52.3**
Under 1 year	3.8	3.3	3.1	3.3	4.4	3.8	3.5	3.1	3.1	2.7	2.6	3.4
1 to 4 years	0.3	0.3	0.4	0.4	0.3	(B)	0.5	0.3	0.3	0.4	0.3	0.4
5 to 14 years	0.2	0.2	0.2	0.2	0.2	0.2	0.3	0.2	0.2	0.2	0.2	0.2
15 to 24 years	0.6	0.5	0.5	0.4	0.7	0.5	0.4	0.5	0.6	0.5	0.5	0.4
25 to 34 years	2.2	1.5	1.4	1.3	2.1	1.5	1.5	1.4	2.2	1.5	1.2	1.2
35 to 44 years	6.4	5.8	5.2	4.8	6.8	5.8	5.2	5.1	6.1	5.7	5.1	4.5
45 to 54 years	18.7	16.0	15.0	13.8	20.5	17.5	16.5	15.3	17.0	14.5	13.6	12.3
55 to 64 years	47.9	41.0	33.0	31.0	54.3	47.2	38.5	36.0	42.2	35.3	27.9	26.4
65 to 74 years	144.2	128.6	101.1	88.9	166.6	145.0	113.6	100.1	126.7	115.1	90.5	79.4
75 to 84 years	498.0	461.3	359.0	314.5	551.1	490.8	372.9	325.4	466.2	442.1	349.5	306.9
85 years and over	1,628.9	1,589.2	1,141.8	972.6	1,528.5	1,484.3	1,023.3	861.3	1,667.6	1,632.0	1,196.1	1,026.3

B Figure too small to meet statistical standards for reliability. [1] See footnote 1, Table 127. [2] The total number of deaths in a given time period divided by the total resident population as of July 1.

Source: U.S. National Center for Health Statistics, *Health, United States, 2011.* See also <http://cdc.gov/nchs/hus.htm>.

Table 129. Death Rates From Malignant Neoplasms by Selected Characteristics: 1990 to 2008

[Rates per 100,000 population. Excludes deaths of nonresidents of the United States. Beginning 1999, deaths classified according to tenth revision of International Classification of Diseases (ICD); for earlier years, causes of death were classified according to the revisions then in use. Changes in classification of causes of death due to these revisions may result in discontinuities in cause-of-death trends. For explanation of age adjustment, see text, this section. See Appendix III]

Characteristic	1990	2000	2004	2005	2006	2007	2008
All ages, age adjusted [1]	**216.0**	**199.6**	**185.8**	**183.8**	**180.7**	**178.4**	**175.3**
All ages, crude rate [2]	**203.2**	**196.5**	**188.6**	**188.7**	**187.0**	**186.6**	**186.0**
Under 1 year	2.3	2.4	1.8	1.8	1.8	1.7	1.6
1 to 4 years	3.5	2.7	2.5	2.3	2.3	2.2	2.4
5 to 14 years	3.1	2.5	2.5	2.5	2.2	2.4	2.2
15 to 24 years	4.9	4.4	4.1	4.1	3.9	3.9	3.9
25 to 34 years	12.6	9.8	9.1	9.0	9.0	8.5	8.6
35 to 44 years	43.3	36.6	33.4	33.2	31.9	30.8	29.9
45 to 54 years	158.9	127.5	119.0	118.6	116.3	114.3	113.6
55 to 64 years	449.6	366.7	333.4	326.9	321.1	315.4	309.0
65 to 74 years	872.3	816.3	755.1	742.7	727.2	715.5	701.5
75 to 84 years	1,348.5	1,335.6	1,280.4	1,274.8	1,263.8	1,256.3	1,235.8
85 years old and over	1,752.9	1,819.4	1,653.3	1,637.7	1,606.1	1,590.2	1,566.1
DEATH RATES FOR MALIGNANT NEOPLASM OF BREASTS FOR FEMALES							
All ages, age adjusted [1]	**33.3**	**29.4**	**24.4**	**24.1**	**23.5**	**22.9**	**22.5**
All ages, crude rate [2]	**34.0**	**31.3**	**27.5**	**27.3**	**26.9**	**26.5**	**26.3**
Under 25 years	(B)	(B)	(B)	(B)	(B)	(B)	(B)
25 to 34 years	2.9	2.6	2.0	1.8	1.8	1.7	1.6
35 to 44 years	17.8	14.1	11.3	11.3	10.8	10.1	10.1
45 to 54 years	45.4	38.3	29.3	28.7	27.6	26.7	26.3
55 to 64 years	78.6	66.8	55.8	54.5	53.7	51.3	49.9
65 to 74 years	111.7	98.3	81.6	79.2	76.9	77.3	76.6
75 to 84 years	146.3	137.6	119.5	119.2	119.2	116.3	113.3
85 years old and over	196.8	201.7	178.6	177.9	169.9	170.4	167.3
DEATH RATES FOR MALIGNANT NEOPLASM OF TRACHEA, BRONCHUS, AND LUNG							
All ages, age adjusted [1]	**37.1**	**41.3**	**40.9**	**40.5**	**40.0**	**50.6**	**49.5**
All ages, crude rate [2]	**39.4**	**45.4**	**45.9**	**45.9**	**45.7**	**52.6**	**52.2**
Under 25 years	(Z)	(Z)	(Z)	(Z)	(Z)	(Z)	(Z)
25 to 34 years	0.5	0.5	0.3	0.3	0.4	0.3	0.4
35 to 44 years	5.2	5.3	5.2	5.1	4.5	4.3	3.8
45 to 54 years	34.5	25.0	24.2	24.5	24.6	28.4	28.2
55 to 64 years	105.0	93.3	83.9	80.7	78.2	95.4	91.4
65 to 74 years	177.6	206.9	205.0	199.6	197.0	248.8	240.0
75 to 84 years	190.1	265.6	277.0	280.9	280.3	371.3	368.1
85 years old and over	138.1	212.8	221.3	226.2	226.9	299.8	302.3

B Base figure too small to meet statistical standards for reliability of a derived figure. Z Less than 0.05. [1] Age adjusted death rates were prepared using the direct method, in which age specific death rates for a population of interest are applied to a standard population distributed by age. Age adjustment eliminates the differences in observed rates between points in time or among compared population groups that result from age differences in population composition. [2] The total number of deaths in a given time period divided by the total population as of July 1.

Source: U.S. National Center for Health Statistics, *Health, United States, 2011.* See also <http://www.cdc.gov/nchs/hus.htm>.

Table 130. Death Rates From Suicide by Selected Characteristics: 1990 to 2008

[Rates per 100,000 population. Excludes deaths of nonresidents of the United States. Beginning 2000, deaths classified according to the tenth revision of International Classification of Diseases. See Appendix III]

Characteristic	1990	2000	2004	2005	2006	2007	2008
All ages, age adjusted [1]	**12.5**	**10.4**	**10.9**	**10.9**	**10.9**	**11.3**	**11.6**
All ages, crude rate [2]	**12.4**	**10.4**	**11.0**	**11.0**	**11.1**	**11.5**	**11.9**
Under 1 year	(X)	(X)	(X)	(X)	(X)	(X)	(X)
1 to 4 years	(X)	(X)	(X)	(X)	(X)	(X)	(X)
5 to 14 years	0.8	0.7	0.7	0.7	0.5	0.5	0.6
15 to 24 years	13.2	10.2	10.3	10.0	9.9	9.7	10.1
25 to 44 years	15.2	13.4	13.9	13.7	13.8	14.3	14.4
45 to 64 years	15.3	13.5	15.4	15.4	16.0	16.8	17.6
65 to 74 years	17.9	12.5	12.3	12.6	12.6	12.6	13.9
75 to 84 years	24.9	17.6	16.3	16.9	15.9	16.3	16.2
85 years and over	22.2	19.6	16.4	16.9	15.9	15.6	14.9
AGE-ADJUSTED RATES							
Male	21.5	17.7	18.0	18.0	18.0	18.4	18.9
Female	4.8	4.0	4.5	4.4	4.5	4.7	4.8
White male	22.8	19.1	19.6	19.6	19.6	20.2	20.8
Black male	12.8	10.0	9.6	9.2	9.4	8.8	9.5
American Indian, Alaska Native male	20.1	16.0	18.7	18.9	18.3	18.1	17.7
Asian, Pacific Islander male	9.6	8.6	8.4	7.3	7.9	9.0	8.2
Hispanic male [3]	13.7	10.3	9.8	9.4	8.8	10.1	9.3
Non-Hispanic, White male [3]	23.5	20.2	21.0	21.2	21.4	21.9	22.9
White female	5.2	4.3	5.0	4.9	5.1	5.2	5.4
Black female	2.4	1.8	1.8	1.9	1.4	1.7	1.7
American Indian, Alaska Native female	3.6	3.8	5.9	4.6	5.1	4.9	5.8
Asian, Pacific Islander female	4.1	2.8	3.5	3.3	3.4	3.5	3.7
Hispanic female [3]	2.3	1.7	2.0	1.8	1.8	1.9	1.9
Non-Hispanic, White female [3]	5.4	4.7	5.4	5.3	5.6	5.7	6.0

X Not applicable. [1] Age-adjusted death rates were prepared using the direct method, in which age-specific death rates for a population of interest are applied to a standard population distributed by age. Age adjustment eliminates the differences in observed rates between points in time or among compared population groups that result from age differences in population composition. [2] The total number of deaths in a given time period divided by the total resident population as of July 1. [3] Persons of Hispanic origin may be any race. Excludes data from states lacking an Hispanic-origin item on their death certificates.

Source: U.S. National Center for Health Statistics, *Health, United States, 2011*. See also <http://www.cdc.gov/nchs/hus.htm>.

Table 131. Death Rates From Human Immunodeficiency Virus (HIV) Disease by Selected Characteristics, 1990 to 2008

[Rates per 100,000 population. Excludes deaths of nonresidents of the United States. Beginning 2000, deaths classified according to tenth revision of International Classification of Diseases. See Appendix III]

Characteristic	1990	2000	2004	2005	2006	2007	2008
All ages, age adjusted [1]	**10.2**	**5.2**	**4.5**	**4.2**	**4.0**	**3.7**	**3.3**
All ages, crude [2]	**10.1**	**5.1**	**4.4**	**4.2**	**4.0**	**3.7**	**3.4**
Under 1 year	2.7	(B)	(B)	(B)	(B)	(B)	(B)
1 to 4 years	0.8	(B)	(B)	(B)	(B)	(B)	(B)
5 to 14 years	0.2	0.1	0.1	(B)	(B)	(B)	(B)
15 to 24 years	1.5	0.5	0.5	0.4	0.5	0.4	0.4
25 to 34 years	19.7	6.1	3.7	3.3	2.9	2.7	2.4
35 to 44 years	27.4	13.1	10.9	9.9	9.2	8.3	6.7
45 to 54 years	15.2	11.0	10.6	10.6	10.1	9.5	8.4
55 to 64 years	6.2	5.1	5.4	5.3	5.5	5.3	5.7
65 to 74 years	2.0	2.2	2.4	2.3	2.5	2.3	2.6
75 to 84 years	0.7	0.7	0.8	0.8	0.8	0.8	0.9
85 years and over	(B)	(B)	(B)	(B)	(B)	(B)	0.5
AGE-ADJUSTED RATES							
Male	18.5	7.9	6.6	6.2	5.9	5.4	4.8
Female	2.2	2.5	2.4	2.3	2.2	2.1	1.9
White male	15.7	4.6	3.8	3.6	3.4	3.1	2.8
Black male	46.3	35.1	29.2	28.2	26.3	24.5	21.9
American Indian, Alaska Native male	3.3	3.5	4.3	4.0	3.3	3.6	3.3
Asian, Pacific Islander male	4.3	1.2	1.2	1.0	1.1	0.8	1.0
Hispanic male [3]	28.8	10.6	8.2	7.5	7.0	6.3	5.4
Non-Hispanic, White male [3]	14.1	3.8	3.1	3.0	2.8	2.5	2.3
White female	1.1	1.0	0.9	0.8	0.7	0.7	0.7
Black female	10.1	13.2	13.0	12.0	12.2	11.3	9.8
American Indian, Alaska Native female	(B)	1.0	1.5	1.5	1.5	1.7	(B)
Asian, Pacific Islander female	(B)	0.2	(B)	(B)	(B)	(B)	0.3
Hispanic female [3]	3.8	2.9	2.4	1.9	1.9	1.8	1.7
Non-Hispanic, White female [3]	0.7	0.7	0.6	0.6	0.6	0.5	0.5

B Base figure too small to meet statistical standards. [1] Age-adjusted death rates were prepared using the direct method, in which age-specific death rates for a population of interest are applied to a standard population distributed by age. Age adjustment eliminates the differences in observed rates between points in time or among compared population groups that result from age differences in population composition. [2] The total number of deaths in a given time period divided by the total resident population as of July 1. [3] Persons of Hispanic origin may be any race. Excludes data from states lacking an Hispanic-origin item on their death certificates.

Source: U.S. National Center for Health Statistics, *Health, United States, 2011*. See also <http://www.cdc.gov/nchs/hus.htm>.

Table 132. Deaths—Life Years Lost and Mortality Costs by Age, Sex, and Cause: 2009

[2,436 represents 2,436,000. Life years lost: Number of years person would have lived in absence of death. Mortality cost: value of lifetime earnings lost by persons who die prematurely]

Characteristics	Number of deaths (1,000)	Life years lost [1] Total (1,000)	Life years lost [1] Per death	Mortality cost [2] Total (mil. dol.)	Mortality cost [2] Per death (dol.)
2009, total [3]	**2,436**	**38,144**	**15.7**	**527,897**	**216,678**
Under 5 years	31	2,409	77.8	35,769	1,154,815
5 to 14 years	6	385	68.5	8,201	1,457,171
15 to 24 years	30	1,752	57.9	52,410	1,732,506
25 to 44 years	117	5,002	42.8	160,080	1,370,198
45 to 64 years	371	12,466	33.6	235,767	634,991
65 years and over	1,881	16,129	8.6	35,670	18,960
Heart disease	599	7,449	12.4	80,032	133,709
Cancer	569	8,906	15.7	105,979	186,378
Cerebrovascular diseases	129	1,501	11.7	13,227	102,861
Accidents and adverse effects	117	3,518	30.0	88,668	756,947
Other	1,023	16,769	16.4	239,991	234,500
Male	**1,217**	**20,281**	**16.7**	**366,978**	**301,476**
Under 5 years	17	1,316	75.6	21,700	1,247,558
5 to 14 years	3	214	66.4	5,057	1,571,498
15 to 24 years	22	1,259	56.7	40,463	1,822,258
25 to 44 years	76	3,140	41.6	113,623	1,504,748
45 to 64 years	299	7,218	24.2	161,893	542,110
65 years and over	800	7,134	8.9	24,242	30,291
Heart disease	307	4,132	13.5	60,640	197,683
Cancer	297	4,380	14.7	63,675	214,059
Cerebrovascular diseases	52	642	12.4	8,321	160,081
Accidents and adverse effects	75	2,351	31.5	67,771	909,176
Other	487	8,776	18.0	166,571	342,366
Female	**1,219**	**17,863**	**14.7**	**160,919**	**132,003**
Under 5 years	14	1,093	80.5	14,069	1,036,025
5 to 14 years	2	172	71.2	3,144	1,304,514
15 to 24 years	8	493	61.3	11,947	1,484,814
25 to 44 years	41	1,862	45.1	46,457	1,124,317
45 to 64 years	73	5,248	72.2	73,874	1,016,751
65 years and over	1,081	8,995	8.3	11,428	10,571
Heart disease	292	3,318	11.4	19,392	66,455
Cancer	271	4,526	16.7	42,304	156,011
Cerebrovascular diseases	77	859	11.2	4,906	64,034
Accidents and adverse effects	43	1,167	27.4	20,897	490,567
Other	537	7,993	14.9	73,420	136,752

[1] Based on life expectancy at year of death. [2] Cost estimates based on the person's age, sex, life expectancy at the time of death, labor force participation rates, annual earnings, value of homemaking services, and a 3 percent discount rate by which to convert to present worth the potential aggregate earnings lost over the years. [3] Total excludes 329 deaths for which age is unknown.

Source: Wendy Max and Yanling Shi, Institute for Health & Aging, University of California San Francisco, CA., unpublished data (copyright).

Table 133. Suicide Deaths by Age, Sex, and Method: 2009

[Deaths based on tenth revision of International Classification of Diseases (ICD). Data are 2007-2009 annual averages. This table replaces Table 127 in the 2012 edition of the Statistical Abstract. That table, prepared by the National Safety Council, included data on suicide rates. It did not include data by sex]

Method	Total	Age 5-14 years [1]	Age 15-17 years	Age 18-24 years	Age 25-44 years	Age 45-64 years	Age 65-74 years	Age 75-84 years	Age 85+ years
Total	**35,847**	**224**	**737**	**3,533**	**12,000**	**13,668**	**2,719**	**2,097**	**862**
MEN									
Total	**28,269**	**153**	**560**	**2,986**	**9,422**	**10,356**	**2,237**	**1,810**	**740**
Knife or other sharp object	532	(D)	(D)	28	162	269	30	26	15
Drowning	243	(D)	(D)	28	83	91	16	15	7
Jumping from a high place	521	(D)	8	71	211	173	26	18	13
Fire/hot object or substance	107	(D)	(D)	12	32	48	8	(S)	(S)
Firearm	15,806	46	268	1,513	4,429	5,766	1,709	1,490	583
Poisoning	3,436	4	21	197	1,224	1,668	182	94	44
Hanging, suffocation, strangulation	6,979	100	237	1,044	3,039	2,118	227	146	68
WOMEN									
Total	**7,578**	**70**	**177**	**547**	**2,578**	**3,313**	**482**	**287**	**122**
Knife or other sharp object	119	(D)	(D)	4	29	66	9	6	4
Drowning	142	(D)	(D)	9	46	56	15	9	6
Jumping from a high place	188	(D)	(D)	19	60	76	13	9	7
Fire/hot object or substance	55	(D)	(D)	(D)	19	28	5	(D)	(D)
Firearm	2,297	9	38	150	768	1,018	180	105	27
Poisoning	2,963	6	20	109	971	1,524	185	105	41
Hanging, suffocation, strangulation	1,601	53	108	235	609	454	62	46	35

D Data withheld to protect confidentiality. S Unreliable data. [1] It is generally accepted that children under 5 years of age cannot commit suicide.

Source: National Center for Health Statistics, "Injury Mortality, Health Data Interactive," <http://205.207.175.93/HDI/ReportFolders/reportFolders.aspx>, accessed September 2012.

Table 134. Marriages and Divorces—Number and Rate by State: 1990 to 2010

[(2,443 represents 2,443,000). Based on provisional counts by State of occurrence. Population enumerated as of April 1. See Appendix III]

State	Marriages [1] Number (1,000) 1990	2000	2010	Rate per 1,000 population [2] 1990	2000	2010	Divorces [3] Number (1,000) 1990	2000	2010	Rate per 1,000 population [2] 1990	2000	2010
United States [4]	2,443	2,329	(NA)	9.8	8.3	6.8	1,182	(NA)	(NA)	4.7	4.1	3.6
Alabama	43.1	45.0	(NA)	10.6	10.1	8.2	25.3	23.5	(NA)	6.1	5.5	4.4
Alaska	5.7	5.6	(NA)	10.2	8.9	8.0	2.9	2.7	(NA)	5.5	3.9	4.7
Arizona [5]	36.8	38.7	(NA)	10.0	7.5	5.9	25.1	21.6	(NA)	6.9	4.6	3.5
Arkansas	36.0	41.1	(NA)	15.3	15.4	10.8	16.8	17.9	(NA)	6.9	6.4	5.7
California	237.1	196.9	(NA)	7.9	5.8	5.8	128.0	(NA)	(NA)	4.3	(NA)	(NA)
Colorado	32.4	35.6	(NA)	9.8	8.3	6.9	18.4	(NA)	(NA)	5.5	4.7	4.3
Connecticut	26.0	19.4	(NA)	7.9	5.7	5.6	10.3	6.5	(NA)	3.2	3.3	2.9
Delaware	5.6	5.1	(NA)	8.4	6.5	5.2	3.0	3.2	(NA)	4.4	3.9	3.5
District of Columbia	5.0	2.8	(NA)	8.2	4.9	7.6	2.7	1.5	(NA)	4.5	3.2	2.8
Florida	141.8	141.9	(NA)	10.9	8.9	7.3	81.7	81.9	(NA)	6.3	5.1	4.4
Georgia	66.8	56.0	(NA)	10.3	6.8	7.3	35.7	30.7	(NA)	5.5	3.3	(NA)
Hawaii	18.3	25.0	(NA)	16.4	20.6	17.6	5.2	4.6	(NA)	4.6	3.9	(NA)
Idaho	14.1	14.0	(NA)	13.9	10.8	8.8	6.6	6.9	(NA)	6.5	5.5	5.2
Illinois	100.6	85.5	(NA)	8.8	6.9	5.7	44.3	39.1	(NA)	3.8	3.2	2.6
Indiana	53.2	34.5	(NA)	9.6	7.9	6.3	(NA)	(NA)	(NA)	(NA)	(NA)	(NA)
Iowa	24.9	20.3	(NA)	9.0	6.9	6.9	11.1	9.4	(NA)	3.9	3.3	2.4
Kansas	22.7	22.2	(NA)	9.2	8.3	6.4	12.6	10.6	(NA)	5.0	3.6	3.7
Kentucky	49.8	39.7	(NA)	13.5	9.8	7.4	21.8	21.6	(NA)	5.8	5.1	4.5
Louisiana	40.4	40.5	(NA)	9.6	9.1	6.9	(NA)	(NA)	(NA)	(NA)	(NA)	(NA)
Maine	11.9	10.5	(NA)	9.7	8.8	7.1	5.3	5.8	(NA)	4.3	5.0	4.2
Maryland	46.3	40.0	(NA)	9.7	7.5	5.7	16.1	17.0	(NA)	3.4	3.3	2.8
Massachusetts	47.7	37.0	(NA)	7.9	5.8	5.6	16.8	18.6	(NA)	2.8	2.5	2.5
Michigan	76.1	66.4	(NA)	8.2	6.7	5.5	40.2	39.4	(NA)	4.3	3.9	3.5
Minnesota	33.7	33.4	(NA)	7.7	6.8	5.3	15.4	14.8	(NA)	3.5	3.2	(NA)
Mississippi	24.3	19.7	(NA)	9.4	6.9	4.9	14.4	14.4	(NA)	5.5	5.0	4.3
Missouri	49.1	43.7	(NA)	9.6	7.8	6.5	26.4	26.5	(NA)	5.1	4.5	3.9
Montana	6.9	6.6	(NA)	8.6	7.3	7.4	4.1	2.1	(NA)	5.1	4.2	3.9
Nebraska	12.6	13.0	(NA)	8.0	7.6	6.6	6.5	6.4	(NA)	4.0	3.7	3.6
Nevada	120.6	144.3	(NA)	99.0	72.2	38.3	13.3	18.1	(NA)	11.4	9.9	5.9
New Hampshire	10.5	11.6	(NA)	9.5	9.4	7.3	5.3	7.1	(NA)	4.7	4.8	3.8
New Jersey	58.7	50.4	(NA)	7.6	6.0	5.1	23.6	25.6	(NA)	3.0	3.0	3.0
New Mexico [5]	13.3	14.5	(NA)	8.8	8.0	7.7	7.7	9.2	(NA)	4.9	5.1	4.0
New York [5]	154.8	162.0	(NA)	8.6	7.1	6.5	57.9	62.8	(NA)	3.2	3.0	2.9
North Carolina	51.9	65.6	(NA)	7.8	8.2	6.6	34.0	36.9	(NA)	5.1	4.5	3.8
North Dakota	4.8	4.6	(NA)	7.5	7.2	6.5	2.3	2.0	(NA)	3.6	3.4	3.1
Ohio	98.1	88.5	(NA)	9.0	7.8	5.8	51.0	49.3	(NA)	4.7	4.2	3.4
Oklahoma	33.2	15.6	(NA)	10.6	(NA)	7.2	24.9	12.4	(NA)	7.7	(NA)	5.2
Oregon	25.3	26.0	(NA)	8.9	7.6	6.5	15.9	16.7	(NA)	5.5	4.8	4.0
Pennsylvania	84.9	73.2	(NA)	7.1	6.0	5.3	40.1	37.9	(NA)	3.3	3.1	2.7
Rhode Island	8.1	8.0	(NA)	8.1	7.6	5.8	3.8	3.1	(NA)	3.7	2.9	3.2
South Carolina	55.8	42.7	(NA)	15.9	10.6	7.4	16.1	14.4	(NA)	4.5	3.8	3.1
South Dakota	7.7	7.1	(NA)	11.1	9.4	7.3	2.6	2.7	(NA)	3.7	3.5	3.4
Tennessee	68.0	88.2	(NA)	13.9	15.5	8.8	32.3	33.8	(NA)	6.5	5.9	4.2
Texas	178.6	196.4	(NA)	10.5	9.4	7.1	94.0	85.2	(NA)	5.5	4.0	3.3
Utah	19.4	24.1	(NA)	11.2	10.8	8.5	8.8	9.7	(NA)	5.1	4.3	3.7
Vermont	6.1	6.1	(NA)	10.9	10.0	9.3	2.6	5.1	(NA)	4.5	4.1	3.8
Virginia	71.0	62.4	(NA)	11.4	8.8	6.8	27.3	30.2	(NA)	4.4	4.3	3.8
Washington	46.6	40.9	(NA)	9.5	6.9	6.0	28.8	27.2	(NA)	5.9	4.6	4.2
West Virginia	13.0	15.7	(NA)	7.2	8.7	6.7	9.7	9.3	(NA)	5.3	5.1	5.1
Wisconsin	38.9	36.1	(NA)	7.9	6.7	5.3	17.8	17.6	(NA)	3.6	3.2	3.0
Wyoming	4.9	4.9	(NA)	10.7	10.0	7.6	3.1	2.8	(NA)	6.6	5.8	5.1

NA Not available. [1] Data are counts of marriages performed, except as noted. [2] Based on total population residing in area; population enumerated as of April 1. [3] Includes annulments. Includes divorce petitions filed or legal separations for some counties or states. [4] U.S. total for the number of divorces is an estimate which includes states not reporting. Beginning 2000, divorce rates based solely on the combined counts and populations for reporting states and the District of Columbia. [5] Some figures for marriages are marriage licenses issued.

Source: U.S. National Center for Health Statistics. "National Vital Statistics System, Marriages and Divorces, Detailed State Tables," http://www.cdc.gov/nchs/mardiv.htm, accessed August 2012. National Vital Statistics Reports (NVSR), *Births, Marriages, Divorces and Deaths: Provisional Data for 2009*, Vol. 58, No. 25, August 2010, and prior reports.

Table 135. People Who Got Married and Divorced in the Past 12 Months by State: 2010

[For 12 month period prior to interview date, which occurred for each month in calendar year. For example, a person interviewed in January 2010 could report they got married between January 2009 and January 2010. Persons 15 years and over. Vital event is counted in state in which respondent lived at the time of survey. Based on 2010 American Community Survey (ACS). The ACS universe includes the household population and the group quarters population. Based on a sample and subject to sampling variability. See Appendix III]

State	People who got married in the past 12 months				People who got divorced in the past 12 months			
	Males	Marriage rate per 1,000 men	Females	Marriage rate per 1,000 women	Males	Divorce rate per 1,000 men	Females	Divorce rate per 1,000 women
United States............	**2,142,639**	**17.7**	**2,113,521**	**16.6**	**1,108,188**	**9.2**	**1,250,086**	**9.8**
Alabama...................	37,747	20.5	37,587	18.8	23,024	12.5	25,806	12.9
Alaska....................	6,761	23.3	6,654	24.9	3,055	10.5	3,158	11.8
Arizona...................	44,832	18.0	43,804	17.1	24,197	9.7	25,517	10.0
Arkansas..................	25,073	22.2	26,131	21.8	13,633	12.1	18,918	15.8
California.................	244,441	16.7	237,878	15.8	105,352	7.2	129,370	8.6
Colorado..................	47,412	23.7	47,266	23.4	22,058	11.0	21,768	10.8
Connecticut...............	19,897	14.2	21,526	14.2	13,397	9.6	13,545	9.0
Delaware..................	7,778	22.2	6,697	17.6	3,377	9.6	4,271	11.2
District of Columbia.......	6,049	24.9	5,507	19.9	1,819	7.5	2,327	8.4
Florida....................	119,719	15.9	117,360	14.6	74,191	9.8	82,022	10.2
Georgia...................	68,329	18.6	69,375	17.5	38,729	10.5	44,365	11.2
Hawaii....................	11,331	20.4	9,721	17.5	4,925	8.9	4,720	8.5
Idaho.....................	13,424	22.3	12,742	20.9	5,578	9.3	9,978	16.4
Illinois...................	80,093	16.1	78,900	14.9	38,646	7.8	43,830	8.3
Indiana...................	48,799	19.4	46,741	17.7	29,089	11.6	28,506	10.8
Iowa......................	23,151	19.3	24,933	19.9	10,807	9.0	12,047	9.6
Kansas....................	22,078	20.0	22,108	19.3	11,763	10.6	12,554	11.0
Kentucky..................	36,529	21.5	38,134	21.3	23,306	13.7	22,772	12.7
Louisiana.................	31,458	18.0	31,297	16.8	19,055	10.9	18,570	10.0
Maine.....................	7,590	14.2	7,834	13.7	5,615	10.5	6,522	11.4
Maryland..................	42,138	18.9	41,971	17.2	19,881	8.9	21,816	8.9
Massachusetts.............	38,946	15.1	39,338	14.0	17,408	6.7	24,126	8.6
Michigan..................	58,120	15.0	56,471	13.8	34,750	9.0	37,463	9.1
Minnesota.................	32,011	15.3	33,314	15.5	15,896	7.6	17,531	8.1
Mississippi................	21,068	18.8	20,660	16.9	13,843	12.3	14,348	11.7
Missouri..................	40,882	17.5	40,175	16.1	27,107	11.6	25,794	10.3
Montana..................	9,596	23.7	8,379	20.8	4,175	10.3	3,080	7.6
Nebraska.................	17,004	24.0	17,227	23.4	7,291	10.3	6,735	9.2
Nevada...................	22,537	20.8	21,466	20.1	15,128	14.0	13,292	12.4
New Hampshire...........	10,821	20.4	10,307	18.5	4,497	8.5	6,748	12.1
New Jersey................	48,816	14.3	48,752	13.2	22,547	6.6	24,796	6.7
New Mexico...............	13,697	17.1	13,628	16.4	8,755	10.9	8,303	10.0
New York..................	119,221	15.7	116,216	14.0	49,289	6.5	54,691	6.6
North Carolina............	67,836	18.4	69,587	17.5	35,646	9.7	35,757	9.0
North Dakota..............	4,709	16.9	4,684	17.3	2,555	9.2	1,905	7.0
Ohio......................	74,209	16.5	70,669	14.7	43,168	9.6	47,478	9.9
Oklahoma.................	29,840	20.5	27,962	18.4	17,849	12.2	19,802	13.0
Oregon...................	28,811	18.8	28,749	18.1	14,592	9.5	20,858	13.1
Pennsylvania..............	76,133	15.1	74,605	13.8	38,734	7.7	43,204	8.0
Rhode Island..............	5,926	14.3	5,433	11.9	3,402	8.2	3,946	8.6
South Carolina............	29,165	16.2	31,721	16.4	14,881	8.3	18,419	9.5
South Dakota.............	6,248	19.4	5,648	17.3	2,918	9.0	3,158	9.7
Tennessee.................	46,122	18.7	46,527	17.5	29,333	11.9	32,805	12.4
Texas.....................	199,676	20.8	195,503	19.7	94,142	9.8	117,633	11.9
Utah......................	26,985	26.6	26,851	26.4	12,345	12.2	13,098	12.9
Vermont...................	3,887	15.3	4,593	17.2	1,982	7.8	2,491	9.3
Virginia...................	62,803	19.9	60,081	18.0	28,326	9.0	34,885	10.5
Washington...............	51,542	19.2	50,993	18.6	24,304	9.0	31,962	11.6
West Virginia..............	12,933	17.2	12,449	15.9	7,817	10.4	9,801	12.5
Wisconsin.................	31,191	13.8	30,612	13.1	21,311	9.4	20,974	9.0
Wyoming..................	7,275	31.8	6,755	30.7	2,700	11.8	2,621	11.9

Source: U.S. Census Bureau, 2010 American Community Survey, B12501, "Marriage in the Last Year by Sex by Marital Status for the Population 15 Years and Over;" B12502, "Marriages Ending in Widowhood in the Last Year by Sex by Marital Status for the Population 15 Years and Over;" and B12503, "Divorces in the Last Year by Sex by Marital Status for the Population 15 Years and Over;" <http://factfinder2.census.gov>.

Table 136. Percent of First Marriages Reaching Stated Anniversary by Sex and Year of Marriage: 2009

[In percent except number of marriages. For currently married couples aged 15 years and over. Based on the second wave (interview) of the 2008 Survey of Income and Program Participation (SIPP), a longitutinal survey, conducted from January through April 2009]

Sex and year of marriage	Number of marriages (1,000)	Anniversary [1]							
		5th	10th	15th	20th	25th	30th	35th	40th
Men									
1960 to 1964................	4,150	94.6	83.4	74.7	70.2	66.9	64.5	62.1	60.1
1965 to 1969................	5,658	91.7	80.0	69.9	65.8	62.7	60.5	57.9	(X)
1970 to 1974................	7,036	88.0	75.0	65.7	60.2	56.8	53.8	(X)	(X)
1975 to 1979................	6,901	88.2	73.4	63.7	58.7	54.4	(X)	(X)	(X)
1980 to 1984................	7,144	90.6	74.3	65.2	60.0	(X)	(X)	(X)	(X)
1985 to 1989................	7,670	87.7	75.4	66.6	(X)	(X)	(X)	(X)	(X)
1990 to 1994................	7,569	89.7	77.3	(X)	(X)	(X)	(X)	(X)	(X)
1995 to 1999................	8,088	89.6	(X)	(X)	(X)	(X)	(X)	(X)	(X)
Women									
1960 to 1964................	5,495	93.0	82.8	73.5	67.0	60.8	57.2	53.6	49.7
1965 to 1969................	6,705	90.7	79.3	69.6	64.0	59.1	55.8	52.1	(X)
1970 to 1974................	7,667	89.2	74.5	66.1	61.3	56.2	52.6	(X)	(X)
1975 to 1979................	7,619	86.9	72.8	63.2	57.4	53.2	(X)	(X)	(X)
1980 to 1984................	8,051	87.8	71.1	62.9	56.6	(X)	(X)	(X)	(X)
1985 to 1989................	8,027	87.9	74.5	66.4	(X)	(X)	(X)	(X)	(X)
1990 to 1994................	8,164	87.1	74.5	(X)	(X)	(X)	(X)	(X)	(X)
1995 to 1999................	8,229	89.5	(X)	(X)	(X)	(X)	(X)	(X)	(X)

X Marriage cohort had not sufficient time to reach stated anniversary at time of the survey. [1] People reaching stated anniversary.

Source: U.S. Census Bureau, Current Population Reports, "Number, Timing, and Duration of Marriages and Divorces: 2009," P70-125, May 2011. See also <http://www.census.gov/hhes/socdemo/marriage/data/sipp/index.html>.

Health and Nutrition

This section presents statistics on health expenditures and insurance coverage, including Medicare and Medicaid, medical personnel, hospitals, nursing homes and other care facilities, injuries, diseases, disability status, nutritional intake of the population, and food consumption. Summary statistics showing recent trends on health care and discussions of selected health issues are published annually by the U.S. National Center for Health Statistics (NCHS) in *Health, United States*. Data on national health expenditures, medical costs, and insurance coverage are compiled by the U.S. Centers for Medicare & Medicaid Services (CMS) and appear on the CMS Web site at <http://www.cms.gov/NationalHealthExpendData/> and in the annual *Medicare and Medicaid Statistical Supplement* to the *Health Care Financing Review*. Statistics on health insurance are also collected by NCHS and are published in Series 10 of *Vital and Health Statistics*. NCHS also conducts periodic surveys of nutrient levels in the population, including estimates of food and nutrient intake, overweight and obesity, hypercholesterolemia, hypertension, and clinical signs of malnutrition. Data are published in Series 10 and 11 of *Vital and Health Statistics*. Statistics on hospitals are published annually by the Health Forum, L.L.C.; an American Hospital Association (AHA) company, in *AHA Hospital Statistics*. Data on nutrition and on annual per capita consumption of food are issued by the U.S. Department of Agriculture, Economic Research Service, and Center for Nutrition Policy and Promotion. Data are available on the Web sites at <http://www.ers.usda.gov/data-products/food-availability-(per-capita)-data-system.aspx> and <http://www.usda.gov/cnpp/>, respectively.

National health expenditures—CMS compiles estimates of national health expenditures (NHE) to measure spending for health care in the United States. The NHE accounts are structured to show spending by type of expenditure (i.e., hospital care, physician and clinical care, dental care, and other professional care; home health care; retail sales of prescription drugs; other medical nondurables; nursing home care and other personal health expenditures; plus other health expenditures such as public health activities, administration, and the net cost of private health insurance; plus medical sector investment, the sum of noncommercial medical research and capital formation in medical sector structures and equipment; and by source of funding (e.g., health insurance, out-of-pocket payments, and other third party payers and programs).

Data used to estimate health expenditures come from existing sources, which are tabulated for other purposes. The type of expenditure estimates rely upon statistics produced by such groups as the AHA, the Census Bureau, and the U.S. Department of Health and Human Services (HHS). Source of funding estimates are constructed using administrative and statistical records from the Medicare and Medicaid programs, the U.S. Department of Defense and VA medical programs, the Social Security Administration, Census Bureau's *Governmental Finances*, state and local governments, other HHS agencies, and other nongovernment sources.

Medicare, Medicaid, and CHIP—Since July 1966, the federal Medicare program has provided two coordinated plans for nearly all people aged 65 and over: (1) a hospital insurance plan, which covers hospital and related services and (2) a voluntary supplementary medical insurance plan, financed partially by monthly premiums paid by participants, which partly covers physicians' and related medical services. Such insurance also applies, since July 1973, to disabled beneficiaries of any age after 24 months of entitlement to cash benefits under the social security or railroad retirement programs and to persons with end stage renal disease. On January 1, 2006, Medicare began to provide coverage for prescription drugs as mandated by the Medicare Prescription Drug, Improvement, and Modernization Act of 2003 (MMA). This benefit is available on a voluntary basis to everyone with Medicare, and beneficiaries pay a monthly premium to enroll in one of Medicare's prescription drug plans.

Medicaid is a health insurance program for certain low-income people. These include: certain low-income families with children; people on supplemental security income; certain low-income pregnant women and children; and people who have very high medical bills. There are special rules for those who live in nursing homes and for disabled children living at home. Medicaid is funded and administered through a state/federal partnership. Although there are broad federal requirements for Medicaid, states have a wide degree of flexibility to design their program. The Children's Health Insurance Program Reauthorization Act of 2009 (CHIPRA or Public Law 111-3) reauthorized the Children's Health Insurance Program (CHIP). The program went into effect on April 1, 2009. CHIP replaces the State Children's Health Insurance Program (SCHIP). It will preserve coverage for the millions of children who rely on CHIP today and provides the resources for states to reach millions of additional uninsured children. CHIP was designed as a federal/state partnership, similar to Medicaid, with the goal of expanding health insurance to children whose families earn too much money to be eligible for Medicaid, but not enough money to purchase private insurance.

Health resources—Hospital statistics based on data from AHA's yearly survey are published annually in *AHA Hospital Statistics* and cover all hospitals accepted for registration by the Association. To be accepted for registration, a hospital must meet certain requirements relating to number of beds, construction, equipment, medical and nursing staff, patient care, clinical records, surgical and obstetrical facilities, diagnostic and treatment facilities, laboratory services, etc. Data obtained from NCHS cover all U.S. hospitals that meet certain criteria for inclusion. The criteria are published in *Vital and Health Statistics* reports, Series 13. Statistics on the demographic characteristics of persons employed in the health occupations are compiled by the U.S. Bureau of Labor Statistics and reported in *Employment and Earnings* (monthly) (see Table 626, Section 12, Labor Force, Employment, and Earnings). Data based on surveys of health personnel and utilization of health facilities providing long-term care, ambulatory care, emergency room care, and hospital care are presented in NCHS Series 13, data from the National Health Interview Survey. Statistics on patient visits to health care providers, as reported in health interviews, appear in NCHS Series 10, data from the National Health Care Survey.

The CMS's *Health Care Financing Review* and its annual *Medicare and Medicaid Statistical Supplement* present data for hospitals and nursing homes as well as extended care facilities and home health agencies. These data are based on records of the Medicare program and differ from those of other sources because they are limited to facilities meeting federal eligibility standards for participation in Medicare.

Disability and illness—General health statistics, including morbidity, disability, injuries, preventive care, and findings from physiological testing are collected by NCHS in its National Health Interview Survey and its National Health and Nutrition Examination Surveys and appear in *Vital and Health Statistics*, Series 10 and 11, respectively. Annual incidence data on notifiable diseases are compiled by the Public Health Service (PHS) at its Centers for Disease Control and Prevention in Atlanta, Georgia, and are published as a supplement to its *Morbidity and Mortality Weekly Report* (MMWR). The list of diseases is revised annually and includes those which, by mutual agreement of the states and PHS, are communicable diseases of national importance.

Statistical reliability—For discussion of statistical collection, estimation, and sampling procedures and measures of reliability applicable to data from NCHS and CMS, see Appendix III.

Table 137. National Health Expenditures—Summary: 1960 to 2010

[In billions of dollars (27.4 represents $27,400,000,000). Excludes Puerto Rico and Island Areas]

Year	Total expenditures [1]	Health consumption expenditures, total [2]	Personal health care expenditures									
			Total [3]	Hospital care	Physician and clinical services	Other professional services	Dental services	Home health care	Nursing care facilities [4]	Prescription drugs	Durable medical equipment	Other nondurable medical equipment
1960.....	27.4	24.8	23.4	9.0	5.6	0.4	2.0	0.1	0.8	2.7	0.7	1.6
1961.....	29.2	26.4	24.8	9.8	5.8	0.4	2.1	0.1	0.8	2.7	0.8	1.8
1962.....	31.9	28.4	26.7	10.4	6.3	0.4	2.2	0.1	0.9	3.0	0.9	1.9
1963.....	34.7	30.9	29.1	11.5	7.1	0.5	2.4	0.1	1.0	3.2	0.9	1.9
1964.....	38.5	34.1	32.1	12.5	8.1	0.5	2.6	0.1	1.2	3.3	1.0	2.1
1965.....	42.0	37.2	34.7	13.5	8.6	0.5	2.8	0.1	1.4	3.7	1.1	2.2
1966.....	46.3	41.2	38.4	15.3	9.3	0.6	3.0	0.1	1.7	4.0	1.2	2.4
1967.....	51.8	46.5	43.5	17.8	10.4	0.6	3.4	0.2	2.2	4.2	1.1	2.5
1968.....	58.8	52.8	49.2	20.5	11.3	0.6	3.7	0.2	2.9	4.7	1.3	2.8
1969.....	66.2	59.1	55.5	23.4	12.7	0.7	4.2	0.3	3.4	5.1	1.5	3.0
1970.....	74.9	67.1	63.1	27.2	14.3	0.7	4.7	0.2	4.0	5.5	1.7	3.3
1971.....	83.2	74.4	69.5	30.2	15.9	0.8	5.2	0.2	4.6	5.9	1.8	3.5
1972.....	93.1	83.4	77.2	33.8	17.7	0.9	5.6	0.2	5.2	6.3	2.0	3.7
1973.....	103.4	93.1	86.2	37.9	19.6	1.0	6.4	0.3	6.0	6.8	2.2	4.0
1974.....	117.2	105.9	98.8	44.1	22.2	1.2	7.1	0.4	6.9	7.4	2.5	4.5
1975.....	133.6	121.2	113.3	51.2	25.3	1.3	8.0	0.6	8.0	8.1	2.8	4.9
1976.....	153.0	139.4	129.4	59.4	28.7	1.6	9.0	0.9	9.1	8.7	3.0	5.4
1977.....	174.0	160.0	146.8	67.0	33.1	2.1	10.1	1.1	10.3	9.2	3.2	6.1
1978.....	195.5	180.1	164.3	75.6	35.8	2.4	11.0	1.6	11.8	9.9	3.4	7.1
1979.....	221.7	204.7	187.2	86.2	41.2	2.8	12.0	1.9	13.3	10.7	3.8	8.5
1980.....	255.8	235.7	217.2	100.5	47.7	3.5	13.4	2.4	15.3	12.0	4.1	9.8
1981.....	296.8	273.7	252.1	117.5	55.6	4.3	15.8	2.9	17.3	13.4	4.3	11.3
1982.....	334.7	308.3	283.4	133.6	61.6	4.9	17.1	3.5	19.5	15.0	4.6	12.6
1983.....	369.0	339.7	312.0	144.7	68.6	5.7	18.4	4.2	21.7	17.3	5.3	13.8
1984.....	406.5	375.5	342.1	154.4	77.4	7.3	20.0	5.1	23.7	19.6	6.1	15.0
1985.....	444.6	413.4	376.9	164.6	90.9	8.1	21.8	5.6	26.3	21.8	7.1	16.0
1986.....	476.9	444.4	409.5	175.6	100.7	9.3	23.3	6.4	28.7	24.3	8.1	17.1
1987.....	519.1	483.1	448.5	189.5	112.9	11.4	25.5	6.7	30.7	26.9	9.5	18.3
1988.....	581.7	541.5	499.5	206.5	128.6	13.8	27.5	8.4	34.3	30.6	11.1	19.4
1989.....	647.5	603.5	551.6	226.0	143.3	14.6	29.5	10.2	38.7	34.8	11.9	20.8
1990.....	724.3	675.6	616.8	250.4	158.9	17.4	31.7	12.6	44.9	40.3	13.8	22.4
1991.....	791.5	739.5	677.6	275.8	176.5	18.7	33.5	15.2	49.4	44.4	13.1	23.2
1992.....	857.9	801.0	733.7	298.5	191.3	21.0	37.3	18.7	53.1	47.0	13.5	23.2
1993.....	921.5	860.3	781.2	315.7	202.7	23.2	39.2	22.8	56.0	49.6	14.1	23.7
1994.....	972.7	908.8	823.1	328.4	212.2	24.2	41.7	27.4	58.6	53.1	15.3	24.3
1995.....	1,027.5	961.6	872.9	339.3	222.3	27.0	44.8	32.4	64.5	59.8	15.8	25.1
1996.....	1,081.9	1,014.1	921.9	350.8	231.3	29.2	47.1	35.8	69.6	68.1	17.4	26.0
1997.....	1,142.6	1,070.4	974.6	363.4	242.9	31.7	50.5	37.0	74.4	77.6	19.2	27.6
1998.....	1,209.0	1,129.6	1,029.3	374.9	258.7	33.8	53.8	34.2	79.4	88.4	21.3	28.6
1999.....	1,286.6	1,201.1	1,089.8	393.6	271.9	35.0	57.4	32.9	80.8	104.7	23.0	30.6
2000.....	1,377.2	1,289.6	1,165.4	415.5	290.9	37.0	62.3	32.4	85.1	120.9	25.1	31.6
2001.....	1,494.1	1,402.8	1,265.3	449.4	315.7	40.6	67.8	34.4	90.8	138.7	25.1	32.3
2002.....	1,636.4	1,534.4	1,372.0	486.5	340.9	43.7	73.7	36.6	94.5	158.2	27.1	33.3
2003.....	1,774.3	1,664.3	1,480.4	526.2	368.1	46.8	76.3	39.8	100.3	176.0	28.2	35.1
2004.....	1,900.0	1,782.6	1,589.3	566.0	393.1	50.3	82.1	43.8	105.7	192.2	29.6	35.8
2005.....	2,029.1	1,902.6	1,697.2	609.4	416.9	53.0	87.0	48.7	112.5	204.8	31.2	37.2
2006.....	2,162.4	2,031.5	1,804.9	651.9	438.8	55.4	91.4	52.6	117.3	224.2	32.9	38.7
2007.....	2,297.1	2,153.4	1,914.6	692.5	461.8	59.5	97.3	57.8	126.4	236.2	34.3	41.0
2008.....	2,403.9	2,250.1	2,010.2	729.3	486.6	63.6	102.4	61.5	132.7	243.6	34.9	42.5
2009.....	2,495.8	2,349.5	2,109.0	776.1	502.7	66.0	102.5	66.1	138.7	256.1	35.2	43.6
2010.....	2,593.6	2,444.6	2,186.0	814.0	515.5	68.4	104.8	70.2	143.1	259.1	37.7	44.8

[1] Includes Health Consumption Expenditures plus medical research, and medical structures and equipment. [2] Includes Personal Health Expenditures plus government administration, net cost of health insurance, and government public health activities. [3] Includes hospital care, physician and clinical services, dental services, other professional services, other health, residential, and personal services, home health care, nursing care facilities and continuing care retirement communities, prescription drugs, durable medical equipment, and other nondurable medical products. [4] Includes care provided in nursing care facilities (NAICS 6231), continuing care retirement communities (623311), state and local government nursing facilities, and nursing facilities operated by the Department of Veterans' Affairs (DVA).

Source: U.S. Centers for Medicare and Medicaid Services, Office of the Actuary, National Health Statistics Group, <http://www.cms.gov/NationalHealthExpendData/>.

Table 138. National Health Expenditures by Source of Funds: 1990 to 2010

[In billions of dollars (724.3 represents $724,300,000,000), except percent. Excludes Puerto Rico and Island Areas]

Type of expenditure	1990	2000	2005	2006	2007	2008	2009	2010
National health expenditure, total.............	**724.3**	**1,377.2**	**2,029.1**	**2,162.4**	**2,297.1**	**2,403.9**	**2,495.8**	**2,593.6**
Annual percent change [1]............	11.0	7.0	6.8	6.6	6.2	4.7	3.8	3.9
Percent of gross domestic product...........	12.5	13.8	16.1	16.2	16.4	16.8	17.9	17.9
Out of pocket.............................	138.7	201.8	263.4	271.9	287.3	294.0	294.4	299.7
Health insurance........................	439.5	920.3	1,415.3	1,520.2	1,610.2	1,700.7	1,793.3	1,870.8
Private health insurance....................	234.3	459.6	702.9	740.2	776.2	807.6	828.8	848.7
Medicare...............................	110.2	224.3	338.8	403.1	432.3	466.9	499.8	524.6
Medicaid (Title XIX).....................	73.7	200.5	309.5	306.8	326.4	343.8	374.4	401.4
CHIP (Title XIX and Title XXI)...........	–	3.0	7.5	8.3	9.1	10.2	11.1	11.7
Department of Defense..................	10.4	13.8	26.7	29.9	32.3	33.9	36.8	38.4
Department of Veterans Affairs............	10.9	19.1	29.8	31.9	34.0	38.2	42.4	46.0
Other third party payers and programs.......	77.5	124.5	167.8	176.8	186.9	182.7	185.6	191.6
Worksite health care.....................	2.2	3.5	4.2	4.3	4.4	4.4	4.4	4.6
Other private revenues [2]...................	29.6	57.5	70.5	77.6	86.0	80.9	85.7	89.4
Indian health services....................	1.0	2.0	2.5	2.6	2.7	2.8	3.2	3.6
Workers' compensation....................	17.5	26.2	41.2	41.6	41.2	40.1	36.7	37.2
General assistance.......................	5.0	3.9	6.2	6.7	6.9	7.1	7.2	7.0
Maternal/Child health....................	1.6	2.7	2.6	2.7	2.8	2.8	2.7	2.8
Vocational rehabilitation.................	0.3	0.4	0.5	0.5	0.5	0.5	0.5	0.5
Other federal programs [3]................	1.5	4.5	6.3	6.4	6.7	6.9	7.3	7.3
Substance abuse and mental health services administration.................	1.4	2.6	3.2	3.2	3.2	3.2	3.3	3.4
Other state and local programs [4]...........	16.0	18.8	27.2	27.7	28.7	29.8	30.4	31.3
School health...........................	1.3	2.5	3.4	3.6	3.9	4.1	4.3	4.5
Public health activity [5]......................	20.0	43.0	56.2	62.5	69.0	72.7	76.2	82.5
Investment................................	**48.7**	**87.5**	**126.5**	**130.9**	**143.7**	**153.8**	**146.3**	**149.0**
Research [6]...............................	12.7	25.5	40.3	41.4	41.9	43.4	45.7	49.3
Structures & equipment [7]...................	36.0	62.1	86.2	89.6	101.7	110.4	100.6	99.8

– Represents zero. [1] Average annual growth from prior year shown. [2] The most common source of other private funds is philanthropy. Philanthropic support may be direct from individuals or may be obtained through philanthropic fund-raising organizations. Support may also be obtained from foundations or corporations. [3] Includes general hospital/medical, general hospital/medical NEC, non-XIX federal, and O.E.O. [4] Includes non-XIX state and local, temporary disability insurance, and state and local subsidies. [5] Governments are involved in organizing and delivering publicly provided health services such as epidemiological surveillance, inoculations, immunization/vaccination services, disease prevention programs, and the operation of public health laboratories. In the NHEA, spending for these activities is reported in government public health activity. [6] Non-profit or government entities. Research and development expenditures by drug and medical supply and equipment manufacturers are not shown, those expenditures are treated as intermediate purchases under the definitions of national income accounting; that is, the value of that research is deemed to be recouped through product sales. [7] Structures are defined as the value of new construction by the medical sector. Includes establishments engaged in providing health care, but does not include retail establishments that sell non-durable or durable medical goods. Construction includes new buildings; additions, alterations, and major replacements; mechanical and electric installations; and site preparation.

Source: U.S. Centers for Medicare and Medicaid Services, Office of the Actuary, National Health Expenditure Group, <http://www.cms.gov/NationalHealthExpendData/>.

Table 139. National Health Expenditures by Source of Funds and Type of Expenditure: 1990 to 2010

[In billions of dollars (724.3 represents $724,300,000,000). Excludes Puerto Rico and Island Areas]

Object of expenditure	1990	2000	2004	2005	2006	2007	2008	2009	2010
Total........	**724.3**	**1,377.2**	**1,900.0**	**2,029.1**	**2,162.4**	**2,297.1**	**2,403.9**	**2,495.8**	**2,593.6**
Source of funds:									
Out-of-pocket.............................	138.7	201.8	248.9	263.4	271.9	287.3	294.0	294.4	299.7
Health insurance [1]........................	439.5	920.3	1,320.6	1,415.3	1,520.2	1,610.2	1,700.7	1,793.3	1,870.8
Other third party payers and programs [2].............	77.5	124.5	159.2	167.8	176.8	186.9	182.7	185.6	191.6
Public health activities [3]................	20.0	43.0	54.0	56.2	62.5	69.0	72.7	76.2	82.5
Investment...............................	48.7	87.5	117.4	126.5	130.9	143.7	153.8	146.3	149.0
Type of expenditure:									
Health consumption expenditures....................	675.6	1,289.6	1,782.6	1,902.6	2,031.5	2,153.4	2,250.1	2,349.5	2,444.6
Personal health care..................	616.8	1,165.4	1,589.3	1,697.2	1,804.9	1,914.6	2,010.2	2,109.0	2,186.0
Hospital care.......................	250.4	415.5	566.0	609.4	651.9	692.5	729.3	776.1	814.0
Physician and clinical services....................	158.9	290.9	393.1	416.9	438.8	461.8	486.6	502.7	515.5
Other professional services [4]...................	17.4	37.0	50.3	53.0	55.4	59.5	63.6	66.0	68.4
Dental services.....................	31.7	62.3	82.1	87.0	91.4	97.3	102.4	102.5	104.8
Other health, residential, and personal care [5].......	24.3	64.6	90.6	96.5	101.7	107.7	113.3	122.0	128.5
Home health care....................	12.6	32.4	43.8	48.7	52.6	57.8	61.5	66.1	70.2
Nursing care facilities and continuing care retirement communities.................	44.9	85.1	105.7	112.5	117.3	126.4	132.7	138.7	143.1
Prescription drugs..................	40.3	120.9	192.2	204.8	224.2	236.2	243.6	256.1	259.1
Durable medical equipment [6]...........	13.8	25.1	29.6	31.2	32.9	34.3	34.9	35.2	37.7
Other nondurable medical products [7].............	22.4	31.6	35.8	37.2	38.7	41.0	42.5	43.6	44.8
Investment...............................	48.7	87.5	117.4	126.5	130.9	143.7	153.8	146.3	149.0
Research [8].............................	12.7	25.5	38.5	40.3	41.4	41.9	43.4	45.7	49.3
Structures & equipment [9]............................	36.0	62.1	78.9	86.2	89.6	101.7	110.4	100.6	99.8

[1] Includes Private Health Insurance, Medicare, Medicaid, CHIP (Titles XIX and XXI), Department of Defense, and Department of Veterans Affairs. [2] See footnote 2, Table 144. [3] See footnote 5, Table 138. [4] Covers services provided in establishments operated by health practitioners other than physicians and dentists. These professional services include those provided by private-duty nurses, chiropractors, podiatrists, optometrists, and physical, occupational and speech therapists, among others. [5] Includes spending for Medicaid home and community based waivers, care provided in residential care facilities, ambulance services, school health and worksite health care. Generally these programs provide payments for services in non-traditional settings such as community centers, senior citizens centers, schools, and military field stations. [6] Covers "retail" sales of items such as contact lenses, eyeglasses and other ophthalmic products, surgical and orthopedic products, hearing aids, wheelchairs, and medical equipment rentals. [7] Covers the "retail" sales of non-prescription drugs and medical sundries. [8] See footnote 6, Table 138. [9] See footnote 7, Table 138.

Source: U.S. Centers for Medicare and Medicaid Services, Office of the Actuary, National Health Statistics Group, <http://www.cms.gov/NationalHealthExpendData/>.

Table 140. Health Consumption Expenditures—Per Capita Spending by Type of Expenditure: 1990 to 2010

[In dollars, except percent. Based on U.S. Census Bureau estimates of total U.S. resident population plus the net Census undercount. Excludes research, structures and equipment. Excludes Puerto Rico and Island Areas]

Type of expenditure and source of funds	1990	2000	2004	2005	2006	2007	2008	2009	2010
Total [1]	**2,662**	**4,568**	**6,087**	**6,440**	**6,812**	**7,151**	**7,405**	**7,671**	**7,919**
Annual percent change [2]	11.1	7.4	7.1	6.7	6.8	6.0	4.5	4.4	4.0
Hospital care	987	1,472	1,933	2,063	2,186	2,299	2,400	2,534	2,637
Physician and clinical services	626	1,030	1,342	1,411	1,471	1,533	1,601	1,641	1,670
Other professional services [3]	69	131	172	179	186	198	209	215	221
Dental services	125	221	280	295	307	323	337	335	339
Other health, residential, and personal care [4]	96	229	309	327	341	358	373	398	416
Home health care	50	115	150	165	176	192	202	216	227
Nursing care facilities and continuing care retirement communities	177	302	361	381	393	420	437	453	464
Prescription drugs	159	428	656	693	752	784	802	836	839
Durable medical equipment [5]	54	89	101	106	110	114	115	115	122
Other nondurable medical products [6]	88	112	122	126	130	136	140	142	145
Public health activities [7]	79	152	184	190	210	229	239	249	267

[1] Includes other items, not shown separately. [2] Average annual growth from prior year shown. [3] See footnote 4, Table 139. [4] Includes spending for Medicaid home and community based waivers, care provided in residential care facilities, ambulance services, school health and worksite health care. Generally these programs provide payments for services in non-traditional settings such as community centers, senior citizens centers, schools, and military field stations. [5] See footnote 6, Table 139. [6] Covers the "retail" sales of non-prescription drugs and medical sundries. [7] See footnote 5, Table 138.

Source: U.S. Centers for Medicare and Medicaid Services, Office of the Actuary, National Health Statistics Group, <http://www.cms.gov/NationalHealthExpendData/>.

Table 141. Health Consumption Expenditures by Type of Expenditure and Source of Funds: 2010

[In billions of dollars (2,444.6 represents $2,444,600,000,000). Excludes Puerto Rico and Island Areas. Excludes research, structures, and equipment]

Type of expenditure	Total	Out–of–pocket	Health insurance					Other third party payers and pro-grams [2]
			Total	Private health insurance	Medicare	Medicaid	Other health insurance pro-grams [1]	
Total	**2,444.6**	**299.7**	**1,870.8**	**848.7**	**524.6**	**401.4**	**96.1**	**191.6**
Personal health care [3]	2,186.0	299.7	1,703.0	746.0	493.8	371.6	91.6	183.3
Hospital care	814.0	25.9	714.4	285.8	226.5	152.5	49.6	73.7
Physician and clinical services	515.5	49.3	418.7	239.4	114.6	43.0	21.7	47.6
Dental services	104.8	43.3	61.0	51.0	0.2	7.4	2.3	0.5
Other health, residential, and personal care [4]	128.5	7.1	81.5	6.3	4.7	67.7	2.7	40.0
Home health care	70.2	5.0	63.0	4.5	31.5	26.2	0.8	2.2
Nursing care facilities and continuing care retirement communities	143.1	40.4	93.7	12.7	31.9	45.1	4.0	8.9
Prescription drugs	259.1	48.8	206.9	117.0	59.5	20.2	10.3	3.4
Durable medical equipment [5]	37.7	20.6	16.6	4.4	7.5	4.6	0.1	0.6
Government administration [6]	30.1	–	29.0	–	7.3	18.1	3.6	1.1
Net cost of health insurance [6]	146.0	–	138.8	102.7	23.4	11.8	0.9	7.3
Public health activities [7]	82.5	–	–	–	–	–	–	–

– Represents zero. [1] Includes CHIP (Titles XIX and XXI), Department of Defense, and Department of Veterans Affairs. [2] See footnote 2, Table 144. [3] Includes other items, not shown separately [4] See footnote 5, Table 139. [5] See footnote 6, Table 139. [6] See source material for definitions. [7] See footnote 5, Table 138.

Source: U.S. Centers for Medicare and Medicaid Services, Office of the Actuary, National Health Statistics Group, <http://www.cms.gov/NationalHealthExpendData/>.

Table 142. Personal Health Care Expenditures by Source of Funds: 1990 to 2010

[In billions of dollars (616.8 represents $616,800,000,000), except percent. Excludes Puerto Rico and Island Areas]

Item	1990	2000	2004	2005	2006	2007	2008	2009	2010
Personal health care expenditures	**616.8**	**1,165.4**	**1,589.3**	**1,697.2**	**1,804.9**	**1,914.6**	**2,010.2**	**2,109.0**	**2,186.0**
Out-of-pocket	138.7	201.8	248.9	263.4	271.9	287.3	294.0	294.4	299.7
Health insurance	403.3	844.8	1,194.8	1,281.4	1,372.0	1,455.0	1,544.9	1,637.1	1,703.0
Private health insurance	205.1	407.1	566.9	607.7	640.6	673.5	707.5	734.0	746.0
Medicare	107.3	215.8	299.4	325.3	381.7	408.2	442.0	471.2	493.8
Medicaid	69.7	186.9	270.9	287.7	283.4	301.9	317.1	345.9	371.6
Other health insurance [1]	21.2	34.9	57.5	60.7	66.3	71.4	78.3	86.1	91.6
Other third party payers and programs [2]	74.9	118.8	145.7	152.5	161.0	172.2	171.4	177.4	183.3

[1] Includes Children's Health Insurance Program (Titles XIX and XXI), Department of Defense, and Department of Veterans Affairs. [2] See footnote 2, Table 144.

Source: U. S. Centers for Medicare and Medicaid Services, Office of the Actuary, National Health Statistics Group, <http://www.cms.gov/NationalHealthExpendData/>.

Table 143. National Health Expenditures by Sponsor: 1990 to 2010

[In billions of dollars (724.3 represents $724,300,000,000). Excludes Puerto Rico and Island Areas.]

Type of sponsor	1990	2000	2005	2006	2007	2008	2009	2010
Total	**724.3**	**1,377.2**	**2,029.1**	**2,162.4**	**2,297.1**	**2,403.9**	**2,495.8**	**2,593.6**
Business, households and other private revenues	488.2	888.5	1,226.8	1,289.0	1,364.3	1,407.8	1,402.8	1,429.9
Private business [1]	178.3	346.3	487.7	502.4	523.5	531.4	529.8	534.5
Household [2,3]	253.0	434.3	596.7	633.3	668.9	703.1	705.5	725.5
Other private revenues	56.9	107.9	142.3	153.3	171.9	173.4	167.4	169.9
Governments	236.1	488.7	802.4	873.4	932.8	996.1	1,093.1	1,163.7
Federal government [4,5]	125.3	261.0	451.8	498.1	529.8	582.4	684.0	742.7
State and local government [6,7]	110.8	227.7	350.6	375.4	403.0	413.6	409.1	421.1

[1] Estimates for 2006–2010 exclude Retiree Drug Subsidy (RDS) payments to private plans. [2] Estimates for 2010 excludes subsidized COBRA payments. [3] Includes one-half of self-employment contribution to Medicare Hospital Insurance Trust Fund and taxation of Social Security benefits. [4] Includes RDS payments to private and state and local plans, 2006-2010. [5] Includes maternal and child health, vocational rehabilitation, Substance Abuse and Mental Health Services Administration, Indian Health Service, Office of Economic Opportunity (1965–74), Federal workers' compensation, and other federal programs, public health activities, Department of Defense, Department of Veterans Affairs, Children's Health Program (CHIP), investment (research, structures and equipment) and COBRA subsidies. [6] Includes Medicaid buy-in premiums for Medicare. [7] Includes other public and general assistance, maternal and child health, vocational rehabilitation, public health activities, hospital subsidies, other state and local programs, state phase-down payments and investment (research, structures and equipment).

Source: U.S. Centers for Medicare and Medicaid Services, Office of the Actuary, "National Health Expenditures, by Type of Sponsors," <http://www.cms.gov/NationalHealthExpendData/>.

Table 144. Hospital Care, Physician and Clinical Services, Nursing Care Facilities and Continuing Care Retirement Communities, and Prescription Drug Expenditures by Source of Funds: 1990 to 2010

[In billions of dollars (250.4 represents $250,400,000,000). Excludes Puerto Rico and Island Areas]

Source of payment	1990	2000	2005	2006	2007	2008	2009	2010
Hospital care, total	**250.4**	**415.5**	**609.4**	**651.9**	**692.5**	**729.3**	**776.1**	**814.0**
Out-of-pocket	11.2	13.5	19.6	20.9	22.4	23.5	24.9	25.9
Health insurance	206.8	357.9	532.4	567.9	601.4	639.8	680.0	714.4
Private health insurance	96.9	141.9	218.4	237.5	250.1	266.8	279.5	285.8
Medicare	67.4	122.9	175.4	184.1	192.6	205.5	216.5	226.5
Medicaid	26.7	71.2	104.8	110.2	119.8	124.1	137.1	152.5
Other health insurance [1]	15.8	21.9	33.7	36.1	38.9	43.3	46.9	49.6
Other third party payers and programs [2]	32.5	44.1	57.4	63.1	68.7	66.0	71.2	73.7
Physician and clinical services, total	**158.9**	**290.9**	**416.9**	**438.8**	**461.8**	**486.6**	**502.7**	**515.5**
Out-of-pocket	30.1	32.5	42.5	44.5	46.8	48.7	47.7	49.3
Health insurance	107.8	222.8	330.0	349.2	367.9	390.6	408.9	418.7
Private health insurance	67.0	138.0	201.9	211.4	222.2	233.0	237.2	239.4
Medicare	30.5	58.7	85.9	91.5	96.0	103.8	111.4	114.6
Medicaid	7.0	19.2	29.8	31.6	33.3	35.7	40.0	43.0
Other health insurance [1]	3.3	6.8	12.4	14.6	16.5	18.1	20.3	21.7
Other third party payers and programs [2]	21.0	35.6	44.4	45.1	47.1	47.3	46.2	47.6
Nursing care facilities and continuing care retirement communities, total	**44.9**	**85.1**	**112.5**	**117.3**	**126.4**	**132.7**	**138.7**	**143.1**
Out-of-pocket	18.1	27.2	32.5	33.9	37.2	38.6	39.5	40.4
Health insurance	21.9	52.0	72.8	75.8	80.3	85.9	90.6	93.7
Private health insurance	2.8	7.5	8.3	9.4	10.2	10.9	11.8	12.7
Medicare	1.7	10.8	20.5	22.4	24.8	27.6	29.9	31.9
Medicaid	16.4	31.9	41.1	41.3	42.1	43.8	44.9	45.1
Other health insurance [1]	1.0	1.9	2.8	2.8	3.3	3.7	4.0	4.0
Other third party payers and programs [2]	4.9	5.9	7.2	7.6	8.9	8.2	8.6	8.9
Prescription drugs, total	**40.3**	**120.9**	**204.8**	**224.2**	**236.2**	**243.6**	**256.1**	**259.1**
Out-of-pocket	22.9	34.0	51.6	51.3	53.0	51.0	50.8	48.8
Health insurance	16.2	84.7	149.3	168.9	179.4	188.9	201.7	206.9
Private health insurance	10.9	60.7	101.6	102.2	106.8	110.1	117.2	117.0
Medicare	0.2	2.1	3.9	39.6	45.9	50.6	54.5	59.5
Medicaid	5.1	19.8	36.3	18.9	18.1	18.9	20.1	20.2
Other health insurance [1]	0.1	2.1	7.5	8.2	8.6	9.2	9.9	10.3
Other third party payers and programs [2]	1.2	2.2	3.8	4.0	3.8	3.6	3.5	3.4

[1] Includes Children's Health Insurance Program (Titles XIX and XXI), Department of Defense, and Department of Veterans Affairs. [2] Includes worksite health care, other private revenues, Indian Health Service, workers' compensation, general assistance, maternal and child health, vocational rehabilitation, other federal programs, Substance Abuse and Mental Health Services Administration, other state and local programs, and school health.

Source: U.S. Centers for Medicare and Medicaid Services, Office of the Actuary, National Health Statistics Group, <http://www.cms.gov/NationalHealthExpendData/>.

Table 145. Consumer Price Indexes of Medical Care Prices: 1980 to 2011

[1982–1984 = 100. Indexes are annual averages of monthly data based on components of consumer price index for all urban consumers; for explanation, see text, Section 14 and Appendix III]

Year	Medical care, total	Medical care services				Medical care commodities		Annual percent change [3]		
		Total [1]	Professional services			Hospital and related services	Total [2]	Pre-scription drugs	Medical care, total	Medical care services	Medical care com-modities
			Total [1]	Physi-cians	Dental						
1980.......	74.9	74.8	77.9	76.5	78.9	69.2	75.4	72.5	11.0	11.3	9.3
1985.......	113.5	113.2	113.5	113.3	114.2	116.1	115.2	120.1	6.3	6.1	7.2
1990.......	162.8	162.7	156.1	160.8	155.8	178.0	163.4	181.7	9.0	9.3	8.4
1995.......	220.5	224.2	201.0	208.8	206.8	257.8	204.5	235.0	4.5	5.1	1.9
2000.......	260.8	266.0	237.7	244.7	258.5	317.3	238.1	285.4	4.1	4.3	3.2
2005.......	323.2	336.7	281.7	287.5	324.0	439.9	276.0	349.0	4.2	4.8	2.5
2006.......	336.2	350.6	289.3	291.9	340.9	468.1	285.9	363.9	4.0	4.1	3.6
2007.......	351.1	369.3	300.8	303.2	358.4	498.9	290.0	369.2	4.4	5.3	1.4
2008.......	364.1	384.9	311.0	311.3	376.9	534.0	296.0	378.3	3.7	4.2	2.1
2009.......	375.6	397.3	319.4	320.8	388.1	567.9	305.1	391.1	3.2	3.2	3.1
2010.......	388.4	411.2	328.2	331.3	398.8	607.7	314.7	407.8	3.4	3.5	3.1
2011.......	400.3	423.8	335.7	340.3	408.0	641.5	324.1	425.0	3.0	3.1	3.0

[1] Includes other services not shown separately. [2] Includes other commodities not shown separately. [3] Percent change from the immediate prior year.

Source: Bureau of Labor Statistics, "CPI Detailed Report," <http://www.bls.gov/cpi/cpi_dr.htm>. See also "Monthly Labor Review Online," <http://www.bls.gov/opub/mlr/>.

Table 146. Average Annual Expenditures Per Consumer Unit for Health Care: 2008 to 2010

[In dollars, except percent. See text, Section 13 and headnote, Table 692. For composition of regions, see map, inside front cover]

Item	Health care, total		Health insur-ance	Medical services	Drugs and medical sup-plies [1]	Percent distribution		
	Amount	Percent of total expendi-tures				Health insur-ance	Medical services	Drugs and medical sup-plies [1]
2008..........................	2,976	5.9	1,653	727	596	55.5	24.4	20.0
2009..........................	3,126	6.4	1,785	736	605	57.1	23.5	19.4
2010..........................	**3,157**	**6.6**	**1,831**	**722**	**604**	**58.0**	**22.9**	**19.1**
Age of reference person:								
Under 25 years old..............	775	2.8	405	236	134	52.3	30.5	17.3
25 to 34 years old................	1,800	3.9	1,086	443	271	60.3	24.6	15.1
35 to 44 years old................	2,583	4.6	1,453	681	449	56.3	26.4	17.4
45 to 54 years old................	3,261	5.6	1,747	879	634	53.6	27.0	19.4
55 to 64 years old................	3,859	7.6	2,110	943	807	54.7	24.4	20.9
65 to 74 years old................	4,922	11.9	3,133	849	941	63.7	17.2	19.1
75 years old and over............	4,754	15.1	3,031	735	987	63.8	15.5	20.8
Race of reference person:								
White and other..................	3,397	6.9	1,937	804	656	57.0	23.7	19.3
Black............................	1,734	4.8	1,156	239	338	66.7	13.8	19.5
Origin of reference person:								
Hispanic.........................	1,842	4.4	971	519	352	52.7	28.2	19.1
Non-Hispanic....................	3,339	6.8	1,950	750	639	58.4	22.5	19.1
Region of residence:								
Northeast........................	3,125	5.9	1,930	630	564	61.8	20.2	18.0
Midwest.........................	3,265	7.2	1,888	726	650	57.8	22.2	19.9
South............................	3,041	6.9	1,798	660	584	59.1	21.7	19.2
West.............................	3,265	6.1	1,746	893	626	53.5	27.4	19.2
Size of consumer unit:								
One person.......................	2,027	7.0	1,176	435	417	58.0	21.5	20.6
Two or more persons.............	3,625	6.5	2,102	841	681	58.0	23.2	18.8
Two persons.....................	4,108	8.1	2,421	885	801	58.9	21.5	19.5
Three persons...................	3,346	5.9	1,902	802	643	56.8	24.0	19.2
Four persons....................	3,286	5.2	1,925	793	567	58.6	24.1	17.3
Five persons or more.............	2,977	4.9	1,636	825	516	55.0	27.7	17.3
Income before taxes:								
Quintiles of income:								
Lowest 20 percent.............	1,524	7.3	886	264	375	58.1	17.3	24.6
Second 20 percent.............	2,649	8.7	1,578	537	533	59.6	20.3	20.1
Third 20 percent..............	3,068	7.4	1,863	631	574	60.7	20.6	18.7
Fourth 20 percent.............	3,715	6.7	2,201	845	670	59.2	22.7	18.0
Highest 20 percent............	4,827	5.2	2,624	1,335	868	54.4	27.7	18.0
Education:								
Less than a high school graduate............	2,129	7.2	1,252	403	475	58.8	18.9	22.3
High school graduate..............	2,820	7.4	1,733	533	554	61.5	18.9	19.6
High school graduate with some college. ...	2,938	6.8	1,685	672	581	57.4	22.9	19.8
Associate's degree...............	3,238	6.4	1,811	805	622	55.9	24.9	19.2
Bachelor's degree................	3,824	6.0	2,194	976	655	57.4	25.5	17.1
Master's, professional, doctoral degree.....	4,497	5.9	2,492	1,173	833	55.4	26.1	18.5

[1] Includes prescription and nonprescription drugs.

Source: U.S. Bureau of Labor Statistics, Consumer Expenditure Survey, annual, <http://www.bls.gov/cex/>.

Table 147. Medicare Disbursements by Type of Beneficiary: 1990 to 2010

[In millions of dollars (109,709 represents $109,709,000,000). For years ending Sept. 30. Distribution of benefits by type is estimated and subject to change. See headnote, Table 152]

Selected type of beneficiary	1990	1995	2000	2005	2007	2008 [1]	2009	2010
Total disbursements	109,709	180,096	219,276	336,876	434,823	455,069	498,213	521,141
HI, Part A disbursements [2]	66,687	114,883	130,284	184,142	202,827	230,240	238,001	248,978
Benefits	65,722	113,394	125,992	181,934	203,990	226,276	234,302	245,180
Aged	58,503	100,107	110,067	155,772	172,847	183,846	196,766	205,180
Disabled	7,218	13,288	15,925	26,161	31,142	33,946	37,536	40,001
SMI, Part B disbursements [2]	43,022	65,213	88,992	151,537	179,651	177,709	203,421	208,380
Benefits	41,498	63,490	88,875	147,449	172,698	174,805	200,169	204,885
Aged	36,837	54,830	76,340	122,905	142,841	151,386	164,266	167,540
Disabled	4,661	8,660	12,535	24,544	29,858	31,903	35,903	37,345
SMI, Part D disbursements [2]	(X)	(X)	(X)	1,198	52,345	47,120	56,791	63,783
Benefits	(X)	(X)	(X)	73	51,331	46,728	56,559	63,525
Transitional assistance benefit payments	(X)	(X)	(X)	1,125	10	–	–	–

– Represents or rounds to zero. X Not applicable. [1] A transfer of expenditures between Parts A and B took place during 2008 that corrected for accounting errors that happened during FY2005–2007. The transfer is reflected in the "Benefits" data and is the sum of "Aged, Disabled, and Transfer." The Part A "Benefits" total increased by $8,484,000,000 while Part B "Benefits" total decreased by the same amount. [2] Other types, not shown separately.

Source: U.S. Centers for Medicare and Medicaid Services, Trustees Report and Trust Funds, and unpublished data. See also <http://www.cms.gov/ReportsTrustFunds/>.

Table 148. Children's Health Insurance Program (CHIP)—Enrollment and Expenditures by State: 2000 and 2010

[3,357.4 represents 3,357,400. For year ending September 30. This program provides health benefits coverage to children living in families whose incomes exceed the eligibility limits for Medicaid. Although it is generally targeted to families with incomes at or below 200 percent of the federal poverty level, each state may set its own income eligibility limits, within certain guidelines. For explanation of poverty level, see text, Section 13. States have three options: they may expand their Medicaid programs, develop a separate child health program that functions independently of Medicaid, or do a combination of both. See text, this section, regarding the change from SCHIP to CHIP]

State	Enrollment [1] (1,000)		Expenditures [2] (mil. dol.)		State	Enrollment [1] (1,000)		Expenditures [2] (mil. dol.)	
	2000	2010	2000	2010		2000	2010	2000	2010
U.S.	3,357.4	7,718.4	1,928.8	7,913.1	MO	72.8	91.4	41.2	107.0
AL	37.6	137.5	31.9	128.4	MT	8.3	25.2	4.3	36.5
AK	13.4	12.6	18.1	18.7	NE	11.4	47.9	6.1	36.7
AZ	59.6	39.6	29.4	57.8	NV	15.9	31.6	9.0	22.7
AR	1.9	100.8	1.5	85.8	NH	4.3	10.6	1.6	12.2
CA	484.4	1,731.6	187.3	1,186.8	NJ	89.0	187.2	46.9	562.4
CO	34.9	106.6	13.9	115.6	NM	8.0	9.7	3.4	230.6
CT	19.9	21.0	12.8	29.7	NY	769.5	539.6	401.0	499.4
DE	4.5	12.9	1.5	12.9	NC	103.6	254.0	65.5	359.2
DC	2.3	8.1	5.8	11.3	ND	2.6	6.7	1.8	14.4
FL	227.5	403.3	125.7	308.5	OH	118.3	253.7	53.1	264.0
GA	120.6	248.3	48.7	225.4	OK	57.7	122.9	51.3	113.0
HI	(Z)	27.3	0.4	31.4	OR	37.1	64.7	12.5	86.1
ID	12.4	42.2	7.5	34.1	PA	119.7	273.2	70.7	305.6
IL	62.5	329.1	32.7	259.4	RI	11.5	23.3	10.4	28.8
IN	44.4	141.5	53.7	89.8	SC	60.4	73.4	46.6	92.5
IA	20.0	64.0	15.5	71.6	SD	5.9	15.9	3.1	18.9
KS	26.3	56.4	12.8	52.7	TN	14.9	89.3	41.7	127.0
KY	55.6	79.4	60.0	122.9	TX	131.1	928.5	41.4	776.3
LA	50.0	157.0	25.3	175.7	UT	25.3	62.1	12.8	59.5
ME	22.7	33.0	11.4	33.7	VT	4.1	7.0	1.4	5.5
MD	93.1	118.9	92.2	160.3	VA	37.7	173.5	18.6	165.4
MA	113.0	142.3	44.2	301.0	WA	2.6	35.9	0.6	42.7
MI	55.4	69.8	36.2	114.9	WV	21.7	37.5	9.7	39.2
MN	(Z)	5.2	(Z)	19.5	WI	47.1	161.5	21.4	97.6
MS	12.2	95.6	21.1	152.4	WY	2.5	8.3	1.0	9.3

Z Less than 50 or $50,000. [1] Number of children ever enrolled during the year in Children's Health Insurance Program. [2] Expenditures for which states are entitled to federal reimbursement under Title XXI and which reconciles any advance of Title XXI federal funds made on the basis of estimates.

Source: U.S. Centers for Medicare & Medicaid Services, *The Children's Health Insurance Program (CHIP), Annual Enrollment Report* and the *Statement of Expenditures for the CHIP Program (CMS-21)*. See also <http://www.medicaid.gov/CHIP/CHIP-Program-Information.html>.

Table 149. Medicare Enrollees: 1990 to 2010

[In millions (34.3 represents 34,300,000). As of July 1. Includes Puerto Rico and Island Areas and enrollees in foreign countries and unknown place of residence. SMI is Supplemental Medical Insurance. See headnote, Table 152]

Item	1990	1995	2000	2005	2006	2007	2008	2009	2010
Total	**34.3**	**37.5**	**39.6**	**42.3**	**43.3**	**44.0**	**45.5**	**46.1**	**47.2**
Aged	30.9	33.4	34.3	35.6	36.3	36.7	37.8	38.5	39.3
Disabled	3.3	4.4	5.4	6.7	7.0	7.3	7.8	7.6	7.9
Hospital insurance, Part A	**33.7**	**37.1**	**39.2**	**42.0**	**42.9**	**43.7**	**45.2**	**45.8**	**46.9**
Aged	30.5	32.7	33.8	35.3	35.9	36.3	37.4	38.1	39.0
Disabled	3.3	4.4	5.4	6.1	7.0	7.4	7.8	7.6	7.9
SMI, Part B	**32.6**	**35.7**	**37.4**	**39.6**	**40.3**	**41.0**	**42.1**	**42.7**	**43.7**
Aged	29.6	31.7	32.6	33.7	34.1	34.4	35.2	35.9	36.5
Disabled	2.9	3.9	4.8	6.0	6.2	6.5	6.9	6.9	7.1
SMI, Part D	(X)	(X)	(X)	1.8	22.9	24.5	25.8	27.0	28.0

X Not applicable. (NA) Not Available.

Source: U.S. Centers for Medicare and Medicaid Services, Office of the Actuary, "Medicare Enrollment Reports" and "Medicare & Medicaid Statistical Supplement". See also <http://www.cms.gov/Research-Statistics-Data-and-Systems/Research-Statistics-Data-and-Systems.html>.

Table 150. Medicare—Enrollment by State and Other Areas: 2000 to 2010

[In thousands (39,620 represents 39,620,000). Hospital (HI) and/or supplementary medical insurance (SMI) enrollment as of July 1]

State and area	2000	2005	2009	2010	State and area	2000	2005	2009	2010
All areas [1]	**39,620**	**42,395**	**46,521**	**47,664**	MT	137	146	165	170
U.S.	**38,762**	**41,003**	**45,467**	**46,585**	NE	254	259	276	279
AL	685	740	828	845	NV	240	294	343	357
AK	42	51	63	66	NH	170	185	217	223
AZ	675	777	899	930	NJ	1,203	1,215	1,304	1,327
AR	439	464	520	531	NM	234	261	304	313
CA	3,901	4,158	4,620	4,757	NY	2,715	2,758	2,937	2,988
CO	467	513	602	625	NC	1,133	1,255	1,448	1,490
CT	515	520	558	568	ND	103	103	108	109
DE	112	125	145	149	OH	1,701	1,731	1,870	1,901
DC	75	72	77	78	OK	508	531	592	603
FL	2,804	3,008	3,289	3,375	OR	489	532	602	621
GA	916	1,016	1,194	1,236	PA	2,095	2,108	2,252	2,283
HI	165	180	200	206	RI	172	171	180	183
ID	165	188	222	230	SC	568	637	749	774
IL	1,635	1,674	1,806	1,839	SD	119	123	134	137
IN	852	893	985	1,006	TN	829	903	1,031	1,058
IA	477	484	512	517	TX	2,265	2,491	2,900	3,001
KS	390	397	425	433	UT	206	231	274	283
KY	623	668	743	760	VT	89	95	108	112
LA	602	630	671	687	VA	893	981	1,110	1,141
ME	216	233	259	265	WA	736	807	938	972
MD	645	687	764	785	WV	338	351	377	382
MA	961	961	1,039	1,061	WI	783	818	892	911
MI	1,403	1,468	1,615	1,651	WY	65	70	78	80
MN	654	691	767	786	Outlying areas [2]	537	622	653	(NA)
MS	419	449	488	497	Pending state				
MO	861	901	985	1,004	designations [3]	321	769	(NA)	(NA)

NA Not available. [1] Includes outlying areas and pending state designation. [2] Includes American Samoa, Federated States of Micronesia, Guam, Marshall Islands, Northern Marianas, Puerto Rico, Virgin Islands, and Wake Island. [3] Include foreign countries and unknown places of residence.

Source: U.S. Centers for Medicare and Medicaid Services, "Data Compendium," <http://www.cms.gov/Research-Statistics-Data-and-Systems/Statistics-Trends-and-Reports/DataCompendium/index.html>.

Table 151. Medicaid—Selected Characteristics of Persons Covered: 2010

[In thousands, except percent (48,302 represents 48,302,000). Represents number of persons as of March of following year who were enrolled at any time in year shown. Excludes unrelated individuals under age 15. Persons did not have to receive medical care paid for by Medicaid in order to be counted. For explanation of poverty level, see text, Section 13. See headnote, Table 577]

Poverty status	Total [1]	White alone [2]	Black alone [3]	Asian alone [4]	His-panic [5]	Under 18 years	18–44 years	45–64 years	65 years and over
Persons covered, total	**48,302**	**33,099**	**10,832**	**1,888**	**13,106**	**25,788**	**12,214**	**6,712**	**3,587**
Below poverty level	21,029	13,278	5,938	630	6,379	11,765	5,519	2,796	948
Above poverty level	27,273	19,821	4,894	1,258	6,727	14,023	6,695	3,916	2,639
Percent of population covered	**15.8**	**13.6**	**27.8**	**13.2**	**26.3**	**34.6**	**11.0**	**8.3**	**9.2**
Below poverty level	45.5	42.0	55.6	36.4	48.2	71.7	30.9	33.3	26.9
Above poverty level	10.5	9.4	17.3	10.0	18.4	24.1	7.2	5.4	7.4

[1] Includes other races, not shown separately. [2] White alone refers to people who reported White and did not report any other race category. [3] Black alone refers to people who reported Black and did not report any other race category. [4] Asian alone refers to people who reported Asian and did not report any other race category. [5] Persons of Hispanic origin may be of any race.

Source: U.S. Census Bureau, Income, Poverty, and Health Insurance Coverage in the United States: 2010, Current Population Reports, P60-238, 2011; Table HI02, "Health Insurance Coverage Status and Type of Coverage by Selected Characteristics for People in the Poverty Universe: 2010;" and Table HI03, "Health Insurance Coverage Status and Type of Coverage by Selected Characteristics for Poor People in the Poverty Universe: 2010." See also <http://www.census.gov/hhes/www/cpstables/032011/health/toc.htm>.

Table 152. Medicare Benefits by Type of Provider: 1990 to 2010

[In millions of dollars (65,721 represents $65,721,000,000). For years ending Sept. 30. Distribution of benefits by type is estimated and subject to change. The Medicare program has two components: Hospital Insurance (HI) or Medicare Part A and Supplementary Medical Insurance (SMI) consisting of Medicare Part B (medical insurance) and Part D (prescription drug plans). See text in this section for details. See footnote 1, Table 147, for 2008 data changes]

Type of provider	1990	1995	2000	2005	2007	2008	2009	2010
Hospital insurance benefits (Part A), total	**65,721**	**113,395**	**125,992**	**181,934**	**203,990**	**217,791**	**234,302**	**245,180**
Inpatient hospital	57,012	81,095	86,561	122,718	125,533	128,851	132,768	137,834
Skilled nursing facility	2,761	8,684	10,269	18,644	22,432	24,117	25,826	27,047
Home health agency	3,295	15,715	4,880	5,892	6,313	6,537	6,942	7,138
Hospice	318	1,854	2,818	7,678	10,482	11,137	11,977	12,910
Managed care	2,335	6,047	21,463	27,001	39,230	47,150	56,789	60,253
Supplementary medical insurance benefits (Part B), total	**41,498**	**63,490**	**88,876**	**147,449**	**172,698**	**183,289**	**200,169**	**204,885**
Physician fee schedule	(NA)	31,110	35,958	57,211	58,780	59,396	62,462	63,442
Durable medical equipment	(NA)	3,576	4,577	7,894	8,188	8,454	8,209	8,131
Carrier lab [1]	(NA)	2,819	2,194	3,521	4,050	4,141	4,639	4,924
Other carrier [2]	(NA)	4,513	7,154	15,195	15,698	16,390	17,269	17,199
Hospital [3]	(NA)	8,448	8,516	18,974	22,882	23,435	26,447	26,800
Home health	(NA)	223	4,281	6,750	9,053	10,100	11,326	12,087
Intermediary lab [4]	(NA)	1,437	1,748	2,820	3,019	2,912	3,274	3,235
Other intermediary [5]	(NA)	5,110	6,099	11,350	13,305	12,775	14,375	14,330
Managed care	(NA)	6,253	18,348	23,735	37,724	45,686	52,167	54,739
Supplementary medical insurance benefits (Part D), total [6]	**(X)**	**(X)**	**(X)**	**1,198**	**51,341**	**46,728**	**56,559**	**63,525**

NA Not available. X Not applicable. [1] Lab services paid under the lab fee schedule performed in a physician's office lab or an independent lab. [2] Includes free-standing ambulatory surgical centers facility costs, ambulance, and supplies. [3] Includes the hospital facility costs for Medicare Part B services which are predominantly in the outpatient department. The physician reimbursement associated with these services is included on the "Physician Fee Schedule" line. [4] Lab fee services paid under the lab fee schedule performed in a hospital outpatient department. [5] Includes End Stage Renal Disease (ESRD) free-standing dialysis facility payments and payments to rural health clinics and federally qualified health centers. [6] Starting with 2006, Part D provides subsidized access to drug insurance coverage on a voluntary basis for all beneficiaries and premium and cost-sharing subsidies for low-income enrollees. Benefits prior to 2006 were for transitional assistance to beneficiaries with low income.

Source: U.S. Centers for Medicare and Medicaid Services, unpublished data. See also <http://www.cms.gov/Research-Statistics-Data-and-Systems/Statistics-Trends-and-Reports/ReportsTrustFunds/index.html>.

Table 153. Medicare Insurance Trust Funds: 1990 to 2010

[In billions of dollars (126.3 represents $126,300,000,000). SMI is Supplemental Medical Insurance. See headnote, Table 152]

Type of trust fund	1990	1995	2000	2005	2006	2007	2008	2009	2010
TOTAL MEDICARE									
Total income	126.3	175.3	257.1	357.5	437.0	462.1	480.8	508.2	486.0
Total expenditures	111.0	184.2	221.8	336.4	408.3	431.7	468.1	509.0	522.8
Assets, end of year	114.4	143.4	221.5	309.8	338.5	368.9	381.6	380.8	344.0
HOSPITAL INSURANCE (Part A)									
Net contribution income [1]	72.1	103.3	154.5	182.6	194.3	205.4	213.5	206.3	199.3
Interest received [2]	8.5	10.8	11.7	16.1	16.4	17.4	16.3	17.0	15.9
Benefit payments [3]	66.2	116.4	126.8	180.0	189.0	200.2	232.3	239.3	244.5
Assets, end of year	98.9	130.3	177.5	285.8	305.4	326.0	321.3	304.2	271.9
SMI (Part B)									
Net premium income	11.3	19.7	20.6	37.5	42.9	46.8	50.2	56.0	52.0
Transfers from general revenue	33.0	39.0	65.9	118.1	132.7	139.6	146.8	162.8	153.5
Interest received [2]	1.6	1.6	3.5	1.4	1.8	2.2	3.5	3.0	3.1
Benefit payments [3]	42.5	65.0	88.9	149.9	166.2	176.4	180.3	202.6	209.7
Assets, end of year	15.5	13.1	44.0	24.0	32.3	42.1	59.4	75.5	71.4
SMI (Part D)									
Net premium income	(X)	(X)	(X)	–	3.5	4.0	5.0	6.3	6.5
Transfers from general revenue [4]	(X)	(X)	(X)	1.1	39.2	38.8	37.3	47.1	51.1
Interest received	(X)	(X)	(X)	–	–	–	–	–	–
Benefit payments [4]	(X)	(X)	(X)	1.1	47.0	48.8	49.0	60.5	61.7
Assets, end of year	(X)	(X)	(X)	–	0.8	0.8	0.9	1.1	0.7

– Represents zero. X Not applicable. [1] Includes income from taxation of benefits beginning in 1994. Includes premiums from aged ineligibles enrolled in Hospital Insurance (HI). [2] Includes recoveries of amounts reimbursed from the trust fund. [3] Beginning 1998, monies transferred to the SMI trust fund for home health agency costs, as provided for by P.L. 105-33, are included in HI benefit payments but excluded from SMI benefit payments. [4] The amount for 2005 includes amounts transferred for transitional assistance for Part D of Medicare.

Source: U.S. Centers for Medicare and Medicaid Services, *2012 Annual Report of the Board of Trustees of the Federal Hospital Insurance and Federal Supplementary Medical Insurance Trust Funds.* See also <http://www.cms.gov/Research-Statistics-Data-and-Systems/Statistics-Trends-and-Reports/ReportsTrustFunds/index.html>.

Table 154. Medicaid—Beneficiaries and Payments: 2000 to 2009

[42,887 represents 42,887,000. For year ending September 30]

Basis of eligibility and type of service	Beneficiaries (1,000) [1]				Payments (mil. dol.)			
	2000	2005	2008	2009 [2]	2000	2005	2008	2009 [2]
Total	42,887	57,651	58,771	60,119	168,443	274,851	296,830	308,238
Age 65 and over	3,730	4,395	4,147	3,937	44,560	63,415	61,131	60,098
Blind/Disabled	6,890	8,211	8,694	8,601	72,772	119,305	129,040	134,419
Children	19,018	26,341	27,111	27,776	23,490	41,863	51,200	55,325
Adults	8,671	12,533	12,903	13,435	17,671	32,162	37,185	(S)
Foster care children	761	874	960	913	3,309	5,286	5,936	(S)
Unknown	3,817	5,268	4,912	5,316	6,639	12,539	11,825	11,393
BCCA WOMEN [3]	(NA)	29	44	48	(NA)	281	513	(S)
All service categories:								
Capitated care [4]	21,292	33,496	38,151	39,864	25,026	46,421	68,130	77,383
Clinic services	7,678	11,918	11,857	12,139	6,138	8,921	9,152	9,749
Dental services	5,922	9,317	9,821	10,296	1,413	3,040	3,819	4,329
Home health services	1,007	1,195	1,144	1,042	3,133	5,362	6,620	6,174
ICF/MR services [5]	119	109	102	98	9,376	11,709	12,558	12,364
Inpatient hospital services	4,913	5,480	5,259	5,250	24,131	35,131	37,245	36,879
Lab and X-ray services	11,439	15,959	15,612	15,534	1,292	2,917	2,931	2,990
Mental health facility services [6]	100	120	108	108	1,769	2,301	2,374	2,363
Nursing facility services	1,706	1,711	1,616	1,557	34,528	44,790	47,718	45,807
Other care [7]	9,022	12,346	12,264	11,998	14,755	26,421	34,257	35,812
Outpatient hospital services	13,170	16,234	14,789	15,795	7,082	10,011	10,881	11,310
Other practitioner services	4,758	5,893	5,165	5,180	664	1,180	884	888
PCCM services [8]	5,649	8,723	8,728	8,223	177	232	276	338
Prescribed drugs	20,325	28,390	24,579	25,220	19,898	42,849	23,515	24,101
Physician services	18,965	24,238	21,661	22,152	6,809	11,269	10,506	11,056
Personal support services [9]	4,559	6,807	6,371	6,471	11,629	20,657	24,539	25,572
Sterilizations	137	178	138	121	128	211	143	140
Unknown	74	73	90	161	496	1,428	1,282	983

NA Not available. S Figure does not meet publication standards. [1] Beneficiaries data do not add due to number of beneficiaries that are reported in more than one category. [2] 2009 data not available for Massachusetts, Utah, and Wisconsin. [3] Women-Breast and Cervical Cancer Assistance. [4] HMO payments and prepaid health plans. [5] Intermediate care facilities for the mentally retarded. [6] Inpatient mental health facilities for individuals under 21 and for individuals 65 years and older. [7] Includes beneficiaries of, and payments for, other care not shown separately. [8] Primary Care Case Management Services. [9] Includes personal care services, rehabilitative services, physical occupational targeted case management services, speech therapies, hospice services, nurse midwife services, nurse practitioner services, private duty nursing services, and religious nonmedical health care institutions.

Source: U.S. Centers for Medicare and Medicaid Services, "Medicaid Program Statistics, Medicaid Statistical Information System," <http://www.cms.gov/Research-Statistics-Data-and-Systems/Computer-Data-and-Systems/MedicaidDataSourcesGenInfo/index.html>.

Table 155. Medicaid—Summary by State: 2000 and 2009

[42,887 represents 42,887,000. For year ending September 30]

State	Beneficiaries [1] (1,000)		Payments [2] (mil. dol.)		State	Beneficiaries [1] (1,000)		Payments [2] (mil. dol.)	
	2000	2009 [3]	2000	2009 [3]		2000	2009 [3]	2000	2009 [3]
U.S.	42,887	60,119	168,443	308,238	MO	890	1,101	3,274	5,771
AL	619	877	2,393	3,626	MT	104	113	422	714
AK	96	119	473	1,067	NE	229	256	960	1,590
AZ	681	1,588	2,112	8,617	NV	138	281	516	1,196
AR	489	825	1,543	3,579	NH	97	141	651	995
CA	7,918	11,519	17,105	35,224	NJ	822	1,151	4,714	8,293
CO	381	678	1,809	3,288	NM	376	562	1,249	2,913
CT	420	558	2,839	5,289	NY	3,420	4,985	26,148	44,883
DE	115	209	529	1,264	NC	1,214	1,782	4,834	9,665
DC	139	175	793	1,940	ND	63	77	358	588
FL	2,373	3,261	7,433	14,054	OH	1,305	2,238	7,115	13,972
GA	1,369	1,805	3,624	7,376	OK	507	809	1,604	3,574
HI	194	261	600	1,201	OR	558	564	1,714	2,797
ID	131	253	594	1,351	PA	1,492	2,716	6,366	14,207
IL	1,519	2,626	7,807	11,774	RI	179	203	1,070	1,556
IN	706	1,109	2,977	5,390	SC	689	906	2,765	4,712
IA	314	482	1,477	2,877	SD	102	141	402	732
KS	263	355	1,227	2,316	TN	1,568	1,479	3,491	7,262
KY	764	942	2,921	5,017	TX	2,633	4,283	9,277	18,543
LA	761	1,184	2,632	5,430	UT	225	(NA)	960	(NA)
ME	194	315	1,310	1,481	VT	139	171	480	970
MD	626	846	3,003	6,325	VA	627	917	2,479	5,548
MA	1,060	(NA)	5,413	(NA)	WA	896	1,177	2,435	5,734
MI	1,352	1,890	4,881	10,171	WV	342	386	1,394	2,589
MN	558	802	3,280	7,029	WI	577	(NA)	2,968	(NA)
MS	605	932	1,808	3,198	WY	46	72	215	552

[1] Persons who had payments made on their behalf at any time during the fiscal year. [2] Payments are for fiscal year and reflect federal and state contribution payments. Data exclude disproportionate share hospital payments. Disproportionate share hospitals receive higher Medicaid reimbursement than other hospitals because they treat a disproportionate share of Medicaid patients. [3] 2009 data not available for Massachusetts, Utah, and Wisconsin.

Source: U.S. Centers for Medicare and Medicaid Services, "Medicaid, Program Statistics, Medicaid Statistical Information System," <http://www.cms.gov/Research-Statistics-Data-and-Systems/Computer-Data-and-Systems/MedicaidDataSourcesGenInfo/index.html>.

Table 156. Medicaid Managed Care Enrollment by State and Other Areas: 1995 to 2010

[33,373 represents 33,373,000. For year ending June 30]

State and other areas	Total enrollment [1] (1,000)	Managed care enrollment [2] Number (1,000)	Percent of total	State and other areas	Total enrollment [1] (1,000)	Managed care enrollment [2] Number (1,000)	Percent of total	State and other areas	Total enrollment [1] (1,000)	Managed care enrollment [2] Number (1,000)	Percent of total
1995......	33,373	9,800	29.4	HI.........	260	255	98.0	NY........	4,741	3,227	68.1
2000......	33,690	18,786	55.8	ID..........	214	187	87.6	NC........	1,465	1,135	77.5
2005......	45,392	28,576	63.0	IL..........	2,430	1,372	56.5	ND........	62	42	67.3
2006......	45,653	29,830	65.3	IN..........	1,035	728	70.4	OH........	2,125	1,562	73.5
2007......	45,962	29,463	64.1	IA..........	430	387	90.1	OK........	669	603	90.1
2008......	47,143	33,428	70.1	KS.........	326	282	86.6	OR........	550	477	86.7
2009......	50,472	36,202	71.7	KY.........	813	717	88.2	PA........	2,030	1,659	81.7
2010, Total...	**54,612**	**39,020**	**71.5**	LA.........	1,181	752	63.7	RI.........	189	128	67.4
U.S.......	**53,566**	**38,277**	**71.5**	ME........	287	194	67.7	SC........	808	808	100.0
AL........	873	520	59.6	MD........	902	716	79.5	SD........	113	91	80.3
AK........	113	–		MA........	1,417	758	53.5	TN........	1,204	1,204	100.0
AZ........	1,322	1,196	90.5	MI.........	1,829	1,577	86.2	TX........	3,764	2,520	67.0
AR........	596	467	78.4	MN........	734	468	63.8	UT........	270	225	83.3
CA........	7,327	4,033	55.0	MS........	703	533	75.9	VT........	177	100	56.7
CO........	554	524	94.6	MO........	892	884	99.1	VA........	884	524	59.2
CT........	543	379	69.9	MT........	101	75	74.6	WA........	1,121	972	86.7
DE........	180	140	77.4	NE........	230	197	85.6	WV........	335	163	48.6
DC........	221	154	69.7	NV........	265	225	85.1	WI........	1,144	714	62.4
FL........	2,853	1,840	64.5	NH........	131	0	0.0	WY........	69	–	–
GA........	1,497	1,362	91.0	NJ........	1,039	798	76.8	PR........	1,038	743	71.6
				NM........	546	399	73.1	VI.........	9	–	–

– Represents zero. [1] The unduplicated Medicaid enrollment figures include individuals in state health care reform programs that expand eligibility beyond traditional Medicaid eligibility standards. [2] The unduplicated managed care enrollment figures include enrollees receiving comprehensive and limited benefits.

Source: U.S. Centers for Medicare and Medicaid Services, "2010 Medicaid Managed Care Enrollment Report," <http://www.cms.gov/Research-Statistics-Data-and-Systems/Computer-Data-and-Systems/MedicaidDataSourcesGenInfo/index.html>.

Table 157. Persons Enrolled in Health Maintenance Organizations (HMOs) by State: 2007 and 2008

[74,698 represents 74,698,000. As of January 1. Data are based on a census of health maintenance organizations]

State	Number 2008 (1,000)	Percent of population 2007	2008	State	Number 2008 (1,000)	Percent of population 2007	2008	State	Number 2008 (1,000)	Percent of population 2007	2008
U.S......	**74,698**	**24.7**	**24.8**	KY........	408	8.1	9.6	ND........	10	0.2	1.5
AL........	201	3.6	4.3	LA........	352	8.6	8.2	OH........	2,466	20.3	21.5
AK........	7	1.0	1.1	ME........	152	29.4	11.5	OK........	263	7.2	7.3
AZ........	1,942	29.2	30.6	MD........	1,701	29.3	30.3	OR........	1,007	25.3	26.9
AR........	106	3.4	3.7	MA........	2,964	48.1	46.0	PA........	3,744	30.6	30.1
CA........	16,415	44.6	44.9	MI........	2,841	28.1	28.2	RI........	223	22.6	21.0
CO........	1,053	23.8	21.7	MN........	939	14.1	18.1	SC........	417	7.8	9.5
CT........	1,349	41.2	38.5	MS........	54	0.9	1.8	SD........	148	17.7	18.5
DE........	201	26.0	23.3	MO........	1,164	23.0	19.8	TN........	1,897	31.1	30.8
DC........	377	64.0	64.1	MT........	62	5.1	6.5	TX........	3,702	12.8	15.5
FL........	4,400	24.1	24.1	NE........	135	6.9	7.6	UT........	970	35.1	36.7
GA........	2,099	26.5	22.0	NV........	608	23.0	23.7	VT........	86	19.9	13.8
HI........	650	46.7	50.6	NH........	219	23.2	16.7	VA........	1,665	21.5	21.6
ID........	86	4.6	5.7	NJ........	2,284	26.5	26.3	WA........	1,423	20.0	22.0
IL........	1,762	13.9	13.7	NM........	591	23.3	30.0	WV........	277	11.3	15.3
IN........	1,098	24.1	17.3	NY........	6,500	32.3	33.7	WI........	1,507	23.8	26.9
IA........	327	9.7	11.0	NC........	838	8.3	9.2	WY........	21	2.6	4.1
KS........	471	14.9	17.0								

Source: HealthLeaders-InterStudy, Nashville, TN, *The Competitive Edge* (copyright). See also <http://hl-isy.com/>.

Table 158. Health Insurance Coverage Status by Selected Characteristics: 2009 and 2010

[304,280 represents 304,280,000. Persons as of following year for coverage in the year shown. Government health insurance includes Medicare, Medicaid, and military plans. Based on Current Population Survey, Annual Social and Economic Supplement (ASEC); see text, Section 1 and Appendix III]

Characteristic	Number (1,000)							Percent			
		Covered by private or government health insurance					Not covered by health insurance	Covered by private or government health insurance			Not covered by health insurance
			Private		Government						
	Total persons	Total [1]	Total	Group health [2]	Medicare	Medicaid		Total [1]	Private	Medicaid	
2009................	**304,280**	**253,606**	**194,545**	**169,689**	**43,440**	**47,758**	**50,674**	**83.3**	**63.9**	**15.7**	**16.7**
2010................	**306,110**	**256,206**	**195,874**	**169,264**	**44,327**	**48,580**	**49,904**	**83.7**	**64.0**	**15.9**	**16.3**
Age:											
Under 18 years......	74,916	67,609	44,620	41,083	602	26,067	7,307	90.2	59.6	34.8	9.8
Under 6 years.....	25,555	23,241	13,866	12,951	233	10,283	2,314	90.9	54.3	40.2	9.1
6 to 11 years.......	24,701	22,400	14,825	13,919	182	8,694	2,301	90.7	60.0	35.2	9.3
12 to 17 years......	24,660	21,968	15,929	14,212	186	7,090	2,692	89.1	64.6	28.7	10.9
18 to 24 years......	29,651	21,573	17,407	13,612	257	4,516	8,078	72.8	58.7	15.2	27.2
25 to 34 years......	41,584	29,780	25,314	23,221	610	4,249	11,804	71.6	60.9	10.2	28.4
35 to 44 years......	39,842	31,149	27,426	25,573	900	3,449	8,692	78.2	68.8	8.7	21.8
45 to 54 years......	43,954	36,035	31,695	29,201	1,901	3,607	7,919	82.0	72.1	8.2	18.0
55 to 64 years......	36,984	31,672	26,743	23,846	3,600	3,105	5,312	85.6	72.3	8.4	14.4
65 years and over...	39,179	38,387	22,668	12,728	36,457	3,587	792	98.0	57.9	9.2	2.0
Sex:											
Male..................	150,643	123,735	95,894	83,886	19,594	22,560	26,908	82.1	63.7	15.0	17.9
Female..............	155,466	132,470	99,980	85,378	24,733	26,020	22,996	85.2	64.3	16.7	14.8
Race: White alone [3]...	243,323	205,938	162,508	139,386	37,634	33,306	37,385	84.6	66.8	13.7	15.4
Black alone [3]........	39,031	30,899	18,867	17,032	4,544	10,868	8,132	79.2	48.3	27.8	20.8
Asian alone [3].......	14,332	11,731	9,473	8,394	1,397	1,890	2,600	81.9	66.1	13.2	18.1
Hispanic origin [4]......	49,972	34,631	20,828	19,068	3,503	13,183	15,340	69.3	41.7	26.4	30.7
Household income:											
Less than $25,000...	60,140	43,974	15,772	9,102	15,142	22,535	16,166	73.1	26.2	37.5	26.9
$25,000–$49,999. ..	70,680	55,245	37,160	29,599	13,926	14,202	15,435	78.2	52.6	20.1	21.8
$50,000–$74,999. ..	57,359	48,528	41,494	36,783	6,683	6,001	8,831	84.6	72.3	10.5	15.4
$75,000 or more.....	117,931	108,458	101,448	93,781	8,576	5,841	9,473	92.0	86.0	5.0	8.0
Persons below											
poverty..............	46,180	31,678	9,214	5,713	5,324	21,029	14,502	68.6	20.0	45.5	31.4

[1] Includes other government insurance, not shown separately. Persons with coverage counted only once in total, even though they may have been covered by more than one type of policy. [2] Related to employment of self or other family members. [3] Refers to people who reported specified race and did not report any other race category. [4] Persons of Hispanic origin may be any race.

Source: U.S. Census Bureau, *Income, Poverty, and Health Insurance Coverage in the United States: 2010*, Current Population Reports, P60-239, 2010, Table HI01, "Health Insurance Coverage Status and Type of Coverage by Selected Characteristics: 2010" and Table HI03, "Health Insurance Coverage Status and Type of Coverage by Selected Characteristics for Poor People in the Poverty Universe: 2010." See also <http://www.census.gov/hhes/www/hlthins/index.html>.

Table 159. Persons With and Without Health Insurance Coverage by State: 2010

[256,206 represents 256,206,000. Based on the Current Population Survey, Annual Social and Economic Supplement (ASEC), see text, Section 1 and Appendix III]

State	Total persons covered (1,000)	Total persons not covered		Children not covered		State	Total persons covered (1,000)	Total persons not covered		Children not covered	
		Number (1,000)	Percent of total	Number (1,000)	Percent of total			Number (1,000)	Percent of total	Number (1,000)	Percent of total
U.S.........	**256,206**	**49,904**	**16.3**	**7,307**	**9.8**	MO..........	5,143	835	14.0	124	8.9
AL...........	3,951	720	15.4	101	8.9	MT...........	795	176	18.1	19	8.8
AK...........	568	125	18.0	25	13.7	NE...........	1,551	237	13.3	47	10.3
AZ...........	5,420	1,283	19.1	267	15.0	NV...........	2,076	563	21.3	117	17.5
AR...........	2,341	539	18.7	52	7.4	NH...........	1,168	134	10.3	15	5.5
CA...........	30,014	7,209	19.4	1,019	10.7	NJ...........	7,334	1,338	15.4	188	9.2
CO...........	4,393	656	13.0	98	7.8	NM...........	1,580	435	21.6	71	13.7
CT...........	3,113	384	11.0	49	6.0	NY...........	16,403	2,886	15.0	350	7.9
DE...........	782	99	11.3	12	6.0	NC...........	7,673	1,575	17.0	213	9.2
DC...........	532	76	12.5	6	5.1	ND...........	552	83	13.1	15	10.2
FL...........	14,677	3,854	20.8	576	14.2	OH...........	9,795	1,554	13.7	222	8.3
GA...........	7,927	1,905	19.4	257	9.9	OK...........	3,049	624	17.0	114	11.9
HI...........	1,160	97	7.7	7	2.3	OR...........	3,165	612	16.2	89	10.4
ID...........	1,238	294	19.2	38	9.0	PA...........	11,085	1,368	11.0	226	8.2
IL...........	10,986	1,914	14.8	239	7.6	RI...........	928	119	11.4	12	5.3
IN...........	5,505	855	13.4	97	6.0	SC...........	3,596	930	20.6	152	14.2
IA...........	2,597	366	12.3	53	7.4	SD...........	701	105	13.0	13	6.6
KS...........	2,407	350	12.7	53	7.5	TN...........	5,381	930	14.7	116	7.9
KY...........	3,653	640	14.9	69	6.8	TX...........	18,973	6,181	24.6	1,153	16.3
LA...........	3,545	886	20.0	105	9.0	UT...........	2,443	386	13.6	101	11.4
ME...........	1,164	121	9.4	12	4.4	VT...........	563	59	9.5	5	4.1
MD...........	4,979	747	13.1	125	9.2	VA...........	6,675	1,096	14.1	154	8.3
MA...........	6,246	370	5.6	54	3.8	WA...........	5,797	927	13.8	95	5.9
MI...........	8,500	1,271	13.0	119	5.1	WV...........	1,564	244	13.5	11	2.7
MN...........	4,678	509	9.8	75	6.0	WI...........	5,084	526	9.4	59	4.6
MS...........	2,311	618	21.1	102	13.4	WY...........	444	93	17.3	14	10.2

Source: U.S. Census Bureau, *Income, Poverty, and Health Insurance Coverage in the United States: 2010*, Current Population Reports, P60-239, 2011, Table HI05, "Health Insurance Coverage Status and Type of Coverage by State for All People: 2010." See also <http://www.census.gov/hhes/www/cpstables/032011/health/toc.htm>.

Table 160. People Without Health Insurance for the Entire Year by Selected Characteristics: 2009 and 2010

[In thousands, except as noted (304,280 represents 304,280,000). Based on the Current Population Survey; Annual Social and Economic Supplement (ASEC); see text, Section 1 and Appendix III]

Characteristic	2009			2010		
		Uninsured Persons			Uninsured Persons	
	Total persons	Number	Percent distribution	Total persons	Number	Percent distribution
Total [1]	**304,280**	**50,674**	**100.0**	**306,110**	**49,904**	**100.0**
Under 18 years	75,040	7,513	14.8	74,916	7,307	14.6
18 to 24 years	29,313	8,923	17.6	29,651	8,078	16.2
25 to 34 years	41,085	11,963	23.6	41,584	11,804	23.7
35 to 44 years	40,447	8,759	17.3	39,842	8,692	17.4
45 to 64 years	79,782	12,840	25.3	80,938	13,231	26.5
65 years and over	38,613	676	1.3	39,179	792	1.6
Male	149,485	27,463	54.2	150,643	26,908	53.9
Female	154,795	23,211	45.8	155,466	22,996	46.1
White alone [2]	242,403	38,399	75.8	243,323	37,385	74.9
White alone or in combination	247,660	39,118	77.2	248,806	38,208	76.6
Black alone [2]	38,624	8,102	16.0	39,031	8,132	16.3
Black alone or in combination	40,957	8,414	16.6	41,577	8,507	17.0
Asian alone [2]	14,011	2,409	4.8	14,332	2,600	5.2
Asian alone or in combination	15,281	2,503	4.9	15,695	2,761	5.5
Hispanic [3]	48,901	15,820	31.2	49,972	15,340	30.7
White alone, not Hispanic	197,436	23,658	46.7	197,423	23,093	46.3

[1] Includes other races, not shown separately. [2] Refers to people who reported specified race and did not report any other race category. [3] Persons of Hispanic origin may be any race.

Source: U.S. Census Bureau, *Income, Poverty, and Health Insurance Coverage in the United States: 2010*, Current Population Reports, P60-238, 2011, and "Health Insurance Coverage Status and Type of Coverage by Selected Characteristics: 2010." See also <http://www.census.gov/prod/www/abs/p60.html> and <http://www.census.gov/hhes/www/cpstables/032011/health/toc.htm>.

Table 161. Percent of Workers Participating in Health Care Benefit Programs and Percent of Participants Required to Contribute: 2011

[Based on National Compensation Survey, a sample survey of 8,727 private industry establishments of all sizes, representing about 101 million workers; see Appendix III. See also Table 668. For more information, see <www.bls.gov/ncs/ebs/benefits/2011/benefits.htm>]

Characteristic	Percent of workers participating—				Single coverage medical plans		Family coverage medical plans	
	Medical care	Dental care	Vision care	Out-patient prescription drug coverage	Employee contributions required (percent)	Average monthly contribution [1] (dol.)	Employee contributions required (percent)	Average monthly contribution [1] (dol.)
Total	**51**	**35**	**20**	**50**	**82**	**104.60**	**90**	**404.03**
Worker characteristics:								
Management, professional, and related	66	50	28	65	84	104.51	92	404.65
Management, business, and financial	72	57	31	71	84	105.09	92	409.33
Professional and related	64	46	26	62	83	104.20	91	402.19
Service	27	18	10	26	83	101.91	92	447.00
Sales and office	50	34	18	49	84	108.63	93	411.08
Sales and related	42	28	14	40	87	115.06	93	424.30
Office and administrative support	55	38	20	54	83	105.33	93	404.53
Natural resources, construction, and maintenance	56	35	23	55	68	111.67	82	434.77
Production, transportation, and material moving	58	38	23	57	80	97.45	88	351.14
Production	65	42	24	64	82	96.47	88	341.60
Transportation, and material moving	52	33	21	51	79	98.72	87	363.24
Full-time [2]	64	44	24	63	82	103.62	91	401.81
Part-time [2]	13	9	6	13	80	118.59	85	437.09
Union [3]	75	60	46	74	57	95.49	65	330.98
Nonunion	48	32	17	47	86	105.59	94	412.03
Average hourly wage: [4]								
Less than $8.25	11	6	4	10	87	115.23	92	438.14
$8.25 to under $10.69	21	11	7	20	85	107.74	92	433.32
$10.69 to under $15.87	53	34	18	51	85	104.60	93	412.76
$15.87 to under $24.81	66	45	24	64	80	104.12	91	399.79
$24.81 to under $37.89	71	55	32	70	79	103.83	87	389.67
$37.89 or greater	73	59	35	72	81	104.59	88	387.47

[1] The average is presented for all covered workers and excludes workers without the plan provision. Averages are for plans stating a flat monthly cost. [2] Employees are classified as working either a full-time or part-time schedule based on the definition used by each establishment. [3] Union workers are those whose wages are determined through collective bargaining. [4] The National Compensation Survey—Benefits program presents wage data in percentiles rather than dollar amounts; see "Technical Note" in source.

Source: U.S. Bureau of Labor Statistics, *National Compensation Survey: Employee Benefits in Private Industry in the United States–March 2011*. See also <http://www.bls.gov/ncs/ebs/publications.htm>.

Table 162. Retail Prescription Drug Sales: 1995 to 2010

[2,125 represents 2,125,000,000]

Sales outlet	Unit	1995	2000	2004	2005	2006	2007	2008	2009	2010
Number of prescriptions.............	**Mil.**	**2,125**	**2,865**	**3,274**	**3,279**	**3,419**	**3,530**	**3,559**	**3,633**	**3,676**
Traditional chain.............	Mil.	908	1,335	1,494	1,513	1,599	1,652	1,677	1,731	1,760
Independent.................	Mil.	672	698	744	719	738	753	739	730	729
Mass merchant.............	Mil.	238	293	353	359	375	390	400	423	433
Supermarkets...............	Mil.	221	394	470	465	476	478	481	488	490
Mail order.....................	Mil.	86	146	214	223	232	257	262	261	264
Percent distribution of brand/generic mix:										
Brand drugs..............	Percent	59.8	57.6	54.1	50.6	44.8	40.8	35.5	32.6	28.8
Generic drugs...............	Percent	40.2	42.4	45.9	49.4	55.2	59.2	64.5	67.4	71.2
Retail sales...............	**Bil. dol.**	**72.2**	**145.6**	**216.7**	**226.1**	**243.2**	**249.2**	**249.2**	**261.3**	**266.4**
Traditional chain.............	Bil. dol.	27.8	59.1	86.7	90.7	96.0	100.5	101.2	105.3	106.6
Independent.................	Bil. dol.	22.0	33.4	44.2	45.4	46.7	45.3	43.3	43.6	44.7
Mass merchant.............	Bil. dol.	7.7	13.5	16.8	17.5	21.6	23.6	24.2	25.6	26.6
Supermarkets...............	Bil. dol.	7.4	17.4	26.4	26.9	28.1	27.3	25.2	25.9	25.9
Mail order.....................	Bil. dol.	7.4	22.1	42.7	45.5	50.9	52.5	55.4	61.3	62.6
Average prices [1]										
All prescriptions.............	Dollars	30.01	45.79	62.64	63.87	66.97	68.77	71.69	75.66	79.39
Brand drugs.................	Dollars	40.22	65.29	91.80	97.65	112.24	121.26	137.98	151.06	166.61
Generic drugs...............	Dollars	14.84	19.33	28.23	29.21	30.17	32.60	35.21	39.25	44.14

[1] Excludes mail order.

Source: National Association of Chain Drug Stores, Alexandria, VA, *NACDS Foundation Chain Pharmacy Industry Profile, 2011-12*, (copyright). See also <http://www.nacds.org>.

Table 163. Annual Revenue for Health Care Industries: 2008 to 2010

[In millions of dollars (1,757,926 represents $1,757,926,000,000). For taxable and tax-exempt employer firms. Estimates have been adjusted to the results of the 2007 Economic Census. Based on the Service Annual Survey and administrative data; see Appendix III. All firms in NAICS 6211, 6212, 6213, and 6215 are defined as taxable]

Kind of business	2002 NAICS code [1]	Total, all firms [2]			Taxable employer firms		
		2008	2009	2010	2008	2009	2010
Health care and social assistance................	**62**	**1,757,926**	**1,842,674**	**1,917,183**	**872,425**	**907,384**	**938,503**
Ambulatory health care services [3]......................	621	707,502	731,930	756,477	641,236	662,037	683,658
Offices of physicians....................................	6211	352,834	361,897	372,579	352,834	361,897	372,579
Offices of dentists......................................	6212	98,917	99,175	101,619	98,917	99,175	101,619
Offices of other health practitioners....................	6213	54,609	57,333	60,003	54,609	57,333	60,003
Offices of chiropractors..............................	62131	10,151	10,383	10,642	10,151	10,383	10,642
Offices of optometrists...............................	62132	11,097	11,414	11,684	11,097	11,414	11,684
Offices of mental health practitioners................	62133	5,575	6,222	6,702	5,575	6,222	6,702
Offices of PT/OT/speech therapy & audiology [4]....	62134	19,973	21,263	22,363	19,973	21,263	22,363
Outpatient care centers................................	6214	79,150	84,234	88,821	39,840	42,452	45,344
Medical & diagnostic laboratories......................	6215	42,533	44,944	45,318	42,533	44,944	45,318
Home health care services..............................	6216	51,200	55,367	58,116	35,224	38,496	40,204
Other ambulatory health care services................	6219	28,259	28,980	30,021	17,279	17,740	18,591
Hospitals [3]...	622	738,197	787,121	822,590	88,993	97,458	99,860
General medical & surgical hospitals..................	6221	689,356	735,136	767,738	72,795	79,159	79,912
Psychiatric & substance abuse hospitals.............	6222	18,029	18,500	19,216	3,986	4,331	4,620
Other specialty hospitals..............................	6223	30,812	33,485	35,636	12,212	13,968	15,328
Nursing and residential care facilities [3].................	623	177,506	183,916	192,035	108,504	112,422	118,453
Nursing care facilities..................................	6231	97,357	100,832	105,297	74,846	77,499	81,648
Residential mental retardation/health facilities.......	6232	29,071	30,490	31,948	8,855	9,348	9,885
Residential mental retardation facilities..............	62321	19,788	20,933	21,807	5,581	5,899	6,184
Community care facilities for the elderly..............	6233	42,641	44,502	46,594	23,446	24,242	25,608
Continuing care retirement communities............	623311	26,914	28,437	29,332	11,044	11,516	11,780
Homes for the elderly..............................	623312	15,727	16,065	17,262	12,402	12,726	13,828
Other residential care facilities........................	6239	8,437	8,092	8,196	1,357	1,333	1,312
Social assistance [3].......................................	624	134,721	139,707	146,081	33,692	35,467	36,532
Individual and family services........................	6241	66,123	68,551	71,847	12,741	13,922	14,832
Community food and housing, and emergency and other relief services............................	6242	25,819	26,709	28,569	500	477	468
Vocational rehabilitation services......................	6243	11,986	12,610	13,220	1,800	1,872	1,980
Child day care services................................	6244	30,793	31,837	32,445	18,651	19,196	19,252

[1] North American Industry Classification System (NAICS), 2002; see text, Section 15. [2] Excludes taxable nonemployer firms. [3] Includes other kinds of business, not shown separately. [4] Offices of physical, occupational, and speech therapists, and audiologists.

Source: U.S. Census Bureau, "2010 Annual Services Report: Health Care and Social Assistance Sector Services," February 2012, <http://www.census.gov/services/index.html>.

Table 164. Revenue for Selected Health Care Industries by Source of Revenue: 2009 and 2010

[In millions of dollars (361,897 represents $361,897,000,000). For taxable and tax-exempt employer firms. Estimates have been adjusted to the results of the 2007 Economic Census. Based on Service Annual Survey and administrative data; see Appendix III]

Source of revenue	Offices of physicians (NAICS 6211)[1]		Offices of dentists (NAICS 6212)[1]		Hospitals (NAICS 622)[1]		Nursing and residential care facilities (NAICS 623)[1]	
	2009	2010	2009	2010	2009	2010	2009	2010
Total..........................	**361,897**	**372,579**	**99,063**	**101,503**	**787,121**	**822,590**	**183,513**	**191,542**
Medicare.........................	73,590	76,322	925	931	197,456	205,009	31,391	33,582
Medicaid.........................	18,277	19,801	4,402	4,709	77,256	81,901	66,269	68,889
Other government[2]..........	5,881	6,276	767	901	40,110	42,287	13,674	14,620
Worker's compensation.......	7,476	7,690	(S)	(S)	7,374	7,172	(S)	(S)
Private insurance..............	186,306	187,950	45,142	46,049	336,708	353,153	9,161	9,580
Patient (out-of-pocket)[3].......	35,922	37,502	42,338	42,603	36,943	39,857	44,214	44,864
Other patient care sources n.e.c[4]..........................	19,342	20,275	4,483	5,392	26,616	24,346	7,294	7,972
Nonpatient care revenue......	15,103	16,763	1,006	918	64,658	68,865	11,510	12,035

S Figure does not meet publication standards. [1] North American Industry Classification System (NAICS), 2002; see text Section 15. [2] Veterans, National Institute of Health, Indian Affairs, etc. [3] Represents payment from patients and their families plus patients' assigned social security benefits for NAICS 623. [4] n.e.c. (not elsewhere classified).

Source: U.S. Census Bureau, "2010 Annual Services Report: Health Care and Social Assistance Sector Services," February 2012, <http://www.census.gov/services/index.html>.

Table 165. Employment in the Health Service Industries: 1990 to 2011

[In thousands (9,296 represents 9,296,000). See headnote, Table 643. Based on the 2007 North American Industry Classification System (NAICS); see text, Section 15. For more information on the NAICS changes, please see <http://stats.bls.gov/ces/cesnaics07.htm>]

Industry	2007 NAICS code	1990	2000	2005	2007	2008	2009	2010	2011
Health care and social assistance[1].........	62	**9,296**	**12,718**	**14,536**	**15,380**	**15,798**	**16,103**	**16,375**	**16,643**
Ambulatory health care services[1]................	621	2,842	4,320	5,114	5,474	5,647	5,793	5,975	6,146
Offices of physicians.............................	6211	1,278	1,840	2,094	2,202	2,253	2,279	2,313	2,355
Offices of dentists................................	6212	513	688	774	808	818	818	828	842
Offices of other health practitioners............	6213	276	438	549	600	627	647	671	697
Medical and diagnostic laboratories...........	6215	129	162	198	211	217	219	228	232
Home health care services......................	6216	288	633	821	914	961	1,027	1,085	1,139
Hospitals[1]...	622	3,513	3,954	4,345	4,515	4,627	4,667	4,679	4,731
General medical and surgical hospitals........	6221	3,305	3,745	4,096	4,242	4,337	4,367	4,357	4,375
Psychiatric and substance abuse hospitals..	6222	113	86	93	99	102	104	109	120
Other hospitals...................................	6223	95	123	156	174	188	196	213	236
Nursing and residential care facilities[1]..........	623	1,856	2,583	2,855	2,958	3,016	3,082	3,124	3,169
Nursing care facilities...........................	6231	1,170	1,514	1,577	1,603	1,619	1,645	1,657	1,668

[1] Includes other industries, not shown separately.

Source: U.S. Bureau of Labor Statistics, Current Employment Statistics, "Employment, Hours, and Earnings—National," <http://www.bls.gov/ces/data.htm>, accessed July 2012.

Table 166. Osteopathic Physicians: 2002 to 2011

[As of May 31. Osteopathic physicians are fully qualified physicians licensed to practice medicine and to perform surgery. Osteopathic medicine has a strong emphasis on the interrelationship of the body's nerves, muscles, bones and organs. Doctors of osteopathic medicine, or D.O.s, apply the philosophy of treating the whole person to the prevention, diagnosis and treatment of illness, disease, and injury]

Characteristics	2002	2006	2011	Characteristics	2002	2006	2011
Total number of DOs	49,210	58,940	73,977				
Female............................	11,832	16,416	24,323	Self-identified practice specialty[1].........	33,452	40,378	58,510
Male...............................	37,378	42,524	49,654	Family and general practice..............	14,929	18,610	22,834
Age:				General internal Medicine................	2,700	3,468	7,481
Less than 35 years old..........	10,528	13,241	16,979	Pediatrics/adolescent medicine[2]........	985	1,325	3,284
35 to 44 years old...............	14,993	16,970	21,243	Obstetrics and gynecology...............	1,293	1,543	2,698
45 to 54 years old...............	13,434	15,391	15,913	Pediatric specialties[3].....................	334	365	NA
55 to 64 years old...............	5,305	7,605	12,237	Osteopathic specialties[4].................	423	498	811
65 years old and over...........	4,915	5,305	7,062	Other specialties...........................	12,292	14,020	21,402
Unknown.........................	35	428	543	Unknown....................................	496	549	NA

NA Not available [1] DOs are assumed to be in active practice if they are under age 65 and have not informed the AOA that they have retired or are inactive. DOs are assumed to be in postdoctoral training (internship, residency or fellowship) if they graduated within the last 3 years or if the AOA has received information that they are in a postdoctoral program. [2] "Pediatric and adolescent medicine" includes all specialties where the patient is a child or adolescent and includes both general pediatricians and pediatric specialties. [3] Beginning in 2009, separate data for "Pediatric specialties" are no longer available. [4] Osteopathic self-identified practice specialties include FOM (Family Practice/OMT), FPO (Family Practice/OMM), NMO (Neuromusculoskeletal Med/OMM), NMS (Neuromusculoskeletal Med/OMT), OM1 (Osteopathic Manipulative Med +1), OMM (Spec Prof in Osteo Manip Med), OMS (Sports Medicine-OMM), and OMT (Osteo Manipulative Medicine). OMT is the therapeutic application of manually guided forces by an osteopathic physician to improve physiologic function and/or support homeostasis that has been altered by somatic dysfunction. OMM is the application of osteopathic philosophy, structural diagnosis, and use of OMT in the patient's diagnosis and management.

Source: American Osteopathic Association, Chicago, IL, AOA Annual Statistics, *Osteopathic Medical Profession Report,* annual, (copyright). See also <http://www.osteopathic.org>.

Table 167. Physicians by Sex and Specialty: 1980 to 2010

[In thousands (467.7 represents 467,700). As of Dec. 31, except 1990 as of Jan. 1, and as noted. Includes Puerto Rico and Island Areas]

Activity	1980 Total	1980 Office-based	1990 Total	1990 Office-based	2000 Total	2000 Office-based	2010 Total	2010 Office-based
Doctors of medicine, total [1]	**467.7**	**272.0**	**615.4**	**361.0**	**813.8**	**490.4**	**985.4**	**565.0**
Place of medical education:								
U.S./Canadian medical graduates [2]	370.0	226.2	483.7	286.2	616.8	376.5	731.0	424.8
International medical graduates [2]	97.7	45.8	131.8	74.8	197.0	113.9	254.4	140.2
Sex:								
Male	413.4	251.4	511.2	311.7	618.2	382.3	688.5	399.4
Female	54.3	20.6	104.2	49.2	195.5	108.1	296.9	165.6
Allergy/immunology	1.5	1.4	3.4	2.5	4.0	3.1	4.3	3.4
Anesthesiology	16.0	11.3	26.0	17.8	35.7	27.6	43.4	31.8
Cardiovascular diseases	9.8	6.7	15.9	10.7	21.0	16.3	22.9	17.5
Child psychiatry	3.3	2.0	4.3	2.6	6.2	4.3	7.4	5.4
Dermatology	5.7	4.4	7.6	6.0	9.7	8.0	11.3	9.3
Diagnostic radiology	7.0	4.2	15.4	9.8	21.1	14.6	26.1	17.5
Emergency medicine	5.7	3.4	14.2	8.4	23.1	14.5	33.3	20.7
Family practice	27.5	18.4	47.6	37.5	71.6	54.2	87.6	69.9
Gastroenterology	4.0	2.7	7.5	5.2	10.6	8.5	13.2	10.5
General practice	32.5	29.6	22.8	20.5	15.2	13.0	8.6	7.2
General surgery	34.0	22.4	38.4	24.5	36.7	24.5	37.1	24.3
Internal medicine	71.5	40.6	98.3	58.0	134.5	89.7	161.3	110.6
Neurological surgery	3.3	2.5	4.4	3.1	5.0	3.7	5.8	4.0
Neurology	5.7	3.3	9.2	5.6	12.3	8.6	15.9	10.5
Obstetrics and gynecology	26.3	19.5	33.7	25.5	40.2	31.7	42.8	34.1
Ophthalmology	13.0	10.6	16.1	13.1	18.1	15.6	18.5	15.7
Orthopedic surgery	14.0	10.7	19.1	14.2	22.3	17.4	25.2	19.3
Otolaryngology	6.6	5.3	8.1	6.4	9.4	7.6	10.3	8.0
Pathology	13.6	6.1	16.6	7.5	18.8	10.6	19.0	10.7
Pediatrics	29.5	18.2	41.9	27.1	63.9	43.2	76.4	53.1
Physical med./rehab.	2.1	1.0	4.1	2.2	6.5	4.3	9.0	6.5
Plastic surgery	3.0	2.4	4.6	3.8	6.2	5.3	7.4	6.2
Psychiatry	27.5	16.0	35.2	20.1	39.5	25.0	39.7	25.7
Pulmonary diseases	3.7	2.0	6.1	3.7	8.7	5.9	11.1	7.8
Radiology	11.7	7.8	8.5	6.1	8.7	6.7	9.4	7.0
Urological surgery	7.7	6.2	9.4	7.4	10.3	8.5	10.7	8.6
Unspecified	12.3	5.0	8.1	1.6	8.3	3.8	9.5	3.6
Not classified	20.6	(X)	12.7	(X)	45.1	(X)	64.2	(X)
Other categories [3]	32.1	(X)	55.4	(X)	75.2	(X)	126.4	(X)

X Not applicable. NA Not available. [1] Includes other categories not shown. [2] International medical graduates received their medical education in schools outside the United States and Canada. [3] Includes inactive and address unknown.

Source: American Medical Association, *Physician Characteristics and Distribution in the U.S.*, Chicago, IL, annual (copyright). For more information, see <http://www.ama-assn.org/>.

Table 168. Active Physicians and Nurses by State: 2010

[As of December 31. Excludes doctors of osteopathy, physicians with inactive status. Includes all physicians not classified according to activity status. As of May. Nurses data comes from the Bureau of Labor Statistics]

State	Physicians Total	Physicians Rate [1]	Nurses Total	Nurses Rate [1]	State	Physicians Total	Physicians Rate [1]	Nurses Total	Nurses Rate [1]
United States	**846,468**	**274**	**2,655,000**	**860**	Missouri	15,071	252	66,810	1,116
Alabama	10,311	216	44,300	927	Montana	2,108	213	8,500	859
Alaska	1,617	228	5,150	725	Nebraska	4,522	248	18,780	1,028
Arizona	14,291	224	41,730	653	Nevada	5,003	185	16,780	621
Arkansas	5,908	203	23,730	814	New Hampshire	3,877	294	13,850	1,052
California	101,206	272	240,030	644	New Jersey	27,151	309	76,680	872
Colorado	13,325	265	41,960	834	New Mexico	4,918	239	13,780	669
Connecticut	13,379	374	35,310	988	New York	76,178	393	169,710	876
Delaware	2,221	247	9,900	1,103	North Carolina	24,425	256	90,730	951
District of Columbia	5,275	877	9,510	1,580	North Dakota	1,616	240	6,880	1,023
Florida	47,251	251	158,390	842	Ohio	31,735	275	122,300	1,060
Georgia	21,608	223	65,390	675	Oklahoma	6,575	175	28,260	753
Hawaii	4,107	302	9,390	690	Oregon	10,925	285	31,950	834
Idaho	2,689	172	10,820	690	Pennsylvania	39,132	308	130,930	1,031
Illinois	37,094	289	120,810	942	Rhode Island	4,098	389	12,430	1,181
Indiana	14,014	216	60,300	930	South Carolina	10,661	230	40,520	876
Iowa	5,770	189	32,090	1,053	South Dakota	1,799	221	10,690	1,313
Kansas	6,505	228	28,070	984	Tennessee	16,858	266	61,890	975
Kentucky	10,133	234	44,920	1,035	Texas	54,887	218	176,330	701
Louisiana	12,191	269	40,780	900	Utah	6,030	218	18,230	660
Maine	3,685	277	14,730	1,109	Vermont	2,311	369	5,980	956
Maryland	24,164	419	50,480	874	Virginia	22,111	276	62,020	775
Massachusetts	31,875	487	85,120	1,300	Washington	18,432	274	52,490	781
Michigan	25,837	261	86,040	871	West Virginia	4,313	233	17,650	953
Minnesota	15,950	301	56,010	1,056	Wisconsin	14,986	264	52,880	930
Mississippi	5,321	179	28,200	950	Wyoming	1,019	181	4,790	850

[1] Per 100,000 resident population. Based on U.S. Census Bureau estimates as of April 1.

Source: Physicians: American Medical Association, *Physician Characteristics and Distribution in the U.S.*, Chicago, IL, annual (copyright). Nurses: Bureau of Labor Statistics, Occupational Employment Statistics, Occupational Employment and Wages, "May 2010 Wage and Employment Statistics," <http://www.bls.gov/oes/home.htm#data>.

Table 169. Percent Distribution of Number of Visits to Health Care Professionals by Selected Characteristics: 2000 and 2010

[Covers ambulatory visits to doctor's offices and emergency departments, and home health care visits during a 12-month period. Based on the redesigned National Health Interview Survey, a sample survey of the civilian noninstitutionalized population]

Characteristic	None 2000	None 2010	1–3 visits 2000	1–3 visits 2010	4–9 visits 2000	4–9 visits 2010	10 or more visits 2000	10 or more visits 2010
All persons [1,2]...............	**16.7**	**15.6**	**45.4**	**45.4**	**24.6**	**25.8**	**13.3**	**13.2**
SEX [2]								
Male............................	21.7	20.4	45.9	46.4	22.3	22.7	10.1	10.5
Female..........................	11.9	10.9	44.8	44.4	27.0	28.8	16.3	15.9
AGE								
Under 18 years old.............	12.3	8.1	53.8	55.6	26.2	28.2	7.6	8.2
18 to 44 years old.............	23.5	24.2	45.2	43.9	19.1	20.6	12.2	11.3
45 to 64 years old.............	15.0	14.8	43.4	42.8	25.7	26.1	15.9	16.4
65 to 74 years old.............	9.0	6.3	34.5	36.1	34.5	35.7	22.1	21.9
75 years old and over..........	5.8	4.1	29.3	31.0	39.3	38.0	25.6	27.0
RACE [2,3]								
Race alone:								
White..........................	16.1	15.3	45.1	44.9	25.2	26.1	13.6	13.7
Black or African American......	17.2	15.7	46.7	47.2	23.4	24.7	12.6	12.4
American Indian or Alaska Native...........	21.3	19.4	43.0	40.3	20.0	28.1	15.7	12.2
Asian..........................	20.3	20.4	49.2	49.9	20.8	22.1	9.7	7.6
Two or more races..............	12.1	13.9	41.7	42.3	28.2	25.2	18.0	18.6
HISPANIC ORIGIN AND RACE [2,3,4]								
Hispanic or Latino.............	26.8	23.5	41.8	43.2	19.8	22.6	11.6	10.7
Mexican........................	31.0	25.2	40.8	43.3	17.8	21.4	10.3	10.1
Not Hispanic or Latino.........	15.2	14.0	45.9	45.8	25.3	26.5	13.6	13.7
White, non-Hispanic............	14.5	13.2	45.4	45.3	25.9	27.1	14.1	14.4
Black, non-Hispanic............	17.1	15.6	46.8	47.3	23.5	24.9	12.6	12.2

[1] Includes other categories not shown separately. [2] Estimates are age adjusted to the year 2000 standard using six age groups: Under 18 years, 18–44 years, 45–54 years, 55–64 years, 65–74 years, and 75 years and over. [3] Estimates by race and Hispanic origin are tabulated using the 1997 standards for federal data on race and ethnicity. Estimates for specific race groups are shown when they meet requirements for statistical reliability and confidentiality. The categories "White only," "Black or African American only," "American Indian and Alaska Native (AI/AN) only," and "Asian only" include persons who reported only one racial group; and the category "2 or more races" includes persons who reported more than one of the five racial groups in the 1997 standards or one of the five racial groups and "Some other race." [4] Persons of Hispanic or Latino origin may be any race.

Source: U.S. National Center for Health Statistics, *Health, United States, 2011*. See also <www.cdc.gov/nchs/hus.htm>.

Table 170. Adults 18 Years and Over Who Used Complementary and Alternative Medicine (CAM) in the Past 12 Months by Type of Therapy: 2002 and 2007

[The denominators for statistics shown exclude persons with unknown CAM information. Estimates were age adjusted to the year 2000 U.S. standard population using four age groups: 18 to 24 years, 25 to 44 years, 45 to 64 years, and 65 years and over]

Therapy	2002 Number (1,000)	2002 Percent	2007 Number (1,000)	2007 Percent
Alternative medical systems:				
Acupuncture........................	2,136	1.1	3,141	1.4
Homeopathic treatment..............	3,433	1.7	3,909	1.8
Biologically based therapies:				
Nonvitamin, nonmineral, natural products [1].............	38,183	18.9	38,797	17.7
Diet-based therapies [2,3].........	7,099	3.5	7,893	3.6
Vegetarian diet....................	3,184	1.6	3,351	1.5
Atkins diet........................	3,417	1.7	2,673	1.2
South Beach........................	(X)	(X)	2,334	1.1
Megavitamin therapy................	5,739	2.8	(X)	(X)
Manipulative and body-based therapies:				
Chiropractic care [4]..............	15,226	7.5	(X)	(X)
Chiropractic or osteopathic manipulation [4]..................	(X)	(X)	18,740	8.6
Massage............................	10,052	5.0	18,068	8.3
Movement therapies.................	(X)	(X)	3,146	1.5
Pilates............................	(X)	(X)	3,015	1.4
Mind-body therapies:				
Meditation.........................	15,336	7.6	20,541	9.4
Guided imagery.....................	4,194	2.1	4,866	2.2
Progressive relaxation.............	6,185	3.0	6,454	2.9
Deep breathing exercises...........	23,457	11.6	27,794	12.7
Yoga...............................	10,386	5.1	13,172	6.1
Tai chi............................	2,565	1.3	2,267	1.0
Energy healing therapy/Reiki.......	1,080	0.5	1,216	0.5

X Not applicable. [1] While questions were asked about nonvitamin, nonmineral, natural products in both 2002 and 2007, the data are not comparable due primarily to question order and the specific nonvitamin, nonmineral, natural product covered. [2] The totals of the numbers and percents of the categories listed under "Diet-based therapies" are greater than the number and percent of their respective category heading because respondents could choose more than one of the categories. [3] While questions were asked about Diet-based therapies in both 2002 and 2007, the data are not comparable because respondents were asked about the South Beach Diet in 2007, but not in 2002. [4] While questions were asked about chiropractic therapy in both 2002 and 2007, the data are not comparable because respondents were asked about chiropractic care in 2002 and chiropractic or osteopathic manipulation in 2007.

Source: U.S. National Center for Health Statistics, *Complementary and Alternative Medicine Use Among Adults and Children: United States, 2007*, National Health Statistics Reports, Number 12, 2008. See also <http://www.cdc.gov/nchs/products/nhsr.htm>.

Table 171. Ambulatory Care Visits to Physicians' Offices and Hospital Outpatient and Emergency Departments: 2009

[1,270.0 represents 1,270,000,000. Based on the annual National Ambulatory Medical Care Survey and National Hospital Ambulatory Medical Care Survey and subject to sampling error; see source for details]

Characteristic	Number of visits (mil.)				Visits per 100 persons			
	Total	Physician offices	Out-patient dept.	Emer-gency dept.	Total	Physician offices	Out-patient dept.	Emer-gency dept.
Total	**1,270.0**	**1,037.8**	**96.1**	**136.1**	**421.1**	**344.1**	**31.9**	**45.1**
Age:								
Under 15 years old	206.2	158.9	19.0	28.3	333.4	257.0	30.7	45.7
15 to 24 years old	105.8	74.1	10.6	21.1	251.7	176.3	25.3	50.1
25 to 44 years old	268.8	208.9	22.3	37.6	332.2	258.1	27.6	46.5
45 to 64 years old	374.8	316.4	29.1	29.3	475.4	401.3	36.9	37.2
65 to 74 years old	153.9	137.5	8.0	8.4	748.9	668.9	39.1	40.9
75 years old and over	160.5	142.1	7.1	11.4	923.2	816.9	40.6	65.7
Sex:								
Male	526.3	426.7	38.0	61.5	356.4	288.9	25.8	41.7
Female	743.7	611.1	58.1	74.5	483.5	397.2	37.8	48.5
Race: [2]								
White	1,044.7	877.2	69.9	97.6	434.4	364.7	29.1	40.6
Black/African American	167.3	113.0	22.1	32.3	438.3	296.0	57.8	84.5
Expected sources of payment: [3]								
Private insurance	758.4	664.4	41.5	52.5	(X)	(X)	(X)	(X)
Medicare	303.6	262.7	17.8	23.1	(X)	(X)	(X)	(X)
Medicaid/SCHIP [4]	208.4	140.3	28.2	39.9	(X)	(X)	(X)	(X)
Worker's compensation	16.6	14.2	0.8	1.6	(X)	(X)	(X)	(X)
No insurance: [5]	72.2	40.1	10.9	21.2	(X)	(X)	(X)	(X)
Self pay	64.3	37.6	6.8	19.8	(X)	(X)	(X)	(X)
No charge	8.5	2.7	[1] 4.3	1.5	(X)	(X)	(X)	(X)
Other	39.4	30.9	3.9	4.6	(X)	(X)	(X)	(X)
Unknown	37.6	25.0	3.5	9.1	(X)	(X)	(X)	(X)

X Not applicable. [1] Figure does not meet standards of reliability or precision. [2] Race data were missing for 24.0 percent of ambulatory care visits, including 24.4 percent of visits to physician offices, 10.4 percent of visits to hospital outpatient departments, and 10.6 percent of visits to emergency departments. Missing data were imputed, and readers are advised to treat the resulting estimates with caution. More information is available at the Web site below. [3] Estimates include all expected sources of payment reported at the visit. [4] SCHIP is State Children's Health Insurance Program. [5] "No insurance" is defined as having only "self-pay" or "no charge/charity" as payment sources.

Source: U.S. National Center for Health Statistics, *National Health Statistics Reports*, <http://www.cdc.gov/nchs/ahcd.htm>.

Table 172. Visits to Office-Based Physicians and Hospital Outpatient Departments by Diagnosis: 2003 and 2008

[405.5 represents 405,500,000. Based on the International Classification of Diseases, 9th Revision, Clinical Modification, (ICD-9-CM). See headnote, Table 171]

Leading diagnosis	Number (mil.)		Rate per 1,000 persons [1]		Leading diagnosis	Number (mil.)		Rate per 1,000 persons [1]	
	2003	2008	2003	2008		2003	2008	2003	2008
Male, all ages	**405.5**	**425.8**	**2,908**	**2,911**	**Female, all ages**	**595.1**	**640.1**	**4,074**	**4,199**
Under 15 years old [2]	**89.1**	**89.6**	**2,870**	**2,869**	**Under 15 years old [2]**	**78.0**	**79.9**	**2,630**	**2,679**
Routine infant or child health check	16.8	23.1	541	740	Routine infant or child health check	14.0	21.9	472	733
Acute upper respiratory infections [3]	7.8	8.1	250	259	Acute upper respiratory infections [3]	7.8	7.1	262	239
Otitis media and Eustachian tube disorders	8.4	7.4	269	236	Otitis media and Eustachian tube disorders	6.4	6.2	217	209
Acute pharyngitis	2.1	3.4	66	107	Acute pharyngitis	3.3	3.1	110	105
15 to 44 years old [2]	**104.0**	**93.4**	**1,710**	**1,524**	**15 to 44 years old [2]**	**208.3**	**212.8**	**3,386**	**3,458**
General medical examination	4.4	4.8	72	78	Normal pregnancy	25.6	24.7	415	401
Acute upper respiratory infections [3]	4.0	3.2	65.0	53.0	Gynecological examination	9.8	10.1	160	165
Spinal disorders	3.4	3.2	56	52	Complications of pregnancy, childbirth, and puerperium	7.4	7.7	121	124
Essential hypertension	2.1	2.8	35	46					
45 to 64 years old [2]	**112.6**	**127.2**	**3,404**	**3,376**	**45 to 64 years old [2]**	**167.9**	**188.1**	**4,781**	**4,720**
Essential hypertension	7.6	8.6	231	227	Essential hypertension	8.2	12.0	234	302
Diabetes mellitus	5.2	6.4	156	171	Arthropathies and related disorders	8.1	7.9	231	198
Spinal disorders	4.7	5.4	143	144	Rheumatism, excluding back	6.0	6.4	170	161
Arthropathies and related disorders	4.5	4.1	135	110					
65 years old and over [2]	**99.8**	**115.5**	**6,881**	**7,211**	**65 years old and over [2]**	**140.9**	**159.3**	**7,123**	**7,509**
Essential hypertension	7.2	8.8	496	546	Essential hypertension	11.1	15.4	563	728
Heart disease [4]	3.7	6.7	256	416	Arthropathies and related disorders	8.1	7.7	408	364
Malignant neoplasms	6.3	6.3	434	392	Heart disease [4]	4.3	6.9	218	328
Ischemic heart disease	3.6	6.0	250	376					

[1] Based on U.S. Census Bureau estimated civilian population as of July 1. [2] Includes other first-listed diagnoses, not shown separately. [3] Excluding pharyngitis. [4] Excluding ischemic.

Source: U.S. National Center for Health Statistics, *National Health Statistics Reports*, <http://www.cdc.gov/nchs/ahcd.htm>.

Table 173. Visits to Hospital Emergency Departments by Diagnosis: 2009

[61,534 represents 61,534,000. See headnote, Tables 171 and 172]

Leading diagnosis	Number (1,000)	Rate per 1,000 persons [1]	Leading diagnosis	Number (1,000)	Rate per 1,000 persons [1]
MALE			**FEMALE**		
All ages	**61,534**	**408**	**All ages**	**74,540**	**478**
Under 15 years old [2]	**15,392**	**493**	**Under 15 years old [2]**	**12,882**	**431**
Acute upper respiratory infections [3]	1,611	52	Acute respiratory infections [3]	1,452	49
Pyrexia of unknown origin	977	31	Pyrexia of unknown origin	886	30
Otitis media and eustachian tube disorders	902	29	Otitis media and Eustachian tube disorders	831	28
Open wound of head	634	20	Unspecified viral and chlamydial infections	410	14
Unspecified viral and chlamydial infections	557	18	Contusion with intact skin surface	397	13
15 to 64 years old [2]	**38,036**	**371**	**15 to 64 years old [2]**	**49,945**	**483**
Open wound, excluding head	1,842	18	Abdominal pain	3,090	30
Chest pain	1,765	17	Chest pain	2,099	20
Contusion with intact skin surfaces	1,592	16	Contusion with intact skin surface	1,753	17
Spinal disorders	1,533	15	Spinal disorders	1,712	17
Abdominal pain	1,385	14	Acute respiratory infections [3]	1,700	16
65 years old and over [2]	**8,106**	**476**	**65 years old and over [2]**	**11,713**	**518**
Heart disease, excluding ischemic	567	33	Chest pain	655	29
Chest pain	422	25	Contusion with intact skin surface	551	24
Cerebrovascular disease	265	16	Urinary tract infection site not specified	440	19
Pneumonia	236	14	Abdominal pain	415	18
Abdominal pain	232	14	Heart disease, excluding ischemic	412	18

[1] Based on U.S. Census Bureau estimated civilian noninstitutional population as of July 1. [2] Includes other first-listed diagnosis, not shown separately. [3] Excluding pharyngitis.

Source: U.S. National Center for Health Statistics, *National Health Statistics Reports*, <http://www.cdc.gov/nchs/ahcd.htm>.

Table 174. Procedures for Inpatients Discharged From Short-Stay Hospitals: 1990 to 2008

[23,051 represents 23,051,000. Procedure categories are based on the International Classification of Diseases, 9th Revision, Clinical Modification. See headnote, Table 179]

Sex and type of procedure	Number of procedures (1,000)				Rate per 1,000 population [1]			
	1990	1995	2000	2008	1990	1995	2000	2008
Surgical procedures, total [2]	**23,051**	**22,530**	**23,244**	**28,704**	**92.4**	**86.2**	**83.6**	**94.8**
Cesarean section	945	785	855	1,351	3.8	3.0	3.1	4.5
Repair of current obstetric laceration	795	964	1,136	1,325	3.2	3.7	4.1	4.4
Cardiac catheterization	995	1,068	1,221	1,108	4.0	4.1	4.4	3.7
Reduction of fracture [3]	609	577	628	716	2.4	2.2	2.3	2.4
Male, total [2]	**8,538**	**8,388**	**8,689**	**11,317**	**70.6**	**65.9**	**63.9**	**76.0**
Cardiac catheterization	620	660	732	648	5.1	5.2	5.4	4.4
Coronary artery bypass graft [4]	286	423	371	329	2.4	3.3	2.7	2.2
Reduction of fracture [3]	300	251	285	362	2.5	2.0	2.1	2.4
Female, total [2]	**14,513**	**14,142**	**14,556**	**17,387**	**113.0**	**105.3**	**102.4**	**112.9**
Cesarean section	945	785	855	1,351	7.4	5.8	6.0	8.8
Repair of current obstetric laceration	795	964	1,136	1,325	6.2	7.2	8.0	8.6
Hysterectomy	591	583	633	584	4.6	4.3	4.5	3.8
Diagnostic and other nonsurgical procedures [5]	**17,455**	**17,278**	**16,737**	**18,634**	**70.0**	**66.1**	**60.2**	**61.5**
Angiocardiography and arteriography [6]	1,735	1,834	2,005	1,996	7.0	7.0	7.2	6.6
Respiratory therapy	1,164	1,127	991	1,182	4.7	4.3	3.6	3.9
Manual assisted delivery	750	866	898	1,308	3.0	3.3	3.2	4.3
Diagnostic ultrasound	1,608	1,181	886	895	6.4	4.5	3.2	3.0
Fetal electrocardiogram (EKG) and fetal monitoring	1,377	935	750	1,024	5.6	3.6	2.7	3.4
Male, total [5]	**7,378**	**7,261**	**6,965**	**7,473**	**61.0**	**57.1**	**51.2**	**50.2**
Angiocardiography and arteriography [6]	1,051	1,076	1,157	1,094	8.7	8.5	8.5	7.3
Respiratory therapy	586	572	507	610	4.9	4.5	3.7	4.1
Computerized Axial Tomographic scan [7]	736	473	345	278	6.1	3.7	2.5	1.9
Female, total [5]	**10,077**	**10,016**	**9,772**	**11,161**	**78.5**	**74.6**	**68.8**	**72.5**
Manual assisted delivery	750	866	898	1,308	5.9	6.5	6.3	8.5
Fetal electrocardiogram (EKG) and fetal monitoring	1,377	935	750	1,024	10.8	7.0	5.5	6.7
Respiratory therapy	578	555	484	572	4.5	4.1	3.4	3.7
Diagnostic ultrasound	941	682	501	476	7.3	3.5	3.5	3.1

[1] Based on Census Bureau estimated civilian population as of July 1. Population estimates based on the 1990 census were used to calculate rates for 1990 through 2000. Population estimates based on the 2000 census were used to calculate rates for 2001 through 2008. [2] Includes other types of surgical procedures, not shown separately. [3] Excluding skull, nose, and jaw. [4] It is possible for a discharge to have more than one of these recorded. [5] Includes other nonsurgical procedures, not shown separately. [6] Using contrast material. [7] Also known as CAT scan.

Source: U.S. National Center for Health Statistics, *Vital and Health Statistics*, Series 13, and unpublished data, <http://www.cdc.gov/nchs/products/series.htm> and <http://www.cdc.gov/nchs/nhds.htm>.

Table 175. Hospitals—Summary Characteristics: 1990 to 2009

[For beds, (1,213 represents 1,213,000). Covers hospitals accepted for registration by the American Hospital Association; see text, this section. Short-term hospitals have an average patient stay of less than 30 days; long-term, an average stay of longer duration. Special hospitals include obstetrics and gynecology; eye, ear, nose, and throat; rehabilitation; orthopedic; chronic and other special hospitals except psychiatric, tuberculosis, alcoholism, and chemical dependency hospitals]

Item	1990	1995	2000	2004	2005	2006	2007	2008	2009
Number:									
All hospitals	6,649	6,291	5,810	5,759	5,756	5,747	5,708	5,815	5,795
With 100 beds or more	3,620	3,376	3,102	2,972	2,942	2,928	2,901	2,884	2,861
Nonfederal [1]	6,312	5,992	5,565	5,520	5,530	5,526	5,495	5,602	5,584
Community hospitals [2]	5,384	5,194	4,915	4,919	4,936	4,927	4,897	5,010	5,008
Nongovernmental nonprofit	3,191	3,092	3,003	2,967	2,958	2,919	2,913	2,923	2,918
For profit	749	752	749	835	868	889	873	982	998
State and local government	1,444	1,350	1,163	1,117	1,110	1,119	1,111	1,105	1,092
Long term general and special	131	112	131	108	115	127	135	128	115
Psychiatric	757	657	496	466	456	462	444	447	444
Tuberculosis	4	3	4	4	3	2	1	1	2
Federal	337	299	245	239	226	221	213	213	211
Beds (1,000): [3]									
All hospitals	1,213	1,081	984	956	947	947	945	951	944
Rate per 1,000 population [4]	4.9	4.1	3.5	3.3	3.2	3.2	3.1	3.1	3.1
Beds per hospital	182	172	169	166	165	165	166	164	163
Nonfederal [1]	1,113	1,004	931	908	901	901	899	905	900
Community hospitals [2]	927	873	824	808	802	802	801	808	806
Rate per 1,000 population [4]	3.7	3.3	2.9	2.8	2.7	2.7	2.7	2.7	2.6
Nongovernmental nonprofit	657	610	583	567	561	559	554	557	556
For profit	102	106	110	112	114	115	116	121	122
State and local government	169	157	131	127	128	128	131	131	127
Long term general and special	25	19	18	15	15	16	17	16	16
Psychiatric	158	110	87	86	82	84	79	79	76
Tuberculosis	(Z)	(Z)	(Z)	(Z)	(Z)	(Z)	(Z)	(Z)	(Z)
Federal	98	78	53	47	46	46	46	46	45
Average daily census (1,000): [5]									
All hospitals	844	710	650	658	656	653	645	649	641
Community hospitals [2]	619	548	526	541	540	538	533	536	528
Nongovernmental nonprofit	455	393	382	388	388	384	380	380	375
For profit	54	55	61	68	68	67	66	70	70
State and local government	111	100	83	84	85	86	87	86	83
Expenses (bil. dol.): [6]									
All hospitals	234.9	320.3	395.4	533.8	570.5	607.3	638.5	690.0	726.7
Nonfederal [1]	219.6	300.0	371.5	499.0	533.7	569.8	599.7	646.1	676.6
Community hospitals [2]	203.7	285.6	356.6	481.2	515.7	551.8	581.0	626.6	656.2
Nongovernmental nonprofit	150.7	209.6	267.1	359.4	386.0	412.8	435.5	468.1	492.9
For profit	18.8	26.7	35.0	48.9	51.8	54.9	55.8	61.8	64.4
State and local government	34.2	49.3	54.5	72.8	77.9	83.9	89.8	96.7	98.9
Long term general and special	2.7	2.2	2.8	3.6	3.6	4.0	3.9	4.5	4.2
Psychiatric	12.9	11.7	11.9	13.8	13.9	15.0	14.5	14.7	15.1
Tuberculosis	0.1	0.4	(Z)	(Z)	(Z)	(Z)	(Z)	(Z)	(Z)
Federal	15.2	20.2	23.9	34.8	36.8	37.5	38.8	44.0	50.1
Personnel (1,000): [7]									
All hospitals	4,063	4,273	4,454	4,695	4,790	4,907	5,024	5,116	5,178
Nonfederal [1]	3,760	3,971	4,157	4,379	4,479	4,569	4,699	4,775	4,814
Community hospitals [2]	3,420	3,714	3,911	4,147	4,260	4,343	4,465	4,550	4,585
Nongovernmental nonprofit	2,533	2,702	2,919	3,076	3,154	3,207	3,286	3,340	3,369
For profit	273	343	378	405	421	423	432	450	464
State and local government	614	670	614	665	681	713	747	760	751
Long term general and special	55	38	41	42	38	43	44	41	37
Psychiatric	280	215	200	185	182	180	187	182	183
Tuberculosis	1	1	1	1	1	1	1	(Z)	(Z)
Federal	303	301	297	315	311	339	325	341	364
Outpatient visits (mil.)	368.2	483.2	592.7	662.1	673.7	690.4	693.5	710.0	742.0
Emergency	92.8	99.9	106.9	116.9	118.9	122.6	124.7	126.7	131.4

Z Less than 500 or $50 million. [1] Includes hospital units of institutions. [2] Short-term (average length of stay less than 30 days) general and special (e.g., obstetrics and gynecology; eye, ear, nose and throat; rehabilitation, etc. except psychiatric, tuberculosis, alcoholism, and chemical dependency). Excludes hospital units of institutions. [3] Number of beds at end of reporting period. [4] Based on Census Bureau estimated resident population as of July 1. 1990 and 2000 based on enumerated resident population as of April 1. Other years are estimates, which reflect revisions based on the 2000 Census of Population. [5] The average number of people served on an inpatient basis on a single day during the reporting period. [6] Excludes new construction. [7] Includes full-time equivalents of part-time personnel.

Source: Health Forum, An American Hospital Association Company, Chicago, IL, *AHA Hospital Statistics 2011 Edition*, and prior years (copyright). See also <www.ahadata.com>.

Table 176. Average Cost to Community Hospitals Per Patient: 1990 to 2009

[In dollars, except percent. Covers non-federal short-term general or special hospitals (excluding psychiatric or tuberculosis hospitals and hospital units of institutions). Total cost per patient based on total hospital expenses (payroll, employee benefits, professional fees, supplies, etc.). Data have been adjusted for outpatient visits]

Type of expense and hospital	1990	1995	2000	2003	2004	2005	2006	2007	2008	2009
Average cost per day, total	**687**	**968**	**1,149**	**1,379**	**1,450**	**1,522**	**1,612**	**1,690**	**1,782**	**1,853**
Annual percent change [1]	7.8	4.0	4.2	6.9	5.1	5.0	5.9	4.8	5.4	4.0
Nongovernmental nonprofit	692	994	1,182	1,429	1,501	1,585	1,686	1,772	1,876	1,957
For profit	752	947	1,057	1,264	1,362	1,412	1,472	1,519	1,556	1,574
State and local government	635	878	1,064	1,238	1,291	1,329	1,400	1,460	1,552	1,611
Average cost per stay, total	**4,947**	**6,216**	**6,649**	**7,796**	**8,166**	**8,793**	**8,970**	**9,342**	**9,788**	**10,043**
Nongovernmental nonprofit	5,001	6,279	6,717	7,905	8,266	8,670	9,190	9,574	10,081	10,379
For profit	4,727	5,425	5,642	6,590	7,139	7,351	7,422	7,740	7,985	8,037
State and local government	4,838	6,445	7,106	8,205	8,473	8,793	9,147	9,446	9,827	10,068

[1] Change from immediate prior year.

Source: Health Forum, An American Hospital Association Company, Chicago, IL, *AHA Hospital Statistics 2011 Edition*, and prior years (copyright). See also <www.ahadata.com>.

Table 177. Community Hospitals—States: 2000 and 2009

[In thousands, (823.6 represents 823,600). For definition of community hospitals see footnote 2, Table 175]

State	Number of hospitals		Beds (1,000)		Patients admitted (1,000)		Average daily census [1] (1,000)		Outpatient visits (mil.)		Average cost per day (dol.)	
	2000	2009	2000	2009	2000	2009	2000	2009	2000	2009	2000	2009
United States	**4,915**	**5,008**	**823.6**	**805.6**	**33,089**	**35,527**	**525.7**	**527.9**	**521.4**	**642.0**	**1,149**	**1,853**
Alabama	108	108	16.4	15.3	680	666	9.8	9.5	8.0	9.2	980	1,319
Alaska	18	22	1.4	1.5	47	57	0.8	0.9	1.3	1.8	1,495	2,163
Arizona	61	72	10.9	13.5	539	705	6.8	8.8	5.3	7.1	1,311	2,106
Arkansas	83	86	9.8	9.6	368	380	5.7	5.4	4.4	5.0	908	1,428
California	389	343	72.7	68.7	3,315	3,433	47.8	48.2	44.9	48.3	1,438	2,419
Colorado	69	81	9.4	10.4	397	445	5.4	6.1	6.7	8.9	1,280	2,156
Connecticut	35	35	7.7	7.9	349	408	5.8	6.4	6.7	8.2	1,373	2,077
Delaware	5	7	1.8	2.2	83	102	1.4	1.6	1.5	1.7	1,311	2,154
District of Columbia	11	10	3.3	3.5	129	138	2.5	2.5	1.3	2.4	1,512	2,514
Florida	202	210	51.2	53.3	2,119	2,453	31.0	33.6	21.8	24.9	1,161	1,776
Georgia	151	152	23.9	25.4	863	957	15.0	16.6	11.2	14.4	978	1,354
Hawaii	21	25	3.1	3.0	100	112	2.3	2.1	2.5	2.2	1,088	1,892
Idaho	42	41	3.5	3.4	123	130	1.8	1.7	2.2	3.1	1,003	1,887
Illinois	196	189	37.3	33.9	1,531	1,558	22.4	21.3	25.1	32.1	1,278	1,948
Indiana	109	123	19.2	17.3	700	713	10.8	10.1	14.1	17.5	1,132	1,955
Iowa	115	118	11.8	10.3	360	355	6.8	6.0	9.2	11.0	740	1,204
Kansas	129	133	10.8	10.1	310	316	5.7	5.5	5.3	6.7	837	1,271
Kentucky	105	104	14.8	14.1	582	597	9.1	8.5	8.7	10.1	929	1,543
Louisiana	123	128	17.5	15.9	654	639	9.8	9.6	10.0	12.4	1,075	1,510
Maine	37	37	3.7	3.6	147	150	2.4	2.3	3.2	5.8	1,148	1,881
Maryland	49	49	11.2	11.9	587	715	8.2	8.9	6.0	8.3	1,315	2,271
Massachusetts	80	78	16.6	15.5	740	820	11.7	11.5	16.7	21.4	1,467	2,351
Michigan	146	158	26.1	25.9	1,106	1,220	16.9	17.3	24.9	29.3	1,211	1,905
Minnesota	135	132	16.7	15.6	571	624	11.2	10.2	7.3	10.8	932	1,667
Mississippi	95	97	13.6	12.9	425	413	8.0	7.1	3.7	4.7	719	1,231
Missouri	119	125	20.1	19.1	773	825	11.7	11.7	14.8	19.2	1,185	1,934
Montana	52	48	4.3	3.8	99	101	2.9	2.4	2.6	3.3	579	1,190
Nebraska	85	87	8.2	7.4	209	210	4.8	4.3	3.4	4.7	743	1,402
Nevada	22	35	3.8	5.1	199	246	2.7	3.6	2.2	2.8	1,285	1,912
New Hampshire	28	28	2.9	2.9	111	123	1.7	1.8	2.8	4.7	1,201	1,980
New Jersey	80	74	25.3	21.1	1,074	1,095	17.3	15.3	16.3	18.4	1,299	2,147
New Mexico	35	37	3.5	3.9	174	183	2.0	2.3	3.1	4.6	1,388	1,989
New York	215	189	66.4	60.4	2,416	2,534	52.1	47.9	46.4	54.2	1,118	1,820
North Carolina	113	115	23.1	22.8	971	1,034	16.0	15.9	12.4	18.3	1,061	1,641
North Dakota	42	41	3.9	3.4	89	93	2.3	2.1	1.7	2.4	747	1,140
Ohio	163	183	33.8	33.9	1,404	1,531	20.6	21.2	26.9	34.2	1,198	2,021
Oklahoma	108	116	11.1	11.3	429	442	6.2	6.6	4.7	5.6	1,031	1,489
Oregon	59	58	6.6	6.5	330	324	3.9	3.9	7.3	8.9	1,461	2,596
Pennsylvania	207	194	42.3	39.2	1,796	1,842	28.8	27.0	31.8	37.9	1,080	1,837
Rhode Island	11	11	2.4	2.5	119	127	1.7	1.8	2.1	2.6	1,313	2,235
South Carolina	63	70	11.5	12.5	495	528	8.0	8.1	7.8	6.3	1,101	1,792
South Dakota	48	53	4.3	4.1	99	102	2.8	2.8	1.7	1.9	476	985
Tennessee	121	137	20.6	21.0	737	859	11.5	13.2	10.3	11.6	1,078	1,464
Texas	403	428	55.9	62.1	2,367	2,621	33.1	37.3	29.4	36.0	1,274	1,923
Utah	42	44	4.3	5.0	194	226	2.4	2.8	4.5	5.5	1,375	2,071
Vermont	14	14	1.7	1.3	52	51	1.1	0.9	1.2	3.4	888	1,586
Virginia	88	90	16.9	17.5	727	793	11.4	12.0	9.5	14.2	1,057	1,747
Washington	84	87	11.1	11.3	505	589	6.6	7.3	9.6	11.5	1,511	2,696
West Virginia	57	56	8.0	7.4	288	280	4.8	4.5	5.2	6.7	844	1,134
Wisconsin	118	126	15.3	13.6	558	609	9.1	8.6	10.9	14.9	1,055	1,935
Wyoming	24	24	1.9	2.0	48	52	1.1	1.1	0.9	1.1	677	1,025

[1] The average number of people served on an inpatient basis on a single day during the reporting period.

Source: Health Forum, An American Hospital Association Company, Chicago, IL, *AHA Hospital Statistics 2011 Edition*, and prior years (copyright). See also <www.ahadata.com>.

Table 178. Hospital Utilization Rates by Type of Hospital: 1990 to 2009

Type of hospital	1990	1995	2000	2005	2006	2007	2008	2009
Community hospitals: [1]								
Admissions per 1,000 population [2]	125	116	117	119	118	117	118	116
Admissions per bed	34	35	40	44	44	43	44	44
Average length of stay (days) [3]	7.2	6.5	5.8	5.6	5.5	5.5	5.5	5.4
Outpatient visits per admission	9.7	13.4	15.8	16.6	16.9	17.1	17.5	18.1
Outpatient visits per 1,000 population [2]	1,207	1,556	1,852	1,976	2,002	2,000	2,053	2,091
Surgical operations (million [4])	21.9	23.2	26.1	27.5	28.1	28.1	27.5	27.5
Number per admission	0.7	0.7	0.8	0.8	0.7	0.8	0.8	0.8
Nonfederal psychiatric:								
Admissions per 1,000 population [2]	2.9	2.7	2.4	2.5	2.3	2.3	2.4	2.5
Days in hospital per 1,000 population [2]	190	122	93	89	83	82	80	80

[1] Short term (average length of stay less than 30 days) general and special (e.g., obstetrics and gynecology; eye, ear, nose and throat; rehabilitation, etc., except psychiatric, tuberculosis, alcoholism and chemical dependency). Excludes hospital units of institutions. [2] Based on U.S. Census Bureau estimated resident population as of July 1. Estimates reflect revisions based on the 2000 Census of Population. 1990 and 2000 based on enumerated resident population as of April 1. [3] Number of inpatient days divided by number of admissions. [4] 21.9 represents 21,900,000.

Source: Health Forum, An American Hospital Association Company, Chicago, IL, *AHA Hospital Statistics 2011 Edition*, and prior years (copyright). See also <www.ahadata.com>.

Table 179. Hospital Utilization Rates by Sex: 1990 to 2009

[30,788 represents 30,788,000. Represents estimates of inpatients discharged from noninstitutional, short-stay hospitals, exclusive of federal hospitals. Excludes newborn infants. Based on sample data collected from the National Hospital Discharge Survey, a sample survey of hospital records of patients discharged in year shown; subject to sampling variability]

Item and sex	1990	1995	2000	2004	2005	2006	2007	2008	2009
Patients discharged (1,000)	30,788	30,722	31,706	34,864	34,667	34,854	34,369	35,697	36,120
Patients discharged per 1,000 persons, total [1]	122	116	113	119	117	117	114	118	118
Male	100	94	91	97	96	95	94	97	98
Female	143	136	134	141	138	138	134	139	138
Days of care per 1,000 persons, total [1]	784	620	555	574	562	558	554	577	575
Male	694	551	486	505	498	495	494	518	518
Female	869	686	620	641	624	619	612	635	630
Average stay (days)	6.4	5.4	4.9	4.8	4.8	4.8	4.8	4.9	4.9
Male	6.9	5.8	5.3	5.2	5.2	5.2	5.3	5.4	5.3
Female	6.1	5.0	4.6	4.5	4.5	4.5	4.6	4.6	4.6

NA Not available. [1] Rates are computed using Census Bureau estimates of the civilian population as of July 1. Rates for 1990 and 1995 were based on population estimates adjusted for the net underenumeration in the 1990 census. Rates for 2000 and later were calculated using 2000-based postcensal estimates.

Source: U.S. National Center for Health Statistics, *Vital and Health Statistics*, Series 13, National Hospital Discharge Survey, <http://www.cdc.gov/nchs/nhds/nhds_tables.htm#average>, and unpublished data.

Table 180. Hospital Utilization Measures for HIV Patients: 1990 to 2008

[HIV represents human immunodeficiency virus. See headnote, Table 179]

Measure of utilization	Unit	1990	1995	2000	2005	2006	2007	2008
Number of patients discharged	1,000	146	249	173	185	223	221	215
Male	1,000	114	183	115	113	145	146	133
Female	1,000	32	66	58	72	78	75	81
Rate of patient discharges [1]	Rate	5.8	9.4	6.2	6.3	7.5	7.4	7.1
Number of days of care	1,000	2,188	2,326	1,257	1,244	1,418	1,483	1,342
Male	1,000	1,777	1,649	895	751	907	1,009	875
Female	1,000	411	677	362	493	511	474	468
Rate of days of care [1]	Rate	86.9	87.6	45.2	42.2	47.6	49.3	44.3
Average length of stay	Days	14.9	9.3	7.3	6.7	6.3	6.7	6.3
Male	Days	15.5	9.0	7.8	6.7	6.2	6.9	6.6
Female	Days	12.9	10.3	6.3	6.8	6.5	6.3	5.7

[1] Per 10,000 population. Based on Census Bureau estimated civilian population as of July 1. Rates for 1990 and 1995 were based on population estimates adjusted for the net undernumeration in the 1990 census. Populations for 2000 and later were 2000-based postcensal estimates.

Source: U.S. National Center for Health Statistics, *Vital and Health Statistics*, Series 13 and unpublished data. See also <http://www.cdc.gov/nchs/products/series.htm#sr13> and <http://www.cdc.gov/nchs/nhds.htm>.

Table 181. Hospital Discharges and Days of Care: 2003 and 2008

[(34,738 represents 34,738,000). See headnote, Table 179. For composition of regions, see map, inside front cover]

Age, race, and region	Discharges Number (1,000) 2003	2008	Discharges Per 1,000 persons [1] 2003	2008	Days of care per 1,000 persons [1] 2003	2008	Average stay (days) 2003	2008
Total [2]	**34,738**	**35,697**	**120**	**118**	**578**	**577**	**4.8**	**4.9**
Age:								
Under 1 year old	833	715	208	166	1,218	940	5.9	5.7
1 to 4 years old	751	563	48	34	149	102	3.1	3.0
5 to 14 years old	986	707	24	18	108	75	4.5	4.3
15 to 24 years old	3,138	2,950	77	70	268	233	3.5	3.3
25 to 34 years old	4,011	4,066	102	100	353	346	3.5	3.4
35 to 44 years old	3,683	3,453	83	82	359	331	4.3	4.0
45 to 64 years old	8,120	9,341	118	120	582	628	4.9	5.2
65 to 74 years old	4,861	5,094	265	253	1,429	1,391	5.4	5.5
75 years old and over	8,356	8,808	475	470	2,776	2,735	5.8	5.8
Race:								
White	21,292	20,487	91	85	437	421	4.8	5.0
Black	4,102	4,665	111	120	611	642	5.5	5.3
Asian/Pacific Islander	550	591	44	42	231	[3] 213	5.2	5.1
American Indian/Eskimo/Aleut	120	[3] 194	43	[3] 63	224	[3] 259	5.2	4.1
Region:								
Northeast	7,267	7,574	134	138	735	771	5.5	5.6
Midwest	7,786	8,062	119	121	520	543	4.4	4.5
South	13,055	13,366	126	120	610	584	4.9	4.9
West	6,631	6,695	100	95	455	450	4.5	4.7

[1] Rates were calculated using U.S. Census Bureau 2000-based postcensal estimates of the civilian population as of July 1. [2] Includes other races not shown separately. [3] Figure does not meet standard of reliability or precision.

Source: U.S. National Center for Health Statistics, *Vital and Health Statistics*, Series 13 and unpublished data. See also <http://www.cdc.gov/nchs/products/series.htm#sr13>.

Table 182. Hospital Discharges and Days of Care by Selected Diagnosis: 2008

[(14,371 represents 14,371,000). Represents estimates of inpatients discharged from noninstitutional, short-stay hospitals, exclusive of federal hospitals. Excludes newborn infants. Diagnostic categories are based on the International Classification of Diseases, Ninth Revision, Clinical Modification. See headnote, Table 179]

Sex, age, and selected first-listed diagnosis [1]	Discharges Number (1,000) [2]	Per 1,000 persons [2]	Average stay (days) [2]	Sex, age, and selected first-listed diagnosis [1]	Discharges Number (1,000) [2]	Per 1,000 persons [2]	Average stay (days) [2]
MALE				**FEMALE**			
All ages [3]	**14,371**	**96.5**	**5.4**	**All ages [3]**	**21,326**	**138.5**	**4.6**
Under 18 years [3]	1,336	35.3	4.7	Under 18 years [3]	1,203	33.3	3.9
Injury	131	3.5	3.4	Childbirth	138	3.8	2.7
Pneumonia	95	2.5	5.2	Injury	76	2.1	2.4
Asthma	82	2.2	2.3	Schizophrenia, mood disorders, delusional disorders, nonorganic psychoses [5]	[4] 67	[4] 1.8	7.5
18-44 years [3]	2,486	43.9	4.7				
Injury	399	7.1	4.6	18-44 years [3]	7,430	133.9	3.2
Schizophrenia, mood disorders, delusional disorders, nonorganic psychoses [5]	263	4.6	7.2	Childbirth	3,998	72.0	2.7
				Schizophrenia, mood disorders, delusional disorders, nonorganic psychoses [5]	293	5.3	7.2
Heart disease	157	2.8	3.7	Injury	175	3.1	4.3
Alcohol and drug [6]	118	2.1	3.8	Uterine fibroids	108	1.9	2.2
45-64 years [3]	4,619	121.4	5.4	45-64 years [3]	4,722	118.2	5.1
Heart disease	774	20.3	3.9	Heart disease	436	10.9	4.3
Injury	271	7.1	5.2	Cancer, all	267	6.7	5.9
Cancer, all	255	6.7	6.3	Osteoarthritis	225	5.6	3.3
65-74 years [3]	2,410	260.2	5.6	65-74 years [3]	2,683	247.1	5.4
Heart disease	491	53.0	4.4	Heart disease	424	39.0	4.5
Cancer, all	152	16.4	6.9	Osteoarthritis	178	16.4	4.0
Stroke	110	11.8	5.1	Cancer, all	141	13.0	6.5
Pneumonia	93	10.0	6.1	Pneumonia	93	8.6	6.0
75-84 years [3]	2,400	449.8	5.8	75-84 years [3]	3,087	401.5	5.8
Heart disease	475	89.0	4.8	Heart disease	526	68.5	5.1
Cancer, all	130	24.4	7.6	Injury	204	26.5	5.2
Pneumonia	130	24.3	5.6	Pneumonia	160	20.8	6.0
Stroke	126	23.6	4.8	Stroke	160	20.8	5.2
85 years and over [3]	1,119	600.4	6.2	85 years and over [3]	2,202	570.6	5.7
Heart disease	230	123.4	4.9	Heart disease	384	99.5	5.3
Pneumonia	90	48.2	6.4	Injury	239	62.0	5.3
Injury	69	37.0	6.6	Pneumonia	123	31.9	5.4

[1] The first-listed diagnosis is the one specified as the principal diagnosis or the first diagnosis listed on the face sheet or discharge summary of the medical record. It is usually the main cause of the hospitalization. The number of first-listed diagnoses is the same as the number of discharges. [2] Crude estimates. [3] Includes discharges with first-listed diagnoses not shown in table. [4] Estimates are considered unreliable. [5] These estimates are for nonfederal short-stay hospitals only and do not include mental illness discharges from other types of facilities such as Veterans Affairs hospitals. [6] Includes abuse, dependence, and withdrawal. These estimates are for non-federal short-stay hospitals only and do not include alcohol and drug discharges from other types of facilities or programs such as the Department of Veterans Affairs or day treatment programs.

Source: Centers for Disease Control and Prevention, National Center for Health Statistics, National Hospital Discharge Survey, <http://www.cdc.gov/nchs/nhds.htm>.

Table 183. Medicare-Certified Hospices, Utilization, and Costs: 1993 to 2010

[215 represents 215,000]

Year	Total Hospices, Number	Persons Served (1,000)	Covered Days of Care		Program Payments [1]	
			Number (1,000)	Per Person Served	Total (mil. dol.)	Per Person Served (dol.) [2]
1993................	1,445	215	12,649	59	1,250	5,817
1994................	1,726	266	16,038	60	1,614	6,071
1995................	1,992	309	18,197	59	1,873	6,058
1996................	2,161	349	18,884	54	1,991	5,704
1997................	2,344	383	19,166	50	2,058	5,374
1998................	2,317	421	20,308	48	2,206	5,242
1999................	2,326	474	21,657	47	2,525	5,324
2000................	2,267	534	25,958	49	2,926	5,476
2001................	2,275	595	30,684	52	3,690	6,208
2002................	2,323	662	36,195	55	4,539	6,863
2003................	2,434	731	45,512	60	5,630	7,724
2004................	2,645	800	50,530	64	6,716	8,428
2005................	2,872	874	57,437	66	7,902	9,118
2006................	3,071	942	64,997	70	9,236	9,837
2007................	3,255	1,000	70,552	71	10,343	10,385
2008................	3,346	1,055	74,017	71	11,196	10,662
2009................	3,405	1,094	77,410	71	12,084	11,089
2010................	3,509	1,163	81,655	71	12,950	11,175

[1] Medicare program payments represent fee-for-service only and exclude amounts paid for managed care services. [2] Excludes persons who received covered services, but for whom no program payments were reported during the reporting year.

Source: Centers for Medicare & Medicaid Services (HHS), Medicare and Medicaid Statistical Supplement, 2011. See also <http://www.cms.gov/>.

Table 184. Organ Transplants: 1990 to 2010

[As of end of year. Based on reports of procurement programs and transplant centers in the United States, except as noted]

Procedure	Number of procedures						Number of centers		Number of people waiting, 2010	1-year patient survival rates, 2009 (percent)
	1990	1995	2000	2005	2009	2010	1990	2010		
Transplant: [1]										
Heart................	2,095	2,342	2,172	2,125	2,212	2,333	148	132	3,182	86.7
Heart-lung..........	52	69	47	35	29	41	79	50	67	67.6
Lung................	203	869	955	1,406	1,661	1,770	70	66	1,774	80.6
Liver................	2,631	3,818	4,816	6,443	6,320	6,291	85	132	16,954	86.4
Kidney..............	9,358	10,957	13,258	16,481	16,829	16,898	232	238	94,598	94.6
Kidney-pancreas. ..	459	915	910	903	854	828	(NA)	(NA)	2,281	94.7
Pancreas...........	60	103	420	541	379	350	84	144	1,385	93.4
Intestine............	1	21	29	178	180	151	(NA)	43	266	74.4
Multi-organ.........	71	124	213	518	(NA)	(NA)	(NA)	(NA)	(NA)	(NA)

NA Not available. [1] Kidney-pancreas and heart-lung transplants are each counted as one procedure. All other multiorgan transplants, excluding kidney-pancreas and heart-lung, are included in the multiorgan row. Based on the Organ Procurement and Transplant Network (OPTN) as of May 20, 2011. The data have been supplied by UNOS under contract with Health and Human Services (HHS). This work was supported in part by Health Resources and Services Administration contract 231-00-0015. The authors alone are responsible for the reporting and interpretation of these data. Data subject to change based on future data submission or correction.

Source: U.S. Department of Health and Human Services, Health Resources and Services Administration, Office of Special Programs, Division of Transplantation, Rockville, MD; United Network for Organ Sharing (UNOS), Richmond, VA; University Renal Research and Education Association, Ann Arbor, MI; American Association of Tissue Banks, McLean, VA; and unpublished data. See also <http://optn.transplant.hrsa.gov/>.

Table 185. Selected Cosmetic Plastic Surgical and Nonsurgical Procedures: 2005 to 2011

[In thousands (11,428.8 represents 11,428,800). As of December 31. The final data are projected to reflect nationwide statistics and are based on a survey of doctors who have been certified by the American Board of Medical Specialties recognized boards, including but not limited to the American Board of Plastic Surgery. Data for the procedures include but are not limited to those performed by American Society for Aesthetic Plastic Surgery (ASAPS) members. ASAPS members are plastic surgeons certified by the American Board of Plastic Surgery who specialize in cosmetic surgery of the face and the entire body]

Procedure	2005	2006	2007	2008	2009	2010	2011
Total all procedures	**11,428.8**	**11,456.8**	**11,701.0**	**10,258.6**	**9,964.4**	**9,183.2**	**9,194.5**
Total surgical procedures [1]	**2,131.0**	**1,922.8**	**2,079.0**	**1,766.7**	**1,491.9**	**1,624.3**	**1,638.5**
Lipoplasty (Liposuction)	455.5	403.7	456.8	341.1	283.7	289.0	325.3
Breast augmentation	364.6	383.9	399.4	355.7	312.0	318.1	316.8
Abdominoplasty (tummy tuck)	169.3	172.5	185.3	147.4	127.9	144.9	149.4
Blepharoplasty (eyelid surgery)	231.5	210.0	240.8	195.1	149.9	152.1	147.5
Rhinoplasty (nose reshaping)	200.9	141.9	151.8	152.4	138.3	133.5	126.1
Total nonsurgical procedures [1]	**9,297.7**	**9,534.0**	**9,622.0**	**8,491.9**	**8,472.6**	**7,558.9**	**7,556.0**
Botox injection [2]	3,294.8	3,181.6	2,775.2	2,464.1	2,557.1	2,437.2	2,619.7
Hyaluronic acid [3]	1,194.2	1,593.6	1,448.7	1,262.8	1,313.0	1,315.1	1,206.2
Laser hair removal	1,566.9	1,475.3	1,412.7	1,281.0	1,280.0	936.3	919.8
Microdermabrasion [4]	1,023.9	993.1	829.7	557.1	621.9	450.7	499.4
Chemical peel	556.2	558.4	575.1	591.8	529.3	493.9	384.2
Total female procedures	**10,443.8**	**10,516.7**	**10,602.5**	**9,394.8**	**9,058.5**	**8,586.7**	**8,398.4**
Total surgical procedures [1]	**1,918.1**	**1,730.5**	**1,877.1**	**1,600.7**	**1,310.7**	**1,479.7**	**1,493.6**
Breast augmentation	364.6	383.9	399.4	355.7	312.0	318.1	316.8
Lipoplasty (Liposuction)	402.9	350.4	398.8	309.7	243.2	251.8	283.7
Abdominoplasty (tummy tuck)	164.1	164.8	180.5	143.0	123.0	137.9	142.7
Blepharoplasty (eyelid surgery)	198.1	182.4	208.2	166.4	124.9	131.4	124.6
Breast reduction	160.5	145.8	153.1	139.9	113.5	138.2	113.0
Total nonsurgical procedures [1]	**8,525.7**	**8,786.2**	**8,725.4**	**7,794.1**	**7,747.8**	**7,107.1**	**6,904.8**
Botox injection [2]	2,990.7	2,881.1	2,445.7	2,239.0	2,299.3	2,211.9	2,355.5
Hyaluronic acid [3]	1,149.2	1,519.9	1,364.5	1,200.4	1,221.8	1,245.3	1,127.2
Laser hair removal	1,334.7	1,308.7	1,227.0	1,101.3	1,114.0	817.4	812.4
Microdermabrasion [4]	939.5	922.0	743.7	517.3	565.0	416.3	468.5
IPL laser treatment [5]	(X)	(X)	584.5	479.9	404.5	345.5	396.9
Chemical peel	533.0	530.1	536.0	554.5	492.3	469.6	360.3
Sclerotherapy (Spider veins)	548.0	541.3	467.8	417.5	442.0	435.0	348.5
Laser skin resurfacing	432.6	528.1	479.8	532.0	463.3	518.3	319.8
Total male procedures	**984.9**	**940.0**	**1,098.6**	**863.7**	**935.2**	**750.1**	**796.1**
Total surgical procedures [1]	**212.9**	**192.3**	**202.0**	**166.0**	**160.9**	**142.6**	**144.9**
Lipoplasty (Liposuction)	52.5	53.3	58.0	31.5	40.5	37.2	41.7
Rhinoplasty (nose reshaping)	45.9	33.1	31.7	30.2	32.7	30.1	24.5
Blepharoplasty (eyelid surgery)	33.4	27.6	32.6	28.7	25.0	20.7	22.9
Gynecomastia (male breast reduction)	17.7	23.7	20.3	19.1	16.8	18.3	17.6
Hair transplantation	11.2	11.2	16.5	18.1	13.1	(NA)	(NA)
Facelift	13.0	14.1	12.4	13.4	10.5	10.4	(NA)
Total nonsurgical procedures [1]	**772.0**	**747.7**	**896.6**	**697.8**	**774.4**	**607.4**	**651.2**
Botox injection [2]	304.1	300.5	329.5	225.1	257.8	225.2	264.3
Laser hair removal	232.2	166.6	185.7	179.7	166.0	118.9	107.5
Hyaluronic acid [3]	45.0	73.6	84.2	62.4	91.2	69.8	79.0
IPL laser treatment [5]	(X)	(X)	63.2	46.9	47.7	35.9	42.3
Microdermabrasion [4]	84.4	71.1	85.9	39.8	56.9	34.4	31.0
Laser skin resurfacing	43.1	48.5	30.1	38.9	49.0	44.4	25.8

X Not applicable. NA Not available. [1] Totals include procedure not shown separately. [2] As of 2009, includes Dysport. [3] In 2003, the FDA has approved hyaluronan injections for filling soft tissue defects such as facial wrinkles. [4] Procedure for reducing fine lines, "crow's feet," age spots, and acne scars. [5] IPL is intense pulse light. One of the procedures available for facial rejuvenation.

Source: The American Society for Aesthetic Plastic Surgery, *Statistics*, annual (copyright), <http://www.surgery.org/media/statistics>.

Table 186. Cancer—Estimated New Cases, 2012, and Survival Rates: 1990–2008

[1,639 represents 1,639,000. The 5-year relative survival rate, which is derived by adjusting the observed survival rate for expected mortality, represents the likelihood that a person will not die from causes directly related to their cancer within 5 years. Survival data shown are based on those patients diagnosed while residents of an area listed below during the time periods shown. Data are based on information collected as part of the National Cancer Institute's Surveillance, Epidemiology and End Results (SEER) program, a collection of 9 population-based registries in 18 areas.]

| Site | Estimated new cases,[1] 2012 (1,000) | | | 5-year relative survival rates (percent) | | | | | | | |
| | | | | White | | | | Black | | | |
	Total	Male	Female	1990–1992	1996–2000	2001–2007	2002-2008	1990–1992	1996–2000	2001–2007	2002-2008
All sites[2]	**1,639**	**848**	**791**	**61.5**	**65.4**	**68.6**	**66.0**	**47.9**	**56.0**	**59.4**	**58.3**
Lung	226	116	110	14.0	15.2	16.7	16.3	10.4	12.6	13.3	13.0
Breast[3]	229	2	227	86.6	90.2	91.4	90.2	71.7	77.5	77.4	77.6
Colon and rectum	143	73	70	62.2	64.5	67.1	65.0	53.0	53.8	56.3	56.8
Colon	103	50	53	63.0	64.4	66.5	64.4	53.5	53.5	54.8	56.1
Rectum	40	24	17	60.2	65.0	68.7	66.5	51.3	54.8	60.9	58.9
Prostate	242	242	(X)	94.4	98.9	99.9	99.6	84.6	95.6	97.9	96.2
Bladder	74	56	18	80.6	80.3	81.1	78.2	63.4	62.6	64.1	64.2
Corpus uteri	47	(X)	47	86.4	86.6	86.3	84.8	56.0	63.4	62.0	61.3
Non-Hodgkin's lymphoma[4]	70	38	32	51.7	61.4	70.7	68.8	42.1	53.6	62.1	61.3
Oral cavity and pharynx	40	29	12	58.1	60.9	65.1	63.3	32.5	39.8	44.7	42.1
Leukemia[4]	47	27	20	46.4	49.0	57.1	55.2	36.0	38.3	50.3	48.0
Melanoma of skin	76	44	32	89.3	91.5	93.0	90.9	61.8	72.7	73.4	72.0
Pancreas	44	22	22	4.4	4.3	5.9	5.7	3.7	4.6	3.8	5.0
Kidney	65	40	25	60.8	63.0	71.0	70.9	57.2	65.6	68.4	68.1
Stomach	21	13	8	18.8	21.0	26.1	25.4	22.9	22.1	27.2	26.5
Ovary	22	(X)	22	40.5	42.9	43.3	43.5	36.2	37.6	36.0	36.0
Cervix uteri[5]	12	(X)	12	70.9	73.8	70.3	69.2	57.9	66.6	60.9	58.5

X Not applicable. [1] Estimates provided by American Cancer Society, <www.cancer.org>, are based on rates from the National Cancer Institute's SEER program. [2] Includes other sites, not shown separately. [3] Survival rates for female only. [4] All types combined. [5] Invasive cancer only.

Source: U.S. National Institutes of Health, National Cancer Institute, <http://seer.cancer.gov/csr/1975_2009/>.

Table 187. Cancer—Estimated New Cases and Deaths by State: 2012

[Excludes basal and squamous cell skin cancers and in situ carcinomas, except urinary bladder]

| State | New cases[1] | | | Deaths | | | State | New cases[1] | | | Deaths | | |
	Total[2]	Female breast	Lung & bronchus	Total[2]	Female breast	Lung & bronchus		Total[2]	Female breast	Lung & bronchus	Total[2]	Female breast	Lung & bronchus
U.S.	1,638,910	226,870	226,160	577,190	39,510	160,340	MO	33,440	4,440	5,370	12,710	900	3,970
AL	26,440	3,450	4,440	10,290	710	3,240	MT	5,550	740	700	2,010	110	580
AK	3,640	470	490	930	70	260	NE	9,030	1,270	1,230	3,450	210	900
AZ	31,990	4,470	3,970	11,090	780	2,850	NV	13,780	1,770	1,930	4,590	350	1,490
AR	16,120	2,150	2,760	6,570	420	2,160	NH	8,350	1,160	1,130	2,700	180	750
CA	165,810	25,040	18,060	56,620	4,110	12,830	NJ	50,650	6,970	5,990	16,650	1,340	4,200
CO	22,820	3,420	2,400	7,190	510	1,690	NM	9,640	1,310	1,090	3,530	240	780
CT	21,530	3,140	2,720	6,940	480	1,780	NY	109,440	14,730	13,620	34,140	2,420	8,880
DE	5,340	740	800	1,930	120	580	NC	51,860	7,090	7,950	18,440	1,290	5,600
DC	2,980	460	370	1,010	80	250	ND	3,510	490	460	1,300	90	320
FL	117,580	15,540	17,860	42,170	2,600	12,200	OH	66,560	8,990	10,270	25,030	1,750	7,350
GA	48,130	6,970	6,570	15,790	1,140	4,650	OK	19,210	2,630	3,370	7,800	500	2,440
HI	6,610	1,120	860	2,380	140	580	OR	21,370	3,200	2,920	7,790	510	2,120
ID	7,720	1,000	920	2,640	170	660	PA	78,340	10,290	10,890	28,790	1,950	7,750
IL	65,750	9,090	9,190	23,970	1,650	6,590	RI	6,310	870	860	2,190	130	620
IN	35,060	4,490	5,460	13,240	850	4,140	SC	26,570	3,570	4,270	9,670	660	2,970
IA	17,010	2,350	2,330	6,410	400	1,790	SD	4,430	600	620	1,630	110	450
KS	14,090	1,990	1,910	5,400	370	1,580	TN	35,610	4,680	6,140	13,880	890	4,570
KY	25,160	3,160	4,430	9,890	570	3,530	TX	110,470	15,050	14,810	36,820	2,650	9,780
LA	23,480	3,320	3,660	9,150	660	2,730	UT	10,620	1,480	880	2,780	250	460
ME	8,990	1,170	1,340	3,230	180	970	VT	4,060	560	550	1,300	80	370
MD	31,000	4,700	4,250	10,440	810	2,850	VA	41,380	6,190	5,550	14,610	1,110	4,150
MA	38,470	5,480	4,920	12,930	800	3,570	WA	35,790	5,240	4,700	12,170	800	3,270
MI	57,790	7,710	8,210	20,430	1,350	5,910	WV	11,610	1,430	2,070	4,600	280	1,460
MN	28,060	4,110	3,750	9,490	600	2,500	WI	31,920	4,270	4,220	11,240	690	3,000
MS	15,190	1,990	2,550	6,330	440	1,960	WY	2,650	360	330	940	60	250

[1] Estimates are offered as a rough guide and should be interpreted with caution. [2] Includes other types of cancer, not shown separately.

Source: American Cancer Society, Inc., *Cancer Facts and Figures—2012*, Atlanta, GA, (copyright). See also <http://www.cancer.org/Research/CancerFactsFigures/index>.

Table 188. Selected Notifiable Diseases—Cases Reported: 1980 to 2010

[190.9 represents 190,900. As of June 1, 2012. Figures should be interpreted with caution. Although reporting of some of these diseases is incomplete, the figures are of value in indicating trends of disease incidence. Includes cases imported from outside the United States]

Disease	1980	1990	1995	2000	2005	2007	2008	2009	2010
AIDS [1]	([2])	41,595	71,547	40,758	41,120	37,503	39,202	([1])	([1])
Botulism [3]	89	92	97	138	135	144	145	118	112
Brucellosis (undulant fever)	183	85	98	87	120	131	80	115	115
Chickenpox (Varicella) [4] (1,000)	190.9	173.1	120.6	27.4	32.2	40.1	30.4	20.5	15.4
Coccidoidomycosis	([2])	([2])	([2])	2,867	6,542	8,121	7,523	12,926	([2])
Cryptosporidiosis	([2])	([2])	([2])	3,128	5,659	11,170	9,113	7,654	8,944
Domestic arboviral diseases: [5]									
West Nile: neuroinvasive	([2])	([2])	([2])	([2])	1,309	1,227	689	386	629
nonneuroinvasive	([2])	([2])	([2])	([2])	1,691	2,403	667	334	392
Enterohemorrhagic Escherichia coli 0157:H7	([2])	([2])	2,139	4,528	2,621	([2])	([2])	([2])	([2])
Giardiasis	([2])	([2])	([2])	([2])	19,733	19,417	18,908	19,399	19,811
Haemophilus influenza	([2])	([2])	1,180	1,398	2,304	2,541	2,886	3,022	3,151
Hansen disease (Leprosy)	223	198	144	91	87	101	80	103	98
Hepatitis: A (infectious) (1,000) [6]	29.1	31.4	31.6	13.4	4.5	3.0	2.6	2.0	1.7
B (serum) (1,000)	19.0	21.1	10.8	8.0	5.1	4.5	4.0	3.4	3.4
C/Non-A, non-B	([2])	2,600	4,576	3,197	652	845	877	782	849
Legionellosis	([2])	1,370	1,241	1,127	2,301	2,716	3,181	3,522	3,346
Lyme disease	([2])	([2])	11,700	17,730	23,305	27,444	35,198	38,468	30,158
Malaria	2,062	1,292	1,419	1,560	1,494	1,408	1,255	1,451	1,773
Meningococcal infections	2,840	2,451	3,243	2,256	1,245	1,077	1,172	980	833
Mumps (1,000)	8.6	5.3	0.9	0.3	0.3	0.8	0.5	2.0	2.6
Pertussis [7] (1,000)	1.7	4.6	5.1	7.9	25.6	10.5	13.3	16.9	27.6
Psittacosis	124	113	64	17	16	12	8	9	4
Rabies, animal	6,421	4,826	7,811	6,934	5,915	5,862	4,196	5,343	4,331
Rocky Mountain spotted fever	1,163	651	590	495	1,936	2,221	2,563	1,815	1,985
Rubella [8]	3,904	1,125	128	176	11	12	16	3	5
Salmonellosis [9] (1,000)	33.7	48.6	46.0	39.6	45.3	48.0	51.0	49.2	54.4
Shigellosis [10] (1,000)	19.0	27.1	32.1	22.9	16.2	19.8	22.6	15.9	14.8
Streptococcal disease, invasive, Group A	([2])	([2])	([2])	3,144	4,715	5,294	5,674	5,279	([2])
Streptococcus pneumoniae, invasive:									
Drug-resistant	([2])	([2])	([2])	4,533	2,996	3,329	3,448	3,370	16,569
Age less than 5 years	([2])	([2])	([2])	([2])	1,495	563	532	583	2,186
Tetanus	95	64	41	35	27	28	19	18	26
Toxic-shock syndrome	([2])	322	191	135	90	92	71	74	82
Trichinosis	131	129	29	16	16	5	39	13	7
Tuberculosis [11] (1,000)	27.7	25.7	22.9	16.4	14.1	13.3	12.9	11.5	11.2
Typhoid fever	510	552	369	377	324	434	449	397	467
Sexually transmitted diseases:									
Chlamydia (1,000)	([2])	([2])	478	702	976	1,108	1,211	1,244	1,308
Gonorrhea (1,000)	1,004	690	393	359	340	356	337	301	309
Syphilis (1,000)	69	134	69	32	33	41	46	45	46

[1] Acquired immunodeficiency syndrome was not a notifiable disease until 1984. Includes all cases reported to the Division of HIV/AIDS Prevention, National Center for HIV/AIDS, Viral Hepatitis, STD, and TB Prevention. In 2008 CDC published a revised HIV case definition, see Table 189. [2] Disease was not notifiable. [3] Includes foodborne, infant, wound, and unspecified cases. [4] Chickenpox was taken off the nationally notifiable list in 1991 but many states continue to report. [5] The national surveillance case definitions for the arboviral diseases was revised in 2005, and nonneuroinvasive arboviral diseases were added to the list of nationally notifiable infectious diseases. [6] Data on chronic hepatitis B and hepatitis C virus infection (past or present) are not included because they are undergoing data quality review. [7] Whooping cough. [8] German measles. Excludes congenital syndrome. [9] Excludes typhoid fever. [10] Bacillary dysentery. [11] Newly reported active cases.

Source: Centers for Disease Control and Prevention, *Summary of Notifiable Diseases, United States, 2010, Morbidity and Mortality Weekly Report*, Vol. 59, No. 53, 2012. See also <http://www.cdc.gov/mmwr/mmwr_nd/index.html>.

Table 189. HIV Diagnoses, Chlamydia, and Lyme Disease Cases Reported by State: 2010

State	HIV diagnoses [1]	Chlamydia [2]	Lyme disease	State	HIV diagnoses [1]	Chlamydia [2]	Lyme disease	State	HIV diagnoses [1]	Chlamydia [2]	Lyme disease
U.S.	35,741	1,307,893	30,158	KS	110	9,601	10	NC	1,324	42,048	82
AL	570	27,041	2	KY	270	16,376	5	ND	11	2,404	33
AK	35	6,019	7	LA	1,164	29,151	3	OH	913	51,150	44
AZ	544	26,861	2	ME	55	2,586	751	OK	247	14,302	–
AR	202	15,424	–	MD	1,195	26,192	1,617	OR	198	12,352	39
CA	3,786	150,443	129	MA	446	21,080	3,263	PA	1,377	47,518	3,805
CO	408	19,447	3	MI	650	49,478	95	RI	108	3,480	181
CT	356	12,649	3,068	MN	336	15,294	1,960	SC	750	26,525	29
DE	122	4,464	656	MS	486	21,417	–	SD	32	3,192	1
DC	638	5,589	42	MO	533	26,049	4	TN	826	28,327	36
FL	4,862	74,744	84	MT	12	3,082	4	TX	3,232	119,872	142
GA	1,170	45,147	10	NE	95	5,114	8	UT	68	6,690	3
HI	51	6,015	(NA)	NV	344	9,666	2	VT	7	1,257	356
ID	36	4,208	9	NH	51	2,462	1,339	VA	918	30,797	1,245
IL	1,068	60,672	135	NJ	941	26,142	3,712	WA	494	21,348	16
IN	413	22,825	78	NM	135	11,706	5	WV	75	3,876	145
IA	108	10,542	85	NY	3,693	99,920	3,425	WI	255	23,236	3,488
								WY	21	2,113	

– Represents zero. NA Not available. [1] Total number of HIV diagnoses reported to the Division of HIV/AIDS Prevention, National Center for HIV/AIDS, Viral Hepatitis, STD, and TB Prevention (NCIRD), as of December 31, 2010. [2] As of June 8, 2011.

Source: Centers for Disease Control and Prevention, Summary of Notifiable Diseases, United States, 2010, *Morbidity and Mortality Weekly Report*, Vol. 59, No. 53, 2012. See also <http://www.cdc.gov/mmwr/mmwr_nd/index.html>.

Table 190. Estimated Numbers of AIDS Diagnoses Among Adults and Adolescents by Sex and Transmission Category: 2007 to 2010

[All data are provisional. Data are included for 50 states, the District of Columbia, Puerto Rico, the U.S. Virgin Islands, Guam, and the U.S. Pacific Islands. Estimated numbers resulted from statistical adjustment that accounted for reporting delays and missing risk-factor information, but not for incomplete reporting. Acquired immunodeficiency syndrome (AIDS) is a specific group of diseases or conditions which are indicative of severe immunosuppression related to infection with the human immunodeficiency virus (HIV). Data are subject to retrospective changes and may differ from those data in Table 188. For information on HIV death rates, go to Table 131]

Transmission category	2007	2008	2009	2010	Cumulative through 2010 [1]
Persons 13 years old and over, total [2]	**35,081**	**34,347**	**33,628**	**33,607**	**1,153,677**
Males, total	**25,534**	**25,278**	**24,992**	**25,186**	**918,581**
Male-to-male sexual contact	16,120	16,067	16,470	16,935	547,061
Injection drug use	3,573	3,346	2,918	2,906	199,428
Male-to-male sexual contact and injection drug use	1,828	1,738	1,577	1,474	81,567
Heterosexual contact [3]	3,863	3,960	3,887	3,738	78,497
Other [4]	150	167	139	133	12,028
Females, total	**9,547**	**9,068**	**8,636**	**8,422**	**235,096**
Injection drug use	2,367	2,145	1,927	1,790	91,415
Heterosexual contact [3]	7,016	6,805	6,576	6,506	137,253
Other [4]	164	118	134	127	6,428

[1] From the beginning of the epidemic through 2010. [2] Because column totals for estimated numbers were calculated independently of the values for the subpopulations, the values in each column may not sum to the column total. [3] Heterosexual contact with a person known to have, or to be at high risk for, HIV infection. [4] Includes hemophilia, blood transfusion, perinatal exposure, and risk factor not reported or not identified.

Source: U.S. Centers for Disease Control and Prevention, Atlanta, GA, *HIV Surveillance Report, 2010*, Vol. 22, <http://www.cdc.gov/hiv/surveillance/resources/reports/2010report>.

Table 191. Estimated Numbers of Persons Living With an AIDS Diagnosis by Selected Characteristics: 2000 to 2009

[See headnote, Table 190]

Age and characteristic	2000	2005	2007	2008	2009
Total [1, 2]	**323,679**	**432,846**	**456,313**	**472,560**	**487,968**
AGE AS OF END OF YEAR					
Less than 13 years old	2,954	1,506	933	711	554
13 and 14 years old	528	811	702	629	491
15 to 24 years old	5,158	7,806	8,791	9,399	10,049
25 to 34 years old	56,129	45,923	43,809	44,290	44,999
35 to 44 years old	146,206	164,551	151,582	144,336	136,107
45 to 54 years old	85,474	149,284	169,788	181,636	191,944
55 to 64 years old	21,717	50,376	64,457	72,976	82,529
65 years old and over	5,513	12,589	16,251	18,584	21,294
RACE/ETHNICITY					
American Indian/Alaska Native	1,035	1,506	1,529	1,602	1,659
Asian [3]	2,293	3,777	4,367	4,751	5,112
Black/African American	131,826	183,083	192,006	199,472	206,488
Hispanic/Latino [4]	66,271	90,836	98,122	102,208	106,396
Native Hawaiian/Other Pacific Islander	174	331	407	437	481
White	118,189	147,585	152,855	156,807	160,402
Multiple races	3,719	5,566	6,925	7,184	7,335
Transmission category:					
MALE ADULT/ADOLESCENT					
Males 13 years old and over, total	251,286	330,239	346,250	358,174	369,674
Male-to-male sexual contact	143,594	196,973	211,381	220,844	230,389
Injection drug use	58,437	65,366	63,309	63,346	63,075
Male-to-male sexual contact and injection drug use	25,635	30,289	30,974	31,281	31,326
Heterosexual contact [5]	20,922	34,563	37,858	39,923	42,076
Other [6]	2,698	3,048	2,728	2,781	2,808
FEMALE ADULT/ADOLESCENT					
Females 13 years old and over, total	68,423	98,500	106,032	110,379	114,322
Injection drug use	28,644	34,207	34,352	34,510	34,679
Heterosexual contact [5]	38,269	62,252	69,846	73,988	77,698
Other [6]	1,510	2,041	1,834	1,881	1,945
CHILD (LESS THAN 13 YEARS OLD AT DIAGNOSIS)					
Total	3,971	4,107	4,031	4,007	3,972
Perinatal	3,756	3,889	3,826	3,801	3,772
Other [6]	215	218	205	206	201

[1] Total numbers include persons of unknown race/ethnicity. [2] Because column totals were calculated independently of the values for the subpopulations, the values in each column may not sum to the column total. [3] Includes Asian/Pacific Islander legacy cases. [4] Hispanics/Latinos can be of any race. [5] Heterosexual contact with a person known to have, or to be at high risk for, HIV infection. [6] Includes hemophilia, blood transfusion, perinatal exposure, and risk factor not reported or not identified.

Source: U.S. Centers for Disease Control and Prevention, Atlanta, GA, *HIV Surveillance Report, 2010*, Vol. 22, <http://www.cdc.gov/hiv/surveillance/resources/reports/2010report>.

Table 192. Learning Disability or Attention Deficit Hyperactivity Disorder for Children 3 to 17 Years of Age by Selected Characteristics: 2010

[In thousands, except percent (61,655 represents 61,655,000). Learning disability is based on the question, "Has a representative from a school or a health professional ever told you that (child's name) had a learning disability?" Attention Deficit Hyperactivity Disorder is based on the question, "Has a doctor or health professional ever told you that (child's name) had Attention Hyperactivity Disorder or Attention Deficit Disorder?"]

| Selected characteristic | Total | Ever told had— | | | |
| | | Learning disability | | Attention deficit hyperactivity disorder | |
		Number [1]	Percent [2]	Number [1]	Percent [2]
Total [3]	**61,655**	**4,838**	**7.9**	**5,161**	**8.4**
SEX [4]					
Male	31,519	2,917	9.3	3,511	11.2
Female	30,137	1,921	6.4	1,649	5.5
AGE					
3 to 4 years old	8,443	267	3.2	139	[6] 1.7
5 to 11 years old	28,666	2,291	8.0	2,181	7.6
12 to 17 years old	24,546	2,280	9.3	2,840	11.6
RACE					
Race Alone [4, 5]	59,155	4,598	7.8	4,948	8.4
White	46,607	3,532	7.6	3,920	8.4
Black or African American	9,106	904	10.0	939	10.5
American Indian or Alaska Native	541	[6] 57	[6] 10.2	[6] 43	[6] 7.6
Asian	2,746	95	3.5	[6] 38	[6] 1.4
Native Hawaiian or Other Pacific Islander	155	(B)	(B)	(B)	(B)
Two or more races [4, 7]	2,500	240	9.3	213	8.9
Black or African American and White	1,082	[6] 142	11.5	144	14.1
American Indian or Alaska Native and White	425	40	[6] 10.6	(B)	[6] 4.3
HISPANIC ORIGIN AND RACE [4, 8]					
Hispanic or Latino	13,846	895	6.7	589	4.4
Mexican or Mexican American	9,480	607	6.6	319	3.5
Not Hispanic or Latino	47,809	3,942	8.2	4,572	9.5
White, single race	34,175	2,765	8.0	3,391	9.8
Black or African American, single race	8,625	860	10.1	917	10.8

B Base figure too small to meet statistical standards for reliability of a derived figure. [1] Unknowns for the columns are not included in the frequencies, but they are included in the "Total" column. [2] Unknowns for the column variables are not included in the denominators when calculating percentages. [3] Includes other races not shown separately. [4] Percents are age-adjusted to the 2000 projected U.S. standard population using age groups 3–4 years, 5–11 years, and 12–17 years. [5] Refers to persons who indicated only a single race group. [6] Figures do not meet standard of reliability or precision. [7] Refers to all persons who indicated more than one race group. [8] Persons of Hispanic or Latino origin may be any race.

Source: National Center for Health Statistics, *Summary Health Statistics for U.S. Children: National Health Interview Survey, 2010*, Vital and Health Statistics, Series 10, Number 250, 2011. See also <http://www.cdc.gov/nchs/nhis.htm>.

Table 193. Children and Youth With Disabilities Served by Type of Disability: 1995 to 2010

[In thousands (5,078.8 represents 5,078,800). As of fall. For children and youth aged 6 to 21 served under the Individuals with Disabilities Education Act (IDEA) Part B. Includes outlying areas]

Disability	1995	2000	2005	2006	2007	2008	2009	2010
Total	**5,078.8**	**5,773.9**	**6,109.6**	**6,081.9**	**6,007.8**	**5,889.8**	**5,882.2**	**5,822.8**
Specific learning disabilities	2,601.8	2,881.6	2,780.2	2,710.5	2,620.2	2,525.9	2,486.4	2,415.6
Speech or language impairments	1,026.9	1,093.4	1,157.2	1,160.9	1,154.2	1,122.0	1,107.4	1,090.4
Mental retardation	585.6	613.4	545.5	523.2	498.2	476.1	461.3	445.3
Emotional disturbance	439.2	474.3	472.4	458.9	440.2	418.1	405.5	387.6
Multiple disabilities	94.5	122.9	133.9	134.2	132.6	124.1	124.5	123.6
Hearing impairments	68.0	70.8	72.4	72.6	72.2	70.8	70.7	69.8
Orthopedic impairments	63.2	73.0	63.1	61.9	60.5	62.4	58.0	55.7
Other health impairments	134.2	294.0	561.0	599.5	631.2	648.4	679.0	704.3
Visual impairments	25.5	26.0	26.0	26.4	26.4	25.8	25.8	25.7
Autism	29.1	79.6	193.6	224.6	258.3	292.8	333.2	370.0
Deaf-blind	1.4	1.3	1.6	1.5	1.4	1.7	1.4	1.3
Traumatic brain injury	9.6	14.9	23.5	23.9	23.9	24.9	24.4	24.6
Developmental delay [1]	(X)	28.6	79.1	83.9	88.6	96.9	104.5	109.1

X Not applicable. [1] States had the option of reporting children aged 3 to 9 under developmental delay beginning 1997.

Source: U.S. Department of Education, Office of Special Education, <http://www.ideadata.org/PartBData.asp>.

Table 194. Children Under 18 Years of Age Receiving Special Education or Early Intervention Services: 2010

[In thousands, except percent (74,625 represents 74,625,000). Receiving special education or early intervention services is based on the question, "Do any of the following (family members under 18 years of age) receive special education or early intervention services?"]

Selected Characteristic	Total	Persons under 18 years who were receiving special education early intervention services	
		Number [1]	Percent [2]
Total [3]	**74,625**	**5,162**	**6.9**
SEX [4]			
Male	38,134	3465	9.1
Female	36,491	1,697	4.7
AGE			
Under 12 years	50,457	3,177	6.3
12 to 17 years	24,168	1,985	8.2
RACE			
Race Alone [4, 5]	71,622	4,962	7.0
White	56,223	3,922	7.0
Black or African American	11,085	862	7.8
American Indian or Alaska Native	772	54	7.0
Asian	3,374	105	3.1
Native Hawaiian or Other Pacific Islander	168	[6] 19	[6] 11.2
Two or more races [4, 7]	3,003	200	7.0
HISPANIC ORIGIN AND RACE [4, 8]			
Hispanic or Latino	17,166	878	5.2
Mexican or Mexican American	11,629	537	4.7
Not Hispanic or Latino	57,459	4,284	7.5
White, single race	40,804	3,151	7.7
Black or African American, single race	10,480	818	7.8

B Base figure too small to meet statistical standards for reliability of a derived figure. [1] Unknowns for the columns are not included in the frequencies, but they are included in the "Total" column. [2] Unknowns for the column variables are not included in the denominators when calculating percentages. [3] Includes other races not shown separately. [4] Percents are age-adjusted to the 2000 projected U.S. standard population using two age groups 0-11 years, and 12-17 years. [5] Refers to persons who indicated only a single race group. [6] Figures do not meet standard of reliability or precision. [7] Refers to all persons who indicated more than one race group. [8] Persons of Hispanic or Latino origin may be any race.

Source: National Center for Health Statistics, *Summary Health Statistics for the U.S. Population: National Health Interview Survey, 2010*, Vital and Health Statistics, Series 10, Number 251, 2011. See also <http://www.cdc.gov/nchs/nhis.htm>.

Table 195. Disabilities Tallied by Age Group and by State: 2010

[In thousands (35,475 represents 35,475,000). Based on data from the American Community Survey (ACS). Disability data limited to civilian noninstitutionalized population. People aged 5 to 14 were classified as having a disability if they were reported to have any one of the five limitations: hearing difficulty, vision difficulty, cognitive difficulty, ambulatory difficulty, or self-care difficulty. People aged 15 and over were classified as having a disability if they reported any one of the five limitations listed above or independent living difficulty. Based on a sample and subject to sampling variability. See text, Section 1 and Appendix III]

State	Total	5 to 17 years	18 to 64 years	65 years and over	State	Total	5 to 17 years	18 to 64 years	65 years and over
U.S.	**35,475**	**2,733**	**18,670**	**14,071**	MO.	811	60	440	311
AL.	758	54	423	281	MT.	125	8	64	52
AK.	74	6	48	20	NE.	205	16	104	85
AZ.	703	52	364	287	NV.	282	19	152	110
AR.	466	37	255	173	NH.	145	14	77	54
CA.	3,620	263	1,818	1,539	NJ.	842	69	398	375
CO.	496	38	273	185	NM.	268	16	140	112
CT.	367	28	179	159	NY.	2,013	142	1,012	858
DE.	108	8	60	39	NC.	1,229	95	673	460
DC.	66	6	37	23	ND.	69	4	32	32
FL.	2,359	148	1,115	1,096	OH.	1,501	128	804	569
GA.	1,108	96	615	397	OK.	574	39	323	212
HI.	140	11	66	63	OR.	521	37	287	198
ID.	194	17	103	74	PA.	1,633	132	824	677
IL.	1,285	101	640	544	RI.	139	12	75	53
IN.	797	66	435	295	SC.	627	37	352	237
IA.	335	25	172	138	SD.	90	6	43	40
KS.	340	26	178	136	TN.	944	66	530	348
KY.	708	51	423	233	TX.	2,851	273	1,549	1,029
LA.	668	58	378	232	UT.	231	22	124	85
ME.	197	15	104	78	VT.	82	7	45	30
MD.	578	48	298	231	VA.	842	59	447	336
MA.	697	57	354	285	WA.	788	56	425	307
MI.	1,320	109	715	496	WV.	344	21	197	126
MN.	520	45	266	209	WI.	603	51	306	246
MS.	471	36	267	168	WY.	65	5	36	25

Source: U.S. Census Bureau, 2010 American Community Survey, B18101, "Sex by Age by Disability Status," <http://www.factfinder.census.gov/>, accessed April 2012.

Table 196. Children Immunized Against Specified Diseases: 1995 to 2010

[In percent. Covers civilian noninstitutionalized population aged 19 months to 35 months. Based on estimates from the National Immunization Survey. The health care providers of the children are contacted to verify and/or complete vaccination information. Results are based on race/ethnic status of the child]

Vaccination	1995, total	2000, total	2010 [1]					
			Total	White [2]	Black [2]	Hispanic [3]	American Indian/ Alaska Native only [2]	Asian [2]
Diphtheria-tetanus-pertussis (DTP) diphtheria-tetanus:								
3+ doses..............................	95.0	94.0	95.0	95.1	95.3	95.1	97.3	95.7
4+ doses..............................	79.0	82.0	84.4	84.5	83.7	84.4	81.8	88.3
Polio: 3+ doses........................	88.0	90.0	93.3	93.2	94.0	93.8	94.6	92.8
Measles, mumps, rubella vaccine..........	90.0	91.0	91.5	90.6	92.1	92.9	93.4	91.7
Hib: 3+ doses [4]......................	92.0	93.0	90.4	90.3	89.4	92.0	93.9	85.7
Hepatitis B: 3+ doses...................	68.0	90.0	91.8	91.4	92.1	92.5	97.2	91.7
Varicella [5]............................	(NA)	68.0	90.4	88.9	91.5	92.3	95.7	92.5
PCV: 3+ doses [6]......................	(X)	(X)	92.6	92.8	92.6	93.4	94.5	87.8
4+ DTP/3+ polio/1+ MMR/3+ Hib [7]........	74.0	76.0	80.3	79.8	79.3	81.6	80.2	80.2
4+ DTP/3+ polio/1+ MMR/3+ Hib/3+ HepB [8].................	55.1	72.8	[9] 76.3	[9] 75	[9] 75.7	[9] 78.3	[9] 77.8	[9] 76.9

NA Not available. X Not applicable. [1] Children in the first quarter 2010—fourth quarter 2010 National Immunization Survey were born between January 2007 and July 2009. [2] Non-Hispanic. [3] Children of Hispanic origin may be any race. [4] Haemophilus influenzae type B. [5] Data collection for varicella (chicken pox) began in July 1996. [6] PCV = Pneumococcal conjugate vaccine. [7] MMR = Measles, mumps, and rubella. [8] Children are considered immunized with this series. [9] 4+ DTP/3+ polio/1+ MMR/3+ Hib/3+ HepB/1+ Varicella

Source: U.S. Centers for Disease Control and Prevention, Atlanta, GA, National Immunization Program, Data and Statistics, *Immunization Coverage in the U.S.* See also <http://www.cdc.gov/vaccines/stats-surv/imz-coverage.htm#nis>.

Table 197. Asthma Incidence Among Children Under 18 Years of Age by Selected Characteristics: 2010

[In thousands, except percent (74,626 represents 74,626,000). Based on the National Health Interview Survey, a sample survey of the civilian noninstitutionalized population; see Appendix III]

Selected characteristic	Total	Ever told had asthma		Still have asthma	
		Number [1]	Percent [2]	Number [1]	Percent [2]
Total [3]...................	**74,626**	**10,133**	**13.6**	**6,976**	**9.4**
SEX [4]					
Male...................	38,135	5,827	15.5	3,991	10.6
Female.................	36,491	4,307	11.9	2,986	8.3
AGE					
0 to 4 years old...........	21,414	1,714	8.0	1,285	6.0
5 to 11 years old..........	28,666	4,200	14.7	3,020	10.5
12 to 17 years old.........	24,546	4,219	17.2	2,672	10.9
RACE					
Race Alone [4,5]............	71,490	9,581	13.5	6,605	9.3
White....................	56,170	6,747	12.1	4,544	8.2
Black or African American......	11,030	2,331	21.4	1,742	16.0
American Indian or Alaska Native......	768	[6] 65	[6] 9.6	[6] 33	[6] 4.9
Asian....................	3,354	428	13.0	281	8.5
Native Hawaiian or Other Pacific Islander.............	168	(B)	(B)	(B)	(B)
Two or more races [4,7].......	3,136	553	18.7	372	12.5
HISPANIC ORIGIN AND RACE [4,8]					
Hispanic or Latino............	17,167	2,099	12.7	1,385	8.3
Mexican or Mexican American.........	11,590	1,243	11.1	793	7.1
Not Hispanic or Latino............	57,460	8,034	14.0	5,591	9.8
White, single race...........	40,766	4,936	12.1	3,347	8.2
Black or African American, single race.............	10,430	2,206	21.4	1,654	16.1

B Figure too small to meet statistical standards for reliability of a derived figure. [1] Unknowns for the columns are not included in the frequencies, but they are included in the "Total" column. [2] Unknowns for the column variables are not included in the denominators when calculating percentages. [3] Includes other races, not shown separately. [4] Estimates are age-adjusted to the 2000 projected U.S. standard population using age groups 0–4 years, 5–11 years, and 12–17 years. [5] Refers to persons who indicated only a single race group. [6] Figures do not meet standard of reliability or precision. [7] Refers to all persons who indicated more than one race group. [8] Persons of Hispanic or Latino origin may be any race or combination of races.

Source: National Center for Health Statistics, *Summary Health Statistics for U.S. Children: National Health Interview Survey, 2010*, Vital and Health Statistics, Series 10, Number 250, 2011. See also <http://www.cdc.gov/nchs/data/series/sr_10/sr10_250.pdf>.

Table 198. Nursing Homes, Beds, Residents, and Occupancy Rate by State: 2010

[Based on a census of certified nursing facilities]

State	Nursing homes	Beds	Residents	Occupancy rate [1]	State	Nursing homes	Beds	Residents	Occupancy rate [1]
U.S.	**15,690**	**1,703,398**	**1,396,473**	**82.0**	MO	514	55,393	37,839	68.3
AL	227	26,656	22,968	86.2	MT	88	6,991	4,943	70.7
AK	15	682	641	94.0	NE	222	16,065	12,630	78.6
AZ	139	16,460	11,878	72.2	NV	50	5,856	4,735	80.9
AR	232	24,548	17,864	72.8	NH	79	7,692	6,932	90.1
CA	1,239	121,167	102,591	84.7	NJ	360	51,101	45,917	89.9
CO	213	20,259	16,302	80.5	NM	70	6,769	5,555	82.1
CT	239	29,255	25,972	88.8	NY	635	117,984	109,044	92.4
DE	47	4,990	4,145	83.1	NC	424	44,392	37,199	83.8
DC	19	2,775	2,595	93.5	ND	85	6,438	5,629	87.4
FL	678	82,226	71,907	87.5	OH	960	93,043	79,234	85.2
GA	360	39,960	34,704	86.8	OK	314	28,932	19,227	66.5
HI	48	4,303	3,880	90.2	OR	137	12,218	7,549	61.8
ID	79	6,153	4,388	71.3	PA	710	88,829	81,014	91.2
IL	787	101,061	75,224	74.4	RI	86	8,802	8,043	91.4
IN	506	57,721	39,167	67.9	SC	184	19,474	17,133	88.0
IA	443	32,842	25,463	77.5	SD	110	7,932	6,497	81.9
KS	340	25,598	18,985	74.2	TN	318	37,279	31,927	85.6
KY	285	26,063	23,252	89.2	TX	1,173	130,665	91,099	69.7
LA	281	36,098	25,198	69.8	UT	99	8,255	5,361	64.9
ME	109	7,127	6,417	90.0	VT	40	3,276	2,931	89.5
MD	231	29,004	24,816	85.6	VA	286	32,152	28,314	88.1
MA	427	49,175	42,880	87.2	WA	229	21,837	18,065	82.7
MI	428	47,054	39,894	84.8	WV	127	10,840	9,557	88.2
MN	385	32,339	29,434	91.0	WI	392	36,113	30,618	84.8
MS	203	18,589	16,489	88.7	WY	38	2,965	2,427	81.9

NA Not available. [1] Percentage of beds occupied (number of nursing home residents per 100 nursing home beds).

Source: U.S. National Center for Health Statistics, *Health, United States, 2011*. See also <http://www.cdc.gov/nchs/hus.htm>.

Table 199. Insufficient Rest or Sleep by Number of Days and Selected Characteristics: 2008

[In percent, except as noted. Age-adjusted to 2000 projected U.S. population. Respondents were asked, "During the past 30 days, for about how many days have you felt you did not get enough sleep?"]

Characteristic	Number [1]	Days without enough rest or sleep			
		0 days	1–13 days	14–29 days	30 days
Total	**403,981**	**30.7**	**41.3**	**16.8**	**11.1**
Sex:					
Male	152,513	33.6	40.9	15.6	9.9
Female	251,468	28.1	41.5	18	12.4
Age:					
18 to 24 years old	13,881	23.2	45.5	19.7	11.6
25 to 34 years old	38,978	21.8	44.1	20.4	13.8
35 to 44 years old	61,350	22.8	45.2	20.1	12.0
45 to 64 years old	169,906	30.5	42.4	16.3	10.9
65 years old or over	119,866	56.7	28.3	7.6	7.4
Race/ethnicity:					
White, non-Hispanic	318,694	27.9	42.7	18.2	11.2
Black, non-Hispanic	31,513	30.4	40.4	16.0	13.3
Other, non-Hispanic [2]	22,108	35.4	37.2	15.8	11.6
Hispanic [3]	28,045	38.8	37.7	13.0	10.5
Employment status:					
Employed	215,127	28.7	44.2	17.1	9.9
Unemployed	16,797	32.5	36.7	16.9	13.9
Retired	106,325	43.8	33.2	13.4	9.5
Unable to work	25,956	24.3	28.4	21.6	25.8
Homemaker or student	38,395	31.3	41.7	15.9	11.1
Education:					
Less than high school	39,395	37.9	33.6	14.2	14.3
High school or GED [4]	121,346	33.8	37.3	15.7	13.2
Some college or college graduate	242,194	28.0	44.5	17.9	9.6
Marital status:					
Married	226,418	30.9	42.1	15.9	11.1
Divorced, widowed, or separated	119,372	30.4	35.1	18.6	16.0
Member of unmarried couple	8,945	28.4	42.8	16.7	12.1
Never married	48,016	31.6	41.0	16.7	10.6

[1] Unweighted sample. Categories may not sum to total due to missing responses. [2] Asian, Hawaiian or other Pacific Islander, American Indian/Alaska Native, or multiracial. [3] Persons of Hispanic origin may be any race. [4] General Education Development certificate.

Source: U.S. Centers for Disease Control and Prevention, Atlanta, GA, *Morbidity and Mortality Weekly Report*, Vol. 58, No. 42, 2009. See also <http://www.cdc.gov/mmwr/index2009.html>.

Table 200. Persons 18 Years of Age and Over With Selected Diseases and Conditions by Selected Characteristics: 2010

[In thousands (229,505 represents 229,505,000). Based on National Health Interview Survey, a sample survey of the civilian noninstitutionalized population; see Appendix III]

Selected characteristics	Total persons	Persons with selected diseases and conditions					
		Diabetes [1,2]	Ulcers [1]	Kidney disease [3,4]	Liver disease [3]	Arthritis diagnosis [5]	Chronic joint symptoms [5]
Total [6]	**229,505**	**20,974**	**14,992**	**3,931**	**3,288**	**51,948**	**67,024**
SEX							
Male	110,929	10,804	6,703	1,775	1,721	21,152	30,141
Female	118,576	10,170	8,289	2,156	1,567	30,796	36,883
AGE							
18 to 44 years	110,615	3,022	4,591	804	978	7,838	18,794
45 to 64 years	80,198	9,676	6,418	1,578	1,835	24,292	30,801
65 to 74 years	21,291	4,563	2,241	740	309	10,426	9,572
75 years and over	17,401	3,713	1,742	809	167	9,391	7,857
RACE							
Race alone [7]	226,314	20,640	14,701	3,904	3,263	51,203	65,868
White	185,330	16,180	12,449	3,093	2,615	43,703	56,151
Black or African American	27,807	3,257	1,620	704	426	5,855	7,364
American Indian or Alaska Native	1,795	266	170	[8] 23	[8] 47	429	598
Asian	11,096	891	449	85	175	1,186	1,717
Native Hawaiian or other Pacific Islander	284	(B)	(B)	–	–	[8] 31	[8] 38
Two or more races [9]	3,191	335	291	[8] 27	(B)	744	1,156
HISPANIC ORIGIN [10]							
Hispanic or Latino	32,094	3,178	1,510	549	569	3,774	6,033
Mexican or Mexican American	19,712	1,977	898	369	342	2,100	3,603

– Represents zero. B Figure too small to meet statistical standards for reliability of a derived figure. [1] Respondents were asked if they had ever been told by a health professional that they had an ulcer or diabetes. A person may be represented in more than one column. [2] Excludes borderline diabetes. [3] Respondents were asked if they had been told in the last 12 months by a health professional that they had weak or failing kidneys or any kind of liver condition. [4] Excludes kidney stones, bladder infections, or incontinence. [5] Respondents were asked if they had ever been told by a health professional that they had some form of arthritis, rheumatoid arthritis, gout, lupus or fibromyalgia. Those that answered "yes" were classified as having an arthritis diagnosis. Respondents with joint symptoms (excluding back and neck) that began more than 3 months prior to interview were classified as having chronic joint symptoms. [6] Total includes other races not shown separately. [7] Refers to persons who indicated only a single race group. [8] Figures do not meet standard of reliability or precision. [9] Refers to all persons who indicated more than one race group. [10] Persons of Hispanic or Latino origin may be of any race or combination of races.

Source: National Center for Health Statistics, *Summary Health Statistics for U.S. Adults: National Health Interview Survey, 2010*, Vital and Health Statistics, Series 10, Number 252, 2012, <http://www.cdc.gov/nchs/nhis.htm>.

Table 201. Persons 18 Years of Age and Over With Selected Circulatory Diseases by Selected Characteristics: 2010

[In thousands (229,505 represents 229,505,000). In separate questions, respondents were asked if they had ever been told by a doctor or other health professional that they had: hypertension (or high blood pressure); coronary heart disease, angina (or angina pectoris); heart attack (or myocardial infarction); any other heart condition or disease not already mentioned; or a stroke. A person may be represented in more than one column. Based on National Health Interview Survey, a sample survey of the civilian noninstitutionalized population; see Appendix III]

Characteristic	Total persons	Selected circulatory diseases			
		Heart disease		Hypertension [3]	Stroke
		All types [1]	Coronary [2]		
Total [4]	**229,505**	**27,066**	**15,262**	**59,259**	**6,226**
SEX					
Male	110,929	13,705	8,872	28,018	3,002
Female	118,576	13,361	6,391	31,241	3,223
AGE					
18 to 44 years	110,615	4,897	1,494	10,303	664
45 to 64 years	80,198	10,568	5,803	27,531	2,403
65 to 74 years	21,291	5,173	3,508	11,485	1,302
75 years and over	17,401	6,428	4,457	9,940	1,856
RACE					
Race alone [5]	226,314	26,664	15,008	58,575	6,130
White	185,330	22,903	12,829	46,999	4,912
Black or African American	27,807	2,798	1,577	8,973	951
American Indian or Alaska Native	1,795	224	104	482	[6] 72
Asian	11,096	696	458	2,040	180
Native Hawaiian or Other Pacific Islander	284	(B)	(B)	[6] 81	(B)
Two or more races [7]	3,191	402	254	684	[6] 96
HISPANIC ORIGIN [8]					
Hispanic or Latino	32,094	2,020	1235	5,681	590
Mexican or Mexican American	19,712	1,178	708	3,395	321

B Figure too small to meet statistical standards for reliability of a derived figure. [1] Heart disease includes coronary heart disease, angina pectoris, heart attack, or any other heart condition or disease. [2] Coronary heart disease includes coronary heart disease, angina pectoris, or heart attack. [3] Persons had to have been told on two or more different visits that they had hypertension, or high blood pressure, to be classified as hypertensive. [4] Includes other races not shown separately. [5] Refers to persons who indicated only a single race group. [6] Figures do not meet standard of reliability or precision. [7] Refers to all persons who indicated more than one race group. [8] Persons of Hispanic or Latino origin may be any race or combination of races.

Source: National Center for Health Statistics, *Summary Health Statistics for the U.S. Population: National Health Interview Survey, 2010*, Vital and Health Statistics, Series 10, Number 252, 2012. See also <http://www.cdc.gov/nchs/nhis.htm>.

Table 202. Selected Respiratory Diseases Among Persons 18 Years of Age and Over by Selected Characteristics: 2010

[In thousands (229,505 represents 229,505,000). Respondents were asked in two separate questions if they had ever been told by a doctor or other health professional that they had emphysema or asthma. Respondents who had been told they had asthma were asked if they still had asthma. Respondents were asked in three separate questions if they had been told by a doctor or other health professional in the past 12 months that they had hay fever, sinusitis, or bronchitis. Based on the National Health Interview Survey, a sample survey of the civilian noninstitutionalized population; see Appendix III]

Selected characteristic	Total persons	Selected respiratory conditions [1]					
		Emphy-sema	Asthma		Hay fever	Sinusitis	Chronic bronchitis
			Ever	Still			
Total [2]...........	**229,505**	**4,314**	**29,057**	**18,734**	**17,937**	**29,821**	**9,883**
SEX							
Male.........	110,929	2,248	11,869	6,418	7,513	11,021	3,399
Female.........	118,576	2,066	17,188	12,316	10,424	18,800	6,484
AGE							
18 to 44 years.........	110,615	361	15,020	8,902	6,656	11,584	3,265
45 to 64 years.........	80,198	1,703	9,723	6,704	8,638	13,025	4,247
65 to 74 years.........	21,291	1,153	2,492	1,849	1,684	3,240	1,279
75 years and over.........	17,401	1,097	1,822	1,279	958	1,973	1,092
RACE							
Race alone [3].........	226,314	4,214	28,406	18,235	17,600	29,309	9,656
White.........	185,330	3,822	22,837	14,528	14,969	24,261	8,324
Black or African American.........	27,807	281	4,285	2,950	1,802	3,929	1,115
American Indian or Alaska Native.........	1,795	(B)	234	202	87	238	[4] 73
Asian.........	11,096	[4] 88	1,014	546	724	862	137
Native Hawaiian or other Pacific Islander....	284	–	[4] 36	(B)	(B)	(B)	(B)
Two or more races [5].........	3,191	[4] 100	651	499	336	511	227
HISPANIC ORIGIN AND RACE [6]							
Hispanic or Latino.........	32,094	231	3,289	2,224	1,440	2,783	878
Mexican or Mexican American.........	19,712	112	1,686	1,173	804	1,545	509
Not Hispanic or Latino.........	197,411	4,083	25,768	16,510	16,497	27,038	9,005
White, single race.........	156,119	3,600	19,926	12,552	13,659	21,752	7,525
Black or African American, single race.......	26,689	279	4,118	2,841	1,744	3,833	1,074

B Figure too small to meet statistical standards for reliability of a derived figure. [1] A person may be represented in more than one column. [2] Total includes other races not shown separately. [3] Refers to persons who indicated only a single race group. [4] Figure does not meet standard of reliability or precision. [5] Refers to all persons who indicated more than one race group. [6] Persons of Hispanic or Latino origin may be any race or combination of races.

Source: National Center for Health Statistics, *Summary Health Statistics for the U.S. Population: National Health Interview Survey, 2010*, Vital and Health Statistics, Series 10, Number 252, 2012. See also <http://www.cdc.gov/nchs/nhis.htm>.

Table 203. Injury and Poisoning Episodes by Age and Sex: 2010

[34,895 represents 34,895,000. Covers all medically attended injuries and poisonings occurring during the 5–week period prior to the survey interview. Age adjustment is used to adjust for differences in the age distribution of populations being compared. There may be more than one condition per episode. Based on the National Health Interview Survey, a sample survey of the civilian noninstitutionalized population; see Appendix III]

External cause and nature of injury	Both sexes							Male	Female
	Total	Total, age-adjusted [1]	Under 12 years	12 to 21 years	22 to 44 years	45 to 64 years	65 years and over		
EPISODES									
Number (1,000).........	34,895	(X)	4,574	4,341	11,686	9,273	5,022	17,943	16,952
Annual rate per 1,000 population, total [2].........	114.7	114.9	90.7	179.6	105.7	115.6	265.4	121.0	108.4
Fall.........	13,042	42.66	2,119	1,485	2,843	3,420	3,175	4,957	8,085
Struck by or against a person or an object.........	4,325	14.42	863	917	1,226	898	[4] 266	2,436	1,889
Transportation [3].........	3,672	12.07	[4] 503	[4] 343	1,454	931	[4] 402	1,971	1,701
Overexertion.........	4,891	15.97	[4] 191	[4] 444	2,183	1,725	[4] 301	2,571	2,321
Cutting, piercing instruments.......	2,517	8.42	185	283	1,292	602	(B)	1,629	888
Poisoning [5].........	[4] 575	[4] 1.82	(B)	(B)	[4] 164	(B)	(B)	(B)	[4] 238

X Not applicable. [1] Data were age-adjusted using the 2000 standard population using five age groups: under 12 years, 12-17 years, 18-44 years, 45-64 years, and 65 years and over. [2] Includes other items not shown separately. [3] Includes the categories "Motor vehicle traffic"; "Pedal cycle, other"; "Pedestrian, other"; and "Transport, other." [4] Figure does not meet standard of reliability or precision. [5] Poisoning episodes are assumed to have a single condition resulting from the episode.

Source: National Center for Health Statistics, *Summary Health Statistics for the U.S. Population: National Health Interview Survey, 2010*, Vital and Health Statistics, Series 10, Number 251, 2012. See also <http://www.cdc.gov/nchs/nhis.htm>.

Table 204. Persons 18 Years of Age and Over With Migraines and Pains in the Neck, Lower Back, Face, or Jaw by Selected Characteristics: 2010

[In thousands (229,505 represents 229,505,000). Based on National Health Interview Survey, a sample survey of the civilian noninstitutionalized population, Appendix III]

Selected characteristic	Total persons	Migraine and pain [1]			
		Migraine or severe headache [2]	Pain in neck [3]	Pain in lower back [3]	Pain in face or jaw [3]
Total [4].................................	**229,505**	**37,529**	**36,177**	**66,106**	**11,460**
SEX					
Male........................	110,929	12,171	14,796	29,577	3,792
Female......................	118,576	25,358	21,381	36,529	7,667
AGE					
18 to 44 years................	110,615	22,580	14,459	27,811	5,460
45 to 64 years................	80,198	12,485	16,002	26,007	4,779
65 to 74 years................	21,291	1,578	3,292	6,923	725
75 years and over.............	17,401	886	2,425	5,365	496
RACE					
Race alone [5]...................	226,314	36,815	35,537	65,046	11,298
White........................	185,330	30,106	30,434	54,857	9,834
Black or African American..........	27,807	5,168	3,725	7,536	1,063
American Indian or Alaska Native........	1,795	355	306	543	102
Asian........................	11,096	1,151	1,061	2,054	298
Native Hawaiian or other Pacific Islander.........	284	[6] 35	(B)	[6] 55	–
Two or more races [7]................	3,191	713	640	1,060	161
HISPANIC ORIGIN AND RACE [8]					
Hispanic or Latino................	32,094	5,475	4,595	8,429	1,411
Mexican or Mexican American...........	19,712	3,274	2,722	4,970	859
Not Hispanic or Latino................	197,411	32,053	31,583	57,677	10,048
White, single race................	156,119	25,135	26,277	47,256	8,562
Black or African American, single race................	26,689	4,999	3,577	7,223	1,024

B Figure to small to meet statistical standards for reliability of a derived figure. [1] A person may be represented in more than one column. [2] Respondents were asked, "During the past 3 months, did you have a severe headache or migraine?" Respondents were instructed to report pain that had lasted a whole day or more and, conversely, not to report fleeting or minor aches or pains. [3] Respondents were asked, "During the past 3 months, did you have a neck pain; or low back pain; or facial ache or pain in the jaw muscles or the joint in front of the ear?" Respondents were instructed to report pain that had lasted a whole day or more and, conversely, not to report fleeting or minor aches or pains. [4] Total includes other races not shown separately. [5] Refers to persons who indicated only a single race group. [6] Figure does not meet standard of reliability or precision. [7] Refers to all persons who indicated more than one race group. [8] Persons of Hispanic or Latino origin may be any race or combination of races.

Source: National Center for Health Statistics, *Summary Health Statistics for the U.S. Adults: National Health Interview Survey, 2010*, Vital and Health Statistics, Series 10, Number 252, 2012. See also http://www.cdc.gov/nchs/nhis.htm>.

Table 205. Use of Mammography for Women 40 Years Old and Over by Patient Characteristics: 2000 to 2010

[Percent of women having a mammogram within the past 2 years. Covers civilian noninstitutional population. Based on National Health Interview Survey; see Appendix III]

Characteristic	2000 [1]	2005 [1]	2010 [1]	Characteristic	2000 [1]	2005 [1]	2010 [1]
Total [2].......................	**70.4**	**66.8**	**67.1**	Years of school completed: No high school diploma or			
40 to 49 years old.............	64.3	63.5	62.3	GED...............................	57.7	52.8	53.0
50 years old and over..........	73.6	68.4	69.2	High school diploma or GED....	69.7	64.9	64.4
50 to 64 years old.............	78.7	71.8	72.6	Some college or more...........	76.2	72.7	72.1
65 years old and over........	67.9	63.8	64.4				
White, non-Hispanic...........	72.2	68.4	67.8	Poverty status: [4]			
Black, non-Hispanic............	67.9	65.2	67.4	Below poverty......................	54.8	48.5	51.4
Hispanic origin [3]...............	61.2	58.8	64.2	At or above poverty..............	72.1	68.8	(NA)

NA Not available. [1] Adjusted data—data have been reweighted using the 2000 Census population controls. [2] Includes other races not shown separately and unknown education level and poverty status. [3] Persons of Hispanic origin may be any race or combination of races. [4] For explanation of poverty level, see text, Section 13.

Source: U.S. National Center for Health Statistics, *Health, United States, 2011*. See also <http://www.cdc.gov/nchs/hus.htm>.

Table 206. Current Cigarette Smoking: 1990 to 2010

[In percent. Prior to 1992, a current smoker is a person who has smoked at least 100 cigarettes and who now smokes. Beginning 1992, definition includes persons who smoke only "some days." Excludes unknown smoking status. For definition of age adjustment, see text, Section 2. Based on National Health Interview Survey; for details, see Appendix III]

Sex, age, and race	1990[1]	2000	2005	2010
Total smokers, age-adjusted[2]	**25.3**	**23.1**	**20.8**	**19.3**
Male	28.0	25.2	23.4	21.2
Female	22.9	21.1	18.3	17.5
White male	27.6	25.4	23.3	21.4
Black male	32.8	25.7	25.9	23.3
White female	23.5	22.0	19.1	18.3
Black female	20.8	20.7	17.1	16.6
Total smokers[3]	**25.5**	**23.2**	**20.9**	**19.3**
Male, total	28.4	25.6	23.9	21.5
18 to 24 years	26.6	28.1	28.0	22.8
25 to 34 years	31.6	28.9	27.7	26.1
35 to 44 years	34.5	30.2	26.0	22.5
45 to 64 years	29.3	26.4	25.2	23.2
65 years and over	14.6	10.2	8.9	9.7
White, total	28.0	25.7	23.6	21.4
18 to 24 years	27.4	30.4	29.7	23.8
25 to 34 years	31.6	29.7	27.7	26.6
35 to 44 years	33.5	30.6	26.3	23.1
45 to 64 years	28.7	25.8	24.5	22.5
65 years and over	13.7	9.8	7.9	9.6
Black, total	32.5	26.2	26.5	24.3
18 to 24 years	21.3	20.9	21.6	18.8
25 to 34 years	33.8	23.2	29.8	25.7
35 to 44 years	42.0	30.7	23.3	22.6
45 to 64 years	36.7	32.2	32.4	31.8
65 years and over	21.5	14.2	16.8	10.0
Female, total	22.8	20.9	18.1	17.3
18 to 24 years	22.5	24.9	20.7	17.4
25 to 34 years	28.2	22.3	21.5	20.6
35 to 44 years	24.8	26.2	21.3	19.0
45 to 64 years	24.8	21.7	18.8	19.1
65 years and over	11.5	9.3	8.3	9.3
White, total	23.4	21.4	18.7	17.9
18 to 24 years	25.4	28.5	22.6	18.4
25 to 34 years	28.5	24.9	23.1	22.0
35 to 44 years	25.0	26.6	22.2	20.5
45 to 64 years	25.4	21.4	18.9	19.5
65 years and over	11.5	9.1	8.4	9.4
Black, total	21.2	20.8	17.3	17.0
18 to 24 years	[4]10.0	14.2	14.2	14.2
25 to 34 years	29.1	15.5	16.9	19.3
35 to 44 years	25.5	30.2	19.0	17.2
45 to 64 years	22.6	25.6	21.0	19.8
65 years and over	11.1	10.2	10.0	9.4

[1] Data prior to 1997 are not strictly comparable with data for later years due to the 1997 questionnaire redesign. [2] Data are age-adjusted to the year 2000 standard using five age groups: 18–24 years, 25–34 years, 35–44 years, 45–64 years, 65 years and over. [3] Crude, not age-adjusted. [4] Figure does not meet standard of reliability or precision.

Source: U.S. National Center for Health Statistics, *Health, United States, 2011*. See also <http://www.cdc.gov/nchs/hus.htm>.

Table 207. Substance Abuse Treatment Facilities and Clients: 1995 to 2010

[As of October 2 (1995), as of October 1 (1997–2000), as of March 31 (2003–2006), as of March 30 (2007), and as of March 31 (2008–2010). Based on the Uniform Facility Data Set (UFDS)/National Survey of Substance Abuse Treatment Services (N-SSATS) survey, a census of all known facilities that provide substance abuse treatment in the United States and associated jurisdictions. Selected missing data for responding facilities were imputed]

Primary focus (FACILITIES)	Number	Primary focus (CLIENTS)	Number	Type of care and type of problem	Number of clients
1995	10,746	1995	1,009,127	**2010, total[1]**	**1,175,462**
2000	13,428	2000	1,000,896	Outpatient	1,056,532
2004	13,454	2004	1,072,251	Regular	593,077
2005	13,371	2005	1,081,049	Intensive	138,188
2006	13,771	2006	1,130,881	Detoxification	13,216
2007	13,648	2007	1,135,425	Residential (non-hospital)	103,692
2008	13,688	2008	1,192,490	Hospital inpatient	15,238
2009	13,513	2009	1,182,077	Detoxification	6,476
2010, total	**13,339**	**2010, total**	**1,175,462**	Treatment	8,762
Substance abuse treatment services	8,100	Substance abuse treatment services	780,098	Drug only	459,069
Mental health services	853	Mental health services	44,564	Alcohol only	215,101
General health care	168	General health care	15,965	Both alcohol & drug	498,671
Both substance abuse and mental health	4,113	Both substance abuse and mental health	330,621	Both substance abuse and mental health disorders	479,699
Other	105	Other	4,214		

[1] Includes clients at facilities that did not provide data on type of substance abuse problem treated.

Source: U.S. Substance Abuse and Mental Health Services Administration, Uniform Facility Data Set (UFDS), 1995–1999, and Center for Behavioral Health Statistics and Quality, Substance Abuse and Mental Health Services Administration, National Survey of Substance Abuse Treatment Services (N-SSATS), 2000–2010, <http://www.samhsa.gov/dataOutcomes/>.

Table 208. Current Cigarette Smoking by Sex and State: 2010

[In percent. Current cigarette smoking is defined as persons 18 years and older who reported having smoked 100 or more cigarettes during their lifetime and who currently smoke every day or some days. Based on the Behavioral Risk Factor Surveillance System, a telephone survey of health behaviors of the civilian, noninstitutionalized U.S. population, 18 years old and over; for details, see source]

State	Total	Male	Female	State	Total	Male	Female	State	Total	Male	Female
U.S. [1]	**17.3**	**18.5**	**15.8**	KS	17.0	18.2	15.9	NC	19.8	23.4	16.4
AL	21.9	25.5	18.7	KY	24.8	26.3	23.4	ND	17.4	18.2	16.6
AK	20.4	22.5	18.1	LA	22.1	25.3	19.1	OH	22.5	23.0	22.1
AZ	15.0	16.1	14.0	ME	18.2	19.2	17.3	OK	23.7	25.1	22.3
AR	22.9	26.2	19.8	MD	15.2	17.3	13.4	OR	15.1	15.5	14.7
CA	12.1	15.0	9.2	MA	14.1	14.8	13.4	PA	18.4	18.5	18.4
CO	16.0	18.0	14.0	MI	18.9	21.0	17.0	RI	15.7	17.9	13.7
CT	13.2	15.4	11.1	MN	14.9	15.5	14.4	SC	21.0	25.5	17.0
DE	17.3	19.9	14.9	MS	22.9	26.5	19.7	SD	15.4	17.1	13.7
DC	15.6	18.0	13.6	MO	21.1	20.7	21.4	TN	20.1	21.7	18.6
FL	17.1	18.4	16.0	MT	18.8	19.7	17.9	TX	15.8	18.3	13.4
GA	17.6	20.0	15.4	NE	17.2	18.3	16.2	UT	9.1	10.6	7.7
HI	14.5	16.0	13.0	NV	21.3	22.4	20.2	VT	15.4	15.7	15.0
ID	15.7	16.8	14.6	NH	16.9	18.0	15.8	VA	18.5	22.2	15.1
IL	16.9	20.3	13.7	NJ	14.4	15.7	13.2	WA	15.2	16.2	14.2
IN	21.2	23.3	19.3	NM	18.5	21.8	15.3	WV	26.8	28.3	25.4
IA	16.1	17.5	14.8	NY	15.5	18.1	13.0	WI	19.1	20.7	17.4
								WY	19.5	20.2	18.9

[1] Represents median value among the states and DC. For definition of median, see Guide to Tabular Presentations.

Source: U.S. Centers for Disease Control and Prevention, "Behavioral Risk Factor Surveillance System," 2010. See also <http://www.cdc.gov/brfss/>.

Table 209. Drug Use by Type of Drug and Age Group: 2008 and 2009

[In percent. Data comes from the National Survey on Drug Use and Health (NSDUH). Current users are those who used drugs at least once within month prior to this study. Based on a representative sample of the U.S. population 12 years old and over, including persons living in households and in some group quarters such as dormitories and homeless shelters. Estimates are based on computer-assisted interviews of about 68,000 respondents. Subject to sampling variability; see source]

Age and type of drug	Ever used		Current user		Age and type of drug	Ever used		Current user	
	2008	2009	2008	2009		2008	2009	2008	2009
12 YEARS OLD AND OVER					**18 TO 25 YEARS OLD**				
Any illicit drug [1]	47.0	47.1	8.0	8.7	Any illicit drug [1]	56.6	58.1	19.6	21.2
Marijuana and hashish	41.0	41.5	6.1	6.6	Marijuana and hashish	50.4	52.2	16.5	18.1
Cocaine	14.7	14.5	0.7	0.7	Cocaine	14.4	14.8	1.5	1.4
Crack	3.4	3.3	0.1	0.2	Hallucinogens	17.7	19.0	1.7	1.8
Heroin	1.5	1.5	0.1	0.1	Inhalants	10.4	10.7	0.3	0.4
Hallucinogens	14.4	14.8	0.4	0.5	Any psychotherapeutic [2,3]	29.2	(NA)	5.9	(NA)
LSD	9.4	9.4	0.1	0.1	Alcohol	85.6	85.8	61.2	61.8
Ecstasy	5.2	5.7	0.2	0.3	"Binge" alcohol use [4]	(NA)	(NA)	41.8	41.7
Inhalants	8.9	8.9	0.3	0.2	Cigarettes	64.2	63.7	35.7	35.8
Any psychotherapeutic [2,3]	20.8	20.6	2.5	2.8	Smokeless tobacco	20.3	21.0	5.4	6.1
Pain relievers	14.0	13.9	1.9	2.1	Cigars	41.4	41.7	11.3	11.4
Tranquilizers	8.6	8.6	0.7	0.8					
Stimulants [3]	8.5	8.7	0.4	0.5	**26 TO 34 YEARS OLD**				
Methamphetamine [3]	5.0	5.1	0.1	0.2	Any illicit drug [1]	58.2	59.3	11.2	12.3
Sedatives	3.6	3.4	0.1	0.1	Marijuana and hashish	51.3	53.0	8.8	9.6
Alcohol	82.2	82.8	51.6	51.9	Cocaine	16.7	18.1	1.5	1.0
"Binge" alcohol use [4]	(NA)	(NA)	23.3	23.7	Hallucinogens	22.2	23.9	0.6	0.9
Cigarettes	65.1	64.6	23.9	23.3	Inhalants	12.8	13.7	0.1	0.2
Smokeless tobacco	18.4	17.8	3.5	3.4	Any psychotherapeutic [2,3]	28.0	29.2	3.2	3.8
Cigars	35.8	35.8	5.3	5.3					
Pipe tobacco	14.6	13.9	0.8	0.8	**35 YEARS OLD AND OVER**				
					Any illicit drug [1]	45.7	45.2	4.7	4.9
					Marijuana and hashish	40.6	40.4	3.2	3.4
12 TO 17 YEARS OLD					Cocaine	16.4	15.7	0.4	0.5
Any illicit drug [1]	26.2	26.8	9.3	10.0	Hallucinogens	13.6	13.5	0.0	0.1
Marijuana and hashish	16.5	17.0	6.7	7.3	Inhalants	7.7	7.4	0.1	0.1
Cocaine	1.9	1.6	0.4	0.3	Any psychotherapeutic [2,3]	18.9	18.2	1.6	1.7
Hallucinogens	3.9	4.1	1.0	0.9					
Inhalants	9.3	9.2	1.1	1.0	**26 YEARS OLD AND OVER**				
Any psychotherapeutic [2,3]	11.1	(NA)	2.9	(NA)	Alcohol	87.3	88.0	54.8	54.9
Alcohol	38.3	38.1	14.6	14.7	"Binge" alcohol use [4]	(NA)	(NA)	22.1	22.4
"Binge" alcohol use [4]	(NA)	(NA)	8.8	8.8	Cigarettes	70.7	70.1	23.8	23.0
Cigarettes	22.9	22.2	9.1	8.9	Smokeless tobacco	19.5	18.5	3.3	3.1
Smokeless tobacco	7.2	7.6	2.2	2.3	Cigars	37.8	37.7	4.4	4.4
Cigars	12.4	12.4	3.8	4.0					

NA Not available. – Represents or rounds to zero. [1] Illicit drugs include marijuana/hashish, cocaine (including crack), heroin, hallucinogens, inhalants, or prescription-type psychotherapeutics used nonmedically. [2] Nonmedical use of prescription-type psychotherapeutics includes the nonmedical use of pain relievers, tranquilizers, stimulants, or sedatives and does not include over-the-counter drugs. [3] Includes data from new methamphetamine items added in 2006 and 2007. Previous estimates have been adjusted to be comparable with new data and differ from those in reports prior to the 2007 data year. [4] Binge alcohol use is defined as drinking five or more drinks on the same occasion (i.e., at the same time or within a couple of hours of each other) on at least 1 day in the past 30 days.

Source: U.S. Substance Abuse and Mental Health Services Administration, *National Survey on Drug Use and Health, 2008 and 2009*, <http://oas.samhsa.gov/nhsda.htm>.

Table 210. Estimated Use of Selected Drugs by State: 2008 to 2009

[20,945 represents 20,945,000. Data in this table cover a 2-year period. Data is based on the National Survey on Drug Use and Health (NSDUH). Current users are those persons 12 years old and over who used drugs at least once within month prior to this study. Based on national sample of respondents (see also headnote, Table 209). The state estimates were produced by combining the prevalence rate based on the state sample data and the prevalence rate based on a national regression model applied to local-area county and census block group/tract-level estimates from the state (i.e., a survey-weighted hierarchical Bayes estimation approach). The parameters of the regression model are estimated from the entire national sample. For comparison purposes, the data shown here display estimates for all 50 states and the District of Columbia utilizing the modeled estimates for all 51 areas]

State	Estimated current users (1,000)					Current users as percent of population				
	Any illicit drug [1]	Mari-juana	Any illicit drug other than mari-juana [1]	Ciga-rettes	Binge alcohol [2]	Any illicit drug [1]	Mari-juana	Any illicit drug other than mari-juana [1]	Ciga-rettes	Binge alcohol [2]
U.S.........	20,945	15,960	8,861	59,217	58,827	8.4	6.4	3.5	23.6	23.5
AL............	272	195	148	1,033	791	7.1	5.1	3.8	26.8	20.5
AK............	74	63	21	133	132	13.5	11.5	3.8	24.2	24.2
AZ............	498	353	219	1,159	1,221	9.5	6.7	4.2	22.0	23.2
AR............	183	142	87	711	482	7.8	6.1	3.7	30.3	20.5
CA............	3,007	2,307	1,207	5,798	6,657	10.0	7.7	4.0	19.3	22.2
CO............	460	399	147	908	1,068	11.3	9.8	3.6	22.3	26.3
CT............	261	212	100	629	792	8.9	7.2	3.4	21.5	27.0
DE............	63	51	29	185	191	8.7	7.0	4.0	25.5	26.2
DC............	54	43	20	122	151	10.6	8.5	4.0	24.0	29.7
FL............	1,239	892	522	3,491	3,377	8.0	5.8	3.4	22.7	21.9
GA............	617	473	245	1,904	1,672	7.9	6.1	3.2	24.4	21.4
HI............	125	89	53	213	240	11.9	8.5	5.1	20.2	22.8
ID............	101	73	47	284	248	8.2	5.9	3.8	23.1	20.2
IL............	823	625	343	2,641	2,800	7.8	5.9	3.2	24.9	26.4
IN............	444	320	209	1,405	1,204	8.5	6.1	4.0	26.8	23.0
IA............	132	111	50	619	710	5.3	4.5	2.0	24.9	28.6
KS............	159	114	75	569	571	7.0	5.0	3.3	25.0	25.1
KY............	262	170	139	1,130	717	7.4	4.8	3.9	32.0	20.3
LA............	259	186	136	957	852	7.2	5.2	3.8	26.5	23.6
ME............	126	111	38	289	249	11.2	9.9	3.4	25.6	22.1
MD............	320	253	125	942	980	6.8	5.4	2.7	20.1	20.9
MA............	602	480	226	1,162	1,374	10.9	8.7	4.1	21.1	24.9
MI............	791	626	316	2,180	2,110	9.5	7.5	3.8	26.2	25.3
MN............	300	259	123	1,019	1,169	6.9	6.0	2.8	23.5	26.9
MS............	147	106	74	622	479	6.2	4.5	3.1	26.4	20.3
MO............	370	291	153	1,291	1,187	7.6	5.9	3.1	26.4	24.2
MT............	78	66	28	200	219	9.6	8.1	3.5	24.7	27.0
NE............	97	78	41	353	376	6.7	5.4	2.8	24.3	25.8
NV............	213	149	103	523	556	10.0	7.0	4.8	24.6	26.1
NH............	126	108	47	261	284	11.2	9.7	4.2	23.3	25.4
NJ............	490	363	201	1,519	1,766	6.8	5.0	2.8	21.0	24.4
NM............	147	107	62	368	371	9.1	6.6	3.8	22.7	22.9
NY............	1,596	1,267	597	3,491	3,943	9.8	7.7	3.7	21.3	24.1
NC............	616	473	275	1,997	1,574	8.2	6.3	3.6	26.4	20.8
ND............	30	25	11	131	159	5.6	4.7	2.1	24.6	29.8
OH............	719	568	309	2,551	2,420	7.5	6.0	3.2	26.7	25.3
OK............	264	166	146	834	660	8.9	5.6	5.0	28.2	22.3
OR............	393	296	156	796	764	12.3	9.3	4.9	25.0	24.0
PA............	711	538	317	2,613	2,529	6.8	5.1	3.0	24.9	24.1
RI............	113	89	49	200	242	12.7	10.0	5.5	22.5	27.2
SC............	330	219	150	993	807	8.9	5.9	4.1	26.9	21.8
SD............	41	34	15	164	195	6.2	5.2	2.2	25.0	29.7
TN............	387	282	184	1,461	967	7.5	5.5	3.6	28.3	18.7
TX............	1,291	918	619	4,365	4,686	6.7	4.7	3.2	22.5	24.2
UT............	133	76	80	349	300	6.3	3.6	3.8	16.4	14.1
VT............	66	58	21	119	139	12.3	10.8	3.9	22.3	26.0
VA............	395	338	170	1,483	1,502	6.2	5.3	2.7	23.3	23.6
WA............	497	395	186	1,252	1,170	9.1	7.2	3.4	22.9	21.4
WV............	121	85	68	472	309	7.9	5.5	4.4	30.7	20.1
WI............	374	292	159	1,209	1,364	8.0	6.2	3.4	25.7	29.0
WY............	28	24	12	117	103	6.4	5.4	2.8	26.5	23.3

[1] Illicit drugs include marijuana/hashish, cocaine (including crack), heroin, hallucinogens, inhalants, or prescription-type psychotherapeutics used nonmedically. [2] Binge alcohol use is defined as drinking five or more drinks on the same occasion (i.e., at the same time or within a couple of hours of each other) on at least 1 day in the past 30 days.

Source: U.S. Substance Abuse and Mental Health Services Administration, *National Survey on Drug Use and Health, 2008 and 2009*. See also <http://www.oas.samhsa.gov/nhsda.htm>.

Table 211. Cumulative Percent Distribution of Population by Height and Sex: 2007 to 2008

[Data are based on National Health and Nutrition Examination Survey (NHANES), a sample of the civilian noninstitutional population. For this survey, the respondent participates in an interview and a physical examination. For persons 20 years old and over. Height was measured without shoes. Based on sample and subject to sampling variability; see source]

Height	Males						Females					
	20–29 years	30–39 years	40–49 years	50–59 years	60–69 years	70–79 years	20–29 years	30–39 years	40–49 years	50–59 years	60–69 years	70–79 years
Percent under—												
4'10"	–	–	–	(B)	–	–	–	¹1.7	–	¹1	–	¹3.3
4'11"	–	–	–	(B)	(B)	–	¹2.6	3.1	¹1.6	2.1	¹3.6	8.7
5'	(B)	–	–	(B)	(B)	–	5.7	6.0	5.0	8.0	9.0	16.0
5'1"	(B)	(B)	(B)	(B)	¹0.4	(B)	12.3	11.6	10.8	16.7	14.7	26.0
5'2"	(B)	(B)	(B)	(B)	(B)	(B)	20.8	19.7	19.8	23.3	23.4	36.9
5'3"	(B)	¹3.1	¹1.9	(B)	¹2.3	(B)	30.4	31.3	30.8	36.3	38.4	51.9
5'4"	3.7	¹4.4	3.8	¹4.3	4.4	5.8	43.5	46.6	46.0	50.7	52.8	69.9
5'5"	7.2	6.7	5.6	7.6	7.8	12.8	54.1	61.2	58.0	68.4	66.6	82.8
5'6"	11.6	13.1	9.8	12.2	14.7	23.0	72.4	74.0	72.2	79.7	83.3	89.3
5'7"	20.6	19.6	19.4	18.6	23.7	35.1	82.3	84.9	83.0	88.4	93.3	95.4
5'8"	33.1	32.2	30.3	30.3	37.7	47.7	90.3	91.8	91.2	95.2	97.0	98.4
5'9"	42.2	45.4	40.4	41.2	50.2	60.3	94.1	96.1	94.7	97.3	97.8	99.6
5'10	58.6	58.1	54.4	54.3	65.2	75.2	97.6	98.9	97.8	98.9	99.6	99.6
5'11"	70.7	69.4	69.6	70.0	75.0	85.8	99.6	98.9	99.4	100.0	99.8	100.0
6'	79.9	78.5	79.1	81.2	84.3	91.0	100.0	99.4	99.5	100.0	99.9	100.0
6'1"	89.0	89.0	87.4	91.6	93.6	94.9	100.0	99.9	99.5	100.0	99.9	100.0
6'2"	94.1	94.0	92.5	93.7	97.8	98.6	100.0	100.0	99.5	100.0	100.0	100.0
6'3"	98.3	95.8	97.7	96.6	99.9	100.0	100.0	100.0	99.5	100.0	100.0	100.0
6'4"	100.0	97.6	99.0	99.5	100.0	100.0	100.0	100.0	99.5	100.0	100.0	100.0
6'5"	100.0	99.4	99.4	99.6	100.0	100.0	100.0	100.0	100.0	100.0	100.0	100.0
6'6"	100.0	99.5	99.9	100.0	100.0	100.0	100.0	100.0	100.0	100.0	100.0	100.0

– Represents zero. B Base figure too small to meet statistical standards of reliability of a derived figure. ¹ Figure does not meet standard for reliability or precision.

Source: U.S. National Center for Health Statistics, unpublished data, <http://www.cdc.gov/nchs/nhanes.htm>.

Table 212. Cumulative Percent Distribution of Population by Weight and Sex: 2007 to 2008

[See headnote, Table 211. Data are based on National Health and Nutrition Examination Survey (NHANES). Weight was measured without shoes. Pregnant females were excluded from the analyses. Based on sample and subject to sampling variability; see source]

Weight	Males						Females					
	20–29 years	30–39 years	40–49 years	50–59 years	60–69 years	70–79 years	20–29 years	30–39 years	40–49 years	50–59 years	60–69 years	70–79 years
Percent under—												
100 lbs	–	–	(B)	(B)	–	–	¹2	1.3	(B)	¹0.4	0.2	(B)
110 lbs	(B)	(B)	(B)	(B)	(B)	(B)	4.9	4.7	3.7	¹4	(B)	6.1
120 lbs	(B)	(B)	(B)	¹1.1	(B)	1.5	16.3	10.5	7.8	7.9	7.2	12.4
130 lbs	4.3	¹2.1	¹2.5	¹2.3	2.8	3.5	27.8	18.9	16.0	17.1	13.5	22.5
140 lbs	11.1	6.4	4.7	5.6	5.3	5.2	39.4	29.8	26.4	27.3	27.4	30.1
150 lbs	20.9	11.5	7.6	8.6	10.0	9.7	49.7	40.6	37.5	38.7	37.4	43.1
160 lbs	31.3	20.4	15.1	13.9	16.5	17.7	57.5	51.1	49.8	49.7	46.1	53.7
170 lbs	43.6	30.5	21.3	22.0	24.9	27.4	63.2	59.8	59.3	56.9	58.9	65.6
180 lbs	55.7	40.9	33.6	33.2	33.4	40.1	72.6	68.7	65.6	63.7	72.4	74.0
190 lbs	65.0	50.6	43.7	44.5	42.6	50.1	76.3	73.6	75.0	70.3	79.4	81.2
200 lbs	73.5	59.3	58.0	55.7	55.5	65.7	80.0	79.4	80.0	75.3	84.6	87.3
210 lbs	79.4	70.0	66.2	64.6	64.4	71.6	82.8	83.7	82.8	81.9	88.4	90.5
220 lbs	83.8	76.1	75.6	74.0	73.4	80.0	84.9	89.0	87.2	85.9	91.1	93.4
230 lbs	86.5	81.7	84.6	78.8	81.2	83.5	88.6	91.3	90.6	89.5	93.7	96.4
240 lbs	89.7	85.5	88.1	85.6	85.1	87.3	90.0	94.1	93.0	91.4	95.6	97.0
250 lbs	93.2	89.6	89.7	88.0	88.2	90.6	92.3	95.2	95.5	92.9	96.7	98.4
260 lbs	94.7	92.0	92.8	91.3	90.7	93.1	93.3	95.8	96.7	96.5	97.6	98.6
270 lbs	95.1	93.3	94.6	93.5	93.0	96.4	95.7	96.4	97.5	97.2	98.0	98.6
280 lbs	96.1	95.1	95.4	94.2	94.8	97.5	97.0	97.2	97.8	98.2	99.0	99.4
290 lbs	96.8	96.4	96.4	95.8	97.2	98.5	97.2	97.5	98.2	98.9	99.0	99.6
300 lbs	97.5	96.9	98.1	98.1	97.8	99.4	97.7	98.4	98.3	99.4	99.3	100.0
320 lbs	98.1	98.2	98.8	99.0	98.5	99.4	98.9	99.1	98.7	99.7	99.9	100.0
340 lbs	99.5	98.8	98.8	99.1	99.0	100.0	99.6	99.5	99.4	99.8	99.9	100.0
360 lbs	99.5	99.4	99.3	99.8	99.0	100.0	99.6	99.7	99.8	99.9	99.9	100.0
380 lbs	99.7	99.7	99.5	99.8	99.1	100.0	99.6	99.9	99.8	100.0	100.0	100.0
400 lbs	99.7	99.7	99.5	99.9	99.5	100.0	99.6	100.0	99.8	100.0	100.0	100.0
420 lbs	99.7	99.7	99.5	100.0	99.5	100.0	99.6	100.0	99.9	100.0	100.0	100.0
440 lbs	99.8	99.9	99.5	100.0	99.5	100.0	99.6	100.0	100.0	100.0	100.0	100.0

– Represents zero. B Base figure too small to meet statistical standards of reliability of a derived figure. ¹ Figure does not meet standard of reliability or precision.

Source: U.S. National Center for Health Statistics, unpublished data, <http://www.cdc.gov/nchs/nhanes.htm>.

Table 213. Age-Adjusted Percent Distribution of Body Mass Index (BMI) Among Persons 18 Years Old and Over by Selected Characteristics: 2007 to 2008

[See headnote, Table 211. Body Mass Index (BMI) is a measure that adjusts body weight for height. It is calculated as weight in kilograms divided by height in meters squared. For both men and women, underweight is indicated by a BMI under 18.5; healthy weight is indicated by a BMI greater than or equal to 18.5 and less than 25.0; overweight is greater than or equal to 25.0 and less than 30.0; obesity is indicated by a BMI greater than or equal to 30.0. BMI is calculated from the measurement of the participants' weight and height during the examination. For definition of age adjustment, see text, Section 2. Based on the National Health and Nutrition Examination Survey (NHANES)]

Selected characteristic	Underweight	Healthy weight	Above healthy weight		
			Total	Overweight	Obese
Total [1] **(age-adjusted)**..	**1.8**	**31.6**	**66.6**	**33.9**	**32.6**
Total [1] **(crude)**..	**1.8**	**31.2**	**67.0**	**34.0**	**33.0**
Age: [2]					
18 to 44 years old..	2.1	35.5	62.4	32.2	30.3
45 to 64 years old..	[3] 1.6	26.9	71.5	34.2	37.3
65 to 74 years old..	(B)	25.7	73.3	36.5	36.8
75 years old and over..	1.7	30.3	68.0	41.7	26.2
Sex:					
Male..	1.1	28.2	70.7	39.9	30.8
Female...	2.5	34.8	62.7	28.2	34.5
Race/ethnicity and sex:					
Not Hispanic or Latino:					
White, male..	[3] 1.2	27.8	71.1	40.5	30.5
White, female..	2.6	37.3	60.0	27.7	32.3
Black alone or African American, male...................	[3] 1.6	31.4	67.0	31.1	36.0
Black alone or African American, female.................	2.8	21.1	76.0	27.9	48.1
Mexican or Mexican American, male.......................	(B)	20.9	78.6	44.0	34.6
Mexican or Mexican American, female....................	(B)	25.2	73.6	31.0	42.6
Education: [4]					
Less than a high school diploma...........................	2.2	25.1	72.6	34.4	38.3
High school diploma or GED [5]............................	1.5	27.6	70.9	36.1	34.8
Some college, bachelor's degree, or higher..............	1.0	31.6	67.4	35.1	32.3

B Base figure too small to meet statistical standards for reliability of a derived figure. [1] Total includes other race/ethnicities not shown separately and persons with unknown race/ethnicity. [2] Estimates for age groups are not age adjusted. [3] Figure does not meet standard of reliability or precision. [4] Education is shown only for persons 25 years old and over. [5] General Education Development certificate.

Source: U.S. National Center for Health Statistics, unpublished data, <http://www.cdc.gov/nchs/nhanes.htm>.

Table 214. Age-Adjusted Percentage of Persons Engaging in Physical Activity and Fitness by Selected Characteristics: 2008

[In percent. Covers persons 18 years old and over. Based on the National Health Interview Survey, a sample survey of the civilian noninstitutionalized population. Leisure-time physical activity is assessed by asking respondents a series of questions about participation in moderate and vigorous-intensity physical activities. For definition of age adjustment, see text, Section 2. To assess muscle-strengthening activities, respondents were asked about leisure-time physical activities specifically designed to strengthen their muscles]

Characteristic	No leisure-time physical activity [1]	Regular physical activity-moderate or vigorous [2]	Muscular strength and endurance [3]	Characteristic	No leisure-time physical activity [1]	Regular physical activity-moderate or vigorous [2]	Muscular strength and endurance [3]
Total......................	**36.2**	**32.5**	**21.9**	Two or more races.......	32.3	29.2	23.0
SEX				HISPANIC ORIGIN AND RACE			
Male.........................	33.9	34.7	25.7	Hispanic or Latino [5].......	47.4	25.1	15.0
Female......................	38.2	30.5	18.3	Not Hispanic or Latino....	34.3	33.8	23.2
				White, non-Hispanic.....	31.9	35.8	24.2
AGE [4]				Black, non-Hispanic.....	47.9	24.8	19.2
18 to 29 years old.........	28.7	38.4	29.3				
30 to 44 years old.........	31.7	35.5	24.6	**EDUCATION** [7]			
45 to 64 years old.........	37.2	31.7	19.9				
65 to 74 years old.........	45.8	26.1	16.3	Less than 9th grade.....	64.3	14.6	6.3
75 years old and over.....	55.9	18.4	11.5	Grades 9 thru 11.........	56.3	18.0	9.2
				High School graduate. ..	47.0	25.0	14.4
RACE				Some college or AA degree [6]................	33.0	31.8	22.4
Race alone				College graduate or above...................	20.7	45.2	31.8
White........................	34.6	33.8	22.6				
Black or African American...............	47.3	25.0	19.4				
American Indian or Alaska Native..........	49.2	25.0	11.2				
Asian or Pacific Islander.................	(NA)	(NA)	(NA)				

NA Not available. [1] Persons with no moderate- or vigorous-intensity activity for at least 10 minutes at a time. [2] Regular physical activity is moderate-intensity physical activity at least 5 times a week for 30 minutes at a time or vigorous-intensity physical activity for at least 3 times a week for 20 minutes at a time. [3] Persons who participated in muscle strengthening activities at least 2 times a week. [4] Age data are not age-adjusted. [5] Persons of Hispanic or Latino origin may be any race. [6] Associate of Arts degree. [7]For persons aged 25 and over.

Source: National Center for Health Statistics, National Health Interview Survey—United States, 2008, Hyattsville, MD. See also <http://wonder.cdc.gov/data2010/>.

Table 215. High School Students Engaged in Physical Activity by Sex: 2011

[In percent. For students in grades 9 to 12. Based on the Youth Risk Behavior Survey, a school-based survey and subject to sampling error; for details, see source]

Characteristic	Participated in 60+ min. of physical activity on 5 of last 7 days [1]	Participated in 60+ min. of physical activity on all 7 days [2]	Did not participate in 60+ min. of physical activity on any day [3]	Attended physical education class		Played on at least one sports team [6]	Used computers 3 or more hours/ day [7]	Watched three or more hours/ day of TV [8]
				Total [4]	Attended daily [5]			
All students.....	**49.5**	**28.7**	**13.8**	**51.8**	**31.5**	**58.4**	**31.1**	**32.4**
Male...............	**59.9**	**38.3**	**10.0**	**56.7**	**35.5**	**64.0**	**35.3**	**33.3**
Grade 9..........	61.0	38.8	8.7	70.8	44.0	65.6	35.5	33.9
Grade 10.........	62.3	42.6	10.0	59.2	36.7	68.2	36.1	35.3
Grade 11.........	58.5	36.2	10.5	49.2	31.6	60.9	36.7	32.3
Grade 12.........	57.3	34.9	10.8	44.7	27.9	60.2	32.4	30.9
Female...........	**38.5**	**18.5**	**17.7**	**46.7**	**27.2**	**52.6**	**26.6**	**31.6**
Grade 9..........	44.5	22.2	13.9	65.3	38.6	57.1	29.5	33.8
Grade 10.........	40.3	18.1	17.9	49.8	29.3	56.1	26.7	31.7
Grade 11.........	35.7	18.0	19.0	36.3	18.4	51.3	24.6	30.4
Grade 12.........	32.0	14.9	20.6	32.1	20.4	44.5	25.0	29.9

[1] Were physically active doing any kind of physical activity that increased their heart rate and made them breathe hard some of the time for a total of at least 60 minutes/day for at least 5 or more days out of the 7 days preceding the survey. [2] Participate in 60 or more minutes of any kind of physical activity that increased their heart rate and made them breathe hard some of the time on all 7 days before the survey. [3] Did not participate in 60 or more minutes of any kind of physical activity that increased their heart rate and made them breathe hard some of the time on at least 1 day during the 7 days before the survey. [4] On one or more days in an average week when they were in school. [5] Five days in an average week when they were in school. [6] Run by their school or community groups during the 12 months before the survey. [7] Played video or computer games or used computer for something that was not school work on an average school day. [8] On an average school day.

Source: U.S. Centers for Disease Control and Prevention, Atlanta, GA, "Youth Risk Behavior Surveillance— United States, 2011," Surveillance Series, June 2012, *Morbidity and Mortality Weekly Report 2012*, Vol. 61 (SS-4). See also <http://www.cdc.gov/mmwr/pdf/ss/ss6104.pdf>.

Table 216. Households and Persons Having Problems With Access to Food: 2005 to 2010

[114,437 represents 114,437,000. Food-secure means that a household had access at all times to enough food for an active healthy life for all household members, with no need for recourse to socially unacceptable food sources or extraordinary coping behaviors to meet their basic food needs. Food-insecure households had limited or uncertain ability to acquire acceptable foods in socially acceptable ways. Households with very low food security (a subset of food-insecure households) were those in which food intake of one or more household members was reduced and normal eating patterns disrupted due to inadequate resources for food. The severity of food insecurity in households is measured through a series of questions about experiences and behaviors known to characterize households that are having difficulty meeting basic food needs. These experiences and behaviors generally occur in an ordered sequence as the severity of food insecurity increases. As resources become more constrained, adults in typical households first worry about having enough food, then they stretch household resources and juggle other necessities, then decrease the quality and variety of household members' diets, then decrease the frequency and quantity of adults' food intake, and finally decrease the frequency and quantity of children's food intake. All questions refer to the previous 12 months and include a qualifying phrase reminding respondents to report only those occurrences that resulted from inadequate financial resources. Restrictions to food intake due to dieting or busy schedules are excluded. The omission of homeless persons may be a cause of underreporting. Data are from the Food Security Supplement to the Current Population Survey (CPS); for details about the CPS, see text, Section 1 and Appendix III]

Household food	Number (1,000)					Percent distribution				
	2005	2007	2008	2009	2010	2005	2007	2008	2009	2010
Households, total....................	**114,437**	**117,100**	**117,565**	**118,174**	**118,756**	**100.0**	**100.0**	**100.0**	**100.0**	**100.0**
Food-secure.................................	101,851	104,089	100,416	100,820	101,527	89.0	88.9	85.4	85.3	85.5
Food-insecure.............................	12,586	13,011	17,149	17,354	17,229	11.0	11.1	14.6	14.7	14.5
With low food security [1]............	8,158	8,262	10,426	10,601	10,872	7.1	7.0	8.9	9.0	9.1
With very low food security [2]...........	4,428	4,749	6,723	6,753	6,357	3.9	4.1	5.7	5.7	5.4
Adult members......................	**217,897**	**223,467**	**225,461**	**227,543**	**229,129**	**100.0**	**100.0**	**100.0**	**100.0**	**100.0**
In food-secure households..............	195,172	199,672	193,026	194,579	196,505	89.6	89.4	85.6	85.5	85.8
In food-insecure households............	22,725	23,795	32,435	32,964	32,624	10.4	10.6	14.4	14.5	14.2
With low food security.....................	15,146	15,602	20,320	20,741	21,357	7.0	7.0	9.0	9.1	9.3
With very low food security [2]..........	7,579	8,193	12,115	12,223	11,267	3.5	3.7	5.4	5.4	4.9
Households with children with very low food security among children [3]..	270	323	506	469	386	0.7	0.8	1.3	1.2	1.0
Child members......................	**73,604**	**73,575**	**74,106**	**74,207**	**74,905**	**100.0**	**100.0**	**100.0**	**100.0**	**100.0**
In food-secure households..............	61,201	61,140	57,433	57,010	58,697	83.1	83.1	77.5	76.8	78.4
In food-insecure households............	12,403	12,435	16,673	17,197	16,208	16.9	16.9	22.5	23.2	21.6
With very low food security among children [3]......................	606	691	1,077	988	976	0.8	0.9	1.5	1.3	1.3

[1] Prior to 2006, USDA described these households as food insecure without hunger. [2] Food intake of one or more members in these households was reduced and normal eating patterns disrupted at some time during the year because of the household's food insecurity. Prior to 2006, USDA described these households as food insecure with hunger. [3] Percentages omit households with no children. The food security survey measures food security status at the household level. Not all children residing in food-insecure households were directly affected by the households' food insecurity. Similarly, not all children in households classified as having very low food security among children were subject to the reductions in food intake and disruptions in eating patterns that characterize this condition. Young children, in particular, are often protected from effects of the households' food insecurity.

Source: U.S. Department of Agriculture, Economic Research Service, *Household Food Security in the United States, 2010*, Economic Research Report Number 125, September 2011. See also <http://www.ers.usda.gov/topics/food-nutrition-assistance/food-security-in-the-us.aspx>.

Table 217. Children Who Are Obese by Age, Sex, Race, and Hispanic Origin: 1976 to 2010

[In percent. For children aged 6-17. Data are from U.S. National Center for Health Statistics, National Health and Nutrition Examination Surveys, a program of studies that combines interviews and physical examinations to assess the health and nutritional status of adults and children. Children classified as obese have a body mass index (BMI) at or above the 95th percentile of the sex-specific BMI growth charts]

Selected characteristic	1976–1980	1988–1994	1999–2000	2001–2002	2003–2004	2005–2006	2007–2008	2009–2010
Total...................................	**5.7**	**11.2**	**15.0**	**16.5**	**18.0**	**16.5**	**19.2**	**18.0**
Race and Hispanic Origin: [1]								
White, non-Hispanic....................	4.9	10.5	11.3	14.6	17.3	13.8	17.4	14.6
Black, non-Hispanic....................	8.2	14.0	21.1	20.4	21.7	21.3	22.4	25.7
Hispanic origin [2,3]...................	(NA)	(NA)	(NA)	(NA)	(NA)	(NA)	24.4	23.1
Mexican-American [2,3]...............	(NA)	15.4	24.1	21.5	19.6	25.6	24.2	23.4
Sex:								
Male...................................	5.5	11.8	15.7	18.0	19.1	17.2	21.0	19.7
Female.................................	5.8	10.6	14.3	15.1	16.8	15.9	17.3	16.2
Ages 6-11...............................	6.5	11.3	15.1	16.3	18.8	15.1	19.6	18.0
Male...................................	6.7	11.6	15.7	17.5	19.9	16.2	21.2	20.1
Female.................................	6.4	11.0	14.3	14.9	17.6	14.1	18.0	15.7
Ages 12-17..............................	5.0	11.1	14.9	16.8	17.2	17.8	18.8	18.0
Male...................................	4.5	12.0	15.6	18.4	18.3	18.1	20.8	19.4
Female.................................	5.4	10.2	14.2	15.2	16.0	17.5	16.7	16.5

NA Not available. [1] Includes other races not shown separately. [2] Persons of Hispanic and Mexican origin may be any race. [3] From 1976 to 2006, the survey sample was designed to provide estimates specifically for persons of Mexican origin. Beginning in 2007, the survey allows for reporting of both total Hispanics and Mexican Americans.

Source: Federal Interagency Forum on Child and Family Statistics. "America's Children in Brief: Key National Indicators of Well-Being, 2012," accessed September 2012, <http://www.childstats.gov/americaschildren/index.asp>.

Table 218. Youth with a Major Depressive Episode in the Past Year by Selected Characteristics: 2004 to 2010

[In percent. Data are from Sustance Abuse and Mental Health Services Administration, National Survey on Drug Use and Health. Data collection is through in-person interviews with sampled persons. Major Depressive Episode is defined as a period of at least 2 weeks when a person experienced a depressed mood or loss of interest or pleasure in daily activities and had at least four additional symptoms (such as problems with sleep, eating, energy, concentration, and feelings of self-worth)]

Item	2004	2005	2006	2007	2008	2009	2010
Total..................................	**9.0**	**8.8**	**7.9**	**8.2**	**8.3**	**8.1**	**8.0**
Age:							
12-13 years...........................	5.4	5.2	4.9	4.3	4.8	4.6	4.3
14-15 years...........................	9.2	9.5	7.9	8.4	8.4	8.8	8.9
16-17 years...........................	12.3	11.5	10.7	11.5	11.1	10.4	10.6
Sex:							
Male..................................	5.0	4.5	4.2	4.6	4.3	4.7	4.4
Female................................	13.1	13.3	11.8	11.9	12.4	11.7	11.8
Race and Hispanic Origin: [1]							
White.................................	9.2	9.1	8.1	8.7	8.7	8.3	8.5
Black.................................	7.7	7.6	6.4	7.8	7.0	7.9	6.8
American Indian or Alaska Native......	7.8	6.1	9.3	4.6	10.1	7.5	7.4
Asian.................................	8.3	6.0	7.6	6.8	7.6	7.6	5.6
Two or more races.....................	11.7	10.5	13.0	10.0	12.0	7.9	9.4
Hispanic..............................	9.1	9.1	8.0	7.1	7.5	7.7	7.8
Poverty status:							
Below 100% poverty....................	(NA)	8.1	7.6	7.6	7.8	7.4	7.2
100-199% poverty......................	(NA)	9.6	9.0	8.9	9.0	8.6	9.0
200% poverty and above................	(NA)	8.7	7.6	8.0	8.1	8.1	7.8

NA Not available. [1] Respondents could choose more than one race. Those reporting more than one race were classified as "Two or more races." Data on Hispanic origin are collected separately. Persons of Hispanic origin may be of any race. Included in the total but not shown separately are persons of Native Hawaiian or Other Pacific Islander origin.

Source: Federal Interagency Forum on Child and Family Statistics. "America's Children in Brief: Key National Indicators of Well-Being, 2012," accessed September 2012, <http://www.childstats.gov/americaschildren/index.asp>.

Table 219. Injuries Associated With Selected Consumer Products: 2010

[Estimates are based on a national probability sample of hospitals in the U.S. and its territories. Patient information is collected from each participating hospital for every emergency visit involving an injury associated with consumer products. From this sample, the total number of product-related injuries treated in hospital emergency rooms nationwide is estimated]

Product Type	Number	Product Type	Number
Items for infants/children:		Housewares:	
All nursery equipment	106,742	Cans, other containers	288,622
Baby strollers	15,294	Drinking glasses	86,665
High chairs	10,620	Knives	413,230
Playground equipment (excl. swings)	248,673	Tableware and flatware	97,980
Swings or swings sets	65,555		
Toys	241,745	Tools & garden equipment:	
		Chain saws	30,928
Sports & recreational equipment		Hand garden tools	79,528
ATV's, mopeds, minibikes, etc.	230,666	Lawn mowers	89,518
Bicycles & accessories	541,746	Power home tools (excl. saws)	23,625
Exercise equipment	61,196	Power home workshop saws	80,688
Nonpowder guns, bb's, pellets	19,221	Workshop Manual Tools	131,762
Skateboards	130,627		
Snowskiing, snowboarding	103,274	Household appliances:	
Trampolines	92,159	Cooking ranges, ovens, etc.	49,745
Water slides	14,235	Heating stoves, space heaters	25,280
		Small kitchen appliances	47,410
Home entertainment equipment		Washers, dryers	22,861
Computers (equipment and electronic games)	38,699		
Television sets & stands	73,040	Home furnishings & fixtures	
		Bathroom structures & fixtures	430,174
Personal use items		Bathtubs or showers	294,865
Crutches, canes or walkers	133,527	Beds, mattresses, pillows	714,873
Grooming devices	43,852	Carpets, rugs	154,240
Razors, shavers, razor blades	42,350	Chairs, sofas, sofa beds	590,118
Wheelchairs	145,850	Hot tubs or home spas	8,371
		Tables [1]	357,613
		Toilets	103,998

[1] Excludes baby-changing and television tables or stands.

Source: Consumer Product Safety Commission, National Electronic Injury Surveillance System (NEISS), <http://www.cpsc.gov/library/neiss.html>, accessed September 2012.

Table 220. Per Capita Consumption of Selected Beverages by Type: 1980 to 2010

[In gallons. See headnote, Table 222. Per capita consumption uses U.S. resident population, July 1, for all beverages except coffee, tea, and fruit juices which use U.S. total population (Resident plus Armed Forces overseas), July 1]

Beverages	1980	1990	1995	2000	2005	2007	2008	2009	2010
Nonalcoholic	104.0	112.6	107.5	114.8	(NA)	(NA)	(NA)	(NA)	(NA)
Milk (plain and flavored)	27.5	25.7	23.9	22.5	21.0	20.6	20.8	20.6	20.1
Whole	17.0	10.5	8.6	8.1	7.0	6.4	6.1	5.9	5.6
Reduced-fat, light, and skim [1]	10.5	15.2	15.3	14.4	14.1	14.3	14.6	14.6	14.6
Tea	7.3	6.9	7.9	7.8	8.0	8.4	8.0	9.0	8.9
Coffee	26.7	26.8	20.2	26.3	24.3	24.6	24.2	23.3	23.2
Carbonated soft drinks	35.1	46.2	47.4	49.3	(NA)	(NA)	(NA)	(NA)	(NA)
Diet	5.1	10.7	10.9	11.6	(NA)	(NA)	(NA)	(NA)	(NA)
Regular	29.9	35.6	36.5	37.7	(NA)	(NA)	(NA)	(NA)	(NA)
Fruit juices	7.4	7.0	8.1	8.9	8.1	7.9	6.9	7.4	7.2

NA Not available. [1] Includes buttermilk.

Source: U.S. Department of Agriculture, Economic Research Service, "Food Availability (Per Capita) Data System," <http://www.ers.usda.gov/data-products/food-availability-(per-capita)-data-system.aspx>.

Table 221. Per Capita Utilization of Selected Commercially Produced Fruits and Vegetables: 1980 to 2010

[In pounds, farm weight. Domestic food use of fresh fruits and vegetables reflects the fresh-market share of commodity production plus imports and minus exports. Based on Census Bureau estimated resident population]

Commodity	1980	1990	1995	2000	2005	2007	2008	2009	2010
Fruits and vegetables, total [1]	**603.0**	**648.4**	**688.2**	**710.5**	**684.3**	**667.6**	**649.0**	**644.2**	**651.4**
Fruits, total	265.0	256.8	273.7	286.0	269.7	261.3	256.6	253.4	258.3
Fresh fruits [2]	106.2	116.6	123.1	128.5	125.0	123.3	126.5	124.1	127.9
Noncitrus [2]	80.1	95.2	99.2	105.0	103.4	105.4	105.8	103.4	106.4
Apples	19.2	19.6	18.7	17.5	16.7	16.4	15.9	16.3	15.5
Avocados	2.1	1.4	1.6	2.2	3.5	3.5	3.8	4.2	3.5
Bananas	20.8	24.3	27.1	28.4	25.2	26.0	25.0	22.0	25.6
Blueberries	0.2	0.1	0.3	0.3	0.4	0.6	0.8	1.0	1.1
Cantaloupes	5.8	9.2	9.0	11.1	9.6	9.6	8.9	9.1	8.5
Cherries	0.7	0.4	0.3	0.6	0.9	1.2	1.0	1.6	1.3
Grapes	4.0	7.8	7.4	7.4	8.6	8.0	8.5	7.9	8.2
Honeydew melons	1.4	2.1	1.9	2.3	1.9	1.8	1.7	1.6	1.5
Mangoes	0.2	0.5	1.1	1.8	1.9	2.1	2.1	2.0	2.2
Papayas	0.2	0.2	0.4	0.7	0.9	1.1	1.0	1.2	1.2
Peaches and nectarines	7.1	5.5	5.3	5.3	4.8	4.5	5.1	4.4	4.7
Pears	2.6	3.2	3.4	3.4	2.9	3.1	3.1	3.2	2.9
Pineapples	1.5	2.0	1.9	3.2	4.9	5.0	5.1	5.1	5.7
Plums and prunes	1.5	1.5	0.9	1.2	1.1	1.0	0.9	0.7	0.8
Strawberries	2.0	3.3	4.1	4.9	5.9	6.3	6.5	7.2	7.3
Watermelons	10.7	13.3	15.2	13.8	13.5	14.4	15.6	14.9	15.5
Fresh citrus	26.1	21.4	23.8	23.5	21.6	17.9	20.6	20.7	21.6
Oranges and temples	14.3	12.4	11.8	11.7	11.4	7.5	9.9	9.1	9.7
Tangerines and tangelos	2.2	1.3	2.0	2.9	2.5	2.6	3.1	3.1	3.8
Lemons	1.9	2.6	2.8	2.4	2.9	2.8	2.0	3.1	2.8
Limes	0.4	0.7	1.2	1.4	2.1	2.3	2.5	2.5	2.6
Grapefruit	7.3	4.4	6.0	5.1	2.6	2.8	3.2	2.8	2.8
Processed fruits	158.8	140.3	150.6	157.5	144.7	138.0	130.1	129.3	130.3
Frozen fruits [3]	3.3	4.3	4.3	4.6	5.2	5.3	4.9	4.9	5.0
Dried fruits [4]	11.3	12.1	12.7	10.4	10.0	9.8	9.8	9.2	9.4
Canned fruits [5]	24.4	20.8	17.2	17.5	16.6	16.0	15.6	15.5	14.8
Fruit juices [6]	119.0	102.7	116.2	124.6	112.3	106.3	99.0	99.1	100.5
Vegetables, total	338.0	391.6	414.5	424.6	414.6	406.3	392.4	390.8	393.1
Fresh vegetables [7]	151.6	176.4	188.1	200.7	196.5	194.0	188.9	184.8	187.1
Asparagus	0.3	0.6	0.6	1.0	1.1	1.2	1.2	1.3	1.4
Bell peppers (all uses)	2.9	5.9	7.0	8.2	9.2	9.4	9.6	9.8	9.9
Broccoli	1.4	3.4	4.3	5.9	5.3	5.6	6.0	6.2	5.6
Cabbage	8.0	8.3	8.1	8.9	7.8	8.0	8.1	7.3	7.5
Carrots	6.2	8.3	11.2	9.2	8.7	8.0	8.1	7.4	7.6
Cauliflower	1.1	2.2	1.6	1.7	1.8	1.7	1.6	1.7	1.3
Celery (all uses)	7.4	7.2	6.9	6.3	5.9	6.3	6.2	6.2	6.2
Corn (sweet)	6.5	6.7	7.8	9.0	8.7	9.2	9.1	9.2	9.2
Cucumbers	3.9	4.7	5.6	6.4	6.2	6.4	6.4	6.8	6.8
Garlic (all uses)	0.9	1.3	1.8	2.2	2.4	2.7	2.8	2.4	2.3
Lettuce, head	25.6	27.7	22.2	23.5	20.9	18.4	16.8	16.1	16.1
Lettuce, Romaine and leaf	(NA)	3.8	5.9	8.4	9.7	11.5	10.4	10.0	10.7
Mushrooms	1.2	2.0	2.0	2.6	2.6	2.5	2.4	2.4	2.5
Onions	11.4	15.1	17.8	18.9	20.9	21.6	20.2	19.6	19.9
Potatoes	51.1	46.7	49.2	47.1	41.3	38.7	37.8	36.4	35.6
Pumpkin (all uses)	(NA)	4.5	6.0	4.7	4.9	5.0	4.8	4.1	4.5
Snap beans	1.3	1.1	1.6	2.0	1.8	2.2	2.0	1.7	1.9
Spinach	0.4	0.8	0.7	1.4	2.3	1.6	1.8	2.1	1.8
Squash (all uses)	2.3	3.5	3.8	4.5	4.4	4.1	4.2	4.4	4.3
Sweet potatoes (all uses)	4.4	4.4	4.2	4.2	4.5	5.1	5.0	5.2	6.3
Tomatoes	12.8	15.5	16.8	19.0	20.2	19.2	18.5	19.6	20.9
Processed vegetables	186.5	215.2	226.4	223.8	218.1	212.3	203.5	206.0	206.0
Selected vegetables for freezing [8]	51.5	66.8	78.8	79.3	76.4	75.8	72.6	71.3	70.2
Selected vegetables for canning [9]	102.5	110.3	108.2	103.2	104.8	96.7	94.6	100.4	99.1
Vegetables for dehydrating [10]	10.5	14.6	14.5	17.3	13.9	14.1	13.9	13.7	12.7
Potatoes for chips	16.5	16.4	16.4	15.6	16.0	18.6	15.7	13.7	15.0
Legumes [11]	5.4	7.2	8.4	8.4	6.9	7.1	6.8	6.8	8.9

NA Not available. [1] Excludes wine grapes. [2] Includes other fruits not shown separately. [3] Apples, apricots, blackberries, blueberries, boysenberries, cherries, loganberries, peaches, plums, prunes, raspberries, and strawberries. [4] Apples, apricots, dates, figs, peaches, pears, prunes, and raisins. [5] Apples, apricots, cherries, olives, peaches, pears, pineapples, plums, and prunes. [6] Apple, cranberry, grape, grapefruit, lemon, lime, orange, pineapple, and prunes. [7] Includes other vegetables not shown separately. [8] Asparagus, snap beans, lima beans, broccoli, carrots, cauliflower, sweet corn, green peas, potatoes, spinach, and miscellaneous vegetables. [9] Asparagus, snap beans, beets, cabbage, carrots, chili peppers, sweet corn, cucumbers for pickling, green peas, lima beans, mushrooms, spinach, and tomatoes. [10] Onions and potatoes. [11] Dry peas, lentils, and dry edible beans.

Source: U.S. Department of Agriculture, Economic Research Service, "Food Availability (Per Capita) Data System," <http://www.ers.usda.gov/data-products/food-availability-(per-capita)-data-system.aspx>.

Table 222. Per Capita Consumption of Major Food Commodities: 1980 to 2010

[In pounds, retail weight, except as indicated. Consumption represents the residual after exports, nonfood use and ending stocks are subtracted from the sum of beginning stocks, domestic production, and imports. Based on Census Bureau estimated resident population plus Armed Forces overseas for most commodities. For commodities not shipped overseas in substantial amounts, such as fluid milk and cream, the resident population is used]

Commodity	Unit	1980	1990	2000	2005	2008	2009	2010
Red meat, total (boneless, trimmed weight) [1,2]	Pounds	126.4	112.2	113.7	110.2	106.6	105.7	102.1
Beef	Pounds	72.1	63.9	64.5	62.5	59.6	58.1	56.7
Veal	Pounds	1.3	0.9	0.5	0.4	0.3	0.3	0.3
Lamb and mutton	Pounds	1.0	1.0	0.8	0.8	0.7	0.7	0.7
Pork	Pounds	52.1	46.4	47.8	46.6	45.9	46.6	44.3
Poultry (boneless, trimmed weight) [2]	Pounds	40.8	56.2	67.9	73.7	72.6	69.4	70.9
Chicken	Pounds	32.7	42.4	54.2	60.5	58.7	56.0	58.0
Turkey	Pounds	8.1	13.8	13.7	13.2	13.9	13.3	12.9
Fish and shellfish (boneless, trimmed weight)	Pounds	12.4	14.9	15.2	16.2	16.0	15.8	15.8
Eggs	Number	271	234	251	256	247	247	246
Shell	Number	236	186	172	173	165	169	167
Processed	Number	35	48	79	83	81	77	79
Dairy products, total [3]	Pounds	543.1	568.0	591.7	597.8	603.1	604.6	610.7
Fluid milk products [4]	Gallons	27.9	26.2	23.2	22.2	22.1	22.1	21.7
Beverage milks	Gallons	27.6	25.7	22.5	21.0	20.7	20.6	20.1
Plain whole milk	Gallons	16.5	10.2	7.7	6.7	5.9	5.7	5.4
Plain reduced-fat milk (2%)	Gallons	6.3	9.1	7.1	6.9	7.3	7.3	7.0
Reduced fat milk (1%) and skim milk	Gallons	3.1	4.9	6.1	5.6	5.7	5.7	5.8
Flavored whole milk	Gallons	0.6	0.3	0.4	0.3	0.2	0.2	0.2
Flavored milks other than whole	Gallons	0.6	0.8	1.0	1.4	1.4	1.4	1.6
Buttermilk	Gallons	0.5	0.4	0.3	0.2	0.2	0.2	0.2
Yogurt (excl. frozen)	1/2 pints	4.6	7.8	12.0	19.1	21.7	23.1	25.0
Fluid cream products [5]	1/2 pints	10.5	14.3	18.3	24.1	23.8	23.6	22.6
Cream [6]	1/2 pints	6.3	8.7	11.6	14.9	15.1	15.0	14.1
Sour cream and dips	1/2 pints	3.4	4.7	6.1	8.3	7.9	7.8	7.7
Condensed and evaporated milks	Pounds	7.0	7.9	5.8	5.9	7.3	7.1	7.0
Whole milk	Pounds	3.8	3.1	2.0	2.2	2.2	2.2	1.8
Skim milk	Pounds	3.3	4.8	3.8	3.7	5.1	5.0	5.2
Cheese [7]	Pounds	17.5	24.6	29.8	32.5	33.1	33.3	33.2
American [8]	Pounds	9.6	11.1	12.7	13.5	13.6	13.9	13.3
Cheddar	Pounds	6.8	9.0	9.7	10.1	10.1	10.4	10.4
Italian [8]	Pounds	4.4	9.0	12.1	13.4	14.0	14.0	14.6
Mozzarella	Pounds	3.0	6.9	9.3	10.2	10.6	10.7	11.3
Other [8]	Pounds	3.3	4.3	5.0	5.7	5.6	5.5	5.1
Swiss	Pounds	1.3	1.4	1.0	1.3	1.1	1.2	1.2
Cream and Neufchatel	Pounds	0.9	1.6	2.4	2.4	2.5	2.5	2.4
Cottage cheese, total	Pounds	4.5	3.4	2.6	2.6	2.3	2.4	2.3
Lowfat	Pounds	0.8	1.2	1.3	1.4	1.3	1.3	1.3
Frozen dairy products	Pounds	23.9	26.1	25.4	23.0	22.6	21.8	21.2
Ice cream	Pounds	16.4	14.8	15.6	14.6	13.7	13.4	13.3
Lowfat ice cream	Pounds	5.8	6.3	6.4	5.8	5.9	6.1	5.8
Sherbet	Pounds	1.2	1.2	1.1	1.1	1.1	1.0	1.0
Frozen yogurt	Pounds	(NA)	2.8	2.0	1.3	1.5	0.9	1.0
Fats and oils:								
Total, fat content only	Pounds	55.6	60.3	81.7	85.5	85.0	77.7	82.1
Butter (product weight)	Pounds	4.5	4.0	4.5	4.6	5.0	5.0	4.9
Margarine (product weight)	Pounds	11.3	10.9	8.2	4.0	4.2	3.7	3.5
Lard (direct use)	Pounds	2.3	0.9	0.8	1.6	1.0	1.5	1.5
Edible beef tallow (direct use)	Pounds	1.1	0.6	4.0	3.8	2.9	0.7	3.3
Shortening	Pounds	16.9	20.6	31.5	29.0	18.0	15.9	15.3
Salad and cooking oils	Pounds	21.2	25.1	33.7	42.7	54.0	51.0	53.6
Other edible fats and oils	Pounds	1.5	1.2	1.5	1.6	1.6	1.7	1.7
Flour and cereal products [9]	Pounds	146.3	180.8	199.2	192.4	196.5	194.6	194.8
Wheat flour	Pounds	116.9	135.6	146.3	134.3	136.5	134.6	134.7
Rice, milled	Pounds	10.9	15.9	18.9	21.0	21.1	21.2	21.2
Corn products	Pounds	12.9	21.4	28.4	31.4	33.0	33.0	33.1
Oat products	Pounds	3.9	6.5	4.3	4.6	4.8	4.7	4.7
Caloric sweeteners, total [10]	Pounds	120.2	132.5	148.9	142.1	135.6	130.5	131.6
Sugar, refined cane and beet	Pounds	83.6	64.4	65.5	63.0	65.0	63.4	65.8
Corn sweeteners [11]	Pounds	35.3	66.8	81.8	77.6	69.1	65.7	64.3
High-fructose corn syrup	Pounds	19.0	49.6	62.6	59.1	53.0	50.1	48.8
Other:								
Cocoa beans	Pounds	3.4	5.4	5.9	6.5	5.6	5.5	5.5
Coffee (green beans)	Pounds	10.3	10.3	10.3	9.5	9.5	9.1	9.0
Peanuts (shelled)	Pounds	5.0	6.1	5.8	6.7	6.4	6.6	6.9
Tree nuts (shelled)	Pounds	1.8	2.5	2.6	2.6	3.5	3.7	4.0

NA Not available. [1] Excludes edible offals. [2] Excludes shipments to Puerto Rico and the other U.S. possessions. [3] Milk-equivalent, milk-fat basis. Includes butter. [4] Fluid milk figures are aggregates of commercial sales and milk produced and consumed on farms. [5] Includes eggnog, not shown separately. [6] Heavy cream, light cream, and half-and-half. [7] Excludes full-skim American, cottage, pot, and baker's cheese. [8] Includes other cheeses, not shown separately. [9] Includes rye flour and barley products, not shown separately. Excludes quantities used in alcoholic beverages. [10] Dry weight. Includes edible syrups (maple, molasses, etc.) and honey, not shown separately. [11] Includes glucose and dextrose, not shown separately.

Source: U.S. Department of Agriculture, Economic Research Service, "Food Availability (Per Capita) Data System," <http://www.ers.usda.gov/data-products/food-availability-(per-capita)-data-system.aspx>.

Table 223. Nutrition—Nutrients in Foods Available for Civilian Consumption Per Capita Per Day: 1970 to 2006

[Computed by the Center for Nutrition Policy and Promotion (CNPP). Based on Economic Research Service (ERS) estimates of per capita quantities of food available for consumption from "Food Consumption, Prices, and, Expenditures," on imputed consumption data for foods no longer reported by ERS, and on CNPP estimates of quantities of produce from home gardens. Food supply estimates do not reflect loss of food or nutrients from further marketing or home processing. Enrichment and fortification levels of iron, zinc, thiamin, riboflavin, niacin, folate, vitamin A, vitamin B6, vitamin B12, and Vitamin C are included]

Nutrient	Unit	1970–79	1980–89	1990–99	2000	2006
Food energy	Kilocalories	3,200	3,400	3,600	3,900	3,900
Carbohydrate	Grams	395	421	478	495	474
Fiber	Grams	20	22	24	24	25
Protein	Grams	96	100	108	111	111
Total fat [1]	Grams	143	151	150	169	178
Saturated	Grams	49	50	48	52	54
Monounsaturated	Grams	57	61	64	75	77
Polyunsaturated	Grams	27	30	31	35	39
Cholesterol	Milligrams	430	420	400	410	420
Vitamin A	Micrograms RAE [2]	1,050	1,050	1,100	1,090	940
Carotene	Micrograms	560	600	710	690	690
Vitamin E	Milligrams a-TE [3]	14	16	17	20	21
Vitamin C	Milligrams	109	115	118	121	106
Thiamin	Milligrams	2	3	3	3	3
Riboflavin	Milligrams	3	3	3	3	3
Niacin	Milligrams	25	29	31	32	32
Vitamin B6	Milligrams	2	2	2	2	2
Folate [4]	Micrograms DFE [5]	341	383	504	902	874
Vitamin B12	Micrograms	9	8	8	8	8
Calcium	Milligrams	930	930	980	980	960
Phosphorus	Milligrams	1,540	1,590	1,690	1,720	1,700
Magnesium	Milligrams	340	360	390	400	400
Iron	Milligrams	17	20	23	23	23
Zinc	Milligrams	13	14	15	15	16
Copper	Milligrams	2	2	2	2	2
Potassium	Milligrams	3,510	3,550	3,720	3,780	3,620
Sodium [6]	Milligrams	1,210	1,210	1,240	1,230	1,150
Selenium	Micrograms	133	143	163	179	181

[1] Includes other types of fat not shown separately. [2] Retinol activity equivalents. [3] Alpha-Tocopherol equivalents. [4] Reflects new terminology from Institute of Medicine's Dietary Reference Intakes reports. [5] Dietary Folate Equivalents (DFE). [6] Does not include amount from processed foods; underestimates actual availability.

Source: U.S. Department of Agriculture, Center for Nutrition Policy and Promotion, *Nutrient Content of the U.S. Food Supply, 1909–2006*, <http://www.cnpp.usda.gov/USFoodSupply.htm>.

Section 4
Education

This section presents data primarily concerning formal education as a whole, at various levels, and for public and private schools. Data shown relate to the school-age population and school enrollment, educational attainment, education personnel, and financial aspects of education. In addition, data are shown for charter schools, homeschooling, security measures used in schools, technology usage in schools, and academic libraries. The chief sources are the decennial census of population and the Current Population Survey (CPS), both conducted by the U.S. Census Bureau (see text, Section 1, Population); annual, biennial, and other periodic surveys conducted by the National Center for Education Statistics (NCES), a part of the U.S. Department of Education; and surveys conducted by the National Education Association.

The censuses of population have included data on school enrollment since 1840 and on educational attainment since 1940. The CPS has reported on school enrollment annually since 1945 and on educational attainment periodically since 1947.

The NCES is continuing the pattern of statistical studies and surveys conducted by the U.S. Office of Education since 1870. The annual *Digest of Education Statistics* provides summary data on pupils, staff, finances, including government expenditures, and organization at the elementary, secondary, and higher education levels. It is also a primary source for detailed information on federal funds for education, projections of enrollment, graduates, and teachers. The *Condition of Education*, issued annually, presents a summary of information on education of particular interest to policymakers. NCES also conducts special studies periodically.

The census of governments, conducted by the Census Bureau every 5 years (for the years ending in "2" and "7"), provides data on school district finances and state and local government expenditures for education. Reports published by the Bureau of Labor Statistics contain data relating civilian labor force experience to educational attainment (see also Tables 603, 629, and 639 in Section 12, Labor Force, Employment, and Earnings).

Types and sources of data— The statistics in this section are of two general types. One type, exemplified by data from the Census Bureau, is based on direct interviews with individuals to obtain information about their own and their family members' education. Data of this type relate to school enrollment and level of education attained, classified by age, sex, and other characteristics of the population. The school enrollment statistics reflect attendance or enrollment in any regular school within a given period; educational attainment statistics reflect the highest grade completed by an individual, or beginning 1992, the highest diploma or degree received.

Beginning in 2001, the CPS used Census 2000 population controls. From 1994 to 2000, the CPS used 1990 census population controls plus adjustment for undercount. Also the survey changed from paper to computer-assisted technology. For years 1981 through 1993, 1980 census population controls were used; 1971 through 1980, 1970 census population controls had been used. These changes had little impact on summary measures (e.g., medians) and proportional measures (e.g., enrollment rates); however, use of the controls may have significant impact on absolute numbers.

The second type, generally exemplified by data from the NCES and the National Education Association, is based on reports from administrators of educational institutions and of state and local agencies having jurisdiction over education. Data of this type relate to enrollment, attendance, staff, and finances for the nation, individual states, and local areas.

Unlike the NCES, the Census Bureau does not regularly include specialized vocational, trade, business, or correspondence schools in its surveys. The NCES includes nursery schools and kindergartens that are part of regular grade schools in their enrollment figures. The Census Bureau includes all nursery schools and kindergartens. At the higher education level, the statistics of both agencies are concerned with institutions granting degrees or offering work acceptable for degree-credit, such as junior colleges.

School attendance—All states require that children attend school. While state laws vary as to the ages and circumstances of compulsory attendance, generally they require that formal schooling begin by age 6 and continue to age 16.

Schools—The NCES defines a school as "a division of the school system consisting of students composing one or more grade groups or other identifiable groups, organized as one unit with one or more teachers to give instruction of a defined type, and housed in a school plant of one or more buildings. More than one school may be housed in one school plant, as is the case when the elementary and secondary programs are housed in the same school plant."

Regular schools are those which advance a person toward a diploma or degree. They include public and private nursery schools, kindergartens, graded schools, colleges, universities, and professional schools.

Public schools are schools controlled and supported by local, state, or federal governmental agencies; private schools are those controlled and supported mainly by religious organizations or by private persons or organizations.

The Census Bureau defines *elementary* schools as including grades 1 through 8; *high* schools as including grades 9 through 12; and *colleges* as including junior or community colleges, regular 4-year colleges, and universities and graduate or professional schools. Statistics reported by the NCES and the National Education Association by type of organization, such as elementary level and secondary level, may not be strictly comparable with those from the Census Bureau because the grades included at the two levels vary, depending on the level assigned to the middle or junior high school by the local school systems.

School year—Except as otherwise indicated in the tables, data refer to the school year which, for elementary and secondary schools, generally begins in September of the preceding year and ends in June of the year stated. For the most part, statistics concerning school finances are for a 12-month period, usually July 1 to June 30. Enrollment data generally refer to a specific point in time, such as fall, as indicated in the tables.

Statistical reliability—For a discussion of statistical collection, estimation, and sampling procedures and measures of statistical reliability applicable to the Census Bureau and the NCES data, see Appendix III.

Table 224. School Enrollment: 1980 to 2020

[In thousands (58,305 represents 58,305,000). As of Fall]

Year	All levels			Pre-kindergarten through grade 8		Grades 9 through 12		College [3]	
	Total	Public	Private	Public	Private [1, 2]	Public	Private [1]	Public	Private
1980....................	58,305	50,335	7,971	27,647	3,992	13,231	1,339	9,457	2,640
1985....................	57,226	48,901	8,325	27,034	4,195	12,388	1,362	9,479	2,768
1990....................	60,683	52,061	8,622	29,876	4,512	11,341	1,136	10,845	2,974
1991....................	62,087	53,357	8,730	30,506	4,518	11,541	1,163	11,310	3,049
1992....................	62,987	54,208	8,779	31,088	4,528	11,735	1,148	11,385	3,102
1993....................	63,438	54,654	8,784	31,504	4,536	11,961	1,132	11,189	3,116
1994....................	64,385	55,245	9,139	31,896	4,856	12,215	1,138	11,134	3,145
1995....................	65,020	55,933	9,087	32,338	4,756	12,502	1,163	11,092	3,169
1996....................	65,911	56,732	9,180	32,762	4,755	12,849	1,178	11,121	3,247
1997....................	66,574	57,323	9,251	33,071	4,759	13,056	1,185	11,196	3,306
1998....................	67,033	57,676	9,357	33,344	4,776	13,195	1,212	11,138	3,369
1999....................	67,667	58,167	9,500	33,486	4,789	13,371	1,229	11,309	3,482
2000....................	68,685	58,956	9,729	33,686	4,906	13,517	1,264	11,753	3,560
2001....................	69,920	59,905	10,014	33,936	5,023	13,736	1,296	12,233	3,695
2002....................	71,015	60,935	10,080	34,114	4,915	14,069	1,306	12,752	3,860
2003....................	71,551	61,399	10,152	34,201	4,788	14,339	1,311	12,859	4,053
2004....................	72,154	61,776	10,379	34,178	4,756	14,618	1,331	12,980	4,292
2005....................	72,674	62,135	10,539	34,204	4,724	14,909	1,349	13,022	4,466
2006....................	73,066	62,496	10,570	34,235	4,631	15,081	1,360	13,180	4,579
2007....................	73,451	62,783	10,668	34,205	4,546	15,087	1,364	13,491	4,757
2008....................	74,076	63,238	10,838	34,286	4,365	14,980	1,342	13,972	5,131
2009....................	75,290	64,184	11,106	34,418	4,179	14,955	1,309	14,811	5,617
2010, proj. [4].....	75,720	64,449	11,271	34,637	4,092	14,668	1,306	15,143	5,873
2011, proj...........	76,321	65,063	11,258	34,892	4,057	14,530	1,266	15,640	5,934
2012, proj...........	76,522	65,309	11,212	35,129	4,034	14,512	1,229	15,668	5,949
2013, proj...........	76,988	65,749	11,238	35,368	4,025	14,545	1,194	15,836	6,019
2014, proj...........	77,708	66,389	11,319	35,579	4,027	14,689	1,160	16,121	6,132
2015, proj...........	78,448	67,037	11,410	35,829	4,042	14,830	1,134	16,378	6,234
2016, proj...........	79,169	67,662	11,507	36,161	4,073	14,877	1,103	16,624	6,331
2017, proj...........	79,879	68,277	11,602	36,491	4,110	14,939	1,077	16,847	6,415
2018, proj...........	80,588	68,881	11,708	36,803	4,146	15,000	1,060	17,078	6,502
2019, proj...........	81,309	69,496	11,813	37,121	4,181	15,083	1,052	17,292	6,579
2020, proj...........	82,014	70,110	11,905	37,444	4,216	15,222	1,056	17,444	6,632

[1] Since the biennial Private School Universe Survey (PSS) is collected in the fall of odd numbered years, even numbered years are estimated based on data from the PSS. [2] Includes private nursery and prekindergarten enrollment in schools that offer kindergarten or higher grades. [3] Data beginning 1996 based on new classification system. See footnote 1, Table 278. [4] Pre-K through 12 are projections; college data are actual.

Source: U.S. National Center for Education Statistics, *Digest of Education Statistics*, annual, and *Projections of Education Statistics*, annual. See also <http://nces.ed.gov/programs/digest/>.

Table 225. School Expenditures by Type of Control and Level of Instruction in Current and Constant (2009 to 2010) Dollars: 1980 to 2011

[In millions of dollars (160,075 represents $160,075,000,000). For school years ending in year shown. Data shown reflect historical revisions. Total expenditures for public elementary and secondary schools include current expenditures, interest on school debt and capital outlay. Based on survey of state education agencies; see source for details]

Year	Current dollars			Constant 2009-10 dollars [1]			
	Total	Elementary and secondary schools	Colleges and universities [2]	Total	Elementary and secondary schools		Colleges and universities [2]
		Total	Total		Total	Public	Total
1980.................	160,075	103,162	56,914	446,896	288,005	267,904	158,891
1985.................	239,351	149,400	89,951	490,472	306,147	280,737	184,326
1990.................	365,825	231,170	134,656	624,431	394,586	363,179	229,845
1993.................	439,676	274,435	165,241	668,607	417,328	384,633	251,279
1994.................	460,757	287,407	173,351	682,973	426,018	393,260	256,955
1995.................	485,169	302,200	182,969	699,119	435,465	402,034	263,654
1996.................	508,523	318,046	190,476	713,363	446,161	411,932	267,203
1997.................	538,854	338,951	[3] 199,903	734,944	462,296	427,107	[3] 272,648
1998.................	570,471	361,615	[3] 208,856	764,434	484,566	447,984	[3] 279,868
1999.................	603,847	384,638	219,209	795,388	506,646	468,710	288,742
2000.................	649,322	412,538	236,784	831,291	528,149	488,846	303,141
2001.................	705,017	444,811	260,206	872,694	550,603	508,516	322,092
2002.................	752,780	472,064	280,715	915,606	574,172	529,534	341,434
2003.................	795,691	492,807	302,884	946,988	586,512	541,405	360,476
2004.................	830,293	513,542	316,751	967,013	598,104	552,333	368,909
2005.................	875,988	540,969	335,019	990,428	611,642	564,833	378,787
2006.................	925,712	572,135	353,577	1,008,252	623,149	575,879	385,103
2007.................	984,034	608,495	375,539	1,044,757	646,044	596,887	398,713
2008.................	1,054,200	645,710	408,490	1,079,263	661,061	610,794	418,201
2009.................	1,089,854	659,110	430,744	1,100,399	665,487	616,013	434,912
2010 [2, 3].........	1,108,483	662,000	446,483	1,108,483	662,000	614,000	446,483
2011 [2, 3].........	1,133,000	673,000	460,000	1,111,000	660,000	614,000	451,000

[1] Constant dollars based on the Consumer Price Index, prepared by the Bureau of Labor Statistics, U.S. Department of Labor, adjusted to a school-year basis. [2] Data beginning 1996 based on new classification system. See footnote 1, Table 278. [3] Estimated. [4] Data for elementary and secondary education are estimated; data for degree-granting institutions are actual.

Source: U.S. National Center for Education Statistics, *Digest of Education Statistics*, annual. See also <http://www.nces.ed.gov/programs/digest/>.

Table 226. School Enrollment, Faculty, Graduates, and Finances—Projections: 2011 to 2017

[54,746 represents 54,746,000. As of Fall, except as indicated]

Item	Unit	2011	2012	2013	2014	2015	2016	2017
ELEMENTARY AND SECONDARY SCHOOLS								
School enrollment, total...............	1,000	54,746	54,905	55,133	55,455	55,836	56,214	56,617
Pre-kindergarten through grade 8........	1,000	38,949	39,163	39,394	39,606	39,872	40,234	40,602
Grades 9 through 12...................	1,000	15,797	15,742	15,739	15,849	15,964	15,980	16,015
Public.....................	1,000	49,422	49,642	49,914	50,268	50,659	51,038	51,430
Pre-kindergarten through grade 8........	1,000	34,892	35,129	35,368	35,579	35,829	36,161	36,491
Grades 9 through 12...................	1,000	14,530	14,512	14,545	14,689	14,830	14,939	14,939
Private....................	1,000	5,324	5,263	5,219	5,187	5,176	5,176	5,187
Pre-kindergarten through grade 8........	1,000	4,057	4,034	4,025	4,027	4,042	4,073	4,110
Grades 9 through 12...................	1,000	1,266	1,229	1,194	1,160	1,134	1,103	1,077
Classroom teachers, total FTE [1]........	1,000	3,679	3,696	3,725	3,752	3,782	3,814	3,846
Public....................	1,000	3,253	3,274	3,274	3,306	3,334	3,364	3,425
Private....................	1,000	426	422	419	419	418	419	420
High school graduates, total [2].........	1,000	3,220	3,197	3,154	3,132	3,165	3,183	3,231
Public....................	1,000	2,926	2,912	2,875	2,867	2,904	2,931	2,983
Public schools: [2]								
Average daily attendance (ADA)........	1,000	46,172	46,377	46,631	46,962	47,328	47,681	48,048
Current dollars: [3]								
Current school expenditure............	Bil. dol.	536	550	570	(NA)	(NA)	(NA)	(NA)
Per pupil in fall enrollment.............	Dollar	10,855	11,081	11,410	(NA)	(NA)	(NA)	(NA)
Constant (2008–2009) dollars: [3, 4]								
Current school expenditure............	Bil. dol.	515	518	525	541	557	572	586
Per pupil in fall enrollment.............	Dollar	10,428	10,434	10,524	10,760	10,987	11,206	11,389
HIGHER EDUCATION								
Enrollment, total...................	1,000	20,688	20,727	20,948	21,320	21,651	21,968	22,251
Male........................	1,000	8,896	8,894	8,941	9,028	9,100	9,172	9,239
Full-time....................	1,000	5,709	5,705	5,730	5,787	5,834	5,883	5,927
Part-time....................	1,000	3,186	3,189	3,211	3,242	3,266	3,289	3,312
Female......................	1,000	11,793	11,833	12,008	12,291	12,551	12,796	13,013
Full-time....................	1,000	7,145	7,151	7,232	7,371	7,495	7,610	7,714
Part-time....................	1,000	4,648	4,682	4,776	4,921	5,056	5,185	5,299
Public......................	1,000	14,998	15,023	15,180	15,445	15,682	15,909	16,115
Four-year institutions...............	1,000	7,817	7,833	7,913	8,048	8,167	8,280	8,379
Two-year institutions...............	1,000	7,181	7,190	7,266	7,397	7,515	7,629	7,736
Private.....................	1,000	5,691	5,704	5,769	5,875	5,970	6,059	6,137
Four-year institutions...............	1,000	5,271	5,285	5,346	5,445	5,533	5,616	5,688
Two-year institutions...............	1,000	420	420	423	430	437	443	449
Undergraduate....................	1,000	17,786	17,801	17,965	18,255	18,512	18,759	18,985
Postbaccalaureate.................	1,000	2,903	2,927	2,984	3,065	3,140	3,209	3,267
Full-time equivalent.................	1,000	15,677	15,692	15,840	16,099	16,329	16,548	16,745
Public......................	1,000	10,867	10,874	10,972	11,148	11,303	11,453	11,589
2-year.....................	1,000	4,326	4,325	4,364	4,437	4,502	4,565	4,626
4-year.....................	1,000	6,541	6,548	6,608	6,711	6,802	6,888	6,963
Private.....................	1,000	4,810	4,818	4,868	4,951	5,025	5,095	5,156
2-year.....................	1,000	389	389	392	398	404	409	415
4-year.....................	1,000	4,421	4,430	4,476	4,553	4,621	4,686	4,741
Degrees conferred, total [2]............	1,000	3,586	3,615	3,656	3,701	3,756	3,816	3,872
Associate's....................	1,000	895	899	906	915	927	940	953
Bachelor's....................	1,000	1,781	1,791	1,805	1,817	1,835	1,858	1,879
Master's.....................	1,000	730	741	756	776	795	813	829
Doctoral.....................	1,000	77	80	83	87	90	93	96
First-professional.................	1,000	103	104	105	107	109	112	114

NA Not available. [1] Full-time equivalent. [2] For school year ending in June the following year. [3] Limited financial projections are shown due to the uncertain behavior of inflation over the long term. [4] Based on the Consumer Price Index (CPI) for all urban consumers, U.S. Bureau of Labor Statistics. CPI adjusted to a school year basis by NCES.

Source: U.S. National Center for Education Statistics, *Projections of Education Statistics to 2020*. See also <http://www.nces.ed.gov/surveys/AnnualReports/>.

Table 227. Federal Funds for Education and Related Programs: 2005 to 2011

[In millions of dollars (146,207.0 represents $146,207,000,000), except percent. For fiscal years ending in September. Figures represent on-budget funds]

Level, agency, and program	2005	2010	2011[1]
Total, all programs	**146,207.0**	**179,860.4**	**(NA)**
Percent of federal budget outlays	5.9	5.2	(NA)
Elementary/secondary education programs	**68,957.7**	**87,548.8**	**78,509.2**
Department of Education[2]	37,477.6	49,621.5	38,693.6
Grants for the disadvantaged	14,635.6	15,864.7	15,535.9
School improvement programs	7,918.1	16,999.9	6,741.7
Indian education	121.9	750.0	733.5
Special education	10,940.3	12,587.0	12,542.9
Vocational and adult education	1,967.1	2,016.4	1,738.9
Education reform—Goals 2000	-35.0	(X)	(X)
Department of Agriculture[2]	12,577.3	17,875.6	19,978.6
Child nutrition programs	11,901.9	16,383.4	18,489.1
Agricultural Marketing Service—commodities[3]	399.3	1,100.0	1,085.0
Department of Defense[2]	1,786.3	1,981.3	2,051.8
Overseas dependents schools	1,060.9	1,186.6	1,224.6
Section VI schools[4]	410.2	435.1	449.7
Department of Health and Human Services	8,003.3	8,547.0	8,539.3
Head Start	6,842.3	7,234.0	7,235.0
Social security student benefits	1,161.0	1,313.0	1,304.3
Department of Homeland Security[2]	0.5	1.9	2.1
Department of the Interior[2]	938.5	783.1	804.2
Mineral Leasing Act and other funds	140.0	73.0	65.7
Indian Education	797.5	709.1	737.5
Department of Justice	554.5	876.2	875.0
Inmate programs	554.5	873.6	873.0
Department of Labor	5,654.0	6,826.0	6,474.0
Job Corps	1,521.0	1,850.0	1,714.0
Department of Veterans Affairs	1,815.0	760.5	821.8
Vocational rehab for disabled veterans	1,815.0	760.5	821.8
Other agencies and programs	153.2	275.8	268.8
Higher education programs	**38,587.3**	**50,166.3**	**64,310.0**
Department of Education[2]	31,420.0	36,539.7	48,880.3
Student financial assistance	15,209.5	25,959.5	43,412.1
Federal Family Education Loans[5]	10,777.5	3,933.0	-123.4
Department of Agriculture	62.0	80.7	81.7
Department of Commerce	(NA)	(NA)	(NA)
Department of Defense	1,858.3	2,550.7	2,297.2
Tuition assistance for military personnel	608.1	669.9	567.4
Service academies[6]	300.8	402.6	348.8
Senior ROTC	537.5	885.5	851.9
Professional development education	411.9	592.6	529.1
Department of Health and Human Services[2]	1,433.5	1,297.7	1,303.4
Health professions training programs	581.7	406.0	408.0
National Health Service Corps scholarships	45.0	41.0	41.0
National Institutes of Health training grants[7]	756.0	775.2	780.9
Department of Homeland Security	36.4	57.5	61.3
Department of the Interior	249.2	160.8	93.0
Shared revenues, Mineral Leasing Act and other receipts—estimated education share	146.2	16.2	13.8
Indian programs	103.0	144.6	79.2
Department of State	424.0	609.0	643.0
Department of Transportation	73.0	95.0	99.0
Department of Veterans Affairs[2]	2,478.6	8,042.4	10,131.5
Post-Vietnam veterans	1.1	0.9	0.7
All-volunteer-force educational assistance	2,071.0	1,854.9	1,535.9
Other agencies and programs[2]	552.2	732.9	719.6
National Endowment for the Humanities	29.3	47.9	47.0
National Science Foundation	490.0	646.0	631.0
Other education programs[2]	**6,908.5**	**9,326.7**	**9,427.3**
Department of Education[2]	3,538.9	5,073.1	5,303.3
Administration	548.8	1,531.2	1,793.9
Rehabilitative services and handicapped research	2,973.3	3,506.9	3,474.7
Department of Agriculture	468.6	567.4	552.0
Department of Health and Human Services	313.0	340.0	341.0
Department of Homeland Security	278.2	341.1	380.5
Department of Justice	26.1	33.6	33.6
Department of State	109.3	120.5	120.0
Other agencies and programs[2]	2,174.3	2,850.9	2,696.7
Agency for International Development	574.0	542.7	771.3
Library of Congress	430.0	516.0	530.0
National Endowment for the Arts	2.5	2.9	2.7
National Endowment for the Humanities	88.0	94.6	94.0
Research programs at universities and related institutions[2]	**31,753.5**	**32,818.5**	**(NA)**
Department of Agriculture	709.7	849.9	(NA)
Department of Commerce	(NA)	2,675.9	(NA)
Department of Defense	2,675.9	2,651.5	(NA)
Department of Energy	4,339.9	4,570.0	(NA)
Department of Health and Human Services	16,358.0	17,857.5	(NA)
National Aeronautics and Space Administration	2,763.1	1,191.5	(NA)
National Science Foundation	3,503.2	4,439.6	(NA)

NA Not available. X Not applicable. [1] Estimated except U.S. Department of Education, which are actual budget reports. [2] Includes other programs and agencies, not shown separately. [3] Purchased under Section 32 of the Act of August 1935 for use in child nutrition programs. [4] Program provides for the education of dependents of federal employees residing on federal property where free public education is unavailable in the nearby community. [5] Includes Federal Direct Loans. [6] Instructional costs only including academics, audiovisual, academic computer center, faculty training, military training, physical education, and libraries. [7] Includes alcohol, drug abuse, and mental health training programs.

Source: U.S. National Center for Education Statistics, Digest of Education Statistics, annual. See also <http://www.nces.ed.gov/programs/digest/>.

Table 228. School Enrollment by Age: 1970 to 2010

[As of October (60,357 represents 60,357,000). Covers civilian noninstitutional population enrolled in nursery school and above. Based on Current Population Survey; see text, Section 1 and Appendix III]

Age	1970	1980	1985	1990	1995	2000	2005	2008	2009	2010
ENROLLMENT (1,000)										
Total, 3 to 34 years old	**60,357**	**57,348**	**58,013**	**60,588**	**66,939**	**69,560**	**72,768**	**73,275**	**73,905**	**78,519**
3 and 4 years old	1,461	2,280	2,801	3,292	4,042	4,097	4,383	4,458	4,475	4,706
5 and 6 years old	7,000	5,853	6,697	7,207	7,901	7,648	7,486	7,651	7,783	7,955
7 to 13 years old	28,943	23,751	22,849	25,016	27,003	28,296	27,936	27,681	27,609	27,984
14 and 15 years old	7,869	7,282	7,362	6,555	7,651	7,885	8,375	7,965	7,789	7,736
16 and 17 years old	6,927	7,129	6,654	6,098	6,997	7,341	8,472	8,202	7,939	7,963
18 and 19 years old	3,322	3,788	3,716	4,044	4,274	4,926	5,109	5,607	5,935	5,904
20 and 21 years old	1,949	2,515	2,708	2,852	3,025	3,314	4,069	4,052	4,163	4,552
22 to 24 years old	1,410	1,931	2,068	2,231	2,545	2,731	3,254	3,488	3,818	3,602
25 to 29 years old	1,011	1,714	1,942	2,013	2,216	2,030	2,340	2,764	2,819	3,088
30 to 34 years old	466	1,105	1,218	1,281	1,284	1,292	1,344	1,407	1,576	1,658
35 years old and over	(NA)	1,290	1,766	2,439	2,830	2,653	3,013	3,079	3,383	3,372
ENROLLMENT RATE										
Total, 3 to 34 years old	**56.4**	**49.7**	**48.3**	**50.2**	**53.7**	**55.8**	**56.5**	**56.2**	**56.5**	**57.3**
3 and 4 years old	20.5	36.7	38.9	44.4	48.7	52.1	53.6	52.8	52.4	53.2
5 and 6 years old	89.5	95.7	96.1	96.5	96.0	95.6	95.4	93.8	94.1	94.5
7 to 13 years old	99.2	99.3	99.2	99.6	98.9	98.2	98.6	98.7	98.2	98.0
14 and 15 years old	98.1	98.2	98.1	99.0	98.9	98.7	98.0	98.6	98.0	98.1
16 and 17 years old	90.0	89.0	91.7	92.5	93.6	92.8	95.1	95.2	94.6	96.1
18 and 19 years old	47.7	46.4	51.6	57.3	59.4	61.2	67.6	66.0	68.9	69.2
20 and 21 years old	31.9	31.0	35.3	39.7	44.9	44.1	48.7	50.1	51.7	52.4
22 to 24 years old	14.9	16.3	16.9	21.0	23.2	24.6	27.3	28.2	30.4	28.9
25 to 29 years old	7.5	9.3	9.2	9.7	11.6	11.4	11.9	13.2	13.5	14.6
30 to 34 years old	4.2	6.4	6.1	5.8	6.0	6.7	6.9	7.3	8.1	8.3
35 years old and over	(NA)	1.4	1.6	2.1	2.2	1.9	2.0	2.0	2.1	2.6

NA Not available.

Source: U.S. Census Bureau, Current Population Reports, PPL-148, P-20, and earlier reports, and "School Enrollment," <http://www.census.gov/hhes/school/index.html>.

Table 229. School Enrollment by Race, Hispanic Origin, and Age: 2000 to 2010

[(54,257 represents 54,257,000). See headnote, Table 228]

Age	White [1]			Black [1]			Hispanic [2]		
	2000	2005	2010	2000	2005	2010	2000	2005	2010
ENROLLMENT (1,000)									
Total, 3 to 34 years old	**54,257**	**55,715**	**56,776**	**11,115**	**10,885**	**11,272**	**9,928**	**12,502**	**15,235**
3 and 4 years old	3,091	3,380	3,439	725	655	776	518	773	1,025
5 and 6 years old	5,959	5,707	5,956	1,219	1,144	1,207	1,390	1,532	1,961
7 to 13 years old	22,061	21,310	21,201	4,675	4,317	4,108	4,373	5,394	6,241
14 and 15 years old	6,176	6,429	5,907	1,260	1,321	1,157	1,093	1,431	1,555
16 and 17 years old	5,845	6,520	6,059	1,106	1,281	1,245	959	1,357	1,448
18 and 19 years old	3,924	4,006	4,566	716	707	837	617	681	1,171
20 and 21 years old	2,688	3,262	3,432	416	430	678	311	447	582
22 to 24 years old	2,101	2,411	2,720	393	475	514	309	419	559
25 to 29 years old	1,473	1,740	2,289	353	307	462	198	310	462
30 to 34 years old	939	950	1,207	252	248	288	160	158	231
35 years old and over	2,087	2,299	2,462	387	499	697	235	307	435
ENROLLMENT RATE									
Total, 3 to 34 years old	**55.1**	**55.9**	**55.8**	**59.0**	**58.4**	**58.4**	**51.3**	**50.9**	**55.1**
3 and 4 years old	50.2	54.2	52.1	52.1	52.2	56.2	35.9	43.0	44.2
5 and 6 years old	95.3	95.3	94.2	94.2	95.9	94.4	94.3	93.8	94.3
7 to 13 years old	98.2	98.6	97.9	97.9	98.6	98.0	97.5	97.6	97.8
14 and 15 years old	98.4	98.3	98.0	98.0	95.8	98.5	96.2	97.3	97.9
16 and 17 years old	92.8	95.4	96.2	96.2	93.1	95.5	87.0	92.6	96.0
18 and 19 years old	61.3	68.0	70.0	70.0	62.8	62.6	49.5	54.3	66.2
20 and 21 years old	44.9	49.3	51.6	51.6	37.6	50.3	26.1	30.0	37.0
22 to 24 years old	23.7	26.0	28.1	28.1	28.0	29.0	18.2	19.5	23.8
25 to 29 years old	10.4	11.3	13.9	13.9	11.7	16.0	7.4	7.8	11.4
30 to 34 years old	6.0	6.2	7.8	7.8	10.0	10.9	5.6	4.2	5.7
35 years old and over	1.8	1.8	1.9	2.6	3.1	4.0	2.0	2.0	2.3

[1] Starting 2005, data are for persons who selected this race group only. See footnote 2, Table 234. [2] Persons of Hispanic origin may be any race.

Source: U.S. Census Bureau, Current Population Reports, PPL-148, P-20, and earlier reports, and "School Enrollment," <http://www.census.gov/hhes/school/index.html>.

Table 230. Enrollment in Public and Private Schools: 1970 to 2009

[In millions (52.2 represents 52,200,000), except percent. As of October. For civilian noninstitutional population. For 1970 to 1985, persons 3 to 34 years old; beginning 1990, for 3 years old and over. For enrollment 35 years old and over, see Table 228]

Year	Public						Private					
	Total	Nursery	Kinder-garten	Elemen-tary	High school	College	Total	Nursery	Kinder-garten	Elemen-tary	High school	College
1970............	52.2	0.3	2.6	30.0	13.5	5.7	8.1	0.8	0.5	3.9	1.2	1.7
1975............	52.8	0.6	2.9	27.2	14.5	7.7	8.2	1.2	0.5	3.3	1.2	2.0
1980............	(NA)	0.6	2.7	24.4	(NA)	(NA)	(NA)	1.4	0.5	3.1	(NA)	(NA)
1985............	49.0	0.9	3.2	23.8	12.8	8.4	9.0	1.6	0.6	3.1	1.2	2.5
1990 [1].........	53.8	1.2	3.3	26.6	11.9	10.7	9.2	2.2	0.6	2.7	0.9	2.9
1993............	56.0	1.2	3.5	27.7	12.6	10.9	9.4	1.8	0.7	2.9	1.0	3.0
1994............	58.6	1.9	3.3	28.1	13.5	11.7	10.7	2.3	0.6	3.4	1.1	3.3
1995............	58.7	2.0	3.2	28.4	13.7	11.4	11.1	2.4	0.7	3.4	1.2	3.3
1996............	59.5	1.9	3.4	28.1	14.1	12.0	10.8	2.3	0.7	3.4	1.2	3.2
1997............	61.6	2.3	3.3	29.3	14.6	12.1	10.5	2.2	0.7	3.1	1.2	3.3
1998............	60.8	2.3	3.1	29.1	14.3	12.0	11.3	2.3	0.7	3.4	1.2	3.6
1999............	60.8	2.3	3.2	29.2	14.4	11.7	11.4	2.3	0.7	3.6	1.3	3.5
2000............	61.2	2.2	3.2	29.4	14.4	12.0	11.0	2.2	0.7	3.5	1.3	3.3
2001............	62.4	2.2	3.1	29.8	14.8	12.4	10.8	2.1	0.6	3.4	1.2	3.5
2002............	62.8	2.2	3.0	29.7	15.1	12.8	11.3	2.2	0.6	3.5	1.3	3.7
2003............	63.8	2.6	3.1	29.2	15.8	13.1	11.1	2.4	0.6	3.4	1.3	3.5
2004............	64.3	2.5	3.4	29.2	15.5	13.7	11.3	2.3	0.6	3.4	1.3	3.7
2005............	64.2	2.5	3.3	29.0	15.8	13.4	11.5	2.1	0.6	3.4	1.4	4.0
2006............	64.1	2.5	3.6	29.0	15.6	13.5	11.1	2.2	0.5	3.1	1.5	3.8
2007............	65.1	2.6	3.7	29.1	15.8	14.1	10.8	2.1	0.5	3.1	1.3	3.9
2008............	65.5	2.6	3.6	29.2	15.4	14.7	10.8	2.0	0.5	3.2	1.3	4.0
2009............	66.9	2.7	3.8	29.4	15.3	15.7	10.4	2.0	0.4	2.9	1.2	4.0
Percent White:												
1970..........	84.5	59.5	84.4	83.1	85.6	90.7	93.4	91.1	88.2	94.1	96.1	92.8
1980..........	(NA)	68.2	80.7	80.9	(NA)	(NA)	(NA)	89.0	87.0	90.7	(NA)	(NA)
1990..........	79.8	71.7	78.3	78.9	79.2	84.1	87.4	89.6	83.2	88.2	89.4	85.0
2000..........	77.0	69.4	77.3	76.7	78.0	78.0	83.5	84.9	82.8	85.9	84.6	79.8
2005 [2]........	75.7	71.3	78.0	75.2	76.0	76.7	81.4	83.6	79.0	83.0	83.6	78.4
2007 [2]........	75.4	73.2	77.6	75.3	75.2	77.1	80.4	80.9	81.3	82.1	86.1	76.6
2008 [2]........	75.7	69.5	76.8	75.4	75.2	77.6	79.9	83.2	79.5	80.6	83.6	76.4
2009 [2]........	75.2	66.8	75.9	75.8	74.8	76.0	79.3	80.0	80.3	80.7	85.5	76.2

NA Not available. [1] Beginning 1990, based on a revised edit and tabulation package. [2] Beginning 2005, for persons who selected this race group only. See footnote 2, Table 234.

Source: U.S. Census Bureau, Current Population Reports, PPL-148, P-20, and earlier reports, and "School Enrollment," <http://www.census.gov/hhes/school/index.html>.

Table 231. School Enrollment by Sex and Level: 1970 to 2010

[In millions (60.4 represents 60,400,000). As of October. For the civilian noninstitutional population. Prior to 1980, persons 3 to 34 years old; beginning 1980, 3 years old and over. Elementary includes kindergarten and grades 1–8; high school, grades 9–12; and college, 2-year and 4-year colleges, universities, and graduate and professional schools. Data for college represent degree-credit enrollment. See headnote, Table 228]

Year	All levels [1]			Elementary			High school			College		
	Total	Male	Female	Total	Male	Female	Total	Male	Female	Total	Male	Female
1970............	60.4	31.4	28.9	37.1	19.0	18.1	14.7	7.4	7.3	7.4	4.4	3.0
1980............	58.6	29.6	29.1	30.6	15.8	14.9	14.6	7.3	7.3	11.4	5.4	6.0
1990 [2]..........	63.0	31.5	31.5	33.2	17.1	16.0	12.8	6.5	6.4	13.6	6.2	7.4
1992............	64.6	32.2	32.3	34.3	17.7	16.6	13.3	6.8	6.5	14.0	6.2	7.8
1993............	65.4	32.9	32.5	34.8	17.9	16.9	13.6	7.0	6.6	13.9	6.3	7.6
1994............	69.3	34.6	34.6	35.4	18.2	17.2	14.6	7.4	7.2	15.0	6.8	8.2
1995............	69.8	35.0	34.8	35.7	18.3	17.4	15.0	7.7	7.3	14.7	6.7	8.0
1996............	70.3	35.1	35.2	35.5	18.3	17.3	15.3	7.9	7.4	15.2	6.8	8.4
1997............	72.0	35.9	36.2	36.3	18.7	17.6	15.8	8.0	7.7	15.4	6.8	8.6
1998............	72.1	36.0	36.1	36.4	18.7	17.7	15.6	7.9	7.6	15.5	6.9	8.6
1999............	72.4	36.3	36.1	36.7	18.8	17.9	15.9	8.2	7.7	15.2	7.0	8.2
2000............	72.2	35.8	36.4	36.7	18.9	17.9	15.8	8.1	7.7	15.3	6.7	8.6
2001............	73.1	36.3	36.9	36.9	19.0	17.9	16.1	8.2	7.8	15.9	6.9	9.0
2002............	74.0	36.8	37.3	36.7	18.9	17.8	16.4	8.3	8.0	16.5	7.2	9.3
2003............	74.9	37.3	37.6	36.3	18.7	17.6	17.1	8.6	8.4	16.6	7.3	9.3
2004............	75.5	37.4	38.0	36.5	19.0	17.6	16.8	8.4	8.4	17.4	7.6	9.8
2005............	75.8	37.4	38.4	36.4	18.6	17.7	17.4	8.9	8.5	17.5	7.5	9.9
2006............	75.2	37.2	38.0	36.1	18.5	17.6	17.1	8.8	8.4	17.2	7.5	9.7
2007............	76.0	37.6	38.4	36.3	18.6	17.7	17.1	8.8	8.3	18.0	7.8	10.1
2008............	76.3	37.8	38.6	36.4	18.6	17.7	16.8	8.5	8.2	18.6	8.3	10.3
2009............	77.3	38.0	39.3	36.4	18.6	17.7	16.4	8.4	8.1	19.8	8.6	11.1
2010............	78.5	38.7	39.8	36.8	18.8	18.1	16.6	8.5	8.0	20.3	9.0	11.3

[1] Includes nursery schools, not shown separately. [2] For data beginning 1990, based on a revised edit and tabulation package.

Source: U.S. Census Bureau, Current Population Reports, PPL-148, P20, and earlier reports, and "School Enrollment," <http://www.census.gov/hhes/school/index.html>.

Table 232. School Enrollment by Control and Level: 1980 to 2011

[In thousands (58,305 represents 58,305,000). As of Fall. Data below college level are for regular day schools and exclude subcollegiate departments of colleges, federal schools, and home-schooled children. College data include degree-credit and nondegree-credit enrollment. Based on survey of state education agencies; see source for details. For more projections, see Tables 224 and 226]

Control of school and level	1980	1990	1995	2000	2005	2007	2008	2009	2010, proj.	2011, proj.
Total	**58,305**	**60,683**	**65,020**	**68,685**	**72,674**	**73,451**	**74,076**	**75,290**	**75,720**	**76,321**
Public	50,335	52,061	55,933	58,956	62,135	62,783	63,238	64,184	64,449	65,062
Private	7,971	8,622	9,087	9,729	10,539	10,668	10,838	11,106	11,271	11,258
Pre-kindergarten through 8	31,639	34,388	37,094	38,592	38,928	38,751	38,651	38,597	38,729	38,949
Public	27,647	29,876	32,338	33,686	34,204	34,205	34,286	34,418	34,637	34,892
Private	3,992	[1] 4,512	4,756	[1] 4,906	4,724	4,546	[1] 4,365	4,179	4,092	4,057
Grades 9 through 12	14,570	12,476	13,665	14,781	16,258	16,451	16,322	16,265	15,975	15,797
Public	13,231	11,341	12,502	13,517	14,909	15,087	14,980	14,955	14,668	14,530
Private	1,339	[1] 1,136	1,163	[1] 1,264	1,349	1,364	[1] 1,342	1,309	1,306	1,266
College [2][3]	12,097	13,819	14,262	15,312	17,487	18,248	19,103	20,428	21,016	21,575
Public	9,457	10,845	11,092	11,753	13,022	13,491	13,972	14,811	15,143	15,640
Private	2,640	2,974	3,169	3,560	4,466	4,757	5,131	5,617	5,873	5,934
Not-for-profit	2,528	2,760	2,929	3,109	3,455	3,571	3,662	3,765	3,855	(NA)
For profit	112	214	240	450	1,011	1,186	1,469	1,852	2,018	(NA)

NA Not available. [1] Estimated. [2] For data beginning 2000, reflects new classification system. See footnote 1, Table 278. [3] Data for 2010 are actual.

Source: U.S. National Center for Education Statistics, *Digest of Education Statistics*, annual, and *Projections of Education Statistics*, annual. See also <http://www.nces.ed.gov/annuals>.

Table 233. Students Who Are Foreign Born or Who Have Foreign-Born Parents: 2009

[In thousands (48,684 represents 48,684,000), except percent. As of October. Covers civilian noninstitutional population enrolled in elementary school and above. Based on Current Population Survey, see text, Section 1 and Appendix III]

Characteristic	All students	Students with at least one foreign-born parent					
		Total		Foreign-born student		Native student	
		Number	Percent	Number	Percent	Number	Percent
ELEMENTARY AND HIGH SCHOOL							
Total [1]	**48,684**	**10,965**	**22.5**	**2,355**	**4.8**	**8,610**	**17.7**
White [2]	37,001	7,584	20.5	1,500	4.1	6,084	16.4
White, non-Hispanic	27,817	1,806	6.5	314	1.1	1,492	5.4
Black [2]	7,429	1,052	14.2	313	4.2	739	9.9
Asian [2][3]	1,878	1,660	88.4	475	25.3	1,185	63.1
Hispanic [4]	10,200	6,287	61.6	1,274	12.5	5,014	49.2
COLLEGE, 1 TO 4 YEARS							
Total [1]	**16,012**	**3,617**	**22.6**	**1,534**	**9.6**	**2,083**	**13.0**
White [2]	12,235	2,198	18.0	879	7.2	1,319	10.8
White, non-Hispanic	10,252	916	8.9	355	3.5	561	5.5
Black [2]	2,410	482	20.0	262	10.9	219	9.1
Asian [2][3]	850	776	91.3	376	44.2	400	47.1
Hispanic [4]	2,169	1,375	63.4	548	25.3	827	38.1
GRADUATE SCHOOL							
Total [1]	**3,752**	**1,068**	**28.5**	**637**	**17.0**	**431**	**11.5**
White [2]	2,792	483	17.3	247	8.8	236	8.5
White, non-Hispanic	2,574	345	13.4	173	6.7	172	6.7
Black [2]	479	167	34.9	109	22.8	58	12.1
Asian [2][3]	381	366	96.1	273	71.7	93	24.4
Hispanic [4]	265	170	64.2	81	30.6	88	33.2

[1] Includes other races not shown separately. [2] For persons who selected this race group only. See footnote 2, Table 234. [3] Data are for Asians only, excludes Pacific Islanders. [4] Persons of Hispanic origin may be of any race.

Source: U.S. Census Bureau, Current Population Survey, unpublished data, <https://www.census.gov/hhes/school/>.

Table 234. Educational Attainment by Race and Hispanic Origin: 1970 to 2011

[In percent. For persons 25 years old and over. 1970 and 1980 data as of April 1 and based on sample data from the censuses of population. Other years as of March and based on the Current Population Survey; see text, Section 1 and Appendix III. See Table 235 for data by sex]

Year	Total [1]	White [2]	Black [2]	Asian and Pacific Islander [2,6]	Hispanic [3] Total [4]	Mexican	Puerto Rican	Cuban
HIGH SCHOOL GRADUATE OR MORE [5]								
1970.	52.3	54.5	31.4	62.2	32.1	24.2	23.4	43.9
1980.	66.5	68.8	51.2	74.8	44.0	37.6	40.1	55.3
1990.	77.6	79.1	66.2	80.4	50.8	44.1	55.5	63.5
1995.	81.7	83.0	73.8	(NA)	53.4	46.5	61.3	64.7
2000.	84.1	84.9	78.5	85.7	57.0	51.0	64.3	73.0
2005.	85.2	85.8	81.1	87.6	58.5	52.2	72.4	73.3
2008.	86.6	87.1	83.0	88.7	62.3	55.2	76.4	80.0
2009.	86.7	87.1	84.1	88.2	61.9	55.7	76.6	78.5
2010.	87.1	87.6	84.2	88.9	62.9	57.4	74.8	81.4
2011.	87.6	88.1	84.5	88.6	64.3	(NA)	(NA)	(NA)
COLLEGE GRADUATE OR MORE [5]								
1970.	10.7	11.3	4.4	20.4	4.5	2.5	2.2	11.1
1980.	16.2	17.1	8.4	32.9	7.6	4.9	5.6	16.2
1990.	21.3	22.0	11.3	39.9	9.2	5.4	9.7	20.2
1995.	23.0	24.0	13.2	(NA)	9.3	6.5	10.7	19.4
2000.	25.6	26.1	16.5	43.9	10.6	6.9	13.0	23.0
2005.	27.7	28.1	17.6	50.2	12.0	8.2	13.8	24.6
2008.	29.4	29.8	19.6	52.6	13.3	9.1	15.5	28.1
2009.	29.5	29.9	19.3	52.3	13.2	9.5	16.5	27.9
2010.	29.9	30.3	19.8	52.4	13.9	10.6	17.5	26.2
2011.	30.4	31.0	19.9	50.4	14.1	(NA)	(NA)	(NA)

NA Not available. [1] Includes other races not shown separately. [2] Beginning 2005, for persons who selected this race group only. The 2003 Current Population Survey (CPS) allowed respondents to choose more than one race. Therefore, beginning with 2003, data represent persons who selected this race group only and exclude persons reporting more than one race. The CPS in prior years only allowed respondents to report one race group. See also comments on race in the text for Section 1. [3] Persons of Hispanic origin may be of any race. [4] Includes persons of other Hispanic origin not shown separately. [5] Through 1990, completed 4 years of high school or more and 4 years of college or more. [6] Starting in 2005, data are for Asians only, excludes Pacific Islanders.

Source: U.S. Census Bureau, U.S. Census of Population, 1970 and 1980, Vol. 1; Current Population Reports, P20-550, and earlier reports; and "Educational Attainment," <http://www.census.gov/hhes/socdemo/education/>.

Table 235. Educational Attainment by Race, Hispanic Origin, and Sex: 1970 to 2011

[In percent. See Table 234 for headnote and totals for both sexes]

Year	All races [1] Male	Female	White [2] Male	Female	Black [2] Male	Female	Asian and Pacific Islander [2,5] Male	Female	Hispanic [3] Male	Female
HIGH SCHOOL GRADUATE OR MORE [4]										
1970.	51.9	52.8	54.0	55.0	30.1	32.5	61.3	63.1	37.9	34.2
1980.	67.3	65.8	69.6	68.1	50.8	51.5	78.8	71.4	45.4	42.7
1990.	77.7	77.5	79.1	79.0	65.8	66.5	84.0	77.2	50.3	51.3
1995.	81.7	81.6	83.0	83.0	73.4	74.1	(NA)	(NA)	52.9	53.8
2000.	84.2	84.0	84.8	85.0	78.7	78.3	88.2	83.4	56.6	57.5
2005.	84.9	85.5	85.2	86.2	81.0	81.2	90.4	85.2	57.9	59.1
2008.	85.9	87.2	86.3	87.8	81.8	84.0	90.8	86.9	60.9	63.7
2009.	86.2	87.1	86.5	87.7	84.0	84.1	90.4	86.2	60.6	63.3
2010.	86.6	87.6	86.9	88.2	83.6	84.6	91.2	87.0	61.4	64.4
2011.	87.1	88.0	87.4	88.6	83.8	85.0	90.4	87.0	63.6	65.1
COLLEGE GRADUATE OR MORE [4]										
1970.	13.5	8.1	14.4	8.4	4.2	4.6	23.5	17.3	7.8	4.3
1980.	20.1	12.8	21.3	13.3	8.4	8.3	39.8	27.0	9.4	6.0
1990.	24.4	18.4	25.3	19.0	11.9	10.8	44.9	35.4	9.8	8.7
1995.	26.0	20.2	27.2	21.0	13.6	12.9	(NA)	(NA)	10.1	8.4
2000.	27.8	23.6	28.5	23.9	16.3	16.7	47.6	40.7	10.7	10.6
2005.	28.9	26.5	29.4	26.8	16.0	18.8	54.0	46.8	11.8	12.1
2008.	30.1	28.8	30.5	29.1	18.7	20.4	55.8	49.8	12.6	14.1
2009.	30.1	29.1	30.6	29.3	17.8	20.6	55.7	49.3	12.5	14.0
2010.	30.3	29.6	30.8	29.9	17.7	21.4	55.6	49.5	12.9	14.9
2011.	30.8	30.1	31.5	30.5	18.0	21.4	53.3	47.7	13.1	15.2

NA Not available. [1] Includes other races not shown separately. [2] Beginning 2005, for persons who selected this race group only. See footnote 2, Table 234 . [3] Persons of Hispanic origin may be of any race. [4] Through 1990, completed 4 years of high school or more and 4 years of college or more. [5] Starting in 2005, data are for Asians only, excludes Pacific Islanders.

Source: U.S. Census Bureau, U.S. Census of Population, 1970 and 1980, Vol. 1; Current Population Reports P20-550, and earlier reports; and "Educational Attainment," <http://www.census.gov/hhes/socdemo/education/index.html>.

Table 236. Educational Attainment by Selected Characteristics: 2011

[201,543 represents 201,543,000. For persons 25 years old and over. As of March. Based on the Current Population Survey; see text, Section 1 and Appendix III]

Characteristic	Population (1,000)	Percent of population—					
		Not a high school graduate	High school graduate	Some college, but no degree	Associate's degree [1]	Bachelor's degree	Advanced degree
Total persons.................	**201,543**	**12.4**	**30.7**	**17.0**	**9.5**	**19.5**	**10.9**
Age:							
25 to 34 years old................	41,584	11.0	27.1	18.9	10.1	23.9	9.1
35 to 44 years old................	39,842	10.9	27.6	16.8	10.4	22.2	12.0
45 to 54 years old................	43,954	10.7	31.9	16.5	10.7	19.6	10.6
55 to 64 years old................	36,984	10.4	30.8	17.6	9.8	18.6	12.8
65 to 74 years old................	21,414	15.6	35.7	15.3	7.0	14.1	12.3
75 years old or over..............	17,764	24.0	37.0	14.7	5.0	11.1	8.1
Sex:							
Male................................	97,220	12.9	31.2	16.6	8.4	19.6	11.3
Female.............................	104,323	12.0	30.2	17.3	10.4	19.4	10.6
Race:							
White [2]...........................	163,979	11.9	30.7	16.9	9.5	19.9	11.1
Black [2]...........................	23,364	15.5	34.8	19.8	9.9	13.2	6.7
Asian [2]...........................	9,723	11.4	21.6	10.2	6.5	30.8	19.5
Hispanic origin:							
Hispanic............................	26,672	35.7	29.8	13.7	6.7	10.0	4.1
Non-Hispanic white..................	139,146	7.6	30.9	17.5	10.0	21.6	12.4
Marital status:							
Never married......................	37,205	13.3	30.2	17.7	8.8	21.1	9.0
Married, spouse present.............	117,727	10.2	29.4	16.0	9.8	21.4	13.1
Married, spouse absent [3]...........	3,265	24.3	30.0	15.5	6.2	15.3	8.6
Separated..........................	4,996	22.2	34.1	18.3	9.0	11.0	5.3
Widowed...........................	14,215	24.8	38.4	15.0	6.1	10.0	5.7
Divorced...........................	24,134	10.8	32.7	21.5	11.0	15.7	8.2
Civilian labor force status:							
Employed...........................	121,646	7.9	27.5	16.9	10.8	23.4	13.5
Unemployed.........................	10,789	16.5	36.9	18.9	8.5	14.1	5.2
Not in the labor force................	69,108	19.8	35.4	16.8	7.2	13.5	7.3

[1] Includes vocational degrees. [2] For persons who selected this race group only. See footnote 2, Table 234. [3] Excludes those separated.

Source: U.S. Census Bureau, "Educational Attainment in the United States: 2011 - Detailed Tables," <http://www.census.gov/hhes/socdemo/education/data/cps/2011/tables.html>.

Table 237. Mean Earnings by Highest Degree Earned: 2010

[In dollars. Persons as of March 2011. For persons 18 years old and over with earnings. Based on Current Population Survey; see text, Section 1 and Appendix III. For definition of mean, see Guide to Tabular Presentation]

Characteristic	Total persons [1]	Mean earnings by level of highest degree (dollars)							
		Ninth to twelfth grade, non-graduate	High school graduate only	Some college, no degree	Asso-ciate's	Bach-elor's	Master's	Profes-sional	Doctorate
All persons [2].................	**42,922**	**21,004**	**31,003**	**31,793**	**39,404**	**57,621**	**71,439**	**125,891**	**106,840**
Age:									
25 to 34 years old..............	36,440	19,558	27,925	30,197	34,357	46,916	53,606	74,667	80,114
35 to 44 years old..............	49,865	25,562	34,517	39,137	42,732	66,196	76,384	138,585	108,826
45 to 54 years old..............	52,093	27,282	37,247	43,216	46,904	67,840	83,208	145,850	109,930
55 to 64 years old..............	51,825	29,726	35,284	41,814	41,863	64,398	76,663	159,598	115,002
65 years old and over..........	38,923	20,475	26,121	32,965	31,164	43,290	52,987	79,376	119,213
Sex:									
Male.............................	50,645	24,850	36,181	38,345	46,524	69,623	87,951	147,310	118,883
Female...........................	34,216	14,972	24,172	25,216	33,470	45,044	57,056	87,185	87,808
White [3].........................	44,142	21,839	32,067	32,439	40,440	59,188	72,344	128,412	108,594
Male.............................	52,304	25,990	37,477	39,399	48,015	71,958	90,064	149,410	121,536
Female...........................	34,561	14,775	24,645	25,111	33,943	45,223	56,893	86,984	87,291
Black [3].........................	32,808	17,415	25,757	28,908	33,507	44,311	62,224	104,425	97,820
Male.............................	35,598	19,130	29,478	32,670	36,798	48,068	66,456	(B)	(B)
Female...........................	30,438	15,552	21,700	26,115	31,330	41,653	59,758	79,460	(B)
Asian [3].........................	49,894	20,491	28,579	28,360	36,869	57,183	72,556	120,686	101,170
Male.............................	57,937	22,477	31,783	31,654	42,966	65,448	85,695	132,400	106,750
Female...........................	40,952	17,788	25,295	24,640	30,923	48,745	55,195	(B)	92,704
Hispanic [4]......................	29,917	20,856	26,381	29,015	34,733	47,980	63,033	88,687	95,104
Male.............................	32,981	23,884	29,620	33,292	41,177	56,774	69,897	106,234	(B)
Female...........................	25,574	15,024	21,234	24,137	29,156	39,321	57,903	(B)	(B)

B Base figure too small to meet statistical standards for reliability of a derived figure. [1] Includes those with less than ninth grade education not shown separately. [2] Includes other races not shown separately. [3] For persons who selected this race group only. See footnote 2, Table 234. [4] Persons of Hispanic origin may be of any race.

Source: U.S. Census Bureau, "Table PINC-04. Educational Attainment--People 18 Years Old and Over, by Total Money Earnings in 2010, Work Experience in 2010, Age, Race, Hispanic Origin, and Sex," <http://www.census.gov/hhes/www/cpstables/032012/perinc/toc.htm>.

Table 238. Educational Attainment by State: 1990 to 2010

[In percent. 1990 and 2000 as of April; 2010 represents annual averages for calendar year. For persons 25 years old and over. Based on the 1990 and 2000 Census of Population and the 2010 American Community Survey, which includes the household population and the population living in institutions, college dormitories, and other group quarters. See text, Section 1 and Appendix III. For margin of error data, see source]

State	1990			2000			2010		
	High school graduate or more	Bachelor's degree or more	Advanced degree or more	High school graduate or more	Bachelor's degree or more	Advanced degree or more	High school graduate or more	Bachelor's degree or more	Advanced degree or more
United States	**75.2**	**20.3**	**7.2**	**80.4**	**24.4**	**8.9**	**85.6**	**28.2**	**10.4**
Alabama	66.9	15.7	5.5	75.3	19.0	6.9	82.1	21.9	8.0
Alaska	86.6	23.0	8.0	88.3	24.7	8.6	91.0	27.9	9.4
Arizona	78.7	20.3	7.0	81.0	23.5	8.4	85.6	25.9	9.2
Arkansas	66.3	13.3	4.5	75.3	16.7	5.7	82.9	19.5	6.3
California	76.2	23.4	8.1	76.8	26.6	9.5	80.7	30.1	11.0
Colorado	84.4	27.0	9.0	86.9	32.7	11.1	89.7	36.4	13.0
Connecticut	79.2	27.2	11.0	84.0	31.4	13.3	88.6	35.5	15.3
Delaware	77.5	21.4	7.7	82.6	25.0	9.4	87.7	27.8	11.3
District of Columbia	73.1	33.3	17.2	77.8	39.1	21.0	87.4	50.1	26.9
Florida	74.4	18.3	6.3	79.9	22.3	8.1	85.5	25.8	9.2
Georgia	70.9	19.3	6.4	78.6	24.3	8.3	84.3	27.3	9.8
Hawaii	80.1	22.9	7.1	84.6	26.2	8.4	89.9	29.5	9.6
Idaho	79.7	17.7	5.3	84.7	21.7	6.8	88.3	24.4	7.7
Illinois	76.2	21.0	7.5	81.4	26.1	9.5	86.9	30.8	11.5
Indiana	75.6	15.6	6.4	82.1	19.4	7.2	87.0	22.7	8.1
Iowa	80.1	16.9	5.2	86.1	21.2	6.5	90.6	24.9	7.9
Kansas	81.3	21.1	7.0	86.0	25.8	8.7	89.2	29.8	10.5
Kentucky	64.6	13.6	5.5	74.1	17.1	6.9	81.9	20.5	8.1
Louisiana	68.3	16.1	5.6	74.8	18.7	6.5	81.9	21.4	7.0
Maine	78.8	18.8	6.1	85.4	22.9	7.9	90.3	26.8	9.5
Maryland	78.4	26.5	10.9	83.8	31.4	13.4	88.1	36.1	16.4
Massachusetts	80.0	27.2	10.6	84.8	33.2	13.7	89.1	39.0	16.7
Michigan	76.8	17.4	6.4	83.4	21.8	8.1	88.7	25.2	9.6
Minnesota	82.4	21.8	6.3	87.9	27.4	8.3	91.8	31.8	10.3
Mississippi	64.3	14.7	5.1	72.9	16.9	5.8	81.0	19.5	7.1
Missouri	73.9	17.8	6.1	81.3	21.6	7.6	86.9	25.6	9.5
Montana	81.0	19.8	5.7	87.2	24.4	7.2	91.7	28.8	9.0
Nebraska	81.8	18.9	5.9	86.6	23.7	7.3	90.4	28.6	9.0
Nevada	78.8	15.3	5.2	80.7	18.2	6.1	84.7	21.7	7.4
New Hampshire	82.2	24.4	7.9	87.4	28.7	10.0	91.5	32.8	12.4
New Jersey	76.7	24.9	8.8	82.1	29.8	11.0	88.0	35.4	13.3
New Mexico	75.1	20.4	8.3	78.9	23.5	9.8	83.3	25.0	10.8
New York	74.8	23.1	9.9	79.1	27.4	11.8	84.9	32.5	14.0
North Carolina	70.0	17.4	5.4	78.1	22.5	7.2	84.7	26.5	8.7
North Dakota	76.7	18.1	4.5	83.9	22.0	5.5	90.3	27.6	7.9
Ohio	75.7	17.0	5.9	83.0	21.1	7.4	88.1	24.6	8.9
Oklahoma	74.6	17.8	6.0	80.6	20.3	6.8	86.2	22.9	7.5
Oregon	81.5	20.6	7.0	85.1	25.1	8.7	88.8	28.8	10.5
Pennsylvania	74.7	17.9	6.6	81.9	22.4	8.4	88.4	27.1	10.4
Rhode Island	72.0	21.3	7.8	78.0	25.6	9.7	83.5	30.2	12.2
South Carolina	68.3	16.6	5.4	76.3	20.4	6.9	84.1	24.5	8.8
South Dakota	77.1	17.2	4.9	84.6	21.5	6.0	89.6	26.3	7.7
Tennessee	67.1	16.0	5.4	75.9	19.6	6.8	83.6	23.1	8.5
Texas	72.1	20.3	6.5	75.7	23.2	7.6	80.7	25.9	8.6
Utah	85.1	22.3	6.8	87.7	26.1	8.3	90.6	29.3	9.4
Vermont	80.8	24.3	8.9	86.4	29.4	11.1	91.0	33.6	13.3
Virginia	75.2	24.5	9.1	81.5	29.5	11.6	86.5	34.2	14.2
Washington	83.8	22.9	7.0	87.1	27.7	9.3	89.8	31.1	11.1
West Virginia	66.0	12.3	4.8	75.2	14.8	5.9	83.2	17.5	6.6
Wisconsin	78.6	17.7	5.6	85.1	22.4	7.2	90.1	24.1	9.0
Wyoming	83.0	18.8	5.7	87.9	21.9	7.0	92.3	22.3	8.4

Source: U.S. Census Bureau, 1990 Census of Population, CPH-L-96; 2000 Census of Population, P37. "Sex by Educational Attainment for the Population 25 Years and Over;" and 2010 American Community Survey, GCT1501, "Percent of Persons 25 Years and Over Who Have Completed High School (Includes Equivalency)," R1502, "Percent of Persons 25 Years and Over Who Have Completed a Bachelor's Degree," and R1503, "Percent of Persons 25 Years and Over Who Have Completed an Advanced Degree," <http://factfinder2.census.gov>, accessed May 2012.

Table 239. Children With Parental Involvement in Home Literacy Activities: 1993 to 2007

[In percent, except number of children (8,579 represents 8,579,000). For children 3 to 5 years old not yet enrolled in kindergarten who participated in activities with a family member. Based on the School Readiness Early Childhood Program Participation Surveys of the National Household Education Surveys Program; see source and Appendix III. See also Table 240]

Characteristic	Children (1,000)		Read to [1]		Told a story [1]		Taught letters, words, or numbers [1]		Visited a library [2]	
	1993	2007	1993	2007	1993	2005	1993	2005	1993	2007
Total	**8,579**	**8,686**	**78**	**83**	**43**	**54**	**58**	**77**	**38**	**36**
Age:										
3 years old	3,889	3,755	79	84	46	54	57	75	34	36
4 years old	3,713	3,738	78	83	41	53	58	77	41	35
5 years old	976	1,193	76	83	36	55	58	80	38	39
Race/ethnicity:										
White, non-Hispanic	5,902	4,664	85	91	44	53	58	76	42	41
Black, non-Hispanic	1,271	1,312	66	78	39	54	63	81	29	25
Hispanic [3]	1,026	1,899	58	68	38	50	54	74	26	27
Other	381	812	73	87	50	64	59	82	43	46
Mother's home language: [4]										
English	7,805	7,244	81	88	44	55	58	78	39	38
Not English	603	1,312	42	57	36	45	52	69	26	24
Mother's highest education: [4]										
Less than high school	1,036	808	60	56	37	39	56	70	22	20
High school	3,268	2,048	76	74	41	51	56	78	31	29
Vocational ed or some college	2,624	2,658	83	86	45	57	60	79	44	33
College degree	912	1,849	90	95	48	56	56	75	55	43
Graduate/professional training or degree	569	1,194	90	95	50	64	60	76	59	53

[1] Three or more times in the past week. [2] At least once in the past month. [3] Persons of Hispanic origin may be of any race. [4] Excludes children with no mother in the household and no female guardian.

Source: U.S. National Center for Education Statistics, Statistical Brief, NCES 2000–026, November 1999; the Early Childhood Program Participation Survey, National Household Education Surveys Program (NHES), 2005, unpublished data; and the NHES School Readiness Survey, 2007, unpublished data, <http://nces.ed.gov/nhes>.

Table 240. Children's School Readiness Skills: 1993 to 2007

[In percent. For children 3 to 5 years old not yet enrolled in kindergarten. Based on the School Readiness Surveys of the National Household Education Survey Program; see source for details. See also Table 239]

Characteristic	Recognizes all letters		Counts to 20 or higher		Writes name		Reads or pretends to read storybooks		Has 3 to 4 skills	
	1993	2007	1993	2007	1993	2007	1993	2005	1993	2005
Total	**21**	**32**	**52**	**63**	**50**	**60**	**72**	**70**	**35**	**42**
Age:										
3 years old	11	17	37	47	22	34	66	67	15	24
4 years old	28	38	62	73	70	76	75	73	49	55
5 years old	36	59	78	84	84	88	81	72	65	66
Sex:										
Male	19	31	49	61	47	56	68	70	32	40
Female	23	33	56	65	53	63	76	71	39	45
Race/ethnicity:										
White, non-Hispanic	23	36	56	69	52	64	76	75	39	47
Black, non-Hispanic	18	37	53	69	45	58	63	67	31	44
Hispanic [1]	10	15	32	41	42	49	59	55	22	26
Other	22	39	49	69	52	61	70	79	36	48
Mother's employment status: [2]										
Employed	23	34	57	66	52	63	75	72	39	46
Unemployed	17	14	41	42	46	41	67	61	29	32
Not in the labor force	18	31	49	60	47	58	68	69	32	39
Family type:										
Two parents	22	33	54	64	51	62	74	72	37	44
None or one parent	18	27	49	57	47	52	65	65	31	36
Poverty status: [3]										
Above threshold	24	35	57	67	53	64	74	75	40	47
Below threshold	12	21	41	48	41	46	64	54	23	26

[1] Persons of Hispanic origin may be of any race. [2] Excludes children with no mother in the household and no female guardian. [3] Children are considered poor if they lived in households with incomes below the poverty threshold, which is a dollar amount determined by the federal government to meet the household's need, given its size and composition. For more information about the poverty threshold, see text, section 13.

Source: U.S. Department of Education, U.S. National Center for Education Statistics, *Home Literacy Activities and Signs of Children's Emerging Literacy, 1993,* NCES 2000–026, November 1999; the Early Childhood Program Participation Survey, National Household Education Surveys Program (NHES), 2005, unpublished data; and the NHES School Readiness Survey, 2007, unpublished data, <http://nces.ed.gov/nhes>.

Table 241. Children Who Speak a Language Other Than English at Home by Region: 2010

[In thousands (11,783 represents 11,783,000), except percent. For children 5 to 17 years old. For more on languages spoken at home, see Tables 54–55. Based on the American Community Survey; see text Section 1, and Appendix III. For composition of regions, see map inside front cover]

Characteristic	U.S.	Northeast	Midwest	South	West
Children who speak another language at home..............................	11,783	1,975	1,450	3,890	4,467
Percent of children 5 to 17 years old..	21.8	21.7	12.3	19.3	34.4
Speak Spanish..	8,457	1,074	868	3,077	3,437
Speak English "very well"...	6,474	843	656	2,322	2,653
Speak English less than "very well"..	1,982	231	213	755	784
Speak other Indo-European languages....................................	1,568	551	295	411	312
Speak English "very well"...	1,280	446	236	339	259
Speak English less than "very well"..	288	105	59	72	53
Speak Asian and Pacific Island languages...............................	1,313	246	173	301	593
Speak English "very well"...	972	183	124	224	440
Speak English less than "very well"..	341	62	49	77	153
Speak other languages..	445	105	113	102	126
Speak English "very well"...	352	81	88	83	100
Speak English less than "very well"..	93	24	25	18	26
Have difficulty speaking English [1]..	2,705	422	346	922	1,015
Language spoken at home in linguistically isolated households [2].............	2,986	492	343	1,024	1,128
Speak only English...	175	38	21	59	57
Speak Spanish..	2,168	274	220	816	857
Speak other Indo-European languages....................................	25	88	41	53	44
Speak Asian and Pacific Island languages...............................	347	74	38	84	151
Speak other languages..	71	17	22	13	18

[1] Children aged 5 to 17 who speak English less than "very well." [2] A household in which no person aged 14 or over speaks English at least "very well."

Source: U.S. Census Bureau, 2010 American Community Survey, B16003, "Age by Language Spoken at Home for the Population 5 Years and Over" and C16004, "Age by Language Spoken at Home by Ability to Speak English for the Population 5 Years and Over," <http://factfinder2.census.gov>, accessed September 2012.

Table 242. Preprimary School Enrollment—Summary: 1970 to 2010

[10,949 represents 10,949,000. As of October. Civilian noninstitutional population. Includes public and nonpublic nursery school and kindergarten programs. Excludes 5-year-olds enrolled in elementary school. Based on Current Population Survey. See text, Section 1 and Appendix III]

Item	1970	1980	1990	1995	2000	2005	2008	2009	2010
NUMBER OF CHILDREN (1,000)									
Population, 3 to 5 years old...............	**10,949**	**9,284**	**11,207**	**12,518**	**11,858**	**12,134**	**12,583**	**12,717**	**12,949**
Total enrolled [1]...........................	**4,104**	**4,878**	**6,659**	**7,739**	**7,592**	**7,801**	**7,928**	**8,075**	**8,493**
Nursery..	1,094	1,981	3,378	4,331	4,326	4,529	4,570	4,648	4,797
Public..	332	628	1,202	1,950	2,146	2,409	2,609	2,703	2,749
Private.......................................	762	1,353	2,177	2,381	2,180	2,120	1,961	1,945	2,048
Kindergarten..................................	3,010	2,897	3,281	3,408	3,266	3,272	3,358	3,428	3,449
Public..	2,498	2,438	2,767	2,799	2,701	2,804	2,982	3,144	3,079
Private.......................................	511	459	513	608	565	468	376	284	369
White [2]..	3,443	3,994	5,389	6,144	5,861	6,025	6,011	5,943	6,160
Black [2]..	586	725	964	1,236	1,265	1,148	1,231	1,338	1,301
Hispanic [3].....................................	(NA)	370	642	1,040	1,155	1,494	1,645	1,721	1,874
3 years old....................................	454	857	1,205	1,489	1,540	1,715	1,654	1,776	1,718
4 years old....................................	1,007	1,423	2,086	2,553	2,556	2,668	2,804	2,698	2,988
5 years old....................................	2,643	2,598	3,367	3,697	3,496	3,418	3,470	3,601	3,787
ENROLLMENT RATE									
Total enrolled [1]...........................	**37.5**	**52.5**	**59.4**	**61.8**	**64.0**	**64.3**	**63.0**	**63.5**	**63.7**
White [2]..	37.8	52.7	59.7	63.0	63.2	65.1	65.1	62.8	63.4
Black [2]..	34.9	51.8	57.8	58.9	68.5	62.0	66.2	66.3	64.1
Hispanic [3].....................................	(NA)	43.3	49.0	51.1	52.6	56.1	57.6	54.1	56.0
3 years old....................................	12.9	27.3	32.6	35.9	39.2	41.3	39.3	40.7	38.2
4 years old....................................	27.8	46.3	56.0	61.6	64.9	66.2	66.1	64.6	68.6
5 years old....................................	69.3	84.7	88.8	87.5	87.6	86.4	83.8	86.1	88.1

NA Not available. [1] Includes races not shown separately. [2] Beginning 2005, for persons who selected this race group only. See footnote 2, Table 224. [3] Persons of Hispanic origin may be of any race. The method of identifying Hispanic children was changed in 1980 from allocation based on status of mother to status reported for each child. The number of Hispanic children using the new method is larger.

Source: U.S. Census Bureau, Current Population Reports, PPL-148; earlier PPL and P-20 reports and unpublished data; and "School Enrollment," accessed May 2012, <http://www.census.gov/hhes/school/index.html>.

Table 243. Type of School Attended by Student and Household Characteristics: 1996 and 2007

[In percent, except total in thousands (34,600 represent 34,600,000). For students in grades 1 to 12. Includes homeschooled students enrolled in public or private school 9 or more hours per week. Based on the Parent and Family Involvement Survey of the National Household Education Survey Program; see source and Appendix III for details]

Characteristic	Public				Private			
	Assigned		Chosen		Church related		Not church related	
	1996	2007	1996	2007	1996	2007	1996	2007
Total students (1,000)...................	**34,600**	**34,700**	**6,200**	**7,400**	**3,700**	**4,100**	**1,000**	**1,200**
Percent distribution........................	76.0	73.2	13.7	15.5	8.0	8.7	2.3	2.6
Grade level:								
1 to 5...............................	74.1	71.4	14.8	17.0	8.9	8.7	2.2	2.8
6 to 8...............................	79.4	77.0	11.2	11.9	7.4	8.6	2.0	2.5
9 to 12..............................	75.9	72.6	14.1	16.4	7.3	8.6	2.7	2.3
Race/ethnicity:								
White, non-Hispanic..................	77.1	73.6	11.1	12.5	9.2	10.8	2.7	3.1
Black, non-Hispanic..................	72.9	68.9	21.5	23.7	4.2	5.5	1.4	1.8
Other, non-Hispanic..................	69.3	72.7	19.0	17.4	9.5	6.4	2.2	3.5
Hispanic [1].........................	76.4	75.8	16.1	17.4	6.3	5.6	1.3	1.2
Family type:								
Two-parent household................	76.3	72.7	11.7	14.4	9.5	10.0	2.4	2.9
One-parent household................	74.6	74.9	18.4	17.7	5.0	5.4	1.9	2.0
Nonparent guardians.................	80.2	72.8	14.6	22.7	2.3	3.9	2.9	0.6
Parents' education:								
Less than high school...............	78.8	85.4	17.4	12.4	2.0	1.5	1.8	0.6
High school diploma or equivalent...	82.1	79.8	12.3	15.4	5.0	3.5	0.7	1.3
Some college, including vocational/technical..........	76.4	75.4	14.7	16.3	7.1	7.3	1.8	1.0
Bachelor's degree...................	70.7	70.7	13.1	15.3	13.0	11.6	3.3	2.4
Graduate/professional degree.........	66.1	62.2	12.6	15.8	15.3	15.1	6.0	6.8
Region: [2]								
Northeast............................	74.3	72.3	12.9	13.3	9.2	10.9	3.6	3.4
South................................	78.7	75.2	12.5	14.0	6.4	8.5	2.4	2.3
Midwest..............................	75.4	73.6	12.4	15.0	10.9	9.9	1.3	1.5
West.................................	74.0	70.6	17.7	20.1	6.3	6.1	2.0	3.3

[1] Persons of Hispanic origin may be of any race. [2] For composition of regions see map, inside front cover.

Source: U.S. National Center for Education Statistics, *Condition of Education, 2009*, NCES 2009-081, June 2009.

Table 244. Public Charter and Traditional Schools—Selected Characteristics: 2007 to 2008

[47,432 represents 47,432,000. For school year ending in 2008. A public charter school is a public school that, in accordance with an enabling state statute, has been granted a charter exempting it from selected state and local rules and regulations]

Characteristic	All schools		Elementary		Secondary		Combined	
	Tradi-tional	Public charter	Tradi-tional	Public charter	Tradi-tional	Public charter	Tradi-tional	Public charter
Number of schools...............................	87,190	3,560	60,390	2,050	20,720	920	6,080	590
Enrollment (1,000)................................	47,432	1,047	29,194	619	16,513	229	1,725	200
PERCENT DISTRIBUTION OF STUDENTS								
Race/ethnicity....................................	100.0	100.0	100.0	100.0	100.0	100.0	100.0	100.0
White, non-Hispanic..........................	58.2	41.0	56.2	35.9	60.3	43.5	71.3	54.0
Black, non-Hispanic..........................	15.7	29.0	15.8	36.1	15.8	(S)	12.2	17.6
Hispanic [1]..................................	20.3	23.8	22.1	21.6	18.0	31.5	11.5	22.0
Asian/Pacific Islander........................	4.4	3.8	4.5	3.8	4.7	3.5	1.3	(S)
American Indian/Alaska Native................	1.4	2.3	1.4	2.6	1.2	1.5	3.8	(S)
PERCENT DISTRIBUTION OF SCHOOLS								
Size of enrollment...............................	100.0	100.0	100.0	100.0	100.0	100.0	100.0	100.0
Less than 300 students.......................	28.1	64.2	24.1	59.3	28.9	81.1	65.8	54.9
300 to 599 students..........................	40.6	25.8	49.2	29.2	20.8	14.8	22.8	31.2
600 to 999 students..........................	20.8	7.4	22.5	10.0	19.9	(S)	7.5	6.9
1,000 students or more.......................	10.5	2.7	4.3	(S)	30.4	(S)	4.0	(S)
Percent minority enrollment......................	100.0	100.0	100.0	100.0	100.0	100.0	100.0	100.0
Less than 10.0...............................	28.7	(S)	27.7	(S)	30.2	(S)	33.8	(S)
10.0 to 24.9.................................	17.9	17.0	18.1	15.7	18.4	(S)	14.5	30.7
25.0 to 49.9.................................	19.7	18.0	19.5	15.1	21.3	20.8	17.4	23.9
50.0 to 74.9.................................	12.6	14.1	13.1	11.8	11.4	20.7	12.2	(S)
75.0 or more.................................	21.0	42.7	21.7	50.4	18.7	39.2	22.1	21.2
Percent of students eligible for free or reduced-price lunch [2]................	100.0	100.0	100.0	100.0	100.0	100.0	100.0	100.0
Less than 15.0...............................	4.0	24.5	1.7	16.2	8.5	35.8	11.0	35.3
15.0 to 29.9.................................	27.6	9.9	27.4	9.4	32.7	(S)	11.9	(S)
30.0 to 49.9.................................	27.7	18.8	26.5	16.6	30.9	28.7	28.6	(S)
50.0 to 74.9.................................	21.4	21.4	23.2	25.9	15.6	(S)	22.6	27.5
75.0 or more.................................	19.4	25.5	21.2	31.9	12.2	16.6	25.9	16.9

S Figure does not meet publication standards. [1] Persons of Hispanic origin may be of any race. [2] Excludes data for schools not providing information on eligibility for free or reduced-price lunch.

Source: U.S. National Center for Education Statistics, School and Staffing Survey (SASS), "Public School Questionnaire," 2007-08 and "Public Teacher Questionnaire," 2007-08; <http://nces.ed.gov/surveys/sass/>.

Table 245. Students Who Are Homeschooled by Selected Characteristics: 2007

[51,135 represents 51,135,000. As of spring. For students 5 to 17 with a grade equivalent of K–12. Homeschoolers are students whose parents reported them to be schooled at home instead of a public or private school. Excludes students who were enrolled in school for more than 25 hours a week or were homeschooled due to a temporary illness. Based on the Parent and Family Involvement Survey of the National Household Education Surveys Program; see source and Appendix III for details]

Characteristic	Number of students			Percent distribution		
	Total (1,000)	Home-schooled (1,000)	Percent home-schooled	Total	Home-schooled	Non-Home-schooled
Total	**51,135**	**1,508**	**2.9**	**100.0**	**100.0**	**100.0**
Grade equivalent: [1]						
K–5	23,529	717	3.0	46.0	47.6	46.0
Kindergarten	3,669	114	3.1	7.2	7.6	7.2
Grades 1 to 3	11,965	406	3.4	23.4	26.9	23.3
Grades 4 to 5	7,895	197	2.5	15.4	13.1	15.5
Grades 6 to 8	12,435	359	2.9	24.3	23.8	24.3
Grades 9 to 12	15,161	422	2.8	29.6	28.0	29.7
Sex:						
Male	26,286	633	2.4	51.4	41.9	51.7
Female	24,849	875	3.5	48.6	58.1	48.3
Race/ethnicity:						
White, non-Hispanic	29,815	1,159	3.9	58.3	76.8	57.7
Black, non-Hispanic	7,523	61	0.8	14.7	4.0	15.0
Hispanic [2]	9,589	147	1.5	18.8	9.8	19.0
Other	4,208	141	3.3	8.2	9.3	8.2
Number of children in the household:						
One child	8,463	187	2.2	16.6	12.4	16.7
Two children	20,694	412	2.0	40.5	27.3	40.9
Three or more children	21,979	909	4.1	43.0	60.3	42.5
Number of parents in the household:						
Two parents	37,262	1,348	3.6	72.9	89.4	72.4
One parent	11,734	115	1.0	22.9	7.6	23.4
Nonparental guardians	2,139	45	2.1	4.2	3.0	4.2
Parents' participation in the labor force:						
Two parents—one in labor force	26,075	509	2.0	51.0	33.8	51.5
Two parents—both in labor force	10,776	808	7.5	21.1	53.6	20.1
One parent in labor force	9,989	127	1.3	19.5	8.4	19.9
No parent in labor force	4,296	64	1.5	8.4	4.3	8.5
Household income:						
$25,000 or less	11,544	239	2.1	22.6	15.9	22.8
$25,001 to 50,000	10,592	364	3.4	20.7	24.1	20.6
$50,001 to 75,000	10,289	405	3.9	20.1	26.8	19.9
$75,001 or more	18,710	501	2.7	36.6	33.2	36.7
Parents' highest educational attainment:						
High school diploma or less	14,303	206	1.4	28.0	13.7	28.4
Voc/tech degree or some college	14,584	549	3.8	28.5	36.4	28.3
Bachelor's degree	12,321	502	4.1	24.1	33.3	23.8
Graduate/professional school	9,927	251	2.5	19.4	16.6	19.5

[1] Excludes those ungraded. [2] Persons of Hispanic origin may be of any race.

Source: U.S. National Center for Education Statistics, "Parent and Family Involvement in Education Survey," National Household Education Surveys Program, 2007, unpublished data. See also <http://nces.ed.gov/nhes>.

Table 246. Public Elementary and Secondary Schools by Type and Size of School: 2009 to 2010

[Enrollment in thousands (49,136 represents 49,136,240), except for average enrollment. For school year ending in 2010. Data reported by schools, rather than school districts. Based on the Common Core of Data Survey; see source for details]

Enrollment size of school	Number of schools					Enrollment [1]				
	Total	Elemen-tary [2]	Second-ary [3]	Com-bined [4]	Other [5]	Total	Elemen-tary [2]	Second-ary [3]	Com-bined [4]	Other [5]
Total	**98,817**	**67,140**	**24,651**	**5,730**	**1,296**	**49,136**	**31,551**	**15,981**	**1,544**	**60**
PERCENT										
Total	**100.00**	**100.00**	**100.00**	**100.00**	**100.00**	**100.00**	**100.00**	**100.00**	**100.00**	**100.00**
Under 100 students	10.63	5.62	18.28	39.75	36.08	0.93	0.60	1.13	5.43	9.41
100 to 199 students	9.37	8.03	11.40	16.55	26.58	2.72	2.58	2.42	7.98	20.37
200 to 299 students	11.29	12.19	8.94	9.95	15.51	5.51	6.53	3.21	8.12	20.01
300 to 399 students	13.74	16.16	7.98	8.32	12.03	9.33	11.98	4.00	9.68	22.06
400 to 499 students	13.92	17.11	6.52	6.29	5.38	12.11	16.23	4.22	9.46	12.39
500 to 599 students	11.36	13.90	5.57	5.03	1.58	12.05	16.08	4.41	9.22	4.61
600 to 699 students	8.45	10.04	5.12	3.26	1.27	10.60	13.73	4.78	7.07	4.22
700 to 799 students	5.83	6.70	4.07	2.62	0.95	8.43	10.57	4.39	6.54	3.67
800 to 999 students	6.43	6.55	6.88	3.28	0.32	11.02	12.20	8.88	9.60	1.44
1,000 to 1,499 students	5.32	3.37	11.49	3.21	0.32	12.36	8.27	20.42	12.78	1.82
1,500 to 1,999 students	2.01	0.29	7.24	1.05	–	6.74	1.01	18.12	6.02	–
2,000 to 2,999 students	1.36	0.04	5.41	0.39	–	6.24	0.20	18.49	3.13	–
3,000 or more students	0.28	–	1.08	0.29	–	1.97	0.02	5.53	4.97	–
Average enrollment [1]	516	473	693	300	191	516	473	693	300	191

– Represents zero. [1] Exclude data for schools not reporting enrollment. [2] Includes schools beginning with grade 6 or below and with no grade higher than 8. [3] Includes schools with no grade lower than 7. [4] Includes schools beginning with grade 6 or below and ending with grade 9 or above. [5] Includes special education, alternative, and other schools not classified by grade span.

Source: U.S. National Center for Education Statistics, *Digest of Education Statistics*, annual. See also <http://www.nces.ed.gov/programs/digest/>.

Table 247. Public Elementary and Secondary Schools—Summary: 1980 to 2010

[48,041 represents 48,041,000. For school year ending in year shown, except as indicated. Data are estimates]

Item	Unit	1980	1990	2000	2005	2008	2009	2010
School districts, total	**Number**	**16,044**	**15,552**	**15,403**	**15,731**	**15,581**	**15,609**	**15,350**
ENROLLMENT								
Population 5-17 years old [1]	1,000	48,041	44,949	53,119	53,606	53,833	53,890	53,980
Percent of resident population	Percent	21.4	18.2	18.9	18.1	17.7	17.6	17.5
Fall enrollment [2]	1,000	41,778	40,527	46,577	48,417	49,011	49,036	49,141
Percent of population 5-17 years old	Percent	87.0	90.2	87.7	90.3	91.0	91.0	91.0
Elementary [3]	1,000	24,397	26,253	29,243	29,632	29,903	30,016	30,117
Secondary [4]	1,000	17,381	14,274	17,334	18,784	19,108	19,020	19,025
Average daily attendance (ADA)	1,000	38,411	37,573	43,313	45,088	45,870	46,374	46,680
High school graduates	1,000	2,762	2,327	2,544	2,803	2,996	3,060	3,118
INSTRUCTIONAL STAFF								
Total [5]	**1,000**	**2,521**	**2,685**	**3,273**	**3,509**	**3,654**	**3,697**	**3,693**
Classroom teachers	1,000	2,211	2,362	2,891	3,072	3,186	3,228	3,215
Average salaries:								
Instructional staff	Dollar	16,715	32,638	43,837	49,135	54,589	56,314	57,146
Classroom teachers	Dollar	15,970	31,367	41,807	47,516	52,800	54,274	55,202
REVENUES								
Revenue receipts	Mil. dol.	97,635	208,656	369,754	477,371	560,140	564,928	581,883
Federal	Mil. dol.	9,020	13,184	26,346	42,908	47,547	57,255	64,849
State	Mil. dol.	47,929	100,787	183,986	225,142	269,993	261,512	263,866
Local	Mil. dol.	40,686	94,685	159,421	209,321	242,599	246,161	253,168
EXPENDITURES								
Total	**Mil. dol.**	**96,105**	**209,698**	**374,782**	**496,199**	**579,683**	**591,785**	**609,954**
Current expenditures (day schools)	Mil. dol.	85,661	186,583	320,954	422,346	495,475	505,694	520,209
Other current expenditures [6]	Mil. dol.	1,859	3,341	6,618	8,710	9,753	11,212	11,994
Capital outlay	Mil. dol.	6,504	16,012	37,552	48,757	57,105	56,111	58,009
Interest on school debt	Mil. dol.	2,081	3,762	9,659	16,385	17,350	18,769	19,742
Current expenditures per pupil enrolled	Dollar	2,050	4,604	6,891	8,723	10,110	10,313	10,586

[1] Estimated resident population as of July 1 of the previous year, except 1980, 1990, 2000, and 2010 population enumerated as of April 1. Estimates reflect revisions based on the 2010 Census of Population. [2] Fall enrollment of the previous year. [3] Kindergarten through grade 6. [4] Grades 7 through 12. [5] Full-time equivalent. [6] Current expenses for summer schools, adult education, post-high school vocational education, personnel retraining, etc., when operated by local school districts and not part of regular public elementary and secondary day-school program.

Source: National Education Association, Washington, DC, "Estimates of School Statistics Database" (copyright). See also <http://www.nea.org/home/32073.htm>.

Table 248. Public Elementary and Secondary School Enrollment by Grade: 1980 to 2009

[In thousands (40,877 represents 40,877,000). As of Fall of year. Based on survey of state education agencies; see source for details]

Grade	1980	1990	1995	2000	2003	2004	2005	2006	2007	2008	2009
Pupils enrolled [1]	**40,877**	**41,217**	**44,840**	**47,204**	**48,540**	**48,795**	**49,113**	**49,299**	**49,293**	**49,266**	**49,373**
Pre-kindergarten to 8 [1]	27,647	29,878	32,341	33,688	34,202	34,178	34,205	34,221	34,205	34,286	34,418
Pre-K and Kindergarten	2,689	3,610	4,173	4,158	4,453	4,534	4,656	4,706	4,691	4,819	4,903
First	2,894	3,499	3,671	3,636	3,613	3,663	3,691	3,750	3,750	3,708	3,730
Second	2,800	3,327	3,507	3,634	3,544	3,560	3,606	3,640	3,704	3,699	3,666
Third	2,893	3,297	3,445	3,676	3,611	3,580	3,586	3,627	3,659	3,708	3,708
Fourth	3,107	3,248	3,431	3,711	3,619	3,612	3,578	3,585	3,624	3,647	3,701
Fifth	3,130	3,197	3,438	3,707	3,685	3,635	3,633	3,601	3,600	3,629	3,653
Sixth	3,038	3,110	3,395	3,663	3,772	3,735	3,670	3,660	3,628	3,614	3,645
Seventh	3,085	3,067	3,422	3,629	3,841	3,818	3,777	3,715	3,701	3,653	3,642
Eighth	3,086	2,979	3,356	3,538	3,809	3,825	3,802	3,765	3,709	3,692	3,652
Grades 9 to 12 [1]	13,231	11,338	12,500	13,340	14,338	14,617	14,909	15,078	15,087	14,980	14,955
Ninth	3,377	3,169	3,704	3,963	4,190	4,281	4,287	4,260	4,200	4,123	4,081
Tenth	3,368	2,896	3,237	3,491	3,675	3,750	3,866	3,881	3,863	3,822	3,810
Eleventh	3,195	2,612	2,826	3,083	3,277	3,369	3,455	3,551	3,558	3,548	3,542
Twelfth	2,925	2,381	2,487	2,803	3,046	3,094	3,180	3,276	3,375	3,400	3,433

[1] Includes unclassified students not shown separately.

Source: U.S. National Center for Education Statistics, *Digest of Education Statistics*, annual. See also <http://www.nces.ed.gov/programs/digest/>.

Table 249. Public Elementary and Secondary Schools and Enrollment—States: 2008 to 2009

[For total number of students (49,136 represents 49,136,000). For school year ending in 2009. Based on the Common Core of Data Program; see source for details]

State	Total number of schools with member-ship [1]	Total number of students (1,000)	Regular — Number of schools	Regular — Percent of students	Special education [2] — Number of schools	Special education [2] — Percent of students	Vocational education [3] — Number of schools	Vocational education [3] — Percent of students	Alternative education [4] — Number of schools	Alternative education [4] — Percent of students
Total...........	98,817	49,136	89,018	98.2	2,089	0.4	1,417	0.3	6,293	1.2
Alabama.............	1,600	749	1,370	99.5	41	0.1	72	(Z)	117	0.4
Alaska..............	506	132	450	89.3	2	0.1	3	0.6	51	10.0
Arizona.............	2,248	1,076	1,939	98.5	20	0.1	207	0.3	82	1.0
Arkansas............	1,120	481	1,082	99.6	4	(Z)	23	–	11	0.3
California...........	10,068	6,177	8,472	96.7	146	0.4	75	(Z)	1,375	2.8
Colorado............	1,793	832	1,683	98.0	9	0.1	6	0.1	95	1.8
Connecticut.........	1,165	564	1,049	96.9	56	0.6	16	1.9	44	0.6
Delaware............	217	125	182	91.9	19	1.4	6	5.7	10	1.0
District of Columbia........	233	69	208	95.5	10	2.2	4	1.4	11	0.9
Florida.............	4,043	2,635	3,398	97.6	170	0.7	53	0.1	422	1.6
Georgia.............	2,461	1,668	2,248	99.3	72	0.5	1	–	140	0.2
Hawaii..............	289	180	285	99.9	3	(Z)	–	(X)	1	0.1
Idaho...............	742	276	633	98.1	15	(Z)	11	(Z)	83	1.8
Illinois..............	4,405	2,097	4,017	99.2	147	0.4	53	(Z)	188	0.4
Indiana.............	1,961	1,047	1,875	99.7	38	0.1	29	–	19	0.2
Iowa...............	1,468	482	1,410	99.2	7	0.1	–	(X)	51	0.7
Kansas.............	1,419	469	1,407	99.9	10	0.1	1	–	1	(Z)
Kentucky...........	1,542	676	1,238	99.0	10	0.1	124	–	170	0.9
Louisiana...........	1,488	691	1,260	94.5	38	0.2	6	–	184	5.4
Maine..............	649	184	619	100.0	1	(Z)	27	–	2	(Z)
Maryland...........	1,447	848	1,321	97.6	40	0.5	24	1.0	62	0.9
Massachusetts.......	1,836	957	1,755	95.4	23	0.5	39	3.7	19	0.4
Michigan...........	3,879	1,618	3,332	95.8	197	1.9	38	0.1	312	2.2
Minnesota..........	2,433	837	1,666	96.3	276	1.8	11	(Z)	480	1.9
Mississippi.........	1,085	492	928	100.0	3	(Z)	90	–	64	–
Missouri............	2,427	917	2,181	98.7	68	0.5	66	0.5	112	0.3
Montana............	828	142	822	99.9	2	(Z)	–	(X)	4	0.1
Nebraska...........	1,120	295	1,087	99.8	28	0.2	–	(X)	5	0.0
Nevada.............	636	429	593	98.4	10	0.2	1	(Z)	32	1.4
New Hampshire......	484	197	484	100.0	–	(X)	–	(X)	–	(X)
New Jersey..........	2,590	1,387	2,359	97.6	73	0.7	55	1.6	103	0.2
New Mexico.........	855	333	808	98.4	6	0.2	1	0.1	40	1.3
New York...........	4,730	2,766	4,591	98.7	105	0.8	6	0.2	28	0.3
North Carolina......	2,550	1,477	2,531	99.9	14	(Z)	1	(Z)	4	(Z)
North Dakota.......	517	93	474	100.0	34	(Z)	9	–	–	(X)
Ohio...............	3,796	1,762	3,653	99.5	64	0.3	73	0.1	6	0.1
Oklahoma..........	1,795	655	1,786	99.8	4	(Z)	–	(X)	5	0.1
Oregon.............	1,301	554	1,256	99.0	2	(Z)	–	(X)	43	1.0
Pennsylvania........	3,244	1,762	3,132	98.8	12	0.1	87	1.0	13	0.1
Rhode Island........	321	144	298	97.3	3	0.1	11	1.2	9	1.4
South Carolina......	1,206	723	1,136	99.8	10	0.1	39	–	21	0.1
South Dakota.......	714	124	676	98.9	7	0.1	4	(Z)	27	1.0
Tennessee..........	1,772	973	1,704	99.4	19	0.2	21	0.1	28	0.2
Texas..............	8,619	4,850	7,518	98.4	25	(Z)	–	(X)	1,076	1.6
Utah...............	1,046	583	862	97.6	86	1.0	6	–	92	1.3
Vermont............	323	86	307	100.0	–	(X)	15	–	1	(Z)
Virginia............	2,164	1,245	1,883	99.7	42	(Z)	49	0.1	190	0.2
Washington.........	2,318	1,035	1,885	95.0	103	0.4	15	(Z)	315	4.5
West Virginia.......	759	283	693	99.6	3	0.1	31	(Z)	32	0.3
Wisconsin..........	2,242	872	2,136	99.3	9	(Z)	8	0.1	89	0.6
Wyoming...........	363	88	336	98.6	3	(Z)	–	(X)	24	1.4

– Represents zero. X Not applicable. Z Less than 0.05 percent. [1] Membership is the count of students enrolled on October 1 of the reported school year. Individual state total number of students is included only if the state or jurisdiction reports data for regular, special education, vocational education, and alternative education school types. [2] Focuses on special education with materials and instructional approaches adapted to meet the students' needs. [3] Focuses on vocational, technical, or career education and provides education and training in at least one semi-skilled or technical occupation. [4] Addresses the needs of students that typically cannot be met in the regular school setting and provides nontraditional education.

Source: U.S. National Center for Education Statistics, Common Core of Data, "Public Elementary/Secondary School Universe Survey," 2009–10, Version 1a; <http://www.nces.ed.gov/ccd/>.

Table 250. Selected Statistics for the Largest Public School Districts: 2007 to 2009

[For the 50 largest districts by enrollment size. For 2008-09 school year, unless otherwise noted. Data from the Common Core Data Program; see source for details. School district boundaries are not necessarily the same as city or county boundaries]

School district	City	County	Number of students [1]	Number of full-time equivalent (FTE) teachers [2]	Number of 2007-08 completers [3]	Number of schools [4]
New York City Public Schools, NY................	New York	New York	981,690	71,824	55,290	1,496
Los Angeles Unified, CA............................	Los Angeles	Los Angeles	687,534	35,084	30,580	860
City of Chicago School District, IL...................	Chicago	Cook	421,430	21,512	20,285	630
Dade County School District, FL...................	Miami	Miami-Dade	345,525	22,384	20,791	496
Clark County School District, NV..................	Las Vegas	Clark	312,761	15,348	13,031	350
Broward County School District, FL...............	Fort Lauderdale	Broward	256,351	18,729	15,742	303
Houston Independent School District, TX.........	Houston	Harris	200,225	11,994	7,976	296
Hillsborough County School District, FL..........	Tampa	Hillsborough	192,007	13,986	10,503	285
Hawaii Department of Education, HI...............	Honolulu	Honolulu	179,478	11,294	11,833	290
Orange County School District, FL................	Orlando	Orange	172,257	10,975	10,672	236
Palm Beach County School District, FL...........	West Palm Beach	Palm Beach	170,757	13,213	10,879	247
Fairfax County Public Schools, VA................	Falls Church	Fairfax	169,030	9,274	12,150	193
Philadelphia City School District, PA.............	Philadelphia	Philadelphia	159,867	10,258	8,732	274
Dallas Independent School District, TX...........	Dallas	Dallas	157,352	10,937	6,371	232
Gwinnett County, GA..............................	Lawrenceville	Gwinnett	157,219	10,978	8,472	115
Montgomery County Public Schools, MD.........	Rockville	Montgomery	139,282	9,401	10,316	204
Wake County Schools, NC.........................	Raleigh	Wake	138,443	9,317	7,717	156
Charlotte-Mecklenburg Schools, NC..............	Charlotte	Mecklenburg	135,064	9,312	6,611	166
San Diego Unified, CA.............................	San Diego	San Diego	132,256	6,855	6,778	218
Prince George's County Public Schools, MD......	Upper Marlboro	Prince George's	127,977	8,870	8,644	215
Duval County School District, FL..................	Jacksonville	Duval	122,606	7,973	6,502	175
Memphis City School District, TN.................	Memphis	Shelby	111,954	7,201	6,547	200
Cobb County, GA..................................	Marietta	Cobb	106,747	8,215	7,090	118
Pinellas County School District, FL...............	Largo	Pinellas	106,061	7,878	6,790	173
Baltimore County Public Schools, MD............	Towson	Baltimore	103,180	7,339	7,571	172
Cypress-Fairbanks Independent School District, TX......................................	Houston	Harris	100,685	6,411	5,294	78
DeKalb County, GA................................	Decatur	Dekalb	99,775	6,902	5,424	146
Jefferson County, KY..............................	Louisville	Jefferson	98,774	6,144	5,396	174
Detroit City School District, MI..................	Detroit	Wayne	97,577	5,953	(NA)	197
Albuquerque Public Schools, NM..................	Albuquerque	Bernalillo	95,934	6,542	5,239	174
Polk County School District, FL...................	Bartow	Polk	94,657	7,548	5,068	156
Northside Independent School District, TX........	San Antonio	Bexar	89,000	5,782	4,704	101
Fulton County, GA................................	Atlanta	Fulton	88,299	6,530	5,087	98
Long Beach Unified, CA...........................	Long Beach	Los Angeles	87,509	4,017	5,054	92
Jefferson County, CO..............................	Golden	Jefferson	85,946	4,959	5,968	162
Milwaukee, WI....................................	Milwaukee	Milwaukee	85,381	5,158	(NA)	215
Austin Independent School District, TX...........	Austin	Travis	83,483	5,890	3,903	120
Baltimore City Public Schools, MD................	Baltimore	Baltimore City	82,266	5,839	4,116	194
Jordan District, UT...............................	Sandy	Salt Lake	81,485	3,221	(NA)	99
Lee County School District, FL....................	Fort Myers	Lee	79,434	5,034	4,491	117
Fort Worth Independent School District, TX.......	Fort Worth	Tarrant	79,285	5,167	3,529	147
Fresno Unified, CA................................	Fresno	Fresno	76,621	3,922	3,870	106
Davidson County School District, TN..............	Nashville	Davidson	74,312	5,307	4,018	139
Denver County, CO................................	Denver	Denver	74,189	4,356	3,190	143
Prince William County, VA........................	Manassas	Prince William	73,917	3,845	4,560	83
Anne Arundel County Public Schools, MD.........	Annapolis	Anne Arundel	73,653	4,939	5,297	124
Brevard School District, FL.......................	Viera	Brevard	73,098	5,290	5,018	121
Guilford County Schools, NC......................	Greensboro	Guilford	72,951	5,091	4,776	119
Virginia Beach City Public Schools, VA...........	Virginia Beach	Virginia Beach	71,554	3,984	5,341	84
Greenville County Schools, SC....................	Greenville	Greenville	70,441	4,542	(NA)	94

NA Not Available. [1] Number of students receiving educational services from the school district. [2] Full-time equivalent is the amount of time required to perform an assignment stated as a proportion of a full-time position. [3] Includes high school diploma recipients and other completers (for example certificates of attendance) but does not include high school equivalents (GEDs). [4] Totals for number of schools may differ from published estimates since they exclude closed, inactive, and future schools.

Source: U.S. Department of Education, National Center for Education Statistics, Common Core of Data (CCD), "Characteristics of the 100 Largest Public Elementary and Secondary School Districts in the United States: 2008-09," <http://nces.ed.gov/ccd/>.

Table 251. Public Elementary and Secondary School Enrollment by State: 1990 to 2009

[In thousands (29,878 represents 29,878,000). As of Fall. Includes unclassified students. Based on survey of state education agencies; see source for details]

State	Prekindergarten through grade 8					Grades 9 through 12				
	1990	2000	2005	2008	2009	1990	2000	2005	2008	2009
United States	**29,878**	**33,688**	**34,205**	**34,286**	**34,418**	**11,338**	**13,515**	**14,908**	**14,980**	**14,955**
Alabama	527	539	529	528	529	195	201	212	218	219
Alaska	85	94	91	89	91	29	39	42	41	41
Arizona	479	641	740	772	760	161	237	355	316	317
Arkansas	314	318	336	342	344	123	132	138	137	136
California	3,615	4,408	4,466	4,306	4,264	1,336	1,733	1,971	2,016	1,999
Colorado	420	517	550	580	591	154	208	230	238	241
Connecticut	347	406	400	392	390	122	156	175	175	174
Delaware	73	81	85	87	88	27	34	36	39	39
District of Columbia	61	54	56	51	52	19	15	21	18	18
Florida	1,370	1,760	1,873	1,849	1,851	492	675	802	782	784
Georgia	849	1,060	1,145	1,186	1,195	303	385	453	470	473
Hawaii	123	132	127	126	127	49	52	55	54	53
Idaho	160	170	183	194	195	61	75	79	81	82
Illinois	1,310	1,474	1,480	1,479	1,464	512	575	631	641	640
Indiana	676	703	724	730	731	279	286	311	316	316
Iowa	345	334	326	336	341	139	161	157	152	151
Kansas	320	323	321	331	333	117	147	147	140	141
Kentucky	459	471	487	472	484	177	194	192	198	196
Louisiana	586	547	482	504	510	199	197	172	181	181
Maine	155	146	133	129	129	60	61	62	64	61
Maryland	527	609	589	576	582	188	244	271	267	267
Massachusetts	604	703	675	667	667	230	273	297	292	291
Michigan	1,145	1,222	1,191	1,119	1,115	440	498	551	541	534
Minnesota	546	578	558	560	565	211	277	281	276	272
Mississippi	372	364	358	352	352	131	134	137	140	141
Missouri	588	645	635	635	638	228	268	283	282	280
Montana	111	105	98	97	98	42	50	48	45	44
Nebraska	198	195	195	203	207	76	91	92	90	89
Nevada	150	251	296	308	306	51	90	116	125	123
New Hampshire	126	147	139	133	133	46	61	67	65	64
New Jersey	784	968	971	957	968	306	346	425	425	428
New Mexico	208	225	230	231	235	94	95	97	99	99
New York	1,828	2,029	1,909	1,843	1,847	770	853	906	898	919
North Carolina	783	945	1,003	1,059	1,054	304	348	413	430	430
North Dakota	85	72	66	64	65	33	37	33	31	30
Ohio	1,258	1,294	1,261	1,239	1,225	514	541	578	578	539
Oklahoma	425	445	457	468	477	154	178	178	177	178
Oregon	340	379	380	395	404	132	167	173	180	178
Pennsylvania	1,172	1,258	1,228	1,194	1,201	496	556	603	581	586
Rhode Island	102	114	104	98	98	37	44	50	47	47
South Carolina	452	493	498	508	512	170	184	204	211	211
South Dakota	95	88	84	87	86	34	41	38	39	38
Tennessee	598	668	677	685	687	226	241	277	287	286
Texas	2,511	2,943	3,268	3,447	3,520	872	1,117	1,257	1,306	1,330
Utah	325	333	358	404	421	122	148	151	155	161
Vermont	71	70	65	63	63	25	32	32	31	30
Virginia	728	816	841	855	864	270	329	372	381	381
Washington	613	694	699	705	705	227	310	333	332	330
West Virginia	224	201	197	199	200	98	85	84	83	82
Wisconsin	566	595	584	590	593	232	285	291	284	279
Wyoming	71	60	57	61	62	27	30	27	27	26

Source: U.S. National Center for Education Statistics, *Digest of Education Statistics*, annual. See also <http://www.nces.ed.gov/programs/digest/>.

Table 252. Parent Participation in School-Related Activities by Selected School, Student, and Family Characteristics: 2007

[In percent, except as noted (51,600 represents 51,600,000). For school year ending in 2007. Covers parents with children in kindergarten through grade 12. Homeschooled students are excluded]

Characteristic	Number of students in grades K through 12 (thousands)	Participation in school activities by parent or other household member				
		Attended a general school or PTO/PTA [1] meeting	Attended regularly scheduled parent-teacher conference	Attended a school or class event	Volunteered or served on school committee	Participated in school fundraising
Total........ [2]	**51,600**	**89**	**78**	**74**	**46**	**65**
School type: [2]						
Public, assigned........	37,168	89	76	72	42	63
Public, chosen........	7,951	88	81	74	45	62
Private, religious........	4,560	96	86	86	73	85
Private, nonreligious........	1,438	97	90	86	68	72
Student's sex:						
Male........	26,875	89	79	71	45	65
Female........	24,725	90	77	78	48	66
Student's race/ethnicity:						
White, non-Hispanic........	29,832	91	78	80	54	72
Black, non-Hispanic........	7,837	87	77	65	35	58
Hispanic [3]........	9,767	87	80	65	32	51
Asian or Pacific Islander, non-Hispanic........	1,566	90	80	72	46	62
Other, non-Hispanic........	2,598	90	74	76	47	62
Student's grade level: [4]						
K–2nd grade........	11,516	93	90	78	63	72
3rd–5th grade........	11,519	94	92	83	57	71
6th–8th grade........	12,058	91	76	72	38	63
9th–12th grade........	16,503	83	61	68	34	57
Parents' highest education level:						
Less than high school........	3,504	75	70	48	20	34
High school graduate or equivalent........	11,070	84	74	65	33	55
Vocational/technical or some college........	14,844	89	77	72	42	67
Bachelor's degree........	11,353	94	81	83	56	72
Graduate or professional school........	10,829	95	82	87	64	77
Parents' language at home:						
Both/only parent(s) speak(s) English........	45,219	90	78	77	49	69
One of two parents speaks English........	1,022	82	75	63	42	54
No parent speaks English........	5,359	84	82	57	22	38

[1] Parent Teacher Organization (PTO) or Parent Teacher Association (PTA) meeting. [2] School type has a certain number of missing cases due to school non-report; therefore, the number of students across the category does not sum to the total number of students. [3] Persons of Hispanic origin may be of any race. [4] Students whose parents reported the student's grade equivalent as "ungraded" were excluded from the analyses of grade level.

Source: U.S. Department of Education, National Center for Education Statistics, Parent and Family Involvement in Education Survey of the National Household Education Surveys Program (NHES), 2007. See also: <http://nces.ed.gov/nhes/>.

Table 253. School Enrollment Below Postsecondary—Summary by Sex, Race, and Hispanic Origin: 2010

[In thousands (58,244 represents 58,244,000), except percent. As of October. Covers civilian noninstitutional population enrolled in nursery school through high school. Based on Current Population Survey, see text, Section 1 and Appendix III]

Characteristic	Total			Race and Hispanic origin				
				White [2]				
	Number [1]	Male	Female	Total	Non-Hispanic	Black [2]	Asian [2]	Hispanic [3]
All students........	58,244	29,734	28,510	43,978	32,355	8,886	2,493	12,791
Nursery........	4,835	2,521	2,315	3,659	2,766	698	223	994
Full day........	2,301	(NA)	(NA)	1,549	1,144	521	102	466
Part day........	2,534	(NA)	(NA)	2,111	1,621	177	121	528
Public schools........	2,776	1,356	1,388	1,992	1,274	522	97	794
Full day........	1,352	(NA)	(NA)	849	525	375	45	371
Part day........	1,424	(NA)	(NA)	1,143	748	147	52	423
Private schools........	2,059	1,165	927	1,668	1,492	175	127	200
Full day........	949	(NA)	(NA)	700	619	146	57	95
Part day........	1,110	(NA)	(NA)	968	873	30	69	105
Kindergarten........	4,172	2,071	2,101	3,069	2,120	736	196	1,050
Elementary........	32,663	16,682	15,981	24,680	17,942	4,795	1,488	7,403
High school........	16,574	8,461	8,113	12,570	9,528	2,657	586	3,344
Population 18 to 24 years old........	29,659	14,886	14,773	22,851	17,693	4,457	1,304	5,685
Percent dropouts [4]........	8.7	9.9	7.6	8.5	5.7	10.1	4.9	18.5
Percent high school graduates........	85.0	83.1	87.0	85.4	89.1	82.3	91.4	72.8
Percent enrolled in college........	41.2	38.3	44.1	40.8	43.3	38.0	62.2	31.9

[1] Includes other races not shown separately. [2] For persons who selected this race group only. See footnote 2, Table 234. [3] Persons of Hispanic origin may be of any race. [4] For persons not in regular school and who have not completed the 12th grade nor received a general equivalency degree.

Source: U.S. Census Bureau, "School Enrollment, Current Population Survey October 2010 -Detailed Tables," <http://www.census.gov/hhes/school/data/cps/2010/tables.html>.

Table 254. Elementary and Secondary Schools—Teachers, Enrollment, and Pupil-Teacher Ratio: 1970 to 2010

[In thousands (2,292 represents 2,292,000), except ratios. As of Fall. Data are for full-time equivalent teachers. Based on surveys of state education agencies and private schools; see source for details]

Year	Teachers			Enrollment			Pupil-teacher ratio		
	Total	Public	Private	Total	Public	Private	Total	Public	Private
1970	2,292	2,059	233	51,257	45,894	5,363	22.4	22.3	23.0
1975	2,453	2,198	255	49,819	44,819	5,000	20.3	20.4	19.6
1980	2,485	2,184	301	46,208	40,877	5,331	18.6	18.7	17.7
1985	2,549	2,206	343	44,979	39,422	5,557	17.6	17.9	16.2
1986	2,592	2,244	348	45,205	39,753	5,452	17.4	17.7	15.7
1987	2,631	2,279	352	45,487	40,008	5,479	17.3	17.6	15.6
1988	2,668	2,323	345	45,430	40,189	5,242	17.0	17.3	15.2
1989	2,713	2,357	356	45,741	40,543	5,198	17.0	17.2	15.7
1990	2,759	2,398	361	46,451	41,217	5,234	17.0	17.2	15.6
1991	2,797	2,432	365	47,728	42,047	5,681	17.1	17.3	15.6
1992	2,827	2,459	368	48,500	42,823	5,677	17.2	17.4	15.4
1993	2,874	2,504	370	49,133	43,465	5,668	17.1	17.4	15.3
1994 [1]	2,925	2,552	373	49,898	44,111	5,787	17.1	17.3	15.5
1995	2,974	2,598	376	50,759	44,840	5,918	17.1	17.3	15.7
1996 [1]	3,051	2,667	384	51,544	45,611	5,933	16.9	17.1	15.5
1997	3,138	2,746	391	52,071	46,127	5,944	16.6	16.8	15.2
1998 [1]	3,230	2,830	400	52,525	46,539	5,988	16.3	16.4	15.0
1999	3,319	2,911	408	52,876	46,857	6,018	15.9	16.1	14.7
2000 [1]	3,366	2,941	424	53,373	47,204	6,169	15.9	16.0	14.5
2001	3,440	3,000	441	53,992	47,672	6,320	15.7	15.9	14.3
2002 [1]	3,476	3,034	442	54,403	48,183	6,220	15.7	15.9	14.1
2003	3,490	3,049	441	54,639	48,540	6,099	15.7	15.9	13.8
2004 [1]	3,536	3,091	445	54,882	48,795	6,087	15.5	15.8	13.7
2005	3,593	3,143	450	55,187	49,113	6,073	15.4	15.6	13.5
2006 [1]	3,622	3,166	456	55,307	49,316	5,991	15.3	15.6	13.2
2007	3,634	3,178	456	55,203	49,293	5,910	15.2	15.5	13.0
2008 [1]	3,670	3,222	448	54,973	49,266	5,707	15.0	15.3	12.8
2009	3,647	3,210	437	54,862	49,373	5,488	15.0	15.4	12.5
2010 [2]	3,668	3,240	428	54,704	49,306	5,398	14.9	15.2	12.6

[1] Private school numbers are estimated based on data from the Private School Universe Survey. [2] Projection.

Source: U.S. National Center for Education Statistics, *Digest of Education Statistics*, annual, See also <http://nces.ed.gov/programs/digest/>.

Table 255. Public Elementary and Secondary School Teachers—Selected Characteristics: 2007 to 2008

[612 represents 612,000. For school year. Based on the 2007-2008 Schools and Staffing Survey and subject to sampling error; for details, see source Web site at <http://nces.ed.gov/surveys/sass/>. Excludes prekindergarten teachers. See Table 265 for similar data on private school teachers]

Characteristic	Unit	Age					Sex		Race/ethnicity		
		Under 30 years old	30 to 39 years old	40 to 49 years old	50 to 59 years old	Over 60 years old	Male	Female	White [1]	Black [1]	His-panic [2]
Total teachers [3]	1,000	612	898	808	879	207	821	2,584	2,829	239	240
Highest degree held:											
Bachelor's	Percent	70.1	46.8	43.7	38.4	35.0	47.0	47.5	46.8	47.0	56.3
Master's	Percent	28.0	46.1	47.3	50.4	51.1	43.9	44.8	45.7	41.4	34.1
Education specialist	Percent	1.5	6.0	7.3	8.7	9.6	5.5	6.7	6.0	8.7	7.7
Doctorate	Percent	(S)	0.4	0.7	1.5	3.2	1.6	0.7	0.8	2.0	1.1
Full-time teaching experience:											
Less than 3 years	Percent	44.1	10.3	7.4	3.4	2.9	13.6	13.4	13.0	13.1	18.0
3 to 9 years	Percent	55.9	53.5	25.1	11.4	8.5	33.2	33.7	32.6	38.0	39.0
10 to 20 years	Percent	(S)	36.3	40.9	26.3	20.0	26.6	27.5	27.6	24.9	26.7
20 years or more	Percent	–	(S)	26.6	59.0	68.6	26.6	25.5	26.8	24.1	16.3
Full-time teachers	1,000	572	828	739	803	185	776	2,351	2,579	229	230
Earned income	Dollars	41,790	48,380	52,850	58,760	59,610	53,910	50,790	51,530	51,110	51,520
Salary	Dollars	39,760	46,320	50,870	56,760	57,910	50,560	49,230	49,570	48,910	49,260

– Represents or rounds to zero. S Reporting standards not met, the standard error for this estimate is 50% or more of the estimate's value. [1] Non-Hispanic. [2] Persons of Hispanic origin may be of any race. [3] Includes teachers with no degrees and associate's degrees not shown separately.

Source: U.S. Department of Education, National Center for Education Statistics, Schools and Staffing Survey (SASS), "Public School Teacher Data Files," 2007–08.

Table 256. Public Elementary and Secondary Schools—Number and Average Salary of Classroom Teachers, 1990 to 2010, and by State, 2010

[2,362 represents 2,362,000. Estimates for school year ending in June of year shown. Schools classified by type of organization rather than by grade-group; elementary includes kindergarten]

Year and state	Teachers [1] (1,000)			Avg. salary ($1,000)		
	Total	Elementary	Secondary	All teachers	Elementary	Secondary
1990	2,362	1,390	972	31.4	30.8	32.0
1995	2,565	1,517	1,048	36.7	36.1	37.5
2000	2,891	1,696	1,195	41.8	41.3	42.5
2002	2,992	1,751	1,240	44.7	44.2	45.3
2003	3,020	1,769	1,251	45.7	45.4	46.1
2004	3,042	1,782	1,260	46.5	46.2	47.0
2005	3,072	1,799	1,273	47.5	47.1	47.7
2006	3,125	1,811	1,313	49.1	48.6	49.5
2007	3,172	1,848	1,324	51.1	50.7	51.5
2008	3,201	1,860	1,341	52.8	52.4	53.3
2009	3,228	1,884	1,344	54.3	53.9	54.8
2010, U.S.	**3,215**	**1,876**	**1,340**	**55.2**	**54.9**	**55.6**
AL	46.3	24.9	21.4	47.6	46.9	48.3
AK	8.9	6.0	2.9	59.7	59.7	59.7
AZ	56.9	40.3	16.7	47.0	47.0	47.0
AR	36.2	17.6	18.5	46.7	46.7	46.7
CA	291.0	200.4	90.6	68.2	68.2	68.2
CO	49.0	25.4	23.5	49.2	48.8	49.6
CT	43.2	29.0	14.2	64.4	64.4	64.4
DE	8.8	4.3	4.4	57.1	57.4	56.8
DC	5.8	3.8	1.9	64.5	64.5	64.5
FL	166.1	85.5	80.6	46.7	46.7	46.7
GA	115.7	70.3	45.4	53.1	52.7	53.7
HI	11.7	6.3	5.4	55.1	55.1	55.1
ID	15.4	8.1	7.3	46.3	46.3	46.3
IL	141.6	97.0	44.6	62.1	62.1	62.1
IN	62.5	33.5	29.0	50.0	50.0	50.0
IA	35.5	23.6	11.9	49.6	50.0	48.9
KS	35.0	17.4	17.5	46.7	46.7	46.7
KY	41.3	29.4	11.9	49.5	48.4	49.2
LA	49.3	34.2	15.2	48.9	48.9	48.9
ME	17.1	11.5	5.6	46.1	46.1	46.1

State	Teachers [1] (1,000)			Avg. salary ($1,000)		
	Total	Elementary	Secondary	All teachers	Elementary	Secondary
MD	59.1	34.8	24.3	64.0	63.6	64.5
MA	70.4	46.5	23.9	69.3	69.3	69.3
MI	97.8	49.8	48.0	58.0	58.0	58.0
MN	52.7	26.8	25.9	52.4	52.4	52.4
MS	35.6	21.1	14.5	45.6	45.6	45.6
MO	67.9	34.4	33.5	45.3	45.3	45.3
MT	10.6	7.1	3.4	45.8	45.8	45.8
NE	22.1	13.7	8.4	46.2	46.2	46.2
NV	24.3	14.1	10.2	51.5	51.5	51.5
NH	15.4	10.5	4.9	51.4	51.4	51.4
NJ	114.5	44.5	70.1	65.1	64.3	66.8
NM	21.9	15.1	6.9	46.3	45.7	46.6
NY	226.1	100.4	125.7	71.6	72.0	71.4
NC	95.4	67.4	28.0	46.9	46.9	46.9
ND	7.8	5.4	2.4	43.0	43.2	42.4
OH	110.6	71.0	39.6	56.0	56.9	55.1
OK	42.4	29.4	13.0	47.7	43.9	56.0
OR	30.0	19.4	10.6	55.2	54.9	55.8
PA	126.8	63.4	63.4	59.2	59.2	59.2
RI	11.1	6.9	4.2	59.7	59.7	59.7
SC	48.3	33.6	14.7	47.5	45.9	46.5
SD	9.2	6.5	2.7	38.8	38.9	38.7
TN	65.0	45.3	19.7	46.3	46.3	46.3
TX	333.1	170.5	162.6	45.9	47.9	48.7
UT	25.2	14.1	11.0	45.9	45.9	45.9
VT	8.9	4.6	4.3	49.1	49.1	49.1
VA	106.7	62.8	43.8	50.0	50.0	50.0
WA	53.6	29.6	24.0	53.0	52.9	53.2
WV	19.8	14.3	5.5	46.0	46.0	46.0
WI	58.8	40.4	18.5	51.3	51.2	51.3
WY	7.1	3.7	3.4	55.9	55.5	56.2

[1] Full-time equivalent.

Source: National Education Association, Washington, DC, *Rankings and Estimates Reports* (copyright). See also <http://www.nea.org/home/32073.htm>.

Table 257. Teacher Stayers, Movers, and Leavers by Selected Characteristics: 2000 to 2001 and 2008 to 2009

[2,994.7 represents 2,994,700. Data compare the teaching status of teacher between one school year and the prior year. Stayers are teachers who were teaching in the same school in both years. Movers are teachers who were still teaching in the current school year but in a different school. Leavers are teachers who left the teaching profession. Based on the School and Staffing Survey; see source for details]

Characteristic	Public				Private			
	Total [1]	Stayers	Movers	Leavers	Total [1]	Stayers	Movers	Leavers
NUMBER (1,000)								
2000-01	2,994.7	2,542.2	231.0	221.4	448.6	354.8	37.6	56.2
2008-09	3,380.3	2,854.9	255.7	269.8	487.3	386.0	24.0	77.3
PERCENT DISTRIBUTION								
Total, 2008-09	100.0	84.5	7.6	8.0	100.0	79.2	4.9	15.9
Age:								
Less than 30 years old	100.0	76.1	14.7	9.2	100.0	68.9	10.0	21.1
30 to 39 years old	100.0	84.4	7.3	8.4	100.0	76.9	4.9	18.2
40 to 49 years old	100.0	89.6	6.6	3.9	100.0	83.7	5.4	10.9
50 to 59 years old	100.0	85.9	5.7	8.4	100.0	85.2	2.4	12.4
60 years old and over	100.0	82.4	[2] 2.0	15.6	100.0	77.7	[2] 2.7	19.6
Sex:								
Male	100.0	84.4	7.8	7.9	100.0	80.0	5.7	14.3
Female	100.0	84.5	7.5	8.0	100.0	78.9	4.7	16.4
Race/ethnicity:								
White, non-Hispanic	100.0	85.0	7.0	8.0	100.0	80.7	4.6	14.7
Black, non-Hispanic	100.0	80.5	10.4	9.0	100.0	67.2	[2] 8.6	[2] 24.2
Hispanic, single or more than one race	100.0	83.8	10.7	[2] 5.6	100.0	69.2	(S)	[2] 23.7
Asian, Native Hawaiian, or Other Pacific Islander, non-Hispanic	100.0	80.1	(S)	[2] 8.0	100.0	[2] 58.7	(S)	(S)
American Indian/Alaska Native, non-Hispanic	100.0	[2] 82.5	(S)	(S)	100.0	(S)	(S)	(S)
More than one race, non-Hispanic	100.0	82.5	(S)	(S)	100.0	100.0	–	–
Years as a teacher:								
3 or fewer	100.0	76.2	14.1	9.7	100.0	70.5	6.5	22.9
4 to 9	100.0	83.4	8.6	7.9	100.0	74.8	7.8	17.4
10 to 19	100.0	90.4	5.2	4.4	100.0	84.3	2.8	12.9
20 or more	100.0	84.0	5.2	10.8	100.0	85.8	2.7	11.4
Main assignment field:								
Early childhood/general elementary	100.0	87.0	7.4	5.6	100.0	79.7	6.5	13.8
Special education	100.0	78.0	9.8	12.3	100.0	62.9	(S)	[2] 27.5
Arts/music	100.0	88.4	7.5	4.1	100.0	87.9	(S)	9.0
English/language arts	100.0	81.8	7.7	10.5	100.0	80.5	[2] 2.9	16.5
Mathematics	100.0	85.6	6.7	7.7	100.0	85.3	(S)	[2] 12.7
Natural sciences	100.0	83.9	7.1	[2] 9.0	100.0	80.6	[2] 4.8	[2] 14.6
Social sciences	100.0	84.2	[2] 8.2	7.6	100.0	83.3	[2] 4.3	[2] 12.4
Other	100.0	84.2	6.7	9.1	100.0	72.3	4.9	22.8

– Represents or rounds to zero. S Reporting standards not met. [1] Total teachers prior school year. [2] Interpret data with caution. The standard error for this estimate is equal to 30 percent or more of the estimate's value.

Source: U.S. National Center for Education Statistics, Teacher Follow-up Survey (TFS), "Current Teacher Data File" and "Former Teacher Data File," 2008–09. See also <http://nces.ed.gov/surveys/sass/index.asp>.

Table 258. Public and Private School Teachers Who Moved to a Different School or Left Teaching by Reason: 2008 to 2009

[In percent. Movers are teachers who were still teaching in the current year but had moved to a different school after the 2007–08 school year. Leavers are teachers who left the teaching profession after the 2007–08 school year. Based on the School and Staffing Survey; see source for details]

Primary reason for moving	Movers		Primary reason for moving	Leavers	
	Public	Private		Public	Private
Contract was not renewed	10.7	12.7	Contract was not renewed	5.3	13.0
Primary reason for moving, other than contract was not renewed:			Primary reason for leaving, other than contract was not renewed:		
Personal life factors	26.2	16.0	Personal life factors	42.9	27.8
Assignment and credential factors	[1] 7.5	(S)	Assignment and credential factors	[1] 1.2	[1] 1.6
Salary and other job benefits	[1] 4.0	23.2	Salary and other job benefits	[1] 4.0	[1] 10.7
Classroom factors	1.8	(S)	Classroom factors	(S)	(S)
School factors	16.1	18.9	School factors	9.8	12.1
Student performance factors	[1] 1.6	(S)	Student performance factors	3.5	(S)
Other factors	32.0	24.3	Other career factors	14.8	22.8
			Other factors	17.1	10.3

S Reporting standards not met. [1] Interpret data with caution. The standard error of this estimate is equal to 30 percent or more of the estimate's value.

Source: U.S. National Center for Education Statistics, Teacher Attrition and Mobility: Results from the 2008-09 Teacher Follow-up Survey, NCES 2010-353, August 2010. See also <http://nces.ed.gov/surveys/btls/index.asp>.

Table 259. Average Salary and Wages Paid in Public School Systems: 1985 to 2011

[In dollars. For school year ending in year shown. Data reported by a stratified sample of school systems enrolling 300 or more pupils. Data represent unweighted means of average salaries paid school personnel reported by each school system]

Position	1985	1990	1995	2000	2005	2008	2009	2010	2011
ANNUAL SALARY									
Central-office administrators:									
Superintendent (contract salary).......	56,954	75,425	90,198	112,158	128,770	148,387	155,634	159,634	161,992
Deputy/assoc. superintendent.........	52,877	69,623	81,266	97,251	116,186	134,245	136,832	139,463	138,061
Assistant superintendent...............	48,003	62,698	75,236	88,913	103,212	116,833	119,755	123,509	122,333
Administrators for—									
Finance and business...............	40,344	52,354	61,323	73,499	83,678	96,490	98,590	100,306	101,347
Instructional services................	43,452	56,359	66,767	79,023	88,950	99,748	102,322	103,974	103,025
Public relations/information..........	35,287	44,926	53,263	60,655	70,502	80,534	83,235	86,567	84,629
Staff personnel services.............	44,182	56,344	65,819	76,608	86,966	98,190	100,620	102,269	101,578
Technology.........................	(X)	(X)	(X)	(X)	76,308	86,085	87,898	90,530	90,914
Subject area supervisors.............	34,422	45,929	54,534	63,103	68,714	78,309	80,290	80,964	80,534
School building administrators:									
Principals:									
Elementary.......................	36,452	48,431	58,589	69,407	76,182	85,907	88,062	89,673	89,591
Junior high/middle..................	39,650	52,163	62,311	73,877	81,514	91,334	93,478	95,003	95,426
Senior high.......................	42,094	55,722	66,596	79,839	86,938	97,486	99,365	102,387	102,191
Assistant principals:									
Elementary.......................	30,496	40,916	48,491	56,419	63,140	71,192	71,893	73,181	71,764
Junior high/middle..................	33,793	44,570	52,942	60,842	67,600	76,053	77,476	79,164	78,131
Senior high.......................	35,491	46,486	55,556	64,811	71,401	79,391	81,083	83,074	82,027
Classroom teachers..................	23,587	31,278	37,264	42,213	45,884	51,329	52,900	54,370	54,220
Auxiliary professional personnel:									
Counselors.........................	27,593	35,979	42,486	48,195	52,500	57,618	58,775	60,142	60,188
Librarians..........................	24,981	33,469	40,418	46,732	50,720	56,933	57,974	59,495	59,093
School nurses......................	19,944	26,090	31,066	35,540	40,520	46,025	46,476	48,032	48,044
Secretarial/clerical personnel:									
Central office:									
Secretaries.......................	15,343	20,238	23,935	28,405	32,716	36,657	37,785	38,601	38,606
Accounting/payroll clerks.............	15,421	20,088	24,042	28,498	33,217	37,732	39,031	39,895	39,790
Typists/data entry clerks.............	12,481	16,125	18,674	22,853	26,214	30,072	31,718	32,555	32,636
School building level:									
Secretaries.......................	12,504	16,184	19,170	22,630	25,381	28,810	29,480	30,474	30,226
Library clerks......................	9,911	12,152	14,381	16,509	18,443	21,004	21,190	21,639	21,142
HOURLY WAGE RATE									
Other support personnel:									
Teacher aides:									
Instructional......................	5.89	7.43	8.77	10.00	11.35	12.86	13.23	13.48	13.55
Noninstructional....................	5.60	7.08	8.29	9.77	11.23	12.70	13.13	13.59	13.58
Custodians..........................	6.90	8.54	10.05	11.35	12.61	14.19	14.59	15.04	14.92
Cafeteria workers....................	5.42	6.77	7.89	9.02	10.33	11.60	11.94	12.18	12.23
Bus drivers.........................	7.27	9.21	10.69	12.48	14.18	16.56	16.44	16.62	16.61

X Not applicable.

Source: Editorial Projects in Education, Bethesda MD, *National Survey of Salaries and Wages in Public Schools*, (copyright). See also: <http://www.edweek.org/ew/marketplace/products/ers/publications.html>.

Table 260. Public School Employment: 1990 and 2008

[In thousands (3,181 represents 3,181,000). Covers all public elementary-secondary school districts with 100 or more full-time employees]

Occupation	1990					2008				
	Total	Male	Female	White [1]	Black [1]	Total	Male	Female	White [1]	Black [1]
All occupations [2]...............	**3,181**	**914**	**2,267**	**2,502**	**463**	**4,772**	**1,213**	**3,559**	**3,562**	**617**
Officials, administrators..............	43	28	15	37	4	76	36	41	60	8
Principals and assistant principals..........................	90	56	34	70	13	190	86	104	125	35
Classroom teachers [3]................	1,746	468	1,278	1,469	192	2,544	613	1,930	2,055	240
Elementary schools.................	875	128	747	722	103	1,218	152	1,066	978	107
Secondary schools.................	662	304	358	570	66	1,007	394	614	828	92
Other professional staff.............	227	58	170	187	30	386	71	315	298	49
Teachers' aides [4]...................	324	54	270	208	69	555	72	483	372	96
Clerical, secretarial staff.............	226	5	221	181	24	323	11	312	230	37
Service workers [5]..................	524	245	279	348	129	761	352	409	454	164

[1] Excludes individuals of Hispanic origin. [2] 2008 Includes other occupations not shown separately. [3] Includes other classroom teachers not shown separately. [4] Includes technicians. [5] Includes craftworkers and laborers.

Source: U.S. Equal Employment Opportunity Commission, *Elementary-Secondary Staff Information (EEO-5)*, biennial.

Table 261. Public Elementary and Secondary School Finances by Enrollment-Size Group: 2009 to 2010

[In millions of dollars (593,682 represents $593,682,000,000). Data are based on the Annual Government Finance Survey. For details, see source. See also Appendix III]

Item	All school systems	\multicolumn{7}{c}{School systems with enrollment of—}
		50,000 or more	25,000 to 49,999	15,000 to 24,999	7,500 to 14,999	5,000 to 7,499	3,000 to 4,999	Under 3,000
TOTAL								
General revenue	593,682	125,058	73,393	52,850	84,690	53,716	70,994	132,981
From federal sources	74,047	16,831	9,928	6,638	10,239	5,596	7,403	17,411
Through state	69,722	16,005	9,521	6,383	9,548	5,302	7,019	15,944
Child nutrition programs	11,856	2,864	1,762	1,209	1,677	940	1,198	2,207
Direct	4,325	827	407	256	691	294	384	1,466
From state sources [1]	258,191	50,154	33,213	25,716	38,412	22,220	29,198	59,278
General formula assistance	176,565	31,921	23,930	18,283	27,069	15,384	19,611	40,367
Compensatory programs	4,604	1,089	703	544	770	331	441	726
Special education	16,673	4,165	1,714	1,325	2,053	1,319	2,010	4,087
From local sources	261,445	58,073	30,252	20,495	36,039	25,900	34,393	56,293
Taxes	176,700	28,897	20,948	14,313	26,272	19,283	25,347	41,640
Contributions from parent government	48,162	22,067	4,780	2,970	4,967	3,529	4,847	5,001
From other local governments	7,507	603	1,172	709	938	727	922	2,436
Current charges	14,439	2,477	1,690	1,252	2,044	1,293	1,743	3,941
School lunch	6,614	981	779	627	1,044	689	899	1,594
Other	14,637	4,029	1,662	1,252	1,818	1,068	1,534	3,274
General expenditure	602,648	129,183	75,700	54,212	85,507	54,138	70,305	133,601
Current spending	523,990	110,757	64,738	46,890	74,332	47,545	62,299	117,428
By function:								
Instruction	317,818	69,859	38,959	28,363	45,139	29,039	37,880	68,581
Support services	179,024	35,178	22,330	15,995	25,422	16,212	21,416	42,472
Other current spending	27,148	5,721	3,450	2,532	3,771	2,295	3,004	6,375
By object:								
Total salaries and wages	312,044	65,344	39,890	28,885	45,076	28,487	37,032	67,330
Total employee benefits	109,516	23,158	12,671	9,735	15,850	10,269	13,457	24,376
Capital outlay	59,355	13,934	8,307	5,561	8,397	4,768	5,935	12,454
Interest on debt	17,630	4,277	2,598	1,733	2,604	1,593	1,886	2,939
Payments to other governments	1,673	215	57	28	175	232	186	781
Debt outstanding	406,903	97,144	56,451	39,822	59,460	36,608	46,270	71,147
Long-term	399,001	95,983	55,791	39,282	58,590	35,784	45,150	68,422
Short-term	7,903	1,161	661	540	871	824	1,121	2,725
Long-term debt issued	48,163	14,661	5,799	4,438	5,948	3,449	5,300	8,568
Long-term debt retired	35,296	8,655	4,437	3,113	4,888	2,992	4,362	6,849
PER PUPIL								
Fall enrollment (1,000)	48,243	10,092	6,706	4,848	7,246	4,298	5,548	9,504
General revenue	12,306	12,392	10,944	10,900	11,688	12,497	12,796	13,992
From federal sources	1,535	1,668	1,480	1,369	1,413	1,302	1,334	1,832
From state sources [1]	5,352	4,970	4,953	5,304	5,301	5,169	5,263	6,237
General formula assistance	3,660	3,163	3,568	3,771	3,736	3,579	3,535	4,247
Special education	346	413	256	273	283	307	362	430
From local sources [1]	5,419	5,754	4,511	4,227	4,974	6,026	6,199	5,923
Taxes	3,663	2,863	3,124	2,952	3,626	4,486	4,569	4,381
Contributions from parent government	998	2,187	713	613	685	821	874	526
Current charges	299	245	252	258	282	301	314	415
School lunch	137	97	116	129	144	160	162	168
General expenditure [1]	12,245	12,523	11,040	11,000	11,590	12,337	12,428	13,787
Current spending	10,615	10,698	9,405	9,490	10,048	10,803	10,985	12,085
By function:								
Instruction	6,478	6,789	5,676	5,790	6,131	6,620	6,712	7,126
Support services	3,711	3,486	3,330	3,299	3,508	3,772	3,860	4,469
By object:								
Total salaries and wages	6,468	6,475	5,948	5,958	6,221	6,627	6,675	7,085
Total employee benefits	2,270	2,295	1,890	2,008	2,187	2,389	2,425	2,565
Capital outlay	1,230	1,381	1,239	1,147	1,159	1,109	1,070	1,310
Interest on debt	365	424	387	358	359	371	340	309
Debt outstanding	8,434	9,626	8,418	8,213	8,206	8,517	8,340	7,486
Long-term	8,271	9,511	8,320	8,102	8,086	8,325	8,138	7,199

[1] Includes other sources not shown separately.

Source: U.S. Census Bureau, *Public Education Finances, 2010*, June 2012, <http://www.census.gov/govs/school>.

Table 262. Public Elementary and Secondary Schools by School Type, Racial/Ethnic Concentration of Students, and Eligibility of Students for Free or Reduced-Price Lunch: 1999 and 2009

[For school year ending in June of year shown]

Characteristic	1999				2009			
	Total	Elementary	Secondary	Combined	Total	Elementary	Secondary	Combined
Total number of schools [1]	90,874	63,382	21,790	5,067	98,706	67,082	24,275	5,623
Percent [1]	100.0	69.7	24.0	5.6	100.0	68.0	24.6	5.7
PERCENT								
School type	100.0	100.0	100.0	100.0	100.0	100.0	100.0	100.0
Regular	92.0	98.5	85.4	49.2	90.0	98.3	79.9	49.7
Special education	2.2	0.8	1.2	17.2	2.3	0.8	1.4	16.7
Vocational	1.2	–	2.9	7.2	1.4	–	4.9	1.5
Alternative	4.6	0.7	10.5	26.3	6.3	0.9	13.8	32.2
Charter school [2]	0.6	0.5	0.5	1.7	4.8	3.7	5.2	15.4
Title I school [3]	–	–	–	–	63.1	72.7	44.9	47.3
Magnet school/program [4]	1.3	1.4	1.3	0.5	3.1	3.3	3.0	1.6
Racial/ethnic concentration: [5]								
More than 50 percent White	72.0	71.2	76.4	62.8	62.7	62.0	66.1	57.1
More than 50 percent Black	10.9	11.4	8.8	13.8	11.5	11.4	10.5	16.4
More than 50 percent Hispanic	8.2	8.7	6.8	6.8	13.4	14.1	11.8	10.3
Percentage of students in school eligible for free or reduced-price lunch	100.0	100.0	100.0	100.0	100.0	100.0	100.0	100.0
0–25 percent	22.1	18.8	31.4	25.6	24.7	23.6	28.6	21.9
26–50 percent	20.9	20.6	23.0	16.2	28.9	27.1	35.2	23.6
51–75 percent	14.5	16.3	9.1	17.2	24.7	25.6	21.7	26.1
76–100 percent	9.7	11.8	3.7	9.4	19.1	21.7	11.2	20.4
Missing/school did not participate	32.8	32.4	32.8	31.5	2.7	2.0	3.3	8.0

– Represents or rounds to zero. [1] Schools reporting membership are those which report at least one student enrolled on October 1 of the school year. In any given year, some small schools will not have any students. The Common Core of Data (CCD) allows a student to be reported for only a single school or agency. For example, a vocational school (identified as a "shared time" school) may provide classes for students from a number of districts and show no membership. [2] A charter school is a school that provides free public elementary and/or secondary education to eligible students under a specific charter granted by the state legislature or other appropriate authority and that is designated by such authority to be a charter school. [3] A Title I School is designated under appropriate state and federal regulations as a high-poverty school that is eligible for participation in programs authorized by Title I of P.L. 107-110. The 1998-99 estimates exclude a large number of schools that did not report whether they were Title I. [4] A magnet school or program is a special school or program designed to attract students of different racial/ethnic backgrounds in an effort to reduce, prevent, or eliminate racial isolation and/or provide an academic or social focus on a particular theme. [5] Race categories exclude persons of Hispanic ethnicity.

Source: U.S. Department of Education, National Center for Education Statistics, Common Core of Data (CCD), Public Elementary/ Secondary School Universe Survey, 1998-99 (version 1c) and 2008-09 (version 1b). See also: *The Condition of Education 2011*, <nces.ed.gov/pubsearch/pubsinfo.asp?pubid=2011033>.

Table 263. Public School Districts Offering Various Technology Resources to All or Some Students by District Characteristics: 2008

[In percent. As of Fall. Percents are based on the percent of public school districts with students at that level (97 percent of districts have elementary students and 88 percent have secondary students). For composition of regions, see map, inside front cover]

Characteristic	Electronic storage space on a server				Online access to the library catalogue				Online curriculum			
	Elementary		Secondary		Elementary		Secondary		Elementary		Secondary	
	All	Some	All	Some	All	Some	All	Some	All	Some	All	Some
All public school districts	62	17	83	7	72	6	82	2	47	19	53	25
District enrollment size:												
Less than 2,500	63	15	85	3	69	5	80	[1] 1	46	17	53	23
2,500 to 9,999	59	22	78	14	79	7	87	3	50	23	54	28
10,000 or more	58	23	74	17	84	7	87	6	49	26	51	34
Community type:												
City	52	32	75	16	80	14	89	5	47	28	46	36
Suburban	67	15	84	7	76	7	87	2	40	23	46	30
Town	63	18	84	7	82	4	88	2	44	26	51	31
Rural	60	16	83	6	66	5	77	1	52	14	57	20
Region:												
Northeast	73	16	90	4	78	8	88	3	41	22	42	36
Southeast	43	20	64	18	74	4	82	3	52	16	59	20
Central	67	14	91	2	71	4	82	(S)	45	20	56	21
West	53	22	75	10	69	6	77	2	55	17	54	23
Poverty concentration:												
Less than 10 percent	76	12	92	3	82	6	92	[1] 1	45	22	51	30
10 to 19 percent	60	19	85	7	69	5	82	2	44	20	51	28
20 percent or more	50	21	72	10	66	6	72	2	54	14	56	18

S Reporting standards not met. [1] Interpret data with caution; the coefficient of variation is greater than 50 percent.

Source: U.S. National Center for Education Statistics, *Educational Technology in Public School Districts: Fall 2008*, NCES 2010-003, December 2009.

Table 264. Private Schools: 2009 to 2010

[5,488 represents 5,488,000. Based on the Private School Survey, conducted every 2 years; see source for details. For composition of regions, see map inside front cover]

Characteristic	Schools				Students (1,000)				Teachers (1,000) [1]			
	Number	Elementary	Secondary	Combined	Total	Elementary	Secondary	Combined	Total	Elementary	Secondary	Combined
Total	**33,366**	**21,425**	**2,776**	**9,165**	**5,488**	**2,937**	**786**	**1,766**	**437**	**194**	**68**	**175**
School type:												
Catholic	7,115	5,679	1,097	339	2,160	1,455	587	118	143	89	43	10
Parochial	3,111	2,893	145	73	856	762	67	28	53	46	5	2
Diocesan	2,969	2,384	487	98	909	613	261	35	58	37	18	3
Private	1,035	402	465	168	395	80	259	55	31	6	20	6
Other religious	15,616	8,903	776	5,937	2,076	884	107	1,086	172	63	11	98
Conservative Christian	4,614	1,645	147	2,823	737	209	18	511	60	15	2	43
Affiliated	2,882	1,789	259	834	516	246	43	226	45	19	5	21
Unaffiliated	8,120	5,470	370	2,280	823	429	46	349	67	29	5	33
Nonsectarian	10,635	6,842	903	2,889	1,252	599	92	562	123	43	13	67
Regular	5,231	3,899	319	1,014	818	361	64	392	76	24	9	43
Special emphasis	3,821	2,703	322	797	328	223	16	89	29	17	2	10
Special education	1,582	240	263	1,079	107	14	12	81	18	2	2	14
Program emphasis:												
Regular elem/sec	22,565	13,812	2,048	6,705	4,648	2,366	742	1,541	367	161	61	144
Montessori	2,653	2,438	8	207	213	193	1	19	15	13	(Z)	2
Special program emphasis	917	411	102	405	128	50	12	66	15	5	1	9
Special education	1,779	278	276	1,225	118	16	12	90	20	3	2	15
Vocational/tech	2	–	1	1	1	–	(Z)	1	(Z)	–	(Z)	(Z)
Alternative	1,327	363	341	623	95	26	19	50	10	3	2	6
Early childhood	4,122	4,122	(X)	–	285	285	(X)	–	10	10	(X)	–
Size:												
Less than 50	11,065	7,113	842	3,110	296	198	19	79	34	17	4	13
50 to 149	10,469	7,160	541	2,767	950	656	48	245	82	46	6	30
150 to 299	6,695	4,742	446	1,506	1,423	1,004	99	320	107	64	10	33
300 to 499	3,013	1,770	382	861	1,155	676	150	329	87	43	13	30
500 to 749	1,276	536	284	456	769	312	176	281	57	18	13	25
750 or more	848	104	279	464	896	91	294	511	70	5	20	44
Region:												
Northeast	7,643	4,982	923	1,739	1,310	686	270	353	115	47	25	43
Midwest	8,419	6,226	636	1,557	1,296	840	212	243	92	53	16	23
South	10,483	5,618	601	4,263	1,842	807	159	876	153	56	14	83
West	6,821	4,600	616	1,605	1,041	604	144	293	77	38	12	27

– Represents zero. X Not applicable. Z Less than 500. [1] Full-time equivalents.

Source: U.S. National Center for Education Statistics, Private School Universe Survey, 2009-2010; <http://nces.ed.gov/surveys/pss/>.

Table 265. Private Elementary and Secondary School Teachers—Selected Characteristics: 2007 to 2008

[80 represents 80,000. For school year. Based on the 2007–08 Schools and Staffing Survey Private School Teacher Questionnaire, and subject to sampling error; for details, see source at <http://nces.ed.gov/surveys/sass/>. Excludes prekindergarten teachers. See Table 255 for similar data on public school teachers]

Characteristic	Unit	Age					Sex		Race/ethnicity		
		Under 30 years old	30 to 39 years old	40 to 49 years old	50 to 59 years old	60 years old and over	Male	Female	White [1]	Black [1]	Hispanic [2]
Total teachers [3]	**1,000**	**80**	**109**	**116**	**128**	**56**	**127**	**362**	**423**	**20**	**29**
Highest degree held:											
Bachelor's	Percent	68.3	52.9	54.4	49.8	43.6	45.7	56.8	53.5	55.3	59.3
Master's	Percent	19.1	33.7	30.1	39.8	39.9	37.6	31.1	34.2	22.2	20.9
Education specialist	Percent	1.2	2.3	2.9	2.7	6.5	4.2	2.4	2.9	1.6	3.7
Doctorate	Percent	–	1.9	3.5	2.0	5.1	5.4	1.3	2.4	(S)	(S)
Full-time teaching experience:											
Less than 3 years	Percent	55.5	24.4	20.4	13.2	7.2	24.1	23.5	22.5	30.2	31.9
3 to 9 years	Percent	44.2	49.7	30.4	17.8	7.5	29.5	31.6	30.6	40.6	29.8
10 to 20 years	Percent	(S)	25.8	34.3	25.8	17.2	22.2	22.8	22.6	16.4	25.9
20 years or more	Percent	–	(S)	14.9	43.2	68.1	24.2	22.2	24.3	12.7	12.3
Full-time teachers	1,000	69	90	89	99	41	99	289	334	17	23
School related income	Dol.	31,800	36,380	36,780	41,310	44,280	42,960	35,940	38,000	32,630	36,120
Annual salary	Dol.	30,090	34,650	35,270	39,850	42,740	40,380	34,700	36,500	30,300	34,070

– Represents or rounds to zero. S Reporting standards not met. The standard error for this estimate is 50 percent or more of the estimate's value. [1] Non-Hispanic. [2] Persons of Hispanic origin may be of any race. [3] Includes teachers with no degrees and associate's degrees, not shown separately.

Source: U.S. Department of Education, National Center for Education Statistics, Schools and Staffing Survey (SASS), "Private School Teacher Data Files," 2007–08. See <http://nces.ed.gov/surveys/sass/>.

Table 266. SAT Scores and Characteristics of College-Bound Seniors: 1970 to 2011

[For school year ending in year shown. Data are for the SAT I: Reasoning Tests. SAT I: Reasoning Test replaced the SAT in March 1994. Scores between the two tests have been equated to the same 200–800 scale and are thus comparable. Scores for 1995 and prior years have been recentered and revised]

Type of test and characteristic	Unit	1970	1980	1990	1995	2000	2005	2008	2009	2010	2011
AVERAGE TEST SCORES [1]											
Critical reading, total [2]	Point	537	502	500	504	505	508	502	501	501	497
Male	Point	536	506	505	505	507	513	504	503	503	500
Female	Point	538	498	496	502	504	505	500	498	498	495
Math, total [2]	Point	512	492	501	506	514	520	515	515	516	514
Male	Point	531	515	521	525	533	538	533	534	534	531
Female	Point	493	473	483	490	498	504	500	499	500	500
Writing	Point	(X)	(X)	(X)	(X)	(X)	(X)	494	493	492	489
Male	Point	(X)	(X)	(X)	(X)	(X)	(X)	488	486	486	482
Female	Point	(X)	(X)	(X)	(X)	(X)	(X)	501	499	498	496
PARTICIPANTS											
Total [3]	1,000	(NA)	922	1,026	1,068	1,260	1,476	1,519	1,530	1,548	1,647
Male	Percent	(NA)	48.2	47.8	46.4	46.2	46.5	46.4	46.5	46.6	46.8
White	Percent	(NA)	82.1	73.0	69.2	66.4	62.3	59.8	58.1	54.1	52.6
Black	Percent	(NA)	9.1	10.0	10.7	11.2	11.6	12.1	12.8	12.7	13.1
Obtaining scores [1] of—											
600 or above:											
Critical reading	Percent	(NA)	(NA)	20.3	21.9	21.1	22.5	21.0	20.5	20.5	20.2
Math	Percent	(NA)	(NA)	20.4	23.4	24.2	26.5	25.0	25.7	25.2	25.3
Writing	Percent	(X)	(X)	(X)	(X)	(X)	(X)	18.3	18.7	18.4	18.1
Below 400:											
Critical reading	Percent	(NA)	(NA)	17.3	16.4	15.9	15.5	17.0	17.4	17.5	18.3
Math	Percent	(NA)	(NA)	15.8	16.0	14.7	13.8	15.0	15.3	14.9	15.2
Writing	Percent	(X)	(X)	(X)	(X)	(X)	(X)	18.5	19.4	19.4	20.6

NA Not available. X Not applicable. [1] Minimum score, 200; maximum score, 800. [2] 1970 estimates based on total number of persons taking SAT. For 2010, based on 1,647,123 test takers. [3] 922 represents 922,000.

Source: The College Board, *College-Bound Seniors 2011* (copyright 1967 to 2011), <http://www.collegeboard.com>. Reproduced with permission.

Table 267. ACT Program Scores and Characteristics of College-Bound Students: 1970 to 2012

[For academic year ending in year shown. Except as indicated, test scores and characteristics of college-bound students. Through 1980, data based on 10 percent sample; thereafter, based on all ACT tested graduating seniors]

Type of test and characteristic	Unit	1970	1980	1990 [1]	1995 [1]	2000 [1]	2008 [1]	2009 [1]	2010 [1]	2011 [1]	2012 [1]
TEST SCORES [2]											
Composite	Point	19.9	18.5	20.6	20.8	21.0	21.1	21.1	21.0	21.1	21.1
Male	Point	20.3	19.3	21.0	21.0	21.2	21.2	21.3	21.2	21.2	21.2
Female	Point	19.4	17.9	20.3	20.7	20.9	21.0	20.9	20.9	21.0	21.0
English	Point	18.5	17.9	20.5	20.2	20.5	20.6	20.6	20.5	20.6	20.5
Male	Point	17.6	17.3	20.1	19.8	20.0	20.1	20.2	20.1	20.2	20.2
Female	Point	19.4	18.3	20.9	20.6	20.9	21.0	20.9	20.8	20.9	20.9
Math	Point	20.0	17.4	19.9	20.2	20.7	21.0	21.0	21.0	21.1	21.1
Male	Point	21.1	18.9	20.7	20.9	21.4	21.6	21.6	21.6	21.6	21.7
Female	Point	18.8	16.2	19.3	19.7	20.2	20.4	20.4	20.5	20.6	20.6
Reading [3]	Point	19.7	17.2	(NA)	21.3	21.4	21.4	21.4	21.3	21.3	21.3
Male	Point	20.3	18.2	(NA)	21.1	21.2	21.2	21.3	21.1	21.1	21.2
Female	Point	19.0	16.4	(NA)	21.4	21.5	21.5	21.4	21.4	21.4	21.4
Science reasoning [4]	Point	20.8	21.1	(NA)	21.0	21.0	20.8	20.9	20.9	20.9	20.9
Male	Point	21.6	22.4	(NA)	21.6	21.6	21.3	21.4	21.4	21.4	21.4
Female	Point	20.0	20.0	(NA)	20.5	20.6	20.4	20.4	20.5	20.5	20.5
PARTICIPANTS [5]											
Total [6]	1,000	788	822	817	945	1,065	1,422	1,480	1,569	1,623	1,666
Male	Percent	52	45	46	44	43	45	45	45	46	46
White	Percent	(NA)	83	73	69	72	63	64	62	60	59
Black	Percent	4	8	9	9	10	13	13	14	14	13
Obtaining composite scores of [7]											
27 or above	Percent	14	13	12	13	14	16	16	16	17	17
18 or below	Percent	21	33	35	34	32	33	34	35	34	34

NA Not available. [1] Beginning 1990, not comparable with previous years because a new version of the ACT was introduced. Estimated average composite scores for prior years: 1989, 20.6; 1988, 1987, and 1986, 20.8. [2] Minimum score, 1; maximum score, 36. [3] Prior to 1990, social studies; data not comparable with previous years. [4] Prior to 1990, natural sciences; data not comparable with previous years. [5] Beginning 1985, data are for seniors who graduated in year shown and had taken the ACT in their junior or senior years. Data by race are for those responding to the race question. [6] 788 represents 788,000. [7] Prior to 1990, 26 or above and 15 or below.

Source: ACT, Inc., Iowa City, IA, *High School Profile Report*, annual (copyright). Reproduced with permission.

Table 268. Proficiency Levels on Selected NAEP Tests for Students in Public Schools by State: 2009

[Represents percent of public school students scoring at or above basic and proficient levels. Basic denotes mastery of the knowledge and skills that are fundamental for proficient work at a given grade level. Proficient represents solid academic performance. Students reaching this level demonstrated competency over challenging subject matter. For more detail, see <http://www.nagb.org/pubs/pubs.html>. Based on the National Assessment of Educational Progress (NAEP) tests which are administered to a representative sample of students in public schools, private schools, and Department of Defense schools. Data shown here are for public school students only]

State	Grade 4 Math		Grade 8 Math		Grade 4 Reading		Grade 8 Reading	
	At or above Basic	At or above Proficient	At or above Basic	At or above Proficient	At or above Basic	At or above Proficient	At or above Basic	At or above Proficient
U.S. average	82	39	73	34	67	33	75	32
Alabama	70	24	58	20	62	28	66	24
Alaska	78	38	75	33	59	27	72	27
Arizona	71	28	67	29	56	25	68	27
Arkansas	80	36	67	27	63	29	69	27
California	72	30	59	23	54	24	64	22
Colorado	84	45	76	40	72	40	78	32
Connecticut	86	46	78	40	76	42	81	43
Delaware	84	36	75	32	73	35	78	31
District of Columbia	56	17	40	11	44	17	51	14
Florida	86	40	70	29	73	36	76	32
Georgia	78	34	67	27	63	29	72	27
Hawaii	77	37	65	25	57	26	67	22
Idaho	85	41	78	38	69	32	77	33
Illinois	80	38	73	33	65	32	77	33
Indiana	87	42	78	36	70	34	79	32
Iowa	87	41	76	34	69	34	77	32
Kansas	89	46	79	39	72	35	80	33
Kentucky	81	37	70	27	72	36	79	33
Louisiana	72	23	62	20	51	18	64	20
Maine	87	45	78	35	70	35	80	35
Maryland	85	44	75	40	70	37	77	36
Massachusetts	92	57	85	52	80	47	83	43
Michigan	78	35	68	31	64	30	72	31
Minnesota	89	54	83	47	70	37	82	38
Mississippi	69	22	54	15	55	22	62	19
Missouri	83	41	77	35	70	36	79	34
Montana	88	45	82	44	73	35	84	38
Nebraska	82	38	75	35	70	35	80	35
Nevada	79	32	63	25	57	24	65	22
New Hampshire	92	56	82	43	77	41	81	39
New Jersey	88	49	80	44	76	40	83	42
New Mexico	72	26	59	20	52	20	66	22
New York	83	40	73	34	71	36	75	33
North Carolina	87	43	74	36	65	32	70	29
North Dakota	91	45	86	43	76	35	86	34
Ohio	85	45	76	36	71	36	80	37
Oklahoma	82	33	68	24	65	28	73	26
Oregon	80	37	75	37	65	31	76	33
Pennsylvania	84	46	78	40	70	37	81	40
Rhode Island	81	39	68	28	69	36	72	28
South Carolina	78	34	69	30	62	28	68	24
South Dakota	86	42	83	42	70	33	84	37
Tennessee	74	28	65	25	63	28	73	28
Texas	85	38	78	36	65	28	73	27
Utah	81	41	75	35	67	31	78	33
Vermont	89	51	81	43	75	41	84	41
Virginia	85	43	76	36	74	38	78	32
Washington	84	43	78	39	68	33	78	36
West Virginia	77	28	61	19	62	26	67	22
Wisconsin	85	45	79	39	67	33	78	34
Wyoming	87	40	78	35	72	33	82	34

Source: National Center for Education Statistics, National Assessment of Educational Progress (NAEP), 2009 Mathematics and Reading Assessments. See also <http://nces.ed.gov/nationsreportcard/>, accessed April 2010.

Table 269. Public High School Graduates by State: 1980 to 2010

[In thousands (2,747.7 represents 2,747,700). For school year ending in year shown]

State	1980	1990	2000	2010, proj.
United States	**2,747.7**	**2,320.3**	**2,553.8**	**3,013.4**
Alabama	45.2	40.5	37.8	40.6
Alaska	5.2	5.4	6.6	8.4
Arizona	28.6	32.1	38.3	60.6
Arkansas	29.1	26.5	27.3	28.5
California	249.2	236.3	309.9	383.7
Colorado	36.8	33.0	38.9	47.7
Connecticut	37.7	27.9	31.6	37.8
Delaware	7.6	5.6	6.1	8.1
District of Columbia [1]	5.0	3.6	2.7	3.0
Florida	87.3	88.9	106.7	144.3
Georgia	61.6	56.6	62.6	85.4
Hawaii	11.5	10.3	10.4	10.7
Idaho	13.2	12.0	16.2	17.2
Illinois	135.6	108.1	111.8	133.7
Indiana	73.1	60.0	57.0	62.4
Iowa	43.4	31.8	33.9	33.5
Kansas	30.9	25.4	29.1	30.1
Kentucky	41.2	38.0	36.8	41.0
Louisiana	46.3	36.1	38.4	34.6
Maine	15.4	13.8	12.2	14.0
Maryland	54.3	41.6	47.8	58.2
Massachusetts	73.8	55.9	53.0	63.7
Michigan	124.3	93.8	97.7	112.7
Minnesota	64.9	49.1	57.4	59.7
Mississippi	27.6	25.2	24.2	26.0
Missouri	62.3	49.0	52.8	63.7
Montana	12.1	9.4	10.9	9.9
Nebraska	22.4	17.7	20.1	20.1
Nevada	8.5	9.5	14.6	18.5
New Hampshire	11.7	10.8	11.8	14.5
New Jersey	94.6	69.8	74.4	94.7
New Mexico	18.4	14.9	18.0	18.1
New York	204.1	143.3	141.7	177.3
North Carolina	70.9	64.8	62.1	85.5
North Dakota	9.9	7.7	8.6	6.8
Ohio	144.2	114.5	111.7	120.2
Oklahoma	39.3	35.6	37.6	38.1
Oregon	29.9	25.5	30.2	34.9
Pennsylvania	146.5	110.5	114.0	121.9
Rhode Island	10.9	7.8	8.5	9.5
South Carolina	38.7	32.5	31.6	38.6
South Dakota	10.7	7.7	9.3	8.6
Tennessee	49.8	46.1	41.6	58.2
Texas	171.4	172.5	212.9	265.7
Utah	20.0	21.2	32.5	26.4
Vermont	6.7	6.1	6.7	7.1
Virginia	66.6	60.6	65.6	78.4
Washington	50.4	45.9	57.6	64.5
West Virginia	23.4	21.9	19.4	17.5
Wisconsin	69.3	52.0	58.5	64.0
Wyoming	6.1	5.8	6.5	5.4

[1] Beginning in 1990, graduates from adult programs are excluded.

Source: U.S. National Center for Education Statistics, *Digest of Education Statistics*, annual. See also <http://www.nces.ed.gov/programs/digest/>.

Table 270. High School Dropouts by Race and Hispanic Origin: 1980 to 2010

[In percent. As of October. Dropouts are persons 18 to 24 years old who have not completed high school and are not enrolled, regardless of when they dropped out]

Item	1980	1985	1990 [1]	1995	2000	2005	2006	2007	2008	2009	2010
Total [2]	15.6	13.9	14.4	13.9	12.4	11.3	11.0	10.2	9.3	9.4	8.7
White [3]	14.4	13.5	14.1	13.6	12.2	11.3	10.8	10.0	8.8	9.1	8.5
Male	15.7	14.7	15.4	14.3	13.5	13.2	12.4	11.7	9.8	10.5	9.7
Female	13.2	12.3	12.8	13.0	10.9	9.4	9.2	8.3	7.8	7.7	7.3
Black [3]	23.5	17.6	16.4	14.4	15.3	12.9	13.0	10.2	12.0	11.6	10.1
Male	26.0	18.8	18.6	14.2	17.4	14.8	11.2	10.0	10.2	13.9	12.1
Female	21.5	16.6	14.5	14.6	13.5	11.2	14.7	10.3	13.7	9.5	8.2
Hispanic [4]	40.3	31.5	37.7	34.7	32.3	27.3	26.2	25.3	22.3	20.8	18.5
Male	42.6	35.8	40.3	34.2	36.8	32.1	31.0	29.2	24.3	22.5	21.3
Female	38.1	27.0	35.0	35.4	27.3	21.8	21.0	21.1	20.2	19.1	15.4

[1] Beginning 1990, reflects new editing procedures for cases with missing data on school enrollment. [2] Includes other races, not shown separately. [3] Beginning 2005, for persons who selected this race group only. See footnote 2, Table 234. [4] Persons of Hispanic origin may be of any race.

Source: U.S. Census Bureau, Current Population Reports, PPL-148, P20 and earlier reports, and "School Enrollment, CPS October 2010, Detailed Tables," <http://www.census.gov/hhes/school/data/cps/2010/tables.html>.

Table 271. High School Dropouts by Age, Race, and Hispanic Origin: 1980 to 2010

[5,212 represents 5,212,000. As of October. For persons 14 to 24 years old. See footnote 2, Table 273 for definition of dropouts. Based on Current Population Survey; see text, Section 1 and Appendix III]

Age and race	Number of dropouts (1,000)					Percent of population				
	1980	1990	2000	2005	2010	1980	1990	2000	2005	2010
Total dropouts [1,2]	**5,212**	**3,854**	**3,883**	**3,597**	**2,952**	**12.0**	**10.1**	**9.1**	**7.9**	**6.4**
16 to 17 years............	709	418	460	303	227	8.8	6.3	5.8	3.4	2.7
18 to 21 years............	2,578	1,921	2,005	1,669	1,445	15.8	13.4	12.9	10.5	8.4
22 to 24 years............	1,798	1,458	1,310	1,485	1,144	15.2	13.8	11.8	12.4	9.2
White [2,3]	4,169	3,127	3,065	2,785	2,232	11.3	10.1	9.1	7.9	6.3
16 to 17 years............	619	334	366	223	181	9.2	6.4	5.8	3.3	2.9
18 to 21 years............	2,032	1,516	1,558	1,299	1,048	14.7	13.1	12.6	10.4	8.0
22 to 24 years............	1,416	1,235	1,040	1,167	893	14.0	14.0	11.7	12.6	9.2
Black [2,3]	934	611	705	616	498	16.0	10.9	10.9	9.2	7.2
16 to 17 years............	80	73	84	64	30	6.9	6.9	7.0	4.7	2.3
18 to 21 years............	486	345	383	281	283	23.0	16.0	16.0	12.4	10.5
22 to 24 years............	346	185	232	231	167	24.0	13.5	14.3	13.6	9.4
Hispanic [2,4]	919	1,122	1,499	1,467	1,122	29.5	26.8	23.5	18.6	12.8
16 to 17 years............	92	89	121	93	40	16.6	12.9	11.0	6.3	2.7
18 to 21 years............	470	502	733	672	506	40.3	32.9	30.0	24.5	15.2
22 to 24 years............	323	523	602	663	543	40.6	42.8	35.5	30.8	23.2

[1] Includes other groups not shown separately. [2] Includes persons 14 to 15 years not shown separately. [3] Beginning 2005, for persons who selected this race group only. See footnote 2, Table 234. [4] Persons of Hispanic origin may be of any race.

Source: U.S. Census Bureau, "Detailed Tables, Table 1. Enrollment Status of the Population 3 Years Old and Over, by Sex, Age, Race, Hispanic Origin, Foreign Born, and Foreign-Born Parentage," <http://www.census.gov/hhes/school/data/cps/index.html>.

Table 272. Enrollment Status by Race, Hispanic Origin, and Sex: 2000 and 2010

[15,553 represents 15,553,000. As of October. For persons 18 to 21 years old. For the civilian noninstitutional population. Based on the Current Population Survey; see text, Section 1 and Appendix III]

Characteristic	Total persons 18 to 21 years old (1,000)		Percent distribution							
			Enrolled in high school		High school graduates				Not high school graduates and not enrolled in high school	
					Total		In college			
	2000	2010	2000	2010	2000	2010	2000	2010	2000	2010
Total [1]	**15,553**	**17,210**	**9.4**	**9.9**	**77.6**	**81.5**	**43.5**	**50.6**	**12.9**	**8.4**
White [2]	12,383	13,176	8.9	9.7	78.5	82.2	44.4	50.8	12.6	8.0
Black [2]	2,389	2,538	12.6	13.9	71.3	73.0	34.7	41.5	16.0	13.0
Hispanic [3]	2,439	3,339	12.5	13.5	57.2	71.3	25.3	38.9	30.0	15.2
Male [1]	7,814	8,824	11.0	11.0	74.7	79.8	38.9	46.7	14.3	9.0
White [2]	6,313	6,867	10.6	10.8	75.7	80.4	39.8	46.6	13.7	8.7
Black [2]	1,096	1,277	14.9	15.5	66.0	69.1	27.4	36.2	19.1	15.4
Hispanic [3]	1,269	1,744	14.4	14.0	51.8	70.0	21.9	35.7	33.7	15.8
Female [1]	7,739	8,386	7.9	8.8	80.6	83.2	48.1	54.8	11.5	7.8
White [2]	6,070	6,308	7.1	8.4	81.3	84.1	49.3	55.5	11.4	7.2
Black [2]	1,293	1,261	10.7	12.3	75.9	76.9	40.9	46.9	13.5	10.5
Hispanic [3]	1,169	1,595	10.6	12.9	63.1	72.7	28.9	42.4	26.1	14.4

[1] Includes other races not shown separately. [2] For 2010, for persons who selected this race group only. See footnote 2, Table 234. [3] Persons of Hispanic origin may be of any race.

Source: U.S. Census Bureau, Current Population Reports, PPL-148, P-20 and earlier reports, and "School Enrollment," <http://www.census.gov/hhes/school/>.

Table 273. Employment Status of High School Graduates and Dropouts Not Enrolled in School by Sex and Race: 1980 to 2010

[In thousands (11,622 represents 11,622,000), except percent. As of October. For civilian noninstitutional population 16 to 24 years old. Based on Current Population Survey; see text, Section 1 and Appendix III]

Employment status, sex, and race	Graduates [1]				Dropouts [3]			
	1980	1990	2000 [2]	2010 [2]	1980	1990	2000 [2]	2010 [2]
Civilian population..........................	**11,622**	**8,370**	**7,351**	**6,999**	**5,254**	**3,800**	**3,776**	**2,816**
In labor force..	9,795	7,107	6,195	5,407	3,549	2,506	2,612	1,817
Percent of population............................	84.3	84.9	84.3	77.3	67.5	66.0	69.2	64.5
Employed...	8,567	6,279	5,632	4,201	2,651	1,993	2,150	1,290
Percent of labor force............................	87.5	88.3	90.9	77.7	74.7	79.5	82.3	71.0
Unemployed..	1,228	828	563	1,206	898	513	463	527
Unemployment rate, total [4].....................	12.5	11.7	9.1	22.3	25.3	20.5	17.7	29.0
Male...	13.5	11.1	9.3	21.7	23.5	18.8	16.3	27.7
Female..	11.5	12.3	8.8	23.3	28.7	23.5	20.3	31.4
White [5]..	10.8	9.0	7.2	19.5	21.6	17.0	15.0	25.5
Black [5]..	26.1	26.0	18.1	33.9	43.9	43.3	33.2	46.6
Not in labor force..................................	1,827	1,262	1,156	1,592	1,705	1,294	1,163	999
Percent of population............................	15.7	15.1	15.7	22.7	32.5	34.1	30.8	35.5

[1] For persons not enrolled in college who have completed 4 years of high school only. [2] Data not strictly comparable with data for earlier years. See text, this section, and February 2000 and 2010 issues of Employment and Earnings. [3] For persons not in regular school and who have not completed the 12th grade nor received a general equivalency degree. [4] Includes other races not shown separately. [5] 2010 data are for persons who selected this race group only. See footnote 2, Table 234.

Source: U.S. Bureau of Labor Statistics, News Release, USDL 11-0462, April 2011, and unpublished data. See also <http://www.bls.gov/news.release/hsgec.toc.htm>.

Table 274. General Educational Development (GED) Credentials Issued: 1980 to 2010

[GEDs issued in thousands (479 represents 479,000). For the 50 states and DC]

Year	GEDs issued	Percent distribution of GED test takers				
		16 to 18 years old [1]	19 to 24 years old [1]	25 to 29 years old	30 to 34 years old	35 years old and over
1980...............................	479	37	27	13	8	15
1985...............................	413	32	26	15	10	16
1990...............................	410	22	39	13	10	15
1995...............................	504	27	36	13	9	15
2000...............................	487	33	37	11	7	13
2004...............................	406	35	38	11	6	10
2005...............................	424	34	37	12	7	11
2006...............................	398	35	36	12	6	11
2007...............................	429	35	35	12	7	11
2008...............................	469	34	35	13	7	11
2009...............................	448	31	36	13	8	12
2010...............................	452	27	37	14	9	14

[1] For 1985 and prior years, 19-year-olds are included with the 16- to 18-year-olds instead of the 19- to 24-year-olds.

Source: U.S. National Center for Education Statistics, *Digest of Education Statistics*, annual. See also <http://www.nces.ed.gov/programs/digest/>.

Table 275. Public Elementary and Secondary School Estimated Finances by State: 2010

[In millions of dollars (593,682 represents $593,682,000,000), except as noted. For the school year ending in June. This table replaces Table 262 in the 2012 edition of the Statistical Abstract. That table, prepared by the National Education Association, included national summary statistics from 1980 and data on non-revenue receipts]

State	Revenue receipts				Expenditures		Current expenditures		
	Total	Source			Total [1]	Per capita [2] (dol.)	Elementary and secondary schools	Average per enrolled public school pupil [3]	
		Federal	State	Local				Amount (dol.)	Rank
Total..........................	593,682	74,047	258,191	261,445	602,648	1,963	523,990	10,681	(X)
Alabama.....................	7,280	1,134	3,800	2,346	7,639	1,622	6,764	9,033	39
Alaska.......................	2,230	367	1,357	506	2,371	3,395	2,080	15,795	4
Arizona......................	8,734	1,580	3,140	4,014	8,813	1,336	7,573	7,043	49
Arkansas....................	5,049	788	3,414	848	5,482	1,897	4,757	9,899	29
California....................	64,982	9,716	34,174	21,092	68,149	1,844	58,918	9,557	32
Colorado....................	8,741	714	3,818	4,209	8,862	1,764	7,370	8,859	42
Connecticut.................	9,544	819	3,238	5,487	9,314	2,647	8,343	14,798	6
Delaware....................	1,696	181	992	523	1,695	1,915	1,480	11,859	15
District of Columbia..........	1,196	81	(X)	1,115	1,290	2,151	993	14,341	9
Florida.......................	26,224	4,200	8,217	13,807	27,267	1,471	23,513	8,925	40
Georgia......................	17,836	2,598	6,739	8,498	17,822	1,813	15,724	9,429	35
Hawaii.......................	2,565	382	2,093	89	2,215	1,711	2,143	11,890	14
Idaho........................	2,177	444	1,232	502	2,099	1,358	1,899	6,873	50
Illinois.......................	27,531	3,810	8,696	15,024	27,511	2,131	24,776	11,824	16
Indiana......................	13,723	1,478	7,343	4,902	11,218	1,746	9,936	9,493	34
Iowa.........................	5,533	728	2,218	2,587	5,720	1,902	4,819	9,995	27
Kansas......................	5,452	674	2,861	1,918	5,970	2,118	4,586	9,773	30
Kentucky....................	6,961	1,140	3,662	2,158	7,090	1,644	6,150	9,093	38
Louisiana....................	8,039	1,550	3,348	3,141	7,990	1,779	7,082	10,258	25
Maine........................	2,669	321	1,084	1,264	2,611	1,981	2,403	13,042	11
Maryland....................	13,322	1,004	5,545	6,773	12,936	2,270	11,677	13,763	10
Massachusetts..............	15,490	1,093	6,450	7,947	15,210	2,307	14,141	14,775	7
Michigan....................	18,409	2,384	9,694	6,330	18,630	1,869	16,565	10,247	26
Minnesota...................	10,225	1,245	5,978	3,001	10,392	1,973	8,976	10,725	22
Mississippi..................	4,455	946	2,109	1,400	4,504	1,526	4,010	8,142	48
Missouri.....................	9,508	1,431	3,472	4,606	10,048	1,678	8,830	9,635	31
Montana.....................	1,609	256	745	608	1,622	1,664	1,496	10,551	24
Nebraska....................	3,644	466	1,185	1,993	3,616	2,013	3,169	10,733	21
Nevada......................	4,261	358	2,342	1,561	4,259	1,611	3,619	8,468	44
New Hampshire..............	2,803	185	1,061	1,557	2,695	2,034	2,525	12,810	12
New Jersey..................	25,785	2,387	9,060	14,339	25,980	2,984	24,403	17,610	2
New Mexico..................	3,639	754	2,308	577	3,807	1,894	3,114	9,363	36
New York....................	55,244	3,694	23,111	28,439	59,536	3,047	52,214	19,258	1
North Carolina...............	16,621	1,928	7,451	7,242	14,093	1,502	12,217	8,269	46
North Dakota................	1,261	278	553	430	1,208	1,868	1,050	11,288	19
Ohio.........................	22,593	2,310	9,988	10,295	22,537	1,952	19,369	10,991	20
Oklahoma...................	5,778	768	2,658	2,351	5,965	1,618	5,427	8,291	45
Oregon......................	6,172	813	2,948	2,411	6,383	1,668	5,520	9,966	28
Pennsylvania................	26,433	2,977	9,431	14,025	25,658	2,036	22,401	12,718	13
Rhode Island................	2,193	247	737	1,210	2,172	2,062	2,086	14,522	8
South Carolina..............	7,742	1,058	3,378	3,306	8,223	1,803	6,633	9,173	37
South Dakota................	1,290	251	399	640	1,271	1,565	1,100	8,891	41
Tennessee..................	8,371	1,094	3,834	3,443	8,732	1,387	7,918	8,142	47
Texas.......................	50,391	7,985	18,900	23,507	53,652	2,165	41,679	8,595	43
Utah........................	4,246	570	2,172	1,504	4,324	1,553	3,429	5,883	51
Vermont.....................	1,572	174	1,327	72	1,527	2,456	1,448	16,809	3
Virginia......................	14,693	1,532	5,490	7,671	14,706	1,866	13,269	10,655	23
Washington..................	11,831	1,401	6,931	3,498	11,784	1,768	9,841	9,505	33
West Virginia................	3,176	514	1,678	985	3,483	1,914	3,278	11,596	17
Wisconsin...................	11,049	1,115	4,952	4,982	10,882	1,924	9,936	11,390	18
Wyoming....................	1,715	124	881	710	1,685	3,095	1,342	15,221	5

X Not applicable. [1] Includes interest on school debt and payments to state and local governments, not shown separately. [2] Based on U.S. Census Bureau estimated resident population, as of July 1, 2009. [3] Based on 2009-2010 enrollment counts, National Center for Education Statistics, Common Core of Data.

Source: U.S. Census Bureau, *Public Education Finances: 2010*, June 2012. See also <http://www.census.gov/govs/school/>.

Table 276. College Enrollment of Recent High School Completers: 1970 to 2010

[2,758 represents 2,758,000. For persons 16 to 24 years old who graduated from high school in the preceding 12 months. Includes persons receiving GEDs. Based on surveys and subject to sampling error; data will not agree with data in other tables]

Year	Number of high school completers (1,000)						Percent enrolled in college [5]					
	Total [1]	Male	Female	White [2]	Black [2,3]	His-panic [3,4]	Total [1]	Male	Female	White [2]	Black [2,3]	His-panic [3,4]
1970..........	2,758	1,343	1,415	2,461	(NA)	(NA)	52	55	49	52	(NA)	(NA)
1975..........	3,185	1,513	1,672	2,701	302	132	51	53	49	51	42	58
1980..........	3,088	1,498	1,589	2,554	350	130	49	47	52	50	43	52
1985..........	2,668	1,287	1,381	2,104	332	141	58	59	57	60	42	51
1990..........	2,362	1,173	1,189	1,819	331	121	60	58	62	63	47	43
1995..........	2,599	1,238	1,361	1,861	349	288	62	63	61	64	51	54
2000..........	2,756	1,251	1,505	1,938	393	300	63	60	66	66	55	53
2002..........	2,796	1,412	1,384	1,903	382	344	65	62	68	69	59	54
2003..........	2,677	1,306	1,372	1,832	327	314	64	61	67	66	58	59
2004..........	2,752	1,327	1,425	1,854	398	286	67	61	72	69	63	62
2005..........	2,675	1,262	1,414	1,799	345	390	69	67	70	73	56	54
2006..........	2,692	1,328	1,363	1,805	318	382	66	66	66	69	55	58
2007..........	2,955	1,511	1,444	2,043	416	355	67	66	68	70	56	64
2008..........	3,151	1,640	1,511	2,091	416	458	69	66	72	72	56	64
2009..........	2,937	1,407	1,531	1,863	415	459	70	66	74	71	70	59
2010..........	3,160	1,679	1,482	1,937	461	507	68	63	74	70	62	60

NA Not available. [1] Includes other races not shown separately. [2] Beginning 2003, for persons of this race group only. See footnote 2, Table 234. [3] Due to small sample size, data are subject to relatively large sampling errors. [4] Persons of Hispanic origin may be of any race. [5] As of October.

Source: U.S. National Center for Education Statistics, *Digest of Education Statistics*, annual. See also <http://www.nces.ed.gov/programs/digest/>.

Table 277. College Enrollment by Sex and Attendance Status: 2005 to 2011

[In thousands (17,487 represents 17,487,000). As of Fall. Includes enrollment at branch campuses, some additional (primarily 2-year) colleges, and excludes a few institutions that did not award degrees. Includes enrollment at institutions that were eligible to participate in Title IV federal financial aid programs. Includes unclassified students (students taking courses for credit, but are not candidates for degrees)]

Sex and age	2005		2008		2009		2010		2011 proj.	
	Total	Part-time	Total	Part-time	Total	Part-time	Total	Part-time	Total	Part-time
Total........................	**17,487**	**6,690**	**19,103**	**7,355**	**20,428**	**7,705**	**21,016**	**7,934**	**21,575**	**8,214**
Male............................	7,456	2,653	8,189	2,955	8,770	3,099	9,045	3,208	9,243	3,311
14 to 17 years old.............	68	15	93	20	103	25	92	29	97	24
18 to 19 years old.............	1,523	184	1,704	188	1,806	226	1,842	249	1,887	261
20 to 21 years old.............	1,658	260	1,695	289	1,876	329	1,931	349	2,014	420
22 to 24 years old.............	1,410	428	1,555	450	1,606	430	1,666	467	1,724	486
25 to 29 years old.............	1,057	551	1,222	625	1,382	717	1,414	706	1,414	706
30 to 34 years old.............	591	365	691	442	709	428	745	438	764	450
35 years old and over.........	1,149	850	1,228	941	1,287	944	1,354	971	1,343	964
Female.........................	10,032	4,038	10,914	4,401	11,658	4,606	11,971	4,726	12,332	4,903
14 to 17 years old.............	119	21	102	7	114	11	119	11	107	13
18 to 19 years old.............	1,920	233	2,109	265	2,236	303	2,276	327	2,408	368
20 to 21 years old.............	1,905	327	1,954	318	2,069	345	2,120	384	2,294	418
22 to 24 years old.............	1,704	564	1,888	646	1,987	629	2,008	611	2,047	701
25 to 29 years old.............	1,413	745	1,618	846	1,713	858	1,783	907	1,789	909
30 to 34 years old.............	847	526	918	595	1,032	651	1,078	636	1,112	655
35 years old and over.........	2,123	1,623	2,326	1,723	2,507	1,810	2,587	1,850	2,575	1,840

Source: U.S. National Center for Education Statistics, *Digest of Education Statistics*, annual. See also <http://www.nces.ed.gov/programs/digest/>.

Table 278. Higher Education—Institutions and Enrollment 1980 to 2010

[686 represents 686,000. As of Fall. Covers universities, colleges, professional schools, junior and teachers' colleges, both publicly and privately controlled, regular session. Includes estimates for institutions not reporting. See also Appendix III]

Item	Unit	1980	1990	2000	2005	2007	2008	2009	2010
ALL INSTITUTIONS									
Number of institutions [1]	**Number**	**3,231**	**3,559**	**4,182**	**4,276**	**4,352**	**4,409**	**4,495**	**4,599**
4-year	Number	1,957	2,141	2,450	2,582	2,675	2,719	2,774	2,870
2-year	Number	1,274	1,418	1,732	1,694	1,677	1,690	1,721	1,729
Instructional staff—									
(lecturer or above) [2]	**1,000**	**686**	**817**	**(NA)**	**1,290**	**1,371**	**(NA)**	**1,439**	**(NA)**
Percent full-time	Percent	66	61	(NA)	52	51	(NA)	51	(NA)
Total enrollment [3, 4]	**1,000**	**12,097**	**13,819**	**15,312**	**17,487**	**18,248**	**19,103**	**20,428**	**21,016**
Male	1,000	5,874	6,284	6,722	7,456	7,816	8,189	8,770	9,045
Female	1,000	6,223	7,535	8,591	10,032	10,432	10,914	11,658	11,971
4-year institutions	1,000	7,571	8,579	9,364	10,999	11,630	12,131	12,906	13,335
2-year institutions	1,000	4,526	5,240	5,948	6,488	6,618	6,971	7,521	7,681
Full-time	1,000	7,098	7,821	9,010	10,797	11,270	11,748	12,723	13,082
Part-time	1,000	4,999	5,998	6,303	6,690	6,978	7,355	7,705	7,934
Public	1,000	9,457	10,845	11,753	13,022	13,491	13,972	14,811	15,143
Private	1,000	2,640	2,974	3,560	4,466	4,757	5,131	5,617	5,873
Not-for-profit	1,000	2,528	2,760	3,109	3,455	3,571	3,662	3,765	3,855
For profit	1,000	112	213	450	1,011	1,186	1,469	1,852	2,018
Undergraduate [4]	1,000	10,475	11,959	13,155	14,964	15,604	16,366	17,565	18,079
Men	1,000	5,000	5,380	5,778	6,409	6,728	7,067	7,595	7,835
Women	1,000	5,475	6,579	7,377	8,555	8,876	9,299	9,970	10,244
First-time freshmen	1,000	2,588	2,257	2,428	2,657	2,776	3,025	3,210	(NA)
First professional	1,000	278	273	307	337	351	(NA)	(NA)	(NA)
Men	1,000	199	167	164	170	178	(NA)	(NA)	(NA)
Women	1,000	78	107	143	167	173	(NA)	(NA)	(NA)
Graduate [4]	1,000	1,343	1,586	1,850	2,186	2,294	(NA)	(NA)	(NA)
Men	1,000	675	737	780	877	910	(NA)	(NA)	(NA)
Women	1,000	670	849	1,071	1,309	1,383	(NA)	(NA)	(NA)
2-YEAR INSTITUTIONS									
Number of institutions [1]	**Number**	**1,274**	**1,418**	**1,732**	**1,694**	**1,677**	**1,690**	**1,721**	**1,729**
Public	Number	945	972	1,076	1,053	1,032	1,024	1,000	978
Private	Number	329	446	656	641	645	666	721	751
Instructional staff—									
(lecturer or above) [2]	**1,000**	**192**	**(NA)**	**(NA)**	**373**	**381**	**(NA)**	**401**	**(NA)**
Enrollment [3, 4]	**1,000**	**4,526**	**5,240**	**5,948**	**6,488**	**6,618**	**6,971**	**7,521**	**7,681**
Public	1,000	4,329	4,996	5,697	6,184	6,324	6,640	7,101	7,218
Private	1,000	198	244	251	304	294	331	420	463
Male	1,000	2,047	2,233	2,559	2,680	2,771	2,936	3,197	3,265
Female	1,000	2,479	3,007	3,390	3,808	3,847	4,035	4,325	4,416
4-YEAR INSTITUTIONS									
Number of institutions [1]	**Number**	**1,957**	**2,141**	**2,450**	**2,582**	**2,675**	**2,719**	**2,774**	**2,870**
Public	Number	552	595	622	640	653	652	672	678
Private	Number	1,405	1,546	1,828	1,942	2,022	2,067	2,102	2,192
Instructional staff—									
(lecturer or above) [2]	**1,000**	**494**	**(NA)**	**(NA)**	**917**	**991**	**(NA)**	**1,038**	**(NA)**
Enrollment [3, 4]	**1,000**	**7,571**	**8,579**	**9,364**	**10,999**	**11,630**	**12,131**	**12,906**	**13,335**
Public	1,000	5,129	5,848	6,055	6,838	7,167	7,332	7,709	7,925
Private	1,000	2,442	2,730	3,308	4,162	4,464	4,800	5,197	5,410
Male	1,000	3,827	4,051	4,163	4,776	5,045	5,253	5,573	5,780
Female	1,000	3,743	4,527	5,201	6,224	6,585	6,878	7,333	7,556

NA Not available. [1] Number of institutions includes count of branch campuses. Due to revised survey procedures, data beginning 1990 are not comparable with previous years. Beginning 2000, data reflect a new classification of institutions; this classification includes some additional, primarily 2-year, colleges and excludes a few institutions that did not award degrees. Includes institutions that were eligible to participate in Title IV federal financial aid programs. Includes schools accredited by the National Association of Trade and Technical Schools. [2] Due to revised survey methods, data beginning 1990 not comparable with previous years. [3] Branch campuses counted according to actual status, e.g., 2-year branch in 2-year category. [4] Includes unclassified students (those taking courses for credit, but not candidates for degrees).

Source: U.S. National Center for Education Statistics, *Digest of Education Statistics*, annual, and unpublished data. See also <http://www.nces.ed.gov/programs/digest/>.

Table 279. College Enrollment by Selected Characteristics: 1990 to 2010

[In thousands (13,818.6 represents 13,818,600). As of Fall. Nonresident alien students are not distributed among racial/ethnic groups]

Characteristic	1990	2000 [1]	2005 [1]	2007 [1]	2008 [1]	2009 [1]	2010 [1]
Total	**13,818.6**	**15,312.3**	**17,487.5**	**18,248.1**	**19,102.8**	**20,427.7**	**21,016.1**
Male	6,283.9	6,721.8	7,455.9	7,815.9	8,188.9	8,769.5	9,044.8
Female	7,534.7	8,590.5	10,031.6	10,432.2	10,913.9	11,658.2	11,971.3
Public	10,844.7	11,752.8	13,021.8	13,490.8	13,972.2	14,810.6	15,142.8
Private	2,973.9	3,559.5	4,465.6	4,757.3	5,130.7	5,617.1	5,873.3
2-year	5,240.1	5,948.4	6,488.1	6,617.9	6,971.4	7,521.4	7,680.9
4-year	8,578.6	9,363.9	10,999.4	11,630.2	12,131.4	12,906.3	13,335.3
Undergraduate	11,959.2	13,155.4	14,964.0	15,603.8	16,365.7	17,565.3	18,078.7
Graduate	1,586.2	1,850.3	2,186.5	2,293.6	(NA)	(NA)	(NA)
First professional	273.4	306.6	337.0	350.8	(NA)	(NA)	(NA)
White [2]	10,722.5	10,462.1	11,495.4	11,756.2	12,088.8	12,730.8	12,722.5
Male	4,861.0	4,634.6	5,007.2	5,146.1	5,302.9	5,594.4	5,606.8
Female	5,861.5	5,827.5	6,488.2	6,610.1	6,785.9	7,136.4	7,115.7
Public	8,385.4	7,963.4	8,518.2	8,640.3	8,817.7	9,234.6	9,187.1
Private	2,337.0	2,498.7	2,977.3	3,116.0	3,271.1	3,496.2	3,535.4
2-year	3,954.3	3,804.1	3,998.6	3,975.2	4,101.6	4,373.4	4,324.4
4-year	6,768.1	6,658.0	7,496.9	7,781.0	7,987.1	8,357.4	8,398.2
Undergraduate	9,272.6	8,983.5	9,828.6	10,046.6	10,339.2	10,915.3	10,897.7
Graduate	1,228.4	1,258.5	1,428.7	1,465.0	(NA)	(NA)	(NA)
First professional	221.5	220.1	238.1	244.7	(NA)	(NA)	(NA)
Black [2]	1,247.0	1,730.3	2,214.6	2,383.4	2,584.5	2,919.8	3,038.8
Male	484.7	635.3	774.1	838.1	911.8	1,037.1	1,089.1
Female	762.3	1,095.0	1,440.4	1,545.3	1,672.7	1,882.7	1,949.7
Public	976.4	1,319.2	1,580.4	1,667.6	1,759.2	1,937.2	1,988.6
Private	270.6	411.1	634.2	715.7	825.3	982.7	1,050.1
2-year	524.3	734.9	901.1	941.7	1,019.5	1,152.8	1,197.7
4-year	722.8	995.4	1,313.4	1,441.7	1,565.0	1,767.0	1,841.0
Undergraduate	1,147.2	1,548.9	1,955.4	2,092.6	2,269.3	2,577.4	2,676.5
Graduate	83.9	157.9	233.2	263.5	(NA)	(NA)	(NA)
First professional	15.9	23.5	26.0	27.3	(NA)	(NA)	(NA)
Hispanic	782.4	1,461.8	1,882.0	2,076.2	2,272.9	2,546.7	2,741.4
Male	353.9	627.1	774.6	861.6	946.7	1,066.3	1,154.6
Female	428.5	834.7	1,107.3	1,214.5	1,326.1	1,480.4	1,586.9
Public	671.4	1,229.3	1,525.6	1,685.4	1,832.4	2,017.7	2,157.4
Private	111.0	232.5	356.4	390.7	440.5	529.0	584.1
2-year	424.2	843.9	981.5	1,067.4	1,180.7	1,309.0	1,386.4
4-year	358.2	617.9	900.5	1,008.7	1,092.2	1,237.7	1,355.1
Undergraduate	724.6	1,351.0	1,733.6	1,915.9	2,103.5	2,362.5	2,543.6
Graduate	47.2	95.4	130.7	140.9	(NA)	(NA)	(NA)
First professional	10.7	15.4	17.7	19.3	(NA)	(NA)	(NA)
American Indian/ Alaska Native	102.8	151.2	176.3	190.0	193.3	207.9	196.4
Male	43.1	61.4	68.4	74.4	76.9	83.4	78.8
Female	59.7	89.7	107.9	115.6	116.4	124.5	117.6
Public	90.4	127.3	143.0	153.3	153.0	161.8	151.0
Private	12.4	23.9	33.3	36.7	40.3	46.1	45.4
2-year	54.9	74.7	80.7	81.4	85.5	90.3	87.4
4-year	47.9	76.5	95.6	108.6	108.6	117.7	109.0
Undergraduate	95.5	138.5	160.4	171.3	175.6	189.4	179.3
Graduate	6.2	10.3	13.4	16.1	(NA)	(NA)	(NA)
First professional	1.1	2.3	2.5	2.6	(NA)	(NA)	(NA)
Asian/Pacific Islander	572.4	978.2	1,134.4	1,217.9	1,302.8	1,337.7	1,282.2
Male	294.9	465.9	522.0	562.5	597.4	621.5	600.8
Female	277.5	512.3	612.4	655.4	705.4	716.1	681.3
Public	461.0	770.5	881.9	942.5	982.9	1,018.5	969.5
Private	111.5	207.7	252.4	275.4	319.9	319.1	312.7
2-year	215.2	401.9	434.4	456.4	479.4	495.7	463.8
4-year	357.2	576.3	700.0	761.5	823.4	842.0	818.4
Undergraduate	500.5	845.5	971.4	1,042.1	1,117.9	1,142.3	1,087.9
Graduate	53.2	95.8	118.4	127.8	(NA)	(NA)	(NA)
First professional	18.7	36.8	44.6	48.0	(NA)	(NA)	(NA)
Nonresident alien	391.5	528.7	584.8	624.5	660.6	684.8	709.6
Male	246.3	297.3	309.5	333.2	353.3	366.7	380.3
Female	145.2	231.4	275.3	291.2	307.3	318.1	329.2
Public	260.0	343.1	372.8	401.7	427.0	440.8	454.3
Private	131.4	185.6	212.0	222.8	233.6	244.0	255.3
2-year	67.1	89.0	91.8	95.8	104.7	100.2	100.6
4-year	324.3	439.7	493.1	528.7	555.9	584.6	608.9
Undergraduate	218.7	288.0	314.7	335.3	360.3	378.4	400.3
Graduate	167.3	232.3	262.1	280.3	(NA)	(NA)	(NA)
First professional	5.4	8.4	8.1	8.8	(NA)	(NA)	(NA)

NA Not available. [1] Data beginning 2000 reflect a new classification of institutions; see footnote 1, Table 278. [2] Non-Hispanic.

Source: U.S. National Center for Education Statistics, *Digest of Education Statistics*, annual. See also <http://www.nces.ed.gov/programs/digest/>.

Table 280. Degree-Granting Institutions, Number and Enrollment by State: 2009

[20,428 represents 20,428,000. Number of institutions beginning in academic year. Opening fall enrollment of resident and extension students attending full-time or part-time. Excludes students taking courses for credit by mail, radio, or TV, and students in branches of U.S. institutions operated in foreign countries. See Appendix III]

State	Num-ber of institu-tions [1]	Enrollment (1,000)							Minority			Non-resi-dent alien
		Total	Male	Female	Public	Private	Full-time	White [2]	Total [3]	Black [2]	His-panic	
United States	**4,495**	**20,428**	**8,770**	**11,658**	**14,811**	**5,617**	**12,723**	**12,731**	**7,012**	**2,920**	**2,547**	**685**
Alabama	72	312	131	181	260	51	207	197	109	94	6	6
Alaska	7	32	13	20	30	2	14	24	8	1	1	1
Arizona	78	829	306	523	350	478	612	497	311	133	125	20
Arkansas	50	168	69	99	149	19	109	121	43	33	5	4
California	436	2,736	1,231	1,504	2,289	446	1,397	1,077	1,569	224	830	90
Colorado	82	352	153	199	255	97	222	254	91	28	43	7
Connecticut	45	192	81	110	123	69	125	132	52	22	20	8
Delaware	10	55	22	33	40	15	37	37	17	12	3	2
District of Columbia	18	137	52	85	5	132	68	59	72	55	7	6
Florida	207	1,053	436	617	759	294	609	557	466	202	221	30
Georgia	131	532	214	319	418	114	365	292	225	182	19	15
Hawaii	20	75	31	43	58	17	43	18	52	2	3	5
Idaho	15	84	37	47	63	21	59	73	9	1	5	2
Illinois	181	901	390	511	589	312	534	560	312	141	115	29
Indiana	106	441	196	245	325	116	305	351	73	46	16	17
Iowa	65	351	138	213	171	180	214	268	71	36	21	11
Kansas	67	211	94	117	183	28	126	164	36	15	12	12
Kentucky	75	278	119	159	222	56	175	236	37	29	4	4
Louisiana	87	252	103	149	216	36	174	151	94	79	7	7
Maine	30	70	29	41	50	21	45	63	5	2	1	1
Maryland	59	359	151	208	298	61	194	196	148	105	16	15
Massachusetts	125	497	214	284	219	278	343	343	122	43	39	33
Michigan	105	686	300	386	553	133	407	509	152	102	21	25
Minnesota	117	442	181	261	270	172	264	340	90	52	13	12
Mississippi	41	173	67	106	156	18	134	97	74	70	2	2
Missouri	132	425	178	247	246	179	260	324	88	60	14	13
Montana	23	52	24	27	47	5	38	43	8	1	1	1
Nebraska	43	139	62	76	104	34	89	115	19	8	7	4
Nevada	21	125	56	69	112	13	60	72	51	11	24	3
New Hampshire	28	74	31	43	44	31	53	64	8	2	3	2
New Jersey	65	432	194	238	349	83	274	245	169	63	68	17
New Mexico	41	153	66	87	143	10	80	62	87	5	65	4
New York	305	1,290	552	738	712	577	905	749	460	183	161	80
North Carolina	137	569	233	336	470	99	362	369	186	143	21	13
North Dakota	22	54	26	28	47	8	39	46	6	1	1	3
Ohio	213	711	310	401	522	189	486	556	135	99	17	21
Oklahoma	61	221	98	123	190	31	141	151	61	22	10	9
Oregon	60	243	109	134	201	42	150	192	44	7	17	7
Pennsylvania	257	778	339	439	426	352	562	591	159	88	34	28
Rhode Island	13	85	37	47	43	41	63	65	16	5	7	4
South Carolina	71	247	99	148	200	46	172	163	80	70	6	4
South Dakota	25	53	23	30	42	12	35	46	6	1	1	1
Tennessee	106	333	138	194	232	101	242	241	86	69	8	6
Texas	240	1,448	631	817	1,259	189	800	683	712	193	430	53
Utah	40	237	118	119	171	66	146	200	30	5	14	7
Vermont	25	45	20	25	27	18	34	41	4	1	1	1
Virginia	119	545	232	313	401	144	339	347	183	119	28	15
Washington	81	383	170	212	328	54	247	277	92	18	29	13
West Virginia	45	142	70	72	95	48	87	119	21	12	5	3
Wisconsin	77	373	163	210	295	78	242	311	54	24	14	9
Wyoming	11	37	17	20	36	1	21	32	4	(Z)	2	1
U.S. military [4]	5	16	13	3	16	(X)	16	12	3	1	2	(Z)

X Not applicable. Z Fewer than 500. [1] Branch campuses counted as separate institutions. [2] Non-Hispanic. [3] Includes other races not shown separately. [4] Service schools.

Source: U.S. National Center for Education Statistics, *Digest of Education Statistics*, annual. See also <http://www.nces.ed.gov/programs/digest/>.

Table 281. College Enrollment by Sex, Age, Race, and Hispanic Origin: 1980 to 2010

[In thousands (11,387 represents 11,387,000). As of October for the civilian noninstitutional population, 14 years old and over. Based on the Current Population Survey; see text, Section 1 and Appendix III]

Characteristic	1980	1990 [1]	1995	2000	2004	2005	2006	2007	2008	2009	2010
Total [2]	**11,387**	**13,621**	**14,715**	**15,314**	**17,383**	**17,472**	**17,020**	**17,770**	**18,632**	**19,764**	**20,275**
Male [3]	5,430	6,192	6,703	6,682	7,575	7,539	7,427	7,749	8,311	8,642	9,007
18 to 24 years	3,604	3,922	4,089	4,342	4,866	4,972	4,874	5,156	5,383	5,640	5,698
25 to 34 years	1,325	1,412	1,561	1,361	1,604	1,486	1,571	1,625	1,806	1,843	2,055
35 years old and over	405	772	985	918	1,033	1,019	982	968	989	1,069	1,161
Female [3]	5,957	7,429	8,013	8,631	9,808	9,933	9,593	10,021	10,321	11,123	11,268
18 to 24 years	3,625	4,042	4,452	5,109	5,742	5,859	5,712	6,004	6,083	6,432	6,515
25 to 34 years	1,378	1,749	1,788	1,846	2,091	2,115	2,087	2,212	2,207	2,450	2,569
35 years old and over	802	1,546	1,684	1,589	1,850	1,838	1,793	1,804	1,922	2,124	2,049
White [3,4]	9,925	11,488	12,021	11,999	13,381	13,467	13,112	13,693	14,405	15,027	15,258
18 to 24 years	6,334	6,635	7,011	7,566	8,354	8,499	8,298	8,780	9,141	9,327	9,324
25 to 34 years	2,328	2,698	2,686	2,339	2,748	2,647	2,725	2,769	2,859	3,163	3,414
35 years old and over	1,051	2,023	2,208	1,978	2,143	2,206	2,090	2,144	2,234	2,377	2,365
Male	4,804	5,235	5,535	5,311	5,944	5,844	5,772	5,989	6,570	6,681	6,883
Female	5,121	6,253	6,486	6,689	7,438	7,624	7,340	7,705	7,834	8,346	8,375
Black [3,4]	1,163	1,393	1,772	2,164	2,301	2,297	2,304	2,473	2,481	2,889	3,083
18 to 24 years	688	894	988	1,216	1,238	1,229	1,321	1,395	1,349	1,604	1,692
25 to 34 years	289	258	426	567	522	520	502	629	646	663	715
35 years old and over	156	207	334	361	502	448	480	449	451	587	642
Male	476	587	710	815	776	864	886	1,006	919	1,058	1,185
Female	686	807	1,062	1,349	1,525	1,435	1,418	1,468	1,562	1,831	1,898
Hispanic origin [3,5]	443	748	1,207	1,426	1,975	1,942	1,914	2,131	2,227	2,434	2,879
18 to 24 years	315	435	745	899	1,223	1,216	1,182	1,375	1,338	1,465	1,814
25 to 34 years	118	168	250	309	460	438	461	487	500	590	652
35 years old and over	(NA)	130	193	195	271	257	271	269	338	336	372
Male	222	364	568	619	852	804	789	864	1,042	1,080	1,302
Female	221	384	639	807	1,123	1,139	1,125	1,267	1,185	1,354	1,576

NA Not available. [1] Beginning 1990, based on a revised edit and tabulation package. [2] Includes other races not shown separately. [3] Includes persons 14 to 17 years old not shown separately. [4] Beginning 2003, for persons who selected this race group only. See footnote 2, Table 234. [5] Persons of Hispanic origin may be of any race.

Source: U.S. Census Bureau, Current Population Reports, "School Enrollment in the United States: 2010," detailed tables, and earlier reports <http://www.census.gov/hhes/school/index.html>.

Table 282. Foreign (Nonimmigrant) Student Enrollment in College: 1980 to 2011

[In thousands (286 represents 286,000). For fall of the previous year]

Region of origin	1980	1990	1995	2000	2001	2002	2003	2004	2005	2006	2007	2008	2009	2010	2011
All regions	**286**	**387**	**453**	**515**	**548**	**583**	**586**	**573**	**565**	**565**	**583**	**624**	**672**	**691**	**723**
Africa	36	25	21	30	34	38	40	38	36	36	36	36	37	37	37
Nigeria	16	4	2	4	4	4	6	6	6	6	6	6	6	7	7
Asia [1,2,3]	165	245	292	315	339	363	367	356	356	346	367	405	444	469	504
China [4]	1	33	39	54	60	63	65	62	63	63	68	81	98	128	158
Taiwan [4]	18	31	36	29	29	29	28	26	26	28	29	29	28	27	25
Hong Kong	10	11	13	8	8	8	8	7	7	8	8	8	8	8	8
India	9	26	34	42	55	67	75	80	80	77	84	95	103	105	104
Indonesia	2	9	12	11	12	12	10	9	8	8	7	8	8	7	7
Iran	51	7	3	2	2	2	2	2	2	2	3	3	4	5	6
Japan	12	30	45	47	46	47	46	41	42	39	35	34	29	25	21
Malaysia	4	14	14	9	8	7	7	6	6	6	5	5	6	6	7
Saudi Arabia	10	4	4	5	5	6	4	4	3	3	8	10	13	16	23
South Korea	5	22	34	41	46	49	52	52	53	59	62	69	75	72	73
Thailand	7	7	11	11	11	12	10	9	9	9	9	9	9	9	8
Europe [5]	23	46	65	78	81	82	78	74	72	85	83	84	88	85	84
Latin America [1,6]	42	48	47	62	64	68	69	66	68	65	65	64	68	66	64
Mexico	6	7	9	11	11	13	13	13	13	14	14	15	15	13	14
Venezuela	10	3	4	5	5	6	5	6	5	5	5	5	5	5	5
North America	16	19	23	24	26	27	27	28	29	29	29	29	30	29	28
Canada	15	18	23	24	25	27	27	28	28	28	28	29	30	28	28
Oceania	4	4	4	5	5	5	5	5	4	5	4	5	5	5	6

[1] Includes countries not shown separately. [2] Includes the Middle East. [3] Beginning 2006, excludes Cyprus and Turkey. [4] With the establishment of diplomatic relations with China on January 1, 1979, the U.S. government recognized the People's Republic of China as the sole legal government of China and acknowledged the Chinese position that there is only one China and that Taiwan is part of China. [5] Beginning 2006, includes Cyprus and Turkey. [6] Includes Mexico, Central America, Caribbean, and South America.

Source: Institute of International Education, New York, NY, *Open Doors Report on International Educational Exchange*, annual (copyright). See also <http://www.iie.org/opendoors>.

Table 283. College Enrollment—by Type of College and Sex: 2010

[In thousands (20,275 represents 20,275,000). As of October. Covers civilian noninstitutional population 15 years old and over enrolled in colleges and graduate schools. Based on Current Population Survey. See text, Section 1 and Appendix III]

Characteristic	Total				Male		Female	
	Total enrolled	Two-year college	Four-year college	Graduate school	Total enrolled [1]	Four-year college	Total enrolled [1]	Four-year college
Total enrollment [2]	**20,275**	**5,904**	**10,450**	**3,921**	**9,007**	**4,607**	**11,268**	**5,844**
15 to 19 years old..................	4,593	1,754	2,793	47	2,103	1,179	2,490	1,614
20 to 24 years old..................	7,849	2,065	4,830	954	3,689	2,290	4,160	2,541
25 to 34 years old..................	4,624	1,170	1,742	1,713	2,055	730	2,569	1,011
35 years old and over..............	3,210	915	1,086	1,209	1,160	408	2,049	678
White [3].................................	15,258	4,385	7,904	2,969	6,883	3,544	8,375	4,359
White non-Hispanic [3].............	12,613	3,294	6,684	2,635	5,673	3,023	6,940	3,660
Black [3]................................	3,083	1,006	1,580	497	1,185	610	1,898	970
Asian [3]...............................	1,322	301	643	377	647	309	676	335
Hispanic [4]..........................	2,879	1,171	1,336	371	1,302	567	1,576	769
Type of school:								
Public.................................	16,153	5,450	8,251	2,453	7,178	3,632	8,975	4,619
Private...............................	4,122	454	2,199	1,468	1,829	975	2,293	1,225
Employed full-time.................	5,119	1,365	1,965	1,790	2,299	848	2,820	1,117
Employed part-time................	5,437	1,619	3,105	714	2,268	1,280	3,169	1,824
Not employed........................	9,718	2,920	5,380	1,418	4,440	2,478	5,278	2,903
Full time students..................	14,600	3,870	8,485	2,246	6,631	3,778	7,969	4,707
15 to 19 years old..................	4,067	1,422	2,610	34	1,836	1,092	2,231	1,518
20 to 24 years old..................	6,541	1,422	4,303	817	3,102	2,055	3,439	2,248
25 to 34 years old..................	2,702	653	1,021	1,027	1,209	410	1,493	611
35 years old and over.............	1,291	373	551	367	485	221	806	330
Part time students.................	5,675	2,034	1,965	1,675	2,376	828	3,299	1,137
15 to 19 years old..................	526	332	182	11	267	87	259	96
20 to 24 years old..................	1,308	644	528	137	587	235	721	293
25 to 34 years old..................	1,922	517	721	686	846	319	1,076	401
35 years old and over.............	1,919	542	535	842	675	187	1,244	348

[1] Includes enrollment in two-year colleges and graduate school not shown separately. [2] Includes other races not shown separately. [3] For persons who selected this race group only. See footnote 2, Table 234. [4] Persons of Hispanic origin may be of any race.

Source: U.S. Census Bureau, "Table 5. Type of College and Year Enrolled for College Students 15 Years Old and Over, by Age, Sex, Race, Attendance Status, Control of School, and Enrollment Status: October 2010," <http://www.census.gov/hhes/school/data/cps/2010/tables.html>.

Table 284. Higher Education Enrollment in Languages Other Than English: 1970 to 2009

[1,111.5 represents 1,111,500. As of Fall. For credit enrollment]

Enrollment	1970	1980	1986	1990	1995	1998	2002	2006	2009
Registrations [1] **(1,000)**......................	**1,111.5**	**924.8**	**1,003.2**	**1,184.1**	**1,138.8**	**1,193.8**	**1,397.3**	**1,577.8**	**1,682.6**
By selected language (1,000):									
Spanish............................	389.2	379.4	411.3	533.9	606.3	656.6	746.3	823.0	865.0
French..............................	359.3	248.4	275.3	272.5	205.4	199.1	202.0	206.4	216.4
German............................	202.6	126.9	121.0	133.3	96.3	89.0	91.1	94.3	96.3
American Sign Language.......	(NA)	(NA)	(NA)	1.6	4.3	11.4	60.8	78.8	91.8
Italian..............................	34.2	34.8	40.9	49.7	43.8	49.3	63.9	78.4	80.8
Japanese..........................	6.6	11.5	23.5	45.7	44.7	43.1	52.2	66.6	73.4
Chinese............................	6.2	11.4	16.9	19.5	26.5	28.5	34.2	51.6	61.0
Arabic..............................	1.3	3.5	3.4	3.5	4.4	5.5	10.6	24.0	35.1
Latin................................	27.6	25.0	25.0	28.2	25.9	26.1	29.8	32.2	32.6
Russian............................	36.2	24.0	34.0	44.6	24.7	23.8	23.9	24.8	26.9
Hebrew.............................	16.6	19.4	15.6	13.0	13.1	15.8	22.8	23.8	22.1
Ancient Greek....................	16.7	22.1	17.6	16.4	16.3	16.4	20.4	22.8	20.7
Portuguese........................	5.1	4.9	5.1	6.2	6.5	6.9	8.4	10.3	11.4
Korean.............................	0.1	0.4	0.9	2.3	3.3	4.5	5.2	7.1	8.5
Index (1965=100)................	107.3	89.3	96.8	114.3	109.9	115.2	134.9	152.3	162.4

NA Not available. [1] Includes other languages, not shown separately.

Source: Modern Language Association, Nelly Furman, David Goldberg, and Natalia Lusin. *Enrollments in Languages Other Than English in United States Institutions of Higher Education, Fall 2009*, December 2010 (copyright). For 1970 to 2006, consult Association of Departments of Foreign Languages (ADFL) Bulletins.

Table 285. Students Reported Disability Status by Selected Characteristic: 2007 to 2008

[20,928 represents 20,928,000. Disabled students reported that they had one or more of the following conditions: a specific learning disability, a visual handicap, hard of hearing, deafness, a speech disability, an orthopedic handicap, or a health impairment. Based on the 2007–2008 National Postsecondary Student-Aid Study; see source for details. Includes Puerto Rico. See also Appendix III]

Student characteristic	Undergraduate			Graduate and first-professional		
	All students	Disabled students	Nondisabled students	All students	Disabled students	Nondisabled students
Total students (1,000)................	20,928	2,266	18,662	3,456	261	3,195
PERCENT DISTRIBUTION						
Total...........................	100.0	10.8	89.2	100.0	7.6	92.4
Age:						
15 to 23 years old.............	59.7	54.0	60.4	11.4	7.8	11.7
24 to 29 years old.............	17.3	20.1	17.0	39.9	36.2	40.2
30 years or older..............	23.0	25.9	22.7	48.7	56.0	48.1
Sex:						
Male............................	43.1	42.7	43.1	40.1	39.2	40.2
Female.........................	56.9	57.3	56.9	59.9	60.8	59.8
Race/ethnicity of student:						
White, non-Hispanic............	61.8	66.3	61.2	66.6	63.6	66.9
Black, non-Hispanic............	14.0	12.7	14.1	11.7	19.0	11.1
Hispanic.......................	14.1	12.3	14.4	8.0	7.4	8.0
Asian/Pacific Islander.........	6.6	4.8	6.8	11.1	7.3	11.4
American Indian/Alaska Native..	0.8	0.8	0.9	0.3	0.5	0.3
Other..........................	2.7	3.2	2.6	2.3	2.3	2.3
Attendance status:						
Full-time, full-year...........	39.3	34.7	39.8	34.1	32.6	34.2
Part-time or part-year.........	60.7	65.3	60.2	65.9	67.4	65.8
Student housing status:						
On-campus......................	14.2	11.1	14.5	(NA)	(NA)	(NA)
Off-campus.....................	54.0	56.3	53.7	(NA)	(NA)	(NA)
With parents or relatives......	31.9	32.6	31.8	(NA)	(NA)	(NA)
Dependency status:						
Dependent......................	53.0	46.8	53.7	(S)	(S)	(S)
Independent, unmarried.........	15.3	19.5	14.7	50.0	52.7	49.8
Independent, married...........	6.4	6.9	6.3	16.9	12.9	17.2
Independent with dependents....	25.4	26.7	25.2	33.1	34.4	33.0

NA Not available. S Figure does not meet publication standards.

Source: U.S. National Center for Education Statistics, *Digest of Education Statistics*, annual. See also <http://nces.ed.gov/programs/digest/>.

Table 286. College Freshmen—Summary Characteristics: 1980 to 2011

[In percent, except as indicated (24.5 represents $24,500). As of fall for first-time full-time freshmen in 4-year colleges and universities. Based on sample survey and subject to sampling error; see source]

Characteristic	1980	1990	1995	2000	2005	2008	2009	2010	2011
Sex:									
Male...........................	48.8	46.9	45.6	45.2	45.0	45.4	45.9	44.3	45.1
Female.........................	51.2	53.1	54.4	54.8	55.0	54.6	54.1	55.7	54.9
Applied to more than three colleges...	31.5	42.9	44.4	50.5	55.4	60.1	61.9	64.1	67.4
Average grade in high school:									
A– to A+.......................	26.6	29.4	36.1	42.9	46.6	47.2	48.1	48.4	49.7
B– to B+.......................	58.2	57.0	54.2	50.5	48.0	48.0	47.5	47.5	46.2
C to C+........................	14.9	13.4	9.6	6.5	5.4	4.7	4.4	4.1	4.1
D..............................	0.2	0.2	0.1	0.1	0.1	0.1	0.1	0.1	0.0
Political orientation:									
Liberal........................	21.0	24.6	22.9	24.8	27.1	31.0	29.0	27.3	27.6
Middle of the road............	57.0	51.7	51.3	51.9	45.0	43.3	44.4	46.4	47.4
Conservative..................	19.0	20.6	21.8	18.9	22.6	20.7	21.8	21.7	20.7
Probable field of study:									
Biological sciences...........	4.5	4.9	8.3	6.6	7.6	9.3	9.7	10.8	10.9
Business......................	21.2	21.1	15.4	16.7	17.4	16.8	14.3	13.7	14.9
Education.....................	8.4	10.3	10.1	11.0	9.9	8.2	8.1	7.2	5.9
Engineering...................	11.2	9.7	8.1	8.7	8.3	9.4	9.7	10.3	12
Physical science..............	3.2	2.8	3.1	2.6	3.1	3.2	3.4	2.7	3.7
Social science................	8.2	11.0	9.9	10.0	10.7	11.5	11.7	8.9	12.1
Data processing/computer programming...	1.7	0.7	0.8	1.5	0.5	0.5	0.6	0.5	0.6
Other [1]......................	41.6	39.5	44.3	42.9	42.5	41.1	42.5	45.9	46.2
Communications................	2.4	2.9	1.8	2.7	2.0	1.8	1.9	1.8	1.6
Computer science..............	2.6	1.7	2.2	3.7	1.1	1.0	1.0	1.0	1.1
Personal objectives—very important or essential:									
Being very well off financially...	62.5	72.3	72.8	73.4	74.5	76.8	78.1	77.4	79.6
Developing a meaningful philosophy of life...	62.5	45.9	45.4	42.4	45.0	51.4	48.0	46.9	46.8
Keeping up to date with political affairs...	45.2	46.6	32.3	28.1	36.4	39.5	36.0	33.2	32.8
Median family income ($1,000)...	24.5	46.6	54.8	64.4	73.2	77.5	76.6	76.1	(NA)

NA Not available. [1] Includes other fields not shown separately.

Source: The Higher Education Research Institute, University of California, Los Angeles, CA, *The American Freshman: National Norms*, annual, (Copyright).

Table 287. Residence and Migration of College Freshmen by State: 2010

[As of fall. Includes first-time postsecondary students who had graduated from high school in the previous 12 months and were enrolled at public and private not-for-profit 4-year degree-granting institutions that participated in Title IV federal financial aid programs. Excludes respondents for whom state residence and/or migration are unknown. Also excludes U.S. Service Academies (Air Force Academy, Coast Guard Academy, Merchant Marine Academy, Military Academy, and Naval Academy)]

State	Total freshmen enrollment in institutions located in the state	Ratio of in-state students to freshmen enrollment	Ratio of in-state students to residents enrolled in any state [1]	State	Total freshmen enrollment in institutions located in the state	Ratio of in-state students to freshmen enrollment	Ratio of in-state students to residents enrolled in any state [1]
U.S.	1,476,522	0.73	0.75	MO	30,204	0.70	0.78
AL	23,817	0.67	0.86	MT	6,037	0.64	0.79
AK	2,633	0.90	0.63	NE	11,071	0.75	0.82
AZ	22,043	0.66	0.80	NV	8,413	0.88	0.75
AR	16,040	0.73	0.89	NH	9,093	0.40	0.45
CA	114,035	0.88	0.79	NJ	27,560	0.85	0.44
CO	23,523	0.74	0.71	NM	7,710	0.81	0.80
CT	19,340	0.53	0.42	NY	106,279	0.71	0.73
DE	1,743	0.44	0.29	NC	46,834	0.73	0.85
DC	8,802	0.06	0.23	ND	6,252	0.48	0.78
FL	93,625	0.86	0.88	OH	70,277	0.80	0.83
GA	49,722	0.83	0.81	OK	19,147	0.72	0.88
HI	3,974	0.64	0.50	OR	15,047	0.59	0.70
ID	7,144	0.56	0.65	PA	86,453	0.64	0.79
IL	50,222	0.77	0.61	RI	10,928	0.26	0.52
IN	45,077	0.72	0.87	SC	23,652	0.65	0.85
IA	19,109	0.55	0.78	SD	5,798	0.64	0.75
KS	13,941	0.73	0.77	TN	30,650	0.77	0.80
KY	23,426	0.74	0.86	TX	91,495	0.92	0.82
LA	23,435	0.78	0.89	UT	19,114	0.68	0.92
ME	6,519	0.62	0.57	VT	6,593	0.27	0.46
MD	18,774	0.65	0.45	VA	39,251	0.69	0.73
MA	49,910	0.50	0.58	WA	23,515	0.76	0.70
MI	50,546	0.85	0.85	WV	12,902	0.60	0.89
MN	27,047	0.73	0.62	WI	35,727	0.73	0.78
MS	10,671	0.62	0.82	WY	1,402	0.57	0.54

[1] Students residing in a particular state when admitted to an institution anywhere, either in their home state or another state.

Source: U.S. Department of Education, National Center for Education Statistics, Integrated Postsecondary Education Data System (IPEDS), Spring 2011 and Digest of Education Statistics, annual. See also <http://nces.ed.gov/programs/digest/>.

Table 288. Average Total Price of Attendance of Undergraduate Education: 2007 to 2008

[In dollars. For school year ending in 2008. Excludes students attending more than one institution. Price of attendance includes tuition and fees, books and supplies, room and board, transportation, and personal and other expenses allowed for federal cost of attendance budgets. Based on the 2007–2008 National Postsecondary Student-Aid Study; see source for details. Includes Puerto Rico. See also Appendix III]

Student characteristic	All institu-tions [1]	Public 2-year	Public 4-year Non-doctorate	Public 4-year Doctorate	Private not-for-profit 4-year Non-doctorate	Private not-for-profit 4-year Doctorate	Private for-profit
Total	14,006	7,033	12,657	16,615	25,194	31,628	20,636
Age: [2]							
18 years or younger	17,065	12,630	16,664	19,888	32,586	38,311	19,868
19 to 23 years	16,059	6,830	10,128	12,513	17,861	22,540	20,376
24 to 29 years	11,551	8,035	11,188	13,833	17,823	21,294	20,275
30 to 39 years	10,994	3,854	5,739	7,319	8,446	10,419	21,305
40 years or older	9,269	8,268	14,912	18,501	31,809	37,581	21,265
Sex:							
Male	13,957	7,406	13,778	17,661	30,099	35,206	21,765
Female	14,044	6,856	10,701	13,005	17,458	20,772	20,133
Race:							
One race:							
White	14,446	6,546	9,690	12,452	15,561	17,839	20,888
Black or African American	13,235	5,992	9,062	10,623	14,722	14,452	20,141
Asian	15,122	7,121	12,668	16,486	25,512	31,163	22,203
American Indian/Alaska Native	12,150	7,013	13,170	16,707	26,717	32,236	25,013
Native Hawaiian or other Pacific Islander	12,904	6,974	12,824	15,891	21,412	26,817	23,122
Other race	12,788	6,990	10,511	15,513	19,548	27,808	24,076
More than one race	15,077	7,313	13,285	18,271	29,162	36,973	23,245
Hispanic or Latino [3]	12,419	6,920	12,644	16,757	24,765	32,182	19,753
Attendance pattern:							
Full-time, full-year	22,368	7,330	10,436	15,078	27,614	(S)	28,638
Full-time, part-year	12,227	6,718	12,988	16,878	18,659	40,521	16,653
Part-time, full-year	10,655	6,759	10,879	15,650	16,534	(S)	19,259
Part-time, part-year	5,231	7,495	13,028	17,256	28,172	34,460	11,810

S Data do not meet publication standards. [1] Includes public less-than-2-year and private not-for-profit less-than-4-year. [2] As of December 31, 2007. [3] Persons of Hispanic origin may be of any race.

Source: U.S. National Center for Education Statistics, "Student Financial Aid Estimates for 2007–08," NCES 2009-166, April 2009, <http://nces.ed.gov/surveys/npsas/>.

Table 289. Average Out-of-Pocket Net Price of Attendance for Undergraduates: 2007 to 2008

[In dollars. For school year ending in 2008. Excludes students attending more than one institution. Net price of attendance is the price that students pay to receive postsecondary education after taking financial aid into account. Based on net tuition and net price for all students. Based on the 2007–2008 National Postsecondary Student-Aid Study; see source for details. Includes Puerto Rico. See also Appendix III]

Student characteristic	All institu-tions [1]	Type of Institution					
		Public 2-year	Public 4-year		Private not-for-profit 4 year		Private for-profit
			Non-doctorate	Doctorate	Non-doctorate	Doctorate	
Total........................	8,769	5,645	7,801	10,627	12,772	18,103	11,647
Age: [2]							
18 years or younger................	10,219	6,612	8,927	11,313	15,067	20,967	9,974
19 to 23 years.....................	9,974	5,995	8,488	11,509	14,672	20,217	11,460
24 to 29 years.....................	7,160	5,303	6,559	7,508	9,755	11,380	11,239
30 to 39 years.....................	7,073	5,168	5,916	7,360	8,858	9,832	12,353
40 years or older..................	6,487	4,998	5,933	7,180	9,365	8,822	12,379
Sex:							
Male.............................	8,985	5,705	8,061	11,042	12,946	19,016	11,942
Female...........................	8,603	5,599	7,586	10,248	12,644	17,313	11,517
Race:							
One race:							
White..........................	9,211	5,674	8,266	11,196	13,550	18,899	11,858
Black or African American.......	7,286	5,192	6,039	7,318	10,564	12,319	11,109
Asian..........................	10,613	6,386	9,518	12,615	17,147	24,543	12,809
American Indian/Alaska Native....	7,715	5,493	6,047	8,115	(S)	(S)	16,623
Native Hawaiian or other Pacific Islander........	8,445	5,627	8,840	9,499	7,855	29,807	11,896
Other race.....................	8,286	5,435	(S)	7,968	(S)	(S)	15,868
More than one race................	8,867	5,854	7,581	10,100	11,828	17,450	13,817
Hispanic or Latino [3]................	7,567	5,638	6,941	8,657	9,761	12,824	11,028
Attendance pattern:							
Full-time, full-year................	13,218	9,428	9,654	12,419	15,659	21,293	16,875
Full-time, part-year................	7,751	5,442	6,672	8,522	10,386	14,220	8,825
Part-time, full-year................	7,410	6,544	7,588	9,030	9,561	12,597	9,174
Part-time, part-year................	3,906	3,348	4,193	5,297	5,498	6,791	5,933

S Data do not meet publication standards. [1] Includes public less-than-2-year and private not-for-profit less-than-4-year. [2] As of December 2007. [3] Persons of Hispanic origin may be of any race.

Source: U.S. National Center for Education Statistics, "Student Financial Aid Estimates for 2007–08," NCES 2009-166, April 2009, <http://nces.ed.gov/surveys/npsas/>.

Table 290. Higher Education Price Indexes: 2003 to 2011

[1983=100. For years ending June 30. The Higher Education Price Index (HEPI), calculated for the July-June academic fiscal year, reflects prices paid by colleges and universities for the following eight cost factors: faculty salaries, administrative salaries, clerical and service employees, fringe benefits, miscellaneous services, supplies and materials, and utilities. Minus sign (-) indicates decrease]

Item and year	Total	Personnel compensation					Contracted services, supplies, and equipment		
		Faculty salaries	Admin-istrative salaries	Clerical salaries	Service employ-ees salaries	Fringe benefits	Miscel-laneous services	Supplies and materials	Utilities
INDEXES									
2003.....................	223.5	229.4	255.7	211.1	193.9	292.3	209.5	132.2	157.6
2004.....................	231.7	234.2	263.3	217.1	197.6	312.8	216.4	135.6	176.4
2005.....................	240.8	240.7	274.0	223.4	201.4	327.2	222.7	145.5	200.2
2006.....................	253.1	248.2	287.7	229.5	205.5	343.7	228.8	158.1	255.7
2007.....................	260.3	257.6	299.2	237.7	213.6	360.8	238.3	165.3	220.6
2008.....................	273.2	268.1	314.0	245.0	220.4	380.7	246.5	180.0	252.0
2009.....................	279.3	277.3	330.9	251.6	226.7	394.4	253.1	181.6	213.8
2010.....................	281.8	280.6	337.6	255.2	230.0	402.8	255.8	179.3	193.6
2011.....................	288.4	284.5	343.2	260.2	233.2	417.6	260.3	193.9	201.6
ANNUAL PERCENT CHANGE [1]									
2003.....................	5.1	3.0	8.2	2.8	2.3	5.5	1.8	3.1	33.5
2004.....................	3.7	2.1	3.0	2.8	1.9	7.0	3.3	2.6	11.9
2005.....................	3.9	2.8	4.1	2.9	1.9	4.6	2.9	7.3	13.5
2006.....................	5.1	3.1	5.0	2.7	2.0	5.0	2.7	8.7	27.7
2007.....................	2.8	3.8	4.0	3.6	4.0	5.0	4.2	4.5	-13.7
2008.....................	5.0	4.1	5.0	3.1	3.2	5.5	3.4	8.9	14.2
2009.....................	2.3	3.4	5.4	2.7	2.9	3.6	2.7	0.9	-15.1
2010.....................	0.9	1.2	2.0	1.4	1.4	2.1	1.1	-1.3	-9.5
2011.....................	2.3	1.4	1.7	2.0	1.4	3.7	1.8	8.2	4.1

[1] Percent change from the immediate prior year.

Source: The Commonfund Institute, Wilton, CT, (copyright), <http://www.commonfund.org>.

Table 291. Federal Student Financial Assistance: 1995 to 2011

[35,477 represents $35,477,000,000. For award years July 1 of year shown to the following June 30. Funds utilized exclude operating costs, etc., and represent funds given to students]

Type of assistance	1995	2000	2005	2008	2009	2010, est.	2011, est.
FUNDS UTILIZED (mil. dol.)							
Total	**35,477**	**44,007**	**72,634**	**97,478**	**130,549**	**144,977**	**155,102**
Federal Pell Grants	5,472	7,956	12,693	18,291	29,992	36,515	35,773
Academic Competitiveness Grants [1]	(X)	(X)	(X)	340	479	548	(X)
SMART Grants [1]	(X)	(X)	(X)	200	359	384	(X)
TEACH Grants [2]	(X)	(X)	(X)	25	72	109	131
Federal Supplemental Educational Opportunity Grant	764	907	1,084	1,039	1,066	959	959
Federal Work-Study	764	939	1,050	1,113	1,246	1,171	1,171
Federal Perkins Loan	1,029	1,144	1,593	961	818	971	971
Federal Direct Student Loan (FDSL)	8,296	10,348	12,930	18,213	29,738	84,704	116,098
Federal Family Education Loans (FFEL)	19,152	22,712	43,284	57,296	66,778	19,618	(X)
NUMBER OF AWARDS (1,000)							
Total	**13,667**	**15,043**	**21,317**	**25,713**	**32,188**	**34,257**	**35,730**
Federal Pell Grants	3,612	3,899	5,167	6,157	8,094	8,873	9,413
Academic Competitiveness Grants [1]	(X)	(X)	(X)	438	613	786	(X)
SMART Grants [1]	(X)	(X)	(X)	64	115	150	(X)
TEACH Grants [2]	(X)	(X)	(X)	8	31	36	44
Federal Supplemental Educational Opportunity Grant	1,083	1,175	1,419	1,451	1,593	1,339	1,339
Federal Work-Study	702	713	710	678	733	713	713
Federal Perkins Loan	688	639	727	488	441	493	493
Federal Direct Student Loan (FDSL)	2,339	2,739	2,971	3,730	6,109	16,647	23,728
Federal Family Education Loans (FFEL)	5,243	5,878	10,323	12,698	14,459	5,220	(X)
AVERAGE AWARD (dol.)							
Total	**2,596**	**2,925**	**3,407**	**3,791**	**4,056**	**4,232**	**4,341**
Federal Pell Grants	1,515	2,041	2,456	2,971	3,706	4,115	3,800
Academic Competitiveness Grants [1]	(X)	(X)	(X)	774	760	697	(X)
SMART Grants [1]	(X)	(X)	(X)	3,107	3,125	2,560	(X)
TEACH Grants [2]	(X)	(X)	(X)	3,125	2,369	2,966	2,966
Federal Supplemental Educational Opportunity Grant	705	772	764	716	669	716	716
Federal Work-Study	1,088	1,318	1,478	1,642	1,700	1,642	1,642
Federal Perkins Loan	1,496	1,790	2,190	1,968	1,852	1,968	1,968
Federal Direct Student Loan (FDSL)	3,547	3,778	4,352	4,882	4,867	5,088	4,893
Federal Family Education Loans (FFEL)	3,653	3,864	4,193	4,512	4,618	3,758	(X)
COHORT DEFAULT RATE [3]							
Federal Perkins Loan	12.6	9.9	8.1	10.4	10.1	(NA)	(NA)

NA Not available. X Not applicable. [1] National Science and Mathematics Access to Retain Talent. Funding for Academic Competitiveness Grants and SMART Grants was terminated in 2011. [2] Teacher Education Assistance for College and Higher Education (TEACH) Grant Program. [3] As of June 30. Represents the percent of borrowers entering repayment status in year shown who defaulted in the following year.

Source: U.S. Department of Education, Office of Postsecondary Education, unpublished data.

Table 292. Institutions of Higher Education—Average Charges: 1985 to 2011

[In dollars. Estimated. For the entire academic year ending in year shown. Figures are average charges per full-time equivalent student. Room and board are based on full-time students]

Academic control and year	Tuition and required fees [1]				Board rates [2]				Dormitory charges			
	All institutions	2-yr. colleges	4-yr. universities	Other 4-yr. schools	All institutions	2-yr. colleges	4-yr. universities	Other 4-yr. schools	All institutions	2-yr. colleges	4-yr. universities	Other 4-yr. schools
Public:												
1985	971	584	1,386	1,117	1,241	1,302	1,276	1,201	1,196	921	1,237	1,200
1990	1,356	756	2,035	1,608	1,635	1,581	1,728	1,561	1,513	962	1,561	1,554
1995	2,057	1,192	2,977	2,499	1,949	1,712	2,108	1,866	1,959	1,232	1,992	2,044
2000	2,504	1,348	3,768	3,091	2,364	1,834	2,628	2,239	2,440	1,549	2,516	2,521
2005	3,629	1,849	5,939	4,512	2,931	2,353	3,222	2,809	3,304	2,174	3,427	3,413
2007	4,102	2,018	6,842	5,020	3,191	2,390	3,498	3,083	3,757	2,407	3,875	3,881
2008	4,291	2,061	7,173	5,285	3,331	2,409	3,668	3,221	3,952	2,506	4,079	4,083
2009	4,512	2,136	7,624	5,610	3,554	2,769	3,911	3,417	4,190	2,664	4,344	4,322
2010	4,751	2,285	8,123	5,964	3,653	2,574	4,018	3,578	4,399	2,845	4,571	4,561
2011	5,706	2,439	8,751	6,325	3,848	2,685	4,200	3,798	4,640	2,960	4,771	4,857
Private:												
1985	5,315	3,485	6,843	5,135	1,462	1,294	1,647	1,405	1,426	1,424	1,753	1,309
1990	8,147	5,196	10,348	7,778	1,948	1,811	2,339	1,823	1,923	1,663	2,411	1,774
1995	11,111	6,914	14,537	10,653	2,509	2,023	3,035	2,362	2,587	2,233	3,469	2,347
2000	14,100	8,225	19,307	13,390	2,877	2,922	3,157	2,788	3,236	3,067	4,070	2,982
2005	18,154	12,122	25,643	17,050	3,485	3,700	3,855	3,370	4,178	4,475	5,263	3,858
2007	20,048	12,708	28,580	18,848	3,785	3,429	4,166	3,672	4,606	4,147	5,691	4,302
2008	20,972	13,126	30,251	19,663	3,992	4,074	4,376	3,875	4,804	4,484	6,006	4,466
2009	21,570	13,562	31,968	20,162	4,209	4,627	4,622	4,080	5,025	4,537	6,254	4,688
2010	21,444	14,876	33,315	19,941	4,331	4,390	4,765	4,205	5,249	5,217	6,539	4,897
2011	22,186	14,467	34,805	20,732	4,434	4,475	4,912	4,298	5,406	4,928	6,802	5,041

[1] For public institutions, data are for in-state students. [2] Beginning 1990, rates reflect 20 meals per week, rather than meals served 7 days a week.

Source: U.S. National Center for Education Statistics, *Digest of Education Statistics*, annual. See also <http://www.nces.ed.gov/programs/digest/>.

Table 293. State and Local Financial Support for Higher Education by State: 2010 to 2011

[11,793.7 represents 11,793,700. For 2010-11 fiscal year. Data for the 50 states]

State	2010-2011		State	2010-2011	
	FTE enrollment [1] (1,000)	Educational appropriations per FTE enrollment [2] (dollars)		FTE enrollment [1] (1,000)	Educational appropriations per FTE enrollment [2] (dollars)
Total............	**11,793.7**	**6,290**			
AL................	213.7	5,315	MT................	41.0	4,631
AK................	21.1	14,837	NE................	84.4	7,345
AZ................	275.1	5,863	NV................	69.2	7,081
AR................	124.2	5,810	NH................	39.5	3,067
CA................	1,738.3	6,596	NJ................	277.1	7,155
CO................	195.6	3,774	NM................	88.1	7,791
CT................	86.3	10,024	NY................	578.4	8,686
DE................	34.9	5,697	NC................	425.8	8,843
FL................	648.8	5,475	ND................	37.9	6,492
GA................	385.6	6,789	OH................	460.7	4,480
HI................	40.7	10,378	OK................	150.2	6,338
ID................	53.2	6,282	OR................	168.9	4,427
IL................	425.1	7,589	PA................	375.0	5,187
IN................	267.2	4,772	RI................	31.7	5,205
IA................	132.7	4,884	SC................	175.7	4,364
KS................	141.8	5,531	SD................	33.3	4,818
KY................	159.8	6,491	TN................	201.4	6,416
LA................	183.6	6,904	TX................	943.7	6,721
ME................	38.3	6,339	UT................	125.1	5,338
MD................	235.9	6,838	VT................	22.5	3,025
MA................	168.7	6,742	VA................	322.0	5,225
MI................	433.0	5,135	WA................	258.3	5,708
MN................	214.3	5,221	WV................	81.1	4,859
MS................	136.5	5,525	WI................	240.6	6,539
MO................	181.2	5,998	WY................	26.4	13,945

[1] Full-time equivalent. Includes degree enrollment and enrollment in public postsecondary programs resulting in a certificate or other formal recognition. Includes summer sessions. Excludes medical enrollments. [2] State and local appropriations for general operating expenses of public postsecondary education. Includes American Recovery and Reinvestment Act of 2009 (ARRA) funds, state-funded financial aid to students attending in-state public institutions. Excludes sums for research, agricultural extension, and teaching hospitals and medical schools.

Source: State Higher Education Executive Officers, Boulder, CO (copyright), <http://www.sheeo.org>.

Table 294. Voluntary Financial Support of Higher Education: 1990 to 2011

[9,800 represents $9,800,000,000. For school years ending in years shown. Voluntary support, as defined in Gift Reporting Standards, excludes income from endowment and other invested funds as well as all support received from federal, state, and local governments and their agencies and contract research]

Item	Unit	1990	1995	2000	2005	2008	2009	2010	2011
Estimated support, total......................	Mil. dol.	9,800	12,750	23,200	25,600	31,600	27,850	28,000	30,300
Individuals.....................................	Mil. dol.	4,770	6,540	12,220	12,100	14,820	12,125	12,020	13,450
Alumni...	Mil. dol.	2,540	3,600	6,800	7,100	8,700	7,130	7,100	7,800
Business corporations........................	Mil. dol.	2,170	2,560	4,150	4,400	4,900	4,620	4,730	5,020
Foundations....................................	Mil. dol.	1,920	2,460	5,080	7,000	9,100	8,235	8,400	8,675
Fundraising consortia and other organizations.................................	Mil. dol.	700	940	1,380	1,730	2,400	2,545	2,545	2,850
Religious organizations......................	Mil. dol.	240	250	370	370	380	325	305	305
Current operations...........................	Mil. dol.	5,440	7,230	11,270	14,200	17,070	16,955	17,000	17,800
Capital purposes..............................	Mil. dol.	4,360	5,520	11,930	11,400	14,530	10,895	11,000	12,500
Support per student...........................	Dollars	724	893	1,568	1,482	1,732	1,458	1,414	1,461
In 2011 dollars...............................	Dollars	1,206	1,319	2,050	1,708	1,810	1,530	1,415	1,461
Expenditures, higher education.............	Bil. dol.	134.7	183.0	236.8	335.0	408.0	432.0	444.8	465.5
Expenditures per student....................	Dollars	9,946	12,814	16,008	19,397	22,358	22,614	22,455	22,446
In 2011 dollars...............................	Dollars	16,114	18,925	20,924	22,911	23,739	23,725	22,475	22,446
Institutions reporting support.................	Number	1,056	1,086	945	997	1,052	1,027	996	1,009
Total support reported........................	Mil. dol.	8,214	10,992	19,419	20,953	27,323	23,693	23,487	25,702
Private 4-year institutions...................	Mil. dol.	5,072	6,500	11,047	11,011	14,296	12,351	12,189	12,517
Public 4-year institutions....................	Mil. dol.	3,056	4,382	8,254	9,780	12,766	11,141	11,114	11,992
2-year colleges...............................	Mil. dol.	85	110	117	163	261	201	185	193

Source: Council for Aid to Education, New York, NY, *Voluntary Support of Education*, annual (copyright). See also: <www.cae.org>.

Table 295. Average Salaries for College Faculty Members: 2010 to 2012

[In thousands of dollars (78.0 represents $78,000). For academic year ending in year shown. Figures are for 9 months teaching for full-time faculty members in 2-year and 4-year institutions with ranks. Fringe benefits averaged in 2010, $22,258 in public institutions and $25,516 in private institutions; in 2011, $23,103 in public institutions and $26,211 in private institutions; and in 2012, $23,600 in public institutions and $27,016 in private institutions]

Type of control and academic rank	2010	2011	2012	Type of control and academic rank	2010	2011	2012
Public: All ranks.............	78.0	78.3	79.5	Private: [1] All ranks.............	92.9	94.6	96.9
Professor......................	105.7	105.8	107.9	Professor......................	128.7	131.6	135.1
Associate professor.........	75.7	76.2	77.2	Associate professor...........	82.9	84.6	86.2
Assistant professor..........	64.0	64.7	65.9	Assistant professor...........	69.5	71.0	72.7
Instructor....................	46.5	45.7	46.3	Instructor......................	52.8	53.6	55.0

[1] Excludes church-related colleges and universities.

Source: American Association of University Professors, Washington, DC, *AAUP Annual Report on the Economic Status of the Profession* (copyright). See also: <http://www.aaup.org/>.

Table 296. Employees in Higher Education Institutions by Sex and Occupation: 1995 to 2009

[In thousands (2,662.1 represents 2,662,100). As of Fall. Based on complete census taken every other year; see source]

Year and status	Total	Professional staff										Non–professional staff, total
		Total	Executive, administrative, and managerial		Faculty [1]		Graduate assistants		Other			
			Male	Female	Male	Female	Male	Female	Male	Female		
1995, total..........	**2,662.1**	**1,744.9**	**82.1**	**65.3**	**562.9**	**368.8**	**124.0**	**91.9**	**177.2**	**272.7**		**917.2**
Full–time...........	1,801.4	1,066.5	79.2	61.8	360.2	190.7	–	–	151.5	223.2		734.9
Part–time..........	860.7	678.4	2.9	3.6	202.7	178.1	124.0	91.9	25.6	49.5		182.3
2005, total [2]........	**3,379.1**	**2,459.9**	**95.2**	**101.1**	**714.5**	**576.0**	**167.5**	**149.6**	**262.8**	**393.2**		**919.2**
Full–time...........	2,179.9	1,432.1	92.9	97.2	401.5	274.1	–	–	231.4	335.0		747.8
Part–time..........	1,199.2	1,027.8	2.4	3.9	312.9	301.9	167.5	149.6	31.4	58.2		171.4
2009, total..........	**3,723.4**	**2,782.1**	**106.9**	**123.7**	**761.0**	**678.1**	**180.9**	**161.5**	**305.0**	**465.0**		**941.3**
Full–time...........	2,381.7	1,619.5	103.8	118.5	415.8	313.2	–	–	268.6	399.7		762.2
Part–time..........	1,341.7	1,162.6	3.1	5.2	345.2	365.0	180.9	161.5	36.4	65.3		179.1

– Represents zero. [1] Instruction and research. [2] Beginning 2005, data reflect the new classification of institutions. See footnote 1, Table 278.

Source: U.S. National Center for Education Statistics, *Digest of Education Statistics*, annual. See also <http://www.nces.ed.gov/programs/digest>.

Table 297. Faculty in Institutions of Higher Education: 1980 to 2009

[In thousands (686 represents 686,000), except percent. As of Fall. Based on complete census taken every other year; see source]

Year	Total	Employment status		Control		Level		Percent		
		Full-time	Part-time	Public	Private	4-Year	2-Year or less	Part-time	Public	2-Year or less
1980 [1]...............	686	450	236	495	191	494	192	34	72	28
1985 [1]...............	715	459	256	503	212	504	211	36	70	30
1991 [2]...............	826	536	291	581	245	591	235	35	70	28
1995.................	932	551	381	657	275	647	285	41	70	31
1999 [3]...............	1,028	591	437	713	315	714	314	43	69	31
2001 [3]...............	1,113	618	495	771	342	764	349	44	69	31
2003 [3]...............	1,174	630	544	792	382	814	359	46	67	31
2005 [3]...............	1,290	676	615	841	449	917	373	48	65	29
2007 [3, 4]............	1,371	703	668	877	494	991	381	49	64	28
2009 [3, 4]............	1,439	729	710	914	525	1,038	401	49	63	28

[1] Estimated on the basis of enrollment. [2] Data beginning 1991 not comparable to prior years. [3] Beginning 1997, data reflect the new classification of institutions. See footnote 1, Table 278. [4] Beginning in 2007, data include institutions with fewer than 15 full-time employees; these institutions did not report staff data prior to 2007.

Source: U.S. National Center for Education Statistics, *Digest of Education Statistics*, annual. See also <http://www.nces.ed.gov/programs/digest/>.

Table 298. Salary Offers to Candidates for Degrees: 2005 to 2010

[In dollars. Data are average beginning salaries based on offers made by business, industrial, government, nonprofit, and educational employers to graduating students. Data from representative colleges throughout the United States]

Field of study	Bachelor's			Master's [1]			Doctoral		
	2005	2009	2010	2005	2009	2010	2005	2009	2010
Accounting.............................	42,940	48,471	48,378	45,992	48,760	[3] 49,254	(NA)	(NA)	(NA)
Business administration/ management [2]	39,480	44,607	43,991	[3] 50,513	[3] 63,615	[3] 49,875	[3] 66,500	[3] 82,429	[3] 103,667
Marketing.............................	36,409	42,260	41,670	[3] 47,000	(NA)	[3] 40,933	(NA)	(NA)	(NA)
Engineering:									
Civil..................................	43,774	52,287	51,321	48,619	[3] 53,311	[3] 57,225	[3] 59,216	[3] 60,351	[3] 58,964
Chemical...........................	53,639	65,675	64,889	62,845	[3] 70,484	[3] 90,333	[3] 73,317	[3] 85,250	[3] 82,488
Computer...........................	52,242	60,844	60,396	58,631	[3] 72,771	[3] 69,389	[3] 69,625	[3] 104,286	[3] 92,556
Electrical...........................	51,773	60,509	59,512	64,781	70,921	[3] 67,844	[3] 75,066	[3] 89,715	[3] 81,188
Mechanical.........................	50,175	59,222	58,110	60,223	66,961	67,234	69,757	[3] 75,186	[3] 73,036
Nuclear [4]	[3] 51,225	60,209	[3] 57,417	[3] 59,059	[3] 69,100	[3] 69,467	(NA)	(NA)	(NA)
Petroleum..........................	62,236	85,417	77,278	[3] 65,000	(NA)	[3] 96,000	(NA)	(NA)	(NA)
Engineering technology...........	45,790	55,023	52,756	(NA)	(NA)	(NA)	(NA)	(NA)	(NA)
Chemistry..........................	38,635	39,354	39,404	(NA)	[3] 49,800	[3] 58,000	55,874	62,785	[3] 64,249
Mathematics......................	43,304	50,461	48,499	[3] 34,500	[3] 58,200	[3] 53,200	[3] 55,047	[3] 70,226	[3] 61,888
Physics............................	[3] 44,700	[3] 53,939	[3] 52,487	[3] 62,500	[3] 98,425	[3] 65,500	[3] 54,897	[3] 74,333	[3] 59,008
Humanities........................	31,565	[3] 38,292	[3] 34,982	[3] 35,212	[3] 42,380	[3] 49,250	[3] 43,728	[3] 47,491	[3] 53,000
Social sciences [5]	31,621	36,217	36,433	[3] 40,575	[3] 47,000	[3] 46,030	[3] 46,838	[3] 54,870	[3] 57,320
Computer science................	50,664	61,467	60,473	64,840	[3] 68,627	[3] 69,753	[3] 84,025	[3] 84,080	[3] 69,112

NA Not available. [1] Candidates with 1 year or less of full-time nonmilitary employment. [2] For master's degree, offers are after nontechnical undergraduate degree. [3] Fewer than 50 offers reported. [4] Includes engineering physics. [5] Excludes economics.

Source: National Association of Colleges and Employers, Bethlehem, PA (copyright). Reprinted with permission from Fall 2005, 2009, and 2010 *Salary Survey*. All rights reserved.

Table 299. Degrees Earned by Level and Sex: 1960 to 2010

[In thousands (477 represents 477,000), except percent. Based on survey; see Appendix III]

Year ending	All degrees		Associate's		Bachelor's		Master's		Doctoral [1]	
	Total	Percent male	Male	Female	Male	Female	Male	Female	Male	Female
1960..............	477	64.0	(NA)	(NA)	[2] 254	[2] 138	51	24	9	1
1970..............	1,271	59.2	117	89	451	341	131	83	54	6
1975..............	1,666	56.0	191	169	505	418	166	131	71	14
1980..............	1,732	51.1	184	217	474	456	157	148	70	26
1985..............	1,828	49.3	203	252	483	497	149	144	66	35
1990..............	1,940	46.6	191	264	492	560	158	172	64	40
1995..............	2,218	44.9	218	321	526	634	183	221	67	47
1996..............	2,248	44.2	220	336	522	642	183	229	67	48
1997..............	2,288	43.6	224	347	521	652	185	240	68	50
1998..............	2,298	43.2	218	341	520	664	189	247	67	52
1999..............	2,323	42.7	218	342	519	682	190	256	65	51
2000..............	2,385	42.6	225	340	530	708	196	267	65	54
2001..............	2,416	42.4	232	347	532	712	198	276	64	55
2002..............	2,494	42.2	238	357	550	742	203	285	63	57
2003..............	2,622	42.1	253	380	573	775	215	304	63	59
2004..............	2,755	41.8	260	405	595	804	233	331	64	62
2005..............	2,850	41.6	268	429	613	826	237	343	67	67
2006..............	2,936	41.3	270	443	631	855	242	358	69	69
2007..............	3,007	41.2	275	453	650	875	242	368	71	73
2008..............	3,093	41.2	283	468	668	895	250	380	73	76
2009..............	3,205	41.3	298	489	685	916	264	399	76	79
2010..............	3,351	41.2	323	527	707	943	275	418	77	82

NA Not available. [1] Includes Ph.D., Ed.D, and comparable degrees at the doctoral level. Includes most degrees formerly classified as first-professional, such as M.D., D.D.S., and law degrees. [2] Includes some degrees classified as master's or doctor's degrees in later years.

Source: U.S. National Center for Education Statistics, *Digest of Education Statistics*, annual. See also <http://www.nces.ed.gov/programs/digest/>.

Table 300. Degrees Earned by Level and Race/Ethnicity: 1990 to 2010

[For school year ending in year shown. Based on survey; see Appendix III]

Level of degree and race/ethnicity	Total 1990	Total 2000 [1]	Total 2005 [1]	Total 2009 [1]	Total 2010 [1]	Percent distribution 1990	Percent distribution 2000 [1]	Percent distribution 2010 [1]
Associate's degrees, total.............	455,102	564,933	696,660	787,325	849,452	100.0	100.0	100.0
White, non-Hispanic....................	376,816	408,772	475,513	522,985	552,863	82.8	72.4	65.1
Black, non-Hispanic...................	34,326	60,221	86,402	101,487	113,905	7.5	10.7	13.4
Hispanic..............................	21,504	51,573	78,557	97,921	112,211	4.7	9.1	13.2
Asian or Pacific Islander..............	13,066	27,782	33,669	40,914	44,021	2.9	4.9	5.2
American Indian/Alaska Native.......	3,430	6,497	8,435	8,834	10,337	0.8	1.2	1.2
Nonresident alien.....................	5,960	10,088	14,084	15,184	16,115	1.3	1.8	1.9
Bachelor's degrees, total.............	1,051,344	1,237,875	1,439,264	1,601,368	1,650,014	100.0	100.0	100.0
White, non-Hispanic....................	887,151	929,106	1,049,141	1,144,612	1,167,499	84.4	75.1	70.8
Black, non-Hispanic...................	61,046	108,013	136,122	156,615	164,844	5.8	8.7	10.0
Hispanic..............................	32,829	75,059	101,124	129,526	140,316	3.1	6.1	8.5
Asian or Pacific Islander..............	39,230	77,912	97,209	112,510	117,422	3.7	6.3	7.1
American Indian/Alaska Native.......	4,390	8,719	10,307	12,222	12,399	0.4	0.7	0.8
Nonresident alien.....................	26,698	39,066	45,361	45,883	47,534	2.5	3.2	2.9
Master's degrees, total...............	324,301	457,056	574,618	656,784	693,025	100.0	100.0	100.0
White, non-Hispanic....................	254,299	320,485	379,350	424,188	445,038	78.4	70.1	64.2
Black, non-Hispanic...................	15,336	35,874	54,482	70,010	76,458	4.7	7.8	11.0
Hispanic..............................	7,892	19,253	31,485	39,439	43,535	2.4	4.2	6.3
Asian or Pacific Islander..............	10,439	23,218	32,783	39,944	42,707	3.2	5.1	6.2
American Indian/Alaska Native.......	1,090	2,246	3,295	3,759	3,960	0.3	0.5	0.0
Nonresident alien.....................	35,245	55,980	73,223	79,444	81,332	10.9	12.2	11.7
Doctoral degrees, total..............	38,371	44,808	52,631	67,716	158,558	100.0	100.0	100.0
White, non-Hispanic....................	26,221	27,843	30,261	39,648	104,426	68.3	62.1	65.9
Black, non-Hispanic...................	1,149	2,246	3,056	4,434	10,417	3.0	5.0	6.6
Hispanic..............................	780	1,305	1,824	2,540	8,085	2.0	2.9	5.1
Asian or Pacific Islander..............	1,225	2,420	2,911	3,875	16,625	3.2	5.4	10.5
American Indian/Alaska Native........	98	160	237	332	952	0.3	0.4	0.6
Nonresident alien.....................	8,898	10,834	14,342	16,887	18,053	23.2	24.2	11.4
First-professional degrees, total.....	70,988	80,057	87,289	92,004	94,103	100.0	100.0	100.0
White, non-Hispanic....................	60,487	59,637	63,429	65,439	66,172	85.2	74.5	70.3
Black, non-Hispanic...................	3,409	5,555	6,313	6,571	6,850	4.8	6.9	7.3
Hispanic..............................	2,425	3,865	4,445	5,089	5,430	3.4	4.8	5.8
Asian or Pacific Islander..............	3,362	8,584	10,501	12,182	12,691	4.7	10.7	13.5
American Indian/Alaska Native.......	257	564	564	659	665	0.4	0.7	0.7
Nonresident alien.....................	1,048	1,852	2,037	2,064	2,295	1.5	2.3	2.4

[1] Beginning 2000, data reflect the new classification of institutions. See footnote 1, Table 278.

Source: U.S. National Center for Education Statistics, *Digest of Education Statistics*, annual. See also <http://www.nces.ed.gov/programs/digest/>.

Table 301. Bachelor's Degrees Earned by Field: 1980 to 2010

[The new Classification of Instructional Programs was introduced in 2009-10. Data for previous years has been reclassified where necessary to conform to the new classifications. Based on survey; see Appendix III]

Field of study	1980	1990	2000	2005	2009	2010
Total [1]..	**929,417**	**1,051,344**	**1,237,875**	**1,439,264**	**1,601,368**	**1,650,014**
Agriculture and natural resources..............	22,802	12,900	24,238	23,002	24,988	26,336
Architecture and related services...............	9,132	9,364	8,462	9,237	10,119	10,051
Area, ethnic, cultural, and gender studies.......	2,840	4,447	6,212	7,569	8,772	8,621
Biological and biomedical sciences.............	46,190	37,204	63,005	64,611	80,756	86,400
Business.......................................	186,264	248,568	256,070	311,574	347,985	358,293
Communication, journalism, and related programs [2]...	28,616	51,572	57,058	75,238	83,109	81,266
Computer and information sciences.............	11,154	27,347	37,788	54,111	37,994	39,589
Education......................................	118,038	105,112	108,034	105,451	101,708	101,265
Engineering and engineering technologies......	69,387	82,480	73,419	79,743	84,636	88,729
English language and literature/letters..........	32,187	46,803	50,106	54,379	55,462	53,231
Family and consumer sciences/human sciences....	18,411	13,514	16,321	20,074	21,905	21,818
Foreign languages, literatures, and linguistics....	12,480	13,113	15,886	18,386	21,158	21,516
Health professions and related clinical sciences....	63,848	58,983	80,863	80,685	120,488	129,634
Homeland security, law enforcement, and firefighting....	15,015	15,354	24,877	30,723	41,800	43,667
Legal professions and studies..................	683	1,632	1,969	3,161	3,822	3,886
Liberal arts and sciences, general studies, and humanities....................................	23,196	27,985	36,104	43,751	47,096	46,953
Mathematics and statistics....................	11,378	14,276	11,418	14,351	15,496	16,030
Multi/interdisciplinary studies..................	11,457	16,557	28,561	30,243	37,444	37,648
Parks, recreation, leisure, and fitness studies....	5,753	4,582	17,571	22,888	31,667	33,318
Philosophy and religious studies...............	7,069	7,034	8,535	11,584	12,444	12,504
Physical sciences and science technologies......	23,407	16,056	18,331	18,905	22,466	23,379
Psychology....................................	42,093	53,952	74,194	85,614	94,271	97,216
Public administration and social services........	16,644	13,908	20,185	21,769	23,851	25,414
Social sciences and history....................	103,662	118,083	127,101	156,892	168,500	172,780
Theology and religious vocations...............	6,170	5,185	6,789	9,284	8,940	8,718
Transportation and materials moving............	213	2,387	3,395	4,904	5,189	4,998
Visual and performing arts....................	40,892	39,934	58,791	80,955	89,140	91,802

[1] Includes other fields of study, not shown separately. [2] Includes technologies.

Source: U.S. National Center for Education Statistics, *Digest of Education Statistics*, annual and unpublished data. See also <http://www.nces.ed.gov/programs/digest/>.

Table 302. Associate Degrees and Certificates Below the Associate's Degree Level by Field, 2010

[For school year ending in 2010. The new Classification of Instructional Programs was introduced in 2009-2010. Data for previous years has been reclassified where necessary to conform to the new classifications. Covers certificates below the associate's degree level based on postsecondary curriculums of less than 4 years in degree- and nondegree-granting institutions of higher education and associate's degrees conferred by degree-granting institutions. Based on survey; see Appendix III]

Field of study	Less than 1-year awards		1- to less than 4-year awards		Associate degree	
	Total	Women	Total	Women	Total	Women
Total [1]	**503,325**	**302,199**	**432,464**	**278,210**	**849,452**	**526,536**
Agriculture and natural resources, total	3,373	1,049	2,189	783	5,894	2,111
Architecture and related services	240	115	118	58	552	286
Area, ethnic, cultural, and gender studies	467	329	101	68	199	124
Biological and biomedical sciences	245	177	95	69	2,664	1,813
Business, management, marketing, and support services	39,464	27,096	20,425	15,016	116,904	76,504
Communications and communications technologies	1,904	590	2,928	676	4,419	1,381
Computer and information sciences and support services	15,866	5,088	8,725	2,405	32,466	7,784
Construction trades	13,613	628	14,171	621	4,617	267
Education	6,019	4,964	3,424	2,978	17,048	14,696
Engineering technologies and engineering-related fields	15,305	2,152	13,398	1,177	31,850	4,288
English language and literature/letters	1,577	995	344	218	1,658	1,097
Family and consumer sciences	11,388	9,831	3,145	2,860	9,573	9,078
Foreign languages, literatures, and linguistics	1,049	800	449	380	1,683	1,365
Health professions and related programs	249,259	201,725	182,604	156,776	177,686	151,782
Homeland security, law enforcement, and firefighting	24,276	5,111	6,018	1,763	37,260	17,384
Legal professions and studies	1,961	1,656	3,255	2,771	10,003	8,800
Liberal arts and sciences, general studies, and humanities	2,314	1,527	14,089	8,538	284,775	174,074
Library science	230	201	54	48	112	92
Mathematics and statistics	34	5	2	–	1,051	326
Mechanics and repair technologies/technicians	30,263	1,548	47,933	1,724	16,305	826
Military technologies and applied sciences	29	5	0	0	668	137
Multi/interdisciplinary studies	1,161	576	1,151	687	17,671	10,711
Parks, recreation, leisure, and fitness studies	548	253	530	228	2,016	793
Personal and culinary services	33,986	27,312	81,956	71,347	16,467	8,699
Philosophy and religion	64	37	25	14	256	93
Physical sciences and science technologies	278	98	682	228	4,140	1,591
Precision production trades	16,202	729	12,915	597	2,787	178
Psychology	88	72	48	37	6,582	5,311
Public administration and social service professions	1,054	869	553	436	4,526	3,864
Social sciences and history	487	218	227	96	10,649	6,840
Theology and religious vocations	196	110	1,057	578	613	307
Transportation and material moving	22,015	1,751	1,213	93	1,444	209
Visual and performing arts	6,047	3,683	7,878	4,677	19,567	11,881

– Represents zero. [1] Includes other fields of study, not shown separately.

Source: U.S. National Center for Education Statistics, *Digest of Education Statistics*, annual. See also <http://www.nces.ed.gov/programs/digest>.

Table 303. Master's and Doctoral Degrees Earned by Field: 1971 to 2010

[For school years ending in years shown. The new Classification of Instructional Programs was introduced in 2009-2010. Data for previous years has been reclassified where necessary to conform to the new classifications. Based on survey; see Appendix III]

Field of study	1971	1981	1991	2001	2009	2010
MASTER'S DEGREES						
Total [1]	**235,564**	**302,637**	**342,863**	**473,502**	**662,079**	**693,025**
Agriculture and natural resources	2,457	4,003	3,295	4,272	4,877	5,211
Architecture and related services	1,705	3,153	3,490	4,302	6,587	7,280
Area, ethnic, cultural, gender, and group studies	1,032	802	1,233	1,555	1,779	1,775
Biological and biomedical sciences	5,625	5,766	4,834	7,017	10,017	10,725
Business	26,490	57,888	78,255	115,602	168,375	177,684
Communication, journalism, and related programs	1,770	2,896	4,123	5,218	7,092	7,636
Communications technologies	86	209	204	427	475	463
Computer and information sciences	1,588	4,218	9,324	16,911	17,907	17,953
Education	87,666	96,713	87,352	127,829	178,564	182,139
Engineering	16,813	16,893	24,454	25,174	34,546	35,088
Engineering technologies	134	323	996	2,013	3,455	4,258
English language and literature/letters	10,441	5,742	6,784	6,763	9,261	9,201
Family and consumer sciences/human sciences	1,452	2,570	1,541	1,838	2,453	2,580
Foreign languages, literatures, and linguistics	5,480	2,934	3,049	3,035	3,592	3,755
Health professions and related programs	5,330	16,176	21,354	43,623	62,620	69,084
Homeland security, law enforcement, and firefighting	194	1,538	1,108	2,514	6,128	6,714
Legal professions and studies	955	1,832	2,057	3,829	5,150	5,734
Liberal arts and sciences, general studies, and humanities	885	2,375	2,213	3,193	3,728	3,804
Library science	7,001	4,859	4,763	4,727	7,091	7,448
Mathematics and statistics	5,191	2,567	3,549	3,209	5,211	5,634
Military technologies and applied sciences	2	43	–	–	3	–
Multi/interdisciplinary studies	924	2,356	2,079	3,413	5,225	5,973
Parks, recreation, leisure, and fitness studies	218	643	483	2,354	4,822	5,617
Philosophy and religious studies	1,326	1,231	1,471	1,386	1,859	2,043
Physical sciences and science technologies	6,336	5,246	5,281	5,134	5,862	6,063
Precision production	–	–	–	2	10	10
Psychology	5,717	10,223	11,349	16,539	23,415	23,752
Public administration and social services	7,785	17,803	17,905	25,268	33,933	35,729
Social sciences and history	16,539	11,945	12,233	13,791	19,240	20,222
Theology and religious vocations	7,747	11,061	10,498	9,876	12,836	12,824
Transportation and materials moving	–	–	406	756	1,048	1,074
Visual and performing arts	6,675	8,629	8,657	11,404	14,918	15,552
DOCTORAL DEGREES						
Total [1]	**64,998**	**98,016**	**105,547**	**119,585**	**154,425**	**158,558**
Agriculture and natural resources	1,086	1,067	1,185	1,127	1,328	1,147
Architecture and related services	36	93	135	153	212	210
Area, ethnic, cultural, gender, and group studies	143	161	159	216	239	253
Biological and biomedical sciences	3,603	3,640	4,152	5,225	7,499	7,666
Business	774	808	1,185	1,180	2,123	2,245
Communication, journalism, and related programs	145	171	259	368	533	570
Communications technologies	–	11	13	2	2	3
Computer and information sciences	128	252	676	768	1,580	1,599
Education	6,041	7,279	6,189	6,284	9,028	9,233
Engineering	3,687	2,598	5,316	5,485	7,742	7,704
Engineering technologies	1	10	14	62	59	67
English language and literature/letters	1,554	1,040	1,056	1,330	1,271	1,332
Family and consumer sciences/human sciences	123	247	229	354	333	296
Foreign languages, literatures, and linguistics	1,084	931	889	1,078	1,111	1,091
Health professions and related programs	15,988	29,595	29,842	39,019	54,709	57746
Homeland security, law enforcement, and firefighting	1	21	28	44	97	106
Legal professions and studies	17,441	36,391	38,035	38,190	44,304	44626
Liberal arts and sciences, general studies, and humanities	32	121	70	102	67	96
Library science	39	71	56	58	35	64
Mathematics and statistics	1,199	728	978	997	1,535	1,592
Multi/interdisciplinary studies	101	236	306	512	731	631
Parks, recreation, leisure, and fitness studies	2	42	28	177	285	266
Philosophy and religious studies	555	411	464	600	686	667
Physical sciences and science technologies	4,324	3,105	4,248	3,968	5,237	5,063
Psychology	2,144	3,576	3,932	5,091	5,477	5,540
Public administration and social services	174	362	430	574	812	838
Social sciences and history	3,660	3,122	3,012	3,930	4,234	4,238
Theology and religious vocations	312	1,273	1,076	1,461	1,587	2,070
Visual and performing arts	621	654	838	1,167	1,569	1,599

– Represents zero. [1] Includes other fields of study, not shown separately.

Source: U.S. National Center for Education Statistics, *Digest of Education Statistics*, annual. See also <http://www.nces.ed.gov/programs/digest/>.

Table 304. First Professional Degrees Earned in Selected Professions: 1970 to 2010

[First professional degrees include degrees which require at least 6 years of college work for completion (including at least 2 years of preprofessional training). Based on survey; see Appendix III]

Type of degree and sex of recipient	1970	1980	1985	1990	1995	2000	2005	2008	2009	2010
Medicine (M.D.):										
Institutions conferring degrees.............	86	112	120	124	119	118	120	120	120	120
Degrees conferred, total.....................	8,314	14,902	16,041	15,075	15,537	15,286	15,461	15,646	15,987	16,356
Percent to women..........................	8.4	23.4	30.4	34.2	38.8	42.7	47.3	49.3	48.9	48.2
Dentistry (D.D.S. or D.M.D.):										
Institutions conferring degrees.............	48	58	59	57	53	54	53	55	55	55
Degrees conferred, total.....................	3,718	5,258	5,339	4,100	3,897	4,250	4,454	4,795	4,918	5,062
Percent to women..........................	0.9	13.3	20.7	30.9	36.4	40.1	43.8	44.5	46.4	45.8
Law (LL.B. or J.D.):										
Institutions conferring degrees.............	145	179	181	182	183	190	198	201	203	205
Degrees conferred, total.....................	14,916	35,647	37,491	36,485	39,349	38,152	43,423	43,769	44,045	44,345
Percent to women..........................	5.4	30.2	38.5	42.2	42.6	45.9	48.7	47.0	45.8	47.2
Theological (B.D., M.Div., M.H.L.):										
Institutions conferring degrees.............	(NA)	(NA)	(NA)	(NA)	192	198	(NA)	(NA)	(NA)	(NA)
Degrees conferred, total.....................	5,298	7,115	7,221	5,851	5,978	6,129	5,533	5,751	5,362	5,672
Percent to women..........................	2.3	13.8	18.5	24.8	25.7	29.2	35.6	34.3	33.1	33.8

NA Not available.

Source: U.S. National Center for Education Statistics, *Digest of Education Statistics*, annual. See also <http://www.nces.ed.gov/programs/digest/>.

Table 305. Mean Student Loan Debt of Households: 1989 to 2010

[In 2011 dollars, unless otherwise noted. Includes education loans that are currently in deferment and loans in scheduled repayment period. Pew Research Center tabulations of Survey of Consumer Finances data. See source for details]

Household Characteristic	1989	1992	1995	1998	2001	2004	2007	2010
All households................................	**9,634**	**11,086**	**11,714**	**17,942**	**17,562**	**20,022**	**23,349**	**26,682**
Age of household head								
Younger than 35.............................	10,304	10,449	11,841	20,682	15,478	19,586	25,795	26,842
35-44..	8,632	12,743	10,056	13,455	26,239	22,651	20,477	27,634
45-54..	11,010	7,659	14,907	17,269	12,717	19,042	22,440	25,152
55-64..	5,488	16,826	11,746	21,203	19,258	17,321	19,778	29,853
65 and older.................................	9,419	10,854	4,794	5,771	2,579	25,145	21,443	17,578
Highest education of household head								
Less than HS diploma.......................	5,156	4,083	5,739	8,104	5,573	9,257	10,260	9,477
HS graduate.................................	6,344	6,280	6,349	7,687	10,745	14,792	13,573	13,227
Some college................................	8,140	6,716	12,475	16,109	10,756	13,837	14,839	20,509
College graduate............................	12,373	15,254	14,359	22,310	24,561	25,405	31,470	36,809
Household annual income								
Lowest fifth.................................	9,126	6,887	9,552	13,444	11,388	18,312	19,018	20,640
Second fifth.................................	5,955	10,328	9,976	16,880	15,861	21,426	17,400	18,659
Middle fifth..................................	12,843	15,474	14,092	19,890	16,610	18,146	20,887	29,953
Fourth fifth..................................	11,083	8,639	9,764	18,157	16,136	19,041	26,283	24,076
80%–89.9%..................................	6,367	10,516	15,804	15,155	19,822	19,678	25,921	31,989
Richest 10%.................................	11,014	17,025	14,756	27,990	33,215	28,855	36,033	44,810
Household wealth								
Lowest fourth...............................	11,623	13,773	14,842	23,703	18,405	21,352	23,121	35,096
Second fourth...............................	6,071	7,598	8,399	11,813	11,923	15,430	20,548	18,071
Third fourth.................................	7,777	8,587	8,319	15,603	14,849	22,800	23,150	21,108
75%–89.9%..................................	15,155	7,797	15,227	9,353	24,981	24,330	27,312	21,564
Wealthiest 10%..............................	6,223	17,883	11,519	19,256	72,373	12,930	37,616	26,145
Percent of student loan debt to household income.....................	**1.2**	**1.9**	**2.1**	**2.8**	**2.3**	**3.2**	**3.9**	**6.3**

Source: Pew Research Center, Social and Demographic Trends, *A Record One-in-Five Households Now Owe Student Loan Debt*, September 2012, <http://pewresearch.org/>.

Table 306. Public Schools Reporting Incidents of Crime by Incident Type and Selected School Characteristics: 2009 to 2010

[For school year ending in 2010. Includes incidents that happen in school buildings, on school grounds, on school buses, and at places that hold school-sponsored events or activities. Based on sample; see source for details]

School characteristic	Total number of schools	Percent of schools with—				Rate per 1,000 students			
		Violent incidents[1]	Serious violent incidents[2]	Theft[3]	Other incidents[4]	Violent incidents[1]	Serious violent incidents[2]	Theft[3]	Other incidents[4]
All public schools[5]	**82,800**	**73.8**	**16.4**	**44.1**	**68.1**	**25.0**	**1.1**	**5.5**	**9.2**
Level:[6]									
Primary	48,900	64.4	13.0	25.7	57.3	21.3	1.0	1.8	4.5
Middle	15,300	90.5	18.9	65.2	81.9	40.0	1.5	7.4	11.1
High school	12,200	90.9	27.6	82.6	92.2	21.4	1.1	10.1	16.2
Enrollment size:									
Less than 300	18,900	62.8	10.4	30.7	55.3	27.2	[7] 1.5	5.2	8.9
300 to 499	25,200	71.3	15.7	36.4	63.3	26.5	1.4	3.9	6.9
500 to 999	29,800	76.4	15.9	46.7	72.5	25.0	0.8	4.2	6.9
1,000 or more	8,900	95.4	32.8	84.9	94.3	23.2	1.2	8.6	14.4
Percent minority enrollment:									
Less than 5 percent	11,700	69.6	12.6	40.8	59.0	23.3	[7] 1.2	4.9	7.4
5 to 20 percent	20,900	67.9	9.9	38.3	61.2	17.2	0.6	4.8	7.1
20 to 50 percent	20,000	75.9	18.6	46.2	69.7	23.1	1.2	5.8	8.9
50 percent or more	30,100	78.2	21.1	48.0	75.5	31.4	1.4	5.8	11.1

[1] Violent incidents include rape, sexual battery other than rape, physical attack or fight with or without a weapon, threat of physical attack with or without a weapon, and robbery with or without a weapon. [2] Serious violent incidents include rape, sexual battery other than rape, physical attack or fight with a weapon, threat of physical attack with a weapon, and robbery with or without a weapon. [3] Theft or larceny (taking things worth over $10 without personal confrontation). Includes pocket picking, stealing purse or backpack (if left unattended or no force was used to take from owner), theft from motor vehicles, etc. [4] Other incidents include possession of a firearm or explosive device, possession of knife or sharp object, distribution of illegal drugs, possession or use of alcohol or illegal drugs, and vandalism. [5] Includes combined schools, not shown separately, which include all other combination of grades, including K–12 schools. [6] Primary schools are defined as schools in which the lowest grade is not higher than grade 3 and the highest grade is not higher than grade 8. Middle schools are defined as schools in which the lowest grade is not lower than grade 4 and the highest grade is not higher than grade 9. High schools are defined as schools in which the lowest grade is not lower than grade 9 and the highest grade is not higher than grade 12. [7] Interpret data with caution.

Source: U.S. Department of Education, National Center for Education Statistics, *Indicators of School Crime and Safety, 2011,* <http://nces.ed.gov/surveys/ssocs/>.

Table 307. Percent of Public Schools Reporting Selected Types of Disciplinary Problems Occurring at School by Selected School Characteristics: 2009 to 2010

[In percent. For school year. "At school" includes activities that happen in school buildings, on school grounds, on school buses, and at places that hold school-sponsored events or activities. Based on sample; see source for details]

School characteristic	Happens at least once a week						Happens at all	
	Student racial tensions	Student bullying	Student sexual harrassment of other students[1]	Student verbal abuse of teachers	Widespread disorder in classrooms	Student acts of disrespect for teachers	Undesirable gang activities[2]	Undesirable cult or extremist group activities[3]
All public schools	**2.8**	**23.1**	**3.2**	**4.8**	**2.5**	**8.6**	**16.4**	**1.7**
Level:[4]								
Primary	2.1	19.6	[5] 1.8	3.4	[5] 1.9	6.1	7.5	[5] 1.4
Middle	5.4	38.6	6.1	6.8	4.1	13.7	29.2	1.4
High school	3.3	19.8	3.2	8.6	4.4	14.3	38.4	3.9
Combined	(S)	18.6	[5] 7.5	(S)	–	[5] 4.4	11.1	(S)
Enrollment size:								
Less than 300	(S)	16.5	[5] 4.5	(S)	(S)	[5] 3.3	6.5	(S)
300 to 499	[5] 2.5	24.0	[5] 2.4	5.2	2.4	[5] 9.5	11.9	(S)
500 to 999	3.0	25.3	2.6	4.3	2.6	8.3	16.4	[5] 1.3
1,000 or more	5.5	27.0	4.7	11.2	4.3	18.2	49.8	5.6
Percent minority enrollment:								
Less than 5 percent	(S)	22.0	[5] 4.5	(S)	(S)	[5] 3.6	1.5	[5] 0.4
5 to 20 percent	1.5	21.3	[5] 1.8	1.8	[5] 0.5	6.1	5.8	[5] 1.8
20 to 50 percent	3.2	22.3	2.6	4.5	[5] 1.1	[5] 9.6	16.9	1.4
50 percent or more	4.3	25.2	[5] 4.1	8.5	5.7	11.7	29.1	2.4

S Figure does not meet publication standards. – Represents zero [1] Sexual harassment includes "unsolicited, offensive behavior that inappropriately asserts sexuality over another person. This behavior may be verbal or nonverbal." [2] Gang includes an "ongoing loosely organized association of three or more persons, whether formal or informal, that has a common name, signs, symbols, or colors, whose members engage, either individually or collectively, in violent or other forms of illegal behavior." [3] Cult or extremist group includes "a group that espouses radical beliefs and practices, which may include a religious component, that are widely seen as threatening the basic values and cultural norms of society at large." [4] Primary schools are defined as schools in which the lowest grade is not higher than grade 3 and the highest grade is not higher than grade 8. Middle schools are defined as schools in which the lowest grade level is not lower than grade 4 and the highest grade is not higher than grade 9. High schools are defined as schools in which the lowest grade is not lower than grade 9 and the highest grade is not higher than grade 12. Combined schools include all other combinations of grades, including K–12 schools. [5] Interpret data with caution.

Source: U.S. Department of Education, National Center for Education Statistics, *Indicators of School Crime and Safety, 2011,* <http://nces.ed.gov/surveys/ssocs/>.

Table 308. Students Who Reported Being Threatened or Injured With a Weapon on School Property by Selected Student Characteristics: 1995 to 2009

[In percent. For students in grades 9 to 12. Data are for previous 12 months. "On school property" was not defined for survey respondents]

Characteristic	1995	1997	1999	2001	2003	2005	2007	2009
Total.....................	**8.4**	**7.4**	**7.7**	**8.9**	**9.2**	**7.9**	**7.8**	**7.7**
Sex:								
Male..........................	10.9	10.2	9.5	11.5	11.6	9.7	10.2	9.6
Female........................	5.8	4.0	5.8	6.5	6.5	6.1	5.4	5.5
Race/ethnicity: [1]								
White.........................	7.0	6.2	6.6	8.5	7.8	7.2	6.9	6.4
Black.........................	11.0	9.9	7.6	9.3	10.9	8.1	9.7	9.4
Hispanic......................	12.4	9.0	9.8	8.9	9.4	9.8	8.7	9.1
Asian.........................	[2]	[2]	7.7	11.3	11.5	4.6	[3] 7.6	5.5
American Indian/Alaska Native.........	[3] 11.4	[3] 2.5	[3] 13.2	[3] 15.2	22.1	9.8	5.9	16.5
Pacific Islander/Native Hawaiian........	[2]	[2]	15.6	24.8	16.3	[3] 14.5	[3] 8.1	12.5
More than one race.....................	[2]	[2]	9.3	10.3	18.7	10.7	13.3	9.2
Grade:								
9th...........................	9.6	10.1	10.5	12.7	12.1	10.5	9.2	8.7
10th..........................	9.6	7.9	8.2	9.1	9.2	8.8	8.4	8.4
11th..........................	7.7	5.9	6.1	6.9	7.3	5.5	6.8	7.9
12th..........................	6.7	5.8	5.1	5.3	6.3	5.8	6.3	5.2

[1] Race categories exclude persons of Hispanic ethnicity. [2] The response categories for race/ethnicity changed in 1999 making comparisons of some categories with earlier years problematic. In 1995 and 1997, Asian students and Pacific Islander students were not categorized separately and students were not given the option of choosing more than one race. [3] Interpret data with caution.

Source: U.S. National Center for Education Statistics, *Indicators of School Crime and Safety: 2011*, February 2012. See also: <http://nces.ed.gov/surveys/ssocs/>.

Table 309. Public Schools Using Selected Safety and Security Measures by School Characteristics: 2000 to 2010

[In percent. For school year ending in year shown. Based on survey of principals or persons knowledgeable about discipline issues at the school. Refers only to those times during normal school hours or when school activities or events were in session. Based on the School Survey on Crime and Safety and subject to sampling error; for details see source]

Measure	2000	2006	2008	2010
Controlled access during school hours:				
Buildings (locked or monitored doors)............	74.6	84.9	89.5	91.7
Grounds (locked or monitored gates).............	33.7	41.1	42.6	46.0
Closed the campus for most students during lunch........	64.6	66.1	65.0	66.9
Drug testing:				
Any students.................................	4.1	(NA)	(NA)	(NA)
Athletes....................................	(NA)	5.0	6.4	6.0
Students in extracurricular activities other than athletes............	(NA)	3.4	4.5	4.6
Any other students...........................	(NA)	3.0	3.0	3.0
Prohibited all tobacco use on school grounds.............	90.1	90.3	91.4	(NA)
Required to wear badges or picture IDs:				
Students....................................	3.9	6.1	7.6	6.9
Faculty and staff.............................	25.4	47.8	58.3	62.9
Metal detector checks on students:				
Random checks [1]............................	7.2	4.9	5.3	5.2
Required to pass through daily..................	0.9	1.1	1.3	1.4
Sweeps and technology:				
Random dog sniffs to check for drugs [1]...............	20.6	23.0	21.5	22.9
Random sweeps for contraband [1,2]................	11.8	13.1	11.4	12.1
Provided telephones in most classrooms............	44.6	66.8	71.6	74.0
Used security cameras to monitor school [1]...........	19.4	42.8	55.0	61.1
Provided two-way radios.......................	(NA)	70.8	73.1	73.3
Limited access to social networking websites from school computers..........	(NA)	(NA)	(NA)	93.4
Prohibited use of cell phones and text messaging devices............	(NA)	(NA)	(NA)	90.9
Visitor requirements:				
Sign-in or check-in...........................	96.6	97.6	98.7	99.3
Pass through metal detectors...................	0.9	1.0	(NA)	(NA)
Dress code:				
Required students to wear uniforms..............	11.8	13.8	17.5	18.9
Enforced a strict dress code....................	47.4	55.3	54.8	56.9
School supplies and equipment:				
Required clear book bags or banned book bags on school grounds........	5.9	6.4	6.0	5.5
Provided school lockers to students.............	46.5	50.6	48.9	52.1

NA Not available. [1] One or more check, sweep, or camera. [2] For example, drugs or weapons. Does not include dog sniffs.

Source: U.S. National Center for Education Statistics, *Indicators of School Crime and Safety, 2011*, February 2012. See also <http://nces.ed.gov/programs/crimeindicators/crimeindicators2011/>.

Table 310. Students Who Reported Being Bullied at School or Cyber-Bullied by Student Characteristics: 2009

[In percent. For school year ending in 2009. For students aged 12 through 18. "At school" includes the school building, on school property, on a school bus, or going to and from school. For more information, see Appendix A of source]

Characteristic	Total [1]	Bullied at school					Cyber-bullying anywhere [2]
		Total bullying at school	Made fun of, called names, or insulted	Subject of rumors	Threatened with harm	Pushed, shoved, tripped, spit on	
Total........................	**29.0**	**28.0**	**18.8**	**16.5**	**5.7**	**9.0**	**6.0**
Sex:							
Male........................	27.8	26.6	18.4	12.8	5.6	10.1	4.9
Female.....................	30.2	29.5	19.2	20.3	5.8	7.9	7.2
Race/ethnicity: [3]							
White.......................	30.3	29.3	20.5	17.4	5.4	9.1	6.8
Black.......................	30.3	29.1	18.4	17.7	7.8	9.9	5.5
Hispanic...................	26.5	25.5	15.8	14.8	5.8	9.1	5.0
Asian.......................	17.8	17.3	9.6	8.1	(S)	[4] 5.5	[4] 2.9
Other.......................	26.7	26.7	17.4	12.9	[4] 9.7	[4] 7.1	[4] 4.2
Grade:							
6th...........................	39.4	39.4	30.6	21.4	9.3	14.5	5.0
7th...........................	33.2	33.1	23.6	17.3	5.7	13.1	4.9
8th...........................	32.3	31.7	22.8	18.1	6.8	12.8	6.5
9th...........................	28.9	28.0	19.2	16.6	7.1	9.7	6.7
10th.........................	28.2	26.6	15.0	17.0	5.8	7.3	7.2
11th.........................	22.6	21.1	13.9	13.9	4.8	4.4	5.6
12th.........................	22.2	20.4	11.1	13.1	2.0	3.0	5.9

S Reporting standards not met. [1] Bullying types do not sum to total because students could have experienced more than one type of bullying. Also, total includes other types of bullying not shown separately. [2] Cyber-bullied includes students who responded that another student "made unwanted contact, for example, threatened or insulted (the respondent) via text (SMS) messaging." This category did not meet reporting standards to be reported separately. [3] Race categories exclude persons of Hispanic ethnicity. Other includes American Indian, Alaska Native, Pacific Islander, and more than one race. [4] Interpret data with caution.

Source: U.S. National Center for Education Statistics, *Indicators of School Crime and Safety: 2011*, February 2012. See also: <http://nces.ed.gov/programs/crimeindicators/crimeindicators2011/>.

Table 311. Academic Libraries by Selected Characteristics: 2010

[As of Fall of year shown. For information on public libraries, see Tables 1169 and 1170]

Institution characteristic	Number of libraries	Circulation (1,000)		Expendi-tures (mil. dol.)	Paid staff [1]			
		General collection	Reserve collection		Total [2]	Librar-ians	Other pro-fessional staff	Student assistants
All U.S. academic libraries............	**3,689**	**136,003**	**40,733**	**6,829**	**88,943**	**26,706**	**7,441**	**22,382**
Control:								
Public........................	1,559	87,090	28,993	4,020	53,606	15,387	4,319	12,700
Private.......................	2,130	48,913	11,740	2,809	35,337	11,319	3,122	9,682
Level: [3]								
Total 4-year and above..................	2,363	118,003	33,100	6,199	76,683	22,563	6,376	19,830
Doctor's.....................	821	87,255	23,309	4,986	56,436	16,072	4,936	13,601
Master's....................	833	20,533	6,878	852	13,934	4,355	961	4,221
Bachelor's..................	709	10,216	2,913	361	6,313	2,135	478	2,008
Less than 4-year........................	1,326	18,000	7,633	630	12,260	4,144	1,065	2,552
Size (FTE enrollment): [4]								
Less than 1,000..........................	1,236	7,208	1,115	295	5,475	2,029	508	1,734
1,000 to 2,999...........................	1,145	18,512	5,594	811	13,329	4,345	1,107	4,050
3,000 to 4,999...........................	470	11,444	3,713	547	8,690	2,813	656	2,238
5,000 to 9,999...........................	428	18,606	7,126	1,055	14,547	4,451	1,089	3,680
10,000 to 19,999........................	277	29,607	10,904	1,627	19,709	5,666	1,568	4,413
20,000 or more...........................	133	50,624	12,280	2,495	27,194	7,402	2,512	6,268

[1] Full-time equivalent (FTE) staff is calculated by dividing the total number of hours for all part-time positions by the number of hours the library defines as a full-time position. [2] Includes other staff not shown separately. [3] Level refers to the highest level of any degree offered by the institution. Doctoral, master's, and bachelor's level institutions do not sum to total number of 4-year and above institutions because there are 4-year and above institutions that grant "other" degrees and are thus not included in the breakdown. [4] Full-time equivalent (FTE) enrollment is calculated by adding one-third of part-time enrollment to full-time enrollment.

Source: U.S. National Center for Education Statistics, Academic Libraries Survey (ALS), 2010. See also <http://nces.ed.gov/surveys/libraries/academic.asp>.

Law Enforcement, Courts, and Prisons

This section presents data on crimes committed, victims of crimes, arrests, and data related to criminal violations and the criminal justice system. The major sources of these data are the Bureau of Justice Statistics (BJS), the Federal Bureau of Investigation (FBI), and the Administrative Office of the U.S. Courts. BJS issues many reports—see our Guide to Sources for a complete listing. The Federal Bureau of Investigation's major annual reports are *Crime in the United States, Law Enforcement Officers Killed and Assaulted*, annual, and *Hate Crimes*, annual, which present data on reported crimes as gathered from state and local law enforcement agencies.

Legal jurisdiction and law enforcement— Law enforcement is, for the most part, a function of state and local officers and agencies. The U.S. Constitution reserves general police powers to the states. By act of Congress, federal offenses include only offenses against the U.S. government and against or by its employees while engaged in their official duties, and offenses which involve the crossing of state lines or an interference with interstate commerce. Excluding the military, there are 52 separate criminal law jurisdictions in the United States: one in each of the 50 states, one in the District of Columbia, and the federal jurisdiction. Each of these has its own criminal law and procedure and its own law enforcement agencies. While the systems of law enforcement are quite similar among the states, there are often substantial differences in the penalties for like offenses.

Law enforcement can be divided into three parts: Investigation of crimes and arrests of persons suspected of committing them; prosecution of those charged with crime; and the punishment or treatment of persons convicted of crime.

Crime—The U.S. Department of Justice administers two statistical programs to measure the magnitude, nature, and impact of crime in the nation: the Uniform Crime Reporting (UCR) Program and the National Crime Victimization Survey (NCVS). Each of these programs produces valuable information about aspects of the nation's crime problem. Because the UCR and NCVS programs are conducted for different purposes, use different methods, and focus on somewhat different aspects of crime, the information they produce together provides a more comprehensive panorama of the nation's crime problem than either could produce alone.

Uniform Crime Reports (UCR)—The FBI's UCR Program, which began in 1929, collects information on the following crimes reported to law enforcement authorities—Part 1 offenses (detailed data reported): murder and nonnegligent manslaughter, forcible rape, robbery, aggravated assault, burglary, larceny-theft, motor vehicle theft, and arson. For Part 2 offenses, law enforcement agencies report only arrest data for 20 additional crime categories. For UCR definitions of criminal offenses (including those listed), please go to: <www.fbi.gov/about-us/cjis/ucr/crime-in-the-u.s/2010/crime-in-the-u.s.-2010/offense-definitions>.

The UCR Program compiles data from monthly law enforcement reports or individual crime incident records transmitted directly to the FBI or to centralized state agencies that then report to the FBI. The Program thoroughly examines each report it receives for reasonableness, accuracy, and deviations that may indicate errors. Large variations in crime levels may indicate modified records procedures, incomplete reporting, or changes in a jurisdiction's boundaries. To identify any unusual fluctuations in an agency's crime counts, the Program compares monthly reports to previous submissions of the agency and with those for similar agencies.

The UCR Program presents crime counts for the nation as a whole, as well as for regions, states, counties, cities, towns, tribal law enforcement, and colleges and universities. This permits studies among neighboring jurisdictions and among those with similar populations and other common characteristics.

The UCR Program annually publishes its findings in a preliminary release in the spring of the following calendar year, followed by a detailed annual report, *Crime in the United States*, issued in the fall. In addition to crime counts and trends, this report includes data on crimes cleared, persons arrested (age, sex, and race), law enforcement personnel (including the number of sworn officers killed or assaulted), and the characteristics of homicides (including age, sex, and race of victims and offenders; victim-offender relationships; weapons used; and circumstances surrounding the homicides). Other periodic reports are also available from the UCR Program.

National Crime Victimization Survey (NCVS)—A second perspective on crime is provided by this survey of the Bureau of Justice Statistics (BJS). The NCVS is an annual data collection (interviews of persons aged 12 or older), conducted by the U.S. Census Bureau for the BJS. As an ongoing survey of households, the NCVS measures crimes of violence and property both reported and not reported to police. It produces national rates and levels of personal and property victimization. No attempt is made to validate the information against police records or any other source.

The NCVS measures rape/sexual assault, robbery, assault, pocket-picking, purse snatching, burglary, and motor vehicle theft. The NCVS includes crimes reported to the police, as well as those not reported. Murder and kidnaping are not covered. The so-called victimless crimes, such as drunkenness, drug abuse, and prostitution, also are excluded, as are crimes for which it is difficult to identify knowledgeable respondents or to locate data records.

Crimes of which the victim may not be aware also cannot be measured effectively. Buying stolen property may fall into this category, as may some instances of embezzlement. Attempted crimes of many types probably are under recorded for this reason. Events in which the victim has shown a willingness to participate in illegal activity also are excluded.

In any encounter involving a personal crime, more than one criminal act can be committed against an individual. For example, a rape may be associated with a robbery, or a household offense, such as a burglary, can escalate into something more serious in the event of a personal confrontation. In classifying the survey measured crimes, each criminal incident has been counted only once, by the most serious act that took place during the incident, and ranked in accordance with the seriousness classification system used by the FBI. The order of seriousness for crimes against persons is as follows: rape, robbery, assault, and larceny. Personal crimes take precedence over household offenses.

A *victimization*, the basic measure of the occurrence of crime, is a specific criminal act as it affects a single victim. The number of victimizations is determined by the number of victims of such acts. Victimization counts serve as key elements in computing rates of victimization. For crimes against persons, the rates are based on the total number of individuals aged 12 and over or on a portion of that population sharing a particular characteristic or set of traits. As general indicators of the danger of having been victimized during the reference period, the rates are not sufficiently refined to represent true measures of risk for specific individuals or households.

An *incident* is a specific criminal act involving one or more victims; therefore the number of incidents of personal crimes is lower than that of victimizations.

Courts—Statistics on criminal offenses and the outcome of prosecutions are incomplete for the country as a whole, although data are available for many states individually.

Since 1986, through its National Judicial Reporting Program, the BJS has surveyed a nationally representative sample of 300 counties every 2 years and collected detailed information on demographic characteristics of felons, conviction offenses, type of sentences, sentence lengths, and time from arrest to conviction and sentencing.

The bulk of civil and criminal litigation in the country is commenced and determined in the various state courts. Only when the U.S. Constitution and acts of Congress specifically confer jurisdiction upon the federal courts may civil or criminal litigation be heard and decided by them. Generally, the federal courts have jurisdiction over the following types of cases: suits or proceedings by or against the United States; civil actions between private parties arising under the Constitution, laws, or treaties of the United States; civil actions between private litigants who are citizens of different states; civil cases involving admiralty, maritime, or private jurisdiction; and all matters in bankruptcy.

There are several types of courts with varying degrees of legal jurisdiction. These jurisdictions include original, appellate, general, and limited or special. A court of original jurisdiction is one having the authority initially to try a case and pass judgment on the law and the facts; a court of appellate jurisdiction is one with the legal authority to review cases and hear appeals; a court of general jurisdiction is a trial court of unlimited original jurisdiction in civil and/or criminal cases, also called a "major trial court"; a court of limited or special jurisdiction is a trial court with legal authority over only a particular class of cases, such as probate, juvenile, or traffic cases.

The 94 federal courts of original jurisdiction are known as the U.S. district courts. One or more of these courts is established in every state and one each in the District of Columbia, Puerto Rico, the Virgin Islands, the Northern Mariana Islands, and Guam. Appeals from the district courts are taken to intermediate appellate courts of which there are 13, known as U.S. courts of appeals and the United States Court of Appeals for the Federal Circuit. The Supreme Court of the United States is the final and highest appellate court in the federal system of courts.

Juvenile offenders—For statistical purposes, the FBI and most states classify as juvenile offenders persons under the age of 18 years who have committed a crime or crimes.

Delinquency cases are all cases of youths referred to a juvenile court for violation of a law or ordinance or for seriously "antisocial" conduct. Several types of facilities are available for those adjudicated delinquents, ranging from the short-term physically unrestricted environment to the long-term very restrictive atmosphere.

Prisoners and jail inmates—BJS started to collect annual data in 1979 on prisoners in federal and state prisons and reformatories. Adults convicted of criminal activity may be given a prison or jail sentence. A *prison* is a confinement facility having custodial authority over adults sentenced to confinement of more than 1 year. A *jail* is a facility, usually operated by a local law enforcement agency, holding persons detained pending adjudication and/or persons committed after adjudication to 1 year or less.

Data on inmates in local jails were collected by the BJS for the first time in 1970. Since then, BJS has conducted censuses of facilities and inmates every 5 to 6 years. In 1984, BJS initiated an annual survey of jails conducted in noncensus years.

Statistical reliability—For discussion of statistical collection, estimation and sampling procedures, and measures of statistical reliability pertaining to the National Crime Victimization Survey and Uniform Crime Reporting Program, see Appendix III.

Table 312. Crimes and Crime Rates by Type of Offense: 1980 to 2010

[(13,408 represents 13,408,000). Data include offenses reported to law enforcement, offense estimations for nonreporting and partially reporting agencies within each state. Rates are based on Census Bureau estimated resident population as of July 1, 1980, 1990, and 2000, enumerated as of April 1. See source for details]

Item and year	All crimes	Violent crime						Property crimes			
		Total	Murder [1]	Forcible rape	Robbery	Aggra-vated assault		Total	Burglary	Larceny/ theft	Motor vehicle theft
Number of offenses (1,000):											
1980	13,408	1,345	23.0	83.0	566	673		12,064	3,795	7,137	1,132
1985	12,430	1,328	19.0	87.7	498	723		11,103	3,073	6,926	1,103
1990	14,476	1,820	23.4	102.6	639	1,055		12,655	3,074	7,946	1,636
1995	13,863	1,799	21.6	97.5	581	1,099		12,064	2,594	7,998	1,472
1998	12,486	1,534	17.0	93.1	447	977		10,952	2,333	7,376	1,243
1999	11,634	1,426	15.5	89.4	409	912		10,208	2,101	6,956	1,152
2000	11,608	1,425	15.6	90.2	408	912		10,183	2,051	6,972	1,160
2001 [2]	11,877	1,439	16.0	90.9	424	909		10,437	2,117	7,092	1,228
2002	11,879	1,424	16.2	95.2	421	891		10,455	2,151	7,057	1,247
2003	11,827	1,384	16.5	93.9	414	859		10,443	2,155	7,027	1,261
2004	11,679	1,360	16.1	95.1	401	847		10,319	2,144	6,937	1,238
2005	11,565	1,391	16.7	94.3	417	862		10,175	2,155	6,783	1,236
2006	11,455	1,435	17.3	94.5	449	874		10,020	2,195	6,626	1,198
2007	11,305	1,423	17.1	92.2	447	866		9,882	2,190	6,592	1,100
2008	11,169	1,394	16.5	90.8	444	844		9,774	2,229	6,586	959
2009	10,663	1,326	15.4	89.2	409	813		9,337	2,203	6,338	796
2010	10,329	1,246	14.7	84.8	368	779		9,083	2,160	6,186	737
Rate per 100,000 population:											
1980	5,950	597	10.2	36.8	251	299		5,353	1,684	3,167	502
1985	5,225	558	8.0	36.8	209	304		4,666	1,292	2,911	464
1990	5,803	730	9.4	41.1	256	423		5,073	1,232	3,185	656
1995	5,276	685	8.2	37.1	221	418		4,591	987	3,043	560
1998	4,619	568	6.3	34.5	166	361		4,053	863	2,730	460
1999	4,267	523	5.7	32.8	150	334		3,744	770	2,551	423
2000	4,125	507	5.5	32.0	145	324		3,618	729	2,477	412
2001 [2]	4,163	505	5.6	31.8	149	319		3,658	742	2,486	431
2002	4,125	494	5.6	33.1	146	310		3,631	747	2,451	433
2003	4,067	476	5.7	32.3	143	295		3,591	741	2,417	434
2004	3,977	463	5.5	32.4	137	289		3,514	730	2,362	422
2005	3,899	469	5.6	31.8	141	291		3,432	727	2,288	417
2006	3,826	479	5.8	31.6	150	292		3,347	733	2,213	400
2007	3,748	472	5.7	30.6	148	287		3,276	726	2,185	365
2008	3,673	459	5.4	29.8	146	278		3,215	733	2,166	315
2009	3,473	432	5.0	29.1	133	265		3,041	718	2,065	259
2010	3,346	404	4.8	27.5	119	252		2,942	700	2,004	239

[1] Includes nonnegligent manslaughter. [2] The murder and nonnegligent homicides that occurred as a result of the events of September 11, 2001, were not included in this table.

Source: U.S. Department of Justice, Federal Bureau of Investigation, "Crime in the United States," September 2011, <http://www.fbi.gov/about-us/cjis/ucr>.

Table 313. Crimes and Crime Rates by Type and Geographic Community: 2010

[In thousands (1,246.2 represents 1,246,200), except rate. Rate per 100,000 population. See headnote, Table 312]

Type of crime	United States		Metropolitan statistical area [1]		Cities outside metropolitan areas		Nonmetropolitan counties	
	Total	Rate	Total	Rate	Total	Rate	Total	Rate
Violent crime	1,246.2	403.6	1,107.0	428.3	80.3	399.7	58.9	195.1
Murder [2]	14.7	4.8	13.1	5.0	.7	3.6	1.0	3.2
Forcible rape	84.8	27.5	69.7	27.0	8.4	41.6	6.7	22.0
Robbery	367.8	119.1	351.6	136.0	11.5	57.1	4.8	15.9
Aggravated assault	778.9	252.3	672.7	260.3	59.8	297.3	46.5	154.0
Property crime	9,032.9	2,941.9	7,874.2	3,046.5	724.1	3,602.3	484.6	1,605.8
Burglary	2,159.9	699.6	1,826.2	706.5	164.8	819.9	168.9	559.7
Larceny-theft	6,185.9	2,003.5	5,369.5	2,077.5	531.3	2,643.5	285.0	944.4
Motor vehicle theft	737.1	238.8	678.5	262.5	27.9	138.9	30.7	101.7

[1] For definition, see Appendix II. [2] Includes nonnegligent manslaughter.

Source: U.S. Department of Justice, Federal Bureau of Investigation, "Crime in the United States," September 2011, <http://www.fbi.gov/about-us/cjis/ucr>.

Table 314. Crime Rates by State, 2009 and 2010, and by Type, 2010

[For year ending December 31. Rates per 100,000 population. Offenses reported to law enforcement. Based on Census Bureau estimated resident population as of July 1]

State	Violent crime						Property crime				
	2009 total	2010					2009 total	2010			
		Total	Murder	Forcible rape	Rob-bery	Aggra-vated assault		Total	Burglary	Larceny/ theft	Motor vehicle theft
United States............	431.9	403.6	4.8	27.5	119.1	252.3	3,041.3	2,941.9	699.6	2,003.5	238.8
Alabama..................	450.1	377.8	5.7	28.2	99.6	244.2	3,780.4	3,516.8	879.4	2,415.6	221.8
Alaska...................	633.4	638.8	4.4	75.0	83.6	475.8	2,940.4	2,852.5	437.2	2,187.3	228.0
Arizona..................	426.5	408.1	6.4	33.9	108.5	259.3	3,589.0	3,534.0	794.3	2,403.2	336.5
Arkansas.................	515.8	505.3	4.7	45.0	81.3	374.3	3,775.0	3,558.9	1,114.9	2,253.8	190.1
California................	473.3	440.6	4.9	22.4	156.0	257.4	2,731.0	2,635.8	614.3	1,612.1	409.4
Colorado.................	338.8	320.8	2.4	43.7	62.3	212.4	2,670.7	2,684.2	520.0	1,940.5	223.6
Connecticut..............	300.9	281.4	3.6	16.3	99.4	162.0	2,348.4	2,193.2	424.5	1,581.0	187.7
Delaware.................	645.4	620.9	5.3	34.7	203.7	377.1	3,353.8	3,448.2	836.9	2,396.5	214.8
District of Columbia [1].....	1,348.9	1,330.2	21.9	31.1	718.8	558.4	4,751.9	4,778.9	703.1	3,238.9	836.9
Florida..................	612.5	542.4	5.2	28.6	138.7	369.8	3,840.8	3,558.4	899.5	2,438.4	220.5
Georgia..................	428.0	403.3	5.8	21.6	127.7	248.2	3,672.6	3,640.5	998.4	2,329.3	312.8
Hawaii...................	274.1	262.7	1.8	26.8	77.5	156.7	3,668.7	3,314.2	636.8	2,302.4	374.9
Idaho....................	246.2	221.0	1.3	33.5	13.7	172.6	2,019.7	1,995.8	414.8	1,496.7	84.3
Illinois [2]................	497.2	435.2	5.5	23.6	156.3	249.7	2,736.9	2,681.0	587.6	1,868.9	224.4
Indiana..................	334.0	314.5	4.5	27.2	95.9	186.9	3,112.3	3,042.4	726.7	2,113.4	202.3
Iowa.....................	282.1	273.5	1.3	27.4	33.2	211.6	2,329.9	2,242.5	546.8	1,571.8	124.0
Kansas...................	406.6	369.1	3.5	38.8	54.1	272.7	3,225.9	3,119.9	680.1	2,229.2	210.6
Kentucky.................	255.0	242.6	4.3	31.8	86.4	120.1	2,524.6	2,551.3	698.5	1,709.7	143.1
Louisiana................	642.9	549.0	11.2	27.2	114.9	395.6	3,842.7	3,647.5	1,002.2	2,427.1	218.2
Maine....................	119.9	122.0	1.8	29.3	31.2	59.8	2,405.1	2,479.3	554.0	1,850.8	74.5
Maryland.................	590.0	547.7	7.4	21.3	191.5	327.5	3,198.5	2,997.3	632.9	2,051.7	312.6
Massachusetts............	462.6	466.6	3.2	26.7	105.0	331.8	2,323.1	2,350.5	576.8	1,598.8	174.9
Michigan.................	499.8	490.3	5.7	47.3	116.3	321.0	2,848.8	2,713.6	747.4	1,689.5	276.8
Minnesota [3].............	(NA)	(NA)	1.8	(NA)	63.9	136.4	2,644.9	2,572.3	460.3	1,950.0	161.9
Mississippi...............	286.3	269.7	7.0	31.2	93.7	137.8	2,958.2	2,985.9	1,026.0	1,778.4	180.6
Missouri.................	492.9	455.0	7.0	23.9	102.4	321.7	3,370.0	3,346.4	735.4	2,343.0	268.0
Montana.................	287.0	272.2	2.6	32.4	15.9	221.2	2,546.3	2,543.8	369.3	2,020.3	154.2
Nebraska.................	289.4	279.5	3.0	36.8	56.1	183.6	2,768.0	2,673.2	455.9	2,019.4	197.9
Nevada..................	705.2	660.2	5.9	35.7	196.2	422.9	3,063.7	2,774.7	823.0	1,574.5	377.1
New Hampshire...........	160.4	167.0	1.0	31.3	34.3	100.4	2,173.5	2,186.3	413.3	1,699.5	73.5
New Jersey...............	311.4	307.7	4.2	11.2	134.4	157.9	2,075.8	2,081.9	440.5	1,464.5	176.9
New Mexico..............	632.4	588.9	6.9	46.5	78.4	457.1	3,714.0	3,435.4	1,020.5	2,160.1	254.8
New York................	384.4	392.1	4.5	14.3	146.9	226.4	1,932.0	1,941.2	335.3	1,500.4	105.4
North Carolina...........	404.5	363.4	5.0	21.1	100.8	236.5	3,663.9	3,447.3	1,076.9	2,178.4	192.0
North Dakota.............	266.4	225.0	1.5	35.2	13.4	174.8	1,980.8	1,768.5	292.3	1,348.5	127.7
Ohio.....................	331.9	315.2	4.1	32.1	142.8	136.2	3,261.3	3,245.2	923.3	2,138.8	183.1
Oklahoma................	503.4	479.5	5.2	38.7	89.0	346.7	3,589.6	3,415.5	999.0	2,144.8	271.6
Oregon..................	260.6	252.0	2.4	31.7	62.4	155.6	3,000.3	3,012.9	512.6	2,267.7	232.6
Pennsylvania.............	382.3	366.2	5.2	26.9	128.8	205.3	2,199.0	2,173.0	434.3	1,607.4	131.2
Rhode Island.............	254.3	256.6	2.8	28.1	74.1	151.6	2,616.6	2,556.6	581.5	1,747.2	227.9
South Carolina...........	675.2	597.7	6.1	31.7	107.7	452.3	3,909.2	3,900.4	997.9	2,617.2	285.3
South Dakota.............	218.7	268.5	2.8	47.9	18.9	198.9	1,769.9	1,852.4	390.7	1,364.1	97.6
Tennessee................	666.0	613.3	5.6	33.7	131.8	442.2	3,766.6	3,657.9	1,012.2	2,411.9	233.8
Texas....................	491.0	450.3	5.0	30.3	130.6	284.4	4,015.3	3,783.0	909.1	2,603.3	270.5
Utah....................	215.4	212.7	1.9	34.3	45.9	130.6	3,295.0	3,179.6	543.3	2,421.0	215.2
Vermont.................	134.6	130.2	1.1	21.1	11.8	96.2	2,414.1	2,282.3	537.9	1,673.9	70.5
Virginia.................	230.8	213.6	4.6	19.1	70.7	119.1	2,461.4	2,327.2	382.8	1,812.5	148.0
Washington..............	336.3	313.8	2.3	38.1	88.2	185.3	3,679.6	3,706.6	820.3	2,503.7	382.6
West Virginia.............	305.2	314.6	3.3	19.1	44.7	247.5	2,539.6	2,239.6	580.5	1,531.7	127.4
Wisconsin................	259.1	248.7	2.7	20.9	79.2	145.9	2,611.8	2,507.7	467.1	1,897.5	143.1
Wyoming.................	219.7	195.9	1.4	29.1	13.5	151.9	2,616.9	2,461.6	381.3	1,975.4	104.9

NA Not available. [1] Includes offenses reported by the Zoological Police and the Metro Transit Police. [2] Because of changes in the state's reporting practices, figures are not comparable to previous years' data. [3] The data collection methodology for the offense of forcible rape used by the the Minnesota state Uniform Crime Reporting (UCR) Programs (with the exception of Minneapolis and St. Paul, Minnesota) does not comply with national UCR guidelines. Consequently, their state figures for forcible rape and violent crime (of which forcible rape is a part) are not published in this table.

Source: U.S. Department of Justice, Federal Bureau of Investigation, "Crime in the United States," September 2011.

ProQuest Statistical Abstract of the United States: 2013

Table 315. Number of Crimes by Type—Selected Large Cities: 2010

[For year ending December 31. Offenses reported to law enforcement]

Selected Large Cities	Violent crime					Property crime			
	Total	Murder	Forcible rape	Robbery	Aggra-vated assault	Total	Burglary	Larceny/ theft	Motor vehicle theft
New York, NY...................	48,489	536	1,036	19,608	27,309	139,615	17,296	111,370	10,319
Los Angeles, CA................	21,484	293	923	10,924	9,344	89,704	17,410	55,248	17,046
Chicago, IL......................	(¹)	432	(¹)	14,213	13,757	120,045	26,203	74,764	19,078
Houston, TX.....................	22,491	269	712	9,449	12,061	115,323	27,924	74,582	865
Phoenix, AZ.....................	8,002	117	522	3,250	4,113	61,362	15,626	38,012	7,724
Philadelphia, PA................	18,535	306	945	8,363	8,921	57,788	10,796	39,924	7,068
Las Vegas MPD, NV............	12,648	107	652	4,003	7,886	43,319	13,824	22,231	7,164
San Antonio, TX................	8,434	79.0	467	2,360	5,528	88,353	17,301	65,395	5,657
San Diego, CA..................	5,616	29	300	1,636	3,651	30,753	6,387	17,977	6,389
Dallas, TX.......................	9,161	148	505	4,487	4,021	64,125	19,594	36,147	8,384
San Jose, CA...................	3,215	20	253	976	1,966	22,081	3,940	12,730	5,411
Detroit, MI......................	16,976	310	405	5,538	10,723	47,787	17,090	18,095	12,602
Honolulu, HI....................	2,548	19	218	891	1,420	31,868	5,760	22,007	3,901
Indianapolis, IN................	(NA)	(NA)	(NA)	(NA)	(NA)	(NA)	(NA)	(NA)	(NA)
Jacksonville, FL.................	5,469	80	316	1,693	3,380	37,424	9,588	25,863	1,973
San Francisco, CA..............	5,747	48	133	3,180	2,386	32,365	4,557	23,905	3,903
Charlotte-Mecklenburg, NC.....	4,891	61	239	1,795	2,796	34,701	9,325	22,711	2,665
Austin, TX.......................	3,790	38	265	1,231	2,256	45,826	8,749	34,827	2,250
Columbus, OH...................	5,451	94	566	3,359	1,432	50,168	15,234	30,784	4,150
Fort Worth, TX..................	4,293	63	318	1,330	2,582	35,090	9,352	23,274	2,464
Memphis, TN....................	10,384	89	422	3,236	6,637	42,138	13,094	25,114	3,930
Baltimore, MD...................	9,316	223	265	3,336	5,492	28,280	7,573	16,298	4,409
Louisville Metro, KY............	3,734	52	229	1,603	1,850	29,551	7,571	20,005	1,975
Boston, MA......................	5,819	73	256	1,926	3,564	20,628	3,587	15,004	2,037
El Paso, TX......................	2,861	5	179	479	2,198	17,404	1,953	13,899	1,552
Nashville, TN....................	6,695	55	367	1,817	4,756	30,517	7,731	20,881	1,905
Denver, CO......................	3,291	22	367	926	1,976	20,671	4,501	12,944	3,226
Milwaukee, WI...................	6,239	94	197	2,932	3,106	31,720	6,181	21,212	4,327
Seattle, WA.....................	3,515	19	96	1,429	1,971	33,186	6,449	23,284	3,453
Washington, DC.................	7,648	132	184	3,914	3,238	27,138	4,224	18,050	4,864
Portland, OR....................	3,051	22	230	1,005	1,794	28,391	4,120	21,026	3,245
Oklahoma City, OK..............	5,304	54	340	1,112	3,798	33,263	9,901	19,760	3,602
Atlanta, GA.....................	5,749	93	89	2,162	3,405	30,800	8,016	17,741	5,043
Tucson, AZ......................	3,331	51	158	1,088	2,034	(²)	5,002	(²)	3,433
Albuquerque, NM................	4,291	42	338	940	2,971	26,372	5,465	18,134	2,773
Kansas City, MO................	5,506	102	234	1,626	3,544	26,919	7,124	16,625	3,170
Fresno, CA......................	3,304	45	70	1,021	1,898	24,460	5,262	14,645	4,553
Mesa, AZ........................	1,790	15	124	511	1,140	14,876	2,711	11,158	1,007
Sacramento, CA.................	5,747	48	133	3,180	2,386	32,365	4,557	23,905	3,903
Long Beach, CA.................	2,720	32	134	1,202	1,352	11,642	2,929	6,254	2,189
Omaha, NE......................	2,263	34	194	723	1,312	17,334	3,046	12,091	2,197
Virginia Beach, VA..............	820	14	55	422	329	13,232	2,151	10,431	650
Cleveland, OH...................	5,525	81	341	3,181	1,922	23,436	9,854	10,079	3,503
Miami, FL........................	4,879	68	46	1,856	2,909	21,218	4,604	14,165	2,449
Raleigh, NC.....................	1,740	14	99	643	984	12,995	3,021	9,104	870
Oakland, CA.....................	6,267	90	318	2,917	2,942	17,325	4,961	7,720	4,620
Colorado Springs, CO..........	1,957	20	319	526	1,092	16,794	3,452	12,054	1,288
Tulsa, OK.......................	4,304	54	252	1,381	2,617	21,355	7,146	11,857	2,352
Minneapolis, MN................	4,064	37	438	1,596	1,993	18,299	4,787	11,609	1,903
Arlington, TX....................	1,925	16	119	532	1,258	19,350	4,763	13,342	1,245
Wichita, KS......................	3,026	16	246	481	2,283	18,241	4,241	12,472	1,528
St. Louis, MO....................	6,205	144	188	2,125	3,748	27,324	6,705	16,356	4,263
Tampa, FL.......................	2,170	27	47	684	1,412	11,453	3,131	7,484	838
Santa Ana, CA..................	1,510	28	88	719	675	6,580	1,116	4,189	1,275
New Orleans, LA................	2,593	175	144	953	1,321	12,645	3,695	6,540	2,410
Anaheim, CA....................	1,161	7	88	492	574	8,473	1,594	5,869	1,010
Cincinnati, OH...................	3,608	68	233	2,116	1,191	20,513	6,490	12,408	1,615
Bakersfield, CA..................	2,104	33	34	641	1,396	15,197	4,235	8,507	2,455
Aurora, CO......................	1,443	23	183	505	732	10,051	2,290	6,873	888
Pittsburgh, PA..................	2,810	55	66	1,190	1,499	11,284	2,949	7,678	657
Riverside, CA....................	1,448	9	78	502	859	9,963	2,068	6,434	1,461
Lexington, KY...................	1,724	18	87	593	1,026	11,024	2,679	7,704	641
Stockton, CA....................	4,033	49	107	1,413	2,464	16,177	4,482	9,654	2,041
Toledo, OH......................	2,854	23	140	1,097	1,594	(²)	7,287	(²)	1,197
Corpus Christi, TX..............	2,068	16	191	389	1,472	15,101	2,626	12,027	448
Anchorage, AK..................	2,432	13	264	454	1,701	10,214	1,223	8,178	813
St. Paul, MN....................	2,112	16	183	665	1,248	11,756	2,883	6,820	2,053
Newark, NJ......................	2,885	90	79	1,604	1,112	9,209	1,928	3,661	3,620
Plano, TX.......................	503	4	53	152	294	6,716	1,237	5,093	386
Buffalo, NY......................	3,599	55	157	1,466	1,921	14,753	4,296	9,027	1,430
Henderson, NV..................	543	8	35	189	311	5,196	1,280	3,406	510
Chandler, AZ....................	691	6	61	195	429	7,516	1,373	5,766	377

NA Not available. ¹ The data collection methodology for the offense of forcible rape used by Chicago, Illinois does not comply with national UCR Program guidelines. Consequently, its figures for forcible rape and violent crime (of which forcible rape is a part) are not published in this table. ² It was determined that the agency did not follow the national UCR program guidelines for reporting an offense. Consequently, this figure is not included in this table.

Source: U.S. Department of Justice, Federal Bureau of Investigation, "Crime in the United States, 2010." Accessed August 2012, <http://www.fbi.gov/about-us/cjis/ucr>.

Table 316. Murder Victims—Circumstances and Weapons Used or Cause of Death: 2000 to 2010

[For year ending December 31. The FBI's Uniform Crime Reporting (UCR) Program defines murder and nonnegligent manslaughter as the willful (nonnegligent) killing of one human being by another. The classification of this offense is based solely on police investigation as opposed to the determination of a court, medical examiner, coroner, jury, or other judicial body. The UCR Program does not include the following situations in this offense classification: deaths caused by negligence, suicide, or accident; justifiable homicides; and attempts to murder, which are scored as aggravated assaults]

Characteristic	2000	2005	2009	2010	Characteristic	2000	2005	2009	2010
Murders, total	**13,230**	**14,965**	**13,752**	**12,996**	Gangland killings	65	96	177	176
					Juvenile gang killings	653	756	715	673
CIRCUMSTANCES					Institutional killings	10	12	12	17
Felonies, total	2,229	2,189	2,052	1,923	Sniper attack	8	2	1	3
Rape	58	45	24	41	Other—not specified	1,901	1,938	1,994	1,781
Robbery	1,077	930	857	780	Unknown	4,070	5,635	4,848	4,656
Burglary	76	91	110	80					
Larceny-theft	23	12	13	20	TYPE OF WEAPON OR				
Motor vehicle theft	25	32	23	37	CAUSE OF DEATH				
Arson	81	39	38	35	Total firearms	8,661	10,158	9,199	8,775
					Handguns	6,778	7,565	6,501	6,009
Prostitution and					Rifles	411	445	351	358
commercialized vice	6	13	6	5	Shotguns	485	522	423	373
Other sex offenses	10	9	10	14	Other not specified or				
Narcotic drug laws	589	597	496	463	type unknown	53	138	96	96
Gambling	12	2	5	7	Firearms, type not stated	934	1,488	1,828	1,939
Other—not specified	272	419	470	441	Knives or cutting				
					instruments	1,782	1,920	1,836	1,704
Suspected felony type	60	45	56	66	Blunt objects [1]	617	608	623	540
Other than felony type	6,871	7,096	6,796	6,351	Personal weapons [2]	927	905	817	745
Romantic triangle	122	118	88	90	Poison	8	9	7	11
Child killed by babysitter	30	26	29	36	Explosives	9	2	2	4
Brawl due to influence of					Fire	134	125	98	74
alcohol	188	123	117	121	Narcotics	20	46	52	39
Brawl due to influence of					Drowning	15	20	8	10
narcotics	99	97	94	58	Strangulation	166	118	122	122
Argument over money or					Asphyxiation	92	96	84	98
property	206	210	205	181	All other [3]	799	958	904	874
Other arguments	3,589	3,718	3,364	3,215					

[1] Refers to club, hammer, etc. [2] Hands, fists, feet, pushed, etc. [3] Includes poison, explosives, narcotics, drowning, and unknown.

Source: U.S. Department of Justice, Federal Bureau of Investigation, Uniform Crime Reporting Program, "Crime in the United States, 2010." Accessed June 2012, <http://www.fbi.gov/about-us/cjis/ucr>.

Table 317. Murder Victims by Age, Sex, and Race: 2010

[See headnote, Table 316]

Age	Total	Sex			Race			
		Male	Female	Unknown	White	Black	Other	Unknown
Murders, total	**12,996**	**1,058**	**2,918**	**20**	**6,043**	**6,470**	**331**	**152**
Percent of total [1]	100.0	77.4	22.5	0.2	46.5	49.8	2.5	1.2
Under 18 years old [2]	1,277	890	386	1	599	622	37	19
18 years old and over [2]	11,566	9,069	2,493	4	5,385	5,797	291	93
Infant (under 1 year old)	186	91	94	1	121	56	5	4
1 to 4 years old	313	192	121	–	174	120	11	8
5 to 8 years old	85	44	41	–	55	26	4	–
9 to 12 years old	43	28	15	–	20	17	3	3
13 to 16 years old	363	288	75	–	140	212	9	2
17 to 19 years old	1,231	1,065	166	–	425	779	20	7
20 to 24 years old	2,256	1,944	312	–	813	1,387	40	16
25 to 29 years old	1,964	1,627	337	–	753	1,157	34	20
30 to 34 years old	1,541	1,286	253	2	626	865	35	15
35 to 39 years old	1,072	820	252	–	495	535	31	11
40 to 44 years old	882	635	247	–	477	366	31	8
45 to 49 years old	838	589	249	–	502	306	26	4
50 to 54 years old	686	508	178	–	426	237	19	4
55 to 59 years old	473	329	143	1	288	154	25	6
60 to 64 years old	325	199	126	–	217	90	17	1
65 to 69 years old	189	125	64	–	132	53	3	1
70 to 74 years old	137	80	56	1	103	26	8	–
75 years old and over	259	109	150	–	217	33	7	2
Age unknown	153	99	39	15	59	51	3	40

– Represents zero. [1] Because of rounding, the percentages may not add to 100.0. [2] Does not include unknown ages.

Source: U.S. Department of Justice, Federal Bureau of Investigation, Uniform Crime Reporting Program, "Crime in the United States, 2010." Accessed June 2012, <http://www.fbi.gov/about-us/cjis/ucr>.

Table 318. Homicide Trends: 1980 to 2008

[Based on Federal Bureau of Investigation's Uniform Crime Reports Supplementary Homicide Reports. Homicide includes murder and nonnegligent manslaughter, which is the willful killing of one human being by another. Excludes deaths caused by negligence, suicide, or accident; justifiable homicides; and attempts to murder. Justifiable homicides based on the reports of law enforcement agencies are analyzed separately. Deaths from the terrorist attacks of 9/11/01 are not included. Data based solely on police investigation, as opposed to the determination of a court, medical examiner, coroner, jury, or other judicial body]

Year	Number of victims						Rate [1]					
	Total	Male	Female	White	Black	Other	Total	Male	Female	White	Black	Other
1980	23,040	17,803	5,237	12,275	9,767	327	10.2	16.1	4.5	6.3	37.7	5.7
1985	18,980	14,095	4,885	10,590	7,891	399	7.9	12.2	4.0	5.2	27.6	5.5
1990	23,440	18,320	5,121	11,278	11,489	400	9.4	15.1	4.0	5.4	37.6	4.2
1995	21,610	16,579	5,030	10,376	10,444	581	8.2	12.7	3.7	4.8	31.6	4.9
1996	19,650	15,175	4,475	9,483	9,476	512	7.4	11.5	3.3	4.3	28.3	4.1
1997	18,210	14,079	4,132	8,620	8,842	524	6.8	10.5	3.0	3.9	26.0	4.1
1998	16,970	12,812	4,158	8,389	7,931	393	6.3	9.5	3.0	3.8	23.0	2.9
1999	15,522	11,718	3,804	7,777	7,139	458	5.7	8.6	2.7	3.5	20.5	3.3
2000	15,586	11,844	3,742	7,560	7,425	399	5.5	8.6	2.6	3.3	20.3	2.7
2001	16,037	12,256	3,782	7,884	7,522	424	5.6	8.8	2.6	3.4	20.2	2.8
2002	16,204	12,432	3,772	7,784	7,759	437	5.6	8.8	2.6	3.3	20.6	2.8
2003	16,528	12,828	3,700	7,932	7,893	468	5.7	9.0	2.5	3.4	20.7	2.9
2004	16,148	12,596	3,552	7,944	7,562	417	5.5	8.7	2.4	3.3	19.6	2.5
2005	16,740	13,169	3,571	8,045	8,015	443	5.6	9.0	2.4	3.3	20.5	2.6
2006	17,030	13,433	3,597	7,906	8,428	461	5.7	9.1	2.4	3.3	21.3	2.6
2007	16,929	13,286	3,643	7,924	8,352	402	5.6	8.9	2.4	3.3	20.9	2.2
2008	16,272	12,731	3,541	7,995	7,901	376	5.4	8.5	2.3	3.3	19.6	2.0

[1] Rate is per 100,000 inhabitants.

Source: U.S. Department of Justice, Bureau of Justice Statistics, "Homicide Trends in the United States, 1980–2008." See also <http://bjs.ojp.usdoj.gov/index.cfm?ty=tp&tid=311#pubs>.

Table 319. Homicide Victims by Race and Sex: 1980 to 2008

[Excludes deaths to nonresidents of United States. Effective with data for 1999, causes of death are classified by The Tenth Revision International Classification of Diseases (ICD-10), replacing the Ninth Revision (ICD-9) used for 1979–98 data. In ICD-9, the category Homicide also includes death as a result of legal intervention. ICD-10 has two separate categories for these two causes of death. Some caution should be used in comparing data. See text, Section 2]

Year	Homicide victims					Homicide rate [2]				
		White		Black			White		Black	
	Total [1]	Male	Female	Male	Female	Total [1]	Male	Female	Male	Female
1980	24,278	10,381	3,177	8,385	1,898	10.7	10.9	3.2	66.6	13.5
1985	19,893	8,122	3,041	6,616	1,666	8.3	8.2	2.9	48.4	11.0
1990	24,932	9,147	3,006	9,981	2,163	10.0	9.0	2.8	69.2	13.5
1995	22,895	8,336	3,028	8,847	1,936	8.7	7.8	2.7	56.3	11.1
1997	19,846	7,343	2,570	7,601	1,652	7.4	6.7	2.3	47.1	9.3
1998	18,272	6,707	2,534	6,873	1,547	6.8	6.1	2.2	42.1	8.6
1999	16,889	6,162	2,466	6,214	1,434	6.2	5.6	2.2	37.5	7.8
2000	16,765	5,925	2,414	6,482	1,385	6.1	5.3	2.1	38.6	7.5
2001	20,308	8,254	3,074	6,780	1,446	7.1	7.2	2.6	38.3	7.4
2002	17,638	6,282	2,403	6,896	1,391	6.1	5.4	2.0	38.4	7.0
2003	17,732	6,337	2,372	7,083	1,309	6.1	5.4	2.0	38.9	6.6
2004	17,357	6,302	2,341	6,839	1,296	5.9	5.3	1.9	37.1	6.4
2005	18,124	6,457	2,313	7,412	1,257	6.1	5.4	1.9	39.7	6.2
2006	18,573	6,514	2,346	7,677	1,355	6.2	5.4	1.9	40.6	6.6
2007	18,361	6,541	2,373	7,584	1,286	6.1	5.4	1.9	39.7	6.2
2008	17,826	6,556	2,337	7,148	1,187	5.9	5.4	1.9	37.1	5.6

[1] Includes races not shown separately. [2] Rates per 100,000 resident population in specified group. Based on enumerated population figures as of April 1 for 1980, 1990, and 2000; estimated resident population as of July 1 for other years.

Source: U.S. National Center for Health Statistics, *Deaths: Final Data for 2008*, Vol. 59, No.10, Dec. 2011, and earlier reports. See <http://www.cdc.gov/nchs/products/nvsr.htm>.

Table 320. Forcible Rape—Number and Rate: 1990 to 2009

[For year ending December 31. Forcible rape, as defined in the FBI's Uniform Crime Reporting (UCR) Program, is the carnal knowledge of a female forcibly and against her will. Attempts or assaults to commit rape by force or threat of force are also included; however, statutory rape (without force) and other sex offenses are excluded]

Item	1990 [1]	2000 [1]	2001	2002	2003	2004	2005	2006	2007	2008	2009
NUMBER											
Total	**102,560**	**90,186**	**79,365**	**81,953**	**80,371**	**82,835**	**82,725**	**83,480**	**82,000**	**81,009**	**81,280**
By force	86,541	81,111	71,626	74,570	73,483	76,015	75,930	76,773	75,545	74,901	75,720
Attempt	16,019	9,075	7,739	7,383	6,888	6,820	6,795	6,707	6,455	6,108	5,560
RATE											
Per 100,000 population	41.1	32.0	32.70	32.9	33.10	33.10	32.50	32.10	30.80	30.10	29.80
Per 100,000 females	80.5	62.7	54.70	56.0	54.40	55.60	55.10	55.10	53.60	52.50	52.30

[1] Estimated. 2002–2009 contain actual reported data; no estimates or annual averages. It is noted that the estimations are considerably higher than actual reported values because estimations are performed against total U.S. population and not just female population.

Source: U.S. Department of Justice, Federal Bureau of Investigation, Uniform Crime Reporting Program, Return A Master Files.

Table 321. Criminal Victimizations and Victimization Rates: 1995 to 2009

[(39,926 represents 39,926,000). Based on National Crime Victimization Survey (NCVS); see text, this section and Appendix III]

Type of crime	Number of victimizations (1,000)				Victimization rates [1]			
	1995	2000	2005	2009	1995	2000	2005	2009
All crimes, total.........................	**39,926**	**25,893**	**23,441**	**20,057**	(X)	(X)	(X)	(X)
Population: Aged 12 or older......................	215,709	226,805	244,505	254,106	(X)	(X)	(X)	(X)
Personal crimes [2].....................	**10,436**	**6,597**	**5,401**	**4,477**	**46.2**	**29.1**	**22.1**	**17.6**
Crimes of violence.............................	10,022	6,323	5,174	4,343	44.5	27.9	21.2	17.1
Completed violence.......................	2,960	2,044	1,659	1,383	12.9	9.0	6.8	5.4
Attempted/threatened violence.........	7,061	4,279	3,515	2,960	31.6	18.9	14.4	11.6
Rape/sexual assault.......................	363	261	192	126	1.6	1.2	0.8	0.5
Rape/attempted rape.....................	252	147	130	88	1.1	0.6	0.5	0.3
Rape........................	153	92	69	37	0.7	0.4	0.3	0.1
Attempted rape....................	99	55	61	50	0.4	0.2	0.2	0.2
Sexual assault.........................	112	114	62	38	0.5	0.5	0.3	0.2
Robbery..........................	1,171	732	625	534	5.3	3.2	2.6	2.1
Completed/property taken.............	753	520	415	368	3.5	2.3	1.7	1.4
With injury........................	224	160	143	153	1.0	0.7	0.6	0.6
Without injury.....................	529	360	272	215	2.4	1.6	1.1	0.8
Attempted to take property.............	418	212	210	166	1.8	0.9	0.9	0.7
With injury........................	84	66	64	63	0.4	0.3	0.3	0.2
Without injury.....................	335	146	145	103	1.4	0.6	0.6	0.4
Assault............................	8,487	5,330	4,357	3,684	37.6	23.5	17.8	14.5
Aggravated...........................	2,050	1,293	1,052	823	8.8	5.7	4.3	3.2
With injury........................	533	346	331	313	2.4	1.5	1.4	1.2
Threatened with weapon...........	1,517	946	722	510	6.4	4.2	3.0	2.0
Simple..............................	6,437	4,038	3,305	2,860	28.9	17.8	13.5	11.3
With minor injury.................	1,426	989	795	638	6.0	4.4	3.3	2.5
Without injury.....................	5,012	3,048	2,510	2,222	22.9	13.4	10.3	8.7
Personal theft [3].............................	414	274	227	133	1.7	1.2	0.9	0.5
Total number of households (1,000)..............	101,888	108,353	117,100	122,328	(X)	(X)	(X)	(X)
Property crimes.............................	**29,490**	**19,297**	**18,040**	**15,581**	**279.5**	**178.1**	**154.0**	**127.4**
Household burglary.........................	5,004	3,444	3,456	3,135	47.4	31.8	29.5	25.6
Completed.........................	4,232	2,909	2,900	2,604	40.0	26.9	24.8	21.3
Attempted forcible entry..........................	773	534	556	531	7.4	4.9	4.7	4.3
Motor vehicle theft.............................	1,717	937	978	736	16.2	8.6	8.4	6.0
Completed.........................	1,163	642	775	570	10.8	5.9	6.6	4.7
Attempted.........................	554	295	203	166	5.5	2.7	1.7	1.4
Theft..............................	22,769	14,916	13,606	11,710	215.9	137.7	116.2	95.7
Completed [4].........................	21,857	14,300	13,116	11,219	207.6	132.0	112.0	91.7
Attempted.........................	911	616	489	491	8.4	5.7	4.2	4.0

X Not applicable. [1] Per 1,000 persons age 12 or older for "Personal crime;" per 1,000 households for "Property crime." [2] The victimization survey cannot measure murder because of the inability to question the victim. [3] Includes pocket picking, purse snatching, and attempted purse snatching. [4] Includes thefts in which the amount taken was not ascertained.

Source: U.S. Department of Justice, Bureau of Justice Statistics, *Criminal Victimization, 2009*, NCJ 231327, October 2010, annual. See also <http://bjs.ojp.usdoj.gov/index.cfm?ty=pbdetail&iid=2217>.

Table 322. Victimization Rates by Type of Crime and Characteristics of the Victim: 2009

[Rate per 1,000 persons age 12 years or older. Based on the National Crime Victimization Survey. See text, this section and Appendix III]

Characteristic of the victim	Personal crimes	Crimes of violence						Personal theft [1]
		Total	Rape/sexual assault	Robbery	Assault			
					Total	Aggravated	Simple	
Total........................	**17.6**	**17.1**	**0.5**	**2.1**	**14.5**	**3.2**	**11.3**	**0.5**
Male.........................	18.8	18.4	[2] 0.2	2.7	15.6	4.3	11.3	0.4
Female.......................	16.5	15.8	0.8	1.6	13.5	2.3	11.2	0.6
12 to 15 years old...........	37.3	36.8	[2] 0.9	3.1	32.8	6.9	25.9	[2] 0.4
16 to 19 years old...........	32.3	30.3	[2] 0.6	5.2	24.6	5.3	19.3	[2] 1.9
20 to 24 years old...........	28.8	28.1	[2] 0.8	3.5	23.8	7.5	16.3	[2] 0.7
25 to 34 years old...........	22.1	21.5	[2] 0.8	2.8	17.9	4.5	13.4	[2] 0.7
35 to 49 years old...........	16.3	16.1	[2] 0.4	2.0	13.7	2.6	11.1	[2] 0.2
50 to 64 years old...........	11.0	10.7	[2] 0.3	1.1	9.3	[2] 1.9	7.5	[2] 0.4
65 years old and over.......	3.7	3.2	[2] 0.2	[2] 0.4	2.5	[2] 0.3	2.2	[2] 0.5
White.........................	16.3	15.8	0.4	1.6	13.7	2.7	11.0	0.5
Black.........................	27.8	26.8	1.2	5.6	19.9	6.8	13.0	[2] 1.0
Other [3].......................	9.8	9.8	(Z)	[2] 0.5	9.3	[2] 1.9	7.4	(Z)
Two or more races.........	43.3	42.1	(Z)	[2] 5.2	36.9	[2] 9.3	27.5	21.2
Hispanic.....................	18.6	18.1	[2] 0.5	3.4	14.2	3.2	11.0	20.5
Non-Hispanic................	17.5	17.0	0.5	1.9	14.6	3.3	11.3	0.5
Household income:								
Less than $7,500.............	49.0	47.7	[2] 3.9	7.3	36.5	15.5	21.0	[2] 1.2
$7,500 to $14,999.........	40.4	40.0	[2] 1.8	5.7	32.6	6.0	26.6	[2] 0.4
$15,000 to $24,999.........	23.3	22.3	[2] 0.9	3.8	17.6	4.0	13.5	[2] 1.0
$25,000 to $34,999.........	18.7	18.6	[2](Z)	2.0	16.6	3.9	12.8	[2] 0.2
$35,000 to $49,999.........	16.7	16.6	[2] 0.3	2.0	14.3	4.5	9.8	[2] 0.1
$50,000 to $74,999.........	13.0	12.6	[2] 0.2	[2] 0.9	11.5	2.0	9.5	[2] 0.4
$75,000 or more...........	12.4	11.5	[2] 0.2	1.1	10.2	2.1	8.1	0.9

Z Rounds to less than 0.05 victimizations per 1,000 persons. [1] Includes pocket picking, completed purse snatching, and attempted purse snatching. [2] Based on 10 or fewer sample cases. [3] Includes American Indians, Alaska Natives, Asians, Native Hawaiians, and other Pacific Islanders.

Source: U.S. Department of Justice, Bureau of Justice Statistics, *Criminal Victimization, 2009*, NCJ 231327, October 2010. See also <http://bjs.ojp.usdoj.gov/index.cfm?ty=pbdetail&iid=2217>.

Table 323. Violent Crimes by Characteristics of Incident: 2009

[In percent, except as indicated. Based on National Crime Victimization Survey; see text, this section, and Appendix III]

Selected characteristics of incident	Number of incidents	Crimes of violence Total	Rape/ sexual assault	Robbery	Assault Total	Aggra-vated [1]	Simple
Total.....................................	**4,343,450**	**100.0**	**100.0**	**100.0**	**100.0**	**100.0**	**100.0**
Victim/offender relationship: [2]							
Relatives................................	523,670	12.1	[3] 6.6	13.3	12.1	[3] 3.7	14.5
Well-known..............................	1,126,240	25.9	39.4	11.5	27.6	27.8	27.5
Casual acquaintance..................	552,530	12.7	[3] 22.4	[3] 2.3	13.9	14.3	13.8
Stranger.................................	1,813,850	41.8	[3] 29.1	56.8	40.0	46.2	38.3
Time of day: [4]							
6 a.m. to 6 p.m........................	2,264,520	54.8	43.9	49.2	56.1	43.0	59.5
6 p.m. to midnight.....................	1,183,920	28.7	[3] 26.8	32.3	28.2	39.0	25.3
Midnight to 6 a.m......................	488,190	11.8	[3] 21.8	13.2	11.2	15.7	10.1
Location of crime:							
At or near victim's home or lodging........	1,649,510	40.0	56.2	43.1	38.9	33.5	40.4
Friend's/relative's/neighbor's home........	323,110	7.8	[3] 11.2	[3] 5.3	8.1	12.5	6.9
Commercial places.....................	397,910	9.7	[3] 1.6	[3] 6.3	10.4	10.9	10.2
Parking lots/garages...................	214,000	5.2	[3] 2.5	8.9	4.7	6.0	4.4
School...................................	540,780	13.1	[3] 3.2	[3] 6.9	14.4	6.3	16.5
Streets other than near victim's home......	575,950	13.9	[3] 11.9	26.7	12.1	20.6	9.9
Other [5].................................	428,870	10.3	[3] 13.4	2.7	11.8	10.1	11.7
Victim's activity: [6]							
At work or traveling to or from work........	668,280	16.2	[3] 9.8	10.0	(NA)	15.1	17.9
School...................................	576,590	14.0	[3] 8.1	11.3	(NA)	9.7	15.9
Activities at home......................	1,151,300	27.9	37.1	20.6	(NA)	20.6	30.8
Shopping/errands.......................	206,430	5.0	[3] 2.5	13.1	(NA)	[3] 3.4	4.0
Leisure activities away from home..........	901,550	21.8	[3] 21.9	23.1	(NA)	34.8	18.1
Traveling................................	292,520	7.1	[3] 6.8	13.6	(NA)	9.0	5.4
Other [7].................................	285,080	6.9	[3] 11.8	7.8	(NA)	6.7	6.6
Distance from victim's home: [8]							
Inside home or lodging.................	884,320	21.4	51.2	25.1	19.8	11.9	21.9
Near victim's home....................	749,310	18.1	[3] 10.8	11.0	19.5	18.6	19.7
1 mile or less..........................	749,020	18.1	[3] 12.9	28.2	16.8	26.3	14.3
5 miles or less.........................	890,500	21.6	[3] 14.7	17.2	22.5	22.6	22.4
50 miles or less........................	709,520	17.2	[3] 10.4	15.7	17.6	15.7	18.2
More than 50 miles.....................	127,840	3.1	[3] –	[3] 2.8	3.2	[3] 4.9	2.8
Weapons:							
No weapons present....................	2,999,560	72.6	84.7	47.5	75.9	11.3	93.2
Weapons present.......................	904,820	21.9	[3] 10.3	46.9	18.6	88.2	[3] –

– Represents zero. NA Not available. [1] An aggravated assault is any assault in which an offender possesses or uses a weapon or inflicts serious injury. [2] Excludes "don't know" relationships. [3] Based on 10 or fewer sample cases. [4] Excludes "not known and not available" time of day. [5] Includes areas on public transportation or inside station, in apartment yard, park, field, playground, or other areas. [6] Excludes "don't know" and "not available" victim activity. [7] Includes sleeping. [8] Excludes "don't know" and "not available" distance from victim's home.

Source: U.S. Department of Justice, Bureau of Justice Statistics, *Criminal Victimization, 2009*, NCJ 231327, October 2010. See also <http://bjs.ojp.usdoj.gov/index.cfm?ty=pbdetail&iid=2217>.

Table 324. Violent Crime Between Intimate Partners by Sex of Victims: 2008

[Violence includes rape and sexual assault, robbery, aggravated assault, simple assault and homicide. Intimate partners are defined as spouses, ex-spouses, current boy/girlfriends, and ex-boy/girlfriends. Based on the National Crime Victimization Survey, for 2000 to 2008, and the Federal Bureau of Investigation's (FBI) Uniform Crime Reporting Program's Supplementary Homicide Reports for 2000 to 2007; see text, this section and Appendix III]

Year and type of crime	All persons Number	Rate per 1,000 [1]	Female victims Number	Rate per 1,000 [1]	Male victims Number	Rate per 1,000 [1]
2000..............................	684,970	3.0	584,390	5.0	100,580	0.9
2005..............................	519,130	2.1	410,970	3.3	108,160	0.9
2006 [2]..........................	823,360	3.3	665,600	5.3	157,760	1.3
2007..............................	663,780	2.7	587,680	4.6	76,100	0.6
2008, total...................	**652,660**	**2.6**	**551,590**	**4.3**	**101,060**	**0.8**
Rape or sexual assault...........	44,000	0.2	(B)	(B)	(B)	(B)
Robbery..........................	(B)	(B)	(B)	(B)	(B)	(B)
Aggravated assault...............	111,530	0.4	70,550	0.5	(B)	(B)
Simple assault....................	458,310	1.8	406,530	3.1	51,770	0.4
Homicide.........................	(NA)	(NA)	(NA)	(NA)	(NA)	(NA)

B Base figure too small to meet statistical standards for reliability of derived figure. NA Not available. [1] Rates are the number of victimizations per 1,000 persons. Rates are not available for all categories. Except for homicide, the number of victimizations is per 100,000 persons aged 12 or older. [2] Due to changes in methodology, the 2006 national crime victimization rates are not comparable to previous years and cannot be used for yearly trend comparisons. However, the overall patterns of victimization at the national level can be examined.

Source: U.S. Department of Justice, Bureau of Justice Statistics, *Female Victims of Violence*, NCJ-228356, September 2009; See also <http://bjs.ojp.usdoj.gov/index.cfm?ty=pbdetail&iid=2020>.

Table 325. Stalking and Harassment Victimization in the United States: 2006

[Survey based on population of persons aged 18 or older. The survey defines stalking as a course of conduct directed at a specific person that would cause a reasonable person to feel fear. The survey characterizes individuals as victims of harassment who experience the behaviors associated with stalking but neither reported feeling fear as a result of such conduct nor experienced actions that would cause a reasonable person to feel fear]

Characteristic	Number			Rate per 1,000 persons		
	All	Stalking	Harassment	All	Stalking	Harassment
All victims [1]	**5,857,030**	**3,424,100**	**2,432,930**	**23.8**	**13.9**	**9.9**
Male	2,032,460	892,340	1,140,120	16.9	7.4	9.5
Female	3,824,570	2,531,770	1,292,800	30.3	20.0	10.2
18 to 19 years old	379,610	238,990	140,620	47.2	29.7	17.5
20 to 24 years old	929,710	576,870	352,840	45.7	28.4	17.3
25 to 34 years old	1,198,195	805,260	392,930	30.1	20.2	9.9
35 to 49 years old	1,971,290	1,139,320	831,970	29.9	17.3	12.6
50 to 64 years old	1,046,650	534,870	511,780	20.4	10.4	10.0
65 years old and over	331,580	128,790	202,790	9.3	3.6	5.7
White	4,835,270	2,860,810	1,974,460	24.1	14.2	9.8
Black	678,230	363,280	314,950	22.7	12.2	10.5
American Indian/ Alaska Native	55,890	[2] 33,150	[2] 22,740	33.0	[2] 19.6	[2] 13.4
Asian/Pacific Islander	151,670	79,790	71,890	13.4	7.0	6.4
More than one race [3]	135,960	87,080	48,880	49.3	31.6	17.7
Hispanic origin						
Hispanic	487,320	312,490	174,830	16.5	10.6	5.9
Non-Hispanic	5,308,010	3,089,570	2,218,440	24.7	14.4	10.3
Marital status						
Never married	2,143,400	1,321,870	821,530	26.9	16.6	10.3
Married	2,078,830	1,071,630	1,007,200	16.8	8.7	8.1
Divorced or separated	1,363,540	895,620	467,920	51.8	34.0	17.8
Widowed	229,450	107,730	121,720	16.0	7.5	8.5
Household Income						
Less than $7,500	395,740	266,800	128,940	47.0	31.7	15.3
$7,500 to $14,999	583,840	399,620	184,210	40.1	27.4	12.6
$15,000 to $24,999	724,270	474,220	250,050	32.3	21.1	11.1
$25,000 to $34,999	625,680	362,180	263,500	27.4	15.8	11.5
$35,000 to $49,999	765,580	480,750	284,830	25.2	15.8	9.4
$50,000 to $74,999	877,660	476,420	401,230	23.1	12.6	10.6
$75,000 or more	1,063,860	542,730	521,130	18.8	9.6	9.2

[1] Table excludes missing data. [2] Based on 10 or fewer sample cases. [3] Includes all persons of any race, including persons who identify two or more races.

Source: U.S. Department of Justice, Bureau of Justice Statistics, National Crime Victimization Survey, Supplemental Victimization Survey, *Stalking Victimization in the United States*, Series NCJ-224527, January 2009. See also <http://bjs.ojp.usdoj.gov/index.cfm?ty=pbdetail&iid=1211>.

Table 326. Property Crime by Selected Household Characteristics: 2010

[(122,885 represents 122,885,000). Households headed by person aged 12 years or older. Based on National Crime Victimization Survey (NCVS); see text, this section and Appendix III]

Characteristic	Number of house-holds (1,000)	Property crimes							
		Number of victimizations (1,000)				Victimization rate per 1,000 households			
		Total	Burglary	Motor vehicle theft	Theft	Total	Burglary	Motor vehicle theft	Theft
Total	**122,885**	**15,412**	**3,176**	**607**	**11,628**	**125.4**	**25.8**	**4.9**	**94.6**
Race:									
White	99,741	11,965	2,310	402	9,252	120.0	23.2	4.0	92.8
Black	15,996	2,427	641	163	1,624	151.8	40.0	10.2	101.5
Other	5,917	656	147	[1] 30	479	110.9	24.9	5.1	80.9
Two or more races	1,231	363	78	[1] 12	274	295.3	63.4	[1] 9.4	222.4
Ethnicity:									
Hispanic	14,006	2,130	415	127	1,588	152.1	29.6	9.1	113.4
Non-Hispanic	108,536	13,274	2,761	480	10,033	122.3	25.4	4.4	92.4
Household income:									
Less than $7,500	4,472	770	213	[1] 18	538	172.1	47.7	[1] 4.0	120.4
$7,500 to $14,999	6,996	1,310	400	42	868	187.3	57.2	5.9	124.1
$15,000 to $24,999	10,134	1,502	333	84	1,085	148.2	32.8	8.3	107.1
$25,000 to $34,999	10,365	1,468	316	77	1,075	141.6	30.5	7.4	103.8
$35,000 to $49,999	13,384	1,802	346	79	1,378	134.6	25.8	5.9	102.9
$50,000 to $74,999	14,550	1,680	278	86	1,316	115.4	19.1	5.9	90.4
$75,000 or more	23,125	2,863	403	117	2,343	123.8	17.4	5.1	101.3
Number of persons in household:									
1	35,569	3,395	975	121	2,300	95.5	27.4	3.4	64.7
2 or 3	61,309	7,404	1,496	271	5,636	120.8	24.4	4.4	91.9
4 or 5	22,149	3,769	566	177	3,026	170.2	25.6	8.0	136.6
6 or more	3,858	843	139	38	667	218.5	35.9	9.8	172.8

[1] Based on 10 or fewer sample cases.

Source: U.S. Department of Justice, Bureau of Justice Statistics, National Crime Victimization Survey, Victimization Analysis Tool, accessed September 2012. See also <http://www.bjs.gov/index.cfm?ty=nvat>.

Table 327. Robbery and Property Crimes by Type and Average Value Lost: 1990 to 2009

[639 represents 639,000. For year ending December 31]

Characteristic of offense	Number of offenses (1,000)				Rate per 100,000 population				Average value lost (dol.)			
	1990	2000	2005	2009	1990	2000	2005	2009	1990	2000	2005	2009
Robbery, total [1]	**639**	**408**	**417**	**342**	**256.3**	**144.9**	**140.7**	**125.1**	**631**	**1,127**	**1,239**	**1,246**
Type of crime:												
Street or highway	359	188	184	146	144.2	66.7	62.1	53.5	511	858	1,020	865
Commercial house	73	57	60	46	29.5	20.1	20.1	16.9	945	1,685	1,662	1,774
Gas station	18	12	12	8	7.1	4.1	4.0	3	423	679	1,104	862
Convenience store	39	26	24	18	15.6	9.3	8.0	6.7	344	566	677	717
Residence	62	50	59	58	25.1	17.7	20.0	21.1	828	1,243	1,332	1,674
Bank	9	9	9	7	3.8	3.1	3.0	2.7	2,885	4,379	4,113	4,202
Weapon used:												
Firearm	234	161	175	131	94.1	57.0	59.0	55.3	(NA)	(NA)	(NA)	(NA)
Knife or cutting instrument	76	36	37	24	30.7	12.8	12.5	9.9	(NA)	(NA)	(NA)	(NA)
Other weapon	61	53	39	27	24.5	18.9	13.2	11.3	(NA)	(NA)	(NA)	(NA)
Strong-arm	268	159	166	126	107.7	56.4	56.0	53.3	(NA)	(NA)	(NA)	(NA)
Burglary, total	**3,074**	**2,050**	**2,154**	**1,955**	**1,232.2**	**728.4**	**726.7**	**715.7**	**1,014**	**1,458**	**1,771**	**2,087**
Forcible entry [2]	2,150	1,297	1,310	1,224	864.5	460.7	440.0	448.1	(NA)	(NA)	(NA)	(NA)
Unlawful entry [2]	678	615	701	655	272.8	218.7	237.5	239.7	(NA)	(NA)	(NA)	(NA)
Attempted forcible entry [2]	245	138	133	129	98.7	49.0	45.2	47.4	(NA)	(NA)	(NA)	(NA)
Residence	2,033	1,335	1,417	1,127	817.4	474.3	477.9	412.9	1,037	1,378	1,813	2,709
Nonresidence	1,041	715	738	407	418.5	254.1	248.8	148.8	967	1,610	1,687	2,521
Occurred during the night [2]	1,135	699	708	625	456.4	248.3	238.9	229.0	(NA)	(NA)	(NA)	(NA)
Occurred during the day [2]	1,151	836	890	910	462.8	297.2	328.8	332.8	(NA)	(NA)	(NA)	(NA)
Larceny-theft, total	**7,946**	**6,972**	**6,783**	**5,560**	**3,185.1**	**2,477.3**	**2,286.3**	**2,035.1**	**426**	**727**	**857**	**865**
Pocket picking	81	36	29	24	32.4	12.7	9.8	8.8	384	437	346	489
Purse snatching	82	37	42	27	32.8	13.2	14.2	9.8	228	387	404	440
Shoplifting	1,291	959	940	1,002	519.1	340.7	317.0	366.9	104	185	184	178
From motor vehicles	1,744	1,754	1,752	1,520	701.3	623.3	590.6	556.5	461	692	704	737
Motor vehicle accessories	1,185	677	693	501	476.3	240.6	233.6	183.2	297	451	482	528
Bicycles	443	312	249	187	178.2	110.9	83.9	67.6	188	273	267	345
From buildings	1,118	914	852	620	449.4	324.6	287.3	226.8	673	1,184	1,738	1,233
From coin-operated machines	63	46	41	22	25.4	16.2	13.8	8.1	144	272	232	348
Other	1,940	2,232	2,184	1,660	780.0	793.0	736.1	607.5	615	957	1,137	1,439
Motor vehicles, total [3]	**1,636**	**1,160**	**1,236**	**731**	**655.8**	**412.2**	**417.4**	**258.6**	**5,117**	**6,581**	**6,204**	**6,495**
Automobiles	1,304	877	907	527	524.3	311.5	304.5	193.0	(NA)	(NA)	(NA)	(NA)
Trucks and buses	238	209	219	205	95.5	74.1	76.2	74.9	(NA)	(NA)	(NA)	(NA)

NA Not available. [1] Includes other crimes, not shown separately. [2] Unknown data not included. [3] Includes other types of motor vehicles, not shown separately.

Source: U.S. Department of Justice, Federal Bureau of Investigation, Uniform Crime Reports, Return A and Supplement to Return A Master Files.

Table 328. Hate Crimes—Number of Incidents, Offenses, Victims, and Known Offenders by Bias Motivation: 2000 to 2010

[The FBI collected statistics on hate crimes from 14,977 law enforcement agencies representing over an estimated 285 million people in 2010. Not all law enforcement agencies participated in the Hate Crimes Statistics Program. Hate crime offenses cover incidents motivated by race, religion, sexual orientation, ethnicity/national origin, and disability. See Source and Appendix III]

Bias motivation	Incidents reported	Offenses	Victims [1]	Known offenders [2]
2000.	8,213	9,619	10,117	7,690
2005.	7,163	8,380	8,804	6,804
2010, total.	**6,628**	**7,699**	**8,208**	**6,008**
Bias motive:				
Race, total.	**3,135**	**3,725**	**3,949**	**2,934**
Anti-White.	575	679	697	649
Anti-Black.	2,201	2,600	2,765	1,974
Anti-American Indian/Alaska native.	44	45	47	43
Anti-Asian/Pacific Islander.	150	190	203	156
Anti-multiracial group.	165	211	237	112
Ethnicity/national origin, total.	**847**	**1,040**	**1,122**	**887**
Anti-Hispanic.	534	681	747	593
Anti-other ethnicity/national origin.	313	359	375	294
Religion, total.	**1,322**	**1,409**	**1,552**	**606**
Anti-Jewish.	887	922	1,040	346
Anti-Catholic.	58	61	65	22
Anti-Protestant.	41	46	47	6
Anti-Islamic.	160	186	197	125
Anti-other religious group.	123	134	141	72
Anti-multi-religious group.	48	53	55	30
Anti-atheism/agnosticism/etc.	5	7	7	5
Sexual orientation, total.	**1,277**	**1,470**	**1,528**	**1,516**
Anti-male homosexual.	739	851	876	904
Anti-female homosexual.	144	167	181	152
Anti-homosexual.	347	403	420	412
Anti-heterosexual.	21	21	22	21
Anti-bisexual.	26	28	29	27
Disability, total.	**43**	**46**	**48**	**58**
Anti-physical.	19	22	24	28
Anti-mental.	24	24	24	30
Multiple bias [3]	**4**	**9**	**9**	**7**

[1] The term "victim" may refer to a person, business, institution, or a society as a whole. [2] The term "known offender" does not imply that the identity of the suspect is known, but only that an attribute of the suspect has been identified which distinguishes him/her from an unknown offender. [3] In a "multiple-bias incident" two conditions must be met: more than one offense type must occur in the incident and at least two offense types must be motivated by different biases.

Source: U.S. Department of Justice, Federal Bureau of Investigation, "Hate Crime Statistics, 2010." <http://www.fbi.gov/about-us/cjis/ucr/hate-crime/2010/index>.

Table 329. Hate Crimes by Bias Motivation and Location of Incident: 2010

[See headnote, Table 328]

Location	Total incidents	Bias motivation					Multiple-bias incidents [1]
		Race	Religion	Sexual orientation	Ethnic/nat'l origin	Disability	
Total.	6,628	3,135	1,322	1,277	847	43	4
Air/bus/train terminal.	70	31	8	21	9	1	–
Bank/savings and loan.	12	7	1	2	2	–	–
Bar/nightclub.	144	54	7	62	20	–	1
Camp/campground.	1	–	–	–	1	–	–
Church/synagogue/temple.	244	26	207	7	4	–	–
Commercial office building.	123	63	20	16	23	1	–
Construction site.	11	7	–	1	3	–	–
Convenience store.	68	33	8	9	17	1	–
Department/discount store.	72	34	15	14	9	–	–
Drug store/Doctor's office/hospital.	55	24	22	5	3	1	–
Field/woods.	65	34	9	14	8	–	–
Gambling facility/casino/race track.	1	1	–	–	–	–	–
Government/public building.	106	58	22	15	11	–	–
Grocery/supermarket.	39	18	4	8	9	–	–
Highway/road/alley/street.	1,127	593	109	268	148	9	–
Hotel/motel/etc.	38	21	3	7	6	1	–
Industrial site.	1	–	1	–	–	–	–
Jail/prison.	52	35	2	10	5	–	–
Lake/waterway.	14	8	3	3	–	–	–
Liquor store.	8	4	1	2	1	–	–
Parking lot/garage.	385	188	45	88	63	1	–
Park/playground.	2	2	–	–	–	–	–
Rental storage facility.	5	1	2	1	1	–	–
Residence/home.	2,079	1,052	352	399	261	14	1
Restaurant.	107	54	8	21	23	1	–
School/college.	724	368	168	107	71	9	1
Service/gas station.	59	30	8	9	12	–	–
Shopping mall.	2	1	–	1	–	–	–
Specialty store (TV, furniture, etc.).	55	21	14	10	10	–	–
Other/unknown.	950	361	283	177	125	4	–
Multiple locations.	9	6	–	–	2	–	1

– Represents zero. [1] See footnote 3, Table 328.

Source: U.S. Department of Justice, Federal Bureau of Investigation, "Hate Crime Statistics, 2010," <http://www.fbi.gov/about-us/cjis/ucr/hate-crime/2010>.

Table 330. Financial Crimes: 2005 to 2011

[For the year ending September 30. The FBI focuses its financial crimes investigations on such criminal activities as corporate fraud, securities and commodities fraud, health care fraud, financial institution fraud, mortgage fraud, insurance fraud, mass marketing fraud, and money laundering]

Type of financial fraud	Unit indicator	2005	2006	2007	2008	2009	2010	2011
Corporate fraud:								
Cases pending...................................	Number	423	486	529	545	592	661	726
Indictments....................................	Number	178	176	183	160	161	(NA)	242
Convictions....................................	Number	150	134	181	134	162	(NA)	241
Restitution.....................................	Bil. dol.	5.6	1.1	12.6	8.2	6.1	(NA)	2.4
Recoveries.....................................	1,000 dol.	68.0	41,400.0	27,400.0	6,590.0	16,100.0	(NA)	(NA)
Fines..	Mil. dol.	122.4	14.2	38.6	193.7	5.3	(NA)	16.1
Seizures.......................................	Mil. dol.	12.6	82.4	70.1	9.3	40.6	(NA)	(NA)
Securities/Commodities fraud:								
Cases pending...................................	Number	1,139	1,165	1,217	1,210	1,510	1,703	1,846
Indictments....................................	Number	327	320	408	359	412	(NA)	520
Convictions....................................	Number	363	279	321	302	309	(NA)	394
Restitution.....................................	Bil. dol.	2.3	2.1	1.5	3.0	2.1	(NA)	8.8
Recoveries.....................................	Mil. dol.	76.3	20.6	25.4	43.7	47.3	(NA)	36.0
Fines..	Mil. dol.	14.8	80.7	202.8	128.5	7.4	(NA)	113.0
Seizures.......................................	Mil. dol.	281.9	41.8	83.0	77.5	85.0	(NA)	751.0
Insurance fraud:								
Cases pending...................................	Number	270	233	209	177	152	156	140
Indictments....................................	Number	72	56	39	73	43	(NA)	19
Convictions....................................	Number	79	66	47	60	42	(NA)	21
Restitution.....................................	Mil. dol.	171.7	30.4	27.6	553.7	22.9	(NA)	87.6
Recoveries.....................................	1,000 dol.	913.0	14.0	21.0	10,400.0	31,400.0	(NA)	(NA)
Fines..	1,000 dol.	112.0	212.0	447.0	31.0	138.0	(NA)	(NA)
Seizures.......................................	Mil. dol.	10.7	3.5	15.9	25.3	2.2	(NA)	(NA)
Mass marketing fraud:								
Cases pending...................................	Number	161	147	127	100	92	86	96
Indictments....................................	Number	28	15	13	50	9	(NA)	(NA)
Convictions....................................	Number	43	46	11	23	23	(NA)	(NA)
Restitution.....................................	Mil. dol.	503.8	273.2	30.6	4.2	4.4	(NA)	(NA)
Recoveries.....................................	1,000 dol.	4.0	468.0	542.0	173.0	–	(NA)	(NA)
Fines..	1,000 dol.	362.0	86,900.0	121.0	23.0	2.1	(NA)	(NA)
Seizures.......................................	Mil. dol.	8.1	12.7	(Z)	–	(Z)	(NA)	(NA)
Health care fraud:								
Cases pending...................................	Number	2,547	2,423	2,493	2,434	2,494	2,573	2,690
Indictments....................................	Number	589	588	847	851	982	(NA)	1,676
Convictions....................................	Number	550	535	642	707	674	(NA)	736
Restitution.....................................	Bil. dol.	1.1	0.4	1.1	1.1	1.3	(NA)	1.2
Recoveries.....................................	Mil. dol.	115.0	1,600.0	439.8	102.4	517.1	(NA)	(NA)
Fines..	Mil. dol.	42.4	172.8	33.7	25.6	68.9	(NA)	1,000.0
Seizures.......................................	Mil. dol.	52.7	28.9	86.1	48.3	55.7	(NA)	96.0
Money laundering:								
Cases pending...................................	Number	507	473	443	404	350	323	303
Indictments....................................	Number	126	264	140	114	63	(NA)	37
Convictions....................................	Number	91	112	115	134	96	(NA)	45
Restitution.....................................	Mil. dol.	313.0	17.1	69.4	222.4	81.9	(NA)	18.4
Recoveries.....................................	Mil. dol.	9.3	3.2	2.7	20.9	0.6	(NA)	0.8
Fines..	Mil. dol.	0.3	0.4	11.4	34.1	1.5	(NA)	1.0
Seizures.......................................	Mil. dol.	7.8	6.4	10.9	24.2	4.5	(NA)	(NA)
Mortgage fraud:								
Cases pending...................................	Number	721	881	1,211	1,644	2,794	3,129	2,691
Indictments....................................	Number	93	138	328	574	822	(NA)	1,233
Convictions....................................	Number	60	123	283	354	494	(NA)	1,082
Restitution.....................................	Mil. dol.	151.2	308.3	600.6	825.2	2,540.0	(NA)	1,380.0
Recoveries.....................................	Mil. dol.	(Z)	1.2	21.8	3.3	7.5	(NA)	7.3
Fines..	Mil. dol.	44.0	300.8	1.6	3.1	58.4	(NA)	116.3
Seizures.......................................	Mil. dol.	(NA)	(NA)	5.1	6.6	5.0	(NA)	15.7
Suspicious Activity Reports (SARs) [1,2]								
Mortgage fraud related—								
Number of violations:								
Mortgage fraud.................................	Number	21,994	35,617	46,717	63,713	67,190	70,533	93,508
Commercial loan................................	Number	2,126	2,409	3,240	4,189	4,514	3,347	2,947
False statement................................	Number	11,611	21,023	28,692	37,622	38,159	(NA)	(NA)
Dollars losses reported on:								
Mortgage fraud SARs...........................	Bil. dol.	1.0	0.9	0.8	1.5	2.8	3.2	3.0
Reported on commercial loan SARs...........	Bil. dol.	0.7	0.5	1.0	1.9	1.7	(NA)	(NA)
False statement SARs..........................	Bil. dol.	1.0	1.4	0.8	2.5	2.1	(NA)	(NA)

– Represents zero. NA Not available. Z represents a value less than 50 thousand. [1] Reports filed by federally-insured financial institutions. [2] SARs are cataloged according to the year in which they are submitted and the information contained within them may describe activity that occurred in previous month or years.

Source: U.S. Department of Justice, Federal Bureau of Investigation, *Financial Crimes Report to the Public* and *2010 Mortgage Fraud Report, Year in Review*. See also <http://www.fbi.gov/stats-services/publications/financial-crimes-report-2010-2011> and <http://www.fbi.gov/stats-services/publications/mortgage-fraud-2010>.

Table 331. Fraud and Identity Theft—Consumer Complaints by State: 2011

[Rate per 100,000 population. As of December 31. Rates based on 2010 Census results. The Consumer Sentinel Network (CSN) is a secure online database of consumer complaints available only to law enforcement. Based on unverified complaints reported by consumers. Excludes complaints outside of the U.S. and the Minnesota Department of Public Safety, the North Carolina Department of Justice, the Tennessee Division of Consumer Affairs, and the Offices of the Attorneys General for Idaho, Michigan, Mississippi, Ohio, Oregon, and Washington]

State	Fraud and other complaints [1]		Identity theft victims [1]		State	Fraud and other complaints [1]		Identity theft victims [1]	
	Number	Rate	Number	Rate		Number	Rate	Number	Rate
U.S.	**1,320,171**	**427.6**	**279,156**	**90.4**	MO	26,863	448.5	4,282	71.5
AL	19,304	403.9	3,942	82.5	MT	4,020	406.3	390	39.4
AK	3,130	440.7	316	44.5	NE	6,824	373.6	869	47.6
AZ	32,195	503.7	6,296	98.5	NV	14,320	530.3	2,427	89.9
AR	10,314	353.7	1,862	63.9	NH	5,948	451.8	617	46.9
CA	155,986	418.7	38,607	103.6	NJ	39,737	452.0	7,599	86.4
CO	28,854	573.7	4,156	82.6	NM	8,023	389.6	1,610	78.2
CT	14,447	404.2	2,413	67.5	NY	75,163	387.9	17,880	92.3
DE	4,958	552.2	750	83.5	NC	38,063	399.2	6,287	65.9
DC	4,736	787.1	999	166.0	ND	1,732	257.5	156	23.2
FL	96,854	515.1	33,595	178.7	OH	54,493	472.4	7,479	64.8
GA	43,395	447.9	11,625	120.0	OK	13,481	359.4	2,115	56.4
HI	5,695	418.7	583	42.9	OR	16,208	423.1	2,226	58.1
ID	6,790	433.2	658	42.0	PA	54,027	425.3	10,061	79.2
IL	52,278	407.4	10,361	80.8	RI	4,004	380.4	614	58.3
IN	25,296	390.1	3,555	54.8	SC	19,720	426.3	3,168	68.5
IA	9,611	315.5	1,208	39.7	SD	2,415	296.6	206	25.3
KS	11,225	393.4	1,914	67.1	TN	26,987	425.3	4,275	67.4
KY	16,053	369.9	1,891	43.6	TX	102,107	406.1	24,162	96.1
LA	18,000	397.1	2,934	64.7	UT	10,895	394.2	1,514	54.8
ME	4,589	345.5	503	37.9	VT	2,328	372.0	259	41.4
MD	31,581	547.0	4,980	86.3	VA	42,165	527.0	5,416	67.7
MA	26,245	400.8	4,128	63.0	WA	31,832	473.4	4,853	72.2
MI	37,007	374.4	8,119	82.1	WV	5,987	323.1	731	39.4
MN	19,679	371.0	2,671	50.4	WI	22,736	399.8	2,782	48.9
MS	9,595	323.4	2,210	74.5	WY	2,276	403.8	280	49.7

[1] Includes non-U.S. residents and people who did not report residence.

Source: U.S. Federal Trade Commission, *Consumer Sentinel Network Data Book*, for January–December 2011, Feb. 2012, <http://www.ftc.gov/sentinel/reports.shtml>.

Table 332. Juvenile Arrests for Drug Abuse Offenses: 1980 to 2009

[For year ending December 31. Juveniles are persons under 18 years of age. Some persons may be arrested more than once during a year. Therefore, this table could, in some cases, represent multiple arrests of the same person]

Offense	1980	1990	2000	2003	2004	2005	2006	2007	2008	2009
Drug arrests, total	**86,685**	**66,300**	**146,594**	**134,746**	**135,056**	**137,809**	**145,153**	**143,270**	**134,661**	**130,317**
Sale and manufacturing	13,004	24,575	26,432	21,987	21,136	21,607	22,466	21,493	19,467	18,840
Heroin/cocaine	1,318	17,511	11,000	7,848	7,852	7,863	8,261	7,334	6,288	4,975
Marijuana	8,876	4,372	11,792	10,463	9,743	9,845	10,333	10,640	9,678	9,871
Synthetic narcotics	465	346	945	1,043	1,119	1,071	1,262	1,162	1,093	1,170
Dangerous nonnarcotic drugs	2,345	2,346	2,695	2,633	2,422	2,828	2,610	2,357	2,408	2,824
Possession	73,681	41,725	120,432	112,759	113,920	116,202	122,687	121,777	115,194	111,477
Heroin/cocaine	2,614	15,194	12,586	9,932	10,805	11,131	12,024	9,756	7,944	6,208
Marijuana	64,465	20,940	95,962	87,909	87,717	88,909	95,120	97,671	93,042	90,927
Synthetic narcotics	1,524	1,155	2,052	2,872	3,279	3,235	3,337	3,142	3,286	3,385
Dangerous nonnarcotic drugs	5,078	4,436	9,832	12,046	12,119	12,927	12,206	11,208	10,922	10,957

Source: U.S. Department of Justice, Federal Bureau of Investigation Uniform Crime Reports, Arrests Master File.

Table 333. Arrests by Race: 2010

[Based on Uniform Crime Reporting (UCR) Program. Represents arrests reported (not charged) by 12,221 agencies with a total population of 240,100,189 as estimated by the FBI. See headnote, Table 338]

Offense charged	Total	White	Black	American Indian/Alaskan Native	Asian Pacific Islander
Total	10,177,907	7,066,154	2,846,862	145,612	119,279
Violent crime	429,166	254,620	163,670	5,776	5,100
Murder and nonnegligent manslaughter	8,641	4,261	4,209	91	80
Forcible rape	15,503	10,178	4,925	214	186
Robbery	87,587	37,906	48,154	617	910
Aggravated assault	317,435	202,275	106,382	4,854	3,924
Property crime	1,288,295	881,420	372,562	17,080	17,233
Burglary	225,775	152,210	69,541	1,961	2,063
Larceny-theft	998,476	687,609	282,246	14,323	14,298
Motor vehicle theft	55,278	35,009	18,797	696	776
Arson	8,766	6,592	1,978	100	96
Other assaults	1,004,273	659,171	318,117	14,848	12,137
Forgery and counterfeiting	60,538	40,167	19,350	342	679
Fraud	144,214	95,126	46,493	1,253	1,342
Embezzlement	12,930	8,568	4,037	88	237
Stolen property; buying, receiving, possessing	74,122	48,303	24,494	598	727
Vandalism	197,015	145,284	46,306	3,279	2,146
Weapons—carrying, possessing, etc	123,278	71,772	49,443	874	1,189
Prostitution and commercialized vice	48,154	26,156	20,405	342	1,251
Sex offenses [1]	56,125	41,406	13,182	744	793
Drug abuse violations	1,270,443	846,736	404,609	8,766	10,332
Gambling	7,512	2,160	5,071	32	249
Offenses against the family and children	84,812	56,233	26,470	1,533	576
Driving under the influence	1,082,301	927,516	124,467	13,980	16,338
Liquor laws	396,942	329,895	47,529	14,129	5,389
Drunkenness	440,688	362,396	66,837	8,583	2,872
Disorderly conduct	480,080	305,154	162,521	8,415	3,990
Vagrancy	24,759	14,092	9,935	567	165
All other offenses (except traffic)	2,877,687	1,905,436	893,018	43,634	35,599
Suspicion	903	582	310	5	6
Curfew and loitering law violations	73,670	43,961	28,036	744	929

[1] Except forcible rape and prostitution.

Source: U.S. Department of Justice, Federal Bureau of Investigation, "Crime in the United States, Arrests," <http://www.fbi.gov/about-us/cjis/ucr/crime-in-the-u.s/2010/crime-in-the-u.s.-2010/persons-arrested>, accessed May 2012.

Table 334. Drug Arrest Rates for Drug Abuse Violations, 1990 to 2005, and by Region: 2009

[Rate per 100,000 population. For year ending December 31. Based on Census Bureau estimated resident population as of July 1, except 1990 and 2000, enumerated as of April 1. For composition of regions, see map, inside front cover]

Offense	1990	2000	2005	2009 Total	North-east	Mid-west	South	West
Drug arrest rate, total	435.3	587.1	600.9	416.0	382.5	295.3	425.8	538.9
Sale and/or manufacture	139.0	122.7	109.9	76.9	85.4	57.9	76.9	87.9
Heroin or cocaine [1]	93.7	60.8	47.8	29.5	48.6	15.0	29.1	28.7
Marijuana	26.4	34.2	29.6	25.2	24.4	26.1	21.7	30.4
Synthetic or manufactured drugs	2.7	6.4	8.6	7.5	5.5	3.9	13.2	3.3
Other dangerous nonnarcotic drugs	16.2	21.3	23.9	14.8	6.9	12.9	13.0	25.5
Possession	296.3	464.4	490.9	339.1	297.1	237.4	348.9	451.0
Heroin or cocaine [1]	144.4	138.7	131.5	72.8	71.8	31.6	71.9	113.5
Marijuana	104.9	244.4	228.9	190.0	179.5	157.7	216.5	186.1
Synthetic or manufactured drugs	6.6	12.0	21.0	15.6	10.8	11.4	21.3	14.2
Other dangerous nonnarcotic drugs	40.4	69.4	109.6	60.7	35.0	36.6	39.2	137.3

[1] Includes other derivatives such as morphine, heroin, and codeine.

Source: U.S. Department of Justice, Federal Bureau of Investigation, Uniform Crime Reports, Arrests Master Files and unpublished data.

Table 335. Federal Drug Arrests and Seizures by Type of Drug: 2000 to 2010

[For fiscal years ending in year shown. The data have all been revised. In years past, the data for the amount of drugs seized at the Federal level was obtained from the Federal-wide Drug Seizure System (FDSS). A new system has been created called the National Seizure System (NSS). This system will broaden the scope of data collected for the amount of drugs seized (in pounds) at the national level. The data for "Seizure in (pounds)" for years shown are from NSS]

Drug	2000	2003	2004	2005	2006	2007	2008	2009	2010
Number of arrests, total [1, 2]	**36,845**	**26,021**	**26,863**	**28,118**	**27,326**	**27,493**	**25,783**	**27,115**	**27,200**
Heroin	3,622	2,527	2,491	2,453	2,361	2,169	2,610	3,063	2,991
Cocaine	16,375	11,389	11,979	13,045	13,104	12,885	12,168	11,738	10,726
Cannabis [3]	8,572	6,032	6,312	6,115	6,003	6,887	6,271	7,511	8,108
Methamphetamine	8,276	6,073	6,081	6,505	5,858	5,552	4,734	4,803	5,375
Seizure in (pounds), total	**1,451,412**	**3,746,766**	**3,248,585**	**2,907,197**	**3,007,207**	**3,973,738**	**3,397,766**	**4,575,249**	**4,499,621**
Cocaine	61,051	106,530	104,836	112,076	142,859	124,713	108,838	127,789	137,823
Heroin	1,590	5,968	4,159	4,005	4,404	3,633	4,114	4,941	6,234
Cannabis [3]	1,383,189	3,622,057	3,126,441	2,777,560	2,847,150	3,832,127	3,271,081	4,428,160	4,333,348
Methamphetamine	5,582	12,211	13,149	13,556	12,794	13,265	13,733	14,359	22,216

[1] Domestic arrests are for the Drug Enforcement Administration only. [2] Includes other drug-related arrests not shown. [3] Includes Hashish.

Source: U.S. Drug Enforcement Administration, "Stats and Facts," <www.justice.gov/dea/>, and unpublished data from the National Seizure System (NSS).

Table 336. Background Checks for Firearm Transfers: 1994 to 2009

[In thousands (12,740 represents 12,740,000), except rates. The Brady Handgun Violence Prevention Act (Brady Act) requires a background check on an applicant for a firearm purchase from a dealer who is a Federal Firearms Licensee]

Inquiries and rejections	Interim period 1994– 1998 [1]	Permanent Brady [2]									
		2000	2001	2002	2003	2004	2005	2006	2007	2008	2009
Applications and denials:											
Applications received	12,740	7,699	7,958	7,806	7,831	8,084	8,278	8,612	8,658	9,901	10,764
Applications denied	312	153	151	136	126	126	132	135	136	147	150
Denied (percent)	2.4	2.0	1.9	1.7	1.6	1.6	1.6	1.6	1.6	1.5	1.4
Selective reasons for rejection:											
Felony indictment/conviction	44	88	87	65	53	53	57	52	49	77	67
Other	18	65	64	71	73	73	75	83	87	70	83
Felony denials per 1,000 applications	(NA)	11.4	10.9	8.3	6.8	6.6	6.9	6.0	5.7	7.2	6.2

NA Not available. [1] Background checks on applicants were conducted by state and local agencies, mainly on handgun transfers. See "Presale Handgun Checks, the Brady Interim Period, 1994–98" (NCJ 175034). [2] The period beginning November 30, 1998 is the effective date for the Brady Handgun Violence Prevention Act, P.L. 103–159, 1993. The National Instant Criminal Background Check System (NICS) began operations. Checks on handgun and long gun transfers are conducted by the Federal Bureau of Investigation (FBI), and by state and local agencies. Totals combine Firearm Inquiry Statistics (FIST) estimates for state and local agencies with transactions and denials reported by the FBI.

Source: U.S. Department of Justice, Office of Justice Programs, Bureau of Justice Statistics, "Background Checks for Firearm Transfers—Statistical Tables, 2009," Series NCJ 231679, October 2010. See also <http://bjs.ojp.usdoj.gov/index.cfm?ty=pbdetail&iid=1706>.

Table 337. Employment by State and Local Law Enforcement Agencies by Type of Agency and Employee: 2008

[As of September 30. Based on census of all state and local law enforcement agencies operating nationwide, conducted every 4 years]

Type of agency	Number of agencies	Number of employees					
		Full-time			Part-time		
		Total	Sworn	Civilian	Total	Sworn	Civilian
Total [1]	**17,985**	**1,133,905**	**765,237**	**368,668**	**100,340**	**44,062**	**56,278**
Local police	12,501	593,003	461,054	131,949	58,129	27,810	30,319
Sheriffs' offices	3,063	353,461	182,979	170,482	26,052	11,334	14,718
Primary State	50	93,148	60,772	32,376	947	54	893
Special jurisdiction	1,733	90,262	56,968	33,294	14,681	4,451	10,230
Constable/marshal	638	4,031	3,464	567	531	413	118

[1] Excludes agencies with less than one full-time officer or the equivalent in part-time officers.

Source: U.S. Bureau of Justice Statistics, "Census of State and Local Law Enforcement Agencies, 2008," <http://bjs.ojp.usdoj.gov/index.cfm?ty=dcdetail&iid=249>.

Table 338. Arrests by Sex and Age: 2010

[In thousands (10,223.6 represents 10,223,558) For year ending December 31. Based on Uniform Crime Reporting (UCR) Program. Represents arrests reported (not charged) by 12,222 agencies with a total population of 240,103,394 as estimated by the FBI. Some persons may be arrested more than once during a year, therefore, the data in this table, in some cases, could represent multiple arrests of the same person. See text, this section and source]

Offense charged	Total			Male			Female		
	Total	Under 18 years	18 years and over	Total	Under 18 years	18 years and over	Total	Under 18 years	18 years and over
Total............................	10,223.6	1,288.6	8,934.9	7,621.1	910.8	6,710.3	2,602.5	377.8	2,224.6
Violent crime..................	430.4	59.1	371.3	346.5	48.3	298.2	83.8	10.8	73.0
Murder and nonnegligent manslaughter............	8.7	0.8	7.9	7.7	0.7	7.0	0.9	0.1	0.9
Forcible rape..............	15.6	2.2	13.4	15.4	2.2	13.3	0.2	–	0.1
Robbery..................	87.8	21.1	66.7	77.1	19.1	58.0	10.7	2.0	8.7
Aggravated assault.........	318.3	35.0	283.3	246.3	26.3	220.0	72.0	8.7	63.4
Property crime................	1,293.0	290.4	1,002.7	807.5	180.0	627.5	485.6	110.4	375.2
Burglary..................	226.3	51.3	175.0	191.7	45.3	146.4	34.7	6.0	28.6
Larceny-theft.............	1,002.5	223.2	779.3	562.8	121.3	441.5	439.7	101.9	337.7
Motor vehicle theft.......	55.4	12.3	43.2	45.7	10.3	35.4	9.7	2.0	7.7
Arson...................	8.8	3.6	5.2	7.3	3.1	4.2	1.5	0.5	1.1
Other assaults..............	1,008.5	163.4	845.1	737.2	105.9	631.3	271.3	57.5	213.8
Forgery and counterfeiting....	60.8	1.3	59.5	38.0	1.0	37.0	22.9	0.4	22.5
Fraud.....................	145.0	4.6	140.4	84.8	3.0	81.8	60.1	1.6	58.6
Embezzlement..............	13.0	0.3	12.7	6.4	0.2	6.2	6.6	0.1	6.4
Stolen property [1]..........	74.3	11.6	62.7	59.6	9.6	50.0	14.7	2.0	12.7
Vandalism.................	197.9	60.6	137.3	160.4	51.7	108.7	37.5	8.9	28.6
Weapons; carrying, possessing, etc...	123.7	24.5	99.2	113.3	21.9	91.4	10.4	2.6	7.8
Prostitution and commercialized vice...	48.3	0.8	47.5	15.1	0.1	14.9	33.2	0.7	32.5
Sex offenses [2]............	56.3	10.1	46.2	52.0	9.1	42.9	4.3	1.0	3.3
Drug abuse violations........	1,274.0	132.9	1,141.0	1,030.1	111.1	919.0	243.9	21.8	222.1
Gambling.................	7.5	1.0	6.5	6.8	1.0	5.8	0.7	–	0.7
Offenses against family and children...	85.2	3.0	82.2	63.7	2.0	61.8	21.5	1.0	20.5
Driving under the influence...........	1,088.0	9.4	1,078.6	830.0	7.0	823.0	258.0	2.4	255.6
Liquor laws................	400.6	75.9	324.7	286.3	46.6	239.7	114.3	29.2	85.1
Drunkenness...............	442.4	10.0	432.4	366.0	7.4	358.6	76.4	2.7	73.7
Disorderly conduct..........	483.0	121.3	361.7	349.0	79.7	269.3	134.0	41.6	92.4
Vagrancy.................	24.8	1.7	23.1	19.9	1.3	18.6	4.9	0.4	4.6
All other offenses (except traffic).......	2,892.0	232.7	2,659.3	2,195.7	171.8	2,023.8	696.3	60.9	635.5
Suspicion.................	0.9	0.1	0.8	0.7	0.1	0.6	0.2	–	0.2
Curfew and loitering law violations.....	73.9	73.9	(X)	52.0	52.0	(X)	21.9	21.9	(X)

– Represents zero. X Not applicable. [1] Buying, receiving, possessing stolen property. [2] Except forcible rape and prostitution.

Source: U.S. Department of Justice, Federal Bureau of Investigation, "Crime in the United States, 2010," accessed May 2012.

Table 339. Law Enforcement Officers Killed and Assaulted: 1990 to 2010

[The statistics presented in this table are based on information collected by the staff of the FBI's Law Enforcement Officers Killed and Assaulted (LEOKA) Program from law enforcement agencies throughout the Nation and U.S. Territories. It contains statistics on line-of-duty felonious deaths, accidental deaths, and assaults of duly sworn local, state, tribal, and federal law enforcement officers. For composition of regions, see map, inside front cover]

Item	1990	1995	2000	2005	2006	2007	2008	2009	2010
OFFICERS KILLED									
Total killed...................	132	133	134	122	114	141	109	96	128
Geographical region:									
Northeast......................	13	16	13	12	12	13	14	13	11
Midwest......................	20	19	32	23	20	20	14	14	24
South........................	68	63	67	58	48	78	52	42	61
West.........................	23	32	19	24	31	28	26	25	29
Puerto Rico.................	8	2	3	5	3	1	2	2	3
Island Areas, foreign countries.......	–	1	–	–	–	1	1	–	–
Total feloniously killed...............	65	74	51	55	48	58	41	48	56
Firearms...................	56	63	47	50	46	56	35	45	55
Handgun..................	47	44	33	42	36	39	25	28	38
Rifle.....................	8	14	10	3	8	8	6	15	15
Shotgun..................	1	5	4	5	2	8	4	2	2
Type of firearm not reported........	–	–	–	–	–	1	–	–	–
Blunt instrument..............	–	–	–	–	–	–	–	–	–
Bomb......................	–	8	–	–	–	–	2	–	–
Knife/cutting instrument..............	3	1	1	–	–	–	–	–	–
Personal weapons [1].................	2	–	–	–	–	–	–	–	–
Vehicle.....................	1	2	3	5	2	2	4	3	1
Other......................	3	–	–	–	–	–	–	–	–
Total accidentally killed.................	67	59	83	67	66	83	68	48	72
OFFICERS ASSAULTED									
Population covered (1,000) [2]..........	197,426	191,759	204,599	222,874	227,361	234,734	238,731	245,926	235,355
Number of—									
Reporting agencies.............	9,343	8,503	8,940	10,119	10,596	10,973	10,835	11,691	11,108
Officers employed........................	410,131	428,379	452,531	489,393	504,147	523,944	541,906	560,387	532,395
Total assaulted......................	72,091	57,762	58,398	57,820	59,396	61,257	61,087	58,364	53,469
Firearm......................	3,651	2,354	1,749	2,157	2,290	2,216	2,292	2,007	1,831
Knife/cutting instrument.................	1,647	1,356	1,015	1,059	1,055	1,028	958	886	884
Other dangerous weapon..............	7,423	6,414	8,132	8,379	8,611	8,692	8,466	7,966	6,990
Personal weapons [1].................	59,370	47,638	47,502	46,225	47,440	49,321	49,371	47,505	43,764

– Represents zero. [1] Includes hands, fists, feet, etc. [2] Represents the number of persons covered by agencies shown.

Source: U.S. Department of Justice, Federal Bureau of Investigation, Crime Statistics Management Unit, LEOKA Program, <http://www.fbi.gov/about-us/cjis/ucr/leoka/leoka-2010>.

Table 340. State and Local Government Expenditures Per Capita by Criminal Justice Function and State: 2008

[In dollars. Based on Census Bureau's Annual Government Finance Survey and Annual Survey of Public Employment. Based on Census Bureau resident population as of July 1. See Appendix III]

State	Total justice system	Police protec- tion	Judicial and legal	Correc- tions	State	Total justice system	Police protec- tion	Judicial and legal	Correc- tions
Total	**669**	**293**	**136**	**239**	Missouri	471	241	82	148
Alabama	465	225	88	151	Montana	579	235	133	211
Alaska	1,054	382	310	363	Nebraska	499	228	90	181
Arizona	739	332	155	253	Nevada	879	414	169	295
Arkansas	425	176	74	175	New Hampshire	468	241	100	127
California	1,031	405	252	373	New Jersey	760	355	167	238
Colorado	630	287	104	238	New Mexico	741	304	157	279
Connecticut	678	285	189	204	New York	911	418	196	297
Delaware	823	324	178	322	North Carolina	506	240	73	192
District of Columbia	1,632	998	182	451	North Dakota	410	185	94	131
Florida	753	367	126	259	Ohio	586	270	144	172
Georgia	579	237	105	237	Oklahoma	488	210	84	194
Hawaii	680	261	249	170	Oregon	647	269	110	268
Idaho	524	210	111	203	Pennsylvania	598	228	125	245
Illinois	584	328	102	153	Rhode Island	632	302	113	216
Indiana	438	190	81	167	South Carolina	452	219	71	162
Iowa	463	204	111	147	South Dakota	449	175	83	191
Kansas	508	244	98	166	Tennessee	487	238	95	154
Kentucky	438	164	102	172	Texas	536	231	90	214
Louisiana	722	302	141	279	Utah	535	232	117	185
Maine	424	177	85	162	Vermont	529	224	114	192
Maryland	763	326	138	299	Virginia	597	258	102	238
Massachusetts	649	284	149	217	Washington	608	221	123	264
Michigan	598	243	109	246	West Virginia	425	174	101	150
Minnesota	594	293	126	175	Wisconsin	637	276	105	257
Mississippi	441	201	74	166	Wyoming	956	319	186	451

Source: U.S. Department of Justice, Bureau of Justice Statistics, "Justice Expenditure and Employment Extracts, 2008," Series NCJ 237912, May 2012, <http://bjs.ojp.usdoj.gov/index.cfm?ty=pbdetail&iid=4333>.

Table 341. Denials of Firearm Transfer Applications by Reason and Agency Type: 1999 to 2009

[In percent. Reasons for denials are based on The Brady Handgun Violence Prevention Act, pursuant to 18 U.S.C. 922 and state laws. Denial occurs when an applicant is prohibited from receiving a firearm or a permit that can be used to receive a firearm because a disqualifying factor was found during a background check. Application for firearm transfer is information submitted by a person to a state or local checking agency to purchase a firearm or obtain a permit that can be used for a purchase. Information may be submitted directly to a checking agency or forwarded by a prospective seller]

Reason for denial	2008			2009			1999-2009		
	FBI [1]	State	Local	FBI [1]	State	Local	FBI [1]	State	Local
Felony indictment/conviction	55.9	45.7	23.8	48.5	39.4	21.7	64.5	52.8	26.4
State law prohibition	6.8	10.5	5.4	11.2	10.7	6.3	2.6	7.7	12.4
Domestic violence	11.4	13.9	16.6	11.5	13.5	15.8	16	13.6	13.5
Misdemeanor conviction	7.3	9.9	14.4	7.2	10.2	13.9	11.6	10.1	11.6
Restraining order	4.1	4.0	2.2	4.3	3.3	1.9	4.4	3.5	1.9
Fugitive	13.4	8.6	1.1	16.8	7.1	1.0	6.6	6.8	1.3
Illegal alien	1.4	0.5	0.5	1.0	0.3	0.7	1.3	0.4	0.5
Mental illness or disability	1.1	3.7	5.3	1.4	6.2	5.3	0.6	2.5	4.4
Drug user/addict	9.5	3.1	12.9	9.3	1.6	15.2	7.7	1.1	8.9
Local law prohibition	(X)	–	4.7	(X)	(NA)	1.5	(X)	(NA)	5.1
Other prohibitions [2]	0.6	13.9	29.7	0.3	21.2	32.5	0.7	15.1	27.5

– Represents zero. NA not available. X not applicable. [1] During 2008 the FBI began a new classification system and reclassified all denials from 1999 to 2008. [2] Includes juveniles, persons dishonorably discharged from the Armed Services, persons who have renounced their U.S. citizenship, and other unspecified persons.

Source: U.S. Department of Justice, Bureau of Justice Statistics, "Background Checks For Firearm Transfers, 2009 - Statistical Tables," October 2010. See also: <http://bjs.ojp.usdoj.gov/index.cfm?ty=pbse&sid=13>.

Table 342. U.S. Supreme Court—Cases Filed and Disposition: 1980 to 2010

[Statutory term of court begins first Monday in October]

Action	1980	1990	1995	2000	2005	2007	2008	2009	2010
Total cases on docket............	**5,144**	**6,316**	**7,565**	**8,965**	**9,608**	**9,602**	**8,966**	**9,302**	**9,066**
Appellate cases on docket.............	2,749	2,351	2,456	2,305	2,025	1,969	1,941	1,908	1,895
From prior term......................	527	365	361	351	354	355	345	328	337
Docketed during present term........	2,222	1,986	2,095	1,954	1,671	1,614	1,596	1,580	1,558
Cases acted upon......................	2,324	2,042	2,130	2,024	1,703	1,666	1,654	1,607	1,618
Granted review.....................	167	114	92	85	63	85	78	69	76
Denied, dismissed, or withdrawn....	1,999	1,802	1,945	1,842	1,554	1,529	1,505	1,452	1,461
Summarily decided..................	90	81	62	63	46	30	29	45	45
Cases not acted upon.................	425	309	326	281	322	303	287	301	277
Pauper cases on docket..............	2,371	3,951	5,098	6,651	7,575	7,628	7,021	7,388	7,167
Cases acted upon [1]...................	2,027	3,436	4,514	5,736	6,533	6,753	6,214	6,524	6,250
Granted review.....................	17	27	13	14	15	10	9	8	14
Denied, dismissed, or withdrawn....	1,968	3,369	4,439	5,658	6,459	6,562	6,136	6,465	6,195
Summarily decided..................	32	28	55	61	58	175	65	46	37
Cases not acted upon.................	344	515	584	915	1,042	875	807	864	917
Original cases on docket.............	24	14	11	9	8	5	4	6	4
Cases disposed of during term........	7	3	5	2	4	1	1	2	2
Total cases available for argument.........................	**264**	**201**	**145**	**138**	**122**	**125**	**136**	**125**	**131**
Cases disposed of.......................	162	131	93	89	87	78	88	86	88
Cases argued...........................	154	125	90	86	88	75	87	82	86
Cases dismissed or remanded without argument....................	8	6	3	3	1	3	1	4	2
Cases remaining........................	102	70	52	49	31	47	48	40	43
Cases decided by signed opinion......	144	121	87	83	82	72	83	77	83
Cases decided by per curiam opinion................................	8	4	3	4	5	2	3	4	3
Number of signed opinions.............	123	112	75	77	69	67	74	73	75

[1] Includes cases granted review and carried over to next term, not shown separately.

Source: Office of the Clerk, Supreme Court of the United States, unpublished data.

Table 343. Judicial Caseloads for the Federal Judiciary: 2000 to 2011

[For 12 month period ending June 30]

Judicial caseload	2000	2005	2007	2008	2009	2010	2011
U.S. Courts of Appeals:							
Cases filed.........................	54,642	67,999	58,809	59,406	59,399	56,097	55,353
Cases terminated...................	56,509	59,577	63,916	59,152	60,144	59,343	58,146
Cases pending......................	40,815	57,349	51,849	52,478	50,954	46,816	44,023
U.S. District Courts Civil:							
Cases filed.........................	263,049	282,758	272,067	256,354	257,204	285,215	289,630
Cases terminated...................	260,277	280,455	249,960	230,930	255,361	295,908	301,773
Cases pending......................	247,973	266,938	260,769	295,414	298,493	285,071	272,934
Criminal (includes transfers):							
Cases filed.........................	62,523	69,876	67,503	70,024	75,324	78,213	78,764
Defendants filed....................	84,147	92,356	88,006	91,782	96,718	100,031	102,605
Cases terminated...................	57,543	65,239	67,791	69,008	74,478	77,633	78,855
Cases pending......................	46,796	70,692	73,419	75,566	78,186	80,506	80,415
U.S. Bankruptcy Courts:							
Cases filed.........................	1,276,922	1,637,254	751,056	967,831	1,306,315	1,572,597	1,529,560
Cases terminated...................	1,271,300	1,583,959	862,382	929,206	1,109,993	1,441,419	1,486,950
Cases pending......................	1,396,916	1,748,038	1,312,016	1,325,220	1,527,073	1,659,399	1,702,005
Post-conviction supervision:							
Persons under supervision.........................	99,577	113,008	115,930	120,051	123,839	126,642	129,319
Pretrial services:							
Total cases activated.............................	86,067	98,946	95,955	98,862	103,610	110,666	113,120
Pretrial services cases activated..............	84,107	97,045	94,384	97,315	102,434	109,711	112,181
Pretrial diversion cases activated.............	1,960	1,901	1,571	1,547	1,176	965	939
Total released on supervision..................	31,607	34,348	32,361	32,460	29,937	29,748	30,265
Pretrial supervision..........................	31,927	32,438	30,865	31,089	28,754	28,440	28,903
Diversion supervision........................	2,166	1,910	1,496	1,371	1,183	1,308	1,362

Source: Administrative Office of the United States Courts, Statistical Tables for the Federal Judiciary, <http://www.uscourts.gov/Statistics/StatisticalTablesForTheFederalJudiciary.aspx>.

Table 344. U.S. District Courts—Civil Cases Filed: by Basis of Jurisdiction and Nature of Suit: 2006 to 2011

[For years ending June 30]

Type of case	Cases filed					
	2006	2007	2008	2009	2010	2011
Cases total [1]	**244,343**	**272,067**	**256,354**	**257,204**	**285,215**	**289,630**
BASIS OF JURISDICTION						
U.S. cases:						
U.S. plaintiff	9,693	9,218	9,868	9,030	8,427	10,282
U.S. defendant	35,194	35,299	35,527	33,286	34,306	36,502
Private cases:						
Federal question	133,656	141,044	134,623	133,697	137,776	141,334
Diversity of citizenship	65,800	86,506	76,284	81,188	104,703	101,508
NATURE OF SUIT						
Contract actions [1]	28,139	34,071	34,818	35,229	31,461	32,366
Recovery of overpayments [2]	2,856	3,053	3,491	3,214	3,079	4,623
Real property actions [1]	4,761	4,456	5,607	5,413	6,809	10,078
Foreclosure	2,982	2,441	2,689	2,639	3,836	6,569
Tort actions	53,809	77,257	59,588	61,936	87,256	79,394
Personal injury	49,834	73,004	55,777	57,332	82,057	74,921
Personal injury product liability [1]	32,515	51,557	39,664	43,055	66,958	60,631
Other personal injury [1]	17,319	21,447	16,113	14,277	15,099	14,290
Medical malpractice	1,158	1,234	1,242	1,076	1,120	1,089
Personal property damage	3,975	4,253	3,811	4,604	5,199	4,473
Actions under statutes [1]	157,536	156,152	156,277	154,572	159,683	167,791
Bankruptcy suits	3,193	3,182	2,630	2,334	2,615	2,597
Civil rights [1]	33,417	31,975	31,632	33,188	34,427	37,000
Employment	14,851	13,608	13,036	13,778	14,343	15,255
Environmental matters	874	763	900	735	826	881
Prisoner petitions	55,775	53,222	55,374	52,237	52,450	53,692
Forfeiture and penalty	2,318	2,221	2,324	2,322	2,297	2,372
Labor laws	16,853	18,630	16,685	17,153	18,878	18,025
Immigration	(NA)	(NA)	1,110	2,166	1,262	1,097
Protected property rights [3]	11,745	11,132	9,636	8,714	8,519	9,944
Securities commodities and exchanges	1,654	1,369	1,669	1,720	1,442	1,394
Social security laws	14,052	12,964	13,329	13,222	13,725	15,697
Tax suits	1,498	1,485	1,448	1,411	1,171	1,217
Freedom of information	309	325	294	279	315	354
Other actions	98	131	64	54	6	1

NA Not available. [1] Includes other types not shown separately. [2] Includes enforcement of judgments in student loan cases, and overpayments of veterans' benefits. [3] Includes copyright, patent, and trademark rights.

Source: Administrative Office of the United States Courts, "Statistical Tables for the Federal Judiciary," <http://www.uscourts.gov/Statistics/StatisticalTablesForTheFederalJudiciary.aspx>.

Table 345. U.S. Courts of Appeals—Nature of Suit or Offense in Cases Arising From the U.S. District Courts: 2000 to 2011

[For 12-month periods ending June 30. Excludes data for the U.S. Court of Appeals for the Federal Circuit. Includes appeals reopened, remanded, and reinstated (after being terminated due to procedural defaults) as well as original appeals]

Nature of suit and offense	2000	2005	2007	2008	2009	2010	2011
Total cases	**46,682**	**48,907**	**43,789**	**43,671**	**45,490**	**43,880**	**43,113**
Criminal cases	10,570	15,831	13,583	13,011	14,259	12,863	12,412
Civil cases	36,112	33,076	30,206	30,660	31,231	31,017	30,701
U.S cases	8,707	9,055	7,541	7,688	8,536	7,772	7,427
U.S. plaintiff	615	356	387	386	382	435	364
U.S. defendant	8,092	8,699	7,154	7,302	8,154	7,337	7,063
Private cases	27,405	24,021	22,665	22,972	22,695	23,245	23,274
Federal question	24,155	21,000	19,998	20,289	20,044	20,599	20,412
Diversity of citizenship	3,239	3,020	2,664	2,678	2,651	2,646	2,860
General local jurisdiction	11	1	3	5	–	–	2
Criminal cases	10,570	15,831	13,583	13,011	14,259	12,863	12,412
Violent offenses	683	768	703	637	653	621	658
Property offenses	1,520	1,974	1,626	1,585	1,526	1,624	1,630
Drug offenses	4,388	5,962	5,237	5,125	6,519	5,066	4,444
Firearms, explosives offenses	1,029	2,488	2,057	1,947	1,997	1,927	1,749
Sex offenses	190	403	520	611	657	651	708
Justice system offenses	179	216	185	166	172	142	147
Immigration offenses	1,109	2,888	2,198	1,663	1,644	1,787	1,736
General offenses	579	553	574	484	432	411	369
Other	893	579	483	793	659	634	971

– Represents or rounds to zero.

Source: Administrative Office of the United States Courts, "Statistical Tables for the Federal Judiciary," <http://www.uscourts.gov/Statistics/StatisticalTablesForTheFederalJudiciary.aspx>.

Table 346. Total Incoming Caseloads in State Trial Courts by Case Category: 2009

[Represents total incoming caseloads (i.e., new filings, plus reopened and reactivated cases when provided) as reported to the Court Statistics Project for 2009. Some figures may be incomplete and/or overinclusive. Since state court caseload statistics should only be viewed in the context of each state's court structure, comparisons of the data reported here should not be made without additional information]

State	Total	Civil [1]	Domestic relations [2]	Criminal [3]	Juvenile [4]	Traffic/ violations [5]
United States.............	105,929,999	19,511,237	5,724,189	20,705,784	1,970,190	58,018,599
Alabama......................	2,011,992	221,044	93,050	282,940	52,361	1,362,597
Alaska........................	154,543	25,487	13,355	37,526	2,620	75,555
Arizona.......................	2,841,926	376,615	140,037	734,871	22,115	1,568,288
Arkansas....................	1,502,986	125,032	53,020	572,790	25,666	726,478
California.....................	10,255,311	1,298,536	458,814	1,673,973	137,960	6,686,028
Colorado.....................	1,034,221	330,115	51,741	185,279	21,426	445,660
Connecticut.................	916,166	261,678	39,081	179,844	27,429	408,134
Delaware....................	548,926	67,450	41,835	399,149	7,554	32,938
District of Columbia......	120,721	68,460	12,052	33,280	4,386	2,543
Florida........................	5,385,408	1,476,089	495,872	1,236,975	180,602	1,995,870
Georgia......................	4,384,245	1,005,587	170,483	655,840	101,526	2,450,809
Hawaii........................	591,660	35,487	13,757	95,567	17,220	429,629
Idaho.........................	480,779	79,546	25,148	120,960	14,700	240,425
Illinois........................	4,106,892	667,160	142,839	479,804	30,257	2,786,832
Indiana.......................	1,988,376	490,237	105,213	302,343	58,995	1,031,588
Iowa..........................	1,055,583	178,725	44,654	92,969	12,940	726,295
Kansas.......................	994,777	195,843	39,175	57,566	18,482	683,711
Kentucky....................	1,004,040	273,496	82,077	240,660	41,669	366,138
Louisiana....................	2,006,950	270,948	58,373	370,146	46,925	1,260,558
Maine.........................	283,010	47,041	15,144	68,515	4,809	147,501
Maryland.....................	2,180,375	1,067,943	99,475	305,324	38,913	668,720
Massachusetts.............	1,115,459	452,054	109,868	269,765	37,926	245,846
Michigan.....................	4,130,019	767,488	123,844	957,817	54,452	2,226,418
Minnesota...................	1,613,389	224,966	48,910	90,117	48,731	1,200,665
Mississippi..................	180,200	106,061	72,887	(NA)	1,252	(NA)
Missouri......................	2,262,008	337,078	129,284	178,958	14,948	1,601,740
Montana......................	354,793	63,388	14,025	51,630	2,309	223,441
Nebraska.....................	465,974	138,483	14,429	129,388	11,514	172,160
Nevada.......................	1,060,201	188,743	57,507	160,342	24,263	629,346
New Hampshire.............	216,595	54,616	4,421	81,900	2,075	73,583
New Jersey..................	7,649,907	922,471	229,932	783,815	68,963	5,644,726
New Mexico..................	443,730	100,759	41,678	118,866	7,011	175,416
New York.....................	4,513,663	1,819,981	672,459	754,171	123,856	1,143,196
North Carolina..............	3,371,327	605,155	116,711	1,843,906	36,633	768,922
North Dakota................	190,066	33,170	17,303	40,998	9,205	89,390
Ohio...........................	3,911,704	840,353	249,310	865,742	139,705	1,816,594
Oklahoma....................	580,655	215,611	36,911	116,697	11,493	199,943
Oregon [6]..................	611,641	202,283	45,318	93,433	17,152	253,455
Pennsylvania [7]..........	3,698,601	416,015	365,443	528,740	55,625	2,332,778
Rhode Island...............	210,778	62,453	13,513	40,139	8,883	85,790
South Carolina.............	1,833,128	334,305	59,840	760,310	17,097	661,576
South Dakota...............	251,026	61,997	17,017	27,639	9,776	134,597
Tennessee...................	469,326	71,577	88,765	170,308	138,676	(NA)
Texas.........................	12,943,692	853,897	383,149	2,497,907	44,257	9,164,482
Utah..........................	879,101	150,985	23,517	120,014	46,967	537,618
Vermont......................	185,542	24,497	21,841	17,831	2,115	119,258
Virginia.......................	4,214,212	994,926	347,970	1,148,499	91,055	1,631,762
Washington..................	2,782,932	295,708	69,435	361,229	41,127	2,015,433
West Virginia................	417,158	83,766	56,439	138,010	9,071	129,872
Wisconsin....................	1,020,385	302,611	53,834	134,345	17,221	512,374
Wyoming.....................	202,644	41,125	8,506	29,682	1,544	121,787
Puerto Rico..................	301,256	182,196	34,928	67,265	6,733	10,134

NA Not available. [1] Includes tort, contract, real property, small claims, probate, mental health, and civil appeals cases. [2] Includes divorce/dissolution, paternity, custody, support, visitation, adoption, and civil protection/restraining order cases. [3] Includes felony, misdemeanor, and appeals from limited jurisdiction courts. [4] Includes delinquency, dependency, and status offense petitions. [5] Includes non-criminal traffic violations (infractions), parking violations, and ordinance violations. [6] Data for Oregon are for 2008. [7] Data for Pennsylvania are preliminary 2009.

Source: National Center for State Courts, Court Statistics Project, "State Court Caseload Statistics," <http://www.courtstatistics.org/Other-Pages/StateCourtCaseloadStatistics.aspx>, accessed May 2012 (copyright).

Table 347. U.S. District Courts—National Petit and Grand Juror Service: 2007 to 2011

[For years ending September 30. Includes data on jury selection days only. Data on juror service after the selection day are not included]

Juror service	2007	2008	2009	2010	2011
PETIT JUROR SERVICE					
Jurors present for jury selection or orientation	307,204	297,820	282,668	262,376	249,266
Percent selected	23.3	23.0	22.2	22.7	23.0
Percent challenged	38.6	39.8	37.9	38.5	39.4
Percent not selected or challenged	38.1	37.3	39.9	38.7	37.7
Voir Dire [1]	24.0	24.2	24.9	24.9	25.0
Non-Voir Dire [2]	13.3	13.2	15.0	13.9	12.7
Total juries selected	6,139	6,039	5,378	5,332	5,565
GRAND JUROR SERVICE					
Juries serving	733	749	766	784	799
Sessions convened	9,279	9,357	9,257	9,277	9,083
Jurors in session	185,083	186,586	186,194	186,020	182,106
Average per session	19.9	19.9	20.1	20.1	20.0
Hours in session	45,197	44,731	44,676	44,845	43,083
Average per session	4.9	4.8	4.8	4.8	4.7

[1] Jurors who completed pre-screening questionnaires or were in the courtroom during the conducting of voir dire. [2] Other jurors not selected or challenged who were not called to the courtroom or otherwise did not participate in the actual voir dire.

Source: Administrative Office of the United States Courts, *Judicial Business of the United States Courts,* annual. See also <http://www.uscourts.gov/Statistics/JudicialBusiness.aspx>.

Table 348. Federal Prosecutions of Public Corruption: 1990 to 2010

[As of December 31. Prosecution of persons who have corrupted public office in violation of Federal Criminal Statutes]

Prosecution status	1990 Charged	1990 Convicted	1990 Awaiting trial	2000 Charged	2000 Convicted	2000 Awaiting trial	2005 Charged	2005 Convicted	2005 Awaiting trial	2010 Charged	2010 Convicted	2010 Awaiting trial
Total [1]	**1,176**	**1,084**	**300**	**1,000**	**938**	**327**	**1,163**	**1,027**	**453**	**1,184**	**1,036**	**554**
Federal officials	615	583	103	441	422	92	445	390	118	422	397	103
State officials	96	79	28	92	91	37	96	94	51	168	108	105
Local officials	257	225	98	211	183	89	309	232	148	296	280	146
Others involved	208	197	71	256	242	109	313	311	136	298	251	200

[1] Includes individuals who are neither public officials nor employees, but were involved with public officials or employees in violating the law, not shown separately.

Source: U.S. Department of Justice, Criminal Division, *Report to Congress on the Activities and Operations of the Public Integrity Section.* See also <http://www.justice.gov/criminal/pin/>.

Table 349. Felony Convictions in State Courts: 2000 to 2006

[In 2006, an estimated 1,205,273 persons were convicted of a felony (federal and state courts). Of that number, 1,132,290 were convicted in state courts, the vast majority (94 percent) of whom pleaded guilty. At the time of sentencing, about 3 out of 4 felons sentenced (77 percent) were sentenced for a single felony]

Most serious conviction	Felony convictions in state courts							
	2000 Number	2000 Percent	2002 Number	2002 Percent	2004 Number	2004 Percent	2006 Number	2006 Percent
All offenses	924,700	100.0	1,051,000	100.0	1,078,920	100.0	1,132,290	100.0
Violent offenses	173,200	18.7	197,030	18.8	194,570	18.0	206,140	18.2
Murder [1]	8,600	0.9	8,990	0.9	8,400	0.8	8,670	0.8
Rape/Sexual assault	31,500	3.4	35,500	3.4	33,190	3.1	33,200	2.9
Robbery	36,800	4.0	38,430	3.7	38,850	3.6	41,740	3.7
Aggravated assault	79,400	8.6	95,600	9.1	94,380	8.7	100,560	8.9
Other violent [2]	17,000	1.8	18,510	1.8	19,750	1.8	21,980	1.9
Property offenses	262,000	28.3	325,200	30.9	310,680	28.8	321,570	28.4
Burglary	79,300	8.6	100,640	9.6	93,870	8.7	99,910	8.8
Larceny [3]	100,000	10.8	124,320	11.8	119,340	11.1	125,390	11.1
Fraud/forgery [4]	82,700	8.9	100,240	9.5	97,470	9.0	96,260	8.5
Drug offenses	319,700	34.6	340,330	32.4	362,850	33.6	377,860	33.4
Possession	116,300	12.6	127,530	12.1	161,090	14.9	165,360	14.6
Trafficking	203,400	22.0	212,810	20.2	201,760	18.7	212,490	18.8
Weapon offenses	28,200	3.1	32,470	3.1	33,010	3.1	38,010	3.4
Other offenses [5]	141,600	15.3	155,970	14.8	177,810	16.5	188,730	16.7

[1] A small number of cases were classified as nonnegligent manslaughter when it was unclear if the conviction offense was murder or nonnegligent manslaughter. [2] Includes offenses such as negligent manslaughter and kidnapping. [3] When vehicle theft could not be distinguished from other theft, the case was coded as "other theft." This results in a conservative estimate of vehicle thefts. [4] Includes embezzlement. [5] Composed of nonviolent offenses such as receiving stolen property and vandalism.

Source: U.S. Department of Justice, Office of Justice Programs, Bureau of Justice Statistics, *Criminal Sentencing Statistics*, Series NCJ 226846, December 2009. See <http://bjs.ojp.usdoj.gov/index.cfm?ty=pbdetail&iid=2152>.

Table 350. Delinquency Cases Disposed by Juvenile Courts by Type of Offense: 1990 to 2009

[In thousands (1,346 represents 1,346,000), except rate. A delinquency offense is an act committed by a juvenile for which an adult could be prosecuted in a criminal court. Disposition of a case involves taking a definite action such as waiving the case to criminal court, dismissing the case, placing the youth on probation, placing the youth in a facility for delinquents, or such actions as fines, restitution, and community service]

Type of offense	1990	1995	2000	2001	2002	2003	2004	2005	2006	2007	2008	2009
All delinquency offenses.............	**1,346**	**1,824**	**1,707**	**1,687**	**1,676**	**1,683**	**1,689**	**1,699**	**1,643**	**1,647**	**1,635**	**1,504**
Case rate [1]............................	52.5	63.6	55.5	54.3	53.4	53.4	53.5	53.8	52.2	52.8	53.0	49.3
Person offenses [2].........................	257	405	399	405	404	411	419	434	415	410	401	366
Criminal homicide.....................	2	3	1	1	1	1	1	1	1	1	1	1
Forcible rape........................	4	6	4	4	4	4	4	5	4	4	4	4
Robbery................................	28	42	22	22	21	21	21	26	30	31	32	30
Aggravated assault....................	54	79	55	53	50	52	52	55	53	52	50	46
Property offenses [2].....................	783	919	698	660	655	645	631	615	588	599	613	567
Burglary..............................	148	152	118	113	111	111	105	102	105	105	108	99
Larceny-theft........................	348	434	323	301	299	292	291	276	248	261	281	273
Motor vehicle theft....................	70	54	38	38	38	38	34	32	29	27	23	20
Arson................................	7	11	9	9	9	8	9	8	9	8	8	7
Drug law violations.....................	71	163	186	191	184	183	185	185	182	183	178	167
Public order offenses [2].................	235	337	424	431	434	445	454	465	458	454	443	404
Obstruction of justice.................	89	133	217	217	212	217	210	213	209	209	206	197
Disorderly conduct....................	57	93	102	108	117	120	131	133	129	129	125	110
Weapons offenses.....................	31	46	34	34	32	35	39	43	44	41	39	33
Liquor law violations..................	17	14	20	19	19	20	21	20	22	23	21	19
Nonviolent sex offenses................	11	10	14	14	14	14	14	13	12	11	11	11

[1] Number of cases disposed per 1,000 juveniles (ages 10 to upper age of juvenile court jurisdiction). The upper age of juvenile court jurisdiction is defined by statute in each state. [2] Total includes other offenses not shown.

Source: National Center for Juvenile Justice, Pittsburgh, PA, *Juvenile Court Statistics*, annual (copyright), <www.ncjj.org>. See also <http://ojjdp.gov/ojstatbb/ezajcs/>.

Table 351. Delinquency Cases Disposed by Juvenile Courts by Type of Offense, Sex, and Race: 1995 to 2009

[See headnote, Table 350]

Sex, race, and offense	Number of cases disposed				Case rate [1]			
	1995	2000	2005	2009	1995	2000	2005	2009
Male, total........................	**1,414,700**	**1,274,600**	**1,232,200**	**1,088,600**	**96.0**	**80.8**	**76.2**	**69.6**
Person..............................	304,800	287,300	304,900	257,000	20.7	18.2	18.8	16.4
Property............................	711,400	520,500	445,200	401,000	48.3	33.0	27.5	25.6
Drugs...............................	139,600	155,600	149,100	137,300	9.5	9.9	9.2	8.8
Public order........................	258,900	311,100	332,900	293,300	17.6	19.7	20.6	18.8
Female, total......................	**409,700**	**432,700**	**466,900**	**415,600**	**29.3**	**28.9**	**30.3**	**27.9**
Person..............................	100,700	111,300	129,300	108,700	7.2	7.4	8.4	7.3
Property............................	207,600	177,900	169,500	166,200	14.9	11.9	11.0	11.2
Drugs...............................	23,800	30,400	36,000	29,800	1.7	2.0	2.3	2.0
Public order........................	77,700	113,100	132,100	110,900	5.6	7.6	8.6	7.4
White, total.......................	**1,230,900**	**1,166,100**	**1,088,600**	**955,400**	**53.9**	**48.3**	**44.4**	**40.3**
Person..............................	242,300	250,300	247,500	208,300	10.6	10.4	10.1	8.8
Property............................	660,300	492,000	415,900	371,300	28.9	20.4	17.0	15.7
Drugs...............................	107,800	136,600	135,500	125,100	4.7	5.7	5.5	5.3
Public order........................	220,600	287,100	289,700	250,700	9.7	11.9	11.8	10.6
Black, total.......................	**544,200**	**492,000**	**561,300**	**505,600**	**125.0**	**101.7**	**108.4**	**103.2**
Person..............................	153,200	138,300	176,100	148,200	35.2	28.6	34.0	30.2
Property............................	230,300	182,000	178,100	177,600	52.9	37.6	34.4	36.3
Drugs...............................	52,800	45,000	44,700	37,400	12.1	9.3	8.6	7.6
Public order........................	107,800	126,800	162,500	142,400	24.8	26.2	31.4	29.1
American Indian, total..........	**26,200**	**25,800**	**25,000**	**21,900**	**69.4**	**56.7**	**54.4**	**50.9**
Person..............................	5,100	5,300	5,700	5,000	13.6	11.6	12.3	11.6
Property............................	15,100	12,500	10,200	8,700	39.9	27.5	22.1	20.2
Drugs...............................	1,500	2,500	2,900	2,500	4.0	5.5	6.3	5.9
Public order........................	4,500	5,500	6,300	5,700	11.9	12.1	13.7	13.2
Asian, total.......................	**23,100**	**23,400**	**24,200**	**21,200**	**20.7**	**18.1**	**17.1**	**14.2**
Person..............................	4,900	4,800	5,000	4,200	4.4	3.7	3.6	2.8
Property............................	13,200	11,900	10,500	9,500	11.9	9.2	7.5	6.4
Drugs...............................	1,200	1,900	2,100	2,100	1.1	1.4	1.5	1.4
Public order........................	3,700	4,800	6,500	5,400	3.3	3.7	4.6	3.6

[1] Cases per 1,000 juveniles (ages 10 to upper age of juvenile court jurisdiction). The upper age of juvenile court jurisdiction is defined by statute in each state.

Source: National Center for Juvenile Justice, Pittsburgh, PA, *Juvenile Court Statistics*, annual, (Copyright), <http://www.ncjj.org/>. See also <http://ojjdp.gov/ojstatbb/ezajcs/>.

Table 352. Child Abuse and Neglect Victims by Selected Characteristics: 2004 to 2010

[Based on State submissions to National Child Abuse and Neglect Data System (NCANDS) of alleged child abuse and neglect. NCANDS collects case level data on children who received child protective services response in the form of an investigative or alternative response. Each state has its own definition of child abuse and neglect based on standards set by federal law. Child abuse is defined as any recent act or failure to act on the part of a parent or caretaker which results in death, serious physical or emotional harm, or sexual abuse or exploitation; or an act or failure to act which presents an imminent risk or serious harm. See source for more information]

Item	FY2004	FY2005	FY2006	FY2007	FY2008	FY2009	FY2010
TYPES OF MALTREATMENT [1]							
Victims, total [2,3,4]................	**714,844**	**792,685**	**809,494**	**690,849**	**704,732**	**693,507**	**688,251**
Neglect................	452,284	505,737	522,914	489,275	504,717	502,417	499,691
Physical abuse................	135,042	139,783	137,678	118,137	121,735	120,510	118,502
Sexual abuse................	71,805	79,486	75,638	68,024	68,156	64,358	62,057
Emotional maltreatment................	46,784	57,420	56,500	49,848	49,947	50,466	53,426
Medical neglect................	14,238	16,728	18,572	15,597	16,067	16,373	15,711
Other and unknown................	110,112	119,728	132,880	58,035	61,083	64,394	68,590
SEX OF VICTIM [2]							
Victims, total................	**714,844**	**792,685**	**809,494**	**690,849**	**704,732**	**693,507**	**688,251**
Male................	344,328	381,364	390,269	332,445	340,300	334,404	333,864
Female................	367,769	408,784	416,591	356,226	361,787	354,677	352,174
AGE OF VICTIM [2]							
Victims, total................	**714,844**	**792,685**	**809,494**	**690,849**	**704,732**	**693,507**	**688,251**
1 year and younger................	121,285	139,541	147,146	132,122	138,231	136,502	136,910
2 to 5 years old................	176,754	197,372	201,295	171,332	175,573	177,126	180,271
6 to 9 years old................	157,043	171,686	176,500	150,593	152,196	147,812	145,354
10 to 13 years old................	144,726	154,171	150,719	123,127	123,805	120,577	119,555
14 to 17 years old................	111,736	125,830	129,686	108,228	111,493	108,633	103,764
18 years old and over................	430	436	500	398	627	638	490

[1] Not all states use this taxonomy, nor do states define the categories in the same way. [2] Total victims is the sum of the states contributing data to the Child File. The number of states not contributing data varies by year. [3] This is a count of the number of distinct victims of the specified types of maltreatment. [4] A child may be a victim of more than one type of maltreatment, so the sum of types is greater than the count of victims.

Source: U.S. Department of Health and Human Services, Administration for Children and Families, Administration on Children, Youth and Families, Children's Bureau, *Child Maltreatment 2010*, annual. See also <http://www.acf.hhs.gov/programs/cb/pubs/cm10/index.htm>.

Table 353. Child Abuse and Neglect Cases Reported, Investigated, and Number of Child Victims by State: 2010

[See headnote, Table 352. Duplicate counts of child victims]

State and outlying area	Population under 18 years old	Number of reports [1]	Number of children subject of an investigation [2,3]	Number of child victims [3]	State and outlying area	Population under 18 years old	Number of reports [1]	Number of children subject of an investigation [2,3]	Number of child victims [3]
U.S.......	**75,512,062**	**1,987,086**	**3,604,100**	**753,655**	MT.........	219,828	7,419	12,904	1,442
AL.........	1,128,864	19,900	29,508	9,586	NE.........	451,641	13,138	30,994	5,051
AK.........	183,546	5,240	9,079	3,147	NV.........	681,033	12,108	24,743	4,947
AZ.........	1,732,019	25,580	59,422	6,258	NH.........	289,071	7,909	11,646	899
AR.........	709,968	34,532	73,257	12,591	NJ.........	2,045,848	60,168	93,833	9,546
CA.........	9,435,682	228,535	439,306	82,879	NM.........	510,238	16,622	27,122	6,018
CO.........	1,227,763	32,969	51,132	11,720	NY.........	4,424,083	169,395	282,132	88,842
CT.........	807,985	25,777	38,814	10,846	NC.........	2,277,967	66,136	137,672	23,938
DE.........	206,993	6,681	15,830	2,204	ND.........	143,971	3,871	6,915	1,144
DC.........	114,036	5,806	14,411	2,810	OH.........	2,714,341	71,811	108,854	33,947
FL.........	4,057,773	151,441	332,469	53,969	OK.........	918,849	28,583	48,895	7,728
GA.........	2,583,792	26,011	64,019	20,567	OR.........	872,811	29021	46,478	11734
HI.........	290,361	2,668	5,096	1,795	PA.........	2,775,132	24,840	24,840	3,706
ID.........	419,190	6,643	10,614	1,664	RI.........	226,825	6,825	10,378	3,620
IL.........	3,177,377	65,761	142,816	28,530	SC.........	1,080,732	18,803	43,155	12,191
IN.........	1,589,365	66,735	104,287	23,095	SD.........	199,616	3,838	7,208	1,435
IA.........	713,155	24,982	39,257	13,449	TN.........	1,493,252	59,487	95,541	9,066
KS.........	704,951	17,379	26,155	1,552	TX.........	6,895,969	175,168	297,188	67,269
KY.........	1,014,323	49,141	74,864	18,332	UT.........	868,824	20,043	32,299	13,712
LA.........	1,123,386	21,822	35,443	8,848	VT.........	126,275	3,795	4,834	705
ME.........	271,176	6,077	10,187	3,483	VA.........	1,847,182	33,996	69,952	6,621
MD.........	1,351,935	26,294	37,109	13,955	WA.........	1,569,592	34,621	51,037	7,108
MA.........	1,433,002	39,825	77,863	26,588	WV.........	386,449	17,686	39,469	4,133
MI.........	2,349,892	77,286	194,719	35,497	WI.........	1,310,250	26,521	39,494	4,876
MN.........	1,260,797	17,803	25,341	4,668	WY.........	132,025	3,213	6,895	744
MS.........	767,742	19,976	32,108	7,968					
MO.........	1,431,338	50,969	74,026	5,509	PR.........	963,847	16,236	32,490	11,723

[1] Once an allegation of abuse and neglect is received by a child protective services (CPS) agency, it is either screened in for further attention by CPS agency or it is screened out. A screened-in referral is called a report. [2] The number of "Children Subject of an Investigation" is based on the total number of children who were included in an investigation or assessment. [3] Maltreatment acted upon by a CPS agency in the form of an investigative or alternative response.

Source: U.S. Department of Health and Human Services, Administration for Children and Families, Administration on Children, Youth and Families, Children's Bureau, *Child Maltreatment 2010*, annual. See also <http://www.acf.hhs.gov/programs/cb/stats_research/index.htm#can>.

Table 354. Prisoners Under Jurisdiction of Federal or State Correctional Authorities—Summary by State: 1990 to 2010

[For years ending December 31. Jurisdiction refers to the legal authority over a prisoner, regardless of where held]

State	1990	2000	2005	2009	2010	State	1990	2000	2005	2009	2010
U.S. [1]	773,919	1,391,261	1,527,929	1,614,355	1,605,127						
Federal	65,526	145,416	187,618	208,118	209,771	MS	8,375	20,241	20,515	21,482	21,067
State	708,393	1,245,845	1,340,311	1,406,237	1,395,356	MO	14,943	27,543	30,823	30,563	30,623
						MT	1,425	3,105	3,532	3,605	3,716
AL	15,665	26,332	27,888	31,874	31,764	NE	2,403	3,895	4,455	4,474	4,587
AK [2]	2,622	4,173	4,812	5,285	5,597	NV	5,322	10,063	11,782	12,482	12,653
AZ [3]	14,261	26,510	33,565	40,627	40,130	NH	1,342	2,257	2,530	2,731	2,761
AR	7,322	11,915	13,541	15,208	16,204	NJ	21,128	29,784	27,359	25,382	25,007
CA	97,309	163,001	170,676	171,275	165,062	NM	3,187	5,342	6,571	6,448	6,659
CO	7,671	16,833	21,456	22,795	22,815	NY	54,895	70,199	62,743	58,687	56,656
CT [2]	10,500	18,355	19,442	19,716	19,321	NC	18,411	31,266	36,365	40,529	40,116
DE [2]	3,471	6,921	6,966	6,794	6,598	ND	483	1,076	1,385	1,486	1,487
DC [4,5]	9,947	7,456	(NA)	(NA)	(NA)	OH	31,822	45,833	45,854	51,606	51,712
FL	44,387	71,319	89,768	103,915	104,306	OK	12,285	23,181	26,676	26,397	26,252
GA [3]	22,411	44,232	48,749	53,371	49,164	OR	6,492	10,580	13,411	14,403	14,014
HI [2]	2,533	5,053	6,146	5,891	5,912	PA	22,290	36,847	42,380	51,429	51,264
ID	1,961	5,535	6,818	7,400	7,431	RI [2]	2,392	3,286	3,654	3,674	3,357
IL	27,516	45,281	44,919	45,161	48,418	SC	17,319	21,778	23,160	24,288	23,578
IN	12,736	20,125	24,455	28,808	28,028	SD	1,341	2,616	3,463	3,434	3,434
IA [3]	3,967	7,955	8,737	8,813	9,455	TN	10,388	22,166	26,369	26,965	27,451
KS	5,775	8,344	9,068	8,641	9,051	TX	50,042	166,719	169,003	171,249	173,649
KY	9,023	14,919	19,662	21,638	20,544	UT	2,496	5,637	6,382	6,538	6,807
LA	18,599	35,207	36,083	39,780	39,445	VT [2]	1,049	1,697	2,078	2,220	2,079
ME	1,523	1,679	2,023	2,206	2,154	VA	17,593	30,168	35,344	38,092	37,410
MD	17,848	23,538	22,737	22,255	22,645	WA	7,995	14,915	17,382	18,233	18,235
MA	8,345	10,722	10,701	11,316	11,312	WV	1,565	3,856	5,312	6,367	6,681
MI	34,267	47,718	49,546	45,478	44,113	WI	7,465	20,754	22,697	23,165	22,724
MN	3,176	6,238	9,281	9,986	9,796	WY	1,110	1,680	2,047	2,075	2,112

NA Not available. [1] U.S. total includes federal prisoners not distributed by state and prison system. [2] Data include both total jail and prison population. Prisons and jails form one integrated system. [3] Numbers are for custody rather than jurisdiction counts. [4] The transfer of responsibility for sentenced felons from the District of Columbia to the federal system was completed by the year end 2001. [5] The District of Columbia inmates sentenced to more than 1 year are now under the responsibility of the Bureau of Prisons.

Source: Source: U.S. Department of Justice, Bureau of Justice Statistics, *Prisoners in 2010*, Series NCJ 236096, and earlier reports. See also <http://bjs.ojp.usdoj.gov/index.cfm?ty=pbdetail&iid=2230>.

Table 355. Adults Under Correctional Supervision: 2000 to 2010

[As of December 31, except jail counts as of June 30]

Year	Total correctional population [1]	Community Supervision			Incarcerated [3]		
		Total [2]	Probation	Parole	Total	Jail [4]	Prison [5]
2000	6,460,000	4,565,100	3,839,532	725,527	1,937,500	621,149	1,316,333
2005	7,051,300	4,946,800	4,162,495	784,354	2,195,900	747,529	1,448,344
2006	7,202,100	5,035,200	4,237,023	798,202	2,258,800	765,819	1,492,973
2007	7,337,900	5,119,300	4,293,163	826,097	2,298,000	780,174	1,517,867
2008 [6]	7,312,400	5,095,200	4,270,917	828,169	2,308,400	785,533	1,522,834
2009	7,232,800	5,018,900	4,203,967	819,308	2,291,900	767,434	1,524,478
2010	7,076,200	4,887,900	4,055,514	840,676	2,266,800	748,728	1,518,104
Average annual percent change, 2000–2009	1.3	1.1	1.0	1.4	1.9	2.4	1.6
Percent change, 2009–2010 [7]	-1.3	-1.3	-1.7	0.3	-1.1	-2.4	-0.4

[1] Estimates were adjusted to account for some offenders with multiple correctional statuses. Details may not sum to total. [2] Estimates include some offenders held in prison or jail but who remained under the authority of a probation or parole agency. The 2007-2010 estimates were adjusted to account for offenders with dual community supervision statuses. Details may not sum to total. [3] Includes jail inmates and prisoners held in privately operated facilities. [4] Estimates were revised to include all inmates confined in local jails, including inmates under the age of 18 who were tried or awaiting trial as an adult and the number held as juveniles. Totals for 2000 and 2006-2010 are estimates based on the Annual Survey of Jails. Total for 2005 is a complete enumeration based on the 2005 Census of Jail Inmates. [5] Includes prisoners held in the custody of state or federal correctional facilities or privately operated facilities under state or federal authority. The custody prison population is not comparable to the jurisdiction prison population. [6] Two jurisdictions changed their method of reporting probation data in 2008 resulting from changes in scope. Decreases in the probation, community supervision, and total correctional populations from 2007-2008 were due to these changes in scope and do not reflect actual declines in the populations. [7] Change in the total correctional population was based on the sum of the differences in the probation, parole, jail, and prison custody populations.

Source: U.S. Department of Justice, Bureau of Justice Statistics (BJS), *Correctional Populations in the United States, 2010*. See also <http://bjs.ojp.usdoj.gov/index.cfm?ty=pbdetail&iid=2237>.

Table 356. Jail Inmates by Sex, Race, and Hispanic Origin: 1990 to 2011

[As of the last week day in June. Data for 2000 and 2009-2011 are based on the Annual Survey of Jails]

Characteristic	1990	1995	2000	2005	2009	2010	2011
Total inmates [1,2]	405,320	507,044	621,149	747,529	767,434	748,728	735,601
Incarceration rate per 100,000							
U.S. residents	163	193	220	252	250	242	236
Rated capacity [3,4]	389,171	545,763	677,787	786,954	849,895	866,782	877,302
Adult	403,019	499,300	613,534	740,770	760,216	741,168	729,700
Male	365,821	448,000	543,120	646,807	667,039	649,284	636,900
Female	37,198	51,300	70,414	93,963	93,176	91,884	92,800
Juveniles [5]	2,301	7,800	7,615	6,759	7,218	7,560	5,900
White, non-Hispanic	169,600	203,300	260,500	331,000	326,400	331,600	329,400
Black, non-Hispanic	172,300	220,600	256,300	290,500	300,500	283,200	276,400
Hispanic/Latino [6]	58,100	74,400	94,100	111,900	124,000	118,100	113,900
Other [7]	5,400	8,800	10,200	13,000	14,800	15,000	14,700

[1] Total does not include offenders who were supervised outside of jail facilities. [2] Race and Hispanic origin data do not include the Two or More Race data. [3] Beginning 1995, rated capacity subject to sampling error. [4] Rated capacity is the number of beds or inmates assigned by a rating official to facilities within each jurisdiction. [5] Juveniles are persons held under the age of 18. Includes juveniles who were tried or awaiting trial as adults. [6] Persons of Hispanic origin may be any race. [7] Excludes persons of Hispanic or Latino origin. Includes American Indians, Alaska Natives, Asians, and Pacific Islanders.

Source: U.S. Department of Justice, Bureau of Justice Statistics, *Jail Inmates at Midyear 2011*, annual, Series NCJ 237961, April 2012. See also: <http://bjs.ojp.usdoj.gov/index.cfm?ty=pbse&sid=38>.

Table 357. Prisoners Under Federal or State Jurisdiction by Sex: 1980 to 2010

[Prisoners, as of December 31. Represents prisoners sentenced to more than one year under jurisdiction of federal or state authorities rather than those in the custody of such authorities]

Year	Total [1]	Rate [2]	State	Male	Female	Year	Total [1]	Rate [2]	State	Male	Female
1980	315,974	139	295,363	303,643	12,331	2002	1,380,516	476	1,237,476	1,291,450	89,066
1985	480,568	202	447,873	459,223	21,345	2003	1,408,361	482	1,256,442	1,315,790	92,571
1990	739,980	297	689,577	699,416	40,564	2004	1,433,728	486	1,274,591	1,337,730	95,998
1995	1,085,022	411	1,001,359	1,021,059	63,963	2005	1,462,866	491	1,296,693	1,364,178	98,688
1997	1,195,498	445	1,100,511	1,121,663	73,835	2006	1,504,660	501	1,331,127	1,401,317	103,343
1998	1,245,402	461	1,141,720	1,167,802	77,600	2007	1,532,850	506	1,353,646	1,427,064	105,786
1999	1,304,074	476	1,189,799	1,221,611	82,463	2008	1,547,742	504	1,365,409	1,441,384	106,358
2000	1,331,278	[3] 470	1,206,234	1,246,234	85,044	2009	1,553,700	504	1,365,814	1,448,344	105,356
2001	1,345,217	470	1,208,708	1,260,033	85,184	2010	1,550,257	500	1,359,616	1,445,628	104,629

[1] Includes prisoners under the legal authority of state or federal correctional officials. [2] Rate per 100,000 estimated population. Based on U.S. Census Bureau estimated resident population. [3] Decrease in incarceration rate from 1999 to 2000 due to use of new Census numbers.

Source: U.S. Department of Justice, Bureau of Justice Statistics, *Prisoners in 2010*, Series NCJ 236096, December 2011. See also <http://bjs.ojp.usdoj.gov/index.cfm?ty=pbdetail&iid=2230>.

Table 358. Prisoners Under Sentence of Death by Characteristic: 1980 to 2009

[As of December 31. Excludes prisoners under sentence of death who remained within local correctional systems pending exhaustion of appellate process or who had not been committed to prison]

Characteristic	1980	1990	2000	2001	2002	2003	2004	2005	2006	2007	2008	2009
Total [1,2]	688	2,346	3,601	3,577	3,562	3,377	3,320	3,245	3,233	3,215	3,210	3,173
White	418	1,368	1,989	1,968	1,939	1,882	1,856	1,802	1,806	1,806	1,795	1,780
Black and other	270	978	1,612	1,609	1,623	1,495	1,464	1,443	1,427	1,409	1,415	1,393
Under 20 years old	11	8	11	4	4	1	1	–	–	1	–	–
20 to 24 years old	173	168	237	192	153	133	95	61	51	42	44	39
25 to 34 years old	334	1,110	1,103	1,099	1,058	965	896	816	735	680	610	564
35 to 54 years old	186	1,006	2,019	2,043	2,069	1,969	1,977	2,012	2,043	2,060	2,076	2,062
55 years old and over	10	64	223	243	273	306	345	365	399	437	477	508
Years of school completed:												
7 years or less	68	178	214	212	215	213	207	192	186	183	176	176
8 years	74	186	233	236	234	227	221	206	195	189	185	180
9 to 11 years	204	775	1,157	1,145	1,130	1,073	1,053	1,030	1,015	989	977	950
12 years	162	729	1,184	1,183	1,173	1,108	1,091	1,105	1,098	1,089	1,094	1,097
More than 12 years	43	209	315	304	294	270	262	256	248	248	247	238
Unknown	163	279	490	501	511	483	480	465	486	522	528	532
Marital status:												
Never married	268	998	1,749	1,763	1,746	1,641	1,622	1,586	1,577	1,558	1,552	1,531
Married	229	632	739	716	709	684	658	649	626	635	630	613
Divorced [3]	217	726	1,105	1,102	1,102	1,049	1,034	1,019	1,025	1,027	1,025	1,029
Time elapsed since sentencing:												
Less than 12 months	185	231	208	151	147	137	117	122	105	110	106	103
12 to 47 months	389	753	786	734	609	495	421	399	382	352	339	329
48 to 71 months	102	438	507	476	468	451	388	299	262	262	244	237
72 months and over	38	934	2,092	2,220	2,333	2,291	2,388	2,434	2,479	2,496	2,518	2,504
Legal status at arrest:												
Not under sentence	384	1,345	2,202	2,189	2,165	2,048	2,026	1,979	1,952	1,963	1,961	1,931
Parole or probation [4]	115	578	921	918	909	845	809	792	778	760	753	739
Prison or escaped	45	128	126	135	141	137	145	144	142	143	146	156
Unknown	170	305	344	339	342	344	334	339	356	354	347	347

– Represents zero. [1] Revisions to the total number of prisoners were not carried to the characteristics except for race. [2] Includes races not shown separately. [3] Includes persons married but separated, widows, widowers, and unknown. [4] Includes prisoners on mandatory conditional release, work release, other leave, AWOL, or bail. Covers 28 prisoners in 1990; 17 in 2001, 2002, and 2003; 15 in 2004; 14 in 2005, 2006, 2007, and 2009; and 12 in 2008.

Source: U.S. Department of Justice, Bureau of Justice Statistics, *Capital Punishment, 2009*, Series NCJ 231676, December 2010. See also: <http://bjs.gov/index.cfm?ty=pbdetail&iid=2215>.

Table 359. Prisoners Executed Under Civil Authority by Sex and Race: 1930 to 2010

[Excludes executions by military authorities]

Year or period	Total [1]	Male	Female	White	Black	Executed for murder Total [1]	Executed for murder White	Executed for murder Black
All years, 1930–2009.............	**5,093**	**5,049**	**44**	**2,544**	**2,492**	**4,568**	**2,457**	**2,056**
1960 to 1967..........................	191	190	1	98	93	155	87	68
1968 to 1976..........................	–	–	–	–	–	–	–	–
1977 to 2010..........................	1,234	1,222	12	793	426	1,234	793	426
1985....................................	18	18	–	11	7	18	11	7
1990....................................	23	23	–	16	7	23	16	7
1995....................................	56	56	–	33	22	56	33	22
2000....................................	85	83	2	49	35	85	49	35
2001....................................	66	63	3	48	17	66	48	17
2002....................................	71	69	2	53	18	71	53	18
2003....................................	65	65	–	44	20	65	44	20
2004....................................	59	59	–	39	19	59	39	19
2005....................................	60	59	1	41	19	60	41	19
2006....................................	53	53	–	32	21	53	32	21
2007....................................	42	42	–	28	14	42	28	14
2008....................................	37	37	–	20	17	37	20	17
2009....................................	52	52	–	31	21	52	31	21
2010....................................	46	45	1	34	12	46	34	12

– Represents zero. [1] Includes races other than White or Black.

Source: Through 1978, U.S. Law Enforcement Assistance Administration; thereafter, U.S. Department of Justice, Bureau of Justice Statistics, *Capital Punishment*, Annual. See also: <http://bjs.ojp.usdoj.gov/index.cfm?ty=pbse&sid=1>.

Table 360. Prisoners Executed Under Civil Authority by State: 1977 to 2010

[Alaska, District of Columbia, Hawaii, Iowa, Maine, Massachusetts, Michigan, Minnesota, New Jersey, North Dakota, Rhode Island, Vermont, West Virginia, and Wisconsin are jurisdictions without a death penalty. New Mexico abolished the death penalty for offenses committed after July 1, 2009; two men under previously imposed death sentences are still subject to execution]

State	1977 to 2010	2000	2005	2008	2009	2010	State	1977 to 2010	2000	2005	2008	2009	2010	State	1977 to 2010	2000	2005	2008	2009	2010
U.S.	**1,234**	**85**	**60**	**37**	**52**	**46**	IL....	12	–	–	–	–	–	OH...	41	–	4	2	5	8
							IN....	20	–	5	–	1	–	OK...	94	11	4	2	3	3
AL....	49	4	4	–	6	–	KY...	3	–	–	1	–	–	OR...	2	–	–	–	–	–
AZ....	24	3	–	–	–	1	LA...	28	1	–	–	–	1	PA...	3	–	–	–	–	–
AR....	27	2	1	–	–	–	MD...	5	–	1	–	–	–	SC...	42	1	3	3	2	–
CA....	13	1	2	–	–	–	MS...	13	–	1	2	–	3	SD...	1	–	–	–	–	–
CO. ..	1	–	–	–	–	–	MO...	67	5	5	–	1	–	TN...	6	1	–	–	2	–
CT....	1	–	1	–	–	–	MT...	3	–	–	–	–	–	TX...	464	40	19	18	24	17
DE....	14	1	1	–	–	–	NE...	3	–	–	–	–	–	UT...	7	–	–	–	–	1
FL....	69	6	1	2	2	1	NV...	12	–	–	–	–	–	VA...	108	8	–	4	3	3
GA. ..	48	–	3	3	3	2	NM...	1	–	–	–	–	–	WA...	5	–	–	–	–	1
ID.....	1	–	–	–	–	–	NC...	43	1	5	–	–	–	WY...	1	–	–	–	–	–

– Represents zero.

Source: Through 1978, U.S. Law Enforcement Assistance Administration; thereafter, U.S. Department of Justice, Bureau of Justice Statistics, *Capital Punishment*, Annual. See also <http://bjs.ojp.usdoj.gov/index.cfm?ty=pbse&sid=1>.

Table 361. Fire Losses—Total and Per Capita: 1980 to 2010

[5,579 represents $5,579,000,000. Includes allowances for FAIR Plan and uninsured losses]

Year	Total (mil. dol.)	Per capita [1] (dol.)	Year	Total (mil. dol.)	Per capita [1] (dol.)	Year	Total (mil. dol.)	Per capita [1] (dol.)
1980...............	5,579	24.56	1995.........	11,887	45.23	2003.........	21,129	72.73
1985...............	7,753	32.70	1996.........	12,544	47.29	2004.........	17,344	59.23
1989...............	9,514	38.33	1997.........	12,940	48.32	2005.........	20,427	69.12
1990...............	9,495	38.07	1998.........	11,510	45.59	2006.........	20,340	68.17
1991...............	11,302	44.82	1999.........	12,428	45.58	2007.........	24,399	81.00
1992...............	13,588	53.28	2000.........	13,457	47.69	2008.........	24,734	81.34
1993...............	11,331	43.96	2001 [2]......	17,118	60.07	2009.........	22,911	74.68
1994...............	12,778	49.08	2002.........	17,586	61.14	2010.........	19,637	63.48

[1] Based on U.S. Census Bureau estimated resident population as of July 1. Enumerated population as of April 1 for 1980, 1990, and 2000. [2] Does not include insured fire losses related to terrorism.

Source: ISO; Insurance Information Institute, New York, NY. *The Insurance Fact Book,* annual (copyright). Data from ISO. See also <http://www.iii.org>.

Table 362. The U.S. Fire Service: Departments and Personnel: 1990 to 2010

[In thousands (1,025.7 represents 1,025,700). A fire department is a public or private organization that provides fire prevention, fire suppression, and associated emergency and non-emergency services to a jurisdiction such as a county, municipality, or organized fire district. For 2010, there was an estimated 30,125 fire departments in the United States. These fire departments have an estimated 51,300 fire stations, 66,800 pumpers, 6,800 aerial apparatus and 72,800 other suppression vehicles. A fire department responds to a fire every 23 seconds]

Items	1990	1995	2000	2005	2006	2007	2008	2009	2010
Total	**30,391**	**31,197**	**30,339**	**30,300**	**30,635**	**30,185**	**30,170**	**30,165**	**30,125**
Fire departments (Number):									
All career	1,949	1,831	2,178	2,087	2,321	2,263	2,315	2,457	2,495
Mostly career	1,338	1,660	1,667	1,766	1,731	1,765	1,790	1,752	1,860
Mostly volunteer	4,000	4,581	4,523	4,902	5,134	4,989	4,830	5,099	5,290
All volunteer	23,104	23,125	21,971	21,575	21,449	21,168	21,235	20,857	20,480
Fire Department personnel (1,000)	1,025.7	1,098.9	1,064.2	1,136.7	1,140.9	1,148.5	1,148.9	1,148.1	1,103.3
Career [1]	253.0	260.9	286.8	313.0	317.0	323.4	321.7	336.0	335.2
Volunteer [2]	772.7	838.0	777.4	823.7	824.0	825.5	827.2	812.1	768.2

[1] Career firefighters include full-time uniform firefighters regardless of assignment (i.e., suppression, administrative, prevention/inspection, etc.). Career firefighters do not include firefighters who work for the state or federal government or in private fire brigades. [2] Volunteer firefighters include any active part-time (call or volunteer) firefighters.

Source: National Fire Protection Association, Quincy, MA, *U.S. Fire Department Profile Through 2010*, October 2011, and prior issues (copyright).

Table 363. Fires—Number and Loss by Type and Property Use: 2007 to 2010

[1,557 represents 1,557,000; property loss of 14,639 represents $14,639,000,000. Based on annual sample survey of fire departments. No adjustments were made for unreported fires and losses]

Type and property use	Number (1,000)				Direct property loss (mil. dol.) [1]			
	2007	2008	2009	2010	2007	2008	2009	2010
Fires, total	**1,557**	**1,451**	**1,349**	**1,331**	**14,639**	**15,478**	**12,531**	**11,593**
Structure	531	515	481	482	10,638	12,361	10,842	9,716
Outside of structure [2]	85	71	69	73	707	129	254	413
Brush and rubbish	561	523	477	477	–	–	–	–
Vehicle	257	236	219	216	1,411	1,494	1,361	1,376
Other	123	106	103	85	[3] 1,883	[4] 1,494	74	88
Structure by property use:								
Public assembly	15	14	14	12	498	518	757	421
Educational	6	6	6	6	100	66	83	76
Institutional	7	7	6	6	41	22	32	37
Stores and offices	21	20	16	18	642	684	713	730
Residential	414	403	377	384	7,546	8,550	7,796	7,079
1–2 family homes [5]	300	291	273	279	6,225	6,892	6,391	5,895
Apartments	99	96	90	91	1,164	1,351	1,225	1,033
Other residential [6]	15	16	14	15	157	307	180	151
Storage	31	30	30	28	670	661	796	756
Industry, utility, defense [7]	12	10	10	9	779	[8] 1,401	572	515
Special structures	25	25	22	20	362	459	98	102

– Represents zero. [1] Direct property damage figures do not include indirect losses, like business interruption and adjustments for inflation. [2] Includes outside storage, crops, timber, etc. [3] Includes California Fire Storm 2007 with an estimated $1.8 billion in property loss. [4] Includes California Wildfires 2008 with an estimated $1.4 billion in property loss. [5] Includes mobile homes. [6] Includes hotels and motels, college dormitories, boarding houses, etc. [7] Data underreported as some incidents were handled by private fire brigades or fixed suppression systems which do not report. [8] Includes three industrial property incidents that resulted in $775 million in property loss.

Source: National Fire Protection Association, Quincy, MA, *Fire Loss in the United States During 2010*, September 2011, and prior issues (copyright). See also <http://www.nfpa.org/categoryList.asp?categoryID=15&URL=Research>.

Table 364. Fires and Property Loss for Incendiary and Suspicious Fires and Civilian Fire Deaths and Injuries by Selected Property Type: 2007 to 2010

[In thousands (531 represents 531,000), except as indicated. Based on sample survey of fire departments]

Characteristic	2007	2008	2009	2010	Characteristic	2007	2008	2009	2010
NUMBER (1,000)					One- and two-family dwellings	2,350	2,365	2,100	2,200
Structure fires, total	**531**	**515**	**481**	**482**	Apartments	515	390	465	440
Structure fires that were intentionally set	32	31	27	28	Vehicles	385	365	280	310
PROPERTY LOSS [1] (mil. dol.)					CIVILIAN FIRE INJURIES				
Structure fires, total	**10,638**	**12,361**	**10,842**	**9,716**	**Injuries, total [2]**	**17,675**	**16,705**	**17,050**	**17,720**
Structure fires that were intentionally set	773	866	684	585	Residential property	14,000	13,560	13,050	13,800
					One- and two-family dwellings	9,650	9,185	9,300	9,400
CIVILIAN FIRE DEATHS					Apartments	3,950	3,975	3,350	3,950
Deaths, total [2]	**3,430**	**3,320**	**3,010**	**3,120**	Vehicles	1,675	1,065	1,610	1,590
Residential property	2,895	2,780	2,590	2,665					

[1] Direct property loss only. [2] Includes other not shown separately.

Source: National Fire Protection Association, Quincy, MA, *Fire Loss in the United States During 2010*, September 2011, and prior issues (copyright). See also <http://www.nfpa.org/categoryList.asp?categoryID=15&URL=Research>.

Section 6
Geography and Environment

This section presents a variety of information on the physical environment of the United States, starting with basic area measurement data and ending with climatic data for selected weather stations around the country. The subjects covered between those points are mostly concerned with environmental trends but include related subjects such as land use, water consumption, air pollutant emissions, toxic releases, oil spills, hazardous waste sites, municipal waste and recycling, threatened and endangered wildlife, and the environmental industry.

The information in this section is selected from a wide range of federal agencies that compile the data for various administrative or regulatory purposes, such as the Environmental Protection Agency (EPA), U.S. Geological Survey (USGS), National Oceanic and Atmospheric Administration (NOAA), Natural Resources Conservation Service (NRCS), and National Atlas® of the United States. New data on 11 coastline counties most frequently hit by hurricanes may be found in Table 369.

Area—2010 Area measurements are the latest available. These measurements were calculated by computer based on the information contained in a single, consistent geographic database, the Topologically Integrated Geographic Encoding & Referencing system (TIGER®) database. The 2010 area measurements may be found in Table 365.

Geography—The USGS conducts investigations, surveys, and research in the fields of geography, geology, topography, geographic information systems, mineralogy, hydrology, and geothermal energy resources as well as natural hazards. The USGS provides United States cartographic data through the Earth Sciences Information Center and water resources data through the *Water Resources of the United States* at <http://water.usgs.gov/pubs/>. In a joint project with the U.S. Census Bureau, during the 1980s, the USGS provided the basic information on geographic features for input into a national geographic and cartographic database prepared by the Census Bureau, called TIGER® database. Since then, using a variety of sources, the Census Bureau has updated these features and their related attributes (names, descriptions, etc.) and inserted current information on the boundaries, names, and codes of legal and statistical geographic entities. The 2010 area measures, land and water, including their classifications, reflect base feature updates made in the Master Address File (MAF)/TIGER database through August 2010. The boundaries of the states and equivalent areas are as of January 1, 2010. Maps prepared by the Census Bureau using the TIGER® database show the names and boundaries of entities and are available on a current basis.

An inventory of the nation's land resources by type of use/cover was conducted by the National Resources Inventory Conservation Services (NRCS) every 5 years beginning in 1977 through 2003. The most recent survey results, which were published for the year 2003, covered all nonfederal land for the contiguous 48 states.

Environment—The principal federal agency responsible for pollution abatement and control activities is the Environmental Protection Agency (EPA). It is responsible for establishing and monitoring national air quality standards, water quality activities, solid and hazardous waste disposal, and control of toxic substances. Many of these series now appear in the Envirofacts portion of the EPA Web site at <http://www.epa.gov/enviro/>.

The Clean Air Act, which was last amended in 1990, requires the EPA to set National Ambient Air Quality Standards (NAAQS) (40 CFR part 50) for pollutants considered harmful to public health and the environment. The Clean Air Act established two types of national air quality standards. **Primary standards** set limits to protect public health, including the health of "sensitive" populations such as asthmatics, children, and the elderly. **Secondary standards** set limits to protect public welfare, including protection against decreased visibility, damage to animals, crops vegetation, and buildings. See <http://www.epa.gov/air/criteria.html>. The EPA Office of Air Quality Planning and Standards (OAQPS) has set National Ambient Air Quality Standards for six principal pollutants, which are called "criteria" pollutants. These pollutants are: Carbon Monoxide, Lead, Nitrogen Dioxide, Particulate Matter (PM2.5 and 10), Ozone, and Sulfur Dioxide. NAAQS are periodically reviewed and revised to include any additional or new health or welfare data. Table 379 gives some of the health-related standards for the six air pollutants having NAAQS. Data gathered from state networks are periodically submitted to EPA's National Aerometric Information Retrieval System (AIRS) for summarization in annual reports on the nationwide status and trends in air quality. For details, see "Air Trends" on the EPA Web site at <http://www.epa.gov/airtrends/index.html>.

The Toxics Release Inventory (TRI), published by the EPA, is a valuable source of information on approximately 650 chemicals that are being used, manufactured, treated, transported, or released into the environment. Sections 313 of the Emergency Planning and Community Right-to-Know Act (EPCRA) and 6607 of the Pollution Prevention Act (PPA), mandate that a publicly-accessible toxic chemical database be developed and maintained by EPA. This database, known as the TRI, contains information concerning waste management activities and the release of toxic chemicals by facilities that manufacture, process, or otherwise use said materials. Data on the release of these chemicals are collected from about 21,000 facilities and facilities added in 1998 that have the equivalent of 10 or more full time employees and meet the established thresholds for manufacturing, processing, or "other use" of listed chemicals. Facilities must report their releases and other waste management quantities. Since 1994 federal facilities have been required to report their data regardless of industry classification. In May 1997, EPA added seven new industry sectors that reported to the TRI for the first time in July 1999 for the 1998 reporting year. More current information on this program can be found at <http://www.epa.gov/tri>.

Climate—NOAA, through the National Weather Service and the National Environmental Satellite, Data, and Information Service, is responsible for climate data. NOAA maintains about 11,600 weather stations, of which over 3,000 produce autographic precipitation records, about 600 take hourly readings of a series of weather elements, and the remainder record data once a day. These data are reported monthly in the Climatological Data and Storm Data, published monthly and annually in the Local Climatological Data (published by location for major cities). Data can be found in tables 394 and 397–402.

Table 365. Land and Water Area of States and Other Entities: 2010

[One square mile = 2.59 square kilometers. The area measurements were derived from the Census Bureau's Master Address File/Topologically Integrated Geographic Encoding and Referencing (MAF/TIGER®) database. The boundaries of the states and equivalent areas are as of January 1, 2010. The land and water areas, including their classifications, reflect base feature updates made in the MAF/TIGER® database through August, 2010. For more details, see <http://www.census.gov/geo/www/tiger/tgrshp2010/tgrshp2010.html>]

State and other areas [2]	Total area		Land area [1]		Water area [1]					
					Total		Inland (sq. mi.)	Coastal (sq. mi.)	Great Lakes (sq. mi.)	Territorial (sq. mi.)
	Sq. mi.	Sq. km.	Sq. mi.	Sq. km.	Sq. mi.	Sq. km.				
Total [3]	3,805,927	9,857,306	3,535,932	9,158,022	269,995	699,284	85,763	42,371	60,094	81,767
United States [4]	3,796,742	9,833,517	3,531,905	9,147,593	264,837	685,924	85,647	42,337	60,094	76,759
Alabama	52,420	135,767	50,645	131,171	1,775	4,597	1,058	517	(X)	199
Alaska	665,384	1,723,337	570,641	1,477,953	94,743	245,383	19,304	26,119	(X)	49,320
Arizona	113,990	295,234	113,594	294,207	396	1,026	396	—	(X)	—
Arkansas	53,179	137,732	52,035	134,771	1,143	2,961	1,143	—	(X)	—
California	163,695	423,967	155,779	403,466	7,916	20,501	2,833	245	(X)	4,837
Colorado	104,094	269,601	103,642	268,431	452	1,170	452	—	(X)	—
Connecticut	5,543	14,357	4,842	12,542	701	1,816	171	530	(X)	—
Delaware	2,489	6,446	1,949	5,047	540	1,399	91	355	(X)	94
District of Columbia	68	177	61	158	7	19	7	—	(X)	—
Florida	65,758	170,312	53,625	138,887	12,133	31,424	5,027	1,349	(X)	5,757
Georgia	59,425	153,910	57,513	148,959	1,912	4,951	1,412	46	(X)	453
Hawaii	10,932	28,313	6,423	16,635	4,509	11,678	42	9	(X)	4,458
Idaho	83,569	216,443	82,643	214,045	926	2,398	926	—	(X)	—
Illinois	57,914	149,995	55,519	143,793	2,395	6,202	820	—	1,575	—
Indiana	36,420	94,326	35,826	92,789	593	1,537	361	—	233	—
Iowa	56,273	145,746	55,857	144,669	416	1,077	416	—	(X)	—
Kansas	82,278	213,100	81,759	211,754	520	1,346	520	—	(X)	—
Kentucky	40,408	104,656	39,486	102,269	921	2,387	921	—	(X)	—
Louisiana	52,378	135,659	43,204	111,898	9,174	23,761	4,562	2,880	(X)	1,732
Maine	35,380	91,633	30,843	79,883	4,537	11,750	2,314	591	(X)	1,633
Maryland	12,406	32,131	9,707	25,142	2,699	6,990	768	1,820	(X)	111
Massachusetts	10,554	27,336	7,800	20,202	2,754	7,134	486	1,177	(X)	1,092
Michigan	96,714	250,487	56,539	146,435	40,175	104,052	2,001	—	38,174	—
Minnesota	86,936	225,160	79,627	206,232	7,309	18,930	4,763	—	2,546	—
Mississippi	48,432	125,438	46,923	121,531	1,509	3,907	769	616	(X)	123
Missouri	69,707	180,540	68,742	178,040	965	2,501	965	—	(X)	—
Montana	147,040	380,831	145,546	376,962	1,494	3,869	1,494	—	(X)	—
Nebraska	77,348	200,330	76,824	198,974	524	1,356	524	—	(X)	—
Nevada	110,572	286,380	109,781	284,332	791	2,048	791	—	(X)	—
New Hampshire	9,349	24,214	8,953	23,187	397	1,027	328	—	(X)	69
New Jersey	8,723	22,591	7,354	19,047	1,368	3,544	436	427	(X)	506
New Mexico	121,590	314,917	121,298	314,161	292	757	292	—	(X)	—
New York	54,555	141,297	47,126	122,057	7,429	19,240	1,989	975	3,986	479
North Carolina	53,819	139,391	48,618	125,920	5,201	13,471	4,052	—	(X)	1,149
North Dakota	70,698	183,108	69,001	178,711	1,698	4,397	1,698	—	(X)	—
Ohio	44,826	116,098	40,861	105,829	3,965	10,269	474	—	3,491	—
Oklahoma	69,899	181,037	68,595	177,660	1,304	3,377	1,304	—	(X)	—
Oregon	98,379	254,799	95,988	248,608	2,391	6,191	1,068	72	(X)	1,251
Pennsylvania	46,054	119,280	44,743	115,883	1,312	3,397	563	—	748	—
Rhode Island	1,545	4,001	1,034	2,678	511	1,324	182	64	(X)	266
South Carolina	32,020	82,933	30,061	77,857	1,960	5,076	1,064	110	(X)	786
South Dakota	77,116	199,729	75,811	196,350	1,305	3,379	1,305	—	(X)	—
Tennessee	42,144	109,153	41,235	106,798	909	2,355	909	—	(X)	—
Texas	268,596	695,662	261,232	676,587	7,365	19,075	5,616	401	(X)	1,347
Utah	84,897	219,882	82,170	212,818	2,727	7,064	2,727	—	(X)	—
Vermont	9,616	24,906	9,217	23,871	400	1,035	400	—	(X)	—
Virginia	42,775	110,787	39,490	102,279	3,285	8,508	1,282	1,565	(X)	438
Washington	71,298	184,661	66,456	172,119	4,842	12,542	1,715	2,468	(X)	660
West Virginia	24,230	62,756	24,038	62,259	192	497	192	—	(X)	—
Wisconsin	65,496	169,635	54,158	140,268	11,339	29,367	1,997	—	9,342	—
Wyoming	97,813	253,335	97,093	251,470	720	1,864	720	—	(X)	—
Puerto Rico	5,325	13,791	3,424	8,868	1,901	4,924	76	13	(X)	1,812
Island Areas:	3,860	9,998	603	1,562	3,257	8,436	40	22	(X)	3,196
American Samoa	581	1,505	76	198	505	1,307	8	—	(X)	497
Guam	571	1,478	210	543	361	935	8	1	(X)	352
No. Mariana Islands	1,976	5,117	182	472	1,793	4,644	6	5	(X)	1,782
U.S. Virgin Islands	733	1,898	134	348	599	1,550	18	16	(X)	565

– Represents or rounds to zero. X Not applicable. [1] Water area calculations in this table include only perennial water. All other water (intermittent, glacier, and marsh/swamp) is included in this table as part of land area calculations. [2] This table does not include area calculations for the U.S. Minor Outlying Islands. [3] Includes all 50 states, the District of Columbia, Puerto Rico, and the Island Areas. [4] Includes all 50 states and the District of Columbia.

Source: U.S. Census Bureau, unpublished data from the MAF/TIGER® database. See <http://www.census.gov/geo/www/tiger/>.

Table 366. Great Lakes Profile

[The Great Lakes contain the largest supply of freshwater in the world, holding about 18% of the world's total freshwater and about 90% of the United States' total freshwater. The Lakes are a series of five interconnecting large lakes, one small lake, four connecting channels, and the St. Lawrence Seaway. Combined, the lakes cover an area of over 94,000 square miles (245,000 square kilometers) and contain over 5,400 cubic miles (23,000 cubic kilometers) of water]

Characteristics	Unit	Lake Superior	Lake Michigan	Lake Huron	Lake Erie	Lake Ontario
Length........	Miles	350	307	206	241	193
Breadth........	Miles	160	118	183	57	53
Depth						
Average........	Feet	489	279	159	62	283
Maximum........	Feet	1,333	923	750	210	802
Volume........	Cubic miles	2,935	1,180	849	116	393
Water Surface Area [1]........	Square miles	31,700	22,300	23,000	9,910	7,340
Surface area in U.S........	Square miles	20,598	22,300	9,111	4,977	3,560
Retention/Replacement Time [2]........	Years	191	99	22	3	6

[1] Includes surface area in both U.S. and Canada. [2] The amount of time it takes for lakes to get rid of pollutants.

Source: Department of Commerce, National Oceanic and Atmospheric Administration, Great Lakes Environmental Research Laboratory, "About Our Great Lakes, Lake by Lake Profiles," June 2004, <http://www.glerl.noaa.gov/pr/ourlakes/intro.html\>.

Table 367. Great Lakes Length of Shoreline in Separate Basin

[In statute miles]

	Total	Canada	U.S.	MI	MN	WI	IL	IN	OH	PA	NY
Total........	**10,368**	**5,127**	**5,241**	**3,288**	**189**	**820**	**63**	**45**	**312**	**51**	**473**
Lake Superior......	2,980	1,549	1,431	917	189	325	–	–	–	–	–
St. Marys River.....	297	206	91	91	–	–	–	–	–	–	–
Lake Michigan......	1,661	–	1,661	1,058	–	495	63	45	–	–	–
Lake Huron.........	3,350	2,416	934	934	–	–	–	–	–	–	–
St. Clair River......	128	47	81	81	–	–	–	–	–	–	–
Lake St. Clair......	160	71	89	89	–	–	–	–	–	–	–
Detroit River........	107	43	64	64	–	–	–	–	–	–	–
Lake Erie...........	860	366	494	54	–	–	–	–	312	51	77
Niagara River.......	99	34	65	–	–	–	–	–	–	–	65
Lake Ontario.......	726	395	331	–	–	–	–	–	–	–	331

– Represents zero.

Source: State of Michigan, Department of Environment Quality, "Great Lakes, Shorelines of the Great Lakes," and U.S. Lake Survey, File no. 3-3284 corrected to 1952. <http://www.michigan.gov/deq/0,4561,7-135-3313_3677-15959--,00.html>.

Table 368. Largest Lakes in the United States

[The list of lakes include manmade lakes and those that are only partially within the United States]

Lake	Location	Area in sq. mi.	Lake	Location	Area in sq. mi.
Lake Superior..........	MI-MN-WI-Ontario.........	31,700	Lake Pontchartrain......	Louisiana..............	631
Lake Huron...........	MI-Ontario..............	23,000	Lake Sakakawea [1].......	North Dakota..........	520
Lake Michigan.........	IL-IN-MI-WI.............	22,300	Lake Champlain.........	NY-VT-Quebec.........	490
Lake Erie............	MI-NY-OH-PA-Ontario.....	9,910	Becharof Lake.........	Alaska...............	453
Lake Ontario..........	NY-Ontario.............	7,340	Lake St. Clair............	MI-Ontario............	430
Great Salt Lake........	Utah.................	2,117	Red Lake.............	Minnesota...........	427
Lake of the Woods......	MN-Manitoba-Ontario.....	1,485	Selawik Lake..........	Alaska...............	404
Iliamna Lake..........	Alaska................	1,014	Fort Peck Lake [1].........	Montana.............	393
Lake Oahe [1]...........	ND-SD..............	685	Salton Sea............	California............	347
Lake Okeechobee........	Florida...............	662	Rainy Lake............	MN-Ontario..........	345

[1] Manmade lakes.

Source: U.S. Geological Survey, 2003, and National Oceanic and Atmospheric Administration, "Great Lakes, 2002" and The National Atlas of the United States of America, *Lakes*, <http://nationalatlas.gov/articles/mapping/a_general.html\>.

Table 369. Coastline Counties Most Frequently Hit by Hurricanes: 1960 to 2008

[Hurricane is a type of tropical cyclone, an intense tropical weather system of strong thunderstorms with a well-defined surface circulation and maximum sustained winds of 74 miles per hour or higher]

County and State	Coastline region	Number of hurricanes	Percent change in population		Percent change in housing units	
			1960 to 2008	2000 to 2008	1960 to 2008	2000 to 2008
Monore Conty, FL..................	Gulf of Mexico......	15	50.8	-9.2	221.8	4.3
Lafourche Parish, LA...............	Gulf of Mexico......	14	67.2	2.9	151.5	8.9
Carteret County, NC...............	Atlantic..............	14	104.3	6.4	366.4	12.4
Dare County, NC..................	Atlantic..............	13	465.9	12.1	709.6	22.8
Hyde County, NC.................	Atlantic..............	13	-10.1	-11.1	83.7	5.8
Jefferson Parish, LA................	Gulf of Mexico......	12	108.9	-4.2	201.4	-3.5
Palm Beach County, FL.............	Atlantic..............	12	454.7	11.9	616.9	15.2
Miami-Dade County, FL.............	Atlantic..............	11	156.5	6.4	180.6	14.9
St. Bernard Parish, LA.............	Gulf of Mexico......	11	17.2	-43.9	-2.6	-67.9
Cameron Parish, LA...............	Gulf of Mexico......	11	4.8	-27.6	87.7	-8.1
Terrebonne Parish, LA.............	Gulf of Mexico......	11	78.7	3.9	179.4	11.0

Source: National Oceanic and Atmospheric Administration (NOAA), Coastal Services Center, Historical Hurricane Tracks: 1851 to to 2008. U.S. Census Bureau, Current Population Reports, P25-1139, Population Estimates and Projections, "Coastline Population Trends in the United States: 1960 to 2008," Issued May 2010.

Table 370. U.S.–Canada and U.S.–Mexico Border Lengths

[In statue miles. Each statue mile equals one mile. For 2011, there were over 59 million personal vehicle passengers entering the United States from Canada, and almost 111 million personal vehicle passengers entering the United States from Mexico]

State	Length of international border	State	Length of international border
United States–Canada total..............	**5,525**	Ohio........................	146
Alaska........................	1,538	Pennsylvania..................	42
Idaho.........................	45	Vermont.......................	90
Maine.........................	611	Washington....................	427
Michigan......................	721		
Minnesota.....................	547	**United States–Mexico total**..............	**1,933**
Montana.......................	545	Arizona.......................	373
New Hampshire.................	58	California....................	140
New York......................	445	New Mexico....................	180
North Dakota..................	310	Texas.........................	1,241

Source: U.S.–Canada lengths: International Boundary Commission, 2003; U.S. Mexico lengths: U.S. Geological Survey; and The National Atlas of the United States, 1976, Borders, <http://nationalatlas.gov/articles/mapping/a_general.html>.

Table 371. Coastline and Shoreline of the United States by State

[In statue miles. Each statue mile equals one mile. The term coastline is United States coastline measurements were made from small-scale maps, and the coastline was generalized. The coastlines of large sounds and used to describe the general outline of the seacoast. For the table below, bays were included. Measurements were made in 1948. Shoreline is the term used to describe a more detailed measure of the seacoast. The tidal shoreline figures in the table below were obtained in 1939–1940 from the largest-scale charts and maps then available. Shoreline of the outer coast, offshore islands, sounds, and bays was included, as well as the tidal portion of rivers and creeks. Only states with coastline or shoreline are included in the following table]

State	General coastline	Tidal shoreline	State	General coastline	Tidal shoreline
United States.................	**12,383**	**88,633**	Mississippi..................	44	359
Alabama.......................	53	607	New Hampshire................	13	131
Alaska........................	6,640	33,904	New Jersey...................	130	1,792
California....................	840	3,427	New York.....................	127	1,850
Connecticut...................	–	618	North Carolina...............	301	3,375
Delaware......................	28	381	Oregon.......................	296	1,410
Florida.......................	1,350	8,426	Pennsylvania.................	–	89
Georgia.......................	100	2,344	Rhode Island.................	40	384
Hawaii........................	750	1,052	South Carolina...............	187	2,876
Louisiana.....................	397	7,721	Texas........................	367	3,359
Maine.........................	228	3,478	Virginia.....................	112	3,315
Maryland......................	31	3,190	Washington...................	157	3,026
Massachusetts.................	192	1,519			

– Represents zero.

Source: National Oceanic Atmospheric Administration, 1975 and The National Atlas of the United States, *Coastline and Shoreline*, <http://nationalatlas.gov/articles/mapping/a_general.html>.

Table 372. Flows of Largest U.S. Rivers—Length, Discharge, and Drainage Area

[A flow of 1,000 cubic ft per second is equal to 646 million gallons per day, 724,000 acre-feet per year, or 28.3 cubic meters per second. One acre-foot is the volume of water that would cover 1 acre to a depth of 1 foot]

River	Location of mouth	Source stream (name and location)	Length (miles) [1]	Average discharge at mouth (1,000 cubic feet per second) [8]	Drainage area (1,000 sq. miles)
Missouri..................	Missouri....................	Red Rock Creek, MT..........	[3] 2,540	76.2	[2] 529
Mississippi..............	Louisiana..................	Mississippi River, MN.......	2,340	[4] 593	[2,5] 1,150
Yukon....................	Alaska.....................	McNeil River, Canada........	1,980	225	[2] 328
St. Lawrence.............	Canada.....................	North River, MN.............	1,900	348	[2] 396
Rio Grande...............	Mexico-Texas...............	Rio Grande, CO..............	1,900	[7]	336
Arkansas.................	Arkansas...................	East Fork Arkansas River, CO........	1,460	41	161
Colorado.................	Mexico.....................	Colorado River, CO..........	1,450	[7]	246
Atchafalaya [6]..........	Louisiana..................	Tierra Blanca Creek, NM.....	1,420	58	95.1
Ohio.....................	Illinois-Kentucky..........	Allegheny River, PA.........	1,310	281	203
Red [6]..................	Louisiana..................	Tierra Blanca Creek, NM.....	1,290	56	93.2
Brazos...................	Texas......................	Blackwater Draw, NM.........	1,280	[7]	45.6
Columbia.................	Oregon-Washington..........	Columbia River, Canada......	1,240	265	[2] 258
Snake....................	Washington.................	Snake River, WY.............	1,040	56.9	108
Platte...................	Nebraska...................	Grizzly Creek, CO...........	990	[7]	84.9
Pecos....................	Texas......................	Pecos River, NM.............	926	[7]	44.3
Canadian.................	Oklahoma...................	Canadian River, CO..........	906	[7]	46.9
Tennessee................	Kentucky...................	Courthouse Creek, NC........	886	68	40.9

[1] From source to mouth. [2] Drainage area includes both the United States and Canada. [3] The length from the source of the Missouri River to the Mississippi River and thence to the Gulf of Mexico is about 3,710 miles. [4] Includes about 167,000 cubic feet per second diverted from the Mississippi into the Atchafalaya River but excludes the flow of the Red River. [5] Excludes the drainage areas of the Red and Atchafalaya Rivers. [6] In east-central Louisiana, the Red River flows into the Atchafalaya River, a distributary of the Mississippi River. Data on average discharge, length, and drainage area include the Red River, but exclude all water diverted into the Atchafalaya from the Mississippi River. [7] Less than 15,000 cubic feet per second.

Source: U.S. Geological Survey, *Largest Rivers in the United States*, September 2005, <http://pubs.usgs.gov/of/1987/ofr87-242/>.

Table 373. Extreme and Mean Elevations by State and Other Areas

[One foot = .305 meter. There are 2,130 square miles of the United States below sea level (Death Valley is the lowest point). There are 20,230 square miles above 10,000 feet (Mount McKinley is the highest point in the United States). Minus sign (–) indicates below sea level]

State and other areas	Highest point Name	Elevation Feet	Elevation Meters	Lowest point Name	Elevation Feet	Elevation Meters	Approximate mean elevation Feet	Approximate mean elevation Meters
U.S.	Mt. McKinley (AK)	20,320	6,198	Death Valley (CA)	-282	-86	2,500	763
AL	Cheaha Mountain	2,407	734	Gulf of Mexico	([1])	([1])	500	153
AK	Mount McKinley	20,320	6,198	Pacific Ocean	([1])	([1])	1,900	580
AZ	Humphreys Peak	12,633	3,853	Colorado River	70	21	4,100	1,251
AR	Magazine Mountain	2,753	840	Ouachita River	55	17	650	198
CA	Mount Whitney	14,494	4,419	Death Valley	-282	-86	2,900	885
CO	Mt. Elbert	14,433	4,402	Arikaree River	3,315	1,011	6,800	2,074
CT	Mt. Frissell on south slope	2,380	726	Long Island Sound	([1])	([1])	500	153
DE [2]	Ebright Road [2]	448	137	Atlantic Ocean	([1])	([1])	60	18
DC	Tenleytown at Reno Reservoir	410	125	Potomac River	1	(Z)	150	46
FL	Britton Hill	345	105	Atlantic Ocean	([1])	([1])	100	31
GA	Brasstown Bald	4,784	1,459	Atlantic Ocean	([1])	([1])	600	183
HI	Pu'u Wekiu, Mauna Kea	13,796	4,208	Pacific Ocean	([1])	([1])	3,030	924
ID	Borah Peak	12,662	3,862	Snake River	710	217	5,000	1,525
IL	Charles Mound	1,235	377	Mississippi River	279	85	600	183
IN	Hoosier Hill	1,257	383	Ohio River	320	98	700	214
IA	Hawkeye Point	1,670	509	Mississippi River	480	146	1,100	336
KS	Mount Sunflower	4,039	1,232	Verdigris River	679	207	2,000	610
KY	Black Mountain	4,145	1,264	Mississippi River	257	78	750	229
LA	Driskill Mountain	535	163	New Orleans	-8	-2	100	31
ME	Mount Katahdin	5,268	1,607	Atlantic Ocean	([1])	([1])	600	183
MD	Hoye Crest	3,360	1,025	Atlantic Ocean	([1])	([1])	350	107
MA	Mount Greylock	3,491	1,065	Atlantic Ocean	([1])	([1])	500	153
MI	Mount Arvon	1,979	604	Lake Erie	571	174	900	275
MN	Eagle Mountain	2,301	702	Lake Superior	601	183	1,200	366
MS	Woodall Mountain	806	246	Gulf of Mexico	([1])	([1])	300	92
MO	Taum Sauk Mountain	1,772	540	St. Francis River	230	70	800	244
MT	Granite Peak	12,799	3,904	Kootenai River	1,800	549	3,400	1,037
NE	Panorama Point	5,424	1,654	Missouri River	840	256	2,600	793
NV	Boundary Peak	13,140	4,007	Colorado River	479	146	5,500	1,678
NH	Mount Washington	6,288	1,918	Atlantic Ocean	([1])	([1])	1,000	305
NJ	High Point	1,803	550	Atlantic Ocean	([1])	([1])	250	76
NM	Wheeler Peak	13,161	4,014	Red Bluff Reservoir	2,842	867	5,700	1,739
NY	Mount Marcy	5,344	1,630	Atlantic Ocean	([1])	([1])	1,000	305
NC	Mount Mitchell	6,684	2,039	Atlantic Ocean	([1])	([1])	700	214
ND	White Butte	3,506	1,069	Red River of the North	750	229	1,900	580
OH	Campbell Hill	1,550	473	Ohio River	455	139	850	259
OK	Black Mesa	4,973	1,517	Little River	289	88	1,300	397
OR	Mount Hood	11,239	3,428	Pacific Ocean	([1])	([1])	3,300	1,007
PA	Mount Davis	3,213	980	Delaware River	([1])	([1])	1,100	336
RI	Jerimoth Hill	812	248	Atlantic Ocean	([1])	([1])	200	61
SC	Sassafras Mountain	3,560	1,086	Atlantic Ocean	([1])	([1])	350	107
SD	Harney Peak	7,242	2,209	Big Stone Lake	966	295	2,200	671
TN	Clingmans Dome	6,643	2,026	Mississippi River	178	54	900	275
TX	Guadalupe Peak	8,749	2,668	Gulf of Mexico	([1])	([1])	1,700	519
UT	Kings Peak	13,528	4,126	Beaverdam Wash	2,000	610	6,100	1,861
VT	Mount Mansfield	4,393	1,340	Lake Champlain	95	29	1,000	305
VA	Mount Rogers	5,729	1,747	Atlantic Ocean	([1])	([1])	950	290
WA	Mount Rainier	14,411	4,395	Pacific Ocean	([1])	([1])	1,700	519
WV	Spruce Knob	4,863	1,483	Potomac River	240	73	1,500	458
WI	Timms Hill	1,951	595	Lake Michigan	579	177	1,050	320
WY	Gannett Peak	13,804	4,210	Belle Fourche River	3,099	945	6,700	2,044
Other areas: Puerto Rico	Cerro de Punta	4,390	1,339	Atlantic Ocean	([1])	([1])	1,800	549
American Samoa	Lata Mountain	3,160	964	Pacific Ocean	([1])	([1])	1,300	397
Guam	Mount Lamlam	1,332	406	Pacific Ocean	([1])	([1])	330	101
U.S. Virgin Islands	Crown Mountain	1,556	475	Atlantic Ocean	([1])	([1])	750	229

Z Less than .5 meter. [1] Sea level. [2] At DE–PA state line.

Source: For highest and lowest points, see U.S. Geological Survey, "Elevations and Distances in the United States," <http://egsc.usgs.gov/isb/pubs/booklets/elvadist/elvadist.html\>, released April 2005. For mean elevations, see *Elevations and Distances in the United States*, 1983 edition.

Table 374. Land Cover/Use by Type: 1982 to 2007

[In millions of acres (1,937.7 represents 1,937,700,000), except percent. Excludes Alaska, Hawaii, and District of Columbia. For inventory-specific glossary of key terms, see <http://www.nrcs.usda.gov/technical/NRI/glossaries.html>]

| Year | Total surface area | Nonfederal rural land | | | | | | Devel-oped land | Water areas | Federal land |
		Rural land total [1]	Crop-land	Pasture-land	Range-land	Forest land	Other rural land			
Land										
1982	1,937.7	1,419.0	420.0	131.0	417.9	403.4	47.2	71.0	48.7	399.1
1992	1,937.7	1,402.8	381.4	125.0	408.9	405.2	48.1	83.9	49.4	401.5
1997	1,937.7	1,391.5	376.1	119.8	407.5	406.6	48.7	94.6	49.9	401.7
2002	1,937.7	1,381.3	367.1	117.8	408.2	407.3	48.9	104.0	50.4	401.9
2007	1,937.7	1,373.7	357.0	118.6	409.1	406.4	49.6	111.3	50.8	401.9
Percent of total land										
1982	100.0	73.2	21.7	6.8	21.6	20.8	2.4	3.7	2.5	20.6
1992	100.0	72.4	19.7	6.5	21.1	20.9	2.5	4.3	2.5	20.7
1997	100.0	71.8	19.4	6.2	21.0	21.0	2.5	4.9	2.6	20.7
2002	100.0	71.3	18.9	6.1	21.1	21.0	2.5	5.4	2.6	20.7
2007	100.0	70.9	18.4	6.1	21.1	21.0	2.6	5.7	2.6	20.7

[1] Includes Conservation Reserve Program (CRP) land not shown separately. CRP is a federal program established under the Food Security Act of 1985 to assist private landowners to convert highly erodible cropland to vegetative cover for 10 years.

Source: U.S. Department of Agriculture, Natural Resources and Conservation Service, *Summary Report: 2007 National Resources Inventory*. See also <http://www.nrcs.usda.gov/technical/NRI>.

Table 375. Wetlands on Nonfederal Land and Water Areas by Land Cover/Use and Farm Production Region: 2003

[In thousands of acres (110,760 represents 110,760,000). Represents palustrine and estuarine wetlands; see source]

Farm production region [1]	Total	Cropland [2]	Forest land	Range-land	Other rural land	Developed land	Water area
Wetlands, total	**110,760**	**16,730**	**65,440**	**7,740**	**15,800**	**1,590**	**3,460**
Lake states	22,460	2,710	15,480	–	3,880	160	230
Southeast	22,360	940	16,010	970	3,460	420	560
Delta states	17,950	3,240	11,020	270	2,730	190	500
Northeast	14,150	1,250	10,890	–	1,550	240	220
Northern plains	7,640	3,020	210	2,870	1,090	80	370
Appalachian	7,460	400	6,080	–	570	110	300
Southern plains	5,590	970	2,350	970	520	230	550
Mountain	4,780	1,570	220	2,010	820	30	130
Corn belt	4,690	1,330	2,440	–	380	100	440
Pacific	3,680	1,300	740	650	800	30	160

– Represents or rounds to zero. [1] Ten regions established by USDA, Economic Research Service, that group states according to differences in soils, slope of land, climate, distance to market, and storage and marketing facilities. [2] Includes pastureland and Conservation Reserve Program (CRP) lands.

Source: U.S. Department of Agriculture, Natural Resources Conservation Service, *2003 Annual National Resources Inventory*. See also <http://www.nrcs.usda.gov/technical/NRI/>.

Table 376. Land Cover/Use by State: 2003

[In thousands of acres (1,937,664 represents 1,937,664,000), except percent. Excludes Alaska, District of Columbia, Hawaii, and Island Areas]

| State | Total surface area | Selected nonfederal rural land, percent of total | | | State | Total surface area | Selected nonfederal rural land, percent of total | | |
		Crop-land	Range-land	Forest land			Crop-land	Range-land	Forest land
United States	**1,937,664**	**19.0**	**20.9**	**20.9**	Montana	94,110	15.4	39.0	5.7
					Nebraska	49,510	39.5	46.6	1.6
Alabama	33,424	7.5	0.2	64.4	Nevada	70,763	0.9	11.7	0.4
Arizona	72,964	1.3	44.2	5.7	New Hampshire	5,941	2.1	–	65.6
Arkansas	34,037	22.1	0.1	44.1	New Jersey	5,216	10.1	–	30.8
California	101,510	9.3	17.5	13.7	New Mexico	77,823	2.0	51.3	7.0
Colorado	66,625	12.5	37.2	4.9	New York	31,361	17.1	–	56.1
Connecticut	3,195	5.4	–	53.4	North Carolina	33,709	16.4	–	45.9
Delaware	1,534	29.8	–	22.2	North Dakota	45,251	53.6	24.5	1.0
Florida	37,534	7.7	7.2	33.9	Ohio	26,445	42.5	–	27.3
Georgia	37,741	11.0	–	58.0	Oklahoma	44,738	20.1	31.6	16.5
Idaho	53,488	10.2	12.0	7.5	Oregon	62,161	6.0	15.1	20.5
Illinois	36,059	66.5	–	11.0	Pennsylvania	28,995	17.7	–	53.9
Indiana	23,158	57.5	–	16.5	Rhode Island	813	2.5	–	45.9
Iowa	36,017	70.8	–	6.4	South Carolina	19,939	11.9	–	56.0
Kansas	52,661	50.3	30.1	2.9	South Dakota	49,358	34.6	44.7	1.0
Kentucky	25,863	21.2	–	40.6	Tennessee	26,974	17.6	–	44.3
Louisiana	31,377	17.3	0.9	42.5	Texas	171,052	14.9	56.2	6.2
Maine	20,966	1.8	–	84.0	Utah	54,339	3.1	19.6	3.5
Maryland	7,870	19.3	–	30.1	Vermont	6,154	9.5	–	67.1
Massachusetts	5,339	4.7	–	49.9	Virginia	27,087	10.6	–	48.7
Michigan	37,349	21.7	–	44.7	Washington	44,035	14.7	13.3	28.9
Minnesota	54,010	39.1	–	30.3	West Virginia	15,508	5.3	–	68.1
Mississippi	30,527	16.3	–	54.9	Wisconsin	35,920	28.7	–	40.4
Missouri	44,614	30.7	0.2	28.1	Wyoming	62,603	3.5	44.0	1.5

– Represents zero.

Source: U.S. Department of Agriculture, Natural Resources and Conservation Service, *Summary Report, 2003 Annual National Resources Inventory*. See also <http://www.nrcs.usda.gov/technical/NRI/>.

Table 377. U.S. Wetland Resources and Deepwater Habitats by Type: 2004 to 2009

[In thousands of acres (153,121.4 represents 153,121,400). Wetlands and deepwater habitats are defined separately because the term wetland does not include permanent water bodies. Deepwater habitats are permanently flooded land lying below the deepwater boundary of wetlands. Deepwater habitats include environments where surface water is permanent and often deep, so that water, rather than air, is the principal medium within which the dominant organisms live, whether or not they are attached to the substrate. As in wetlands, the dominant plants are hydrophytes; however, the substrates are considered nonsoil because the water is too deep to support emergent vegetation. In general terms, wetlands are lands where saturation with water is the dominant factor determining the nature of soil development and the types of plant and animal communities living in the soil and on its surface. The single feature that most wetlands share is soil or substrate that is at least periodically saturated with or covered by water. Wetlands are lands transitional between terrestrial and aquatic systems where the water table is usually at or near the surface or the land is covered by shallow water. For more information on wetlands, see the "Classification of Wetlands and Deepwater Habitats of the United States" at <http://www.npwrc.usgs.gov/resource/wetlands/classwet/index.htm>]

Wetland or deepwater category	Estimated area, 2004	Estimated area, 2009	Change, 2004 to 2009
All wetlands and deepwater habitats, total	**153,121.4**	**153,206.4**	**85.0**
All deepwater habitats, total	42,999.4	43,146.6	147.2
Lacustrine [1]	16,786.0	16,859.6	73.6
Riverine [2]	7,517.9	7,510.5	-7.4
Estuarine Subtidal [3]	18,695.4	18,776.5	81.1
All wetlands, total	110,122.1	110,059.8	-62.3
Intertidal wetlands [4]	5,869.3	5,785.2	-84.1
Marine intertidal	219.2	227.8	8.5
Estuarine intertidal nonvegetated	999.4	1,017.7	18.3
Estuarine intertidal vegetated	4,650.7	4,539.7	-110.9
Freshwater wetlands	104,252.7	104,274.6	21.9
Freshwater nonvegetated	6,502.1	6,709.3	207.2
Freshwater vegetated	97,750.6	97,565.3	-185.3
Freshwater emergent [5]	27,162.7	27,430.5	267.8
Freshwater forested [6]	52,256.5	51,623.3	-633.1
Freshwater shrub [7]	18,331.4	18,511.5	180.1

[1] The lacustrine system includes deepwater habitats with all of the following characteristics: (1) situated in a topographic depression or a dammed river channel; (2) lacking trees, shrubs, persistent emergents, emergent mosses or lichens with greater than 30 percent coverage; and (3) total area exceeds 20 acres (8 hectares). [2] The riverine system includes deepwater habitats contained within a channel, with the exception of habitats with water containing ocean derived salts in excess of 0.5 parts per thousand. [3] The estuarine system consists of deepwater tidal habitats and adjacent tidal wetlands that are usually semi-enclosed by land but have open, partly obstructed, or sporadic access to the open ocean, and in which ocean water is at least occasionally diluted by freshwater runoff from the land. Subtidal is where the substrate is continuously submerged by marine or estuarine waters. [4] Intertidal is where the substrate is exposed and flooded by tides. Intertidal includes the splash zone of coastal waters. [5] Emergent wetlands are characterized by erect, rooted, herbaceous hydrophytes, excluding mosses and lichens. This vegetation is present for most of the growing season in most years. These wetlands are usually dominated by perennial plants. [6] Forested wetlands are characterized by woody vegetation that is 20 feet tall or taller. [7] Shrub wetlands include areas dominated by woody vegetation less than 20 feet tall. The species include true shrubs, young trees, and trees or shrubs that are small or stunted because of environmental conditions.

Source: U.S. Fish and Wildlife Service, *Status and Trends of Wetlands in the Conterminous United States, 2004 to 2009*, September 2011. See also <http://www.fws.gov/wetlands/Status-And-Trends-2009/index.html>.

Table 378. U.S. Water Withdrawals Per Day by End Use: 1950 to 2005

[(180 represents 180,000,000,000). Includes the District of Columbia, Puerto Rico and U.S. Virgin Islands. Withdrawal signifies water physically withdrawn from a source. Includes fresh and saline water; excludes water used for hydroelectric power. For information on changes for the 2005 report, see source report *Estimated Use of Water in the United States in 2005*, Table 14]

Year	Total with-drawals	Public supply	Rural domestic and livestock		Irri-gation	Thermo electric power	Other			
			Self supplied domestic	Live-stock			Self supplied domestic	Mining	Com-mercial	Aqua-culture
1950 [1]	180	14	2.1	1.5	89	40	37	(5)	(5)	(5)
1955 [2]	240	17	2.1	1.5	110	72	39	(5)	(5)	(5)
1960 [3]	270	21	2.0	1.6	110	100	38	(5)	(5)	(5)
1965 [4]	310	24	2.3	1.7	120	130	46	(5)	(5)	(5)
1970 [4]	370	27	2.6	1.9	130	170	47	(5)	(5)	(5)
1975 [3]	420	29	2.8	2.1	140	200	45	(5)	(5)	(5)
1980 [3]	430	33	3.4	2.2	150	210	45	(5)	(5)	(5)
1985 [3]	397	36.4	3.32	2.23	135	187	25.9	3.44	1.23	2.24
1990 [3]	404	38.8	3.39	2.25	134	194	22.6	4.93	2.39	2.25
1995 [3]	399	40.2	3.39	2.28	130	190	22.4	3.72	2.89	3.22
2000 [3]	413	43.2	3.58	2.38	139	195	19.7	4.50	(NA)	5.77
2005 [3]	410	44.2	3.83	2.14	128	201	18.2	4.02	(NA)	8.78

NA Not available. [1] Population covered: 48 states, District of Columbia, and Hawaii. [2] Population covered: 48 states. [3] Population covered: 50 states, District of Columbia, Puerto Rico, and the Virgin Islands. [4] Population covered: 50 states, District of Columbia, and Puerto Rico. [5] Included in "Self-Supplied Industrial."

Source: 1940–1960, U.S. Bureau of Domestic Business Development, based principally on committee prints, *Water Resources Activities in the United States*, for the Senate Committee on National Water Resources, U.S. Senate, thereafter, U.S. Geological Survey, *Estimated Use of Water in the United States in 2005*, circular 1344, October 2009. See also <http://pubs.usgs.gov/circ/1344/>.

Table 379. National Ambient Air Pollutant Concentrations by Type of Pollutant: 2003 to 2009

[Data represent annual composite averages of pollutant based on daily 24-hour averages of monitoring stations, except carbon monoxide which is based on the second-highest, nonoverlapping, 8-hour average; ozone, the fourth-highest maximum 8-hour value; and lead, the maximum quarterly average of ambient lead levels. Based on data from the Air Quality System. µmg/m [3] = micrograms of pollutant per cubic meter of air; ppm = parts per million]

Pollutant	Unit	Moni-toring stations, number	Air quality stan-dard [1]	2003	2004	2005	2006	2007	2008	2009
Carbon monoxide............	ppm	300	9 [2]	2.7	2.5	2.3	2.2	2.0	1.9	1.8
Ozone...........................	ppm	1,011	0.075 [3]	0.080	0.074	0.079	0.077	0.077	0.073	0.069
Sulfur dioxide................	ppm	384	0.03 [4]	0.0043	0.0041	0.0041	0.0037	0.0035	0.0032	0.0027
Particulates (PM-10).........	µmg/m [3]	722	150 [5]	90.5	70.4	69.4	76.0	69.4	67.3	59.7
Fine particulates (PM2.5) annual average..............	µmg/m [3]	741	15 [6]	12.3	11.9	12.8	11.6	11.9	10.9	9.9
Fine particulates (PM2.5) daily average................	µmg/m [3]	741	35 [7]	31.1	31.0	33.6	28.8	31.3	27.1	24.9
Nitrogen dioxide...............	ppm	311	0.053 [8]	0.014	0.013	0.013	0.013	0.012	0.011	0.011
Lead.............................	µmg/m [3]	109	0.15 [9]	0.16	0.20	0.15	0.14	0.15	0.19	0.11

[1] Refers to the primary National Ambient Air Quality Standard. [2] Based on 8-hour standard of 9 ppm. [3] Based on 8-hour standard of 0.075 ppm. On March 12, 2008, EPA revised the level of the primary and secondary 8-hour ozone standards to 0.075 ppm. [4] Based on annual standard of 0.03 ppm. [5] Based on 24-hour (daily) standard of 150 mg/m [3]. The particulates (PM-10) standard replaced the previous standard for total suspended particulates in 1987. In 2006, EPA revoked the annual PM-10 standard. [6] Based on annual standard of 15 mg/m [3]. The PM-2.5 national monitoring network was deployed in 1999. National trend data prior to that time is not available. [7] Based on daily standard of 35 mg/m [3]. The PM-2.5 national monitoring network was deployed in 1999. National trend data prior to that time is not available. [8] Based on annual standard of 0.053 ppm. [9] Based on 3-month standard of 1.5 µmg/m [3]. On October 15, 2008, EPA revised the form of the primary and secondary lead standards and revised the level to 0.15 mg/m [3].

Source: U.S. Environmental Protection Agency, *Latest Findings on National Air Quality—Status and Trends through 2009*, <http://www.epa.gov/airtrends/reports.html>.

Table 380. Selected National Air Pollutant Emissions: 1970 to 2010

[In thousands of tons (4,320 represents 4,320,000), except as indicated. The methodology used to estimate emission data for 1970 thru 1984 and for 1985 thru the current year is different. Beginning with 1985, the methodology for more recent years is described in the document available at <http://www.epa.gov/ttn/chief/net/2011inventory.html>]

Year	Ammonia	Carbon monoxide	Nitrogen oxide	PM-10 [1]	PM-10 [2]	PM-2.5 [1]	PM-2.5 [2]	Sulfur dioxide	V.O.C. [3]
1970..............	(NA)	204,042	26,882	13,022	13,022	(NA)	(NA)	31,218	34,659
1980..............	(NA)	185,408	27,080	7,013	7,013	(NA)	(NA)	25,926	31,107
1990..............	4,320	154,188	25,527	27,753	27,753	7,560	7,560	23,077	24,108
2000..............	4,907	114,467	22,598	23,747	22,961	7,288	6,502	16,347	17,512
2006..............	4,153	87,535	18,429	21,170	15,670	5,544	2,778	13,330	17,804
2007..............	4,224	82,656	17,812	21,197	16,964	5,635	3,066	11,834	17,267
2008..............	4,364	82,076	17,198	21,577	18,258	6,052	3,354	10,352	17,709
2009..............	4,356	80,190	15,683	21,538	18,238	6,030	3,332	8,288	17,492
2010..............	4,343	76,221	14,717	21,489	18,199	5,984	3,286	7,578	17,021

NA Not available. [1] PM=Particular Matter; PM-10 is equal to or less than ten microns in diameter; PM-2.5 to or less than 2.5 microns effective diameter. [2] Without condensibles. [3] Volatile organic compound.

Source: U.S. Environmental Protection Agency, *National Emissions Inventory (NEI) Air Pollutant Emissions Trends Data*, 1970–2012 Average annual emissions, all criteria pollutants, <http://www.epa.gov/ttn/chief/trends/index.html#tables>.

Table 381. Selected Air Pollutant Emissions by Pollutant and Source: 2010

[In thousands of tons, except as indicated (4,343 represents 4,343,000). See headnote, Table 380]

Source	Ammonia	Carbon monoxide	Nitrogen oxide	PM-10 [1]	PM-2.5 [1]	Sulfur dioxide	V.O.C. [2]
Total emissions...............	**4,343**	**76,221**	**14,717**	**21,538**	**5,984**	**7,578**	**17,021**
Fuel combustion, stationary sources................	103	4,320	4,080	967	819	6,486	530
Electric utilities................	27	722	2,106	398	303	5,147	43
Industrial........................	13	894	1,391	191	147	1,055	107
Other fuel combustion.............	63	2,704	582	377	370	283	381
Industrial processes.............	151	3,111	1,081	1,513	686	789	6,879
Chemical and allied product manufacturing........	19	186	55	27	21	185	87
Metals processing..............	2	840	79	82	63	177	38
Petroleum and related industries....................	1	261	424	30	23	147	1,742
Other............................	56	425	412	1,083	349	253	364
Solvent utilization................	–	5	5	4	4	–	3,274
Storage and transport............	5	18	9	48	22	6	1,189
Waste disposal and recycling.......	68	1,377	97	239	205	21	185
Highway vehicles..................	116	32,000	5,951	337	246	66	2,661
Off highway [3]...................	4	15,826	3,344	241	223	99	2,257
Miscellaneous [4]..................	3,968	20,964	262	18,480	4,010	139	4,694

– Rounds to zero. [1] See footnote 1, Table 380. [2] Volatile organic compound. [3] Includes emissions from farm tractors and other farm machinery, construction equipment, industrial machinery, recreational marine vessels, and small general utility engines such as lawn mowers. [4] Includes emissions such as from forest fires and other kinds of burning, various agricultural activities, fugitive dust from paved and unpaved roads, and other construction and mining activities, and natural sources.

Source: U.S. Environmental Protection Agency, *National Emissions Inventory (NEI) Air Pollutant Emissions Trends Data*, 1970–2012 Average annual emissions, all criteria pollutants, <http://www.epa.gov/ttn/chief/trends/index.html#tables>.

Table 382. Emissions of Greenhouse Gases by Type and Source: 1990 to 2009

[In millions of metric tons (6,133.2 represents 6,133,200,000). Metric ton = 2,204.6 lbs. Emission estimates were mandated by Congress through Section 1605(a) of the Energy Policy Act of 1992 (Title XVI). Data shown below, by type and source, are measured in terms of their carbon dioxide equivalent]

Type and source	1990	2000	2004	2005	2006	2007	2008	2009 [1]
Total emissions	**6,133.2**	**6,935.3**	**7,071.9**	**7,109.4**	**7,027.4**	**7,150.4**	**6,983.1**	**6,575.5**
Carbon dioxide, total	5,040.9	5,900.3	6,031.3	6,055.2	5,961.6	6,059.5	5,865.5	5,446.8
From energy use by sector								
Residential	963.4	1,185.1	1,227.8	1,261.5	1,192.0	1,242.0	1,229.0	1,162.2
Commercial	792.6	1,022.0	1,053.5	1,069.0	1,043.4	1,078.6	1,073.5	1,003.6
Industrial	1,695.1	1,788.1	1,731.1	1,675.2	1,661.1	1,661.6	1,597.6	1,405.4
Transportation	1,587.7	1,872.0	1,962.3	1,990.7	2,021.9	2,039.6	1,937.9	1,854.5
Adjustments to energy [2]	-82.9	-64.7	-45.3	-44.6	-62.7	-67.5	-76.1	-66.0
Adjusted energy subtotal	4,955.9	5,802.6	5,929.3	5,951.8	5,855.7	5,954.2	5,761.9	5,359.6
Other sources	85.1	97.8	102.0	103.5	105.9	105.3	103.6	87.3
Methane	768.8	663.1	661.6	669.2	678.5	690.9	724.2	730.9
Energy sources	293.1	281.7	280.0	277.0	279.8	285.8	299.3	303.0
Agricultural sources	190.6	201.2	204.0	209.9	211.8	212.3	219.7	215.9
Waste management	280.6	174.6	172.0	177.3	181.9	187.6	200.6	207.9
Industrial processes	4.5	5.6	5.6	5.0	5.1	5.1	4.6	4.2
Nitrous oxide	221.4	217.8	222.0	223.6	223.7	228.6	223.5	219.6
Agricultural sources	148.7	144.3	154.1	156.9	157.8	162.1	161.1	161.0
Energy use	40.2	52.1	49.7	48.2	47.2	47.3	45.1	42.5
Industrial processes	28.5	16.7	13.3	13.6	13.6	14.1	12.1	10.8
Waste management	4.0	4.7	4.9	5.0	5.1	5.2	5.2	5.3
High-GWP gases [3]	102.1	154.0	157.0	161.3	163.6	171.4	169.9	178.2

[1] 2009 preliminary data. [2] Carbon dioxide emissions from U.S. Territories are added to the U.S. total, and carbon dioxide emissions from fuels used for international transport (both ocean-going vessels and airplanes) are subtracted to derive total U.S. greenhouse as emissions. [3] High global warming potential gases: hyrdofluorocarbons (HFCs), perfluorocarbons (PFCs), and sulfur hexafluoride (SF6).

Source: U.S. Energy Information Administration, Environment, *Greenhouse Gas Emissions in the United States, 2009*, Series DOE/EIA-0573 (2009), annual. See also <http://www.eia.gov/environment/emissions/ghg_report/>.

Table 383. Carbon Dioxide Emissions by Sector and Source: 1990 to 2009

[In million metric tons (5,040.9 represents 5,040,900,000), except as noted. Data below measured in terms of carbon dioxide equivalent. Data have been revised for years shown]

Sector	1990	2000	2004	2005	2006	2007	2008	2009 [1]
Total [2]	5,040.9	5,900.3	6,031.3	6,055.2	5,961.6	6,059.5	5,865.5	5,446.8
Total [3]	**5,038.7**	**5,867.2**	**5,974.7**	**5,996.4**	**5,918.3**	**6,021.8**	**5,838.0**	**5,425.6**
Petroleum	2,186.6	2,460.6	2,608.6	2,627.6	2,602.5	2,603.2	2,443.5	2,318.8
Coal	1,821.4	2,155.5	2,160.2	2,181.9	2,146.9	2,172.2	2,139.4	1,876.8
Natural gas	1,024.8	1,240.6	1,194.4	1,175.2	1,157.0	1,234.7	1,243.0	1,218.0
Residential	**963.4**	**1,185.1**	**1,227.8**	**1,261.5**	**1,192.0**	**1,242.0**	**1,229.0**	**1,162.2**
Petroleum	98.4	108.0	106.0	100.9	85.0	86.8	84.9	82.9
Coal	3.0	1.1	1.1	0.8	0.6	0.7	0.7	0.6
Natural gas	238.3	270.8	264.3	262.4	237.5	257.3	265.8	259.1
Electricity [4]	623.7	805.2	856.4	897.3	868.9	897.2	877.5	819.5
Commercial	**792.6**	**1,022.0**	**1,053.5**	**1,069.0**	**1,043.4**	**1,078.6**	**1,073.5**	**1,003.6**
Petroleum [5]	72.5	57.9	58.3	54.9	47.6	46.6	46.1	43.6
Coal	12.0	8.8	9.8	9.3	6.2	6.7	6.5	5.8
Natural gas	142.3	172.5	169.8	163.1	154.0	164.2	171.3	169.1
Electricity [4]	565.9	782.8	815.6	841.8	835.6	861.1	849.5	785.1
Industrial [6]	**1,695.1**	**1,788.1**	**1,731.1**	**1,675.2**	**1,661.1**	**1,661.6**	**1,597.6**	**1,405.4**
Petroleum	365.5	370.4	418.6	416.8	430.4	415.4	376.2	343.1
Coal	258.4	210.8	190.5	182.9	179.4	174.6	168.2	130.9
Natural gas	432.4	480.8	431.5	397.5	394.2	406.3	406.9	383.1
Electricity [4]	638.3	718.6	674.7	672.8	650.2	662.3	641.8	55.1
Transportation [6]	**1,587.7**	**1,872.0**	**1,962.3**	**1,990.7**	**2,021.9**	**2,039.6**	**1,937.9**	**1,854.5**
Petroleum	1,548.4	1,832.8	1,925.6	1,952.7	1,984.0	1,999.0	1,896.3	1,815.7
Natural gas	36.1	35.7	31.9	33.1	33.2	35.3	36.7	34.1
Electricity [4]	3.2	3.6	4.8	5.0	4.7	5.3	4.9	4.7
Electric power sector [7]	**1,831.0**	**2,310.2**	**2,351.5**	**2,416.9**	**2,359.5**	**2,425.9**	**2,373.7**	**2,160.3**
Petroleum	101.8	91.5	100.1	102.3	55.6	55.3	40.0	33.6
Coal	1,547.6	1,927.4	1,943.1	1,983.8	1,953.7	1,987.3	1,959.4	1,742.2
Natural gas	175.5	280.9	296.8	319.1	338.2	371.7	362.3	372.6

[1] Preliminary. [2] Emissions from nonfuel uses, adjustments to energy, and other sources are included. [3] Emissions from renewables are included in total. [4] Share of total electric power sector carbon dioxide emissions weighted by sales to this sector. [5] Includes small amounts of petroleum coke. [6] Includes emissions from nonfuel uses of fossil fuels. [7] Emissions from the electric power sector are apportioned to each end-use sector according to their share of electricity sales.

Source: U.S. Energy Information Administration, Environment, *Greenhouse Gas Emissions in the United States, 2009*, Series DOE/EIA-0573 (2009), annual. See also <http://www.eia.doe.gov/environment.html>.

Table 384. Municipal Solid Waste Generation, Materials Recovery, Combustion With Energy Recovery, and Discards: 1980 to 2010

[In millions of tons (151.6 represents 151,600,000), except as indicated. Covers post-consumer residential and commercial solid wastes which comprise the major portion of typical municipal collections. Excludes mining, agricultural and industrial processing, demolition and construction wastes, sewage sludge and junked autos and obsolete equipment wastes. Based on material-flows estimating procedure and wet weight as generated]

Item and material	1980	1990	2000	2005	2008	2009	2010
Waste generated..................	151.6	208.3	242.5	252.7	251.4	243.7	249.9
Per person per day (lb.)............	3.7	4.6	4.7	4.7	4.5	4.4	4.4
Total materials recovery.............	14.5	33.2	69.5	79.9	83.8	82.3	85.1
Per person per day (lb.)............	0.4	0.7	1.4	1.5	1.5	1.5	1.5
Recovery for recycling.............	14.5	29.0	53.0	59.3	61.7	61.5	65.0
Per person per day (lb.)...........	0.4	0.6	1.0	1.1	1.1	1.1	1.2
Recovery for composting [1].........	(Z)	4.2	16.5	20.6	22.1	20.8	20.2
Per person per day (lb.)...........	(Z)	0.1	0.3	0.4	0.4	0.4	0.4
Combustion with energy recovery..........	2.7	29.7	33.7	31.6	31.6	29.0	29.3
Per person per day (lb.)...........	0.1	0.7	0.7	0.6	0.6	0.5	0.5
Discards to landfill, other disposal.............	134.4	145.3	139.4	141.2	136.0	132.4	135.5
Per person per day (lb.)...........	3.2	3.2	2.7	2.6	2.4	2.4	2.4
PERCENT DISTRIBUTION OF GENERATION							
Percent of total generation............	71.8	70.3	73.7	73.2	72.1	70.7	71.2
Paper and paperboard............	36.4	34.9	36.2	33.6	30.8	28.1	28.5
Glass............	10.0	6.3	5.3	5.0	4.8	4.8	4.6
Metals............	10.2	7.9	7.8	8.1	8.5	8.8	9.0
Plastics............	4.5	8.2	10.5	11.6	12.0	12.2	12.4
Rubber and leather............	2.8	2.8	2.8	2.9	3.0	3.1	3.1
Textiles............	1.7	2.8	3.9	4.6	5.1	5.3	5.3
Wood............	4.6	5.9	5.6	5.9	6.1	6.5	6.4
Other............	1.7	1.5	1.6	1.7	1.9	1.9	1.9
Total other waste............	28.2	29.7	26.3	26.8	27.9	29.3	28.8
Food scraps............	8.6	11.5	12.3	12.7	13.3	14.1	13.9
Yard trimmings............	18.1	16.8	12.6	12.7	13.1	13.6	13.4
Miscellaneous inorganic wastes............	1.5	1.4	1.4	1.5	1.5	1.6	1.5

Z Less than 5,000 tons or 0.05 percent. [1] Composting of yard trimmings, food scraps, and other municipal solid waste organic material. Does not include backyard composting.

Source: Franklin Associates, a Division of ERG, Prairie Village, KS, *Municipal Solid Waste in the United States: 2010 Facts and Figures.* Prepared for the U.S. Environmental Protection Agency. See also <www.epa.gov/osw/nonhaz/municipal/msw99.htm>.

Table 385. Generation and Recovery of Selected Materials in Municipal Solid Waste: 1980 to 2010

[In millions of tons (151.6 represents 151,600,000), except as indicated. Covers post-consumer residential and commercial solid wastes which comprise the major portion of typical municipal collections. Excludes mining, agricultural and industrial processing, demolition and construction wastes, sewage sludge, and junked autos and obsolete equipment wastes. Based on material-flows estimating procedure and wet weight as generated]

Item and material	1980	1990	2000	2005	2008	2009	2010
Waste generated, total [1]............	**151.6**	**205.2**	**242.6**	**252.4**	**251.4**	**243.7**	**249.9**
Paper and paperboard............	55.2	72.7	87.7	84.8	77.4	68.4	71.3
Glass............	15.1	13.1	12.8	12.5	12.2	11.8	11.5
Metals: Ferrous............	12.6	12.6	14.1	15.0	16.0	15.9	16.9
Aluminum............	1.7	2.8	3.2	3.3	3.4	3.4	3.4
Other nonferrous............	1.2	1.1	1.6	1.9	2.0	2.0	2.1
Plastics............	6.8	17.1	25.5	29.3	30.1	29.8	31.0
Food scraps............	13.0	20.8	26.8	32.0	33.3	34.3	34.8
Yard trimmings............	27.5	35.0	30.5	32.1	32.9	33.2	33.4
Materials recovered, total [1]............	**14.5**	**33.2**	**69.5**	**79.9**	**83.8**	**82.3**	**85.1**
Paper and paperboard............	11.7	20.2	37.6	42.0	42.9	42.5	44.6
Glass............	0.8	2.6	2.9	2.6	2.8	3.0	3.1
Metals: Ferrous............	0.4	2.2	4.7	5.0	5.3	5.3	5.7
Aluminum............	0.3	1.0	0.9	0.7	0.7	0.7	0.7
Other nonferrous............	0.5	0.7	1.1	1.3	1.4	1.4	1.5
Plastics............	0.2	0.4	1.5	1.8	2.1	2.1	2.6
Food scraps............	(Z)	(Z)	0.7	0.7	0.8	0.9	1.0
Yard trimmings............	(Z)	4.2	15.8	19.9	21.3	19.9	19.2
Percent of generation recovered, total [1]............	**9.6**	**16.2**	**28.6**	**31.6**	**33.3**	**33.8**	**34.1**
Paper and paperboard............	21.3	27.8	42.8	49.5	55.5	62.1	62.5
Glass............	5.0	20.1	22.6	20.7	23.1	25.5	27.1
Metals: Ferrous............	2.9	17.6	33.1	33.1	33.2	33.1	33.8
Aluminum............	17.9	35.9	26.9	20.7	21.1	20.1	19.9
Other nonferrous............	46.6	66.4	66.3	68.8	69.4	69.5	70.5
Plastics............	0.3	2.2	5.8	6.0	7.1	7.2	8.2
Food scraps............	(Z)	(Z)	2.5	2.2	2.4	2.5	2.8
Yard trimmings............	(Z)	12.0	51.7	61.9	64.7	59.9	57.5

Z Less than 5,000 tons or 0.05 percent. [1] Includes products not shown separately.

Source: Franklin Associates, a Division of ERG, Prairie Village, KS, *Municipal Solid Waste in the United States: 2010 Facts and Figures.* Prepared for the U.S. Environmental Protection Agency. See also <www.epa.gov/osw/nonhaz/municipal/msw99.htm>.

Table 386. Municipal Solid Waste—Generation, Recovery, and Discards by Selected Type of Product: 2010

[See headnote, Table 385]

Type of product	Generation (1,000 tons)	Recovery Products recovered (1,000 tons)	Recovery Percent of generation	Discards (1,000 tons)
Paper and paperboard products [1]	71,310	44,570	62.5	26,680
Nondurable goods	33,570	17,720	52.8	15,850
Newspapers/Mechanical Papers	9,880	7,070	71.6	2,810
Other paper nondurable goods	23,690	10,650	45.0	13,040
Containers and packaging	37,680	26,850	71.3	10,830
Corrugated boxes	29,050	24,690	85.0	4,360
Other paper and paperboard packaging	8,630	2,160	25.0	6,470
Glass products [1]	11,530	3,130	27.1	8,400
Containers and packaging	9,360	3,130	33.4	6,230
Beer and soft drink bottles	5,670	2,350	41.4	3,320
Wine and liquor bottles	1,700	420	24.7	1,280
Food and other bottles and jars	1,990	360	18.1	1,630
Metal products [1]	22,410	7,870	35.1	14,540
Ferrous	14,160	3,820	27.0	10,340
Aluminum	1,310	(Z)	(Z)	1,310
Other nonferrous	2,100	1,480	70.5	620
Plastics [1]	31,040	2,550	8.2	28,490
Plastics in durable goods	10,960	700	6.4	10,260
Plastics in nondurable goods	6,400	(Z)	(Z)	6,400
Plastics in containers and packaging	13,680	1,850	13.5	11,830
Rubber and leather [1]	7,780	1,170	15.0	6,610
Rubber in tires	3,300	1,170	35.5	2,130

Z Less than 5,000 tons or 0.05 percent. [1] Includes products not shown separately.

Source: Franklin Associates, a Division of ERG, Prairie Village, KS, *Municipal Solid Waste in the United States: 2010 Facts and Figures.* Prepared for the U.S. Environmental Protection Agency. See also <www.epa.gov/osw/nonhaz/municipal/msw99.htm>.

Table 387. Environmental Industry—Revenues and Employment by Industry Segment: 2000 to 2010

[211.2 represents $211,200,000,000. Covers approximately 30,000 private and public companies engaged in revenue-generating environmental activities]

Industry segment	Revenue (bil. dol.) 2000	2005	2009	2010	Employment 2000	2005	2009	2010
Industry total	211.2	255.0	304.6	316.3	1,371,600	1,469,600	1,621,300	1,657,300
Analytical services [1]	1.8	1.8	1.9	1.8	20,200	20,000	19,600	19,200
Wastewater treatment works [2]	28.7	35.6	44.1	46.9	118,800	141,100	169,000	178,900
Solid waste management [3]	39.4	47.8	51.1	52.4	221,400	256,500	265,300	271,200
Hazardous waste management [4]	8.2	8.7	8.6	8.7	44,800	45,000	42,100	42,000
Remediation/industrial services	10.1	11.0	11.9	12.2	100,200	96,600	99,600	101,000
Consulting and engineering	17.4	22.4	25.7	26.2	184,000	220,800	240,500	242,900
Water equipment and chemicals	19.8	24.8	26.6	27.2	130,500	153,000	157,300	159,300
Instrument manufacturing	3.8	4.7	5.2	5.5	30,200	34,600	36,100	37,500
Air pollution control equipment [5]	19.0	18.8	15.8	14.9	129,600	123,400	101,800	95,600
Waste management equipment [6]	10.0	10.1	11.0	11.1	75,500	72,900	73,800	73,700
Process and prevention technology	1.2	1.5	1.8	1.9	29,000	28,100	26,500	26,400
Water utilities [7]	29.9	35.1	40.6	42.1	130,000	145,200	162,000	167,200
Resource recovery [8]	16.0	21.0	24.5	25.2	127,000	78,900	88,200	91,500
Clean energy systems and power [9]	5.9	11.9	35.8	40.1	30,400	53,500	139,500	150,900

[1] Covers environmental laboratory testing and services. [2] Mostly revenues collected by municipal entities for sewage or wastewater plants. [3] Covers such activities as collection, transportation, transfer stations, disposal, landfill ownership and management for solid waste and recyclables. [4] Transportation and disposal of hazardous, medical, and nuclear waste. [5] Includes stationary and mobile sources. [6] Includes vehicles, containers, liners, processing, and remediation equipment. [7] Revenues generated from the sale of water, majority in public sector. [8] Revenues generated from the sale of recovered metals, paper, plastic, etc. [9] Revenues generated from the sale of equipment and systems and electricity.

Source: Environmental Business International, Inc., San Diego, CA, publisher of *Environmental Business Journal;* (copyright) 2012 EBI Inc. See also <http://www.ebionline.org>.

Table 388. Toxic Chemical Releases and Transfers by Media: 2005 to 2010

[In millions of pounds (4,444.7 represents 4,444,700,000), except as indicated. Based on reports filed as required by Section 313 of the Emergency Planning and Community Right-to-Know Act (EPCRA, or Title III of the Superfund Amendments and Reauthorization Act of 1986), Public Law 99-499. The Pollution Prevention Act (PPA) of 1990 mandates collection of data on toxic chemicals that are treated on-site, recycled, and combusted for energy recovery. Owners and operators of facilities that are classified within North American Industrial Classification Code groups 31 through 33, 2121, 2122, 2211, 4246, 4247 and 562; have 10 or more full-time employees, and that manufacture, process, or otherwise use any listed toxic chemical in quantities greater than the established threshold in the course of a calendar year are covered and required to report. Includes all Persistent, Toxic (PBT) chemicals and vanadium and vanadium compounds. Does not include off-site disposal or other releases transferred to other TRI facilities that reported the amounts as on-site disposal or other releases]

Media	2005	2006	2007	2008	2009	2010
Total facilities reporting............................	24,312	23,823	23,198	22,504	21,328	20,973
Total on- and off-site disposal or other releases.................	4,444.7	4,397.1	4,152.9	3,881.9	3,393.8	3,847.8
On-site releases............................	3,843.3	3,801.4	3,575.2	3,391.7	3,037.0	3,419.3
Air emissions [1]............................	1,519.7	1,418.2	1,334.5	1,152.5	924.0	860.3
Surface water discharges.......................	257.7	253.0	241.8	249.9	208.0	226.1
Underground injection class I..................	215.6	204.0	188.9	174.1	155.0	201.8
Underground injection class II-V...............	20.2	20.1	21.6	18.3	26.3	27.7
RCRA subtitle C landfills [2]...................	159.3	154.0	154.2	127.5	83.9	67.4
Other landfills............................	269.8	264.9	270.4	282.3	240.4	282.1
Land treatment/application farming............	23.7	27.1	22.1	24.8	17.0	15.0
Surface impoundments........................	782.3	823.7	769.3	740.1	799.6	834.2
Other land disposal........................	595.0	636.4	572.4	622.4	582.8	904.6
Off-site releases............................	601.5	595.7	577.7	490.2	356.8	428.5
Total transfers offsite for further waste management...............	3,962.3	4,007.6	3,871.8	3,514.0	2,837.5	3,244.3
Tranfers to recycling........................	2,112.6	2,197.9	2,125.2	1,976.5	1,630.8	1,889.4
Transfers to energy recovery..................	609.3	556.2	525.8	451.2	367.0	428.8
Transfers to treatment.......................	349.8	337.4	296.3	257.4	229.1	250.4
Transfers to POTWs (non metals) [3]............	265.0	260.7	253.7	255.3	217.5	230.6
Transfers to POTWs metal and metal compounds [3]...	1.6	1.6	1.8	1.1	0.8	0.8
Other off-site transfers......................	0.4	0.5	0.2	0.2	0.0	0.2
Transfers off-site for disposal or other releases.....	623.6	653.3	668.8	572.3	392.1	443.9
Total production-related waste managed.....................	24,873.1	24,333.2	24,146.6	23,038.4	20,392.3	21,735.6
Recycled on-site..........................	6,720.7	6,823.9	6,883.4	6,822.1	6,056.6	6,014.1
Recycled off-site...........................	2,118.0	2,201.7	2,132.6	1,975.0	1,616.9	1,889.8
Energy recovery on-site......................	2,436.0	2,391.5	2,283.3	2,269.5	1,870.3	1,969.0
Energy recovery off-site.....................	609.1	555.6	523.9	450.1	369.2	428.9
Treated on-site............................	7,921.9	7,307.1	7,538.6	7,074.0	6,610.0	7,103.2
Treated off-site............................	575.9	558.6	518.5	481.6	423.8	456.9
Quantity disposed or otherwise release of on- and off-site.............	4,491.5	4,494.7	4,266.3	3,966.2	3,445.6	3,873.7
Non-production-related waste managed.................	24.0	18.3	14.2	34.0	11.3	13.6

[1] Air emissions include both fugitive and point source. [2] RCRA=Resource Conservation and Recovery Act. [3] POTW (Publicly Owned Treatment Work) is a wastewater treatment facility that is owned by a state or municipality.

Source: U.S. Environmental Protection Agency, Toxic Release Inventory (TRI) Program, *2010 TRI National Analysis*. See also <http://www.epa.gov/tri/tridata/tri10/nationalanalysis/index.htm>. Data as of September 2012.

Table 389. Toxic Chemical Releases by Industry: 2010

[In millions of pounds (3,929.3 represents 3,929,300,000), except as indicated. See headnote, Table 388]

Industry	2002 NAICS [1] code	Total on- and off-site releases	On-site releases Total	Air emissions	Other surface impound- ments	Off-site releases/ transfers to [2] disposal
Total [3]............................	(X)	3,929.3	3,519.5	860.0	831.6	409.8
Coal mining..............................	2121	10.5	10.5	0.6	0.9	(Z)
Metal mining............................	2122	1,622.5	1,620.2	3.3	659.3	2.3
Electric utilities.........................	2211	697.5	622.7	312.9	113.5	74.8
Food/beverages/tobacco..................	311/312	143.7	133.4	43.1	0.1	10.3
Textiles..................................	313/314	2.7	2.2	1.5	0.1	0.6
Apparel..................................	315	(Z)	(Z)	(Z)	(Z)	(Z)
Leather..................................	316	0.7	0.3	0.2	–	0.4
Wood products..........................	321	8.4	7.9	7.7	(Z)	0.6
Paper....................................	322	178.0	170.7	133.6	3.4	7.3
Printing and publishing..................	323/51	10.4	10.2	10.2	0.0	0.2
Petroleum...............................	324	65.2	60.2	36.0	(Z)	5.0
Chemicals...............................	325	501.8	449.3	161.6	19.2	52.5
Plastics and rubber......................	326	35.3	28.2	28.1	(Z)	7.1
Stone/clay/glass.........................	327	23.5	20.6	16.3	(Z)	2.9
Cement..................................	32731	5.3	5.2	4.0	(Z)	0.1
Primary metals..........................	331	368.7	190.9	34.5	30.2	177.8
Fabricated metals.......................	332	40.6	22.1	20.4	(Z)	18.4
Machinery...............................	333	4.8	2.8	2.8	–	2.0
Computers/electronic products............	334	5.3	3.0	1.3	(Z)	2.2
Electrical equipment.....................	335	5.6	1.6	1.5	(Z)	4.0
Transportation equipment................	336	34.4	27.2	26.9	(Z)	7.2
Furniture................................	337	4.2	4.2	4.2	–	0.1
Miscellaneous Manufacturing.............	339	3.9	3.1	3.1	–	0.8
Chemical wholesalers....................	4246	1.6	1.4	1.4	–	0.2
Petroleum bulk terminals.................	4247	2.4	2.3	2.3	(Z)	0.1
Hazardous waste........................	562	118.3	87.2	0.4	3.8	31.1
No codes [3].............................	(X)	34.0	32.1	2.0	0.9	1.9

– Represents zero. X Not applicable. Z less than 50,000 lbs. [1] North American Industry Classification System, see text, Section 12. [2] Includes off-site disposal to underground injection for Class I wells, Class II to V wells, other surface impoundments, land releases, and other releases, not shown separately. [3] Includes industries with no specific industry identified.

Source: U.S. Environmental Protection Agency, *2010 TRI National Analysis*. See also <http://www.epa.gov/tri/tridata/tri10/national_analysis/index.htm>. Data as of November 18, 2011.

Table 390. Toxic Chemical Releases by State and Outlying Area: 2010

[In millions of pounds (3,929.3 represents 3,929,300,000). Based on reports filed as required by Section 313 of the EPCRA. See headnote, Table 388]

State and outlying areas	Total on-and off-site releases	On-site releases or other disposal Total [1]	Air emissions	Other surface impoundments	Off-site releases/transfers to disposal	State and outlying areas	Total on-and off-site releases	On-site releases or other disposal Total [1]	Air emissions	Other surface impoundments	Off-site releases/transfers to disposal
Total	3,929.3	3,519.5	940.4	831.6	409.8	MO	76.7	74.8	11.5	44.7	1.8
U.S. total	3,922.8	3,513.9	935.5	831.6	408.8	MT	38.3	36.8	1.7	4.7	1.5
AL	93.1	75.6	35.7	15.5	17.5	NE	31.9	28.6	19.8	(Z)	3.2
AK	835.7	835.5	0.3	303.8	0.3	NV	476.9	474.9	1.8	173.6	1.9
AZ	79.9	78.8	2.1	10.4	1.1	NH	3.3	3.1	3.0	0.0	0.2
AR	36.8	32.9	16.1	1.9	3.8	NJ	16.0	13.1	11.6	(Z)	2.9
CA	35.2	31.5	9.7	(Z)	3.7	NM	12.5	12.4	0.7	1.0	0.1
CO	23.0	18.6	2.5	2.5	4.4	NY	22.9	15.6	13.1	(Z)	7.3
CT	2.7	1.7	1.2	–	1.1	NC	65.9	59.8	39.9	4.9	6.0
DE	8.8	4.3	4.0	–	4.5	ND	21.1	13.7	3.9	5.6	7.4
DC	(Z)	(Z)	(Z)	(Z)	(Z)	OH	154.8	121.6	67.9	9.4	33.2
FL	80.2	75.3	31.0	0.4	4.9	OK	36.7	35.2	19.3	0.6	1.5
GA	78.0	75.8	49.9	14.5	2.3	OR	18.0	17.4	6.8	(Z)	0.6
HI	2.5	2.4	1.9	0.0	0.1	PA	116.4	68.0	50.4	3.8	48.4
ID	66.8	65.7	5.7	12.3	1.1	RI	0.4	0.2	0.1	–	0.2
IL	101.8	57.9	32.6	11.2	43.9	SC	59.5	44.5	30.5	4.4	15.1
IN	155.3	107.6	67.8	7.4	47.7	SD	6.1	5.8	3.8	(Z)	0.4
IA	41.4	33.0	21.5	0.9	8.3	TN	88.3	75.5	29.2	18.5	12.8
KS	22.0	19.1	7.5	0.2	2.9	TX	205.9	187.6	53.9	5.3	18.3
KY	95.1	83.2	58.5	10.4	11.9	UT	212.0	210.8	7.3	127.5	1.2
LA	135.5	126.2	45.5	5.8	9.3	VT	0.3	0.2	0.1	–	0.1
ME	9.6	8.5	6.1	–	1.1	VA	52.1	48.2	41.7	1.2	3.9
MD	12.0	8.4	6.9	–	3.6	WA	20.1	18.5	8.1	3.1	1.6
MA	4.3	2.7	2.3	–	1.6	WV	45.8	36.8	24.6	2.4	9.0
MI	76.4	46.9	27.8	4.8	29.6	WI	37.2	20.3	15.3	–	16.9
MN	22.8	20.5	8.9	4.9	2.3	WY	22.7	21.3	1.5	2.2	1.4
MS	62.1	57.1	22.4	11.7	5.0	PR	5.3	4.4	4.1	–	0.9

– Represents zero. Z Less than 50,000 lbs. [1] Includes other types of release, not shown separately.

Source: U.S. Environmental Protection Agency, Toxic Release Inventory (TRI) Program, *2010 TRI National Analysis*. See also <http://www.epa.gov/tri/tridata/tri10/national_analysis/index.htm>. Data as of November 18, 2011.

Table 391. Hazardous Waste Sites on the National Priority List by State and Outlying Area: 2008

[As of December 31. Includes both proposed and final sites listed on the National Priorities List for the Superfund program as authorized by the Comprehensive Environmental Response, Compensation, and Liability Act (CERCLA) of 1980 and the Superfund Amendments and Reauthorization Act (SARA) of 1986. For information on CERCLA and SARA, see also <http://www.epa.gov/superfund/policy/cercla.htm>]

State and outlying areas	Total sites	Rank	Percent distribution	Federal	Non-federal	State and outlying areas	Total sites	Rank	Percent distribution	Federal	Non-federal
Total	1,318	(X)	(X)	163	1,155	Missouri	29	16	2.3	3	26
United States	1,301	(X)	(X)	161	1,140	Nebraska	13	32	1.0	1	12
Alabama	15	26	1.2	3	12	Nevada	1	49	0.1	–	1
Alaska	5	45	0.4	5	–	New Hampshire	21	19	1.7	1	20
Arizona	9	39	0.7	2	7	New Jersey	116	1	9.3	8	108
Arkansas	9	40	0.7	–	9	New Mexico	14	29	1.1	1	13
California	97	2	7.8	24	73	New York	86	4	6.9	4	82
Colorado	20	20	1.6	3	17	North Carolina	32	13	2.6	2	30
Connecticut	15	24	1.2	1	14	North Dakota	–	50	–	–	–
Delaware	14	27	1.1	1	13	Ohio	40	10	3.2	5	35
District of Columbia	1	(X)	0.1	1	–	Oklahoma	9	42	0.7	1	8
Florida	52	6	4.2	6	46	Oregon	12	36	1.0	2	10
Georgia	16	23	1.3	2	14	Pennsylvania	96	3	7.7	6	90
Hawaii	3	46	0.2	2	1	Rhode Island	12	37	1.0	2	10
Idaho	9	41	0.7	2	7	South Carolina	26	17	2.1	2	24
Illinois	49	7	3.9	5	44	South Dakota	2	47	0.2	1	1
Indiana	31	14	2.5	–	31	Tennessee	14	30	1.1	4	10
Iowa	12	33	1.0	1	11	Texas	49	8	3.9	4	45
Kansas	12	34	1.0	1	11	Utah	19	22	1.5	4	15
Kentucky	14	28	1.1	1	13	Vermont	11	38	0.9	0	11
Louisiana	13	31	1.0	1	12	Virginia	30	15	2.4	11	19
Maine	12	35	1.0	3	9	Washington	48	9	3.8	13	35
Maryland	19	21	1.5	10	9	West Virginia	9	43	0.7	2	7
Massachusetts	32	12	2.6	6	26	Wisconsin	38	11	3.0	–	38
Michigan	67	5	5.4	1	66	Wyoming	2	48	0.2	1	1
Minnesota	25	18	2.0	2	23						
Mississippi	6	44	0.5	–	6	Puerto Rico	13	(X)	(X)	1	12

– Represents zero. X Not applicable.

Source: U.S. Environmental Protection Agency, Supplementary Materials: CERCLIS3/WasteLan Database, published July 2009. See also <http://www.epa.gov/osw/inforesources/data/biennialreport/>.

Table 392. Hazardous Waste Generated, Shipped, and Received by State and Other Areas: 2009

[In thousands of tons (35,331.4 represents 35,331,400). Covers hazardous waste regulated under the Resource Conservation and Recovery Act (RCRA) of 1976 as amended. The data have been revised. See source for exclusions of data from the 2009 National Biennial RCRA Hazardous Waste Report]

State and other areas	Hazardous waste quantity (1,000) tons			State and other areas	Hazardous waste quantity (1,000) tons		
	Generated	Shipped	Received		Generated	Shipped	Received
Total...............	**35,331.4**	**6,144.7**	**7,282.7**	Missouri.......................	238.2	69.5	143.4
				Montana......................	37.8	6.3	–
United States..............	**35,285.3**	**6,098.0**	**7,281.0**	Nebraska.....................	28.2	31.2	32.8
				Nevada........................	11.1	17.2	62.7
Alabama.......................	2,063.6	166.6	220.0	New Hampshire.............	4.5	4.5	–
Alaska.........................	1.9	1.3	–	New Jersey...................	555.8	546.5	349.7
Arizona........................	21.1	18.0	16.2	New Mexico..................	1,078.7	6.2	5.0
Arkansas......................	273.2	235.3	289.1	New York......................	1,032.6	218.8	185.9
California......................	699.6	828.5	1,143.4	North Carolina..............	71.8	72.7	10.7
Colorado......................	41.5	31.6	38.8	North Dakota................	530.5	1.3	0.3
Connecticut...................	21.1	27.2	13.2	Ohio............................	1,300.8	463.1	583.1
Delaware......................	19.8	19.5	0.1	Oklahoma.....................	41.9	26.0	82.8
District of Columbia..........	0.9	0.9	–	Oregon........................	61.9	51.5	88.4
Florida.........................	168.9	31.3	9.4	Pennsylvania................	290.8	210.2	442.5
Georgia........................	4,024.5	90.2	5.0	Rhode Island................	4.5	9.2	6.6
Hawaii.........................	1.0	1.0	0.2	South Carolina..............	102.0	106.7	128.6
Idaho..........................	4.8	8.3	334.0	South Dakota................	1.2	1.3	0.1
Illinois.........................	1,045.4	182.7	472.9	Tennessee...................	78.6	49.3	1.3
Indiana........................	778.5	313.1	367.7	Texas.........................	13,461.9	581.4	637.9
Iowa...........................	40.3	40.1	0.7	Utah...........................	59.4	79.3	111.5
Kansas........................	222.8	111.1	195.0	Vermont.......................	1.5	2.1	1.3
Kentucky......................	132.7	162.3	70.2	Virginia........................	51.0	50.4	3.6
Louisiana......................	3,878.8	527.7	475.9	Washington...................	317.2	97.6	33.6
Maine..........................	3.7	3.7	0.2	West Virginia.................	92.4	68.7	9.3
Maryland.......................	33.7	42.0	34.6	Wisconsin.....................	223.4	152.7	45.8
Massachusetts................	32.5	41.5	11.8	Wyoming......................	3.5	3.5	–
Michigan.......................	284.3	189.1	341.8	Guam..........................	0.4	0.4	0.1
Minnesota.....................	106.8	34.5	249.6	Navajo Nation................	–	–	–
Mississippi....................	1,702.4	63.4	24.4	Puerto Rico..................	43.0	43.2	1.6
				Virgin Islands...............	2.6	3.0	–

– Represents or rounds to zero.

Source: U.S. Environmental Protection Agency, *The National Biennial RCRA Hazardous Waste Report* (Based on 2009 data), Series EPA530-R-10-014a, November 2010. See also <http://www.epa.gov/epawaste/inforesources/data/biennialreport/index.htm>.

Table 393. Oil Spills in U.S. Water—Number and Volume: 2000 to 2009

[These summary statistics are based on reported discharges of oil and petroleum based products into U.S. navigable waters, including territorial waters (extending 3 to 12 miles from the coastline), tributaries, the contiguous zone, onto shoreline, or into other waters that threaten the marine environment. Spills associated with Hurricanes Katrina and Rita have been excluded]

Spill characteristic	Number of spills				Spill volume (millions)			
	2000	2005	2008	2009	2000	2005	2008	2009
Total........................	**8,354**	**4,073**	**3,633**	**3,492**	**1,431,370**	**2,364,169**	**777,039**	**195,189**
Size of spill (gallons):								
1 to 100...........................	8,058	3,857	3,474	3,351	39,355	33,041	25,335	24,428
101 to 1,000.....................	219	166	130	123	78,779	62,357	50,486	46,062
1,001 to 3,000...................	37	26	12	9	67,529	46,019	22,130	20,907
3,001 to 5,000...................	12	9	8	2	45,512	36,803	30,396	6,872
5,001 to 10,000.................	16	7	3	3	112,415	58,453	21,800	21,400
10,001 to 50,000...............	6	5	3	4	108,400	106,870	73,600	75,520
50,001 to 100,000..............	4	1	1	–	266,380	84,000	82,274	–
100,001 to 1,000,000...........	2	1	2	–	713,000	110,000	471,018	–
1,000,000 and over.............	–	1	–	–	–	1,826,626	–	–
Source:								
Tankship.......................	111	40	36	34	608,176	2,975	1,338	14,415
Tankbarge......................	229	130	184	166	133,540	2,006,774	288,029	5,678
All other vessels................	5,220	1,789	1,577	1,585	291,927	115,906	263,632	92,388
Facilities........................	1,054	996	1,048	963	311,604	92,399	170,299	38,299
Pipelines........................	25	20	18	17	17,021	111,253	14,494	1,739
All other nonvessels...........	566	264	297	312	45,136	13,422	29,056	27,557
Unknown........................	1,149	834	473	415	23,966	21,440	10,191	15,113

– Represents zero.

Source: U.S. Coast Guard, *Pollution Incidents In and Around U.S. Waters, A Spill/Release Compendium: 1969–2004,* and *2004–2009: U.S. Coast Guard Marine Information for Safety and Law Enforcement (MISLE).* Data are unpublished. See <http://homeport.uscg.mil/mycg/portal/ep/home.do\>.

Table 394. Tornadoes, Floods, Tropical Storms, and Lightning: 2000 to 2011

Weather type	2000	2003	2004	2005	2006	2007	2008	2009	2010	2011
Tornadoes: [1]										
Number............................	1,072	1,374	1,820	1,262	1,117	1,102	1,685	1,305	1,543	1,894
Lives lost............................	41	54	35	38	67	81	126	21	45	553
Injuries............................	882	1,087	396	537	990	659	1,714	351	699	5,483
Property loss (mil. dol.).............	424	1,266	537	422	752	1,401	1,846	566	1,107	9,463
Floods and flash floods:										
Lives lost............................	38	85	82	43	76	87	82	56	103	113
Injuries............................	47	65	128	38	23	59	46	27	310	40
Property loss (mil. dol.).............	1,255	2,541	1,696	1,538	3,768	1,740	3,406	1,050	3,927	7,978
North Atlantic tropical cyclones and hurricanes: [2]..........	15	21	16	27	9	17	17	11	21	20
Hurricanes............................	8	7	9	15	5	6	8	3	12	7
Lives lost............................	–	14	34	1,016	0	1	12	2	0	9
Property loss (mil.dol.).............	8	1,880	18,902	93,064	2	39	7,619	1	15	344
Lightning:										
Deaths............................	51	44	32	38	48	45	27	34	29	26
Injuries............................	364	237	280	309	246	138	216	201	182	187

– Represents zero. [1] Source: U.S. National Weather Service, <http://www.spc.noaa.gov/climo/torn/monthlytornstats.html>. A violent, rotating column of air descending from a cumulonimbus cloud in the form of a tubular- or funnel-shaped cloud, usually characterized by movements along a narrow path and wind speeds from 100 to over 300 miles per hour. Also known as a "twister" or "waterspout." [2] Tropical cyclones include depressions, storms and hurricanes. For data on individual hurricanes, see National Hurricane Center (NHC) at <http://www.nhc.noaa.gov/>.

Source: Except as noted, U.S. National Oceanic and Atmospheric Administration (NOAA), National Weather Service (NWS), *Office of Climate, Water, and Weather Services, Natural Hazard Statistics,* monthly. See also <http://www.nws.noaa.gov/om/hazstats.shtml>.

Table 395. Number of Earthquakes in the United States: 2000 to 2011

[The United States Geological Survey (USGS) detects but does not generally locate mine blasts (explosions) throughout the United States on any given business day. For more information, see "Routine United States Mining Seismicity." For information on "Top Earthquake States," see <http://earthquake.usgs.gov/earthquakes/states/top_states.php>]

Magnitude	2000	2003	2004	2005	2006	2007	2008	2009	2010	2011 [1]	Top earth-quake states	1974–2003 [2]
Total...............	**2,342**	**2,946**	**3,550**	**3,685**	**2,783**	**2,791**	**3,618**	**4,262**	**8,499**	**5,237**	**Total**	**21,080**
8.0 to 9.9..........	–	–	–	–	–	–	–	–	–	–	AK [3]	1,2053
7.0 to 7.9..........	–	2	–	1	–	1	–	–	1	1	CA	4,895
6.0 to 6.9..........	6	7	2	4	7	9	9	4	8	3	HI	1,533
5.0 to 5.9..........	63	54	25	47	51	72	85	58	84	51	NE	778
4.0 to 4.9..........	281	541	284	345	346	366	432	288	637	347	WA	424
3.0 to 3.9..........	917	1,303	1,362	1,475	1,213	1,137	1,486	1,492	3,588	1,838	ID	404
2.0 to 2.9..........	660	704	1,336	1,738	1,145	1,173	1,573	2,379	4,130	2,941	WY	217
1.0 to 1.9..........	–	2	1	2	7	11	13	26	39	47	MT	186
0.1 to 0.9..........	–	–	–	–	1	–	–	1	–	1	UT	139
No magnitude......	415	333	540	73	13	22	20	14	12	8	OR	73

– Represents zero. [1] Data are as of August 10, 2012. [2] The total number represents earthquakes of a magnitude range of 3.5 and greater. [3] The number of earthquakes is underreported. Events in the magnitude range of 3.5 to 4.0 in the Aleutian Islands are not recorded on enough seismograph stations to be located.

Source: U.S. Geological Survey, *Earthquake Facts and Statistics.* See <http://earthquake.usgs.gov/earthquakes/eqarchives>.

Table 396. Wildland Fires, Number, and Acres: 1970 to 2011

[In thousands (3,279 represents 3,279,000), except as indicated. As of December 31. There are three distinct types of wildland fires: wildfire, wildland fire use, and prescribed fire. Wildland fire is any nonstructure fire that occurs in the wildland]

Year	Total [1] Fires (number)	Total [1] Acres (1,000)	Year	Total [1] Fires (number)	Total [1] Acres (1,000)	State	Top states ranked by wildland acres burned for 2011 — Wildland [1] Fires	Wildland [1] Acres	Prescribed [2] Fires	Prescribed [2] Acres
1970...........	121,736	3,279	2001........	84,079	3,571	**Total**...	**74,126**	**8,711,367**	**8,672**	**2,112,811**
1975...........	134,872	1,791	2002........	73,457	7,185	TX.....	3,470	2,722,623	20	13,969
1980...........	234,892	5,261	2003........	63,629	3,961	NM......	1,875	1,286,487	75	254,762
1985...........	82,591	2,896	2004 [3]......	65,461	8,098	AZ.....	1,988	1,016,428	204	61,170
1990...........	66,481	4,622	2005........	66,753	8,689	NV......	817	424,170	32	5,995
1995...........	82,234	1,841	2006........	96,385	9,874	ID......	1,094	384,103	347	43,333
1996...........	96,363	6,066	2007........	85,705	9,328	FL......	5,102	299,991	473	327,178
1997...........	66,196	2,857	2008........	78,979	5,292	OK.....	2,486	293,381	7	2,217
1998...........	81,043	1,330	2009........	78,792	5,922	AK.....	515	293,018	20	8,982
1999...........	92,487	5,626	2010........	71,971	3,423	OR.....	1,511	285,712	703	73,855
2000...........	92,250	7,393	2011........	74,126	8,711	MT.....	1,335	168,010	384	39,635

[1] Data are for wildland fires only. The data do not include wildland fire use and prescribed fires. [2] Prescribed fire is any fire which are ignited by management action under certain predetermined conditions to meet specific objectives related to hazardous fuels or habitat improvement. [3] 2004 fires and acres do not include state lands for North Carolina.

Source: National Interagency Coordination Center, *Wildland Fire Summary and Statistics Annual Report, 2011.* See also <http://www.predictiveservices.nifc.gov/intelligence/2011_statssumm/fires_acres.pdf>, accessed August 2012.

Table 397. Highest and Lowest Temperatures by State Through 2011

State	Highest temperatures			Lowest temperatures		
	Station	Temperature (F)	Date	Station	Temperature (F)	Date
AL.............	Centerville................	112	Sep. 5, 1925	New Market.............	-27	Jan. 30, 1966
AK.............	Fort Yukon................	100	[1] Jun. 27, 1915	Prospect Creek Camp...	-80	Jan. 23, 1971
AZ.............	Lake Havasu City.......	128	Jun. 29, 1994	Hawley Lake.............	-40	Jan. 7, 1971
AR.............	Ozark......................	120	Aug. 10, 1936	Pond......................	-29	Feb. 13, 1905
CA.............	Greenland Ranch........	134	Jul. 10, 1913	Boca......................	-45	Jan. 20, 1937
CO.............	Sedgwick..................	114	[1] Jul. 11, 1954	Maybell..................	-61	Feb. 1, 1985
CT.............	Danbury....................	106	[1] Jul. 15, 1995	Coventry.................	-32	[1] Jan. 22, 1961
DE.............	Millsboro..................	110	Jul. 21, 1930	Millsboro................	-17	Jan. 17, 1893
FL.............	Monticello.................	109	Jun. 29, 1931	Tallahassee..............	-2	Feb. 13, 1899
GA.............	Greenville 2 NNW.......	112	[1] Aug. 20, 1983	CCC Camp F-16.........	-17	[1] Jan. 27, 1940
HI.............	Pahala.....................	100	Apr. 27, 1931	Mauna Kea Obs. 111.2...	12	May 17, 1979
ID.............	Orofino....................	118	Jul. 28, 1934	Island Park Dam.........	-60	Jan. 18, 1943
IL.............	East St. Louis............	117	Jul. 14, 1954	Congerville..............	-36	Jan. 5, 1999
IN.............	Collegeville...............	116	Jul. 14, 1936	New Whiteland..........	-36	Jan. 19, 1994
IA.............	Keokuk....................	118	Jul. 20, 1934	Elkader...................	-47	[1] Feb. 3, 1996
KS.............	Alton......................	121	Jul. 24, 1936	Lebanon..................	-40	Feb. 13, 1905
KY.............	Greensburg...............	114	Jul. 28, 1930	Shelbyville..............	-37	Jan. 19, 1994
LA.............	Plain Dealing.............	114	Aug. 10, 1936	Minden...................	-16	Feb. 13, 1899
ME.............	North Bridgton...........	105	Jul. 10, 1911	Van Buren...............	-48	Jan. 16, 2009
MD.............	Cumberland & Frederick..................	109	[1] Jul. 10, 1936	Oakland..................	-40	Jan. 13, 1912
MA.............	New Bedford & Chester....................	107	[1] Aug. 2, 1975	Chester...................	-35	[1] Jan. 12, 1981
MI.............	Mio........................	112	Jul. 13, 1936	Vanderbilt...............	-51	Feb. 9, 1934
MN.............	Moorhead..................	115	Jul. 29, 1917	Tower.....................	-60	Feb. 2, 1996
MS.............	Holly Springs.............	115	Jul. 29, 1930	Corinth...................	-19	Jan. 30, 1966
MO.............	Warsaw & Union.........	118	[1] Jul. 14, 1954	Warsaw...................	-40	Feb. 13, 1905
MT.............	Medicine Lake...........	117	[1] Jul. 5, 1937	Rogers Pass..............	-70	Jan. 20, 1954
NE.............	Minden....................	118	[1] Jul. 24, 1936	Oshkosh..................	-47	[1] Dec. 22, 1989
NV.............	Laughlin...................	125	[1] Jun. 29, 1994	San Jacinto..............	-50	Jan. 8, 1937
NH.............	Nashua....................	106	Jul. 4, 1911	Mt. Washington.........	-47	Jan. 22, 1885
NJ.............	Runyon....................	110	Jul. 10, 1936	River Vale...............	-34	Jan. 5, 1904
NM.............	Waste Isolat Pilot Plt.....	122	Jun. 27, 1994	Gavilan..................	-50	Feb. 1, 1951
NY.............	Troy.......................	108	Jul. 22, 1926	Old Forge................	-52	Feb. 18, 1979
NC.............	Fayetteville...............	110	Aug. 21, 1983	Mt. Mitchell.............	-34	Jan. 21, 1985
ND.............	Steele.....................	121	Jul. 6, 1936	Parshall..................	-60	Feb. 15, 1936
OH.............	Gallipolis (near)..........	113	Jul. 21, 1934	Milligan..................	-39	Feb. 10, 1899
OK.............	Tipton.....................	120	[1] Jun. 27, 1994	Nowata...................	-31	Feb. 10, 2011
OR.............	Pendleton.................	119	[1] Aug. 10, 1898	Seneca...................	-54	[1] Feb. 10, 1933
PA.............	Phoenixville...............	111	Jul. 10, 1936	Smethport................	-42	[1] Jan. 5, 1904
RI.............	Providence.................	104	Aug. 2, 1975	Greene....................	-25	Jan. 11, 1942
SC.............	Camden....................	111	[1] Jun. 28, 1954	Caesars Head............	-19	Jan. 21, 1985
SD.............	Fort Pierre................	120	[1] Jul. 15, 2006	McIntosh.................	-58	Feb. 17, 1936
TN.............	Perryville.................	113	Aug. 9, 1930	Mountain City...........	-32	Dec. 30, 1917
TX.............	Monahans.................	120	[1] Jun. 28, 1994	Seminole.................	-23	Feb. 8, 1933
UT.............	Saint George.............	117	Jul. 5, 1985	Peter's Sink.............	-69	Jan. 5, 1913
VT.............	Vernon....................	107	Jul. 7, 1912	Bloomfield...............	-50	Dec. 30, 1933
VA.............	Balcony Falls.............	110	[1] Jul. 15, 1954	Mtn. Lake Bio. Stn........	-30	Jan. 22, 1985
WA.............	Ice Harbor Dam..........	118	[1] Aug. 5, 1961	Mazama & Winthrop.....	-48	[1] Dec. 30, 1968
WV.............	Martinsburg................	112	[1] Jul. 10, 1936	Lewisburg................	-37	Dec. 30, 1917
WI.............	Wisconsin Dells...........	114	Jul. 13, 1936	Couderay.................	-55	Feb. 4, 1996
WY.............	Diversion Dam...........	115	[1] Mar. 5, 1998	Riverside R.S.............	-66	Feb. 9, 1933

[1] Also on earlier dates at the same or other places.

Source: U.S. National Oceanic and Atmospheric Administration, National Environmental Satellite, Data, and Information Services (NESDIS), National Climatic Data Center (NCDC), *Temperature Extremes and Drought*, <http://www.ncdc.noaa.gov /Extremes/scec/searchrecs.php>.

Table 398. Major U.S. Weather Disasters: 2011

[12.0 represents $12,000,000,000. Covers only weather-related disasters costing $1 billion or more]

Event	Description	Time period	Estimated cost [1] (bil.dol.)	Deaths (number)
Southern Plains/Southwest Drought & Heat Wave.	Drought and heat wave conditions created major impacts across TX, OK, NM, AZ, southern KS, and western LA. In TX and OK, a majority of range and pastures were classified in "very poor" condition for much of the 2011 crop growing season.	2011	Over 12.0	95
Southeast/Ohio Valley/Midwest.	Outbreak of an estimated 343 tornadoes over central and southern states (AL, AR, LA, MS, GA, TN, VA, KY, IL, MO, OH, TX,OK), the deadliest tornado being an EF-5, hitting northern AL, killing 78 people. Several major metropolitan areas were directly impacted by strong tornadoes in AL and TN, causing the estimated damage costs to soar.	April, 2011	Over 10.0	321
Hurricane Irene.	Category 1 hurricane made landfall over coastal NC and moved northward along the Mid-Atlantic Coast (NC, VA, MD, NJ, NY, CT, RI, MA, VT) causing torrential rainfall and flooding across the Northeast. Wind damage in coastal NC, VA, and MD was moderate with considerable damage resulting from falling trees and power lines, while flooding caused extensive flood damage across NJ, NY, and VT. Over seven million homes and businesses lost power during the storm. Numerous tornadoes were also reported in several states further adding to the damage.	August, 2011	10.0	45
Midwest/Southeast.	Outbreak of tornadoes over central and southern states (MO, TX, OK, KS, AR, GA, TN, VA, KY, IN, IL, OH, WI, MN, PA, with an estimated 180 tornadoes, included an EF-5 tornado in Joplin, MO that resulted in at least 160 deaths, making it the deadliest single tornado to strike the U.S. since modern tornado record keeping began in 1950.	May, 2011	9.3	177
Mississippi River flooding.	Persistent rainfall (nearly 300 percent normal precipitation amounts in the OH Valley) combined with melting snowpack caused historical flooding along the MS River and its tributaries. Examples of economic damage include: $500 million to agriculture in AR; $320 million in damage to Memphis, TN; $800 million to agriculture in MS; $317 million to agriculture and property in MO's Birds Point-New Madrid Spillway; $80 million for the first 30 days of flood fighting efforts in LA.	May, 2011	Over 3.0	7
Midwest/Southeast Tornadoes.	Outbreak of tornadoes over central and southern states (KS, MO, IA, IL, WI, KY, GA, TN, NC, SC) with an estimated 46 tornadoes.	April, 2011	2.9	9
Southeast/Midwest Tornadoes.	Outbreak of tornadoes over central and southern states (NC, SC, TN, AL, TX, OK, KS, IA, WI) with an estimated 59 tornadoes.	April, 2011	2.2	–
Midwest/Southeast Tornadoes.	Outbreak of tornadoes over central and southern states (OK, TX, AR, MS, AL, GA, NC, SC, VA, PA) with an estimated 177 tornadoes.	April, 2011	2.1	38
Missouri River flooding.	Melting of an above-average snow pack across the Northern Rocky Mountains combined with above-average precipitation causes the Missouri and Souris Rivers to swell beyond their banks across the Upper Midwest (MT, ND, SD, NE, IA, KS, MO). An estimated 11,000 people were forced to evacuate Minot, North Dakota due to the record high water level of the Souris River, where 4,000 homes were flooded. Numerous levees were breached along the Missouri River, flooding thousands of acres of farmland.	Summer 2011	2.0	5
Groundhog Day Blizzard.	A large winter storm impacted many central, eastern and northeastern states. The city of Chicago was brought to a virtual standstill as between 1 and 2 feet of snow fell over the area.	February, 2011	1.8	36
Midwest/Southeast Tornadoes and Severe Weather.	Outbreak of tornadoes over central states (OK, TX, KS, NE, MO, IA, IL) with an estimated 81 tornadoes. Additional wind and hail damage across the Southeast (TN, GA, NC, SC).	June, 2011	1.3	3
Tropical Storm Lee.	Wind and flood damage across the southeast (LA, MS, AL, GA, TN) but considerably more damage from record flooding across the northeast (PA, NY, NJ, CT, VA, MD). Pennsylvania and New York were most affected.	September, 2011	1.3	21
Texas, New Mexico, Arizona Wildfires.	Continued drought conditions and periods of extreme heat provided conditions favorable for a series of historic wildfires across TX, NM and AZ. The Bastrop Fire in TX was the most destructive fire in TX history destroying over 1,500 homes. The Wallow Fire consumed over 500,000 acres in AZ making it the largest on record in AZ. The Las Conchas Fire in NM was also the state's largest wildfire on record scorching over 150,000 acres while threatening the Los Alamos National Laboratory. Over 3 million acres have burned across TX this wildfire season.	Summer 2011	1.0	5
Rockies and Midwest Severe Weather.	An outbreak of tornadoes, hail, and high wind caused damage east of the Rockies and across the central plains (CO, WY, IA, IL, MI, MN, OH).	July, 2011	1.0	2

– Represents zero. [1] Represents actual dollar costs at the time of event and is not adjusted for inflation.

Source: U.S. National Oceanic and Atmospheric Administration, National Climatic Data Center, "Billion Dollar U.S. Weather Disasters, 1980–2011" (released January 2012). See also <http://www.ncdc.noaa.gov/billions>.

Table 399. Highest Temperature of Record—Selected Cities

[In Fahrenheit degrees. Airport data, except as noted. For period of record through 2011]

State	Station	Length of record (years)	Jan.	Feb.	Mar.	Apr.	May	June	July	Aug.	Sept.	Oct.	Nov.	Dec.	An-nual[1]
AL....	Mobile	70	84	82	90	94	100	103	104	105	99	93	87	81	105
AK....	Juneau	67	57	57	61	74	82	86	90	84	73	61	56	54	90
AZ....	Phoenix	74	88	92	100	105	113	122	121	117	118	107	96	88	122
AK....	Little Rock	70	83	85	91	95	98	105	112	114	106	97	86	80	112
CA....	Los Angeles	76	91	92	95	102	97	104	97	98	110	106	101	94	110
	Sacramento	61	74	76	88	95	105	115	114	110	108	104	87	73	115
	San Diego	71	88	90	93	98	96	101	99	98	111	107	100	88	111
	San Francisco	84	72	78	85	92	97	106	105	100	103	99	85	75	106
CO....	Denver	69	73	77	84	90	96	104	105	104	97	89	80	75	105
CT....	Hartford	57	72	73	89	96	99	100	103	102	99	91	81	76	102
DE....	Wilmington	64	75	78	86	94	96	100	103	101	100	91	85	75	103
DC...	Washington	70	79	82	89	95	99	102	104	105	101	94	86	79	105
FL....	Jacksonville	70	85	88	91	95	100	103	105	102	100	96	88	84	105
	Miami	69	88	89	93	96	96	98	98	98	97	95	91	89	98
GA...	Atlanta	63	79	80	89	93	95	101	105	104	98	95	84	79	105
HI.....	Honolulu	42	88	88	88	91	93	92	94	93	95	94	93	89	95
ID.....	Boise	72	63	71	81	92	99	109	111	110	102	94	78	65	111
IL.....	Chicago	53	65	72	88	91	93	104	104	101	99	91	78	71	104
	Peoria	72	70	72	86	92	94	105	104	103	100	93	81	71	105
IN.....	Indianapolis	72	71	76	85	89	93	102	104	102	100	91	81	74	104
IA.....	Des Moines	72	67	73	91	93	98	103	105	108	101	95	81	69	108
KS....	Wichita	59	75	87	89	96	100	110	113	111	108	97	86	83	113
KY....	Louisville	64	77	77	86	91	95	102	106	105	104	93	84	76	106
LA....	New Orleans	65	83	85	89	92	96	101	101	102	101	94	87	84	102
ME...	Portland	71	67	64	88	92	94	98	100	103	95	88	74	71	103
MD...	Baltimore	61	75	79	89	94	98	101	106	105	100	94	83	77	105
MA...	Boston	60	69	70	89	94	95	100	103	102	100	90	79	76	102
MI....	Detroit	53	64	70	81	89	93	104	102	100	98	91	77	69	104
	Sault Ste. Marie	71	45	49	75	85	89	93	97	98	95	81	68	62	98
MN...	Duluth	70	52	55	78	88	90	94	97	97	95	86	71	55	97
	Minneapolis-St. Paul	73	58	61	83	95	97	103	105	102	98	90	77	68	105
MS...	Jackson	48	83	85	89	94	99	105	106	107	104	95	88	84	107
MO...	Kansas City	39	71	78	86	93	95	105	107	109	106	95	82	74	109
	St. Louis	54	76	85	89	93	94	102	107	107	104	94	85	76	107
MT...	Great Falls	74	67	70	78	89	93	101	105	106	98	91	76	69	106
NE....	Omaha	75	69	78	89	97	99	105	114	110	104	96	83	72	114
NV....	Reno	70	71	75	83	89	97	103	108	105	101	93	77	70	108
NH....	Concord	70	69	67	89	95	97	98	102	101	98	90	80	73	102
NJ....	Atlantic City	68	78	75	87	94	99	106	105	103	99	90	84	77	106
NM...	Albuquerque	72	69	76	85	89	98	107	105	101	100	91	77	72	107
NY....	Albany	65	71	68	89	92	94	99	100	99	100	89	82	71	100
	Buffalo	68	72	71	81	94	91	96	97	99	98	87	80	74	99
	New York[2]	143	72	75	86	96	99	101	106	104	102	94	84	75	106
NC...	Charlotte	72	79	82	90	93	100	103	103	104	104	98	85	80	104
	Raleigh	67	80	84	92	95	97	104	105	105	104	98	88	81	105
ND...	Bismarck	72	63	69	81	93	98	111	112	109	105	95	79	65	112
OH...	Cincinnati	50	69	75	84	89	93	102	103	102	100	91	81	75	103
	Cleveland	70	73	74	83	88	92	104	103	102	101	90	82	77	104
	Columbus	72	74	75	85	89	94	102	100	101	100	91	80	76	102
OK...	Oklahoma City	58	80	92	93	100	104	105	110	110	108	96	87	86	110
OR...	Portland	71	66	71	80	90	100	102	107	107	105	92	73	65	107
PA....	Philadelphia	70	74	74	87	95	97	100	104	101	100	96	81	73	104
	Pittsburgh	59	72	76	82	89	91	98	103	100	97	87	82	74	103
RI.....	Providence	58	69	72	85	98	96	97	102	104	100	86	78	77	104
SC....	Columbia	64	84	84	91	94	101	107	107	107	101	101	90	83	107
SD....	Sioux Falls	66	66	70	87	94	100	110	108	108	104	94	81	63	110
TN....	Memphis	70	79	81	86	94	99	104	108	107	103	95	86	81	108
	Nashville	72	78	84	86	91	97	106	107	106	105	94	84	79	107
TX....	Dallas-Fort Worth	58	88	95	96	101	103	113	110	110	111	102	89	89	113
	El Paso	72	80	83	89	98	105	114	112	108	104	96	87	80	114
	Houston	42	84	91	91	95	99	105	104	109	109	96	89	85	109
UT....	Salt Lake City	83	63	69	78	89	99	104	107	106	100	89	75	69	107
VT....	Burlington	68	66	62	84	91	93	100	100	101	98	85	75	67	101
VA....	Norfolk	63	80	82	88	97	100	101	105	104	99	95	86	80	105
	Richmond	82	81	83	93	96	100	104	105	104	103	99	86	81	105
WA...	Seattle-Tacoma	67	64	70	78	85	93	96	103	99	98	89	74	64	103
	Spokane	64	59	63	71	90	96	101	103	108	98	86	67	56	108
WV...	Charleston	64	79	79	89	94	94	98	104	104	102	93	85	80	104
WI....	Milwaukee	71	63	68	82	91	93	101	103	103	98	89	77	68	103
WY...	Cheyenne	76	66	71	74	83	91	100	100	98	95	84	75	69	100
PR....	San Juan	57	92	96	96	97	96	97	95	97	97	98	96	94	98

[1] Represents the highest observed temperature in any month. [2] City office data.

Source: U.S. National Oceanic and Atmospheric Administration, *Comparative Climatic Data*. See also <http://www.ncdc.noaa.gov/statistical-weather-and-climate-information>.

Table 400. Lowest Temperature of Record—Selected Cities

[In Fahrenheit degrees. Airport data, except as noted. For period of record through 2011]

State	Station	Length of record (years)	Jan.	Feb.	Mar.	Apr.	May	June	July	Aug.	Sept.	Oct.	Nov.	Dec.	Annual [1]
AL.....	Mobile	70	3	11	21	32	43	49	60	59	42	30	22	8	3
AK.....	Juneau	67	-22	-22	-15	6	25	31	36	27	23	11	-5	-21	-22
AZ.....	Phoenix	74	17	22	25	32	40	50	61	60	47	34	25	22	17
AR....	Little Rock	70	-4	-5	11	28	40	46	54	52	37	29	17	-1	-5
CA....	Los Angeles	76	23	32	34	39	43	48	49	51	47	41	34	32	23
	Sacramento	61	21	23	26	31	36	41	48	49	42	36	26	18	18
	San Diego	71	29	36	39	41	48	51	55	57	51	43	38	34	29
	San Francisco	84	24	25	30	31	36	41	43	42	38	34	25	20	20
CO....	Denver	69	-25	-30	-11	-2	21	30	43	41	17	3	-8	-25	-30
CT....	Hartford	57	-26	-21	-6	9	28	35	44	36	30	17	1	-14	-26
DE....	Wilmington	64	-14	-6	2	18	30	41	48	43	36	24	14	-7	-14
DC....	Washington	70	-5	4	11	24	34	47	54	49	39	29	16	1	-5
FL.....	Jacksonville	70	7	19	23	31	45	47	61	59	48	33	21	11	7
	Miami	69	30	32	32	46	53	60	69	68	68	51	39	30	30
GA....	Atlanta	63	-8	5	10	26	37	46	53	55	36	28	3	0	-8
HI.....	Honolulu	42	53	53	55	57	60	65	66	65	66	61	57	54	53
ID.....	Boise	72	-17	-15	6	19	22	31	35	34	23	11	-3	-25	-25
IL.....	Chicago	53	-27	-19	-8	7	24	36	40	41	28	17	1	-25	-27
	Peoria	72	-25	-19	-10	14	25	39	47	41	26	19	-2	-23	-25
IN.....	Indianapolis	72	-27	-21	-7	16	28	37	44	41	28	17	-2	-23	-27
IA.....	Des Moines	72	-24	-26	-22	9	30	38	47	40	26	14	-4	-22	-26
KS....	Wichita	59	-12	-21	-2	15	31	43	51	48	31	18	1	-16	-21
KY....	Louisville	64	-22	-19	-1	22	31	42	50	46	33	23	-1	-15	-22
LA.....	New Orleans	65	14	16	25	32	41	50	60	60	42	35	24	11	11
ME....	Portland	71	-26	-39	-21	8	23	33	40	33	23	15	3	-21	-39
MD....	Baltimore	61	-7	-3	6	20	32	40	50	45	35	25	13	0	-7
MA....	Boston	60	-12	-4	5	16	34	45	50	47	38	28	15	-7	-12
MI.....	Detroit	53	-21	-15	-4	10	25	36	41	38	29	17	9	-10	-21
	Sault Ste. Marie	71	-36	-35	-24	-2	18	26	36	29	25	16	-10	-31	-36
MN....	Duluth	70	-39	-39	-29	-5	17	27	35	32	22	8	-23	-34	-39
	Minneapolis-St. Paul	73	-34	-32	-32	2	18	34	43	39	26	13	-17	-29	-34
MS....	Jackson	48	2	10	15	27	38	47	51	54	35	26	17	4	2
MO....	Kansas City	39	-17	-19	-10	12	30	42	51	43	31	17	1	-23	-23
	St. Louis	54	-18	-12	-5	22	31	43	51	47	36	23	1	-16	-18
MT....	Great Falls	74	-37	-35	-29	-8	12	31	36	30	16	-11	-25	-43	-43
NE....	Omaha	75	-23	-21	-16	5	27	38	44	43	25	13	-9	-23	-23
NV....	Reno	70	-16	-16	-2	13	18	21	33	24	20	8	1	-16	-16
NH....	Concord	70	-33	-37	-16	8	21	30	35	29	21	10	-5	-22	-37
NJ....	Atlantic City	68	-10	-11	3	12	25	37	42	40	32	20	10	-7	-11
NM....	Albuquerque	72	-17	-7	8	19	16	40	52	50	37	21	-7	-7	-17
NY....	Albany	65	-28	-21	-21	10	26	36	40	34	24	16	5	-22	-28
	Buffalo	68	-16	-20	-7	12	26	35	43	38	32	20	9	-10	-20
	New York [2]	143	-6	-15	3	12	32	44	52	50	39	28	5	-13	-15
NC....	Charlotte	72	-5	5	4	21	32	45	53	50	39	24	11	2	-5
	Raleigh	67	-9	0	11	23	31	38	48	46	37	19	11	4	-9
ND....	Bismarck	72	-44	-43	-31	-12	15	30	35	33	11	-10	-30	-43	-44
OH....	Cincinnati	50	-25	-11	-11	15	27	39	47	43	31	16	1	-20	-25
	Cleveland	70	-20	-15	-5	10	25	31	41	38	32	19	3	-15	-20
	Columbus	72	-22	-13	-6	14	25	35	43	39	31	20	5	-17	-22
OK....	Oklahoma City	58	-4	-5	3	20	36	47	53	51	36	16	11	-8	-8
OR....	Portland	71	-2	-3	19	29	29	39	43	44	34	26	13	6	-3
PA.....	Philadelphia	70	-7	-4	7	19	28	44	51	44	35	25	15	1	-7
	Pittsburgh	59	-22	-12	-1	14	26	34	42	39	31	16	-1	-12	-22
RI.....	Providence	58	-13	-7	1	14	29	41	48	40	33	20	6	-10	-13
SC....	Columbia	64	-1	5	4	26	34	44	54	53	40	23	12	4	-1
SD....	Sioux Falls	66	-36	-31	-23	5	17	33	38	34	22	9	-17	-28	-36
TN....	Memphis	70	-4	-11	12	28	38	48	52	48	36	25	9	-13	-13
	Nashville	72	-17	-13	2	23	34	42	51	47	36	26	-1	-10	-17
TX.....	Dallas-Fort Worth	58	4	7	15	29	41	51	59	56	43	29	20	-1	-1
	El Paso	72	-8	1	14	23	31	46	57	56	41	25	1	5	-8
	Houston	42	12	3	22	31	44	52	62	60	48	29	19	7	3
UT....	Salt Lake City	83	-22	-30	2	14	25	35	40	37	27	16	-14	-21	-30
VT.....	Burlington	68	-30	-30	-20	2	24	33	39	35	25	15	-2	-26	-30
VA.....	Norfolk	63	-3	8	18	28	36	45	54	49	45	27	20	7	-3
	Richmond	82	-12	-10	10	23	31	40	51	46	35	21	10	-1	-12
WA....	Seattle-Tacoma	67	0	1	11	29	28	38	43	44	35	28	6	6	0
	Spokane	64	-22	-24	-7	17	24	33	37	35	22	7	-21	-25	-25
WV....	Charleston	64	-16	-12	0	19	26	33	46	41	34	17	6	-12	-16
WI.....	Milwaukee	71	-26	-26	-10	12	21	33	40	44	28	18	-5	-20	-26
WY....	Cheyenne	76	-29	-34	-21	-8	16	25	38	36	8	-1	-16	-28	-34
PR....	San Juan	57	61	62	60	64	66	69	69	70	69	46	66	59	46

[1] Represents the lowest observed temperature in any month. [2] City office data.

Source: U.S. National Oceanic and Atmospheric Administration, *Comparative Climatic Data*. See also <http://www.ncdc.noaa.gov/oa/climate/climateproducts.html>.

Table 401. Snow, Hail, Ice Pellets, and Sleet—Selected Cities

[In inches. Airport data, except as noted. For period of record through 2011. T denotes trace. Stations may show snowfall (hail) during the warm months]

State	Station	Length of record (years)	Jan.	Feb.	Mar.	Apr.	May	June	July	Aug.	Sept.	Oct.	Nov.	Dec.	Annual
AL....	Mobile	69.0	0.1	0.1	0.1	T	T	–	T	–	–	–	T	0.1	0.4
AK....	Juneau	67.0	26.4	18.8	15.3	3.5	T	T	–	–	T	1.1	12.8	21.1	98.8
AZ....	Phoenix	62.0	T	–	T	T	T	–	–	–	–	T	–	T	–
AR. ..	Little Rock	60.0	2.5	1.7	0.5	T	T	T	–	–	–	T	0.2	0.6	5.3
CA. ..	Los Angeles	62.0	T	T	T	–	–	–	–	–	–	–	–	T	–
	Sacramento	50.0	T	T	T	–	T	–	–	–	–	–	–	T	–
	San Diego	60.0	T	–	T	T	–	–	–	–	–	–	T	T	–
	San Francisco	69.0	–	T	T	T	–	–	–	–	–	–	T	T	–
CO. ..	Denver	67.0	7.9	7.4	12.1	8.4	1.6	–	T	T	1.6	4.1	8.6	7.9	59.7
CT....	Hartford	54.0	13.9	12.4	9.8	1.5	–	T	–	–	–	0.3	2.1	11.0	50.1
DE. ..	Wilmington	61.0	6.8	7.2	3.3	0.2	T	T	T	–	–	0.1	0.9	3.6	22.0
DC. ..	Washington	68.0	5.2	5.7	2.3	2.3	T	T	T	T	–	–	0.8	3.2	19.6
FL....	Jacksonville	60.0	T	–	–	T	–	T	T	–	–	–	–	–	–
	Miami	59.0	–	–	–	–	T	–	–	–	–	–	–	–	–
GA. ..	Atlanta	72.0	1.0	0.5	0.5	T	–	–	T	–	–	T	T	0.2	2.2
HI. ...	Honolulu	52.0	–	–	–	–	–	–	–	–	–	–	–	–	–
ID. ...	Boise	72.0	6.3	3.7	1.7	0.6	0.1	T	T	T	T	0.1	2.4	5.8	20.9
IL.....	Chicago	52.0	11.4	8.8	6.3	1.6	0.1	T	T	T	T	0.4	2.1	8.8	39.3
	Peoria	68.0	6.7	5.7	4.2	0.8	T	T	T	–	T	0.1	2.1	6.5	25.9
IN. ...	Indianapolis	80.0	7.1	5.8	3.5	0.5	T	T	–	T	–	0.2	1.9	5.6	24.5
IA.....	Des Moines	68.0	8.6	7.7	6.0	1.9	T	T	T	–	T	0.3	3.1	6.9	34.5
KS....	Wichita	58.0	4.0	4.3	2.8	0.2	T	T	T	T	T	–	1.4	3.5	16.1
KY....	Louisville	64.0	5.3	4.3	3.2	0.1	T	T	T	T	–	0.1	1.0	2.6	16.6
LA....	New Orleans	51.0	T	0.1	T	T	T	–	–	–	–	–	T	0.1	0.2
ME. ..	Portland	71.0	19.2	16.5	13.0	3.1	0.2	–	T	–	T	0.3	3.3	14.9	70.5
MD. ..	Baltimore	61.0	6.1	7.6	3.6	0.1	T	T	T	–	–	T	1.0	3.6	22.0
MA. ..	Boston	74.0	13.2	11.9	7.9	0.9	–	T	T	T	–	T	1.3	8.5	43.4
MI. ...	Detroit	53.0	11.4	10.1	7.0	2.0	T	–	–	–	T	0.2	2.5	10.1	42.9
	Sault Ste. Marie	64.0	28.8	18.5	14.4	5.9	0.5	T	T	T	0.1	2.4	15.4	30.7	117.3
MN. ..	Duluth	68.0	17.6	12.0	13.9	6.9	0.8	T	T	T	0.1	1.7	12.4	16.1	81.8
	Minneapolis-St. Paul	69.0	10.4	8.3	10.6	2.8	0.1	T	T	T	T	0.5	7.5	10.2	50.3
MS. ..	Jackson	38.0	0.5	0.2	0.2	T	–	–	–	T	–	–	T	0.1	1.0
MO. ..	Kansas City	77.0	5.5	4.8	3.5	0.8	T	T	T	T	T	0.1	1.3	4.5	20.2
	St. Louis	75.0	5.4	4.5	3.8	0.5	T	T	T	–	T	T	1.4	4.2	19.7
MT. ..	Great Falls	74.0	9.5	8.9	10.4	8.0	1.9	0.4	T	0.1	1.5	3.5	7.6	8.5	60.0
NE. ..	Omaha	76.0	7.7	6.9	6.1	1.1	0.1	T	T	T	T	0.3	2.6	6.0	30.7
NV. ..	Reno	62.0	5.8	5.5	4.2	1.2	0.8	–	–	–	–	0.3	2.5	4.8	25.0
NH. ..	Concord	70.0	18.5	14.6	11.5	2.8	0.1	T	–	–	T	0.4	3.8	14.2	65.4
NJ....	Atlantic City	62.0	5.2	6.1	2.6	0.3	T	T	T	–	–	T	0.4	2.9	17.4
NM. ..	Albuquerque	72.0	2.5	2.1	1.8	0.6	T	T	T	T	T	0.1	1.2	3.0	11.3
NY. ..	Albany	65.0	17.0	13.9	11.3	2.8	0.1	T	T	–	T	0.3	3.9	14.7	63.5
	Buffalo	68.0	24.6	18.0	12.5	3.2	0.2	T	T	T	T	0.7	10.8	24.2	94.2
	New York [1]	143.0	7.9	8.9	5.1	0.9	T	–	T	–	–	–	0.9	5.7	29.2
NC. ..	Charlotte	72.0	2.2	1.8	1.2	T	T	T	T	–	–	T	0.1	0.5	5.8
	Raleigh	67.0	2.8	2.6	1.3	T	T	T	T	–	–	–	0.1	0.9	7.7
ND. ..	Bismarck	72.0	7.9	7.0	8.6	4.0	0.9	T	T	T	T	0.2	1.9	6.7	7.7	44.8
OH. ..	Cincinnati	64.0	7.3	5.9	4.2	0.5	–	T	T	T	–	0.3	2.0	4.0	24.1
	Cleveland	70.0	14.9	13.1	10.9	2.9	0.1	T	T	T	–	T	0.6	4.9	12.4	59.8
	Columbus	64.0	9.0	6.6	4.7	1.0	T	T	T	T	–	T	0.1	2.2	5.3	28.9
OK. ..	Oklahoma City	72.0	3.2	2.6	1.5	T	T	T	T	T	T	T	0.6	2.1	9.8
OR. ..	Portland	55.0	3.2	1.1	0.4	T	–	T	–	T	T	–	0.4	1.4	6.5
PA....	Philadelphia	69.0	6.3	7.7	3.5	0.3	T	T	T	–	–	–	0.7	3.8	22.0
	Pittsburgh	59.0	12.3	10.3	8.0	1.8	0.1	T	T	T	T	0.4	3.4	8.3	44.4
RI. ...	Providence	58.0	10.0	9.6	7.2	0.7	0.2	–	–	–	–	0.1	1.3	7.6	36.4
SC. ..	Columbia	63.0	0.6	0.9	0.2	T	T	–	T	T	–	–	T	0.3	2.0
SD. ..	Sioux Falls	66.0	7.0	8.0	9.1	3.3	T	T	T	T	T	0.9	5.8	7.5	41.8
TN....	Memphis	54.0	2.3	1.5	0.9	T	T	T	–	–	–	T	0.1	0.6	5.3
	Nashville	65.0	3.6	3.0	1.5	–	–	T	–	T	–	–	0.4	1.4	9.9
TX....	Dallas-Fort Worth	53.0	1.1	1.3	0.2	T	T	–	–	–	–	T	0.1	0.3	2.9
	El Paso	62.0	1.3	0.8	0.4	0.3	T	T	T	–	T	–	1.0	1.7	5.5
	Houston	77.0	0.2	0.2	T	T	T	T	–	–	–	–	T	–	0.4
UT....	Salt Lake City	83.0	13.2	9.9	9.0	4.9	0.6	T	T	T	T	0.1	1.3	7.0	12.2	58.4
VT....	Burlington	68.0	19.9	17.4	13.8	4.0	0.2	–	T	T	T	0.2	6.5	18.9	80.4
VA....	Norfolk	61.0	3.1	2.9	1.0	–	T	T	–	T	–	–	–	1.3	8.3
....	Richmond	72.0	5.0	3.8	2.5	0.1	T	–	T	–	–	T	0.4	2.2	14.1
WA. ..	Seattle-Tacoma	55.0	4.9	1.6	1.3	0.1	T	–	T	–	T	–	1.1	2.4	11.4
	Spokane	64.0	15.2	7.3	4.1	0.8	0.1	T	–	–	T	0.4	6.5	14.6	49.2
WV. ..	Charleston	57.0	10.9	8.8	5.1	0.9	–	T	T	T	T	0.2	2.4	5.6	34.0
WI....	Milwaukee	71.0	13.9	10.1	8.4	2.0	0.1	T	T	–	T	0.2	3.0	11.0	48.5
WY...	Cheyenne	76.0	6.0	6.6	11.8	9.5	3.5	0.2	T	T	1.1	4.1	7.3	6.8	56.7
PR. ..	San Juan	56.0	–	–	–	–	–	–	–	–	T	–	–	–	–

– Represents zero. [1] City office data.

Source: U.S. National Oceanic and Atmospheric Administration, *Comparative Climatic Data*, annual. See also <http://www.ncdc.noaa.gov/statistical-weather-and-climate-information>.

Table 402. Cloudiness, Average Wind Speed, Heating and Cooling Degree Days, and Average Relative Humidity—Selected Cities

[Airport data, except as noted. For period of record through 2011, except as noted. M=morning. A=afternoon]

State	Station	Cloudiness—average percentage of days [1] Length of record (yr.)	Annual	Average wind speed (miles per hour, m.p.h.) Length of record (yr.)	An-nual	Jan.	July	Heating degree days	Cooling degree days	Length of record (yr.)	Average relative humidity (percent) Annual M	Annual A	Jan. M	Jan. A	July M	July A
AL.....	Mobile	47	72.1	63	8.7	10.0	6.9	1,681	2,539	49	86	66	81	67	89	69
AK.....	Juneau	47	87.9	66	8.1	7.9	7.5	8,574	–	45	81	71	79	75	79	68
AZ.....	Phoenix	57	42.3	66	6.2	5.3	7.1	1,027	4,364	51	49	22	63	31	42	19
AR....	Little Rock	35	67.5	69	7.7	8.4	6.7	3,084	2,086	47	82	64	78	66	84	63
CA....	Los Angeles	60	59.8	63	7.5	6.7	7.9	1,274	679	52	79	66	71	60	85	68
	Sacramento	49	48.5	61	7.8	6.7	8.9	2,666	1,248	25	83	46	90	69	77	29
	San Diego	55	60.0	71	7.0	6.0	7.1	1,063	866	51	77	63	71	57	82	67
	San Francisco	68	56.2	84	10.6	7.2	13.6	2,862	142	52	84	63	86	68	86	60
CO....	Denver	61	68.5	55	8.7	8.7	8.3	6,128	696	43	67	41	62	50	67	34
CT.....	Hartford	41	77.5	57	8.4	8.9	7.3	6,104	759	52	77	52	72	56	77	51
DE.....	Wilmington	47	73.4	63	9.0	9.8	7.8	4,888	1,125	64	78	55	75	59	78	54
DC....	Washington	48	73.8	63	9.4	10.0	8.3	4,055	1,531	51	74	53	70	55	75	52
FL.....	Jacksonville	47	74.2	62	7.8	8.1	7.0	1,354	2,627	75	88	56	87	57	88	58
	Miami	46	79.7	62	9.2	9.5	7.9	149	4,361	47	82	61	83	59	81	63
GA....	Atlanta	61	69.9	73	9.1	10.4	7.7	2,827	1,810	51	82	55	78	58	86	58
HI.....	Honolulu	47	75.3	62	11.2	9.4	13.1	–	4,561	42	71	56	79	61	66	51
ID.....	Boise	56	67.1	72	8.7	7.9	8.4	5,727	807	72	68	43	80	70	53	20
IL......	Chicago	37	77.0	53	10.3	11.6	8.4	6,498	830	53	79	65	77	71	80	62
	Peoria	52	73.9	68	9.8	10.7	7.8	6,097	998	52	82	68	79	72	85	66
IN.....	Indianapolis	64	76.0	63	9.6	10.9	7.5	5,521	1,042	52	83	61	81	70	85	58
IA......	Des Moines	46	71.3	62	10.7	11.4	8.9	6,436	1,052	50	79	66	76	70	82	65
KS.....	Wichita	39	64.9	58	12.2	11.9	11.2	4,765	1,658	58	79	62	78	67	77	57
KY.....	Louisville	47	74.6	64	8.3	9.5	6.8	4,352	1,443	51	80	58	77	64	83	57
LA.....	New Orleans	47	72.3	63	8.2	9.3	6.1	1,417	2,773	63	86	68	83	69	89	70
ME....	Portland	54	72.3	71	8.7	9.0	7.6	7,318	347	71	78	59	75	60	79	59
MD....	Baltimore	45	71.2	61	8.7	9.1	7.5	4,720	1,147	58	77	53	72	56	78	52
MA....	Boston	60	73.2	54	12.3	13.6	11.0	5,630	777	47	72	58	68	57	72	56
MI.....	Detroit	37	79.5	53	10.1	11.6	8.5	6,422	736	53	81	59	80	69	80	53
	Sault Ste. Marie	54	81.9	70	9.1	9.4	7.8	9,224	145	70	84	66	80	73	87	61
MN....	Duluth	47	79.0	62	11.0	11.5	9.4	9,724	189	50	80	69	77	73	84	66
	Minneapolis-St. Paul	57	74.0	73	10.5	10.5	9.4	7,876	699	52	77	65	75	70	78	61
MS....	Jackson	30	69.6	48	6.8	8.0	5.2	2,401	2,264	48	88	67	84	70	91	68
MO....	Kansas City	23	67.1	39	10.6	11.0	9.1	5,249	1,325	39	79	68	76	69	83	68
	St. Louis	47	72.4	62	9.6	10.6	8.0	4,758	1,561	51	80	65	79	69	81	63
MT....	Great Falls	57	78.4	70	12.5	14.7	10.0	7,828	288	50	68	46	66	61	67	30
NE....	Omaha	49	69.6	75	10.5	10.9	8.8	6,311	1,095	47	80	67	78	70	83	66
NV....	Reno	53	56.7	69	6.6	5.6	7.2	5,600	493	48	67	31	79	50	56	17
NH....	Concord	54	75.3	69	6.7	7.2	5.7	7,478	442	46	80	53	76	58	82	51
NJ.....	Atlantic City	37	74.2	53	9.7	10.6	8.3	5,113	935	47	80	56	77	58	81	56
NM....	Albuquerque	56	54.2	72	8.9	8.0	8.9	4,281	1,290	51	58	29	66	38	58	27
NY....	Albany	57	81.1	73	8.9	9.8	7.5	6,860	544	46	79	57	77	63	80	55
	Buffalo	52	85.2	72	11.8	13.8	10.2	6,692	548	51	79	63	79	72	78	55
	New York [2]	42	70.8	74	9.1	10.3	7.5	4,754	1,151	77	72	56	67	58	74	55
NC....	Charlotte	49	70.2	62	7.4	7.8	6.6	3,162	1,681	51	82	53	77	54	84	55
	Raleigh	47	69.7	62	7.5	8.1	6.7	3,465	1,521	47	84	53	78	53	86	56
ND....	Bismarck	56	74.5	72	10.2	10.0	9.2	8,802	471	52	80	64	76	72	82	58
OH....	Cincinnati	44	77.8	64	9.0	10.4	7.2	5,148	1,064	49	82	59	80	68	84	57
	Cleveland	54	81.9	70	10.5	12.2	8.6	6,121	702	51	79	62	78	70	80	56
	Columbus	46	80.3	62	8.3	9.8	6.5	5,492	951	52	80	58	77	67	82	55
OK....	Oklahoma City	44	61.9	63	12.2	12.5	10.8	3,663	1,907	46	78	63	76	64	78	59
OR....	Portland	47	81.3	63	7.9	9.8	7.6	4,400	390	71	85	59	85	75	81	44
PA.....	Philadelphia	55	74.5	71	9.5	10.3	8.2	4,759	1,235	52	76	54	72	58	77	52
	Pittsburgh	43	83.8	59	8.9	10.3	7.3	5,829	726	51	79	57	77	65	82	54
RI.....	Providence	42	73.2	58	10.4	10.8	9.4	5,754	714	48	75	55	71	56	76	55
SC....	Columbia	48	68.5	63	6.8	7.2	6.3	2,594	2,074	45	85	50	81	52	86	52
SD....	Sioux Falls	50	71.2	63	11.0	10.9	9.8	7,812	747	48	81	68	78	72	83	64
TN.....	Memphis	43	67.7	63	8.8	10.0	7.5	3,041	2,187	72	79	61	77	65	82	62
	Nashville	54	72.0	70	7.9	9.0	6.5	3,677	1,652	46	81	65	77	68	85	65
TX.....	Dallas-Fort Worth	42	63.0	58	10.7	11.0	9.7	2,370	2,568	48	78	63	76	65	76	57
	El Paso	53	47.1	69	8.8	8.3	8.3	2,543	2,254	51	55	27	63	33	60	29
	Houston	26	75.3	42	7.6	8.1	6.6	1,525	2,893	42	88	69	83	71	90	68
UT....	Salt Lake City	69	65.8	82	8.8	7.5	9.5	5,631	1,066	51	67	44	79	70	50	21
VT....	Burlington	52	84.1	68	9.0	9.6	8.0	7,665	489	46	77	58	73	64	77	53
VA.....	Norfolk	47	71.0	63	10.4	11.3	8.1	3,368	1,612	63	78	57	74	58	80	54
	Richmond	50	72.7	63	7.7	8.1	6.9	3,919	1,435	77	82	53	79	56	83	55
WA....	Seattle-Tacoma	51	84.2	63	8.8	9.5	8.1	4,797	173	52	84	62	82	75	81	48
	Spokane	48	76.4	64	8.9	8.7	8.6	6,820	394	52	78	52	86	80	64	26
WV....	Charleston	47	82.2	64	5.8	6.9	4.8	4,644	978	64	83	56	78	63	89	59
WI.....	Milwaukee	55	75.3	71	11.5	12.6	9.7	7,087	616	51	79	68	75	70	80	66
WY....	Cheyenne	60	71.0	54	12.8	15.0	10.4	7,388	273	52	65	45	57	50	68	37
PR....	San Juan	40	80.0	56	8.3	8.3	9.6	–	5,426	56	79	66	81	65	78	67

– Represents zero. [1] Percent of days that are either partly cloudy or cloudy. [2] Airport data for sunshine.

Source: U.S. National Oceanic and Atmospheric Administration, *Comparative Climatic Data*, annual. See also <http://www.ncdc.noaa.gov/statistical-weather-and-climate-information>.

Table 403. Significant Flood Event Losses Covered by the National Flood Insurance Program: 1978 to 2012

[In nominal dollars. Covers period 1978-March 31, 2012. Data are from U.S. Department of Homeland Security, Federal Emergency Management Agency]

Event	Date	Number of Paid Losses	Amount Paid ($)	Average Paid Loss ($)
Hurricane Katrina............................	Aug. 2005	167,856	16,247,530,180	96,950
Hurricane Ike.................................	Sept. 2008	46,219	2,629,409,589	56,890
Hurricane Ivan...............................	Sept. 2004	27,637	1,586,783,563	57,390
Tropical Storm Allison......................	June 2001	30,663	1,103,877,235	36,000
Louisiana Flood.............................	May 1995	31,343	585,071,593	18,667
Hurricane Isabel.............................	Sept. 2003	19,866	493,376,315	24,835
Hurricane Rita...............................	Sept. 2005	9,513	472,268,681	49,645
Hurricane Floyd.............................	Sept. 1999	20,438	462,281,156	22,619
Hurricane Opal..............................	Oct. 1995	10,343	405,527,543	39,208
Hurricane Hugo.............................	Sept. 1989	12,840	376,433,739	29,317
Hurricane Wilma............................	Oct. 2005	9,615	365,061,170	37,968
Nor'Easter....................................	Dec. 1992	25,142	346,150,356	13,768
Midwest Flood..............................	June 1993	10,472	272,819,515	26,052
PA, NJ, NY Floods..........................	June 2006	6,410	228,414,752	35,579
Nor'Easter....................................	Apr. 2007	8,637	225,708,711	26,133

Source: Congressional Research Service, *National Flood Insurance Program: Background, Challenges, and Financial Status*, May 2012.

Table 404. Threatened and Endangered Wildlife and Plant Species: 2012

[As of June 2012. Endangered species: One in danger of becoming extinct throughout all or a significant part of its natural range. Threatened species: One likely to become endangered in the foreseeable future]

Item	Mammals	Birds	Reptiles	Amphibians	Fishes	Snails	Clams	Crustaceans	Insects	Arachnids	Plants
Total listings..............	**361**	**309**	**118**	**34**	**161**	**40**	**78**	**22**	**66**	**12**	**797**
Endangered species, total.........................	**326**	**280**	**79**	**23**	**91**	**28**	**70**	**19**	**56**	**12**	**645**
United States..............	70	77	13	15	80	27	68	19	52	12	644
Foreign.....................	256	203	66	8	11	1	2	–	4	–	1
Threatened species, total.........................	**35**	**29**	**39**	**11**	**70**	**12**	**8**	**3**	**10**	**–**	**152**
United States..............	15	15	23	10	69	12	8	3	10	–	150
Foreign.....................	20	14	16	1	1	–	–	–	–	–	2

– Represents zero.

Source: U.S. Fish and Wildlife Service, *Endangered Species Bulletin*, bimonthly. See also <http://ecos.fws.gov/tess_public/pub/boxScore.jsp>, accessed June 2012.

Elections

This section relates primarily to presidential, congressional, and gubernatorial elections. Also presented are summary tables on congressional legislation; state legislatures; Hispanic and female officeholders; population of voting age; voter participation; and campaign finances.

Official statistics on federal elections, collected by the Clerk of the House, are published biennially in *Statistics of the Presidential and Congressional Election* and *Statistics of the Congressional Election*. Federal elections data also appear in the U.S. Congress, *Congressional Directory*, and in official state documents. Data on reported registration and voting for social and economic groups are obtained by the U.S. Census Bureau as part of the Current Population Survey (CPS) and are published in Current Population Reports, Series P20 (see text, Section 1).

Almost all federal, state, and local governmental units in the United States conduct elections for political offices and other purposes. The conduct of elections is regulated by state laws or, in some cities and counties, by local charter. An exception is that the U.S. Constitution prescribes the basis of representation in Congress and the manner of electing the president and grants to Congress the right to regulate the times, places, and manner of electing federal officers. Amendments to the Constitution have prescribed national criteria for voting eligibility. The 15th Amendment, adopted in 1870, gave all citizens the right to vote regardless of race, color, or previous condition of servitude. The 19th Amendment, adopted in 1920, further extended the right to vote to all citizens regardless of sex. The payment of poll taxes as a prerequisite to voting in federal elections was banned by the 24th Amendment in 1964. In 1971, as a result of the 26th Amendment, eligibility to vote in national elections was extended to all citizens, 18 years old and over.

Presidential election— The Constitution specifies how the president and vice president are selected. Each state elects, by popular vote, a group of electors equal in number to its total of members of Congress. The 23rd Amendment, adopted in 1961, grants the District of Columbia three presidential electors, a number equal to that of the least populous state. Subsequent to the election, the electors meet in their respective states to vote for president and vice president. Usually, each elector votes for the candidate receiving the most popular votes in his or her state. A majority vote of all electors is necessary to elect the president and vice president. If no candidate

receives a majority, the House of Representatives, with each state having one vote, is empowered to elect the president and vice president, again, with a majority of votes required.

The 22nd Amendment to the Constitution, adopted in 1951, limits presidential tenure to two elective terms of 4 years each or to one elective term for any person who, upon succession to the presidency, has held the office or acted as President for more than 2 years.

Congressional election— The Constitution provides that representatives be apportioned among the states according to their population, that a census of population be taken every 10 years as a basis for apportionment, and that each state have at least one representative. At the time of each apportionment, Congress decides what the total number of representatives will be. Since 1912, the total has been 435, except during 1960 to 1962 when it increased to 437, adding one representative each for Alaska and Hawaii. The total reverted to 435 after reapportionment following the 1960 census. Members are elected for 2-year terms, all terms covering the same period. The District of Columbia, American Samoa, Guam, and the Virgin Islands each elect one nonvoting delegate, and Puerto Rico elects a nonvoting resident commissioner.

The Senate is composed of 100 members, two from each state, who are elected to serve for a term of 6 years. One-third of the Senate is elected every 2 years. Senators were originally chosen by the state legislatures. The 17th Amendment to the Constitution, adopted in 1913, prescribed that senators be elected by popular vote.

Voter eligibility and participation—The Census Bureau publishes estimates of the population of voting age and the percent casting votes in each state for presidential and congressional election years. These voting-age estimates include a number of persons who meet the age requirement but are not eligible to vote, (e.g. aliens and some institutionalized persons). In addition, since 1964, voter participation and voter characteristics data have been collected during November of election years as part of the CPS. These survey data include noncitizens in the voting- age population estimates, but exclude members of the Armed Forces and the institutional population.

Statistical reliability— For a discussion of statistical collection and estimation, sampling procedures, and measures of statistical reliability applicable to Census Bureau data, see Appendix III.

Table 405. Participation in Elections for President and U.S. Representatives: 1932 to 2010

[75,768 represents 75,768,000. As of November, except as noted. Estimated resident population 21 years old and over, 1932–70, except as noted, and 18 years old and over thereafter; includes Armed Forces stationed in the U.S. Prior to 1958, excludes Alaska and prior to 1960, excludes Hawaii. District of Columbia is included in votes cast for President beginning 1964]

| Year | Resident population (includes aliens) of voting age [1] (1,000) | Votes cast | | | |
		For President (1,000)	Percent of voting-age population	For U.S. Representatives (1,000)	Percent of voting-age population
1932	75,768	39,817	52.6	(NA)	(NA)
1934	77,997	(X)	(X)	32,804	42.1
1936	80,174	45,647	56.9	(NA)	(NA)
1938	82,354	(X)	(X)	(NA)	(NA)
1940	84,728	49,815	58.8	(NA)	(NA)
1942	86,465	(X)	(X)	28,074	32.5
1944	85,654	48,026	56.1	45,110	52.7
1946	92,659	(X)	(X)	34,410	37.1
1948	95,573	48,834	51.1	46,220	48.4
1950	98,134	(X)	(X)	40,430	41.2
1952	99,929	61,552	61.6	57,571	57.6
1954	102,075	(X)	(X)	42,583	41.7
1956	104,515	62,027	59.3	58,886	56.3
1958	106,447	(X)	(X)	45,719	43.0
1960	109,672	68,836	62.8	64,124	58.5
1962	112,952	(X)	(X)	51,242	45.4
1964	114,090	70,098	61.4	65,879	57.7
1966	116,638	(X)	(X)	52,902	45.4
1968	120,285	73,027	60.7	66,109	55.0
1970	124,498	(X)	(X)	54,259	43.6
1972	140,777	77,625	55.1	71,188	50.6
1974	146,338	(X)	(X)	52,313	35.7
1976	152,308	81,603	53.6	74,259	48.8
1978	158,369	(X)	(X)	54,584	34.5
1980	163,945	86,497	52.8	77,874	47.5
1982	169,643	(X)	(X)	63,881	37.7
1984	173,995	92,655	53.3	82,422	47.4
1986	177,922	(X)	(X)	59,758	33.6
1988	181,956	91,587	50.3	81,682	44.9
1990	185,812	(X)	(X)	62,355	33.6
1992	189,493	104,600	55.2	97,198	51.3
1994	193,010	(X)	(X)	70,494	36.5
1996	196,789	96,390	49.0	90,233	45.9
1998	201,270	(X)	(X)	66,605	33.1
2000	[2] 209,787	105,594	50.3	98,800	47.1
2002	[2] 214,755	(X)	(X)	74,707	34.8
2004	[2] 219,553	122,349	55.7	113,192	51.6
2006	[2] 224,583	(X)	(X)	80,976	36.1
2008	[2] 229,945	131,407	57.1	122,586	53.3
2010	[3] 235,206	(X)	(X)	86,785	36.9

NA Not available. X Not applicable. [1] Population 18 and over in Georgia, 1944-70, and in Kentucky, 1956–70; 20 and over in Alaska and 20 and over in Hawaii, 1960–70. Source: Through 1990, U.S. Census Bureau, "Table 4. Participation in Elections for President and U.S. Representatives: 1930 to 1992," May 1994, <http://www.census.gov/population/socdemo/voting/p25-1117/tab03-04.pdf>. For 1992–1998, "Estimates and Projections of the Voting-Age Population, 1992 to 2000, and Percent Casting Votes for President, by State: November 1992 and 1996," July 2000, <http://www.census.gov/population/socdemo/voting/proj00/tab03.txt>. For 2000-2008, "Annual Estimates of the Resident Population by Sex and Selected Age Groups for the United States: April 1, 2000 to July 1, 2009, (NC-EST2009-02)," June 2010, <http://www.census.gov/popest/national/asrh/NC-EST2009/NC-EST2009-02.xls>. Starting 2010, "Annual Estimates of the Resident Population by Sex and Selected Age Groups for the United States: April 1, 2010 to July 1, 2011," May 2012, <http://www.census.gov/popest/data/national/asrh/2011/index.html>. [2] As of July 1. Based on results of the 2000 Census. [3] As of July 1. Based on results of the 2010 Census.

Source: Except as noted, U.S. House of Representatives, Office of the Clerk, *Statistics of the Presidential and Congressional Election*, biennial. See also <http://clerk.house.gov/member_info/election.aspx>.

Table 406. Resident Population of Voting Age and Percent Casting Votes— States: 2000 to 2010

[219,553 represents 219,553,000. Estimated population, 18 years old and over. 2010 based on 2010 Census as of April 1. Includes Armed Forces stationed in each state, aliens, and institutional population]

| State | Voting-age population (1,000) [1] | | | | Percent casting votes for— | | | | | |
| | | | | | Presidential electors | | | U.S. Representatives | | |
	2004 [2]	2006 [2]	2008 [2]	2010	2000 [2]	2004 [2]	2008 [2]	2006 [2]	2008 [2]	2010
U.S.	**219,553**	**224,583**	**229,945**	**234,564**	**50.3**	**55.7**	**57.1**	**36.1**	**53.3**	**37.0**
AL...............	3,403	3,476	3,548	3,647	50.0	55.3	59.2	32.8	52.3	37.5
AK...............	475	493	508	523	65.3	65.8	64.3	47.6	62.5	48.6
AZ...............	4,232	4,550	4,782	4,763	40.4	47.6	48.0	32.8	45.1	35.7
AR...............	2,063	2,117	2,161	2,204	46.1	51.1	50.3	36.0	36.4	35.1
CA...............	26,078	26,534	27,156	27,959	44.4	47.6	49.9	31.3	45.4	34.5
CO...............	3,448	3,576	3,725	3,804	54.1	61.8	64.5	43.0	61.3	46.4
CT...............	2,632	2,656	2,689	2,757	56.8	60.0	61.3	40.5	56.8	41.3
DE...............	627	649	669	692	55.4	59.9	61.6	38.8	57.6	44.2
DC...............	464	469	477	501	44.2	49.1	55.7	(X)	(X)	(X)
FL...............	13,455	14,023	14,353	14,799	48.1	56.6	58.5	27.5	51.7	34.6
GA...............	6,550	6,852	7,132	7,196	42.7	50.4	55.0	30.2	51.2	34.3
HI...............	959	985	998	1,056	40.1	44.7	45.7	34.3	45.7	34.1
ID...............	1,010	1,064	1,112	1,139	54.0	59.3	58.9	41.8	57.4	39.3
IL...............	9,417	9,514	9,660	9,701	51.6	56.0	57.2	36.3	54.3	38.1
IN...............	4,639	4,715	4,796	4,876	48.7	53.2	57.4	35.4	55.8	35.8
IA...............	2,229	2,253	2,281	2,318	61.6	67.6	67.4	45.9	64.9	47.7
KS...............	2,031	2,060	2,097	2,126	54.2	58.5	58.9	41.0	57.6	39.3
KY...............	3,153	3,213	3,272	3,316	50.6	57.0	55.8	39.0	53.5	40.8
LA...............	3,319	3,175	3,331	3,415	54.3	58.6	58.9	28.9	31.4	30.3
ME...............	1,017	1,031	1,044	1,054	66.8	72.8	70.0	52.0	68.0	53.6
MD...............	4,158	4,236	4,302	4,421	51.2	57.3	61.2	40.2	58.1	41.3
MA...............	4,966	5,009	5,105	5,129	56.2	58.9	60.8	44.8	60.8	43.4
MI...............	7,548	7,598	7,610	7,540	57.5	64.1	65.7	48.0	63.2	42.4
MN...............	3,808	3,883	3,968	4,020	66.9	74.3	73.3	56.1	70.6	52.0
MS...............	2,122	2,137	2,173	2,212	47.9	53.7	59.4	28.1	58.2	35.7
MO...............	4,335	4,429	4,521	4,563	56.5	63.0	64.7	47.4	62.4	42.1
MT...............	706	727	748	766	61.0	63.8	65.6	55.9	64.3	47.1
NE...............	1,296	1,315	1,334	1,367	55.2	60.0	60.1	45.3	58.1	35.5
NV...............	1,729	1,848	1,939	2,036	40.6	48.0	49.9	31.1	46.8	34.5
NH...............	985	1,009	1,028	1,029	61.2	68.9	69.2	39.9	65.6	43.7
NJ...............	6,495	6,536	6,610	6,727	50.3	55.6	58.5	32.7	52.0	31.5
NM...............	1,394	1,442	1,481	1,541	45.6	54.3	56.1	38.9	55.0	38.7
NY...............	14,677	14,819	15,015	15,053	48.6	50.7	51.4	31.6	51.4	31.5
NC...............	6,446	6,703	6,993	7,254	47.7	54.3	61.5	29.0	60.3	36.7
ND...............	489	493	498	523	59.9	63.9	63.5	44.1	63.0	45.2
OH...............	8,642	8,710	8,789	8,806	55.5	65.1	64.9	45.5	61.1	43.4
OK...............	2,633	2,682	2,737	2,822	48.2	55.6	53.4	33.8	48.9	28.1
OR...............	2,725	2,817	2,912	2,965	59.4	67.4	62.8	48.2	57.8	48.2
PA...............	9,530	9,641	9,771	9,910	52.4	60.5	61.5	41.6	59.2	39.9
RI...............	825	823	824	829	51.0	53.0	57.3	45.3	53.2	40.5
SC...............	3,172	3,289	3,428	3,545	45.9	51.0	56.0	33.0	54.7	37.8
SD...............	578	591	606	611	57.2	67.2	63.0	56.4	62.5	52.2
TN...............	4,486	4,622	4,749	4,850	48.2	54.3	54.7	37.1	48.5	32.1
TX...............	16,159	16,851	17,538	18,280	42.6	45.9	46.1	24.6	42.9	26.0
UT...............	1,679	1,781	1,877	1,893	50.6	55.2	50.7	32.0	49.9	33.8
VT...............	479	486	492	497	63.6	65.2	66.0	54.0	60.5	48.0
VA...............	5,662	5,818	5,957	6,147	51.1	56.4	62.5	39.5	58.7	35.6
WA...............	4,662	4,835	5,008	5,143	56.6	61.3	60.6	42.5	58.2	48.2
WV...............	1,414	1,419	1,427	1,466	46.1	53.5	50.0	32.0	45.2	35.1
WI...............	4,170	4,243	4,311	4,347	64.9	71.9	69.2	48.6	64.4	49.2
WY...............	380	389	404	428	58.5	64.1	63.1	50.4	61.8	44.6

X Not applicable. [1] As of July 1. Source: U.S. Census Bureau, "Annual Estimates of the Resident Population by Sex and Age for States: April 1, 2000 to July 1, 2009, (SC-EST2009-02)," June 2010, <http://www.census.gov/popest/data/index.html>. [2] Based on results of the 2000 Census.

Source: Except as noted, U.S. House of Representatives, Office of the Clerk, *Statistics of the Presidential and Congressional Election*, biennial. See also <http://clerk.house.gov/member_info/electionInfo/index.html>.

Table 407. Voting-Age Population—Reported Registration and Voting by Selected Characteristics: 1996 to 2010

[198.2 represents 198,200,000. As of November. Covers civilian noninstitutional population 18 years old and over. Includes aliens. Figures are based on Current Population Survey (see text, Section 1 and Appendix III) and differ from those in Table 405 based on population estimates and official vote counts]

| Characteristic | Voting-age population (mil.) | | | | | | | Percent reporting they registered | | | | | | | Percent reporting they voted | | | | | | |
| | | | | | | | | Presidential election years | | | | Congressional election years | | | Presidential election years | | | | Congressional election years | | |
	1998	2000	2002	2004	2006	2008	2010	1996	2000	2004	2008	2002	2006	2010	1996	2000	2004	2008	2002	2006	2010
Total[1]	**198.2**	**202.6**	**210.4**	**215.7**	**220.6**	**225.5**	**229.7**	**65.9**	**63.9**	**65.9**	**64.9**	**60.9**	**61.6**	**59.8**	**54.2**	**54.7**	**58.3**	**58.2**	**42.3**	**43.6**	**41.8**
18 to 20 years old	11.4	11.9	11.7	11.5	11.6	11.7	12.2	45.6	40.5	50.7	49.3	32.6	37.0	34.4	31.2	28.4	41.0	41.0	15.1	17.1	16.4
21 to 24 years old	14.1	14.9	15.6	16.4	16.4	16.6	16.7	51.2	52.1	52.1	56.2	42.5	44.9	47.2	33.4	35.4	42.5	46.6	18.7	21.9	22.0
25 to 34 years old	38.6	37.3	38.5	39.0	39.4	40.2	41.2	56.9	54.7	55.6	56.5	50.2	50.3	49.8	43.1	43.7	46.9	48.5	27.1	28.3	26.9
35 to 44 years old	44.4	44.5	43.7	43.1	42.6	41.5	39.9	66.5	63.8	64.2	61.4	60.0	59.3	57.3	54.9	55.0	56.9	55.2	40.2	40.1	37.7
45 to 64 years old	57.4	61.4	66.9	71.0	75.0	78.1	80.7	73.5	71.2	72.7	70.4	69.4	69.6	66.3	64.4	64.1	66.6	65.0	53.1	54.3	51.1
65 years old and over	32.3	32.8	33.9	34.7	35.8	37.5	39.0	77.0	76.1	76.9	75.0	75.8	75.4	72.5	67.0	67.6	68.9	68.1	61.0	60.5	58.9
Male	95.2	97.1	100.9	103.8	106.5	109.0	111.1	64.4	62.2	64.0	62.6	58.9	59.5	57.9	52.8	53.1	56.3	55.7	41.4	42.4	40.9
Female	103.0	105.5	109.5	111.9	114.1	116.5	118.6	67.3	65.6	67.6	67.0	62.8	63.5	61.5	55.5	56.2	60.1	60.4	43.0	44.7	42.7
White[2]	165.8	168.7	174.1	176.6	179.9	183.2	185.8	67.7	65.6	67.9	66.6	63.1	64.0	61.6	56.0	56.4	60.3	59.6	44.1	45.8	43.4
Black[2,3]	23.3	24.1	24.4	24.9	25.7	26.5	27.4	63.5	63.6	64.4	65.5	58.8	57.4	58.8	50.6	53.5	56.3	60.8	39.7	38.6	40.7
Asian[2,3]	(NA)	8.0	9.6	9.3	9.9	10.5	11.0	(NA)	30.7	34.9	37.3	30.7	32.9	34.1	(NA)	25.4	29.8	32.1	19.4	21.8	21.3
Hispanic[4]	20.3	21.6	25.2	27.1	29.0	30.9	32.5	35.7	34.9	34.3	37.6	32.6	32.1	33.8	26.7	27.5	28.0	31.6	18.9	19.3	20.5
Region:[5]																					
Northeast	38.5	38.9	41.1	41.0	41.2	41.5	42.3	64.7	63.7	65.3	63.7	60.8	60.3	59.7	54.5	55.2	58.6	57.4	41.4	42.8	41.6
Midwest	45.9	46.4	48.8	48.4	49.1	49.4	50.1	71.6	70.2	72.8	70.6	66.5	68.3	65.0	59.3	60.9	65.0	63.4	47.1	50.7	45.1
South	70.1	71.8	74.2	77.2	80.0	82.4	84.2	65.9	64.5	65.5	65.5	61.6	62.0	59.4	52.2	53.5	56.4	57.7	41.6	40.3	39.3
West	43.7	45.5	46.3	49.1	50.4	52.2	53.2	60.8	56.9	60.1	59.4	54.0	55.4	55.5	51.8	49.9	54.4	54.6	39.0	42.4	42.7
School years completed:																					
8 years or less	13.3	12.9	12.3	12.6	12.1	11.1	11.1	40.7	36.1	32.5	30.1	32.4	29.5	27.0	28.1	26.8	23.6	23.4	19.4	17.1	15.8
High school:																					
Less than high school graduate	21.0	20.1	20.9	20.7	20.2	19.1	18.8	47.9	45.9	45.8	43.2	41.6	39.6	37.8	33.8	33.6	34.6	33.7	23.3	22.8	20.8
High school graduate or GED[6]	65.6	66.3	68.9	68.5	70.0	70.4	71.0	62.2	60.1	61.5	59.5	57.1	57.5	54.0	49.1	49.4	52.4	50.9	37.1	37.6	35.2
College:																					
Some college or Associate's degree	52.9	55.3	57.3	58.9	60.2	63.8	65.3	72.9	70.0	73.7	72.0	66.7	68.3	65.5	60.5	60.3	66.1	65.0	45.8	47.3	44.4
Bachelor's or advanced degree	45.4	48.0	51.0	54.9	58.2	61.1	63.5	80.4	77.3	78.1	76.8	74.4	73.9	72.5	73.0	72.0	74.2	73.3	58.5	59.5	57.1
Employed	130.5	133.4	134.9	138.8	143.8	143.2	138.3	67.0	64.7	67.1	66.4	61.7	62.7	61.5	55.2	55.5	60.0	60.1	42.1	43.9	42.5
Unemployed	5.2	4.9	7.7	7.3	6.2	9.5	13.9	52.5	46.1	56.3	57.2	48.1	48.5	52.3	37.2	35.1	46.4	48.8	27.2	28.0	31.6
Not in labor force	62.5	64.2	67.8	69.6	70.5	72.8	77.5	65.1	63.8	64.4	62.9	60.9	60.7	58.0	54.1	54.5	56.2	55.5	44.2	44.3	42.3

NA Not available. [1] Includes other races, not shown separately. [2] Beginning with the 2003 Current Population Survey (CPS), respondents could choose more than one race. 2004, 2006, 2008, and 2010 data represent persons who selected this race group only and exclude persons reporting more than one race. The CPS in prior years only allowed respondents to report one race group. See also comment on race in the text for Section 1. [3] Prior to 2004, this category was "Asian and Pacific Islanders," therefore rates are not comparable with prior years. [4] Persons of Hispanic origin may be any race. [5] For composition of regions, see map, inside cover. [6] The General Educational Development (GED) Test measures how well a non-high school graduate has mastered the skills and general knowledge that are acquired in a 4-year high school education. Successfully passing the exam is a credential generally considered to be equivalent to a high school diploma.

Source: U.S. Census Bureau, *Voting and Registration in the Election of November 2010*, Current Population Reports, P20-562, 2010, and earlier reports, and unpublished data, <http://www.census.gov/hhes/www/socdemo/voting/index.html>.

Table 408. Persons Reported Registered and Voted by State: 2010

[229,690 represents 229,690,000. As of November. See headnote, Table 407]

State	Voting-age population (1,000)	Percent of voting-age population Registered	Percent of voting-age population Voted	State	Voting-age population (1,000)	Percent of voting-age population Registered	Percent of voting-age population Voted
U.S.............	229,690	59.8	41.8	MO.............	4,506	66.9	44.5
AL.................	3,526	63.1	42.8	MT.............	753	65.2	51.3
AK.................	498	63.8	48.6	NE.............	1,323	60.8	38.7
AZ.................	4,831	60.7	44.9	NV.............	1,957	50.9	37.3
AR.................	2,140	58.7	39.3	NH.............	1,024	65.0	45.9
CA.................	27,381	50.6	39.2	NJ.............	6,581	55.6	36.2
CO.................	3,768	61.0	48.4	NM.............	1,489	50.1	38.9
CT.................	2,648	62.0	45.9	NY.............	14,974	56.1	38.4
DE.................	667	62.6	48.5	NC.............	6,998	63.7	43.0
DC.................	489	60.3	40.8	ND.............	488	73.9	54.5
FL.................	14,227	56.2	39.2	OH.............	8,642	64.8	44.2
GA.................	7,119	57.2	40.2	OK.............	2,695	59.5	39.4
HI.................	965	48.3	39.9	OR.............	2,974	67.4	53.6
ID.................	1,114	59.8	44.7	PA.............	9,631	62.6	42.6
IL.................	9,619	60.5	41.5	RI.............	812	62.8	42.9
IN.................	4,777	59.4	38.2	SC.............	3,453	66.7	49.2
IA.................	2,278	67.9	50.2	SD.............	602	67.4	53.5
KS.................	2,059	65.5	45.2	TN.............	4,745	60.1	36.1
KY.................	3,250	65.0	45.5	TX.............	17,847	53.2	31.4
LA.................	3,314	73.2	48.8	UT.............	1,929	56.8	36.0
ME.................	1,034	75.4	58.4	VT.............	490	72.7	54.0
MD.................	4,279	58.6	42.1	VA.............	5,873	60.4	38.4
MA.................	5,097	63.4	48.1	WA.............	5,095	66.1	52.8
MI.................	7,513	68.2	45.2	WV.............	1,420	62.2	40.9
MN.................	3,982	69.2	52.8	WI.............	4,291	67.8	52.6
MS.................	2,113	72.5	46.5	WY.............	411	58.2	46.1

Source: U.S. Census Bureau, Current Population Reports, *Voting and Registration in the Election of November 2010* and unpublished data, <http://www.census.gov/hhes/www/socdemo/voting/index.html>.

Table 409. Reported Voting and Registration Among Native and Naturalized Citizens by Race and Hispanic Origin: 2010

[In thousands, except percent. (210,800 represents 210,800,000). As of November]

Nativity status, race, and Hispanic origin	Total citizen population (1,000)	U.S. Citizen Reported registered Number (1,000)	Reported registered Percent	Not registered Number (1,000)	Not registered Percent	Reported voted Number (1,000)	Reported voted Percent	Did not vote Number (1,000)	Did not vote Percent
Total:									
All races [1].............	210,800	137,263	65.1	73,537	34.9	95,987	45.5	114,813	54.5
White alone [2].............	172,447	114,482	66.4	57,965	33.6	80,554	46.7	91,893	53.3
Black alone [2].............	25,632	16,101	62.8	9,531	37.2	11,149	43.5	14,483	56.5
Asian alone [2].............	7,639	3,765	49.3	3,874	50.7	2,354	30.8	5,285	69.2
Hispanic [3].............	21,285	10,982	51.6	10,303	48.4	6,646	31.2	14,639	68.8
Native citizen:									
All races [1].............	193,897	128,098	66.1	65,799	33.9	89,740	46.3	104,157	53.7
White alone [2].............	162,609	109,074	67.1	53,535	32.9	76,696	47.2	85,913	52.8
White alone, non-Hispanic........	148,465	101,758	68.5	46,707	31.5	72,495	48.8	75,970	51.2
Black alone [2].............	23,780	15,003	63.1	8,777	36.9	10,385	43.7	13,395	56.3
Asian alone [2].............	2,748	1,273	46.3	1,475	53.7	842	30.6	1,906	69.4
Hispanic [3].............	15,535	7,938	51.1	7,597	48.9	4,541	29.2	10,994	70.8
White alone or in combination [4].....	165,166	110,661	67.0	54,505	33.0	77,715	47.1	87,451	52.9
Black alone or in combination [4].....	24,713	15,562	63.0	9,151	37.0	10,717	43.4	13,996	56.6
Asian alone or in combination [4].....	3,333	1,628	48.9	1,705	51.1	1,089	32.7	2,244	67.3
Naturalized citizen:									
All races [1].............	16,903	9,165	54.2	7,738	45.8	6,247	37.0	10,656	63.0
White alone [2].............	9,838	5,408	55.0	4,430	45.0	3,858	39.2	5,980	60.8
White alone, non-Hispanic........	4,464	2,558	57.3	1,906	42.7	1,877	42.0	2,587	58.0
Black alone [2].............	1,852	1,098	59.3	754	40.7	763	41.2	1,089	58.8
Asian alone [2].............	4,890	2,492	51.0	2,398	49.0	1,512	30.9	3,378	69.1
Hispanic [3].............	5,750	3,044	52.9	2,706	47.1	2,106	36.6	3,644	63.4
White alone or in combination [4].....	9,924	5,454	55.0	4,470	45.0	3,899	39.3	6,025	60.7
Black alone or in combination [4].....	1,889	1,122	59.4	767	40.6	781	41.3	1,108	58.7
Asian alone or in combination [4].....	4,913	2,508	51.1	2,405	48.9	1,525	31.0	3,388	69.0

[1] Includes other races, not shown separately. [2] Beginning with the 2003 Current Population Survey (CPS), respondents could choose more than one race. Data shown represent persons who selected this race group only and exclude persons reporting more than one race. [3] Persons of Hispanic origin may be any race. [4] In combination with one or more races.

Source: U.S. Census Bureau, *Voting and Registration in the Election of November 2010*, Current Population Reports P20-562, 2010. See also <http://www.census.gov/hhes/www/socdemo/voting/index.html>.

Table 410. Vote Cast for President by Major Political Party: 1952 to 2008

[In thousands (61,552 represents 61,552,000), except percent and electoral vote. Prior to 1960, excludes Alaska and Hawaii; prior to 1964, excludes DC. Vote cast for major party candidates includes the votes of minor parties cast for those candidates]

Year	Candidates for President		Vote cast for President						
			Total popular vote [1] (1,000)	Democratic			Republican		
				Popular vote		Electoral vote	Popular vote		Electoral vote
	Democratic	Republican		Number (1,000)	Percent		Number (1,000)	Percent	
1952..........	Stevenson	Eisenhower	61,552	27,315	44.4	89	33,779	54.9	442
1956..........	Stevenson	Eisenhower	62,027	26,739	43.1	73	35,581	57.4	457
1960..........	Kennedy	Nixon	68,836	34,227	49.7	303	34,108	49.5	219
1964..........	Johnson	Goldwater	70,098	42,825	61.1	486	27,147	38.7	52
1968..........	Humphrey	Nixon	73,027	30,989	42.4	191	31,710	43.4	301
1972..........	McGovern	Nixon	77,625	28,902	37.2	17	46,740	60.2	520
1976..........	Carter	Ford	81,603	40,826	50.0	297	39,148	48.0	240
1980..........	Carter	Reagan	86,497	35,481	41.0	49	43,643	50.5	489
1984..........	Mondale	Reagan	92,655	37,450	40.4	13	54,167	58.5	525
1988..........	Dukakis	Bush	91,587	41,717	45.5	111	48,643	53.1	426
1992..........	Clinton	Bush	104,600	44,858	42.9	370	38,799	37.1	168
1996..........	Clinton	Dole	96,390	47,402	49.2	379	39,198	40.7	159
2000..........	Gore	Bush	105,594	50,996	48.3	266	50,465	47.8	271
2004..........	Kerry	Bush	122,349	58,895	48.1	251	61,873	50.6	286
2008..........	Obama	McCain	131,407	69,498	52.9	365	59,948	45.6	173

[1] Include votes for minor party candidates, independents, unpledged electors, and scattered write-in votes.

Source: U.S. House of Representatives, Office of the Clerk, *Statistics of the Presidential and Congressional Election*, biennial. See also <http://clerk.house.gov/member_info/election.html>.

Table 411. Vote Cast for Leading Minority Party Candidates for President: 1952 to 2008

[In thousands (135 represents 135,000). See headnote, Table 410. Data do not include write-ins, scatterings, or votes for candidates who ran on party tickets not shown]

Year	Candidate	Party	Popular vote (1,000)	Candidate	Party	Popular vote (1,000)
1952..........	Vincent Hallinan	Progressive	135	Stuart Hamblen	Prohibition	73
1956 [1]........	T. Coleman Andrews	States' Rights	91	Eric Hass	Socialist Labor	41
1960..........	Eric Hass	Socialist Labor	46	Rutherford Decker	Prohibition	46
1964..........	Eric Hass	Socialist Labor	43	Clifton DeBerry	Socialist Workers	22
1968..........	George Wallace	American Independent	9,446	Henning Blomen	Socialist Labor	52
1972 [1]........	John Schmitz	American	993	Benjamin Spock	People's	9
1976..........	Eugene McCarthy	Independent	680	Roger McBride	Libertarian	172
1980..........	John Anderson	Independent	5,251	Ed Clark	Libertarian	920
1984..........	David Bergland	Libertarian	227	Lyndon H. LaRouche	Independent	79
1988..........	Ron Paul	Libertarian	410	Lenora B. Fulani	New Alliance	129
1992..........	H. Ross Perot	Independent	19,722	Andre Marrou	Libertarian	281
1996..........	H. Ross Perot	Reform	7,137	Ralph Nader	Green	527
2000..........	Ralph Nader	Green	2,530	Pat Buchanan	Reform	324
2004..........	Ralph Nader	Independent	156	Michael Badnarik	Libertarian	369
2008..........	Ralph Nader	Independent	739	Bob Barr	Libertarian	515

[1] Data include write-ins, scatterings, and/or votes for candidates who ran on party tickets not shown.

Source: U.S. House of Representatives, Office of the Clerk, *Statistics of the Presidential and Congressional Election*, biennial. See also <http://clerk.house.gov/member_info/election.html>.

Table 412. Democratic and Republican Percentages of Two-Party Presidential Vote by Selected Characteristics of Voters: 2004 and 2008

[In percent. Covers citizens of voting age living in private housing units in the contiguous United States. Percentages for Democratic Presidential vote are computed by subtracting the percentage Republican vote from 100 percent; third-party or independent votes are not included as valid data. Data are from the National Election Studies and are based on a sample and subject to sampling variability; for details, see source]

Characteristic	2004		2008		Characteristic	2004		2008	
	Demo-cratic	Republi-can	Demo-cratic	Republi-can		Demo-cratic	Republi-can	Demo-cratic	Republi-can
Total [1]..................	**50**	**50**	**55**	**45**	Race:				
Year of birth:					White.................	42	58	44	56
1975 or later.............	66	34	65	35	Black.................	90	10	99	1
1959 to 1974.............	45	55	56	44	Education:				
					Less than high				
1943 to 1958.............	44	56	54	46	school.................	69	31	72	28
1927 to 1942.............	51	49	41	59	High school diploma/				
1911 to 1926.............	52	48	52	48	equivalent.........	46	54	57	43
1895 to 1910.............	–	–	–	–	Some college,				
Sex:					no degree.........	47	53	53	47
Male.................	46	54	52	48	College.................	50	50	51	49
Female.................	53	47	57	43	Union household......	64	36	60	40
					Nonunion				
					household.............	46	54	54	46

– Represents zero. [1] Includes other characteristics, not shown separately.

Source: American National Election Studies, <http://www.electionstudies.org/> (copyright).

Table 413. Electoral Vote Cast for President by Major Political Party—States: 1968 to 2008

[D = Democratic, R = Republican. For composition of regions, see map, inside front cover]

State	1968 [1]	1972 [2]	1976 [3]	1980	1984	1988 [4]	1992	1996	2000 [5]	2004 [6]	2008 [7]
Democratic	**191**	**17**	**297**	**49**	**13**	**111**	**370**	**379**	**266**	**251**	**365**
Republican	**301**	**520**	**240**	**489**	**525**	**426**	**168**	**159**	**271**	**286**	**173**
Northeast:											
Democratic	102	14	86	4	–	53	106	106	102	101	101
Republican	24	108	36	118	113	60	–	–	4	–	–
Midwest:											
Democratic	31	–	58	10	10	29	100	100	68	57	97
Republican	118	145	87	135	127	108	29	29	61	66	27
South:											
Democratic	45	3	149	31	3	8	68	80	15	16	71
Republican	77	165	20	138	174	168	116	104	168	173	118
West:											
Democratic	13	–	4	4	–	21	96	93	81	77	96
Republican	82	102	97	98	111	90	23	26	38	47	28
AL	([1])	R-9	D-9	R-9	R-9	R-9	R-9	R-9	R-9	R-9	R-9
AK	R-3	R-3	R-3	R-3	R-3	R-3	R-3	R-3	R-3	R-3	R-3
AZ	R-5	R-6	R-6	R-6	R-7	R-7	R-8	D-8	R-8	R-10	R-10
AR	([1])	R-6	D-6	R-6	R-6	R-6	D-6	D-6	R-6	R-6	R-6
CA	R-40	R-45	R-45	R-45	R-47	R-47	D-54	D-54	D-54	D-55	D-55
CO	R-6	R-7	R-7	R-7	R-8	R-8	D-8	R-8	R-8	R-9	D-9
CT	D-8	R-8	R-8	R-8	R-8	R-8	D-8	D-8	D-8	D-7	D-7
DE	R-3	R-3	D-3	R-3	R-3	R-3	D-3	D-3	D-3	D-3	D-3
DC	D-3	D-3	D-3	D-3	D-3	D-3	D-3	D-3	[5] D-2	D-3	D-3
FL	R-14	R-17	D-17	R-17	R-21	R-21	R-25	D-25	R-25	R-27	D-27
GA	([1])	R-12	D-12	D-12	R-12	R-12	D-13	R-13	R-13	R-15	R-15
HI	D-4	R-4	D-4	D-4	R-4	D-4	D-4	D-4	D-4	D-4	D-4
ID	R-4	R-4	R-4	R-4	R-4	R-4	R-4	R-4	R-4	R-4	R-4
IL	R-26	R-26	R-26	R-26	R-24	R-24	D-22	D-22	D-22	D-21	D-21
IN	R-13	R-13	R-13	R-13	R-12	R-12	R-12	R-12	R-12	R-11	D-11
IA	R-9	R-8	R-8	R-8	R-8	D-8	D-7	D-7	D-7	R-7	D-7
KS	R-7	R-7	R-7	R-7	R-7	R-7	R-6	R-6	R-6	R-6	R-6
KY	R-9	R-9	D-9	R-9	R-9	R-9	D-8	D-8	R-8	R-8	R-8
LA	([1])	R-10	D-10	R-10	R-10	R-10	D-9	D-9	R-9	R-9	R-9
ME	D-4	R-4	R-4	R-4	R-4	R-4	D-4	D-4	D-4	D-4	D-4
MD	D-10	R-10	D-10	D-10	R-10	R-10	D-10	D-10	D-10	D-10	D-10
MA	D-14	D-14	D-14	D-14	R-13	D-13	D-12	D-12	D-12	D-12	D-12
MI	D-21	R-21	R-21	R-21	R-20	R-20	D-18	D-18	D-18	D-17	D-17
MN	D-10	R-10	D-10	D-10	D-10	D-10	D-10	D-10	D-10	[6] D-9	D-10
MS	([1])	R-7	D-7	R-7	R-7	R-7	R-7	R-7	R-7	R-6	R-6
MO	R-12	R-12	D-12	R-12	R-11	R-11	D-11	D-11	R-11	R-11	R-11
MT	R-4	R-4	R-4	R-4	R-4	R-4	D-3	R-3	R-3	R-3	R-3
NE	R-5	R-5	R-5	R-5	R-5	R-5	R-5	R-5	R-5	R-5	[7] R-4
NV	R-3	R-3	R-3	R-3	R-4	R-4	D-4	D-4	R-4	R-5	D-5
NH	R-4	R-4	R-4	R-4	R-4	R-4	D-4	D-4	R-4	D-4	D-4
NJ	R-17	R-17	R-17	R-17	R-16	R-16	D-15	D-15	D-15	D-15	D-15
NM	R-4	R-4	R-4	R-4	R-5	R-5	D-5	D-5	D-5	R-5	D-5
NY	D-43	R-41	D-41	R-41	R-36	D-36	D-33	D-33	D-33	D-31	D-31
NC	[1] R-12	R-13	D-13	R-13	R-13	R-13	R-14	R-14	R-14	R-15	D-15
ND	R-4	R-3	R-3	R-3	R-3	R-3	R-3	R-3	R-3	R-3	R-3
OH	R-26	R-25	D-25	R-25	R-23	R-23	D-21	D-21	R-21	R-20	D-20
OK	R-8	R-8	R-8	R-8	R-8	R-8	R-8	R-8	R-8	R-7	R-7
OR	R-6	R-6	R-6	R-6	R-7	D-7	D-7	D-7	D-7	D-7	D-7
PA	D-29	R-27	D-27	R-27	R-25	R-25	D-23	D-23	D-23	D-21	D-21
RI	D-4	R-4	D-4	D-4	R-4	D-4	D-4	D-4	D-4	D-4	D-4
SC	R-8	R-8	D-8	R-8	R-8	R-8	R-8	R-8	R-8	R-8	R-8
SD	R-4	R-4	R-4	R-4	R-3	R-3	R-3	R-3	R-3	R-3	R-3
TN	R-11	R-10	D-10	R-10	R-11	R-11	D-11	D-11	R-11	R-11	R-11
TX	D-25	R-26	D-26	R-26	R-29	R-29	R-32	R-32	R-32	R-34	R-34
UT	R-4	R-4	R-4	R-4	R-5	R-5	R-5	R-5	R-5	R-5	R-5
VT	R-3	R-3	R-3	R-3	R-3	R-3	D-3	D-3	D-3	D-3	D-3
VA	R-12	[2] R-11	R-12	R-12	R-12	R-12	R-13	R-13	R-13	R-13	D-13
WA	D-9	R-9	[3] R-8	R-9	R-10	D-10	D-11	D-11	D-11	D-11	D-11
WV	D-7	R-6	D-6	D-6	R-6	[4] D-5	D-5	D-5	R-5	R-5	R-5
WI	R-12	R-11	D-11	R-11	R-11	D-11	D-11	D-11	D-11	D-10	D-10
WY	R-3	R-3	R-3	R-3	R-3	R-3	R-3	R-3	R-3	R-3	R-3

– Represents zero. [1] Excludes 46 electoral votes cast for American Independent George C. Wallace as follows: AL 10, AR 6, GA 12, LA 10, MS 7, and NC 1. [2] Excludes one electoral vote cast for Libertarian John Hospers in Virginia. [3] Excludes one electoral vote cast for Ronald Reagan in Washington. [4] Excludes one electoral vote cast for Lloyd Bentsen for President in West Virginia. [5] Excludes one electoral vote left blank by a Democratic elector in the District of Columbia. [6] Excludes one electoral vote cast for Democratic vice presidential nominee John Edwards in Minnesota. [7] Excludes one electoral vote for Barack Obama in Nebraska.

Source: U.S. House of Representatives, Office of the Clerk, *Statistics of the Presidential and Congressional Election*, biennial. See also <http://clerk.house.gov/member_info/election.html>.

Table 414. Popular Vote Cast for President by Political Party—States: 2004 and 2008

[In thousands (122,349 represents 122,349,000), except percent]

State	2004					2008				
				Percent of total vote					Percent of total vote	
	Total [1]	Demo-cratic party	Republi-can party	Demo-cratic party	Republi-can party	Total [1]	Demo-cratic party	Republi-can party	Demo-cratic party	Republi-can party
United States.........	122,349	58,895	61,873	48.1	50.6	131,407	69,498	59,948	52.9	45.6
Alabama..................	1,883	694	1,176	36.8	62.5	2,100	813	1,267	38.7	60.3
Alaska....................	313	111	191	35.5	61.1	326	124	194	37.9	59.4
Arizona..................	2,013	894	1,104	44.4	54.9	2,293	1,035	1,230	45.1	53.6
Arkansas................	1,055	470	573	44.5	54.3	1,087	422	638	38.9	58.7
California................	12,421	6,745	5,510	54.3	44.4	13,562	8,274	5,012	61.0	37.0
Colorado................	2,130	1,002	1,101	47.0	51.7	2,401	1,289	1,074	53.7	44.7
Connecticut............	1,579	857	694	54.3	43.9	1,647	998	629	60.6	38.2
Delaware...............	375	200	172	53.3	45.8	412	255	152	61.9	36.9
District of Columbia.....	228	203	21	89.2	9.3	266	246	17	92.5	6.5
Florida...................	7,610	3,584	3,965	47.1	52.1	8,391	4,282	4,046	51.0	48.2
Georgia..................	3,302	1,366	1,914	41.4	58.0	3,924	1,844	2,049	47.0	52.2
Hawaii...................	429	232	194	54.0	45.3	456	326	121	71.5	26.4
Idaho....................	598	181	409	30.3	68.4	655	236	403	36.1	61.5
Illinois...................	5,274	2,892	2,346	54.8	44.5	5,522	3,419	2,031	61.9	36.8
Indiana..................	2,468	969	1,479	39.3	59.9	2,751	1,374	1,346	49.9	48.9
Iowa.....................	1,507	742	752	49.2	49.9	1,537	829	682	53.9	44.4
Kansas..................	1,188	435	736	36.6	62.0	1,236	515	700	41.7	56.6
Kentucky................	1,796	713	1,069	39.7	59.5	1,827	752	1,048	41.2	57.4
Louisiana...............	1,943	820	1,102	42.2	56.7	1,961	783	1,148	39.9	58.6
Maine...................	741	397	330	53.6	44.6	731	422	295	57.7	40.4
Maryland................	2,384	1,334	1,025	56.0	43.0	2,632	1,629	960	61.9	36.5
Massachusetts..........	2,927	1,804	1,071	61.6	36.6	3,103	1,904	1,109	61.4	35.7
Michigan................	4,839	2,479	2,314	51.2	47.8	5,002	2,873	2,049	57.4	41.0
Minnesota..............	2,828	1,445	1,347	51.1	47.6	2,910	1,573	1,275	54.1	43.8
Mississippi.............	1,140	458	673	40.2	59.0	1,290	555	725	43.0	56.2
Missouri.................	2,731	1,259	1,456	46.1	53.3	2,925	1,442	1,446	49.3	49.4
Montana................	450	174	266	38.6	59.1	490	232	243	47.3	49.5
Nebraska...............	778	254	513	32.7	65.9	801	333	453	41.6	56.5
Nevada..................	830	397	419	47.9	50.5	968	534	413	55.1	42.7
New Hampshire.........	678	341	331	50.2	48.8	711	385	317	54.1	44.5
New Jersey..............	3,612	1,911	1,670	52.9	46.2	3,868	2,215	1,613	57.3	41.7
New Mexico.............	756	371	377	49.0	49.8	830	472	347	56.9	41.8
New York................	7,448	4,181	2,807	56.1	37.7	7,722	4,805	2,753	62.2	35.6
North Carolina..........	3,501	1,526	1,961	43.6	56.0	4,298	2,143	2,128	49.8	49.5
North Dakota............	313	111	197	35.5	62.9	317	141	169	44.6	53.3
Ohio.....................	5,628	2,741	2,860	48.7	50.8	5,708	2,940	2,678	51.5	46.9
Oklahoma...............	1,464	504	960	34.4	65.6	1,463	502	960	34.4	65.6
Oregon..................	1,837	943	867	51.3	47.2	1,828	1,037	738	56.7	40.4
Pennsylvania...........	5,770	2,938	2,794	50.9	48.4	6,013	3,276	2,656	54.5	44.2
Rhode Island............	437	260	169	59.4	38.7	472	297	165	62.9	35.1
South Carolina..........	1,618	662	938	40.9	58.0	1,921	862	1,035	44.9	53.9
South Dakota...........	388	149	233	38.4	59.9	382	171	203	44.7	53.2
Tennessee..............	2,437	1,036	1,384	42.5	56.8	2,600	1,087	1,479	41.8	56.9
Texas...................	7,411	2,833	4,527	38.2	61.1	8,078	3,529	4,479	43.7	55.5
Utah.....................	928	241	664	26.0	71.5	952	328	596	34.4	62.6
Vermont.................	312	184	121	58.9	38.8	325	219	99	67.5	30.4
Virginia..................	3,195	1,455	1,717	45.5	53.7	3,723	1,960	1,725	52.6	46.3
Washington.............	2,859	1,510	1,305	52.8	45.6	3,037	1,751	1,229	57.7	40.5
West Virginia............	756	327	424	43.2	56.1	713	304	397	42.6	55.7
Wisconsin...............	2,997	1,490	1,478	49.7	49.3	2,983	1,677	1,262	56.2	42.3
Wyoming................	244	71	168	29.0	68.7	255	83	165	32.5	64.7

[1] Includes other parties.

Source: U.S. House of Representatives, Office of the Clerk, *Statistics of the Presidential and Congressional Election*, biennial. See also <http://clerk.house.gov/member_info/election.html>.

Table 415. Vote Cast for U.S. Senators, 2008 and 2010, and Incumbent Senators, 2012—States

[2,060 represents 2,060,000. D = Democrat, R = Republican, I = Independent]

State	2008 Total [2] (1,000)	2008 Percent for leading party	2010 Total [2] (1,000)	2010 Percent for leading party	Incumbent senators and year term expires [1] Name, party, and year	Incumbent senators and year term expires [1] Name, party, and year
Alabama	2,060	R-63.4	1,485	R-65.2	Jeff Sessions (R) 2015	Richard C. Shelby (R) 2017
Alaska	318	D-47.8	256	R-35.6	Lisa Murkowski (R) 2017	Mark Begich (D) 2015
Arizona	(X)	(X)	1,708	R-58.9	Jon Kyl (R) 2013	John McCain (R) 2017
Arkansas	1,012	D-79.5	780	R-57.9	John Boozman (R) 2017	Mark L. Pryor (D) 2015
California	(X)	(X)	10,000	D-52.2	Barbara Boxer (D) 2017	Dianne Feinstein (D) 2013
Colorado	2,332	D-52.8	1,772	D-48.1	Mark Udall (D) 2015	Michael F. Bennett (D) 2017
Connecticut	(X)	(X)	1,153	D-52.5	Richard Blumenthal (D) 2017	Joseph I. Lieberman (I) 2013
Delaware	398	D-64.7	307	D-56.6	Christopher Coons (D) 2015	Thomas R. Carper (D) 2013
Florida	(X)	(X)	5,411	R-48.9	Marco Rubio (R) 2017	Bill Nelson (D) 2013
Georgia	2,266	R-54.2	2,555	R-58.3	Saxby Chambliss (R) 2015	Johnny Isakson (R) 2017
Hawaii	(X)	(X)	371	D-74.8	Daniel K. Akaka (D) 2013	Daniel K. Inouye (D) 2017
Idaho	645	R-57.7	450	R-71.2	James E. Risch (R) 2015	Mike Crapo (R) 2017
Illinois	5,330	D-67.8	3,704	R-48.0	Richard J. Durbin (D) 2015	Mark Kirk (R) 2017
Indiana	(X)	(X)	1,744	R-54.6	Daniel Coats (R) 2017	Richard G. Lugar (R) 2013
Iowa	1,503	D-62.7	1,116	R-64.4	Chuck Grassley (R) 2017	Tom Harkin (D) 2015
Kansas	1,211	R-60.1	838	R-70.1	Jerry Moran (R) 2017	Pat Roberts (R) 2015
Kentucky	1,801	R-53.0	1,356	R-55.7	Rand Paul (R) 2017	Mitch McConnell (R) 2015
Louisiana [3]	1,897	D-52.1	1,265	R-56.6	Mary L. Landrieu (D) 2015	David Vitter (R) 2017
Maine	724	R-61.3	(X)	(X)	Susan M. Collins (R) 2015	Olympia J. Snowe (R) 2013
Maryland	(X)	(X)	1,834	D-62.2	Barbara A. Mikulski (D) 2017	Benjamin L. Cardin (D) 2013
Massachusetts	3,103	D-63.6	(X)	(X)	Scott P. Brown [4] (R) 2013	John F. Kerry (D) 2015
Michigan	4,849	D-62.7	(X)	(X)	Carl Levin (D) 2015	Debbie Stabenow (D) 2013
Minnesota	2,888	D-42.0	(X)	(X)	Al Franken (D) 2015	Amy Klobuchar (D) 2013
Mississippi	1,247	R-61.4	(X)	(X)	Thad Cochran (R) 2015	Roger F. Wicker (R) 2013
Missouri	(X)	(X)	1,944	R-54.2	Roy Blunt (R) 2017	Claire McCaskill (D) 2013
Montana	478	D-72.9	(X)	(X)	Max Baucus (D) 2015	John Tester (D) 2013
Nebraska	793	R-57.5	(X)	(X)	Mike Johanns (R) 2015	Ben Nelson (D) 2013
Nevada	(X)	(X)	721	D-50.3	Dean Heller [5] (R) 2013	Harry Reid (D) 2017
New Hampshire	695	D-51.6	455	R-60.1	Kelly Ayotte (R) 2017	Jeanne Shaheen (D) 2015
New Jersey	3,482	D-56.0	(X)	(X)	Robert Menendez (D) 2013	Frank R. Lautenberg (D) 2015
New Mexico	824	D-61.3	(X)	(X)	Jeff Bingaman (D) 2013	Tom Udall (D) 2015
New York	(X)	(X)	4,764	D-64.0	Kirsten Gillibrand [6] (D) 2013	Charles E. Schumer (D) 2017
North Carolina	4,272	D-52.7	2,660	R-54.8	Richard Burr (R) 2017	Kay R. Hagan (D) 2015
North Dakota	(X)	(X)	239	R-76.2	Kent Conrad (D) 2013	John Hoeven (R) 2017
Ohio	(X)	(X)	3,815	R-56.8	Sherrod Brown (D) 2013	Rob Portman (R) 2017
Oklahoma	1,347	R-56.7	1,017	R-70.6	Tom Coburn (R) 2017	James M. Inhofe (R) 2015
Oregon	1,768	D-48.9	1,443	D-57.2	Jeff Merkley (D) 2015	Ron Wyden (D) 2017
Pennsylvania	(X)	(X)	3,978	R-51.0	Robert P. Casey Jr. (D) 2013	Patrick J. Toomey (R) 2017
Rhode Island	439	D-73.1	(X)	(X)	Sheldon Whitehouse (D) 2013	Jack Reed (D) 2015
South Carolina	1,871	R-57.5	1,319	R-61.5	Jim DeMint (R) 2017	Lindsey Graham (R) 2015
South Dakota	381	D-62.5	228	R-100	Tim Johnson (D) 2015	John Thune (R) 2017
Tennessee	2,425	R-65.1	(X)	(X)	Lamar Alexander (R) 2015	Bob Corker (R) 2013
Texas	7,912	R-54.8	(X)	(X)	John Cornyn (R) 2015	Kay Hutchinson (R) 2013
Utah	(X)	(X)	585	R-61.6	Mike Lee (R) 2017	Orrin G. Hatch (R) 2013
Vermont	(X)	(X)	235	D-64.3	Bernard Sanders (I) 2013	Patrick J. Leahy (D) 2017
Virginia	3,643	D-65.0	(X)	(X)	Jim Webb (D) 2013	Mark R. Warner (D) 2015
Washington	(X)	(X)	2,511	D-52.4	Maria Cantwell (D) 2013	Patty Murray (D) 2017
West Virginia	702	D-63.7	(X)	(X)	Joe Manchin III (D) 2013	John D. Rockefeller IV (D) 2015
Wisconsin	(X)	(X)	2,171	R-51.9	Ronald H. Johnson (R) 2017	Herb Kohl (D) 2013
Wyoming	250	D-75.6	(X)	(X)	Michael B. Enzi (R) 2015	John Barrasso (R) 2013

X Not applicable. [1] As of March 20, 2012. See source note, Table 419. [2] Includes vote cast for minor parties. [3] Louisiana holds an open-primary election with candidates from all parties running on the same ballot. Any candidate who receives a majority is elected. [4] Elected in the January 19, 2010 special election to fill seat previously held by appointed Senator Paul G. Kirk, Jr. 2006 data represents votes cast for Edward M. Kennedy. [5] Appointed April 27, 2011, to fill vacancy due to resignation of John Ensign, May 3, 2011. [6] Appointed January 23, 2009, to fill vacancy due to resignation of Hillary Rodham Clinton, January 21, 2009.

Source: U.S. House of Representatives, Office of the Clerk, *Statistics of the Presidential and Congressional Election*, biennial. See also <http://clerk.house.gov/member_info/election.html>.

Table 416. Apportionment of Membership in House of Representatives by State: 1800 to 2010

[Total membership includes Representatives assigned to newly admitted States after the apportionment acts. Population figures used for apportionment purposes are those determined for States by each decennial census. No reapportionment based on 1920 population census. For method of calculating apportionment and a short history of apportionment, see House Report 91-1314, 91st Congress, 2d session, The Decennial Population Census and Congressional Apportionment]

State	Membership based on census of—																				
	1800	1820	1830	1840	1850	1860	1870	1880	1890	1900	1910	1920	1930	1940	1950	1960	1970	1980	1990	2000	2010
U.S....	142	213	242	232	237	243	293	332	357	391	435	435	435	435	437	435	435	435	435	435	435
AL	(X)	3	5	7	7	6	8	8	9	9	10	10	9	9	9	8	7	7	7	7	
AK	(X)	(X)	(X)	(X)	(X)	(X)	(X)	(X)	(X)	(X)	(X)	(X)	(X)	(X)	[1]1	1	1	1	1	1	
AZ	(X)	(X)	(X)	(X)	(X)	(X)	(X)	(X)	(X)	(X)	[2]1	1	1	2	2	3	4	5	6	8	
AR	(X)	(X)	[1]1	1	2	3	4	5	6	7	7	7	7	7	6	4	4	4	4	4	
CA	(X)	(X)	(X)	[1]2	2	3	4	6	7	8	11	11	20	23	30	38	43	45	52	53	
CO	(X)	(X)	(X)	(X)	(X)	(X)	[1]1	1	2	3	4	4	4	4	4	4	5	6	6	7	
CT	7	6	6	4	4	4	4	4	4	5	5	5	6	6	6	6	6	6	6	5	
DE	1	1	1	1	1	1	1	1	1	1	1	1	1	1	1	1	1	1	1	1	
FL	(X)	(X)	(X)	[1]1	1	1	2	2	2	3	4	4	5	6	8	12	15	19	23	25	
GA	4	7	9	8	8	7	9	10	11	11	12	12	10	10	10	10	10	10	11	13	
HI	(X)	(X)	(X)	(X)	(X)	(X)	(X)	(X)	(X)	(X)	(X)	(X)	(X)	(X)	[1]1	2	2	2	2	2	
ID	(X)	(X)	(X)	(X)	(X)	(X)	(X)	[1]1	1	2	2	2	2	2	2	2	2	2	2	2	
IL	(X)	1	3	7	9	14	19	20	22	25	27	27	27	26	25	24	24	22	20	19	
IN	(X)	3	7	10	11	11	13	13	13	13	13	13	12	11	11	11	11	10	10	9	
IA	(X)	(X)	(X)	[1]2	2	6	9	11	11	11	11	11	9	8	8	7	6	6	5	5	
KS	(X)	(X)	(X)	(X)	(X)	1	3	7	8	8	8	8	7	6	6	5	5	5	4	4	
KY	6	12	13	10	10	9	10	11	11	11	11	11	9	9	8	7	7	7	6	6	
LA	(X)	3	3	4	4	5	6	6	6	7	8	8	8	8	8	8	8	8	7	7	
ME	(X)	7	8	7	6	5	5	4	4	4	4	4	3	3	3	2	2	2	2	2	
MD	9	9	8	6	6	5	6	6	6	6	6	6	6	6	7	8	8	8	8	8	
MA	17	13	12	10	11	10	11	12	13	14	16	16	15	14	14	12	12	11	10	10	
MI	(X)	(X)	[1]1	3	4	6	9	11	12	12	13	13	17	17	18	19	19	18	16	15	
MN	(X)	(X)	(X)	(X)	[1]2	2	3	5	7	9	10	10	9	9	9	8	8	8	8	8	
MS	(X)	1	2	4	5	5	6	7	7	8	8	8	7	7	6	5	5	5	5	4	
MO	(X)	1	2	5	7	9	13	14	15	16	16	16	13	13	11	10	10	9	9	9	
MT	(X)	(X)	(X)	(X)	(X)	(X)	(X)	[1]1	1	1	2	2	2	2	2	2	2	2	1	1	
NE	(X)	(X)	(X)	(X)	(X)	(X)	[1]1	1	3	6	6	6	5	4	4	3	3	3	3	3	
NV	(X)	(X)	(X)	(X)	(X)	[1]1	1	1	1	1	1	1	1	1	1	1	1	2	2	3	
NH	5	6	5	4	3	3	3	2	2	2	2	2	2	2	2	2	2	2	2	2	
NJ	6	6	6	5	5	5	7	7	8	10	12	12	14	14	14	15	15	14	13	13	
NM	(X)	(X)	(X)	(X)	(X)	(X)	(X)	(X)	(X)	(X)	[2]1	1	1	2	2	2	2	3	3	3	
NY	17	34	40	34	33	31	33	34	34	37	43	43	45	45	43	41	39	34	31	29	
NC	12	13	13	9	8	7	8	9	9	10	10	10	11	12	12	11	11	11	12	13	
ND	(X)	(X)	(X)	(X)	(X)	(X)	(X)	[1]1	1	2	3	3	2	2	2	2	1	1	1	1	
OH	[1]1	14	19	21	21	19	20	21	21	21	22	22	24	23	23	24	23	21	19	18	
OK	(X)	(X)	(X)	(X)	(X)	(X)	(X)	(X)	(X)	[1]5	8	8	9	8	6	6	6	6	6	5	
OR	(X)	(X)	(X)	(X)	[1]1	1	1	1	2	2	3	3	4	4	4	4	5	5	5	5	
PA	18	26	28	24	25	24	27	28	30	32	36	36	34	33	30	27	25	23	21	19	
RI	2	2	2	2	2	2	2	2	2	2	3	3	2	2	2	2	2	2	2	2	
SC	8	9	9	7	6	4	5	7	7	7	7	7	6	6	6	6	6	6	6	6	
SD	(X)	(X)	(X)	(X)	(X)	(X)	(X)	[1]2	2	2	3	3	2	2	2	2	2	1	1	1	
TN	3	9	13	11	10	8	10	10	10	10	10	10	9	10	9	9	8	9	9	9	
TX	(X)	(X)	(X)	[1]2	2	4	6	11	13	16	18	18	21	21	22	23	24	27	30	32	
UT	(X)	(X)	(X)	(X)	(X)	(X)	(X)	(X)	[1]1	1	2	2	2	2	2	2	2	3	3	3	
VT	4	5	5	4	3	3	3	2	2	2	2	2	1	1	1	1	1	1	1	1	
VA	22	22	21	15	13	11	9	10	10	10	10	10	9	9	10	10	10	10	11	11	
WA	(X)	(X)	(X)	(X)	(X)	(X)	(X)	[1]1	2	3	5	5	6	6	6	7	7	7	8	9	
WV	(X)	(X)	(X)	(X)	(X)	(X)	3	4	4	5	6	6	6	6	6	5	4	4	3	3	
WI	(X)	(X)	(X)	[1]2	3	6	8	9	10	11	11	11	10	10	10	10	9	9	9	8	
WY	(X)	(X)	(X)	(X)	(X)	(X)	(X)	[1]1	1	1	1	1	1	1	1	1	1	1	1	1	

X Not applicable. [1] Assigned after apportionment. [2] Included in apportionment in anticipation of statehood.

Source: U.S. Census Bureau, Congressional Apportionment, Census 2010, <http://www.census.gov/population/apportionment/>.

Table 417. Vote Cast for U.S. Representatives by Major Political Party— States: 2006 to 2010

[In thousands (80,976 represents 80,976,000), except percent. R = Republican, D = Democrat, and I = Independent. In each state, totals represent the sum of votes cast in each Congressional District or votes cast for Representative-at-Large in states where only one member is elected. In all years there are numerous districts within the state where either the Republican or Democratic party had no candidate. In some states the Republican and Democratic vote includes votes cast for the party candidate by endorsing parties]

State	2006 Total [1]	Demo-cratic	Republi-can	Percent for leading party	2008 Total [1]	Demo-cratic	Republi-can	Percent for leading party	2010 Total [1]	Demo-cratic	Republi-can	Percent for leading party
U.S.	80,976	42,082	35,675	D-52.0	122,586	64,888	51,953	D-52.9	86,785	38,854	44,594	R-51.4
AL	1,140	502	628	R-55.0	1,855	718	1,121	R-60.4	1,368	419	914	R-66.9
AK	235	94	133	R-56.6	317	143	159	R-50.1	254	78	175	R-69.0
AZ	1,493	627	771	R-51.7	2,156	1,055	1,022	D-49.0	1,698	712	901	R-53.0
AR	763	457	306	D-59.8	787	415	215	D-52.8	774	318	435	R-56.2
CA	8,296	4,720	3,314	D-56.9	12,322	7,381	4,516	D-59.9	9,648	5,149	4,195	D-53.4
CO	1,539	833	624	D-54.1	2,284	1,260	991	D-55.2	1,763	801	884	R-50.1
CT	1,075	649	420	D-60.4	1,527	909	505	D-59.5	1,138	635	458	D-55.8
DE	252	98	144	R-57.2	385	146	235	R-61.1	306	174	125	D-56.8
FL [2]	3,852	1,600	2,183	R-56.7	7,421	3,435	3,792	R-51.1	5,117	1,854	3,004	R-58.7
GA	2,070	932	1,138	R-55.0	3,655	1,858	1,797	D-50.8	2,469	940	1,528	R-61.9
HI	338	220	118	D-65.0	456	320	83	D-70.2	360	226	129	D-62.9
ID	445	177	248	R-55.7	638	260	377	R-59.2	447	151	264	R-59.0
IL	3,453	1,986	1,423	D-57.5	5,248	3,176	1,961	D-60.5	3,696	1,876	1,720	D-50.8
IN	1,667	812	832	R-49.9	2,677	1,389	1,241	D-51.9	1,748	679	973	R-55.7
IA	1,033	493	522	R-50.6	1,482	759	698	D-51.3	1,107	480	597	R-54.0
KS	845	369	459	R-54.3	1,208	470	690	R-57.1	836	275	528	R-63.2
KY [2]	1,254	602	612	R-48.8	1,750	761	955	R-54.6	1,354	506	844	R-62.3
LA [2]	916	309	580	R-63.3	1,046	398	594	R-56.8	1,036	311	675	R-65.2
ME	536	351	163	D-65.4	710	432	278	D-60.8	564	316	248	D-56.0
MD	1,701	1,099	547	D-64.6	2,498	1,677	763	D-67.2	1,825	1,104	674	D-60.5
MA	2,244	1,632	199	D-72.7	3,103	2,246	318	D-72.4	2,224	1,336	808	D-60.1
MI	3,646	1,923	1,625	D-52.7	4,811	2,517	2,114	D-52.3	3,195	1,415	1,672	R-52.3
MN	2,179	1,153	925	D-52.9	2,803	1,612	1,069	D-57.5	2,091	1,002	971	D-47.9
MS	601	260	304	R-50.7	1,265	732	527	D-57.9	789	351	424	R-53.7
MO	2,097	992	1,049	R-50.0	2,821	1,413	1,313	D-50.1	1,921	708	1,103	R-57.4
MT	406	159	239	R-58.9	481	156	308	R-64.1	360	122	218	R-60.4
NE	596	262	334	R-56.1	775	265	511	R-65.8	486	138	328	R-67.5
NV	575	288	260	D-50.1	908	457	384	D-50.4	703	318	357	R-50.9
NH	403	209	190	D-52.0	675	365	295	D-54.1	450	201	230	R-51.2
NJ	2,137	1,208	903	D-56.5	3,438	1,912	1,462	D-55.6	2,122	1,025	1,055	R-49.7
NM	561	313	248	D-55.8	815	457	321	D-56.1	597	308	289	D-51.6
NY	4,687	2,538	1,160	D-54.1	7,722	4,006	1,800	D-51.9	4,744	2,515	1,613	D-53.0
NC	1,941	1,027	914	D-52.9	4,215	2,294	1,902	D-54.4	2,663	1,205	1,441	R-54.1
ND	218	143	75	D-65.7	314	195	119	D-62.0	236	107	130	R-54.9
OH	3,961	2,082	1,870	D-52.6	5,374	2,752	2,491	D-51.2	3,825	1,611	2,053	R-53.7
OK [2]	905	373	518	R-57.2	1,337	504	803	R-60.0	793	222	520	R-65.5
OR	1,357	766	557	D-56.4	1,683	1,036	436	D-61.6	1,429	733	657	D-51.3
PA	4,013	2,229	1,732	D-55.5	5,788	3,209	2,521	D-55.4	3,956	1,882	2,034	R-51.4
RI	373	265	42	D-71.0	438	304	119	D-69.3	335	186	127	D-55.4
SC	1,086	473	600	R-55.2	1,874	920	940	R-50.1	1,340	537	754	R-56.3
SD	334	230	98	D-69.1	379	256	123	D-67.6	319	147	154	R-48.1
TN	1,715	861	800	D-50.2	2,302	1,196	978	D-51.9	1,559	542	955	R-61.3
TX	4,141	1,831	2,094	R-50.6	7,529	2,979	4,204	R-55.8	4,746	1,450	3,058	R-64.4
UT	570	244	292	R-51.3	937	394	504	R-53.8	640	218	391	R-61.0
VT	263	140	117	D-53.2	298	248	(X)	D-83.2	239	154	76	D-64.6
VA	2,297	947	1,223	R-53.2	3,495	1,853	1,591	D-53.0	2,190	911	1,186	R-54.2
WA	2,054	1,244	798	D-60.6	2,914	1,725	1,189	D-59.2	2,479	1,297	1,135	D-52.3
WV	455	264	191	D-58.0	646	432	213	D-66.9	514	228	283	R-55.0
WI	2,063	1,003	1,040	R-50.4	2,775	1,384	1,275	D-49.9	2,140	939	1,166	R-54.5
WY	196	92	93	R-47.6	250	107	131	R-52.6	191	46	132	R-69.0

X Not applicable. [1] Includes votes cast for minor parties. [2] State law does not require tabulation of votes for unopposed candidates.

Source: U.S. House of Representatives, Office of the Clerk, *Statistics of the Presidential and Congressional Election*, biennial. See also <http://clerk.house.gov/member_info/election.html>.

Table 418. Vote Cast for U.S. Representatives by Major Political Party— Congressional Districts: 2010

[As of December 2010. Does not include special elections, see <http://clerk.house.gov/member_info/vacancies.html>. In some states the Democratic and Republican vote includes votes cast for the party candidate by endorsing parties]

State and district	Democratic candidate Name	Percent of total	Republican candidate Name	Percent of total	State and district	Democratic candidate Name	Percent of total	Republican candidate Name	Percent of total
AL..........	(X)	(X)	(X)	(X)	5th.........	Bradley	29.27	Lamborn	65.75
1st.........	(1)	(1)	Bonner	82.58	6th.........	Flerlage	31.46	Coffman	65.68
2d.........	Bright	48.79	Roby	50.97	7th.........	Perlmutter	53.44	Fraizer	41.76
3d.........	Segrest	40.48	Rogers	59.42	CT..........	(X)	(X)	(X)	(X)
4th.........	(1)	(1)	Aderholt	98.82	1st.........	Larson	57.75	Brickley	37.20
5th.........	Raby	42.03	Brooks	57.89	2d.........	Courtney	57.08	Peckinpaugh	38.76
6th.........	(1)	(1)	Bachus	98.05	3d.........	DeLauro	60.97	Labriola	33.58
7th.........	Sewell	72.43	Chamberlain	27.50	4th.........	Himes	50.94	Debicella	46.93
AK..........	**Crawford**	**30.51**	**Young**	**68.96**	5th.........	Murphy	52.01	Caligiuri	44.91
AZ..........	(X)	(X)	(X)	(X)	DE..........	**Carney**	**56.78**	**Urquhart**	**41.04**
1st.........	Kirkpatrick	43.73	Gosar	49.72	FL..........	(X)	(X)	(X)	(X)
2d.........	Thrasher	31.06	Franks	64.88	1st.........	(1)	(1)	Miller	80.00
3d.........	Hulburd	41.14	Quayle	52.24	2d.........	Boyd	41.35	Southerland	53.60
4th.........	Pastor	66.94	Contreras	27.53	3d.........	Brown	63.04	Yost	33.89
5th.........	Mitchell	43.23	Schweikert	52.00	4th.........	(1)	(1)	Crenshaw	77.21
6th.........	Schneider	29.12	Flake	66.42	5th.........	Piccillo	32.57	Nugent	67.43
7th.........	Grijalva	50.23	McClung	44.23	6th.........	(1)	(1)	Stearns	71.46
8th.........	Giffords	48.76	Kelly	47.30	7th.........	Beaven	30.97	Mica	69.03
AR..........	(X)	(X)	(X)	(X)	8th.........	Grayson	38.22	Webster	56.11
1st.........	Causey	43.48	Crawford	51.79	9th.........	Palma	28.57	Bilirakis	71.43
2d.........	Elliot	38.27	Griffin	57.90	10th.........	Justice	34.08	Young	65.92
3d.........	Whitaker	27.56	Womack	72.44	11th.........	Castor	59.63	Prendergast	40.37
4th.........	Ross	57.53	Rankin	40.15	12th.........	Edwards	41.14	Ross	48.14
CA..........	(X)	(X)	(X)	(X)	13th.........	Golden	31.14	Buchanan	68.86
1st.........	Thompson	62.79	Hanks	31.03	14th.........	Roach	27.13	Mack	68.56
2d.........	Reed	42.85	Herger	57.15	15th.........	Roberts	35.27	Posey	64.73
3d.........	Bera	43.19	Lungren	50.08	16th.........	Horn	33.09	Rooney	66.85
4th.........	Curtis	31.44	McClintock	61.27	17th.........	Wilson	86.21	(1)	(1)
5th.........	Matsui	72.05	Smith	25.28	18th.........	Banciella	31.11	Ros-Lehtinen	68.89
6th.........	Woolsey	65.94	Judd	29.62	19th.........	Deutch	62.59	Budd	37.30
7th.........	Miller	68.32	Tubbs	31.68	20th.........	Schultz	60.15	Harrington	38.10
8th.........	Pelosi	80.10	Dennis	15.12	21st.........	(1)	(1)	Diaz-Balart	(2)
9th.........	Lee	84.27	Hashimoto	10.77	22d.........	Klein	45.64	West	54.36
10th.........	Garamendi	58.84	Clift	37.86	23d.........	Hastings	79.12	Sansaricq	20.88
11th.........	McNerney	47.97	Harmer	46.86	24th.........	Kosmas	40.32	Adams	59.64
12th.........	Speier	75.58	Moloney	22.11	25th.........	Garcia	42.59	Rivera	52.15
13th.........	Stark	71.95	Baker	27.73	GA..........	(X)	(X)	(X)	(X)
14th.........	Eshoo	69.09	Chapman	27.83	1st.........	Harris II	28.37	Kingston	71.63
15th.........	Honda	67.60	Kirkland	32.40	2d.........	Bishop, Jr	51.44	Keown	48.56
16th.........	Lofgren	67.82	Sahagun	24.29	3d.........	Saunders	30.52	Westmoreland	69.48
17th.........	Farr	66.65	Taylor	29.85	4th.........	Johnson, Jr	74.67	Carter	25.33
18th.........	Cardoza	58.48	Berryhill	41.52	5th.........	Lewis	73.72	Little	26.28
19th.........	Goodwin	35.15	Denham	64.55	6th.........	(1)	(1)	Price	99.91
20th.........	Costa	51.70	Vidak	48.30	7th.........	Heckman	32.93	Woodall	67.07
21st.........	(1)	(1)	Nunes	100.00	8th.........	Marshall	47.30	Scott	52.70
22d.........	(1)	(1)	McCarthy	98.76	9th.........	(1)	(1)	Graves	100.00
23d.........	Capps	57.77	Watson	37.60	10th.........	Edwards	32.64	Broun	67.36
24th.........	Allison	40.06	Gallegly	59.94	11th.........	(1)	(1)	Gingrey	100.00
25th.........	Conaway	38.17	McKeon	61.83	12th.........	Barrow	56.59	McKinney	43.41
26th.........	Warner	36.52	Dreier	54.13	13th.........	Scott	69.43	Crane	30.57
27th.........	Sherman	65.15	Reed	34.85	HI..........	(X)	(X)	(X)	(X)
28th.........	Berman	69.54	Froyd	22.42	1st.........	Hanabusa	53.23	Djou	46.77
29th.........	Schiff	64.78	Colbert	31.98	2d.........	Hirono	72.19	Willoughby	25.32
30th.........	Waxman	64.63	Wilkerson	31.94	ID..........	(X)	(X)	(X)	(X)
31st.........	Becerra	83.82	Smith	16.18	1st.........	Minnick	41.28	Labrador	51.02
32d.........	Chu	71.04	Schmerling	28.96	2d.........	Crawford	24.41	Simpson	68.83
33d.........	Bass	86.08	Andion	13.92	IL..........	(X)	(X)	(X)	(X)
34th.........	Roybal-Allard	77.23	Miller	22.77	1st.........	Rush	80.36	Wardingley	15.87
35th.........	Waters	79.33	Brown	20.66	2d.........	Jackson, Jr	80.52	Hayes	13.83
36th.........	Harman	59.62	Fein	34.74	3d.........	Lipinski	69.69	Bendas	24.29
37th.........	Richardson	68.36	Parker	23.23	4th.........	Gutierrez	77.36	Vasquez	14.32
38th.........	Napolitano	73.45	Vaughn	26.55	5th.........	Quigley	70.62	Ratowitz	25.38
39th.........	Sanchez	63.27	Andre	32.60	6th.........	Lowe	36.35	Roskam	63.65
40th.........	Avalos	33.21	Royce	66.79	7th.........	Davis	81.50	Weiman	16.09
41st.........	Meagher	36.78	Lewis	63.21	8th.........	Bean	48.32	Walsh	48.47
42d.........	Williamson	31.86	Miller	62.21	9th.........	Schakowsky	66.34	Pollak	31.14
43d.........	Baca	65.50	Folkens	34.50	10th.........	Seals	48.92	Dold	51.08
44th.........	Hedrick	44.39	Calvert	55.61	11th.........	Halvorson	42.65	Kinzinger	57.35
45th.........	Pougnet	42.14	Mack	51.49	12th.........	Costello	59.83	Newman	36.53
46th.........	Arnold	37.79	Rohrabacher	62.20	13th.........	Harper	36.19	Biggert	63.81
47th.........	Sanchez	52.98	Tran	39.27	14th.........	Foster	45.04	Hultgren	51.31
48th.........	Krom	36.45	Campbell	59.94	15th.........	Gill	35.68	Johnson	64.32
49th.........	Katz	31.48	Issa	62.78	16th.........	Gaulrapp	31.04	Manzullo	65.00
50th.........	Busby	38.96	Bilbray	56.65	17th.........	Hare	42.96	Schilling	52.58
51st.........	Filner	60.05	Popaditch	39.95	18th.........	Hirner	25.79	Schock	69.12
52d.........	Lutz	32.06	Hunter	63.09	19th.........	Bagwell	28.78	Shimkus	71.22
53d.........	Davis	62.26	Crimmins	34.00	IN..........	(X)	(X)	(X)	(X)
CO..........	(X)	(X)	(X)	(X)	1st.........	Visclosky	58.56	Leyva	38.63
1st.........	DeGette	67.42	Fallon	28.76	2d.........	Donnelly	48.18	Walorski	46.84
2d.........	Polis	57.41	Bailey	37.90	3d.........	Hayhurst	33.11	Stutzman	62.76
3d.........	Salazar	45.76	Tipton	50.10	4th.........	Sanders	26.28	Rokita	68.57
4th.........	Markey	41.35	Gardner	52.48	5th.........	Crawford	25.39	Burton	62.14

See footnotes at end of table.

Table 418. Vote Cast for U.S. Representatives by Major Political Party—Congressional Districts: 2010-Continued.

See headnote on page 268.

State and district	Democratic candidate Name	Percent of total	Republican candidate Name	Percent of total
6th.........	Welsh	29.92	Pence	66.57
7th.........	Carson	58.90	Scott	37.81
8th.........	VanHaaften	37.43	Bucshon	57.55
9th.........	Hill	42.28	Young	52.34
IA............	(X)	(X)	(X)	(X)
1st.........	Braley	49.51	Lange	47.52
2d..........	Loebsack	50.99	Miller-Meeks	45.92
3d..........	Boswell	50.73	Zaun	46.49
4th.........	Maske	31.95	Latham	65.62
5th.........	Campbell	32.35	King	65.75
KS............	(X)	(X)	(X)	(X)
1st.........	Jilka	22.85	Huelskamp	73.76
2d..........	Hudspeth	32.33	Jenkins	63.13
3d..........	Moore	38.66	Yoder	58.40
4th.........	Goyle	36.45	Pompeo	58.79
KY............	(X)	(X)	(X)	(X)
1st.........	Hathett	28.75	Whitfield	71.25
2d..........	Marksberry	32.11	Guthrie	67.89
3d..........	Yarmuth	54.68	Lally	44.01
4th.........	Waltz	30.52	Davis	69.48
5th.........	Holbert	22.58	Rogers	77.42
6th.........	Chandler	50.08	Barr	49.81
LA [3].......	(X)	(X)	(X)	(X)
1st.........	Katz	19.19	Scalise	78.52
2d..........	Richmond	64.59	Cao	33.47
3d..........	Sangisetty	36.23	Landry	63.77
4th.........	Melville	32.35	Fleming	62.34
5th.........	([1])	([1])	Alexander	78.57
6th.........	McDonald,Sr	34.37	Cassidy	65.63
7th.........	([1])	([1])	Boustany, Jr	([2])
ME............	(X)	(X)	(X)	(X)
1st.........	Pingree	56.82	Scontras	43.17
2d..........	Michaud	55.13	Levesque	44.87
MD............	(X)	(X)	(X)	(X)
1st.........	Kratovil, Jr	41.98	Harris	54.08
2d..........	Ruppersberger	64.21	Cardarelli	33.28
3d..........	Sarbanes	61.07	Wilhelm	36.01
4th.........	Edwards	83.44	Broadus	16.39
5th.........	Hoyer	64.26	Lollar	34.62
6th.........	Duck	33.22	Bartlett	61.45
7th.........	Cummings	75.18	Mirabile	22.84
8th.........	Hollen	73.27	Philips	25.00
MA............	(X)	(X)	(X)	(X)
1st.........	Olver	60.00	Gunn	34.88
2d..........	Neal	57.33	Wesley	42.60
3d..........	McGovern	56.46	Lamb	39.16
4th.........	Frank	53.90	Bielat	43.36
5th.........	Tsongas	54.84	Golnik	42.25
6th.........	Tierney	56.85	Hudak	42.99
7th.........	Markey	66.42	Dembrowski	33.49
8th.........	Capuano	98.05	([1])	([1])
9th.........	Lynch	68.30	Harrison	26.08
10th........	Keating	46.87	Perry	42.38
MI............	(X)	(X)	(X)	(X)
1st.........	McDowell	40.87	Benishek	51.94
2d..........	Johnson	31.62	Huizenga	65.27
3d..........	Miles	37.47	Amash	59.68
4th.........	Campbell	30.51	Camp	66.20
5th.........	Kildee	53.04	Kupiec	44.33
6th.........	Cooney	33.58	Upton	61.98
7th.........	Schauer	45.38	Walberg	50.16
8th.........	Enderle	34.33	Rogers	64.08
9th.........	Peters	49.76	Reczkowski	47.23
10th........	Yanez	25.02	Miller	71.97
11th........	Mosher	38.49	McCotter	59.27
12th........	Levin	61.08	Volaric	34.97
13th........	Clarke	79.39	Hauler	18.46
14th........	Conyers, Jr	76.76	Ukrainec	19.87
15th........	Dingell	56.81	Steele	40.08
MN............	(X)	(X)	(X)	(X)
1st.........	Walz	49.34	Demmer	44.05
2d..........	Madore	36.59	Kline	63.31
3d..........	Meffert	36.57	Paulsen	58.80
4th.........	McCollum	59.09	Collett	34.63
5th.........	Ellison	67.69	Demos	24.14
6th.........	Clark	39.79	Bachmann	52.51
7th.........	Peterson	55.20	Byberg	37.60
8th.........	Oberstar	46.59	Cravaack	48.18
MS............	(X)	(X)	(X)	(X)
1st.........	Childers	40.80	Nunnelee	55.26
2d..........	Thompson	61.47	Marcy	37.64
3d..........	Gill	31.19	Harper	67.99
4th.........	Taylor	46.83	Palazzo	51.93
MO............	(X)	(X)	(X)	(X)

State and district	Democratic candidate Name	Percent of total	Republican candidate Name	Percent of total
1st.........	Clay	73.55	Hamlin	23.62
2d..........	Lieber	29.16	Akin	67.94
3d..........	Carnahan	48.94	Martin	46.66
4th.........	Skelton	45.11	Hartzler	50.43
5th.........	Cleaver	53.32	Turk	44.18
6th.........	Hylton	30.54	Graves	69.44
7th.........	Eckersley	30.37	Long	63.39
8th.........	Sowers	28.76	Emerson	65.56
9th.........	([1])	([1])	Luetkemeyer	77.36
MT............	**McDonald**	**33.84**	**Rehberg**	**60.41**
NE............	(X)	(X)	(X)	(X)
1st.........	Harper	28.73	Fortenberry	71.27
2d..........	White	39.19	Terry	60.81
3d..........	Davis	17.90	Smith	70.12
NV............	(X)	(X)	(X)	(X)
1st.........	Berkley	61.75	Wegner	35.28
2d..........	Price	32.66	Heller	63.30
3d..........	Titus	47.47	Heck	48.13
NH............	(X)	(X)	(X)	(X)
1st.........	Shea-Porter	42.42	Guinta	54.04
2d..........	Kuster	46.76	Bass	48.34
NJ............	(X)	(X)	(X)	(X)
1st.........	Andrews	63.19	Glading	34.80
2d..........	Stein	30.93	LoBiondo	65.50
3d..........	Adler	47.32	Runyan	50.03
4th.........	Kleinhendler	27.88	Smith	69.41
5th.........	Theise	32.79	Garrett	64.94
6th.........	Pallone, Jr	54.75	Little	43.71
7th.........	Potosnak	40.63	Lance	59.37
8th.........	Pascrell, Jr	62.66	Straten	36.13
9th.........	Rothman	60.72	Agosta	37.84
10th........	Payne	85.18	Alonso	12.83
11th........	Herbert	30.51	Frelinghuysen	67.19
12th........	Holt	53.05	Sipprelle	45.90
13th........	Sires	74.11	Dwyer	23.04
NM............	(X)	(X)	(X)	(X)
1st.........	Heinrich	51.80	Barela	48.20
2d..........	Teague	44.60	Pearce	55.40
3d..........	Lujan	56.99	Mullins	43.01
NY............	(X)	(X)	(X)	(X)
1st.........	Bishop	48.67	Altschuler	38.76
2d..........	Israel	54.21	Gomez	33.54
3d..........	Kudler	27.64	King	70.88
4th.........	McCarthy	53.61	Becker, Jr.	39.33
5th.........	Ackerman	59.74	Milano	30.48
6th.........	Meeks	76.27	Taub	9.01
7th.........	Crowley	72.72	Reynolds	14.04
8th.........	Nadler	69.06	Kone	20.62
9th.........	Weiner	56.98	Turner	32.10
10th........	Towns	79.66	Muniz	6.19
11th........	Clarke	83.50	Carr	7.30
12th........	Velazquez	79.10	([1])	([1])
13th........	McMahon	46.24	Grimm	42.47
14th........	Maloney	71.32	Brumberg	21.31
15th........	Rangel	71.80	Faulkner	8.40
16th........	Serrano	86.40	Della Valle	3.16
17th........	Engel	68.53	Mele	21.41
18th........	Lowey	61.71	Russell	32.30
19th........	Hall	45.78	Hayworth	41.13
20th........	Murphy	43.75	Gibson	45.27
21st........	Tonko	56.92	Danz, Jr	32.00
22d.........	Hinchey	51.03	Phillips	39.08
23d.........	Owens	45.06	Doheny	40.35
24th........	Arcuri	45.25	Hanna	43.19
25th........	Maffei	48.21	Buerkle	37.74
26th........	Fedele	24.49	Lee	68.29
27th........	Higgins	57.84	Roberto	30.61
28th........	Slaughter	61.00	Rowland	27.15
29th........	([1])	([1])	Reed II	44.33
NC............	(X)	(X)	(X)	(X)
1st.........	Butterfield	59.31	Woolard	40.69
2d..........	Etheridge	48.69	Ellmers	49.47
3d..........	Rouse	25.75	Jones	71.86
4th.........	Price	57.16	Lawson	42.84
5th.........	Kennedy	34.11	Foxx	65.89
6th.........	Turner	24.79	Coble	75.21
7th.........	McIntyre	53.68	Pantano	46.32
8th.........	Kissell	53.02	Johnson	43.67
9th.........	Doctor	31.03	Myrick	68.97
10th........	Gregory	28.82	McHenry	71.18
11th........	Shuler	54.34	Miller	45.66
12th........	Watt	63.88	Dority	34.14
13th........	Miller	55.50	Randall	44.50
ND............	**Pomeroy**	**45.08**	**Berg**	**54.92**

See footnotes at end of table.

Table 418. Vote Cast for U.S. Representatives by Major Political Party— Congressional Districts: 2010-Continued.

See headnote on page 268.

State and district	Democratic candidate Name	Percent of total	Republican candidate Name	Percent of total	State and district	Democratic candidate Name	Percent of total	Republican candidate Name	Percent of total
OH..........	(X)	(X)	(X)	(X)	2d........	(1)	(1)	Poe	88.61
1st........	Driehaus	45.99	Chabot	51.49	3d........	Lingenfelder	31.34	Johnson	66.28
2d........	Yalamanchili	34.66	Schmidt	58.45	4th........	Hathcox	22.00	Hall	73.19
3d........	Roberts	31.89	Turner	68.11	5th........	Berry	27.52	Hensarling	70.53
4th........	Litt	24.74	Jordan	71.49	6th........	Cozad	31.20	Barton	65.91
5th........	Finkenbiner	26.47	Latta	67.82	7th........	(1)	(1)	Culberson	81.45
6th........	Wilson	45.15	Johnson	50.19	8th........	Hargett	17.25	Brady	80.27
7th........	Conner	32.25	Austria	62.17	9th........	Green	75.74	Mueller	22.88
8th........	Coussoule	30.30	Boehner	65.64	10th........	Ankrum	33.05	McCaul	64.67
9th........	Kaptur	59.35	Iott	40.65	11th........	Quillian	15.44	Conaway	80.84
10th........	Kucinich	53.05	Corrigan	43.87	12th........	Smith	25.13	Granger	71.86
11th........	Fudge	82.93	Pekarek	17.07	13th........	(1)	(1)	Thornberry	87.05
12th........	Brooks	40.98	Tiberi	55.79	14th........	Pruett	24.01	Paul	75.99
13th........	Sutton	55.73	Ganley	44.27	15th........	Hinojosa	55.73	Zamora	41.59
14th........	O'Neill	31.45	LaTourette	64.92	16th........	Reyes	58.07	Besco	36.58
15th........	Kilroy	41.29	Stivers	54.16	17th........	Edwards	36.57	Flores	61.80
16th........	Boccieri	41.26	Renacci	52.08	18th........	Jackson-Lee	70.15	Faulk	27.26
17th........	Ryan	53.89	Graham	30.08	19th........	Wilson	19.06	Neugebauer	77.78
18th........	Space	40.49	Gibbs	53.86	20th........	Gonzalez	63.62	Trotter	34.45
OK..........	(X)	(X)	(X)	(X)	21st........	Melnick	27.87	Smith	68.88
1st........	(1)	(1)	Sullivan	76.80	22d........	Rogers	29.82	Olson	67.49
2d........	Boren	56.52	Thompson	43.48	23d........	Rodriguez	44.44	Canseco	49.40
3d........	Robbins	22.01	Lucas	77.99	24th........	(1)	(1)	Marchant	81.57
4th........	(1)	(1)	Cole	(2)	25th........	Doggett	52.82	Campbell	44.84
5th........	Coyle	34.54	Lankford	62.52	26th........	Durrance	30.70	Burgess	67.05
OR..........	(X)	(X)	(X)	(X)	27th........	Ortiz	47.10	Farenthold	47.85
1st........	Wu	54.75	Cornilles	41.94	28th........	Cuellar	56.35	Underwood	41.96
2d........	Segers	25.87	Walden	73.91	29th........	Green	64.61	Morales	34.09
3d........	Blumenauer	70.02	Lopez	24.55	30th........	Johnson	75.74	Broden	21.64
4th........	DeFazio	54.49	Robinson	43.58	31st........	(1)	(1)	Carter	82.54
5th........	Schrader	51.25	Bruun	45.96	32d........	Raggio	34.88	Sessions	62.61
PA..........	(X)	(X)	(X)	(X)	UT..........	(X)	(X)	(X)	(X)
1st........	Brady	100.00	(1)	(1)	1st........	Bowen	23.93	Bishop	69.19
2d........	Fattah	89.30	Hellberg	10.70	2d........	Matheson	50.49	Philpot	46.06
3d........	Dahlkemper	44.28	Kelly	55.72	3d........	Hyer	22.94	Chaffetz	72.32
4th........	Altmire	50.81	Rothfus	49.19	VT..........	Welch	64.57	Beaudry	32.03
5th........	Pipe	28.23	Thompson	68.69	VA..........	(X)	(X)	(X)	(X)
6th........	Trivedi	42.90	Gerlach	57.10	1st........	Ball	34.78	Wittman	63.87
7th........	Lentz	43.98	Meehan	54.94	2d........	Nye	42.45	Ringell	53.12
8th........	Murphy	46.48	Fitzpatrick	53.52	3d........	Scott	70.01	Smith	27.18
9th........	Conners	26.94	Shuster	73.06	4th........	LeGrow	37.45	Forbes	62.33
10th........	Carney	44.82	Marino	55.18	5th........	Perriello	46.99	Hurt	50.81
11th........	Kanjorski	45.30	Barletta	54.70	6th........	(1)	(1)	Goodlatte	76.27
12th........	Critz	50.78	Burns	49.22	7th........	Waugh, Jr	34.11	Cantor	59.22
13th........	Schwartz	56.34	Adcock	43.66	8th........	Moran	61.03	Murray	37.30
14th........	Doyle	68.79	Haluszczak	28.17	9th........	Boucher	46.41	Griffith	51.21
15th........	Callahan	39.00	Dent	53.55	10th........	Barnett	34.81	Wolf	62.87
16th........	Herr	34.61	Pitts	65.39	11th........	Connolly	49.23	Fimian	48.79
17th........	Holden	55.50	Argall	44.50	WA..........	(X)	(X)	(X)	(X)
18th........	Connolly	32.67	Murphy	67.33	1st........	Inslee	57.67	Watkins	42.33
19th........	Sanders	23.31	Platts	71.91	2d........	Larsen	51.07	Koster	48.93
RI..........	(X)	(X)	(X)	(X)	3d........	Heck	47.03	Herrera	52.97
1st........	Cicilline	50.54	Loughlin	44.49	4th........	Clough	32.36	Hastings	67.64
2d........	Langevin	59.79	Zaccaria	31.72	5th........	Romeyn	36.33	McMorris	63.67
SC..........	(X)	(X)	(X)	(X)	6th........	Dicks	58.04	Cloud	41.96
1st........	Fraiser	28.67	Scott	65.37	7th........	McDermott	82.97	(1)	(1)
2d........	Miller	43.76	Wilson	53.48	8th........	DelBene	47.95	Reichert	52.05
3d........	Dyer	32.90	Duncan	62.46	9th........	Smith	54.85	Muri	45.15
4th........	Corden	28.79	Gowdy	63.45	WV..........	(X)	(X)	(X)	(X)
5th........	Spratt, Jr	44.81	Mulvaney	55.15	1st........	Oliverio	49.60	McKinley	50.40
6th........	Clyburn	62.86	Pratt	36.41	2d........	Graf	29.69	Capito	68.46
SD..........	Sandlin	45.89	Noem	48.12	3d........	Rahall II	56.04	Maynard	43.96
TN..........	(X)	(X)	(X)	(X)	WI..........	(X)	(X)	(X)	(X)
1st........	Clark	17.12	Roe	80.84	1st........	Heckenlively	30.10	Ryan	68.21
2d........	Hancock	14.65	Duncan, Jr	81.78	2d........	Baldwin	61.77	Lee	38.16
3d........	Wolfe	28.01	Fleischmann	56.79	3d........	Kind	50.28	Kapanke	46.49
4th........	Davis	38.56	DesJarlais	57.07	4th........	Moore	68.98	Sebring	29.57
5th........	Cooper	56.23	Hall	42.07	5th........	Kolosso	27.36	Sensenbrenner, Jr.	69.32
6th........	Carter	29.38	Black	67.26	6th........	Kallas	29.27	Petri	70.66
7th........	Rabidoux	24.75	Blackburn	72.37	7th........	Lassa	44.43	Duffy	52.11
8th........	Herron	38.80	Fincher	58.99	8th........	Kagen	45.12	Ribble	54.77
9th........	Cohen	74.00	Bergmann	25.11	WY..........	Wendt	23.98	Lummis	69.00
TX..........	(X)	(X)	(X)	(X)					
1st........	(1)	(1)	Gohmert	89.73					

X Not applicable. [1] No candidate. [2] According to state law, it is not required to tabulate votes for unopposed candidates. [3] Louisiana holds an open-primary election with candidates from all parties running on the same ballot. Any candidate who receives a majority is elected; if no candidate receives 50 percent, there is a run-off election in November between the top two finishers.

Source: U.S. House of Representatives, Office of the Clerk, *Statistics of the Presidential and Congressional Election*, biennial. See also <http://clerk.house.gov/member_info/election.html>.

Table 419. Composition of Congress by Political Party Affiliation—States: 2005 to 2011

[Figures are for the beginning of the first session, except as noted. Dem. = Democratic; Rep. = Republican]

State	Representatives 109th Cong.,[1,2,3] 2005 Dem.	Rep.	110th Cong., 2007 Dem.	Rep.	111th Cong.,[4] 2009 Dem.	Rep.	112th Cong., 2011 Dem.	Rep.	Senators 109th Cong.,[5] 2005 Dem.	Rep.	110th Cong.,[6] 2007 Dem.	Rep.	111th Cong.,[6,7] 2009 Dem.	Rep.	112th Cong.,[6] 2011 Dem.	Rep.
U.S......	202	231	233	202	256	178	193	242	44	55	49	49	55	41	51	47
AL........	2	5	2	5	3	4	1	6	–	2	–	2	–	2	–	2
AK........	–	1	–	1	–	1	–	1	–	2	–	2	1	1	1	1
AZ........	2	6	4	4	5	3	3	5	–	2	–	2	–	2	–	2
AR........	3	1	3	1	3	1	1	3	2	–	2	–	2	–	1	1
CA........	33	20	34	19	34	19	34	19	2	–	2	–	2	–	2	–
CO........	3	4	4	3	5	2	3	4	1	1	1	1	2	–	2	–
CT........	2	3	4	1	5	–	5	–	2	–	1	–	1	–	1	–
DE........	–	1	–	1	–	1	1	–	2	–	2	–	2	–	2	–
FL........	7	18	9	16	10	15	6	19	1	1	1	1	1	1	1	1
GA........	6	7	6	7	6	7	5	8	–	2	–	2	–	2	–	2
HI........	2	–	2	–	2	–	2	–	2	–	2	–	2	–	2	–
ID........	–	2	–	2	1	1	–	2	–	2	–	2	–	2	–	2
IL........	10	9	10	9	11	7	8	11	2	–	2	–	1	–	1	1
IN........	2	7	5	4	5	4	3	6	1	1	1	1	1	1	–	2
IA........	1	4	3	2	3	2	3	2	1	1	1	1	1	1	1	1
KS........	1	3	2	2	1	3	–	4	–	2	–	2	–	2	–	2
KY........	1	5	2	4	2	4	2	4	–	2	–	2	–	2	–	2
LA........	2	5	2	5	1	6	1	6	1	1	1	1	1	1	1	1
ME........	2	–	2	–	2	–	2	–	–	2	–	2	–	2	–	2
MD........	6	2	6	2	7	1	6	2	2	–	2	–	2	–	2	–
MA........	10	–	10	–	10	–	10	–	2	–	2	–	2	–	1	1
MI........	6	9	6	9	8	7	6	9	2	–	2	–	2	–	2	–
MN........	4	4	5	3	5	3	4	4	1	1	1	1	1	–	2	–
MS........	2	2	2	2	3	1	1	3	–	2	–	2	–	2	–	2
MO........	4	5	4	5	4	5	3	6	–	2	1	1	1	1	1	1
MT........	–	1	–	1	–	1	–	1	1	1	2	–	2	–	2	–
NE........	–	3	–	3	–	3	–	3	1	1	1	1	1	1	1	1
NV........	1	2	1	2	2	1	1	2	1	1	1	1	1	1	1	1
NH........	–	2	2	–	2	–	–	2	–	2	–	2	1	1	1	1
NJ........	7	6	7	6	8	5	7	6	2	–	2	–	2	–	2	–
NM........	1	2	1	2	3	–	2	1	1	1	1	1	2	–	2	–
NY........	20	9	23	6	26	3	21	8	2	–	2	–	2	–	2	–
NC........	6	7	7	6	8	5	7	6	–	2	–	2	1	1	1	1
ND........	1	–	1	–	1	–	–	1	2	–	2	–	2	–	1	1
OH........	6	11	7	11	10	8	5	13	–	2	1	1	1	1	1	1
OK........	1	4	1	4	1	4	1	4	–	2	–	2	–	2	–	2
OR........	4	1	4	1	4	1	4	1	1	1	1	1	2	–	2	–
PA........	7	12	11	8	12	7	7	12	–	2	1	1	1	1	1	1
RI........	2	–	2	–	2	–	2	–	1	1	2	–	2	–	2	–
SC........	2	4	2	4	2	4	1	5	–	2	–	2	–	2	–	2
SD........	1	–	1	–	1	–	–	1	1	1	1	1	1	1	1	1
TN........	5	4	5	4	5	4	2	7	–	2	–	2	–	2	–	2
TX........	11	21	13	19	12	20	9	23	–	2	–	2	–	2	–	2
UT........	1	2	1	2	1	2	1	2	–	2	–	2	–	2	–	2
VT........	–	–	1	–	1	–	1	–	1	–	1	–	1	–	1	–
VA........	3	8	3	8	6	5	3	8	–	2	1	1	2	–	2	–
WA........	6	3	6	3	6	3	5	4	2	–	2	–	2	–	2	–
WV........	2	1	2	1	2	1	1	2	2	–	2	–	2	–	2	–
WI........	4	4	5	3	5	3	3	5	2	–	2	–	2	–	1	2
WY........	–	1	–	1	–	1	–	1	–	2	–	2	–	2	–	2

– Represents zero. [1] Vermont had one Independent-Socialist representative. [2] Ohio had one vacancy due to the resignation of Rob Portman, April 29, 2005. [3] As of June 28, 2005. [4] One vacancy due to the resignation of Rahm Emanuel, January 6, 2009. [5] Vermont had one Independent senator. [6] Vermont and Connecticut both had one Independent senator. [7] Two vacancies—one in Illinois due to the resignation of Barack Obama, November 16, 2008, and one in Minnesota due to election dispute between Norm Coleman and Al Franken.

Source: U.S. House of Representatives, Office of the Clerk, *Official List of Members*, annual. See also <http://clerk.house.gov/member_info/>.

Table 420. Composition of Congress by Political Party: 1975 to 2011

[D = Democratic, R = Republican. As of beginning of first session of each Congress. Data reflect immediate result of elections. Vacancies and third party candidates are noted]

Year	Party and president	Congress	House Majority party	House Minority party	House Other	Senate Majority party	Senate Minority party	Senate Other
1975 [1]	R (Ford)	94th	D-291	R-144	–	D-61	R-37	2
1977 [2]	D (Carter)	95th	D-292	R-143	–	D-61	R-38	1
1979 [2]	D (Carter)	96th	D-277	R-158	–	D-58	R-41	1
1981 [3]	R (Reagan)	97th	D-242	R-192	1	R-53	D-46	1
1983	R (Reagan)	98th	D-269	R-166	–	R-54	D-46	–
1985	R (Reagan)	99th	D-253	R-182	–	R-53	D-47	–
1987	R (Reagan)	100th	D-258	R-177	–	D-55	R-45	–
1989	R (Bush)	101st	D-260	R-175	–	D-55	R-45	–
1991 [4]	R (Bush)	102d	D-267	R-167	1	D-56	R-44	–
1993 [4]	D (Clinton)	103d	D-258	R-176	1	D-57	R-43	–
1995 [4]	D (Clinton)	104th	R-230	D-204	1	R-52	D-48	–
1997 [5]	D (Clinton)	105th	R-226	D-207	2	R-55	D-45	–
1999 [4]	D (Clinton)	106th	R-223	D-211	1	R-55	D-45	–
2001 [5]	R (Bush)	107th	R-221	D-212	2	D-50	R-50	–
2003 [3,6]	R (Bush)	108th	R-229	D-204	1	R-51	D-48	1
2005 [3]	R (Bush)	109th	R-232	D-202	1	R-55	D-44	1
2007 [7]	R (Bush)	110th	D-233	R-202	–	D-49	R-49	2
2009 [6,7,8]	D (Obama)	111th	D-256	R-178	–	D-55	R-41	2
2011 [7]	D (Obama)	112th	R-242	D-193	–	D-51	R-47	2

– Represents zero. [1] Senate had one Independent and one Conservative-Republican. [2] Senate had one Independent. [3] House and Senate each had one Independent. [4] House had one Independent-Socialist. [5] House had one Independent-Socialist and one Independent. [6] House had one vacancy. [7] Senate had two Independents. [8] Senate had two vacancies.

Source: U.S. House of Representatives, Office of the Clerk, *Official List of Members, 2011*, annual. See also <http://clerk.house.gov/member_info/>.

Table 421. Members of Congress—Selected Characteristics: 1995 to 2011

[As of beginning of first session of each Congress, except as noted. Figures for Representatives exclude vacancies]

Members of Congress and year	Male	Female	Black	[4] API	Hispanic	Age [1] (in years) Under 40	40 to 49	50 to 59	60 to 69	70 and over	Seniority [2,3] Less than 2 yrs.	2 to 9 yrs.	10 to 19 yrs.	20 to 29 yrs.	30 yrs. or more
REPRESENTATIVES															
104th Cong., 1995	388	47	[5] 40	7	17	53	155	135	79	13	92	188	110	36	9
107th Cong., 2001	376	59	[5] 39	7	19	14	97	167	117	35	44	155	158	63	14
108th Cong., 2003	376	59	[5] 39	5	22	19	86	174	121	32	54	178	140	48	13
109th Cong., 2005	369	65	[5] 42	4	23	22	96	175	113	28	37	173	158	48	18
110th Cong., 2007	362	73	[5] 42	4	23	20	91	172	118	34	62	159	160	37	17
111th Cong., 2009	361	74	[5] 41	8	(NA)	24	84	156	126	44	66	166	142	42	18
112th Cong., 2011	364	71	[5] 42	9	29	(NA)	(NA)	(NA)	(NA)	(NA)	100	140	131	42	22
SENATORS															
104th Cong., 1995	92	8	1	2	0	1	14	41	27	17	12	38	30	15	5
107th Cong., 2001	87	13	0	2	0	0	8	39	33	18	11	34	30	14	9
108th Cong., 2003	86	14	0	2	0	1	12	29	34	24	9	42	29	13	7
109th Cong., 2005	86	14	1	2	2	0	17	29	33	21	9	41	29	14	7
110th Cong., 2007	84	16	1	2	3	0	11	31	34	24	12	42	24	13	9
111th Cong., 2009	83	17	1	1	(NA)	0	7	31	38	22	9	34	28	17	10
112th Cong., 2011	83	17	0	1	2	(NA)	(NA)	(NA)	(NA)	(NA)	20	35	24	13	8

NA Not available. [1] Some members do not provide date of birth. [2] Represents consecutive years of service. [3] Some members do not provide years of service. [4] Asian and Pacific Islander. [4] Includes District of Columbia and Virgin Islands delegate.

Source: Congressional Research Service, *Membership of 112th Congress: A Profile*, April 2011; and compiled by ProQuest from data published in *Congressional Directory*, biennial. See also <http://www.gpoaccess.gov/cdirectory/browse.html>.

Table 422. U.S. Congress—Measures Introduced and Enacted and Time in Session: 1995 to 2011

[Excludes simple and concurrent resolutions]

Item	104th Cong., 1995–96	105th Cong., 1997–98	106th Cong., 1999–00	107th Cong., 2001–02	108th Cong., 2003–04	109th Cong., 2005–06	110th Cong., 2007–08	111th Cong., 2009–10	112th Cong., 2011
Measures introduced.............	6,808	7,732	9,158	9,130	8,625	10,703	11,228	10,778	5,917
Bills..................................	6,545	7,532	8,968	8,953	8,468	10,560	11,081	10,629	5,787
Joint resolutions..................	263	200	190	177	157	143	147	149	130
Measures enacted.................	337	404	604	337	504	590	460	385	90
Public [1]............................	333	394	580	331	498	589	460	383	90
Private [2]...........................	4	10	24	6	6	1	0	2	0
HOUSE OF REPRESENTATIVES									
Number of days....................	290	251	272	265	243	241	283	286	175
Number of hours...................	2,445	2,001	2,179	1,694	1,894	1,917	2,138	2,126	993
Number of hours per day..........	8.4	8.0	8.0	6.4	7.8	8.0	7.6	7.4	5.7
SENATE									
Number of days....................	343	296	303	322	300	297	374	349	170
Number of hours...................	2,876	2,188	2,200	2,279	2,486	2,250	2,364	2,495	1,102
Number of hours per day..........	8.4	7.4	7.3	7.1	8.3	7.6	6.3	7.1	6.5

[1] Laws on public matters that apply to all persons. [2] Laws designed to provide legal relief to specified persons or entities adversely affected by laws of general applicability.

Source: U.S. Congress, *Résumé of Congressional Activity*, selected issues. See <http://www.senate.gov/pagelayout/reference/two_column_table/Resumes.htm>.

Table 423. Congressional Bills Vetoed: 1961 to 2012

Period	President	Total vetoes	Regular vetoes	Pocket vetoes	Vetoes sustained	Bills passed over veto
1961–63.....................	John F. Kennedy..............	21	12	9	21	–
1963–69.....................	Lyndon B. Johnson...........	30	16	14	30	–
1969–74.....................	Richard M. Nixon.............	43	26	17	36	7
1974–77.....................	Gerald R. Ford................	66	48	18	54	12
1977–81.....................	Jimmy Carter.................	31	13	18	29	2
1981–89.....................	Ronald W. Reagan...........	78	39	39	69	9
1989–93.....................	George Bush.................	44	29	15	43	1
1993–2001..................	William J. Clinton............	37	36	1	34	2
2001–2009..................	George W. Bush..............	10	10	–	7	3
2009–2012 [1]...............	Barack Obama...............	2	2	–	2	–

– Represents zero. [1] For the period January 20, 2009 through June 27, 2012.

Source: U.S. Congress, Senate Library, *Presidential Vetoes . . . 1789–1968*; U.S. Congress, *Calendars of the U.S. House of Representatives and History of Legislation*, annual. See also <http://artandhistory.house.gov/house_history/vetoes.aspx>.

Table 424. Number of Governors by Political Party Affiliation: 1975 to 2012

[Reflects figures after inaugurations for each year]

Year	Democratic	Republican	Independent/ other	Year	Democratic	Republican	Independent/ other	Year	Democratic	Republican	Independent/ other
1975..............	36	13	1	2001.....	19	29	2	2007.....	28	22	–
1980..............	31	19	–	2002.....	22	27	1	2008.....	28	22	–
1985..............	34	16	–	2003.....	23	27	–	2009.....	28	22	–
1990..............	29	21	–	2004.....	22	28	–	2010.....	26	24	–
1995..............	19	30	1	2005.....	22	28	–	2011.....	20	29	1
2000..............	18	30	2	2006.....	22	28	–	2012.....	20	29	1

– Represents zero.

Source: ProQuest research.

Table 425. Vote Cast for and Governor Elected by State: 2008 to 2011

[D = Democratic, R = Republican, I = Independent]

State	Current governor [1]	Year of election	Total vote [2]	Republican	Democratic	Percent leading party
Alabama..................	Robert Bentley	2010	1,485,324	860,272	625,052	R-57.9
Alaska....................	Sean Parnell	2010	256,192	151,318	96,519	R-59.1
Arizona...................	Jan Brewer	2010	1,728,081	938,934	733,935	R-54.3
Arkansas.................	Mike Beebe	2010	781,333	262,784	503,336	D-64.4
California................	Jerry Brown	2010	10,095,185	4,127,391	5,428,149	D-53.8
Colorado.................	John Hickenlooper	2010	1,787,730	199,034	912,005	D-51.0
Connecticut..............	Dan Malloy	2010	1,145,799	560,874	567,278	D-49.5
Delaware.................	Jack Markell	2008	395,204	126,662	266,861	D-67.5
Florida...................	Rick Scott	2010	5,359,735	2,619,335	2,557,785	R-48.9
Georgia..................	Nathan Deal	2010	2,576,161	1,365,832	1,107,011	R-53.0
Hawaii...................	Neil Abercrombie	2010	382,583	157,311	222,724	D-58.2
Idaho....................	C.L. "Butch" Otter	2010	452,535	267,483	148,680	R-59.1
Illinois...................	Patrick Quinn	2010	3,729,989	1,713,385	1,745,219	D-46.8
Indiana..................	Mitch Daniels	2008	2,703,752	1,563,885	1,082,463	R-57.8
Iowa.....................	Terry Branstad	2010	1,122,013	592,494	484,798	R-52.8
Kansas...................	Sam Brownback	2010	838,790	530,760	270,166	R-63.3
Kentucky.................	Steven L. Beshear	2011	833,139	294,034	464,245	D-55.7
Louisiana................	Bobby Jindal	2011	1,023,163	673,239	288,161	R-65.8
Maine....................	Paul LePage	2010	572,766	218,065	109,387	R-38.1
Maryland.................	Martin O'Malley	2010	1,857,880	776,319	1,044,961	D-56.2
Massachusetts............	Deval L. Patrick	2010	2,297,039	964,866	1,112,283	D-48.4
Michigan.................	Rick Snyder	2010	3,226,088	1,874,834	1,287,320	R-58.1
Minnesota................	Mark Dayton	2010	2,107,021	910,462	919,232	D-43.6
Mississippi...............	Phil Bryant	2011	893,468	544,851	348,617	R-61.0
Missouri..................	Jay Nixon	2008	2,877,778	1,136,364	1,680,611	D-58.4
Montana..................	Brian Schweitzer	2008	486,734	158,268	318,670	D-65.5
Nebraska.................	Dave Heineman	2010	487,988	360,645	127,343	R-73.9
Nevada...................	Brian Sandoval	2010	716,529	382,350	298,171	R-53.4
New Hampshire..........	John Lynch	2010	456,588	205,616	240,346	D-52.6
New Jersey..............	Chris Christie	2009	2,423,684	1,174,445	1,087,731	R-48.5
New Mexico..............	Susana Martinez	2010	602,827	321,219	280,614	R-53.3
New York................	Andrew Cuomo	2010	4,654,352	1,548,184	2,911,721	D-62.6
North Carolina...........	Beverly Perdue	2008	4,268,941	2,001,168	2,146,189	D-50.3
North Dakota............	Jack Dalrymple [3]	2008	315,692	235,009	74,279	R-74.4
Ohio.....................	John Kasich	2010	3,852,469	1,889,186	1,812,059	R-49.0
Oklahoma................	Mary Fallin	2010	1,034,767	625,506	409,261	R-60.4
Oregon..................	John Kitzhaber	2010	1,453,548	694,287	716,525	D-49.3
Pennsylvania.............	Tom Corbett	2010	3,987,551	2,172,763	1,814,788	R-54.5
Rhode Island............	Lincoln Chafee	2010	342,290	114,911	78,896	I-43.4
South Carolina...........	Nikki Haley	2010	1,344,198	690,525	630,534	R-51.4
South Dakota............	Dennis Daugaard	2010	317,083	195,046	122,037	R-61.5
Tennessee...............	Bill Haslam	2010	1,601,549	1,041,545	529,851	R-65.0
Texas....................	Rick Perry	2010	4,979,870	2,737,481	2,106,395	R-55.0
Utah.....................	Gary R. Herbert [4]	2010	643,307	412,151	205,246	R-64.1
Vermont..................	Peter Shumlin	2010	241,605	115,212	119,543	D-49.5
Virginia..................	Robert McDonnell	2009	1,982,424	1,163,523	818,901	R-58.7
Washington..............	Christine Gregoire	2008	3,002,862	1,404,124	1,598,738	D-53.2
West Virginia............	Earl Ray Tomblin [5]	2011	301,084	141,656	149,202	D-49.6
Wisconsin................	Scott Walker	2010	2,133,244	1,128,941	1,004,303	R-52.3
Wyoming.................	Matt Mead	2010	188,463	123,780	43,240	R-65.7

[1] As of January 2012. [2] Includes minor party and scattered votes. [3] North Dakota Lt. Governor Jack Dalrymple became governor 7 December 2010, completing the unexpired term of Governor John Hoeven following his election to the U.S. Senate. [4] Utah Lt. Governor Gary Herbert became governor 11 August 2009, following Governor Jon Huntsman Jr.'s appointment as U.S. Ambassador to China. [5] West Virginia Senate President Earl Ray Tomblin became governor 15 November 2010, following the election of Governor Joe Manchin III to the U.S. Senate. Tomblin won a special election held Oct. 4, 2011 to complete the unexpired term.

Source: The Council of State Governments, Lexington, KY, *The Book of the States 2012*, annual (copyright). See <http://www.csg.org/CSG/default.htm>.

Table 426. Political Party Control of State Legislatures by Party: 1985 to 2012

[As of beginning of year. Nebraska has a nonpartisan legislature]

Year	Legislatures under— Democratic control	Legislatures under— Split control or tie	Legislatures under— Republican control	Year	Legislatures under— Democratic control	Legislatures under— Split control or tie	Legislatures under— Republican control	Year	Legislatures under— Democratic control	Legislatures under— Split control or tie	Legislatures under— Republican control
1985......	27	11	11	1999......	20	12	17	2006......	19	10	20
1990......	29	11	9	2000......	16	15	18	2007......	22	12	15
1993......	25	16	8	2001......	16	15	18	2008......	23	14	12
1994......	24	17	8	2002......	17	15	17	2009......	27	8	14
1995......	18	12	19	2003......	16	12	21	2010......	27	8	14
1996......	16	15	18	2004......	17	11	21	2011......	15	8	26
1997......	20	11	18	2005......	19	10	20	2012......	15	8	26

Source: National Conference of State Legislatures, Denver, CO, *State Legislatures*. See <ncsl.org>.

Table 427. Composition of State Legislatures by Political Party Affiliation: 2011 and 2012

[2011 data are as of March; 2012 data are as of February. Figures reflect immediate results of elections, including holdover members in state houses which do not have all of their members running for reelection. Dem. = Democrat, Rep. = Republican, Vac. = Vacancies. In general, Lower House refers to body consisting of state representatives and Upper House of state senators]

State	Lower House 2011				Lower House 2012				Upper House 2011				Upper House 2012			
	Dem.	Rep.	Other	Vac.	Dem.	Rep.	Other	Vac.	Dem.	Rep.	Other	Vac.	Dem.	Rep.	Other	Vac.
U.S.	2,453	2,924	22	12	2,430	2,939	18	24	881	1,032	5	4	875	1,039	5	3
AL [1]	39	65	–	1	40	65	–	–	12	22	1	–	12	22	1	–
AK [2]	16	24	–	–	16	24	–	–	10	10	–	–	10	10	–	–
AZ [3]	20	40	–	–	20	40	–	–	9	21	–	–	9	21	–	–
AR [2]	54	44	–	2	54	46	–	–	20	15	–	–	20	15	–	–
CA [2]	52	27	–	1	52	28	–	–	25	15	–	–	25	15	–	–
CO [2]	32	33	–	–	32	33	–	–	20	15	–	–	20	15	–	–
CT [3]	98	52	–	1	99	52	–	–	22	14	–	–	22	14	–	–
DE [2]	26	15	–	–	26	15	–	–	14	7	–	–	14	7	–	–
FL [2]	38	81	–	1	39	81	–	–	12	28	–	–	12	28	–	–
GA [3]	63	116	1	–	63	115	1	1	20	36	–	–	20	36	–	–
HI [2]	43	8	–	–	42	8	–	1	24	1	–	–	24	1	–	–
ID [3]	13	57	–	–	13	57	–	–	7	28	–	–	7	28	–	–
IL [4]	64	54	–	–	64	54	–	–	34	24	–	1	35	24	–	–
IN [2]	40	60	–	–	40	60	–	–	13	37	–	–	13	37	–	–
IA [2]	40	60	–	–	40	60	–	–	26	24	–	–	26	24	–	–
KS [2]	33	92	–	–	33	92	–	–	8	32	–	–	8	32	–	–
KY [2]	58	42	–	–	59	40	–	1	15	22	1	–	15	22	1	–
LA [1]	47	52	4	2	45	58	2	–	19	20	–	–	15	24	–	–
ME [3]	72	78	1	–	72	77	1	1	14	20	1	–	14	20	1	–
MD [1]	98	43	–	–	98	43	–	–	35	12	–	–	35	12	–	–
MA [3]	128	31	–	1	125	33	–	2	36	4	–	–	36	4	–	–
MI [2]	47	63	–	–	46	62	–	2	12	26	–	–	12	26	–	–
MN [2]	62	72	–	–	62	72	–	0	30	37	–	–	30	37	–	–
MS [1]	69	53	–	–	58	64	–	0	25	27	–	–	21	31	–	–
MO [2]	57	106	–	–	56	106	–	1	7	26	–	1	8	26	–	–
MT [2]	32	68	–	–	32	68	–	–	22	28	–	–	22	28	–	–
NE [5]	([5])	([5])	([5])	([5])	([5])	([5])	([5])	([5])	([5])	([5])	([5])	([5])	([5])	([5])	([5])	([5])
NV [2]	26	16	–	–	26	16	–	–	11	10	–	–	11	10	–	–
NH [3]	102	296	1	1	104	292	–	4	5	19	–	–	5	19	–	–
NJ [2]	47	33	–	–	47	32	–	1	24	16	–	–	24	16	–	–
NM [2]	37	33	–	–	36	33	1	0	27	15	–	–	28	14	–	–
NY [3]	98	51	1	–	96	49	1	4	30	32	–	–	29	32	–	1
NC [3]	51	67	1	1	52	68	–	–	19	31	–	–	19	31	–	–
ND [1]	25	69	–	–	25	69	–	–	12	35	–	–	12	35	–	–
OH [2]	40	59	–	–	40	59	–	–	10	23	–	–	10	23	–	–
OK [2]	31	70	–	–	33	68	–	–	16	32	–	–	15	31	–	2
OR [2]	30	30	–	–	30	30	–	–	16	14	–	–	16	14	–	–
PA [2]	91	112	–	–	87	110	–	6	19	30	–	1	20	30	–	–
RI [3]	65	10	–	–	65	10	–	–	29	8	1	–	29	8	1	–
SC [2]	48	76	–	–	48	76	–	–	19	26	–	1	19	27	–	–
SD [3]	19	50	1	–	19	50	1	–	5	30	–	–	5	30	–	–
TN [2]	34	64	1	–	34	64	1	–	13	20	–	–	13	20	–	–
TX [2]	49	101	–	–	49	101	–	–	12	19	–	–	12	19	–	–
UT [2]	17	58	–	–	17	58	–	–	7	22	–	–	7	22	–	–
VT [3]	94	48	8	–	94	48	8	–	21	8	1	–	21	8	1	–
VA [2]	39	58	2	1	32	67	1	–	22	18	–	–	20	20	–	–
WA [2]	56	42	–	–	56	42	–	–	27	22	–	–	27	22	–	–
WV [2]	65	35	–	–	65	35	–	–	28	6	–	–	28	6	–	–
WI [2]	38	60	1	–	39	59	1	–	14	19	–	–	16	17	–	–
WY [2]	10	50	–	–	10	50	–	–	4	26	–	–	4	26	–	–

– Represents zero. [1] Members of both houses serve 4-year terms. [2] Upper House members serve 4-year terms and Lower House members serve 2-year terms. [3] Members of both houses serve 2-year terms. [4] Illinois—4- and 2-year term depending on district. [5] Nebraska—4-year term and only state to have a nonpartisan legislature.

Source: The Council of State Governments, Lexington, KY, *The Book of the States 2012*, annual (copyright). See <http://www.csg.org/>.

Table 428. Women Holding State Public Offices by Office and State: 2012

[As of January. For data on women in U.S. Congress, see Table 421]

State	Total	Statewide elective executive office[1]	State legislature Total	Percent	State	Total	Statewide elective executive office[1]	State legislature Total	Percent
U.S.	**1,822**	**73**	**1,749**	**24**	MO	48	1	47	24
					MT	40	4	36	24
AL	24	5	19	14	NE	12	1	11	22
AK	15	–	15	25	NV	19	3	16	25
AZ	33	3	30	33	NH	105	–	105	25
AR	31	1	30	22	NJ	36	1	35	29
CA	36	2	34	28	NM	34	3	31	28
CO	40	–	40	40	NY	47	–	47	22
CT	59	3	56	30	NC	44	6	38	22
DE	17	1	16	26	ND	22	1	21	15
FL	43	2	41	26	OH	32	1	31	23
GA	56	–	56	24	OK	23	4	19	13
HI	27	–	27	36	OR	28	2	26	29
ID	30	1	29	28	PA	43	–	43	17
IL	58	3	55	31	RI	31	2	29	26
IN	34	2	32	21	SC	18	1	17	10
IA	33	1	32	21	SD	22	1	21	20
KS	46	1	45	27	TN	24	–	24	18
KY	27	1	26	19	TX	40	2	38	21
LA	16	–	16	11	UT	17	–	17	16
ME	54	–	54	29	VT	71	1	70	39
MD	58	–	58	31	VA	24	–	24	17
MA	51	2	49	25	WA	48	1	47	32
MI	32	1	31	21	WV	25	1	24	18
MN	69	3	66	33	WI	34	1	33	25
MS	31	2	29	17	WY	15	2	13	14

– Represents zero. [1] Excludes women elected to the judiciary, women appointed to state cabinet-level positions, women elected to executive posts by the legislature, and elected members of university Board of Trustees or Board of Education.

Source: Center for the American Woman and Politics, Eagleton Institute of Politics, Rutgers University, New Brunswick, NJ, information releases, (copyright). See <http://www.cawp.rutgers.edu.>.

Table 429. Hispanic Public Elected Officials by Office, 1985 to 2012, and State, 2012

[As of January of year shown. For states not shown, no Hispanic public officials had been identified]

State	Total	State executives and legislators 1	County and municipal officials	Judicial and law enforcement	Education and school boards	State	Total	State executives and legislators 1	County and municipal officials	Judicial and law enforcement	Education and school boards
1985	3,147	129	1,316	517	1,185	LA	7	1	2	3	1
1990	4,004	144	1,819	583	1,458	MD	8	3	5	0	0
2000	5,019	217	1,852	447	2,503	MA	32	5	14	0	13
2005	4,853	266	2,149	678	1,760	MI	15	2	1	5	7
2006	4,932	244	2,151	693	1,835	MN	6	2	1	3	0
2007	4,954	270	2,152	685	1,847	MO	3	2	1	0	0
2008	5,240	283	2,266	738	1,952	MT	4	0	2	1	1
2009	5,670	252	2,264	842	2,037	NE	1	0	0	0	1
2010	5,739	251	2,270	874	2,072	NV	20	11	1	5	3
2011	5,850	260	2,282	864	2,173	NH	4	4	0	0	0
2012	**5,928**	**266**	**2,293**	**881**	**2,225**	NJ	119	7	65	0	45
AK	2	0	2	0	0	NM	701	50	325	132	154
AZ	345	13	129	47	148	NY	143	22	55	38	26
AR	1	0	0	0	1	NC	2	2	0	0	0
CA	1,353	23	424	84	687	OH	12	1	8	1	2
CO	165	9	96	19	34	OK	1	1	0	0	0
CT	40	9	22	0	9	OR	13	1	3	6	3
DE	3	1	1	1	0	PA	10	1	5	2	2
FL	164	16	93	44	7	RI	12	5	7	0	0
GA	7	2	3	2	0	TN	4	1	3	0	0
HI	2	2	0	0	0	TX	2,518	38	917	471	1,038
ID	3	1	0	1	0	UT	9	5	3	1	0
IL	109	11	62	7	20	VT	1	1	0	0	0
IN	17	2	10	3	2	VA	5	1	2	0	2
IA	2	0	2	0	0	WA	41	3	19	0	18
KS	12	5	6	0	1	WI	8	1	2	5	0
						WY	4	2	2	0	0

[1] Includes U.S. Senators and Representatives, not shown separately.

Source: National Association of Latino Elected and Appointed Officials (NALEO) Educational Fund, Washington, DC, *National Directory of Latino Elected Officials*, annual. See also <http://www.naleo.org/>.

Table 430. Political Action Committees—Number by Committee Type: 1980 to 2011

[As of December 31]

Committee type	1980	1990	2000	2005	2007	2008	2009	2010	2011
Total	**2,551**	**4,172**	**3,907**	**4,210**	**4,234**	**4,611**	**4,578**	**4,859**	**4,657**
Corporate	1,206	1,795	1,545	1,622	1,601	1,598	1,628	1,683	1,652
Labor	297	346	317	290	273	272	280	283	280
Trade/membership/health	576	774	860	925	925	995	968	1,004	985
Nonconnected	374	1,062	1,026	1,233	1,300	1,594	1,567	1,747	1,601
Cooperative	42	59	41	37	38	49	40	39	35
Corporation without stock	56	136	118	103	97	103	95	103	104

Source: U.S. Federal Election Commission, January 2012, <http://www.fec.gov/press/cf_summaries.shtml>.

Table 431. Political Action Committees—Financial Activity Summary by Committee Type: 2005 to 2010

[In millions of dollars (1,085.5 represents $1,085,500,000). Covers financial activity during 2-year calendar period indicated]

Committee type	Receipts			Disbursements [1]			Contributions to candidates		
	2005–06	2007–08	2009–10	2005–06	2007–08	2009–10	2005–06	2007–08	2009–10
Total	**1,085.5**	**1,212.4**	**1,279.5**	**1,055.3**	**1,180.0**	**1,264.1**	**372.1**	**412.8**	**431.5**
Corporate	278.3	313.4	317.0	277.8	298.6	305.7	135.9	158.3	165.5
Labor	218.2	262.1	259.1	197.4	265.0	254.2	55.8	62.7	64.2
Trade/membership/health	218.4	241.0	227.4	208.9	229.5	223.4	101.8	112.9	115.3
Nonconnected	352.9	372.7	451.7	354.5	364.6	457.1	70.2	66.6	74.1
Cooperative	6.2	10.3	10.1	5.6	9.9	9.8	3.5	6.9	5.0
Corporation without stock	11.4	13.0	14.3	11.1	12.4	13.8	4.9	5.5	7.5

[1] Comprises contributions to candidates, independent expenditures, and other disbursements.

Source: U.S. Federal Election Commission, 2009-2010 PAC Financial Activity, biennial data sheet. See <http://www.fec.gov/>.

Table 432. Presidential Campaign Finances—Federal Funds for General Election: 1996 to 2008

[In millions of dollars (152.6 represents $152,600,000). Based on FEC certifications, audit reports, and Dept. of Treasury reports]

1996		2000		2004		2008	
Candidate	Amount	Candidate	Amount	Candidate	Amount	Candidate	Amount
Total	**152.6**	**Total**	**147.7**	**Total**	**150.1**	**Total**	**84.2**
Clinton	61.8	Bush	67.6	Bush	74.6	Obama	–
Dole	61.8	Gore	67.6	Kerry	74.6	McCain	84.1
Perot	29.0	Buchanan	12.6	Nader	0.9	Nader	0.1

– Represents zero.

Source: U.S. Federal Election Commission, periodic press releases. See also <http://www.fec.gov/press/press.shtml>.

Table 433. Presidential Campaign Finances—Primary Campaign Receipts and Disbursements: 1999 to 2008

[In millions of dollars (351.6 represents $351,600,000). Covers campaign finance activity during 2-year calendar period indicated. Covers candidates who received federal matching funds or who had significant financial activity]

Item	Total [1]			Democratic			Republican		
	1999–00	2003–04	2007–08 [2,3]	1999–00	2003–04	2007–08 [2]	1999–00	2003–04	2007–08 [3]
Receipts, total [4]	**351.6**	**673.9**	**1,550.3**	**96.6**	**401.8**	**1,073.8**	**236.7**	**269.6**	**472.4**
Individual contributions	238.2	611.4	1,325.6	66.7	351.0	932.6	159.1	258.9	390.0
Federal matching funds	61.6	28.0	21.0	29.3	27.2	17.5	26.5	–	2.6
Disbursements	**343.5**	**661.1**	**1,498.0**	**92.2**	**389.7**	**1,043.9**	**233.2**	**268.9**	**450.2**

– Represents zero. [1] Includes other parties, not shown separately. [2] Obama activity includes both Primary and General election funds because he used a single committee for both elections. Dodd received $1,961,742 in matching funds; however his committee reported the receipt of $1,447,568. Gravel received an additional $115,966 in matching funds in early 2009. [3] Tancredo received an additional $83,775 in matching funds in early 2009. [4] Includes other types of receipts, not shown separately.

Source: U.S. Federal Election Commission, periodic press releases. See also <http://www.fec.gov>.

Table 434. Congressional Campaign Finances—Receipts and Disbursements: 2005 to 2010

[875.4 represents $875,400,000. Covers all campaign finance activity during 2-year calendar period indicated for primary, general, run-off, and special elections. Data have been adjusted to eliminate transfers between all committees within a campaign. For further information on legal limits of contributions, see Federal Election Campaign Act of 1971, as amended]

Item	House of Representatives						Senate					
	Amount (mil. dol.)			Percent distribution			Amount (mil. dol.)			Percent distribution		
	2005–06	2007–08	2009–10	2005–06	2007–08	2009–10	2005–06	2007–08	2009–10	2005–06	2007–08	2009–10
Total receipts [1]...	**875.4**	**983.8**	**1,101.8**	**100**	**100**	**100**	**564.6**	**436.2**	**757.6**	**100**	**100**	**100**
Individual contributions......	478.9	528.8	640.2	55	54	58	383.2	270.1	466.1	68	62	62
Other committees...	279.8	300.7	313.6	32	31	28	68.9	79.3	89.4	12	18	12
Candidate loans.....	56.1	75.8	89.7	6	8	8	47.0	24.2	146.9	8	6	19
Candidate contributions......	14.7	29.7	19.3	2	3	2	37.5	6.5	3.9	7	1	1
Democrats..........	417.5	539.6	510.2	48	55	46	291.8	239.5	318.4	52	55	42
Republicans.........	453.6	440.8	588.2	52	45	53	245.8	196.0	424.2	44	45	56
Others...............	4.2	3.4	3.4	(Z)	(Z)	(Z)	26.9	.7	15.0	5	(Z)	2
Incumbents..........	532.6	579.5	626.2	61	59	57	278.4	234.5	238.4	49	54	31
Challengers..........	188.7	233.1	336.3	22	24	31	186.6	136.7	182.1	33	31	24
Open seats [2]........	154.1	171.1	139.3	18	17	13	99.6	65.0	337.2	18	15	45
Total disbursements...	**854.8**	**941.5**	**1,094.1**	**100**	**100**	**100**	**562.9**	**433.7**	**751.2**	**100**	**100**	**100**
Democrats..........	395.5	496.7	534.3	46	53	49	288.6	231.1	328.9	51	53	44
Republicans.........	455.2	441.5	556.7	53	47	51	249.3	201.9	407.5	44	47	54
Others...............	4.1	3.2	3.1	(Z)	(Z)	(Z)	25.0	.6	14.8	4	(Z)	2
Incumbents..........	519.2	543.2	627.8	61	58	57	274.3	234.2	242.1	49	54	32
Challengers..........	185.6	229.3	328.8	22	24	30	187.1	134.2	176.9	33	31	24
Open seats [2]........	150.0	169.0	137.5	18	18	13	101.5	65.3	332.3	18	15	44

Z Less than 0.5 percent. [1] Includes other types of receipts, not shown separately. [2] Elections in which an incumbent did not seek reelection.

Source: U.S. Federal Election Commission, *Financial Activity of All Senate and House Campaigns*, biennial data sheet. See also <http://www.fec.gov/>.

Table 435. Contributions to Congressional Campaigns by Political Action Committees (PAC) by Type of Committee: 1999 to 2010

[In millions of dollars (193.4 represents $193,400,000). Covers amounts given to candidates in primary, general, run-off, and special elections during the 2-year calendar period indicated. For number of political action committees, see Table 430]

Type of committee	Total [1]	Democrats	Republicans	Incumbents	Challengers	Open seats [2]
HOUSE OF REPRESENTATIVES						
1999–00................................	193.4	98.2	94.7	150.5	19.9	23.0
2001–02................................	206.9	102.6	104.2	161.0	13.8	32.1
2003–04................................	225.4	98.6	126.6	187.3	15.6	22.5
2005–06................................	279.2	124.9	154.2	229.3	26.2	23.6
2007–08................................	308.1	185.6	122.4	253.5	35.8	18.8
2009–10, total [3]...................	**313.6**	**184.4**	**129.2**	**262.8**	**30.0**	**20.7**
Corporate................................	113.7	58.0	55.7	102.1	6.4	5.3
Trade association [4].....................	86.4	45.6	40.8	74.2	6.7	5.5
Labor....................................	54.2	50.8	3.5	46.6	3.7	3.9
Nonconnected [5].........................	49.8	25.1	24.7	31.8	12.4	5.6
SENATE						
1999–00................................	51.9	18.7	33.2	33.5	7.1	11.3
2001–02................................	59.2	25.4	33.8	37.0	14.2	8.1
2003–04................................	63.7	28.4	35.3	39.3	5.6	18.8
2005–06................................	66.1	28.6	37.5	47.7	10.0	8.3
2007–08................................	79.8	33.9	45.9	57.7	13.0	9.1
2009–10, total [3]...................	**88.8**	**39.9**	**49.0**	**48.9**	**10.4**	**29.5**
Corporate................................	36.8	13.6	23.2	22.6	3.2	11.0
Trade association [4].....................	21.4	8.3	13.1	12.6	2.2	6.6
Labor....................................	7.7	7.1	0.6	2.9	1.4	3.4
Nonconnected [5].........................	20.8	9.9	10.9	9.6	3.4	7.8

[1] Includes other parties, not shown separately. [2] Elections in which an incumbent did not seek reelection. [3] Includes other types of political action committees, not shown separately. [4] Includes membership organizations and health organizations. [5] Represents "ideological" groups as well as other issue groups not necessarily ideological in nature.

Source: U.S. Federal Election Commission, campaign finance summary data, <http://www.fec.gov>.

State and Local Government Finances and Employment

This section presents data on revenues, expenditures, debt, and employment of state and local governments. Nationwide statistics relating to state and local governments, their numbers, finances, and employment are compiled primarily by the U.S. Census Bureau through a program of censuses and surveys. Every fifth year (for years ending in "2" and "7"), the Census Bureau conducts a census of governments involving collection of data for all governmental units in the United States. In addition, the Census Bureau conducts annual surveys which cover all the state governments and a sample of local governments.

Annually, the Census Bureau releases information on the Internet which presents financial data for the federal government, nationwide totals for state and local governments, and state-local data by states. Also released annually is a series on state, city, county, and school finances and on state and local public employment. There is also a series of quarterly data releases covering tax revenue and finances of major public employee retirement systems.

Basic information for Census Bureau statistics on governments is obtained by mail canvass from state and local officials; however, financial data for each state government and for many of the large local governments are compiled from their official records and reports by Census Bureau personnel. In over two-thirds of the states, all or part of local government financial data are obtained through central collection arrangements with state governments. Financial data on the federal government are primarily based on the *Budget* published by the Office of Management and Budget.

Governmental units—The governmental structure of the United States includes, in addition to the federal government and the states, thousands of local governments—counties, municipalities, townships, school districts, and many "special districts." In 2007, 89,476 local governments were identified by the census of governments (see Tables 436-437). As defined by the census, governmental units include all agencies or bodies having an organized existence, governmental character, and substantial autonomy. While most of these governments can impose taxes, many of the special districts—such as independent public housing authorities and numerous local irrigation, power, and other types of districts—are financed from rentals, charges for services, benefit assessments, grants from other governments, and other nontax sources. The count of governments excludes semi-autonomous agencies through which states, cities, and counties sometimes provide for certain functions—for example, "dependent" school systems, state institutions of higher education, and certain other "authorities" and special agencies which are under the administrative or fiscal control of an established governmental unit.

Finances—The financial statistics relate to government fiscal years ending June 30 or at some date within the 12 previous months. The following governments are exceptions and are included as though they were part of the June 30 group; ending September 30, the state governments of Alabama and Michigan, the District of Columbia, and Alabama school districts; and ending August 31, the state government of Texas and the Chicago school district. New York State ends its fiscal year on March 31. The federal government ended the fiscal year June 30 until 1976 when its fiscal year, by an act of Congress, was revised to extend from Oct. 1 to Sept. 30. A 3-month quarter (July 1 to Sept. 30, 1976) bridged the transition.

Nationwide government finance statistics have been classified and presented in terms of uniform concepts and categories, rather than according to the highly diverse terminology, organization, and fund structure utilized by individual governments.

Statistics on governmental finances distinguish among general government, utilities, liquor stores, and insurance trusts. *General government* comprises all activities except utilities, liquor stores, and insurance trusts. Utilities include government water supply, electric light and power, gas supply, and transit systems. Liquor stores are operated by 17 states and by local governments in 6 states. Insurance trusts relate to employee retirement, unemployment compensation, and other social insurance systems administered by the federal, state, and local governments.

Data for cities or counties relate only to municipal or county and their dependent agencies and do not include amounts for other local governments in the same geographic location. Therefore, expenditure figures for "education" do not include spending by the separate school districts which administer public schools within most municipal or county areas. Variations in the assignment of governmental responsibility for public assistance, health, hospitals, public housing, and other functions to a lesser degree also have an important effect upon reported amounts of city or county expenditure, revenue, and debt.

Employment and payrolls—These data are based mainly on mail canvassing of state and local governments. Payroll includes all salaries, wages, and individual fee payments for the month specified, and employment relates to all persons on governmental payrolls during a pay period of the month covered—including paid officials, temporary help, and (unless otherwise specified) part-time as well as full-time personnel. Effective with the 1997 Census of Governments, the reference period for measuring government employment was changed from October of the calendar year to March of the calendar year. As a result, there was no annual survey of government employment covering the October 1996 period. The prior reference month of October was used from 1958 to 1995. Figures shown for individual governments cover major dependent agencies such as institutions of higher education, as well as the basic central departments and agencies of the government.

Statistical reliability—For a discussion of statistical collection and estimation, sampling procedures, and measures of statistical reliability applicable to Census Bureau data, see Appendix III.

Table 436. Number of Governmental Units by Type: 1962 to 2007

Type of government	1962	1967	1972	1977	1982	1987	1992	1997	2002	2007
Total units	**91,237**	**81,299**	**78,269**	**79,913**	**81,831**	**83,237**	**85,006**	**87,504**	**87,576**	**89,527**
U.S. government	1	1	1	1	1	1	1	1	1	1
State governments	50	50	50	50	50	50	50	50	50	50
Local governments	91,186	81,248	78,218	79,862	81,780	83,186	84,955	87,453	87,525	89,476
County	3,043	3,049	3,044	3,042	3,041	3,042	3,043	3,043	3,034	3,033
Municipal	18,000	18,048	18,517	18,862	19,076	19,200	19,279	19,372	19,429	19,492
Township and town	17,142	17,105	16,991	16,822	16,734	16,691	16,656	16,629	16,504	16,519
School district	34,678	21,782	15,781	15,174	14,851	14,721	14,422	13,726	13,506	13,051
Special district	18,323	21,264	23,885	25,962	28,078	29,532	31,555	34,683	35,052	37,381

Source: U.S. Census Bureau, *Census of Governments*, Volume 1, Number 1, Government Organization, Series GC07(1)-1), quinquennial. See also <http://www.census.gov/govs/cog/>.

Table 437. Number of Local Governments by Type—States: 2007

[Governments in existence in January. Limited to governments actually in existence. Excludes, therefore, a few counties and numerous townships and "incorporated places" existing as areas for which statistics can be presented as to population and other subjects, but lacking any separate organized county, township, or municipal government. See Appendix III]

State	All governmental units [1]	County	Municipal	Township [1]	School district	Special district [2] Total [3]	Natural resources	Fire protection	Housing [4]
United States	**89,476**	**3,033**	**19,492**	**16,519**	**13,051**	**37,381**	**7,227**	**5,873**	**3,463**
Alabama	1,185	67	458	–	131	529	69	11	150
Alaska	177	14	148	–	–	15	–	–	14
Arizona	645	15	90	–	239	301	78	150	–
Arkansas	1,548	75	502	–	247	724	250	81	119
California	4,344	57	478	–	1,044	2,765	473	353	70
Colorado	2,416	62	270	–	180	1,904	180	252	89
Connecticut	649	–	30	149	17	453	1	72	114
Delaware	338	3	57	–	19	259	238	–	3
District of Columbia	2	–	1	–	–	– 1	–	–	–
Florida	1,623	66	411	–	95	1,051	125	61	94
Georgia	1,439	154	535	–	180	570	38	2	191
Hawaii	19	3	1	–	–	15	14	–	–
Idaho	1,240	44	200	–	116	880	174	150	10
Illinois	6,994	102	1,299	1,432	912	3,249	1,026	841	113
Indiana	3,231	91	567	1,008	293	1,272	139	1	65
Iowa	1,954	99	947	–	380	528	247	66	23
Kansas	3,931	104	627	1,353	316	1,531	258	1	197
Kentucky	1,346	118	419	–	175	634	126	156	13
Louisiana	526	60	303	–	68	95	8	3	–
Maine	850	16	22	466	98	248	15	–	34
Maryland	256	23	157	–	–	76	38	–	20
Massachusetts	861	5	45	306	82	423	16	16	252
Michigan	2,893	83	533	1,242	579	456	79	25	–
Minnesota	3,526	87	854	1,788	341	456	144	–	162
Mississippi	1,000	82	296	–	164	458	249	33	55
Missouri	3,723	114	952	312	536	1,809	329	357	124
Montana	1,273	54	129	–	332	758	132	220	13
Nebraska	2,659	93	530	454	288	1,294	83	417	168
Nevada	198	16	19	–	17	146	33	18	5
New Hampshire	545	10	13	221	164	137	10	16	21
New Jersey	1,383	21	324	242	549	247	15	196	–
New Mexico	863	33	101	–	96	633	576	–	6
New York	3,403	57	618	929	680	1,119	3	891	–
North Carolina	963	100	548	–	–	315	145	–	94
North Dakota	2,699	53	357	1,320	198	771	78	281	35
Ohio	3,702	88	938	1,308	668	700	106	85	77
Oklahoma	1,880	77	594	–	567	642	100	30	137
Oregon	1,546	36	242	–	234	1,034	204	271	21
Pennsylvania	4,871	66	1,016	1,546	515	1,728	5	–	90
Rhode Island	134	–	8	31	4	91	4	37	25
South Carolina	698	46	268	–	85	299	48	83	43
South Dakota	1,983	66	309	916	166	526	103	84	49
Tennessee	928	92	347	–	14	475	109	1	96
Texas	4,835	254	1,209	–	1,081	2,291	442	139	387
Utah	599	29	242	–	40	288	82	18	17
Vermont	733	14	45	237	293	144	14	16	10
Virginia	511	95	229	–	1	186	47	–	–
Washington	1,845	39	281	–	296	1,229	178	375	43
West Virginia	663	55	232	–	55	321	14	–	37
Wisconsin	3,120	72	592	1,259	441	756	251	–	177
Wyoming	726	23	99	–	55	549	131	64	–

– Represents zero. [1] Includes "town" governments in the six New England States and in Minnesota, New York, and Wisconsin. [2] Single function districts. [3] Includes other special districts not shown separately. [4] Includes community development.

Source: U.S. Census Bureau, *Census of Governments*, Volume 1, Number 1, Government Organization, Series GC07(1)–1), quinquennial. See also <http://www.census.gov/cog/>.

Table 438. State and Local Government Current Receipts and Expenditures in the National Income and Product Accounts: 1990 to 2011

[In billions of dollars (738.0 represents $738,000,000,000). For explanation of national income, see text, Section 13. Minus sign (–) indicates net loss]

Item	1990	1995	2000	2005	2007	2008	2009	2010	2011
Current receipts.........................	**738.0**	**991.9**	**1,322.6**	**1,730.4**	**1,923.1**	**1,944.8**	**1,961.4**	**2,042.4**	**2,064.4**
Current tax receipts........................	519.1	672.1	893.2	1,163.1	1,313.6	1,326.4	1,264.9	1,304.6	1,360.8
Personal current taxes....................	122.6	158.1	236.7	276.7	323.1	334.4	287.6	300.6	322.8
Income taxes..............................	109.6	141.7	217.4	251.7	295.9	307.7	259.3	270.1	291.2
Other.....................................	13.0	16.4	19.4	25.0	27.2	26.7	28.3	30.4	31.6
Taxes on production and imports..........	374.1	482.4	621.3	831.4	932.7	944.6	931.8	959.5	990.4
Sales taxes..............................	184.3	242.7	316.8	402.2	447.1	444.0	422.3	442.6	461.5
Property taxes...........................	161.5	202.6	254.7	346.9	396.0	408.3	431.2	433.5	439.8
Other.....................................	28.3	37.0	49.8	82.3	89.7	92.3	78.3	83.4	89.2
Taxes on corporate income...............	22.5	31.7	35.2	54.9	57.8	47.4	45.5	44.5	47.6
Contributions for government social insurance.................................	10.0	13.6	10.8	24.8	18.9	19.0	19.0	18.4	18.3
Income receipts on assets.................	68.5	68.5	94.3	88.3	114.5	106.8	95.0	88.8	86.4
Interest receipts.........................	64.1	63.0	86.7	76.4	100.6	91.9	81.8	75.7	73.0
Dividends................................	0.2	1.0	1.4	2.1	2.4	2.9	2.1	2.2	2.2
Rents and royalties......................	4.2	4.5	6.3	9.8	11.5	12.0	11.1	10.9	11.2
Current transfer receipts..................	133.5	224.2	313.9	454.3	485.1	505.0	593.6	643.2	612.7
Federal grants-in-aid.....................	111.4	184.2	247.3	361.2	380.8	395.5	482.6	531.1	497.8
From business (net)......................	7.1	13.5	28.6	36.5	41.3	44.3	45.0	44.8	45.5
From persons............................	14.9	26.5	38.0	56.5	63.1	65.2	66.0	67.3	69.4
Current surplus of government enterprises...............................	6.9	13.5	10.4	0.1	-9.1	-12.3	-11.1	-12.5	-13.8
Current expenditures...................	**731.8**	**982.7**	**1,281.3**	**1,704.5**	**1,910.8**	**2,017.0**	**2,074.6**	**2,132.1**	**2,166.3**
Consumption expenditures................	547.0	701.3	930.6	1,212.0	1,368.9	1,449.2	1,473.3	1,496.2	1,518.0
Government social benefit payments to persons..................................	127.7	217.6	271.4	404.8	433.7	456.7	495.1	528.3	538.5
Interest payments.........................	56.8	63.5	78.8	87.3	101.1	108.1	104.8	106.0	109.2
Subsidies.................................	0.4	0.3	0.5	0.4	7.1	3.0	1.4	1.6	0.5
Net state and local government saving.................................	**6.2**	**9.2**	**41.3**	**25.9**	**12.2**	**-72.2**	**-113.2**	**-89.7**	**-102.0**
Social insurance funds....................	2.0	4.0	2.0	7.4	1.9	1.2	1.7	2.2	2.8
Other.....................................	4.2	5.1	39.3	18.5	10.4	-73.4	-115.0	-91.9	-104.7

Source: U.S. Bureau of Economic Analysis, National Income and Product Accounts Tables, July 2012. See also <http://www.bea.gov/itable/>.

Table 439. Federal Grants–in–Aid to State and Local Governments: 1990 to 2012

[135,325 represents $135,325,000,000, except as indicated. For fiscal year ending Sept. 30. Minus sign (–) indicates decrease]

Year	Current dollars							Constant (2005) dollars	
			Grants to individuals		Grants as percent of—				
	Total grants (mil. dol.)	Annual percent change [1]	Grants to individuals, total (mil. dol.)	Percent of total grants	State and local government expenditures from own sources [2]	Federal outlays	Gross domestic product	Total grants (bil. dol.)	Annual percent change [1]
1990..............	135,325	11.0	77,264	57.1	25.2	10.8	2.4	198.1	6.2
1995..............	224,991	6.8	144,427	64.2	31.5	14.8	3.1	283.5	3.9
1998..............	246,128	5.1	160,305	65.1	30.3	14.9	2.8	293.8	3.8
1999..............	267,886	8.8	172,384	64.3	31.2	15.7	2.9	314.7	7.1
2000..............	285,874	6.7	182,592	63.9	27.4	16.0	2.9	326.7	3.8
2001..............	318,542	11.4	203,920	64.0	28.4	17.1	3.1	354.8	8.6
2002..............	352,895	10.8	227,373	64.4	29.5	17.5	3.3	387.3	9.2
2003..............	388,542	10.1	246,570	63.5	30.5	18.0	3.5	416.1	7.4
2004..............	407,512	4.9	262,177	64.3	30.9	17.8	3.5	424.2	1.9
2005..............	428,018	5.0	273,898	64.0	30.8	17.3	3.4	428.0	0.9
2006..............	434,099	1.4	272,585	62.8	29.7	16.3	3.3	417.3	-2.5
2007..............	443,797	2.2	284,362	64.1	28.4	16.3	3.2	412.5	-1.2
2008..............	461,317	3.9	300,820	65.2	27.4	15.5	3.2	411.2	-0.3
2009..............	537,991	16.6	356,692	66.3	33.1	15.3	3.9	476.6	15.9
2010..............	608,390	13.1	384,480	63.2	37.5	17.6	4.2	531.7	11.6
2011..............	606,766	-0.3	387,806	63.9	(NA)	16.8	4.1	514.6	-3.2
2012, est..........	612,419	0.9	368,552	60.2	(NA)	16.1	3.9	504.4	-2.0

NA Not available. [1] Average annual percent change from prior year shown; For 1990, change from 1989. For explanation, see Guide to Tabular Presentation. [2] Expenditures from own sources as defined in the national income and product accounts.

Source: U.S. Office of Management and Budget, *Budget of the United States Government, Historical Tables*, annual. See also <http://www.whitehouse.gov/omb/budget>.

Table 440. Total Outlays for Grants to State and Local Governments—Selected Agencies and Programs: 1990 to 2011

[In millions of dollars (135,325 represents $135,325,000,000). For fiscal year ending Sept. 30. Includes trust funds]

Program	1990	2000	2005	2008	2009	2010	2011	2012, est.
Total outlays for grants	**135,325**	**285,874**	**428,018**	**461,317**	**537,991**	**608,390**	**606,766**	**612,419**
Energy	461	433	636	524	999	2,656	5,128	4,030
Natural resources and environment	3,745	4,595	5,858	5,902	6,285	9,132	8,259	7,083
Environmental Protection Agency [1]	2,874	3,490	3,734	3,854	3,580	6,883	5,979	4,809
Agriculture	1,285	724	933	862	937	843	938	1,084
Transportation	19,174	32,222	43,370	51,216	55,438	60,981	60,986	66,695
Grants for airports [1]	1,220	1,624	3,530	3,808	3,759	3,156	3,095	3,713
Federal-aid highways [2]	13,854	24,711	30,915	35,429	36,049	30,385	35,754	38,598
Urban mass transportation [1]	3,728	5,262	8,114	9,847	11,182	12,939	11,783	12,513
Community and regional development	4,965	8,665	20,167	19,221	17,368	18,818	19,935	17,662
Rural Community Advancement Program	139	479	814	5	–	–	-	-
Community Development Fund	2,818	4,955	4,985	8,935	6,408	7,043	7,037	7,946
Homeland Security	1,184	2,439	13,541	8,630	9,068	8,393	9,456	5,948
State and local programs	–	–	2,116	2,870	2,529	3,247	3,252	4,188
Firefighter assistance grants	–	–	1,185	–	–	–	-	-
Operations, planning, and support	11	192	132	–	–	–	-	-
Mitigation grants	–	13	39	33	11	–	-	-
Disaster relief	1,173	2,234	10,069	5,724	6,525	5,141	6,201	1,156
Education, training, employment, social services	21,780	36,672	57,247	58,904	73,986	97,586	89,147	114,769
Accelerating Achievement & Ensuring Equity [3, 4]	4,437	8,511	14,539	14,799	15,797	19,515	19,486	20,143
School improvement programs [4]	1,080	2,394	6,569	5,208	5,247	5,184	5,309	4,949
Special education	1,485	4,696	10,661	12,078	12,536	17,075	16,832	14,274
Social Services Block Grant	2,749	1,827	1,822	1,843	1,854	2,035	1,787	1,908
Children and family services programs	2,618	5,843	8,490	8,633	8,793	10,473	10,141	9,677
Training and employment services	3,042	2,957	3,372	3,052	3,768	4,592	3,666	3,046
Health	43,890	124,843	197,848	218,025	268,320	290,168	292,847	275,199
Substance abuse and mental health services [4]	1,241	1,931	3,203	2,847	2,888	2,846	2,964	2,941
Grants to states for Medicaid [4]	41,103	117,921	181,720	201,426	250,924	272,771	274,964	255,263
State children's health insurance fund [4]	–	1,220	5,129	6,900	7,547	7,887	8,629	9,778
Income security	36,768	68,653	90,885	96,102	103,169	115,156	113,625	106,151
SNAP (formerly Food Stamp Program) [4]	2,130	3,508	4,385	4,935	5,624	5,739	5,973	6,832
Child nutrition programs [4]	4,871	9,060	11,726	13,761	15,083	16,259	17,112	19,436
Temporary Assistance for Needy Families [4]	–	15,464	17,357	17,532	17,861	17,513	17,116	16,538
Veterans benefits and services [4]	134	434	552	695	809	836	996	1,027
Administration of justice	574	5,263	4,784	4,201	4,810	5,086	4,876	7,749

– Represents zero. [1] Grants include trust funds. [2] Trust funds. [3] Formerly Education for the Disadvantaged. [4] Includes grants for payments to individuals.

Source: U.S. Office of Management and Budget, *Budget of the United States Government, Historical Tables*, annual. See also <http://www.whitehouse.gov/omb/budget>.

Table 441. Federal Aid to State and Local Governments by State: 2005 to 2010

[In millions of dollars (403,660 represents $403,660,000,000). For fiscal year ending September 30]

State	2005	2008	2009	2010	State	2005	2008	2009	2010
U.S. [1]	**403,660**	**469,773**	**552,108**	**630,170**	MO	7,407	8,273	10,293	12,717
AL	6,306	6,994	7,610	8,609	MT	2,021	2,109	2,566	2,810
AK	2,671	2,604	3,624	3,326	NE	2,256	2,439	2,826	3,122
AZ	7,965	9,940	12,997	13,370	NV	2,213	2,450	3,143	3,610
AR	4,179	4,733	5,598	6,418	NH	1,483	1,692	1,986	2,355
CA	46,029	53,818	61,971	66,565	NJ	10,479	11,580	13,515	16,309
CO	4,538	5,321	6,333	7,651	NM	4,097	5,381	6,635	6,811
CT	4,539	5,279	6,759	7,673	NY	43,438	44,454	52,183	61,341
DE	1,142	1,363	1,679	3,325	NC	11,568	12,906	15,308	15,522
DC	3,450	11,946	9,659	9,942	ND	1,394	1,402	1,806	2,169
FL	19,046	20,659	22,686	27,731	OH	13,726	15,230	19,115	23,072
GA	8,914	10,675	12,953	15,879	OK	4,935	5,922	7,828	8,022
HI	1,731	2,120	2,560	2,520	OR	4,808	5,498	6,807	7,849
ID	1,814	2,688	2,458	3,057	PA	18,103	18,832	21,796	26,291
IL	14,616	16,267	20,941	23,194	RI	1,937	2,037	2,310	2,944
IN	6,483	8,272	10,194	10,400	SC	5,326	6,035	6,863	8,296
IA	3,594	4,014	5,033	5,871	SD	1,336	1,473	2,068	2,145
KS	2,872	3,514	3,965	4,980	TN	9,083	9,201	10,210	12,514
KY	5,779	6,867	8,245	9,756	TX	25,622	30,580	35,330	43,732
LA	7,148	12,457	11,534	13,437	UT	2,633	3,160	3,942	4,212
ME	2,623	2,695	3,399	3,581	VT	1,213	1,441	1,671	2,044
MD	6,800	7,473	9,405	10,832	VA	6,330	7,724	8,970	10,647
MA	9,989	11,402	15,200	15,121	WA	7,681	8,668	10,631	11,945
MI	12,113	13,587	16,580	19,646	WV	3,482	3,557	4,031	4,830
MN	5,878	7,533	9,304	10,872	WI	6,563	7,000	9,556	10,710
MS	5,168	7,484	7,642	8,611	WY	2,243	2,334	2,214	2,356

[1] Total includes U.S. Island Areas.

Source: U.S. Census Bureau, *Federal Aid to States for Fiscal Year 2010*. <http:www.census.gov/prod/www/abs/fas.html>.

Table 442. Federal Aid Total from Dept. of Agriculture and Dept. of Eduction to State and Local Governments—Selected Programs by State: 2010

[In millions of dollars (630,170 represents 630,170,000,000). For fiscal year ending September 30. Negative amounts (–) are refunds (from the recipients) of advances from a prior year, or represent reductions in the amount of funds originally obligated to the recipients for the particular program or program category during the fiscal year. For similar data from other Federal agencies, see tables 443-444]

State and Island Areas	Federal aid total [1]	Department of Agriculture					Department of Education				
		Total	Food and Nutrition Service				Total	Special educa-tion pro-grams	Office of Elementary and Secondary Education		Other
			Child nutri-tion pro-grams	Supple-mental Nutrition Assis-tance Program (SNAP) [2]	Special mental food program (WIC)	Other			No Child Left Behind Act	Title 1 programs	
United States, total	630,170	32,793	16,281	5,619	6,457	4,435	73,209	16,695	5,014	18,110	33,390
Alabama	8,609	525	290	45	108	82	904	274	79	343	208
Alaska	3,326	159	46	12	25	76	401	57	29	50	266
Arizona	13,370	665	359	59	141	106	1,480	261	86	374	759
Arkansas	6,418	383	211	37	68	68	757	176	51	186	344
California	66,565	4,165	1,990	632	1,117	426	6,165	1,792	516	2,236	1,620
Colorado	7,651	363	172	48	76	66	1,067	217	66	195	589
Connecticut	7,673	224	119	34	43	29	840	229	46	165	400
Delaware	3,325	93	48	14	13	17	220	44	24	48	105
District of Columbia	9,942	76	38	14	15	9	225	19	26	40	139
Florida	27,731	1,591	947	133	354	158	4,011	953	236	905	1,917
Georgia	15,879	1,179	686	90	254	150	2,663	480	140	602	1,441
Hawaii	2,520	125	51	14	32	28	319	50	26	53	190
Idaho	3,057	180	77	11	29	64	469	86	25	65	294
Illinois	23,194	1,099	620	126	237	117	3,066	769	212	830	1,256
Indiana	10,400	570	335	54	108	73	1,201	374	79	311	438
Iowa	5,871	301	143	29	48	81	796	217	43	121	415
Kansas	4,980	302	156	19	45	82	688	182	34	129	343
Kentucky	9,756	516	260	64	96	96	1,238	261	82	303	591
Louisiana	13,437	637	346	78	122	91	1,410	293	134	392	591
Maine	3,581	125	55	18	18	34	337	87	33	76	141
Maryland	10,832	414	211	54	98	52	1,346	300	70	264	712
Massachusetts	15,121	439	247	56	88	48	547	14	8	3	522
Michigan	19,646	894	436	157	175	126	2,641	603	185	705	1,148
Minnesota	10,872	544	235	90	99	120	1,484	315	74	196	899
Mississippi	8,611	481	261	40	90	91	913	171	73	244	425
Missouri	12,717	555	301	66	87	100	1,535	364	81	294	796
Montana	2,810	133	47	16	15	54	315	59	32	61	162
Nebraska	3,122	195	102	18	31	44	444	108	34	76	226
Nevada	3,610	185	91	19	44	30	572	104	32	113	323
New Hampshire	2,355	71	34	8	12	17	366	69	26	46	225
New Jersey	16,309	635	327	119	127	61	2,277	537	106	354	1,280
New Mexico	6,811	326	162	32	40	93	783	141	49	169	424
New York	61,341	1,942	1,000	359	419	166	5,552	1,019	433	1,518	2,582
North Carolina	15,522	914	520	89	191	114	1,473	486	126	489	372
North Dakota	2,169	88	36	11	12	28	285	44	26	48	167
Ohio	23,072	960	513	158	179	110	2,880	710	190	725	1,255
Oklahoma	8,022	531	262	62	96	111	984	205	78	174	528
Oregon	7,849	519	172	110	72	165	848	218	65	194	370
Pennsylvania	26,291	1,081	483	192	197	208	3,173	659	189	732	1,592
Rhode Island	2,944	85	44	9	20	12	269	67	26	71	106
South Carolina	8,296	457	276	24	89	68	1,078	256	85	249	488
South Dakota	2,145	118	47	15	18	38	113	1	2	–	110
Tennessee	12,514	617	343	69	119	85	1,424	353	92	353	627
Texas	43,732	2,924	1,907	210	532	276	6,965	1,503	450	1,810	3,202
Utah	4,212	249	129	31	43	45	573	149	38	81	304
Vermont	2,044	93	25	28	14	26	213	43	26	48	97
Virginia	10,647	517	239	100	92	86	1,050	386	88	279	297
Washington	11,945	559	265	69	125	100	1,469	356	88	250	775
West Virginia	4,830	207	99	19	37	51	496	124	41	130	202
Wisconsin	10,710	471	232	67	87	84	1,208	323	82	270	534
Wyoming	2,356	59	25	8	9	17	157	36	27	39	55
Island Areas:											
American Samoa	198	32	18	5	7	1	31	8	1	–	23
Micronesia	117	–	–	–	–	–	–	–	–	–	–
Guam	319	23	9	2	9	3	36	16	1	–	20
Marshall Islands	98	–	–	–	–	–	–	–	–	–	–
Northern Marianas	140	27	9	12	5	1	21	6	–	–	14
Palau	24	–	–	–	–	–	3	1	–	–	2
Puerto Rico	6,886	2,218	202	1,749	225	42	1,424	121	124	702	477
Virgin Islands	412	45	21	12	7	4	2	–	–	–	2
Undistributed	1,231	-95	–	–	–	-95	–	–	–	–	–

– Represents or rounds to zero. [1] Total includes programs, not shown separately. [2] For Puerto Rico, amount shown is for nutritional assistance grant program, all other amounts are grant payments for food stamp administration.

Source: U.S. Census Bureau, *Federal Aid to States for Fiscal Year 2010*. See also <http://www.census.gov/prod/www/abs/fas.html>.

Table 443. Federal Aid from FEMA, HUD, and Dept. of Labor to State and Local Governments—Selected Programs by State: 2010

[See headnote, Table 442. For similar data from other Federal agencies, see tables 442 and 444]

State and Island Areas	FEMA [1] total	Department of Housing and Urban Development						Department of Labor			
		Total	Community development block grants	Public housing programs			Other	State unemployment insurance and employment Total	employment service	Workforce investment	Other
				Low rent housing assistance	Housing certificate program	Capital program					
United States, total.............	4,972	55,272	7,361	30,699	1,292	5,686	10,234	11,362	4,727	4,370	2,265
Alabama.............	50	764	99	410	6	141	109	126	57	42	27
Alaska..............	10	260	15	58	2	6	178	65	38	18	9
Arizona.............	5	627	74	240	4	20	290	178	69	66	43
Arkansas............	78	311	39	185	5	42	40	107	45	37	26
California............	169	6,901	1,268	4,272	91	182	1,087	1,478	672	660	146
Colorado............	12	573	52	366	10	34	112	139	67	49	23
Connecticut.........	11	900	55	595	64	73	113	147	82	39	26
Delaware............	2	141	13	71	15	12	29	29	14	11	5
District of Columbia..........	7	2,890	202	816	9	784	1,079	225	15	17	194
Florida..............	362	2,210	212	1,263	21	141	573	426	173	199	54
Georgia.............	51	1,474	128	808	9	157	373	257	116	116	26
Hawaii..............	4	239	22	160	2	18	37	48	22	12	14
Idaho...............	1	111	19	59	3	3	26	71	40	12	19
Illinois..............	51	2,580	202	1,597	90	330	361	528	221	218	89
Indiana.............	20	757	120	430	9	61	138	249	93	103	52
Iowa...............	169	340	107	156	3	18	56	108	46	33	29
Kansas.............	343	256	35	134	4	25	58	74	35	25	15
Kentucky............	161	594	46	365	6	83	93	175	55	82	39
Louisiana...........	1,335	1,338	644	484	7	90	112	127	45	65	18
Maine..............	10	262	29	147	24	15	48	63	28	20	16
Maryland............	30	1,361	80	752	35	169	324	264	93	44	127
Massachusetts......	42	2,250	144	1,610	114	134	248	222	106	85	31
Michigan............	31	1,250	150	642	116	93	249	633	221	306	106
Minnesota..........	35	766	67	385	74	95	146	197	78	80	39
Mississippi..........	349	1,080	699	263	6	45	68	128	39	74	15
Missouri............	123	737	105	410	10	74	137	204	71	91	42
Montana............	8	152	19	58	–	7	67	48	20	10	18
Nebraska...........	17	181	25	97	2	23	35	40	24	6	10
Nevada.............	3	308	31	172	1	15	89	105	57	36	11
New Hampshire.....	12	231	23	139	7	14	48	39	25	9	6
New Jersey..........	30	1,814	125	1,226	99	172	192	304	185	87	32
New Mexico.........	7	240	32	114	3	18	73	62	23	15	23
New York...........	129	6,641	691	4,383	72	645	850	634	269	283	82
North Carolina......	26	999	82	621	12	125	159	323	128	128	67
North Dakota.......	124	103	9	50	–	6	39	29	15	7	6
Ohio................	9	1,928	187	1,187	23	181	350	462	175	211	77
Oklahoma...........	77	488	45	231	4	34	175	95	44	33	18
Oregon.............	24	481	41	293	2	29	117	219	102	72	45
Pennsylvania.......	22	2,207	251	1,168	110	321	357	459	231	139	89
Rhode Island........	7	373	24	259	5	33	52	53	25	19	9
South Carolina......	8	512	54	302	7	54	95	181	62	100	18
South Dakota.......	20	154	18	50	10	7	70	31	14	7	9
Tennessee..........	22	801	57	472	14	121	137	199	68	108	22
Texas..............	610	2,715	515	1,519	20	245	416	620	237	262	121
Utah...............	11	195	29	103	2	7	53	72	40	14	18
Vermont............	2	119	11	69	7	8	24	33	12	10	10
Virginia............	201	1,115	71	605	64	166	208	317	84	52	181
Washington.........	70	957	85	552	2	84	234	313	161	88	65
West Virginia.......	11	245	47	144	4	20	29	61	27	18	16
Wisconsin...........	22	652	119	284	51	47	151	232	106	64	63
Wyoming............	2	57	6	26	–	3	22	29	15	8	5
Island Areas:											
American Samoa..	9	–	–	–	–	–	–	2	–	–	1
Micronesia........	1	–	–	–	–	–	–	–	–	–	–
Guam.............	-1	52	7	39	–	3	3	7	–	4	3
Marshall Islands. ..	–	–	–	–	–	–	–	–	–	–	–
Northern Marianas..........	1	6	–	5	–	–	1	2	–	2	1
Palau..............	–	–	–	–	–	–	–	–	–	–	–
Puerto Rico........	22	961	125	506	28	199	103	109	34	66	8
Virgin Islands......	6	69	3	46	1	16	3	10	4	4	2
Undistributed........	–	-458	1	-698	–	241	-1	–	–	–	–

– Represents or rounds to zero. [1] FEMA = Federal Emergency Management Agency. FEMA is part of the U.S. Department of Homeland Security.

Source: U.S. Census Bureau, *Federal Aid to States for Fiscal Year 2010*. See also <http://www.census.gov/prod/www/abs/fas.html>.

Table 444. Federal Aid from Dept. of Health and Human Services, Dept. of Transportation, and Other Aid to State and Local Governments—Selected Programs by State: 2010

[See headnotes, Table 442. For similar data from other Federal agencies, see tables 442-443]

State and Island Areas	Department of Health and Human Services						Department of Transportation				Other, federal aid [1]
		Administration for Children and Families			Centers for Medicare and Medicaid Services						
	Total	Children & family services (Head Start)	Foster care and adoption assistance	Temporary Assistance for Needy Families		Other	Total	Highway trust fund	Federal Transit Administration	Other	
United States, total	**348,197**	**10,388**	**6,958**	**19,868**	**278,041**	**32,942**	**63,882**	**30,273**	**13,041**	**20,568**	**40,482**
Alabama	4,853	176	42	150	3,980	505	834	675	57	102	553
Alaska	1,221	50	26	49	911	184	711	352	80	280	499
Arizona	8,582	206	164	255	7,403	553	810	512	184	113	1,023
Arkansas	3,897	109	57	87	3,338	306	573	341	43	189	311
California	39,605	1,257	1,697	4,251	29,247	3,153	4,809	1,881	1,553	1,376	3,273
Colorado	3,807	260	81	226	2,723	517	997	416	240	340	692
Connecticut	4,354	88	96	288	3,464	419	889	584	157	148	308
Delaware	1,018	22	5	50	834	108	1,633	1,547	26	60	188
District of Columbia	2,054	71	62	112	1,493	315	3,083	154	480	2,449	1,382
Florida	15,358	414	265	669	12,297	1,713	2,360	1,269	357	735	1,412
Georgia	7,728	266	132	394	6,075	861	1,723	1,135	200	388	803
Hawaii	1,312	41	34	148	933	156	239	138	35	66	233
Idaho	1,430	53	16	22	1,179	160	446	286	23	137	348
Illinois	12,488	402	248	729	9,835	1,274	2,070	859	618	593	1,311
Indiana	5,615	149	149	200	4,570	547	1,353	722	150	481	637
Iowa	3,121	92	63	172	2,469	325	672	349	70	253	363
Kansas	2,364	87	46	145	1,823	263	644	398	36	209	308
Kentucky	5,613	182	101	220	4,666	444	876	497	86	293	583
Louisiana	6,691	229	80	235	5,538	610	1,086	604	89	394	812
Maine	2,219	49	35	95	1,840	199	271	151	21	99	294
Maryland	5,933	129	105	351	4,574	774	863	418	257	187	622
Massachusetts	9,650	189	103	553	7,860	944	1,157	623	302	233	814
Michigan	11,470	366	223	992	8,701	1,188	1,724	809	205	710	1,004
Minnesota	6,023	152	72	315	4,842	641	1,169	511	247	411	655
Mississippi	4,503	231	20	130	3,715	407	697	377	27	292	459
Missouri	7,315	204	89	255	6,152	615	1,584	939	193	451	664
Montana	1,103	56	21	49	807	171	562	342	26	194	489
Nebraska	1,601	72	31	50	1,232	216	321	131	31	160	322
Nevada	1,416	43	54	66	1,020	232	565	290	106	169	457
New Hampshire	1,092	28	21	50	835	158	264	161	18	85	280
New Jersey	8,704	186	138	606	6,840	935	1,751	622	713	415	795
New Mexico	3,795	101	45	176	3,187	287	565	305	42	218	1,032
New York	39,344	656	566	2,741	32,737	2,644	4,876	1,632	2,684	560	2,224
North Carolina	10,135	326	129	348	8,369	964	973	376	128	469	680
North Dakota	723	46	17	28	523	109	411	192	17	202	406
Ohio	14,034	397	375	877	11,299	1,087	1,707	968	276	464	1,092
Oklahoma	4,113	167	72	185	3,218	471	1,067	653	57	357	667
Oregon	4,124	143	138	247	3,193	403	1,041	513	256	272	593
Pennsylvania	15,516	374	363	762	12,688	1,328	2,498	1,235	599	664	1,336
Rhode Island	1,597	44	27	93	1,280	153	312	175	44	93	248
South Carolina	4,848	122	50	111	4,119	446	779	456	50	273	433
South Dakota	845	61	11	23	626	124	389	214	17	158	475
Tennessee	7,415	193	82	251	6,346	542	1,177	660	118	399	859
Texas	24,184	783	353	665	20,095	2,288	3,435	1,611	661	1,162	2,279
Utah	1,930	73	30	75	1,490	261	695	248	267	180	487
Vermont	1,107	30	20	55	890	111	288	163	24	100	189
Virginia	5,287	170	87	171	4,221	639	1,292	854	249	189	868
Washington	6,192	214	148	553	4,474	804	1,390	479	427	484	994
West Virginia	2,819	86	53	193	2,224	262	606	396	41	169	387
Wisconsin	6,121	160	112	316	4,942	592	1,228	660	108	459	776
Wyoming	499	30	4	24	365	75	405	239	11	155	1,148
Island Areas:											
American Samoa	31	5	–	–	13	12	40	9	–	30	54
Micronesia	7	–	–	–	–	7	–	–	–	–	109
Guam	57	7	–	4	18	28	56	33	1	22	89
Marshall Islands	5	–	–	–	–	5	25	–	–	25	68
Northern Marianas	22	4	–	–	10	8	17	–	1	16	43
Palau	7	2	–	–	–	6	–	–	–	–	13
Puerto Rico	1,233	319	2	50	501	361	221	91	78	52	698
Virgin Islands	64	15	–	4	18	28	17	7	1	9	199
Undistributed	3	–	–	–	–	3	1,639	16	250	1,374	141

– Represents or rounds to zero. [1] Represents aid for other programs, not shown in Tables 442-444.

Source: U.S. Census Bureau, *Federal Aid to States for Fiscal Year 2010*. See also <http://www.census.gov/prod/www/abs/fas.html>.

Table 445. State and Local Governments—Summary of Finances: 1990 to 2009

[In millions of dollars (1,032,115 represents $1,032,115,000,000). For fiscal year ending in year shown; see text, this section. Local government amounts are estimates subject to sampling variation; see Appendix III and source]

Item	1990	2000	2005	2007	2008	2009
Revenue [1]	1,032,115	1,942,328	2,528,546	3,067,232	2,654,134	2,066,666
From federal government	136,802	291,950	438,558	464,585	477,983	536,760
Public welfare	59,961	148,549	(NA)	(NA)	(NA)	(NA)
Highways	14,368	24,414	(NA)	(NA)	(NA)	(NA)
Education	23,233	45,873	(NA)	(NA)	(NA)	(NA)
Health and hospitals	5,904	15,611	(NA)	(NA)	(NA)	(NA)
Housing and community development	9,655	17,690	(NA)	(NA)	(NA)	(NA)
Other and unallocable	23,683	39,812	(NA)	(NA)	(NA)	(NA)
From state and local sources	895,313	1,650,379	2,089,988	2,602,647	2,176,151	1,529,905
General, net intergovernmental	712,700	1,249,373	1,587,476	1,864,771	1,945,042	1,876,624
Taxes	501,619	872,351	1,098,513	1,283,263	1,331,012	1,271,356
Property	155,613	249,178	335,779	388,701	408,972	424,014
Sales and gross receipts	177,885	309,290	384,266	440,331	451,776	433,556
Individual income	105,640	211,661	242,273	290,278	304,901	270,518
Corporation net income	23,566	36,059	43,256	60,626	56,932	45,980
Other	38,915	66,164	92,939	103,326	108,430	97,288
Charges and miscellaneous	211,081	377,022	488,963	581,508	614,030	605,268
Utility and liquor stores	58,642	89,546	119,608	140,756	145,768	151,260
Water supply system	17,674	30,515	37,378	43,401	44,840	45,489
Electric power system	29,268	42,436	59,157	70,346	72,677	76,016
Gas supply system	5,216	8,049	6,937	8,614	8,878	9,304
Transit system	3,043	3,954	10,146	11,571	12,130	12,994
Liquor stores	3,441	4,592	5,990	6,823	7,242	7,457
Insurance trust revenue [2]	123,970	311,460	382,904	597,120	85,342	-497,978
Employee retirement	94,268	273,881	316,576	533,735	26,875	-563,836
Unemployment compensation	18,441	23,366	35,367	34,186	34,489	42,115
Direct expenditure	972,695	1,742,914	2,363,696	2,659,141	2,832,090	2,961,794
By function:						
Direct general expenditure [2]	831,573	1,502,768	2,007,490	2,255,229	2,399,788	2,475,076
Education [2]	288,148	521,612	688,314	773,676	825,486	850,674
Elementary and secondary	202,009	365,181	473,843	534,980	565,717	577,597
Higher education	73,418	134,352	182,003	203,933	222,631	234,387
Highways	61,057	101,336	126,350	144,714	153,734	152,067
Public welfare	107,287	233,350	360,730	383,652	403,697	431,098
Health	24,223	51,366	66,637	74,051	79,820	81,939
Hospitals	50,412	75,976	103,555	118,793	129,370	136,461
Police protection	30,577	56,798	74,131	83,978	89,267	92,999
Fire protection	13,186	23,102	30,830	36,688	39,500	40,312
Natural resources	12,330	20,235	23,519	28,638	29,876	30,563
Sanitation and sewerage	28,453	45,261	57,940	66,872	70,443	72,009
Housing and community development	15,479	26,590	40,014	45,884	50,965	47,489
Parks and recreation	14,326	25,038	31,925	37,498	40,652	40,578
Financial administration	16,217	29,300	36,695	39,757	40,462	40,319
Interest on general debt [3]	49,739	69,814	81,122	93,535	100,242	103,478
Utility and liquor stores [3]	77,801	114,916	160,470	189,835	198,673	211,239
Water supply system	22,101	35,789	45,695	54,177	54,950	57,366
Electric power system	30,997	39,719	58,612	69,625	75,184	79,498
Gas supply system	2,989	3,724	7,075	12,007	10,537	9,762
Transit system	18,788	31,883	44,203	48,423	52,072	58,491
Liquor stores	2,926	3,801	4,885	5,603	5,931	6,122
Insurance trust expenditure [2]	63,321	125,230	195,735	214,078	233,629	275,479
Employee retirement	38,355	95,679	145,796	167,416	180,007	190,964
Unemployment compensation	16,499	18,648	29,849	28,934	35,568	66,159
By character and object:						
Current operation	700,131	1,288,746	1,760,283	1,973,964	2,094,167	2,166,533
Capital outlay	123,102	217,063	278,063	325,267	349,170	357,274
Construction	89,144	161,694	218,691	254,702	269,873	280,210
Equipment, land, and existing structures	33,958	55,369	59,372	70,565	79,297	77,064
Assistance and subsidies	27,227	31,375	37,755	39,816	42,024	45,352
Interest on debt (general and utility)	58,914	80,499	91,859	106,017	113,100	117,157
Insurance benefits and repayments	63,321	125,230	195,735	214,078	233,629	275,479
Expenditure for salaries and wages [4]	340,654	548,796	694,583	762,158	801,543	827,816
Debt outstanding, year end	858,006	1,451,815	2,085,026	2,404,698	2,552,522	2,683,668
Long-term	838,700	1,427,524	2,054,268	2,373,330	2,507,913	2,648,645
Short-term	19,306	24,291	30,758	31,369	44,609	35,023
Long-term debt:						
Issued	108,468	184,831	323,739	381,835	372,610	368,562
Retired	64,831	121,897	224,639	228,383	243,450	258,112

NA Not available. [1] Aggregates exclude duplicative transactions between state and local governments; see source. [2] Includes amounts not shown separately. [3] Interest on utility debt included in "utility and liquor stores expenditure." For total interest on debt, see "Interest on debt (general and utility)." [4] Included in items above.

Source: U.S. Census Bureau; "Federal, State and Local Governments, State and Local Government Finances," June 2011, <http://www.census.gov/govs/>.

Table 446. State and Local Governments—Revenue and Expenditures by Function: 2008 and 2009

[In millions of dollars (2,654,134 represents $2,654,134,000,000) For fiscal year ending in year shown; see text, this section. Local government amounts are estimates subject to sampling variation; see Appendix III and source]

Item	2008			2009 [1]		
	Total	State	Local	Total	State	Local
Revenue [2]	**2,620,868**	**1,578,851**	**1,530,595**	**2,066,666**	**1,123,226**	**1,433,818**
Intergovernmental revenue [2]	477,441	441,733	524,285	536,760	495,624	531,515
Total revenue from own sources [2]	2,143,427	1,137,118	1,006,309	1,529,905	627,602	902,303
General revenue from own sources	1,944,536	1,067,648	876,889	1,876,624	1,000,107	876,517
Taxes [3]	1,329,599	779,720	549,878	1,271,356	715,496	555,860
Property	409,540	12,689	396,850	424,014	12,964	411,050
Individual income	304,902	277,996	26,906	270,518	245,881	24,637
Corporation income	57,231	49,860	7,370	45,980	39,278	6,702
Sales and gross receipts	449,945	358,825	91,120	433,556	344,568	88,988
General sales	304,739	240,165	64,574	291,045	228,729	62,316
Selective sales [3]	145,205	118,660	26,546	142,511	115,839	26,672
Motor fuel	38,961	37,632	1,329	37,816	36,471	1,344
Alcoholic beverages	5,748	5,290	458	5,865	5,348	517
Tobacco products	16,583	16,068	515	17,157	16,690	467
Public utilities	28,099	14,818	13,281	28,376	14,898	13,478
Motor vehicle and operators' licenses	21,197	19,558	1,640	21,296	19,627	1,670
Death and gift	(NA)	(NA)	(NA)	(NA)	(NA)	(NA)
Charges and miscellaneous [3]	614,938	287,927	327,010	605,268	284,610	320,657
Current charges [3]	375,694	153,863	221,831	388,766	161,239	227,527
Education [3]	108,805	83,716	25,089	115,642	89,846	25,795
School lunch sales	6,999	31	6,968	6,963	35	6,928
Higher education	92,977	82,557	10,420	99,740	88,604	11,136
Natural resources	3,938	2,543	1,395	3,986	2,497	1,489
Hospitals	97,983	37,123	60,861	103,975	39,236	64,739
Sewerage	38,146	388	37,758	39,453	507	38,947
Solid waste management	15,240	520	14,720	15,015	486	14,529
Parks and recreation	9,611	1,593	8,018	9,017	1,517	7,500
Housing and community development	5,826	802	5,024	5,853	799	5,053
Airports	17,787	1,326	16,461	18,074	1,277	16,797
Sea and inland port facilities	4,133	1,221	2,912	3,921	1,080	2,841
Highways	11,323	6,574	4,750	11,843	6,770	5,073
Interest earnings	94,186	47,689	46,497	72,938	38,311	34,627
Special assessments	7,470	631	6,838	7,795	595	7,199
Sale of property	4,340	1,049	3,291	3,576	960	2,616
Utility and liquor store revenue	145,844	22,650	123,194	151,260	22,848	128,412
Insurance trust revenue	53,047	46,820	6,227	-497,978	-395,352	-102,626
Expenditure [2]	**2,839,548**	**1,738,743**	**1,590,333**	**2,966,614**	**1,827,126**	**1,641,392**
Intergovernmental expenditure [2]	4,766	479,091	15,202	4,820	491,322	15,403
Direct expenditure [2]	2,834,782	1,259,651	1,575,131	2,961,794	1,335,804	1,625,990
General expenditure [3]	2,401,417	1,028,334	1,373,084	2,475,076	1,064,596	1,410,479
Education [3]	826,061	232,087	593,974	850,674	242,608	608,066
Elementary and secondary education	565,618	8,243	557,375	577,597	8,284	569,313
Higher education	222,932	186,333	36,599	234,387	195,634	38,753
Public welfare	404,198	353,720	50,477	431,098	379,211	51,886
Hospitals	130,113	53,641	76,472	136,461	55,774	80,687
Health	79,791	40,666	39,125	81,939	41,326	40,613
Highways	153,831	90,955	62,876	152,067	90,623	61,443
Police protection	89,463	12,058	77,405	92,999	12,186	80,814
Fire protection	39,305	-	39,305	40,312	-	40,312
Corrections	72,753	47,222	25,530	74,503	47,840	26,663
Natural resources	29,766	20,023	9,744	30,563	20,225	10,337
Sewerage	46,716	1,273	45,443	47,619	1,188	46,430
Solid waste management	23,662	2,439	21,223	24,390	2,639	21,751
Housing and community development	51,071	10,979	40,093	47,489	8,431	39,058
Governmental administration	125,789	51,631	74,158	127,424	51,930	75,494
Parks and recreation	40,614	5,550	35,064	40,578	5,277	35,301
Interest on general debt	101,008	44,838	56,170	103,478	45,202	58,276
Utility	192,234	24,693	167,541	205,117	26,539	178,578
Liquor store expenditure	5,931	4,945	986	6,122	5,175	948
Insurance trust expenditure	235,200	201,680	33,520	275,479	239,494	35,985
By character and object:						
Current operation	2,094,115	865,840	1,228,275	2,166,533	896,786	1,269,747
Capital outlay	349,710	112,695	237,014	357,274	116,578	240,696
Construction	270,360	92,779	177,581	280,210	97,526	182,683
Equipment, land, and existing structures	79,350	19,916	59,434	77,064	19,051	58,013
Assistance and subsidies	42,021	32,600	9,421	45,352	35,703	9,649
Interest on debt (general and utility)	113,736	46,836	66,900	117,157	47,244	69,913
Insurance benefits and repayments	235,200	201,680	33,520	275,479	239,494	35,985
Expenditure for salaries and wages [4]	801,811	229,862	571,949	827,816	237,797	590,018

NA Not available. – Represents or rounds to zero. [1] Data are preliminary. [2] Aggregates exclude duplicative transactions between levels of government; see source. [3] Includes other items, not shown separately. [4] Included in items shown above.

Source: U.S. Census Bureau, "Federal, State, and Local Governments, State and Local Government Finances," October 2011, <http://www.census.gov/govs/>.

Table 447. State and Local Governments—Capital Outlays: 1990 to 2008

[In millions of dollars (123,102 represents $123,102,000,000), except percent. For fiscal year ending in year shown; see text, this section. Local government amounts are subject to sampling variation; see Appendix III and source]

Level and function	1990	2000	2003	2004	2005	2006	2007	2008
State & local governments: Total	**123,102**	**217,063**	**263,198**	**269,976**	**277,200**	**295,368**	**324,467**	**348,827**
Percent of direct expenditure	12.7	12.5	12.2	11.9	11.7	11.8	12.2	12.3
By function:								
Education [1]	25,997	60,968	70,813	74,597	77,779	82,505	91,466	97,855
Elementary and secondary	18,057	45,150	51,118	52,977	54,509	59,256	65,467	70,283
Higher education	7,441	15,257	19,044	21,121	22,782	22,798	25,356	26,953
Highways	33,867	56,439	65,523	65,964	69,642	76,371	83,289	88,218
Health and hospitals	3,848	5,502	7,158	7,241	7,711	8,538	9,737	11,217
Natural resources	2,545	4,347	4,244	4,657	4,543	4,473	6,372	6,755
Housing and community development	3,997	6,184	7,660	7,578	7,880	8,130	7,991	9,191
Air transportation	3,434	6,717	9,066	9,731	9,326	9,064	9,851	10,386
Sea and inland port facilities [2]	924	1,618	3,721	1,798	1,598	1,850	2,140	2,149
Sewerage	8,356	10,093	12,467	14,068	14,170	15,336	17,683	18,777
Parks and recreation	3,877	6,916	9,224	7,866	8,151	9,267	10,085	11,672
Utilities	16,601	24,847	34,538	37,432	34,879	36,795	38,230	41,348
Water	6,873	10,542	13,536	13,651	14,402	14,356	16,960	16,295
Electric	3,976	4,177	6,438	7,173	6,055	7,793	7,981	11,637
Gas	310	400	422	582	544	520	508	520
Transit	5,443	9,728	14,142	16,026	13,879	14,126	12,781	12,897
Other	19,657	33,431	38,784	39,044	41,520	43,039	47,624	51,260
State governments: Total	**45,524**	**76,233**	**91,943**	**90,950**	**94,181**	**101,432**	**110,044**	**113,021**
Percent of direct expenditure	11.5	10.1	9.4	8.9	8.8	9.0	9.4	9.0
By function:								
Education [1]	7,253	14,077	17,727	19,632	20,632	20,623	23,752	24,705
Elementary and secondary	388	521	643	716	442	580	1,734	1,592
Higher education	6,366	12,995	16,433	18,417	19,702	19,593	21,375	22,494
Highways	24,850	41,651	48,719	48,566	51,578	57,025	61,218	61,705
Health and hospitals	1,531	2,228	2,930	2,763	3,278	3,469	3,972	4,500
Natural resources	1,593	2,758	2,788	2,957	2,670	2,588	3,324	3,024
Housing and community development	119	860	774	222	338	196	505	321
Air transportation	339	561	846	795	615	519	655	764
Sea and inland port facilities [2]	202	310	410	388	367	493	573	524
Sewerage	333	403	405	881	486	650	740	601
Parks and recreation	601	1,044	1,098	945	931	1,146	1,176	1,192
Utilities	2,605	4,232	7,084	5,211	4,319	5,907	4,859	5,936
Water	20	197	174	321	83	83	89	57
Electric	464	296	964	1,089	685	1,826	983	2,738
Gas	–	–	–	–	–	–	–	–
Transit	2,121	3,740	5,945	3,800	3,550	3,998	3,788	3,140
Other	6,098	8,108	9,163	8,589	8,967	8,817	9,272	9,749
Local governments: Total	**77,578**	**140,830**	**171,255**	**179,026**	**183,020**	**193,936**	**214,423**	**235,806**
Percent of direct expenditure	13.5	14.3	14.5	14.4	14.1	14.1	14.4	15.0
By function:								
Education [1]	18,744	46,890	53,087	54,965	57,147	61,882	67,714	73,150
Elementary and secondary	17,669	44,629	50,475	52,261	54,068	58,677	63,733	68,691
Higher education	1,076	2,261	2,612	2,704	3,079	3,205	3,981	4,459
Highways	9,017	14,789	16,804	17,398	18,064	19,346	22,071	26,513
Health and hospitals	2,316	3,274	4,228	4,478	4,433	5,069	5,765	6,717
Natural resources	952	1,589	1,456	1,699	1,873	1,885	3,048	3,731
Housing and community development	3,878	5,324	6,886	7,356	7,542	7,934	7,486	8,871
Air transportation	3,095	6,156	8,221	8,936	8,712	8,545	9,196	9,622
Sea and inland port facilities [2]	722	1,308	3,310	1,410	1,231	1,357	1,567	1,626
Sewerage	8,023	9,690	12,062	13,186	13,684	14,687	16,943	18,176
Parks and recreation	3,276	5,872	8,126	6,921	7,221	8,122	8,909	10,479
Utilities	13,996	20,615	27,455	32,221	30,560	30,888	33,371	35,412
Other	13,559	25,323	29,621	30,454	32,553	34,222	38,352	41,510

– Represents or rounds to zero. [1] Includes other education, not shown separately. [2] Includes terminals.

Source: U.S Census Bureau, "State and Local Government Finances," June 2011, and unpublished data. See also <http://www.census.gov/govs/>.

Table 448. State and Local Governments—Indebtedness: 1990 to 2009

[In billions of dollars (858.0 represents $858,000,000,000). For fiscal year ending in year shown; see text, this section. Local government amounts are estimates subject to sampling variation; see Appendix III and source]

Item	Debt outstanding						Long-term		
	Total	Cash and security holdings	Long-term			Short-term	Net long-term [1]	Debt issued	Debt retired
			Total	Public debt for private purposes	All other				
1990: Total......	**858.0**	**1,490.8**	**838.7**	**294.1**	**544.6**	**19.3**	**474.4**	**108.5**	**64.8**
State...........	318.3	963.3	315.5	154.4	161.1	2.8	125.5	43.5	22.9
Local...........	539.8	527.5	523.2	139.7	383.5	16.5	348.9	65.0	42.0
1995: Total......	**1,115.4**	**2,058.5**	**1,088.3**	**300.6**	**787.7**	**27.0**	**697.3**	**129.3**	**95.1**
State...........	427.2	1,393.9	421.1	176.8	244.4	6.1	205.3	52.6	37.5
Local...........	688.1	664.6	667.2	123.9	543.3	20.9	491.9	76.8	57.6
1998: Total......	**1,283.6**	**2,890.2**	**1,266.3**	**335.8**	**930.5**	**17.3**	**842.6**	**204.4**	**144.6**
State...........	483.1	2,058.6	480.9	202.3	278.7	2.2	237.2	83.4	58.1
Local...........	800.4	831.6	785.4	133.6	651.8	15.1	605.4	120.9	86.5
1999: Total......	**1,369.3**	**3,168.5**	**1,351.4**	**351.1**	**1,000.3**	**17.8**	**907.3**	**229.4**	**153.1**
State...........	510.5	2,265.9	507.8	213.9	293.9	2.7	249.4	83.2	55.6
Local...........	858.8	902.5	843.6	137.2	706.4	15.2	657.9	146.2	97.5
2000: Total......	**1,451.8**	**3,503.7**	**1,427.5**	**372.6**	**1,054.9**	**24.3**	**959.6**	**184.8**	**121.9**
State...........	547.9	2,518.9	541.5	227.3	314.2	6.4	266.9	75.0	44.4
Local...........	903.9	984.8	886.0	145.3	740.7	17.9	692.7	109.8	77.5
2001: Total......	**1,554.0**	**3,592.1**	**1,531.9**	**395.1**	**1,136.8**	**22.1**	**1,038.6**	**199.6**	**130.6**
State...........	576.5	2,537.7	572.8	238.2	334.7	3.7	287.4	81.3	50.7
Local...........	977.5	1,054.3	959.1	157.0	802.1	18.5	751.2	118.3	79.9
2002: Total......	**1,681.4**	**3,650.7**	**1,638.1**	**417.7**	**1,220.5**	**43.2**	**1,121.0**	**262.7**	**161.9**
State...........	636.8	2,555.4	618.2	258.5	359.6	18.6	311.8	104.2	64.9
Local...........	1,044.6	1,095.3	1,020.0	159.2	860.8	24.6	809.2	158.5	97.0
2003: Total......	**1,812.7**	**3,696.1**	**1,772.2**	**431.4**	**1,340.8**	**40.5**	**1,242.7**	**345.8**	**215.2**
State...........	697.9	2,594.2	681.8	267.3	414.5	16.1	366.2	148.8	85.9
Local...........	1,114.7	1,101.9	1,090.4	164.1	926.3	24.3	876.5	196.9	129.3
2004: Total......	**1,976.6**	**4,137.8**	**1,938.3**	**459.3**	**1,479.0**	**38.3**	**(NA)**	**359.8**	**242.1**
State...........	779.5	2,944.9	766.0	279.1	486.9	13.6	(NA)	170.8	107.4
Local...........	1,197.0	1,192.9	1,172.3	180.2	992.1	24.7	(NA)	189.0	134.7
2005: Total......	**2,085.0**	**4,439.2**	**2,054.3**	**483.3**	**1,571.0**	**30.8**	**(NA)**	**323.7**	**224.6**
State...........	810.9	3,153.8	805.3	297.4	507.9	5.6	(NA)	131.6	93.6
Local...........	1,274.2	1,285.4	1,249.0	185.9	1,063.0	25.2	(NA)	192.2	131.1
2006: Total......	**2,204.0**	**4,818.1**	**2,170.8**	**509.6**	**1,661.3**	**33.2**	**(NA)**	**341.9**	**229.5**
State...........	870.0	3,443.2	859.4	318.0	541.5	10.6	(NA)	148.2	95.9
Local...........	1,334.0	1,374.8	1,311.4	191.6	1,119.8	22.6	(NA)	193.7	133.6
2007: Total......	**2,404.7**	**5,457.7**	**2,373.3**	**553.3**	**1,820.0**	**31.4**	**(NA)**	**381.8**	**228.4**
State...........	936.0	3,918.8	929.4	353.9	575.6	6.6	(NA)	161.6	93.4
Local...........	1,468.7	1,538.9	1,443.9	199.5	1,244.4	24.8	(NA)	220.3	135.0
2008: Total......	**2,552.5**	**5,376.1**	**2,507.9**	**593.8**	**1,914.1**	**44.6**	**(NA)**	**372.6**	**243.5**
State...........	1,005.3	3,828.0	991.1	378.9	612.2	14.2	(NA)	151.3	93.0
Local...........	1,547.2	1,548.2	1,516.8	214.9	1,301.9	30.4	(NA)	221.3	150.5
2009: Total......	**2,683.7**	**4,568.4**	**2,648.6**	**610.8**	**2,037.9**	**35.0**	**(NA)**	**368.6**	**258.1**
State...........	1,045.3	3,100.4	1,038.2	393.5	644.7	7.2	(NA)	152.3	108.8
Local...........	1,638.3	1,468.1	1,610.5	217.3	1,393.2	27.9	(NA)	216.2	149.3

NA Not available. [1] Net long-term debt outstanding is the amount of long-term debt held by a government for which no funds have been set aside for its repayment.

Source: U.S. Census Bureau, 1990, Government Finances, Series GF, No. 5, annual; thereafter, "Federal, State, and Local Governments, Government Finance Statistics," Annual Surveys of State and Local Finances, and unpublished data. See also <http://www.census.gov/govs/>.

Table 449. State and Local Governments—Expenditures for Public Works: 2000 to 2009

[In millions of dollars (230,569 represents $230,569,000,000), except percent. Public works include expenditures for current operations and capital outlays on highways, airports, sea and inland port facilities, sewerage, solid waste management, water supply, and mass transit systems. Represents direct expenditures excluding intergovernmental grants]

Item	Total	Highways	Air trans-portation	Sea and inland port facilities	Sewerage	Solid waste manage-ment	Water supply	Mass transit
2000, Total............................	230,569	101,336	13,160	3,141	28,052	17,208	35,789	31,883
State................................	74,974	61,942	1,106	863	955	2,347	354	7,407
Local................................	155,595	39,394	12,054	2,277	27,098	14,861	35,435	24,476
Capital expenditures (percent).....	41.9	55.7	51.0	51.5	36.0	8.9	29.5	30.5
2005, Total............................	296,054	126,350	17,970	3,896	36,478	21,462	45,695	44,203
State................................	94,569	78,316	1,405	1,156	1,118	3,177	319	9,077
Local................................	201,484	48,034	16,565	2,740	35,360	18,285	45,375	35,125
Capital expenditures (percent).....	(NA)	55.9	(NA)	(NA)	38.6	9.3	(NA)	(NA)
2009, Total............................	368,012	152,067	22,861	5,219	47,619	24,390	57,366	58,491
State................................	108,867	90,623	1,651	1,486	1,188	2,639	343	10,936
Local................................	259,145	61,443	21,209	3,733	46,430	21,751	57,023	47,555
Capital expenditures (percent).....	(NA)	56.4	(NA)	(NA)	40.3	10.1	(NA)	(NA)

NA Not available.

Source: U.S. Census Bureau, Federal, State, and Local Governments, Government Finance Statistics, "Annual Surveys of State and Local Government Finances," and unpublished data. See also <http://www.census.gov/govs>.

Table 450. New Security Issues, State and Local Governments: 1990 to 2011

[In billions of dollars (122.9 represents 122,900,000,000)]

Type of issue, issuer, or use	1990	1995	2000	2005	2006	2007	2008	2009	2010	2011
All issues, new and refunding [1].........	122.9	145.7	180.4	409.6	389.5	426.2	394.5	437.1	461.7	315.9
By type of issue:										
General obligation.........................	39.5	57.0	64.5	145.8	115.1	130.5	115.5	142.0	137.4	95.4
Revenue..................................	83.3	88.7	115.9	263.8	274.4	295.7	279.0	295.1	324.3	220.5
By type of issuer:										
State.....................................	15.0	14.7	19.9	31.6	28.3	35.0	35.1	63.5	55.2	119.0
Special district or statutory authority [2].....	75.9	93.5	121.2	298.6	293.4	315.3	286.2	270.8	294.9	568.1
Municipality, county, or township...........	32.0	37.5	39.3	79.4	67.9	75.9	73.2	80.5	86.6	167.8
Issues for new capital.....................	97.9	102.4	154.3	223.8	262.5	275.3	217.4	279.0	280.6	166.4
By use of proceeds:										
Education................................	17.1	24.0	38.7	71.0	70.3	70.9	56.4	60.3	61.4	37.4
Transportation...........................	11.8	11.9	19.7	25.4	30.2	27.9	25.0	23.7	32.3	18.2
Utilities and conservation..................	10.0	9.6	11.9	9.9	7.8	11.4	14.5	14.9	22.6	13.4
Industrial aid.............................	6.6	6.6	7.1	18.6	35.0	38.1	24.9	27.5	36.0	16.1
Other purposes...........................	31.7	30.8	47.3	60.6	72.7	82.9	66.1	105.1	92.3	50.6

[1] Par amounts of long-term issues based on date of sale. [2] Includes school districts.

Source: Board of Governors of the Federal Reserve System, *Statistical Supplement to the Federal Reserve Bulletin*, monthly. Based on data from Securities Data Company. See also <http://www.federalreserve.gov/econresdata/releases/govsecure/current.htm>.

Table 451. State and Local Governments—Total Revenue and Expenditures by State: 2000 to 2009

[In millions of dollars (1,942,328 represents $1,942,328,000,000). For fiscal year ending in year shown; see text, this section. These data cannot be used to compute the deficit or surplus for any single government, as these are estimates for all state and local governments within a state area. For further information, see the "2006 Government Finance and Employment Classification Manual" at <http://http://www.census.gov/govs/pubs/>]

State	Revenue				Expenditures			
	2000	2005	2008	2009	2000	2005	2008	2009
United States	**1,942,328**	**2,528,546**	**2,654,134**	**2,066,666**	**1,746,943**	**2,368,316**	**2,836,852**	**2,966,614**
Alabama	25,726	33,377	30,974	33,107	25,319	31,752	37,893	39,799
Alaska	10,525	11,404	19,334	11,730	8,628	10,027	12,904	14,325
Arizona	27,778	41,057	46,996	42,239	27,293	39,458	52,419	53,571
Arkansas	13,833	18,866	19,615	16,947	12,245	16,682	20,187	20,585
California	270,380	381,059	352,122	232,176	236,645	342,546	415,210	430,703
Colorado	29,603	38,915	47,184	28,777	26,173	35,063	42,533	44,560
Connecticut	25,828	30,490	32,690	31,633	24,011	29,631	35,152	37,463
Delaware	6,224	7,637	8,405	7,436	5,153	7,595	9,073	9,345
District of Columbia	6,383	10,046	11,790	9,608	6,527	8,947	12,957	12,589
Florida	92,402	135,491	148,484	118,273	84,301	130,860	158,513	159,584
Georgia	49,310	60,297	73,036	63,465	43,517	60,730	77,693	76,487
Hawaii	8,488	11,000	11,969	9,551	8,254	10,534	13,378	14,366
Idaho	7,590	10,004	10,493	8,987	6,404	8,915	10,738	11,530
Illinois	80,695	99,670	104,418	75,909	74,727	97,723	115,807	123,150
Indiana	32,716	44,302	46,950	46,199	31,250	42,164	49,121	51,302
Iowa	17,220	23,204	24,961	22,590	17,275	21,486	25,786	28,041
Kansas	16,235	19,990	22,610	20,570	14,419	18,948	23,438	25,448
Kentucky	25,200	28,069	29,426	28,137	21,473	27,308	34,600	36,040
Louisiana	27,109	35,858	44,234	36,815	25,018	32,578	45,992	46,440
Maine	8,554	11,383	10,796	9,557	7,652	10,207	11,194	11,853
Maryland	33,949	45,076	44,555	38,328	30,598	41,373	51,195	54,064
Massachusetts	46,103	62,019	73,622	55,065	44,362	57,862	67,846	71,336
Michigan	70,112	81,138	68,583	66,991	61,506	76,063	83,681	86,192
Minnesota	38,785	45,465	45,653	38,755	35,424	42,936	50,895	54,041
Mississippi	16,672	21,113	23,524	21,570	15,379	20,041	25,164	25,917
Missouri	31,635	41,340	41,796	32,500	27,953	37,186	44,658	47,793
Montana	5,643	7,438	8,515	7,101	4,983	6,412	8,127	8,449
Nebraska	11,650	15,905	17,100	15,864	10,831	14,332	17,607	18,526
Nevada	11,885	18,953	19,991	17,204	11,230	17,405	21,454	22,507
New Hampshire	6,948	8,911	9,627	9,072	6,222	8,679	9,963	10,592
New Jersey	62,331	79,126	85,921	74,417	54,590	78,522	91,705	95,618
New Mexico	13,073	16,656	16,465	13,736	11,195	15,427	19,269	20,734
New York	188,907	234,689	242,029	175,634	171,858	226,867	262,218	276,141
North Carolina	50,542	64,813	76,986	57,301	46,135	60,080	72,042	76,251
North Dakota	4,495	5,239	6,577	5,997	4,041	4,794	5,610	6,003
Ohio	80,074	102,498	100,932	58,560	68,418	91,972	102,739	107,249
Oklahoma	18,760	24,552	26,820	25,654	15,962	22,044	27,470	29,628
Oregon	28,644	32,406	29,209	18,966	24,086	29,084	34,617	37,477
Pennsylvania	80,546	103,692	109,650	72,294	75,624	101,484	111,826	117,221
Rhode Island	7,427	9,731	9,444	7,464	6,432	9,226	10,566	10,660
South Carolina	23,467	33,278	35,998	32,352	23,436	33,012	39,771	41,636
South Dakota	4,277	5,857	5,207	4,614	3,760	4,973	5,868	6,428
Tennessee	33,625	44,888	48,204	40,810	32,010	42,800	49,572	51,373
Texas	120,666	162,806	196,442	159,272	109,634	151,960	189,827	201,572
Utah	14,954	19,183	22,981	16,443	13,044	17,247	22,198	23,899
Vermont	4,019	5,393	6,084	5,485	3,766	5,172	6,066	6,321
Virginia	44,175	56,658	58,106	46,994	38,092	51,529	63,333	64,901
Washington	46,372	57,510	63,026	50,505	41,794	55,800	66,533	71,484
West Virginia	10,760	14,587	13,680	14,093	9,990	12,110	13,620	14,417
Wisconsin	43,003	48,235	41,538	22,494	34,559	43,146	49,303	52,691
Wyoming	7,030	7,269	9,384	7,423	3,743	5,619	7,520	8,314

Source: U.S. Census Bureau, 2009 Annual Survey of State and Local Government Finances, October 2011. See also <http://www.census.gov/govs/>.

Table 452. State and Local Governments—Revenue by State: 2009

[In millions of dollars (2,066,666 represents $2,066,666,000,000). For fiscal year ending in year shown; see text, this section]

State	Total revenue	General revenue — Total	Intergovernmental from federal government	General revenue from own sources	Select taxes — Total[1]	Property	Sales and gross receipt	Individual income	Corporation income	Other taxes	Current charges and miscellaneous revenue — Total[1]	Current charges — Total[1]	Education	Hospitals	Sewerage	Miscellaneous revenue — Total[1]	Interest earnings	Special assessments	Utility and liquor stores	Insurance trust revenue
U.S...	2,066,666	2,413,384	536,760	1,876,624	1,271,356	424,014	433,556	270,518	45,980	97,288	605,268	388,766	115,642	103,975	39,453	216,502	72,938	7,795	151,260	−497,978
AL...	33,107	31,475	8,037	23,437	13,349	2,384	6,289	2,795	494	1,387	10,088	7,723	2,652	3,728	397	2,365	683	26	2,871	−1,239
AK...	11,730	14,073	2,655	11,418	6,359	1,198	530	-	632	3,999	5,059	1,199	199	245	71	3,860	1,070	6	312	−2,655
AZ...	42,239	41,426	11,234	30,192	20,645	7,061	9,561	2,576	592	855	9,547	5,495	2,157	722	666	4,052	1,167	76	3,824	−3,012
AR...	16,947	18,877	5,149	13,729	9,425	1,584	4,822	2,239	346	435	4,303	2,983	1,181	1,000	230	1,321	416	31	868	−2,798
CA...	232,176	317,574	66,665	250,909	169,594	53,879	49,186	44,356	9,536	12,637	81,315	54,718	8,634	15,027	5,670	26,597	8,962	1,585	26,672	−112,070
CO...	28,777	36,896	6,543	30,353	18,748	6,298	6,545	4,403	330	1,172	11,605	7,475	2,856	1,604	700	4,130	1,647	192	2,386	−10,506
CT...	31,633	31,790	5,907	25,883	21,092	8,789	5,429	5,609	444	821	4,790	2,973	1,350	443	317	1,817	706	48	795	−952
DE...	7,436	8,036	1,579	6,458	3,594	632	486	967	213	1,297	2,864	1,406	635	17	146	1,457	291	476	418	−1,018
DC...	9,608	9,753	3,470	6,283	5,013	1,790	1,343	1,126	343	411	1,270	460	23	17	206	810	90	-	904	−1,049
FL...	118,273	134,039	24,548	109,491	68,605	29,537	32,020	-	1,837	5,211	40,886	26,863	4,464	5,950	2,544	14,023	3,936	1,845	9,249	−25,015
GA...	63,465	60,630	13,796	46,834	31,510	10,439	11,687	7,801	695	888	15,325	10,687	2,880	3,624	1,061	4,638	1,109	53	4,558	−1,723
HI...	9,551	11,679	2,459	9,220	6,389	1,316	3,333	1,339	79	323	2,831	1,879	351	480	300	951	212	18	286	−2,413
ID...	8,987	9,646	2,261	7,385	4,521	1,255	1,600	1,176	142	348	2,865	2,110	846	169	315	755	287	49	315	−974
IL...	75,909	97,035	20,006	77,029	56,771	22,764	19,672	9,223	1,710	3,402	20,259	11,913	4,651	1,258	1,018	8,345	3,018	609	3,451	−24,577
IN...	46,199	46,135	9,718	36,417	23,876	7,238	8,993	5,701	839	1,104	12,540	8,042	3,454	2,628	871	4,499	1,468	44	2,028	−1,964
IA...	22,590	24,724	5,953	18,771	11,892	3,946	4,068	2,798	264	816	6,879	5,093	1,794	2,172	378	1,786	560	16	1,128	−3,261
KS...	20,570	21,626	4,021	17,605	11,471	3,816	3,988	2,734	371	565	6,134	4,113	1,374	1,645	315	2,021	737	105	1,232	−2,288
KY...	28,137	29,131	7,953	21,177	13,859	2,854	5,203	4,339	505	958	7,318	4,926	1,710	1,599	448	2,392	1,122	13	1,550	−2,544
LA...	36,815	40,177	13,559	26,617	17,478	3,135	9,218	2,941	613	1,571	9,140	5,360	1,226	2,359	339	3,780	1,581	18	1,332	−4,694
ME...	9,557	11,109	3,238	7,871	5,651	2,182	1,646	1,371	143	310	2,220	1,195	484	78	157	1,025	287	9	123	−1,676
MD...	38,328	45,575	9,533	36,042	26,977	6,876	6,735	10,757	749	1,860	9,064	5,817	2,798	185	753	3,247	836	17	789	−8,036
MA...	55,065	59,670	13,558	46,112	32,271	12,161	6,294	10,599	1,790	1,422	13,841	7,633	2,492	980	1,338	6,208	2,431	23	3,374	−7,979
MI...	66,991	73,340	17,755	55,585	35,914	14,411	12,759	6,274	703	1,766	19,671	13,629	5,497	3,184	1,558	6,042	1,898	223	3,091	−9,440
MN...	38,755	43,419	8,676	34,743	24,024	7,084	7,644	6,948	779	1,568	10,719	6,811	2,454	1,495	648	3,908	1,296	415	2,269	−6,933
MS...	21,570	23,231	8,485	14,745	9,001	2,343	4,240	1,486	324	607	5,744	4,620	1,179	2,722	202	1,125	395	7	1,042	−2,702
MO...	32,500	38,819	9,973	28,846	19,219	5,520	7,095	5,074	327	1,203	9,626	6,356	2,475	1,898	652	3,271	1,427	54	1,901	−8,220
MT...	7,101	7,867	2,326	5,541	3,488	1,275	534	827	164	687	2,053	1,055	488	83	78	998	290	74	185	−951
NE...	15,864	13,895	2,975	10,920	7,352	2,593	2,427	1,602	198	532	3,568	2,376	903	724	136	1,191	480	36	3,360	−1,391
NV...	17,204	18,219	3,041	15,178	10,133	3,519	5,260	-	-	1,353	5,045	3,187	652	616	386	1,858	653	60	970	−1,985
NH...	9,072	9,090	1,866	7,223	4,988	3,211	830	98	493	355	2,236	1,224	629	11	110	1,011	469	5	598	−616
NJ...	74,417	79,663	12,673	66,990	50,920	23,260	11,852	10,664	2,397	2,746	16,070	10,197	3,788	1,334	1,423	5,873	1,703	6	1,848	−7,095
NM...	13,736	17,090	5,316	11,774	6,999	1,227	3,410	959	163	1,241	4,775	2,099	681	767	142	2,676	785	8	493	−3,846
NY...	175,634	229,363	47,935	181,428	135,495	41,140	33,705	44,504	10,458	5,688	45,933	25,561	4,776	7,157	2,001	20,372	6,159	112	14,069	−67,798
NC...	57,301	64,831	16,441	48,389	31,658	8,137	11,103	9,560	901	1,957	16,732	11,994	3,397	5,160	1,109	4,738	1,622	15	4,384	−11,914
ND...	5,997	6,459	1,460	4,999	3,314	770	1,061	370	130	983	1,685	1,021	477	6	48	663	336	76	124	−585
OH...	58,560	86,181	20,759	65,422	43,949	13,080	14,032	12,603	628	3,606	21,473	14,035	5,894	3,269	1,792	7,438	2,765	242	3,321	−30,941
OK...	25,654	26,064	6,785	19,278	12,237	2,206	4,927	2,545	343	2,216	7,042	4,614	1,918	1,303	286	2,427	703	19	1,479	−1,888
OR...	18,966	27,925	6,878	21,046	12,474	4,441	1,215	5,165	287	1,366	8,573	5,263	1,566	1,328	778	3,310	760	84	1,702	−10,661
PA...	72,294	94,925	21,002	73,923	51,916	15,505	15,813	13,421	1,753	5,427	22,005	14,027	5,251	2,065	1,949	7,978	2,846	105	4,241	−26,871
RI...	7,464	9,235	2,462	6,773	4,766	2,128	1,398	961	108	170	2,007	970	487	5	97	1,037	396	8	207	−1,978
SC...	32,352	32,542	8,116	24,426	13,087	4,423	4,541	2,812	249	1,062	11,338	8,594	2,285	4,539	475	2,745	878	60	3,124	−3,314
SD...	4,614	5,696	1,688	4,007	2,555	892	1,382	-	49	232	1,453	758	363	44	66	695	317	24	295	−1,377
TN...	40,810	38,065	9,106	28,959	17,887	4,698	10,374	222	816	1,777	11,072	7,315	2,013	2,708	604	3,757	840	101	9,175	−6,430
TX...	159,272	167,101	38,337	128,764	86,232	36,219	39,885	-	-	10,129	42,532	26,846	8,796	7,799	2,928	15,686	7,243	288	11,484	−19,313
UT...	16,443	18,688	4,329	14,359	8,729	2,323	3,296	2,320	246	544	5,630	3,881	1,295	1,120	301	1,749	555	78	2,066	−4,311

See footnotes at end of table.

Table 452. State and Local Governments—Revenue by State: 2009-Continued.

See headnote on page 292.

State	Total revenue	General revenue Total	Intergovernmental from federal government Total	General revenue from own sources Total	Select taxes Total[1]	Property	Sales and gross receipt	Individual income	Corporation income	Other taxes	Current charges and miscellaneous revenue Total	Current charges Total[1]	Education	Hospitals	Sewerage	Miscellaneous revenue Total[1]	Interest earnings	Special assessments	Utility and liquor stores	Insurance trust revenue
VT...	5,485	5,709	1,639	4,070	2,904	1,284	836	533	87	164	1,166	744	522	-	59	422	172	4	254	-478
VA...	46,994	55,917	8,588	47,329	31,464	11,274	8,038	9,194	633	2,325	15,865	10,637	3,725	2,911	1,042	5,227	1,751	131	2,355	-11,279
WA...	50,505	52,714	10,992	41,722	26,981	8,107	16,486	-	-	2,387	14,741	10,516	2,704	2,918	1,593	4,225	1,463	182	6,712	-8,920
WV...	14,093	13,914	3,897	10,017	6,407	1,307	2,346	1,557	421	776	3,611	2,129	859	352	205	1,481	223	13	266	-87
WI...	22,494	43,834	9,191	34,643	24,125	9,233	7,039	5,971	657	1,226	10,518	6,955	2,524	1,053	644	3,563	1,342	97	1,539	-22,879
WY...	7,423	8,517	2,227	6,290	4,045	1,263	1,381	-	-	1,400	2,245	1,288	204	794	50	957	557	9	83	-1,335

- Represents or rounds to zero. [1] Includes items not shown separately.

Source: U.S. Census Bureau, Federal, State and Local Governments, "Annual Survey of State and Local Government Finances," October 2011, <http://www.census.gov/govs>.

State and Local Government Finances and Employment   293

Table 453. State and Local Governments—Expenditures and Debt by State: 2009

[In millions of dollars (2,966,614 represents $2,966,614,000,000), except as indicated. For fiscal year ending in year shown; see text, this section]

State	Total expenditures	General expenditures — Total [1]	Direct general expenditures — Total [1]	Education	Public welfare	Health	Hospitals	Highways	Police protection	Corrections	Natural resources	Parks and recreation	Housing and community development	Sewerage	Solid waste	Governmental administration	Interest on general debt	Other direct general expenditures	Utility and liquor store expenditures	Insurance trust expenditures	Total debt outstanding
U.S.	2,966,614	2,479,895	2,475,076	850,674	431,098	81,939	136,461	152,067	92,999	74,503	30,563	40,578	47,489	47,619	24,390	127,424	103,478	233,794	211,239	275,479	2,683,668
AL	39,799	33,966	33,966	13,362	5,432	899	3,626	2,230	1,070	715	285	477	439	290	260	1,405	1,050	2,425	2,858	2,975	25,966
AK	14,325	12,434	12,434	3,120	1,520	212	297	1,625	275	264	315	147	275	88	89	825	417	2,967	557	1,334	10,253
AZ	53,571	43,939	43,939	13,998	8,040	1,921	983	3,109	2,156	1,844	679	1,061	549	1,184	399	2,442	1,818	3,757	5,731	3,901	48,333
AR	20,585	18,014	18,014	7,378	3,844	243	1,028	1,207	519	429	232	189	163	304	193	869	465	949	918	1,653	12,684
CA	430,703	345,162	341,552	104,093	52,644	13,375	19,921	14,818	16,221	14,349	5,988	5,756	9,908	6,676	4,102	21,985	14,229	37,485	38,681	46,860	373,694
CO	44,560	36,506	36,501	12,752	4,170	1,255	2,070	2,282	1,450	1,207	377	1,098	670	915	126	2,419	1,922	3,788	3,596	4,459	50,415
CT	37,463	31,905	31,905	11,521	5,663	834	1,437	1,484	988	725	135	264	694	453	404	1,780	1,765	3,758	1,352	4,207	38,058
DE	9,345	8,182	8,181	2,934	1,507	412	147	623	290	273	97	77	128	174	91	596	358	562	528	635	8,232
DC	12,589	10,138	10,138	2,217	2,649	434	147	403	573	262	28	234	521	301	157	609	412	1,190	2,092	359	9,720
FL	159,584	137,890	137,890	39,432	19,866	4,773	8,092	9,664	7,061	4,545	4,618	3,025	2,309	2,803	2,423	7,383	5,075	16,822	11,517	10,177	147,178
GA	76,487	64,321	64,321	25,834	9,677	2,068	4,316	3,245	2,315	2,264	482	1,049	1,203	1,421	691	3,436	1,472	4,847	6,312	5,855	52,977
HI	14,366	12,639	12,638	3,557	1,763	701	569	727	368	231	128	294	234	361	290	784	621	2,011	580	1,147	11,474
ID	11,530	10,180	10,180	3,304	1,791	212	850	870	359	334	232	138	61	189	170	696	275	700	338	1,011	5,858
IL	123,150	100,864	100,864	34,600	17,514	3,063	2,448	7,525	4,301	1,968	570	2,815	1,981	1,664	514	4,692	5,618	11,591	7,236	15,050	128,100
IN	51,302	45,456	45,441	16,586	7,899	782	3,141	2,883	1,192	1,054	372	846	705	1,029	250	1,893	1,791	5,018	2,472	3,374	51,081
IA	28,041	24,836	24,836	9,209	4,228	520	2,505	2,130	898	478	624	323	211	405	189	1,010	567	1,839	1,213	1,992	15,465
KS	25,448	22,365	22,365	8,426	3,322	460	1,711	1,854	695	478	295	303	207	381	143	1,093	1,026	1,970	1,332	1,750	24,176
KY	36,040	30,314	30,313	10,719	6,781	960	1,747	2,145	647	711	335	294	355	506	201	1,384	1,730	1,798	1,875	3,852	40,843
LA	46,440	41,232	41,223	12,223	6,072	871	3,253	3,494	1,353	1,262	829	669	2,531	542	362	2,102	1,671	3,998	1,566	3,642	34,160
ME	11,853	10,825	10,813	3,254	2,854	581	141	764	242	215	199	71	237	104	125	502	363	1,091	139	888	7,765
MD	54,064	48,004	48,004	17,365	8,407	1,823	540	3,116	1,980	1,780	777	705	1,221	777	606	2,669	1,670	4,570	1,669	4,390	38,751
MA	71,336	58,228	58,026	17,969	12,953	1,149	1,874	2,553	1,922	1,347	384	402	1,857	1,037	406	2,751	4,264	7,161	4,891	8,217	97,612
MI	86,192	72,805	72,805	28,119	12,480	3,599	3,443	3,778	2,470	2,436	400	848	975	1,959	532	2,908	2,965	5,895	3,910	9,477	77,976
MN	54,041	46,401	46,401	15,964	11,020	3,064	1,861	3,452	1,647	907	677	1,166	768	650	410	2,213	1,754	2,809	2,690	4,951	43,426
MS	25,917	23,014	23,014	7,415	4,861	445	3,061	1,542	610	509	281	235	222	206	150	927	472	2,078	1,027	1,877	13,444
MO	47,793	40,689	40,689	14,322	7,128	1,646	2,642	3,070	1,485	898	415	918	576	792	167	1,536	1,652	3,443	2,755	4,350	42,346
MT	8,449	7,447	7,446	2,567	1,255	222	120	812	232	229	255	86	112	103	85	537	223	607	227	775	6,338
NE	18,526	13,890	13,857	5,483	2,212	395	748	1,242	368	342	268	205	184	174	87	598	328	1,223	3,944	692	13,373
NV	22,507	18,805	18,804	5,829	2,130	362	1,006	1,714	1,152	804	339	774	263	272	27	1,582	889	1,662	1,603	2,099	25,901
NH	10,592	9,352	9,352	3,486	1,920	129	55	695	305	180	71	111	186	104	135	502	497	975	545	694	11,025
NJ	95,618	80,758	80,758	31,645	13,348	1,663	2,498	3,702	3,133	2,145	564	1,165	1,309	1,434	1,143	3,608	3,594	9,807	3,820	11,040	92,624
NM	20,734	18,452	18,452	6,400	3,975	555	985	1,356	614	571	300	314	161	179	161	1,076	485	1,321	708	1,574	14,330
NY	276,141	221,572	220,886	68,857	44,483	6,945	14,203	10,196	8,472	5,816	734	3,025	4,092	4,297	2,848	10,471	10,696	25,750	27,774	26,795	293,510
NC	76,251	65,312	65,312	23,310	11,020	3,064	6,204	3,257	2,186	1,833	859	1,184	856	1,124	731	2,780	1,995	4,908	4,668	6,271	50,178
ND	6,003	5,407	5,407	1,909	856	93	18	676	131	92	199	111	68	153	46	257	227	670	163	432	4,071
OH	107,249	88,433	88,418	31,440	17,643	3,955	4,975	3,855	3,274	2,033	400	1,142	2,204	2,438	490	4,841	3,325	6,403	3,911	14,905	73,943
OK	29,628	25,335	25,288	9,585	5,105	746	1,300	2,109	782	715	244	382	252	349	268	1,316	672	1,462	1,940	2,353	18,357
OR	37,477	30,395	30,395	10,595	4,672	930	1,504	1,861	1,044	1,031	558	590	529	962	127	1,799	1,168	3,026	2,218	4,863	33,249
PA	117,221	98,063	97,905	34,143	21,502	4,212	2,585	8,375	2,908	3,050	731	975	1,763	1,689	721	5,682	4,662	4,908	5,847	13,311	117,684
RI	10,660	8,943	8,918	2,931	2,111	186	65	330	330	197	41	47	207	129	88	586	548	1,120	325	1,392	11,738
SC	41,636	34,303	34,303	12,488	6,160	1,173	4,273	1,340	983	780	250	446	435	455	368	1,939	1,266	1,948	4,251	3,082	35,550
SD	6,428	5,710	5,710	1,926	901	157	114	711	153	161	161	159	107	82	41	365	198	474	321	396	5,494
TN	51,373	39,823	39,823	12,653	8,293	1,649	3,252	2,555	1,507	988	413	538	703	617	1,243	1,978	1,199	3,137	9,115	2,434	36,657
TX	201,572	172,357	172,357	70,630	26,259	4,123	11,155	10,420	6,097	5,548	1,625	2,489	2,017	3,127	1,243	6,248	8,503	12,873	15,375	13,840	228,282
UT	23,899	19,710	19,710	7,836	2,529	553	979	1,667	633	517	231	511	303	391	145	1,422	500	1,493	2,744	1,445	17,739

See footnotes at end of table.

Table 453. State and Local Governments—Expenditures and Debt by State: 2009-Continued.

See headnote on page 294.

State	Total expendi-tures	General expenditures Total [1]	Direct general expenditures Total [1]	Educa-tion	Public welfare	Health	Hospi-tals	High-ways	Police protec-tion	Correc-tions	Natural resour-ces	Parks and recre-ation	Hous-ing and com-munity devel-opment	Sewer-age	Solid waste	Govern-mental adminis-tration	Inter-est on general debt	Other direct general expendi-tures	Utility and liquor store expendi-tures	Insur-ance trust expendi-tures	Total debt out-standing
VT....	6,321	5,657	5,657	2,273	1,360	171	20	459	141	119	76	44	125	73	47	253	194	301	317	347	4,534
VA....	64,901	57,801	57,799	22,402	8,618	1,454	3,244	3,408	2,058	2,166	262	976	941	1,096	664	3,174	2,100	5,237	2,680	4,419	59,018
WA....	71,484	56,509	56,504	19,082	8,305	2,335	4,135	3,849	1,470	1,717	1,022	987	1,192	1,976	589	2,354	2,259	5,231	8,452	6,523	66,757
WV....	14,417	13,069	13,069	4,893	2,830	288	376	1,282	350	288	186	159	111	237	69	817	380	804	309	1,040	9,824
WI....	52,691	45,023	45,023	16,166	8,848	1,795	1,142	3,760	1,631	1,519	768	592	341	892	400	1,786	2,054	3,329	1,836	5,831	41,212
WY....	8,314	7,399	7,461	2,454	730	390	862	725	233	222	252	163	25	88	75	545	93	605	310	543	2,295

[1] Includes items not shown separately.

Source: U.S. Census Bureau; Federal, State and Local Governments, "Annual Survey of State and Local Government Finances," October 2011. See also <http://www.census.gov/govs/>.

Table 454. State Resources, Expenditures, and Balances: 2010 and 2011

[In millions of dollars (1,621,370 represents $1,621,370,000,000). For fiscal year ending in year shown; see text; this section. General funds exclude special funds earmarked for particular purposes, such as highway trust funds and federal funds; they support most on-going broad-based state services, and are available for appropriation to support any governmental activity. Minus sign (–) indicates deficit]

State	Total, 2010 actual	Expenditures by fund source 2011[1] estimated Total[2]	General fund	Federal fund	State general fund Resources[3,4] 2010	2011[1]	Expenditures[4] 2010	2011[1]	Balance[5,6] 2010	2011[1]
United States......	**1,621,370**	**1,687,096**	**636,257**	**574,760**	**638,360**	**676,870**	**623,401**	**648,095**	**8,014**	**18,925**
Alabama..............	20,584	20,843	6,507	9,067	6,751	6,981	7,457	7,356	72	38
Alaska...............	9,759	13,923	8,878	3,174	5,635	5,307	6,603	6,075	-1,429	-785
Arizona..............	27,680	29,264	8,676	10,499	7,846	8,376	7,852	8,372	-6	3
Arkansas.............	19,922	20,333	4,442	7,026	4,323	4,479	4,323	4,479	0	0
California............	206,089	227,353	91,480	91,459	81,894	90,012	87,237	91,480	-5,342	-1,206
Colorado.............	31,064	28,462	6,984	8,813	6,853	7,373	6,716	6,921	137	451
Connecticut...........	19,694	20,545	11,969	2,520	17,689	18,083	17,208	17,845	481	238
Delaware.............	8,720	8,412	3,271	1,848	3,614	4,069	3,077	3,271	537	798
Florida..............	62,049	70,518	24,046	24,999	22,796	24,487	21,223	24,054	1,573	433
Georgia..............	40,441	39,166	15,954	14,217	17,110	18,195	15,971	17,064	1,138	1,131
Hawaii...............	10,948	11,222	4,969	2,554	4,816	5,095	4,838	4,969	-22	126
Idaho................	6,393	7,050	2,388	3,014	2,336	2,519	2,507	2,384	0	69
Illinois..............	60,653	56,222	22,902	16,185	32,609	36,710	25,165	25,933	453	971
Indiana..............	26,662	27,042	13,037	10,596	13,656	14,161	12,877	13,050	831	1,124
Iowa.................	17,637	18,538	5,348	6,088	5,634	5,834	5,298	5,283	287	482
Kansas...............	14,045	14,778	5,727	3,865	5,241	5,763	5,268	5,727	-27	36
Kentucky.............	25,941	25,528	8,787	9,763	8,604	9,136	8,452	8,789	80	290
Louisiana............	29,134	30,174	7,951	12,406	8,575	7,768	8,683	7,731	-108	-13
Maine................	8,257	8,171	2,858	3,000	2,921	2,990	2,849	2,873	0	19
Maryland.............	33,104	34,795	13,262	10,621	13,773	14,228	13,429	13,238	344	990
Massachusetts.......	50,424	51,761	28,468	3,739	31,327	33,978	30,424	32,078	903	1,901
Michigan.............	47,758	50,020	8,386	22,415	7,892	8,891	7,705	8,630	187	260
Minnesota............	30,133	32,082	16,478	9,468	15,067	16,265	14,627	15,540	440	725
Mississippi..........	18,283	19,777	4,344	9,578	4,499	4,605	4,320	4,528	5	76
Missouri.............	25,526	24,728	7,616	10,294	7,755	8,084	7,570	7,705	185	379
Montana..............	6,049	6,164	1,701	2,380	2,026	2,092	1,716	1,747	311	340
Nebraska.............	9,606	9,802	3,322	3,220	3,610	3,824	3,313	3,322	297	502
Nevada...............	8,284	8,549	3,401	2,642	3,362	3,609	3,212	3,337	314	225
New Hampshire......	5,466	5,435	1,322	1,938	1,436	1,462	1,405	1,302	75	36
New Jersey..........	47,764	48,235	29,322	13,518	29,284	29,718	28,480	29,025	804	693
New Mexico.........	15,246	14,829	5,203	5,716	5,930	5,480	5,358	5,203	572	277
New York............	128,937	132,765	53,313	44,707	54,504	56,749	52,202	55,373	2,302	1,376
North Carolina.......	48,745	51,124	18,503	17,605	18,750	19,394	18,513	18,503	237	584
North Dakota........	4,845	4,974	1,585	1,801	1,898	2,710	1,585	1,651	313	997
Ohio.................	57,640	60,314	27,649	14,431	25,685	28,274	25,175	27,429	510	845
Oklahoma.............	21,607	22,067	6,475	10,048	5,163	5,759	5,119	5,417	42	93
Oregon...............	32,554	33,455	6,107	9,334	5,982	6,142	6,371	6,107	-390	35
Pennsylvania.........	68,108	70,089	25,142	29,977	27,346	29,213	27,641	28,321	-294	1,073
Rhode Island.........	7,810	8,292	2,974	3,085	2,881	3,021	2,864	2,959	18	65
South Carolina.......	20,302	25,691	5,080	12,844	5,363	5,879	5,117	5,167	245	712
South Dakota........	3,820	3,781	1,148	1,671	1,132	1,148	1,132	1,148	0	0
Tennessee............	28,449	30,904	11,227	13,930	10,004	11,189	9,451	10,508	240	372
Texas................	93,121	94,443	40,541	35,901	40,916	41,641	39,465	41,149	1,533	1,100
Utah.................	14,991	13,372	4,710	3,954	4,435	4,724	4,441	4,710	-28	0
Vermont..............	4,667	4,827	822	1,864	1,090	1,228	1,088	1,162	0	0
Virginia..............	40,773	42,470	16,435	9,832	14,919	15,723	14,787	15,458	132	265
Washington...........	33,587	32,430	14,825	8,543	14,475	14,739	15,036	14,823	-561	-84
West Virginia.........	20,356	21,492	3,793	4,638	4,240	4,616	3,677	3,772	552	793
Wisconsin............	40,086	42,844	13,565	12,236	12,963	13,580	12,824	13,565	71	86
Wyoming.............	7,657	8,041	3,364	1,737	1,750	1,567	1,750	1,562	0	5

[1] Estimated. [2] Includes bonds and other state funds, not shown separately. [3] Includes funds budgeted, adjustments, and balances from previous year. [4] May or may not include budget stabilization fund transfers, depending on state accounting practices. [5] Resources less expenditures, minus adjustments. [6] Ending balance is held in a budget stabilization fund.

Source: National Association of State Budget Officers, Washington, DC, *2010 State Expenditure Report*, and *Fiscal Survey of the States*, semiannual (copyright), <http://www.nasbo.org>.

Table 455. Estimated State and Local Taxes Paid by a Family of Three for Largest City in Selected States: 2010

[Data based on average family of three (two wage earners and one school age child) owning their own home and living in a city where taxes apply. Comprises state and local sales, income, auto, and real estate taxes. For definition of median, see Guide to Tabular Presentation]

City	Total taxes paid by gross family income level (dollars)					Total taxes paid as percent of income				
	$25,000	$50,000	$75,000	$100,000	$150,000	$25,000	$50,000	$75,000	$100,000	$150,000
Albuquerque, NM.......	2,521	4,090	6,079	7,980	11,386	10.1	8.2	8.1	8.0	7.6
Anchorage, AK.........	2,236	2,438	2,971	3,343	4,133	8.9	4.9	4.0	3.3	2.8
Atlanta, GA...........	3,391	4,962	7,607	10,077	14,861	13.6	9.9	10.1	10.1	9.9
Baltimore, MD.........	2,148	4,890	7,471	10,083	15,180	8.6	9.8	10.0	10.1	10.1
Boston, MA...........	3,009	5,266	7,233	8,919	12,426	12.0	10.5	9.6	8.9	8.3
Charlotte, NC.........	3,134	4,767	7,455	10,031	15,002	12.5	9.5	9.9	10.0	10.0
Chicago, IL...........	3,154	5,068	6,830	8,402	11,152	12.6	10.1	9.1	8.4	7.4
Columbus, OH.........	2,968	5,793	8,222	10,838	15,928	11.9	11.6	11.0	10.8	10.6
Denver, CO...........	2,770	3,603	5,447	7,175	10,693	11.1	7.2	7.3	7.2	7.1
Detroit, MI...........	2,869	5,960	8,502	11,354	16,109	11.5	11.9	11.3	11.4	10.7
Honolulu, HI..........	3,160	3,184	5,211	7,341	11,506	12.6	6.4	6.9	7.3	7.7
Houston, TX..........	2,451	3,051	4,188	5,028	6,310	9.8	6.1	5.6	5.0	4.2
Indianapolis, IN.......	3,258	4,749	6,833	8,913	12,787	13.0	9.5	9.1	8.9	8.5
Jacksonville, FL.......	2,627	2,751	3,693	4,466	5,797	10.5	5.5	4.9	4.5	3.9
Kansas City, MO.......	3,246	5,067	7,906	10,037	14,741	13.0	10.1	10.5	10.0	9.8
Las Vegas, NV........	2,421	3,229	4,066	4,796	5,836	9.7	6.5	5.4	4.8	3.9
Los Angeles, CA.......	2,788	5,409	7,704	9,740	15,539	11.2	10.8	10.3	9.7	10.4
Memphis, TN..........	2,725	3,054	4,206	4,945	6,092	10.9	6.1	5.6	4.9	4.1
Milwaukee, WI.........	2,470	5,407	7,686	10,207	14,698	9.9	10.8	10.2	10.2	9.8
New Orleans, LA.......	2,684	3,272	4,910	6,507	9,338	10.7	6.5	6.5	6.5	6.2
New York City, NY.....	2,909	4,857	7,833	10,984	18,077	11.6	9.7	10.4	11.0	12.1
Oklahoma City, OK.....	2,496	3,722	5,787	7,748	11,419	10.0	7.4	7.7	7.7	7.6
Omaha, NE...........	2,406	4,484	6,766	9,396	14,267	9.6	9.0	9.0	9.4	9.5
Philadelphia, PA.......	4,112	6,928	9,378	11,749	16,302	16.4	13.9	12.5	11.7	10.9
Phoenix, AZ..........	3,327	3,683	5,143	6,857	9,748	13.3	7.4	6.9	6.9	6.5
Portland, OR..........	2,497	4,484	6,806	9,117	14,100	10.0	9.0	9.1	9.1	9.4
Seattle, WA..........	2,825	4,020	5,173	5,651	6,502	11.3	8.0	6.9	5.7	4.3
Virginia Beach, VA....	2,427	3,684	5,782	7,637	11,205	9.7	7.4	7.7	7.6	7.5
Washington, DC........	2,549	3,647	6,055	8,345	13,330	10.2	7.3	8.1	8.3	8.9
Wichita, KS...........	2,471	3,595	6,071	8,562	13,115	9.9	7.2	8.1	8.6	8.7
Average [1]...........	2,727	4,414	6,471	8,402	12,244	10.9	8.8	8.6	8.4	8.2
Median [1]............	2,684	4,484	6,766	8,586	12,947	10.7	9.0	9.0	8.6	8.6

[1] Based on selected cities and District of Columbia. For complete list of cities, see Table 456.

Source: Government of the District of Columbia, Office of the Chief Financial Officer, *Tax Rates and Tax Burdens in the District of Columbia - A Nationwide Comparison*, annual. See also <http://cfo.dc.gov/>.

Table 456. Residential Property Tax Rates for Largest City in Each State: 2010

[The real property tax is a function of housing values, real estate tax rates, assessment levels, homeowner exemptions and credits. Effective rate is the amount each jurisdiction considers based upon assessment level used. Assessment level is ratio of assessed value to assumed market value. Nominal rates represent the "announced" rates levied by the jurisdiction]

City	Effective tax rate per $100		Assessment level (percent)	Nominal rate per $100	City	Effective tax rate per $100		Assessment level (percent)	Nominal rate per $100
	Rank	Rate				Rank	Rate		
Providence, RI.........	1	3.04	100.0	3.04	Kansas City, MO........	27	8.56	19.0	1.63
Louisville, KY..........	2	2.86	100.0	2.86	Anchorage, AL.........	28	1.57	96.0	1.51
Indianapolis, IN........	3	2.84	100.0	2.84	Little Rock, AR.........	29	7.05	20.0	1.41
Bridgeport, CT.........	4	3.96	70.0	2.77	Wichita, KS............	30	12.20	11.5	1.40
Philadelphia, PA.......	5	8.26	32.0	2.64	New Orleans, LA.......	31	13.98	10.0	1.40
Detroit, MI...........	6	6.73	38.7	2.60	Albuquerque, NM.......	32	4.11	33.3	1.37
Columbus, OH.........	7	7.36	35.0	2.58	Sioux Falls, SD........	33	1.58	85.0	1.34
Salt Lake City, UT......	8	2.53	100.0	2.53	Oklahoma City, OK.....	34	11.43	11.0	1.26
Milwaukee, WI.........	9	2.53	100.0	2.53	Minneapolis, MN.......	35	1.27	96.8	1.23
Houston, TX..........	10	2.52	100.0	2.52	Portland, OR..........	36	2.08	57.6	1.20
Baltimore, MD.........	11	2.27	100.0	2.27	Boston, MA...........	37	1.19	100.0	1.19
Omaha, NE...........	12	2.18	96.0	2.09	Charlotte, NC..........	38	1.30	88.9	1.15
Burlington, VT.........	13	2.03	100.0	2.03	Las Vegas, NV.........	39	3.29	35.0	1.15
Columbia, SC..........	14	48.93	4.0	1.96	Los Angeles, CA.......	40	1.12	100.0	1.12
Jacksonville, FL.......	15	1.83	100.0	1.83	Phoenix, AZ..........	41	9.73	10.0	0.97
Portland, ME..........	16	1.83	100.0	1.83	Washington, DC........	42	0.85	100.0	0.85
Wilmington, DE........	17	3.83	47.2	1.81	Seattle, WA..........	43	1.01	83.9	0.85
Billings, MT...........	18	6.40	28.2	1.81	Charleston, WV........	44	1.40	60.0	0.84
Memphis, TN..........	19	7.22	25.0	1.80	Virginia Beach, VA.....	45	0.89	92.9	0.83
Newark, NJ...........	20	3.18	56.2	1.79	Birmingham, AL........	46	6.95	10.0	0.70
Manchester, NH.......	21	1.79	100.0	1.79	Cheyenne, WY........	47	7.10	9.5	0.67
Atlanta, GA...........	22	4.42	40.0	1.77	New York City, NY......	48	17.36	3.7	0.64
Boise, ID.............	23	1.72	98.9	1.70	Denver, CO..........	49	7.04	8.0	0.56
Des Moines, IA........	24	3.45	48.5	1.67	Chicago, IL............	50	4.73	10.0	0.47
Jackson, MS..........	25	16.71	10.0	1.67	Honolulu, HI..........	51	0.34	100.0	0.34
Fargo, ND............	26	38.51	4.3	1.67	Unweighted average...	(X)	6.22	58.6	1.62
					Median................	(X)	3.18	57.6	1.67

X Not applicable.

Source: Government of the District of Columbia, Office of the Chief Financial Officer, *Tax Rates and Tax Burdens in the District of Columbia - A Nationwide Comparison,* annual. See also <http://cfo.dc.gov/>.

Table 457. Gross Revenue From Parimutuel and Amusement Taxes and Lotteries by State: 2007 to 2009

[In millions of dollars (57,767.7 represents $57,767,700,000). For fiscal years; see text, this section]

State	2007, total gross revenue	2008, total gross revenue	2009 Total gross revenue	2009 Amuse-ment taxes [1]	2009 Pari-mutuel taxes	2009 Lottery revenue Total [2]	2009 Lottery revenue Apportionment of funds Prizes	2009 Lottery revenue Apportionment of funds Adminis-tration	2009 Lottery revenue Apportionment of funds Proceeds available from ticket sales
United States	**57,767.7**	**59,553.5**	**58,933.1**	**6,424.2**	**181.2**	**52,327.6**	**32,211.5**	**2,444.2**	**17,671.8**
Alabama	3.1	2.8	2.5	0.1	2.4	-	-	-	-
Alaska	2.4	9.5	9.2	9.2	(X)	-	-	-	-
Arizona	432.1	442.6	452.8	0.5	0.3	452.0	282.5	42.5	127.0
Arkansas	8.1	12.0	12.4	7.1	5.3	-	-	-	-
California	3,123.3	2,872.4	2,777.9	0.0	30.7	2,747.1	1,556.1	175.1	1,015.9
Colorado	568.9	578.4	553.2	95.7	0.6	456.9	301.5	37.9	117.5
Connecticut	1,377.8	1,402.3	1,388.4	445.3	7.6	935.5	604.7	39.3	291.5
Delaware	444.8	438.5	429.8	(X)	0.1	429.7	66.8	48.3	314.6
Florida	3,923.4	4,090.3	3,851.8	114.1	14.1	3,723.6	2,340.4	130.4	1,252.9
Georgia	2,957.8	3,045.6	3,158.2	(X)	(X)	3,158.2	2,148.7	148.4	861.1
Hawaii	(X)	(X)	(X)	(X)	(X)	-	-	-	-
Idaho	121.9	128.0	130.6	(X)	1.3	129.2	85.0	5.3	38.9
Illinois	2,839.6	2,798.9	2,659.5	575.5	6.9	2,077.2	1,225.9	65.1	786.2
Indiana	1,557.2	1,585.2	1,567.1	881.0	4.0	682.2	453.2	50.9	178.0
Iowa	499.2	532.1	521.7	289.9	3.8	228.0	138.4	30.8	58.9
Kansas	229.3	225.3	211.8	0.5	0.3	211.0	130.9	20.6	59.5
Kentucky	702.5	734.0	719.4	0.2	4.4	714.8	470.4	38.3	206.1
Louisiana	1,065.3	1,100.1	1,078.9	715.5	6.0	357.5	193.3	30.8	133.3
Maine	235.6	237.7	226.2	26.2	2.9	197.1	131.5	14.7	50.9
Maryland	1,474.7	1,571.8	1,597.7	19.9	1.6	1,576.2	1,025.9	58.7	491.6
Massachusetts	4,196.0	4,424.5	4,168.5	3.4	2.8	4,162.4	3,217.8	99.6	845.0
Michigan	2,511.1	2,468.1	2,506.3	121.4	7.5	2,377.4	1,436.4	74.8	866.2
Minnesota	429.6	455.2	467.5	37.8	0.7	429.0	310.4	24.0	94.7
Mississippi	185.8	194.0	172.4	172.4	(X)	-	-	-	-
Missouri	1,217.0	1,280.4	1,279.4	370.4	(X)	908.9	629.3	34.1	245.6
Montana	94.4	104.5	103.9	62.5	0.1	41.3	23.1	8.0	10.2
Nebraska	113.1	120.4	122.0	6.2	0.2	115.6	71.9	15.1	28.6
Nevada	1,089.1	1,047.8	905.7	905.7	(X)	-	-	-	-
New Hampshire	253.0	250.0	229.1	0.3	2.0	226.9	142.1	16.5	68.3
New Jersey	2,669.8	2,810.1	2,739.5	375.7	(X)	2,363.8	1,421.3	71.9	870.6
New Mexico	214.9	201.2	197.4	62.2	0.6	134.6	79.9	14.0	40.7
New York	6,608.5	6,871.8	6,849.5	0.8	27.9	6,820.8	4,003.3	311.2	2,506.4
North Carolina	839.5	1,017.0	1,217.4	14.7	(X)	1,202.7	741.3	54.8	406.6
North Dakota	30.8	30.8	31.4	10.4	0.3	20.7	11.3	3.7	5.7
Ohio	2,131.6	2,191.9	2,277.2	(X)	9.5	2,267.6	1,459.0	122.5	686.1
Oklahoma	214.6	213.6	208.8	14.0	1.6	193.2	95.9	13.5	83.7
Oregon	971.5	997.0	889.6	0.1	2.1	887.4	211.9	80.1	595.3
Pennsylvania	3,103.4	3,655.8	3,884.9	1,006.6	13.9	2,864.4	1,852.5	74.1	937.8
Rhode Island	475.1	510.5	496.8	(X)	2.5	494.3	144.9	9.1	340.4
South Carolina	956.2	960.0	967.4	33.5	(X)	933.9	633.2	42.5	258.1
South Dakota	157.1	161.1	157.1	8.0	0.3	148.8	23.3	7.1	118.4
Tennessee	989.2	995.2	1,016.4	(X)	(X)	1,016.4	705.8	50.2	260.3
Texas	3,618.3	3,534.0	3,579.9	37.3	10.6	3,532.0	2,299.8	192.2	1,040.1
Utah	(X)	(X)	(X)	(X)	(X)	-	-	-	-
Vermont	98.4	96.0	90.3	(X)	(X)	90.3	60.7	8.5	21.0
Virginia	1,286.0	1,386.5	1,288.8	.1	(X)	1,288.7	781.0	71.8	435.9
Washington	463.5	492.0	459.9	.1	2.9	457.0	301.3	42.4	113.3
West Virginia	823.0	813.3	802.3	(X)	2.4	799.9	119.4	33.2	647.3
Wisconsin	460.0	463.1	474.4	.3	.7	473.4	279.6	32.2	161.7
Wyoming	.2	.2	.2	(X)	.2	-	-	-	-

– Represents or rounds to zero. X Not applicable. [1] Represents nonlicense taxes. [2] Excludes commissions.

Source: U.S. Census Bureau, "Federal, State and Local Governments: State Government Finances, Lottery" and "State Government Tax Collections," <http://www.census.gov/govs/state/> and <http://www.census.gov/govs/>.

Table 458. Lottery Sales—Type of Game and Proceeds: 1990 to 2011

[In millions of dollars (20,137 represents $20,137,000,000). For fiscal years]

Game	1990	1995	2000	2005	2008	2009	2010	2011
Total ticket sales	**20,137**	**32,147**	**37,201**	**52,055**	**59,857**	**59,630**	**60,846**	**62,546**
Instant [1]	5,204	11,511	15,387	26,006	30,491	30,328	30,665	32,101
Three-digit [2]	4,572	5,738	5,780	5,858	5,985	5,970	5,861	5,854
Four-digit [2]	1,302	1,918	2,273	2,869	3,163	3,315	3,424	3,435
Lotto [3]	8,563	10,594	9,339	9,828	10,426	10,053	10,879	10,566
Other [4]	497	2,388	4,423	7,493	9,792	9,964	10,017	10,590
State proceeds (net income) [5]	7,703	11,100	11,871	15,792	17,877	17,596	17,957	18,484

[1] Player scratches a latex section on ticket which reveals instantly whether ticket is a winner. [2] Players choose and bet on three or four digits, depending on game, with various payoffs for different straight order or mixed combination bets. [3] Players typically select six digits out of a large field of numbers. Varying prizes are offered for matching three through six numbers drawn by lottery. [4] Includes break-open tickets, spiel, keno, video lottery, etc. [5] Sales minus prizes and expenses equal net government income.

Source: TLF Publications, Inc., Boyds, MD, *2011 World Lottery Almanac* (copyright). See <http://www.lafleurs.com>.

Table 459. State Governments—Summary of Finances: 1990 to 2009

[In millions of dollars (632,172 represents $632,172,000,000). For fiscal year ending in year shown; see text, this section]

Item	1990	2000	2004	2005	2006	2007	2008	2009
Total Revenue	**632,172**	**1,260,829**	**1,586,764**	**1,642,469**	**1,774,649**	**1,995,162**	**1,613,002**	**1,123,226**
General revenue	517,429	984,783	1,192,741	1,286,901	1,391,134	1,451,715	1,511,123	1,495,730
Taxes [1]	300,489	539,655	591,832	650,629	715,973	757,467	779,717	713,983
Sales and gross receipts	147,069	252,147	293,287	312,602	337,949	352,706	358,825	342,667
General	99,702	174,461	197,949	212,921	229,630	238,304	240,165	226,782
Motor fuels	19,379	29,968	33,762	34,567	35,710	36,543	37,632	36,471
Alcoholic beverages	3,191	4,104	4,593	4,706	4,925	5,166	5,290	5,348
Tobacco products	5,541	8,391	12,303	12,917	14,537	15,299	16,068	16,690
Other	19,256	35,222	44,680	47,491	53,147	57,393	59,669	57,377
Licenses	18,842	32,598	39,722	42,584	44,949	46,697	49,067	49,304
Motor vehicles	9,848	15,099	17,336	18,221	18,997	19,470	19,558	19,627
Corporations in general	3,099	6,460	6,339	7,148	7,497	8,570	10,437	10,195
Other	5,895	11,039	16,047	17,216	18,456	18,657	19,072	19,482
Individual income	96,076	194,573	196,958	221,597	245,646	265,863	277,996	246,153
Corporation net income	21,751	32,522	30,229	38,691	47,469	52,915	49,860	39,293
Property	5,848	10,996	11,425	11,342	12,284	12,618	12,686	12,983
Other	10,902	16,819	20,211	23,813	27,676	26,668	31,283	23,584
Charges and miscellaneous	90,612	170,747	208,870	228,497	255,520	267,215	286,975	284,610
Intergovernmental revenue	126,329	274,382	393,467	407,792	419,641	427,030	442,361	495,624
From Federal Government	118,353	259,114	373,513	386,314	398,200	406,934	419,760	475,953
Public welfare	59,397	147,150	(NA)	(NA)	(NA)	(NA)	(NA)	(NA)
Education	21,271	42,086	(NA)	(NA)	(NA)	(NA)	(NA)	(NA)
Highways	13,931	23,790	(NA)	(NA)	(NA)	(NA)	(NA)	(NA)
Health and hospitals	5,475	14,223	(NA)	(NA)	(NA)	(NA)	(NA)	(NA)
Other	18,279	31,865	(NA)	(NA)	(NA)	(NA)	(NA)	(NA)
From local governments	7,976	15,268	19,954	21,478	21,440	20,096	22,600	19,671
Utility revenue	3,305	4,513	13,755	14,628	15,817	16,736	16,522	16,471
Liquor store revenue	2,907	3,895	4,941	5,118	5,475	5,799	6,128	6,377
Insurance trust revenue [2]	108,530	267,639	375,327	335,822	362,223	520,912	79,228	-395,352
Employee retirement	78,898	230,166	308,950	269,617	295,603	457,650	20,890	-461,072
Unemployment compensation	18,370	23,260	38,230	35,243	36,864	34,063	34,360	41,976
Borrowing	40,948	75,968	(NA)	(NA)	(NA)	(NA)	(NA)	(NA)
Total expenditure	**572,318**	**1,084,097**	**1,404,968**	**1,472,542**	**1,554,533**	**1,634,809**	**1,734,251**	**1,827,126**
General expenditure [3]	508,284	964,723	1,207,987	1,278,434	1,349,968	1,422,831	1,504,121	1,555,918
Education	184,935	346,465	430,011	454,348	483,477	514,124	546,875	567,104
Public welfare	104,971	238,890	340,370	368,765	376,675	392,796	411,158	438,395
Health	20,029	42,066	50,251	48,634	50,703	57,212	60,850	62,345
Hospitals	22,637	32,578	40,349	43,623	45,960	48,983	53,749	56,957
Highways	44,249	74,415	84,931	92,816	100,842	103,201	107,368	107,077
Police protection	5,166	9,788	10,793	11,395	12,221	12,856	13,594	13,646
Correction	17,266	35,129	39,230	40,562	42,794	46,485	49,881	50,381
Natural resources	9,909	15,967	18,868	18,822	20,036	22,038	22,524	22,586
Housing and community development	2,856	4,726	(NA)	(NA)	(NA)	(NA)	(NA)	(NA)
Other and unallocable	96,267	164,698	193,183	199,467	217,260	225,135	238,122	237,427
Utility expenditure	7,131	10,723	21,481	21,827	24,922	24,530	24,946	26,539
Liquor store expenditure	2,452	3,195	3,924	4,082	4,338	4,664	4,945	5,175
Insurance trust expenditure [2]	54,452	105,456	171,576	168,200	175,304	182,784	200,239	239,494
Employee retirement	29,562	75,971	111,497	118,333	127,501	136,201	146,714	155,165
Unemployment compensation	16,423	18,583	43,174	29,776	28,009	28,854	35,471	65,974
By character and object:								
Intergovernmental expenditure	175,028	327,070	388,559	405,925	432,265	460,184	479,010	491,322
Direct expenditure	397,291	757,027	1,016,409	1,066,617	1,122,268	1,174,625	1,255,241	1,335,804
Current operation	258,046	523,114	692,255	738,886	774,003	807,565	863,426	896,786
Capital outlay	45,524	76,233	89,320	95,155	103,253	110,044	112,252	116,578
Construction	34,803	59,681	71,016	78,049	85,713	90,788	92,346	97,526
Land and existing structures	3,471	4,681	18,304	17,106	17,540	19,256	19,906	19,051
Equipment	7,250	11,871	(NA)	(NA)	(NA)	(NA)	(NA)	(NA)
Assistance and subsidies	16,902	22,136	28,677	28,403	29,565	30,652	32,603	35,703
Interest on debt	22,367	30,089	34,581	35,974	40,143	43,580	46,721	47,244
Insurance benefits [4]	54,452	105,456	171,576	168,200	175,304	182,784	200,239	239,494
Debt redemption	19,895	41,730	(NA)	(NA)	(NA)	(NA)	(NA)	(NA)
Debt outstanding, year end	**318,254**	**547,876**	**779,542**	**810,852**	**870,032**	**936,008**	**1,005,311**	**1,045,340**
Long term [5]	315,490	541,497	765,987	805,300	859,430	929,431	991,130	1,038,171
Full-faith and credit	74,972	138,525	(NA)	(NA)	(NA)	(NA)	(NA)	(NA)
Nonguaranteed	240,518	402,972	(NA)	(NA)	(NA)	(NA)	(NA)	(NA)
Short-term	2,764	6,379	13,555	5,551	10,602	6,577	14,181	7,169
Net long term [6]	125,524	266,870	(NA)	(NA)	(NA)	(NA)	(NA)	(NA)
Full-faith and credit only	63,481	128,384	(NA)	(NA)	(NA)	(NA)	(NA)	(NA)

NA Not available. [1] Tax data are from U.S. Census Bureau, Annual Surveys of State Government Tax Collections. [2] Includes other items not shown separately. [3] Data on general expenditures are from U.S. Census Bureau, Annual Surveys of State Government Finances. [4] Includes repayments. [5] As of fiscal year 2005, the Census Bureau no longer collects government debt information by the character of long-term debt. For further information, see the 2006 Government Finance and Employment Classification Manual at <http://www.census.gov/govs/pubs/>. [6] Less cash and investment assets specifically held for redemption of long-term debt.

Source: U.S. Census Bureau, "Survey of State Government Finances." See also <http://www.census.gov/govs>.

Table 460. State Government Tax Collections by State: 2011

[In millions of dollars (757,255 represents $757,255,000,000)]

State	All taxes, Total	Total property taxes	Selective sales and gross receipts, Total	Total general sales and gross receipts, Total	Selective sales tax, Total[1]	Alcoholic beverage sales	Insurance premiums	Motor fuels sales	Public utilities	Tobacco products	Other	License taxes, Total[1]	Corporation	Motor vehicle operators	Occupancy & business, n.e.c.[2]	Income taxes, Total	Individual income	Corporation net income	Other taxes, Total[1]	Death and gift	Severance
U.S.	757,255	13,935	365,912	234,480	131,432	5,728	16,421	39,889	14,676	17,129	37,590	51,835	10,024	2,571	13,080	299,340	259,144	40,196	26,233	4,489	14,693
AL	8,636	319	4,575	2,175	2,400	168	272	548	772	137	504	496	109	21	129	3,097	2,796	301	148	—	116
AK	5,538	184	256	—	256	36	56	40	—	71	50	138	—	—	42	721	—	721	4,239	—	4,239
AZ	10,848	758	6,206	4,463	1,744	63	444	769	23	328	116	419	11	28	120	3,424	2,864	560	41	—	40
AR	7,738	723	3,877	2,737	1,140	47	154	469	—	245	226	362	25	17	119	2,647	2,270	377	129	—	80
CA	116,695	3,207	45,148	30,996	14,151	334	2,307	5,706	791	905	4,109	8,186	52	269	4,220	60,122	50,508	9,614	32	—	32
CO	9,468	—	3,797	2,174	1,623	37	192	623	12	199	562	599	16	28	42	4,924	4,541	384	147	—	147
CT	13,432	—	5,523	3,252	2,271	49	196	478	275	401	873	447	28	39	161	7,142	6,469	673	321	227	—
DE	3,018	—	493	—	493	17	88	114	59	129	87	1,172	691	5	258	1,285	962	323	67	16	—
FL	32,558	—	27,156	19,353	7,803	560	698	2,268	3,122	394	760	2,132	274	346	182	1,870	—	1,870	1,399	1	59
GA	16,003	77	7,109	5,081	2,028	162	361	933	—	229	344	477	43	30	74	8,329	7,659	670	12	—	—
HI	4,858	—	3,336	2,496	840	48	143	95	118	126	309	152	1	—	27	1,315	1,247	68	55	7	—
ID	3,262	—	1,613	1,187	426	8	69	239	2	50	58	298	2	11	66	1,339	1,169	170	12	1	8
IL	29,433	58	13,614	7,421	6,193	268	339	1,314	1,845	588	1,838	2,525	336	105	371	13,076	11,225	1,851	160	122	—
IN	14,909	—	8,832	6,270	2,562	43	185	775	209	470	879	626	12	206	33	5,301	4,584	717	151	149	2
IA	7,236	—	3,326	2,232	1,094	14	97	448	—	227	308	732	39	11	109	3,102	2,851	250	77	66	—
KS	6,828	72	3,333	2,487	845	113	160	437	—	102	33	334	42	21	46	2,967	2,721	247	122	—	122
KY	10,203	515	4,894	2,896	1,998	113	129	733	62	300	661	473	99	16	114	3,934	3,418	517	387	41	342
LA	8,865	52	5,131	2,813	2,318	56	536	608	11	142	967	351	85	12	106	2,601	2,404	197	730	—	729
ME	3,676	46	1,683	1,010	672	17	90	239	32	145	149	249	—	9	103	1,630	1,421	209	69	49	—
MD	16,003	793	6,654	3,897	2,757	30	410	752	132	408	1,025	739	94	26	156	7,421	6,645	776	395	216	—
MA	22,090	6	7,109	4,921	2,188	74	320	661	26	577	530	854	24	87	235	13,529	11,597	1,932	591	310	—
MI	23,540	1,897	12,920	9,477	3,442	143	265	975	27	977	1,055	1,404	21	61	170	7,111	6,392	720	209	—	80
MN	18,953	775	8,236	4,657	3,578	78	354	848	—	422	1,877	1,114	8	45	346	8,486	7,482	1,004	342	161	28
MS	6,714	24	4,320	2,933	1,387	42	180	429	2	160	574	455	124	38	90	1,801	1,448	353	114	—	112
MO	10,110	27	4,627	2,973	1,655	33	284	719	—	106	513	573	79	15	137	4,858	4,534	324	25	2	—
MT	2,304	244	533	—	533	25	69	209	51	86	93	308	3	8	99	937	813	124	282	—	278
NE	4,153	—	2,033	1,385	647	28	53	318	57	43	149	227	3	12	82	1,876	1,722	155	16	—	4
NV	6,332	320	4,689	2,932	1,758	40	236	291	23	108	1,059	613	71	21	243	—	—	—	710	—	272
NH	2,320	394	904	—	904	13	71	163	89	232	336	271	49	7	64	667	83	583	84	2	—
NJ	27,183	4	11,922	8,144	3,777	131	465	524	943	788	925	1,498	246	51	517	12,833	10,617	2,216	925	642	—
NM	4,980	66	2,574	1,880	693	45	135	239	32	64	178	240	18	4	27	1,296	1,066	230	805	—	805
NY	67,945	—	22,368	11,581	10,787	230	1,282	1,609	954	1,613	5,098	1,834	73	129	227	40,225	36,209	4,016	3,519	1,219	2
NC	22,406	—	9,935	6,185	3,750	311	501	1,663	401	290	585	1,449	500	128	212	10,962	9,869	1,092	60	27	—
ND	3,822	2	1,169	776	393	8	37	171	38	25	114	173	—	4	61	594	433	161	1,884	—	1,884
OH	25,177	—	12,591	7,768	4,824	94	467	1,757	1,194	856	455	3,445	1,496	91	848	9,057	8,820	237	83	72	11
OK	7,766	—	3,236	2,177	1,059	95	184	448	34	259	39	942	40	15	91	2,739	2,385	354	848	6	831
OR	8,112	22	1,097	—	1,097	16	60	442	91	263	225	940	27	29	230	5,962	5,493	469	91	76	13
PA	32,352	48	16,784	8,952	7,832	308	927	2,064	1,231	1,126	2,176	2,578	633	62	847	11,809	9,831	1,978	1,133	779	—
RI	2,738	—	1,448	825	624	12	67	126	105	137	175	96	4	1	29	1,164	1,016	148	28	21	—
SC	7,687	8	4,066	2,794	1,272	151	158	528	49	25	361	461	90	43	152	3,124	2,908	216	29	—	—
SD	1,380	—	1,153	808	345	19	65	127	—	63	68	200	4	4	88	15	—	15	11	—	11
TN	10,859	—	8,228	6,186	2,041	123	667	845	11	291	104	1,099	451	45	292	1,258	190	1,069	274	113	2
TX	43,188	—	33,798	21,794	12,005	871	1,350	3,108	631	1,502	4,542	6,712	3,962	171	609	—	—	—	2,678	—	2,678
UT	5,476	—	2,543	1,844	699	42	96	370	28	124	38	285	4	14	47	2,546	2,298	248	102	—	102
VT	2,688	956	904	326	578	21	58	105	13	73	309	100	2	8	18	661	556	105	67	36	—

See footnotes at end of table.

Table 460. State Government Tax Collections by State: 2011-Continued.
See headnote on page 300.

State	All taxes	Total property taxes	Selective sales and gross receipts — Total general sales and gross receipts Total	Selective sales tax Total [1]	Alcoholic beverage sales	Insurance premiums	Motor fuels sales	Public utilities	Tobacco products	Other	License taxes Total [1]	Selected license taxes — Corporation	Motor vehicle operators	Occupancy & business n.e.c. [2]	Income taxes Total	Individual income	Corporation net income	Other taxes — Total [1]	Selected other taxes — Death and gift	Severance
VA......	17,409	39	3,461	2,390	183	406	897	158	174	572	775	57	59	180	10,329	9,531	798	416	3	2
WA......	17,411	1,858	10,580	3,523	332	413	1,206	473	494	606	931	29	71	222	–	–	–	518	123	27
WV......	5,143	6	1,210	1,209	18	146	398	165	111	373	150	7	103	16	1,973	1,666	307	594	–	586
WI......	15,347	147	4,109	2,700	55	157	990	375	646	478	1,058	18	42	397	7,280	6,429	–	53	–	6
WY......	2,462	284	863	124	2	22	70	3	26	1	141	12	2	23	–	–	–	1,049	–	1,044

– Represents zero or rounds to zero. [1] Includes other items not shown separately. [2] n.e.c. means not elsewhere classified.

Source: U.S. Census Bureau, *State Government Tax Collections Summary Report*, annual. See also <http://www.census.gov/govs/statetax>.

Table 461. State Governments—Expenditures and Debt by State: 2009

[In millions of dollars (1,827,126 represents $1,827,126,000,000) except as indicated. For fiscal year ending in year shown; see text, this section]

State	Total expenditures	General exp.: Total[1]	General exp.: Intergovernmental[1]	Direct: Total	Education	Public welfare	Health	Hospitals	Highways	Police protection	Corrections	Parks and recreation	Housing and community development	Sewerage	Solid waste management	Governmental administration	Interest on general debt	Other	Utility and liquor store	Insurance trust	Cash and security holdings	Total debt outstanding
U.S...	1,827,126	1,555,918	491,322	1,335,804	242,608	379,211	41,326	55,774	90,623	12,186	47,840	5,277	8,431	1,188	2,639	51,930	45,202	351,570	31,714	239,494	3,100,372	1,045,340
AL...	26,422	23,335	6,536	19,886	5,514	5,386	552	1,282	1,420	155	509	38	14	—	2	582	341	4,092	240	2,847	33,862	8,156
AK...	11,338	9,896	1,617	9,721	1,296	1,514	151	34	1,335	80	260	23	140	—	5	585	303	4,000	135	1,307	60,168	6,590
AZ...	31,517	27,819	9,619	21,898	3,626	7,718	1,659	62	1,587	256	1,086	77	85	—	5	666	506	4,564	32	3,666	42,251	12,325
AR...	16,169	14,553	4,699	11,470	2,631	3,831	207	838	753	64	305	42	9	—	9	504	161	2,115	—	1,616	20,535	4,135
CA...	254,334	211,083	94,909	159,425	24,578	36,221	2,517	7,259	6,998	1,664	8,827	372	373	175	1,361	8,407	5,840	54,834	4,673	38,578	440,921	134,572
CO...	24,886	20,818	6,846	18,041	4,431	3,408	969	514	922	127	919	77	78	3	2	820	784	4,986	23	4,046	55,701	17,202
CT...	25,684	21,377	4,351	21,332	3,139	5,535	673	1,437	949	210	725	22	177	—	192	1,146	1,433	5,696	513	3,794	34,027	28,394
DE...	7,361	6,634	1,205	6,156	1,224	1,507	377	59	520	104	273	44	56	—	63	438	284	1,206	135	592	12,002	5,985
FL...	75,469	66,809	17,678	57,791	8,259	18,511	3,643	893	5,627	424	2,671	175	68	—	205	2,281	1,481	13,555	108	8,552	146,628	38,885
GA...	41,452	35,956	10,817	30,636	7,183	9,448	985	622	1,779	261	1,394	210	207	12	84	775	660	7,018	37	5,460	65,073	13,455
HI...	11,200	10,051	159	11,040	3,557	1,688	636	569	456	26	231	84	141	4	—	500	433	2,717	2	1,147	13,168	6,880
ID...	8,217	7,119	2,077	6,140	1,156	1,760	150	50	606	53	249	44	12	—	—	368	181	1,510	89	1,010	14,643	3,502
IL...	68,624	57,281	15,235	53,389	7,402	16,944	2,258	1,116	4,569	395	1,290	122	279	18	40	1,178	2,964	14,813	—	11,343	102,094	56,962
IN...	32,182	28,856	8,204	23,978	6,277	7,345	559	205	2,036	252	674	82	284	7	8	605	899	4,744	65	3,261	53,141	23,712
IA...	18,304	16,172	4,661	13,643	2,949	4,115	145	1,189	1,180	92	290	34	66	1	3	560	253	2,767	142	1,990	27,429	6,353
KS...	15,832	14,156	4,315	11,517	2,236	3,281	213	1,002	1,081	98	308	33	78	—	5	446	347	2,390	30	1,676	14,909	5,857
KY...	26,853	23,019	4,770	22,083	4,914	6,738	511	1,256	1,736	157	488	111	160	—	26	770	525	4,691	—	3,804	36,442	13,364
LA...	32,355	28,906	6,505	25,850	4,682	6,012	672	1,050	2,597	272	682	256	1,950	—	—	935	954	5,787	6	3,444	51,118	17,505
ME...	8,775	7,886	1,326	7,450	955	2,826	553	59	499	74	148	12	120	2	3	304	269	1,625	1	888	14,753	5,297
MD...	36,023	31,665	8,655	27,368	4,498	8,130	1,372	540	2,049	386	1,392	161	280	105	22	1,274	1,045	6,115	821	3,538	49,434	23,473
MA...	47,911	40,909	8,891	39,020	5,137	12,888	1,032	490	1,695	454	1,099	182	428	278	11	1,764	3,648	9,916	235	6,767	91,835	74,598
MI...	58,754	50,110	19,630	39,125	8,517	11,331	997	2,366	1,520	288	1,741	101	538	—	8	765	1,148	9,805	634	8,011	77,420	29,591
MN...	36,309	31,550	11,199	25,110	5,443	9,309	485	367	1,329	282	484	170	82	—	17	864	527	5,751	144	4,615	47,854	10,524
MS...	19,246	17,162	5,157	14,089	2,251	4,835	348	1,042	975	107	336	45	15	—	18	347	219	3,568	207	1,877	24,819	6,209
MO...	28,651	24,819	5,888	22,762	3,607	6,973	1,272	1,352	1,925	211	720	44	179	—	11	509	848	5,110	—	3,831	57,600	19,217
MT...	6,269	5,420	1,276	4,992	936	1,202	124	47	623	40	180	18	49	—	1	352	168	1,251	73	775	14,818	4,724
NE...	9,034	8,548	2,064	6,970	1,753	2,139	329	248	698	67	229	31	1	5	11	210	108	1,141	—	486	12,199	2,517
NV...	12,056	9,870	3,864	8,192	1,543	1,757	224	257	688	106	393	35	9	—	7	365	209	2,600	88	2,099	22,532	4,445
NH...	6,956	5,847	1,279	5,678	953	1,715	100	55	439	55	108	27	91	4	18	226	392	1,494	425	684	11,348	8,412
NJ...	62,044	48,208	11,136	50,908	9,027	12,255	1,271	1,984	2,472	448	1,422	427	379	3	50	1,856	2,135	17,179	2,807	11,029	99,693	56,898
NM...	17,112	15,512	4,741	12,371	2,178	3,860	509	833	1,000	129	380	76	65	—	1	620	325	2,398	26	1,574	37,972	8,002
NY...	163,706	133,941	55,107	108,599	12,223	34,048	3,081	5,898	4,524	775	2,978	565	471	—	138	5,490	4,231	34,177	12,586	17,180	274,762	122,652
NC...	48,586	42,306	13,562	35,024	7,408	9,483	1,462	1,501	2,684	430	1,351	253	179	1	13	1,418	637	8,204	35	6,245	80,395	19,911
ND...	4,487	4,069	934	3,553	845	806	58	15	408	29	65	23	22	—	7	134	146	1,001	—	417	11,717	1,888
OH...	71,600	56,355	18,988	52,612	9,249	14,639	1,337	2,452	2,532	275	1,585	103	327	419	32	1,330	1,446	16,885	472	14,774	157,209	27,949
OK...	21,383	18,159	4,506	16,876	3,736	5,066	603	230	1,374	165	611	88	17	1	77	543	431	3,935	932	2,292	31,408	9,855
OR...	24,381	19,388	5,704	18,677	3,129	4,394	331	1,221	1,097	164	602	76	101	2	6	942	456	6,156	225	4,767	57,176	12,679
PA...	77,564	64,612	19,111	58,454	9,063	17,583	799	2,569	6,628	785	1,649	210	59	—	23	2,860	1,824	14,399	1,439	11,513	111,349	41,924
RI...	7,347	5,964	964	6,383	813	2,101	182	65	221	67	180	7	42	34	39	358	437	1,838	149	1,234	13,801	9,181
SC...	28,664	22,932	5,521	23,143	4,536	6,107	1,027	1,398	972	174	484	91	139	—	—	991	580	6,644	2,654	3,078	31,131	15,313
SD...	4,114	3,732	708	3,406	646	887	129	60	442	29	113	43	47	—	15	218	135	656	—	382	10,551	3,626
TN...	27,815	25,870	6,798	21,018	4,238	8,138	1,274	466	1,815	182	609	139	43	23	15	856	236	2,984	—	1,946	33,365	4,848
TX...	110,921	98,299	29,252	81,668	18,491	25,895	2,231	3,760	6,333	742	3,561	147	55	4	62	1,732	1,243	17,412	96	12,526	228,829	30,438

See footnotes at end of table.

Table 461. State Governments—Expenditures and Debt by State: 2009-Continued.

See headnote on page 302.

State	Total expend-itures	General expenditures		Direct expenditures															Expenditures		Cash and security holdings	Total debt out-stand-ing
		Total[1]	Inter-govern-mental[1]	Total	Educa-tion	Public welfare	Health	Hospi-tals	High-ways	Police protec-tion	Correc-tions	Parks and recre-ation	Hous-ing and com-munity devel-opment	Sewer-age	Solid waste man-age-ment	Gov-ern-men-tal admin-istra-tion	Inter-est on gen-eral debt	Other	Utility and liquor store	Insur-ance trust		
UT...	15,568	13,961	3,121	12,448	3,526	2,432	352	927	1,215	124	334	53	84	13	–	771	244	2,375	167	1,440	24,733	6,268
VT...	5,449	5,035	1,533	3,916	847	1,359	161	20	281	71	119	17	76	10	13	165	164	613	74	340	6,034	3,427
VA...	42,053	37,871	11,811	30,242	7,643	7,166	615	2,992	2,534	298	1,198	106	175	30	4	1,046	920	5,515	474	3,707	65,217	24,301
WA...	43,443	36,537	10,044	33,400	7,300	8,153	1,337	1,859	2,233	236	1,158	75	135	–	15	745	1,111	9,045	564	6,342	65,657	24,603
WV...	11,482	10,398	2,233	9,249	1,994	2,825	237	114	1,199	102	256	55	15	34	8	427	246	1,737	77	1,006	16,208	6,502
WI...	35,646	30,177	10,200	25,447	4,501	7,242	318	1,142	1,587	129	1,026	28	23	–	25	635	1,262	7,528	9	5,461	77,112	20,913
WY...	5,578	4,963	1,919	3,659	567	704	296	3	483	73	148	27	10	–	6	248	64	1,030	72	543	17,328	1,321

– Represents or rounds to zero. [1] Duplicative intergovernmental transactions are excluded.

Source: U.S. Census Bureau, 2009 Annual Survey of State and Local Government Finances, October 2011; except as noted. See also <http://www.census.gov/govs/>.

Table 462. Local Governments—Revenue by State: 2009

[In millions of dollars (1,433,818 represents $1,433,818,000,000), except as noted. For fiscal year ending in year shown; see text, this section. Minus sign (−) indicates decrease]

State	Total revenue	General revenue, total	Inter-govern-mental revenue	General revenue from own sources — Taxes: Total	Taxes: Prop-erty	Taxes: Sales and gross receipt	Taxes: Indi-vidual income	Taxes: Corpo-ration income	Other taxes	Current charges and miscel-laneous general revenue	Current charges: Total [1]	Current charges: Educa-tion	Current charges: Hospi-tals	Current charges: Sewer-age	Misc. general revenue: Total [1]	Misc.: Interest earn-ings	Misc.: Special assess-ment	Utility revenue	Liquor store reve-nue	Insur-ance trust revenue
U.S...	1,433,818	1,408,032	531,515	876,517	411,050	88,988	24,637	6,702	24,482	320,657	227,527	25,795	64,739	38,947	93,130	34,627	7,199	127,332	1,080	−102,626
AL...	18,994	16,763	6,702	10,061	2,068	2,086	132	–	757	5,018	4,049	332	2,625	397	970	303	26	2,619	–	−388
AK...	4,123	3,936	1,658	1,403	1,086	280	–	–	37	875	648	29	242	71	226	118	6	295	–	−107
AZ...	27,861	24,734	9,687	15,047	6,226	2,851	–	–	434	5,536	3,596	566	722	666	1,940	767	76	3,794	–	−667
AR...	8,382	7,981	4,513	3,468	851	1,071	–	–	36	1,510	960	148	173	230	549	211	31	868	–	−467
CA...	211,551	224,024	98,913	125,111	51,544	12,805	–	–	4,238	56,524	40,502	2,765	9,516	5,670	16,022	6,065	1,479	22,020	–	−34,492
CO...	23,874	23,028	6,400	16,628	6,298	3,246	–	–	522	6,562	4,492	445	1,251	700	2,070	772	192	2,386	–	−1,540
CT...	15,235	15,244	4,923	10,322	8,789	3	–	–	140	1,389	969	133	–	317	420	120	48	766	–	−775
DE...	2,949	2,636	1,303	1,333	632	11	56	4	85	545	349	18	–	146	196	40	27	404	–	−92
DC...	9,608	9,753	3,470	6,283	1,790	1,343	1,126	343	411	1,270	460	23	17	206	810	90	–	904	–	−1,049
FL...	92,184	86,935	22,978	63,957	29,536	5,042	–	–	1,961	27,417	18,401	2,192	5,459	2,544	9,016	2,874	1,845	9,231	–	−3,982
GA...	40,534	36,947	11,647	25,299	10,356	4,685	–	–	390	9,868	7,448	530	3,392	1,061	2,420	819	53	4,551	–	−964
HI...	3,077	2,791	510	2,281	1,316	208	–	–	153	605	490	–	–	300	115	64	9	286	–	–
ID...	5,566	5,353	2,224	3,129	1,255	25	–	–	68	1,780	1,505	100	818	169	275	95	49	214	–	−1
IL...	52,722	58,621	19,937	38,684	22,700	3,892	–	–	816	11,276	7,199	1,424	748	1,018	4,077	1,224	609	3,451	–	−9,350
IN...	27,503	25,442	9,587	15,854	7,231	137	1,388	–	220	6,880	4,581	353	2,619	871	2,298	451	44	2,028	–	33
IA...	13,854	12,949	4,754	8,195	3,946	796	95	–	71	3,287	2,671	537	1,217	378	616	197	16	920	–	−14
KS...	12,996	12,131	4,286	7,845	3,736	940	2	–	98	3,069	1,931	396	665	315	1,138	526	105	1,232	–	−367
KY...	13,584	12,098	4,906	7,193	2,341	539	1,023	116	99	3,074	1,966	131	499	448	1,108	797	13	1,550	–	−65
LA...	20,007	19,258	7,331	11,928	3,071	4,015	–	–	190	4,652	3,303	69	1,885	339	1,349	632	18	1,325	–	−576
ME...	4,506	4,383	1,554	2,829	2,140	5	–	–	17	666	517	38	75	157	149	49	9	123	–	–
MD...	22,053	23,695	8,554	15,141	6,187	512	4,279	–	713	3,449	2,612	758	–	641	838	189	17	465	206	−2,313
MA...	27,455	27,747	11,078	16,669	12,162	181	–	–	228	4,098	3,225	307	978	971	872	203	18	3,163	–	−3,455
MI...	37,523	42,191	19,718	22,473	12,247	255	418	–	236	9,317	6,984	1,258	960	1,558	2,333	828	223	2,309	–	−6,977
MN...	26,436	24,838	11,131	13,707	6,371	282	–	–	209	6,844	4,480	484	1,342	648	2,364	851	415	1,985	284	−671
MS...	11,720	10,936	4,801	6,134	2,338	102	–	–	89	3,605	3,100	424	2,093	202	506	196	7	785	–	–
MO...	20,512	20,359	6,342	14,017	5,490	2,496	303	49	580	5,100	3,807	717	1,296	652	1,293	537	54	1,901	–	−1,747
MT...	3,482	3,365	1,438	1,926	1,040	5	–	–	35	846	552	76	76	78	294	85	74	118	–	–
NE...	10,495	7,503	2,217	5,287	2,591	412	–	–	348	1,936	1,405	239	524	136	531	204	36	3,360	–	−368
NV...	14,177	13,293	5,035	8,258	3,288	905	–	–	329	3,737	2,461	133	592	386	1,275	455	58	884	–	–
NH...	5,076	5,013	1,559	3,454	2,819	–	–	–	43	592	401	55	–	110	191	53	4	106	–	−43
NJ...	44,412	43,429	13,189	30,240	23,258	126	–	–	349	6,507	4,685	1,254	470	1,400	1,822	392	6	980	–	−696
NM...	8,246	7,754	4,396	3,357	1,162	925	–	–	83	1,187	773	107	119	142	415	118	8	493	2	−125
NY...	139,476	150,367	54,801	95,566	41,140	13,466	7,664	6,030	2,438	24,828	17,199	1,502	4,146	2,001	7,629	2,457	112	5,765	563	−16,656
NC...	39,932	35,620	14,566	21,054	8,137	2,667	–	–	328	9,922	7,944	716	4,217	1,109	1,978	583	15	3,821	–	−71
ND...	2,434	2,355	920	1,435	768	116	–	–	15	535	289	48	–	48	247	72	76	124	–	−44
OH...	53,250	51,391	21,144	30,247	13,080	1,883	4,280	106	650	10,248	6,715	1,152	1,157	1,790	3,533	1,713	242	2,555	–	−696
OK...	12,540	11,687	4,547	7,141	2,206	1,769	–	–	74	3,092	2,404	315	1,047	286	688	219	19	978	–	−125
OR...	16,898	15,611	6,450	9,161	4,419	330	2	43	565	3,803	2,717	526	264	778	1,086	390	84	1,287	–	−1
PA...	54,292	54,993	23,481	31,512	15,450	716	3,871	12	1,798	9,665	6,527	941	37	1,949	3,137	1,648	105	2,749	–	−3,449
RI...	3,935	3,889	1,223	2,666	2,126	14	–	–	39	486	330	33	–	96	157	25	8	173	–	−127
SC...	17,998	16,454	5,464	10,989	4,413	462	–	–	575	5,539	4,446	250	2,998	475	1,093	409	60	1,550	–	−6
SD...	2,886	2,658	854	1,804	892	299	–	–	30	583	418	84	44	66	166	62	24	269	26	−68
TN...	28,208	20,558	6,748	13,810	4,698	2,373	–	–	382	6,356	4,965	432	2,659	604	1,391	585	101	9,175	–	−1,525

See footnotes at end of table.

Table 462. Local Governments—Revenue by State: 2009-Continued.

See headnote on page 304.

State	Total revenue	General revenue, total revenue	General revenue from own sources Inter-govern-mental revenue	General revenue from own sources Total	Taxes Total	Taxes Property	Taxes Sales and gross receipt	Taxes Indi-vidual income	Taxes Corpo-ration income	Taxes Other taxes	Current charges and miscel-laneous general revenue	Current charges Total [1]	Current charges Educa-tion	Current charges Hospi-tals	Current charges Sewer-age	Miscellaneous general revenue Total [1]	Interest earn-ings	Special assess-ment	Utility revenue	Liquor store reve-nue	Insur-ance trust revenue
TX...	105,395	99,122	31,029	68,093	44,453	36,219	7,250	–	–	984	23,640	16,080	2,228	4,514	2,927	7,560	3,855	288	11,484	–	-5,210
UT...	10,750	8,941	3,566	5,376	3,306	2,323	898	–	–	85	2,070	1,352	86	50	301	717	236	77	1,839	–	-30
VT...	2,414	2,220	1,553	666	399	372	14	–	–	12	268	183	27	–	59	84	20	4	210	–	-15
VA...	31,926	32,051	11,687	20,364	14,857	11,242	2,400	–	–	1,215	5,507	3,839	403	281	1,042	1,668	680	131	1,804	–	-1,929
WA...	36,812	30,977	11,946	19,031	10,573	6,322	3,376	–	–	875	8,458	6,496	344	1,873	1,593	1,962	738	182	6,151	–	-316
WV...	5,103	4,923	2,243	2,680	1,619	1,302	120	–	–	197	1,061	786	36	286	203	275	99	13	186	–	-6
WI...	24,204	24,580	10,623	13,957	9,678	9,099	391	–	–	188	4,279	3,219	556	–	644	1,061	442	75	1,539	–	-1,915
WY...	4,667	4,508	1,926	2,581	1,281	976	261	–	–	44	1,300	1,098	78	793	50	202	71	9	159	–	–

– Represents or rounds to zero. [1] Includes items not shown separately.

Source: U.S. Census Bureau; Federal, State and Local Governments, 2009 Annual Survey of State and Local Government Finances, October 2011. See also <http://www.census.gov/govs/>.

State and Local Government Finances and Employment

Table 463. Local Governments—Expenditures and Debt by State: 2009

[In millions of dollars (1,641,392 represents $1,641,392,000,000), except as indicated. For fiscal year ending in year shown; see text, this section]

General expenditures group spans *Total* through *Other*; *Direct expenditures* sub-group spans *Education* through *Other*.

State	Total expendi-tures[1]	Total[1]	Total (general exp.)	Educa-tion	Public welfare	Health	Hospi-tals	High-ways	Police protec-tion	Correc-tions	Sewer-age	Solid waste	Parks and recrea-tion	Housing and community develop-ment	Govern-mental admini-stration	Interest on general debt	Other	Utility expen-ditures	Insurance trust expen-ditures	Debt out-stand-ing
U.S.	1,641,392	1,425,882	1,410,479	608,066	51,886	40,613	80,687	61,443	80,814	26,663	46,430	21,751	35,301	39,058	75,494	58,276	183,995	178,578	35,985	1,638,328
AL	19,930	17,184	17,167	7,848	47	347	2,343	810	915	206	290	259	439	426	823	710	1,705	2,618	128	17,810
AK	4,605	4,155	4,155	1,824	6	60	263	289	195	4	88	89	125	135	241	114	723	422	27	3,663
AZ	31,896	25,962	25,739	10,372	322	262	921	1,522	1,900	758	1,184	394	984	463	1,775	1,313	3,570	5,699	235	36,008
AR	9,123	8,168	8,159	4,747	13	36	190	454	454	125	304	183	147	154	365	304	682	918	37	8,549
CA	268,118	225,828	225,378	79,515	16,424	10,859	12,662	7,821	14,557	5,522	6,502	2,741	5,383	9,535	13,579	8,389	31,890	34,008	8,282	239,122
CO	26,562	22,577	22,530	8,321	762	286	1,556	1,359	1,323	288	912	124	1,021	592	1,599	1,138	3,249	3,572	413	33,213
CT	16,138	14,887	14,880	8,382	128	161	—	536	778	—	453	212	242	517	634	332	2,505	839	412	9,664
DE	3,196	2,759	2,752	1,709	—	—	—	103	186	—	174	28	34	72	158	74	179	394	43	2,247
DC	12,589	10,138	10,138	2,217	2,649	434	147	403	573	262	301	157	234	521	609	412	1,217	2,092	359	9,720
FL	102,116	89,082	88,759	31,172	1,355	1,130	7,199	4,037	6,637	1,874	2,803	2,218	2,851	2,241	5,103	3,594	16,544	11,410	1,625	108,292
GA	45,891	39,221	39,181	18,652	229	1,083	3,695	1,466	2,055	871	1,410	607	839	996	2,661	811	3,808	6,275	396	39,522
HI	3,325	2,747	2,747	1,281	76	66	800	271	342	84	357	290	210	93	284	188	570	578	—	4,594
ID	5,393	5,142	5,138	2,147	31	62	—	264	306	—	189	170	94	49	328	94	521	250	2	2,356
IL	69,764	58,821	58,818	27,198	570	805	1,331	2,955	3,906	679	1,645	475	2,693	1,702	3,514	2,654	8,691	7,236	3,707	71,138
IN	27,434	24,913	24,789	10,309	554	223	2,936	848	940	379	1,022	242	765	421	1,288	891	3,971	2,407	113	27,369
IA	14,496	13,422	13,324	6,281	113	374	1,316	949	531	142	405	186	289	145	450	314	1,828	1,072	2	9,112
KS	13,940	12,524	12,524	6,190	41	247	709	774	597	170	381	139	270	129	647	679	1,551	1,332	73	18,319
KY	13,964	12,072	12,064	5,805	43	449	491	408	490	223	506	175	183	194	614	1,205	1,275	1,844	48	27,479
LA	20,604	18,846	18,831	7,542	60	199	2,203	896	1,081	579	542	362	413	582	1,166	717	2,489	1,561	198	16,655
ME	4,392	4,254	4,252	2,299	28	29	82	265	168	67	172	122	59	117	198	94	553	138	—	2,467
MD	26,847	25,145	24,994	12,867	277	451	1,384	1,067	1,594	387	671	584	545	941	1,395	625	3,591	701	853	15,278
MA	33,003	26,896	26,008	12,832	65	117	1,078	858	1,468	248	759	395	221	1,430	986	616	4,631	4,656	1,450	23,014
MI	47,315	42,573	42,325	19,602	1,149	2,602	1,494	2,258	2,181	694	1,959	523	747	437	2,143	1,817	5,136	3,276	1,466	48,385
MN	29,061	26,179	26,050	10,521	1,658	671	2,019	2,123	1,365	423	650	393	997	686	1,348	1,227	2,493	2,261	336	32,902
MS	11,828	11,009	11,008	5,164	26	97	—	567	503	173	206	150	189	207	580	253	875	820	—	7,236
MO	25,032	21,758	21,758	10,714	155	373	1,290	1,145	1,274	178	1,019	156	874	397	1,027	804	2,579	2,755	518	23,129
MT	3,457	3,303	3,303	1,631	53	98	73	189	192	49	103	83	68	63	185	55	460	153	—	1,614
NE	11,526	7,376	7,372	3,730	74	65	500	544	301	113	169	76	174	183	389	220	836	3,944	206	10,856
NV	14,326	12,810	12,798	4,286	373	138	749	1,026	1,046	411	272	19	739	254	1,217	680	1,587	1,516	—	21,456
NH	4,996	4,865	4,784	2,532	205	30	—	256	250	72	100	117	85	95	275	105	662	120	10	2,613
NJ	45,091	44,067	43,685	22,617	1,093	392	513	1,230	2,685	722	1,431	1,093	738	930	1,751	1,459	7,028	1,013	11	35,727
NM	8,391	7,708	7,680	4,222	114	46	152	356	485	192	179	161	238	96	456	161	822	683	—	6,328
NY	176,119	151,316	142,053	56,634	10,435	3,864	8,305	5,672	7,697	2,838	4,297	2,709	2,460	3,621	4,981	6,466	22,073	15,188	9,616	170,858
NC	41,852	37,194	36,568	15,950	1,537	1,602	4,703	573	1,755	483	1,123	718	931	677	1,362	1,358	3,844	4,140	25	30,267
ND	2,459	2,280	2,272	1,064	50	35	—	268	103	27	53	46	80	46	122	80	286	163	15	2,182
OH	55,048	51,477	51,051	22,191	3,004	2,618	1,404	2,443	2,999	449	2,019	458	1,039	1,877	3,510	1,879	5,162	3,439	132	45,994
OK	12,707	11,638	11,636	5,849	39	143	1,070	735	617	104	348	192	293	236	773	241	995	1,008	61	8,501
OR	18,813	16,724	16,711	7,465	278	599	283	764	880	430	960	121	513	428	857	712	2,421	1,993	96	20,570
PA	58,613	52,408	52,404	25,080	3,918	3,414	16	1,746	2,123	1,400	1,687	698	765	1,704	2,822	2,838	4,191	4,407	1,799	75,760
RI	4,252	3,918	3,918	2,118	11	5	—	110	263	17	95	49	41	165	227	111	707	176	158	2,557
SC	18,533	16,932	16,892	7,952	53	146	2,874	368	810	295	455	368	355	296	948	686	1,285	1,597	4	20,237
SD	3,022	2,686	2,686	1,281	14	27	54	269	123	48	82	41	116	60	147	63	360	299	15	1,868
TN	30,359	20,755	20,751	8,415	155	374	2,786	740	1,325	379	594	327	399	660	1,122	963	2,512	9,115	489	31,809
TX	121,382	104,789	103,310	52,138	364	1,892	7,395	4,087	5,355	1,987	3,123	1,181	2,342	1,962	4,516	7,260	9,707	15,280	1,314	197,844
UT	11,492	8,910	8,869	4,310	97	201	52	452	509	184	378	145	458	219	651	257	956	2,577	5	11,471

See footnotes at end of table.

Table 463. Local Governments—Expenditures and Debt by State: 2009-Continued.

See headnote on page 306.

State	Total expendi-tures [1]	General expenditures Total [1]	Direct expenditures Total	Educa-tion	Public welfare	Health	Hospi-tals	High-ways	Police protec-tion	Correc-tions	Sewer-age	Solid waste	Parks and recre-ation	Housing and com-munity devel-opment	Gov-ern-mental admini-stration	Interest on general debt	Other	Utility expen-ditures	Insur-ance trust expen-ditures	Debt out-stand-ing
VT....	2,405	2,155	2,154	1,427	1	10	29	177	70	–	63	34	27	49	88	30	178	243	8	1,107
VA....	34,709	31,791	31,739	14,759	1,452	838	252	875	1,760	967	1,066	659	870	766	2,128	1,181	4,166	2,206	712	34,716
WA....	38,169	30,100	30,010	11,783	152	997	2,276	1,616	1,234	559	1,976	575	912	1,058	1,610	1,148	4,113	7,888	181	42,154
WV....	5,176	4,911	4,903	2,899	5	51	262	83	248	33	203	60	104	97	390	134	335	231	34	3,322
WI....	27,275	25,077	25,046	11,665	1,605	1,477	–	2,173	1,502	493	892	375	565	318	1,152	792	2,038	1,828	371	20,298
WY....	4,657	4,418	4,417	1,887	25	94	859	242	161	74	88	70	136	15	296	29	441	238	–	974

– Represents or rounds to zero. [1] Includes other items not shown separately.

Source: U.S. Census Bureau; Federal, State and Local Governments, "2009 Annual Survey of State and Local Government Finances," October 2011. See also <http://www.census.gov/govs>.

Table 464. City Governments—Revenue for Largest Cities: 2006

[In millions of dollars (83,520 represents $83,520,000,000). For fiscal years ending in year shown; see text, this section. Cities ranked by estimated resident population as of July 1. Data reflect inclusion of fiscal activity of dependent school systems where applicable. Regarding intercity comparisons, see text, this section. See Appendix III]

2006 population	Total revenue	General revenue — Total [1]	Intergovernmental — Total	Intergov. — From federal government	Intergov. — From state/local government	Intergov. — From local government	Own sources — Total [1]	Taxes — Total [1]	Taxes — Property	Sales and gross receipts — Total [1]	Sales — General sales	Sales — Public utilities	Current charges — Total [1]	Current charges — Parks and recreation	Current charges — Sewerage	Miscellaneous — Total [1]	Misc. — Interest earnings	Utility revenue [2]	Insurance trust revenue
New York, NY [3]	83,520	70,823	25,957	3,722	22,045	191	44,866	35,104	12,754	5,953	4,439	516	6,380	63	1,151	3,382	1,153	3,472	9,224
Los Angeles, CA	14,199	7,863	952	282	670	–	6,911	3,233	1,090	1,362	552	673	2,413	105	599	1,264	461	3,143	3,193
Chicago, IL	8,812	7,257	1,325	449	876	–	5,933	2,179	429	1,454	275	555	2,872	–	144	881	248	347	1,207
Houston, TX	4,449	3,119	550	195	328	27	2,569	1,492	781	664	423	187	808	26	330	269	153	341	989
Phoenix, AZ	3,377	2,903	1,115	581	488	46	1,788	1,023	261	692	537	84	581	26	232	184	137	288	186
Philadelphia, PA [3]	7,345	5,809	2,478	653	1,712	113	3,332	2,450	394	225	125	–	698	24	240	184	105	1,007	529
San Antonio, TX	3,283	1,469	191	54	120	17	1,278	612	292	287	200	27	431	24	280	234	107	1,573	242
San Diego, CA	3,266	2,101	411	175	216	20	1,690	744	313	323	173	45	694	63	396	252	110	332	833
Dallas, TX	3,027	2,277	164	123	36	6	2,113	857	488	329	198	89	861	35	240	394	144	207	543
San Jose, CA	1,924	1,498	217	50	141	27	1,281	660	285	238	106	112	440	15	185	181	100	20	406
Honolulu, HI [3]	1,483	1,337	197	117	79	–	1,140	807	591	114	–	62	284	23	241	50	29	146	–
Detroit, MI	3,184	2,132	694	97	543	54	1,438	867	309	218	–	61	452	4	351	119	47	314	739
Jacksonville, FL [3]	3,292	1,829	323	72	251	–	1,506	745	365	371	213	106	383	16	158	379	207	1,187	276
Indianapolis, IN [3]	3,749	3,014	646	86	550	10	2,368	1,638	1,486	47	–	1	506	26	74	224	94	687	48
San Francisco, CA [3]	7,955	5,647	2,155	87	1,664	404	3,492	2,047	923	598	327	91	1,045	25	165	400	178	426	1,882
Columbus, OH	1,227	1,058	198	82	103	13	860	560	40	20	–	7	228	11	172	72	26	169	–
Austin, TX	2,272	1,037	108	54	30	24	929	457	255	186	124	30	378	23	166	94	26	1,032	203
Louisville/Jefferson, KY [3]	1,090	975	170	73	89	8	805	515	124	55	–	4	117	11	102	173	93	115	–
Memphis, TN	3,777	1,882	1,149	63	557	529	733	449	301	135	99	5	150	11	120	134	86	1,587	308
Ft. Worth, TX [3]	1,132	712	56	–	56	–	656	417	236	144	102	32	153	5	149	85	32	184	237
Baltimore, MD [3]	3,339	2,922	1,504	262	1,205	38	1,418	1,023	558	87	–	56	261	10	199	134	48	109	308
Charlotte City, NC	1,613	1,507	351	76	114	161	1,156	366	286	39	2	32	398	3	71	392	50	80	26
El Paso, TX	822	627	91	74	17	3	535	339	178	141	107	32	134	3	122	62	20	81	115
Boston, MA	3,626	3,103	1,368	100	1,264	3	1,735	1,333	1,255	40	–	2	194	42	288	209	48	112	411
Seattle, WA	2,481	1,424	144	41	100	3	1,279	784	284	307	146	–	387	26	178	108	23	882	176
Washington, DC	9,248	8,674	2,589	2,589	–	–	6,085	4,545	1,214	1,257	817	124	574	4	178	966	205	96	478
Milwaukee, WI	1,392	931	442	69	306	67	489	250	237	–	–	214	191	45	109	48	17	59	402
Denver, CO [3]	2,472	2,121	237	17	219	2	1,884	849	226	534	460	26	810	11	70	225	72	166	185
Las Vegas, NV	883	882	401	22	272	107	481	233	121	60	–	54	185	9	78	63	15	–	1
Nashville-Davidson, TN [3]	3,237	1,955	446	8	438	–	1,509	1,101	720	327	271	15	236	9	82	172	99	1,008	275
Oklahoma City, OK	1,069	950	96	56	39	–	854	451	45	358	319	31	268	12	84	135	33	78	41
Portland, OR	1,053	961	181	54	112	15	780	419	254	65	–	49	294	24	205	67	33	91	1
Tucson, AZ	953	756	265	79	170	16	491	305	54	243	196	28	149	21	38	37	6	126	72
Albuquerque, NM	1,146	1,047	321	28	260	33	727	414	102	248	219	19	239	15	98	74	43	98	–
Atlanta, GA	1,696	1,517	323	118	115	90	1,194	354	186	110	–	38	650	31	148	190	155	146	34

– Represents or rounds to zero. [1] Includes revenue sources not shown separately. [2] Includes water, electric, gas, and transit. [3] Represents, in effect, city-county consolidated government.

Source: U.S. Census Bureau, "Federal, State, and Local Governments," Survey of State & Local Government Finances, 2006, July 2009. See also <http://www.census.gov/govs/>.

Table 465. City Governments—Expenditures and Debt for Largest Cities: 2006

[In millions of dollars (82,454 represents $82,454,000,000). For fiscal year ending in year shown; see headnote, Table 464]

Cities ranked by 2006 population	Total expenditures [1]	Total direct expenditures [1]	General expenditures														Utility expenditures [3]	Insurance trust expenditures	Debt outstanding
			Total [1]	Education	Housing and community development	Public welfare	Health and hospitals	Police protection	Fire protection	Corrections	Highways	Parks and recreation	Sewerage	Solid waste management	Governmental administration [2]	Interest on general debt			
New York, NY [4]	82,454	77,456	66,237	17,472	3,710	9,811	8,976	3,971	1,519	1,314	1,526	559	2,161	1,100	1,178	3,205	8,699	7,517	85,234
Los Angeles, CA	12,315	12,315	7,252	–	275	–	202	1,659	589	–	561	332	498	238	842	410	3,675	1,388	15,723
Chicago, IL	7,622	7,544	6,033	1	257	135	178	1,175	390	–	454	77	101	183	153	756	316	1,272	15,862
Houston, TX	3,982	3,953	3,295	–	255	–	98	571	381	20	139	129	384	67	139	357	307	381	11,403
Phoenix, AZ	3,362	3,349	2,592	18	100	–	–	367	187	13	127	577	198	99	114	251	672	97	7,373
Philadelphia, PA [4]	6,745	6,660	5,077	23	234	555	1,292	510	172	350	71	94	189	98	332	114	1,054	614	5,825
San Antonio, TX	3,625	3,625	1,546	45	35	43	43	242	161	–	112	157	248	57	52	81	2,010	70	6,055
San Diego, CA	2,431	2,418	1,803	–	339	–	44	336	160	9	82	142	290	52	88	70	413	215	2,795
Dallas, TX	2,713	2,704	2,194	–	41	7	27	268	143	8	121	124	196	67	80	229	276	242	8,557
San Jose, CA	1,894	1,866	1,703	–	186	–	15	227	116	–	95	138	144	79	192	204	36	156	4,368
Honolulu, HI [4]	1,473	1,473	1,228	–	46	16	26	180	82	–	107	100	159	137	98	100	246	–	3,155
Detroit, MI	3,349	3,248	2,168	35	98	47	66	447	192	–	146	79	402	107	157	147	627	554	7,515
Jacksonville, FL [4]	3,474	3,343	1,847	–	33	–	84	206	96	62	200	77	198	86	97	217	1,447	180	11,022
Indianapolis, IN	3,412	3,398	2,592	–	268	91	619	188	70	75	110	149	301	40	173	193	741	79	4,125
San Francisco, CA [4]	6,908	6,908	5,305	102	148	605	1,246	317	211	170	143	200	155	34	714	406	1,008	595	8,738
Columbus, OH	1,152	1,144	1,012	–	8	10	32	212	144	10	94	60	193	43	72	93	140	–	1,703
Austin, TX	2,304	2,304	1,159	–	35	17	75	176	88	–	83	96	137	18	58	80	1,036	110	3,887
Louisville/Jefferson, KY [4]	925	924	868	–	39	–	124	130	47	41	15	38	–	43	31	102	57	191	2,520
Memphis, TN	3,508	3,479	1,815	999	36	–	11	180	132	–	65	56	33	35	45	62	1,502	83	2,747
Ft. Worth, TX	1,047	1,047	766	–	21	–	15	161	81	–	85	58	76	69	31	26	197	259	1,231
Baltimore, MD [4]	3,289	3,212	2,930	1,029	86	2	147	348	134	–	192	391	147	40	128	58	101	16	2,287
Charlotte City, NC	1,448	1,436	1,019	–	42	–	5	151	77	–	96	52	253	13	21	44	413	61	2,665
El Paso, TX	725	476	476	–	22	–	16	81	52	–	35	25	44	58	27	25	187	–	1,459
Boston, MA	3,341	3,038	2,813	950	82	150	184	279	160	106	51	34	215	114	55	57	171	357	
Seattle, WA	2,424	2,311	1,400	–	45	36	14	190	135	13	113	195	175	266	67	52	932	93	3,465
Washington, DC	8,543	8,291	8,256	1,478	560	1,846	669	493	176	206	96	332	237	76	434	320	169	118	7,824
Milwaukee, WI	1,302	1,274	1,026	–	123	–	32	218	99	–	132	4	66	5	37	37	72	203	1,199
Denver, CO [4]	2,415	2,357	2,110	–	103	98	55	165	87	75	86	216	79	21	132	289	199	106	5,845
Las Vegas, NV	747	600	745	–	18	–	3	124	105	39	90	80	40	31	117	16	1	–	352
Nashville-Davidson, TN [4]	3,270	3,269	2,046	679	9	28	168	158	101	52	38	72	109	3	105	148	1,084	140	3,837
Oklahoma City, OK	1,115	1,115	960	–	54	–	–	125	111	–	91	83	146	36	137	30	138	17	1,049
Portland, OR	1,210	1,210	1,059	–	43	–	–	137	79	–	162	89	192	45	52	85	71	80	2,524
Tucson, AZ	874	874	694	–	32	–	–	134	56	–	70	71	–	45	71	46	146	35	1,090
Albuquerque, NM	843	843	760	–	5	19	9	122	66	49	55	107	29	–	31	37	83	–	777
Atlanta, GA	2,025	1,979	1,552	–		–	–	152	66	36	43	103	185	–	61	87	407	65	6,425

– Represents or rounds to zero. [1] Includes expenditure categories, not shown separately. [2] Excludes public buildings. [3] Includes water, electric, and transit. [4] Represents, in effect, city-county consolidated government.

Source: U.S. Census Bureau, Survey of State & Local Government Finances, 2006, July 2009. See also <http://www.census.gov/govs/>.

Table 466. County Governments—Revenue for Largest Counties: 2006

[In millions of dollars (21,586 represents $21,586,000,000). For fiscal year ending in year shown; see text, this section. See Appendix III]

Counties ranked by 2006 population	Total revenue [1]	General revenue — Total	Intergovernmental — Total	From federal govt — Total [1]	From federal govt — Housing and community development	From state govt — Total [1]	From state govt — Public welfare	From state govt — Health and hospitals	From local government	Taxes — Total [1]	Taxes — Property	Sales and gross receipts — Total	Sales and gross receipts — General sales	Current charges — Total [1]	Current charges — Parks and recreation	Current charges — Sanitation [2]	Current charges — Hospitals	Miscellaneous general revenue — Total [1]	Misc. — Interest earnings
Los Angeles, CA	21,586	17,015	9,177	386	4	8,556	4,815	1,311	235	3,285	3,009	127	42	3,802	95	83	2,220	751	235
Cook, IL	3,378	2,851	606	41	–	564	287	–	1	1,536	810	702	358	577	47	–	333	132	49
Harris, TX	3,165	3,165	647	91	23	471	174	216	85	1,318	1,232	56	–	815	3	–	256	385	245
Maricopa, AZ	2,015	2,015	952	55	9	869	167	27	28	781	604	144	144	80	4	–	–	202	128
Orange, CA	4,439	3,464	1,926	51	8	1,800	650	172	75	626	536	46	43	622	42	114	–	289	181
San Diego, CA	5,117	4,027	2,880	167	120	2,447	986	473	266	686	585	27	18	259	3	24	–	201	110
Dade, FL	6,528	6,263	1,353	896	254	413	–	55	44	1,871	1,283	480	119	2,477	36	508	1,084	562	289
Dallas, TX	1,662	1,623	254	9	–	233	150	19	12	649	597	12	–	608	–	71	545	111	29
Riverside, CA	3,399	3,399	1,898	61	13	1,683	904	208	154	666	534	43	35	581	7	73	184	255	99
San Bernardino, CA	3,919	3,290	2,043	134	18	1,826	918	240	83	383	326	25	17	680	7	75	331	183	62
Wayne, MI	1,991	1,848	1,117	122	8	862	14	522	134	448	423	16	–	229	4	–	10	54	19
King, WA	2,239	2,108	520	135	16	266	–	6	119	1,005	446	534	431	499	7	333	–	84	51
Broward, FL	2,326	2,270	466	119	10	203	38	23	144	927	780	124	–	676	16	172	475	201	111
Clark, NV	4,446	3,980	1,051	87	16	792	971	180	173	1,333	577	484	113	1,082	66	3	688	513	83
Santa Clara, CA	3,497	3,497	1,717	37	3	1,603	7	189	78	800	605	143	140	872	4	24	146	107	37
Tarrant, TX	1,150	1,150	273	51	24	219	–	–	4	515	478	15	–	203	–	83	–	158	124
Bexar, TX	1,113	1,113	203	6	2	188	101	44	9	396	363	27	–	421	–	2	389	93	70
Suffolk, NY	2,744	2,592	580	29	7	538	275	153	13	1,701	556	1,119	1,114	174	10	5	–	137	50
Alameda, CA	3,198	2,696	1,468	31	3	1,399	737	311	38	480	399	26	15	609	–	199	341	139	66
Sacramento, CA	3,235	2,559	1,563	46	–	1,457	811	202	60	428	275	89	63	373	13	18	–	195	65
Nassau, NY	3,347	3,347	769	73	21	696	397	136	–	1,903	906	965	953	431	23	78	247	244	39
Cuyahoga, OH	2,170	2,170	964	20	19	940	503	260	4	565	336	184	169	383	–	70	341	258	198
Palm Beach, FL	1,873	1,823	239	102	47	136	–	–	2	967	685	154	–	421	13	3	–	196	37
Allegheny, PA	1,486	1,419	1,026	63	6	961	282	467	155	302	262	38	23	64	4	–	4	27	6
Oakland, MI	1,162	1,051	574	201	32	218	6	61	–	350	326	9	–	85	9	–	–	42	15
Hillsborough, FL	1,836	1,663	259	75	8	183	45	–	19	901	605	274	199	395	2	146	284	108	44
Hennepin, MN	1,843	1,843	727	50	4	785	353	169	26	605	459	–	–	388	2	24	–	123	30
Franklin, OH	1,158	1,156	459	14	–	419	193	128	–	459	334	104	85	97	–	–	–	140	124
Orange, FL	1,753	1,704	720	85	102	199	5	–	81	506	506	225	–	322	4	–	404	156	95
Contra Costa, CA	2,506	2,071	899	113	68	705	391	113	28	406	342	24	10	670	47	232	–	96	33
Fairfax, VA	5,137	4,343	1,024	122	11	874	146	76	–	2,673	2,117	326	155	426	45	4	–	220	127
St Louis, MO	727	683	71	17	–	54	–	5	9	512	152	347	312	78	1	12	–	21	6
Salt Lake, UT	532	532	76	15	15	51	–	–	2	346	203	112	79	70	7	–	–	40	5
Fulton, GA	1,162	1,000	102	29	23	70	32	14	–	733	522	178	164	71	–	46	–	94	37
Westchester, NY	2,468	2,459	508	14	–	484	245	116	10	1,041	607	426	407	838	31	30	563	73	46

– Represents or rounds to zero. [1] Includes revenue sources, not shown separately. [2] Includes fee for sewerage and solid waste management.

Source: U.S. Census Bureau, *Survey of State & Local Government Finances 2006*, July 2009, <http://www.census.gov/govs/>.

Table 467. County Governments—Expenditures and Debt for Largest Counties: 2006

[In millions of dollars (18,720 represents $18,720,000,000). For fiscal year ending in year shown; see text, this section and Appendix III]

Counties ranked by 2006 population	Total expenditures [1]	Total direct expenditures	General expenditures: Total [1]	Education	Housing and community development	Public welfare	Health	Hospitals	Police protection	Correction	Highways	Parks and recreation	Natural resources	Sewage and solid waste management	Governmental administration	General public building	Interest on general debt	Utility expenditures [2]	Employee retirement expenditures	Debt outstanding
Los Angeles, CA	18,720	18,439	16,859	890	5	4,515	1,925	2,454	1,213	1,128	273	248	424	66	1,572	114	63	1,798	2,713	3
Cook, IL	3,048	3,036	2,665	–	10	8	41	916	85	350	119	118	142	–	620	149	–	383	3,246	3
Harris, TX	3,207	3,207	3,207	–	12	43	208	888	364	70	266	24	90	–	329	450	–	–	8,538	8
Maricopa, AZ	1,813	1,517	1,813	34	13	376	81	–	69	354	138	8	–	6	391	108	–	–	1,856	2
Orange, CA	3,482	3,428	3,879	244	14	764	328	–	282	263	54	–	67	100	433	174	–	265	2,856	3
San Diego, CA	4,205	3,843	6,344	425	102	989	518	1,380	207	297	175	20	20	29	523	125	587	326	1,845	2
Dade, FL	6,931	6,921	1,533	–	295	298	71	1,010	425	229	153	278	47	502	273	620	–	–	10,985	10
Dallas, TX	1,547	1,547	3,156	4	32	7	42	–	32	99	43	3	–	1	131	22	–	13	423	1
Riverside, CA	3,156	2,994	3,131	367	78	660	325	271	265	177	162	10	66	66	277	74	–	–	1,298	1
San Bernardino, CA	3,335	3,187	1,717	379	9	799	219	376	242	203	74	18	56	71	247	116	–	204	1,912	2
Wayne, MI	1,828	1,771	1,785	–	8	153	474	49	35	250	124	67	46	67	330	50	–	111	643	1
King, WA	2,226	2,180	2,068	–	30	46	344	–	121	127	112	53	9	413	246	163	441	–	3,167	3
Broward, FL	2,215	2,160	3,487	–	15	187	99	–	353	190	43	127	19	149	183	165	147	–	3,225	3
Clark, NV	4,013	3,953	3,350	214	22	624	60	495	467	136	483	319	11	42	268	218	526	–	5,865	5
Santa Clara, CA	3,350	3,274	1,034	–	9	7	365	905	105	258	102	31	4	3	336	58	–	–	910	2
Tarrant, TX	1,034	1,034	1,029	–	23	43	95	446	34	98	35	2	1	–	136	114	–	–	1,981	1
Bexar, TX	1,029	1,004	2,568	–	1	504	52	578	42	73	11	43	–	–	89	67	–	–	933	2
Suffolk, NY	2,750	2,454	2,303	161	7	557	337	–	431	124	42	32	36	79	116	65	182	216	1,797	3
Alameda, CA	2,563	2,559	2,603	39	6	741	319	394	87	271	27	1	36	94	281	41	44	183	1,327	3
Sacramento, CA	2,804	2,741	3,631	154	10	573	430	–	224	233	133	34	4	111	240	81	18	–	2,167	3
Nassau, NY	3,633	3,243	2,131	181	23	438	298	380	688	215	127	61	2	13	189	153	2	–	3,532	2
Cuyahoga, OH	2,131	2,112	1,777	–	20	72	327	576	26	94	54	7	7	169	260	201	–	60	3,338	1
Palm Beach, FL	1,777	1,690	1,686	–	57	351	50	–	216	102	112	92	37	98	193	63	91	36	1,818	2
Allegheny, PA	1,477	1,385	1,416	32	63	7	461	–	32	76	29	62	–	75	106	24	–	–	613	1
Oakland, MI	988	964	926	10	9	89	266	8	52	102	123	9	30	52	131	13	27	–	339	1
Hillsborough, FL	1,911	1,781	1,718	–	32	458	134	–	165	132	109	78	55	–	222	56	193	–	2,174	2
Hennepin, MN	1,856	1,847	1,849	–	23	289	288	480	85	83	108	3	–	–	112	25	7	–	544	1
Franklin, OH	1,164	1,126	1,160	–	7	79	320	–	30	58	47	20	–	6	162	118	3	–	2,178	3
Orange, FL	1,689	1,652	1,675	30	30	379	42	–	142	153	159	36	20	232	128	128	14	198	3,074	3
Contra Costa, CA	2,253	2,198	2,054	127	106	227	189	437	89	116	100	28	9	23	155	58	1	306	1,106	1
Fairfax, VA	4,831	4,759	4,328	2,195	162	24	178	–	196	37	37	144	30	259	174	177	197	25	3,701	4
St Louis, MO	725	495	696	–	10	46	47	–	77	20	83	30	78	4	66	16	4	–	410	1
Salt Lake, UT	519	519	519	–	1	62	26	78	32	63	25	78	5	14	92	6	–	59	197	1
Fulton, GA	1,111	909	952	–	8	–	35	–	65	83	26	4	1	62	259	14	100	–	749	1
Westchester, NY	2,629	2,311	2,586	95	–	455	277	591	41	134	43	56	1	146	107	53	44	–	1,594	1

– Represents or rounds to zero. [1] Includes expenditure categories, not shown separately. [2] Includes water, gas, electric, and transit.

Source: U.S. Census Bureau, Federal, State, and Local Governments, *State & Local Government Finances, 2006*, July 2009, <http://www.census.gov/govs/>.

Table 468. State Governments—Revenue by State: 2010

[In millions of dollars (2,035,700 represents $2,035,700,000,000), except as noted. For fiscal year ending in year shown. See text, this section. Includes local shares of state imposed taxes. Minus sign (–) indicates decrease]

State	Total revenue [1,2]	General revenue							Utilities and liquor store revenue	Insurance trust revenue
		Total	Intergovernmental revenue		General revenue from own sources					
			Total [1]	From federal govern-ment	Total	Total taxes	Current charges	Miscel-laneous general revenue		
United States........	2,035,700	1,563,629	575,562	555,297	988,067	702,221	169,575	116,270	21,617	450,455
Alabama................	26,824	22,990	9,370	8,841	13,620	8,186	4,106	1,328	252	3,582
Alaska..................	12,375	11,036	2,962	2,955	8,074	4,518	558	2,999	19	1,320
Arizona................	32,842	26,324	12,577	12,338	13,747	10,199	2,091	1,457	30	6,488
Arkansas..............	19,595	16,221	5,978	5,961	10,243	7,279	2,146	817	–	3,374
California..............	278,495	196,643	67,805	62,958	128,838	104,841	15,479	8,518	4,053	77,799
Colorado..............	27,991	19,931	6,371	6,294	13,560	8,586	2,982	1,991	–	8,060
Connecticut...........	26,840	21,924	6,230	6,218	15,695	12,286	2,010	1,398	29	4,887
Delaware..............	7,976	7,234	2,035	1,977	5,199	2,770	1,143	1,286	15	727
Florida.................	91,653	71,341	25,448	24,997	45,894	31,499	8,399	5,996	21	20,291
Georgia...............	44,878	36,480	16,193	15,939	20,286	14,783	3,535	1,968	7	8,392
Hawaii.................	11,566	9,627	2,592	2,587	7,035	4,838	1,414	783	–	1,938
Idaho..................	8,859	6,727	2,673	2,659	4,054	2,952	616	486	118	2,015
Illinois.................	73,275	55,674	19,346	18,956	36,329	27,512	4,523	4,294	–	17,601
Indiana................	35,575	29,802	10,401	10,277	19,401	13,796	3,544	2,061	–	5,773
Iowa...................	21,265	17,113	6,743	6,536	10,370	6,809	2,417	1,144	214	3,938
Kansas................	16,546	14,215	4,624	4,581	9,591	6,493	2,200	898	–	2,330
Kentucky..............	26,993	22,862	9,149	9,118	13,713	9,531	2,924	1,258	–	4,131
Louisiana.............	32,188	27,441	13,255	13,174	14,186	8,758	3,094	2,334	11	4,736
Maine..................	9,539	8,248	3,213	3,202	5,035	3,490	697	848	–	1,291
Maryland..............	37,394	31,185	10,534	10,163	20,651	15,224	3,156	2,270	124	6,085
Massachusetts........	50,472	42,209	13,326	13,127	28,883	20,050	4,271	4,561	211	8,052
Michigan..............	65,972	52,667	19,528	19,320	33,140	22,206	7,050	3,884	780	12,524
Minnesota............	39,887	31,462	10,025	9,930	21,438	17,209	2,534	1,695	–	8,425
Mississippi............	20,979	17,427	8,808	8,646	8,619	6,269	1,687	664	257	3,294
Missouri...............	33,916	26,112	11,798	11,445	14,313	9,708	2,657	1,948	–	7,804
Montana...............	7,141	6,009	2,505	2,498	3,504	2,143	579	782	68	1,065
Nebraska..............	10,063	8,676	3,203	3,146	5,473	3,809	978	686	-	1,387
Nevada................	14,053	9,937	2,917	2,759	7,020	5,836	675	509	84	4,032
New Hampshire.......	7,828	6,222	2,361	2,138	3,861	2,125	950	786	514	1,092
New Jersey............	66,740	51,183	15,477	14,753	35,706	25,928	5,969	3,808	881	14,677
New Mexico...........	17,567	14,011	6,247	6,065	7,763	4,414	1,448	1,901	–	3,556
New York..............	195,460	139,966	55,726	49,619	84,240	63,529	8,882	11,829	7,427	48,067
North Carolina........	57,467	44,058	15,699	15,350	28,359	21,517	4,240	2,602	–	13,410
North Dakota..........	6,118	5,415	1,742	1,687	3,673	2,646	651	376	–	703
Ohio...................	89,664	57,508	22,462	21,953	35,046	23,584	7,754	3,708	779	31,377
Oklahoma.............	23,692	19,486	8,007	7,892	11,479	7,080	2,334	2,066	491	3,714
Oregon................	28,703	19,001	6,858	6,844	12,143	7,289	3,024	1,829	421	9,282
Pennsylvania..........	83,287	63,884	21,339	21,116	42,545	30,169	7,939	4,437	1,511	17,892
Rhode Island..........	8,809	7,088	2,967	2,851	4,121	2,569	694	858	28	1,694
South Carolina........	28,868	21,512	7,934	7,499	13,578	7,313	4,360	1,906	1,689	5,667
South Dakota.........	4,493	3,974	1,794	1,767	2,180	1,304	334	542	–	518
Tennessee.............	29,720	25,517	11,371	11,321	14,146	10,514	2,184	1,448	–	4,202
Texas..................	120,390	99,924	41,450	40,780	58,474	39,399	11,479	7,595	–	20,466
Utah...................	16,022	13,228	4,374	4,370	8,854	5,092	2,716	1,045	237	2,558
Vermont...............	6,001	5,331	1,905	1,903	3,426	2,511	608	306	45	626
Virginia................	46,357	37,103	9,780	9,221	27,323	16,411	7,233	3,680	559	8,695
Washington...........	44,299	33,711	11,176	10,891	22,534	16,106	4,175	2,253	579	10,009
West Virginia..........	13,564	11,561	4,426	4,353	7,135	4,655	1,319	1,161	82	1,921
Wisconsin.............	48,088	30,845	10,403	10,230	20,442	14,369	3,633	2,440	–	17,243
Wyoming..............	7,411	5,586	2,457	2,093	3,129	2,117	182	830	82	1,744

– Represents or rounds to zero. [1] Includes amounts for categories not shown separately. [2] Duplicate intergovernmental transactions are excluded.

Source: U.S. Census Bureau, Federal, State, and Local Governments, "State Government Finances Summary: 2010." See also <http://www.census.gov/govs/>.

Table 469. Governmental Employment and Payrolls: 1982 to 2010

[Employees in thousands (15,841 represents 15,841,000), payroll in millions of dollars (23,173 represents $23,173,000,000). Data are for the month of October through 1992. Beginning with the 1997 survey, data are for the month of March. Covers both full-time and part-time employees. Local government data are estimates subject to sampling variation; see Appendix III and source]

Type of government	1982	1987	1992	1997	2000	2005	2007	2008	2009	2010
EMPLOYEES (1,000)										
Total...........	**15,841**	**17,212**	**18,745**	**19,540**	**20,876**	**21,725**	**22,116**	**22,462**	**22,668**	**22,607**
Federal (civilian) [1]...........	2,848	3,091	3,047	2,807	2,899	2,720	2,730	2,769	2,824	3,008
State and local...........	12,993	14,121	15,698	16,733	17,976	19,004	19,386	19,693	19,844	19,599
Percent of total...........	82	82	84	86	86	87	88	88	88	87
State...........	3,744	4,116	4,595	4,733	4,877	5,078	5,200	5,270	5,346	5,326
Local...........	9,249	10,005	11,103	12,000	13,099	13,926	14,186	14,423	14,498	14,274
Counties...........	1,824	1,963	2,253	2,425	(NA)	(NA)	(NA)	(NA)	(NA)	(NA)
Municipalities...........	2,397	2,493	2,665	2,755	(NA)	(NA)	(NA)	(NA)	(NA)	(NA)
School districts...........	4,194	4,627	5,134	5,675	(NA)	(NA)	(NA)	(NA)	(NA)	(NA)
Townships...........	356	393	424	455	(NA)	(NA)	(NA)	(NA)	(NA)	(NA)
Special districts...........	478	529	627	691	(NA)	(NA)	(NA)	(NA)	(NA)	(NA)
PAYROLLS (mil. dol.)										
Total...........	**23,173**	**32,669**	**43,120**	**49,156**	**58,166**	**71,599**	**78,583**	**83,268**	**85,281**	**86,643**
Federal (civilian) [1]...........	5,959	7,924	9,937	9,744	11,485	13,475	14,427	15,472	15,106	16,238
State and local...........	17,214	24,745	33,183	39,412	46,681	58,123	64,156	67,796	70,175	70,404
Percent of total...........	74	76	77	80	80	81	82	81	82	81
State...........	5,022	7,263	9,828	11,413	13,279	16,062	17,789	18,726	19,425	19,579
Local...........	12,192	17,482	23,355	27,999	33,402	42,062	46,368	49,070	50,750	50,825
Counties...........	2,287	3,270	4,698	5,750	(NA)	(NA)	(NA)	(NA)	(NA)	(NA)
Municipalities...........	3,428	4,770	6,207	7,146	(NA)	(NA)	(NA)	(NA)	(NA)	(NA)
School districts...........	5,442	7,961	10,394	12,579	(NA)	(NA)	(NA)	(NA)	(NA)	(NA)
Townships...........	370	522	685	869	(NA)	(NA)	(NA)	(NA)	(NA)	(NA)
Special districts...........	665	959	1,370	1,654	(NA)	(NA)	(NA)	(NA)	(NA)	(NA)

NA Not available. [1] Includes employees outside the United States.

Source: U.S. Census Bureau, Governments Division, "Annual Survey of Public Employment and Payroll Summary Report," January 2012. <http://www.census.gov/govs/apes/>.

Table 470. All Governments—Employment and Payroll by Function: 2010

[Employees in thousands (22,607 represents 22,607,000), payroll in millions of dollars (86,643 represents $86,643,000,000). See headnote, Table 469]

Function	Employees, total	Federal (civilian) [1]	State and local Total	State and local State	State and local Local	Total	Federal (civilian) [1]	State and local Total	State and local State	State and local Local
	Employees (1,000)					Payrolls (mil. dol.)				
Total........	**22,607**	**3,008**	**19,599**	**5,326**	**14,274**	**86,643**	**16,238**	**70,404**	**19,579**	**50,825**
National defense [2]........	774	774	(X)	(X)	(X)	3,057	3,057	(X)	(X)	(X)
Postal Service........	658	658	(X)	(X)	(X)	3,646	3,646	(X)	(X)	(X)
Space research and technology........	19	19	(X)	(X)	(X)	174	174	(X)	(X)	(X)
Elem. and secondary education........	7,917	(X)	7,917	64	7,853	26,601	(X)	26,601	227	26,375
Higher education........	3,121	(X)	3,121	2,511	611	9,532	(X)	9,532	7,915	1,617
Other education........	104	10	94	94	–	455	80	374	374	–
Health........	640	158	481	200	282	2,969	1,135	1,834	801	1,033
Hospitals........	1,278	201	1,077	438	638	5,826	1,307	4,519	1,837	2,682
Public welfare........	543	8	535	241	294	2,005	71	1,935	875	1,059
Social insurance administration........	160	69	92	92	(X)	777	415	361	361	(X)
Police protection........	1,192	183	1,010	109	901	6,105	1,220	4,885	561	4,324
Fire protection........	421	(X)	421	(X)	421	1,947	(X)	1,947	(X)	1,947
Correction........	781	38	743	477	267	3,214	216	2,997	1,915	1,083
Streets & highways........	550	3	547	235	311	2,168	23	2,145	983	1,161
Air transportation........	98	49	49	3	46	661	434	227	16	212
Water transport/terminals. ..	19	5	14	5	9	84	14	70	24	45
Solid waste management. ..	119	(X)	119	2	117	408	(X)	408	11	396
Sewerage........	133	(X)	133	2	131	568	(X)	568	10	558
Parks & recreation........	436	27	409	42	367	1,029	142	887	115	772
Natural resources........	391	187	204	155	49	1,924	1,181	743	576	167
Housing & community development........	134	15	118	–	118	576	110	466	(X)	466
Water supply........	181	–	181	1	181	764	–	764	4	760
Electric power........	80	–	80	4	76	485	–	485	27	458
Gas supply........	12	–	12	–	12	50	–	50	(X)	50
Transit........	244	(X)	244	33	211	1,209	(X)	1,209	197	1,012
Libraries........	193	4	189	1	188	460	28	432	2	431
State liquor stores........	12	(X)	12	12	(X)	30	(X)	30	30	(X)
Financial administration.....	551	128	423	169	254	2,499	804	1,694	707	987
Other government administration........	444	25	419	59	359	1,379	166	1,214	245	969
Judicial and legal........	513	63	450	181	269	2,495	444	2,051	901	1,150
Other & unallocable........	890	384	507	197	310	3,543	1,571	1,972	863	1,109

– Represents or rounds to zero. X Not applicable. [1] Includes employees outside the United States. [2] Includes international relations.

Source: U.S. Census Bureau, Governments Division, "Annual Survey of Public Employment and Payroll Summary Report," January 2012. See also <http://www.census.gov/govs/apes/>.

Table 471. State and Local Government—Employer Costs Per Hour Worked: 2012

[In dollars. As of March. Based on a sample; see source for details. Collection of severance pay and supplemental unemployment plans, which comprised "other benefits" and was published in all tables, was discontinued beginning with the March 2006 estimates]

Occupation and industry	Total compensation	Wages and salaries	Benefit cost					
			Total	Paid leave	Supplemental pay	Insurance	Retirement and savings	Legally required benefits
Total workers	**41.16**	**26.85**	**14.31**	**3.02**	**0.33**	**4.94**	**3.49**	**2.52**
Occupational group:								
Management, professional, and related	49.85	33.82	16.03	3.32	0.23	5.49	4.10	2.88
Professional and related	48.90	33.39	15.52	2.99	0.23	5.48	4.05	2.77
Teachers [1]	56.14	39.60	16.54	2.70	0.14	5.94	4.70	3.07
Primary, secondary, and special education school teachers	57.01	39.87	17.14	2.52	0.16	6.60	4.91	2.95
Sales and office	28.43	17.27	11.16	2.50	0.20	4.37	2.19	1.90
Office and administrative support	28.62	17.34	11.28	2.53	0.20	4.44	2.22	1.90
Service	30.74	18.27	12.48	2.71	0.57	4.03	3.10	2.07
Industry group:								
Education and health services	42.98	29.06	13.92	2.68	0.20	5.13	3.44	2.46
Educational services	44.00	29.99	14.01	2.59	0.15	5.21	3.60	2.46
Elementary and secondary schools	43.58	29.73	13.85	2.26	0.16	5.42	3.62	2.39
Junior colleges, colleges, and universities	45.57	30.99	14.58	3.72	0.11	4.47	3.58	2.71
Health care and social assistance	35.84	22.57	13.27	3.28	0.59	4.60	2.35	2.46
Hospitals	38.67	24.33	14.34	3.62	0.74	4.97	2.51	2.51
Public administration	39.43	23.89	15.54	3.74	0.57	4.78	3.80	2.66

[1] Includes postsecondary teachers; primary, secondary, and special education teachers; and other teachers and instructors.

Source: U.S. Bureau of Labor Statistics, *National Compensation Survey, Benefits, Archives, 2012 National Survey Compensation Publications List, Employer Costs for Employee Compensation*, News Release, March 2012, <http://www.bls.gov/schedule/archives/ecec_nr.htm>.

Table 472. State and Local Government—Full-Time Employment and Salary by Sex and Race and Ethnic Group: 1980 to 2009

[2,350 represents 2,350,000. As of June 30. Excludes school systems and educational institutions. Based on reports from state governments (42 in 1980; 47 in 1983; 42 in 1990; 47 in 1984 through 1987; 49 in 1981 and 1984 through 1987; 49 in 1981 and 1984 through 1987; and 50 in 1989 through 1991) and a sample of county, municipal, township, and special district jurisdictions employing 15 or more nonelected, nonappointed full-time employees. Beginning 1993, only for state and local governments with 100 or more employees. For definition of median, see Guide to Tabular Presentation]

Year and occupation	Employment (1,000)						Median annual salary ($1,000)					
				Minority						Minority		
	Male	Female	White [1]	Total [2]	Black [1]	His-panic [3]	Male	Female	White [1]	Total [2]	Black [1]	His-panic [3]
1980	2,350	1,637	3,146	842	619	163	15.2	11.4	13.8	11.8	11.5	12.3
1983	2,674	1,818	3,423	1,069	768	219	20.1	15.3	18.5	15.9	15.6	17.3
1984	2,700	1,880	3,458	1,121	799	233	21.4	16.2	19.6	17.4	16.5	18.4
1985	2,789	1,952	3,563	1,179	835	248	22.3	17.3	20.6	18.4	17.5	19.2
1986	2,797	1,982	3,549	1,230	865	259	23.4	18.1	21.5	19.6	18.7	20.2
1987	2,818	2,031	3,600	1,249	872	268	24.2	18.9	22.4	20.9	19.3	21.1
1989	3,030	2,227	3,863	1,394	961	308	26.1	20.6	24.1	22.1	20.7	22.7
1990	3,071	2,302	3,918	1,456	994	327	27.3	21.8	25.2	23.3	22.0	23.8
1991	3,110	2,349	3,965	1,494	1,011	340	28.4	22.7	26.4	23.8	22.7	24.5
1993	2,820	2,204	3,588	1,436	948	341	30.6	24.3	28.5	25.9	24.2	26.8
1995	2,960	2,355	3,781	1,534	993	379	33.5	27.0	31.4	26.3	26.8	28.6
1997	2,898	2,307	3,676	1,529	973	392	34.6	27.9	32.2	30.2	27.4	29.5
1999	2,939	2,393	3,723	1,609	1,012	417	37.0	29.9	34.8	31.1	29.6	31.2
2001	3,080	2,554	3,888	1,746	1,077	471	39.8	32.1	37.5	34.0	31.5	33.8
2003	3,134	2,610	3,919	1,826	1,097	508	42.2	34.7	40.0	35.9	33.6	36.6
2005	3,185	2,644	3,973	1,856	1,100	532	44.1	36.4	41.5	37.7	35.3	38.9
2007	3,383	2,823	4,156	(NA)	(NA)	(NA)	(NA)	(NA)	(NA)	(NA)	(NA)	(NA)
2009, total	3,239	2,742	3,978	2,004	1,145	601	50.3	41.5	47.6	(NA)	40.3	44.8
Officials/administrators	230	153	303	79	45	22	71.9	69.6	71.2	(NA)	70.8	71.3
Professionals	671	923	1,109	484	261	117	62.4	53.0	57.2	(NA)	50.7	55.8
Technicians	268	206	324	151	76	48	49.9	40.4	46.5	(NA)	39.8	44.7
Protective service	998	239	857	380	217	134	51.3	41.2	50.3	(NA)	42.2	54.2
Paraprofessionals	(NA)	(NA)	(NA)	(NA)	(NA)	(NA)	(NA)	(NA)	(NA)	(NA)	32.0	36.6
Administrative support	125	774	562	337	183	116	37.3	35.0	34.9	(NA)	35.0	36.3
Skilled craft	407	23	305	125	68	43	45.0	38.7	34.9	(NA)	42.0	46.9
Service/maintenance	434	142	299	277	180	79	37.3	29.1	29.1	(NA)	29.1	35.9

NA Not available [1] Non-Hispanic. [2] Includes other minority groups, not shown separately. [3] Persons of Hispanic origin may be of any race.

Source: U.S. Equal Employment Opportunity Commission, 1980–1991, "State and Local Government Information Report," annual; beginning 1993, biennial, <www.eeoc.gov>.

Table 473. State and Local Government Full-Time Equivalent Employment by Selected Function and State: 2010

[In thousands (1,824.0 represents 1,824,000). For March. Local government amounts are estimates subject to sampling variation; see Appendix III and source]

State	Total[1] State	Total[1] Local	Education: Elementary and secondary State	Elementary and secondary Local	Higher education State	Higher education Local	Public welfare State	Public welfare Local	Health State	Health Local	Hospitals State	Hospitals Local	Highways State	Highways Local	Police protection State	Police protection Local	Fire protection State	Fire protection Local	Corrections State	Corrections Local	Parks and recreation State	Parks and recreation Local
U.S.	1,824.0	7,144.5	51.7	6,802.0	1,685.9	342.5	235.9	275.1	193.5	250.2	409.2	577.3	230.4	295.5	106.9	833.5	(X)	342.7	472.3	259.4	34.3	232.7
AL	41.4	103.7		103.7	38.4	—	4.3	1.5	6.0	.4	12.1	25.9	4.6	6.8	1.6	12.1	(X)	5.8	5.5	3.4	.5	3.7
AK	8.9	17.3	3.1	17.2	5.5	.1	1.9	—	.7	.5	.2	—	3.1	.6	.7	1.3	(X)	.8	1.9	.6	.1	.6
AZ	31.6	134.2		121.3	28.6	12.9	4.6	2.1	2.7	2.9	.7	4.2	2.7	4.6	2.0	18.8	(X)	8.1	9.7	5.9	.3	5.5
AR	27.2	74.8		74.7	25.8	.2	4.1	.1	4.4	.4	6.8	1.7	3.4	4.0	1.2	7.5	(X)	3.0	5.2	2.5	.8	1.2
CA	162.4	722.8		653.3	158.1	69.6	4.0	64.9	13.2	43.1	41.7	66.3	21.1	20.7	11.9	90.3	(X)	33.3	61.7	31.9	3.6	34.6
CO	38.7	107.6		105.6	37.4	2.0	2.3	6.2	1.3	4.1	5.2	10.1	3.1	5.5	1.5	13.7	(X)	5.9	7.3	3.6	.3	6.9
CT	21.1	88.6		86.6	18.7	—	5.8	1.7	4.3	—	6.8	—	3.0	3.5	1.9	8.6	(X)	4.6	7.2	—	.2	2.1
DE	8.4	15.6		15.6	8.0	—	1.6	—	2.0	.3	1.7	—	1.6	1.2	1.0	2.3	(X)	.1	2.9	—	.3	.2
DC	(X)	9.1	(X)	8.2	(X)	.9	(X)	2.1	(X)	.8	(X)	1.5	(X)	.9	(X)	4.7	(X)	1.9	(X)	1.4	(X)	.8
FL	57.2	389.7		360.2	54.1	29.5	10.0	5.5	20.6	5.5	3.9	49.8	7.6	13.7	4.4	61.2	(X)	31.1	30.7	16.6	1.4	17.7
GA	56.7	243.7		243.7	53.6	—	8.5	1.5	4.5	10.2	7.4	19.0	5.6	8.1	2.0	25.7	(X)	12.4	19.2	9.9	1.5	5.8
HI	37.2	—	27.4	—	9.7	—	.5	—	2.1	.2	4.3	—	.9	1.1	.4	3.9	—	1.9	2.4	—	.2	2.0
ID	8.7	33.5		31.6	8.3	1.9	1.7	4.8	1.1	1.0	.7	—	1.6	1.6	.4	3.6	(X)	1.3	1.9	1.4	.2	.8
IL	64.1	299.6		276.8	62.1	22.9	9.3	6.2	2.5	7.2	11.1	11.8	6.8	11.8	3.7	41.7	(X)	16.9	11.1	10.1	.5	17.2
IN	57.7	147.4		147.4	56.6	—	4.7	1.1	1.8	3.2	2.5	25.9	4.0	5.7	2.0	15.2	(X)	8.0	6.8	6.1	.5	3.4
IA	24.1	80.0		71.1	22.9	8.9	3.1	1.2	.5	2.1	7.9	11.1	2.4	5.6	1.0	6.2	(X)	2.0	3.2	1.4	.1	2.0
KS	20.2	102.2		93.1	19.5	9.1	2.2	.6	1.2	4.0	3.1	8.8	3.2	5.6	1.1	8.4	(X)	3.5	3.4	3.2	.6	2.5
KY	39.2	112.1		112.1	37.2	—	5.7	.5	2.9	5.5	5.0	4.5	4.5	2.9	2.3	7.7	(X)	4.2	4.1	3.6	1.2	1.8
LA	35.0	101.0	1.7	101.0	29.8	—	5.9	.3	3.9	1.7	14.5	19.7	4.8	5.2	1.7	15.8	(X)	5.3	7.0	5.9	1.0	4.2
ME	7.5	36.1	.4	36.1	7.3	—	3.0	.4	1.0	.4	.4	.7	2.2	1.6	.6	2.4	(X)	1.6	.7	.7	.4	
MD	29.2	135.3		123.8	27.1	11.5	6.6	3.5	6.4	4.7	4.3	—	4.7	5.3	2.4	16.6	(X)	6.8	12.6	3.6	.4	6.9
MA	32.4	149.0	.1	148.9	31.2	.1	7.0	2.5	7.2	3.0	6.5	3.3	3.6	5.9	6.3	17.8	(X)	12.8	6.2	5.6	.6	2.3
MI	74.9	210.8		195.6	74.3	15.2	10.8	2.9	1.8	9.2	18.8	10.0	2.9	8.8	2.6	19.3	(X)	7.3	15.1	5.3	.3	4.3
MN	40.8	117.7		117.7	36.8	—	2.9	10.1	2.5	3.6	4.9	9.0	4.8	7.2	1.2	10.7	(X)	2.6	4.2	2.0	.6	4.5
MS	20.4	81.1		75.2	18.8	5.9	3.0	.4	3.1	.3	4.9	19.9	3.4	4.9	1.2	8.1	(X)	3.4	4.2	2.0	.4	1.2
MO	30.2	145.7		137.9	28.5	7.8	7.6	3.3	3.1	3.7	11.1	12.5	6.1	6.6	2.4	16.1	(X)	6.8	12.5	3.3	.5	4.6
MT	7.6	24.4		24.0	7.2	.4	1.6	.6	.9	.9	.6	.8	2.1	1.3	.5	2.2	(X)	.8	1.3	.7	.1	.4
NE	13.2	52.3		48.9	12.5	3.4	2.5	.7	.7	.7	3.9	4.9	2.1	3.0	.8	4.3	(X)	1.5	2.9	1.5	.3	1.1
NV	10.3	45.2		45.2	10.1	—	1.7	.9	1.5	1.0	1.4	4.6	1.9	1.3	.8	7.6	(X)	2.9	3.7	2.9	.2	3.7
NH	7.2	36.6		36.6	6.8	—	1.5	2.7	.9	.2	—	—	1.9	1.7	.5	3.4	(X)	2.0	1.2	.7	.2	.5
NJ	55.6	224.9	18.8	213.9	33.8	11.0	9.0	11.1	4.5	4.5	18.5	2.5	6.3	10.8	4.3	32.4	(X)	8.1	9.5	6.9	2.0	6.0
NM	20.1	51.3		47.8	19.1	3.5	1.8	.9	2.6	.6	7.6	1.0	2.3	1.9	.7	5.4	(X)	2.3	4.0	5.1	.7	2.3
NY	57.4	513.0		489.4	53.0	23.6	4.9	48.6	9.6	18.8	43.9	52.4	12.1	27.6	6.5	81.2	(X)	24.4	31.8	24.9	2.3	12.2
NC	61.4	231.0		210.2	59.1	21.1	4.2	15.7	2.7	16.6	19.5	40.5	10.9	3.9	3.5	23.9	(X)	8.8	21.2	5.1	2.0	6.4
ND	9.1	16.7		16.7	8.8	—	.5	1.0	1.4	—	.9	—	1.0	1.2	.2	1.4	(X)	.4	.8		.2	.9
OH	72.0	255.7		250.7	69.7	4.9	2.7	22.8	3.5	17.5	15.2	11.7	6.9	12.6	2.6	29.5	(X)	16.6	15.5	8.8	.6	8.7
OK	32.3	92.7		92.3	30.3	.4	6.9	.2	5.7	1.5	2.6	10.0	3.0	5.6	2.0	9.3	(X)	3.7	5.4	3.6	.4	1.8
OR	23.7	78.5		70.1	23.0	8.4	8.2	.9	1.5	4.4	5.5	2.4	3.9	3.7	1.4	7.9	(X)	4.7	5.5	3.6	.4	3.3
PA	63.1	269.3	.5	262.4	59.0	6.9	12.0	19.7	1.8	5.4	11.7	.7	14.8	10.9	6.6	27.0	(X)	5.7	18.9	13.1	2.6	3.7
RI	6.6	19.8		19.8	5.6	—	1.2	.1	.9	.1	.7	—	.7	.9	.3	3.0	(X)	2.2	1.6	—	.1	.6
SC	32.4	100.6		100.6	29.3	—	4.3	.4	5.6	2.3	7.0	21.5	4.9	2.5	1.9	11.6	(X)	4.6	7.4	3.1	.5	3.0
SD	5.6	20.6		20.1	5.2	.5	1.1	.4	.7	.3	1.0	—	1.8	6.9	.3	1.7	(X)	.5	.9		.6	.6
TN	35.9	134.0		134.0	33.7	—	8.1	2.3	4.7	4.5	5.2	21.0	4.2	6.9	1.6	17.4	(X)	7.8	7.0	6.3	1.1	3.5
TX	131.2	747.2		701.8	126.2	45.4	23.0	3.7	26.5	25.8	31.4	52.6	14.3	23.0	6.6	67.0	(X)	25.6	44.8	28.5	1.3	15.5
UT	25.4	54.9		54.9	24.3	—	2.9	.7	1.8	2.7	6.9	.4	1.6	1.9	.8	5.4	(X)	2.4	3.1	2.1	.3	3.0
VT	5.6	20.6		20.6	5.1	—	1.3	—	.5	—	.3	—	1.0	1.2	.7	.9	(X)	.4	1.1	.3	.2	.2
VA	57.5	199.9		198.1	54.6	1.9	2.8	8.4	5.6	5.9	14.8	2.4	7.6	4.2	2.9	18.7	(X)	10.5	13.9	9.1	.9	7.9

See footnotes at end of table.

Table 473. State and Local Government Full-Time Equivalent Employment by Selected Function and State: 2010-Continued.

See headnote on page 315.

State	Total [1]		Education				Public welfare		Health		Hospitals		Highways		Police protection		Fire protection		Corrections		Parks and recreation	
			Elementary and secondary		Higher education																	
	State	Local	State	Local	State	Local	State	Local	State	Local	State	Local	State	Local	State	Local	State	Local	State	Local	State	Local
WA....	57.5	104.0	–	104.0	55.5	–	9.5	1.7	5.7	4.0	10.7	15.8	5.9	7.2	2.2	13.0	(X)	9.5	9.6	5.1	.7	5.6
WV....	14.6	42.5	–	42.5	13.3	–	3.3	–	.8	1.2	1.8	2.5	5.1	.9	1.0	2.9	(X)	1.0	3.3	.2	.6	.8
WI.....	39.3	129.2	–	118.2	38.3	11.1	1.9	12.2	1.6	6.2	3.3	1.3	1.4	9.0	.9	15.0	(X)	4.8	10.2	4.0	.1	3.0
WY....	4.2	20.6	–	18.7	3.9	1.9	.8	.1	.8	.5	.7	6.3	1.9	.9	.3	1.8	(X)	.5	1.4	.7	.2	.8

– Represents or rounds to zero. X Not applicable. [1] Includes other categories, not shown separately.

Source: U.S. Census Bureau, 2010 Annual Survey of Public Employment and Payroll, January 2012. See also <http://www.census.gov/govs/apes/>.

Table 474. State and Local Government Employment and Average Monthly Earnings by State: 2000 to 2010

[4,083 represents 4,083,000. As of March. Full-time equivalent employment is a derived statistic that provides an estimate of a government's total full-time employment by converting part-time employees to a full-time amount]

State	Full-time equivalent employment (1,000) State 2000	State 2009	State 2010	Local [1] 2000	Local [1] 2009	Local [1] 2010	Average monthly earnings [2] (dol.) State 2000	State 2009	State 2010	Local [1] 2000	Local [1] 2009	Local [1] 2010
United States...	**4,083**	**4,408**	**4,378**	**10,995**	**12,392**	**12,204**	**3,374**	**4,565**	**4,620**	**3,169**	**4,233**	**4,308**
Alabama................	80	89	90	182	200	197	2,841	4,067	4,099	2,431	3,201	3,240
Alaska.................	23	26	27	25	28	28	3,842	5,078	5,176	3,818	4,822	4,979
Arizona...............	65	69	67	182	241	228	3,055	4,215	4,365	2,942	4,108	4,106
Arkansas.............	49	61	63	96	108	112	2,842	3,663	3,795	2,175	3,047	3,016
California.............	355	411	411	1,322	1,437	1,375	4,451	5,714	5,740	4,062	5,780	5,783
Colorado.............	66	73	71	164	203	202	3,779	5,033	5,033	3,076	4,122	4,235
Connecticut.........	66	66	63	111	128	124	3,909	5,825	5,632	3,856	4,752	5,071
Delaware............	24	27	26	21	23	23	3,222	4,227	4,113	3,163	4,496	4,486
District of Columbia.......	(X)	(X)	(X)	45	45	44	(X)	(X)	(X)	3,923	5,025	5,900
Florida...............	185	186	184	580	701	724	3,149	3,859	3,861	2,865	4,092	3,992
Georgia..............	120	123	124	334	411	393	2,899	3,915	3,794	2,677	3,459	3,439
Hawaii................	55	60	58	14	16	15	2,926	4,249	3,943	3,352	4,901	5,045
Idaho.................	23	23	22	51	56	56	3,022	4,202	4,280	2,478	3,321	3,381
Illinois................	128	137	131	493	525	508	3,441	5,077	5,324	3,307	4,450	4,685
Indiana...............	83	92	90	232	257	255	2,990	4,175	4,023	2,711	3,503	3,548
Iowa..................	55	52	51	121	131	127	3,656	5,376	5,326	2,727	3,735	3,838
Kansas...............	43	45	44	128	158	159	3,071	4,112	4,178	2,491	3,349	3,365
Kentucky............	74	81	81	149	163	162	3,051	3,946	3,940	2,339	3,022	3,106
Louisiana............	95	92	89	185	186	189	2,807	4,131	4,282	2,278	3,348	3,390
Maine.................	21	21	21	51	52	51	2,983	4,141	4,063	2,609	3,403	3,542
Maryland.............	91	90	88	182	212	214	3,312	4,606	4,650	3,535	5,129	5,191
Massachusetts. ..	96	97	95	232	246	234	3,683	4,924	4,973	3,403	4,772	4,822
Michigan.............	142	143	146	351	338	331	3,934	5,023	5,208	3,518	4,515	4,623
Minnesota...........	73	81	80	206	204	199	3,892	5,282	5,338	3,255	4,304	4,446
Mississippi..........	56	58	57	133	137	136	2,752	3,450	3,537	2,121	2,982	2,989
Missouri.............	91	90	89	208	238	236	2,678	3,398	3,518	2,678	3,441	3,526
Montana.............	18	21	20	34	36	38	2,931	3,949	4,016	2,546	3,489	3,498
Nebraska............	30	32	33	78	87	89	2,514	3,868	4,013	2,779	3,765	3,802
Nevada..............	22	30	28	61	87	86	3,444	5,016	4,891	3,817	5,027	5,150
New Hampshire...	19	20	19	46	53	54	3,079	4,453	4,584	2,830	3,744	3,815
New Jersey.........	133	154	152	316	361	359	4,075	5,686	5,767	3,967	5,177	5,445
New Mexico.........	48	49	48	70	82	80	2,811	3,938	3,978	2,494	3,460	3,453
New York............	251	257	251	924	997	973	3,859	5,282	5,484	3,961	5,051	5,320
North Carolina....	123	148	146	328	412	403	3,012	4,032	3,886	2,708	3,589	3,686
North Dakota......	16	18	18	23	25	26	2,826	3,952	4,103	2,778	3,488	3,548
Ohio..................	136	143	140	459	476	467	3,369	4,902	4,995	3,118	4,011	4,107
Oklahoma...........	64	72	71	134	149	146	2,821	3,774	3,864	2,280	3,129	3,122
Oregon..............	53	63	65	124	136	133	3,269	4,524	4,452	3,332	4,222	4,385
Pennsylvania......	150	173	168	388	440	431	3,436	4,338	4,564	3,296	4,082	4,290
Rhode Island.......	20	20	19	36	33	31	3,772	5,184	5,298	3,550	4,693	4,958
South Carolina....	79	77	77	155	179	175	2,741	3,579	3,810	2,474	3,484	3,475
South Dakota.....	13	14	14	28	33	32	2,777	3,749	3,938	2,359	3,129	3,148
Tennessee.........	81	84	83	218	244	246	2,786	3,794	3,822	2,631	3,359	3,359
Texas................	269	300	318	909	1,127	1,134	3,095	4,208	4,280	2,643	3,545	3,604
Utah..................	49	52	51	73	89	90	2,880	4,293	4,409	2,836	3,798	3,698
Vermont.............	14	15	14	23	25	26	3,153	4,389	4,645	2,534	3,611	3,585
Virginia..............	119	126	125	269	323	318	3,229	4,246	4,384	2,928	3,900	3,912
Washington........	112	125	123	193	241	228	3,551	4,772	4,913	3,835	5,368	5,505
West Virginia......	32	40	39	61	63	62	2,694	3,479	3,554	2,517	3,130	3,230
Wisconsin..........	64	70	72	220	214	214	3,710	4,878	4,901	3,210	4,233	4,238
Wyoming............	11	14	14	29	38	37	2,589	3,922	4,240	2,660	4,098	4,143

X Not applicable. [1] Estimates subject to sampling variation; see Appendix III and source. [2] For full-time employees.

Source: U.S. Census Bureau; *2010 Annual Survey of Public Employment and Payroll Summary Report*, January 2012. . See also <http://www.census.gov/govs/apes/>.

Table 475. City Government Employment and Payroll—Largest Cities: 2000 to 2010

[In thousands (458.1 represents 458,100), except as noted. As of March. See headnote, Table 474 for full-time equivalent employment definition]

Cities ranked by 2010 population [1]	Total employment (1,000)			Full-time equivalent employment total (1,000)			Payroll (mil. dol.)			Average monthly earnings for full-time employees (dol.)		
	2000	2009	2010	2000	2009	2010	2000	2009	2010	2000	2009	2010
New York, NY............	458.1	453.9	444.0	429.3	423.6	413.0	1,708.8	2,315.1	2,407.5	4,150	5,535	5,918
Los Angeles, CA........	49.4	57.6	55.1	48.4	53.2	51.0	230.1	393.4	385.2	4,793	7,675	7,850
Chicago, IL..............	41.3	38.7	34.9	40.7	37.8	34.1	171.3	192.2	202.5	4,239	5,102	5,959
Houston, TX.............	25.2	23.0	22.8	24.9	22.6	22.6	75.2	98.6	99.0	3,037	4,353	4,389
Philadelphia, PA........	31.1	31.3	30.8	30.0	30.4	29.9	109.2	142.8	144.7	3,637	4,705	4,867
Phoenix, AZ.............	13.0	16.2	14.9	12.7	15.6	14.4	50.3	82.7	80.7	4,024	5,413	5,718
San Antonio, TX........	16.9	16.0	16.5	15.7	15.5	15.4	48.0	63.8	64.9	3,160	4,184	4,293
San Diego, CA..........	12.3	11.3	10.8	11.4	10.5	10.2	46.9	61.3	63.0	4,201	6,022	6,288
Dallas, TX..............	15.6	17.2	15.5	15.2	16.7	15.1	50.4	75.4	72.8	3,332	4,576	4,884
San Jose, CA...........	7.6	7.9	7.6	6.9	7.0	6.7	36.3	52.9	52.5	5,569	7,966	8,401
Jacksonville, FL........	10.1	9.8	9.7	9.7	9.6	9.4	35.6	40.1	41.8	3,815	4,230	4,487
Indianapolis, IN........	12.4	14.0	14.2	12.0	13.4	13.7	36.7	52.3	54.8	3,115	3,878	4,050
San Francisco, CA......	27.7	28.5	30.7	27.7	27.2	27.3	141.6	195.5	207.2	5,112	7,465	7,666
Austin, TX..............	10.6	13.1	12.6	10.1	12.7	12.3	31.2	59.9	59.5	3,128	4,731	4,863
Columbus, OH..........	9.1	8.4	8.2	8.8	8.1	7.9	30.1	40.8	40.6	3,478	5,093	5,210
Ft Worth, TX............	6.1	6.5	6.3	5.7	6.5	6.2	18.9	29.2	28.7	3,394	4,538	4,618
Charlotte, NC...........	5.2	7.3	7.4	5.1	6.8	6.9	17.1	31.2	31.2	3,408	4,613	4,570
Detroit, MI..............	40.7	13.8	13.1	36.1	13.7	12.9	132.1	60.9	58.4	3,693	4,487	4,570
El Paso, TX.............	5.9	6.2	5.9	5.8	6.0	5.6	15.6	22.5	21.2	2,701	3,796	3,836
Memphis, TN............	28.2	25.8	24.5	26.9	24.6	23.5	80.3	91.0	87.1	3,024	3,770	3,746
Baltimore, MD..........	30.8	30.1	27.9	29.2	28.4	26.7	95.3	129.9	121.8	3,361	4,675	4,597
Boston, MA.............	23.3	21.8	19.9	22.0	21.1	19.3	80.2	110.5	104.0	3,734	5,319	5,452
Seattle, WA.............	11.4	13.7	13.9	10.3	12.4	12.5	48.3	71.5	72.4	4,726	5,918	5,948
Washington, DC........	37.7	36.6	35.2	36.5	35.1	34.0	139.4	166.7	197.8	3,863	4,842	5,893
Denver, CO.............	14.5	13.4	13.0	13.7	12.6	12.3	47.3	64.6	65.2	3,534	5,227	5,388
Nashville, TN...........	20.6	23.3	23.9	19.6	21.6	21.7	62.3	91.0	91.4	3,235	4,399	4,311
Louisville, KY...........	4.6	8.5	8.9	4.3	8.2	8.6	11.8	32.3	33.9	2,844	4,001	4,028
Milwaukee, WI..........	7.9	7.1	6.9	7.7	6.8	6.7	28.5	34.4	33.3	3,706	5,097	5,020
Portland, OR............	6.2	6.8	6.8	5.4	5.9	5.8	23.4	33.9	35.1	4,416	5,989	6,253
Las Vegas, NV..........	2.6	3.1	3.2	2.5	2.9	2.9	11.2	21.1	19.3	4,681	7,499	7,162
Oklahoma City, OK.....	5.1	4.8	4.7	4.8	4.6	4.4	16.0	22.9	21.0	3,457	5,149	4,858
Albuquerque, NM.......	7.1	7.1	7.0	6.6	6.8	6.5	18.3	23.7	22.9	2,868	3,612	3,654
Tucson, AZ.............	7.1	6.0	5.6	5.8	5.6	5.3	16.0	25.4	23.5	2,787	4,740	4,545
Fresno, CA.............	3.2	4.6	4.1	3.1	4.3	4.0	12.7	22.2	20.2	4,073	5,403	5,260
Sacramento, CA.........	4.4	5.6	5.7	4.0	4.9	5.0	17.0	24.8	28.1	4,400	5,469	6,061
Long Beach, CA.........	6.1	6.8	6.6	5.7	6.3	6.1	25.7	36.1	35.0	4,855	5,973	5,982
Kansas City, MO........	6.8	6.8	6.4	6.6	6.8	6.3	21.3	29.3	27.3	3,246	4,349	4,324
Mesa, AZ...............	3.5	3.7	3.6	3.3	3.6	3.5	13.4	20.6	19.2	4,072	5,845	5,532
Virginia Beach, VA......	19.7	19.4	19.2	17.4	18.0	17.7	43.4	62.2	61.1	2,679	3,778	3,775
Atlanta, GA.............	8.8	7.9	8.1	8.6	7.9	8.1	25.6	30.9	31.5	2,974	3,901	3,872
Colorado Springs, CO...	7.4	8.6	8.3	6.9	7.9	7.6	25.3	38.4	39.8	3,747	4,941	5,307
Omaha, NE..............	3.4	3.1	3.1	2.9	2.9	2.9	10.6	14.0	14.8	3,874	5,193	5,491
Raleigh, NC.............	3.2	4.3	5.1	2.9	3.8	4.2	8.9	15.2	16.3	3,114	4,248	4,166
Miami, FL...............	3.8	4.5	4.3	3.6	4.2	4.1	15.1	24.4	21.2	4,276	5,992	5,378
Cleveland, OH..........	10.1	7.8	8.4	9.4	7.7	7.9	27.8	34.2	35.2	2,989	4,472	4,462
Tulsa, OK...............	4.5	4.4	4.0	4.5	4.3	3.9	13.7	17.8	16.8	3,126	4,204	4,376
Oakland, CA............	4.2	5.4	4.1	4.2	5.3	3.6	24.8	37.7	28.4	5,861	7,109	8,702
Minneapolis, MN........	6.3	5.5	5.5	5.8	5.2	5.1	21.3	25.8	25.7	3,866	5,084	5,159
Wichita, KS.............	3.6	3.9	3.1	3.1	3.4	3.1	9.3	13.7	13.0	3,072	4,175	4,198
Arlington, TX............	3.0	2.9	2.9	2.4	2.6	2.6	7.1	12.2	12.1	3,090	4,975	4,878
Bakersfield, CA..........	1.3	1.5	1.5	1.2	1.5	1.5	5.3	8.3	8.2	4,469	5,586	5,691
New Orleans, LA........	(NA)	6.8	6.9	(NA)	6.6	6.8	(NA)	25.2	25.9	(NA)	3,788	3,815
Honolulu, HI.............	9.8	10.0	9.5	9.1	9.3	8.8	30.9	45.1	45.8	3,435	4,937	5,266
Anaheim, CA............	3.2	3.6	3.2	2.5	2.7	2.6	11.5	17.8	17.4	5,267	7,797	7,982
Tampa, FL..............	4.3	4.3	4.5	4.2	4.2	4.4	14.1	22.3	23.2	3,370	5,387	5,376
Aurora, CO..............	2.5	2.6	2.6	2.5	2.6	2.6	9.0	13.6	13.8	3,682	5,271	5,374
Santa Ana, CA..........	2.5	2.1	1.7	2.2	1.8	1.5	10.1	13.8	12.1	5,606	8,101	8,623
St Louis, MO............	8.0	6.8	6.9	7.6	6.5	6.8	24.1	26.9	26.8	3,176	4,122	3,973
Pittsburgh, PA...........	4.4	4.2	3.3	4.3	4.2	3.3	15.3	18.2	13.8	3,593	4,374	4,210
Riverside, CA...........	2.1	2.6	2.4	1.9	2.3	2.2	8.0	14.5	13.8	4,625	6,575	6,536
Corpus Christi, TX......	3.5	3.3	2.8	3.3	3.3	2.8	8.6	12.0	10.5	2,675	3,707	3,848
Cincinnati, OH..........	6.5	6.0	5.9	6.4	5.7	5.6	21.3	24.9	27.9	3,504	4,518	5,122
Lexington, KY...........	4.0	5.1	4.1	3.6	4.4	3.8	10.2	16.6	16.6	2,910	4,099	4,575
Anchorage, AK..........	10.1	11.1	11.1	9.0	10.0	9.9	34.6	48.5	50.6	3,973	4,938	5,142
Stockton, CA............	2.3	2.0	1.8	1.9	1.8	1.6	7.1	9.7	9.4	4,054	5,759	6,160
Toledo, OH.............	2.8	2.9	2.6	2.8	2.9	2.6	10.0	12.7	11.7	3,628	4,406	4,551
St Paul, MN.............	4.2	3.3	3.2	3.2	3.0	3.0	13.3	15.3	16.4	4,189	5,356	5,751
Newark, NJ.............	5.5	4.3	4.7	5.2	3.6	4.5	22.3	17.7	26.6	4,371	5,104	6,061
Greensboro, NC.........	0.0	3.4	3.4	0.0	3.1	3.1	0.0	12.0	11.6	0	3,994	3,837
Plano, TX...............	2.0	2.6	2.5	1.8	2.2	2.2	6.4	10.6	10.2	3,702	4,934	4,927
Buffalo, NY.............	11.4	10.5	11.3	10.5	9.9	10.0	43.4	45.4	45.9	4,457	4,694	4,569
Lincoln, NE.............	2.7	2.8	2.9	2.5	2.6	2.6	8.2	12.1	12.4	3,382	4,869	4,982
Henderson, NV..........	0.0	2.8	2.7	0.0	2.3	2.2	0.0	14.1	13.7	0	6,957	7,007
Ft Wayne, IN............	0.0	2.1	2.1	0.0	2.0	2.0	0.0	8.0	8.6	0	4,109	4,319
Jersey City, NJ..........	(NA)	4.0	3.6	(NA)	3.7	3.4	(NA)	22.0	20.2	(NA)	6,142	6,122
Chula Vista, CA.........	(NA)	1.7	1.4	(NA)	1.4	1.3	(NA)	8.6	7.9	(NA)	6,276	6,314

NA Not applicable. [1] Based on estimated resident population as of July 1.

Source: U.S. Census Bureau, *2010 Annual Survey of Public Employment and Payroll*, January 2012. See also <http://www.census.gov/govs/apes/>.

Table 476. County Government Employment and Payroll—Largest Counties: 1999 to 2010

[In thousands (93.3 represents 93,300). As of March. See text, this section. See headnote, Table 474, for full-time equivalent employment definition]

Counties ranked by 2010 population [1]	Total employment (1,000)			Total full-time equivalent employment (1,000)		Payroll (mil. dol.)			Average monthly earnings for full-time employees (dol.)	
	1999	2009	2010	1999	2010	1999	2009	2010	1999	2010
Los Angeles, CA..........	93.3	109.7	107.5	89.7	103.9	368.6	610.1	610.3	4,165	5,679
Cook, IL..................	27.4	22.8	22.8	27.4	22.8	91.2	110.1	120.7	3,333	5,305
Harris, TX................	19.4	26.7	27.8	19.1	26.4	56.8	111.5	119.8	2,981	4,537
Maricopa, AZ.............	14.6	13.9	13.2	14.5	13.1	36.9	56.3	54.2	2,562	4,188
San Diego, CA............	19.1	22.1	20.9	18.1	19.5	62.8	104.8	101.1	3,513	5,201
Orange, CA...............	22.8	19.2	17.7	21.4	16.9	71.1	108.1	102.9	3,358	6,103
Dade, FL.................	36.6	47.3	51.1	35.6	49.9	123.3	288.6	285.0	3,546	5,794
Dallas, TX................	12.5	16.7	18.1	11.9	16.8	34.2	76.2	76.6	2,881	4,536
Riverside, CA.............	14.7	21.3	21.0	14.3	20.1	51.9	116.8	110.8	3,688	5,517
San Bernardino, CA......	18.1	21.5	21.2	16.8	19.9	58.2	102.4	101.7	3,553	5,269
Clark, NV................	15.6	22.1	22.4	14.2	20.3	54.8	120.8	121.5	3,982	6,155
King, WA.................	16.1	14.4	14.1	14.2	13.4	52.9	78.1	82.3	3,867	6,321
Tarrant, TX...............	6.6	11.6	11.0	6.4	10.7	17.1	47.1	46.0	2,717	4,307
Wayne, MI................	6.7	5.3	4.7	6.6	4.7	24.0	24.8	21.5	3,658	4,645
Santa Clara, CA..........	15.2	19.2	19.0	14.6	18.2	62.3	128.5	129.6	4,342	7,297
Broward, FL..............	10.7	13.2	12.1	10.5	11.7	33.5	59.2	61.4	3,220	5,313
Bexar, TX................	9.2	10.9	11.0	8.9	10.6	22.4	41.0	41.3	2,545	3,865
Alameda, CA.............	11.5	13.2	12.1	10.6	11.5	45.4	87.2	77.2	4,263	6,885
Suffolk, NY..............	12.7	17.0	15.0	11.8	13.2	49.1	84.5	74.7	4,300	5,813
Sacramento, CA..........	12.7	13.8	13.1	11.7	12.7	46.7	78.0	72.5	3,963	5,736
Nassau, NY..............	18.5	17.6	18.0	17.4	16.0	73.5	85.0	88.5	4,518	5,748
Palm Beach, FL..........	8.4	11.6	11.3	8.2	10.9	26.0	60.1	60.7	3,193	5,634
Cuyahoga, OH...........	15.7	16.1	14.6	15.7	14.2	46.2	70.4	62.1	2,939	4,305
Hillsborough, FL..........	14.5	11.9	10.5	12.4	10.1	30.2	48.2	45.7	2,640	4,583
Allegheny, PA............	7.3	6.9	7.1	7.2	7.0	18.0	24.6	26.3	2,530	3,853
Oakland, MI..............	4.7	4.7	4.3	4.4	4.0	15.2	20.5	18.8	3,537	4,764
Franklin, OH.............	7.1	6.7	6.7	6.8	6.4	18.1	25.0	25.3	2,727	3,957
Hennepin, MN............	12.9	7.6	7.7	10.9	7.6	40.0	38.8	40.3	3,705	5,449
Orange, FL...............	9.4	11.8	11.3	8.8	10.4	26.1	44.7	43.8	2,986	4,235
Fairfax, VA...............	34.3	47.3	47.6	31.5	39.2	107.5	204.8	200.7	3,514	5,170
Contra Costa, CA.........	9.9	9.0	8.6	9.1	7.9	41.0	50.2	49.8	4,620	6,337
Salt Lake, UT............	5.6	6.1	6.5	4.2	4.9	12.2	17.3	18.2	3,176	4,010
Travis, TX................	3.6	5.2	5.3	3.5	5.2	10.4	21.6	22.0	2,949	4,228
St. Louis, MO............	4.1	4.1	4.1	4.0	4.0	12.0	16.0	15.9	3,052	4,042
Pima, AZ................	7.9	7.9	7.7	7.1	7.2	18.8	28.7	28.3	2,717	4,056
Montgomery, MD........	36.8	42.6	43.3	28.5	36.3	116.3	220.8	232.5	4,401	6,859
Westchester, NY.........	10.4	11.8	11.6	9.8	10.3	40.0	48.3	66.5	4,067	6,463
Milwaukee, WI...........	8.2	7.6	7.3	7.8	6.8	25.9	30.7	30.1	3,374	4,436
Fresno, CA...............	7.5	8.9	9.0	7.2	8.4	22.3	37.7	37.6	3,190	4,513
Shelby, TN...............	13.6	14.5	13.9	12.9	13.4	36.2	51.0	48.5	2,825	3,641
Fulton, GA...............	7.9	9.0	6.0	7.6	6.0	23.5	37.4	23.1	3,203	3,890
Mecklenburg, NC........	23.1	28.6	28.3	20.4	26.2	54.0	92.8	104.4	2,722	4,040
Erie, NY.................	12.3	11.7	11.2	10.6	10.0	35.5	42.4	44.2	3,538	4,583
Du Page, IL..............	3.6	3.6	3.0	3.4	2.9	10.3	12.9	12.5	3,097	4,403
Pinellas, FL..............	5.7	6.5	6.2	5.6	6.1	16.2	28.9	26.9	2,915	4,430
Wake, NC................	16.9	25.8	25.5	14.9	21.9	39.5	90.3	88.1	2,686	4,018
Bergen, NJ...............	5.7	5.8	6.0	4.1	4.9	13.2	25.0	26.8	3,273	5,674
Prince Georges, MD......	30.0	34.7	35.7	27.2	29.4	84.6	155.6	155.6	3,195	5,489
Kern, CA................	9.0	11.2	11.3	8.7	10.7	29.4	55.0	55.6	3,426	5,263
Macomb, MI.............	3.0	3.4	3.1	2.8	2.9	8.7	13.1	11.7	3,245	4,241
Ventura, CA..............	8.3	9.5	9.3	8.1	8.9	30.2	56.7	57.0	3,754	6,584
Middlesex, NJ............	5.5	5.1	4.6	4.9	3.7	16.9	22.1	19.5	3,528	5,448
Gwinnett, GA.............	3.7	5.4	5.3	3.5	4.9	10.7	21.9	20.4	3,090	4,200
Baltimore, MD............	25.7	29.7	30.6	22.6	26.2	66.5	118.2	122.2	3,172	4,979
El Paso, TX..............	3.7	5.1	5.1	3.6	5.0	9.0	20.1	20.4	2,573	4,173
Hamilton, OH.............	6.0	5.4	5.1	5.8	5.0	15.0	19.8	19.0	2,604	3,838
Montgomery, PA.........	3.7	4.1	3.6	3.5	3.5	9.0	12.9	13.0	2,690	3,824
Pierce, WA...............	3.4	3.9	3.5	3.2	3.3	13.7	21.3	20.2	4,367	6,108
Collin, TX................	1.0	2.0	2.0	1.0	2.0	2.7	7.6	7.6	2,617	3,875
Essex, NJ................	6.5	5.4	5.2	5.8	4.6	20.2	24.8	24.3	3,573	5,351
Hidalgo, TX..............	1.6	2.7	2.9	1.6	2.9	3.3	8.6	9.1	2,040	3,140
Monroe, NY..............	6.9	6.9	7.1	6.0	6.2	18.9	25.7	25.6	3,157	4,279
Multnomah, OR..........	5.7	4.8	4.9	4.6	4.6	12.6	22.4	22.4	2,990	4,998
Oklahoma, OK...........	2.4	2.4	2.4	2.3	2.2	4.2	6.5	6.5	1,834	2,977
San Mateo, CA..........	6.1	7.7	7.3	5.8	6.9	23.9	42.4	41.7	4,346	7,042
Snohomish, WA..........	2.4	2.9	2.7	2.4	2.7	8.6	15.1	14.9	3,643	5,481
Dekalb, GA..............	6.2	7.6	7.5	6.1	7.4	18.1	27.8	27.9	3,000	3,827
Cobb, GA................	4.0	5.1	5.0	3.8	4.5	10.7	17.5	18.7	2,933	4,235
San Joaquin, CA.........	7.1	8.2	8.3	6.5	7.2	20.7	37.7	37.6	3,364	5,334
Will, IL..................	1.9	2.4	2.4	1.8	2.3	5.5	10.0	9.7	3,052	4,259
Jackson, MO.............	1.9	2.0	2.0	1.8	2.0	4.4	6.1	6.7	2,403	3,417
Lake, IL.................	2.9	3.3	3.3	2.7	3.0	8.5	13.8	14.2	3,180	4,809
Norfolk, MA..............	0.9	0.5	0.1	0.9	0.1	2.5	2.2	0.6	2,810	5,406
Denton, TX..............	(NA)	1.9	1.9	(NA)	1.9	(NA)	6.9	7.0	(NA)	3,763

NA Not available. [1] Based on estimated resident population as of July 1.

Source: U.S. Census Bureau, "2010 Annual Survey of Public Employment and Payroll," January 2012. See also <http://www.census.gov/govs/apes/>.

Section 9
Federal Government Finances and Employment

This section presents statistics relating to the financial structure and the civilian employment of the federal government. The fiscal data cover taxes, other receipts, outlays, and debt. The principal sources of fiscal data are the *Budget of the United States Government* and related documents, published annually by the Office of Management and Budget (OMB), and the U.S. Department of the Treasury's *Combined Statement of Receipts, Outlays, and Balances of the United States Government*. Detailed data on tax returns and collections are published annually by the Internal Revenue Service. The personnel data relate to staffing and payrolls. They are published by the Office of Personnel Management and the Bureau of Labor Statistics. Data on federally owned land and real property are collected by the General Services Administration and presented in its annual *Federal Real Property Report*.

Budget concept—Under the unified budget concept, all federal monies are included in one comprehensive budget. These monies comprise both federal funds and trust funds. Federal funds are derived mainly from taxes and borrowing and are not restricted by law to any specific government purpose. Trust funds, such as the Unemployment Trust Fund, collect certain taxes and other receipts for use in carrying out specific purposes or programs in accordance with the terms of the trust agreement or statute. Fund balances include both cash balances with the Treasury and investments in U.S. securities. Part of the balance is obligated, part unobligated. Prior to 1985, the budget totals, under provisions of law, excluded some federal activities—including the Federal Financing Bank, the Postal Service, the Synthetic Fuels Corporation, and the lending activities of the Rural Electrification Administration. The Balanced Budget and Emergency Deficit Control Act of 1985 (P.L.99-177) repealed the off-budget status of these entities and placed Social Security (Federal Old-Age and Survivors Insurance and the Federal Disability Insurance Trust Funds) off-budget. Though Social Security is now off-budget and, by law, excluded from coverage of the congressional budget resolutions, it continues to be a federal program. Receipts arising from the government's sovereign powers are reported as governmental receipts and all other receipts, i.e., from business or market-oriented activities, are offset against outlays. Outlays are reported on a checks-issued (net) basis (i.e., outlays are recorded at the time the checks to pay bills are issued).

Debt concept—For most of U.S. history, the total debt consisted of debt borrowed by the Treasury (i.e., public debt). The present debt series includes both public debt and agency debt. The *gross federal debt* includes money borrowed by the Treasury and by various federal agencies; it is the broadest generally used measure of the federal debt. *Total public debt* is covered by a statutory debt limitation and includes only borrowing by the Treasury.

Treasury receipts and outlays—All receipts of the government, with a few exceptions, are deposited to the credit of the U.S. Treasury regardless of ultimate disposition. Under the Constitution, no money may be withdrawn from the Treasury unless appropriated by the Congress.

The day-to-day cash operations of the federal government clearing through the accounts of the U.S. Treasury are reported in the *Daily Treasury Statement*. Extensive detail on the public debt is published in the *Monthly Statement of the Public Debt of the United States*.

Budget receipts such as taxes, customs duties, and miscellaneous receipts, which are collected by government agencies, and outlays represented by checks issued and cash payments made by disbursing officers as well as government agencies are reported in the *Monthly Treasury Statement of Receipts and Outlays of the United States Government* and in the Treasury's *Combined Statement of Receipts, Outlays, and Balances of the United States Government*. These deposits in and payments from accounts maintained by government agencies are on the same basis as the unified budget.

The quarterly *Treasury Bulletin* contains data on fiscal operations and related Treasury activities, including financial statements of government corporations and other business-type activities.

Income tax returns and tax collections—Tax data are compiled by the Internal Revenue Service of the Treasury Department. The annual *Internal Revenue Service Data Book* gives a detailed account of tax collections by kind of tax. The agency's annual *Statistics of Income* reports present detailed data from individual income tax returns and corporation income tax returns. The quarterly *Statistics of Income Bulletin* presents data on such diverse subjects as tax-exempt organizations, unincorporated businesses, fiduciary income tax and estate tax returns, sales of capital assets by individuals, international income and taxes reported by corporations and individuals, and estate tax wealth.

Employment and payrolls—The Office of Personnel Management collects employment and payroll data from all departments and agencies of the federal government, except the Central Intelligence Agency, the National Security Agency, and the Defense Intelligence Agency. Employment figures represent the number of persons who occupied civilian positions at the end of the report month shown and who are paid for services rendered to the federal government, regardless of the nature of appointment or method of payment. Federal payrolls include all payments for personal services rendered during the report month and payments for accumulated annual leave of employees who separate from the service. Since most federal employees are paid on a biweekly basis, the calendar month earnings are partially estimated on the basis of the number of work days in each month where payroll periods overlap.

Federal employment and payroll figures are published by the Office of Personnel Management in its *Federal Civilian Workforce Statistics—Employment and Trends*. It also publishes employment data on minority groups, white- and blue-collar workers, employment by geographic area, and salary and wage distribution of federal employees. General schedule is primarily white-collar; wage system primarily blue-collar. Data on federal employment are also issued by the Bureau of Labor Statistics in its *Monthly Labor Review* and *Employment and Earnings Online* and by the U.S. Census Bureau in its annual report series *Federal, State, and Local Governments: Public Employment and Payroll Data.*

Table 477. Federal Budget—Receipts and Outlays: 1960 to 2012

[92.5 represents $92,500,000,000. For fiscal years ending in year shown; See text, Section 8. See also headnote, Table 479]

Fiscal year	In current dollars (bil. dol.)			In constant (2005) dollars (bil. dol.)			As percentage of GDP [1]		
	Receipts	Outlays	Surplus or deficit (−)	Receipts	Outlays	Surplus or deficit (−)	Receipts	Outlays	Surplus or deficit (−)
1960	92.5	92.2	0.3	630.5	628.4	2.0	17.8	17.8	0.1
1970	192.8	195.6	-2.8	967.9	982.2	-14.3	19.0	19.3	-0.3
1980	517.1	590.9	-73.8	1,197.3	1,368.2	-170.9	19.0	21.7	-2.7
1990	1,032.0	1,253.0	-221.0	1,508.3	1,831.3	-323.1	18.0	21.9	-3.9
1995	1,351.8	1,515.7	-164.0	1,690.8	1,895.9	-205.1	18.4	20.6	-2.2
1996	1,453.1	1,560.5	-107.4	1,774.8	1,906.1	-131.2	18.8	20.2	-1.4
1997	1,579.2	1,601.1	-21.9	1,889.3	1,915.4	-26.2	19.2	19.5	-0.3
1998	1,721.7	1,652.5	69.3	2,040.2	1,958.1	82.1	19.9	19.1	0.8
1999	1,827.5	1,701.8	125.6	2,135.4	1,988.6	146.8	19.8	18.5	1.4
2000	2,025.2	1,789.0	236.2	2,309.2	2,039.9	269.4	20.6	18.2	2.4
2001	1,991.1	1,862.8	128.2	2,214.3	2,071.7	142.6	19.5	18.2	1.3
2002	1,853.1	2,010.9	-157.8	2,027.9	2,200.6	-172.6	17.6	19.1	-1.5
2003	1,782.3	2,159.9	-377.6	1,900.5	2,303.2	-402.6	16.2	19.7	-3.4
2004	1,880.1	2,292.8	-412.7	1,949.3	2,377.2	-427.9	16.1	19.6	-3.5
2005	2,153.6	2,472.0	-318.3	2,153.6	2,472.0	-318.3	17.3	19.9	-2.6
2006	2,406.9	2,655.0	-248.2	2,324.6	2,564.3	-239.7	18.2	20.1	-1.9
2007	2,568.0	2,728.7	-160.7	2,413.1	2,564.1	-151.0	18.5	19.7	-1.2
2008	2,524.0	2,982.5	-458.6	2,288.1	2,703.8	-415.7	17.6	20.8	-3.2
2009	2,105.0	3,517.7	-1,412.7	1,899.0	3,173.4	-1,274.4	15.1	25.2	-10.1
2010	2,162.7	3,456.2	-1,293.5	1,927.9	3,081.0	-1,153.0	15.1	24.1	-9.0
2011	2,303.5	3,603.1	-1,299.6	1,998.7	3,126.3	-1,127.6	15.4	24.1	-8.7
2012, est	2,468.6	3,795.5	-1,326.9	2,089.4	3,212.5	-1,123.1	15.8	24.3	-8.5

[1] Gross domestic product; see text, Section 13.

Source: U.S. Office of Management and Budget, *Budget of the United States Government, Historical Tables*, annual. See also <http://www.whitehouse.gov/omb/budget>.

Table 478. Federal Budget Debt: 1960 to 2012

[290.5 represents $290,500,000,000. As of the end of the fiscal year. See text, Section 8]

Fiscal year	Total (bil. dol.)					As percentages of GDP [1]				
	Gross federal debt	Federal govern- ment accounts	Held by the public			Gross federal debt	Federal govern- ment accounts	Held by the public		
			Total	Federal Reserve System	Other			Total	Federal Reserve System	Other
1960	290.5	53.7	236.8	26.5	210.3	56.0	10.3	45.6	5.1	40.5
1970	380.9	97.7	283.2	57.7	225.5	37.6	9.6	28.0	5.7	22.3
1980	909.0	197.1	711.9	120.8	591.1	33.4	7.2	26.1	4.4	21.7
1985	1,817.4	310.2	1,507.3	169.8	1,337.5	43.8	7.5	36.4	4.1	32.3
1988	2,601.1	549.5	2,051.6	229.2	1,822.4	51.9	11.0	41.0	4.6	36.4
1989	2,867.8	677.1	2,190.7	220.1	1,970.6	53.1	12.5	40.6	4.1	36.5
1990	3,206.3	794.7	2,411.6	234.4	2,177.1	55.9	13.9	42.1	4.1	38.0
1991	3,598.2	909.2	2,689.0	258.6	2,430.4	60.7	15.3	45.3	4.4	41.0
1992	4,001.8	1,002.1	2,999.7	296.4	2,703.3	64.1	16.1	48.1	4.7	43.3
1993	4,351.0	1,102.6	3,248.4	325.7	2,922.7	66.1	16.7	49.3	4.9	44.4
1994	4,643.3	1,210.2	3,433.1	355.2	3,077.9	66.6	17.3	49.2	5.1	44.1
1995	4,920.6	1,316.2	3,604.4	374.1	3,230.3	67.0	17.9	49.1	5.1	44.0
1996	5,181.5	1,447.4	3,734.1	390.9	3,343.1	67.1	18.8	48.4	5.1	43.3
1997	5,369.2	1,596.9	3,772.3	424.5	3,347.8	65.4	19.4	45.9	5.2	40.8
1998	5,478.2	1,757.1	3,721.1	458.2	3,262.9	63.2	20.3	43.0	5.3	37.7
1999	5,605.5	1,973.2	3,632.4	496.6	3,135.7	60.9	21.4	39.4	5.4	34.1
2000	5,628.7	2,218.9	3,409.8	511.4	2,898.4	57.3	22.6	34.7	5.2	29.5
2001	5,769.9	2,450.3	3,319.6	534.1	2,785.5	56.4	24.0	32.5	5.2	27.2
2002	6,198.4	2,658.0	3,540.4	604.2	2,936.2	58.8	25.2	33.6	5.7	27.8
2003	6,760.0	2,846.6	3,913.4	656.1	3,257.3	61.6	25.9	35.6	6.0	29.7
2004	7,354.7	3,059.1	4,295.5	700.3	3,595.2	63.0	26.2	36.8	6.0	30.8
2005	7,905.3	3,313.1	4,592.2	736.4	3,855.9	63.6	26.7	36.9	5.9	31.0
2006	8,451.4	3,622.4	4,829.0	768.9	4,060.0	64.0	27.4	36.6	5.8	30.7
2007	8,950.7	3,915.6	5,035.1	779.6	4,255.5	64.6	28.2	36.3	5.6	30.7
2008	9,986.1	4,183.0	5,803.1	491.1	5,311.9	69.7	29.2	40.5	3.4	37.1
2009	11,875.9	4,331.1	7,544.7	769.2	6,775.5	85.2	31.1	54.1	5.5	48.6
2010	13,528.8	4,509.9	9,018.9	811.7	8,207.2	94.2	31.4	62.8	5.7	57.2
2011	14,764.2	4,636.0	10,128.2	1,664.7	8,463.5	98.7	31.0	67.7	11.1	56.6
2012, est	16,350.9	4,772.8	11,578.1	(NA)	(NA)	104.8	30.6	74.2	(NA)	(NA)

NA Not available. [1] Gross domestic product; see text, Section 13.

Source: U.S. Office of Management and Budget, *Budget of the United States Government, Historical Tables*, annual. See also <http://www.whitehouse.gov/omb/budget>.

Table 479. Federal Budget Outlays by Type: 1990 to 2012

[1,253.0 represents $1,253,000,000,000. For fiscal years ending September 30. Given the inherent imprecision in adjusting outlays for inflation, the data shown in constant dollars present a reasonable perspective—not precision. The deflators and the categories that are deflated are as comparable over time as feasible. Minus sign (–) indicates offset]

Type	Unit	1990	2000	2005	2009	2010	2011	2012, est.
Current dollar outlays	**Bil. dol.**	**1,253.0**	**1,789.0**	**2,472.0**	**3,517.7**	**3,456.2**	**3,603.1**	**3,795.5**
National defense [1]	Bil. dol.	299.3	294.4	495.3	661.0	693.6	705.6	716.3
Nondefense, total	Bil. dol.	953.7	1,494.6	1,976.7	2,856.6	2,762.6	2,897.4	3,079.2
Payments for individuals	Bil. dol.	585.7	1,054.5	1,490.2	2,093.0	2,285.6	2,344.3	2,366.3
Direct payments [2]	Bil. dol.	507.0	867.7	1,212.1	1,732.2	1,893.3	1,948.9	1,993.8
Grants to State and local governments	Bil. dol.	78.7	186.8	278.1	360.7	392.3	395.4	372.4
All other grants	Bil. dol.	56.4	99.1	149.9	177.2	216.0	211.3	239.8
Net interest [2]	Bil. dol.	184.3	222.9	184.0	186.9	196.2	230.0	224.8
All other [2]	Bil. dol.	163.9	160.7	217.8	492.2	146.9	198.3	347.3
Undistributed offsetting receipts [2]	Bil. dol.	-36.6	-42.6	-65.2	-92.6	-82.1	-86.5	-98.9
Constant (2005) dollar outlays	**Bil. dol.**	**1,831.3**	**2,039.9**	**2,472.0**	**3,173.4**	**3,081.0**	**3,126.3**	**3,212.5**
National defense [1]	Bil. dol.	461.1	361.3	495.3	588.2	614.1	612.0	610.9
Nondefense, total	Bil. dol.	1,370.0	1,678.6	1,976.6	2,585.2	2,466.6	2,514.3	2,601.6
Payments for individuals	Bil. dol.	815.0	1,171.8	1,490.2	1,908.7	2,046.8	2,038.4	2,002.5
Direct payments [2]	Bil. dol.	705.4	964.0	1,212.1	1,580.1	1,696.1	1,695.2	1,687.7
Grants to state and local governments	Bil. dol.	109.6	207.8	278.1	328.6	350.7	343.2	314.9
All other grants	Bil. dol.	87.9	118.5	149.9	148.3	181.4	171.8	189.6
Net interest [2]	Bil. dol.	255.5	250.6	184.0	169.1	175.9	202.2	194.1
All other [2]	Bil. dol.	278.8	190.5	217.8	441.3	134.5	176.1	298.7
Undistributed offsetting receipts [2]	Bil. dol.	-67.1	-52.9	-65.2	-82.1	-71.8	-74.2	-83.3
Outlays as percent of GDP [3]	**Percent**	**21.9**	**18.2**	**19.9**	**25.2**	**24.1**	**24.1**	**24.3**
National defense [1]	Percent	5.2	3.0	4.0	4.7	4.8	4.7	4.6
Nondefense, total	Percent	16.6	15.2	15.9	20.5	19.2	19.4	19.7
Payments for individuals	Percent	10.2	10.7	12.0	15.0	15.9	15.7	15.2
Direct payments [2]	Percent	8.8	8.8	9.8	12.4	13.2	13.0	12.8
Grants to state and local governments	Percent	1.4	1.9	2.2	2.6	2.7	2.6	2.4
All other grants	Percent	1.0	1.0	1.2	1.3	1.5	1.4	1.5
Net interest [2]	Percent	3.2	2.3	1.5	1.3	1.4	1.5	1.4
All other [2]	Percent	2.9	1.6	1.8	3.5	1.0	1.3	2.2
Undistributed offsetting receipts [2]	Percent	-0.6	-0.4	-0.5	-0.7	-0.6	-0.6	-0.6

[1] Includes a small amount of grants to state and local governments and direct payments for individuals. [2] Includes some off-budget amounts; most of the off-budget amounts are direct payments for individuals (social security benefits). [3] Gross domestic product; see text, Section 13.

Source: U.S. Office of Management and Budget, *Budget of the United States Government, Historical Tables*, annual. See also <http://www.whitehouse.gov/omb/budget>.

Table 480. Federal Budget Outlays by Agency: 1990 to 2012

[In billions of dollars (1,253.0 represents $1,253,000,000,000). For fiscal years ending September 30]

Department or other unit	1990	2000	2005	2009	2010	2011	2012, est.
Outlays, total [1]	**1,253.0**	**1,789.0**	**2,472.0**	**3,517.7**	**3,456.2**	**3,603.1**	**3,795.5**
Legislative branch	2.2	2.9	4.0	4.7	5.8	4.6	5.3
Judicial branch	1.6	4.1	5.5	6.6	7.2	7.3	7.6
Agriculture	45.9	75.1	85.3	114.4	129.5	139.4	150.7
Commerce	3.7	7.8	6.1	10.7	13.2	9.9	11.3
Defense—Military	289.7	281.0	474.4	636.8	666.7	678.1	688.3
Education	23.0	33.5	72.9	53.4	92.9	65.5	98.5
Energy	12.1	15.0	21.3	23.7	30.8	31.4	39.0
Health and Human Services	175.5	382.3	581.4	796.3	854.1	891.2	871.8
Homeland Security	7.2	13.2	38.7	51.7	44.5	45.7	60.4
Housing and Urban Development	20.2	30.8	42.5	61.0	60.1	57.0	56.8
Interior	5.8	8.0	9.3	11.8	13.2	13.5	11.2
Justice	5.9	16.8	22.4	27.7	29.6	30.5	34.6
Labor	26.1	31.9	46.9	138.2	173.1	132.0	127.2
State	4.8	6.7	12.7	21.4	23.8	24.4	29.9
Transportation	25.6	41.6	56.6	73.0	77.8	77.3	84.1
Treasury	253.9	390.5	410.2	701.8	444.3	536.7	579.6
Veterans Affairs	29.0	47.0	69.8	95.5	108.3	126.9	129.2
Army Corps of Engineers	3.3	4.2	4.7	6.8	9.9	10.1	9.2
Other Defense—Civil Programs	21.7	32.8	43.5	57.3	54.0	54.8	52.0
Environmental Protection Agency	5.1	7.2	7.9	8.1	11.0	10.8	9.4
Executive Office of the President	0.2	0.3	7.7	0.7	0.6	0.5	0.4
International Assistance Programs	10.1	12.1	15.0	14.8	20.0	20.6	25.6
National Aeronautics and Space Administration	12.4	13.4	15.6	19.2	18.9	17.6	17.6
National Science Foundation	1.8	3.4	5.4	6.0	6.7	7.1	8.3
Office of Personnel Management	31.9	48.7	59.5	72.3	69.9	74.1	87.5
Social Security Administration (on-budget)	17.3	45.1	54.6	78.7	70.8	155.3	188.6
Social Security Administration (off-budget)	245.0	396.2	506.8	648.9	683.4	628.9	638.5
Undistributed offsetting receipts [2]	-98.9	-173.0	-226.2	-274.2	-267.9	-274.5	-279.3

[1] Includes other agencies, not shown separately. [2] See footnote 2, Table 479.

Source: U.S. Office of Management and Budget, *Budget of the United States Government, Historical Tables*, annual. See also <http://www.whitehouse.gov/omb/budget>.

Table 481. Federal Budget Outlays by Detailed Function: 1990 to 2012

[In billions of dollars (1,253.0 represents $1,253,000,000,000). For fiscal years ending September 30. Minus sign (–) indicates decrease]

Superfunction and function	1990	2000	2005	2007	2008	2009	2010	2011	2012, est.
Total outlays	**1,253.0**	**1,789.0**	**2,472.0**	**2,728.7**	**2,982.5**	**3,517.7**	**3,456.2**	**3,603.1**	**3,795.5**
National defense [1]	299.3	294.4	495.3	551.3	616.1	661.0	693.6	705.6	716.3
Department of Defense—Military	289.7	281.0	474.1	528.5	594.6	636.7	666.7	678.1	688.3
Military personnel	75.6	76.0	127.5	127.5	138.9	147.3	155.7	161.6	156.2
Operation and maintenance	88.3	105.8	188.1	216.6	244.8	259.3	276.0	291.0	294.5
Procurement	81.0	51.7	82.3	99.6	117.4	129.2	133.6	128.0	139.9
Research, development, test, and evaluation	37.5	37.6	65.7	73.1	75.1	79.0	77.0	74.9	75.9
Military construction	5.1	5.1	5.3	7.9	11.6	17.6	21.2	19.9	18.1
Atomic energy defense activities	9.0	12.1	18.0	17.1	17.1	17.6	19.3	20.4	19.8
International affairs [1]	13.8	17.2	34.6	28.5	28.9	37.5	45.2	45.7	56.3
International development and humanitarian assistance	5.5	6.5	17.7	15.5	14.1	22.1	19.0	21.3	24.2
International security assistance	8.7	6.4	7.9	8.0	9.5	6.2	11.4	12.0	12.5
Conduct of foreign affairs	3.0	4.7	9.1	8.4	10.4	12.2	13.6	12.5	15.8
General science, space, and technology	14.4	18.6	23.6	24.4	26.8	28.4	30.1	29.5	31.0
General science and basic research	2.8	6.2	8.8	9.1	9.6	10.0	11.7	12.4	13.9
Space flight, research, and supporting activities	11.6	12.4	14.8	15.3	17.2	18.4	18.4	17.0	17.1
Energy	3.3	-0.8	0.4	-0.9	0.6	4.7	11.6	12.2	23.3
Energy supply	2.0	-1.8	-0.9	-2.0	-0.4	2.0	5.8	8.1	12.9
Natural resources and environment [1]	17.1	25.0	28.0	31.7	31.8	35.6	43.7	45.5	42.8
Water resources	4.4	5.1	5.7	5.1	6.1	8.1	11.7	11.6	10.9
Conservation and land management	4.0	6.8	6.2	9.6	8.7	9.8	10.8	12.0	11.9
Recreational resources	1.4	2.5	3.0	3.0	3.2	3.6	3.9	4.2	3.6
Pollution control and abatement	5.2	7.4	8.1	8.4	8.1	8.3	10.8	10.9	9.5
Agriculture	11.8	36.5	26.6	17.7	18.4	22.2	21.4	20.7	19.2
Farm income stabilization	9.7	33.4	22.0	13.1	13.8	17.6	16.6	16.0	13.4
Agricultural research and services	2.1	3.0	4.5	4.6	4.6	4.6	4.8	4.6	5.8
Commerce and housing credit [1]	67.6	3.2	7.6	0.5	27.9	291.5	-82.3	-12.6	79.6
Mortgage credit	3.8	-3.3	-0.9	-5.0	0.0	99.8	35.8	14.2	16.2
Postal service	2.1	2.1	-1.2	-3.2	-3.1	-1.0	-0.7	0.9	-5.8
Deposit insurance	57.9	-3.1	-1.4	-1.5	18.8	22.6	-32.0	-8.7	26.9
Transportation [1]	29.5	46.9	67.9	72.9	77.6	84.3	92.0	93.0	102.6
Ground transportation	19.0	31.7	42.3	46.8	50.0	54.1	60.8	60.9	65.3
Air transportation	7.2	10.6	18.8	18.1	19.4	20.8	21.4	21.4	25.9
Water transportation	3.2	4.4	6.4	7.7	8.1	9.1	9.4	10.4	10.5
Community and regional development [1]	8.5	10.6	26.3	29.6	24.0	27.7	23.8	23.8	31.7
Community development	3.5	5.5	5.9	11.8	10.2	7.7	9.9	9.6	10.6
Disaster relief and insurance	2.1	2.6	17.7	15.2	11.2	16.7	10.7	10.2	18.4
Education, training, employment, and social services [1]	37.2	53.8	97.6	91.7	91.3	79.7	127.7	101.2	139.2
Elementary, secondary, and vocational education	9.9	20.6	38.3	38.4	38.9	53.2	73.3	66.5	87.8
Higher education	11.1	10.1	31.4	24.6	23.6	-3.3	20.0	1.1	13.2
Research and general education aids	1.6	2.5	3.1	3.2	3.2	3.5	3.6	3.7	3.7
Training and employment	5.6	6.8	6.9	7.1	7.2	7.7	9.9	9.1	13.4
Social services	8.1	12.6	16.3	16.7	16.8	17.0	19.2	18.9	19.1
Health	57.7	154.5	250.5	266.4	280.6	334.3	369.1	372.5	361.6
Health care services	47.6	136.2	219.6	233.9	247.7	300.0	330.7	332.2	323.9
Health research and training	8.6	16.0	28.1	29.3	29.9	30.6	34.2	36.2	33.0
Consumer and occupational health and safety	1.5	2.3	2.9	3.2	3.0	3.8	4.1	4.1	4.7
Medicare	98.1	197.1	298.6	375.4	390.8	430.1	451.6	485.7	484.5
Income security [1]	148.7	253.7	345.8	366.0	431.3	533.2	622.2	597.4	579.6
General retirement and disability insurance (excluding social security)	5.1	5.2	7.0	7.8	8.9	8.2	6.6	6.7	8.3
Federal employee retirement and disability	52.0	77.2	93.4	103.9	109.0	118.1	119.9	124.5	127.6
Unemployment compensation	18.9	23.0	35.4	35.1	45.3	122.5	160.1	120.6	109.0
Housing assistance	15.9	28.9	37.9	39.7	40.6	50.9	58.7	55.4	59.6
Food and nutrition assistance	24.0	32.5	50.8	54.5	60.7	79.1	95.1	103.2	113.5
Social security	248.6	409.4	523.3	586.2	617.0	683.0	706.7	730.8	778.6
Veterans benefits and services [1]	29.0	47.0	70.1	72.8	84.7	95.4	108.4	127.2	129.6
Income security for veterans	15.3	24.9	35.8	35.7	41.3	46.0	49.2	58.7	57.5
Veterans education, training, and rehabilitation	0.2	1.3	2.8	2.7	2.7	3.5	8.1	10.7	12.2
Hospital and medical care for veterans	12.1	19.5	28.8	32.3	37.0	41.9	45.7	50.1	52.3
Veterans housing	0.5	0.4	0.9	-0.9	-0.4	-0.6	0.5	1.3	1.6
Administration of justice	10.2	28.5	40.0	42.4	48.1	52.6	54.4	56.1	62.0
Federal law enforcement activities	4.8	12.1	19.9	20.7	25.6	28.6	28.7	29.8	32.1
Federal litigative and judicial activities	3.6	7.8	9.6	11.0	11.8	12.1	13.1	13.6	14.2
Federal correctional activities	1.3	3.7	5.9	6.3	6.9	7.3	7.7	8.1	8.3
Criminal justice assistance	0.5	4.9	4.6	4.3	3.9	4.6	4.8	4.6	7.4
General government	10.5	13.0	17.0	17.4	20.3	22.0	23.0	25.5	31.8
Net interest [1]	184.3	222.9	184.0	237.1	252.8	186.9	196.2	230.0	224.8
Interest on Treasury debt securities (gross)	264.7	361.9	352.3	430.0	451.1	383.1	413.9	454.0	450.3
Interest received by on-budget trust funds	-46.3	-69.3	-69.2	-72.0	-77.8	-63.6	-67.3	-72.0	-67.8
Interest received by off-budget trust funds	-16.0	-59.8	-91.8	-106.0	-113.7	-118.0	-118.5	-116.0	-112.6
Allowances	–	–	–	–	–	–	–	–	0.1
Undistributed offsetting receipts [2]	-36.6	-42.6	-65.2	-82.2	-86.2	-92.6	-82.1	-86.5	-98.9

– Represents or rounds to zero. [1] Includes functions not shown separately. [2] See footnote 2, Table 479.

Source: U.S. Office of Management and Budget, *Budget of the United States Government, Historical Tables*, annual. See also <http://www.whitehouse.gov/omb/budget>.

Federal Government Finances and Employment 325

Table 482. Outlays for Payments for Individuals by Category and Major Program: 1990 to 2012

[In billions of dollars (585.7 represents 585,700,000,000). For fiscal years ending September 30]

Category and program	1990	2000	2005	2008	2009	2010	2011	2012, est.
Total, payments for individuals	**585.7**	**1,054.5**	**1,490.9**	**1,825.8**	**2,094.1**	**2,286.7**	**2,345.6**	**2,367.6**
Social security and railroad retirement	250.5	410.5	523.4	617.4	681.0	706.5	730.6	779.1
Social security:								
Old age and survivors insurance	221.9	351.4	434.0	506.6	561.4	576.6	595.6	635.2
Disability insurance	24.4	54.4	84.2	104.7	115.5	123.5	128.6	136.9
Railroad retirement (excl. social security)	4.1	4.6	5.3	6.1	4.1	6.5	6.4	7.1
Federal employees retirement and insurance	64.1	100.3	126.9	148.2	161.7	166.5	181.4	183.5
Military retirement	21.5	32.8	39.0	45.8	50.0	50.6	54.9	48.5
Civil service retirement	31.0	45.1	54.7	63.5	67.5	69.4	70.4	79.6
Veterans service-connected compensation	10.7	20.8	30.9	36.3	40.4	43.4	52.9	52.0
Other	0.8	1.7	2.4	2.7	3.8	3.1	3.3	3.3
Unemployment assistance	17.4	21.1	33.1	43.4	119.8	158.3	118.6	106.4
Medical care	164.3	362.7	562.5	714.9	813.8	865.5	913.0	900.3
Medicare:								
Hospital insurance	65.9	127.9	182.8	223.6	240.0	250.2	260.9	264.0
Supplementary medical insurance	41.5	87.2	151.0	231.1	257.6	268.9	297.4	296.3
State children's health insurance	–	1.2	5.1	6.9	7.5	7.9	8.6	9.9
Medicaid	41.1	117.9	181.7	201.4	250.9	272.8	275.0	255.3
Indian health	1.1	2.4	3.1	3.3	3.6	4.4	4.2	5.0
Hospital and medical care for veterans	12.0	19.3	23.1	31.1	35.3	38.2	41.3	43.3
Health resources and services	1.4	3.9	5.9	6.3	6.5	7.1	7.5	8.0
Substance abuse and mental health services	1.2	2.5	3.2	3.1	3.4	3.3	3.4	3.4
Health care tax credit	–	–	0.1	0.1	0.1	0.2	(NA)	(NA)
Uniformed Services retiree health care fund	–	–	6.3	7.9	8.4	8.4	8.6	10.0
Other	(Z)	0.3	0.3	0.3	0.6	4.3	2.7	0.9
Assistance to students	11.2	10.9	32.1	31.1	30.6	55.5	58.6	65.1
Veterans education benefits	0.8	1.6	3.2	3.6	4.3	8.7	11.1	12.5
Student assistance, Department of Education and other	10.4	9.2	28.9	27.5	26.3	46.8	47.5	52.6
Housing assistance	15.9	24.1	31.8	33.4	43.6	50.0	45.9	51.1
Food and nutrition assistance	23.9	32.4	50.7	60.5	78.9	95.0	103.1	113.3
Food stamp program (including Puerto Rico)	15.9	18.3	32.6	39.3	55.6	70.5	77.6	85.2
Child nutrition and special milk programs	5.0	9.2	11.9	13.9	15.3	16.4	17.3	19.6
Supplemental feeding programs (WIC [1] and CSFP [2])	2.1	4.0	5.0	6.2	6.5	6.5	6.8	7.1
Commodity donations and other	0.8	0.9	1.2	1.1	1.6	1.6	1.3	1.5
Public assistance and related programs	34.9	88.3	123.3	168.6	156.0	183.1	188.4	162.7
Supplemental security income program	11.5	29.5	35.3	38.0	41.4	43.9	49.6	44.7
Family support payments to states and TANF [3]	12.2	18.4	21.3	21.8	22.2	21.9	21.3	20.4
Low income home energy assistance	1.3	1.5	2.1	2.7	4.5	4.6	4.4	3.7
Earned income tax credit	4.4	26.1	34.6	40.6	42.4	54.7	55.7	52.2
Legal services	0.3	0.3	0.3	0.3	–	–	(NA)	(NA)
Payments to states for daycare assistance	–	3.3	4.9	5.0	5.3	5.9	6.1	5.2
Veterans non-service-connected pensions	3.6	3.0	3.7	3.8	4.2	4.4	4.7	4.2
Payments to states for foster care/adoption assistance	1.6	5.5	6.4	6.8	6.9	7.0	6.9	6.8
Payment where child credit exceeds tax liability	–	0.8	14.6	34.0	24.3	22.7	22.7	22.5
Other public assistance	0.3	0.3	0.4	16.0	4.1	17.1	16.7	2.8
All other payments for individuals	3.5	4.3	7.1	8.1	8.7	6.3	6.0	6.1
Coal miners and black lung benefits	1.5	1.0	0.7	0.6	3.0	0.5	0.5	0.5
Veterans insurance and burial benefits	1.4	1.4	1.4	1.4	1.4	1.3	1.1	1.1
D.C. employee retirement	–	0.4	2.2	0.5	–	–	(NA)	(NA)
Aging services programs	–	0.9	1.4	1.4	1.5	1.5	1.6	1.5
Energy employees compensation fund	–	–	0.6	1.1	1.0	1.1	1.2	1.3
September 11th victim compensation	–	–	(Z)	–	–	–	–	0.2
Refugee assistance and other	0.6	1.0	3.0	3.7	1.8	1.9	1.6	1.6

NA Not Available – Represents zero. Z Less than $50,000,000. [1] WIC means Women, Infants, and Children. [2] CSFP means Commodity Supplemental Food Program. [3] TANF means Temporary Assistance for Needy Families.

Source: U.S. Office of Management and Budget, *Budget of the United States Government, Historical Tables*, annual. See also <http://www.whitehouse.gov/omb/budget>.

Table 483. Federal Budget Receipts by Source: 1990 to 2012

[In billions of dollars (1,032.0 represents $1,032,000,000,000). For fiscal years ending September 30. Receipts reflect collections. Covers both federal funds and trust funds; see text, this section. Minus sign (-) indicates decrease]

Source	1990	2000	2005	2008	2009	2010	2011	2012, est.
Total federal receipts....................................	**1,032.0**	**2,025.2**	**2,153.6**	**2,524.0**	**2,105.0**	**2,162.7**	**2,303.5**	**2,468.6**
Individual income taxes................................	466.9	1,004.5	927.2	1,145.7	915.3	898.5	1,091.5	1,164.7
Corporation income taxes.............................	93.5	207.3	278.3	304.3	138.2	191.4	181.1	236.8
Social insurance and retirement receipts.................	380.0	652.9	794.1	900.2	890.9	864.8	818.8	840.7
Excise taxes..	35.3	68.9	73.1	67.3	62.5	66.9	72.4	79.4
Other...	56.2	91.7	80.9	106.4	98.1	141.0	139.7	147.1
Social insurance and retirement receipts..	**380.0**	**652.9**	**794.1**	**900.2**	**890.9**	**864.8**	**818.8**	**840.7**
Employment and general retirement:								
Old–age and survivors insurance (off–budget).........................	255.0	411.7	493.6	562.5	559.1	540.0	483.7	489.1
Disability insurance (off–budget)......................	26.6	68.9	83.8	95.5	94.9	91.7	82.1	83.1
Hospital insurance....................................	68.6	135.5	166.1	194.0	190.7	180.1	188.5	202.5
Railroad retirement/pension fund......................	2.3	2.7	2.3	2.4	2.3	2.3	2.4	2.5
Unemployment insurance funds.........................	21.6	27.6	42.0	39.5	37.9	44.8	56.2	57.1
Other retirement.......................................	4.5	4.8	4.5	4.2	4.1	4.1	4.0	4.3
Federal employees retirement—employee share.....................................	4.4	4.7	4.4	4.1	4.1	4.1	4.0	4.3
Excise taxes, total..................................	**35.3**	**68.9**	**73.1**	**67.3**	**62.5**	**66.9**	**72.4**	**79.4**
Federal funds [1].......................................	15.6	22.7	22.5	15.7	13.9	18.3	18.9	23.0
Alcohol..	5.7	8.1	8.1	9.3	9.9	9.2	9.3	9.5
Tobacco...	4.1	7.2	7.9	7.6	12.8	17.2	16.7	16.5
Telephone...	3.0	5.7	6.0	1.0	1.1	1.0	0.9	0.7
Ozone–depleting chemicals/products.................	0.4	0.1	–	–	–	–	–	–
Transportation fuels..................................	–	0.8	-0.8	-5.1	-10.3	-11.0	-8.6	-5.2
Trust funds [1]...	19.8	46.2	50.5	51.6	48.6	48.7	53.5	56.5
Highway..	13.9	35.0	37.9	36.4	35.0	35.0	36.9	38.7
Airport and airway.....................................	3.7	9.7	10.3	12.0	10.6	10.6	11.5	11.6
Black lung disability...................................	0.7	0.5	0.6	0.7	0.6	0.6	0.6	0.6
Inland waterway.......................................	0.1	0.1	0.1	0.1	0.1	0.1	0.1	0.1
Oil spill liability..	0.1	0.2	–	0.3	0.4	0.5	0.5	0.5
Aquatic resources.....................................	0.2	0.3	0.4	0.6	0.6	0.6	0.6	0.6
Tobacco assessments.................................	–	–	0.9	1.1	1.0	0.9	0.9	1.0
Vaccine injury compensation...........................	0.2	0.1	0.1	0.3	0.2	0.2	0.3	0.3

– Represents zero. [1] Includes other funds, not shown separately.

Source: U.S. Office of Management and Budget, *Budget of the United States Government, Historical Tables*, annual. See also <http://www.whitehouse.gov/omb/budget>.

Table 484. Federal Trust Fund Income, Outlays, and Balances: 2011 to 2013

[In billions of dollars (11.8 represents $11,800,000,000). For fiscal years ending September 30. Income reflects receipts deposited. Outlays are on a checks-issued basis less refunds collected. Balances reflect funds that not been spent. See text, this section, for discussion of the budget concept and trust funds. Minus sign (-) indicates negative balance]

Description	Income			Outlays			Balances [1]		
	2011	2012, est.	2013, est.	2011	2012, est.	2013, est.	2011	2012, est.	2013, est.
Airport and airway trust fund.....................	11.8	11.9	13.1	10.9	12.2	13.7	10.3	10.1	9.5
Federal civilian employees' retirement funds...	94.0	95.1	94.2	70.5	79.8	83.2	803.8	819.2	830.2
Federal employees' health benefits fund........	43.6	44.7	47.3	40.6	43.5	47.3	19.1	20.3	20.4
Foreign military sales trust fund.................	23.9	25.5	27.7	23.0	28.3	30.9	18.5	15.6	12.5
Medicare:									
Hospital insurance (HI) trust fund..............	233.5	248.3	261.2	266.6	267.7	285.0	245.7	226.3	202.6
Supplemental medical insurance trust fund...	302.9	294.8	344.8	302.1	300.2	343.6	72.8	67.4	68.6
Military retirement fund.........................	104.9	109.2	112.1	54.9	48.5	54.6	368.6	429.2	486.8
Railroad retirement trust funds..................	9.8	11.1	10.5	11.3	11.8	12.2	18.6	17.9	16.4
Social security: Old-age, survivors and disability insurance trust funds.................	810.9	852.3	876.3	742.9	790.5	837.6	2,653.5	2,715.7	2,754.4
Transportation trust fund.......................	37.1	39.1	78.1	44.7	49.2	53.9	21.6	11.5	35.7
Unemployment trust funds......................	110.0	106.7	78.8	121.4	110.8	78.8	-26.7	-27.2	-30.4
Veterans' life insurance trust funds.............	0.9	0.8	0.7	1.5	1.5	1.4	9.5	8.8	8.1
Other trust funds................................	17.7	17.9	21.2	13.4	14.2	15.5	82.4	85.7	91.2

[1] Balances available on a cash basis (rather than an authorization basis) at the end of the year. Balances are primarily invested in federal debt securities.

Source: U.S. Office of Management and Budget, *Budget of the United States Government, Analytical Perspectives*, annual. See also <http://www.whitehouse.gov/omb/budget>.

Table 485. Tax Expenditure Estimates Relating to Individual and Corporate Income Taxes by Selected Function: 2011 to 2014

[In millions of dollars (13,250 represents $13,250,000,000). For fiscal years ending September 30. Tax expenditures are defined as revenue losses attributable to provisions of the federal tax laws which allow a special exclusion, exemption, or deduction from gross income or which provide a special credit, a preferential rate of tax, or a deferral of liability. Minus sign (-) indicates decrease]

Function and provision	2011	2012	2013	2014
National defense:				
Exclusion of benefits and allowances to armed forces personnel	13,250	14,270	14,900	15,380
International affairs:				
Exclusion of income earned abroad by U.S. citizens	5,550	5,400	5,800	6,140
Exclusion of certain allowances for Federal employees abroad	1,020	1,070	1,120	1,180
Inventory property sales source rules exception	3,160	3,430	3,730	4,050
Deferral of income from controlled foreign corporations (normal tax method)	41,410	42,000	41,810	41,770
Deferred taxes for financial firms on certain income earned overseas	6,180	2,510	–	–
General science, space, and technology:				
Expensing of research and experimentation expenditures (normal tax method)	800	3,060	5,070	6,190
Credit for increasing research activities	8,760	6,420	4,230	3,380
Energy:				
Alternative fuel production credit	10	10	10	–
Energy production credit	1,560	1,710	1,900	1,960
Energy investment credit	700	920	1,510	2,290
Bio–diesel and small agri–biodiesel producer tax credits	20	10	–	–
Commerce and housing:				
Financial institutions and insurance:				
Exclusion of interest on life insurance savings	22,060	23,570	25,150	26,810
Housing:				
Deductibility of mortgage interest on owner–occupied homes	72,240	86,910	100,910	110,830
Deductibility of state and local property tax on owner–occupied homes	23,210	16,150	22,320	27,900
Capital gains exclusion on home sales	15,060	16,040	23,440	31,610
Exclusion of net imputed rental income	46,950	50,640	51,080	58,740
Exception from passive loss rules for $25,000 of rental loss	11,080	12,550	15,380	18,450
Credit for low–income housing investments	6,150	6,530	7,380	7,830
Commerce:				
Capital gains (except agriculture, timber, iron ore, and coal)	47,390	66,210	62,040	48,300
Step–up basis of capital gains at death	3,940	19,940	23,860	36,200
Accelerated depreciation of machinery and equipment (normal tax method)	118,530	76,280	33,180	48,730
Graduated corporation income tax rate (normal tax method)	3,280	3,220	3,300	3,590
Deduction for U.S. production activities	13,130	13,750	14,500	15,330
Transportation:				
Exclusion of reimbursed employee parking expenses	3,060	3,170	3,290	3,440
Education, training, employment, and social services:				
Education:				
HOPE tax credit	–	–	580	5,780
Lifetime Learning tax credit	2,800	3,250	3,920	5,750
Exclusion of interest on bonds for private nonprofit educational facilities	2,100	2,320	2,900	3,430
Parental personal exemption for students age 19 years or over	5,600	3,120	2,800	3,060
Deductibility of charitable contributions (education)	3,520	3,910	4,610	5,060
Training, employment, and social services:				
Child credit	23,410	24,470	18,390	9,280
Credit for child and dependent care expenses	4,200	3,400	1,620	1,460
Deductibility of charitable contributions, other than education and health	29,820	33,290	39,770	43,900
Health:				
Exclusion of employer contributions for medical insurance premiums [1]	163,040	170,650	180,580	189,670
Self–employed medical insurance premiums	5,170	5,520	5,970	6,970
Deductibility of medical expenses	8,280	9,320	9,910	10,710
Exclusion of interest on hospital construction bonds	3,100	3,440	4,280	5,050
Deductibility of charitable contributions (health)	3,370	3,760	4,490	4,960
Income security:				
Exclusion of workers' compensation benefits	7,050	7,410	7,790	8,170
Net exclusion of pension contributions and earnings:				
Employer plans	36,390	44,490	52,330	56,650
401(k) plans	53,360	60,090	72,740	81,030
Individual Retirement Accounts (IRAs)	12,840	15,410	19,650	18,450
Keogh (self–employed) plans	15,030	17,070	19,580	20,940
Exclusion of other employee benefits:				
Premiums on group term life insurance	1,980	2,080	2,120	2,150
Earned income tax credit	1,172	1,128	3,155	3,265
Social security:				
Exclusion of social security benefits:				
Social security benefits for retired workers	25,360	25,970	25,620	27,580
Social security benefits for disabled	7,690	8,030	8,230	8,590
Social security benefits for dependents and survivors	4,710	4,470	3,890	3,960
Veterans' benefits and services:				
Exclusion of veterans' death benefits and disability compensation	5,200	5,880	5,650	6,060
General purpose fiscal assistance:				
Exclusion of interest on public purpose state and local bonds	26,190	29,080	36,210	42,770
Deductibility of nonbusiness state and local tax, other than owner-occupied homes	41,060	33,180	46,260	56,980
Interest:				
Deferral of interest on U.S. savings bonds	1,190	1,200	1,250	1,330
Addendum: Aid to state and local governments:				
Deductibility of:				
Property taxes on owner–occupied homes	23,210	16,150	22,320	27,900
Nonbusiness state and local taxes other than on owner–occupied homes	41,060	33,180	46,260	56,980
Exclusion of interest on state and local bonds for:				
Public purposes	26,190	29,080	36,210	42,770
Private nonprofit educational facilities	2,100	2,320	2,900	3,430
Hospital construction	3,100	3,440	4,280	5,050

– Represents zero. [1] Includes medical care.

Source: U.S. Office of Management and Budget, *Budget of the United States Government, Supplemental Materials*, annual. See also <http://www.whitehouse.gov/omb/budget/>.

Table 486. Federal Funds—Summary Distribution by State: 2010

[In millions of dollars (3,276,422 represents $3,276,422,000,000), except as indicated. For fiscal year ending September 30. Data for grants, salaries and wages, and direct payments to individuals are on an expenditure basis; procurement data are on an obligation basis]

State and Island Areas	Federal funds Total	Per capita [1] (dollars)	Agency Defense	Non-defense	Object category Direct payments	Procure-ment	Grants	Salaries and wages
United States [2]	**3,276,422**	**10,460**	**556,959**	**2,719,463**	**818,570**	**516,714**	**683,361**	**342,933**
Alabama	56,496	11,820	13,029	43,466	13,151	10,482	9,273	5,613
Alaska	12,615	17,762	5,211	7,404	1,040	2,464	3,465	4,055
Arizona	64,427	10,079	14,263	50,164	13,738	12,813	14,361	4,980
Arkansas	28,904	9,912	2,968	25,936	7,529	1,751	6,843	2,418
California	333,809	8,960	55,750	278,059	87,976	57,537	78,869	24,585
Colorado	49,687	9,880	12,211	37,476	9,169	10,367	8,793	8,519
Connecticut	55,978	15,662	11,980	43,998	23,672	11,957	8,299	1,903
Delaware	8,076	8,994	817	7,259	1,895	363	2,055	708
District of Columbia	61,920	102,904	8,699	53,221	3,982	21,250	10,872	23,030
Florida	186,704	9,930	22,647	164,056	63,317	17,981	28,066	12,964
Georgia	92,387	9,537	22,794	69,594	19,744	12,461	16,751	17,372
Hawaii	20,855	15,331	10,003	10,852	2,819	2,745	3,026	7,898
Idaho	14,252	9,092	1,079	13,173	2,835	2,633	2,980	1,245
Illinois	109,967	8,571	10,442	99,525	32,513	11,601	24,060	7,949
Indiana	58,603	9,038	7,147	51,456	17,098	5,498	11,965	4,360
Iowa	28,379	9,316	2,581	25,797	8,246	2,373	6,394	1,902
Kansas	29,046	10,180	6,921	22,124	6,845	3,060	4,736	5,818
Kentucky	57,271	13,198	13,252	44,018	16,241	7,486	9,502	9,205
Louisiana	53,214	11,738	9,297	43,917	13,101	7,291	15,088	4,703
Maine	14,644	11,024	2,152	12,492	3,094	1,736	3,787	1,134
Maryland	96,261	16,673	18,677	77,584	21,137	26,522	14,441	15,041
Massachusetts	82,454	12,593	14,562	67,892	21,196	15,987	22,352	4,506
Michigan	90,921	9,199	6,057	84,865	26,675	6,467	20,577	4,798
Minnesota	44,376	8,367	3,114	41,261	13,256	2,950	10,528	3,368
Mississippi	31,419	10,588	4,070	27,349	8,081	2,666	7,871	3,017
Missouri	70,348	11,746	15,133	55,215	16,801	13,002	14,003	7,321
Montana	10,758	10,874	946	9,812	2,401	819	2,939	1,195
Nebraska	16,532	9,052	2,112	14,420	4,478	1,307	3,507	1,783
Nevada	19,771	7,321	2,896	16,875	4,475	2,407	3,702	1,942
New Hampshire	11,335	8,610	1,603	9,732	2,405	1,435	2,311	880
New Jersey	80,990	9,212	10,351	70,639	24,895	10,236	15,457	5,578
New Mexico	27,959	13,578	3,236	24,723	4,343	7,499	6,720	2,768
New York	202,266	10,438	15,244	187,023	57,533	13,883	63,104	13,936
North Carolina	90,737	9,516	17,607	73,130	19,587	6,091	20,099	15,349
North Dakota	8,696	12,930	1,039	7,657	2,485	685	2,237	1,083
Ohio	106,449	9,227	9,954	96,495	31,106	8,829	24,399	6,975
Oklahoma	38,475	10,256	7,008	31,466	9,098	3,375	7,855	5,575
Oregon	33,974	8,868	2,160	31,814	8,586	2,047	8,694	2,569
Pennsylvania	145,934	11,489	16,254	129,680	44,909	19,352	29,411	8,803
Rhode Island	11,759	11,172	1,488	10,271	3,276	1,001	3,152	997
South Carolina	46,578	10,070	8,853	37,726	9,653	8,171	8,210	4,618
South Dakota	9,507	11,676	1,180	8,327	2,688	913	2,250	1,031
Tennessee	68,866	10,852	5,647	63,219	19,677	10,141	14,094	3,837
Texas	225,725	8,977	54,249	171,476	50,157	40,594	44,624	29,926
Utah	23,545	8,519	4,782	18,764	5,580	3,758	4,987	3,195
Vermont	7,405	11,834	1,101	6,304	1,362	932	2,380	724
Virginia	136,083	17,008	58,115	77,968	16,101	58,338	12,228	21,112
Washington	70,437	10,475	14,964	55,474	13,650	10,041	14,725	11,539
West Virginia	21,511	11,609	1,129	20,382	5,081	1,783	4,970	1,936
Wisconsin	54,866	9,648	9,980	44,886	13,310	9,805	11,992	2,926
Wyoming	6,211	11,019	621	5,590	1,034	569	2,254	709

[1] Based on U.S. Census Bureau estimated resident population as of Apr. 1. [2] Includes Island Areas, not shown separately.

Source: U.S. Census Bureau, *Consolidated Federal Funds Report for Fiscal Year 2010*, Sept. 2011. See also <http://www.census.gov/govs/cffr/>.

Table 487. U.S. Savings Bonds: 1990 to 2011

[In billions of dollars (122.5 represents $122,500,000,000), except percent. For fiscal years ending September 30]

Item	Unit	1990	1995	2000	2004	2005	2006	2007	2008	2009	2010	2011
Amounts outstanding, total [1]	Bil. dol	122.5	181.5	177.7	194.1	189.9	189.2	181.5	177.8	175.6	172.3	169.0
Sales	Bil. dol	7.8	7.2	5.6	10.3	6.5	8.5	3.6	3.6	3.0	2.6	1.8
Accrued discounts	Bil. dol	8.0	9.5	6.9	6.9	6.7	7.5	7.2	7.1	6.9	5.2	5.6
Redemptions [2]	Bil. dol	7.5	11.8	14.5	14.6	13.8	16.0	17.4	13.6	11.7	11.5	11.0
Percent of total outstanding	Percent	6.1	6.5	8.2	7.5	7.3	8.5	9.6	7.6	6.7	6.7	6.5

[1] Interest-bearing debt only for amounts at end of year. [2] Matured and unmatured bonds.

Source: U.S. Department of the Treasury, Bureau of Public Debt, <http://www.treasurydirect.gov/govt/reports/pd/pd.htm>.

Table 488. Internal Revenue Gross Collections by Type of Tax: 2005 to 2011

[2,269 represents $2,269,000,000,000, except percent. For fiscal years ending September 30. See text, this section, for information on taxes]

Type of tax	Gross collections (bil. dol.)						Percent of total					
	2005	2007	2008	2009	2010	2011	2005	2007	2008	2009	2010	2011
United States, total............	**2,269**	**2,692**	**2,745**	**2,345**	**2,345**	**2,415**	**100.0**	**100.0**	**100.0**	**100.0**	**100.0**	**100.0**
Individual income taxes............	1,108	1,366	1,400	1,175	1,164	1,331	48.8	50.8	51.0	50.2	49.7	55.1
Withheld by employers............	787	929	971	881	900	1,010	34.7	34.5	35.4	37.6	38.4	41.8
Tax payments [1]...................	321	438	430	295	264	321	14.1	16.3	15.7	12.6	11.3	13.3
Estate and trust income tax.......	(NA)	(NA)	26	15	12	15	(NA)	(NA)	0.9	0.6	0.5	0.6
Employment taxes.................	771	850	883	858	824	768	34.0	31.6	32.2	36.6	35.1	31.8
Old-age and disability insurance.........................	760	838	871	847	813	756	33.5	31.1	31.7	36.1	34.7	31.3
Unemployment insurance........	7	7	7	7	7	7	0.3	0.3	0.3	0.3	0.3	0.3
Railroad retirement...............	5	5	5	5	5	5	0.2	0.2	0.2	0.2	0.2	0.2
Business income taxes [2].........	307	396	354	225	278	243	13.5	14.7	12.9	9.6	11.9	10.1
Estate and gift taxes...............	26	27	30	25	20	9	1.1	1.0	1.1	1.1	0.8	0.4
Excise taxes......................	57	53	52	47	47	49	2.5	2.0	1.9	2.0	2.0	2.0

NA Not available. [1] Includes estimated income tax collections and payments made with tax filings. Also includes estate and trust income tax for 2005–2007. [2] Includes corporate income tax and tax-exempt organization unrelated business income tax.

Source: U.S. Internal Revenue Service, *IRS Data Book* (Publication 55B), annual. See also <http://www.irs.gov/uac/Tax-Stats-2>.

Table 489. Individual Income Tax Returns Filed—Examination Coverage: 1995 to 2011

[114,683 represents 114,683,000, except percent. See the annual *IRS Data Book* (Publication 55B) for a detailed explanation]

Year	Returns filed [1] (1,000)	Returns examined		Total recommended additional tax [3] ($1,000)	Average recommended additional tax per return (dol.) [3]
		Total [2] (1,000)	Percent coverage		
1995.........................	114,683	1,919	1.7	7,756,954	4,041
1998.........................	120,342	1,193	1.0	6,095,698	5,110
1999.........................	122,547	1,100	0.9	4,458,474	4,052
2000.........................	124,887	618	0.5	3,388,905	5,486
2001.........................	127,097	732	0.6	3,301,860	4,512
2002.........................	129,445	744	0.6	3,636,486	4,889
2003.........................	130,341	849	0.7	4,559,902	5,369
2004.........................	130,134	997	0.8	6,201,693	6,220
2005.........................	130,577	1,199	0.9	13,355,087	11,138
2006.........................	132,276	1,284	1.0	13,045,221	10,160
2007.........................	134,543	1,385	1.0	15,705,155	11,343
2008.........................	137,850	1,392	1.0	12,462,770	8,956
2009 [4].....................	138,950	1,426	1.0	14,940,892	10,478
2010.........................	142,823	1,581	1.1	15,066,486	9,527
2011.........................	140,837	1,565	1.1	14,652,239	9,364

[1] Returns generally filed in previous calendar year. [2] Includes taxpayer examinations by correspondence. [3] For 1995 to 1997, amount includes associated penalties. [4] Excludes returns filed by individuals only to receive an economic stimulus payment and who had no other reason to file.

Source: U.S. Internal Revenue Service, *IRS Data Book* (Publication 55B), annual. See also <http://www.irs.gov/uac/Tax-Stats-2>.

Table 490. Federal Individual Income Tax Returns—Adjusted Gross Income, Taxable Income, and Total Income Tax: 2008 and 2009

[142,451 represents 142,451,000. For tax years. Based on a sample of returns, see source and Appendix III]

Year	2008		2009		Percent change in amount, 2008-09
	Number of returns (1,000)	Amount (mil. dol.)	Number of returns (1,000)	Amount (mil. dol.)	
Adjusted gross income (less deficit)......................	142,451	8,262,860	140,494	7,626,431	-7.7
Exemptions [1]......................................	282,929	980,977	282,240	1,029,070	4.9
Taxable income......................................	107,995	5,652,925	104,161	5,088,388	-10.0
Total income tax.....................................	90,660	1,031,581	81,890	865,949	-16.1
Alternative minimum tax...............................	3,935	25,649	3,828	22,580	-12.0

[1] The number of returns columns represent the number of exemptions.

Source: U.S. Internal Revenue Service, Statistics of Income Bulletin, fall issues. See also <http://www.irs.gov/uac/Tax-Stats-2>.

Table 491. Federal Individual Income Tax Returns—Adjusted Gross Income (AGI) by Selected Source of Income and Income Class: 2009

[In millions of dollars (7,626,431 represents $7,626,431,000,000), except as indicated. For the tax year. Minus sign (–) indicates net loss was greater than net income. Based on sample; see Appendix III]

Item	Total [1]	Under $10,000	$10,000 to $19,999	$20,000 to $29,999	$30,000 to $39,999	$40,000 to $49,999	$50,000 to $99,999	$100,000 and over
Number of all returns (1,000)..............	140,494	25,180	23,845	18,696	14,372	10,796	30,159	17,447
Adjusted gross income [2]...................	7,626,431	-79,333	354,483	463,162	499,880	483,089	2,139,407	3,765,743
Salaries and wages......................	5,707,088	116,213	256,073	370,133	409,417	389,508	1,685,992	2,479,753
Interest received........................	241,575	19,424	10,007	9,755	9,011	9,247	43,167	140,965
Dividends in AGI........................	163,459	8,088	5,104	4,434	4,327	4,888	23,885	112,734
Business, profession, net profit less loss......................	244,983	-4,328	30,563	17,045	12,309	11,275	45,501	132,617
Sales of property, net gain less loss [3]......................	231,187	8,089	-696	-380	-155	20	7,190	217,120
Pensions and annuities in AGI...........	523,296	12,244	34,756	38,818	40,748	41,238	190,075	165,416
Rents and royalties, net income less loss [4]...................	22,473	-7,767	-346	-559	-706	-777	-1,464	34,093

[1] Includes a small number of returns with no adjusted gross income. [2] Includes other sources, not shown separately. [3] Includes sales of capital assets and other property. [4] Excludes rental passive losses disallowed in the computation of AGI.

Source: U.S. Internal Revenue Service, *Statistics of Income*, Fall issues. See also <http://www.irs.gov/uac/Tax-Stats-2>.

Table 492. Federal Individual Income Tax Returns—Total and Selected Sources of Adjusted Gross Income: 2008 and 2009

[142,451 represents 142,451,000. For tax years. Based on a sample of returns, see source and Appendix III. Minus sign (–) indicates decrease]

Item	2008 Number of returns (1,000)	2008 Amount (mil. dol.)	2009 Number of returns (1,000)	2009 Amount (mil. dol.)	Change in amount, 2008-09 Net change (mil. dol.)	Change in amount, 2008-09 Percent change
Adjusted gross income (less deficit) [1]...........................	142,451	8,262,860	140,494	7,626,431	-636,429	-7.7
Salaries and wages.................................	119,579	5,950,635	116,669	5,707,088	-243,547	-4.1
Taxable interest....................................	62,450	223,291	57,811	168,001	-55,290	-24.8
Ordinary dividends.................................	31,043	219,331	29,288	163,459	-55,872	-25.5
Qualified dividends...............................	26,409	158,975	25,413	123,570	-35,405	-22.3
Business or profession net income (less loss).................	22,112	264,234	22,112	244,983	-19,251	-7.3
Net capital gain....................................	23,731	469,273	20,291	231,548	-237,725	-50.7
Capital gain distributions [2].........................	11,544	21,954	4,191	2,411	-19,543	-89.0
Sales of property other than capital assets, net gain (less loss).................................	1,723	-7,811	1,788	-18,027	-10,216	-130.8
Sales of property other than capital assets, net gain..	773	12,953	675	11,898	-1,055	-8.1
Taxable social security benefits...........................	15,015	168,110	15,320	174,650	6,540	3.9
Total rental and royalty net income (less net loss) [3].............	10,545	32,940	10,636	22,473	-10,467	-31.8
Partnership and S corporation net income (less loss)...........	7,909	366,965	8,013	345,097	-21,868	-6.0
Estate and trust net income (less loss).........................	604	18,150	652	17,382	-768	-4.2
Farm net income (less loss).................................	1,948	-14,847	1,924	-14,095	751	5.1
Farm net income.................................	549	11,749	523	11,616	-133	-1.1
Unemployment compensation..................................	9,533	43,675	11,299	83,538	39,863	91.3
Taxable pensions and annuities...............................	25,540	506,269	26,020	523,296	17,027	3.4
Taxable Individual Retirement Account (IRA) distributions......	11,259	162,150	9,659	135,203	-26,948	-16.6
Other net income (less loss) [4]...............................	(NA)	34,267	(NA)	31,316	-2,951	-8.6
Gambling earnings....................................	1,890	27,197	1,768	23,776	-3,421	-12.6

NA Not available. [1] Includes other sources of income, not shown separately. [2] Includes both Schedule D and non-Schedule D capital gain distributions. [3] Includes farm rental net income (less loss). [4] Other net income (less loss) represents data reported on Form 1040, line 21, except net operating loss, the foreign-earned income exclusion, and gambling earnings.

Source: U.S. Internal Revenue Service, *Statistics of Income Bulletin*, Fall issues. See also <http://www.irs.gov/uac/Tax-Stats-2>.

Federal Government Finances and Employment

Table 493. Federal Individual Income Tax Returns—Net Capital Gains and Capital Gain Distributions From Mutual Funds: 1990 to 2009

[14,288 represents 14,288,000. For tax years. Based on a sample of returns, see source and Appendix III. Minus sign (–) indicates decrease]

Tax year	Net capital gain (less loss)				Capital gain distributions [2]			
	Number of returns (1,000)	Current dollars (mil. dol.)	Constant (1982–1984) dollars [1]		Number of returns (1,000)	Current dollars (mil. dol.)	Constant (1982–1984) dollars [1]	
			Amount (mil. dol.)	Percent change			Amount (mil. dol.)	Percent change
1990	14,288	114,231	87,400	-25.6	5,069	3,905	2,988	-32.4
1991	15,009	102,776	75,460	-13.7	5,796	4,665	3,425	14.6
1992	16,491	118,230	84,269	11.7	5,917	7,426	5,293	54.5
1993	18,409	144,172	99,773	18.4	9,998	11,995	8,301	56.8
1994	18,823	142,288	96,011	-3.8	9,803	11,322	7,640	-8.0
1995	19,963	170,415	111,821	16.5	10,744	14,391	9,443	23.6
1996	22,065	251,817	160,495	43.5	12,778	24,722	15,757	66.9
1997	24,240	356,083	221,859	38.2	14,969	45,132	28,120	78.5
1998	25,690	446,084	273,671	23.4	16,070	46,147	28,311	0.7
1999	27,701	542,758	325,785	19.0	17,012	59,473	35,698	26.1
2000	29,521	630,542	366,169	12.4	17,546	79,079	45,923	28.6
2001	25,956	326,527	184,375	-49.6	12,216	13,609	7,685	-83.3
2002	24,189	238,789	132,734	-28.0	7,567	5,343	2,970	-61.4
2003	22,985	294,354	159,975	20.5	7,265	4,695	2,552	-14.1
2004	25,267	473,662	250,747	56.7	10,733	15,336	8,119	218.1
2005	26,196	668,015	342,046	36.4	13,393	35,581	18,219	124.4
2006	26,668	779,462	386,638	13.0	14,511	59,417	29,473	61.8
2007	27,156	907,656	437,758	13.2	15,714	86,397	41,669	41.4
2008	23,731	469,273	217,959	-50.2	11,544	21,954	10,197	-75.5
2009	20,291	231,548	107,929	-50.5	4,191	2,411	1,124	-89.0

[1] Constant dollars were calculated using the U.S. Bureau of Labor Statistics consumer price index for urban consumers (CPI-U, 1982–84 = 100). See Table 737. [2] Capital gain distributions are included in net capital gain (less loss). For 1989–1996, and 1999 and later years, capital gain distributions from mutual funds are the sum of the amounts reported on the Form 1040 and Schedule D. For 1997 and 1998, capital gain distributions were reported entirely on the Schedule D.

Source: U.S. Internal Revenue Service, *Statistics of Income Bulletin*, Fall issues. See also <http://www.irs.gov/uac/Tax-Stats-2>.

Table 494. Alternative Minimum Tax: 1986 to 2009

[609 represents 609,000. For tax years. Based on a sample of returns, see source and Appendix III]

Tax year	Highest statutory alternative minimum tax rate (percent)	Alternative minimum tax		Tax year	Highest statutory alternative minimum tax rate (percent)	Alternative minimum tax	
		Number of returns (1,000)	Amount (mil. dol.)			Number of returns (1,000)	Amount (mil. dol.)
1986	20	609	6,713	1998	[1] 28	853	5,015
1987	21	140	1,675	1999	[1] 28	1,018	6,478
1988	21	114	1,028	2000	[1] 28	1,304	9,601
1989	21	117	831	2001	[1] 28	1,120	6,757
1990	21	132	830	2002	[1] 28	1,911	6,854
1991	24	244	1,213	2003	[1] 28	2,358	9,470
1992	24	287	1,357	2004	[1] 28	3,096	13,029
1993	28	335	2,053	2005	[1] 28	4,005	17,421
1994	28	369	2,212	2006	[1] 28	3,967	21,565
1995	28	414	2,291	2007	[1] 28	4,109	24,110
1996	28	478	2,813	2008	[1] 28	3,935	25,649
1997	[1] 28	618	4,005	2009	[1] 28	3,828	22,580

[1] Top rate on most long-term capital gains was 20 percent; beginning 2003, the rate was 15 percent.

Source: U.S. Internal Revenue Service, *Statistics of Income Bulletin*, Winter issues. See also <http://www.irs.gov/uac/Tax-Stats-2>.

Table 495. Federal Individual Income Tax Returns—Sources of Net Losses Included in Adjusted Gross Income: 2007 to 2009

[5,697 represents 5,697,000. For tax years. Based on a sample of returns, see source and Appendix III]

Item	2007 Number of returns (1,000)	2007 Amount (mil. dol.)	2008 Number of returns (1,000)	2008 Amount (mil. dol.)	2009 Number of returns (1,000)	2009 Amount (mil. dol.)
Total net losses	**(NA)**	**390,035**	**(NA)**	**477,538**	**(NA)**	**493,543**
Business or profession net loss	5,697	54,849	5,677	60,646	5,572	63,905
Net capital loss [1]	7,558	16,508	12,357	28,568	13,532	31,912
Net loss, sales of property other than capital assets	858	10,756	949	20,764	1,113	29,926
Total rental and royalty net loss [2]	4,886	56,288	4,936	57,145	5,002	55,406
Partnership and S corporation net loss	2,799	132,696	2,959	175,489	3,006	152,676
Estate and trust net loss	47	2,505	48	3,748	52	3,106
Farm net loss	1,422	24,625	1,399	26,596	1,401	25,711
Net operating loss [3]	923	86,369	920	97,019	1,120	124,079
Other net loss [4]	228	5,438	244	7,564	250	6,822

NA Not available. [1] Includes only the portion of capital losses allowable in the calculation of adjusted gross income. Only $3,000 of net capital loss per return ($1,500 for married filing separately) are allowed to be included in negative total income. Any excess is carried forward to future years. [2] Includes farm rental net loss. [3] Net operating loss is a carryover of the loss from a business when taxable income from a prior year was less than zero. [4] Other net loss represents losses reported on Form 1040, line 21, except net operating loss and the foreign-earned income exclusion.

Source: U.S. Internal Revenue Service, *Statistics of Income Bulletin*, Fall issues. See also <http://www.irs.gov/uac/Tax-Stats-2>.

Table 496. Federal Individual Income Tax Returns—Number, Income Tax, and Average Tax by Size of Adjusted Gross Income: 2000 and 2009

[129,374 represents 129,374,000. Based on sample of returns; see Appendix III. Minus sign (–) indicates net loss was greater than net income]

Size of adjusted gross income	Number of returns (1,000) 2000	Number of returns (1,000) 2009	Adjusted gross income (AGI) (bil. dol.) 2000	Adjusted gross income (AGI) (bil. dol.) 2009	Income tax total [1] (bil. dol.) 2000	Income tax total [1] (bil. dol.) 2009	Taxes as percent of AGI (for taxable returns only) 2000	Taxes as percent of AGI (for taxable returns only) 2009	Average tax (for taxable returns only) (dol.) 2000	Average tax (for taxable returns only) (dol.) 2009
Total	**129,374**	**140,494**	**6,365**	**7,626**	**981**	**866**	**16**	**13**	**10,129**	**10,575**
Less than $1,000 [2]	2,966	4,311	-58	-198	–	–	(X)	(X)	648	20
$1,000 to $2,999	5,385	4,140	11	8	–	–	7	4	134	66
$3,000 to $4,999	5,599	4,508	22	18	–	–	4	6	179	219
$5,000 to $6,999	5,183	4,623	31	28	1	–	5	1	297	90
$7,000 to $8,999	4,972	5,024	40	40	1	–	4	3	331	242
$9,000 to $10,999	5,089	5,012	51	50	1	–	5	3	470	344
$11,000 to $12,999	4,859	5,035	58	60	2	–	6	3	704	335
$13,000 to $14,999	4,810	4,972	67	69	3	–	6	2	883	263
$15,000 to $16,999	4,785	4,702	76	75	3	1	7	2	1,052	399
$17,000 to $18,999	4,633	4,553	83	82	4	1	7	3	1,279	540
$19,000 to $21,999	6,502	6,337	133	130	7	2	8	4	1,565	809
$22,000 to $24,999	5,735	5,842	135	137	8	3	8	5	1,815	1,097
$25,000 to $29,999	8,369	8,662	229	238	16	7	8	5	2,248	1,483
$30,000 to $39,999	13,548	14,372	471	500	40	20	9	6	3,094	2,101
$40,000 to $49,999	10,412	10,796	466	483	46	25	10	7	4,462	3,031
$50,000 to $74,999	17,076	18,695	1,045	1,149	116	78	11	8	6,824	4,740
$75,000 to $99,999	8,597	11,464	738	990	100	80	14	8	11,631	7,326
$100,000 to $199,999	8,083	13,522	1,066	1,801	184	212	17	12	22,783	15,873
$200,000 to $499,999	2,136	3,195	614	905	146	176	24	20	68,628	55,475
$500,000 to $999,999	396	493	269	332	76	80	28	24	192,092	164,233
$1,000,000 or more	240	237	817	727	226	178	28	24	945,172	753,994

– Represents or rounds to zero. X Not applicable. [1] Consists of income tax after credits (including alternative minimum tax). [2] In addition to low-income taxpayers, this size class (and others) includes taxpayers with "tax preferences," not reflected in adjusted gross income or taxable income, which are subject to the "alternative minimum tax" (included in total income tax).

Source: U.S. Internal Revenue Service, *Statistics of Income Bulletin*, Fall issues. See also <http://www.irs.gov/uac/Tax-Stats-2>.

Table 497. Federal Individual Income Tax Returns—Selected Itemized Deductions and the Standard Deduction: 2008 and 2009

[48,167 represents 48,167,000. For tax years. Based on a sample of returns, see source and Appendix III. Minus sign (–) indicates decrease]

Item	2008		2009		Percent change, 2008–09	
	Number of returns [1] (1,000)	Amount (mil. dol.)	Number of returns [1] (1,000)	Amount (mil. dol.)	Number of returns [1] (1,000)	Amount (percent)
Total itemized deductions before limitation...............	**48,167**	**1,339,354**	**45,696**	**1,216,313**	**-5.1**	**-9.2**
Medical and dental expenses after 7.5 percent Adjusted Gross Income (AGI) limitation.....................	10,155	76,387	10,090	79,866	-0.6	4.6
Taxes paid [2]...	47,836	467,212	45,424	432,032	-5.0	-7.5
State and local income taxes................................	35,403	270,958	33,755	236,096	-4.7	-12.9
State and local general sales taxes........................	11,045	17,686	10,262	15,563	-7.1	-12.0
Interest paid [3]...	39,200	497,618	37,004	442,051	-5.6	-11.2
Home mortgage interest....................................	38,684	470,408	36,542	420,813	-5.5	-10.5
Charitable contributions [4]................................	39,250	172,936	37,243	158,017	-5.1	-8.6
Other than cash contributions.............................	23,027	40,421	21,867	31,816	-5.0	-21.3
Casualty and theft losses...................................	337	4,348	134	2,330	-60.1	-46.4
Miscellaneous deductions after 2-percent AGI limitation...	12,437	89,924	11,868	80,903	-4.6	-10.0
Total unlimited miscellaneous deductions.....................	1,642	30,929	1,411	21,114	-14.0	-31.7
Itemized deductions in excess of limitation....................	6,783	17,077	5,706	12,504	-15.9	-26.8
Total itemized deductions after limitation.....................	48,167	1,322,276	45,696	1,203,808	-5.1	-9.0
Total standard deduction....................................	91,781	695,488	92,269	747,780	0.5	7.5
Total deductions (after itemized deduction limitation)..	139,948	2,017,764	137,965	1,951,588	-1.4	-3.3

[1] Returns with no adjusted gross income are excluded from the deduction counts. For this reason, the sum of the number of returns with total itemized deductions and the number of returns with total standard deduction is less than the total number of returns for all filers. [2] Includes real estate taxes, personal property taxes, and other taxes, not shown separately. [3] Includes investment interest and deductible mortgage "points," not shown separately. [4] For more information, see Table 594.

Source: U.S. Internal Revenue Service, *Statistics of Income Bulletin*, Fall issues. See also <http://www.irs.gov/uac/Tax-Stats-2>.

Table 498. Federal Individual Income Tax Returns—Statutory Adjustments: 2008 and 2009

[35,774 represents 35,774,000. For tax years. Based on a sample of returns, see source and Appendix III. Minus sign (–) indicates decrease]

Item	2008		2009		Percent change in amount, 2008–09
	Number of returns (1,000)	Amount (mil. dol.)	Number of returns (1,000)	Amount (mil. dol.)	
Total statutory adjustments.............................	**35,774**	**121,599**	**34,764**	**112,967**	**-7.1**
Payments to an Individual Retirement Account (IRA)................	2,740	11,666	2,588	11,215	-3.9
Educator expenses deduction................................	3,753	947	3,841	970	2.5
Moving expenses adjustment................................	1,113	3,003	856	2,100	-30.1
Student loan interest deduction..............................	9,136	7,731	9,719	8,340	7.9
Tuition and fees deduction..................................	4,577	11,002	2,423	5,453	-50.4
Self-employment tax deduction..............................	17,411	24,286	17,436	23,834	-1.9
Self-employment health insurance deduction...................	3,618	21,194	3,626	21,820	3.0
Payments to a self-employed retirement (Keogh) plan..............	1,010	20,262	923	18,857	-6.9
Forfeited interest penalty...................................	1,311	389	1,205	339	-12.9
Alimony paid...	580	9,621	570	9,844	2.3
Other adjustment [1].......................................	(NA)	1,862	(NA)	1,350	-27.5

NA Not available. [1] Includes foreign housing adjustment, medical savings accounts deduction, jury duty pay deduction, and other adjustments for 2008 and 2009.

Source: U.S. Internal Revenue Service, *Statistics of Income Bulletin*, Fall issues. See also <http://www.irs.gov/uac/Tax-Stats-2>.

Table 499. Federal Individual Income Tax Returns—Itemized Deductions and Statutory Adjustments by Size of Adjusted Gross Income: 2009

[45,696 represents 45,696,000. Based on a sample of returns; see Appendix III]

Item	Unit	Total	Under $10,000	$10,000 to $19,999	$20,000 to $29,999	$30,000 to $39,999	$40,000 to $49,999	$50,000 to $99,999	$100,000 and over
Returns with itemized deductions:									
Number of returns [1]	1,000	45,696	1,069	2,092	2,853	3,620	3,995	16,856	15,212
Amount [1,2]	Mil. dol	1,203,808	17,953	32,829	45,499	57,101	68,331	345,050	637,045
Medical and dental expenses: [3]									
Returns	1,000	10,090	737	1,296	1,285	1,297	1,098	3,319	1,058
Amount	Mil. dol	79,866	6,303	10,316	10,050	8,710	8,185	24,627	11,676
Taxes paid:									
Returns	1,000	45,424	1,010	2,047	2,807	3,587	3,960	16,815	15,197
Amount	Mil. dol	432,032	3,599	6,370	9,227	13,148	16,752	105,048	277,888
State and local taxes: [4]									
Returns	1,000	44,017	867	1,887	2,657	3,429	3,803	16,401	14,972
Amount	Mil. dol	251,658	793	1,471	2,756	4,828	7,087	51,099	183,625
Real estate taxes:									
Returns	1,000	39,988	800	1,582	2,174	2,831	3,253	15,078	14,270
Amount	Mil. dol	167,779	2,661	4,582	5,999	7,675	8,880	49,712	88,270
Interest paid:									
Returns	1,000	37,004	634	1,259	1,974	2,621	3,084	14,178	13,254
Amount	Mil. dol	442,051	5,975	10,934	17,078	22,170	27,889	144,980	213,025
Home mortgage interest:									
Returns	1,000	36,542	614	1,238	1,950	2,602	3,059	14,062	13,016
Amount	Mil. dol	420,813	5,811	10,679	16,684	21,523	26,842	140,278	198,996
Charitable contributions:									
Returns	1,000	37,243	604	1,373	1,965	2,581	2,988	13,884	13,849
Amount	Mil. dol	158,017	696	2,666	4,098	5,485	7,131	38,533	99,407
Unreimbursed employee business expenses:									
Returns	1,000	14,942	79	317	743	1,206	1,407	6,311	4,880
Amount	Mil. dol	75,607	297	1,324	3,881	6,373	7,585	30,420	25,727
Returns with statutory adjustments:									
Number of returns	1,000	34,764	4,759	4,529	3,361	3,106	2,748	9,451	6,812
Amount of adjustments [2]	Mil. dol	112,967	7,257	6,480	5,927	5,928	5,823	23,753	57,799
Payments to IRAs: [5]									
Returns	1,000	2,588	59	140	223	291	300	955	621
Amount	Mil. dol	11,215	209	469	699	985	1,163	4,053	3,638
Deduction for self-employment tax:									
Returns	1,000	17,436	3,530	3,234	1,656	1,260	1,035	3,541	3,179
Amount	Mil. dol	23,834	1,656	2,591	1,682	1,380	1,196	4,919	10,409
Self-employment health insurance:									
Returns	1,000	3,626	458	363	317	268	251	822	1,146
Amount	Mil. dol	21,820	1,851	1,563	1,334	1,179	1,204	4,525	10,165
Payments to Keogh plans:									
Returns	1,000	923	19	16	21	20	32	154	662
Amount	Mil. dol	18,857	128	96	123	138	226	1,610	16,536

[1] After limitations. [2] Includes other deductions and adjustments, not shown separately. [3] Before limitation. [4] State and local taxes include income taxes and sales taxes. [5] IRA means Individual Retirement Account.

Source: U.S. Internal Revenue Service, *Statistics of Income Bulletin*, Fall issues. See also <http://www.irs.gov/uac/Tax-Stats-2>.

Table 500. Federal Individual Income Tax Returns—Selected Tax Credits: 2007 to 2009

[48,091 represents 48,091,000. For tax years. Based on a sample of returns, see source and Appendix III]

Item	2007 Number of returns (1,000)	2007 Amount (mil. dol.)	2008 Number of returns (1,000)	2008 Amount (mil. dol.)	2009 Number of returns (1,000)	2009 Amount (mil. dol.)
Total tax credits [1]	**48,091**	**63,779**	**55,229**	**75,352**	**87,501**	**110,076**
Child care credit	6,492	3,483	6,587	3,527	6,286	3,317
Earned income credit [2]	3,420	934	3,382	971	1,489	489
Foreign tax credit	7,643	15,435	6,708	16,572	6,310	13,060
General business credit	231	846	304	1,649	293	1,601
Minimum tax credit	395	1,035	416	945	320	759
Child tax credit [3]	25,889	31,556	25,174	30,538	23,563	28,417
Education credits	7,435	6,910	7,741	7,633	10,599	10,837
Retirement savings contribution credit	5,862	977	5,961	977	6,253	1,040

[1] Includes credits not shown separately. [2] Represents portion of earned income credit used to offset income tax before credits. [3] Excludes refundable portion.

Source: U.S. Internal Revenue Service, *Statistics of Income Bulletin*, Fall issues. See also <http://www.irs.gov/uac/Tax-Stats-2>.

Table 501. Federal Individual Income Tax Returns by State: 2009

[141,459 represents 141,459,000. For tax year. Data may not agree with data in other tables due to differing survey methodology used to derive state data]

State	Total number of returns (1,000)	Adjusted gross income (mil. dol.)			Itemized deductions (mil. dol.)				Income tax (mil. dol.)
		Total [1]	Salaries and wages	Net capital gain [2]	Total [1]	State and local income tax	Real estate taxes	Mortgage interest paid	
U.S.	141,459	7,801,041	5,710,910	224,063	1,250,733	243,410	172,123	425,428	916,513
AL.	2,049	95,602	71,313	1,707	12,918	2,115	660	4,304	9,766
AK.	358	20,210	14,647	387	1,938	27	318	932	2,529
AZ.	2,671	135,328	99,457	3,242	23,859	3,045	2,153	9,961	14,118
AR.	1,212	54,628	39,532	1,175	6,805	1,584	383	1,862	5,418
CA.	16,384	996,256	724,744	29,379	207,982	47,226	24,578	80,111	120,456
CO.	2,332	137,053	100,025	5,642	23,012	3,818	1,985	9,983	16,023
CT.	1,712	135,993	95,462	5,172	24,473	6,137	4,577	7,039	20,426
DE.	420	23,454	17,131	612	3,618	753	309	1,509	2,570
DC.	312	23,249	16,108	937	4,067	1,223	321	1,304	3,606
FL.	8,911	452,703	302,770	21,295	64,923	2,143	9,769	24,489	54,966
GA.	4,448	211,991	161,261	4,547	37,943	7,128	3,950	13,313	22,504
HI.	649	33,438	23,955	770	6,027	1,117	323	2,477	3,576
ID.	658	29,903	21,455	911	5,032	997	419	1,863	2,727
IL.	6,008	350,438	256,867	10,835	51,887	7,184	10,892	18,297	43,333
IN.	2,951	138,570	104,192	2,077	16,452	3,545	1,533	5,571	13,992
IA.	1,392	69,595	51,000	1,453	8,890	2,076	1,037	2,491	6,933
KS.	1,310	68,321	49,993	1,497	9,298	2,132	1,088	2,581	7,369
KY.	1,841	84,009	62,469	1,652	11,290	3,004	948	3,513	8,178
LA.	1,960	96,308	70,948	2,157	11,573	2,074	674	3,275	10,791
ME.	625	29,157	21,432	691	4,215	1,052	633	1,401	2,832
MD.	2,751	183,271	139,180	3,729	40,786	10,109	4,562	13,741	22,040
MA.	3,172	217,427	159,415	6,394	35,735	8,694	5,679	12,270	29,586
MI.	4,535	218,495	158,069	2,723	31,805	5,617	5,146	11,033	22,654
MN.	2,542	145,272	109,197	3,076	24,550	5,933	3,060	8,782	16,330
MS.	1,241	51,047	38,530	787	6,583	1,369	419	1,784	4,708
MO.	2,684	131,802	97,563	2,317	18,341	3,838	1,910	5,927	14,248
MT.	472	21,250	14,163	972	3,170	622	308	1,058	2,134
NE.	846	42,706	31,713	1,021	5,722	1,240	816	1,553	4,414
NV.	1,244	67,548	47,490	3,357	11,441	323	1,113	4,632	8,186
NH.	659	39,361	29,353	1,052	6,304	428	1,395	2,188	4,503
NJ.	4,237	299,574	224,537	5,950	57,109	13,076	13,492	17,117	40,660
NM.	912	40,772	29,420	699	5,176	801	458	2,034	4,572
NY.	9,117	602,715	421,675	28,036	110,566	36,662	18,177	24,461	83,890
NC.	4,145	201,873	150,527	3,876	33,861	7,907	3,216	11,508	20,527
ND.	323	16,662	11,486	502	1,399	225	182	379	1,864
OH.	5,410	257,359	192,758	3,247	34,954	8,684	5,187	11,176	26,771
OK.	1,586	77,281	55,604	2,381	9,915	1,887	754	2,568	8,283
OR.	1,733	85,986	60,848	2,402	17,692	4,073	2,067	6,280	8,565
PA.	6,059	324,849	239,864	7,467	43,740	9,283	7,307	14,000	37,723
RI.	502	27,102	20,003	470	4,497	978	833	1,565	3,058
SC.	2,024	91,092	66,816	1,881	14,594	2,971	1,010	4,952	8,730
SD.	385	18,983	12,723	689	1,749	58	208	524	2,088
TN.	2,795	130,485	98,380	3,095	15,391	431	1,440	5,568	13,977
TX.	10,785	588,290	441,542	19,744	66,435	1,254	12,274	20,734	71,963
UT.	1,125	58,508	44,090	2,142	11,129	1,919	838	4,093	5,506
VT.	316	15,391	11,114	566	2,429	456	431	688	1,579
VA.	3,686	234,321	177,334	5,222	41,379	8,475	4,687	16,634	28,445
WA.	3,145	186,217	136,298	5,815	27,918	718	4,121	13,083	21,975
WV.	778	34,934	25,770	1,070	3,183	859	187	993	3,445
WI.	2,728	139,548	103,413	2,821	22,100	5,498	3,917	6,632	14,815
WY.	269	16,035	10,774	1,074	1,671	75	141	599	1,955
Other [3]	1,054	48,677	46,497	3,347	3,208	568	236	597	5,206

[1] Includes other items, not shown separately. [2] Less loss. [3] Includes returns filed from Army Post Office and Fleet Post Office addresses by members of the armed forces stationed overseas; returns by other U.S. citizens abroad; and returns filed by residents of Puerto Rico with income from sources outside of Puerto Rico or with income earned as U.S. government employees.

Source: U.S. Internal Revenue Service, *Statistics of Income Bulletin, Historical Tables.* See also <http://www.irs.gov/uac/Tax-Stats-2>.

Table 502. Federal Individual Income Tax—Tax Liability and Effective and Marginal Tax Rates for Selected Income Groups: 2000 to 2010

[Refers to income after exclusions but before deductions for itemized or standard deductions and for personal exemptions. Tax liability is after reductions for tax credits. As a result of the tax credits, tax liability can be negative, which means that the taxpayer receives a payment from the government. The effective rate represents tax liability, which may be negative as a result of the tax credits, divided by stated income. The marginal tax rate is the percentage of the first additional dollar of income which would be paid in income tax. Tax credits which increase with income can result in negative marginal tax rates. Computations assume itemized deductions (in excess of floors) of 18 percent of adjusted gross income or the standard deduction, whichever is greater. All income is assumed to be from wages and salaries. Does not include Social Security and Medicare taxes imposed on most wages and salaries]

Adjusted gross income	2000	2005	2007	2008 [1]	2009	2010
TAX LIABILITY (dol.)						
Single person, no dependents:						
$5,000	[2] -353	[2] -383	[2] -383	[1,2] -683	[2,5] -693	[2,5] -693
$10,000	[2] 391	[2] 46	[2] -73	[1,2] -415	[2,5] -598	[2,5] -600
$20,000	1,920	1,405	1,296	[1] 656	[5] 780	[5] 779
$30,000	3,270	2,845	2,789	2,156	[5] 2,280	[5] 2,279
$40,000	4,988	4,075	4,019	3,394	[5] 3,555	[5] 3,554
$50,000	7,284	6,115	5,824	5,119	[5] 5,125	[5] 5,119
$75,000	13,024	11,240	10,949	10,244	[5] 10,250	[5] 10,244
$100,000	19,233	16,571	16,119	15,969	[5] 15,775	[5] 15,769
Married couple, two dependents, with one spouse working:						
$5,000	-2,000	[2] -2,000	[2] -2,000	[1,2] -3,200	-2,610	[2,4,5] -2,610
$10,000	-3,888	[2] -4,000	[2] -4,000	[1,2,4] -5,425	-5,670	[2,4,5] -5,670
$20,000	-2,349	[2,4] -4,986	[2,5] -5,404	[1,2,4] -7,484	-7,828	[2,4,5] -7,836
$30,000	475	[2,3,4] -2,810	[2,4,5] -3,490	[1,2,3,4] -5,143	-5,621	[2,3,4,5] -5,637
$40,000	2,218	[3,4] -150	[4,5] -428	[1,2,3,4] -2,637	-2,515	[2,3,4,5] -2,531
$50,000	3,470	[3] 1,350	[4] 1,073	[1,3] -838	-35	[3,5] -37
$75,000	7,384	[3] 4,575	[4] 4,403	[1,3] 2,523	3,400	[3,5] 3,398
$100,000	13,124	[3] 8,630	[4] 7,948	[1,3] 5,888	6,475	[3,5] 6,473
EFFECTIVE RATE (percent)						
Single person, no dependents:						
$5,000	-7.1	[2] -7.7	[2] -7.7	[1,2] -13.7	[2,5] -13.9	[2,5] -13.9
$10,000	3.9	[2] 0.5	[2] -0.7	[1,2] -4.2	[2,5] -6.0	[2,5] -6.0
$20,000	9.6	7.0	6.5	[1] 3.3	[5] 3.9	[5] 3.9
$30,000	10.9	9.5	9.3	[1] 7.2	[5] 7.6	[5] 7.6
$40,000	12.5	10.2	10.1	[1] 8.5	[5] 8.9	[5] 8.9
$50,000	14.6	12.2	11.6	[1] 10.2	[5] 10.3	[5] 10.2
$75,000	17.4	15.0	14.6	[1] 13.7	[5] 13.7	[5] 13.7
$100,000	19.2	16.6	16.1	16.0	15.8	15.8
Married couple, two dependents, with one spouse working:						
$5,000	[2] -40.0	[2] -40.0	[2] -40.0	[1,2] -64.0	[2,4,5] -52.2	[2,4,5] -52.2
$10,000	[2] -38.9	[2] -40.0	[2] -40.0	[1,2,4] -54.3	[2,4,5] -56.7	[2,4,5] -56.7
$20,000	[2,3] -11.7	[2,4] -24.9	[2,5] -27.0	[1,2,4] -37.4	[2,4,5] -39.1	[2,4,5] -39.2
$30,000	[2,3] 1.6	[2,3,4] -9.4	[2,4,5] -11.6	[1,2,3,4] -17.1	[2,3,4,5] -18.7	[2,3,4,5] -18.8
$40,000	[3] 5.5	[3,4] -0.4	[4,5] -1.1	[1,2,3,4] -6.6	[2,3,4,5] -6.3	[2,3,4,5] -6.3
$50,000	[3] 6.9	[3] 2.7	[4] 2.1	[1,3] -1.7	[3,5] -0.1	[3,5] -0.1
$75,000	[3] 9.8	[3] 6.1	[4] 5.9	[1,3] 3.4	[3,5] 4.5	[3,5] 4.5
$100,000	[3] 13.1	[3] 8.6	[4] 7.9	[1,3] 5.9	[3,5] 6.5	[3,5] 6.5
MARGINAL TAX RATE (percent)						
Single person, no dependents:						
$5,000	–	[2] -7.7	[2] -7.7	[2] -7.7	[2,5] -13.9	[2,5] -13.9
$10,000	[2] 22.7	[2] 17.7	[2] 17.7	[2] 17.7	[2] 17.7	[2] 17.7
$20,000	15.0	15.0	15.0	15.0	15.0	15.0
$30,000	15.0	15.0	15.0	15.0	15.0	15.0
$40,000	28.0	15.0	15.0	15.0	15.0	15.0
$50,000	28.0	25.0	25.0	25.0	25.0	25.0
$75,000	28.0	25.0	25.0	25.0	[5] 27.0	[5] 27.0
$100,000	31.0	28.0	28.0	25.0	25.0	25.0
Married couple, two dependents, with one spouse working:						
$5,000	[2] -40.0	[2] -40.0	[2] -40.0	[2] -40.0	[2,4,5] -61.2	[2,4,5] -61.2
$10,000	–	[2] -40.0	[2] -40.0	[2,4] -55.0	[2,4,5] -61.2	[2,4,5] -61.2
$20,000	[2,3] 21.1	[2,4] 6.1	[2,5] 6.1	[2,4] 6.1	–	–
$30,000	[2] 36.1	[2,3,4] 31.1	[2,4,5] 31.1	[2,3,4] 31.1	[2] 31.1	[2] 31.1
$40,000	15.0	[3,4] 15.0	[4,5] 15.0	[2,3,4] 31.1	[2] 31.1	[2] 31.1
$50,000	15.0	15.0	15.0	15.0	15.0	15.0
$75,000	28.0	15.0	15.0	15.0	15.0	15.0
$100,000	28.0	25.0	25.0	25.0	15.0	15.0

– Represents zero. [1] Includes effect of the Recovery Rebate paid in 2008 under the Economic Stimulus Act of 2008 (P.L. 110–185). [2] Includes effect from the refundable earned income tax credit. [3] Includes effect from the child tax credit. [4] Includes effect from the additional (refundable) child tax credit. [5] Includes effect from the (refundable) Making Work Pay tax credit.

Source: U.S. Department of the Treasury, Office of Tax Analysis, unpublished data.

Table 503. Federal Individual Income Tax—Current Income Equivalent to 2000 Constant Income for Selected Income Groups: 2000 to 2010

[Constant 2000 incomes are calculated by using the U.S. Bureau of Labor Statistics Consumer Price Index for Urban Consumers (CPI–U); see Table 737, Section 14. See also headnote, Table 502]

Adusted gross income (constant 2000 dollars)	2000	2005	2007	2008 [1]	2009	2010
REAL INCOME EQUIVALENT (dol.)						
$5,000	5,000	5,670	6,020	6,250	6,230	6,330
$10,000	10,000	11,340	12,040	12,500	12,460	12,660
$20,000	20,000	22,680	24,080	25,010	24,920	25,330
$30,000	30,000	34,020	36,120	37,510	37,380	37,990
$40,000	40,000	45,370	48,160	50,010	49,830	50,650
$50,000	50,000	56,710	60,200	62,520	62,290	63,310
$75,000	75,000	85,060	90,310	93,770	93,440	94,970
$100,000	100,000	113,410	120,410	125,030	124,590	126,630
TAX LIABILITY (dol.)						
Single person, no dependents:						
$5000	[2] -353	[2] -399	[2] -428	[1,2] -738	[2,5] -843	[2,5] -850
$10,000	[2] 391	[2] 283	[2] 287	[1,2] -29	[2,5] -164	[2,5] -130
$20,000	1,920	1,807	1,908	[1] 1,408	[5] 1,518	[5] 1,578
$30,000	3,270	3,339	3,542	[1] 3,087	[5] 3,233	[5] 3,307
$40,000	4,988	5,166	5,447	[1] 5,121	[5] 5,090	[5] 5,252
$50,000	7,284	7,491	7,915	[1] 7,685	[5] 7,644	[5] 7,847
$75,000	13,024	13,302	14,087	[1] 14,692	[5] 14,399	[5] 14,737
$100,000	19,233	19,649	20,805	[1] 21,705	[5] 21,304	21,761
Married couple, 2 dependents with one spouse working:						
$5,000	[2] -2,000	[2] -2,268	[2] -2,408	[1,2] -3,700	[2,4,5] -3,363	[2,4,5] -3,424
$10,000	[2] -3,888	[2,4] -4,451	[2] -4,760	[1,2,4] -6,624	[2,4,5] -7,176	[2,4,5] -7,270
$20,000	[2,3] -2,349	[2,4] -4,823	[2,4] -5,157	[1,2,3,4] -6,693	[2,4,5] -7,091	[2,4,5] -7,021
$30,000	[2,3] 475	[2,3,4] -1,561	[2,3,4] -1,589	[1,2,3,4] -3,410	[2,3,4,5] -3,329	[2,4,5] -3,156
$40,000	[3] 2,218	[3] 656	[3,4] 797	[1,3] -836	[3,5] -60	3,560
$50,000	[3] 3,470	[3] 2,325	[3] 2,582	[1,3] 987	[3,5] 1,809	[3,5] 1,959
$75,000	[3] 7,384	[3] 5,812	[3] 6,286	[1,3] 4,831	[3,5] 5,668	[3,5] 5,854
$100,000	[3] 13,124	[3] 11,579	[3] 12,682	[1,3] 11,819	[3,5] 12,216	[3,5] 12,722
EFFECTIVE TAX RATE (percent)						
Single person, no dependents:						
$5,000	[2] -7.1	[2] -7.0	[2] -7.1	[1,2] -11.8	[2,5] -13.5	[2,5] -13.4
$10,000	[2] 3.9	[2] 2.5	[2] 2.4	[1,2] -0.2	[2,5] -1.3	[2,5] -1.0
$20,000	9.6	8.0	7.9	[1] 5.6	[5] 6.1	[5] 6.2
$30,000	10.9	9.8	9.8	[1] 8.2	[5] 8.6	[5] 8.7
$40,000	12.5	11.4	11.3	[1] 10.2	[5] 10.2	[5] 10.4
$50,000	14.6	13.2	13.1	[1] 12.3	[5] 12.3	[5] 12.4
$75,000	17.4	15.6	15.6	[1] 15.7	[5] 15.4	[5] 15.5
$100,000	19.2	17.3	17.3	[1] 17.4	17.1	17.2
Married couple, 2 dependents with one spouse working:						
$5,000	[2] -40.0	[2] -40.0	[2] -40.0	[1,2] -59.2	[2,4,5] -54.0	[2,4,5] -54.1
$10,000	[2] -38.9	[2,4] -39.3	[2] -39.5	[1,2,4] -53.0	[2,4,5] -57.6	[2,4,5] -57.4
$20,000	[2,3] -11.7	[2,4] -21.3	[2,4] -21.4	[1,2,3,4] -26.8	[2,4,5] -28.5	[2,4,5] -27.7
$30,000	[2,3] 1.6	[2,3,4] -4.6	[2,3,4] -4.4	[1,2,3,4] -9.1	[2,3,4,5] -8.9	[2,4,5] -8.3
$40,000	[3] 5.5	[3] 1.4	[3,4] -1.7	[1,3] -1.7	[3,5] -0.1	[3,5] 0.1
$50,000	[3] 6.9	[3] 4.1	[3] 4.3	[1,3] 1.6	[3,5] 2.9	[3,5] 3.1
$75,000	[3] 9.8	[3] 6.8	[3] 7.0	[1,3] 5.2	[3,5] 6.1	[3,5] 6.2
$100,000	[3] 13.1	[3] 10.2	[3] 10.5	[1,3] 9.5	[3,5] 9.8	[3,5] 10.0
MARGINAL TAX RATE (percent)						
Single person, no dependents:						
$5,000	–	–	–	–	[5] -6.2	[5] -6.2
$10,000	[2] 22.7	[2] 17.7	[2] 17.7	[2] 7.7	[2] 17.7	[2] 17.7
$20,000	15.0	15.0	15.0	15.0	15.0	15.0
$30,000	15.0	15.0	15.0	15.0	15.0	15.0
$40,000	28.0	25.0	25.0	25.0	25.0	25.0
$50,000	28.0	25.0	25.0	25.0	25.0	25.0
$75,000	28.0	25.0	25.0	25.0	[5] 27.0	[5] 27.0
$100,000	31.0	28.0	28.0	28.0	28.0	28.0
Married couple, 2 dependents with one spouse working:						
$5,000	[2] -40.0	[2] -40.0	[2] -40.0	[2] -40.0	[2,4,5] -61.2	[2,4,5] -61.2
$10,000	–	[4] -15.0	[4] -15.0	[4] -15.0	[2,4,5] -61.2	[2,4,5] -21.2
$20,000	[2,3] 21.1	[2,4] 6.1	[2,3,4] 31.1	[2,3,4] 31.1	[2] 21.1	[2] 21.1
$30,000	[2] 36.1	[2,3,4] 31.1	[2,3,4] 31.1	[2,3,4] 31.1	[2] 31.1	[2] 31.1
$40,000	15.0	15.0	15.0	15.0	15.0	15.0
$50,000	15.0	15.0	15.0	15.0	15.0	15.0
$75,000	28.0	15.0	15.0	15.0	15.0	15.0
$100,000	28.0	[3] 30.1	[3] 30.1	[3] 30.1	[3] 30.1	[3] 30.1

– Represents zero. [1] Includes effect of the Recovery Rebate paid in 2008 under the Economic Stimulus Act of 2008 (P.L. 110–185). [2] Includes effect from the refundable earned income tax credit. [3] Includes effect from the child tax credit. [4] Includes effect from the additional (refundable) child tax credit. [5] Includes effect from the (refundable) Making Work Pay tax credit.

Source: U.S. Department of the Treasury, Office of Tax Analysis, unpublished data.

Table 504. Federal Civilian Employment and Annual Payroll by Branch: 1970 to 2010

[2,997 represents 2,997,000. For fiscal year ending in year shown. See text, Section 8. Includes employees in U.S. territories and foreign countries. Data represent employees in active-duty status, including intermittent employees. Annual employment figures are averages of monthly figures. Excludes Central Intelligence Agency, National Security Agency and as of November 1984, Defense Intelligence Agency; and as of October 1996, National Imagery and Mapping Agency]

| Year | Employment | | | | | | Payroll (mil. dol.) | | | | |
| | Total (1,000) | Percent U.S. employed [1] | Executive (1,000) | | Legis-lative (1,000) | Judicial (1,000) | | Executive | | Legis-lative | Judicial |
			Total	Defense			Total	Total	Defense		
1970.............	[2] 2,997	3.81	2,961	1,263	29	7	27,322	26,894	11,264	338	89
1975.............	2,877	3.35	2,830	1,044	37	10	39,126	38,423	13,418	549	154
1980.............	[2] 2,987	3.01	2,933	971	40	14	58,012	56,841	18,795	883	288
1985.............	3,001	2.80	2,944	1,080	39	18	80,599	78,992	28,330	1,098	509
1990.............	[2] 3,233	2.72	3,173	1,060	38	23	99,138	97,022	31,990	1,329	787
1995.............	2,943	2.36	2,880	852	34	28	118,304	115,328	31,753	1,598	1,379
2003.............	2,743	1.99	2,677	669	31	34	143,380	139,506	29,029	1,908	1,966
2004.............	2,713	1.95	2,649	668	30	34	148,037	144,134	29,128	1,977	1,927
2005.............	2,701	1.91	2,636	671	31	34	152,222	148,275	29,331	2,048	1,900
2006.............	2,700	1.87	2,637	676	29	34	160,570	156,543	29,580	2,109	1,918
2007.............	2,699	1.85	2,636	673	30	33	161,394	157,010	29,025	2,119	2,265
2008.............	2,758	1.90	2,694	694	30	34	167,166	162,675	29,749	2,162	2,328
2009.............	2,838	2.03	2,774	737	31	34	174,804	170,349	30,995	2,203	2,252
2010.............	2,841	2.04	2,777	773	31	34	152,321	147,554	32,377	2,515	2,251

[1] Civilian employment only. See Table 596, Section 12. [2] Includes temporary census workers.

Source: U.S. Office of Personnel Management, *Federal Civilian Workforce Statistics—Employment and Trends*, and unpublished data, <http://www.opm.gov/feddata>.

Table 505. Full-Time Federal Civilian Employment—Employees and Average Pay by Pay System: 2000 to 2010

[(1,671 represents 1,671,000).As of March 31. Excludes employees of Congress and federal courts, maritime seamen of U.S. Department of Commerce, and small number for whom rates were not reported. See text, this section, for explanation of general schedule and wage system]

| Pay system | Employees (1,000) | | | | Average annual pay (dol.) | | | |
	2000	2008	2009	2010	2000	2008	2009	2010
Total, excluding postal..........	**1,671**	**1,885**	**1,798**	**1,865**	**50,429**	**69,061**	**63,678**	**73,908**
General Schedule...................	1,216	1,265	1,083	1,162	49,428	68,674	59,330	70,426
Wage system......................	205	200	189	196	37,082	47,652	50,223	50,862
Other.............................	250	420	526	507	66,248	80,444	77,433	90,383
Postal pay system [1]..............	788	663	623	584	37,627	50,294	49,951	53,304

[1] Career employees—U.S. Postal Service, *Annual Report of the Postmaster General*. See also <http://about.usps.com/news/welcome.htm>. Average pay—U.S. Postal Service, *Comprehensive Statement of Postal Operations*, annual.

Source: Except as noted, U.S. Office of Personnel Management, *Pay Structure of the Federal Civil Service*, annual (publication discontinued) and unpublished data, <http://www.opm.gov/feddata>.

Table 506. Federal Government Civilian Employment and Annuitants by State: 2010

[In thousands (1,832 represents 1,832,000). As of September 30. Employment data are for full-time permanent employees. Includes all non-postal executive branch agencies as well as Government Printing Office, U.S. Tax Court, Medicare Payment Advisory Commission, U.S. Commission on International Religious Freedom, U.S.-China Economic & Security Review Commission, Dwight D. Eisenhower Memorial Commission, and Federal Bureau of Investigation.]

State	Employment	Annuitants	State	Employment	Annuitants	State	Employment	Annuitants
U.S. [1]........	**1,832**	**2,512**	KS.............	15	24	NC............	38	71
AL.............	39	58	KY.............	23	33	ND............	6	6
AK.............	11	8	LA.............	19	26	OH............	49	74
AZ.............	37	53	ME............	10	14	OK............	36	48
AR.............	13	25	MD............	111	154	OR............	17	33
CA.............	150	214	MA............	25	43	PA............	65	107
CO.............	35	48	MI.............	27	43	RI............	6	8
CT.............	8	15	MN............	16	28	SC............	19	43
DE.............	3	9	MS............	17	25	SD............	7	10
DC.............	145	44	MO............	34	53	TN............	25	45
FL.............	81	165	MT............	9	12	TX............	128	165
GA.............	72	81	NE............	10	13	UT............	27	35
HI.............	23	25	NV............	10	22	VT............	4	4
ID.............	7	14	NH............	4	12	VA............	141	140
IL.............	47	67	NJ............	29	55	WA............	49	65
IN.............	22	36	NM............	23	28	WV............	18	17
IA.............	8	21	NY............	62	96	WI............	13	26
						WY............	5	6

[1] Includes employees outside the United States and in states not specified, not shown separately.

Source: U.S. Office of Personnel Management, *Federal Civilian Employment by Major Geographic Area, State, and Selected Agency Executive Branch and Selected Other Agencies, Non-Postal, Full-Time, Permanent Employees and All Annuitants: September 2010*, <http://www.opm.gov/feddata>.

Table 507. Federal Civilian Employment by Branch and Agency: 1990 to 2010

[For years ending September 30. Annual averages of monthly figures. Excludes Central Intelligence Agency, National Security Agency; Defense Intelligence Agency; and as of October 1996, National Imagery and Mapping Agency]

Agency	1990	2000	2005	2008	2009	2010
Total, all agencies	**3,128,267**	**2,708,101**	**2,700,965**	**2,757,872**	**2,838,491**	**2,841,143**
Legislative branch	37,495	31,157	30,816	30,293	30,859	30,643
Judicial branch	23,605	32,186	34,064	33,754	33,754	33,756
Executive branch	3,067,167	2,644,758	2,636,085	2,693,825	2,773,878	2,776,744
Executive Office of the President	1,731	1,658	1,693	1,701	1,769	1,965
Executive departments	2,065,542	1,592,200	1,685,211	1,782,079	1,905,137	1,937,291
State	25,288	27,983	33,948	36,421	37,464	39,016
Treasury	158,655	143,508	107,950	105,971	109,189	110,099
Defense	1,034,152	676,268	671,364	694,149	736,592	772,601
Justice	83,932	125,970	105,458	109,331	113,495	117,916
Interior	77,679	73,818	75,973	72,702	75,381	70,231
Agriculture	122,594	104,466	107,852	103,753	104,460	106,867
Commerce [1]	69,920	47,652	39,836	42,155	80,167	56,856
Labor	17,727	16,040	15,383	16,243	16,909	17,592
Health & Human Services [2]	123,959	62,605	60,736	64,732	67,149	69,839
Housing & Urban Development	13,596	10,319	9,941	9,818	9,585	9,585
Transportation [3]	67,364	63,598	55,559	55,439	57,277	57,972
Energy	17,731	15,692	15,010	15,246	16,145	16,145
Education	4,771	4,734	4,321	4,207	4,101	4,452
Veterans Affairs	248,174	219,547	235,210	279,049	297,318	304,665
Homeland Security [3]	(X)	(X)	146,670	172,863	179,905	183,455
Independent agencies [4]	999,894	1,050,900	949,181	910,045	866,972	837,488
Board of Governors Federal Reserve System	1,525	2,372	1,860	1,873	1,873	1,873
Environmental Protection Agency	17,123	18,036	17,824	18,209	18,399	18,740
Equal Employment Opportunity Commission	2,880	2,780	2,360	2,189	2,351	2,543
Federal Communications Commission	1,778	1,965	1,885	1,824	1,877	1,838
Federal Deposit Insurance Corporation	17,641	6,958	4,635	4,940	6,436	6,436
Federal Trade Commission	988	1,019	1,007	1,131	1,131	1,131
General Services Administration	20,277	14,334	12,769	11,981	12,524	12,820
National Archives & Records Administration	3,120	2,702	3,029	3,138	3,386	3,523
National Aeronautics & Space Administration	24,872	18,819	18,752	18,533	18,539	18,664
National Labor Relations Board	2,263	2,054	1,869	1,641	1,644	1,715
National Science Foundation	1,318	1,247	1,305	1,397	1,447	1,474
Nuclear Regulatory Commission	3,353	2,858	3,242	4,107	4,169	4,240
Office of Personnel Management	6,636	3,780	4,939	5,440	5,440	5,892
Peace Corps	1,178	1,065	1,072	1,001	1,003	1,082
Railroad Retirement Board	1,772	1,176	1,008	967	971	981
Securities & Exchange Commission	2,302	2,955	3,907	3,632	3,728	3,917
Small Business Administration	5,128	4,150	4,343	3,826	3,575	4,037
Smithsonian Institution	5,092	5,065	4,901	4,961	4,977	4,984
Social Security Administration [2]	(X)	64,474	66,144	64,007	67,631	69,975
Tennessee Valley Authority	28,392	13,145	12,703	11,584	12,200	12,457
U.S. Information Agency	8,555	2,436	2,175	1,975	1,958	1,953
U.S. International Development Cooperation Agency	4,698	2,552	2,493	2,515	2,515	2,515
U.S. Postal Service	816,886	860,726	764,165	728,276	678,020	643,420

X Not applicable. [1] Includes enumerators for the 1990 and 2000 censuses. [2] The Social Security Administration was separated from the Department of Health and Human Services to become an independent agency effective April 1995. [3] See text, Section 10, National Security and Veteran Affairs, concerning the development of the Department of Homeland Security. [4] Includes agencies with fewer than 1,000 employees in 2005, not shown separately.

Source: U.S. Office of Personnel Management, "Federal Civilian Workforce Statistics—Employment and Trends," <http://www.opm.gov/feddata/html/empt.asp>, accessed August 2012.

Table 508. Federal Employees—Summary Characteristics: 1990 to 2009

[In percent, except as indicated. As of September 30. For civilian employees of executive branch agencies participating in Office of Personnel Management's Central Personnel Data File (CPDF)]

Characteristics	1990	1995	2000	2005	2006	2007	2008	2009	2010
Average age (years) [1]	42.3	44.3	46.3	46.9	46.9	47.0	46.8	46.8	46.8
Average length of service (years)	13.4	15.5	17.1	16.4	16.3	16.1	15.5	15.1	14.3
Retirement eligible: [2]									
Civil Service Retirement System	8	10	17	33	37	41	46	51	57
Federal Employees Retirement System	3	5	11	13	13	13	13	(NA)	(NA)
Bachelor's degree or higher	35	39	41	43	43	45	44	45	46
Sex: Male	57	56	55	56	56	56	56	56	56
Female	43	44	45	44	44	44	44	44	44
Race and national origin:									
Total minorities	27.4	28.9	30.4	31.7	32.1	32.5	33.0	33.0	33.3
Black	16.7	16.8	17.1	17.0	17.2	17.3	17.5	17.5	17.5
Hispanic	5.4	5.9	6.6	7.4	7.5	7.6	7.7	7.7	7.7
Asian/Pacific Islander	3.5	4.2	4.5	5.1	5.1	5.4	5.2	5.6	5.6
American Indian/Alaska Native	1.8	2.0	2.2	2.1	2.1	2.1	2.1	2.1	2.1
Disabled	7.0	7.0	7.0	7.0	7.0	7.0	6.8	6.9	7.0
Veterans preference	30.0	26.0	24.0	22.0	22.0	22.0	22.4	22.7	23.1
Vietnam era veterans	17.0	17.0	14.0	11.0	10.0	9.0	8.0	7.1	8.0
Retired military	4.9	4.2	3.9	5.4	5.7	6.0	6.2	6.6	7.0
Retired officers	0.5	0.5	0.5	1.0	1.1	1.2	1.3	1.4	1.6

NA Not available. [1] For full-time permanent employees. [2] Represents full-time permanent employees under the Civil Service Retirement System (excluding hires since January 1984), and the Federal Employees Retirement System (since January 1984).

Source: U.S. Office of Personnel Management, Office of Workforce Information, *The Fact Book, Federal Civilian Workforce Statistics*, annual. Beginning 2008, Central Personnel Data File, "Profile of Federal Civilian Non-Postal Employees."

Table 509. Federal Executive Branch (Non-postal) Employment by Race and National Origin: 1990 to 2008

[As of September 30. Covers total employment for executive branch agencies participating in Office of Personnel Management's Central Personnel Data File(CPDF). For information on the CPDF, see <http://www.opm.gov/feddata/acpdf.pdf>]

Pay system	1990	1995	2000	2005	2006	2007	2008
All personnel [1]	**2,150,359**	**1,960,577**	**1,755,689**	**1,856,966**	**1,848,339**	**1,862,404**	**1,916,726**
White, non-Hispanic	1,562,846	1,394,690	1,224,836	1,267,922	1,254,308	1,254,131	1,297,772
General schedule and related	1,218,188	1,101,108	961,261	973,767	948,740	878,182	858,050
Grades 1 to 4	132,028	79,195	55,067	46,671	43,450	42,135	44,324
Grades 5 to 8	337,453	288,755	239,128	227,387	219,168	208,180	211,004
Grades 9 to 12	510,261	465,908	404,649	408,111	399,400	367,195	351,302
Grades 13 to 15	238,446	267,250	262,417	291,598	286,722	260,672	251,420
Total executive/senior pay levels	9,337	13,307	14,332	16,409	16,118	20,718	21,793
Wage pay system	244,220	186,184	146,075	135,383	133,942	132,290	134,933
Other pay systems	91,101	94,091	103,168	142,363	155,508	222,941	282,996
Black	356,867	327,302	298,701	315,644	317,697	323,470	337,742
General schedule and related	272,657	258,586	241,135	246,691	246,248	236,721	236,525
Grades 1 to 4	65,077	41,381	26,895	19,774	18,326	17,692	18,286
Grades 5 to 8	114,993	112,962	99,937	94,655	93,717	89,903	90,410
Grades 9 to 12	74,985	79,795	82,809	90,809	91,869	88,042	86,054
Grades 13 to 15	17,602	24,448	31,494	41,453	42,336	41,084	41,775
Total executive/senior pay levels	479	942	1,180	1,270	1,218	1,510	1,565
Wage pay system	72,755	55,637	42,590	37,666	37,378	37,685	38,540
Other pay systems	10,976	12,137	13,796	30,017	32,853	47,554	61,973
Hispanic	115,170	115,964	115,247	138,507	138,596	141,968	136,167
General schedule and related	83,218	86,762	89,911	104,927	105,236	102,613	95,016
Grades 1 to 4	15,738	11,081	8,526	7,768	6,854	6,454	5,459
Grades 5 to 8	28,727	31,152	31,703	33,653	33,834	33,738	31,261
Grades 9 to 12	31,615	34,056	36,813	46,268	46,951	45,309	42,542
Grades 13 to 15	7,138	10,473	12,869	17,238	17,597	17,112	15,754
Total executive/senior pay levels	154	382	547	682	699	1,070	1,109
Wage pay system	26,947	22,128	16,926	15,945	15,822	15,652	15,639
Other pay systems	4,851	6,692	7,863	16,953	16,839	22,633	28,646
American Indian, Alaska Native, Asian, and Pacific Islander	115,476	122,621	116,905	134,893	136,593	141,138	145,045
General schedule and related	81,499	86,768	86,074	97,866	97,870	95,008	93,197
Grades 1 to 4	15,286	11,854	9,340	8,357	7,877	7,938	7,608
Grades 5 to 8	24,960	26,580	25,691	27,417	26,986	26,292	26,046
Grades 9 to 12	31,346	33,810	33,167	38,276	38,492	36,664	35,259
Grades 13 to 15	9,907	14,524	17,876	23,816	24,515	24,114	24,284
Total executive/senior pay levels	148	331	504	804	873	2,630	2,851
Wage pay system	24,927	21,553	17,613	16,938	16,728	16,661	17,022
Other pay systems	8,902	13,969	12,714	19,285	21,122	26,839	33,834

[1] Beginning 2006, includes persons classified as multiracial, not shown separately.

Source: U.S. Office of Personnel Management, "Central Personnel Data File," <http://www.opm.gov/feddata>.

Table 510. Area of Federally Owned Buildings in the United States by State: 2010

[2,914.0 represents 2,914,000,000. As of September 30. For executive branch agencies. For data on federal land by state, see Table 365]

State	Total building area [1] (mil. sq. ft.)	Owned building area (mil. sq. ft.)	Leased building area (mil. sq. ft.)	State	Total building area [1] (mil. sq. ft.)	Owned building area (mil. sq. ft.)	Leased building area (mil. sq. ft.)
U.S. [2]	**2,914.0**	**2,487.5**	**308.4**	MO	53.2	42.4	8.5
AL	55.8	48.1	4.5	MT	18.4	15.5	2.2
AK	48.3	44.3	3.3	NE	15.1	12.3	1.6
AZ	55.5	50.5	3.9	NV	32.6	29.7	2.1
AR	24.2	19.3	1.6	NH	4.1	2.6	0.6
CA	295.4	269.4	21.2	NJ	46.5	39.1	5.1
CO	58.2	50.3	7.3	NM	61.6	55.4	4.8
CT	14.1	11.4	1.0	NY	95.6	81.0	9.7
DE	6.2	5.1	0.4	NC	85.4	77.5	5.3
DC	91.2	65.7	24.9	ND	23.1	20.5	1.0
FL	110.9	95.5	11.8	OH	68.6	60.7	5.0
GA	116.7	104.0	10.8	OK	65.3	51.5	11.5
HI	50.6	49.0	0.8	OR	25.2	19.9	2.6
ID	22.3	18.8	2.8	PA	81.7	68.6	9.8
IL	71.8	62.0	6.0	RI	13.9	13.0	0.5
IN	37.2	31.5	3.2	SC	53.5	48.9	2.3
IA	17.1	12.1	1.9	SD	18.2	14.8	2.0
KS	37.1	32.7	2.8	TN	66.3	58.2	5.0
KY	52.5	44.7	5.6	TX	202.0	175.9	22.3
LA	45.6	32.9	6.0	UT	37.4	32.1	3.3
ME	13.3	11.6	0.9	VT	4.4	2.6	1.2
MD	126.0	101.6	22.2	VA	174.4	142.3	30.5
MA	36.0	30.4	3.1	WA	86.6	77.8	7.1
MI	31.3	22.5	4.6	WV	20.7	16.0	2.9
MN	21.5	14.7	2.0	WI	24.2	18.9	2.6
MS	43.8	33.5	2.6	WY	15.2	13.4	0.8

[1] Includes otherwised managed square feet, not shown separately. [2] Includes location not reported, not shown separately.

Source: U.S. General Services Administration, Federal Real Property Council, "Federal Real Property Report 2010." See also <http://www.gsa.gov/portal/content/102880>.

National Security and Veterans Affairs

This section displays data for national security (national defense and homeland security) and benefits for veterans. Data are presented on national defense and its human and financial costs; active and reserve military personnel; federally sponsored programs and benefits for veterans; and funding, budget and selected agencies for homeland security. The principal sources of these data are the annual *Selected Manpower Statistics* and the *Atlas/Data Abstract for the United States*, U.S. Department of Defense; *Annual Report of Secretary of Veterans Affairs*, U.S. Department of Veterans Affairs (VA); *Budget in Brief*, U.S. Department of Homeland Security; and *The Budget of the United States Government*, Office of Management and Budget. For data on international expenditures and personnel, see Table 1420, Section 30.

Department of Defense (DoD)—The U.S. Department of Defense is responsible for providing the military forces of the United States. It includes the Office of the Secretary of Defense, the Joint Chiefs of Staff, the Army, the Navy, the Air Force, and the defense agencies. The President serves as Commander-in-Chief of the Armed Forces; from him, the authority flows to the Secretary of Defense and through the Joint Chiefs of Staff to the commanders of unified and specified commands (e.g., U.S. Strategic Command).

Reserve components—The Reserve Components of the Armed Forces consist of the Army National Guard of the United States, Army Reserve, Naval Reserve, Marine Corps Reserve, Air National Guard, Air Force Reserve, and Coast Guard Reserve. They provide trained personnel and units available for active duty in the Armed Forces during times of war or national emergency, and at such other times as national security may require. The National Guard has dual federal/state responsibilities and uses jointly provided equipment, facilities, and budget support. The President is empowered to mobilize the National Guard and to use such of the Armed Forces as he considers necessary to enforce federal authority in any state. There is in each Armed Force a ready reserve, a standby reserve, and a retired reserve. The Ready Reserve includes the Selected Reserve, which provides trained and ready units and individuals to augment the active forces during times of war or national emergency, or at other times when required; and the Individual Ready Reserve, which is a manpower pool that can be called to active duty during times of war or national emergency and would normally be used as individual fillers for active, guard, and reserve units, and as a source of combat replacements. Most of the Ready Reserve serves in an active status. See Table 521 for Standby Reserve and Retired Reserve detail.

Department of Veterans Affairs (VA)—A veteran is someone 18 years and older (there are a few 17-year-old veterans) who is not currently on active duty, but who once served on active duty in the United States Army, Navy, Air Force, Marine Corps, or Coast Guard, or who served in the Merchant Marine during World War II. There are many groups whose active service makes them veterans including: those who incurred a service-connected disability during active duty for training in the Reserves or National Guard, even though that service would not otherwise have counted for veteran status and members of a national guard or reserve component who have been ordered to active duty by order of the President or those who have a full-time military job. The latter are called AGRs (Active Guard and Reserve). No one who has received a dishonorable discharge is a veteran.

The VA administers laws authorizing benefits for eligible former and present members of the Armed Forces and for the beneficiaries of deceased members. Veterans' benefits available under various acts of Congress include compensation for service-connected disability or death; pensions for non-service-connected disability or death; vocational rehabilitation, education and training; home loan insurance; life insurance; health care; special housing and automobiles or other conveyances for certain disabled veterans; burial and plot allowances; and educational assistance to families of deceased or totally disabled veterans, servicemen missing in action, or prisoners of war. Since these benefits are legislated by Congress, the dates they were enacted and the dates they apply to veterans may be different from the actual dates the conflicts occurred. VA estimates of veterans cover all persons discharged from active U.S. military service under conditions other than dishonorable.

Department of Homeland Security (DHS)—The creation of DHS, which began operations in March 2003, represents a fusion of 22 federal agencies (legacy agencies, Coast Guard and Secret Service remained intact) to coordinate and centralize the leadership of many homeland security activities under a single department. The largest organizations under DHS include: Customs and Border Protection (CBP), Immigration and Customs Enforcement (ICE), Transportation Security Administration (TSA), Federal Emergency Management Agency (FEMA), and the Coast Guard.

Coast Guard—With more than 218 years of service to the Nation, the Coast Guard is a military, multi-mission, maritime organization that promotes safety and safeguards U.S. economic and security interests throughout the maritime environment. As one of the five Armed Services of the United States, it is the only military organization within the DHS. Unlike its sister services in the Department of Defense (DoD), the Coast Guard is also a law enforcement and regulatory agency with broad domestic authorities.

Federal Emergency Management Agency (FEMA)—FEMA manages and coordinates the federal response to and recovery from major domestic disasters and emergencies of all types in accordance with the Robert T. Stafford Disaster Relief and Emergency Assistance Act. The agency ensures the effectiveness of emergency response providers at all levels of government in responding to terrorist attacks, major disasters, and other emergencies. Through the Disaster Relief Fund, FEMA provides individual and public assistance to help families and communities impacted by declared disasters rebuild and recover. FEMA is also the principal component for preparing state and local governments to prevent or respond to threats or incidents of terrorism and other catastrophic events, through their state and local programs.

The Customs and Border Protection (CBP) is responsible for managing, securing, and controlling U.S. borders. This includes carrying out traditional border-related responsibilities, such as stemming the tide of illegal drugs and illegal aliens; securing and facilitating legitimate global trade and travel; and protecting the food supply and agriculture industry from pests and disease. CBP is composed of the Border Patrol and Inspections (both moved from INS) along with Customs (absorbed from the U.S. Department of Treasury) and Animal and Plant Health Inspections Services (absorbed from the U.S. Department of Agriculture).

The Immigration and Customs Enforcement (ICE) mission is to protect America and uphold public safety by targeting the people, money, and materials crossing the nation's borders that support terrorist and criminal activities. ICE is the largest investigation arm of DHS. ICE is composed of five law enforcement divisions: Investigations, Intelligence, Federal Protective Service, International Affairs, and Detention and Removal Operations. ICE investigates a wide range of national security, financial, and smuggling violations including drug smuggling, human trafficking, illegal arms exports, financial crimes, commercial fraud, human smuggling, document fraud, money laundering, child pornography/exploitation, and immigration fraud.

The Transportation Security Administration (TSA) was created as part of the Aviation and Transportation Security Act on November 19, 2001. TSA was originally part of the U.S. Department of Transportation, but was moved to DHS. TSA's mission is to provide security to our nation's transportation systems with a primary focus on aviation security.

Table 511. National Defense Outlays and Veterans' Benefits: 1960 to 2013

[In billions of dollars (53.6 represents $53,600,000,000), except percent. For fiscal year ending in year shown, see text, Section 8. Includes outlays of Department of Defense, Department of Veterans Affairs, and other agencies for activities primarily related to national defense and veterans programs. For explanation of average annual percent change, see Guide to Tabular Presentation. Minus sign (–) indicates decrease]

Year	National defense and veterans' outlays				Annual percent change [1]			Defense outlays, percent of—	
	Total outlays	Defense outlays		Veterans' outlays	Total outlays	Defense outlays	Veterans' outlays	Federal outlays	Gross domestic product [2]
		Current dollars	Constant (FY2005) dollars						
1960	53.6	48.1	369.4	5.4	2.50	2.40	3.10	52.2	9.3
1970	90.4	81.7	463.8	8.7	0.26	-0.98	13.60	41.8	8.1
1980	155.2	134.0	330.1	21.2	13.88	15.17	6.30	22.7	4.9
1985	279.0	252.7	433.1	26.3	10.28	11.14	2.64	26.7	6.1
1990	328.4	299.3	461.1	29.0	-1.56	-1.39	-3.23	23.9	5.2
1995	309.9	272.1	375.5	37.9	-2.91	-3.40	0.81	17.9	3.7
1997	309.8	270.5	354.6	39.3	2.34	1.79	6.30	16.9	3.3
1998	309.9	268.2	346.1	41.7	0.05	-0.85	6.26	16.2	3.1
1999	317.9	274.8	347.6	43.2	2.58	2.45	3.39	16.1	3.0
2000	341.4	294.4	361.3	47.0	7.37	7.13	8.88	16.5	3.0
2001	349.7	304.7	363.0	45.0	2.45	3.52	-4.29	16.4	3.0
2002	399.4	348.5	401.7	50.9	14.21	14.35	13.24	17.3	3.3
2003	461.7	404.7	444.6	57.0	15.61	16.15	11.89	18.7	3.7
2004	515.6	455.8	480.3	59.7	11.66	12.62	4.85	19.9	3.9
2005	565.4	495.3	495.3	70.1	9.67	8.66	17.36	20.0	4.0
2006	591.6	521.8	499.3	69.8	4.64	5.35	-0.44	19.7	3.9
2007	624.1	551.3	509.2	72.8	5.48	5.64	4.31	20.2	4.0
2008	700.7	616.1	547.7	84.7	12.28	11.76	16.25	20.7	4.3
2009	756.5	661.0	588.2	95.4	7.96	7.30	12.73	18.8	4.7
2010	802.0	693.6	614.1	108.4	6.01	4.92	13.58	20.1	4.8
2011	832.8	705.6	611.9	127.2	3.84	1.73	17.36	19.6	4.7
2012, est	845.9	716.3	611.0	129.6	1.57	1.52	1.89	18.9	4.5
2013, est	841.9	701.8	587.9	140.1	-0.47	-2.02	8.10	18.5	4.2

[1] Change from immediate prior year; for 1960, change from 1955. [2] Represents fiscal year GDP; for definition, see text, Section 13.

Source: U.S. Office of Management and Budget, "Budget of the United States Government, Historical Tables," annual, <http://www.whitehouse.gov/omb/budget/>.

Table 512. National Defense Budget Authority and Outlays for Defense Functions: 1990 to 2012

[In billions of dollars (303.3 represents $303,300,000,000). For year ending September 30. Data includes defense budget authority and outlays by other departments. Minus sign (–) indicates decrease]

Function	1990	1995	2000	2005	2006	2007	2008	2009	2010	2011	2012 est.
Total budget authority	303.3	266.4	304.0	505.8	556.3	625.8	696.2	697.8	721.3	717.4	676.7
Department of Defense—military	293.0	255.7	290.3	483.8	532.9	603.0	674.7	667.5	695.6	691.5	650.5
Military personnel	78.9	71.6	73.8	121.3	128.5	131.8	139.0	149.3	157.1	158.4	158.5
Operation and maintenance	88.4	93.7	108.7	179.2	213.5	240.2	256.2	271.6	293.6	305.2	284.9
Procurement	81.4	43.6	55.0	96.6	105.4	133.8	165.0	135.4	135.8	131.9	120.5
Research, development, test, and evaluation	36.5	34.5	38.7	68.8	72.9	77.5	79.6	80.0	80.2	76.7	71.9
Military construction	5.1	5.4	5.1	7.3	9.5	14.0	22.1	26.8	22.6	16.0	11.4
Family housing	3.1	3.4	3.5	4.1	4.4	4.0	2.9	3.9	2.3	1.8	1.7
Other	-0.4	3.4	5.5	6.6	-1.3	1.6	9.9	0.6	4.0	1.4	1.6
Atomic energy defense activities	9.7	10.1	12.4	17.9	17.4	17.2	16.6	23.0	18.2	18.5	18.4
Defense-related activities	0.7	1.0	1.3	4.0	5.9	5.7	4.9	7.3	7.4	7.4	7.8
Total outlays	299.3	272.1	294.4	495.3	521.8	551.3	616.1	661.0	693.6	705.6	716.3
Department of Defense—military	289.8	259.4	281.1	474.1	499.3	528.5	594.6	636.7	666.7	678.1	688.3
Military personnel	75.6	70.8	76.0	127.5	127.5	127.5	138.9	147.3	155.7	161.6	156.2
Operation and maintenance	88.3	91.0	105.8	188.1	203.8	216.6	244.8	259.3	276.0	291.0	294.5
Procurement	81.0	55.0	51.7	82.3	89.8	99.6	117.4	129.2	133.6	128.0	139.9
Research, development, test, and evaluation	37.5	34.6	37.6	65.7	68.6	73.1	75.1	79.0	77.0	74.9	75.9
Military construction	5.1	6.8	5.1	5.3	6.2	7.9	11.6	17.6	21.2	19.9	18.1
Family housing	3.5	3.6	3.4	3.7	3.7	3.5	3.6	2.7	3.2	3.4	2.1
Other	-1.2	-2.4	1.5	1.5	-0.4	0.2	3.2	1.5	0.1	-0.8	1.6
Atomic energy activities	9.0	11.8	12.1	18.0	17.5	17.1	17.1	17.6	19.3	20.4	19.8
Defense-related activities	0.6	0.9	1.2	3.2	5.1	5.7	4.3	6.8	7.6	7.2	8.3

Source: U.S. Office of Management and Budget, "Budget of the United States Government, Historical Tables, Budget Authority by Function and Subfunction, Outlay by Function and Subfunction," annual, <http://www.whitehouse.gov/omb/budget>.

Table 513. Military Expenditures: 2000 to 2009

[In millions of dollars (229,072 represents $229,072,000,000). For year ending September 30. For definitions, see headnote, Tables 514 and 516]

Item	2000	2005	2006	2007	2008	2009
Expenditures, total	229,072	381,290	408,249	455,769	501,032	527,824
Payroll outlays	103,447	141,018	146,858	154,326	146,781	195,170
Active duty military pay	36,872	50,482	55,829	61,918	52,159	84,460
Civilian pay	29,935	43,798	45,105	43,587	46,170	49,736
Reserve and National Guard pay	4,646	11,087	10,123	12,325	11,068	22,759
Retired military pay	31,994	35,651	35,801	36,496	37,384	38,216
Total contracts [1]	123,295	236,986	257,456	297,363	349,557	327,462
Army	32,615	74,432	79,962	98,171	139,437	109,995
Navy & Marine Corps	38,963	62,775	70,351	82,321	92,679	91,868
Air Force	35,369	51,671	58,552	66,240	59,262	63,946
Other defense activities	16,348	48,108	48,592	50,630	58,178	61,653
Grants	2,330	3,285	3,934	4,080	4,694	5,192

[1] Represents contract awards over $25,000.

Source: U.S. Department of Defense, Statistical Information Analysis Division, *Atlas/Data Abstract for the United States and Selected Areas*, annual, <http://siadapp.dmdc.osd.mil/personnel/Pubs.htm>.

Table 514. Department of Defense Payroll and Contract Awards by State: 2009

[In millions of dollars (195,170 represents $195,170,000,000). For year ending September 30. Payroll outlays include the gross earnings of civilian, active duty military, reserve and national guard, and retired military personnel for services rendered to the government and for cash allowances for benefits. Excludes employer's share of employee benefits, accrued military retirement benefits and most permanent change of station costs. Contracts refer to awards made in year specified; expenditures relating to awards may extend over several years. Includes awards for supplies, services, and construction with a net value of contracts of over $25,000 for work in each state and DC. Figures reflect impact of prime contracting on state distribution of defense work. The state in which a prime contractor is located is often not the state where the subcontracted work is done. Undistributed civilian and military payrolls, and prime contract awards for performance in classified locations are excluded]

State	Payroll Total	Payroll Active duty military	Contract awards	Grants	State	Payroll Total	Payroll Active duty military	Contract awards	Grants
U.S.	195,170	84,460	327,462	5,192	MO	3,787	1,311	10,454	40
AL	4,724	1,255	9,502	66	MT	541	188	289	24
AK	2,660	2,078	2,180	49	NE	1,152	435	931	59
AZ	3,138	1,263	12,065	106	NV	1,415	600	1,819	35
AR	1,622	435	986	66	NH	411	73	1,568	36
CA	14,568	5,183	41,698	477	NJ	2,671	543	8,227	122
CO	5,125	2,966	5,544	56	NM	1,626	571	1,604	40
CT	720	198	11,818	100	NY	4,819	2,701	8,545	199
DE	537	216	315	24	NC	10,558	7,012	3,995	125
DC	3,599	1,907	4,741	66	ND	631	336	437	32
FL	9,418	2,816	13,189	195	OH	3,834	640	6,249	172
GA	11,495	6,668	7,039	74	OK	4,100	1,679	2,880	124
HI	6,344	4,529	2,377	79	OR	1,051	141	1,546	99
ID	709	262	166	59	PA	4,210	574	12,363	216
IL	3,129	738	5,937	172	RI	743	120	662	26
IN	2,338	351	6,795	55	SC	3,683	1,530	5,299	39
IA	747	140	1,285	57	SD	514	198	445	68
KS	3,668	2,465	3,158	42	TN	2,235	282	3,083	44
KY	5,681	4,339	6,534	70	TX	19,299	11,128	22,484	300
LA	2,688	1,417	6,408	54	UT	2,116	432	2,206	39
ME	847	113	1,407	128	VT	262	64	550	17
MD	6,538	2,013	12,912	477	VA	18,071	6,214	38,372	131
MA	1,491	320	13,347	244	WA	8,224	4,407	5,174	127
MI	1,827	264	5,332	130	WV	617	107	396	50
MN	1,208	206	1,530	69	WI	1,152	222	7,674	72
MS	2,224	629	3,447	18	WY	405	177	140	21

Source: U.S. Department of Defense, Statistical Information Analysis Division, *Atlas/Data Abstract for the United States and Selected Areas*, annual, <http://siadapp.dmdc.osd.mil/personnel/Pubs.htm>.

Table 515. Expenditures and Personnel for Selected Major Locations: 2009

[In thousands of dollars (8,406,173 represents $8,406,173,000), except for personnel. For year ending September 30. See headnote, Table 516]

Major locations	Expenditures Total	Expenditures Payroll outlays	Expenditures Contracts/grants	Major locations	Military and civilian personnel Total	Military and civilian personnel Active duty military	Military and civilian personnel Civilian
Washington, DC	8,406,173	3,599,245	4,806,928	Fort Hood, TX	60,309	54,309	6,000
Fort Hood, TX	6,478,403	6,075,895	402,508	Camp Pendleton, CA	49,114	46,242	2,872
San Diego, CA	6,413,361	1,884,891	4,528,470	Camp Lejeune, NC	44,286	40,789	3,497
Oshkosh, WI	5,780,785	20,929	5,759,856	Fayetteville, NC	36,223	36,198	25
Huntsville, AL	5,744,462	366,537	5,377,925	Fort Lewis, WA	35,250	32,220	3,030
Arlington, VA	5,279,716	2,946,069	2,333,647	Fort Campbell, KY	33,971	32,799	1,172
Tucson, AZ	4,879,568	326,019	4,553,549	Fort Carson, CO	26,759	23,796	2,963
Fayetteville, NC	4,658,633	4,623,376	35,257	Arlington, VA	26,335	9,305	17,030
St. Louis, MO	4,623,210	203,614	4,419,596	Fort Benning, GA	26,101	22,123	3,978
Louisville, KY	4,436,075	167,250	4,268,825	Fort Bragg, NC	23,843	15,580	8,263

Source: U.S. Department of Defense, Statistical Information Analysis Division, *Atlas/Data Abstract for the United States and Selected Areas*, annual, <http://siadapp.dmdc.osd.mil/personnel/Pubs.htm>.

Table 516. Military and Civilian Personnel in Installations: 2009

[As of September 30. Civilian personnel includes United States citizens and foreign national direct-hire civilians subject to Office of Management and Budget (OMB) ceiling controls and civilian personnel involved in civil functions in the United States. Excludes indirect-hire civilians and those direct-hire civilians not subject to OMB ceiling controls. Military personnel include active duty personnel based ashore or afloat, excluding personnel temporarily shore-based in a transient status]

State	Active duty military personnel				Reserve and National Guard, total [1]	Civilian personnel			
	Total [1]	Army	Navy/ Marine Corps	Air Force		Total [1]	Army	Navy/ Marine Corps	Air Force
United States.........	1,088,465	537,407	264,375	286,683	819,318	709,265	274,140	186,135	160,339
Alabama................	11,896	8,121	403	3,372	22,099	24,794	19,768	84	2,472
Alaska.................	23,178	14,087	113	8,978	4,747	5,356	3,049	20	1,938
Arizona................	21,343	5,531	4,118	11,694	13,728	9,591	4,471	637	3,408
Arkansas..............	6,717	1,219	109	5,389	13,051	4,168	3,073	6	973
California..............	117,806	11,097	88,370	18,339	57,792	61,365	9,278	34,798	10,720
Colorado..............	35,404	25,471	715	9,218	12,491	11,585	4,187	65	5,675
Connecticut...........	1,914	624	1,172	118	6,369	2,625	618	1,120	257
Delaware..............	3,870	246	15	3,609	4,881	1,622	292	5	1,248
District of Columbia....	13,424	7,831	3,040	2,553	6,378	16,088	4,708	9,617	853
Florida.................	42,642	5,363	13,782	23,497	34,653	28,429	4,070	11,871	10,297
Georgia...............	73,988	59,892	3,724	10,372	29,358	37,012	14,169	4,757	15,222
Hawaii.................	40,874	22,435	13,642	4,797	9,276	18,400	5,532	9,605	2,188
Idaho..................	4,967	526	41	4,400	5,892	1,716	893	51	711
Illinois.................	10,111	2,212	2,805	5,094	25,084	15,770	9,016	1,842	3,688
Indiana................	3,108	2,612	209	287	21,073	10,932	2,403	3,243	952
Iowa...................	1,296	997	118	181	12,390	1,733	1,157	8	525
Kansas................	25,482	21,994	117	3,371	11,479	7,800	6,296	6	1,103
Kentucky..............	43,138	42,532	279	327	13,126	8,962	7,655	164	248
Louisiana.............	17,398	10,223	1,553	5,622	18,011	6,647	4,045	793	1,476
Maine.................	730	334	265	131	4,153	6,946	402	5,580	287
Maryland..............	29,160	8,239	12,652	8,269	16,000	34,966	14,460	15,826	2,384
Massachusetts........	3,205	1,157	574	1,474	15,335	6,918	2,632	192	3,171
Michigan..............	2,858	1,708	743	407	17,618	8,972	6,456	46	892
Minnesota............	1,897	1,291	378	228	19,256	2,752	1,766	23	798
Mississippi............	9,895	1,443	1,394	7,058	17,332	9,124	3,878	2,428	2,515
Missouri...............	17,925	12,053	2,028	3,844	23,769	9,982	7,569	490	1,246
Montana...............	3,623	397	12	3,214	4,748	1,596	686	1	862
Nebraska..............	6,845	653	450	5,742	7,498	3,785	1,468	15	2,197
Nevada................	10,034	545	584	8,905	6,087	2,319	561	285	1,316
New Hampshire........	675	307	198	170	4,251	1,047	568	34	304
New Jersey............	6,673	1,538	277	4,858	17,312	15,217	10,798	2,122	1,575
New Mexico...........	11,038	1,094	166	9,778	5,199	7,029	3,041	46	3,460
New York..............	29,553	26,568	1,676	1,309	30,362	12,318	7,561	151	2,528
North Carolina.........	116,073	53,231	54,942	7,900	22,542	20,426	8,975	7,669	1,472
North Dakota..........	7,209	416	14	6,779	4,669	1,910	617	3	1,214
Ohio...................	8,261	1,939	684	5,638	28,523	25,001	1,884	91	13,671
Oklahoma..............	21,673	12,216	926	8,531	15,640	22,115	5,739	91	14,794
Oregon................	1,615	815	336	464	10,470	3,561	2,893	26	615
Pennsylvania..........	5,215	3,270	1,443	502	32,297	27,107	10,606	6,469	1,290
Rhode Island..........	1,490	420	905	165	4,438	4,372	289	3,777	209
South Carolina........	32,518	11,074	12,613	8,831	19,102	10,406	3,875	3,868	1,912
South Dakota..........	3,910	406	1	3,503	4,982	1,388	565	3	775
Tennessee............	3,511	1,610	1,422	479	20,606	7,967	4,767	1,202	1,227
Texas.................	131,548	88,346	4,606	38,596	56,367	48,057	27,585	1,404	15,271
Utah...................	6,237	1,614	170	4,453	11,999	14,818	2,470	45	11,244
Vermont...............	565	347	32	186	3,952	729	403	3	290
Virginia................	63,160	24,386	25,171	13,603	25,109	89,713	23,532	39,844	4,983
Washington............	46,161	34,557	4,907	6,697	19,470	27,980	9,471	15,577	1,980
West Virginia..........	1,199	677	317	205	9,303	2,146	1,431	97	605
Wisconsin.............	2,046	1,522	163	361	15,833	2,810	2,138	34	522
Wyoming..............	3,407	221	1	3,185	3,218	1,193	374	1	776

[1] Includes Other Defense Activities (ODA), not shown separately.

Source: U.S. Department of Defense, Statistical Information Analysis Division, *Atlas/Data Abstract for the United States and Selected Areas*, annual, <http://siadapp.dmdc.osd.mil/personnel/Pubs.htm>.

Table 517. Military Personnel on Active Duty by Location: 1980 to 2011

[In thousands (2,051 represents 2,051,000). As of September 30]

Location	1980	1990	1995	2000	2005	2007	2008	2009	2010	2011
Total..........................	2,051	2,046	1,518	1,384	1,389	1,380	1,402	1,419	1,431	1,425
Shore-based [1]....................	1,840	1,794	1,351	1,237	1,262	1,264	1,294	1,313	1,328	1,325
Afloat [2]..........................	211	252	167	147	127	115	108	105	103	101
United States [3]..................	1,562	1,437	1,280	1,127	1,098	1,085	1,113	1,156	1,134	1,220
Foreign countries................	489	609	238	258	291	295	289	263	297	205

[1] Includes Navy personnel temporarily on shore. [2] Includes Marine Corps. [3] Includes Puerto Rico and Island Areas.

Source: U.S. Department of Defense, Statistical Information Analysis Division, *Active Duty Military Personnel By Service By Region/Country*, annual, <http://siadapp.dmdc.osd.mil>.

Table 518. Department of Defense Personnel: 1960 to 2011

[In thousands (2,475 represents 2,475,000). As of end of fiscal year; see text, Section 8. Includes National Guard, Reserve, and retired regular personnel on extended or continuous active duty. Excludes Coast Guard. Other officer candidates are included under enlisted personnel]

Year	Total [1,2]	Army Total [1]	Army Male Officers	Army Male Enlisted	Army Female Officers	Army Female Enlisted	Navy [2] Total [1]	Navy Male Officers	Navy Male Enlisted	Navy Female Officers	Navy Female Enlisted	Marine Corps Total [1]	MC Male Officers	MC Male Enlisted	MC Female Officers	MC Female Enlisted	Air Force Total [1]	AF Male Officers	AF Male Enlisted	AF Female Officers	AF Female Enlisted
1960	2,475	873	97	762	4.3	8.3	617	67	540	2.7	5.4	171	16	153	0.1	1.5	815	126	677	3.7	5.7
1965	2,654	969	108	846	3.8	8.5	670	75	583	2.6	5.3	190	17	172	0.1	1.4	825	128	685	4.1	4.7
1970	3,065	1,323	162	1,142	5.2	11.5	691	78	600	2.9	5.8	260	25	233	0.3	2.1	791	125	648	4.7	9.0
1975	2,128	784	98	640	4.6	37.7	535	62	449	3.7	17.5	196	19	174	0.3	2.8	613	100	478	5.0	25.2
1980	2,051	777	91	612	7.6	61.7	527	58	430	4.9	30.1	189	18	164	0.5	6.2	558	90	404	8.5	51.9
1983	2,123	780	97	602	9.5	66.5	558	62	444	6.3	40.8	194	19	166	0.6	8.3	592	94	428	10.6	55.3
1984	2,138	780	98	601	10.2	67.1	565	62	448	6.6	42.6	196	19	167	0.6	8.6	597	95	430	11.2	55.9
1985	2,151	781	99	599	10.8	68.4	571	64	449	6.9	45.7	198	19	169	0.7	9.0	602	96	431	11.9	58.1
1986	2,169	781	99	597	11.3	69.7	581	65	457	7.3	47.2	200	19	170	0.6	9.2	608	97	434	12.4	61.2
1987	2,174	781	96	596	11.6	71.6	587	65	462	7.2	47.7	200	19	170	0.6	9.1	607	94	432	12.6	63.2
1988	2,138	772	95	588	11.8	72.0	593	65	466	7.3	49.7	197	19	168	0.7	9.0	576	92	405	12.9	61.5
1989	2,130	770	95	584	12.2	74.3	593	65	464	7.5	52.1	197	19	168	0.7	9.0	571	91	399	13.4	63.7
1990	2,044	732	92	553	12.4	71.2	570	64	451	7.8	52.1	197	19	168	0.7	8.7	535	87	370	13.3	60.8
1991	1,986	711	91	535	12.5	67.8	542	63	444	8.0	51.4	194	19	166	0.7	8.3	510	84	350	13.3	59.1
1992	1,807	610	83	449	11.7	61.7	510	61	417	8.3	51.0	185	18	157	0.6	7.9	470	77	320	12.7	56.1
1993	1,705	572	77	420	11.1	60.2	469	58	390	8.3	49.3	178	17	153	0.6	7.2	444	72	302	12.3	54.5
1994	1,610	541	74	394	10.9	59.0	435	54	355	8.0	47.9	174	17	149	0.6	7.0	426	69	287	12.3	54.0
1995	1,518	509	72	365	10.8	57.3	417	51	324	7.9	47.9	175	17	150	0.7	7.4	400	66	266	12.1	52.1
1996	1,472	491	70	347	10.6	59.0	396	50	308	7.8	46.9	175	17	149	0.8	7.8	389	64	256	12.0	52.8
1997	1,439	492	69	346	10.4	62.4	382	48	290	7.8	44.8	174	17	148	0.8	8.5	377	62	246	12.0	53.8
1998	1,407	484	68	340	10.4	61.4	373	47	280	7.7	42.9	173	17	146	0.9	8.9	368	60	237	12.0	54.2
1999	1,386	479	67	337	10.5	61.5	373	46	271	7.7	43.9	173	17	145	0.9	9.3	361	58	232	11.8	54.6
2000	1,384	482	66	339	10.8	62.9	373	46	272	7.8	43.8	173	17	146	0.9	9.5	356	57	227	11.8	55.0
2001	1,385	481	65	337	11.0	63.4	378	46	273	8.0	46.6	173	17	145	1.0	9.6	354	57	224	12.0	55.6
2002	1,414	487	66	341	11.5	63.2	385	47	279	8.2	47.3	174	17	146	1.0	9.5	368	59	233	12.9	58.6
2003	1,434	499	68	352	12.0	63.5	382	47	276	8.2	47.3	178	18	149	1.1	9.6	375	61	237	13.5	60.0
2004	1,427	500	69	358	12.3	61.0	373	46	273	8.1	46.1	178	18	149	1.1	9.7	377	61	242	13.6	60.2
2005	1,389	493	69	353	12.4	57.9	363	45	266	7.8	44.5	180	18	151	1.0	9.8	354	60	225	13.4	55.6
2006	1,385	505	69	365	12.5	58.5	350	44	255	7.6	43.2	180	18	151	1.1	10.0	349	58	223	12.8	55.8
2007	1,380	522	71	379	13.0	58.8	338	44	244	7.6	42.2	186	18	156	1.1	10.5	333	54	214	11.8	53.4
2008	1,402	544	74	392	13.5	59.7	332	44	235	7.7	41.4	199	19	167	1.1	11.1	327	53	207	11.9	51.4
2009	1,419	553	76	399	14.3	59.4	329	44	231	7.9	42.2	203	19	170	1.2	11.7	333	53	211	12.1	52.0
2010	1,431	566	79	407	15.1	60.3	328	44	228	8.2	43.4	202	18	169	3.0	12.2	334	54	212	12.4	50.9
2011	1,425	565	82	403	15.7	60.2	325	44	224	8.5	44.0	201	21	167	1.3	12.4	333	53	213	12.3	50.3

[1] Includes cadets, midshipmen, and others, not shown separately. [2] Beginning 1980, excludes Navy Reserve personnel on active duty for Training and Administration of Reserves (TARS).

Source: U.S. Department of Defense, Statistical Information Analysis Division, *Selected Manpower Statistics*, annual; and "Active Duty Military Personnel by Service by Rank/Grade," September 2011, <http://siadapp.dmdc.osd.mil/>.

Table 519. Military Personnel on Active Duty by Rank or Grade: 1990 to 2011

[In thousands (2,043.7 represents 2,043,700). As of September 30]

Rank/grade	1990	2000	2005	2008	2009	2010	2011
Total	**2,043.7**	**1,384.3**	**1,389.4**	**1,401.8**	**1,418.5**	**1,431.0**	**1,425.1**
Total Officers	**296.6**	**217.2**	**226.6**	**223.7**	**228.3**	**234.0**	**237.4**
General-Admiral	(Z)	(Z)	(Z)	(Z)	(Z)	(Z)	(Z)
Lieutenant General-Vice Admiral	0.1	0.1	0.1	0.1	0.2	0.2	0.2
Major General-Rear Admiral (U)	0.4	0.3	0.3	0.3	0.3	0.3	0.3
Brigadier General-Rear Admiral (L)	0.5	0.4	0.4	0.5	0.5	0.5	0.5
Colonel-Captain	14.0	11.3	11.4	11.6	12.0	12.2	12.1
Lieutenant Colonel-Commander	32.3	27.5	28.1	28.1	28.4	28.8	28.8
Major-LT Commander	53.2	43.2	44.4	43.4	43.9	45.3	46.2
Captain-Lieutenant	106.6	68.1	72.5	71.0	72.5	75.0	76.5
1st Lieutenant-Lieutenant (JG)	37.9	24.7	27.5	23.9	24.9	25.5	27.0
2nd Lieutenant-Ensign	31.9	26.4	25.9	26.4	26.9	27.1	26.1
Chief Warrant Officer W-5	(Z)	0.1	0.5	0.6	0.7	0.7	0.8
Chief Warrant Officer W-4	3.0	2.0	2.2	3.1	3.1	3.2	3.3
Chief Warrant Officer W-3	5.0	3.8	4.6	4.7	4.7	4.8	4.7
Chief Warrant Officer W-2	8.4	6.7	6.2	6.4	7.1	7.5	8.1
Warrant Officer W-1	3.2	2.1	2.5	3.4	3.2	2.9	2.6
Total Enlisted	**1,733.8**	**1,154.6**	**1,149.9**	**1,164.7**	**1,176.7**	**1,183.2**	**1,174.2**
E-9	15.3	10.2	10.5	10.5	10.4	10.2	10.3
E-8	38.0	26.0	27.1	27.4	27.4	27.3	27.3
E-7	134.1	97.7	97.8	97.2	98.5	97.1	96.2
E-6	239.1	164.9	172.4	170.3	170.5	170.9	168.7
E-5	361.5	229.5	248.5	249.0	248.5	250.0	244.0
E-4	427.8	251.0	261.7	266.1	280.2	279.3	290.0
E-3	280.1	196.3	201.7	194.9	205.9	228.2	223.6
E-2	140.3	99.0	70.8	83.6	84.8	75.2	69.7
E-1	97.6	80.0	59.5	65.6	50.4	45.1	44.3
Cadets and Midshipmen	**13.3**	**12.5**	**12.9**	**13.4**	**13.6**	**13.8**	**13.5**

Z Fewer than 50.

Source: U.S. Department of Defense, Statistical Information Analysis Division, *Military Personnel Statistics*, annual; and "Active Duty Military Personnel by Rank/Grade," September 2011, <http://siadapp.dmdc.osd.mil/>.

Table 520. Military Retirement System: 2011

[Payment in thousands of dollars (2,051,939 represents $2,051,939,000). As of September 30. The data published in the source report are produced from files maintained by the Defense Manpower Data Center (DMDC). This report compiles data primarily from the "Retiree Pay and Survivor Pay" files. Any grouping of members by address reflects mailing, not necessarily residence address. Only those members in plans administered by the Department of Defense (DoD) are included in this table. The data are preliminary because of reporting delays about members who retired or died within one month of the September 30 reporting date. These data were not processed in time to be included in this report. For more information, see Introduction and Overview of source publication, *Statistical Report on the Military Retirement System; Fiscal Year 2011*]

State	Retired military personnel [1]			Monthly payment	State	Retired military personnel [1]			Monthly payment
	Total	Disabled [2]	Non-disabled			Total	Disabled [2]	Non-disabled	
Total [3]	**2,051,939**	**190,234**	**1,861,705**	**3,932,166**	MO	37,272	3,985	33,287	62,390
U.S.	2,010,671	186,640	1,824,031	3,859,121	MT	8,908	849	8,059	15,729
AL	57,726	4,741	52,985	109,035	NE	14,169	1,094	13,075	27,785
AK	9,967	734	9,233	18,717	NV	27,462	1,890	25,572	53,557
AZ	54,540	4,706	49,834	107,687	NH	9,512	832	8,680	18,189
AR	25,770	2,551	23,219	44,020	NJ	20,021	2,621	17,400	30,842
CA	164,180	15,658	148,522	319,383	NM	21,465	1,713	19,752	43,539
CO	49,648	4,325	45,323	110,168	NY	38,775	6,061	32,714	54,152
CT	10,597	1,320	9,277	17,632	NC	87,578	7,837	79,741	170,625
DE	8,493	592	7,901	14,898	ND	5,025	385	4,640	8,042
DC	2,620	384	2,236	5,590	OH	45,164	5,787	39,377	76,133
FL	187,224	15,564	171,660	383,663	OK	35,225	3,099	32,126	61,871
GA	91,390	8,118	83,272	172,043	OR	21,012	2,566	18,446	36,340
HI	16,701	1,144	15,557	34,625	PA	50,275	5,960	44,315	82,587
ID	13,115	1,167	11,948	23,685	RI	5,463	527	4,936	10,210
IL	36,391	4,664	31,727	63,816	SC	56,486	4,464	52,022	105,509
IN	24,635	3,206	21,429	37,996	SD	7,616	617	6,999	13,277
IA	12,268	1,348	10,920	18,325	TN	52,273	4,849	47,424	93,137
KS	21,177	1,879	19,298	40,071	TX	192,192	17,590	174,602	388,489
KY	27,469	3,019	24,450	47,406	UT	15,669	1,221	14,448	28,567
LA	25,795	2,801	22,994	45,206	VT	3,785	352	3,433	5,875
ME	12,110	1,148	10,962	20,334	VA	149,888	8,248	141,640	384,474
MD	52,928	4,034	48,894	112,010	WA	71,264	5,461	65,803	140,568
MA	19,052	2,526	16,526	29,637	WV	11,015	1,384	9,631	17,248
MI	28,595	4,273	24,322	42,434	WI	20,441	2,466	17,975	30,467
MN	18,248	2,119	16,129	26,921	WY	5,137	434	4,703	9,033
MS	26,940	2,327	24,613	45,184					

[1] Represents military personnel (officers and enlisted) receiving and not receiving pay from DoD. [2] A disabled military member is entitled to disability retired pay if the disability is not the result of the member's intentional misconduct or willful neglect, was not incurred during a period of unauthorized absence, and either: (1) the member has at least 20 years of service; or (2) at the time of determination, the disability is at least 30 percent (under a standard schedule of rating disabilities by the Veterans Administration) and one of four additional conditions are met. For details on these conditions and additional information, see the Overview in the source publication, *Statistical Report on the Military Retirement System, Fiscal Year 2011*. [3] Includes states, U.S. territories, and retirees living in foreign countries.

Source: U.S. Department of Defense, Office of the Actuary, *Statistical Report on the Military Retirement System, Fiscal Year 2011* (issued May 2012), <http://www.defenselink.mil/actuary/>.

Table 521. Military Reserve Personnel: 1995 to 2010

[As of September 30. The Ready Reserve includes the Selected Reserve, which is scheduled to augment active forces during times of war or national emergency, and the Individual Ready Reserve, which during times of war or national emergency would be used to fill out active duty, National Guard, and Reserve units, and which would also be a source for casualty replacements. Ready Reservists serve in an active status (except for the Inactive National Guard—a very small pool within the Army National Guard). The Standby Reserve cannot be called to active duty, other than for training, unless authorized by Congress under "full mobilization," and a determination is made that there are not enough qualified members in the Ready Reserve in the required categories who are readily available. The Retired Reserve represents a lower potential for involuntary mobilization]

Reserve status and branch of service	1995	2000	2005	2007	2008	2009	2010
Total reserves [1]	**1,674,164**	**1,276,843**	**1,136,200**	**1,109,805**	**1,099,915**	**1,094,071**	**1,102,863**
Ready Reserve	**1,648,388**	**1,251,452**	**1,113,427**	**1,088,587**	**1,080,617**	**1,079,627**	**1,078,621**
Army [2]	999,462	725,771	636,355	621,422	626,892	645,394	651,098
Navy	267,356	184,080	140,821	128,421	123,159	109,271	102,349
Marine Corps	103,668	99,855	99,820	100,787	95,748	95,199	97,087
Air Force [3]	263,011	229,009	223,551	226,806	224,545	220,364	218,350
Coast Guard	14,891	12,737	12,880	11,151	10,273	9,399	9,737
Standby Reserve	**25,776**	**25,391**	**22,773**	**21,218**	**19,298**	**25,808**	**24,242**
Army	1,128	701	1,668	[4] 5,294	2,136	2,072	1,673
Navy	12,707	7,213	4,038	3,046	3,310	[4] 10,036	9,742
Marine Corps	216	895	1,129	1,372	1,691	1,205	1,278
Air Force	11,453	16,429	15,897	10,154	10,384	10,530	10,213
Coast Guard	272	153	41	1,352	1,777	1,965	1,336
Retired Reserve	**505,905**	**573,305**	**627,424**	**648,346**	**658,251**	**707,060**	**716,228**
Army	259,553	296,004	321,312	330,121	334,258	378,603	383,220
Navy	97,532	109,531	117,093	120,859	122,000	123,292	124,870
Marine Corps	11,319	12,937	14,693	15,264	15,558	15,948	16,277
Air Force	137,501	154,833	174,326	182,102	186,435	189,217	191,861

[1] Less Retired Reserves. [2] Includes Army National Guard. [3] Includes Air National Guard. [4] The Army for FY2007 and the Navy for FY2009 modified their Individual Ready Reserve (IRR) category and reclassified personnel awaiting retirement or discharge into the Standby Reserve. This action was done in order to give them a better perspective on actual IRR members cleared for mobilization, if required.

Source: U.S. Department of Defense, *Fiscal Year 2010 Official Guard and Reserve Manpower Strengths and Statistics*. See also <http://siadapp.dmdc.osd.mil/index.html>.

Table 522. Ready Reserve Personnel by Race, Hispanic Origin, and Sex: 1990 to 2010

[In thousands (1,658.7 represents 1,658,700). As of September 30]

Year	Total [1]	Race						His-panic [2]	Sex			
		White	Black	Asian	Ameri-can Indian	Pacific Islander	Other/ Unknown		Officer		Enlisted	
									Male	Female	Male	Female
1990	1,658.7	1,304.6	272.3	14.9	7.8	(NA)	59.1	83.1	226.8	40.5	1,204.7	186.7
1995	1,648.4	1,267.7	274.5	22.0	8.8	(NA)	75.4	96.2	209.9	44.7	1,196.8	196.9
1999	1,288.8	980.0	202.6	22.6	7.6	(NA)	76.0	88.9	166.2	38.4	911.2	173.1
2000	1,251.5	942.2	199.6	26.7	8.4	(NA)	74.6	91.8	159.4	36.9	879.9	175.3
2001	1,224.1	912.7	198.4	27.9	8.5	(NA)	76.7	94.3	158.0	36.6	852.2	177.3
2002	1,199.3	891.3	193.2	27.9	8.8	(NA)	78.2	96.0	152.1	35.6	835.2	176.4
2003	1,167.1	865.7	187.5	25.4	8.5	(NA)	80.1	98.0	145.1	34.0	813.7	174.3
2004	1,145.0	845.3	181.3	26.2	9.1	3.6	79.6	100.2	141.9	33.6	799.7	169.8
2005	1,113.4	825.4	169.9	26.9	9.5	4.1	77.6	99.8	139.2	33.3	778.0	162.9
2006	1,101.6	822.4	163.5	27.7	10.1	4.5	73.4	101.1	136.7	33.1	769.4	162.3
2007	1,088.6	818.1	156.6	28.1	10.8	4.8	70.3	102.7	130.0	31.8	766.5	160.2
2008	1,080.7	815.2	153.4	29.0	10.9	5.3	66.9	102.6	128.0	31.2	760.8	160.6
2009	1,070.2	810.6	149.4	30.1	10.8	5.8	63.7	99.9	126.4	30.8	754.3	158.7
2010	1,068.9	809.8	148.2	31.0	10.9	6.1	62.8	99.6	125.9	30.7	754.2	158.1

[1] Includes other races, not shown separately. [2] Persons of Hispanic origin may be any race.

Source: U.S. Department of Defense, *Fiscal Year 2010 Official Guard and Reserve Manpower Strengths and Statistics*. See also <http://siadapp.dmdc.osd.mil/index.html>.

Table 523. National Guard by Sex and Race: 1995 to 2010

[In thousands (375 represents 375,000). As of September 30]

Year	Army National Guard					Air National Guard				
	Total	Male [1]	Female	White	Black	Total	Male [1]	Female	White	Black
1995	375	344	31	299	59	110	94	16	96	9
2000	353	313	40	278	55	106	88	18	90	10
2004	343	299	44	271	50	107	88	19	89	10
2005	333	290	43	264	46	106	87	19	89	9
2006	346	300	47	276	47	106	87	19	88	9
2007	353	304	49	283	47	106	87	19	88	9
2008	360	309	51	288	49	108	88	20	89	9
2009	358	308	50	288	47	109	89	20	90	9
2010	362	310	52	291	48	108	88	20	89	9

[1] Male population includes unknown sex.

Source: U.S. Department of Defense, Statistical Information Analysis Division, *Atlas/Data Abstract for the United States and Selected Areas, Selected Manpower Statistics*, annual, <http://siadapp.dmdc.osd.mil>.

Table 524. U.S. Active Duty Military Deaths by Manner of Death: 1980 to 2011
[As of Nov. 2, 2011]

Manner of death	1980–2011	1980	1990	1995	2000	2004	2005	2006	2007	2008	2009	2010	2011
Deaths, total	**50,085**	**2,392**	**1,507**	**1,040**	**832**	**1,874**	**1,929**	**1,882**	**1,953**	**1,440**	**1,515**	**1,485**	**1,251**
Accident	25,382	1,556	880	538	429	605	646	561	561	506	467	424	309
Hostile action	5,166	–	–	–	–	735	739	769	847	352	346	456	352
Homicide	2,353	174	74	67	37	46	54	47	52	47	77	39	24
Illness	8,761	419	277	174	180	256	280	257	237	244	277	238	182
Pending	249	–	–	–	–	–	1	8	22	6	19	22	170
Self-inflicted	7,097	231	232	250	153	197	182	213	211	259	302	289	186
Terrorist attack	422	1	1	7	17	–	–	–	–	1	–	–	2
Undetermined	655	11	43	4	16	8	27	27	23	25	27	17	26
Deaths per 100,000 of personnel strength	**(X)**	**110.8**	**66.7**	**62.6**	**54.4**	**107.9**	**115.9**	**116.8**	**121.4**	**85.6**	**92.3**	**88.1**	**77.9**
Accident	(X)	72.0	39.0	32.4	28.0	35.3	38.8	34.8	34.9	30.1	28.5	25.2	19.2
Hostile action	(X)	–	–	–	–	42.9	44.4	47.7	52.7	20.9	21.1	27.1	21.9
Homicide	(X)	8.1	3.3	4.0	2.4	2.7	3.2	2.9	3.2	2.8	4.7	2.3	1.5
Illness	(X)	19.4	12.3	10.5	11.8	15.0	16.8	15.9	14.7	14.5	16.9	14.1	11.3
Pending	(X)	–	–	–	–	–	0.1	0.5	1.4	0.4	1.2	1.3	10.6
Self-inflicted	(X)	10.7	10.3	15.0	10.0	11.5	10.9	13.2	13.1	15.4	18.4	17.1	11.6
Terrorist attack	(X)	–	–	0.4	1.1	–	–	–	–	0.1	–	–	0.1
Undetermined	(X)	0.5	1.9	0.2	1.0	0.5	1.6	1.7	1.4	1.5	1.6	1.0	1.6

– Represents zero. X Not applicable.

Source: Department of Defense Personnel and Procurement, "DoD Personnel and Military Casualty Statistics, Military Casualty Information," <https://www.dmdc.osd.mil/dcas/pages/main.xhtml>.

Table 525. U.S. Military Personnel on Active Duty in Selected Foreign Countries: 1995 to 2011
[As of September 30]

Country	1995	2000	2005	2007	2008	2009	2010	2011
Total in foreign countries [1]	**238,064**	**257,817**	**290,997**	**295,003**	**288,550**	**262,793**	**297,286**	**205,118**
Ashore	208,836	212,858	268,214	272,124	269,260	242,291	277,151	186,476
Afloat	29,228	44,959	22,783	22,879	19,290	20,502	20,135	18,642
Australia	314	175	196	140	140	139	130	198
Bahrain	618	949	1,641	1,495	1,545	1,507	1,349	2,142
Belgium	1,689	1,554	1,366	1,328	1,266	1,267	1,252	1,205
Bosnia and Herzegovina	1	5,708	263	209	14	11	8	9
Canada	214	156	150	141	134	128	127	130
Colombia	44	224	52	123	114	77	62	63
Cuba (Guantanamo)	5,129	688	950	932	969	926	913	929
Diego Garcia [2]	897	625	683	260	244	253	238	292
Djibouti	7	2	622	2,100	1,780	1,207	1,379	335
Egypt	1,123	499	410	250	284	265	275	251
Germany	73,280	69,203	66,418	57,080	55,140	52,658	53,951	53,766
Greece	489	678	428	363	366	361	338	382
Greenland	131	125	146	126	134	144	133	142
Honduras	193	351	438	403	429	416	403	354
Italy	12,007	11,190	11,841	9,855	9,601	9,707	9,646	10,801
Japan	39,134	40,159	35,571	32,803	33,286	35,965	34,385	39,222
Korea, South	36,016	36,565	30,983	27,014	25,062	(NA)	(NA)	(NA)
Kuwait	771	4,602	([3])	([3])	([3])	([3])	([3])	([3])
Netherlands	687	659	583	579	547	510	442	405
Portugal	1,066	1,005	970	826	783	716	703	723
Qatar	2	52	463	411	433	463	555	621
Saudi Arabia	1,077	7,053	258	243	284	269	239	274
Senegal	13	10	42	11	7	9	9	13
Singapore	166	411	169	125	129	125	132	163
Spain	2,799	2,007	1,660	1,286	1,220	1,365	1,240	1,479
Turkey	3,111	2,006	1,780	1,594	1,575	1,616	1,530	1,491
United Kingdom	12,131	11,207	10,752	9,825	9,426	9,199	9,229	9,382
DEPLOYMENTS								
Operation Enduring Freedom (OEF) [4]	(X)	(X)	19,500	25,240	32,300	66,400	105,900	109,200
Operation New Dawn (OND) [5]	(X)	(X)	192,600	218,500	190,400	164,100	96,200	92,200

X Not applicable. NA Not available. [1] Includes items not shown separately. [2] British Indian Ocean Territory. [3] Military personnel data for Kuwait are included with the Operation New Dawn (OND) data. [4] Total (in/around Afghanistan as of September 30) includes Reserve/National Guard. [5] Total (in/around Iraq as of September 30) includes Reserve/National Guard.

Source: U.S. Department of Defense, Statistical Information Analysis Division, "Active Duty Military Personnel Strengths by Regional Area and by Country," <http://siadapp.dmdc.osd.mil>.

Table 526. U.S. Military Sales and Assistance to Foreign Governments: 1995 to 2010

[In millions of dollars (8,495 represents $8,495,000,000). For year ending September 30. Department of Defense (DoD) sales deliveries cover deliveries against sales orders authorized under Arms Export Control Act, as well as earlier and applicable legislation. For details regarding individual programs, see source]

Item	1995	2000	2004	2005	2006	2007	2008	2009	2010
Military sales agreements.................	8,495	10,685	13,261	9,387	17,585	17,988	28,533	29,886	24,447
Military construction sales agreements...	24	284	682	308	171	430	186	980	928
Military sales deliveries [1]	12,100	10,867	11,400	11,148	11,519	12,506	11,814	12,440	13,619
Military construction sales deliveries......	(NA)	183	281	349	323	197	267	204	459
Military financing program.................	3,712	4,333	4,584	4,956	4,450	4,519	4,506	4,580	5,016
Commercial exports licensed under Arms Export Control Act [2]...........	(NA)	478	7,895	30,146	31,605	8,874	33,510	(NA)	(NA)
Military assistance program delivery [3]....	20	5	45	71	11	(NA)	(NA)	(NA)	(NA)
IMET program/deliveries [4].................	26	50	89	86	85	83	83	90	108

NA Not available. [1] Includes military construction sales deliveries. [2] The total dollar value of deliveries made for purchases of munitions-controlled items by foreign governments directly from U.S. manufacturers. [3] Includes Military Assistance Service Funded (MASF) program data and Section 506(a) drawdown authority. [4] International Military Education and Training. Includes military assistance services and emergency drawdowns.

Source: U.S. Department of Defense, Defense Security Cooperation Agency, "DSCA Data and Statistics." See <http://www.dsca.osd.mil/data_stats.htm>.

Table 527. U.S. Military Sales Deliveries by Selected Country: 1995 to 2010

[In millions of dollars (12,100 represents $12,100,000,000). For year ending September 30. Represents Department of Defense military sales]

Country	1995	2000	2004	2005	2006	2007	2008	2009	2010
Total [1]..............	12,100	10,886	11,400	11,148	11,519	12,506	11,814	12,440	13,619
Afghanistan...............	(NA)	–	110	169	173	18	7	2	11
Argentina.................	(NA)	10	4	4	6	8	23	10	26
Australia.................	303	332	193	350	350	780	916	375	918
Bahrain..................	40	55	88	65	55	84	42	101	119
Belgium..................	8	61	42	49	53	49	44	39	26
Brazil...................	(NA)	61	14	11	28	62	54	46	32
Canada..................	127	84	144	150	183	240	468	527	391
Colombia................	(NA)	14	53	41	86	199	124	110	455
Denmark................	54	43	22	40	49	63	57	43	44
Ecuador.................	(NA)	1	3	4	6	7	3	2	3
Egypt...................	1,479	1,092	1,513	1,422	1,195	1,222	856	878	884
El Salvador.............	(NA)	13	3	3	2	2	6	10	6
Finland.................	(NA)	690	46	38	74	28	86	83	127
France..................	64	217	99	69	42	45	57	59	112
Georgia.................	(NA)	3	7	12	11	25	72	18	10
Germany................	257	131	264	208	149	205	173	161	296
Greece.................	220	389	1,224	467	180	204	198	1,291	542
India....................	(NA)	–	7	100	49	92	40	15	32
Iraq....................	(NA)	–	–	–	2	177	683	693	377
Israel..................	327	585	1,202	1,524	1,284	1,314	1,407	739	901
Italy...................	54	52	280	127	288	153	76	93	179
Japan..................	693	448	392	410	766	647	609	859	813
Jordan.................	47	52	104	140	102	170	263	170	173
Kenya.................	(NA)	1	4	7	2	2	1	6	2
Korea, South...........	442	1,399	601	591	599	728	797	478	614
Kuwait................	471	321	209	278	542	463	245	252	243
Malaysia...............	(NA)	411	11	49	22	19	17	23	45
Mexico................	(NA)	9	6	4	8	6	4	5	59
Morocco...............	(NA)	5	9	17	41	8	4	10	30
Netherlands............	153	278	277	178	231	240	252	249	207
Nigeria................	(NA)	–	3	7	3	4	–	3	5
Norway................	25	64	80	106	92	163	88	296	127
Pakistan...............	(NA)	–	36	61	121	196	265	117	1,229
Poland................	(NA)	13	64	84	393	1,483	731	157	75
Portugal...............	88	20	30	84	57	39	45	94	30
Saudi Arabia...........	3,567	1,968	1,223	981	978	1,014	895	1,716	1,587
Singapore.............	59	131	205	229	355	173	167	182	308
Spain.................	193	141	432	126	104	144	169	176	156
Taiwan [2].............	1,332	784	917	1,400	1,068	777	618	646	713
Thailand..............	356	114	180	92	82	46	40	47	42
Turkey................	368	216	290	189	247	183	306	307	253
United Arab Emirates....	345	42	155	165	192	70	83	119	602
United Kingdom.........	419	347	453	381	294	424	297	754	293
Venezuela.............	(NA)	13	12	8	8	1	–	–	–

NA Not available. – Represents or rounds to zero. [1] Includes countries not shown. [2] See footnote 4, Table 1348.

Source: U.S. Department of Defense, Defense Security Cooperation Agency, "DSCA Data and Statistics." See also <http://www.dsca.osd.mil/data_stats.htm>.

Table 528. Arms Transfer Agreements with Developing Nations by Supplier: 2004 to 2011

[In millions of current U.S. dollars (6,783 is 6,783,000,000) Developing nations category excludes the United States, Europe, Canada, Japan, Australia, and New Zealand. All data are for the calendar year given except for U.S. MAP (Military Assistance Program), IMET (International Military Education and Training), and Excess Defense Article data, which are included for the particular fiscal year. All amounts given include the values of all categories of weapons, spare parts, construction, all associated services, military assistance, excess defense articles, and training programs. Statistics for foreign countries are based upon estimated selling prices. All foreign data are rounded to the nearest $100 million]

Supplier	2004	2005	2006	2007	2008	2009	2010	2011	2004-2011
Total............................	26,983	30,193	39,035	41,218	52,923	50,582	32,279	71,503	344,716
United States................	6,783	5,493	8,435	11,518	28,023	14,582	14,079	56,303	145,216
Russia..........................	8,500	8,000	15,300	9,600	6,400	13,000	7,600	4,100	72,500
France..........................	1,100	5,400	500	1,400	3,600	9,200	1,800	2,700	25,700
United Kingdom...............	4,100	2,800	4,000	9,500	200	1,100	1,200	300	23,200
China...........................	1,000	2,700	2,000	2,500	2,100	2,300	1,600	2,100	16,300
Germany........................	200	700	2,400	1,700	4,700	500	0	0	10,200
Italy............................	300	500	600	1,000	1,600	1,300	1,800	1,100	8,200
All other European.............	2,400	3,600	2,700	2,100	4,400	4,700	2,700	2,400	25,000
All others......................	2,600	1,000	3,100	1,900	1,900	3,900	1,500	2,500	18,400

Source: Congressional Research Service, *Conventional Arms Transfers to Developing Nations, 2004-2011*, August 2012.

Table 529. Veterans by Selected Period of Service and State: 2011

[In thousands (22,032 represents 22,032,000). As of September 30. "Veteran Population 2007" is the Department of Veterans Affairs (VA) latest official estimate and projection of the veteran population. It is based on tabulations of Census 2000 data (prepared for the VA Office of the Actuary by the Census Bureau) and on recent American Community Survey data. "Veteran Population 2007" also uses administrative data and projections of service member separations from active duty provided by the Department of Defense (the Defense Manpower Data Center and the Office of the Actuary), as well as VA data on veterans benefits]

State	Total [1,2]	Gulf War era [3]	Vietnam era [4]	State	Total [1,2]	Gulf War era [3]	Vietnam era [4]
United States........	22,032	5,854	7,326	Missouri..................	497	124	169
Alabama..................	401	118	135	Montana..................	101	26	35
Alaska....................	77	28	27	Nebraska.................	142	38	49
Arizona...................	551	143	179	Nevada...................	242	65	85
Arkansas..................	251	68	86	New Hampshire.........	126	26	45
California.................	1,918	517	621	New Jersey..............	423	80	135
Colorado..................	418	120	150	New Mexico..............	173	52	56
Connecticut..............	222	42	76	New York.................	913	181	297
Delaware..................	77	20	25	North Carolina..........	761	232	249
District of Columbia....	37	11	11	North Dakota............	55	16	17
Florida....................	1,617	412	504	Ohio......................	867	199	296
Georgia...................	773	250	257	Oklahoma................	320	98	106
Hawaii....................	115	37	35	Oregon...................	327	74	116
Idaho.....................	136	38	46	Pennsylvania............	933	189	313
Illinois....................	763	196	245	Rhode Island............	69	15	23
Indiana...................	482	115	163	South Carolina..........	404	120	137
Iowa......................	229	53	78	South Dakota............	71	20	23
Kansas...................	221	64	73	Tennessee...............	489	130	173
Kentucky.................	331	92	112	Texas.....................	1,683	541	557
Louisiana.................	298	95	92	Utah......................	152	41	50
Maine.....................	136	31	49	Vermont..................	51	10	18
Maryland..................	466	142	147	Virginia...................	823	311	256
Massachusetts..........	379	71	125	Washington..............	627	178	221
Michigan..................	684	141	244	West Virginia............	163	42	55
Minnesota................	372	71	138	Wisconsin................	408	90	139
Mississippi...............	202	62	65	Wyoming.................	56	16	20

[1] Veterans serving in more than one period of service are counted only once in the total. [2] Current civilians discharged from active duty, other than for training only without service-connected disability. [3] Service from August 2, 1990 to the present. [4] Service from August 5, 1964 to May 7, 1975.

Source: U.S. Department of Veterans Affairs, National Center for Veterans Analysis and Statistics, "Veteran Population 2007," <http://www.va.gov/VETDATA/Demographics/Demographics.asp>, accessed April 2012.

Table 530. Veterans Benefits—Expenditures by Program and Compensation for Service-Connected Disabilities: 1990 to 2011

[In millions of dollars (28,998 represents $28,998,000,000). For years ending September 30]

Program	1990	1995	2000	2005	2008	2009	2010	2011
Total expenditures...................................	28,998	37,775	47,086	69,667	85,153	97,144	108,635	122,859
Medical programs...	11,582	16,255	19,637	29,433	35,301	40,079	42,372	43,085
Construction...	661	641	466	483	907	1,191	1,618	1,813
General operating expenses..........................	811	954	1,016	1,294	4,242	4,962	6,101	6,655
Compensation and pension...........................	14,674	17,765	22,012	34,694	39,166	44,608	47,785	57,596
Vocational rehabilitation and education.............	452	1,317	1,610	2,937	3,228	4,270	8,260	10,630
All other [1]..	818	844	2,345	826	2,309	2,034	2,499	3,080
Compensation for service-connected disabilities...	9,284	11,644	15,511	24,515	30,274	34,103	36,486	39,374

[1] Includes insurance, indemnities, and miscellaneous funds and expenditures and offsets from public receipts. (Excludes expenditures from personal funds of patients.)

Source: U.S. Department of Veterans Affairs, "Summary of Expenditures By State" and *Annual Benefits Report*. See <http://www.va.gov/vetdata/>.

Table 531. Veterans' Status by Sex, Race, and Hispanic Origin: 2010

[Data are based on the American Community Survey (ACS). The survey universe includes the household population and the population living in institutions, college dormitories, and other group quarters. Based on a sample and subject to sampling variability; see text, this section and Appendix III]

Characteristics	Total number	18 to 64 years	65 years and over
Total	**21,798,077**	**12,662,865**	**9,135,212**
Male	20,230,784	11,345,824	8,884,960
Female	1,567,293	1,317,041	250,252
White alone	18,381,236	10,034,549	8,346,687
Male	17,231,186	9,112,242	8,118,944
Female	1,150,050	922,307	227,743
Black or African American alone	2,398,602	1,861,870	536,732
Male	2,095,030	1,573,213	521,817
Female	303,572	288,657	14,915
American Indian/Alaska Native alone	156,515	114,015	42,500
Male	138,891	97,722	41,169
Female	17,624	16,293	1,331
Asian alone	265,198	173,099	92,099
Male	240,444	150,675	89,769
Female	24,754	22,424	2,330
Native Hawaiian and Other Pacific Islander alone	27,773	22,087	5,686
Male	23,640	18,262	5,378
Female	4,133	3,825	308
Some other race alone	241,487	202,315	39,172
Male	217,918	179,510	38,408
Female	23,569	22,805	764
Two or more races	322,266	254,930	67,336
Male	278,675	214,200	64,475
Female	43,591	40,730	2,861
Hispanic or Latino origin [1]	1,163,091	884,256	278,835
Male	1,048,419	776,630	271,789
Female	114,672	107,626	7,046

[1] Persons of Hispanic or Latino origin may be any race.

Source: U.S. Census Bureau, 2009 American Community Survey, B21001, B21001A, B21001B, B21001C, B21001D, B21001E, B21001F, B21001G, and B21001I (accessed June 2012), <http://www.census.gov/acs/www/data_documentation/data_main/>.

Table 532. Veterans Living by Period of Service, Age, and Sex: 2011

[In thousands (22,658 represents 22,658,000). As of September 30. Includes those veterans living outside the United States]

Age	Total veterans	Wartime veterans					Peacetime veterans
		Total [1]	Gulf War era [2]	Vietnam era [3]	Korean conflict [4]	World War II	
Total	**22,234**	**16,546**	**5,946**	**7,391**	**2,275**	**1,711**	**5,688**
Under 20 years old	8	8	8	–	–	–	–
20 to 24 years old	302	302	302	–	–	–	–
25 to 29 years old	745	745	745	–	–	–	–
30 to 34 years old	907	907	907	–	–	–	–
35 to 39 years old	963	951	951	–	–	–	12
40 to 44 years old	1,419	1,117	1,117	–	–	–	303
45 to 49 years old	1,724	746	746	–	–	–	978
50 to 54 years old	1,905	581	520	66	–	–	1,324
55 to 59 years old	1,957	1,381	339	1,160	–	–	576
60 to 64 years old	2,943	2,806	206	2,737	–	–	137
65 to 69 years old	2,776	2,423	77	2,408	–	–	353
70 to 74 years old	1,901	711	19	665	51	–	1,190
75 to 79 years old	1,773	1,088	7	203	982	–	685
80 to 84 years old	1,481	1,374	2	109	1,081	352	107
85 years & over	1,430	1,406	–	43	160	1,359	24
Female, total	**1,854**	**1,312**	**952**	**248**	**58**	**86**	**542**

– Represents or rounds to zero. [1] Veterans who served in more than one wartime period are counted only once in the total. [2] Service from August 2, 1990 to the present. [3] Service from August 5, 1964 to May 7, 1975. [4] Service during period June 27, 1950 to January 31, 1955.

Source: U.S. Department of Veterans Affairs, National Center for Veterans Analysis and Statistics, "Veteran Population 2007," <http://www.va.gov/VETDATA/Demographics/Demographics.asp>, accessed April 2012.

Table 533. Veterans Compensation and Pension Benefits—Number on Rolls by Period of Service and Status: 1990 to 2010

[In thousands (3,584 represents 3,584,000), except as indicated. As of September 30. Living refers to veterans receiving compensation for disability incurred or aggravated while on active duty and war veterans receiving pension and benefits for nonservice-connected disabilities. Deceased refers to deceased veterans whose dependents were receiving pensions and compensation benefits]

Period of service and veteran status	1990	1995	2000	2005	2007	2008	2009	2010
Total	**3,584**	**3,330**	**3,236**	**3,503**	**3,691**	**3,801**	**3,919**	**4,070**
Living veterans	2,746	2,669	2,672	2,973	3,167	3,268	3,384	3,524
Service-connected	2,184	2,236	2,308	2,637	2,844	2,952	3,070	3,210
Nonservice-connected	562	433	364	336	323	316	314	314
Deceased veterans	838	662	564	530	524	533	535	546
Service-connected	320	307	307	323	330	338	341	347
Nonservice-connected	518	355	257	207	195	196	194	199
World War I	198	89	34	13	9	8	7	6
Living	18	3	(Z)	(Z)	(Z)	(Z)	(Z)	(Z)
World War II	1,723	1,307	968	718	634	598	559	529
Living	1,294	961	676	466	397	362	329	298
Korean conflict [1]	390	368	323	295	287	282	276	275
Living	305	290	255	231	223	218	213	209
Vietnam era [2]	774	868	969	1,218	1,305	1,347	1,393	1,447
Living	685	766	848	1,068	1,142	1,175	1,214	1,261
Gulf War era [3]	(X)	138	334	630	819	923	1,028	1,140
Living	(X)	134	326	617	802	904	1,007	1,117
Peacetime	495	559	607	627	637	644	655	673
Living	444	514	567	591	602	609	621	638

X Not applicable. Z Fewer than 500. [1] Service during period June 27, 1950 to January 31, 1955. [2] Service from August 5, 1964 to May 7, 1975. [3] Service from August 2, 1990 to the present.

Source: U.S. Department of Veterans Affairs, 1990 to 1995, *Annual Report of the Secretary of Veterans Affairs*; beginning 2000, *Annual Accountability Report* and unpublished data, see also <http://www.va.gov/vetdata/>.

Table 534. Federal Funding Obligations for Selected Homeless Veterans Programs: 1988 to 2011

[In thousands of dollars, except as indicated (12,932 represents 12,932,000). For year ending September 30]

Year	Number of homeless veterans (estimated) [1]	Federal funding obligations for selected programs					Department of Labor
		Department of Veterans Affairs					
		Health care for homeless veterans [2]	Domiciliary care for homeless veterans	Compensated work therapy/ therapeutic residence	Grant and per diem program	HUD-VA Supported Housing (Supportive Services) [3]	Homeless Veterans Reintegration Program
1988	(NA)	12,932	15,000	(NA)	(NA)	(NA)	1,915
1989	(NA)	13,252	10,367	(NA)	(NA)	(NA)	1,877
1990	(NA)	15,000	15,000	(NA)	(NA)	(NA)	1,920
1991	(NA)	15,461	15,750	([4])	(NA)	(NA)	2,018
1992	(NA)	16,500	16,500	([4])	(NA)	2,300	1,366
1993	(NA)	22,150	22,300	400	(NA)	2,000	5,055
1994	(NA)	24,513	27,140	3,051	8,000	3,235	5,055
1995	(NA)	[5] 38,585	38,948	3,387	([5])	4,270	[6] 107
1996	(NA)	[5] 38,433	41,117	3,886	([5])	4,829	0
1997	(NA)	[5] 38,063	37,214	3,628	([5])	4,958	0
1998	256,872	36,407	38,489	8,612	5,886	5,084	3,000
1999	344,983	32,421	39,955	4,092	20,000	5,223	3,000
2000	292,105	38,381	34,434	8,068	19,640	5,137	9,636
2001	294,840	58,602	34,576	8,144	31,100	5,219	17,500
2002	299,321	54,135	45,443	8,028	22,431	4,729	18,250
2003	313,087	45,188	49,213	8,371	43,388	4,603	18,131
2004	192,368	42,905	51,829	10,240	62,965	3,375	18,888
2005	194,254	40,357	57,555	10,004	62,180	3,243	20,832
2006	195,827	56,998	63,592	19,529	63,621	5,297	21,780
2007	153,584	71,925	77,633	21,514	81,187	7,487	21,809
2008	131,230	77,656	96,098	21,497	114,696	4,854	23,620
2009	106,558	80,219	115,373	22,206	128,073	26,601	26,330
2010	(NA)	109,727	175,979	61,205	175,057	71,137	36,330
2011 [7]	(NA)	135,932	140,949	52,788	217,639	151,069	(NA)

NA Not available. [1] Estimates for 1988 to 2003 are of number of veterans experiencing homelessness at any time during the year. Beginning in 2004 estimates are of the highest number of veterans who are homeless on any given day of the year. [2] Through 1991 the program was called the Homeless Chronically Ill Veterans program. [3] Covers funding allocated for supportive services, but not the cost of providing housing. [4] For 1991 and 1992, funds from Homeless Chronically Mentally Ill Veterans program as well as substance abuse treatment funds were used for the program. [5] For 1995 through 1997, funds were obligated with funds for the Health Care for Veterans program. Department of Veterans Affairs budget documents do not provide a separate breakdown for grant and per diem obligations. [6] Congress appropriated $5.011 million for the program in 1995. A subsequent rescission reduced the amount. [7] Obligations for 2011 are estimates.

Source: Congressional Research Service, *Veterans and Homelessness*, April 1, 2011.

Table 535. Homeland Security Funding by Agency: 2005 to 2012

[In millions of dollars. (52,657 represents 52,657,000,000). A total of 31 agencies comprise federal homeland security funding. Department of Homeland Security (DHS) is the designated department to coordinate and centralize the leadership of many homeland security activities under a single department. In addition to DHS, the Departments of Defense (DoD), Energy (DoE), Justice (DoJ), Health and Human Services (HHS), and the U.S. State Department account for most of the total government-wide homeland security funding]

Agency	2005	2008	2009	2010	2011	2012
Total budget authority, excluding BioShield [1, 2]	52,657	61,228	70,445	70,009	66,983	67,988
Department of Agriculture	596	575	513	614	580	570
Department of Commerce	167	207	259	284	262	290
Department of Defense	16,108	17,374	19,414	19,054	16,994	17,358
Department of Education	24	27	32	29	30	31
Department of Energy	1,562	1,827	1,939	2,016	1,994	1,923
Department of Health and Human Services	4,229	4,301	4,627	7,196	4,182	4,147
Department of Homeland Security [3]	23,980	29,756	36,037	32,609	34,901	35,125
Department of Housing and Urban Development	2	2	5	5	3	3
Department of the Interior	65	50	50	52	58	58
Department of Justice	2,691	3,278	3,650	4,094	3,966	4,055
Department of Labor	56	48	49	40	43	46
Department of State	824	1,719	1,809	1,793	1,949	2,283
Department of Transportation	219	205	221	228	243	247
Department of the Treasury	101	120	133	125	126	123
Department of Veterans Affairs	249	309	310	427	413	395
Army Corps of Engineers	89	42	40	36	36	36
Environmental Protection Agency	106	138	157	154	108	102
Executive Office of the President	30	21	19	12	9	10
General Services Administration	65	143	125	214	19	38
National Aeronautics and Space Administration	221	205	214	218	228	229
National Science Foundation	342	365	377	390	386	444
Office of Personnel Management	3	2	2	2	2	1
Social Security Administration	155	184	182	190	213	234
District of Columbia	15	3	39	15	15	15
Federal Communications Commission	2	2	2	1	3	(NA)
Intelligence Community Management Account	72	122	33	14	13	9
National Archives and Records Administration	17	18	20	20	22	23
Nuclear Regulatory Commission	59	72	73	65	73	78
Securities and Exchange Commission	5	13	15	6	6	8
Smithsonian Institution	75	91	92	99	98	97
United States Holocaust Memorial Museum	8	8	9	10	10	11

NA Not available. [1] The federal spending estimates are for the executive branch's homeland security activities. These estimates do not include the activities of the legislative or judicial branches. [2] The Department of Homeland Security Appropriations Act, 2004, provided $5.6 billion for Project BioShield, to remain available through 2013. Including this uneven funding stream can distort year-over-year comparisons. [3] Not all activities carried out by DHS constitute homeland security funding (e.g. response to natural disasters and Coast Guard search and rescue activities). DHS estimates in this table do not represent the entire DHS budget. See Table 536.

Source: U.S. Office of Management and Budget, "Budget of the United States Government Fiscal Year 2013," *The Budget Documents, Analytical Perspectives*, and "Budget of the United States Government Fiscal Year 2013," *Crosscutting Programs, Homeland Security Funding Analysis*, <http://www.whitehouse.gov/omb/budget/>.

Table 536. Department of Homeland Security Total Budget Authority and Personnel by Organization: 2011 and 2012

[In thousands of dollars (55,331,462 represents $55,331,462,000). For the fiscal year ending September 30. Not all activities carried out by the Department of Homeland Security (DHS) constitute homeland security funding (e.g., Coast Guard search and rescue activities)]

Organization	Budget authority		Full-time employees	
	2011 [1]	2012	2011 [1]	2012
Total	55,331,462	59,914,091	220,601	223,675
Departmental operations [2]	839,292	802,885	1,882	2,079
Analysis and operations	334,360	338,068	793	851
Office of the Inspector General	129,614	141,000	665	676
U.S. Customs & Border Protection	11,245,410	11,737,569	58,954	60,888
U.S. Immigration & Customs Enforcement	5,805,420	5,862,453	20,417	20,271
Transportation Security Administration	7,687,552	7,841,019	54,831	55,722
U.S. Coast Guard	10,193,685	10,348,886	49,995	50,711
U.S. Secret Service	1,755,299	1,911,617	7,055	7,055
National Protection and Program Directorate	2,331,197	2,531,339	2,777	3,072
Office of Health Affairs	139,455	167,449	95	99
Federal Emergency Management Agency (FEMA) [3]	7,073,862	11,549,247	10,042	10,027
FEMA Grants [4]	3,372,741	2,374,681	([5])	([5])
U.S. Citizenship & Immigration Services	2,983,422	3,078,465	11,421	10,500
Federal Law Enforcement Training Center	270,832	271,413	1,103	1,103
Science & Technology Directorate (S&T)	827,578	668,000	441	491
Domestic Nuclear Detection Office	341,744	290,000	130	130

[1] Continuing resolution. [2] Departmental operations is comprised of the Office of the Secretary & Executive Management, the Office of the Federal Coordinator for Gulf Coast Rebuilding, the Office of the Undersecretary for Management, the Office of the Chief Financial Officer, and the Office of the Chief Information Officer. [3] Supplemental appropriations funding was added to the 2010 budget. [4] Includes the following FEMA appropriations: State and Local Programs and Emergency Management Performance Grants, and Assistance to Firefighters Grants. [5] Employee data are included among FEMA full-time employees.

Source: U.S. Department of Homeland Security, "Budget-in-Brief, Fiscal Year 2013," <http://www.dhs.gov/dhs-budget>, accessed April 2012.

Table 537. Homeland Security Grants by State/Territory: 2010 and 2011

[In thousands of dollars (1,726,360 represents 1,726,360,000). For years ending September 30. Grants consist of the following programs: State Homeland Security Program (SHSP), Urban Areas Security Initiative (UASI), Metropolitan Medical Response System (MMRS), and Citizen Corps Program (CCP). Data for Operation Stone Garden (OPSG) funding not included]

State/territory	2010	2011	State/territory	2010	2011	State/territory	2010	2011
Total........	1,726,360	1,234,406	KY.............	11,045	5,858	OK.............	13,999	5,847
U.S.............	1,710,436	1,224,383	LA.............	23,694	8,191	OR.............	15,402	10,593
AL.............	11,294	6,429	ME.............	6,739	5,237	PA.............	57,856	42,240
AK.............	7,358	5,789	MD.............	27,342	16,189	RI.............	11,814	5,514
AZ.............	30,087	15,693	MA.............	35,713	27,769	SC.............	8,412	5,582
AR.............	7,094	5,549	MI.............	34,076	20,200	SD.............	6,726	5,228
CA.............	268,685	220,441	MN.............	19,908	12,251	TN.............	19,564	6,841
CO.............	19,210	11,476	MS.............	7,096	5,550	TX.............	143,037	99,331
CT.............	14,955	5,561	MO.............	28,169	12,255	UT.............	9,991	5,548
DE.............	6,728	5,229	MT.............	6,730	5,231	VT.............	6,722	5,224
DC.............	69,574	64,764	NE.............	8,398	5,810	VA.............	30,915	16,418
FL.............	71,140	37,723	NV.............	16,493	11,250	WA.............	30,616	18,187
GA.............	33,716	20,193	NH.............	7,056	5,519	WV.............	6,751	5,247
HI.............	11,810	5,519	NJ.............	62,036	50,000	WI.............	14,610	5,884
ID.............	6,744	5,242	NM.............	7,072	5,533	WY.............	6,720	5,223
IL.............	87,934	75,470	NY.............	277,151	244,630	AS [1]	1,502	1,184
IN.............	19,314	6,425	NC.............	21,273	12,055	GU [1]	1,505	1,186
IA.............	7,097	5,552	ND.............	6,722	5,225	NM [1]	1,502	1,184
KS.............	7,410	5,830	OH.............	40,438	19,842	PR [1]	9,911	5,285
						VI [1]	1,503	1,185

[1] AS—American Samoa, GU—Guam, NM—Northern Mariana Islands, PR—Puerto Rico, VI—Virgin Islands.

Source: U.S. Department of Homeland Security, "FY 2011 Homeland Security Grant Program," *HSGP Guidance and Application Kit* <http://www.fema.gov/fy-2011-homeland-security-grant-program>, released May 2011.

Table 538. Urban Areas Security Initiative (UASI) Grant Program: 2011

[In thousands of dollars (662,622 represents $662,622,000). For year ending September 30. The UASI Program provides financial assistance to address the unique multi-disciplinary planning, operations, equipment, training, and exercise needs of high-threat, high-density urban areas. The 31 highest risk urban areas were eligible for funding. The top eleven highest risk urban areas are designated Tier 1. For a listing of all grant programs and their descriptions, see <http://www.fema.gov/preparedness-non-disaster-grants>]

State/ territory	Urban area	Amount	State/ territory	Urban area	Amount
Total.............		662,622			
TIER 1			TIER 2 (cont.)		
CA.............	Bay Area	42,828	FL................	Miami/Fort Lauderdale	9,646
	Los Angeles/Long Beach	69,922		Orlando	3,697
	San Diego Area	16,209		Tampa	5,471
DC.............	National Capital Region	59,392	GA................	Atlanta	9,751
IL................	Chicago	54,654	MD................	Baltimore	7,813
MA.............	Boston	18,934	MI................	Detroit	9,437
NJ.............	Jersey City/Newark	37,292	MN................	Twin Cities	6,117
NY.............	New York City	151,579	MI................	St. Louis	5,973
PA.............	Philadelphia	23,336	NV................	Las Vegas	5,705
TX.............	Dallas/Fort Worth/Arlington	25,097	NC................	Charlotte	3,244
	Houston	41,453	OH................	Cincinnati	3,491
				Cleveland	3,590
TIER 2			OR................	Portland	5,025
AZ.............	Phoenix	7,755	PA................	Pittsburgh	4,479
CA.............	Anaheim/Santa Ana	8,941	VA................	Norfolk	5,160
	Riverside	3,700	WA................	Seattle	7,959
CO	Denver	4,969			

Source: Department of Homeland Security, FEMA, "FY 2011 Homeland Security Grant Program (HSGP)," <http://www.fema.gov/fy-2011-homeland-security-grant-program>, released May 2011.

Table 539. Preparedness Grant Programs: 2009 to 2011

[In dollars. For years ending September 30]

Program	2009	2010	2011
Total [1]...........	968,585,000	2,967,879,947	2,191,248,008
Homeland Security Grant Program [1].....................	(X)	1,786,359,956	1,289,296,132
State Homeland Security Program..............	(X)	842,000,000	526,874,100
Urban Areas Security Initiative................	(X)	832,520,000	662,622,100
Operation Stonegarden......................	(X)	60,000,000	54,890,000
Emergency Management Performance Grants Program............	(X)	329,799,991	329,040,400
Transit Security Grant Program [1].....................	348,600,000	253,437,597	200,079,000
Port Security Grant Program.......................	388,600,000	288,000,000	235,029,000

X Not applicable. [1] Includes programs not listed separately.

Source: U.S. Department of Homeland Security, State Contracts and Grants Award Administration, <http://www.fema.gov/preparedness-non-disaster-grants>.

Table 540. Deportable Aliens Located by Program and Border Patrol Sector: 2000 to 2010

[As of the end of September. For purposes of statistical reporting there is no difference between the terms "apprehension" and "deportable alien located." For definitions for immigration statistics, see <http://www.dhs.gov/files/statistics/dtadefstd.shtm>]

Program and sector	2000	2005	2007	2008	2009	2010
Total	1,814,729	1,291,142	960,756	791,568	613,003	516,992
Investigations [1]	138,291	102,034	53,562	33,573	21,877	17,836
Detention and Removal Operations [2]	(X)	(X)	30,407	34,155	35,094	35,774
Border Patrol	1,676,438	1,189,108	876,787	723,840	556,032	463,382
All Southwest sectors	1,643,679	1,171,428	858,722	705,022	540,851	447,731
San Diego, CA	151,681	126,909	152,459	162,392	118,712	68,565
El Centro, CA	238,126	55,726	55,881	40,962	33,520	32,562
Yuma, AZ	108,747	138,438	37,994	8,363	6,952	7,116
Tucson, AZ	616,346	439,090	378,323	317,709	241,667	212,202
El Paso, TX	115,696	122,689	75,464	30,310	14,998	12,251
Marfa, TX	13,689	10,536	5,537	5,390	6,357	5,288
Del Rio, TX	157,178	68,510	22,919	20,761	17,082	14,694
Laredo, TX	108,973	75,342	56,715	43,659	40,571	35,287
Rio Grande Valley, TX	133,243	134,188	73,430	75,476	60,992	59,766
All other sectors	32,759	17,680	18,065	18,818	15,181	15,651
Blaine, WA	2,581	1,001	749	951	844	673
Buffalo, NY	1,570	400	2,190	3,338	2,672	2,422
Detroit, MI	2,057	1,792	902	961	1,157	1,669
Grand Forks, ND	562	754	500	542	472	543
Havre, MT	1,568	949	486	427	283	290
Houlton, ME	489	233	95	81	60	56
Livermore, CA [3]	6,205	117	(X)	(X)	(X)	(X)
Miami, FL	6,237	7,243	7,121	6,020	4,429	4,651
New Orleans, LA	6,478	1,358	4,018	4,303	3,527	3,171
Ramey, PR	1,731	1,619	548	572	418	398
Spokane, WA	1,324	279	337	340	277	356
Swanton, VT	1,957	1,935	1,119	1,283	1,042	1,422

X Not applicable. [1] The Immigration and Customs Enforcement (ICE) Office of Investigations focuses on the enforcement of a wide variety of laws that include immigration and customs statutes. [2] Includes arrests of fugitive and nonfugitive aliens under the Office of Detention and Removal Operations (DRO), National Fugitive Operations Program. [3] Livermore sector closed July 30, 2004.

Source: U.S. Department of Homeland Security, Office of Immigration Statistics, *Yearbook of Immigration Statistics, 2009*. See also <http://www.dhs.gov/publications>.

Table 541. U.S. Border Patrol Apprehensions by Border, Gender, Age, and Country of Nationality: 2007 to 2010

[As of the end of September. See headnote, Table 540]

Characteristic	2007		2008		2009		2010	
	Number	Percent	Number	Percent	Number	Percent	Number	Percent
Border total	876,803	100.0	723,840	100.0	556,032	100.0	463,382	100.0
Southwest	858,737	97.9	705,022	97.4	540,851	97.3	447,731	96.6
Coastal	11,687	1.3	10,895	1.5	8,374	1.5	8,220	1.8
Northern	6,379	0.7	7,923	1.1	6,807	1.2	7,431	1.6
Gender								
Total	876,803	100.0	723,840	100.0	556,032	100.0	463,382	100.0
Male	730,217	83.3	606,761	83.8	469,994	84.5	397,198	85.7
Female	146,574	16.7	117,061	16.2	86,023	15.5	66,173	14.3
Unknown	12	–	18	–	15		11	–
Age								
Total	876,803	100.0	723,840	100.0	556,032	100.0	463,382	100.0
17 years and under	77,778	8.9	59,578	8.2	40,461	7.3	31,291	6.8
18 to 24 years	325,901	37.2	257,409	35.6	182,740	32.9	148,969	32.1
25 to 34 years	301,002	34.3	255,261	35.3	205,173	36.9	173,763	37.5
35 to 44 years	127,285	14.5	112,941	15.6	95,922	17.3	82,236	17.7
45 to 54 years	36,661	4.2	32,003	4.4	26,668	4.8	22,981	5.0
55 years and over	7,384	0.8	6,235	0.9	5,029	0.9	4,125	0.9
Unknown	792	0.1	413	0.1	39	–	17	–
Country of Nationality								
Total	876,803	100.0	723,840	100.0	556,032	100.0	463,382	100.0
Mexico	808,773	92.2	661,773	91.4	503,379	90.5	404,365	87.3
Honduras [1]	22,914	2.6	19,351	2.7	14,630	2.6	13,580	2.9
Guatemala	17,337	2.0	16,395	2.3	15,575	2.8	18,406	4.0
El Salvador [1]	14,114	1.6	12,684	1.8	11,693	2.1	13,723	3.0
Cuba	4,295	0.5	3,351	0.5	910	0.2	712	0.2
Ecuador	958	0.1	1,579	0.2	1,313	0.2	1,777	0.4
Nicaragua	1,646	0.2	1,467	0.2	975	0.2	909	0.2
Brazil [1]	1,214	0.1	977	0.1	798	0.1	812	0.2
China, People's Republic	837	0.1	836	0.1	1,499	0.3	1,157	0.2
Dominican Republic	562	0.1	819	0.1	865	0.2	1,330	0.3
Canada	554	0.1	610	0.1	490	0.1	690	0.1
Other	3,599	0.4	3,998	0.6	3,905	0.7	5,921	1.3

– Represents zero. [1] Between 2005 and 2008, the percentage of persons apprehended who were from Honduras, El Salvador, and Brazil declined substantially. These decreases reflect the end of "catch and release," the practice of apprehending illegal aliens from countries other than Mexico and releasing them on their own recognizance pending a removal hearing.

Source: U.S. Dept. of Homeland Security, Office of Immigration Statistics, "Apprehensions by the U.S. Border Patrol: 2005-2010," *Fact Sheets*; see also <http://www.dhs.gov/publications>.

Table 542. Deportable Aliens Located: 1925 to 2010

[See headnote, Table 540. Detention and Removal Operations (DRO) data are included beginning in fiscal year 2006]

Year	Number	Year	Number	Year	Number	Year	Number
1925	22,199	1975	766,600	1987	1,190,488	1999	1,714,035
1930	20,880	1976 [1]	1,097,739	1988	1,008,145	2000	1,814,729
1935	11,016	1977	1,042,215	1989	954,243	2001	1,387,486
1940	10,492	1978	1,057,977	1990	1,169,939	2002	1,062,279
1945	69,164	1979	1,076,418	1991	1,197,875	2003	1,046,422
1950	468,339	1980	910,361	1992	1,258,481	2004	1,264,232
1955	254,096	1981	975,780	1993	1,327,261	2005	1,291,142
1960	70,684	1982	970,246	1994	1,094,719	2006	1,206,457
1965	110,371	1983	1,251,357	1995	1,394,554	2007	960,756
1970	345,353	1984	1,246,981	1996	1,649,986	2008	791,568
1973	655,968	1985	1,348,749	1997	1,536,520	2009	613,003
1974	788,145	1986	1,767,400	1998	1,679,439	2010	516,992

[1] Includes the 15 months from July 1, 1975 to September 30, 1976, because the end date of fiscal years was changed from June 30 to September 30.

Source: U.S. Department of Homeland Security, Office of Immigration Statistics, *Yearbook of Immigration Statistics, 2010*. See also <http://www.dhs.gov/publications>.

Table 543. Aliens Returned or Removed by Crime Categories and Country of Nationality: 2005 to 2010

[For definitions of immigration enforcement terms, see *Immigration Enforcement Actions, 2010* and *Yearbook of Immigration Statistics*; "Crime categories" and "Countries of nationality" ranked by latest data year]

Crime category and country of nationality	2005	2006	2007	2008	2009	2010
Total aliens returned or removed:	**1,343,351**	**1,324,355**	**1,210,772**	**1,177,058**	**981,329**	**863,647**
Returns [1]	1,096,920	1,043,381	891,390	811,263	586,164	476,405
Removals [2]	246,431	280,974	319,382	359,795	395,165	387,242
Noncriminal	154,210	182,484	216,988	254,529	263,325	218,710
Criminal [3]	92,221	98,490	102,394	105,266	131,840	168,532
Leading crime categories:						
Dangerous drugs	34,215	33,485	33,449	34,882	37,993	42,692
Immigration	17,106	23,176	21,538	17,542	19,807	31,585
Assault	9,633	9,574	11,048	7,485	9,436	12,105
Larceny	2,742	2,757	2,878	3,282	4,228	5,406
Burglary	3,351	3,506	3,466	3,292	3,795	4,188
Robbery	3,023	2,915	2,908	3,101	3,252	3,628
Family offenses	2,172	2,262	2,410	2,343	2,611	3,318
Sexual assault	2,649	2,571	2,786	2,929	2,792	3,252
Stolen vehicles	1,806	1,934	1,875	(NA)	(NA)	(NA)
Sex offenses	1,922	1,868	1,874	(NA)	(NA)	(NA)
Other	13,106	13,371	15,692	18,170	21,161	27,701
Leading country of nationality of criminals removed:						
Mexico	70,779	73,171	76,967	77,531	99,619	127,728
Honduras	2,704	5,752	5,236	5,476	6,998	10,358
Guatemala	2,143	3,850	3,917	5,138	6,547	9,359
El Salvador	2,827	3,850	4,949	5,558	6,344	8,315
Dominican Republic	2,308	2,206	2,044	2,046	2,207	2,215
Colombia	1,367	1,307	1,191	1,081	1,124	1,223
Jamaica	1,475	1,234	1,139	1,214	1,246	1,161
Canada	356	592	508	533	620	794
Brazil	1,431	563	352	368	388	481
Nicaragua	462	423	411	347	418	445

NA Not available. [1] Returns are the confirmed movement of an inadmissible or deportable alien out of the United States not based on an order of removal. Most of the voluntary departures are of Mexican nationals who have been apprehended by the U.S. Border Patrol and are returned to Mexico. [2] Removals are the compulsory and confirmed movement of an inadmissible or deportable alien out of the United States based on an order of removal. An alien who is removed has administrative or criminal consequences placed on subsequent reentry owing to the fact of the removal. [3] Refers to persons removed based on a criminal charge or those with a criminal conviction.

Source: U.S. Department of Homeland Security, Office of Immigration Statistics, *2010 Yearbook of Immigration Statistics* and *Immigration Enforcement Actions 2010*. Deportable Alien Control System (DACS), Enforcement Case Tracking System (ENFORCE), July 2009. See also <http://www.dhs.gov/publications>.

Table 544. Coast Guard Migrant Interdictions by Nationality of Alien: 2000 to 2011

[For the year ending September 30]

Year	Total	Haiti	Dominican Republic	China	Cuba	Mexico	Ecuador	Other
2000	4,210	1,113	499	261	1,000	49	1,244	44
2005	9,455	1,850	3,612	32	2,712	55	1,149	45
2007	6,338	1,610	1,469	73	2,868	26	125	167
2008	4,825	1,583	688	1	2,216	47	220	65
2009	3,467	1,782	727	35	799	77	6	41
2010	2,088	1,377	140	–	422	61	–	88
2011	2,474	1,137	222	11	985	68	1	50

– Represents zero.

Source: U.S. Department of Homeland Security, United States Coast Guard, "USCG Migrant Interdiction Statistics," accessed April 10, 2012. See also <http://www.uscg.mil>.

Table 545. Customs and Border Protection (CBP)—Processed and Cleared Passengers, Planes, Vehicles, and Containers: 2000 to 2007

[In thousands (80,519 represents 80,519,000). For year ending September 30]

Characteristic	2000	2001	2002	2003	2004	2005	2006	2007
Air								
Passengers...................	80,519	79,676	71,608	72,959	80,866	86,123	87,906	91,574
Commercial planes [1].................	829	839	769	790	824	866	881	916
Private planes...................	146	126	129	132	140	135	139	139
Land								
Passengers [2, 3]...................	397,312	381,477	333,652	329,998	326,693	317,765	289,048	299,004
Autos [2]...................	127,095	129,603	118,307	120,376	121,419	121,654	119,372	112,428
Rail containers...................	2,157	2,257	2,430	2,472	2,588	2,655	2,735	2,737
Truck containers [4]...................	10,397	11,001	11,129	11,163	11,252	11,308	11,489	11,459
Sea								
Passengers [5]...................	10,990	11,291	12,224	15,127	22,234	26,228	26,223	27,059
Vessels [6]...................	211	215	212	204	142	113	168	170
Vessel containers [7]...................	5,813	5,944	7,248	9,092	9,796	11,341	11,622	11,703

[1] A commercial aircraft is any aircraft transporting passengers and/or cargo for some payment or other consideration, including money or services rendered. [2] See Table 1285 for more details. [3] Includes pedestrians. [4] Truck containers—number of trucks entering the U.S. [5] Does not include passengers on ferries. [6] Includes every description of water craft or other contrivance used or capable of being used as a means of transportation on water, does not include aircraft. [7] Number of vessel containers.

Source: U.S. Department of Homeland Security, Customs and Border Protection, "About CBP, Statistics and Accomplishments, National Workload Statistics, 2000–2007," <http://www.cbp.gov/xp/cgov/about/accomplish/previous_year/national_workload_stats.xml>.

Table 546. Prohibited Items Intercepted at U.S. Airport Screening Checkpoints: 2004 to 2008

[Passengers boarding aircraft in thousands (703,692 represents 703,692,000). For the calendar year. Transportation Security Administration (TSA) assumed responsibility for airport security on February 17, 2002, and by November 19, 2002, TSA assumed control over all passenger screenings from private contractors]

Year	2004	2005	2006	2007	2008
Passengers boarding aircraft, total [1]...................	**703,692**	**738,628**	**744,728**	**769,622**	**743,313**
Domestic...................	641,470	670,417	671,799	693,372	665,734
International...................	62,222	68,211	72,929	76,250	77,580
Total prohibited items (number)...................	**7,104,095**	**15,886,404**	**13,709,684**	**6,516,026**	**(NA)**
Knife [2]...................	2,055,404	1,822,892	1,607,125	1,056,691	([9])
Other cutting items [3]...................	3,409,888	3,276,941	163,419	101,387	([9])
Club [4]...................	28,998	20,531	12,296	9,443	([9])
Box cutter...................	22,430	21,319	15,999	11,908	([9])
Firearm [5]...................	254	850	820	1,416	902
Incendiary [6]...................	697,606	374,487	94,097	73,670	116,200
Lighters [7]...................	178	9,420,991	11,616,688	5,124,344	([9])
Other [8]...................	889,337	949,243	200,060	137,167	([9])

NA Not available. [1] Data come from Airlines for America (formerly the Air Transport Association). Data are for U.S. passenger and cargo airlines only. [2] Knife includes any length and type except round-bladed, butter, and plastic cutlery. [3] Other cutting instruments refer to scissors, screwdrivers, swords, sabers, and ice picks, etc. [4] Club refers to baseball bats, night sticks, billy clubs, bludgeons, etc. [5] Firearm refers to items like pistols, revolvers, rifles, automatic weapons, shotguns, parts of guns and firearms. [6] Incendiaries refer to categories of ammunition and gunpowder, flammables/irritants, and explosives. [7] As of April 14, 2005, passengers are prohibited from carrying all lighters on their person or in carry-on luggage or onboard an airplane. [8] Other refers to categories of ammunition and gunpower, dangerous objects, fireworks, replica weapons, and tools. [9] The data for this prohibited item category are no longer collected as of August 8, 2008.

Source: U.S. Department of Homeland Security, Transportation Security Administration, unpublished data, June 2009, <http://www.tsa.gov>; Airlines for America, Washington, DC; "Annual Traffic and Operations: U.S. Airlines" (copyright), <http://www.airlines.org/pages/home.aspx/>.

Table 547. Seizure Statistics for Intellectual Property Rights (IPR) Violations by Commodity and Trading Partner: 2010 and 2011

[In thousands of dollars (188,125 represents $188,125,000, except as indicated). Customs and Border Protection (CBP) is dedicated to protecting against the importation of goods which infringe/violate Intellectual Property Rights (IPR) by devoting substantial resources toward identifying and seizing shipments of infringing articles]

Commodity	2010	2011	Trading partner	2010	2011
Number of IPR seizures...................	19,959	24,792	China...................	124,681	109,996
Total domestic value of IPR seizures [1]...........	188,125	178,323	Hong Kong...................	26,173	32,156
Consumer electronics [2]...................	33,588	38,993	India...................	1,571	4,535
Footwear...................	45,750	25,253	Pakistan...................	(NA)	3,955
Pharmaceuticals...................	5,662	16,848	Taiwan...................	1,138	2,288
Media [3]...................	12,681	15,567	Switzerland...................	(NA)	1,407
Wearing apparel...................	18,682	14,756	Malaysia...................	1,286	1,286
Watches /parts...................	7,848	8,435	Korea, South...................	1,049	714
Computers/technology components...........	9,502	7,814	Jordan...................	7,713	(NA)
Toys/electronic games...................	(NA)	7,597	Canada...................	609	(NA)
Handbags/wallets/backpacks...................	15,422	(NA)	Vietnam...................	742	(NA)
All other commodities...................	38,990	43,060	All other countries...................	23,163	21,986

NA Not available. [1] Domestic value is the cost of the seized goods, plus the costs of shipping and importing the goods into the U.S. and an amount for profit. [2] Consumer electronics include cell phones and accessories, radios, power strips, electrical tools and appliances. [3] Includes motion pictures on tape, laser disc, and DVD; interactive and computer software on CD-ROM and floppy discs; and music on CD or tape.

Source: U.S. Department of Homeland Security, Customs and Border Protection, "Import, Commercial Enforcement, Intellectual Property Rights, Seizure Statistics," <http://www.cbp.gov/xp/cgov/trade/priority_trade/ipr/ipr_communications/seizure/>.

Social Insurance and Human Services

This section presents data related to government expenditures for social insurance and human services; government programs for Old-Age, Survivors, Disability, and Health Insurance (OASDHI); government employee retirement; private pension plans; government unemployment and temporary disability insurance; federal supplemental security income payments and aid to the needy; child and other welfare services; and federal food programs. Also included here are selected data on workers' compensation and vocational rehabilitation, child support, child care, charity contributions, and philanthropic trusts and foundations.

The principal source for these data is the Social Security Administration's *Annual Statistical Supplement to the Social Security Bulletin* which presents current data on many of the programs.

Social insurance under the Social Security Act—Programs established by the Social Security Act provide protection against wage loss resulting from retirement, prolonged disability, death, or unemployment, and protection against the cost of medical care during old age and disability. The federal OASDI program provides monthly benefits to retired or disabled insured workers and their dependents and to survivors of insured workers. To be eligible, a worker must have had a specified period of employment in which OASDI taxes were paid. The age of eligibility for full retirement benefits had been 65 years old for many years. However, for persons born in 1938 or later that age gradually increases until it reaches age 67 for those born after 1959. Reduced benefits may be obtained as early as age 62. The worker's spouse is under the same limitations. Survivor benefits are payable to dependents of deceased insured workers. Disability benefits are payable to an insured worker under full retirement age with a prolonged disability and to the disabled worker's dependents on the same basis as dependents of retired workers. Disability benefits are provided at age 50 to the disabled widow or widower of a deceased worker who was fully insured at the time of death. Disabled children, aged 18 or older, of retired, disabled, or deceased workers are also eligible for benefits. A lump sum benefit is generally payable on the death of an insured worker to a spouse or minor children. For information on the Medicare program, see Section 3, Health and Nutrition.

Retirement, survivors, disability, and hospital insurance benefits are funded by a payroll tax on annual earnings (up to a maximum share of earnings set by law) of workers, employers, and the self-employed. The maximum taxable earnings are adjusted annually to reflect increasing wage levels (see Table 554). Effective January 1994, there is no dollar limit on wages and self-employment income subject to the hospital insurance tax. Tax receipts and benefit payments are administered through federal trust funds. Special benefits for uninsured persons; hospital benefits for persons aged 65 and over with specified amounts of social security coverage less than that required for cash benefit eligibility; and that part of the cost of supplementary medical insurance not financed by contributions from participants are all financed from federal general revenues.

Unemployment insurance is presently administered by the U.S. Employment and Training Administration and each state's employment security agency. By agreement with the U.S. Secretary of Labor, state agencies also administer unemployment compensation for eligible ex-military personnel and federal employees. Under state unemployment insurance laws, benefits related to an individual's past earnings are paid to unemployed eligible workers. State laws vary concerning the length of time benefits are paid and their amount. In most states, benefits are payable for 26 weeks and, during periods of high unemployment, extended benefits are payable under a federal-state program to those who have exhausted their regular state benefits. Some states also supplement the basic benefit with allowances for dependents.

Unemployment insurance is funded by a federal unemployment tax levied on the taxable payrolls of most employers. Taxable payroll under the federal act and three state or territory laws is the first $7,000 in wages paid each worker during a year. Fifty states or territories have taxable payrolls above $7,000. Employers are allowed a percentage credit of taxable payroll for contributions paid to states under state unemployment insurance laws. The remaining percent of the federal tax finances administrative costs, the federal share of extended benefits, and advances to states. About 97 percent of wage and salary workers are covered by unemployment insurance.

Retirement programs for government employees—The Civil Service Retirement System (CSRS) and the Federal Employees' Retirement System (FERS) are the two major programs providing old-age, disability, and survivor annuities for federal civilian employees. In general, employees hired after December 31, 1983, are covered under FERS and the Social Security program (OASDHI), and employees on staff prior to that date are members of CSRS and are covered under Medicare. CSRS employees were offered the option of transferring to FERS during 1987 and 1998. There are separate retirement systems for the uniformed services (supplementing OASDHI) and for certain special groups of federal employees. State and local government employees are covered for the most part by state and local retirement systems similar to the federal programs. In many jurisdictions these benefits supplement OASDHI coverage.

Workers' compensation—All states provide protection against work-connected injuries and deaths, although some states exclude certain workers (e.g., domestic workers). Federal laws cover federal employees, private employees in the District of Columbia, and longshoremen and harbor workers. In addition, the Department of Labor administers "black lung" benefit programs for coal miners disabled by pneumoconiosis and for specified dependents and survivors. Specified occupational diseases are compensable to some extent. In most states, benefits are related to the worker's salary. The benefits may or may not be augmented by dependents' allowances or automatically adjusted to prevailing wage levels.

Income support—Income support programs are designed to provide benefits for persons with limited income and resources. The Supplemental Security Income (SSI) program and Temporary Assistance for Needy Families (TANF) program are the major programs providing monthly payments. In addition, a number of programs provide money payments or in-kind benefits for special needs or purposes. Several programs offer food and nutritional services. Also, various federal-state programs provide energy assistance, public housing, and subsidized housing to individuals and families with low incomes. General assistance may also be available at the state or local level.

The SSI program, administered by the Social Security Administration, provides income support to persons aged 65 or older and to blind or disabled adults and children. Eligibility requirements and federal payment standards are nationally uniform. Most states supplement the basic SSI payment for all or selected categories of persons.

The Personal Responsibility and Work Opportunity Reconciliation Act of 1996 contained provisions that replaced the Aid to Families With Dependent Children (AFDC), Job Opportunities and Basic Skills (JOBS), and Emergency Assistance programs with the TANF block grant program. This law contains strong work requirements, comprehensive child support enforcement, support for families moving from welfare to work, and other features. The TANF program became effective as soon as each state submitted a complete implementation plan, but no later than July 1, 1997. The older AFDC program provided cash assistance based on need, income, resources, and family size.

Federal food stamp program—Under the Supplemental Nutrition Assistance Program (SNAP), formerly known as the food stamp program, single persons and those living in households meeting nationwide standards for income and assets may receive benefit payments redeemable for food at most retail food stores through electronic benefit transfer. The monthly amount of benefits or allotments a unit receives is determined by household size and income. Households without income receive the determined monthly cost of a nutritionally adequate diet for their household size. This amount is updated to account for food price increases. Households with income receive

the difference between the amount of a nutritionally adequate diet and 30 percent of their income, after certain allowable deductions.

To qualify for the program, a household must have less than $2,000 in disposable assets ($3,250 if one member is aged 60 or older), gross income below 130 percent of the official poverty guidelines for the household size, and net income below 100 percent of the poverty guidelines. Households with a person aged 60 or older or a disabled person receiving SSI, social security, state general assistance, or veterans' disability benefits may have gross income exceeding 130 percent of the poverty guidelines. All households in which all members receive TANF or SSI are categorically eligible for SNAP without meeting these income or resource criteria. Households are certified for varying lengths of time, depending on their income sources and individual circumstances.

Health and welfare services—Programs providing health and welfare services are aided through federal grants to states for child welfare services, vocational rehabilitation, activities for the aged, maternal and child health services, maternity and infant care projects, comprehensive health services, and a variety of public health activities. For information about the Medicaid program, see Section 3, Health and Nutrition.

Noncash benefits—The U.S. Census Bureau annually collects data on the characteristics of recipients of noncash (in-kind) benefits to supplement the collection of annual money income data in the Current Population Survey (see text, Section 1, Population, and Section 13, Income, Expenditures, Poverty, and Wealth). Noncash benefits are those benefits received in a form other than money which serve to enhance or improve the economic well-being of the recipient. As for money income, the data for noncash benefits are for the calendar year prior to the date of the interview. The major categories of noncash benefits covered are public transfers (e.g., food stamps, school lunch, public housing, and Medicaid) and employer or union-provided benefits to employees.

Statistical reliability—For discussion of statistical collection, estimation, and sampling procedures and measures of statistical reliability applicable to Social Security Administration and Census Bureau data, see Appendix III.

Table 548. Selected Benefit Payments to Individuals by Function: 1970 to 2010

[In billions of dollars (108 represents $108,000,000,000).The employee benefit system is composed of voluntary and mandatory programs which are employment-based and financed primarily from employment-based contributions]

Source and sector	1970	1980	1990	1995	2000	2002	2003	2004	2005	2006	2007	2008	2009	2010
All benefits	**108**	**422**	**1,027**	**1,493**	**1,909**	**2,251**	**2,393**	**2,559**	**2,721**	**2,912**	**3,107**	**3,289**	**3,613**	**3,820**
Retirement income benefits	51	202	482	660	864	977	1,023	1,092	1,158	1,265	1,359	1,386	1,478	1,537
Social security—old-age, survivors, and disability insurance	31	119	244	328	401	447	464	486	513	544	576	606	665	690
Private employer pension and profit sharing	7	35	136	191	271	311	323	355	376	433	476	454	465	479
Public employer retirement plans	12	48	102	141	192	219	237	252	269	287	308	326	348	368
Federal civilian employee retirement [1]	3	16	32	39	50	53	55	58	62	67	72	74	78	81
State and local government retirement	4	15	41	65	100	121	133	142	151	162	174	186	200	216
Military retirement [2]	3	13	22	28	33	36	41	43	46	49	52	56	59	60
Railroad retirement	2	5	7	8	8	9	9	9	9	10	10	10	11	11
Health benefits	22	99	300	456	596	705	767	834	901	986	1,044	1,109	1,173	1,231
Medicare hospital insurance and supplementary medical insurance	7	36	108	181	219	259	277	305	332	399	428	462	494	518
Group health insurance	15	62	191	274	376	444	488	528	567	585	614	645	676	709
Military health insurance [3]	–	–	2	1	1	2	2	2	2	3	2	3	3	4
Other employee benefits	17	51	88	103	113	156	162	148	147	148	155	180	271	286
Unemployment insurance [4]	4	16	18	22	21	54	53	36	32	30	33	51	131	139
Workers' compensation [5]	3	13	38	43	48	53	56	57	56	55	57	59	59	60
Group life insurance [6]	3	7	12	16	17	18	18	18	19	20	20	20	24	25
Miscellaneous disability [6]	1	3	4	3	4	4	4	5	5	5	6	6	6	6
Veterans' benefits [7]	7	13	16	19	23	28	30	32	35	37	40	44	50	56
Public assistance [8]	18	70	157	275	336	413	441	485	515	513	549	614	691	765

– Represents or rounds to zero. [1] Consists of civil service, foreign service, Public Health Service officers, Tennessee Valley Authority, and several small retirement programs. [2] Includes the U.S. Coast Guard. [3] Consists of payments for medical services for dependents of active duty military personnel at nonmilitary facilities. [4] Consists of state, railroad employee, and federal employee unemployment benefits; special unemployment benefits; and supplemental unemployment benefits. [5] Includes payments from private, federal, and state and local workers' compensation funds. [6] Includes federal black-lung payments and payments from state and local temporary disability insurance. [7] Consists of pension and disability, readjustment, and other veterans' benefits. [8] Consists of federal benefits (food stamp benefits, Supplemental Security Income, direct relief, earned income tax credit, payments to nonprofit institutions, aid to students, and payments for medical services for retired military personnel and their dependents at nonmilitary facilities) and state benefits (medical care, Aid to Families with Dependent Children, Supplemental Security Income, general assistance, energy assistance, emergency assistance, and medical insurance premium payments on behalf of indigents). Financed from state and federal general revenues.

Source: Employee Benefit Research Institute, Washington, DC, *EBRI Databook on Employee Benefits*, and unpublished data (copyright). EBRI tabulations based on U.S. Department of Commerce, Bureau of Economic Analysis. See also <http://www.ebri.org/>.

Table 549. Government Transfer Payments to Individuals—Summary: 1990 to 2010

[In billions of dollars (566.1 represents $566,100,000,000)]

Year	Transfer payments, total	Retirement and disability insurance benefits	Medical payments	Income maintenance benefits	Unemployment insurance benefits	Veterans benefits	Federal education and training assistance payments [1]	Other [2]
1990	566.1	263.9	188.8	63.5	18.2	17.7	12.3	1.7
1995	849.8	350.0	338.6	100.4	21.8	20.5	17.2	1.2
1998	940.9	391.2	383.4	101.1	19.9	23.3	20.5	1.6
1999	975.7	402.4	400.7	104.8	20.7	24.1	21.3	1.7
2000	1,027.8	424.5	427.2	106.3	21.0	25.0	21.9	2.0
2002	1,232.1	474.4	523.8	120.7	53.7	29.5	27.9	2.1
2003	1,299.0	493.5	555.8	133.2	53.6	31.8	28.5	2.7
2004	1,381.2	517.1	610.3	144.2	37.1	34.0	31.2	7.3
2005	1,465.1	545.4	653.2	159.6	32.3	36.4	33.8	4.5
2006	1,565.6	576.9	717.0	163.4	30.9	38.9	35.9	2.7
2007	1,669.8	609.1	771.4	172.3	33.4	41.7	39.5	2.6
2008	1,823.5	639.7	821.2	216.7	51.8	45.0	45.1	4.0
2009	2,079.5	699.2	890.4	223.3	131.4	51.5	56.6	27.1
2010	2,220.9	725.9	948.3	264.5	139.5	57.9	67.9	16.9

[1] See footnote 9, Table 550. [2] See footnote 10, Table 550.

Source: U.S. Bureau of Economic Analysis, "Regional Accounts Data, Annual State Personal Income," <http://www.bea.gov/iTable/index_nipa.cfm>, accessed July 2012. See also <http://www.bea.gov/regional/spi/>.

Table 550. Government Transfer Payments to Individuals by Type: 1990 to 2010

[In millions of dollars (566,100 represents $566,100,000,000)]

Item	1990	2000	2005	2007	2008	2009	2010
Total	566,100	1,027,827	1,465,125	1,669,795	1,823,460	2,079,548	2,220,915
Retirement & disability insurance benefit payments	263,888	424,461	545,361	609,100	639,718	699,189	725,926
Old-age, survivors, & disability insurance	244,135	401,393	512,728	575,648	605,542	664,471	690,177
Railroad retirement and disability	7,221	8,267	9,191	9,813	10,068	10,630	10,778
Workers' compensation payments (federal & state)	8,618	10,898	15,866	15,794	15,831	15,670	16,108
Other government disability insurance & retirement [1]	3,914	3,903	7,576	7,845	8,277	8,418	8,863
Medical payments	188,808	427,194	653,193	771,361	821,180	890,416	948,254
Medicare	107,638	219,117	331,924	427,556	461,634	493,827	518,431
Public assistance medical care [2]	78,176	205,021	315,032	336,884	352,028	388,258	420,466
Military medical insurance [3]	2,994	3,056	6,237	6,921	7,518	8,331	9,357
Income maintenance benefit payments	63,481	106,285	159,624	172,255	216,660	223,320	264,544
Supplemental Security Income (SSI)	16,670	31,675	38,285	42,285	44,102	47,641	48,952
Family assistance [4]	19,187	18,440	18,216	18,334	19,255	20,554	20,668
Supplemental Nutrition Assistance Program	14,741	14,565	29,492	30,920	37,034	54,763	66,514
Other income maintenance [5]	12,883	41,605	73,631	80,716	116,269	100,362	128,410
Unemployment insurance benefit payments	18,208	20,989	32,276	33,381	51,800	131,391	139,495
State unemployment insurance compensation	17,644	20,223	31,001	32,006	50,096	129,103	136,829
Unemployment compensation for federal civilian employees	215	226	224	216	255	439	537
Unemployment compensation for railroad employees	89	81	72	83	84	179	116
Unemployment compensation for veterans	144	181	446	406	467	840	1154
Other unemployment compensation [6]	116	278	533	670	898	830	859
Veterans benefit payments	17,687	25,004	36,371	41,676	45,008	51,486	57,853
Veterans pension and disability	15,550	21,966	32,505	37,721	40,715	45,533	48,437
Veterans readjustment [7]	257	1,322	2,256	2,421	2,749	4,432	7,939
Veterans life insurance benefits	1,868	1,706	1,596	1,517	1,523	1,494	1,445
Other assistance to veterans [8]	12	10	14	17	21	27	32
Federal education & training assistance payments [9]	12,286	21,851	33,796	39,450	45,057	56,604	67,895
Other payments to individuals [10]	1,742	2,043	4,504	2,572	4,037	27,142	16,948

[1] Consists largely of temporary disability payments, pension benefit guaranty payments, and black lung payments. [2] Consists of Medicaid and other medical vendor payments. [3] Consists of payments made under the TriCare Management Program (formerly called CHAMPUS) for the medical care of dependents of active duty military personnel and of retired military personnel and their dependents at nonmilitary medical facilities. [4] Through 1990, consists of emergency assistance and aid to families with dependent children. Beginning with 2000, consists of benefits—generally known as temporary assistance for needy families—provided under the Personal Responsibility and Work Opportunity Reconciliation Act of 1996. [5] Consists largely of general assistance, expenditures for food under the supplemental program for women, infants, and children; refugee assistance; foster home care and adoption assistance; earned income tax credits; and energy assistance. [6] Consists of trade readjustment allowance payments, Redwood Park benefit payments, public service employment benefit payments, and transitional benefit payments. [7] Consists largely of veterans' readjustment benefit payments, educational assistance to spouses and children of disabled or deceased veterans, payments to paraplegics, and payments for autos and conveyances for disabled veterans. [8] Consists largely of state and local government payments to veterans. [9] Excludes veterans. Consists largely of federal fellowship payments (National Science Foundation fellowships and traineeships, subsistence payments to state maritime academy cadets, and other federal fellowships), interest subsidy on higher education loans, basic educational opportunity grants, and Job Corps payments. [10] Consists largely of Bureau of Indian Affairs payments, education exchange payments, Alaska Permanent Fund dividend payments, compensation of survivors of public safety officers, compensation of victims of crime, disaster relief payments, compensation for Japanese internment, and other special payments to individuals.

Source: U.S. Bureau of Economic Analysis, "Regional Accounts Data, Annual State Personal Income," <http://www.bea.gov/iTable/index_nipa.cfm>, accessed July 2012. See also <http://www.bea.gov/regional/spi/>.

Table 551. Government Transfer Payments to Individuals by State: 2000 to 2010

[In millions of dollars (1,027,827 represents $1,027,827,000,000)]

State	2000, total	2009, total	2010							
			Total	Retire-ment and disability insurance benefits	Medical payments	Income mainte-nance benefits	Unem-ployment insurance benefits	Veterans benefits	Federal educa-tion and training assistance pay-ments [1]	Other [2]
U.S.	1,027,827	2,079,548	2,220,915	725,926	948,254	264,544	139,495	57,853	67,895	16,948
AL.	16,803	34,112	36,885	13,061	14,826	5,049	1,162	1,362	1,243	183
AK.	2,950	4,540	4,885	987	1,948	591	270	208	61	820
AZ.	15,948	42,568	45,884	14,917	19,587	4,878	1,899	1,336	2,837	431
AR.	10,168	21,524	22,778	8,020	9,456	2,680	938	852	715	117
CA.	114,879	231,145	252,818	72,843	110,045	33,393	22,150	5,009	7,106	2,271
CO.	11,144	25,009	27,622	9,518	10,747	2,789	2,216	1,166	970	215
CT.	14,222	26,745	28,140	9,053	12,997	2,406	2,426	391	636	231
DE.	2,908	6,433	6,872	2,459	3,092	598	329	159	196	39
DC.	2,695	4,745	5,325	914	3,009	740	333	86	215	28
FL.	64,580	134,582	145,252	50,518	61,280	16,612	6,574	4,466	4,784	1,018
GA.	24,190	54,163	58,290	19,287	21,546	9,195	3,375	2,170	2,307	410
HI.	3,887	8,015	8,814	2,995	3,458	1,230	597	342	143	49
ID.	3,868	8,938	9,691	3,671	3,661	1,060	598	327	308	65
IL.	42,291	83,048	89,271	28,484	38,097	10,519	7,189	1,366	2,847	768
IN.	20,472	42,543	44,487	16,720	17,169	4,747	2,894	920	1,727	309
IA.	10,242	19,781	20,788	7,868	8,068	2,005	1,082	451	1,195	118
KS.	9,091	17,470	18,294	6,843	7,251	1,976	1,144	483	474	123
KY.	16,058	32,536	34,050	11,569	13,826	4,375	1,715	1,017	1,366	182
LA.	16,744	31,795	33,637	9,867	15,908	4,925	862	890	1,044	141
ME.	5,351	10,808	10,719	3,715	4,692	1,160	420	467	215	51
MD.	17,140	35,040	37,551	12,055	17,369	3,991	1,902	1,006	1,046	182
MA.	26,575	52,208	54,356	15,317	25,780	6,050	4,835	944	1,018	412
MI.	36,987	75,351	79,210	27,910	31,120	9,708	5,853	1,339	2,475	805
MN.	16,106	34,868	36,862	12,129	16,152	3,526	2,572	985	1,256	242
MS.	10,916	21,787	23,435	7,385	10,443	3,550	637	587	715	118
MO.	21,121	41,849	43,963	15,517	19,219	4,551	1,928	1,178	1,315	256
MT.	3,197	6,309	6,783	2,681	2,606	635	329	293	192	47
NE.	5,753	10,654	11,221	4,272	4,610	1,104	357	500	331	48
NV.	5,580	14,634	15,842	5,478	5,605	1,701	1,977	530	342	208
NH.	4,003	8,070	8,376	3,461	3,408	629	364	264	207	43
NJ.	33,512	63,331	67,602	22,404	28,398	5,882	7,614	943	1,713	648
NM.	6,035	14,167	15,163	4,506	6,524	2,089	764	654	455	170
NY.	96,578	168,485	177,201	47,545	91,382	21,642	9,260	2,083	4,283	1,006
NC.	28,335	63,807	66,749	23,004	26,295	8,284	4,605	2,371	1,598	592
ND.	2,339	4,096	4,338	1,701	1,782	419	119	145	139	33
OH.	43,906	83,935	87,558	30,558	36,306	10,381	4,700	1,679	3,351	583
OK.	12,064	25,338	26,793	9,346	10,977	3,241	950	1,382	769	128
OR.	12,330	26,330	28,009	10,230	10,182	3,095	2,570	971	700	261
PA.	55,370	101,106	107,197	36,380	47,324	9,785	8,267	1,865	2,769	808
RI.	4,702	8,709	9,138	2,897	4,080	966	705	184	246	60
SC.	14,601	32,456	34,756	12,331	13,339	4,356	1,689	1,294	1,494	254
SD.	2,499	4,757	5,041	1,920	2,086	540	86	206	145	58
TN.	21,977	44,475	48,249	16,325	20,476	6,604	1,709	1,410	1,463	263
TX.	60,244	136,608	149,399	44,638	65,849	21,387	7,023	5,421	4,266	816
UT.	5,025	11,509	12,444	4,558	4,450	1,591	768	333	647	96
VT.	2,308	4,911	5,116	1,672	2,322	577	224	130	166	26
VA.	20,239	43,481	46,595	17,330	18,283	5,356	1,598	2,319	1,521	188
WA.	21,190	43,918	47,704	17,082	16,721	5,835	4,311	1,688	1,488	578
WV.	8,909	15,637	16,277	6,088	6,758	1,813	523	603	433	59
WI.	18,185	37,954	40,048	14,481	16,441	4,069	2,873	961	856	366
WY.	1,613	3,267	3,437	1,414	1,304	258	212	119	106	24

[1] Excludes veterans. Consists largely of federal fellowship payments (National Science Foundation, fellowships and traineeships, subsistence payments to state maritime academy cadets, and other federal fellowships), interest subsidy on higher education loans, basic educational opportunity grants, and Job Corps payments. [2] Consists largely of Bureau of Indian Affairs payments, education exchange payments, Alaska Permanent Fund dividend payments, compensation of survivors of public safety officers, compensation of victims of crime, disaster relief payments, compensation for Japanese internment, and other special payments to individuals.

Source: U.S. Bureau of Economic Analysis, "Regional Accounts Data, Annual State Personal Income," <http://www.bea.gov/iTable/index_nipa.cfm>, accessed July 2012. See also <http://www.bea.gov/regional/spi/>.

Table 552. Number of Persons With Income by Specified Source of Income: 2010

[In thousands (211,492 represents 211,492,000). Persons 15 years old and over as of March of following year. Based on Current Population Survey (CPS); see text, Sections 1 and 13, and Appendix III]

Source of income	Total persons with income	Under 65 years	65 years and over	White [1]	Black [2]	Hispanic origin [3]
Total...	**211,492**	**173,621**	**37,872**	**172,954**	**24,263**	**27,087**
Earnings...	153,298	145,298	8,000	125,428	16,997	21,772
Wages and salary..............................	144,301	137,478	6,823	117,588	16,459	20,687
Nonfarm self-employment....................	11,899	10,664	1,235	10,285	820	1,344
Farm self-employment.........................	2,025	1,755	270	1,807	128	107
Unemployment compensation....................	12,448	11,944	505	9,814	1,819	1,684
State or local only.............................	11,750	11,281	469	9,257	1,720	1,615
Combinations..................................	699	663	36	557	99	70
Workers' compensation..........................	1,469	1,347	121	1,174	179	208
State payments................................	521	493	27	428	47	75
Employment insurance........................	626	581	46	479	91	90
Own insurance.................................	39	36	3	36	1	5
Other..	337	286	51	279	44	53
Social Security....................................	44,515	11,338	33,177	38,074	4,540	3,088
SSI (Supplemental Security Income)..........	5,562	4,493	1,069	3,644	1,480	868
Public assistance, total..........................	2,224	2,121	103	1,360	676	564
TANF/welfare (AFDC) only [4]...............	1,503	1,469	35	889	486	420
Other assistance only.........................	660	591	69	442	162	131
Both...	61	61	–	29	29	12
Veterans' benefits................................	2,883	1,789	1,094	2,334	383	158
Disability only.................................	1,742	1,220	523	1,421	223	95
Survivors only.................................	241	79	162	208	24	12
Pension only...................................	585	261	324	464	85	36
Education only.................................	74	74	–	58	4	7
Other only......................................	140	86	54	104	27	3
Combinations..................................	101	71	31	79	19	5
Means-tested..................................	585	365	220	446	106	50
Nonmeans-tested..............................	2,298	1,424	874	1,888	277	108
Survivors benefits [5]............................	2,942	1,041	1,901	2,634	203	137
Company or union..............................	1,297	311	987	1,191	73	59
Federal government............................	211	60	151	172	26	10
Military retirement.............................	238	60	178	202	14	3
Disability benefits [5]............................	1,547	1,338	210	1,219	231	194
Workers' compensation........................	79	65	14	55	21	13
Company or union..............................	385	336	50	317	53	41
Federal government............................	146	114	32	118	23	11
Military retirement.............................	73	55	18	52	19	3
State or local government.....................	306	287	20	249	28	62
Pension income [5]...............................	16,975	5,464	11,511	14,844	1,497	683
Company or union retirement.................	11,081	3,286	7,795	9,772	945	490
Federal government retirement...............	1,858	664	1,194	1,572	193	77
Military retirement.............................	1,319	693	627	1,072	173	40
State or local government retirement........	4,840	1,868	2,972	4,256	388	238
Property income [6]...............................	92,885	72,981	19,904	81,711	5,408	5,709
Interest...	86,887	68,362	18,525	76,574	4,985	5,292
Dividends.......................................	30,134	22,958	7,176	27,385	1,051	1,011
Rents, royalties, estates or trusts...........	10,707	7,573	3,134	9,572	501	671
Educational assistance [5].......................	9,578	9,544	34	7,049	1,710	1,192
Pell grant only.................................	3,165	3,155	9	2,128	803	471
Other government only........................	1,442	1,437	5	1,070	262	202
Scholarships only.............................	2,439	2,426	13	1,906	280	251
Child support.....................................	4,749	4,719	29	3,604	910	642
Alimony...	392	334	58	355	19	32
Financial assistance from outside the household.................	2,407	2,223	184	1,809	318	301
Other income, not elsewhere classified........	1,070	871	199	890	84	63
Combinations of income types:						
Government transfer payments................	70,548	35,812	34,736	57,456	9,387	6,753
Public assistance or SSI or both.............	7,568	6,418	1,150	4,884	2,081	1,389

– Represents or rounds to zero. [1] Beginning with the 2003, CPS respondents could choose one or more races. "White" refers to people who reported White and did not report any other race category. The use of this single-race population does not imply that it is the preferred method of presenting or analyzing data. Information on people who reported more than one race, such as "Asian and Black or African American," is available from Census 2000 through American FactFinder. [2] "Black" refers to people who reported Black and did not report any other race category. [3] Persons of Hispanic origin may be of any race. [4] TANF— Temporary Assistance for Needy Families Program; AFDC—Aid to Families With Dependent Children Program. [5] Includes other sources not shown separately. [6] Includes estates and trusts that it is the preferred method of presenting or analyzing data. Information on people who reported as survivor benefits.

Source: U.S. Census Bureau: "Table PINC-09. Source of Income in 2010—Number With Income and Mean Income of Specified Type in 2010 of People 15 Years Old and Over, by Age, Race, Hispanic Origin and Sex," published September 2011; <http://www.census.gov/hhes/www/cpstables/032011/perinc/new09_000.htm>.

Table 553. Persons Living in Households Receiving Selected Noncash Benefits: 2010

[In thousands (305,688 represents 305,688,000), except percent. Persons, as of March 2011, who lived with someone (a nonrelative or a relative) who received aid. Not every person tallied here received the aid themselves. Persons living in households receiving more than one type of aid are counted only once. Excludes members of the Armed Forces except those living off post or with their families on post. Population controls for 2010 based on Census 2000 and an expanded sample of households. Based on Current Population Survey (CPS); see text, Section 1 and Appendix III. SNAP = Supplemental Nutrition Assistance Program]

Age, sex, and race	Total	In household that received means-tested assistance [1]		In household that received means-tested cash assistance		In household that received food stamps (SNAP)		In household in which one or more persons were covered by Medicaid		Lived in public or authorized housing	
		Number	Percent	Number	Percent	Number	Percent	Number	Percent	Number	Percent
Total....................	305,688	94,432	30.9	20,256	6.6	38,912	12.7	76,232	24.9	11,208	3.7
Under 18 years...........	74,494	34,557	46.4	5,958	8.0	15,437	20.7	28,499	38.3	4,079	5.5
18 to 24 years............	29,651	10,270	34.6	2,150	7.3	4,408	14.9	8,312	28.0	1,294	4.4
25 to 34 years............	41,584	13,160	31.6	2,437	5.9	5,689	13.7	10,889	26.2	1,446	3.5
35 to 44 years............	39,842	11,792	29.6	2,199	5.5	4,445	11.2	9,354	23.5	974	2.4
45 to 54 years............	43,954	10,248	23.3	2,679	6.1	3,833	8.7	8,125	18.5	1,014	2.3
55 to 59 years............	19,554	3,852	19.7	1,403	7.2	1,438	7.4	3,053	15.6	487	2.5
60 to 64 years............	17,430	3,290	18.9	1,244	7.1	1,211	6.9	2,580	14.8	437	2.5
65 years and over........	39,179	7,264	18.5	2,186	5.6	2,451	6.3	5,420	13.8	1,476	3.8
65 to 74 years...........	21,414	3,865	18.1	1,193	5.6	1,323	6.2	2,946	13.8	710	3.3
75 years and over.......	17,764	3,399	19.1	993	5.6	1,128	6.3	2,475	13.9	766	4.3
Male......................	150,413	44,583	29.6	9,407	6.3	17,673	11.7	35,904	23.9	4,613	3.1
Female....................	155,275	49,850	32.1	10,849	7.0	21,239	13.7	40,328	26.0	6,595	4.2
White alone [2]...........	243,013	66,232	27.3	12,819	5.3	25,640	10.6	53,387	22.0	5,731	2.4
Black alone [2]...........	38,965	20,068	51.5	5,541	14.2	10,156	26.1	16,014	41.1	4,533	11.6
Asian alone [2]...........	14,324	3,817	26.7	754	5.3	1,081	7.5	3,277	22.9	393	2.7
Hispanic [3]................	49,869	26,659	53.5	4,498	9.0	10,271	20.6	21,516	43.1	2,467	4.9
White alone, Non-Hispanic [2].........	197,203	41,900	21.2	8,925	4.5	16,455	8.3	33,840	17.2	3,614	1.8

[1] Means-tested assistance includes means-tested cash assistance, food stamps, Medicaid, and public or authorized housing. [2] Refers to people who reported specific race and did not report any other race category. [3] People of Hispanic origin may be of any race.

Source: U.S. Census Bureau, Current Population Reports, P60-239. See also <http://www.census.gov/hhes/www/poverty/index.html>.

Table 554. Social Security—Covered Employment, Earnings, and Contribution Rates: 1990 to 2011

[164.4 represents 164,400,000. Includes Puerto Rico, Virgin Islands, American Samoa, and Guam. Represents all reported employment. Data are estimated. OASDHI = Old-age, survivors, disability, and health insurance; SMI = Supplementary medical insurance]

Item	Unit	1990	1995	2000	2005	2007	2008	2009	2010	2011
Workers with insured status [1].........	Million	164.4	173.3	185.2	195.3	200.1	202.3	204.0	205.7	207.4
Male....................	Million	86.7	90.4	95.6	99.9	102.0	103.0	103.7	104.4	105.1
Female..................	Million	77.7	82.9	89.6	95.5	98.1	99.3	100.3	101.3	102.3
Under 25 years....................	Million	21.2	18.9	20.8	20.1	20.2	20.1	19.8	19.4	19.0
25 to 34 years....................	Million	41.6	39.4	36.6	36.4	36.8	37.2	37.7	38.2	38.6
35 to 44 years....................	Million	36.4	40.6	42.5	40.9	39.9	39.2	38.5	38.1	37.8
45 to 54 years....................	Million	23.0	29.6	35.8	40.2	41.5	42.0	42.2	42.3	42.1
55 to 59 years....................	Million	8.9	9.8	12.3	16.2	16.9	17.4	17.9	18.4	19.0
60 to 64 years....................	Million	8.7	8.6	9.5	11.9	13.5	14.2	14.7	15.4	15.9
65 to 69 years....................	Million	8.1	8.0	7.9	8.9	9.8	10.4	10.7	11.0	11.7
70 years and over....................	Million	16.5	18.5	19.8	20.9	21.5	21.9	22.4	22.9	23.4
Workers reported with—										
Taxable earnings [2]....................	Million	133	141	155	159	163	162	158	157	158
Maximum earnings [2].................	Million	8	8	10	10	10	10	8	8	9
Earnings in covered employment [2]...	Bil. dol.	2,716	3,407	4,840	5,693	6,381	6,491	6,193	6,322	6,595
Reported taxable [2]....................	Bil. dol.	2,359	2,920	4,009	4,764	5,268	5,434	5,276	5,320	5,466
Percent of total.....................	Percent	86.8	85.7	82.8	83.7	82.6	83.7	85.2	84.2	82.9
Average per worker:										
Total earnings [2]....................	Dollars	20,413	24,187	31,317	35,888	39,166	39,984	39,292	40,273	41,809
Taxable earnings [2]....................	Dollars	17,727	20,727	25,942	30,033	32,334	33,472	33,476	33,893	34,651
Annual maximum taxable earnings [3]............................	Dollars	51,300	61,200	76,200	90,000	97,500	102,000	106,800	106,800	106,800
Contribution rates for OASDHI: [4]										
Each employer and employee......	Percent	7.65	7.65	7.65	7.65	7.65	7.65	7.65	7.65	7.65
Self-employed [5]......................	Percent	15.30	15.30	15.30	15.30	15.30	15.30	15.30	15.30	15.30
SMI, monthly premium [6].............	Dollars	28.60	46.10	45.50	78.20	93.50	96.40	96.40	110.50	115.40

[1] Estimated number fully insured for retirement and/or survivor benefits as of end of year. [2] Includes self-employment. Averages per worker computed with unrounded earnings and worker amounts and may not agree with rounded table and amounts. [3] Beginning 1995, upper limit on earnings subject to health insurance taxes was repealed. [4] As of January 1, 2006, each employee and employer pays 7.65 percent and the self-employed pay 15.3 percent. [5] Self-employed pays 15.3 percent and half of the tax is deductible for income tax purposes and for computing self-employment income subject to social security tax. [6] As of January 1.

Source: U.S. Social Security Administration, *Annual Statistical Supplement to the Social Security Bulletin*. February 2012, See also <http://www.ssa.gov/policy/docs/statcomps/supplement/2012>.

Table 555. Social Security (OASDI)—Benefits by Type of Beneficiary: 1990 to 2011

[39,832 represents 39,832,000. A person eligible to receive more than one type of benefit is generally classified or counted only once as a retired-worker beneficiary. OASDI = Old-age, survivors, and disability insurance. See also headnote, Table 556, and Appendix III]

Type of beneficiary	1990	1995	2000	2005	2006	2007	2008	2009	2010	2011
Number of benefits [1] (1,000)	**39,832**	**43,387**	**45,415**	**48,434**	**49,123**	**49,865**	**50,898**	**52,523**	**54,032**	**55,404**
Retired workers [2] (1,000)	24,838	26,673	28,499	30,461	30,976	31,528	32,274	33,514	34,593	35,600
Disabled workers [3] (1,000)	3,011	4,185	5,042	6,519	6,807	7,099	7,427	7,788	8,204	8,576
Wives and husbands [2,4] (1,000)	3,367	3,290	2,963	2,680	2,632	2,585	2,525	2,502	2,477	2,456
Children (1,000)	3,187	3,734	3,803	4,025	4,041	4,051	4,132	4,231	4,313	4,375
Under age 18	2,497	2,956	2,976	3,130	3,133	3,120	3,118	3,158	3,209	3,245
Disabled children [5]	600	686	729	769	777	795	871	921	949	977
Students [6]	89	92	98	127	131	136	142	152	155	153
Of retired workers	422	442	459	488	490	494	525	561	580	594
Of deceased workers	1,776	1,884	1,878	1,903	1,899	1,892	1,915	1,921	1,913	1,907
Of disabled workers	989	1,409	1,466	1,633	1,652	1,665	1,692	1,748	1,820	1,874
Widowed mothers [7] (1,000)	304	275	203	178	171	165	160	160	158	158
Widows and widowers [2,8] (1,000)	5,111	5,226	4,901	4,569	4,494	4,436	4,380	4,327	4,286	4,239
Parents [2] (1,000)	6	4	3	2	2	2	2	2	2	2
Special benefits [9] (1,000)	7	1	(Z)	(Z)	(Z)	(Z)	(Z)	(Z)	(Z)	(Z)
AVERAGE MONTHLY BENEFIT, CURRENT DOLLARS										
Retired workers [2]	603	720	844	1,002	1,044	1,079	1,153	1,164	1,176	1,229
Retired worker and wife [2]	1,027	1,221	1,420	1,660	1,726	1,776	1,894	1,913	1,930	2,019
Disabled workers [3]	587	682	786	938	978	1,004	1,063	1,064	1,068	1,111
Wives and husbands [2,4]	298	354	416	485	502	516	551	556	561	587
Children of retired workers	259	322	395	493	518	538	568	570	577	603
Children of deceased workers	406	469	550	656	684	704	745	747	752	783
Children of disabled workers	164	183	228	279	290	299	318	318	318	330
Widowed mothers [7]	409	478	595	725	757	782	835	842	849	884
Widows and widowers, nondisabled [2]	556	680	810	967	1,008	1,040	1,112	1,124	1,134	1,185
Parents [2]	482	591	704	851	892	918	979	988	998	1,045
Special benefits [9]	167	192	217	247	256	261	276	276	276	286
AVERAGE MONTHLY BENEFIT, CONSTANT (2011) DOLLARS [10]										
Retired workers [2]	1,017	1,059	1,095	1,149	1,168	1,159	1,238	1,217	1,210	1,229
Retired worker and wife [2]	1,732	1,795	1,842	1,904	1,930	1,908	2,033	1,999	1,987	2,019
Disabled workers [3]	990	1,003	1,019	1,076	1,094	1,079	1,141	1,112	1,099	1,111
Wives and husbands [2,4]	503	520	540	556	561	554	592	581	578	587
Children of deceased workers	685	690	713	753	765	757	800	781	774	783
Widowed mothers [7]	690	703	772	831	847	840	896	879	874	884
Widows and widowers, nondisabled [2]	938	999	1,051	1,108	1,127	1,118	1,194	1,174	1,167	1,185
Number of benefits awarded (1,000)	**3,717**	**3,882**	**4,290**	**4,672**	**4,621**	**4,711**	**5,135**	**5,728**	**5,697**	**5,567**
Retired workers [2]	1,665	1,609	1,961	2,000	1,999	2,036	2,279	2,740	2,634	2,578
Disabled workers [3]	468	646	622	830	799	805	877	971	1,027	999
Wives and husbands [2,4]	379	322	385	379	378	364	395	429	409	399
Children	695	809	777	908	897	902	961	1,008	1,045	1,017
Widowed mothers [7]	58	52	40	38	36	34	33	33	32	30
Widows and widowers [2,8]	452	445	505	517	512	570	590	547	550	545
Parents [2]	(Z)	(Z)	(Z)	(Z)	(Z)	(Z)	(Z)	(Z)	(Z)	(Z)
Special benefits [9]	(Z)	(Z)	(Z)	(Z)	(Z)	(Z)	(Z)	(Z)	(Z)	(Z)
BENEFIT PAYMENTS DURING YEAR (bil. dol.)										
Total [11]	**247.8**	**332.6**	**407.6**	**520.8**	**552.8**	**585.0**	**615.4**	**675.5**	**701.6**	**725.1**
Monthly benefits [12]	247.6	332.4	407.4	520.6	552.6	584.8	615.2	675.3	701.4	724.9
Retired workers [2]	156.8	205.3	253.5	321.7	342.9	364.3	384.0	424.0	443.4	461.2
Disabled workers [3]	22.1	36.6	49.8	78.4	85.0	91.3	98.1	109.5	115.1	119.6
Wives and husbands [2,4]	14.5	17.9	19.4	20.5	21.5	22.1	22.6	24.2	24.6	24.8
Children	12.0	16.1	19.3	24.5	25.8	27.0	28.2	30.2	30.7	31.2
Under age 18	9.0	11.9	14.1	17.9	18.8	19.5	20.1	21.2	21.4	21.2
Disabled children [5]	2.5	3.6	4.6	5.8	6.1	6.5	6.9	7.8	8.0	8.7
Students [6]	0.5	0.6	0.7	0.8	1.0	1.0	1.1	1.2	1.3	1.3
Of retired workers	1.3	1.7	2.1	2.9	3.1	3.3	3.5	3.9	4.1	4.3
Of deceased workers	8.6	10.7	12.5	15.1	15.8	16.5	17.0	18.1	18.0	18.1
Of disabled workers	2.2	3.7	4.7	6.5	6.9	7.3	7.7	8.2	8.5	8.8
Widowed mothers [7]	1.4	1.6	1.4	1.5	1.6	1.6	1.6	1.6	1.6	1.6
Widows and widowers [2,8]	40.7	54.8	63.9	73.4	75.9	78.5	80.7	85.6	86.0	86.5
Parents [2]	(Z)	(Z)	(Z)	(Z)	(Z)	(Z)	(Z)	(Z)	(Z)	(Z)
Special benefits [9]	(Z)	(Z)	(Z)	(Z)	(Z)	(Z)	(Z)	(Z)	(Z)	(Z)
Lump sum	0.2	0.2	0.2	0.2	0.2	0.2	0.2	0.2	0.2	0.2

Z Fewer than 500 or less than $50 million. [1] Number of benefit payments in current-payment status, i.e., actually being made at a specified time with no deductions or with deductions amounting to less than a month's benefit. [2] 62 years and over. [3] Disabled workers under age 65. [4] Includes wife beneficiaries with entitled children in their care and entitled divorced wives. [5] 18 years old and over. Disability began before age 22. [6] Full-time students aged 18 and 19. [7] Includes surviving divorced mothers with entitled children in their care and widowed fathers with entitled children in their care. [8] Includes widows aged 60–61, surviving divorced wives aged 60 and over, disabled widows and widowers aged 50 and over; and widowers aged 60–61. [9] Benefits for persons aged 72 and over not insured under regular or transitional provisions of Social Security Act. [10] Constant dollar figures are based on the consumer price index (CPI-U) for December as published by the U.S. Bureau of Labor Statistics. [11] Represents total disbursements of benefit checks by the U.S. Department of the Treasury during the years specified. [12] Distribution by type estimated.

Source: U.S. Social Security Administration, *Annual Statistical Supplement to the Social Security Bulletin*. See also <http://www.ssa.gov/policy/docs/statcomps/supplement/2012>.

Table 556. Social Security—Beneficiaries, Annual Payments, and Average Monthly Benefit, 1990 to 2011, and by State and Other Areas, 2011

[Number of beneficiaries in current-payment status (39,832 represents 39,832,000) and annual and average monthly benefit as of December. Data based on 10-percent sample of administrative records. See also headnote, Table 555, and Appendix III]

Year, state, and other area	Number of beneficiaries (1,000)				Annual payments [2] (mil. dol.)				Average monthly benefit (dol.)		
	Total	Retired workers and dependents [1]	Survivors	Disabled workers and dependents	Total	Retired workers and dependents [1]	Survivors	Disabled workers and dependents	Retired workers [3]	Disabled workers	Widows and widowers [4]
1990................	39,832	28,369	7,197	4,266	247,796	172,042	50,951	24,803	603	587	557
2000................	45,417	31,761	6,981	6,675	407,431	274,645	77,848	54,938	845	787	810
2005................	48,446	33,488	6,650	8,307	520,561	345,094	90,073	85,394	1,002	938	967
2008................	50,898	35,169	6,456	9,273	615,152	409,503	99,348	106,301	1,153	1,063	1,112
2009................	52,523	36,419	6,410	9,694	685,299	451,579	105,380	118,329	1,164	1,064	1,124
2010................	54,032	37,489	6,358	10,184	701,436	471,505	105,740	124,191	1,176	1,068	1,134
2011, total [5, 6]	**55,404**	**38,486**	**6,305**	**10,613**	**724,943**	**489,698**	**106,310**	**128,935**	**1,229**	**1,111**	**1,185**
United States............	**53,972**	**37,536**	**6,082**	**10,354**	**712,932**	**482,835**	**103,815**	**126,282**	**(NA)**	**(NA)**	**(NA)**
Alabama................	1,037	623	132	282	13,156	7,753	2,058	3,345	1,199	1,091	1,126
Alaska..................	82	56	10	16	1,010	672	149	189	1,170	1,093	1,137
Arizona................	1,105	808	111	185	14,744	10,490	1,908	2,346	1,254	1,154	1,227
Arkansas..............	647	397	76	174	7,964	4,807	1,158	1,999	1,161	1,058	1,100
California..............	5,130	3,745	546	838	66,661	46,693	9,375	10,593	1,216	1,137	1,197
Colorado..............	721	525	76	121	9,382	6,572	1,317	1,493	1,215	1,118	1,206
Connecticut..........	630	471	62	98	9,111	6,684	1,174	1,253	1,347	1,152	1,329
Delaware..............	177	127	18	32	2,482	1,736	321	425	1,309	1,174	1,290
District of Columbia......	76	52	9	15	904	606	123	175	1,114	982	1,012
Florida................	3,894	2,884	383	628	50,986	36,668	6,580	7,738	1,221	1,119	1,211
Georgia................	1,524	1,016	182	326	19,578	12,752	2,886	3,940	1,210	1,112	1,149
Hawaii................	234	184	22	29	3,056	2,327	367	362	1,218	1,142	1,154
Idaho..................	279	199	29	51	3,549	2,460	496	593	1,197	1,082	1,214
Illinois................	2,065	1,470	246	349	28,189	19,388	4,421	4,380	1,264	1,135	1,259
Indiana................	1,220	830	144	246	16,709	11,189	2,550	2,970	1,290	1,117	1,271
Iowa..................	592	434	68	90	7,840	5,562	1,217	1,061	1,226	1,059	1,223
Kansas................	499	352	57	90	6,705	4,643	1,007	1,055	1,259	1,082	1,260
Kentucky..............	914	534	120	259	11,379	6,456	1,861	3,062	1,171	1,084	1,099
Louisiana..............	809	482	136	192	9,941	5,626	2,090	2,225	1,148	1,084	1,094
Maine................	307	204	30	72	3,740	2,430	502	808	1,138	1,030	1,143
Maryland..............	873	628	98	147	11,879	8,310	1,699	1,870	1,268	1,143	1,224
Massachusetts........	1,161	803	114	244	15,439	10,479	2,036	2,924	1,244	1,099	1,234
Michigan..............	2,017	1,366	231	419	28,270	18,801	4,215	5,254	1,324	1,166	1,287
Minnesota............	905	665	92	148	12,123	8,686	1,645	1,792	1,255	1,101	1,228
Mississippi............	610	363	82	165	7,415	4,346	1,184	1,885	1,151	1,058	1,067
Missouri..............	1,188	792	136	260	15,416	10,058	2,268	3,090	1,212	1,082	1,199
Montana..............	198	143	22	33	2,485	1,731	367	387	1,165	1,059	1,185
Nebraska..............	313	227	36	51	4,093	2,883	623	587	1,214	1,052	1,214
Nevada................	425	314	40	71	5,607	3,995	688	924	1,225	1,174	1,227
New Hampshire..........	263	182	23	58	3,554	2,444	415	695	1,280	1,132	1,275
New Jersey..............	1,500	1,105	154	241	21,865	15,731	2,902	3,232	1,360	1,219	1,304
New Mexico............	371	253	43	75	4,524	2,990	659	875	1,152	1,063	1,099
New York..............	3,337	2,362	342	633	45,819	31,710	6,115	7,994	1,289	1,150	1,241
North Carolina..........	1,808	1,230	187	391	23,505	15,722	2,977	4,806	1,223	1,105	1,152
North Dakota..........	121	88	17	17	1,519	1,042	282	195	1,149	1,034	1,136
Ohio..................	2,166	1,474	285	407	28,618	18,835	4,998	4,785	1,230	1,077	1,217
Oklahoma..............	717	474	90	153	9,136	5,868	1,457	1,811	1,188	1,074	1,162
Oregon................	735	540	72	122	9,743	6,922	1,299	1,522	1,233	1,112	1,245
Pennsylvania............	2,618	1,829	305	484	35,656	24,278	5,495	5,883	1,268	1,114	1,244
Rhode Island..........	207	144	19	44	2,739	1,889	328	522	1,239	1,075	1,239
South Carolina..........	956	640	105	211	12,453	8,176	1,659	2,618	1,226	1,125	1,144
South Dakota............	156	115	19	22	1,934	1,375	303	256	1,148	1,035	1,123
Tennessee..............	1,288	837	153	298	16,512	10,561	2,427	3,524	1,213	1,082	1,149
Texas..................	3,552	2,385	469	699	44,966	29,149	7,600	8,217	1,198	1,093	1,148
Utah..................	335	241	38	57	4,385	3,074	647	664	1,242	1,100	1,264
Vermont................	132	93	13	27	1,710	1,184	220	306	1,229	1,039	1,199
Virginia................	1,319	917	146	255	17,400	11,795	2,449	3,156	1,238	1,119	1,172
Washington............	1,127	814	111	202	15,317	10,773	2,021	2,523	1,279	1,123	1,268
West Virginia............	451	266	65	121	5,867	3,291	1,067	1,509	1,211	1,140	1,150
Wisconsin..............	1,086	784	113	189	14,657	10,347	2,029	2,281	1,263	1,104	1,254
Wyoming..............	94	68	10	15	1,240	876	181	183	1,231	1,101	1,227

See footnotes at end of table.

Table 556. Social Security—Beneficiaries, Annual Payments, and Average Monthly Benefit, 1990 to 2011, and by State and Other Areas, 2011-Continued.

See headnote on page 369.

Year, state, and other area	Number of beneficiaries (1,000)				Annual payments [2] (mil. dol.)				Average monthly benefit (dol.)		
	Total	Retired workers and dependents [1]	Survivors	Disabled workers and dependents	Total	Retired workers and dependents [1]	Survivors	Disabled workers and dependents	Retired workers [3]	Disabled workers	Widows and widowers [4]
Puerto Rico............	821	474	113	234	7,465	3,856	1,219	2,390	822	981	725
Guam...................	15	10	3	2	129	78	30	21	821	961	805
American Samoa.......	6	3	2	2	48	19	13	16	799	858	706
Virgin Islands..........	20	15	2	2	226	169	30	27	1,080	1,100	934
Northern Mariana Islands................	3	2	1	(Z)	17	10	5	2	683	724	570
Abroad.................	567	446	103	18	4,131	2,733	1,200	198	653	1,027	725

NA Not available. Z Less than 500. [1] Data for 1990-2006 include special benefits for persons aged 72 years and over not insured under regular or transitional provisions of Social Security Act. [2] Unnegotiated checks not deducted. 1990 data include lump-sum payments to survivors of deceased workers. [3] Excludes persons with special benefits. [4] Nondisabled only. [5] Includes those with state or area unknown. [6] 2011 data are preliminary.

Source: U.S. Social Security Administration, *Annual Statistical Supplement to the Social Security Bulletin*, 2012. See also <http://www.ssa.gov/policy/docs/statcomps/supplement/2012>.

Table 557. Social Security Trust Funds: 1990 to 2011

[In billions of dollars (272.4 represents $272,400,000,000)]

Type of trust fund	1990	1995	2000	2005	2007	2008	2009	2010	2011
Old-age and survivors insurance (OASI):									
Net contribution income [1, 2]...................	272.4	310.1	433.0	520.7	578.1	590.2	590.3	568.9	592.4
Interest received [2]............................	16.4	32.8	57.5	84.0	97.0	105.3	107.9	108.2	106.5
Benefit payments [3]...........................	223.0	291.6	352.7	435.4	489.1	509.3	557.2	577.4	596.2
Assets, end of year..........................	214.2	458.5	931.0	1,663.0	2,023.6	2,202.9	2,336.8	2,429.0	2,524.1
Disability insurance (DI):									
Net contribution income [1, 2]...................	28.7	54.7	71.8	87.2	96.6	98.9	98.9	94.8	98.4
Interest received [2]............................	0.9	2.2	6.9	10.3	13.2	11.0	10.5	9.3	7.9
Benefit payments [3]...........................	24.8	40.9	55.0	85.4	95.9	106.0	118.3	124.2	128.9
Assets, end of year..........................	11.1	37.6	118.5	195.6	214.9	215.8	203.6	179.9	153.9

[1] Includes deposits by states and deductions for refund of estimated employee tax overpayment. Includes government contributions to deemed wage credits for military service 1957–2001. Includes taxation of benefits. Includes reimbursements from Treasury General Fund in 2010-11. [2] In 1990, includes interest on advance tax transfers. Includes interest on reimbursement for unnegotiated checks. [3] Includes payments for vocational rehabilitation services furnished to disabled persons receiving benefits because of their disabilities. Amounts reflect deductions for unnegotiated benefit checks.

Source: U.S. Social Security Administration, *Annual Report of Board of Trustees, OASI, DI, HI, and SMI Trust Funds*; <http://www.ssa.gov/OACT/TR/2012/index.html>. Also published in *Social Security Bulletin*, quarterly.

Table 558. Percent of Workers Participating in Retirement Benefits by Worker Characteristics: 2005 to 2011

[Based on National Compensation Survey, a sample survey of over 15,500 private industry establishments of all sizes, representing over 100 million workers; see Appendix III. Survey covers all 50 states and the District of Columbia. For a definition of defined benefit and defined contribution, see headnote, Table 562. See also Table 668]

Characteristic	Total [1]				Defined benefit				Defined contribution			
	2005	2009	2010	2011	2005	2009	2010	2011	2005	2009	2010	2011
Total............................	**50**	**51**	**50**	**49**	**21**	**20**	**19**	**18**	**42**	**43**	**41**	**41**
White-collar occupations.........	61	69	68	68	24	28	25	25	53	60	60	60
Blue-collar occupations..........	51	53	51	49	26	26	26	24	38	41	40	39
Service occupations..............	22	26	23	22	7	8	7	7	18	21	18	18
Full-time.......................	60	61	59	59	25	24	22	22	50	51	50	50
Part-time.......................	19	22	21	20	9	9	8	8	14	16	15	14
Union..........................	85	82	82	83	72	66	67	67	43	44	44	42
Nonunion.......................	46	48	46	45	15	15	13	13	41	43	41	41

[1] Total is less than the sum of the individual retirement items because many employees participated in both types of plans.

Source: U.S. Bureau of Labor Statistics, *Employee Benefits in Private Industry in the United States*, March 2011. See also <http://www.bls.gov/ncs/ebs/benefits>.

Table 559. Federal Civil Service Retirement: 1990 to 2010

[As of September 30 or for fiscal year ending September 30 (2,945 represents 2,945,000). Covers both Civil Service Retirement System and Federal Employees Retirement System]

Item	Unit	1990	1995	2000	2005	2006	2007	2008	2009	2010
Employees covered [1]	1,000	2,945	2,668	2,764	2,674	2,611	2,618	2,613	2,672	2,756
Annuitants, total	**1,000**	**2,143**	**2,311**	**2,376**	**2,433**	**2,449**	**2,463**	**2,471**	**2,481**	**2,479**
Age and service	1,000	1,288	1,441	1,501	1,568	1,602	1,625	1,643	1,662	1,674
Disability	1,000	297	263	242	229	226	222	218	216	210
Survivors	1,000	558	607	633	636	621	616	610	603	595
Receipts, total [2]	**Mil. dol**	**52,689**	**65,684**	**75,967**	**83,691**	**87,164**	**89,860**	**90,892**	**93,061**	**95,662**
Employee contributions	Mil. dol	4,501	4,498	4,637	4,353	4,304	4,205	4,111	4,083	4,015
Federal government contributions	Mil. dol	27,368	33,130	37,722	43,093	46,427	48,397	49,547	51,789	55,019
Disbursements, total [3]	**Mil. dol**	**31,416**	**38,435**	**45,194**	**54,790**	**57,983**	**78,146**	**63,687**	**67,669**	**69,452**
Age and service annuitants [4]	Mil. dol	26,495	32,070	37,546	46,029	48,895	68,776	54,202	57,782	59,594
Survivors	Mil. dol	4,366	5,864	7,210	8,338	8,642	8,905	9,011	9,463	9,532
Average monthly benefit:										
Age and service	Dollars	1,369	1,643	1,885	2,240	2,363	2,473	2,550	2,710	2,723
Disability	Dollars	1,008	1,164	1,240	1,327	1,366	1,394	1,409	1,469	1,453
Survivors	Dollars	653	819	952	1,106	1,157	1,200	1,232	1,309	1,315
Cash and security holdings	Bil. dol	238.0	366.2	508.1	660.8	690.0	701.7	728.9	754.3	780.4

[1] Excludes employees in leave-without-pay status. [2] Includes interest on investments. [3] Includes refunds, death claims, and administration. [4] Includes disability annuitants.

Source: U.S. Office of Personnel Management, *Civil Service Retirement and Disability Trust Fund Annual Report*. For more information, see <http://www.opm.gov/feddata/>.

Table 560. State and Local Government Retirement Systems—Beneficiaries and Finances: 1990 to 2009

[In billions of dollars (111.3 represents $111,300,000,000), except as indicated. For fiscal years closed during the 12 months ending June 30. Minus sign (–) indicates negative earnings on investment]

Year and level of government	Number of beneficiaries (1,000)	Receipts					Benefits and withdrawals			Cash and security holdings
		Total	Employee contributions	Government contributions		Earnings on investments	Total	Benefits	Withdrawals	
				State	Local					
1990: All systems	4,026	111.3	13.9	14.0	18.6	64.9	38.4	36.0	2.4	721
State-administered	3,232	89.2	11.6	14.0	11.5	52.0	29.6	27.6	2.0	575
Locally administered	794	22.2	2.2	(Z)	7.0	12.9	8.8	8.4	0.4	145
1995: All systems	4,979	148.8	18.6	16.6	24.4	89.2	61.5	58.8	2.7	1,118
State-administered	4,025	123.3	15.7	16.2	15.4	76.0	48.0	45.8	2.2	914
Locally administered	954	25.5	2.9	0.4	9.0	13.3	13.5	13.0	0.5	204
2000: All systems	6,292	297.0	25.0	17.5	22.6	231.9	95.7	91.3	4.4	2,169
State-administered	4,786	247.4	20.7	17.2	16.7	192.8	76.0	72.2	3.8	1,798
Locally administered	1,506	49.7	4.3	0.4	5.9	39.1	19.8	19.1	0.7	371
2005: All systems	6,946	354.3	31.0	24.4	36.2	262.7	156.1	142.1	3.7	2,675
State-administered	5,847	293.6	26.2	24.0	22.5	220.9	126.8	115.2	3.1	2,226
Locally administered	1,100	60.7	4.8	0.4	13.7	41.8	29.3	26.9	0.5	449
2008: All systems	7,773	48.4	37.2	36.5	46.1	-71.4	194.8	176.8	4.8	3,140
State-administered	6,617	24.5	31.9	36.0	28.3	-71.7	158.4	144.8	3.4	2,617
Locally administered	1,156	23.9	5.3	0.5	17.8	0.3	36.4	32.0	1.4	523
2009: All systems	8,005	-496.6	39.3	35.1	50.1	-621.1	201.7	188.9	4.0	2,418
State-administered	6,771	-414.6	33.4	34.6	28.9	-511.5	163.4	153.5	3.3	2,006
Locally administered	1,234	-82.0	6.0	0.5	21.2	-109.6	38.4	35.5	0.6	411

Z Less than $50 million.

Source: U.S. Census Bureau, through 1990, *Finances of Employee-Retirement Systems of State and Local Governments*, Series GF, No. 2, annual; beginning 2000, "Federal, State, and Local Governments, State and Local Government Public Employee Retirement Systems," <http://www.census.gov/govs/retire>.

Table 561. Public Employee Retirement Systems—Participants and Finances: 1980 to 2009

[For participants 4,629 represents 4,629,000. For finances, 258 represents $258,000,000,000 For fiscal year of retirement system, except data for the Thrift Savings Plan are for calendar year. For a definition of defined benefit, see headnote, Table 562]

Retirement plan	Unit	1980	1990	2000	2004	2005	2006	2007	2008	2009, proj.
TOTAL PARTICIPANTS [1]										
Federal retirement systems:										
Defined benefit:										
Civil Service Retirement System...........	1,000	4,629	4,167	3,256	3,035	2,958	2,878	2,789	2,650	2,575
Federal Employees Retirement System [2]...................	1,000	(X)	1,180	1,935	2,104	2,196	2,290	2,371	2,572	2,748
Military Service Retirement System [3]......	1,000	3,380	3,763	3,397	3,545	3,536	3,560	3,585	3,657	3,676
Thrift Savings Plan [4]......................	1,000	(X)	1,625	2,500	3,400	3,600	3,700	3,900	4,000	4,300
State and local retirement systems [5, 6]........	1,000	(NA)	16,858	23,126	24,594	24,997	25,781	26,071	26,841	27,470
ACTIVE PARTICIPANTS										
Federal retirement systems:										
Defined benefit:										
Civil Service Retirement System...........	1,000	2,700	1,826	978	788	722	650	580	477	426
Federal Employees Retirement System [2]...................	1,000	(X)	1,136	1,668	1,882	1,952	2,014	2,066	2,195	2,330
Military Service Retirement System [3]......	1,000	2,050	2,130	1,437	1,480	1,445	1,443	1,438	1,461	1,480
Thrift Savings Plan [4]......................	1,000	(X)	1,419	1,900	2,500	2,800	2,600	2,600	2,700	2,800
State and local retirement systems [5, 6]........	1,000	(NA)	11,345	13,917	14,181	14,116	14,529	14,422	14,701	14,830
ASSETS										
Total............	Bil. dol.	258	1,047	2,951	3,472	3,695	4,022	4,533	4,380	3,758
Federal retirement systems...................	Bil. dol.	73	326	783	977	1,037	1,110	1,156	1,190	1,292
Defined benefit................	Bil. dol.	73	318	685	825	864	903	924	987	1,048
Civil Service Retirement System...........	Bil. dol.	73	220	395	433	438	442	426	423	422
Federal Employees Retirement System [2]...................	Bil. dol.	(X)	18	127	204	228	253	280	311	348
Military Service Retirement System [3]......	Bil. dol.	([7])	80	163	188	198	208	218	253	278
Thrift Savings Plan [4]......................	Bil. dol.	(X)	8	98	152	173	207	232	203	244
State and local retirement systems [5]..........	Bil. dol.	185	721	2,168	2,495	2,658	2,912	3,377	3,190	2,466
CONTRIBUTIONS										
Total........	Bil. dol.	83	103	143	187	196	206	224	260	274
Federal retirement systems..................	Bil. dol.	19	61	78	95	105	109	117	141	148
Defined benefit..................	Bil. dol.	19	59	69	79	86	89	96	119	125
Civil Service Retirement System...........	Bil. dol.	19	28	33	34	33	35	36	35	36
Federal Employees Retirement System [2]...................	Bil. dol.	(X)	4	9	13	15	15	17	19	20
Military Service Retirement System [3]......	Bil. dol.	([7])	27	27	32	38	39	43	65	69
Thrift Savings Plan [4]......................	Bil. dol.	(X)	2	9	16	19	20	21	22	23
State and local retirement systems [5]..........	Bil. dol.	64	42	65	92	91	97	107	119	126
BENEFITS										
Total........	Bil. dol.	39	89	172	226	240	258	274	295	311
Federal retirement systems..................	Bil. dol.	27	53	81	93	99	106	112	120	124
Defined benefit................	Bil. dol.	27	53	78	89	94	99	104	112	117
Civil Service Retirement System...........	Bil. dol.	15	31	44	50	52	55	57	59	63
Federal Employees Retirement System [2]...................	Bil. dol.	(X)	(Z)	1	2	3	3	4	4	5
Military Service Retirement System [3]......	Bil. dol.	12	22	33	37	39	41	43	49	49
Thrift Savings Plan [4]......................	Bil. dol.	(X)	(Z)	3	4	5	7	8	8	7
State and local retirement systems [5]..........	Bil. dol.	12	36	91	133	141	152	162	175	187

NA Not available. X Not applicable. Z Less than $500 million. [1] Includes active, separated, vested, and retired employees and survivors. [2] The Federal Employees Retirement System was established June 6, 1986. [3] Includes nondisability and disability retirees, surviving families, and all active personnel with the exception of active reserves. [4] The Thrift Savings Plan (a defined contribution plan) was established April 1, 1987. [5] Excludes state and local plans that are fully supported by employee contributions. [6] Not adjusted for double counting of individuals participating in more than one plan. [7] The Military Retirement System was unfunded until October 1, 1984.

Source: Employee Benefit Research Institute, Washington, DC, *EBRI Databook on Employee Benefits*, and unpublished data (copyright). See also <http://www.ebri.org>.

Table 562. Private Pension Plans—Summary by Type of Plan: 1990 to 2009

[712.3 represents 712,300. "Pension plan" is defined by the Employee Retirement Income Security Act (ERISA) as "any plan, fund, or program which was heretofore or is hereafter established or maintained by an employer or an employee organization, or by both, to the extent that such plan (a) provides retirement income to employees, or (b) results in a deferral of income by employees for periods extending to the termination of covered employment or beyond, regardless of the method of calculating the contributions made to the plan, the method of calculating the benefits under the plan, or the method of distributing benefits from the plan." A defined benefit plan provides a definite benefit formula for calculating benefit amounts—such as a flat amount per year of service or a percentage of salary times years of service. A defined contribution plan is a pension plan in which the contributions are made to an individual account for each employee. The retirement benefit is dependent upon the account balance at retirement. The balance depends upon amounts contributed, investment outcomes, and, in the case of profit sharing plans, amounts which may be allocated to the account due to forfeitures by terminating employees. Employee Stock Ownership Plans (ESOP) and 401(k) plans are included among defined contribution plans. Data are based on Form 5500 series reports filed with the U.S. Department of Labor and exclude (1) most pension plans qualified under sections 403(b), 457(b) and 457(f) of the Internal Revenue Code, (2) most SARSEP, SEP and SIMPLE IRA plans, (3) unfunded excess benefit plans, (4) most church plans, (5) top hat plans, (6) individual retirement accounts (IRAs), and (7) governmental plans]

Item	Unit	Total				Defined contribution plan				Defined benefit plan			
		1990	2000	2005	2009	1990	2000	2005	2009	1990	2000	2005	2009
Number of plans [1].........	1,000	712.3	735.7	679.1	706.7	599.2	686.9	631.5	659.5	113.1	48.8	47.6	47.1
Total participants [2]........	Million	76.9	103.3	117.4	129.3	38.6	61.7	75.5	87.4	38.8	41.6	41.9	41.8
Active participants [3].....	Million	61.5	73.1	82.7	90.1	35.6	50.9	62.4	72.0	26.2	22.2	20.3	18.1
Assets [4]....................	Bil. dol	1,674	4,203	5,062	5,511	834	2,216	2,808	3,317	962	1,986	2,254	2,194
Contributions [5].............	Bil. dol	98.8	231.9	341.4	413.5	80.9	198.5	248.8	298.7	24.7	33.4	92.7	114.8
Benefits [6]..................	Bil. dol	129.4	341.0	354.5	409.1	64.0	213.5	218.0	241.4	66.4	127.5	136.6	167.8

[1] Excludes all plans covering only one participant. [2] Includes active, retired, and separated vested participants not yet in pay status. Also includes double counting of workers in more than one plan. [3] Includes any workers currently in employment covered by a plan and who are earning or retaining credited service under a plan. Also includes any nonvested former employees who have not yet incurred breaks in service. [4] Asset amounts shown exclude funds held by life insurance companies under allocated group insurance contracts for payment of retirement benefits. These excluded funds make up roughly 10 to 15 percent of total private fund assets. [5] Includes both employer and employee contributions. [6] Includes benefits paid directly from trust and premium payments made from plans to insurance carriers. Excludes benefits paid directly by insurance carriers.

Source: U.S. Department of Labor, Employee Benefits Security Administration, *Private Pension Plan Bulletin*. See also <http://www.dol.gov/ebsa/>.

Table 563. Defined Benefit Retirement Plans—Selected Features: 2010

[In percent. Covers full-time employees in private industry. Based on National Compensation Survey, a sample survey of 9,018 private industry establishments of all sizes, representing nearly 99 million workers; see Appendix III. For definition of defined benefit, see headnote, Table 562. See also Table 668]

Feature	All workers	Goods producing	Service producing	1 to 99 workers	100 workers or more	Union	Nonunion
Benefit formula:							
Percent of terminal earnings..............	32	27	34	38	30	22	38
Percent of career earnings................	11	(NA)	13	(NA)	(NA)	10	12
Dollar amount formula....................	18	40	(NA)	(NA)	20	45	(NA)
Percent of contribution formula...........	3	(NA)	(NA)	(NA)	(NA)	7	(NA)
Cash balance.............................	31	19	34	30	31	11	41
Pension equity...........................	5	(NA)	6	(NA)	6	(NA)	(NA)

NA Not available.

Source: U.S. Bureau of Labor Statistics, *National Compensation Survey: Employee Benefits in Private Industry in theUnited States*, <http://www.bls.gov/ncs/ebs/detailedprovisions/2010/basic_retirement.htm>. See also <http://www.bls.gov/ncs/ebs/home.htm>.

Table 564. Percent of U.S. Households Owning Individual Retirement Accounts (IRAs): 2000 to 2011

[Incidence of IRA ownership is based on an annual tracking survey of 4,200 randomly selected, representative U.S. households; see source for details]

Year and characteristic	Any type of IRA [1]	Traditional IRA	Roth IRA	Employer-sponsored IRA [2]	Year and characteristic	Any type of IRA [1]	Traditional IRA	Roth IRA	Employer-sponsored IRA [2]
2000......................	35.7	28.7	9.2	6.8	2009....................	39.3	31.2	14.5	8.2
2002......................	34.8	28.2	10.8	7.7	2010....................	41.4	32.8	16.6	8.0
2003......................	36.7	29.6	12.5	7.5	**2011, total [3]........**	**38.8**	**31.2**	**15.7**	**7.5**
2004......................	36.5	29.6	11.6	8.0	Under 35 years........	23.0	15.0	11.0	7.0
2005......................	37.9	30.0	12.8	7.4	35 to 44 years........	37.0	26.0	18.0	9.0
2006......................	38.3	31.7	13.4	7.7	45 to 54 years........	43.0	33.0	19.0	10.0
2007......................	39.8	32.5	14.9	7.9	55 to 64 years........	50.0	43.0	23.0	9.0
2008......................	40.5	32.1	15.9	8.6	65 years and over....	42.0	40.0	9.0	3.0

[1] Excludes ownership of Coverdell Education Savings Accounts, which were referred to as Education IRAs before July 2001. [2] Employer-sponsored IRAs include SEP IRAs, SARSEP IRAs, and SIMPLE IRAs. [3] Age is based on the age of the sole or co-decision maker for household saving and investing.

Source: Investment Company Institute, Washington, DC, *Research Perspective*, "Appendix: Additional Data on IRA Ownership in 2011," Vol. 17, No. 8A, November 2011 (copyright). See also <http://www.ici.org>.

Table 565. Characteristics of U.S. Households Owning Individual Retirement Accounts (IRAs): 2011

[Incidence of IRA ownership is based on an annual tracking survey of 4,200 randomly selected, representative U.S. households; see source for details]

Characteristic	Unit	Households owning IRAs				House-holds not own-ing IRAs
		Total [1]	Tradi-tional IRA	Roth IRA	Employer-spon-sored [1]	
MEDIAN PER HOUSEHOLD						
Age of household sole or co-decision maker for investing..........	Years	53	55	49	51	47
Household income [2]........	Dollars	75,000	80,000	90,000	85,000	35,000
Household financial assets [3]........	Dollars	200,000	225,000	250,000	240,000	25,000
Household financial assets in all types of IRAs........	Dollars	42,500	56,000	45,000	62,500	(X)
Share of household financial assets in type of IRA indicated.......	Percent	30	25	10	19	(X)
PERCENT OF HOUSEHOLDS						
Household has defined contribution account or defined benefit plan coverage (total) [4]........	Percent	81	82	85	77	49
Defined contribution retirement plan account........	Percent	70	71	77	71	40
Defined benefit plan coverage........	Percent	49	50	52	44	22
Types of IRAs owned: [4]						
Traditional IRA........	Percent	80	100	68	58	(X)
Roth IRA........	Percent	40	34	100	33	(X)
Employer-sponsored IRA [1]........	Percent	19	14	16	100	(X)

X Not applicable. [1] Employer-sponsored IRAs include SIMPLE IRAs, SEP IRAs, and SARSEP IRAs. [2] Total reported is household income before taxes in 2010. [3] Household financial assets include assets in employer-sponsored retirement plans but exclude the household's primary residence. [4] Multiple responses are included.

Source: Investment Company Institute, Washington, DC, *Research Perspective*, "Appendix: Additional Data on IRA Ownership in 2011," Vol. 17, No. 8A, November 2011 (copyright). See also <http://www.ici.org>.

Table 566. Percent Distribution of Assets in Individual Retirement Accounts (IRAs) by Type of IRA: 2011

[Incidence of IRA ownership is based on an annual tracking survey of 4,200 randomly selected, representative U.S. households; see source for details]

Assets by type of IRA	Unit	Total assets in IRAs	Type of IRA owned	
			Traditional IRAs	Roth IRAs
PERCENT DISTRIBUTION OF ASSETS IN IRAs				
Less than $10,000........	Percent	18	18	33
$10,000 to $24,999........	Percent	20	20	27
$25,000 to $49,999........	Percent	14	14	15
$50,000 to $99,999........	Percent	15	16	13
$100,000 to $249,999........	Percent	18	19	10
$250,000 or more........	Percent	15	13	2
TOTAL ASSETS IN IRAs				
Mean........	Dollars	122,100	118,000	44,100
Median........	Dollars	42,500	42,500	20,000

Source: Investment Company Institute, Washington, DC, *Research Perspective*, "Appendix: Additional Data on IRA Ownership in 2011," Vol. 17, No. 8A, November 2011 (copyright). See also <http://www.ici.org>.

Table 567. 401(k) Plans—Participants, Assets, Contributions, and Benefits by Type of Plan: 2009

Type of plan [1]	Total plans [2]	Total participants (1,000) [3]	Total assets (dol.)	Total contributions (dol.) [4]	Total benefits (dol.) [5]
Total........	**512,464**	**72,499**	**2,734,064**	**258,357**	**208,467**
Profit sharing and thrift-savings........	508,614	71,033	2,661,426	253,004	203,584
Stock bonus........	237	610	38,904	2,713	2,798
Target benefit........	45	2	83	10	4
Money purchase........	663	308	11,663	872	671
Annuity—403(b)(1)........	700	157	5,036	452	216
Custodial account—403(b)(7)........	294	70	1,022	172	78

[1] About 1 percent of defined contribution plans report more than one plan type. [2] Excludes plans covering only one participant. [3] Includes active, retired, and separated vested participants not yet in pay status. [4] Includes both employer and employee contributions. [5] Amounts shown include benefits paid directly from trust funds and premium payments made by plans to insurance carriers.

Source: U.S. Department of Labor, *Private Pension Plan Bulletin: 2009*, December 2011. See also <http://www.dol.gov/ebsa/>.

Table 568. State Unemployment Insurance—Summary: 1990 to 2009

[2,522 represents 2,522,000. Includes unemployment compensation for state and local government employees where covered by state law]

Item	Unit	1990	1995	2000	2004	2005	2006	2007	2008	2009
Insured unemployment, average weekly........	1,000	2,522	2,572	2,110	2,950	2,661	2,476	2,572	3,306	5,724
Percent of covered employment [1]........	Percent	2.4	2.3	1.7	2.3	2.1	1.9	1.9	2.5	4.5
Percent of civilian unemployed.................	Percent	35.8	34.7	37.1	36.2	35.1	35.4	36.3	37.0	40.1
Unemployment benefits, average weekly........	Dollars	162	187	221	263	267	277	288	297	310
Percent of weekly wage........................	Percent	36.0	35.5	32.9	35.2	34.6	34.3	34.1	34.4	35.8
Weeks compensated..............................	Million	116.0	118.3	96.0	135.1	121.2	112.1	116.3	149.5	266.0
Beneficiaries, first payments.....................	1,000	8,629	8,035	7,033	8,369	7,917	7,351	7,642	10,053	14,173
Average duration of benefits [2]...................	Weeks	13.4	14.7	13.7	16.1	15.3	15.2	15.2	14.9	18.8
Claimants exhausting benefits...................	1,000	2,323	2,662	2,144	3,532	2,856	2,677	2,671	3,424	7,530
Percent of first payment [3]......................	Percent	29.4	34.3	31.8	39.0	35.9	35.3	35.6	41.5	55.3
Contributions collected [4].........................	Bil. dol.	15.2	22.0	19.9	31.2	34.8	34.1	31.7	30.0	28.2
Benefits paid....................................	Bil. dol.	17.3	20.1	19.4	32.3	29.3	28.0	30.5	40.7	75.9
Funds available for benefits [5]....................	Bil. dol.	38.4	35.4	54.1	23.4	29.0	36.0	38.3	30.0	11.1
Average employer contribution rate [6]............	Percent	1.95	2.44	1.75	2.68	2.86	2.68	2.44	2.25	2.29

[1] Insured unemployment as percent of average covered employment in preceding year. [2] Weeks compensated during the year divided by the number of first payments. May include more than one period of continuous unemployment. [3] Based on first payments for 12-month period ending June 30. [4] Contributions from employers; also employees in states which tax workers. [5] End of year. Sum of balances in state clearing accounts, benefit-payment accounts, and state accounts in federal unemployment trust funds. [6] As percent of taxable wages.

Source: U.S. Department of Labor, Employment and Training Administration, *Unemployment Insurance Financial Data Handbook*. See also <http://www.ows.doleta.gov/unemploy/hb394.asp>.

Table 569. State Unemployment Insurance by State and Other Areas: 2010

[10,739 represents 10,739,000. See headnote, Table [568]. For state data on insured unemployment, see Table 641]

State and other areas	Beneficiaries, first payments (1,000)	Benefits paid (mil. dol.)	Avg. weekly unemploy- ment benefits (dol.)	State and other areas	Beneficiaries, first payments (1,000)	Benefits paid (mil. dol.)	Avg. weekly unemploy- ment benefits (dol.)
Total....................	10,739	54,455	299	MT.............	34	168	272
AL........................	140	444	206	NE.............	54	188	252
AK........................	35	167	239	NV.............	128	784	318
AZ........................	179	698	214	NH.............	42	174	272
AR........................	103	407	278	NJ.............	385	2,707	397
CA........................	1,524	8,505	301	NM.............	54	328	316
CO........................	153	918	347	NY.............	666	3,535	307
CT........................	174	943	327	NC.............	379	1,717	298
DE........................	27	147	247	ND.............	18	78	310
DC........................	28	170	299	OH.............	308	1,679	297
FL........................	522	2,108	231	OK.............	76	393	276
GA........................	300	1,090	273	OR.............	200	1,023	290
HI........................	41	305	416	PA.............	599	3,329	338
ID........................	75	266	255	RI.............	49	312	380
IL........................	476	2,896	317	SC.............	149	547	236
IN........................	222	978	295	SD.............	13	50	251
IA........................	126	567	321	TN.............	194	684	223
KS........................	91	425	326	TX.............	545	2,770	316
KY........................	135	655	289	UT.............	75	354	316
LA........................	107	333	209	VT.............	29	134	297
ME........................	48	199	274	VA.............	178	725	288
MD........................	155	848	316	WA.............	264	1,786	384
MA........................	270	1,807	392	WV.............	58	237	255
MI........................	387	1,976	297	WI.............	325	1,291	275
MN........................	185	1,123	356	WY.............	22	120	337
MS........................	80	268	190	PR.............	119	298	118
MO........................	189	793	244	VI.............	2	12	302

Source: U.S. Employment and Training Administration, *Unemployment Insurance Financial Data Handbook*. See also <http://www.ows.doleta.gov/unemploy/hb394.asp>.

Table 570. Persons With Work Disability by Selected Characteristics: 2009

[In thousands, except percent (21,476 represents 21,476,000). As of March. Covers civilian noninstitutional population and members of Armed Forces living off post or with their families on post. Persons are classified as having a work disability if they (1) have a health problem or disability which prevents them from working or which limits the kind or amount of work they can do; (2) have a service-connected disability or ever retired or left a job for health reasons; (3) did not work in survey reference week or previous year because of long-term illness or disability; or (4) are under age 65, and are covered by Medicare or receive supplemental security income. Based on Current Population Survey; see text, Section 1 and Appendix III]

Age	Total [1]	Male	Female	White alone [2]	Black alone [3]	Hispanic [4]
Persons with work disability...................	**21,476**	**10,624**	**10,852**	**16,063**	**4,132**	**2,434**
16 to 24 years old...............	1,737	883	854	1,174	428	253
25 to 34 years old...............	2,448	1,199	1,248	1,740	546	346
35 to 44 years old...............	3,518	1,740	1,778	2,567	726	519
45 to 54 years old...............	6,152	3,033	3,119	4,596	1,197	646
55 to 64 years old...............	7,622	3,769	3,853	5,987	1235	670
Percent work-disabled of total population—						
16 to 24 years old...............	4.6	4.6	4.6	4.0	7.5	3.8
25 to 34 years old...............	6.0	5.9	6.2	5.5	10.1	4.3
35 to 44 years old...............	8.5	8.5	8.5	7.8	14.0	7.4
45 to 54 years old...............	13.9	13.9	13.8	12.7	22.6	12.6
55 to 64 years old...............	22.2	22.8	21.7	20.8	35.0	22.6

[1] Includes other races, not shown separately. [2] Beginning in 2003 Current Population Survey asked respondents to choose one or more races. White alone refers to people who reported only the White race category. The use of this single-race population does not imply that it is the preferred method of presenting or analyzing data. Information on people who reported more than one race is available from Census 2000 through American FactFinder. [3] Black alone refers to people who reported Black and did not report any other race category. [4] Hispanic persons may be of any race.

Source: U.S. Census Bureau. Retrieved from CPS Table Creator on July 24, 2012. See also <http://www.census.gov/cps/data/>.

Table 571. Workers' Compensation Payments: 1990 to 2009

[In billions of dollars, except as indicated (53.1 represents $53,100,000,000). See headnote, Table 573]

Item	1990	1995	2000	2003	2004	2005	2006	2007	2008	2009
Workers covered (mil.)......................	105.5	112.8	127.1	124.7	125.9	128.2	130.3	131.7	130.6	124.9
Premium amounts paid [1]...............	**53.1**	**57.1**	**60.1**	**80.5**	**84.2**	**89.3**	**87.2**	**85.5**	**79.9**	**73.9**
Private carriers [1].............................	35.1	31.6	35.7	45.3	47.4	50.7	51.4	51.2	46.6	42.2
State funds.............................	8.0	10.5	8.8	16.4	17.5	18.2	15.7	13.7	12.6	11.0
Federal programs [2].........................	2.2	2.6	3.6	4.0	4.1	4.1	4.1	4.2	4.3	4.1
Self-insurers.............................	7.9	12.5	11.9	14.9	15.2	16.4	15.9	16.3	16.4	16.5
Annual benefits paid [1]...................	**38.2**	**42.1**	**47.7**	**54.7**	**56.1**	**57.1**	**55.1**	**56.0**	**58.1**	**58.3**
By private carriers [1]........................	22.2	20.1	26.9	28.4	28.6	29.0	28.1	28.7	30.2	30.5
From state funds [3].........................	5.9	7.7	7.4	10.4	11.1	11.1	10.6	10.3	10.4	10.1
Federal employees [3]......................	2.9	3.1	3.0	3.2	3.3	3.3	3.3	3.3	3.4	3.5
Employers' self-insurance [4]...............	7.2	11.2	10.5	12.7	13.1	13.7	13.2	13.6	14.1	14.2
Type of benefit:										
Medical/hospitalization....................	15.2	16.7	20.9	25.7	26.1	26.4	26.3	27.0	29.3	28.9
Compensation payments..................	23.1	25.4	26.8	29.0	30.1	30.7	28.8	29.0	28.8	29.4
Percent of covered payroll: [1]										
Workers' compensation costs.............	2.18	1.83	1.34	1.71	1.70	1.71	1.57	1.46	1.34	1.30
Benefits....................................	1.57	1.35	1.06	1.16	1.13	1.09	0.99	0.96	0.98	1.03

[1] Premium and benefit amounts include estimated payments under insurance policy deductible provisions. Deductible benefits are allocated to private carriers and state funds. [2] Years 1990–1995 include federal employer compensation program and that portion of federal black lung benefits program financed from employer contributions. Years 2000–2009 include federal employer compensation program only due to changes in reporting methods. [3] Net cash and medical benefits paid by competitive and exclusive state funds and by federal workers' compensation programs. [4] Cash and medical benefits paid by self-insurers, plus value of medical benefits paid by employers carrying workers' compensation policies that exclude standard medical coverage.

Source: National Academy of Social Insurance, Washington, DC, *Workers' Compensation: Benefits, Coverage, and Costs*, annual (copyright). See also <http://www.nasi.org>.

Table 572. Supplemental Security Income—Recipients and Payments: 1990 to 2010

[In thousands (4,817 represents 4,817,000), except as noted. Recipients and monthly payment as of December. Total payments for calendar year. Includes persons with a federal SSI payment and/or federally administered state supplementation. See also Appendix III]

Program	Unit	1990	1995	2000	2005	2006	2007	2008	2009	2010
Recipients, total...............	1,000	**4,817**	**6,514**	**6,602**	**7,114**	**7,236**	**7,360**	**7,521**	**7,677**	**7,912**
Aged...........................	1,000	1,454	1,446	1,289	1,214	1,212	1,205	1,203	1,186	1,184
Blind..........................	1,000	84	84	79	75	73	72	70	69	69
Disabled.......................	1,000	3,279	4,984	5,234	5,825	5,951	6,083	6,247	6,421	6,659
Payments, total [1].............	Mil. dol.	**16,133**	**27,037**	**30,672**	**37,236**	**38,889**	**41,205**	**43,040**	**46,592**	**48,195**
Aged...........................	Mil. dol.	3,559	4,239	4,540	4,965	5,116	5,301	5,379	5,569	5,454
Blind..........................	Mil. dol.	329	367	386	414	409	419	416	427	423
Disabled.......................	Mil. dol.	12,245	22,431	25,746	31,857	33,364	35,485	37,246	40,597	42,317
Average monthly payment, total...............	Dollars	**276**	**335**	**379**	**439**	**455**	**468**	**478**	**499**	**501**
Aged...........................	Dollars	208	250	300	360	373	384	393	399	400
Blind..........................	Dollars	319	355	413	475	488	500	508	520	522
Disabled.......................	Dollars	303	358	398	455	471	485	494	517	518

[1] Includes payments not distributed by reason of ineligibility.

Source: U.S. Social Security Administration, *Annual Statistical Supplement to the Social Security Bulletin, 2011*, released February 2012 (copyright). See also <http://www.ssa.gov/policy/docs/statcomps/>.

Table 573. Workers' Compensation Payments by State: 2000 to 2009

[In millions of dollars (47,699 represents $47,699,000,000). Calendar-year data. Payments represent compensation and medical benefits and include insurance losses paid by private insurance carriers (compiled from state workers' compensation agencies and A.M. Best Co.); disbursements of state funds (compiled from the A.M. Best Co. and state workers' compensation agencies); and self-insurance payments (compiled from state workers' compensation agencies and authors' estimates)]

State	2000	2005	2007	2008	2009	State	2000	2005	2007	2008	2009
Total	**47,699**	**57,067**	**55,998**	**58,104**	**58,327**	Montana	155	227	243	253	254
Alabama	529	620	635	657	626	Nebraska	230	306	284	324	304
Alaska	139	183	188	205	213	Nevada	347	457	414	430	433
Arizona	498	571	696	691	651	New Hampshire	177	229	208	241	231
Arkansas	214	227	244	233	216	New Jersey	1,378	1,702	1,849	1,952	2,003
California	9,449	10,868	9,551	9,466	9,318	New Mexico	144	259	273	271	283
Colorado	810	932	879	917	884	New York	2,761	3,378	3,389	3,859	4,147
Connecticut	638	720	730	778	835	North Carolina	865	1,382	1,345	1,456	1,409
Delaware	118	215	213	218	206	North Dakota	70	82	92	106	111
District of Columbia	78	92	86	80	92	Ohio	2,099	2,447	2,478	2,490	2,353
Florida	2,577	3,474	2,915	2,835	2,977	Oklahoma	485	638	700	772	825
Georgia	965	1,409	1,494	1,577	1,493	Oregon	425	555	589	607	623
Hawaii	231	251	247	246	244	Pennsylvania	2,379	2,741	2,804	2,902	2,901
Idaho	114	243	268	281	266	Rhode Island	127	137	152	159	158
Illinois	1,944	2,419	2,739	2,922	2,979	South Carolina	515	925	886	917	892
Indiana	545	569	599	626	612	South Dakota	63	86	120	111	94
Iowa	343	487	496	555	557	Tennessee	774	862	751	783	784
Kansas	323	390	394	415	419	Texas	2,160	1,597	1,426	1,539	1,595
Kentucky	584	703	648	702	737	Utah	172	257	285	302	296
Louisiana	547	705	733	855	840	Vermont	101	122	119	128	144
Maine	245	281	277	264	264	Virginia	597	852	1,071	1,112	873
Maryland	641	784	850	936	896	Washington	1,527	1,848	1,996	2,193	2,312
Massachusetts	801	922	903	856	950	West Virginia	661	765	511	488	491
Michigan	1,474	1,474	1,511	1,407	1,510	Wisconsin	765	1,170	1,094	1,155	1,113
Minnesota	798	949	959	1,026	1,083	Wyoming	89	117	127	137	137
Mississippi	293	290	323	336	318	**Federal total** [1]	**2,957**	**3,258**	**3,340**	**3,424**	**3,543**
Missouri	780	892	871	906	834	Federal employees	2,119	2,462	2,587	2,676	2,764

[1] Federal benefits include: those paid under the Federal Employees' Compensation Act for civilian employees; the portion of the black lung benefit program that is financed by employers; and a portion of benefits under the Longshore and Harbor Workers' Compensation Act (LHWCA) that are not reflected in state data, namely, benefits paid by self-insured employers and by special funds under the LHWCA. See Appendix H of source for more information about federal programs.

Source: National Academy of Social Insurance, Washington, DC, *Workers' Compensation: Benefits, Coverage, and Costs*, annual. See also <http://www.nasi.org>.

Table 574. Supplemental Security Income (SSI)—Recipients and Payments by State and Other Area: 2000 to 2010

[Recipients as of December (6,602 represents 6,602,000); payments for calendar year ($30,672 represents $30,672,000,000). Data cover federal SSI payments and/or federally administered state supplementation. For explanation of methodology, see Appendix III]

State and other area	Recipients (1,000)		Payments for the year (mil. dol.)			State and other area	Recipients (1,000)		Payments for the year (mil. dol.)		
	2000	2010	2000	2005	2010		2000	2010	2000	2005	2010
Total [1]	**6,602**	**7,912**	**30,672**	**37,236**	**48,195**	MO	112	134	471	573	785
U.S.	**6,601**	**7,911**	**30,669**	**37,232**	**48,189**	MT	14	18	57	70	98
AL	159	172	659	776	996	NE	21	26	85	103	144
AK	9	12	37	53	70	NV	25	41	108	163	241
AZ	81	110	355	482	644	NH	12	18	49	67	103
AR	85	107	333	407	603	NJ	146	169	672	763	1,001
CA	1,088	1,269	6,386	8,146	8,870	NM	47	60	193	248	340
CO	54	66	228	264	377	NY	617	681	3,197	3,561	4,445
CT	49	58	216	260	340	NC	191	219	732	894	1,243
DE	12	16	50	66	91	ND	8	8	30	33	43
DC	20	24	93	113	153	OH	240	286	1,114	1,295	1,784
FL	377	484	1,621	2,031	2,760	OK	72	94	302	381	541
GA	197	228	785	944	1,317	OR	52	75	228	298	439
HI	21	25	104	119	157	PA	284	358	1,367	1,659	2,229
ID	18	27	76	106	155	RI	28	33	130	161	201
IL	249	273	1,174	1,337	1,662	SC	107	112	429	488	635
IN	88	118	382	488	716	SD	13	14	48	55	75
IA	40	48	158	193	266	TN	164	175	664	752	1,023
KS	36	46	151	187	269	TX	409	617	1,575	2,191	3,316
KY	174	192	741	862	1,116	UT	20	28	87	110	160
LA	166	175	715	771	989	VT	13	15	51	63	87
ME	30	35	116	146	196	VA	132	148	535	632	832
MD	88	107	400	481	658	WA	101	137	484	616	881
MA	168	193	807	902	1,211	WV	71	80	318	376	472
MI	210	254	988	1,157	1,581	WI	85	107	357	437	625
MN	64	86	272	355	516	WY	6	6	23	26	35
MS	129	126	512	572	699	N. Marianas	1	1	3	4	6

[1] Includes Northern Mariana Islands.

Source: U.S. Social Security Administration, *Annual Statistical Supplement to the Social Security Bulletin*, Feb. 2012, see also <http://www.ssa.gov/policy/docs/statcomps/>.

Table 575. Temporary Assistance for Needy Families (TANF)—Families and Recipients: 1980 to 2010

[In thousands (3,712 represents 3,712,000). Average monthly families and recipients for calendar year. Prior to TANF, the cash assistance program to families was called Aid to Families with Dependent Children (1980–1996). Under the new welfare law (Personal Responsibility and Work Opportunity Reconciliation Act of 1996), the program became TANF. See text, this section. Includes Puerto Rico, Guam, and Virgin Islands]

Year	Families	Recipients	Year	Families	Recipients	Year	Families	Recipients
1980	3,712	10,774	1995	4,791	13,418	2003	2,024	4,929
1985	3,701	10,855	1996	4,434	12,321	2004	1,979	4,748
1989	3,799	10,993	1997	3,740	10,376	2005	1,894	4,469
1990	4,057	11,695	1998	3,050	8,347	2006	1,777	4,148
1991	4,497	12,930	1999	2,554	6,824	2007	1,674	3,897
1992	4,829	13,773	2000	2,215	5,778	2008	1,633	3,795
1993	5,012	14,205	2001	2,104	5,359	2009	1,769	4,154
1994	5,033	14,161	2002	2,048	5,069	2010	1,858	4,403

Source: U.S. Department of Health and Human Services, Administration for Children and Families. For more information, see <http://www.acf.hhs.gov/programs/ofa/>.

Table 576. Temporary Assistance for Needy Families (TANF)—Recipients by State and Other Areas: 2000 to 2010

[In thousands (2,215 represents 2,215,000). Average monthly families and recipients for calendar year. See headnote, Table 575]

State or other area	Families			Recipients			State or other area	Families			Recipients		
	2000	2005	2010	2000	2005	2010		2000	2005	2010	2000	2005	2010
Total [1]	2,215	1,894	1,858	5,778	4,469	4,403	MT	5	4	4	13	12	9
U.S.	2,181	1,876	1,843	5,678	4,418	4,361	NE	9	10	8	24	25	18
AL	19	20	22	45	47	53	NV	6	6	11	16	15	27
AK	7	4	3	21	11	9	NH	6	6	5	14	14	11
AZ	33	42	28	84	96	60	NJ	50	43	34	125	104	81
AR	12	8	8	29	18	19	NM	23	18	20	69	45	54
CA	489	461	584	1,262	1,078	1,437	NY	250	140	122	695	321	272
CO	11	15	11	28	39	29	NC	45	33	24	98	64	46
CT	27	19	17	64	39	34	ND	3	3	2	7	7	5
DE	6	6	5	12	13	15	OH	95	82	104	235	177	238
DC	17	17	8	45	41	19	OK	14	11	9	35	26	21
FL	65	58	58	142	100	105	OR	17	19	28	38	44	72
GA	52	39	20	125	82	38	PA	88	97	54	241	254	130
HI	14	8	9	46	19	26	RI	16	10	7	44	26	17
ID	1	2	2	2	3	3	SC	18	16	19	42	36	44
IL	78	38	23	234	96	66	SD	3	3	3	7	6	7
IN	37	44	35	101	124	86	TN	57	70	61	147	184	157
IA	20	17	18	53	42	46	TX	129	82	51	347	189	117
KS	13	18	15	32	46	38	UT	8	9	6	21	22	18
KY	38	34	30	87	74	62	VT	6	5	3	16	11	6
LA	27	15	11	71	36	24	VA	31	10	35	69	28	79
ME	11	9	11	28	25	26	WA	56	57	67	148	136	162
MD	29	23	25	71	53	60	WV	13	12	10	33	26	23
MA	43	48	50	100	102	97	WI	17	19	23	38	44	53
MI	72	81	68	198	215	179	WY	1	–	–	1	1	1
MN	39	28	23	114	71	50	PR	30	15	14	88	41	37
MS	15	15	12	34	33	25	GU	3	3	1	10	9	3
MO	47	40	36	125	96	86	VI	1	–	1	3	1	2

– Represents or rounds to zero. [1] Includes Puerto Rico, Guam, and the Virgin Islands.

Source: U.S. Department of Health and Human Services, Administration for Children and Families. See also <http://www.acf.hhs.gov/programs/ofa/>.

Table 577. Temporary Assistance for Needy Families (TANF)—Expenditures by State: 2000 to 2010

[In millions of dollars (24,781 represents $24,781,000,000). Represents federal and state funds expended in fiscal year]

State	2000, Total	2005, Total	2010 Total [1]	2010 Expenditures on assistance	State	2000, Total	2005, Total	2010 Total [1]	2010 Expenditures on assistance
U.S.	**24,781**	**25,580**	**33,255**	**12,253**	MO	321	299	405	106
AL	96	123	191	55	MT	44	44	47	22
AK	93	74	62	49	NE	79	78	98	31
AZ	261	299	350	107	NV	69	70	108	46
AR	139	67	233	16	NH	73	63	86	44
CA	6,481	5,882	7,239	4,478	NJ	321	994	1,446	309
CO	205	214	323	77	NM	149	127	237	117
CT	436	459	500	99	NY	3,512	3,970	5,347	2,032
DE	55	61	75	11	NC	440	448	563	76
DC	157	156	251	66	ND	33	34	37	20
FL	781	868	901	211	OH	995	990	1,331	506
GA	386	520	563	83	OK	130	174	179	73
HI	162	128	378	85	OR	169	269	392	240
ID	43	40	35	6	PA	1,327	1,190	964	213
IL	879	998	1,255	76	RI	172	168	149	44
IN	342	307	344	92	SC	245	230	180	51
IA	163	162	194	86	SD	21	30	31	22
KS	151	154	207	92	TN	293	233	338	153
KY	203	216	281	159	TX	727	851	908	159
LA	118	186	264	43	UT	100	108	132	46
ME	108	127	141	100	VT	62	68	78	26
MD	336	349	564	124	VA	418	290	299	127
MA	690	689	1,022	337	WA	535	525	1,494	369
MI	1,264	1,175	1,703	593	WV	134	124	199	103
MN	381	392	475	96	WI	382	446	524	130
MS	62	79	106	34	WY	34	32	29	12

[1] Includes other items not shown separately.

Source: U.S. Administration for Children and Families, Temporary Assistance for Needy Families (TANF) Program. See also <http://www.acf.hhs.gov/programs/ofa/>.

Table 578. Federal Food Programs: 1990 to 2011

[20.0 represents 20,000,000, except as noted. For fiscal years ending September 30. Program data include Puerto Rico, Virgin Islands, Guam, American Samoa, Northern Marianas, and the former Trust Territory when a federal food program was operated in these areas. Participation data are average monthly figures except as noted. Participants are not reported for programs. Cost data are direct federal benefits to recipients; they exclude federal administrative payments and applicable state and local contributions. Federal costs for commodities and cash in-lieu of commodities are shown separately from direct cash benefits for those programs receiving both]

Program	Unit	1990	2000	2005	2007	2008	2009	2010	2011
Supplemental nutrition assistance program (SNAP): [1]									
Participants	Million	20.0	17.2	25.6	26.3	28.2	33.5	40.3	44.7
Federal cost	Mil. dol.	14,143	14,983	28,568	30,373	34,608.0	50,360	64,703	71,813
Monthly average coupon value per recipient	Dollars	58.78	72.62	92.89	96.18	102.19	125.31	133.79	133.85
Nutrition assistance program for Puerto Rico: [2]									
Federal cost	Mil. dol.	937	1,268	1,495	1,551	1,623	2,001	2,001	2,001
National school lunch program (NSLP):									
Free lunches served	Million	1,662	2,205	2,477	2,506	2,611	2,724	2,948	3,066
Reduced-price lunches served	Million	273	409	479	502	521	520	498	445
Children participating [3]	Million	24.1	27.3	29.6	30.6	31.0	31.3	31.7	31.8
Federal cost	Mil. dol.	3,214	5,493	7,055	7,706	8,265	8,873	9,750	10,104
School breakfast (SB):									
Children participating [3]	Million	4.1	7.6	9.4	10.1	10.6	11.1	11.7	12.2
Federal cost	Mil. dol.	596	1,393	1,927	2,163	2,366	2,583	2,859	3,034
Special supplemental food program (WIC): [4]									
Participants	Million	4.5	7.2	8.0	8.3	8.7	9.1	9.2	9.0
Federal cost	Mil. dol.	1,637	2,853	3,603	3,881	4,534	4,641	4,563	5,018
Child and adult care (CAC): [5]									
Participants [6]	Million	1.5	2.7	3.1	3.2	3.3	3.3	3.4	3.4
Federal cost	Mil. dol.	719	1,500	1,904	2,023	2,169	2,289	2,398	2,472
Federal cost of commodities donated to— [7]									
Child nutrition (NSLP, CACFP, SFS, and SBP) [8]	Mil. dol.	644	704	1,045	1,110	1,139	1,214	1,222	1,303
Emergency feeding [9]	Mil. dol.	282	182	314	198	226	553	566	462

[1] The program name was changed from Food Stamp to Supplemental Nutrition Assistance (SNAP) in October 2008. [2] Puerto Rico receives a grant in lieu of SNAP benefits. [3] Average monthly participation (excluding summer months of June through August). Includes children in public and private elementary and secondary schools and in residential child care institutes. [4] WIC serves pregnant and postpartum women, infants, and children up to age 5. [5] CACFP provides year-round subsidies to feed preschool children in child care centers and family day care homes. Certain care centers serving disabled or elderly adults also receive meal subsidies. [6] Average quarterly daily attendance at participating institutions. [7] Includes the federal cost of commodity entitlements, cash-in-lieu of commodities, and bonus foods. [8] May include NSLP, CACFP, and Summer Food Service. [9] Provides free (bonus) commodities to needy persons for home consumption through food banks, hunger centers, soup kitchens, and similar nonprofit agencies. Includes The Emergency Food Assistance Program (TEFAP), the Commodity Purchases for Soup Kitchens/Food Banks Program (FY 1989–96), and commodity disaster relief. Does not include SNAP disaster assistance.

Source: U.S. Department of Agriculture, Food and Nutrition Service, "Food and Nutrition Service, Program Data," <http://www.fns.usda.gov/fns/>, updated monthly. Accessed June 2012.

Table 579. Federal Supplemental Nutrition Assistance Program (SNAP) by State: 2000 to 2011

[17,194 represents 17,194,000. Participation data are average monthly number participating in year ending September 30.]

State	Persons (1,000)			Benefits (mil.dol.)			State	Persons (1,000)			Benefits (mil.dol.)		
	2000	2005	2011	2000	2005	2011		2000	2005	2011	2000	2005	2011
Total [1]	**17,194**	**25,628**	**44,709**	**14,983**	**28,568**	**71,813**	MO	423	677	943	358	736	1,438
U.S.	**17,156**	**25,588**	**44,645**	**14,927**	**28,493**	**71,660**	MT	59	81	124	51	89	193
AL	396	559	920	344	616	1,493	NE	82	117	174	61	120	256
AK	38	56	86	46	80	176	NV	61	122	333	57	129	497
AZ	259	550	1,068	240	634	1,649	NH	36	52	113	28	51	163
AR	247	374	486	206	401	722	NJ	345	392	759	304	437	1,214
CA	1,831	1,992	3,673	1,639	2,315	6,484	NM	169	241	414	140	251	632
CO	156	246	453	127	313	763	NY	1,439	1,755	3,000	1,361	2,136	5,351
CT	165	204	379	138	223	647	NC	488	800	1,590	403	856	2,377
DE	32	62	135	31	65	205	ND	32	42	61	25	45	96
DC	81	89	135	77	103	229	OH	610	1,007	1,779	520	1,155	2,986
FL	882	1,382	3,075	771	1,598	5,149	OK	253	424	615	208	440	947
GA	559	921	1,780	489	1,048	2,892	OR	234	429	773	198	456	1,189
HI	118	94	160	166	156	413	PA	777	1,043	1,718	656	1,105	2,647
ID	58	93	229	46	103	362	RI	74	76	160	59	79	275
IL	817	1,158	1,794	777	1,400	2,995	SC	295	521	844	249	566	1,340
IN	300	556	878	268	627	1,386	SD	43	56	102	37	61	162
IA	123	207	374	100	220	567	TN	496	850	1,276	415	942	2,049
KS	117	178	299	83	180	453	TX	1,333	2,442	3,977	1,215	2,659	5,993
KY	403	570	823	337	611	1,261	UT	82	133	284	68	141	401
LA	500	808	885	448	979	1,386	VT	41	45	92	32	45	135
ME	102	153	248	81	162	382	VA	336	488	859	263	500	1,335
MD	219	289	668	199	320	1,035	WA	295	508	1,055	241	539	1,603
MA	232	368	814	182	363	1,292	WV	227	262	346	185	258	497
MI	603	1,048	1,928	457	1,099	3,151	WI	193	346	801	129	317	1,118
MN	196	260	506	165	275	698	WY	22	25	36	19	27	53
MS	276	435	623	226	463	921							

[1] Includes Guam and the Virgin Islands. Several outlying areas receive nutrition assistance grants in lieu of SNAP (Puerto Rico, American Samoa, and the Northern Marianas).

Source: U.S. Department of Agriculture, Food and Nutrition Service, "Food and Nutrition Service, Program Data," <http://www.fns.usda.gov/pd>, updated monthly. Accessed June 2012.

Table 580. Selected Characteristics of Supplemental Nutrition Assistance Program (SNAP) Households and Participants: 1990 to 2010

[7,811 represents 7,811,000. For fiscal years ending September 30. Data for 1990 exclude Guam and the Virgin Islands. Based on a sample of households from the SNAP Quality Control System]

Year	Households				Participants		
	Total [1] (1,000)	Percent of total			Total (1,000)	Percent of total	
		With children	With elderly [2]	With disabled [3]		Children	Elderly [2]
1990	7,811	60.3	18.1	8.9	20,440	49.6	7.7
1995	10,883	59.7	16.0	18.9	26,955	51.5	7.1
2000	7,335	53.9	21.0	27.5	17,091	51.3	10.0
2005	10,852	53.7	17.1	23.0	24,794	49.9	8.2
2007	11,561	51.0	17.8	23.8	25,775	48.9	8.8
2008	12,464	50.6	18.5	22.6	27,607	48.4	9.1
2009	14,981	49.9	16.6	21.2	32,889	47.5	8.3
2010	18,369	48.7	15.5	19.8	39,759	46.6	7.9

[1] Total does not include those who are ineligible or those receiving disaster benefits. [2] Persons 60 years old and over. [3] The substantial increase in 1995 and decrease in 2005 are due in part to the changes in definition of a disabled household. Prior to 1995, disabled households were defined as households with SSI income but no members over age 59. In 1995, that definition changed to households with at least one member under 65 who received SSI, or at least one member aged 18–61 who received Social Security, veterans' benefits, or other government benefits as a result of a disability. In 2003, the definition of a disabled household changed to households with either SSI income or a medical expense deduction and without an elderly person, and households containing a nonelderly adult who does not appear to be working and who is receiving Social Security, veterans' benefits, or workers' compensation.

Source: U.S. Department of Agriculture, Food and Nutrition Service. Percentages obtained from *Characteristics of SNAP Households: Fiscal Year 2010*, September 2011. See also <http://www.fns.usda.gov/ora/MENU/Published/snap/SNAPParthh.htm>.

Table 581. Supplemental Nutrition Assistance Program (SNAP) Households and Participants—Summary: 2010

[18,369 represents 18,369,000. For fiscal year ending September 30. Based on a sample of households from the Supplemental Nutrition Assistance Program Quality Control (QC) System. Figures are lower than official participation counts because they do not include ineligible participants or those receiving disaster food stamp assistance]

Household type and income source	Households Number (1,000)	Percent	Age, sex, race, and Hispanic origin	Participants Number (1,000)	Percent
Total.................................	18,369	100.0	Total.................................	39,759	100.0
With children..........................	8,947	48.7	Children...........................	18,516	46.6
Single-parent households.............	4,996	27.2	Under 5 years old..................	6,317	15.9
Married-couple households............	1,702	9.3	5 to 17 years old..................	12,199	30.7
Other................................	2,249	12.2	Adults.............................	21,242	53.5
With elderly..........................	2,852	15.5	18 to 35 years old.................	9,424	23.7
Living alone.......................	2,286	12.4	36 to 59 years old.................	8,697	21.9
Not living alone...................	567	3.1	60 years old and over.............	3,121	7.9
Nonelderly disabled..................	3,633	19.8			
Living alone.......................	2,125	11.6	Male...............................	17,354	43.6
Not living alone...................	1,509	8.2	Female.............................	22,405	56.4
Earned income........................	5,498	29.9	White, non-Hispanic................	13,395	33.7
Wages and salaries.................	4,834	26.3	Black, non-Hispanic................	8,909	22.4
			Hispanic...........................	6,637	16.7
Unearned income......................	11,074	60.3	Asian..............................	1,120	2.8
TANF [1].............................	1,471	8.0	Native American....................	1,696	4.3
Supplemental security income........	3,841	20.9	Other [2]..........................	8,002	20.2
Social security....................	3,933	21.4			
No income............................	3,627	19.7			

[1] Temporary Assistance for Needy Families (TANF) program. [2] For FY 2010, this category includes respondents who recorded more than one race, and those with no racial/ethnic data.

Source: U.S. Department of Agriculture, Food and Nutrition Service, *Characteristics of SNAP Households: Fiscal Year 2010*, September 2011. See also <http://www.fns.usda.gov/ora//MENU/Published/snap/snapparthh.htm>.

Table 582. Child Support—Award and Recipient Status of Custodial Parents: 2009

[In thousands except as noted (13,672 represents 13,672,000). Custodial parents 15 years and older with own children under 21 years of age as of spring 2010. Covers civilian noninstitutionalized population. Based on Current Population Survey; see text, Section 1 and Appendix III. For definition of mean, see Guide to Tabular Presentation]

Award and recipient status	All custodial parents				Custodial parents below poverty level			
	Total Number	Percent distribu-tion	Mothers	Fathers	Total Number	Percent distribu-tion	Mothers	Fathers
Total..	**13,672**	**(X)**	**11,237**	**2,435**	**3,876**	**(X)**	**3,420**	**457**
With child support agreement or award [1]........	6,914	(X)	6,174	740	1,823	(X)	1,676	146
Supposed to receive payments in 2009........	5,897	100.0	5,278	619	1,524	100.0	1,398	125
Actually received payments in 2009..........	4,174	70.8	3,723	451	1,011	66.3	920	91
Received full amount.........................	2,428	41.2	2,217	211	550	36.1	498	52
Received partial payments....................	1,745	29.6	1,506	240	461	30.2	421	39
Did not receive payments in 2009.............	1,724	29.2	1,555	168	513	33.7	478	34
Child support not awarded........................	6,759	(X)	5,063	1,695	2,054	(X)	1,743	310
MEAN INCOME AND CHILD SUPPORT Received child support payments in 2009:								
Mean total money income (dol.)................	31,991	(X)	30,018	48,288	8,642	(X)	8,858	6,453
Mean child support received (dol.).............	5,135	(X)	5,248	4,202	3,909	(X)	3,822	4,792
Received the full amount due:								
Mean total money income (dol.)...............	33,337	(X)	32,042	46,948	8,486	(X)	8,835	(NA)
Mean child support received (dol.)...........	6,928	(X)	6,917	7,036	5,314	(X)	5,073	(NA)
Received partial payments:								
Mean total money income (dol.)...............	30,119	(X)	27,036	49,466	8,828	(X)	8,885	(NA)
Mean child support received (dol.)...........	2,642	(X)	2,790	1,712	2,231	(X)	2,342	(NA)
Received no payments in 2009:								
Mean total money income (dol.)................	30,210	(X)	29,056	40,869	9,317	(X)	9,139	11,791
Without child support agreement or award:								
Mean total money income (dol.)................	28,957	(X)	23,894	44,079	7,537	(X)	7,515	7,661

X Not applicable. NA Not available. [1] As of April of following year (e.g., 2009 data is as of April 2010).

Source: U.S. Census Bureau, <http://www.census.gov/hhes/www/childsupport/reports.html>.

Table 583. Child Support Enforcement Program—Caseload and Collections: 1990 to 2010

[For fiscal years ending September 30 (12,796 represents 12,796,000). Includes Puerto Rico, Guam, and the Virgin Islands. The child support enforcement program locates absent parents, establishes paternity of children born out of wedlock, and establishes and enforces support orders. By law, these services are available to all families that need them. The program is operated at the state and local government level, but 66 percent of administrative costs are paid by the federal government. Child support (CS) collected for families not receiving Temporary Assistance for Needy Families (TANF) goes to the family to help it remain self–sufficient. Most of the child support collected on behalf of TANF families goes to federal and state governments to offset TANF payments. Some states pass–through a portion of the CS collections to help families become self–sufficient. Based on data reported by state agencies. Minus sign (–) indicates net outlay]

Item	Unit	1990	2000	2005	2006	2007	2008	2009	2010, prel.
Total cases [1]	**1,000**	**12,796**	**17,334**	**15,861**	**15,844**	**15,755**	**15,676**	**15,798**	**15,859**
Paternities established, total [2]	1,000	393	867	690	675	640	629	643	620
Support orders established, total [3]	1,000	1,022	1,175	1,180	1,159	1,178	1,193	1,267	1,297
FINANCES									
Collections, total	**Mil. dol.**	**6,010**	**17,854**	**23,006**	**23,933**	**24,855**	**26,561**	**26,386**	**26,556**
TANF/FC collections [4]	Mil. dol.	1,750	2,593	2,191	2,112	2,050	2,254	1,971	1,925
State share	Mil. dol.	620	1,080	911	875	852	928	741	716
Estimated incentive payments to states	Mil. dol.	264	353	365	402	431	615	446	448
Federal share [5]	Mil. dol.	533	968	1,129	1,086	1,054	1,170	945	891
Current assistance medical support collections	Mil. dol.	(NA)	27	11	12	11	12	13	19
Current assistance payments to families or foster care	Mil. dol.	(NA)	165	140	139	133	124	155	165
Non–TANF collections	Mil. dol.	4,260	15,261	20,815	21,822	22,804	24,307	24,415	24,630
Administrative expenditures, total	Mil. dol.	1,606	4,526	5,353	5,561	5,594	5,870	5,850	5,776
State share	Mil. dol.	545	1,519	1,813	1,884	1,902	2,200	1,963	1,964
Federal share	Mil. dol.	1,061	3,006	3,540	3,677	3,692	3,671	3,887	3,811
Program savings, total	Mil. dol.	-190	-2,125	-3,312	-3,600	-3,687	-3,780	(NA)	(NA)
State share	Mil. dol.	338	-87	-537	-607	-619	-700	(NA)	(NA)
Federal share	Mil. dol.	-528	-2,038	-2,776	-2,993	-3,068	-3,080	(NA)	(NA)

NA Not available. [1] Passage of the Personal Responsibility and Work Opportunity Reconciliation Act of 1996 (PRWORA) mandated new categories in 1999 and cases were no longer double counted resulting in a 2 million case reduction. [2] Does not include in–hospital paternities. [3] Includes modifications to orders. [4] Collections for current assistance cases where the children are: (1) recipients of TANF under Title IV–A of the Social Security Act or (2) entitled to foster care (FC) maintenance under Title IV–E of the Social Security Act plus collections distributed as assistance reimbursements. Includes assistance reimbursements, which are collections that will be divided between the state and federal governments to reimburse their respective shares of either Title IV–A assistance payments or Title IV–E foster care maintenance payments. [5] Prior to fiscal year 2002, incentives were paid out of the federal share of collections and the net federal share was reported.

Source: U.S. Department of Health and Human Services, Office of Child Support Enforcement, *Annual Report to Congress* and *Preliminary Report*. See <http://www.acf.hhs.gov/programs/cse/pubs/>.

Table 584. Head Start—Summary: 1980 to 2009

[For years ending September 30 (376 represents 376,000)]

Year	Enrollment (1,000)	Appropriation (mil. dol.)	Age and race	Enrollment, 2009 (percent)	Item	Number
1980	376	735	Under 3 years old	10	Average cost per child:	
1990	541	1,552	3 years old	36	1995	$4,534
1995	751	3,534	4 years old	51	2000	$5,951
1999	826	4,658	5 years old and over	3	2009	$7,600
2000	858	5,267				
2001	905	6,200	White	40	Paid staff (1,000):	
2002	912	6,537	Black	30	1995	147
2003	910	6,668	Hispanic	36	2000	180
2004	906	6,775	American Indian/		2009	212
2005	907	6,843	Alaska Native	4	Volunteers (1,000):	
2006	909	6,872	Asian	2	1995	1,235
2007	908	6,888	Hawaiian/		2000	1,252
2008	907	6,878	Pacific Islander	1	2009	1,274
2009	904	7,113				

Source: U.S. Department of Health and Services, Administration for Children and Families, "Head Start Statistical Fact Sheet;" <http://www.acf.hhs.gov/programs/ohs/about>.

Table 585. Number of Emergency and Transitional Beds in Homeless Assistance Systems Nationwide: 2010

[Data include beds located in Puerto Rico, Guam, and the Virgin Islands. Data are based on a nationally representative sample of 102 jurisdictions that collect data from emergency shelters and transitional providers. The data estimate homeless persons who used emergency shelters or transitional housing from October 2009 through September 2010. As a complement to the survey, a "Continuum of Care" community was derived from each jurisdiction in order to estimate the number of unsheltered homeless persons and the number of emergency shelter and transitional housing beds available on a single night in January 2010. The data do not include homeless individuals living outside a sampled jurisdiction or homeless individuals not using an emergency shelter or a transitional housing program. For more information on data collection and methodology, see Appendix B of *2010 Annual Homeless Assessment Report to Congress*]

Homeless programs	Year-round units/beds [1]			Total year-round beds	Other beds	
	Family units	Family beds	Individual beds		Seasonal beds [2]	Overflow/ voucher [3]
Emergency shelters.............................	32,878	107,950	113,660	221,610	19,668	32,393
Transitional housing..........................	35,185	109,512	91,111	200,623	(NA)	(NA)
Total inventory....................................	68,063	217,462	206,970	424,432	19,668	32,393
Permanent supportive housing.................	33,060	95,353	141,445	236,798	(NA)	(NA)

NA Not available. [1] Year-round beds are available for use throughout the year and are considered part of the stable inventory of beds for homeless persons. [2] Seasonal beds are typically available during particularly high-demand seasons of the year (e.g. winter months in the North or summer months in the South) to accommodate increased need for emergency shelters to prevent illness or death due to the weather. [3] Overflow beds are typically used during unanticipated emergencies (e.g., precipitous temperature drops or a natural disaster that displaces residents). Voucher beds are made available in a hotel or motel, and often function like overflow beds.

Source: U.S. Department of Housing and Urban Development, *2010 Annual Homeless Assessment Report to Congress* and *2010 Continuum of Care Homeless Assistance Programs: Housing Inventory Chart Report*. See also <http://www.hudhre.info/>.

Table 586. Children in Foster Care and Awaiting Adoption: 2000 to 2010

[Data cover the period from October 1 of prior year through September 30 of year shown]

Characteristic	In foster care		Entered foster care		Exited foster care		Waiting to be adopted		Adopted from foster care	
	2000	2010 [1]	2000	2010 [1]	2000	2010 [1]	2000	2010 [1]	2000	2010 [1]
Total..........................	**552,000**	**408,425**	**293,000**	**254,375**	**272,000**	**254,114**	**131,000**	**107,011**	**51,000**	**52,891**
AGE										
Under 1 year..................	22,839	24,634	37,996	40,857	11,025	11,561	3,957	3,795	939	1,126
1 to 5 years..................	134,378	125,307	72,365	77,564	70,667	84,087	44,126	41,357	23,135	28,402
6 to 10 years.................	136,003	80,590	63,346	47,356	63,228	51,107	44,980	27,764	17,831	14,221
11 to 15 years................	160,077	94,981	86,555	58,232	65,550	45,872	33,143	25,769	7,946	7,374
16 to 20 years................	98,701	82,372	32,737	29,455	61,531	61,011	4,793	8,326	1,149	1,761
RACE										
White [2]..........................	207,970	165,135	136,214	113,510	121,322	109,169	44,898	42,059	19,462	22,764
Black [2]..........................	217,615	117,610	84,460	61,375	84,065	68,101	57,345	30,812	19,566	12,795
Asian [2]..........................	4,370	2,469	3,565	1,839	3,307	1,890	664	464	290	219
Hispanic [3].....................	81,823	84,727	42,769	51,805	39,909	50,974	17,050	23,389	7,430	11,192
Two or more..................	8,043	21,830	5,362	13,038	4,026	13,177	2,277	6,771	951	3,464
SEX										
Male..........................	289,187	214,354	(NA)	(NA)	(NA)	(NA)	68,620	56,404	25,472	26,750
Female.......................	262,813	193,998	(NA)	(NA)	(NA)	(NA)	62,380	50,596	25,528	26,132
LENGTH OF STAY										
Mean months...............	32.3	25.3	(X)	(X)	22.7	21.7	43.5	37.3	(X)	(X)
Median months..............	19.8	14.0	(X)	(X)	12.0	13.5	35.1	28.3	(X)	(X)

NA Not available. X Not applicable. [1] Preliminary data. [2] Beginning with the 2000 census, respondents could choose more than one race. Data represent persons who selected this race group only and exclude persons reporting more than one race. The census in prior years only allowed respondents to report one race group. See also comments on race in the text for Section 1. [3] Persons of Hispanic origin may be any race.

Source: U.S. Department of Health and Human Services, Administration for Children and Families, *Adoption and Foster Care Analysis and Reporting System Reports*, annual. See also <http://www.acf.hhs.gov/programs/cb/stats_research/index.htm#afcars>.

Table 587. Social Assistance Services—Revenue for Employer Firms: 2000 to 2010

[In millions of dollars (77,032 represents $77,032,000,000). Estimates have been adjusted to the results of the 2007 Economic Census. Based on the Service Annual Survey and administrative data; see Appendix III]

Kind of business	2002 NAICS code [1]	2000, Total	2005, Total	2010		
				Total	Taxable firms	Tax-exempt firms
Social assistance, total..	**624**	**77,032**	**112,644**	**146,081**	**36,532**	**109,549**
Individual and family services.....................................	6241	37,311	53,703	71,847	14,832	57,015
Child and youth services......................................	62411	7,517	10,471	11,725	1,125	10,600
Services for elderly and disabled persons......................	62412	12,804	20,223	30,466	9,592	20,874
Other individual and family services...........................	62419	16,990	23,009	29,656	4,115	25,541
Community, emergency and other relief services...............	6242	12,281	21,462	28,569	468	28,101
Community food services..	62421	2,835	4,352	6,720	(S)	6,585
Community housing services....................................	62422	4,888	7,811	12,071	275	11,796
Emergency and other relief services............................	62423	4,558	9,299	9,778	58	9,720
Vocational rehabilitation services.................................	6243	9,458	12,785	13,220	1,980	11,240
Child day care services...	6244	17,982	24,694	32,445	19,252	13,193

S Estimate does not meet publication standards because of high sampling variability or poor response quality. [1] Based on the North American Industry Classification System, 2002; see text, Section 15.

Source: U.S. Census Bureau, "Service Annual Survey" 2010, February 2012, <http://www.census.gov/services/index.html>.

Table 588. Social Assistance Services—Nonemployer Establishments and Receipts: 2000 to 2009

[Receipts in millions of dollars (7,539 represents $7,539,000,000). Includes only firms subject to federal income tax. Nonemployers are businesses with no paid employees. Data for 2000 based on the North American Industry Classification System (NAICS), 1997; 2005 data based on NAICS 2002; 2009 data based on NAICS 2007; see text, Section 15]

Kind of business	NAICS code	Establishments			Receipts		
		2000	2005	2009	2000	2005	2009
Social assistance, total..................................	624	642,946	807,729	881,050	7,539	10,265	12,258
Individual and family services..............................	6241	72,433	112,909	133,317	1,106	1,920	2,409
Community/emergency and other relief services..........	6242	3,560	5,533	6,121	54	81	92
Vocational rehabilitation services...........................	6243	7,314	11,022	11,451	151	245	277
Child day care services......................................	6244	559,639	678,265	730,161	6,228	8,018	9,480

Source: U.S. Census Bureau, "Nonemployer Statistics," July 2011, <http://www.census.gov/econ/nonemployer/index.html>.

Table 589. Child Care Arrangements of Preschool Children by Type of Arrangement: 1991 to 2005

[In percent, except as indicated (8,428 represents 8,428,000). Estimates are based on children 3 to 5 years old who have not entered kindergarten. Based on interviews from a sample survey of the civilian, noninstitutionalized population in households with telephones; see source for details. See also Appendix III]

Characteristic	Children		Type of nonparental arrangement [1] (percent)			With parental care only (percent)
	Number (1,000)	Percent distribution	In relative care	In non-relative care	In center-based program [2]	
1991, total...	8,428	100.0	16.9	14.8	52.8	31.0
1995, total...	9,232	100.0	19.4	16.9	55.1	25.9
2005, total...	**9,066**	**100.0**	**22.6**	**11.6**	**57.2**	**26.3**
Age:						
3 years old.......................................	4,070	44.9	24.0	14.4	42.5	33.4
4 years old.......................................	3,873	42.7	20.8	9.2	69.2	20.6
5 years old.......................................	1,123	12.4	23.8	9.9	68.7	20.4
Race-ethnicity:						
White, non-Hispanic............................	5,177	57.1	21.4	15.0	59.1	24.1
Black, non-Hispanic............................	1,233	13.6	25.0	5.2	66.5	19.5
Hispanic..	1,822	20.1	22.7	8.1	43.4	38.0
Other..	834	9.2	26.4	8.1	61.5	24.7
Household income:						
Less than $10,001..............................	795	8.8	25.1	8.6	53.4	33.4
$10,001 to $20,000............................	978	10.8	26.0	7.8	49.2	27.2
$20,001 to $30,000............................	1,183	13.1	25.4	6.3	43.9	38.5
$30,001 to $40,000............................	1,124	12.4	23.8	6.9	48.7	33.4
$40,001 to $50,000............................	808	8.9	21.8	11.6	50.0	35.4
$50,001 to $75,000............................	1,849	20.4	21.1	13.3	57.1	25.5
$75,001 or more................................	2,329	25.7	19.8	18.0	75.1	11.4

[1] Columns do not add to 100.0 because some children participated in more than one type of nonparental arrangement. [2] Center-based programs include day care centers, Head Start programs, preschools, prekindergarten, and nursery schools.

Source: U.S. Department of Education, National Center for Education Statistics, *Early Childhood Program Participation Survey of the National Household Education Surveys Program (NHES), 2005*. See also <http://nces.ed.gov/>.

Table 590. Private Philanthropy Funds by Source and Allocation: 1990 to 2011

[In billions of dollars (100.5 represents $100,500,000,000). Estimates for sources of funds based on U.S. Internal Revenue Service reports of individual charitable deductions and household surveys of giving conducted by Independent Sector and the Center on Philanthropy at Indiana University. For corporate giving, data are corporate charitable deductions from the U.S. Internal Revenue Service and the contributions made by corporate foundations as reported by the Foundation Center. Data about foundation donations are based upon surveys of foundations and data provided by the Foundation Center. Estimates of the allocation of funds were derived from surveys of nonprofits conducted by various sources]

Source and allocation	1990	1995	2000	2003	2004	2005	2006	2007	2008	2009	2010	2011
Total funds	**100.5**	**123.7**	**229.7**	**238.1**	**262.5**	**287.6**	**293.0**	**309.8**	**290.9**	**278.7**	**286.9**	**298.4**
Individuals	81.0	95.4	174.5	182.0	203.0	222.0	224.8	233.1	213.8	200.7	209.6	217.8
Foundations [1]	7.2	10.6	24.6	26.8	28.4	32.4	34.9	40.0	42.2	41.1	41.0	41.7
Corporations	5.5	7.4	10.7	11.1	11.4	15.2	14.5	14.2	12.4	13.8	14.6	14.6
Charitable bequests	6.8	10.4	17.9	18.2	19.8	18.0	18.8	22.4	22.6	23.1	21.8	24.4
Allocation:												
Religion	49.8	58.1	77.0	84.1	87.5	90.9	94.6	97.8	98.2	99.6	97.5	95.9
Health	7.8	17.9	15.3	17.5	18.6	20.2	23.9	25.1	24.2	23.8	24.1	24.8
Education	11.9	16.5	28.8	29.6	31.7	35.1	40.1	42.3	35.8	35.3	37.4	38.9
Human service	6.7	10.6	20.8	23.6	26.3	30.2	30.8	31.9	35.9	31.5	34.5	35.4
Arts, culture, and humanities	3.7	5.2	10.6	11.1	10.9	12.4	13.9	14.8	12.3	12.1	12.6	13.1
Public/societal benefit	6.9	9.2	14.6	16.3	18.0	21.0	23.9	20.8	18.7	19.2	20.5	21.4
Environment/wildlife	1.3	2.2	4.9	5.0	5.9	6.6	7.4	8.0	7.7	7.2	7.5	7.8
International	2.1	2.6	6.3	9.5	11.5	12.6	13.3	14.9	20.0	19.7	21.1	22.7
Gifts to foundations [1]	3.8	8.5	24.7	21.6	20.3	24.5	27.1	37.7	30.1	32.4	27.5	25.8
Unallocated [2]	6.7	-7.1	26.8	19.7	30.0	31.1	14.1	13.1	4.5	-6.2	0.7	9.0

[1] Data are from the Foundation Center through 2001. [2] Money deducted as a charitable contribution by donors but not allocated to sources. May include gifts to governmental entities, in-kind giving, or gifts to new charities.

Source: Giving USA Foundation, Glenview, IL, researched and written by the Center on Philanthropy at Indiana University, *Giving USA*, annual (copyright). For more information <http://givingusareports.org/>.

Table 591. Foundations—Number and Finances by Asset Size: 1990 to 2009

[Figures are for latest year reported by foundations. In millions of dollars (142,500 represents $142,500,000,000), except number of foundations. Covers nongovernmental nonprofit organizations with funds and programs managed by their own trustees or directors, whose goals were to maintain or aid social, educational, religious, or other activities deemed to serve the common good. Excludes organizations that make general appeals to the public for funds, act as trade associations for industrial or other special groups, or do not currently award grants]

Asset size	Number	Assets (million dollars)	Gifts received (million dollars)	Total giving [1] (million dollars)
1990	32,401	142,500	5,000	8,700
2000	56,582	486,100	27,600	27,600
2005	71,095	550,600	31,500	36,400
2008	75,595	564,951	39,554	46,781
Total, 2009	**76,544**	**590,188**	**40,862**	**45,778**
Under $50,000	12,551	193	2,354	2,590
$50,000 to $99,999	4,958	367	154	207
$100,000 to $249,999	10,153	1,703	409	573
$250,000 to $499,999	9,738	3,557	396	589
$500,000 to $999,999	10,980	7,952	968	1,345
$1,000,000 to $4,999,999	17,887	40,844	2,790	4,098
$5,000,000 to $9,999,999	4,214	29,857	2,194	2,660
$10,000,000 to $49,999,999	4,558	96,565	7,185	8,659
$50,000,000 to $99,999,999	762	52,417	3,920	4,530
$100,000,000 to $249,999,999	483	71,981	4,876	4,749
$250,000,000 or more	260	284,754	15,616	15,777

[1] Includes grants, scholarships, and employee matching gifts; excludes set-asides, loans, program-related investments (PRIs), and program expenses.

Source: The Foundation Center, New York, NY, *Foundation Yearbook 2011*, annual (copyright). See also: <http://foundationcenter.org/>.

Table 592. Domestic Private Foundations—Financial Information: 1990 to 2008

[In billions (122.4 represents $122,400,000,000), except for number of returns. Minus sign (−) indicates loss]

Item	1990	1995	2000	2001	2002	2003	2004	2005	2006	2007	2008
Number of tax returns	40,105	47,917	66,738	70,787	73,255	76,348	76,897	79,535	81,850	84,613	90,850
Nonoperating foundations [1]	36,880	43,966	61,501	63,650	67,101	70,004	70,613	72,800	74,364	77,457	83,024
Operating foundations [2]	3,226	3,951	5,238	7,137	6,154	6,344	6,284	6,734	7,486	7,156	7,826
Total assets, book value [3]	122.4	195.6	409.5	413.6	383.5	418.5	455.5	481.8	569.3	591.2	531.4
Total assets, fair market value [3]	151.0	242.9	471.6	455.4	413.0	475.0	509.9	545.9	645.8	652.4	526.5
Investments in securities	115.0	190.7	361.4	329.4	294.4	344.3	361.2	373.1	403.7	400.3	287.6
Total revenue	19.0	30.8	72.8	45.3	27.8	48.4	58.7	76.4	94.1	107.3	49.7
Total expenses	11.3	17.2	37.4	36.7	34.4	35.1	36.6	42.8	48.8	58.8	60.3
Contributions, gifts, and grants paid	8.6	12.3	27.6	27.4	26.3	26.7	27.6	31.9	34.9	42.6	42.8
Excess of revenue over expenses (net)	7.7	13.6	35.3	8.6	-6.6	13.3	22.1	33.5	45.3	48.6	-10.6
Net investment income [4]	11.9	20.4	48.8	25.7	17.6	25.2	34.0	44.3	54.2	62.8	23.1

[1] Generally provide charitable support through grants and other financial means to charitable organizations; the majority of foundations are nonoperating. [2] Generally conduct their own charitable activities, e.g., museums. [3] For Tax Years 2007 and 2008, data shown for book and fair market assets were reduced by $38.7 billion and $29.6 billion, respectively, to avoid overstating joint assets of Bill and Melinda Gates Foundation and Bill and Melinda Gates Foundation Trust. [4] Represents income not considered related to a foundation's charitable purpose, e.g., interest, dividends, and capital gains. Foundations could be subject to an excise tax on such income.

Source: Source: Internal Revenue Service, *Statistics of Income Bulletin*, "SOI Tax Stats—Domestic Private Foundation and Charitable Trust Statistics, "<http://www.irs.gov/uac/Tax-Stats-2>, accessed April 2012.

Table 593. Nonprofit Charitable Organizations—Financial Information: 2000 and 2008

[In billions of dollars (1,562.5 represents $1,562,500,000,000), except as indicated. Categories based on The National Taxonomy of Exempt Entities (NTEE), a classification system that uses 26 major field areas that are aggregated into 10 categories. Includes data reported by organizations described in Internal Revenue Code, Section 501(3), excluding private foundations and most religious organizations. Organizations with receipts under $25,000 were not required to file]

Year and major category	Number of tax returns (1,000)	Total assets	Total fund balance or net worth	Revenue Total	Revenue Program service revenue [1]	Revenue Contributions, gifts, and grants	Total expenses	Excess of revenue over expenses (net)
2000.	230.2	1,562.5	1,023.2	866.2	579.1	199.1	796.4	69.8
2008, total.	**315.2**	**2,521.2**	**1,434.7**	**1,378.3**	**1,038.0**	**320.7**	**1,396.4**	**-18.1**
Arts, culture, and humanities.	33.8	95.8	74.7	28.4	9.9	16.8	29.7	-1.3
Education.	54.8	840.8	540.6	240.3	164.2	79.7	263.2	-23.0
Environment, animals.	13.9	38.7	32.4	13.9	3.4	9.7	12.8	1.1
Health.	36.5	990.7	459.1	803.9	730.0	61.9	797.6	6.3
Human services.	119.6	288.1	131.7	191.9	108.0	76.8	189.9	1.9
International, foreign affairs.	6.1	21.9	15.5	27.9	2.0	25.5	28.6	-0.7
Mutual, membership benefit.	0.7	14.5	5.7	0.9	1.3	0.1	1.8	-0.9
Public, societal benefit.	29.2	206.9	155.9	61.7	17.5	42.9	63.1	-1.4
Religion related.	20.5	23.9	19.0	9.4	1.6	7.2	9.5	-0.1

[1] Represents fees collected by organizations in support of their tax-exempt purposes, and income such as tuition and fees at educational institutions, hospital patient charges, and admission and activity fees collected by museums and other nonprofit organizations or institutions.

Source: Internal Revenue Service, *Statistics of Income Bulletin* "Charities, Fraternal Beneficiary Societies, and Other Tax-Exempt Organizations, 2008," Fall 2011, <http://www.irs.gov/uac/SOI-Tax-Stats-SOI-Bulletins>. See also <http://www.irs.gov/uac/Tax-Stats-2>.

Table 594. Individual Charitable Contributions by State: 2009

[In millions of dollars (157,644 represents $157,644,000,000), except as indicated. For tax year. Data will not agree with data in other tables due to differing survey methodology used to derive state data]

State	Number of returns (1,000)	Amount (mil. dol.)	State	Number of returns (1,000)	Amount (mil. dol.)	State	Number of returns (1,000)	Amount (mil. dol.)	State	Number of returns (1,000)	Amount (mil. dol.)
U.S. [1,2]	**37,615**	**157,644**	ID.	170	764	MO.	635	2,705	PA.	1,492	5,438
AL.	511	2,736	IL.	1,664	6,497	MT.	108	456	RI.	151	395
AK.	66	296	IN.	623	2,542	NE.	207	898	SC.	522	2,410
AZ.	759	2,606	IA.	339	1,221	NV.	320	1,135	SD.	57	429
AR.	232	1,266	KS.	319	1,602	NH.	176	479	TN.	538	3,191
CA.	4,848	19,045	KY.	427	1,699	NJ.	1,551	4,883	TX.	2,074	11,671
CO.	724	2,778	LA.	362	1,794	NM.	175	656	UT.	376	2,685
CT.	621	2,596	ME.	141	382	NY.	2,791	13,678	VT.	68	209
DE.	124	452	MD.	1,122	4,570	NC.	1,196	5,038	VA.	1,218	4,927
DC.	104	590	MA.	1,029	3,625	ND.	47	217	WA.	865	3,371
FL.	1,957	8,752	MI.	1,204	4,397	OH.	1,291	4,356	WV.	102	515
GA.	1,319	6,074	MN.	836	2,923	OK.	337	1,950	WI.	772	2,327
HI.	169	533	MS.	244	1,345	OR.	537	1,807	WY.	44	330

[1] The sum for the states does not add to the total because other components are not shown in this table. [2] U.S. totals do not agree with Table [497] in Section 9 because this table also includes (1) "substitutes for returns," whereby the IRS constructs returns for certain nonfilers on the basis of available information and imposes an income tax on the resulting estimate of the tax base and (2) returns of nonresident or departing aliens. In addition, in this table, income tax includes the alternative minimum tax, but differs from total income tax in Table [497] in that it is after subtraction of all tax credits except a portion of the earned income credit.

Source: Internal Revenue Service, *Statistics of Income Bulletin*, Historical Tables. See also <http://www.irs.gov/uac/Tax-Stats-2>.

Table 595. Volunteers by Selected Characteristics: 2011

[In percent, except as noted. Data on volunteers relate to persons who performed unpaid volunteer activities for an organization at any point from September 1, 2010 through September 2011. Data represent the percent of the population involved in the activity]

Type of main organization [1]	Total, both sexes	Sex Male	Sex Female	Educational attainment [2] Less than a high school diploma	Educational attainment [2] High school graduate, no college [3]	Educational attainment [2] Less than a bachelor's degree [4]	Educational attainment [2] College graduates
Total volunteers (1,000).	**64,252**	**27,354**	**36,898**	**2,461**	**11,049**	**15,946**	**26,218**
Percent of population.	26.8	23.5	29.9	9.8	18.2	29.5	42.4
Median annual hours [5].	51	52	50	45	50	52	56
Civic and political [6].	5.4	7.0	4.3	4.9	5.0	5.6	6.0
Educational or youth service.	25.7	23.9	27.0	22.7	22.3	24.7	26.7
Environmental or animal care.	2.3	2.1	2.4	1.5	1.4	2.4	2.5
Hospital or other health.	7.7	5.7	9.2	4.4	7.1	7.5	8.2
Public safety.	1.3	2.4	0.5	1.5	2.2	1.6	0.7
Religious.	33.2	32.8	33.5	47.8	39.0	33.5	31.3
Social or community service.	14.3	14.9	13.8	10.7	14.4	15.0	13.9
Sport and hobby [7].	3.8	4.9	3.1	1.4	3.4	3.5	4.4

[1] Main organization is defined as the organization for which the volunteer worked the most hours during the year. [2] Data refer to persons 25 years and over. [3] Includes high school diploma or equivalent. [4] Includes the categories "some college, no degree" and "associate degree." [5] At all organizations. For those reporting annual hours. [6] Includes professional and/or international activities. [7] Includes cultural and/or arts activities.

Source: U.S. Bureau of Labor Statistics, News release, USDL 12-0329, February 2012. See also <http://www.bls.gov/bls/newsrels.htm>.

Section 12
Labor Force, Employment, and Earnings

This section presents statistics on the labor force; its distribution by occupation and industry affiliation; and the supply of, demand for, and conditions of labor. The chief source of these data is the Current Population Survey (CPS) conducted by the U.S. Census Bureau for the Bureau of Labor Statistics (BLS). Comprehensive historical and current data are available from the BLS Internet site at <http://www.bls.gov/cps/>. These data are published on a current basis in the BLS monthly publication *Employment and Earnings Online.* Detailed data on the labor force are also available from the Census Bureau's decennial census of population.

Types of data—Most statistics in this section are obtained by two methods: household interviews or questionnaires and reports of establishment payroll records. Each method provides data that the other cannot suitably supply. Population characteristics, for example, are readily obtainable only from the household survey, while detailed industrial classifications can be readily derived only from establishment records.

CPS data are obtained from a monthly sample survey of the population. The CPS is used to gather data for the calendar week, generally the week including the 12th of the month, and provides current comprehensive data on the labor force (see text, Section 1, Population). The CPS provides information on the work status of the population without duplication since each person is classified as employed, unemployed, or not in the labor force. Employed persons holding more than one job are counted only once, according to the job at which they worked the most hours during the survey week.

Monthly, quarterly, and annual data from the CPS are published by the BLS in *Employment and Earnings Online.* Data presented include national totals of the number of persons in the civilian labor force by sex, disability status, race, Hispanic origin, and age; the number employed; hours of work; industry and occupational groups; usual weekly earnings; and the number unemployed, reasons for, and duration of unemployment. Annual data shown in this section are averages of monthly figures for each calendar year, unless otherwise specified. Historical national CPS data are available at <http://www.bls.gov/cps/>.

The CPS also produces annual estimates of employment and unemployment for each state, 50 large metropolitan statistical areas, and selected cities. These estimates are published by the BLS in its annual *Geographic Profile of Employment and Unemployment* available at <http://www.bls.gov/gps/>.

Data based on establishment records are compiled by the BLS and cooperating state agencies as part of an ongoing Current Employment Statistics program. The BLS collects survey data monthly from a probability-based sample of nonfarm, business establishments through Internet electronic data interchange, touchtone data entry, and computer-assisted telephone interviews, Internet, other electronic media, fax, transcript, or mail. CES data are adjusted annually to data from government unemployment insurance administrative records, which are supplemented by data from other government agencies. The estimates exclude self-employed persons, private household workers, unpaid family workers, agricultural workers, and members of the Armed Forces.

The establishment survey counts workers each time they appear on a payroll during the reference period (the payroll period that includes the 12th of the month). Thus, unlike the CPS, a person with two jobs is counted twice. The establishment survey is designed to provide estimates of nonfarm wage and salary employment, average weekly hours, and average hourly and weekly earnings by detailed industry for the nation, states, and selected metropolitan areas. Establishment survey data also are published in *Employment and Earnings Online.* Historical national data are available at <http://www.bls.gov/ces/>. Historical data for states and metropolitan areas are available at <http://www.bls.gov/sae/>. CES estimates are currently classified by the 2007 North American Industry Classification System (NAICS). All published series for the nation have a NAICS–based history extending back to at least 1990. Employment series for total nonfarm and other high-level aggregates start in 1939.

For more information on data concepts, sample design, and estimating methods for the CES Survey, see the BLS Handbook of Methods, Chapter 2 <http://bls.gov/opub/hom/homch2.htm>.

The completion of the sample redesign and the conversion to NAICS for state and metropolitan area establishment survey data were implemented in March 2003 with the release of January 2003 estimates. For a discussion of the changes to the state and area establishment survey data, see "Revisions to the Current Employment Statistics State and Area Estimates Effective January 2003" in the March 2003 issue of *Employment and Earnings Online.*

Labor force—According to the CPS definitions, the civilian labor force comprises all civilians in the noninstitutionalized population 16 years and over classified as "employed" or "unemployed" according to the following criteria: Employed civilians comprise (a) all civilians, who, during the reference week, did any work for pay or profit (minimum of an hour's work) or worked 15 hours or more as unpaid workers in a family enterprise and (b) all civilians who were not working but who had jobs or businesses from which they were temporarily absent for noneconomic reasons (illness, weather conditions, vacation, labor-management dispute, etc.) whether they were paid for the time off or were seeking other jobs. Unemployed persons comprise all civilians who had no employment during the reference week, who made specific efforts to find a job within the previous 4 weeks (such as applying directly to an employer or to a public employment service or checking with friends) and who were available for work during that week, except for temporary illness. Persons on layoff from a job and expecting recall also are classified as unemployed. All other civilian persons, 16 years old and over, are classified as "not in the labor force."

Various breaks in the CPS data series have occurred over time due to the introduction of population adjustments and other changes. For details on these breaks in series and the effect that they had on the CPS data, see the BLS Web site at <http://www.bls.gov/cps/documentation.htm#concepts>.

Beginning in January of each year, the CPS data reflect the introduction of revised population controls. For additional information on the effects of revised population controls on estimates from the CPS, see <http://www.bls.gov/cps/documentation.htm#pop>.

Hours and earnings—Average hourly earnings, based on establishment data, are gross earnings (i.e., earnings before payroll deductions) and include overtime premiums; they exclude irregular bonuses and value of payments in kind. Hours are those for which pay was received. Annual wages and salaries from the CPS consist of total monies received for work performed by an employee during the income year. It includes wages, salaries, commissions, tips, piece-rate payments, and cash bonuses earned before deductions were made for taxes, bonds, union dues, etc. Persons who worked 35 hours or more are classified as working full-time.

Industry and occupational groups—Industry data derived from the CPS for 1983 to 1991 utilize the 1980 census industrial classification developed from the 1972 SIC. CPS data from 1971 to 1982 were based on the 1970 census classification system, which was developed from the 1967 SIC. Most of the industry categories were not affected by the change in classification.

The occupational classification system used in the 1980 census and in the CPS for 1983 to 1991, evolved from the 1980 Standard Occupational Classification (SOC) system, first introduced in 1977. Occupational categories used in the 1980 census classification system are so radically different from the 1970 census system used in the CPS through 1982 that their implementation represented a break in historical data series.

Beginning in January 1992, the occupational and industrial classification systems used in the 1990 census were introduced into the CPS. (These systems were largely based on the 1980 SOC and the 1987 SIC systems, respectively.)

Beginning in 2003, the 2002 occupational and industrial classification systems were introduced into the CPS. These systems were derived from the 2000 SOC and the 2002 NAICS. The composition of detailed occupational and industrial classifications in the new classification systems was substantially changed from the previous systems in use, as was the structure for aggregating them into broad groups. Consequently, the use of the new classification systems created breaks in existing data series at all levels of aggregation. CPS data using the new classification systems are available beginning 2000. Additional information on the occupational and industrial classifications systems used in the CPS, including changes over time, appears on the BLS Web site at <www.bls.gov/cps/documentation.htm#oi>. Establishments responding to the establishment survey are classified according to the 2007 NAICS. Previously they were classified according to the SIC manual. See text, Section 15, Business Enterprise, for information about the SIC manual and NAICS.

Productivity—BLS publishes data on productivity as measured by output per hour (labor productivity), output per combined unit of labor and capital input (multifactor productivity), and, for industry groups and industries, output per combined unit of capital, labor, energy, materials, and purchased service inputs. Labor productivity and related indexes are published for the business sector as a whole and its major subsectors: nonfarm business, manufacturing, and nonfinancial corporations, and for over 200 detailed industries. Productivity indexes that take into account capital, labor, energy, materials, and service inputs are published for 18 major manufacturing industry groups, 86 detailed manufacturing industries, utility services, and air and railroad transportation. The major sector data are published in the BLS quarterly news release *Productivity and Costs* and in the annual *Multifactor Productivity Trends* release. Industry productivity measures are updated and published annually in the news releases *Productivity and Costs by Industry* and *Multifactor Productivity Trends by Industry*. The latest data are available at the Labor Productivity and Costs Web site at <http://www.bls.gov/lpc/> and the Multifactor Productivity Web site at <http://www.bls.gov/mfp>. Detailed information on methods, limitations, and data sources appears in the BLS *Handbook of Methods*, BLS Bulletin 2490 (1997), Chapters 10 and 11 at <http://www.bls.gov/opub/hom/home.htm> and <http://www.bls.gov/lpc/lpcmethods.pdf>.

Unions—As defined here, unions include traditional labor unions and employee associations similar to labor unions. Data on union membership status provided by BLS are for employed wage and salary workers and relate to their principal job. Earnings by union membership status are usual weekly earnings of full-time wage and salary workers. The information is collected through the Current Population Survey.

Work stoppages—Work stoppages include all strikes and lockouts known to BLS that last for at least 1 full day or shift and involve 1,000 or more workers. All stoppages, whether or not authorized by a union, legal or illegal, are counted. Excluded are work slowdowns and instances where employees report to work late or leave early to attend mass meetings or mass rallies.

Seasonal adjustment—Many economic statistics reflect a regularly recurring seasonal movement that can be estimated on the basis of past experience. By eliminating that part of the change which can be ascribed to usual seasonal variation (e.g., climate or school openings and closings), it is possible to observe the cyclical and other nonseasonal movements in the series. However, in evaluating deviations from the seasonal pattern—that is, changes in a seasonally adjusted series—it is important to note that seasonal adjustment is merely an approximation based on past experience. Seasonally adjusted estimates have a broader margin of possible error than the original data on which they are based, since they are subject not only to sampling and other errors, but also are affected by the uncertainties of the adjustment process itself. Consistent with BLS practices, annual estimates will be published only for not seasonally-adjusted data.

Statistical reliability—For discussion of statistical collection, estimation, sampling procedures, and measures of statistical reliability applicable to Census Bureau and BLS data, see Appendix III.

Table 596. Civilian Population—Employment Status: 1970 to 2011

[In thousands (137,085 represents 137,085,000), except as indicated. Annual averages of monthly figures. Civilian noninstitutionalized population 16 years old and over. Based on Current Population Survey; see text, Section 1 and Appendix III]

Year	Civilian noninsti- tutional population	Civilian labor force				Unemployed		Not in labor force	
		Total	Percent of population	Employed	Employ- ment/ population ratio [1]	Number	Percent of labor force	Number	Percent of population
1970.............	137,085	82,771	60.4	78,678	57.4	4,093	4.9	54,315	39.6
1980.............	167,745	106,940	63.8	99,303	59.2	7,637	7.1	60,806	36.2
1990 [2].............	189,164	125,840	66.5	118,793	62.8	7,047	5.6	63,324	33.5
1995.............	198,584	132,304	66.6	124,900	62.9	7,404	5.6	66,280	33.4
1998 [2].............	205,220	137,673	67.1	131,463	64.1	6,210	4.5	67,547	32.9
1999 [2].............	207,753	139,368	67.1	133,488	64.3	5,880	4.2	68,385	32.9
2000 [2].............	212,577	142,583	67.1	136,891	64.4	5,692	4.0	69,994	32.9
2001.............	215,092	143,734	66.8	136,933	63.7	6,801	4.7	71,359	33.2
2002.............	217,570	144,863	66.6	136,485	62.7	8,378	5.8	72,707	33.4
2003 [2].............	221,168	146,510	66.2	137,736	62.3	8,774	6.0	74,658	33.8
2004 [2].............	223,357	147,401	66.0	139,252	62.3	8,149	5.5	75,956	34.0
2005 [2].............	226,082	149,320	66.0	141,730	62.7	7,591	5.1	76,762	34.0
2006 [2].............	228,815	151,428	66.2	144,427	63.1	7,001	4.6	77,387	33.8
2007 [2].............	231,867	153,124	66.0	146,047	63.0	7,078	4.6	78,743	34.0
2008 [2].............	233,788	154,287	66.0	145,362	62.2	8,924	5.8	79,501	34.0
2009 [2].............	235,801	154,142	65.4	139,877	59.3	14,265	9.3	81,659	34.6
2010 [2].............	237,830	153,889	64.7	139,064	58.5	14,825	9.6	83,941	35.3
2011 [2].............	239,618	153,617	64.1	139,869	58.4	13,747	8.9	86,001	35.9

[1] Civilian employed as a percent of the civilian noninstitutional population. [2] Data not strictly comparable with data for earlier years. See text, this section, and February 1994, March 1996, February 1997–99, and February 2003–12 issues of Employment and Earnings.

Source: U.S. Bureau of Labor Statistics, "Employment and Earnings Online," January 2012 issue, March 2012, <http://www.bls.gov/opub/ee/home.htm> and <http://www.bls.gov/cps/home.htm>.

Table 597. Civilian Labor Force and Participation Rates With Projections: 1980 to 2020

[106.9 represents 106,900,000. Civilian noninstitutionalized population 16 years old and over. Annual averages of monthly figures. Rates are based on annual average civilian noninstitutional population of each specified group and represent proportion of each specified group in the civilian labor force. Based on Current Population Survey; see text, Section 1 and Appendix III]

Race, Hispanic origin, sex, and age	Civilian labor force (mil.)						Participation rate (percent) [1]					
	1980	1990 [2]	2000 [2]	2005 [2]	2010 [2]	2020, proj.	1980	1990 [2]	2000 [2]	2005 [2]	2010 [2]	2020, proj.
Total [3]................	106.9	125.8	142.6	149.3	153.9	164.4	63.8	66.5	67.1	66.0	64.7	62.5
White [4]...................	93.6	107.4	118.5	122.3	125.1	130.5	64.1	66.9	67.3	66.3	65.1	62.8
Male.................	54.5	59.6	64.5	66.7	67.7	70.4	78.2	77.1	75.5	74.1	72.0	69.0
Female.................	39.1	47.8	54.1	55.6	57.4	60.1	51.2	57.4	59.5	58.9	58.5	56.9
Black [4]...................	10.9	13.7	16.4	17.0	17.9	19.7	61.0	64.0	65.8	64.2	62.2	60.3
Male.................	5.6	6.8	7.7	8.0	8.4	9.4	70.3	71.0	69.2	67.3	65.0	63.1
Female.................	5.3	6.9	8.7	9.0	9.4	10.3	53.1	58.3	63.1	61.6	59.9	57.9
Asian [4,5]................	(NA)	(NA)	6.3	6.5	7.2	9.4	(NA)	(NA)	67.2	66.1	64.7	63.1
Male.................	(NA)	(NA)	3.4	3.5	3.9	5.0	(NA)	(NA)	76.1	74.8	73.2	71.0
Female.................	(NA)	(NA)	2.9	3.0	3.4	4.5	(NA)	(NA)	59.2	58.2	57.0	56.1
Hispanic [6]................	6.1	10.7	16.7	19.8	22.7	30.5	64.0	67.4	69.7	68.0	67.5	66.2
Male.................	3.8	6.5	9.9	12.0	13.5	17.9	81.4	81.4	81.5	80.1	77.8	75.9
Female.................	2.3	4.2	6.8	7.8	9.2	12.6	47.4	53.1	57.5	55.3	56.5	56.1
Male.................	61.5	69.0	76.3	80.0	82.0	87.1	77.4	76.4	74.8	73.3	71.2	68.2
16 to 19 years..........	5.0	4.1	4.3	3.6	3.0	2.4	60.5	55.7	52.8	43.2	34.9	27.9
20 to 24 years..........	8.6	7.9	7.5	8.1	7.9	7.3	85.9	84.4	82.6	79.1	74.5	69.4
25 to 34 years..........	17.0	19.9	17.8	17.8	18.4	19.7	95.2	94.1	93.4	91.7	89.7	86.9
35 to 44 years..........	11.8	17.5	20.1	19.5	18.1	19.3	95.5	94.3	92.7	92.1	91.5	91.3
45 to 54 years..........	9.9	11.1	16.3	18.1	18.9	17.4	91.2	90.7	88.6	87.7	86.8	86.0
55 to 64 years..........	7.2	6.6	7.8	10.0	12.1	14.7	72.1	67.8	67.3	69.3	70.0	71.1
65 years and over......	1.9	2.0	2.5	3.0	3.7	6.4	19.0	16.3	17.7	19.8	22.1	26.7
Female...................	45.5	56.8	66.3	69.3	71.9	77.2	51.5	57.5	59.9	59.3	58.6	57.1
16 to 19 years..........	4.4	3.7	4.0	3.6	2.9	2.1	52.9	51.6	51.2	44.2	35.0	25.2
20 to 24 years..........	7.3	6.8	6.7	7.1	7.2	6.5	68.9	71.3	73.1	70.1	68.3	62.3
25 to 34 years..........	12.3	16.1	14.9	14.5	15.3	16.8	65.5	73.5	76.1	73.9	74.7	74.2
35 to 44 years..........	8.6	14.7	17.5	16.5	15.2	15.8	65.5	76.4	77.2	75.8	75.2	74.0
45 to 54 years..........	7.0	9.1	14.8	16.3	17.1	15.6	59.9	71.2	76.8	76.0	75.7	75.7
55 to 64 years..........	4.7	4.9	6.6	8.9	11.2	14.6	41.3	45.2	51.9	57.0	60.2	66.6
65 years and over......	1.2	1.5	1.8	2.3	3.0	5.7	8.1	8.6	9.4	11.5	13.8	19.2

NA Not available. [1] Civilian labor force as a percent of the civilian noninstitutional population. [2] See footnote 2, Table 596. [3] Includes other races, not shown separately. [4] The 2005 Current Population Survey (CPS) allowed respondents to choose more than one race. Beginning 2005, data represent persons who selected this race group only and exclude persons reporting more than one race. Prior to 2005 the CPS only allowed respondents to report one race group. See also comments on race in the text for Section 1. [5] Prior to 2005, includes Pacific Islanders. [6] Persons of Hispanic origin may be any race.

Source: U.S. Bureau of Labor Statistics, "Employment and Earnings Online," January 2012; "Monthly Labor Review," November 2011; and "Employment Projections Program," <http://www.bls.gov/emp/ep_data_labor_force.htm>.

Table 598. Civilian Population—Employment Status by Sex, Race, and Ethnicity: 1980 to 2011

[In thousands (79,398 represents 79,398,000), except as indicated. Annual averages of monthly figures. See Table 596 for U.S. totals and coverage]

Year, sex, race, and Hispanic origin	Civilian noninstitutionalized population	Civilian labor force				Unemployed		Not in labor force	
		Total	Percent of population	Employed	Employment/population ratio [1]	Number	Percent of labor force	Number	Percent of population
Male:									
1980................	79,398	61,453	77.4	57,186	72.0	4,267	6.9	17,945	22.6
1990 [2]............	90,377	69,011	76.4	65,104	72.0	3,906	5.7	21,367	23.6
2000 [2]............	101,964	76,280	74.8	73,305	71.9	2,975	3.9	25,684	25.2
2005 [2]............	109,151	80,033	73.3	75,973	69.6	4,059	5.1	29,119	26.7
2009 [2]............	114,136	82,123	72.0	73,670	64.5	8,453	10.3	32,013	28.0
2010 [2]............	115,174	81,985	71.2	73,359	63.7	8,626	10.5	33,189	28.8
2011 [2]............	116,317	81,975	70.5	74,290	63.9	7,684	9.4	34,343	29.5
Female:									
1980................	88,348	45,487	51.5	42,117	47.7	3,370	7.4	42,861	48.5
1990 [2]............	98,787	56,829	57.5	53,689	54.3	3,140	5.5	41,957	42.5
2000 [2]............	110,613	66,303	59.9	63,586	57.5	2,717	4.1	44,310	40.1
2005 [2]............	116,931	69,288	59.3	65,757	56.2	3,531	5.1	47,643	40.7
2009 [2]............	121,665	72,019	59.2	66,208	54.4	5,811	8.1	49,646	40.8
2010 [2]............	122,656	71,904	58.6	65,705	53.6	6,199	8.6	50,752	41.4
2011 [3]............	123,300	71,642	58.1	65,579	53.2	6,063	8.5	51,658	41.9
White: [3]									
1980................	146,122	93,600	64.1	87,715	60.0	5,884	6.3	52,523	35.9
1990 [2]............	160,625	107,447	66.9	102,261	63.7	5,186	4.8	53,178	33.1
2000 [2]............	176,220	118,545	67.3	114,424	64.9	4,121	3.5	57,675	32.7
2005 [2]............	184,446	122,299	66.3	116,949	63.4	5,350	4.4	62,148	33.7
2009 [2]............	190,902	125,644	65.8	114,996	60.2	10,648	8.5	65,258	34.2
2010 [2]............	192,075	125,084	65.1	114,168	59.4	10,916	8.7	66,991	34.9
2011 [2]............	193,077	124,579	64.5	114,690	59.4	9,889	7.9	68,498	35.5
Black: [3]									
1980................	17,824	10,865	61.0	9,313	52.2	1,553	14.3	6,959	39.0
1990 [2]............	21,477	13,740	64.0	12,175	56.7	1,565	11.4	7,737	36.0
2000 [2]............	24,902	16,397	65.8	15,156	60.9	1,241	7.6	8,505	34.2
2005 [2]............	26,517	17,013	64.2	15,313	57.7	1,700	10.0	9,504	35.8
2009 [2]............	28,241	17,632	62.4	15,025	53.2	2,606	14.8	10,609	37.6
2010 [2]............	28,708	17,862	62.2	15,010	52.3	2,852	16.0	10,846	37.8
2011 [2]............	29,114	17,881	61.4	15,051	51.7	2,831	15.8	11,233	38.6
Asian: [3, 4]									
2000................	9,330	6,270	67.2	6,043	64.8	227	3.6	3,060	32.8
2005 [2]............	9,842	6,503	66.1	6,244	63.4	259	4.0	3,339	33.9
2009 [2]............	10,842	7,156	66.0	6,635	61.2	522	7.3	3,685	34.0
2010 [2]............	11,199	7,248	64.7	6,705	59.9	543	7.5	3,951	35.3
2011 [2]............	11,439	7,386	64.6	6,867	60.0	518	7.0	4,054	35.4
Hispanic: [5]									
1980................	9,598	6,146	64.0	5,527	57.6	620	10.1	3,451	36.0
1990 [2]............	15,904	10,720	67.4	9,845	61.9	876	8.2	5,184	32.6
2000 [2]............	23,938	16,689	69.7	15,735	65.7	954	5.7	7,249	30.3
2005 [2]............	29,133	19,824	68.0	18,632	64.0	1,191	6.0	9,310	32.0
2009 [2]............	32,891	22,352	68.0	19,647	59.7	2,706	12.1	10,539	32.0
2010 [2]............	33,713	22,748	67.5	19,906	59.0	2,843	12.5	10,964	32.5
2011 [2]............	34,438	22,898	66.5	20,269	58.9	2,629	11.5	11,540	33.5
Mexican:									
1990 [2]............	9,752	6,707	68.8	6,146	63.0	561	8.4	3,045	31.2
2000 [2]............	15,333	10,783	70.3	10,144	66.2	639	5.9	4,550	29.7
2005 [2]............	18,523	12,671	68.4	11,887	64.2	784	6.2	5,851	31.6
2009 [2]............	20,923	14,210	67.9	12,478	59.6	1,732	12.2	6,713	32.1
2010 [2]............	21,267	14,403	67.7	12,622	59.4	1,781	12.4	6,864	32.3
2011 [2]............	21,519	14,360	66.7	12,697	59.0	1,663	11.6	7,159	33.3
Puerto Rican:									
1990 [2]............	1,718	960	55.9	870	50.6	91	9.5	758	44.1
2000 [2]............	2,193	1,411	64.3	1,318	60.1	92	6.6	783	35.7
2005 [2]............	2,654	1,619	61.0	1,492	56.2	126	7.8	1,035	39.0
2009 [2]............	2,962	1,850	62.4	1,594	53.8	256	13.8	1,113	37.6
2010 [2]............	3,110	1,906	61.3	1,612	51.8	293	15.4	1,204	38.7
2011 [2]............	3,201	1,893	59.2	1,627	50.8	266	14.1	1,307	40.8
Cuban:									
1990 [2]............	918	603	65.7	559	60.9	44	7.2	315	34.3
2000 [2]............	1,174	740	63.1	707	60.3	33	4.5	434	37.0
2005 [2]............	1,259	755	60.0	730	58.0	25	3.3	503	40.0
2009 [2]............	1,442	877	60.8	795	55.1	82	9.4	565	39.2
2010 [2]............	1,549	970	62.6	850	54.9	120	12.4	579	37.4
2011 [2]............	1,533	976	63.6	867	56.5	109	11.2	558	36.4

[1] Civilian employed as a percent of the civilian noninstitutional population. [2] See footnote 2, Table 596. [3] The 2005 Current Population Survey (CPS) allowed respondents to choose more than one race. Beginning 2005, data represent persons who selected this race group only and exclude persons reporting more than one race. The CPS in prior years only allowed respondents to report one race group. See also comments on race in the text for Section 1. [4] Prior to 2005, includes Pacific Islanders. [5] Persons of Hispanic origin may be any race. Includes persons of other Hispanic or Latino ethnicity, not shown separately.

Source: U.S. Bureau of Labor Statistics, "Employment and Earnings Online," January 2012 issue, March 2012, <www.bls.gov/opub/ee/home.htm> and <http://www.bls.gov/cps/home.htm>.

Table 599. Foreign-Born and Native-Born Populations—Employment Status by Selected Characteristics: 2011

[239,618 represents 239,618,000. For civilian noninstitutional population 16 years old and over, except as indicated. The foreign born are persons who reside in the United States but who were born outside the country or in one of its outlying areas to parents who were not U.S. citizens. The foreign born include legally admitted immigrants, refugees, temporary residents such as students and temporary workers and undocumented immigrants. Annual averages of monthly figures. Based on Current Population Survey; see text, Section 1 and Appendix III]

| Characteristic | Civilian noninstitu- tionalized population (1,000) | Civilian labor force | | | | | Not in the labor force |
| | | Total (1,000) | Participa- tion rate [1] | Employed (1,000) | Unemployed | | |
					Number (1,000)	Unemploy- ment rate	
Total..	**239,618**	**153,617**	**64.1**	**139,869**	**13,747**	**8.9**	**86,001**
Male..	116,317	81,975	70.5	74,290	7,684	9.4	34,342
Female..	123,300	71,642	58.1	65,579	6,063	8.5	51,658
FOREIGN BORN							
Total [2]..	**36,420**	**24,391**	**67.0**	**22,183**	**2,208**	**9.1**	**12,029**
Male..	18,090	14,379	79.5	13,120	1,260	8.8	3,711
Female..	18,331	10,012	54.6	9,063	949	9.5	8,319
Age:							
16 to 24 years old........................	3,631	1,971	54.3	1,695	276	14.0	1,660
25 to 34 years old........................	7,562	5,758	76.1	5,255	503	8.7	1,804
35 to 44 years old........................	8,492	6,843	80.6	6,301	542	7.9	1,649
45 to 54 years old........................	7,089	5,799	81.8	5,274	525	9.1	1,290
55 to 64 years old........................	4,737	3,161	66.7	2,870	290	9.2	1,576
65 years old and over.....................	4,909	860	17.5	788	72	8.3	4,049
Race and Hispanic ethnicity:							
White non-Hispanic........................	7,617	4,583	60.2	4,237	346	7.6	3,034
Black non-Hispanic........................	3,002	2,137	71.2	1,870	267	12.5	865
Asian non-Hispanic........................	8,306	5,449	65.6	5,086	363	6.7	2,857
Hispanic [3]........................	17,132	11,963	69.8	10,751	1,212	10.1	5,169
Educational attainment:							
Total, 25 years old and over.............	32,790	22,420	68.4	20,488	1,932	8.6	10,370
Less than a high school diploma.........	9,532	5,721	60.0	5,086	634	11.1	3,811
High school graduates, no college [4]......	8,488	5,674	66.8	5,145	529	9.3	2,814
Some college or associate's degree......	5,389	3,927	72.9	3,584	343	8.7	1,462
Bachelor's degree and higher [5]...........	9,381	7,098	75.7	6,673	425	6.0	2,283
NATIVE BORN							
Total [2]..	**203,197**	**129,226**	**63.6**	**117,686**	**11,539**	**8.9**	**73,971**
Male..	98,228	67,595	68.8	61,170	6,425	9.5	30,633
Female..	104,970	61,630	58.7	56,516	5,115	8.3	43,340
Age:							
16 to 24 years old........................	34,567	19,026	55.0	15,668	3,358	17.7	15,541
25 to 34 years old........................	33,801	27,967	82.7	25,282	2,685	9.6	5,834
35 to 44 years old........................	31,006	25,817	83.3	23,970	1,847	7.2	5,189
45 to 54 years old........................	36,753	29,560	80.4	27,593	1,967	6.7	7,193
55 to 64 years old........................	32,250	20,604	63.9	19,315	1,289	6.3	11,646
65 years old and over.....................	34,819	6,252	18.0	5,858	393	6.3	28,567
Race and Hispanic ethnicity:							
White non-Hispanic........................	153,541	98,751	64.3	91,609	7,142	7.2	54,790
Black non-Hispanic........................	24,911	14,973	60.1	12,526	2,447	16.3	9,938
Asian non-Hispanic........................	2,917	1,793	61.5	1,647	147	8.2	1,124
Hispanic [3]........................	17,306	10,934	63.2	9,518	1,417	13.0	6,372
Educational attainment:							
Total, 25 years and over.................	168,630	110,200	65.4	102,019	8,181	7.4	58,430
Less than a high school diploma.........	15,590	5,878	37.7	4,881	998	17.0	9,712
High school graduates, no college [4]......	53,444	31,670	59.3	28,679	2,992	9.4	21,774
Some college or associate's degree......	47,700	32,904	69.0	30,310	2,594	7.9	14,796
Bachelor's degree and higher [5]...........	51,896	39,747	76.6	38,149	1,598	4.0	12,149

[1] Civilian labor force as a percent of the civilian noninstitutionalized population. [2] Includes other races, not shown separately. [3] Persons of Hispanic origin may be any race. [4] Includes persons with a high school diploma or equivalent. [5] Includes persons with bachelor's, master's, professional, and doctoral degrees.

Source: U.S. Bureau of Labor Statistics, *Foreign-Born Workers: Labor Force Characteristics in 2011*, News Release, USDL-12-1019, May 2012. See also <http://www.bls.gov/news.release/forbrn.toc.htm>.

Table 600. Employment Status of Veterans by Period of Service and Sex: 2011

[In thousands (230,891 represents 230,891,000). For civilian noninstitutional population 18 years old and over. Veterans are defined as men and women who have previously served on active duty in the U.S. Armed Forces and who were civilians at the time they were surveyed. See text, Section 10. Annual averages of monthly figures. Based on Current Population Survey; see text, Section 1 and Appendix III]

Veteran status, period of service, and sex	Civilian non-institu-tionalized popula-tion	Civilian labor force							Not in labor force
				Employed			Unemployed		
		Total	Percent of popula-tion	Total	Percent of popula-tion	Total	Percent of labor force		
Total, 18 years and over...........	**230,891**	**151,743**	**65.7**	**138,515**	**60.0**	**13,229**	**8.7**		**79,147**
Veterans...........................	21,613	11,320	52.4	10,375	48.0	945	8.3		10,293
Gulf War era, total.................	5,323	4,397	82.6	3,992	75.0	405	9.2		925
Gulf War era I [1].................	2,387	1,937	81.2	1,704	71.4	234	12.1		450
Gulf War era II [2]................	2,936	2,460	83.8	2,289	78.0	172	7.0		476
WWII, Korean War, and Vietnam era [3]......	10,436	3,549	34.0	3,280	31.4	269	7.6		6,887
Other service periods [4].............	5,853	3,374	57.6	3,102	53.0	271	8.0		2,480
Nonveterans [5]......................	209,278	140,424	67.1	128,140	61.2	12,284	8.7		68,854
Male, 18 years and over............	**111,831**	**81,058**	**72.5**	**73,641**	**65.8**	**7,417**	**9.2**		**30,773**
Veterans...........................	19,812	10,204	51.5	9,360	47.2	844	8.3		9,608
Gulf War era, total.................	4,457	3,777	84.7	3,428	76.9	349	9.2		680
Gulf War era I [1].................	1,982	1,656	83.5	1,457	73.5	199	12.0		327
Gulf War era II [2]................	2,475	2,121	85.7	1,971	79.6	150	7.1		353
WWII, Korean War, and Vietnam era [3]......	10,106	3,441	34.0	3,181	31.5	260	7.6		6,665
Other service periods [4].............	5,248	2,986	56.9	2,751	52.4	235	7.9		2,262
Nonveterans [5]......................	92,019	70,854	77.0	64,280	69.9	6,573	9.3		21,166
Female, 18 years and over..........	**119,060**	**70,685**	**59.4**	**64,874**	**54.5**	**5,811**	**8.2**		**48,374**
Veterans...........................	1,801	1,116	62.0	1,015	56.3	101	9.1		685
Gulf War era, total.................	865	620	71.7	564	65.2	56	9.1		245
Gulf War era I [1].................	405	281	69.5	246	60.9	35	12.4		123
Gulf War era II [2]................	461	339	73.5	318	68.9	21	6.3		122
WWII, Korean War, and Vietnam era [3]......	330	108	32.7	99	30.1	9	7.9		222
Other service periods [4].............	605	388	64.1	351	58.1	36	9.4		217
Nonveterans [5]......................	117,259	69,570	59.3	63,859	54.5	5,710	8.2		47,689

[1] Gulf War era I: August 1990–August 2001. [2] Gulf War era II: September 2001–present. [3] World War II: December 1941–December 1946. Korean War: July 1950–January 1955. Vietnam era: August 1964–April 1975. [4] Other service periods; all other time periods. [5] Nonveterans are men and women who never served on active duty in the U.S. Armed Forces.

Source: Bureau of Labor Statistics, Employment Situation of Veterans - 2011, News Release, USDL-12-0493, March 2012. See also <http://www.bls.gov/news.release/vet.nr0.htm>.

Table 601. Labor Force Status of Persons With and Without a Disability: 2011

[27,382 represents 27,382,000. For civilian noninstitutionalized population 16 years old and over, except as indicated. Persons with a disability are those who have a physical, mental, or emotional condition that causes serious difficulty with their daily activities. Annual averages of monthly figures. Based on Current Population Survey; see text, Section 1 and Appendix III]

Characteristic	Civilian non-institutional-ized popula-tion (1,000)	Civilian labor force					Not in the labor force
		Total (1,000)	Participation rate [1]	Employed (1,000)	Unemployed		
					Number (1,000)	Unemploy-ment rate	
WITH DISABILITY							
Total................................	**27,382**	**5,722**	**20.9**	**4,861**	**861**	**15.0**	**21,659**
Male...............................	12,633	3,152	24.9	2,670	482	15.3	9,481
Female.............................	14,749	2,571	17.4	2,192	379	14.7	12,178
Both Sexes 65 and over............	12,335	868	7.0	794	74	8.5	11,467
WITHOUT DISABILITY							
Total................................	**212,236**	**147,894**	**69.7**	**135,008**	**12,886**	**8.7**	**65,342**
Male...............................	103,684	78,823	76.0	71,621	7,202	9.1	24,861
Female.............................	108,552	69,071	63.6	63,387	5,684	8.2	39,480
Both Sexes 65 and over............	27,394	6,244	22.8	5,853	391	6.3	21,150

[1] Civilian labor force as a percent of the civilian noninstitutionalized population.

Source: U.S. Bureau of Labor Statistics, Current Population Survey, "Data on the Employment Status of People With a Disability," <http://www.bls.gov/cps/cpsdisability.htm>.

Table 602. Civilian Labor Force—Percent Distribution by Sex and Age: 1980 to 2011

[106,940 represents 106,940,000. Civilian noninstitutionalized population 16 years old and over. Annual averages of monthly figures. Based on Current Population Survey; see text, Section 1 and Appendix III]

Year and sex	Civilian labor force (1,000)	Percent distribution						
		16 to 19 years	20 to 24 years	25 to 34 years	35 to 44 years	45 to 54 years	55 to 64 years	65 years and over
Total: 1980...................	106,940	8.8	14.9	27.3	19.1	15.8	11.2	2.9
1990 [1]................	125,840	6.2	11.7	28.6	25.5	16.1	9.2	2.7
2000 [1]................	142,583	5.8	10.0	23.0	26.3	21.8	10.1	3.0
2010 [1]................	153,889	3.8	9.8	21.8	21.7	23.4	15.1	4.4
2011 [1]................	153,617	3.7	9.9	22.0	21.3	23.0	15.5	4.6
Male: 1980................	61,453	8.1	14.0	27.6	19.3	16.1	11.8	3.1
1990 [1]................	69,011	5.9	11.4	28.8	25.3	16.1	9.6	2.9
2000 [1]................	76,280	5.6	9.9	23.4	26.3	21.3	10.2	3.3
2010 [1]................	81,985	3.6	9.6	22.4	22.1	23.0	14.8	4.5
2011 [1]................	81,975	3.5	9.9	22.5	21.6	22.5	15.1	4.9
Female: 1980.............	45,487	9.6	16.1	26.9	19.0	15.4	10.4	2.6
1990 [1]................	56,829	6.5	12.0	28.3	25.8	16.1	8.7	2.6
2000 [1]................	66,303	6.0	10.2	22.5	26.4	22.3	9.9	2.7
2010 [1]................	71,904	4.1	10.0	21.2	21.2	23.8	15.6	4.2
2011 [1]................	71,642	4.0	10.0	21.3	20.9	23.6	15.9	4.4

[1] See footnote 2, Table 596.

Source: U.S. Bureau of Labor Statistics, "Employment and Earnings Online," January 2012 issue, March 2012, <http://www.bls.gov/opub/ee/home.htm> and <http://www.bls.gov/cps/home.htm>.

Table 603. Civilian Labor Force and Participation Rates by Educational Attainment, Sex, Race, and Hispanic Origin: 2000 to 2011

[120,061 represents 120,061,000. Civilian noninstitutional population 25 years old and over. Annual averages of monthly figures. See Table 639 for unemployment data. Rates are based on annual average civilian noninstitutional population of each specified group and represent proportion of each specified group in the civilian labor force]

Year, sex, and race	Civilian labor force					Participation rate (percent) [1]				
		Percent distribution								
	Total (1,000)	Less than a high school diploma	High school graduate, no college	Less than a bachelor's degree	College graduate	Total	Less than a high school diploma	High school graduate, no college	Less than a bachelor's degree	College graduate
Total: [2]										
2000 [3]............	120,061	10.4	31.4	27.7	30.5	67.3	43.5	64.4	73.9	79.4
2005 [3]............	127,030	10.0	30.1	27.5	32.4	67.1	45.5	63.2	72.5	77.9
2010 [3]............	132,955	8.9	28.8	27.7	34.6	66.5	46.3	61.6	70.5	76.7
2011 [3]............	132,620	8.7	28.2	27.8	35.3	65.8	46.2	60.3	69.4	76.4
Male:										
2000 [3]............	64,490	11.8	31.1	25.9	31.2	76.1	56.0	75.1	80.9	84.4
2005 [3]............	68,389	11.7	30.9	25.4	32.1	75.4	58.6	73.6	79.3	82.9
2010 [3]............	71,129	10.6	30.4	25.6	33.4	74.1	59.1	71.4	76.7	81.3
2011 [3]............	70,979	10.4	29.8	25.7	34.1	73.3	58.9	69.9	75.0	81.3
Female:										
2000 [3]............	55,572	8.8	31.8	29.7	29.7	59.4	32.3	55.5	68.0	74.0
2005 [3]............	58,641	8.0	29.2	30.0	32.8	59.4	32.9	53.8	66.8	72.9
2010 [3]............	61,825	7.0	26.9	30.1	36.0	59.5	33.5	52.4	65.4	72.4
2011 [3]............	61,641	6.8	26.2	31.2	36.8	59.0	33.5	51.1	64.6	71.9
White: [4]										
2000 [3]............	99,964	10.1	31.4	27.5	31.0	67.0	44.1	63.6	73.1	79.0
2005 [3]............	104,240	9.8	29.9	27.6	32.7	66.9	46.4	62.5	72.0	77.5
2010 [3]............	108,274	8.9	28.7	27.5	34.9	66.5	47.7	61.2	70.1	76.5
2011 [3]............	107,745	8.8	27.9	27.6	35.7	65.8	47.8	59.8	68.9	76.2
Black: [4]										
2000 [3]............	13,582	12.4	36.0	31.2	20.5	68.2	39.3	69.9	79.3	84.4
2005 [3]............	14,252	11.2	36.4	30.2	22.2	67.2	39.8	67.9	75.6	82.0
2010 [3]............	15,114	9.4	33.3	32.8	24.5	65.8	38.8	63.8	73.5	79.5
2011 [3]............	15,129	8.9	33.6	32.8	24.7	64.8	37.9	62.2	72.1	78.6
Asian: [4, 5]										
2000 [3]............	5,402	9.1	20.7	20.2	50.1	70.9	46.0	65.6	76.4	79.1
2005 [3]............	5,805	8.0	17.7	17.3	57.0	69.4	45.3	61.8	71.6	77.5
2010 [3]............	6,601	7.3	18.8	17.1	56.7	68.7	44.1	62.8	70.6	75.9
2011 [3]............	6,726	6.9	18.8	17.4	57.0	68.3	42.2	61.1	70.6	76.2
Hispanic: [6]										
2000 [3]............	12,975	36.7	29.3	20.6	13.4	71.5	61.9	75.0	80.8	83.5
2005 [3]............	16,135	35.5	29.4	20.9	14.2	70.8	61.4	74.3	78.8	81.7
2010 [3]............	18,987	31.4	30.8	21.7	16.0	71.4	61.9	73.9	77.8	81.7
2011 [3]............	18,916	31.0	30.7	22.3	16.0	70.5	61.0	72.7	77.1	80.6

[1] See footnote 1, Table 597. [2] Includes other races, not shown separately. [3] See footnote 2, Table 596. [4] Beginning 2005, for persons in this race group only. See footnote 4, Table 597. [5] 2000 data include Pacific Islanders. [6] Persons of Hispanic origin may be any race.

Source: U.S. Bureau of Labor Statistics, "Employment and Earnings Online," January 2012 issue, March 2012, <http://www.bls.gov/opub/ee/home.htm> and <http://www.bls.gov/cps/home.htm>.

Table 604. Characteristics of the Civilian Labor Force by State: 2010

[In thousands (153,889 represents 153,889,000), except ratio and rate. Civilian noninstitutionalized population 16 years old and over. Annual averages of monthly figures. Data for states may not sum to national totals due to rounding]

State	Total Number	Total Female	Employed Total	Employed Female	Employment/ population ratio [1]	Unemployed Total Number	Unemployed Total Female	Unemployed Rate [2] Total	Unemployed Rate [2] Male	Unemployed Rate [2] Female	Participation rate [3] Male	Participation rate [3] Female
United States.........	**153,889**	**71,904**	**139,064**	**65,705**	**58.5**	**14,825**	**6,199**	**9.6**	**10.5**	**8.6**	**71.2**	**58.6**
Alabama..............	2,180	1,042	1,952	943	53.5	228	99	10.5	11.3	9.5	65.8	54.3
Alaska...............	360	167	331	155	64.0	29	11	8.0	9.0	6.8	73.7	65.3
Arizona..............	3,180	1,430	2,850	1,296	56.7	331	134	10.4	11.2	9.4	70.4	56.3
Arkansas............	1,343	632	1,228	577	55.3	116	55	8.6	8.6	8.7	66.5	54.9
California............	18,195	8,197	15,976	7,271	56.5	2,219	926	12.2	12.9	11.3	71.9	57.0
Colorado............	2,720	1,236	2,482	1,133	63.7	238	103	8.7	9.1	8.3	76.7	63.0
Connecticut..........	1,892	902	1,719	827	62.2	173	76	9.2	9.9	8.4	74.5	62.8
Delaware............	428	207	392	192	56.5	37	15	8.5	9.7	7.3	67.3	56.8
District of Columbia......	341	172	310	157	62.5	31	15	9.2	9.7	8.6	74.1	64.4
Florida..............	9,089	4,278	8,083	3,863	54.9	1,006	415	11.1	12.3	9.7	67.8	56.0
Georgia.............	4,744	2,210	4,238	2,000	57.3	506	211	10.7	11.7	9.5	71.8	57.2
Hawaii..............	623	296	579	278	58.6	43	18	7.0	7.8	6.1	67.9	58.3
Idaho...............	759	342	691	314	59.4	68	28	9.0	9.7	8.1	72.4	58.2
Illinois.............	6,645	3,073	5,970	2,801	60.1	675	271	10.2	11.3	8.8	74.1	60.1
Indiana.............	3,153	1,472	2,818	1,330	57.1	334	142	10.6	11.4	9.7	70.1	57.9
Iowa...............	1,673	797	1,571	754	66.9	102	44	6.1	6.6	5.5	76.1	66.6
Kansas.............	1,497	702	1,385	655	64.6	111	47	7.4	8.1	6.7	75.7	64.0
Kentucky............	2,056	978	1,844	886	55.0	212	92	10.3	11.1	9.4	67.0	56.1
Louisiana............	2,092	1,007	1,928	927	56.4	164	80	7.8	7.7	8.0	67.1	55.9
Maine..............	690	338	633	314	59.4	57	24	8.2	9.3	7.1	68.6	61.0
Maryland............	3,055	1,477	2,819	1,368	63.5	236	109	7.7	8.0	7.4	75.1	63.1
Massachusetts..........	3,493	1,703	3,194	1,576	60.5	298	127	8.5	9.6	7.5	70.6	62.0
Michigan............	4,821	2,276	4,232	2,052	54.4	589	224	12.2	14.3	9.9	67.6	56.7
Minnesota...........	2,935	1,390	2,721	1,310	66.2	214	80	7.3	8.6	5.8	76.0	66.9
Mississippi...........	1,296	624	1,155	564	52.2	141	60	10.9	12.1	9.6	64.7	53.2
Missouri.............	3,032	1,477	2,745	1,347	59.1	287	130	9.5	10.1	8.8	69.9	61.1
Montana.............	490	231	452	218	58.5	38	14	7.7	9.3	5.9	67.6	59.2
Nebraska............	976	471	929	450	67.5	47	21	4.8	5.2	4.4	74.8	67.2
Nevada.............	1,322	580	1,131	507	56.1	191	74	14.4	15.8	12.7	73.1	58.0
New Hampshire.........	747	357	702	338	66.1	44	18	5.9	6.7	5.1	75.1	65.6
New Jersey...........	4,520	2,102	4,100	1,917	60.2	420	185	9.3	9.7	8.8	73.6	59.6
New Mexico...........	921	429	843	400	54.9	79	29	8.5	10.1	6.8	66.3	54.1
New York............	9,654	4,596	8,832	4,242	57.2	822	353	8.5	9.3	7.7	68.6	57.1
North Carolina..........	4,573	2,165	4,094	1,968	56.9	479	197	10.5	11.7	9.1	70.3	57.4
North Dakota...........	372	175	358	169	70.2	14	6	3.8	4.1	3.5	77.7	68.4
Ohio................	5,853	2,812	5,263	2,572	58.6	590	239	10.1	11.5	8.5	70.5	60.3
Oklahoma............	1,745	815	1,621	761	57.8	125	53	7.2	7.7	6.6	68.9	56.2
Oregon..............	2,000	943	1,780	852	58.5	221	91	11.0	12.3	9.7	71.0	60.8
Pennsylvania...........	6,317	2,968	5,774	2,743	57.8	543	226	8.6	9.5	7.6	69.9	57.1
Rhode Island...........	572	281	508	251	60.1	65	30	11.3	12.0	10.5	72.1	63.7
South Carolina..........	2,134	1028	1,899	930	53.8	235	99	11.0	12.3	9.6	66.3	55.2
South Dakota...........	443	212	420	203	67.2	23	9	5.1	6.0	4.2	75.1	66.8
Tennessee............	3,077	1,443	2,788	1,332	56.7	289	111	9.4	10.9	7.7	69.6	56.3
Texas...............	12,122	5,391	11,149	4,967	60.5	974	424	8.0	8.2	7.9	74.6	57.4
Utah................	1,385	603	1,271	564	63.3	114	40	8.2	9.5	6.6	77.8	60.2
Vermont.............	361	175	339	166	66.4	22	9	6.2	7.1	5.2	74.6	67.1
Virginia.............	4,108	1,972	3,800	1,839	62.5	308	133	7.5	8.2	6.7	73.6	62.1
Washington...........	3,541	1,662	3,180	1,514	60.6	361	148	10.2	11.4	8.9	72.7	62.4
West Virginia..........	795	362	724	336	49.6	71	26	9.0	10.5	7.1	61.2	48.2
Wisconsin............	3,082	1,481	2,813	1,368	63.4	268	114	8.7	9.7	7.7	73.3	65.6
Wyoming............	298	136	278	128	65.9	20	8	6.6	7.0	6.1	76.2	64.8

[1] Civilian employment as a percent of civilian noninstitutionalized population. [2] Percent unemployed of the civilian labor force. [3] Percent of civilian noninstitutionalized population of each specified group in the civilian labor force.

Source: U.S. Bureau of Labor Statistics, Local Area Unemployment Statistics, "Geographic Profile of Employment and Unemployment, 2010 Annual Averages," <http://www.bls.gov/gps/>.

Table 605. Civilian Labor Force Status by Selected Metropolitan Areas: 2011

[153,617 represents 153,617,000. Civilian noninstitutional population 16 years old and over. Annual averages of monthly figures. Data are derived from the Local Area Unemployment Statistics program, a Federal-State cooperative effort in which monthly estimates of total employment and unemployment are prepared for approximately 7,300 areas. For metro areas with a Census 2010 population of 1 million or more. For definitions of metropolitan areas, see Appendix II.]

Metropolitan area ranked by population, 2010	Civilian labor force (1,000)	Unemployment rate [1]	Metropolitan area ranked by population, 2010	Civilian labor force (1,000)	Unemployment rate [1]
U.S. total, 2011............	**153,617**	**8.9**	San Antonio-New Braunfels, TX....................	1,012	7.4
New York-Northern New Jersey-Long Island, NY-NJ-PA..	9,440	8.5	Orlando-Kissimmee-Sanford, FL...............	1,122	10.4
Los Angeles-Long Beach-Santa Ana, CA........	6,528	11.4	Cincinnati-Middletown, OH-KY-IN..............	1,100	8.6
Chicago-Joliet-Naperville, IL-IN-WI..............	4,831	9.8	Cleveland-Elyria-Mentor, OH..................	1,083	7.7
Dallas-Fort Worth-Arlington, TX..................	3,287	7.8	Kansas City, MO-KS........................	1,056	8.1
Philadelphia-Camden-Wilmington, PA-NJ-DE-MD..	2,976	8.6	Las Vegas-Paradise, NV.....................	994	13.9
Houston-Sugar Land-Baytown, TX..............	2,983	8.1	San Jose-Sunnyvale-Santa Clara, CA............	923	9.9
Washington-Arlington-Alexandria, DC-VA-MD-WV..	3,173	5.8	Columbus, OH.............................	957	7.5
Miami-Fort Lauderdale-Pompano Beach, FL.....	2,875	10.5	Charlotte-Gastonia-Rock Hill, NC-SC..............	896	10.9
Atlanta-Sandy Springs-Marietta, GA...........	2,687	9.6	Indianapolis-Carmel, IN......................	903	8.4
Boston-Cambridge-Quincy, MA-NH NECTA [2]..	2,524	6.6	Austin-Round Rock-San Marcos, TX.............	940	6.8
San Francisco-Oakland-Fremont, CA..............	2,263	9.4	Virginia Beach-Norfolk-Newport News, VA-NC....	847	7.0
Detroit-Warren-Livonia, MI....................	2,018	11.5	Providence-Fall River-Warwick, RI-MA NECTA [2]..	699	11.2
Riverside-San Bernardino-Ontario, CA...........	1,799	13.4	Nashville-Davidson-Murfreesboro-Franklin, TN. ..	841	8.0
Phoenix-Mesa-Glendale, AZ...................	2,035	8.6	Milwaukee-Waukesha-West Allis, WI.............	797	7.9
Seattle-Tacoma-Bellevue, WA.................	1,878	8.7	Jacksonville, FL..........................	693	10.1
Minneapolis-St. Paul-Bloomington, MN-WI.......	1,852	6.3	Memphis, TN-MS-AR........................	625	9.9
San Diego-Carlsbad-San Marcos, CA...........	1,584	10.0	Louisville-Jefferson County, KY-IN...............	634	9.7
St. Louis, MO-IL.............................	1,450	8.9	Richmond, VA.............................	675	6.9
Tampa-St. Petersburg-Clearwater, FL..............	1,308	10.9	Oklahoma City, OK........................	580	5.7
			Hartford-West Hartford-East Hartford, CT NECTA [2]..	608	8.8
Baltimore-Towson, MD.........................	1,441	7.5	New Orleans-Metairie-Kenner, LA.................	541	7.2
Denver-Aurora-Broomfield, CO..................	1,400	8.3	Buffalo-Niagara Falls, NY.....................	571	8.0
Pittsburgh, PA..............................	1,232	7.2	Birmingham-Hoover, AL......................	530	8.3
Portland-Vancouver-Hillsboro, OR-WA............	1,198	9.1	Rochester, NY............................	521	7.7
Sacramento--Arden-Arcade--Roseville, CA......	1,039	11.9			

[1] Percent unemployed of the civilian labor force. [2] New England City and Town Areas. See Appendix II.

Source: U.S. Bureau of Labor Statistics, Local Area Unemployment Statistics (LAUS), <http://www.bls.gov/lau/home.htm>.

Table 606. School Enrollment and Labor Force Status: 2011

[In thousands (38,276 represents 38,276,000), except percent. As of October. Based on Current Population Survey; see text, Section 1 and Appendix III]

Characteristic	Population	Civilian labor force	Employed	Unemployed Total	Unemployed Rate [1]	Not in labor force
Total, 16 to 24 years [2].....................	**38,276**	**21,386**	**17,932**	**3,454**	**16.2**	**16,890**
Enrolled in school [2]......................	22,403	8,744	7,501	1,243	14.2	13,659
Enrolled in high school......................	9,618	2,116	1,582	534	25.2	7,502
Male..................................	5,010	976	704	272	27.9	4,034
Female...............................	4,608	1,140	878	262	23.0	3,468
Enrolled in college........................	12,785	6,628	5,919	709	10.7	6,158
Enrolled in 2 year college................	3,685	2,252	1,941	311	13.8	1,433
Enrolled in 4 year college................	9,101	4,375	3,977	398	9.1	4,725
Race/ethnicity:						
White: [3]						
Enrolled in high school................	7,232	1,764	1,365	399	22.6	5,468
Enrolled in college....................	9,970	5,435	4,911	524	9.6	4,536
Black or African American: [3]						
Enrolled in high school................	1,598	263	161	102	38.8	1,334
Enrolled in college....................	1,670	736	619	117	15.9	934
Asian: [3]						
Enrolled in high school................	372	37	28	9	([5])	335
Enrolled in college....................	772	261	223	38	14.5	511
Hispanic: [4]						
Enrolled in high school................	1,981	300	192	108	36.1	1,681
Enrolled in college....................	2,112	1,088	926	162	14.9	1,023
Not enrolled [2]...........................	15,873	12,642	10,431	2,212	17.5	3,231
White [3].................................	12,265	9,935	8,414	1,521	15.3	2,330
Black [3].................................	2,467	1,838	1,315	523	28.5	630
Asian [3].................................	467	353	300	53	15.1	114
Hispanic [4].............................	3,600	2,834	2,309	525	18.5	766

[1] Percent unemployed of civilian labor force in each category. [2] Includes other races, not shown separately. [3] Data for persons in this race group only. See footnote 4, Table 597. [4] Persons of Hispanic origin may be any race. [5] Data not shown where base is less than 75,000.

Source: U.S. Bureau of Labor Statistics, *College Enrollment and Work Activity of High School Graduates*, News Release, USDL 12-0716, April 2012. See also <http://www.bls.gov/news.release/hsgec.toc.htm>.

Table 607. Labor Force Participation Rates by Marital Status, Sex, and Age: 1970 to 2011

[In percent. For the civilian noninstitutional population 16 years old and over. Annual averages of monthly figures. Participation rate is the civilian labor force as a percent of the civilian noninstitutional population. Based on Current Population Survey; see text, Section 1 and Appendix III]

Marital status and year	Male participation rate							Female participation rate						
	Total	16–19 years	20–24 years	25–34 years	35–44 years	45–64 years	65 years and over	Total	16–19 years	20–24 years	25–34 years	35–44 years	45–64 years	65 years and over
Single: [1]														
1970	65.5	54.6	73.8	87.9	86.2	75.7	25.2	56.8	44.7	73.0	81.4	78.6	73.0	19.7
1980	72.6	59.9	81.3	89.2	82.2	66.9	16.8	64.4	53.6	75.2	83.3	76.9	65.6	13.9
1990 [2]	74.8	55.1	81.6	89.9	84.5	67.3	15.7	66.7	51.7	74.5	80.9	80.8	66.2	12.1
2000 [2]	73.6	52.5	80.5	89.4	82.9	69.7	17.3	68.9	51.1	76.1	83.9	80.9	69.9	10.8
2004 [2]	70.2	43.6	77.7	87.9	82.7	67.8	20.3	65.9	43.8	73.1	81.8	80.5	70.9	14.7
2005 [2]	70.1	42.9	77.0	87.9	82.9	68.6	18.8	66.0	44.2	72.6	81.4	80.7	70.9	15.5
2006 [2]	70.7	43.4	77.8	87.7	83.5	69.9	19.3	65.7	43.7	71.8	81.4	79.8	70.5	15.0
2007 [2]	70.1	40.8	76.9	88.5	84.0	70.3	22.6	65.3	41.4	72.6	82.1	78.0	70.4	18.4
2008 [2]	69.9	39.8	77.1	87.9	84.3	69.5	24.7	65.3	40.3	71.9	82.6	79.6	70.4	20.5
2009 [2]	68.3	37.1	74.6	86.5	83.7	68.5	26.1	64.2	37.5	71.4	81.6	79.5	69.3	19.7
2010 [2]	67.3	34.6	73.1	85.8	83.7	67.6	25.0	63.3	34.9	69.8	81.3	78.2	69.4	20.1
2011 [2]	67.0	33.4	73.3	85.4	82.6	67.4	23.8	62.8	34.3	69.1	79.9	77.8	67.8	21.7
Married: [3]														
1970	86.1	92.3	94.7	98.0	98.1	91.2	29.9	40.5	37.8	47.9	38.8	46.8	44.0	7.3
1980	80.9	91.3	96.9	97.5	97.2	84.3	20.5	49.8	49.3	61.4	58.8	61.8	46.9	7.3
1990 [2]	78.6	92.1	95.6	96.9	96.7	82.6	17.5	58.4	49.5	66.1	69.6	74.0	56.5	8.5
2000 [2]	77.3	79.5	94.1	96.7	95.8	83.0	19.2	61.1	53.2	63.8	70.3	74.8	65.4	10.1
2004 [2]	77.1	77.4	92.4	95.6	95.1	83.1	20.4	60.5	41.1	60.9	67.6	72.7	67.0	11.6
2005 [2]	77.2	71.4	93.4	95.3	95.2	83.6	21.4	60.7	44.1	61.1	68.4	73.0	67.0	12.5
2006 [2]	77.1	79.2	93.3	95.5	95.2	83.6	21.8	61.0	39.6	59.8	69.0	73.3	67.8	12.4
2007 [2]	76.9	86.9	92.9	95.7	95.3	83.6	21.8	61.0	43.3	61.7	68.6	73.1	67.7	13.6
2008 [2]	76.8	83.4	92.0	95.3	95.2	84.0	22.8	61.4	38.0	62.3	69.5	73.8	68.3	14.1
2009 [2]	76.3	75.8	91.2	94.7	94.8	83.8	23.3	61.4	44.7	61.8	69.4	73.7	68.6	14.9
2010 [2]	75.8	78.2	89.3	94.3	94.5	83.6	23.5	61.0	40.2	60.9	68.8	72.8	68.8	15.2
2011 [2]	74.9	75.9	90.2	93.9	94.3	82.8	24.5	60.2	44.7	60.6	68.2	72.5	68.0	15.3
Other: [4]														
1970	60.7	(B)	90.4	93.7	91.1	78.5	19.3	40.3	48.6	60.3	64.6	68.8	61.9	10.0
1980	67.5	(B)	92.6	94.1	91.9	73.3	13.7	43.6	50.0	68.4	76.5	77.1	60.2	8.2
1990 [2]	68.9	(B)	93.1	93.0	90.7	74.9	12.0	47.2	53.9	65.4	77.0	82.1	65.0	8.4
2000 [2]	66.8	60.5	88.1	93.2	89.9	73.9	12.9	49.0	46.0	74.0	83.1	82.9	69.8	8.7
2004 [2]	64.9	53.1	87.2	90.6	88.6	72.8	14.3	49.6	48.7	70.0	79.4	81.7	69.8	10.4
2005 [2]	64.9	54.9	86.4	90.4	89.4	72.7	15.1	49.4	46.8	67.4	78.1	80.9	69.4	10.5
2006 [2]	65.6	47.8	86.0	91.5	88.9	73.8	16.3	49.6	45.3	71.5	78.2	80.9	69.3	10.9
2007 [2]	65.6	43.4	82.5	92.1	89.4	73.7	16.1	49.5	44.6	63.8	78.4	81.4	69.3	11.4
2008 [2]	65.0	43.2	84.9	90.7	89.4	73.2	16.8	49.2	39.7	64.9	77.4	81.4	69.1	12.1
2009 [2]	63.7	42.6	78.6	88.5	88.5	71.8	17.0	49.3	39.0	68.3	78.2	80.5	68.8	12.1
2010 [2]	63.0	37.6	78.8	89.0	88.5	71.8	17.2	48.8	35.2	66.3	77.7	80.7	68.8	12.1
2011 [2]	62.4	39.7	76.2	88.3	87.2	71.1	17.8	48.8	39.9	65.6	77.1	79.2	68.3	12.3

B Percentage not shown where base is less than 50,000. [1] Never married. [2] See footnote 2, Table 596. [3] Spouse present. [4] Widowed, divorced, and married (spouse absent).

Source: U.S. Bureau of Labor Statistics, Bulletin 2217 and Basic Tabulations, Table 12.

Table 608. Marital Status of Women in the Civilian Labor Force: 1970 to 2011

[31,543 represents 31,543,000. For civilian noninstitutional population 16 years and over. Annual averages of monthly figures. Based on the Current Population Survey; see text, Section 1 and Appendix III]

Year	Female civilian labor force (1,000)				Female participation rate (percent) [3]			
	Total	Never married	Married [1]	Other [2]	Total	Never married	Married [1]	Other [2]
1970	31,543	7,265	18,475	5,804	43.3	56.8	40.5	40.3
1980	45,487	11,865	24,980	8,643	51.5	64.4	49.8	43.6
1990 [4]	56,829	14,612	30,901	11,315	57.5	66.7	58.4	47.2
2000 [4]	66,303	17,849	35,146	13,308	59.9	68.9	61.1	49.0
2002	67,363	18,203	35,477	13,683	59.6	67.4	61.0	49.2
2003 [4]	68,272	18,397	36,046	13,828	59.5	66.2	61.0	49.6
2004 [4]	68,421	18,616	35,845	13,961	59.2	65.9	60.5	49.6
2005 [4]	69,288	19,183	35,941	14,163	59.3	66.0	60.7	49.4
2006 [4]	70,173	19,474	36,314	14,385	59.4	65.7	61.0	49.6
2007 [4]	70,988	19,745	36,881	14,362	59.3	65.3	61.0	49.5
2008 [4]	71,767	20,231	37,194	14,342	59.5	65.3	61.4	49.2
2009 [4]	72,019	20,224	37,264	14,531	59.2	64.2	61.4	49.3
2010 [4]	71,904	20,592	36,742	14,570	58.6	63.3	61.0	48.8
2011 [4]	71,642	20,878	36,141	14,623	58.1	62.8	60.2	48.8

[1] Husband present. [2] Widowed, divorced, or separated. [3] Civilian labor force as a percent of the civilian noninstitutional population. [4] See footnote 2, Table 596.

Source: U.S. Bureau of Labor Statistics, Basic Tabulations, Table 12.

Table 609. Employment Status of Women by Marital Status and Presence and Age of Children: 1970 to 2011

[As of March (7.0 represents 7,000,000). Annual Social and Economic Supplement (ASEC) includes civilian noninstitutionalized population, age 16 years old and over. Based on the Current Population Survey; see text, Section 1 and Appendix III]

Item	Total			With any children								
				Total			Children 6 to 17 years only			Children under 6 years		
	Single [1]	Married [2]	Other [3]	Single [1]	Married [2]	Other [3]	Single [1]	Married [2]	Other [3]	Single [1]	Married [2]	Other [3]
IN LABOR FORCE (mil.)												
1970	7.0	18.4	5.9	(NA)	10.2	1.9	(NA)	6.3	1.3	(NA)	3.9	0.6
1980	11.2	24.9	8.8	0.6	13.7	3.6	0.2	8.4	2.6	0.3	5.2	1.0
1990	14.0	31.0	11.2	1.5	16.5	4.2	0.6	9.3	3.0	0.9	7.2	1.2
2000	17.8	35.0	13.2	3.1	18.2	4.5	1.2	10.8	3.4	1.8	7.3	1.1
2005 [4]	18.6	35.7	14.3	3.4	18.0	4.6	1.4	10.8	3.4	1.9	7.2	1.2
2010 [4]	20.0	37.2	14.7	3.6	17.6	4.5	1.6	10.4	3.3	2.1	7.2	1.2
2011 [4]	20.6	36.4	14.6	3.8	17.1	4.5	1.6	10.0	3.3	2.2	7.1	1.2
PARTICIPATION RATE [5]												
1970	53.0	40.8	39.1	(NA)	39.7	60.7	(NA)	49.2	66.9	(NA)	30.3	52.2
1980	61.5	50.1	44.0	52.0	54.1	69.4	67.6	61.7	74.6	44.1	45.1	60.3
1990	66.4	58.2	46.8	55.2	66.3	74.2	69.7	73.6	79.7	48.7	58.9	63.6
2000	68.6	62.0	50.2	73.9	70.6	82.7	79.7	77.2	84.9	70.5	62.8	76.6
2005 [4]	65.1	60.2	49.8	72.9	68.1	79.8	79.7	75.0	82.2	68.5	59.8	73.5
2010 [4]	62.3	61.7	49.2	70.1	69.7	79.2	77.0	75.9	81.8	65.6	62.5	73.1
2011 [4]	62.3	60.5	48.9	70.0	69.1	79.7	76.4	74.9	81.9	65.8	62.3	74.2
EMPLOYMENT (mil.)												
1970	6.5	17.5	5.6	(NA)	9.6	1.8	(NA)	6.0	1.2	(NA)	3.6	0.6
1980	10.1	23.6	8.2	0.4	12.8	3.3	0.2	8.1	2.4	0.2	4.8	0.9
1990	12.9	29.9	10.5	1.2	15.8	3.8	0.5	8.9	2.7	0.7	6.9	1.1
2000	16.4	34.0	12.7	2.7	17.6	4.3	1.1	10.6	3.2	1.6	7.1	1.1
2005 [4]	17.0	34.6	13.5	2.9	17.4	4.3	1.3	10.4	3.2	1.6	7.0	1.1
2010 [4]	17.5	35.0	13.3	3.0	16.5	4.0	1.3	9.8	2.9	1.6	6.7	1.1
2011 [4]	18.1	34.3	13.2	3.1	16.1	4.0	1.4	9.4	3.0	1.7	6.6	1.0
UNEMPLOYMENT RATE [6]												
1970	7.1	4.8	4.8	(NA)	6.0	7.2	(NA)	4.8	5.9	(NA)	7.9	9.8
1980	10.3	5.3	6.4	23.2	5.9	9.2	15.6	4.4	7.9	29.2	8.3	12.8
1990	8.2	3.5	5.7	18.4	4.2	8.5	14.5	3.8	7.7	20.8	4.8	10.2
2000	7.3	2.7	4.3	11.0	2.9	5.1	8.7	2.6	4.8	12.6	3.5	5.9
2005 [4]	8.9	3.0	5.3	15.1	3.1	6.9	10.9	2.9	5.8	18.2	3.4	9.8
2010 [4]	12.3	6.0	9.7	18.1	6.3	11.1	14.4	6.0	10.3	20.9	6.7	13.4
2011 [4]	12.0	5.6	9.5	18.9	5.9	11.9	13.5	5.6	10.5	22.9	6.4	15.7

NA Not available. [1] Never married. [2] Husband present. [3] Widowed, divorced, or separated (including married, spouse absent). [4] See footnote 2, Table 596. [5] Percent of women in each specific category in the labor force. [6] Unemployed as a percent of civilian labor force in specified group.

Source: U.S. Bureau of Labor Statistics, Bulletin 2307 and unpublished data.

Table 610. Labor Force Participation Rates for Wives, Husband Present, by Age of Own Youngest Child: 1990 to 2011

[In percent. As of March. Annual Social and Economic Supplement (ASEC) includes Civilian noninstitutionalized population, 16 years old and over, and military personnel who live in households with at least one other civilian adult. Armed Forces includes only those Armed Forces members living on or off post with their families; all other members of the Armed Forces are excluded. Data refer to persons in primary families. Based on Current Population Survey; see text, Section 1 and Appendix III]

Presence and age of child	1990	2000 [1]	2005 [1]	2010 [1]	2011 [1]				
					Total	White [2]	Black [2]	Asian [2,3]	Hispanic [4]
Wives, total	**58.3**	**62.2**	**60.4**	**61.9**	**60.9**	**60.4**	**65.8**	**62.5**	**56.5**
No children under 18 years	51.1	54.8	54.1	56.0	54.9	54.4	58.0	57.6	55.4
With children under 18 years	66.5	70.9	68.3	70.1	69.6	69.3	76.1	67.1	57.2
Under 6 years, total	59.1	63.1	60.3	62.9	62.8	62.6	69.3	59.5	50.7
Under 3 years	55.9	59.4	57.3	59.5	60.6	60.8	65.1	53.0	46.0
under 1 year	53.9	58.4	55.8	59.0	58.1	59.0	56.7	50.2	42.4
1 year	NA	NA	NA	57.6	62.1	62.5	66.9	54.1	43.8
2 years	60.9	61.9	60.8	62.4	61.5	60.9	71.0	54.9	51.2
3 to 5 years	64.1	68.6	64.8	67.7	66.0	65.2	74.8	67.4	56.5
3 years	63.0	66.0	62.7	66.4	64.0	64.3	61.7	66.6	59.1
4 years	65.0	69.6	64.9	68.9	67.0	65.8	80.6	72.4	50.2
5 years	64.4	70.7	67.5	68.2	67.4	65.7	82.6	62.9	60.5
6 to 13 years	73.1	76.0	73.2	74.8	73.7	73.3	81.0	71.2	62.4
14 to 17 years	75.0	80.8	79.6	79.0	78.6	78.3	82.4	81.0	67.8

[1] See footnote 2, Table 596. [2] Beginning 2005, for persons in this race group only. See footnote 4, Table 597. [3] Excludes Pacific Islanders. [4] Persons of Hispanic origin may be any race.

Source: U.S. Bureau of Labor Statistics, Bulletin 2307 and unpublished data.

Table 611. Married Couples by Labor Force Status of Spouses: 1990 to 2011

[As of March. (52,317 represents 52,317,000). Annual Social and Economic Supplement (ASEC). Based on the Current Population Survey, for details see source and Appendix III]

Year	Number (1,000)					Percent distribution				
	All married couples	In labor force			Husband and wife not in labor force	All married couples	In labor force			Husband and wife not in labor force
		Husband and wife	Husband only	Wife only			Husband and wife	Husband only	Wife only	
TOTAL										
1990	52,317	28,056	13,013	2,453	8,794	100.0	53.6	24.9	4.7	16.8
2000	55,311	31,095	11,815	3,301	9,098	100.0	56.2	21.4	6.0	16.4
2004	57,719	31,536	12,980	3,684	9,519	100.0	54.6	22.5	6.4	16.5
2005	57,975	31,398	13,385	3,641	9,551	100.0	54.2	23.1	6.3	16.5
2006	58,179	31,783	12,990	3,754	9,652	100.0	54.6	22.3	6.5	16.6
2007	60,676	33,337	13,351	4,031	9,958	100.0	54.9	22.0	6.6	16.4
2008	60,129	32,988	13,141	4,118	9,882	100.0	54.8	21.8	6.8	16.4
2009	60,844	33,249	13,207	4,314	10,074	100.0	54.6	21.7	7.1	16.6
2010	60,384	32,731	13,074	4,526	10,053	100.0	53.6	21.7	7.5	16.6
2011	60,155	31,994	13,241	4,455	10,464	100.0	53.2	22.0	7.4	17.4
WITH CHILDREN UNDER 18										
1990	24,537	15,768	7,667	558	544	100.0	64.3	31.2	2.3	2.2
2000	25,248	17,116	6,950	795	387	100.0	67.8	27.5	3.1	1.5
2004	25,793	16,691	7,715	952	433	100.0	64.7	29.9	3.7	1.7
2005	25,919	16,789	7,806	925	400	100.0	64.8	30.1	3.6	1.5
2006	25,982	16,909	7,754	900	420	100.0	65.1	29.9	3.5	1.6
2007	26,802	17,670	7,743	920	469	100.0	65.9	28.9	3.4	1.7
2008	25,778	16,977	7,398	932	471	100.0	65.9	28.7	3.6	1.8
2009	25,799	17,054	7,284	963	501	100.0	66.1	28.2	3.7	1.9
2010	25,317	16,710	7,220	962	425	100.0	66.0	28.5	3.8	1.7
2011	24,739	16,109	7,173	999	459	100.0	65.1	29.0	4.0	1.9
WITH CHILDREN UNDER 6										
1990	12,051	6,932	4,692	192	235	100.0	57.5	38.9	1.6	2.0
2000	11,393	6,984	4,077	211	121	100.0	61.3	35.8	1.9	1.1
2004	11,711	6,657	4,579	158	158	100.0	56.8	39.1	2.7	1.3
2005	11,802	6,813	4,553	299	137	100.0	57.7	38.6	2.5	1.2
2006	11,984	6,939	4,572	324	149	100.0	57.9	38.2	2.7	1.2
2007	12,468	7,337	4,633	331	167	100.0	58.8	37.2	2.7	1.3
2008	11,848	6,976	4,382	321	168	100.0	58.9	37.1	2.7	1.4
2009	11,760	6,917	4,330	329	185	100.0	58.8	36.8	2.8	1.6
2010	11,599	6,924	4,181	335	159	100.0	59.7	36.0	2.9	1.4
2011	11,352	6,709	4,101	368	174	100.0	59.1	36.1	3.2	1.5

Source: U.S. Census Bureau, Families and Living Arrangements, Detailed Table MC-1, "Married Couples by Labor Force Status of Spouses: 1986 to Present," October 2011, <http://www.census.gov/hhes/families/>.

Table 612. Employed Civilians and Weekly Hours: 1980 to 2010

[In thousands (99,303 represents 99,303,000), except as indicated. Annual averages of monthly figures. Civilian noninstitutionalized population 16 years old and over. Based on Current Population Survey; see text, Section 1 and Appendix III]

Item	1980	1990 [1]	2000 [1]	2005 [1]	2008 [1]	2009 [1]	2010 [1]
Total employed	**99,303**	**118,793**	**136,891**	**141,730**	**145,362**	**139,877**	**139,064**
Age:							
16 to 19 years old	7,710	6,581	7,189	5,978	5,573	4,837	4,378
20 to 24 years old	14,087	13,401	13,229	13,792	13,629	12,764	12,699
25 to 34 years old	27,204	33,935	31,549	30,680	31,383	30,014	30,229
35 to 44 years old	19,523	30,817	36,433	34,630	33,457	31,517	30,663
45 to 54 years old	16,234	19,525	30,310	33,207	34,529	33,613	33,191
55 to 64 years old	11,586	11,189	14,002	18,349	20,812	21,019	21,636
65 years old and over	2,960	3,346	4,179	5,094	5,979	6,114	6,268
Class of worker:							
Nonagricultural industries	95,938	115,570	134,427	139,532	143,194	137,775	136,858
Wage and salary worker [2]	88,525	106,598	125,114	129,931	133,882	128,713	127,914
Self-employed	7,000	8,719	9,205	9,509	9,219	8,995	8,860
Unpaid family workers	413	253	108	93	93	66	84
Agriculture and related industries	3,364	3,223	2,464	2,197	2,168	2,103	2,206
Wage and salary worker [2]	1,425	1,740	1,421	1,212	1,279	1,242	1,353
Self-employed	1,642	1,378	1,010	955	860	836	821
Unpaid family workers	297	105	33	30	28	25	33
Weekly hours:							
Nonagricultural industries:							
Wage and salary workers [2]	38.1	39.2	39.6	39.1	39.0	38.0	38.3
Self-employed	41.2	40.8	39.7	38.4	37.0	35.6	35.6
Unpaid family workers	34.7	34.0	32.5	32.2	33.4	30.7	33.3
Agriculture and related industries:							
Wage and salary workers [2]	41.6	41.2	43.2	43.6	42.3	41.8	41.6
Self-employed	49.3	46.8	45.3	44.0	44.2	42.6	42.0
Unpaid family workers	38.6	38.5	38.3	41.1	41.0	36.1	42.1

[1] See footnote 2, Table 596. [2] Includes the incorporated self-employed.

Source: U.S. Bureau of Labor Statistics, "Employment and Earnings Online," January 2011 issue, March 2011, <http://www.bls.gov/opub/ee/home.htm> and <http://www.bls.gov/cps/home.htm>.

Table 613. Persons at Work by Hours Worked: 2011

[In thousands (134,879 represents 134,879,000), except as indicated. Annual averages of monthly figures. Persons "at work" are a subgroup of employed persons "at work," excluding those absent from their jobs during reference period for reasons such as vacation, illness, or industrial dispute. Civilian noninstitutionalized population 16 years old and over. Based on Current Population Survey; see text, Section 1, and Appendix III. See headnote Table 616, regarding industries]

Hours of work	Persons at work (1,000)			Perent distribution		
	Total	Agriculture and related industries	Non-agricultural industries	Total	Agriculture and related industries	Non-agricultural industries
Total...................	**134,879**	**2,162**	**132,717**	**100.0**	**100.0**	**100.0**
1 to 34 hours..................	34,898	627	34,271	25.9	29.0	25.8
1 to 4 hours..................	1,516	50	1,466	1.1	2.3	1.1
5 to 14 hours.................	5,426	150	5,275	4.0	7.0	4.0
15 to 29 hours................	17,223	290	16,933	12.8	13.4	12.8
30 to 34 hours................	10,733	136	10,597	8.0	6.3	8.0
35 hours and over.............	99,981	1,535	98,446	74.1	71.0	74.2
35 to 39 hours................	9,528	100	9,428	7.1	4.6	7.1
40 hours.....................	57,064	603	56,461	42.3	27.9	42.5
41 hours and over.............	33,389	832	32,557	24.8	38.5	24.5
41 to 48 hours................	11,449	137	11,312	8.5	6.4	8.5
49 to 59 hours................	12,913	248	12,665	9.6	11.5	9.5
60 hours and over.............	9,027	447	8,580	6.7	20.7	6.5
Average weekly hours: Persons at work..........	38.3	41.7	38.2	(X)	(X)	(X)
Persons usually working full-time [1]...............	42.4	48.2	42.3	(X)	(X)	(X)

X Not applicable. [1] Full-time workers are those who usually worked 35 hours or more (at all jobs).

Source: U.S. Bureau of Labor Statistics, "Employment and Earnings Online," January 2012 issue, March 2012, <http://www.bls.gov/opub/ee/home.htm> and <http://www.bls.gov/cps/home.htm>.

Table 614. Persons With a Job, But Not at Work: 1980 to 2011

[In thousands (5,881 represents 5,881,000), except percent. For civilian noninstitutionalized population 16 years old and over. Annual averages of monthly figures. Based on Current Population Survey; see text, Section 1 and Appendix III]

Reason for not working	1980	1990 [1]	2000 [1]	2004 [1]	2005 [1]	2006 [1]	2007 [1]	2008 [1]	2009 [1]	2010 [1]	2011 [1]
All industries, number.........	**5,881**	**6,160**	**5,681**	**5,482**	**5,511**	**5,746**	**5,719**	**5,539**	**5,434**	**5,060**	**4,990**
Percent of employed...........	5.9	5.2	4.2	3.9	3.9	4.0	3.9	3.8	3.9	3.6	3.6
Reason for not working:											
Vacation.......................	3,320	3,529	3,109	2,923	2,892	3,101	3,056	2,916	2,806	2,487	2,500
Illness........................	1,426	1,341	1,156	1,058	1,088	1,096	1,064	1,026	993	942	921
Bad weather....................	155	90	89	133	145	117	140	141	126	172	169
Industrial dispute..............	105	24	14	10	6	7	10	7	6	8	9
All other......................	876	1,177	1,313	1,358	1,381	1,425	1,449	1,449	1,503	1,451	1,392

[1] Data not strictly comparable with data for earlier years. See text, this section, and February 1994, March 1996, February 1997–99, and February 2003–11 issues of "Employment and Earnings Online."

Source: U.S. Bureau of Labor Statistics, unpublished data, <http://www.bls.gov/cps/home.htm>.

Table 615. Class of Worker by Sex and Selected Characteristics: 2011

[In percent, except as indicated (9,449 represents 9,449,000). Civilian noninstitutionalized population 16 years old and over. Annual averages of monthly figures. Based on Current Population Survey; see text, Section 1 and Appendix III]

Characteristic	Unincorporated self-employed			Incorporated self-employed			Wage and salary workers [1]		
	Total	Male	Female	Total	Male	Female	Total	Male	Female
Total (1,000).....................	**9,449**	**5,894**	**3,555**	**5,127**	**3,670**	**1,456**	**125,187**	**64,686**	**60,502**
PERCENT DISTRIBUTION........	100.0	100.0	100.0	100.0	100.0	100.0	100.0	100.0	100.0
Age:									
16 to 19 years old.................	0.9	0.9	0.8	0.2	0.2	0.1	3.4	3.1	3.6
20 to 24 years old.................	2.9	2.9	2.9	1.1	1.3	0.8	10.1	10.2	10.1
25 to 34 years old.................	13.9	13.9	13.8	10.3	10.5	9.9	22.9	23.9	21.8
35 to 44 years old.................	20.2	19.6	21.0	21.9	21.7	22.3	21.8	22.3	21.2
45 to 54 years old.................	27.2	26.9	27.5	31.0	30.2	33.0	22.9	22.3	23.6
55 to 64 years old.................	22.7	22.7	22.6	24.9	24.9	24.7	15.0	14.2	15.8
65 years old and over.............	12.4	13.0	11.4	10.7	11.3	9.2	3.9	3.9	3.9
Race/ethnicity:									
White [2]............................	87.5	87.6	87.3	88.7	89.6	86.4	81.3	82.6	79.9
Black [2]............................	6.0	6.0	6.1	4.4	4.3	4.8	11.4	10.0	12.9
Asian [2]............................	4.3	4.2	4.5	5.8	5.1	7.3	4.7	5.0	4.8
Hispanic [3].........................	12.5	13.9	10.3	6.9	7.1	6.3	15.0	17.0	12.8
Country of birth: U.S. born.........	82.4	81.0	84.6	84.3	84.5	83.6	84.3	82.4	86.4
Foreign-born....................	17.6	19.0	15.4	15.7	15.4	16.4	15.7	17.7	13.6

[1] Excludes the incorporated self-employed. [2] For persons in this race group only. [3] Persons of Hispanic origin may be any race.

Source: U.S. Bureau of Labor Statistics, Current Population Survey, unpublished data.

Table 616. Self-Employed Workers by Industry and Occupation: 2000 to 2011

[In thousands (10,214 represents 10,214,000). Civilian noninstitutionalized population 16 years old and over. Annual averages of monthly figures. Data represent the unincorporated self-employed; the incorporated self-employed are considered wage and salary workers. Based on the occupational and industrial classification derived from those used in the 2000 census. See text, this section. Based on the Current Population Survey; see text, Section 1 and Appendix III]

Item	2000	2005 [1]	2008 [1]	2009 [1]	2010 [1]	2011 [1]
Total self-employed	**10,214**	**10,464**	**10,080**	**9,831**	**9,681**	**8,603**
Industry:						
Agriculture and related industries	1,010	955	860	836	821	846
Mining	12	11	15	18	20	20
Construction	1,728	1,830	1,817	1,701	1,699	1,585
Manufacturing	334	327	308	324	304	273
Wholesale and retail trade	1,221	1,251	1,059	963	962	949
Transportation and utilities	348	442	405	402	360	352
Information	139	126	125	145	139	131
Financial activities [2]	735	785	749	667	641	615
Professional and business services [2]	1,927	1,957	1,980	1,996	1,999	2,011
Education and health services [2]	1,107	1,071	1,071	1,102	1,100	1,077
Leisure and hospitality [2]	660	674	693	636	610	636
Other services [3]	993	1,036	997	1,039	1,028	956
Occupation:						
Management, professional, and related occupations	4,169	4,085	4,043	4,079	3,928	(NA)
Service occupations	1,775	1,774	1,847	1,879	1,885	(NA)
Sales and office occupations	1,982	1,986	1,771	1,663	1,586	(NA)
Natural resources, construction, and maintenance occupations	1,591	1,864	1,707	1,535	1,635	(NA)
Production, transportation, and material moving occupations	698	756	712	674	647	(NA)

[1] Data not strictly comparable with data for earlier years. See text, this section, and February 1994, March 1996, February 1997–99, and February 2003–11 issues of "Employment and Earnings." [2] For composition of industries, see Table 637. [3] Includes private households.

Source: U.S. Bureau of Labor Statistics, "Employment and Earnings Online," January 2012 issue, March 2012, <http://www.bls.gov/opub/ee/home.htm> and <http://www.bls.gov/cps/home.htm>.

Table 617. Type of Work Flexibility Provided to Employees: 2012

[In percent. The National Study of Employers does not ask employers to report on whether they have "written policies," but rather whether their organization "allows employees to" or "provides the following benefits or programs." The wording is used for two reasons. First, employers may have written policies, but not "allow" employees to use them. Second, smaller employers are less likely to have written policies than larger ones. For methodology, see source]

Type of work flexibility provided (to employee)	Employer allows all or most employees	Employer size	
		50 to 99 employees	1,000 or more employees
FLEX TIME AND PLACE			
Periodically change starting and quitting times within some range of hours	27	32	16
Change starting and quitting times on a daily basis	9	10	3
Compress workweek by working longer hours on fewer days for at least part of the year	7	9	5
Work some regular paid hours at home occasionally	6	10	3
Work some regular paid hours at home on regular basis	2	3	0
CHOICES IN MANAGING TIME			
Have control over when to take breaks	62	70	42
Have choices about and control over which shifts to work	7	8	11
Have control over paid and unpaid overtime hours	20	20	16
REDUCED TIME			
Move from full time to part time and back again while remaining in same position or level	6	7	7
Work part year (work reduced time on annual basis)	2	2	2
CAREGIVING LEAVE			
Return to work gradually after childbirth or adoption	44	48	29
TIME OFF			
Family or personal time off without loss of pay	55	62	38
Do volunteer work during regular work hours	20	21	203
FLEX CAREERS			
Phase into retirement by working reduced hours over time prior to full retirement	17	21	10
Take sabbaticals (paid or unpaid for six months or more)	9	11	6
Take extended career breaks for caregiving or other personal or family reasons	30	33	20
Receive special consideration when returning to the organization after an extended career break	11	12	7

Source: Families and Work Institute, "2012 National Study of Employers" (copyright), <http://familiesandwork.org/site/research/reports/main.html>.

Table 618. Persons on Flexible Schedules: 2004

[In thousands (99,778 represents 99,778,000), except percent. As of May. For employed full-time wage and salary workers 16 years old and over. Excludes all self-employed persons, regardless of whether their businesses were incorporated. Data related to the primary job. Based on the Current Population Survey; see text, Section 1 and Appendix III]

Item	Total	With flexible schedules [2]		Male	With flexible schedules [2]		Female	With flexible schedules [2]	
	Total [1]	Number	Percent	Total [1]	Number	Percent	Total [1]	Number	Percent
Total....................	**99,778**	**27,411**	**27.5**	**56,412**	**15,853**	**28.1**	**43,366**	**11,558**	**26.7**
AGE									
16 to 19 years old.......................	1,427	336	23.6	903	185	20.5	524	151	28.9
20 years and over.......................	98,351	27,075	27.5	55,509	15,668	28.2	42,842	11,406	26.6
20 to 24 years old.....................	9,004	2,058	22.9	5,147	1,065	20.7	3,856	993	25.8
25 to 34 years old.....................	24,640	6,902	28.0	14,358	4,051	28.2	10,283	2,851	27.7
35 to 44 years old.....................	26,766	7,807	29.2	15,424	4,605	29.9	11,342	3,202	28.2
45 to 54 years old.....................	24,855	6,651	26.8	13,440	3,769	28.0	11,415	2,882	25.2
55 to 64 years old.....................	11,745	3,181	27.1	6,383	1,865	29.2	5,361	1,316	24.5
65 years old and over................	1,341	475	35.4	757	314	41.4	585	161	27.6
RACE AND HISPANIC ORIGIN									
White [3]................................	80,498	23,121	28.7	46,222	13,582	29.4	34,276	9,539	27.8
Black [3]................................	12,578	2,476	19.7	6,447	1,193	18.5	6,131	1,283	20.9
Asian [3]................................	4,136	1,132	27.4	2,300	720	31.3	1,836	412	22.4
Hispanic [4]................................	14,110	2,596	18.4	8,621	1,430	16.6	5,489	1,166	21.2
MARITAL STATUS									
Married, spouse present..............	57,630	16,270	28.2	34,926	10,382	29.7	22,704	5,888	25.9
Not married........................	42,148	11,141	26.4	21,486	5,471	25.5	20,662	5,670	27.4
Never married........................	25,144	6,693	26.6	14,469	3,605	24.9	10,676	3,088	28.9
Other marital status..................	17,004	4,448	26.2	7,018	1,866	26.6	9,986	2,582	25.9
PRESENCE AND AGE OF CHILDREN									
Without own children under 18.......	61,761	16,759	27.1	34,680	9,410	27.1	27,081	7,349	27.1
With own children under 18..........	38,018	10,652	28.0	21,733	6,443	29.6	16,285	4,209	25.8
With youngest child 6 to 17..........	21,739	5,960	27.4	11,477	3,341	29.1	10,262	2,619	25.5
With youngest child under 6.........	16,279	4,692	28.8	10,256	3,102	30.2	6,023	1,590	26.4

[1] Includes persons who did not provide information on flexible schedules. [2] Allowed to vary or make changes in time work begins or ends. [3] For persons in the race group only. See footnote 4, Table 597. [4] Persons of Hispanic origin may be any race.

Source: U.S. Bureau of Labor Statistics, *Workers on Flexible and Shift Schedules in May 2004*, News Release, USDL 05-1198, July 2005. See also <http://www.bls.gov/bls/newsrels.htm#OEUS>.

Table 619. Employed Workers With Alternative and Traditional Work Arrangements: 2005

[In thousands (138,952 represents 138,952,000). As of February. For employed workers 16 years old and over. Based on the Current Population Survey; see text, Section 1 and Appendix III]

Characteristic	Total employed [1]	Workers with alternative arrangements				Workers with traditional arrangements
		Independent contractors	On-call workers	Temporary help agency workers	Workers provided by contract firms	
Total employed........................	**138,952**	**10,342**	**2,454**	**1,217**	**813**	**123,843**
16 to 19 years old..................	5,510	89	133	33	7	5,194
20 to 24 years old..................	13,114	356	355	202	87	12,055
25 to 34 years old..................	30,103	1,520	535	362	205	27,427
35 to 44 years old..................	34,481	2,754	571	253	196	30,646
45 to 54 years old..................	32,947	2,799	417	200	186	29,324
55 to 64 years old..................	17,980	1,943	267	135	114	15,496
65 years old and over...............	4,817	881	175	33	18	3,701
Male...........................	73,946	6,696	1,241	574	561	64,673
16 to 19 years old..................	2,579	32	82	24	7	2,389
20 to 24 years old..................	6,928	194	200	107	61	6,331
25 to 34 years old..................	16,624	1,006	299	185	138	14,950
35 to 44 years old..................	18,523	1,824	252	120	140	16,130
45 to 54 years old..................	17,193	1,764	209	71	143	15,003
55 to 64 years old..................	9,485	1,287	108	52	70	7,954
65 years old and over...............	2,615	589	91	16	3	1,917
Female...........................	65,006	3,647	1,212	643	252	59,170
16 to 19 years old..................	2,931	57	52	9	–	2,805
20 to 24 years old..................	6,186	162	155	95	27	5,724
25 to 34 years old..................	13,480	514	236	177	67	12,477
35 to 44 years old..................	15,958	930	319	133	57	14,516
45 to 54 years old..................	15,754	1,035	208	129	43	14,322
55 to 64 years old..................	8,495	656	158	83	44	7,542
65 years old and over...............	2,202	292	84	17	15	1,785
Full-time workers.....................	113,798	7,732	1,370	979	695	102,889
Part-time workers.....................	25,154	2,611	1,084	238	119	20,954

– Represents zero. [1] Includes day laborers (an alternative arrangement) and a small number of workers who were both "on call" and "provided by contract firms," not shown separately.

Source: U.S. Bureau of Labor Statistics, *Contingent and Alternative Employment Arrangements, February 2005*, News Release, USDL 05–1443, July 2005. See also <http://www.bls.gov/bls/newsrels.htm#OEUS>.

Table 620. Multiple Jobholders: 2011

[Annual average of monthly figures (6,880 represents 6,880,000). Civilian noninstitutionalized population 16 years old and over. Multiple jobholders are employed persons who either 1) had jobs as wage or salary workers with two employers or more; 2) were self-employed and also held a wage and salary job; or 3) were unpaid family workers and also held a wage and salary job. Based on the Current Population Survey; see text, Section 1 and Appendix III]

Characteristic	Total		Male		Female	
	Number (1,000)	Percent of employed	Number (1,000)	Percent of employed	Number (1,000)	Percent of employed
Total [1]................................	**6,880**	**4.9**	**3,384**	**4.6**	**3,496**	**5.3**
Age:						
16 to 19 years old.............................	183	4.2	78	3.7	104	4.7
20 to 24 years old.............................	697	5.3	294	4.3	403	6.5
25 to 54 years old.............................	4,676	5.0	2,341	4.7	2,335	5.4
55 to 64 years old.............................	1,083	4.9	523	4.6	561	5.2
65 years old and over........................	241	3.6	148	4.0	93	3.2
Race and Hispanic ethnicity:						
White [2]..	5,812	5.1	2,883	4.7	2,929	5.6
Black [2]..	679	4.5	328	4.7	351	4.3
Asian [2]..	212	3.1	100	2.7	112	3.5
Hispanic [3].....................................	611	3.0	358	3	253	3.1
Marital status:						
Married, spouse present......................	3,646	4.7	2,044	4.7	1,602	4.7
Widowed, divorced, or separated..........	1,209	5.3	402	4.2	806	6.1
Single, never married.........................	2,026	5.1	939	4.4	1,087	6
Full- or part-time status:						
Primary job full-time, secondary job part-time.............	3,620	(X)	1,979	(X)	1,640	(X)
Both jobs part-time...........................	1,811	(X)	619	(X)	1,193	(X)
Both jobs full-time............................	234	(X)	147	(X)	88	(X)
Hours vary on primary or secondary job..................	1,172	(X)	619	(X)	552	(X)

X Not applicable. [1] Includes a small number of persons who work part-time on their primary job and full-time on their secondary job(s), not shown separately. Includes other races, not shown separately. [2] For persons who selected this race group only. See footnote 4, Table 597. [3] Persons of Hispanic origin may be any race.

Source: U.S. Bureau of Labor Statistics, "Employment and Earnings Online," January 2012 issue, March 2012, <http://www.bls.gov/opub/ee/home.htm> and <http://www.bls.gov/cps/home.htm>.

Table 621. Average Number of Jobs Held From Ages 18 to 46: 1978 to 2010

[For persons ages 45 to 53 in 2010-11 (and who were ages 14 to 22 when first interviewed in 1979). A job is an uninterrupted period of work with a particular employer. Educational attainment as of 2010-11. Based on the National Longitudinal Survey of Youth 1979; see source for details]

Sex and educational attainment	Total [1]	Number of jobs held by age				
		18 to 24 years	25 to 29 years	30 to 34 years	35 to 39 years	40 to 46 years
Total [2]................................	**11.3**	**5.5**	**3.0**	**2.4**	**2.1**	**2.1**
Less than a high school diploma........................	11.9	5.0	3.0	2.5	2.1	2.0
High school graduates, no college..................	10.5	5.0	2.8	2.4	2.0	2.0
Some college or associate's degree..................	11.8	5.7	3.1	2.5	2.2	2.2
Bachelor's degree or more....................	11.8	6.2	3.1	2.4	2.1	2.1
Male................................	11.5	5.7	3.1	2.6	2.1	2.1
Less than a high school diploma......................	13.1	5.9	3.6	2.8	2.2	2.2
High school graduate, no college..................	10.9	5.3	3.1	2.5	2.0	2.1
Some college or associate's degree................	11.8	6.0	3.2	2.6	2.1	2.1
Bachelor's degree or more................	11.4	5.9	2.9	2.5	2.2	2.1
Female................................	11.1	5.3	2.8	2.3	2.0	2.1
Less than a high school diploma......................	10.1	3.8	2.3	2.2	2.0	1.8
High school graduate, no college..................	10.2	4.7	2.5	2.2	2.0	2.0
Some college or associate's degree................	11.8	5.5	3.0	2.4	2.2	2.3
Bachelor's degree or more................	12.2	6.4	3.2	2.3	1.9	2.1
White, non-Hispanic.........................	11.4	5.7	3.0	2.4	2.1	2.1
Less than a high school diploma......................	12.5	5.5	3.2	2.7	2.2	2.1
High school graduate, no college..................	10.5	5.2	2.8	2.4	2.0	2.0
Some college or associate's degree................	11.9	5.9	3.0	2.4	2.1	2.1
Bachelor's degree or more................	11.8	6.3	3.1	2.4	2.0	2.1
Black, non-Hispanic.........................	10.9	4.6	2.9	2.5	2.1	2.2
Less than a high school diploma......................	10.3	3.8	2.6	2.1	1.9	1.8
High school graduate, no college..................	10.8	4.3	2.8	2.5	2.1	2.1
Some college or associate's degree................	11.5	5.2	3.1	2.6	2.4	2.4
Bachelor's degree or more................	11.1	5.4	3.1	2.7	2.1	2.4
Hispanic [3]................................	11.2	4.9	2.8	2.3	2.1	2.1
Less than a high school diploma......................	11.2	4.5	2.8	2.2	2.0	2.2
High school graduate, no college..................	10.7	5.0	2.7	2.4	2.0	2.2
Some college or associate's degree................	11.6	5.1	3.1	2.3	2.2	2.4
Bachelor's degree or more................	12.2	5.4	2.9	2.6	2.1	2.0

[1] Jobs held in more than one age category were counted in each category, but only once in the total. [2] Includes other races, not shown separately. [3] Persons of Hispanic origin may be any race.

Source: U.S. Bureau of Labor Statistics, "Number of Jobs Held, Labor Market Activity, and Earnings Growth Among the Youngest Baby Boomers: Results from a Longitudinal Survey," News Release, USDL 10-1489, July 25, 2012. See also <http://www.bls.gov/news.release/nlsoy.nr0.htm>.

Table 622. Distribution of Workers by Tenure With Current Employer by Selected Characteristics: 2010

[121,931 represents 121,931,000. As of January from the 2010 Displaced Worker Supplement. For employed wage and salary workers 16 years old and over. Data exclude the incorporated and unincorporated self-employed. Based on the Current Population Survey; see source and Appendix III]

Characteristic	Number employed (1,000)	Percent distribution by tenure with current employer								Median years [1]
		12 months or less	13 to 23 months	2 years	3 to 4 years	5 to 9 years	10 to 14 years	15 to 19 years	20 years or more	
Total [2]	121,931	19.0	7.0	5.8	18.9	20.5	12.2	6.1	10.5	4.4
AGE AND SEX										
16 to 19 years old	3,984	66.7	12.7	10.7	9.6	0.3	–	–	–	–
20 to 24 years old	11,835	45.1	13.3	12.1	22.4	7.0	0.1	–	–	1.5
25 to 34 years old	27,756	23.3	9.8	7.5	27.7	24.4	6.6	0.8	–	3.1
35 to 44 years old	27,205	14.4	6.3	4.8	19.2	24.7	18.2	8.0	4.3	5.1
45 to 54 years old	28,841	10.6	4.4	4.1	14.6	21.5	16.0	9.8	18.9	7.8
55 to 64 years old	17,740	7.8	3.6	2.9	12.8	19.7	15.6	9.6	27.9	10.0
65 years old and over	4,570	6.9	2.9	2.7	12.9	21.4	15.3	9.8	28.0	9.9
Male	61,495	18.5	6.6	5.7	18.3	20.8	12.4	6.1	11.5	4.6
16 to 19 years old	1,850	65.8	12.4	10.2	11.3	0.3	–	–	–	–
20 to 24 years old	5,746	44.2	12.7	11.9	22.8	8.3	0.1	–	–	1.6
25 to 34 years old	14,604	22.9	9.2	7.3	26.6	25.4	7.6	1.0	–	3.2
35 to 44 years old	14,160	14.0	5.8	4.7	18.4	24.7	19.4	8.3	4.7	5.3
45 to 54 years old	14,239	10.8	3.9	4.1	13.1	20.7	15.4	10.5	21.4	8.5
55 to 64 years old	8,655	7.2	3.4	2.7	12.3	19.4	14.5	9.0	31.4	10.4
65 years old and over	2,242	6.8	4.0	2.5	13.9	20.9	15.3	7.0	29.6	9.7
Female	60,435	19.4	7.4	5.9	19.5	20.2	12.0	6.0	9.5	4.2
16 to 19 years old	2,135	67.4	12.9	11.2	8.2	0.3	–	–	–	–
20 to 24 years old	6,089	46.0	13.9	12.2	22.0	5.8	0.1	–	–	1.5
25 to 34 years old	13,151	23.8	10.4	7.7	28.8	23.2	5.5	0.5	–	3.0
35 to 44 years old	13,045	14.8	7.0	4.8	20.1	24.7	17.0	7.7	3.9	4.9
45 to 54 years old	14,602	10.5	4.9	4.1	16.1	22.3	16.6	9.2	16.4	7.1
55 to 64 years old	9,085	8.2	3.7	3.1	13.3	20.0	16.7	10.2	24.6	9.7
65 years old and over	2,328	7.0	1.9	2.8	12.0	21.9	15.4	12.5	26.5	10.1
RACE AND HISPANIC ORIGIN										
White [3]	99,768	18.6	7.1	5.7	18.4	20.4	12.4	6.4	11.1	4.5
Male	51,081	18.1	6.7	5.6	17.7	20.6	12.6	6.5	12.3	4.8
Female	48,687	19.2	7.6	5.8	19.1	20.1	12.1	6.3	9.8	4.3
Black [3]	13,508	20.7	6.1	6.1	20.9	20.4	11.6	4.9	9.3	4.1
Male	5,969	20.4	5.1	6.6	20.7	21.1	11.9	4.8	9.4	4.2
Female	7,539	20.9	6.9	5.8	21.0	19.8	11.3	5.0	9.2	4.0
Asian [3]	5,598	18.1	7.0	6.8	22.1	25.4	11.8	3.3	5.5	4.0
Male	2,922	18.7	7.1	5.8	23.6	25.1	11.5	3.5	4.7	3.9
Female	2,677	17.4	6.8	7.8	20.5	25.7	12.2	3.2	6.4	4.1
Hispanic [4]	18,016	22.5	7.0	7.4	23.2	20.4	9.8	4.2	5.6	3.4
Male	10,279	22.5	6.7	7.0	23.1	19.9	10.2	4.3	6.3	3.5
Female	7,737	22.4	7.4	7.8	23.3	21.1	9.1	4.1	4.7	3.3

– Represents zero. [1] For definition of median, see Guide to Tabular Presentation. [2] Includes other races, not shown separately. [3] For persons in this race group only. See footnote 4, Table 597. [4] Persons of Hispanic origin may be any race.

Source: U.S. Bureau of Labor Statistics, *Employee Tenure in 2010*, News Release, USDL 10–1278, September 2010. See also <http://www.bls.gov/news.release/tenure.toc.htm>.

Table 623. Part-Time Workers by Reason: 2011

[In thousands (34,898 represents 34,898,000), except hours. For persons working 1 to 34 hours per week. For civilian noninstitutionalized population 16 years old and over. Annual average of monthly figures. Based on the Current Population Survey; see text, Section 1 and Appendix III]

Reason	All industries			Nonagricultural industries		
		Usually work—			Usually work—	
	Total	Full-time	Part-time	Total	Full-time	Part-time
Total working fewer than 35 hours	34,898	10,047	24,851	34,271	9,874	24,397
Economic reasons	8,560	2,043	6,517	8,423	1,983	6,440
Slack work or business conditions	5,711	1,791	3,920	5,617	1,749	3,868
Could find only part time work	2,514	(S)	2,514	2,494	(S)	2,494
Seasonal work	224	140	84	201	123	79
Job started or ended during the week	112	112	(S)	111	111	(S)
Noneconomic reasons	26,337	8,003	18,334	25,848	7,892	17,957
Child-care problems	812	53	759	806	52	754
Other family or personal obligations	4,533	596	3,938	4,463	587	3,875
Health or medical limitations	786	(S)	786	763	(S)	763
In school or training	5,607	81	5,526	5,539	80	5,459
Retired or social security limit on earnings	2,180	(S)	2,180	2,059	(S)	2,059
Vacation or personal day	3,437	3,437	(S)	3,391	3,391	(S)
Holiday, legal, or religious	838	838	(S)	833	833	(S)
Weather-related curtailment	749	749	(S)	724	724	(S)
Other	7,395	2,250	5,145	7,270	2,224	5,047
Average hours per week:						
Economic reasons	22.5	24	22.1	22.6	24	22.1
Noneconomic reasons	21.3	25	19.7	21.4	25.1	19.8

S No data or data do not meet publication standards.

Source: U.S. Bureau of Labor Statistics, Labor Force Statistics from the Current Population Survey, Characteristics of the Employed, <http://www.bls.gov/cps/tables.htm>.

Table 624. Displaced Workers by Selected Characteristics: 2012

[In percent, except total (6,121 represents 6,121,000). As of January, from the Displaced Worker: 2009-2011 News Release. For persons 20 years old and over with tenure of 3 years or more who lost or left a job between January 2009 and December 2011 because of plant closings or moves, slack work, or the abolishment of their positions. Based on Current Population Survey; see source and Appendix III]

Characteristic	Total (1,000)	Employment status in January 2012			Reason for job loss, 2009-2011		
		Employed	Unemployed	Not in the labor force	Plant or company closed down or moved	Slack/ insufficient work	Position or shift abolished
Total [1]	**6,121**	**56.0**	**26.7**	**17.4**	**30.8**	**39.5**	**29.7**
20 to 24 years old	128	61.7	22.4	15.9	40.5	39.3	20.3
25 to 54 years old	4,268	61.5	26.2	12.3	31.8	40.2	28.0
55 to 64 years old	1,338	47.4	28.1	24.5	27.8	37.0	35.2
65 years old and over	386	23.5	27.5	49.0	26.7	40.8	32.5
Males	3,440	60.9	23.4	15.7	31.1	43.2	25.7
20 to 24 years old	78	70.6	15.0	14.4	40.2	36.7	23.1
25 to 54 years old	2,438	66.7	22.7	10.6	32.6	43.4	24.0
55 to 64 years old	727	50.8	25.6	23.7	27.6	43.0	29.4
65 years old and over	197	23.5	27.3	49.2	21.7	44.2	34.2
Females	2,681	47.9	30.8	19.5	30.4	34.8	34.8
20 to 24 years old	50	([2])	([2])	([2])	([2])	([2])	([2])
25 to 54 years old	1,831	54.6	30.9	14.5	30.8	35.9	33.3
55 to 64 years old	611	43.3	31.1	25.6	28.1	29.9	42.0
65 years old and over	189	23.5	27.7	48.8	31.9	37.3	30.8
White [3]	5,027	57.4	26.1	16.5	30.2	38.9	30.9
Male	2,920	61.9	23.1	14.9	30.5	42.5	27.0
Female	2,107	51.2	30.2	18.7	29.8	34.0	36.2
Black [3]	662	46.1	31.2	22.7	33.5	41.0	25.5
Male	284	52.7	24.8	22.4	35.5	44.9	19.6
Female	378	41.2	35.9	22.9	32.0	38.0	30.0
Asian [3]	230	60.3	26.7	13.1	30.5	46.9	22.7
Male	121	61.5	27.6	10.9	24.3	56.8	18.9
Female	109	58.9	25.6	15.5	37.3	35.9	26.8
Hispanic [4]	901	54.9	27.7	17.4	35.9	50.1	14.0
Male	594	60.3	25.7	14.0	37.3	52.4	10.3
Female	307	44.3	31.6	24.1	33.3	45.6	21.1

[1] Includes other races, not shown separately. [2] Data not shown where base is less than 75,000. [3] For persons in this race group only. See footnote 3, Table 597. [4] Persons of Hispanic origin may be of any race.

Source: U.S. Bureau of Labor Statistics, Worker Displacement, 2009-2011, News Release, USDL 12-1719, August 2012. See also <http://www.bls.gov/news.release/disp.toc.htm>.

Table 625. Persons Not in the Labor Force: 2011

[In thousands (86,001 represents 86,001,000). For civilian noninstitutional population 16 years old and over. Annual average of monthly figures. Based on the Current Population Survey; see text, Section 1, and Appendix III]

Status and reason	Total	Age			Sex	
		16 to 24 years old	25 to 54 years old	55 years old and over	Male	Female
Total not in the labor force	**86,001**	**17,201**	**22,961**	**45,839**	**34,343**	**51,658**
Do not want a job now [1]	79,564	15,177	20,107	44,280	31,298	48,266
Want a job now	6,437	2,023	2,854	1,560	3,045	3,392
In the previous year—						
Did not search for a job	3,268	1,010	1,303	955	1,463	1,804
Did search for a job [2]	3,169	1,014	1,551	605	1,582	1,587
Not available for work now	597	262	262	73	236	361
Available for work now, not looking for work [3]	2,573	752	1,289	532	1,346	1,227
Reason for not currently looking for work:						
Discouraged over job prospects [4]	989	222	519	248	579	410
Family responsibilities	215	30	139	45	48	166
In school or training	323	245	75	4	183	140
Ill health or disability	169	18	93	58	86	83
Other [5]	877	238	463	177	449	428

[1] Includes some persons who are not asked if they want a job. [2] Persons who had a job in the prior 12 months must have searched since the end of that job. [3] Persons who have searched for work in the previous year and are available to work now also are referred to as "marginally attached to the labor force." [4] Includes such things as believes no work available, could not find work, lacks necessary schooling or training, employer thinks too young or old, and other types of discrimination. [5] Includes such things as child care and transportation problems.

Source: U.S. Bureau of Labor Statistics, Labor Force Statistics from the Current Population Survey, Annual average data, Persons Not in the Labor Force, <http://www.bls.gov/cps/tables.htm>.

Table 626. Employed Civilians by Occupation, Sex, Race, and Hispanic Origin: 2011

[139,869 represents 139,869,000. Civilian noninstitutionalized population 16 years old and over. Annual average of monthly figures. Based on Current Population Survey; see text, Section 1 and Appendix III. Occupational classifications are those used in the 2010 Census]

Occupation	Total employed (1,000)	Percent of total			
		Female	Black [1]	Asian [1]	Hispanic [2]
Total, 16 years and over...............	**139,869**	**46.9**	**10.8**	**4.9**	**14.5**
Management, professional and related occupations...................	**52,547**	**51.4**	**8.4**	**6.1**	**7.5**
Management, business, and financial operations occupations.............	21,589	43.1	7.3	5.1	7.7
Management occupations [3].............	15,250	38.1	6.3	4.6	7.7
Chief executives.............	1,515	24.2	2.7	3.0	4.1
General and operations managers.............	978	30.4	6.6	2.7	7.6
Marketing and sales managers.............	1009	45.8	5.6	5.6	6.6
Administrative services managers.............	128	39.5	6.9	2.2	7.3
Computer and information systems managers.............	553	25.3	5.7	12.9	3.8
Financial managers.............	1,107	54.2	6.5	5.8	8.7
Human resources managers.............	243	73.6	11.3	2.1	9.5
Industrial production managers.............	259	16.5	3.9	5.1	8.9
Purchasing managers.............	204	47.3	8.8	2.1	8.8
Transportation, storage, and distribution managers.............	254	14.1	8.7	3.0	8.9
Farmers, ranchers, and other agricultural managers.............	978	23.0	0.9	0.8	4.1
Construction managers.............	926	6.1	3.0	1.5	9.7
Education administrators.............	853	65.2	13.3	2.9	6.5
Engineering managers.............	106	8.5	1.3	5.9	4.7
Food service managers.............	1051	45.7	9.2	9.2	13.9
Lodging managers.............	148	52.4	7.0	13.4	8.1
Medical and health services managers.............	529	71.4	11.2	5.0	8.4
Property, real estate, and community association managers.............	587	48.0	8.8	3.1	8.8
Social and community service managers.............	329	71.3	11.3	2.6	6.9
Business and financial operations occupations [3].............	6,339	55.3	9.8	6.6	7.8
Wholesale and retail buyers, except farm products.............	170	46.4	4.2	4.7	11.8
Purchasing agents, except wholesale, retail, and farm products.........	259	54.0	8.7	3.5	5.3
Claims adjusters, appraisers, examiners, and investigators.............	296	58.6	16.5	2.3	9.5
Compliance officers, except agriculture, construction, health and safety, and transportation.............	198	43.8	10.9	3.8	9.4
Cost estimators.............	119	15.0	2.7	2.3	6.0
Human resources workers.............	595	74.5	15.1	4.4	10.5
Management analysts.............	707	41.9	6.8	8.5	4.5
Accountants and auditors.............	1,653	61.3	8.5	10.3	7.6
Appraisers and assessors of real estate.............	88	34.4	3.7	1.6	0.0
Financial analysts.............	84	34.8	6.0	13.4	2.7
Personal financial advisors.............	371	31.2	6.8	5.6	6.7
Insurance underwriters.............	117	62.7	10.7	3.0	3.0
Loan counselors and officers.............	326	53.7	12.1	5.5	11.4
Tax preparers.............	110	65.8	9.8	5.8	11.9
Professional and related occupations............. [3]	30,957	57.1	9.1	6.8	7.4
Computer and mathematical occupations [3].............	3,608	25.0	6.9	16.6	5.7
Computer programmers.............	459	20.8	4.3	15.4	5.8
Software developers, applications and systems software.............	1,044	19.0	4.8	27.1	4.6
Computer support specialists.............	461	26.3	11.8	8.7	7.5
Database administrators.............	134	37.3	9.2	11.8	9.0
Network and computer systems administrators.............	233	22.8	6.2	10.0	7.2
Operations research analysts.............	116	45.1	14.5	6.5	4.1
Architecture and engineering occupations [3].............	2,785	13.6	5.2	8.8	6.4
Architects, except naval.............	181	20.7	1.6	5.5	4.1
Aerospace engineers.............	144	12.4	5.7	8.0	8.2
Civil engineers.............	383	13.1	4.3	7.8	4.7
Computer hardware engineers.............	77	13.2	3.1	19.1	5.2
Electrical and electronics engineers.............	309	8.8	4.8	12.0	7.4
Industrial engineers, including health and safety.............	174	17.8	2.3	7.0	8.6
Mechanical engineers.............	322	5.5	5.7	12.0	3.9
Drafters.............	147	20.8	2.1	3.9	8.4
Engineering technicians, except drafters.............	376	16.3	11.3	6.7	9.4
Life, physical, and social science occupations [3].............	1,303	47.3	7.3	9.8	5.9
Biological scientists.............	114	48.2	7.7	13.5	6.8
Medical scientists.............	156	54.4	5.2	25.1	7.0
Chemists and materials scientists.............	88	45.9	9.5	11.5	4.6
Environmental scientists and geoscientists.............	98	28.9	4.9	0.6	3.0
Psychologists.............	197	71.2	5.1	2.9	5.9
Community and social services occupations [3].............	2,352	64.5	18.1	2.8	10.7
Counselors.............	732	69.9	18.7	2.8	11.2
Social workers.............	769	81.6	22.8	2.4	11.2
Miscellaneous community and social service specialists.............	83	67.5	17.6	2.9	10.9
Clergy.............	414	17.7	11.3	4.1	6.8
Legal occupations.............	1,770	49.8	7.3	3.9	5.4
Lawyers.............	1,085	31.9	5.3	4.2	3.2
Judges, magistrates, and other judicial workers.............	67	44.4	11.5	1.1	8.3
Paralegals and legal assistants.............	404	84.3	11.0	3.0	8.3
Miscellaneous legal support workers.............	209	76.7	9.3	4.3	10.5
Education, training, and library occupations [3].............	8,619	73.6	9.7	3.5	8.3
Postsecondary teachers.............	1,355	46.2	7.3	10.1	4.8
Preschool and kindergarten teachers.............	707	97.7	14.5	2.8	12.7
Elementary and middle school teachers.............	2,848	81.7	9.8	1.6	8.0
Secondary school teachers.............	1,136	58.0	7.4	2.1	6.9
Special education teachers.............	388	85.4	8.0	1.8	6.8
Other teachers and instructors.............	812	62.6	8.0	3.9	7.3
Librarians.............	198	86.2	10.1	2.6	3.9
Teacher assistants.............	950	92.2	14.3	2.6	14.9

See footnotes at end of table.

Table 626. Employed Civilians by Occupation, Sex, Race, and Hispanic Origin:
2011-Continued.
See headnote on page 405.

Occupation	Total employed (1,000)	Female	Black [1]	Asian [1]	Hispanic [2]
			Percent of total		
Arts, design, entertainment, sports, and media occupations [3]	2,779	46.1	6.0	3.6	9.1
Artists and related workers	180	48.0	3.8	3.8	2.8
Designers	766	51.3	3.6	3.2	10.5
Producers and directors	149	40.7	8.2	3.2	7.3
Athletes, coaches, umpires, and related workers	272	34.5	5.4	2.6	9.7
Musicians, singers, and related workers	191	29.8	15.1	1.2	6.6
News analysts, reporters and correspondents	70	34.1	9.3	5.0	11.4
Public relations specialists	158	61.6	6.3	2.7	9.8
Editors	166	54.2	4.6	3.8	3.4
Writers and authors	218	57.0	4.5	3.1	3.7
Miscellaneous media and communication workers	89	64.9	7.9	12.5	30.6
Broadcast and sound engineering technicians and radio operators	106	9.9	9.1	6.0	10.2
Photographers	148	51.3	3.5	2.8	9.6
Healthcare practitioner and technical occupations [3]	7,740	74.4	10.0	7.8	6.7
Dentists	181	22.2	1.0	11.0	5.8
Dietitians and nutritionists	102	90.6	15.2	4.5	8.4
Pharmacists	274	55.7	7.1	15.3	4.4
Physicians and surgeons	822	33.8	5.3	16.1	6.6
Physician assistants	82	69.8	9.6	2.7	10.1
Registered nurses	2,706	91.1	10.4	7.3	5.1
Occupational therapists	112	92.0	2.7	7.6	4.6
Physical therapists	222	67.8	5.2	8.9	5.0
Speech-language pathologists	125	95.6	1.5	1.5	6.4
Clinical laboratory technologists and technicians	321	73.6	15.3	8.9	9.4
Dental hygienists	148	97.5	0.5	5.5	7.2
Diagnostic-related technologists and technicians	342	73.0	9.0	4.0	7.2
Emergency medical technicians and paramedics	185	36.0	4.5	0.9	6.4
Health practitioner support technologists and technicians	511	78.6	15.1	5.6	11.0
Licensed practical and licensed vocational nurses	560	90.5	23.7	3.9	8.3
Medical records and health information technicians	116	89.7	10.6	9.5	19.6
Service occupations	**24,787**	**55.9**	**15.4**	**4.9**	**21.0**
Healthcare support occupations [3]	3,359	87.7	24.6	4.3	13.9
Nursing, psychiatric, and home health aides	1,981	87.8	33.1	4.3	13.3
Massage therapists	146	86.5	5.5	5.5	7.0
Dental assistants	307	97.9	8.3	5.1	16.3
Medical assistants and other healthcare support occupations	395	93.4	14.3	5.2	20.2
Protective service occupations [3]	3,210	20.7	17.4	2.1	12.6
First-line supervisors of police and detectives	107	17.5	9.3	4.0	6.7
Fire-fighters	305	4.5	2.9	0.6	10.0
Bailiffs, correctional officers, and jailers	446	27.9	25.1	1.9	13.0
Detectives and criminal investigators	151	16.7	8.9	1.2	14.9
Police and sheriff's patrol officers	668	12.0	11.5	2.0	12.7
Private detectives and investigators	92	35.3	8.3	1.2	11.5
Security guards and gaming surveillance officers	963	19.2	27.2	3.6	15.4
Lifeguards and other protective service workers	146	58.1	6.2	0.3	6.3
Food preparation and serving related occupations	7,747	54.4	12.6	5.9	21.8
Chefs and head cooks	347	18.7	9.1	15.3	18.0
First-line supervisors of food preparation and serving workers	505	59.1	18.2	3.2	15.1
Cooks	1,990	39.2	17.9	5.9	30.4
Food-preparation workers	784	58.0	14.4	5.7	23.0
Bartenders	392	55.7	5.1	2.1	10.1
Combined food preparation and serving workers, including fast food	326	66.0	16.3	3.7	15.4
Counter attendants, cafeteria, food concession, and coffee shop	255	68.3	9.1	3.5	16.9
Waiters and waitresses	2,059	69.5	7.8	6.6	17.1
Food servers, nonrestaurant	181	67.7	21.0	6.1	17.1
Dining room and cafeteria attendants and bartender helpers	347	46.8	9.8	4.9	31.5
Dishwashers	273	19.9	11.9	7.4	34.4
Hosts and hostesses, restaurant, lounge, and coffee shop	286	83.0	6.9	3.3	16.4
Building and grounds cleaning and maintenance occupations	5,492	38.8	13.7	3.1	34.8
First-line supervisors of housekeeping and janitorial workers	292	41.0	17.3	3.5	16.0
First-line supervisors of landscaping, lawn service, and groundskeeping workers	274	9.9	4.9	1.4	19.1
Janitors and building cleaners	2,186	30.3	16.6	3.1	30.4
Maids and housekeeping cleaners	1,419	88.6	16.5	4.5	39.9
Pest control workers	75	3.7	7.0	0.0	20.3
Grounds maintenance workers	1,247	5.2	7.1	1.8	45.2
Personal care and service occupations [3]	4,979	78.4	14.1	7.6	14.7
First-line supervisors of gaming workers	120	46.4	3.7	9.1	8.4
First-line supervisors of personal service workers	192	73.5	9.9	13.8	11.0
Nonfarm animal caretakers	179	75.9	2.7	1.4	11.0
Gaming services workers	113	44.9	5.6	23.3	16.4
Barbers	89	24.0	27.7	2.6	17.6
Hairdressers, hairstylists, and cosmetologists	758	93.0	11.6	4.1	12.8
Miscellaneous personal appearance workers	251	84.1	5.9	55.1	5.3
Baggage porters, bellhops, and concierges	81	14.0	20.7	9.1	28.4
Child care workers	1,231	94.5	15.0	3.4	18.1
Personal and home care aides	1057	85.6	21.9	5.8	19.3
Recreation and fitness workers	390	64.1	10.5	3.4	7.2
Sales and office occupations	**33,066**	**62.3**	**11.3**	**4.4**	**13.2**
Sales and related occupations [3]	15,330	49.6	9.8	4.9	12.6

See footnotes at end of table.

Table 626. Employed Civilians by Occupation, Sex, Race, and Hispanic Origin: 2011-Continued.

Occupation	Total employed (1,000)	Percent of total			
		Female	Black [1]	Asian [1]	Hispanic [2]
First-line supervisors of retail sales workers........................	3,217	43.5	8.8	5.4	10.9
First-line supervisors of non retail sales workers......................	1,088	26.7	5.8	4.9	10.1
Cashiers...	3,158	73.6	15.6	6.5	18.1
Counter and rental clerks..	139	48.6	10.2	8.6	13.0
Parts salespersons..	131	15.5	6.5	0.3	10.3
Retail salespersons...	3,224	51.2	11.5	4.4	14.3
Advertising sales agents...	254	55.6	10.8	1.6	8.8
Insurance sales agents...	531	47.3	8.2	3.2	9.1
Securities, commodities, and financial services sales agents..............	267	29.9	4.7	6.5	5.6
Travel agents...	69	79.4	5.9	5.3	9.5
Sales representatives, services, all other...........................	503	31.2	7.6	4.6	10.9
Sales representatives, wholesale and manufacturing....................	1,297	25.9	2.9	3.4	7.9
Real estate brokers and sales agents...............................	811	56.8	4.6	4.2	8.8
Telemarketers..	108	59.4	14.9	1.2	17.4
Door-to-door sales workers, news and street vendors, and related workers..	201	59.2	12.6	3.0	17.8
Office and administrative support occupations [3].....................	17,736	73.4	12.6	4.1	13.7
First-line supervisors of office and administrative support workers...........................	1,423	68.2	9.6	3.7	11.7
Bill and account collectors.......................................	211	70.6	17.3	3.8	18.4
Billing and posting clerks and machine operators.....................	471	90.1	12.3	4.5	15.2
Bookkeeping, accounting, and auditing clerks........................	1,300	89.9	7.7	4.1	8.4
Payroll and timekeeping clerks...................................	168	89.3	14.2	3.7	12.0
Tellers..	413	85.3	8.7	3.9	14.8
Court, municipal, and license clerks...............................	86	79.5	16.6	3.5	7.3
Customer service representatives.................................	1,916	66.5	15.7	4.5	16.9
File clerks...	334	83.9	13.7	6.4	15.3
Hotel, motel, and resort desk clerks...............................	135	64.4	19.6	7.8	16.9
Interviewers, except eligibility and loan...........................	153	84.4	17.2	4.5	18.3
Library assistants, clerical.......................................	113	81.6	8.6	5.2	8.5
Loan interviewers and clerks.....................................	117	82.7	11.9	4.2	10.4
Order clerks..	113	67.1	5.9	5.4	11.5
Receptionists and information clerks...............................	1,259	92.1	11.3	3.9	17.0
Reservation and transportation ticket agents and travel clerks.............	99	59.5	23.2	5.8	8.8
Couriers and messengers..	249	16.4	16.7	2.5	14.4
Dispatchers..	239	57.9	17.8	1.9	12.0
Postal service clerks..	146	50.9	26.4	10.9	10.1
Postal service mail carriers......................................	348	36.0	13.7	6.9	10.0
Postal service mail sorters, processors, and processing machine operators................................	60	40.5	30.5	8.9	16.2
Production, planning, and expediting clerks..........................	236	53.5	8.9	2.9	9.5
Shipping, receiving, and traffic clerks..............................	559	28.5	14.2	3.7	24.3
Stock clerks and order fillers.....................................	1,503	34.8	15.5	3.4	18.8
Weighers, measurers, checkers, and samplers, recordkeeping............	70	55.7	17.6	5.0	22.1
Secretaries and administrative assistants...........................	2,871	95.9	8.2	2.6	9.7
Computer operators...	126	49.9	11.1	5.9	11.1
Data entry keyers...	334	83.2	16.0	4.9	12.6
Word processors and typists......................................	136	88.5	18.8	6.2	10.0
Insurance claims and policy processing clerks........................	246	83.0	17.4	2.1	10.1
Mail clerks and mail machine operators, except postal service.............	93	53.0	18.0	3.3	15.0
Office clerks, general..	1061	85.4	13.5	5.0	15.5
Natural resources, construction, and maintenance occupations........	**13,009**	**4.2**	**6.5**	**2.0**	**25.3**
Farming, fishing, and forestry occupations [3].......................	1,001	21.6	4.3	1.4	43.0
Construction and extraction occupations [3].........................	7,125	2.3	5.9	1.5	29.4
First-line supervisors of construction trades and extraction workers..	634	2.2	5.2	0.7	16.5
Brickmasons, blockmasons, and stonemasons........................	146	0.9	5.0	1.9	39.3
Carpenters...	1,330	1.9	5.3	1.6	26.7
Carpet, floor, and tile installers and finishers........................	189	0.5	6.3	2.4	43.2
Cement masons, concrete finishers, and terrazzo workers...............	70	0.0	9.3	0.6	47.8
Construction laborers...	1,253	2.1	7.3	1.8	42.9
Operating engineers and other construction equipment operators.........	369	0.8	5.0	0.2	16.6
Drywall installers, ceiling tile installers, and tapers..................	150	1.7	2.0	0.6	59.7
Electricians..	682	1.5	6.1	2.4	14.0
Painters, construction and maintenance............................	528	6.8	6.5	2.5	41.8
Pipelayers, plumbers, pipefitters, and steamfitters....................	519	1.7	6.4	1.4	22.5
Roofers...	222	1.1	4.9	0.8	47.3
Sheet metal workers..	126	2.3	2.2	0.6	18.9
Construction and building inspectors...............................	75	4.7	5.0	0.2	11.6
Highway maintenance workers....................................	105	2.5	11.0	0.5	13.2
Installation, maintenance, and repair occupations [3]..................	4,883	3.5	7.9	2.9	15.8
First-line supervisors of mechanics, installers, and repairers...	313	6.8	6.4	0.9	9.7
Computer, automated teller, and office machine repairers..............	305	9.0	11.0	6.3	9.9
Radio and telecommunications equipment installers and repairers........	150	7.7	10.1	3.2	10.6
Aircraft mechanics and service technicians..........................	164	3.1	8.9	3.1	17.2
Automotive body and related repairers.............................	140	1.2	6.9	2.9	18.1
Automotive service technicians and mechanics.......................	855	1.4	7.8	4.2	19.7
Bus and truck mechanics and diesel engine specialists.................	312	0.7	4.0	2.5	15.1
Heavy vehicle and mobile equipment service technicians and mechanics..	199	1.3	5.0	1.2	11.1
Heating, air conditioning, and refrigeration mechanics and installers..	338	0.8	5.8	1.9	16.9
Industrial and refractory machinery mechanics.......................	433	2.5	7.1	3.8	15.2

See footnotes at end of table.

Occupation	Total employed (1,000)	Percent of total			
		Female	Black [1]	Asian [1]	Hispanic [2]
Maintenance and repair workers, general...................................	422	3.2	12.2	1.9	17.4
Electrical power-line installers and repairers...........................	124	0.2	8.6	0.4	11.5
Telecommunications line installers and repairers......................	201	4.3	12.2	1.1	17.3
Production, transportation, and material moving occupations...........	**16,461**	**21.6**	**13.7**	**4.3**	**21.0**
Production occupations [3]...	8,142	28.4	11.0	5.9	21.6
First-line supervisors of production and operating workers...	727	18.6	7.7	5.6	12.7
Electrical, electronics, and electromechanical assemblers..................	156	51.9	13.5	21.5	20.4
Bakers..	207	55.0	13.3	5.0	32.9
Butchers and other meat, poultry, and fish processing workers............	342	26.6	17.2	10.6	38.0
Food batchmakers...	90	53.3	15.3	4.3	29.3
Cutting, punching, and press machine setters, operators, and tenders, metal and plastic.............................	100	14.8	10.7	3.3	18.2
Machinists...	419	4.4	3.7	4.2	14.1
Welding, soldering, and brazing workers.................................	505	7.8	7.6	3.8	20.9
Printing machine operators..	217	18.7	12.0	2.2	16.9
Laundry and dry-cleaning workers.......................................	174	60.7	15.2	10.4	33.8
Sewing machine operators...	169	78.5	9.7	12.0	36.9
Tailors, dressmakers, and sewers..	94	74.9	4.2	10.7	27.5
Stationary engineers and boiler operators................................	95	2.2	13.5	3.4	17.4
Water and wastewater treatment plant and system operators............	71	5.2	11.1	0.8	10.8
Crushing, grinding, polishing, mixing, and blending workers..............	94	13.5	8.1	3.9	21.0
Inspectors, testers, sorters, samplers, and weighers.....................	647	34.9	8.1	6.0	16.4
Medical, dental, and ophthalmic laboratory technicians...................	87	53.1	7.3	9.8	13.0
Packaging and filling machine operators and tenders.....................	288	50.6	13.3	5.6	40.9
Painting workers...	120	13.4	10.8	3.1	23.1
Transportation and material-moving occupations [3].......................	8,318	14.9	16.3	2.7	20.3
Supervisors, transportation and material-moving workers..................	228	22.1	16.5	2.3	13.7
Aircraft pilots and flight engineers.......................................	121	4.3	2.9	2.4	3.9
Bus drivers..	573	43.4	24.6	1.6	12.7
Driver/sales workers and truck drivers..................................	3,059	4.8	13.7	1.6	17.6
Taxi drivers and chauffeurs...	342	12.5	26.7	15.6	16.0
Parking lot attendants...	73	13.2	26.6	4.1	28.7
Automotive and water craft attendants..................................	76	10.6	7.1	2.3	17.1
Industrial truck and tractor operators....................................	528	6.7	22.7	1.3	27.9
Cleaners of vehicles and equipment.....................................	331	12.0	14.2	1.3	33.4
Laborers and freight, stock, and material movers, hand....................	1,787	16.9	17.4	3.1	21.8
Packers and packagers, hand..	393	53.5	14.1	3.6	45.8
Refuse and recyclable material collectors................................	92	7.7	17.1	0.7	30.0

– Represents or rounds to zero. [1] The Current Population Survey (CPS) allows respondents to choose more than one race. Data represent persons who selected this race group only and exclude persons reporting more than one race. The CPS in prior years only allowed respondents to report one race group. See also comments on race in the text for Section 1. [2] Persons of Hispanic origin may be any race. [3] Includes other occupations, not shown separately.

Source: U.S. Bureau of Labor Statistics, "Employment and Earnings Online," January 2012 issue, March 2012, <http://www.bls.gov/opub/ee/home.htm> and <http://www.bls.gov/cps/home.htm>.

Table 627. Employed Civilians by Occupation—States: 2010

[In thousands (139,064 represents 139,064,000). Based on the Current Population Survey see text, Section 1 and Appendix III]

State	Total	Management, professional, and related occupations		Service occupa-tions	Sales and office occupations		Natural resources, construc-tion, and maintenance occupations			Production, transportation, and material-moving occupations	
		Manage-ment, business, and financial opera-tions	Profes-sional and related occupa-tions		Sales and related occupa-tions	Office and admin-istrative occupa-tions	Farming, fishing, and forestry occupa-tions	Construc-tion and extraction occupa-tions	Instal-lation, mainte-nance, and repair occupa-tions	Produc-tion occupa-tions	Transpor-tation and material-moving occupa-tions
Total.......	139,064	20,938	30,805	24,634	15,386	18,047	987	7,175	4,911	7,998	8,182
AL............	1,952	215	408	316	198	262	14	128	87	183	142
AK............	331	49	66	62	32	44	4	24	18	12	22
AZ............	2,850	454	617	506	371	392	6	165	93	124	120
AR............	1,228	161	245	193	129	164	16	65	51	117	88
CA............	15,976	2,507	3,597	2,909	1,838	2,014	222	747	500	812	830
CO...........	2,482	441	623	392	274	295	10	133	81	100	132
CT............	1,719	297	443	288	191	211	3	73	56	84	73
DE............	392	59	81	69	42	61	3	21	13	18	25
DC............	310	79	114	50	19	30	(Z)	5	3	3	7
FL............	8,083	1,231	1,763	1,554	1,022	1,069	36	389	308	250	458
GA............	4,238	696	860	696	531	528	19	236	159	218	296
HI............	579	75	110	134	70	79	4	38	22	18	29
ID............	691	100	125	123	85	97	18	37	31	37	38
IL............	5,970	894	1,249	1,049	693	784	17	231	180	435	437
IN............	2,818	382	555	473	317	346	13	143	103	287	200
IA............	1,571	219	309	265	165	211	13	82	60	136	111
KS............	1,385	234	308	235	137	173	12	68	50	88	80
KY............	1,844	244	396	320	189	220	20	104	69	143	138
LA............	1,928	280	394	337	218	262	20	111	72	110	125
ME............	633	93	143	112	66	82	8	35	25	35	35
MD...........	2,819	487	767	470	275	376	9	145	93	82	117
MA...........	3,194	557	875	531	320	382	8	137	88	149	148
MI............	4,232	589	1,006	749	441	568	45	161	130	311	230
MN...........	2,721	458	635	434	279	366	31	112	84	165	158
MS...........	1,155	133	231	190	105	168	16	72	52	106	82
MO...........	2,745	386	534	486	295	417	8	159	104	185	170
MT...........	452	78	90	90	47	53	9	28	16	17	23
NE...........	929	153	206	139	100	119	11	46	31	76	48
NV...........	1,131	156	183	305	138	143	4	56	41	36	69
NH...........	702	115	177	108	82	83	2	31	26	44	33
NJ............	4,100	700	962	688	463	551	10	179	127	158	261
NM...........	843	124	203	156	78	106	4	66	32	34	40
NY...........	8,832	1,230	2,134	1,800	951	1,186	8	428	246	362	486
NC...........	4,094	602	958	703	447	481	18	231	163	281	210
ND...........	358	63	70	64	36	42	7	24	15	18	19
OH...........	5,263	702	1,074	966	558	730	24	257	199	426	328
OK...........	1,621	244	316	281	176	222	17	109	77	86	93
OR...........	1,780	292	390	325	204	213	32	75	48	97	104
PA...........	5,774	854	1,291	978	607	770	50	285	210	340	389
RI............	508	72	131	95	53	63	1	20	16	32	25
SC...........	1,899	227	393	346	230	244	10	82	97	157	113
SD...........	420	73	77	73	42	57	9	21	15	29	25
TN...........	2,788	384	556	499	313	373	15	141	111	215	181
TX...........	11,149	1,541	2,204	2,014	1,243	1,415	69	805	490	645	722
UT............	1,271	193	264	186	153	186	5	82	42	84	76
VT............	339	53	87	54	36	40	4	20	11	19	16
VA...........	3,800	680	968	598	413	432	21	196	124	174	192
WA...........	3,180	499	783	546	313	383	52	162	101	158	182
WV...........	724	99	157	132	73	98	1	48	32	38	46
WI............	2,813	420	588	468	287	395	22	124	88	240	181
WY........	278	39	52	48	22	36	3	29	16	12	22

Z Less than 500.

Source: U.S. Bureau of Labor Statistics, *Geographic Profile of Employment and Unemployment, 2010*, Bulletin 2748, July 2011. See also <http://www.bls.gov/opub/gp/laugp.htm>.

Labor Force, Employment, and Earnings 409

Table 628. Employment Projections by Occupation: 2010 to 2020

[In thousands (861.0 represents 861,000), except percent and rank. Estimates based on the Current Employment Statistics Program; the Occupational Employment Statistics Survey; and the Current Population Survey. See source for methodological assumptions. Occupations based on the 2000 Standard Occupational Classification system]

Occupation	Employment (1,000)		Change, 2010–2020		Quartile rank by 2010 median annual earnings [1]	Typical Education Needed for Entry
	2010	2020	Number (1,000)	Percent		
FASTEST GROWING						
Personal care aides............................	861.0	1,468.0	607.0	70.5	VL	Less than high school
Home health aides..............................	1,017.7	1,723.9	706.3	69.4	VL	Less than high school
Biomedical engineers...........................	15.7	25.4	9.7	61.7	VH	Bachelor's degree
Helpers-brickmasons, blockmasons, stonemasons, and tile and marble setters..............	29.4	47.0	17.6	60.1	L	Less than high school
Helpers-carpenters.............................	46.5	72.4	25.9	55.7	L	Less than high school
Veterinary technologists and technicians................	80.2	121.9	41.7	52.0	L	Associate's degree
Reinforcing iron and rebar workers.......................	19.1	28.4	9.3	48.6	H	High school diploma or equivalent
Physical therapist assistants.......................	67.4	98.2	30.8	45.7	H	Associate's degree
Helpers-pipelayers, plumbers, pipefitters, and steamfitters........................	57.9	84.2	26.3	45.4	L	High school diploma or equivalent
Meeting, convention, and event planners.................	71.6	102.9	31.3	43.7	H	Bachelor's degree
Diagnostic medical sonographers.......................	53.7	77.1	23.4	43.5	VH	Associate's degree
Occupational therapy assistants....................	28.5	40.8	12.3	43.3	H	Associate's degree
Physical therapist aides.........................	47.0	67.3	20.3	43.1	L	High school diploma or equivalent
Glaziers.......................................	41.9	59.6	17.7	42.4	H	High school diploma or equivalent
Interpreters and translators.......................	58.4	83.1	24.6	42.2	H	Bachelor's degree
Medical secretaries............................	508.7	718.9	210.2	41.3	L	High school diploma or equivalent
Market research analysts and marketing specialists.................................	282.7	399.3	116.6	41.2	VH	Bachelor's degree
Marriage and family therapists....................	36.0	50.8	14.8	41.2	H	Master's degree
Brickmasons and blockmasons.......................	89.2	125.3	36.1	40.5	H	High school diploma or equivalent
Physical therapists.............................	198.6	276.0	77.4	39.0	VH	Doctoral or professional degree
Dental hygienists..............................	181.8	250.3	68.5	37.7	VH	Associate's degree
Bicycle repairers...............................	9.9	13.6	3.7	37.6	L	High school diploma or equivalent
Audiologists...................................	13.0	17.8	4.8	36.8	VH	Doctoral or professional degree
Health educators...............................	63.4	86.6	23.2	36.5	H	Bachelor's degree
Stonemasons...................................	15.6	21.4	5.7	36.5	H	High school diploma or equivalent
Cost estimators................................	185.4	252.9	67.5	36.4	VH	Bachelor's degree
Medical scientists, except epidemiologists..............	100.0	136.5	36.4	36.4	VH	Doctoral or professional degree
Mental health counselors.........................	120.3	163.9	43.6	36.3	H	Master's degree
Pile-driver operators............................	4.1	5.6	1.5	36.0	H	High school diploma or equivalent
Veterinarians..................................	61.4	83.4	22.0	35.9	VH	Doctoral or professional degree
LARGEST JOB GROWTH						
Registered nurses..............................	2,737.4	3,449.3	711.9	26.0	VH	Associate's degree
Retail salespersons............................	4,261.6	4,968.4	706.8	16.6	VL	Less than high school
Home health aides..............................	1,017.7	1,723.9	706.3	69.4	VL	Less than high school
Personal care aides............................	861.0	1,468.0	607.0	70.5	VL	Less than high school
Office clerks, general...........................	2,950.7	3,440.2	489.5	16.6	L	High school diploma or equivalent
Combined food preparation and serving workers, including fast food..............	2,682.1	3,080.1	398.0	14.8	VL	Less than high school
Customer service representatives..................	2,187.3	2,525.6	338.4	15.5	L	High school diploma or equivalent
Heavy and tractor-trailer truck drivers.................	1,604.8	1,934.9	330.1	20.6	H	High school diploma or equivalent
Laborers and freight, stock, and material movers, hand........................	2,068.2	2,387.3	319.1	15.4	L	Less than high school
Postsecondary teachers.........................	1,756.0	2,061.7	305.7	17.4	H	Doctoral or professional degree
Nursing aides, orderlies, and attendants...............	1,505.3	1,807.2	302.0	20.1	L	Postsecondary nondegree award
Childcare workers..............................	1,282.3	1,544.3	262.0	20.4	VL	High school diploma or equivalent
Bookkeeping, accounting, and auditing clerks..........	1,898.3	2,157.4	259.0	13.6	H	High school diploma or equivalent
Cashiers......................................	3,362.6	3,612.8	250.2	7.4	VL	Less than high school
Elementary school teachers, except special education..............................	1,476.5	1,725.3	248.8	16.8	VH	Bachelor's degree
Receptionists and information clerks..................	1048.5	1297.0	248.5	23.7	L	High school diploma or equivalent
Janitors and cleaners, except maids and housekeeping cleaners....................	2310.4	2556.8	246.4	10.7	L	Less than high school
Landscapers and groundskeepers.....................	1151.5	1392.3	240.8	20.9	L	Less than high school
Sales representatives, wholesale and manufacturing, except technical and scientific products................	1430.0	1653.4	223.4	15.6	VH	High school diploma or equivalent
Construction laborers...........................	998.8	1211.2	212.4	21.3	L	Less than high school
Medical secretaries............................	508.7	718.9	210.2	41.3	L	High school diploma or equivalent
First-line supervisors of office and administrative support workers........................	1,424.4	1,627.8	203.4	14.3	H	High school diploma or equivalent
Carpenters....................................	1,001.7	1,197.6	196.0	19.6	H	High school diploma or equivalent
Waiters and waitresses..........................	2,260.3	2,456.2	195.9	8.7	VL	Less than high school
Security guards................................	1,035.7	1,230.7	195.0	18.8	L	High school diploma or equivalent
Teacher assistants.............................	1,288.3	1,479.3	191.1	14.8	L	High school diploma or equivalent
Accountants and auditors........................	1,216.9	1,407.6	190.7	15.7	VH	Bachelor's degree
Licensed practical and licensed vocational nurses..............................	752.3	920.8	168.5	22.4	H	Postsecondary nondegree award
Physicians and surgeons.........................	691.0	859.3	168.3	24.4	VH	Doctoral or professional degree
Medical assistants.............................	527.6	690.4	162.9	30.9	L	High school diploma or equivalent

[1] Quartile ranks based on the Occupational Employment Statistics annual wages. VH = very high ($51,540 and over), H = high ($32,390 to $51,530), L = low ($21,590 to $32,380), and VL = very low (under $21,590). The rankings were based on quartiles using one-fourth of total employment to define each quartile. Wages are for wage and salary workers.

Source: U.S. Bureau of Labor Statistics "Occupational Employment Projections to 2020," *Monthly Labor Review*, Volume 135, Number 12, January 2012, <http://www.bls.gov/opub>.

Table 629. Occupations of the Employed by Selected Characteristic: 2010

[In thousands (121,987 represents 121,987,000). Annual averages of monthly figures. Civilian noninstitutional population 25 years old and over. Based on Current Population Survey; see text, Section 1 and Appendix III. See headnote, Table 616, regarding occupations]

Race and educational attainment	Total employed	Managerial, professional, and related	Service	Sales and office	Natural resources, construction, and maintenance	Production, transportation, and material-moving
Total [1].	**121,987**	**48,913**	**19,226**	**27,833**	**11,675**	**14,339**
Less than a high school diploma.	10,115	655	3,292	1,280	2,310	2,578
High school graduates, no college.	34,293	5,639	7,334	9,235	5,150	6,935
Less than a bachelor's degree.	33,747	11,138	5,899	9,866	3,243	3,601
College graduates.	43,832	31,481	2,701	7,452	972	1,225
White [2].	100,100	40,920	14,448	23,027	10,343	11,362
Less than a high school diploma.	8,290	548	2,523	1,008	2,099	2,112
High school graduates, no college.	28,128	4,891	5,319	7,801	4,593	5,525
Less than a bachelor's degree.	27,506	9,352	4,473	8,054	2,826	2,802
College graduates.	36,176	26,130	2,133	6,165	826	923
Black [2].	13,092	4,118	3,164	2,980	810	2,021
Less than a high school diploma.	1,103	54	490	170	118	271
High school graduates, no college.	4,234	517	1,388	947	357	1,025
Less than a bachelor's degree.	4,346	1,211	1,018	1,274	261	582
College graduates.	3,409	2,336	268	589	74	143
Asian [2].	6,155	2,993	1,070	1,234	240	618
Less than a high school diploma.	431	33	185	56	29	129
High school graduates, no college.	1,149	130	421	286	81	232
Less than a bachelor's degree.	1,037	305	220	312	74	125
College graduates.	3,538	2,525	244	580	57	132
Hispanic [3].	16,946	3,449	4,325	3,266	2,907	2,999
Less than a high school diploma.	5,183	174	1,813	463	1,398	1,336
High school graduates, no college.	5,175	534	1,425	1,141	986	1,088
Less than a bachelor's degree.	3,725	981	771	1,163	391	419
College graduates.	2,862	1,760	316	499	132	155

[1] Includes other races, not shown separately. [2] For persons in this race group only. See footnote 4, Table 597. [3] Persons of Hispanic origin may be any race.

Source: U.S. Bureau of Labor Statistics, Current Population Survey, unpublished data.

Table 630. Employment by Industry: 2000 to 2011

[In thousands (136,891 represents 136,891,000), except percent. See headnote, Table 616]

Industry	2000	2005 [1]	2010 [1]	2011 [1]	2011, percent [1]			
					Female	Black [2]	Asian [2]	Hispanic [3]
Total employed.	**136,891**	**141,730**	**139,064**	**139,869**	**46.9**	**10.8**	**4.9**	**14.5**
Agriculture and related industries.	2,464	2,197	2,206	2,254	24.7	2.3	1.0	23.2
Mining.	475	624	731	817	12.1	4.5	1.6	16.0
Construction.	9,931	11,197	9,077	9,039	9.2	5.5	1.5	24.4
Manufacturing.	19,644	16,253	14,081	14,336	28.7	8.7	6.0	15.0
Durable goods.	12,519	10,333	8,789	9,007	24.8	7.2	6.5	12.7
Nondurable goods.	7,125	5,919	5,293	5,329	35.2	11.1	5.2	18.9
Wholesale trade.	4,216	4,579	3,805	3,798	28.5	7.5	4.6	15.6
Retail trade.	15,763	16,825	15,934	15,927	48.6	10.8	4.5	14.6
Transportation and utilities.	7,380	7,360	7,134	7,200	22.6	15.6	3.9	15.1
Transportation and warehousing.	6,096	6,184	5,880	5,957	22.6	17.0	4.3	16.0
Utilities.	1,284	1,176	1,253	1,243	22.2	9.0	2.1	10.7
Information.	4,059	3,402	3,149	3,150	40.2	10.8	5.6	9.5
Financial activities.	9,374	10,203	9,350	9,386	54.7	9.4	5.5	10.6
Finance and insurance.	6,641	7,035	6,605	6,613	57.6	9.3	6.2	9.7
Real estate and rental and leasing.	2,734	3,168	2,745	2,773	47.6	9.6	4.0	12.8
Professional and business services.	13,649	14,294	15,253	15,819	41.0	8.7	6.1	14.7
Professional and technical services.	8,266	8,584	9,115	9,461	42.5	5.9	8.3	6.9
Management, administrative, and waste services.	5,383	5,709	6,138	6,358	38.6	12.8	2.9	26.3
Education and health services.	26,188	29,174	32,062	31,867	74.4	13.8	4.8	10.5
Educational services.	11,255	12,264	13,155	12,965	68.4	10.7	3.7	9.6
Health care and social assistance.	14,933	16,910	18,907	18,902	78.5	16.0	5.5	11.1
Hospitals.	5,202	5,719	6,249	6,315	75.8	15.3	7.2	8.7
Health services, except hospitals.	7,009	8,332	9,406	9,367	78.1	15.9	5.1	11.2
Social assistance.	2,722	2,860	3,252	3,221	85.0	17.7	3.5	15.7
Leisure and hospitality.	11,186	12,071	12,530	12,697	50.4	11.2	6.4	19.6
Arts, entertainment, and recreation.	2,539	2,765	2,966	2,922	45.3	8.6	5.1	11.1
Accommodation and food services.	8,647	9,306	9,564	9,775	51.9	12.0	6.8	22.1
Other services.	6,450	7,020	6,769	6,724	52.0	9.1	6.6	16.6
Other services, except private households.	5,731	6,208	6,102	6,002	47.5	9.2	6.9	14.3
Private households.	718	812	667	722	89.3	8.4	3.7	35.2
Public administration.	6,113	6,530	6,983	6,853	44.7	15.3	3.2	10.1

[1] See footnote 2, Table 596. [2] Persons in this race group only. See footnote 4, Table 597. [3] Persons of Hispanic origin may be any race.

Source: U.S. Bureau of Labor Statistics, "Employment and Earnings Online," January 2012 issue, March 2012, <http://www.bls.gov/opub/ee/home.htm> and <http://www.bls.gov/cps/home.htm>.

Table 631. Employment Projections by Industry: 2010 to 2020

[5,525.6 represents 5,525,600. Estimates based on the Current Employment Statistics program. See source for methodological assumptions. Minus sign (–) indicates decline]

Industry	2007 NAICS code [1]	Employment 2010 (1,000)	Employment 2020 (1,000)	Change, 2010–2020 (1,000)	Average annual rate of change 2010–2020
LARGEST GROWTH					
Construction..............................	23	5,525.6	7,365.1	1,839.5	2.9
Retail trade..............................	44, 45	14,413.7	16,182.2	1,768.5	1.2
Offices of health practitioners.................	6211, 6212, 6213	3,818.2	5,209.6	1,391.4	3.2
Hospitals..............................	622	4,685.3	5,563.6	878.3	1.7
Home health care services.................	6216	1,080.6	1,952.4	871.8	6.1
Food services and drinking places.............	722	9,351.8	10,212.2	860.4	0.9
Individual and family services.............	6241	1,215.0	2,066.4	851.4	5.5
Nursing and residential care facilities.............	623	3,129.0	3,951.0	822.0	2.4
Wholesale trade..............................	42	5,456.1	6,200.2	744.1	1.3
General local government educational services compensation.............	(X)	8,010.4	8,751.4	741.0	0.9
Computer systems design and related services.............	5415	1,441.5	2,112.8	671.3	3.9
Employment services..............................	5613	2,716.7	3,348.0	631.3	2.1
Management, scientific, and technical consulting services.............	5416	991.4	1,567.0	575.6	4.7
Junior colleges, colleges, universities, and professional schools...........	6112, 6113	1,694.0	2,171.1	477.1	2.5
Outpatient, laboratory, and other ambulatory care services.................	6214, 6215, 6219	1,077.1	1,471.2	394.1	3.2
Architectural, engineering, and related services.............	5413	1,276.6	1,635.1	358.5	2.5
Services to buildings and dwellings.............	5617	1,742.5	2,044.8	302.3	1.6
Truck transportation..............................	484	1,244.0	1,544.0	300.0	2.2
General state government educational services compensation.............	(X)	2,377.1	2,661.7	284.6	1.1
Child day care services..............................	6244	851.8	1,101.3	249.5	2.6
FASTEST GROWTH					
Home health care services.................	6216	1,080.6	1,952.4	871.8	6.1
Individual and family services.................	6241	1,215.0	2,066.4	851.4	5.5
Management, scientific, and technical consulting services.............	5416	991.4	1,567.0	575.6	4.7
Veneer, plywood, and engineered wood product manufacturing...........	3212	64.7	94.9	30.2	3.9
Computer systems design and related services.............	5415	1,441.5	2,112.8	671.3	3.9
Cement and concrete product manufacturing.............	3273	171.8	236.1	64.3	3.2
Outpatient, laboratory, and other ambulatory care services.................	6214, 6215, 6219	1,077.1	1,471.2	394.1	3.2
Offices of health practitioners.................	6211, 6212, 6213	3,818.2	5,209.6	1,391.4	3.2
Software publishers..............................	5112	259.8	351.6	91.8	3.1
Construction..............................	23	5,525.6	7,365.1	1,839.5	2.9
Commercial and industrial machinery and equipment rental and leasing..	5324	113.5	151.2	37.7	2.9
Other professional, scientific, and technical services.............	5419	573.1	760.2	187.1	2.9
Facilities support services..............................	5612	134.0	177.6	43.6	2.9
Community and vocational rehabilitation services.............	6242, 6243	557.5	738.4	180.9	2.9
Lessors of nonfinancial intangible assets (except copyrighted works).....	533	25.2	33.4	8.2	2.9
Other educational services.............	6114–7	604.2	787.1	182.9	2.7
Automotive repair and maintenance.............	8111	799.7	1,037.2	237.5	2.6
Grantmaking and giving services and social advocacy organizations......	8132, 8133	394.5	510.7	116.2	2.6
Sawmills and wood preservation.............	3211	81.3	105.1	23.8	2.6
Child day care services.............	6244	851.8	1,101.3	249.5	2.6
MOST RAPIDLY DECLINING					
Apparel knitting mills...........................	3151	157.7	66.1	–91.6	–8.3
Leather and hide tanning and finishing, and other leather and allied product manufacturing...........................	3161, 3169	27.8	12.7	–15.1	–7.6
Postal Service..............................	491	656.4	474.6	–181.8	–3.2
Communications equipment manufacturing.............	3342	118.0	85.7	–32.3	–3.1
Computer and peripheral equipment manufacturing.............	3341	161.6	117.5	–44.1	–3.1
Pipeline transportation..............................	486	42.4	32.6	–9.8	–2.6
Metal ore mining..............................	2122	36.4	28.1	–8.3	–2.5
Pesticide, fertilizer, and other agricultural chemical manufacturing.........	3253	35.3	27.5	–7.8	–2.5
Federal enterprises except the Postal Service and electric utilities.........	(X)	76.6	60.2	–16.4	–2.4
Other miscellaneous manufacturing.............	3399	266.0	210.3	–55.7	–2.3
Other chemical product and preparation manufacturing.............	3259	82.9	68.6	–14.3	–1.9
Metalworking machinery manufacturing.............	3335	153.2	130.5	–22.7	–1.6
Glass and glass product manufacturing.............	3272	80.7	68.8	–11.9	–1.6
Basic chemical manufacturing.............	3251	142.4	121.6	–20.8	–1.6
Electrical equipment manufacturing.............	3353	136.3	116.9	–19.4	–1.5
Pulp, paper, and paperboard mills.............	3221	112.7	97.4	–15.3	–1.4
Fiber, yarn, and thread mills.............	3131	237.8	206.1	–31.7	–1.4
Iron and steel mills and ferroalloy manufacturing.............	3311	85.4	74.3	–11.1	–1.4
Petroleum and coal products manufacturing.............	324	114.0	100.0	–14.0	–1.3
Newspaper, periodical, book, and directory publishers.............	5111	501.3	439.7	–61.6	–1.3

X Not applicable. [1] Based on the North American Industry Classification System, 2007; see text, Section 15.

Source: U.S. Bureau of Labor Statistics, "Industry Employment and Output Projections to 2020," *Monthly Labor Review*, Vol. 135, No. 1, January 2012, <http://www.bls.gov/opub/mlr/2012/01/art4exc.htm>.

Table 632. Export-Supported Jobs for Largest Metropolitan Areas: 2010

[(1,562.9 represents $1,562,900,000). Direct export-production jobs are jobs supported by exports in the industries producing the exported good or service; these are in the metropolitan area where the export is produced. Total export-supported jobs include direct export-production jobs as well as jobs supported by exports in the suppliers to the exporting industry, and in the case of goods exports, in the transportation and wholesale trade industries; some portion of these jobs are outside the metro area producing the export and in other parts of the United States]

Metropolitan areas ranked by 2010 export value	Exports		Direct Export-Production Jobs (1,000)	Total Export-Supported Jobs (1,000)
	Value (bil. dol.)	Percent of Metro GDP		
United States................	**1,562.9**	**10.7**	**5,542.3**	**10,719.9**
Los Angeles-Long Beach-Santa Ana, CA................	79.8	10.9	312.7	540.7
New York-Northern New Jersey-Long Island, NY-NJ-PA..............	78.0	6.6	329.0	539.3
Chicago-Joliet-Naperville, IL-IN-WI................	53.9	10.9	197.6	376.1
Houston-Sugar Land-Baytown, TX................	47.9	14.0	141.3	307.0
Dallas-Fort Worth-Arlington, TX................	41.1	12.7	147.2	279.7
San Francisco-Oakland-Fremont, CA................	31.8	11.2	110.0	194.3
Seattle-Tacoma-Bellevue, WA................	29.0	13.7	104.4	188.4
Detroit-Warren-Livonia, MI................	26.6	14.9	79.1	186.3
Philadelphia-Camden-Wilmington, PA-NJ-DE-MD................	26.6	8.5	97.0	174.1
Boston-Cambridge-Quincy, MA-NH................	26.4	8.9	118.9	196.0
San Jose-Sunnyvale-Santa Clara, CA................	22.8	18.0	72.9	144.8
Portland-Vancouver-Hillsboro, OR-WA................	21.3	18.2	70.3	142.4
Atlanta-Sandy Springs-Marietta, GA................	20.0	8.0	88.3	151.7
Minneapolis-St. Paul-Bloomington, MN-WI................	17.6	9.8	63.2	117.2
Phoenix-Mesa-Glendale, AZ................	16.6	9.1	66.7	117.1
Washington-Arlington-Alexandria, DC-VA-MD-WV................	16.4	4.2	100.2	146.2
San Diego-Carlsbad-San Marcos, CA................	16.0	9.3	65.5	113.4
Indianapolis-Carmel, IN................	15.9	17.2	35.7	81.0
Miami-Fort Lauderdale-Pompano Beach, FL................	14.7	6.2	75.1	115.4
St. Louis, MO-IL................	14.4	11.5	49.0	94.9
Cleveland-Elyria-Mentor, OH................	12.1	12.4	35.6	76.8
Cincinnati-Middletown, OH-KY-IN................	11.6	12.2	35.2	74.4
Pittsburgh, PA................	11.1	9.5	38.2	74.6
Riverside-San Bernardino-Ontario, CA................	10.9	8.3	39.4	73.6
Denver-Aurora-Broomfield, CO................	10.2	7.2	44.5	72.8
Charlotte-Gastonia-Rock Hill, NC-SC................	9.8	10.7	33.1	68.4
Baltimore-Towson, MD................	9.7	6.7	40.0	67.6
Milwaukee-Waukesha-West Allis, WI................	9.3	12.3	29.6	61.0
Hartford-West Hartford-East Hartford, CT................	8.9	9.3	31.7	59.8
New Orleans-Metairie-Kenner, LA................	8.7	14.3	21.6	46.0
Austin-Round Rock-San Marcos, TX................	8.5	10.5	31.3	58.0
Kansas City, MO-KS................	8.1	8.6	30.2	57.5
Rochester, NY................	8.1	13.6	23.0	47.8
Tampa-St. Petersburg-Clearwater, FL................	8.0	6.8	34.2	57.5
Columbus, OH................	7.9	8.9	29.5	55.5
Las Vegas-Paradise, NV................	7.4	8.4	43.7	64.4
Orlando-Kissimmee-Sanford, FL................	7.3	7.0	37.8	58.0
Baton Rouge, LA................	7.3	18.3	16.6	46.0
Bridgeport-Stamford-Norwalk, CT................	7.0	10.6	23.5	45.0
Nashville-Davidson-Murfreesboro-Franklin, TN................	7.0	9.6	24.6	48.2
Virginia Beach-Norfolk-Newport News, VA-NC................	6.8	8.0	21.9	40.2
San Antonio-New Braunfels, TX................	6.7	7.9	26.7	46.8
Salt Lake City, UT................	6.6	10.8	27.0	52.4
Greensboro-High Point, NC................	6.5	17.3	17.9	40.7
Providence-New Bedford-Fall River, RI-MA................	6.4	9.1	25.3	46.5
Buffalo-Niagara Falls, NY................	6.4	9.9	23.0	45.2
Louisville-Jefferson County, KY-IN................	6.4	11.5	19.2	43.8
Oxnard-Thousand Oaks-Ventura, CA................	6.2	15.7	16.6	34.2
Sacramento-Arden-Arcade-Roseville, CA................	6.0	5.9	26.8	44.3
Tulsa, OK................	5.5	13.8	18.9	36.4

Source: Brookings Institution, *Export Nation 2012: How U.S. Metropolitan Areas Are Driving National Growth*, March 2012. See also <http://www.brookings.edu/research/reports/2012/03/08-exports>.

Table 633. Green Goods and Services Employment by Industry: 2010

[Covers employment in 333 of the 1,193 detailed industries in the 2007 North American Industry Classification System (NAICS) identified by BLS as potentially providing goods and services that directly benefit the environment or conserve natural resources. Data compiled through the Green Goods and Services (GGS) survey under the Quarterly Census of Employment and Wages (QCEW) program. Data may not add to total or sub-total due to rounding. Industries may not add to total because of unclassified employment in the QCEW, not shown separately]

Industry	2007 NAICS code [1]	Private		Federal government		State government		Local government	
		Number	Per-cent	Number	Per-cent	Number	Per-cent	Number	Per-cent
Total, all industries		**2,268,824**	**2.1**	**156,707**	**5.3**	**227,103**	**4.9**	**476,479**	**3.4**
Natural resources and mining..................	11,21	65,050	3.6	(S)	(S)	1,740	77.2	(S)	(S)
Utilities..	22	65,664	11.9	9,998	74	(S)	(S)	99,790	41.1
Construction...................................	23	372,077	6.8	(S)	(S)	(S)	(S)	(S)	(S)
Manufacturing.................................	31-33	461,847	4	(S)	(S)	(S)	(S)	(S)	(S)
Wholesale & retail trade......................	42,44-45	202,370	1	(S)	(S)	(S)	(S)	(S)	(S)
Transportation and warehousing...............	48-49	245,057	6.2	(S)	(S)	22,038	41.5	228,874	85.1
Information....................................	51	37,163	1.4	(S)	(S)	166	2.2	5,418	4.2
Financial activities...........................	52,53	190	0	(S)	(S)	(S)	(S)	(S)	(S)
Professional, scientific, and technical services...............................	54	349,024	4.7	(S)	(S)	1,573	8	(S)	(S)
Management of companies and enterprises...	55	34,711	1.9	(NA)	(NA)	(NA)	(NA)	(NA)	(NA)
Administrative and waste services.............	56	319,915	4.3	(S)	(S)	(S)	(S)	30,732	43.1
Education and health services.................	61,62	37,069	0.2	(S)	(S)	50,076	2	18,317	0.2
Leisure and hospitality.........................	71,72	22,510	0.2	13,549	22.6	6,611	27.2	11,613	3
Other services, except public administration...	81	56,174	1.3	(S)	(S)	(S)	(S)	2,574	5.7
Public administration...........................	92	(NA)	(NA)	128,304	7.6	141,689	7.6	77,696	1.9

S Data does not meet disclosure standards. NA Not available. [1] North American Industry Classification System, 2007; see text, Section 15.

Source: Department of Labor, Bureau of Labor Statistics, *Employment in Green Goods and Services, 2010*, March 2012. See also <http://www.bls.gov/ggs/>.

Table 634. Unemployed Persons by Sex and Reason: 1990 to 2011

[In thousands (3,906 represents 3,906,000). For civilian noninstitutionalized population 16 years old and over. Annual averages of monthly figures. Based on Current Population Survey; see text, Section 1 and Appendix III]

Sex and reason	1990 [1]	2000 [1]	2002	2003 [1]	2004 [1]	2005 [1]	2006 [1]	2007 [1]	2008 [1]	2009 [1]	2010 [1]	2011 [1]
Male, total..............	**3,906**	**2,975**	**4,597**	**4,906**	**4,456**	**4,059**	**3,753**	**3,882**	**5,033**	**8,453**	**8,626**	**7,684**
Job losers [2]..............	2,257	1,516	2,820	3,024	2,603	2,188	2,021	2,175	3,055	5,967	5,919	4,968
Job leavers................	528	387	434	422	437	445	406	408	458	438	457	494
Reentrants................	806	854	1,068	1,141	1,070	1,067	1,015	956	1,128	1,504	1,608	1545
New entrants.............	315	217	274	320	346	359	312	343	393	545	641	678
Female, total..........	**3,140**	**2,717**	**3,781**	**3,868**	**3,694**	**3,531**	**3,247**	**3,196**	**3,891**	**5,811**	**6,199**	**6,063**
Job losers [2]..............	1,130	1,001	1,787	1,814	1,595	1,479	1,300	1,340	1,735	3,193	3,331	3,139
Job leavers................	513	393	432	397	421	427	421	385	438	444	432	463
Reentrants................	1,124	1,107	1,300	1,336	1,338	1,319	1,223	1,186	1,345	1,683	1,858	1,857
New entrants.............	373	217	262	321	340	306	304	285	374	491	579	605

[1] Data not strictly comparable with data for earlier years. See text, this section, and February 1994, March 1996, February 1997–99, and February 2003–11 issues of *Employment and Earnings*. [2] Beginning 2000, persons who completed temporary jobs are identified separately and are included as job losers.

Source: U.S. Bureau of Labor Statistics, "Employment and Earnings Online," January 2012 issue, March 2012, <http://www.bls.gov/opub/ee/home.htm> and <http://www.bls.gov/cps/home.htm>.

Table 635. Unemployed Jobseekers' Job Search Activities: 2011

[13,747 represents 13,747,000. For the civilian noninstitutionalized population 16 years old and over. Annual averages of monthly data. Based on the Current Population Survey; see text, Section 1 and Appendix III]

Characteristic	Population (1,000)		Jobseekers' job search methods (percent)							Average number of methods used
	Total unem-ployed	Total jobseek-ers [1]	Em-ployer directly	Sent out a resume or filled out applica-tions	Placed or answer-ed ads	Friends or relatives	Public employ-ment agency	Private employ-ment agency	Other activi-ties	
Total, 16 years and over [2]....	**13,747**	**12,517**	**51.5**	**55.6**	**18.5**	**28.8**	**21.0**	**8.6**	**15.4**	**2.00**
16 to 19 years old..............	1,400	1,349	48.7	61.3	12.5	20.5	10.7	3.7	10.2	1.70
20 to 24 years old..............	2,234	2,082	51.6	58.0	16.0	24.3	18.3	6.9	13.8	1.90
25 to 34 years old..............	3,187	2,920	52.3	57.3	18.2	28.1	22.7	8.8	15.5	2.00
35 to 44 years old..............	2,389	2,141	51.8	53.9	20.7	32.1	24.0	10.8	16.7	2.10
45 to 54 years old..............	2,493	2,224	52.9	53.1	21.2	33.7	24.5	10.5	17.1	2.10
55 to 64 years old..............	1,579	1,408	50.4	53.4	21.4	31.2	23.0	9.8	17.9	2.10
65 years old and over........	465	394	48.7	43.2	16.5	32.8	14.2	5.8	15.8	1.80
Male...........................	7,684	6,875	52.4	53.0	18.0	30.4	22.0	9.0	15.7	2.00
16 to 19 years old..............	786	759	48.1	59.0	12.6	22.3	12.2	3.8	9.7	1.70
20 to 24 years old..............	1,275	1,165	52.7	55.0	15.5	25.3	20.1	7.9	13.6	1.90
25 to 34 years old..............	1,795	1,605	53.3	55.5	18.1	30.3	23.9	9.3	15.7	2.10
35 to 44 years old..............	1,316	1,150	53.8	49.9	20.7	35.8	25.4	11.3	17.5	2.20
45 to 54 years old..............	1,370	1,198	54.0	50.2	20.4	35.4	24.8	10.6	18.1	2.10
55 to 64 years old..............	882	777	50.1	51.6	20.2	30.9	23.6	9.6	18.6	2.10
65 years old and over........	261	222	50.6	41.5	13.9	30.8	13.2	6.7	15.4	1.70
Female.........................	6,063	5,642	50.4	58.8	19.1	26.9	19.8	8.2	15.1	2.00
16 to 19 years old..............	613	589	49.4	64.2	12.4	18.2	8.9	3.5	11.0	1.70
20 to 24 years old..............	960	917	50.2	61.9	16.7	23.1	16.1	5.6	14.2	1.90
25 to 34 years old..............	1,392	1,315	51.1	59.5	18.3	25.4	21.2	8.3	15.2	2.00
35 to 44 years old..............	1,073	991	49.5	58.7	20.8	27.8	22.4	10.3	15.9	2.10
45 to 54 years old..............	1,123	1,026	51.7	56.5	22.3	31.7	24.1	10.5	16.0	2.10
55 to 64 years old..............	697	631	50.8	55.6	22.8	31.6	22.3	10.1	17.1	2.10
65 years old and over........	204	172	46.2	45.4	19.9	35.5	15.6	4.8	16.2	1.80
White [3].........................	9,889	8,874	51.9	55.7	19.0	29.3	19.8	8.5	15.8	2.00
Male...........................	5,631	4,947	52.7	53.2	18.5	31.1	20.8	8.9	16.1	2.00
Female.........................	4,257	3,927	50.8	58.9	19.6	27.0	18.4	8.1	15.4	2.00
Black [3].........................	2,831	2,686	50.9	55.1	17.5	27.1	25.6	8.6	13.7	2.00
Male...........................	1,502	1,418	51.6	52.6	16.8	28.2	26.8	8.6	13.4	2.00
Female.........................	1,329	1,268	50.3	57.9	18.3	25.9	24.4	8.7	14.1	2.00
Asian [3].........................	518	486	48.5	54.1	18.3	34.9	17.6	11.6	19.3	2.10
Male...........................	269	253	49.9	52.9	16.7	37.2	18.1	12.4	21.1	2.10
Female.........................	250	233	47.0	55.5	20.0	32.4	17.0	10.8	17.3	2.00
Hispanic [4].....................	2,629	2,370	53.6	48.1	14.1	34.3	20.5	9.0	13.0	1.90
Male...........................	1,527	1,341	55.1	45.3	13.5	35.7	21.5	9.0	13.4	1.90
Female.........................	1,102	1,028	51.7	51.8	14.9	32.4	19.2	9.1	12.5	1.90

[1] Excludes persons on temporary layoff. The percent using each method will always total more than 100 because many jobseekers use more than one method. [2] Includes other races not shown separately. [3] Data for this race group only. See footnote 4, Table 597. [4] Persons of Hispanic or Latino origin may be any race.

Source: U.S. Bureau of Labor Statistics, "Employment and Earnings Online," January 2012 issue, March 2012, <http://www.bls.gov/opub/ee/home.htm> and <http://www.bls.gov/cps/home.htm>.

Table 636. Unemployed Workers—Summary: 1990 to 2011

[In thousands (7,047 represents 7,047,000), except as indicated. For civilian noninstitutionalized population 16 years old and over. Annual averages of monthly figures. Based on the Current Population Survey; see text, Section 1 and Appendix III. For data on unemployment insurance, see Table 641]

Item	1990 [1]	2000 [1]	2005 [1]	2007 [1]	2008 [1]	2009 [1]	2010 [1]	2011 [1]
UNEMPLOYED								
Total [2]	**7,047**	**5,692**	**7,591**	**7,078**	**8,924**	**14,265**	**14,825**	**13,747**
16 to 19 years old	1,212	1,081	1,186	1,101	1,285	1,552	1,528	1,400
20 to 24 years old	1,299	1,022	1,335	1,241	1,545	2,207	2,329	2,234
25 to 34 years old	1,995	1,207	1,661	1,544	1,949	3,284	3,386	3,187
35 to 44 years old	1,328	1,133	1,400	1,225	1,604	2,722	2,703	2,389
45 to 54 years old	723	762	1,195	1,135	1,473	2,592	2,769	2,493
55 to 64 years old	386	355	630	642	803	1,487	1,660	1,579
65 years and over	105	132	184	190	264	421	449	465
Male	3,906	2,975	4,059	3,882	5,033	8,453	8,626	7,684
16 to 19 years old	667	599	667	623	736	898	863	786
20 to 24 years old	715	547	775	721	920	1,329	1,398	1,275
25 to 34 years old	1,092	602	844	856	1,119	1,988	1,993	1,795
35 to 44 years old	711	557	715	634	875	1,600	1,534	1,316
45 to 54 years old	413	398	624	591	804	1,558	1,614	1,370
55 to 64 years old	249	189	331	349	425	840	962	882
65 years and over	59	83	102	108	153	241	262	261
Female	3,140	2,717	3,531	3,196	3,891	5,811	6,199	6,063
16 to 19 years old	544	483	519	478	549	654	665	613
20 to 24 years old	584	475	560	520	625	878	931	960
25 to 34 years old	902	604	817	688	830	1,296	1,392	1,392
35 to 44 years old	617	577	685	591	730	1,121	1,169	1,073
45 to 54 years old	310	364	571	544	669	1,034	1,156	1,123
55 to 64 years old	137	165	299	293	377	647	698	697
65 years and over	46	50	82	81	111	180	187	204
White [3]	5,186	4,121	5,350	5,143	6,509	10,648	10,916	9,889
Black [3]	1,565	1,241	1,700	1,445	1,788	2,606	2,852	2,831
Asian [3, 4]	(NA)	227	259	229	285	522	543	518
Hispanic [5]	876	954	1,191	1,220	1,678	2,706	2,843	2,629
UNEMPLOYMENT RATE [6] **(percent)**								
Total [2]	**5.6**	**4.0**	**5.1**	**4.6**	**5.8**	**9.3**	**9.6**	**8.9**
16 to 19 years old	15.5	13.1	16.6	15.7	18.7	24.3	25.9	24.4
20 to 24 years old	8.8	7.2	8.8	8.2	10.2	14.7	15.5	14.6
25 to 34 years old	5.6	3.7	5.1	4.7	5.8	9.9	10.1	9.5
35 to 44 years old	4.1	3.0	3.9	3.4	4.6	7.9	8.1	7.3
45 to 54 years old	3.6	2.5	3.5	3.2	4.1	7.2	7.7	7.1
55 to 64 years old	3.3	2.5	3.3	3.1	3.7	6.6	7.1	6.6
65 years and over	3.0	3.1	3.5	3.3	4.2	6.4	6.7	6.5
Male	5.7	3.9	5.1	4.7	6.1	10.3	10.5	9.4
16 to 19 years old	16.3	14.0	18.6	17.6	21.2	27.8	28.8	27.2
20 to 24 years old	9.1	7.3	9.6	8.9	11.4	17.0	17.8	15.7
25 to 34 years old	5.5	3.4	4.7	4.7	6.1	10.9	10.9	9.7
35 to 44 years old	4.1	2.8	3.7	3.3	4.6	8.6	8.5	7.4
45 to 54 years old	3.7	2.4	3.5	3.1	4.2	8.2	8.6	7.4
55 to 64 years old	3.8	2.4	3.3	3.2	3.8	7.2	8.0	7.1
65 years and over	3.0	3.3	3.4	3.4	4.5	6.7	7.1	6.5
Female	5.5	4.1	5.1	4.5	5.4	8.1	8.6	8.5
16 to 19 years old	14.7	12.1	14.5	13.8	16.2	20.7	22.8	21.7
20 to 24 years old	8.5	7.1	7.9	7.3	8.8	12.3	13.0	13.4
25 to 34 years old	5.6	4.1	5.6	4.6	5.5	8.6	9.1	9.1
35 to 44 years old	4.2	3.3	4.1	3.6	4.5	7.1	7.7	7.2
45 to 54 years old	3.4	2.5	3.5	3.2	3.9	6.0	6.8	6.7
55 to 64 years old	2.8	2.5	3.3	3.0	3.7	6.0	6.2	6.1
65 years and over	3.1	2.7	3.5	3.1	3.9	6.1	6.2	6.5
White [3]	4.8	3.5	4.4	4.1	5.2	8.5	8.7	7.9
Black [3]	11.4	7.6	10.0	8.3	10.1	14.8	16.0	15.8
Asian [3, 4]	(NA)	3.6	4.0	3.2	4.0	7.3	7.5	7.0
Hispanic [5]	8.2	5.7	6.0	5.6	7.6	12.1	12.5	11.5
Percent without work for—								
Fewer than 5 weeks	46.3	44.9	35.1	35.9	32.8	22.2	18.7	19.5
5 to 14 weeks	32.0	31.9	30.4	31.5	31.4	26.8	22.0	21.8
15 weeks and over	21.6	23.2	34.5	32.5	35.7	51.0	59.3	58.8
15 to 26 weeks	11.7	11.8	14.9	15.0	16.0	19.5	16.0	15.0
27 weeks and over	10.0	11.4	19.6	17.6	19.7	31.5	43.3	43.8
Unemployment duration, average (weeks)	12.0	12.6	18.4	16.8	17.9	24.4	33.0	(NA)

NA Not available. [1] See footnote 2, Table 596. [2] Includes other races not shown separately. [3] See footnote 4, Table 597. [4] Prior to 2004, includes Pacific Islanders. [5] Persons of Hispanic or Latino origin may be any race. [6] Unemployed as percent of civilian labor force in specified group.

Source: U.S. Bureau of Labor Statistics, "Employment and Earnings Online," January 2012 issue, March 2012, <http://www.bls.gov/opub/ee/home.htm> and <http://www.bls.gov/cps/home.htm>.

Table 637. Unemployment Rates by Industry and by Sex: 2000 to 2011

[In percent. Civilian noninstitutionalized population 16 years old and over. Annual averages of monthly figures. Rate represents unemployment as a percent of labor force in each specified group. Based on Current Population Survey; see text, Section 1 and Appendix III. See also headnote, Table 616, regarding industries]

Industry	2000	2005 [1]	2010 [1]	2011 [1]	Male 2010 [1]	Male 2011 [1]	Female 2010 [1]	Female 2011 [1]
All employed [2]	**4.0**	**5.1**	**9.6**	**8.9**	**10.5**	**9.4**	**8.6**	**8.5**
Wage and salary workers:								
Agriculture and related industries	9.0	8.3	13.9	12.5	13.2	11.5	16.4	15.6
Mining, quarrying, and oil and gas extraction	4.4	3.1	9.4	6.1	9.5	6.1	8.4	6.8
Construction	6.2	7.4	20.6	16.4	21.1	17.0	16.0	11.3
Manufacturing	3.5	4.9	10.6	9.0	9.9	8.4	12.4	10.2
Wholesale trade	3.3	4.0	7.3	6.9	7.2	6.3	7.7	8.4
Retail trade	4.6	5.7	10.0	9.4	10.0	8.8	10.1	10.1
Transportation and utilities	3.4	4.1	8.4	8.2	8.3	8.0	8.8	8.8
Transportation and warehousing	3.8	4.5	9.4	8.8	9.3	8.7	9.8	9.1
Utilities	1.9	1.9	3.4	4.9	3.3	4.0	3.7	7.4
Information	3.2	5.0	9.7	7.3	9.4	7.0	10.2	7.8
Telecommunications	2.3	5.2	9.2	7.3	8.3	6.7	10.8	8.4
Financial activities	2.4	2.9	6.9	6.4	7.0	6.6	6.8	6.2
Finance and insurance	2.2	2.7	6.6	5.9	6.6	5.9	6.6	5.9
Real estate and rental and leasing	3.1	3.3	7.6	7.7	7.8	8.0	7.3	7.3
Professional and business services	4.8	6.2	10.8	9.7	10.6	9.2	11.1	10.4
Professional and technical services	2.5	3.5	6.5	5.8	5.7	4.8	7.5	7.1
Management, administrative, and waste services	8.1	10.2	16.8	15.0	16.7	14.7	17.0	15.5
Education and health services	2.5	3.4	5.8	5.6	5.9	5.3	5.7	5.7
Educational services	2.4	3.7	6.4	6.4	6.9	6.4	6.2	6.5
Health care and social assistance	2.5	3.3	5.6	5.4	5.4	4.9	5.7	5.6
Leisure and hospitality	6.6	7.8	12.2	11.6	12.4	11.3	11.9	11.8
Arts, entertainment, and recreation	5.9	6.9	11.6	11.5	13.4	12.1	9.4	10.7
Accommodation and food services	6.8	8.0	12.3	11.6	12.1	11.1	12.5	12.1
Other services [3]	3.9	4.8	8.5	8.8	9.3	9.3	7.8	8.3
Government workers	2.1	2.6	4.4	4.7	4.5	4.6	4.3	4.7

[1] See footnote 2, Table 596. [2] Includes the self-employed, unpaid family workers, and persons with no previous work experience, not shown separately. [3] Includes private household workers.

Source: U.S. Bureau of Labor Statistics, "Employment and Earnings Online," January 2012 issue, March 2012, <http://www.bls.gov/opub/ee/home.htm> and <http://www.bls.gov/cps/home.htm>.

Table 638. Unemployment by Occupation: 2000 to 2011

[5,692 represents 5,692,000. Civilian noninstitutionalized population 16 years old and over. Annual averages of monthly data. Rate represents unemployment as a percent of the labor force for each specified group. Based on Current Population Survey; see text, Section 1 and Appendix III. See also headnote, Table 616, regarding occupations]

Occupation	Number (1,000) 2000	Number (1,000) 2010 [1]	Number (1,000) 2011 [1]	Unemployment rate 2000	Unemployment rate 2010 [1]	2011 [1] Total	2011 [1] Male	2011 [1] Female
Total [2]	**5,692**	**14,825**	**13,747**	**4.0**	**9.6**	**8.9**	**9.4**	**8.5**
Management, professional, and related occupations	827	2,566	2,458	1.8	4.7	4.5	4.4	4.5
Management, business, and financial operations	320	1,117	1,067	1.6	5.1	4.7	4.5	5.0
Management	214	762	700	1.5	4.8	4.4	4.2	4.8
Business and financial operations	106	355	366	2.0	5.6	5.5	5.5	5.4
Professional and related occupations	507	1,449	1,392	1.9	4.5	4.3	4.4	4.3
Computer and mathematical	74	195	155	2.2	5.2	4.1	3.8	5.0
Architecture and engineering	51	173	149	1.7	6.2	5.1	4.9	6.2
Life, physical, and social science	18	69	51	1.4	4.6	3.8	4.3	3.2
Community and social services	40	114	122	2.0	4.6	4.9	3.9	5.5
Legal	18	48	68	1.2	2.7	3.7	2.6	4.7
Education, training, and library	136	379	410	1.8	4.2	4.5	4.7	4.5
Arts, design, entertainment, sports, and media	97	269	225	3.5	8.9	7.5	8.1	6.7
Healthcare practitioner and technical	73	203	212	1.2	2.5	2.7	2.0	2.9
Service occupations	1,132	2,819	2,727	5.2	10.3	9.9	10.0	9.8
Healthcare support	101	276	284	4.0	7.6	7.8	8.2	7.7
Protective service	70	207	206	2.7	5.9	6.0	5.1	9.3
Food preparation and serving-related	469	1,079	1,037	6.6	12.4	11.8	12.2	11.5
Building and grounds cleaning and maintenance	301	780	725	5.8	12.8	11.7	11.8	11.4
Personal care and service	190	477	474	4.4	8.7	8.7	8.9	8.6
Sales and office occupations	1,446	3,315	3,135	3.8	9.0	8.7	8.2	8.9
Sales and related	673	1,596	1,481	4.1	9.4	8.8	7.2	10.4
Office and administrative support	773	1,719	1,653	3.6	8.7	8.5	9.8	8.0
Natural resources, construction, and maintenance	758	2,504	2,000	5.3	16.1	13.3	13.1	17.5
Farming, fishing, and forestry	133	193	181	10.2	16.3	15.3	13.4	21.8
Construction and extraction	507	1,809	1,414	6.2	20.1	16.6	16.5	17.7
Installation, maintenance, and repair	119	503	406	2.4	9.3	7.7	7.5	11.4
Production, transportation, and material moving occupations	1,081	2,365	2,099	5.1	12.8	11.3	10.9	12.9
Production	575	1,206	1,025	4.8	13.1	11.2	10.4	13.0
Transportation and material moving	505	1,159	1,073	5.6	12.4	11.4	11.2	12.6

[1] See footnote 2, Table 596. [2] Includes persons with no previous work experience and those whose last job was in the Armed Forces.

Source: U.S. Bureau of Labor Statistics, "Employment and Earnings Online," January 2012 issue, March 2012, <http://www.bls.gov/opub/ee/home.htm> and <http://www.bls.gov/cps/home.htm>.

Table 639. Unemployed and Unemployment Rates by Educational Attainment, Sex, Race, and Hispanic Origin: 2000 to 2011

[3,589 represents 3,589,000. Annual averages of monthly figures. Civilian noninstitutionalized population 25 years old and over. See Table 603 for civilian labor force and participation rate data. Based on Current Population Survey; see text, Section 1 and Appendix III]

Year, sex, and race	Unemployed (1,000)					Unemployment rate [1]				
	Total	Less than a high school diploma	High school graduate, no college	Some college or associate's degree	Bachelor's degree or more	Total	Less than a high school diploma	High school graduate, no college	Some college or associate's degree	Bachelor's degree or more
Total: [2]										
2000 [3]	3,589	791	1,298	890	610	3.0	6.3	3.4	2.7	1.7
2010 [3]	10,968	1,765	3,943	3,093	2,167	8.2	14.9	10.3	8.4	4.7
2011 [3]	10,114	1,632	3,521	2,937	2,024	7.6	14.1	9.4	8.0	4.3
Male:										
2000 [3]	1,829	411	682	427	309	2.8	5.4	3.4	2.6	1.5
2010 [3]	6,365	1,137	2,452	1,646	1,130	8.9	15.0	11.3	9.0	4.8
2011 [3]	5,622	1,009	2,110	1,458	1,045	7.9	13.6	10.0	8.0	4.3
Female:										
2000 [3]	1,760	380	616	463	301	3.2	7.8	3.5	2.8	1.8
2010 [3]	4,603	628	1,492	1,447	1,037	7.4	14.6	9.0	7.8	4.7
2011 [3]	4,490	623	1,411	1,478	978	7.3	14.8	8.7	7.9	4.3
White: [4]										
2000 [3]	2,644	564	924	667	489	2.6	5.6	2.9	2.4	1.6
2010 [3]	8,174	1,337	2,937	2,278	1,622	7.5	13.9	9.5	7.6	4.3
2011 [3]	7,318	1,195	2,524	2,083	1,516	6.8	12.7	8.4	7.0	3.9
Black: [4]										
2000 [3]	731	179	315	169	68	5.4	10.7	6.4	4.0	2.5
2010 [3]	2,022	321	795	614	292	13.4	22.5	15.8	12.4	7.9
2011 [3]	2,033	330	790	649	264	13.4	24.6	15.5	13.1	7.1
Asian: [4,5]										
2000 [3]	146	28	34	35	49	2.7	5.7	3.0	3.2	1.8
2010 [3]	446	54	95	92	205	6.8	11.1	7.6	8.1	5.5
2011 [3]	425	44	96	86	199	6.3	9.5	7.6	7.4	5.2
Hispanic: [6]										
2000 [3]	569	297	150	85	38	4.4	6.2	3.9	3.2	2.2
2010 [3]	2,041	787	674	399	182	10.8	13.2	11.5	9.7	6.0
2011 [3]	1,857	703	597	384	173	9.8	12.0	10.3	9.1	5.7

[1] Percent unemployed of the civilian labor force. [2] Includes other races, not shown separately. [3] See footnote 2, Table 596. [4] Beginning 2005 data are for persons in this race group only. See footnote 4, Table 597. [5] 2000 data include Pacific Islanders. [6] Persons of Hispanic origin may be any race.

Source: U.S. Bureau of Labor Statistics, "Employment and Earnings Online," January 2012 issue, March 2012, <http://www.bls.gov/opub/ee/home.htm> and <http://www.bls.gov/cps/home.htm>.

Table 640. Unemployed Persons by Reason for Unemployment: 2011

[13,747 represents 13,747,000. Annual averages of monthly data. Based on Current Population Survey; see text, Section 1 and Appendix III]

Age, sex, and reason	Total unemployed (1,000)	Percent distribution by duration				
		Less than 5 weeks	5 to 14 weeks	15 weeks and over		
				Total	15 to 26 weeks	27 weeks or longer
Total 16 years old and over	**13,747**	**19.5**	**21.8**	**58.8**	**15.0**	**43.8**
16 to 19 years old	1,400	30.6	30.9	38.5	15.7	22.8
Total 20 years old and over	**12,348**	**18.2**	**20.8**	**61.0**	**14.9**	**46.1**
Males	**6,898**	**18.2**	**20.3**	**61.5**	**15.0**	**46.5**
Job losers and persons who completed temporary jobs	4,856	19.3	20.2	60.6	14.9	45.7
On temporary layoff	782	49.7	31.2	19.1	12.0	7.1
Not on temporary layoff	4,074	13.4	18.0	68.6	15.5	53.1
Permanent job losers	3,197	11.5	16.3	72.1	15.1	57.0
Persons who completed temporary jobs	877	20.3	24.3	55.4	16.7	38.7
Job leavers	464	19.8	23.7	56.5	17.0	39.4
Reentrants	1,312	14.6	20.2	65.2	14.8	50.5
New entrants	267	13.7	17.9	68.4	14.3	54.1
Females	**5,450**	**18.2**	**21.3**	**60.5**	**14.8**	**45.7**
Job losers and persons who completed temporary jobs	3,070	18.5	20.7	60.8	14.6	46.1
On temporary layoff	397	55.1	29.7	15.3	8.4	6.9
Not on temporary layoff	2,673	13.1	19.4	67.5	15.5	52.0
Permanent job losers	2,202	11.7	17.9	70.4	15.0	55.4
Persons who completed temporary jobs	471	19.6	26.4	54.1	18.1	35.9
Job leavers	441	22.4	25.1	52.6	16.5	36.0
Reentrants	1,661	17.0	21.4	61.7	15.0	46.7
New entrants	279	16.4	20.9	62.7	12.9	49.8

Source: U.S. Bureau of Labor Statistics, "Employment and Earnings Online," January 2012 issue, March 2012, <http://www.bls.gov/opub/ee/home.htm> and <http://www.bls.gov/cps/home.htm>.

Table 641. Total Unemployed and Insured Unemployed by State: 2000 to 2010

[5,692 represents 5,692,000. Civilian noninstitutionalized population 16 years old and over. Annual averages of monthly figures. State total unemployment estimates come from the Local Area Unemployment Statistics program, while U.S. totals come from the Current Population Survey; see text, Section 1 and Appendix III. U.S. totals derived by independent population controls; therefore state data may not add to U.S. totals. Unemployment data are based on population controls from Census 2000]

State	Total unemployed								Insured unemployed [1]			
	Number (1,000)				Percent [2]				Number (1,000)		Percent [3]	
	2000 [4]	2005 [4]	2009 [4]	2010 [4]	2000 [4]	2005 [4]	2009 [4]	2010 [4]	2000	2010	2000	2010
United States......	5,692	7,591	14,265	14,825	4.0	5.1	9.3	9.6	2,130.2 [5]	4,543.1 [5]	1.7 [5]	3.6 [5]
Alabama.............	87	81	211	202	4.1	3.8	9.7	9.5	29.4	53.3	1.6	3.0
Alaska...............	20	24	28	29	6.2	6.9	7.8	8.0	12.2	17.3	4.9	5.8
Arizona.............	100	134	306	316	4.0	4.7	9.7	10.0	20.5	80.0	1.0	3.3
Arkansas...........	53	69	100	107	4.2	5.1	7.4	7.9	24.2	44.1	2.2	4.0
California...........	833	953	2,063	2,260	4.9	5.4	11.3	12.4	339.6	662.4	2.4	4.6
Colorado...........	65	133	226	240	2.7	5.1	8.3	8.9	14.7	65.0	0.7	3.0
Connecticut........	39	88	157	173	2.3	4.9	8.3	9.1	28.9	70.1	1.8	4.4
Delaware...........	14	17	35	36	3.3	4.0	8.0	8.5	6.0	13.0	1.5	3.2
District of Columbia....	18	21	32	33	5.7	6.5	9.6	9.9	5.5	11.9	1.3	2.5
Florida...............	300	330	930	1,065	3.8	3.8	10.2	11.5	70.8	225.9	1.1	3.2
Georgia.............	148	241	464	480	3.5	5.2	9.7	10.2	34.8	117.7	0.9	3.2
Hawaii..............	24	17	43	42	4.0	2.8	6.8	6.6	8.4	17.4	1.7	3.1
Idaho...............	31	27	58	71	4.6	3.7	7.7	9.3	12.3	26.2	2.3	4.3
Illinois..............	291	371	660	681	4.5	5.8	10.0	10.3	105.7	223.5	1.8	4.1
Indiana.............	92	172	332	320	2.9	5.4	10.4	10.2	32.3	79.4	1.1	2.9
Iowa................	45	70	94	103	2.8	4.3	5.6	6.1	19.5	40.8	1.4	2.8
Kansas..............	53	75	107	106	3.8	5.1	7.1	7.0	15.9	38.2	1.3	2.9
Kentucky...........	83	121	222	218	4.2	6.0	10.7	10.5	25.4	49.9	1.5	3.0
Louisiana...........	101	139	136	155	5.0	6.7	6.6	7.5	24.2	56.1	1.3	3.1
Maine...............	22	34	57	55	3.3	4.9	8.2	7.9	8.9	18.1	1.6	3.2
Maryland...........	100	122	215	223	3.6	4.1	7.1	7.5	29.0	72.4	1.3	3.1
Massachusetts.........	92	164	286	297	2.7	4.8	8.2	8.5	59.9	117.0	1.9	3.8
Michigan...........	190	346	648	597	3.7	6.8	13.3	12.5	83.3	161.3	1.9	4.3
Minnesota..........	87	120	238	217	3.1	4.2	8.1	7.3	31.8	80.1	1.3	3.1
Mississippi.........	74	103	125	137	5.7	7.8	9.6	10.4	19.9	37.2	1.8	3.5
Missouri............	98	162	283	289	3.3	5.4	9.3	9.6	43.8	83.2	1.7	3.2
Montana............	22	17	31	36	4.8	3.6	6.3	7.2	7.7	17.7	2.2	4.3
Nebraska...........	27	38	47	45	2.8	3.9	4.8	4.7	7.4	18.7	0.9	2.1
Nevada.............	48	55	170	201	4.5	4.5	12.5	14.9	19.6	53.9	2.1	4.7
New Hampshire........	19	26	47	45	2.7	3.6	6.3	6.1	3.1	17.9	0.5	3.0
New Jersey..........	157	197	410	426	3.7	4.5	9.1	9.5	84.6	164.4	2.3	4.4
New Mexico.........	42	47	66	80	5.0	5.2	7.0	8.4	9.5	26.3	1.4	3.4
New York...........	416	474	813	824	4.5	5.0	8.4	8.6	147.4	291.9	1.8	3.5
North Carolina.........	155	229	490	476	3.7	5.3	10.8	10.6	55.0	157.6	1.5	4.1
North Dakota...........	10	12	16	15	2.9	3.4	4.3	3.9	3.9	5.2	1.3	1.5
Ohio................	234	344	601	595	4.0	5.9	10.1	10.1	72.8	153.3	1.4	3.1
Oklahoma...........	52	77	116	124	3.1	4.5	6.6	7.1	12.2	34.5	0.9	2.4
Oregon.............	93	115	221	215	5.1	6.2	11.1	10.8	41.6	83.9	2.7	5.3
Pennsylvania.........	255	312	514	549	4.2	5.0	8.0	8.7	131.4	266.0	2.5	4.9
Rhode Island...........	23	28	61	67	4.2	5.1	10.8	11.6	12.3	18.4	2.8	4.2
South Carolina.........	71	140	247	242	3.6	6.8	11.3	11.2	27.6	71.8	1.6	4.1
South Dakota...........	11	16	22	21	2.7	3.7	5.0	4.8	2.1	4.7	0.6	1.2
Tennessee..........	115	164	317	297	4.0	5.6	10.4	9.7	42.9	68.4	1.7	2.7
Texas...............	452	599	900	994	4.4	5.4	7.6	8.2	107.4	221.5	1.2	2.2
Utah................	38	53	98	106	3.4	4.1	7.1	7.7	10.7	29.6	1.1	2.7
Vermont............	9	12	25	22	2.7	3.5	6.9	6.2	4.8	10.4	1.7	3.6
Virginia.............	82	138	284	289	2.3	3.5	6.8	6.9	22.5	64.2	0.7	1.9
Washington.........	151	180	329	340	5.0	5.5	9.3	9.6	70.1	111.5	2.7	4.0
West Virginia...........	44	39	62	71	5.5	4.9	7.7	9.1	14.2	21.8	2.1	3.2
Wisconsin...........	101	146	271	255	3.4	4.8	8.7	8.3	54.1	123.1	2.0	4.7
Wyoming............	10	10	19	20	3.8	3.7	6.5	7.0	2.9	6.9	1.3	2.5

[1] Number of jobless workers who are receiving state unemployment benefits. Source: U.S. Employment and Training Administration, Unemployment Insurance, Financial Handbook, annual updates. See <http://www.ows.doleta.gov/unemploy/claims.asp>. [2] Total unemployment as percent of civilian labor force. [3] Those currently collecting unemployment insurance as a percent of the total number of eligible workers. [4] See footnote 2, Table 596. [5] U.S. totals include Puerto Rico and the Virgin Islands.

Source: Except as noted, U.S. Bureau of Labor Statistics, Local Area Unemployment Statistics program <http://www.bls.gov/lau/>.

Table 642. Nonfarm Establishments—Employees, Hours, and Earnings by Industry: 1990 to 2011

[Annual averages of monthly data. (109,487 represents 109,487,000). Based on data from establishment reports. Includes all full- and part-time employees who worked during, or received pay for, any part of the pay period reported. Excludes proprietors, the self-employed, farm workers, unpaid family workers, private household workers, and Armed Forces. Establishment data shown here conform to industry definitions in the 2007 North American Industry Classification System (NAICS) and are adjusted to March 2010 employment benchmarks. Based on the Current Employment Statistics Program; see source and Appendix III]

Item and year	Total nonfarm	Private industry																Government
		Total [1]	Construction	Manufacturing	Wholesale trade	Retail trade	Transportation and warehousing	Utilities	Information	Finance and insurance	Real estate and rental and leasing	Professional, scientific, and technical services	Administrative and waste services	Educational services	Health care and social assistance	Arts, entertainment, and recreation	Accommodations and food services	
EMPLOYEES (1,000)																		
1990	109,487	91,072	5,263	17,695	5,268	13,182	3,476	740	2,688	4,976	1,637	4,538	4,643	1,688	9,296	1,132	8,156	18,415
2000	131,785	110,995	6,787	17,263	5,933	15,280	4,410	601	3,630	5,677	2,011	6,702	8,168	2,390	12,718	1,788	10,074	20,790
2005	133,703	111,899	7,336	14,226	5,764	15,280	4,361	554	3,061	6,019	2,134	7,025	8,170	2,836	14,536	1,892	10,923	21,804
2008	136,790	114,281	7,162	13,406	5,943	15,283	4,508	559	2,984	6,015	2,130	7,799	8,032	3,040	15,798	1,970	11,466	22,509
2009	130,807	108,252	6,016	11,847	5,587	14,522	4,236	560	2,804	5,775	1,994	7,509	7,203	3,090	16,103	1,916	11,162	22,555
2010	129,874	107,384	5,518	11,528	5,452	14,440	4,191	553	2,707	5,718	1,934	7,441	7,414	3,155	16,375	1,913	11,135	22,490
2011	131,359	109,254	5,504	11,733	5,529	14,643	4,292	555	2,659	5,752	1,929	7,691	7,724	3,241	16,643	1,910	11,410	22,104
WEEKLY EARNINGS [2] (dol.)																		
1990	(NA)	349.75	513.43	436.16	444.48	235.62	471.72	670.40	479.50	(NA)	(NA)	504.83	273.60	(NA)	319.80	219.02	147.89	(NA)
2000	(NA)	481.01	685.78	590.77	631.40	333.38	562.31	955.66	700.86	(NA)	(NA)	745.77	387.49	(NA)	449.27	273.79	207.44	(NA)
2005	(NA)	544.33	750.22	673.33	685.00	377.58	618.58	1,095.90	805.08	(NA)	(NA)	862.79	431.92	(NA)	560.43	330.19	226.48	(NA)
2008	(NA)	607.95	842.61	724.46	769.62	386.21	670.37	1,230.69	908.99	(NA)	(NA)	995.66	500.14	(NA)	630.06	354.52	259.93	(NA)
2009	(NA)	617.18	851.76	726.12	784.49	388.57	677.56	1,239.37	931.08	(NA)	(NA)	1,036.36	517.27	(NA)	643.19	359.71	261.87	(NA)
2010	(NA)	636.92	891.83	765.15	816.50	400.05	710.85	1,262.89	939.85	(NA)	(NA)	1,073.70	535.79	(NA)	661.03	363.91	266.78	(NA)
2011	(NA)	654.87	921.66	784.68	845.36	412.10	737.37	1,296.85	963.99	(NA)	(NA)	1,090.79	551.95	(NA)	686.56	373.81	269.08	(NA)
WEEKLY HOURS [2]																		
1990	(NA)	34.3	38.3	40.5	38.4	30.6	37.7	41.5	35.8	(NA)	(NA)	36.1	32.3	(NA)	31.8	26.1	25.9	(NA)
2000	(NA)	34.3	39.2	41.3	38.8	30.7	37.4	42.0	36.8	(NA)	(NA)	36.2	33.1	(NA)	32.1	25.6	26.2	(NA)
2005	(NA)	33.8	38.6	40.7	37.7	30.6	37.0	41.1	36.5	(NA)	(NA)	35.7	32.8	(NA)	32.9	25.7	25.7	(NA)
2008	(NA)	33.6	38.5	40.8	38.2	30.0	36.4	42.7	36.7	(NA)	(NA)	35.8	33.6	(NA)	32.8	24.1	25.4	(NA)
2009	(NA)	33.1	37.6	39.8	37.6	29.9	36.0	42.0	36.6	(NA)	(NA)	35.7	33.4	(NA)	32.4	23.8	25.0	(NA)
2010	(NA)	33.4	38.4	41.1	37.9	30.2	37.1	42.0	36.3	(NA)	(NA)	35.9	33.9	(NA)	32.3	23.8	25.0	(NA)
2011	(NA)	33.6	39.0	41.4	38.5	30.5	37.8	42.1	36.2	(NA)	(NA)	36.0	34.0	(NA)	32.5	23.8	24.9	(NA)
HOURLY EARNINGS [2] (dol.)																		
1990	(NA)	10.20	13.42	10.78	11.58	7.71	12.50	16.14	13.40	(NA)	(NA)	13.99	8.48	(NA)	10.05	8.41	5.70	(NA)
2000	(NA)	14.02	17.48	14.32	16.28	10.86	15.05	22.75	19.07	(NA)	(NA)	20.61	11.69	(NA)	13.98	10.68	7.92	(NA)
2005	(NA)	16.13	19.46	16.56	18.16	12.36	16.70	26.68	22.06	(NA)	(NA)	24.15	13.16	(NA)	17.05	12.85	8.80	(NA)
2008	(NA)	18.08	21.87	17.75	20.13	12.87	18.41	28.83	24.78	(NA)	(NA)	27.82	14.87	(NA)	19.23	14.73	10.23	(NA)
2009	(NA)	18.63	22.66	18.24	20.84	13.01	18.81	29.48	25.45	(NA)	(NA)	29.03	15.51	(NA)	19.83	15.08	10.49	(NA)
2010	(NA)	19.07	23.22	18.61	21.54	13.24	19.16	30.04	25.87	(NA)	(NA)	29.94	15.80	(NA)	20.44	15.27	10.68	(NA)
2011	(NA)	19.47	23.64	18.94	21.97	13.51	19.50	30.82	26.61	(NA)	(NA)	30.28	16.23	(NA)	21.12	15.68	10.79	(NA)

NA Not available. [1] Includes other industries not shown separately. [2] Average hours and earnings of production workers for mining and logging, manufacturing, and construction; average hours and earnings of nonsupervisory workers for the service-providing industries.

Source: U.S. Bureau of Labor Statistics, Current Employment Statistics, "Employment, Hours, and Earnings—National," <http://www.bls.gov/ces/home.htm>.

Table 643. Employees in Nonfarm Establishments—States: 2011

[In thousands (131,337 represents 131,337,000). Includes all full- and part-time employees who worked during, or received pay for, any part of the pay period reported. Excludes proprietors, the self-employed, farm workers, unpaid family workers, private household workers, and Armed Forces. National totals differ from the sum of the state figures because of differing benchmarks among states and differing industrial and geographic stratification. Compiled from data supplied by cooperating state agencies. Based on North American Industry Classification System, 2007; see text, Section 15]

State	Total [1]	Con-struction	Manu-facturing	Trade, transpor-tation and utilities	Infor-mation	Fin-ancial activi-ties [2]	Profes-sional and business ser-vices [3]	Educa-tion and health ser-vices [4]	Leisure and hospita-lity [5]	Other ser-vices [6]	Govern-ment
U.S............	131,337	5,096	11,712	24,969	2,685	7,631	17,279	19,893	13,274	5,285	22,263
AL..............	1,866.5	78.9	237.3	364.3	23.3	92.5	212.7	216.1	168.8	79.9	380.4
AK..............	328.8	15.2	13.2	63.3	6.4	14.8	27.3	44.5	32.4	11.0	84.8
AZ..............	2,405.5	111.7	149.7	472.6	36.6	166.0	343.4	354.9	259.1	89.6	410.4
AR..............	1,160.0	46.9	158.3	235.2	14.6	48.1	117.9	166.8	99.0	43.4	218.9
CA..............	14,060.5	553.7	1,245.8	2,662.9	432.4	761.5	2,126.3	1,833.6	1,530.3	486.9	2,398.7
CO..............	2,255.3	112.6	129.0	400.9	71.5	143.6	339.8	272.9	271.5	93.5	392.8
CT..............	1,623.5	51.2	166.4	293.7	31.5	134.9	195.0	314.6	136.5	60.5	238.8
DE..............	417.3	19.6 [7]	25.7	75.2	5.7	42.7	55.6	66.7	42.7	19.5	64.1
DC..............	727.8	12.0 [7]	1.0	27.2	18.6	26.8	150.1	115.2	61.8	67.4	247.7
FL..............	7,271.5	330.1	311.2	1,495.0	134.3	482.9	1,051.6	1,104.4	954.0	307.0	1,095.5
GA..............	3,880.0	145.5	350.2	821.0	97.3	208.8	547.1	499.0	379.6	153.4	669.2
HI..............	592.1	\7 28.3	13.2	111.0	8.2	26.9	74.8	75.5	103.7	25.8	124.7
ID..............	606.8	30.1	55.0	121.7	9.4	29.4	74.8	86.7	58.7	21.0	116.4
IL..............	5,663.1	195.3	574.0	1,139.5	100.4	361.9	829.5	849.7	518.8	247.9	836.7
IN..............	2,830.3	120.5	464.2	548.2	34.2	131.4	286.7	426.3	278.2	109.3	424.7
IA..............	1,477.8	62.3	207.4	301.3	27.9	100.4	123.6	215.9	130.6	56.5	249.6
KS..............	1,337.0	53.0	161.0	253.2	27.8	72.8	151.0	183.9	115.4	52.3	257.9
KY..............	1,790.4	67.6	212.6	364.0	26.7	84.3	187.8	255.4	169.4	70.2	329.9
LA..............	1,916.7	121.9	139.3	373.1	23.7	94.9	196.3	292.3	198.8	63.1	360.0
ME..............	593.4	24.7	50.4	117.6	8.2	31.7	57.1	120.2	59.5	20.1	101.3
MD..............	2,548.8	146.2 [7]	113.1	441.9	42.3	142.7	396.2	409.8	232.9	115.6	507.4
MA..............	3,210.6	107.9	254.2	549.0	83.0	205.8	474.9	669.6	309.4	121.2	434.6
MI..............	3,935.7	124.7	506.1	719.9	53.4	193.2	549.4	620.5	375.5	167.3	618.5
MN..............	2,675.7	90.9	300.7	495.9	52.8	174.3	327.9	468.2	234.9	115.4	408.1
MS..............	1,090.0	48.8	134.4	214.2	11.9	44.8	93.9	135.1	117.6	34.1	246.1
MO..............	2,650.3	102.3	247.4	512.6	58.4	159.3	331.3	415.8	269.3	112.3	437.4
MT..............	426.1	23.0	16.8	86.2	7.3	20.9	40.8	64.2	55.7	16.5	86.8
NE..............	944.0	41.1 [7]	93.1	195.8	16.9	69.5	103.5	137.1	82.3	36.6	168.2
NV..............	1,125.1	52.7	38.0	212.3	12.6	52.0	139.2	103.7	317.8	33.4	149.5
NH..............	626.4	21.9	66.5	133.9	11.1	34.7	65.5	113.7	63.6	22.8	92.6
NJ..............	3,856.2	129.7	254.1	816.0	74.2	250.9	601.9	609.8	334.8	163.6	619.9
NM..............	804.1	42.7	29.5	133.0	14.2	33.0	100.1	123.0	84.4	27.4	195.9
NY..............	8,683.4	306.8	458.0	1,458.0	254.9	683.7	1,134.5	1,731.8	765.7	369.8	1,488.1
NC..............	3,922.4	175.6	433.6	724.8	68.5	203.0	510.5	546.5	399.6	155.8	699.0
ND..............	394.2	24.0	23.6	85.5	7.1	21.1	30.2	56.5	34.9	15.6	79.1
OH..............	5,083.1	173.9	638.4	953.7	76.4	278.1	646.9	850.1	477.7	210.1	766.2
OK..............	1,550.3	68.3	129.0	281.1	24.2	79.6	172.9	206.2	142.2	59.9	336.0
OR..............	1,618.1	68.8	166.5	312.4	32.3	92.0	186.0	235.1	165.3	57.5	295.4
PA..............	5,687.1	221.8	563.9	1,093.5	90.2	309.5	709.9	1,156.7	509.6	254.3	744.1
RI..............	460.2	15.7	40.7	73.1	10.2	30.7	54.2	103.5	49.2	22.1	60.6
SC..............	1,832.1	76.3	216.2	350.4	25.9	96.1	227.9	216.9	209.6	68.8	340.2
SD..............	406.2	20.9 [7]	38.9	82.2	6.4	28.0	28.5	65.4	42.4	15.5	78.0
TN..............	2,656.3	109.6 [7]	304.1	559.0	44.1	135.5	321.9	365.9	265.8	101.4	431.9
TX..............	10,557.3	559.5	835.5	2,103.3	195.5	639.0	1,339.2	1,422.2	1,043.7	369.3	1,814.1
UT..............	1,208.1	65.3	114.1	232.9	29.4	69.0	159.6	158.9	113.7	33.9	219.6
VT..............	299.6	13.7	30.9	56.4	5.0	12.1	24.9	60.2	32.7	9.8	53.1
VA..............	3,680.4	178.6	229.0	629.1	74.0	182.5	662.6	468.5	348.0	186.7	710.4
WA..............	2,820.5	137.5	269.2	526.0	103.7	137.4	337.7	382.1	271.9	107.2	541.9
WV..............	753.9	33.0	49.5	135.2	10.5	27.3	62.3	123.2	72.9	54.8	151.8
WI..............	2,740.7	90.5	442.8	508.4	46.4	158.1	282.8	410.7	249.4	135.8	412.9
WY..............	285.7	20.8	9.0	52.5	3.9	10.7	17.5	26.7	32.4	11.8	73.3

[1] Includes mining and logging, not shown separately. [2] Finance and insurance; real estate and rental and leasing. [3] Professional, scientific, and technical services; management of companies and enterprises; administrative and support and waste management and remediation services. [4] Education services; health care and social assistance. [5] Arts, entertainment, and recreation; accommodations and food services. [6] Includes repair and maintenance; personal and laundry services; and membership associations and organizations. [7] Mining and logging included with construction.

Source: U.S. Bureau of Labor Statistics, Current Employment Statistics, "State and Metro Area Employment, Hours, and Earnings (SAE)," <http://www.bls.gov/sae/data.htm>.

Table 644. Nonfarm Industries—Employees and Earnings: 1990 to 2011

[Annual averages of monthly figures (109,487 represents 109,487,000). Covers all full- and part-time employees who worked during, or received pay for, any part of the pay period including the 12th of the month. See also headnote, Table 642]

Industry	2007 NAICS code [1]	All employees (1,000)					Average hourly earnings [2] (dol.)		
		1990	2000	2005	2010	2011	2000	2005	2011
Total nonfarm	(X)	**109,487**	**131,785**	**133,703**	**129,874**	**131,359**	**(NA)**	**(NA)**	**(NA)**
Goods-producing [3]	(X)	23,723	24,649	22,190	17,751	18,021	15.27	17.60	20.66
Service-providing [4]	(X)	85,764	107,136	111,513	112,123	113,338	(NA)	(NA)	(NA)
Total private	(X)	**91,072**	**110,995**	**111,899**	**107,384**	**109,254**	**14.02**	**16.13**	**19.47**
Mining and logging	(X)	**765**	**599**	**628**	**705**	**784**	**16.55**	**18.72**	**24.51**
Logging	1133	85	79	65	50	48	13.70	15.74	19.41
Mining	21	**680**	**520**	**562**	**655**	**735**	**16.94**	**19.04**	**24.84**
Oil and gas extraction	211	190	125	126	159	174	19.43	19.34	27.27
Mining, except oil and gas	212	302	225	213	205	217	18.07	20.18	25.39
Support activities for mining	213	188	171	224	81	86	14.55	17.89	23.75
Construction	23	**5,263**	**6,787**	**7,336**	**5,518**	**5,504**	**17.48**	**19.46**	**23.64**
Construction of buildings	236	1,413	1,633	1,712	1,230	1,219	16.74	19.05	22.94
Residential building	2361	673	823	960	572	563	15.18	17.72	19.63
Nonresidential building	2362	741	809	752	658	656	18.18	20.55	25.57
Heavy and civil engineering construction [5]	237	813	937	951	825	829	16.80	19.60	24.44
Highway, street, and bridge construction	2373	289	340	351	287	282	18.17	20.12	24.14
Specialty trade contractors	238	3,037	4,217	4,673	3,463	3,455	17.91	19.55	23.64
Building foundation and exterior contractors	2381	703	919	1,083	680	661	16.93	18.44	21.56
Building equipment contractors	2382	1,282	1,897	1,918	1,634	1,644	19.52	21.01	25.35
Building finishing contractors	2383	665	857	992	634	621	16.44	18.82	22.57
Manufacturing	31-33	**17,695**	**17,263**	**14,226**	**11,528**	**11,733**	**14.32**	**16.56**	**18.94**
Durable goods	(X)	10,737	10,877	8,956	7,064	7,274	14.92	17.33	20.12
Wood products	321	541	613	559	342	335	11.63	13.16	14.81
Nonmetallic mineral products	327	528	554	505	371	367	14.53	16.61	18.16
Cement and concrete products	3273	195	234	240	170	164	14.64	16.68	18.87
Primary metals	331	689	622	466	362	390	16.64	18.94	19.96
Iron and steel mills and ferroalloy production	3311	187	135	96	87	94	20.97	23.55	29.64
Foundries	3315	214	217	164	112	121	14.72	17.50	17.91
Fabricated metal products	332	1,610	1,753	1,522	1,282	1,344	13.77	15.80	18.13
Architectural and structural metals	3323	357	428	398	321	328	13.43	15.10	17.94
Machine shops and threaded products	3327	309	365	345	313	341	14.53	16.43	18.63
Machinery	333	1,410	1,457	1,166	996	1,057	15.21	17.02	19.53
Agricultural, construction, and mining machinery	3331	229	222	208	208	226	14.21	15.91	19.60
Heating, ventilation and air conditioning, and commercial refrigeration equipment	3334	165	194	154	125	131	13.10	14.60	16.73
Metalworking machinery	3335	267	274	202	155	167	16.66	17.86	20.59
Computer and electronic products	334	1,903	1,820	1,316	1,095	1,107	14.73	18.39	23.32
Computer and peripheral equipment	3341	367	302	205	158	159	18.39	22.75	23.92
Communications equipment	3342	223	239	141	117	115	14.39	18.05	24.41
Semiconductors and electronic components	3344	574	676	452	369	384	13.46	17.03	20.37
Electronic instruments	3345	635	488	441	406	404	15.80	17.71	25.53
Electrical equipment and appliances	335	633	591	434	360	367	13.23	15.24	17.96
Household appliances	3352	114	106	85	60	57	(NA)	(NA)	(NA)
Electrical equipment	3353	244	210	152	136	139	13.28	15.31	17.99
Transportation equipment	336	2,135	2,057	1,772	1,333	1,382	18.89	22.09	25.36
Motor vehicles	3361	271	291	248	153	160	24.45	29.01	28.91
Motor vehicle parts	3363	653	840	678	419	443	17.95	21.10	20.70
Aerospace products and parts	3364	841	517	455	478	488	20.52	24.82	33.85
Ship and boat building	3366	174	154	154	125	121	14.84	17.26	23.81
Furniture and related products	337	604	683	568	357	353	11.73	13.45	15.24
Household and institutional furniture	3371	401	443	383	223	220	11.39	13.15	14.94
Miscellaneous manufacturing	339	686	728	647	567	573	11.93	14.07	16.83
Medical equipment and supplies	3391	283	305	300	303	309	12.70	14.71	17.83
Nondurable goods	(X)	6,958	6,386	5,271	4,464	4,460	13.31	15.27	17.07
Food manufacturing	311	1,507	1,553	1,478	1,451	1,456	11.77	13.04	14.63
Fruit and vegetable preserving and specialty	3114	218	197	174	173	172	11.89	12.81	14.81
Dairy products	3115	145	136	132	130	134	14.85	16.73	19.57
Animal slaughtering and processing	3116	427	507	504	489	488	10.27	11.47	12.92
Bakeries and tortilla manufacturing	3118	292	306	280	277	281	11.45	12.57	14.33
Beverages and tobacco products [5]	312	218	207	192	165	167	17.40	18.76	20.02
Beverages	3121	173	175	167	183	188	(NA)	(NA)	(NA)
Textile mills	313	492	378	218	167	172	11.23	12.38	13.79
Textile product mills	314	236	230	176	119	121	10.31	11.61	12.66
Apparel	315	903	484	251	119	117	8.61	10.26	11.96
Cut and sew apparel	3152	750	380	193	157	152	8.40	10.06	16.86
Leather and allied products	316	133	69	40	124	124	10.35	11.50	13.48
Paper and paper products	322	647	605	484	28	29	15.91	17.99	20.26
Pulp, paper, and paperboard mills	3221	238	191	142	112	109	20.62	22.99	25.75
Converted paper products	3222	409	413	343	282	282	13.58	15.71	17.84
Printing and related support activities	323	809	807	646	488	469	14.09	15.74	17.28
Petroleum and coal products	324	153	123	112	114	112	22.80	24.47	31.71
Chemicals	325	1,036	980	872	787	788	17.09	19.67	21.46
Basic chemicals	3251	249	188	150	142	142	21.06	23.80	24.16
Resin, rubber, and artificial fibers	3252	158	136	108	89	91	17.09	19.03	21.12
Pharmaceuticals and medicines	3254	207	274	288	277	273	17.27	21.31	23.77
Plastics and rubber products	326	825	951	802	625	636	12.70	14.80	15.95
Plastics products	3261	618	737	634	502	509	12.04	14.01	15.60
Rubber products	3262	207	214	168	123	127	14.83	17.58	17.20
Trade, transportation, and utilities	(X)	**22,666**	**26,225**	**25,959**	**24,636**	**25,019**	**13.31**	**14.92**	**17.15**
Wholesale trade	42	**5,268**	**5,933**	**5,764**	**5,452**	**5,529**	**16.28**	**18.16**	**21.97**
Durable goods	423	2,834	3,251	2,999	2,714	2,753	16.71	18.88	21.44
Motor vehicles and parts	4231	309	356	344	309	312	14.27	16.18	17.96
Lumber and construction supplies	4233	181	227	254	188	183	13.61	16.78	18.91

See footnotes at end of table.

Table 644. Nonfarm Industries—Employees and Earnings: 1990 to 2011-Continued.

See headnote on page 422.

Industry	2007 NAICS code [1]	All employees (1,000)						Average hourly earnings [2] (dol.)		
		1990	2000	2005	2010	2011	2000	2005	2011
Commercial equipment........................	4234	597	722	639	604	616	20.29	23.67	25.14
Electric goods...............................	4236	357	425	342	309	311	19.43	21.78	23.80
Hardware and plumbing.....................	4237	216	247	245	218	220	15.07	16.47	20.90
Machinery and supplies.....................	4238	690	725	659	608	615	16.47	18.71	21.59
Nondurable goods.............................	424	1,900	2,065	2,022	1,928	1,940	14.33	16.15	19.60
Paper and paper products..................	4241	162	177	152	124	121	15.65	17.23	22.35
Druggists' goods............................	4242	136	192	213	190	185	18.98	19.20	24.21
Apparel and piece goods..................	4243	152	163	148	137	139	14.58	17.53	20.71
Grocery and related products..............	4244	623	689	699	704	715	13.57	15.38	18.96
Alcoholic beverages........................	4248	115	128	147	120	122	15.72	18.30	19.69
Electronic markets and agents and brokers.........	425	535	618	743	811	836	20.79	20.71	29.35
Retail trade..................................	**44,45**	**13,182**	**15,280**	**15,280**	**14,440**	**14,643**	**10.86**	**12.36**	**13.51**
Motor vehicle and parts dealers.............	441	1,494	1,847	1,919	1,629	1,688	14.94	16.33	17.47
Automobile dealers.........................	4411	983	1,217	1,261	1,012	1,055	16.95	17.85	18.61
Auto parts, accessories, and tire stores......	4413	418	499	491	489	506	11.04	12.74	14.95
Furniture and home furnishings stores...........	442	432	544	576	438	442	12.33	14.23	15.15
Furniture stores............................	4421	244	289	298	217	215	13.37	14.87	16.19
Home furnishings stores....................	4422	188	254	278	221	227	11.06	13.46	13.79
Electronics and appliance stores...........	443	382	564	536	522	526	13.67	17.73	18.68
Building material and garden supply stores.........	444	891	1,142	1,276	1,132	1,141	11.25	13.14	14.21
Building material and supplies dealers........	4441	753	982	1,134	1,005	1,006	11.30	13.24	14.21
Food and beverage stores...................	445	2,779	2,993	2,818	2,808	2,829	9.76	10.85	12.02
Grocery stores.............................	4451	2,406	2,582	2,446	2,461	2,477	9.71	10.80	12.07
Specialty food stores.......................	4452	232	270	236	211	215	9.97	11.04	11.14
Beer, wine, and liquor stores...............	4453	141	141	136	136	138	10.40	11.48	12.47
Health and personal care stores............	446	792	928	954	981	981	11.68	14.03	17.35
Gasoline stations..........................	447	910	936	871	819	828	8.05	8.92	10.17
Clothing & clothing accessories stores.........	448	1,313	1,322	1,415	1,353	1,356	9.96	11.07	11.47
Clothing stores............................	4481	930	954	1,066	1,040	1,041	9.88	10.63	10.98
Shoe stores...............................	4482	216	193	180	182	183	8.96	10.05	11.40
Jewelry, luggage, and leather goods stores.......	4483	167	175	169	131	132	11.48	14.10	14.64
Sporting goods, hobby, book, and music stores................................	451	532	686	647	579	574	9.33	10.35	11.57
Sporting goods and musical instrument stores..................................	4511	352	437	447	459	475	9.55	10.68	11.71
Book, periodical, and music stores.........	4512	180	249	200	120	100	8.91	9.59	10.88
General merchandise stores.................	452	2,500	2,820	2,934	2,998	3,080	9.22	10.53	11.27
Department stores.........................	4521	1,494	1,755	1,595	1,502	1,547	(NA)	(NA)	(NA)
Miscellaneous store retailers..............	453	738	1,007	900	762	767	10.20	11.22	13.52
Florists....................................	4531	121	130	101	69	65	8.95	9.88	11.45
Office supplies, stationery, and gift stores........	4532	358	471	391	303	302	10.46	11.65	14.45
Used merchandise stores...................	4533	56	107	113	125	133	8.07	8.96	10.92
Nonstore retailers..........................	454	419	492	435	421	432	13.22	14.56	18.15
Electronic shopping and mail-order houses.......	4541	157	257	240	247	261	13.38	14.52	18.90
Transportation and warehousing..............	**48,49**	**3,476**	**4,410**	**4,361**	**4,191**	**4,292**	**15.05**	**16.70**	**19.50**
Air transportation...........................	481	529	614	501	458	456	13.57	17.77	26.02
Scheduled air transportation..............	4811	503	570	456	417	415	(NA)	(NA)	(NA)
Rail transportation..........................	482	272	232	228	216	229	(NA)	(NA)	(NA)
Water transportation........................	483	57	56	61	62	63	18.07	19.04	23.07
Truck transportation........................	484	1,122	1,406	1,398	1,250	1,299	15.86	16.74	19.40
General freight trucking...................	4841	807	1,013	981	868	900	16.37	17.20	19.46
Specialized freight trucking...............	4842	315	393	417	383	399	14.51	15.60	19.26
Transit and ground passenger transportation..............................	485	274	372	389	430	436	11.88	13.00	15.17
Urban, interurban, rural, and charter bus transportation..........................	4851, 2,5	72	97	91	94	93	(NA)	(NA)	(NA)
Taxi and limousine service.................	4853	57	72	66	68	71	(NA)	(NA)	(NA)
School and employee bus transportation.........	4854	114	152	169	186	184	11.42	12.74	15.49
Pipeline transportation.....................	486	60	46	38	42	43	19.86	24.33	31.89
Scenic and sightseeing transportation........	487	16	28	29	27	29	12.49	13.75	19.85
Support activities for transportation..........	488	364	537	552	543	564	14.57	17.67	21.06
Support activities for air transportation........	4881	96	141	148	154	160	13.42	15.07	17.45
Support activities for water transportation......	4883	91	97	94	91	91	19.57	27.07	34.91
Support activities for road transportation........	4884	35	66	79	80	82	13.98	15.41	15.90
Freight transportation arrangement.........	4885	111	178	177	169	179	13.46	16.94	21.12
Couriers and messengers...................	492	375	605	571	528	529	13.51	15.33	16.14
Couriers and express delivery services......	4921	340	546	522	480	477	(NA)	(NA)	(NA)
Warehousing and storage...................	493	407	514	595	633	646	14.46	15.06	15.92
Utilities....................................	**22**	**740**	**601**	**554**	**553**	**555**	**22.75**	**26.68**	**30.82**
Power generation and supply................	2211	550	434	401	398	400	23.13	27.63	32.01
Natural gas distribution....................	2212	155	121	107	108	109	23.41	26.86	29.12
Water, sewage and other systems.........	2213	35	46	45	47	47	16.93	17.70	24.23
Information.................................	**51**	**2,688**	**3,630**	**3,061**	**2,707**	**2,659**	**19.07**	**22.06**	**26.61**
Publishing industries, except Internet.........	511	871	1,035	904	759	749	20.18	24.20	28.62
Newspaper, book, and directory publishers........	5111	773	774	666	498	479	15.06	18.57	21.68
Software publishers........................	5112	98	261	238	261	270	28.48	38.11	39.54
Motion picture and sound recording industries......	512	255	383	378	370	361	21.25	18.75	22.69
Broadcasting, except Internet...............	515	284	344	328	290	282	16.74	21.22	24.22
Radio and television broadcasting..........	5151	232	253	239	210	208	(NA)	(NA)	(NA)
Cable and other subscription programming........	5152	52	91	89	80	74	(NA)	(NA)	(NA)
Telecommunications........................	517	1,009	1,397	1,071	903	865	18.59	22.13	25.82
Wired telecommunications carriers.........	5171	760	922	690	603	577	18.62	22.46	25.75
Wireless telecommunications carriers (except satellite)........................	5172	36	186	191	170	164	14.40	20.40	23.92

See footnotes at end of table.

Industry	2007 NAICS code [1]	All employees (1,000)					Average hourly earnings [2] (dol.)		
		1990	2000	2005	2010	2011	2000	2005	2011
Data processing, hosting and related services......	518	211	316	263	243	243	16.97	19.97	25.98
Financial activities............................	**(X)**	**6,614**	**7,687**	**8,153**	**7,652**	**7,681**	**14.98**	**17.95**	**21.91**
Finance and insurance.........................	**52**	**4,976**	**5,677**	**6,019**	**5,718**	**5,752**	**(NA)**	**(NA)**	**(NA)**
Monetary authorities—central bank...........	521	24	23	21	20	19	(NA)	(NA)	(NA)
Credit intermediation and related activities......	522	2,425	2,548	2,869	2,550	2,559	13.14	15.85	18.46
Depository credit intermediation [5].............	5221	1,909	1,681	1,769	1,729	1,738	11.97	14.13	17.61
Commercial banking..........................	52211	1,362	1,251	1,296	1,306	1,315	11.83	13.79	17.55
Nondepository credit intermediation...........	5222	398	644	770	562	562	15.30	19.24	20.76
Activities related to credit intermediation.....	5223	119	222	330	259	258	15.39	16.48	18.69
Securities, commodity contracts, investments......	523	458	805	786	801	807	20.20	26.59	32.18
Securities and commodity contracts brokerage and exchanges.........................	5231,2	338	566	499	468	464	20.07	27.68	30.98
Other financial investment activities...........	5239	120	239	287	330	343	20.48	24.69	33.97
Insurance carriers and related activities...........	524	2,016	2,221	2,259	2,261	2,282	17.37	20.66	25.29
Insurance carriers..........................	5241	1,338	1,433	1,386	1,386	1,398	17.92	21.67	26.52
Insurance agencies, brokerages, and related services..................................	5242	678	788	874	875	884	16.28	18.88	23.15
Funds, trusts, and other financial vehicles.........	525	54	81	84	87	85	17.68	21.09	21.43
Insurance and employee benefit funds...........	5251	33	46	46	49	46	(NA)	(NA)	(NA)
Other investment pools and funds...............	5259	20	35	37	38	39	(NA)	(NA)	(NA)
Real estate and rental and leasing..............	**53**	**1,637**	**2,011**	**2,134**	**1,934**	**1,929**	**(NA)**	**(NA)**	**(NA)**
Real estate...................................	**531**	**1,109**	**1,316**	**1,461**	**1,396**	**1,402**	**12.26**	**14.69**	**17.47**
Lessors of real estate.........................	5311	566	610	603	565	561	11.19	13.81	16.76
Offices of real estate agents and brokers.......	5312	217	281	356	286	284	12.57	14.90	17.43
Activities related to real estate...............	5313	327	424	502	544	557	13.60	15.64	18.18
Rental and leasing services.....................	532	514	667	646	514	503	11.69	14.05	16.12
Automotive equipment rental and leasing........	5321	163	208	199	161	165	10.70	13.64	13.43
Consumer goods rental.........................	5322	220	292	275	198	178	9.53	12.39	14.57
Machinery and equipment rental and leasing.....	5324	84	103	111	114	121	14.95	17.12	20.62
Lessors of nonfinancial intangible assets............	533	14	28	27	25	24	17.68	20.06	(NA)
Professional and business services...........	**(X)**	**10,848**	**16,666**	**16,954**	**16,728**	**17,331**	**15.52**	**18.08**	**23.12**
Professional and technical services [5].............	**54**	**4,538**	**6,702**	**7,025**	**7,441**	**7,691**	**20.61**	**24.15**	**30.28**
Legal services................................	5411	944	1,066	1,168	1,114	1,115	21.38	23.96	31.11
Accounting and bookkeeping services............	5412	664	866	849	887	921	14.42	17.45	21.38
Architectural and engineering services..........	5413	942	1,238	1,311	1,275	1,294	20.49	23.96	29.81
Specialized design services.....................	5414	82	132	131	113	115	15.32	20.29	23.59
Computer systems design and related services....	5415	410	1,254	1,195	1,449	1,530	27.13	31.64	37.22
Management and technical consulting services....	5416	305	673	824	999	1,070	20.83	23.97	29.81
Scientific research and development services......	5417	494	515	577	621	630	21.39	28.33	36.20
Advertising and related services................	5418	382	497	446	408	425	16.99	19.49	26.34
Management of companies and enterprises.......	**55**	**1,667**	**1,796**	**1,759**	**1,872**	**1,915**	**15.28**	**18.08**	**24.04**
Administrative and waste services..............	**56**	**4,643**	**8,168**	**8,170**	**7,414**	**7,724**	**11.69**	**13.16**	**16.23**
Administrative and support services [5].............	561	4,413	7,855	7,833	7,057	7,359	11.53	12.93	16.02
Office administrative services..................	5611	211	264	345	407	419	14.68	17.82	24.71
Facilities support services......................	5612	58	97	120	133	130	16.73	18.02	19.65
Employment services [5].........................	5613	1,512	3,849	3,607	2,723	2,952	11.89	13.04	16.73
Temporary help services.......................	56132	1,156	2,636	2,549	2,094	2,316	11.79	12.00	15.27
Business support services.......................	5614	505	787	766	809	812	11.08	13.14	14.61
Travel arrangement and reservation services.....	5615	250	299	224	186	190	12.72	14.55	17.70
Investigation and security services..............	5616	507	689	737	781	800	9.78	11.64	14.59
Services to buildings and dwellings..............	5617	1,175	1,571	1,738	1,745	1,777	10.02	11.44	13.20
Waste management and remediation services [5].....	562	229	313	338	357	365	15.29	17.69	19.79
Waste collection...............................	5621	82	100	124	141	146	12.97	15.54	17.35
Waste treatment and disposal...................	5622	77	119	103	96	95	15.02	17.76	22.16
Education and health services....................	**(X)**	**10,984**	**15,109**	**17,372**	**19,531**	**19,884**	**13.95**	**16.71**	**20.78**
Educational services.............................	**61**	**1,688**	**2,390**	**2,836**	**3,155**	**3,241**	**(NA)**	**(NA)**	**(NA)**
Elementary and secondary schools..............	6111	461	716	837	849	867	(NA)	(NA)	(NA)
Junior colleges................................	6112	44	79	100	99	100	(NA)	(NA)	(NA)
Colleges and universities.......................	6113	939	1,196	1,393	1,591	1,628	(NA)	(NA)	(NA)
Business, computer, and management training....	6114	60	86	77	78	76	(NA)	(NA)	(NA)
Technical and trade schools.....................	6115	72	91	102	126	128	(NA)	(NA)	(NA)
Other schools and instruction...................	6116	96	184	250	309	334	(NA)	(NA)	(NA)
Educational support services....................	6117	17	39	78	103	108	(NA)	(NA)	(NA)
Health care and social assistance..................	**62**	**9,296**	**12,718**	**14,536**	**16,375**	**16,643**	**13.98**	**17.05**	**21.12**
Health care...................................	621,2,3	8,211	10,858	12,314	13,777	14,046	14.63	17.98	22.44
Ambulatory health care services...............	621	2,842	4,320	5,114	5,975	6,146	14.99	17.86	22.57
Offices of physicians.........................	6211	1,278	1,840	2,094	2,313	2,355	15.65	18.95	25.75
Offices of dentists...........................	6212	513	688	774	828	842	15.96	19.40	23.06
Offices of other health practitioners...........	6213	276	438	549	671	697	14.24	16.70	21.05
Outpatient care centers......................	6214	261	386	473	600	624	15.29	18.96	23.22
Medical and diagnostic laboratories...........	6215	129	162	198	228	232	15.74	18.67	22.80
Home health care services...................	6216	288	633	821	1,085	1,139	12.86	14.42	17.02
Hospitals....................................	622	3,513	3,954	4,345	251	4,731	16.71	21.30	27.01
General medical and surgical hospitals.........	6221	3,305	3,745	4,096	4,679	4,375	16.75	21.40	27.31
Psychiatric and substance abuse hospitals.......	6222	113	86	93	109	120	14.97	17.79	20.26
Nursing and residential care facilities..............	623	1,856	2,583	2,855	3,124	3,169	10.67	12.37	14.24
Nursing care facilities........................	6231	1,170	1,514	1,577	1,657	1,668	11.08	13.08	15.26
Residential mental health facilities............	6232	269	437	497	565	571	9.96	11.30	12.80
Community care facilities for the elderly.........	6233	330	478	615	741	769	9.83	11.33	13.06
Social assistance..............................	624	1,085	1,860	2,222	2,599	2,597	9.78	11.35	13.10
Individual and family services.................	6241	389	678	921	1,220	1,263	10.57	12.44	13.91
Emergency and other relief services...........	6242	67	117	129	143	145	10.95	13.48	15.12
Vocational rehabilitation services..............	6243	242	370	383	388	345	9.57	10.67	12.53

See footnotes at end of table.

Table 644. Nonfarm Industries—Employees and Earnings: 1990 to 2011-Continued.

See headnote on page 422.

Industry	2007 NAICS code [1]	All employees (1,000)						Average hourly earnings [2] (dol.)		
		1990	2000	2005	2010	2011	2000	2005	2011	
Child day care services..........................	6244	388	696	790	848	844	8.88	10.14	11.82	
Leisure and hospitality..............................	(X)	**9,288**	**11,862**	**12,816**	**13,049**	**13,320**	**8.32**	**9.38**	**11.45**	
Arts, entertainment, and recreation.................	**71**	**1,132**	**1,788**	**1,892**	**1,913**	**1,910**	**10.68**	**12.85**	**15.68**	
Performing arts and spectator sports................	711	273	382	376	406	394	13.11	18.67	22.78	
Museums, historical sites, zoos, and parks.........	712	68	110	121	139	128	12.20	13.67	15.87	
Amusements, gambling, and recreation.............	713	791	1,296	1,395	1,379	1,383	9.86	11.08	13.45	
Accommodation and food services................	**72**	**8,156**	**10,074**	**10,923**	**11,135**	**11,410**	**7.92**	**8.80**	**10.79**	
Accommodation..	721	1,616	1,884	1,819	1,760	1,797	9.48	10.75	12.74	
Traveler accommodation and other longer-term accommodation..	7211	1,582	1,837	1,765	1,703	1,734	9.49	10.78	12.78	
Food services and drinking places..................	722	6,540	8,189	9,104	9,376	9,613	7.49	8.34	10.36	
Full-service restaurants.............................	7221	3,070	3,845	4,316	4,482	4,597	7.78	8.84	11.17	
Limited-service eating places.......................	7222	2,765	3,462	3,889	4,001	NA	6.87	7.49	8.94	
Special food services...............................	7223	392	491	538	543	552	9.45	10.48	12.69	
Drinking places, alcoholic beverages..............	7224	312	391	361	341	346	7.24	7.89	10.79	
Other services...	**81**	**4,261**	**5,168**	**5,395**	**5,331**	**5,342**	**12.73**	**14.34**	**17.32**	
Repair and maintenance...............................	811	1,009	1,242	1,236	1,139	1,160	13.28	14.82	17.05	
Automotive repair and maintenance..................	8111	659	888	886	801	813	12.45	14.11	16.03	
Electronic equipment repair and maintenance......	8112	100	107	103	98	97	16.31	16.65	19.40	
Commercial machinery repair and maintenance. ...	8113	161	161	170	172	183	15.53	16.89	20.22	
Personal and laundry services.......................	812	1,120	1,243	1,277	1,265	1,285	10.18	11.81	13.34	
Personal care services...............................	8121	430	490	577	601	613	10.18	12.44	13.99	
Death care services..................................	8122	123	136	137	131	128	13.04	15.34	17.71	
Dry-cleaning and laundry services..................	8123	371	388	347	302	298	9.17	10.18	11.50	
Dry-cleaning and laundry services, except coin-operated..............................	81232	215	211	180	146	143	8.14	9.14	10.41	
Other personal services.............................	8129	196	229	216	232	246	10.52	11.29	12.19	
Pet care services, except veterinary...............	81291	23	31	44	63	69	12.12	10.61	12.85	
Parking lots and garages...........................	81293	68	93	103	111	115	8.81	9.89	10.74	
Membership associations & organizations............	813	2,132	2,683	2,882	2,926	2,897	13.66	15.20	19.20	
Grantmaking and giving services....................	8132	113	116	137	178	164	14.65	18.80	24.16	
Social advocacy organizations......................	8133	126	143	174	202	206	12.08	13.89	17.71	
Civic and social organizations......................	8134	377	404	409	392	391	9.85	11.16	12.77	
Professional and similar organizations..............	8139	379	473	492	477	468	15.98	18.60	22.88	
Government..	(X)	**18,415**	**20,790**	**21,804**	**22,490**	**22,104**	(NA)	(NA)	(NA)	
Federal...	(X)	3,196	2,865	2,732	2,977	2,858	(NA)	(NA)	(NA)	
State..	(X)	4,305	4,786	5,032	5,137	5,082	(NA)	(NA)	(NA)	
Local..	(X)	10,914	13,139	14,041	14,376	14,165	(NA)	(NA)	(NA)	

NA Not available. X Not applicable. [1] Based on the North American Industry Classification System, 2007. See text, Section 15. [2] Production employees in the goods-producing industries and nonsupervisory employees in service-providing industries. See footnotes 3 and 4. [3] Mining and logging, construction, and manufacturing. [4] Trade, transportation and utilities, information, financial activities, professional and business services, education and health services, leisure and hospitality, other services, and government. [5] Includes other industries, not shown separately.

Source: U.S. Bureau of Labor Statistics, Current Employment Statistics, "Employment, Hours, and Earnings—National," <http://www.bls.gov/ces/data.htm\>.

Table 645. Women Employees on Nonfarm Payrolls by Major Industry: 1980 to 2011

[37,813 represents 37,813,000. Annual averages of monthly data. For coverage, see headnote, Table 642]

Industry	Women employees (1,000)				Percent of total employees			
	1980	1990	2000	2011	1980	1990	2000	2011
Total nonfarm [1]...............	**37,813**	**51,587**	**63,223**	**64,939**	**41.8**	**47.1**	**48.0**	**49.4**
Total private.........................	29,783	41,732	51,452	52,377	40.2	45.8	46.4	47.9
Construction........................	458	656	846	708	10.3	12.5	12.5	12.9
Manufacturing......................	5,676	5,702	5,359	3,243	30.3	32.2	31.0	27.6
Trade, transportation, and utilities.................	6,799	9,363	10,859	10,028	36.9	41.3	41.4	40.1
Wholesale trade..................	1,179	1,611	1,827	1,664	25.9	30.6	30.8	30.1
Retail trade.......................	4,980	6,696	7,680	7,224	48.6	50.8	50.3	49.3
Transportation and warehousing..........	506	879	1,202	1,006	17.1	25.3	27.3	23.4
Utilities............................	134	177	151	136	20.6	24.0	25.1	24.4
Information.........................	1,118	1,324	1,697	1,079	47.4	49.3	46.7	40.6
Financial activities................	2,848	4,055	4,638	4,481	56.7	61.3	60.3	58.3
Professional and business services.........	3,096	5,105	7,680	7,693	41.0	47.1	46.1	44.4
Professional and technical services...........	(NA)	2,209	3,146	3,614	(NA)	48.7	46.9	47.0
Management of companies and enterprises......	(NA)	849	924	942	(NA)	50.9	51.4	49.2
Administrative and waste services.............	(NA)	2,048	3,610	3,137	(NA)	44.1	44.2	40.6
Education and health services.................	5,459	8,422	11,586	15,278	77.2	76.7	76.7	76.8
Educational services..............	(NA)	958	1,417	1,979	(NA)	56.8	59.3	61.1
Health care and social assistance...........	(NA)	7,464	10,168	13,299	(NA)	80.3	79.9	79.9
Leisure and hospitality............	3,021	4,829	6,082	6,947	44.9	52.0	51.3	52.2
Arts, entertainment, and recreation................	(NA)	516	815	887	(NA)	45.6	45.6	46.4
Accommodation and food services...........	(NA)	4,312	5,267	6,060	(NA)	52.9	52.3	53.1
Other services.....................	1,185	2,164	2,614	2,815	43.0	50.8	50.6	52.7
Government.........................	8,029	9,855	11,771	12,562	49.0	53.5	56.6	56.8
Federal.............................	1,136	1,378	1,231	1,203	37.9	43.1	43.0	42.1
State government..................	1,641	2,137	2,464	2,645	45.5	49.6	51.5	52.0
Local government.................	5,252	6,340	8,076	8,713	53.8	58.1	61.5	61.5

NA Not available [1] Includes other industries, not shown separately.

Source: U.S. Bureau of Labor Statistics, Current Employment Statistics, "Employment, Hours, and Earnings—National," <http://www.bls.gov/ces/data.htm>.

Table 646. Private Nonfarm Extended Mass Layoff Activity by Industry and Reason for Layoff: 2000 to 2010

[Covers layoffs of at least 31 days duration that involve 50 or more individuals from a single employer. Based on administrative records of unemployment filings and establishment classifications, supplemented with employer confirmation of layoffs, plant closings, and additional employer provided data. See source for more information]

Industry	2007 NAICS code [1]	Extended mass layoff events	Separations	Initial claimants [2]
2000.......................	(X)	4,591	915,962	846,267
2005.......................	(X)	4,881	884,661	834,533
2006.......................	(X)	4,885	935,969	951,155
2007.......................	(X)	5,363	965,935	978,712
2008.......................	(X)	8,259	1,516,978	1,670,042
2009.......................	(X)	11,824	2,108,202	2,442,000
Total, 2010..............	**(X)**	**7,247**	**1,256,606**	**1,412,386**
Mining, quarrying, and gas extraction.............	21	59	7,940	8,246
Utilities........................	22	17	2,795	3,266
Construction.................	23	1,623	197,436	251,417
Manufacturing...............	31–33	1,412	224,173	257,712
Wholesale trade.............	42	149	17,274	17,319
Retail trade..................	44,45	479	122,576	152,959
Transportation and warehousing...........	48,49	486	95,564	105,099
Information..................	51	220	54,081	76,222
Finance and Insurance......	52	251	47,888	53,291
Real estate and rental and leasing..........	53	68	10,035	9,575
Professional and technical services...........	54	298	58,797	63,189
Management of companies and enterprises.............	55	30	5,338	4,815
Administrative and waste services...........	56	747	150,042	172,897
Educational services........	61	87	11,817	13,284
Health care and social assistance.............	62	384	48,501	49,243
Arts, entertainment, and recreation...........	71	228	48,590	34,023
Accommodation and food services...........	72	564	134,814	120411
Other services...............	81	145	18,945	19,418
Unclassified.................	(X)	–	–	–
Reason for layoff:				
Business demand...........	(X)	2,515	384,564	509,089
Disaster/safety..............	(X)	24	3,202	3,225
Financial issues.............	(X)	511	86,637	103,762
Organizational changes......	(X)	397	79,784	80,192
Production specific..........	(X)	54	7,830	8,459
Seasonal.....................	(X)	2,417	429,846	442,596
Other/miscellaneous........	(X)	1,329	264,743	265,063

– Represents zero. X Not applicable. [1] Based on North American Industry Classification System, 2007. See text, Section 15. [2] A person who files any notice of unemployment to initiate a request either for a determination of entitlement to and eligibility for compensation, or for a subsequent period of unemployment within a benefit year or period of eligibility.

Source: U.S. Bureau of Labor Statistics, "Mass Layoff Statistics," May 2011, <http://www.bls.gov/mls/home.htm>.

Table 647. Private Sector Gross Job Gains and Job Losses: 2001 to 2011

[In thousands (15,177 represents 15,177,000). For year ending in March. Based on the Quarterly Census of Employment and Wages (QCEW). Excludes self-employed and certain nonprofit organizations. Minus sign (–) indicates a decrease in employment and comes from either closing establishments or contracting establishments. See source]

Year and industry	Gross job gains			Gross job losses			Net change[1]
	Total	Expanding establishments	Opening establishments	Total	Contracting establishments	Closing establishments	
2001	15,177	10,147	5,028	14,328	9,249	5,081	847
2002	13,579	8,635	4,944	16,308	11,041	5,332	-2,729
2003	13,191	8,599	4,592	13,923	9,290	4,638	-732
2004	13,307	8,953	4,354	12,428	8,237	4,191	879
2005	13,759	9,403	4,356	11,767	7,672	4,095	1,992
2006	14,019	9,625	4,394	11,438	7,711	3,727	2,581
2007	13,441	9,238	4,203	11,941	8,246	3,695	1,500
2008	12,704	8,714	3,990	12,609	8,772	3,837	95
2009	10,048	6,664	3,384	15,912	11,703	4,209	-5,864
2010	9,985	6,834	3,151	12,683	9,137	3,546	-2,698
2011, Total private	**11,509**	**8,281**	**3,228**	**9,638**	**6,615**	**3,023**	**1,871**
Goods producing	2,208	1,755	453	1,976	1,415	561	232
Natural resources and mining	268	205	63	190	136	54	78
Construction	985	705	283	1,040	702	338	-55
Manufacturing	955	848	107	746	577	169	209
Service providing	9,298	6,526	2,772	7,662	5,200	2,462	1,636
Wholesale trade	563	426	137	479	315	164	84
Retail trade	1,267	890	377	1,116	783	333	151
Transportation and warehousing	406	308	98	316	218	98	90
Utilities	23	19	4	24	20	4	-1
Information	242	185	57	278	211	67	-36
Financial activities	700	511	189	735	484	251	-35
Professional and business services	2,486	1,884	602	1,867	1,287	580	619
Education and health services	1,447	1,099	348	1,113	799	314	334
Leisure and hospitality	1,549	900	649	1,288	818	470	261
Other services	440	295	145	409	260	149	31

[1] Net change is the difference between total gross job gains and total gross job losses.

Source: Bureau of Labor Statistics, Business Employment Dynamics, "Annual Business Employment Dynamics Data," <http://www.bls.gov/bdm/bdmann.htm#TOTAL>.

Table 648. Private Sector Gross Job Gains and Job Losses by State: 2011

[In thousands (11,509 represents 11,509,000). For year ending in March. Based on the Quarterly Census of Employment and Wages (QCEW). Excludes self-employed and certain nonprofit organizations. Minus sign (–) indicates a decrease in employment and come from either closing establishments or contracting establishments. For more information, see source]

State	Gross job gains			Gross job losses			Net change[1]	State	Gross job gains			Gross job losses			Net change[1]
	Total	Expanding establishments	Opening establishments	Total	Contracting establishments	Closing establishments			Total	Expanding establishments	Opening establishments	Total	Contracting establishments	Closing establishments	
U.S.	**11,509**	**8,281**	**3,228**	**9,638**	**6,615**	**3,023**	**1,871**	MO	213	151	62	201	136	65	13
AL	158	113	45	151	108	43	7	MT	35	25	10	32	22	11	2
AK	25	19	6	19	14	5	6	NE	66	48	18	58	43	15	8
AZ	221	157	64	198	131	67	22	NV	108	75	32	98	69	28	10
AR	97	68	28	92	60	31	5	NH	50	38	13	43	30	14	7
CA	1,398	976	422	1,185	819	366	213	NJ	328	227	101	305	206	98	24
CO	208	145	63	176	117	59	31	NM	63	44	19	59	41	18	4
CT	123	92	31	97	78	20	26	NY	732	507	225	592	403	189	140
DE	39	25	13	30	21	9	8	NC	366	259	107	306	203	103	60
DC	52	38	15	42	28	14	10	ND	39	29	9	21	16	5	18
FL	777	498	278	700	417	283	77	OH	411	318	94	335	249	86	76
GA	379	260	120	322	201	121	57	OK	138	98	40	113	74	40	24
HI	48	35	13	41	27	15	7	OR	138	101	37	116	80	37	21
ID	53	36	17	50	33	17	2	PA	446	337	109	355	260	94	91
IL	437	330	107	354	247	107	83	RI	34	24	10	33	24	10	1
IN	248	187	61	185	132	53	63	SC	163	119	44	131	91	40	32
IA	106	82	24	95	70	25	11	SD	29	22	7	24	18	6	5
KS	105	76	30	95	66	29	11	TN	230	174	56	188	134	54	42
KY	144	106	38	125	90	35	19	TX	987	732	255	749	534	215	238
LA	185	131	53	156	109	47	28	UT	112	79	33	93	63	30	19
ME	43	31	12	40	27	13	3	VT	23	17	6	19	13	6	4
MD	219	155	64	193	133	60	26	VA	313	222	91	267	187	80	46
MA	241	182	58	206	145	61	34	WA	237	178	59	202	145	57	36
MI	353	274	79	254	161	94	98	WV	61	46	15	53	37	16	8
MN	206	154	52	167	113	53	40	WI	205	157	48	166	119	47	39
MS	94	67	27	83	58	24	11	WY	24	17	7	21	14	7	3

[1] Net change is the difference between total gross job gains and total gross job losses.

Source: Bureau of Labor Statistics, Business Employment Dynamics, "Annual Business Employment Dynamics Data," <http://www.bls.gov/bdm/bdmann.htm#TOTAL>.

Table 649. Hires and Separations Affecting Establishment Payrolls: 2008 to 2011

[55,166 represents 55,166,000. Hires represent any additions to payrolls, including new and rehired employees, full- and part-time workers, short-term and seasonal workers, etc. Separations represent terminations of employment, including quits, layoffs, and discharges, etc. Based on a monthly survey of private nonfarm establishments and governmental entities]

Industry	Annual hires (1,000)				Annual separations (1,000)			
	2008	2009	2010	2011	2008	2009	2010	2011
Total	**55,166**	**46,398**	**48,647**	**50,083**	**58,601**	**51,527**	**47,641**	**48,242**
Total private industry	51,606	43,052	44,826	46,869	55,216	48,095	43,518	44,774
Mining and logging	357	185	286	328	324	295	219	241
Construction	4,479	3,679	3,996	4,096	5,228	4,764	4,195	3,962
Manufacturing	3,592	2,755	3,134	3,082	4,452	4,172	3,036	2,831
Durable goods	2,064	1,409	1,797	1,792	2,688	2,519	1,679	1,541
Nondurable goods	1,526	1,344	1,337	1,289	1,765	1,654	1,356	1,290
Trade, transportation, and utilities	11,413	9,440	9,681	9,942	12,499	10,526	9,401	9,531
Wholesale trade	1,765	1,453	1,411	1,504	2,000	1,777	1,406	1,416
Retail trade	7,882	6,333	6,697	6,752	8,599	6,872	6,475	6,517
Transportation, warehousing, and utilities	1,768	1,659	1,576	1,686	1,900	1,878	1,521	1,601
Information	753	667	651	708	867	840	709	752
Financial activities	2,502	1,995	2,046	1,861	2,716	2,325	2,047	1,852
Finance and insurance	1,604	1,192	1,359	1,178	1,753	1,397	1,328	1,168
Real estate and rental and leasing	897	801	687	685	962	925	718	686
Professional and business services	9,966	8,256	9,330	10,391	10,787	9,011	8,801	9,807
Education and health services	6,352	5,952	5,770	5,730	5,881	5,641	5,459	5,319
Educational services	910	862	887	924	814	830	808	828
Health care and social assistance	5,441	5,091	4,882	4,807	5,070	4,811	4,647	4,489
Leisure and hospitality	9,820	7,779	7,822	8,453	10,038	8,087	7,576	8,204
Arts, entertainment, and recreation	1,449	1,198	1,317	1,455	1,477	1,267	1,271	1,491
Accommodation and food services	8,369	6,580	6,507	6,995	8,564	6,822	6,304	6,714
Other services	2,372	2,338	2,102	2,279	2,418	2,434	2,075	2,271
Government workers	3,558	3,346	3,821	3,213	3,382	3,433	4,124	3,470
Federal	321	460	1,048	330	302	409	995	374
State and local	3,238	2,886	2,772	2,883	3,082	3,023	3,129	3,094

Source: U.S. Bureau of Labor Statistics, *Job Openings and Labor Turnover*, News Release, USDL 12-0447, March 2012. See also <http://www.bls.gov/jlt/news.htm>.

Table 650. Type of Separations Affecting Establishment Payrolls: 2011

[23,578 represents 23,578,000. Covers all private nonfarm establishments. Separations are the total number of terminations of employment occurring at any time during the reference month, and are reported by type of separation—quits, layoffs and discharges, and other separations. Annual rate estimates are computed by dividing annual levels by the Current Employment Statistics (CES) annual average employment level, see Table 644, and multiplying that quotient by 100]

Industry	Number (1,000)			Rate (percent) [1]		
	Annual quits level [2]	Annual layoffs and discharge levels [3]	Annual other separations [4]	Annual quits level [2]	Annual layoffs and discharge levels [3]	Annual other separations [4]
Total	**23,578**	**20,718**	**3,943**	**17.9**	**15.8**	**3.0**
Private industry	22,191	19,394	3,188	20.3	17.8	2.9
Mining and logging	140	84	17	17.9	10.7	2.2
Construction	945	2,865	154	17.2	52.1	2.8
Manufacturing	1,254	1,327	250	10.7	11.3	2.1
Durable goods	640	747	157	8.8	10.3	2.2
Nondurable goods	615	581	94	13.8	13.0	2.1
Trade, transportation, and utilities	5,247	3,400	883	21.0	13.6	3.5
Wholesale trade	634	591	193	11.5	10.7	3.5
Retail trade	3,880	2,154	481	26.5	14.7	3.3
Transportation, warehousing, and utilities	734	655	213	15.1	13.5	4.4
Information	405	284	62	15.2	10.7	2.3
Financial activities	995	650	211	13.0	8.5	2.7
Finance and insurance	667	344	156	11.6	6.0	2.7
Real estate and rental and leasing	328	307	55	17.0	15.9	2.9
Professional and business services	4,485	4,720	600	25.9	27.2	3.5
Education and health services	2,965	1,814	538	14.9	9.1	2.7
Educational services	384	369	75	11.8	11.4	2.3
Health care and social assistance	2,582	1,445	466	15.5	8.7	2.8
Leisure and hospitality	4,729	3,145	327	35.5	23.6	2.5
Arts, entertainment, and recreation	509	953	29	26.6	49.9	1.5
Accommodation and food services	4,220	2,197	299	37.0	19.3	2.6
Other services	1,026	1,101	142	19.2	20.6	2.7
Government workers	1,389	1,324	756	6.3	6.0	3.4
Federal	113	133	130	4.0	4.7	4.5
State and local	1,276	1,194	627	6.6	6.2	3.3

[1] As a percent of total employment. [2] Quits are voluntary separations by employees (except for retirements, which are reported as other separations). [3] Layoffs and discharges are involuntary separations initiated by the employer and include layoffs with no intent to rehire; formal layoffs lasting or expected to last more than seven days; discharges resulting from mergers, downsizing, or closings, firings or other discharges for cause; terminations of permanent or short term employees; and terminations of seasonal employees. [4] Other separations include retirements, transfers to other locations, deaths, and separations due to disability.

Source: U.S. Bureau of Labor Statistics, *Job Openings and Labor Turnover*, News Release, USDL 12-0447, Jan. 2012. See also <http://www.bls.gov/jlt>.

Table 651. Productivity and Related Measures for Selected NAICS Industries: 1987 to 2010 and 2009 to 2010

[For a discussion of productivity measures and methodology, see text, this section and BLS Handbook of Methods, <http://www.bls.gov/opub/hom/homch11.htm>. Minus sign (–) indicates decrease]

| Industry | 2007 NAICS code [1] | Average annual percent change [2] | | | | | | | |
| | | 1987–2010 [3, 4] | | | | 2009–2010 | | | |
		Output per hour	Output	Hours	Unit labor costs	Output per hour	Output	Hours	Unit labor costs
Mining	21	0.1	-0.1	-0.2	4.9	-2.0	2.5	4.6	5.8
Oil and gas extraction	2111	1.1	-0.4	-1.4	5.7	8.7	2.8	-5.5	5.3
Mining, except oil and gas	212	1.8	0.3	-1.5	1.7	1.2	1.7	0.5	3.1
Support activities for mining	213	2.1	4.1	1.9	3.4	12.7	27.3	12.9	-12.7
Utilities:									
Power generation and supply	2211	2.3	0.9	-1.3	1.9	3.3	1.5	-1.8	-0.8
Power generation and supply	2212	2.6	1.2	-1.4	2.1	5.7	2.9	-2.7	-3.1
Manufacturing:									
Food	311	1.1	1.3	0.2	1.7	-1.2	-0.4	0.8	3.5
Animal slaughtering and processing	3116	1.0	2.1	1.1	1.4	-	-0.6	-0.6	2.6
Bakeries and tortilla manufacturing	3118	0.5	0.2	-0.3	1.8	0.4	0.9	0.5	1.0
Beverages and tobacco products	312	0.9	-0.3	-1.2	1.6	-2.4	-	2.5	-0.1
Textile mills	313	3.5	-2.8	-6.1	-0.4	6.0	9.5	3.3	-8.0
Textile product mills	314	0.9	-1.9	-2.8	2.0	10.0	3.9	-5.6	-0.9
Apparel	315	-1.1	-8.1	-7.1	2.3	3.8	-	-3.7	-2.4
Leather and allied products	316	2.0	-4.6	-6.5	1.5	8.5	11.9	3.2	-7.3
Wood products	321	1.5	-0.9	-2.3	2.0	9.2	6.3	-2.7	-5.9
Paper and paper products	322	1.9	-0.2	-2.0	1.3	2.7	2.5	-0.2	-0.6
Converted paper products	3222	1.3	-	-1.3	1.8	0.8	2.1	1.3	0.4
Printing and related support activities	3231	1.3	-0.6	-1.9	1.3	4.3	-0.3	-4.4	-4.4
Petroleum and coal products	3241	2.7	1.2	-1.5	2.5	5.2	4.0	-1.1	-3.0
Chemicals	325	1.6	0.7	-0.9	2.3	6.1	6.4	0.3	-3.3
Pharmaceuticals and medicines	3254	-	2.0	2.1	3.9	-8.2	-8.3	-0.1	10.9
Plastics and rubber products	326	2.0	1.1	-0.9	1.1	5.4	9.2	3.6	-4.3
Plastics products	3261	1.9	1.4	-0.5	1.3	4.9	8.6	3.5	-4.5
Nonmetallic mineral products	327	1.0	-0.4	-1.4	1.7	6.3	3.2	-2.9	-3.6
Primary metals	331	2.5	-0.2	-2.6	0.8	15.5	23.2	6.6	-11.3
Fabricated metal products	332	1.3	0.5	-0.9	1.7	5.1	6.6	1.4	-3.6
Architectural and structural metals	3323	0.7	0.3	-0.4	2.4	2.3	-3.8	-5.9	-0.4
Machine shops and threaded products	3327	2.0	2.3	0.3	1.3	7.5	14.7	6.7	-5.8
Other fabricated metal products	3329	1.2	-	-1.2	1.6	1.1	5.1	4.0	-1.5
Machinery	333	2.4	1.1	-1.3	0.7	9.3	11.8	2.3	-7.4
Agriculture, construction, and mining machinery	3331	2.8	2.8	-	-0.1	11.3	15.6	3.9	-12.7
Other general purpose machinery	3339	2.6	1.1	-1.5	1.3	6.4	7.9	1.4	-3.5
Computer and electronic products	334	11.2	8.3	-2.6	-6.9	11.6	8.1	-3.1	-3.9
Semiconductors and electronic components	3344	16.5	14.2	-1.9	-11.4	32.8	32.1	-0.5	-17.3
Electronic instruments	3345	4.0	1.8	-2.1	0.2	9.4	6.4	-2.7	-1.1
Electrical equipment and appliances	335	2.4	-0.4	-2.7	1.2	5.6	5.3	-0.3	-2.9
Transportation equipment	336	3.1	1.1	-2.0	-0.4	15.7	17.8	1.8	-13.3
Motor vehicles	3361	3.9	0.9	-2.9	-1.2	26.1	39.9	11.0	-21.2
Motor vehicle parts	3363	3.4	1.7	-1.6	-1.7	17.1	27.4	8.8	-18.4
Aerospace products and parts	3364	2.0	-0.3	-2.3	1.1	7.5	2.6	-4.5	-2.3
Furniture and related products	337	1.5	-0.9	-2.4	1.7	6.7	-1.6	-7.9	-3.0
Household and institutional furniture	3371	1.6	-1.2	-2.8	1.8	10.5	0.1	-9.4	-5.2
Miscellaneous manufacturing	339	3.1	2.5	-0.6	1.4	8.3	4.0	-4.0	-0.3
Medical equipment and supplies	3391	3.6	4.6	1.0	0.9	6.5	2.6	-3.6	1.4
Other miscellaneous manufacturing	3399	2.4	0.6	-1.8	1.8	10.7	5.9	-4.4	-2.7
Wholesale trade	42	3.1	3.4	0.3	0.7	9.0	7.2	-1.7	-5.5
Durable goods	423	5.0	4.9	-	-0.9	14.4	11.5	-2.5	-10.3
Nondurable goods	424	1.4	1.5	0.1	2.8	3.7	2.8	-0.8	-1.5
Electronic markets and agents and brokers	4251	1.4	3.9	2.4	0.8	9.2	8.5	-0.6	-2.5
Retail trade	44–45	2.8	3.2	0.4	-	3.9	4.5	0.5	-3.2
Motor vehicle and parts dealers	441	1.9	2.3	0.4	0.8	4.4	4.6	0.2	-1.0
Automobile dealers	4411	2.0	2.3	0.4	0.8	6.6	5.5	-1.0	-1.3
Other motor vehicle dealers	4412	2.4	2.8	0.4	1.1	7.1	-1.5	-8.1	-3.1
Auto parts, accessories, and tire stores	4413	1.4	2.0	0.6	1.2	-3.1	1.5	4.8	3.3
Furniture and home furnishings stores	442	3.8	3.3	-0.5	-0.9	5.2	6.0	0.7	-5.7
Furniture stores	4421	3.1	2.8	-0.3	-0.8	3.9	6.8	2.8	-6.5
Home furnishings stores	4422	4.7	3.9	-0.7	-1.1	6.8	5.1	-1.6	-4.9
Electronics and appliance stores	4431	12.5	13.8	1.1	-8.4	5.7	11.6	5.6	-4.2
Building material and garden supply stores	444	2.6	3.2	0.6	-	10.6	6.9	-3.4	-9.1
Building material and supplies dealers	4441	2.3	3.1	0.9	0.2	9.9	6.8	-2.9	-9.3
Lawn and garden equipment and supplies stores	4442	4.3	3.7	-0.6	-1.3	16.0	7.7	-7.2	-7.3
Food and beverage stores	445	0.4	0.2	-0.2	2.7	1.6	1.3	-0.3	-1.1
Grocery stores	4451	0.3	0.2	-0.1	2.9	1.2	1.2	-	-0.8
Specialty food stores	4452	-	-0.6	-0.7	2.1	-0.5	0.4	0.9	3.3
Beer, wine, and liquor stores	4453	2.3	0.9	-1.4	1.0	11.7	2.9	-7.9	-10.3
Health and personal care stores	4461	2.2	3.4	1.2	1.4	1.3	1.3	-	-0.6
Gasoline stations	4471	1.7	1.0	-0.8	1.3	1.5	1.0	-0.5	-1.3
Clothing and clothing accessories stores	448	4.4	4.0	-0.4	-1.2	4.9	4.8	-0.1	-3.2
Clothing stores	4481	4.7	4.6	-0.1	-1.7	3.2	5.1	1.8	-3.5
Shoe stores	4482	3.4	2.2	-1.1	-0.6	5.8	5.0	-0.8	0.7
Jewelry, luggage, and leather goods stores	4483	3.6	2.8	-0.8	0.4	11.2	2.9	-7.5	-4.1
Sporting goods, hobby, book, and music stores	451	4.1	4.0	-0.1	-0.8	9.3	5.6	-3.4	-2.6
Sporting goods and musical instrument stores	4511	4.7	5.1	0.4	-1.4	8.6	8.1	-0.4	-1.7
Book, periodical, and music stores	4512	2.9	1.4	-1.4	0.7	11.7	-1.9	-12.2	-5.0
General merchandise stores	452	3.0	4.9	1.8	-1.1	0.3	4.2	3.9	-3.4
Department stores	4521	0.3	1.6	1.3	0.8	-2.8	1.2	4.2	-

See footnotes at end of table.

Table 651. Productivity and Related Measures for Selected NAICS Industries: 1987 to 2010 and 2009 to 2010-Continued.

See headnote on page 429.

Industry	2007 NAICS code [1]	Average annual percent change [2]							
		1987–2010 [3, 4]				2009–2010			
		Output per hour	Output	Hours	Unit labor costs	Output per hour	Output	Hours	Unit labor costs
Other general merchandise stores..............	4529	6.0	8.5	2.3	-3.0	1.9	5.6	3.6	-5.2
Miscellaneous store retailers......................	453	4.0	3.5	-0.4	-1.4	6.9	5.6	-1.2	-3.8
Florists..	4531	3.8	-	-3.7	-0.4	17.9	10.8	-6.1	-3.3
Office supplies, stationery, and gift stores.......	4532	6.2	5.0	-1.1	-3.0	4.0	0.2	-3.6	0.1
Used merchandise stores.......................	4533	4.8	6.0	1.1	-2.2	16.5	19.3	2.4	-16.8
Other miscellaneous store retailers..........	4539	1.6	2.5	0.8	-0.2	5.4	5.8	0.4	-3.2
Nonstore retailers.................................	454	8.8	9.0	0.1	-5.0	8.3	12.2	3.5	-10.0
Electronic shopping and mail-order houses.....	4541	11.2	15.0	3.4	-6.5	10.9	16.2	4.8	-7.8
Vending machine operators......................	4542	1.1	-1.9	-2.9	2.4	11.5	5.8	-5.1	-16.4
Direct selling establishments...................	4543	3.3	1.4	-1.8	-0.6	-4.0	-0.1	4.0	-5.6
Transportation and warehousing:									
Air transportation.................................	481	3.0	2.7	-0.2	0.1	6.6	4.4	-2.1	-0.9
Line-haul railroads...............................	482111	4.2	1.9	-2.2	-0.8	8.1	12.8	4.4	-6.1
Truck transportation.............................	484	0.6	1.5	0.9	0.8	8.8	6.5	-2.1	-6.3
General freight trucking.........................	4841	1.3	2.1	0.8	0.8	11.0	7.9	-2.8	-9.1
Used household and office goods moving.......	48421	-0.7	-1.0	-0.3	2.8	-3.6	-1.2	2.5	0.2
Postal service....................................	4911	0.9	-0.2	-1.1	3.8	1.5	-5.7	-7.1	13.1
Couriers and messengers........................	492	-0.9	1.3	2.2	3.2	1.8	-5.5	-7.2	18.9
Warehousing and storage........................	4931	2.9	5.6	2.7	-0.4	8.7	9.5	0.7	-7.1
General warehousing and storage...............	49311	5.1	7.9	2.7	-2.0	7.9	9.4	1.3	-7.1
Refrigerated warehousing and storage..........	49312	0.5	3.4	2.9	0.8	21.9	15.2	-5.5	-12.1
Information:									
Publishing..	511	3.9	3.5	-0.3	1.4	7.2	1.6	-5.2	-
Newspaper, book, and directory publishers.....	5111	-	-1.8	-1.8	4.1	3.8	-5.2	-8.7	-1.3
Software publishers..............................	5112	13.5	20.3	6.0	-7.3	5.9	7.9	1.9	2.1
Motion picture and video exhibition.............	51213	1.4	1.8	0.4	1.6	0.3	-0.2	-0.5	-
Broadcasting, except Internet..................	515	2.0	2.6	0.5	1.9	12.0	4.4	-6.7	-4.1
Radio and television broadcasting...............	5151	1.0	0.7	-0.4	2.7	15.0	6.6	-7.2	-7.8
Cable and other subscription programming......	5152	3.7	7.6	3.8	2.5	8.5	2.4	-5.6	2.0
Wired telecommunications carriers.............	5171	4.1	3.3	-0.8	-0.9	4.6	0.9	-3.5	-2.9
Wireless telecommunications carriers..........	5172	10.5	21.3	9.7	-7.0	16.0	10.1	-5.0	-13.8
Finance and insurance:									
Commercial banking............................	52211	3.9	3.8	-0.1	1.7	-3.1	-4.0	-0.8	7.9
Real estate and rental and leasing:									
Passenger car rental............................	532111	2.0	2.2	0.2	2.5	8.5	4.4	-3.8	2.1
Truck, trailer, and RV rental and leasing........	53212	2.8	1.9	-0.8	0.9	-0.3	-2.9	-2.6	0.2
Video tape and disc rental......................	53223	5.1	2.6	-2.4	-1.7	24.5	-11.2	-28.7	-13.0
Professional and technical services:									
Tax preparation services........................	541213	0.4	2.6	2.2	1.4	3.4	-1.9	-5.1	0.3
Architectural services...........................	54131	1.1	1.9	0.8	2.2	-4.1	-10.9	-7.1	3.4
Engineering services............................	54133	1.0	2.7	1.7	3.4	-2.3	-3.3	-1.0	5.1
Advertising agencies............................	54181	2.3	2.4	0.1	2.0	9.4	8.2	-1.1	-5.0
Photography studios, portrait...................	541921	0.3	1.8	1.4	2.1	12.5	-2.0	-12.9	-4.5
Administrative and waste services:									
Employment placement agencies...............	561311	6.2	6.7	0.5	-1.3	-3.3	2.7	6.2	5.1
Travel agencies.................................	56151	6.0	4.1	-1.8	-1.2	13.7	10.8	-2.5	-8.0
Janitorial services..............................	56172	1.9	3.6	1.6	1.7	2.6	2.2	-0.4	1.8
Health care and social assistance:									
Medical and diagnostic laboratories............	6215	3.2	6.3	3.0	-0.2	-4.3	1.0	5.6	4.5
Arts, entertainment, and recreation:									
Amusement and theme parks....................	71311	-0.5	2.2	2.7	3.7	-2.0	0.3	2.3	5.7
Bowling centers.................................	71395	0.2	-1.9	-2.1	2.9	2.5	-1.7	-4.1	-0.9
Accommodation and food services..............	72	0.9	2.0	1.2	2.8	2.2	1.7	-0.5	1.2
Accommodation.................................	721	0.9	2.0	1.2	2.8	2.1	1.4	-0.7	1.3
Traveler accommodation.......................	7211	1.6	2.3	0.7	2.2	2.1	1.4	-0.7	1.4
Food services and drinking places.............	722	0.7	2.0	1.3	3.1	2.3	1.8	-0.5	1.2
Full-service restaurants........................	7221	0.6	1.9	1.3	3.9	1.3	0.8	-0.5	2.7
Limited-service eating places..................	7222	0.8	2.3	1.4	2.6	4.3	3.1	-1.1	-0.6
Special food services..........................	7223	1.3	2.4	1.0	1.1	-0.7	1.3	2.0	0.4
Drinking places, alcoholic beverages..........	7224	-0.4	-0.8	-0.3	3.1	-2.0	-0.9	1.1	5.1
Other services:									
Automotive repair and maintenance.............	8111	0.7	1.0	0.3	2.5	2.3	1.0	-1.3	-0.8
Reupholstery and furniture repair...............	81142	-1.0	-3.4	-2.4	3.6	-4.8	-4.9	-0.1	3.5
Hair, nail, and skin care services...............	81211	1.7	2.7	1.0	2.3	-1.0	1.9	2.9	-0.9
Funeral homes and funeral services............	81221	-0.5	-0.5	-	4.3	2.0	0.7	-1.2	-
Drycleaning and laundry services..............	8123	1.3	0.3	-1.0	2.1	3.0	0.7	-2.3	-2.4
Photofinishing...................................	81292	2.3	-4.8	-7.0	1.8	22.3	-1.0	-19.0	-5.3

– Represents or rounds to zero. [1] North American Industry Classification System, 2007 (NAICS); see text, Section 15. [2] Average annual percent changes based on compound rate formula. Rates of change are calculated using index numbers to three decimal places. [3] For NAICS industries 484, 4841, 48411, 4931, 49311, and 49312, annual percent changes are for 1992-2010. [4] For NAICS industries 561311 and 6215, average annual percent changes are for 1994-2010.

Source: U.S. Bureau of Labor Statistics, Labor Productivity and Costs, <http://www.bls.gov/lpc/home.htm>, accessed August 2012.

Table 652. Productivity and Related Measures: 1980 to 2011

[See text, this section. Minus sign (–) indicates decrease]

Item	1980	1990	2000	2005	2007	2008	2009	2010	2011
INDEXES (2005=100)									
Output per hour, business sector.............	58.0	69.0	85.6	100.0	102.4	103.2	106.3	109.5	110.0
Nonfarm business...............................	59.4	69.6	85.9	100.0	102.5	103.1	106.1	109.4	110.2
Manufacturing................................	(NA)	53.8	80.4	100.0	104.8	104.2	104.4	111.1	113.8
Output, [1] business sector.....................	42.7	60.0	87.7	100.0	105.1	103.7	99.2	102.2	104.6
Nonfarm business...............................	42.9	60.0	87.7	100.0	105.3	103.7	99.0	102.0	104.7
Manufacturing................................	(NA)	67.0	98.9	100.0	103.8	99.1	86.3	91.9	96.3
Hours, [2] business sector.....................	73.6	86.9	102.4	100.0	102.6	100.5	93.3	93.3	95.1
Nonfarm business...............................	72.2	86.3	102.2	100.0	102.7	100.6	93.3	93.3	95.1
Manufacturing................................	(NA)	124.5	123.1	100.0	99.1	95.1	82.7	82.7	84.6
Compensation per hour, [3] business sector......	33.1	55.2	82.3	100.0	108.1	111.7	113.2	115.4	118.4
Nonfarm business...............................	33.4	55.5	82.5	100.0	107.9	111.6	113.2	115.5	118.6
Manufacturing................................	(NA)	55.2	81.2	100.0	105.3	109.8	114.3	115.6	118.6
Real hourly compensation, [3] business sector....	74.6	80.0	93.3	100.0	101.8	101.2	103.0	103.3	102.8
Nonfarm business...............................	75.4	80.3	93.5	100.0	101.6	101.2	103.0	103.6	102.9
Manufacturing................................	(NA)	80.0	92.0	100.0	99.1	99.6	104.0	103.5	103.0
Unit labor costs, [4] business sector.............	57.0	80.0	96.1	100.0	105.5	108.2	106.5	105.4	107.7
Nonfarm business...............................	56.2	79.7	96.1	100.0	105.3	108.2	106.7	105.6	107.6
Manufacturing................................	(NA)	102.7	101.0	100.0	100.5	105.3	109.5	104.1	104.2
ANNUAL PERCENT CHANGE [5]									
Output per hour, business sector.................	-0.2	2.1	3.5	1.7	1.5	0.7	3.1	3.0	0.4
Nonfarm business...............................	-0.3	1.8	3.4	1.6	1.5	0.6	2.9	3.1	0.7
Manufacturing................................	(NA)	2.2	4.4	4.8	3.9	-0.6	0.1	6.4	2.5
Output, [1] business sector.....................	-1.1	1.5	4.5	3.4	2.0	-1.3	-4.3	3.0	2.4
Nonfarm business...............................	-1.1	1.4	4.4	3.4	2.1	-1.5	-4.5	3.1	2.6
Manufacturing................................	(NA)	-0.3	3.1	3.6	2.1	-4.5	-12.9	6.4	4.8
Hours, [2] business sector.....................	-0.9	-0.6	1.0	1.7	0.5	-2.0	-7.2	0.0	1.9
Nonfarm business...............................	-0.8	-0.4	1.0	1.7	0.5	-2.1	-7.2	0.0	1.9
Manufacturing................................	(NA)	-2.5	-1.3	-1.1	-1.7	-4.0	-13.0	0.0	2.2
Compensation per hour, [3] business sector......	10.7	6.4	7.4	3.9	4.1	3.3	1.4	2.0	2.6
Nonfarm business...............................	10.7	6.2	7.4	3.9	4.0	3.4	1.4	2.0	2.7
Manufacturing................................	(NA)	4.8	7.7	3.3	3.2	4.3	4.1	1.1	2.6
Real hourly compensation, [3] business sector....	-0.4	1.4	3.9	0.5	1.2	-0.5	1.8	0.3	-0.5
Nonfarm business...............................	-0.4	1.1	4.0	0.6	1.1	-0.4	1.8	0.4	-0.5
Manufacturing................................	(NA)	-0.1	4.2	0.0	0.4	0.4	4.5	-0.5	-0.5
Unit labor costs, [4] business sector.............	10.9	4.2	3.7	2.2	2.6	2.6	-1.6	-1.0	2.2
Nonfarm business...............................	11.0	4.3	3.9	2.3	2.4	2.8	-1.5	-1.0	2.0
Manufacturing................................	(NA)	2.6	3.2	-1.4	-0.6	4.9	4.0	-5.0	0.1

– Represents zero. NA Not available. [1] Refers to gross sectoral product, a chain–type, current–weighted index. [2] Hours at work of all persons engaged in the business and nonfarm business sectors (employees, proprietors, and unpaid family workers); employees' and proprietors' hours in manufacturing. [3] Wages and salaries of employees plus employers' contributions for social insurance and private benefit plans. Also includes an estimate of same for self–employed. Real compensation deflated by the Consumer Price Index research series, see text, Section 14. [4] Hourly compensation divided by output per hour. [5] All changes are from the immediate prior year.

Source: U.S. Department of Labor, Bureau of Labor Statistics, *Productivity and Costs*, News Release, USDL 12-1123, June 2012. See also <http://www.bls.gov/lpc/home.htm>.

Table 653. Average Hours Worked Per Day by Employed Persons: 2011

[149,386 represents 149,386,000. Civilian noninstitutionalized population 15 years old and over, except as indicated. Includes work at main and any other job(s). Excludes travel related to work. Based on the American Time Use Survey. See source for details]

Characteristic	Total em-ployed (1,000)	Employed persons who worked on their diary day [1]								
		Number (1,000)	Percent of employed	Hours of work	Worked at workplace			Worked at home [2]		
					Number (1,000)	Percent of employed [3]	Hours of work	Number (1,000)	Percent of employed [3]	Hours of work
Total......................	**149,386**	**101,723**	**68.1**	**7.64**	**86,637**	**85.2**	**7.86**	**21,699**	**21.3**	**2.88**
Work status: [4]										
Full-time workers [5].......	115,758	83,389	72.0	8.10	72,057	86.4	8.27	17,276	20.7	3.00
Part-time workers [5].......	33,628	18,334	54.5	5.55	14,580	79.5	5.84	4,423	24.1	2.41
Male [4].......................	80,057	56,108	70.1	8.00	48,166	85.8	8.21	11,568	20.6	2.72
Full-time workers [5].......	67,465	49,523	73.4	8.30	42,976	86.8	8.47	10,150	20.5	2.75
Part-time workers [5].......	12,592	6,585	52.3	5.72	5,190	78.8	6.02	1,418	21.5	2.47
Female [4].....................	69,329	45,616	65.8	7.21	38,471	84.3	7.43	10,131	22.2	3.06
Full-time workers [5].......	48,292	33,866	70.1	7.81	29,081	85.9	7.97	7,126	21.0	3.34
Part-time workers [5].......	21,036	11,750	55.9	5.46	9,390	79.9	5.74	3,005	25.6	2.39
Jobholding status:										
Single jobholders............	135,219	90,504	66.9	7.59	77,549	85.7	7.82	18,268	20.2	2.82
Multiple jobholders.........	14,167	11,219	79.2	8.05	9,088	81.0	8.19	3,431	30.6	3.20
Educational attainment: [6]										
Less than high school....	9,665	6,104	63.2	7.72	5,645	92.5	7.49	669	11.0	4.10
High school diploma [7]...	35,501	23,603	66.5	7.96	21,327	90.4	8.14	2,640	11.2	3.48
Some college.............	33,149	23,383	70.5	7.83	20,192	86.4	8.01	4,693	20.1	2.94
Bachelor's degree or higher...................	49,050	35,610	72.6	7.59	27,754	77.9	7.99	12,662	35.6	2.71

[1] Individuals may have worked at more than one location. [2] "Working at home" includes any time persons did work at home and is not restricted to persons whose usual workplace is their home. [3] Percent of employed who worked on their diary day. [4] Includes workers whose hours vary. [5] Full-time workers usually worked 35 or more hours per week at all jobs combined; part-time workers fewer than 35 hours per week. [6] For those 25 years old and over. [7] Includes persons with a high school diploma or equivalent.

Source: U.S. Bureau of Labor Statistics, *American Time Use Survey—2011 Results*, News Release, USDL 12-1246, June 2012. See also <http://www.bls.gov/tus/home.htm#news>.

Table 654. Average Hours Per Week Spent Doing Unpaid Household Work and Paid Work by Sex and Age: 2003 to 2007

[In hours. Data for persons in the civilian noninstitutionalized population 15 years old and over for 2003 through 2007. Unpaid household work is defined as activities that are unpaid, for which market substitutes exist, and done for one's own household]

Type of work	Total, 15 years and over	Age						
		15–24 years	25–34 years	35–44 years	45–54 years	55–64 years	65–74 years	75 years and over
MEN								
Total paid work and unpaid household work	**47.4**	**29.9**	**57.2**	**60.0**	**57.6**	**47.9**	**30.2**	**21.2**
Unpaid household work	15.9	8.9	15.8	18.3	17.0	17.8	19.9	18.1
Household activities	9.2	4.6	7.4	9.1	10.6	12.3	13.4	12.8
Food and drink preparation	1.9	0.8	1.7	2.2	2.1	2.2	2.3	3.0
Cleaning	1.2	0.9	1.2	1.3	1.2	1.2	1.2	1.4
Laundry and sewing	0.4	0.3	0.5	0.5	0.5	0.4	0.4	0.4
Household management	0.8	0.4	0.6	0.8	0.9	1.1	1.2	1.2
Lawn and garden care	1.9	0.5	1.0	1.5	2.2	3.2	3.9	3.6
Maintenance and repair	2.4	1.4	1.8	2.3	2.8	3.2	3.5	2.3
Caring for and helping household members	2.0	0.7	3.4	4.1	1.6	0.6	0.6	0.7
Purchasing goods and services	2.4	1.9	2.5	2.4	2.2	2.6	3.3	2.7
Travel related to unpaid household work	2.4	1.8	2.4	2.7	2.5	2.3	2.6	1.9
Paid work	31.4	20.9	41.4	41.7	40.6	30.1	10.3	3.1
WOMEN								
Total paid work and unpaid household work	**47.7**	**33.4**	**58.0**	**60.4**	**55.8**	**48.0**	**33.7**	**25.1**
Unpaid household work	26.7	15.9	31.7	33.1	26.7	26.2	28.1	23.8
Household activities	15.5	7.1	13.9	17.0	17.3	18.1	20.9	18.8
Food and drink preparation	5.3	2.2	5.3	6.1	5.6	5.9	7.0	6.4
Cleaning	4.0	2.3	4.2	4.4	4.0	4.3	5.0	4.5
Laundry and sewing	2.5	0.9	2.0	2.8	3.0	2.9	3.6	3.1
Household management	1.1	0.8	0.8	1.1	1.2	1.3	1.6	1.5
Lawn and garden care	0.9	0.2	0.5	0.8	1.1	1.5	1.7	1.6
Maintenance and repair	0.8	0.4	0.5	0.8	1.1	1.1	0.9	0.7
Caring for and helping household members	4.4	3.1	10.3	8.1	2.4	1.1	0.8	0.5
Purchasing goods and services	3.7	3.3	3.8	4.1	3.8	4.1	3.9	2.8
Travel related to unpaid household work	3.1	2.4	3.7	4.0	3.1	2.9	2.5	1.7
Paid work	21.0	17.4	26.3	27.3	29.1	21.8	5.7	1.2

Source: U.S. Bureau of Labor Statistics, "Measuring Time Spent in Unpaid Household Work: Results from the American Time Use Survey," Monthly Labor Review, July 2009, Vol. 132, No. 7, <http://www.bls.gov/opub/mlr/2009/07/contents.htm>.

Table 655. Annual Total Compensation and Wages and Salary Accruals Per Full-Time Equivalent Employee by Industry: 2000 to 2011

[In dollars. Wage and salary accruals include executives' compensation, bonuses, tips, and payments-in-kind; total compensation includes in addition to wages and salaries, employer contributions for social insurance, employer contributions to private and welfare funds, director's fees, jury and witness fees, etc. Based on the 2002 North American Industry Classification System (NAICS); see text, Section 15]

Industry	Total annual compensation				Annual salary and wages			
	2000	2005	2010	2011	2000	2005	2010	2011
Compensation of employees	47,059	56,620	66,249	68,129	39,243	45,729	53,237	54,710
Domestic industries	46,946	56,371	65,908	67,743	39,157	45,537	52,974	54,413
Private industries	45,772	54,139	62,664	64,560	38,862	44,717	51,896	53,463
Agriculture, forestry, fishing, and hunting	25,799	34,322	38,095	39,134	22,154	28,600	31,391	32,157
Mining	69,644	86,560	107,759	112,852	57,983	73,161	91,758	97,152
Utilities	80,304	104,284	125,731	130,881	64,742	77,409	89,571	93,558
Construction	46,145	53,139	64,252	65,825	38,563	43,948	52,733	53,748
Manufacturing	53,285	64,534	76,484	78,991	43,933	50,909	59,987	61,680
Wholesale trade	59,059	68,006	78,350	81,591	50,853	57,922	67,132	69,940
Retail trade	31,110	35,468	38,406	39,273	26,585	29,230	32,031	32,602
Transportation and warehousing	47,985	55,737	63,122	64,899	39,057	43,865	49,796	51,376
Information	71,023	83,067	98,823	103,654	62,582	68,330	81,298	84,864
Finance and insurance	75,339	92,949	105,348	109,561	64,561	77,981	88,112	91,904
Real estate and rental and leasing	43,195	50,768	57,954	60,274	37,146	43,708	49,041	51,131
Professional, scientific, and technical services	71,541	81,862	95,883	99,218	62,568	69,767	82,477	85,297
Management of companies and enterprises [1]	89,918	106,577	124,248	130,930	74,201	87,971	103,851	110,115
Administrative and waste management services	28,934	36,942	44,183	45,317	25,035	31,370	37,390	38,006
Educational services	34,085	41,730	49,465	50,778	29,243	34,844	41,377	42,405
Health care and social assistance	41,701	51,850	60,226	60,883	35,269	42,286	49,005	49,931
Arts, entertainment, and recreation	37,296	43,210	50,224	51,524	32,479	37,149	43,075	44,240
Accommodation and food services	20,801	24,809	28,055	28,776	18,047	21,018	24,282	24,875
Other services, except government	30,118	35,781	41,914	43,320	25,989	30,465	36,009	37,083
Government	53,344	68,229	81,870	83,896	40,767	49,894	58,279	59,229
Federal	69,842	99,230	122,321	125,455	46,470	64,184	76,252	77,414
State and local	48,707	60,161	71,063	72,673	39,164	46,174	53,476	54,319

[1] Consists of offices of bank and other holding companies and of corporate, subsidiary, and regional managing offices.

Source: U.S. Bureau of Economic Analysis, Survey of Current Business, April 2012. See also <http://www.bea.gov/itable/index.cfm>.

Table 656. Average Hourly and Weekly Earnings by Private Industry Group: 1990 to 2011

[In dollars. Average earnings include overtime. Data are for production employees in mining and logging, manufacturing, and construction, and nonsupervisory employees in the service providing industries. See headnote, Table 642]

Private industry group	Current dollars					Constant (1982–84) dollars [1]				
	1990	2000	2005	2010	2011	1990	2000	2005	2010	2011
AVERAGE HOURLY EARNINGS										
Total private	**10.20**	**14.02**	**16.13**	**19.07**	**19.47**	**7.91**	**8.30**	**8.45**	**8.91**	**8.79**
Mining and logging	13.40	16.55	18.72	23.82	24.51	10.39	9.80	9.80	11.13	11.06
Construction	13.42	17.48	19.46	23.22	23.64	10.40	10.35	10.19	10.85	10.67
Manufacturing	10.78	14.32	16.56	18.61	18.94	8.36	8.48	8.67	8.70	8.55
Trade, transportation, and utilities [2]	9.83	13.31	14.92	16.82	17.15	7.62	7.88	7.81	7.86	7.74
Information	13.40	19.07	22.06	25.87	26.61	10.39	11.29	11.55	12.09	12.01
Financial activities [2]	9.99	14.98	17.95	21.52	21.91	7.74	8.87	9.40	10.06	9.89
Professional and business services [2]	11.14	15.52	18.08	22.78	23.12	8.64	9.19	9.47	10.65	10.43
Education and health services [2]	10.00	13.95	16.71	20.12	20.78	7.75	8.26	8.75	9.40	9.38
Leisure and hospitality [2]	6.02	8.32	9.38	11.31	11.45	4.67	4.93	4.91	5.29	5.17
Other services	9.08	12.73	14.34	17.06	17.32	7.04	7.54	7.51	7.97	7.82
AVERAGE WEEKLY EARNINGS										
Total private	**350**	**481**	**544**	**637**	**655**	**271**	**285**	**285**	**298**	**296**
Mining and logging	603	735	854	1,063	1,144	467	435	447	497	516
Construction	513	686	750	892	922	398	406	393	417	416
Manufacturing	436	591	673	765	785	338	350	353	358	354
Trade, transportation, and utilities	332	450	498	560	578	257	266	261	262	261
Information	480	701	805	940	964	372	415	422	439	435
Financial activities [2]	355	537	645	778	798	275	318	338	364	360
Professional and business services [2]	381	535	619	799	814	295	317	324	373	367
Education and health services [2]	319	449	545	647	671	248	266	285	302	303
Leisure and hospitality [2]	156	217	241	281	284	121	129	126	131	128
Other services	298	413	443	524	532	231	245	232	245	240

[1] Earnings in current dollars divided by the Consumer Price Index (CPI-W) on a 1982–84 base; see text, Section 14. [2] For composition of industries, see Table 637.

Source: U.S. Bureau of Labor Statistics, Current Employment Statistics, "Employment, Hours, and Earnings—National." See also <http://www.bls.gov/ces/data.htm>.

Table 657. Mean Hourly Earnings and Weekly Hours by Selected Characteristics: 2010

[Based on the National Compensation Survey (NCS). Covers civilian workers in private industry establishments and state and local governments in the 50 states and D.C. Excludes private households, federal government and agriculture. The NCS obtained data from 35,408 establishments representing over 121 million workers. See source and Appendix III]

Item	Mean hourly earnings (dollars) [1]			Mean weekly hours [2]		
	Total	Private industry	State and local government	Total	Private industry	State and local government
Total	**21.29**	**20.47**	**26.08**	**35.1**	**34.9**	**36.2**
WORKER CHARACTERISTIC						
Management, professional and related	34.49	34.99	33.02	36.7	37.0	35.9
Management, business, and financial	38.81	39.42	35.32	39.3	39.7	37.4
Professional and related	32.55	32.57	32.50	35.6	35.7	35.6
Service	12.14	10.62	19.32	30.7	29.7	36.4
Sales and office	16.44	16.35	17.39	34.7	34.5	36.4
Sales and related	17.11	17.11	16.65	32.3	32.3	33.9
Office and administrative support	16.09	15.90	17.42	36.1	36.0	36.5
Natural resources, construction, and maintenance	21.21	21.24	20.97	39.0	39.0	38.8
Construction and extraction	21.18	21.31	20.13	39.0	39.0	38.7
Installation, maintenance, and repair	21.40	21.34	21.98	39.2	39.2	39.2
Production, transportation, and material moving	16.00	15.88	19.52	37.1	37.2	34.4
Production	16.26	16.18	21.69	38.9	38.8	39.5
Transportation and material moving	15.73	15.55	18.86	35.4	35.6	33.1
Full-time [3]	22.77	22.02	26.75	39.5	39.6	38.9
Part-time [3]	12.10	11.78	16.39	20.7	21.0	18.3
Union [4]	26.04	23.13	29.72	36.6	36.3	37.0
Nonunion	20.46	20.19	23.12	34.8	34.8	35.6
Time [5]	21.06	20.16	26.07	34.9	34.7	36.2
Incentive [5]	26.04	26.03	(S)	38.4	38.4	(S)
ESTABLISHMENT CHARACTERISTIC						
Goods producing [6]	(S)	22.04	(S)	(NA)	39.4	(NA)
Service providing [6]	(S)	20.09	(S)	(NA)	34.0	(NA)
1 to 49 workers	17.86	17.80	19.61	33.5	33.6	33.0
50 to 99 workers	19.24	19.10	21.40	34.3	34.2	35.8
100 to 499 workers	20.88	20.42	24.31	35.9	35.8	36.0
500 workers or more	27.02	26.65	27.68	36.9	37.0	36.7

NA Not available. S Figure does not meet publication standards. [1] Earnings are straight time hourly wages or salary, including incentive pay, cost-of-living adjustments, and hazard pay. Excludes premium pay for overtime, vacations and holidays, nonproduction bonuses and tips. [2] Mean weekly hours are the hours an employee is scheduled to work in a week exclusive of overtime [3] Based on definition used by each establishment. [4] Workers whose wages are determined through collective bargaining. [5] Time worker wages are based solely on an hourly rate or salary. Incentive workers wages are based at least in part on productivity payments such as piece rates or commissions. [6] For private industry only. See footnotes 3 and 4, Table 644, for composition of goods and service producing industries.

Source: U.S. Bureau of Labor Statistics, National Compensation Survey: Occupational Earnings in the United States, 2010, Bulletin 2753, May 2011. See also <http://www.bls.gov/ncs/ncswage2010.htm>.

Table 658. Employment and Wages: 2000 to 2010

[(7,879 represents 7,879,000). See headnote, Table 659]

Employment and wages	Unit	2000	2005	2006	2007	2008	2009	2010
Establishments:								
Total	1,000	7,879	8,571	8,784	8,972	9,082	9,003	8,993
Excluding federal	1,000	7,829	8,518	8,731	8,908	9,018	8,938	8,926
Private	1,000	7,622	8,295	8,505	8,681	8,789	8,709	8,696
State government	1,000	65	66	67	67	68	67	67
Local governments	1,000	141	157	159	160	161	161	164
Federal government	1,000	50	53	53	64	64	66	67
Average annual employment:								
Total	1,000	129,877	131,572	133,834	135,366	134,806	128,608	127,820
Excluding federal	1,000	127,006	128,838	131,105	132,640	132,044	125,781	124,840
Private	1,000	110,015	110,611	112,719	114,012	113,189	106,947	106,201
State government	1,000	4,370	4,528	4,566	4,611	4,643	4,640	4,606
Local governments	1,000	12,620	13,699	13,820	14,016	14,212	14,194	14,032
Federal government	1,000	2,871	2,734	2,729	2,726	2,762	2,827	2,981
Annual wages:								
Total	Bil. dol.	4,588	5,352	5,693	6,018	6,142	5,859	5,976
Excluding federal	Bil. dol.	4,455	5,188	5,523	5,841	5,959	5,668	5,769
Private	Bil. dol.	3,888	4,480	4,781	5,058	5,135	4,829	4,934
State government	Bil. dol.	159	191	200	212	223	226	226
Local governments	Bil. dol.	409	517	541	572	601	612	610
Federal government	Bil. dol.	133	164	170	177	183	192	206
Average annual wage per employee:								
Total	Dol.	35,323	40,677	42,535	44,458	45,563	45,559	46,751
Excluding federal	Dol.	35,077	40,270	42,124	44,038	45,129	45,060	46,215
Private	Dol.	35,337	40,505	42,414	44,362	45,371	45,155	46,455
State government	Dol.	36,296	42,249	43,875	45,903	47,980	48,742	48,960
Local governments	Dol.	32,387	37,718	39,179	40,790	42,274	43,140	43,493
Federal government	Dol.	46,228	59,864	62,274	64,871	66,293	67,756	69,198
Average weekly wage per employee:								
Total	Dol.	679	782	818	855	876	876	899
Excluding federal	Dol.	675	774	810	847	868	867	889
Private	Dol.	680	779	816	853	873	868	893
State government	Dol.	698	812	844	883	923	937	942
Local governments	Dol.	623	725	753	784	813	830	836
Federal government	Dol.	889	1,151	1,198	1,248	1,275	1,303	1,331

Source: U.S. Bureau of Labor Statistics, "Employment and Wages Annual Averages, 2010," <http://www.bls.gov/cew/cewbultn10.htm>.

Table 659. Average Annual Wage, by State: 2009 and 2010

[In dollars, except percent change. Based on federal-state cooperative program, The Quarterly Census of Employment and Wages (QCEW), also referenced as ES-202. Includes workers covered by state unemployment insurance laws and for federal civilian workers covered by unemployment compensation for federal employees, approximately 97 percent of employees on nonfarm payrolls in 2010. Excludes most agricultural workers on small farms, all Armed Forces, elected officials in most states, railroad employees, most domestic workers, most student workers at school, value of meals and lodging, and tips and other gratuities. Minus sign (–) indicates decrease]

State	Average wage per employee 2009	Average wage per employee 2010	Percent change, 2009–2010	State	Average wage per employee 2009	Average wage per employee 2010	Percent change, 2009–2010
United States	**45,559**	**46,751**	**2.62**	Missouri	40,022	40,679	1.64
Alabama	39,422	40,289	2.20	Montana	33,762	34,596	2.47
Alaska	47,103	48,230	2.39	Nebraska	36,644	37,324	1.85
Arizona	42,832	43,299	1.09	Nevada	42,743	42,512	-0.54
Arkansas	35,692	36,254	1.58	New Hampshire	44,932	45,957	2.28
California	51,566	53,285	3.33	New Jersey	55,168	56,382	2.20
Colorado	46,861	47,868	2.15	New Mexico	38,529	39,264	1.91
Connecticut	57,771	59,465	2.93	New York	57,739	60,291	4.42
Delaware	47,770	48,669	1.88	North Carolina	39,844	41,119	3.20
District of Columbia	77,483	80,200	3.51	North Dakota	35,970	38,128	6.00
Florida	40,970	41,581	1.49	Ohio	40,900	41,788	2.17
Georgia	42,902	43,899	2.32	Oklahoma	37,238	38,237	2.68
Hawaii	41,328	41,709	0.92	Oregon	40,757	41,675	2.25
Idaho	34,124	34,900	2.27	Pennsylvania	44,829	45,733	2.02
Illinois	48,358	49,497	2.36	Rhode Island	43,439	44,645	2.78
Indiana	38,270	39,256	2.58	South Carolina	36,759	37,553	2.16
Iowa	37,158	38,146	2.66	South Dakota	33,352	34,331	2.93
Kansas	38,154	38,936	2.05	Tennessee	40,242	41,572	3.31
Kentucky	37,996	38,720	1.90	Texas	45,692	46,952	2.76
Louisiana	40,579	41,461	2.17	Utah	38,614	39,389	2.01
Maine	36,617	37,338	1.97	Vermont	38,778	39,434	1.69
Maryland	50,579	51,739	2.29	Virginia	48,239	49,651	2.93
Massachusetts	56,267	57,770	2.67	Washington	47,470	48,516	2.20
Michigan	43,645	44,439	1.82	West Virginia	36,897	37,675	2.11
Minnesota	45,319	46,787	3.24	Wisconsin	39,131	39,966	2.13
Mississippi	33,847	34,343	1.47	Wyoming	40,709	41,963	3.08

Source: U.S. Bureau of Labor Statistics, "Employment and Wages Online Annual Averages, 2010," <http://www.bls.gov/cew/cewbultn10.htm>.

Table 660. Full-Time Wage and Salary Workers—Number and Earnings: 2000 to 2011

[In current dollars of usual weekly earnings. Data represent annual averages (101,210 represents 101,210,000). Full time workers are those who usually worked 35 hours or more at all jobs combined. Based on the Current Population Survey; see text, Section 1 and Appendix III. For definition of median, see Guide to Tabular Presentation]

Characteristic	Number of workers (1,000)			Median weekly earnings (dollars)		
	2000	2005 [1]	2011 [1]	2000	2005 [1]	2011 [1]
All workers [2].........................	**101,210**	**103,560**	**100,457**	**576**	**651**	**756**
Male.....................................	57,107	58,406	55,971	641	722	832
Female..................................	44,103	45,154	44,486	493	585	684
White [3]................................	83,228	84,110	81,336	590	672	775
Black [3, 4]..............................	12,410	12,388	11,604	474	520	615
Asian [3, 4].............................	4,598	4,651	5,197	615	753	866
Hispanic [5].............................	12,761	14,673	15,147	399	471	549
OCCUPATION						
Management, professional and related occupations..............	34,831	36,908	39,791	810	937	1,082
Management, business, and financial operations..............	14,240	14,977	16,061	877	997	1,160
Professional and related occupations.............................	20,590	21,931	23,730	770	902	1,029
Computer and mathematical occupations.....................	3,051	2,924	3,296	938	1,132	1,305
Architecture and engineering occupations.....................	2,781	2,509	2,494	949	1,105	1,315
Life, physical, and social science occupations..................	989	1,164	1,043	811	965	1,108
Community and social services occupations..................	1,641	1,797	1,931	629	725	813
Legal occupations.......................	1,039	1,162	1,259	919	1,052	1,277
Education, training, and library occupations...................	5,467	6,066	6,518	704	798	919
Arts, design, entertainment, sports, and media..............	1,488	1,488	1,464	724	819	929
Healthcare practitioner and technical occupations.............	4,134	4,821	5,725	727	878	995
Service occupations......................	12,595	14,123	14,378	365	413	486
Healthcare support occupations...........	1,731	2,085	2,190	358	410	487
Protective service occupations...........	2,281	2,549	2,798	591	678	757
Food preparation and serving-related occupations.............	3,483	4,007	3,930	317	356	409
Building and grounds cleaning and maintenance...............	3,354	3,425	3,339	351	394	465
Personal care and service occupations.....	1,746	2,057	2,121	351	409	453
Sales and office occupations...............	25,606	25,193	22,989	492	575	638
Sales and related occupations............	9,650	10,031	9,294	525	622	670
Office and administrative support occupations.............	15,956	15,161	13,695	480	550	623
Natural resources, construction, and maintenance occupations..............	10,958	12,086	9,965	582	623	732
Farming, fishing, and forestry occupations.....................	842	755	775	310	372	430
Construction and extraction occupations.........................	5,852	6,826	5,031	580	604	717
Installation, maintenance, and repair occupations..............	4,263	4,504	4,159	628	705	806
Production, transportation, and material-moving occupations..............	17,221	15,251	13,333	475	540	609
Production occupations...................	10,378	8,403	7,058	471	538	605
Transportation and material-moving occupations................	6,843	6,848	6,275	481	543	614

[1] See footnote 2, Table 596. [2] Includes other races, not shown separately. [3] Beginning 2005, for persons in this race group only. See footnote 4, Table 597. [4] 2000, includes Pacific Islanders. [5] Persons of Hispanic origin may be any race.

Source: U.S. Bureau of Labor Statistics, "Employment and Earnings Online," January 2012 issue, March 2012, <http://www.bls.gov/opub/ee/home.htm> and <http://www.bls.gov/cps/home.htm>.

Table 661. Median Usual Weekly Earnings of Full-Time Wage and Salary Workers, by Sex and Education: 1980 to 2011

[In current dollars, except as indicated. For wage and salary workers 25 years and over. Based on Current Population Survey; see text, Section 1 and Appendix III. Wages and salaries are collected before taxes and other deductions and include overtime pay, commissions, or tips usually received at principal job. Earnings reported on basis other than weekly are converted to a weekly equivalent. Excludes all incorporated and unincorporated self employed]

Year and sex	Total	Less than a high school diploma	High school, no college [1]	Some college or associate's degree	Bachelor's degree and higher [2]
CURRENT DOLLARS					
Male:					
1980..............................	339	267	327	358	427
1990 [3]...........................	512	349	459	542	741
2000 [3]...........................	693	406	591	691	1,020
2011 [3]...........................	866	488	720	840	1,332
Female:					
1980..............................	213	164	201	231	290
1990 [3]...........................	369	240	315	395	535
2000 [3]...........................	516	304	420	505	756
2011 [3]...........................	718	395	554	645	998
WOMEN'S EARNINGS AS PERCENT OF MEN'S					
1980..............................	62.8	61.4	61.5	64.5	67.9
1990 [3]...........................	72.1	68.8	68.6	72.9	72.2
2000 [3]...........................	74.5	74.9	71.1	73.1	74.1
2011 [3]...........................	82.9	80.9	76.9	76.8	74.9

[1] Includes persons with a high school diploma or equivalent. [2] Includes persons with a bachelor's, master's, professional, or doctoral degree. [3] Data not strictly comparable to data for earlier years. See text this section and <http://www.bls.gov/cps/eetech_methods.pdf>.

Source: U.S. Bureau of Labor Statistics, Labor Force Statistcs from the Current Population Survey, <http://www.bls.gov/cps/earnings.htm> database accessed Aug. 2012.

Table 662. Workers With Earnings by Occupation of Longest Held Job and Sex: 2010

[As of March. 72,118 represents 72,118,000. For definition of median, see Guide to Tabular Presentation. Beginning with 2009 income data, the Census Bureau expanded the income intervals used to calculate medians to $250,000 or more. Medians falling in the upper open-ended interval are plugged with "$250,000." Before 2009, the upper open-ended interval was $100,000 and a plug of "$100,000" was used. Based on Annual Social and Economic Supplement (ASEC) of Current Population Survey; includes Civilian noninstitutional population, 15 years old and over, and military personnel who live in households with at least one other civilian adult. See text, Section 1, and Appendix III]

Major occupation group of longest job held in 2010	All workers				Full-time, year-round			
	Female		Male		Female		Male	
	Number (1,000)	Median earnings (dol.)	Number (1,000)	Median earnings (dol.)	Number (1,000)	Median earnings (dol.)	Number (1,000)	Median earnings (dol.)
Total............................	**72,118**	**26,552**	**81,180**	**36,676**	**42,834**	**36,931**	**56,412**	**47,715**
Management, business, and financial occupations.......................	9,697	46,909	12,760	65,479	7,607	52,236	10,708	72,013
Professional and related occupations................................	19,027	40,698	13,850	59,788	12,069	49,244	10,681	67,339
Service occupations...........................	15,646	14,829	12,111	20,306	7,031	22,906	6,695	31,433
Sales and office occupations...............	8,617	23,889	13,603	31,811	13,318	32,248	9,442	42,165
Natural resources, construction, and maintenance.................	718	19,347	14,146	31,399	398	30,804	9,894	40,884
Production, transportation, and material-moving occupations..............	4,003	20,180	13,964	29,835	2,347	25,548	9,527	36,620
Armed Forces...............................	90	37,170	746	42,745	78	50,597	649	46,953

Source: U.S. Census Bureau, *Income, Poverty and Health Insurance in the United States: 2010*, Current Population Reports, P60-239, and Detailed Tables—Table PINC-06, September 2011. See also <http://www.census.gov/hhes/www/income/data/incpovhlth/2010/index.html>.

Table 663. Employment Cost Index (ECI) by Total Compensation and Occupation and Industry: 2008 to 2011

[As of December (2005 = 100). The ECI is a measure of the rate of change in compensation (wages, salaries, and employer costs for employee benefits). Data are not seasonally adjusted. Based on North American Industry Classification System (NAICS) for classifying by industry. Based on the 2000 Standard Occupational Classification (SOC) for classifying by occupation]

Occupational group and industry	Indexes (December 2005 = 100)				Percent change for 12 months ending December			
	2008	2009	2010	2011	2008	2009	2010	2011
Civilian workers [1]............................	**109.5**	**111.0**	**113.2**	**115.5**	**2.6**	**1.4**	**2.0**	**2.0**
State and local government.........................	**111.6**	**114.2**	**116.2**	**117.7**	**3.0**	**2.3**	**1.8**	**1.3**
Workers, by occupational group:								
Management, professional and related occupations...	111.6	113.8	115.5	116.9	3.0	2.0	1.5	1.2
Sales and office occupations.............................	111.3	114.4	116.6	118.4	2.5	2.8	1.9	1.5
Service occupations....................................	112.4	115.3	118.0	119.5	3.0	2.6	2.3	1.3
Workers, by industry division:								
Service-providing industries: [2]								
Education and health services..........................	111.5	113.9	115.6	117.0	3.0	2.2	1.5	1.2
Schools..	111.2	113.7	115.3	116.5	3.0	2.2	1.4	1.0
Health care and social assistance......................	113.2	115.4	117.9	120.1	3.6	1.9	2.2	1.9
Hospitals..	111.3	114.3	117.0	119.2	2.9	2.7	2.4	1.9
Public administration [3].............................	112.0	114.6	116.8	118.2	2.7	2.3	1.9	1.2
Private industry workers [4]........................	**108.9**	**110.2**	**112.5**	**115.0**	**2.4**	**1.2**	**2.1**	**2.2**
Workers, by occupational group:								
Management, professional, and related occupations...	109.9	110.7	113.0	115.4	2.9	0.7	2.1	2.1
Sales and office occupations.............................	107.9	109.2	111.6	114.2	1.7	1.2	2.2	2.3
Natural resources, construction, and maintenance occupations.........................	109.6	111.2	113.3	115.8	2.7	1.5	1.9	2.2
Production, transportation, and material moving occupations................................	106.9	108.9	111.5	114.2	2.3	1.9	2.4	2.4
Service occupations....................................	109.8	111.8	113.5	115.4	2.6	1.8	1.5	1.7
Workers, by industry division:								
Goods-producing industries [5].........................	107.5	108.6	111.1	113.8	2.4	1.0	2.3	2.4
Construction......................................	110.9	111.7	112.7	114.5	3.1	0.7	0.9	1.6
Manufacturing.....................................	105.9	107.0	110.0	113.1	2.0	1.0	2.8	2.8
Service-providing industries [2]........................	109.4	110.8	113.0	115.3	2.5	1.3	2.0	2.0
Trade, transportation, and utilities......................	107.5	108.8	111.4	114.1	1.9	1.2	2.4	2.4
Information..	107.4	108.3	110.0	112.5	1.2	0.8	1.6	2.3
Financial activities.................................	107.1	108.6	111.4	114.2	1.4	1.4	2.6	2.5
Professional and business services...................	111.6	112.4	114.6	117.1	3.8	0.7	2.0	2.2
Education and health services.......................	110.6	112.8	114.7	116.5	2.7	2.0	1.7	1.6
Leisure and hospitality.............................	111.4	112.7	114.1	115.2	3.1	1.2	1.2	1.0
Bargaining status:								
Union...	108.0	111.1	114.8	117.9	2.8	2.9	3.3	2.7
Nonunion..	109.1	110.1	112.1	114.5	2.4	0.9	1.8	2.1

[1] Includes private industry and state and local government workers and excludes farm, household, and federal government workers. [2] Includes all other service industries not shown seperately. For a description of NAICS industries, see text, this section. [3] Consists of executive, legislative, judicial, administrative, and regulatory activities. [4] Excludes farm and household workers. [5] Includes the following NAICS industries: construction and manufacturing.

Source: U.S. Bureau of Labor Statistics, "Employment Cost Index Historical Listing Current-Dollar," <http://www.bls.gov/ncs/ect/home.htm>.

Table 664. Federal and State Minimum Wage Rates: 1940 to 2012

[In current dollars. Where an employee is subject to both the state and federal minimum wage laws, the employee is entitled to the higher minimum wage rate]

Year	Federal minimum wage rates per hour	State	2012 minimum wage rates per hour	State	2012 minimum wage rates per hour	State	2012 minimum wage rates per hour
1940	0.30	AL	(¹)	KY	7.25	ND	7.25
1945	0.40	AK	7.75	LA	(¹)	OH	7.70 [8]
1950	0.75	AZ	7.65	ME	7.50	OK	7.25/2.00 [9]
1955	0.75	AR	6.25 [2]	MD	7.25	OR	8.50
1960	1.00	CA	8.00	MA	8.00	PA	7.25
1965	1.25	CO	7.64	MI	7.40 [4]	RI	7.40
1970	1.60	CT	8.25	MN	6.15/5.25 [5]	SC	(¹)
1975	2.10	DE	7.25	MS	(¹)	SD	7.25
1980	3.10	DC	8.25	MO	7.25	TN	(¹)
1985	3.35	FL	7.67	MT	7.65 [6]	TX	7.25
1990	3.80	GA	5.15 [3]	NE	7.25 [2]	UT	7.25
1995	4.25	HI	7.25	NV	7.25/8.25 [7]	VT	8.46 [2]
2000	5.15	ID	7.25	NH	7.25	VA	7.25 [2]
2005	5.15	IL	8.25 [2]	NJ	7.25	WA	9.04
2007	5.85	IN	7.25 [4]	NM	7.50	WV	7.25 [3]
2008	6.55	IA	7.25	NY	7.25	WI	7.25
2009	7.25	KS	7.25	NC	7.25	WY	5.15
2010	7.25						
2011	7.25						
2012	7.25						

[1] No state minimum wage law. [2] Employers of 4 or more, Illinois excluding family members. [3] Employers of 6 or more. [4] Employers of 2 or more. [5] Large employer (receipts of $625,000 or more) and small employer (with annual receipts of less than $625,000). [6] Except businesses with gross annual sales of $110,000 or less. [7] $8.25 with no health insurance benefits provided by employer. $7.25 with health insurance provided by employer and received by employee. [8] $7.25 for those employers grossing $271,000 or less. [9] Employees of 10 or more full time employees at any one location and employers with gross sales over $100,000 regardless of number of full-time employees. All other employers $2.00.

Source: U.S. Department of Labor, Wage and Hour Division, "Minimum Wage Laws in the States—January 1, 2012," <http://www.dol.gov/esa/minwage/america.htm>.

Table 665. Workers Paid Hourly Rates by Selected Characteristics: 2011

[Data are annual averages (73,926 represents 73,926,000). For employed wage and salary workers, excluding the incorporated self-employed. Based on the Current Population Survey; see text, Section 1 and Appendix III]

Characteristic	Number of workers paid hourly rates (1,000)				Percent of workers paid hourly rates			
		At or below federal minimum wage				At or below federal minimum wage		
	Total	Total	Below prevailing federal minimum wage	At prevailing federal minimum wage	Total	Total	Below prevailing federal minimum wage	At prevailing federal minimum wage
Total, 16 years and over [1]	73,926	3,829	2,152	1,677	5.2	2.9	2.3	
16 to 24 years	14,436	1,896	1,003	893	13.1	6.9	6.2	
25 years and over	59,490	1,933	1,149	784	3.2	1.9	1.3	
Male, 16 years old and over	36,457	1,433	785	648	3.9	2.2	1.8	
16 to 24 years	7,290	787	399	388	10.8	5.5	5.3	
25 years and over	29,167	647	387	260	2.2	1.3	0.9	
Female, 16 years old and over	37,469	2,395	1,366	1,029	6.4	3.6	2.7	
16 to 24 years	7,147	1,109	604	505	15.5	8.5	7.1	
25 years and over	30,323	1,286	762	524	4.2	2.5	1.7	
White [2]	59,314	3,006	1,748	1,258	5.1	2.9	2.1	
Men	29,743	1,108	624	484	3.7	2.1	1.6	
Women	29,571	1,898	1,124	774	6.4	3.8	2.6	
Black [2]	9,523	577	253	324	6.1	2.7	3.4	
Men	4,252	222	105	117	5.2	2.5	2.8	
Women	5,271	356	148	208	6.8	2.8	3.9	
Asian [2]	3,037	99	63	36	3.3	2.1	1.2	
Men	1,425	41	28	13	2.9	2.0	0.9	
Women	1,612	58	35	23	3.6	2.2	1.4	
Hispanic [3]	13,264	720	380	340	5.4	2.9	2.6	
Men	7,703	326	172	154	4.2	2.2	2.0	
Women	5,561	394	208	186	7.1	3.7	3.3	
Full-time workers	53,594	1,274	752	522	2.4	1.4	1.0	
Men	29,292	501	296	205	1.7	1.0	0.7	
Women	24,302	773	456	317	3.2	1.9	1.3	
Part-time workers [4]	20,199	2,545	1,392	1,153	12.6	6.9	5.7	
Men	7,103	932	489	443	13.1	6.9	6.2	
Women	13,096	1,615	904	711	12.3	6.9	5.4	
Private sector industries	64,525	3,625	2,048	1,577	5.6	3.2	2.4	
Public sector industries	9,401	204	104	100	2.2	1.1	1.1	

[1] Includes races not shown separately. Also includes a small number of multiple jobholders whose full- or part-time status cannot be determined for their principal job. [2] For persons in this race group only. See footnote 4, Table 597. [3] Persons of Hispanic or Latino origin may be any race. [4] Working fewer than 35 hours per week.

Source: U.S. Bureau of Labor Statistics, CPS Reports and Summaries, "Characteristics of Minimum Wage Workers: 2011," March 2012, <http://www.bls.gov/cps/minwage2011.htm>.

Table 666. Employer Costs for Employee Compensation Per Hour Worked: 2011

[In dollars. As of December. Based on the National Compensation Survey (NCS). See Appendix III]

Compensation component	Total civilian workers	State and local government workers	Private Industry workers						
			Total	Goods producing [1]	Service providing [2]	Union workers	Non-union workers	1–99 workers	100 workers or more
Total compensation	**30.45**	**40.90**	**28.57**	**33.64**	**27.54**	**38.23**	**27.58**	**23.68**	**34.30**
Wages and salaries	21.14	26.75	20.14	22.40	19.68	23.04	19.84	17.50	23.23
Total benefits	9.30	14.16	8.43	11.24	7.86	15.19	7.74	6.18	11.07
Paid leave	2.13	3.02	1.97	2.19	1.92	2.76	1.89	1.36	2.68
Vacation	1.03	1.13	1.01	1.16	0.98	1.41	0.97	0.69	1.39
Holiday	0.65	0.88	0.61	0.77	0.58	0.81	0.59	0.44	0.80
Sick	0.33	0.78	0.25	0.19	0.26	0.39	0.23	0.16	0.35
Supplemental pay	0.73	0.33	0.80	1.34	0.70	1.18	0.77	0.52	1.14
Overtime [3]	0.24	0.17	0.25	0.54	0.19	0.72	0.20	0.17	0.33
Insurance	2.70	4.89	2.31	3.15	2.14	5.21	2.01	1.61	3.13
Health insurance	2.56	4.73	2.17	2.97	2.01	4.91	1.89	1.52	2.94
Retirement and savings	1.39	3.41	1.02	1.64	0.90	2.85	0.84	0.60	1.52
Defined benefit	0.83	3.08	0.43	0.95	0.33	2.08	0.26	0.21	0.69
Defined contributions	0.55	0.33	0.59	0.70	0.57	0.77	0.58	0.39	0.83
Legally required	2.36	2.51	2.33	2.92	2.21	3.18	2.24	2.10	2.60
Social Security and Medicare	1.71	1.88	1.67	1.90	1.63	2.01	1.64	1.44	1.95
Social Security [4]	1.36	1.46	1.34	1.52	1.31	1.62	1.31	1.16	1.56
Medicare	0.35	0.43	0.33	0.37	0.32	0.39	0.33	0.28	0.39
Federal unemployment	0.02	[5]	0.02	0.02	0.03	0.02	0.02	0.03	0.02
State unemployment	0.20	0.13	0.21	0.29	0.20	0.28	0.21	0.22	0.21
Workers' compensation	0.43	0.50	0.41	0.71	0.35	0.86	0.37	0.41	0.42

– Represents or rounds to zero. [1] Based on the North American Industry Classification System, 2002 (NAICS). See text, this section. Includes mining, construction, and manufacturing. The agriculture, forestry, farming, and hunting sector is excluded. [2] Based on the 2002 NAICS. Includes utilities; wholesale and retail trade; transportation and warehousing; information; finance and insurance; real estate and rental and leasing; professional and technical services; management of companies and enterprises, administrative and waste services; education services; health care and social assistance; arts, entertainment, and recreation; accommodations and food services; and other services, except public administration. [3] Includes premium pay for work in addition to regular work schedule, such as, overtime, weekends, and holidays. [4] Comprises the Old-Age, Survivors, and Disability Insurance Program (OASDI). [5] Cost per hour worked is $0.01 or less.

Source: U.S. Bureau of Labor Statistics, *Employer Costs for Employee Compensation—December 2011*, News Release, USDL 12-0450, March 2012. See also <http://www.bls.gov/schedule/archives/ecec_nr.htm#2011>.

Table 667. Percent of Workers in Private Industry With Access to Retirement and Health Care Benefits by Selected Characteristics: 2011

[In percent (All workers = 100 percent). As of March. Based on National Compensation Survey (NCS). See headnote, Table 668, and Appendix III]

Characteristic	Retirement benefits			Healthcare benefits			
	All plans [1]	Defined benefit [2]	Defined contribution [2]	Medical care	Dental care	Vision care	Outpatient prescription coverage
Total	**64**	**20**	**58**	**69**	**45**	**26**	**68**
WORKER CHARACTERISTICS							
Management, professional, and related occupations	80	27	75	87	61	36	85
Service occupations	40	8	36	42	25	15	41
Sales and office occupations	69	18	64	71	45	23	69
Natural resources, construction, and maintenance occupations	62	24	54	75	43	29	73
Production, transportation, and material moving occupations	66	24	55	75	47	29	74
Full-time [3]	73	23	68	85	56	32	84
Part-time [3]	37	10	31	23	14	9	22
Union [4]	90	70	53	92	72	57	90
Nonunion [4]	61	14	59	67	42	23	66
AVERAGE HOURLY WAGE [5]							
Less than $8.25	39	7	35	36	18	10	34
$8.25 to under $10.69	28	5	25	20	11	7	20
$10.69 to under$15.87	66	15	61	74	46	24	73
$15.87 to under $24.81	74	24	66	85	55	31	83
$24.81 to under $37.89	84	37	77	91	66	42	89
$37.89 or greater	87	38	82	93	71	44	91
ESTABLISHMENT CHARACTERISTIC							
1 to 99 workers	49	9	46	56	29	17	55
100 or more workers	81	32	73	84	64	36	83
Goods producing [6]	73	28	66	85	54	32	83
Service producing [6]	62	18	57	66	43	25	65

[1] Employees may have access to both defined benefit and defined contribution plans. Total excludes duplication. [2] A defined benefit plan is a retirement plan that uses a specific, predetermined formula to calculate the amount of an employee's guaranteed future benefit. A defined contribution plan is a type of retirement plan in which the employer makes specified contributions to individual employee accounts, but the amount of the retirement benefit is not specified. [3] Employees are classified as working either a full-time or part-time schedule based on the definition used by each establishment. [4] See footnote 6, Table 668. [5] The National Compensation Survey—Benefits program presents wage data in percentiles rather than dollar amounts; for calculation detail, see "Technical Note" in source. [6] See Table 644 for composition of goods- and service-producing industries.

Source: U.S. Bureau of Labor Statistics, *Employee Benefits in the United States, March 2011*, News Release, USDL 11-1112, July 2011. See also <http://www.bls.gov/ncs/ebs/home.htm>.

Table 668. Percent of Workers In Private Industry With Access to Selected Employee Benefits: 2011

[As of March. Based on National Compensation Survey (NCS). The NCS benefits survey obtained data from 8,727 private industry establishments of all sizes, representing over 100 million workers. Excludes agricultural establishments, private households, and the self-employed. An employee has access to a benefit plan if the plan is made available by the employer, regardless of whether the employee participates in the plan. See Appendix III]

Characteristic	Leave benefits						Quality of life benefits			Nonproduction bonuses	
					Family leave [1]		Employer assistance for child care [2]	Flexible workplace [3]	Subsidized commuting [4]	All non-production bonuses [5]	End of year bonus
	Paid holidays	Paid sick leave	Paid vacation	Paid jury duty leave	Paid	Unpaid					
Total	**77**	**63**	**77**	**66**	**11**	**85**	**9**	**5**	**5**	**44**	**11**
WORKER CHARACTERISTIC											
Management, professional, and related occupations	89	86	87	83	19	89	17	13	11	52	13
Service occupations	53	43	58	46	7	79	8	(Z)	2	29	6
Sales and office occupations	81	66	79	69	11	87	6	5	5	47	12
Natural resources, construction, and maintenance occupations	79	51	80	54	8	78	3	1	3	45	13
Production, transportation, and material moving occupations	84	54	83	67	6	85	4	1	2	43	10
Full-time [6]	90	75	91	75	13	88	10	6	7	50	12
Part-time [6]	40	27	37	38	6	75	6	2	2	27	5
Union [7]	89	71	90	86	10	91	14	1	6	37	4
Nonunion [7]	76	62	76	64	11	84	8	5	5	44	11
AVERAGE HOURLY WAGE [8]											
Less than $8.25	51	32	51	41	5	77	4	(Z)	1	29	6
$8.25 to under $10.69	34	21	38	32	4	74	5	–	1	24	6
$10.69 to under $15.87	85	66	84	70	10	86	7	2	4	46	10
$15.87 to under $24.81	89	74	90	75	12	87	9	6	6	48	13
$24.81 to under $37.89	90	85	89	84	19	90	16	13	11	55	14
$37.89 or greater	90	87	90	86	21	91	18	17	14	58	15
ESTABLISHMENT CHARACTERISTIC											
Goods producing [9]	88	56	88	68	9	86	7	4	3	51	14
Service producing [9]	75	64	75	65	11	84	9	5	6	42	10
GEOGRAPHIC AREA [10]											
New England	75	70	75	77	12	87	9	7	9	43	8
Middle Atlantic	80	67	76	76	10	82	9	7	7	43	11
East North Central	79	58	78	66	11	83	11	5	4	45	12
West North Central	74	61	78	61	10	87	8	5	4	43	12
South Atlantic	77	60	79	66	11	83	8	5	4	46	10
East South Central	79	58	78	68	7	91	–	4	3	47	9
West South Central	80	64	80	64	13	85	9	4	4	46	11
Mountain	75	63	77	60	9	84	7	4	6	47	11
Pacific	73	65	75	56	12	86	9	5	9	37	11

NA Not available. Z Less than 0.5 percent. (-) Dash indicates no workers in this category or data did not meet publication criteria. [1] Some workers may have access to both types of plans. [2] A workplace program that provides for either the full or partial cost of caring for an employee's children in a nursery, day care center, or a baby sitter in facilities either on or off the employer's premises. [3] Permits employees to set their own schedules within a general set of parameters. Employees generally are required to work a minimum number of core hours each day. [4] Employers subsidize employees' cost of commuting to and from work via public transportation, company-sponsored van pool, discounted subway fares, for example. [5] All nonproduction bonuses include cash profit sharing bonuses, employee recognition bonuses, holiday bonuses, end of year bonuses, referral bonuses, and other bonuses. [6] Employees are classified as working either a full-time or part-time schedule based on the definition used by each establishment. [7] Union workers are those whose wages are determined through collective bargaining. [8] The National Compensation Survey—Benefits program presents wage data in percentiles rather than dollar amounts; see "Technical Note" in source. [9] See Table 644, for composition of goods- and service-producing industries. [10] Composition of divisions: New England = Connecticut, Maine, Massachusetts, New Hampshire, Rhode Island, and Vermont; Middle Atlantic = New Jersey, New York, and Pennsylvania; East North Central = Illinois, Indiana, Michigan, Ohio, and Wisconsin; West North Central = Iowa, Kansas, Minnesota, Missouri, Nebraska, North Dakota, and South Dakota; South Atlantic = Delaware, District of Columbia, Florida, Georgia, Maryland, North Carolina, South Carolina, Virginia, and West Virginia; East South Central = Alabama, Kentucky, Mississippi, and Tennessee; West South Central = Arkansas, Louisiana, Oklahoma, and Texas; Mountain = Arizona, Colorado, Idaho, Montana, Nevada, New Mexico, Utah, and Wyoming; and Pacific = Alaska, California, Hawaii, Oregon, and Washington.

Source: U.S. Bureau of Labor Statistics, *Employee Benefits in the United States, March 2011*, Bulletin 2771, September 2011. See also <http://www.bls.gov/ncs/ebs/benefits/2011/>.

Table 669. Industries With the Highest Total Case Incidence Rates for Nonfatal Injuries and Illnesses: 2010

[Rates per 100 full-time employees. Private industry unless otherwise noted. Incidence rates refer to any Occupational Safety & Health Administration (OSHA)-recordable occupational injury or illness, whether or not it resulted in days away from work, job transfer, or restriction. Incidence rates were calculated as: number of injuries and illnesses divided by total hours worked by all employees during the year multiplied by 200,000 as base for 100 full-time equivalent workers (working 40 hours per week, 50 weeks per year)]

Industry	2007 NAICS code [1]	Inci- dence rate	Industry	2007 NAICS code [1]	Inci- dence rate
All Industries, including State and local... government [2]	**(X)**	**3.8**			
			Elevator and moving stairway manufacturing.....	333921	9.5
Nursing and residential care facilities [4]..........	623	15.3	Other concrete product manufacturing.............	32739	9.5
Fire protection [3]...............................	92216	13.6	Heavy and civil engineering construction [3].......	237	9.4
Travel trailer and camper manufacturing.........	336214	13.1	Light truck and utility vehicle manufacturing.......	336112	9.4
Iron foundries.................................	331511	12.7	Veterinary services.............................	54194	9.3
Hospitals [4]....................................	622	11.3	Ship building and repairing......................	336611	9.1
Skiing facilities...............................	71392	11.1	Iron and steel forging..........................	332111	9.0
Nursing and residential care facilities [3]..........	623	11.0	Aluminum foundries (except die-casting)..........	331524	8.9
Police protection [3]............................	92212	10.5	Animal (except poultry) slaughtering.............	311611	8.6
Aluminum die-casting foundries.................	331521	10.2	Scheduled passenger air transportation..........	481111	8.6
Ambulance services...........................	62191	10.0	Soft drink manufacturing........................	312111	8.5
Steel foundries (except investment).............	331513	9.9	Nursing care facilities..........................	6231	8.4
Sugar manufacturing...........................	31131	10.1	Pet and pet supplies stores.....................	45391	8.4

X Not applicable [1] Based on the North American Industry Classification System, 2007 (NAICS). See text, this section. [2] Excludes farms with fewer than 11 employees. [3] Local Government. [4] State Government.

Source: U.S. Bureau of Labor Statistics, News Release, *Industry Injury and Illness Data-2010*, Supplemental News Release Tables SNR01, October 2011. See also <http://www.bls.gov/iif/oshsum.htm>.

Table 670. Nonfatal Occupational Injuries and Illnesses by Industry: 2010

[3,883.6 represents 3,883,600. Rates per 100 full-time employees. Except as noted, data refer to any Occupational Safety and Health Administration (OSHA) recordable occupational injury or illness, whether or not it resulted in days away from work, job transfer, or restriction. Incidence rates were calculated as: number of injuries and illnesses divided by total hours worked by all employees during the year multiplied by 200,000 as base for 100 full-time equivalent workers (working 40 hours, per week, 50 weeks per year)]

Industry	2007 NAICS code [1]	Annual average employment [2]	Number of cases (1,000)	Incidence rate of cases
Total [3]...	**(X)**	**124,868.5**	**3,883.6**	**3.8**
Private industry..	(X)	106,444.4	3,063.4	3.5
Agriculture, forestry, fishing, hunting......................	11	967.8	40.2	4.8
Mining [4]...	21	612.0	15.5	2.3
Construction..	23	5,701.5	202.1	4.0
Manufacturing..	31–33	11,446.6	501.8	4.4
Wholesale trade..	42	5,487.5	179.7	3.4
Retail trade..	44–45	14,521.5	453.8	4.1
Transportation and warehousing [5]........................	48–49	3,937.4	202.1	5.2
Utilities..	22	557.1	16.9	3.1
Information...	51	2,725.6	46.3	1.8
Finance and insurance.....................................	52	5,542.9	40.7	0.8
Real estate and rental and leasing.........................	53	1,965.6	48.1	2.9
Professional, scientific, and technical services..............	54	7,525.9	70.5	1.0
Management of companies and enterprises.................	55	1,887.6	26.0	1.5
Administrative and support and waste management and remediation services.............................	56	7,231.4	127.6	2.8
Educational services......................................	61	2,464.5	37.3	2.2
Health care and social assistance..........................	62	16,132.2	653.9	5.2
Arts, entertainment, and recreation........................	71	2,049.9	56.4	4.8
Accommodation and food services.........................	72	11,182.6	265.4	3.7
Other services, except public administration................	81	4,504.8	79.1	2.7
State and local government [3].............................	(X)	18,424.1	820.3	5.7
State government......................................	(X)	4,624.5	183.9	4.6
Local government......................................	(X)	13,799.6	636.4	6.1

X Not applicable. [1] North American Industry Classification System, 2007; see text, this section. [2] Employment figure primarily derived from Quarterly Census of Employment and Wages (QCEW). [3] Excludes farms with fewer than 11 employees. [4] Data for Mining (Sector 21 in the North American Industry Classification System—United States, 2007) include establishments not governed by the Mine Safety and Health Administration rules and reporting, such as those in Oil and Gas Extraction and related support activities. Data for mining operators in coal, metal, and nonmetal mining are provided to BLS by the Mine Safety and Health Administration, U.S. Department of Labor. Independent mining contractors are excluded from the coal, metal, and nonmetal mining industries. These data do not reflect the changes the Occupational Safety and Health Administration made to its recordkeeping requirements effective January 1, 2002; therefore, estimates for these industries are not comparable to estimates in other industries. [5] Data for employers in railroad transportation are provided to BLS by the Federal Railroad Administration, U.S. Department of Transportation.

Source: U.S. Bureau of Labor Statistics, News Release, *Workplace Injuries and Illnesses—2010*, News Release, USDL-11-1502, October 2011. See also <http://www.bls.gov/iif/home.htm>.

Table 671. Fatal Work Injuries by Event or Exposure: 2010

[For the 50 states and the District of Columbia. Based on the Census of Fatal Occupational Injuries. For details, see source]

Event or exposure	Number of fatalities	Percent distribu- tion	Event or exposure	Number of fatalities	Percent distribu- tion
Total..	**4,690**	**100**	Contacts with objects and equipment [1]........	738	16
			Struck by object or equipment [1]...............	404	9
Transportation incidents [1]......................	1,857	40	Struck by falling object or equipment.......	265	6
Highway incident [1]...........................	1044	22	Struck by flying object........................	34	1
Collision between vehicles, mobile			Caught in or compressed by equipment		
equipment.................................	535	11	or objects...................................	228	5
Noncollision incidents.......................	233	5	Caught in or crushed in collapsing		
Nonhighway incident (farm, industrial			materials...................................	91	2
premises).................................	276	6	Falls..	646	14
Aircraft accidents.............................	152	3	Exposure to harmful substances or		
Pedestrians struck by a vehicle, mobile			environments [1]...........................	414	9
equipment.................................	280	6	Contact with electric current................	164	3
Water vehicle accidents......................	60	1	Exposure to caustic, noxious or allergenic		
Railway accidents.............................	45	1	substances................................	140	3
Assaults and violent acts [1]....................	832	18	Oxygen deficiency...........................	61	1
Homicides [1]..................................	518	11	Drowning, submersion......................	45	1
Shooting...................................	405	9	Fires and explosions..........................	191	4
Stabbing...................................	37	1	Other events and exposures..................	3	(Z)
Self-inflicted injury............................	270	6			

Z Less than 0.5 percent. [1] Includes other causes, not shown separately.

Source: U.S. Bureau of Labor Statistics, "Census of Fatal Occupational Injuries (CFOI)—Current and Revised Data," <http://www.bls.gov/iif/oshcfoi1.htm>.

Table 672. Workplace Violence Incidents and Security Measures: 2005

[In percent. Covers period September 2004 to June 2006. Based on establishment survey; see source for details]

Incident or security measure	Total	Industry			Employment size				
		Private indus- try [1]	State govern- ment	Local govern- ment	1 to 10 employ- ees	11 to 49 employ- ees	50 to 249 employ- ees	250 to 999 or employ- ees	1,000 more employ- ees
Any workplace violence incidents........	5.3	4.8	32.2	14.7	2.4	9.1	16.0	28.8	49.9
Criminal...............................	2.2	2.1	8.7	3.7	1.4	3.5	4.7	6.8	17.2
Customer or client.....................	2.2	1.9	15.4	10.3	1.0	3.9	6.4	12.2	28.3
Co-worker.............................	2.3	2.1	17.7	4.3	0.6	4.6	8.1	16.8	34.1
Domestic violence.....................	0.9	0.8	5.5	2.1	0.1	2.0	2.9	9.0	24.1
No incident..............................	92.1	92.5	65.3	85.1	95.6	87.8	77.8	63.9	43.8
Selected types of security provided:									
Intruder/burglar systems...............	41.8	42.1	29.1	35.5	35.7	53.9	57.5	54.2	61.0
Surveillance cameras...................	22.6	22.2	45.2	32.7	17.0	29.2	47.9	69.1	77.9
Motion detectors.......................	26.9	27.1	14.8	21.3	24.0	32.9	33.7	28.3	36.4
Metal detectors........................	0.9	0.7	16.0	4.3	0.5	1.1	2.5	7.2	15.7
Electronic badges [2]....................	6.3	6.0	35.6	9.0	3.9	7.2	20.8	45.1	60.1
Security guards........................	9.5	9.1	48.6	10.5	6.4	11.7	24.8	53.9	65.3
Limited access [3].......................	30.7	30.0	58.0	50.7	26.0	35.9	52.5	68.3	83.2
Physical barriers [4].....................	13.4	13.1	27.2	23.6	10.2	18.2	24.5	33.5	46.5
Lighting of work areas..................	39.1	38.7	55.8	48.5	32.2	50.0	62.1	71.9	80.4
Workplace violence training provided:									
Any training...........................	20.8	20.2	58.0	32.3	14.6	29.1	45.7	64.2	67.8
No training............................	78.4	78.9	42.0	67.6	84.3	70.5	54.0	35.6	32.0

[1] Excludes farms with fewer than 11 employees. [2] Or ID scanner at entry or exit. [3] Secured entry/locked doors. [4] Between work areas and the public.

Source: U.S. Bureau Labor Statistics, *Survey of Workplace Violence and Prevention—2005*, News Release, USDL 06- 1860, October 2006. See also <http://www.bls.gov/iif/home.htm>.

Table 673. Workers Killed on the Job by Industry and Occupation: 2010

[Excludes homicides and suicides. Replaces Table 657 in the 2012 edition of the Statistical Abstract. That table, prepared by the National Safety Council, included estimates of workers disabled on the job but did include data on occupations]

Industry group	Deaths		Occupations with highest fatal work injury rates	Deaths	
	Number	Rate [1]		Number	Rate
Total.................................	4,690	3.6	Fishers and fishing workers.............	38	152
			Logging workers..........................	60	93.5
Agriculture [2]...........................	621	27.9	Aircraft pilots and flight engineers......	78	70.6
Mining [3]...............................	172	19.8	Mine workers, misc extraction..........	26	64.2
Construction............................	774	9.8	Farmers and ranchers...................	308	42.5
Manufacturing..........................	329	2.3	Mining machine operators..............	22	37.0
Wholesale trade........................	191	4.9	Roofers..................................	57	32.4
Retail trade.............................	311	2.2	Refuse & recyclables collectors........	26	29.8
			Truck drivers and driver/sales		
Transportation and warehousing.......	661	13.7	workers..................................	718	23.0
Utilities..................................	26	2.8	Agricultural workers, misc.............	161	21.4
Information.............................	43	1.5	Industrial machinery installers, repair		
Financial activities [4].................	113	1.3	and maintenance workers..............	98	20.7
Professional & business services [4]....	364	2.6	Police and sheriff's parole officers......	134	18.1
Educational & health services..........	171	0.9	Construction laborers...................	202	16.3
Leisure & hospitality [4]..................	238	2.3	Electrical power line installers		
Other services [5].......................	192	3	and repairers...........................	22	16.3
Government.............................	484	2.2			

[1] The rate represents the number of fatal occupational injuries per 100,000 full-time equivalent workers. [2] Includes forestry, fishing, and hunting. [3] Includes oil and gas extraction. [4] For composition of industry, see Table 644. [5] Excludes public service administration.

Source: Bureau of Labor Statistics, "Census of Fatal Occupational Injuries," <http://stats.bls.gov/iif/oshcfoi1.htm#2010>, accessed September 2012.

Table 674. Nonfatal Occupational Injury and Illness Cases in Private Industry by Type of Injury or Illness and Days Away from Work: 2010

[(933.2 represents 933,200). Covers work-related injuries and illnesses involving one or more days of missed work]

Type of work-related injury or illness	Number of injury or illness cases (1,000)								Median number of days away from work
	All cases	1 day	2 days	3-5 days	6-10 days	11-20 days	21-30 days	31 days or more	
Total [1].................................	**933.20**	**134.08**	**101.56**	**167.01**	**109.69**	**104.22**	**60.03**	**256.59**	**8**
Traumatic injuries and disorders..............	872.32	125.59	96.18	158.29	103.64	96.25	54.68	237.69	8
Fractures.......................................	69.38	4.24	4.09	6.81	6.38	8.41	6.12	33.32	30
Sprains, strains, tears........................	370.13	41.55	35.76	66.69	47.93	44.14	24.49	109.57	10
Concussions...................................	5.87	0.89	0.86	1.11	0.84	0.72	0.20	1.25	6
Back pain, hurt back..........................	33.24	3.84	3.61	7.22	3.98	3.17	1.85	9.57	7
Systemic diseases and disorders.............	42.00	5.02	3.05	5.15	4.21	6.48	4.61	13.48	16
Carpal tunnel syndrome.....................	8.49	0.37	0.32	0.77	0.87	1.51	0.95	3.70	27
Hernia...	13.68	0.49	0.29	1.07	1.19	2.94	2.72	4.98	24
Vision disorders..............................	3.20	1.50	0.80	0.50	0.20	0.10	0.10	0.10	2
Infectious and parasitic diseases.............	1.49	0.24	0.23	0.37	0.34	0.12	0.04	0.16	5
Mental disorders or syndromes...............	2.73	1.10	0.70	0.31	0.22	0.33	0.11	1.59	35

[1] Total includes unclassified and ill-defined conditions.

Source: Bureau of Labor Statistics, Survey of Occupational Injuries and Illnesses, 2010 Supplemental Tables <http://stats.bls.gov/iif/oshcdnew2010.htm#10Supplemental_Tables>, accessed September 2012.

Table 675. Work Stoppages: 1960 to 2011

[896 represents 896,000. Excludes work stoppages involving fewer than 1,000 workers and lasting less than 1 day. The term "major work stoppage" includes both worker-initiated strikes and employer-initiated lockouts that involve 1,000 workers or more. Information is based on reports of labor disputes appearing in daily newspapers, trade journals, and other public sources. The parties to the disputes are contacted by telephone, when necessary, to clarify details of the stoppages]

Year	Number of work stoppages [1]	Workers involved [2] (1,000)	Days idle Number [3] (1,000)	Days idle Percent estimated working time [4]	Year	Number of work stoppages [1]	Workers involved [2] (1,000)	Days idle Number [3] (1,000)	Days idle Percent estimated working time [4]
1960.......	222	896	13,260	0.09	1993......	35	182	3,981	0.01
1970.......	381	2,468	52,761	0.29	1994......	45	322	5,021	0.02
1975.......	235	965	17,563	0.09	1995......	31	192	5,771	0.02
1977.......	298	1,212	21,258	0.10	1996......	37	273	4,889	0.02
1978.......	219	1,006	23,774	0.11	1997......	29	339	4,497	0.01
1979.......	235	1,021	20,409	0.09	1998......	34	387	5,116	0.02
1980.......	187	795	20,844	0.09	1999......	17	73	1,996	0.01
1981.......	145	729	16,908	0.07	2000......	39	394	20,419	0.06
1982.......	96	656	9,061	0.04	2001......	29	99	1,151	(Z)
1983.......	81	909	17,461	0.08	2002......	19	46	660	(Z)
1984.......	62	376	8,499	0.04	2003......	14	129	4,091	0.01
1985.......	54	324	7,079	0.03	2004......	17	171	3,344	0.01
1986.......	69	533	11,861	0.05	2005......	22	100	1,736	0.01
1987.......	46	174	4,481	0.02	2006......	20	70	2,688	0.01
1988.......	40	118	4,381	0.02	2007......	21	189	1,265	(Z)
1989.......	51	452	16,996	0.07	2008......	15	72	1,954	0.01
1990.......	44	185	5,926	0.02	2009......	5	13	124	(Z)
1991.......	40	392	4,584	0.02	2010......	11	45	302	(Z)
1992.......	35	364	3,989	0.01	2011........	19	113	1,020	(Z)

Z Less than 0.005 percent. [1] Beginning in year indicated. [2] Workers counted more than once if involved in more than one stoppage during the year. [3] Resulting from all stoppages in effect in a year, including those that began in an earlier year. [4] Agricultural and government employees are included in the total working time; private household and forestry and fishery employees are excluded.

Source: U.S. Bureau of Labor Statistics, *Major Work Stoppages in 2011*, News Release, USDL 12-0215, February 2012. See also <http://www.bls.gov/news.release/wkstp.toc.htm>.

Table 676. Labor Union Membership by Sector: 1985 to 2011

[Annual averages of monthly figures (16,996 represents 16,996,000). For wage and salary workers in agriculture and non-agriculture. Data represent union members by place of residence. Based on the Current Population Survey and subject to sampling error. For methodological details, see source]

Sector	1985	1990	1995	2000	2005	2008	2009	2010	2011
TOTAL (1,000)									
Wage and salary workers:									
Union members......................	16,996	16,740	16,360	16,258	15,685	16,098	15,327	14,715	14,755
Covered by unions...................	19,358	19,058	18,346	17,944	17,223	17,761	16,904	16,290	16,281
Public sector workers:									
Union members......................	5,743	6,485	6,927	7,111	7,430	7,832	7,897	7,623	7,550
Covered by unions...................	6,921	7,691	7,987	7,976	8,262	8,676	8,678	8,406	8,309
Private sector workers:									
Union members......................	11,253	10,255	9,432	9,148	8,255	8,265	7,431	7,092	7,205
Covered by unions...................	12,438	11,366	10,360	9,969	8,962	9,084	8,226	7,884	7,972
PERCENT									
Wage and salary workers:									
Union members......................	18.0	16.1	14.9	13.5	12.5	12.4	12.3	11.9	11.8
Covered by unions...................	20.5	18.3	16.7	14.9	13.7	13.7	13.6	13.1	13.0
Public sector workers:									
Union members......................	35.7	36.5	37.7	37.5	36.5	36.8	37.4	36.2	37.0
Covered by unions...................	43.1	43.3	43.5	42.0	40.5	40.7	41.1	40.0	40.7
Private sector workers:									
Union members......................	14.3	11.9	10.3	9.0	7.8	7.6	7.2	6.9	6.9
Covered by unions...................	15.9	13.2	11.3	9.8	8.5	8.4	8.0	7.7	7.6

Source: The Bureau of National Affairs, Inc., Arlington, VA, *Union Membership and Earnings Data Book: Compilations from the Current Population Survey* (2012 edition), authored by Barry Hirsch of Georgia State University and David Macpherson of Trinity University. See also <http://www.bna.com/union-membership-earnings-p12884903659/> and <http://unionstats.gsu.edu>. Copyright 2012 by The Bureau of National Affairs, Inc., Research & Custom Solutions (800-372-1033).

Table 677. Union Members by Selected Characteristics: 2011

[Annual averages of monthly data (125,187 represents 125,187,000). Covers employed wage and salary workers 16 years old and over. Excludes self-employed workers whose businesses are incorporated although they technically qualify as wage and salary workers. Based on Current Population Survey, see text, Section 1 and Appendix III]

Characteristic	Employed wage and salary workers			Median usual usual weekly earnings [3] (dollars)			
		Percent					
	Total (1,000)	Union members [1]	Repre-sented by union [2]	Total	Union members [1]	Repre-sented by union [2]	Not repre-sented by union
Total [4]............................	**125,187**	**11.8**	**13.0**	**756**	**938**	**934**	**729**
AGE							
16 to 24 years old......................	16,910	4.4	5.0	440	552	550	432
25 to 34 years old......................	28,682	9.9	11.0	693	852	848	671
35 to 44 years old......................	27,231	12.7	14.0	837	992	983	805
45 to 54 years old......................	28,693	14.9	16.4	866	988	987	832
55 to 64 years old......................	18,751	15.7	17.2	881	992	992	845
65 years and over......................	4,920	10.0	11.4	742	849	855	728
SEX							
Men..	64,686	12.4	13.5	832	982	981	798
Women....................................	60,502	11.2	12.5	684	879	871	653
RACE							
White [5].................................	101,768	11.6	12.8	775	961	956	747
Men.....................................	53,418	12.3	13.4	856	1,004	1,001	821
Women..................................	48,351	10.9	12.2	703	903	897	670
Black [5].................................	14,249	13.5	15.0	615	771	768	595
Men.....................................	6,440	14.6	15.8	653	802	803	619
Women..................................	7,808	12.6	14.3	595	744	741	577
Asian [5].................................	6,153	10.1	11.2	866	961	962	846
Men.....................................	3,269	9.1	10.1	970	964	983	969
Women..................................	2,884	11.4	12.4	751	959	943	727
HISPANIC OR LATINO ETHNICITY							
Hispanic [6].............................	18,733	9.7	10.8	549	811	804	520
Men.....................................	10,980	9.8	10.8	571	859	856	538
Women..................................	7,754	9.6	10.7	518	743	733	501
INDUSTRY [7]							
Private sector............................	104,737	6.9	7.6	729	878	875	716
Mining...................................	780	7.2	7.8	1,064	1,030	1,005	1,069
Construction............................	6,244	14.0	14.9	746	1,059	1,037	698
Manufacturing..........................	13,599	10.5	11.2	787	836	835	780
Wholesale and retail trade...........	18,002	4.8	5.3	613	622	622	612
Transportation and utilities...........	5,239	21.1	22.1	805	987	985	762
Information..............................	2,756	10.1	10.8	940	1,122	1,117	916
Financial activities....................	8,086	1.6	2.0	866	824	822	866
Professional and business services.........................	12,171	2.1	2.6	880	872	883	880
Education and health services......	19,855	8.6	10.0	736	870	878	722
Leisure and hospitality...............	11,355	2.7	3.0	479	607	605	473
Other services.........................	5,467	3.4	3.8	626	917	901	619
Public sector............................	20,450	37.0	40.7	895	981	977	810

[1] Members of a labor union or an employee association similar to a labor union. [2] Members of a labor union or an employee association similar to a union as well as workers who report no union affiliation but whose jobs are covered by a union or an employee association contract. [3] For full-time employed wage and salary workers. [4] Includes races not shown separately. Also includes a small number of multiple jobholders whose full- and part-time status cannot be determined for their principal job. [5] For persons in this race group only. See footnote 4, Table 597. [6] Persons of Hispanic origin may be any race. [7] For composition of industries, see Table 644.

Source: U.S. Bureau of Labor Statistics, *Union Members in 2011*, News Release, USDL-12-0094, January 2012. See also <http://www.bls.gov/news.release/union2.toc.htm>.

Table 678. Labor Union Membership by State: 1985 and 2011

[Annual averages of monthly figures (16,996.1 represents 16,996,100). For wage and salary workers in agriculture and non-agriculture. Data represent union members by place of residence. Based on the Current Population Survey and subject to sampling error. For methodological details, see source]

| State | Union members (1,000) | | Workers covered by unions (1,000) | | Percent of workers | | | | | |
| | | | | | Union members | | Covered by unions | | Private sector union members | |
	1985	2011	1985	2011	1985	2011	1985	2011	1985	2011
United States......	**16,996.1**	**14,754.7**	**19,358.1**	**16,281.0**	**18.0**	**11.8**	**20.5**	**13.0**	**14.3**	**6.9**
Alabama [1]...........	226.6	178.1	254.9	192.2	15.7	10.0	17.6	10.8	13.5	6.7
Alaska................	47.7	67.6	53.4	72.7	25.0	22.1	28.0	23.8	17.0	11.0
Arizona [1]...........	115.6	149.1	145.7	183.2	9.5	6.0	12.0	7.3	7.9	3.9
Arkansas [1]..........	91.6	47.0	108.4	57.1	11.2	4.2	13.3	5.1	9.5	2.5
California.............	2,123.1	2,375.6	2,485.8	2,528.5	20.4	17.1	23.9	18.2	15.8	9.0
Colorado.............	165.2	179.5	191.1	202.8	11.8	8.2	13.7	9.3	8.9	4.9
Connecticut..........	306.5	258.7	325.9	271.8	20.9	16.8	22.2	17.7	14.4	8.5
Delaware.............	45.6	38.6	50.9	41.4	16.6	10.4	18.5	11.2	12.8	5.5
District of Columbia..	45.2	23.5	58.2	27.9	16.5	8.3	21.2	9.9	13.9	4.7
Florida [1].............	395.2	460.7	515.7	557.1	9.1	6.3	11.9	7.7	5.3	2.8
Georgia [1]...........	239.5	153.6	273.1	186.4	10.0	4.0	11.4	4.8	9.1	2.7
Hawaii................	109.6	112.8	121.2	118.4	27.8	21.5	30.8	22.5	19.7	14.1
Idaho [1].............	41.7	30.6	48.4	36.3	11.7	5.1	13.6	6.1	9.8	3.2
Illinois...............	1,031.7	875.9	1,124.9	929.2	22.2	16.2	24.3	17.2	19.2	10.6
Indiana [3]...........	476.7	300.7	524.4	331.4	21.3	11.2	23.4	12.4	20.8	8.9
Iowa [1]..............	181.7	155.6	212.8	187.8	17.0	11.2	20.0	13.5	14.5	6.5
Kansas [1]............	129.0	96.6	157.3	128.0	12.8	7.6	15.6	10.1	11.4	4.6
Kentucky.............	219.2	149.6	250.8	172.7	16.5	8.9	18.8	10.3	16.4	6.7
Louisiana [1]..........	147.9	76.2	172.8	90.2	9.6	4.4	11.2	5.3	7.9	3.4
Maine................	77.5	62.7	90.0	74.6	17.1	11.3	19.8	13.4	11.2	4.6
Maryland.............	329.9	315.9	412.9	348.2	16.7	12.4	20.9	13.7	13.0	6.6
Massachusetts.......	495.4	422.1	548.4	445.5	18.5	14.6	20.4	15.5	13.0	7.1
Michigan.............	1,004.5	670.9	1,071.0	702.6	28.4	17.5	30.3	18.3	23.5	11.9
Minnesota............	407.5	370.5	452.7	389.2	22.6	15.1	25.1	15.8	16.7	7.8
Mississippi [1].........	81.3	53.7	94.5	73.4	9.3	5.0	10.8	6.8	8.4	3.4
Missouri..............	378.3	275.0	418.9	315.7	18.7	10.9	20.7	12.5	19.1	9.2
Montana..............	57.3	48.8	66.9	54.7	19.4	13.0	22.7	14.5	14.9	5.4
Nebraska [1]..........	78.8	65.4	99.0	82.7	12.7	7.9	16.0	10.0	10.3	3.8
Nevada [1]............	89.7	153.6	102.1	174.5	21.6	14.6	24.6	16.6	19.5	10.8
New Hampshire......	48.8	68.4	54.8	77.0	10.7	11.1	12.0	12.5	6.9	4.4
New Jersey..........	821.0	615.7	937.2	641.8	24.9	16.1	28.4	16.8	19.0	8.7
New Mexico..........	49.4	49.3	62.4	65.1	10.0	6.8	12.7	9.0	8.9	2.9
New York............	2,102.3	1,904.4	2,298.3	2,068.0	30.2	24.1	33.0	26.1	21.3	13.5
North Carolina [1].....	167.0	104.5	209.5	148.4	6.4	2.9	8.0	4.1	4.7	1.6
North Dakota [1]......	27.9	20.1	34.2	27.3	11.4	6.3	14.0	8.6	6.4	3.8
Ohio.................	999.0	646.4	1,090.9	705.7	23.6	13.4	25.7	14.7	20.7	8.6
Oklahoma [2]..........	128.4	93.5	151.0	112.2	10.5	6.4	12.3	7.7	8.2	3.8
Oregon..............	231.6	269.2	260.8	285.3	22.7	17.1	25.6	18.1	16.7	8.8
Pennsylvania.........	1,055.4	778.6	1,174.7	845.0	22.8	14.5	25.4	15.8	19.1	9.3
Rhode Island........	90.2	78.7	97.7	80.9	21.1	17.4	22.9	17.8	12.7	9.2
South Carolina [1].....	58.8	59.5	72.5	86.3	4.5	3.4	5.6	5.0	3.8	1.8
South Dakota [1]......	27.9	18.3	34.5	23.1	11.2	5.1	13.8	6.4	7.5	2.7
Tennessee [1].........	236.8	115.5	281.8	139.5	13.1	4.6	15.6	5.6	10.9	2.5
Texas [1]..............	474.8	533.0	626.2	642.3	7.4	5.2	9.7	6.3	5.6	3.0
Utah [1]...............	69.9	66.5	91.9	81.6	11.4	5.8	14.9	7.1	8.0	3.5
Vermont..............	28.5	34.9	35.4	39.2	12.8	12.0	15.9	13.5	7.1	4.4
Virginia [1]............	236.0	163.1	296.7	197.6	9.7	4.6	12.2	5.6	8.6	2.1
Washington...........	405.8	517.1	469.2	557.2	25.0	18.9	28.9	20.4	18.6	11.1
West Virginia.........	134.7	92.9	148.3	102.4	22.7	13.8	25.0	15.2	22.2	9.7
Wisconsin............	435.9	338.7	463.9	357.7	22.3	13.3	23.8	14.1	17.8	7.0
Wyoming [1]...........	26.8	18.0	34.2	21.0	13.8	7.2	17.6	8.4	11.2	5.0

[1] Right to work state. [2] Passed right to work law in 2001. [3] Passed right to work law in 2012.

Source: The Bureau of National Affairs, Inc., Arlington, VA, *Union Membership and Earnings Data Book: Compilations from the Current Population Survey* (2012 edition), authored by Barry Hirsch of Georgia State University and David Macpherson of Trinity University. See also <http://www.bna.com/union-membership-earnings-p12884903659/> and <http://unionstats.gsu.edu>. Copyright 2012 by The Bureau of National Affairs, Inc., Research & Custom Solutions (800-372-1033).

Section 13
Income, Expenditures, Poverty, and Wealth

This section presents data on gross domestic product (GDP), gross national product (GNP), national and personal income, saving and investment, money income, poverty, and national and personal wealth. The data on income and expenditures measure two aspects of the U.S. economy. One aspect relates to the National Income and Product Accounts (NIPA), a summation reflecting the entire complex of the nation's economic income and output and the interaction of its major components; the other relates to the distribution of money income to families and individuals, or consumer income.

The primary source for data on GDP, GNP, national and personal income, gross saving and investment, and fixed assets and consumer durables is the *Survey of Current Business*, published monthly by the Bureau of Economic Analysis (BEA). These data are also available in tables accessible through an interactive tool on the BEA's Web site, <http://www.bea.gov/itable/index.cfm>. A comprehensive revision to the NIPA was released beginning in July 2009. Discussions of the revision appeared in the March, August, September, October, and November 2009 issues of the *Survey of Current Business*. Comprehensive revisions are conducted approximately every 5 years. Summary historical estimates appeared in the August 2012 issue of the *Survey of Current Business*. Detailed historical data can be found on BEA's Web site at <http://www.bea.gov/>.

Sources of income distribution data are the decennial censuses of population, the Current Population Survey (CPS), and the American Community Survey, all products of the U.S. Census Bureau (see text, Section 1). Annual data on income of families, individuals, and households are presented in *Current Population Reports, Consumer Income: Income, Poverty, and Health Insurance Coverage in the United States,* P60-239, in print. Many data series are also found on the Census Web site at <http://www.census.gov/hhes/www/income/>. Data on the household sector's saving and assets are published by the Board of Governors of the Federal Reserve System in the quarterly statistical release *Flow of Funds Accounts*. The Federal Reserve Board also periodically conducts the *Survey of Consumer Finances*, which presents financial information on family assets and net worth. The most recent survey is available at <http://www.federalreserve.gov/econresdata/scf/scfindex.htm>. Detailed information on personal wealth is published periodically by the Internal Revenue Service (IRS) in *SOI Bulletin*.

National income and product—GDP is the total output of goods and services produced by labor and property located in the United States, valued at market prices. GDP can be viewed in terms of the expenditure categories that comprise its major components: personal consumption expenditures, gross private domestic investment, net exports of goods and services, and government consumption expenditures and gross investment. The goods and services included are largely those bought for final use (excluding illegal transactions) in the market economy. A number of inclusions, however, represent imputed values, the most important of which is the rental value of owner-occupied housing. GDP, in this broad context, measures the output attributable to the factors of production located in the United States. GDP by state is the gross market value of the goods and services attributable to labor and property located in a state. It is the state counterpart of the nation's GDP.

The featured measure of real GDP is an index based on chain-type annual weights. Changes in this measure of real output and prices are calculated as the average of changes based on weights for the current and preceding years. (Components of real output are weighted by price, and components of prices are weighted by output.) These annual changes are "chained" (multiplied) together to form a time series that allows for the effects of changes in relative prices and changes in the composition of output over time. Quarterly and monthly changes are based on quarterly and monthly weights, respectively.

The output indexes are expressed as 2005 = 100, and for recent years, in 2005 dollars; the price indexes are also based to 2005 = 100. For more information on chained-dollar indexes, see the article on this subject in the November 2003 issue of the *Survey of Current Business*.

Chained (2005) dollar estimates of most components of GDP are not published for periods prior to 1990, because during periods far from the base period, the levels of the components may provide misleading information about their contributions to an aggregate. Values are published in index form (2005 = 100) for 1929 to the present to allow users to calculate the percent changes for all components, which are accurate for all periods. In addition, BEA publishes estimates of contributions of major components to the percent change in GDP for all periods.

Gross national product measures the output attributable to all labor and property supplied by United States residents. GNP differs from "national income" mainly in that GNP includes allowances for depreciation—that is, consumption of fixed capital.

National income includes all net incomes, net of consumption of fixed capital (CFC), earned in production. National income is the sum of compensation of employees, proprietors' income with inventory valuation adjustment (IVA) and capital consumption adjustment (CCAdj), rental income of persons with CCAdj, corporate profits with IVA and CCAdj, net interest and miscellaneous payments, taxes on production and imports, business current transfer payments (net), and current surplus of government enterprises, less subsidies.

Capital consumption adjustment for corporations and for nonfarm sole proprietorships and partnerships is the difference between capital consumption based on income tax returns and capital consumption measured using empirical evidence on prices of used equipment and structures in resale markets, which have shown that depreciation for most types of assets approximates a geometric pattern. The tax return data are valued at historical costs and reflect changes over time in service lives and depreciation patterns as permitted by tax regulations. Inventory valuation adjustment represents the difference between the book value of inventories used up in production and the cost of replacing them.

Personal income is the current income received by persons from all sources minus their personal contributions for government social insurance. Classified as "persons" are individuals (including owners of unincorporated firms), nonprofit institutions that primarily serve individuals, private trust funds, and private noninsured welfare funds. Personal income includes personal current transfer receipts (payments not resulting from current production) from government and business such as social security benefits, public assistance, etc., but excludes transfers among persons. Also included are certain nonmonetary types of income; chiefly, estimated net rental value to owner-occupants of their homes and the value of services furnished without payment by financial intermediaries. Capital gains (and losses) are excluded.

Disposable personal income is personal income less personal current taxes. It is the income available to persons for spending or saving. Personal current taxes are tax payments (net of refunds) by persons (except personal contributions for government social insurance) that are not chargeable to business expense. Personal taxes include income taxes, personal property taxes, motor vehicle licenses, and other miscellaneous taxes.

Gross domestic product by industry—The BEA also prepares estimates of value added by industry. *Value added* is a measure of the contribution of each private industry and of government to the nation's GDP. It is defined as an industry's gross output (which consists of sales or receipts and other operating income, commodity taxes, and inventory change) minus its intermediate inputs (which consist of energy, raw materials, semi-finished goods, and services that are purchased from domestic industries or from foreign sources). These estimates of value added are produced for 61 private industries and for 4 government classifications—federal general government and government enterprises, and state and local general government and government enterprises.

The estimates by industry are available in current dollars and are derived from the estimates of gross domestic income, which consists of three components—the compensation of employees, gross operating surplus, and taxes on production and imports, less subsidies. Real, or inflation-adjusted, estimates are also prepared.

Regional Economic Accounts—These accounts consist of estimates of state and local area personal income and of gross domestic product by state and are consistent with estimates of personal income and gross domestic product in the Bureau's national economic accounts. BEA's estimates of state and local area personal income provide a framework for analyzing individual state and local economies, and they show how the economies compare with each other. The *personal income* of a state and/or local area is the income received by, or on behalf of, the residents of that state or area. Estimates of labor and proprietors' earnings by place of work indicate the economic activity of business and government within that area, and estimates of personal income by place of residence indicate the income within the area that is

available for spending. BEA prepares estimates for states, counties, metropolitan areas, and BEA economic areas.

Gross domestic product by state estimates measure the value added to the nation's production by the labor and property in each state. GDP by state is often considered the state counterpart of the nation's GDP. The GDP by state estimates provide the basis for analyzing the regional impacts of national economic trends. GDP by state is measured as the sum of the distributions by industry and state of the components of gross domestic income; that is, the sum of the costs incurred and incomes earned in the production of GDP by state. The GDP estimates are presented in current dollars and in real (chained dollars) for 63 industries.

Consumer Expenditure Survey—The Consumer Expenditure Survey program began in 1980. The principal objective of the survey is to collect current consumer expenditure data, which provide a continuous flow of data on the buying habits of American consumers. The data are necessary for future revisions of the Consumer Price Index.

The survey conducted by the Census Bureau for the Bureau of Labor Statistics consists of two components: (1) an interview panel survey in which the expenditures of consumer units are obtained in five interviews conducted every 3 months, and (2) a diary or recordkeeping survey completed by participating households for two consecutive 1-week periods.

Each component of the survey queries an independent sample of consumer units. Data are collected in 91 areas of the country that are representative of the U.S. civilian noninstitutional population. The survey includes students in student housing. For the diary survey, the Census Bureau selects 12,000 addresses each year for participation; usable diaries are collected from approximately 7,100 households. The placement of diaries is spread out equally over the 52 weeks of the year. The interview survey contacts 15,000 addresses each quarter; usable interviews are obtained from approximately 7,100 households each quarter. Data from the two surveys are combined; integration is necessary to permit analysis of total family expenditures because neither the diary nor quarterly interview survey was designed to collect a complete account of consumer spending.

Distribution of money income to families and individuals—Money income statistics are based on data collected in various field surveys of income conducted since 1936. Since 1947, the Census Bureau has collected the data on an annual basis and published them in *Current Population Reports*, P60 Series. In each of the surveys, field representatives interview samples of the population with respect to income received during the previous year. *Money income* as defined by the Census Bureau differs from the BEA concept of "personal income." Data on consumer income collected in the CPS by the Census Bureau cover money income received (exclusive of certain money receipts such as capital gains) before payments for personal income taxes, social security, union dues, Medicare deductions, etc. Therefore, money income does not reflect the fact that some families receive part of their income in the form of noncash benefits (see Section 11) such as food stamps, health benefits, and subsidized housing; that some farm families receive noncash benefits in the form of rent-free housing and goods produced and consumed on the farm; or that noncash benefits are also received by some nonfarm residents, which often take the form of the use of business transportation and facilities, full or partial payments by business for retirement programs, medical and educational expenses, etc. These elements should be considered when comparing income levels. None of the aggregate income concepts (GDP, national income, or personal income) is exactly comparable with money income, although personal income is the closest. For a definition of families and households, see text, Section 1.

Poverty—Families and unrelated individuals are classified as being above or below poverty following the Office of Management and Budget's Statistical Policy Directive 14. The Census Bureau uses a set of thresholds that vary by family size and composition.

The poverty calculation is based solely on money income and does not reflect the fact that many low-income persons receive noncash benefits such as food stamps, Medicaid, and public housing.

The original thresholds were based on the U.S. Department of Agriculture's 1961 Economy Food Plan and reflected the different consumption requirements of families. The poverty thresholds are updated every year to reflect changes in the Consumer Price Index. The following technical changes to the thresholds were made in 1981: (1) distinctions based on sex of householder were eliminated, (2) separate thresholds for farm families were dropped, and (3) the matrix was expanded to families of nine or more persons from the old cutoff of seven or more persons. These changes were incorporated in the calculation of poverty data beginning with 1981. Besides the Census Bureau Web site at <http://www.census.gov/hhes/www/poverty/methods/measure.html>, information on poverty guidelines and research may be found at the U.S. Department of Human Services Web site at <http://aspe.hhs.gov/poverty/index.shtml>.

In the recent past, the Census Bureau has published a number of technical papers and reports that presented experimental poverty estimates based on income definitions that counted the value of selected government noncash benefits. The Census Bureau has also published reports on after-tax income.

Statistical reliability—For a discussion of statistical collection and estimation, sampling procedures, and measures of statistical reliability pertaining to Census Bureau data, see Appendix III.

Table 679. Gross Domestic Product in Current and Chained (2005) Dollars: 1970 to 2011

[In billions of dollars (1,038 represents $1,038,000,000,000). For explanation of gross domestic product and chained dollars, see text, this section. Minus sign (−) indicates decline in inventories or net imports]

Item	1970	1980	1990	1995	1999	2000	2001	2002	2003	2004	2005	2006	2007	2008	2009	2010	2011
CURRENT DOLLARS																	
Gross domestic product	**1,038**	**2,788**	**5,801**	**7,415**	**9,354**	**9,952**	**10,286**	**10,642**	**11,142**	**11,853**	**12,623**	**13,377**	**14,029**	**14,292**	**13,939**	**14,527**	**15,094**
Personal consumption expenditures	648	1,756	3,836	4,987	6,343	6,830	7,149	7,439	7,804	8,271	8,804	9,301	9,772	10,036	9,866	10,246	10,726
Durable goods	90	226	497	636	857	916	946	992	1,015	1,073	1,123	1,155	1,188	1,109	1,030	1,086	1,163
Nondurable goods	229	573	994	1,180	1,433	1,543	1,588	1,618	1,713	1,819	1,953	2,070	2,176	2,273	2,168	2,302	2,484
Services	330	956	2,344	3,172	4,053	4,371	4,615	4,829	5,077	5,379	5,727	6,076	6,408	6,654	6,669	6,859	7,079
Gross private domestic investment	152	479	861	1,144	1,642	1,772	1,662	1,647	1,730	1,969	2,172	2,327	2,295	2,088	1,547	1,795	1,916
Fixed investment	150	486	846	1,113	1,581	1,718	1,700	1,635	1,713	1,904	2,122	2,267	2,266	2,129	1,708	1,728	1,870
Change in private inventories	2	−6	15	31	61	55	−38	12	16	65	50	60	29	−41	−161	67	46
Net exports of goods and services	4	−13	−78	−91	−262	−382	−371	−427	−504	−619	−723	−769	−713	−710	−392	−517	−579
Exports	60	281	552	812	989	1,093	1,028	1,003	1,041	1,180	1,305	1,471	1,662	1,847	1,583	1,840	2,086
Imports	56	294	630	903	1,251	1,475	1,399	1,430	1,545	1,799	2,028	2,240	2,375	2,557	1,975	2,357	2,664
Government consumption expenditures and gross investment	234	566	1,182	1,374	1,631	1,731	1,846	1,983	2,113	2,233	2,370	2,518	2,674	2,878	2,918	3,003	3,031
Federal	113	244	508	519	555	571	612	681	757	825	876	932	976	1,080	1,143	1,223	1,233
National defense	88	168	374	349	361	371	393	438	498	551	589	625	662	738	775	819	825
Nondefense	26	76	134	170	194	205	219	243	259	274	287	307	314	342	368	404	408
State and local	120	322	674	855	1,076	1,155	1,235	1,303	1,356	1,408	1,494	1,587	1,698	1,798	1,775	1,780	1,798
CHAINED (2005) DOLLARS																	
Gross domestic product	**4,270**	**5,839**	**8,034**	**9,094**	**10,780**	**11,226**	**11,347**	**11,553**	**11,841**	**12,247**	**12,623**	**12,959**	**13,206**	**13,162**	**12,703**	**13,088**	**13,315**
Personal consumption expenditures	2,740	3,766	5,316	6,079	7,241	7,608	7,814	8,022	8,248	8,516	8,804	9,055	9,263	9,212	9,038	9,221	9,421
Durable goods	(NA)	(NA)	(NA)	512	754	820	864	930	986	1,061	1,123	1,174	1,232	1,172	1,108	1,188	1,285
Nondurable goods	(NA)	(NA)	(NA)	1,438	1,661	1,715	1,746	1,780	1,846	1,893	1,953	2,005	2,043	2,019	1,983	2,041	2,076
Services	(NA)	(NA)	(NA)	4,208	4,853	5,093	5,219	5,318	5,418	5,563	5,727	5,876	5,990	6,017	5,936	5,992	6,076
Gross private domestic investment	475	718	994	1,259	1,844	1,970	1,832	1,807	1,856	2,058	2,172	2,232	2,160	1,940	1,454	1,715	1,797
Fixed investment	(NA)	(NA)	(NA)	1,236	1,782	1,914	1,878	1,798	1,856	1,993	2,122	2,173	2,131	1,979	1,606	1,648	1,761
Change in private inventories	(NA)	(NA)	(NA)	32	69	60	−42	13	17	66	50	59	28	−36	−145	59	35
Net exports of goods and services	(NA)	(NA)	(NA)	−99	−357	−452	−472	−549	−604	−688	−723	−729	−649	−495	−359	−422	−414
Exports	176	352	600	846	1,094	1,188	1,122	1,099	1,117	1,223	1,305	1,422	1,554	1,649	1,494	1,663	1,774
Imports	237	345	673	945	1,451	1,640	1,594	1,648	1,721	1,910	2,028	2,152	2,203	2,144	1,853	2,085	2,188
Government consumption expenditures and gross investment	1,234	1,359	1,864	1,889	2,056	2,098	2,178	2,280	2,331	2,362	2,370	2,402	2,434	2,497	2,540	2,557	2,503
Federal	(NA)	(NA)	(NA)	704	695	698	727	780	831	865	876	895	906	971	1,030	1,076	1,055
National defense	(NA)	(NA)	(NA)	477	456	454	471	505	549	580	589	598	612	658	696	718	702
Nondefense	(NA)	(NA)	(NA)	228	239	244	256	274	282	285	287	297	294	313	334	358	353
State and local	(NA)	(NA)	(NA)	1,184	1,362	1,400	1,452	1,501	1,500	1,497	1,494	1,507	1,528	1,528	1,514	1,487	1,454
Residual	−118	−11	−67	−176	−50	−24	−29	−20	−12	−4	0	−2	−1	16	34	9	−26

− Represents or rounds to zero. NA Not available.

Source: U.S. Bureau of Economic Analysis, *Survey of Current Business*, May 2012. See also <http://www.bea.gov/itable/>.

Table 680. Real Gross Domestic Product, Chained (2005) Dollars—Annual Percent Change: 1990 to 2011

[Change from immediate previous year; for example, 1990, change from 1989. Minus sign (–) indicates decrease]

Component	1990	2000	2004	2005	2006	2007	2008	2009	2010	2011
Gross domestic product (GDP)	**1.9**	**4.1**	**3.5**	**3.1**	**2.7**	**1.9**	**-0.3**	**-3.5**	**3.0**	**1.7**
Personal consumption expenditures	2.0	5.1	3.3	3.4	2.9	2.3	-0.6	-1.9	2.0	2.2
Durable goods	-0.4	8.8	7.3	5.9	4.5	5.0	-4.9	-5.4	7.2	8.2
Nondurable goods	1.2	3.2	2.8	3.2	2.6	1.9	-1.2	-1.8	2.9	1.7
Services	3.0	5.0	2.7	3.0	2.6	1.9	0.4	-1.4	0.9	1.4
Gross private domestic investment	-3.4	6.8	10.1	5.5	2.7	-3.2	-10.2	-25.0	17.9	4.8
Fixed investment	-2.1	7.4	7.4	6.5	2.4	-1.9	-7.1	-18.8	2.6	6.8
Nonresidential	0.5	9.8	6.2	6.7	8.0	6.5	-0.8	-17.8	4.4	8.8
Structures	1.5	7.8	1.1	1.4	9.2	14.1	6.4	-21.2	-15.8	4.6
Equipment and software	–	10.5	7.9	8.5	7.6	3.3	-4.3	-16.0	14.6	10.4
Residential	-8.6	1.0	9.8	6.2	-7.3	-18.7	-23.9	-22.2	-4.3	-1.3
Exports	9.0	8.6	9.5	6.7	9.0	9.3	6.1	-9.4	11.3	6.7
Goods	8.4	11.1	8.5	7.5	9.4	9.7	6.3	-12.0	14.4	7.4
Services	10.5	2.7	11.9	5.0	7.9	8.3	5.6	-3.5	5.0	4.9
Imports	3.6	13.0	11.1	6.1	6.1	2.4	-2.7	-13.6	12.5	4.9
Goods	2.9	13.4	11.1	6.8	5.9	2.6	-3.8	-15.6	14.8	5.7
Services	6.5	11.0	11.2	2.8	7.1	1.4	3.6	-3.5	2.9	1.1
Government consumption expenditures and gross investment	3.2	2.0	1.4	0.3	1.4	1.3	2.6	1.7	0.7	-2.1
Federal	2.0	0.5	4.1	1.3	2.1	1.2	7.2	6.0	4.5	-1.9
National defense	–	-0.5	5.7	1.5	1.6	2.2	7.5	5.8	3.3	-2.3
Nondefense	8.2	2.4	1.0	0.9	3.2	-0.8	6.5	6.5	7.1	-1.2
State and local	4.1	2.8	-0.2	-0.2	0.9	1.4	–	-0.9	-1.8	-2.2

– Represents or rounds to zero.

Source: U.S. Bureau of Economic Analysis, *Survey of Current Business*, May 2012. See also <http://www.bea.gov/National/Index.htm>.

Table 681. Gross Domestic Product in Current and Chained (2005) Dollars by Type of Product and Sector: 1990 to 2011

[In billions of dollars (5,801 represents $5,801,000,000,000). For explanation of chained dollars, see text, this section]

Type of product and sector	1990	2000	2005	2006	2007	2008	2009	2010	2011
CURRENT DOLLARS									
Gross domestic product	**5,801**	**9,952**	**12,623**	**13,377**	**14,029**	**14,292**	**13,939**	**14,527**	**15,094**
PRODUCT									
Goods	1,923	3,125	3,476	3,664	3,844	3,759	3,617	4,010	4,259
Durable goods	981	1,770	1,909	1,999	2,098	2,020	1,798	2,052	2,186
Nondurable goods	942	1,355	1,567	1,664	1,746	1,739	1,819	1,958	2,073
Services [1]	3,344	5,878	7,784	8,261	8,752	9,174	9,212	9,509	9,812
Structures	534	949	1,363	1,453	1,433	1,359	1,110	1,008	1,023
SECTOR									
Business [2]	4,454	7,716	9,680	10,262	10,738	10,788	10,339	10,879	11,387
Nonfarm [3]	4,377	7,642	9,578	10,169	10,623	10,657	10,226	10,747	11,234
Farm	77	74	102	93	115	131	113	133	153
Households and institutions	624	1,157	1,506	1,603	1,686	1,806	1,836	1,838	1,868
General government [4]	723	1,079	1,437	1,512	1,605	1,698	1,764	1,809	1,839
Federal	259	315	439	461	486	518	553	590	608
State and local	464	764	998	1,051	1,119	1,180	1,211	1,220	1,230
CHAINED (2005) DOLLARS									
Gross domestic product	**8,027**	**11,216**	**12,623**	**12,959**	**13,206**	**13,162**	**12,703**	**13,088**	**13,315**
PRODUCT									
Goods	1,914	3,047	3,476	3,659	3,820	3,790	3,567	3,984	4,163
Durable goods	(NA)	1,617	1,909	2,015	2,143	2,105	1,873	2,177	2,335
Nondurable goods	(NA)	1,429	1,567	1,645	1,678	1,685	1,684	1,807	1,836
Services [1]	5,270	6,919	7,784	7,961	8,132	8,217	8,173	8,261	8,339
Structures	942	1,245	1,363	1,341	1,267	1,170	972	887	871
SECTOR									
Business [2]	5,809	8,491	9,680	9,974	10,173	10,038	9,550	9,924	10,154
Nonfarm [3]	5,753	8,408	9,578	9,875	10,082	9,934	9,431	9,805	10,056
Farm	56	84	102	99	90	102	117	117	100
Households and institutions	1,010	1,376	1,506	1,540	1,572	1,629	1,623	1,631	1,636
General government [4]	1,266	1,349	1,437	1,445	1,463	1,492	1,520	1,528	1,523
Federal	484	411	439	438	442	459	486	504	509
State and local	789	939	998	1,007	1,021	1,033	1,035	1,025	1,015

NA Not available. [1] Includes government consumption expenditures, which are for services (such as education and national defense) produced by government. In current dollars, these services are valued at their cost of production. [2] Equals gross domestic product excluding gross value added of households and institutions and of general government. [3] Equals gross domestic business value added excluding gross farm value added. [4] Equals compensation of general government employees plus general government consumption of fixed capital.

Source: U.S. Bureau of Economic Analysis, *Survey of Current Business*, May 2012. See also <http://www.bea.gov/national/index.htm>.

Table 682. Gross Domestic Product in Current and Chained (2005) Dollars by Industry: 2000 to 2011

[In billions of dollars (9,952 represents $9,952,000,000,000). Data are based on the 2002 North American Industry Classification System (NAICS); see text, Section 15. Data include nonfactor charges (capital consumption allowances, indirect business taxes, etc.) as well as factor charges against gross product; corporate profits and capital consumption allowances have been shifted from a company to an establishment basis]

Industry	Current dollars				Chained (2005) dollars			
	2000	2005	2010	2011	2000	2005	2010	2011
Gross domestic product.....................	**9,952**	**12,623**	**14,527**	**15,094**	**11,216**	**12,623**	**13,088**	**13,315**
Private industries..........................	8,736	11,037	12,558	13,097	9,786	11,037	11,354	11,555
Agriculture, forestry, fishing, and hunting..................	96	127	157	178	104	127	138	121
Farms..........................	74	102	133	(NA)	84	102	117	(NA)
Forestry, fishing, and related activities..................	22	25	24	(NA)	21	25	21	(NA)
Mining..........................	109	192	240	288	233	192	234	249
Oil and gas extraction..................	68	129	148	(NA)	155	129	168	(NA)
Mining, except oil and gas..................	28	36	49	(NA)	46	36	31	(NA)
Mining support activities..................	14	27	43	(NA)	29	27	34	(NA)
Utilities..........................	174	206	265	251	223	206	205	192
Construction..........................	467	613	512	520	655	613	442	441
Manufacturing..........................	1,416	1,569	1,702	1,837	1,390	1,569	1,606	1,675
Durable goods..........................	839	878	915	989	742	878	953	1,028
Wood products..........................	28	33	22	(NA)	33	33	30	(NA)
Nonmetallic mineral products..................	42	45	35	(NA)	45	45	31	(NA)
Primary metals..........................	46	54	43	(NA)	62	54	40	(NA)
Fabricated metal products..................	121	121	121	(NA)	130	121	103	(NA)
Machinery..........................	111	110	140	(NA)	111	110	125	(NA)
Computer and electronic products..................	172	184	265	(NA)	78	184	403	(NA)
Electrical equipment, appliances, and components........	44	40	44	(NA)	43	40	38	(NA)
Motor vehicles, bodies & trailers, & parts..................	117	113	55	(NA)	94	113	52	(NA)
Other transportation equipment..................	66	76	72	(NA)	79	76	66	(NA)
Furniture and related products..................	34	34	30	(NA)	35	34	26	(NA)
Miscellaneous manufacturing..................	58	70	89	(NA)	60	70	84	(NA)
Nondurable goods..........................	577	691	787	848	649	691	657	659
Food & beverage & tobacco..................	165	172	207	(NA)	176	172	185	(NA)
Textile mills and textile product mills..................	28	24	16	(NA)	27	24	15	(NA)
Apparel and leather and allied products..................	21	16	12	(NA)	20	16	12	(NA)
Paper products..........................	62	54	57	(NA)	58	54	43	(NA)
Printing and related support activities..................	40	38	32	(NA)	37	38	32	(NA)
Petroleum and coal products..................	44	139	172	(NA)	74	139	139	(NA)
Chemical products..........................	152	183	226	(NA)	170	183	178	(NA)
Plastics and rubber products..................	65	66	67	(NA)	66	66	56	(NA)
Wholesale trade..........................	618	726	797	845	606	726	700	723
Retail trade..........................	686	838	885	917	753	838	869	886
Transportation and warehousing..................	301	370	403	419	319	370	357	358
Air transportation..........................	53	56	63	(NA)	43	56	51	(NA)
Rail transportation..........................	23	27	32	(NA)	27	27	24	(NA)
Water transportation..........................	8	9	15	(NA)	8	9	21	(NA)
Truck transportation..........................	97	120	116	(NA)	106	120	113	(NA)
Transit & ground passenger transport..................	18	21	26	(NA)	21	21	23	(NA)
Pipeline transportation..........................	9	10	15	(NA)	9	10	11	(NA)
Other transportation & support..................	68	92	93	(NA)	76	92	80	(NA)
Warehousing and storage..................	26	35	42	(NA)	29	35	39	(NA)
Information..........................	418	587	624	662	398	587	647	680
Publishing industries (includes software)..................	100	150	144	(NA)	102	150	143	(NA)
Motion picture and sound recording..................	37	55	58	(NA)	43	55	54	(NA)
Broadcasting and telecommunications..................	257	311	347	(NA)	228	311	371	(NA)
Information and data processing services..................	24	71	74	(NA)	24	71	81	(NA)
Finance and insurance..........................	762	1,019	1,242	1,256	841	1,019	1,112	1,132
Real estate and rental and leasing..................	1,236	1,579	1,765	1,752	1,422	1,579	1,625	1,583
Professional, scientific, and technical services..................	662	870	1,096	1,171	745	870	967	1,015
Legal services..........................	139	191	220	(NA)	176	191	172	(NA)
Computer systems design, related services..................	114	131	184	(NA)	102	131	194	(NA)
Miscellaneous services..........................	410	548	691	(NA)	468	548	607	(NA)
Management of companies & enterprises..................	171	218	264	283	215	218	207	211
Admin/support waste management/remediation services....	283	371	423	444	311	371	384	398
Educational services..........................	86	120	163	169	116	120	127	125
Health care and social assistance..................	592	833	1,109	1,151	711	833	961	986
Ambulatory health care services..................	288	406	549	(NA)	327	406	485	(NA)
Hospitals, nursing, residential care..................	253	355	466	(NA)	323	355	395	(NA)
Social assistance..........................	52	73	94	(NA)	62	73	82	(NA)
Arts, entertainment, and recreation..................	99	119	139	144	115	119	125	129
Performing arts, spectator sports, museums, and related activities..................	48	66	80	(NA)	59	66	70	(NA)
Amusements, gambling, & recreation..................	50	53	59	(NA)	55	53	55	(NA)
Accommodation and food services..................	283	367	417	442	328	367	360	372
Accommodation..........................	89	110	116	(NA)	100	110	111	(NA)
Food services and drinking places..................	194	256	301	(NA)	227	256	250	(NA)
Other services, except government..................	278	313	357	369	347	313	295	295
Government..........................	1,215	1,586	1,969	1,997	1,509	1,586	1,658	1,650
Federal..........................	378	502	650	668	482	502	551	555
State and local..........................	837	1,084	1,319	1,329	1,027	1,084	1,107	1,096

NA Not available.

Source: U.S. Bureau of Economic Analysis, *Survey of Current Business*, May 2012. See also <http://www.bea.gov/iTable/iTable.cfm?ReqID=9&step=1>.

Table 683. Gross Domestic Product by State in Current and Chained (2005) Dollars: 2000 to 2010

[In billions of dollars (9,884.2 represents $9,884,200,000,000). For definition of gross domestic product by state or chained dollars, see text, this section]

State	Current dollars					Chained (2005) dollars				
	2000	2005	2008	2009	2010	2000	2005	2008	2009	2010
United States [1]	9,884.2	12,554.5	14,270.5	14,014.8	14,551.8	11,223.1	12,554.5	13,100.0	12,773.9	13,099.7
Alabama	116.0	151.1	169.7	166.8	172.6	132.6	151.1	155.7	151.0	154.1
Alaska	25.9	37.8	49.2	45.9	49.1	34.1	37.8	40.6	44.2	45.0
Arizona	161.9	223.0	260.5	249.7	253.6	179.3	223.0	240.6	226.8	228.5
Arkansas	68.1	88.2	99.5	98.8	102.6	77.3	88.2	91.1	89.7	91.8
California	1,317.3	1,692.0	1,911.7	1,847.0	1,901.1	1,470.4	1,692.0	1,766.5	1,701.3	1,731.8
Colorado	171.9	217.4	254.2	250.7	257.6	195.2	217.4	233.0	231.8	235.2
Connecticut	163.9	197.1	226.0	227.6	237.3	185.3	197.1	208.7	205.0	211.3
Delaware	41.0	54.7	58.7	60.7	62.3	46.9	54.7	54.3	55.5	56.2
District of Columbia	58.3	82.8	97.4	98.9	103.3	69.8	82.8	88.3	87.6	90.7
Florida	481.1	680.3	747.8	732.8	747.7	548.8	680.3	689.9	664.1	673.4
Georgia	294.5	363.2	405.3	394.1	403.1	329.7	363.2	375.5	357.2	362.0
Hawaii	41.4	56.9	66.1	65.4	66.8	48.7	56.9	60.2	58.6	59.3
Idaho	36.1	48.7	55.2	53.7	55.4	39.4	48.7	51.5	49.7	50.7
Illinois	474.4	569.5	637.0	632.0	651.5	537.1	569.5	586.0	570.3	581.3
Indiana	198.0	239.6	263.6	259.9	275.7	221.9	239.6	244.7	234.8	245.4
Iowa	93.3	120.3	135.0	136.1	142.7	105.3	120.3	125.0	123.8	127.7
Kansas	85.7	105.2	125.3	122.5	127.2	97.9	105.2	115.3	111.7	114.0
Kentucky	113.1	139.3	155.6	155.8	163.3	128.3	139.3	142.8	140.1	144.6
Louisiana	131.4	197.2	213.4	205.1	218.9	168.0	197.2	182.7	190.1	195.2
Maine	36.4	45.6	50.0	50.0	51.6	41.6	45.6	46.1	45.0	46.0
Maryland	183.0	248.1	281.7	285.1	295.3	209.7	248.1	259.4	257.4	264.9
Massachusetts	272.7	323.3	365.6	360.5	378.7	301.3	323.3	339.5	328.2	342.1
Michigan	336.8	375.3	375.4	369.7	384.2	371.2	375.3	352.5	335.0	344.9
Minnesota	188.4	238.4	262.8	258.5	270.0	211.2	238.4	243.0	236.0	243.4
Mississippi	65.6	81.5	96.7	94.4	97.5	76.0	81.5	88.3	86.1	87.1
Missouri	181.0	216.6	241.3	238.0	244.0	204.8	216.6	222.7	214.3	217.3
Montana	21.6	30.1	35.8	35.0	36.1	25.8	30.1	31.9	31.5	31.8
Nebraska	57.2	72.5	84.9	86.4	89.8	65.2	72.5	77.7	78.2	79.7
Nevada	75.9	114.8	132.3	125.0	125.7	88.1	114.8	119.9	111.9	111.6
New Hampshire	44.1	53.7	58.8	59.1	60.3	48.7	53.7	54.8	53.9	54.6
New Jersey	349.3	430.0	483.6	471.9	487.3	393.3	430.0	445.5	428.2	438.7
New Mexico	50.3	67.8	77.2	76.9	79.7	58.5	67.8	69.2	71.6	72.8
New York	770.6	961.9	1,109.1	1,094.1	1,159.5	863.2	961.9	1,014.7	984.4	1,034.3
North Carolina	281.4	355.0	403.9	407.0	424.9	316.4	355.0	375.6	368.0	380.6
North Dakota	18.3	24.7	31.7	31.6	34.7	21.2	24.7	28.6	29.2	31.3
Ohio	381.2	444.7	470.6	462.0	477.7	429.1	444.7	435.7	417.3	426.1
Oklahoma	91.3	120.7	151.9	142.4	147.5	110.3	120.7	133.4	132.1	133.5
Oregon	113.0	143.3	174.5	167.5	174.2	121.2	143.3	169.6	161.2	166.7
Pennsylvania	395.8	482.3	545.2	546.5	569.7	452.4	482.3	499.5	491.0	505.9
Rhode Island	33.5	44.2	47.4	47.5	49.2	38.4	44.2	43.6	42.8	44.0
South Carolina	115.4	141.9	159.5	158.8	164.4	130.8	141.9	146.6	141.4	145.1
South Dakota	24.0	31.6	38.3	38.3	39.9	26.9	31.6	35.3	35.5	36.3
Tennessee	177.6	224.5	247.8	243.8	254.8	198.1	224.5	231.1	220.9	228.7
Texas	733.0	971.0	1,202.1	1,146.6	1,207.5	872.6	971.0	1,070.8	1,076.4	1,106.2
Utah	69.5	90.7	112.4	111.3	114.5	79.6	90.7	102.6	101.1	102.8
Vermont	18.0	22.8	24.6	24.6	25.6	20.0	22.8	23.0	22.4	23.1
Virginia	261.9	356.9	402.9	409.7	423.9	298.2	356.9	371.9	370.9	380.6
Washington	227.8	279.4	334.5	331.6	340.5	259.1	279.4	309.2	301.9	306.6
West Virginia	41.4	52.0	59.0	61.0	64.6	49.6	52.0	52.4	53.8	56.0
Wisconsin	177.6	218.9	239.2	239.6	248.3	199.2	218.9	222.1	215.9	221.3
Wyoming	17.0	26.2	38.9	36.8	38.5	23.1	26.2	31.4	34.5	34.4

[1] For chained (2005) dollar estimates, states will not add to U.S. total.

Source: U.S. Bureau of Economic Analysis, "Gross Domestic Product by State," Sept. 2011, <http://www.bea.gov/itable/>.

Table 684. Gross Domestic Product by Selected Industries and State: 2011

[In billions of dollars (14,981.0 represents $14,981,000,000,000). For definition of gross domestic product by state, see text, this section. Industries based on 2002 North American Industry Classification System, see text, Section 15]

State	Total [1]	Manu- facturing	Whole- sale trade	Retail trade	Infor- mation	Finance and insur- ance	Real estate, rental, and leasing	Profes- sional and technical services	Health care and social assis- tance	Govern- ment [2]
United States........	14,981.0	1,837.0	844.9	917.0	662.3	1,256.2	1,751.7	1,171.1	1,151.2	1,883.7
Alabama..................	173.1	25.9	9.6	13.1	4.0	10.9	15.1	11.5	13.4	30.3
Alaska....................	51.4	2.1	1.1	2.1	1.1	1.9	3.9	2.2	3.0	9.9
Arizona..................	258.4	21.8	14.0	19.4	6.6	22.8	37.2	16.0	22.0	32.6
Arkansas.................	105.8	15.4	7.2	7.8	2.7	5.1	11.2	4.4	8.8	15.0
California.................	1,958.9	229.9	106.9	121.4	136.0	111.5	293.8	185.1	129.4	224.7
Colorado.................	264.3	20.6	13.7	15.2	22.7	17.5	31.1	25.7	16.7	34.0
Connecticut..............	230.1	25.0	12.3	11.9	9.1	44.6	29.9	16.9	18.8	21.0
Delaware.................	65.8	4.4	2.2	2.5	1.1	25.6	6.4	4.4	4.0	6.0
District of Columbia......	107.6	0.3	0.9	1.2	5.3	5.1	7.9	23.6	5.0	37.6
Florida...................	754.3	38.3	47.7	58.2	31.5	52.9	117.4	54.7	66.3	97.3
Georgia..................	418.9	47.0	30.8	26.2	25.7	31.2	44.8	31.0	28.1	58.9
Hawaii...................	67.0	1.4	2.0	4.6	1.5	2.4	10.9	3.3	4.5	16.5
Idaho....................	57.9	7.9	3.0	4.4	1.1	2.8	6.5	4.2	4.7	7.9
Illinois...................	670.7	86.6	46.1	39.7	22.3	68.6	81.6	58.8	48.1	66.2
Indiana..................	278.1	74.2	14.2	17.0	5.6	18.9	24.7	12.0	22.7	28.1
Iowa.....................	149.0	27.6	8.2	8.7	4.1	18.7	14.1	4.9	10.3	16.8
Kansas...................	130.9	18.4	8.0	8.6	5.8	8.7	12.0	7.0	10.0	20.0
Kentucky.................	164.8	27.2	10.3	10.6	4.4	9.3	13.9	7.2	14.6	28.0
Louisiana................	247.7	63.0	9.9	13.8	4.0	9.1	19.8	11.1	14.8	25.9
Maine....................	51.6	5.9	2.5	4.5	1.0	3.6	6.7	2.8	6.2	7.3
Maryland.................	301.1	19.5	13.6	16.8	11.5	18.3	44.7	34.1	24.5	55.7
Massachusetts...........	391.8	43.3	20.2	17.9	19.1	38.7	50.1	47.8	39.0	37.1
Michigan.................	385.2	61.0	23.6	26.7	10.2	25.4	44.8	30.5	35.2	45.7
Minnesota...............	281.7	40.0	18.4	15.3	10.1	28.4	32.0	18.0	25.0	27.4
Mississippi..............	97.8	15.1	4.4	7.9	2.0	5.2	8.5	3.6	7.6	18.0
Missouri.................	249.5	31.9	15.1	16.5	14.0	16.5	23.4	16.3	22.5	32.0
Montana.................	38.0	2.3	1.9	2.6	0.9	1.9	4.5	1.9	3.6	6.1
Nebraska................	94.2	11.2	4.8	5.5	2.8	9.3	7.8	4.7	7.1	12.4
Nevada..................	130.4	5.2	4.6	8.4	2.4	15.8	16.7	6.6	7.1	13.6
New Hampshire..........	63.6	8.5	3.7	4.9	2.2	5.9	8.5	4.6	6.2	6.5
New Jersey..............	487.0	38.1	37.5	30.9	21.6	40.6	76.3	46.9	38.7	54.7
New Mexico..............	79.4	5.9	2.5	5.2	2.2	3.2	9.2	6.6	6.1	15.5
New York................	1,158.0	67.2	58.1	60.9	83.2	198.7	133.9	112.3	91.3	125.3
North Carolina...........	439.9	86.6	22.2	24.0	13.0	52.6	38.5	23.8	29.6	63.8
North Dakota............	40.3	2.8	3.0	2.4	1.1	3.3	4.2	1.3	3.2	5.0
Ohio.....................	484.0	80.7	29.7	32.2	13.7	39.1	49.9	30.4	45.2	55.7
Oklahoma................	155.0	18.6	7.6	10.2	4.1	7.6	14.0	7.1	11.4	26.4
Oregon..................	194.7	56.0	10.7	9.1	5.6	8.9	22.2	9.4	14.7	22.4
Pennsylvania............	578.8	71.0	34.0	33.3	22.6	47.9	64.6	46.3	59.9	59.2
Rhode Island............	50.1	3.9	2.4	2.7	2.2	6.3	6.9	2.8	5.2	6.9
South Carolina..........	165.8	26.4	9.0	12.6	4.2	8.8	16.7	9.3	11.3	29.2
South Dakota............	40.1	3.6	2.3	2.8	0.9	6.2	3.3	1.2	3.6	5.1
Tennessee...............	266.5	40.7	16.5	20.3	8.0	18.1	25.1	15.7	27.9	33.2
Texas....................	1,308.1	192.0	85.8	76.6	44.9	89.8	109.7	92.1	82.0	146.2
Utah.....................	124.5	17.6	5.8	8.4	4.5	13.9	13.6	7.8	7.0	16.3
Vermont..................	25.9	2.9	1.2	2.2	0.7	1.6	3.3	1.8	2.8	3.7
Virginia..................	428.9	39.0	16.9	22.5	18.0	29.4	51.0	60.4	26.4	80.0
Washington..............	355.1	44.1	19.6	25.1	31.3	17.3	43.1	25.5	24.8	52.8
West Virginia............	66.8	6.1	3.0	4.8	1.6	2.6	5.5	2.8	6.2	11.8
Wisconsin................	254.8	50.1	14.5	15.3	7.6	22.7	27.5	11.9	23.3	27.0
Wyoming................	37.6	2.6	1.3	2.0	0.5	0.9	3.4	1.1	1.5	5.2

[1] Includes industries not shown separately. [2] Includes federal civilian and military and state and local government.

Source: U.S. Bureau of Economic Analysis, "Gross Domestic Product by State," June 2012, <http://www.bea.gov/regional/index.htm>.

Table 685. Relation of GDP, GNP, Net National Product, National Income, Personal Income, Disposable Personal Income, and Personal Saving: 1990 to 2011

[In billions of dollars (5,801 represents $5,801,000,000,000). For definitions, see text, this section. Minus sign (–) indicates deficit or net disbursement]

Item	1990	2000	2005	2007	2008	2009	2010	2011
Gross domestic product (GDP)...............	**5,801**	**9,952**	**12,623**	**14,029**	**14,292**	**13,939**	**14,527**	**15,094**
Plus: Income receipts from the rest of the world..	189	381	573	871	856	640	703	779
Less: Income payments to the rest of the world...	154	343	476	748	687	488	514	534
Equals: Gross national product (GNP).........	**5,835**	**9,989**	**12,720**	**14,152**	**14,461**	**14,091**	**14,716**	**15,340**
Less: Consumption of fixed capital................	691	1,184	1,541	1,768	1,854	1,866	1,875	1,950
Equals: Net national product....................	**5,144**	**8,805**	**11,179**	**12,384**	**12,607**	**12,225**	**12,841**	**13,389**
Less: Statistical discrepancy........................	84	-134	-95	-12	-2	77	1	-48
Equals: National income..........................	**5,060**	**8,939**	**11,274**	**12,396**	**12,609**	**12,148**	**12,840**	**13,437**
Less: Corporate profits [1]...........................	434	819	1,456	1,511	1,248	1,362	1,800	1,943
Taxes on production and imports less subsidies...	398	663	869	973	986	958	997	1,035
Contributions for government social insurance..	410	706	873	960	987	964	987	926
Net interest and miscellaneous payments on assets..	444	539	543	732	870	657	564	535
Business current transfer payments (net).......	40	87	96	103	123	132	137	134
Current surplus of government enterprises......	2	9	-4	-12	-16	-15	-16	-15
Wage accruals less disbursements...............	0	0	5	-6	-5	5	0	0
Plus: Personal income receipts on assets.........	921	1,361	1,542	2,057	2,165	1,708	1,721	1,790
Personal current transfer receipts..............	595	1,083	1,509	1,719	1,879	2,138	2,281	2,336
Equals: Personal income..........................	**4,847**	**8,559**	**10,486**	**11,912**	**12,460**	**11,930**	**12,374**	**13,005**
Less: Personal current taxes......................	593	1,232	1,209	1,489	1,436	1,141	1,194	1,400
Equals: Disposable personal income..........	**4,254**	**7,327**	**9,277**	**10,424**	**11,025**	**10,789**	**11,180**	**11,605**
Less: Personal outlays.............................	3,977	7,114	9,134	10,175	10,432	10,236	10,587	11,055
Equals: Personal saving..........................	**277**	**213**	**143**	**249**	**592**	**553**	**593**	**550**

[1] Corporate profits with inventory valuation and capital consumption adjustments.

Source: U.S. Bureau of Economic Analysis, *Survey of Current Business*, May 2012. See also <http://www.bea.gov/itable/>.

Table 686. Gross Saving and Investment: 1990 to 2011

[In billions of dollars (918 represents $918,000,000,000)]

Item	1990	2000	2005	2007	2008	2009	2010	2011
Gross saving.......................................	**918**	**1,800**	**1,919**	**2,048**	**1,908**	**1,597**	**1,821**	**1,964**
Net saving..	226	616	378	280	54	-269	-55	14
Net private saving..................................	397	389	635	513	740	1,027	1,245	1,263
Personal saving..................................	277	213	143	249	592	553	593	550
Undistributed corporate profits with IVA and CCA [1]...	120	176	486	271	153	470	652	713
Wage accruals less disbursements...............	–	–	5	-6	-5	5	–	–
Net government saving.............................	-170	227	-257	-233	-686	-1,296	-1,299	-1,249
Federal...	-176	185	-283	-245	-614	-1,218	-1,274	-1,183
State and local....................................	6	41	26	12	-72	-78	-25	-66
Consumption of fixed capital......................	691	1,184	1,541	1,768	1,854	1,866	1,875	1,950
Private...	560	987	1,291	1,476	1,543	1,542	1,541	1,598
Domestic business...............................	470	824	1,046	1,191	1,248	1,250	1,246	1,294
Households and institutions....................	91	163	245	286	295	293	295	303
Government..	131	198	251	291	311	324	334	352
Federal...	68	88	100	113	120	125	130	138
State and local....................................	63	110	150	179	191	199	204	214
Gross domestic investment, capital acct. transactions, and net lending..................	**1,002**	**1,666**	**1,824**	**2,036**	**1,906**	**1,675**	**1,821**	**1,916**
Gross domestic investment.........................	1,077	2,077	2,564	2,752	2,585	2,052	2,300	2,400
Gross private domestic investment...............	861	1,772	2,172	2,295	2,088	1,547	1,795	1,916
Gross government investment.....................	216	304	392	457	497	505	505	483
Capital account transactions (net) [2].............	7	–	-13	–	-5	1	1	1
Net lending or net borrowing......................	-82	-411	-728	-716	-674	-378	-480	-484
Statistical discrepancy.............................	84	-134	-95	-12	-2	77	1	-48
Addenda:								
Gross private saving...............................	957	1,376	1,925	1,989	2,283	2,570	2,785	2,861
Gross government saving..........................	-40	424	-7	58	-375	-972	-965	-896
Federal...	-109	273	-183	-133	-494	-1,093	-1,144	-1,045
State and local....................................	69	151	176	191	119	121	179	149
Net domestic investment...........................	386	892	1,023	984	731	186	426	449
Gross saving as a percentage of gross national income....................................	16.0	17.8	15.0	14.5	13.2	11.4	12.4	12.8
Net saving as a percentage of gross national income....................................	3.9	6.1	2.9	2.0	–	-1.9	–	–

– Represents or rounds to zero. [1] IVA and CCA = Inventory valuation adjustment and capital consumption adjustment. [2] Consists of capital transfers and the acquisition and disposal of nonproduced nonfinancial assets. Prior to 1982, reflects only capital grants paid to the U.S. territories and the Commonwealths of Puerto Rico and Northern Mariana Islands.

Source: U.S. Bureau of Economic Analysis, *Survey of Current Business*, May 2012. See also <http://www.bea.gov/itable/>.

Table 687. Flow of Funds Accounts—Composition of Individuals' Savings: 1990 to 2011

[In billions of dollars (532.6 represents $532,600,000,000). Combined statement for households, farm business, and nonfarm noncorporate business. Minus sign (–) indicates decrease]

Composition of savings	1990	2000	2005	2007	2008	2009	2010	2011
Net acquisition of financial assets	**532.6**	**375.8**	**1,233.6**	**1,520.2**	**762.5**	**142.0**	**458.4**	**860.0**
Foreign deposits	1.4	7.6	2.4	15.4	-23.7	-6.4	4.3	-3.8
Checkable deposits and currency	-9.2	-95.3	-37.6	-7.7	228.2	44.4	-45.4	314.9
Time and savings deposits	47.9	347.9	506.0	496.0	203.0	122.8	188.1	400.3
Money market fund shares	39.2	171.8	35.6	234.4	236.2	-270.4	-186.3	-22.3
Securities	200.9	-625.8	42.1	-105.3	-126.5	273.3	319.3	-138.4
Open market paper	5.8	12.4	14.7	-10.2	-101.3	28.7	28.8	-5.3
U.S. savings bonds	8.5	-1.7	0.7	-6.0	-2.4	-2.8	-3.3	-2.7
Treasury bills and other Treasury securities	88.8	-205.8	-90.9	-41.0	151.7	419.6	452.7	-88.9
Agency and GSE-backed securities [1]	35.3	34.1	110.8	320.2	96.8	-566.7	-4.7	-32.9
Municipal securities	34.7	4.5	77.4	43.6	41.4	129.5	57.9	-62.7
Corporate and foreign bonds	47.1	88.6	122.1	219.8	-216.3	-127.7	-281.5	-69.0
Corporate equities [2]	-50.8	-637.5	-368.3	-845.9	-108.4	88.0	-132.6	-174.8
Mutual fund shares	31.5	79.5	175.6	214.2	12.0	304.8	202.0	297.9
Life insurance reserves	26.5	50.2	16.1	18.0	61.7	23.7	9.0	63.6
Pension fund reserves	191.8	263.0	275.7	201.1	125.7	135.4	208.9	146.5
Miscellaneous and other assets	34.1	256.5	393.2	668.3	57.9	-180.8	-39.6	99.3
Gross investment in nonfinancial assets	**797.3**	**1,517.3**	**2,094.7**	**2,063.9**	**1,826.4**	**1,576.1**	**1,622.8**	**1,715.5**
Minus: Consumption of fixed capital	571.2	907.7	1,197.7	1,346.1	1,412.4	1,420.5	1,420.3	1,423.7
Equals: Net investment in nonfinancial assets	**226.1**	**609.6**	**897.0**	**717.8**	**414.0**	**155.6**	**202.5**	**291.8**
Net increase in liabilities	**237.2**	**918.8**	**1,695.1**	**1,478.5**	**289.7**	**-278.2**	**-380.9**	**-163.1**
Home mortgages	207.1	423.9	1,106.2	708.5	-103.1	-185.8	-338.2	-255.3
Other mortgages	-4.4	106.7	117.7	286.4	230.8	22.0	-107.7	-23.8
Consumer credit	15.1	176.5	100.4	141.4	20.1	-115.8	-30.6	96.6
Policy loans	4.1	2.8	0.8	3.6	5.9	0.7	3.4	2.5
Security credit	-3.7	7.2	-31.6	33.4	-160.7	38.1	75.2	-39.7
Other liabilities	19.1	201.6	401.6	305.2	296.7	-37.3	16.9	56.6
Personal saving, FOF concept (FOF [3])	537.2	102.3	400.5	762.5	874.9	523.1	991.5	1,284.1
Personal saving, NIPA concept (FOF [3])	457.4	-135.6	150.4	529.6	740.8	474.5	892.3	1,099.7
Personal saving, NIPA concept (NIPA [4])	276.7	213.1	143.2	248.7	592.3	552.6	592.8	538.5

[1] GSE = government-sponsored enterprises. [2] Only directly held and those in closed-end and exchange-traded funds. Other equities are included in mutual funds and life insurance and pension reserves. [3] Flow of Funds measure. [4] National Income and Product Accounts measure.

Source: Board of Governors of the Federal Reserve System, "Federal Reserve Statistical Release, Z.1, Flow of Funds Accounts of the United States," June 7, 2012, <http://www.federalreserve.gov/apps/fof/>.

Table 688. Government Consumption Expenditures and Gross Investment by Level of Government and Type: 2000 to 2011

[In billions of dollars (1,731.0 represents $1,731,000,000,000). Government consumption expenditures are services (such as education and national defense) produced by government that are valued at their cost of production. Excludes government sales to other sectors and government own-account investment (construction and software). Gross government investment consists of general government and government enterprise expenditures for fixed assets; inventory investment is included in government consumption expenditures. For explanation of national income and chained dollars, see text, Section 13]

Item	Current Dollars				Chained (2005) dollars			
	2000	2005	2010	2011	2000	2005	2010	2011
Government consumption expenditures and gross investment, total	**1,731.0**	**2,369.9**	**3,002.8**	**3,030.6**	**2,097.8**	**2,369.9**	**2,556.8**	**2,502.7**
Consumption expenditures	1,426.6	1,977.9	2,497.5	2,547.3	1,750.6	1,977.9	2,126.3	2,101.1
Gross investment	304.3	392.0	505.3	483.3	347.5	392.0	430.6	401.5
Structures	189.6	246.5	304.3	284.6	239.4	246.5	238.4	215.2
Equipment and software	114.7	145.5	201.0	198.7	109.8	145.5	197.5	193.2
Federal	**576.1**	**876.3**	**1,222.8**	**1,232.9**	**698.1**	**876.3**	**1,075.9**	**1,055.0**
Consumption expenditures	496.0	765.8	1,054.0	1,072.1	616.4	765.8	916.4	905.1
Gross investment	80.1	110.5	168.8	160.8	82.0	110.5	160.6	150.3
Structures	13.7	15.7	33.6	30.4	17.2	15.7	28.5	25.0
Equipment and software	66.4	94.7	135.2	130.3	65.2	94.7	131.3	124.7
National defense	**371.0**	**589.0**	**819.2**	**824.9**	**453.5**	**589.0**	**718.3**	**701.6**
Consumption expenditures	321.8	514.8	702.1	716.9	403.9	514.8	609.0	602.2
Gross investment	49.2	74.2	117.1	108.1	50.3	74.2	110.2	99.6
Structures	5.4	7.5	17.3	14.8	6.9	7.5	14.7	12.3
Equipment and software	43.8	66.8	99.8	93.3	43.6	66.8	94.9	87.0
Nondefense	**205.0**	**287.3**	**403.6**	**407.9**	**244.4**	**287.3**	**357.7**	**353.4**
Consumption expenditures	174.2	251.0	351.9	355.2	212.4	251.0	307.5	302.9
Gross investment	30.9	36.3	51.7	52.7	31.6	36.3	50.4	50.9
Structures	8.3	8.3	16.3	15.6	10.4	8.3	13.7	12.8
Equipment and software	22.6	28.0	35.4	37.1	21.5	28.0	36.3	38.0
State and local	**1,154.9**	**1,493.6**	**1,780.0**	**1,797.7**	**1,400.1**	**1,493.6**	**1,487.0**	**1,453.8**
Consumption expenditures	930.6	1,212.0	1,443.5	1,475.2	1,133.7	1,212.0	1,213.0	1,199.1
Gross investment	224.3	281.6	336.5	322.5	266.6	281.6	274.3	255.4
Structures	176.0	230.8	270.8	254.2	222.2	230.8	210.6	190.8
Equipment and software	48.3	50.8	65.7	68.3	44.3	50.8	66.2	68.6

Source: U.S. Bureau of Economic Analysis, *Survey of Current Business*, April 2012. See also <http://www.bea.gov/iTable/iTable.cfm?ReqID=9&step=1>.

Table 689. Personal Consumption Expenditures by Function: 2000 to 2010

[In billions of dollars (6,830.4 represents $6,830,400,000,000). For definition of "chained" dollars, see text, this section. Minus sign (-) indicates decrease]

Function	Current dollars				Chained (2005) dollars			
	2000	2005	2009	2010	2000	2005	2009	2010
Personal consumption expenditures [1]	**6,830.4**	**8,803.5**	**9,866.1**	**10,245.5**	**7,604.6**	**8,803.5**	**9,037.5**	**9,220.9**
Food and nonalcoholic beverages purchased for off-premises consumption	463.1	558.2	645.3	659.4	519.0	558.2	566.3	577.1
Alcoholic beverages purchased for off-premises consumption	74.0	86.0	100.4	106.6	81.1	86.0	90.7	95.8
Clothing, footwear, and related services	297.3	330.2	334.8	350.7	276.8	330.2	336.3	354.1
Clothing	250.4	276.9	278.3	290.9	230.4	276.9	281.8	296.9
Footwear [2]	46.9	53.3	56.4	59.8	46.6	53.3	54.5	57.2
Housing [1]	1,010.5	1,328.9	1,574.9	1,583.8	1,174.2	1,328.9	1,403.7	1,410.7
Rental of tenant-occupied nonfarm housing [3]	227.9	264.7	353.2	359.4	267.9	264.7	308.9	313.9
Imputed rental of owner-occupied nonfarm housing [4]	768.9	1,044.5	1,201.0	1,203.1	890.7	1,044.5	1,077.2	1,079.2
Household utilities and fuels	204.0	273.7	317.0	332.1	265.1	273.7	269.3	275.5
Water supply and sanitation	50.4	63.7	81.3	85.7	61.9	63.7	65.6	65.0
Electricity, gas, and other fuels	153.5	209.9	235.7	246.5	203.1	209.9	203.8	210.9
Furnishings, household equipment, and routine household maintenance [1]	342.5	418.7	403.1	413.1	332.5	418.7	396.1	416.9
Furniture, furnishings, and floor coverings [5]	114.4	141.9	125.5	129.7	106.2	141.9	131.6	142.3
Household appliances [6]	37.6	47.2	43.4	44.5	36.6	47.2	40.2	42.8
Tools and equipment for house and garden	17.1	22.3	20.2	20.7	17.0	22.3	20.0	21.2
Medical products, appliances, and equipment	191.2	296.3	367.0	385.5	223.7	296.3	332.1	338.7
Pharmaceutical and other medical products [7]	159.0	254.7	316.8	330.6	189.3	254.7	284.8	286.9
Therapeutic appliances and equipment	32.2	41.5	50.2	54.9	34.0	41.5	47.3	52.0
Outpatient services	436.6	625.9	750.2	767.0	490.3	625.9	679.1	679.4
Physician services [8]	229.2	330.5	387.8	391.9	248.7	330.5	356.6	351.7
Dental services	63.6	89.1	104.4	106.0	79.7	89.1	87.1	86.1
Paramedical services	143.8	206.3	258.0	269.1	162.6	206.3	235.9	242.3
Hospital and nursing home services	481.8	683.0	854.0	900.4	592.7	683.0	743.9	762.9
Transportation	798.4	978.0	882.7	967.0	901.1	978.0	839.5	849.8
Motor vehicles	321.4	361.6	270.1	290.9	311.4	361.6	282.8	288.6
New motor vehicles	210.7	248.9	165.9	178.5	202.8	248.9	169.6	178.7
Net purchases of used motor vehicles	110.7	112.7	104.2	112.4	108.5	112.7	113.7	110.3
Motor vehicle operation [1]	404.0	540.0	535.2	592.3	525.0	540.0	483.0	486.2
Motor vehicle parts and accessories	41.8	46.6	46.4	49.2	45.2	46.6	39.5	41.0
Motor vehicle fuels, lubricants, and fluids	172.9	283.8	279.1	331.4	261.3	283.8	263.1	264.2
Motor vehicle maintenance and repair	127.4	155.1	151.2	153.0	148.7	155.1	128.6	127.7
Public transportation	73.0	76.3	77.4	83.9	72.7	76.3	68.8	70.3
Telephone and facsimile equipment	5.5	9.4	13.5	14.0	3.3	9.4	17.4	18.8
Postal and delivery services	9.9	8.6	8.8	8.4	11.9	8.6	7.3	6.7
Telecommunication services	130.2	145.9	159.1	161.1	125.3	145.9	150.8	153.5
Internet access	16.4	29.9	48.0	53.8	16.3	29.9	60.1	66.9
Recreation [1]	639.9	817.7	879.4	918.3	598.7	817.7	923.3	990.7
Video and audio equipment	83.1	111.0	111.9	113.3	58.6	111.0	182.3	212.6
Information processing equipment	44.1	67.0	83.0	91.3	(NA)	(NA)	(NA)	(NA)
Services related to video and audio goods and computers	57.2	74.6	91.1	93.2	66.9	74.6	83.0	84.1
Sports and recreational goods and related service	147.9	186.4	179.3	186.1	135.4	186.4	185.0	198.0
Membership clubs, sports centers, parks, theaters, and museums	91.9	115.2	131.6	136.3	106.9	115.2	118.5	122.2
Magazines, newspapers, books, and stationery	81.0	85.6	87.8	95.0	84.6	85.6	82.1	88.7
Pets, pet products, and related services	39.7	55.6	71.0	75.7	45.8	55.6	57.1	60.6
Education [1]	134.3	181.9	234.4	249.3	188.2	181.9	186.4	189.4
Higher education	76.8	108.7	144.3	154.9	109.9	108.7	113.0	115.3
Food services	354.9	461.3	526.7	547.4	408.0	461.3	455.7	467.3
Accommodations [9]	55.2	72.7	83.6	90.6	62.4	72.7	78.6	84.0
Financial services	370.0	424.0	481.5	514.5	404.9	424.0	441.7	441.1
Insurance	199.9	274.4	266.3	265.8	260.7	274.4	234.7	227.1
Personal care [10]	132.2	167.8	184.5	191.1	142.7	167.8	167.0	171.9
Personal items [11]	63.7	78.6	84.8	89.6	57.2	78.6	73.3	76.6
Social services and religious activities [12]	85.0	121.0	147.6	154.1	98.8	121.0	133.0	136.4
Legal services	65.4	87.2	96.1	96.8	81.7	87.2	82.6	80.3
Funeral and burial services	15.8	18.9	18.7	19.0	19.2	18.9	15.5	15.4
Tobacco	68.5	71.1	87.9	94.4	80.3	71.1	60.7	58.8
Net foreign travel and expenditures abroad by U.S. residents [1]	-13.3	0.0	-13.0	-16.3	-3.0	0.0	-13.4	-17.8
Foreign travel by U.S. residents	84.3	99.8	106.1	115.4	106.8	99.8	94.5	97.1
Less: Expenditures in the United States by nonresidents	100.8	104.7	126.9	138.2	115.0	104.7	114.0	120.0
Final consumption expenditures of nonprofit institutions serving households NPISHs) [13]	165.4	211.7	280.3	280.2	177.8	211.7	277.1	280.0

NA Not available. [1] Includes other expenditures not shown separately. [2] Consists of shoes and other footwear, and of repair and hire of footwear. [3] Consists of space rent (see footnote 4) and rent for appliances, furnishings, and furniture. [4] Consists of rent for space and for heating and plumbing facilities, water heaters, lighting fixtures, kitchen cabinets, linoleum, storm windows and doors, window screens, and screen doors, but excludes rent for appliances and furniture and purchases of fuel and electricity. [5] Includes clocks, lamps, lighting fixtures, and other household decorative items; also includes repair of furniture, furnishings, and floor coverings. [6] Consists of major household appliances, small electric household appliances, and repair of household appliances. [7] Excludes drug preparations and related products dispensed by physicians, hospitals, and other medical services. [8] Consists of offices of physicians, health maintenance organization medical centers, and freestanding ambulatory surgical and emergency centers. [9] Consists of transient hotels, motels, other traveler accommodations, clubs, and housing at schools. [10] Consists of cosmetics and toiletries, electric appliances for personal care, hairdressing salons, and miscellaneous personal care services. [11] Consists of jewelry, watches, luggage, and similar personal items. [12] Consists of household purchases of goods and services from business, government, and nonprofit institutions providing social services and religious activities. Purchases from nonprofit establishments exclude unrelated sales, secondary sales, and sales to businesses, government, and the rest of the world, but include membership dues and fees. [13] Net expenses of NPISHs, defined as their gross operating expenses less primary sales to households.

Source: U.S. Bureau of Economic Analysis, *Survey of Current Business*, Aug. 2011. See also <http://www.bea.gov/iTable/iTable. cfm?ReqID=9&step=1>.

Table 690. Personal Income and Its Disposition: 1990 to 2011

[In billions of dollars (4,847 represents $4,847,000,000,000), except as indicated. For definition of personal income and chained dollars, see text, this section]

Item	1990	2000	2005	2007	2008	2009	2010	2011
Personal income...................	**4,847**	**8,559**	**10,486**	**11,912**	**12,460**	**11,930**	**12,374**	**13,005**
Compensation of employees, received................	3,326	5,789	7,060	7,862	8,073	7,801	7,971	8,293
Wage and salary disbursements.....................	2,741	4,828	5,701	6,422	6,551	6,270	6,408	6,683
Supplements to wages and salaries.................	585	961	1,359	1,440	1,523	1,531	1,563	1,610
Proprietors' income [1]...................	365	818	1,070	1,090	1,098	941	1,036	1,109
Farm........................	32	30	44	38	52	39	52	66
Nonfarm.....................	333	788	1,026	1,053	1,046	902	984	1,043
Rental income of persons [2].................	50	215	178	144	232	306	350	404
Personal income receipts on assets..................	921	1,361	1,542	2,057	2,165	1,708	1,721	1,790
Personal interest income..................	752	984	987	1,265	1,382	1,109	1,003	998
Personal dividend income...............	169	377	555	792	783	599	718	792
Personal current transfer receipts.....................	595	1,083	1,509	1,719	1,879	2,138	2,281	2,336
Government social benefits to persons..............	573	1,041	1,483	1,688	1,842	2,100	2,243	2,297
Social security [3]...................	244	401	513	576	606	665	690	714
Other current transfer receipts, from business (net)........................	22	42	26	31	37	38	38	40
Less: Contributions for government social insurance........................	410	706	873	960	987	964	987	926
Less: Personal current taxes.........................	593	1,232	1,209	1,489	1,436	1,141	1,194	1,400
Equals: Disposable personal income...............	**4,254**	**7,327**	**9,277**	**10,424**	**11,025**	**10,789**	**11,180**	**11,605**
Less: Personal outlays..........................	3,977	7,114	9,134	10,175	10,432	10,236	10,587	11,055
Personal consumption expenditures...................	3,836	6,830	8,804	9,772	10,036	9,866	10,246	10,726
Personal interest payments [4]..................	111	200	211	261	246	214	173	158
Personal current transfer payments...................	31	83	120	142	151	157	168	171
Equals: Personal saving........................	**277**	**213**	**143**	**249**	**592**	**553**	**593**	**550**
Personal saving as a percentage of disposable personal income..........................	6.5	2.9	1.5	2.4	5.4	5.1	5.3	4.7
Addenda:								
Disposable personal income:								
Total, billions of chained (2005) dollars [5]...............	5,894	8,158	9,277	9,880	10,120	9,883	10,062	10,193
Per capita:								
Current dollars..........................	17,004	25,946	31,343	34,550	36,200	35,115	36,090	37,191
Chained (2005) dollars............................	23,557	28,888	31,343	32,749	33,229	32,166	32,481	32,667

[1] With inventory valuation adjustments and capital consumption adjustment. [2] Includes capital consumption adjustment. [3] Social security benefits include old-age, survivors, and disability insurance benefits that are distributed from the federal Old-Age and Survivors Insurance Trust Fund and the Disability Insurance Trust Fund. [4] Consists of nonmortgage interest paid by households. [5] The current-dollar measure is deflated by the implicit price deflator for personal consumption expenditures.

Source: U.S. Bureau of Economic Analysis, *Survey of Current Business*, May 2012. See also <http://www.bea.gov/National/Index.htm>.

Table 691. Selected Per Capita Income and Product Measures in Current and Chained (2005) Dollars: 1960 to 2011

[In dollars. Based on U.S. Census Bureau estimated population including Armed Forces abroad; based on quarterly averages. For explanation of chained dollars, see text, this section]

Year	Current dollars					Chained (2005) dollars			
	Gross domestic product	Gross national product	Personal income	Disposable personal income	Personal consumption expenditures	Gross domestic product	Gross national product	Disposable personal income	Personal consumption expenditures
1960.............	2,912	2,930	2,275	2,020	1,836	15,648	15,757	10,860	9,867
1970.............	5,063	5,094	4,089	3,586	3,161	20,802	20,946	15,151	13,355
1975.............	7,583	7,643	6,180	5,497	4,786	22,573	22,767	17,083	14,874
1980.............	12,243	12,394	10,107	8,794	7,710	25,618	25,945	18,855	16,531
1985.............	17,683	17,794	14,661	12,911	11,394	28,693	28,880	21,561	19,028
1990.............	23,185	23,323	19,373	17,004	15,331	32,085	32,276	23,557	21,240
1994.............	26,893	26,985	22,299	19,678	18,033	33,642	33,755	24,505	22,456
1995.............	27,813	27,924	23,260	20,470	18,708	34,082	34,216	24,939	22,793
1996.............	29,062	29,180	24,439	21,355	19,553	34,948	35,086	25,463	23,315
1997.............	30,526	30,612	25,648	22,255	20,408	36,071	36,172	26,049	23,888
1998.............	31,843	31,905	27,251	23,534	21,432	37,207	37,281	27,287	24,850
1999.............	33,486	33,585	28,321	24,356	22,707	38,559	38,675	27,792	25,911
2000.............	35,239	35,373	30,310	25,946	24,187	39,718	39,870	28,888	26,929
2001.............	36,063	36,245	31,145	26,816	25,064	39,749	39,951	29,297	27,383
2002.............	36,958	37,129	31,464	27,816	25,835	40,087	40,274	29,981	27,846
2003.............	38,339	38,575	32,269	28,827	26,853	40,727	40,980	30,453	28,368
2004.............	40,419	40,730	33,885	30,312	28,202	41,761	42,084	31,211	29,038
2005.............	42,646	42,974	35,426	31,343	29,742	42,646	42,974	31,343	29,742
2006.............	44,767	45,009	37,709	33,183	31,126	43,366	43,599	32,303	30,301
2007.............	46,499	46,908	39,484	34,550	32,391	43,774	44,157	32,749	30,703
2008.............	46,928	47,483	40,914	36,200	32,953	43,219	43,728	33,229	30,248
2009.............	45,368	45,864	38,830	35,115	32,112	41,346	41,802	32,166	29,415
2010.............	46,894	47,505	39,944	36,090	33,074	42,250	42,809	32,481	29,767
2011.............	48,372	49,159	41,678	37,191	34,374	42,671	43,370	32,667	30,193

Source: U.S. Bureau of Economic Analysis, *Survey of Current Business*, May 2012. See also <http://www.bea.gov/national/index.htm>.

Table 692. Personal Income in Current and Constant (2005) Dollars by State: 2000 to 2011

[In billions of dollars (8,554.9 represents $8,554,900,000,000). Represents a measure of income received from all sources during the calendar year by residents of each state. Data exclude federal employees overseas and U.S. residents employed by private U.S. firms on temporary foreign assignment. Totals may differ from those in Tables 685, 690, and 691]

State	Current dollars					Constant (2005) dollars [1]				
	2000	2005	2009	2010	2011, prel.	2000	2005	2009	2010	2011, prel.
United States............	8,554.9	10,476.7	11,916.8	12,353.6	12,981.7	9,524.7	10,476.7	10,932.4	11,120.6	11,408.5
Alabama....................	107.2	135.6	155.4	160.3	166.4	119.3	135.6	142.6	144.3	146.2
Alaska......................	19.2	24.6	30.2	31.6	32.9	21.3	24.6	27.7	28.4	28.9
Arizona....................	135.7	188.2	215.4	221.5	232.6	151.1	188.2	197.6	199.4	204.4
Arkansas..................	60.5	77.5	92.9	95.8	99.9	67.3	77.5	85.2	86.3	87.8
California..................	1,135.3	1,387.7	1,526.5	1,587.4	1,676.6	1,264.0	1,387.7	1,400.4	1,429.0	1,473.4
Colorado...................	147.1	179.7	205.8	213.5	225.6	163.7	179.7	188.8	192.2	198.3
Connecticut...............	143.0	168.8	188.8	193.9	203.7	159.2	168.8	173.2	174.6	179.0
Delaware..................	24.4	31.1	34.8	36.1	37.8	27.1	31.1	31.9	32.5	33.2
District of Columbia........	23.1	32.0	40.5	42.8	45.2	25.8	32.0	37.1	38.5	39.7
Florida.....................	466.6	633.2	697.3	719.8	754.0	519.5	633.2	639.7	648.0	662.6
Georgia....................	234.8	292.5	327.6	337.5	354.4	261.4	292.5	300.5	303.8	311.4
Hawaii.....................	35.2	45.3	54.6	56.6	59.2	39.2	45.3	50.1	51.0	52.0
Idaho......................	32.1	42.2	48.2	50.1	52.8	35.7	42.2	44.2	45.1	46.4
Illinois.....................	405.9	472.1	525.2	539.9	568.0	451.9	472.1	481.9	486.0	499.2
Indiana....................	167.3	195.5	215.2	220.6	231.7	186.2	195.5	197.5	198.5	203.6
Iowa.......................	79.9	95.5	112.5	116.0	123.9	89.0	95.5	103.2	104.4	108.9
Kansas....................	76.7	90.9	108.5	111.4	116.2	85.4	90.9	99.5	100.3	102.1
Kentucky..................	100.4	119.2	137.8	140.5	147.1	111.7	119.2	126.4	126.5	129.3
Louisiana.................	105.3	135.3	162.5	168.4	176.5	117.3	135.3	149.1	151.6	155.1
Maine.....................	34.1	42.0	48.0	48.8	50.4	38.0	42.0	44.0	43.9	44.3
Maryland..................	184.2	237.1	272.8	283.6	297.5	205.1	237.1	250.3	255.3	261.4
Massachusetts.............	243.1	282.4	324.5	336.3	353.2	270.7	282.4	297.7	302.8	310.4
Michigan..................	292.6	325.7	332.1	342.9	360.8	325.8	325.7	304.6	308.7	317.1
Minnesota.................	160.8	194.0	217.6	227.3	238.8	179.1	194.0	199.6	204.6	209.8
Mississippi................	61.4	77.7	88.9	92.3	95.8	68.4	77.7	81.6	83.1	84.2
Missouri...................	156.4	186.8	215.2	220.6	229.9	174.1	186.8	197.5	198.6	202.0
Montana...................	21.2	28.2	33.2	34.7	36.5	23.6	28.2	30.4	31.3	32.1
Nebraska..................	49.0	60.1	70.1	72.4	76.6	54.6	60.1	64.3	65.1	67.3
Nevada....................	62.5	91.8	98.1	99.9	104.0	69.6	91.8	90.0	89.9	91.4
New Hampshire.............	42.3	50.0	56.0	57.5	60.4	47.1	50.0	51.4	51.8	53.0
New Jersey................	326.0	379.7	433.8	450.0	469.1	362.9	379.7	398.0	405.1	412.3
New Mexico...............	41.4	55.3	66.0	68.9	72.0	46.1	55.3	60.5	62.0	63.3
New York..................	657.9	786.5	904.0	942.5	983.9	732.5	786.5	829.4	848.5	864.6
North Carolina.............	225.5	277.7	322.7	334.7	349.2	251.1	277.7	296.0	301.3	306.9
North Dakota..............	16.4	20.5	26.5	28.9	31.3	18.3	20.5	24.3	26.0	27.5
Ohio.......................	326.1	371.9	405.2	417.2	436.3	363.0	371.9	371.8	375.6	383.4
Oklahoma.................	85.0	107.6	126.4	133.1	141.3	94.6	107.6	116.0	119.8	124.2
Oregon....................	98.5	117.6	135.1	139.4	146.8	109.7	117.6	123.9	125.5	129.0
Pennsylvania..............	369.9	432.2	499.7	516.4	541.3	411.9	432.2	458.4	464.9	475.7
Rhode Island..............	31.0	38.6	42.8	44.2	46.2	34.5	38.6	39.2	39.8	40.6
South Carolina.............	100.9	124.4	145.3	150.5	157.6	112.4	124.4	133.3	135.5	138.5
South Dakota..............	20.0	25.8	30.9	32.3	34.3	22.2	25.8	28.4	29.1	30.1
Tennessee.................	152.2	187.7	213.0	222.0	233.9	169.5	187.7	195.4	199.8	205.6
Texas......................	597.0	756.7	905.3	953.3	1,016.5	664.7	756.7	830.5	858.1	893.3
Utah.......................	55.0	71.5	86.9	90.3	95.2	61.3	71.5	79.7	81.2	83.7
Vermont...................	17.2	20.7	24.3	25.1	26.2	19.1	20.7	22.3	22.6	23.0
Virginia....................	224.8	294.7	342.3	355.2	371.8	250.3	294.7	314.1	319.7	326.7
Washington................	191.6	230.1	278.9	287.2	302.5	213.3	230.1	255.9	258.5	265.9
West Virginia..............	40.1	48.1	57.5	59.4	62.2	44.6	48.1	52.8	53.5	54.6
Wisconsin..................	156.6	186.5	209.6	217.6	228.9	174.4	186.5	192.3	195.8	201.1
Wyoming..................	14.5	20.0	24.4	25.4	26.9	16.1	20.0	22.4	22.8	23.6

[1] Constant dollar estimates are computed by ProQuest using the national implicit price deflator for personal consumption expenditures from the Bureau of Economic Analysis. Any regional differences in the rate of inflation are not reflected in these constant dollar estimates.

Source: Except as noted, U.S. Bureau of Economic Analysis, *Survey of Current Business*, May 2012, and unpublished data. See also <http://www.bea.gov/itable/>.

Table 693. Personal Income Per Capita in Current and Constant (2005) Dollars by State: 1990 to 2011

[In dollars, except as indicated. 2011 preliminary. See headnote, Table 692]

State	Current dollars				Constant (2005) dollars [1]				Income rank	
	1990	2000	2010	2011, prel.	1990	2000	2010	2011, prel.	2000	2011
United States..................	**19,354**	**30,319**	**39,937**	**41,663**	**26,814**	**33,756**	**35,951**	**36,614**	**(X)**	**(X)**
Alabama........................	15,618	24,067	33,504	34,650	21,638	26,795	30,160	30,451	44	42
Alaska..........................	22,594	30,508	44,233	45,529	31,302	33,966	39,818	40,011	15	10
Arizona.........................	16,806	26,293	34,539	35,875	23,283	29,274	31,092	31,527	37	40
Arkansas.......................	14,402	22,574	32,805	34,014	19,953	25,133	29,531	29,892	48	44
California.......................	21,380	33,404	42,514	44,481	29,620	37,191	38,271	39,090	8	12
Colorado.......................	19,377	33,986	42,295	44,088	26,845	37,839	38,074	38,745	7	15
Connecticut....................	26,198	41,920	54,239	56,889	36,295	46,672	48,826	49,995	1	1
Delaware.......................	21,209	31,009	40,097	41,635	29,383	34,524	36,095	36,589	13	20
District of Columbia.............	26,015	40,462	70,710	73,105	36,042	45,049	63,653	64,246	(X)	(X)
Florida..........................	19,437	29,079	38,210	39,563	26,929	32,375	34,396	34,768	21	27
Georgia........................	17,563	28,541	34,747	36,104	24,332	31,776	31,279	31,729	26	39
Hawaii..........................	21,818	29,024	41,550	43,053	30,227	32,314	37,403	37,835	22	17
Idaho...........................	15,603	24,685	31,897	33,326	21,617	27,483	28,714	29,287	41	49
Illinois..........................	20,835	32,645	42,040	44,140	28,865	36,346	37,844	38,791	9	14
Indiana.........................	17,454	27,459	33,981	35,550	24,181	30,572	30,590	31,242	32	41
Iowa............................	17,350	27,285	38,039	40,470	24,037	30,378	34,243	35,566	33	24
Kansas.........................	18,034	28,486	38,977	40,481	24,985	31,695	35,087	35,575	28	23
Kentucky.......................	15,360	24,785	32,316	33,667	21,280	27,595	29,091	29,587	40	47
Louisiana.......................	15,171	23,554	37,039	38,578	21,018	26,224	33,342	33,903	45	28
Maine..........................	17,211	26,699	36,763	37,973	23,845	29,726	33,094	33,371	34	31
Maryland.......................	22,681	34,678	49,023	51,038	31,423	38,609	44,130	44,853	4	4
Massachusetts.................	22,797	38,222	51,304	53,621	31,584	42,555	46,184	47,123	3	2
Michigan.......................	18,719	29,400	34,714	36,533	25,934	32,733	31,249	32,106	18	37
Minnesota......................	19,710	32,599	42,798	44,672	27,307	36,295	38,527	39,258	10	11
Mississippi.....................	13,117	21,555	31,071	32,176	18,173	23,999	27,970	28,277	50	50
Missouri........................	17,582	27,885	36,799	38,248	24,359	31,046	33,126	33,613	31	29
Montana........................	15,346	23,457	35,053	36,573	21,261	26,116	31,555	32,141	46	35
Nebraska.......................	17,948	28,590	39,534	41,584	24,866	31,831	35,588	36,545	25	22
Nevada.........................	20,042	30,977	36,938	38,173	27,767	34,489	33,251	33,547	14	30
New Hampshire.................	20,236	34,102	43,698	45,787	28,035	37,968	39,337	40,238	6	8
New Jersey.....................	24,354	38,667	51,139	53,181	33,741	43,050	46,035	46,736	2	3
New Mexico....................	14,823	22,746	33,342	34,575	20,536	25,325	30,014	30,385	47	43
New York.......................	23,710	34,623	48,596	50,545	32,848	38,548	43,746	44,420	5	5
North Carolina..................	17,194	27,906	35,007	36,164	23,821	31,069	31,513	31,781	30	38
North Dakota...................	15,866	25,592	42,890	45,747	21,981	28,493	38,609	40,203	38	9
Ohio............................	18,638	28,695	36,162	37,791	25,822	31,948	32,553	33,211	24	33
Oklahoma......................	16,077	24,602	35,389	37,277	22,273	27,391	31,857	32,759	42	34
Oregon.........................	17,895	28,728	36,317	37,909	24,792	31,985	32,692	33,315	23	32
Pennsylvania...................	19,433	30,113	40,604	42,478	26,923	33,527	36,552	37,330	16	18
Rhode Island...................	19,821	29,498	41,995	43,992	27,461	32,842	37,804	38,661	17	16
South Carolina.................	15,844	25,076	32,462	33,673	21,951	27,919	29,222	29,592	39	46
South Dakota..................	16,075	26,421	39,519	41,590	22,271	29,416	35,575	36,550	36	21
Tennessee.....................	16,574	26,689	34,921	36,533	22,962	29,715	31,436	32,106	35	36
Texas..........................	17,260	28,506	37,747	39,593	23,912	31,738	33,980	34,795	27	26
Utah............................	14,847	24,515	32,517	33,790	20,569	27,294	29,272	29,695	43	45
Vermont........................	17,643	28,196	40,134	41,832	24,443	31,392	36,128	36,762	29	19
Virginia.........................	20,312	31,634	44,267	45,920	28,141	35,220	39,849	40,355	12	7
Washington....................	19,637	32,410	42,589	44,294	27,206	36,084	38,338	38,926	11	13
West Virginia...................	14,436	22,173	32,042	33,513	20,000	24,687	28,844	29,452	49	48
Wisconsin......................	17,986	29,141	38,225	40,073	24,918	32,444	34,410	35,217	20	25
Wyoming.......................	17,910	29,261	44,961	47,301	24,813	32,578	40,474	41,569	19	6

X Not applicable. [1] Constant dollar estimates are computed by ProQuest using the national implicit price deflator for personal consumption expenditures from the Bureau of Economic Analysis. Any regional differences in the rate of inflation are not reflected in these constant dollar estimates.

Source: Except as noted, U.S. Bureau of Economic Analysis, *Survey of Current Business*, May 2012, and unpublished data. See also <http://www.bea.gov/iTable/index_regional.cfm>.

Table 694. Disposable Personal Income Per Capita in Current and Constant (2005) Dollars by State: 1990 to 2011

[In dollars, except percent. Disposable personal income is the income available to persons for spending or saving; it is calculated as personal income less personal tax and nontax payments. See headnote, Table 692]

State	Current dollars				Constant (2005) dollars [1]				Index, compared to U.S. average	
	1990	2000	2010	2011, prel.	1990	2000	2010	2011, prel.	2000	2011, prel.
United States	**16,985**	**25,956**	**36,081**	**37,167**	**23,531**	**28,898**	**32,480**	**32,663**	**100.0**	**100.0**
Alabama	13,943	21,355	30,905	31,655	19,317	23,776	27,821	27,819	82.3	85.2
Alaska	19,937	27,081	40,597	41,258	27,621	30,151	36,545	36,258	104.3	111.0
Arizona	14,932	22,966	31,946	32,828	20,687	25,569	28,758	28,850	88.5	88.3
Arkansas	12,928	20,031	30,202	31,020	17,911	22,302	27,188	27,261	77.2	83.5
California	18,614	27,669	37,883	39,186	25,788	30,806	34,102	34,437	106.6	105.4
Colorado	17,003	28,865	38,210	39,336	23,556	32,137	34,396	34,569	111.2	105.8
Connecticut	22,815	33,837	46,813	47,992	31,608	37,673	42,141	42,176	130.4	129.1
Delaware	18,262	26,428	35,883	36,750	25,301	29,424	32,302	32,296	101.8	98.9
District of Columbia	22,400	33,441	62,782	63,938	31,034	37,232	56,516	56,189	128.8	172.0
Florida	17,398	25,392	35,284	36,124	24,104	28,271	31,762	31,746	97.8	97.2
Georgia	15,424	24,614	31,682	32,514	21,369	27,404	28,520	28,574	94.8	87.5
Hawaii	18,901	25,454	37,908	38,904	26,186	28,340	34,125	34,189	98.1	104.7
Idaho	13,868	21,577	29,446	30,510	19,213	24,023	26,507	26,813	83.1	82.1
Illinois	18,180	27,885	37,981	39,206	25,187	31,046	34,190	34,455	107.4	105.5
Indiana	15,331	23,983	30,900	31,970	21,240	26,702	27,816	28,096	92.4	86.0
Iowa	15,330	24,129	34,772	36,688	21,239	26,864	31,302	32,242	93.0	98.7
Kansas	15,921	24,833	35,383	36,410	22,057	27,648	31,852	31,998	95.7	98.0
Kentucky	13,544	21,725	29,442	30,371	18,764	24,188	26,504	26,690	83.7	81.7
Louisiana	13,687	21,059	34,245	35,307	18,962	23,446	30,827	31,028	81.1	95.0
Maine	15,222	23,230	33,566	34,326	21,089	25,863	30,216	30,166	89.5	92.4
Maryland	19,420	29,229	43,451	44,699	26,905	32,542	39,114	39,282	112.6	120.3
Massachusetts	19,549	30,795	45,013	46,235	27,084	34,286	40,520	40,632	118.6	124.4
Michigan	16,368	25,293	31,779	32,970	22,677	28,160	28,607	28,974	97.4	88.7
Minnesota	17,123	27,781	38,334	39,404	23,723	30,930	34,508	34,629	107.0	106.0
Mississippi	11,938	19,491	29,035	29,863	16,539	21,701	26,137	26,244	75.1	80.3
Missouri	15,492	24,330	33,608	34,593	21,463	27,088	30,254	30,401	93.7	93.1
Montana	13,693	20,770	32,024	33,069	18,971	23,125	28,828	29,061	80.0	89.0
Nebraska	15,996	25,063	36,189	37,664	22,161	27,904	32,577	33,100	96.6	101.3
Nevada	17,562	26,875	33,947	34,667	24,331	29,922	30,559	30,466	103.5	93.3
New Hampshire	18,016	29,286	40,057	41,473	24,960	32,606	36,059	36,447	112.8	111.6
New Jersey	21,163	32,334	45,391	46,562	29,320	35,999	40,861	40,919	124.6	125.3
New Mexico	13,313	20,196	30,672	31,520	18,444	22,485	27,611	27,700	77.8	84.8
New York	20,371	28,618	41,971	42,835	28,222	31,862	37,782	37,644	110.3	115.3
North Carolina	15,145	24,246	31,850	32,568	20,982	26,995	28,671	28,621	93.4	87.6
North Dakota	14,380	23,092	39,427	41,213	19,922	25,710	35,492	36,218	89.0	110.9
Ohio	16,341	24,758	32,815	33,869	22,639	27,565	29,540	29,764	95.4	91.1
Oklahoma	14,170	21,721	32,504	33,857	19,631	24,183	29,260	29,754	83.7	91.1
Oregon	15,709	24,544	32,688	33,720	21,764	27,326	29,426	29,634	94.6	90.7
Pennsylvania	17,091	26,002	36,538	37,773	23,678	28,950	32,891	33,195	100.2	101.6
Rhode Island	17,453	25,351	38,115	39,454	24,180	28,225	34,311	34,673	97.7	106.2
South Carolina	14,044	22,161	29,950	30,771	19,457	24,673	26,961	27,042	85.4	82.8
South Dakota	14,725	23,876	36,875	38,493	20,400	26,583	33,195	33,828	92.0	103.6
Tennessee	15,004	24,009	32,684	33,879	20,787	26,731	29,422	29,773	92.5	91.2
Texas	15,463	25,168	34,867	36,130	21,423	28,021	31,387	31,751	97.0	97.2
Utah	13,131	21,453	29,715	30,541	18,192	23,885	26,749	26,840	82.7	82.2
Vermont	15,527	24,535	36,731	37,848	21,511	27,316	33,065	33,261	94.5	101.8
Virginia	17,735	26,775	39,497	40,417	24,571	29,810	35,555	35,519	103.2	108.7
Washington	17,449	27,954	39,273	40,364	24,174	31,123	35,353	35,472	107.7	108.6
West Virginia	12,908	19,815	29,357	30,362	17,883	22,061	26,427	26,682	76.3	81.7
Wisconsin	15,716	25,079	34,503	35,763	21,773	27,922	31,059	31,429	96.6	96.2
Wyoming	16,056	25,312	41,265	42,929	22,244	28,181	37,147	37,727	97.5	115.5

[1] Constant dollar estimates are computed by ProQuest using the national implicit price deflator for personal consumption expenditures from the Bureau of Economic Analysis. Any regional differences in the rate of inflation are not reflected in these constant dollar estimates.

Source: Except as noted, U.S. Bureau of Economic Analysis, *Survey of Current Business*, May 2012, earlier reports and unpublished data. See also <http://www.bea.gov/iTable/index_regional.cfm>.

Table 695. Personal Income by Selected Large Metropolitan Area: 2005 to 2010

[9,152,380 represents $9,152,380,000,000. Metropolitan areas as defined December 2009. MSA = Metropolitan Statistical Area. See Appendix II. Minus sign (–) indicates decrease]

Metropolitan areas ranked by 2010 population	Personal income				Personal income per capita			
	2005 (mil. dol.)	2009 (mil. dol.)	2010 (mil. dol.)	Annual percent change, 2009–2010	2005 (dol.)	2009 (dol.)	2010 (dol.)	Index (U.S.= 100), 2010
United States, metro portion...............	9,152,380	10,372,056	10,749,602	3.6	37,177	40,442	41,524	100.0
New York-Northern New Jersey-Long Island, NY-NJ-PA MSA..........	863,632	986,036	1,028,560	4.3	46,510	52,448	54,365	130.9
Los Angeles-Long Beach-Santa Ana, CA MSA..........	496,595	541,033	561,142	3.7	39,021	42,352	43,688	105.2
Chicago-Joliet-Naperville, IL-IN-WI MSA........	375,515	408,690	420,051	2.8	40,481	43,342	44,344	106.8
Dallas-Fort Worth-Arlington, TX MSA............	220,482	252,935	264,223	4.5	38,494	40,227	41,282	99.4
Philadelphia-Camden-Wilmington, PA-NJ-DE-MD MSA..........	236,491	272,509	281,764	3.4	40,571	45,865	47,184	113.6
Houston-Sugar Land-Baytown, TX MSA........	209,655	250,562	262,968	5.0	39,868	42,815	44,001	106.0
Washington-Arlington-Alexandria, DC-VA-MD-WV MSA..........	262,193	307,389	321,644	4.6	50,187	55,947	57,343	138.1
Miami-Fort Lauderdale-Pompano Beach, FL MSA..........	210,605	226,021	232,992	3.1	38,921	41,060	41,769	100.6
Atlanta-Sandy Springs-Marietta, GA MSA..........	179,145	196,729	202,577	3.0	37,683	37,667	38,321	92.3
Boston-Cambridge-Quincy, MA-NH MSA.........	212,251	243,699	252,729	3.7	48,042	53,830	55,431	133.5
San Francisco-Oakland-Fremont, CA MSA..........	227,850	247,646	257,540	4.0	55,065	57,554	59,295	142.8
Detroit-Warren-Livonia, MI MSA..........	164,087	159,500	163,893	2.8	37,031	36,992	38,197	92.0
Riverside-San Bernardino-Ontario, CA MSA..........	108,598	120,805	124,840	3.3	28,020	29,035	29,409	70.8
Phoenix-Mesa-Glendale, AZ MSA..........	131,597	147,839	151,725	2.6	34,863	35,593	36,047	86.8
Seattle-Tacoma-Bellevue, WA MSA..........	138,212	165,239	169,344	2.5	43,215	48,389	49,115	118.3
Minneapolis-St. Paul-Bloomington, MN-WI MSA..........	133,840	147,623	153,844	4.2	42,740	45,262	46,819	112.8
San Diego-Carlsbad-San Marcos, CA MSA..........	122,030	135,953	141,678	4.2	41,530	44,412	45,627	109.9
St. Louis, MO-IL MSA..........	101,082	113,930	116,891	2.6	36,697	40,624	41,528	100.0
Tampa-St. Petersburg-Clearwater, FL MSA..........	91,393	100,202	103,171	3.0	34,467	36,253	37,003	89.1
Baltimore-Towson, MD MSA..........	111,453	128,354	133,362	3.9	42,150	47,609	49,129	118.3
Denver-Aurora-Broomfield, CO MSA..........	101,788	115,201	119,734	3.9	43,634	45,907	46,871	112.9
Pittsburgh, PA MSA..........	84,956	97,150	100,656	3.6	35,779	41,245	42,688	102.8
Portland-South Portland-Biddeford, ME MSA........	18,631	21,077	21,526	2.1	36,510	40,948	41,901	100.9
Sacramento-Arden-Arcade-Roseville, CA MSA......	75,029	83,913	86,154	2.7	36,872	39,347	39,987	96.3
San Antonio-New Braunfels, TX MSA..........	58,670	71,292	75,320	5.7	30,939	33,857	34,969	84.2
Orlando-Kissimmee-Sanford, FL MSA..........	64,007	71,115	73,535	3.4	32,727	33,673	34,368	82.8
Cincinnati-Middletown, OH-KY-IN MSA..........	75,148	81,903	84,600	3.3	36,294	38,572	39,673	95.5
Cleveland-Elyria-Mentor, OH MSA..........	76,110	81,240	84,078	3.5	36,042	39,038	40,509	97.6
Kansas City, MO-KS MSA..........	70,738	82,973	84,767	2.2	36,558	41,061	41,557	100.1
Las Vegas-Paradise, NV MSA..........	64,181	68,791	69,800	1.5	37,109	35,470	35,723	86.0
San Jose-Sunnyvale-Santa Clara, CA MSA..........	89,629	98,182	105,605	7.6	51,810	53,959	57,338	138.1
Columbus, OH MSA..........	60,968	68,120	70,319	3.2	35,307	37,384	38,205	92.0
Charlotte-Gastonia-Rock Hill, NC-SC MSA..........	57,216	65,344	68,610	5.0	37,678	37,562	38,895	93.7
Indianapolis-Carmel, IN MSA..........	60,018	66,185	68,314	3.2	36,550	37,997	38,796	93.4
Austin-Round Rock-San Marcos, TX MSA...........	51,047	63,323	66,945	5.7	35,124	37,640	38,736	93.3
Virginia Beach-Norfolk-Newport News, VA-NC MSA..........	56,595	65,410	67,373	3.0	34,413	39,325	40,234	96.9
Providence-New Bedford-Fall River, RI-MA MSA..........	57,418	64,335	66,483	3.3	35,589	40,185	41,524	100.0
Nashville-Davidson-Murfreesboro-Franklin, TN MSA..........	52,294	60,784	64,016	5.3	36,382	38,629	40,138	96.7
Milwaukee-Waukesha-West Allis, WI MSA.........	58,251	65,010	66,720	2.6	38,263	41,952	42,853	103.2
Jacksonville, FL MSA..........	45,618	51,261	53,341	4.1	36,521	38,398	39,550	95.2
Memphis, TN-MS-AR MSA..........	44,057	47,608	49,519	4.0	34,865	36,369	37,569	90.5
Louisville-Jefferson County, KY-IN MSA..........	41,228	46,641	47,567	2.0	33,820	36,576	36,992	89.1
Richmond, VA MSA..........	44,587	50,498	52,004	3.0	37,749	40,384	41,260	99.4
Oklahoma City, OK MSA..........	38,462	44,927	47,221	5.1	33,120	36,297	37,533	90.4
Hartford-West Hartford-East Hartford, CT MSA..........	51,428	59,428	61,297	3.2	43,292	49,130	50,555	121.7
New Orleans-Metairie-Kenner, LA MSA..........	43,498	47,648	49,859	4.6	31,866	41,592	42,485	102.3
Buffalo-Niagara Falls, NY MSA..........	36,232	41,987	43,449	3.5	31,546	36,981	38,271	92.2
Raleigh-Cary, NC MSA..........	35,209	43,001	44,899	4.4	37,269	38,737	39,479	95.1
Birmingham-Hoover, AL MSA..........	39,199	42,653	43,733	2.5	36,084	37,905	38,734	93.3
Salt Lake City, UT MSA..........	35,347	41,575	43,154	3.8	34,273	37,460	38,248	92.1
Rochester, NY MSA..........	35,256	40,555	42,103	3.8	33,728	38,527	39,919	96.1
Tucson, AZ MSA..........	28,574	33,449	34,361	2.7	31,048	34,286	34,987	84.3
Honolulu, HI MSA..........	34,264	41,664	43,210	3.7	37,437	44,174	45,216	108.9
Tulsa, OK MSA..........	30,734	35,072	36,565	4.3	34,812	37,719	38,894	93.7
Fresno, CA MSA..........	24,078	27,788	28,839	3.8	27,598	30,156	30,905	74.4
Bridgeport-Stamford-Norwalk, CT MSA..........	61,073	64,179	65,907	2.7	68,036	70,494	71,768	172.8
Albuquerque, NM MSA..........	25,338	29,899	30,688	2.6	31,299	34,114	34,482	83.0
Albany-Schenectady-Troy, NY MSA..........	30,672	35,948	36,985	2.9	35,890	41,350	42,464	102.3
Omaha-Council Bluffs, NE-IA MSA..........	31,077	35,708	36,559	2.4	38,164	41,703	42,115	101.4
New Haven-Milford, CT MSA..........	33,857	39,309	40,270	2.4	39,965	45,707	46,693	112.4

Source: U.S. Bureau of Economic Analysis, *Survey of Current Business*, April 2012. See also <http://www.bea.gov/regional/index.htm>.

Table 696. Household Income—Distribution by Income Level and State: 2010

[In thousands (114,567 represents 114,567,000), except as indicated. The American Community Survey universe includes the household population and the population living in institutions, college dormitories, and other group quarters. Based on a sample and subject to sampling variability; see text, Section 1 and Appendix III. For definition of median, see Guide to Tabular Presentation]

State	Number of households (1,000)								Median income (dollars)
	Total	Under $25,000	$25,000 to $49,999	$50,000 to $74,999	$75,000 to $99,999	$100,000 to $149,999	$150,000 to $199,999	$200,000 or more	
United States.......	**114,567**	**28,591**	**28,636**	**20,941**	**13,527**	**13,545**	**4,810**	**4,518**	**50,046**
Alabama..............	1,815	580	493	308	178	164	54	39	40,474
Alaska................	255	43	54	49	34	46	16	13	64,576
Arizona...............	2,334	589	641	438	264	256	76	70	46,789
Arkansas.............	1,115	361	328	191	105	87	24	20	38,307
California.............	12,406	2,669	2,771	2,169	1,531	1,770	753	744	57,708
Colorado.............	1,961	435	472	362	248	266	94	84	54,046
Connecticut..........	1,359	261	279	231	180	212	92	104	64,032
Delaware.............	329	69	77	64	43	47	16	12	55,847
District of Columbia. ..	252	61	46	40	29	33	18	26	60,903
Florida................	7,035	1,919	1,967	1,285	751	678	216	219	44,409
Georgia..............	3,482	954	891	634	386	373	130	114	46,430
Hawaii................	446	82	93	82	64	75	25	23	63,030
Idaho.................	577	154	169	119	65	47	13	10	43,490
Illinois................	4,753	1,096	1,141	873	601	615	219	208	52,972
Indiana................	2,471	656	702	474	287	239	61	51	44,613
Iowa..................	1,223	297	338	250	153	126	34	25	47,961
Kansas................	1,102	270	297	219	132	119	35	29	48,257
Kentucky.............	1,684	547	455	294	175	141	38	33	40,062
Louisiana.............	1,690	523	428	288	184	171	50	45	42,505
Maine.................	545	145	147	109	65	53	15	11	45,815
Maryland.............	2,127	346	412	388	287	372	167	156	68,854
Massachusetts........	2,520	543	490	429	323	403	165	167	62,072
Michigan.............	3,807	1,047	1,019	720	428	383	119	90	45,413
Minnesota............	2,092	442	500	413	290	278	93	76	55,459
Mississippi............	1,080	384	292	180	107	80	20	18	36,851
Missouri..............	2,351	654	641	437	261	235	64	59	44,301
Montana..............	403	112	117	74	47	36	9	7	42,666
Nebraska.............	719	176	193	145	92	76	20	17	48,408
Nevada...............	990	227	257	196	126	118	36	30	51,001
New Hampshire.......	515	90	120	100	74	80	29	23	61,042
New Jersey...........	3,172	576	609	542	414	527	247	258	67,681
New Mexico...........	765	230	206	132	81	75	24	17	42,090
New York.............	7,196	1,735	1,595	1,232	849	967	395	424	54,148
North Carolina........	3,671	1,046	1,019	675	396	332	106	98	43,326
North Dakota..........	280	71	73	56	38	31	7	6	48,670
Ohio..................	4,525	1,241	1,223	850	520	452	131	109	45,090
Oklahoma.............	1,433	415	406	272	149	123	36	31	42,072
Oregon...............	1,507	390	411	285	173	161	47	40	46,560
Pennsylvania..........	4,936	1,252	1,243	929	590	564	190	167	49,288
Rhode Island..........	402	101	90	73	52	51	19	16	52,254
South Carolina........	1,761	538	475	320	189	156	44	38	42,018
South Dakota.........	319	82	89	63	39	31	7	7	45,904
Tennessee............	2,441	736	682	443	248	209	61	62	41,461
Texas.................	8,739	2,227	2,235	1,589	999	1,003	352	333	48,615
Utah..................	880	175	222	194	121	115	29	25	54,744
Vermont..............	257	64	65	51	33	27	9	7	49,406
Virginia...............	2,993	583	668	533	377	449	194	190	60,674
Washington...........	2,607	548	621	509	351	356	124	98	55,631
West Virginia..........	742	251	208	130	75	56	12	10	38,218
Wisconsin.............	2,280	550	608	457	293	251	66	54	49,001
Wyoming.............	223	48	54	47	31	29	8	6	53,512

Source: U.S. Census Bureau, 2010 American Community Survey, B19001, "Household Income in the Past 12 Months" and B19013, "Median Household Income in the Past 12 Months (In 2010 Inflation-Adjusted Dollars)," <http://factfinder.census.gov/>, accessed April 2011.

Table 697. Family Income—Distribution by Income Level and State: 2010

[In thousands (76,089 represents 76,089,000), except as indicated. The American Community Survey universe includes the household population and the population living in institutions, college dormitories, and other group quarters. Based on a sample and subject to sampling variability; see text, Section 1 and Appendix III. For definition of median, see Guide to Tabular Presentation]

State	Number of families (1,000)								Median income (dollars)
	Total	Less than $25,000	$25,000 to $49,000	$50,000 to $74,999	$75,000 to $99,999	$100,000 to $149,999	$150,000 to $199,999	$200,000 and over	
United States.......	76,089	13,256	17,910	14,991	10,639	11,262	4,131	3,901	60,609
Alabama.............	1,228	280	328	239	151	145	49	36	50,429
Alaska..............	171	20	31	32	26	37	14	12	76,962
Arizona.............	1,548	294	399	318	202	209	65	61	55,353
Arkansas............	761	177	224	153	91	78	22	17	47,049
California...........	8,508	1,435	1,837	1,499	1,124	1,383	616	614	65,481
Colorado............	1,259	182	270	241	190	219	83	75	67,800
Connecticut..........	891	102	155	151	137	176	77	92	81,246
Delaware............	221	29	49	44	35	39	14	11	68,746
District of Columbia. ..	102	19	17	14	10	15	10	17	77,514
Florida................	4,557	889	1,233	921	587	559	183	187	53,093
Georgia..............	2,386	492	590	464	306	317	116	101	55,209
Hawaii..............	303	35	57	56	53	62	22	18	76,134
Idaho...............	402	72	115	95	56	41	12	9	52,342
Illinois..............	3,134	482	691	608	468	512	193	180	65,417
Indiana..............	1,656	289	452	361	241	214	54	46	55,368
Iowa................	794	112	199	189	128	113	30	23	60,917
Kansas..............	722	110	174	163	111	107	31	26	61,013
Kentucky............	1,127	256	302	225	151	128	35	29	50,392
Louisiana............	1,129	257	279	211	150	147	46	39	52,456
Maine...............	345	58	89	80	52	44	13	10	58,197
Maryland............	1,432	149	240	250	215	295	144	139	83,137
Massachusetts........	1,590	211	273	275	231	316	141	144	78,653
Michigan............	2,509	462	639	529	352	337	108	81	56,101
Minnesota............	1,354	170	281	288	229	237	82	67	69,625
Mississippi............	746	202	202	142	94	72	19	15	45,484
Missouri.............	1,524	272	395	330	213	204	57	52	56,214
Montana.............	255	48	68	54	40	31	8	6	54,507
Nebraska............	468	68	114	108	76	69	18	15	60,812
Nevada..............	640	108	159	134	96	94	27	24	60,192
New Hampshire.......	344	34	70	68	59	67	25	20	74,634
New Jersey..........	2,186	261	361	361	312	442	218	231	82,427
New Mexico..........	501	119	126	95	63	64	20	16	51,020
New York...........	4,633	787	974	822	618	765	323	344	65,897
North Carolina........	2,442	507	643	499	326	284	94	88	52,920
North Dakota..........	172	24	38	40	31	27	6	5	65,207
Ohio................	2,960	541	754	629	431	392	117	97	56,518
Oklahoma............	955	195	260	209	126	106	32	26	51,958
Oregon.............	963	169	251	199	137	131	41	34	56,661
Pennsylvania..........	3,198	490	759	677	473	484	167	148	61,890
Rhode Island..........	246	36	52	48	37	42	17	13	67,814
South Carolina........	1,181	260	308	241	159	138	39	34	51,704
South Dakota.........	204	31	50	49	34	28	6	6	59,987
Tennessee............	1,645	354	448	339	208	185	54	57	51,083
Texas................	6,092	1,203	1,487	1,161	797	846	305	293	56,575
Utah................	666	93	159	157	106	101	27	23	61,618
Vermont.............	160	23	39	35	26	23	8	6	62,575
Virginia.............	2,014	265	404	369	287	356	165	167	72,476
Washington..........	1,681	240	350	348	266	289	104	85	67,328
West Virginia.........	486	108	140	103	64	50	11	9	48,927
Wisconsin............	1,453	217	342	329	239	220	59	48	62,088
Wyoming.............	147	18	31	36	25	25	8	5	65,841

Source: U.S. Census Bureau, 2010 American Community Survey, B19101, "Family Income in the Past 12 Months" and B19113, "Median Family Income in the Past 12 Months (In 2010 Inflation-Adjusted Dollars)," <http://factfinder.census.gov/>, accessed April 2012.

Table 698. Average Annual Expenditures of All Consumer Units by Selected Major Types of Expenditure: 1990 to 2010

[In dollars, except as indicated (96,968 represents 96,968,000). Based on Consumer Expenditure Survey. Data are averages for the noninstitutional population. Expenditures reported here are out-of-pocket. Consumer units include families, single persons living alone or sharing a household with others but who are financially independent, or two or more persons living together who share expenses]

Type of expenditure	1990	1995	2000	2005	2007	2008	2009	2010
Number of consumer units (1,000).............	96,968	103,123	109,367	117,356	120,171	120,770	120,847	121,107
Expenditures, avg. (dol.) [1]..................	**28,381**	**32,264**	**38,045**	**46,409**	**49,638**	**50,486**	**49,067**	**48,109**
Food..........................	4,296	4,505	5,158	5,931	6,133	6,443	6,372	6,129
Food at home [1]...........................	2,485	2,803	3,021	3,297	3,465	3,744	3,753	3,624
Meats, poultry, fish, and eggs..............	668	752	795	764	777	846	841	784
Dairy products.....................	295	297	325	378	387	430	406	380
Fruits and vegetables.....................	408	457	521	552	600	657	656	679
Other food at home..........................	746	856	927	1,158	1,241	1,305	1,343	1,278
Food away from home.....................	1,811	1,702	2,137	2,634	2,668	2,698	2,619	2,505
Alcoholic beverages...........................	293	277	372	426	457	444	435	412
Housing [1].........................	8,703	10,458	12,319	15,167	16,920	17,109	16,895	16,557
Shelter.........................	4,836	5,928	7,114	8,805	10,023	10,183	10,075	9,812
Utilities, fuels, and public services...........	1,890	2,191	2,489	3,183	3,477	3,649	3,645	3,660
Apparel and services........................	1,618	1,704	1,856	1,886	1,881	1,801	1,725	1,700
Transportation [1]........................	5,120	6,014	7,417	8,344	8,758	8,604	7,658	7,677
Vehicle purchases.....................	2,129	2,638	3,418	3,544	3,244	2,755	2,657	2,588
Gasoline and motor oil........................	1,047	1,006	1,291	2,013	2,384	2,715	1,986	2,132
Other vehicle expenses.....................	1,642	2,015	2,281	2,339	2,592	2,621	2,536	2,464
Health care........................	1,480	1,732	2,066	2,664	2,853	2,976	3,126	3,157
Entertainment..........................	1,422	1,612	1,863	2,388	2,698	2,835	2,693	2,504
Reading........................	153	162	146	126	118	116	110	100
Tobacco products, smoking supplies...........	274	269	319	319	323	317	380	362
Personal insurance and pensions..............	2,592	2,964	3,365	5,204	5,336	5,605	5,471	5,373
Life and other personal insurance............	345	373	399	381	309	317	309	318
Pensions and Social Security.................	2,248	2,591	2,966	4,823	5,027	5,288	5,162	5,054

[1] Includes expenditures not shown separately.

Source: U.S. Bureau of Labor Statistics, *Consumer Expenditure Survey, 2010*. See also <http://www.bls.gov/cex/home.htm>.

Table 699. Average Annual Expenditures of All Consumer Units by Metropolitan Area: 2009 to 2010

[In dollars. Covers 2-year period, 2009-2010. Metropolitan areas defined June 30, 1983: CMSA = Consolidated Metropolitan Statistical Area; MSA = Metropolitan Statistical Area; PMSA = Primary Metropolitan Statistical Area. See text, Section 1 and Appendix II. See headnote, Table 698]

Metropolitan area	Total expenditures [1]	Food	Housing			Transportation			Health care
			Total [1]	Shelter	Utility fuels [2]	Total [1]	Vehicle purchases	Gasoline and motor oil	
Atlanta, GA MSA.............................	47,502	5,399	17,932	10,849	4,078	7,164	[3] 2,330	2,249	2,668
Baltimore, MD MSA...........................	52,815	6,158	20,642	13,293	4,276	6,566	[3] 1,937	2,123	3,043
Boston-Lawrence-Salem, MA-NH CMSA..	63,063	8,066	20,959	12,866	4,177	9,104	3,324	2,056	4,004
Chicago-Gary-Lake County, IL-IN-WI CMSA..............................	57,022	7,200	20,537	13,218	3,969	8,662	3,025	2,157	3,500
Cleveland-Akron-Lorain, OH CMSA........	44,561	5,534	14,720	8,337	3,680	6,931	2,032	1,706	2,824
Dallas-Fort Worth, TX CMSA................	52,977	6,673	18,181	10,183	4,346	8,016	2,257	2,452	3,182
Detroit-Ann Arbor, MI CMSA................	50,608	6,058	16,489	9,665	3,911	9,460	3,414	2,212	2,871
Houston-Galveston-Brazoria, TX CMSA...	56,764	6,610	19,323	10,903	4,539	9,410	3,351	2,471	3,413
Los Angeles-Long Beach, CA PMSA.......	54,576	7,182	20,584	14,126	3,049	8,540	2,260	2,334	2,478
Miami-Fort Lauderdale, FL CMSA..........	42,266	5,381	18,407	12,274	3,737	6,569	[3] 1,585	2,149	1,629
Minneapolis-St. Paul, MN-WI MSA........	54,420	6,927	18,291	11,045	3,336	7,482	2,173	2,134	3,668
New York-Northern New Jersey-Long Island, NY-NJ-CT CMSA..................	58,942	7,412	23,238	15,321	4,323	7,944	2,098	1,741	3,016
Philadelphia-Wilmington-Trenton, PA-NJ-DE-MD CMSA......................	52,041	6,217	19,690	12,268	4,316	6,960	1,788	1,802	2,950
Phoenix-Mesa, AZ MSA......................	49,016	6,583	16,480	9,476	3,742	8,008	2,561	2,202	2,995
San Diego, CA MSA..........................	52,012	5,831	21,679	15,305	3,114	6,963	1,819	2,246	2,370
San Francisco-Oakland-San Jose, CA CMSA.................................	67,360	7,920	26,268	19,190	3,207	8,509	2,457	1,931	3,461
Seattle-Tacoma, WA CMSA.................	65,317	7,174	21,627	13,453	3,611	10,054	4,463	2,046	3,922
Washington, DC-MD-VA MSA...............	70,075	7,693	25,427	16,398	4,103	10,067	3,363	2,139	3,554

[1] Includes expenditures not shown separately. [2] Includes public services. [3] Data are likely to have large sampling errors.

Source: U.S. Bureau of Labor Statistics, *Consumer Expenditure Survey, 2010*. See also <http://www.bls.gov/cex/csxmsa.htm>.

Table 700. Average Annual Expenditures of All Consumer Units by Race, Hispanic Origin, and Age of Householder: 2010

[In dollars. See headnote, Table 698]

Type	All consumer units [1]	White and all other races	Asian	Black or African American	Hispanic [2]	Age of householder Under 25 years	Age of householder 65 years old and over
Expenditures, total	**48,109**	**49,395**	**58,376**	**35,863**	**41,456**	**27,483**	**36,802**
Food	6,129	6,253	7,656	4,796	6,486	4,073	4,558
Food at home	3,624	3,689	3,953	3,075	4,012	2,197	2,950
Cereals and bakery products	502	511	563	419	519	312	416
Cereals and cereal products	165	162	269	151	188	103	123
Bakery products	337	349	294	268	331	209	293
Meats, poultry, fish, and eggs [3]	784	776	891	813	964	447	660
Beef	217	226	174	167	267	136	206
Pork	149	146	156	169	176	83	134
Poultry	138	131	154	182	192	84	94
Fish and seafood	117	108	251	139	142	45	97
Dairy products	380	400	350	255	421	218	316
Fresh milk and cream	141	145	171	102	170	88	110
Other dairy products	240	255	179	153	251	130	206
Fruits and vegetables [3]	679	683	958	572	820	395	577
Fresh fruits	232	235	330	182	287	119	199
Fresh vegetables	210	211	385	156	255	131	184
Processed fruits	113	112	120	117	134	68	96
Other food at home [3]	1,278	1,320	1,190	1,016	1,287	826	982
Sugar and other sweets	132	137	99	107	114	63	116
Nonalcoholic beverages	333	341	290	291	384	223	232
Food away from home	2,505	2,564	3,703	1,721	2,474	1,876	1,608
Alcoholic beverages	412	446	322	203	260	406	295
Housing	16,557	16,712	20,549	14,102	15,432	9,553	13,015
Shelter	9,812	9,851	13,875	8,132	9,518	6,166	7,027
Owned dwellings	6,277	6,572	8,099	3,630	4,676	1,123	4,881
Mortgage interest and charges	3,351	3,451	4,582	2,242	2,911	686	1,317
Property taxes	1,814	1,920	2,385	894	1,218	252	1,919
Maintenance, repair, insurance, other expenses	1,112	1,202	1,132	495	547	185	1,645
Rented dwellings	2,900	2,604	4,922	4,216	4,526	4,813	1,514
Other lodging	635	675	853	286	317	231	632
Utilities, fuels, and public services	3,660	3,666	3,285	3,749	3,471	1,818	3,402
Natural gas	440	428	447	517	379	186	460
Electricity	1,413	1,413	1,108	1,513	1,330	716	1,348
Fuel oil and other fuels	140	159	44	49	40	20	212
Telephone	1,178	1,173	1,143	1,221	1,244	713	883
Water and other public services	489	492	543	449	477	184	498
Household operations	1,007	1,037	1,298	704	673	416	827
Personal services	340	341	567	256	263	154	90
Other household expenses	667	696	731	448	410	261	737
Housekeeping supplies [3]	612	638	542	449	549	279	664
Laundry and cleaning supplies	150	152	97	157	195	90	139
Postage and stationery	132	140	147	73	79	34	153
Household furnishings and equipment [3]	1,467	1,520	1,549	1,068	1,222	874	1,095
Household textiles	102	108	89	71	91	53	91
Furniture	355	359	378	324	301	268	229
Major appliances	209	216	185	173	153	92	195
Miscellaneous household equipment	657	690	766	389	570	409	465
Apparel and services [3]	1,700	1,663	3,414	1,429	1,998	1,559	964
Men and boys	382	385	613	289	415	260	211
Women and girls	663	668	881	558	696	670	419
Footwear	303	292	493	323	476	305	149
Other apparel products and services	261	227	1,295	180	261	177	157
Transportation	7,677	7,915	8,673	5,724	6,629	4,692	5,242
Vehicle purchases (net outlay) [3]	2,588	2,734	2,599	1,591	1,907	1,591	1,495
Cars and trucks, new	1,219	1,264	1,646	764	637	393	696
Cars and trucks, used	1,318	1,411	909	827	1,213	1,107	795
Gasoline and motor oil	2,132	2,186	2,098	1,775	2,185	1,493	1,396
Other vehicle expenses	2,464	2,509	2,885	2,025	2,134	1,333	1,959
Vehicle finance charges	243	253	189	193	233	137	108
Maintenance and repair	787	815	788	602	621	480	608
Vehicle insurance	1,010	1,005	1,336	946	926	498	933
Vehicle rental, leases, licenses, other charges	423	436	572	285	354	217	311
Public transportation	493	486	1,092	333	402	275	391
Health care [5]	3,157	3,397	2,525	1,734	1,842	775	4,843
Entertainment [6]	2,504	2,687	2,192	1,352	1,644	1,221	1,891
Personal care products and services	582	590	593	525	565	347	517
Reading	100	109	89	41	37	39	141
Education	1,074	1,077	2,854	441	803	1,906	193
Tobacco products and smoking supplies	362	392	146	231	165	283	227
Miscellaneous	849	907	546	549	507	277	772
Cash contributions	1,633	1,700	1,178	1,334	1,074	314	2,272
Personal insurance and pensions	5,373	5,546	7,640	3,401	4,014	2,036	1,872
Life and other personal insurance	318	333	333	212	149	22	314
Pensions and social security	5,054	5,213	7,306	3,189	3,865	2,013	1,557
Personal taxes	**1,769**	**1,811**	**4,873**	**407**	**446**	**104**	**660**

[1] Includes other races not shown separately. [2] People of Hispanic origin may be any race. [3] Includes other types, not shown separately. [4] Data are likely to have large sampling errors. [5] For additional health care expenditures, see Table 146. [6] For additional recreation expenditures, see Section 26.

Source: U.S. Bureau of Labor Statistics, *Consumer Expenditure Survey 2010*. See also <http://www.bls.gov/cex/home.htm>.

Table 701. Average Annual Expenditures of All Consumer Units by Region and Size of Unit: 2010

[In dollars. For composition of regions, see map, inside front cover. See headnote, Table 698]

Type	Region				Size of consumer unit				
	North-east	Mid-west	South	West	One person	Two persons	Three persons	Four persons	Five or more
Expenditures, total	**52,802**	**45,278**	**44,217**	**53,429**	**29,149**	**50,967**	**56,413**	**63,268**	**61,086**
Food	6,755	5,738	5,645	6,804	3,450	5,958	7,297	8,778	9,083
Food at home	3,910	3,577	3,335	3,914	1,877	3,480	4,431	5,219	5,746
Cereals and bakery products	558	501	454	535	257	464	602	756	833
Cereals and cereal products	185	160	148	181	82	143	190	254	310
Bakery products	373	341	307	354	175	321	412	501	523
Meats, poultry, fish, and eggs [1]	860	717	763	826	382	762	985	1,105	1,276
Beef	216	219	194	251	90	226	288	285	347
Pork	148	143	158	140	71	150	181	208	241
Poultry	160	112	143	139	66	120	180	203	253
Fish and seafood	149	86	113	129	67	115	141	165	170
Dairy products	432	386	341	397	193	366	450	561	618
Fresh milk and cream	157	136	132	148	71	126	163	216	254
Other dairy products	275	251	209	249	122	240	287	345	364
Fruits and vegetables [1]	753	669	589	779	365	659	810	968	1,063
Fresh fruits	255	232	192	280	128	222	269	343	361
Fresh vegetables	233	198	181	253	116	211	250	286	318
Processed fruits	130	113	97	123	58	110	137	162	177
Other food at home [1]	1,307	1,303	1,188	1,377	681	1,229	1,585	1,830	1,955
Sugar and other sweets	132	144	120	140	66	131	150	192	215
Nonalcoholic beverages	349	318	332	339	181	326	419	464	491
Food away from home	2,845	2,161	2,310	2,891	1,573	2,478	2,866	3,559	3,338
Alcoholic beverages	528	380	325	492	322	545	388	441	248
Housing	19,034	14,762	14,890	19,019	11,223	16,876	18,794	21,684	20,702
Shelter	11,772	8,514	8,123	12,237	7,246	9,859	10,709	12,541	12,050
Owned dwellings	7,429	5,903	5,229	7,412	3,477	6,765	7,004	8,895	8,212
Mortgage interest and charges	3,240	2,840	2,870	4,723	1,551	3,270	3,904	5,455	5,135
Property taxes	2,839	1,961	1,315	1,646	1,063	2,078	1,954	2,411	2,137
Maintenance, repair, insurance, other expenses	1,349	1,102	1,043	1,042	863	1,417	1,146	1,029	940
Rented dwellings	3,636	1,947	2,353	4,127	3,404	2,232	2,998	2,929	3,349
Other lodging	708	664	542	699	365	863	707	717	489
Utilities, fuels, and public services	3,985	3,415	3,847	3,334	2,331	3,764	4,229	4,671	4,955
Natural gas	624	619	260	406	292	443	486	586	591
Electricity	1,314	1,175	1,785	1,123	906	1,456	1,590	1,796	1,950
Fuel oil and other fuels	424	102	71	61	106	166	162	143	125
Telephone	1,233	1,104	1,222	1,135	720	1,190	1,447	1,515	1,606
Water and other public services	389	416	510	609	307	508	543	630	683
Household operations	1,093	859	940	1,192	518	881	1,398	1,742	1,254
Personal services	360	307	291	434	60	100	638	977	607
Other household expenses	733	552	649	758	458	781	760	766	647
Housekeeping supplies [1]	619	634	586	624	349	687	660	829	762
Laundry and cleaning supplies	139	162	150	148	85	145	175	215	232
Postage and stationery	142	135	124	135	81	162	133	163	142
Household furnishings and equipment [1]	1,566	1,340	1,393	1,632	779	1,686	1,799	1,901	1,681
Household textiles	108	94	92	124	51	115	139	123	128
Furniture	382	333	341	378	219	406	431	431	376
Major appliances	197	187	210	240	102	234	286	284	228
Miscellaneous household equipment	716	604	610	739	320	766	748	909	804
Apparel and services [1]	2,084	1,474	1,506	1,932	804	1,704	2,089	2,515	2,588
Men and boys	491	329	308	466	185	368	465	569	613
Women and girls	700	604	620	762	302	639	859	1,048	974
Footwear	333	259	295	338	151	273	337	449	584
Other apparel products and services	468	199	193	267	148	375	253	276	216
Transportation	7,754	7,222	7,590	8,206	4,011	8,439	9,523	9,897	10,133
Vehicle purchases (net outlay) [1]	2,353	2,403	2,719	2,749	1,036	2,965	3,508	3,262	3,616
Cars and trucks, new	1,325	974	1,328	1,198	481	1,576	1,585	1,408	1,438
Cars and trucks, used	983	1,379	1,331	1,509	516	1,329	1,895	1,780	2,118
Gasoline and motor oil	1,903	2,108	2,229	2,186	1,164	2,190	2,504	2,926	3,115
Other vehicle expenses	2,785	2,285	2,315	2,623	1,495	2,694	2,986	3,067	2,944
Vehicle finance charges	202	224	276	242	100	270	305	353	330
Maintenance and repair	826	782	721	869	483	850	976	980	932
Vehicle insurance	1,134	875	1,032	1,009	669	1,088	1,225	1,166	1,215
Vehicle rental, leases, licenses, other charges	623	405	286	502	244	486	480	568	467
Public transportation	713	426	327	648	316	589	525	641	457
Health care [2]	3,125	3,265	3,041	3,265	2,027	4,108	3,346	3,286	2,977
Entertainment [3]	2,688	2,548	2,347	2,568	1,441	2,707	2,810	3,396	3,276
Personal care products and services	602	518	566	655	360	612	727	769	669
Reading	124	101	80	111	81	128	100	98	68
Education	1,618	1,153	697	1,167	600	827	1,536	1,833	1,524
Tobacco products/smoking supplies	380	381	401	266	268	368	437	393	462
Miscellaneous	910	773	716	1,090	752	866	920	960	821
Cash contributions	1,444	1,589	1,633	1,830	1,242	2,046	1,487	1,487	1,584
Personal insurance and pensions	5,756	5,371	4,780	6,023	2,570	5,784	6,758	7,732	6,950
Life and other personal insurance	350	384	286	279	143	380	413	402	376
Pensions and social security	5,406	4,987	4,494	5,744	2,427	5,404	6,345	7,330	6,574
Personal taxes	**2,242**	**1,499**	**1,495**	**2,096**	**1,117**	**2,252**	**2,000**	**2,145**	**1,304**

[1] Includes other types not shown separately. [2] For additional health care expenditures, see Table 146. [3] For additional recreation expenditures, see Section 26.

Source: U.S. Bureau of Labor Statistics, *Consumer Expenditure Survey, 2010*. See also <http://stats.bls.gov/cex/csxstnd.htm>.

Table 702. Average Annual Expenditures of All Consumer Units by Income Level: 2010

[In dollars. See headnote, Table 698]

Income level	Total expenditures [1]	Food	Housing			Transportation			Health care	Pensions and Social Security
			Total [1]	Shelter	Utilities, fuels [2]	Total [1]	Vehicle purchases	Gasoline and motor oil		
All consumer units........	**48,109**	**6,129**	**16,557**	**9,812**	**3,660**	**7,677**	**2,588**	**2,132**	**3,157**	**5,054**
Consumer units with complete reporting:										
Less than $70,000............	33,269	4,661	12,254	7,187	3,089	5,390	1,634	1,708	2,555	2,076
$70,000 to $79,999...........	57,024	6,979	18,589	10,604	4,164	10,706	4,222	2,686	3,785	6,483
$80,000 to $99,999...........	62,966	7,819	20,962	12,475	4,543	10,392	3,717	2,899	4,003	8,163
$100,000 and over............	97,737	11,161	30,999	18,732	5,336	14,493	5,285	3,260	4,942	14,948
$100,000 to $119,999........	74,797	9,372	23,326	13,794	4,777	12,557	4,799	3,248	4,550	10,867
$120,000 to $149,999........	89,614	10,463	27,723	16,320	5,125	14,967	5,806	3,231	4,491	13,174
$150,000 and over............	123,064	13,317	39,787	24,557	5,952	15,808	5,313	3,291	5,594	19,603

[1] Includes expenditures not shown separately. [2] Includes public service.

Source: U.S. Bureau of Labor Statistics, *Consumer Expenditure Survey, 2010.* See also <http://stats.bls.gov/cex/tables.htm>.

Table 703. Annual Expenditure Per Child by Husband-Wife Families by Family Income and Expenditure Type: 2011

[In dollars. Data are for a child in a two-child family. Excludes expenses for college. Expenditures based on before-tax income data from the 2005–2006 Consumer Expenditure Survey updated to 2011 dollars using the Consumer Price Index. For more on the methodology, see report cited below]

Family income and age of child	Total	Expenditure type						
		Housing	Food	Transportation	Clothing	Health care	Child care and education [1]	Miscellaneous [2]
INCOME: LESS THAN $57,600								
Less than 2 years old......................	9,050	2,990	1,160	1,170	640	630	2,040	420
3 to 5 years old............................	9,100	2,990	1,260	1,230	500	590	1,910	620
6 to 8 years old............................	8,760	2,990	1,710	1,350	570	660	850	630
9 to 11 years old..........................	9,520	2,990	1,970	1,350	580	710	1,290	630
12 to 14 years old........................	9,960	2,990	2,130	1,480	690	1,090	880	700
15 to 17 years old........................	9,970	2,990	2,120	1,630	730	1,010	910	580
INCOME: $57,600 TO $99,730								
Less than 2 years old......................	12,370	3,920	1,400	1,690	760	850	2,860	980
3 to 5 years old............................	12,390	3,920	1,490	1,740	610	800	2,740	1,090
6 to 8 years old............................	12,290	3,920	2,100	1,860	680	940	1,680	1,110
9 to 11 years old..........................	13,110	3,920	2,400	1,870	710	1,000	2,110	1,100
12 to 14 years old........................	13,820	3,920	2,580	1,990	840	1,410	1,910	1,170
15 to 17 years old........................	14,320	3,920	2,570	2,150	900	1,330	2,400	1,050
INCOME: MORE THAN $99,730								
Less than 2 years old......................	20,460	7,100	1,900	2,550	1,050	980	5,090	1,790
3 to 5 years old............................	20,480	7,100	2,000	2,610	880	930	4,970	1,990
6 to 8 years old............................	20,420	7,100	2,630	2,730	970	1,080	3,910	2,000
9 to 11 years old..........................	21,320	7,100	2,980	2,730	1,010	1,150	4,350	2,000
12 to 14 years old........................	22,700	7,100	3,190	2,860	1,170	1,610	4,700	2,070
15 to 17 years old........................	24,510	7,100	3,180	3,020	1,280	1,520	6,460	1,950

[1] Includes only families with child care and education expenses. [2] Expenses include personal care items, entertainment, and reading materials.

Source: U.S. Department of Agriculture, Center for Nutrition Policy and Promotion, *Expenditures on Children by Families, 2011*, June 2012. See also <http://www.cnpp.usda.gov/Publications.htm>.

Table 704. Money Income of Households—Percent Distribution by Income Level, Race, and Hispanic Origin, in Constant (2010) Dollars: 1990 to 2010

[Constant dollars based on CPI-U-RS deflator. Households as of March of following year. (94,312 represents 94,312,000). Based on Current Population Survey, Annual Social and Economic Supplement (ASEC); see text, this section and Section 1, and Appendix III. For definition of median, see Guide to Tabular Presentation]

Year	Number of house-holds (1,000)	Percent distribution							Median income (dollars)
		Under $15,000	$15,000 to $24,999	$25,000 to $34,999	$35,000 to $49,999	$50,000 to $74,999	$75,000 to $99,999	$100,000 and over	
ALL HOUSEHOLDS [1]									
1990................	94,312	13.8	11.7	11.0	15.5	20.1	12.3	15.6	48,423
2000 [2]............	108,209	11.5	10.9	10.6	14.2	18.4	13.0	21.4	53,164
2009 [3]............	117,538	12.9	11.8	11.0	14.1	18.0	11.7	20.7	50,599
2010................	118,682	13.7	12.0	10.9	13.9	17.7	11.4	20.5	49,445
WHITE									
1990................	80,968	11.8	11.3	10.9	15.8	20.7	13.0	16.6	49,686
2000 [2]............	90,030	10.8	10.8	10.3	14.4	18.6	13.2	21.9	50,506
2009 [3,4,5]........	95,489	11.2	11.4	10.7	14.1	18.5	12.2	21.9	52,717
2010................	96,144	11.8	11.6	10.7	13.9	18.2	12.1	21.7	51,846
BLACK									
1990................	10,671	28.8	14.8	12.4	14.0	15.7	7.6	6.7	30,202
2000 [2]............	13,174	20.1	14.3	13.1	15.2	17.6	9.0	10.6	37,562
2009 [3,4,6]........	14,730	23.3	15.3	13.4	14.5	15.2	8.8	9.6	33,122
2010................	15,065	25.8	14.7	12.7	14.6	15.2	7.6	9.4	32,068
ASIAN AND PACIFIC ISLANDER									
1990................	1,958	10.6	9.1	8.3	12.2	20.2	14.1	25.5	62,180
2000 [2]............	3,963	9.0	7.1	7.9	11.5	17.1	15.0	32.4	70,595
2009 [3,4,7]........	4,687	11.6	7.8	8.1	11.1	16.7	11.8	32.8	66,550
2010................	4,747	10.8	9.7	7.4	10.6	18.0	11.3	32.2	64,308
HISPANIC [8]									
1990................	6,220	19.3	16.4	12.9	17.3	18.5	7.8	7.8	36,111
2000 [2]............	10,034	13.6	14.6	13.2	17.2	19.2	10.7	11.6	41,994
2009 [3]............	13,298	16.3	15.2	14.3	15.4	17.4	9.4	12.0	38,667
2010................	13,665	17.4	14.8	13.8	15.7	17.2	9.6	11.5	37,759

[1] Includes other races not shown separately. [2] Data reflect implementation of Census 2000-based population controls and a 28,000 household sample expansion to 78,000 households. [3] Median income is calculated using $2,500 income intervals. Beginning with 2009 income data, the Census Bureau expanded the upper income intervals used to calculate medians to $250,000 or more. Medians falling in the upper open-ended interval are plugged with "$250,000." Before 2009, the upper open-ended interval was $100,000 and a plug of "$100,000" was used. [4] Beginning with the 2003 Current Population Survey (CPS), the questionnaire allowed respondents to choose more than one race. For 2002 and later, data represent persons who selected this race group only and exclude persons reporting more than one race. The CPS in prior years allowed respondents to report only one race group. See also comments on race in the text for Section 1. [5] Data represent White alone, which refers to people who reported White and did not report any other race category. [6] Data represent Black alone, which refers to people who reported Black and did not report any other race category. [7] Data represent Asian alone, which refers to people who reported Asian and did not report any other race category. [8] People of Hispanic origin may be any race.

Source: U.S. Census Bureau, *Income, Poverty, and Health Insurance Coverage in the United States: 2010*, P60-239, and "Historical Tables—Table H17," <http://www.census.gov/hhes/www/income/data/historical/index.html>. See also <http://www.census.gov/hhes/www/income/>.

Table 705. Money Income of Households—Median Income by Race and Hispanic Origin, in Current and Constant (2010) Dollars: 1980 to 2010

[In dollars. See headnote, Table 704]

Year	Median income in current dollars					Median income in constant (2010) dollars				
	All house-holds [1]	White [2]	Black [3]	Asian, Pacific Islander [4]	His-panic [5]	All house-holds [1]	White [2]	Black [3]	Asian, Pacific Islander [4]	His-panic [5]
1980................	17,710	18,684	10,764	(NA)	13,651	44,616	47,070	27,117	(NA)	34,391
1990................	29,943	31,231	18,676	38,450	22,330	48,423	50,506	30,202	62,180	36,111
1995 [6]............	34,076	35,766	22,393	40,614	22,860	48,408	50,809	31,811	57,696	32,475
2000 [7,8].........	41,990	43,916	29,667	55,757	33,168	53,164	55,603	37,562	70,595	41,994
2005 [9]............	46,326	48,554	30,858	61,094	35,967	51,739	54,227	34,464	68,233	40,170
2007................	50,233	52,115	33,916	66,103	38,679	52,823	54,802	35,665	69,511	40,673
2008................	50,303	52,312	34,218	65,637	37,913	50,939	52,974	34,651	66,467	38,393
2009 [10]...........	49,777	51,861	32,584	65,469	38,039	50,599	52,717	33,122	66,550	38,667
2010................	49,445	51,846	32,068	64,308	37,759	49,445	51,846	32,068	64,308	37,759

NA Not available. [1] Includes other races, not shown separately. [2] Beginning with 2002, data represents White alone, which refers to people who reported White and did not report any other race category. [3] Beginning with 2002, data represents Black alone, which refers to people who reported Black and did not report any other race category. [4] Beginning with 2002, data represents Asian alone, which refers to people who reported Asian and did not report any other race category. [5] People of Hispanic origin may be any race. [6] Data reflect full implementation of the 1990 Census-based sample design and metropolitan definitions, 7,000 household sample reduction, and revised race edits. [7] Implementation of Census 2000-based population controls. [8] Implementation of a 28,000 household sample expansion. [9] See footnote 3, Table 704. See also comments on race in the text for Section 1. [10] Median income is calculated using $2,500 income intervals. Beginning with 2009 income data, the Census Bureau expanded the upper income intervals used to calculate medians to $250,000 or more. Before 2009, the upper open-ended interval was $100,000 and a plug of "$100,000" was used.

Source: U.S. Census Bureau, *Income, Poverty and Health Insurance Coverage in the United States: 2010*, Current Population Reports, P60-239, and "Historical Tables—Table H-5," September 2011. See also <http://www.census.gov/hhes/www/income/income.html> and <http://www.census.gov/hhes/www/income/data/historical/household/index.html>.

Table 706. Money Income of Households—Distribution by Income Level and Selected Characteristics: 2010

[118,682 represents 118,682,000. Households as of March of the following year. Based on Current Population Survey, Annual Social and Economic Supplement (ASEC); see text, this section and Section 1, and Appendix III. For definition of median, see Guide to Tabular Presentation. Median income is calculated using $2,500 income intervals. Beginning with 2009 income data, the Census Bureau expanded the upper income intervals used to calculate medians to $250,000 or more. Medians falling in the upper open-ended interval are plugged with "$250,000." Before 2009, the upper open-ended interval was $100,000 and a plug of "$100,000" was used]

Characteristic	Total house-holds	Under $15,000	$15,000 to $24,999	$25,000 to $34,999	$35,000 to $49,999	$50,000 to $74,999	$75,000 to $99,999	$100,000 and over	Median house-hold income (dollars)
Total...............	**118,682**	**16,292**	**14,197**	**12,878**	**16,464**	**21,051**	**13,567**	**24,234**	**49,445**
Age of householder:									
15 to 24 years..................	6,140	1,667	1,062	841	955	895	325	396	28,322
25 to 34 years..................	19,572	2,311	2,139	2,109	3,211	4,106	2,523	3,174	50,059
35 to 44 years..................	21,250	1,971	1,764	1,961	2,824	4,127	2,987	5,618	61,644
45 to 54 years..................	24,530	2,658	2,056	2,115	2,894	4,555	3,317	6,933	62,485
55 to 64 years..................	21,828	2,809	2,041	2,008	2,880	3,857	2,699	5,535	56,575
65 years and over..........	25,362	4,874	5,135	3,843	3,699	3,512	1,715	2,583	31,408
Region: [1]									
Northeast..............	21,597	2,861	2,359	2,206	2,716	3,780	2,406	5,267	53,283
Midwest................	26,669	3,487	3,322	3,000	3,877	4,951	3,146	4,886	48,445
South..................	44,161	6,783	5,651	4,937	6,321	7,512	4,919	8,035	45,492
West....................	26,254	3,159	2,864	2,736	3,550	4,808	3,094	6,044	53,142
Size of household:									
One person..............	32,723	9,494	6,572	4,488	4,567	4,223	1,591	1,787	25,538
Two people..............	39,718	3,395	4,051	4,548	6,173	7,921	5,141	8,489	54,617
Three people............	18,529	1,595	1,564	1,623	2,441	3,631	2,719	4,954	62,791
Four people.............	15,910	976	1,065	1,202	1,832	2,984	2,463	5,383	73,884
Five people.............	7,346	493	573	587	884	1,419	1,007	2,383	69,368
Six people..............	2,773	202	212	252	337	586	391	791	66,060
Seven or more people.........	1,684	135	159	177	229	284	254	447	60,572
Type of household:									
Family household..........	78,613	6,184	6,917	7,699	10,767	15,194	10,968	20,885	61,544
Married-couple..............	58,036	2,359	3,739	4,797	7,301	11,653	9,246	18,940	72,751
Male householder, spouse absent..............	5,559	524	653	675	942	1,261	651	852	49,718
Female householder, spouse absent..............	15,019	3,302	2,525	2,226	2,526	2,280	1,071	1,091	32,031
Nonfamily household..........	40,069	10,106	7,281	5,179	5,696	5,858	2,600	3,348	29,730
Male householder..........	18,835	3,979	2,948	2,329	2,857	3,144	1,554	2,024	35,627
Female householder.........	21,234	6,127	4,333	2,851	2,839	2,715	1,047	1,324	25,456
Educational attainment of householder: [2]									
Total...............	**112,542**	**14,624**	**13,135**	**12,037**	**15,509**	**20,156**	**13,242**	**23,839**	**50,813**
Less than 9th grade.............	5,092	1,758	1,163	752	591	489	164	174	21,254
9th to 12th grade (no diploma)...................	8,059	2,376	1,679	1,232	1,119	959	352	343	24,787
High school graduate.......	32,720	5,270	5,074	4,378	5,330	5,902	3,293	3,475	38,976
Some college, no degree.......	20,223	2,472	2,331	2,393	3,149	4,054	2,550	3,274	48,722
Associate's degree.............	10,953	1,031	971	1,147	1,614	2,241	1,738	2,213	56,811
Bachelor's degree or more.....	35,496	1,716	1,916	2,135	3,707	6,509	5,148	14,365	82,109
Bachelor's degree.............	22,458	1,232	1,411	1,489	2,572	4,417	3,361	7,974	75,568
Master's degree.............	9,436	379	397	480	924	1,620	1,378	4,257	90,802
Professional degree..........	1,761	53	64	87	122	217	187	1,031	119,825
Doctoral degree...............	1,841	54	45	78	88	255	221	1,102	118,714
Number of earners:									
No earners.....................	27,388	10,940	6,425	3,690	2,960	1,949	699	727	18,484
One earner....................	44,922	4,805	6,423	6,796	8,428	8,952	3,997	5,518	41,711
Two earners and more........	46,373	547	1,350	2,392	5,075	10,150	8,871	17,988	84,525
Two earners..................	37,470	521	1,243	2,145	4,471	8,481	7,143	13,466	80,884
Three earners................	6,705	23	100	214	521	1,378	1,325	3,143	96,120
Four earners or more........	2,197	3	7	32	83	291	404	1,377	117,034
Work experience of householder:									
Total...............	**118,682**	**16,292**	**14,197**	**12,878**	**16,464**	**21,051**	**13,567**	**24,234**	**49,445**
Worked.......................	78,542	4,543	6,414	7,576	11,292	16,322	11,397	20,997	63,148
Worked at full-time jobs......	64,763	2,168	4,452	5,883	9,332	14,100	10,115	18,713	68,037
50 weeks or more...........	54,312	945	3,036	4,656	7,632	12,165	8,935	16,945	71,928
27 to 49 weeks............	6,215	399	746	721	1,039	1,248	798	1,266	53,458
26 weeks or less...........	4,235	825	670	506	660	687	381	504	37,584
Worked at part-time jobs. . . .	13,779	2,375	1,962	1,693	1,961	2,221	1,282	2,283	40,645
50 weeks or more...........	7,408	920	1,015	895	1,084	1,273	767	1,454	46,491
27 to 49 weeks............	2,909	494	444	401	395	473	264	438	39,434
26 weeks or less..............	3,461	959	504	397	480	478	253	389	30,786
Did not work.................	40,141	11,748	7,783	5,302	5,171	4,729	2,170	3,239	25,843
Tenure:									
Owner occupied................	78,573	6,591	7,308	7,316	10,346	15,059	10,828	21,126	61,601
Renter occupied..............	38,472	9,181	6,551	5,363	5,904	5,788	2,668	3,018	31,034
Occupier paid no cash rent. ..	1,637	518	338	199	214	204	72	92	23,269

[1] For composition of regions, see map, inside front cover. [2] People 25 years old and over.

Source: U.S. Census Bureau, *Income, Poverty and Health Insurance Coverage in the United States: 2010*, Current Population Reports, P60-239, and Detailed Tables—Table HINC-01, September 2011. See also <http://www.census.gov/hhes/www/income/data/index.html>.

Table 707. Money Income of Households—Number and Distribution by Race and Hispanic Origin: 2010

[Households as of March of the following year. (118,682 represents 118,682,000). Based on Current Population Survey, Annual Social and Economic Supplement (ASEC); see text, this section and Section 1, and Appendix III. The 2009 CPS allowed respondents to choose more than one race. Data represent persons who selected this race group only and excludes persons reporting more than one race. See also comments on race in the text for Section 1]

Income interval	Number of households (1,000)					Percent distribution				
	All races	White alone	Black alone	Asian alone	His-panic [1]	All races	White alone	Black alone	Asian alone	His-panic [1]
All households	**118,682**	**96,144**	**15,065**	**4,747**	**13,665**	**100.0**	**100.0**	**100.0**	**100.0**	**100.0**
Under $10,000	9,231	6,082	2,478	342	1,363	7.8	6.3	16.4	7.2	10.0
$10,000 to $14,999	7,061	5,309	1,404	171	1,018	5.9	5.5	9.3	3.6	7.4
$15,000 to $19,999	7,260	5,763	1,094	209	949	6.1	6.0	7.3	4.4	6.9
$20,000 to $24,999	6,937	5,390	1,127	249	1,067	5.8	5.6	7.5	5.2	7.8
$25,000 to $29,999	6,730	5,361	1,001	182	1,033	5.7	5.6	6.6	3.8	7.6
$30,000 to $34,999	6,148	4,910	916	170	856	5.2	5.1	6.1	3.6	6.3
$35,000 to $39,999	5,907	4,834	788	162	822	5.0	5.0	5.2	3.4	6.0
$40,000 to $44,999	5,624	4,537	766	168	707	4.7	4.7	5.1	3.5	5.2
$45,000 to $49,999	4,933	4,007	638	173	622	4.2	4.2	4.2	3.6	4.6
$50,000 to $59,999	9,291	7,710	1,031	354	1,132	7.8	8.0	6.8	7.5	8.3
$60,000 to $74,999	11,760	9,769	1,253	499	1,224	9.9	10.2	8.3	10.5	9.0
$75,000 to $84,999	6,261	5,293	596	230	678	5.3	5.5	4.0	4.8	5.0
$85,000 to $99,999	7,306	6,305	550	308	627	6.2	6.6	3.7	6.5	4.6
$100,000 to $149,999	14,302	2,828	973	803	1,055	12.1	2.9	6.5	16.9	7.7
$150,000 to $199,999	5,305	1,102	277	91	75	4.5	1.1	1.8	1.9	0.5
$200,000 to $249,999	2,143	1,845	88	185	98	1.8	1.9	0.6	3.9	0.7
$250,000 and above	2,484	2,208	84	161	103	2.1	2.3	0.6	3.4	0.8

[1] Persons of Hispanic origin may be any race.

Source: U.S. Census Bureau, *Income, Poverty and Health Insurance Coverage in the United States: 2010*, Current Population Reports, P60-239, and Detailed Tables—Table HINC-06, September 2011. See also <http://www.census.gov/hhes/www/income/index.html>.

Table 708. Share of Aggregate Income Received by Each Fifth and Top 5 Percent of Households: 1970 to 2010

[Households as of March of the following year. (64,778 represents 64,778,000). Income in constant 2010 CPI-U-RS-adjusted dollars. The shares method ranks households from highest to lowest on the basis of income and then divides them into groups of equal population size, typically quintiles. The aggregate income of each group is then divided by the overall aggregate income to derive shares. Based on the Current Population Survey, Annual Social and Economic Supplement (ASEC); see text, this section and Section 1, and Appendix III. For data collection changes over time, see <http://www.census.gov/hhes/www/income/data /historical/history.html>]

Year	Number of house-holds (1,000)	Income at selected positions in constant (2010) dollars					Percent distribution of aggregate income					
		Upper limit of each fifth				Top 5 percent	Lowest 5th	Second 5th	Third 5th	Fourth 5th	Highest 5th	Top 5 percent
		Lowest	Second	Third	Fourth							
1970	64,778	18,480	35,402	51,493	73,466	116,129	4.1	10.8	17.4	24.5	43.3	16.6
1980	82,368	18,839	35,330	54,164	79,307	127,629	4.2	10.2	16.8	24.7	44.1	16.5
1990	94,312	20,215	38,266	58,542	89,276	153,224	3.8	9.6	15.9	24.0	46.6	18.5
1995 [1]	99,627	20,456	38,234	59,667	92,514	160,526	3.7	9.1	15.2	23.3	48.7	21.0
2000 [2,3]	108,209	22,689	41,782	66,058	103,525	183,865	3.6	8.9	14.8	23.0	49.8	22.1
2003	112,000	21,320	40,307	64,553	102,980	182,707	3.4	8.7	14.8	23.4	49.8	21.4
2004 [4]	113,343	21,338	40,025	63,751	101,580	181,399	3.4	8.7	14.7	23.2	50.1	21.8
2005	114,384	21,419	40,206	64,397	102,420	185,397	3.4	8.6	14.6	23.0	50.4	22.2
2006	116,011	21,666	40,848	64,883	104,930	188,175	3.4	8.6	14.5	22.9	50.5	22.3
2007	116,783	21,337	41,116	65,197	105,156	186,126	3.4	8.7	14.8	23.4	49.7	21.2
2008	117,181	20,974	39,493	63,518	101,508	182,277	3.4	8.6	14.7	23.3	50.0	21.5
2009	117,538	20,791	39,186	62,821	101,651	182,972	3.4	8.6	14.6	23.2	50.3	21.7
2010	118,682	20,000	38,043	61,735	100,065	180,810	3.3	8.5	14.6	23.4	50.2	21.3

[1] Data reflect full implementation of the 1990 Census-based sample design and metropolitan definitions, 7,000 household sample reduction, and revised race edits. [2] Implementation of Census 2000-based population controls. [3] Implementation of a 28,000 household sample expansion. [4] Data have been revised to reflect a correction to the weights in the 2005 ASEC.

Source: U.S. Census Bureau, *Income, Poverty and Health Insurance Coverage in the United States: 2010*, Current Population Reports, P60-239, and "Historical Tables—Tables H1 and H2," September 2011. See also <http://www.census.gov/hhes/www/income/income.html> and <http://www.census.gov/hhes/www/income/data/historical/household/index.html>.

Table 709. Money Income of Families—Number and Distribution by Race and Hispanic Origin: 2010

[Families as of March of the following year. (78,633 represents 78,633,000). Based on Current Population Survey, Annual Social and Economic Supplement (ASEC); see text, this section, Section 1, and Appendix III. The 2010 CPS allowed respondents to choose more than one race. Data represent persons who selected this race group only and excludes persons reporting more than one race. See also comments on race in the text for Section 1]

Income interval	Number of families (1,000)					Percent distribution				
	All races	White alone	Black alone	Asian alone	His-panic [1]	All races	White alone	Black alone	Asian alone	His-panic [1]
All families [1]	**78,633**	**63,837**	**9,419**	**3,537**	**10,668**	**100.0**	**100.0**	**100.0**	**100.0**	**100.0**
Under $10,000	4,242	2,718	1,188	166	1,002	5.4	4.3	12.6	4.7	9.4
$10,000 to $14,999	2,743	1,957	636	70	662	3.5	3.1	6.8	2.0	6.2
$15,000 to $19,999	3,273	2,456	576	134	727	4.2	3.8	6.1	3.8	6.8
$20,000 to $24,999	3,861	2,874	724	148	826	4.9	4.5	7.7	4.2	7.7
$25,000 to $29,999	3,957	3,101	632	118	828	5.0	4.9	6.7	3.3	7.8
$30,000 to $34,999	3,771	2,939	603	126	678	4.8	4.6	6.4	3.6	6.4
$35,000 to $39,999	3,785	3,096	485	117	656	4.8	4.8	5.1	3.3	6.1
$40,000 to $44,999	3,677	2,960	495	135	530	4.7	4.6	5.3	3.8	5.0
$45,000 to $49,999	3,291	2,644	429	129	498	4.2	4.1	4.6	3.6	4.7
$50,000 to $59,999	6,417	5,338	701	238	924	8.2	8.4	7.4	6.7	8.7
$60,000 to $74,999	8,472	7,045	877	377	995	10.8	11.0	9.3	10.7	9.3
$75,000 to $84,999	409	310	66	21	77	0.5	0.5	0.7	0.6	0.7
$85,000 to $99,999	489	415	49	16	62	0.6	0.7	0.5	0.5	0.6
$100,000 to $149,999	11,907	10,194	809	677	867	15.1	16.0	8.6	19.1	8.1
$150,000 to $199,999	4,494	3,865	226	338	260	5.7	6.1	2.4	9.6	2.4
$200,000 to $249,999	1,852	1,595	69	166	83	2.4	2.5	0.7	4.7	0.8
$250,000 and above	2,178	1,934	69	147	89	2.8	3.0	0.7	4.2	0.8

[1] Persons of Hispanic origin may be any race.

Source: U.S. Census Bureau, *Income, Poverty and Health Insurance Coverage in the United States: 2010*, Current Population Reports, P60-239, and Detailed Tables—Table FINC-07, September 2011. See also <http://www.census.gov/hhes/www/income/>.

Table 710. Money Income of Families—Percent Distribution by Income Level in Constant (2010) Dollars: 1990 to 2010

[Constant dollars based on CPI-U-RS deflator. Families as of March of following year. (66,322 represents 66,322,000). Based on Current Population Survey, Annual Social and Economic Supplement (ASEC); see text, this section, Section 1, and Appendix III. For data collection changes over time, see <http://www.census.gov/hhes/www/income/data/historical/history.html>. For definition of median, see Guide to Tabular Presentation]

Year	Number of families (1,000)	Percent distribution							Median income (dollars)
		Under $15,000	$15,000 to $24,999	$25,000 to $34,999	$35,000 to $49,999	$50,000 to $74,999	$75,000 to $99,999	$100,000 and over	
ALL FAMILIES [1]									
1990	66,322	8.5	9.2	10.0	15.3	22.5	14.6	19.8	57,172
2000 [2]	73,778	6.6	8.4	9.3	14.0	19.6	15.3	26.8	64,232
2009 [3]	78,867	8.5	9.0	9.8	13.7	19.1	13.8	26.1	61,080
2010	78,633	8.9	9.1	9.8	13.7	18.9	13.6	25.9	60,395
WHITE									
1990	56,803	6.5	8.6	9.7	15.6	23.2	15.4	21.0	59,698
2000 [2]	61,330	5.4	7.6	8.9	13.9	19.8	16.0	28.3	67,141
2009 [3, 4, 5]	54,461	5.7	7.1	8.5	13.3	19.9	15.2	30.3	68,453
2010	53,918	5.8	7.2	8.6	13.2	19.6	15.1	30.3	68,961
BLACK									
1990	7,471	23.5	14.5	12.6	14.1	17.8	9.0	8.3	34,645
2000 [2]	8,731	14.9	13.8	12.9	15.8	18.8	10.5	13.3	42,638
2009 [3, 4, 6]	9,367	17.8	14.3	13.4	15.0	16.5	10.7	12.5	39,043
2010	9,419	19.4	13.8	13.1	15.0	16.8	9.6	12.5	38,500
ASIAN AND PACIFIC ISLANDER									
1990	1,536	8.1	7.3	8.3	11.4	20.0	15.4	29.4	68,319
2000 [2]	2,982	5.8	6.0	6.8	10.7	17.5	15.9	37.2	79,280
2009 [3, 4, 7]	3,592	6.9	6.9	7.8	10.5	17.5	12.2	38.2	76,266
2010	3,537	6.6	8.0	6.9	10.8	17.4	12.8	37.6	75,486
HISPANIC ORIGIN [8]									
1990	4,981	16.7	16.2	13.5	17.1	19.3	8.6	8.5	37,892
2000 [2]	8,017	11.7	14.2	13.4	17.9	19.6	10.9	12.3	43,607
2009 [3]	10,422	15.1	14.6	14.2	16.1	17.7	9.7	12.8	40,386
2010	10,668	15.6	14.6	14.1	15.8	18.0	9.8	12.1	39,538

[1] Includes other races not shown separately. [2] Data reflect implementation of Census 2000-based population controls and a 28,000 household sample expansion to 78,000 households. [3] Median income is calculated using $2,500 income intervals. Beginning with 2009 income data, the Census Bureau expanded the upper income intervals used to calculate medians to $250,000 or more. Medians falling in the upper open-ended interval are plugged with "$250,000." Before 2009, the upper open-ended interval was $100,000 and a plug of "$100,000" was used. [4] Beginning with the 2003 Current Population Survey (CPS), the questionnaire allowed respondents to choose more than one race. For 2002 and later, data represent persons who selected this race group only and exclude persons reporting more than one race. The CPS in prior years allowed respondents to report only one race group. See also comments on race in the text for Section 1. [5] Data represent White alone, which refers to people who reported White and did not report any other race category. [6] Data represent Black alone, which refers to people who reported Black and did not report any other race category. [7] Data represent Asian alone, which refers to people who reported Asian and did not report any other race category. [8] People of Hispanic origin may be any race.

Source: U.S. Census Bureau, *Income, Poverty and Health Insurance Coverage in the United States: 2010*, Current Population Reports, P60-239, and "Historical Tables—Table F-23," September 2011. See also <http://www.census.gov/hhes/www/income/income.html> and <http://www.census.gov/hhes/www/income/data/historical/families/index.html>.

Table 711. Money Income of Families—Median Income by Race and Hispanic Origin in Current and Constant (2010) Dollars: 1990 to 2010

[In dollars. See headnote, Table 710]

Year	Median income in current dollars					Median income in constant (2010) dollars				
	All families [1]	White [2]	Black [3]	Asian, Pacific Islander [4]	His-panic [5]	All families [1]	White [2]	Black [3]	Asian, Pacific Islander [4]	His-panic [5]
1990.............	35,353	36,915	21,423	42,246	23,431	57,172	59,698	34,645	68,319	37,892
1995 [6]...........	40,611	42,646	25,970	46,356	24,570	57,691	60,582	36,893	65,853	34,904
2000 [7,8].........	50,732	53,029	33,676	62,617	34,442	64,232	67,141	42,638	79,280	43,607
2005.............	56,194	59,317	35,464	68,957	37,867	62,760	66,248	39,608	77,014	42,292
2006.............	58,407	61,280	38,269	74,612	40,000	63,161	66,268	41,384	80,685	43,256
2007.............	61,355	64,427	40,143	77,133	40,566	64,518	67,749	42,213	81,110	42,658
2008.............	61,521	65,000	39,879	73,578	40,466	62,299	65,822	40,383	74,509	40,978
2009 [9]...........	60,088	62,545	38,409	75,027	39,730	61,080	63,577	39,043	76,266	40,386
2010.............	60,395	63,146	38,500	75,486	39,538	60,395	63,146	38,500	75,486	39,538

[1] Includes other races not shown separately. [2] Beginning with 2002, data represent White alone, which refers to people who reported White and did not report any other race category. [3] Beginning with 2002, data represent Black alone, which refers to people who reported Black and did not report any other race category. [4] Beginning with 2002, data represent Asian alone, which refers to people who reported Asian and did not report any other race category. [5] People of Hispanic origin may be any race. [6] Data reflect full implementation of the 1990 Census-based sample design and metropolitan definitions, 7,000 household sample reduction, and revised race edits. [7] Implementation of Census 2000-based population controls. [8] Implementation of 28,000 household sample expansion. [9] Median income is calculated using $2,500 income intervals. Beginning with 2009 income data, the Census Bureau expanded the upper income intervals used to calculate medians to $250,000 or more. Medians falling in the upper open-ended interval are plugged with "$250,000." Before 2009, the upper open-ended interval was $100,000 and a plug of "$100,000" was used. See also comments on race in the text for Section 1.

Source: U.S. Census Bureau, *Income, Poverty and Health Insurance Coverage in the United States: 2010*, Current Population Reports, P60-239, and "Historical Tables—Table F-05," September 2011. See also <http://www.census.gov/hhes/www/income/income.html> and <http://www.census.gov/hhes/www/income/data/historical/families/index.html>.

Table 712. Money Income of Families—Distribution by Family Characteristics and Income Level: 2010

[78,633 represents 78,633,000. See headnote, Table 710. Median income is calculated using $2,500 income intervals. Beginning with 2009 income data, the Census Bureau expanded the upper income intervals used to calculate medians to $250,000 or more. Medians falling in the upper open-ended interval are plugged with "$250,000." Before 2009, the upper open-ended interval was $100,000 and a plug of "$100,000" was used. For composition of regions, see map inside front cover]

Characteristic	Number of families (1,000)								Median income (dollars)
	Total	Under $15,000	$15,000 to $24,999	$25,000 to $34,999	$35,000 to $49,999	$50,000 to $74,999	$75,000 to $99,999	$100,000 and over	
All families.....................	78,633	6,985	7,132	7,729	10,753	14,889	10,715	20,431	60,395
Age of householder:									
15 to 24 years old.................	3,316	990	579	428	472	437	180	231	26,688
25 to 34 years old.................	13,068	1,770	1,436	1,325	1,965	2,526	1,742	2,305	50,241
35 to 44 years old.................	16,715	1,360	1,289	1,420	2,058	3,188	2,496	4,905	66,769
45 to 54 years old.................	17,790	1,202	1,170	1,309	1,897	3,346	2,746	6,119	74,739
55 to 64 years old.................	14,275	814	866	1,050	1,831	2,783	2,199	4,732	72,840
65 years old and over.............	13,469	850	1,793	2,198	2,529	2,610	1,352	2,140	45,763
Region:									
Northeast........................	13,862	1,043	1,093	1,266	1,637	2,586	1,840	4,394	67,256
Midwest.........................	17,395	1,449	1,407	1,653	2,530	3,472	2,568	4,319	61,017
South...........................	29,763	3,043	3,065	3,097	4,289	5,460	3,965	6,847	55,286
West............................	17,612	1,450	1,568	1,713	2,295	3,371	2,344	4,874	61,840
Type of family:									
Married-couple families............	58,047	2,381	3,769	4,808	7,348	11,667	9,230	18,846	72,426
Male householder, no spouse present.............................	5,560	708	741	729	986	1,133	559	705	43,058
Female householder, no spouse present.............................	15,026	3,896	2,623	2,193	2,419	2,087	928	880	29,220
Unrelated subfamilies.............	641	256	128	87	80	41	24	26	20,596
Educational attainment of householder:									
Persons 25 years old and over, total................................	75,317	5,995	6,554	7,301	10,281	14,450	10,537	20,202	61,776
Less than 9th grade.................	3,358	719	794	624	493	435	145	148	27,122
9th to 12th grade (no diploma).....	5,194	1,094	957	855	920	767	291	310	31,020
High school graduate (includes equivalency)......................	21,808	2,127	2,513	2,821	3,834	4,612	2,835	3,065	48,332
Some college, no degree...........	13,369	1,046	1,085	1,373	2,037	2,969	2,096	2,763	58,685
Associate's degree.................	7,580	393	473	649	1,034	1,681	1,406	1,938	67,854
Bachelor's degree or more.........	24,010	615	732	978	1,963	3,986	3,761	11,973	99,716
Bachelor's degree.................	15,058	428	549	687	1,396	2,809	2,514	6,676	90,636
Master's degree..................	6,418	142	133	208	446	921	972	3,594	107,611
Professional degree...............	1,223	25	22	42	67	112	130	823	136,862
Doctoral degree..................	1,311	22	27	42	53	145	147	876	135,313
Number of earners:									
No earners.......................	12,545	3,749	2,418	2,061	1,953	1,351	496	520	25,447
One earner.......................	26,524	2,821	3,706	3,834	4,723	5,107	2,522	3,810	42,863
Two earners or more..............	39,564	415	1,008	1,834	4,076	8,430	7,699	16,100	87,136

Source: U.S. Census Bureau, *Income, Poverty and Health Insurance Coverage in the United States: 2010*, Current Population Reports, P60-239, and Detailed Tables—Table FINC-01, September 2011. See also <http://www.census.gov/hhes/www/income/>.

Table 713. Median Income of Families by Type of Family in Current and Constant (2010) Dollars: 1990 to 2010

[In dollars. See headnote, Table 710. For definition of median, see Guide to Tabular Presentation]

Year	Current dollars						Constant (2010) dollars					
	All families	Married-couple families			Male house-holder, no spouse present	Female house-holder, no spouse present	All families	Married-couple families			Male house-holder, no spouse present	Female house-holder, no spouse present
		Total	Wife in paid labor force	Wife not in paid labor force				Total	Wife in paid labor force	Wife not in paid labor force		
1990.............	35,353	39,895	46,777	30,265	29,046	16,932	57,172	64,517	75,646	48,944	46,972	27,382
1995 [1]...........	40,611	47,062	55,823	32,375	30,358	19,691	57,691	66,856	79,301	45,991	43,126	27,973
2000 [2,3].........	50,732	59,099	69,235	39,982	37,727	25,716	64,232	74,826	87,659	50,622	47,767	32,559
2006.............	58,407	69,404	82,788	45,757	41,844	28,829	63,161	75,053	89,526	49,481	45,250	31,175
2007.............	61,355	72,589	86,435	47,329	44,358	30,296	64,518	76,332	90,892	49,769	46,645	31,858
2008.............	61,521	72,743	86,621	48,502	43,571	30,129	62,299	73,663	87,717	49,116	44,122	30,510
2009 [4]..........	60,088	71,627	85,948	47,649	41,501	29,770	61,080	72,809	87,367	48,436	42,186	30,261
2010.............	60,395	72,426	87,485	48,858	43,058	29,220	60,395	72,426	87,485	48,858	43,058	29,220

[1] Data reflect full implementation of the 1990 Census-based sample design and metropolitan definitions, 7,000 household sample reduction, and revised race edits. [2] Implementation of Census 2000-based population controls. [3] Implementation of a 28,000 household sample expansion. [4] Median income is calculated using $2,500 income intervals. Beginning with 2009 income data, the Census Bureau expanded the upper income intervals used to calculate medians to $250,000 or more. Before 2009, the upper open-ended interval was $100,000.

Source: U.S. Census Bureau, *Income, Poverty and Health Insurance Coverage in the United States: 2010*, Current Population Reports, P60-239, and "Historical Tables—Table F-7," September 2011. See also <http://www.census.gov/hhes/www/income/income.html> and <http://www.census.gov/hhes/www/income/data/historical/families/index.html>.

Table 714. Married-Couple Families—Number and Median Income by Work Experience of Husbands and Wives and Presence of Related Children: 2010

[58,047 represents 58,047,000. See headnote, Table 710. For definition of median, see Guide to Tabular Presentation]

Work experience of husband or wife	Number (1,000)					Median income (dollars)				
	All married-couple families	With no related children	One or more related children under 18 years old			All married-couple families	With no related children	One or more related children under 18 years old		
			Total	One child	Two children or more			Total	One child	Two children or more
All married-couple families........	**58,047**	**32,562**	**25,485**	**10,047**	**15,437**	**72,426**	**68,650**	**77,749**	**80,044**	**76,683**
Husband worked.......................	44,022	20,764	23,258	8,981	14,277	84,834	87,564	81,861	84,243	80,638
Wife worked...........................	31,427	15,047	16,380	6,870	9,511	92,829	95,395	91,221	91,513	91,028
Wife did not work.....................	12,595	5,717	6,878	2,111	4,766	60,351	65,622	55,261	56,884	54,493
Husband year-round, full-time worker.....	34,596	15,481	19,116	7,374	11,742	91,513	95,372	88,708	91,231	86,968
Wife worked...........................	25,210	11,678	13,532	5,661	7,871	99,499	101,246	97,343	98,459	96,664
Wife did not work.....................	9,386	3,803	5,584	1,713	3,871	67,108	73,087	62,151	63,059	61,811
Husband did not work..................	14,025	11,798	2,227	1,067	1,160	39,700	40,262	36,520	40,497	31,804
Wife worked...........................	4,650	3,289	1,361	644	717	54,573	58,005	44,678	51,339	40,122
Wife did not work.....................	9,375	8,509	866	423	443	33,990	34,947	20,903	23,106	17,164

Source: U.S. Census Bureau, *Income, Poverty and Health Insurance Coverage in the United States: 2010*, Current Population Reports, P60-239, and Detailed Tables—Table FINC-04, September 2011. See also <http://www.census.gov/hhes/www/income/index.html>.

Table 715. Median Income of People in Constant (2010) Dollars by Sex, Race, and Hispanic Origin: 1990 to 2010

[In dollars. People as of March of following year. People 15 years old and over. Constant dollars based on CPI-U-RS deflator. Based on the Current Population Survey, Annual Social and Economic Supplement (ASEC); see text, this section and Section 1 and Appendix III. For data collection changes over time, see <http://www.census.gov/hhes/www/income/data/historical/history.html>]

Race and Hispanic Origin	Male					Female				
	1990	2000 [1]	2005 [2]	2009 [3]	2010	1990	2000 [1]	2005 [2]	2009 [3]	2010
All races [4]..................	**32,817**	**35,885**	**34,929**	**32,715**	**32,137**	**16,285**	**20,338**	**20,747**	**21,303**	**20,831**
White [5]......................	34,236	37,726	35,939	34,305	34,047	16,684	20,358	20,850	21,467	20,947
Black [6]......................	20,810	27,023	25,300	24,130	23,203	13,468	20,107	19,691	19,791	19,700
Asian [7]......................	31,363	39,038	38,213	37,946	36,267	17,928	21,975	24,170	24,745	23,612
Hispanic [8]...................	21,783	24,687	24,670	22,623	22,233	12,181	15,507	16,793	16,478	16,269
White non-Hispanic...........	35,510	39,893	39,475	37,392	37,037	17,111	21,100	21,724	22,301	21,754

[1] Implementation of Census 2000-based population controls and sample expanded by 28,000 households. [2] Beginning with the 2003 Current Population Survey (CPS), the questionnaire allowed respondents to choose more than one race. For 2005 and later, data represent persons who selected this race group only and excludes persons reporting more than one race. The CPS in prior years allowed respondents to report only one race group. See also comments on race in the text for Section 1. [3] Median income is calculated using $2,500 income intervals. Beginning with 2009 income data, the Census Bureau expanded the upper income intervals used to calculate medians to $250,000 or more. Before 2009, the upper open ended interval was $100,000. [4] Includes other races not shown separately. [5] Beginning with 2005, data represent White alone, which refers to people who reported White and did not report any other race category. [6] Beginning with 2005, data represent Black alone, which refers to people who reported Black and did not report any other race category. [7] Beginning with 2005, data represent Asian alone, which refers to people who reported Asian and did not report any other race category. [8] People of Hispanic origin may be any race.

Source: U.S. Census Bureau, *Income, Poverty and Health Insurance Coverage in the United States: 2010*, Current Population Reports, P60-239, and "Historical Tables—Table P-2," September 2011. See also <http://www.census.gov/hhes/www/income/income.html> and <http://www.census.gov/hhes/www/income/data/historical/people/index.html>.

Table 716. Money Income of People—Selected Characteristics by Income Level: 2010

[People as of March 2010 (118,871 represents 118,871,000). Covers people 15 years old and over. For definition of median, see Guide to Tabular Presentation. Median income is calculated using $2,500 income intervals. Beginning with 2009 income data, the Census Bureau expanded the upper income intervals used to calculate medians to $250,000 or more. Medians falling in the upper open-ended interval are plugged with "$250,000." Before 2009, the upper open-ended interval was $100,000 and a plug of "$100,000" was used. For composition of regions, see map, inside front cover. Based on the Current Population Survey, Annual Social and Economic Supplement (ASEC), see Appendix III]

Characteristic	All persons (1,000)	People with income Total (1,000)	Number (1,000) Under $5,000 [1]	$5,000 to $9,999	$10,000 to $14,999	$15,000 to $24,999	$25,000 to $34,999	$35,000 to $49,999	$50,000 to $74,999	$75,000 and over	Median income (current dollars)
MALE											
Total	**118,871**	**105,351**	**7,350**	**7,741**	**8,933**	**17,439**	**13,979**	**15,879**	**16,191**	**17,838**	**32,137**
15 to 24 years old	21,651	13,038	3,986	2,551	1,667	2,434	1,178	713	343	168	9,959
25 to 34 years old	20,985	19,435	951	1,339	1,515	3,553	3,130	3,743	3,192	2,014	31,793
35 to 44 years old	19,714	18,671	633	816	1,027	2,370	2,460	3,389	3,736	4,242	42,252
45 to 54 years old	21,495	20,399	720	962	1,307	2,496	2,374	3,183	4,034	5,323	45,420
55 to 64 years old	17,946	17,140	607	869	1,162	2,382	2,248	2,633	3,077	4,162	41,197
65 years old and over	17,081	16,667	452	1,205	2,254	4,203	2,591	2,220	1,814	1,930	25,704
Region:											
Northeast	21,578	19,242	1,428	1,355	1,492	2,883	2,366	2,816	3,064	3,838	35,363
Midwest	25,756	23,360	1,718	1,700	1,783	3,888	3,274	3,689	3,813	3,492	32,275
South	43,374	38,040	2,447	3,090	3,445	6,598	5,084	5,854	5,481	6,040	31,173
West	28,162	24,708	1,758	1,595	2,214	4,072	3,255	3,517	3,833	4,464	32,361
Educational attainment of householder: [2]											
Total	**97,220**	**92,313**	**3,364**	**5,190**	**7,266**	**15,005**	**12,802**	**15,166**	**15,851**	**17,670**	**36,772**
Less than 9th grade	5,117	4,709	236	833	1,046	1,349	592	375	190	89	16,237
9th to 12th grade [3]	7,443	6,628	422	916	1,048	1,843	1,027	727	430	216	19,243
High school graduate [4]	30,370	28,365	1,111	1,764	2,616	5,937	5,099	5,330	4,268	2,241	30,232
Some college, no degree	16,137	15,426	658	754	1,145	2,517	2,343	2,995	2,927	2,085	36,082
Associate's degree	8,182	7,955	275	302	479	984	1,170	1,637	1,799	1,307	40,918
Bachelor's degree or more	29,971	29,230	662	621	932	2,374	2,571	4,101	6,241	11,729	61,388
Bachelor's degree	19,017	18,455	477	425	651	1,704	1,905	2,898	4,144	6,254	55,038
Master's degree	7,181	7,059	130	144	203	447	460	908	1,498	3,270	69,378
Professional degree	1,862	1,841	29	26	38	123	97	150	243	1,135	96,363
Doctoral degree	1,911	1,875	25	26	40	101	108	145	358	1,071	85,963
Tenure:											
Owner-occupied	83,046	74,649	5,002	4,361	5,258	10,763	9,308	11,543	12,892	15,524	37,552
Renter-occupied	34,365	29,481	2,219	3,213	3,537	6,363	4,513	4,182	3,206	2,247	23,581
Occupier paid no cash rent	1,460	1,221	129	166	140	313	158	154	94	67	19,889
FEMALE											
Total	**125,084**	**106,142**	**12,538**	**14,061**	**13,672**	**19,813**	**13,810**	**13,922**	**10,998**	**7,328**	**20,831**
15 to 24 years old	20,761	12,376	4,089	2,685	13,672	2,100	838	547	205	66	8,765
25 to 34 years old	20,599	17,645	1,916	1,695	13,672	3,321	2,916	3,169	2,042	925	25,655
35 to 44 years old	20,128	17,552	1,832	1,406	13,672	2,949	2,516	2,944	2,626	1,737	29,447
45 to 54 years old	22,459	20,100	1,969	1,649	13,672	3,554	2,886	3,243	2,723	2,212	27,748
55 to 64 years old	19,038	17,263	1,717	1,887	13,672	2,908	2,417	2,482	2,269	1,621	25,502
65 years old and over	22,098	21,204	1,014	4,738	13,672	4,982	2,238	1,535	1,136	764	15,072
Region:											
Northeast	23,170	20,008	2,336	2,612	2,527	3,457	2,480	2,492	2,411	1,692	21,498
Midwest	27,168	23,830	2,781	2,998	3,129	4,731	3,204	3,262	2,430	1,296	20,777
South	46,229	38,607	4,339	5,408	5,030	7,318	5,234	5,242	3,660	2,372	20,547
West	28,517	23,697	3,083	3,044	2,986	4,309	2,891	2,924	2,497	1,964	20,835
Educational attainment of householder: [2]											
Total	**104,323**	**93,765**	**8,449**	**11,376**	**11,824**	**17,713**	**12,973**	**13,375**	**10,795**	**7,261**	**23,011**
Less than 9th grade	5,160	3,800	445	1,288	1,025	728	192	69	35	18	10,658
9th to 12th grade 3	7,320	5,899	725	1,568	1,284	1,489	467	239	88	43	12,063
High school graduate 4	31,541	27,976	2,556	4,355	4,704	6,977	4,243	3,140	1,493	510	17,830
Some college, no degree	18,065	16,516	1,520	1,793	1,995	3,541	2,924	2,597	1,467	679	22,772
Associate's degree	10,865	10,132	749	849	1,014	1,845	1,811	1,818	1,461	585	28,193
Bachelor's degree or more	31,372	29,442	2,455	1,525	1,801	3,133	3,337	5,511	6,251	5,429	41,132
Bachelor's degree	20,269	18,816	1,743	1,164	1,316	2,335	2,404	3,695	3,607	2,553	36,381
Master's degree	8,834	8,460	597	311	405	659	789	1,569	2,155	1,976	48,556
Professional degree	1,118	1,044	72	35	33	82	74	122	245	384	60,551
Doctoral degree	1,151	1,122	45	16	49	56	70	126	246	515	70,375
Tenure:											
Owner-occupied	86,439	74,875	8,793	8,961	8,837	13,076	9,602	10,487	8,828	6,291	22,492
Renter-occupied	37,228	30,073	3,580	4,884	4,625	6,468	4,067	3,345	2,096	1,007	17,309
Occupier paid no cash rent	1,417	1,193	165	216	210	269	140	89	76	29	15,166

[1] Includes persons with income deficit. [2] Persons 25 years and over. [3] No diploma attained. [4] Includes high school equivalency.

Source: U.S. Census Bureau, *Income, Poverty and Health Insurance Coverage in the United States: 2010*, Current Population Reports, P60-239, and Detailed Tables—Table PINC-01, September 2011. See also <http://www.census.gov/hhes/www/income/index.html>.

Table 717. Average Earnings of Year-Round, Full-Time Workers by Educational Attainment: 2010

[In dollars. For people 18 years old and over as of March 2011. See headnote, Table 715]

Sex and age	All workers	Less than 9th grade	High school 9th to 12th grade (no diploma)	High school graduate [1]	College Some college, no degree	College Associate degree	College Bachelor's degree or more
Male, total............	**62,518**	**28,766**	**33,524**	**44,281**	**51,241**	**54,540**	**91,566**
18 to 24 years old..........	28,230	21,237	25,619	24,328	28,254	31,647	42,936
25 to 34 years old..........	48,250	25,083	29,186	38,663	43,036	45,679	64,060
35 to 44 years old..........	66,379	28,615	32,778	45,774	53,525	58,049	96,118
45 to 54 years old..........	71,116	31,114	37,754	50,216	59,852	60,980	104,490
55 to 64 years old..........	74,517	31,481	41,139	50,177	58,637	58,155	106,221
65 years old and over......	67,994	35,500	33,467	48,520	63,522	56,133	90,746
Female, total............	**45,315**	**20,510**	**23,514**	**32,099**	**36,409**	**41,953**	**62,626**
18 to 24 years old..........	25,080	(B)	17,172	20,480	22,675	27,086	35,718
25 to 34 years old..........	40,313	19,739	20,943	27,731	31,748	37,615	51,212
35 to 44 years old..........	48,754	19,873	22,596	32,746	37,811	41,569	68,074
45 to 54 years old..........	48,939	19,996	23,775	34,410	41,117	47,723	69,263
55 to 64 years old..........	48,326	21,962	28,043	35,141	40,697	42,569	68,105

B Base figure too small to meet statistical standards for reliability of derived figure. [1] Includes equivalency.

Source: U.S. Census Bureau, *Income, Poverty and Health Insurance Coverage in the United States: 2010*, Current Population Reports, series P60-239, and Detailed Tables—Table PINC-04, September 2011. See also <http://www.census.gov/hhes/www/income/index.html>.

Table 718. Per Capita Money Income in Current and Constant (2010) Dollars by Race and Hispanic Origin: 1990 to 2010

[In dollars. Constant dollars based on CPI-U-RS deflator. People as of March of following year. Based on the Current Population Survey, Annual Social and Economic Supplement (ASEC); see text, this section, Section 1, and Appendix III. For data collection changes over time, see <http://www.census.gov/hhes/www/income/data/historical/history.html>]

Year	Current dollars All races [1]	Current dollars White [2]	Current dollars Black [3]	Current dollars Asian and Pacific Islander [4]	Current dollars His-panic [5]	Constant (2010) dollars All races [1]	Constant (2010) dollars White [2]	Constant (2010) dollars Black [3]	Constant (2010) dollars Asian and Pacific Islander [4]	Constant (2010) dollars His-panic [5]
1990...............	14,387	15,265	9,017	(NA)	8,424	23,266	24,686	14,582	(NA)	13,623
1995 [6]...........	17,227	18,304	10,982	16,567	9,300	24,472	26,002	15,601	23,535	13,211
2000 [7,8]...........	22,346	23,582	14,796	23,350	12,651	28,293	29,857	18,733	29,564	16,018
2005 [9,10]...........	25,036	26,496	16,874	27,331	14,483	27,961	29,592	18,846	30,525	16,175
2007...............	26,804	28,325	18,428	29,901	15,603	28,186	29,785	19,378	31,443	16,407
2008...............	26,964	28,502	18,406	30,292	15,674	27,305	28,863	18,639	30,675	15,872
2009 [11]...........	26,530	28,034	18,135	30,653	15,063	26,968	28,497	18,434	31,159	15,312
2010...............	26,487	28,144	17,919	28,648	14,831	26,487	28,144	17,919	28,648	14,831

NA Not available. [1] Includes other races, not shown separately. [2] Beginning with 2002, data represents White alone, which refers to people who reported White and did not report any other race category. [3] Beginning with 2002, data represents Black alone, which refers to people who reported Black and did not report any other race category. [4] Beginning with 2002, data represents Asian alone, which refers to people who reported Asian and did not report any other race category. [5] People of Hispanic origin may be any race. [6] Data reflect full implementation of the 1990 Census-based sample design and metropolitan definitions, 7,000 household sample reduction, and revised race edits. [7] Implementation of Census 2000-based population controls. [8] Implementation of a 28,000 household sample expansion. [9] See footnote 4, Table 710. See also comments on race in the text for Section 1. [10] Data have been revised to reflect a correction to the weights in the 2005 ASEC. [11] Median income is calculated using $2,500 income intervals. Beginning with 2009 income data, the Census Bureau expanded the upper income intervals used to calculate medians to $250,000 or more. Before 2009, the upper open-ended interval was $100,000.

Source: U.S. Census Bureau, *Income, Poverty and Health Insurance Coverage in the United States: 2010*, Current Population Reports, P60-239, and Historical Tables—Table P-1, September 2011. See also <http://www.census.gov/hhes/www/income/income.html> and <http://www.census.gov/hhes/www/income/data/historical/index.html>.

Table 719. Money Income of People—Number by Income Level and by Sex, Race, and Hispanic Origin: 2010

[In thousands (118,871 represents 118,871,000). People as of March of the following year. Based on Current Population Survey, Annual Social and Economic Supplement (ASEC); see text, this section, Section 1, and Appendix III]

Income interval	Male All races [1]	Male White alone	Male Black alone	Male Asian alone	Male His-panic [2]	Female All races [1]	Female White alone	Female Black alone	Female Asian alone	Female His-panic [2]
All households...............	**118,871**	**96,931**	**13,534**	**5,424**	**18,105**	**125,084**	**99,672**	**16,228**	**6,076**	**16,964**
Under $10,000 [3].................	28,611	21,080	5,108	1,395	5,808	45,541	35,264	6,326	2,557	8,555
$10,000 to $19,999............	17,847	14,420	2,218	682	3,820	24,643	19,978	3,250	866	3,343
$20,000 to $29,999............	15,658	12,791	1,828	667	2,974	16,070	12,766	2,284	626	1,994
$30,000 to $39,999............	12,686	10,500	1,383	507	1,821	12,025	9,601	1,602	523	1,283
$40,000 to $49,999............	10,039	8,479	966	378	1,214	8,479	6,923	1,031	370	667
$50,000 to $59,999............	8,069	7,029	602	297	791	5,766	4,744	631	282	403
$60,000 to $74,999............	8,122	6,931	633	401	667	5,232	4,326	503	312	322
$75,000 to $84,999............	4,019	3,514	243	195	296	2,031	1,645	211	138	115
$85,000 to $99,999............	3,433	3,015	164	201	204	1,713	1,411	153	116	94
$100,000 to $149,999............	6,323	5,524	261	456	335	2,488	2,083	165	206	132
$150,000 to $199,999............	2,033	1,808	56	138	87	606	522	39	40	34
$200,000 to $249,999............	792	714	33	38	33	245	193	17	29	8
$250,000 and above............	1,238	1,127	36	67	56	245	217	14	10	12

[1] Includes races not shown separately. [2] Persons of Hispanic origin may be of any race. [3] Includes persons without income.

Source: U.S. Census Bureau, *Income, Poverty and Health Insurance Coverage in the United States: 2010*, Current Population Reports, P60-239, and Detailed Tables—Table PINC-11, September 2011. See also <http://www.census.gov/hhes/www/income/>.

Table 720. Household, Family, and Per Capita Income and Individuals, and Families Below Poverty Level by City: 2010

[The American Community Survey universe includes the household population and the population living in institutions, college dormitories, and other group quarters. Based on a sample and subject to sampling variability; see text, Section 1 and Appendix III. For definition of median, see Guide to Tabular Presentation]

City	Median household income (dol.)	Median family income (dol.)	Per capita income (dol.)	Number below poverty level [1] Individuals	Number below poverty level [1] Families	Percent below poverty level [1] Individuals	Percent below poverty level [1] Families
Albuquerque, NM	46,079	59,469	25,358	94,330	19,465	17.4	14.6
Anaheim, CA	54,157	56,012	21,813	51,979	9,325	15.5	12.4
Anchorage municipality, AK	72,128	85,829	34,516	25,799	5,039	9.0	7.2
Arlington, TX	48,752	54,653	22,618	54,893	11,252	15.0	12.2
Atlanta, GA	41,631	50,113	30,688	102,297	16,949	26.1	22.4
Aurora, CO	50,358	58,652	23,178	53,877	10,417	16.7	13.5
Austin, TX	47,434	61,605	28,449	162,072	25,798	20.8	15.1
Bakersfield, CA	53,038	57,800	22,208	66,891	12,113	19.4	14.9
Baltimore, MD	38,346	45,715	22,120	153,961	26,017	25.6	20.0
Boston, MA	49,893	60,254	31,982	136,467	20,752	23.3	17.6
Buffalo, NY	28,490	34,063	19,117	76,558	14,767	30.2	25.9
Charlotte, NC	49,616	57,917	28,911	124,172	23,513	17.2	13.7
Chicago, IL	44,776	50,995	25,650	596,975	102,555	22.5	18.2
Cincinnati, OH	34,110	42,472	23,682	86,312	15,263	30.6	24.6
Cleveland, OH	25,977	31,182	15,635	131,624	26,865	34.0	30.4
Colorado Springs, CO	49,929	61,897	26,459	56,874	11,556	13.7	10.9
Columbus, OH	41,397	50,561	22,495	175,157	31,196	22.6	18.1
Corpus Christi, TX	41,845	49,306	22,572	60,636	11,649	20.1	15.7
Dallas, TX	40,650	43,132	24,557	277,959	51,676	23.6	20.0
Denver, CO	45,074	55,651	30,243	127,754	20,804	21.6	16.2
Detroit, MI	25,787	31,011	14,118	263,864	47,901	37.6	32.3
El Paso, TX	37,278	41,449	18,231	139,993	28,077	21.6	18.1
Fort Wayne, IN	42,609	53,275	22,670	41,017	7,181	16.5	11.7
Fort Worth, TX	48,224	55,727	22,613	129,716	23,979	17.9	13.7
Fresno, CA	41,144	46,517	17,817	147,481	26,347	30.2	24.4
Honolulu, HI [2]	54,828	71,644	28,885	36,797	4,466	11.3	6.1
Houston, TX	42,355	45,977	24,623	474,346	90,487	22.8	19.5
Indianapolis, IN [3]	38,502	47,287	22,022	170,660	32,156	21.1	16.8
Jacksonville, FL	45,584	54,182	23,703	133,888	24,118	16.7	12.2
Kansas City, MO	42,780	53,474	24,756	92,965	16,529	20.4	15.4
Las Vegas, NV	50,783	58,730	24,360	92,058	16,348	16.0	12.0
Lexington-Fayette, KY	44,895	63,086	25,561	58,733	8,978	20.4	12.9
Long Beach, CA	51,426	59,765	25,138	89,447	14,591	19.7	15.1
Los Angeles, CA	47,031	51,029	26,226	806,811	139,954	21.6	17.6
Memphis, TN	37,045	41,271	20,237	167,059	33,518	26.5	21.9
Mesa, AZ	44,747	52,899	21,918	65,662	12,364	15.1	11.5
Miami, FL	27,291	31,519	18,269	128,116	21,235	32.4	26.4
Milwaukee, WI	32,911	38,316	17,912	171,521	31,721	29.5	25.2
Minneapolis, MN	46,508	61,725	29,558	86,153	11,845	23.3	16.9
Nashville-Davidson, TN [3]	42,813	51,094	24,932	120,354	22,048	20.8	16.3
New Orleans, LA	37,726	44,196	25,082	92,045	17,516	27.2	22.6
New York, NY	48,743	53,593	29,326	1,621,327	314,679	20.1	17.0
Newark, NJ	32,043	36,277	15,933	79,243	15,908	30.2	27.7
Oakland, CA	49,190	54,625	28,660	86,682	14,667	22.3	18.0
Oklahoma City, OK	44,043	52,705	24,595	96,240	19,003	16.8	13.5
Omaha, NE	43,813	57,940	25,008	70,282	11,745	17.6	12.1
Philadelphia, PA	34,400	43,147	20,170	397,083	65,956	26.7	21.3
Phoenix, AZ	42,260	50,027	22,429	321,560	57,217	22.5	17.5
Pittsburgh, PA	36,196	49,558	24,365	62,909	9,689	22.3	15.6
Plano, TX	79,234	95,335	38,778	20,736	3,475	7.9	5.0
Portland, OR	47,185	59,504	28,678	105,852	16,907	18.5	13.4
Raleigh, NC	49,931	63,098	28,053	70,750	12,096	18.4	13.9
Riverside, CA	53,847	61,762	20,829	55,254	7,604	18.6	12.3
Sacramento, CA	46,731	51,978	24,142	99,347	17,098	21.5	16.4
San Antonio, TX	43,758	51,499	21,425	249,857	46,584	19.1	15.0
San Diego, CA	60,037	71,498	30,747	219,516	35,113	17.4	12.7
San Francisco, CA	71,745	82,213	44,079	100,230	11,358	12.5	7.6
San Jose, CA	76,794	84,798	30,757	118,538	18,877	12.6	8.7
Santa Ana, CA	51,467	49,144	15,235	67,295	10,864	21.3	18.5
Seattle, WA	60,212	88,904	39,167	86,737	9,574	14.7	7.8
St. Louis, MO	32,688	40,683	21,069	86,635	13,399	27.8	20.6
St. Paul, MN	44,057	55,254	23,550	67,209	11,460	24.2	18.8
St. Petersburg, FL	43,728	56,430	27,012	39,702	6,070	16.5	10.6
Stockton, CA	45,606	47,797	18,994	65,688	13,110	23.0	19.7
Tampa, FL	40,883	49,368	27,034	69,950	12,179	21.3	16.7
Toledo, OH	31,708	39,292	17,427	72,525	14,274	25.8	21.4
Tucson, AZ	36,428	45,883	19,259	117,317	20,053	23.5	17.4
Tulsa, OK	38,220	47,105	24,342	77,275	14,772	20.1	15.5
Virginia Beach, VA	64,212	75,757	30,420	32,384	6,161	7.5	5.5
Washington, DC	60,903	77,514	41,240	109,423	14,285	19.2	14.1
Wichita, KS	42,694	55,385	23,339	64,514	11,456	17.0	12.5

[1] See headnote, Table 721. [2] Data shown for census designated place (CDP). [3] Represents the portion of a consolidated city that is not within one or more separately incorporated places.

Source: U.S. Census Bureau, 2010 American Community Survey, 2010 ACS 1-year estimates: B01003, B19019, B17019, B17001, B19113, DP03, and B17010, <http://factfinder.census.gov/>, accessed August 2012.

Income, Expenditures, Poverty, and Wealth   477

Table 721. Individuals and Families Below Poverty Level—Number and Rate by State: 2000 and 2010

[In thousands (33,311 represents 33,311,000), except as indicated. Represents number and percent below poverty in the past 12 months. Prior to 2006, the American Community Survey universe was limited to the household population and excluded the population living in institutions, college dormitories, and other group quarters. Poverty status was determined for all people except institutionalized people, people in military group quarters, people in college dormitories, and unrelated individuals under 15 years old. These groups were excluded from the numerator and denominator when calculating poverty rates. Based on a sample and subject to sampling variability; see Appendix III]

State	Number below poverty (1,000)				Percent below poverty			
	Individuals		Families		Individuals		Families	
	2000	2010	2000	2010	2000	2010	2000	2010
United States	**33,311**	**46,216**	**6,615**	**8,580**	**12.2**	**15.3**	**9.3**	**11.3**
Alabama	672	888	146	181	15.6	19.0	12.4	14.7
Alaska	55	69	11	12	9.1	9.9	6.8	7.2
Arizona	780	1,094	150	194	15.6	17.4	11.6	12.5
Arkansas	439	535	96	107	17.0	18.8	13.0	14.1
California	4,520	5,783	832	1,003	13.7	15.8	10.7	11.8
Colorado	363	660	64	118	8.7	13.4	5.7	9.4
Connecticut	254	350	51	64	7.7	10.1	5.8	7.2
Delaware	70	103	14	18	9.3	11.8	6.7	8.1
District of Columbia	94	109	17	14	17.5	19.2	15.4	14.1
Florida	1,987	3,047	387	549	12.8	16.5	9.3	12.0
Georgia	999	1,689	206	326	12.6	17.9	10.0	13.7
Hawaii	103	142	19	22	8.8	10.7	6.8	7.4
Idaho	144	242	26	47	11.4	15.7	7.7	11.6
Illinois	1,335	1,732	262	315	11.1	13.8	8.6	10.1
Indiana	592	963	113	182	10.1	15.3	7.1	11.0
Iowa	281	371	53	65	10.0	12.6	7.0	8.2
Kansas	247	378	43	68	9.5	13.6	6.2	9.5
Kentucky	640	800	148	163	16.4	19.0	13.5	14.5
Louisiana	862	825	182	164	20.0	18.7	16.0	14.5
Maine	124	167	22	30	10.1	12.9	6.6	8.8
Maryland	477	557	89	95	9.3	9.9	6.6	6.6
Massachusetts	586	725	110	131	9.6	11.4	7.1	8.2
Michigan	975	1,618	196	303	10.1	16.8	7.7	12.1
Minnesota	328	600	66	102	6.9	11.6	5.1	7.5
Mississippi	498	644	104	132	18.2	22.4	14.2	17.8
Missouri	606	889	118	162	11.2	15.3	7.7	10.6
Montana	117	141	23	26	13.4	14.6	9.5	10.0
Nebraska	158	230	28	41	9.6	12.9	6.5	8.8
Nevada	194	398	34	71	9.9	14.9	6.9	11.1
New Hampshire	63	106	11	18	5.3	8.3	3.5	5.3
New Jersey	651	885	126	170	7.9	10.3	6.0	7.8
New Mexico	320	414	64	79	18.0	20.4	14.2	15.7
New York	2,391	2,821	491	530	13.1	14.9	10.7	11.5
North Carolina	1,018	1,628	203	325	13.1	17.5	9.6	13.3
North Dakota	71	85	14	13	11.6	13.0	8.1	7.8
Ohio	1,216	1,779	246	348	11.1	15.8	8.4	11.8
Oklahoma	459	617	100	121	13.8	16.9	11.0	12.7
Oregon	439	596	84	106	13.2	15.8	9.5	11.0
Pennsylvania	1,240	1,648	247	298	10.5	13.4	7.8	9.3
Rhode Island	108	142	23	23	10.7	14.0	8.5	9.2
South Carolina	557	816	123	163	14.4	18.2	11.7	13.8
South Dakota	83	114	16	19	11.5	14.4	8.4	9.2
Tennessee	745	1,095	158	220	13.5	17.7	10.5	13.4
Texas	3,056	4,414	639	843	15.1	17.9	12.3	13.8
Utah	192	359	40	65	8.8	13.2	7.2	9.7
Vermont	63	76	12	13	10.7	12.7	7.5	8.4
Virginia	630	862	124	156	9.2	11.1	6.8	7.7
Washington	667	889	127	154	11.6	13.4	8.6	9.2
West Virginia	327	327	72	64	18.6	18.1	14.7	13.2
Wisconsin	461	731	75	133	8.9	13.2	5.6	9.1
Wyoming	55	62	10	11	11.4	11.2	7.9	7.2

Source: U.S. Census Bureau, 2010 American Community Survey, B17001, "Poverty Status in the Past 12 Months by Sex and Age" and B17010, "Poverty Status in the Past 12 Months of Families by Family Type by Presence of Related Children under 18 Years by Age of Related Children," <http://factfinder2.census.gov/faces/nav/jsf/pages/index.xhtml>, accessed July 2012.

Table 722. Poverty Thresholds by Size of Family Unit: 1980 to 2010

[In dollars per year. For information on the official poverty thresholds, see text, this section. For more on poverty, see <http://www.census.gov/hhes/www/poverty/about/overview/measure.html>]

Size of family unit	1980	1990	1995	2000 [1]	2005	2007	2008	2009	2010
One person (unrelated individual) [2]......	4,190	6,652	7,763	8,791	9,973	10,590	10,991	10,956	11,139
Under 65 years old.......................	4,290	6,800	7,929	8,959	10,160	10,787	11,201	11,161	11,344
65 years old and over....................	3,949	6,268	7,309	8,259	9,367	9,944	10,326	10,289	10,458
Two persons................................	5,363	8,509	9,933	11,235	12,755	13,540	14,051	13,991	14,218
Householder under 65 years old........	5,537	8,794	10,259	11,589	13,145	13,954	14,417	14,366	14,676
Householder 65 years old and over.....	4,983	7,905	9,219	10,418	11,815	12,550	13,014	12,968	13,194
Three persons..............................	6,565	10,419	12,158	13,740	15,577	16,530	17,163	17,098	17,374
Four persons...............................	8,414	13,359	15,569	17,604	19,971	21,203	22,025	21,954	22,314
Five persons...............................	9,966	15,792	18,408	20,815	23,613	25,080	26,049	25,991	26,439
Six persons................................	11,269	17,839	20,804	23,533	26,683	28,323	29,456	29,405	29,897
Seven persons.............................	12,761	20,241	23,552	26,750	30,249	32,233	33,529	33,372	34,009
Eight persons..............................	14,199	22,582	26,237	29,701	33,610	35,816	37,220	37,252	37,934
Nine or more persons.....................	16,896	26,848	31,280	35,150	40,288	42,739	44,346	44,366	45,220

[1] Implementation of Census 2000-based population controls and sample expanded by 28,000 households. [2] A person living alone or with non-relatives.

Source: U.S. Census Bureau, *Income, Poverty, and Health Insurance Coverage in the United States: 2010*, Current Population Reports, P60-239, and Historical Tables—Table 1, September 2011. See also <http://www.census.gov/hhes/www/poverty/poverty.html> and <http://www.census.gov/hhes/www/poverty/data/historical/index.html>.

Table 723. People Below Poverty Level and Below 125 Percent of Poverty Level by Race and Hispanic Origin: 1980 to 2010

[29,272 represents 29,272,000. People as of March of the following year. Based on Current Population Survey, Annual Social and Economic Supplement (ASEC); see text, this section, Section 1, and Appendix III. For data collection changes over time, see <http://www.census.gov/hhes/www/income/data/historical/history.html>]

Year	Number of persons below poverty (1,000)					Percent of persons below poverty					Below 125 percent [1] of poverty level	
	All races [2]	White [3]	Black [4]	Asian and Pacific Islander [5]	His-panic [6]	All races [2]	White [3]	Black [4]	Asian and Pacific Islander [5]	His-panic [6]	Number (1,000)	Percent of total population
1980.........	29,272	19,699	8,579	(NA)	3,491	13.0	10.2	32.5	(NA)	25.7	40,658	18.1
1985.........	33,064	22,860	8,926	(NA)	5,236	14.0	11.4	31.3	(NA)	29.0	44,166	18.7
1989.........	31,528	20,785	9,302	939	5,430	12.8	10.0	30.7	14.1	26.2	42,653	17.3
1990.........	33,585	22,326	9,837	858	6,006	13.5	10.7	31.9	12.2	28.1	44,837	18.0
1991.........	35,708	23,747	10,242	996	6,339	14.2	11.3	32.7	13.8	28.7	47,527	18.9
1992 [7].......	38,014	25,259	10,827	985	7,592	14.8	11.9	33.4	12.7	29.6	50,592	19.7
1993 [8].......	39,265	26,226	10,877	1,134	8,126	15.1	12.2	33.1	15.3	30.6	51,801	20.0
1994.........	38,059	25,379	10,196	974	8,416	14.5	11.7	30.6	14.6	30.7	50,401	19.3
1995.........	36,425	24,423	9,872	1,411	8,574	13.8	11.2	29.3	14.6	30.3	48,761	18.5
1996.........	36,529	24,650	9,694	1,454	8,697	13.7	11.2	28.4	14.5	29.4	49,310	18.5
1997.........	35,574	24,396	9,116	1,468	8,308	13.3	11.0	26.5	14.0	27.1	47,853	17.8
1998.........	34,476	23,454	9,091	1,360	8,070	12.7	10.5	26.1	12.5	25.6	46,036	17.0
1999 [9].......	32,791	22,169	8,441	1,285	7,876	11.9	9.8	23.6	10.7	22.7	45,030	16.3
2000 [10]......	31,581	21,645	7,982	1,258	7,747	11.3	9.5	22.5	9.9	21.5	43,612	15.6
2001.........	32,907	22,739	8,136	1,275	7,997	11.7	9.9	22.7	10.2	21.4	45,320	16.1
2002 [11].......	34,570	23,466	8,602	1,161	8,555	12.1	10.2	24.1	10.1	21.8	47,084	16.5
2003.........	35,861	24,272	8,781	1,401	9,051	12.5	10.5	24.4	11.8	22.5	48,687	16.9
2004 [12]......	37,040	25,327	9,014	1,201	9,122	12.7	10.8	24.7	9.8	21.9	49,693	17.1
2005.........	36,950	24,872	9,168	1,402	9,368	12.6	10.6	24.9	11.1	21.8	49,327	16.8
2006.........	36,460	24,416	9,048	1,353	9,243	12.3	10.3	24.3	10.3	20.6	49,688	16.8
2007.........	37,276	25,120	9,237	1,349	9,890	12.5	10.5	24.5	10.2	21.5	50,876	17.0
2008.........	39,829	26,990	9,379	1,576	10,987	13.2	11.2	24.7	11.8	23.2	53,805	17.9
2009.........	43,569	29,830	9,944	1,746	12,350	14.3	12.3	25.8	12.5	25.3	56,840	18.7
2010.........	46,180	31,650	10,675	1,729	13,243	15.1	13.0	27.4	12.1	26.6	60,443	19.8

NA Not available. [1] Includes those in poverty, plus those who have income above poverty but less than 1.25 times their poverty threshold. [2] Includes other races, not shown separately. [3] Beginning 2002, data represent White alone, which refers to people who reported White and did not report any other race category. [4] Beginning 2002, data represent Black alone, which refers to people who reported Black and did not report any other race category. [5] Beginning 2002, data represent Asian alone, which refers to people who reported Asian and did not report any other race category. [6] People of Hispanic origin may be any race. [7] Implementation of 1990 Census population controls. [8] The March 1994 income supplement was revised to allow for the coding of different income amounts on selected questionnaire items. Limits either increased or decreased in the following categories: earnings increased to $999,999; Social Security increased to $49,999; Supplemental Security Income and public assistance increased to $24,999; veterans' benefits increased to $99,999; child support and alimony decreased to $49,999. [9] Implementation of Census-2000-based population controls. [10] Implementation of sample expansion by 28,000 households. [11] Beginning with the 2003 Current Population Survey (CPS), the questionnaire allowed respondents to choose more than one race. For 2002 and later, data represent persons who selected this race group only and exclude persons reporting more than one race. The CPS in prior years allowed respondents to report only one race group. See also comments on race in the text for Section 1. [12] Data have been revised to reflect a correction to the weights in the 2005 ASEC.

Source: U.S. Census Bureau, *Income, Poverty, and Health Insurance Coverage in the United States: 2010*, Current Population Reports, series P60-239, and Historical Tables—Tables 2 and 6, September 2011. See also <http://www.census.gov/hhes/www/poverty/poverty.html>.

Table 724. Children Below Poverty Level by Race and Hispanic Origin: 1980 to 2010

[11,114 represents 11,114,000. Persons as of March of the following year. Covers only related children in families under 18 years old. Based on Current Population Survey, Annual Social and Economic Supplement (ASEC); see text, this section, Section 1, and Appendix III. For data collection changes over time, see <http://www.census.gov/hhes/www/income/data/historical/history.html>]

Year	Number of children below poverty level (1,000)					Percent of children below poverty level				
	All races [1]	White [2]	Black [3]	Asian and Pacific Islander [4]	His-panic [5]	All races [1]	White [2]	Black [3]	Asian and Pacific Islander [4]	His-panic [5]
1980	11,114	6,817	3,906	(NA)	1,718	17.9	13.4	42.1	(NA)	33.0
1985	12,483	7,838	4,057	(NA)	2,512	20.1	15.6	43.1	(NA)	39.6
1990	12,715	7,696	4,412	356	2,750	19.9	15.1	44.2	17.0	37.7
1992 [6]	14,521	8,752	5,015	352	3,440	21.6	16.5	46.3	16.0	39.0
1993 [7]	14,961	9,123	5,030	358	3,666	22.0	17.0	45.9	17.6	39.9
1994	14,610	8,826	4,787	308	3,956	21.2	16.3	43.3	17.9	41.1
1995	13,999	8,474	4,644	532	3,938	20.2	15.5	41.5	18.6	39.3
1996	13,764	8,488	4,411	553	4,090	19.8	15.5	39.5	19.1	39.9
1997	13,422	8,441	4,116	608	3,865	19.2	15.4	36.8	19.9	36.4
1998	12,845	7,935	4,073	542	3,670	18.3	14.4	36.4	17.5	33.6
1999 [8]	11,678	7,194	3,698	367	3,561	16.6	13.1	32.8	11.5	29.9
2000 [9]	11,005	6,834	3,495	407	3,342	15.6	12.4	30.9	12.5	27.6
2001	11,175	7,086	3,423	353	3,433	15.8	12.8	30.0	11.1	27.4
2002 [10]	11,646	7,203	3,570	302	3,653	16.3	13.1	32.1	11.4	28.2
2003	12,340	7,624	3,750	331	3,982	17.2	13.9	33.6	12.1	29.5
2004 [11]	12,473	7,876	3,702	265	3,985	17.3	14.3	33.4	9.4	28.6
2005	12,335	7,652	3,743	312	3,977	17.1	13.9	34.2	11.0	27.7
2006	12,299	7,522	3,690	351	3,959	16.9	13.6	33.0	12.0	26.6
2007	12,802	8,002	3,838	345	4,348	17.6	14.4	34.3	11.8	28.3
2008	13,507	8,441	3,781	430	4,888	18.5	15.3	34.4	14.2	30.3
2009	14,774	9,440	3,919	444	5,419	20.1	17.0	35.3	13.6	32.5
2010	15,730	9,982	4,282	459	5,881	21.5	18.1	39.2	14.0	34.5

NA Not available. [1] Includes other races, not shown separately. [2] Beginning 2002, data represent White alone, which refers to people who reported White and did not report any other race category. [3] Beginning 2002, data represent Black alone, which refers to people who reported Black and did not report any other race category. [4] Beginning 2002, data represent Asian alone, which refers to people who reported Asian and did not report any other race category. [5] People of Hispanic origin may be of any race. [6] Implementation of 1990 Census population controls. [7] The March 1994 income supplement was revised to allow for the coding of different income amounts on selected questionnaire items. Limits either increased or decreased in the following categories: earnings increased to $999,999; Social Security increased to $49,999; Supplemental Security Income and public assistance increased to $24,999; veterans' benefits increased to $99,999; child support and alimony decreased to $49,999. [8] Implementation of Census 2000-based population controls. [9] Implementation of sample expansion to 28,000 households. [10] Beginning with the 2003 Current Population Survey (CPS), the questionnaire allowed respondents to choose more than one race. For 2002 and later, data represent persons who selected this race group only and excludes persons reporting more than one race. The CPS in prior years allowed respondents to report only one race group. See also comments on race in the text for Section 1. [11] Data have been revised to reflect a correction to the weights in the 2005 Annual Social and Economic Supplement (ASEC).

Source: U.S. Census Bureau, *Income, Poverty, and Health Insurance Coverage in the United States: 2010*, Current Population Reports, P60-239, and Historical Tables—Table 3, September 2011. See also <http://www.census.gov/hhes/www/poverty/poverty.html> and <http://www.census.gov/hhes/www/poverty/data/historical/people.html>.

Table 725. People Below Poverty Level by Selected Characteristics: 2010

[46,180 represents 46,180,000. People as of March 2011. Based on Current Population Survey (CPS); see text, this section and Section 1, and Appendix III. The 2009 CPS allowed respondents to choose more than one race. For 2010, data represent persons who selected this race group only and exclude persons reporting more than one race. The CPS in prior years allowed respondents to report only one race group. See also comments on race in the text for Section 1. For composition of regions, see map, inside front cover]

Sex, age, region, nativity	Number below poverty level (1,000)					Percent below poverty level				
	All races [1]	White alone	Black alone	Asian alone	His-panic [2]	All races [1]	White alone	Black alone	Asian alone	His-panic [2]
Total	46,180	31,650	10,675	1,729	13,243	15.1	13.0	27.4	12.1	26.6
Male	21,012	14,580	4,643	794	6,420	14.0	12.1	25.5	11.6	25.0
Female	25,167	17,069	6,032	935	6,824	16.2	14.0	29.1	12.5	28.2
Under 18 years old	16,401	10,492	4,362	474	6,110	22.0	18.7	39.1	14.4	35.0
18 to 24 years old	6,507	4,532	1,448	279	1,547	21.9	19.9	32.5	21.4	26.8
25 to 34 years old	6,333	4,425	1,398	235	1,917	15.2	13.7	24.8	10.2	23.6
35 to 44 years old	5,028	3,638	1,012	214	1,618	12.6	11.6	20.0	8.8	22.9
45 to 54 years old	4,662	3,302	1,021	176	968	10.6	9.3	19.1	8.7	18.1
55 to 59 years old	1,972	1,380	432	86	308	10.1	8.5	20.3	10.3	17.1
60 to 64 years old	1,755	1,273	390	53	261	10.1	8.7	21.5	7.7	18.0
65 years old and over	3,520	2,608	612	213	514	9.0	7.7	18.0	14.6	18.0
65 to 74 years old	1,737	1,248	322	117	296	8.1	6.9	16.2	13.3	17.3
75 years old and over	1,784	1,361	290	96	218	10.0	8.7	20.7	16.7	19.0
Northeast	6,987	4,648	1,646	441	1,837	12.8	10.5	24.3	14.9	26.6
Midwest	9,148	6,307	2,225	197	1,189	13.9	11.3	33.0	11.8	28.0
South	19,072	12,263	5,895	370	5,039	16.9	14.4	27.0	11.4	27.9
West	10,973	8,432	909	721	5,179	15.3	14.6	25.4	11.2	25.1
Native	38,568	26,028	9,924	697	8,403	14.4	11.9	28.0	12.6	26.3
Foreign born	7,611	5,622	751	1,032	4,841	19.9	22.5	21.0	11.8	26.9
Naturalized citizen	1,906	1,227	256	374	846	11.3	12.4	14.8	7.8	15.0
Not a citizen	5,706	4,395	496	658	3,995	26.7	29.0	27.0	16.7	32.3

[1] Includes other races, not shown separately. [2] Persons of Hispanic origin may be any race.

Source: U.S. Census Bureau, *Income, Poverty, and Health Insurance Coverage in the United States: 2010*, Current Population Reports, P60-239, and Detailed Tables—Tables POV01, POV29, and POV41. See also <http://www.census.gov/hhes/www/poverty/index.html>.

Table 726. Work Experience of People During 2010 by Poverty Status, Sex, and Age: 2010

[99,250 represents 99,250,000. Covers only persons 16 years old and over. Based on Current Population Survey, Annual Social and Economic Supplement (ASEC); see text, this section, Section 1, and Appendix III]

Sex and age	Worked full-time year-round			Did not work full-time year-round			Did not work		
	Number (1,000)	Below poverty level		Number (1,000)	Below poverty level		Number (1,000)	Below poverty level	
		Number (1,000)	Percent		Number (1,000)	Percent		Number (1,000)	Percent
BOTH SEXES									
Total................	**99,250**	**2,608**	**2.6**	**53,891**	**8,057**	**15.0**	**86,776**	**20,717**	**23.9**
16 to 17 years old........	67	11	(B)	1,482	104	7.0	7,175	1,488	20.7
18 to 64 years old........	95,549	2,569	2.7	48,032	7,823	16.3	48,434	15,867	32.8
18 to 24 years old.......	6,084	378	6.2	12,363	2,378	19.2	11,204	3,752	33.5
25 to 34 years old.......	22,565	749	3.3	10,783	2,256	20.9	8,236	3,329	40.4
35 to 54 years old.......	49,673	1,264	2.5	17,498	2,559	14.6	16,626	5,867	35.3
55 to 64 years old.......	17,228	179	1.0	7,388	630	8.5	12,368	2,919	23.6
65 years old and over.....	3,634	28	0.8	4,377	130	3.0	31,167	3,362	10.8
MALE									
Total................	**56,416**	**1,419**	**2.5**	**24,659**	**3,668**	**14.9**	**35,729**	**8,263**	**23.1**
16 to 17 years old........	37	3	(B)	724	40	5.6	3,743	748	20.0
18 to 64 years old........	54,235	1,399	2.6	21,633	3,562	16.5	19,352	6,445	33.3
18 to 24 years old.......	3,477	159	4.6	6,115	1,017	16.6	5,489	1,655	30.2
25 to 34 years old.......	12,956	407	3.1	5,095	1,086	21.3	2,934	1,135	38.7
35 to 54 years old.......	28,247	734	2.6	7,178	1,184	16.5	5,784	2,340	40.5
55 to 64 years old.......	9,555	99	1.0	3,245	275	8.5	5,146	1,315	25.6
65 years old and over.....	2,144	17	0.8	2,303	66	2.9	12,634	1,070	8.5
FEMALE									
Total................	**42,834**	**1,189**	**2.8**	**29,232**	**4,389**	**15.0**	**51,047**	**12,454**	**24.4**
16 to 17 years old........	29	8	(B)	758	64	8.4	3,432	740	21.6
18 to 64 years old........	41,314	1,169	2.8	26,399	4,261	16.1	29,082	9,422	32.4
18 to 24 years old.......	2,607	218	8.4	6,247	1,361	21.8	5,716	2,097	36.7
25 to 34 years old.......	9,609	341	3.6	5,688	1,170	20.6	5,302	2,193	41.4
35 to 54 years old.......	21,425	530	2.5	10,320	1,375	13.3	10,842	3,528	32.5
55 to 64 years old.......	7,673	80	1.0	4,143	355	8.6	7,222	1,604	22.2
65 years old and over.....	1,490	12	0.8	2,075	65	3.1	18,533	2,292	12.4

B Base figure too small to meet statistical standards for reliability of a derived figure.

Source: U.S. Census Bureau, *Income, Poverty, and Health Insurance Coverage in the United States: 2010*, Current Population Reports, P60-239, and Detailed Tables—Table POV22, September 2011. See also <http://www.census.gov/hhes/www/poverty/index.html>.

Table 727. Families Below Poverty Level and Below 125 Percent of Poverty by Race and Hispanic Origin: 1980 to 2010

[6,217 represents 6,217,000. Families as of March of the following year. Based on Current Population Survey, Annual Social and Economic Supplement (ASEC); see text, this section and Section 1, and Appendix III. For data collection changes over time, see <http://www.census.gov/hhes/www/income/data/historical/history.html>]

Year	Number of families below poverty (1,000)					Percent of persons below poverty					Below 125 percent[1] of poverty level	
	All races[2]	White[3]	Black[4]	Asian and Pacific Islander[5]	His-panic[6]	All races[2]	White[3]	Black[4]	Asian and Pacific Islander[5]	His-panic[6]	Number (1,000)	Percent
1980........	6,217	4,195	1,826	(NA)	751	10.3	8.0	28.9	(NA)	23.2	8,764	14.5
1985........	7,223	4,983	1,983	(NA)	1,074	11.4	9.1	28.7	(NA)	25.5	9,753	15.3
1990........	7,098	4,622	2,193	169	1,244	10.7	8.1	29.3	11.0	25.0	9,564	14.4
1995........	7,532	4,994	2,127	264	1,695	10.8	8.5	26.4	12.4	27.0	10,223	14.7
2000[7]......	6,400	4,333	1,686	233	1,540	8.7	7.1	19.3	7.8	19.2	9,032	12.2
2002[8]......	7,229	4,862	1,923	210	1,792	9.6	7.8	21.5	7.4	19.7	9,998	13.2
2003........	7,607	5,058	1,986	311	1,925	10.0	8.1	22.3	10.2	20.8	10,360	13.6
2004[9]......	7,835	5,293	2,035	232	1,953	10.2	8.4	22.8	7.4	20.5	10,499	13.7
2005........	7,657	5,068	1,997	289	1,948	9.9	8.0	22.1	9.0	19.7	10,442	13.5
2006........	7,668	5,118	2,007	260	1,922	9.8	8.0	21.6	7.8	18.9	10,531	13.4
2007........	7,623	5,046	2,045	261	2,045	9.8	7.9	22.1	7.9	19.7	10,551	13.5
2008........	8,147	5,414	2,055	341	2,239	10.3	8.4	22.0	9.8	21.3	11,164	14.2
2009........	8,792	5,994	2,125	337	2,369	11.1	9.3	22.7	9.4	22.7	11,620	14.7
2010........	9,221	6,268	2,279	329	2,557	11.7	9.8	24.2	9.3	24.0	12,217	15.5

NA Not available. [1] See footnote 1, Table 723. [2] Includes other races, not shown separately. [3] Beginning 2002, data represent White alone, which refers to people who reported White and did not report any other race category. [4] Beginning 2002, data represent Black alone, which refers to people who reported Black and did not report any other race category. [5] Beginning 2002, data represent Asian alone, which refers to people who reported Asian and did not report any other race category. [6] People of Hispanic origin may be any race. [7] Implementation of a 28,000 household sample expansion. [8] Beginning with the 2003 Current Population Survey (CPS), the questionnaire allowed respondents to choose more than one race. For 2002 and later, data represent persons who selected this race group only and excludes persons reporting more than one race. The CPS in prior years allowed respondents to report only one race group. See also comments on race in the text for Section 1, Population. [9] Data have been revised to reflect a correction to the weights in the 2005 Annual Social and Economic Supplement (ASEC).

Source: U.S. Census Bureau, *Income, Poverty, and Health Insurance Coverage in the United States: 2010*, Current Population Reports, P60-239, and Historical and Detailed Tables—Tables 4 and POV04, September 2011. See also <http://www.census.gov/hhes/www/poverty/index.html> and <http://www.census.gov/hhes/www/poverty/data/historical/index.html>.

Table 728. Families Below Poverty Level by Selected Characteristics: 2010

[9,221 represents 9,221,000. Families as of March 2011. Based on Current Population Survey (CPS), Annual Social and Economic Supplement (ASEC); see text, this section and Section 1, and Appendix III. As of 2003, the CPS allowed respondents to choose more than one race. Data below represent persons who selected each race group only and exclude persons reporting more than one race. See also comments on race in the text for Section 1. For composition of regions, see map, inside front cover]

Characteristic	Number below poverty level (1,000)					Percent below poverty level				
	All races [1]	White alone	Black alone	Asian alone	His-panic [2]	All races [1]	White alone	Black alone	Asian alone	His-panic [2]
Total families..................	**9,221**	**6,268**	**2,279**	**329**	**2,557**	**11.7**	**9.8**	**24.2**	**9.3**	**24.0**
Age of householder:										
18 to 24 years old...............	1,152	760	320	20	317	36.7	33.3	51.7	15.9	39.4
25 to 34 years old...............	2,557	1,674	699	65	794	19.6	16.6	36.0	10.2	30.9
35 to 44 years old...............	2,131	1,468	509	82	726	12.8	11.1	23.8	9.1	25.1
45 to 54 years old...............	1,590	1,105	370	68	395	8.9	7.6	17.9	7.9	17.7
55 to 64 years old...............	958	687	210	31	174	6.7	5.7	14.5	5.4	14.1
65 years old and over..........	770	532	156	59	119	5.7	4.6	13.4	13.8	13.7
Region:										
Northeast......................	1,330	874	339	83	357	9.6	7.6	21.6	11.7	23.9
Midwest........................	1,845	1,263	479	40	231	10.6	8.4	29.4	9.5	26.6
South..........................	3,997	2,563	1,273	69	988	13.4	11.2	23.7	8.3	24.6
West...........................	2,049	1,569	189	138	981	11.6	10.9	22.1	8.7	22.9
Type of family:										
Married couple..................	3,596	2,894	367	207	1,152	6.2	5.8	8.8	7.4	17.1
Male householder, no spouse present...........	880	562	233	29	238	15.8	13.5	25.9	10.7	20.2
Female householder, no spouse present...........	4,745	2,812	1,679	93	1,167	31.6	28.8	38.7	20.9	42.3

[1] Includes other races, not shown separately. [2] Hispanic persons may be any race.

Source: U.S. Census Bureau, *Income, Poverty, and Health Insurance Coverage in the United States: 2010*, Current Population Reports, P60-239, and Detailed Tables—Tables POV04 and POV44, September 2011. See also <http://www.census.gov/hhes/www/poverty/index.html>.

Table 729. Top Wealth Holders With Gross Assets of $2.0 Million or More— Debts, Mortgages, and Net Worth: 2007

[2,290 represents 2,290,000. Net worth is defined as assets minus liabilities. Figures are estimates based on a sample of federal estate tax returns (Form 706). Based on the estate multiplier technique; for more information on this methodology, see source]

Sex and net worth	Total assets		Debts and mortgages		Net worth	
	Number of top wealth holders (1,000)	Amount [1] (mil. dol.)	Number of top wealth holders (1,000)	Amount (mil. dol.)	Number of top wealth holders (1,000)	Amount (mil. dol.)
Both sexes, total........................	**2,290**	**13,221,799**	**1,792**	**1,124,478**	**2,290**	**12,097,321**
Size of net worth:						
Under $2.0 million [2]........................	449	860,731	403	390,799	449	469,932
$2.0 million under $3.5 million..............	1,008	2,810,250	744	196,440	1,008	2,613,810
$3.5 million under $5.0 million..............	364	1,607,665	275	96,621	364	1,511,044
$5.0 million under $10.0 million............	286	2,091,670	222	141,875	286	1,949,794
$10.0 million under $20.0 million...........	116	1,687,934	95	97,133	116	1,590,801
$20.0 million or more.......................	66	4,163,549	54	201,609	66	3,961,939
Males, total.............................	**1,320**	**8,062,977**	**1,038**	**872,850**	**1,320**	**7,190,127**
Size of net worth:						
Under $2.0 million [2]........................	324	613,092	284	325,369	324	287,723
$2.0 million under $3.5 million..............	526	1,502,230	385	134,813	526	1,367,417
$3.5 million under $5.0 million..............	190	846,527	146	62,021	190	784,506
$5.0 million under $10.0 million............	169	1,257,007	131	107,010	169	1,149,997
$10.0 million under $20.0 million...........	71	1,029,068	58	67,473	71	961,595
$20.0 million or more.......................	41	2,815,052	35	176,164	41	2,638,888
Females, total...........................	**970**	**5,158,822**	**754**	**251,629**	**970**	**4,907,194**
Size of net worth:						
Under $2.0 million [2]........................	125	247,639	119	65,430	125	182,209
$2.0 million under $3.5 million..............	482	1,308,020	359	61,627	482	1,246,393
$3.5 million under $5.0 million..............	175	761,139	129	34,600	175	726,538
$5.0 million under $10.0 million............	117	834,663	91	34,866	117	799,797
$10.0 million under $20.0 million...........	46	658,866	37	29,660	46	629,206
$20.0 million or more.......................	26	1,348,496	20	25,445	26	1,323,051

[1] Includes other types of assets, not shown separately. [2] Includes individuals with zero net worth.

Source: U.S. Internal Revenue Service, Statistics of Income Division, "SOI Data Tables," January 2012. <http://www.irs.gov/uac/SOI-Tax-Stats---Personal-Wealth-Statistics>.

Table 730. Top Wealth Holders With Gross Assets of $2.0 Million or More by Type of Property, Sex, and Size of Net Worth: 2007

[2,290 represents 2,290,000. Net worth is defined as assets minus liabilities. Figures are estimates based on a sample of federal estate tax returns (Form 706). Based on the estate multiplier technique; for more information on this methodology, see source]

Sex and net worth	Number of top wealth holders (1,000)	Assets (mil. dol.)				
		Total [1]	Personal residences	Other real estate	Closely held stock	Publicly traded stock
Both sexes, total	**2,290**	**13,221,799**	**1,247,026**	**1,659,926**	**1,577,715**	**2,553,437**
Size of net worth:						
Under $2.0 million [2]	449	860,731	181,133	208,138	56,760	63,121
$2.0 million under $3.5 million	1,008	2,810,250	413,215	435,218	140,964	467,856
$3.5 million under $5.0 million	364	1,607,665	193,726	236,360	115,070	311,686
$5.0 million under $10.0 million	286	2,091,670	195,830	310,222	242,341	384,644
$10.0 million under $20.0 million	116	1,687,934	134,600	195,331	203,913	361,193
$20.0 million or more	66	4,163,549	128,522	274,657	818,667	964,936
Males, total	**1,320**	**8,062,977**	**656,699**	**978,024**	**1,142,747**	**1,445,410**
Size of net worth:						
Under $2.0 million [2]	324	613,092	117,898	144,801	46,276	42,054
$2.0 million under $3.5 million	526	1,502,230	192,820	232,863	95,870	215,697
$3.5 million under $5.0 million	190	846,527	91,968	121,207	77,869	143,539
$5.0 million under $10.0 million	169	1,257,007	114,668	175,414	193,956	205,132
$10.0 million under $20.0 million	71	1,029,068	68,834	119,681	155,875	197,680
$20.0 million or more	41	2,815,052	70,510	184,059	572,901	641,308
Females, total	**970**	**5,158,822**	**590,327**	**681,902**	**434,968**	**1,108,027**
Size of net worth:						
Under $2.0 million [2]	125	247,639	63,235	63,337	10,484	21,068
$2.0 million under $3.5 million	482	1,308,020	220,395	202,355	45,094	252,159
$3.5 million under $5.0 million	175	761,139	101,757	115,153	37,201	168,148
$5.0 million under $10.0 million	117	834,663	81,162	134,808	48,385	179,512
$10.0 million under $20.0 million	46	658,866	65,765	75,650	48,038	163,513
$20.0 million or more	26	1,348,496	58,012	90,599	245,766	323,628

[1] Includes other types of assets, not shown separately. [2] Includes individuals with zero net worth.

Source: U.S. Internal Revenue Service, Statistics of Income Division, "SOI Data Tables," January 2012, <http://www.irs.gov/uac/SOI-Tax-Stats---Personal-Wealth-Statistics>.

Table 731. Top Wealth Holders With Net Worth of $2.0 Million or More— Number and Net Worth by State: 2007

[1,841 represents 1,841,000. Estimates based on a sample of federal estate tax returns (Form 706). Estimates of wealth by state can be subject to significant year-to-year fluctuations, especially for individuals at the extreme tail of the net worth distribution and for states with relatively small decedent populations. Based on the estate multiplier technique; for more information on this methodology, see source]

State	Number of top wealth holders (1,000)	Net worth (mil. dol.)	State	Number of top wealth holders (1,000)	Net worth (mil. dol.)
Total [1]	**1,841**	**11,627,389**	Montana	7	34,794
Alabama	17	94,464	Nebraska	6	36,643
Alaska	3	11,579	Nevada	16	226,904
Arizona	34	196,438	New Hampshire	13	68,492
Arkansas	8	91,058	New Jersey	71	332,456
California	329	1,941,513	New Mexico	10	40,482
Colorado	32	243,210	New York	159	1,201,654
Connecticut	36	286,124	North Carolina	45	240,370
Delaware	5	23,788	North Dakota	4	13,673
District of Columbia	3	30,140	Ohio	50	237,826
Florida	155	1,105,649	Oklahoma	17	76,728
Georgia	41	213,487	Oregon	24	90,338
Hawaii	7	75,601	Pennsylvania	57	323,679
Idaho	8	52,888	Rhode Island	6	29,640
Illinois	83	493,809	South Carolina	25	189,396
Indiana	25	115,056	South Dakota	7	78,126
Iowa	14	56,740	Tennessee	26	116,288
Kansas	11	58,061	Texas	100	662,518
Kentucky	15	76,777	Utah	9	49,879
Louisiana	16	129,584	Vermont	6	23,205
Maine	8	39,673	Virginia	49	269,648
Maryland	43	331,467	Washington	41	359,004
Massachusetts	51	394,752	West Virginia	5	27,085
Michigan	39	217,591	Wisconsin	32	165,770
Minnesota	24	158,224	Wyoming	6	45,258
Mississippi	9	37,101			
Missouri	26	145,218	Other areas [1]	8	67,541

[1] Includes U.S. territories and possessions.

Source: U.S. Internal Revenue Service, Statistics of Income Division, "SOI Data Tables," January 2012, <http://www.irs.gov/uac/SOI-Tax-Stats---Personal-Wealth-Statistics>.

Income, Expenditures, Poverty, and Wealth

Table 732. Nonfinancial Assets Held by Families by Type of Asset: 2010

[187.2 represents $187,200. Families include one-person units and, as used in this table, are more comparable to the U.S. Census Bureau's household concept. Based on Survey of Consumer Finance; see Appendix III and <http://www.federalreserve.gov/pubs/oss/oss2/papers/measurement.pdf>. For definition of median, see Guide to Tabular Presentation. For data on financial assets, see Table 1182]

Family characteristic	Any financial or non-financial asset	Any non-financial asset	Vehicles	Primary residence	Other resi-dential property	Equity in nonresi-dential property	Bus-iness equity	Other asset
PERCENT OF FAMILIES HOLDING ASSET								
All families, total...................	**97.4**	**91.3**	**86.7**	**67.3**	**14.3**	**7.7**	**13.3**	**7.0**
Age of family head:								
Under 35 years old.................	95.5	82.8	79.4	37.5	4.5	2.3	8.4	6.1
35 to 44 years old..................	97.4	92.7	88.9	63.8	9.7	3.9	11.2	4.2
45 to 54 years old..................	98.3	94.7	91.0	75.2	17.0	7.5	16.8	6.6
55 to 64 years old..................	98.3	94.4	90.3	78.1	22.1	12.6	19.6	9.6
65 to 74 years old..................	97.1	92.6	86.5	82.6	22.8	11.0	15.9	11.1
75 years old and over..............	98.7	93.0	83.4	81.9	14.6	13.4	6.0	6.0
Race or ethnicity of respondent:								
White non-Hispanic.................	99.1	94.9	90.9	75.3	16.5	9.4	15.6	8.8
Non-White or Hispanic..............	94.1	84.0	78.1	50.6	9.9	4.2	8.3	3.3
Tenure:								
Owner occupied....................	100.0	100.0	93.9	100.0	19.1	10.5	17.0	8.4
Renter occupied or other..........	92.2	73.6	71.9	(B)	4.6	1.9	5.5	4.2
MEDIAN VALUE [1] ($1,000)								
All families, total...................	**187.2**	**154.6**	**15.3**	**170.0**	**120.0**	**65.0**	**78.7**	**15.0**
Age of family head:								
Under 35 years old.................	35.7	34.2	12.4	140.0	72.0	24.0	30.0	5.0
35 to 44 years old..................	156.3	142.8	16.5	170.0	75.0	50.0	50.0	10.0
45 to 54 years old..................	248.4	191.4	18.4	200.0	103.5	50.0	80.0	15.0
55 to 64 years old..................	286.6	206.6	17.8	185.0	165.0	102.0	100.0	20.0
65 to 74 years old..................	281.7	199.8	16.0	165.0	125.0	60.0	100.0	28.1
75 years old and over..............	237.7	168.2	10.6	150.0	125.0	65.0	220.9	26.0
Race or ethnicity of respondent:								
White non-Hispanic.................	238.9	183.5	16.7	175.0	140.0	75.0	97.2	15.0
Non-White or Hispanic..............	76.8	86.0	12.3	139.0	70.0	50.0	43.0	10.0
Tenure:								
Owner occupied....................	296.2	217.0	18.8	170.0	120.0	70.0	95.0	20.0
Renter occupied or other..........	12.6	9.7	8.5	(B)	120.0	22.5	25.0	5.3

B Base too small to meet statistical standards for reliability of derived figure. [1] Median value of asset for families holding such assets.

Source: Source: Board of Governors of the Federal Reserve System, "2010 Survey of Consumer Finances," July 2010, <http://www.federalreserve.gov/econresdata/scf/scf_2010.htm>.

Table 733. Family Net Worth—Median and Mean Net Worth in Constant (2010) Dollars by Selected Family Characteristics: 2001 to 2010

[Net worth in thousands of constant (2010) dollars (106.1 represents $106,100). Constant dollar figures are based on Consumer Price Index for all urban consumers published by U.S. Bureau of Labor Statistics. Families include one-person units and as used in this table are comparable to the U.S. Census Bureau's household concept. Based on Survey of Consumer Finance; see Appendix III. For definition of mean and median, see Guide to Tabular Presentation]

Family characteristic	2001		2004		2007		2010	
	Median	Mean	Median	Mean	Median	Mean	Median	Mean
All families............................	**106.1**	**487.0**	**107.2**	**517.1**	**126.4**	**584.6**	**77.3**	**498.8**
Age of family head:								
Under 35 years old.................	14.3	111.2	16.3	84.6	12.4	111.1	9.3	65.3
35 to 44 years old..................	95.1	318.6	79.9	345.2	92.4	341.9	42.1	217.4
45 to 54 years old..................	164.9	595.9	167.1	625.8	193.7	694.6	117.9	573.0
55 to 64 years old..................	227.2	898.6	290.0	976.4	266.2	986.7	179.4	880.5
65 to 74 years old..................	217.8	831.4	218.8	795.1	250.8	1,064.1	206.7	848.4
75 years old and over..............	190.3	574.8	187.7	607.7	223.7	668.8	216.8	677.9
Race or ethnicity of respondent:								
White non-Hispanic.................	150.4	599.0	162.2	648.3	179.4	727.4	130.5	654.5
Non-White or Hispanic..............	22.0	144.1	28.5	176.2	29.7	240.3	20.4	175.9
Tenure:								
Owner occupied....................	211.5	687.2	212.6	720.9	246.0	817.6	174.5	713.4
Renter occupied or other.............	5.9	67.7	4.6	62.3	5.4	74.7	5.1	57.2

Source: Board of Governors of the Federal Reserve System, "2010 Survey of Consumer Finances," Tables 1 and 4, July 2012, <http://www.federalreserve.gov/econresdata/scf/scf_2010.htm>.

Table 734. Household and Nonprofit Organization Sector Balance Sheet: 1990 to 2011

[In billions of dollars (24,425 represents $24,425,000,000,000). As of December 31. For details of financial assets and liabilities, see Table 1180]

Item	1990	1995	2000	2005	2008	2009	2010	2011
Assets	**24,425**	**33,252**	**50,634**	**73,367**	**67,649**	**69,467**	**72,853**	**73,518**
Nonfinancial assets [1]	9,730	11,472	16,867	28,478	24,787	23,740	23,448	23,289
Real estate	7,613	8,844	13,528	24,156	19,937	18,874	18,557	18,183
Households [2,3]	6,808	8,055	12,198	22,049	17,545	17,138	16,561	16,050
Consumer durable goods [4]	2,039	2,531	3,196	4,098	4,567	4,572	4,582	4,769
Financial assets [1]	14,695	21,780	33,767	44,889	42,861	45,727	49,404	50,229
Deposits [1]	3,366	3,399	4,440	6,232	8,107	7,969	7,966	8,651
Time and savings deposits	2,512	2,317	3,049	4,937	6,119	6,232	6,434	6,833
Money market fund shares	389	472	937	949	1,582	1,313	1,130	1,107
Credit market instruments [1]	1,741	2,380	2,564	4,298	4,974	5,244	5,423	5,148
Treasury securities	504	828	579	471	257	816	1,207	1,115
Municipal securities	648	533	531	1,639	1,767	1,897	1,955	1,892
Corporate and foreign bonds	238	617	657	1,429	2,066	2,227	1,956	1,887
Corporate equities [2]	1,961	4,434	8,140	8,084	5,742	7,398	8,579	8,357
Mutual fund shares [5]	512	1,253	2,708	3,676	3,347	4,165	4,613	4,652
Security credit	62	128	412	575	743	669	694	752
Life insurance reserves	392	566	819	1,083	1,050	1,109	1,137	1,201
Pension fund reserves	3,310	5,725	9,171	11,460	10,408	11,915	13,091	13,147
Equity in noncorporate business [6]	3,097	3,567	5,133	8,873	7,724	6,472	7,070	7,444
Liabilities [1]	**3,694**	**5,043**	**7,353**	**12,142**	**14,094**	**13,872**	**13,693**	**13,481**
Credit market instruments [1]	3,572	4,846	6,964	11,701	13,666	13,394	13,116	12,930
Home mortgages [7]	2,489	3,319	4,814	8,891	10,497	10,353	10,051	9,819
Consumer credit	824	1,168	1,741	2,321	2,549	2,439	2,412	2,508
Net worth	**20,731**	**28,209**	**43,281**	**61,224**	**53,554**	**55,595**	**59,160**	**60,037**
Replacement cost value of structures:								
Residential [1]	4,618	6,091	8,469	13,475	14,410	14,130	14,194	14,358
Households	4,512	5,975	8,326	13,276	14,195	13,918	13,984	14,146
Nonresidential (nonprofits)	479	600	819	1,196	1,490	1,437	1,450	1,507
Owners' equity in household real estate	4,319	4,736	7,384	13,158	7,048	6,785	6,510	6,231
Owners' equity as percentage of household real estate	63.4	58.8	60.5	59.7	40.2	39.6	39.3	38.8

[1] Includes types of assets and/or liabilities not shown separately. [2] At market value. [3] Includes all types of owner-occupied housing including farm houses and mobile homes, as well as second homes that are not rented, vacant homes for sale, and vacant land. [4] At replacement (current) cost. [5] Value based on the market values of equities held and the book value of other assets held by mutual funds. [6] Net worth of nonfinancial noncorporate business and owners' equity in unincorporated security brokers and dealers. [7] Includes loans made under home equity lines of credit and home equity loans secured by junior liens.

Source: Board of Governors of the Federal Reserve System, "Federal Reserve Statistical Release, Z.1, Flow of Funds Accounts of the United States," Table B.100, June 2012. See also <http://www.federalreserve.gov/apps/fof/FOFTables.aspx>.

Table 735. Net Stock of Fixed Assets and Consumer Durable Goods in Current and Chained (2005) Dollars: 1990 to 2010

[In billions of dollars (18,307 represents $18,307,000,000,000). Estimates as of December 31. For explanation of chained dollars, see text, this section]

Item	1990	1995	2000	2005	2007	2008	2009	2010
CURRENT DOLLARS								
Net stock, total	18,307	22,846	30,129	42,610	48,032	49,625	48,655	49,324
Fixed assets	16,268	20,315	26,932	38,512	43,564	45,059	44,083	44,743
Private	12,671	15,811	21,230	30,593	34,081	34,869	33,887	34,201
Nonresidential	6,564	7,990	10,563	14,063	16,125	17,185	16,541	16,804
Equipment and software	2,507	3,100	4,134	4,937	5,513	5,766	5,686	5,740
Structures	4,057	4,890	6,429	9,127	10,611	11,419	10,855	11,064
Residential	6,107	7,821	10,668	16,530	17,956	17,685	17,346	17,397
Government	3,598	4,504	5,702	7,919	9,483	10,189	10,196	10,542
Nonresidential	3,449	4,316	5,473	7,587	9,140	9,856	9,871	10,213
Equipment and software	551	675	704	802	895	956	992	1,046
Structures	2,898	3,641	4,769	6,785	8,245	8,900	8,879	9,167
Residential	149	188	229	332	343	333	325	329
Federal	1,077	1,292	1,432	1,744	1,948	2,036	2,024	2,092
Defense	734	868	904	1,081	1,204	1,255	1,260	1,307
State and local	2,521	3,213	4,271	6,175	7,535	8,153	8,172	8,450
Consumer durable goods	2,039	2,531	3,196	4,098	4,468	4,567	4,572	4,582
Motor vehicles and parts	650	811	1,042	1,302	1,318	1,261	1,274	1,263
Furnishings and durable household equipment	649	787	977	1,242	1,365	1,415	1,397	1,373
Other	322	392	449	568	700	755	781	821
CHAINED (2005) DOLLARS								
Net stock, total	(NA)	30,357	35,726	41,144	43,403	44,186	44,532	44,943
Fixed assets	(NA)	28,414	32,883	37,021	38,824	39,476	39,773	40,088
Private	(NA)	22,082	25,959	29,364	30,876	31,374	31,514	31,679
Nonresidential	(NA)	10,216	12,327	13,584	14,297	14,615	14,673	14,769
Equipment and software	(NA)	3,044	4,205	4,906	5,309	5,424	5,372	5,429
Structures	(NA)	7,361	8,149	8,678	9,000	9,203	9,304	9,345
Residential	(NA)	11,898	13,626	15,780	16,578	16,751	16,834	16,902
Government	(NA)	6,334	6,926	7,657	7,950	8,102	8,248	8,385
Nonresidential	(NA)	6,058	6,628	7,339	7,628	7,778	7,920	8,052
Equipment and software	(NA)	714	734	796	853	891	926	962
Structures	(NA)	5,328	5,891	6,543	6,777	6,892	7,003	7,101
Residential	(NA)	281	298	318	322	324	327	332
Consumer durable goods	(NA)	2,174	2,942	4,123	4,604	4,743	4,794	4,901

NA Not available.

Source: U.S. Bureau of Economic Analysis, *Survey of Current Business*, August 2011. See also <http://www.bea.gov/national/index.htm>.

Prices

The Prices section contains producer and consumer prices indexes and actual prices for selected commodities. The primary sources of the data are monthly publications of the U.S. Department of Labor, Bureau of Labor Statistics (BLS), which include *Monthly Labor Review, Consumer Price Index, Detailed Report, Producer Price Indexes*, and *U.S. Import and Export Price Indexes*. The Bureau of Economic Analysis is the source for gross domestic product measures. Cost of living data for many urban and metropolitan areas are provided by The Council for Community and Economic Research, a private organization in Arlington, VA. Table 741 on housing price indexes appears in this edition from the Federal Housing Finance Agency, Housing Price Index. Other commodity, housing, and energy prices may be found in the Energy and Utilities; Forestry, Fishing and Mining; and Construction and Housing sections.

Most price data is measured by an index. An index is a tool that simplifies the measurement of movements in a numerical series. An index allows you to properly compare two or more values in different time periods or places by comparing both to a base year. An index of 110, for example, means there has been a 10-percent increase in price since the reference period; similarly, an index of 90 means a 10-percent decrease. Movements of the index from one date to another can be expressed as changes in index points (simply, the difference between index levels), but it is more useful to express the movements as percent changes. This is because index points are affected by the level of the index in relation to its reference period, while percent changes are not.

Consumer price indexes (CPI)—The CPI is a measure of the average change in prices over time in a "market basket" of goods and services purchased either by urban wage earners and clerical workers or by all urban consumers. The all urban consumer group represents 87 percent of the total U.S. population and is based on the expenditures of residents of urban or metropolitan areas, including professionals, the self-employed, the poor, the unemployed, and retired people, as well as urban wage earners and clerical workers. Not included in the CPI are the spending patterns of people living in rural nonmetropolitan areas, farm families, people in the Armed Forces, and those in institutions, such as prisons and mental hospitals. Consumer inflation for all urban consumers is measured by two indexes, the Consumer Price Index for All Urban Consumers (CPI-U) and the Chained Consumer Price Index for All Urban Consumers (C-CPI-U). The broadest and most comprehensive CPI is called the All Items Consumer Price Index for All Urban Consumers (CPI-U) for the U.S. City Average. All CPIs in this section have a base of 1982–84 = 100.

The CPI is a product of a series of interrelated samples. Data from the 1990 Census of Population determines the urban areas from which data on prices are collected and the housing units within each area that are eligible for use in the shelter component of the CPI. The Census of Population also provides data on the number of consumers represented by each area selected as a CPI price collection area. A sample (of about 14,500 families each year) serves as the basis for a Point-of-Purchase Survey that identified the

places where households purchased various types of goods and services. The CPI market basket is developed from detailed expenditure information provided by families and individuals on what they actually bought. In calculating the index, each item is assigned a weight to account for its relative importance in consumers' budgets. Price changes for the various items in each location are then averaged and local data are combined to obtain a U.S. city average. For the current CPI, this information was collected from the Consumer Expenditure Surveys for 2007 and 2008. In each of those years, about 7,000 families from around the country provided information each quarter on their spending habits in the interview survey. To collect information on frequently purchased items, such as food and personal care products, another 7,000 families in each of these years kept diaries listing everything they bought during a 2-week period. Over the 2 year period, expenditure information came from approximately 28,000 weekly diaries and 60,000 quarterly interviews used to determine the importance, or weight, of the more than 200 item categories in the CPI index structure.

The CPI represents all goods and services purchased for consumption by the reference population. BLS has classified all expenditure items into more than 200 categories, arranged into eight major groups which are food and beverages, housing, apparel, transportation, medical care, recreation, education and communication, and other goods. The CPI does not include investment items, such as stocks, bonds, real estate, and life insurance. (These items relate to savings and not to day-to-day consumption expenses.)

Producer price index (PPI)— Dating from 1890, the PPI is the oldest continuous statistical series published by BLS. The PPI is a family of indexes that measures the average change over time in the selling prices received by domestic producers of goods and services. Imports are excluded. The target set of goods and services included in the PPI is the entire marketed output of U.S. producers. The set includes both goods and services purchased by other producers as inputs to their operations or as capital investment, as well as goods and services purchased by consumers either directly from the service producer or indirectly from a retailer. Over 10,000 PPIs for individual products and groups of products are released each month.

Prices used in constructing the index are collected from sellers and generally apply to the first significant large-volume commercial transaction for each commodity. The weights used in the index represent the total net selling value of commodities produced or processed in this country. Most producer price indexes have a reference base year of 1982 = 100. The reference year of the PPI shipment weights has been taken primarily from the 2002 Census of Manufactures. For further detail regarding the PPI, see the *BLS Handbook of Methods*, Chapter 14, <http://www.bls.gov/opub/hom/homch14.htm>.

BEA price indexes—BEA chain-weighted price indexes are weighted averages of the detailed price indexes used in the deflation of the goods and services that make up the gross domestic product (GDP) and its major components. Growth rates are constructed for years and quarters using quantity weights for the current and preceding year or quarter; these growth rates are used to move the index for the preceding period forward a year or quarter at a time. All chain-weighted price indexes are expressed in terms of the reference year value 2005 = 100.

Personal consumption expenditures (PCE) price and quantity indexes are based on market transactions for which there are corresponding price measures. The price index provides a measure of the prices paid by persons for domestic purchases of goods and services. PCEs are defined as market value of spending by individuals and not-for-profit institutions on all goods and services. Personal consumption expenditures also include the value of certain imputed goods and services—such as the rental value of owner-occupied homes and compensation paid in kind—such as employer-paid health and life insurance premiums. More information on this index may be found at <http://www.bea.gov/national/index.htm>.

Measures of inflation—Inflation is a period of rising price levels for goods and factors of production. Inflation results in a decline in the purchasing power of the dollar. It is suggested that changes in price levels be compared from the same month of the prior year and not as a change from the prior month. The BLS offers several indexes that measure different aspects of inflation, three of which are included in this section. The CPI measures inflation as experienced by consumers in their day-to-day living expenses. The PPI measures prices at the producer level only. The International Price Program measures change in the prices of imports and exports of nonmilitary goods between the United States and other countries.

Whereas the CPI and PPI measure a benchmark approach to price levels, the BEA's Personal Consumption Expenditures uses a chain-weight approach which links weighted averages from adjoining years.

Other measures of inflation include the futures price and spot market price indexes from the Commodity Research Bureau and the employment cost, hourly compensation, and unit labor cost indexes from the BLS. Found in Section 12, Labor Force, Employment, and Earnings, these BLS indexes are used as a measure of the change in cost of the labor factor of production and changes in long-term interest rates that are often used to measure changes in the cost of the capital factor of production.

International price indexes—The BLS International Price Program produces export and import price indexes for nonmilitary goods traded between the United States and the rest of the world.

The export price index provides a measure of price change for all products sold by U.S. residents to foreign buyers. The import price index provides a measure of price change for goods purchased from other countries by U.S. residents. The reference period for the indexes is 2000 = 100, unless otherwise indicated. The product universe for both the import and export indexes includes raw materials, agricultural products, semifinished manufactures, and finished manufactures, including both capital and consumer goods. Price data for these items are collected primarily by mail questionnaire. In nearly all cases, the data are collected directly from the exporter or importer.

To the extent possible, the data gathered refer to prices at the U.S. border for exports and at either the foreign border or the U.S. border for imports. For nearly all products, the prices refer to transactions completed during the first week of the month. Survey respondents are asked to indicate all discounts, allowances, and rebates applicable to the reported prices, so that the price used in the calculation of the indexes is the actual price for which the product was bought or sold.

Table 736. Purchasing Power of the Dollar: 1950 to 2011

[Indexes: PPI, 1982 = $1.00; CPI, 1982-84 = $1.00. Producer prices prior to 1961, and consumer prices prior to 1964, exclude Alaska and Hawaii. Producer prices based on finished goods index. Obtained by dividing the average price index for the 1982 = 100, PPI; 1982-84 = 100, CPI base periods (100.0) by the price index for a given period and expressing the result in dollars and cents. Annual figures are based on average of monthly data]

Year	Annual average as measured by—		Year	Annual average as measured by—	
	Producer prices	Consumer prices		Producer prices	Consumer prices
1950.................	3.546	4.151	1982.................	1.000	1.035
1953.................	3.300	3.735	1983.................	0.984	1.003
1954.................	3.289	3.717	1984.................	0.964	0.961
1955.................	3.279	3.732	1985.................	0.955	0.928
1956.................	3.195	3.678	1986.................	0.969	0.913
1957.................	3.077	3.549	1987.................	0.949	0.880
1958.................	3.012	3.457	1988.................	0.926	0.846
1959.................	3.021	3.427	1989.................	0.880	0.807
1960.................	2.994	3.373	1990.................	0.839	0.766
1961.................	2.994	3.340	1991.................	0.822	0.734
1962.................	2.985	3.304	1992.................	0.812	0.713
1963.................	2.994	3.265	1993.................	0.802	0.692
1964.................	2.985	3.220	1994.................	0.797	0.675
1965.................	2.933	3.166	1995.................	0.782	0.656
1966.................	2.841	3.080	1996.................	0.762	0.638
1967.................	2.809	2.993	1997.................	0.759	0.623
1968.................	2.732	2.873	1998.................	0.765	0.613
1969.................	2.632	2.726	1999.................	0.752	0.600
1970.................	2.545	2.574	2000.................	0.725	0.581
1971.................	2.469	2.466	2001.................	0.711	0.565
1972.................	2.392	2.391	2002.................	0.720	0.556
1973.................	2.193	2.251	2003.................	0.698	0.543
1974.................	1.901	2.029	2004.................	0.673	0.529
1975.................	1.718	1.859	2005.................	0.642	0.512
1976.................	1.645	1.757	2006.................	0.623	0.496
1977.................	1.546	1.649	2007.................	0.600	0.482
1978.................	1.433	1.532	2008.................	0.565	0.464
1979.................	1.289	1.380	2009.................	0.579	0.466
1980.................	1.136	1.215	2010.................	0.556	0.459
1981.................	1.041	1.098	2011.................	0.525	0.445

Source: Bureau of Labor Statistics, CPI Detailed Report, monthly, and at <http://www.bls.gov/cpi/cpi_dr.htm>; and Producer Price Indexes, monthly and at <http://www.bls.gov/ppi/>.

Table 737. Consumer Price Indexes (CPI-U) by Major Groups: 1990 to 2011

[1982-84 = 100, except as indicated. Represents annual averages of monthly figures. Reflects buying patterns of all urban consumers. Minus sign (–) indicates decrease. See text, this section]

Year	All items	Com-mod-ities	Ser-vices	Food	Energy	All items less food and energy	Food and bever-ages	Hous-ing	Apparel	Trans-porta-tion	Medical care	Educa-tion and com-munica-tion [1]
1990.................	130.7	122.8	139.2	132.4	102.1	135.5	132.1	128.5	124.1	120.5	162.8	(NA)
1995.................	152.4	136.4	168.7	148.4	105.2	161.2	148.9	148.5	132.0	139.1	220.5	92.2
1999.................	166.6	144.4	188.8	164.1	106.6	177.0	164.6	163.9	131.3	144.4	250.6	101.2
2000.................	172.2	149.2	195.3	167.8	124.6	181.3	168.4	169.6	129.6	153.3	260.8	102.5
2001.................	177.1	150.7	203.4	173.1	129.3	186.1	173.6	176.4	127.3	154.3	272.8	105.2
2002.................	179.9	149.7	209.8	176.2	121.7	190.5	176.8	180.3	124.0	152.9	285.6	107.9
2003.................	184.0	151.2	216.5	180.0	136.5	193.2	180.5	184.8	120.9	157.6	297.1	109.8
2004.................	188.9	154.7	222.8	186.2	151.4	196.6	186.6	189.5	120.4	163.1	310.1	111.6
2005.................	195.3	160.2	230.1	190.7	177.1	200.9	191.2	195.7	119.5	173.9	323.2	113.7
2006.................	201.6	164.0	238.9	195.2	196.9	205.9	195.7	203.2	119.5	180.9	336.2	116.8
2007.................	207.3	167.5	246.8	202.9	207.7	210.7	203.3	209.6	119.0	184.7	351.1	119.6
2008.................	215.3	174.8	255.5	214.1	236.7	215.6	214.2	216.3	118.9	195.5	364.1	123.6
2009.................	214.5	169.7	259.2	218.0	193.1	219.2	218.2	217.1	120.1	179.3	375.6	127.4
2010.................	218.1	174.6	261.3	219.6	211.4	221.3	220.0	216.3	119.5	193.4	388.4	129.9
2011.................	224.9	183.9	265.8	227.8	243.9	225.0	227.9	219.1	122.1	212.4	400.4	131.5
PERCENT CHANGE [2]												
1990.................	5.4	5.2	5.5	5.8	8.3	5.0	5.8	4.5	4.6	5.6	9.0	(NA)
1995.................	2.8	1.9	3.4	2.8	0.6	3.0	2.8	2.6	-1.0	3.6	4.5	3.8
1999.................	2.2	1.8	2.5	2.1	3.6	2.1	2.2	2.2	-1.3	2.0	3.5	0.9
2000.................	3.4	3.3	3.4	2.3	16.9	2.4	2.3	3.5	-1.3	6.2	4.1	1.3
2001.................	2.8	1.0	4.1	3.2	3.8	2.6	3.1	4.0	-1.8	0.7	4.6	2.6
2002.................	1.6	-0.7	3.1	1.8	-5.9	2.4	1.8	2.2	-2.6	-0.9	4.7	2.6
2003.................	2.3	1.0	3.2	2.2	12.2	1.4	2.1	2.5	-2.5	3.1	4.0	1.8
2004.................	2.7	2.3	2.9	3.4	10.9	1.8	3.4	2.5	-0.4	3.5	4.4	1.6
2005.................	3.4	3.6	3.3	2.4	17.0	2.2	2.5	3.3	-0.7	6.6	4.2	1.9
2006.................	3.2	2.4	3.8	2.4	11.2	2.5	2.4	3.8	–	4.0	4.0	2.7
2007.................	2.8	2.1	3.3	4.0	5.5	2.3	3.9	3.1	-0.4	2.1	4.4	2.4
2008.................	3.8	4.3	3.5	5.5	13.9	2.3	5.4	3.2	-0.1	5.9	3.7	3.4
2009.................	-0.4	-2.9	1.4	1.8	-18.4	1.7	1.9	0.4	1.0	-8.3	3.2	3.0
2010.................	1.6	2.9	0.8	0.8	9.5	1.0	0.8	-0.4	-0.5	7.9	3.4	2.0
2011.................	3.2	5.3	1.7	3.7	15.4	1.7	3.6	1.3	2.2	9.8	3.0	1.2

– Represents zero. NA Not available. [1] Dec. 1997 = 100. [2] Change from immediate prior year. 1990 change from 1989.

Source: U.S. Bureau of Labor Statistics, CPI Detailed Report, monthly, <http://www.bls.gov/cpi/cpi_dr.htm>. See also Monthly Labor Review, <http://www.bls.gov/opub/mlr/welcome.htm>.

Table 738. Annual Percent Changes From Prior Year in Consumer Price Indexes (CPI-U)—Selected Areas: 2011

[Percent changes computed from annual averages of monthly figures published by source. Local area CPI indexes are by-products of the national CPI program. Each local index has a smaller sample size than the national index and is therefore subject to substantially more sampling and other measurement error. As a result, local area indexes show greater volatility than the national index, although their long-term trends are similar. Area definitions are those established by the Office of Management and Budget in 1983. For further detail, see the U.S. Bureau of Labor Statistics Handbook of Methods, Bulletin 2285, Chapter 19, the Consumer Price Index, and Report 751, the CPI: 1987 Revision. Minus sign (–) indicates decrease. See also text, this section and Appendix III]

Area	All items	Food and beverage	Food	Housing	Apparel	Transportation	Medical care	Fuel and other utilities
U.S. city average	**3.2**	**3.6**	**3.7**	**1.3**	**2.2**	**9.8**	**3.0**	**2.9**
Anchorage, AK MSA	3.2	3.6	4.1	2.9	2.2	4.7	5.3	3.4
Atlanta, GA MSA	2.8	3.3	3.4	0.2	1.4	12.2	1.8	7.2
Boston, MA MSA	2.7	3.0	3.3	1.6	1.1	10.6	2.4	8.6
Chicago-Gary, IL-IN CMSA	2.7	3.2	3.3	1.3	0.6	9.9	2.4	1.4
Cincinnati-Hamilton, OH-KY-IN CMSA	3.1	2.7	2.9	1.2	2.6	10.6	2.4	-0.7
Cleveland-Akron-Lorain, OH CMSA	3.2	4.3	4.7	0.8	2.0	9.9	4.1	-0.3
Dallas-Fort Worth, TX CMSA	3.1	3.3	3.5	1.1	0.4	11.0	0.9	1.0
Denver-Boulder-Greely, CO CMSA	3.7	4.0	4.2	2.2	2.7	10.1	1.3	7.7
Detroit-Ann Arbor-Flint, MI CMSA	3.3	3.5	3.7	0.4	7.9	9.7	2.1	0.1
Honolulu, HI MSA	3.7	3.5	3.8	3.4	1.7	6.9	1.3	19.6
Houston-Galveston-Brazoria, TX CMSA	3.3	3.6	3.7	0.2	3.2	10.9	4.1	-0.2
Kansas City, MO-KS CMSA	4.0	5.4	5.9	1.6	1.3	10.5	3.5	1.8
Los Angeles-Anaheim-Riverside, CA CMSA	2.7	3.7	4.0	0.8	2.4	8.9	3.9	3.0
Miami-Fort Lauderdale, FL CMSA	3.5	4.4	4.6	0.7	2.8	11.9	4.1	1.3
Milwaukee, WI PMSA	3.5	3.5	3.8	1.5	2.4	9.7	4.9	3.8
Minneapolis-St. Paul, MN-WI MSA	3.6	6.3	4.9	0.9	5.4	10.3	2.0	3.8
NY-Northern New Jersey-Long Island, NY-NJ-CT CMSA	2.8	3.2	3.3	1.3	3.6	9.9	3.1	1.3
Philadelphia-Wilmington-Trenton, PA-NJ-DE-MD CMSA	2.7	3.7	3.7	1.4	1.7	9.3	2.0	3.9
Pittsburgh, PA MSA	4.5	5.2	5.6	2.5	7.4	11.1	5.5	4.6
Portland, OR MSA	2.9	3.2	3.2	1.7	5.6	6.9	3.7	5.8
San Diego, CA MSA	3.0	4.2	4.7	0.8	4.3	11.1	2.0	3.5
San Francisco-Oakland-San Jose, CA CMSA	2.6	2.7	2.9	1.5	4.5	7.1	2.5	2.7
Seattle-Tacoma, WA CMSA	2.7	3.6	4.3	1.3	-3.0	8.2	(NA)	4.3
St. Louis-East St. Louis, MO-IL CMSA	3.2	3.0	3.1	2.1	4.4	8.7	1.9	8.5
Tampa-St. Petersburg-Clearwater, FL MSA	2.8	3.9	4.1	-0.2	-1.3	11.8	3.1	-0.7
Washington-Baltimore, DC-MD-VA-WV CMSA	3.3	4.0	4.1	1.6	7.1	10.1	3.7	-1.8

NA Not available.

Source: U.S. Bureau of Labor Statistics, *CPI Detailed Report*, monthly, <http://www.bls.gov/cpi/>.

Table 739. Consumer Price Indexes for All Urban Consumers (CPI-U) for Selected Items and Groups: 2000 to 2011

[1982-84 = 100, except as noted. Annual averages of monthly figures. Minus sign (–) indicates decrease. See headnote, Table 737]

Item	2000	2005	2007	2008	2009	2010	2011	Annual percent change, 2010-11
All items	**172.2**	**195.3**	**207.3**	**215.3**	**214.5**	**218.1**	**225.0**	**3.2**
Food and beverages	**168.4**	**191.2**	**203.3**	**214.2**	**218.2**	**220.0**	**227.9**	**3.6**
Food	167.8	190.7	202.9	214.1	218.0	219.6	227.8	3.7
Food at home	167.9	189.8	201.2	214.1	215.1	215.8	226.2	4.8
Cereals and bakery products	188.3	209.0	222.1	244.9	252.6	250.4	260.3	3.9
Cereals and cereal products	175.9	186.7	194.7	214.4	221.8	217.6	227.2	4.4
Rice, pasta, and cornmeal	150.7	165.3	181.4	218.8	229.9	224.4	234.1	4.3
Rice [1, 2]	99.3	108.8	120.1	152.8	161.0	156.9	163.9	4.5
Bakery products [2]	194.1	220.5	236.6	261.0	268.9	268.0	278.0	3.7
Bread [2]	107.4	126.2	140.1	160.6	162.6	159.8	168.7	5.6
Cakes, cupcakes, and cookies	187.9	209.8	221.7	239.9	250.7	251.7	256.0	1.7
Other bakery products	191.5	211.4	220.5	236.5	245.9	247.1	253.1	2.4
Meats, poultry, fish and eggs	154.5	184.7	195.6	204.7	203.8	207.7	223.2	7.4
Meats, poultry, and fish	155.5	186.7	195.4	203.6	204.6	208.6	223.9	7.4
Meats	150.7	187.5	195.0	201.8	200.5	206.2	224.4	8.8
Beef and veal	148.1	200.4	211.1	220.6	218.3	224.5	247.4	10.2
Uncooked ground beef	125.2	175.1	184.3	196.4	198.5	203.6	226.7	11.3
Uncooked beef steaks [2]	109.1	145.1	151.8	155.3	150.1	153.3	166.5	8.6
Pork	156.5	177.7	180.9	185.0	181.4	190.0	206.1	8.5
Other meats	152.0	177.5	184.8	190.6	194.9	194.8	207.3	6.4
Poultry	159.8	185.3	191.4	200.9	204.2	204.0	210.0	2.9
Chicken [2]	102.5	120.6	124.4	130.7	132.6	131.8	134.3	1.8
Fish and seafood	190.4	200.1	219.1	232.1	240.6	243.2	260.5	7.1
Dairy products [2]	160.7	182.4	194.8	210.4	197.0	199.2	212.7	6.8
Milk [2]	107.8	127.0	140.1	148.5	129.0	133.6	145.8	9.2
Cheese and related products	162.8	183.3	191.5	214.5	203.5	204.8	217.5	6.2
Ice cream and related products	164.4	177.6	183.4	192.8	196.6	195.0	209.1	7.2
Fruits and vegetables	204.6	241.4	262.6	278.9	272.9	273.5	284.7	4.1
Fresh fruits and vegetables	238.8	285.3	312.1	328.3	312.7	314.8	328.9	4.5
Fresh fruits	258.3	297.4	329.5	345.4	324.4	322.3	333.1	3.3
Fresh vegetables	219.4	271.7	293.5	309.8	299.3	305.5	322.5	5.6
Processed fruits and vegetables [2]	105.6	119.3	127.2	139.3	148.6	146.6	150.9	2.9
Nonalcoholic beverages and beverage materials	137.8	144.4	153.4	160.0	163.0	161.6	166.8	3.2
Juices and nonalcoholic drinks [2]	105.6	110.6	117.9	123.1	126.3	124.5	126.7	1.8
Carbonated drinks	123.4	131.9	140.1	147.0	154.1	154.7	158.8	2.6
Nonfrozen noncarbonated juices and drinks [2]	104.2	106.5	112.9	117.5	118.0	114.8	116.0	7.6
Beverage materials including coffee and tea [2]	97.9	102.4	108.2	112.8	113.3	114.0	122.5	7.5
Other food at home	155.6	167.0	173.3	184.2	191.2	191.1	197.4	3.3
Sugar and sweets	154.0	165.2	176.8	186.6	196.9	201.2	207.8	3.3
Candy and chewing gum [2]	103.8	109.5	116.1	123.2	130.2	132.5	136.0	2.6
Fats and oils	147.4	167.7	172.9	196.8	201.2	200.6	219.2	9.3
Frozen and freeze dried prepared food	148.5	153.2	156.7	163.5	168.1	165.3	167.8	1.5
Snacks	166.3	178.5	184.9	199.8	213.2	216.6	224.3	3.5
Spices, seasonings, condiments, sauces	175.8	188.0	195.5	204.6	214.7	214.4	219.9	2.6
Other miscellaneous food [2]	107.5	111.3	115.1	119.9	122.4	121.7	124.0	1.9
Food away from home	169.0	193.4	206.7	215.8	223.3	226.1	231.4	2.3
Full service meals and snacks [2]	106.8	121.9	130.2	135.4	139.2	141.1	144.4	2.3
Limited service meals and snacks [2]	106.3	122.4	130.6	136.9	142.6	143.9	147.1	2.2
At employee sites and schools [2]	104.4	118.6	126.8	131.8	137.3	141.0	145.7	3.4
From vending machines and mobile vendors [2]	102.4	112.6	118.3	124.1	129.7	133.1	135.8	2.0
Other food away from home [2]	109.0	131.3	144.1	150.6	155.9	159.3	162.8	2.2
Alcoholic beverages	174.7	195.9	207.0	214.5	220.8	223.3	226.7	1.5
Alcoholic beverages at home	158.1	172.3	179.1	184.9	190.3	191.0	191.8	0.4
Beer, ale, and other malt beverages at home	156.8	176.4	184.1	190.3	197.4	201.0	203.9	1.4
Distilled spirits at home	162.3	177.4	181.0	185.0	189.2	188.8	188.8	0.1
Wine at home	151.6	156.2	162.9	168.7	172.1	169.7	168.5	-0.8
Alcoholic beverages away from home	207.1	244.5	266.0	277.4	285.6	291.9	300.9	3.1
Housing	**169.6**	**195.7**	**209.6**	**216.3**	**217.1**	**216.3**	**219.1**	**1.3**
Shelter	193.4	224.4	240.6	246.7	249.4	248.4	251.6	1.3
Rent of primary residence	183.9	217.3	234.7	243.3	248.8	249.4	253.6	1.7
Lodging away from home [2]	117.5	130.3	142.8	143.7	134.2	133.7	137.4	2.8
Other lodging away from home including hotels and motels	252.4	274.2	299.9	301.0	279.2	280.4	287.4	2.5
Owners' equivalent rent of primary residence [3]	198.7	230.2	246.2	252.4	256.6	256.6	259.6	1.2
Tenants' and household insurance [2]	103.7	117.6	117.0	118.8	121.5	125.7	127.4	1.4
Fuels and utilities	137.9	179.0	200.6	220.0	210.7	214.2	220.4	2.9
Household energy	122.8	161.6	181.7	200.8	188.1	189.3	193.6	2.3
Fuel oil and other fuels	129.7	208.6	251.5	334.4	239.8	275.1	337.1	22.5
Fuel oil	130.3	216.4	262.6	365.0	240.2	282.9	367.8	30.0
Propane, kerosene and firewood [4]	155.5	240.6	286.0	344.2	293.1	320.6	348.1	8.6
Energy services	**128.0**	**166.5**	**186.3**	**202.2**	**193.6**	**192.9**	**194.4**	**0.8**
Electricity	128.5	150.8	175.8	187.1	192.7	193.1	196.7	1.9
Utility (piped) gas service	132.0	215.4	217.7	247.8	193.7	189.7	184.3	-2.8
Water and sewer and trash collection services [2]	106.5	130.3	143.7	152.1	161.1	170.9	179.6	5.1
Water and sewerage maintenance	227.5	283.4	312.6	331.3	354.4	380.7	402.9	5.8
Garbage and trash collection [5]	269.8	314.0	345.6	364.7	376.4	384.4	395.1	2.8
Household furnishings and operations	**128.2**	**126.1**	**126.9**	**127.8**	**128.7**	**125.5**	**124.9**	**-0.4**
Furniture and bedding	134.4	125.9	125.8	124.5	124.8	119.7	118.6	-1.0
Bedroom furniture	138.4	142.7	144.7	143.7	143.0	136.4	136.1	-0.2
Living room, kitchen, and dining room furniture [2]	102.4	92.7	91.6	90.5	90.7	88.9	88.9	-0.1
Appliances [2]	96.3	86.9	89.8	89.9	91.1	86.9	85.9	-1.2
Other household equipment and furnishings [2]	98.0	85.5	76.9	75.6	74.0	70.8	68.5	-3.3
Clocks, lamps, and decorator items	111.7	88.0	73.6	69.9	67.2	62.9	59.5	-5.4

See footnotes at end of table.

Table 739. Consumer Price Indexes for All Urban Consumers (CPI-U) for Selected Items and Groups: 2000 to 2011-Continued.

Item	2000	2005	2007	2008	2009	2010	2011	Annual percent change, 2010-11
Nonelectric cookware and tableware [2]	98.4	91.3	93.1	95.9	97.1	96.6	97.9	1.3
Tools, hardware, outdoor equipment and supplies [2]	97.0	94.4	94.6	93.5	94.2	91.6	91.6	(Z)
Tools, hardware, and supplies [2]	97.3	98.1	99.7	99.0	99.2	96.5	98.1	1.6
Outdoor equipment and supplies [2]	96.8	92.4	92.0	90.7	91.4	88.9	88.3	-0.6
Housekeeping supplies	153.4	159.9	169.4	176.5	183.1	183.3	185.4	1.2
Household cleaning products [2]	105.1	107.9	112.3	115.9	121.4	120.6	121.4	0.6
Household paper products [2]	113.8	125.4	135.6	146.8	156.1	158.0	161.7	2.3
Miscellaneous household products [2]	104.3	106.4	113.6	116.3	116.8	116.9	117.9	0.9
Household operations [2]	110.5	130.3	140.6	147.5	150.3	150.3	151.8	1.0
Domestic services [2]	109.7	128.3	138.1	142.8	144.1	144.4	145.4	0.7
Gardening and lawncare services [2]	111.4	127.9	140.5	(NA)	156.5	155.3	156.9	1.0
Apparel	**129.6**	**119.5**	**119.0**	**118.9**	**120.1**	**119.5**	**122.1**	**2.2**
Men's and boy's apparel	129.7	116.1	112.4	113.0	113.6	111.9	114.7	2.5
Men's apparel	133.1	121.4	118.2	118.4	118.6	117.5	119.8	1.9
Men's shirts and sweaters [2]	98.3	84.2	82.5	80.4	81.0	78.6	79.6	1.2
Boys' apparel	116.2	97.0	91.7	93.5	95.2	91.5	95.9	4.8
Women's and girl's apparel	121.5	110.8	110.3	107.5	108.1	107.1	109.2	1.9
Women's apparel	121.9	111.8	112.1	109.3	109.9	109.5	111.3	1.7
Women's suits and separates [2]	98.2	87.3	88.9	85.7	84.9	83.9	84.2	0.3
Women's underwear, nightwear, sportswear, and accessories [2]	101.8	95.4	91.8	90.4	93.1	96.0	98.6	2.7
Girls' apparel	119.7	105.3	101.1	98.5	99.0	95.4	98.5	3.3
Footwear	123.8	122.6	122.4	124.2	126.9	128.0	128.5	0.4
Men's footwear	129.5	121.3	120.9	122.9	126.4	127.6	129.2	1.3
Women's footwear	119.6	121.9	122.5	122.6	123.4	125.3	123.7	-1.3
Jewelry and watches [4]	137.0	127.6	137.1	146.5	149.2	152.4	165.2	8.4
Jewelry [4]	141.2	131.3	142.4	153.8	157.0	161.2	176.6	9.5
Transportation	**153.3**	**173.9**	**184.7**	**195.5**	**179.3**	**193.4**	**212.4**	**9.8**
Private transportation	149.1	170.2	180.8	191.0	174.8	188.7	207.6	10.0
New and used motor vehicles [2]	100.8	95.6	94.3	93.3	93.5	97.1	99.8	2.7
New vehicles	142.8	137.9	136.3	134.2	135.6	138.0	141.9	2.8
Used cars and trucks	155.8	139.4	135.7	134.0	127.0	143.1	149.0	4.1
Leased cars and trucks [7]	(NA)	92.7	92.6	95.1	102.4	97.0	94.4	-2.7
Motor fuel	129.3	195.7	239.1	279.7	202.0	239.2	302.6	26.5
Gasoline (all types)	128.6	194.7	238.0	277.5	201.6	238.6	301.7	26.4
Motor vehicle parts and equipment	101.5	111.9	121.6	128.7	134.1	137.0	143.9	5.0
Motor vehicle maintenance and repair	177.3	206.9	223.0	233.9	243.3	248.0	253.1	2.1
Motor vehicle insurance	256.7	329.2	333.1	341.5	357.0	375.2	388.7	3.6
Motor vehicle fees [2]	107.3	134.7	141.2	145.8	155.7	165.5	167.3	1.1
Public transportation	209.6	217.3	230.0	250.5	236.3	251.4	269.4	7.2
Airline fare	239.4	236.6	251.7	282.0	258.0	278.2	304.0	9.3
Medical care	**260.8**	**323.2**	**351.1**	**364.1**	**375.6**	**388.4**	**400.3**	**3.0**
Medical care commodities	238.1	276.0	290.0	296.0	305.1	314.7	324.1	3.0
Prescription drugs	285.4	349.0	369.2	378.3	391.1	407.8	425.0	4.2
Nonprescription drugs and medical supplies [4]	149.5	151.7	156.8	158.3	161.4	(NA)	(NA)	(NA)
Medical care services	266.0	336.7	369.3	384.9	397.3	411.2	423.8	3.1
Professional medical services	237.7	281.7	300.8	311.0	319.4	328.2	335.7	2.3
Physicians' services	244.7	287.5	303.2	311.3	320.8	331.3	340.3	2.7
Dental services	258.5	324.0	358.4	376.9	388.1	398.8	408.0	2.3
Eyeglasses and eye care [4]	149.7	163.2	171.6	174.1	175.5	176.7	178.3	0.9
Services by other medical professionals [4]	161.9	186.8	197.4	205.5	209.8	214.4	217.4	1.4
Hospital and related services	317.3	439.9	498.9	534.0	567.9	607.7	641.5	5.6
Hospital services [9]	115.9	161.6	183.6	197.2	210.7	227.2	241.2	6.2
Recreation [2]	**103.3**	**109.4**	**111.4**	**113.3**	**114.3**	**113.3**	**113.4**	**(Z)**
Video and audio [2]	101.0	104.2	102.9	102.6	101.3	99.1	98.4	-0.7
Cable and satellite television and radio service [5]	266.8	331.9	351.5	359.9	367.6	372.4	379.0	1.8
Pets, pet products and services [2]	106.1	123.6	133.8	144.5	153.4	154.4	158.7	2.8
Sporting goods	119.0	115.5	116.4	118.4	119.9	118.8	118.5	-0.3
Other recreational goods [2]	87.8	69.5	64.3	62.1	60.2	57.8	55.9	-3.2
Other recreation services [2]	111.7	130.5	139.4	142.9	144.6	145.1	145.3	0.1
Club membership dues and fees for participant sports [2]	108.9	117.4	123.7	125.8	125.7	123.5	122.1	-1.1
Admissions	230.5	282.3	303.8	312.3	317.8	322.8	325.0	0.7
Education and communication [2]	**102.5**	**113.7**	**119.6**	**123.6**	**127.4**	**129.9**	**131.5**	**1.2**
Education [2]	112.5	152.7	171.4	181.3	190.9	199.3	207.8	4.2
Tuition, other school fees, and childcare	324.0	440.9	494.1	522.1	549.0	573.2	597.2	4.2
College tuition and fees	331.9	475.1	538.7	572.3	606.7	638.2	670.3	5.0
Communication [2]	93.6	84.7	83.4	84.2	85.0	84.7	83.3	-1.6
Information and information processing [2]	92.8	82.6	80.7	81.4	81.9	81.5	80.0	-1.9
Telephone services [2]	98.5	94.9	98.2	100.5	102.4	102.4	101.2	-1.1
Land-line telephone services, local charges	175.6	209.6	222.1	230.0	236.6	(NA)	(NA)	(NA)
Land-line telephone services, long distance charges [2]	91.8	67.5	71.5	74.8	78.1	(NA)	(NA)	(NA)
Wireless telephone services [2]	76.0	65.0	64.4	64.2	64.3	62.4	60.1	-3.6
Information technology, hardware, and services [10]	25.9	13.6	10.6	10.1	9.7	9.4	9.0	-4.1
Other goods and services	**271.1**	**313.4**	**333.3**	**345.4**	**368.6**	**381.3**	**387.2**	**1.6**
Tobacco and smoking products	394.9	502.8	554.2	588.7	730.3	807.3	834.8	3.4
Cigarettes [2]	159.9	203.5	224.8	239.0	297.4	329.0	340.0	3.3
Personal care	165.6	185.6	195.6	201.3	204.6	206.6	208.6	0.9
Personal care products	153.7	154.4	158.3	159.3	162.6	161.1	160.5	-0.3
Hair, dental, shaving, and miscellaneous personal care products [2]	103.3	101.8	103.6	104.3	105.4	104.3	102.4	-1.8

See footnotes at end of table.

Item	2000	2005	2007	2008	2009	2010	2011	Annual percent change, 2010-11
Cosmetics, perfume, bath, nail preparations and implements	166.8	171.3	177.0	178.0	183.6	182.2	184.3	1.2
Personal care services	178.1	203.9	216.6	223.7	227.6	229.6	230.8	0.5
Haircuts and other personal care services [2]	108.7	124.4	132.1	136.5	138.9	140.1	140.8	0.5
Miscellaneous personal services	252.3	303.0	325.0	338.9	344.5	354.1	362.9	2.5
Legal services [4]	189.3	241.8	260.3	270.7	278.1	288.1	297.4	3.2
Funeral expenses [4]	187.8	228.8	252.6	265.4	275.7	282.0	288.3	2.2
SPECIAL AGGREGATE INDEXES								
Commodities	**149.2**	**160.2**	**167.5**	**174.8**	**169.7**	**174.6**	**183.9**	**5.3**
Commodities less food and beverages	137.7	142.5	147.5	153.0	144.4	150.4	159.9	6.4
Nondurables less food and beverages	147.4	168.4	182.5	196.2	179.0	189.9	208.4	9.7
Nondurables less food, beverages, and apparel	162.5	202.6	226.2	248.8	219.6	238.1	267.0	12.1
Durables	125.4	115.3	112.5	110.9	109.9	111.3	112.6	1.1
Services	195.3	230.1	246.8	255.5	259.2	261.3	265.8	1.7
Rent of shelter [3]	201.3	233.7	250.8	257.2	259.9	258.8	262.2	1.3
Transportation services	196.1	225.7	233.7	244.1	251.0	259.8	268.0	3.1
Other services	229.9	268.4	285.6	295.8	304.0	309.6	314.4	1.6
All items less food	173.0	196.0	208.1	215.5	214.0	217.8	224.5	3.1
All items less shelter	165.7	186.1	196.6	205.5	203.3	208.6	217.0	4.0
All items less medical care	167.3	188.7	200.1	207.8	206.6	209.7	216.3	3.2
Commodities less food	139.2	144.5	149.7	155.3	147.1	153.0	162.4	6.2
Nondurables less food	149.1	170.1	184.0	197.3	181.5	191.9	209.6	9.2
Nondurables less food and apparel	162.9	201.2	223.4	244.4	218.7	235.6	262.1	11.3
Nondurables	158.2	180.2	193.5	205.9	198.5	205.3	219.0	6.7
Apparel less footwear	126.2	114.4	113.8	113.4	114.2	113.3	116.2	2.6
Services less rent of shelter [3]	202.9	243.2	260.8	273.0	278.1	284.4	290.6	2.2
Services less medical care services	188.9	221.2	236.8	245.0	248.1	249.6	253.6	1.6
Energy	124.6	177.1	207.7	236.7	193.1	211.4	243.9	15.4
All items less energy	178.6	198.7	208.9	214.8	218.4	220.5	224.8	2.0
All items less food and energy	181.3	200.9	210.7	215.6	219.2	221.3	225.0	1.7
Commodities less food and energy commodities	144.9	140.3	140.1	140.2	142.0	143.6	145.5	1.3
Energy commodities	129.5	197.4	241.0	284.4	205.3	242.6	306.4	26.3
Services less energy services	202.1	236.6	253.1	261.0	265.9	268.3	273.1	1.8
Domestically produced farm food	170.1	195.0	206.5	220.1	220.4	221.6	232.5	4.9
Utilities and public transportation	152.6	176.6	191.3	202.8	200.3	203.1	206.5	1.7

NA Not available. Z Less than 0.05 percent. [1] Special indexes based on a substantially smaller sample. [2] December 1997=100. [3] December 1982=100. [4] December 1986=100. [5] December 1983=100. [6] December 1990=100. [7] December 2001=100. [8] December 1993=100. [9] December 1996=100. [10] December 1988=100.

Source: Bureau of Labor Statistics, *CPI Detailed Report*, monthly, <http://www.bls.gov/cpi/>. See also Monthly Labor Review, <http://www.bls.gov/opub/mlr/welcome.htm>.

Table 740. Cost of Living Index-Selected Urban Areas, Annual Average: 2011

[Data are for a selected urban area within the larger metropolitan area shown. Measures relative price levels for consumer goods and services in participating areas for a mid-management standard of living. The nationwide average equals 100 and each index is read as a percent of the national average. The index does not measure inflation, but compares prices at a single point in time. Excludes taxes. Metropolitan areas as defined by the Office of Management and Budget. For definitions, urban areas, and components of MSAs, see source. Beginning February 2008, data are based on an annual average survey compiled from data submitted in the first 3 quarters of the year. To calculate the annual average index, actual and estimated prices are collected to calculate an annual average price for each item used to represent the various spending categories. The share of consumer spending devoted to the category determines that category's importance, or weight, in the Index. Weights are based on the Bureau of Labor Statistics' most recent Consumer Expenditure Survey]

Urban Area	Composite Index (100%)	Grocery items (13%)	Housing (29%)	Utilities (10%)	Trans- portation (11%)	Health care (4%)	Misc. goods and services (32%)
Akron, OH............................	99.9	104.5	102.9	98.1	103.7	86.7	96.6
Albany, GA...........................	92.5	109.4	77.3	84.7	102.0	93.7	98.2
Albany, NY...........................	111.3	106.3	117.2	105.2	103.0	106.1	113.4
Amarillo, TX..........................	93.0	91.5	94.3	82.4	95.2	95.4	94.7
Ames, IA.............................	96.1	93.0	101.1	81.0	105.2	100.5	94.2
Anchorage, AK.......................	130.6	137.4	149.8	98.2	112.0	139.4	126.3
Anderson, SC........................	91.0	105.1	73.7	98.9	93.7	97.0	96.3
Ann Arbor, MI........................	100.9	98.7	105.1	107.7	100.4	97.5	96.4
Anniston-Calhoun County, AL.......	91.8	103.2	79.1	102.4	88.4	94.1	95.7
Appleton, WI.........................	94.2	92.9	75.5	110.9	108.7	108.1	99.3
Asheville, NC.........................	101.7	102.0	99.9	111.9	97.3	104.4	100.9
Atlanta, GA..........................	97.3	101.6	89.2	93.4	102.1	101.2	101.8
Auburn-Opelika, AL..................	98.1	105.9	84.1	103.5	95.2	90.4	107.5
Augusta-Aiken, GA-SC..............	94.1	104.6	80.2	96.8	93.5	93.0	101.5
Austin, TX...........................	92.7	84.9	82.0	99.2	101.0	102.3	99.3
Bakersfield, CA......................	98.5	106.7	92.7	104.2	103.0	107.6	95.6
Baltimore, MD........................	119.1	109.2	159.9	115.3	103.8	96.7	96.5
Baton Rouge, LA.....................	93.6	101.2	91.9	86.0	90.8	99.1	94.7
Beaumont, TX........................	96.4	89.2	99.1	90.8	98.0	93.9	98.6
Bellingham, WA......................	115.3	116.6	136.8	83.3	115.6	116.8	105.8
Bergen-Passaic, NJ..................	131.6	105.4	174.3	131.4	103.6	105.0	117.4
Bethesda-Gaithersburg-Frederick, MD...........	128.9	110.7	182.5	123.7	108.9	101.8	101.2
Birmingham, AL......................	88.6	90.6	73.3	104.4	84.8	81.8	98.6
Blacksburg, VA......................	95.8	90.1	93.4	97.0	98.1	104.2	97.9
Boise, ID.............................	96.1	101.2	83.4	97.2	101.3	101.6	102.3
Boston, MA...........................	137.3	118.8	160.2	147.3	106.7	121.3	133.7
Bradenton, FL........................	95.3	104.4	86.8	87.5	101.9	98.2	99.1
Brazoria County, TX.................	87.7	84.0	78.5	91.2	92.7	99.4	93.1
Brownsville, TX......................	87.5	89.0	74.4	94.7	96.1	97.5	92.0
Buffalo, NY..........................	98.6	93.0	108.6	109.0	103.1	89.4	88.6
Burlington, NC.......................	95.5	102.8	84.8	81.3	96.5	101.2	105.5
Burlington-Chittenden Co., VT......	122.0	108.4	146.3	126.6	102.9	105.9	113.2
Camden, SC..........................	97.4	103.8	88.3	108.4	87.5	90.9	103.5
Cape Coral-Fort Myers, FL..........	95.5	105.1	90.3	81.1	101.7	99.3	98.2
Cedar Rapids, IA....................	93.6	97.3	78.7	101.3	96.6	94.7	101.6
Champaign-Urbana, IL...............	97.0	92.8	90.2	112.1	97.9	104.6	98.5
Chapel Hill, NC......................	114.0	107.3	127.9	83.9	98.1	103.4	120.9
Charleston, WV.......................	94.2	89.3	92.2	99.7	96.6	97.1	95.1
Charleston-N Charleston, SC........	99.7	107.5	90.1	107.5	98.3	109.0	101.8
Charlotte, NC........................	93.3	100.1	81.9	92.8	98.2	105.2	97.4
Charlottesville, VA...................	106.3	100.9	119.7	100.2	96.3	98.0	103.0
Chattanooga, TN.....................	94.1	99.5	86.5	89.6	101.3	94.0	97.7
Cheyenne, WY........................	96.6	101.7	98.1	91.4	91.3	98.5	96.4
Chicago, IL...........................	114.7	114.4	133.8	97.6	114.5	107.1	104.6
Cincinnati, OH.......................	93.3	104.1	78.9	99.4	96.4	101.1	97.6
Clarksville, TN.......................	97.5	90.8	89.2	93.6	93.0	100.0	110.0
Cleveland, OH.......................	101.4	110.4	91.4	99.1	101.7	111.1	105.9
Cleveland, TN........................	92.6	100.8	88.6	95.7	96.2	93.0	90.4
Colorado Springs, CO...............	92.5	94.0	89.1	89.8	96.8	102.5	93.1
Columbia, MO........................	91.2	95.5	80.4	90.7	96.1	96.3	96.7
Columbia, SC........................	95.5	104.6	78.5	106.6	104.0	101.4	99.7
Columbus, OH.......................	90.3	94.3	76.8	99.9	99.0	102.1	92.9
Conroe, TX...........................	90.7	87.3	79.7	97.1	97.7	97.0	96.6
Conway, AR..........................	87.7	94.8	78.3	93.1	95.3	85.6	89.2
Corpus Christi, TX...................	89.6	79.3	77.4	113.9	96.7	91.8	93.9
Covington, KY........................	89.5	90.4	77.5	99.5	99.3	93.9	92.6
Dallas, TX...........................	96.2	100.6	75.2	108.1	105.0	104.7	105.0
Danville City, VA....................	91.8	93.8	81.6	94.2	99.8	100.1	95.3
Danville, IL..........................	90.5	92.6	70.6	116.5	113.5	97.6	90.3
Davenport-Moline-Rock Is., IA-IL...	99.0	98.9	107.7	81.0	102.3	101.6	95.8
Dayton, OH..........................	93.1	92.0	74.1	110.7	98.1	90.5	103.4
Decatur, IL..........................	89.8	90.2	81.2	98.4	94.4	88.1	93.1
Decatur-Hartselle, AL................	91.8	100.1	74.6	98.8	99.2	88.1	99.3
Denton, TX...........................	91.8	90.5	78.4	83.1	106.5	100.5	100.9
Denver, CO...........................	105.0	102.6	112.9	90.0	95.0	106.8	106.9
Des Moines, IA......................	91.2	93.7	88.9	91.3	98.5	88.0	90.4
Detroit, MI...........................	93.7	95.8	84.6	104.0	100.5	95.7	95.1
Dothan, AL..........................	91.4	99.2	82.0	84.4	92.5	82.4	99.6
Dover, DE............................	102.1	114.5	89.1	111.1	100.6	108.2	105.3
Dubuque, IA.........................	96.2	99.6	88.9	97.5	101.7	99.9	98.6
Durham, NC..........................	92.7	98.7	78.3	92.7	103.9	100.8	98.0
Dutchess County, NY................	121.0	110.8	133.7	130.2	110.4	111.5	115.7
Eau Claire, WI.......................	90.2	96.9	84.1	79.9	101.0	105.9	90.6
Edmond, OK..........................	92.5	90.9	88.6	92.5	99.0	97.4	93.8
El Paso, TX..........................	90.9	100.7	90.7	81.8	94.0	92.7	88.8
Elkhart-Goshen, IN..................	93.1	94.7	93.8	87.5	100.6	97.6	90.7
Erie, PA.............................	96.2	97.9	99.0	89.5	100.0	94.2	94.1

See footnotes at end of table.

Table 740. Cost of Living Index-Selected Urban Areas, Annual Average:
2011-Continued.
See headnote on page 494.

Urban Area	Composite Index (100%)	Grocery items (13%)	Housing (29%)	Utilities (10%)	Trans- portation (11%)	Health care (4%)	Misc. goods and services (32%)
Eugene, OR....................................	107.7	93.8	128.1	89.0	108.0	116.2	100.0
Evansville, IN.................................	93.4	92.4	86.9	105.7	95.7	95.3	94.6
Everett, WA....................................	110.2	107.4	126.5	89.1	107.7	129.1	102.1
Fairbanks, AK.................................	137.0	132.4	140.3	211.5	109.9	142.5	120.2
Fargo-Moorhead, ND-MN.................	93.2	103.8	84.2	89.3	96.9	102.8	95.5
Farmington, NM..............................	99.0	100.2	98.2	91.9	98.6	102.7	101.1
Fayetteville, AR..............................	86.4	92.1	75.9	93.9	88.4	92.3	89.6
Fayetteville, NC.............................	96.7	109.4	79.2	102.1	98.9	108.9	102.9
Flagstaff, AZ..................................	113.3	110.3	141.7	95.2	104.0	103.0	99.6
Florence, AL..................................	91.0	97.6	80.6	95.8	96.8	85.9	94.8
Fort Lauderdale, FL.........................	111.0	106.7	128.3	94.4	108.2	103.4	104.9
Fort Wayne-Allen County, IN............	95.6	94.7	92.1	84.3	103.2	95.7	100.1
Fort Worth, TX...............................	93.1	92.0	79.0	110.9	102.1	96.6	96.9
Fresno, CA....................................	109.1	109.9	113.2	113.5	110.0	103.5	104.2
Gainesville, FL...............................	99.7	106.7	101.6	95.1	102.4	98.2	95.8
Gastonia, NC.................................	92.9	100.9	74.7	101.7	96.3	91.2	102.0
Glenwood Springs, CO....................	115.1	101.7	147.0	90.3	103.3	110.6	104.9
Grand Junction, CO........................	99.6	98.8	106.7	92.1	99.1	102.9	95.8
Grand Rapids, MI............................	89.4	97.8	76.0	90.9	95.0	95.6	94.5
Greenville, NC...............................	96.7	107.5	80.9	105.7	95.5	112.3	101.4
Greenville, SC................................	92.3	103.0	75.2	94.8	97.7	104.1	99.0
Gunnison, CO.................................	110.6	108.6	137.9	91.3	97.6	94.3	100.0
Hampton Roads-SE Virginia, VA.......	105.3	100.2	113.6	110.9	97.7	102.6	101.1
Harlingen, TX.................................	81.0	79.4	72.0	104.3	89.1	93.9	77.7
Harrisburg, PA...............................	102.9	98.0	99.1	113.6	104.2	95.6	105.6
Harrisonburg, VA............................	96.7	94.6	97.8	100.0	93.2	100.0	96.3
Hartford, CT..................................	123.8	122.1	138.8	118.0	110.9	111.7	119.0
Hattiesburg, MS.............................	92.6	102.1	77.1	98.4	97.2	90.4	99.1
Honolulu, HI..................................	167.8	155.6	251.8	161.9	125.9	123.7	120.5
Hot Springs, AR.............................	96.4	103.2	86.1	93.5	94.4	93.0	104.8
Houma-Terrebonne Parish, LA..........	96.2	91.9	109.3	79.6	106.5	89.2	89.2
Houston, TX..................................	89.8	80.7	83.1	89.3	95.2	98.3	96.8
Huntsville, AL................................	93.6	95.8	78.5	96.2	101.8	95.2	102.4
Idaho Falls, ID...............................	89.3	98.2	76.2	89.0	97.8	93.4	93.9
Iowa City, IA..................................	100.3	99.3	100.1	88.1	107.0	97.1	103.0
Ithaca, NY.....................................	102.8	100.5	104.9	111.3	107.0	108.1	97.1
Jackson, MS..................................	96.6	91.2	94.8	124.4	94.9	98.6	91.7
Jackson-Madison County, TN...........	91.1	94.1	74.7	100.6	99.3	90.3	98.7
Jacksonville, FL.............................	93.9	100.4	82.7	101.5	106.3	88.7	95.2
Jacksonville, NC............................	97.4	102.7	86.3	103.6	96.3	97.7	103.2
Janesville, WI................................	98.2	94.5	90.2	110.6	101.1	101.9	101.3
Jefferson City, MO.........................	96.8	95.7	83.0	97.3	98.8	96.9	108.7
Johnson City, TN...........................	87.8	93.5	76.7	91.9	87.3	91.6	93.5
Johnstown, PA...............................	93.7	96.9	78.7	103.8	100.5	96.1	99.7
Joliet-Will County, IL......................	99.9	98.0	98.8	103.3	106.4	104.6	97.7
Jonesboro, AR...............................	89.1	95.4	79.7	83.0	90.1	87.9	96.5
Joplin, MO....................................	90.8	95.3	75.3	116.0	97.1	96.9	91.7
Kalamazoo, MI...............................	87.3	93.6	71.2	100.3	99.1	92.8	90.1
Kansas City, MO-KS.......................	99.4	98.8	89.9	110.1	98.7	97.2	105.2
Kennewick-Richland-Pasco, WA.......	96.1	96.4	96.7	88.9	104.1	110.3	93.2
Knoxville, TN.................................	89.3	90.2	84.9	100.4	84.7	91.4	90.6
Lafayette, IN..................................	94.3	95.7	80.0	105.0	106.6	104.1	97.5
Lafayette, LA.................................	97.9	93.5	106.5	85.0	105.9	87.7	95.1
Lake Charles, LA............................	94.0	93.7	99.7	85.8	94.6	93.4	91.8
Las Cruces, NM.............................	98.5	102.8	101.6	96.4	97.3	93.5	95.6
Las Vegas, NV...............................	100.1	105.0	92.2	91.5	103.8	106.6	105.9
Lawton, OK...................................	95.6	95.0	98.2	93.1	104.2	94.6	91.7
Lexington, KY................................	91.9	91.8	82.6	94.5	97.1	99.1	96.6
Lexington-Buena Vista-Rockbridge, VA..........	93.1	92.5	94.9	95.2	97.9	90.8	89.9
Lima, OH......................................	93.6	99.2	74.7	96.5	95.7	108.7	104.3
Lincoln, NE...................................	93.4	95.1	84.4	103.8	106.8	95.0	92.8
Little Rock-North Little Rock, AR.......	95.7	94.4	89.1	105.4	95.0	91.0	99.8
Los Angeles-Long Beach, CA...........	132.8	107.4	196.7	112.3	108.9	110.3	104.5
Louisville, KY................................	91.7	87.9	83.4	102.3	98.9	87.5	95.5
Lubbock, TX..................................	89.4	93.9	81.0	75.5	101.1	99.0	94.2
Lynchburg, VA...............................	93.4	90.4	88.8	106.5	87.6	97.5	95.7
Madison, WI..................................	108.1	100.7	112.4	103.6	109.7	117.7	107.0
Manchester, NH.............................	119.8	101.6	126.3	127.1	99.7	111.1	127.2
Marietta, GA..................................	96.7	102.8	86.6	90.7	100.2	106.3	102.7
Marion-McDowell County, NC...........	92.2	103.4	89.6	99.1	90.6	105.5	86.2
McAllen, TX...................................	85.4	79.5	75.1	99.3	97.0	92.6	87.8
Memphis, TN.................................	85.9	91.3	72.4	88.2	93.2	99.3	90.6
Miami-Dade County, FL...................	107.1	107.3	111.7	94.4	109.0	106.5	106.4
Middlesex-Monmouth, NJ................	126.0	110.2	154.3	131.3	102.3	110.4	115.6
Midland, TX...................................	93.3	91.3	95.9	94.0	106.2	98.1	86.8
Milwaukee-Waukesha, WI................	99.3	94.4	104.2	109.6	101.2	110.5	91.5
Minneapolis, MN............................	110.6	108.1	118.7	100.7	104.8	103.2	110.6
Missoula, MT.................................	99.9	106.6	92.1	101.3	98.9	107.2	102.8
Mobile, AL....................................	92.0	98.0	80.0	100.8	93.1	85.1	98.0
Monroe, LA...................................	93.4	94.3	88.1	78.5	99.7	94.3	100.4
Montgomery, AL............................	97.3	101.5	96.4	98.5	100.3	88.0	96.1
Morgantown, WV...........................	103.7	95.1	116.7	94.7	102.3	91.3	100.8
Morristown, TN..............................	91.5	93.0	78.2	88.9	95.7	90.5	102.3

See footnotes at end of table.

Table 740. Cost of Living Index-Selected Urban Areas, Annual Average: 2011-Continued.

See headnote on page 494.

Urban Area	Composite Index (100%)	Grocery items (13%)	Housing (29%)	Utilities (10%)	Trans- portation (11%)	Health care (4%)	Misc. goods and services (32%)
Muncie, IN....................................	90.2	94.5	82.3	84.9	100.0	89.4	93.8
Murfreesboro-Smyrna, TN.........................	88.2	94.6	78.2	84.0	95.5	89.4	93.0
Myrtle Beach, SC...........................	95.7	106.7	80.0	113.0	92.6	99.8	100.0
Nashville-Franklin, TN.........................	90.2	97.4	70.4	87.1	93.4	91.8	104.5
Nassau County, NY...........................	138.4	118.7	188.0	138.6	109.8	110.8	116.0
New Haven, CT.............................	127.8	117.6	142.8	129.2	114.6	114.8	124.3
New York (Brooklyn), NY......................	182.7	125.4	334.2	141.7	106.5	115.0	120.0
New York (Manhattan), NY.....................	218.8	148.7	413.5	143.7	122.9	128.0	144.0
New York (Queens), NY.......................	153.9	126.8	235.6	142.5	108.7	117.4	116.5
Newark-Elizabeth, NJ........................	131.2	106.1	170.5	135.0	103.9	104.0	118.4
Norman, OK...............................	91.5	94.0	85.4	81.8	104.1	93.4	94.7
Oakland, CA..............................	136.0	114.0	195.5	94.1	109.7	116.3	117.3
Odessa, TX...............................	91.1	90.5	89.8	90.9	96.4	97.3	90.0
Ogden, UT................................	91.5	92.5	81.5	103.7	94.7	88.0	95.5
Oklahoma City, OK.........................	90.5	91.4	85.4	84.6	95.3	100.2	93.5
Olympia, WA..............................	105.3	107.0	105.3	89.0	110.1	115.9	106.8
Omaha, NE...............................	89.4	94.1	80.2	92.4	100.6	98.5	89.7
Orange County, CA.........................	142.7	108.0	229.6	112.8	112.0	109.2	104.4
Orlando, FL...............................	97.3	100.1	79.5	107.8	99.2	94.4	108.2
Palm Springs, CA..........................	121.8	111.4	149.6	112.1	109.2	99.6	111.8
Pascagoula, MS............................	91.8	101.3	81.5	93.7	95.7	96.2	94.6
Peoria, IL................................	92.9	91.1	84.4	99.9	106.0	93.4	94.4
Philadelphia, PA...........................	125.0	124.5	140.2	129.9	107.7	104.8	118.6
Phoenix, AZ...............................	96.5	103.7	87.2	100.3	102.9	102.8	97.7
Pittsburgh, PA............................	94.8	104.8	76.7	100.6	111.2	93.9	99.6
Pittsfield, MA.............................	104.1	114.6	95.4	109.1	100.5	118.2	105.1
Plano, TX................................	96.7	101.7	84.9	106.3	102.3	103.4	99.2
Portland, ME..............................	113.0	105.7	127.9	103.0	111.6	112.5	106.5
Portland, OR..............................	113.6	111.2	130.6	88.4	113.7	114.0	107.6
Prescott-Prescott Valley, AZ....................	103.7	104.3	116.1	95.8	92.3	99.8	99.3
Providence, RI............................	125.6	111.3	134.2	129.7	104.3	112.1	131.5
Pryor Creek, OK...........................	86.4	94.9	73.8	86.9	86.7	92.7	92.8
Pueblo, CO...............................	85.4	93.2	72.9	85.8	91.9	92.5	89.9
Punta Gorda-Charlotte Co., FL.................	92.8	103.0	74.3	93.0	100.9	111.6	99.6
Raleigh, NC...............................	93.8	101.3	79.7	104.5	96.6	100.5	97.8
Reno-Sparks, NV...........................	94.0	100.6	87.1	87.4	103.9	102.7	95.1
Richmond, VA.............................	100.1	104.4	95.1	108.5	101.9	108.8	98.3
Rio Rancho, NM...........................	94.6	94.4	86.7	98.7	94.4	101.1	99.6
Riverside City, CA..........................	112.4	106.6	135.5	110.2	108.8	102.8	97.5
Roanoke, VA..............................	92.4	90.9	90.4	96.1	93.7	95.1	92.9
Rochester, MN............................	104.7	93.3	103.1	114.6	107.9	108.7	105.9
Rochester, NY............................	98.6	94.9	93.5	112.7	104.1	99.5	98.1
Rockford, IL..............................	90.3	92.2	74.6	90.9	106.1	102.3	96.5
Round Rock, TX...........................	88.6	82.0	75.9	104.9	88.6	94.1	96.6
Salt Lake City, UT..........................	94.6	94.1	94.1	77.3	96.6	96.1	100.0
San Angelo, TX............................	90.2	85.7	79.9	105.4	98.8	95.5	92.8
San Antonio, TX...........................	93.1	84.5	91.2	85.8	102.2	97.4	97.2
San Diego, CA.............................	130.6	107.3	188.6	113.0	111.2	112.7	103.7
San Francisco, CA..........................	162.7	115.8	283.0	91.3	111.5	112.6	122.4
San Jose, CA..............................	150.3	114.6	244.6	131.9	114.6	116.5	103.9
San Marcos, TX...........................	90.4	87.1	86.1	87.3	94.8	96.5	94.3
Sarasota, FL..............................	99.9	104.3	99.1	97.0	100.0	107.7	98.7
Savannah, GA.............................	91.6	97.0	76.9	100.7	97.7	93.5	97.1
Seattle, WA..............................	117.1	111.6	129.2	90.4	112.4	118.7	118.8
Sherman-Denison, TX.......................	86.4	90.2	74.7	92.7	96.8	90.5	89.0
Shreveport-Bossier City, LA...................	97.5	94.3	95.4	94.2	94.6	94.2	103.1
Sioux Falls, SD............................	97.1	94.9	86.0	102.3	92.5	94.6	108.1
Slidell-St. Tammany Parish, LA.................	95.6	95.8	94.9	89.3	99.1	91.4	97.7
South Bend, IN............................	92.4	92.5	83.2	86.2	98.1	97.3	99.8
Spokane, WA.............................	92.9	94.6	85.9	79.0	100.9	105.8	98.6
Springfield, IL............................	88.1	89.9	72.4	78.3	111.1	102.0	94.8
Springfield, MO...........................	88.8	95.3	75.3	83.6	94.3	95.3	96.9
St. Cloud, MN.............................	95.6	103.9	78.5	102.2	101.1	103.3	102.4
St. George, UT............................	92.9	99.0	84.2	88.4	94.4	88.5	99.6
St. Joseph, MO............................	93.7	98.1	83.5	98.0	95.0	92.9	99.2
St. Louis, MO-IL...........................	91.1	95.1	75.3	104.4	98.3	98.9	95.6
St. Paul, MN..............................	110.5	107.1	115.4	101.4	107.6	104.0	112.5
Stamford, CT.............................	147.4	116.3	207.4	139.7	116.5	114.6	124.2
Sumter, SC...............................	93.2	104.4	85.7	100.4	90.5	91.7	93.8
Tacoma, WA..............................	107.3	107.2	110.0	96.2	102.6	107.9	110.1
Tampa, FL................................	91.8	98.1	78.7	96.8	102.8	93.8	95.2
Temple, TX...............................	85.6	83.6	73.1	92.6	99.2	90.3	90.1
Texarkana, TX-AR..........................	91.2	98.8	80.7	102.2	93.6	96.1	92.2
Topeka, KS...............................	93.3	94.5	83.8	82.9	97.3	94.5	103.1
Tucson, AZ...............................	95.0	97.2	85.8	87.2	102.4	100.4	101.5
Tulsa, OK................................	90.0	92.2	68.9	96.9	101.3	99.5	100.5
Tuscaloosa, AL............................	94.2	101.4	80.5	104.9	102.2	89.2	97.9
Tyler, TX.................................	95.2	90.0	92.2	95.7	100.1	93.2	98.3
Valdosta, GA..............................	95.7	105.1	88.9	95.3	98.6	104.9	95.6
Vancouver, WA............................	95.5	94.5	83.9	99.8	106.0	113.1	98.9
Vero Beach-Indian River, FL..................	97.6	113.9	82.3	100.6	96.8	102.1	103.0
Waco, TX.................................	86.3	81.4	84.2	92.3	103.6	85.7	82.7
Washington-Arlington-Alexandria, DC-VA........	143.3	111.3	240.5	103.9	108.1	101.2	100.7

See footnotes at end of table.

Table 740. Cost of Living Index-Selected Urban Areas, Annual Average: 2011-Continued.

See headnote on page 494.

Urban Area	Composite Index (100%)	Grocery items (13%)	Housing (29%)	Utilities (10%)	Trans-portation (11%)	Health care (4%)	Misc. goods and services (32%)
Waterloo-Cedar Falls, IA............	93.4	92.1	90.8	88.1	99.7	94.7	95.9
Wausau, WI............	96.2	100.5	87.5	106.1	98.1	103.5	97.3
Weatherford, TX............	92.2	96.2	79.4	104.7	105.4	101.1	92.3
Wichita Falls, TX............	88.5	91.2	88.0	86.0	82.8	92.8	89.8
Wichita, KS............	92.2	90.1	84.0	92.2	97.2	95.8	98.2
Williamsport-Lycoming Co., PA............	96.8	91.9	92.5	124.5	96.3	96.0	94.0
Wilmington, DE............	109.0	109.1	110.0	117.6	101.5	109.8	107.7
Wilmington, NC............	99.5	106.4	89.7	111.4	101.9	103.0	100.1
Winchester, VA-WV............	104.3	103.7	91.0	102.0	102.3	104.3	117.7
Winston-Salem, NC............	91.2	101.4	74.5	90.5	84.3	102.8	102.6
Yakima, WA............	92.6	100.0	85.8	83.8	98.1	114.4	93.6
York County, PA............	102.9	99.1	107.4	107.1	95.8	96.7	102.1
Youngstown-Warren, OH............	91.3	90.0	81.2	105.6	95.3	82.8	96.1
Yuma, AZ............	103.5	109.3	100.9	115.3	105.7	104.6	98.6

Source: C2ER, Arlington, VA, ACCRA Cost of Living Index, Annual Average 2011 (copyright). See also: <http://www.c2er.org>.

Table 741. Single-Family Housing Price Indexes by State: 2000 to 2011

[Index 1991, 1st quarter = 100. Purchase only indexes. Data are seasonally adjusted. The index reflects average price changes in repeat sales or refinancings on the same properties. Since the data are for the fourth quarter, the index represents the annual percentage change in home values in the fourth quarter of the year shown relative to the fourth quarter of the previous year. The information is obtained by reviewing repeat mortgage transactions on single-family properties whose mortgages have been purchased or securitized by either Fannie Mae or Freddie Mac; for more information on methodology, see Appendix III. Minus sign (–) indicates decrease]

State	2000	2005	2010	2011	Percent Change 2010-11	State	2000	2005	2010	2011	Percent Change 2010-11
U.S.....	**143.7**	**216.3**	**184.8**	**180.0**	**-2.6**	MO.......	149.9	197.6	181.4	178.1	-1.8
AL........	142.4	182.3	176.2	174.2	-1.1	MT.......	179.6	276.7	284.8	290.9	2.1
AK........	136.3	207.0	218.6	225.7	3.3	NE.......	162.5	194.6	189.1	193.7	2.4
AZ........	155.1	301.8	170.5	165.8	-2.7	NV.......	128.1	269.8	125.9	109.2	-13.3
AR........	141.2	185.0	174.6	179.5	2.8	NH.......	146.6	238.4	197.0	192.7	-2.2
CA........	123.1	280.6	158.4	150.8	-4.8	NJ........	133.2	253.3	222.1	208.8	-6.0
CO.......	216.6	270.8	265.8	259.1	-2.5	NM.......	145.6	214.8	211.0	201.5	-4.5
CT........	117.7	194.8	170.1	165.7	-2.6	NY.......	128.6	214.3	209.4	202.6	-3.2
DE........	121.1	207.8	189.2	176.1	-6.9	NC.......	146.1	182.4	185.2	177.5	-4.1
DC........	136.2	325.0	335.0	348.1	3.9	ND......	137.9	191.7	225.5	235.2	4.3
FL........	139.3	296.7	174.2	168.8	-3.1	OH.......	148.2	175.0	154.1	150.7	-2.2
GA........	151.2	190.8	152.7	148.8	-2.5	OK.......	143.7	177.3	191.7	193.4	0.9
HI........	91.9	204.8	175.8	169.9	-3.4	OR.......	184.0	297.0	255.3	247.9	-2.9
ID........	154.4	228.6	188.6	183.9	-2.5	PA.......	121.3	190.0	189.3	183.9	-2.8
IL........	145.5	203.7	179.4	167.1	-6.8	RI........	119.7	235.2	189.7	176.1	-7.1
IN........	142.0	165.4	158.2	158.1	-0.1	SC.......	144.6	184.7	180.6	175.7	-2.7
IA........	157.3	191.1	196.0	194.7	-0.7	SD.......	160.7	209.7	219.9	224.5	2.1
KS........	153.2	187.5	190.9	186.9	-2.1	TN.......	146.8	185.4	182.2	181.6	-0.4
KY........	150.1	183.9	189.2	183.6	-3.0	TX.......	142.9	172.1	187.3	190.0	1.4
LA........	156.6	212.2	226.7	225.6	-0.5	UT.......	194.2	255.9	248.1	237.9	-4.1
ME......	133.5	220.9	205.8	205.7	-0.1	VT........	126.4	206.5	203.6	208.4	2.4
MD......	122.1	253.4	209.4	204.1	-2.5	VA.......	130.9	233.4	209.2	207.4	-0.9
MA......	157.3	254.2	219.2	214.1	-2.3	WA.......	154.3	242.6	224.0	204.8	-8.6
MI.......	173.5	202.2	143.8	141.8	-1.4	WV.......	137.9	179.0	188.5	187.2	-0.7
MN......	172.3	253.2	208.8	199.0	-4.7	WI........	166.3	223.3	209.4	200.2	-4.4
MS.......	142.3	177.5	172.2	175.1	1.7	WY.......	169.1	258.0	281.9	279.5	-0.9

Source: Federal Housing Finance Agency, *Housing Price Index, 4th quarter 2011*. See also <http://www.fhfa.gov/Default.aspx?Page=87>.

Table 742. Average Prices of Selected Fuels and Electricity: 1990 to 2011

[In dollars per unit, except electricity, in cents per kWh. Represents price to end-users, except as noted]

Item	Unit	1990	2000	2004	2005	2006	2007	2008	2009	2010	2011
Crude oil, composite [1]............	Barrel	22.22	28.26	36.98	50.24	60.24	67.94	94.74	59.29	76.69	101.93
Motor gasoline: [2]											
Unleaded regular...................	Gallon	1.16	1.51	1.88	2.30	2.59	2.80	3.27	2.35	2.79	3.53
Unleaded premium................	Gallon	1.35	1.69	2.07	2.49	2.81	3.03	3.52	2.61	3.05	3.79
No. 2 heating oil...................	Gallon	0.73	0.93	1.17	1.71	1.98	2.24	2.99	1.96	2.46	3.19
No. 2 diesel fuel.....................	Gallon	0.73	0.94	1.24	1.79	2.10	2.27	3.15	1.83	2.31	3.12
Propane, consumer grade.........	Gallon	0.75	0.60	0.84	1.09	1.36	1.49	1.89	1.22	1.48	1.71
Residual fuel oil......................	Gallon	0.44	0.60	0.74	1.05	1.22	1.37	1.96	1.34	1.71	2.40
Natural gas, residential............	1,000 cu/ft	5.80	7.76	10.75	12.70	13.73	13.08	13.89	12.14	11.39	10.80
Electricity, residential...............	kWh	7.83	8.24	8.95	9.45	10.40	10.65	11.26	11.51	11.54	11.80

[1] Refiner acquisition cost. [2] Average, all service.

Source: U.S. Energy Information Administration, "Monthly Energy Review," April 2012. See also <http://www.eia.gov/totalenergy/data/monthly/>.

Table 743. Retail Gasoline Prices—Selected Areas: 2000 to 2011

[In dollars per gallon. Prices are annual averages]

Area	Regular				Midgrade				Premium			
	2000	2005	2010	2011	2000	2005	2010	2011	2000	2005	2010	2011
Boston, MA	(NA)	2.26	2.74	3.53	(NA)	2.36	2.87	3.67	(NA)	2.46	2.98	3.79
Chicago, IL	1.57	2.32	2.94	3.74	1.67	2.42	3.05	3.86	1.78	2.52	3.16	3.97
Cleveland, OH	(NA)	2.22	2.75	3.48	(NA)	2.32	2.86	3.60	(NA)	2.43	2.96	3.71
Denver, CO	1.54	2.24	2.65	3.38	1.67	2.35	2.77	3.50	1.78	2.45	2.89	3.61
Houston, TX	1.45	2.17	2.59	3.34	1.56	2.27	2.74	3.51	1.65	2.37	2.87	3.63
Los Angeles, CA	1.62	2.49	3.11	3.85	1.72	2.59	3.21	3.95	1.81	2.68	3.31	4.05
Miami, FL	(NA)	2.39	2.86	3.62	(NA)	2.49	3.01	3.79	(NA)	2.59	3.11	3.89
New York, NY	1.63	2.30	2.81	3.61	1.73	2.42	2.96	3.77	1.80	2.51	3.07	3.88
San Francisco, CA	1.88	2.48	3.12	3.83	1.98	2.59	3.23	3.95	2.09	2.69	3.34	4.05
Seattle, WA	(NA)	2.36	3.00	3.72	(NA)	2.47	3.12	3.85	(NA)	2.58	3.23	3.96

NA Not available.

Source: U.S. Energy Information Administration, *Weekly U.S. Retail Gasoline Prices*, Gasoline Historical Data. See also <http://www.eia.gov/petroleum/gasdiesel/>.

Table 744. Weekly Food Cost of a Nutritious Diet by Type of Family and Individual: 2010 and 2011

[In dollars, As of December. Assumes that food for all meals and snacks is purchased at the store and prepared at home. See source for details on estimation procedures]

Family type	Thrifty plan		Low-cost plan		Moderate plan		Liberal plan	
	2010	2011	2010	2011	2010	2011	2010	2011
FAMILIES								
Family of two:								
19 to 50 years	81.10	86.10	103.40	110.00	128.40	136.90	160.80	171.50
51 to 70 years	76.90	81.70	99.20	105.50	122.60	130.20	148.00	157.00
Family of four:								
Couple, 19 to 50 years and children—								
2 to 3 and 4 to 5 years	118.10	125.40	150.20	159.60	185.50	197.30	229.90	244.60
6 to 8 and 9 to 11 years	135.60	144.00	176.60	188.00	221.00	234.90	268.50	285.20
INDIVIDUALS [1]								
Child:								
1 year	20.10	21.10	26.80	28.30	30.60	32.10	37.10	39.00
2 to 3 years	21.70	23.10	27.50	29.20	33.30	35.40	40.50	43.10
4 to 5 years	22.70	24.00	28.70	30.40	35.50	37.50	43.30	45.70
6 to 8 years	28.80	30.70	39.20	42.10	48.20	51.10	56.90	60.20
9 to 11 years	33.00	35.00	43.40	45.90	56.10	59.30	65.50	69.10
Male:								
12 to 13 years	35.10	37.40	49.50	52.80	61.70	65.90	72.70	77.30
14 to 18 years	36.20	38.50	50.80	54.00	63.80	68.10	73.40	78.10
19 to 50 years	39.00	41.50	50.30	53.50	62.90	67.00	77.10	82.50
51 to 70 years	35.60	37.90	47.60	50.50	58.60	62.20	71.10	75.40
71 years and over	35.80	38.10	47.00	50.30	58.50	62.00	71.90	76.50
Female:								
12 to 13 years	35.30	37.50	42.90	45.70	51.90	54.80	63.00	66.90
14 to 18 years	34.80	37.00	43.10	45.90	52.00	55.60	63.90	68.50
19 to 50 years	34.70	36.80	43.70	46.50	53.80	57.40	69.00	73.40
51 to 70 years	34.30	36.40	42.50	45.40	52.90	56.20	63.50	67.30
71 years and over	33.80	35.70	42.10	45.10	52.50	55.80	63.40	67.20

[1] The costs given are for individuals in 4-person families. For individuals in other size families, the following adjustments are suggested: 1-person, add 20 percent; 2-person, add 10 percent; 3-person, add 5 percent; 5- or 6-person, subtract 5 percent; 7-or-more person, subtract 10 percent.

Source: U.S. Department of Agriculture, *Official USDA Food Plans: Cost of Food at Home at Four Levels*, monthly. See also <http://www.cnpp.usda.gov/USDAFoodCost-Home.htm>.

Table 745. Food—Retail Prices of Selected Items: 2000 to 2011

[In dollars per pound, except as indicated. As of December. See Appendix III]

Food	2000	2010	2011	Food	2000	2010	2011
Cereals and bakery products:				**Fresh fruits and vegetables:**			
Flour, white, all purpose.................	0.28	0.44	0.51	Apples, Red Delicious....................	0.82	1.20	1.27
Rice, white, lg. grain, raw................	(NA)	0.73	0.73	Bananas.................................	0.49	0.59	0.60
Spaghetti and macaroni..................	0.88	1.19	1.31	Oranges, navel.........................	0.62	1.02	0.98
Bread, white, pan.......................	0.99	1.39	1.42	Grapefruit..............................	0.58	0.99	0.89
Bread, whole wheat.....................	1.36	1.88	2.07	Grapes, Thompson seedless............	2.36	2.87	2.86
Beef:				Lemons.................................	1.11	1.60	1.54
Ground beef, 100% beef................	1.63	2.38	2.92	Pears, Anjou............................	(NA)	1.42	1.33
Ground chuck, 100% beef...............	1.98	2.93	3.27	Potatoes, white.........................	0.35	0.58	0.67
Ground beef, lean and extra lean.......	2.33	3.49	3.84	Lettuce, iceberg........................	0.85	0.99	0.95
Round steak, USDA Choice.............	3.28	4.30	4.72	Tomatoes, field grown..................	1.57	1.59	1.53
Sirloin steak, boneless..................	4.81	6.07	6.16				
Pork:				**Processed fruits and vegetables:**			
Bacon, sliced..........................	3.03	4.16	4.55	Orange juice, frozen concentrate,			
Chops, center cut, bone-in..............	3.46	3.58	3.66	12 oz. can, per 16 oz...................	1.88	2.46	2.76
Ham, boneless, excluding				**Sugar and sweets:**			
canned..............................	2.75	3.47	3.66	Sugar, white, all sizes..................	0.41	0.64	0.70
Poultry, fish, and eggs:				Sugar, white, 33–80 oz. pkg............	0.40	0.62	0.70
Chicken, fresh, whole...................	1.08	1.28	1.34	**Fats and oils:**			
Chicken legs, bone-in...................	1.26	1.48	1.46	Margarine, stick........................	(NA)	1.12	1.24
Turkey, frozen, whole...................	0.99	1.38	1.57	Margarine, tubs, soft...................	0.84	1.62	1.91
Eggs, Grade A, large, (dozen)..........	0.96	1.79	1.87	Peanut butter, creamy, all sizes........	1.96	1.99	2.43
Dairy products:							
Milk, fresh, whole, fortified				**Nonalcoholic beverages:**			
(per gal.)............................	2.79	3.32	3.57	Coffee, 100% ground roast,			
Butter, salted, grade AA, stick..........	2.80	3.42	3.32	all sizes..............................	3.21	4.15	5.44
American processed cheese............	3.69	3.80	4.30				
Cheddar cheese, natural...............	3.76	4.93	5.43	**Other prepared foods:**			
Ice cream, prepack., bulk, reg.				Potato chips, per 16 oz.................	3.44	4.74	5.03
(1/2 gal.)............................	3.66	4.58	5.25				

NA Not available.

Source: U.S. Bureau of Labor Statistics, *CPI Detailed Report*, monthly, <http://www.bls.gov/cpi/cpi_dr.htm>.

Table 746. Indexes of Spot Primary Market Prices: 1990 to 2011

[1967 = 100. Represents unweighted geometric average of price quotations of 23 commodities. Computed daily and therefore much more sensitive to changes in market conditions than is a monthly producer price index]

Items and number	1990	1995	2000	2003	2004	2005	2006	2007	2008	2009	2010	2011
All commodities (23).....	**258.1**	**289.1**	**224.0**	**283.6**	**293.0**	**303.3**	**362.4**	**413.4**	**313.0**	**424.2**	**520.3**	**481.8**
Foodstuffs (10)..............	206.4	236.4	184.7	250.2	256.0	241.7	276.0	335.9	294.2	344.7	440.3	435.5
Raw industrials (13).........	301.2	332.2	255.8	309.1	321.5	354.7	437.3	477.0	326.5	489.4	583.8	516.5
Livestock and products (5)..	292.7	307.4	265.5	365.9	365.0	326.6	378.6	402.6	310.8	461.6	528.0	575.4
Metals (5)...................	283.2	300.6	214.0	276.7	357.7	440.9	693.9	811.9	390.9	809.1	1,006.2	837.8
Textiles and fibers (4)......	257.6	274.3	245.7	255.2	237.9	252.5	254.4	267.5	241.3	294.0	342.1	290.2
Fats and oils (4).............	188.7	226.7	163.6	297.2	262.6	223.4	273.9	363.4	268.0	339.7	478.3	497.7

Source: Commodity Research Bureau, Chicago, IL *CRB Commodity Index Report*, weekly (copyright). See also: <http://www.crbtrader.com>.

Table 747. Commodity Research Bureau Futures Price Index: 1990 to 2011

[1967 = 100. Index computed daily. Represents unweighted geometric average of commodity futures prices (through 6 months forward) of 17 major commodity futures markets. Represents end of year index]

Commodity	1990	1995	2000	2003	2004	2005	2006	2007	2008	2009	2010	2011
All commodities...........	**222.6**	**243.2**	**227.8**	**255.3**	**283.9**	**347.9**	**394.9**	**476.1**	**363.1**	**484.4**	**629.5**	**563.0**
Softs [1]........................	276.0	354.4	254.4	250.5	343.5	420.5	475.9	467.5	487.2	(NA)	(NA)	(NA)
Industrials.....................	245.5	272.5	211.0	256.6	232.1	302.5	368.8	418.3	475.4	(NA)	(NA)	(NA)
Grains and Oilseeds [2]........	171.2	218.6	174.9	225.8	177.0	193.8	279.1	427.0	545.5	(NA)	(NA)	(NA)
Energy.........................	246.0	180.0	355.8	358.7	457.3	705.3	591.6	825.1	1263.2	(NA)	(NA)	(NA)
Oilseeds [3]....................	223.6	277.5	([3])	([3])	([3])	([3])	([3])	([3])	([3])	([3])	([3])	([3])
Livestock and Meats..........	226.2	192.4	253.6	237.3	303.6	300.3	294.6	297.7	337.0	(NA)	(NA)	(NA)
Metals (precious).............	257.8	276.0	265.7	364.1	396.6	478.1	611.9	773.6	894.6	(NA)	(NA)	(NA)

NA Not available. [1] Prior to 1997, reported as imported. Softs include commodities that are grown and not mined such as coffee, cocoa, lumber, cotton, and sugar. [2] Prior to 1997, reported as grains. [3] Incorporated into grains and oilseeds beginning 1997.

Source: Commodity Research Bureau (CRB), Chicago, IL, *CRB Commodity Index Report*, weekly (copyright). See also: <http://www.crbtrader.com>.

Table 748. Producer Price Indexes by Stage of Processing: 1990 to 2011

[1982 = 100, except as indicated. Minus sign (−) indicates decrease. For information on producer prices, see Bureau of Labor Statistics, <http://stats.bls.gov/opub/hom/homch14_itc.htm>. Also see Appendix III]

Year	Crude materials				Inter-mediate materials and supplies, compo-nents	Finished goods		Consumer foods		Finished consumer goods, excluding food
	Total	Food-stuffs and feed-stuffs	Fuel	Crude nonfood materials, except fuel		Con-sumer goods	Capital equip-ment	Crude	Pro-cessed	
1990	108.9	113.1	84.8	107.3	114.5	118.2	122.9	123.0	124.4	115.3
1995	102.7	105.8	72.1	105.8	124.9	125.6	136.7	118.8	129.8	124.0
1999	98.2	98.7	91.2	91.1	123.2	132.0	137.6	125.5	135.9	130.5
2000	120.6	100.2	136.9	118.0	129.2	138.2	138.8	123.5	138.3	138.4
2001	121.0	106.1	151.4	101.5	129.2	141.5	139.7	127.7	142.4	141.4
2002	108.1	99.5	117.3	101.0	127.8	139.4	139.1	128.5	141.0	138.8
2003	135.3	113.5	185.7	116.9	133.7	145.3	139.5	130.0	147.2	144.7
2004	159.0	127.0	211.4	149.2	142.6	151.7	141.4	138.2	153.9	150.9
2005	182.2	122.7	279.7	176.7	154.0	160.4	144.6	140.2	156.9	161.9
2006	184.8	119.3	241.5	210.0	164.0	166.0	146.9	151.3	157.1	169.2
2007	207.1	146.7	236.8	238.7	170.7	173.5	149.5	170.2	166.7	175.6
2008	251.8	163.4	298.3	308.5	188.3	186.3	153.8	175.5	178.6	189.1
2009	175.2	134.5	166.3	211.1	172.5	179.1	156.7	157.8	177.3	179.4
2010	212.2	152.4	188.0	280.8	183.4	189.1	157.3	172.6	183.3	190.4
2011	249.4	188.4	181.5	342.0	199.8	203.3	159.7	182.3	195.0	205.5
PERCENT CHANGE [1]										
1990	5.6	1.7	−0.6	12.0	2.2	5.4	3.5	2.8	4.9	5.9
1995	0.9	−0.7	−12.5	9.1	5.4	1.9	1.9	6.7	1.5	2.0
1999	1.4	−5.0	5.2	7.8	0.2	2.4	0.0	−1.3	0.8	3.2
2000	22.8	1.5	50.1	29.5	4.9	4.7	0.9	−1.6	1.8	6.1
2001	0.3	5.9	10.6	−14.0	0.4	2.4	0.6	3.4	3.0	2.2
2002	−10.7	−6.2	−22.5	−0.5	−1.5	−1.5	−0.4	0.6	−1.0	−1.8
2003	25.2	14.1	58.3	15.7	4.6	4.2	0.3	1.2	4.4	4.3
2004	17.5	11.9	13.8	27.6	6.7	4.4	1.4	6.3	4.6	4.3
2005	14.6	−3.4	32.3	18.4	8.0	5.7	2.3	1.4	1.9	7.3
2006	1.4	−2.8	−13.7	18.8	6.5	3.5	1.6	7.9	0.1	4.5
2007	12.1	23.0	−1.9	13.7	4.1	4.5	1.8	12.5	6.1	3.8
2008	21.6	11.4	26.0	29.2	10.3	7.4	2.9	3.1	7.1	7.7
2009	−30.4	−17.7	−44.3	−31.6	−8.4	−3.9	1.9	−10.1	−0.7	−5.1
2010	21.1	13.3	13.0	33.0	6.3	5.6	0.4	9.4	3.4	6.1
2011	17.5	23.6	−3.5	21.8	8.9	7.5	1.5	5.6	6.4	7.9

[1] Change from immediate prior year. 1990, change from 1989.

Source: U.S. Bureau of Labor Statistics, *Producer Price Indexes*, monthly and annual, <http://www.bls.gov/ppi/>. See also *Monthly Labor Review*.

Table 749. Producer Price Indexes by Stage of Processing and Commodity: 1990 to 2011

[1982=100, except as indicated. See Appendix III]

Stage of processing	1990	1995	2000	2005	2008	2009	2010	2011
Finished goods................................	**119.2**	**127.9**	**138.0**	**155.7**	**177.1**	**172.5**	**179.8**	**190.5**
Finished consumer goods.......................	**118.2**	**125.6**	**138.2**	**160.4**	**186.3**	**179.1**	**189.1**	**203.3**
Finished consumer foods........................	**124.4**	**129.0**	**137.2**	**155.7**	**178.3**	**175.5**	**182.4**	**193.9**
Fresh fruits and melons.................	118.1	85.8	91.4	102.8	122.9	110.4	123.8	117.7
Fresh and dry vegetables..............	118.1	144.4	126.7	142.6	172.3	162.2	178.5	195.1
Eggs for fresh use (Dec. 1991 = 100)......	(NA)	86.3	84.9	79.6	152.4	123.3	123.4	138.4
Bakery products........................	141.0	164.3	182.3	201.1	237.5	245.8	244.8	253.6
Milled rice.............................	102.5	113.1	101.2	120.1	251.9	205.8	183.6	200.2
Pasta products (June 1985 = 100).........	114.1	125.0	121.6	127.9	183.5	180.3	170.7	185.8
Beef and veal..........................	116.0	100.9	113.7	147.4	153.7	142.4	157.1	180.7
Pork...................................	119.8	101.5	113.4	131.9	130.7	115.7	142.6	160.4
Processed young chickens..............	111.0	113.5	110.4	136.2	143.2	147.7	149.0	143.5
Processed turkeys.....................	107.6	104.9	98.7	105.1	120.3	119.9	132.1	148.7
Finfish and shellfish...................	147.2	170.8	198.1	222.6	255.4	250.9	272.4	287.6
Dairy products.........................	117.2	119.7	133.7	154.5	182.7	157.1	174.0	195.9
Processed fruits and vegetables........	124.7	122.4	128.6	140.4	166.8	176.2	176.6	183.2
Soft drinks............................	122.3	133.1	144.1	159.1	174.9	181.8	183.9	186.9
Roasted coffee........................	113.0	146.5	133.5	151.1	179.0	179.2	190.2	223.9
Shortening and cooking oils...........	123.2	142.5	132.4	176.7	293.2	225.6	233.6	301.1
Finished consumer goods excluding foods.....	**115.3**	**124.0**	**138.4**	**161.9**	**189.1**	**179.4**	**190.4**	**205.5**
Alcoholic beverages...................	117.2	128.5	140.6	158.5	166.0	172.0	175.1	180.8
Apparel...............................	117.5	124.2	127.4	125.6	128.0	129.3	129.5	133.7
Women's/girls/infants' cut & sew apparel (Dec. 2003 = 100).................	(NA)	(NA)	(NA)	100.3	101.1	102.1	101.6	103.0
Men's and boy's cut and sew apparel Dec. 2003 = 100)..................	(NA)	(NA)	(NA)	98.7	99.7	101.2	101.5	106.6
Textile house furnishings...............	109.5	119.5	122.0	122.9	127.0	129.1	131.7	138.8
Footwear..............................	125.6	139.2	144.9	148.1	156.9	159.9	162.4	168.0
Residential electric power (Dec. 1990 = 100)......	(NA)	111.8	110.8	126.4	146.1	150.5	154.7	158.9
Residential gas (Dec. 1990 = 100).......	(NA)	104.4	135.5	216.8	250.6	205.1	201.7	199.1
Gasoline...............................	78.7	63.7	94.6	168.6	263.0	178.4	225.3	295.7
Fuel oil No. 2..........................	73.3	56.6	93.5	178.4	305.2	162.7	207.5	279.3
Soaps and synthetic detergents........	117.7	122.9	128.2	134.6	153.8	161.4	161.2	166.0
Cosmetics and other toilet preparations..........	121.6	129.0	137.4	143.0	147.9	148.1	149.9	152.1
Tires, tubes, and tread.................	96.8	100.2	93.0	108.1	128.0	131.0	138.1	154.0
Sanitary papers and health products....	135.3	144.4	146.7	154.6	171.5	179.7	181.8	184.1
Sale of books..........................	153.4	185.0	218.2	264.0	296.5	306.9	317.1	324.7
Household furniture....................	125.1	141.8	152.7	166.5	181.0	186.9	187.4	191.6
Floor coverings........................	119.0	123.7	129.6	146.4	160.6	167.5	169.3	176.1
Household appliances..................	110.8	112.4	107.3	103.3	107.2	111.1	110.5	111.8
Home electronic equipment............	82.7	78.9	71.8	62.6	56.7	53.6	52.9	52.4
Household glassware...................	132.5	153.2	166.0	174.7	190.7	198.1	(NA)	(NA)
Household flatware....................	122.1	138.3	142.6	147.7	194.7	193.0	(NA)	(NA)
Lawn and garden equipment, except tractors........	123.0	130.4	132.0	134.5	140.4	142.3	141.7	140.5
Passenger cars........................	118.3	134.1	132.8	131.8	128.9	130.9	129.0	129.9
Toys, games, and children's vehicles..............	118.1	124.3	121.9	127.0	134.3	143.1	140.7	143.9
Sporting and athletic goods............	112.6	122.0	126.1	124.6	129.8	132.2	133.9	133.0
Tobacco products.....................	221.4	231.3	397.2	457.8	508.8	539.3	570.5	604.9
Mobile homes.........................	117.5	145.6	161.3	200.8	218.7	222.3	228.5	236.4
Jewelry, platinum, and karat gold.......	122.8	127.8	127.2	138.6	164.7	169.7	187.8	219.7
Costume jewelry and novelties.........	125.3	135.1	141.6	153.5	159.6	158.7	158.8	161.6
Capital Equipment......................	**122.9**	**136.7**	**138.8**	**144.6**	**153.8**	**156.7**	**157.3**	**159.7**
Agricultural machinery and equipment...............	121.7	142.9	153.7	174.7	192.9	199.9	203.5	209.6
Construction machinery and equipment.............	121.6	136.7	148.6	168.3	185.3	191.0	191.4	197.4
Metal cutting machine tools............	129.8	148.0	161.9	155.1	170.3	173.8	174.6	179.3
Metal forming machine tools...........	128.7	145.7	161.8	178.9	192.5	198.5	200.4	202.4
Pumps, compressors, and equipment...	119.2	139.4	154.1	178.5	205.4	212.6	215.1	223.4
Electronic computers (Dec. 2004 = 100)............	(NA)	850.1	261.6	85.5	40.8	34.0	30.3	26.8
Textile machinery.....................	128.8	146.7	156.2	160.5	164.9	166.3	165.9	166.9
Paper industries machinery (June 1982 = 100)....	134.8	151.0	164.7	178.1	188.5	193.7	197.2	200.7
Printing trades machinery..............	124.9	133.6	142.1	144.3	152.7	157.1	155.4	156.5
Transformers and power regulators.....	120.9	128.9	135.8	150.3	216.2	210.6	223.1	229.8
Communication/related equip.(Dec. 1985 = 100)....	106.1	112.1	110.6	102.5	104.8	105.7	105.8	106.1
X-ray and electromedical equipment....	109.8	111.8	101.5	95.7	91.6	90.1	89.4	88.3
Mining machinery and equipment.......	121.0	135.6	146.1	175.9	205.8	217.3	221.5	233.7
Office and store machines and equipment...........	109.5	111.5	112.7	115.1	122.1	123.5	121.0	122.2
Commercial furniture..................	133.4	148.2	158.4	172.7	190.1	196.1	196.3	201.2
Light motor trucks.....................	130.0	159.0	157.6	148.4	146.0	151.8	153.3	154.6
Heavy motor trucks...................	120.3	144.1	148.0	162.4	182.2	190.3	195.7	200.0
Truck trailers..........................	110.8	131.7	139.4	157.1	177.0	177.7	181.5	190.0
Civilian aircraft (Dec. 1985 = 100)......	115.3	141.8	159.6	202.2	230.2	235.4	238.0	244.3
Ships (Dec. 1985 = 100)................	110.1	132.8	146.9	176.6	199.4	210.0	215.1	220.2
Railroad equipment...................	118.6	134.8	135.7	160.4	180.2	181.9	184.4	187.0
Intermediate materials, supplies, and components.................	**114.5**	**124.9**	**129.2**	**154.0**	**188.3**	**172.5**	**183.4**	**199.8**
Intermediate foods and feeds..................	**113.3**	**114.8**	**111.7**	**133.8**	**181.6**	**166.0**	**171.7**	**192.3**
Flour.................................	103.6	123.0	103.8	133.6	239.8	182.9	182.4	224.5
Refined sugar.........................	122.7	119.3	110.6	124.9	137.2	157.8	185.7	206.9
Soft drink beverage bases (Dec. 1985 = 100)......	126.2	148.3	167.1	180.4	210.3	223.5	223.3	227.0
Prepared animal feeds................	107.4	109.1	102.9	115.6	182.7	175.2	171.6	202.1
Intermediate materials less foods and feeds...	**114.5**	**125.5**	**130.1**	**155.1**	**188.7**	**173.0**	**184.4**	**200.4**
Synthetic fibers.......................	106.7	109.4	107.2	112.3	116.3	113.3	111.6	117.7
Processed yarns and threads...........	112.6	112.8	107.9	111.7	123.7	119.9	130.0	157.6
Leather...............................	177.5	191.4	182.2	219.6	234.3	221.1	233.0	261.8

See footnotes at end of table.

Table 749. Producer Price Indexes by Stage of Processing and Commodity: 1990 to 2011-Continued.

See headnote on page 501.

Stage of processing	1990	1995	2000	2005	2008	2009	2010	2011
Liquefied petroleum gas............................	77.4	65.1	127.1	244.7	375.9	224.7	301.8	374.1
Commercial electric power.........................	115.3	131.7	131.5	149.8	173.3	178.6	182.5	183.9
Industrial electric power............................	119.6	130.8	131.5	156.2	189.1	190.6	193.1	203.5
Commercial natural gas (Dec. 1990 = 100).........	(NA)	96.5	134.7	232.5	272.1	211.9	208.0	200.1
Industrial natural gas (Dec. 1990 = 100)............	(NA)	90.9	139.0	249.4	283.1	210.2	202.0	195.5
Natural gas to electric utilities (Dec. 1990 = 100)....	(NA)	87.7	120.7	204.0	203.4	164.0	174.8	166.1
Jet fuels..	76.0	55.0	88.5	169.6	300.1	169.3	225.5	307.3
No. 2 Diesel fuel...................................	74.1	57.0	93.3	189.1	324.9	180.6	232.9	316.2
Residual fuel.......................................	57.7	52.6	84.7	148.9	229.7	156.6	212.5	277.5
Industrial chemicals................................	113.2	128.4	129.1	188.5	274.6	234.1	269.2	324.7
Prepared paint.....................................	124.8	142.1	160.8	187.9	223.0	236.4	237.1	248.1
Fats and oils, inedible..............................	88.1	126.9	70.1	146.9	288.3	210.3	244.3	344.9
Mixed fertilizers....................................	103.3	111.1	112.4	138.9	249.2	192.8	177.2	197.3
Plastic resins and materials.........................	124.1	143.5	141.6	193.0	215.0	190.8	210.1	229.7
Synthetic rubber....................................	111.9	126.3	119.1	151.3	206.6	185.9	215.5	269.9
Plastic construction products.......................	117.2	133.8	135.8	158.8	185.6	186.2	190.9	199.0
Unsupported plastic film, sheet, and shapes.........	119.0	135.6	133.2	164.8	194.2	191.7	200.9	209.5
Plastic parts and components for manufacturing....	112.9	115.9	117.3	119.8	132.8	135.8	135.6	138.2
Softwood lumber...................................	123.8	178.5	178.6	203.6	156.3	141.4	160.8	160.5
Hardwood lumber..................................	131.0	167.0	185.9	196.6	184.5	171.2	187.3	185.8
Plywood...	114.2	165.3	157.6	186.8	174.7	163.7	176.7	171.3
Paper..	128.8	159.0	149.8	159.6	184.3	179.6	182.1	191.2
Paperboard..	135.7	183.1	176.7	175.5	217.9	207.2	224.9	230.5
Paper boxes and containers........................	129.9	163.8	172.6	183.7	208.3	211.9	219.4	225.6
Building paper and board...........................	112.2	144.9	138.8	184.9	163.9	156.5	168.4	163.6
Commercial printing (June 1982 = 100).............	128.0	144.5	155.2	161.6	169.2	167.8	168.2	170.0
Foundry and forge shop products....................	117.2	129.3	136.5	156.2	189.6	185.2	191.2	201.7
Primary nonferrous metals..........................	133.4	146.8	113.6	158.2	269.1	177.6	210.3	238.9
Nonferrous wire and cable..........................	142.6	151.5	143.7	169.4	249.2	222.4	258.1	282.3
Metal containers....................................	114.0	117.2	106.8	123.9	144.0	155.4	156.4	151.8
Hardware...	125.9	141.1	151.2	168.0	189.9	194.0	194.0	199.3
Plumbing fixtures and brass fittings.................	144.3	166.0	180.4	197.6	226.7	228.9	231.4	237.0
Heating equipment.................................	131.6	147.5	155.6	179.9	208.8	219.1	221.5	227.6
Fabricated ferrous wire products (June 1982 = 100)..	114.6	125.7	130.0	157.1	200.7	200.0	203.8	215.7
Mechanical power transmission equipment..........	125.3	146.9	163.9	189.5	219.7	231.0	232.0	240.9
Air conditioning and refrigeration equipment........	122.1	130.2	135.3	146.2	162.7	164.7	163.8	168.3
Ball and roller bearings.............................	130.6	152.0	168.8	187.1	211.9	222.8	227.1	235.2
Wiring devices.....................................	132.2	147.2	152.9	176.6	206.4	206.8	211.2	218.1
Motors, generators, motor generator sets...........	132.9	143.9	146.2	157.8	181.7	187.0	190.6	202.1
Switchgear and switchboard equipment.............	124.4	140.3	153.0	170.2	195.5	201.0	205.5	210.3
Electronic components and accessories.............	118.4	113.6	97.1	87.0	77.0	75.4	73.5	71.0
Internal combustion engines........................	120.2	135.6	143.8	147.7	157.2	162.3	161.7	164.5
Flat glass..	107.5	113.2	109.7	111.0	115.9	115.0	111.2	112.8
Cement..	103.7	128.1	150.1	176.4	209.7	206.8	193.5	187.8
Concrete products..................................	113.5	129.4	147.8	177.2	210.6	214.0	210.6	210.8
Asphalt felts and coatings..........................	97.1	100.0	104.1	130.8	187.2	220.6	222.7	233.5
Gypsum products..................................	105.2	154.5	201.4	229.6	213.2	213.8	206.6	201.9
Glass containers...................................	120.4	130.5	127.4	146.4	171.8	178.7	181.2	184.3
Motor vehicle parts.................................	111.2	116.0	113.6	113.1	119.7	120.7	121.8	123.9
Aircraft engines and engine parts (Dec. 1985 = 100)..	113.5	132.8	141.0	165.9	185.9	193.1	197.4	204.0
Photographic supplies..............................	127.6	126.8	125.2	120.1	125.5	127.8	124.4	130.4
Medical/surgical/personal aid devices...............	127.3	141.3	146.0	159.2	165.7	167.5	169.0	171.6
Crude materials for further processing........	**108.9**	**102.7**	**120.6**	**182.2**	**251.8**	**175.2**	**212.2**	**249.4**
Crude foodstuffs and feedstuffs.....................	113.1	105.8	100.2	122.7	163.4	134.5	152.4	188.4
Wheat..	87.6	118.6	80.3	102.7	235.1	149.3	157.2	216.2
Corn...	100.9	109.0	76.4	75.9	199.1	146.9	160.8	267.3
Slaughter cattle....................................	122.5	99.5	104.1	131.5	136.1	122.0	139.8	170.7
Slaughter hogs.....................................	94.1	70.2	72.7	82.7	78.1	68.9	92.6	110.6
Slaughter broilers/fryers............................	119.5	129.1	127.6	181.0	210.7	202.6	221.3	210.0
Slaughter turkeys..................................	116.9	120.3	120.7	131.1	165.9	146.7	173.0	200.6
Fluid milk..	100.8	93.6	92.0	113.5	137.2	95.9	121.9	150.6
Soybeans..	100.8	102.2	83.4	102.6	203.9	175.9	177.1	219.6
Crude nonfood materials............................	101.5	96.8	130.4	223.4	313.9	197.5	249.3	284.0
Raw cotton...	118.2	156.2	95.2	78.9	98.0	82.6	117.9	145.5
Coal...	97.5	95.0	87.9	116.8	161.7	182.5	189.5	207.1
Natural gas..	80.4	66.6	155.5	335.4	344.0	160.0	185.8	171.4
Crude petroleum...................................	71.0	51.1	85.2	150.1	275.7	161.7	218.6	275.5
Logs and timber....................................	142.8	220.4	196.4	197.4	216.7	187.8	213.4	228.2
Wastepaper..	138.9	371.1	282.5	230.9	372.5	237.0	421.5	482.5
Iron ore..	83.3	91.8	94.8	116.9	142.5	145.0	147.1	165.4
Iron and steel scrap................................	166.0	202.7	142.1	289.8	566.8	338.1	541.1	646.8
Nonferrous metal ores (Dec. 1983 = 100)...........	98.3	101.6	68.0	150.0	251.0	215.4	298.6	373.2
Copper base scrap.................................	181.3	193.5	123.7	258.6	494.3	375.4	548.2	638.2
Aluminum base scrap...............................	172.6	209.4	177.0	210.1	272.8	166.8	241.6	268.2
Construction sand, gravel, and crushed stone.......	125.4	142.3	163.1	195.8	247.7	259.1	262.2	266.5
Industrial sand.....................................	117.6	132.5	146.0	174.4	217.7	238.1	239.8	247.0

NA Not available.

Source: U.S. Bureau of Labor Statistics, *Producer Price Indexes*, monthly and annual. See also <http://www.bls.gov/ppi/>.

Table 750. Chain-Type Price Indexes for Personal Consumption Expenditures by Type of Expenditure: 1990 to 2010

[2005 = 100. For explanation of "chain-type," see text, Section 13. See also Table 689]

Type of Expenditure	1990	1995	2000	2007	2008	2009	2010
Personal consumption expenditures	**72.2**	**82.1**	**89.8**	**105.5**	**108.9**	**109.2**	**111.1**
Household consumption expenditures [1]	71.8	82.2	89.7	105.6	109.1	109.4	111.4
Food and beverages purchased for off-premises consumption	73.9	80.9	89.5	105.6	112.1	113.5	113.9
Food and nonalcoholic beverages purchased for off-premises consumption	74.1	80.6	89.2	105.9	112.8	113.9	114.3
Alcoholic beverages purchased for off-premises consumption	72.2	83.0	91.3	103.8	107.6	110.7	111.3
Food produced and consumed on farms	93.6	81.6	78.4	104.4	103.0	89.6	104.6
Clothing, footwear, and related services	113.9	112.6	107.4	99.0	98.6	99.6	99.0
Clothing	115.8	113.7	108.7	98.9	98.0	98.8	98.0
Garments	120.1	116.6	110.6	98.4	97.2	97.7	96.7
Women's and girls' clothing	125.4	119.4	109.7	99.5	97.1	97.6	96.7
Men's and boys' clothing	113.2	113.3	111.7	96.7	97.3	97.8	96.4
Children's and infants' clothing	113.9	111.4	111.7	97.7	97.4	98.0	97.8
Footwear [2]	104.2	106.9	100.8	99.9	101.4	103.6	104.5
Housing, utilities, and fuels	64.1	73.4	84.4	108.1	112.4	113.1	113.7
Housing	64.4	74.3	86.1	107.3	110.2	112.2	112.3
Rental of tenant-occupied nonfarm housing [3]	64.2	73.5	85.1	108.0	111.9	114.3	114.5
Imputed rental of owner-occupied nonfarm housing [4]	64.6	74.4	86.3	107.0	109.7	111.5	111.5
Household utilities and fuels	62.0	69.1	76.9	112.5	123.3	117.7	120.6
Water supply and sanitation	53.8	71.0	81.4	110.3	116.7	123.9	131.8
Electricity, gas, and other fuels	64.2	68.5	75.6	113.2	124.5	115.6	116.9
Electricity	78.0	86.0	85.2	116.7	124.2	128.0	128.2
Natural gas	45.2	47.7	62.0	102.6	115.8	90.4	88.7
Fuel oil and other fuels	45.8	40.4	60.6	123.5	168.4	114.1	133.9
Furnishings, household equipment, and routine household maintenance	95.3	100.7	103.0	100.4	101.1	101.8	99.1
Furniture, furnishings, and floor coverings [5]	101.1	107.8	107.7	97.6	95.9	95.4	91.1
Household textiles	133.1	132.2	120.2	91.1	87.8	84.2	79.6
Household appliances [6]	105.8	105.8	102.8	106.1	106.8	107.9	103.9
Glassware, tableware, and household utensils [7]	111.7	115.1	111.8	95.6	97.0	97.3	94.9
Health	58.5	75.8	85.0	106.6	109.3	112.3	115.2
Medical products, appliances, and equipment	62.5	75.0	85.5	105.2	107.4	110.5	113.8
Pharmaceutical and other medical products [8]	60.2	72.8	84.0	105.4	107.8	111.2	115.2
Pharmaceutical products	60.0	72.6	83.8	105.5	107.9	111.3	115.4
Other medical products	79.1	93.2	98.6	102.4	102.7	104.1	101.9
Therapeutic appliances and equipment	74.9	87.5	94.5	104.0	104.9	106.0	105.5
Outpatient services	62.8	79.6	89.1	105.6	108.0	110.5	112.9
Physician services	65.6	85.0	92.2	105.1	106.2	108.8	111.4
Dental services	48.4	63.9	79.8	110.7	116.3	119.8	123.1
Paramedical services	65.9	78.7	88.4	104.4	107.4	109.3	111.1
Hospital and nursing home services	54.0	72.8	81.3	108.0	111.4	114.8	118.0
Hospitals	54.6	74.9	81.3	108.0	111.2	114.6	118.0
Nursing homes	52.1	64.2	81.2	107.9	112.0	115.8	118.1
Transportation	72.2	80.8	88.6	108.7	115.9	105.2	113.8
Motor vehicles	82.7	100.7	103.2	98.6	95.8	95.5	100.8
New motor vehicles	87.5	101.9	103.9	98.3	96.8	97.8	99.9
Net purchases of used motor vehicles	73.0	98.4	102.0	99.2	93.8	91.7	101.9
Motor vehicle operation	62.6	66.3	76.9	115.6	128.9	110.8	121.8
Motor vehicle parts and accessories	94.2	93.9	92.4	107.6	113.2	117.6	119.9
Motor vehicle fuels, lubricants, and fluids	51.8	51.5	66.2	123.9	144.9	106.1	125.4
Public transportation	87.2	92.0	100.3	107.6	116.0	112.6	119.2
Ground transportation	64.4	72.6	81.9	106.3	111.3	116.1	121.0
Air transportation	100.9	102.6	110.4	108.7	119.9	111.7	119.7
Water transportation	113.1	131.5	126.0	99.4	97.0	88.0	89.1
Recreation	110.4	115.6	106.9	97.2	96.9	95.3	92.7
Video and audio equipment, computers, and related services	254.6	215.3	138.2	86.6	81.5	75.6	70.2
Video and audio equipment	210.6	184.9	141.9	78.8	70.9	61.4	53.3
Sports and recreational goods and related services	112.3	118.6	109.2	97.6	97.7	96.9	94.0
Sports and recreational vehicles	84.5	93.6	97.9	102.1	103.1	104.1	104.5
Other sporting and recreational goods	123.3	128.4	113.4	96.1	95.9	94.5	90.9
Magazines, newspapers, books, and stationery	71.6	87.5	95.7	102.0	103.9	106.9	107.2
Education	40.1	56.1	71.4	112.5	119.1	125.8	131.7
Higher education	36.8	55.7	69.9	113.4	120.4	127.7	134.3
Net foreign travel and expenditures abroad by U.S. residents							
Foreign travel by U.S. residents	63.2	75.1	78.9	111.4	120.9	112.2	118.8
Less: Expenditures in the United States by nonresidents	67.4	76.5	87.7	109.0	114.3	111.3	115.1

[1] Consists of household purchases of goods and services from business, government, nonprofit institutions, and the rest of the world. [2] Consists of shoes and other footwear, and of repair and hire of footwear. [3] Consists of space rent (see footnote 4) and rent for appliances, furnishings, and furniture. [4] Consists of rent for space and for heating and plumbing facilities, water heaters, lighting fixtures, kitchen cabinets, linoleum, storm windows and doors, window screens, and screen doors, but excludes rent for appliances and furniture and purchases of fuel and electricity. [5] Includes clocks, lamps, lighting fixtures, and other household decorative items; also includes repair of furniture, furnishings, and floor coverings. [6] Consists of major household appliances, small electric household appliances, and repair of household appliances. [7] Consists of dishes, flatware, and non-electric cookware and tableware. [8] Excludes drug preparations and related products dispensed by physicians, hospitals, and other medical services.

Source: U.S. Bureau of Economic Analysis, National Income and Product Accounts Table; Table 2.5.4 Price Indexes for Personal Consumption Expenditures by Function; <http://www.bea.gov/national/index.htm>.

Table 751. Chain-Type Price Indexes for Gross Domestic Product: 1990 to 2011

[2005 = 100. For explanation of "chain-type," see text, Section 13]

Component	1990	1995	2000	2007	2008	2009	2010	2011
Gross domestic product	**72.3**	**81.6**	**88.7**	**106.2**	**108.6**	**109.7**	**111.0**	**113.3**
Personal consumption expenditures	**72.2**	**82.1**	**89.8**	**105.5**	**108.9**	**109.2**	**111.1**	**113.8**
Durable goods	117.5	124.5	112.0	96.4	94.6	92.9	91.3	90.4
Nondurable goods	76.7	82.1	90.0	106.5	112.6	109.3	112.7	119.7
Services	63.8	75.4	85.8	107.0	110.6	112.4	114.5	116.5
Gross private domestic investment	**87.1**	**91.2**	**90.3**	**106.3**	**107.5**	**106.4**	**104.7**	**106.4**
Fixed investment	86.1	90.4	90.1	106.4	107.6	106.3	104.8	106.2
Nonresidential	101.3	102.8	96.8	105.6	107.7	107.1	105.4	106.7
Structures	53.5	60.6	72.3	119.8	125.7	122.5	121.1	126.6
Equipment and software	126.3	123.2	106.9	100.5	101.0	101.5	99.6	99.8
Residential	58.0	66.4	77.4	107.6	106.3	102.6	102.2	103.4
Net exports of goods and services:								
Exports	92.1	96.1	92.1	106.9	112.0	106.0	110.6	117.6
Goods	100.3	101.5	93.0	106.8	112.1	104.5	109.7	117.8
Services	74.4	83.9	89.9	107.1	111.6	109.1	112.7	117.0
Imports	93.6	95.6	90.0	107.8	119.2	106.6	113.0	121.8
Goods	99.2	99.0	91.2	107.8	120.3	105.4	112.6	122.4
Services	71.0	80.2	84.2	107.8	114.0	111.5	114.6	118.0
Government consumption expenditures and gross investment	**63.4**	**72.8**	**82.5**	**109.9**	**115.2**	**114.9**	**117.4**	**121.1**
Federal	63.5	73.7	82.5	107.8	111.2	111.0	113.7	116.9
National defense	63.9	73.2	81.8	108.2	112.2	111.4	114.0	117.6
Nondefense	62.6	74.8	83.9	106.7	109.2	110.2	112.9	115.4
State and local	63.5	72.3	82.5	111.1	117.7	117.2	119.7	123.7

Source: U.S. Bureau of Economic Analysis, National Income and Product Account Tables; Table 1.1.4: Price Indexes for Gross Domestic Product. See <http://www.bea.gov/iTable/index_nipa.cfm> (accessed May 2012).

Table 752. Import and Export Price Indexes by End-Use Category: 1990 to 2011

[As of June. Import indexes are weighted by the 2000 Tariff Schedule of the United States Annotated, a scheme for describing and reporting product composition and value of U.S. imports. Import prices are based on U.S. dollar prices paid by importer. Export indexes are weighted by 2000 export values according to the Schedule B classification system of the U.S. Census Bureau. Prices used in these indexes were collected from a sample of U.S. manufacturers of exports and are factory transaction prices, except as noted. Minus sign (–) indicates decrease]

Year	Index (2000 = 100)						Percent change [1]					
	Imports			Exports			Imports			Exports		
	Total	Petro-leum imports	Non–petro-leum imports	Total	Agri-cultural exports	Non–agri-cultural exports	Total	Petro-leum imports	Non–petro-leum imports	Total	Agri-cultural exports	Non–agri-cultural exports
1990	90.8	55.4	96.4	95.1	107.7	93.5	-0.8	-13.4	0.5	-0.1	-4.0	0.5
1991	93.4	63.2	98.3	96.1	104.3	95.3	2.9	14.1	2.0	1.1	-3.2	1.9
1992	94.8	66.0	99.5	96.5	104.0	95.8	1.5	4.4	1.2	0.4	-0.3	0.5
1993	95.0	60.4	100.5	96.9	100.3	96.7	0.2	-8.5	1.0	0.4	-3.6	0.9
1994	96.3	57.6	102.6	98.5	109.3	97.5	1.4	-4.6	2.1	1.7	9.0	0.8
1995	101.4	62.9	107.6	104.5	117.0	103.3	5.3	9.2	4.9	6.1	7.0	5.9
1996	100.7	66.4	106.2	105.4	140.8	101.7	-0.7	5.6	-1.3	0.9	20.3	-1.5
1997	98.8	62.5	104.3	103.2	120.5	101.5	-1.9	-5.9	-1.8	-2.1	-14.4	-0.2
1998	93.1	44.3	100.5	99.9	110.8	98.8	-5.8	-29.1	-3.6	-3.2	-8.0	-2.7
1999	92.9	54.5	98.8	98.2	101.1	97.9	-0.2	23.0	-1.7	-1.7	-8.8	-0.9
2000	100.2	101.9	99.9	100.1	100.5	100.0	7.9	87.0	1.1	1.9	-0.6	2.1
2001	97.6	89.4	98.9	99.4	100.9	99.3	-2.6	-12.3	-1.0	-0.7	0.4	-0.7
2002	94.1	85.3	96.2	98.0	100.7	97.8	-3.6	-4.6	-2.7	-1.4	-0.2	-1.5
2003	96.2	96.4	97.3	99.5	110.0	98.7	2.2	13.0	1.1	1.5	9.2	0.9
2004	101.7	129.7	99.7	103.4	127.4	101.5	5.7	34.5	2.5	3.9	15.8	2.8
2005	109.2	181.5	102.0	106.7	123.9	105.4	7.4	39.9	2.3	3.2	-2.7	3.8
2006	117.3	242.6	104.2	111.2	124.1	110.3	7.4	33.7	2.2	4.2	0.2	4.6
2007	120.0	245.6	107.1	116.0	146.7	113.8	2.3	1.2	2.8	4.3	18.2	3.2
2008	145.5	450.3	114.9	126.1	195.2	121.2	21.3	83.3	7.3	8.7	33.1	6.5
2009	120.0	241.5	107.4	117.8	169.7	114.1	-17.5	-46.4	-6.5	-6.6	-13.1	-5.9
2010	125.2	267.4	110.7	122.2	165.3	119.1	4.3	10.7	-6.5	3.7	-2.6	4.4
2011	142.2	400.6	116.1	134.3	216.8	128.4	13.6	49.8	4.9	9.9	31.2	7.8

[1] Percent change from immediate prior year.

Source: U.S. Bureau of Labor Statistics, *U.S. Import and Export Price Indexes*, monthly. See also <http://www.bls.gov/mxp/>.

Table 753. Export Price Indexes—Selected Commodities: 2000 to 2011

[2000 = 100. As of June. Indexes are weighted by 2000 export values according to the Schedule B classification system of the U.S. Census Bureau. Prices used in these indexes were collected from a sample of U.S. manufacturers of exports and are factory transaction prices, except as noted]

Commodity	2000 [1]	2005	2006	2007	2008	2009	2010	2011
All commodities	**100.1**	**106.7**	**111.2**	**116.0**	**126.1**	**117.8**	**122.2**	**134.5**
Animal products	102.2	130.9	125.1	153.2	174.5	158.8	172.2	192.9
Fish	99.1	114.2	122.8	124.3	149.1	145.1	152.3	184.6
Vegetable products	100.0	130.3	131.0	159.3	239.3	205.5	177.5	255.5
Fruit and nuts	94.8	126.5	114.5	117.5	123.0	102.3	131.0	128.4
Cereals	100.0	118.1	136.9	179.2	293.6	222.1	171.4	319.2
Wheat	99.4	130.0	154.3	180.4	276.7	228.5	151.6	290.0
Corn (maize)	101.0	111.8	127.1	189.8	286.4	212.1	174.3	348.0
Oilseeds	102.8	136.2	121.5	157.4	259.3	238.1	196.2	268.4
Beverages and tobacco	100.0	110.3	112.5	120.5	136.3	142.1	139.3	152.0
Mineral products	97.8	182.3	238.4	243.4	360.5	203.9	247.9	335.2
Fuels	97.4	172.8	219.6	230.5	361.9	198.3	239.2	330.9
Chemicals and related products	100.3	122.8	130.1	130.1	145.4	135.7	144.5	153.1
Plastics and rubber products	101.5	118.4	128.7	131.3	142.2	129.8	136.8	150.7
Hides, skins, and leather products	95.7	113.0	116.8	122.6	117.3	79.1	121.2	139.6
Wood products	100.0	104.3	113.5	113.5	112.3	102.5	111.1	110.0
Woodpulp and paper products	101.6	101.9	110.6	110.6	117.5	107.3	117.6	128.1
Textiles	100.2	100.8	101.9	101.9	108.0	101.9	115.7	149.2
Stone and glass products	100.7	103.5	110.1	110.1	111.1	115.9	115.9	115.8
Gems and precious metals	98.1	106.5	162.7	162.7	183.1	171.3	211.0	276.9
Base metals	100.5	131.8	169.3	169.3	181.2	143.5	160.4	187.4
Iron and steel	101.7	164.0	173.7	209.2	243.3	150.0	194.3	244.9
Articles of iron and steel	100.2	124.8	148.5	148.5	156.6	163.6	158.1	170.9
Copper	98.7	143.1	243.9	243.9	261.2	172.0	217.0	278.0
Aluminum	98.4	113.2	149.5	149.5	150.6	100.5	117.8	139.3
Machinery	99.9	94.9	93.8	94.3	95.3	95.3	95.5	96.2
Nonelectrical machinery	100.0	100.5	101.5	102.7	103.7	105.1	106.8	108.6
Electrical machinery	99.8	88.6	85.3	85.2	86.2	84.7	83.2	82.8
Transportation equipment	100.0	108.8	111.5	113.8	116.6	120.5	121.4	123.4
Motor vehicles	100.0	103.2	104.6	105.6	106.7	107.7	108.5	109.6
Instruments	100.0	101.3	102.4	103.3	107.1	107.8	106.2	105.6
Miscellaneous manufactured articles	100.4	100.6	101.1	104.7	108.6	106.9	108.1	109.7

[1] June 2000 may not equal 100 because indexes were reweighted to an "average" trade value in 2000.

Source: U.S. Bureau of Labor Statistics, *U.S. Import and Export Price Indexes*, monthly. See also <http://www.bls.gov/mxp/>.

Table 754. Import Price Indexes—Selected Commodities: 2000 to 2011

[2000 = 100. As of June. Indexes are weighted by the 2000 Tariff Schedule of the United States Annotated, a scheme for describing and reporting product composition and value of U.S. imports. Import prices are based on U.S. dollar prices paid by importer]

Commodity	2000 [1]	2004	2005	2006	2007	2008	2009	2010	2011
All commodities	**100.2**	**101.7**	**109.2**	**117.1**	**120.0**	**145.5**	**120.0**	**125.2**	**142.2**
Animal products	99.9	107.8	112.7	118.2	127.4	141.6	129.0	143.0	167.9
Meat	100.5	130.8	138.7	137.2	146.8	165.4	150.8	183.2	211.7
Fish	100.2	83.4	88.3	96.6	100.2	106.3	99.8	107.1	126.9
Vegetable products	97.1	103.0	116.9	108.6	129.3	159.5	161.2	169.5	206.9
Vegetables	93.9	113.8	136.8	143.6	175.3	202.6	293.1	326.2	291.9
Fruit and nuts	96.9	96.3	89.7	81.7	90.9	112.8	103.8	106.8	124.4
Beverages and tobacco	100.0	108.9	114.0	119.8	124.3	140.0	134.4	141.2	156.5
Mineral products	101.3	130.9	178.1	229.2	234.0	418.5	224.5	248.5	362.1
Fuels	101.3	130.0	177.5	229.0	233.7	421.6	221.3	244.9	358.1
Chemicals and related products	99.8	103.6	111.3	114.5	123.8	139.2	131.3	139.3	147.9
Organic chemicals	100.6	100.1	109.6	118.0	120.5	132.9	124.6	133.8	137.3
Pharmaceutical products	99.8	106.9	111.0	106.5	107.6	114.1	113.3	117.9	112.4
Plastics and rubber products	99.9	105.9	113.5	120.1	121.7	133.2	129.7	136.7	151.6
Hides, skins, and leather products	100.2	101.5	104.0	105.2	107.0	112.4	113.7	114.5	120.9
Wood products	100.5	129.5	124.2	120.7	113.5	118.5	110.2	134.3	128.9
Woodpulp and paper products	100.0	98.2	102.3	107.9	108.0	115.3	108.1	112.5	115.7
Textiles	99.7	100.3	100.4	100.7	102.1	103.5	102.6	103.1	113.0
Footwear and clothing accessories	99.6	99.8	99.9	100.6	101.5	105.8	108.0	106.9	(NA)
Footwear	99.6	100.2	100.3	101.0	101.3	104.7	107.2	106.1	111.8
Stone and glass products	99.5	103.8	105.4	108.6	110.4	115.4	125.3	123.8	129.1
Gems and precious metals	99.3	93.5	98.3	125.1	132.8	157.1	140.6	161.5	197.6
Gold	98.3	137.1	150.7	241.2	238.2	317.4	331.7	430.5	539.4
Platinum	(NA)	116.2	125.7	230.1	257.2	368.6	196.6	292.6	336.5
Base metals	101.5	118.9	132.1	157.9	176.7	206.9	151.1	180.2	200.3
Iron and steel	104.1	155.1	170.6	173.8	206.2	308.8	174.8	238.8	262.4
Articles of iron and steel	100.6	109.0	122.7	125.1	129.0	159.7	139.6	149.9	160.7
Copper	97.2	119.0	142.7	291.6	307.5	326.2	234.4	313.8	392.5
Aluminum	97.9	110.5	113.2	150.0	146.8	155.8	105.7	132.8	156.9
Machinery	100.2	90.7	89.7	88.1	87.8	88.9	86.9	86.5	85.9
Nonelectrical machinery	99.8	90.9	90.1	88.3	88.2	89.3	87.9	87.9	88.6
Electrical machinery	100.5	90.5	89.4	87.9	87.5	88.5	85.8	85.2	82.8
Transportation equipment	100.0	102.8	104.4	104.9	105.9	109.5	109.7	109.7	112.6
Motor vehicles	100.1	102.3	103.8	104.3	105.1	108.7	108.6	108.8	111.7
Instruments	99.8	99.1	100.1	99.6	99.4	101.5	102.0	100.8	102.7
Miscellaneous manufactured articles	99.7	97.4	99.4	99.5	101.1	106.4	107.7	106.5	109.2
Furniture	99.5	99.7	103.4	103.3	104.6	111.9	112.2	109.4	112.2

NA Not available. [1] June 2000 may not equal 100 because indexes were reweighted to an "average" trade value in 2000.

Source: U.S. Bureau of Labor Statistics, *U.S. Import and Export Price Indexes*, monthly. See also <http://stats.bls.gov/mxp/>.

Section 15
Business Enterprise

This section relates to the place and behavior of the business firm and to business initiative in the American economy. It includes data on the number, type, and size of businesses; financial data of domestic and multinational U.S. corporations; business investments, expenditures, and profits; and sales and inventories.

The principal sources of these data are the *Survey of Current Business*, published by the Bureau of Economic Analysis (BEA); the Web site of the Board of Governors of the Federal Reserve System at <http://www.federalreserve.gov/econresdata/default. htm>; the annual *Statistics of Income (SOI)* reports of the Internal Revenue Service (IRS); and the U.S. Census Bureau's Economic Census, *County Business Patterns, Quarterly Financial Report for Manufacturing, Mining, and Trade Corporations (QFR), Survey of Business Owners*, and *Annual Capital Expenditures Survey*. See also BEA Interactive Tables <http://www.bea.gov/ interactive.htm>.

Business firms—A firm is generally defined as a business organization under a single management and may include one or more establishments. The terms firm, business, company, and enterprise are used interchangeably throughout this section. A firm doing business in more than one industry is classified by industry according to the major activity of the firm as a whole.

The IRS concept of a business firm relates primarily to the legal entity used for tax reporting purposes. A sole proprietorship is an unincorporated business owned by one person and may include large enterprises with many employees and hired managers and part-time operators. A partnership is an unincorporated business owned by two or more persons, each of whom has a financial interest in the business. A corporation is a business that is legally incorporated under state laws. While many corporations file consolidated tax returns, most corporate tax returns represent individual corporations, some of which are affiliated through common ownership or control with other corporations filing separate returns.

Economic census—The economic census is the major source of facts about the structure and functioning of the nation's economy. It provides essential information for government, business, industry, and the general public. It furnishes an important part of the framework for such composite measures as the gross domestic product estimates, input/output measures, production and price indexes, and other statistical series that measure short–term changes in economic conditions. The Census Bureau takes the economic census every 5 years, covering years ending in "2" and "7."

The economic census is collected on an establishment basis. A company operating at more than one location is required to file a separate report for each store, factory, shop, or other location. Each establishment is assigned a separate industry classification based on its primary activity and not that of its parent company. Establishments responding to the establishment survey are classified into industries on the basis of their principal product or activity (determined by

annual sales volume). The statistics issued by industry in the 2007 Economic Census are classified primarily on the 2007 North American Industry Classification System (NAICS), and, to a lesser extent, on the 2002 NAICS used in the previous census (see below).

More detailed information about the scope, coverage, methodology, classification system, data items, and publications for each of the economic censuses and related surveys is published in the 2007 *Economic Census User Guide* at <http://www.census.gov/econ/ census07/www/user_guide.html>.

Data from the 2007 Economic Census are released through the Census Bureau's American FactFinder® service on the Census Bureau Web site. For more information, see <http://www.census.gov/econ/ census07/>.

Survey of Business Owners—The Survey of Business Owners (SBO) provides statistics that describe the composition of U.S. businesses by gender, ethnicity, race and veteran status. Data from SBO are published in a series of releases: *American Indian- and Alaska Native-Owned Firms, Asian-Owned Firms, Black-Owned Firms, Hispanic-Owned Firms, Native Hawaiian- and Other Pacific Islander-Owned Firms, Women-Owned Firms, Veteran-Owned Firms, Characteristics of Business Owners* and *Company Summary*. Data are presented by industry classifications, geographic area, and size of firm (employment and receipts). Each owner had the option of selecting more than one race and therefore is included in each race selected. For more information, see <http://www.census.gov/econ/ sbo/>.

North American Industry Classification System (NAICS)—NAICS is the standard used by federal statistical agencies in classifying business establishments for the purpose of collecting, analyzing, and publishing statistical data related to the U.S. business economy. NAICS was developed under the auspices of the Office of Management and Budget (OMB), and adopted in 1997 to replace the Standard Industrial Classification (SIC) system. The official *2007 U.S. NAICS Manual* includes definitions for each industry, background information, tables showing changes between 2002 and 2007, and a comprehensive index. For more information, see <http://www.census.gov/eos/www/naics/>.

Changes between 2002 NAICS and 2007 NAICS are relatively minor, but do affect totals for sectors 52 (finance and insurance), 53 (real estate, rental, and leasing), 54 (professional, scientific, and technical services), and 56 (admin., support, waste mgt., and remediation services). Nearly all industries are comparable from 2002 to 2007 NAICS classifications. Several industries in the Information sector have been consolidated.

Quarterly Financial Report—The Quarterly Financial Report (QFR) program publishes quarterly aggregate statistics on the financial conditions of U.S. corporations. The QFR requests companies to report estimates from their statements of income and retained earnings, and balance sheets. The statistical data are classified and aggregated by type of industry and asset size. The QFR sample includes manufacturing companies with assets of $250,000 and above, and mining, wholesale, retail, and selected service companies with assets of $50 million and above. The data are available quarterly in the *Quarterly Financial Report for Manufacturing, Mining, and Trade Corporations* at <http://www.census.gov/econ/qfr/index.html>.

Multinational companies—BEA collects financial and operating data on U.S. multinational companies. These data provide a picture of the overall activities of foreign affiliates and U.S. parent companies, using a variety of indicators of their financial structure and operations. The data on foreign affiliates cover the entire operations of the affiliate, irrespective of the percentage of U.S. ownership. These data cover items such as sales, value added, employment and compensation of employees, capital expenditures, exports and imports, and research and development expenditures. Separate tabulations are available for all affiliates and for affiliates that are majority-owned by their U.S. parent(s). More information is available at <http://www.bea.gov/international/index.htm#omc>.

Statistical reliability—For a discussion of statistical collection, estimation, and sampling procedures and measures of reliability applicable to data from the Census Bureau and the Internal Revenue Service, see Appendix III.

Table 755. Number of Tax Returns, Receipts, and Net Income by Type of Business: 1990 to 2009

[14,783 represents 14,783,000. Covers active enterprises only. Figures are estimates based on sample of unaudited tax returns; see Appendix III]

Item	Number of returns (1,000) Nonfarm proprietorships	Partnerships	Corporations	Business receipts [1] (bil. dol.) Nonfarm proprietorships	Partnerships	Corporations	Net income (less loss) [2] (bil. dol.) Nonfarm proprietorships	Partnerships	Corporations
1990	14,783	1,554	3,717	731	541	10,914	141	17	371
1991	15,181	1,515	3,803	713	539	10,963	142	21	345
1992	15,495	1,485	3,869	737	571	11,272	154	43	402
1993	15,848	1,468	3,965	757	627	11,814	156	67	498
1994	16,154	1,494	4,342	791	732	12,858	167	82	577
1995	16,424	1,581	4,474	807	854	13,969	169	107	714
1996	16,955	1,654	4,631	843	1,042	14,890	177	145	806
1997	17,176	1,759	4,710	870	1,297	15,890	187	168	915
1998	17,409	1,855	4,849	918	1,534	16,543	202	187	838
1999	17,576	1,937	4,936	969	1,829	18,009	208	228	929
2000	17,905	2,058	5,045	1,021	2,316	19,593	215	269	928
2001	18,338	2,132	5,136	1,017	2,569	19,308	217	276	604
2002	18,926	2,242	5,267	1,030	2,669	18,849	221	271	564
2003	19,710	2,375	5,401	1,050	2,818	19,755	230	301	780
2004	20,591	2,547	5,558	1,140	3,142	21,717	248	385	1,112
2005	21,468	2,764	5,671	1,223	3,719	24,060	270	546	1,949
2006	22,075	2,947	5,841	1,278	4,131	26,070	278	667	1,933
2007	23,122	3,098	5,869	1,324	4,541	27,335	281	683	1,837
2008	22,614	3,146	5,847	1,317	4,963	27,266	265	458	984
2009	22,660	3,169	5,825	1,178	4,814	24,773	245	410	919

[1] Excludes investment income except for partnerships and corporations in finance, insurance, and real estate before 1998. Beginning 1998, finance and insurance, real estate, and management of companies included investment income for partnerships and corporations. Excludes investment income for S corporations; for definition, see footnote 1, Table 764. [2] Net income (less loss) is defined differently by form of organization, basically as follows: (a) Proprietorships: Total taxable receipts less total business deductions, including cost of sales and operations, depletion, and certain capital expensing, excluding charitable contributions and owners' salaries; (b) Partnerships: Total taxable receipts (including investment income except capital gains) less deductions, including cost of sales and operations and certain payments to partners, excluding charitable contributions, oil and gas depletion, and certain capital expensing; (c) Corporations: Total taxable receipts (including investment income, capital gains, and income from foreign subsidiaries deemed received for tax purposes, except for S corporations) less business deductions, including cost of sales and operations, depletion, certain capital expensing, and officers' compensation excluding S corporation charitable contributions and investment expenses; net income is before income tax.

Source: U.S. Internal Revenue Service, *Statistics of Income*, various publications. See also <http://www.irs.ustreas.gov/taxstats/>.

Table 756. Number of Tax Returns and Business Receipts by Size of Receipts: 2000 to 2009

[5,045 represents 5,045,000. Covers active enterprises only. Figures are estimates based on sample of unaudited tax returns; see Appendix III. Minus sign (–) indicates loss]

Size-class of receipts	Returns (1,000) 2000	2006 [3]	2007 [3]	2008 [3]	2009	Business receipts [1] (bil. dol.) 2000	2006 [3]	2007 [3]	2008 [3]	2009
Corporations	**5,045**	**5,841**	**5,869**	**5,847**	**5,825**	**19,593**	**26,070**	**27,335**	**27,266**	**23,614**
Under $25,000 [2]	1,220	1,363	1,391	1,444	1,501	4	3	-2	-17	-3
$25,000 to $49,999	302	341	356	368	399	10	13	13	14	15
$50,000 to $99,999	477	554	570	556	576	35	41	42	41	42
$100,000 to $499,999	1,515	1,780	1,766	1,733	1,714	397	443	445	432	423
$500,000 to $999,999	582	668	657	663	641	407	473	465	453	453
$1,000,000 or more	946	1,135	1,128	1,084	994	18,738	25,097	26,372	26,324	22,684
Partnerships	**2,058**	**2,947**	**3,098**	**3,146**	**3,169**	**2,316**	**4,131**	**4,541**	**4,963**	**3,169**
Under $25,000 [2]	1,105	1,568	1,650	1,705	1,746	5	6	6	6	1,746
$25,000 to $49,999	183	240	233	230	241	7	9	8	8	241
$50,000 to $99,999	187	245	275	266	279	13	18	20	19	279
$100,000 to $499,999	353	498	530	537	511	82	118	125	125	511
$500,000 to $999,999	92	149	149	147	148	66	106	107	104	148
$1,000,000 or more	137	248	261	260	244	2,143	3,875	4,275	4,701	244
Nonfarm proprietorships	**17,905**	**22,075**	**23,122**	**22,614**	**22,660**	**1,021**	**1,278**	**1,324**	**1,317**	**(NA)**
Under $25,000 [2]	11,997	14,867	15,752	15,532	15,951	82	104	111	109	(NA)
$25,000 to $49,999	2,247	2,721	2,796	2,729	2,722	80	96	99	97	(NA)
$50,000 to $99,999	1,645	1,983	2,027	1,936	1,825	117	140	144	136	(NA)
$100,000 to $499,999	1,733	2,139	2,173	2,051	1,834	355	437	440	418	(NA)
$500,000 to $999,999	190	236	242	229	211	126	161	165	156	(NA)
$1,000,000 or more	92	128	132	137	116	261	340	364	401	(NA)

NA Not available. [1] Finance and insurance, real estate, and management of companies included investment income for partnerships and corporations. [2] Includes firms with no receipts. [3] Data for 2006 to 2008 are under review.

Source: U.S. Internal Revenue Service, *Statistics of Income Bulletin* and Corporation Income Tax Returns, <http://www.irs.gov/taxstats/index.html>; and unpublished data.

Table 757. Number of Tax Returns, Receipts, and Net Income by Type of Business and Industry: 2009

[22,660 represents 22,660,000. Covers active enterprises only. Figures are estimates based on sample of unaudited tax returns; see Appendix III. Based on the North American Industry Classification System (NAICS), 2007; see text, this section. Minus sign (–) indicates net loss]

Industry	2007 NAICS code	Number of returns (1,000)			Business receipts [1] (bil. dol.)			Net income (less loss) [2] (bil. dol.)		
		Non-farm propri-etor-ships	Part-ner-ships	Corpo-rations	Non-farm propri-etor-ships	Part-ner-ships	Corpo-rations	Non-farm propri-etor-ships	Part-ner-ships	Corpo-rations
Total	(X)	22,660	3,169	5,825	1,178	3,562	21,585	245	410	919
Agriculture, forestry, fishing, and hunting [3]	11	282	130	139	16	21	141	(Z)	(Z)	1
Mining	21	124	32	38	10	100	315	1	26	9
Utilities	22	9	6	6	(Z)	119	571	(Z)	-3	-4
Construction	23	2,696	181	742	173	213	1,157	27	-7	16
Special trade contractors	238	2,151	69	458	121	60	502	22	4	18
Manufacturing	31–33	335	45	260	24	748	5,957	2	33	301
Wholesale and retail trade [4]	(X)	2,608	231	973	223	871	6,556	12	18	143
Wholesale trade	42	335	55	376	44	529	3,361	3	13	96
Retail trade [5]	44–45	2,272	177	597	179	341	3,195	8	4	74
Motor vehicle and parts dealers	441	146	19	85	34	93	595	1	(Z)	4
Food and beverage stores	445	99	22	79	28	77	485	1	(Z)	9
Gasoline stations	447	21	11	40	23	61	253	(Z)	(Z)	2
Transportation and warehousing	48–49	1,077	51	196	71	118	656	9	2	6
Information [5]	51	331	43	117	10	244	924	2	33	47
Broadcasting (except Internet)	515	84	3	7	35	89	1	1	2	1
Telecommunications	517	(6)	5	17	161	456	(6)	(6)	30	17
Finance and insurance	52	659	313	240	154	2,048	10	10	207	330
Real estate and rental and leasing	53	1,246	1,524	647	119	110	13	13	-12	13
Professional, scientific, and technical services [5]	54	258	189	865	361	1,027	67	67	79	40
Legal services	5411	336	24	12	135	92	17	17	48	10
Accounting, tax preparation, bookkeeping, and payroll services	5412	379	19	81	59	98	5	5	13	5
Management, scientific, and technical consulting services	5416	1,011	48	234	61	185	24	24	9	10
Management of companies and enterprises	55	(NA)	17	48	19	215	(NA)	(NA)	13	-46
Administrative and support and waste management and remediation services	56	2,415	75	274	67	430	18	18	3	12
Educational services	61	685	11	55	4	56	3	3	(Z)	6
Health care and social assistance	62	2,081	70	429	195	642	48	48	27	37
Arts, entertainment, and recreation	71	1,345	58	122	47	87	7	7	-3	2
Accommodation and food services	72	423	113	298	139	413	1	1	-8	7
Accommodation	721	48	29	34	57	78	(Z)	(Z)	-10	-6
Food services and drinking places	722	374	85	264	83	335	2	2	1	14
Other services [5]	81	2,670	74	375	22	183	21	21	(Z)	5
Auto repair and maintenance	8111	356	35	108	10	64	3	3	(Z)	2
Personal and laundry services	812	1,654	38	160	9	73	14	14	(Z)	2
Religious, grantmaking, civic, professional, and similar organizations	813	253	(Z)	47	(Z)	10	2	2	(Z)	(Z)
Unclassified	(X)	483	6	(Z)	(Z)	(Z)	2	2	(Z)	(Z)

NA Not available. X Not applicable. Z Less than $500 million. [1] Includes investment income for partnerships and corporations in finance and insurance, real estate, and management of companies' industries. Excludes investment income for S corporations; for definition, see footnote 1, Table 764. [2] See footnote 2, Table 755. [3] For corporations, represents agricultural services only. [4] For corporations, includes trade business not identified as wholesale or retail. [5] Includes other industries, not shown separately. [6] Broadcasting includes telecommunications.

Source: U.S. Internal Revenue Service, *Statistics of Income*, various publications, http://www.irs.gov/taxstats/index.html, accessed June 2012.

Table 758. Nonfarm Sole Proprietorships—Selected Income and Deduction Items: 1990 to 2009

[In billions of dollars (731 represents $731,000,000,000), except as indicated. All figures are estimates based on samples. Tax law changes have affected the comparability of the data over time; see Statistics of Income reports for a description. See Appendix III]

Item	1990	1995	2000	2004	2005	2006	2007	2008	2009
Number of returns (1,000)	14,783	16,424	17,905	20,591	21,468	22,075	23,122	22,614	22,626
Returns with net income (1,000)	11,222	12,213	13,308	15,053	15,750	16,207	16,929	16,434	16,528
Business receipts	731	807	1,021	1,140	1,223	1,278	1,324	1,317	1,178
Income from sales and operations	719	797	1,008	1,122	1,205	1,259	1,304	1,296	1,159
Business deductions [1]	589	638	806	892	953	1,001	1,044	1,054	935
Cost of goods sold/operations [1]	291	307	387	371	397	410	423	435	366
Purchases	210	219	269	239	253	260	264	281	239
Labor costs	23	24	29	32	32	32	35	31	28
Materials and supplies	30	34	43	53	56	60	62	57	45
Advertising	(NA)	(NA)	10	13	14	15	16	15	14
Car and truck expenses	22	33	46	59	71	75	82	85	75
Commissions	9	10	12	13	15	16	15	13	12
Contract labor	(NA)	(NA)	(NA)	25	28	35	37	35	32
Depreciation	24	27	32	43	39	39	40	41	1
Insurance	13	13	14	19	19	19	19	18	17
Interest paid [2]	13	10	12	11	12	14	15	15	13
Office expenses	(NA)	(NA)	10	12	13	13	13	13	12
Rent paid [3]	23	28	33	37	39	41	43	44	41
Repairs	9	10	12	15	15	16	16	15	14
Salaries and wages (net)	47	54	63	71	75	77	79	79	75
Supplies	(NA)	(NA)	22	27	29	32	32	32	30
Taxes paid	10	13	14	16	17	18	18	18	17
Utilities	14	17	19	21	23	24	25	25	24
Net income (less loss) [4]	141	169	215	248	270	278	281	265	245
Net income [4]	162	192	245	291	315	327	335	325	309
Constant (2000) Dollars [5]									
Business receipts	896	877	1,021	1,045	1,085	1,097	1,105	1,076	1,075
Business deductions	722	693	806	818	846	859	871	861	853
Net income (less loss)	173	184	215	227	239	239	234	216	223
Net income	198	208	245	266	279	280	280	266	282

NA Not available. [1] Includes other amounts not shown separately. [2] Interest paid includes "mortgage interest" and "other interest paid on business indebtedness." [3] Rent paid includes "Rent on machinery and equipment" and "Rent on other business property." [4] After adjustment for the passive loss carryover from prior years. Therefore, "business receipts" minus "total deductions" do not equal "net income." [5] Based on the overall implicit price deflator for gross domestic product. Data for 2009 are in 2005 constant dollars.

Source: U.S. Internal Revenue Service, *Statistics of Income Bulletin*, <http://www.irs.gov/taxstats/index.html>.

Table 759. Partnerships—Selected Income and Balance Sheet Items: 1990 to 2009

[In billions of dollars (1,735 represents $1,735,000,000,000), except as indicated. Covers active partnerships only. All figures are estimates based on samples. See Appendix III]

Item	1990	1995	2000	2004	2005	2006	2007	2008	2009
Number of returns (1,000)	1,554	1,581	2,058	2,547	2,764	2,947	3,098	3,146	3,169
Returns with net income (1,000)	854	955	1,261	1,441	1,580	1,623	1,659	1,609	1,608
Number of partners (1,000)	17,095	15,606	13,660	15,557	16,212	16,728	18,516	19,300	21,142
Assets [1, 2]	1,735	2,719	6,694	11,608	13,734	17,146	20,386	19,260	18,798
Depreciable assets (net)	681	767	1,487	1,988	2,176	2,490	2,865	3,254	4,555
Inventories, end of year	57	88	150	276	315	446	339	431	277
Land	215	221	359	509	607	731	820	885	892
Liabilities [1, 2]	1,415	1,886	3,696	6,248	7,483	9,350	10,440	10,167	18,798
Accounts payable	67	91	230	336	400	505	430	513	444
Short-term debt [3]	88	124	252	296	373	456	565	582	432
Long-term debt [4]	498	544	1,132	1,546	1,772	2,227	2,556	2,767	2,737
Nonrecourse loans	470	466	639	854	914	1,103	1,210	1,283	1,282
Partners' capital accounts [2]	320	832	2,999	5,360	6,251	7,796	9,946	9,092	9,713
Receipts [1]	566	890	2,405	3,260	3,863	4,301	4,727	5,169	3,740
Business receipts [5]	483	854	2,316	3,142	3,719	4,131	4,541	4,963	3,562
Interest received	21	31	82	88	134	193	260	245	178
Deductions [1]	550	784	2,136	2,876	3,317	3,634	4,043	4,711	3,749
Cost of goods sold/operations	243	395	1,226	1,666	1,976	2,109	2,310	2,717	2,055
Salaries and wages	56	80	201	269	293	332	373	403	390
Taxes paid	9	13	31	42	47	53	56	63	62
Interest paid	30	43	93	64	103	137	174	143	94
Depreciation	60	23	59	90	71	79	86	130	125
Net income (less loss)	17	107	269	385	546	667	683	458	410
Net income	116	179	410	566	724	871	976	929	796

[1] Includes items not shown separately. [2] Assets, liabilities, and partners' capital accounts are understated because not all partnerships file complete balance sheets. [3] Mortgages, notes, and bonds payable in less than 1 year. [4] Mortgages, notes, and bonds payable in 1 year or more. [5] Excludes investment income except for partnerships in finance, insurance, and real estate in 1995. Beginning 2000, finance and insurance, real estate, and management of companies included investment income for partnerships.

Source: U.S. Internal Revenue Service, *Statistics of Income*, various issues <http://www.irs.gov/taxstats/article/0,,id=117514,00.html>.

Table 760. Partnerships—Selected Items by Industry: 2009

[In billions of dollars (18,798 represents $18,798,000,000,000), except as indicated. Covers active partnerships only. Figures are estimates based on samples. Based on the North American Industry Classification System (NAICS), 2007; see text, this section. See Appendix III. Minus sign (−) indicates net loss]

Industry and year	2007 NAICS code	Number of partnerships (1,000)			Total assets [1]	Business receipts [2]	Total deductions	Net income less loss	Net income	Net loss
		Total	With net income	With net loss						
Total [3]	(X)	**3,169**	**1,608**	**1,561**	**18,798**	**3,562**	**3,749**	**409.9**	**795.9**	**386.1**
Agriculture, forestry, fishing, and hunting	11	130	66	64	169	21	33	−	9.6	9.6
Mining	21	32	19	13	315	100	86	26.3	39.0	12.7
Utilities	22	6	2	4	251	119	125	-2.7	6.1	8.8
Construction	23	181	90	92	251	213	228	-6.9	15.1	22.1
Manufacturing	31–33	45	23	22	719	748	748	33.3	59.9	26.6
Wholesale trade	42	55	37	17	192	529	523	13.3	21.0	7.7
Retail trade	44–45	177	77	99	131	341	346	4.4	10.6	6.2
Transportation and warehousing	48–49	51	19	31	233	118	120	2.1	9.3	7.3
Information	51	43	17	26	630	244	236	32.9	48.1	15.1
Finance and insurance	52	313	209	104	10,219	154	302	207.4	280.1	72.6
Real estate and rental and leasing	53	1,524	735	790	4,457	119	175	-12.0	128.3	140.3
Professional, scientific, and technical services	54	189	109	80	185	361	299	78.9	87.6	8.6
Management of companies and enterprises	55	17	10	7	515	19	43	13.1	28.5	15.4
Administrative and support and waste management and remediation services	56	75	36	38	57	67	71	3.3	6.3	3.0
Educational services	61	11	5	6	4	4	4	0.2	0.5	0.3
Health care and social assistance	62	70	45	25	123	195	180	26.7	31.9	5.3
Arts, entertainment, and recreation	71	58	24	34	87	47	56	-2.5	5.1	7.6
Accommodation and food services	72	113	51	62	239	139	152	-8.2	7.2	15.4
Other services	81	74	18	56	20	22	22	0.3	1.7	1.4

X Not applicable. − Represents or rounds to zero. [1] Total assets are understated because not all partnerships file complete balance sheets. [2] Finance and insurance, real estate, and management of companies include investment income for partnerships. [3] Includes businesses not allocable to individual industries.

Source: U.S. Internal Revenue Service, "Statistics of Income Tax Stats-Partnership Statistics," <http://www.irs.gov/uac/SOI-Tax-Stats-Partnership-Statistics>.

Table 761. Nonfinancial Noncorporate Business-Sector Balance Sheet: 1990 to 2011

[In billions of dollars (4,546 represents $4,546,000,000,000), except as noted. Represents year-end (4th quarter) outstandings]

Item	1990	1995	2000	2005	2007	2008	2009	2010	2011
Assets	**4,546**	**5,081**	**7,918**	**13,041**	**14,673**	**13,509**	**12,155**	**12,564**	**12,995**
Nonfinancial assets	4,154	4,489	6,445	10,444	11,077	9,816	8,562	9,108	9,525
Real estate [1]	3,662	3,958	5,786	9,635	10,165	8,876	7,649	8,148	8,558
Residential	2,100	2,391	3,479	6,251	5,864	4,921	4,522	4,663	4,880
Nonresidential	1,562	1,568	2,308	3,384	4,300	3,956	3,127	3,485	3,678
Equipment and software [2]	347	387	474	594	667	702	693	702	688
Residential [3]	28	32	35	43	47	49	46	44	45
Nonresidential	319	355	438	551	620	653	647	658	642
Inventories [2]	145	143	185	216	245	238	220	258	279
Financial assets	391	592	1,473	2,597	3,596	3,693	3,592	3,456	3,470
Checkable deposits and currency	83	120	181	374	516	519	540	520	523
Time and savings deposits	51	71	248	324	359	358	353	340	341
Money market fund shares	7	17	49	69	74	75	74	71	71
Treasury securities	13	24	40	56	59	52	46	44	44
Municipal securities	−	2	2	4	5	5	5	5	5
Mortgages	31	22	23	36	42	39	38	36	37
Trade receivables	98	140	342	431	526	523	496	477	479
Miscellaneous assets	109	196	587	1,302	2,014	2,122	2,040	1,963	1,971
Insurance receivables	60	71	77	99	107	111	112	113	119
Equity investment in GSEs [4]	2	3	3	4	5	6	6	7	7
Other	47	122	506	1,198	1,902	2,004	1,921	1,843	1,846
Liabilities	**1,453**	**1,520**	**2,796**	**4,180**	**5,349**	**5,795**	**5,695**	**5,508**	**5,562**
Credit market instruments	1,191	1,175	1,912	2,898	3,775	4,093	3,959	3,762	3,773
Depository institution loans n.e.c. [5]	167	201	402	670	927	1,046	930	859	912
Other loans and advances	99	104	129	135	165	177	172	177	177
Mortgages	925	870	1,381	2,093	2,683	2,870	2,857	2,725	2,685
Trade payables	66	97	267	335	375	381	388	369	373
Taxes payable	32	33	65	87	99	106	100	95	95
Miscellaneous liabilities	164	215	552	861	1,100	1,214	1,247	1,282	1,319
Net worth	**3,093**	**3,561**	**5,122**	**8,861**	**9,324**	**7,714**	**6,460**	**7,056**	**7,434**
Debt/net worth (percent)	38.5	33.0	37.3	32.7	40.5	53.1	61.3	53.3	50.8

− Represents or rounds to zero. [1] At market value. [2] At replacement (current) cost. [3] Durable goods in rental properties. [4] GSEs = government-sponsored enterprises. Equity in the Farm Credit System. [5] Not elsewhere classified.

Source: Board of Governors of the Federal Reserve System, "Federal Reserve Statistical Release, Z.1, Flow of Funds Accounts of the United States," June 2012, <http://www.federalreserve.gov/releases/z1/20120607/>.

Table 762. Nonfinancial Corporate Business-Sector Balance Sheet: 1990 to 2011

[In billions of dollars (9,794 represents $9,794,000,000,000). Represents year-end (4th quarter) outstandings]

Item	1990	1995	2000	2005	2007	2008	2009	2010	2011
Assets	**9,794**	**11,615**	**19,659**	**25,269**	**30,516**	**28,860**	**26,173**	**28,348**	**30,045**
Nonfinancial assets	6,204	6,640	9,897	13,360	16,754	15,923	12,832	14,158	14,971
Real estate [1]	3,432	3,222	5,439	8,170	10,909	9,945	7,050	8,189	8,768
Equipment and software [2]	1,862	2,339	3,119	3,602	4,012	4,191	4,119	4,142	4,231
Inventories [2]	910	1,079	1,339	1,588	1,833	1,787	1,664	1,827	1,972
Financial assets [3]	3,589	4,975	9,762	11,909	13,762	12,938	13,341	14,191	15,074
Checkable deposits and currency	167	207	226	268	143	31	170	326	380
Time and savings deposits	75	100	272	450	441	382	489	511	537
Money market fund shares	20	60	214	352	548	711	642	485	452
Commercial paper	14	20	58	111	69	57	56	68	57
Treasury securities	38	57	18	52	38	30	43	48	46
Consumer credit	67	85	81	60	59	56	52	53	53
Trade receivables	967	1,185	1,939	2,108	2,252	2,085	2,056	2,187	2,388
Mutual fund shares [1]	10	46	118	134	178	106	162	187	167
Liabilities [3]	**4,740**	**6,023**	**9,632**	**11,182**	**12,916**	**13,225**	**12,898**	**13,364**	**13,739**
Credit market instruments	2,577	3,106	4,766	5,742	7,102	7,445	7,232	7,533	8,032
Commercial paper	117	157	278	90	124	131	58	83	116
Municipal securities [4]	115	135	154	218	341	410	448	482	497
Corporate bonds [5]	1,008	1,507	2,376	3,156	3,676	3,881	4,269	4,691	5,077
Depository institution loans n.e.c. [6]	588	629	900	591	716	780	560	545	619
Other loans and advances	463	467	701	903	1,316	1,365	1,139	1,041	1,100
Mortgages	286	210	357	783	929	878	758	690	623
Trade payables	627	879	1,542	1,701	1,898	1,673	1,587	1,751	1,935
Taxes payable	38	40	78	86	36	39	36	43	47
Net worth (market value)	**5,054**	**5,592**	**10,027**	**14,087**	**17,600**	**15,635**	**13,275**	**14,985**	**16,305**
Debt/net worth (percent)	51.0	55.6	47.5	40.8	40.4	47.6	54.5	50.3	49.3

[1] At market value. [2] At replacement (current) cost. [3] Includes items not shown separately. [4] Industrial revenue bonds. Issued by state and local governments to finance private investment and secured in interest and principal by the industrial user of the funds. [5] Through 1992, corporate bonds include net issues by Netherlands Antillean financial subsidiaries. [6] Not elsewhere classified.

Source: Board of Governors of the Federal Reserve System, "Federal Reserve Statistical Release, Z.1, Flow of Funds Accounts of the United States," June 2012, <http://www.federalreserve.gov/releases/z1/20120607/>.

Table 763. Corporate Funds—Sources and Uses: 1990 to 2011

[In billions of dollars (243 represents $243,000,000,000). As of 4th quarter 2011, includes farm and nonfarm nonfinancial corporate businesses. Minus sign (–) indicates a deficit]

Item	1990	1995	2000	2005	2007	2008	2009	2010	2011
Profits before tax	243	431	432	957	1,042	831	693	943	1,003
– Taxes on corporate income	98	140	170	272	294	227	175	229	247
– Net dividends	118	178	251	171	485	474	349	399	443
+ Capital consumption allowance [1]	367	465	640	614	682	832	809	902	1,015
= U.S. internal funds, book	394	577	651	1,128	945	961	978	1,217	1,328
+ Foreign earnings retained abroad	45	53	103	-18	169	184	208	211	208
+ Inventory valuation adjustment (IVA)	-13	-18	-17	-31	-47	-44	1	-39	-60
– Net capital transfers	0	(-Z)	0	-16	(-Z)	-4	38	21	-6
= Internal funds + IVA	426	612	737	1,095	1,067	1,104	1,148	1,368	1,482
Gross investment	376	661	916	937	941	169	1,324	1,138	1,343
Capital expenditures	435	628	950	957	1,147	1,112	761	987	1,071
Fixed investment [2]	424	584	898	911	1,120	1,136	908	926	1,025
Inventory change + IVA	12	39	53	47	28	-40	-151	65	50
Nonproduced nonfinancial assets	-1	5	-2	-1	-2	16	4	-3	-3
Net lending (+) or net borrowing (-) [3]	-59	33	-34	-20	-206	-943	563	151	272
Net acquisition of financial assets [3]	125	425	1,205	946	1,075	-604	309	781	889
Checkable deposits and currency	6	5	35	61	-8	-113	140	156	54
Time and savings deposits	-6	3	35	50	-56	-59	107	23	26
Money market fund shares	9	23	17	53	127	162	-69	-157	-33
Credit market instruments [3]	-26	-9	26	42	-78	-36	8	11	-19
Commercial paper	(-Z)	1	10	16	-53	-12	-1	12	-11
Mutual fund shares	-1	5	(Z)	1	-5	-17	35	11	-11
Trade receivables	29	78	282	278	162	-168	-29	135	200
Miscellaneous assets [3]	114	318	818	444	938	-347	109	587	677
U.S. direct investment abroad [4]	36	90	138	25	307	263	280	322	383
Insurance receivables	13	9	(Z)	21	8	11	-1	3	16
Net increase in liabilities [3]	184	392	1,238	966	1,281	339	-255	630	617
Net funds raised in markets	68	147	256	23	50	12	-194	6	25
Net new equity issues	-63	-58	-118	-342	-787	-336	-65	-278	-473
Credit market instruments [3]	131	205	375	365	837	348	-129	284	498
Commercial paper	10	18	48	-8	11	8	-73	25	33
Corporate bonds [4]	47	79	168	54	311	205	388	423	385
Depository institution loans n.e.c [5]	-11	77	55	-27	96	64	-220	-33	73
Other loans and advances [6]	62	29	78	110	288	48	-142	-96	59
Mortgages	23	-1	24	193	61	-46	-120	-69	-68
Trade payables	28	81	313	199	85	-225	-85	163	185
Miscellaneous liabilities [3]	88	164	662	745	1,196	549	28	453	403
Foreign direct investment in U.S.	59	55	249	99	212	190	112	186	202

Z Less than $500 million. [1] Consumption of fixed capital plus capital consumption adjustment. [2] Nonresidential fixed investment plus residential fixed investment. [3] Includes other items not shown separately. [4] Through 1992 fourth quarter, corporate bonds include net issues by Netherlands Antillean financial subsidiaries, and U.S. direct investment abroad excludes net inflows from those bond issues. [5] Not elsewhere classified. [6] Loans from rest of the world, U.S. government, and nonbank financial institutions.

Source: Board of Governors of the Federal Reserve System, "Federal Reserve Statistical Release, Z.1, Flow of Funds Accounts of the United States," June 2012, <http://www.federalreserve.gov/releases/z1/20120607/>.

Table 764. Corporations—Selected Financial Items: 1990 to 2009

[In billions of dollars (18,190 represents $18,190,000,000,000), except as noted. Covers active corporations only. All corporations are required to file returns except those specifically exempt. See source for changes in law affecting comparability of historical data. Based on samples; see Appendix III]

Item	1990	1995	2000	2004	2005	2006	2007	2008	2009
Number of returns (1,000)	3,717	4,474	5,045	5,558	5,671	5,841	5,869	5,847	5,825
Number with net income (1,000)	1,911	2,455	2,819	3,116	3,324	3,367	3,368	3,184	3,149
S Corporation returns [1] (1,000)	1,575	2,153	2,860	3,518	3,684	3,873	3,990	4,050	4,095
Assets [2]	18,190	26,014	47,027	60,118	66,445	73,081	81,486	76,799	75,965
Cash	771	962	1,820	2,730	2,823	2,902	3,625	4,384	4,853
Notes and accounts receivable	4,198	5,307	8,754	10,691	11,962	13,611	15,315	13,855	12,544
Inventories	894	1,045	1,272	1,386	1,505	1,613	1,656	1,619	1,474
Investments in government obligations	921	1,363	1,236	1,571	1,613	1,714	1,785	2,193	2,501
Mortgage and real estate	1,538	1,713	2,822	4,627	4,777	5,232	5,177	5,450	4,847
Other investments	4,137	7,429	17,874	22,657	25,162	27,903	30,939	27,169	27,574
Depreciable assets	4,318	5,571	7,292	7,974	8,416	8,817	9,222	9,467	9,613
Depletable assets	129	154	191	270	310	382	497	587	629
Land	210	242	303	363	407	457	493	509	517
Liabilities [2]	18,190	26,014	47,027	60,118	66,445	73,081	81,486	76,799	75,965
Accounts payable	1,094	1,750	3,758	5,645	6,029	7,779	7,724	6,822	5,694
Short-term debt [3]	1,803	2,034	4,020	4,399	4,192	4,709	4,735	4,726	4,542
Long-term debt [4]	2,665	3,335	6,184	8,154	8,332	9,399	10,786	11,062	10,718
Net worth [5]	4,739	8,132	17,349	20,814	23,525	25,996	28,812	25,469	24,567
Capital stock	1,585	2,194	3,966	2,308	2,482	2,513	2,775	3,184	3,019
Paid-in or capital surplus	2,814	5,446	12,265	16,160	17,828	19,142	21,792	23,574	24,110
Retained earnings [6]	1,410	2,191	3,627	3,278	4,331	5,764	5,970	613	2,024
Receipts [2, 7]	11,410	14,539	20,606	22,712	25,505	27,402	28,763	28,590	24,773
Business receipts [7, 8]	9,860	12,786	17,637	19,976	21,800	23,310	24,217	24,718	21,585
Interest [9]	977	1,039	1,628	1,368	1,773	2,307	2,640	2,179	1,540
Rents and royalties	133	145	254	274	290	299	314	317	296
Deductions [2, 7]	11,033	13,821	19,692	21,636	23,613	25,502	26,974	27,687	23,944
Cost of sales and operations [8]	6,611	8,206	11,135	12,498	13,816	14,800	15,513	16,080	13,286
Compensation of officers	205	304	401	417	445	474	479	467	428
Rent paid on business property	185	232	380	420	439	462	477	491	476
Taxes paid	251	326	390	447	473	497	509	469	473
Interest paid	825	744	1,272	939	1,287	1,787	2,085	1,659	1,070
Depreciation	333	437	614	691	531	564	599	759	712
Advertising	126	163	234	239	253	277	277	267	241
Net income (less loss) [7, 10]	371	714	928	1,112	1,949	1,933	1,837	984	919
Net income	553	881	1,337	1,456	2,235	2,240	2,253	1,807	1,615
Deficit	182	166	409	344	286	306	416	823	696
Income subject to tax	366	565	760	857	1,201	1,291	1,248	978	895
Income tax before credits [11]	119	194	266	300	419	453	437	342	313
Tax credits	32	42	62	75	107	100	106	114	108
Foreign tax credit	25	30	49	57	82	78	87	100	94
Income tax after credits [12]	96	156	204	224	312	353	331	229	205

[1] Represents certain small corporations with a limit on the number of shareholders, mostly individuals, electing to be taxed at the shareholder level. [2] Includes items not shown separately. [3] Payable in less than 1 year. [4] Payable in 1 year or more. [5] Net worth is the sum of "capital stock," "additional paid-in capital," "retained earnings, appropriated," "retained earnings, unappropriated" minus "cost of treasury stock." [6] Appropriated and unappropriated and "adjustments to shareholders' equity." [7] Receipts, deductions, and net income of S corporations are limited to those from trade or business. Those from investments are excluded. [8] Includes gross sales and cost of sales of securities, commodities, and real estate by exchanges, brokers, or dealers selling on their own accounts. Excludes investment income. [9] Includes tax-exempt interest in state and local government obligations. [10] Excludes regulated investment companies. [11] Consists of regular (and alternative tax) only. [12] Includes minimum tax, alternative minimum tax, adjustments for prior year credits, and other income-related taxes.

Source: U.S. Internal Revenue Service, *Statistics of Income, Corporation Income Tax Returns*, annual, <http://www.irs.gov/uac/Tax-Stats-2>.

Table 765. Corporations by Receipt-Size Class and Industry: 2009

[Number of returns in thousands (5,825 represents 5,825,000); receipts and net income in billions of dollars (21,585 represents $21,585,000,000,000). Covers active enterprises only. Figures are estimates based on a sample of unaudited tax returns; see Appendix III. Numbers in parentheses represent North American Industry Classification System 2007 codes; see text, this section]

Industry	Total	Under $1 mil. [1]	$1 to $4.9 mil.	$5 to $9.9 mil.	$10 to $49.9 mil.	$50 mil. or more
Total: [2]						
Number of returns..............................	5,825	4,831	734	119	111	29
Business receipts [3]..............................	21,585	936	1,551	806	2,147	16,145
Net income (less loss)..............................	919	1	37	19	67	796
Agriculture, forestry, fishing, and hunting (11):						
Returns..............................	139	122	14	2	1	(Z)
Business receipts [3]..............................	141	21	29	12	26	53
Mining (21):						
Returns..............................	38	31	5	1	1	(Z)
Business receipts [3]..............................	315	5	12	8	19	271
Utilities (22):						
Returns..............................	6	5	1	(Z)	(Z)	(Z)
Business receipts [3]..............................	571	1	1	1	2	565
Construction (23):						
Returns..............................	742	604	106	16	14	2
Business receipts [3]..............................	1,157	133	227	111	277	409
Manufacturing (31–33):						
Returns..............................	260	170	54	14	16	6
Business receipts [3]..............................	5,957	42	126	99	329	5,361
Wholesale and retail trade (42, 44–45):						
Returns..............................	973	678	202	42	41	10
Business receipts [3]..............................	6,556	171	453	296	863	4,772
Transportation and warehousing (48–49):						
Returns..............................	196	160	25	5	4	1
Business receipts [3]..............................	656	31	55	36	79	455
Information (51):						
Returns..............................	117	100	11	3	3	1
Business receipts [3]..............................	924	15	24	18	57	810
Finance and insurance (52):						
Returns..............................	240	205	21	4	6	3
Business receipts [3]..............................	2,048	34	32	14	44	1,924
Real estate and rental and leasing (53):						
Returns..............................	647	626	18	2	1	(Z)
Business receipts [3]..............................	207	47	38	12	24	86
Professional, scientific, and technical services (54):						
Returns..............................	865	764	80	10	9	2
Business receipts [3]..............................	1,027	127	168	70	164	498
Management of companies and enterprises (55):						
Returns..............................	48	41	2	1	2	1
Business receipts [3]..............................	215	1	1	2	9	203
Administrative and support and waste management and remediation services (56):						
Returns..............................	274	233	34	4	3	1
Business receipts [3]..............................	430	46	70	25	69	220
Educational services (61):						
Returns..............................	55	51	4	(Z)	(Z)	(Z)
Business receipts [3]..............................	56	7	8	3	5	33
Health care and social assistance (62):						
Returns..............................	429	337	78	8	6	1
Business receipts [3]..............................	642	99	154	54	109	226
Arts, entertainment, and recreation (71):						
Returns..............................	122	113	7	1	1	(Z)
Business receipts [3]..............................	87	17	15	9	10	36
Accommodation and food services (72):						
Returns..............................	298	249	43	3	2	(Z)
Business receipts [3]..............................	413	75	83	21	41	192
Other services (81):						
Returns..............................	375	342	29	2	1	(Z)
Business receipts [3]..............................	183	66	52	15	20	29

Z Less than 500 returns. [1] Includes businesses without receipts. [2] Includes businesses not allocable to individual industries. [3] Includes investment income for corporations in finance and insurance and management of companies' industries. Excludes investment income for S corporations (certain small corporations with up to 75 shareholders, mostly individuals, electing to be taxed at the shareholder level).

Source: U.S. Internal Revenue Service, *Statistics of Income, Corporation Income Tax Returns*, annual, <http://www.irs.gov/uac/Tax-Stats-2>.

Table 766. Corporations by Asset-Size Class and Industry: 2009

[In billions of dollars (157 represents $157,000,000,000), except number of returns. Covers active corporations only. Excludes corporations not allocable by industry. Numbers in parentheses represent North American Industry Classification System 2007 codes; see text, this section]

Industry	Total	Under $10 mil. [1]	$10 to $24.9 mil.	$25 to $49.9 mil.	$50 to $99.9 mil.	$100 to $249.9 mil.	$250 mil. and over
Agriculture, forestry, fishing, and hunting (11):							
Returns	138,792	137,544	792	251	104	67	34
Total receipts	157	94	12	8	8	13	23
Mining (21):							
Returns	38,348	36,567	802	359	195	176	251
Total receipts	355	36	8	7	7	13	285
Utilities (22):							
Returns	6,072	5,649	99	53	47	45	178
Total receipts	605	5	1	3	3	5	588
Construction (23):							
Returns	742,436	734,830	5,249	1,305	580	284	188
Total receipts	1,175	661	135	71	65	59	184
Manufacturing (31–33):							
Returns	259,859	245,068	7,021	2,947	1,775	1,310	1,737
Total receipts	6,513	477	182	154	168	248	5,285
Wholesale and retail trade (42, 44–45):							
Returns	973,378	956,476	10,411	3,240	1,495	882	873
Total receipts	6,692	1,765	487	318	257	308	3,557
Transportation and warehousing (48–49):							
Returns	195,594	193,570	1,121	370	206	140	186
Total receipts	679	193	29	21	19	22	394
Information (51):							
Returns	116,514	113,938	1,109	473	336	255	403
Total receipts	1,047	95	19	15	18	26	874
Finance and insurance (52):							
Returns	239,864	220,563	3,757	2,536	2,597	3,441	6,970
Total receipts	3,379	242	22	20	31	60	3,003
Real estate and rental and leasing (53):							
Returns	647,037	639,045	4,725	1,418	755	550	544
Total receipts	302	112	13	9	10	14	144
Professional, scientific, and technical services (54):							
Returns	864,803	860,073	2,619	900	527	367	317
Total receipts	1,059	551	64	43	41	51	308
Management of companies and enterprises (55):							
Returns	47,729	40,560	1,333	1,012	1,177	1,728	1,919
Total receipts	913	7	2	2	7	17	878
Administrative and support and waste management and remediation services (56):							
Returns	273,900	272,561	660	265	149	112	151
Total receipts	442	206	25	15	16	23	157
Educational services (61):							
Returns	55,309	55,036	124	56	31	33	28
Total receipts	57	21	2	3	3	5	23
Health care and social assistance (62):							
Returns	429,339	428,176	560	233	151	109	111
Total receipts	667	426	21	16	18	24	162
Arts, entertainment, and recreation (71):							
Returns	122,225	121,439	419	182	74	50	60
Total receipts	95	47	5	4	3	6	30
Accommodation and food services (72):							
Returns	297,986	296,570	803	257	141	79	136
Total receipts	444	210	14	10	14	16	181
Other services (81):							
Returns	375,059	374,436	412	107	57	23	24
Total receipts	190	151	7	4	6	4	18

[1] Includes returns with zero assets.

Source: U.S. Internal Revenue Service, *Statistics of Income, Corporation Income Tax Returns*, annual, <http://www.irs.gov/uac/Tax-Stats-2>.

Table 767. Economic Census Summary (NAICS 2002 Basis): 2002 and 2007

[24 represents 24,000. Covers establishments with payroll. Data are based on the 2002 and 2007 economic censuses which are subject to nonsampling error. Data for the construction sector are also subject to sampling errors. For details on survey methodology and nonsampling and sampling errors, see Appendix III]

Kind of business	2002 NAICS code [1]	Establish- ments (1,000)		Sales, receipts, or shipments (bil. dol.)		Annual payroll (bil. dol.)		Paid employees [2] (1,000)	
		2002	2007	2002	2007	2002	2007	2002	2007
Mining.................................	21	24	21	183	369	21	37	475	703
Oil & gas extraction....................	211	8	6	113	231	5	10	99	162
Mining (except oil & gas)...............	212	7	6	48	81	9	11	196	220
Mining support activities...............	213	9	8	22	57	7	16	180	322
Utilities................................	22	17	17	399	582	42	51	663	632
Construction...........................	23	710	725	1,209	1,782	254	348	7,193	7,399
Manufacturing..........................	31–33	351	294	3,915	5,339	568	612	14,664	13,333
Wholesale trade........................	42	436	432	4,635	6,039	260	336	5,878	6,295
Merchant wholesalers, durable goods...........	423	260	253	2,171	2,709	157	206	3,357	3,637
Merchant wholesalers, nondurable goods......	424	143	133	1,980	2,754	93	117	2,273	2,367
Wholesale electronic markets and agents and brokers...........................	425	32	46	483	576	10	14	249	292
Retail trade............................	44–45	1,115	1,123	3,056	3,932	302	365	14,648	15,611
Motor vehicle & parts dealers....................	441	125	126	802	893	65	73	1,845	1,916
Furniture & home furnishings stores............	442	65	65	92	110	13	15	535	589
Electronics & appliance stores....................	443	47	50	82	111	9	11	391	484
Bldg. material & garden equipment & supplies dealers.............................	444	(NA)	90	(NA)	323	(NA)	38	(NA)	1,340
Food & beverage stores....................	445	149	147	457	541	49	56	2,839	2,879
Health & personal care stores....................	446	82	87	178	239	20	59	1,024	1,012
Gasoline stations.......................	447	121	117	249	447	14	15	927	887
Clothing & clothing accessories stores..........	448	150	155	168	213	21	27	1,427	1,689
Sporting goods, hobby, book, & music stores....	451	62	57	73	82	9	10	611	626
General merchandise stores.................	452	41	46	445	578	43	55	2,525	2,770
Miscellaneous store retailers....................	453	129	120	91	103	13	14	792	791
Nonstore retailers........................	454	55	61	173	292	17	23	571	628
Transportation & warehousing [3]	48-49	200	218	382	656	116	172	3,651	4,436
Information............................	51	138	141	892	1,075	195	223	3,736	3,428
Publishing industries (except Internet)...........	511	32	30	242	273	66	76	1,090	1,028
Motion picture & sound recording industries....	512	22	24	78	95	13	17	303	326
Broadcasting (except Internet)....................	515	10	10	74	99	14	18	291	291
Internet publishing and broadcasting...........	516	2	3	6	15	2	5	40	55
Telecommunications.....................	517	49	49	412	485	72	72	1,440	1,210
Internet service providers, Web search portals, and data processing.....................	518	19	21	75	101	26	34	514	463
Other information services.....................	519	3	4	5	7	2	2	58	55
Finance & insurance [4]....................	52	440	503	2,804	3,641	378	494	6,579	6,563
Real estate & rental & leasing [4]..........	53	323	377	336	452	60	85	1,949	2,249
Professional, scientific, & technical services.....	54	771	852	887	1,352	376	515	7,244	8,121
Management of companies & enterprises........	55	49	(S)	107	(S)	179	(S)	2,605	(S)
Admin/support waste management/remediation services.............................	56	351	382	433	629	206	291	8,742	10,154
Administrative & support services...............	561	332	360	381	556	194	275	8,410	9,787
Waste management & remediation services....	562	19	21	51	73	12	16	332	367
Educational services.......................	61	49	61	31	47	10	15	430	562
Health care and social assistance...............	62	705	779	1,207	1,697	496	666	15,052	16,860
Ambulatory health care services...............	621	489	545	489	692	203	280	4,925	5,791
Hospitals.............................	622	6	7	500	713	197	263	5,174	5,536
Nursing & residential care facilities..............	623	69	76	127	168	59	74	2,831	3,056
Social assistance......................	624	140	152	91	124	36	48	2,123	2,477
Arts, entertainment, & recreation..................	71	110	124	142	189	45	58	1,849	2,071
Performing arts, spectator sports, & related industries......................	711	38	44	58	76	21	27	423	441
Museums, historical sites, & like institutions....	712	7	7	9	13	3	4	123	129
Amusement, gambling, & recreation industries...........................	713	66	73	75	99	21	27	1,303	1,500
Accommodation & food services.................	72	566	627	449	613	128	170	10,121	11,588
Accommodation........................	721	61	63	128	180	35	46	1,813	1,980
Food services & drinking places.................	722	505	564	321	433	93	124	8,308	9,608
Other services (except public administration)....	81	538	538	307	418	83	100	3,475	3,516
Repair & maintenance...................	811	231	222	118	143	35	42	1,285	1,305
Personal and laundry services....................	812	201	208	72	84	23	27	1,297	1,341
Religious/grantmaking/prof/like organizations...	813	106	107	117	190	25	31	893	870

NA Not available. S Figure does not meet publication standards. [1] Based on North American Industry Classification System, 2002; see text, this section. [2] For pay period including March 12. [3] For detailed industries, see Table 1074. [4] For detailed industries, see Table 1175.

Source: U.S. Census Bureau, "2007 Economic Census, Comparative Statistics for United States, Summary Statistics by 2002 NAICS," <http://factfinder2.census.gov/faces/nav/jsf/pages/index.xhtml>.

Table 768. Nonemployer Establishments and Receipts by Industry: 2000 to 2009

[Establishments: 16,530 represents 16,530,000. Includes only firms subject to federal income tax. Nonemployers are businesses with no paid employees. Data originate chiefly from administrative records of the Internal Revenue Service; see Appendix III. Data for 2000 based on the North American Industry Classification System (NAICS), 1997. Data for 2008 and 2009 based on NAICS 2007. See text, this section]

Kind of business	NAICS code	Establishments (1,000)			Receipts (mil. dol.)		
		2000	2008	2009	2000	2008	2009
All industries...	(X)	**16,530**	**21,351**	**21,696**	**709,379**	**962,792**	**923,018**
Forestry, fishing & hunting, & agricultural support services.........................	113–115	223	231	229	9,196	10,883	9,010
Mining, quarrying, and oil and gas extraction.............	21	86	109	102	5,227	11,609	6,139
Utilities...	22	14	18	17	504	760	708
Construction...	23	2,014	2,528	2,455	107,538	143,954	121,298
Manufacturing...	31–33	285	314	313	13,022	15,697	13,811
Wholesale trade...	42	388	388	390	31,684	35,558	32,825
Retail trade...	44–45	1,743	1,875	1,826	73,810	83,978	74,433
Transportation & warehousing............................	48–49	747	1,039	1,002	37,824	67,026	54,453
Information...	51	238	306	306	7,620	11,060	10,250
Finance & insurance.....................................	52	692	734	734	49,058	56,434	51,579
Real estate & rental & leasing...........................	53	1,696	2,130	2,373	133,398	163,461	208,306
Professional, scientific, & technical services.............	54	2,420	3,029	3,067	90,272	131,521	123,437
Admin/support waste mgt/remediation services..........	56	1,032	1,826	1,865	23,754	40,415	37,429
Educational services....................................	61	283	552	561	3,736	7,569	7,335
Health care & social assistance..........................	62	1,317	1,812	1,870	36,550	57,888	56,078
Arts, entertainment, & recreation........................	71	782	1,121	1,124	17,713	27,837	25,623
Accommodation & food services.........................	72	218	308	314	13,418	16,100	14,014
Other services (except public administration)............	81	2,350	3,029	3,149	55,056	81,042	76,290

X Not applicable.

Source: U.S. Census Bureau, "Nonemployer Statistics," August 2012 <http://www.census.gov/econ/nonemployer/>.

Table 769. Establishments, Employees, and Payroll by Employment-Size Class: 1990 to 2009

[6,176 represents 6,176,000. Excludes most government employees, railroad employees, and self-employed persons. Employees are for the week including March 12. Covers establishments with payroll. An establishment is a single physical location where business is conducted or where services or industrial operations are performed. For statement on methodology, see Appendix III]

Employment-size class	Unit	1990	1995	2000	2005	2006	2007	2008	2009
Establishments, total...............	**1,000**	**6,176**	**6,613**	**7,070**	**7,500**	**7,601**	**7,705**	**7,601**	**7,433**
Under 20 employees...................	1,000	5,354	5,733	6,069	6,468	6,533	6,633	6,528	6,413
20 to 99 employees...................	1,000	684	730	826	856	886	892	890	852
100 to 499 employees................	1,000	122	135	157	157	163	161	164	151
500 to 999 employees................	1,000	10	10	12	12	12	12	12	11
1,000 or more employees............	1,000	6	6	7	7	7	7	7	7
Employees, total....................	**1,000**	**93,476**	**100,335**	**114,065**	**116,317**	**119,917**	**120,604**	**120,904**	**114,510**
Under 20 employees...................	1,000	24,373	25,785	27,569	28,874	29,429	30,057	29,839	29,099
20 to 99 employees...................	1,000	27,414	29,202	33,147	34,302	35,504	35,615	35,508	33,895
100 to 499 employees................	1,000	22,926	25,364	29,736	29,591	30,616	30,453	30,850	28,249
500 to 999 employees................	1,000	6,551	7,021	8,291	8,053	8,248	8,284	8,236	7,770
1,000 or more employees............	1,000	12,212	12,962	15,322	15,497	16,120	16,196	16,471	15,496
Annual payroll, total...............	**Bil. dol.**	**2,104**	**2,666**	**3,879**	**4,483**	**4,792**	**5,027**	**5,131**	**4,856**
Under 20 employees...................	Bil. dol.	485	608	818	970	1,021	1,067	1,078	1,037
20 to 99 employees...................	Bil. dol.	547	696	1,006	1,177	1,260	1,313	1,334	1,267
100 to 499 employees................	Bil. dol.	518	675	1,031	1,176	1,264	1,310	1,348	1,253
500 to 999 employees................	Bil. dol.	174	219	336	376	401	428	432	414
1,000 or more employees............	Bil. dol.	381	467	690	784	848	910	939	885

Source: U.S. Census Bureau, "County Business Patterns," June 2011, <http://www.census.gov/econ/cbp/>.

Table 770. Establishments, Employees, and Payroll by Employment-Size Class and Industry: 2000 to 2009

[Establishments and employees in thousands (7,070.0 represents 7,070,000); payroll in billions of dollars. See headnote, Table 769. Data for 2000 based on the North American Industry Classification System (NAICS), 1997; 2008 and 2009 data based on NAICS 2007. Svcs = services. See text, this section]

Industry	NAICS code	2000, total	2008, total	2009 Total	Under 20 employ-ees	20 to 99 employ-ees	100 to 499 employ-ees	500 to 999 or employ-ees	1,000 more employ-ees
Establishments, total [1]	(X)	7,070.0	7,601.2	7,433.5	6,412.6	852.3	150.5	11.4	6.7
Forestry, fishing & hunting, & ag support svcs.	113–115	26.1	22.7	21.7	20.4	1.1	0.2	(Z)	(Z)
Mining, quarrying, and oil and gas extraction.	21	23.7	27.4	26.9	21.5	4.3	1.0	0.1	(Z)
Utilities.	22	17.3	17.0	17.3	12.0	4.0	1.2	0.1	(Z)
Construction.	23	709.6	773.6	713.0	654.6	51.6	6.3	0.3	0.1
Manufacturing.	31–33	354.5	326.2	308.9	217.4	67.0	21.6	2.0	0.9
Wholesale trade.	42	446.2	429.5	419.8	359.5	52.2	7.5	0.5	0.2
Retail trade.	44–45	1,113.6	1,100.9	1,076.6	930.4	120.4	25.3	0.5	(Z)
Transportation and warehousing.	48–49	190.0	217.1	210.1	175.4	27.6	6.2	0.6	0.3
Information.	51	133.6	141.6	135.7	108.7	21.0	5.1	0.6	0.2
Finance and insurance.	52	423.7	501.9	488.9	446.2	34.7	6.5	0.9	0.5
Real estate and rental and leasing.	53	300.2	365.7	351.0	336.1	13.2	1.6	0.1	(Z)
Professional, scientific, and technical services.	54	722.7	848.3	842.6	778.8	53.9	8.7	0.7	0.4
Management of companies and enterprises.	55	55 47.4	51.8	51.6	34.5	11.7	4.4	0.6	0.4
Admin/support waste mgt/remediation svcs.	56	351.5	393.5	383.6	322.9	45.8	12.8	1.3	0.8
Educational services.	61	68.0	88.6	88.8	68.1	16.5	3.4	0.4	0.4
Health care and social assistance.	62	658.6	791.0	799.3	673.1	99.5	22.9	1.8	2.0
Arts, entertainment, and recreation.	71	103.8	124.3	122.9	103.2	16.1	3.1	0.2	0.1
Accommodation and food services.	72	542.4	636.6	635.2	457.5	168.0	9.1	0.4	0.2
Other services [2].	81	723.3	730.7	722.7	675.3	43.6	3.6	0.2	0.1
Unclassified establishments.	99	99.0	12.9	16.9	16.9	(Z)	(Z)	(Z)	(Z)
Employees, total [1]	(X)	114,065	120,904	114,510	29,099	33,895	28,249	7,770	15,496
Forestry, fishing & hunting, & ag support svcs.	113–115	184	167	154	71	43	29	4	7
Mining, quarrying, and oil and gas extraction.	21	456	629	605	104	175	192	59	75
Utilities.	22	655	639	642	64	175	229	103	70
Construction.	23	6,573	7,044	5,967	2,356	1,990	1,141	206	275
Manufacturing.	31–33	16,474	13,096	11,633	1,239	2,931	4,289	1,368	1,806
Wholesale trade.	42	6,112	6,165	5,828	1,733	2,046	1,406	302	342
Retail trade.	44–45	14,841	15,615	14,803	5,034	4,765	4,610	304	90
Transportation and warehousing.	48–49	3,790	4,439	4,160	730	1,141	1,179	442	668
Information.	51	3,546	3,434	3,288	501	886	1,013	391	497
Finance and insurance.	52	5,963	6,512	6,171	1,900	1,340	1,297	654	981
Real estate and rental and leasing.	53	1,942	2,196	2,037	1,109	496	288	72	71
Professional, scientific, and technical services.	54	6,816	8,033	7,840	2,661	2,092	1,668	506	913
Management of companies and enterprises.	55	2,874	2,887	2,853	188	520	926	432	787
Admin/support waste mgt/remediation svcs.	56	9,138	10,225	9,061	1,259	1,965	2,515	865	2,458
Educational services.	61	2,532	3,141	3,201	333	696	642	314	1,214
Health care and social assistance.	62	14,109	17,217	17,531	3,591	3,974	4,221	1,243	4,502
Arts, entertainment, and recreation.	71	1,741	2,069	2,010	387	682	574	145	222
Accommodation and food services.	72	9,881	11,926	11,443	2,968	6,399	1,432	253	391
Other services [2].	81	5,293	5,453	5,264	2,852	1,580	599	107	127
Unclassified establishments.	99	144	15	6	5	1	–	–	–
Annual payroll, total [1]	(X)	3,879	5,131	4,856	1,037	1,267	1,253	414	885
Forestry, fishing & hunting, & ag support svcs.	113–115	5	6	5	2	2	1	(Z)	(Z)
Mining, quarrying, and oil and gas extraction.	21	22	48	42	6	11	15	5	6
Utilities.	22	41	55	54	4	13	19	10	7
Construction.	23	240	333	281	90	99	64	12	16
Manufacturing.	31–33	644	622	550	45	122	197	70	116
Wholesale trade.	42	270	353	334	85	109	83	22	34
Retail trade.	44–45	303	369	355	115	118	111	8	4
Transportation and warehousing.	48–49	126	176	165	27	44	46	17	31
Information.	51	209	234	225	29	53	73	28	42
Finance and insurance.	52	347	522	461	102	106	111	53	89
Real estate and rental and leasing.	53	59	89	81	39	22	13	3	3
Professional, scientific, and technical services.	54	362	539	527	139	145	132	41	71
Management of companies and enterprises.	55	211	273	265	18	44	83	40	79
Admin/support waste mgt/remediation svcs.	56	210	314	290	45	64	73	25	84
Educational services.	61	62	102	105	8	20	22	8	47
Health care and social assistance.	62	431	707	736	155	148	141	56	235
Arts, entertainment, and recreation.	71	43	62	61	15	14	20	6	6
Accommodation and food services.	72	126	183	179	44	90	27	6	12
Other services [2].	81	110	143	139	68	42	20	4	4
Unclassified establishments.	99	4	(Z)	–	(Z)	(Z)	–	–	–

– Represents zero. X Not applicable. Z Less than 50 establishments or $500 million. [1] Totals for 2000 include auxiliaries. Beginning 2007, cases previously classified under NAICS code 95 (auxiliaries) are coded in the operating NAICS sector of the establishment. [2] Except public administration.

Source: U.S. Census Bureau, "American FactFinder," <http://factfinder2.census.gov/faces/nav/jsf/pages/index.xhtml>.

Table 771. Employer Firms, Employment, and Annual Payroll by Employment Size of Firm and Industry: 2009

[7,433 represents 7,433,000. A firm is an aggregation of all establishments owned by a parent company (within a geographic location and/or industry) with some annual payroll. A firm may be a single location or it can include multiple locations. Employment is measured in March and payroll is annual leading to some firms with zero employment. Numbers in parentheses represent North American Industry Classification System codes, 2007; see text, this section]

Industry and data type	Unit	Total	All industries—employment size of firm						
			0 to 4	5 to 9	10 to 19	20 to 99	100 to 499	Less than 500	500 or more
Total [1]:									
Firms................................	1,000	7,433	4,061	1,403	949	852	151	7,415	18
Employment.........................	1,000	114,510	7,035	9,287	12,778	33,895	28,249	91,243	23,266
Annual payroll.....................	Bil. dol	4,856	283	312	442	1,267	1,253	3,556	1,299
Construction (23):									
Firms................................	1,000	713	479	110	65	52	6	713	(Z)
Employment.........................	1,000	5,967	756	722	878	1,990	1,141	5,487	480
Annual payroll.....................	Bil. dol	281	26	26	37	99	64	253	28
Manufacturing (31–33):									
Firms................................	1,000	309	116	54	48	67	22	306	3
Employment.........................	1,000	11,633	221	364	654	2,931	4,289	8,459	3,174
Annual payroll.....................	Bil. dol	550	8	12	24	122	197	364	185
Wholesale trade (42):									
Firms................................	1,000	420	220	81	59	52	8	419	1
Employment.........................	1,000	5,828	401	535	797	2,046	1,406	5,184	644
Annual payroll.....................	Bil. dol	334	20	26	40	109	83	278	56
Retail trade (44–45):									
Firms................................	1,000	1,077	489	271	171	120	25	1,076	1
Employment.........................	1,000	14,803	972	1,806	2,256	4,765	4,610	14,409	394
Annual payroll.....................	Bil. dol	355	25	39	51	118	111	344	12
Transportation & warehousing (48–49):									
Firms................................	1,000	210	120	32	24	28	6	209	1
Employment.........................	1,000	4,160	191	209	330	1,141	1,179	3,050	1,110
Annual payroll.....................	Bil. dol	165	7	7	12	44	46	116	48
Information (51):									
Firms................................	1,000	136	69	21	19	21	5	135	1
Employment.........................	1,000	3,288	110	141	250	886	1,013	2,400	888
Annual payroll.....................	Bil. dol	225	8	8	13	53	73	155	70
Finance & insurance (52):									
Firms................................	1,000	489	291	101	54	35	7	487	1
Employment.........................	1,000	6,171	530	663	706	1,340	1,297	4,537	1,634
Annual payroll.....................	Bil. dol	461	30	32	40	106	111	319	141
Professional, scientific and technical services (54):									
Firms................................	1,000	843	588	118	73	54	9	841	1
Employment.........................	1,000	7,840	900	775	986	2,092	1,668	6,421	1,419
Annual payroll.....................	Bil. dol	527	47	38	54	145	132	416	111
Management of companies and enterprises (55):									
Firms................................	1,000	52	20	8	7	12	4	51	1
Employment.........................	1,000	2,853	36	51	101	520	926	1,634	1,220
Annual payroll.....................	Bil. dol	265	4	5	9	44	83	146	119
Admin/support waste mgt/ remediation services (56):									
Firms................................	1,000	384	227	56	39	46	13	382	2
Employment.........................	1,000	9,061	355	372	532	1,965	2,515	5,738	3,323
Annual payroll.....................	Bil. dol	290	14	12	18	64	73	181	108
Educational services (61):									
Firms................................	1,000	89	41	14	12	16	3	88	1
Employment.........................	1,000	3,201	67	95	171	696	642	1,672	1,529
Annual payroll.....................	Bil. dol	105	2	2	4	20	22	50	55
Health care and social assistance (62):									
Firms................................	1,000	799	364	185	124	100	23	796	4
Employment.........................	1,000	17,531	696	1,238	1,658	3,974	4,221	11,786	5,745
Annual payroll.....................	Bil. dol	736	36	51	68	148	141	444	291
Accommodation and food services (72):									
Firms................................	1,000	635	216	110	131	168	9	635	1
Employment.........................	1,000	11,443	369	745	1,854	6,399	1,432	10,799	644
Annual payroll.....................	Bil. dol	179	9	10	25	90	27	161	19
Other services (except public administration) (81):									
Firms................................	1,000	723	446	154	75	44	4	722	(Z)
Employment.........................	1,000	5,264	854	1,003	995	1,580	599	5,030	234
Annual payroll.....................	Bil. dol	139	20	23	25	42	20	131	8

Z Less than $500 million. [1] Includes other industries, not shown separately.

Source: U.S. Census Bureau, "County Business Patterns," June 2011, <http://www.census.gov/econ/cbp/>.

Table 772. Employer Firms, Employment, and Payroll by Employment Size of Firm and State: 2000 and 2009

[5,652.5 represents 5,652,500. A firm is an aggregation of all establishments owned by a parent company (within a state) with some annual payroll. A firm may be a single location or it can include multiple locations. Employment is measured in March and payroll is annual leading to some firms with zero employment]

State	Employer firms (1,000) 2000 Total	Employer firms (1,000) 2000 Less than 20 employees	Employer firms (1,000) 2009 Total	Employer firms (1,000) 2009 Less than 20 employees	Employer firms (1,000) 2009 Less than 500 employees	Employment, 2009 (mil.) Total	Employment, 2009 (mil.) Less than 20 employees	Employment, 2009 (mil.) Less than 500 employees	Annual payroll, 2009 (bil. dol.) Total	Annual payroll, 2009 (bil. dol.) Less than 20 employees	Annual payroll, 2009 (bil. dol.) Less than 500 employees
U.S..........	5,652.5	5,035.0	5,767.3	5,170.8	5,749.8	114.5	20.7	56.3	4,855.5	711.0	2,084.8
AL............	79.9	68.2	77.0	65.4	74.7	1.6	0.3	0.8	57.0	8.5	25.4
AK............	15.9	14.0	16.4	14.4	15.8	0.3	0.1	0.1	12.4	2.4	5.8
AZ............	93.0	79.3	104.2	89.5	101.2	2.1	0.3	1.0	82.9	11.4	33.1
AR............	52.4	45.4	51.4	44.2	49.8	1.0	0.2	0.5	33.1	5.1	13.9
CA............	664.6	581.1	697.1	618.6	691.5	12.8	2.4	6.5	621.7	96.4	271.7
CO............	116.2	101.5	126.8	112.0	123.8	2.0	0.4	1.0	87.5	13.9	37.3
CT............	78.5	67.2	73.5	62.8	71.4	1.5	0.3	0.7	78.0	11.1	34.3
DE............	20.2	16.6	19.7	15.9	18.3	0.4	0.1	0.2	16.8	2.2	6.6
DC............	16.3	12.4	16.7	12.3	15.5	0.5	0.1	0.2	30.2	3.4	12.7
FL............	354.0	319.3	399.8	364.4	395.5	6.9	1.2	2.9	253.4	41.0	101.4
GA............	160.4	138.3	171.7	149.1	167.9	3.4	0.6	1.5	136.6	18.7	53.2
HI............	24.3	20.8	25.7	21.8	24.8	0.5	0.1	0.3	17.7	3.1	9.1
ID............	32.2	28.0	37.5	32.8	36.3	0.5	0.1	0.3	16.3	3.4	8.3
IL............	254.1	218.1	254.0	220.6	249.6	5.1	0.9	2.5	234.0	32.1	99.3
IN............	116.3	98.1	112.0	95.2	109.1	2.4	0.4	1.2	88.4	12.0	37.7
IA............	65.6	56.2	63.7	54.4	62.0	1.3	0.2	0.7	43.8	6.3	20.2
KS............	61.6	52.4	59.7	50.3	57.7	1.1	0.2	0.6	42.1	6.2	19.4
KY............	72.3	61.0	69.6	58.7	67.3	1.5	0.3	0.7	51.7	7.2	21.9
LA............	81.7	69.5	81.5	68.8	79.4	1.6	0.3	0.9	61.4	9.6	29.8
ME............	34.1	30.1	33.8	29.7	32.8	0.5	0.1	0.3	17.2	3.4	9.0
MD............	106.0	90.4	109.1	93.2	106.4	2.1	0.4	1.1	96.6	14.7	45.7
MA............	148.2	127.8	138.4	119.4	135.4	3.0	0.5	1.4	153.8	20.3	63.8
MI............	193.9	167.2	176.3	153.2	173.3	3.4	0.6	1.8	135.8	20.7	61.1
MN............	116.2	99.4	118.7	102.2	116.2	2.4	0.4	1.2	102.2	13.1	42.5
MS............	48.3	41.5	46.1	39.2	44.5	0.9	0.2	0.4	28.5	4.6	12.7
MO............	118.1	101.1	118.5	101.9	115.7	2.4	0.4	1.1	88.8	12.0	36.8
MT............	28.0	25.0	31.7	28.3	30.9	0.3	0.1	0.2	10.7	2.9	6.6
NE............	41.4	35.5	41.9	35.7	40.5	0.8	0.1	0.4	27.5	4.0	12.3
NV............	40.3	33.4	47.9	40.0	45.8	1.0	0.2	0.4	39.1	5.7	15.8
NH............	32.1	27.3	31.4	26.5	30.2	0.6	0.1	0.3	23.6	4.0	11.3
NJ............	202.2	178.4	195.4	172.4	192.2	3.4	0.7	1.7	177.1	26.5	75.3
NM............	35.5	30.1	36.3	30.6	34.8	0.6	0.1	0.3	21.4	3.8	10.5
NY............	424.8	379.2	441.2	396.6	437.0	7.3	1.4	3.8	400.8	58.5	175.1
NC............	163.6	142.0	169.8	147.5	166.4	3.4	0.6	1.6	124.3	18.0	50.5
ND............	17.2	14.7	17.8	15.0	17.1	0.3	0.1	0.2	10.0	1.8	5.4
OH............	212.5	180.5	192.8	164.1	189.1	4.5	0.7	2.1	171.9	22.4	71.3
OK............	70.2	61.0	72.2	62.2	70.3	1.3	0.3	0.7	45.2	7.6	21.7
OR............	85.1	74.2	88.8	77.9	86.7	1.4	0.3	0.8	53.4	9.2	25.2
PA............	237.5	204.6	232.8	200.8	228.8	5.0	0.9	2.4	209.8	28.1	87.4
RI............	25.2	21.5	24.8	21.1	23.8	0.4	0.1	0.2	16.8	2.9	8.2
SC............	78.4	67.2	80.1	68.7	77.8	1.5	0.3	0.8	51.7	8.1	22.4
SD............	20.6	17.7	21.6	18.5	20.8	0.3	0.1	0.2	10.5	2.0	5.8
TN............	102.4	86.7	99.1	83.6	96.1	2.3	0.4	1.0	86.2	11.4	35.4
TX............	369.0	321.3	392.4	339.9	387.1	8.9	1.4	4.1	376.6	51.0	151.6
UT............	46.2	39.3	58.1	50.2	56.3	1.1	0.2	0.5	37.8	5.7	16.3
VT............	19.1	16.7	18.7	16.2	18.0	0.3	0.1	0.2	9.1	2.0	5.2
VA............	139.7	120.3	150.1	129.7	146.9	3.1	0.5	1.5	137.1	18.6	57.7
WA............	138.2	120.9	145.6	128.3	142.9	2.4	0.5	1.3	110.4	16.9	48.0
WV............	33.5	28.8	30.1	25.3	28.9	0.6	0.1	0.3	18.9	2.9	8.8
WI............	115.6	98.2	111.8	95.0	109.3	2.4	0.4	1.2	89.4	12.3	40.0
WY............	15.9	13.9	17.7	15.3	17.0	0.2	0.1	0.1	8.2	1.9	4.7

Source: U.S. Small Business Administration, Office of Advocacy, "Statistics of U.S. Businesses," <http://www.sba.gov/advo/research/data.html>, accessed June 2012.

Table 773. Employer Firms, Establishments, Employment, and Annual Payroll by Firm Size: 1990 to 2009

[In thousands except as noted (5,074 represents 5,074,000). Firms are an aggregation of all establishments owned by a parent company with some annual payroll. Establishments are locations with active payroll in any quarter. This table illustrates the changing importance of enterprise sizes over time, not job growth, as enterprises can grow or decline and change enterprise size cells over time]

Item	Total	All industries—employment size of firm						
		0 to 4 [1]	5 to 9	10 to 19	20 to 99	100 to 499	Less than 500	500 or more
Firms:								
1990	5,074	3,021	952	563	454	70	5,060	14
1995	5,369	3,250	981	577	470	76	5,354	15
2000	5,653	3,397	1,021	617	516	84	5,635	17
2005	5,984	3,678	1,050	630	521	87	5,966	17
2006	6,022	3,670	1,061	647	536	91	6,004	18
2007	6,050	3,705	1,060	645	532	89	6,031	18
2008	5,930	3,618	1,044	633	526	90	5,912	18
2009	5,767	3,559	1,001	611	496	83	5,750	18
Establishments:								
1990	6,176	3,032	971	600	590	255	5,448	728
1995	6,613	3,260	998	618	639	284	5,799	814
2000	7,070	3,406	1,035	652	674	312	6,080	990
2005	7,500	3,684	1,063	662	679	332	6,421	1,079
2006	7,601	3,677	1,073	679	698	346	6,473	1,129
2007	7,705	3,711	1,074	682	723	356	6,546	1,159
2008	7,601	3,625	1,057	667	705	360	6,414	1,187
2009	7,433	3,565	1,015	646	673	354	6,253	1,180
Employment:								
1990	93,469	5,117	6,252	7,543	17,710	13,545	50,167	43,302
1995	100,315	5,395	6,440	7,734	18,422	14,660	52,653	47,662
2000	114,065	5,593	6,709	8,286	20,277	16,260	57,124	56,941
2005	116,317	5,937	6,898	8,454	20,444	16,911	58,645	57,672
2006	119,917	5,960	6,974	8,676	21,077	17,537	60,224	59,693
2007	120,604	6,139	6,975	8,656	20,923	17,174	59,867	60,737
2008	120,904	6,086	6,878	8,497	20,685	17,548	59,694	61,210
2009	114,510	5,966	6,581	8,191	19,390	16,153	56,282	58,228
Annual payroll (bil. dol.):								
1990	2,104	117	114	144	352	279	1,007	1,097
1995	2,666	142	137	175	437	361	1,252	1,414
2000	3,879	186	174	231	608	528	1,727	2,152
2005	4,483	220	206	269	700	617	2,013	2,470
2006	4,792	230	214	282	742	661	2,129	2,664
2007	5,027	235	222	292	769	687	2,205	2,822
2008	5,131	232	223	294	775	706	2,229	2,901
2009	4,856	220	213	278	719	655	2,085	2,771

[1] Employment is measured in March, thus some firms (start-ups after March, closures before March, and seasonal firms) will have zero employment and some annual payroll.

Source: U.S. Small Business Administration, Office of Advocacy, "Statistics of U.S. Businesses," <http://www.sba.gov/advo/research/data. html>, accessed June 2012.

Table 774. Number of Active Establishments by Firm Age and Size of Employer: 2010

[In thousands (2,664 represents 2,664,000). A firm may have one establishment (a single unit establishment) or many establishments (a multi-unit firm). Firms are defined at the enterprise level such that all establishments under the operational control of the enterprise are considered part of the firm. These data include nearly all nonfarm private establishments with paid employees as well as some public sector activities. The Business Dynamics Statistics data measure the net change in employment at the establishment level. Data are not to be compared with Table 771, which is shown by industry based on North American Industry Classification System codes. Data are also not comparable to U.S. Small Business Administration data (Tables 772 and 773) due to differing survey methodologies. For more information about concepts and methodology, see <http://www.ces.census.gov/index.php/bds/bds_overview>]

Firm age [1]	Firm size							Share of employ-ment	Share of job creation	Share of job destruc-tion
	1 to 4	5 to 9	10 to 19	20 to 99	100 to 499	Less than 500	500 or more			
Total	2,664	938	532	388	54	4,576	9	1.00	1.00	1.00
Startups	339	35	12	7	1	395	(Z)	0.04	0.24	0.00
1 to 5 years	888	269	138	87	8	1,391	1	0.18	0.21	0.29
6 to 10 years	504	194	109	77	9	895	1	0.15	0.13	0.18
11 to 20 years	579	251	151	111	15	1,107	2	0.25	0.19	0.25
21 years and over	354	188	121	105	21	789	5	0.38	0.24	0.28
Share of employment	0.05	0.06	0.07	0.17	0.14	0.50	0.50	(X)	(X)	(X)
Share of job creation	0.12	0.09	0.09	0.17	0.13	0.60	0.40	(X)	(X)	(X)

X Not applicable. Z Less than 500. [1] Establishment age is computed by taking the difference between the current year of operation and the birth year. Firm age is computed from the age of the establishments belonging to that particular firm. For more information, see <http://www.ces.census.gov/index.php/bds/bds_overview>.

Source: U.S. Census Bureau, Center for Economic Studies, "Business Dynamics Statistics," <http://www.ces.census.gov/index.php/bds/ bds_database_list>, accessed June 2012.

Table 775. Establishment Births, Deaths, and Employment by Sector and Firm Type—Startups, Young, and Mature Firms: 2010

[In thousands (401 represents 401,000). A firm may have one establishment (a single unit establishment) or many establishments (a multi-unit firm). Firms are defined at the enterprise level such that all establishments under the operational control of the enterprise are considered part of the firm. Sectors based on the Standard Industrial Classification System (SIC); see <http://www.osha.gov/pls/imis/sic_manual.html>. These data include nearly all nonfarm private establishments with paid employees as well as some public sector activities. The Business Dynamics Statistics data measure the net change in employment at the establishment level. Data are not comparable to Tables 771, 773, and 776, which are shown by industry based on North American Industry Classification System codes. Data are also not comparable to U.S. Small Business Administration data due to differing survey methodologies. For more information about concepts and methodology, see <http://www.census.gov/ces/dataproducts/bds/overview.html>. Minus sign (–) indicates decrease]

Sector and firm type [1]	Establishments			Number of employees	Change in employment				
	Number	Births [2]	Deaths [3]		Net total	Due to births [2]	Due to deaths [3]	Due to birth and expansion [4]	Due to death and contraction [4]
All sectors: [5]									
Startups [6]	401	401	-	2,345	2,335	2,345	-	2,345	-
Young firms [7]	2,382	106	437	20,555	-1,636	518	2,149	3,225	4,861
Mature firms [8]	2,419	95	185	39,034	-1,332	925	1,373	4,089	5,421
Agriculture:									
Startups [6]	10	10	-	42	42	(D)	-	(D)	-
Young firms [7]	58	4	11	390	-62	14	38	61	133
Mature firms [8]	48	2	4	512	-18	13	27	67	86
Mining:									
Startups [6]	1	1	-	13	13	(D)	-	(D)	-
Young firms [7]	9	-	2	121	-15	5	16	19	36
Mature firms [8]	9	-	1	170	-11	7	10	24	35
Construction:									
Startups [6]	17	17	-	71	71	(D)	-	(D)	-
Young firms [7]	144	10	39	920	-164	31	133	163	345
Mature firms [8]	211	10	29	2,269	-283	41	116	306	589
Transportation, communication, and utilities:									
Startups [6]	16	16	-	84	84	84	-	84	-
Young firms [7]	93	5	19	754	-55	25	84	127	182
Mature firms [8]	101	4	9	2,105	-94	48	81	208	302
Wholesale:									
Startups [6]	19	19	-	85	85	85	-	85	-
Young firms [7]	123	4	20	915	-58	22	85	141	199
Mature firms [8]	165	5	12	2,274	-110	39	79	210	320
Manufacturing:									
Startups [6]	10	10	-	107	107	107	-	107	-
Young firms [7]	82	3	14	1,070	-118	25	121	150	268
Mature firms [8]	118	3	9	3,202	-224	44	114	261	484
Retail:									
Startups [6]	94	94	-	739	739	739	-	739	-
Young firms [7]	499	17	89	4,712	-492	106	544	610	1,103
Mature firms [8]	477	15	30	7,459	-240	174	240	682	921
Finance, insurance, and real estate:									
Startups [6]	33	33	-	134	134	134	-	134	-
Young firms [7]	216	12	39	1,153	-108	42	136	178	286
Mature firms [8]	224	11	17	2,039	-71	87	102	264	336
Services: [6]									
Startups [6]	181	181	-	988	988	988	-	988	-
Young firms [7]	1,116	47	189	10,234	-512	222	926	1,676	2,188
Mature firms [8]	1,043	40	70	18,676	-288	434	585	1,990	2,277

– Represents zero. D Figure withheld to avoid disclosure pertaining to a specific organization or individual. [1] Firm type is computed from the age of the establishments belonging to that particular firm. Establishment age is computed by taking the difference between the current year of operation and the birth year. For more information, see <http://www.ces.census.gov/index.php/bds/bds_overview>. [2] Birth year is defined as the year an establishment first reports positive employment. [3] Death year is defined as the year an establishment permanently shuts down. [4] For explanation of expansions and contractions, see <http://www.ces.census.gov/index.php/bds/bds_overview>. [5] Excludes government and those sectors not elsewhere classified. [6] Less than 1 year old. [7] 1–10 years old. [8] More than 10 years old.

Source: U.S. Census Bureau, Center for Economic Studies, "Business Dynamics Statistics," <http://www.census.gov/ces/dataproducts/bds/>, accessed July 2012.

Table 776. Firm Births and Deaths by Employment Size of Enterprise: 1990 to 2009

[In thousands (541.1 represents 541,100). Data represent activity from March of the beginning year to March of the ending year. Establishments with no employment in the first quarter of the beginning year were excluded. This table provides the number of births and deaths of initial establishments (based on Census ID) as an approximation of firm births and deaths]

Item	Births (initial locations)				Deaths (initial locations)			
	Total	Less than 20 employees	Less than 500 employees	500 employees or more	Total	Less than 20 employees	Less than 500 employees	500 employees or more
Firms:								
1990 to 1991.......	541.1	515.9	540.9	0.3	546.5	517.0	546.1	0.4
1995 to 1996.......	597.8	572.4	597.5	0.3	512.4	485.5	512.0	0.4
2000 to 2001.......	585.1	558.0	584.8	0.3	553.3	524.0	552.8	0.5
2004 to 2005 [1].....	644.1	616.0	643.9	0.3	565.7	539.1	565.5	0.3
2005 to 2006.......	670.1	640.7	669.8	0.2	599.3	573.3	599.1	0.3
2006 to 2007.......	668.4	639.1	668.2	0.2	592.4	564.3	592.1	0.3
2007 to 2008.......	597.1	570.3	596.8	0.2	641.4	613.8	641.2	0.2
2008 to 2009 [2].....	518.5	497.5	518.4	0.1	680.7	655.9	680.5	0.2
Employment:								
1990 to 1991.......	3,105	1,713	2,907	198	3,208	1,723	3,044	164
1995 to 1996.......	3,256	1,845	3,056	200	3,100	1,560	2,808	291
2000 to 2001.......	3,418	1,821	3,109	310	3,262	1,701	3,050	212
2004 to 2005 [1].....	3,609	1,931	3,279	330	3,307	1,685	2,981	326
2005 to 2006.......	3,682	1,999	3,412	270	3,220	1,711	2,964	256
2006 to 2007.......	3,554	1,945	3,325	229	3,482	1,734	3,126	356
2007 to 2008.......	3,376	1,784	3,058	318	3,413	1,846	3,174	240
2008 to 2009 [2].....	2,697	1,545	2,523	173	3,459	1,928	3,195	264

[1] A change in methodology ("based on Census ID" rather than "plant number") has affected the allocation of firms by employment size. [2] Methodology from 2008 forward is defining firm births/deaths as establishment births/deaths for single location firms.

Source: U.S. Small Business Administration, Office of Advocacy, "Firm Size Data, Statistics of U.S. Businesses and Nonemployer Statistics," <http://www.sba.gov/advo/research/data.html>, accessed June 2012.

Table 777. Establishments and Employment Changes from Births, Deaths, Expansions, and Contractions by Employment Size of Enterprise: 2008 to 2009

[In thousands (6,878 represents 6,878,000), except percent. See headnote, Table 776. An establishment is a single physical location at which business is conducted or where services or industrial operations are performed. An enterprise is a business organization consisting of one or more domestic establishments under common ownership or control. Minus sign (–) indicates decrease]

Employment size of firm	Establish-ments	Births [1]	Deaths [2]	Employ-ment	Change in employ-ment	Percent change in employment due to—			
						Births [1]	Deaths [2]	Births and expan-sions [3]	Deaths and con-tractions [4]
Total.....................	6,878	642	813	120,881	-6,372	4.3	-4.9	11.3	-16.6
1–4.........................	2,937	404	543	6,081	425	11.9	-15.5	30.4	-23.5
5–9.........................	1,056	62	79	6,873	-344	5.9	-7.3	15.9	-21.0
10–19.....................	667	33	40	8,493	-513	5.2	-5.9	13.0	-19.0
20–99.....................	705	26	32	20,679	-1,459	3.8	-4.5	10.0	-17.0
100–499.................	356	18	17	17,545	-1,384	3.2	-4.1	8.9	-16.8
Less than 500.........	5,721	544	711	59,672	-3,275	4.9	-6.1	12.9	-18.4
500 or more............	1,157	98	102	61,210	-3,097	3.7	-3.8	9.8	-14.8

[1] Births are establishments that have zero employment in the first quarter of the initial year and positive employment in the first quarter of the subsequent year. [2] Deaths are establishments that have positive employment in the first quarter of the initial year and zero employment in the first quarter of the subsequent year. [3] Expansions are establishments that have positive first quarter employment in both the initial and subsequent years and increase employment during the time period between the first quarter of the initial year and the first quarter of the subsequent year. [4] Contractions are establishments that have positive first quarter employment in both the initial and subsequent years and decrease employment during the time period between the first quarter of the initial year and the first quarter of the subsequent year.

Source: U.S. Census Bureau, "Statistics of U.S. Businesses," <http://www.census.gov/econ/susb/index.html>, accessed June 2012.

Table 778. Small Business Administration Loans to Minority-Owned Small Businesses: 2000 to 2011

[3,675 represents $3,675,000,000. For year ending September 30. A small business must be independently owned and operated, must not be dominant in its particular industry, and must meet standards set by the Small Business Administration as to its annual receipts or number of employees]

Minority group	Number of loans					Amount (mil. dol.)				
	2000	2005	2009	2010	2011	2000	2005	2009	2010	2011
Total minority loans..........	12,041	30,226	11,182	11,871	13,140	3,675	6,294	3,322	4,004	5,973
African American.................	2,183	7,302	2,861	1,764	1,558	415	756	525	334	400
Asian American.................	5,827	13,353	5,295	6,132	7,113	2,390	4,072	2,123	2,760	4,378
Hispanic American..............	3,491	8,748	2,648	3,531	3,983	767	1,341	609	3,061	1,063
Native American.................	540	823	325	433	478	102	125	50	90	132

Source: U.S. Small Business Administration, "SBA Lending Statistics for Major Programs," <http://www.sba.gov/about-sba-services/7571>.

Table 779. U.S. Firms—Ownership by Gender, Ethnicity, Race, and Veteran Status: 2007

[27,093 represents 27,093,000. Based on the 2007 Survey of Business Owners; see text, this section and Appendix III]

Group	All firms [1]		Firms with paid employees			
	Firms (1,000)	Sales and receipts (bil. dol.)	Firms (1,000)	Sales and receipts (bil. dol.)	Employees (1,000)	Annual payroll (bil. dol.)
All firms..........................	27,093	30,032	5,736	29,059	117,310	4,823
Female............................	7,792	1,197	910	1,014	7,520	215
Male..............................	13,901	8,478	3,230	7,909	41,051	1,510
Equally male/female.............	4,602	1,275	1,050	1,092	8,055	215
Hispanic [2].......................	2,260	351	249	280	1,908	54
Equally Hispanic [2]/non-Hispanic.	243	56	47	47	378	11
Non-Hispanic.....................	23,792	10,543	4,895	9,688	54,341	1,875
Minority..........................	5,759	1,025	767	860	5,816	164
Equally minority/nonminority.....	435	108	86	92	696	22
Nonminority......................	20,101	9,816	4,338	9,063	50,114	1,754
Veteran...........................	2,448	1,220	491	1,126	5,793	210
Equally veteran/nonveteran......	1,220	414	271	365	2,448	75
Nonveteran.......................	22,628	9,316	4,428	8,525	48,386	1,656
White.............................	22,595	10,241	4,640	9,407	52,518	1,824
Black or African American........	1,922	136	107	97	910	23
American Indian and Alaska Native.	237	34	24	27	185	6
Asian..............................	1,550	506	397	454	2,808	79
Native Hawaiian and Other Pacific Islander...........	38	6	4	5	38	1
Some other race..................	81	17	13	14	84	2
Publicly held and other firms [3]...	798	19,082	546	19,044	60,684	2,882
Classifiable firms [4]...............	26,295	10,949	5,190	10,015	56,627	1,941

[1] Both firms with paid employees and firms with no paid employees. [2] An Hispanic firm may be of any race and therefore may be included in more than one race group. [3] Publicly held and other firms not classifiable by gender, ethnicity, race, and veteran status. [4] All firms classifiable by gender, ethnicity, race, and veteran status.

Source: U.S. Census Bureau, 2007 Economic Census, *Survey of Business Owners*, <http://www.census.gov/econ/sbo/>, accessed July 2012.

Table 780. Women-Owned Firms by Kind of Business: 2007

[7,792 represents 7,792,000. See headnote, Table 779]

Kind of business	2007 NAICS code [1]	All firms [2]		Firms with paid employees			
		Firms (1,000)	Sales and receipts (mil. dol.)	Firms (1,000)	Sales and receipts (mil. dol.)	Employees (1,000)	Annual payroll (mil. dol.)
Total [3]............................	(X)	7,792	1,196,608	910	1,014,366	7,520	214,673
Forestry, fishing and hunting, and agricultural support services.....	113–115	27	2,033	2	1,309	10	264
Mining.............................	21	18	11,545	2	10,694	23	1,012
Utilities............................	22	4	1,773	(Z)	1,707	2	80
Construction.......................	23	269	96,889	54	87,884	492	21,127
Manufacturing.....................	31–33	113	113,527	34	111,281	568	20,481
Wholesale trade...................	42	133	245,269	39	240,320	378	15,680
Retail trade........................	44–45	919	190,162	126	171,031	836	17,835
Transportation and warehousing [4].	48–49	143	32,849	19	27,867	216	7,050
Information........................	51	97	25,839	9	23,772	118	6,153
Finance and insurance [5]...........	52	200	32,062	35	24,683	160	6,911
Real estate and rental and leasing...	53	658	58,622	57	29,127	183	5,734
Professional, scientific, and technical services........	54	1,097	107,075	143	77,436	632	28,217
Management of companies and enterprises...........	55	2	2,630	2	2,630	51	3,481
Administrative and support and waste management and remediation services..............	56	786	65,609	64	53,875	1,151	26,691
Educational services...............	61	276	9,798	16	6,795	127	2,556
Health care and social assistance....	62	1,232	92,334	127	69,214	1,130	28,887
Arts, entertainment, and recreation.	71	376	16,452	19	9,717	114	3,045
Accommodation and food services...	72	192	47,184	86	43,907	957	12,223
Other services (except public administration) [6]........	81	1,252	44,777	77	20,939	367	7,195
Industries not classified............	99	3	179	3	179	4	50

X Not applicable. Z Less than 500. [1] Based on the 2007 North American Industry Classification System (NAICS); see text, this section. [2] Both firms with paid employees and firms with no paid employees. [3] Firms with more than one establishment are counted in each industry in which they operate, but only once in the total. [4] Excludes scheduled passenger air transportation (NAICS 481111), rail transportation (NAICS 482), and the postal service (NAICS 491). [5] Excludes funds, trusts, and other financial vehicles (NAICS 525). [6] Excludes religious, grantmaking, civic, professional, and similar organizations (NAICS 813) and private households (NAICS 814).

Source: U.S. Census Bureau, 2007 Economic Census, *Survey of Business Owners*, <http://www.census.gov/econ/sbo/>, accessed July 2012.

Table 781. Minority-Owned Firms by Kind of Business: 2007

[1,024,802 represents $1,024,802,000,000. See headnote, Table 779. A minority-owned firm is one in which Blacks or African Americans, American Indians and Alaska Natives, Asians, Native Hawaiians and Other Pacific Islanders, and/or Hispanics own 51 percent or more of the interest or stock of the business]

Kind of business	2007 NAICS code [1]	All firms [2]		Firms with paid employees			
		Firms	Sales and receipts (mil. dol.)	Firms	Sales and receipts (mil. dol.)	Employees	Annual payroll (mil. dol.)
Total [3]	(X)	**5,759,209**	**1,024,802**	**766,533**	**860,492**	**5,816,114**	**164,065**
Forestry, fishing and hunting, and agricultural support services	113–115	24,420	1,966	1,053	988	13,836	257
Mining	21	4,757	2,026	585	1,761	8,629	389
Utilities	22	3,684	413	163	341	832	29
Construction	23	551,209	96,203	62,747	74,195	425,949	15,699
Manufacturing	31–33	81,949	65,651	24,813	63,367	342,183	11,278
Wholesale trade	42	126,845	215,611	46,919	208,760	333,551	13,221
Retail trade	44–45	525,859	191,647	117,905	174,798	627,792	13,135
Transportation and warehousing [4]	48–49	432,204	42,717	23,247	20,572	153,207	4,583
Information	51	63,789	14,700	6,004	13,093	56,066	3,246
Finance and insurance [5]	52	137,969	26,164	21,912	20,157	100,519	4,314
Real estate and rental and leasing	53	345,806	28,293	24,962	12,760	88,492	2,694
Professional, scientific, and technical services	54	575,857	80,515	78,385	64,747	452,297	24,903
Management of companies and enterprises	55	963	2,182	963	2,182	33,552	2,381
Administrative and support and waste management and remediation services	56	606,667	42,679	41,089	32,849	619,762	14,508
Educational services	61	111,860	4,562	6,761	3,339	51,883	1,208
Health care and social assistance	62	754,919	83,869	104,295	69,722	797,444	27,027
Arts, entertainment, and recreation	71	196,639	8,853	6,671	5,116	46,619	1,676
Accommodation and food services	72	241,031	78,325	134,775	73,913	1,408,938	18,522
Other services (except public administration) [6]	81	972,980	38,229	63,480	17,635	252,740	4,955
Industries not classified	99	1,534	198	1,534	198	1,820	39

X Not applicable. [1] Based on the 2007 North American Industry Classification System (NAICS); see text, this section. [2] Both firms with paid employees and firms with no paid employees. [3] Firms with more than one establishment are counted in each industry in which they operate, but only once in the total. [4] Excludes scheduled passenger air transportation (NAICS 481111), rail transportation (NAICS 482), and the postal service (NAICS 491). [5] Excludes funds, trusts, and other financial vehicles (NAICS 525). [6] Excludes religious, grantmaking, civic, professional, and similar organizations (NAICS 813) and private households (NAICS 814).

Source: U.S. Census Bureau, 2007 Economic Census, *Survey of Business Owners*, <http://www.census.gov/econ/sbo/>, accessed July 2012.

Table 782. Hispanic-Owned Firms by Kind of Business: 2007

[350,661 represents $350,661,000,000. See headnote, Table 779]

Kind of business	2007 NAICS code [1]	All firms [2]		Firms with paid employees			
		Firms	Sales and receipts (mil. dol.)	Firms	Sales and receipts (mil. dol.)	Employees	Annual payroll (mil. dol.)
Total [3]	(X)	**2,260,269**	**350,661**	**248,852**	**279,921**	**1,908,161**	**54,296**
Forestry, fishing and hunting, and agricultural support services	113-115	10,201	936	576	595	11,161	179
Mining	21	2,328	1,021	309	899	5,400	242
Utilities	22	1,866	81	41	41	187	9
Construction	23	340,770	56,770	38,319	41,512	260,420	8,919
Manufacturing	31-33	36,619	22,317	10,547	21,159	135,019	4,395
Wholesale trade	42	43,971	63,998	13,112	61,589	98,064	3,777
Retail trade	44-45	186,417	60,974	29,714	54,777	186,781	4,415
Transportation and warehousing [4]	48-49	200,567	21,268	11,903	9,697	70,873	2,069
Information	51	21,435	3,275	2,134	2,684	14,213	710
Finance and insurance [5]	52	51,715	10,888	8,850	8,821	40,381	1,580
Real estate and rental and leasing	53	130,365	10,196	9,240	4,564	31,489	948
Professional, scientific, and technical services	54	185,420	22,394	24,736	17,137	129,693	6,305
Management of companies and enterprises	55	282	911	282	911	15,801	1,156
Administrative and support and waste management and remediation services	56	313,313	19,833	20,874	14,311	262,892	6,168
Educational services	61	33,144	1,378	1,596	1,011	13,992	372
Health care and social assistance	62	234,824	19,260	23,171	15,174	181,742	6,027
Arts, entertainment, and recreation	71	63,918	2,767	2,315	1,394	13,559	507
Accommodation and food services	72	65,602	18,472	31,164	17,277	354,305	4,697
Other services (except public administration) [6]	81	337,637	13,826	20,093	6,273	81,709	1,803
Industries not classified	99	425	95	425	95	480	17

X Not applicable. [1] Based on the 2007 North American Industry Classification System (NAICS); see text, this section. [2] Both firms with paid employees and firms with no paid employees. [3] Firms with more than one establishment are counted in each industry in which they operate, but only once in the total. [4] Excludes scheduled passenger air transportation (NAICS 481111), rail transportation (NAICS 482), and the postal service (NAICS 491). [5] Excludes funds, trusts, and other financial vehicles (NAICS 525). [6] Excludes religious, grantmaking, civic, professional, and similar organizations (NAICS 813) and private households (NAICS 814).

Source: U.S. Census Bureau, 2007 Economic Census, *Survey of Business Owners*, <http://www.census.gov/econ/sbo/>, accessed July 2012.

Table 783. Black-Owned Firms by Kind of Business: 2007

[135,740 represents $135,740,000,000. See headnote, Table 779]

Kind of business	2007 NAICS code [1]	All firms [2]		Firms with paid employees			
		Firms	Sales and receipts (mil. dol.)	Firms	Sales and receipts (mil. dol.)	Employ-ees	Annual payroll (mil dol.)
Total [3]	(X)	1,921,864	135,740	106,566	97,145	909,552	23,335
Forestry, fishing and hunting, and agricultural support services	113–115	4,347	335	230	137	1,254	27
Mining	21	(S)	(S)	(S)	(S)	(S)	(S)
Utilities	22	1,316	68	18	48	92	4
Construction	23	125,818	13,188	9,605	9,808	56,088	1,977
Manufacturing	31–33	16,041	6,848	1,854	6,501	28,399	1,014
Wholesale trade	42	19,384	15,153	2,300	14,497	17,976	743
Retail trade	44–45	148,181	20,512	11,142	17,486	57,335	1,432
Transportation and warehousing [4]	48–49	168,386	11,158	5,827	3,961	40,111	1,040
Information	51	23,442	2,532	1,204	2,120	11,094	731
Finance and insurance [5]	52	42,100	3,148	4,737	2,032	15,982	605
Real estate and rental and leasing	53	92,655	3,957	3,323	1,301	10,972	296
Professional, scientific, and technical services	54	163,761	12,600	12,916	9,129	79,597	3,671
Management of companies and enterprises	55	196	351	196	351	3,318	191
Administrative and support and waste management and remediation services	56	216,763	9,937	9,630	7,175	167,507	3,490
Educational services	61	47,727	1,121	1,457	675	11,895	253
Health care and social assistance	62	365,140	16,752	24,372	11,447	226,145	4,965
Arts, entertainment, and recreation	71	86,357	3,401	2,156	2,022	11,385	567
Accommodation and food services	72	40,959	6,790	7,347	6,105	139,491	1,695
Other services (except public administration) [6]	81	358,443	7,619	8,023	2,105	29,548	590
Industries not classified	99	487	37	487	37	486	6

X Not applicable. S Withheld because estimate did not meet publication standards. [1] Based on the 2007 North American Industry Classification System (NAICS); see text, this section. [2] Both firms with paid employees and firms with no paid employees. [3] Firms with more than one establishment are counted in each industry in which they operate, but only once in the total. [4] Excludes scheduled passenger air transportation (NAICS 481111), rail transportation (NAICS 482), and the postal service (NAICS 491). [5] Excludes funds, trusts, and other financial vehicles (NAICS 525). [6] Excludes religious, grantmaking, civic, professional, and similar organizations (NAICS 813) and private households (NAICS 814).

Source: U.S. Census Bureau, 2007 Economic Census, *Survey of Business Owners*, <http://www.census.gov/econ/sbo/>, accessed July 2012.

Table 784. Asian–Owned Firms by Kind of Business: 2007

[506,048 represents $506,048,000,000. See headnote, Table 779]

Kind of business	2007 NAICS code [1]	All firms [2]		Firms with paid employees			
		Firms	Sales and receipts (mil. dol.)	Firms	Sales and receipts (mil. dol.)	Employ-ees	Annual payroll (mil. dol.)
Total [3]	(X)	1,549,559	506,048	397,426	453,574	2,807,771	79,230
Forestry, fishing and hunting, and agricultural support services	113–115	5,125	429	122	165	798	27
Mining	21	3	(D)	1	(D)	([4])	(D)
Utilities	22	474	119	63	108	375	11
Construction	23	70,752	18,664	10,542	16,005	77,302	3,353
Manufacturing	31–33	26,375	33,723	11,856	33,022	166,307	5,399
Wholesale trade	42	60,458	130,742	30,525	127,076	208,221	8,272
Retail trade	44–45	190,830	106,981	77,357	99,408	375,276	7,021
Transportation and warehousing [5]	48–49	74,117	10,105	5,284	6,487	37,094	1,314
Information	51	17,428	8,561	2,501	8,023	28,752	1,755
Finance and insurance [6]	52	42,099	11,343	7,579	8,648	39,133	1,907
Real estate and rental and leasing	53	116,035	13,196	11,467	6,345	41,566	1,280
Professional, scientific, and technical services	54	213,705	42,339	38,190	35,918	225,756	13,842
Management of companies and enterprises	55	441	847	441	847	13,182	941
Administrative and support and waste management and remediation services	56	75,485	11,239	9,932	9,758	157,040	4,086
Educational services	61	29,515	1,943	3,545	1,545	24,201	541
Health care and social assistance	62	164,224	44,662	54,839	39,999	362,344	14,672
Arts, entertainment, and recreation	71	40,220	2,202	1,964	1,367	19,445	434
Accommodation and food services	72	133,729	52,073	96,015	49,556	891,886	11,844
Other services (except public administration) [7]	81	287,831	16,350	35,310	8,816	137,171	2,450
Industries not classified	99	613	62	613	62	730	14

X Not applicable. D Withheld to avoid disclosing data for individual companies; data are included in higher level totals. [1] Based on the 2007 North American Industry Classification System (NAICS); see text, this section. [2] Both firms with paid employees and firms with no paid employees. [3] Firms with more than one establishment are counted in each industry in which they operate, but only once in the total. [4] 20 to 99 employees. [5] Excludes scheduled passenger air transportation (NAICS 481111), rail transportation (NAICS 482), and the postal service (NAICS 491). [6] Excludes funds, trusts, and other financial vehicles (NAICS 525). [7] Excludes religious, grantmaking, civic, professional, and similar organizations (NAICS 813) and private households (NAICS 814).

Source: U.S. Census Bureau, 2007 Economic Census, *Survey of Business Owners*, <http://www.census.gov/econ/sbo/>, accessed July 2012.

Table 785. Native Hawaiian- and Other Pacific Islander-Owned Firms by Kind of Business: 2007

[6,319 represents $6,319,000,000. See headnote, Table 779]

Kind of business	2007 NAICS code [1]	All firms [2]		Firms with paid employees			
		Firms	Sales and receipts (mil. dol.)	Firms	Sales and receipts (mil. dol.)	Employ-ees	Annual payroll (mil.dol.)
Total [3]	(X)	**37,687**	**6,319**	**4,151**	**5,250**	**37,801**	**1,217**
Forestry, fishing and hunting, and agricultural support services	113–115	(S)	(S)	(S)	(S)	(S)	(S)
Mining	21	31	(D)	1	(D)	(⁴)	(D)
Utilities	22	186	8	31	(D)	(⁴)	(D)
Construction	23	4,991	1,555	847	1,354	5,993	284
Manufacturing	31–33	623	295	99	280	1,714	53
Wholesale trade	42	631	488	156	432	923	44
Retail trade	44–45	3,880	1,258	464	1,116	3,278	100
Transportation and warehousing [5]	48–49	2,274	261	133	162	896	32
Information	51	414	120	31	108	610	31
Finance and insurance [6]	52	1,030	101	179	79	491	16
Real estate and rental and leasing	53	2,528	227	189	110	613	22
Professional, scientific, and technical services	54	3,619	606	464	499	3,930	226
Management of companies and enterprises	55	13	(D)	13	(D)	(⁷)	(D)
Administrative and support and waste management and remediation services	56	3,542	385	293	339	7,948	166
Educational services	61	614	40	29	34	524	11
Health care and social assistance	62	3,723	290	460	225	2,332	89
Arts, entertainment, and recreation	71	2,625	113	(S)	(S)	(S)	(S)
Accommodation and food services	72	1,316	380	558	369	6,030	92
Other services (except public administration) [8]	81	5,264	168	182	57	759	18
Industries not classified	99	(S)	(S)	(S)	(S)	(S)	(S)

D Withheld to avoid disclosing data for individual companies; data are included in higher level totals. S Withheld because estimate did not meet publication standards. X Not applicable. [1] Based on the 2007 North American Industry Classification System (NAICS); see text, this section. [2] Both firms with paid employees and firms with no paid employees. [3] Firms with more than one establishment are counted in each industry in which they operate, but only once in the total. [4] 0 to 19 employees. [5] Excludes scheduled passenger air transportation (NAICS 481111), rail transportation (NAICS 482), and the postal service (NAICS 491). [6] Excludes funds, trusts, and other financial vehicles (NAICS 525). [7] 100 to 249 employees. [8] Excludes religious, grantmaking, civic, professional, and similar organizations (NAICS 813) and private households (NAICS 814).

Source: U.S. Census Bureau, 2007 Economic Census, *Survey of Business Owners*, <http://www.census.gov/econ/sbo/>, accessed July 2012.

Table 786. American Indian- and Alaska Native-Owned Firms by Kind of Business: 2007

[34,354 represents $34,354,000,000. See headnote, Table 779]

Kind of business	2007 NAICS code [1]	All firms [2]		Firms with paid employees			
		Firms	Sales and receipts (mil. dol.)	Firms	Sales and receipts (mil. dol.)	Employ-ees	Annual payroll (mil. dol.)
Total [3]	(X)	**236,691**	**34,354**	**23,662**	**27,494**	**185,037**	**5,930**
Forestry, fishing and hunting, and agricultural support services	113–115	5,026	279	153	84	493	23
Mining	21	814	293	159	228	1,111	43
Utilities	22	248	(D)	13	(D)	(⁴)	(D)
Construction	23	37,693	8,450	5,178	7,026	37,722	1,529
Manufacturing	31–33	4,985	2,664	1,011	2,558	13,947	512
Wholesale trade	42	4,810	4,288	955	4,124	7,275	296
Retail trade	44–45	19,776	5,396	2,546	4,777	18,312	409
Transportation and warehousing [5]	48–49	12,916	1,519	871	805	6,116	195
Information	51	3,002	383	261	309	2,720	88
Finance and insurance [6]	52	4,573	675	1,013	484	5,485	203
Real estate and rental and leasing	53	12,410	887	894	377	3,402	106
Professional, scientific, and technical services	54	23,886	2,583	2,869	1,805	14,252	699
Management of companies and enterprises	55	31	34	31	34	789	60
Administrative and support and waste management and remediation services	56	22,714	1,935	1,405	1,465	25,928	675
Educational services	61	5,193	133	140	82	1,454	34
Health care and social assistance	62	25,112	1,663	2,324	1,214	16,912	467
Arts, entertainment, and recreation	71	13,506	604	265	327	1,103	175
Accommodation and food services	72	5,385	1,172	2,012	1,091	21,283	251
Other services (except public administration) [7]	81	34,545	1,250	1,498	562	6,538	159
Industries not classified	99	132	8	132	8	120	3

D Withheld to avoid disclosing data for individual companies; data are included in higher level totals. X Not applicable. [1] Based on the 2007 North American Industry Classification System (NAICS); see text, this section. [2] Both firms with paid employees and firms with no paid employees. [3] Firms with more than one establishment are counted in each industry in which they operate, but only once in the total. [4] 20 to 99 employees. [5] Excludes scheduled passenger air transportation (NAICS 481111), rail transportation (NAICS 482), and the postal service (NAICS 491). [6] Excludes funds, trusts, and other financial vehicles (NAICS 525). [7] Excludes religious, grantmaking, civic, professional, and similar organizations (NAICS 813) and private households (NAICS 814).

Source: U.S. Census Bureau, 2007 Economic Census, *Survey of Business Owners*, <http://www.census.gov/econ/sbo/>, accessed July 2012.

Table 787. Bankruptcy Petitions Filed and Pending by Type and Chapter: 1990 to 2011

[For years ending June 30. Covers only bankruptcy cases filed under the Bankruptcy Reform Act of 1978. Bankruptcy: legal recognition that a company or individual is insolvent and must restructure or liquidate. Petitions "filed" means the commencement of a proceeding through the presentation of a petition to the clerk of the court; "pending" is a proceeding in which the administration has not been completed]

Item	1990	1995	2000	2006	2007	2008	2009	2010	2011
Total filed............	725,484	858,104	1,276,922	1,484,570	751,056	967,831	1,306,315	1,572,597	1,529,560
Business [1].............	64,688	51,288	36,910	31,562	23,889	33,822	55,021	59,608	52,134
Nonbusiness [2]..........	660,796	806,816	1,240,012	1,453,008	727,167	934,009	1,251,294	1,512,989	1,477,426
Chapter 7 [3].............	468,171	552,244	864,183	1,142,958	435,064	592,376	870,266	1,091,322	1,047,131
Chapter 11 [4]...........	2,116	1,755	722	749	540	780	1,088	1,827	1,884
Chapter 13 [5]...........	190,509	252,817	375,107	309,298	291,560	340,852	379,939	419,836	428,410
Voluntary...............	723,886	856,991	1,276,146	1,484,085	750,577	967,248	1,305,349	1,571,619	(NA)
Involuntary.............	1,598	1,113	776	485	479	583	966	978	(NA)
Chapter 7 [3].............	505,337	581,390	885,447	1,164,815	450,332	615,748	907,603	1,133,320	1,083,671
Chapter 9 [6].............	7	12	8	10	7	4	6	12	7
Chapter 11 [4]...........	19,591	13,221	9,947	6,224	5,586	7,293	13,951	14,272	12,714
Chapter 12 [7]...........	1,351	904	732	360	386	314	422	660	717
Chapter 13 [5]...........	199,186	262,551	380,770	313,085	294,693	344,421	384,187	424,242	432,333
Section 304 [8]...........	12	26	18	[9]36	(X)	(X)	(X)	(X)	(X)
Chapter 15 [9]...........	(X)	(X)	(X)	40	52	51	146	91	118
Total pending.........	961,919	1,090,446	1,400,416	1,411,212	1,312,016	1,325,220	1,527,073	1,659,399	1,702,005

X Not applicable. NA Not available. [1] Business bankrupties include those filed under Chapters 7, 9, 11, 12, 13, or 15. [2] Includes other petitions, not shown separately. [3] Chapter 7, liquidation of nonexempt assets of businesses or individuals. [4] Chapter 11, individual or business reorganization. [5] Chapter 13, adjustment of debts of an individual with regular income. [6] Chapter 9, adjustment of debts of a municipality. [7] Chapter 12, adjustment of debts of a family farmer with regular income, effective November 26, 1986. [8] Chapter 11, U.S.C., Section 304, cases ancillary to foreign proceedings. [9] Chapter 15 was added and Section 304 was terminated by changes in the Bankruptcy Laws effective October 17, 2005.

Source: Administrative Office of the U.S. Courts, *Bankruptcy Statistics*, <http://www.uscourts.gov/Statistics/BankruptcyStatistics.aspx>, accessed July 2012.

Table 788. Bankruptcy Cases Filed by State: 2000 to 2011

[In thousands (1,276.9 represents 1,276,900). For years ending June 30. Covers only bankruptcy cases filed under the Bankruptcy Reform Act of 1978. Bankruptcy: legal recognition that a company or individual is insolvent and must restructure or liquidate. Petitions "filed" means the commencement of a proceeding through the presentation of a petition to the clerk of the court]

State	2000	2005	2010	2011	State	2000	2005	2010	2011
Total [1]....................	1,276.9	1,637.3	1,572.6	1,529.6	Missouri..................	26.3	39.2	32.9	31.6
Alabama.................	31.4	42.6	34.9	32.3	Montana.................	3.3	4.4	3.1	2.8
Alaska..................	1.4	1.6	1.1	1.1	Nebraska................	5.6	9.6	7.9	7.4
Arizona.................	21.7	32.4	40.7	41.4	Nevada.................	14.3	16.3	31.0	28.0
Arkansas...............	16.3	25.5	16.9	15.9	New Hampshire.........	3.9	4.9	5.7	5.4
California...............	160.6	122.6	242.0	260.6	New Jersey.............	38.7	40.7	39.7	41.1
Colorado................	15.6	30.2	31.9	32.1	New Mexico............	7.1	10.1	6.6	6.3
Connecticut.............	11.4	11.8	11.3	10.8	New York..............	61.7	81.7	58.2	53.2
Delaware...............	4.9	3.6	4.5	4.2	North Carolina.........	25.8	37.5	27.7	25.4
District of Columbia.....	2.6	1.9	1.3	1.1	North Dakota...........	2.0	2.5	1.6	1.5
Florida.................	74.0	85.8	107.4	105.0	Ohio....................	53.6	95.8	72.9	65.3
Georgia.................	57.9	77.3	77.8	77.7	Oklahoma..............	19.3	28.2	15.1	14.0
Hawaii..................	5.0	3.2	3.7	3.8	Oregon.................	18.1	25.3	20.1	19.0
Idaho...................	7.3	9.7	8.3	8.2	Pennsylvania...........	43.8	62.3	38.8	37.5
Illinois.................	62.3	83.6	80.8	78.8	Rhode Island...........	4.8	4.4	5.4	5.4
Indiana.................	37.5	55.9	49.3	43.4	South Carolina.........	11.7	15.2	9.7	8.9
Iowa...................	8.2	14.3	10.4	8.9	South Dakota...........	2.1	2.9	2.0	2.0
Kansas.................	11.4	17.3	11.4	10.7	Tennessee.............	47.1	60.8	52.5	49.1
Kentucky...............	20.8	29.2	26.0	23.5	Texas.................	62.9	97.5	57.8	56.1
Louisiana...............	23.1	31.1	19.5	18.5	Utah..................	14.4	20.5	17.0	19.2
Maine..................	4.1	4.7	4.1	4.0	Vermont................	1.6	1.7	1.7	1.4
Maryland...............	31.1	28.5	29.1	28.5	Virginia................	37.1	38.8	37.8	35.6
Massachusetts..........	16.7	19.6	22.9	22.2	Washington............	31.2	37.7	33.5	33.8
Michigan...............	36.4	68.5	71.0	63.4	West Virginia...........	8.2	12.6	6.6	5.5
Minnesota..............	15.4	19.4	22.6	21.1	Wisconsin..............	18.0	29.0	30.0	29.1
Mississippi.............	17.9	21.8	14.8	14.0	Wyoming................	2.0	2.5	1.5	1.5

[1] Includes Island Areas, not shown separately.

Source: Administrative Office of the U.S. Courts, *Statistical Tables for the Federal Judiciary*, <http://www.uscourts.gov/Statistics.aspx>.

Table 789. Patents and Trademarks: 1990 to 2011

[In thousands (99.2 represents 99,200). Calendar year data. Covers U.S. patents issued to citizens of the United States and residents of foreign countries. For data on foreign countries, see Table 1406]

Type	1990	1995	2000	2005	2007	2008	2009	2010	2011
Patents issued	**99.2**	**113.8**	**176.0**	**157.7**	**182.9**	**185.2**	**191.9**	**244.3**	**247.7**
Inventions	90.4	101.4	157.5	143.8	157.3	157.8	167.3	219.6	224.5
Individuals	17.3	17.4	22.4	14.7	14.0	12.6	12.6	16.6	15.6
Corporations:									
United States	36.1	44.0	70.9	65.2	70.5	70.0	74.8	97.8	99.5
Foreign [1]	36.0	39.1	63.3	63.2	72.0	74.5	79.3	104.3	108.5
U.S. government	1.0	1.0	0.9	0.7	0.7	0.7	0.7	0.9	0.9
Designs	8.0	11.7	17.4	13.0	24.1	25.6	23.1	22.8	21.4
Botanical plants	0.3	0.4	0.5	0.7	1.0	1.2	1.0	1.0	1.0
Reissues	0.4	0.3	0.5	0.2	0.5	0.6	0.5	0.9	1.0
U.S. residents	52.8	64.4	96.9	82.6	93.7	92.0	95.0	121.2	121.2
Foreign country residents	46.2	49.4	79.1	75.2	89.2	93.2	96.9	123.2	126.5
Percent of total	46.7	43.4	44.9	47.6	48.8	50.3	50.5	50.4	51.1
Trademarks:									
Applications filed	127.3	181.0	361.8	334.7	401.0	390.8	351.9	370.2	(NA)
Issued	60.8	92.5	115.2	154.8	218.8	233.9	222.1	210.6	(NA)
Trademarks	53.6	85.6	106.4	121.6	170.8	194.4	177.4	165.2	(NA)
Trademark renewals	7.2	6.9	8.8	33.3	48.1	39.5	44.7	45.4	(NA)

NA Not available. [1] Includes patents to foreign governments.

Source: U.S. Patent and Trademark Office, "Statistical Reports Available For Viewing, Calendar Year Patent Statistics," <http://www.uspto.gov/web/offices/ac/ido/oeip/taf/reports.htm> and unpublished sources.

Table 790. Patents by State and Island Areas: 2011

[Includes only U.S. patents granted to residents of the United States and territories]

State	Total	Inventions	Designs	Botanical plants	Reissues	State	Total	Inventions	Designs	Botanical plants	Reissues
Total	**121,247**	**108,626**	**11,756**	**308**	**557**	Missouri	1,003	878	119	2	4
						Montana	114	96	18	–	–
Alabama	416	352	59	4	1	Nebraska	247	208	39	–	–
Alaska	32	27	5	–	–	Nevada	674	554	116	–	4
Arizona	2,248	2,069	172	2	5	New Hampshire	805	724	70	–	11
Arkansas	188	134	52	–	2	New Jersey	4,277	3,852	394	6	25
California	30,748	28,148	2,364	94	142	New Mexico	412	389	18	1	4
Colorado	2,397	2,102	285	–	10	New York	7,842	6,956	839	22	25
Connecticut	2,121	1,939	170	1	11	North Carolina	2,884	2,607	257	6	14
Delaware	457	418	39	–	–	North Dakota	95	84	10	–	1
District of Columbia	102	97	4	–	1	Ohio	3,903	3,177	712	1	13
Florida	3,841	3,136	658	22	25	Oklahoma	529	484	38	1	6
Georgia	2,206	1,932	246	15	13	Oregon	2,371	1,977	341	43	10
Hawaii	128	101	23	2	2	Pennsylvania	3,652	3,219	411	7	15
Idaho	1,089	1,032	51	–	6	Rhode Island	351	306	44	–	1
Illinois	4,594	3,806	767	3	18	South Carolina	793	656	132	2	3
Indiana	1,633	1,437	187	2	7	South Dakota	106	96	10	–	–
Iowa	856	811	44	–	1	Tennessee	1,080	969	101	4	6
Kansas	805	707	92	–	6	Texas	8,044	7,584	420	1	39
Kentucky	551	488	59	1	3	Utah	1,215	1,066	144	–	5
Louisiana	368	308	52	6	2	Vermont	536	504	31	–	1
Maine	202	183	18	–	1	Virginia	1,737	1,600	127	–	10
Maryland	1,638	1,511	115	1	11	Washington	5,266	4,767	464	5	30
Massachusetts	5,526	5,191	310	10	15	West Virginia	109	94	15	–	–
Michigan	4,397	3,964	382	36	15	Wisconsin	2,154	1,784	352	5	13
Minnesota	4,227	3,860	347	2	18	Wyoming	74	65	8	–	1
Mississippi	172	147	23	1	1	Island areas	32	30	2	–	–

– Represents zero.

Source: U.S. Patent and Trademark Office, "Statistical Reports Available For Viewing, Calendar Year Patent Statistics," <http://www.uspto.gov/web/offices/ac/ido/oeip/taf/reports.htm>.

Table 791. Copyright Registration by Subject Matter: 2000 to 2010

[In thousands (497.6 represents 497,600). For years ending September 30. Comprises claims to copyrights registered for both U.S. and foreign works. Semiconductor chips and renewals are not considered copyright registration claims]

Subject matter	2000	2005	2010	2011	Subject matter	2000	2005	2010	2011
Total copyright claims	**497.6**	**515.2**	**636.0**	**669.5**	Musical works [2]	138.9	133.7	124.5	146.8
Monographs [1]	169.7	191.4	245.8	265.8	Works of the visual arts [3]	85.8	82.5	97.2	91.2
Serials	69.0	57.7	90.5	58.0	Semiconductor chip products	0.7	0.5	0.3	0.3
Sound recordings	34.2	49.9	77.9	107.7	Renewals	16.8	15.8	0.1	0.2

[1] Includes computer software and machine readable works. [2] Includes dramatic works, accompanying music, choreography, pantomimes, motion pictures, and filmstrips. [3] Two-dimensional works of fine and graphic art, including prints and art reproductions; sculptural works; technical drawings and models; photographs; commercial prints and labels; works of applied arts, cartographic works, and multimedia works.

Source: The Library of Congress, Copyright Office, *Annual Report of the Registrar of Copyrights*, <http://www.copyright.gov/reports/>, and *Annual Report of the Librarian of Congress*, <http://www.loc.gov/about/reports/annualreports/index.html>.

Table 792. Net Stock of Private Fixed Assets by Industry: 2000 to 2010

[In billions of dollars (21,230 represents $21,230,000,000,000). Estimates as of Dec. 31. Net stock estimates are presented in terms of current cost and cover equipment, software, and structures. Fixed assets are assets that are used repeatedly, or continuously, in processes of production for an extended period of time. (pt) = part]

Industry	NAICS code [1]	2000	2005	2009	2010
Private fixed assets	(X)	**21,230**	**30,593**	**33,887**	**34,201**
Agriculture, forestry, fishing, and hunting	11	338	431	481	490
Farms [2]	111, 112	310	396	438	446
Forestry, fishing, and related activities	113-115	27	35	42	44
Mining	21	535	1,018	1,308	1,404
Oil and gas extraction	211	405	860	1,102	1,190
Mining, except oil and gas	212	89	100	118	120
Support activities for mining	213	42	57	89	94
Utilities	22	1,038	1,379	1,723	1,825
Construction	23	172	232	280	276
Manufacturing	31-33	1,763	1,988	2,229	2,229
Durable goods	(X)	996	1,109	1,217	1,206
Wood products	321	31	35	37	36
Nonmetallic mineral products	327	56	67	76	75
Primary metals	331	125	131	150	152
Fabricated metal products	332	113	127	145	145
Machinery	333	134	140	152	152
Computer and electronic products	334	247	274	296	288
Electrical equipment, appliances, and components	335	45	47	51	50
Motor vehicles, bodies and trailers, and parts	3361-3363	109	134	141	139
Other transportation equipment	3364, 3365, 3369	75	79	87	87
Furniture and related products	337	16	19	20	20
Miscellaneous manufacturing	339	45	56	63	63
Nondurable goods	(X)	767	879	1,012	1,023
Food and beverage and tobacco products	311, 312	186	223	260	264
Textile mills and textile product mills	313, 314	44	41	40	39
Apparel and leather and allied products	315, 316	17	17	17	17
Paper products	322	100	102	106	103
Printing and related support activities	323	40	46	48	47
Petroleum and coal products	324	93	118	166	176
Chemical products	325	221	256	295	298
Plastics and rubber products	326	67	76	82	81
Wholesale trade	42	338	429	494	495
Retail trade	44-45	654	960	1,133	1,130
Transportation and warehousing [3]	48-49	819	961	1,079	1,096
Air transportation	481	184	209	216	214
Railroad transportation	482	284	316	355	363
Water transportation	483	37	38	41	41
Truck transportation	484	72	98	108	106
Transit and ground passenger transportation	485	37	40	42	43
Pipeline transportation	486	73	112	154	167
Warehousing and storage	493	22	30	39	39
Information	51	888	1,119	1,286	1,294
Publishing industries (includes software)	511, 516 (pt)	60	89	113	115
Motion picture and sound recording industries	512	33	43	45	44
Broadcasting and telecommunications	515, 517	766	929	1,055	1,062
Information and data processing services	516 (pt), 518, 519	28	57	73	73
Finance and insurance	52	843	1,164	1,349	1,342
Federal Reserve banks	521	9	9	10	10
Credit intermediation and related activities	522	480	638	692	680
Securities, commodity contracts, and investments	523	88	117	152	155
Insurance carriers and related activities	524	169	221	248	248
Funds, trusts, and other financial vehicles	525	97	178	248	248
Real estate and rental and leasing	53	11,513	17,610	18,531	18,567
Real estate	531	11,289	17,318	18,212	18,252
Rental and leasing services and lessors of intangible assets [4]	532, 533	224	292	319	315
Professional, scientific, and technical services [3]	54	211	318	404	415
Legal services	5411	23	35	40	41
Computer systems design and related services	5415	45	48	56	58
Management of companies and enterprises [5]	55	268	340	403	409
Admin/support waste mgt	56	153	207	242	248
Administrative and support services	561	87	127	150	155
Waste management and remediation services	562	66	80	92	93
Educational services	61	213	327	444	458
Health care and social assistance	62	681	979	1,167	1,194
Ambulatory health care services	621	201	266	308	312
Hospitals	622	423	617	744	764
Nursing and residential care facilities	623	32	55	68	69
Social assistance	624	25	40	48	49
Arts, entertainment, and recreation	71	128	199	245	247
Performing arts, spectator sports, museums, and related activities	711, 712	48	76	96	97
Amusements, gambling, and recreation industries	713	80	124	149	151
Accommodation and food services	72	342	457	555	552
Accommodation	721	188	263	337	333
Food services and drinking places	722	154	193	219	219
Other services, except government	81	336	477	534	532

X Not applicable. [1] Based on North American Industry Classification System, 2002; see text this section. [2] NAICS crop and animal production. [3] Includes other activities, not shown separately. [4] Intangible assets include patents, trademarks, and franchise agreements, but not copyrights. [5] Consists of bank and other holding companies.

Source: U.S. Bureau of Economic Analysis, "Table 3.1ES. Current-Cost Net Stock of Private Fixed Assets by Industry," August 2011, <http://www.bea.gov/iTable/iTable.cfm?ReqID=10&step=1>.

Table 793. Private Domestic Investment in Current and Chained (2005) Dollars: 1990 to 2010

[In billions of dollars (861 represents $861,000,000,000). Covers equipment, software, and structures. Minus sign (–) indicates decrease. For explanation of chained dollars; see text, Section 13]

Item	1990	2000	2005	2006	2007	2008	2009	2010
CURRENT DOLLARS								
Gross private domestic investment	**861**	**1,772**	**2,172**	**2,327**	**2,295**	**2,088**	**1,547**	**1,795**
Less: Consumption of fixed capital	560	987	1,291	1,391	1,476	1,543	1,542	1,541
Equals: Net private domestic investment	301	785	882	936	819	545	4	254
Fixed investment	846	1,718	2,122	2,267	2,266	2,129	1,708	1,728
Less: Consumption of fixed capital	560	987	1,291	1,391	1,476	1,543	1,542	1,541
Equals: Net fixed investment	286	731	832	876	790	586	165	187
Nonresidential	622	1,269	1,347	1,505	1,638	1,656	1,353	1,390
Residential	224	449	775	762	629	472	355	338
Change in private inventories	15	55	50	60	29	-41	-161	67
CHAINED (2005) DOLLARS								
Gross private domestic investment	**990**	**1,963**	**2,172**	**2,232**	**2,160**	**1,940**	**1,454**	**1,715**
Less: Consumption of fixed capital	627	1,063	1,291	1,341	1,396	1,437	1,455	1,464
Equals: Net private domestic investment	363	900	882	891	764	503	-1	251
Fixed investment	984	1,907	2,122	2,173	2,131	1,979	1,606	1,648
Nonresidential	615	1,311	1,347	1,456	1,550	1,538	1,263	1,319
Residential	386	580	775	718	584	444	346	331
Change in private inventories	17	60	50	59	28	-36	-145	59

Source: U.S. Bureau of Economic Analysis, National Income and Product Accounts Interactive Data, <http://www.bea.gov/iTable/index_nipa.cfm>, accessed July 2012.

Table 794. Information and Communications Technology (ICT) Equipment and Computer Software Expenditures: 2009 and 2010

[In millions of dollars (88,346 represents $88,346,000,000). Covers only companies with employees. The Information and Communication Technology Survey collects noncapitalized and capitalized data on information and communication technology equipment, including computer software. This survey is sent to a sample of approximately 46,500 private nonfarm employer businesses operating in the United States]

Type of expenditure and industry	NAICS code [1]	Noncapitalized expenditures [2]		Capitalized expenditures [3]	
		2009	2010	2009	2010
Total expenditures for ICT equipment and computer software	(X)	**88,346**	**93,586**	**166,940**	**169,542**
Total equipment expenditures	(X)	32,557	33,685	(NA)	(NA)
Purchases	(X)	16,939	17,828	101,904	106,054
Computer and peripheral equipment	(X)	11,118	11,736	48,513	53,478
Information and communication technology equipment	(X)	5,597	5,790	47,924	47,397
Electromedical and electrotherapeutic apparatus	(X)	224	302	5,468	5,179
Operating leases and rental payments	(X)	15,619	15,858	(NA)	(NA)
Computer and peripheral equipment	(X)	10,465	10,314	(NA)	(NA)
Information and communication technology equipment	(X)	4,156	4,144	(NA)	(NA)
Electromedical and electrotherapeutic apparatus	(X)	999	1,400	(NA)	(NA)
Total computer software expenditures	(X)	55,788	59,901	(NA)	(NA)
Purchases and payroll for developing software	(X)	25,866	28,531	65,036	63,847
Software licensing and service/maintenance agreements	(X)	29,922	31,369	(NA)	(NA)
Forestry, fishing, and agricultural services	113–115	62	59	101	94
Mining	21	2,001	1,204	1,045	1,044
Utilities	22	1,513	1,694	4,157	4,300
Construction	23	924	796	1,204	1,287
Manufacturing	31–33	14,068	15,716	15,813	15,125
Durable goods industries	321, 327, 33	9,382	10,173	9,123	8,774
Nondurable goods industries	31, 322-326	4,687	5,543	6,690	6,350
Wholesale trade	42	3,023	2,895	6,582	6,014
Retail trade	44–45	4,067	5,407	10,776	11,243
Transportation and warehousing	48–49	1,721	1,800	2,905	3,102
Information	51	13,864	13,370	52,516	57,917
Finance and insurance	52	20,719	22,026	25,968	26,123
Real estate and rental and leasing	53	1,377	1,206	2,360	1,750
Professional, scientific, and technical services	54	10,669	10,620	11,317	12,079
Management of companies and enterprises	55	955	1,154	2,097	1,994
Admin/support and waste management/remediation services	56	2,413	2,333	3,901	4,183
Educational services	61	1,881	1,897	2,430	2,503
Health care and social assistance	62	7,116	7,839	14,494	15,121
Arts, entertainment, and recreation	71	500	502	951	1,041
Accommodation and food services	72	937	826	1,532	1,414
Other services (except public administration)	81	1,311	1,427	2,666	2,403
Equipment expenditures serving multiple industry codes	(X)	530	816	1,365	807

NA Not available. X Not applicable. [1] Based on North American Industry Classification System, 2002; see text, this section. [2] Expenses for ICT equipment including computer software not charged to asset accounts for which depreciation or amortization accounts are ordinarily maintained. [3] Expenses for ICT equipment including computer software chargeable to asset accounts for which depreciation or amortization accounts are ordinarily maintained.

Source: U.S. Census Bureau, "2010 Information and Communication Technology Survey," March 2012, <http://www.census.gov/econ/ict/>.

Table 795. Capital Expenditures: 2000 to 2010

[In billions of dollars (1,161 represents $1,161,000,000,000). Based on a sample survey and subject to sampling error; see source for details]

Item	All companies				Companies with employees				Companies without employees			
	2000	2008	2009	2010	2000	2008	2009	2010	2000	2008	2009	2010
Capital expenditures, total............	1,161	1,374	1,090	1,106	1,090	1,294	1,015	1,036	71	80	75	70
Structures.................................	364	562	448	429	338	529	413	396	26	33	35	33
New.......................................	329	523	421	395	309	500	393	367	20	23	28	28
Used......................................	35	39	27	34	29	29	19	29	6	10	8	6
Equipment and software.................	797	812	642	677	752	765	602	641	45	47	40	36
New.......................................	751	765	607	639	718	728	577	612	32	37	30	27
Used......................................	46	47	35	38	34	37	25	28	12	10	10	10
Capital leases............................	20	20	17	16	19	19	17	15	(Z)	1	1	1

Z Less than $500 million.

Source: U.S. Census Bureau, "2010 Annual Capital Expenditures Survey," February 2012, <http://www.census.gov/econ/aces/>, and earlier reports.

Table 796. Capital Expenditures by Industry: 2000 and 2010

[In billions of dollars (1,090 represents $1,090,000,000,000). Covers only companies with employees. Data for 2000 based on the North American Industry Classification System (NAICS), 1997; 2010 based on NAICS, 2007; see text this section. Based on a sample survey and subject to sampling error; see source for details]

Industry	NAICS code	2000	2010	Industry	NAICS code	2000	2010
Total expenditures......................	(X)	1,090	1,036				
Forestry, fishing, and agricultural services...................................	113–115	1	3	Professional, scientific, and technical services...	54	34	29
Mining.......................................	21	43	115	Management of companies and enterprises..................................	55	5	5
Utilities.....................................	22	61	95	Admin/support waste mgt/remediation			
Construction...............................	23	25	18	services.......................................	56	18	17
Manufacturing.............................	31–33	215	160				
Durable goods..........................	321, 327, 33	134	85	Educational services.........................	61	18	23
Nondurable goods......................	31, 322–326	81	74	Health care and social assistance..........	62	52	79
Wholesale trade...........................	42	34	31	Arts, entertainment, and recreation.........	71	19	12
Retail trade.................................	44–45	70	66	Accommodation and food services.........	72	26	20
Transportation and warehousing..........	48–49	60	59	Other services (except public			
Information.................................	51	160	97	administration)...............................	81	21	21
Finance and insurance....................	52	134	103	Structure and equipment expenditures			
Real estate and rental and leasing........	53	92	81	serving multiple industry categories........	(X)	2	2

X Not applicable.

Source: U.S. Census Bureau, "2010 Annual Capital Expenditures Survey," February 2012, <http://www.census.gov/econ/aces/>, and earlier reports.

Table 797. Business Cycle Expansions and Contractions—Months of Duration: 1945 to 2009

[A trough is the low point of a business cycle; a peak is the high point. Contraction, or recession, is the period from peak to subsequent trough; expansion is the period from trough to subsequent peak. Business cycle reference dates are determined by the National Bureau of Economic Research, Inc]

Business cycle reference date				Contraction (Peak to trough)	Expansion (Previous trough to peak)	Length of cycle	
Peak		Trough				Trough from previous trough	Peak from previous peak
Month	Year	Month	Year				
February.............................	1945	October.....	1945	8	[1]80	[1]88	[2]93
November............................	1948	October.....	1949	11	37	48	45
July.................................	1953	May.........	1954	10	45	55	56
August..............................	1957	April.........	1958	8	39	47	49
April................................	1960	February....	1961	10	24	34	32
December...........................	1969	November...	1970	11	106	117	116
November...........................	1973	March.......	1975	16	36	52	47
January.............................	1980	July.........	1980	6	58	64	74
July.................................	1981	November...	1982	16	12	28	18
July.................................	1990	March.......	1991	8	92	100	108
March...............................	2001	November...	2001	8	120	128	128
December...........................	2007	June.........	2009	18	73	91	81
Average, all cycles: 1945 to 2009 (11 cycles).........				11	59	73	66

[1] Previous trough: June 1938. [2] Previous peak: May 1937.

Source: National Bureau of Economic Research, Inc., Cambridge, MA, "Business Cycle Expansions and Contractions," <http://www.nber.org/cycles.html>, accessed August 2012 (copyright).

Table 798. The Conference Board Leading, Coincident, and Lagging Economic Indexes®

[299.4 represents 299,400]

Item	Unit	2000	2006	2007	2008	2009	2010	2011
The Conference Board Leading Economic Index® (LEI) for the U.S., composite	2004 = 100	92.7	107.3	105.9	94.9	82.8	89.1	93.7
Average weekly hours, manufacturing	Hours	41.2	41.1	41.2	40.8	39.8	41.1	41.4
Average weekly initial claims for unemployment insurance	1,000	299.4	312.7	321.5	420.6	573.7	458.9	408.8
Manufacturers' new orders, consumer goods and materials (1982 dollars)	Million dollars	152,066	150,373	151,442	136,314	112,028	122,936	126,566
ISM New Orders Index [1]	Percent	50.2	49.9	52.9	58.7	51.8	57.9	51.9
Manufacturers' new orders, nondefense capital goods excl. aircraft (1982 dollars)	Million dollars	45,990	44,200	43,961	42,343	31,326	36,560	39,710
Building permits, new private housing units	1,000	1,598	1,844	1,392	896	582	604	624
Stock prices, 500 common stocks [1]	1941-43 = 10	1,426.8	1,310.0	1,476.7	1,220.9	946.7	1,139.3	1,268.9
Leading Credit Index™ (std. dev.)	Standard Deviation above or below the mean	1.26	-0.57	1.09	5.35	0.59	-0.80	-0.48
Interest rate spread, 10-year Treasury bonds less federal funds	Percent	-0.21	-0.17	-0.39	1.74	3.10	3.04	2.68
Avg. consumer expectations for business conditions (std. dev.) [1]	Standard Deviation above or below the mean	1.24	-0.10	-0.32	-2.15	-1.19	-0.63	-1.03
The Conference Board Coincident Economic Index® (CEI) for the U.S., composite	2004 = 100	96.5	106.2	107.8	105.0	96.9	99.3	102.0
Employees on nonagricultural payrolls	1,000	131,794	136,091	137,595	136,794	130,787	129,856	131,359
Personal income less transfer payments (chain 2005 dollars)	Billion dollars	8,324	9,408	9,656	9,708	8,975	9,083	9,359
Industrial production	2007 = 100	92.3	97.6	100.0	96.5	85.4	90.1	93.7
Manufacturing and trade sales (chain 2005 dollars)	Million dollars	920,306	1,043,668	1,056,680	1,012,203	921,443	959,078	992,008
The Conference Board Lagging Economic Index® (LAG) for the U.S., composite	2004 = 100	96.8	107.0	110.3	113.9	112.8	109.5	111.5
Average duration of unemployment	Weeks	12.7	16.8	16.9	17.8	24.4	33.1	39.4
Inventories to sales ratio, manufacturing and trade (chain 2005 dollars)	Ratio	1.36	1.31	1.32	1.39	1.41	1.34	1.35
Change in labor cost per unit of output, manufacturing (six-month change, annual rate)	Percent	2.5	0.0	-1.6	9.2	0.8	-2.6	-0.4
Average prime rate	Percent	9.2	8.0	8.1	5.1	3.3	3.3	3.3
Commercial and industrial loans outstanding (chain 2005 dollars)	Million dollars	982,718	734,867	817,726	902,164	808,921	677,456	728,481
Consumer installment credit to personal income ratio	Percent	18.9	20.8	20.7	20.6	20.9	19.5	18.9
Change in consumer price index for services (six-month change, annual rate)	Percent	3.8	3.7	3.3	3.6	0.8	0.9	2.0

[1] Data are from private sources and provided through the courtesy of the compilers and are subject to their copyrights: stock prices, Standard & Poor's Corporation; index of consumer expectations, University of Michigan's Survey Research Center; ISM New Orders Index, Institute for Supply Management.

Source: The Conference Board, New York, NY 10022-6601, *Business Cycle Indicators*, monthly. Reproduced with permission from The Conference Board, Inc. © 2012, The Conference Board, Inc. For more information, see <http://www.conference-board.org/data/>.

Table 799. Manufacturing and Trade—Sales and Inventories: 1993 to 2011

[In billions of dollars (568 represents $568,000,000,000), except ratios. Based on North American Industry Classification System (NAICS), 2002; see text, this section]

Year	Sales, average monthly [1]				Inventories [2]				Inventory-sales ratio [3]			
	Total	Manufac-turing	Retail trade	Mer-chant whole-salers	Total	Manufac-turing	Retail trade	Mer-chant whole-salers	Total	Manufac-turing	Retail trade	Mer-chant whole-salers
1993......	568	252	162	154	864	380	280	205	1.50	1.50	1.68	1.30
1994......	610	270	176	165	927	400	305	222	1.46	1.44	1.66	1.29
1995......	655	290	185	180	986	425	323	238	1.48	1.44	1.72	1.29
1996......	687	300	197	190	1,005	430	334	241	1.46	1.43	1.67	1.27
1997......	724	320	206	198	1,047	444	345	259	1.42	1.37	1.64	1.26
1998......	743	325	216	202	1,079	449	357	272	1.43	1.39	1.62	1.32
1999......	787	336	234	217	1,139	464	385	290	1.40	1.35	1.59	1.30
2000......	834	351	249	235	1,197	481	407	309	1.41	1.35	1.59	1.29
2001......	819	331	256	232	1,120	428	395	298	1.43	1.38	1.58	1.32
2002......	1,320	823	261	236	1,856	1,139	415	301	1.39	1.36	1.55	1.26
2003......	1,374	854	272	248	1,887	1,147	431	308	1.38	1.34	1.56	1.23
2004......	1,491	925	289	276	2,040	1,241	460	339	1.35	1.30	1.56	1.18
2005......	1,612	1,004	308	301	2,152	1,313	472	368	1.32	1.27	1.51	1.18
2006......	1,714	1,066	323	325	2,292	1,407	486	399	1.32	1.28	1.49	1.18
2007......	1,806	1,124	333	348	2,412	1,487	500	425	1.32	1.29	1.48	1.18
2008......	1,852	1,154	329	369	2,381	1,461	477	442	1.35	1.32	1.51	1.22
2009......	1,589	979	302	308	2,143	1,324	429	390	1.39	1.39	1.46	1.31
2010......	1,739	1,074	320	344	2,318	1,434	455	429	1.28	1.28	1.38	1.18
2011......	1,930	1,194	346	390	2,487	1,544	472	472	1.26	1.26	1.34	1.17

[1] Averages of monthly not-seasonally-adjusted figures. [2] Seasonally adjusted end-of-year data. [3] Averages of seasonally adjusted monthly ratios.

Source: U.S. Council of Economic Advisors, *Economic Indicators*, <http://www.gpo.gov/fdsys/browse/collection.action?collectionCode=ECONI>, May 2012.

Table 800. Industrial Production Indexes by Industry: 1990 to 2011

[2007 = 100. Except as noted, based on the North American Industry Classification System (NAICS); 2002; see text, this section]

Industry	NAICS code [1]	1990	2000	2005	2007	2008	2009	2010	2011
Total index....................................	([2])	**62.3**	**92.3**	**95.5**	**100.0**	**96.5**	**85.4**	**90.1**	**93.7**
Manufacturing (SIC) [3]............................	([4])	**58.8**	**91.3**	**95.0**	**100.0**	**95.2**	**82.0**	**86.7**	**90.5**
Manufacturing (NAICS).....................	31–33	56.8	89.9	94.4	100.0	95.2	82.1	87.2	91.4
Durable goods................................	([5])	42.8	84.9	91.2	100.0	96.3	78.0	86.0	92.6
Wood products...........................	321	80.7	99.3	105.9	100.0	85.4	65.3	67.9	69.5
Nonmetallic mineral products..............	327	76.0	94.9	99.4	100.0	88.4	66.6	68.9	70.9
Primary metals...........................	331	87.1	100.3	95.2	100.0	100.0	74.0	90.8	96.8
Fabricated metal products.................	332	70.0	96.9	90.9	100.0	96.4	74.2	79.3	87.2
Machinery................................	333	71.9	97.7	91.6	100.0	97.3	75.8	84.5	94.3
Computers and electronic products................................	334	7.2	53.9	77.0	100.0	106.1	92.9	103.0	111.1
Electrical equipment, appliances, and components................	335	82.0	113.9	95.3	100.0	96.3	75.6	79.3	81.9
Motor vehicles and parts..................	3361–3	54.4	97.4	102.3	100.0	80.0	58.6	77.7	86.9
Aerospace and other misc transportation equipment..................	3364–9	94.4	76.0	80.2	100.0	101.9	92.8	93.1	97.7
Furniture and related products.............	337	75.6	103.6	105.5	100.0	90.3	65.5	64.3	67.4
Miscellaneous products...................	339	60.1	86.8	99.5	100.0	101.6	94.2	98.0	100.9
Nondurable goods...........................	([6])	82.4	95.9	98.3	100.0	94.1	86.8	88.7	90.1
Food, beverage, and tobacco products................................	311,2	84.7	95.3	99.8	100.0	97.2	96.5	96.5	98.1
Textile and product mills...................	313,4	128.5	144.2	124.5	100.0	87.9	69.7	74.8	75.5
Apparel and leather.......................	315,6	266.5	235.2	126.1	100.0	80.6	59.4	61.2	62.0
Paper....................................	322	100.1	107.7	100.7	100.0	95.8	85.4	87.2	86.0
Printing and related support...............	323	97.8	107.8	98.6	100.0	93.8	78.8	78.9	75.4
Petroleum and coal products...............	324	77.1	85.2	95.6	100.0	95.6	94.3	93.6	98.5
Chemical.................................	325	67.5	81.9	92.9	100.0	92.5	83.4	86.3	86.7
Plastics and rubber products..............	326	66.8	102.3	102.3	100.0	90.6	75.8	82.5	89.4
Other manufacturing (non-NAICS) [7].........	1133, 5111	111.2	121.9	107.5	100.0	93.6	80.7	76.5	71.6
Mining...	21	**106.4**	**102.9**	**97.0**	**100.0**	**101.0**	**95.8**	**100.7**	**107.0**
Utilities..	2211,2	**71.9**	**89.9**	**97.3**	**100.0**	**99.9**	**97.5**	**100.9**	**100.6**
Electric power generation, transmission, and distribution.................	2211	69.4	87.9	97.0	100.0	99.4	96.9	100.7	100.2
Natural gas distribution........................	2212	87.1	100.3	98.9	100.0	102.3	100.4	101.8	102.5

[1] Based on North American Industry Classification System, 2002; see text, this section. [2] Includes NAICS codes 31–33, 1133, 5111, 21, 2211, and 2212. [3] Standard Industrial Classification (SIC); see text, this section. [4] Includes NAICS codes 31–33, 1133, and 5111. [5] Includes NAICS codes 321, 327, 331–339. [6] Includes NAICS codes 311–316, 322–326. [7] Those industries—logging and newspaper, periodical, book, and directory publishing—that have traditionally been considered to be manufacturing.

Source: Board of Governors of the Federal Reserve System, *Industrial Production and Capacity Utilization*, Statistical Release G.17, Data Download Program, <http://www.federalreserve.gov/datadownload/default.htm>, accessed October 2012.

Table 801. Index of Industrial Capacity: 1990 to 2011

[2007 output = 100. Annual figures are averages of monthly data. Capacity represents estimated quantity of output relative to output that the current stock of plant and equipment was capable of producing, as a proportion of 2007 actual output]

Year	Index of capacity		Relation of output to capacity (percent)				
			Total industry	Stage of process			Manufacturing
	Total industry	Manufacturing		Crude [1]	Primary and semifinished [2]	Finished [3]	
1990.............	75.3	71.8	82.5	87.6	82.7	80.8	81.7
1995.............	85.2	82.4	84.1	88.7	86.5	80.1	83.3
2000.............	113.1	114.3	81.4	88.6	83.9	76.7	79.7
2002.............	119.1	120.1	74.8	82.9	77.0	70.7	72.9
2003.............	118.8	120.1	75.9	84.7	77.9	71.6	73.9
2004.............	118.6	119.8	77.9	86.1	79.9	73.1	76.1
2005.............	119.2	121.2	79.9	86.4	81.9	75.3	78.2
2006.............	121.2	123.6	80.4	87.8	81.4	76.1	78.6
2007.............	123.5	126.3	81.0	88.6	81.5	77.4	79.2
2008.............	123.8	126.9	77.8	87.0	76.8	74.5	74.9
2009.............	123.7	124.2	69.2	79.3	66.6	68.7	66.2
2010.............	121.0	120.8	74.5	85.3	71.8	73.4	71.7
2011.............	121.4	120.8	77.3	88.4	74.3	76.3	75.0

[1] Crude processing covers a relatively small portion of total industrial capacity and consists of logging (NAICS 1133), much of mining (excluding stone, sand, and gravel mining, and oil and gas drilling, which are NAICS 21231, 21221–2, and 213111) and some basic manufacturing industries, including basic chemicals (NAICS 3251); fertilizers, pesticides, and other agricultural chemicals (NAICS 32531,2); pulp, paper, and paperboard mills (NAICS 3221); and alumina, aluminum, and other nonferrous production and processing mills (NAICS 3313,4). [2] Primary and semifinished processing loosely corresponds to the previously published aggregate, primary processing. Includes utilities and portions of several 2-digit SIC industries included in the former advanced processing group. These include printing and related support activities (NAICS 3231); paints and adhesives (NAICS 3255); and newspaper, periodical, book, and directory publishers (NAICS 5111). [3] Finished processing generally corresponds to the previously published aggregate, advanced processing. Includes oil and gas well drilling and carpet and rug mills.

Source: Board of Governors of the Federal Reserve System, *Industrial Production and Capacity Utilization*, Statistical Release G.17, monthly <http://www.federalreserve.gov/releases/g17/>.

Table 802. Corporate Profits, Taxes, and Dividends: 1990 to 2011

[In billions of dollars (434 represents $434,000,000,000). Covers corporations organized for profit and other entities treated as corporations. Represents profits to U.S. residents, without deduction of depletion charges and exclusive of capital gains and losses; intercorporate dividends from profits of domestic corporations are eliminated; net receipts of dividends, reinvested earnings of incorporated foreign affiliates, and earnings of unincorporated foreign affiliates are added]

Item	1990	2000	2005	2008	2009	2010	2011
Corporate profits with IVA and CCA [1]...........................	434	819	1,456	1,248	1,362	1,800	1,943
Taxes on corporate income..........................	145	265	412	309	272	411	416
Profits after tax with IVA and CCA [1]...........................	289	554	1,044	939	1,090	1,389	1,527
Net dividends....................................	169	378	557	787	620	737	814
Undistributed profits with IVA and CCA [1]....................	120	176	486	153	470	652	713
Cash flow:							
Net cash flow with IVA and CCA [1]................................	493	861	1,337	1,245	1,584	1,699	1,820
Undistributed profits with IVA and CCA [1]................	120	176	486	153	470	652	713
Consumption of fixed capital..................................	373	685	863	1,029	1,030	1,027	1,069
Less: Inventory valuation adjustment (IVA)...................	-13	-17	-31	-45	1	-39	-60
Equals: Net cash flow with CCA....................	506	878	1,368	1,290	1,583	1,738	1,880

[1] Inventory valuation adjustment and capital consumption adjustment.

Source: U.S. Bureau of Economic Analysis, *Survey of Current Business* and National Income and Product Accounts Interactive Tables, <http://www.bea.gov/iTable/index_nipa.cfm>, accessed June 2012. See also <http://www.bea.gov/national/index.htm>.

Table 803. Corporate Profits With Inventory Valuation and Capital Consumption Adjustments—Financial and Nonfinancial Industries: 2000 to 2011

[In billions of dollars (819 represents $819,000,000,000). Based on the North American Industry Classification System, 2002; see text, this section. Minus sign (–) indicates loss. See headnote, Table 802]

Industry group	2000	2005	2008	2009	2010	2011
Corporate profits with IVA/CCA [1]...................	**819**	**1,456**	**1,248**	**1,362**	**1,800**	**1,943**
Domestic industries..	674	1,217	842	1,002	1,418	1,514
Rest of the world..	146	239	407	360	382	429
Corporate profits with IVA [1]...........................	**756**	**1,610**	**1,316**	**1,456**	**1,780**	**1,836**
Domestic industries..	610	1,370	909	1,096	1,399	1,407
Financial [2]...	190	444	122	402	495	465
Nonfinancial..	420	926	787	694	904	943
Utilities..	26	30	31	22	25	15
Manufacturing...	144	247	196	125	217	254
Wholesale trade...	59	92	86	83	86	84
Retail trade...	61	123	82	106	123	117
Transportation and warehousing......................	15	29	32	24	34	31
Information..	-16	81	75	81	88	101
Other nonfinancial [3]...................................	132	324	286	253	331	340
Rest of the world..	146	239	407	360	382	429

[1] Inventory valuation adjustment and capital consumption adjustment. [2] Consists of finance and insurance and bank and other holding companies. [3] Consists of agriculture, forestry, fishing, and hunting; mining; construction; real estate and rental and leasing; professional, scientific, and technical services; administrative and waste management services; educational services; health care and social assistance; arts, entertainment, and recreation; accommodation and food services; and other services, except government.

Source: U.S. Bureau of Economic Analysis, *Survey of Current Business* and National Income and Product Accounts Interactive Tables, <http://www.bea.gov/iTable/index_nipa.cfm>, accessed June 2012. See also <http://www.bea.gov/national/index.htm>.

Table 804. Corporate Profits Before Taxes by Industry: 2000 to 2010

[In billions of dollars (772 represents $772,000,000,000). Profits are without inventory valuation and capital consumption adjustments. Minus sign (–) indicates loss. See headnote, Table 802]

Industry	2002 NAICS code [1]	2000	2005	2008	2009	2010
Corporate profits before tax	(X)	**772**	**1,640**	**1,360**	**1,456**	**1,819**
Domestic industries	(X)	627	1,401	953	1,095	1,438
Agriculture, forestry, fishing, and hunting	11	1	5	3	4	4
Mining	21	15	43	54	16	34
Utilities	221	26	31	31	22	25
Construction	23	42	85	43	32	40
Manufacturing	31-33	154	260	217	122	234
Wholesale trade	42	62	101	96	83	100
Retail trade	44–45	63	128	89	108	128
Transportation and warehousing	48–49	15	30	31	24	35
Information	51	-16	81	76	81	88
Finance and insurance	52	102	282	-15	238	339
Real estate and rental and leasing	53	10	29	7	5	8
Professional, scientific, and technical services	54	2	42	59	58	68
Management of companies and enterprises [2]	551111, 551112	88	161	138	164	155
Administrative and waste management services	56	9	24	24	24	28
Educational services	61	2	5	6	8	12
Health care and social assistance	62	26	54	63	73	92
Arts, entertainment, and recreation	71	2	7	6	7	10
Accommodation and food services	72	15	22	15	12	22
Other services, except public administration	81	9	12	11	12	15
Rest of the world [3]	(X)	146	239	407	360	382

X Not applicable. [1] Based on North American Industry Classification System, 2002; see text, this section. [2] Consists of bank and other holding companies. [3] Consists of receipts by all U.S. residents, including both corporations and persons, of dividends from foreign corporations, and, for U.S. corporations, their share of reinvested earnings of their incorporated foreign affiliates, and earnings of unincorporated foreign affiliates, net of corresponding payments.

Source: U.S. Bureau of Economic Analysis, National Income and Product Accounts Interactive Data, <http://www.bea.gov/iTable/index_nipa.cfm>, accessed July 2012.

Table 805. Manufacturing, Mining, and Trade Corporations—Profits and Stockholders' Equity by Industry: 2010 and 2011

[Averages of quarterly figures at annual rates. Manufacturing data exclude estimates for corporations with less than $250,000 in assets at time of sample selection. Mining, wholesale and retail trade data excludes estimates for corporations with less than $50 million in assets at time of sample selection. Based on sample; see source for discussion of methodology. Based on North American Industry Classification System (NAICS), 2002; see text, this section. Minus sign (–) indicates loss]

Industry	2002 NAICS code	Ratio of profits after taxes to stockholders' equity (percent)		Profits after taxes per dollar of sales (cents)		Ratio of stockholders' equity to debt	
		2010	2011	2010	2011	2010	2011
Manufacturing	**31–33**	**15.0**	**17.0**	**8.3**	**9.2**	**1.8**	**1.9**
Nondurable manufacturing	(X)	15.2	17.6	8.1	8.8	1.5	1.6
Food	311	16.1	11.2	5.6	3.9	1.1	1.1
Beverage and tobacco products	312	25.2	23.4	20.7	20.6	1.6	1.5
Textile mills and textile product mills	313, 314	8.3	6.8	3.5	2.8	2.2	2.1
Apparel and leather products	315, 316	19.9	19.3	8.3	8.0	2.4	2.2
Paper	322	16.0	13.2	5.6	4.9	0.9	1.0
Printing and related support activities	323	13.3	13.3	2.5	2.8	0.5	0.6
Petroleum and coal products	324	11.8	21.2	5.1	7.7	2.5	2.9
Chemicals	325	15.1	16.4	13.2	14.1	1.4	1.5
Plastics and rubber products	326	12.7	16.2	3.8	4.9	1.1	1.1
Durable manufacturing	(X)	14.9	16.5	8.6	9.8	2.1	2.3
Wood products	321	4.9	1.9	1.7	0.7	1.0	1.1
Nonmetallic mineral products	327	5.1	2.6	3.2	1.6	1.2	1.5
Primary metals	331	11.9	13.5	5.5	6.1	1.8	1.9
Fabricated metal products	332	15.2	19.1	6.2	7.2	1.6	1.6
Machinery	333	12.8	15.3	7.2	8.3	2.1	2.2
Computer and electronic products	334	17.2	16.8	15.6	16.9	3.2	3.3
Electrical equipment, appliances, & components	335	10.9	11.5	10.5	12.7	4.1	3.8
Transportation equipment	336	21.2	27.6	5.8	8.2	1.4	1.7
Furniture and related products	337	1.7	9.0	0.6	3.1	1.1	1.2
Miscellaneous manufacturing	339	14.1	13.5	12.3	11.9	2.2	2.1
All mining	**21**	**11.1**	**11.1**	**20.0**	**18.7**	**2.1**	**2.1**
All wholesale trade	**42**	**9.9**	**11.2**	**1.5**	**1.6**	**1.5**	**1.4**
Durable goods	421	8.8	11.1	1.8	2.3	1.7	1.6
Nondurable goods	422	11.9	11.4	1.2	1.1	1.2	1.1
All retail trade	**44–45**	**15.3**	**15.2**	**3.1**	**2.9**	**1.7**	**1.6**
Food and beverage stores	445	9.0	11.5	1.0	1.3	1.1	1.2
Clothing and general merchandise stores	448, 452	17.7	16.6	4.2	3.8	1.8	1.7
All other retail trade	(X)	14.4	14.7	3.1	2.9	1.7	1.7

X Not applicable.

Source: U.S. Census Bureau, *Quarterly Financial Report for Manufacturing, Mining, and Trade Corporations*, <http://www.census.gov/econ/overview/mu1400.html>.

Table 806. Value Added, Employment, and Capital Expenditures of U.S. Multinational Companies: 2000 to 2009

[Data for 2009 are preliminary. Value added and capital expenditures in billions of dollars (2,748 represents $2,748,000,000,000); employees in thousands. Data through 2006 include only non-bank multinational companies; beginning in 2007, data include bank companies. See headnote, Table 807. MNC = Multinational company. MOFA = Majority-owned foreign affiliate]

Item	2000	2001	2002	2003	2004	2005	2006	2007 [1]	2008 [1]	2009 [1]
VALUE ADDED										
MNCs worldwide:										
Parents and MOFAs..............	2,748	2,478	2,460	2,656	2,992	3,233	3,538	3,866	3,741	3,593
Parents..............................	2,141	1,892	1,859	1,958	2,173	2,321	2,537	2,705	2,501	2,452
MOFAs...............................	607	586	602	698	818	911	1,001	1,161	1,240	1,140
EMPLOYEES										
MNCs worldwide:										
Parents and all affiliates..........	33,598	32,539	31,894	30,762	31,245	32,094	32,766	34,991	34,892	36,082
Parents and MOFAs...............	32,057	30,929	30,373	29,347	29,843	30,573	31,233	33,203	32,737	33,922
Parents..............................	23,885	22,735	22,118	21,105	21,177	21,472	21,616	22,832	22,273	23,121
Affiliates, total.......................	9,713	9,804	9,776	9,658	10,068	10,622	11,150	12,160	12,619	12,962
MOFAs.............................	8,171	8,194	8,256	8,242	8,667	9,101	9,617	10,372	10,463	10,801
Other................................	1,542	1,610	1,520	1,415	1,402	1,520	1,533	1,788	2,155	2,160
CAPITAL EXPENDITURES										
MNCs worldwide:										
Parents and all affiliates..........	(NA)	(NA)	(NA)	(NA)	487	(NA)	(NA)	(NA)	(NA)	623
Parents and MOFAs...............	548	561	478	444	463	507	600	670	685	580
Parents..............................	438	450	367	335	339	377	445	495	502	410
Affiliates, total.......................	(NA)	(NA)	(NA)	(NA)	147	(NA)	(NA)	(NA)	(NA)	213
MOFAs.............................	111	111	110	110	123	130	155	174	184	170
Other................................	(NA)	(NA)	(NA)	(NA)	24	(NA)	(NA)	(NA)	(NA)	43

NA Not available. [1] Beginning with 2007, data include bank companies.

Source: U.S. Bureau of Economic Analysis, *Survey of Current Business*, November 2011. See also <http: www.bea.gov/international/index.htm>.

Table 807. U.S. Multinational Companies—Selected Characteristics: 2009

[In billions of dollars (27,775 represents $27,775,000,000,000), except as indicated. Consists of U.S. parent companies and their foreign affiliates. U.S. parent comprises the domestic operations of a multinational and is a U.S. person that owns or controls, directly or indirectly, 10 percent or more of the voting securities of an incorporated foreign business enterprise, or an equivalent interest in an unincorporated foreign business enterprise. A U.S. person can be an incorporated business enterprise. A majority-owned foreign affiliate (MOFA) is a foreign business enterprise in which a U.S. parent company owns or controls more than 50 percent of the voting securities]

Industry	2002 NAICS code [1]	U.S. parents [2]				MOFAs [3]		
		Total assets	Capital expendi-tures	Value added	Employ-ment (1,000)	Capital expendi-tures	Value added	Employ-ment (1,000)
All industries......................	(X)	27,775	409.6	2,453	23,121	169.9	1,140	10,801
Mining..................................	21	417	36.2	74	180	59.4	161	201
Utilities..................................	22	470	26.9	62	158	3.3	8	32
Manufacturing [4]......................	31-33	5,784	142.2	959	6,899	54.3	474	4,587
Petroleum and coal products.......	324	688	30.8	70	295	3.7	64	40
Chemicals.............................	325	1,248	17.5	188	820	14.1	113	638
Transportation equipment...........	336	1,385	41.2	187	1,570	7.3	45	852
Wholesale trade......................	42	957	37.0	149	1,134	8.0	156	788
Information [4].........................	51	1,503	50.0	260	1,749	7.1	49	395
Broadcasting (except Internet) and telecommunications..........	515, 517	985	39.3	152	963	5.1	14	91
Finance and insurance...............	52, 522	16,329	37.2	205	2,513	8.9	78	644
Professional, scientific, and technical services....................	54	436	7.4	177	1,222	4.3	79	807
Other industries [4].....................	(X)	1,880	72.7	568	9,267	24.6	134	3,348
Retail trade...........................	44–45	486	16.0	235	4,393	5.9	59	1,146

X Not applicable. [1] Based on North American Industry Classification System, 2002; see text, this section. [2] Data are by industry of U.S. parent. [3] Data are by industry of foreign affiliate. [4] Includes other industries, not shown separately.

Source: U.S. Bureau of Economic Analysis, *U.S. Direct Investment Abroad: Financial and Operating Data for U.S. Multinational Companies*, <http://www.bea.gov/international/di1usdop.htm>, accessed July 2012.

Table 808. U.S. Multinational Companies—Value Added: 2000 and 2009

[In billions of dollars (2,748 represents $2,748,000,000,000). Data for years prior to 2009 consist of non-bank multinational companies; data for 2009 consist of all multinationals including banking companies. See headnote, Table 807. Data are by industry of U.S. parent. Based on the North American Industry Classification System (NAICS), 2002; see text, this section]

Industry	2002 NAICS code [1]	U.S. multinationals		U.S. parents		Majority-owned foreign affiliates	
		2000	2009 [2]	2000	2009 [2]	2000	2009 [2]
All industries................................	(X)	**2,748**	**3,593**	**2,141**	**2,453**	**607**	**1,140**
Mining................................	21	39	111	28	74	11	37
Utilities................................	22	86	65	81	62	5	3
Manufacturing [3]................................	31–33	1,410	1,627	995	959	415	668
Petroleum and coal products................	324	232	274	112	70	120	204
Chemicals................................	325	212	328	141	188	71	140
Transportation equipment................	336	271	263	209	187	62	76
Wholesale trade................................	42	133	197	99	149	34	48
Information [3]................................	51	325	311	302	260	22	51
Broadcasting (except Internet) and telecommunications................	515, 517	(NA)	169	(NA)	152	(NA)	17
Finance and insurance................	52	181	280	157	205	24	75
Professional, scientific, and technical services........	54	141	252	101	177	41	75
Other industries [3]................................	(X)	433	750	379	568	54	182
Retail trade................................	44–45	166	282	149	235	18	47

NA Not available. X Not applicable. [1] See footnote 1, Table 807. [2] Data for 2009 include bank companies. [3] Includes other industries, not shown separately.

Source: U.S. Bureau of Economic Analysis, Interactive Tables, Direct Investment and Multinational Corporations, <http://www.bea.gov/iTable /index_MNC.cfm>, accessed July 2012.

Table 809. U.S. Majority-Owned Foreign Affiliates—Value Added by Industry of Affiliate and Country: 2009

[Preliminary. In millions of dollars (1,139,594 represents $1,139,594,000,000). See headnote, Table 807. Numbers in parentheses represent North American Industry Classification System 2002 codes; see text, this section]

Country	All industries [1]	Mining (21)	Manufacturing (31-33)			Wholesale trade (42)	Professional, scientific, and technical services (54)
			Total [1]	Chemicals (325)	Transportation equipment (336)		
All countries [2]............	**1,139,594**	**161,180**	**474,475**	**113,111**	**44,541**	**156,293**	**79,157**
United Kingdom..............	153,298	10,224	50,799	7,150	4,467	15,942	16,388
Canada.......................	111,106	15,831	40,582	7,415	2,994	11,890	7,509
Germany.....................	87,612	1,095	55,478	9,368	9,198	11,209	6,060
France.......................	51,102	28	27,350	6,160	1,941	6,982	3,670
Ireland.......................	49,682	237	28,284	17,964	25	8,353	913
Australia.....................	44,901	8,892	13,026	1,957	1,320	6,371	4,058
Japan........................	53,054	8	19,696	5,584	484	8,382	7,059
Italy..........................	30,175	90	17,343	3,404	727	4,221	2,815
Mexico.......................	25,285	1,523	16,655	3,045	(D)	1,869	961
Netherlands.................	25,048	1,142	18,119	6,628	612	3,365	3,124

[1] Includes other industries, not shown separately. [2] Includes other countries, not shown separately. (D) Data withheld to avoid disclosure.

Source: U.S. Bureau of Economic Analysis, Foreign Direct Investment in the U.S. (FDIUS), <http://www.bea.gov/international/ fdius2009_preliminary.htm>, accessed July 2012.

Section 16
Science and Technology

This section presents statistics on scientific, engineering, and technological resources, with emphasis on patterns of research and development (R&D) funding and on scientific, engineering, and technical personnel; education; and employment.

The National Science Foundation (NSF) gathers data chiefly through recurring surveys. Current NSF publications containing data on funds for research and development and on scientific and engineering personnel include detailed statistical tables; info briefs; and annual, biennial, and special reports, see <http://www.nsf.gov/statistics>. Titles or the areas of coverage of these reports include the following: *Science and Engineering Indicators; National Patterns of R&D Resources; Women, Minorities, and Persons with Disabilities in Science and Engineering, Federal Funds for Research and Development;* Federal R&D Funding by Budget Function; Federal Support to Universities, Colleges, and Selected Nonprofit Institutions; *Research and Development in Industry;* R&D expenditures and graduate enrollment and support in academic science and engineering; and characteristics of doctoral scientists and engineers and of recent graduates in the United States. Statistical surveys in these areas pose problems of concept and definition and the data should therefore be regarded as broad estimates rather than precise, quantitative statements. See sources for methodological and technical details.

The National Science Board's biennial *Science and Engineering Indicators* at <http://www.nsf.gov/statistics/seind12/> contains data and analysis of international and domestic science and technology, including measures of inputs and outputs.

Research and development outlays—NSF defines research as "systematic study directed toward fuller scientific knowledge of the subject studied" and development as "the systematic use of scientific knowledge directed toward the production of useful materials, devices, systems, or methods, including design and development of prototypes and processes."

National coverage of R&D expenditures is developed primarily from periodic surveys in four principal economic sectors: (1) *Government*, made up primarily of federal executive agencies; (2) *Industry*, consisting of manufacturing and nonmanufacturing firms and the federally funded research and development centers (FFRDCs) they administer; (3) *Universities and colleges*, composed of universities, colleges, and their affiliated institutions, agricultural experiment stations, and associated schools of agriculture and of medicine, and FFRDCs administered by educational institutions; and (4) *Other nonprofit institutions*, consisting of such organizations as private philanthropic foundations, nonprofit research institutes, voluntary health agencies, and FFRDCs administered by nonprofit organizations.

The R&D funds reported consist of current operating costs, including planning and administration costs, except as otherwise noted. They exclude funds for routine testing, mapping and surveying, collection of general purpose data, dissemination of scientific information, and training of scientific personnel.

Scientists, engineers, and technicians—Scientists and engineers are defined as persons engaged in scientific and engineering work at a level requiring a knowledge of sciences equivalent at least to that acquired through completion of a 4-year college course. Technicians are defined as persons engaged in technical work at a level requiring knowledge acquired through a technical institute, junior college, or other type of training less extensive than 4-year college training. Craftsmen and skilled workers are excluded.

Table 810. Research and Development (R&D) Expenditures by Source and Objective: 1980 to 2009

[In millions of dollars (63,224 represents $63,224,000,000), except as indicated]

Year	Total	Sources of funds					Objective (percent of total)			Character of work		
		Federal govern-ment	Industry	Universi-ties\ colleges	Non-profit	Non-federal govern-ment [1]	Defense related [2]	Space related [3]	Other	Basic research	Applied research	Develop-ment
1980.....	63,224	29,986	30,929	920	871	519	24.3	5.3	70.4	8,745	13,714	40,765
1981.....	72,292	33,739	35,948	1,058	967	581	24.4	5.2	70.4	9,658	16,329	46,305
1982.....	80,748	37,133	40,692	1,207	1,095	621	26.1	4.9	69.0	10,651	18,218	51,879
1983.....	89,950	41,451	45,264	1,357	1,220	658	27.7	4.2	68.1	11,880	20,298	57,771
1984.....	102,244	46,470	52,187	1,514	1,351	721	28.7	3.0	68.3	13,332	22,451	66,461
1985.....	114,671	52,641	57,962	1,743	1,491	834	29.9	3.1	67.0	14,748	25,401	74,522
1986.....	120,249	54,622	60,991	2,019	1,647	969	31.4	3.0	65.6	17,154	27,240	75,855
1987.....	126,360	58,609	62,576	2,262	1,849	1,065	31.7	3.2	65.1	18,481	27,951	79,929
1988.....	133,881	60,131	67,977	2,527	2,081	1,165	30.2	3.5	66.3	19,787	29,528	84,567
1989.....	141,891	60,466	74,966	2,852	2,333	1,274	27.6	3.9	68.5	21,891	32,277	87,723
1990.....	151,993	61,610	83,208	3,187	2,589	1,399	25.1	4.3	70.6	23,029	34,897	94,067
1991.....	160,876	60,783	92,300	3,458	2,852	1,483	22.4	4.5	73.1	27,140	38,631	95,105
1992.....	165,350	60,915	96,229	3,569	3,113	1,525	21.6	4.3	74.1	27,604	37,936	99,811
1993.....	165,730	60,528	96,549	3,709	3,388	1,557	21.2	4.4	74.4	28,743	37,283	99,705
1994.....	169,207	60,777	99,204	3,938	3,665	1,623	19.7	4.5	75.8	29,651	36,618	102,938
1995.....	183,625	62,969	110,871	4,110	3,925	1,751	18.6	4.5	76.9	29,610	40,936	113,079
1996.....	197,346	63,394	123,417	4,436	4,239	1,861	17.6	4.1	78.3	32,799	43,170	121,377
1997.....	212,152	64,574	136,228	4,838	4,590	1,922	16.7	4.1	79.2	36,921	46,554	128,677
1998.....	226,457	66,383	147,825	5,163	5,114	1,972	15.8	3.8	80.4	35,372	46,362	144,723
1999.....	245,007	67,055	164,606	5,619	5,628	2,098	14.6	3.2	82.2	38,935	52,007	154,356
2000.....	267,983	66,936	186,038	6,232	6,530	2,247	13.4	2.3	84.3	42,759	56,685	169,412
2001.....	279,755	74,983	188,337	6,827	7,211	2,397	14.0	2.4	83.6	47,751	64,188	167,817
2002.....	278,744	80,056	180,625	7,344	8,162	2,557	15.6	2.4	82.0	51,383	50,688	176,672
2003.....	291,239	86,107	186,076	7,650	8,664	2,742	16.5	2.3	81.2	54,611	61,135	175,493
2004.....	302,503	91,656	191,266	7,936	8,761	2,883	17.2	2.1	80.7	56,092	69,183	177,228
2005.....	324,993	96,276	207,680	8,578	9,538	2,922	17.1	2.0	80.9	59,686	69,588	195,720
2006.....	350,162	100,768	227,057	9,285	10,031	3,021	16.8	1.8	81.4	61,199	76,277	212,686
2007.....	376,960	105,822	246,679	9,959	11,235	3,265	16.2	1.5	82.3	66,206	83,069	227,685
2008.....	403,040	117,611	258,626	10,707	12,578	3,518	15.3	1.4	83.3	70,220	74,321	258,499
2009.....	400,458	124,432	247,357	11,436	13,559	3,675	20.3	2.1	77.6	75,969	71,328	253,160

[1] Nonfederal R&D expenditures to university and college performers. [2] R&D spending by the Department of Defense, including space activities, and a portion of the Department of Energy funds. [3] For the National Aeronautics and Space Administration only.

Source: U.S. National Science Foundation, *National Patterns of R&D Resources*, NSF 10-323, 2011. See also <www.nsf.gov/statistics/nsf10323/>.

Table 811. National Research and Development (R&D) Expenditures as a Percent of Gross Domestic Product by Country: 1990 to 2010

Year	United States	Japan [1]	Germany [2]	France	United Kingdom	Italy	Canada	South Korea	OECD Total [3]	Russia [4]	China [5]
1990.....	2.65	2.81	2.61	2.32	2.10	1.25	1.51	(NA)	2.25	2.03	(NA)
1995.....	2.50	2.71	2.19	2.29	1.91	0.97	1.70	2.27	2.06	0.85	0.57
2000.....	2.71	3.00	2.47	2.15	1.81	1.04	1.91	2.30	2.20	1.05	0.90
2001.....	2.72	3.07	2.47	2.20	1.79	1.08	2.09	2.47	2.24	1.18	0.95
2002.....	2.62	3.12	2.50	2.24	1.79	1.12	2.04	2.40	2.21	1.25	1.07
2003.....	2.61	3.14	2.54	2.18	1.75	1.10	2.04	2.49	2.21	1.29	1.13
2004.....	2.55	3.13	2.50	2.16	1.68	1.09	2.07	2.68	2.18	1.15	1.23
2005.....	2.59	3.31	2.51	2.11	1.73	1.09	2.04	2.79	2.22	1.07	1.32
2006.....	2.64	3.41	2.54	2.11	1.75	1.13	2.00	3.01	2.25	1.07	1.39
2007.....	2.70	3.46	2.53	2.08	1.78	1.17	1.96	3.21	2.28	1.12	1.40
2008.....	2.84	3.47	2.69	2.12	1.79	1.21	1.90	3.36	2.35	1.04	1.47
2009.....	2.90	3.36	2.82	2.26	1.86	1.26	1.92	3.56	2.40	1.25	1.70
2010.....	(NA)	3.26	2.82	2.25	1.76	1.26	1.81	3.74	(NA)	1.16	1.77

NA Not Available [1] Data on Japanese research and development after 1995 may not be consistent with data in earlier years because of changes in methodology. [2] Data for 1990 are for West Germany only. [3] Organization for Economic Cooperation and Development. [4] As of May 16, 2007 Russia is an OECD accession candidate country. [5] As of 2007 China is an OECD enhanced engagement country.

Source: Organization for Economic Cooperation and Development, *Main Science and Technology Indicators*, 2012 (copyright). See also <http://www.oecd.org/>.

Table 812. Performance Sector of Research and Development (R&D) Expenditures: 2000 to 2009

[In millions of dollars (267,983 represents $267,983,000,000). For calendar year. FFRDCs are federally funded research and development centers]

Year	Total	Federal government	Industry				Universities and colleges							Other nonprofit institutions			
			Total	Funded by—			Total	Funded by—					University & college FFRDCs[3]	Total	Funded by—		
				Federal government	Industry[1]	Industry FFRDC's		Federal government	Non-federal government[2]	Industry	Universities colleges	Non-profits			Federal government	Industry	Non-profits
RESEARCH AND DEVELOPMENT TOTAL																	
2000	267,983	18,374	199,961	17,117	182,844	2,001	30,705	17,727	2,247	2,174	6,232	2,326	5,742	9,506	4,447	1,118	3,941
2005	324,993	26,322	226,159	21,909	204,250	2,601	45,197	28,260	2,922	2,323	8,579	3,113	7,817	13,032	5,932	1,253	5,846
2006	350,162	28,240	247,669	24,304	223,365	3,122	46,983	28,815	3,021	2,515	9,307	3,325	7,306	13,469	5,992	1,374	6,103
2007	376,960	29,859	269,267	26,585	242,682	5,165	49,021	29,328	3,249	2,748	9,993	3,703	5,567	14,341	5,954	1,497	6,890
2008	403,040	29,839	290,681	36,360	254,321	6,346	51,650	30,341	3,518	3,004	10,707	4,080	4,766	16,035	6,236	1,301	8,498
2009	400,458	30,901	282,393	39,573	242,820	6,446	54,382	31,575	3,675	3,279	11,436	4,418	4,968	17,531	7,133	1,258	9,141
BASIC RESEARCH																	
2000	42,759	3,765	7,040	925	6,115	547	22,917	13,966	1,550	1,499	4,298	1,604	2,874	4,908	2,099	621	2,188
2005	59,686	4,770	8,667	1,108	7,559	136	34,028	22,186	2,042	1,624	5,999	2,177	3,820	7,084	2,903	614	3,568
2006	61,199	4,716	8,384	1,444	6,940	652	35,635	22,690	2,155	1,791	6,624	2,376	3,344	7,227	2,849	656	3,721
2007	66,206	4,621	11,268	2,780	8,488	2,258	37,271	23,043	2,363	1,983	7,207	2,674	1,724	7,714	2,829	698	4,187
2008	70,220	4,957	12,368	1,475	10,893	2,423	38,840	23,500	2,533	2,162	7,708	2,937	1,672	8,514	3,073	722	4,719
2009	75,969	5,507	14,784	1,340	13,444	2,550	40,543	24,242	2,627	2,344	8,173	3,158	1,808	9,270	3,496	698	5,075
APPLIED RESEARCH																	
2000	56,685	6,105	39,176	2,682	36,494	269	6,498	3,196	572	553	1,585	592	1,291	3,155	1,831	258	1,066
2005	69,588	7,557	45,284	5,289	39,995	1,414	9,077	4,900	721	573	2,115	768	1,637	4,340	2,432	280	1,628
2006	76,277	7,435	51,173	6,140	45,033	1,314	9,440	5,176	710	589	2,182	782	1,827	4,590	2,592	300	1,699
2007	83,069	7,222	57,570	8,945	48,625	1,168	9,849	5,396	740	621	2,256	837	1,354	4,812	2,583	318	1,911
2008	74,321	7,316	46,864	5,397	41,467	1,975	10,875	5,980	808	690	2,460	937	855	5,083	2,600	330	2,154
2009	71,328	8,006	41,055	7,797	33,258	1,930	11,912	6,577	860	767	2,675	1,033	1,289	5,697	3,062	319	2,317
DEVELOPMENT																	
2000	169,412	9,377	153,745	13,510	140,235	1,185	1,290	565	125	121	348	130	1,577	1,579	580	195	804
2005	195,720	13,994	172,208	15,512	156,696	1,052	2,085	1,168	158	126	464	169	2,360	2,652	1,211	212	1,229
2006	212,686	16,089	188,112	16,720	171,392	1,156	1,880	944	156	129	479	172	2,136	2,111	603	226	1,282
2007	227,685	18,016	200,429	14,860	185,569	1,738	1,891	913	162	136	495	184	2,488	2,251	568	240	1,443
2008	258,499	17,566	231,449	29,488	201,961	1,948	1,935	861	177	152	540	206	2,239	2,437	562	249	1,626
2009	253,160	17,389	226,554	30,436	196,118	1,967	1,927	756	189	168	587	227	1,872	2,564	575	241	1,749

[1] Includes all nonfederal sources of industry R&D expenditures. [2] Includes all nonfederal sources. [3] Includes all R&D expenditures of FFRDCs administered by academic institutions and funded by the federal government.

Source: National Science Foundation, National Center for Science and Engineering Statistics, *National Patterns of R&D Resources: 2009 Data Update*, NSF 12-321, June 2012. See also <http://www.nsf.gov/statistics/natlpatterns/>.

Table 813. Federal Obligations for Research in Current and Constant (2005) Dollars by Field of Science: 2005 to 2009

[In millions of dollars (53,738 represents $53,738,000,000). For years ending September 30. Excludes R&D plant]

Field of science	Current dollars				Constant (2005) dollars [1]			
	2005	2007	2008	2009, prel.	2005	2007	2008	2009, prel.
Research, total...................	**53,738**	**54,094**	**53,894**	**59,430**	**53,738**	**50,923**	**49,634**	**54,260**
Basic..........................	27,140	26,866	27,154	30,935	27,140	25,291	25,008	28,244
Applied.......................	26,598	27,228	26,740	28,494	26,598	25,632	24,627	26,015
Life sciences................	28,128	29,464	28,919	30,466	28,128	27,736	26,633	27,815
Psychology..................	1,892	1,838	1,741	1,842	1,892	1,730	1,603	1,682
Physical sciences...........	5,494	5,136	5,073	6,071	5,494	4,835	4,672	5,543
Environmental sciences......	3,503	3,171	2,985	3,646	3,503	2,985	2,749	3,329
Mathematics and computer sciences.......	2,983	2,946	3,047	3,707	2,983	2,773	2,806	3,384
Engineering..................	8,553	8,990	8,976	9,872	8,553	8,463	8,267	9,013
Social sciences..............	1,097	1,147	977	1,261	1,097	1,080	900	1,151
Other sciences, n.e.c. [2].....	2,089	1,403	2,177	2,564	2,089	1,321	2,005	2,341

[1] Based on gross domestic product implicit price deflator. [2] Not elsewhere classified.

Source: U.S. National Science Foundation, *Federal Funds for Research and Development*, NSF 12-308, April 2012. See also <http://www.nsf.gov/statistics/fedfunds/>.

Table 814. Federal Budget Authority for Research and Development (R&D) in Current and Constant (2005) Dollars by Selected Budget Functions: 2008 to 2011

[In millions of dollars (140,113 represents $140,113,000,000). For year ending September 30. Excludes R&D plant. Represents budget authority. Functions shown are those for which $1 billion or more was authorized since 2001]

Function	Current dollars				Constant (2005) dollars [1]			
	2008	2009 [2]	2010	2011 [3]	2008	2009 [2]	2010	2011 [3]
Total [4]....................	**140,113**	**156,009**	**146,596**	**141,399**	**129,039**	**142,436**	**134,208**	**126,480**
National defense.............	84,713	85,166	86,517	81,790	78,018	77,757	78,193	72,434
Health........................	29,063	40,389	31,488	31,138	26,766	36,875	28,554	27,596
Space research and technology..........	8,323	6,891	8,232	8,398	7,665	6,291	7,417	7,416
Energy........................	1,896	3,318	2,455	2,134	1,746	3,029	2,315	1,957
General science..............	8,234	11,840	9,280	9,327	7,583	10,810	9,468	9,270
Natural resources and environment......	2,106	2,245	2,237	2,490	1,940	2,050	2,189	2,053
Transportation...............	1,394	1,440	1,496	1,440	1,284	1,315	1,367	1,287
Agriculture...................	1,864	2,302	2,043	1,891	1,717	2,102	1,988	1,544

[1] Based on gross domestic product implicit price deflator. [2] Includes ARRA (American Recovery and Reinvestment Act) funds. [3] Preliminary. [4] Includes other functions, not shown separately.

Source: U.S. National Science Foundation, *Federal R&D Funding by Budget Function*, NSF 12-322, August 2012. See also <http://www.nsf.gov/statistics/nsf12322/>.

Table 815. Federal Research and Development (R&D) by Federal Agency: Fiscal Year 2011 and 2012

[In millions of dollars (144,368 represents $144,368,000,000). For fiscal years ending September 30. R&D refers to actual research and development activities as well as R&D facilities. R&D facilities (also known as R&D plants) includes construction, repair, or alteration of physical plant used in the conduct of R&D. Based on Office of Management and Budget data]

Federal agency	2011	2012	Federal agency	2011	2012
Total research and development..............	**144,368**	**140,565**			
Defense R&D.........................	83,193	78,745	Department of Veterans Affairs..............	1,160	1,164
Nondefense R&D.....................	61,176	61,820	Department of Homeland Security...........	760	617
			Department of Transportation.................	954	945
Department of Defense..............	79,112	74,464	Department of Interior........................	757	796
Science and technology...........	12,751	13,530	U.S. Geological Survey...................	640	675
All other Department of Defense R&D...........	66,361	60,935	Environmental Protection Agency...........	582	568
Health and Human Services.................	31,183	31,143	Department of Education...................	362	392
National Institute of Health...........	29,831	30,046	Smithsonian..........................	259	243
All other Health and Human Services R&D.......	1,352	1,097	International Assistance Programs..........	121	121
			Department of Housing and Urban Development........................	79	57
Department of Energy...............	10,673	11,019	Department of State......................	75	75
Atomic Energy Defense.............	4,081	4,281	Nuclear Regulatory Commission.............	99	83
Office of Science.................	4,461	4,463	Department of Justice.....................	109	92
Energy R&D........................	2,131	2,275	Social Security Administration...............	42	8
NASA..................................	9,099	9,399	U.S. Postal Service......................	14	14
National Science Foundation...............	5,494	5,614	Tennessee Valley Authority...............	18	15
Department of Agriculture..............	2,135	2,331	Army Corps of Engineers..................	11	11
Department of Commerce.............	1,217	1,263	Telecommunications Development Agency.......................	7	4
National Oceanic and Atmospheric Administration.......................	629	581			
National Institute of Standards and Technology........................	532	555	Department of Labor..........................	4	4

Source: American Association for the Advancement of Science (AAAS), *AAAS Report XXXVI: Research and Development FY2013*, annual (copyright). See also <http://www.aaas.org/spp/rd/rdreport2013/>.

Table 816. Funds for Domestic Business Research and Development (R&D) Performed by Manufacturing and Nonmanufacturing Companies by Industry: 2007 to 2009

[Based on the Business R&D Innovation Survey. For information about the survey, see http://www.nsf.gov/statistics/srvyindustry/about/brdis/]

Industry	NAICS [1] code	Total R&D funds as a percent of net sales			Company R&D funds as a percent of net sales		
		2007	2008	2009	2007	2008	2009
All industries, total.	(X)	**3.8**	**3.7**	**3.8**	**3.5**	**3.0**	**3.0**
All manufacturing industries, total.	(X)	**4.1**	**4.4**	**4.5**	**3.7**	**3.5**	**3.7**
Food.	311	(D)	0.4	(NA)	0.7	0.4	(NA)
Paper, printing, and support activities.	322, 323	(D)	1.4	(NA)	1.3	1.3	(NA)
Petroleum and coal products.	324	(D)	(D)	(D)	0.3	(D)	(D)
Chemicals.	325	(D)	6.5	6.6	7.9	6.1	6.1
Plastic and rubber products.	326	(D)	1.1	(NA)	1.5	1.1	(NA)
Nonmetallic mineral products.	327	1.8	2.0	(NA)	1.8	1.9	(NA)
Primary metals.	331	0.6	0.4	(NA)	0.6	0.4	(NA)
Fabricated metal products.	332	1.7	1.6	(NA)	1.6	1.6	(NA)
Machinery.	333	3.7	3.6	4.0	3.7	3.5	3.9
Computer and electronic products.	334	9.9	11.6	11.4	8.4	10.1	9.2
Electrical equipment, appliances, and components.	335	3.1	2.9	3.4	3.0	2.7	3.2
Transportation equipment.	336	(D)	5.7	5.9	3.1	2.6	3.0
All nonmanufacturing industries, total.	(X)	**3.4**	**2.8**	**2.8**	**3.0**	**2.2**	**2.1**
Information.	51	(D)	4.9	4.6	5.1	4.8	4.4
Software publishing.	5112	(D)	10.8	10.1	19.6	10.6	9.8
Internet service and data processing providers.	518	(D)	6.3	(D)	9.6	6.2	(D)
Professional, scientific, and technical services.	54	11.7	8.4	9.9	9.5	4.5	5.7
Architectural, engineering, and related services.	5413	12.0	8.2	(NA)	8.1	3.3	(NA)
Computer systems design and related services.	5415	7.0	5.9	6.8	6.6	4.2	5.8
Scientific research and development services.	5417	42.0	13.2	18.1	30.0	6.4	8.4

NA Not Available D Figure withheld to avoid disclosure of information pertaining to a specific organization or individual. X Not applicable. [1] North American Industry Classification System (NAICS); see text, Section 15.

Source: U.S. National Science Foundation, National Center for Science and Engineering Statistics, *Business R&D Performed in the United States*, NSF 12-309, 2012. See also <http://www.nsf.gov/statistics/>.

Table 817. Funds for Domestic Performance of Business Research and Development (R&D) in Current and Constant (2005) Dollars by Source of Funds and Selected Industries: 2005 to 2009

[In millions of dollars (226,159 represents $226,159,000,000). For calendar years. Covers basic research, applied research, and development. Based on the Survey of Industry Research and Development and the Business R&D and Innovation Survey; for information about the surveys and methodology, see http://www.nsf.gov/statistics/srvyindustry/sird.cfm]

Industry	NAICS [1] code	2005	2007	2008	2009
CURRENT DOLLARS					
Total funds.	(X)	**226,159**	**269,267**	**290,681**	**282,393**
Company and other funds.	(X)	204,250	242,682	254,321	242,819
Federal funds.	(X)	21,909	26,585	36,360	39,573
Petroleum and coal products.	324	(D)	(D)	(D)	(D)
Chemicals and allied products.	325	42,995	(D)	58,249	53,328
Pharmaceuticals and medicines.	3254	34,839	(D)	48,131	44,936
Machinery.	333	8,531	9,865	10,104	9,138
Computer and electronic products.	334	(D)	58,599	60,463	60,464
Navigational, measuring, electromedical, and control instruments.	3345	15,204	20,438	15,460	(NA)
Electrical equipment, appliances, and components.	335	2,424	(D)	3,143	3,334
Motor vehicles, trailers, and parts.	3361-3363	(D)	(D)	13,140	(D)
Aerospace products and parts.	3364	15,055	18,436	36,941	34,554
Information.	51	23,836	(D)	37,964	33,806
Professional, scientific, and technical services.	54	32,021	40,533	37,594	44,946
Computer systems design and related services.	5415	13,592	14,407	12,146	12,560
Scientific R&D services.	5417	12,299	16,849	17,913	17,270
CONSTANT (2005) DOLLARS [2]					
Total funds.	(X)	**226,159**	**253,483**	**267,706**	**257,825**
Company and other funds.	(X)	204,250	228,456	234,220	221,694
Federal funds.	(X)	21,909	25,027	33,486	36,130
Petroleum and coal products.	324	(D)	(D)	(D)	(D)
Chemicals.	325	42,995	(D)	53,645	48,688
Pharmaceuticals and medicines.	3254	34,839	(D)	44,327	41,027
Machinery.	333	8,531	9,287	9,305	8,343
Computer and electronic products.	334	(D)	55,164	55,684	55,204
Navigational, measuring, electromedical, and control instruments.	3345	15,204	19,240	14,238	(NA)
Electrical equipment, appliances, and components.	335	2,424	(D)	2,895	3,044
Motor vehicles, trailers, and parts.	3361-3363	(D)	(D)	12,101	(D)
Aerospace products and parts.	3364	15,055	17,355	34,021	31,548
Information.	51	23,836	(D)	34,963	30,865
Professional, scientific, and technical services.	54	32,021	38,157	34,623	41,036
Computer systems design and related services.	5415	13,592	13,562	11,186	11,467
Scientific R&D services.	5417	12,299	15,861	16,497	15,768

NA Not Available D Figure withheld to avoid disclosure of information pertaining to a specific organization or individual. X Not applicable. [1] North American Industry Classification System; see text, Section 15. [2] Based on gross domestic product implicit price deflator. Updated Nov. 6, 2012 (1.15031).

Source: U.S. National Science Foundation, *Federal Funds for Research and Development*, NSF 12-308, April 2012. See also <http://www.nsf.gov/statistics/>.

Table 818. Academic and Industrial Research and Development (R&D) Performed by State: 2008

[In millions of dollars (51,650 represents 51,650,000,000). For definition of Research and Development, see text, this section]

State	Academic R&D (mil. dol.)	Academic R&D per $1,000 of state GDP	Industry-performed R&D (mil. dol.)	Industry R&D per $1,000 of state GDP
U.S.[1]	51,650	3.62	290,681	20.37
AL	708	4.15	3,099	18.16[2]
AK	111	2.23	69	1.39
AZ	831	3.18	5,232	20.00
AR	247	2.46	443	4.42
CA	7,026	3.65	67,532	35.07
CO	924	3.62	4,019	15.75
CT	732	3.29	10,518	47.34
DE	133	2.28	1,441	24.69
DC	369	3.81	571	5.90
FL	1,592	2.13	4,178	5.59
GA	1,521	3.78	3,344	8.32
HI	279	4.22	269	4.07
ID	113	2.04	961	17.33
IL	1,973	3.11	8,900	14.01
IN	954	3.62	4,991	18.92
IA	528	3.88	1,509	11.10
KS	404	3.23	1,600	12.81
KY	506	3.25	933	5.99
LA	660	3.12	411	1.94[2]
ME	128	2.54	308	6.10
MD	2,747	9.79	4,333	15.45
MA	2,272	6.26	15,028	41.39
MI	1,594	4.24	13,742	36.53
MN	699	2.67	5,728	21.87
MS	406	4.24	252	2.63
MO	960	4.00	2,857	11.92
MT	186	5.19	148	4.13
NE	376	4.44	561	6.63
NV	191	1.45	677	5.12
NH	302	5.14	2,169	36.88[2]
NJ	877	1.81	19,054	39.34
NM	417	5.35	735	9.43
NY	4,045	3.64	11,455	10.31
NC	1,981	4.90	6,246	15.45
ND	181	5.82	303	9.74
OH	1,827	3.87	7,405	15.68
OK	333	2.20	595	3.93
OR	595	3.51	4,074	24.03[2]
PA	2,604	4.77	9,735	17.82
RI	237	4.98	538	11.31
SC	576	3.61	1,221	7.65
SD	92	2.42	133	3.50
TN	787	3.19	1,608	6.53
TX	3,744	3.13	16,166	13.51
UT	426	3.78	1,945	17.25
VT	117	4.68	422	16.88
VA	1,058	2.63	6,142	15.34
WA	1,058	3.15	13,876	41.26
WV	171	2.79	334	5.45
WI	1,117	4.63	3,798	15.75
WY	75	1.93	63	21.62

[1] National totals for calendar year 2008. Includes $3.3 billion of industrial R&D expenditures that year that could not be allocated to specific states. [2] Estimated, more than 50 percent of the industrial R&D value is imputed due to raking of state data. [3] More than 50 percent of the industrial R&D value is imputed.

Source: National Science Foundation, *National Patterns of R&D Resources*, NSF-12-321, June 2012. See also <http://www.nsf.gov/statistics/nsf12321/>.

Table 819. Research and Development (R&D) Expenditures in Science and Engineering at Universities and Colleges in Current and Constant (2005) Dollars: 2000 to 2010

[In millions of dollars (30,084 represents $30,084,000,000). Totals may not add due to rounding]

Characteristic	Current dollars				Constant (2005) dollars [1]			
	2000	2005	2009	2010	2000	2005	2009	2010
Total................	**30,084**	**45,799**	**54,935**	**58,338**	**33,908**	**45,799**	**50,156**	**52,560**
Basic research [2]...............	22,547	34,368	40,955	(NA)	25,413	34,367	37,392	(NA)
Applied R&D [2]...............	7,537	11,432	13,980	(NA)	8,495	11,432	12,764	(NA)
Source of funds:								
Federal government.....................	17,548	29,209	32,588	37,488	19,778	29,209	29,753	33,775
State and local government...............	2,200	2,940	3,647	3,854	2,480	2,940	3,330	3,472
Institutions' own funds..................	5,925	8,266	11,198	11,897	6,678	8,266	10,224	10,719
Industry.............................	2,156	2,291	3,197	3,209	2,430	2,291	2,919	2,891
Other...............................	2,255	3,093	4,305	4,787	2,542	3,093	3,930	4,313
Fields:								
Physical sciences......................	2,713	3,704	4,294	4,625	3,058	3,704	3,920	4,167
Environmental sciences................	1,766	2,555	2,940	2,990	1,990	2,555	2,684	2,694
Mathematical sciences..................	342	495	553	599	385	494	505	540
Computer sciences.....................	877	1,406	1,592	1,658	988	1,406	1,453	1,494
Life sciences..........................	17,471	27,605	32,791	34,903	19,692	27,605	29,938	31,446
Psychology...........................	517	826	979	1,077	582	826	894	970
Social sciences........................	1,300	1,685	2,075	1,993	1,465	1,685	1,894	1,796
Other sciences........................	543	778	1,060	(NA)	612	778	968	(NA)
Engineering...........................	4,557	6,746	8,651	9,344	5,136	6,746	7,898	8,419

NA Not available. [1] Based on gross domestic product implicit price deflator (updated November 2012). [2] Basic research and applied R&D statistics were re-estimated for FY1998 and forward. These data are not directly comparable to those from earlier years.

Source: U.S. National Science Foundation, *Survey of Research and Development Expenditures at Universities and Colleges*, annual. See also <http://www.nsf.gov/statistics/srvyrdexpenditures/>.

Table 820. Federal Research and Development (R&D) Obligations to Selected Universities and Colleges: 2007 and 2008

[In millions of dollars (24,991.8 represents $24,991,800,000). For fiscal years ending September 30. For the top 40 institutions receiving federal R&D funds in 2008. Awards to the administrative offices of university systems are excluded from totals for individual institutions because that allocation of funds is unknown, but those awards are included in "total all institutions"]

Major institution ranked by total 2008 federal R&D obligations	2007	2008	Major institution ranked by total 2008 federal R&D obligations	2007	2008
Total, all institutions [1]...........................	**24,998.0**	**25,482.0**	University of Colorado......................	330.0	318.4
Johns Hopkins University...........................	1,054.9	1,034.2	Pennsylvania State University...............	320.8	314.3
University of Washington..........................	608.0	568.5	University of Chicago......................	248.6	274.8
University of Michigan............................	501.5	542.1	Case Western Reserve University.........	278.9	268.0
University of California—San Francisco..........	433.4	498.0	Emory University......................	247.9	266.2
University of California—Los Angeles............	480.0	490.1	University Southern California............	260.3	261.2
University of Pennsylvania.......................	498.5	486.4	University of California—Davis............	243.1	258.2
University of California—San Diego..............	432.7	475.4	University of Rochester....................	255.2	248.9
Duke University..................................	470.7	412.8	University of California—Berkeley.........	214.2	247.2
Harvard University...............................	429.3	411.3	Baylor College of Medicine.................	227.9	246.3
University of Pittsburgh..........................	425.9	409.6	Northwestern University...................	254.2	241.5
Washington University............................	407.8	403.6	Ohio State University.....................	217.2	230.6
Columbia University—City of New York...........	425.7	400.4	Boston University........................	208.5	227.3
Stanford University...............................	424.0	396.6	University of Arizona.....................	212.0	217.0
University of Wisconsin—Madison................	369.2	394.2	University of Alabama—Birmingham......	235.1	212.4
Yale University..................................	387.3	393.4	University of Illinois—		
Massachusetts Institute of Technology...........	380.8	388.2	Urbana Champaign......................	210.5	212.0
University of North Carolina at Chapel Hill........	353.5	385.7	University of Iowa........................	208.4	209.4
University of Minnesota..........................	370.7	353.7	The Scripps Research Institute.............	199.0	208.5
Cornell University................................	326.1	338.6	Mt. Sinai School of Medicine..............	187.3	188.1
Vanderbilt University.............................	329.6	319.6	New York University.......................	177.4	181.5

[1] Includes other institutions, not shown separately.

Source: U.S. National Science Foundation, *Federal S&E Support to Universities and Colleges and Nonprofit Institutions*, NSF12-316, May 2012. See also <http://www.nsf.gov/statistics/fedsupport/>.

Table 821. Graduate Science/Engineering Students in Doctorate-Granting Colleges by Characteristic and Field: 1990 to 2010

[In thousands (409.4 represents 409,400). As of fall. Includes outlying areas]

Field of science or engineering	Total			Characteristic								
				Female			Foreign			Part-time		
	1990	2000	2010	1990	2000	2010	1990	2000	2010	1990	2000	2010
Total, all surveyed fields	**409.4**	**443.5**	**575.8**	**155.5**	**201.8**	**265.0**	**103.0**	**123.3**	**165.9**	**130.8**	**123.6**	**142.5**
Science/engineering	360.6	374.8	508.1	117.9	150.3	215.3	98.9	118.0	158.3	107.5	99.3	121.7
Engineering, total	101.0	98.8	141.8	13.8	19.7	32.9	36.9	46.3	64.2	36.7	28.2	35.4
Sciences, total [1]	259.6	275.9	366.3	104.2	130.7	182.4	62.0	71.7	94.1	70.8	71.1	86.4
Physical sciences	32.9	29.6	37.9	7.7	8.8	12.4	12.2	11.5	15.0	3.9	3.5	3.6
Environmental	13.1	13.0	14.8	3.8	5.3	6.7	2.6	2.6	2.9	3.2	2.8	2.9
Math sciences	18.1	14.4	21.3	5.6	5.2	7.4	6.4	5.9	8.4	4.7	3.0	4.4
Computer sciences	29.2	40.3	45.9	6.8	11.7	11.2	9.7	19.7	22.6	14.1	16.7	15.8
Agricultural sciences	11.0	11.3	14.6	3.2	4.8	7.2	3.2	2.4	3.2	2.0	2.4	4.1
Biological sciences	46.7	53.1	69.5	21.4	27.8	39.3	11.2	11.6	16.9	7.2	7.6	9.5
Psychology [2]	38.5	40.3	45.2	25.5	29.0	33.8	1.7	2.1	2.9	12.0	10.8	11.7
Social sciences	70.0	73.9	95.9	30.1	38.1	51.0	15.0	15.8	18.8	23.8	24.3	28.1
Health fields, total [2]	48.8	68.8	67.7	37.6	51.5	49.8	4.1	5.4	7.6	23.3	24.3	20.8

[1] Total in 2010 includes newly eligible fields (communication, family and consumer science/human science, and multidisciplinary/interdisciplinary studies) and neuroscience, previously reported under health field "neurology," not shown separately. [2] Counts in psychology and health declined in 2010, potentially due to more rigorous follow-up with institutions regarding the exclusion of practitioner-oriented graduate degree programs. These decreases may not reflect changes in actual enrollments.

Source: U.S. National Science Foundation, *Survey of Graduate Science Engineering Students and Postdoctorates*, annual. See also <http://www.nsf.gov/statistics/gradpostdoc>.

Table 822. Non-U.S. Citizens Awarded Doctorates in Science and Engineering by Visa Type and Country of Citizenship: 2000 to 2010

[For description of science and engineering fields, see Table 826]

Visa and country	2000	2002	2003	2004	2005	2006	2007	2008	2009	2010
All non-U.S. citizens	**7,664**	**7,707**	**8,393**	**9,164**	**10,427**	**11,587**	**12,369**	**12,626**	**12,211**	**11,302**
Canada	243	251	280	337	312	315	341	354	373	325
Mexico	190	175	198	164	193	169	166	160	169	165
Brazil	121	113	99	124	140	128	111	123	121	124
United Kingdom	64	86	77	73	68	77	82	83	76	69
France	64	81	68	82	98	106	120	120	112	95
Germany	169	164	154	153	145	128	126	137	166	154
China	2,034	2,121	2,263	2,718	3,281	4,056	4,211	4,071	3,674	3,366
Japan	166	141	170	166	183	187	201	196	187	163
Korea	695	807	915	1,003	1,118	1,167	1,093	1,110	1,155	1,055
Taiwan	611	428	407	359	401	403	433	414	510	460
Thailand	149	258	307	263	248	194	218	274	193	172
India	726	601	688	788	1,033	1,415	1,839	2,061	2,030	1,901
Iran	40	35	45	45	112	124	127	129	137	142
Turkey	248	320	348	319	321	321	410	466	446	412
Science	5,213	5,057	5,475	5,852	6,664	7,289	7,768	8,136	7,998	7,451
Engineering	2,451	2,650	2,918	3,312	3,762	4,298	4,601	4,490	4,213	3,851
Permanent visa	1,409	1,173	1,099	1,003	1,113	1,252	1,222	(NA)	(NA)	(NA)
Temporary visa	7,661	7,694	8,384	9,155	10,406	11,525	12,323	(NA)	(NA)	(NA)

NA Not available.

Source: U.S. National Science Foundation, *Science and Engineering Doctorate Awards*, NSF 12-305, 2010. See also <http://www.nsf.gov/statistics/sed/>.

Table 823. Science and Engineering (S&E) Degrees Awarded by Degree Level and Sex of Recipient: 1990 to 2010

[For a description of science and engineering degree categories, see source, Appendix B, <http://www.nsf.gov/statistics/nsf11316/content.cfm?pub_id=4062&id=4>]

Academic year ending	Bachelor's degree				Master's degree				Doctoral degree			
	Total S&E	Men	Women	Percent women	Total S&E	Men	Women	Percent women	Total S&E	Men	Women	Percent women
1990	329,094	189,082	140,012	42.5	77,788	51,230	26,558	34.1	22,867	16,498	6,369	27.9
2000	398,602	197,650	200,952	50.4	96,230	54,560	41,670	43.3	25,966	16,518	9,394	36.2
2005	470,214	233,924	236,290	50.3	120,870	67,244	53,626	44.4	27,984	17,404	10,539	37.7
2006	478,858	238,029	240,829	50.3	120,999	66,249	54,750	45.2	29,867	18,371	11,477	38.4
2007	485,772	241,697	244,075	50.2	120,278	65,353	54,925	45.7	31,831	19,542	12,277	38.6
2008	496,168	246,719	249,449	50.3	126,404	68,810	57,594	45.6	32,836	19,857	12,972	39.5
2009	505,435	250,742	254,693	50.4	134,517	73,489	61,028	45.4	33,466	19,842	13,596	40.6
2010	525,374	261,091	264,283	50.3	139,926	76,266	63,660	45.5	33,141	19,584	13,548	40.9

Source: U.S. National Science Foundation, *Science and Engineering Degrees: 1966–2008*, NSF-11-316, 2011, and unpublished data. See also <http://www.nsf.gov/statistics/degrees/>.

Table 824. Science and Engineering (S&E) Degrees as Share of Higher Education Degrees Conferred by State: 2009

[S&E degrees include physical, computer, agricultural, biological, earth, atmospheric, ocean, and social sciences; psychology; mathematics; and engineering]

State	S&E degrees conferred [1]	All higher education degrees [1]	S&E higher education degrees (percent)	State	S&E degrees conferred [1]	All higher education degrees [1]	S&E higher education degrees (percent)	State	S&E degrees conferred [1]	All higher education degrees [1]	S&E higher education degrees (percent)
U.S.........	667,790	2,322,054	28.8								
AL............	8,899	35,725	24.9	KY.........	6,481	28,070	23.1	ND........	1,610	7,128	22.6
AK...........	802	2,267	35.4	LA.........	7,199	28,256	25.5	OH........	21,129	83,813	25.2
AZ...........	13,432	72,140	18.6	ME.......	2,749	8,717	31.5	OK........	6,384	25,995	24.6
AR...........	3,390	16,089	21.1	MD........	16,514	44,369	37.2	OR........	7,975	24,858	32.1
CA...........	84,579	230,605	36.7	MA.......	26,712	83,467	32.0	PA........	34,537	119,761	28.8
CO...........	14,280	43,834	32.6	MI........	22,804	78,332	29.1	RI........	3,783	13,002	29.1
CT...........	9,615	29,078	33.1	MN.......	13,887	52,323	26.5	SC........	7,279	26,666	27.3
DE...........	2,241	8,118	27.6	MS.......	3,937	17,023	23.1	SD........	1,990	6,377	31.2
DC...........	8,469	22,525	37.6	MO.......	13,464	59,466	22.6	TN........	9,601	40,553	23.7
FL............	29,004	112,165	25.9	MT.......	2,298	6,559	35.0	TX........	38,196	142,321	26.8
GA...........	15,775	57,165	27.6	NE.......	4,193	17,411	24.1	UT........	8,339	27,003	30.9
HI............	2,656	8,001	33.2	NV.......	2,585	9,884	26.2	VT........	3,144	8,031	39.1
ID............	2,797	10,816	25.9	NH.......	3,684	12,375	29.8	VA........	20,822	60,840	34.2
IL............	28,725	111,875	25.7	NJ........	16,535	49,544	33.4	WA.......	13,215	40,136	32.9
IN............	13,251	54,032	24.5	NM.......	3,255	11,366	28.6	WV.......	3,772	15,787	23.9
IA............	9,079	33,315	27.3	NY........	54,412	193,777	28.1	WI........	12,881	43,694	29.5
KS...........	5,920	24,284	24.4	NC........	18,671	60,854	30.7	WY.......	839	2,262	37.1

[1] Includes bachelor's, master's, and doctorate degrees.

Source: National Science Foundation, *Science and Engineering Indicators, 2012*, January 2012. See also <http://www.nsf.gov/statistics/seind12/>.

Table 825. Doctorates Conferred by Characteristics of Recipients: 2000 and 2010

[In percent, except as indicated. Based on the Survey of Earned Doctorate Awards. For description of methodology, see source]

Characteristic	2000, total [1]	2010									
		All fields [1]	Engineering	Physical sciences [2]	Earth sciences [3]	Mathematics	Computer sciences	Biological sciences [4]	Agricultural	Social sciences [5]	Psychology
Total conferred (number)....................	41,365	48,069	7,552	4,201	864	1,589	1,665	8,052	1,102	4,350	3,421
Male............................	56.0	53.1	76.9	69.7	57.5	70.6	78.8	47.6	55.4	52.3	30.2
Female.........................	43.8	46.8	23.1	30.3	42.5	29.4	21.2	52.4	44.6	47.7	69.8
RACE/ETHNICITY [6]											
Total conferred (number)....................	29,936	31,573	3,303	2,329	572	839	786	5,577	620	2,816	2,867
White [7]........................	79.2	74.5	68.5	78.1	85.3	78.1	70.0	73.8	80.2	75.2	76.2
Black [7].........................	5.8	6.3	4.2	3.0	2.1	2.6	3.8	3.9	5.6	6.5	5.9
Asian/Pacific [7]...............	7.6	9.0	16.9	9.8	2.7	11.1	17.4	11.9	6.0	7.3	5.9
Indian/Alaskan [7].............	0.6	0.4	0.2	0.4	0.0	0.4	0.3	0.3	0.5	0.6	0.7
Hispanic........................	4.4	5.9	5.8	4.5	4.1	4.4	3.1	6.3	5.0	6.3	6.7
Other/unknown [8]..............	2.4	1.9	2.4	2.0	3.1	1.7	3.1	1.8	1.6	1.7	1.6

[1] Includes other fields, not shown separately. [2] Astronomy, physics, and chemistry. [3] Includes earth, atmospheric and ocean sciences. [4] Biochemistry, botany, microbiology, physiology, zoology, and related fields. [5] Anthropology, sociology, political science, economics, international relations, and related fields. [6] Excludes those with temporary visas. [7] Non-Hispanic. [8] Data 2001 and after includes Native Hawaiians and Other Pacific Islanders, respondents choosing multiple races (excluding those selecting an Hispanic ethnicity), and respondents with unknown race/ethnicity.

Source: U.S. National Science Foundation, *Science and Engineering Doctorate Awards*, NSF-12-305, annual. See also <http://www.nsf.gov/statistics/sed/start.cfm/>.

Table 826. Doctorates Awarded by Field of Study and Year of Doctorate: 2000 to 2010

[Based on the Survey of Earned Doctorates; for information, see source]

Field of Study	2000	2005	2006	2007	2008	2009	2010
Total, all fields................................	41,372	43,382	45,620	48,133	48,774	49,554	48,069
Science and engineering, total................	7,247	7,745	8,035	8,827	9,262	9,604	9,406
Engineering, total..........................	5,323	6,427	7,185	7,750	7,864	7,646	7,552
Aeronautical/astronautical................	214	219	238	267	266	297	252
Chemical................................	619	774	799	817	873	807	821
Civil....................................	480	622	655	703	713	709	645
Electrical...............................	1,330	1,547	1,786	1,967	1,888	1,695	1,776
Industrial/manufacturing..................	176	221	234	279	280	252	214
Materials/metallurgical...................	404	493	583	646	636	625	670
Mechanical...............................	807	892	1,044	1,071	1,082	1,094	987
Other....................................	1,293	1,659	1,846	2,000	2,126	2,167	2,187
Science, total.............................	31,776	32,291	33,320	35,036	35,251	36,147	34,688
Biological/agricultural sciences...........	7,033	7,526	7,797	8,560	8,996	9,307	9,154
Agricultural sciences....................	1,180	1,160	1,146	1,322	1,199	1,283	1,102
Biological sciences......................	5,853	6,366	6,651	7,238	7,797	8,024	8,052
Earth, atmospheric, and ocean sciences, total........	694	714	757	875	865	877	864
Atmospheric.............................	143	145	146	167	188	167	171
Earth/ocean sciences....................	551	569	611	708	677	710	693
Mathematical/computer sciences, total.....	1,911	2,334	2,778	3,043	3,187	3,162	3,254
Computer sciences.......................	861	1,129	1,453	1,655	1,787	1,609	1,665
Mathematics.............................	1,050	1,205	1,325	1,388	1,400	1,553	1,589
Physical sciences, total...................	3,378	3,643	3,928	4,081	4,081	4,284	4,201
Astronomy...............................	185	186	197	223	249	262	266
Chemistry...............................	1,989	2,126	2,363	2,318	2,246	2,392	2,306
Physics.................................	1,204	1,331	1,368	1,540	1,586	1,630	1,629
Psychology................................	3,615	3,322	3,258	3,271	3,355	3,472	3,421
Social sciences, total.....................	3,723	3,723	3,864	3,920	4,157	4,359	4,350
Economics...............................	933	1,031	996	973	1,055	1,088	1,038
Political science........................	669	618	616	588	628	682	728
Sociology...............................	617	536	579	576	601	662	638
Other social sciences....................	1,504	1,538	1,673	1,783	1,873	1,927	1,946
Non-science and engineering, total............	15,695	15,693	16,053	16,633	16,269	16,447	15,273
Education.................................	6,442	6,227	6,121	6,448	6,561	6,528	5,294
Health....................................	1,591	1,784	1,907	2,143	2,090	2,096	2,112
Humanities................................	5,404	5,141	5,326	5,093	4,719	4,891	4,979
Professional/other/unknown................	2,258	2,541	2,699	2,949	2,899	2,932	2,888

Source: U.S. National Science Foundation, *Science and Engineering Doctorate Awards*, annual. See also <http://www.nsf.gov/sed/start.cfm>.

Table 827. Scientists and Engineers by Selected Demographic Characteristics: 2008

[In thousands (23,279 represents 23,279,000). Scientists and engineers refer to all persons who have received a bachelor's degree or higher in science and engineering (S&E), or S&E related field, plus persons holding a non-S&E degree or higher, employed in S&E or S&E related field. Detail may not add to total due to rounding]

Characteristic	Both sexes	Female	Male	Characteristic	Both sexes	Female	Male
All scientists and engineers.....	23,279	10,718	12,561	Highest degree attained:			
				Bachelor's.....................	13,193	6,246	6,947
Age:				Master's.......................	6,893	3,375	3,518
29 or younger.....................	2,722	1,545	1,176	Doctorate......................	1,091	351	741
30-39 years.......................	5,367	2,681	2,685	Professional...................	2,101	746	1,355
40-49 years.......................	5,788	2,701	3,087				
50-59 years.......................	5,575	2,491	3,084	Citizenship status:			
60-69 years.......................	3,017	1,050	1,967	U.S. citizen, native...........	19,657	9,152	10,506
70 or older.......................	810	249	561	U.S. citizen, naturalized......	2,691	1,222	1,470
				Non-U.S. citizen, permanent resident......	675	264	411
Race/ethnicity:				Non-U.S. citizen, temporary resident...............	254	80	174
American Indian/Alaska Native...	93	46	47				
Asian.............................	2,389	1,056	1,333	Marital status:			
Black.............................	1,305	775	530	Married........................	16,668	7,015	9,654
Native Hawaiian/Other Pacific Islander............................	89	35	54	Living in marriage-like relationship..................	978	550	428
White.............................	17,757	7,972	9,785	Widowed........................	351	247	103
Multiple race.....................	383	197	186	Separated......................	251	144	108
Hispanic, any race...............	1,263	637	626	Divorced.......................	1,533	910	623
				Never married..................	3,497	1,852	1,645
Children in the home?							
Yes...............................	10,854	5,038	5,816				
No................................	12,424	5,680	6,745				

Source: National Science Foundation, Natioanl Center for Science and Engineering Statistics, Scientists and Engineers Statistical Data System (SESTAT), <http://www.nsf.gov/statistics/sestat/>, accessed August 2012.

Table 828. Civilian Employment of Scientists, Engineers, and Related Occupations by Occupation and Industry: 2010

[In thousands (307.9 represents 307,900). Standard Occupational Classification system categorizes workers in 1 of 801 detailed occupations. Industry classifications correspond to 2007 North American Industry Classification (NAICS) industrial groups. For definition of scientists and engineers, see text this section]

Occupation	Total employ-ment, all workers	Wage and salary workers						Self employ-ed [2]
		Mining (NAICS 21) [1]	Con-struction (NAICS 23)	Manu-facturing (NAICS 31–33)	Informa-tion (NAICS 51)	Profes-sional, scientific and technical services (NAICS 54)	Govern-ment (NAICS 99)	
Computer and information systems managers....................	307.9	0.4	0.6	27.2	34.4	78.1	21.2	8.3
Engineering managers........................	176.8	0.4	4.2	67.3	4.4	56.8	17.5	0.1
Natural science managers....................	49.3	0.2	(NA)	7.8	(NA)	15.5	16.1	1.2
Computer and mathematical scientists.........	3,542.8	5.4	8.9	270.4	411.5	1,122.1	259.0	155.0
Computer specialists....................	3,246.0	5.3	8.9	263.9	405.3	1,096.8	237.5	153.0
Mathematical science occupations...........	116.8	(NA)	(NA)	6.6	6.2	25.3	21.6	2.0
Surveyors, cartographers, and photogrammetrists..............................	65.0	0.8	3.2	0.5	0.4	39.0	9.8	9.0
Engineers [3]................................	1,519.0	32.9	39.3	514.6	37.7	453.2	203.5	38.4
Aerospace engineers..........................	81.0	(NA)	(NA)	38.8	(NA)	26.4	10.5	0.9
Civil engineers................................	262.8	0.9	24.4	2.5	0.5	132.8	75.3	10.0
Computer and hardware engineers............	70.0	(NA)	(NA)	26.0	3.7	26.2	5.1	0.9
Electrical and electronics engineers...........	294.0	0.8	4.1	97.7	30.5	75.0	28.8	6.3
Industrial engineers [4]............................	227.6	1.8	5.7	146.5	1.0	32.4	6.2	0.2
Mechanical engineers.......................	243.2	1.3	3.0	118.0	0.2	69.9	15.4	5.6
Drafters, engineering, and mapping technicians [5]................................	714.0	6.2	20.6	204.7	12.5	256.1	106.5	13.4
Engineering technicians.....................	451.9	5.2	4.6	153.2	10.5	112.9	90.2	2.1
Surveying and mapping technicians..........	56.9	0.1	(NA)	0.1	0.5	35.7	11.6	2.7
Life, physical, and social science occupations...................................	1,228.8	18.9	0.7	116.8	1.6	306.3	331.8	91.4
Life scientists........................	285.9	(NA)	(NA)	33.9	0.1	74.7	73.5	11.1
Physical scientists....................	282.0	0.7	0.2	37.4	1.1	98.8	79.5	11.0
Social scientists and related occupations...................................	306.1	0.1	NA	0.5	0.3	39.8	85.7	68.2
Life, physical, and social science technicians................................	354.8	9.4	0.4	45.0	0.1	93.0	93.1	1.1

NA Not available. [1] Includes oil and gas extraction. [2] Includes secondary jobs and unpaid private household employment. [3] Includes kinds of engineers not shown separately. [4] Includes health and safety engineers. [5] Includes other drafters, technicians, and mapping technicians.

Source: U.S. Bureau of Labor Statistics, National Employment Matrix, December 2011 (data collected biennially). See also <http://www.bls.gov/emp/empoils.htm>.

Table 829. Employment, Mean Earnings, and Growth in Science and Engineering (S&E) Occupations: 2004 to 2008

[Minus sign (–) represents a decrease. Based on data derived from Bureau of Labor Statistics' Occupational Employment Survey (OES)]

Occupation	Employment					Mean earnings	
	2004, total	2008, total	Total growth	Total growth (percent)	Average annual growth rate (percent)	2008 annual earnings (dol.)	Average annual growth rate (percent)
All occupations.....................	**128,127,360**	**135,185,230**	**7,057,870**	**5.5**	**1.3**	**42,270**	**3.4**
STEM [1].................................	7,160,770	7,852,710	691,940	9.7	2.3	74,950	3.6
S&E.................................	5,085,740	5,781,460	695,720	13.7	3.3	76,680	3.5
Engineers.....................	1,487,810	1,626,330	138,520	9.3	2.3	84,120	3.7
Mathematical and computer scientists................	2,566,170	2,972,940	406,770	15.9	3.7	74,420	3.4
Life scientists........................	275,500	319,520	44,020	16.0	3.8	75,130	3.7
Physical scientists...................	273,360	301,500	28,140	10.3	2.5	76,710	3.8
Social scientists....................	482,900	561,160	78,260	16.2	3.8	67,980	2.9
Technicians, programmers, and S&E managers.................	2,075,020	2,071,260	-3,760	-0.2	(Z)	70,170	3.6
S&E related........................	6,914,070	7,737,490	823,420	11.9	2.9	(NA)	(NA)
Healthcare practitioners and technicians......................	6,769,900	7,569,040	799,140	11.8	2.8	(NA)	(NA)
Other S&E related....................	144,170	168,450	24,280	16.8	4.0	(NA)	(NA)
Not STEM or S&E related.............	114,052,530	119,595,020	5,542,490	4.9	1.2	(NA)	(NA)

NA Not available. Z Less than 0.05. [1] STEM = science, technology, engineering, and mathematics.

Source: National Science Foundation, *Employment in Science and Engineering Occupations Reached 5.8 Million in 2008*, NSF 10-315, 2010. See also <http://www.nsf.gov/statistics/infbrief/nsf10315/>.

Table 830. Research and Development (R&D) Scientists and Engineers—Employment and Cost by Industry: 2005 to 2007

[In thousands (1,104.5 represents 1,104,500). Data are estimates on full-time-equivalent (FTE) basis. Based on the Survey of Industrial Research and Development. The Business R&D and Innovation Survey replaces the Survey of Industrial Research and Development for data available as of December 2010; see <http://www.nsf.gov/statistics/srvyindustry/about/brdis/>]

Industry	NAICS [1] code	Employed scientists and engineers [2] (1,000)			Cost per scientist or engineer, constant (2000) dollars [3, 4] ($1,000)		
		2005	2006	2007	2005	2006	2007
All industries [5]	(X)	**1,104.5**	**1,116.6**	**1,133.0**	**192.4**	**201.6**	**211.9**
Chemicals	325	118.3	123.2	134.0	328.5	330.1	356.4
Machinery	333	61.1	62.3	61.9	125.2	141.1	144.4
Electrical equipment, appliances, and components	335	18.7	16.9	15.8	(D)	(D)	(D)
Motor vehicles, trailers, and parts	3361–3363	42.0	42.0	(NA)	(D)	(D)	(D)
Aerospace products and parts	3364	39.7	39.5	40.2	335.4	359.4	380.5
Software publishing	5112	93.4	46.5	(NA)	162.5	174.0	175.4
Architectural, engineering, and related services	5413	35.8	41.2	48.5	129.3	146.4	113.9
Computer systems design and related services	5415	82.4	93.1	88.1	158.5	157.2	160.3
Scientific R&D services	5417	43.7	44.3	50.4	264.0	298.2	308.7
NOTE: Constant 2000 dollar deflator	(X)	(X)	(X)	(X)	1.1303	1.1668	1.1982

D Withheld to avoid disclosure. NA Not available. X Not applicable. [1] North American Industry Classification System 2002 (NAICS); see text, Section 15. [2] The mean number of full-time equivalent (R&D) scientists and engineers employed in January of the year shown and the following January. [3] Based on gross domestic product implicit price deflator. [4] Represents the arithmetic mean of the numbers of R&D scientists and engineers reported in each industry for January in 2 consecutive years divided into total R&D expenditures in each industry. [5] Includes other industries not shown separately.

Source: National Science Foundation, *Research and Development in Industry*, NSF 10-319, 2010, and unpublished data. See also <http://www.nsf.gov/statistics/industry/>.

Table 831. Workers in Science and Engineering (S&E) and Science, Technology, Engineering and Mathematics (STEM) Occupations in Largest Metropolitan Statistical Areas: May 2010

[Includes only metropolitan statistical areas with multiple metropolitan divisions. Data are from BLS's Occupational Employment Statistics Survey. Differences among employment estimates may not be statistically significant, see source for details]

Metropolitan statistical area	Workers employed			Percent of workforce	
	All occupations	S&E occupations	STEM occupations	S&E occupations	STEM occupations
U.S. total	**127,097,160**	**5,549,980**	**7,427,350**	**4.4**	**5.8**
New York-Northern New Jersey-Long Island, NY-NJ-PA	8,101,890	(D)	443,200	(D)	5.5
Washington-Arlington-Alexandria, DC-VA-MD-WV	2,840,740	298,180	360,580	10.5	12.7
Los Angeles-Long Beach-Santa Ana, CA	5,191,880	237,430	308,090	4.6	5.9
Boston-Cambridge-Quincy, MA-NH	2,413,780	190,260	244,740	7.9	10.1
Chicago-Naperville-Joliet, IL-IN-WI	4,169,840	155,760	214,310	3.7	5.1
Dallas-Fort Worth-Arlington, TX	2,832,560	151,090	198,860	5.3	7.0
Seattle-Tacoma-Bellevue, WA	1,601,010	138,350	174,920	8.6	10.9
San Francisco-Oakland-Fremont, CA	1,900,110	138,280	177,380	7.3	9.3
Philadelphia-Camden-Wilmington, PA-NJ-DE-MD	2,619,360	129,910	168,720	5.0	6.4
Detroit-Warren-Livonia, MI	1,686,920	102,210	135,190	6.1	8.0
Miami-Fort Lauderdale-Pompano Beach, FL	2,143,470	63,060	83,940	2.9	3.9

D Figure suppressed for reasons of confidentiality and/or reliability.

Source: National Science Foundation, *Science and Engineering Indicators, 2012*. See also <http://www.nsf.gov/statistics/seind/>.

Table 832. Employment and Median Salary in Science and Engineering (S&E) Occupations by Sex: 2008

[Rounded to the nearest 1,000. Percents based on unrounded numbers. Data are for full-time workers who typically work 35 or more hours weekly in their principal job. Data are from National Science Foundation's Scientists and Engineers Statistical Data System (SESTAT)]

Occupation	Total		Female			Male		
	Number	Median salary (dollars)	Number	Percent	Median salary (dollars)	Number	Percent	Median salary (dollars)
All occupations	**8,869,000**	**70,000**	**3,018,000**	**34.0**	**52,000**	**5,851,000**	**66.0**	**80,000**
S&E	3,554,000	80,000	837,000	23.5	70,000	2,718,000	76.5	85,000
Engineers	1,293,000	87,000	162,000	12.5	75,000	1,131,000	87.5	89,000
Computer and mathematical scientists	1,345,000	85,000	302,000	22.4	78,000	1,044,000	77.6	87,000
Biological, agricultural, and other life scientists	365,000	59,000	156,000	42.7	50,000	210,000	57.3	65,000
Physical scientists	269,000	70,000	74,000	27.3	60,000	196,000	72.7	76,000
Social scientists	281,000	68,000	143,000	50.9	63,000	138,000	49.1	73,000
S&E related occupations	1,139,000	65,000	454,000	39.9	51,000	685,000	60.1	80,000
Health-related occupations	353,000	50,000	217,000	61.5	48,000	136,000	38.5	60,000

Non-S&E related occupations

Source: National Science Foundation, National Center for Science and Engineering Statistics, *Science and Engineering Indicators 2012*, January 2012. See also <http://www.nsf.gov/statistics/seind/>.

Table 833. Federal Outlays for General Science, Space, and Other Technology, 1970 to 2011, and Projections, 2012 and 2013

[In billions of dollars (4.5 represents $4,500,000,000). For fiscal years ending in year shown; see text, Section 8]

Year	Current dollars			Constant (2005) dollars		
	Total	General science/basic research	Space and other technologies	Total	General science/basic research	Space and other technologies
1970..................	4.5	0.9	3.6	23.4	4.9	18.5
1980..................	5.8	1.4	4.5	14.6	3.5	11.2
1985..................	8.6	2.0	6.6	16.7	3.9	12.8
1990..................	14.4	2.8	11.6	24.5	4.8	19.7
1995 [1]...............	16.7	4.1	12.6	22.0	5.4	16.6
2000..................	18.6	6.2	12.4	22.1	7.3	14.7
2001..................	19.8	6.5	13.2	22.7	7.5	15.2
2002..................	20.7	7.3	13.5	23.1	8.1	15.1
2003..................	20.8	8.0	12.9	22.6	8.6	14.0
2004..................	23.0	8.4	14.6	23.9	8.7	15.2
2005..................	23.6	8.8	14.8	23.6	8.8	14.8
2006..................	23.6	9.1	14.5	22.7	8.7	14.0
2007..................	24.4	9.1	15.3	22.9	8.6	14.3
2008..................	26.8	9.6	17.2	24.4	8.7	15.7
2009..................	28.4	10.0	18.4	25.4	8.9	16.5
2010..................	30.1	11.7	18.4	27.4	10.6	16.8
2011..................	29.5	12.4	17.0	26.1	11.0	15.1
2012, proj.............	31.0	13.9	17.1	26.5	11.8	14.7
2013, proj.............	31.3	13.9	17.3	26.4	11.7	14.7

[1] Due to the effects of the Credit Reform Act of 1990 on the measurement and classification of federal credit activities, the discretionary outlays for years prior to 1995 are not strictly comparable to those for 1995 and after. However, the discretionary outlays shown for 1995 are no more than $1 billion higher than they would have been if measured on the same (pre-credit reform) basis as the 1990 outlays.

Source: U.S. Office of Management and Budget, *Budget of the United States Government: Historical Tables, Fiscal Year 2013*, annual. See also <http://www.gpo.gov/fdsys/pkg/BUDGET-2013-TAB/pdf/BUDGET-2013-TAB.pdf>.

Table 834. Worldwide Space Launch Events: 2000 to 2011

[In millions of dollars (2,729 represents $2,729,000,000)]

Country	Non-commercial launches				Commercial launches				Launch revenues for commercial launch events (mil. dol.)			
	2000	2005	2010	2011	2000	2005	2010	2011	2000	2005	2010	2011
Total.............	**50**	**37**	**51**	**66**	**35**	**18**	**23**	**18**	**2,729**	**1,190**	**2,453**	**1,927**
United States......	21	11	11	18	7	1	4	–	370	70	307	–
Russia.............	23	18	18	21	13	8	13	10	671	350	826	707
Europe............	–	–	0	3	12	5	6	4	1,433	490	1,320	880
China [1]...........	5	5	15	17	–	–	–	2	(X)	(X)	(X)	140
India..............	–	1	3	3	–	–	–	–	(X)	(X)	(X)	(X)
Japan..............	1	2	2	3	–	–	–	–	(X)	(X)	(X)	(X)
Israel.............	–	–	1	–	–	–	–	–	(X)	(X)	(X)	(X)
Ukraine............	–	–	–	–	–	–	–	–	(X)	(X)	(X)	(X)
Iran...............	–	–	–	1	–	–	–	–	(X)	(X)	(X)	(X)
Brazil.............	–	–	–	–	–	–	–	–	(X)	(X)	(X)	(X)
Korea, North.......	–	–	–	–	–	–	–	–	(X)	(X)	(X)	(X)
Korea, South......	–	–	1	–	–	–	–	–	(X)	(X)	(X)	(X)
Multinational.......	–	–	–	–	3	4	–	2	255	280	(X)	200

– Represents zero. X Not applicable. [1] See footnote 4, Table 1348.

Source: Federal Aviation Administration, *Commercial Space Transportation: 2011 Year in Review*, January 2012, and prior years. See also <http://www.faa.gov/about/office_org/headquarters_offices/ast/reports_studies/year_review>.

Section 17
Agriculture

This section presents statistics on farms and farm operators; farm income, expenditures, and debt; farm output, productivity, and marketings; foreign trade in agricultural products; specific crops; and livestock, poultry, and their products.

The principal sources are the reports issued by the National Agricultural Statistics Service (NASS), the Economic Research Service (ERS), and the Foreign Agricultural Service (FAS) of the U.S. Department of Agriculture (USDA). The information from the 2007 Census of Agriculture is available in printed form in the Volume 1, Geographic Area Series; in electronic format on CD-ROM; and on the Internet at <http://www.agcensus.usda.gov/Publications/2007/Full_Report/index.asp>. The Department of Agriculture publishes annually *Agricultural Statistics*, a general reference book on agricultural production, supplies, consumption, facilities, costs, and returns. The ERS publishes data on farm assets, debt, and income on the Internet at <http://www.ers.usda.gov/briefing/farmincome/>. Sources of current data on agricultural exports and imports include the Global Agricultural Trade System database provided by the FAS at <http://www.fas.usda.gov/gats/default.aspx> and the "Foreign Agricultural Trade of the United States (FATUS)" data, published by the ERS, available on the the ERS Internet site at <http://www.ers.usda.gov/data-products/foreign-agricultural-trade-of-the-united-states-(fatus).aspx>.

The field offices of the NASS collect data on crops, livestock and products, agricultural prices, farm employment, and other related subjects mainly through sample surveys. Information is obtained on crops and livestock items as well as scores of items pertaining to agricultural production and marketing. State estimates and supporting information are sent to the Agricultural Statistics Board of NASS, which reviews the estimates and issues reports containing state and national data. Among these reports are annual summaries such as *Crop Production, Crop Values, Agricultural Prices*, and *Meat Animals Production, Disposition and Income*.

Farms and farmland—The definitions of a farm have varied through time. Since 1850, when minimum criteria defining a farm for census purposes first were established, the farm definition has changed nine times. The current definition, first used for the 1974 census, is any place from which $1,000 or more of agricultural products were produced and sold, or normally would have been sold, during the census year.

Acreage designated as "land in farms" consists primarily of agricultural land used for crops, pasture, or grazing. It also includes woodland and wasteland not actually under cultivation or used for pasture or grazing, provided it was part of the farm operator's total operation. Land in farms includes acres set aside under annual commodity acreage programs as well as acres in the Conservation Reserve and Wetlands Reserve Programs for places meeting the farm definition. Land in farms is an operating unit concept and includes land owned and operated as well as land rented from others. All grazing land, except land used

under government permits on a per-head basis, was included as "land in farms" provided it was part of a farm or ranch.

An evaluation of coverage has been conducted for each census of agriculture since 1945 to provide estimates of the completeness of census farm counts. Beginning with the 1997 Census of Agriculture, census farm counts and totals were statistically adjusted for coverage and reported at the county level. The size of the adjustments varies considerably by state. In general, farms not on the census mail list tended to be small in acreage, production, and sales of farm products. The response rate for the 2007 Census of Agriculture was 85.2 percent as compared with a response rate of 88.0 for the 2002 Census of Agriculture and 86.2 percent for the 1997 Census of Agriculture.

For more explanation about census mail list compilation, collection methods, coverage measurement, and adjustments, see Appendix A, 2007 Census of Agriculture, Volume 1 reports <http://www.agcensus.usda.gov/Publications/2007/Full_Report/index.asp>.

Farm income—The final agricultural sector output comprises cash receipts from farm marketings of crops and livestock, federal government payments made directly to farmers for farm-related activities, rental value of farm homes, value of farm products consumed in farm homes, and other farm-related income such as machine hire and custom work. Farm marketings represent quantities of agricultural products sold by farmers multiplied by prices received per unit of production at the local market. Information on prices received for farm products is generally obtained by the NASS Agricultural Statistics Board from surveys of firms (such as grain elevators, packers, and processors) purchasing agricultural commodities directly from producers. In some cases, the price information is obtained directly from the producers.

Crops—Estimates of crop acreage and production by the NASS are based on current sample survey data obtained from individual producers and objective yield counts, reports of carlot shipments, market records, personal field observations by field statisticians, and reports from other sources. Prices received by farmers are marketing year averages. These averages are based on U.S. monthly prices weighted by monthly marketings during specific periods. U.S. monthly prices are state average prices weighted by marketings during the month. Marketing year average prices do not include allowances for outstanding loans, government purchases, deficiency payments or disaster payments.

All state prices are based on individual state marketing years, while U.S. marketing year averages are based on standard marketing years for each crop. For a listing of the crop marketing years and the participating states in the monthly program, see *Crop Values*. Value of production is computed by multiplying state prices by each state's production. The U.S. value of production is the sum of state values for all states. Value of production figures shown in

Tables 870 through 874 and 876 should not be confused with cash receipts from farm marketings which relate to sales during a calendar year, irrespective of the year of production.

Livestock—Annual inventory numbers of livestock and estimates of livestock, dairy, and poultry production prepared by the Department of Agriculture are based on information from farmers and ranchers obtained by probability survey sampling methods.

Statistical reliability—For a discussion of statistical collection and estimation, sampling procedures, and measures of statistical reliability pertaining to Department of Agriculture data, see Appendix III.

Table 835. Selected Characteristics of Farms by North American Industry Classification System (NAICS): 2007

[297,220,491 represents $297,220,491,000. See text this section and Appendix III]

Industry	2007 NAICS code [1]	Farms	Land in farms (acres)	Harvested cropland (acres)	Market value of agricultural products sold (1,000) Total	Crops	Livestock [2]
Total................................	(X)	**2,204,792**	**922,095,840**	**309,607,601**	**297,220,491**	**143,657,928**	**153,562,563**
Crop production................................	111	1,051,889	416,961,540	244,213,836	141,921,405	135,806,093	6,115,312
Oilseed and grain farming................	1111	338,237	266,831,616	194,191,397	74,559,692	69,851,934	4,707,758
Soybean farming................	11111	62,923	22,094,100	17,599,156	5,637,504	5,532,934	104,570
Oilseed (except soybean) farming.........	11112	515	458,591	306,033	62,238	61,081	1,157
Dry pea and bean farming................	11113	526	382,071	269,759	79,297	78,454	844
Wheat farming................	11114	35,232	55,992,672	29,062,744	6,157,944	5,821,678	336,267
Corn farming................	11115	161,874	103,071,231	86,627,715	39,675,674	38,524,804	1,150,870
Rice farming................	11116	3,853	4,233,156	3,396,230	1,936,574	1,915,447	21,127
Other grain farming................	11119	73,314	80,599,795	56,929,760	21,010,459	17,917,536	3,092,923
Vegetable and melon farming................	11121	40,589	9,272,945	6,018,702	14,975,322	14,850,087	125,235
Potato farming................	111211	2,182	2,577,795	1,992,430	2,885,906	2,854,320	31,586
Other vegetable (except potato) and melon farming................	111219	38,407	6,695,150	4,026,272	12,089,416	11,995,767	93,649
Fruit and tree nut farming................	1113	98,281	12,141,683	5,339,755	18,351,629	18,225,583	126,046
Orange groves................	11131	8,771	1,535,483	800,921	2,423,976	2,382,844	41,131
Citrus (except orange) groves................	11132	3,429	402,617	205,522	783,426	778,099	5,326
Noncitrus fruit and tree nut farming................	11133	86,081	10,203,583	4,333,312	15,144,228	15,064,639	79,589
Apple orchards................	111331	11,550	2,078,125	488,273	2,259,839	2,251,555	8,284
Grape vineyards................	111332	17,036	2,067,987	1,061,070	3,890,152	3,883,341	6,811
Strawberry farming................	111333	1,503	149,972	55,461	1,185,736	1,182,263	3,473
Berry (except strawberry) farming.........	111334	8,535	870,154	220,530	1,211,820	1,209,450	2,370
Tree nut farming................	111335	22,821	3,239,199	1,652,915	3,655,251	3,626,067	29,184
Fruit and tree nut combination farming................	111336	995	292,842	106,488	301,611	286,946	14,666
Other noncitrus fruit farming................	111339	23,641	1,505,304	748,575	2,639,819	2,625,018	14,801
Greenhouse, nursery, and floriculture production................	1114	54,889	3,974,530	1,698,564	16,967,123	16,930,975	36,147
Food crops grown under cover................	11141	2,044	85,809	18,712	1,552,287	1,550,756	1,531
Nursery and floriculture production.........	11142	52,845	3,888,721	1,679,852	15,414,835	15,380,219	34,616
Nursery and tree production................	111421	34,532	3,287,008	1,505,323	8,901,860	8,875,417	26,443
Floriculture production................	111422	18,313	601,713	174,529	6,512,975	6,504,801	8,173
Other crop farming................	1119	519,893	124,740,766	36,965,418	17,067,639	15,947,514	1,120,126
Tobacco farming................	11191	9,626	2,518,697	1,219,827	1,147,173	1,077,481	69,692
Cotton farming................	11192	9,968	13,081,671	9,778,279	4,357,082	4,300,124	56,958
Sugarcane farming................	11193	614	1,299,318	969,321	885,028	881,698	3,330
Hay farming................	11194	254,042	49,923,443	18,606,436	6,488,172	5,807,594	680,578
All other crop farming................	11199	245,643	57,917,637	6,391,555	4,190,184	3,880,617	309,568
Animal production................	112	1,152,903	505,134,300	65,393,765	155,299,086	7,851,835	147,447,251
Cattle ranching and farming................	1121	744,858	413,261,549	55,185,767	92,538,429	5,109,567	87,428,862
Beef cattle ranching and farming including feedlots................	11211	687,540	391,990,769	41,893,929	57,784,399	3,895,789	53,888,610
Beef cattle ranching and farming.........	112111	656,475	376,170,540	36,675,357	27,535,096	2,626,582	24,908,514
Cattle feedlots................	112112	31,065	15,820,229	5,218,572	30,249,303	1,269,207	28,980,096
Dairy cattle and milk production................	11212	57,318	21,270,780	13,291,838	34,754,031	1,213,778	33,540,252
Hog and pig farming................	1122	30,546	6,949,176	4,747,504	18,127,114	1,614,030	16,513,083
Poultry and egg production................	1123	64,570	7,040,000	2,140,320	37,797,542	547,736	37,249,806
Chicken egg production................	11231	35,651	2,259,774	477,371	7,546,997	104,546	7,442,452
Broilers and other meat-type chicken production................	11232	17,888	3,370,828	1,209,528	22,400,358	306,268	22,094,090
Turkey production................	11233	3,405	836,551	396,096	4,643,075	127,009	4,516,067
Poultry hatcheries................	11234	775	69,558	9,985	2,777,612	1,790	2,775,822
Other poultry production................	11239	6,851	503,289	47,340	429,499	8,124	421,375
Sheep and goat farming................	1124	67,254	11,963,667	429,300	554,107	21,374	532,732
Sheep farming................	11241	30,974	8,971,952	324,835	435,107	18,396	416,711
Goat farming................	11242	36,280	2,991,715	104,465	119,000	2,979	116,021
Animal aquaculture................	1125	4,777	2,451,244	70,954	1,407,750	18,384	1,389,366
Other animal production................	1129	240,898	63,468,664	2,819,920	4,874,144	540,743	4,333,401
Apiculture................	11291	7,979	503,609	92,280	263,268	19,827	243,440
Horse and other equine production.........	11292	168,694	22,370,495	675,383	2,088,845	17,332	2,071,512
Fur-bearing animal and rabbit production................	11293	2,252	89,224	16,894	154,325	2,744	151,581
All other animal production................	11299	61,973	40,505,336	2,035,363	2,367,706	500,839	1,866,867

X Not applicable [1] North American Industry Classification System (NAICS) 2007; see text, Section 15. [2] Includes poultry, and their products sold.

Source: U.S. Department of Agriculture, National Agricultural Statistics Service, *2007 Census of Agriculture*, Vol. 1, February 2009. See also <http://www.agcensus.usda.gov/Publications/index.php>.

Table 836. Farms—Number and Acreage: 1990 to 2011

[As of June 1 (2,146 represents 2,146,000). Based on 1974 census definition; for definition of farms and farmland, see text, this section. Activities included as agriculture have undergone changes in recent years. Data for period 2000 to 2011 are not directly comparable with data for 1990. See source for more detail. Data for 2007 have been adjusted for underenumeration]

Year	Unit	1990	2000	2005	2006	2007	2008	2009	2010	2011
Number of farms.........	1,000	2,146	2,167	2,099	2,089	2,205	2,200	2,200	2,192	2,181
Land in farms............	Mil. acres	987	945	928	926	921	920	920	919	917
Average per farm.......	Acres	460	436	442	443	418	418	418	419	420

Source: U.S. Department of Agriculture, National Agricultural Statistics Service, *Farms and Land in Farms, Final Estimates, 1988–1992*; *Farms and Land in Farms, Final Estimates, 1993–1997*; *Farm Numbers and Land in Farms, Final Estimates, 1998–2002*; *Farms and Land in Farms, Final Estimates, 2003-2007*; and *Farms, Land in Farms, and Livestock Operations 2011 Summary, February 2012*. See also <http://www.nass.usda.gov/Publications/index.asp>.

Table 837. Farms—Number and Acreage by State: 2000 to 2011

[As of June 1 (2,167 represents 2,167,000). See headnote, Table 836]

State	Farms (1,000) 2000	Farms (1,000) 2011	Land in farms (mil. acres) 2000	Land in farms (mil. acres) 2011	Acreage per farm 2000	Acreage per farm 2011	State	Farms (1,000) 2000	Farms (1,000) 2011	Land in farms (mil. acres) 2000	Land in farms (mil. acres) 2011	Acreage per farm 2000	Acreage per farm 2011
United States......	**2,167**	**2,181**	**945**	**917**	**436**	**420**							
Alabama.............	47	48	9	9	191	188	Montana............	28	29	59	61	2,133	2,065
Alaska...............	1	1	1	1	1,569	1,294	Nebraska...........	52	47	46	46	887	972
Arizona.............	11	16	27	26	2,514	1,684	Nevada.............	3	3	6	6	2,065	1,983
Arkansas............	48	48	15	14	304	280	New Hampshire....	3	4	(Z)	(Z)	133	113
California............	83	82	28	25	337	312	New Jersey.........	10	10	1	1	86	71
Colorado............	30	37	32	31	1,053	853	New Mexico........	18	23	45	43	2,494	1,887
Connecticut.........	4	5	(Z)	(Z)	86	82	New York...........	38	36	8	7	205	194
Delaware............	3	3	1	(Z)	215	196	North Carolina......	56	50	9	9	166	169
Florida..............	44	48	10	9	236	195	North Dakota.......	31	32	39	40	1,279	1,241
Georgia.............	49	47	11	10	222	219	Ohio...............	79	74	15	14	187	185
Hawaii..............	6	8	1	1	251	148	Oklahoma..........	85	86	34	35	400	406
Idaho...............	25	25	12	11	486	462	Oregon.............	40	38	17	16	433	426
Illinois..............	77	75	28	27	357	357	Pennsylvania.......	59	62	8	8	130	123
Indiana.............	63	62	15	15	240	237	Rhode Island.......	1	1	(Z)	(Z)	75	57
Iowa................	94	92	33	31	346	333	South Carolina.....	24	27	5	5	203	185
Kansas..............	65	66	48	46	736	702	South Dakota......	32	31	44	44	1,358	1,395
Kentucky............	90	85	14	14	152	164	Tennessee.........	88	77	12	11	134	140
Louisiana............	29	29	8	8	277	274	Texas..............	228	245	131	130	573	531
Maine...............	7	8	1	1	190	167	Utah...............	16	17	12	11	748	669
Maryland............	12	13	2	2	172	160	Vermont............	7	7	1	1	192	174
Massachusetts.......	6	8	1	1	89	68	Virginia............	49	46	9	8	180	171
Michigan............	53	55	10	10	192	182	Washington.........	37	40	16	15	420	375
Minnesota...........	81	80	28	27	344	336	West Virginia.......	21	23	4	4	173	162
Mississippi..........	42	42	11	11	266	263	Wisconsin..........	78	77	16	15	206	195
Missouri.............	109	107	30	29	277	271	Wyoming...........	9	11	35	30	3,750	2,745

Z Less than 500,000 acres.

Source: U.S. Department of Agriculture, National Agricultural Statistics Service, *Farm Numbers and Land in Farms, Final Estimates, 1998–2002* and *Farms, Land in Farms, and Livestock Operations 2011 Summary*, February 2012. See also <http://www.nass.usda.gov/Publications/index.asp>.

Table 838. Farms by Size and Type of Organization: 1978 to 2007

[2,258 represents 2,258,000. For comments on adjustment, see text, this section]

Size and type of organization	Unit	Not adjusted for coverage					Adjusted for coverage		
		1978	1982	1987	1992	1997	1997 [1]	2002 [1]	2007 [1]
Farms..............................	1,000	2,258	2,241	2,088	1,925	1,912	2,216	2,129	2,205
Land in farms......................	Mil. acres	1,015	987	964	946	932	955	938	922
Average size of farm...............	Acres	449	440	462	491	487	431	441	418
Farms by size:									
1 to 9 acres.....................	1,000	151	188	183	166	154	205	179	233
10 to 49 acres...................	1,000	392	449	412	388	411	531	564	620
50 to 179 acres..................	1,000	759	712	645	584	593	694	659	661
180 to 499 acres.................	1,000	582	527	478	428	403	428	389	368
500 to 999 acres.................	1,000	213	204	200	186	176	179	162	150
1,000 to 1,999 acres.............	1,000	98	97	102	102	101	103	99	93
2,000 acres or more..............	1,000	63	65	67	71	75	74	78	80
Farms by type of organization:									
Family or individual..............	1,000	1,966	1,946	1,809	1,653	1,643	1,923	1,910	1,906
Partnership......................	1,000	233	223	200	187	169	186	130	174
Corporation.....................	1,000	50	60	67	73	84	90	74	96
Other [2].........................	1,000	9	12	12	12	15	17	16	28

[1] Data have been adjusted for coverage; see text, this section. [2] Cooperative, estate or trust, institutional, etc.

Source: U.S. Department of Agriculture, National Agricultural Statistics Service, *2007 Census of Agriculture*, Vol. 1. See also <http://www.agcensus.usda.gov/Publications/index.php>.

Table 839. Farms—Number and Acreage by Size of Farm: 2002 and 2007

[2,129 represents 2,129,000. Data have been adjusted for coverage; see text, this section]

Size of farm	Number of farms (1,000) 2002	Number of farms (1,000) 2007	Land in farms (mil. acres) 2002	Land in farms (mil. acres) 2007	Cropland harvested (mil. acres) 2002	Cropland harvested (mil. acres) 2007	Percent distribution, 2007 Number of farms	Percent distribution, 2007 All land in farms	Percent distribution, 2007 Cropland harvested
Total..........................	**2,129**	**2,205**	**938.3**	**922.1**	**302.7**	**309.6**	**100.0**	**100.0**	**100.0**
Under 10 acres.................	179	233	0.8	1.1	0.2	0.3	10.6	0.1	0.1
10 to 49 acres.................	564	620	14.7	15.9	4.1	4.3	28.1	1.7	1.4
50 to 69 acres.................	152	154	8.8	8.9	2.5	2.5	7.0	1.0	0.8
70 to 99 acres.................	191	192	15.7	15.8	4.7	4.5	8.7	1.7	1.5
100 to 139 acres.............	175	175	20.2	20.3	6.1	5.8	7.9	2.2	1.9
140 to 179 acres.............	142	139	22.3	22.0	7.3	6.6	6.3	2.4	2.1
180 to 219 acres.............	91	88	18.0	17.3	6.2	5.6	4.0	1.9	1.8
220 to 259 acres.............	72	68	17.1	16.3	6.5	5.7	3.1	1.8	1.9
260 to 499 acres.............	226	213	80.6	75.9	34.1	30.4	9.6	8.2	9.8
500 to 999 acres.............	162	150	112.4	104.1	56.7	51.6	6.8	11.3	16.7
1,000 to 1,999 acres...........	99	93	135.7	127.6	72.8	69.8	4.2	13.8	22.6
2,000 acres or more...........	78	80	491.9	496.9	101.6	122.5	3.6	53.9	39.6

Source: U.S. Department of Agriculture, National Agricultural Statistics Service, *2007 Census of Agriculture*, Vol. 1. See also
<http://www.agcensus.usda.gov/Publications/index.php>.

Table 840. Farms—Number, Acreage, and Value by Tenure of Principal Operator and Type of Organization: 2002 and 2007

[2,129 represents 2,129,000. Full owners own all the land they operate. Part owners own a part and rent from others the rest of the land they operate. A principal operator is the person primarily responsible for the on-site, day-to-day operation of the farm or ranch business. Data have been adjusted for coverage; see text, this section]

Item and year	Unit	Total [1]	Tenure of operator Full owner	Tenure of operator Part owner	Tenure of operator Tenant	Type of organization Family or individual	Type of organization Partner- ship	Type of organization Corpora- tion
NUMBER OF FARMS								
2002....................................	1,000	2,129	1,428	551	150	1,910	130	74
2007....................................	1,000	2,205	1,522	542	141	1,906	174	96
Under 50 acres.....................	1,000	853	739	70	44	774	45	26
50 to 179 acres.....................	1,000	661	492	130	38	588	45	18
180 to 499 acres...................	1,000	368	198	143	27	312	34	16
500 to 999 acres...................	1,000	150	51	84	14	118	18	12
1,000 acres or more...............	1,000	173	41	114	17	114	32	24
LAND IN FARMS								
2002....................................	Mil. acres	938	357	495	87	622	146	108
2007....................................	Mil. acres	922	344	496	82	574	161	125
Value of land and buildings, 2007 [2].................	Bil. dol.	1,744	726	868	150	1,203	277	227
Value of farm products sold, 2007...................	Bil. dol.	297	117	148	32	148	62	84

[1] Includes other types, not shown separately. [2] Based on a sample of farms.

Source: U.S. Department of Agriculture, National Agricultural Statistics Service, *2007 Census of Agriculture*, Vol. 1. See also
<http://www.agcensus.usda.gov/Publications/2007/Full_Report/index.asp>.

Table 841. Corporate Farms—Characteristics by Type: 2007

[125.3 represents 125,300,000. Data have been adjusted for coverage; see text, this section and Appendix III]

Item	Unit	All corpora- tions	Family held corporations Total	Family held corporations 1 to 10 stock- holders	Family held corporations 11 or more stock- holders	Other corporations Total	Other corporations 1 to 10 stock- holders	Other corporations 11 or more stock- holders
Farms..	Number	96,074	85,837	83,796	2,041	10,237	9,330	907
Percent distribution.....................	Percent	100	89	87	2	11	10	1
Land in farms.............................	Mil. acres	125.3	114.3	106.4	7.8	11.1	7.7	3.3
Average per farm........................	Acres	1,304	1,331	1,270	3,834	1,080	829	3,657
Value of—								
Land and buildings [1].....................	Bil. dol.	226.6	200.6	189.5	11.0	26.0	20.2	5.8
Average per farm........................	$1,000	2,358	2,336	2,262	5,399	2,542	2,170	6,371
Farm products sold......................	Bil. dol.	84.1	65.8	58.9	6.9	18.3	12.2	6.2
Average per farm........................	$1,000	876	766	703	3,378	1,791	1,305	6,787

[1] Based on a sample of farms.

Source: U.S. Department of Agriculture, National Agricultural Statistics Service, *2007 Census of Agriculture*, Vol. 1. See also
<http://www.agcensus.usda.gov/Publications/index.php>.

Table 842. Family Farm Household Income and Wealth, 2006 to 2010, and by Farm Type, 2010

[In dollars, except for number of farms. Based on Agricultural Resource Management Survey (ARMS) Phase III. A family farm is defined as one in which the majority of the ownership of the farm business is held by related individuals. Nearly all farms (98 percent in 2010) are family farms. The farm operator is the person who runs the farm, making the day-to-day management decisions. The operator could be an owner, hired manager, cash tenant, share tenant, and/or a partner. If land is rented or worked on shares, the tenant or renter is the operator. For multiple-operator farms, a principal operator is identified as the individual making most of the day-to-day decisions about the operation. About 40 percent of farms have more than one operator, but three-quarters of these are operated by a husband-wife team. Therefore, both operators are considered part of the principal operator household. Minus sign (–) indicates loss]

Item	2006	2007	2008	2009	2010 Total	2010 ERS farm typology Rural residence farms [1]	2010 ERS farm typology Intermediate farms [2]	2010 ERS farm typology Commercial farms [3]
Number of family farms....................	2,021,903	2,143,398	2,129,869	2,131,007	2,143,063	1,311,117	617,876	214,070
INCOME PER FAMILY FARM HOUSEHOLD								
Net earnings from farming activities.......................	8,541	11,364	9,764	6,866	11,769	-3,501	1,593	134,668
Off-farm income of the household.........	72,502	77,432	70,032	70,302	72,671	87,240	49,461	50,430
Earned income...........................	51,674	58,933	50,761	50,852	52,161	(NA)	(NA)	(NA)
Off-farm wages and salaries............	38,481	48,947	42,606	43,852	(NA)	(NA)	(NA)	(NA)
Off-farm business income..............	13,193	9,986	8,155	7,000	(NA)	(NA)	(NA)	(NA)
Unearned income........................	20,827	18,499	19,271	19,450	20,510	(NA)	(NA)	(NA)
Total household income, mean [4].........	81,043	88,796	79,796	77,169	84,440	83,738	51,054	185,098
WEALTH PER FAMILY FARM HOUSEHOLD								
Assets, mean [4]............................	1,026,389	1,006,020	988,156	1,031,000	1,082,121	812,983	1,050,299	2,822,360
Farm assets................................	764,485	739,905	749,190	761,894	799,317	506,768	822,186	2,525,084
Non-farm assets..........................	261,905	266,115	238,966	269,106	282,804	306,214	228,113	297,276
Debt, mean [4].............................	99,766	106,874	112,705	115,981	123,640	89,264	84,599	446,865
Farm debt................................	59,731	56,859	61,131	66,149	67,404	27,489	44,063	379,242
Non-farm debt.............................	40,035	50,015	51,574	49,832	56,235	61,775	40,535	67,623
Net worth, mean [4].........................	926,623	899,146	875,451	915,019	958,481	723,718	965,700	2,375,495
Farm net worth...........................	704,754	683,046	688,059	695,745	731,912	479,279	778,123	2,145,842
Non-farm net worth.......................	221,869	216,101	187,392	219,274	226,568	244,440	187,578	229,653

NA Not available. [1] Farms in which the principal operator is retired or has a major occupation other than farming. [2] Farms with farming as the operator's major occupation, but with less than $250,000 in gross sales. [3] Farms with more than $250,000 in gross sales. [4] For definition of mean see Guide to Tabular Presentation.

Source: U.S. Department of Agriculture, Economic Research Service, *Agricultural Income and Finance Situation and Outlook*, December 2011; and "USDA Agricultural Resource Management Survey," <http://www.ers.usda.gov/Briefing/ARMS/Access.htm>, accessed June 2012. See also <http://www.ers.usda.gov/data-products/farm-household-income-and-characteristics.aspx>.

Table 843. Farm Type, Acreage, and Production: 2000 to 2010

[2,166 represents 2,166,000. Based on Agricultural Resource Management Survey (ARMS) Phase III]

Type of farm	Unit	2000	2003	2004	2005	2006	2007	2008	2009	2010
Total farms										
Number of farms......................	1,000	2,166	2,121	2,108	2,095	2,083	2,197	2,192	2,192	2,193
Total value of production.............	Mil dol.	177,286	186,644	225,698	215,295	226,045	289,530	299,066	278,051	286,753
Total acres operated..................	Mil.	995	912	990	916	893	878	894	913	912
Acres operated per farm..............	Acres	459	430	470	437	429	400	408	417	416
Commercial farms [1]										
Number of farms......................	1,000	178	188	205	216	219	257	272	271	264
Total value of production.............	Mil dol.	121,202	134,627	170,130	166,566	178,104	241,728	249,759	230,717	240,751
Total acres operated..................	Mil.	392	341	429	418	382	424	429	443	482
Acres operated per farm..............	Acres	2,205	1,815	2,096	1,939	1,747	1,650	1,580	1,635	1,829
Intermediate farms [2]										
Number of farms......................	1,000	668	607	624	550	566	546	583	577	618
Total value of production.............	Mil dol.	41,813	37,894	38,438	33,872	32,533	30,933	32,718	30,830	30,286
Total acres operated..................	Mil.	392	349	342	307	318	237	253	270	242
Acres operated per farm..............	Acres	587	576	547	558	561	434	434	469	392
Rural residence farms [3]										
Number of farms......................	1,000	1,320	1,326	1,279	1,329	1,298	1,394	1,338	1,344	1,311
Total value of production.............	Mil dol.	14,272	14,124	17,130	14,856	15,408	16,869	16,589	16,521	15,716
Total acres operated..................	Mil.	211	221	219	191	193	217	212	200	187
Acres operated per farm..............	Acres	160	167	172	144	149	156	158	149	143

[1] Includes farms with sales of $250,000 or more. [2] Small family farms whose operators report farming as their major occupation. [3] Includes retirement and residential farms.

Source: U.S. Department of Agriculture, Economic Research Service, ARMS Phase III—"Structural Characteristics Report," <http://www.ers.usda.gov/Data/ARMS/beta.htm>. For more information: <http://www.ers.usda.gov/data/arms/FarmsOverview.htm>.

Table 844. Organic Agriculture—Number of Farms, Acreage, and Value of Sales: 2007

[2,577 represents 2,577,000. Data have been adjusted for coverage; see text, this section and Appendix III]

Size and usage	Number of farms	Acreage (1,000)	Sales value of organically produced commodities and commodity	Number of farms	Value (mil. dol.)
Total acres used for organic production........	20,437	2,577	Organic product sales, total...................	18,211	1,709
1 to 9 organic acres....................	9,251	29	$1 to $4,999..........................	8,285	13
10 to 49 organic acres....................	4,994	115	$5,000 to $9,999....................	1,935	13
50 to 179 organic acres....................	3,498	348	$10,000 to $24,999...................	2,318	37
180 to 499 organic acres....................	1,808	528	$25,000 to $49,999...................	1,515	54
500 organic acres or more....................	886	1,557	$50,000 or more....................	4,158	1,593
Acres from which organic crops harvested......	16,778	1,288	Crops [1].........................	14,968	1,122
Acres of organic pastureland....................	7,268	975	Livestock and poultry....................	2,496	110
Acres being converted to organic production....................	11,901	616	Livestock and poultry products.................	3,191	477

[1] Includes nursery and greenhouse crops.

Source: U.S. Department of Agriculture, National Agricultural Statistics Service, *2007 Census of Agriculture*, Vol. 1. See also <http://www.agcensus.usda.gov/Publications/index.php>.

Table 845. Certified Organic Farmland, Crops, and Livestock: 2000 to 2008

[1,776 represents 1,776,000. Economic Research Service collaborates with over 50 state and private certifiers to calculate U.S. and state-level estimates of certified organic acreage and livestock]

Item	Unit	2000	2001	2002	2003	2004	2005	2006	2007	2008
Farm operations [1]...................	Number	6,592	6,949	7,323	8,035	8,021	8,493	9,469	11,352	12,941
Average farm size...................	acres	269	301	263	273	380	477	310	378	372
Total farmland......................	1,000 acres	1,776	2,094	1,926	2,197	3,045	4,054	2,936	4,290	4,816
Total cropland......................	1,000 acres	557	790	626	745	1,593	2,331	1,051	2,005	2,161
Total pasture/rangeland..............	1,000 acres	1,219	1,305	1,300	1,452	1,452	1,723	1,885	2,285	2,655
Grains...........................	1,000 acres	416	455	496	548	491	608	624	789	908
Corn............................	1,000 acres	78	94	96	106	99	131	138	172	195
Wheat..........................	1,000 acres	181	195	218	234	214	277	225	330	416
Oats...........................	1,000 acres	30	33	53	46	43	46	65	59	57
Beans...........................	1,000 acres	166	211	145	153	144	156	157	150	164
Soybeans.......................	1,000 acres	136	174	127	122	114	122	115	100	126
Oilseeds.........................	1,000 acres	55	44	33	28	54	46	45	42	69
Hay and silage...................	1,000 acres	231	254	268	328	357	411	508	677	793
Vegetables.......................	1,000 acres	62	72	70	79	80	99	107	132	169
Fruits..........................	1,000 acres	43	56	61	78	81	97	96	97	121
Herbs, nursery, and greenhouse.......................	1,000 acres	41	15	29	25	8	9	18	18	15
Other cropland.......................	1,000 acres	204	197	198	214	239	298	330	380	415
Livestock [2]..........................	1,000	56	72	108	124	157	197	257	363	476
Milk cows.......................	1,000	38	49	67	74	75	87	130	166	250
Poultry [3]...........................	1,000	3,159	5,014	6,270	8,780	7,305	13,757	9,195	12,185	15,518
Layer hens.....................	1,000	1,114	1,612	1,052	1,591	1,788	2,415	3,072	3,872	5,538
Broilers (meat chicken)...........	1,000	1,925	3,286	3,032	6,301	4,769	10,406	5,530	7,436	9,016

[1] Number does not include subcontracted organic farm operations. [2] Total livestock includes other and unclassified livestock animals. [3] Total poultry includes other and unclassified poultry animals.

Source: U.S. Department of Agriculture, Economic Research Service, "Briefing Rooms, Organic Agriculture," <http://www.ers.usda.gov/Briefing/Organic/>.

Table 846. Farm Production Expenses: 2002 and 2007

[2,129 represents 2,129,000. Data have been adjusted for coverage; see text, this section and Appendix III]

Production expenses	2002			2007		
	Farms (1,000)	Expenses (mil. dol.)	Percent of total	Farms (1,000)	Expenses (mil. dol.)	Percent of total
Total.......	**2,129**	**173,199**	**100.0**	**2,205**	**241,114**	**100.0**
Fertilizer................	1,190	9,751	5.6	1,148	18,107	7.5
Chemicals................	947	7,609	4.4	919	10,075	4.2
Seeds, plants, vines, and trees....................	875	7,599	4.4	776	11,741	4.9
Livestock and poultry [1]............	554	27,421	15.8	491	38,004	15.8
Feed........................	1,241	31,695	18.3	1,136	49,095	20.4
Gasoline and fuel................	2,024	6,675	3.9	2,149	12,912	5.4
Utilities..................	1,241	4,874	2.8	1,103	5,918	2.5
Supplies, repairs, and maintenance................	1,899	13,387	7.7	1,992	15,897	6.6
Farm labor [2]................	783	22,020	12.7	665	26,392	11.0
Customwork and custom hauling................	450	3,314	1.9	362	4,091	1.7
Cash rent for land, buildings and grazing fees................	498	9,046	5.2	490	13,275	5.5
Rent and lease for machinery, equipment, and farm share..	151	1,468	0.8	109	1,385	0.6
Interest expense................	758	9,572	5.5	667	10,881	4.5
Property taxes................	1,963	5,351	3.1	1,996	6,223	2.6
Other production expenses................	1,254	13,418	7.7	1,116	17,119	7.1

[1] Purchased or leased. 2002 does not include breeding livestock leased. [2] Includes hired and contract labor.

Source: U.S. Department of Agriculture, National Agricultural Statistics Service, *2007 Census of Agriculture*, Vol. 1. See also <http://www.agcensus.usda.gov/Publications/index.php>.

Table 847. Farms—Number, Acreage, and Value of Sales by Size of Sales: 2002 and 2007

[2,129 represents 2,129,000. Data have been adjusted for coverage; see text, this section and Appendix III]

Market value of agricultural products sold	Farms (1,000)	Acreage Total (mil.)	Acreage Average per farm	Value of sales Total (mil. dol.)	Value of sales Average per farm (dol.)	Percent distribution Farms	Percent distribution Acreage	Percent distribution Value of sales
2002								
Total...................	**2,129**	**938.3**	**441**	**200,646**	**94,244**	**100.0**	**100.0**	**100.0**
Less than $2,500......................	827	107.0	129	485	586	38.8	11.4	0.2
$2,500 to $4,999.....................	213	23.1	108	763	3,582	10.0	2.5	0.4
$5,000 to $9,999.....................	223	34.8	156	1,577	7,072	10.5	3.7	0.8
$10,000 to $24,999..................	256	69.5	271	4,068	15,891	12.0	7.4	2.0
$25,000 to $49,999..................	158	77.9	494	5,594	35,405	7.4	8.3	2.8
$50,000 to $99,999..................	140	110.1	784	10,024	71,600	6.6	11.7	5.0
$100,000 to $249,999..............	159	189.4	1,191	25,401	159,755	7.5	20.2	12.7
$250,000 to $499,999..............	82	140.8	1,723	28,530	347,927	3.9	15.0	14.2
$500,000 to $999,999..............	42	94.0	2,241	28,944	689,143	2.0	10.0	14.4
$1,000,000 or more.................	29	91.7	3,198	95,259	3,284,793	1.4	9.8	47.5
2007								
Total...................	**2,205**	**922.1**	**418**	**297,220**	**134,807**	**100.0**	**100.0**	**100.0**
Less than $2,500......................	900	121.5	135	435	483	40.8	13.2	0.1
$2,500 to $4,999.....................	200	17.5	87	718	3,585	9.1	1.9	0.2
$5,000 to $9,999.....................	219	27.6	126	1,553	7,104	9.9	3.0	0.5
$10,000 to $24,999..................	248	65.8	265	3,960	15,949	11.3	7.1	1.3
$25,000 to $49,999..................	155	59.8	386	5,480	35,419	7.0	6.5	1.8
$50,000 to $99,999..................	125	78.2	623	8,961	71,429	5.7	8.5	3.0
$100,000 to $249,999..............	148	147.6	1,000	24,213	164,156	6.7	16.0	8.1
$250,000 to $499,999..............	93	140.7	1,507	33,410	357,811	4.2	15.3	11.2
$500,000 to $999,999..............	61	119.4	1,965	42,691	702,417	2.8	13.0	14.4
$1,000,000 or more.................	56	144.0	2,593	175,800	3,167,050	2.5	15.6	59.1

Source: U.S. Department of Agriculture, National Agricultural Statistics Service, *2007 Census of Agriculture*, Vol. 1. See also <http://www.agcensus.usda.gov/Publications/index.php>.

Table 848. Farms—Number, Value of Sales, and Government Payments by Economic Class of Farm: 2002 and 2007

[2,129 represents 2,129,000. Economic class of farm is a combination of market value of agricultural products sold and federal farm program payments. Data have been adjusted for coverage; see text, this section and Appendix III]

Economic class	Number of farms (1,000) 2002, total	Number of farms (1,000) 2007 Total	Number of farms (1,000) 2007 Receiving government payments	Market value (mil. dol.) 2002, total	Market value (mil. dol.) 2007 Total	Market value (mil. dol.) 2007 Agricultural products sold	Market value (mil. dol.) 2007 Government payments
Total..............................	**2,129**	**2,205**	**838**	**207,192**	**305,204**	**297,220**	**7,984**
Less than $1,000..................	431	500	42	72	96	77	19
$1,000 to $2,499...................	307	271	85	508	448	332	116
$2,500 to $4,999...................	243	246	80	870	884	685	199
$5,000 to $9,999...................	247	255	87	1,746	1,811	1,488	323
$10,000 to $24,999................	272	274	110	4,320	4,364	3,810	554
$25,000 to $49,999................	164	164	87	5,804	5,795	5,286	508
$50,000 to $99,999................	143	129	83	10,202	9,219	8,644	575
$100,000 to $249,999.............	163	149	110	26,119	24,401	23,256	1,145
$250,000 to $499,999.............	86	96	75	30,084	34,367	32,980	1,387
$500,000 to $999,999.............	44	64	46	30,598	44,578	43,156	1,422
$1,000,000 to $2,499,999........	21	42	27	31,701	62,751	61,508	1,243
$2,500,000 to $4,999,999........	5	10	6	16,056	33,190	32,839	352
$5 million or more..................	3	6	2	49,112	83,300	83,159	141

Source: U.S. Department of Agriculture, National Agricultural Statistics Service, *2007 Census of Agriculture*, Vol. 1. See also <http://www.agcensus.usda.gov/Publications/index.php>.

Table 849. Adoption of Genetically Engineered Crops: 2000 to 2011

[In percent. As of June. Based on June Agricultural Survey conducted by National Agricultural Statistical Services (NASS). Excludes conventionally bred herbicide resistant varieties. Insect resistant varieties include only those containing bacillus thuringiensis (Bt). The Bt varieties include those that contain more than one gene that can resist different types of insects. Stacked gene varieties include only those varieties containing biotech traits for both herbicide and insect resistance]

Genetically engineered crop	2000	2002	2003	2004	2005	2006	2007	2008	2009	2010	2011
Corn............................	25	34	40	47	52	61	73	80	85	86	88
Insect resistant...................	18	22	25	27	26	25	21	17	17	16	16
Herbicide resistant...............	6	9	11	14	17	21	24	23	22	23	23
Stacked gene......................	1	2	4	6	9	15	28	40	46	47	49
Cotton..........................	61	71	73	76	79	83	87	86	88	93	90
Insect resistant...................	15	13	14	16	18	18	17	18	17	15	17
Herbicide resistant...............	26	36	32	30	27	26	28	23	23	20	15
Stacked gene......................	20	22	27	30	34	39	42	45	48	58	58
Soybean........................	54	75	81	85	87	89	91	92	91	93	94
Insect resistant...................	(X)	(X)	(X)	(X)	(X)	(X)	(X)	(X)	(X)	(X)	(X)
Herbicide resistant...............	54	75	81	85	87	89	91	92	91	93	94
Stacked gene......................	(X)	(X)	(X)	(X)	(X)	(X)	(X)	(X)	(X)	(X)	(X)

X Not applicable.

Source: U.S. Department of Agriculture, Economic Research Service, "Adoption of Genetically Engineered Crops in the U.S.," July 2011, <http://www.ers.usda.gov/Data/>.

Table 850. Farms—Number, Acreage, and Value by State: 2002 and 2007

[2,129 represents 2,129,000. Data have been adjusted for coverage; see text, this section and Appendix III]

State	Number of farms (1,000)		Land in farms (mil. acres)		Average size of farm (acres)		Total value of land and buildings [1] (bil. dol.)		Market value of agricultural products sold and government payments, 2007 (mil.dol.)	Total number of operators, 2007 (1,000)
	2002	2007	2002	2007	2002	2007	2002	2007		
U.S..............	2,129	2,205	938.3	922.1	441	418	1,144.9	1,744.3	305,204	3,337
AL..............	45	49	8.9	9.0	197	185	15.1	20.7	4,540	71
AK..............	1	1	0.9	0.9	1,479	1,285	0.3	0.3	59	1
AZ..............	7	16	26.6	26.1	3,645	1,670	10.6	19.5	3,290	26
AR..............	47	49	14.5	13.9	305	281	21.2	32.5	7,778	75
CA..............	80	81	27.6	25.4	346	313	96.1	162.5	34,125	131
CO..............	31	37	31.1	31.6	991	853	23.8	33.1	6,217	61
CT..............	4	5	0.4	0.4	85	83	3.5	5.1	556	8
DE..............	2	3	0.5	0.5	226	200	2.3	5.3	1,092	4
FL..............	44	47	10.4	9.2	236	195	29.3	52.1	7,831	73
GA..............	49	48	10.7	10.2	218	212	22.6	31.6	7,337	69
HI..............	5	8	1.3	1.1	241	149	4.6	8.6	516	11
ID..............	25	25	11.8	11.5	470	454	15.3	22.7	5,788	40
IL..............	73	77	27.3	26.8	374	348	66.7	101.5	13,816	111
IN..............	60	61	15.1	14.8	250	242	38.4	52.9	8,532	92
IA..............	91	93	31.7	30.7	350	331	64.2	104.2	21,124	136
KS..............	64	66	47.2	46.3	733	707	32.6	42.2	14,840	97
KY..............	87	85	13.8	14.0	160	164	25.5	37.5	4,928	124
LA..............	27	30	7.8	8.1	286	269	12.2	16.7	2,787	44
ME..............	7	8	1.4	1.3	190	166	2.3	3.0	626	13
MD..............	12	13	2.1	2.1	170	160	8.5	14.4	1,868	20
MA..............	6	8	0.5	0.5	85	67	4.6	6.4	494	12
MI..............	53	56	10.1	10.0	190	179	27.1	34.2	5,872	85
MN..............	81	81	27.5	26.9	340	332	41.8	69.2	13,626	120
MS..............	42	42	11.1	11.5	263	273	15.6	21.4	5,108	61
MO..............	107	108	29.9	29.0	280	269	45.3	63.2	7,832	164
MT..............	28	30	59.6	61.4	2,139	2,079	23.3	47.6	3,025	47
NE..............	49	48	45.9	45.5	930	953	35.7	52.7	15,893	72
NV..............	3	3	6.3	5.9	2,118	1,873	2.8	3.6	517	5
NH..............	3	4	0.4	0.5	132	113	1.4	2.3	202	7
NJ..............	10	10	0.8	0.7	81	71	7.4	11.3	994	16
NM..............	15	21	44.8	43.2	2,954	2,066	10.6	14.6	2,218	32
NY..............	37	36	7.7	7.2	206	197	12.9	16.3	4,481	58
NC..............	54	53	9.1	8.5	168	160	28.0	34.7	10,461	77
ND..............	31	32	39.3	39.7	1,283	1,241	15.8	30.6	6,444	45
OH..............	78	76	14.6	14.0	187	184	39.6	49.2	7,302	114
OK..............	83	87	33.7	35.1	404	405	23.8	40.6	6,016	131
OR..............	40	39	17.1	16.4	427	425	20.4	31.0	4,463	65
PA..............	58	63	7.7	7.8	133	124	26.3	37.3	5,885	95
RI..............	1	1	0.1	0.1	71	56	0.6	1.1	67	2
SC..............	25	26	4.8	4.9	197	189	10.1	14.0	2,420	37
SD..............	32	31	43.8	43.7	1,380	1,401	19.6	39.1	6,841	47
TN..............	88	79	11.7	11.0	133	138	28.5	37.1	2,713	117
TX..............	229	247	129.9	130.4	567	527	100.5	165.6	21,722	373
UT..............	15	17	11.7	11.1	768	664	9.0	13.9	1,438	26
VT..............	7	7	1.2	1.2	189	177	2.5	3.6	680	11
VA..............	48	47	8.6	8.1	181	171	23.3	34.1	2,961	71
WA..............	36	39	15.3	15.0	426	381	22.4	29.8	6,931	64
WV..............	21	24	3.6	3.7	172	157	4.8	8.8	595	35
WI..............	77	78	15.7	15.2	204	194	35.8	49.0	9,163	123
WY..............	9	11	34.4	30.2	3,651	2,726	10.2	15.5	1,186	19

[1] Based on reports for a sample of farms.

Source: U.S. Department of Agriculture, National Agricultural Statistics Service, *2007 Census of Agriculture*, Vol. 1. See also <http://www.agcensus.usda.gov/Publications/index.php>.

Table 851. Balance Sheet of the Farming Sector: 1990 to 2010

[In billions of dollars, except as indicated (841 represents $841,000,000,000). As of December 31]

Item	1990	2000	2002	2003	2004	2005	2006	2007	2008	2009	2010
Assets	841	1,203	1,260	1,383	1,588	1,779	1,924	2,055	2,023	2,054	2,191
Real estate	619	946	999	1,112	1,305	1,487	1,626	1,751	1,703	1,724	1,854
Livestock and poultry [1]	71	77	76	79	79	81	81	81	81	80	81
Machinery, motor vehicles [2]	86	90	96	100	108	113	114	115	123	126	128
Crops [3]	23	28	23	24	24	24	23	23	28	33	36
Purchased inputs	3	5	6	6	6	6	6	7	7	7	7
Financial assets	38	57	60	62	66	67	74	79	82	84	85
Debt [4]	131	164	177	164	182	196	204	214	242	242	252
Real estate debt	68	85	95	83	96	105	108	113	135	131	141
Farm Credit System	23	30	38	33	37	41	43	47	58	57	64
Farm Service Agency	7	3	3	2	2	2	2	2	2	2	3
Commercial banks	15	30	33	29	35	38	40	42	51	50	54
Life insurance companies	9	11	11	10	11	11	12	13	15	13	13
Individuals and others	14	11	10	9	11	12	10	9	9	8	7
Non-real estate debt	63	79	82	81	86	92	96	101	107	111	111
Farm Credit System	10	17	20	20	22	24	28	32	37	40	41
Farm Service Agency	10	4	4	4	3	3	3	3	3	3	3
Commercial banks	31	45	44	44	46	48	51	54	57	57	57
Individuals and others	12	13	13	14	15	16	14	13	10	11	10
Equity	709	1,039	1,082	1,219	1,406	1,583	1,720	1,841	1,782	1,812	2,039
FINANCIAL RATIOS (percent)											
Farm debt/equity ratio	18.5	15.8	16.4	13.5	12.9	12.4	11.8	11.6	13.6	13.3	13.0
Farm debt/asset ratio	15.6	13.6	14.1	11.9	11.5	11.0	10.6	10.4	11.9	11.8	11.5

[1] Excludes horses and mules. [2] Includes only farm share value for trucks and autos. [3] All non-CCC crops held on farms plus the value above loan rate for crops held under Commodity Credit Corporation (CCC). [4] Includes CCC storage and drying facility loans but excludes debt on operator dwellings and for nonfarm purposes.

Source: U.S. Department of Agriculture, Economic Research Service, "Farm Balance Sheet," <http://www.ers.usda.gov/data-products/farm-income-and-wealth-statistics.aspx>.

Table 852. Farm Sector Output and Value Added: 1990 to 2010

[In billions of dollars (179.9 represents $179,900,000,000). For definition of value added, see text, Section 13. Minus sign (–) indicates decrease]

Item	1990	2000	2002	2003	2004	2005	2006	2007	2008	2009	2010
CURRENT DOLLARS											
Farm output	**179.9**	**204.3**	**201.9**	**229.8**	**262.0**	**251.5**	**252.7**	**302.8**	**337.7**	**304.7**	**331.0**
Cash receipts from farm marketings	171.9	197.6	195.8	218.5	240.4	240.0	242.5	290.4	320.6	293.5	319.0
Farm products consumed on farms	0.6	0.3	0.3	0.3	0.3	0.3	0.4	0.4	0.4	0.3	0.3
Other farm income	4.9	8.4	9.6	10.7	12.3	11.3	13.1	12.5	14.6	12.7	12.8
Change in farm finished goods inventories	2.4	-2.0	-3.7	0.3	9.0	-0.2	-3.3	-0.5	2.1	-1.9	-1.1
Less: Intermediate goods and services consumed	102.6	130.7	129.6	137.4	143.7	149.5	159.6	187.9	207.3	191.5	198.3
Equals: Gross farm value added	**77.3**	**73.6**	**72.3**	**92.4**	**118.3**	**102.0**	**93.1**	**114.9**	**130.5**	**113.1**	**132.6**
Less: Consumption of fixed capital	17.9	23.3	24.7	25.8	27.4	29.5	31.3	32.9	32.5	33.6	34.2
Equals: Net farm value added	59.3	50.4	47.7	66.7	90.9	72.5	61.8	82.0	97.9	79.5	98.4
Compensation of employees	13.4	19.7	20.8	20.5	22.3	22.6	23.1	26.0	26.6	27.5	27.8
Taxes on production and imports	3.8	4.7	4.8	5.1	5.2	5.2	5.7	6.6	6.6	6.7	7.1
Less: Subsidies to operators	7.6	20.0	10.8	14.2	11.1	20.9	13.5	10.2	10.3	10.4	10.3
Net operating surplus	49.8	45.9	32.8	55.2	74.4	65.6	46.4	59.5	75.1	55.7	73.9
CHAINED (2000) DOLLARS [1]											
Farm output, total	**(NA)**	**240.6**	**236.2**	**246.1**	**250.2**	**251.5**	**251.9**	**255.4**	**255.0**	**265.7**	**266.9**
Cash receipts from farm marketings	(NA)	234.8	231.2	235.5	230.1	240.0	242.1	244.8	243.0	257.5	258.2
Farm products consumed on farms	(NA)	0.4	0.4	0.3	0.3	0.3	0.4	0.3	0.4	0.4	0.3
Other farm income	(NA)	9.3	9.9	10.6	11.7	11.3	12.3	10.1	9.9	9.4	9.2
Change in farm finished goods inventories	(NA)	-2.5	-4.5	0.4	8.1	-0.2	-3.4	-0.6	1.4	-1.6	-1.0
Less: Intermediate goods and services consumed	(NA)	159.2	157.2	156.0	152.7	149.5	152.6	164.7	152.9	150.4	151.9
Equals: Gross farm value added	**(NA)**	**83.5**	**81.2**	**91.6**	**97.9**	**102.0**	**99.1**	**90.3**	**101.7**	**117.1**	**116.5**
Less: Consumption of fixed capital	(NA)	26.0	26.9	27.7	28.5	29.5	30.3	31.0	29.5	30.0	30.6
Equals: Net farm value added	(NA)	57.8	54.5	64.1	69.4	72.5	68.7	59.2	71.0	85.9	84.6

NA Not available. [1] See text, Section 13.

Source: U.S. Bureau of Economic Analysis, *Survey of Current Business* and "Interactive Tables," <http://www.bea.gov/itable/index.cfm>, accessed July 2012.

Table 853. Value Added to Economy by Agricultural Sector: 1990 to 2010

[In billions of dollars (188.5 represents $188,500,000,000). Data are consistent with the net farm income accounts and include income and expenses related to the farm operator dwellings. Value of agricultural sector production is the gross value of the commodities and services produced within a year. Net value-added is the sector's contribution to the national economy and is the sum of the income from production earned by all factors-of-production. Net farm income is the farm operators' share of income from the sector's production activities. The concept presented is consistent with that employed by the Organization for Economic Cooperation and Development. Minus sign (–) indicates decrease]

Item	1990	2000	2002	2003	2004	2005	2006	2007	2008	2009	2010
Value of agricultural production	**188.5**	**218.4**	**218.2**	**242.2**	**281.9**	**274.1**	**275.4**	**327.7**	**365.7**	**330.6**	**352.3**
Value of crop production	83.2	95.0	97.9	108.6	125.1	114.4	118.7	151.1	183.3	168.0	172.1
Food grains	7.5	6.5	6.8	8.0	8.9	8.6	9.1	13.6	18.7	14.8	13.9
Feed crops	18.7	20.5	24.0	24.7	27.4	24.6	29.4	42.3	58.6	50.6	52.5
Cotton	5.5	2.9	3.4	6.4	4.8	6.4	5.5	6.5	5.2	4.0	6.3
Oil crops	12.3	13.5	15.0	18.0	17.9	18.4	18.5	24.6	28.6	35.5	35.1
Fruits and tree nuts	9.4	12.3	12.7	13.5	15.1	17.1	17.3	18.7	19.2	19.2	21.5
Vegetables	11.3	15.8	16.7	17.2	16.6	17.3	18.1	19.3	19.9	20.3	19.9
All other crops	12.9	18.6	20.2	20.9	22.1	22.4	23.1	23.9	23.4	22.5	22.5
Home consumption	0.1	0.2	0.2	0.1	0.1	0.1	0.1	0.1	0.1	0.1	0.1
Value of inventory adjustment [1]	2.8	2.2	-2.9	-1.8	10.6	-1.7	-3.6	0.9	8.2	-0.4	-0.9
Value of livestock production	90.0	99.1	93.5	105.0	124.3	126.5	119.3	138.4	140.4	119.8	140.7
Meat animals	51.1	53.0	48.1	56.5	62.3	64.8	63.7	65.1	65.0	59.0	69.9
Dairy products	20.2	20.6	20.6	21.2	27.4	26.7	23.4	35.5	34.8	24.3	31.4
Poultry and eggs	15.3	21.9	21.1	23.7	29.5	28.8	26.6	33.1	36.8	32.4	35.5
Miscellaneous livestock	2.5	4.1	4.1	4.2	4.4	4.6	4.8	4.9	5.0	4.5	4.7
Home consumption	0.5	0.1	0.1	0.1	0.2	0.3	0.3	0.3	0.3	0.3	0.3
Value of inventory adjustment [1]	0.4	-0.6	-0.6	-0.8	0.6	1.3	0.5	-0.4	-1.6	-0.7	-1.0
Services and forestry	15.3	24.4	26.8	28.6	32.5	33.2	36.4	38.1	42.0	42.7	39.5
Machine hire and custom work	1.8	2.2	2.2	2.9	3.4	2.8	2.6	2.7	3.0	4.0	3.5
Forest products sold	1.8	0.8	0.8	0.9	1.0	0.9	1.0	0.7	0.7	0.7	0.6
Other farm income	4.5	8.7	10.2	10.5	11.3	10.7	13.2	14.2	17.7	17.3	14.1
Gross imputed rental value of farm dwellings	7.2	12.7	13.6	14.3	16.8	18.8	19.5	20.6	20.5	20.7	21.2
Less: Purchased inputs	92.2	121.8	123.3	130.4	137.4	144.1	153.7	184.3	202.9	190.0	192.6
Farm origin	39.5	47.9	48.3	53.7	57.5	57.1	61.1	73.4	79.8	77.3	81.3
Feed purchased	20.4	24.5	24.9	27.5	29.7	28.0	31.4	41.9	46.9	45.0	45.4
Livestock and poultry purchased	14.6	15.9	14.4	16.7	18.2	18.7	18.6	18.8	17.7	16.7	19.6
Seed purchased	4.5	7.5	8.9	9.4	9.6	10.4	11.0	12.6	15.1	15.5	16.3
Manufactured inputs	22.0	28.7	28.5	28.8	31.6	35.4	37.5	46.3	55.0	49.0	49.5
Fertilizers and lime	8.2	10.0	9.6	10.0	11.4	12.8	13.3	17.7	22.5	20.1	21.0
Pesticides	5.4	8.5	8.3	8.4	8.6	8.8	9.0	10.5	11.7	11.5	10.6
Petroleum fuel and oils	5.8	7.2	6.6	6.8	8.2	10.3	11.3	13.8	16.2	12.7	13.2
Electricity	2.6	3.0	3.9	3.5	3.4	3.5	3.8	4.3	4.5	4.6	4.6
Other purchased inputs	30.7	45.2	46.6	48.0	48.3	51.6	55.2	64.6	68.1	63.8	61.8
Repair and maintenance of capital items	8.6	10.9	10.5	11.0	11.9	11.9	12.5	14.3	14.8	14.7	14.8
Machine hire and custom work	3.0	4.1	4.0	3.5	3.6	3.5	3.5	3.8	4.1	3.9	4.3
Marketing, storage, and transportation expenses	4.2	7.5	7.6	7.2	7.2	8.9	9.1	10.3	10.1	10.3	10.3
Contract labor	1.6	2.7	2.7	3.3	3.1	3.1	3.0	4.4	4.7	3.9	3.9
Miscellaneous expenses	13.4	19.9	21.7	23.0	22.4	24.3	27.1	31.7	34.3	31.0	28.5
Plus: Net government transactions [2]	3.1	15.8	5.2	9.2	5.4	15.8	6.2	0.9	0.9	1.1	0.9
Direct Government payments [3]	9.3	23.2	12.4	16.5	13.0	24.4	15.8	11.9	12.2	12.2	12.4
Motor vehicle registration and licensing fees	0.4	0.5	0.4	0.5	0.5	0.6	0.6	0.6	0.6	0.6	0.6
Property taxes	5.8	6.9	6.8	6.8	7.0	8.0	9.0	10.3	10.7	10.4	10.8
Equals: Gross value added	**99.3**	**112.5**	**100.0**	**121.0**	**149.9**	**145.8**	**126.9**	**144.3**	**163.7**	**141.7**	**160.6**
Less: Capital consumption	18.1	20.1	20.9	21.4	23.1	24.9	26.2	27.0	28.7	30.1	30.7
Equals: Net value added	**81.2**	**92.4**	**79.1**	**99.5**	**126.8**	**120.9**	**100.7**	**117.3**	**135.0**	**111.6**	**129.9**
Less: Employee compensation	12.4	17.9	19.1	18.7	20.2	20.5	21.2	24.5	25.3	25.0	23.7
Less: Net rent received by nonoperator landlords	9.0	9.2	8.0	8.8	8.5	9.0	7.6	7.6	9.6	9.8	12.6
Less: Real estate and nonreal estate interest	13.5	14.6	12.8	11.0	10.7	12.6	14.4	15.1	15.4	15.2	14.5
Equals: Net farm income	**46.3**	**50.7**	**39.1**	**61.0**	**87.4**	**78.8**	**57.4**	**70.0**	**84.7**	**61.6**	**79.1**

[1] A positive value of inventory change represents current-year production not sold by December 31. A negative value is an offset to production from prior years included in current-year sales. [2] Direct government payments minus motor vehicle registration and licensing fees and property taxes. [3] Government payments reflect payments made directly to all recipients in the farm sector, including landlords. The nonoperator landlords share is offset by its inclusion in rental expenses paid to these landlords and thus is not reflected in net farm income or net cash income.

Source: U.S. Department of Agriculture, Economic Research Service, "Farm Income: Data Files—Value Added to the U.S. Economy by the Agricultural Sector via the Production of Goods and Services, 2000-2010" <http://www.ers.usda.gov/data-products/farm-income-and-wealth-statistics.aspx>.

Table 854. Value of Agricultural Production, Income, and Government Payments: 2009 and 2010

[In millions of dollars (330,567 represents $330,567,000,000). Farm income data are after inventory adjustment and include income and expenses related to the farm operator's dwelling. Minus sign (–) indicates decrease]

State	Value of agricultural production		Net farm income		Government payments, 2010	State	Value of agricultural production		Net farm income		Government payments, 2010
	2009	2010	2009	2010			2009	2010	2009	2010	
U.S.	**330,567**	**352,270**	**61,643**	**79,063**	**12,398**	MT	3,409	3,639	354	698	327
AL	4,950	5,256	1,095	901	135	NE	17,194	18,184	3,270	3,951	510
AK	40	38	8	10	10	NV	650	665	112	138	10
AZ	3,557	3,952	209	776	70	NH	217	217	4	14	20
AR	8,017	8,527	1,485	1,340	389	NJ	1,230	1,185	290	265	22
CA	37,484	40,856	8,456	10,711	365	NM	2,933	3,444	395	1,021	92
CO	6,609	6,794	708	1,035	272	NY	4,220	5,001	598	1,147	66
CT	623	592	85	66	15	NC	10,475	10,604	2,827	3,337	438
DE	1,176	1,195	186	188	24	ND	7,315	7,630	1,958	2,602	845
FL	7,658	8,312	1,354	1,965	93	OH	8,798	8,813	2,051	2,159	373
GA	8,136	8,574	2,244	2,141	262	OK	5,965	6,846	74	1,240	319
HI	711	711	207	207	16	OR	4,718	4,553	423	458	151
ID	5,905	6,246	904	1,408	164	PA	6,050	6,618	951	1,306	81
IL	16,227	16,182	3,626	3,359	698	RI	76	75	9	8	6
IN	10,408	10,496	2,393	2,387	373	SC	2,588	2,746	577	495	125
IA	24,014	24,623	4,768	5,082	1,025	SD	8,224	8,256	2,318	2,581	401
KS	13,899	15,126	2,620	2,944	632	TN	3,932	3,920	617	458	153
KY	5,583	5,108	1,310	781	320	TX	20,335	24,285	2,166	5,579	1,019
LA	3,001	3,248	828	828	210	UT	1,462	1,645	-85	165	39
ME	665	724	120	200	49	VT	581	704	84	156	21
MD	2,085	2,073	267	236	54	VA	3,555	3,731	355	425	111
MA	626	679	88	156	20	WA	7,351	8,326	802	1,914	315
MI	6,669	7,264	1,151	1,822	185	WV	667	710	-27	-7	17
MN	15,698	16,985	3,111	4,601	566	WI	9,276	10,483	802	2,067	259
MS	5,090	5,785	1,300	1,407	251	WY	1,264	1,374	14	126	43
MO	9,250	9,260	2,182	2,201	436						

Source: U.S. Department of Agriculture, Economic Research Service, "U.S. and State Farm Income: and Wealth Statistics: Data Files," accessed July 2012, <http://www.ers.usda.gov/data-products/farm-income-and-wealth-statistics.aspx>.

Table 855. Farm Income—Cash Receipts From Farm Marketings: 2000 to 2010

[In millions of dollars (192,098 represents $192,098,000,000). Represents gross receipts from commercial market sales as well as net Commodity Credit Corporation loans. The source estimates and publishes individual cash receipt values only for major commodities and major producing states. The U.S. receipts for individual commodities, computed as the sum of the reported states, may understate the value of sales for some commodities, with the balance included in the appropriate category labeled "other" or "miscellaneous." The degree of underestimation in some of the minor commodities can be substantial]

Commodities	2000	2005	2009	2010	Commodities	2000	2005	2009	2010
Total	**192,098**	**240,898**	**288,598**	**314,353**	Broccoli	622	539	794	649
Livestock and products	99,597	124,931	120,258	141,444	Carrots	390	592	582	639
Meat animals	53,012	64,813	58,951	69,935	Corn, sweet	709	800	1,181	992
Cattle and calves	40,783	49,283	43,839	51,531	Lettuce	1,996	1,855	2,207	2,265
Hogs	11,758	14,970	14,674	17,872	Head	1,341	1,012	1,122	1,206
Sheep and lambs	470	560	438	532	Onions	713	810	900	1,204
Dairy products	20,587	26,705	24,339	31,361	Peppers, green, fresh	531	535	585	637
Poultry/eggs	21,854	28,834	32,446	35,465	Tomatoes	1,845	2,225	(NA)	2,320
Broilers	13,989	20,878	21,823	23,696	Fresh	1,195	1,604	1,350	(NA)
Chicken eggs	4,289	4,067	6,136	6,473	Misc. vegetables	2,153	2,994	2,675	2,655
Turkeys	2,771	3,026	3,573	4,371	Watermelons	240	429	451	492
Miscellaneous livestock	4,144	4,579	4,522	4,682	Fruits/nuts	12,284	17,138	19,150	21,516
Horses/mules	1,218	1,104	846	759	Grapefruit	377	417	(NA)	279
Aquaculture [1]	798	1,063	1,186	1,319	Lemons	267	345	318	373
Catfish	501	458	373	403	Oranges	1,775	1,901	1,954	1,963
Other livestock	1,970	2,219	2,246	2,286	Apples	1,466	1,712	1,979	2,258
Crops	92,501	115,967	168,340	172,909	Cherries	327	548	575	762
Food grains	6,525	8,611	14,785	13,911	Grapes	3,100	3,491	3,677	3,627
Rice	837	1,589	3,046	3,014	Wine	1,909	2,317	2,447	2,257
Wheat	5,672	7,005	11,710	10,866	Raisins	487	595	562	724
Feed crops	20,546	24,590	50,629	52,465	Peaches	470	511	594	615
Corn	15,162	18,486	42,508	44,769	Pears	288	296	374	361
Hay	3,855	4,697	5,596	5,402	Strawberries	1,045	1,399	2,130	2,246
Cotton	2,950	6,403	4,009	6,267	Blueberries	223	382	520	647
Tobacco	2,316	1,097	1,467	1,247	Raspberries	79	256	422	259
Oil crops	13,478	18,388	35,545	35,102	Almonds	666	2,526	2,294	2,839
Peanuts	897	843	771	878	Pistachios	245	580	593	1,159
Soybeans	12,047	16,918	33,698	33,170	All other crops	18,645	22,449	22,460	22,495
Vegetables	15,758	17,291	20,295	19,906	Sugar beets	1,113	1,193	1,500	1,637
Beans, dry	436	488	757	807	Cane for sugar	881	815	912	998
Potatoes	2,369	2,655	3,358	3,053	Greenhouse/nursery	13,710	16,992	15,418	15,585
Beans, snap	393	414	439	447	Mushrooms	860	899	944	925

NA Not available. [1] See also Table 910.

Source: U.S. Department of Agriculture, Economic Research Service, "Farm Income: Data Files—Cash Receipts by Commodity Groups 2000–2010," <http://www.ers.usda.gov/data-products/farm-income-and-wealth-statistics.aspx>.

Table 856. Cash Receipts for Selected Commodities—Leading States: 2010

[In millions of dollars (51,531 represents $51,531,000,000). See headnote Table 855]

State	Value	State	Value	State	Value	State	Value
Cattle and calves......	**51,531**	**Corn**.................	**44,769**	**Soybeans**...........	**33,170**	**Dairy products**......	**31,361**
Texas......................	7,564	Iowa.....................	8,026	Iowa.....................	4,802	California...............	5,928
Nebraska.................	7,194	Illinois..................	7,343	Illinois..................	4,455	Wisconsin..............	4,147
Kansas...................	6,554	Nebraska.............	5,347	Minnesota.............	2,963	New York..............	2,206
Oklahoma................	2,985	Minnesota............	4,014	Indiana.................	2,715	Pennsylvania..........	1,954
Iowa......................	2,920	Indiana................	3,503	Nebraska..............	2,648	Idaho...................	1,899

Source: U.S. Department of Agriculture, Economic Research Service, "Farm Income: Data Files–Leading Producer States by Commodity, 2010" <http://www.ers.usda.gov/data-products.aspx>.

Table 857. Farm Marketings, 2009 and 2010, and Principal Commodities, 2010, by State

[In millions of dollars (288,598 represents $288,598,000,000). Cattle include calves; sheep include lambs; and greenhouse includes nursery]

State	2009 Total	2009 Crops	2009 Livestock and products	2010 Total	2010 Crops	2010 Livestock and products	2010 State rank for total farm marketings and three principal commodities in order of marketing receipts
U.S..........	288,598	168,340	120,258	314,353	172,909	141,444	**Cattle and calves, Corn, Soybeans**
AL............	4,185	840	3,346	4,553	819	3,734	25-Broilers, cattle and calves, chicken eggs
AK............	31	25	6	31	24	7	50-Greenhouse/nursery, hay, cattle and calves
AZ............	2,971	1,792	1,179	3,375	1,960	1,415	29- Dairy products, cattle and calves, lettuce
AR............	7,277	3,314	3,963	7,688	3,272	4,416	14-Broilers, rice, soybeans
CA............	34,554	26,692	7,862	37,521	27,675	9,846	1-Dairy products, greenhouse/nursery, grapes
CO............	5,565	2,227	3,338	6,018	2,268	3,749	21-Cattle, corn, wheat
CT............	510	363	147	500	341	159	46-Greenhouse/nursery, dairy products, chicken eggs
DE............	1,014	242	772	1,063	232	831	39-Broilers, corn, soybeans
FL............	7,165	6,060	1,105	7,805	6,457	1,349	13-Greenhouse/nursery, oranges, tomatoes
GA............	6,803	2,510	4,293	7,337	2,812	4,525	17-Broilers, cotton, chicken eggs
HI............	631	560	71	631	557	74	41-Greenhouse/nursery, cane for sugar, cattle and calves
ID............	5,125	2,626	2,499	5,733	2,498	3,234	22-Dairy products, cattle and calves, potatoes
IL............	14,914	13,065	1,849	14,857	12,589	2,268	6-Corn, soybeans, hogs
IN............	8,933	6,564	2,370	9,589	6,728	2,862	9-Corn, soybeans, hogs
IA............	21,896	13,374	8,522	23,246	13,109	10,137	2-Corn, hogs, soybeans
KS............	12,591	6,248	6,343	13,958	6,413	7,545	7-Cattle and calves, corn, wheat
KY............	4,344	1,914	2,430	4,440	1,844	2,596	26-Broilers, horses, cattle and calves
LA............	2,708	1,838	870	2,913	1,936	977	33-Soybeans, cane for sugar, rice
ME............	556	306	251	614	323	290	42-Potatoes, dairy products, aquaculture
MD............	1,641	732	909	1,719	692	1,028	36-Broilers, greenhouse/nursery, dairy products
MA............	463	368	94	469	363	106	47-Greenhouse/nursery, cranberries, dairy products
MI............	5,607	3,700	1,907	6,486	4,022	2,464	19-Dairy products, corn, soybeans
MN............	13,788	8,606	5,182	15,138	8,957	6,181	5-Corn, soybeans, hogs
MS............	4,498	1,766	2,732	4,807	1,781	3,027	24-Broilers, soybeans, corn
MO............	7,636	4,342	3,294	8,301	4,627	3,673	11-Soybeans, corn, cattle and calves
MT............	2,732	1,663	1,069	3,050	1,782	1,267	32-Cattle and calves, wheat, hay
NE............	16,068	8,797	7,271	17,283	8,829	8,453	4-Cattle and calves, corn, soybeans
NV............	528	256	273	555	217	338	44-Cattle, dairy products, hay
NH............	169	94	75	175	89	86	48-Dairy products, greenhouse/nursery, apples
NJ............	1,009	876	133	1,042	917	125	40-Greenhouse/nursery, blueberries, horses/mules
NM............	2,637	647	1,991	3,240	780	2,460	30-Dairy products, cattle and calves, pecans
NY............	3,717	1,712	2,005	4,382	1,802	2,581	27-Dairy products, greenhouse/nursery, corn
NC............	9,104	3,409	5,695	9,659	3,293	6,366	8-Broilers, hogs, greenhouse/nursery
ND............	6,638	5,853	785	6,614	5,656	957	18-Wheat, soybeans, cattle and calves
OH............	7,119	4,881	2,238	7,885	5,152	2,732	12-Soybeans, corn, dairy products
OK............	4,879	1,239	3,640	6,150	1,416	4,734	20-Cattle and calves, broilers, hogs, 28-Greenhouse/nursery, cattle and calves, dairy products
OR............	3,790	2,884	907	3,750	2,702	1,048	products
PA............	5,002	1,941	3,061	5,690	2,017	3,673	23-Dairy products, corn, cattle and calves
RI............	58	49	9	59	50	9	49-Greenhouse/nursery, dairy products, sweet corn
SC............	2,189	939	1,250	2,385	1,015	1,370	35-Broilers, turkeys, greenhouse/nursery
SD............	7,384	5,045	2,338	7,687	4,662	3,025	15-Corn, cattle and calves, soybeans
TN............	2,997	1,849	1,148	3,082	1,755	1,328	31-Cattle and calves, soybeans, broilers
TX............	17,074	6,434	10,640	19,927	8,168	11,759	3-Cattle and calves, cotton, broilers
UT............	1,094	337	758	1,329	360	970	37-Dairy products, cattle and calves, hogs
VT............	510	111	399	610	105	505	43-Dairy products, cattle and calves, maple products
VA............	2,691	1,054	1,637	2,899	936	1,962	34-Broilers, cattle and calves, dairy products
WA............	6,654	5,009	1,646	7,448	5,460	1,988	16-Apples, dairy products, wheat
WV............	504	94	410	520	90	430	45-Broilers, cattle and calves, turkeys
WI............	7,592	2,792	4,800	8,968	3,071	5,897	10-Dairy products, corn, cattle and calves
WY............	1,048	298	751	1,172	282	890	38-Cattle and calves, hay, hogs

Source: U.S. Department of Agriculture, Economic Research Service, "Farm Income: Data Files, 2009 Sector Financial Indicators Cash Receipts Ranking Data," "Farm Income: Data Files, Leading Commodities by State, 2010," and "Farm Income: Data Files, Annual Cash Receipts, by Commodity Groups and Selected Commodities, by State, 2000-2010" <http://www.ers.usda.gov/data-products.aspx>.

Table 858. Indexes of Prices Received and Paid by Farmers: 2000 to 2011

[1990–1992 = 100, except as noted]

Item	2000	2005	2010	2011	Item	2000	2005	2010	2011
Prices received, all products.....	96	114	141	178	Feed.............................	102	117	180	225
Crops............................	96	110	153	202	Livestock and poultry..........	110	138	133	154
Food grains...................	85	111	177	239	Seed............................	124	168	310	332
Feed grains and hay...........	86	95	165	252	Fertilizer........................	110	164	252	328
Cotton.........................	82	70	117	145	Agricultural chemicals..........	120	123	144	145
Tobacco........................	107	94	103	83	Fuels...........................	129	216	284	362
Oil-bearing crops..............	85	106	172	223	Supplies and repairs...........	120	140	160	166
Fruits and nuts................	98	128	148	158	Autos and trucks...............	119	114	113	116
Commercial vegetables [1]......	121	130	162	169	Farm machinery................	139	173	230	244
Potatoes and dry beans.......	93	109	140	175	Building materials..............	121	142	166	171
All other crops.................	110	113	126	131	Farm services..................	118	133	161	164
Livestock and products.........	97	119	130	152	Rent............................	110	129	190	205
Meat animals..................	94	118	123	151	Interest.........................	113	111	132	135
Dairy products................	94	116	125	154	Taxes..........................	123	155	211	222
Poultry and eggs..............	106	123	152	152	Wage rates.....................	140	165	189	192
Prices paid, total [2].............	119	142	183	203					
Production......................	115	140	188	215	Parity ratio (1910–14 = 100) [3]. ..	39	38	37	42

[1] Excludes potatoes and dry beans. [2] Includes production items, interest, taxes, wage rates, and a family living component. The family living component is the Consumer Price Index for all urban consumers from the Bureau of Labor Statistics. See text, Section 14 and Table 736. [3] Ratio of prices received by farmers to prices paid.

Source: U.S. Department of Agriculture, National Agricultural Statistics Service, *Agricultural Prices: Annual Summary*, and beginning 2009, "Quick Stats U.S. & All States Data—Prices," <http://quickstats.nass.usda.gov/>.

Table 859. Civilian Consumer Expenditures for Farm Foods: 1990 to 2008

[In billions of dollars, except percent (449.8 represents $449,800,000,000). Excludes imported and nonfarm foods, such as coffee and seafood, as well as food consumed by the military, or exported]

Item	1990	1995	2000	2001	2002	2003	2004	2005	2006	2007	2008
Consumer expenditures, total........	**449.8**	**529.5**	**661.1**	**687.5**	**709.4**	**744.2**	**788.9**	**830.7**	**880.7**	**925.2**	**958.9**
Farm value, total.....................	106.2	113.8	123.3	130.0	132.5	140.2	155.5	157.8	163.2	194.3	192.3
Marketing bill, total [1]..................	343.6	415.7	537.8	557.5	576.9	604.0	633.4	672.9	717.5	731.0	766.6
Percent of total consumer expenditures.........................	76.4	78.5	81.3	81.1	81.3	81.2	80.3	81.0	81.5	79.0	79.9
At-home expenditures [2]..................	276.2	316.9	390.2	403.9	416.8	437.2	463.5	488.1	517.5	543.7	563.5
Farm value..........................	80.2	76.1	79.6	83.9	85.7	91.4	98.5	99.3	103.2	128.3	129.0
Marketing bill [1].....................	196.0	240.8	310.6	320.0	331.1	345.8	365.0	388.8	414.3	415.4	434.5
Away-from-home expenditures..........	173.6	212.6	270.9	283.6	292.6	307.0	325.4	342.6	363.2	381.5	395.4
Farm value..........................	26.0	37.7	43.7	46.1	46.8	48.8	57.0	58.5	60.0	66.0	63.3
Marketing bill [1].....................	147.6	174.9	227.2	237.5	245.8	258.2	268.4	284.1	303.2	315.5	332.1
Marketing bill cost components:											
Labor cost [3]........................	154.0	196.6	252.9	263.8	273.1	285.9	303.7	319.8	341.0	347.4	364.3
Packaging materials.................	36.5	48.2	53.5	55.0	56.8	59.5	63.1	66.5	70.5	71.8	75.3
Rail and truck transport [4]............	19.8	22.3	26.4	27.5	28.4	29.7	31.6	33.2	35.2	35.9	37.6
Corporate profits before taxes.......	13.2	19.5	31.1	32.0	33.0	34.6	35.5	37.4	39.7	40.4	38.9
Fuels and electricity.................	15.2	18.6	23.1	24.1	24.9	26.1	27.6	31.6	33.5	34.1	37.4
Advertising..........................	17.1	19.8	26.1	27.5	28.1	29.4	30.8	32.7	34.9	35.6	37.3
Depreciation.........................	16.3	18.9	24.2	24.5	25.3	26.5	27.8	29.5	31.5	32.1	33.7
Net interest.........................	13.5	11.6	16.9	18.6	19.2	20.1	21.1	22.4	23.9	24.3	25.5
Net rent............................	13.9	19.8	26.7	29.4	30.3	31.7	33.2	35.3	37.6	38.3	40.2
Repairs.............................	6.2	7.9	10.1	10.6	10.9	11.4	12.0	12.7	13.5	13.8	14.5
Taxes..............................	15.7	19.1	23.5	24.1	24.9	26.1	27.4	29.1	31.0	31.6	33.1
Other..............................	22.2	13.4	23.3	20.4	22.0	23.0	19.6	22.7	25.2	25.7	28.8

[1] The difference between expenditures for domestic farm-originated food products and the farm value or payment farmers received for the equivalent farm products. [2] Food primarily purchased from retail food stores for use at home. [3] Covers employee wages and salaries and their health and welfare benefits. Also includes imputed earnings of proprietors, partners, and family workers not receiving stated remuneration. [4] Excludes local hauling.

Source: U.S. Department of Agriculture, Economic Research Service, *Food Cost Review, 1950–97*, ERS Agricultural Economic Report No. AER780, June 1999, and "ERS/USDA Briefing Room—Food Marketing and Price Spreads: USDA Marketing Bill," <http://ers.usda.gov/topics/food-markets-prices.aspx>.

Table 860. Agricultural Exports and Imports—Volume by Principal Commodities: 1990 to 2011

[In thousands (7,703 represents 7,703,000). 1,000 hectoliters equals 264.18 gallons. Includes Puerto Rico, U.S. territories, and shipments under foreign aid programs. Excludes fish, forest products, distilled liquors, manufactured tobacco, and products made from cotton; but includes raw tobacco, raw cotton, rubber, beer and wine, and processed agricultural products]

Commodity	Unit	1990	2000	2005	2008	2009	2010	2011
EXPORTS								
Fruit juices and wine...................	Hectoliters	7,703	14,356	13,982	14,871	13,675	14,982	17,276
Beef, pork, lamb, and poultry meats [1]...............	Metric tons	1,451	4,935	4,343	6,437	6,151	6,368	7,103
Wheat, unmilled..........................	Metric tons	27,384	27,568	27,040	30,021	21,920	27,613	32,771
Wheat products........................	Metric tons	863	844	313	389	404	446	447
Rice, paddy, milled.......................	Metric tons	2,534	3,241	4,388	3,800	3,426	4,481	3,660
Feed grains..............................	Metric tons	61,066	54,946	50,865	59,659	51,388	54,622	49,265
Feed grain products.....................	Metric tons	1,430	2,062	3,442	1,286	1,228	1,081	1,042
Feeds and fodders [2]...................	Metric tons	10,974	13,065	11,422	14,372	14,594	19,046	18,158
Fresh fruits and nuts....................	Metric tons	2,648	3,450	3,675	4,037	4,101	4,311	4,596
Fruit products...........................	Metric tons	390	471	394	540	506	570	620
Vegetables, fresh.......................	Metric tons	1,297	2,029	2,077	2,020	1,972	2,141	2,246
Vegetables, frozen and canned........	Metric tons	529	1,112	1,086	1,604	1,397	1,409	1,656
Oilcake and meal........................	Metric tons	5,079	6,462	6,905	8,405	9,251	10,003	8,264
Oilseeds................................	Metric tons	15,820	28,017	26,462	35,011	41,210	43,172	35,098
Vegetable oils..........................	Metric tons	1,226	2,043	1,937	2,900	3,036	3,544	2,874
Tobacco, unmanufactured..............	Metric tons	223	180	154	169	173	179	184
Cotton, excluding linters................	Metric tons	1,696	1,485	3,405	3,001	2,540	2,959	2,773
IMPORTS								
Fruit juices.............................	Hectoliters	33,116	31,154	41,488	47,299	44,234	42,734	42,127
Wine....................................	Hectoliters	2,510	4,584	7,262	8,487	9,460	9,592	10,381
Malt beverages.........................	Hectoliters	10,382	23,464	29,947	33,668	30,278	31,607	32,019
Coffee, including products..............	Metric tons	1,214	1,370	1,307	1,393	1,348	1,390	1,494
Rubber and allied gums, crude........	Metric tons	840	1,232	1,169	1,053	704	945	1,049
Beef, pork, lamb, and poultry meats [1]...............	Metric tons	1,169	1,579	1,778	1,394	1,430	1,351	1,249
Grains [3]...............................	Metric tons	2,071	4,622	3,726	6,384	5,587	5,166	4,929
Biscuits, pasta, and noodles...........	Metric tons	300	711	1,001	1,038	1,019	1,097	1,154
Feeds and fodders [2]..................	Metric tons	959	1,224	963	1,298	1,330	1,423	1,867
Fruits, nuts, and preparations [4].......	Metric tons	5,401	8,354	9,570	10,547	10,302	10,919	11,234
Vegetables, fresh or frozen............	Metric tons	1,898	3,763	5,183	6,124	6,118	6,861	7,153
Tobacco, unmanufactured..............	Metric tons	173	216	233	221	199	164	164
Oilseeds and oilnuts....................	Metric tons	509	1,056	818	1,555	1,249	1,223	1,362
Vegetable oils and waxes..............	Metric tons	1,204	1,846	2,386	3,708	3,523	3,730	4,350
Oilcake and meal.......................	Metric tons	316	1,254	1,541	1,964	1,539	1,504	2,489

[1] Includes variety meats. [2] Excluding oil meal. [3] Includes wheat, corn, oats, barley, and rice. [4] Includes bananas and plantains.

Source: U.S. Department of Agriculture, Economic Research Service, "Foreign Agricultural Trade of the United States (FATUS)," <http://www.ers.usda.gov/data/fatus/> and "Global Agricultural Trade System," <http://www.fas.usda.gov/gats>.

Table 861. Agricultural Exports and Imports—Value: 1990 to 2011

[In billions of dollars, except percent (16.6 represents $16,600,000,000). Includes Puerto Rico, U.S. territories, and shipments under foreign aid programs. Excludes fish, forest products, distilled liquors, manufactured tobacco, and products made from cotton; but includes raw tobacco, raw cotton, rubber, beer and wine, and processed agricultural products]

Year	Trade balance	Exports, domestic products	Percent of all exports	Imports for consumption	Percent of all imports	Year	Trade balance	Exports, domestic products	Percent of all exports	Imports for consumption	Percent of all imports
1990..........	16.6	39.5	11	22.9	5	2005.......	3.9	63.2	8	59.3	4
1995..........	26.0	56.3	10	30.3	4	2006.......	5.6	70.9	8	65.3	4
2000..........	12.3	51.3	7	39.0	4	2007.......	18.1	90.0	9	71.9	4
2001..........	14.3	53.7	8	39.4	3	2008.......	34.3	114.8	10	80.5	4
2002..........	11.2	53.1	8	41.9	4	2009.......	26.8	98.5	11	71.7	5
2003..........	12.0	59.4	9	47.4	4	2010.......	33.9	115.8	10	81.9	4
2004..........	7.4	61.4	8	54.0	4	2011.......	37.4	136.3	10	98.9	4

Source: U.S. Department of Agriculture, Economic Research Service, "Foreign Agricultural Trade of the United States (FATUS)," <http://www.ers.usda.gov/data/fatus/> and U.S. Department of Agriculture, Foreign Agricultural Service, "Global Agricultural Trade System," <http://www.fas.usda.gov/gats>.

Table 862. Agricultural Imports—Value by Selected Commodity: 1990 to 2011

[In millions of dollars (22,918 represents $22,918,000,000). For calender year. Includes Puerto Rico, U.S. territories, and shipments under foreign aid programs. Excludes fish, forest products, distilled liquors, manufactured tobacco, and products made from cotton; but includes raw tobacco, raw cotton, rubber, beer and wine, and processed agricultural products]

Commodity	Value (mil. dol.)							Percent distribution		
	1990	2000	2005	2008	2009	2010	2011	1990	2000	2011
Total [1]	22,918	38,974	59,291	80,488	71,681	81,858	98,946	100.0	100.0	100.0
Cattle, live	978	1,152	1,039	1,761	1,299	1,575	1,449	4.3	3.0	1.5
Beef and veal	1,872	2,399	3,651	3,058	2,725	2,828	3,161	8.2	6.2	3.2
Pork	938	997	1,281	1,060	978	1,185	1,288	4.1	2.6	1.3
Dairy products	891	1,671	2,686	3,142	2,528	2,619	2,934	3.9	4.3	3.0
Grains and feeds	1,188	3,075	4,527	8,258	7,435	7,787	8,931	5.2	7.9	9.0
Fruits and preparations	2,167	3,851	5,842	7,899	8,210	9,167	9,952	9.5	9.9	10.1
Vegetables and preparations [2]	1,979	3,958	6,410	8,314	8,044	9,318	10,289	8.6	10.2	10.4
Sugar and related products	1,213	1,555	2,494	2,976	3,075	4,047	5,144	5.3	4.0	5.2
Wine	917	2,207	3,762	4,634	4,020	4,279	4,856	4.0	5.7	4.9
Malt beverages	923	2,179	3,096	3,668	3,339	3,506	3,566	4.0	5.6	3.6
Oilseeds and products	952	1,773	2,998	6,766	4,799	5,390	8,252	4.2	4.5	8.3
Coffee and products	1,915	2,700	2,976	4,412	4,070	4,943	8,092	8.4	6.9	8.2
Cocoa and products	1,072	1,404	2,751	3,299	3,476	4,295	4,681	4.7	3.6	4.7
Rubber, crude natural	707	842	1,552	2,857	1,274	2,820	4,772	3.1	2.2	4.8

[1] Includes other commodities, not shown separately. [2] Includes pulses.

Source: U.S. Department of Agriculture, Economic Research Service, "Foreign Agricultural Trade of the United States (FATUS)," <http://ers.usda.gov/Data/FATUS>, and U.S. Department of Agriculture, Foreign Agricultural Service, "Global Agricultural Trade System," <http://www.fas.usda.gov/gats>.

Table 863. Agricultural Imports—Value by Selected Countries of Origin: 1990 to 2011

[In millions of dollars (22,918 represents $22,918,000,000). See headnote Table 861]

Country	Value (mil. dol.)							Percent distribution		
	1990	2000	2005	2008	2009	2010	2011	1990	2000	2011
Total	22,918	38,974	59,291	80,488	71,681	81,858	98,946	100.0	100.0	100.0
Canada	3,171	8,661	12,270	18,009	14,710	16,244	18,918	13.8	22.2	19.1
European Union [1]	5,016	8,303	13,410	15,510	13,378	14,353	16,069	21.9	21.3	16.2
Mexico	2,614	5,077	8,331	10,907	11,373	13,578	15,835	11.4	13.0	16.0
China [2]	273	812	1,872	3,451	2,877	3,367	3,992	1.2	2.1	4.0
Brazil	1,563	1,144	1,952	2,615	2,433	2,892	4,056	6.8	2.9	4.1
Indonesia	683	998	1,702	2,815	1,787	2,886	4,288	3.0	2.6	4.3
Australia	1,174	1,592	2,421	2,425	2,316	2,307	2,362	5.1	4.1	2.4
Chile	481	1,026	1,521	2,049	2,145	2,293	2,370	2.1	2.6	2.4
Thailand	470	779	1,094	1,917	1,567	2,034	2,630	2.0	2.0	2.7
Colombia	790	1,123	1,437	1,769	1,772	1,977	2,462	3.4	2.9	2.5
Malaysia	308	353	666	1,867	1,295	1,729	2,424	1.3	0.9	2.4
New Zealand	855	1,132	1,712	1,833	1,608	1,665	1,968	3.7	2.9	2.0
India	285	826	923	1,601	1,236	1,592	2,676	1.2	2.1	2.7
Guatemala	497	710	920	1,314	1,297	1,386	1,888	2.2	1.8	1.9
Costa Rica	400	812	916	1,207	1,102	1,295	1,449	1.7	2.1	1.5
Argentina	389	672	831	1,257	1,091	1,159	1,625	1.7	1.7	1.6
Peru	90	196	448	818	807	974	1,320	0.4	0.5	1.3
Vietnam	(NA)	200	422	760	727	970	1,284	(NA)	0.5	1.3
Philippines	418	468	568	916	724	884	1,375	1.8	1.2	1.4
Ecuador	482	451	596	746	928	869	1,070	2.1	1.2	1.1
Rest of world	2,958	3,636	5,281	6,701	6,509	7,406	8,885	12.9	9.3	9.0

NA Not available. [1] For consistency, data for all years are shown on the basis of 27 countries in the European Union; see footnote 5, Table 1391. [2] See footnote 4, Table 1348.

Source: U.S. Department of Agriculture, Foreign Agricultural Trade of the United States (FATUS), "Global Agricultural Trade System Online (GATS)," <http://www.fas.usda.gov/gats/default.aspx>.

Table 864. Selected Farm Products—U.S. and World Production and Exports: 2000 to 2011

[Metric tons, except as indicated (60.6 represents 60,600,000). Metric ton = 1.102 short tons or .984 long tons]

Commodity	Unit	Amount United States			Amount World			United States as percent of world		
		2000	2005	2011	2000	2005	2011	2000	2005	2011
PRODUCTION [1]										
Wheat..................	Million	60.6	57.2	54.4	583.1	618.8	695.2	10.4	9.3	7.8
Corn for grain..............	Million	251.9	282.3	313.9	591.4	699.7	876.8	42.6	40.3	35.8
Soybeans..................	Million	75.1	83.5	83.2	175.8	220.6	236.0	42.7	37.8	35.2
Rice, milled...............	Million	5.9	7.1	5.9	399.3	417.3	465.0	1.5	1.7	1.3
Cotton [2]	Million bales [3]	17.2	23.9	15.6	89.1	116.4	122.7	19.3	20.5	12.7
EXPORTS [4]										
Wheat [5]............	Million	28.9	27.3	28.6	101.5	117.2	153.9	28.5	23.3	18.6
Corn........................	Million	49.3	54.2	39.4	76.9	81.1	101.3	64.2	66.9	38.9
Soybeans..................	Million	27.1	25.6	36.7	53.8	63.8	90.5	50.4	40.1	40.6
Rice, milled basis...........	Million	2.6	3.7	3.2	24.1	29.7	35.5	10.7	12.3	9.1
Cotton [2]...................	Million bales [3]	6.7	17.7	11.7	26.2	44.9	44.3	25.7	39.4	26.4

[1] Production years vary by commodity. In most cases, includes harvests from July 1 of the year shown through June 30 of the following year. [2] For production and trade years ending in year shown. [3] Bales of 480 lb. net weight. [4] Trade years may vary by commodity. Wheat, corn, and soybean data are for trade year beginning in year shown. Rice data are for calendar year. [5] Includes wheat flour on a grain equivalent.

Source: U.S. Department of Agriculture, Foreign Agricultural Service, "Production, Supply and Distribution Online," <http://www.fas.usda.gov/psdonline/>, accessed August 2012.

Table 865. Percent of U.S. Agricultural Commodity Output Exported: 1990 to 2010

[In percent. All export shares are estimated from export and production volumes]

Commodity group	1990	1995	2000	2005	2007	2008	2009	2010
Total agriculture [1]......................	**19.0**	**23.4**	**20.0**	**19.3**	**21.7**	**19.9**	**20.1**	**22.1**
Livestock [2]...............................	4.5	8.2	7.0	6.2	8.2	9.9	8.2	8.6
Red meat.............................	3.2	6.0	8.1	7.4	9.4	13.2	12.2	13.3
Poultry.................................	4.3	11.6	12.4	11.8	13.0	14.7	14.8	14.4
Dairy..................................	1.3	2.8	1.1	1.2	2.4	3.9	1.8	2.2
Crops [3].................................	21.3	26.1	22.2	21.5	24.0	21.7	22.1	24.5
Food grains...........................	37.5	51.9	44.6	45.8	57.9	38.8	38.1	54.1
Feed grains...........................	22.5	30.5	20.8	20.1	20.0	15.8	15.9	15.5
Oilseeds..............................	25.8	34.6	33.0	27.8	40.1	40.0	42.2	41.7
Fruit and nuts.........................	17.0	16.1	17.6	17.2	20.5	21.9	19.7	21.8
Vegetables............................	7.6	9.9	10.8	11.9	11.6	14.5	15.5	16.7
Sweeteners............................	5.3	4.4	3.9	5.3	7.8	7.2	7.2	10.8
Wine and beer.........................	3.3	5.1	6.7	8.1	10.4	11.3	8.6	(NA)

NA Not available [1] All export shares are computed from physical weights or weight equivalents. [2] Includes animal fats; excludes live farm animals and fish/shellfish. [3] Exports include vegetable oils and oilseed meal. Excludes nursery crops.

Source: U.S. Department of Agriculture, Economic Research Service, Global Agricultural Trade System, "Production, Supply, and Distribution" database, <http://www.fas.usda.gov/gats>.

Table 866. Top 10 U.S. Export Markets for Selected Commodities: 2011

[In thousands of metric tons (45,722 represents 45,722,000)]

Corn Country	Amount	Wheat [1] Country	Amount	Soybeans Country	Amount	Poultry meat Country	Amount
World, total..........	**45,722**	**World, total...........**	**32,771**	**World, total............**	**34,288**	**World, total...........**	**3,566**
Japan....................	12,963	Japan....................	3,685	China [2]....................	20,603	Mexico....................	657
Mexico...................	8,618	Nigeria..................	3,632	Mexico...................	3,158	Hong Kong...............	252
Korea, South...........	5,989	Mexico..................	3,260	Japan....................	1,785	Russia....................	218
China [2]...................	2,728	Egypt....................	2,489	Indonesia................	1,692	Canada..................	177
Taiwan...................	2,718	Philippines..............	2,067	Taiwan..................	1,357	Angola..................	167
Egypt....................	2,326	Iraq.....................	1,502	Egypt....................	582	Korea, South...........	111
Canada..................	953	Korea, South...........	1,396	Germany..................	555	China [2]..................	106
Venezuela...............	833	Peru.....................	1,007	Korea, South...........	490	Taiwan..................	104
Dominican Republic...	712	Taiwan..................	963	Spain....................	362	Iraq.....................	103
Guatemala.............	695	Indonesia................	816	Malaysia.................	350	Cuba....................	98
Rest of world..........	7,188	Rest of world...........	11,954	Rest of world...........	3,355	Rest of world...........	1,573

[1] Unmilled. [2] See footnote 4, Table 1348.

Source: U.S. Department of Agriculture, Foreign Agricultural Service, "Global Agricultural Trade System Online (GATS)-FATUS Commodity Aggregations," <http://www.fas.usda.gov/>.

Table 867. Agricultural Exports—Value by Principal Commodities: 1990 to 2011

[In millions of dollars (39,495 represents $39,495,000,000). Includes Puerto Rico, U.S. territories, and shipments under foreign aid programs. Excludes fish, forest products, distilled liquors, manufactured tobacco, and products made from cotton; but includes raw tobacco, raw cotton, rubber, beer and wine, and processed agricultural products]

Commodity	Value (mil. dol.)							Percent distribution		
	1990	2000	2005	2008	2009	2010	2011	1990	2000	2011
Total agricultural exports......	**39,495**	**51,265**	**63,182**	**114,761**	**98,454**	**115,820**	**136,345**	**100.0**	**100.0**	**100.0**
Animals and animal products [1]....	6,636	11,600	12,226	21,306	18,047	22,346	27,828	16.8	22.6	20.4
Meat and meat products..........	2,558	5,276	4,299	8,269	7,722	9,338	12,081	6.5	10.3	8.9
Poultry and poultry products......	910	2,235	3,138	5,053	4,775	4,808	5,633	2.3	4.4	4.1
Grains and feeds [1]................	14,386	13,620	16,364	36,913	25,293	29,254	38,643	36.4	26.6	28.3
Wheat and products..............	4,035	3,578	4,520	11,599	5,681	7,062	11,464	10.2	7.0	8.4
Corn..........................	6,037	4,469	4,789	13,431	8,746	9,808	13,676	15.3	8.7	10.0
Fruits and preparations............	2,007	2,743	3,468	4,839	4,661	5,263	6,053	5.1	5.4	4.4
Nuts and preparations.............	978	1,322	2,992	3,780	4,075	4,799	5,698	2.5	2.6	4.2
Vegetables and preparations [2].....	1,836	3,112	3,571	5,124	5,008	5,376	5,825	4.6	6.1	4.3
Oilseeds and products [1]...........	5,725	8,584	10,229	23,671	24,081	27,219	26,027	14.5	16.7	19.1
Soybeans......................	3,550	5,258	6,274	15,431	16,423	18,564	17,540	9.0	10.3	12.9
Vegetable oils and waxes........	832	1,259	1,656	3,900	3,092	3,903	4,014	2.1	2.5	2.9
Tobacco, unmanufactured.........	1,441	1,204	990	1,238	1,159	1,167	1,149	3.6	2.3	0.8
Cotton, excluding linters...........	2,783	1,873	3,921	4,798	3,316	5,739	8,424	7.0	3.7	6.2
Other................................	3,702	7,207	9,421	13,093	12,814	14,657	16,698	9.4	14.1	12.2

[1] Includes commodities not shown separately. [2] Includes pulses.

Source: U.S. Department of Agriculture, Economic Research Service, "Foreign Agricultural Trade of the United States (FATUS)," <http://ers.usda.gov/Data/FATUS>, and U.S. Department of Agriculture, Foreign Agricultural Service, "Global Agricultural Trade System," <http://www.fas.usda.gov/gats>.

Table 868. Agricultural Exports—Value by Selected Countries of Destination: 1990 to 2011

[39,495 represents $39,495,000,000. Includes Puerto Rico, U.S. territories, and shipments under foreign aid programs. Excludes fish, forest products, distilled liquors, manufactured tobacco, and products made from cotton; but includes raw tobacco, raw cotton, rubber, beer and wine, and processed agricultural products]

Country	Value (mil. dol.)							Percent distribution		
	1990	2000	2005	2008	2009	2010	2011	1990	2000	2011
Total agricultural exports [1]......	**39,495**	**51,265**	**63,182**	**114,761**	**98,454**	**115,820**	**136,345**	**100.0**	**100.0**	**100.0**
Canada................................	4,214	7,643	10,618	16,254	15,726	16,899	18,996	10.7	14.9	13.9
Mexico................................	2,560	6,410	9,429	15,508	12,932	14,598	18,367	6.5	12.5	13.5
Caribbean............................	1,015	1,408	1,913	3,592	3,082	3,177	3,411	2.6	2.7	2.5
Central America......................	483	1,121	1,589	3,106	2,553	2,905	3,734	1.2	2.2	2.7
South America [2].....................	1,063	1,704	1,943	5,334	3,459	4,247	5,278	2.7	3.3	3.9
Asia, excluding Middle East [2]........	15,857	19,877	22,543	44,209	40,614	49,736	58,292	40.1	38.8	42.8
Japan..............................	8,142	9,292	7,931	13,223	11,072	11,797	14,069	20.6	18.1	10.3
Korea, South.......................	2,650	2,546	2,233	5,561	3,917	5,307	6,967	6.7	5.0	5.1
Taiwan [3]..........................	1,663	1,996	2,301	3,419	2,988	8,990	3,624	4.2	3.9	2.7
China [3,4].........................	818	1,716	5,233	12,115	13,109	17,518	18,855	2.1	3.3	13.8
Indonesia..........................	275	668	958	2,195	1,796	2,245	2,820	0.7	1.3	2.1
Europe/Eurasia [2]...................	8,140	7,654	8,361	12,262	9,377	11,367	12,558	20.6	14.9	9.2
European Union [5]..................	7,474	6,515	7,052	10,080	7,445	8,906	9,634	18.9	12.7	7.1
Russia.............................	(X)	580	972	1,838	1,429	1,133	1,241	(X)	1.1	0.9
Middle East [2]......................	1,728	2,323	2,844	6,650	4,745	5,998	7,690	4.4	4.5	5.6
Africa [2]............................	1,848	2,308	2,773	2,649	1,930	2,311	2,973	4.7	4.5	2.2
Egypt..............................	687	1,050	819	2,050	1,354	2,095	2,508	1.7	2.0	1.8
Oceania..............................	343	490	742	1,189	1,282	1,389	1,600	0.9	1.0	1.2

X Not applicable. [1] Totals include transshipments through Canada, but transshipments are not distributed by country after 2000. [2] Includes areas not shown separately. [3] See footnote 4, Table 1348. [4] China includes Macao. However Hong Kong remains separate economically until 2050 and is not included. [5] For consistency, data for all years are shown on the basis of 27 countries in the European Union; see footnote 4, Table 1391.

Source: U.S. Department of Agriculture, Economic Research Service, "Foreign Agricultural Trade of the United States (FATUS);"<http://ers.usda.gov/Data/FATUS>, and U.S. Department of Agriculture, Foreign Agricultural Service, "Global Agricultural Trade System," <http://www.fas.usda.gov/gats>.

Table 869. Cropland Used for Crops and Acreages of Crops Harvested: 1990 to 2011

[In millions of acres, except as indicated (341 represents 341,000,000)]

Item	1990	1995	2000	2005	2006	2007	2008	2009	2010	2011 [3]
Cropland used for crops....................	**341**	**332**	**345**	**336**	**330**	**335**	**337**	**333**	**335**	**328**
Index (1977 = 100)...........................	90	88	91	89	87	89	89	88	89	87
Cropland harvested [1]........................	310	302	314	314	303	312	315	310	315	302
Crop failure...................................	6	8	11	7	11	8	9	8	5	13
Cultivated summer fallow......................	25	22	20	16	15	15	14	15	14	14
Cropland idled by all federal programs.......	62	55	31	35	36	37	35	34	31	31
Acres of crops harvested [2].................	**322**	**314**	**325**	**321**	**312**	**322**	**327**	**319**	**322**	**311**

[1] Land supporting one or more harvested crops. [2] Area in principal crops harvested as reported by Crop Reporting Board plus acreages in fruits, vegetables for sale, tree nuts, and other minor crops. Acres are counted twice for land that is doublecropped. [3] Preliminary.

Source: U.S. Department of Agriculture, Economic Research Service, "Major Uses of Land in the United States," see <http://www.ers.usda.gov/data-products/major-land-uses.asp>. Also, "CRP Enrollment and Rental Payments by State, 1986-2011."

Table 870. Crops—Supply and Use: 2000 to 2011

[72.4 represents 72,400,000. Marketing year beginning January 1 for potatoes, May 1 for hay, June 1 for wheat, August 1 for cotton, September 1 for soybeans and corn. Acreage, production, and yield of all crops periodically revised on basis of census data]

Item	Unit	2000	2005	2007	2008	2009	2010	2011
CORN								
Acreage harvested...............	Million	72.4	75.1	86.5	78.6	79.5	81.4	84.0
Yield per acre....................	Bushel	136.9	147.9	150.7	153.9	164.7	152.8	147.2
Production........................	Mil. bu.	9,915	11,112	13,038	12,092	13,092	12,447	12,358
Imports...........................	Mil. bu.	6.82	8.81	20.02	13.53	8.34	27.67	22.00
Total supply [1]................	Mil. bu.	11,639	13,235	14,362	13,729	14,774	14,182	13,508
Ethanol...........................	Mil. bu.	628	1,603	3,049	3,709	4,591	5,021	5,050
Exports...........................	Mil. bu.	1,941	2,134	2,437	1,849	1,980	1,835	1,600
Total use [2].....................	Mil. bu.	9,740	11,268	12,737	12,056	13,066	13,055	12,605
Ending stocks....................	Mil. bu.	1,899	1,967	1,624	1,673	1,708	1,128	903
Price per unit [3].................	Dol./bu.	1.85	2.00	4.20	4.06	3.55	5.18	6.20
Value of production..............	Mil. dol.	18,499	22,198	54,667	49,313	46,734	64,643	76,464
SOYBEANS								
Acreage harvested...............	Million	72.4	71.3	64.1	74.7	76.4	76.6	73.6
Yield per acre....................	Bushel	38.1	43.1	41.7	39.7	44.0	43.5	41.5
Production........................	Mil. bu.	2,758	3,068	2,677	2,967	3,359	3,329	3,056
Imports...........................	Mil. bu.	4	3	10	13	15	14	15
Total supply [1]................	Mil. bu.	3,052	3,327	3,261	3,185	3,512	3,495	3286
Crushings........................	Mil. bu.	1,640	1,739	1,803	1,662	1,752	1,648	1675
Exports...........................	Mil. bu.	996	940	1,159	1,279	1,499	1,501	1340
Total use [2].....................	Mil. bu.	2,804	2,878	3,056	3,047	3,361	3,280	3116
Ending stocks....................	Mil. bu.	248	449	205	138	151	215	170
Price per unit [3].................	Dol./bu.	4.54	5.66	10.10	9.97	9.59	11.30	11.70
Value of production..............	Mil. dol.	12,520	17,367	27,039	29,458	32,145	37,547	35,784
WHEAT								
Acreage harvested...............	Million	53.1	50.1	51.0	55.7	49.9	47.6	45.7
Yield per acre....................	Bushel	42.0	42.0	40.2	44.9	44.5	46.3	43.7
Production........................	Mil. bu.	2,228	2,103	2,051	2,499	2,218	2,207	1,999
Imports...........................	Mil. bu.	89.8	81.4	112.6	127.0	118.6	96.9	115
Total supply [1, 4]................	Mil. bu.	3,268	2,725	2,620	2,932	2,993	3,280	2977
Exports...........................	Mil. bu.	1,062	1,003	1,263	1,015	879	1,289	1048
Total use [2].....................	Mil. bu.	2,392	2,154	2,314	2,275	2,018	2,417	2234
Ending stocks....................	Mil. bu.	876	571	306	657	976	862	743
Price per unit [3].................	Dol./bu.	2.62	3.42	6.48	6.78	4.87	5.70	7.30
Value of production..............	Mil. dol.	5,782	7,171	13,289	16,626	10,654	12,827	14,368
COTTON								
Acreage harvested...............	Million	13.1	13.8	10.5	7.6	7.5	10.7	9.2
Yield per acre....................	Pounds	632	831	879	813	777	812	772
Production [5].....................	Mil. bales [6]	17.2	23.9	19.2	12.8	12.2	18.1	14.7
Imports...........................	Mil. bales [6]	–	–	–	–	–	–	0.01
Total supply [1]................	Mil. bales [6]	21.1	29.4	28.7	22.9	18.5	21.1	17.307
Exports...........................	Mil. bales [6]	6.7	17.5	13.7	13.3	12.0	15.8	11.12
Total use [2].....................	Mil. bales [6]	15.6	23.4	18.2	16.9	15.5	19.5	14.398
Ending stocks....................	Mil. bales [6]	6.0	6.1	10.0	6.3	3.0	2.6	3.081
Price per unit [3].................	Cents/lb.	51.6	47.7	61.3	49.1	64.8	84.6	96.5
Value of production..............	Mil. dol.	4,260	5,695	5,653	3,021	3,788	7,348	7,263
HAY								
Acreage harvested...............	Million	60.4	61.6	61.0	60.2	59.8	59.9	55.6
Yield per acre....................	Sh. tons	2.54	2.44	2.41	2.43	2.47	2.43	2.36
Production........................	Mil. sh. tons	154	150	147	146	148	146	131
Price per unit [7, 8]...............	Dol./ton	84.60	98.20	128.00	152.00	108.00	114.00	175.00
Value of production..............	Mil. dol.	11,557	12,534	16,842	18,639	14,716	14,656	17,746
POTATOES								
Acreage harvested...............	Million	1.3	1.1	1.1	1.0	1.0	1.0	1.1
Yield per acre....................	Cwt. [9]	381	390	396	396	414	401	397
Production........................	Mil. cwt. [9]	514	424	445	415	432	404	427
Price per unit [3].................	Dol./cwt. [9]	5.08	7.06	7.51	9.09	8.25	9.2	9.37
Value of production..............	Mil. dol.	2,590	2,992	3,340	3,770	3,558	3,722	4,006

– Represents zero or rounds to less than half the unit of measurement shown. [1] Comprises production, imports, and beginning stocks. [2] Includes feed, residual, and other domestic uses not shown separately. [3] Marketing year average price. U.S. prices are computed by weighting U.S. monthly prices by estimated monthly marketings and do not include an allowance for outstanding loans and government purchases and payments. [4] Includes flour and selected other products expressed in grain-equivalent bushels. [5] State production figures, which conform with annual ginning enumeration with allowance for cross-state ginnings, rounded to thousands and added for U.S. totals. [6] Bales of 480 pounds, net weight. [7] Prices are for hay sold baled. [8] Season average prices received by farmers. U.S. prices are computed by weighting state prices by estimated sales. [9] Cwt = hundredweight (100 pounds).

Source: Production and prices—U.S. Department of Agriculture, National Agricultural Statistics Service, *Crop Production*, annual, and *Crop Values*, annual; <http://www.nass.usda.gov/Publications/index.asp>. Supply and disappearance--U.S. Department of Agriculture, Economic Research Service, "Feed Grains Yearbook Data Files," "Oil Crops Yearbook Data Files," "Wheat Outlook Data Files," and "Cotton and Wool Outlook Data Files," <http://www.ers.usda.gov/topics/farm-economy/commodity-outlook/ers-outlook-reports-and-data.aspx>. All data are also in *Agricultural Statistics*, annual, and "Agricultural Outlook: Statistical Indicators," <http://www.ers.usda.gov/data-products/agricultural-outlook-statistical-indicators.aspx/>.

Table 871. Corn—Acreage, Production, and Value by Leading States: 2009 to 2011

[79,490 represents 79,490,000. One bushel of corn (bu.) = 56 pounds]

State	Acreage harvested (1,000 acres)			Yield per acre (bu.)			Production (mil. bu.)			Price per unit ($/bu.)			Value of production (mil. dol.)		
	2009	2010	2011	2009	2010	2011	2009	2010	2011	2009	2010	2011	2009	2010	2011
U.S. [1]....	79,490	81,446	83,981	165	153	147	13,092	12,447	12,358	3.55	5.18	6.20	46,734	64,643	76,464
IA.........	13,300	13,050	13,700	182	165	172	2,421	2,153	2,356	3.59	5.23	6.15	8,690	11,261	14,492
IL.........	11,800	12,400	12,400	174	157	157	2,053	1,947	1,947	3.53	5.24	6.30	7,248	10,201	12,265
NE........	8,850	8,850	9,600	178	166	160	1,575	1,469	1,536	3.58	5.09	6.10	5,640	7,478	9,370
MN.......	7,150	7,300	7,700	174	177	156	1,244	1,292	1,201	3.47	5.01	5.85	4,317	6,473	7,027
IN.........	5,460	5,720	5,750	171	157	146	934	898	840	3.66	5.38	6.25	3,417	4,831	5,247
SD........	4,680	4,220	4,950	151	135	132	707	570	653	3.23	5.09	6.05	2,283	2,900	3,953
KS........	3,860	4,650	4,200	155	125	107	598	581	449	3.49	4.95	6.30	2,088	2,877	2,831
WI........	2,930	3,100	3,320	153	162	156	448	502	518	3.57	5.27	6.00	1,600	2,647	3,108
OH........	3,140	3,270	3,220	174	163	158	546	533	509	3.55	5.45	6.40	1,940	2,905	3,256
MO........	2,920	3,000	3,070	153	123	114	447	369	350	3.58	5.35	6.40	1,599	1,974	2,240
MI........	2,090	2,100	2,190	148	150	153	309	315	335	3.53	5.56	6.05	1,092	1,751	2,027
ND........	1,740	1,880	2,060	115	132	105	200	248	216	3.18	5.01	5.75	636	1,243	1,244
TX........	1,960	2,080	1,470	130	145	93	255	302	137	4.01	4.67	6.55	1,022	1,408	895
CO........	990	1,210	1,300	153	151	133	151	183	173	3.68	4.98	6.20	557	910	1,072
KY........	1,150	1,230	1,300	165	124	139	190	153	181	3.74	5.15	6.40	710	785	1,156
PA........	920	910	960	143	128	111	132	116	107	3.84	6.12	7.10	505	713	757
NC........	800	840	815	117	91	84	94	76	68	3.90	5.18	7.20	365	396	493
MS........	695	670	740	126	136	128	88	91	95	3.72	4.37	6.20	326	398	587
TN........	590	640	735	148	117	131	87	75	96	3.65	4.74	6.50	319	355	626
NY........	595	590	620	134	150	133	80	89	82	4.02	6.30	6.55	321	558	540

[1] Includes other states, not shown separately.

Source: U.S. Department of Agriculture, National Agricultural Statistics Service, *Crop Production Annual Summary*, January 2012, and *Crop Values Annual Summary*, February 2012. See also <http://www.nass.usda.gov/Publications/index.asp>.

Table 872. Soybeans—Acreage, Production, and Value by Leading States: 2009 to 2011

[76,372 represents 76,372,000. One bushel of soybeans = 60 pounds]

State	Acreage harvested (1,000 acres)			Yield per acre (bu.)			Production (mil. bu.)			Price per unit ($/bu.)			Value of production (mil. dol.)		
	2009	2010	2011	2009	2010	2011	2009	2010	2011	2009	2010	2011	2009	2010	2011
U.S. [1]...	76,372	76,610	73,636	44	44	42	3,359	3,329	3,056	9.59	11.30	11.70	32,145	37,547	35,784
IA.........	9,530	9,730	9,230	51	51	51	486	496	466	9.52	11.20	11.80	4,627	5,558	5,500
IL.........	9,350	9,050	8,860	46	52	47	430	466	416	9.80	11.80	11.90	4,215	5,500	4,955
MN.......	7,120	7,310	7,020	40	45	39	285	329	270	9.39	10.90	11.50	2,674	3,586	3,108
IN.........	5,440	5,330	5,290	49	49	45	267	259	238	9.80	11.50	11.60	2,612	2,973	2,761
MO......	5,300	5,070	5,200	44	42	37	231	210	190	9.61	11.70	11.90	2,216	2,462	2,259
NE.......	4,760	5,100	4,830	55	53	54	259	268	258	9.48	11.00	11.50	2,459	2,945	2,972
OH......	4,530	4,590	4,540	49	48	48	222	220	216	9.78	11.50	11.90	2,171	2,534	2,566
SD.......	4,190	4,140	4,070	42	38	37	176	157	151	9.18	10.90	11.40	1,615	1,715	1,717
ND.......	3,870	4,070	3,950	30	34	29	116	138	113	9.26	10.90	11.40	1,075	1,508	1,283
KS.......	3,650	4,250	3,750	44	33	27	161	138	101	9.38	11.50	11.40	1,506	1,588	1,154
AR.......	3,270	3,150	3,270	38	35	38	123	110	124	9.66	10.90	12.00	1,185	1,202	1,491
MI.......	1,990	2,040	1,940	40	44	44	80	89	85	9.54	11.10	11.60	759	985	990
MS.......	2,030	1,980	1,800	38	39	39	77	76	70	9.24	10.40	11.90	713	793	835
WI.......	1,620	1,630	1,600	40	51	46	65	82	74	9.62	10.80	11.70	623	889	861

[1] Includes other states, not shown separately.

Source: U.S. Department of Agriculture, National Agricultural Statistics Service, *Crop Production Annual Summary*, January 2012, and *Crop Values Annual Summary*, February 2012. See also <http://www.nass.usda.gov/Publications/index.asp>.

Table 873. Wheat—Acreage, Production, and Value by Leading States: 2009 to 2011

[49,893 represents 49,893,000. One bushel of wheat = 60 pounds]

State	Acreage harvested (1,000 acres)			Yield per acre (bu.)			Production (mil. bu.)			Price per unit ($/bu.)			Value of production (mil. dol.)		
	2009	2010	2011	2009	2010	2011	2009	2010	2011	2009	2010	2011	2009	2010	2011
U.S. [1]......	49,893	47,619	45,705	45	46	44	2,218	2,207	1,999	4.87	5.70	7.30	10,654	12,827	14,368
KS..........	8,800	8,000	7,900	42	45	35	370	360	277	4.79	5.14	7.10	1,770	1,850	1,963
ND.........	8,415	8,400	6,590	45	43	30	377	362	200	4.82	6.61	8.40	1,816	2,391	1,664
MT.........	5,305	5,210	4,975	33	41	35	177	215	175	5.18	6.29	7.75	918	1,369	1,339
OK.........	3,500	3,900	3,200	22	31	22	77	121	70	4.89	5.06	7.45	377	612	524
SD.........	3,009	2,725	2,817	43	45	37	129	123	105	5.07	6.43	7.70	663	778	800
WA.........	2,225	2,285	2,345	55	65	72	123	148	168	4.85	6.24	6.80	594	925	1,135
CO.........	2,479	2,377	2,044	41	46	40	101	108	82	4.57	5.54	6.65	460	601	546
TX.........	2,450	3,750	1,900	25	34	26	61	128	49	5.27	5.25	7.30	323	669	361

[1] Includes other states, not shown separately.

Source: U.S. Department of Agriculture, National Agricultural Statistics Service, *Crop Production Annual Summary*, January 2012, and *Crop Values Annual Summary*, February 2012. See also <http://www.nass.usda.gov/Publications/index.asp>.

Table 874. Commercial Vegetable and Other Specified Crops—Area, Production, and Value, 2009 to 2011, and Leading Producing States, 2011

[285 represents 285,000. Except as noted, relates to commercial production for fresh market and processing combined. Includes market garden areas but excludes minor producing acreage in minor producing states. Excludes production for home use in farm and nonfarm gardens. Value is for season or crop year and should not be confused with calendar-year income. Hundredweight (cwt.) is the unit used for fresh market yield and production and is equal to one hundred pounds]

Crop	Area harvested (1,000 acres) [1]			Production (1,000 cwt.) [2]			Value of production (mil. dol.) [3]			Leading states in order of production, 2011
	2009	2010	2011	2009	2010	2011	2009	2010	2011	
Beans, snap..............	285	282	259	21,554	20,383	18,986	415	452	464	(NA)
Fresh market...........	92	89	95	5,225	5,062	5,367	283	304	303	FL, CA, GA
Processed..............	196	193	164	16,329	15,321	13,619	156	148	161	WI, OR, MI
Beans, dry edible..........	1,464	1,843	1,156	25,427	31,801	19,833	790	899	827	ND, MI, MN
Broccoli.................	126	130	131	19,890	19,289	21,183	794	727	743	CA, AZ
Cabbage [4].............	65	67	62	22,467	23,238	21,129	342	396	368	CA, NY, FL
Cantaloupes [4].........	75	75	71	19,279	19,228	18,840	350	319	350	CA, AZ, GA
Carrots.................	82	79	84	29,252	29,580	28,784	589	647	759	CA, MI, TX
Cauliflower..............	39	38	37	7,167	7,087	7,169	316	295	330	CA, AZ, NY
Celery..................	29	28	28	20,074	19,923	19,098	404	371	382	CA, MI
Corn, sweet..............	613	585	569	93,521	83,512	80,636	1,171	989	1,050	(NA)
Fresh market...........	237	250	242	28,839	29,628	28,089	846	759	747	FL, CA, GA
Processed..............	380	335	327	64,682	53,884	52,547	336	230	303	WA, MN, WI
Cucumbers..............	144	132	123	20,332	19,412	16,740	402	378	362	FL, MI, NC
Garlic..................	22	23	25	3,878	3,752	4,204	193	267	287	CA, OR, NV
Lettuce, head [4]........	135	132	141	50,180	50,120	48,810	1,122	1,056	1,126	CA, AZ
Lettuce, leaf [4].........	49	51	49	11,845	13,004	12,296	459	500	421	CA, AZ
Lettuce, Romaine [4].......	76	79	80	22,355	27,389	24,635	613	656	795	CA, AZ
Onions.................	151	149	148	75,599	73,599	73,294	1,054	1,050	762	CA, OR, WA
Peas, green [5]...........	205	173	159	8,834	6,913	5,898	141	99	118	WA, WI, MN
Peppers, bell.............	52	53	54	16,997	16,156	17,618	585	649	685	CA, FL, GA
Spinach.................	50	43	43	8,734	5,767	9,083	249	268	269	CA, AZ, NJ
Squash.................	44	44	47	7,219	6,728	7,437	203	209	283	FL, MI, CA
Tomatoes................	434	392	368	312,646	283,487	278,329	2,533	2,279	2,229	(NA)
Fresh market...........	109	103	100	33,235	27,961	30,406	1,344	1,352	1,292	CA, FL, NC
Processed..............	328	289	268	279,411	255,526	247,923	1,219	927	937	CA, IN, OH
Watermelons [5]...........	124	134	125	38,911	41,736	39,005	451	500	544	CA, TX, FL

NA Not available. [1] Area of crops for harvest for fresh market, including any partially harvested or not harvested because of low prices or other factors, plus area harvested for processing. [2] Excludes some quantities not marketed. [3] Fresh market vegetables valued at f.o.b. shipping point. Processing vegetables are equivalent returns at packinghouse door. [4] Fresh market only. [5] Processed only.

Source: U.S. Department of Agriculture, National Agricultural Statistics Service, *Vegetables 2011 Summary*, January 2012, and <http://quickstats.nass.usda.gov/>. See also <http://www.nass.usda.gov/Surveys/Guide_to_NASS_Surveys/Vegetables/index.asp>.

Table 875. Fresh Fruits and Vegetables—Supply and Use: 2000 to 2011

[In millions of pounds, except per capita in pounds (8,355 represents 8,355,000,000)]

Year	Utilized production [1]	Imports [2]	Supply, [1] total	Exports [2]	Consumption		Ending stocks
					Total	Per capita [3]	
FRUITS							
Citrus:							
2000...................	8,355	720	9,075	2,445	6,630	23.5	(NA)
2005...................	7,321	1,109	8,430	2,040	6,390	21.6	(NA)
2008...................	7,313	1,321	8,633	2,363	6,271	20.6	(NA)
2009...................	6,857	1,392	8,249	1,902	6,347	20.7	(NA)
2010...................	7,532	1,434	8,965	2,286	6,679	21.6	(NA)
Noncitrus: [4, 5]							
2000...................	13,327	11,367	24,694	3,235	21,459	75.8	(NA)
2005...................	13,639	12,355	25,994	3,294	22,700	76.5	(NA)
2008...................	13,775	13,551	27,326	3,585	23,741	77.8	(NA)
2009...................	14,176	12,436	26,612	3,416	23,196	75.3	(NA)
2010 [P]................	13,914	13,948	27,862	3,546	24,316	78.3	(NA)
VEGETABLES AND MELONS							
2000...................	46,995	7,461	55,800	4,262	49,316	174.6	1,266
2005...................	46,510	9,784	57,785	4,324	51,439	173.7	1,280
2008...................	45,141	11,432	58,045	4,033	51,804	170.0	1,463
2009...................	44,396	11,753	57,612	3,802	51,529	167.6	1,555
2010...................	44,170	13,284	59,009	3,966	52,827	170.5	1,381
2011 [P]................	43,935	13,504	58,820	4,011	52,513	168.3	1,483
POTATOES							
2000...................	13,185	806	13,990	677	13,313	47.2	(NA)
2005...................	12,076	788	12,863	639	12,224	41.3	(NA)
2008...................	10,996	1,072	12,068	616	11,451	37.6	(NA)
2009...................	11,069	795	11,864	682	11,182	36.4	(NA)
2010...................	11,353	763	12,116	813	11,303	36.5	(NA)
2011 [P]................	11,016	910	11,926	953	10,973	35.1	(NA)

NA Not available. p Preliminary data. [1] Crop-year basis for fruits. Supply data for vegetables include ending stocks of previous year. [2] Fiscal year for fruits; calendar year for vegetables and potatoes. [3] Based on Census Bureau estimates as of April 1 for census years and estimates as of July 1 for all other years. [4] Noncitrus fruit data series has been revised and replaces all years of data from previous issues of the Statistical Abstract. [5] Noncitrus fruit data includes apples, apricots, avocados, bananas, blueberries, grapes, kiwifruit, mango, papayas, peaches, pears, pineapples, raspberries, and strawberries.

Source: U.S. Department of Agriculture, Economic Research Service, *Fruit and Tree Nuts Situation and Outlook Yearbook*, *Vegetables and Melons Situation and Outlook Yearbook*, and *Vegetables and Pulses Yearbook*. See also <http://www.ers.usda.gov/topics/crops.aspx>.

Table 876. Fruits and Nuts—Utilized Production and Value, 2009 to 2011, and Leading Producing States: 2011

[4,727 represents 4,727,000]

Fruits and nuts	Unit	Utilized production [1]			Value of production (mil. dol.)			Leading states in order of production, 2011
		2009	2010	2011	2009	2010	2011	
FRUITS								
Apples [2]	1,000 tons	4,727	4,602	4,657	2,187	2,318	2,723	WA, NY, MI
Avocados	1,000 tons	299	174	227	430	479	492	CA, FL, HI
Blackberries, cultivated (OR)	1,000 tons	28	22	26	31	33	43	OR
Blueberries	1,000 tons	227	247	255	517	644	864	ME, MI, OR
Cranberries	1,000 tons	346	340	386	306	299	344	WI, MA, NJ
Dates (CA)	1,000 tons	24	29	33	28	37	45	CA
Figs (fresh) (CA)	1,000 tons	44	41	39	30	22	20	CA
Grapefruit	1,000 tons	1,304	1,238	1,256	224	297	279	FL, TX, CA
Grapes (13 states)	1,000 tons	7,280	7,469	7,370	3,675	3,635	4,293	CA, WA, NY
Kiwifruit (CA)	1,000 tons	25	33	41	21	25	31	CA
Lemons	1,000 tons	912	882	940	335	395	401	CA, AZ
Nectarines	1,000 tons	220	233	229	139	129	133	CA, WA
Olives (CA)	1,000 tons	46	206	71	32	137	54	CA
Oranges [3]	1,000 tons	9,128	8,243	8,857	1,970	1,999	1,977	FL, CA, TX
Papayas (Hawaii)	1,000 tons	16	15	14	14	11	10	HI
Peaches	1,000 tons	1,083	1,131	1,043	594	619	588	CA, SC, GA
Pears	1,000 tons	956	813	954	356	387	372	WA, CA, OR
Plums (CA)	1,000 tons	112	141	160	58	78	64	CA
Plums and prunes (fresh) [4]	1,000 tons	18	11	13	6	5	5	OR, WA, ID
Prunes (dried basis) (CA)	1,000 tons	496	390	444	204	176	164	CA
Raspberries	1,000 tons	99	75	94	422	259	279	CA,
Strawberries	1,000 tons	1,401	1,427	1,447	2,130	2,262	2,399	CA, FL, OR
Tangelos (FL)	1,000 tons	52	41	52	6	7	10	FL
Tangerines	1,000 tons	443	596	629	207	275	317	CA, FL, AZ
NUTS								
Almonds (shelled basis) (CA)	1,000 tons	1,181	1,414	1,692	2,294	2,903	3,867	CA
Hazelnuts (in the shell) (OR)	1,000 tons	47	28	39	79	67	90	OR
Macadamia nuts (HI)	1,000 tons	21	20	25	29	30	38	HI
Pecans (in the shell) (11 states)	1,000 tons	151	147	135	430	675	656	GA, NM, TX
Pistachios (CA)	1,000 tons	178	261	222	593	1,159	879	CA
Walnuts(in the shell) (CA)	1,000 tons	437	504	461	747	1,028	1,323	CA

NA Not available. [1] Excludes quantities not harvested or not marketed. Utilized production is the amount sold plus the quantities used at home or held in storage [2] Production in commercial orchards with 100 or more bearing-age trees. [3] Includes temples and Navel varieties beginning with the 2006–2007 season. [4] Idaho, Michigan, Oregon and Washington.

Source: U.S. Department of Agriculture, National Agricultural Statistics Service, *Citrus Fruits 2011 Summary*, September 2011; and *Noncitrus Fruits and Crops 2011 Summary*, July 2012. See also <http://www.nass.usda.gov/Publications/index.asp>.

Table 877. Nuts—Supply and Use: 2000 to 2010

[In thousands of pounds (shelled) (331,466 represents 331,466,000). For marketing season beginning July 1 for almonds, hazelnuts, and pecans; August 1 for walnuts; and September 1 for pistachios]

Year	Beginning stocks	Marketable [1] production	Imports	Supply, total	Consumption	Exports	Ending stocks
Total nuts: [2]							
2000	331,466	1,127,940	293,172	1,752,577	733,921	780,988	237,669
2005	262,995	1,472,240	431,881	2,167,117	776,517	1,123,446	267,153
2008	405,897	2,259,507	439,516	3,104,613	1,090,855	1,471,198	542,560
2009	542,560	2,113,945	467,327	3,123,832	1,155,329	1,546,654	421,849
2010, total [2, 3]	**421,849**	**2,478,896**	**482,441**	**3,383,187**	**1,315,840**	**1,711,460**	**355,887**
Almonds	321,355	1,612,084	8,112	1,941,551	499,353	1,188,239	253,959
Pecans	39,522	(NA)	82,780	262,710	167,432	54,405	40,873
Pistachios	21,211	250,125	467	271,804	169,404	79,578	22,822
Hazelnuts	2,440	21,322	11,032	34,795	15,581	16,838	2,376
Walnuts	37,321	436,785	501	474,607	216,000	301,665	35,856

NA Not available. [1] Utilized production minus inedibles and noncommercial usage. [2] Includes macadamia nuts, Brazil nuts, cashew nuts, pine nuts, chestnuts, and mixed nuts not shown separately. [3] Data are preliminary.

Source: U.S. Department of Agriculture, Economic Research Service, *Fruit and Tree Nuts Situation and Outlook Yearbook*. See also <http://www.ers.usda.gov/publications/fts/#yearbook>.

Table 878. Honey—Number of Bee Colonies, Yield, and Production: 1990 to 2011

[Includes only beekeepers with five or more colonies. Colonies were not included if honey was not harvested]

Year	Honey-producing colonies [1] (1,000)	Yield per colony (pounds)	Production (1,000 pounds)	Average price per pound (cents)	Value of production (1,000 dollars)
1990	3,220	61.7	198,674	54	106,688
1995	2,655	79.5	211,073	69	144,585
2000	2,622	84.0	220,286	60	132,865
2005	2,409	72.5	174,614	92	160,994
2008	2,342	69.9	163,789	142	232,744
2009	2,498	58.6	146,416	147	215,671
2010	2,692	65.6	176,462	162	285,692
2011	2,491	59.6	148,357	173	256,509

[1] Honey producing colonies are the maximum number of colonies from which honey was taken during the year. It is possible to take honey from colonies which did not survive the entire year.

Source: U.S. Department of Agriculture, National Agricultural Statistics Service, *Honey*, March 2012. See also <http://www.nass.usda.gov/Surveys/Guide_to_NASS_Surveys/Bee_and_Honey/index.asp>.

Table 879. Farmers Markets Characteristics: 2005

[In percent. Based on 2006 National Farmers Market Survey. A farmers market is defined as a retail outlet in which two or more vendors sell agricultural products directly to customers through a common marketing channel. Markets included were in business in the 2005 season and conducted 51 percent of their retail sales directly with consumers]

Characteristic	Total, U.S.	Region [1] North-east	Mid-Atlantic	South-east	North Central	South-west	Rocky Mountain	Far West
Number of vendors:								
Less than 10	23.9	42.4	37.4	24.1	17.8	32.3	15.9	9.4
10 to 19	25.3	27.9	28.4	22.8	29.4	29.0	19.3	12.5
20 to 39	29.0	23.6	22.6	29.7	32.3	17.7	28.4	35.6
40 or more	21.8	6.1	11.6	23.4	20.5	21.0	36.4	42.5
Vendor sales:								
$1 to $5,000	71.4	70.0	61.2	68.1	81.4	71.6	80.4	56.1
$5,001 to $25,000	22.1	26.2	22.8	25.2	15.5	23.0	18.3	31.5
$25,000 to $100,000	5.9	3.8	15.4	4.3	2.9	5.3	1.3	11.8
$100,001 and above	0.6	–	0.7	2.4	0.2	0.2	–	0.6
Months of operation:								
Year-round	12.1	3.5	13.7	19.6	4.1	17.5	4.3	35.4
Seasonal	87.9	96.5	86.3	80.4	95.9	82.5	95.7	64.6
Less than 4 months	20.0	26.3	15.5	16.9	19.2	22.2	39.6	11.4
4 to 6 months	59.5	68.0	57.4	42.6	72.0	47.6	52.7	42.9
7 to 9 months	7.6	2.3	12.9	18.2	4.6	9.5	3.3	8.6
More than 9 months	12.9	3.4	14.2	22.3	4.2	20.6	4.4	37.1
Source of goods sold:								
Grew products sold (their own products)	(NA)	65.0	72.3	69.8	76.8	78.0	60.3	68.6
Organic products	47.0	67.3	37.2	35.5	39.8	30.4	56.8	74.5
Locally grown	87.9	89.3	84.8	90.5	91.2	80.6	88.1	82.1
Pasture raised/free range	38.4	33.6	40.2	21.6	42.5	32.3	34.3	46.3
Natural	46.9	39.3	41.1	45.9	50.9	32.3	55.2	50.4
Hormone or antibiotic free	29.3	20.5	27.7	20.3	34.4	19.4	28.4	36.6
Chemical free/pesticide free	47.6	36.9	39.3	45.9	46.9	41.9	56.7	65.0
Other	12.3	13.9	13.4	12.2	7.3	19.4	16.4	17.1

– Represents zero. NA Not available. [1] Composition of regions—Northeast: Connecticut, Maine, Massachusetts, New Hampshire, New York, Rhode Island, and Vermont. Mid-Atlantic: Delaware, District of Columbia, Maryland, New Jersey, Pennsylvania, Virginia, and West Virginia. Southeast: Alabama, Florida, Georgia, Kentucky, Mississippi, North Carolina, South Carolina, and Tennessee. North Central: Illinois, Indiana, Iowa, Kansas, Minnesota, Missouri, Nebraska, North Dakota, Ohio, South Dakota, and Wisconsin. Southwest: Arkansas, Louisiana, Oklahoma, and Texas. Rocky Mountain: Arizona, Colorado, Idaho, New Mexico, Montana, Utah, and Wyoming. Far West: Alaska, California, Hawaii, Nevada, Oregon, and Washington.

Source: U.S. Department of Agriculture, Agricultural Marketing Service, *National Farmers Market Manager Survey 2006*, May 2009, <http://www.ams.usda.gov/AMSv1.0/FARMERSMARKETS>.

Table 880. Horticultural Specialty Crop Operations, Value of Sales, and Total Land Area Used to Grow Horticultural Crops: 2009

[Horticultural specialty operation is defined as any place that produced and sold $10,000 or more of horticultural specialty products]

Item	Operations	Value of sales (1,000)	Total land area [1]			
			Green-houses (1,000 square feet)	Shade structures (1,000 square feet)	Natural shade (acres)	Area in open (acres)
Horticultural specialty crops, total [2]	**21,585**	**11,687,323**	**859,063**	**406,072**	**8,160**	**572,269**
Annual bedding/garden plants	7,989	2,305,913	258,823	13,858	140	6,815
Herbaceous perennial plants	6,416	843,788	27,101	4,330	314	3,981
Potted flowering plants for indoor or patio use	4,043	871,474	62,208	23,893	41	1,693
Foliage plants for indor or patio use	2,728	509,873	39,583	76,645	144	2,314
Cut flowers	1,703	403,254	53,495	14,248	76	12,068
Cut cultivated greens	634	84,148	5,443	152,512	2,835	2,998
Nursery stock sold	8,441	3,850,363	217,482	87,228	4,184	323,539
Propagative material [3]	1,178	601,657	29,733	3,208	53	8,169
Sod, sprigs, or plugs	1,403	876,847	419	36	(D)	85,842
Dried bulbs, corms, rhizomes, and tubers	223	48,512	183	(D)	(D)	3,736
Food crops grown under protection	1,476	553,270	61,324	1,562	19	5,863
Transplants for commercial vegetable production [4]	502	330,647	32,095	467	4	7,250
Vegetable seeds	340	89,031	163	(D)	–	38,819
Flower seeds	141	30,825	289	308	2	5,695
Aquatic plants	375	26,000	1,373	134	1	1,320
Cut Christmas trees	2,699	249,821	1,010	95	84	45,091
Other	212	11,901	68,340	27,519	227	17,075

D Withheld to avoid disclosure. – Represents zero [1] Total land area represents the land utilized on the operation as the area used for horticultural production. Includes volume of stacked benches and stacked pots and the area used to produce multiple crop types. [2] Excludes acres in production for Christmas trees or sod, sprigs, or plugs. [3] Includes cuttings, liners, tissue cultured plantlets, and prefinished plants. [4] Includes strawberries.

Source: U.S. Department of Agriculture, National Agricultural Statistics Service, 2009 Census of Horticultural Specialties, Vol. 3, AC-07-SS-3. See also <http://www.agcensus.usda.gov/Publications/2007/Online_Highlights/>.

Table 881. Meat Supply and Use: 2000 to 2011

[In millions of pounds (carcass weight equivalent) (82,372 represents 82,372,000,000). Carcass weight equivalent is the weight of the animal minus entrails, head, hide, and internal organs; includes fat and bone. Covers federal and state inspected, and farm slaughtered]

Year and type of meat	Production	Imports	Supply [1]	Exports	Consumption [2]	Ending stocks
RED MEAT AND POULTRY						
2000	82,372	4,136	88,480	9,344	77,067	2,069
2005	86,781	4,846	93,807	9,275	82,334	2,199
2008	93,597	3,646	99,393	14,352	82,590	2,451
2009	90,632	3,735	96,818	13,498	81,327	1,994
2010	91,778	3,439	97,211	13,977	81,120	2,114
2011 [P]	92,214	3,507	97,835	14,411	81,441	1,983
ALL RED MEATS						
2000	46,299	4,127	51,340	3,760	46,559	1,021
2005	45,846	4,804	51,837	3,373	47,385	1,080
2008	50,362	3,553	55,084	6,566	47,211	1,307
2009	49,412	3,631	54,350	6,046	47,191	1,114
2010	49,189	3,321	53,624	6,542	45,937	1,145
2011 [P]	49,065	3,383	53,593	7,116	45,392	1,085
Beef:						
2000	26,888	3,032	30,332	2,468	27,338	525
2005	24,952	3,598	29,191	697	27,919	575
2008	26,664	2,538	29,832	1,887	27,303	642
2009	26,068	2,626	29,336	1,935	26,836	565
2010	26,419	2,297	29,281	2,299	26,397	585
2011 [P]	26,177	2,295	29,057	2,425	26,117	515
Pork:						
2000	18,952	965	20,406	1,287	18,642	478
2005	20,706	1,025	22,274	2,665	19,115	494
2008	23,367	832	24,717	4,667	19,415	635
2009	23,020	834	24,489	4,095	19,870	525
2010	22,458	859	23,842	4,227	19,074	541
2011 [P]	22,586	920	24,047	4,675	18,822	550
Veal:						
2000	225	(NA)	230	(NA)	225	5
2005	165	(NA)	169	(NA)	164	5
2008	152	(NA)	159	(NA)	150	9
2009	147	(NA)	156	(NA)	147	9
2010	142	(NA)	151	(NA)	147	4
2011 [P]	140	(NA)	144	(NA)	137	7
Lamb and mutton:						
2000	234	130	372	5	354	13
2005	191	180	374	9	355	10
2008	180	183	376	12	343	21
2009	177	171	369	16	338	15
2010	171	165	351	16	320	15
2011 [P]	162	168	345	16	316	13
POULTRY, TOTAL						
2000	36,073	9	37,140	5,584	30,508	1,048
2005	40,935	42	41,970	5,902	34,949	1,119
2008	43,235	92	44,309	7,785	35,379	1,144
2009	41,220	104	42,468	7,452	34,136	880
2010	42,589	118	43,586	7,435	35,182	969
2011 [P]	43,149	124	44,242	7,295	36,049	898
Broilers:						
2000	30,209	6	31,011	25,295	4,918	798
2005	34,987	33	35,721	5,203	29,608	910
2008	36,511	79	37,309	6,961	29,603	745
2009	35,131	86	35,961	6,818	28,527	616
2010	36,516	98	37,230	6,773	29,684	773
2011 [P]	37,044	96	37,913	6,650	30,593	670
Mature chicken:						
2000	531	2	540	220	312	9
2005	516	1	520	130	388	2
2008	559	5	566	148	415	3
2009	500	3	509	100	406	2
2010	503	3	508	79	425	4
2011 [P]	504	4	512	85	424	3
Turkeys:						
2000	5,333	1	5,589	445	4,902	241
2005	5,432	7	5,728	569	4,952	207
2008	6,165	8	6,434	676	5,361	396
2009	5,589	13	5,998	534	5,202	262
2010	5,569	17	5,848	583	5,073	192
2011 [P]	5,601	24	5,817	560	5,032	225

NA Not available. p Preliminary data. [1] Total supply equals production plus imports plus ending stocks of previous year. [2] Includes shipments to territories.

Source: U.S. Department of Agriculture, Economic Research Service, *Food Consumption, Prices, and Expenditures, 1970–1997* and "Agricultural Outlook: Statistical Indicators," <http://www.ers.usda.gov/publications/agoutlook/aotables/>; and "Data Files: Livestock, Dairy, and Poultry Outlook," accessed July 2012, <http://www.ers.usda.gov/publications/ldpm-livestock,-dairy,-and-poultry-outlook.aspx>.

Table 882. Livestock Inventory and Production: 1990 to 2011

[95.8 represents 95,800,000. Production in live weight; includes animals-for-slaughter market, younger animals shipped to other states for feeding or breeding purposes, farm slaughter and custom slaughter consumed on farms where produced, minus livestock shipped into states for feeding or breeding with an adjustment for changes in inventory]

Type of livestock	Unit	1990	1995	2000	2005	2006	2007	2008	2009	2010	2011
ALL CATTLE [1]											
Inventory: [2] Number on farms.............	Mil.	95.8	102.8	98.2	95.0	96.3	96.6	96.0	94.5	93.9	92.7
Total value.............................	Bil. dol.	59.0	63.2	67.1	87.0	97.2	89.1	95.1	82.4	78.2	87.8
Value per head.....................	Dol.	616	615	683	916	1,009	922	990	872	832	947
Production: Quantity.....................	Bil. lb.	39.2	42.5	43.0	41.2	41.8	41.4	41.6	41.2	41.6	41.6
Beef, price per 100 pounds......................	Dol.	74.60	61.80	68.60	89.70	87.20	89.90	89.10	80.30	92.20	113.00
Calves, price per 100 pounds......................	Dol.	95.60	73.10	104.00	135.00	133.00	119.00	110.00	105.00	117.00	142.00
Value of production..................	Bil. dol.	29.3	24.7	28.5	36.3	35.5	36.0	35.6	32.0	37.0	45.2
HOGS AND PIGS											
Inventory: [3] Number on farms.............	Mil.	53.8	59.7	59.3	61.0	61.5	62.5	68.2	64.8	64.9	66.4
Total value.............................	Bil. dol.	4.3	3.2	4.3	6.3	5.6	5.0	6.0	5.4	6.9	8.0
Value per head.....................	Dol.	79	53	72	103	90	90	73	83	83	106
Production: Quantity.....................	Bil. lb.	21.3	24.4	25.7	27.4	28.2	29.6	31.4	31.4	30.4	31.0
Price per 100 pounds..............	Dol.	53.70	40.50	42.30	50.20	46.00	46.60	47.00	41.60	54.10	65.30
Value of production..................	Bil. dol.	11.3	9.8	10.8	13.6	12.7	13.5	14.5	12.6	16.1	20.1
SHEEP AND LAMBS											
Inventory: [2] Number on farms.............	Mil.	11.4	9.0	7.0	6.1	6.2	6.1	6.0	5.7	5.6	5.5
Total value.............................	Mil. dol.	901	663	670	798	872	818	823	765	761	931
Value per head.....................	Dol.	79	75	95	130	141	134	138	133	135	170
Production: Quantity.....................	Mil. lb.	781	602	512	472	461	440	417	422	405	(NA)
Value of production..................	Mil. dol.	374	414	365	451	368	363	351	365	443	(NA)

NA Not available. [1] Includes milk cows. [2] As of January 1. [3] As of December 1 of preceding year.

Source: U.S. Department of Agriculture, National Agricultural Statistics Service, *Meat Animals—Production, Disposition, and Income Final Estimates 1998–2002*, May 2004; *Meat Animals—Production, Disposition, and Income Final Estimates 2003–2007*, May 2009; *Meat Animals Production, Disposition, and Income 2011 Summary*, April 2012; and <http://quickstats.nass.usda.gov/>. See also <http://www.nass.usda.gov/Publications/index.asp>.

Table 883. Livestock Operations by Size of Herd: 2000 to 2011

[In thousands (1,076 represents 1,076,000). An operation is any place having one or more head on hand at any time during the year]

Size of herd	2000	2005	2010	2011	Size of herd	2000	2005	2010	2011
CATTLE [1]					MILK COWS [2]				
Total operations...............	**1,076**	**983**	**935**	**922**	**Total operations**...............	**105**	**78**	**63**	**60**
1 to 49 head........................	671	612	635	627	1 to 49 head........................	53	37	31	30
50 to 99 head.......................	186	164	129	127	50 to 99 head.......................	31	23	16	15
100 to 499 head..................	192	178	142	139	100 head or more..............	21	15	16	16
500 to 999 head..................	19	19	19	19					
1,000 head or more..............	10	10	11	11	HOGS AND PIGS				
					Total operations...............	**87**	**67**	**69**	**69**
					1 to 99 head........................	50	41	49	49
BEEF COWS [2]					100 to 499 head..................	17	10	5	5
Total operations...............	**831**	**770**	**742**	**734**	500 to 999 head..................	8	5	3	2
1 to 49 head........................	655	597	588	583	1,000 to 1,999 head..............	6	4	4	3
50 to 99 head.......................	100	95	82	81	2,000 to 4,999 head..............	5	5	5	6
100 to 499 head..................	71	73	66	64	5,000 head or more..............	2	2	3	3
500 head or more................	6	5	6	6					

[1] Includes calves. [2] Included in operations with cattle.

Source: U.S. Department of Agriculture, National Agricultural Statistics Service, *Livestock Operations Final Estimates 2003–2007*, March 2009; and *Farms, Land in Farms, and Livestock Operations 2011 Summary*, February 2012. See also <http://www.nass.usda.gov/Publications/index.asp>.

Table 884. Hogs and Pigs—Number, Production, and Slaughter by States: 2009 to 2011

[Production in live weight (64,887 represents 64,887,000). See headnote Table 882]

State	Number on farms [1] (1,000)			Quantity produced (mil. lb.)			Value of production (mil. dol.)			Commercial slaughter [2] (mil. lb.)	
	2009	2010	2011	2009	2010	2011	2009	2010	2011	2010	2011
U.S. [3] ...	**64,887**	**64,925**	**66,361**	**31,359**	**30,437**	**30,982**	**12,590**	**16,095**	**20,121**	**30,005**	**30,422**
IA........	19,000	19,100	20,000	9,608	9,244	9,793	3,580	4,521	5,929	8,144	8,177
NC........	9,600	9,000	8,900	4,071	3,767	3,653	1,824	2,178	2,486	3,069	2,997
MN........	7,200	7,700	7,800	3,678	3,699	3,689	1,257	1,856	2,305	2,692	2,782
IL........	4,250	4,400	4,650	1,839	1,926	1,899	908	1,121	1,343	2,582	2,701
IN........	3,600	3,650	3,850	1,739	1,754	1,755	728	901	1,094	2,265	2,281
NE........	3,100	3,150	3,150	1,360	1,367	1,319	626	811	907	2,064	2,105
MO........	3,100	2,900	2,750	1,694	1,288	1,323	674	711	935	2,196	2,270

[1] As of December 1. [2] Includes slaughter in federally inspected and other slaughter plants; excludes animals slaughtered on farms. [3] Includes other states, not shown separately.

Source: U.S. Department of Agriculture, National Agricultural Statistics Service, *Meat Animals Production, Disposition and Income 2011 Summary*, April 2012, and *Livestock Slaughter 2011 Summary*, April 2012. See also <http://www.nass.usda.gov/Publications/index.asp>.

Table 885. Cattle and Calves—Number, Production, and Value by State: 2009 to 2012

[93,881 represents 93,881,000. Includes milk cows. See headnote, Table 882]

State	Number on farms [1] (1,000)			Production (mil. lb.)			Value of production (mil. dol.)			Commercial slaughter [2] (mil. lb.)	
	2010	2011	2012	2009	2010	2011	2009	2010	2011	2010	2011
U.S. [3]	93,881	92,682	90,769	41,161	41,569	41,598	31,990	36,969	45,176	43,662	43,402
TX	13,300	13,300	11,900	6,924	6,789	7,164	5,481	6,097	8,089	8,179	8,323
NE	6,300	6,200	6,450	4,615	4,553	4,584	3,746	4,137	4,978	9,109	9,056
KS	6,000	6,300	6,100	3,916	4,090	4,010	2,965	3,444	4,233	8,347	8,257
OK	5,500	5,100	4,500	2,149	2,216	2,270	1,890	2,178	2,649	26	26
CO	2,600	2,650	2,750	1,817	1,725	1,677	1,598	1,770	1,932	3,269	3,278
IA	3,850	3,900	3,900	1,787	1,809	1,757	1,437	1,672	1,967	(⁴)	(⁴)
SD	3,800	3,700	3,650	1,471	1,481	1,468	1,326	1,559	1,758	(⁴)	(⁴)
CA	5,150	5,200	5,350	1,899	1,974	2,095	1,099	1,338	2,015	2,204	2,228
MO	4,150	3,950	3,900	1,348	1,256	1,282	1,170	1,249	1,587	77	78
MT	2,550	2,500	2,500	965	1,112	1,020	777	1,042	1,108	25	23
ID	2,170	2,200	2,220	1,047	1,158	1,037	800	1,018	1,114	346	132

[1] As of January 1. [2] Data cover cattle only. Includes slaughter in federally inspected and other slaughter plants; excludes animals slaughtered on farms. [3] Includes other states, not shown separately. [4] Included in U.S. total. Not printed to avoid disclosing individual operation.

Source: U.S. Department of Agriculture, National Agricultural Statistics Service, *Meat Animals—Production, Disposition and Income 2011 Summary*, April 2012, and *Livestock Slaughter 2011 Summary*, April 2012, annual. See also <http://www.nass.usda.gov/Publications/index.asp>.

Table 886. Milk Cows—Number, Production, and Value by State: 2009 to 2011

[9,203 represents 9,203,000]

State	Number on farms [1] (1,000)			Milk produced on farms [2] (mil. lb.)			Milk produced per milk cow (pounds) [2]			Value of production [3] (mil. dol.)		
	2009	2010	2011	2009	2010	2011	2009	2010	2011	2009	2010	2011
U.S. [4]	9,203	9,119	9,194	189,334	192,848	196,245	20,573	21,148	21,345	24,473	31,531	39,736
CA	1,796	1,754	1,769	39,512	40,385	41,462	22,000	23,025	23,438	4,540	5,933	7,687
WI	1,257	1,262	1,265	25,239	26,035	26,117	20,079	20,630	20,646	3,306	4,192	5,302
NY	619	611	610	12,424	12,713	12,826	20,071	20,807	21,026	1,690	2,212	2,745
ID	550	564	578	12,150	12,779	13,256	22,091	22,658	22,934	1,434	1,904	2,439
PA	545	541	541	10,551	10,737	10,604	19,360	19,847	19,601	1,519	1,965	2,343
MN	469	470	468	9,019	9,102	8,890	19,230	19,366	18,996	1,209	1,465	1,822
TX	423	413	431	8,840	8,828	9,582	20,898	21,375	22,232	1,176	1,510	1,993
MI	355	358	366	7,968	8,333	8,478	22,445	23,277	23,164	1,068	1,417	1,780

[1] Average number during year. Represents cows and heifers that have calved, kept for milk; excluding heifers not yet fresh. [2] Excludes milk sucked by calves. [3] Valued at average returns per 100 pounds of milk in combined marketings of milk and cream. Includes value of milk fed to calves. [4] Includes other states, not shown separately.

Source: U.S. Department of Agriculture, National Agricultural Statistics Service, *Milk Production, Disposition, and Income 2010*; and *Milk Production, Disposition, and Income 2011 Summary*, April 2011. See also <http://www.nass.usda.gov/Publications/index.asp>.

Table 887. Milk Production and Manufactured Dairy Products: 1990 to 2011

[193 represents 193,000]

Item	Unit	1990	2000	2005	2006	2007	2008	2009	2010	2011
Number of farms with milk cows	1,000	193	105	78	75	70	67	65	63	60
Cows and heifers that have calved, kept for milk	Mil. head	10.0	9.2	9.1	9.1	9.2	9.3	9.2	9.1	9.2
Milk produced on farms	Bil. lb.	148	167	177	182	186	190	189	193	196
Production per cow	1,000 lb.	14.8	18.2	19.6	19.9	20.2	20.4	20.6	21.1	21.3
Milk marketed by producers [1]	Bil. lb.	146	166	176	181	185	189	188	192	195
Value of milk produced	Bil. dol.	20.4	20.8	26.9	23.6	35.7	35.1	24.5	31.5	39.7
Cash receipts from marketing of milk and cream [1]	Bil. dol.	20.1	20.6	26.7	23.4	35.5	34.8	24.3	31.4	39.5
Number of dairy manufacturing plants	Number	1,723	1,164	1,088	1,094	1,123	1,125	1,203	1,250	1,278
Manufactured dairy products:										
Butter (including whey butter)	Mil. lb.	1,302	1,256	1,347	1,448	1,533	1,644	1,572	1,564	1,810
Cheese, total [2]	Mil. lb.	6,059	8,258	9,149	9,525	9,777	9,913	10,074	10,433	10,597
American (excl. full-skim American)	Mil. lb.	2,894	3,642	3,808	3,913	3,877	4,109	4,203	4,289	4,267
Cream and Neufchatel	Mil. lb.	431	687	715	756	773	764	767	745	716
All Italian varieties	Mil. lb.	2,207	3,289	3,803	3,973	4,199	4,121	4,181	4,416	4,560
Cottage cheese—creamed and lowfat	Mil. lb.	832	735	784	778	774	714	731	719	704
Nonfat dry milk [3]	Mil. lb.	902	1,457	1,210	1,244	1,298	1,519	1,512	1,563	1,514
Dry whey [4]	Mil. lb.	1,143	1,188	1,041	1,110	1,134	1,082	1,001	1,013	1,010
Yogurt, plain and fruit-flavored	Mil. lb.	(NA)	1,837	3,058	3,301	3,476	3,570	3,839	4,181	4,272
Ice cream, regular	Mil. gal.	824	980	960	982	956	931	918	929	900
Ice cream, lowfat [5]	Mil. gal.	352	373	360	377	383	384	400	415	440

NA Not available. [1] Comprises sales to plants and dealers, and retail sales by farmers direct to consumers. [2] Includes varieties not shown separately. Beginning 1974, includes full-skim. [3] Includes dry skim milk for animal feed through 2000. [4] Includes animal but excludes modified whey production. [5] Includes freezer-made milkshake in most states.

Source: U.S. Department of Agriculture, National Agricultural Statistics Service, *Milk Disposition and Income Final Estimates 2003-2007*, May 2009; *Dairy Products 2011 Summary*, April 2012; *Milk Production, Disposition, and Income 2011 Summary*, April 2012; and *Farms, Land in Farms, And Livestock Operations, 2011 Summary*, April 2012. See also <http://www.nass.usda.gov/Publications/index.asp>.

Table 888. Milk Production and Commercial Use: 1990 to 2011

[In billions of pounds milkfat basis (147.7 represents 147,700,000,000) except as noted]

Year	Production	Farm use	Commercial Farm marketings	Commercial Beginning stocks	Imports	Commercial supply, total	Commodity Credit Corporation net removals [1]	Commercial Ending stocks	Exports	Disappearance [2]	Milk price per 100 pounds [3] (dollars)
1990.....	147.7	2.0	145.7	4.1	2.7	152.5	8.5	5.1	(NA)	138.8	13.68
2000.....	167.4	1.3	166.1	6.1	4.4	176.7	0.8	6.9	(NA)	169.0	12.40
2005.....	176.9	1.1	175.8	7.2	7.5	190.5	–	8.0	3.3	179.2	15.13
2008.....	190.0	1.1	188.9	10.4	5.3	204.6	–	10.1	8.7	185.7	18.33
2009.....	189.3	1.0	188.3	10.1	5.6	204.0	0.7	11.3	4.5	187.3	12.83
2010.....	192.8	1.0	191.8	11.3	4.1	207.2	0.2	10.9	8.3	187.8	16.29
2011......	196.0	1.0	195.0	10.9	3.2	209.1	0.0	11.2	9.2	188.6	20.15

– Represents zero. NA Not available. [1] Removals from commercial supply by Commodity Credit Corporation (CCC) on a fat basis. [2] Prior to 2005, disappearance represents domestic disappearance plus exports. [3] Wholesale price received by farmers for all milk delivered to plants and dealers.

Source: U.S. Department of Agriculture, Economic Research Service, "Agricultural Outlook: Statistical Indicators," <http://www.ers.usda.gov/publications/agoutlook/aotables/>, accessed June 2012.

Table 889. Broiler, Turkey, and Egg Production: 1990 to 2011

[353 represents 353,000,000. For year ending November 30, except as noted]

Item	Unit	1990	1995	2000	2005	2006	2007	2008	2009	2010	2011
Chickens: [1]											
Number [2]...............	Million	353	388	437	456	458	459	447	452	455	447
Value per head [2]........	Dollars	2.29	2.41	2.44	2.52	2.60	2.95	3.39	3.34	3.59	3.80
Value, total [2]............	Mil. dol.	808	935	1,064	1,150	1,190	1,352	1,517	1,508	1,633	1,698
Number sold............	Million	208	180	218	194	174	168	176	176	173	181
Price per pound........	Cents	9.6	6.5	5.7	6.5	5.9	5.6	6.6	(NA)	(NA)	(NA)
Value of sales..........	Mil. dol.	94	60	64	65	54	51	62	65	73	81
PRODUCTION											
Broilers: [3]											
Number.................	Million	5,864	7,326	8,284	8,872	8,868	8,907	9,009	8,550	8,624	8,607
Weight.................	Bil. lb.	25.6	34.2	41.6	47.9	48.8	49.3	50.4	47.8	49.2	49.7
Price per pound........	Cents	32.6	34.4	33.6	43.6	36.3	43.6	(NA)	(NA)	(NA)	(NA)
Production value........	Mil. dol.	8,366	11,762	13,989	20,878	17,739	21,514	23,203	21,823	23,692	23,161
Turkeys:											
Number.................	Million	282	292	270	250	256	267	273	247	244	249
Weight.................	Bil. lb.	6.0	6.8	7.0	7.0	7.2	7.6	7.9	7.1	7.1	7.3
Price per pound........	Cents	39.6	41.0	40.6	44.5	48.0	52.3	56.5	(NA)	(NA)	(NA)
Production value........	Mil. dol.	2,393	2,769	2,828	3,108	3,468	3,952	4,477	3,573	4,374	4,992
Eggs:											
Average number of layers.................	Thousand	(NA)	294,350	327,908	345,027	349,700	346,498	339,131	337,848	340,335	338,428
Eggs per layer.........	Number	(NA)	254	257	262	263	263	266	268	269	271
Total production........	Billion	68.1	74.8	84.4	90.3	91.8	91.1	90.0	90.5	91.5	91.9
Price per dozen........	Cents	70.8	62.5	61.6	54.0	58.3	88.5	109.0	(NA)	(NA)	(NA)
Production value........	Mil. dol.	4,021	3,893	4,346	4,067	4,460	6,719	8,216	6,166	6,535	7,365

NA Not available. [1] Excludes commercial broilers. [2] As of December 1. [3] Young chickens of the heavy breeds and other meat-type birds, to be marketed at 2–5 lbs. live weight and from which no pullets are kept for egg production. Not included in sales of chickens.

Source: U.S. Department of Agriculture, National Agricultural Statistics Service, *Poultry Production and Value Final Estimates 1998–2002*, April 2004; *Turkeys Final Estimates 1998–2002*, April 2004; *Poultry Production and Value Final Estimates 2003–2007*, May 2009; *Chickens and Eggs Final Estimates 1998–2002*, April 2004; *Chickens and Eggs Final Estimates 2003–2007*, March 2009; and *Poultry—Production and Value*, annual; and *Chickens and Eggs*, annual. See also <http://www.nass.usda.gov/Publications/index.asp>.

Table 890. Broiler and Turkey Production by State: 2009 to 2011

[In millions of pounds, live weight production (47,752 represents 47,752,000,000)]

State	Broilers 2009	Broilers 2010	Broilers 2011	Turkeys 2009	Turkeys 2010	Turkeys 2011	State	Broilers 2009	Broilers 2010	Broilers 2011	Turkeys 2009	Turkeys 2010	Turkeys 2011
U.S. [1]....	47,752	49,153	49,702	7,149	7,111	7,319	MS......	4,602	4,766	4,626	(NA)	(NA)	(NA)
AL..........	5,513	5,787	5,718	(NA)	(NA)	(NA)	MO......	(NA)	(NA)	1,369	611	583	569
AR..........	5,780	5,938	5,856	568	552	604	NC......	5,317	5,419	5,587	1,090	969	1,133
CA..........	(NA)	(NA)	(NA)	390	409	422	OH......	338	377	376	203	193	210
DE..........	1,599	1,625	1,525	(NA)	(NA)	(NA)	OK......	1,220	1,503	1,524	(NA)	(NA)	(NA)
FL..........	252	314	383	(NA)	(NA)	(NA)	PA.......	875	839	871	182	175	175
GA..........	6,874	6,883	7,426	(NA)	(NA)	(NA)	SC.......	1,522	1,557	1,497	433	428	449
IL...........	(NA)	(NA)	(NA)	(NA)	(NA)	(NA)	SD......	(NA)	(NA)	(NA)	187	191	180
IN...........	(NA)	(NA)	(NA)	543	574	579	TN......	968	987	990	(NA)	(NA)	(NA)
IA...........	(NA)	(NA)	(NA)	(NA)	(NA)	(NA)	TX......	3,611	3,645	3,594	(NA)	(NA)	(NA)
KY..........	1,658	1,673	1,705	(NA)	(NA)	(NA)	UT......	(NA)	(NA)	(NA)	82	117	98
MD.........	1,399	1,433	1,556	(NA)	(NA)	(NA)	VA......	1,204	1,292	1,292	449	449	460
MI..........	(NA)	(NA)	(NA)	(NA)	(NA)	(NA)	WV......	331	346	342	97	88	92
MN.........	246	231	235	1,161	1,175	1,172	WI.......	192	198	200	(NA)	(NA)	(NA)

NA Not available. [1] Includes other states, not shown separately.

Source: U.S. Department of Agriculture, National Agricultural Statistics Service, *Poultry Production and Value Final Estimates 2003–2007*, May 2009, and *Poultry—Production and Value*, annual. See also <http://www.nass.usda.gov/Publications/index.asp>.

This section presents data on the area, ownership, production, trade, reserves, and disposition of natural resources. Natural resources is defined here as including forestry, fisheries, and mining and mineral products.

Forestry—Presents data on the area, ownership, and timber resource of commercial timberland; forestry statistics covering the National Forests and Forest Service cooperative programs; product data for lumber, pulpwood, woodpulp, paper and paperboard, and similar data.

The principal sources of data relating to forests and forest products are *Forest Resources of the United States, 2007; Timber Demand and Technology Assessment; U.S. Timber Production, Trade, Consumption, and Price Statistics, 1965 to 2005; Land Areas of the National Forest System*, issued annually by the Forest Service of the U.S. Department of Agriculture; *Agricultural Statistics* issued by the Department of Agriculture; and reports of the Annual Survey of Manufactures issued by the U.S. Census Bureau, see <http://www.census.gov/manufacturing/asm/>. Further sources used in this section and issued by the U.S. Census Bureau include the annual *County Business Patterns* reports, and the 2007 Economic Census. Additional information is published in the annual *Wood Pulp and Fiber Statistics* and *The Annual Statistics of Paper, Paperboard, and Wood Pulp* of the American Forest and Paper Association, Washington, DC.

The completeness and reliability of statistics on forests and forest products vary considerably. The data for forest land area and stand volumes are much more reliable for areas that have been recently surveyed than for those for which only estimates are available. In general, more data are available for lumber and other manufactured products such as particle board and softwood panels, etc., than for the primary forest products such as poles and piling and fuelwood.

Fisheries—The principal source of data relating to fisheries is *Fisheries of the United States*, issued annually by the National Marine Fisheries Service (NMFS), National Oceanic and Atmospheric Administration (NOAA). The NMFS collects and disseminates data on commercial landings of fish and shellfish. Annual reports include quantity and value of commercial landings of fish and shellfish disposition of landings and number and kinds of fishing vessels and fishing gear. Reports for the fish-processing industry include annual output for the wholesaling and fish processing establishments, annual and seasonal employment. The principal source for these data is the annual *Fisheries of the United States*. Additional

government sources include Agricultural Statistics, issued by the Department of Agriculture; and *Trout Production, Catfish Production*, and *Catfish Processing*, issued by the National Agricultural Statistics service of the U.S. Department of Agriculture.

Mining and mineral products—Presents data relating to mineral industries and their products, general summary measures of production and employment, and more detailed data on production, prices, imports and exports, consumption, and distribution for specific industries and products. Data on mining and mineral products may also be found in Sections 19, 21, and 28 of this *Abstract*; data on mining employment may be found in Section 12.

Mining comprises the extraction of minerals occurring naturally (coal, ores, crude petroleum, natural gas) and quarrying, well operation, milling, refining and processing, and other preparation customarily done at the mine or well site or as a part of extraction activity. (Mineral preparation plants are usually operated together with mines or quarries.) Exploration for minerals is included as is the development of mineral properties.

The principal governmental sources of these data are the *Minerals Yearbook* and *Mineral Commodity Summaries*, published by the U.S. Geological Survey, U.S. Department of the Interior, and various monthly and annual publications of the Energy Information Administration, U.S. Department of Energy. See text, Section 19, for a list of Department of Energy publications. In addition, the Census Bureau conducts a census of mineral industries every 5 years.

Mineral statistics, with principal emphasis on commodity detail, have been collected by the U.S. Geological Survey and the former Bureau of Mines since 1880. Current data in U.S. Geological Survey publications include quantity and value of nonfuel minerals produced, sold, or used by producers, or shipped; quantity of minerals stocked; crude materials treated and prepared minerals recovered; and consumption of mineral raw materials.

The Economic Census, conducted by the Census Bureau at various intervals since 1840, collects data on mineral industries. Beginning with the 1967 census, legislation provides for a census to be conducted every 5 years for years ending in "2" and "7." The most recent results, published for 2007, are based on the North American Industry Classification System (NAICS). The censuses provide, for the various types of mineral establishments, information on operating costs, capital expenditures, labor, equipment, and energy requirements in relation to their value of shipments and other receipts.

Table 891. Natural Resource–Related Industries—Establishments, Sales, Payroll, and Employees by Industry: 2002 and 2007

[183 represents $183,000,000,000. Includes only establishments of firms with payroll. Data are based on the 2002 and 2007 economic censuses, which are subject to nonsampling error. For details on methodology and nonsampling and sampling errors, see Appendix III]

Industry	2002 NAICS code [1]	Establishments (number)		Value of shipments (bil. dol.)		Annual payroll (bil. dol.)		Paid employees [2] (1,000)	
		2002	2007	2002	2007	2002	2007	2002	2007
Mining..............................	21	24,087	21,169	183	369	21	37	475	703
Oil & gas extraction......................	211	7,730	6,293	113	231	5	10	99	162
Mining (except oil & gas)..................	212	7,253	6,465	48	81	9	11	196	220
Mining support activities.................	213	9,104	8,411	22	57	7	16	180	322
Manufacturing [3].........................	31–33	350,728	293,919	3,915	5,339	568	612	15	13
Wood product mfg..................	321	17,192	14,862	89	102	16	17	540	520
Paper mfg.......................	322	5,520	4,803	154	176	21	21	491	417
Petroleum & coal products manufacturing...	324	2,268	2,284	216	606	6	8	104	105

[1] 2002 data based on North American Industry Classification System (NAICS), 2002. 2007 data based on 2007 NAICS. [2] For pay period including March 12. [3] Includes other industries, not shown separately.

Source: U.S. Census Bureau, 2007 Economic Census, "Comparative Statistics," March 2009, <http://www.census.gov/econ/census07/>.

Table 892. Natural Resource–Related Industries—Establishments, Employees, and Annual Payroll by Industry: 2000 and 2009

[1,791.3 represents 1,791,300. Excludes most government employees, railroad employees, self-employed persons, etc. See "General Explanation" in source for definitions and statement on reliability of data. An establishment is a single physical location where business is conducted or where services or industrial operations are performed. See Appendix III]

Industry	2007 NAICS Code [1]	Establishments (number)		Number of employees [2] (1,000)		Annual payroll (bil. dol.)	
		2000	2009	2000	2009	2000	2009
Natural resource–related industries, total...............	(X)	**72,932**	**68,424**	**1,791.3**	**1,530.6**	**66.58**	**78.75**
Forestry, fishing, hunting, and agriculture support...........	11	26,076	21,679	183.6	158.8	4.68	5.12
Forestry and logging..........................	113	13,347	8,982	83.1	53.0	2.26	1.86
Timber tract operations......................	1131	469	371	3.3	2.1	0.13	0.10
Forest nurseries and gathering forest products...........	1132	258	176	1.7	1.6	0.07	0.05
Logging.............................	1133	12,620	8,435	78.1	49.3	2.06	1.72
Fishing, hunting and trapping...............	114	2,671	2,298	10.0	7.3	0.34	0.33
Fishing.............................	1141	2,308	1,994	7.5	5.5	0.27	0.27
Hunting and trapping.................	1142	363	304	2.5	1.8	0.08	0.06
Agriculture and forestry support activities...................	115	10,058	10,399	90.4	93.6	2.08	2.93
Crop production support activities................	1151	5,061	4,533	57.6	62.8	1.35	2.01
Animal production support activities.............	1152	3,450	4,242	18.2	20.1	0.38	0.58
Forestry support activities.................	1153	1,547	1,624	14.7	10.7	0.35	0.35
Mining, quarrying and oil, and gas extraction...............	21	23,738	26,897	456.1	604.7	22.09	41.86
Oil and gas extraction....................	211	7,740	7,891	83.0	107.4	5.39	11.18
Mining (except oil and gas)..................	212	7,231	6,689	204.3	202.7	9.34	12.20
Coal mining...........................	2121	1,253	1,086	70.7	84.0	3.54	5.65
Metal ore mining.........................	2122	522	313	34.8	34.6	1.72	2.32
Nonmetallic mineral mining and quarrying...............	2123	5,456	5,290	98.8	84.2	4.08	4.23
Mining support activities...................	213	8,767	12,317	168.8	294.6	7.35	18.47
Timber–related manufacturing...................	(X)	23,118	19,848	1,151.6	767.1	39.80	31.77
Wood product manufacturing..................	321	17,328	15,142	597.7	385.8	16.51	12.38
Sawmills and wood preservation................	3211	4,695	3,665	131.4	84.2	3.78	2.79
Veneer, plywood and engineered wood product manufacturing..........................	3212	1,904	1,745	120.6	71.8	3.75	2.51
Other wood product manufacturing........................	3219	10,729	9,732	345.8	229.8	8.95	7.09
Paper manufacturing..........................	322	5,790	4,706	553.9	381.3	23.29	19.39
Pulp, paper and paperboard mills........................	3221	597	492	177.1	116.3	9.48	7.60
Converted paper product manufacturing..................	3222	5,193	4,214	376.8	265.0	13.82	11.79

X Not applicable. [1] 2000 data based on North American Industry Classification System (NAICS), 1997. 2009 data based on 2007 NAICS. [2] Covers full- and part-time employees who are on the payroll in the pay period including March 12.

Source: U.S. Census Bureau, "County Business Patterns," June 2011, <http://www.census.gov/econ/cbp/index.html>.

Table 893. Gross Domestic Product of Natural Resource-Related Industries in Current and Real (2005) Dollars by Industry: 2000 to 2011

[In billions of dollars (9,951.5 represents $9,951,500,000,000). Data are based on the 2002 North American Industry Classification System (NAICS); see text, Section 15. Data include nonfactor charges (capital consumption allowances, indirect business taxes, etc.) as well as factor charges against gross product; corporate profits and capital consumption allowances have been shifted from a company to an establishment basis]

Industry	Current dollars				Chained (2005) dollars			
	2000	2005	2010	2011	2000	2005	2010	2011
All industries, total [1]	**9,951.5**	**12,623.0**	**14,526.5**	**15,094.0**	**11,216.4**	**12,623.0**	**13,088.0**	**13,315.1**
Industries covered	294.5	406.3	475.4	(NA)	427.4	406.3	444.5	(NA)
Percent of all industries	3.0	3.2	3.3	(NA)	3.8	3.2	3.4	(NA)
Agriculture, forestry, fishing, and hunting	95.6	127.1	157.0	177.8	103.7	127.1	138.3	121.2
Farms	73.6	102.0	132.6	(NA)	83.5	102.0	116.5	(NA)
Forestry, fishing, and related activities	22.0	25.1	24.4	(NA)	20.5	25.1	21.2	(NA)
Mining	108.9	192.3	239.5	287.6	232.7	192.3	234.0	248.8
Oil and gas extraction	67.5	128.7	147.5	(NA)	155.0	128.7	168.3	(NA)
Mining, except oil and gas	27.8	36.3	49.2	(NA)	45.5	36.3	31.3	(NA)
Support activities for mining	13.7	27.3	42.8	(NA)	29.4	27.3	34.4	(NA)
Timber-related manufacturing	90.0	86.9	78.9	(NA)	91.0	86.9	72.2	(NA)
Wood products	28.3	33.0	22.3	(NA)	32.8	33.0	29.6	(NA)
Paper products	61.7	53.9	56.6	(NA)	58.2	53.9	42.6	(NA)

NA Not available. [1] Includes industries not shown separately.

Source: U.S. Bureau of Economic Analysis, *Survey of Current Business*, and BEA Interactive Tables, accessed August 2012. See also <http://www.bea.gov/itable/>.

Table 894. Timber–Based Manufacturing Industries—Establishments, Shipments, Payroll, and Employees: 2007

[101,711,917 represents $101,711,917,000. Includes only establishments or firms with payroll. Data for industries with NAICS codes less than 6–digits were derived by summing values with the corresponding 6–digit NAICS codes. See Appendix III]

Industry	2007 NAICS code [1]	Establishments (number)	Value of shipments ($1,000)	Annual payroll ($1,000)	Paid employees [2]
Wood product manufacturing	321	16,868	101,711,917	17,426,832	523,899
Sawmills and wood preservation	3211	4,102	27,911,240	3,642,165	103,413
Sawmills	321113	3,589	22,075,666	3,144,796	90,044
Wood preservation	321114	513	5,835,574	497,369	13,369
Veneer, plywood, and engineered wood product manufacturing	3212	1,958	22,258,829	3,829,184	106,848
Other wood product manufacturing	3219	10,810	51,777,100	9,993,940	314,393
Millwork	32191	4,713	28,300,862	5,201,356	153,739
Wood container and pallet manufacturing	32192	2,909	7,235,876	1,519,970	58,467
All other wood product manufacturing	32199	3,151	16,339,726	3,274,866	102,353
Paper manufacturing	322	4,988	176,687,641	20,858,769	418,241
Pulp, paper, and paperboard mills	3221	486	80,550,214	7,925,398	125,483
Pulp mills	32211	39	5,027,395	504,602	7,268
Paper mills	32212	262	49,732,085	4,919,950	80,838
Paperboard mills	32213	187	25,354,745	2,451,849	36,641
Converted paper product manufacturing	3222	4,502	96,137,427	12,933,371	292,758
Paperboard container manufacturing	32221	2,402	50,900,190	7,387,042	165,839
Paper bag and coated and treated paper manufacturing	32222	891	21,737,348	2,798,096	60,373
Stationery product manufacturing	32223	549	8,242,007	1,197,456	31,628
Other converted paper product manufacturing	32229	654	15,024,475	1,545,024	34,780

[1] North American Industry Classification System, 2007. [2] For pay period including March 12.

Source: U.S. Census Bureau, 2007 Economic Census, "Economy–Wide Key Statistics," August 2010. See also <http://www.census.gov/econ/census07/>.

Table 895. Timber-Based Manufacturing Industries—Employees, Payroll, and Shipments: 2010

[In thousands (10,567 represents 10,567,000). Based on the Annual Survey of Manufactures, see Appendix III]

Selected industry	2007 NAICS code [1]	All employees			Produc-tion workers, total (1,000)	Value added by manufactures		Value of ship-ments (mil. dol.)
		Number (1,000)	Payroll				Per produc-tion worker (dol.)	
			Total (mil. dol.)	Per employee (dol.)		Total (mil. dol.)		
Manufacturing, all industries [2].........	31–33	10,567	540,001	51,101	7,319	2,185,326	298,597	4,916,647
Timber-based manufacturing, total......	**321–322**	**682**	**30,926**	**45,378**	**539**	**108,125**	**200,514**	**239,911**
Percent of total manufacturing........	(X)	6.45	5.73	(X)	7.37	4.95	(X)	4.88
Wood product manufacturing...............	321	330	11,767	35,703	264	29,013	109,702	69,957
Sawmills and wood preservation.........	3211	73	2,908	39,727	61	8,357	137,520	22,209
Veneer, plywood, and engineered wood product....................	3212	59	2,277	38,860	47	5,564	119,387	14,014
Other wood product.......................	3219	198	6,582	33,278	157	15,092	96,069	33,733
Millwork.........................	32191	93	3,297	35,286	74	7,694	103,891	17,240
Wood container and pallet...............	32192	45	1,325	29,282	37	2,810	75,201	6,245
All other wood products.................	32199	59	1,960	33,166	46	4,588	100,457	10,248
Paper manufacturing.......................	322	352	19,159	54,439	275	79,111	287,925	169,954
Pulp, paper, and paperboard mills.......	3221	110	7,509	68,226	88	40,706	464,163	79,324
Pulp mills........................	32211	6	464	73,662	5	2,035	412,650	4,238
Paper mills........................	32212	69	4,536	66,151	55	25,208	456,544	47,712
Paperboard mills..................	32213	35	2,509	71,299	28	13,463	488,654	27,374
Converted paper product..................	3222	242	11,650	48,166	187	38,405	205,303	90,630
Paperboard container.................	32221	138	6,773	49,057	107	20,013	186,871	50,219
Paper bag and coated and treated paper........................	32222	50	2,485	49,359	38	8,709	229,048	19,579
Stationery product..................	32223	21	870	41,958	16	2,126	131,411	5,939
Other converted paper products........	32229	33	1,523	46,509	26	7,557	293,256	14,893

X Not applicable. [1] North American Industry Classification System, 2007; see text, Section 15. [2] Includes other industries, not shown separately.

Source: U.S. Census Bureau, "Annual Survey of Manufactures, 2010," Nov. 2011, <http://www.census.gov/manufacturing/asm/index.html>.

Table 896. Forest Land and Timberland by Type of Owner and Region: 2007

[In thousands of acres (751,228 represents 751,228,000). As of January 1. Forest land is land at least 10 percent stocked by forest trees of any size, including land that formerly had such tree cover and that will be naturally or artificially regenerated. The minimum area for classification of forest land is 1 acre or strips of timber with a crown width of at least 120 feet wide. Timberland is forest land that is producing or is capable of producing crops of industrial wood and that is not withdrawn from timber utilization by statute or administrative regulation]

Region	Forest land, total	Timberland					
		Total	Federal			State, county, and municipal	Private [1]
			Total	National forest	Other		
Total............................	751,228	514,213	112,733	98,721	14,015	44,994	356,485
North............................	172,039	164,018	11,897	10,126	1,771	25,252	126,868
Northeast......................	84,796	79,803	2,971	2,401	570	9,308	67,523
North Central..................	87,243	84,215	8,926	7,725	1,201	15,944	59,345
South............................	214,644	204,030	17,164	12,225	4,940	7,880	178,986
Southeast......................	87,889	85,665	7,559	4,970	2,590	4,689	73,417
South Central..................	126,756	118,365	9,605	7,255	2,350	3,191	105,569
Rocky Mountains.................	150,661	70,968	48,612	45,386	3,228	3,185	19,169
Great Plains....................	5,757	5,287	1,294	1,056	239	198	3,795
Intermountain...................	144,905	65,681	47,318	44,330	2,989	2,987	15,374
Pacific Coast....................	213,883	75,197	35,060	30,984	4,076	8,677	31,462
Alaska..........................	126,869	11,865	4,750	3,772	978	4,344	2,771
Pacific Northwest...............	52,449	43,489	20,403	17,937	2,466	3,704	19,383
Pacific Southwest [2]...........	34,565	19,843	9,907	9,275	632	629	9,308

[1] Includes Indian lands. [2] Includes Hawaii.

Source: U.S. Forest Service, "RPA Assessment Tables," 2007, <http://www.fs.fed.us/research/rpa/>.

Table 897. National Forest System Lands by State: 2011

[In thousands of acres (233,045 represents 233,045,000). As of September 30, 2011. Data do not include Delaware, District of Columbia, Iowa, Maryland, Massachusetts, New Jersey, or Rhode Island]

State	Total lands	National Forest System lands [1]	Other lands [2]	State	Total lands	National Forest System lands [1]	Other lands [2]
U.S.	**233,045**	**193,092**	**39,962**	NE.	560	352	208
				NV.	6,276	5,766	510
AL.	1,289	671	618	NH.	828	736	93
AK.	24,359	21,957	2,402	NM.	10,455	9,411	1,045
AZ.	11,891	11,265	627	NY.	16	16	–
AR.	3,553	2,599	954	NC.	3,165	1,256	1,910
CA.	24,444	20,824	3,619	ND.	1,106	1,106	4
CO.	16,021	14,521	1,500	OH.	834	241	593
CT.	24	24	–	OK.	755	401	354
FL.	1,435	1,176	259	OR.	17,580	15,691	1,889
GA.	1,858	867	991	PA.	743	513	230
HI.	1	1	–	SC.	1,379	631	748
ID.	21,659	20,465	1,193	SD.	2,452	2,017	435
IL.	923	298	626	TN.	1,276	719	557
IN.	644	203	441	TX.	1,994	755	1,239
KS.	116	108	8	UT.	9,213	8,208	1,005
KY.	2,208	814	1,394	VT.	823	401	422
LA.	1,025	604	421	VA.	3,223	1,664	1,559
ME.	93	54	40	WA.	10,114	9,290	823
MI.	4,894	2,876	2,018	WV.	1,896	1,045	852
MN.	5,467	2,842	2,625	WI.	2,023	1,534	489
MS.	2,318	1,174	1,144	WY.	9,706	9,242	465
MO.	3,060	1,493	1,567	PR.	56	28	28
MT.	19,143	17,086	2,057	VI.	147	147	–

– Represents zero. [1] National Forest System is a national significant system of federally owned units of forest, range, and related land consisting of national forests, purchase units, national grasslands, land utilization project areas, experimental forest areas, experimental range areas, designated experimental areas, and other land areas; water areas; and interests in lands that are administered by USDA Forest Service or designated for administration through the Forest Service. [2] Other lands are lands within the unit boundaries in private, state, county, and municipal ownership and the federal lands over which the Forest Service has no jurisdiction. Also includes lands offered to the United States and approved for acquisition and subsequent Forest Service administration, but to which title has not yet been accepted by the United States.

Source: U.S. Forest Service, *Land Areas of the National Forest System*. See also <http://www.fs.fed.us/land/staff/lar>.

Table 898. Timber Volume, Growth, and Removal on Timberland by Species, Group, and Region: 2007

[932,096 represents 932,096,000,000]

Region	Net volume [1]						Timber growth [4] (mil. cu. ft.)			Timber removals [5] (mil. cu. ft.)		
	Growing stock [2] (mil. cu. ft.)			Sawtimber [3] (bil. board ft.)								
	All species	Soft-woods	Hard-woods	All spe-cies	Soft-woods	Hard-woods	All spe-cies	Soft-woods	Hard-woods	All spe-cies	Soft-woods	Hard-woods
Total	**932,096**	**529,203**	**402,893**	**1,013**	**558**	**455**	**26,744**	**15,241**	**11,503**	**15,533**	**9,859**	**5,675**
North	248,007	55,866	192,141	268	60	209	6,576	1,489	5,087	2,820	677	2,143
Northeast	137,585	34,252	103,333	146	37	109	3,249	836	2,412	1,169	353	815
North Central	110,422	21,614	88,808	122	23	99	3,327	652	2,675	1,651	324	1,328
South	288,522	118,471	170,051	325	123	202	13,272	7,632	5,640	9,696	6,317	3,379
Southeast	126,747	56,722	70,025	143	58	84	6,115	3,876	2,239	4,306	2,961	1,345
South Central	161,775	61,749	100,026	182	64	118	7,157	3,756	3,401	5,391	3,357	2,034
Rocky Mountains.	137,263	124,809	12,454	159	144	15	1,761	1,577	184	543	521	22
Great Plains	4,539	1,641	2,898	7	2	5	72	27	45	41	25	16
Intermountain	132,724	123,168	9,556	153	142	11	1,689	1,550	139	502	496	6
Pacific Coast	258,304	230,057	28,247	261	232	29	5,135	4,543	593	2,474	2,344	131
Alaska	31,998	29,125	2,873	34	31	3	248	130	118	66	59	7
Pacific Northwest	158,896	146,006	12,890	159	146	13	3,340	3,039	301	1,939	1,818	121
Pacific Southwest [6]	67,410	54,926	12,484	68	55	13	1,548	1,374	174	469	466	3

[1] As of January 1. [2] Live trees of commercial species meeting specified standards of quality or vigor. Cull trees are excluded. Includes only trees 5.0-inches in diameter or larger at 4 1/2 feet above ground. [3] Live trees of commercial species containing at least one 12-foot sawlog or two noncontiguous 8-foot logs, and meeting regional specifications for freedom from defect. Softwood trees must be at least 9.0 inches in diameter and hardwood trees must be at least 11.0-inches in diameter at 4 1/2 feet above ground. [4] The net increase in the volume of trees during a specified year. Components include the increment in net volume of trees at the beginning of the specific year surviving to its end, plus the net volume of trees reaching the minimum size class during the year, minus the volume of trees that died during the year, and minus the net volume of trees that became cull trees during the year. [5] The net volume of trees removed from the inventory during a specified year by harvesting, cultural operations such as timber stand improvement, or land clearing. [6] Includes Hawaii.

Source: U.S. Forest Service, "RPA Assessment Tables," 2007, <http://www.fs.fed.us/research/rpa/>.

Table 899. Timber Removals—Roundwood Product Output by Source and Species Group: 2006

[In million cubic feet (14,990 represents 14,990,000,000)]

Source and species group	Total	Sawlogs	Pulpwood	Veneer logs	Other products [1]	Fuelwood [2]
Total	**14,990**	**7,179**	**4,394**	**1,211**	**798**	**1,408**
Softwoods	9,948	5,289	2,634	1,068	479	477
Hardwoods	5,042	1,890	1,760	143	319	931
Growing stock [3]	13,002	6,781	3,872	1,156	703	490
Softwoods	8,897	5,030	2,345	1,020	417	86
Hardwoods	4,105	1,752	1,527	136	286	404
Other sources [4]	1,988	398	522	55	95	918
Softwoods	1,051	260	289	48	63	391
Hardwoods	937	138	233	7	33	526

[1] Includes such items as cooperage, pilings, poles, posts, shakes, shingles, board mills, charcoal, and export logs. [2] Downed and dead wood volume left on the ground after trees have been cut on timberland. [3] Includes live trees of commercial species meeting specified standards of quality or vigor. Cull trees are excluded. Includes only trees 5.0-inches in diameter or larger at 4 1/2 feet above the ground. [4] Includes salvable dead trees, rough and rotten trees, trees of noncommercial species, trees less than 5.0-inches in diameter at 4 1/2 feet above the ground, tops, and roundwood harvested from nonforest land (for example, fence rows).

Source: U.S. Forest Service, "RPA Assessment Tables," 2007, <http://www.fs.fed.us/research/rpa/>.

Table 900. Timber Products—Production, Foreign Trade, and Consumption by Type of Product: 1990 to 2010

[In millions of cubic feet, roundwood equivalent (15,577 represents 15,577,000,000)]

Type of Product	1990	1995	2000	2003	2004	2005	2006	2007	2008	2009	2010
Industrial roundwood:											
Domestic production	15,577	15,537	15,436	14,571	15,139	15,465	14,836	13,932	12,493	11,264	11,933
Softwoods	10,968	10,191	10,201	10,290	10,710	11,002	10,413	9,566	8,389	7,213	7,302
Hardwoods	4,609	5,347	5,235	4,282	4,428	4,463	4,423	4,366	4,104	4,052	4,631
Imports	3,091	3,907	4,529	5,096	5,805	5,802	5,292	4,147	3,065	1,986	1,722
Exports	2,307	2,282	1,996	1,535	1,604	1,646	1,596	1,481	1,517	1,248	1,291
Consumption	16,361	17,161	17,969	18,132	19,339	19,622	18,841	16,598	14,041	12,002	13,279
Softwoods	11,779	11,961	12,659	13,398	14,357	14,652	13,732	12,009	9,845	7,941	8,451
Hardwoods	4,582	5,200	5,310	4,734	4,983	4,970	4,799	4,589	4,197	4,062	4,728
Lumber:											
Domestic production	7,317	6,815	7,199	7,131	7,510	7,889	7,552	6,964	5,928	5,020	4,800
Imports	1,909	2,522	2,845	3,193	3,704	3,737	3,415	2,743	1,922	1,336	1,440
Exports	589	460	428	347	348	389	390	359	345	272	224
Consumption	8,637	8,877	9,616	9,977	10,866	11,237	10,577	9,347	7,506	6,084	5,906
Plywood and veneer:											
Domestic production	1,423	1,303	1,187	1,054	1,086	1,068	1,003	912	743	617	177
Imports	97	107	155	240	354	373	339	265	185	177	104
Exports	109	89	42	35	43	37	35	40	45	37	58
Consumption	1,410	1,321	1,300	1,259	1,397	1,403	1,308	1,136	882	757	780
Pulp products:											
Domestic production	5,313	6,079	5,881	5,557	5,692	5,679	5,470	5,176	4,926	4,818	4,841
Imports	1,038	1,248	1,459	1,579	1,669	1,570	1,440	1,071	918	434	566
Exports	646	905	842	643	680	708	681	526	556	423	492
Consumption	5,704	6,422	6,498	6,493	6,680	6,541	6,229	5,721	5,288	4,829	4,915
Logs:											
Imports	4	13	68	80	73	114	94	67	35	29	32
Exports	674	451	331	356	366	345	339	350	313	321	407
Pulpwood chips, exports	288	377	353	155	168	166	151	205	257	195	195
Fuelwood consumption	3,019	2,937	2,561	1,515	1,540	1,550	1,555	1,605	1,510	1,400	1,134

Source: U.S. Forest Service, *U.S. Timber Production, Trade, Consumption, and Price Statistics*, Research Paper RP-FPL-637, and unpublished data. See also <http://www.treesearch.fs.fed.us/pubs/28972>.

Table 901. Selected Timber Products—Imports and Exports: 1990 to 2010

[In million board feet (13,063 represents 13,063,000,000), except as indicated]

Product	Unit	1990	1995	2000	2005	2006	2007	2008	2009	2010
IMPORTS [1]										
Lumber, total [2]	Mil. bd. ft.	13,063	17,524	19,906	25,738	23,037	18,906	13,042	9,172	6,101
From Canada	Percent	91	97	92	85	86	89	72	54	93
Logs, total	Mil. bd. ft. [3]	23	80	435	710	585	418	253	179	198
From Canada	Percent	84	70	96	85	85	91	(NA)	(NA)	(NA)
Paper and board [4]	1,000 tons	12,195	14,292	17,555	20,438	20,293	18,634	16,872	12,133	11,546
Woodpulp	1,000 tons	4,893	5,969	7,227	6,762	6,939	6,793	6,272	5,044	6,136
Plywood	Mil. sq. ft. [5]	1,687	1,951	2,917	6,325	6,324	4,969	3,722	2,778	3,350
EXPORTS										
Lumber, total [2]	Mil. bd. ft.	4,623	2,958	2,700	2,348	2,359	2,193	2,148	1,690	2,133
To: Canada	Percent	14	22	26	28	28	27	27	27	26
Japan	Percent	28	33	12	3	4	4	5	4	–
Europe	Percent	15	17	19	19	16	16	5	7	–
Logs, total	Mil. bd. ft. [3]	4,213	2,820	2,068	2,157	2,120	2,189	2,240	2,005	2,541
To: Canada	Percent	9	25	41	54	52	34	33	32	27
Japan	Percent	62	61	45	27	26	26	28	28	16
China	Percent	9	1	–	4	5	7	9	12	30
Paper and board [4]	1,000 tons	5,163	7,621	10,003	13,434	13,349	14,582	12,907	12,569	13,185
Woodpulp	1,000 tons	5,905	8,261	6,409	6,413	6,606	6,831	7,790	7,519	8,265
Plywood	Mil. sq. ft. [5]	1,766	1,517	754	568	749	501	621	473	418

– Represents zero. NA Not available. [1] Customs value of imports; see text, Section 28. [2] Includes railroad ties. [3] Log scale. [4] Includes paper and board products. Excludes hardboard. [5] 3/8 inch basis.

Source: U.S. Forest Service, *U.S. Timber Production, Trade, Consumption, and Price Statistics*, Research Paper RP-FPL-637, and unpublished data. See also <http://www.treesearch.fs.fed.us/pubs/28972>.

Table 902. Lumber Consumption by Species Group and End Use: 1995 to 2010

[In billion board feet (59.3 represents 59,300,000,000), except per capita in board feet. Per capita consumption based on estimated resident population as of July 1]

Item	1995	2000	2002	2003	2004	2005	2006	2007	2008	2009	2010
Consumption, total	**59.3**	**66.1**	**67.5**	**67.0**	**73.1**	**75.6**	**71.3**	**62.7**	**49.7**	**40.3**	**39.6**
Per capita	225	240	235	230	249	255	238	208	163	131	129
SPECIES GROUP											
Softwoods	47.6	54.0	56.4	56.5	62.0	64.4	60.4	52.6	40.7	31.2	33.1
Hardwoods	11.7	12.2	11.1	10.5	11.1	11.2	10.9	10.2	9.0	9.1	6.5
END USE											
New housing	18.1	21.1	22.5	24.0	25.4	27.7	23.8	17.5	11.2	(NA)	(NA)
Residential upkeep and improvements	15.0	15.3	16.4	16.2	17.6	18.3	18.6	17.8	16.1	(NA)	(NA)
New nonresidential construction [1]	4.7	5.5	4.8	4.4	4.5	4.7	5.2	4.9	5.2	(NA)	(NA)
Shipping	6.9	7.6	7.1	7.0	7.7	8.1	8.6	7.9	6.8	(NA)	(NA)
Other [2]	7.2	8.7	9.9	9.8	13.2	11.3	9.8	10.0	6.0	(NA)	(NA)

NA Not available. [1] In addition to new construction, includes railroad ties laid as replacements in existing track and lumber used by railroads for railcar repair. [2] Includes upkeep and improvement of nonresidential buildings and structures; made-at-home projects, such as furniture, boats, and picnic tables; made-on-the-job items such as advertising and display structures; and miscellaneous products and uses.

Source: U.S. Forest Service, *U.S. Timber Production, Trade, Consumption, and Price Statistics*, Research Paper RP-FPL-637, and unpublished data. See also <http://www.treesearch.fs.fed.us/pubs/28972>.

Table 903. Selected Species—Stumpage Prices in Current and Constant (1996) Dollars: 2000 to 2010

[In dollars per 1,000 board feet. Stumpage prices are based on sales of sawtimber from national forests]

Species	Current dollars				Constant (1996) dollars [1]			
	2000	2005	2009	2010	2000	2005	2009	2010
Softwoods:								
Douglas fir [2]	433	321	(NA)	(NA)	397	260	(NA)	(NA)
Southern pine [3]	258	193	105	105	237	157	71	70
Sugar pine [4]	187	114	63	100	172	93	46	50
Ponderosa pine [4,5]	155	103	38	30	142	84	25	22
Western hemlock [6]	46	70	(NA)	(NA)	42	57	(NA)	(NA)
Hardwoods:								
All eastern hardwoods [7]	341	415	(NA)	(NA)	313	337	(NA)	(NA)
Oak, white, red, and black [7]	258	329	(NA)	(NA)	237	267	(NA)	(NA)
Maple, sugar [8]	314	648	(NA)	(NA)	288	526	(NA)	(NA)

NA Not available. [1] Deflated by the producer price index, all commodities. [2] Western Washington and western Oregon. [3] Southern region. [4] Pacific Southwest region (formerly California region). [5] Includes Jeffrey pine. [6] Pacific Northwest region. [7] Eastern and Southern regions. [8] Eastern region.

Source: U.S. Forest Service, "RPA Assessment Tables," <http://www.fs.fed.us/research/rpa/>.

Table 904. Selected Timber Products—Producer Price Indexes: 1990 to 2011

[1982 = 100. For information about producer prices, see text, Section 14]

Product	1990	1995	2000	2005	2007	2008	2009	2010	2011
Lumber and wood products [1]	**129.7**	**178.1**	**178.2**	**196.5**	**192.4**	**191.3**	**182.8**	**192.7**	**194.7**
Lumber	124.6	173.4	178.8	198.6	174.7	163.5	149.4	167.3	166.6
Softwood lumber	123.8	178.5	178.6	203.6	170.5	156.3	141.4	160.8	160.5
Hardwood lumber	131.0	167.0	185.9	196.6	192.4	184.5	171.2	187.3	185.8
Millwork [1]	130.4	163.8	176.4	197.2	201.4	204.8	205.4	207.0	210.1
General millwork	132.0	165.4	178.0	196.1	203.9	207.7	210.3	211.2	214.2
Prefabricated structural members	122.3	163.5	175.1	206.9	189.5	189.0	181.1	185.6	189.4
Plywood	114.2	165.3	157.6	186.8	176.1	174.7	163.7	176.7	171.3
Softwood plywood	119.6	188.1	173.3	223.5	197.8	193.1	171.9	197.1	185.8
Hardwood plywood and related products	102.7	122.2	130.2	138.1	(NA)	(NA)	(NA)	(NA)	(NA)
Other wood products [1]	114.7	143.7	130.5	139.2	142.1	144.7	141.8	142.5	144.1
Boxes	119.1	145.0	155.2	164.9	170.3	174.6	176.5	183.0	191.1
Pulp, paper, and allied products [1]	**141.2**	**172.2**	**183.7**	**202.6**	**216.9**	**226.8**	**225.6**	**236.9**	**245.1**
Pulp, paper, and prod., excl. bldg. paper [1]	132.9	163.4	161.4	169.8	186.7	199.1	194.1	206.8	216.0
Woodpulp	151.3	183.2	145.3	138.0	161.5	171.4	150.2	186.0	194.8
Wastepaper	138.9	371.1	282.5	230.9	368.7	372.5	237.0	421.5	482.5
Paper [1]	128.8	159.0	149.8	159.6	169.3	184.3	179.6	182.1	191.2
Writing and printing papers	129.1	158.4	146.6	156.1	166.7	181.6	180.5	179.5	185.8
Newsprint	119.6	161.8	127.5	138.5	131.6	148.0	126.4	125.6	137.2
Paperboard	135.7	183.1	176.7	175.5	201.7	217.9	207.2	224.9	230.5
Converted paper and paperboard products [1]	135.2	157.0	162.7	176.1	187.8	199.2	202.9	209.0	216.6
Office supplies and accessories	121.4	134.9	133.8	143.1	151.0	158.3	158.9	159.9	164.7
Building paper & building board mill prods	112.2	144.9	138.8	184.9	155.2	163.9	156.5	168.4	163.6

NA Not available. [1] Includes other products not shown separately.

Source: U.S. Bureau of Labor Statistics, *Producer Price Indexes*, <http://www.bls.gov/ppi/>.

Table 905. Pulpwood Consumption, Woodpulp Production, and Paper and Board Production and Consumption: 1995 to 2010

[Revised to match data from American Forest and Paper Association and American Pulpwood Association]

Item	Unit	1995	2000	2004	2005	2006	2007	2008	2009	2010
Pulpwood consumption [1]	1,000 cords [2]	97,052	95,904	87,110	88,595	86,284	84,076	77,442	70,401	72,321
Woodpulp production [3]	1,000 tons	67,103	62,758	54,301	60,267	60,568	56,636	52,899	44,990	52,607
Paper and board: [4]										
Production	1,000 tons	89,509	94,491	83,612	91,031	91,800	91,570	87,619	71,219	82,469
Consumption or new supply [5]	1,000 tons	96,126	103,147	95,068	101,864	102,948	99,825	93,640	79,141	84,968
Per capita	Pounds	731	731	627	687	688	661	613	515	548

[1] Includes changes in stocks. [2] One cord equals 128 cubic feet. [3] Excludes defibrated and exploded woodpulp used for hard pressed board. [4] Excludes hardboard. [5] Production plus imports, minus exports (excludes products); changes in inventories not taken into account.

Source: U.S. Forest Service, *U.S. Timber Production, Trade, Consumption and Price Statistics*, Research Paper FP-FPL-637, and unpublished data. See also <http://www.treesearch.fs.fed.us/>.

Table 906. Paper and Paperboard—Production and New Supply: 1990 to 2011

[In millions of short tons (80.55 represents 80,550,000). 1 short ton = 2,000 lbs]

Item	1990	1995	2000	2005	2007	2008	2009	2010	2011
Production, total	**80.55**	**91.21**	**96.05**	**92.61**	**92.96**	**88.45**	**79.06**	**83.70**	**82.73**
Paper, total	39.36	42.90	45.52	41.40	41.27	38.96	33.81	35.51	34.34
Paperboard, total	39.42	46.55	48.97	49.71	50.40	48.45	44.49	47.46	47.66
Unbleached kraft	20.36	22.73	21.80	22.58	23.54	22.17	20.55	21.36	21.62
Semichemical	5.64	5.67	5.95	6.41	6.16	5.82	5.21	5.44	5.43
Bleached kraft	4.26	5.16	5.30	5.58	5.72	5.69	5.29	5.62	5.52
Recycled	9.03	12.84	15.79	15.06	14.89	14.69	13.44	15.05	15.12
Wet machine board and Construction grades	1.82	1.82	1.56	1.50	1.29	1.04	0.76	0.73	0.72
New supply, all grades, excluding products	**87.68**	**98.08**	**105.02**	**101.81**	**98.85**	**91.99**	**80.36**	**84.16**	**82.48**
Paper, total	49.49	52.77	57.13	53.69	50.88	46.71	39.37	40.34	38.50
Newsprint	13.41	12.76	12.92	10.12	8.35	7.25	5.26	5.00	4.57
Printing/writing papers	25.46	29.55	32.99	31.99	31.05	28.06	23.03	23.73	22.46
Packaging and ind. conv. papers	4.72	4.24	4.27	4.05	4.07	4.05	3.66	4.18	4.00
Tissue	5.90	6.22	6.95	7.54	7.42	7.36	7.43	7.43	7.48
Paperboard, total	36.30	43.39	46.02	46.51	46.61	44.25	40.19	43.06	43.22

Source: American Forest and Paper Association, Washington, DC, *Annual Statistics of Paper, Paperboard and Wood Pulp*, (copyright).

Table 907. Fishery Products—Domestic Catch, Imports, and Disposition: 1990 to 2010

[Live weight, in millions of pounds (16,349 represents 16,349,000,000)]

Item	1990	1995	2000	2005	2006	2007	2008	2009	2010
Total	**16,349**	**16,484**	**17,340**	**20,612**	**20,960**	**20,561**	**19,199**	**18,899**	**19,748**
For human food	12,662	13,584	14,738	18,147	18,594	18,253	17,037	16,637	17,560
For industrial use	3,687	2,900	2,599	2,382	2,366	2,308	2,163	2,262	2,188
Domestic catch	**9,404**	**9,788**	**9,069**	**9,707**	**9,483**	**9,309**	**8,325**	**8,031**	**8,232**
For human food	7,041	7,667	6,912	7,997	7,842	7,490	6,633	6,198	6,526
For industrial use	2,363	2,121	2,157	1,710	1,641	1,819	1,692	1,833	1,705
Imports [1]	**6,945**	**6,696**	**8,271**	**10,905**	**11,477**	**11,252**	**10,874**	**10,868**	**11,517**
For human food	5,621	5,917	7,828	10,158	10,752	10,763	10,404	10,439	11,034
For industrial use [2]	1,324	779	443	747	725	489	471	430	483
Exports [1]	**4,627**	**5,166**	**5,758**	**8,420**	**7,710**	**7,057**	**6,353**	**5,738**	**6,129**
For human food	3,832	4,175	4,587	6,385	6,250	5,761	5,253	4,760	5,170
For industrial use [2]	795	991	1,171	2,035	1,459	1,296	1,100	978	959
Disposition of domestic catch	**9,404**	**9,788**	**9,069**	**9,707**	**9,483**	**9,309**	**8,325**	**8,031**	**8,231**
Fresh and frozen	6,501	7,099	6,657	7,776	7,627	7,450	6,538	6,204	6,515
Canned	751	769	530	563	573	514	336	392	373
Cured	126	90	119	160	117	121	138	103	102
Reduced to meal, oil, etc.	2,026	1,830	1,763	1,208	1,166	1,224	1,313	1,332	1,241

[1] Excludes imports of edible fishery products consumed in Puerto Rico; includes landings of tuna caught by foreign vessels in American Samoa. [2] Processed into meal, oil, solubles, and shell products, or used as bait and animal food.

Source: U.S. National Oceanic and Atmospheric Administration, National Marine Fisheries Service, *Fisheries of the United States*, annual, August 2011. See also <http://www.st.nmfs.noaa.gov/st1/publications.html>.

Table 908. Fisheries—Quantity and Value of Domestic Catch: 1980 to 2010

[In millions of pounds (6,482 represents 6,482,000,000), except as noted]

Year	Quantity (mil. lbs. [1])			Value (mil. dol.)	Average price per lb. (cents)	Year	Quantity (mil. lbs. [1])			Value (mil. dol.)	Average price per lb. (cents)
	Total	For human food	For industrial products [2]				Total	For human food	For industrial products [2]		
1980	6,482	3,654	2,828	2,237	34.5	2003	9,507	7,521	1,986	3,347	35.2
1985	6,258	3,294	2,964	2,326	37.2	2004	9,683	7,794	1,889	3,756	38.8
1990	9,404	7,041	2,363	3,522	37.5	2005	9,707	7,997	1,710	3,942	40.6
1995	9,788	7,667	2,121	3,770	38.5	2006	9,483	7,842	1,641	4,024	42.4
1999	9,339	6,832	2,507	3,467	37.1	2007	9,309	7,490	1,819	4,192	45.0
2000	9,069	6,912	2,157	3,550	39.1	2008	8,325	6,633	1,692	4,383	52.6
2001	9,489	7,311	2,178	3,218	33.9	2009	8,031	6,198	1,833	3,891	48.4
2002	9,397	7,205	2,192	3,092	32.9	2010	8,231	6,526	1,705	4,520	54.9

[1] Live weight. [2] Meal, oil, solubles, shell products, bait, and animal food.

Source: U.S. National Oceanic and Atmospheric Administration, National Marine Fisheries Service, *Fisheries of the United States*, annual, August 2011. See also <http://www.st.nmfs.noaa.gov/st1/publications.htm>.

Table 909. Domestic Fish and Shellfish Catch and Value by Major Species Caught: 2000 to 2010

[In thousands (9,068,985 represents 9,068,985,000)]

Species	Quantity (1,000 lbs.)				Value ($1,000)			
	2000	2005	2009	2010	2000	2005	2009	2010
Total [1]	**9,068,985**	**9,707,275**	**8,030,703**	**8,230,587**	**3,549,481**	**3,942,376**	**3,891,028**	**4,519,510**
Fish, total [1]	**7,689,661**	**8,462,473**	**6,765,220**	**6,918,013**	**1,594,815**	**1,836,448**	**1,852,658**	**2,155,953**
Cod: Atlantic	25,060	13,920	19,708	17,714	26,384	20,828	25,220	28,119
Pacific	530,505	548,746	491,143	539,635	142,330	150,738	133,714	146,941
Flounder	412,723	419,430	575,119	624,358	109,910	135,176	153,261	146,243
Halibut	75,190	76,263	59,716	56,497	143,826	177,593	139,415	206,553
Herring, Atlantic	160,269	215,565	224,328	144,513	9,972	20,467	26,564	21,275
Herring, Pacific	74,835	87,295	88,723	108,868	12,043	13,799	29,759	23,308
Menhaden	1,760,498	1,243,723	1,404,259	1,471,803	112,403	62,465	97,887	107,193
Pollock, Alaska	2,606,802	3,411,307	1,866,203	1,947,580	160,525	306,972	270,597	282,399
Salmon	628,638	899,457	705,202	787,740	270,213	330,699	370,052	554,816
Tuna	50,779	44,316	49,064	48,047	95,176	85,922	96,434	108,453
Whiting (Atlantic, silver)	26,855	16,561	17,131	17,564	11,370	8,284	8,659	10,862
Whiting (Pacific, hake)	452,718	569,381	253,062	355,272	18,809	29,145	14,105	27,316
Shellfish, total [1]	**1,379,324**	**1,244,802**	**1,227,646**	**1,276,366**	**1,954,666**	**2,105,928**	**2,015,992**	**2,341,902**
Clams	118,482	105,640	101,137	88,891	153,973	173,655	191,074	200,657
Crabs	299,006	299,137	326,217	349,604	405,006	415,057	485,372	572,797
Lobsters: American	83,180	88,032	96,890	115,433	301,300	416,597	299,512	396,757
Oysters	41,146	33,963	35,571	28,080	90,667	110,679	136,493	117,590
Scallops, sea	32,747	56,702	58,000	57,454	164,609	433,512	382,217	455,088
Shrimp	332,486	260,884	301,077	258,972	690,453	406,344	370,240	413,980
Squid, Pacific	259,508	126,107	203,661	286,403	27,077	31,601	56,450	70,706

[1] Includes other species not shown separately.

Source: U.S. National Oceanic and Atmospheric Administration, National Marine Fisheries Service, *Fisheries of the United States*, annual, August 2011. See also <http://www.st.nmfs.noaa.gov/st1/fus/fus10/index.html>.

Table 910. U.S. Private Aquaculture—Trout and Catfish Production and Value: 1990 to 2011

[67.8 represents 67,800,000. Data are for calendar year and foodsize fish (those over 12 inches long)]

Item	Unit	1990	1995	2000	2005	2008	2009	2010	2011
TROUT FOODSIZE									
Number sold...........................	Mil.	67.8	60.2	58.4	55.6	40.4	40.8	38.7	38.4
Total weight...........................	Mil. lb.	56.8	55.6	59.0	59.9	52.4	48.7	45.3	45.4
Total value of sales..................	Mil. dol.	64.6	60.8	63.3	63.5	72.4	67.2	63.2	69.5
Avg. price received by processors..........................	Dol./lb.	1.14	1.09	1.07	1.06	1.38	1.38	1.40	1.53
Percent sold to processors...........	Percent	58	68	70	66	58	63	63	48
CATFISH FOODSIZE									
Number sold...........................	Mil.	272.9	321.8	420.1	395.6	304.0	266.3	263.4	202.1
Total weight...........................	Mil. lb.	392.4	481.5	633.8	605.5	514.9	476.0	478.9	348.2
Total value of sales...................	Mil. dol.	305.1	378.1	468.8	427.8	389.3	352.0	375.1	391.0
Avg. price received by processors....	Dol./lb.	0.78	0.79	0.74	0.71	0.76	0.74	0.78	1.1
Fish sold to processors...............	Mil. lb.	360.4	446.9	593.6	600.7	509.6	466.1	471.7	334.1
Avg. price paid by processors........	Cents/lb.	75.8	78.6	75.1	72.5	78.0	77.1	80.2	117.7
Processor sales.......................	Mil. lb.	183.1	227.0	297.2	300.0	251.2	229.2	231.6	167.2
Avg. price received by processors..........................	Dol./lb.	2.24	2.40	2.36	2.29	2.44	2.53	2.51	3.43
Inventory (Jan. 1).....................	Mil. lb.	9.4	10.9	13.6	13.7	15.5	14.5	12.3	12.9

Source: U.S. Department of Agriculture, National Agricultural Statistics Service, *Trout Production*, February 2012; *Catfish Production*, January 2012; and *Catfish Processing*, August 2012. See also <http://www.nass.usda.gov/Publications/index.asp>. Also in *Agricultural Statistics*, annual.

Table 911. Supply of Selected Fishery Items: 1990 to 2010

[In millions of pounds (734 represents 734,000,000). Totals available for U.S. consumption are supply minus exports plus imports. Round weight is the complete or full weight as caught]

Species	Unit	1990	1995	2000	2005	2006	2007	2008	2009	2010
Shrimp...........................	Heads-off weight	734	832	1,173	1,559	1,879	1,743	1,722	1,746	1,731
Tuna, canned..................	Canned weight	856	875	980	895	858	812	848	762	834
Snow crab......................	Round weight	37	42	122	171	187	208	197	224	197
Clams...........................	Meat weight	152	144	133	120	125	127	121	116	105
Salmon, canned...............	Canned weight	148	147	95	123	56	51	26	67	73
American lobster..............	Round weight	95	94	125	144	150	128	144	159	186
Spiny lobster...................	Round weight	89	89	99	83	77	78	83	57	58
Scallops.........................	Meat weight	74	62	78	86	94	92	88	90	85
Sardines, canned..............	Canned weight	61	44	(NA)	(NA)	(NA)	(NA)	(NA)	(NA)	(NA)
Oysters.........................	Meat weight	56	63	71	65	65	70	54	59	57
King crab.......................	Round weight	19	21	41	78	110	134	71	62	44
Crab meat, canned............	Canned weight	9	12	29	59	58	66	68	59	66

NA Not available.

Source: U.S. National Oceanic and Atmospheric Administration, National Marine Fisheries Service, *Fisheries of the United States*, annual, August, 2011. See also <http://www.st.nmfs.noaa.gov/st1/fus/fus10/index.html>.

Table 912. Canned, Fresh, and Frozen Fishery Products—Production and Value: 1990 to 2010

[In millions of pounds (1,178 represents 1,178,000,000). Fresh fishery products exclude Alaska and Hawaii. Canned fishery products data are for natural pack only]

Product	Production (mil. lbs.)					Value (mil. dol.)				
	1990	2000	2005	2009	2010	1990	2000	2005	2009	2010
Canned, total......................	**1,178**	**1,747**	**1,082**	**934**	**954**	**1,562**	**1,626**	**1,211**	**1,408**	**1411**
Tuna.................................	581	671	446	369	395	902	856	628	756	724
Salmon..............................	196	171	219	142	146	366	288	301	322	356
Clam products......................	110	127	123	100	109	76	120	127	89	97
Sardines, Maine....................	13	(Z)	(NA)	(NA)	(NA)	17	(Z)	(NA)	(NA)	(NA)
Shrimp..............................	1	2	1	[1](D)	[1](D)	3	11	3	[1](D)	[1](D)
Crabs...............................	1	(Z)	(Z)	(Z)	(Z)	4	(Z)	(Z)	(Z)	(Z)
Oysters [2].........................	1	(Z)	(Z)	(Z)	(Z)	1	1	(Z)	(Z)	(Z)
Other...............................	275	776	293	323	304	193	350	152	241	234
Fish fillets and steaks [3]........	**441**	**368**	**615**	**511**	**579**	**843**	**823**	**1,136**	**1,223**	**1449**
Cod..................................	65	56	47	36	50	132	167	116	102	135
Flounder............................	54	27	20	18	33	154	71	65	57	56
Haddock............................	7	6	24	14	23	24	24	89	60	89
Ocean perch, Atlantic..............	1	(Z)	1	1	1	1	1	4	3	4
Rockfish............................	33	11	3	3	2	53	25	8	6	6
Pollock, Atlantic....................	12	2	3	3	2	21	4	6	8	7
Pollock, Alaska.....................	164	160	383	277	290	174	178	404	341	368
Other...............................	105	106	134	159	178	284	353	444	646	784

D Figure withheld to avoid disclosure pertaining to a specific organization or individual. NA Not available. Z Less than 500,000 pounds or $500,000. [1] Included with "other." [2] Includes oyster specialties. [3] Fresh and frozen.

Source: U.S. National Oceanic and Atmospheric Administration, National Marine Fisheries Service, *Fisheries of the United States*, annual, August 2011. See also <http://www.st.nmfs.noaa.gov/st1/fus/fus10/index.html>.

Table 913. Mineral Industries—Employment, Hours, and Earnings: 1990 to 2011

[In thousands (680 represents 680,000), except as noted. Based on the Current Employment Statistics Program, see Appendix III]

Industry and item	Unit	1990	1995	2000	2005	2008	2009	2010	2011
All mining: [1]									
All employees...............	1,000	680	558	520	562	710	643	655	735
Production workers.................	1,000	469	391	383	419	526	466	483	549
Avg. weekly hours.............	Number	46.1	46.8	45.5	46.4	45.3	43.5	44.8	47.1
Avg. weekly earnings.............	Dollars	630	711	771	884	1,043	1,037	1,086	1,170
Oil and gas extraction:									
All employees...............	1,000	190	152	125	126	161	160	159	174
Production workers.................	1,000	84	73	67	72	89	85	89	98
Avg. weekly hours.............	Number	44.4	43.6	41.3	44.3	41.1	40.6	39.0	43.3
Avg. weekly earnings.............	Dollars	591	677	802	856	1,120	1,119	1,066	1,179
Coal mining:									
All employees...............	1,000	136	97	72	74	81	82	81	86
Production workers.................	1,000	110	78	59	61	71	71	70	77
Avg. weekly hours.............	Number	44.7	45.7	45.6	48.5	49.0	47.8	48.4	49.3
Avg. weekly earnings.............	Dollars	822	929	945	1,071	1,140	1,249	1,366	1,403
Metal ore mining:									
All employees...............	1,000	53	48	38	29	40	35	37	42
Production workers.................	1,000	43	39	29	22	32	28	28	(NA)
Avg. weekly hours.............	Number	42.5	43.4	43.4	44.2	46.1	42.3	42.5	(NA)
Avg. weekly earnings.............	Dollars	646	788	871	1,001	1,195	1,095	1,158	(NA)
Nonmetallic minerals mining, and quarrying:									
All employees...............	1,000	113	108	115	110	105	92	87	89
Production workers.................	1,000	85	81	87	84	79	71	65	(NA)
Avg. weekly hours.............	Number	45.0	46.3	46.1	45.9	43.9	41.9	43.8	(NA)
Avg. weekly earnings.............	Dollars	532	632	722	830	839	808	848	(NA)

NA Not available. [1] Includes other industries not shown separately.

Source: U.S. Bureau of Labor Statistics, Current Employment Statistics, "Employment, Hours, and Earnings—National," <http://www.bls.gov/ces/home.htm\>, accessed August 2012.

Table 914. Mine Safety: 2000 to 2011

[Reported injury rates per 200,000 employee hours]

Item	All Mines			Coal			Metal and non-metal		
	2000	2010	2011 [1]	2000	2010	2011 [1]	2000	2010 [1]	2011 [1]
Number of mines...........................	14,413	14,283	14,176	2,124	1,944	1,973	12,289	12,339	12,203
Number of miners........................	348,548	361,176	381,209	108,098	135,500	143,437	240,450	225,676	237,772
Fatalities..............................	85	71	37	38	48	21	47	23	16
Fatal injury rate.......................	0.03	0.02	0.01	0.04	0.04	0.02	0.02	0.01	0.01
All injury rate.........................	5.13	2.81	2.73	6.64	3.43	3.38	4.45	2.37	2.28
Coal production (mil. tons)...............	1,078	1,086	1,095	1,078	1,086	1,095	(X)	(X)	(X)
Total mining area inspection hours/mine..............................	57	63	62	178	259	258	28	23	23
Citations and orders.....................	120,269	170,909	157,613	58,394	96,814	93,630	61,875	74,095	63,983
S&S [2] citations and orders (percent).....	36	33	32	42	34	35	31	33	28
Amount assessed [3] (mil. dol.)............	24.7	162.1	154.3	12.0	110.1	115.1	12.7	52.0	39.2

X Not applicable. [1] Preliminary. [2] A violation that "significantly and substantially" contributes to the cause and effect of a coal or other mine safety or health hazard. [3] Government penalties or fines.

Source: U.S. Mine Safety and Health Administration, Office of Program Education and Outreach Services, "Mine Safety and Health At a Glance," July 2012, <http://www.msha.gov/MSHAINFO/FactSheets/MSHAFCT10.HTM>.

Table 915. Mining and Primary Metal Production Indexes: 1990 to 2011

[Index 2007 = 100]

Industry group	NAICS [1] code	1990	1995	2000	2005	2007	2008	2009	2010	2011
Mining [2]........................	**21**	**106.4**	**104.0**	**102.9**	**97.0**	**100.0**	**101.0**	**95.8**	**100.7**	**107.0**
Oil and gas extraction [2]...............	211	113.8	110.3	107.0	97.8	100.0	100.9	106.5	109.8	116.4
Crude oil and natural gas.............	211111	115.9	111.2	106.9	97.9	100.0	100.9	106.5	109.5	116.2
Coal mining............................	2121	95.2	93.7	96.1	99.3	100.0	102.0	93.5	93.9	93.6
Metal ore mining......................	2122	110.1	120.4	117.3	100.5	100.0	103.0	90.4	96.4	98.7
Iron ore..............................	21221	107.9	119.7	120.1	103.4	100.0	102.1	50.0	94.5	102.4
Gold ore and silver ore...............	21222	124.4	133.1	148.3	107.2	100.0	97.9	93.8	97.1	98.3
Copper, nickel, lead, and zinc........	21223	119.1	136.5	119.8	96.7	100.0	108.3	98.7	93.9	94.7
Oil and gas drilling...................	213111	60.1	52.6	67.2	83.7	100.0	104.4	61.4	82.3	99.2
Primary metal manufacturing [2]........	**331**	**87.1**	**95.6**	**100.3**	**95.2**	**100.0**	**100.0**	**74.0**	**90.8**	**96.8**
Iron and steel........................	3311	83.9	93.3	97.3	94.3	100.0	106.4	68.5	89.0	97.1
Aluminum.............................	3313	102.0	97.9	103.6	106.9	100.0	92.6	75.8	90.2	96.4
Nonferrous metals [2]...................	3314	88.8	98.9	91.7	84.2	100.0	102.6	93.9	112.5	109.9

[1] Based on the 2007 North American Industry Classification System (NAICS). [2] Includes other industries not shown separately.

Source: Board of Governors of the Federal Reserve System, *Industrial Production and Capacity Utilization*, Statistical Release G.17, <http://www.federalreserve.gov/datadownload/default.htm>, accessed July 2012.

Table 916. Mineral Production: 1990 to 2011

[1,029.1 represents 1,029,100,000. Data represent production as measured by mine shipments, mine sales, or marketable production; see Appendix IV]

Minerals and metals	Unit	1990	2000	2009	2010	2011, est.
FUEL MINERALS						
Coal, total [1]	Mil. sh. tons	1,029.1	1,073.6	1,074.9	1,084.4	1,094.3
Bituminous [1]	Mil. sh. tons	693.2	574.3	504.1	489.5	500.5
Subbituminous	Mil. sh. tons	244.3	409.2	496.4	514.8	510.5
Lignite	Mil. sh. tons	88.1	85.6	72.5	78.2	81.0
Anthracite [1]	Mil. sh. tons	3.5	4.6	1.9	1.8	2.3
Natural gas (marketed production)	Tril. cu. ft.	18.59	20.20	21.65	22.40	24.2
Petroleum (crude)	Mil. bbl. [2]	2,685	2,131	1,957	1,999	2,067
Uranium (recoverable content)	Mil. lb.	8.9	4.0	3.7	4.2	4.0
NONFUEL MINERALS						
Asbestos (sales)	1,000 metric tons	(D)	5	–	–	–
Barite, primary, sold/used by producers	1,000 metric tons	430	392	383	662	640
Boron minerals, sold or used by producers	1,000 metric tons	1,090	1,070	(D)	(D)	(D)
Bromine, sold or used by producers	1,000 metric tons	177	228	(D)	(D)	(D)
Cement (excludes Puerto Rico):						
Portland [3, 16]	Mil. metric tons	67	84	62	61	66
Masonry [3, 16]	Mil. metric tons	3	4	2	2	2
Clays	1,000 metric tons	42,900	40,800	24,500	25,300	25,900
Diatomite	1,000 metric tons	631	677	575	595	600
Feldspar [4]	1,000 metric tons	630	790	550	670	690
Fluorspar, finished shipments	1,000 metric tons	64	–	(NA)	(NA)	(NA)
Garnet (industrial)	1,000 metric tons	47	60	46	53	53
Gypsum, crude	Mil. metric tons	15	20	10	9	9
Helium [5]	Mil. cu. meters	65	98	78	75	83
Lime, sold or used by producers	Mil. metric tons	16	20	16	18	19
Mica, scrap/flake, sold/used by producers	1,000 metric tons	109	101	51	53	64
Peat, sales by producers	1,000 metric tons	721	847	644	605	525
Perlite, processed, sold or used	1,000 metric tons	576	672	348	414	400
Phosphate rock (marketable)	Mil. metric tons	46	39	26	26	28
Potash (K2O equivalent) sales	1,000 metric tons	1,710	1,300	720	930	1,100
Pumice & pumicite, producer sales	1,000 metric tons	443	1,050	410	390	380
Salt, common, sold/used by producers	Mil. metric tons	37	46	43	44	44
Sand & gravel, sold/used by producer:	Mil. metric tons	855	1,148	861	790	820
Construction	Mil. metric tons	829	1,120	836	760	790
Industrial	Mil. metric tons	26	28	25	30	30
Silica, sales [6]	Metric tons	(NA)	312	(D)	(D)	(D)
Sodium carbonate (natural, soda ash)	1,000 metric tons	9,100	10,200	9,310	10,600	10,700
Sodium sulfate (natural and synthetic)	1,000 metric tons	349	(NA)	260	297	300
Stone: [7]	Mil. metric tons	2,230	2,810	2,780	2,830	2,750
Crushed and broken	Mil. metric tons	1,110	1,560	1,160	1,160	1,110
Dimension [8]	1,000 metric tons	1,120	1,250	1,620	1,670	1,640
Sulfur: Total shipments	1,000 metric tons	11,500	10,700	8,860	9,140	8,800
Sulfur: Frasch mines (shipments)	1,000 metric tons	3,680	900	–	–	–
Talc and pyrophyllite, crude [9]	1,000 metric tons	1,270	851	511	604	615
Vermiculite concentrate	1,000 metric tons	209	150	100	100	100
METALS						
Antimony ore and concentrate	Metric tons	(D)	(D)	–	–	–
Aluminum	1,000 metric tons	4,048	3,668	1,727	1,726	1,990
Bauxite (dried)	1,000 metric tons	(D)	(NA)	(NA)	(NA)	(NA)
Copper (recoverable content)	1,000 metric tons	1,590	1,450	1,180	1,110	1,120
Gold (recoverable content)	Metric tons	294	353	223	231	237
Iron ore (gross weight) [10]	Mil. metric tons	57	61	27	50	54
Lead (recoverable content)	1,000 metric tons	484	449	406	369	345
Magnesium metal	1,000 metric tons	139	(D)	(D)	(D)	(D)
Manganiferous ore (gross weight) [11]	1,000 metric ton	(D)	–	–	–	–
Mercury [12]	Metric tons	(NA)	(NA)	(NA)	(NA)	(NA)
Molybdenum (concentrate)	1,000 metric tons	62	41	48	59	64
Nickel ore (recovered Ni content)	1,000 metric tons	330	–	–	–	–
Palladium metal	Kilograms	5,930	10,300	12,700	11,600	12,500
Platinum metal	Kilograms	1,810	3,110	3,830	3,450	3,700
Silicon (Si content) [13]	1,000 metric tons	418	367	139	176	(D)
Silver (recoverable content)	Metric tons	2,120	1,860	1,250	1,270	1,160
Titanium concentrate, (TiO2 content) [14]	1,000 metric tons	(D)	300	200	200	300
Tungsten ore and concentrate [15]	Metric tons	(D)	–	(D)	(D)	(D)
Vanadium (recoverable content)	Metric tons	2,310	–	(D)	(D)	(D)
Zinc (recoverable content)	1,000 metric tons	508	796	736	748	760

D Withheld to avoid disclosing individual company data. NA Not available. [1] Included with bituminous. [2] 42-gal. bbl. [3] Excludes Puerto Rico. [4] Excludes attapulgite. [5] Beginning 1995, includes aplite. [6] Refined. [7] Includes grindstones, oilstones, whetstones, and deburring media. Excludes grinding pebbles and tubemill liners. [8] Includes Puerto Rico. [9] Includes only talc after 1990. [10] Represents shipments; includes byproduct ores. [11] From 5 to 35 percent manganiferous ore. [12] Mercury recovered as a byproduct of gold ores only, 1995. [13] 2006–2011 ferrosilicon only; silicon metal withheld to avoid disclosing proprietary data. [14] U.S. production rounded to one significant digit. [15] Content of ore and concentrate. [16] Data for 2010 and 2011 are estimates.

Source: Nonfuels, through 1994, U.S. Bureau of Mines, thereafter, U.S. Geological Survey, *Minerals Yearbook* and *Mineral Commodity Summaries*, annual, and *Historical Statistics for Mineral Commodities in the United States*; fuels, U.S. Energy Information Administration, *Annual Energy Review*. See also <http://www.eia.gov/totalenergy/data/annual/index.cfm>.

Table 917. Nonfuel Mineral Commodities—Summary: 2011

[1,990 represents 1,990,000. Preliminary estimates. Average price in dollars per metric tons except as noted. < = Less than]

Mineral	Unit	Mineral disposition				Average price per unit (dollars)	Employ-ment (number)
		Produc-tion	Exports	Net import reliance [1,2] (percent)	Con-sumption, apparent		
Aluminum	1,000 metric tons	1,990	3,350	13	3,900	[4] 1.2	30,000
Antimony (contained)	Metric tons	[5] _	2,350	87	26,600	[4] 6.85	15
Asbestos	1,000 metric tons	–	60	100	1,100	[6] 940	(NA)
Barite	1,000 metric tons	640	94	78	2,700	[6] 61	350
Bauxite and alumina (metal equivalent)	1,000 metric tons	(NA)	1,876	100	2,660	[6,7] 31	(NA)
Beryllium (contained)	Metric tons	210	25	21	270	[4] 205	(NA)
Bismuth (contained)	Metric tons	–	500	89	744	[4] 11.6	(NA)
Boron (B2O3 content)	1,000 metric tons	(D)	250	([3,8])	(D)	[6,9] 300	1,200
Bromine (contained)	1,000 metric tons	(D)	7	<25	(D)	[10,11] (NA)	950
Cadmium (contained)	Metric tons	[5] 160	200	60	400	[10,13] 330	(NA)
Cement	1,000 metric tons	[14] 67,700	1,700	6	72,300	[6] 91	12,000
Chromium	1,000 metric tons	[15] 160	200	60	400	[16] 330	(NA)
Clays	1,000 metric tons	[17] 25,900	4,390	([3])	21,900	(NA)	5,010
Cobalt (contained)	Metric tons	[15] 2,200	3,400	75	8,700	[4] 18	(NA)
Copper (mine, recoverable)	1,000 metric tons	1,120	255	[5] 35	1,750	[4] 4.03	10,500
Diamond, stones (industrial)	Million carats	57	–	3	59	[18] 26.7	(NA)
Diatomite	1,000 metric tons	600	120	([3])	490	[6] 300	660
Feldspar	1,000 metric tons	690	10	([3])	680	[6] 63	450
Fluorspar	1,000 metric tons	(NA)	23	100	520	(NA)	(NA)
Garnet (industrial)	Metric tons	53,000	13,700	39	87,500	[6] 50-2,000	160
Gemstones	Million dollars	11.0	20,000	98	1,900	(NA)	1,100
Germanium (contained)	Kilograms	3,000	5,000	90	(NA)	[10] 1,650	100
Gold (contained)	Metric tons	237	470	36	(NA)	[19] 1,600	10,300
Graphite (crude)	1,000 metric tons	–	7	100	63	[6,20] 1,170	(NA)
Gypsum (crude)	1,000 metric tons	9,400	300	13	23,400	[6] 7	4,500
Iodine	Metric tons	(D)	660	99	(D)	[10,21] 27	30
Iron ore (usable)	Million metric tons	[22] 54	10	([3])	48	[6] 120	5,260
Iron and steel scrap (metal)	Million metric tons	84	24	([3])	55	[6,23] 500	30,000
Iron and steel slag (metal)	1,000 metric tons	[24] 17	<0.1	8	16.9	[6] 17	2,100
Lead (contained)	1,000 metric tons	345	285	([3])	1,500	[4] 1.24	3,390
Lime	1,000 metric tons	19,300	230	1	19,600	[6,25] 112	5,000
Magnesium compounds	1,000 metric tons	272	20	53	582	(NA)	300
Magnesium metal	1,000 metric tons	(D)	12	35	110	[4] 2.35	400
Manganese (gross weight)	1,000 metric tons	–	1	100	810	[26] 9.1	(NA)
Mercury	Metric tons	[15] (NA)	200	([3])	(NA)	[27] 1,950	(NA)
Mica, scrap and flake	1,000 metric tons	160	9	20	80	[6] 154	(NA)
Molybdenum (contained)	Metric tons	64,000	33,000	([3])	50,000	[10] 34.9	940
Nickel (contained) [28]	Metric tons	(D)	78,000	47	228,000	[2] 22,800	(NA)
Niobium (contained)	Metric tons	–	430	100	8,800	[6] 41,000	(NA)
Nitrogen (fixed)-ammonia	1,000 metric tons	8,100	22	41	13,800	[6,30] 520	1,050
Peat	1,000 metric tons	605	39	63	1,640	[6] 24.4	610
Perlite	1,000 metric tons	400	40	27	540	[6] 51	92
Phosphate rock	1,000 metric tons	28,400	–	13	(NA)	[6] 94	2,200
Platinum-group metals	Kilograms	[31] 16,200	45,900	[31] 88	[32] (NA)	[19,33] 1,720	1,360
Potash (K2O equivalent)	1,000 metric tons	1,100	5,600	83	6,500	[6,34] 700	1,190
Pumice and pumicite	1,000 metric tons	380	15	5	400	[6] 20.3	145
Salt	1,000 metric tons	44,000	400	22	57,000	[6,35] 180	4,100
Silicon (contained)	1,000 metric tons	[36] (D)	[37] 200	[36] 50	(D)	[39] 110	(NA)
Silver (contained)	Metric tons	1,160	1,000	75	7,850	[17] 34.5	850
Sodium carbonate (soda ash)	1,000 metric tons	10,700	5,500	([3])	5,200	[40] 260	2,400
Sodium sulfate	1,000 metric tons	300	200	([3])	180	[41] 140	225
Stone (crushed)	Million metric tons	1,110	1	1	1,150	[6] 9.48	79,000
Sulfur (all forms)	1,000 metric tons	8,800	1,430	24	11,600	[6,42] 200	2,600
Talc	1,000 metric tons	615	220	([3])	670	[6] 157	300
Thallium (contained)	Kilograms	–	700	100	(NA)	[10] 6,000	(NA)
Tin (contained)	Metric tons	[15] 12,500	6,200	76	42,100	[4] 16.4	(NA)
Titanium dioxide	1,000 metric tons	1,420	815	([3])	785	[6,43] 2,187	3,400
Tungsten (contained)	Metric tons	[15] 10,000	6,950	36	18,200	[44] 250	(NA)
Vermiculite	1,000 metric tons	100	3	20	150	[6] 160	90
Zinc (contained)	1,000 metric tons	760	650	73	924	[4,45] 1.06	2,435
Zirconium (ZrO2)	Metric tons	(D)	15,500	([3])	(D)	[6,46] 2,500	(NA)

– Represents or rounds to zero. D Withheld to avoid disclosing company proprietary data. NA Not available. [1] Data are rounded to no more than three significant digits; except prices. [2] Calculated as a percent of apparent consumption. [3] Net exporter. [4] Dollars per pound. [5] Refinery production. [6] Dollars per metric ton. [7] Bauxite, average value U.S. imports (f.a.s.). [8] Boric acid, gross weight. [9] Granulated pentahydrate borax in bulk, f.o.b mine. [10] Dollars per kilogram. [11] Bulk, purified bromine. [12] Metal only. [13] Average New York dealer price for 99.95% purity in 5-short-ton lots. Source: Platts Metals Week. [14] Excludes Puerto Rico. [15] Secondary production. [16] Unit value of imported chromite ore. Dollars per metric ton gross weight. [17] Excludes attapulgite. [18] Value of imports, dollars per carat. [19] Dollars per troy ounce. [20] Price of flake imports. [21] C.i.f. value, crude, per kilogram. [22] Shipments of usable ore. [23] Delivered, No. 1 Heavy Melting composite price. [24] Sales include imports and reprocessed slag from past years and decades, and only some from current production. [25] Quicklime only. [26] 46%-48% Mn metallurgical ore, per unit contained Mn, c.i.f. U.S. ports. [27] Dollars per 76-pound flask. [28] Primary and secondary materials. [29] London Metal Exchange cash price; dollars per metric ton. [30] F.o.b. Gulf Coast. [31] Platinum and palladium. [32] Platinum. [33] Dealer price of platinum. [34] Price of K2O, muriate. [35] Vacuum and open pan, bulk, pellets and packaged, f.o.b. mine and plant. [36] Silicon metal only. [37] Ferrosilicon statistics include: Production (170,000 t), exports (15,000 t), and net import reliance (44%). [38] Ferrosilicon only. [39] Ferrosilicon, 50% Si; cents per pound. [40] Quoted year-end price, dense, bulk, f.o.b. Green River, WY, dollars per short ton. [41] Quoted price, bulk, f.o.b. works, East, dollars per short ton. [42] Elemental sulfur, f.o.b. plant. [43] Year-end. Unit value based on landed-duty-paid U.S. imports for consumption of pigment with 80% or more TiO2. [44] Dollars per metric ton unit WO3 (7.93 kilograms of contained tungsten per metric ton unit). [45] Platts Metals Week North American price for Special High Grade zinc. [46] Price for domestic zircon.

Source: U.S. Geological Survey, *Mineral Commodity Summaries*, annual, January 2012. See also <http://minerals.er.usgs.gov/minerals/pubs/mcs/>.

Table 918. Selected Mineral Products—Average Prices: 1990 to 2011

[Excludes Alaska and Hawaii, except as noted]

Year	Nonfuels									Fuels		
	Copper, cathode [1] (cents per lb.)	Platinum [2] (dol./troy oz.)	Gold (dol./troy oz. [3])	Silver (dol./troy oz. [3])	Lead [4] (cents per lb.)	Nickel [5] (cents per pound)	Tin (New York) [5] (cents per lb.)	Zinc [6] (cents per lb.)	Sulfur, crude [7] (dol./metric ton)	Bituminous coal [8] (dol./short ton)	Crude petroleum [8] (dol./bbl.)	Natural gas [8] (dol./1,000 cu. ft.)
1990.........	123	467	385	4.82	46	402	386	75	80.14	27.43	20.03	1.71
1995.........	138	425	386	5.15	42	373	416	56	44.46	25.56	14.62	1.55
1998.........	79	375	295	5.54	45	210	373	51	29.14	24.87	10.87	1.96
1999.........	76	379	280	5.25	44	273	366	53	37.81	23.92	15.56	2.19
2000.........	88	549	280	5.00	44	392	370	56	24.73	24.15	26.72	3.69
2001.........	77	533	272	4.39	44	270	315	44	10.01	25.36	21.84	4.12
2002.........	76	543	311	4.62	44	307	292	39	11.84	26.57	22.51	2.95
2003.........	85	694	365	4.91	44	437	340	41	28.70	26.57	27.56	4.98
2004.........	134	849	411	6.69	55	627	547	52	32.62	30.56	36.77	5.46
2005.........	174	900	446	7.34	61	669	483	67	30.88	36.80	50.28	7.33
2006.........	315	1,144	606	11.61	77	1,100	565	159	32.85	39.32	59.69	6.39
2007.........	328	1,308	699	13.43	124	1,688	899	154	36.49	40.80	66.52	6.25
2008.........	319	1,578	874	15.02	120	957	1,130	89	264.04	51.39	94.04	7.96
2009.........	241	1,208	975	14.69	87	665	837	78	1.73	55.44	56.35	3.67
2010.........	348	1,616	1,227	20.20	109	989	1,240	102	70.48	60.88	74.71	4.48
2011.........	405	1,720	1,600	34.50	124	1,030	1,640	106	200	57.64	95.73	3.95

[1] U.S. producer price. [2] Average annual dealer prices. [3] 99.95 percent purity. [4] Nationwide delivered basis. [5] Composite price. [6] Platt's Metals Week price for North American Special High Grade zinc. Average prices for 1990 are for U.S. High Grade Zinc. [7] F.o.b. (Free on Board) works. [8] Average value at the point of production or domestic first purchase price.

Source: Nonfuels, 1990, U.S. Bureau of Mines, thereafter, U.S. Geological Survey, *Minerals Yearbook* and *Mineral Commodities Summaries*, annual. See also <http://minerals.er.usgs.gov/minerals/pubs/mcs/>. Fuels, U.S. Energy Information Administration, *Annual Energy Review*. See also <http://www.eia.gov/totalenergy/data/annual/index.cfm>.

Table 919. Value of Domestic Nonfuel Mineral Production by State: 2000 to 2011

[In millions of dollars (39,400 represents $39,400,000,000)]

State	2000	2010	2011 [1]	State	2000	2010	2011 [1]
United States [2]........	39,400	66,400	74,000				
Alabama....................	930	969	964	Montana...............	596	1,140	1,360
Alaska.....................	1,140	3,400	3,790	Nebraska.............	[3] 84	234	259
Arizona....................	2,510	6,790	8,250	Nevada................	2,980	7,700	10,400
Arkansas..................	484	709	771	New Hampshire.......	57	[3] 94	[3] 79
California..................	3,270	2,890	2,870	New Jersey...........	[3] 291	[3] 258	[3] 221
Colorado...................	592	1,850	1,940	New Mexico...........	786	1,020	1,290
Connecticut................	[3] 112	[3] 148	[3] 125	New York.............	1,020	1,310	1,140
Delaware...................	[3] 14	[3] 12	[3] 74	North Carolina.......	744	880	883
Florida.....................	1,820	2,680	3,270	North Dakota.........	35	[3] 70	[3] 98
Georgia....................	1,620	1,430	1,440	Ohio.................	999	1,170	1,160
Hawaii.....................	392	106	95	Oklahoma.............	473	702	749
Idaho......................	358	1,180	1,290	Oregon...............	299	312	297
Illinois....................	913	924	894	Pennsylvania.........	[3] 1,250	[3] 1,670	1,590
Indiana....................	695	782	772	Rhode Island.........	[3] 20	[3] 33	[3] 28
Iowa.......................	503	583	565	South Carolina.......	[3] 551	[3] 468	[3] 502
Kansas.....................	629	1,090	1,180	South Dakota.........	233	258	320
Kentucky...................	501	762	836	Tennessee............	737	831	848
Louisiana..................	325	549	498	Texas................	1,950	2,780	2,810
Maine......................	96	110	[3] 94	Utah.................	1,430	4,380	4,570
Maryland...................	[3] 358	[3] 305	[3] 276	Vermont..............	[3] 67	[3] 121	[3] 123
Massachusetts.............	[3] 200	[3] 233	[3] 196	Virginia.............	710	1,040	1,030
Michigan...................	1,640	2,190	2,470	Washington...........	607	712	727
Minnesota..................	1,460	[3] 4,180	[3] 5,120	West Virginia........	172	272	350
Mississippi................	149	198	195	Wisconsin............	[3] 372	509	[3] 599
Missouri...................	1,370	2,010	2,220	Wyoming..............	978	1,860	1,950

[1] Preliminary. [2] Includes undistributed not shown separately. [3] Partial data only; excludes values withheld to avoid disclosing individual company data.

Source: U.S. Geological Survey, *Minerals Yearbook*, annual, September 2012, and *Mineral Commodities Summaries*, annual. See also <http://minerals.er.usgs.gov/minerals/pubs/mcs/>.

Table 920. Principal Fuels, Nonmetals, and Metals—World Production and the U.S. Share: 2000 to 2011

[In millions of short tons (4,894 represents 4,894,000,000), except as indicated; see Appendix IV]

Mineral	Unit	World production 2000	World production 2005	World production 2010	World production 2011 [1]	Percent U.S. of world 2000	Percent U.S. of world 2005	Percent U.S. of world 2010	Percent U.S. of world 2011 [1]
Fuels: [2]									
Coal................................	Mil. sh. tons	4,894	6,554	7984.9	(NA)	22	17	14	(NA)
Petroleum (crude) [8]..............	Bil. bbl.	25.0	26.9	27.0	27.0	8	7	7	8
Natural gas (dry, marketable)....	Tril. cu. ft.	87.1	98.4	111.8	(NA)	22	18	19	(NA)
Natural gas plant liquids.........	Bil. bbl.	2.3	2.8	3.1	3.1	30	23	25	25
Nonmetals:									
Asbestos.........................	1,000 metric tons	2,110	2,210	2,010	2,000	–	–	–	–
Barite............................	1,000 metric tons	6,470	7,870	7,850	7,800	6	6	8	8
Cement, hydraulic...............	Mil. metric tons	1,660	2,350	3,310	3,400	(NA)	4	2	2
Feldspar.........................	1,000 metric tons	9,580	16,800	20,500	20,700	8	4	3	3
Fluorspar........................	1,000 metric tons	4,470	5,360	6,010	6,200	–	–	(NA)	(NA)
Gypsum..........................	Mil. metric tons	106	147	147	148	19	13	6	6
Mica (incl. scrap)...............	1,000 metric tons	328	354	1,070	1,090	(NA)	(NA)	5	6
Nitrogen (N content)............	Mil. metric tons	108	122	131	136	11	7	6	6
Phosphate rock (gross wt.)......	Mil. metric tons	132	152	181	191	30	24	14	15
Potash (K2O equivalent)........	Mil. metric tons	27	34	34	37	4	4	3	3
Sulfur, elemental basis..........	Mil. metric tons	59	69	68	69	19	14	13	13
Metals, mine basis:									
Bauxite..........................	Mil. metric tons	136	178	212	220	(NA)	(NA)	(NA)	(NA)
Copper..........................	1,000 metric tons	13,300	15,000	16,000	(NA)	11	8	7	(NA)
Gold.............................	Metric tons	2,570	2,470	2,560	2,700	14	10	9	9
Iron ore (gross wt.).............	Mil. metric tons	1,079	1,550	2,590	2,800	6	3	2	2
Lead [3].........................	1,000 metric tons	3,170	3,470	4,140	4,500	15	13	9	8
Mercury.........................	Metric tons	1,350	1,520	2,250	1,930	(NA)	(NA)	(NA)	(NA)
Molybdenum.....................	1,000 metric tons	133	186	242	250	31	31	25	26
Nickel [3].......................	1,000 metric tons	1,290	1,460	1,620	1,800	(Z)	–	–	–
Silver...........................	1,000 metric tons	18	21	23	24	11	6	6	5
Tantalum concentrates (Ta content).................	Metric tons	1,040	1,380	681	790	–	–	–	–
Titanium mineral concentrates (titanium content) [4].............	1,000 metric tons	(NA)	5,200	6,400	6,700	(NA)	6	3	4
Tungsten [3]....................	1,000 metric tons	44	59	69	72	–	–	(D)	(D)
Vanadium [3]....................	1,000 metric tons	56	56	58	60	10	–	(D)	(D)
Zinc [3].........................	1,000 metric tons	8,788	10,000	12,000	12,400	–	7	6	6
Metals, smelter basis:									
Aluminum........................	1,000 metric tons	24,400	31,900	40,800	44,100	15	8	4	5
Cadmium........................	1,000 metric tons	20	20	21	22	10	7	3	5
Copper..........................	1,000 metric tons	11,000	13,500	15,600	(NA)	9	4	4	(NA)
Iron, pig.........................	Mil. metric tons	573	802	1,026	(NA)	8	5	3	(NA)
Lead [4].........................	1,000 metric tons	6,580	7,660	9,490	(NA)	22	17	13	(NA)
Magnesium [5, 6]................	1,000 metric tons	428	622	757	780	(D)	(D)	(D)	(NA)
Raw Steel.......................	Mil. metric tons	850	1,140	1,420	1,500	12	8	6	6
Tin [7]..........................	1,000 metric tons	278	296	350	253	2	(NA)	3	3
Zinc.............................	1,000 metric tons	9,137	10,300	12,700	(NA)	4	3	2	(NA)

– Represents or rounds to zero. D Withheld to avoid disclosing company data. NA Not available. Z Less than 0.05 percent. [1] Preliminary. [2] Source: Energy Information Administration, "International Energy Statistics." [3] Content of ore and concentrate. [4] Refinery production. [5] Primary production; no smelter processing necessary. [6] Starting 2005, excludes U.S. production. [7] Production from primary sources only. [8] Crude oil including lease condensate.

Source: Mineral fuels, U.S. Energy Information Administration, "International Energy Statistics" database, accessed July 2012; and U.S. Geological Survey, *Minerals Yearbook, 2010*, annual, and *Mineral Commodity Summaries, 2012*, annual.

Table 921. Supply, Disposition, and Ending Stocks of Crude Oil and Petroleum Products: 2011

[In millions of barrels (2,065.2 represents 2,065,200,000). Minus sign (–) indicates decrease]

Commodity	Supply: Field production	Supply: Refinery and blender net production	Supply: Imports	Supply: Adjustments [1]	Disposition: Stock change	Disposition: Refinery and blender net inputs	Disposition: Exports	Disposition: Products supplied [2]	Ending stocks
Crude oil.......................	2,065.2	(X)	3,261.4	61.6	-33.3	5,404.3	17.2	–	1,026.6
Natural gas liquids and LRG [3]...	808.9	226.0	91.4	(X)	8.6	178.9	91.0	841.0	129.4
Pentanes plus...................	106.3	(X)	17.7	(X)	5.1	63.4	36.8	11.8	17.6
Liquefied petroleum gases.....	702.6	226.0	73.8	(X)	3.5	115.5	54.1	829.2	111.8
Ethane/ethylene................	338.0	7.1	0.1	(X)	-1.4	(NA)	(NA)	346.7	22.9
Propane/propylene.............	230.2	201.5	57.8	(X)	5.7	(NA)	45.2	438.6	55.0
Normal butane/butylene......	57.4	17.4	12.0	(X)	-0.9	47.6	8.9	31.3	26.8
Isobutane/isobutylene.........	77.0	-0.1	3.8	(X)	0.1	67.9	(NA)	12.7	7.1
Finished motor gasoline........	(X)	3,306.0	38.2	22.4	-2.6	(X)	174.8	3,194.8	60.6
Kerosene-type jet fuel..........	(X)	528.8	25.0	(X)	-1.7	(X)	35.3	520.3	41.5
Distillate fuel oil [4].............	(X)	1,639.6	65.2	14.9	-15.1	(X)	311.7	1,423.1	149.2

– Represents or rounds to zero. NA Not available. X Not applicable. [1] Includes an adjustment for crude oil, previously referred to as "Unaccounted For Crude Oil." Also included is an adjustment for motor gasoline blending components, fuel ethanol, and distillate fuel oil. See Appendix B of source for more details. [2] Products supplied is equal to field production, plus refinery and blender net production, plus imports, plus adjustments, minus stock change, minus refinery and blender net inputs, minus exports. [3] Liquified Refinery Gases (LRGs) are liquefied petroleum gases fractionated from refinery or still gases through compression and/or refrigeration. They are retained in the liquid state. Excludes still gas. [4] Distillate stocks located in the "Northeast Heating Oil Reserve" are not included. For details, see Appendix C of source.

Source: U.S. Energy Information Administration, "Petroleum Supply Annual, Volume 1;" <http://www.eia.gov/petroleum/supply/annual/volume1/>.

Table 922. Petroleum Industry—Summary: 1990 to 2010

[602 represents 602,000. Includes all costs incurred for drilling and equipping wells to point of completion as productive wells or abandonment after drilling becomes unproductive. Based on sample of operators of different size drilling establishments]

Item	Unit	1990	1995	2000	2005	2007	2008	2009	2010 [1]
Crude oil producing wells, (Dec. 31)	1,000	602	574	534	498	500	526	526	520
Daily output per well [2]	Bbl.	12.2	11.4	10.9	10.4	10.1	9.4	10.2	10.5
Completed wells drilled, total	1,000	32.33	21.14	29.29	44.02	51.06	54.35	33.05	37.50
Crude oil	1,000	12.84	8.25	8.09	10.78	13.36	16.65	11.26	16.25
Natural gas	1,000	11.25	8.08	17.05	28.59	32.72	32.27	18.23	16.97
Dry holes	1,000	8.25	4.81	4.15	4.65	4.98	5.43	3.55	4.28
Average depth per well	Feet	4,827	5,542	4,932	5,459	5,904	6,154	7,247	7,183
Average cost per well	$1,000	384	513	755	1,721	4,172	(NA)	(NA)	(NA)
Average cost per foot	Dollars	76.07	87.22	142.16	306.50	688.30	(NA)	(NA)	(NA)
Crude oil production, total [3]	Mil. bbl.	2,685	2,394	2,131	1,890	1,848	1,812	1,957	1,999
Value at wells [3, 4]	Bil. dol.	53.77	35.00	56.93	95.03	122.96	170.38	110.25	150.31
Average price per barrel	Dollars	20.03	14.62	26.72	50.28	66.52	94.04	56.35	74.71
Lower 48 states [5]	Mil. bbl.	2,037	1,853	1,776	1,575	1,585	1,562	1,721	1,779
Alaska	Mil. bbl.	647	542	355	315	264	250	236	220
Onshore	Mil. bbl.	2,290	1,838	1,482	1,265	1,244	1,263	1,322	1,367
Offshore	Mil. bbl.	395	556	649	625	605	548	634	632
Imports: Crude oil [3, 6]	Mil. bbl.	2,151	2,639	3,320	3,696	3,661	3,581	3,290	3,363
Refined petroleum products	Mil. bbl.	775	586	874	1,310	1,255	1,146	977	942
Exports: Crude oil [3]	Mil. bbl.	39.7	34.5	18.4	11.6	10.0	10.5	16.0	15.2
Proved reserves	Bil. bbl.	26.3	22.4	22.0	21.8	21.3	19.1	20.7	23.3
Operable refineries	Number	205	175	158	148	149	150	150	148
Daily Capacity (Jan. 1)	1,000 bbl.	15,572	15,434	16,512	17,125	17,443	17,594	17,672	17,584
Refinery input, total	Mil. bbl.	5,325	5,555	5,964	6,136	6,205	6,278	6,170	6,345
Crude oil [3]	Mil. bbl.	4,894	5,100	5,514	5,555	5,532	5,361	5,233	5,374
Natural gas plant liquids	Mil. bbl.	171	172	139	161	184	178	177	161
Other liquids [7]	Mil. bbl.	260	283	311	420	488	739	760	810
Refinery output, total [8]	Mil. bbl.	5,574	5,838	6,311	6,497	6,568	6,641	6,527	6,735
Motor gasoline [9]	Mil. bbl.	2,540	2,722	2,910	3,036	3,051	3,129	3,207	3,306
Jet fuel [10]	Mil. bbl.	543	517	588	564	528	546	510	517
Distillate fuel oil	Mil. bbl.	1,067	1,152	1,310	1,443	1,509	1,572	1,478	1,542
Residual fuel oil	Mil. bbl.	347	288	255	229	246	227	218	213
Liquefied petroleum gases	Mil. bbl.	182	239	258	209	239	230	227	240
Utilization rate	Percent	87.1	92.0	92.6	90.6	88.5	85.3	82.9	86.4

NA Not available. [1] Preliminary. [2] Based on number of wells producing at end of year. [3] Includes lease condensate. [4] Values based on domestic first purchase price. [5] Excluding Alaska and Hawaii. [6] Includes imports for the Strategic Petroleum Reserve. [7] Unfinished oils (net), other hydrocarbons, hydrogen, aviation and motor gasoline blending components (net). Beginning 1995, also includes oxygenates (net). [8] Includes other products not shown separately. [9] Finished motor gasoline. Beginning 1995, also includes ethanol blended into motor gasoline. [10] Prior to 2005, kerosene-type jet fuel is included with kerosene in "Other products." Beginning 2005, naphtha-type jet fuel is also included in "Other products."

Source: U.S. Energy Information Administration, *Annual Energy Review 2010*. See also <http://www.eia.gov/totalenergy/data/annual/index.cfm>.

Table 923. Net U.S. Imports of Selected Minerals and Metals as Percent of Apparent Consumption: 1980 to 2011

[In percent. Based on net imports which equal the difference between imports and exports plus or minus government stockpile and industry stock changes]

Minerals and metals	1980	1990	1995	2000	2005	2008	2009	2010	2011 [1]
Bauxite [2]	(NA)	98	99	100	100	100	100	100	100
Fluorspar	87	91	92	100	100	100	100	100	100
Manganese	98	100	100	100	100	100	100	100	100
Strontium	100	100	100	100	100	100	100	100	100
Tantalum	90	86	80	80	100	100	100	100	100
Vanadium	35	(D)	84	100	100	91	78	80	80
Mica (sheet)	100	100	100	100	100	100	100	100	100
Platinum	(NA)	(NA)	(NA)	78	93	89	95	91	88
Tin	79	71	84	88	78	70	74	74	76
Barite	44	71	65	84	84	80	78	75	78
Zinc	60	64	71	72	67	72	77	73	73
Cobalt	93	84	79	78	83	81	76	81	75
Potash	65	68	75	80	80	84	73	83	83
Titanium	(NA)	(NA)	70	79	71	78	68	65	68
Tungsten	53	81	90	66	68	60	68	63	36
Silver	7	(NA)	(NA)	43	72	68	59	72	75
Nickel	76	64	60	54	48	33	21	34	47
Iron and steel	13	13	21	18	15	13	11	6	9
Aluminum	([3])	([3])	23	33	41	([3])	10	14	13

D Withheld to avoid disclosure. NA Not available. [1] Preliminary. [2] Includes alumina. [3] Net exporter.

Source: Through 1990, U.S. Bureau of Mines; thereafter, U.S. Geological Survey, *Mineral Commodity Summaries* and *Minerals Yearbook*, annual, and *Historical Statistics for Mineral and Material Commodities in the United States*; and import and export data from U.S. Census Bureau.

Table 924. Crude Petroleum and Natural Gas—Production and Value by Major Producing States: 2009 to 2011

[1,954 represents 1,954,000,000 barrels]

State	Crude petroleum Quantity (mil. bbl.)			Value (mil. dol.)			Natural gas marketed production [1] Quantity (bil. cu. ft.)			Value (mil. dol.)		
	2009	2010	2011	2009	2010	2011	2009	2010	2011	2009	2010	2011
Total [2]	1,954	2,000	2,060	110,097	149,400	197,217	21,648	22,402	24,170	79,349	100,273	(NA)
AL	7	7	8	397	536	888	236	223	(NA)	1,021	995	(NA)
AK [3]	235	220	205	12,813	15,879	20,235	397	374	364	1,164	1,185	(NA)
AR	6	6	6	305	407	515	680	927	(NA)	2,331	3,557	(NA)
CA	207	201	196	11,620	15,005	20,109	277	287	(NA)	1,095	1,397	(NA)
CO	30	33	38	1,578	2,370	3,348	1,499	1,578	(NA)	4,812	6,250	(NA)
FL	1	2	2	(NA)	(NA)	(NA)	–	12	(NA)	(NA)	(NA)	(NA)
IL	9	9	9	505	664	820	1	1	(NA)	(NA)	(NA)	(NA)
IN	2	2	2	100	134	175	5	7	(NA)	20	28	(NA)
KS	39	40	42	2,147	2,931	3,674	354	325	(NA)	1,119	1,372	(NA)
KY	3	3	2	144	178	200	113	135	(NA)	(NA)	605	(NA)
LA	69	67	69	4,074	5,271	7,322	1,549	2,210	3,050	5,920	9,345	(NA)
MI	6	7	7	345	509	606	154	152	(NA)	603	575	(NA)
MS	24	24	24	1,379	1,840	2,432	88	74	(NA)	329	308	(NA)
MT	28	25	24	1,474	1,779	2,140	98	88	(NA)	310	318	(NA)
NE	2	2	3	114	162	217	3	2	(NA)	9	9	(NA)
NM	61	65	71	3,491	4,946	6,494	1,383	1,292	1,270	5,762	6,879	(NA)
NY	–	–	(NA)	(NA)	(NA)	(NA)	45	36	(NA)	189	167	(NA)
ND	80	113	153	4,285	7,942	13,576	59	82	(NA)	222	321	(NA)
OH	5	5	5	275	350	444	89	78	(NA)	387	362	(NA)
OK	67	68	75	3,769	5,092	6,788	1,902	1,827	1,899	6,704	8,607	(NA)
PA	3	3	3	167	225	288	274	573	(NA)	(NA)	(NA)	(NA)
TX	399	427	530	22,904	32,580	48,750	6,819	6,715	7,016	25,957	31,535	(NA)
UT	23	25	26	1,152	1,680	2,169	444	432	(NA)	1,503	1,826	(NA)
WV	2	2	2	84	130	186	264	265	(NA)	(NA)	(NA)	(NA)
WY	52	53	55	2,697	3,626	4,567	2,335	2,306	2,176	7,947	9,914	(NA)
Federal offshore	593	588	500	(NA)	(NA)	(NA)	(NA)	(NA)	(NA)	(NA)	(NA)	(NA)
Lower 48 states	1,718	1,780	1,855	(NA)	(NA)	(NA)	21,251	22,028	23,805	78,185	99,087	(NA)

– Represents zero. NA Not available. [1] Excludes nonhydrocarbon gases. [2] Includes other states, not shown separately. State production includes state offshore production, as well as extractions from the Gulf not distributed to states. U.S. level totals shown in Tables 922 and 929 may contain revisions not carried to state level. [3] Price data are for North Slope only. Value data were calculated using price data.

Source: U.S. Energy Information Administration, "Petroleum Navigator" and "Natural Gas Navigator," <http://www.eia.gov/petroleum/index.cfm> and <http://www.eia.gov/naturalgas/index.cfm>, accessed October 2012.

Table 925. Crude Oil, Natural Gas, and Natural Gas Liquids—Reserves by State: 2008 to 2010

[19,121 mil. bbl. represents 19,121,000,000 bbl. As of December 31. Proved reserves are estimated quantities of the mineral, which geological and engineering data demonstrate with reasonable certainty, to be recoverable in future years from known reservoirs under existing economic and operating conditions. Based on a sample of operators of oil and gas wells]

Area	2008 Crude oil proved reserves (mil. bbl.)	Natural gas (bil. cu. ft.)	Natural gas liquids (mil. bbl.)	2009 Crude oil proved reserves (mil. bbl.)	Natural gas (bil. cu. ft.)	Natural gas liquids (mil. bbl.)	2010 Crude oil proved reserves (mil. bbl.)	Natural gas (bil. cu. ft.)	Natural gas liquids (mil. bbl.)
United States [1]	19,121	244,656	9,275	20,682	272,509	(NA)	23,267	304,625	(NA)
Alabama	38	3,290	106	37	2,871	(NA)	42	2,629	(NA)
Alaska	3,507	7,699	312	3,566	9,101	(NA)	3,722	8,838	(NA)
Arkansas	30	5,626	2	28	10,869	(NA)	40	14,178	(NA)
California	2,705	2,406	113	2,835	2,773	(NA)	2,938	2,647	(NA)
Colorado	288	23,302	716	279	23,058	(NA)	386	24,119	(NA)
Florida	3	1	–	9	7	(NA)	18	56	(NA)
Illinois	54	(NA)	(NA)	66	(NA)	(NA)	64	(NA)	(NA)
Indiana	15	(NA)	(NA)	8	(NA)	(NA)	8	(NA)	(NA)
Kansas	243	3,557	181	259	3,279	(NA)	295	3,673	(NA)
Kentucky	17	2,714	100	20	2,782	(NA)	15	2,613	(NA)
Louisiana	388	11,573	300	370	20,688	(NA)	424	29,277	(NA)
Michigan	48	3,174	62	33	2,763	(NA)	40	2,919	(NA)
Mississippi	249	1,030	9	244	917	(NA)	247	853	(NA)
Montana	321	1,000	11	343	976	(NA)	369	944	(NA)
Nebraska	8	(NA)	(NA)	9	(NA)	(NA)	10	(NA)	(NA)
New Mexico	654	16,285	804	700	15,598	(NA)	823	15,412	(NA)
New York	(NA)	389	(NA)	(NA)	196	(NA)	(NA)	281	(NA)
North Dakota	573	541	55	1,046	1,079	(NA)	1,814	1,667	(NA)
Ohio	38	985	(NA)	38	896	(NA)	42	832	(NA)
Oklahoma	581	20,845	1,034	622	22,769	(NA)	710	26,345	(NA)
Pennsylvania	14	3,577	(NA)	10	6,985	(NA)	22	13,960	(NA)
Texas	4,555	77,546	3,560	5,006	80,424	(NA)	5,674	88,997	(NA)
Utah	286	6,643	116	398	7,257	(NA)	449	6,981	(NA)
Virginia	(NA)	2,378	(NA)	(NA)	3,091	(NA)	(NA)	3,215	(NA)
West Virginia	23	5,136	100	19	5,946	(NA)	17	7,000	(NA)
Wyoming	556	31,143	1,121	583	35,283	(NA)	567	35,074	(NA)
Federal offshore	3,903	13,546	548	4,129	12,552	(NA)	4,496	11,765	(NA)
Lower 48 states	15,614	236,957	8,963	17,116	263,408	(NA)	19,545	295,787	(NA)

– Represents zero. NA Not available. [1] Includes other states, not shown separately.

Source: U.S. Energy Information Administration, "Petroleum Navigator" and "Natural Gas Navigator," <http://www.eia.gov/petroleum/index.cfm> and <http://www.eia.gov/naturalgas/index.cfm>, accessed August 2012.

Table 926. Federal Offshore Leasing, Exploration, Production, and Revenue: 1990 to 2011

[In millions (56.79 represents 56,790,000), except as indicated. Data presented by fiscal year. See source for explanation of terms and for reliability statement]

Item	Unit	1990	1995	2000	2005	2008	2009	2010	2011
Tracts offered................	Number	10,459	10,995	7,992	11,447	19,812	9,893	6,958	3,913
Tracts leased.................	Number	825	835	553	989	2,121	483	446	181
Acres offered................	Millions	56.79	59.70	42.89	61.08	106.76	52.98	36.96	21.01
Acres leased.................	Millions	4.30	4.34	2.92	5.24	11.73	2.66	2.37	1.04
New wells being drilled:									
Active......................	Number	120	237	236	135	122	54	48	(NA)
Suspended.................	Number	266	155	139	59	67	67	76	(NA)
Cumulative wells (since 1953):									
Wells completed............	Number	13,167	13,423	13,733	13,398	12,157	11,384	10,404	(NA)
Wells plugged and abandoned......	Number	14,677	21,478	26,893	31,884	34,613	35,544	36,695	(NA)
Revenue, total [1]...............	Bil. dol.	3.4	2.7	5.2	6.3	18.0	5.8	5.3	6.5
Bonuses....................	Bil. dol.	0.8	0.4	0.4	0.6	9.5	1.2	1.0	0.4
Oil and gas royalties.........	Bil. dol.	2.6	2.1	4.1	5.5	8.3	4.4	3.6	6.0
Rentals....................	Bil. dol.	0.09	0.09	0.21	0.22	0.24	0.23	0.25	0.22
Sales value [2]................	Bil. dol.	17.0	13.8	27.4	37.2	57.2	32.6	25.1	39.0
Oil........................	Bil. dol.	7.0	6.3	11.5	15.4	35.9	23.5	21.3	36.7
Natural gas................	Bil. dol.	9.5	7.5	15.9	21.8	21.3	9.2	3.7	2.2
Sales volume: [3]									
Oil........................	Mil. bbl.	324	409	566	332	358	425	261	385
Natural gas................	Bil. cu. ft.	5,093	4,692	4,723	3,504	1,573	3,539	1,043	1,870

NA Not available. [1] Includes condensate royalties. Excludes gas plant product royalties. [2] Sales value is value at time of sale, not current value. [3] Excludes sales volumes for gas plant products and sulfur.

Source: U.S. Department of the Interior, Bureau of Ocean Energy Management, Regulation and Enforcement, *Federal Offshore Statistics*, annual; for revenue, sales value, and sales volume data after 2000, Office of Natural Resources Revenue, *Annual Reported Royalty Revenue Statistical Information*, <http://www.onrr.gov/ONRRWebStats/Home.aspx>.

Table 927. Oil and Gas Extraction Industry—Establishments, Employees, and Payroll by State: 2009

[10,406,010 represents 10,406,010,000. See headnote, Table 892]

State	Crude petroleum and natural gas extraction (211111) [1]			State	Natural gas liquid extraction (211112) [1]		
	Establish-ments	Number of employees [2]	Annual pay-roll ($1,000)		Establish-ments	Number of employees [2]	Annual pay-roll ($1,000)
United States [3].......	7,568	98,516	10,406,010	United States [3].......	323	8,878	777,090
Alabama.................	31	506	41,520	Alabama.................	2	([4])	(D)
Arkansas.................	100	1,440	110,891	Alaska.................	1	([4])	(D)
California.................	214	5,869	739,609	Arkansas.................	1	([5])	(D)
Colorado.................	380	5,458	617,749	California.................	5	135	12,609
Florida.................	25	([6])	(D)	Colorado.................	15	1,157	138,033
Illinois.................	153	914	37,810	Florida.................	1	([5])	(D)
Indiana.................	43	166	6,524	Illinois.................	2	([4])	(D)
Kansas.................	393	2,562	150,281	Kansas.................	12	([6])	(D)
Kentucky.................	92	843	50,688	Kentucky.................	6	([4])	(D)
Louisiana.................	381	7,646	636,613	Louisiana.................	38	820	70,379
Michigan.................	92	1,049	89,395	Michigan.................	8	([4])	2,267
Mississippi.................	75	916	76,286	Minnesota.................	1	([5])	(D)
Montana.................	82	588	49,692	Mississippi.................	4	([4])	(D)
Nevada.................	18	([4])	5,666	Missouri.................	(NA)	(NA)	(NA)
New Mexico.................	170	2,943	231,282	Montana.................	5	42	2,635
New York.................	55	321	22,771	New Mexico.................	16	608	50,271
North Dakota.................	41	1,359	117,688	North Dakota.................	3	([4])	(D)
Ohio.................	200	1,432	63,729	Ohio.................	3	([5])	371
Oklahoma.................	1,155	13,385	1,367,118	Oklahoma.................	51	1,108	93,865
Pennsylvania.................	201	2,557	212,611	Pennsylvania.................	17	([6])	(D)
Texas.................	3,081	38,901	4,856,555	South Dakota.................	(NA)	(NA)	(NA)
Utah.................	52	1,180	103,548	Texas.................	95	2,460	188,418
Virginia.................	23	292	30,676	Utah.................	3	([4])	(D)
West Virginia.................	228	2,909	198,430	West Virginia.................	7	([7])	(D)
Wyoming.................	163	2,512	232,653	Wyoming.................	22	1,031	94,335

D Withheld to avoid disclosing data for individual companies; data are included in higher level totals. NA Not available. [1] North American Industry Classification System, 2007. [2] Covers full- and part-time employees who are on the payroll in the pay period including March 12. [3] Includes other states, not shown separately. [4] 20 to 99 employees. [5] 0 to 19 employees. [6] 250 to 499 employees. [7] 100 to 249 employees.

Source: U.S. Census Bureau, "County Business Patterns," accessed August 2012, <http://censtats.census.gov/cgi-bin/cbpnaic/cbpdetl.pl>.

Table 928. Natural Gas Plant Liquids—Production and Value: 1990 to 2011

[Barrels of 42 gallons (569 represents 569,000,000)]

Item	Unit	1990	1995	2000	2005	2007	2008	2009	2010	2011
Field production [1]........................	Mil. bbl.	569	643	699	627	651	653	697	757	797
Pentanes plus........................	Mil. bbl.	113	122	112	97	96	97	99	101	108
Liquefied petroleum gases............	Mil. bbl.	456	521	587	529	555	556	598	656	689
Natural gas processed.................	Tril. cu. ft.	15	17	17	15	16	15	(NA)	(NA)	(NA)

NA Not available. [1] Includes other finished petroleum products, not shown separately.

Source: U.S. Energy Information Administration, "Natural Gas Navigator," <http://www.eia.gov/naturalgas/index.cfm>, accessed August 2012.

Table 929. Natural Gas—Supply, Consumption, Reserves, and Marketed Production: 1990 to 2011

[270 represents 270,000. Data are for natural gas, plus a small amount of supplemental gaseous fuels. Minus sign (−) indicates debit]

Item	Unit	1990	1995	2000	2005	2007	2008	2009	2010	2011 [8]
Producing wells (year-end).........	1,000	270	299	342	426	453	477	493	488	504
Production value at wells............	Bil. of dol.	31.8	30.3	74.3	138.8	126.2	168.3	79.3	100.3	(NA)
Avg. per 1,000 cu. ft................	Dollars	1.71	1.55	3.68	7.33	6.25	7.97	3.67	4.48	3.95
Proved reserves [1].....................	Tril. cu. ft.	169	165	177	204	238	245	273	305	(NA)
Marketed production [2]............	**Bil. cu. ft.**	**18,594**	**19,506**	**20,198**	**18,927**	**20,196**	**21,112**	**21,648**	**22,402**	**24,170**
Minus: Extraction losses [3]..........	Bil. cu. ft.	784	908	1,016	876	930	953	1,024	1,070	1,169
Equals: Dry production............	Bil. cu. ft.	17,810	18,599	19,182	18,051	19,266	20,159	20,624	21,332	23,000
Plus: Supplemental gas supplies...	Bil. cu. ft.	123	110	90	64	63	61	65	65	61
Equals: Dry production with supplemental gas...................	Bil. cu. ft.	17,932	18,709	19,272	18,114	19,329	20,219	20,689	21,397	23,062
Plus: Withdrawals from storage....	Bil. cu. ft.	1,986	3,025	3,550	3,107	3,375	3,420	3,007	3,311	3,175
Plus: Imports.....................	Bil. cu. ft.	1,532	2,841	3,782	4,341	4,608	3,984	3,751	3,741	3,453
Plus: Balancing item [4]...............	Bil. cu. ft.	307	396	−306	236	−203	2	−103	−213	−290
Equals: Total supply..............	Bil. cu. ft.	21,758	24,971	26,298	25,798	27,109	27,626	27,345	28,236	29,400
Minus: Exports...................	Bil. cu. ft.	86	154	244	729	822	963	1,072	1,137	1,507
Minus: Additions to storage [5]......	Bil. cu. ft.	2,499	2,610	2,721	3,055	3,183	3,385	3,362	3,324	3,523
Equals: Consumption, total.......	**Bil. cu. ft.**	**19,174**	**22,207**	**23,333**	**22,014**	**23,104**	**23,277**	**22,910**	**23,775**	**24,369**
Lease and plant fuel.............	Bil. cu. ft.	1,236	1,220	1,151	1,112	1,226	1,220	1,275	1,282	1,383
Pipeline fuel [6]......................	Bil. cu. ft.	660	700	642	584	621	648	670	669	686
Residential......................	Bil. cu. ft.	4,391	4,850	4,996	4,827	4,722	4,892	4,779	4,787	4,735
Commercial [7].....................	Bil. cu. ft.	2,623	3,031	3,182	2,999	3,013	3,153	3,119	3,102	3,161
Industrial.......................	Bil. cu. ft.	8,255	9,384	9,293	7,713	7,881	7,890	7,443	7,800	8,153
Vehicle fuel.....................	Bil. cu. ft.	(Z)	5	13	23	25	26	27	31	33
Electric power sector..............	Bil. cu. ft.	3,245	4,237	5,206	5,869	6,841	6,668	6,873	7,387	7,602
World production (dry).............	Tril. cu. ft.	73.8	78.1	87.1	98.4	104.2	107.9	104.8	111.8	(NA)
U.S. production (dry).............	Tril. cu. ft.	17.8	18.6	19.2	18.1	19.3	20.2	20.6	21.3	23.0
Percent U.S. of world............	Percent	24.1	23.8	22.0	18.3	18.5	18.7	19.7	19.1	(NA)

NA Not available. Z Less than 500 million cubic feet. [1] Estimated, end of year. [2] Marketed production includes gross withdrawals from reservoirs less quantities used for reservoir repressuring and quantities vented or flared. Excludes nonhydrocarbon gases subsequently removed. [3] Volumetric reduction in natural gas resulting from the removal of natural gas plant liquids, which are transferred to petroleum supply. [4] Quantities lost and imbalances in data due to differences among data sources. Since 1980, excludes intransit shipments that cross U.S.-Canada border (i.e., natural gas delivered to its destination via the other country). [5] Underground storage. Through 2004, includes liquefied natural gas (LNG) storage in above-ground tanks. [6] Natural gas consumed in the operation of pipelines and delivery to consumers. [7] Includes deliveries to municipalities and public authorities for institutional heating and other purposes. [8]Data for 2011 are preliminary.

Source: Except as noted, U.S. Energy Information Administration, *Annual Energy Review*; "International Energy Annual;" "U.S. Crude Oil, Natural Gas, and Natural Gas Liquids Reserves;" "Natural Gas Annual;" and "International Energy Statistics." See <http://www.eia.gov>.

Table 930. Unconventional Dry Natural Gas Production and Proved Reserves: 2009 and 2010

[In billions of cubic feet (1,914 represents 1,914,000). For states not shown, no production or reserves were reported]

State	Production				Proved reserves [1]			
	Coalbed methane [2]		Shale gas [3]		Coalbed methane [2]		Shale gas [3]	
	2009	2010	2009	2010	2009	2010	2009	2010
U.S.....................	**1,914**	**1,886**	**3,110**	**5,336**	**18,578**	**17,508**	**60,644**	**97,449**
Alabama...............	105	102	–	–	1,342	1,298	–	–
Alaska.................	–	–	–	–	–	–	–	–
Arkansas..............	3	3	527	794	22	28	9,070	12,526
California..............	–	–	(NA)	(NA)	–	–	(NA)	(NA)
Colorado..............	498	533	1	1	7,348	6,485	4	4
Florida.................	–	–	(NA)	(NA)	–	–	(NA)	(NA)
Kansas................	43	41	(NA)	(NA)	163	258	(NA)	(NA)
Kentucky..............	–	–	5	4	–	–	55	10
Louisiana..............	1	–	293	1,232	–	–	9,307	20,070
Michigan..............	–	–	132	120	–	–	2,499	2,306
Mississippi............	–	–	(NA)	(NA)	–	–	(NA)	(NA)
Montana...............	12	10	7	13	37	64	137	186
New Mexico...........	432	402	2	6	3,646	3,532	36	123
New York..............	–	–	(NA)	(NA)	–	–	(NA)	(NA)
North Dakota..........	–	–	25	64	–	–	368	1,185
Ohio...................	–	–	–	–	–	–	–	–
Oklahoma.............	55	45	249	403	338	325	6,389	9,670
Pennsylvania..........	16	3	65	396	131	129	3,790	10,708
Texas.................	–	–	1,789	2,218	–	–	28,167	38,048
Utah..................	71	66	(NA)	(NA)	725	718	(NA)	(NA)
Virginia...............	111	97	(NA)	(NA)	2,261	1,752	(NA)	(NA)
West Virginia..........	31	17	11	80	220	220	688	2,491
Wyoming..............	535	566	–	–	2,328	2,683	–	1

– Represents or rounds to zero. NA Not Available. [1] Proved reserves of natural gas as of December 31 of the report year are the estimated quantities which analysis of geological and engineering data demonstrate with reasonable certainty to be recoverable in future years from known reservoirs under existing economic and operating conditions. [2] Methane is generated during coal formation and is contained in the coal microstructure. Typical recovery entails pumping water out of the coal to allow the gas to escape. Methane is the principal component of natural gas. Coal bed methane can be added to natural gas pipelines without any special treatment. [3] Natural gas produced from low permeability shale formations.

Source: U.S. Energy Information Administration, "Natural Gas Navigator," <http://www.eia.gov/naturalgas/data.cfm>, accessed August 2012.

Table 931. Coal Supply, Disposition, and Prices: 2000 to 2010

[In millions of short tons (1,073.6 represents 1,073,600,000). 1 short ton = 2,000 lbs.]

Item	2000	2005	2006	2007	2008	2009	2010
United States, total supply...............	**1,073.6**	**1,131.5**	**1,162.8**	**1,146.6**	**1,171.8**	**1,074.9**	**1,085.3**
Consumption by sector:							
Total........	1,084.1	1,126.0	1,112.3	1,128.0	1,120.5	997.5	1,048.3
Electric power...............	985.8	1,037.5	1,026.6	1,045.1	1,040.6	933.6	975.6
Coke plants......................	28.9	23.4	23.0	22.7	22.1	15.3	21.1
Other industrial plants..............	65.2	60.3	59.5	56.6	54.4	45.3	48.5
Combined heat and power (CHP).........	28.0	25.9	25.3	22.5	23.6	(NA)	(NA)
Noncombined heat and power............	37.2	34.5	34.2	34.1	31.0	(NA)	(NA)
Residential/commercial users..............	4.1	4.7	3.2	3.5	3.5	3.2	3.1
Year-end coal stocks:							
Total [1]............	140.0	144.3	186.9	192.8	205.1	233.0	224.3
Electric power....................	102.0	101.1	141.0	151.2	161.6	189.5	175.2
Coke plants......................	1.5	2.6	2.9	1.9	2.3	2.0	1.9
Other industrial plants..............	4.6	5.6	6.5	5.6	6.0	5.1	4.5
Producers/distributors...............	31.9	35.0	36.5	34.0	34.7	35.9	42.2
U.S. coal trade:							
Net exports [2]................	46.0	19.5	13.4	22.8	47.3	36.5	62.3
Exports..........................	58.5	49.9	49.6	59.2	81.5	59.1	81.7
Steam coal....................	25.7	21.3	22.1	27.0	39.0	21.8	25.6
Metallurgical coal.............	32.8	28.7	27.5	32.2	42.5	37.3	56.1
Imports.............................	12.5	30.5	36.2	36.3	34.2	22.6	19.4
Average delivered price (dollars per short ton):							
Electric utilities..................	24.28	31.22	34.26	36.06	41.32	44.47	45.09
Independent power producers.............	(NA)	30.39	33.04	33.11	38.98	39.94	41.49
Coke plants......................	44.38	83.79	92.87	94.97	118.09	143.01	153.59
Other industrial plants............	31.46	47.63	51.67	54.42	63.44	64.87	64.24
Average free alongside ship (f.a.s.):							
Exports.......................	34.90	67.10	70.93	70.25	97.68	101.44	120.41
Steam coal....................	29.67	47.64	46.25	47.90	57.35	73.63	65.54
Metallurgical coal.............	38.99	81.56	90.81	88.99	134.62	117.73	145.44
Imports.............................	30.10	46.71	49.10	47.64	59.83	63.91	71.77

NA Not available. [1] Includes other stocks, not shown separately. [2] Exports minus imports.

Source: U.S. Energy Information Administration, "U.S. Coal Supply and Demand: 2010 Review," annual, June 2011, <http://www.eia.gov/coal/review/>.

Table 932. Coal and Coke—Summary: 1990 to 2010

[In millions of short tons (1,029 represents 1,029,000,000), except as indicated. Includes coal consumed at mines. Recoverability varies between 40 and 90 percent for individual deposits; 50 percent or more of overall U.S. coal reserve base is believed to be recoverable]

Item	Unit	1990	1995	2000	2005	2007	2008	2009	2010
COAL									
Coal production, total [1,2]............	**Mil. sh. tons**	**1,029**	**1,033**	**1,074**	**1,131**	**1,147**	**1,172**	**1,075**	**1,084**
Value [3]......................	Bil. dol.	22.39	19.45	18.02	26.69	30.04	36.62	35.73	38.67
Anthracite production [2]..................	Mil. sh. tons	3.5	4.7	4.6	1.7	1.6	1.7	1.7	1.7
Bituminous coal and lignite [4]..........	Mil. sh. tons	1,026	1,028	1,069	1,130	1,145	1,170	1,071	1,083
Underground....................	Mil. sh. tons	425	396	374	369	352	357	332	337
Surface [2]......................	Mil. sh. tons	605	637	700	762	795	815	743	745
Exports........................	Mil. sh. tons	106	89	58	50	59	82	59	82
Imports........................	Mil. sh. tons	3	9	13	30	36	34	23	19
Consumption [5]...................	Mil. sh. tons	904	962	1,084	1,126	1,128	1,121	997	1,049
Electric power sector [6]..................	Mil. sh. tons	783	850	986	1,037	1,045	1,041	934	975
Industrial.......................	Mil. sh. tons	115	106	94	84	79	77	61	70
Number of mines..................	Number	3,243	2,104	1,453	1,415	1,374	1,458	1,407	1,285
Daily employment..................	1,000	131	90	72	79	81	87	88	86
Production, by state:									
Alabama..............................	Mil. sh. tons	29	25	19	21	19	21	19	20
Illinois..............................	Mil. sh. tons	60	48	33	32	32	33	34	33
Indiana..............................	Mil. sh. tons	36	26	28	34	35	36	36	35
Kentucky............................	Mil. sh. tons	173	154	131	120	115	120	107	105
Montana............................	Mil. sh. tons	38	39	38	40	43	45	39	45
Ohio...............................	Mil. sh. tons	35	26	22	25	23	26	28	27
Pennsylvania.......................	Mil. sh. tons	71	62	75	67	65	65	58	59
Virginia............................	Mil. sh. tons	47	34	33	28	25	25	21	22
West Virginia.......................	Mil. sh. tons	169	163	158	154	153	158	137	135
Wyoming...........................	Mil. sh. tons	184	264	339	404	454	468	431	443
Other states.......................	Mil. sh. tons	187	192	192	206	181	176	165	161
World production.....................	Mil. sh. tons	5,347	5,077	4,893	6,554	7,053	7,460	7,546	7,985
Percent U.S. of world..................	Percent	19.2	20.3	21.9	17.3	16.3	15.7	14.2	13.6
COKE									
Production.........................	Mil. sh. tons	27.6	20.0	20.8	16.7	16.2	15.6	11.1	15.0
Imports............................	Mil. sh. tons	0.8	3.8	3.8	3.5	2.5	3.6	0.0	1.2
Exports............................	Mil. sh. tons	0.6	1.4	1.1	1.7	1.4	2.0	1.3	1.5
Consumption [7]......................	Mil. sh. tons	27.8	25.8	23.2	18.2	17.3	17.0	10.3	14.8

NA Not available. [1] Includes bituminous coal, subbituminous coal, lignite, and anthracite. [2] Beginning 2005, includes a small amount of refuse recovery. [3] Coal values are based on free-on-board rail/barge prices, which are the free-on-board prices of coal at the point of first sale, excluding freight or shipping and insurance costs. [4] Includes subbituminous. [5] Includes some categories not shown separately. [6] Electricity-only and combined-heat-and-power (CHP) plants whose primary business is to sell electricity and/or heat to the public. [7] Consumption is calculated as the sum of production and imports minus exports and stock change.

Source: U.S. Energy Information Administration, *Annual Energy Review*, "International Energy Annual," "Annual Coal Report," "Monthly Coal Report," and "International Energy Statistics," <http://www.eia.doe.gov>.

Table 933. Demonstrated Coal Reserves by Major Producing State: 2009 and 2010

[In millions of short tons (486,102 represents 486,102,000,000), except as number of mines. As of January 1. The demonstrated reserve base represents the sum of coal in both measured and indicated resource categories of reliability. Measured resources of coal are estimates that have a high degree of geologic assurance from sample analyses and measurements from closely spaced and geological well-known sample sites. Indicated resources are estimates based partly from sample and analyses and measurements and partly from reasonable geologic projections]

| State | 2009 | | | | 2010 | | | |
| | Number of mines | Total reserves | Method of mining | | Number of mines | Total reserves | Method of mining | |
			Under-ground	Surface			Under-ground	Surface
United States [1]	1,407	486,102	331,882	154,220	1,285	485,511	331,202	153,309
Alabama	57	4,074	915	3,158	50	4,039	890	3,149
Alaska	1	6,102	5,423	680	1	6,100	5,423	677
Arkansas	2	416	272	144	2	416	272	144
Colorado	11	15,981	11,222	4,760	10	15,935	11,175	4,759
Illinois	22	104,222	87,700	16,522	22	104,160	87,644	16,516
Indiana	33	9,271	8,649	623	29	9,217	8,620	597
Iowa	(NA)	2,189	1,732	457	(NA)	2,189	1,732	457
Kansas	1	971	–	971	1	971	(NA)	971
Kentucky	449	29,234	16,505	12,729	392	29,055	16,377	12,678
Kentucky, Eastern	425	9,952	828	9,124	367	9,841	759	9,082
Kentucky, Western	24	19,282	15,677	3,605	25	19,214	15,618	3,596
Maryland	22	623	568	55	22	620	567	53
Missouri	2	5,988	1,479	4,508	2	5,987	1,479	4,508
Montana	6	119,017	70,955	48,062	6	118,958	70,946	48,012
New Mexico	5	11,984	6,101	5,883	4	11,954	6,091	5,863
North Dakota	4	8,903	–	8,903	4	8867	–	8,867
Ohio	46	23,127	17,415	5,712	42	23,080	17,380	5,700
Oklahoma	10	1,545	1,227	318	10	1,544	1,227	317
Pennsylvania	244	26,998	22,802	4,195	240	26,889	22,707	4,182
Anthracite	64	7,190	3,842	3,348	59	7,188	3,842	3,347
Bituminous	180	19,807	18,960	847	181	19,701	18,865	835
Tennessee	25	759	503	256	19	757	502	255
Texas	12	12,183	(NA)	12,183	12	12,132	(NA)	12,132
Utah	8	5,203	4,935	268	8	5,164	4,897	268
Virginia	108	1,519	1,004	515	106	1,481	976	505
Washington	(NA)	1,340	1,332	8	(NA)	1,340	1,332	8
West Virginia	283	31,955	28,507	3,448	252	31,723	28,338	3,385
Wyoming	20	61,563	42,479	19,084	19	61,007	42,472	18,535

– Represents zero. NA Not available. [1] Includes other states not shown separately.

Source: U.S. Energy Information Administration, *Annual Coal Report, 2010*, November 2011. See also <http://www.eia.gov/coal/annual/>.

Table 934. Uranium Concentrate Industry—Summary: 1990 to 2011

[In millions of feet (1.7 represents 1,700,000), except as indicated. See also Section 19, Table 955]

Item	Unit	1990	1995	2000	2006	2007	2008	2009	2010	2011
Exploration and development, surface drilling	Mil. ft.	1.7	1.3	1.0	2.7	5.2	5.1	3.7	4.9	6.3
Expenditures	Mil. dol.	(NA)	2.6	5.6	40.1	67.5	81.9	35.4	44.6	53.6
Number of mines operated	Number	39	12	10	11	12	17	20	9	11
Underground	Number	27	–	1	5	6	10	14	4	5
Openpit	Number	2	–	–	–	–	–	–	–	–
In situ leaching	Number	7	5	4	5	5	6	4	4	5
Other sources [1]	Number	3	7	5	1	1	1	2	1	1
Mine production	1,000 pounds	5,876	3,528	3,123	4,692	4,541	3,879	4,145	4,237	4,114
Underground	1,000 pounds	(D)	–	(D)	(D)	(D)	(D)	(D)	(D)	(D)
Openpit	1,000 pounds	1,881	–	–	–	–	–	–	–	–
In situ leaching	1,000 pounds	(D)	3,372	2,995	4,259	(D)	(D)	(D)	(D)	(D)
Other sources [1]	1,000 pounds	3,995	156	128	(D)	(D)	(D)	(D)	(D)	(D)
Uranium concentrate production	1,000 pounds	8,886	6,043	3,958	4,106	4,534	3,092	3,708	4,228	3,991
Concentrate shipments from mills and plants	1,000 pounds	12,957	5,500	3,187	3,838	4,050	4,130	3,620	5,137	4,000
Employment	Person-years	1,335	1,107	627	755	1,231	1,563	1,096	1,073	1,191

– Represents zero. D Data withheld to avoid disclosing figures for individual companies. NA Not available. [1] Includes mine water, mill site cleanup and mill tailings, and well field restoration as sources of uranium.

Source: U.S. Energy Information Administration, through 2002, *Uranium Industry*, annual. Thereafter, "Domestic Uranium Production Report," annual, May 2012. See also <http://www.eia.doe.gov/cneaf/nuclear/dupr/dupr.html>.

Energy and Utilities

This section presents statistics on fuel resources, energy production and consumption, electric energy, hydroelectric power, nuclear power, solar and wind energy, biomass, and the electric and gas utility industries. The principal sources are the U.S. Department of Energy's Energy Information Administration (EIA), the Edison Electric Institute, Washington, DC, and the American Gas Association, Arlington, VA. The Department of Energy was created in October 1977 and assumed and centralized the responsibilities of all or part of several agencies including the Federal Power Commission (FPC), the U.S. Bureau of Mines, the Federal Energy Administration, and the U.S. Energy Research and Development Administration. For additional data on transportation, see Section 23; on fuels, see Section 18; and on energy–related housing characteristics, see Section 20.

The EIA, in its *Annual Energy Review*, provides statistics and trend data on energy supply, demand, and prices. Information is included on petroleum and natural gas, coal, electricity, hydroelectric power, nuclear power, solar, wind, wood, and geothermal energy. Additional EIA Annual reports include the *Electric Power Annual*; *Natural Gas Annual*; *Petroleum Supply Annual*; *U.S. Crude Oil, Natural Gas, and Natural Gas Liquids Reserves Annual Report*; *Electric Sales, Revenue, and Price*; *State Energy Consumption, Price, and Expenditure Data*; *Annual Energy Outlook*; and *International Energy Statistics*. These various reports contain state, national, and international data on the production of electricity, net summer capability of generating plants, fuels used in energy production, energy sales and consumption, and hydroelectric power. The EIA also issues the *Monthly Energy Review*, which presents current supply, disposition, and price data and monthly publications on petroleum, coal, natural gas, and electric power.

Data on residential energy consumption, expenditures, and conservation activities are available from EIA's Residential Energy Consumption Survey (RECS) and are published every 4 years. The Commercial Buildings Energy Consumption Survey (CBECS), conducted on a quadrennial basis, collects information on the stock of U.S. commercial buildings, their energy-related characteristics, and their energy consumption and expenditures. Data on manufacturing energy consumption, use, and expenditures are also collected every 4 years from EIA's Manufacturing Energy Consumption Survey (MECS). Due to the long gaps between the RECS, CBECS, and MECS, tables are rotated in and out of Section 19 in an effort to keep the data as current as possible. The results from these surveys are published at <http://www.eia.gov/consumption/>.

The Edison Electric Institute's monthly bulletin and annual *Statistical Year Book of the Electric Power Industry* contain data on the distribution of electric energy by public utilities. The American Gas Association, in its monthly and quarterly bulletins and its yearbook, *Gas Facts*, presents data on gas utilities and financial and operating statistics.

Btu conversion factors—Various energy sources are converted from original units to the thermal equivalent using British thermal units (Btu). A Btu is the amount of energy required to raise the temperature of 1 pound of water 1 degree Fahrenheit (F) at or near 39.2 degrees F. Factors are calculated annually from the latest final annual data available; some are revised as a result.

Electric power industry—In recent years, EIA has restructured the industry categories it once used to gather and report electricity statistics. The electric power industry, previously divided into electric utilities and non–utilities, now consists of the Electric Power Sector, the Commercial Sector, and the Industrial Sector.

The Electric Power Sector is composed of electricity-only and combined-heat-and-power plants (CHPs) whose primary business is to sell electricity, or electricity and heat, to the public.

Electricity-only plants are composed of traditional electric utilities, and nontraditional participants, including energy service providers, power marketers, independent power producers (IPPs), and the portion of CHPs that produce only electricity.

A utility is defined as a corporation, person, agency, authority, or other legal entity or instrumentality aligned with distribution facilities for delivery of electric energy for use primarily by the public. Electric utilities include investor-owned electric utilities, municipal and state utilities, federal electric utilities, and rural electric cooperatives.

An independent power producer is an entity defined as a corporation, person, agency, authority, or other legal entity or instrumentality that owns or operates facilities whose primary business is to produce electricity for use by the public. They are not generally aligned with distribution facilities and are not considered electric utilities.

Combined-heat-and-power producers are plants designed to produce both heat and electricity from a single heat source. These types of electricity producers can be independent power producers or industrial or commercial establishments. As some independent power producers are CHPs, their information is included in the data for the combined-heat-and-power sector.

The Commercial Sector consists of commercial CHPs and commercial electricity–only plants. Industrial CHPs and industrial electricity–only plants make up the Industrial Sector. For more information, please refer to the *Electric Power Annual 2010* Web site at <http://www.eia.gov/electricity/annual/>.

Table 935. Utilities—Establishments, Revenue, Payroll, and Employees by Kind of Business: 2007

[584,193 represents $584,193,000,000. Includes only establishments or firms with payroll. Data based on the 2007 Economic Census. See headnote, Table 766 and Appendix III]

Kind of business	2007 NAICS code [1]	Establishments (number)	Revenue Total (mil. dol.)	Revenue Per paid employee (dol.)	Annual payroll Total (mil. dol.)	Annual payroll Per paid employee (dol.)	Paid employees for pay period including March 12 (number)
Utilities.......................	22	16,578	584,193	916,744	51,654	81,057	637,247
Electric power generation, transmission, & distribution....................	2211	9,554	445,693	871,368	43,618	85,277	511,487
Electric power generation..................	22111	1,934	120,968	985,134	11,297	92,001	122,793
Hydroelectric power generation............	221111	295	2,185	534,773	290	71,092	4,086
Fossil fuel electric power generation......	221112	1,248	85,362	1,140,283	6,413	85,667	74,860
Nuclear electric power generation.........	221113	79	28,996	763,603	4,083	107,525	37,972
Other electric power generation...........	221119	312	4,425	753,252	511	86,927	5,875
Electric power transmission, control & distribution...................	22112	7,620	324,726	835,428	32,321	83,153	388,694
Electric bulk power transmission & control.......................	221121	74	4,268	697,997	543	88,795	6,114
Electric power distribution.................	221122	7,546	320,458	837,625	31,778	83,063	382,580
Natural gas distribution........................	2212	2,377	128,555	1,542,000	6,038	72,420	83,369
Water, sewage, & other systems............	2213	4,647	9,944	234,582	1,998	47,125	42,391
Water supply & irrigation systems..........	22131	3,889	7,623	225,070	1,596	47,115	33,871
Sewage treatment facilities.................	22132	689	1,309	187,718	297	42,634	6,974
Steam & air-conditioning supply............	22133	69	1,012	654,375	105	67,603	1,546

[1] North American Industry Classification System, 2007; see text, Section 15.

Source: U.S. Census Bureau, "2007 Economic Census." See also <http://www.census.gov/econ/census07/>, accessed September 2010.

Table 936. Utilities—Employees, Annual Payroll, and Establishments by Industry: 2010

[55,396 represents $55,396,000,000. Excludes most government employees, railroad employees, and self-employed persons, etc. An establishment is a single physical location where business is conducted or where services or industrial operations are performed. See Appendix III]

Industry	2007 NAICS code [1]	Number of employees [2]	Annual payroll (mil. dol.)	Average payroll per employee (dol.)	Establishments by employment size-class Total	Under 20 employees	20 to 99 employees	100 to 499 employees	500 employees and over
Utilities, total............................	22	638,058	55,396	86,819	17,600	12,286	3,995	1,126	193
Electric power generation, transmission and distribution............	2211	511,538	46,520	90,942	10,314	6,188	3,062	882	182
Electric power generation................	22111	132,774	13,059	98,352	2,429	1,545	588	238	58
Hydroelectric power generation........	221111	3,670	300	81,764	350	309	38	3	–
Fossil fuel electric power generation.............	221112	73,137	6,741	92,167	1,330	670	436	217	7
Nuclear electric power generation.............	221113	49,174	5,361	109,021	147	64	22	10	51
Other electric power generation.............	221119	6,793	657	96,673	602	502	92	8	0
Electric power transmission, control & distribution.................	22112	378,764	33,461	88,344	7,885	4,643	2,474	644	124
Electric bulk power transmission & control.......	221121	10,124	1,000	98,776	194	125	44	21	4
Electric power distribution...............	221122	368,640	32,461	88,057	7,691	4,518	2,430	623	120
Natural gas distribution....................	2212	84,546	6,668	78,864	2,458	1,680	570	197	11
Water, sewage, & other systems.........	2213	41,974	2,208	52,604	4,828	4,418	363	47	–
Water supply & irrigation systems..............	22131	33,079	1,722	52,070	4,030	3,736	255	39	–
Sewage treatment facilities..............	22132	6,627	306	46,116	686	604	76	6	–
Steam & air-conditioning supply........	22133	2,268	180	79,347	112	78	32	2	–

– Represents zero. [1] North American Industry Classification System, 2007; see text, Section 15. [2] Covers full- and part-time employees who are on the payroll in the pay period including March 12.

Source: U.S. Census Bureau, "County Business Patterns," June 2012, <http://www.census.gov/econ/cbp/index.html>.

Table 937. Energy Supply and Disposition by Type of Fuel: 1975 to 2011

[In quadrillion British thermal units (Btu) (61.32 represents 61,320,000,000,000,000). For definition of Btu, see source and text, this section]

Year	Production Total [1]	Crude oil [2]	Dry natural gas	Coal [3]	Nuclear electric power	Renewable energy [4] Total [1]	Hydro-electric power [5]	Bio-mass [6]	Solar/photo-voltaic	Wind	Net imports, total [7]	Consumption Total [1,8]	Petro-leum [9]	Dry natural gas [10]	Coal	Nuclear electric power	Renewable energy [4] total
1975	61.32	17.73	19.64	14.99	1.90	4.69	3.15	1.50	(NA)	(NA)	11.71	71.96	32.73	19.95	12.66	1.90	4.69
1980	67.18	18.25	19.91	18.60	2.74	5.43	2.90	2.48	(NA)	(NA)	12.10	78.07	34.20	20.24	15.42	2.74	5.43
1985	67.70	18.99	16.98	19.33	4.08	6.08	2.97	3.02	(Z)	(Z)	7.58	76.39	30.92	17.70	17.48	4.08	6.08
1990	70.70	15.57	18.33	22.49	6.10	6.04	3.05	2.74	0.06	0.03	14.06	84.49	33.55	19.60	19.17	6.10	6.04
1995	71.17	13.89	19.08	22.13	7.08	6.56	3.21	3.10	0.07	0.03	17.75	91.03	34.44	22.67	20.09	7.08	6.56
1996	72.49	13.72	19.34	22.79	7.09	7.01	3.59	3.16	0.07	0.03	19.07	94.02	35.68	23.08	21.00	7.09	7.01
1997	72.47	13.66	19.39	23.31	6.60	7.02	3.64	3.11	0.07	0.03	20.70	94.60	36.16	23.22	21.45	6.60	7.02
1998	72.88	13.24	19.61	24.05	7.07	6.49	3.30	2.93	0.07	0.03	22.28	95.02	36.82	22.83	21.66	7.07	6.49
1999	71.74	12.45	19.34	23.30	7.61	6.52	3.27	2.97	0.07	0.05	23.54	96.65	37.84	22.91	21.62	7.61	6.52
2000	71.33	12.36	19.66	22.74	7.86	6.10	2.81	3.01	0.07	0.06	24.97	98.81	38.26	23.82	22.58	7.86	6.11
2001	71.73	12.28	20.17	23.55	8.03	5.16	2.24	2.62	0.06	0.07	26.39	96.17	38.19	22.77	21.91	8.03	5.16
2002	70.72	12.16	19.38	22.73	8.15	5.73	2.69	2.71	0.06	0.11	25.74	97.65	38.22	23.51	21.90	8.15	5.73
2003	70.04	12.03	19.63	22.09	7.96	5.98	2.82	2.81	0.06	0.11	27.01	97.98	38.81	22.83	22.32	7.96	5.98
2004	70.19	11.50	19.07	22.85	8.22	6.08	2.69	3.00	0.06	0.14	29.11	100.16	40.29	22.92	22.47	8.22	6.08
2005	69.43	10.96	18.56	23.19	8.16	6.23	2.70	3.10	0.06	0.18	30.15	100.28	40.39	22.57	22.80	8.16	6.24
2006	70.78	10.80	19.02	23.79	8.22	6.60	2.87	3.22	0.07	0.26	29.81	99.63	39.96	22.24	22.45	8.22	6.65
2007	71.37	10.72	19.79	23.49	8.46	6.51	2.45	3.46	0.08	0.34	29.22	101.30	39.77	23.66	22.75	8.46	6.52
2008	73.11	10.51	20.70	23.85	8.43	7.20	2.51	3.86	0.09	0.55	25.93	99.27	37.28	23.84	22.39	8.43	7.19
2009	72.66	11.35	21.14	21.62	8.36	7.62	2.67	3.93	0.10	0.72	22.74	94.56	35.40	23.42	19.69	8.36	7.60
2010	74.81	11.59	21.82	22.04	8.43	8.14	2.54	4.34	0.13	0.92	21.64	97.72	36.01	24.26	20.85	8.43	8.09
2011	78.10	11.99	23.51	22.18	8.26	9.24	3.17	4.51	0.16	1.17	18.23	97.30	35.28	24.84	19.64	8.26	9.14

NA Not available. Z Less than 5 trillion. [1] Includes other types of fuel, not shown separately. [2] Includes lease condensate. [3] Beginning 1989, includes waste coal supplied. Beginning 2001, also includes a small amount of refuse recovery. [4] Electricity net generation from conventional hydroelectric power, geothermal, solar, and wind; consumption of electricity from wood, waste, and alcohol fuels; geothermal heat pump and direct use energy; and solar thermal direct use energy. [5] Conventional hydroelectricity net generation. [6] Organic nonfossil material of biological origin constituting a renewable energy source. [7] Imports minus exports. [8] Includes coal coke net imports and electricity net imports, not shown separately. [9] Petroleum products supplied, including natural gas plant liquids and crude oil burned as fuel. Does not include biofuels that have been blended with petroleum—biofuels are included in "Biomass." [10] Excludes supplemental gaseous fuels. [11] Preliminary.

Source: U.S. Energy Information Administration, "Monthly Energy Review," May 2012, <http://www.eia.gov/totalenergy/>.

Table 938. Energy Supply and Disposition by Type of Fuel— Estimates, 2009 and 2010, and Projections, 2015 to 2030

[Quadrillion Btu (72.97 represents 72,970,000,000,000,000) per year. Btu = British thermal unit. For definition of Btu, see source and text, this section. Mcf = 1,000 cubic feet. Projections are "reference" or mid-level forecasts. See report for methodology and assumptions used in generating projections]

Type of Fuel	2009	2010	Projections			
			2015	2020	2025	2030
Production, total.................................	**72.97**	**75.50**	**79.64**	**84.80**	**88.61**	**91.87**
Crude oil and lease condensate...........................	11.35	11.59	13.23	14.40	13.77	13.71
Natural gas plant liquids.............................	2.57	2.78	3.33	3.79	3.93	3.98
Natural gas, dry..................................	21.09	22.10	24.22	25.69	26.91	27.58
Coal [1]..	21.63	22.06	20.24	20.74	22.25	23.22
Nuclear power...................................	8.36	8.44	8.68	9.28	9.60	9.56
Renewable energy [2].............................	7.50	7.90	9.34	10.25	11.47	13.03
Other [3].......................................	0.47	0.64	0.60	0.64	0.69	0.79
Imports, total....................................	**29.56**	**29.49**	**27.37**	**24.25**	**24.14**	**23.86**
Crude oil [4]....................................	19.70	20.14	18.87	16.00	16.23	16.04
Petroleum products [5]............................	5.40	5.02	4.32	4.03	4.08	4.04
Natural gas.....................................	3.85	3.81	3.73	3.49	2.75	3.00
Other imports [6]................................	0.61	0.52	0.44	0.72	1.07	0.78
Exports, total....................................	**6.79**	**8.06**	**9.66**	**9.84**	**10.79**	**11.38**
Petroleum [7]...................................	4.20	4.81	5.00	4.39	4.46	4.67
Natural gas.....................................	1.08	1.15	1.93	3.09	3.51	3.86
Coal...	1.51	2.10	2.73	2.36	2.82	2.85
Consumption, total................................	**94.71**	**98.16**	**97.43**	**99.32**	**101.99**	**104.32**
Petroleum products [8]............................	36.50	37.25	36.72	36.38	36.58	36.99
Natural gas.....................................	23.43	24.71	26.00	26.07	26.14	26.72
Coal...	19.62	20.76	17.80	18.73	20.02	20.59
Nuclear power...................................	8.36	8.44	8.68	9.28	9.60	9.56
Renewable energy [9].............................	6.50	6.73	7.93	8.57	9.38	10.21
Other [10]......................................	0.32	0.29	0.30	0.29	0.28	0.25
Net imports of petroleum..........................	**20.90**	**20.35**	**18.19**	**15.64**	**15.85**	**15.41**
Prices (2010 dollars per unit):						
Imported crude oil price [11]........................	59.72	75.87	113.97	115.74	121.21	126.51
Gas wellhead price (dol. per 1,000 cu. ft.) [12]........	3.85	4.16	3.94	4.19	5.12	5.69
Coal minemouth price (dol. per ton) [13]..............	33.62	35.61	42.08	40.96	44.05	47.28
Average electric price (cents per kWh)...............	9.90	9.80	9.70	9.60	9.70	9.80

[1] Includes waste coal. [2] Includes grid-connected electricity from conventional hydroelectric; wood and wood waste; landfill gas; municipal solid waste; other biomass; wind; photovoltaic and solar thermal sources; nonelectric energy from renewable sources, such as active and passive solar systems, and wood. Excludes electricity imports using renewable sources and nonmarketed renewable energy. [3] Includes nonbiogenic municipal solid waste, liquid hydrogen, methanol, and some domestic inputs to refineries. [4] Includes imports of crude oil for the Strategic Petroleum Reserve. [5] Includes imports of finished petroleum products, imports of unfinished oils, alcohols, ethers, blending components, and renewable fuels such as ethanol. [6] Includes coal, coal coke (net), and electricity (net). [7] Includes crude oil and petroleum products. [8] Includes petroleum-derived fuels and non-petroleum-derived fuels, such as ethanol, biodiesel, and coal-based synthetic liquids. Petroleum coke, which is a solid, is included. Also included are natural gas plant liquids, crude oil consumed as a fuel, and liquid hydrogen. [9] Includes grid-connected electricity from wood and wood waste, non-electric energy from wood, and biofuels heat and coproducts used in the production of liquid fuels, but excludes the energy content of the liquid fuels. Also includes non-biogenic municipal solid waste and net electricity imports. [10] Includes non-biogenic municipal solid waste and net electricity imports. [11] Weighted average price delivered to U.S. refiners. [12] Represents lower 48 onshore and offshore supplies. [13] Includes reported prices for both open market and captive mines.

Source: U.S. Energy Information Administration, *Annual Energy Outlook 2012*, June 2012. See also <http://www.eia.gov/forecasts/aeo/index.cfm>.

Table 939. Fossil Fuel Production Prices by Type of Fuel: 1980 to 2010

[In dollars per million British thermal units (Btu), except as indicated. For definition of Btu and mineral fuel conversions, see source and text, this section. All fuel prices taken as close to the point of production as possible]

Fuel	1980	1990	1995	2000	2004	2005	2006	2007	2008	2009	2010 [1]
CURRENT DOLLARS											
Composite [2]..................	2.04	1.84	1.47	2.60	3.61	4.74	4.73	4.95	6.52	3.97	4.83
Crude oil [3]..................	3.72	3.45	2.52	4.61	6.34	8.67	10.29	11.47	16.21	9.72	12.88
Natural gas [4]..................	1.45	1.55	1.40	3.32	4.95	6.64	5.79	5.66	7.25	3.33	3.78
Coal [5]..................	1.10	1.00	0.88	0.80	0.98	1.16	1.24	1.29	1.55	1.67	1.77
CONSTANT (2005) DOLLARS											
Composite [2]..................	4.28	2.55	1.81	2.93	3.73	4.74	4.58	4.65	6.01	3.62	4.37
Crude oil [3]..................	7.80	4.78	3.09	5.20	6.55	8.67	9.97	10.79	14.93	8.86	11.64
Natural gas [4]..................	3.03	2.14	1.72	3.75	5.11	6.64	5.61	5.33	6.67	3.04	3.41
Coal [5]..................	2.30	1.38	1.08	0.90	1.01	1.16	1.20	1.21	1.42	1.52	1.60

[1] Preliminary. [2] Derived by multiplying the price per Btu of each fossil fuel by the total Btu content of the production of each fossil fuel and dividing this accumulated value of total fossil fuel production by the accumulated Btu content of total fossil fuel production. [3] Domestic first purchase prices. [4] Wellhead prices. [5] Free-on-board (f.o.b.) rail/barge prices, which are the f.o.b. prices of coal at the point of first sale, excluding freight or shipping and insurance costs. Includes bituminous coal, subbituminous coal, and lignite.

Source: U.S. Energy Information Administration, *Annual Energy Review 2010*, October 2011. See also <http://www.eia.gov/totalenergy/data/annual>.

Table 940. Energy Consumption by Mode of Transportation: 2000 to 2010

[40 represents 40,000,000,000,000. Btu = British thermal unit. For conversion rates for each fuel type, see source]

Mode	Trillion Btu			Physical units			
	2000	2005	2010	Unit	2000	2005	2010
AIR [1]							
Aviation gasoline....................	40	35	26	mil. gal.	333	295	221
Jet fuel.........................	2,008	1,999	1,686	mil. gal.	14,876	14,811	12,491
HIGHWAY							
Light duty vehicle, short wheel base and motorcycle [2].........................	9,159	9,701	10,833	mil. gal.	73,275	77,608	86,666
Light duty vehicle, long wheel base [2]...........	6,617	7,359	4,517	mil. gal.	52,939	58,869	36,133
Single-unit 2-axle 6-tire or more truck...........	1,195	1,188	1,884	mil. gal.	9,563	9,501	15,072
Combination truck [3].....................	3,208	3,461	3,736	mil. gal.	25,666	27,689	29,885
Bus..............................	139	140	240	mil. gal.	1,112	1,120	1,924
TRANSIT [4]							
Electricity........................	18	20	22	mil. kWh	5,382	5,765	6,414
Diesel..............................	82	74	81	mil. gal.	591	532	633
Gasoline and other nondiesel fuels [5].............	3	4	18	mil. gal.	24	29	98
Compressed natural gas.................	6	13	18	mil. gal.	44	94	126
RAIL [6]							
Distillate/diesel fuel...................	513	568	485	mil. gal.	3,700	4,098	3,494
Electricity........................	2	2	2	mil. kWh	470	531	559
WATER							
Residual fuel oil.....................	960	775	630	mil. gal.	6,410	5,179	4,206
Distillate/diesel fuel oil...................	314	278	186	mil. gal.	2,261	2,006	1,343
Gasoline..........................	141	158	146	mil. gal.	1,124	1,261	1,167
PIPELINE							
Natural gas........................	662	602	690	mil. cu. ft.	642,210	584,026	668,847

[1] Includes general aviation and certified carriers, domestic operations only. Also includes fuel used in air taxi operations, but not commuter operations. [2] Data for 2010 were calculated using a new methodology developed by FHWA. Data for 2010 are based on new categories and are not comparable to previous years. The new category "Light duty vehicle, short wheel base" includes passenger cars, light trucks, vans and sport utility vehicles with a wheelbase (WB) equal to or less than 121 inches. The new category "Light duty vehicle, long wheel base" includes large passenger cars, vans, pickup trucks, and sport/utility vehicles with wheelbases (WB) larger than 121 inches. [3] A power unit (truck tractor) and one or more trailing units (a semitrailer or trailer). [4] Includes light, heavy, and commuter rail; motor bus; trolley bus; van pools; automated guideway; and demand-responsive vehicles. [5] Gasoline and all other nondiesel fuels such as liquefied natural gas, methanol, and propane, except compressed natural gas. [6] Includes Amtrak and freight service carriers that have an annual operating revenue of $250 million or more.

Source: U.S. Department of Transportation, Bureau of Transportation Statistics, "National Transportation Statistics, 2012," <http://www.bts.gov/publications/national_transportation_statistics/>, accessed July 2012.

Table 941. Energy Consumption by End-Use Sector: 1975 to 2011

[71.96 represents 71,960,000,000,000,000 Btu. Btu = British thermal units. For definition of Btu, see source and text, this section. See Appendix III. Total energy consumption in the end-use sectors consists of primary energy consumption, electricity retail sales, and electrical system energy losses]

Year	Total (quad. Btu)	Residential and commercial [1] (quad. Btu)	Industrial [2] (quad. Btu)	Transportation (quad. Btu)	Percent of total		
					Residential and commercial [1]	Industrial [2]	Transportation
1975................	71.96	24.31	29.41	18.25	33.8	40.9	25.4
1980................	78.07	26.33	32.04	19.70	33.7	41.0	25.2
1985................	76.40	27.49	28.82	20.09	36.0	37.7	26.3
1990................	84.50	30.27	31.81	22.42	35.8	37.6	26.5
1995................	91.03	33.21	33.97	23.85	36.5	37.3	26.2
2000................	98.81	37.60	34.66	26.55	38.1	35.1	26.9
2002................	97.69	38.17	32.68	26.84	39.1	33.5	27.5
2003................	97.98	38.45	32.53	26.99	39.2	33.2	27.6
2004................	100.15	38.75	33.51	27.90	38.7	33.5	27.9
2005................	100.28	39.48	32.44	28.35	39.4	32.4	28.3
2006................	99.62	38.41	32.40	28.83	38.5	32.5	28.9
2007................	101.34	39.83	32.39	29.12	39.3	32.0	28.7
2008................	99.28	39.98	31.29	28.01	40.3	31.5	28.2
2009................	94.56	38.96	28.53	27.07	41.2	30.2	28.6
2010................	97.72	39.94	30.31	27.47	40.9	31.0	28.1
2011................	97.31	39.64	30.59	27.08	40.7	31.4	27.8

[1] Commercial sector fuel use, including that at commercial combined-heat-and-power (CHP) and commercial electricity-only plants. [2] Industrial sector fuel use, including that at industrial combined-heat-and-power (CHP) and industrial electricity-only plants.

Source: U.S. Energy Information Administration, "Monthly Energy Review," May 2012, <http://www.eia.gov/totalenergy/data/monthly/>.

Table 942. Energy Consumption–End-Use Sector and Selected Source by State: 2009

[In trillions of Btu (94,447 represents 94,447,000,000,000,000), except as indicated. For definition of Btu, see source and text, this section. Data are preliminary. U.S. totals may not equal sum of states due to independent rounding and/or interstate flows of electricity that are not allocated to the states. For technical notes and documentation, see source <http://www.eia.gov/state/seds/seds-technical-notes-updates.cfm>]

| State | Total [1,2] | Per capita [3] (mil.Btu) | End-use sector [4] | | | | Source | | | | |
			Resi-dential	Com-mercial	Indus-trial [2]	Trans-portation	Petro-leum [5]	Natural gas (dry) [6]	Coal	Hydro-electric power [7]	Nuclear electric power
U.S.	94,447	308	21,027	17,896	28,559	26,966	35,411	23,348	19,693	2,669	8,356
AL	1,907	401	383	266	789	469	584	474	631	122	415
AK	630	902	53	61	325	191	256	344	15	13	–
AZ	1,454	229	401	352	208	494	521	377	413	63	321
AR	1,055	364	226	167	373	289	343	248	264	41	159
CA	8,006	217	1,527	1,579	1,770	3,130	3,508	2,391	52	272	332
CO	1,452	292	333	292	410	418	472	522	350	18	–
CT	788	221	262	198	84	245	341	188	26	5	174
DE	255	286	64	59	60	71	91	52	34	–	–
DC	182	308	35	125	4	19	19	34	–	–	–
FL	4,295	230	1,294	1,062	487	1,453	1,624	1,082	582	2	305
GA	2,949	307	723	553	720	953	1,028	475	723	32	331
HI	270	200	36	42	63	129	231	–	19	1	–
ID	509	327	130	84	170	125	151	87	8	102	–
IL	3,815	298	944	774	1,108	990	1,243	946	1,015	1	999
IN	2,623	406	523	357	1,150	592	768	511	1,365	5	–
IA	1,419	468	235	199	683	303	415	284	445	10	49
KS	1,084	383	225	197	386	276	384	289	356	–	92
KY	1,877	435	358	242	811	465	663	214	937	32	–
LA	3,366	749	358	282	2,079	647	1,375	1,300	253	12	176
ME	431	324	94	73	140	124	201	73	2	41	–
MD	1,429	249	404	404	155	467	527	204	267	18	152
MA	1,426	219	440	290	243	454	576	409	92	12	56
MI	2,697	272	754	595	612	736	826	747	736	13	229
MN	1,810	343	408	352	577	472	604	406	329	8	130
MS	1,139	385	228	165	389	357	408	371	142	–	115
MO	1,818	305	507	398	348	565	658	267	766	18	107
MT	412	418	88	78	140	106	172	76	173	93	–
NE	759	419	153	134	301	171	210	165	250	4	99
NV	708	264	173	129	191	215	243	284	84	24	–
NH	303	230	88	70	39	106	159	62	33	16	92
NJ	2,394	273	577	624	292	902	1,079	638	60	–	359
NM	670	329	118	122	227	202	247	247	306	3	–
NY	3,819	198	1,128	1,233	366	1,091	1,423	1,166	156	270	455
NC	2,545	269	712	578	547	708	840	251	679	51	427
ND	427	642	66	63	210	88	126	52	423	14	–
OH	3,634	315	906	678	1,124	925	1,165	768	1,267	5	159
OK	1,491	401	304	247	519	421	489	678	373	35	–
OR	1,067	280	274	208	252	332	362	255	33	322	–
PA	3,654	288	919	685	1,072	979	1,281	834	1,224	26	809
RI	219	208	69	57	30	64	96	95	–	(Z)	–
SC	1,581	344	352	257	516	456	542	197	372	23	546
SD	360	446	69	60	139	92	117	66	38	43	–
TN	2,136	339	515	363	667	592	752	223	478	100	282
TX	11,297	456	1,612	1,460	5,502	2,724	5,446	3,462	1,498	10	434
UT	755	277	165	152	202	236	267	224	365	8	–
VT	158	253	48	32	24	54	82	9	–	15	56
VA	2,386	301	611	590	440	746	834	330	335	14	295
WA	2,033	305	502	390	529	612	757	319	84	712	69
WV	716	387	165	111	274	165	213	114	743	16	–
WI	1,745	308	419	347	548	430	532	393	426	14	133
WY	520	929	48	61	290	121	165	146	474	9	–

– Represents zero. Z Less than 50 billion Btu. [1] Includes other sources, not shown separately. [2] U.S. total energy and U.S. industrial sector include net imports of coal coke that are not allocated to the states. [3] Based on estimated resident population as of July 1. [4] End-use sector data include electricity sales and associated electrical system energy losses. [5] Includes fuel ethanol blended into motor gasoline. [6] Includes supplemental gaseous fuels. [7] Conventional hydroelectric power. Does not include pumped-storage hydroelectricity.

Source: U.S. Energy Information Administration, "State Energy Data, 2009," June 2011, <http://www.eia.gov/state/seds/>.

Table 943. Renewable Energy Consumption Estimates by Source: 1990 to 2011

[In quadrillion Btu (6.04 represents 6,040,000,000,000,000). For definition of Btu, see source and text, this section. Renewable energy is obtained from sources that are essentially inexhaustible, unlike fossil fuels of which there is a finite supply]

Source and sector	1990	2000	2005	2008	2009	2010	2011 [1]
Consumption, total	**6.04**	**6.11**	**6.24**	**7.19**	**7.60**	**8.09**	**9.14**
Conventional hydroelectric power [2]	3.05	2.81	2.70	2.51	2.67	2.54	3.17
Geothermal energy [3]	0.17	0.16	0.18	0.19	0.20	0.21	0.23
Biomass [4]	2.74	3.01	3.12	3.85	3.91	4.29	4.41
Solar energy [5]	0.06	0.07	0.06	0.09	0.10	0.13	0.16
Wind energy [6]	0.03	0.06	0.18	0.55	0.72	0.92	1.17
Residential [7]	0.64	0.49	0.50	0.56	0.55	0.57	0.61
Biomass [4]	0.58	0.42	0.43	0.45	0.43	0.42	0.43
Geothermal [3]	0.01	0.01	0.02	0.03	0.03	0.04	0.04
Solar [5]	0.06	0.06	0.06	0.08	0.09	0.11	0.14
Commercial [8]	0.10	0.13	0.12	0.12	0.13	0.13	0.13
Biomass [4]	0.09	0.12	0.11	0.11	0.11	0.11	0.11
Geothermal [3]	0.03	0.01	0.01	0.01	0.02	0.02	0.02
Hydroelectric [2]	(Z)	(Z)	(Z)	(Z)	(Z)	(Z)	(Z)
Industrial [9]	1.72	1.93	1.87	2.05	2.02	2.25	2.30
Biomass [4]	1.68	1.88	1.84	2.03	1.99	2.23	2.27
Geothermal [3]	(Z)	(Z)	(Z)	(Z)	(Z)	(Z)	(Z)
Hydroelectric [2]	0.03	0.04	0.03	0.02	0.02	0.02	0.02
Transportation	0.06	0.13	0.34	0.83	0.94	1.07	1.15
Fuel ethanol [10]	0.06	0.13	0.33	0.79	0.89	1.04	1.04
Biodiesel [11]	(NA)	(NA)	0.01	0.04	0.04	0.03	0.11
Electric power [12]	3.52	3.43	3.41	3.63	3.97	4.06	4.95
Biomass [4]	0.32	0.45	0.41	0.44	0.44	0.46	0.44
Geothermal [3]	0.16	0.14	0.15	0.15	0.15	0.15	0.16
Hydroelectric [2]	3.01	2.77	2.67	2.49	2.65	2.52	3.15
Solar [5]	(Z)	0.01	0.01	0.01	0.01	0.01	0.02
Wind [6]	0.03	0.06	0.18	0.55	0.72	0.92	1.17

NA Not available. Z Less than 5 trillion Btu. [1] Preliminary. [2] Power produced from natural stream flow as regulated by available storage. [3] As used at electric power plants, hot water or steam extracted from geothermal reservoirs in the Earth's crust that is supplied to steam turbines at electric power plants that drive generators to produce electricity. [4] Wood and wood-derived fuels, municipal solid waste (from biogenic sources, landfill gas, sludge waste, agricultural by products, and other biomass), fuel ethanol, and biodiesel. [5] The radiant energy of the sun, which can be converted into other forms of energy, such as heat or electricity. Solar thermal and photovoltaic electricity net generation and solar thermal direct use energy. [6] Energy present in wind motion that can be converted to mechanical energy for driving pumps, mills, and electric power generators. Wind pushes against sails, vanes, or blades radiating from a central rotating shaft. [7] Consists of living quarters for private households, but excludes institutional living quarters. [8] Consists of service-providing facilities and equipment of businesses, governments, and other private and public organizations. Includes institutional living quarters and sewage treatment facilities. Includes commercial combined-heat-and-power and commercial electricity-only plants. [9] Consists of all facilities and equipment used for producing, processing, or assembling goods. Includes industrial combined-heat- and-power and industrial electricity-only plants. [10] Ethanol primarily derived from corn. [11] Any liquid biofuel suitable as a diesel fuel substitute, additive, or extender. [12] Consists of electricity-only and combined-heat-and-power plants whose primary business is to sell electricity and/or heat to the public. Includes sources not shown separately.

Source: U.S. Energy Information Administration, "Monthly Energy Review," June 2012, <http://www.eia.gov/totalenergy/data/monthly/>.

Table 944. Energy Expenditures and Average Fuel Prices by Source and Sector: 1980 to 2009

[In millions of dollars (374,244 represents $374,244,000,000), except as indicated. For definition of Btu, see text, this section. End-use sector and electric utilities exclude expenditures and prices on energy sources such as hydropower, solar, wind, and geothermal. Also excludes expenditures for reported amounts of energy consumed by the energy industry for production, transportation, and processing operations]

Source and Sector	1980	1990	1995	2000	2005	2006	2007	2008	2009
EXPENDITURES (mil. dol.)									
Total [1,2,3]	374,244	472,444	513,947	685,922	1,046,843	1,159,485	1,234,240	1,408,685	1,061,252
Natural gas [4]	51,061	65,278	75,020	119,094	200,303	190,382	196,868	230,305	159,235
Petroleum products	237,573	235,284	236,803	357,475	597,285	682,465	740,628	870,993	578,496
Motor gasoline [5]	124,408	126,558	136,647	192,153	312,047	357,286	389,282	438,237	317,088
Coal	22,607	28,602	27,431	28,080	36,932	40,005	42,717	49,438	45,824
Retail electricity	98,095	176,691	205,876	231,577	295,787	323,962	340,925	360,570	350,438
Residential sector [6]	69,174	110,696	127,961	155,319	215,186	225,277	237,970	257,448	240,768
Commercial sector [2,3]	47,074	79,605	92,106	113,423	155,164	167,628	174,797	192,541	175,027
Industrial sector [2,3]	94,316	102,411	107,067	140,090	208,849	228,144	236,403	270,673	184,248
Transportation sector [2]	163,680	179,732	186,813	277,090	467,644	538,436	585,070	688,024	461,209
Motor gasoline [5]	121,809	123,845	134,641	189,836	304,875	348,695	381,201	430,705	311,605
Electric utilities [3]	38,027	40,626	39,073	60,054	95,975	90,104	100,719	118,545	84,496
AVERAGE FUEL PRICES (dol. per mil. Btu)									
All sectors	6.89	8.25	8.28	10.28	15.55	17.36	18.24	21.37	17.03
Residential sector [6]	7.46	11.87	12.62	14.26	19.20	21.54	21.62	23.13	22.13
Commercial sector [3]	7.83	11.88	12.63	13.92	18.61	20.65	20.75	22.47	20.69
Industrial sector [3]	4.71	5.23	4.97	6.42	10.39	11.37	11.92	14.29	11.04
Transportation sector	8.61	8.27	8.09	10.72	16.89	19.13	20.61	25.23	17.54
Electric utilities [3]	1.77	1.48	1.29	1.71	2.61	2.48	2.68	3.21	2.44

[1] Includes other sources not shown separately. [2] Through 1990, total also includes ethanol blended into gasoline that is not included in motor gasoline for those years. [3] There are no direct fuel costs for hydroelectric, geothermal, wind, photovoltaic, or solar thermal energy. [4] Excludes supplemental gaseous fuels. [5] Beginning 1995, includes fuel ethanol blended into motor gasoline. [6] There are no direct fuel costs for geothermal, photovoltaic, or solar thermal energy.

Source: U.S. Energy Information Administration, "State Energy Data: Prices and Expenditures," annual, June 2011, <http://www.eia.gov/state/seds/>.

Table 945. Fuel Ethanol and Biodiesel—Summary: 1990 to 2011

[110.9 represents 110,900,000,000,000. Data for 1990 are estimates. Beginning 1995, only feedstock data are estimates. Minus sign (−) indicates an excess of exports over imports, except where noted]

Fuel	1990	1995	2000	2005	2007	2008	2009	2010	2011 [1]
FUEL ETHANOL									
Feedstock [2] (tril. Btu)	110.9	197.7	233.1	552.4	914.3	1,299.5	1,517.5	1,839.3	1,921.9
Production:									
1,000 bbl.	17,802	32,325	38,627	92,961	155,263	221,637	260,424	316,617	332,107
Tril. Btu	63.4	115.2	137.6	331.2	553.2	789.7	927.9	1,127.5	1,182.3
Net imports [3] (1,000 bbl.)	(NA)	387	116	3,234	10,457	12,610	4,720	-9,115	-25,322
Stocks [4] (1,000 bbl.)	(NA)	2,186	3,400	5,563	10,535	14,226	16,594	17,941	18,261
Stock change [5,6] (1,000 bbl.)	(NA)	-207	-624	-439	1,775	3,691	2,368	1,347	321
Consumption:									
1,000 bbl.	17,802	32,919	39,367	96,634	163,945	230,556	262,776	306,155	306,464
Tril. Btu	63.4	117.3	140.3	344.3	584.1	821.5	936.3	1,090.2	1,091.0
BIODIESEL									
Feedstock [7] (tril. Btu)	(NA)	(NA)	(NA)	11.7	63.4	87.7	66.7	44.4	125.1
Production:									
1,000 bbl.	(NA)	(NA)	(NA)	2,162	11,662	16,145	12,281	8,177	23,034
Tril. Btu	(NA)	(NA)	(NA)	11.6	62.5	86.5	65.8	43.8	123.4
Net imports (1,000 bbl.)	(NA)	(NA)	(NA)	1	-3,135	-8,626	-4,489	-1,958	-879
Consumption:									
1,000 bbl.	(NA)	(NA)	(NA)	2,163	8,528	7,519	7,750	6,258	20,915
Tril. Btu	(NA)	(NA)	(NA)	11.6	45.7	40.3	41.5	33.5	112.1

NA Not available. [1] Preliminary. [2] Total corn and other biomass inputs to the production of fuel ethanol. [3] Through 2009, data are for fuel ethanol imports only; data for fuel ethanol exports are not available. Beginning in 2010, data are for fuel ethanol imports minus fuel ethanol exports. [4] Imports minus exports. Stocks are at end of year. [5] A negative number indicates a decrease in stocks. [6] Data for 2011 derived using the preliminary December 2010 stock value, not the final December 2010 value shown under "Stocks." [7] Total vegetable oil and other biomass inputs to the production of biodiesel.

Source: U.S. Energy Information Administration, "Monthly Energy Review," June 2012, <http://www.eia.gov/totalenergy/data/monthly/>.

Table 946. Energy Expenditures—End-Use Sector and Selected Source by State: 2009

[In millions of dollars (1,061,252 represents $1,061,252,000,000). Data are preliminary. End-use sector and electric utilities exclude expenditures on energy sources such as hydroelectric, photovoltaic, solar thermal, wind, and geothermal. Also excludes expenditures for reported amounts of energy consumed by the energy industry for production, transportation, and processing operations. For technical notes and documentation, see source, <http://www.eia.gov/state/seds/seds-technical-notes-complete.cfm>]

State	Total [1,2]	End-use sector				Source			
		Residential	Commercial	Industrial [2]	Transportation	Petroleum products [3]	Natural gas [4]	Coal	Electricity sales
U.S.	1,061,252	240,768	175,027	184,248	461,209	578,496	159,235	45,824	350,438
AL	19,020	4,217	2,695	4,247	7,862	9,668	2,710	1,774	7,115
AK	5,338	759	720	520	3,339	4,095	480	41	937
AZ	17,539	4,315	3,247	1,644	8,334	9,279	2,274	754	7,017
AR	10,554	2,165	1,376	2,162	4,850	5,803	1,746	456	3,171
CA	104,712	18,738	18,717	11,656	55,602	59,783	14,166	140	34,114
CO	14,539	3,170	2,277	2,114	6,977	8,021	2,759	555	4,196
CT	13,349	4,820	2,912	1,051	4,567	6,739	1,601	91	5,366
DE	3,594	945	736	668	1,245	1,627	664	111	1,367
DC	2,364	463	1,534	37	330	357	431	1	1,582
FL	54,553	14,911	10,981	3,968	24,693	27,686	8,702	1,976	25,825
GA	32,196	7,794	4,895	4,299	15,208	16,849	4,116	2,625	11,516
HI	4,652	802	861	713	2,276	3,266	77	44	2,112
ID	4,899	1,083	593	1,031	2,192	2,688	693	21	1,481
IL	40,474	9,451	6,688	7,203	17,132	20,480	7,617	1,741	12,306
IN	24,598	5,106	2,940	6,347	10,205	12,315	3,963	3,273	7,478
IA	13,102	2,484	1,634	3,715	5,269	7,561	2,213	630	3,215
KS	10,912	2,244	1,571	2,610	4,487	6,310	1,695	512	3,029
KY	17,477	3,140	1,887	4,471	7,979	10,047	1,560	2,123	5,713
LA	24,197	2,980	2,186	9,523	9,508	15,188	4,450	594	5,397
ME	5,658	1,529	967	859	2,303	3,730	511	6	1,477
MD	20,200	5,790	4,541	1,487	8,383	9,811	2,253	795	8,186
MA	22,617	7,026	4,062	3,201	8,328	10,881	4,120	321	8,400
MI	31,289	8,559	5,257	4,587	12,886	15,407	6,736	1,649	9,158
MN	18,287	3,946	2,761	3,287	8,293	10,351	2,780	566	5,166
MS	11,441	2,333	1,524	1,973	5,612	6,374	1,802	479	3,962
MO	19,933	4,691	2,931	2,560	9,752	11,366	2,736	1,187	5,857
MT	4,245	847	653	844	1,902	2,536	603	238	1,070
NE	6,977	1,340	957	1,661	3,019	3,807	1,114	338	2,050
NV	8,866	2,134	1,319	1,557	3,856	4,405	2,007	185	3,494
NH	4,900	1,470	981	487	1,963	2,964	515	120	1,619
NJ	33,333	8,764	7,550	2,711	14,309	16,862	6,388	239	10,952
NM	6,454	1,166	976	777	3,536	4,193	793	582	1,710
NY	56,400	17,821	16,541	3,251	18,787	24,719	11,770	450	21,728
NC	29,011	7,373	4,805	3,952	12,881	15,673	2,432	2,451	10,821
ND	3,576	568	446	1,091	1,472	2,146	251	725	832
OH	40,900	10,021	6,404	7,896	16,579	20,032	7,459	3,264	13,070
OK	14,486	2,701	1,801	3,284	6,700	7,521	4,253	640	3,760
OR	11,994	2,549	1,649	1,726	6,070	6,779	2,023	60	3,558
PA	43,319	11,674	6,710	7,574	17,361	22,466	7,480	3,126	13,638
RI	3,429	1,133	768	353	1,175	1,777	842	–	1,084
SC	16,554	3,675	2,210	2,928	7,741	8,882	1,391	1,356	6,432
SD	3,354	625	435	674	1,620	2,102	435	68	813
TN	22,892	4,863	3,390	4,690	9,949	12,498	1,916	1,265	8,159
TX	115,217	18,784	13,270	40,041	43,123	74,155	13,059	2,836	33,311
UT	7,357	1,385	1,066	857	4,050	4,453	1,246	580	1,846
VT	2,502	815	431	237	1,019	1,673	111	–	701
VA	26,739	6,663	4,719	2,724	12,633	14,535	2,673	1,106	9,631
WA	21,019	4,369	2,949	2,544	11,157	12,363	3,078	197	5,893
WV	7,010	1,445	906	1,833	2,826	3,951	844	2,063	1,984
WI	19,373	4,678	3,133	3,484	8,077	9,848	3,312	905	6,161
WY	3,895	449	469	1,184	1,794	2,478	387	563	983

– Represents or rounds to zero. [1] Total expenditures are the sum of purchases for each source (including retail electricity sales) less electric power sector purchases of fuel. [2] Includes sources not shown separately, such as electricity imports and exports and coal coke net imports, which are not allocated to the states. [3] Includes fuel ethanol blended into motor gasoline. [4] Includes supplemental gaseous fuels.

Source: U.S. Energy Information Administration, "State Energy Data, 2009," June 2011, <http://www.eia.gov/state/seds/>.

Table 947. Energy Imports and Exports by Type of Fuel: 1980 to 2010

[In quadrillion of Btu. (12.10 represents 12,100,000,000,000,000 Btu). For definition of Btu, see source and text, this section]

Type of fuel	1980	1990	1995	2000	2004	2005	2006	2007	2008	2009	2010 [1]
Net imports, total [2]	**12.10**	**14.06**	**17.75**	**24.97**	**29.11**	**30.15**	**29.81**	**29.22**	**25.93**	**22.74**	**21.62**
Coal	-2.39	-2.70	-2.08	-1.21	-0.57	-0.51	-0.36	-0.60	-1.22	-0.95	-1.62
Natural gas (dry)	0.96	1.46	2.74	3.62	3.50	3.71	3.56	3.89	3.11	2.76	2.68
Petroleum [3]	13.50	15.29	16.89	22.38	25.99	26.81	26.42	25.77	23.89	20.84	20.48
Other [4]	0.04	0.01	0.20	0.18	0.19	0.14	0.19	0.15	0.15	0.08	0.07
Imports, total	15.80	18.82	22.26	28.97	33.54	34.71	34.68	34.70	32.99	29.71	29.79
Coal	0.03	0.07	0.24	0.31	0.68	0.76	0.91	0.91	0.86	0.57	0.48
Natural gas (dry)	1.01	1.55	2.90	3.87	4.37	4.45	4.29	4.72	4.08	3.85	3.83
Petroleum [3]	14.66	17.12	18.88	24.53	28.20	29.25	29.17	28.78	27.69	25.08	25.29
Other [4]	0.10	0.08	0.24	0.26	0.30	0.25	0.31	0.29	0.37	0.21	0.19
Exports, total	3.69	4.75	4.51	4.01	4.43	4.56	4.87	5.48	7.06	6.96	8.17
Coal	2.42	2.77	2.32	1.53	1.25	1.27	1.26	1.51	2.07	1.51	2.10
Natural gas (dry)	0.05	0.09	0.16	0.25	0.86	0.74	0.73	0.83	0.97	1.08	1.15
Petroleum	1.16	1.82	1.99	2.15	2.21	2.44	2.75	3.01	3.80	4.24	4.81
Other [4]	0.07	0.07	0.05	0.08	0.11	0.11	0.13	0.14	0.22	0.13	0.12

[1] Preliminary. [2] Net imports equals imports minus exports. Minus sign (–) indicates exports are greater than imports. [3] Includes imports into the Strategic Petroleum Reserve. [4] Coal coke, small amounts of electricity transmitted across U.S. borders with Canada and Mexico, and small amounts of biodiesel.

Source: U.S. Energy Information Administration, *Annual Energy Review 2010*, October 2011. See also <http://www.eia.gov/totalenergy/>.

Table 948. U.S. Foreign Trade in Selected Mineral Fuels: 1980 to 2011

[985 represents 985,000,000,000 cu. ft. Minus sign (–) indicates trade deficit]

Mineral fuel	Unit	1980	1990	1995	2000	2005	2008	2009	2010	2011 [1]
Natural gas:										
Imports	Bil. cu. ft.	985	1,532	2,841	3,782	4,341	3,984	3,751	3,741	3,456
Exports	Bil. cu. ft.	49	86	154	244	729	963	1,072	1,137	1,507
Net trade [2]	Bil. cu. ft.	-936	-1,446	-2,687	-3,538	-3,612	-3,021	-2,679	-2,604	-1,949
Crude oil: [3]										
Imports [4]	Mil. bbl.	1,926	2,151	2,639	3,320	3,696	3,581	3,290	3,363	3,261
Exports	Mil. bbl.	105	40	35	18	12	10	16	15	17
Net trade [2]	Mil. bbl.	-1,821	-2,112	-2,604	-3,301	-3,684	-3,570	-3,274	-3,348	-3,244
Petroleum products:										
Imports	Mil. bbl.	601	775	586	874	1,310	1,146	977	942	937
Exports	Mil. bbl.	94	273	312	362	414	649	723	843	1,073
Net trade [2]	Mil. bbl.	-507	-502	-274	-512	-896	-497	-255	-98	135
Coal:										
Imports	Mil. sh. tons	1	3	9	13	30	34	23	19	13
Exports	Mil. sh. tons	92	106	89	58	50	82	59	82	107
Net trade [2]	Mil. sh. tons	90.5	103.1	79.1	46.0	19.5	47.3	36.5	62.4	94.2

[1] Preliminary. [2] Exports minus imports. [3] Includes lease condensate. [4] Includes Strategic Petroleum Reserve imports.

Source: U.S. Energy Information Administration, "Monthly Energy Review," July 2011, <http://www.eia.gov/totalenergy/data/monthly/> and "Petroleum & Other Liquids, Imports/Exports & Movements," <http://www.eia.gov/petroleum/data.cfm#imports>.

Table 949. Crude Oil Imports Into the U.S. by Country of Origin: 1980 to 2011

[In millions of barrels (1,921 represents 1,921,000,000). Barrels contain 42 gallons. Crude oil imports are reported by the Petroleum Administration for Defense (PAD) District in which they are to be processed. A PAD District is a geographic aggregation of the 50 states and D.C. into 5 districts. Includes crude oil imported for storage in the Strategic Petroleum Reserve (SPR). Total OPEC excludes, and Non-OPEC includes, petroleum imported into the United States indirectly from members of OPEC, primarily from Caribbean and West European areas, as petroleum products that were refined from crude oil produced by OPEC]

Country of origin	1980	1990	1995	2000	2005	2006	2007	2008	2009	2010	2011
Total imports	**1,921**	**2,151**	**2,639**	**3,311**	**3,670**	**3,685**	**3,656**	**3,571**	**3,307**	**3,344**	**3,256**
OPEC, total [1, 2, 3, 4]	1,410	1,283	1,219	1,659	1,738	1,745	1,969	1,984	1,594	1,654	1,531
Algeria [2]	166	23	10	(Z)	83	130	162	114	101	119	65
Angola [2]	(NA)	86	131	108	164	187	181	184	164	139	122
Ecuador [3]	6	(NA)	35	46	101	99	72	78	64	71	69
Iraq	10	188	–	226	190	202	177	229	164	151	168
Kuwait [5]	10	29	78	96	79	65	64	75	68	71	70
Nigeria	307	286	227	319	387	381	395	338	281	360	280
Saudi Arabia [5]	456	436	460	556	525	519	530	551	361	394	433
Venezuela	57	243	420	446	449	416	420	381	352	333	317
Non-OPEC, total [2, 3, 4, 6]	511	869	1,419	1,652	1,932	1,940	1,687	1,587	1,713	1,690	1,725
Brazil	(NA)	–	–	2	34	49	61	84	107	93	84
Canada	73	235	380	492	600	651	681	707	707	720	806
Colombia	(NA)	51	76	116	57	52	50	65	93	124	141
Congo (Brazzaville) [7]	(NA)	(NA)	(NA)	(NA)	9	10	23	25	24	26	21
Mexico	185	251	375	479	566	575	514	434	400	416	402
Russia	(NA)	(Z)	5	3	70	39	41	41	85	92	93
United Kingdom	63	57	124	106	80	47	37	27	38	44	13

– Represents zero. NA Not available. Z Represents less than 500,000 barrels. [1] OPEC (Organization of Petroleum Exporting Countries) includes the nations shown, as well as Iran, Libya, Qatar, United Arab Emirates, and Indonesia. [2] Angola joined OPEC at the beginning of 2007. Prior to 2007, it is included in the non-OPEC total. [3] Ecuador withdrew from OPEC on Dec. 31, 1992; therefore, it is included under OPEC prior to 1995. From 1995 through 2007, it is included in the Non-OPEC total. In Nov. 2007, Ecuador rejoined OPEC; imports for 2008 are included in the OPEC total. [4] Gabon withdrew from OPEC on Dec. 31, 1994; therefore, it is included under OPEC prior to 1995. Beginning 1995, it is included in the Non-OPEC total. [5] Imports from the Neutral Zone between Kuwait and Saudi Arabia are included in Saudi Arabia. [6] Non-OPEC total includes nations not shown. [7] See footnote 5, Table 1348.

Source: U.S. Energy Information Administration, "Petroleum Supply Monthly," February 2012, <http://www.eia.gov/petroleum/supply/monthly/>.

Table 950. Crude Oil and Refined Products—Summary: 1980 to 2011

[13,481 represents 13,481,000 bbl. Barrels (bbl.) of 42 gallons. Data are averages]

Year	Crude oil [1] (1,000 bbl. per day)					Refined oil products (1,000 bbl. per day)			Total oil imports [5] (1,000 bbl. per day)	Crude oil stocks [1,2] (mil. bbl.)	
	Input to refiner-ies	Domestic produc-tion	Imports		Exports	Domestic demand	Imports	Exports		Total [7]	Strategic reserve [6]
			Total [3]	Strategic reserve [4]							
1980....	13,481	8,597	5,263	44	287	17,056	1,646	258	6,909	466	108
1985....	12,002	8,971	3,201	118	204	15,726	1,866	577	5,067	814	493
1990....	13,409	7,355	5,894	27	109	16,988	2,123	748	8,018	908	586
1995....	13,973	6,560	7,230	–	95	17,725	1,605	855	8,835	895	592
2000....	15,067	5,822	9,071	8	50	19,701	2,389	990	11,459	826	541
2005....	15,220	5,178	10,126	52	32	20,802	3,588	1,133	13,714	1,008	685
2007....	15,156	5,064	10,031	7	27	20,680	3,437	1,405	13,468	983	697
2008....	14,648	4,950	9,783	19	29	19,498	3,132	1,773	12,915	1,028	702
2009....	14,336	5,361	9,013	56	44	18,771	2,678	1,980	11,691	1,052	727
2010....	14,724	5,482	9,213	(NA)	42	19,180	2,580	2,311	11,793	1,060	727
2011....	14,833	5,676	8,921	(NA)	47	18,835	2,439	2,877	11,360	1,027	696

– Represents zero. NA Not available. [1] Includes lease condensate. [2] Crude oil at end of period. Includes commercial and Strategic Petroleum Reserve stocks. [3] Includes Strategic Petroleum Reserve. [4] SPR is the Strategic Petroleum Reserve. Through 2000, includes imports by SPR only; beginning in 2004, includes imports by SPR, and imports into SPR by others. [5] Crude oil (including Strategic Petroleum Reserve imports) plus refined products. [6] Crude oil stocks in the Strategic Petroleum Reserve include non-U.S. stocks held under foreign or commercial storage agreements. [7] Stocks of Alaskan crude oil in transit are included from January 1985 forward.

Source: U.S. Energy Information Administration, "Monthly Energy Review," July 2012, <http://www.eia.gov/totalenergy/>.

Table 951. Petroleum and Coal Products Corporations—Sales, Net Profit, and Profit Per Dollar of Sales: 1990 to 2011

[318.5 represents $318,500,000,000. Represents SIC group 29 (NAICS group 324). Through 2000, based on Standard Industrial Classification (SIC) code; beginning 2001, based on North American Industry Classification System (NAICS). Profit rates are averages of quarterly figures at annual rates. Beginning 1987, excludes estimates for corporations with less than $250,000 in assets]

Item	Unit	1990	1995	2000	2004	2005	2006	2007	2008	2009	2010	2011
Sales............................	Bil. dol.	318.5	283.1	455.2	767.7	956.0	1,037.8	1,113.2	1,369.1	846.0	1,077.1	1,409.7
Net profit:												
Before income taxes..........	Bil. dol.	23.1	16.5	55.5	89.7	120.2	139.8	127.0	101.6	41.9	56.0	125.8
After income taxes............	Bil. dol.	17.8	13.9	42.6	71.8	96.3	111.0	105.4	81.0	43.1	54.2	108.1
Depreciation [1]...................	Bil. dol.	18.7	16.7	15.5	18.5	18.6	20.0	22.6	22.9	28.0	30.8	29.4
Profits per dollar of sales:												
Before income taxes..........	Cents	7.3	5.8	12.2	11.6	12.6	13.4	11.6	5.8	5.1	5.3	8.9
After income taxes............	Cents	5.6	4.9	9.4	9.3	10.1	10.6	9.6	4.4	5.2	5.1	7.7
Profits on stockholders' equity:												
Before income taxes...........	Percent	16.4	12.6	29.4	32.9	38.0	36.3	30.7	21.8	10.2	12.2	24.7
After income taxes..............	Percent	12.7	10.6	22.6	26.3	30.4	28.8	25.5	17.3	10.5	11.8	21.2

[1] Includes depletion and accelerated amortization of emergency facilities.

Source: U.S. Census Bureau, *Quarterly Financial Report for Manufacturing, Mining and Selected Service Industries*. See also <http://www.census.gov/econ/qfr/>.

Table 952. Major Petroleum Companies—Financial Summary: 1980 to 2010

[32.9 represents $32,900,000,000. Data represent a composite of approximately 42 major worldwide petroleum companies aggregated on a consolidated total company basis. Minus sign (–) indicates deficit]

Item	1980	1990	1995	2000	2005	2006	2007	2008	2009	2010
FINANCIAL DATA (bil. dol.)										
Net income............................	32.9	26.8	24.3	76.4	170.6	187.6	237.6	198.1	92.6	185.0
Depreciation, depletion, etc....................	32.5	38.7	43.1	53.3	76.5	85.8	114.3	156.8	170.2	186.8
Cash flow [1]..........................	65.4	65.5	67.4	129.7	239.9	261.2	327.1	440.7	279.6	362.4
Dividends paid........................	9.3	15.9	17.6	23.0	37.5	39.2	62.2	74.8	72.1	70.5
Net internal funds available for investment or debt repayment [2]..............	56.1	49.6	49.8	106.7	202.4	222.0	264.9	365.9	207.5	291.9
Capital and exploratory expenditures.................	62.1	59.6	59.8	72.8	140.4	193.1	221.7	328.0	268.0	344.3
Long-term capitalization.....................	211.4	300.0	304.3	516.9	800.4	910.6	1,211.8	1,362.0	1,449.3	1,621.1
Long-term debt........................	49.8	90.4	85.4	112.8	165.2	177.4	240.1	299.4	365.7	444.2
Preferred stock.....................	2.0	5.2	5.7	5.4	3.5	3.4	1.9	1.4	1.2	5.0
Common stock and retained earnings [3].........	159.6	204.4	213.2	398.7	631.7	729.8	969.8	1,061.2	1,082.4	1,171.9
Excess of expenditures over cash income [4].......................	6.0	10.0	10.0	-33.9	-62.0	-28.9	-43.2	-37.9	60.5	52.4
RATIOS [5] (percent)										
Long-term debt to long-term capitalization..........	23.6	30.1	28.1	21.8	23.5	19.4	19.1	22.0	25.3	24.1
Net income to total average capital..................	17.0	9.1	8.1	15.7	23.0	22.3	21.2	15.2	6.6	10.8
Net income to average common equity.............	22.5	13.5	11.6	20.5	29.3	27.8	26.3	19.2	8.7	14.4

[1] Generally represents internally generated funds from operations: Sum of net income, changes in working capital and noncash items such as depreciation, depletion, amortization, impairments, and unrealized hedging gains/losses. [2] Cash flow minus dividends paid. [3] Includes common stock, capital surplus, and earned surplus accounts after adjustments. [4] Capital and exploratory expenditures plus dividends paid minus cash flow. [5] Represents approximate year-to-year comparisons because of changes in the makeup of the group due to mergers and other corporate changes.

Source: Carl H. Pforzheimer & Co., New York, NY, *Comparative Oil Company Statements*, annual (copyright).

Table 953. Nuclear Power Plants—Number, Capacity, and Generation: 1980 to 2011

[51.8 represents 51,800,000 kW]

Item	1980	1990	1995	2000	2004	2005	2006	2007	2008	2009	2010	2011 [5]
Operable generating units [1, 2]	71	112	109	104	104	104	104	104	104	104	104	104
Net summer capacity [2, 3] (mil. kW)	51.8	99.6	99.5	97.9	99.6	100.0	100.3	100.3	100.8	101.0	101.2	101.4
Net generation (bil. kWh)	251.1	576.9	673.4	753.9	788.5	782.0	787.2	806.4	806.2	798.9	807.0	790.2
Percent of total electricity net generation	11.0	19.0	20.1	19.8	19.9	19.3	19.4	19.4	19.6	20.2	19.6	19.2
Capacity factor [4] (percent)	56.3	66.0	77.4	88.1	90.1	89.3	89.6	91.8	91.1	90.3	91.1	89.1

[1] Total of nuclear generating units holding full-power licenses, or equivalent permission to operate, at the end of the year. For example, although Browns Ferry 1 was shut down in 1985, the unit remained fully licensed and thus continued to be counted as operable. It was eventually reopened in 2007. [2] As of year-end. [3] Net summer capacity is the peak steady hourly output that generating equipment is expected to supply to system load, exclusive of auxiliary and other power plant, as demonstrated by test at the time of summer peak demand. [4] Weighted average of monthly capacity factors. Monthly factors are derived by dividing actual monthly generation by the maximum possible generation for the month (number of hours in the month multiplied by the net summer capacity at the end of the month). [5] Data for 2011 are preliminary.

Source: U.S. Energy Information Administration, "Monthly Energy Review," July 2012, <http://www.eia.gov/totalenergy/data/monthly/#nuclear>.

Table 954. Nuclear Power Plants—Number of Units, Net Generation, and Net Summer Capacity by State: 2010

[806,968 represents 806,968,000,000 kWh]

State	Number of units	Nuclear net generation Total (mil. kWh)	Nuclear net generation Percent of total [1]	Nuclear net summer capability Total (mil. kW)	Nuclear net summer capability Percent of total [1]	State	Number of units	Nuclear net generation Total (mil. kWh)	Nuclear net generation Percent of total [1]	Nuclear net summer capability Total (mil. kW)	Nuclear net summer capability Percent of total [1]
U.S.	104	806,968	19.6	101.2	9.7	MS	1	9,643	17.7	1.3	8.0
AL	5	37,941	24.9	5.0	15.6	MO	1	8,996	9.7	1.2	5.5
AZ	3	31,200	27.9	3.9	14.9	NE	2	11,054	30.2	1.2	15.8
AR	2	15,023	24.6	1.8	11.5	NH	1	10,910	49.2	1.2	29.8
CA	4	32,201	15.8	4.4	6.5	NJ	1	32,771	49.9	4.1	22.3
CT	2	16,750	50.2	2.1	25.4	NY	6	41,870	30.6	5.3	13.4
FL	5	23,936	10.4	3.9	6.6	NC	5	40,740	31.7	5.0	17.9
GA	4	33,512	24.4	4.1	11.1	OH	3	15,805	11.0	2.1	6.5
IL	11	96,190	47.8	11.4	25.9	PA	9	77,828	33.9	9.5	20.9
IA	1	4,451	7.7	0.6	4.1	SC	7	51,988	49.9	6.5	27.0
KS	1	9,556	19.9	1.2	9.2	TN	3	27,739	33.7	3.4	15.9
LA	2	18,639	18.1	2.1	8.0	TX	4	41,335	10.0	5.0	4.6
MD	2	13,994	32.1	1.7	13.6	VT	1	4,782	72.2	0.6	55.0
MA	1	5,918	13.8	0.7	5.0	VA	4	26,572	36.4	3.5	14.5
MI	3	29,625	26.6	3.9	13.2	WA	1	9,241	8.9	1.1	3.6
MN	3	13,478	25.1	1.6	10.8	WI	3	13,281	20.7	1.6	8.9

[1] For total generation and capacity, see Table 961.

Source: U.S. Energy Information Administration, "Electric Power Annual 2010," January 2012, <http://www.eia.gov/electricity/data/state/>. See also <http://www.eia.gov/cneaf/nuclear/page/nuc_generation/gensum.html>.

Table 955. Uranium Concentrate—Supply, Inventories, and Average Prices: 1990 to 2010

[8.89 represents 8,890,000 pounds (lbs.). Years ending Dec. 31. For additional data on uranium, see Section 18]

Item	Unit	1990	1995	2000	2005	2006	2007	2008	2009	2010
Production [1]	Mil. lb.	8.89	6.04	3.96	2.69	4.11	4.53	3.90	3.71	4.23
Exports [2]	Mil. lb.	2.0	9.8	13.6	20.5	18.7	14.8	17.2	23.5	23.1
Imports [2]	Mil. lb.	23.7	41.3	44.9	65.5	64.8	54.1	57.1	58.9	55.3
Electric plant purchases from domestic suppliers	Mil. lb.	20.5	22.3	24.3	27.3	27.9	18.5	20.4	17.6	16.2
Loaded into U.S. nuclear reactors [3, 4]	Mil. lb.	(NA)	51.1	51.5	58.3	51.7	45.5	51.3	49.4	44.3
Inventories, total [4]	Mil. lb.	129.1	72.5	111.3	93.8	106.6	112.4	110.0	111.5	112.3
At domestic suppliers	Mil. lb.	26.4	13.7	56.5	29.1	29.1	31.2	27.0	26.8	25.7
At electric plants	Mil. lb.	102.7	58.7	54.8	64.7	77.5	81.2	83.0	84.8	86.5
Average price per pound:										
Purchased imports	Dollars	12.55	10.20	9.84	14.83	19.31	34.18	41.30	41.23	47.01
Domestic purchases	Dollars	15.70	11.11	11.45	13.98	18.54	33.13	43.43	44.53	44.88

NA Not available. [1] Data are for uranium concentrate, a yellow or brown powder obtained by the milling of uranium ore, processing of in situ leach mining solutions, or as a by-product of phosphoric acid production. [2] Includes transactions by uranium buyers (consumers). Buyer imports and exports prior to 1990 are believed to be small. [3] Does not include any fuel rods removed from reactors and later reloaded into the reactor. [4] Data for 2010 are preliminary.

Source: U.S. Energy Information Administration, Annual Energy Review 2010, October 2011. See also <http://www.eia.doe.gov/emeu/aer/nuclear.html>.

Table 956. Renewable Energy Generating Capacity and Generation: Projections 2010-2035

[In gigawatts, unless otherwise noted. Reference case projections are business-as-usual trend estimates, given known technology, as well as market, demographic, and technological trends. Based on results from EIA's National Energy Modeling System. Minus sign (-) indicates decrease]

Net summer capacity and generation	Reference case								Annual growth 2010-2035 (percent)
	2010	2011	2012	2015	2020	2025	2030	2035	
Electric power sector [1]									
Net summer capacity:									
Conventional hydropower...................	78.0	78.1	78.0	78.6	79.1	80.1	80.7	81.3	0.2
Geothermal [2].............................	2.4	2.4	2.6	2.9	3.6	4.5	5.5	6.3	4.0
Municipal waste [3]........................	3.3	3.4	3.4	3.4	3.4	3.4	3.4	3.4	0.1
Wood and other biomass [4]................	2.5	2.5	2.7	2.7	2.7	2.7	2.7	2.9	0.7
Solar thermal...........................	0.5	0.5	0.7	1.4	1.4	1.4	1.4	1.4	4.3
Solar photovoltaic [5].....................	0.4	0.9	1.4	2.0	2.0	2.3	3.0	8.2	13.0
Wind.....................................	39.1	46.4	53.2	54.3	54.3	57.6	60.3	66.7	2.2
Offshore wind...........................	0.0	0.0	0.0	0.2	0.2	0.2	0.2	0.2	(X)
Total electric power sector capacity........	**126.1**	**134.1**	**142.0**	**145.3**	**146.7**	**152.1**	**157.1**	**170.2**	**1.2**
Generation (bil. kWh):									
Conventional hydropower..................	255.3	312.5	271.7	295.4	300.5	305.0	307.4	310.1	0.8
Geothermal [2].............................	15.7	16.0	16.4	18.7	24.4	31.5	39.9	46.5	4.5
Biogenic municipal waste [6]..............	16.6	14.4	14.7	14.7	14.7	14.7	14.7	14.7	-0.5
Wood and other biomass..................	11.5	10.4	10.6	21.3	51.6	63.9	57.1	49.3	6.0
Dedicated plants.......................	10.2	9.0	9.3	10.1	13.2	13.3	11.8	10.4	0.1
Cofiring................................	1.4	1.4	1.3	11.2	38.4	50.6	45.3	38.9	14.4
Solar thermal...........................	0.8	1.0	1.1	2.9	2.9	2.9	2.9	2.9	5.1
Solar photovoltaic [5].....................	0.5	1.1	2.2	3.6	3.6	4.4	6.2	20.2	16.4
Wind.....................................	94.5	115.8	130.4	150.2	150.3	160.7	169.6	189.9	2.8
Offshore wind...........................	0.0	0.0	0.0	0.8	0.8	0.8	0.8	0.8	(X)
Total electric power sector generation......	**394.8**	**471.0**	**447.1**	**507.5**	**548.8**	**583.8**	**598.5**	**634.3**	**1.9**
End-use sectors [7]									
Net summer capacity:									
Conventional hydropower [8]...............	0.3	0.3	0.3	0.3	0.3	0.3	0.3	0.3	0.0
Geothermal...............................	0.0	0.0	0.0	0.0	0.0	0.0	0.0	0.0	(X)
Municipal waste [3]........................	0.4	0.4	0.4	0.4	0.4	0.4	0.4	0.4	0.0
Biomass..................................	4.6	4.6	4.6	5.7	6.7	8.4	11.3	13.8	4.5
Solar photovoltaic [5].....................	2.1	3.0	4.4	9.0	11.2	11.7	12.4	13.3	7.8
Wind.....................................	0.4	0.7	1.1	2.3	2.6	2.6	2.7	2.7	8.5
Total end-use sector capacity.............	**7.7**	**8.9**	**10.8**	**17.6**	**21.1**	**23.4**	**27.1**	**30.6**	**5.7**
Generation (bil. kWh):									
Conventional hydropower [8]...............	1.8	1.8	1.8	1.8	1.8	1.8	1.8	1.8	0.0
Geothermal...............................	0.0	0.0	0.0	0.0	0.0	0.0	0.0	0.0	(X)
Municipal waste [3]........................	2.0	2.8	2.8	2.8	2.8	2.8	2.8	2.8	1.3
Biomass..................................	26.1	26.2	26.2	33.3	39.5	52.3	76.0	96.2	5.4
Solar photovoltaic [5].....................	3.2	4.7	6.7	13.9	17.4	18.2	19.4	20.9	7.8
Wind.....................................	0.5	0.8	1.4	2.9	3.3	3.4	3.4	3.6	8.5
Total end-use sector generation...........	**33.6**	**36.2**	**38.9**	**54.6**	**64.8**	**78.5**	**103.4**	**125.2**	**5.4**
Total, all sectors									
Net summer capacity:									
Conventional hydropower..................	78.4	78.4	78.4	78.9	79.5	80.5	81.0	81.6	0.2
Geothermal...............................	2.4	2.4	2.6	2.9	3.6	4.5	5.5	6.3	4.0
Municipal waste..........................	3.7	3.7	3.7	3.7	3.7	3.7	3.7	3.7	0.1
Wood and other biomass [4]................	7.0	7.1	7.3	8.5	9.4	11.2	14.0	16.7	3.5
Solar [5]..................................	2.9	4.4	6.5	12.4	14.6	15.4	16.7	22.9	8.6
Wind.....................................	39.4	47.1	54.4	56.7	57.1	60.4	63.2	69.6	2.3
Total capacity, all sectors..................	**133.7**	**143.0**	**152.8**	**163.0**	**167.8**	**175.5**	**184.1**	**200.8**	**1.6**
Generation (bil. kWh):									
Conventional hydropower..................	257.1	314.2	273.5	297.2	302.3	306.8	309.2	311.8	0.8
Geothermal...............................	15.7	16.0	16.4	18.7	24.4	31.5	39.9	46.5	4.5
Municipal waste..........................	18.6	17.2	17.5	17.5	17.5	17.5	17.5	17.5	-0.3
Wood and other biomass..................	37.6	36.5	36.8	54.6	91.1	116.2	133.1	145.5	5.6
Solar [5]..................................	4.5	6.8	10.0	20.4	23.9	25.4	28.4	44.0	9.6
Wind.....................................	95.0	116.6	131.8	153.9	154.4	164.8	173.8	194.2	2.9
Total generation, all sectors...............	**428.4**	**507.2**	**486.0**	**562.1**	**613.6**	**662.3**	**701.9**	**759.5**	**2.3**

X Not applicable. [1] Includes electricity-only and combined-heat-and-power plants whose primary business is to sell electricity to the public. [2] Includes both hydrothermal resources and near-field enhanced geothermal systems(EGS). [3] Includes municipal waste, landfill gas, and municipal sewage sludge. [4] Facilities co-firing biomass and coal are classified as coal. [5] Does not include off-grid photovoltaics(PV). [6] Includes biogenic municipal waste, landfill gas, and municipal sewage sludge. [7] Includes combined heat and power plants and electricity-only plants in the commercial and industrial sectors; and small on-site generating systems in the residential, commercial, and industrial sectors used primarily for own-use generation, but which may also sell some power to the grid. [8] Represents own-use industrial hydroelectric power.

Source: U.S. Energy Information Administration, "Annual Energy Outlook 2012," June 2012, <http://www.eia.gov/forecasts/aeo/>.

Table 957. Solar Collector Shipments by Type, End Use, and Market Sector: 1980 to 2009

[Shipments in thousands of square feet (19,398 represents 19,398,000). Solar collector is a device for intercepting sunlight, converting the light to heat, and carrying the heat to where it will be either used or stored. 1985 data are not available. Based on the Annual Solar Thermal Collector Manufacturers Survey]

Year	Number of manufacturers	Total shipments [1,2,3]	Collector type		End use			Market sector		
			Low temperature [1,2]	Medium temperature, special/ other [2]	Pool heating	Hot water	Space heating	Residential	Commerical	Industrial
1980.............	233	19,398	12,233	7,165	12,029	4,790	1,688	16,077	2,417	488
1990.............	51	11,409	3,645	2,527	5,016	1,091	2	5,835	294	22
1995.............	36	7,666	6,813	840	6,763	755	132	6,966	604	82
2000.............	26	8,354	7,948	400	7,863	367	99	7,473	810	57
2005.............	25	16,041	15,224	702	15,041	640	228	14,681	1,160	31
2008.............	74	16,963	14,015	2,560	11,973	1,978	186	13,000	1,294	128
2009.............	88	13,798	10,511	2,307	8,934	1,992	150	10,239	974	634

[1] Includes shipments of high temperature collectors to the government, including some military, but excluding space applications. Also includes end uses such as process heating, utility, and other market sectors, not shown separately. [2] Includes imputation of shipment data to account for nonrespondents. [3] Total shipments include all domestic and export shipments and may include imported collectors that subsequently were shipped to domestic or foreign customers.

Source: U.S. Energy Information Administration, 1980–1990, "Solar Collector Manufacturing Activity," annual reports; 1995–2002, "Renewable Energy Annual;" and, thereafter, "Solar Thermal Collector Manufacturing Activities 2009," January 2011, <http://www.eia.gov/renewable/annual/solar_thermal/>.

Table 958. Electricity Net Generation by Sector and Fuel Type: 1990 to 2011

[3,037.8 represents 3,037,800,000,000 kWh. Data are for fuels consumed to produce electricity. Also includes fuels consumed to produce useful thermal output at a small number of electric utility combined-heat-and-power (CHP) plants]

Source and sector	Unit	1990	1995	2000	2005	2010	2011 [1]
Net generation, total................................	Bil. kWh.	**3,037.8**	**3,353.5**	**3,802.1**	**4,055.4**	**4,125.1**	**4,105.7**
Electric power sector, total............................	Bil. kWh.	2,901.3	3,194.2	3,637.5	3,902.2	3,972.4	3,955.1
Commercial sector [2]................................	Bil. kWh.	5.8	8.2	7.9	8.5	8.6	8.4
Industrial sector [3]................................	Bil. kWh.	130.8	151.0	156.7	144.7	144.1	142.3
Net generation by source, all sectors:							
Fossil fuels, total................................	Bil. kWh.	2,103.6	2,293.9	2,692.5	2,909.5	2,883.4	2,790.3
Coal [4]................................	Bil. kWh.	1,594.0	1,709.4	1,966.3	2,012.9	1,847.3	1,734.3
Petroleum [5]................................	Bil. kWh.	126.5	74.6	111.2	122.2	37.1	28.2
Natural gas [6]................................	Bil. kWh.	372.8	496.1	601.0	761.0	987.7	1,016.6
Other gases [7]................................	Bil. kWh.	10.4	13.9	14.0	13.5	11.3	11.3
Nuclear electric power............................	Bil. kWh.	576.9	673.4	753.9	782.0	807.0	790.2
Hydroelectric pumped storage [8]................	Bil. kWh.	-3.5	-2.7	-5.5	-6.6	-5.5	-5.9
Renewable energy, total............................	Bil. kWh.	357.2	384.8	356.5	357.7	427.4	520.1
Conventional hydroelectric power................	Bil. kWh.	292.9	310.8	275.6	270.3	260.2	325.1
Biomass, total................................	Bil. kWh.	45.8	56.9	60.7	54.3	56.1	56.7
Wood [9]................................	Bil. kWh.	32.5	36.5	37.6	38.9	37.2	36.9
Waste [10]................................	Bil. kWh.	13.3	20.4	23.1	15.4	18.9	19.8
Geothermal................................	Bil. kWh.	15.4	13.4	14.1	14.7	15.2	16.7
Solar [11]................................	Bil. kWh.	0.4	0.5	0.5	0.6	1.2	1.8
Wind................................	Bil. kWh.	2.8	3.2	5.6	17.8	94.7	119.7
Other [12]................................	Bil. kWh.	3.6	4.1	4.8	12.8	12.9	11.1
Consumption of fuels for electricity generation:							
Coal [4]................................	Mil. sh. tons.	792.5	860.6	994.9	1,041.4	979.7	932.9
Petroleum, total................................	Mil. bbl.	218.8	132.6	195.2	206.8	65.1	49.5
Distillate fuel oil [13]................................	Mil. bbl.	18.1	19.6	31.7	20.7	14.1	10.8
Residual fuel oil [14]................................	Mil. bbl.	190.7	95.5	143.4	141.5	24.0	14.2
Other liquids [15]................................	Mil. bbl.	0.4	0.7	1.4	3.0	2.1	1.7
Petroleum coke................................	Mil. sh. tons [16]	1.9	3.4	3.7	8.3	5.0	4.6
Natural gas [6]................................	Bil. cu. ft.	3.7	4.7	5.7	6.0	7.7	7.9
Other gases [7]................................	Tril. Btu.	0.1	0.1	0.1	0.1	0.1	0.1
Biomass................................	Tril. Btu.	0.7	0.8	0.8	0.6	0.6	0.6
Wood [9]................................	Tril. Btu.	0.4	0.5	0.5	0.4	0.3	0.3
Waste [10]................................	Tril. Btu.	0.2	0.3	0.3	0.2	0.3	0.3
Other [12]................................	Tril. Btu.	0.0	0.0	0.0	0.2	0.2	0.2

[1] Preliminary. [2] Commercial combined-heat-and-power (CHP) and commercial electricity-only plants. [3] Industrial CHP and industrial electricity-only plants. [4] Anthracite, bituminous coal, subbituminous coal, lignite, waste coal, and coal synfuel. [5] Distillate fuel oil, residual fuel oil, petroleum coke, jet fuel, kerosene, other petroleum, and waste oil. [6] Includes a small amount of supplemental gaseous fuels that cannot be identified separately. [7] Blast furnace gas, propane gas, and other manufactured and waste gases derived from fossil fuels. [8] Pumped storage facility production minus energy used for pumping. [9] Wood and wood-derived fuels. [10] Municipal solid waste from biogenic sources, landfill gas, sludge waste, tires, agricultural byproducts, and other biomass. Through 2000, also includes nonrenewable waste (municipal solid waste from non-biogenic sources and tire-derived fuels). [11] Solar thermal and photovoltaic energy. [12] Batteries, chemicals, hydrogen, pitch, purchased steam, sulfur, miscellaneous technologies, and beginning 2001, nonrenewable waste (municipal solid waste from nonbiogenic sources, and tire-derived fuels). [13] Fuel oil numbers 1, 2, and 4. For 1990 through 2000, electric utility data also include small amounts of kerosene and jet fuel. [14] Fuel oil numbers 5 and 6. For 1990 through 2000, electric utility data also include a small amount of fuel oil number 4. [15] Jet fuel, kerosene, other petroleum liquids, and waste oil. [16] Short tons.

Source: U.S. Energy Information Administration, "Monthly Energy Review," August 2012, <http://www.eia.gov/totalenergy/data/monthly/>.

Table 959. Total Electric Net Summer Capacity, All Sectors: 1990 to 2010

[In million kilowatts (734.1 represents 734,100,000). Data are at end of year. For plants that use multiple sources of energy, capacity is assigned to the predominant energy source]

Source	1990	1995	2000	2005	2006	2007	2008	2009	2010 [10]
Net summer capacity, total............	**734.1**	**769.5**	**811.7**	**978.0**	**986.2**	**994.9**	**1,010.2**	**1,025.4**	**1,039.2**
Fossil fuels, total.....................	527.8	554.2	598.9	757.1	761.6	764.0	770.2	774.3	784.2
Coal [1].............................	307.4	311.4	315.1	313.4	313.0	312.7	313.3	314.3	319.4
Petroleum [2]........................	77.9	66.6	61.8	58.5	58.1	56.1	57.4	56.8	56.7
Natural gas [3].......................	140.8	174.5	219.6	383.1	388.3	392.9	397.5	401.3	406.1
Dual fired [4]........................	113.6	122.0	149.8	174.7	(NA)	(NA)	(NA)	(NA)	(NA)
Other gases [5]......................	1.6	1.7	2.3	2.1	2.3	2.3	2.0	1.9	2.0
Nuclear electric power.................	99.6	99.5	97.9	100.0	100.3	100.3	100.8	101.0	101.0
Hydroelectric pumped storage..........	19.5	21.4	19.5	21.3	21.5	21.9	21.9	22.2	22.5
Renewable energy, total...............	86.8	93.9	94.9	98.7	101.9	108.0	116.4	127.1	130.7
Conventional hydroelectric power.......	73.9	78.6	79.4	77.5	77.8	77.9	77.9	78.5	78.5
Biomass, total.......................	8.1	10.3	10.0	9.8	10.1	10.8	11.1	11.3	11.4
Wood [6]............................	5.5	6.7	6.1	6.2	6.4	6.7	6.9	6.9	7.0
Waste [7]...........................	2.5	3.5	3.9	3.6	3.7	4.1	4.2	4.3	4.4
Geothermal..........................	2.7	3.0	2.8	2.3	2.3	2.2	2.2	2.4	2.4
Solar [8]............................	0.3	0.3	0.4	0.4	0.4	0.4	0.5	0.6	0.9
Wind................................	1.8	1.7	2.4	8.7	11.3	16.5	24.7	34.3	37.6
Other [9]............................	0.5	0.5	0.5	0.9	0.9	0.8	0.9	0.9	0.8

NA Not available. [1] Anthracite, bituminous coal, subbituminous coal, lignite, waste coal, and coal synfuel. [2] Distillate fuel oil, residual fuel oil, petroleum coke, jet fuel, kerosene, other petroleum, and waste oil. [3] Includes a small amount of supplemental gaseous fuels that cannot be identified separately. [4] Petroleum and natural gas. [5] Blast furnace gas, propane gas, and other manufactured and waste gases derived from fossil fuels. [6] Wood and wood-derived fuels. [7] Municipal solid waste from biogenic sources, landfill gas, sludge waste, tires, agricultural byproducts, and other biomass. Also includes nonrenewable waste (municipal solid waste from nonbiogenic sources, and tire-derived fuels). [8] Solar thermal and photovoltaic energy. [9] Batteries, chemicals, hydrogen, pitch, purchased steam, sulfur, and miscellaneous technologies. [10] Preliminary data.

Source: U.S. Energy Information Administration, *Annual Energy Review 2010*, October 2011. See also <http://www.eia.gov/totalenergy/>.

Table 960. Electricity—End Use and Average Retail Prices: 1990 to 2010

[Beginning 2003, the category "other" has been replaced by "transportation," and the categories "commercial" and "industrial" have been redefined. Data represent revenue from electricity retail sales divided by the amount of retail electricity sold (in kilowatt-hours). Prices include state and local taxes, energy or demand charges, customer service charges, environmental surcharges, franchise fees, fuel adjustments, and other miscellaneous charges applied to end-use customers during normal billing operations. Prices do not include deferred charges, credits, or other adjustments, such as fuel or revenue from purchased power, from previous reporting periods. Data are for a census of electric utilities. Beginning in 2000 data also include energy service providers selling to retail customers]

Item	1990	1995	2000	2005	2006	2007	2008	2009	2010 [1]
END USE (Billion kilowatt-hours)									
Total end use [2]..................	**2,837.1**	**3,164.0**	**3,592.4**	**3,811.0**	**3,816.8**	**3,890.2**	**3,865.2**	**3,723.8**	**3,884.4**
Direct use [3]........................	124.5	150.7	170.9	150.0	146.9	125.7	132.2	126.9	134.4
Retail sales, total [4]..............	**2,712.6**	**3,013.3**	**3,421.4**	**3,661.0**	**3,669.9**	**3,764.6**	**3,733.0**	**3,596.9**	**3,750.0**
Residential.........................	924.0	1,042.5	1,192.4	1,359.2	1,351.5	1,392.2	1,380.0	1,364.5	1,450.8
Commercial [5]......................	838.3	953.1	1,159.3	1,275.1	1,299.7	1,336.3	1,336.0	1,307.2	1,329.3
Industrial [6]........................	945.5	1,012.7	1,064.2	1,019.2	1,011.3	1,027.8	1,009.3	917.4	962.2
Transportation [7]...................	4.8	5.0	5.4	7.5	7.4	8.2	7.7	7.8	7.7
AVERAGE RETAIL PRICES (Cents per kilowatt-hour)									
Total:									
Nominal............................	6.57	6.89	6.81	8.14	8.90	9.13	9.74	9.82	9.88
Real................................	9.10	8.45	7.68	8.14	8.62	8.59	8.97	8.96	8.93
Residential:									
Nominal............................	7.83	8.40	8.24	9.45	10.40	10.65	11.26	11.51	11.58
Real................................	10.84	10.30	9.30	9.45	10.07	10.02	10.37	10.50	10.46
Commercial: [8]									
Nominal............................	7.34	7.69	7.43	8.67	9.46	9.65	10.36	10.17	10.26
Real................................	10.17	9.43	8.38	8.67	9.16	9.08	9.54	9.28	9.27
Industrial: [6]									
Nominal............................	4.74	4.66	4.64	5.73	6.16	6.39	6.83	6.81	6.79
Real................................	6.57	5.72	5.23	5.73	5.97	6.01	6.29	6.21	6.14
Transportation: [7]									
Nominal............................	(NA)	(NA)	(NA)	8.57	9.54	9.70	10.74	10.65	10.96
Real................................	(NA)	(NA)	(NA)	8.57	9.24	9.13	9.89	9.72	9.90
Other: [9]									
Nominal............................	6.40	6.88	6.56	(X)	(X)	(X)	(X)	(X)	(X)
Real................................	8.86	8.44	7.40	(X)	(X)	(X)	(X)	(X)	(X)

NA Not available. X Not applicable. [1] Preliminary. [2] The sum of "total retail sales" and "direct use." [3] Use of electricity that is 1) self-generated, 2) produced by either the same entity that consumes the power or an affiliate, and 3) used in direct support of a service or industrial process located within the same facility or group of facilities that house the generating equipment. Direct use is exclusive of station use. [4] Electricity retail sales to ultimate customers reported by electric utilities and, beginning in 2000, other energy service providers. [5] Includes public street and highway lighting, interdepartmental sales, and other sales to public authorities. [6] Beginning 2003, includes agriculture and irrigation. [7] Includes sales to railroads and railways. [8] Beginning 2003, includes public street and highway lighting, interdepartmental sales, and other sales to public authorities. [9] Public street and highway lighting, interdepartmental sales, other sales to public authorities, agriculture and irrigation, and transportation including railroads and railways.

Source: U.S. Energy Information Administration, *Annual Energy Review 2010*, October 2011. See also <http://www.eia.gov/totalenergy/>.

Table 961. Electric Power Industry—Net Generation and Net Summer Capacity by State: 2000 to 2010

[3,802.1 represents 3,802,100,000,000. Capacity as of December 31. Covers utilities for public use]

State	Net generation (bil. kWh)									Net summer capacity (mil. kW)	
				2010							
				Total (bil. kWh)	Percent from—						
					Petro-leum	Natural gas	Hydro-electric	Nuclear	Coal		
	2000	2005	2009							2000	2010
U.S...	3,802.1	4,055.4	3,950.3	4,127.6	0.9	23.9	6.3	19.6	44.8	811.7	1,039.1
AL.......	124.4	137.9	143.3	152.2	0.1	25.8	5.7	24.9	41.4	23.5	32.4
AK.......	6.2	6.6	6.7	6.8	13.9	55.5	21.2	–	9.2	2.1	2.1
AZ.......	88.9	101.5	112.0	111.8	0.1	26.6	5.9	27.9	39.1	15.3	26.4
AR.......	43.9	47.8	57.5	61.0	0.1	20.4	6.0	24.6	46.2	9.7	16.0
CA.......	208.1	200.3	204.8	204.1	0.5	52.7	16.4	15.8	1.0	52.3	67.3
CO.......	44.2	49.6	50.6	50.7	(Z)	21.8	3.1	–	68.1	8.4	13.8
CT.......	33.0	33.5	31.2	33.3	1.2	35.1	1.2	50.2	7.8	6.4	8.3
DE.......	6.0	8.1	4.8	5.6	1.0	50.9	0.0	–	45.6	2.4	3.4
DC.......	0.1	0.2	(Z)	0.2	100.0	–	–	–	–	0.8	0.8
FL.......	191.8	220.3	218.0	229.1	4.0	56.1	0.1	10.4	26.1	41.5	59.2
GA.......	123.9	136.7	128.7	137.6	0.5	17.4	2.4	24.4	53.3	27.8	36.6
HI.......	10.6	11.5	11.0	10.8	74.6	–	0.6	–	14.3	2.4	2.5
ID.......	11.9	10.8	13.1	12.0	(Z)	14.0	76.1	–	0.7	3.0	4.0
IL.......	178.5	194.1	193.9	201.4	0.1	2.8	0.1	47.8	46.5	36.3	44.1
IN.......	127.8	130.4	116.7	125.2	0.1	5.2	0.4	–	89.7	23.9	27.6
IA.......	41.5	44.2	51.9	57.5	0.3	2.3	1.6	7.7	71.8	9.1	14.6
KS.......	44.8	45.9	46.7	47.9	0.2	4.8	(Z)	19.9	67.8	10.1	12.5
KY.......	93.0	97.8	90.6	98.2	2.3	1.9	2.6	–	92.7	16.8	20.5
LA.......	92.9	92.6	91.0	102.9	3.2	49.9	1.1	18.1	23.3	21.1	26.7
ME.......	14.0	18.8	16.3	17.0	1.6	49.2	22.4	–	0.5	4.2	4.4
MD.......	51.1	52.7	43.8	43.6	0.7	6.6	3.8	32.1	54.3	10.5	12.5
MA.......	38.7	47.5	39.0	42.8	0.7	59.8	2.3	13.8	19.4	12.4	13.7
MI.......	104.2	121.6	101.2	111.6	0.3	11.0	1.1	26.6	58.8	25.8	29.8
MN.......	51.4	53.0	52.5	53.7	0.1	8.1	1.6	25.1	52.3	10.3	14.7
MS.......	37.6	45.1	48.7	54.5	0.1	54.4	–	17.7	25.0	9.0	15.7
MO.......	76.6	90.8	88.4	92.3	0.1	5.1	1.7	9.7	81.3	17.3	21.7
MT.......	26.5	27.9	26.7	29.8	1.4	0.2	31.6	–	62.4	5.2	5.9
NE.......	29.1	31.5	34.0	36.6	0.1	1.0	3.6	30.2	63.8	6.0	7.9
NV.......	35.5	40.2	37.7	35.1	(Z)	67.4	6.1	–	19.9	6.7	11.4
NH.......	15.0	24.5	20.2	22.2	0.3	24.2	6.7	49.2	13.9	2.9	4.2
NJ.......	58.1	60.5	61.8	65.7	0.4	37.9	(Z)	49.9	9.8	16.6	18.4
NM.......	34.0	35.1	39.7	36.3	0.1	23.5	0.6	–	70.7	5.6	8.1
NY.......	138.1	146.9	133.2	137.0	1.5	35.7	18.6	30.6	9.9	35.6	39.4
NC.......	122.3	129.7	118.4	128.7	0.2	6.6	3.7	31.7	55.9	24.5	27.7
ND.......	31.3	31.9	34.2	34.7	0.1	(Z)	5.9	0.0	81.9	4.7	6.2
OH.......	149.1	157.0	136.1	143.6	1.0	5.0	0.3	11.0	82.1	28.5	33.1
OK.......	55.6	68.6	75.1	72.3	(Z)	47.0	3.9	–	43.6	14.2	21.0
OR.......	51.8	49.3	56.7	55.1	(Z)	28.4	55.4	–	7.5	11.3	14.3
PA.......	201.7	218.1	219.5	229.8	0.2	14.7	1.0	33.9	48.0	36.8	45.6
RI.......	6.0	6.1	7.7	7.7	0.2	98.0	(Z)	–	–	1.2	1.8
SC.......	93.3	102.5	100.1	104.2	0.2	10.5	2.3	49.9	36.2	18.7	24.0
SD.......	9.7	6.5	8.2	10.0	0.1	1.3	52.1	–	32.8	2.8	3.6
TN.......	95.8	97.1	79.7	82.3	0.3	2.8	9.9	33.7	53.0	19.5	21.4
TX.......	377.7	396.7	397.2	411.7	0.2	45.4	0.3	10.0	36.5	81.9	108.3
UT.......	36.6	38.2	43.5	44.8	0.1	14.4	1.6	–	76.0	5.2	7.5
VT.......	6.3	5.7	7.3	6.6	0.1	0.1	20.3	72.2	–	1.0	1.1
VA.......	77.2	78.9	70.1	73.0	1.8	23.3	2.1	36.4	34.9	19.4	24.1
WA.......	108.2	102.0	104.5	103.5	(Z)	10.0	66.0	8.9	8.2	26.1	30.5
WV.......	92.9	93.6	70.8	80.8	0.2	0.2	1.7	–	96.7	15.1	16.5
WI.......	59.6	61.8	60.0	64.3	1.1	8.5	3.3	20.7	62.5	13.6	17.8
WY.......	45.5	45.6	46.0	48.1	0.1	1.0	2.1	–	89.3	6.2	8.0

– Represents zero. Z Represents less than 50 million kWh or 50,000 kW.

Source: U.S. Energy Information Administration, "Electric Power Annual 2010," January 2012, <http://www.eia.gov/electricity/data/state/>.

Table 962. Electric Power Industry—Capability, Peak Load, and Capacity Margin: 1980 to 2010

[558,237 represents 558,237,000 kW. Excludes Alaska and Hawaii. Capability represents the maximum kilowatt output with all power sources available and with hydraulic equipment under actual water conditions, allowing for maintenance, emergency outages, and system operating requirements. Capacity margin is the difference between capability and peak load. Minus sign (–) indicates decrease]

Year	Capability at the time of— Summer peak load (1,000 kW) Amount	Change from prior year	Winter peak load (1,000 kW) Amount	Change from prior year	Noncoincident peak load Summer (1,000 kW)	Winter (1,000 kW)	Capacity margin Summer Amount (1,000 kW)	Percent of capability	Winter Amount (1,000 kW)	Percent of capability
1980...........	558,237	13,731	572,195	17,670	427,058	384,567	131,179	23.5	187,628	32.8
1985...........	621,597	17,357	636,475	14,350	460,503	423,660	161,094	25.9	212,815	33.4
1990...........	685,091	11,775	696,757	11,508	546,331	484,231	138,760	20.3	212,526	30.5
1991...........	690,915	5,824	703,212	6,455	551,418	485,761	139,497	20.2	217,451	30.9
1992...........	695,436	4,521	707,752	4,540	548,707	492,983	146,729	21.1	214,769	30.3
1993...........	694,250	-1,186	711,957	4,205	575,356	521,733	118,894	17.1	190,224	26.7
1994...........	702,985	8,735	715,090	3,133	585,320	518,253	117,665	16.7	196,837	27.5
1995...........	714,222	11,237	727,679	12,589	620,249	544,684	93,973	13.2	182,995	25.1
1996...........	730,376	16,154	737,637	9,958	616,790	554,081	113,586	15.6	183,556	24.9
1997...........	737,855	7,479	736,666	-971	637,677	529,874	100,178	13.6	206,792	28.1
1998...........	744,670	6,815	735,090	-1,576	660,293	567,558	84,377	11.3	167,532	22.8
1999...........	765,744	21,074	748,271	13,181	682,122	570,915	83,622	10.9	177,356	23.7
2000...........	808,054	42,310	767,505	19,234	678,413	588,426	129,641	16.0	179,079	23.3
2001...........	788,990	-19,064	806,598	39,093	687,812	576,312	101,178	12.8	230,286	28.6
2002...........	833,380	44,390	850,984	44,386	714,565	604,986	118,815	14.3	245,998	28.9
2003...........	856,131	22,751	882,120	31,136	709,375	593,874	146,756	17.1	288,246	32.7
2004...........	875,870	19,739	864,849	-17,271	704,459	618,701	171,411	19.6	246,148	28.5
2005...........	882,125	6,255	878,110	13,261	758,876	626,365	123,249	14.0	251,745	28.7
2006...........	891,226	9,101	899,551	21,441	789,475	640,981	101,751	11.4	258,570	28.7
2007...........	914,397	23,171	913,650	14,099	782,227	637,905	132,170	14.5	275,745	30.2
2008...........	909,504	-4,893	927,781	14,131	752,470	643,557	157,034	17.3	284,224	30.6
2009...........	916,449	6,945	920,002	-7,779	725,958	668,818	190,491	20.8	251,184	27.3
2010 [1]........	934,894	18,445	948,326	28,324	772,089	639,073	162,805	17.4	309,253	32.6

[1] Preliminary.

Source: Edison Electric Institute, Washington, DC, *Statistical Yearbook of the Electric Power Industry*, annual (copyright). See also <http://www.eei.org>.

Table 963. Electric Energy Retail Sales by Class of Service and State: 2010

[In billions of kilowatt-hours (3,754.5 represents 3,754,500,000,000). Data include both bundled and unbundled consumers]

State	Total [1]	Resi-dential	Com-mercial	Indus-trial	State	Total [1]	Resi-dential	Com-mercial	Indus-trial
United States......	**3,754.5**	**1,445.7**	**1,330.2**	**970.9**	Missouri..............	86.1	37.3	31.4	17.3
Alabama................	90.9	35.5	23.0	32.4	Montana...............	13.4	4.7	4.8	3.9
Alaska.................	6.2	2.1	2.8	1.3	Nebraska..............	29.8	10.1	9.5	10.2
Arizona................	72.8	32.4	28.9	11.4	Nevada................	33.8	11.6	9.0	13.2
Arkansas...............	48.2	19.2	12.2	16.8	New Hampshire.........	10.9	4.5	4.5	1.9
California..............	258.5	87.3	121.2	49.3	New Jersey............	79.2	30.3	40.1	8.4
Colorado...............	52.9	18.1	19.6	15.2	New Mexico............	22.4	6.8	9.0	6.7
Connecticut............	30.4	13.1	13.4	3.7	New York..............	144.6	50.9	77.3	13.5
Delaware...............	11.6	4.8	4.3	2.5	North Carolina........	136.4	62.2	47.9	26.3
District of Columbia.....	11.9	2.1	9.2	.2	North Dakota..........	13.0	4.4	4.7	3.9
Florida................	231.2	122.2	91.6	17.3	Ohio..................	154.1	54.5	46.5	53.1
Georgia................	140.7	61.6	47.9	31.0	Oklahoma..............	57.8	23.7	19.0	15.2
Hawaii.................	10.0	3.0	3.4	3.7	Oregon................	46.0	18.8	15.5	11.7
Idaho..................	22.8	8.1	5.9	8.8	Pennsylvania..........	149.0	55.3	47.4	45.5
Illinois................	144.8	48.6	51.4	44.2	Rhode Island..........	7.8	3.1	3.7	1.0
Indiana................	106.0	35.1	24.4	46.6	South Carolina........	82.5	32.9	22.3	27.3
Iowa...................	45.4	14.6	12.0	18.9	South Dakota..........	11.4	4.6	4.4	2.4
Kansas.................	40.4	14.3	15.4	10.7	Tennessee.............	103.5	45.2	29.4	28.9
Kentucky...............	93.6	29.1	19.4	45.0	Texas.................	358.5	137.2	121.5	99.8
Louisiana..............	85.1	32.7	24.2	28.2	Utah..................	28.0	8.8	10.4	8.8
Maine..................	11.5	4.4	4.1	3.1	Vermont...............	5.6	2.1	2.0	1.4
Maryland...............	65.3	28.9	30.8	5.1	Virginia..............	113.8	48.4	48.0	17.1
Massachusetts..........	57.1	21.4	18.2	17.1	Washington............	90.4	34.9	28.8	26.6
Michigan...............	103.6	34.7	38.1	30.8	West Virginia.........	32.0	12.4	8.0	11.6
Minnesota..............	67.8	22.5	22.5	22.8	Wisconsin.............	68.8	22.3	23.0	23.5
Mississippi............	49.7	20.2	13.8	15.7	Wyoming...............	17.1	2.7	4.3	10.1

[1] Includes transportation, not shown separately.

Source: U.S. Energy Information Administration, "Electric Sales, Revenue, and Average Price 2010," November 2011, <http://www.eia.gov/electricity/sales_revenue_price/index.cfm>.

Table 964. Electric Energy Average Retail Price by Class of Service and State: 2010

[Revenue (in cents) per kilowatt-hour (kWh). Data include both bundled and unbundled consumers]

State	Total [1]	Resi-dential	Com-mercial	Indus-trial	State	Total [1]	Resi-dential	Com-mercial	Indus-trial
United States	**9.83**	**11.54**	**10.19**	**6.77**	Missouri	7.78	9.08	7.50	5.50
Alabama	8.89	10.67	10.18	6.01	Montana	7.88	9.16	8.55	5.49
Alaska	14.76	16.26	13.95	14.14	Nebraska	7.52	8.94	7.63	6.00
Arizona	9.69	10.97	9.47	6.63	Nevada	9.73	12.36	9.78	7.37
Arkansas	7.28	8.86	7.31	5.44	New Hampshire	14.84	16.32	14.26	12.75
California	13.01	14.75	13.10	9.80	New Jersey	14.68	16.57	13.89	11.81
Colorado	9.15	11.04	9.13	6.90	New Mexico	8.40	10.52	8.57	6.01
Connecticut	17.39	19.25	16.45	14.50	New York	16.41	18.74	16.31	8.78
Delaware	11.97	13.80	11.36	9.57	North Carolina	8.67	10.12	8.16	6.17
District of Columbia	13.35	14.01	13.42	7.78	North Dakota	7.11	8.13	7.21	5.81
Florida	10.58	11.44	9.76	8.85	Ohio	9.14	11.32	9.73	6.40
Georgia	8.87	10.07	9.06	6.22	Oklahoma	7.59	9.14	7.45	5.35
Hawaii	25.12	28.10	25.93	21.94	Oregon	7.56	8.87	7.59	5.41
Idaho	6.54	7.99	6.64	5.15	Pennsylvania	10.31	12.70	10.10	7.66
Illinois	9.13	11.52	8.88	6.82	Rhode Island	14.08	15.92	13.11	11.82
Indiana	7.67	9.56	8.38	5.87	South Carolina	8.49	10.50	8.90	5.74
Iowa	7.66	10.42	7.91	5.36	South Dakota	7.82	8.97	7.55	6.07
Kansas	8.35	10.03	8.25	6.23	Tennessee	8.61	9.23	9.66	6.58
Kentucky	6.73	8.57	7.88	5.05	Texas	9.34	11.60	9.19	6.44
Louisiana	7.80	8.98	8.50	5.84	Utah	6.94	8.71	7.15	4.93
Maine	12.84	15.71	12.51	9.17	Vermont	13.24	15.57	13.44	9.53
Maryland	12.70	14.32	11.75	9.57	Virginia	8.69	10.45	7.65	6.66
Massachusetts	14.26	14.59	14.53	13.71	Washington	6.66	8.04	7.37	4.07
Michigan	9.88	12.46	9.81	7.08	West Virginia	7.45	8.79	7.66	5.86
Minnesota	8.41	10.59	8.38	6.29	Wisconsin	9.78	12.65	9.98	6.85
Mississippi	8.59	9.87	9.32	6.32	Wyoming	6.20	8.77	7.42	4.98

[1] Includes transportation, not shown separately.

Source: U.S. Energy Information Administration, "Electric Sales, Revenue, and Average Price 2010," November 2011, <http://www.eia.gov/electricity/sales_revenue_price/index.cfm>.

Table 965. Total Electric Power Industry—Generation, Sales, Revenue, and Customers: 1990 to 2010

[2,808 represents 2,808,000,000,000 kWh. Sales and revenue are to and from ultimate customers. Commercial and Industrial are not wholly comparable on a year-to-year basis due to changes from one classification to another. For the 2005 period forward, the Energy Information Administration replaced the "Other" sector with the Transportation sector. The Transportation sector consists entirely of electrified rail and urban transit systems. Data previously reported in "Other" have been relocated to the Commercial sector, except for Agriculture (i.e., irrigation load), which have been relocated to the Industrial sector]

Class	Unit	1990	1995	2000	2005	2006	2007	2008	2009	2010 [1]
Generation [2]	Bil. kWh	2,808	3,353	3,802	4,055	4,065	4,157	4,119	3,950	4,120
Sales [3]	**Bil kWh**	**2,713**	**3,013**	**3,421**	**3,661**	**3,670**	**3,765**	**3,733**	**3,597**	**3,750**
Residential or domestic	Bil. kWh	924	1,043	1,192	1,359	1,352	1,392	1,380	1,364	1,451
Percent of total	Percent	34.1	34.6	34.9	37.1	36.8	37.0	37.0	37.9	38.7
Commercial [4]	Bil. kWh	751	863	1,055	1,275	1,300	1,336	1,336	1,307	1,329
Industrial [5]	Bil. kWh	946	1,013	1,064	1,019	1,011	1,028	1,009	917	962
Revenue [3]	**Bil. dol.**	**178.2**	**207.7**	**233.2**	**298.0**	**326.5**	**343.7**	**363.7**	**353.3**	**370.5**
Residential or domestic	Bil. dol.	72.4	87.6	98.2	128.4	140.6	148.3	155.4	157.0	168.0
Percent of total	Percent	40.6	42.2	42.1	43.1	43.1	43.1	42.7	44.4	45.3
Commercial [4]	Bil. dol.	55.1	66.4	78.4	110.5	122.9	128.9	138.5	132.9	136.4
Industrial [5]	Bil. dol.	44.9	47.2	49.4	58.4	62.3	65.7	68.9	62.5	65.3
Ultimate customers, Dec. 31 [3]	**Million**	**110.6**	**118.3**	**127.6**	**138.4**	**140.4**	**142.1**	**143.3**	**143.5**	**144.2**
Residential or domestic	Million	97.1	103.9	111.7	120.8	122.5	123.9	124.9	125.2	125.9
Commercial [4]	Million	12.1	12.9	14.3	16.9	17.2	17.4	17.6	17.6	17.6
Industrial [5]	Million	0.5	0.6	0.5	0.7	0.8	0.8	0.8	0.8	0.7
Avg. kWh used per customer	**1,000**	**24.5**	**25.5**	**26.8**	**26.5**	**26.1**	**26.5**	**26.1**	**25.1**	**26.0**
Residential	1,000	9.5	10.0	10.7	11.3	11.0	11.2	11.0	10.9	11.5
Commercial [4]	1,000	62.2	66.6	73.5	75.6	75.7	76.9	76.1	74.4	75.6
Avg. annual bill per customer	**Dollar**	**1,612**	**1,756**	**1,828**	**2,154**	**2,325**	**2,418**	**2,538**	**2,462**	**2,570**
Residential	Dollar	745	843	879	1,063	1,148	1,196	1,244	1,254	1,335
Commercial [4]	Dollar	4,562	5,124	5,464	6,551	7,158	7,418	7,884	7,570	7,754
Avg. revenue per kWh sold	**Cents**	**6.57**	**6.89**	**6.81**	**8.14**	**8.9**	**9.13**	**9.74**	**9.82**	**9.88**
Residential	Cents	7.83	8.40	8.24	9.45	10.40	10.65	11.26	11.51	11.58
Commercial [4]	Cents	7.34	7.69	7.43	8.67	9.46	9.65	10.36	10.17	10.26
Industrial [5]	Cents	4.74	4.66	4.64	5.73	6.16	6.39	6.83	6.81	6.79

[1] Preliminary. [2] "Generation" includes batteries, chemicals, hydrogen, pitch, sulfur, purchased steam, and miscellaneous technologies, which are not separately displayed. [3] Includes other types, not shown separately. Data for 1990 are as of December 31, data for following years are average yearly customers. [4] Small light and power. [5] Large light and power.

Source: Edison Electric Institute, Washington, DC, *Statistical Yearbook of the Electric Power Industry*, annual (copyright). See also <http://www.eei.org>.

Table 966. Revenue and Expense Statistics for Major U.S. Investor-Owned Electric Utilities: 1995 to 2010

[In millions of nominal dollars (199,967 represents $199,967,000,000). Covers approximately 180 investor-owned electric utilities that during each of the last 3 years met any one or more of the following conditions—1 mil. megawatt-hours of total sales, 100 megawatt-hours of sales for resale, 500 megawatt-hours of gross interchange out, and 500 megawatt-hours of wheeling for other. Missing or erroneous respondent data may result in slight imbalances in some of the expense account subtotals]

Item	1995	2000	2005	2007	2008	2009	2010
Utility operating revenues	**199,967**	**233,915**	**265,652**	**270,964**	**298,962**	**276,124**	**284,373**
Electric utility	183,655	213,634	234,909	240,864	266,124	249,303	260,113
Other utility	16,312	20,281	30,743	30,100	32,838	26,822	24,260
Utility operating expenses	**165,321**	**210,250**	**236,786**	**241,198**	**267,263**	**244,243**	**250,122**
Electric utility	150,599	191,564	207,830	213,076	236,572	219,544	226,845
Operation	91,881	132,607	150,645	153,885	175,887	154,925	159,585
Production	68,983	107,554	120,586	121,700	140,974	118,816	128,808
Cost of fuel	29,122	32,407	36,106	39,548	47,337	40,242	44,115
Purchased power	29,981	62,608	77,902	74,112	84,724	67,630	67,284
Other	9,880	12,561	6,599	8,058	8,937	10,970	13,013
Transmission	1,425	2,713	5,664	6,051	6,950	6,742	6,948
Distribution	2,561	3,092	3,502	3,765	3,997	3,947	4,007
Customer accounts	3,613	4,239	4,229	4,652	5,286	5,203	5,091
Customer service	1,922	1,826	2,291	2,939	3,567	3,857	4,741
Sales	348	405	219	239	225	178	185
Administrative and general	13,028	12,768	14,130	14,346	14,718	15,991	17,115
Maintenance	11,767	12,064	12,033	13,181	14,192	14,092	14,962
Depreciation	19,885	20,636	17,123	17,936	19,049	20,095	20,930
Taxes and other	27,065	24,479	26,805	27,000	26,202	29,081	27,646
Other utility	14,722	18,686	28,956	28,122	30,692	24,698	23,277
Net utility operating income	**34,646**	**23,665**	**28,866**	**29,766**	**31,699**	**31,881**	**34,251**

Source: U.S. Energy Information Administration, "Electric Power Annual 2010," November 2011, <http://www.eia.gov/electricity/>.

Table 967. Total Renewable Energy Net Generation of Electricity by Source and State: 2009

[In millions of kilowatt-hours (417,724 represents 417,724,000,000). MSW = municipal solid waste. For more on net generation, see Table 961]

State	Total [1]	Hydro-electric	Bio-mass [2]	Wind	Wood and derived fuels [3]	State	Total [1]	Hydro-electric	Bio-mass [2]	Wind	Wood and derived fuels [3]
U.S.	**417,724**	**273,445**	**18,443**	**73,886**	**36,050**	MO	2,391	1,817	73	499	2
AL	15,585	12,535	14	(NA)	3,035	MT	10,422	9,506	(NA)	821	95
AK	1,337	1,324	7	7	(NA)	NE	883	434	66	383	(NA)
AZ	6,630	6,427	22	30	137	NV	4,269	2,461	(NA)	(NA)	1
AR	5,778	4,193	57	(NA)	1,529	NH	2,878	1,680	151	62	984
CA	53,428	27,888	2,468	5,840	3,732	NJ	992	32	928	21	(NA)
CO	5,132	1,886	56	3,164	(Z)	NM	1,851	271	34	1,547	(NA)
CT	1,268	510	758	(NA)	1	NY	32,082	27,615	1,665	2,266	536
DE	126	(NA)	126	(NA)	(NA)	NC	7,065	5,171	131	(NA)	1,757
DC	(NA)	(NA)	(NA)	(NA)	(NA)	ND	4,484	1,475	12	2,998	(NA)
FL	4,549	208	2,377	(NA)	1,954	OH	1,161	528	210	14	410
GA	6,085	3,260	80	(NA)	2,746	OK	6,482	3,553	163	2,698	68
HI	817	113	284	251	(NA)	OR	37,306	33,034	128	3,470	674
ID	11,302	10,434	(NA)	313	478	PA	6,035	2,683	1,579	1,075	694
IL	3,666	136	710	2,820	(Z)	RI	149	5	145	(NA)	(NA)
IN	2,209	503	303	1,403	(NA)	SC	4,080	2,332	137	(NA)	1,611
IA	8,560	971	168	7,421	(Z)	SD	4,859	4,432	6	421	(NA)
KS	2,876	13	(NA)	2,863	(NA)	TN	11,162	10,212	36	52	862
KY	3,681	3,318	101	(NA)	263	TX	22,133	1,029	429	20,026	649
LA	3,600	1,236	67	(NA)	2,297	UT	1,322	835	48	160	(NA)
ME	8,150	4,212	273	299	3,367	VT	1,915	1,486	24	12	393
MD	2,440	1,889	376	(NA)	175	VA	3,896	1,479	709	(NA)	1,708
MA	2,430	1,201	1,108	6	115	WA	77,977	72,933	167	3,572	1,305
MI	3,995	1,372	834	300	1,489	WV	2,388	1,646	(-Z)	742	-1
MN	7,546	809	887	5,053	796	WI	3,734	1,394	519	1,052	769
MS	1,424	(NA)	7	(NA)	1,417	WY	3,193	967	(NA)	2,226	(NA)

NA Not available. Z Less than 500,000 million kilowatt-hours. [1] Includes types not shown separately. [2] Includes landfill gas and municipal solid waste biogenic (paper and paper board, wood, food, leather, textiles, and yard trimmings). Also includes agriculture by-products/crops, sludge waste, and other biomass solids, liquids, and gases. Excludes wood and wood waste. [3] Black liquor and wood/woodwaste solids and liquids.

Source: Energy Information Administration, "Trends in Renewable Energy Consumption and Electricity 2009," March 2011, <http://www.eia.gov/renewable/annual/trends/>.

Table 968. Major Weather-Related Power Outages by Duration: 2011

[Data shown for power outages lasting longer than 48 hours]

Type of Disturbance	Month	Area Affected	Duration	Power Loss (megawatts)	Number of Customers Affected [1]
Severe Weather.....	October	Pennsylvania	226 Hours, 59 Minutes	(NA)	312,359
Severe Weather.....	October	Pennsylvania	222 Hours, 1 Minutes	(NA)	50,000
Severe Weather.....	October	Northwest and Central New Jersey	219 Hours, 1 Minutes	(NA)	379,000
Severe Weather.....	October	Connecticut; Maine; Massachusetts; New Hampshire; Rhode Island	215 Hours, 46 Minutes	(NA)	1,418,100
Severe Weather.....	May	Joplin, Sarcoxie, and Wentworth, Missouri	210 Hours, 52 Minutes	200	20,000
Severe Weather.....	August	Maryland	195 Hours, 0 Minutes	1,114	760,113
Severe Weather.....	October	New Jersey	189 Hours, 30 Minutes	125	197,000
Severe Weather.....	December	Southern California	164 Hours, 15 Minutes	(NA)	91,690
Severe Weather.....	August	Borough's and Westshester County New York	144 Hours, 0 Minutes	(NA)	50,000
Severe Weather.....	July	Southeast Michigan	140 Hours, 30 Minutes	(NA)	197,166
Severe Weather.....	August	New York	137 Hours, 1 Minutes	(NA)	99,700
Severe Weather.....	October	Southeast New York	132 Hours, 42 Minutes	(NA)	161,151
Severe Weather.....	October	Harrisburg, Lehigh Valley, Lancaster Region Pennsylvania	130 Hours, 3 Minutes	(NA)	146,721
Severe Weather.....	April	Alabama, Florida, Georgia, Mississippi	128 Hours, 3 Minutes	1,422	426,640
Severe Weather.....	September	Southeast Lower Peninsula, Michigan	124 Hours, 0 Minutes	(NA)	105,000
Major Storm..........	March	Northern and Central California	115 Hours, 14 Minutes	91	128,000
Winter Storm.........	January	Montgomery and Prince George's County, Maryland and District of Columbia	111 Hours, 0 Minutes	(NA)	210,000
Severe Weather.....	October	New York City area	101 Hours, 14 Minutes	(NA)	50,000
Severe Weather.....	July	South East, Lower Peninsula, Michigan	97 Hours, 45 Minutes	(NA)	182,000
Severe Weather.....	August	Cleveland area, Ohio	91 Hours, 30 Minutes	(NA)	107,833
Severe Weather.....	October	Mid-Hudson Valley Region, New York	89 Hours, 15 Minutes	(NA)	145,000
Severe Weather.....	April	Memphis, Tennessee	84 Hours, 14 Minutes	359	63,000
Severe Weather.....	April	Davidson Count, Tennessee	82 Hours, 1 Minutes	300	73,000
Winter Storm.........	February	Northern and Central California	81 Hours, 30 Minutes	91	80,000
Severe Weather.....	August	Southeastern Michigan	74 Hours, 18 Minutes	254	65,000
Winter Storm.........	February	Southern Lower Peninsula, Michigan	72 Hours, 0 Minutes	262	160,000
Winter Storm.........	January	Maryland	70 Hours, 32 Minutes	(NA)	234,326
Severe Weather.....	April	North Carolina, South Carolina	69 Hours, 0 Minutes	1,200	256,000
Winter Storm.........	February	Philadelphia area, Pennsylvania	68 Hours, 59 Minutes	(NA)	213,000
Severe Weather.....	August	Eastern North Carolina	68 Hours, 33 Minutes	(NA)	285,465
Ice Storm.............	January	Southwestern Ohio and Indiana	62 Hours, 0 Minutes	996	272,880
Severe Weather.....	April	Cleveland area, Ohio	61 Hours, 30 Minutes	(NA)	86,000
Severe Weather.....	May	Central Indiana	60 Hours, 46 Minutes	200	141,000
Major Storm..........	February	Northern and Central California	56 Hours, 48 Minutes	91	80,000
Severe Weather.....	July	Central New Jersey	55 Hours, 39 Minutes	(NA)	67,900
Severe Weather.....	May	Central, Indiana	55 Hours, 14 Minutes	1,024	215,387
Severe Weather.....	April	Alabama, Georgia, Mississippi, Tennessee	54 Hours, 29 Minutes	(NA)	612,000
Severe Weather.....	August	District of Columbia; Maryland	52 Hours, 25 Minutes	(NA)	220,000
Severe Weather.....	May	Mid and Southern Lower Peninsula, Michigan	51 Hours, 30 Minutes	250	113,000
Severe Weather.....	August	North Carolina; Virginia	51 Hours, 27 Minutes	(NA)	1,000,000
Severe Weather.....	July	Southwest and South Central Minnesota	51 Hours, 0 Minutes	(NA)	70,000
Severe Weather.....	February	Maryland	50 Hours, 37 Minutes	(NA)	93,000
Severe Thunderstorms....	June	Illinois; Missouri	49 Hours, 0 Minutes	(NA)	80,000
Severe Weather.....	April	Arkasas, Louisiana, Mississippi	48 Hours, 30 Minutes	(NA)	141,700
Severe Weather.....	May	Central Oklahoma	48 Hours, 15 Minutes	(NA)	54,000
Severe Weather.....	April	Alabama, Georgia, Mississippi, Tennessee	48 Hours, 0 Minutes	(NA)	55,000
Severe Weather.....	May	St. Louis County, Missouri	48 Hours, 0 Minutes	(NA)	70,000
Severe Weather.....	August	Puerto Rico	48 Hours, 0 Minutes	2,200	931,000
Severe Weather.....	August	Pennsylvania	48 Hours, 0 Minutes	(NA)	200,717
Severe Weather.....	August	Delaware; Maryland	48 Hours, 0 Minutes	(NA)	165,000
Severe Weather.....	August	Pennsylvania	48 Hours, 0 Minutes	(NA)	264,000
Severe Weather.....	August	Mid-Hudson, New York	48 Hours, 0 Minutes	(NA)	180,000
Severe Weather.....	August	New Jersey	48 Hours, 0 Minutes	500	665,000
Severe Weather.....	August	Northern and Central New Jersey	48 Hours, 0 Minutes	(NA)	650,000
Severe Weather.....	August	Eastern and Northeastern Pennsylvania	48 Hours, 0 Minutes	110	284,000
Severe Weather.....	August	Long Island, New York	48 Hours, 0 Minutes	(NA)	152,261
Severe Weather.....	October	Southeast Pennsylvania	48 Hours, 0 Minutes	(NA)	109,335
Severe Weather.....	October	New Jersey; New York	48 Hours, 0 Minutes	(NA)	74,000

NA Not available. [1]Number of customers affected are preliminary estimates.

Source: U.S. Energy Information Administration, *Electric Power Monthly*, August 2012. See also <http://www.eia.gov/electricity/monthly/>.

Table 969. Gas Utility Industry—Summary: 1990 to 2010

[54,261 represents 54,261,000. Covers natural, manufactured, mixed, and liquid petroleum gas. Based on a questionnaire mailed to all privately and municipally owned gas utilities in the United States, except those with annual revenues less than $25,000]

Item	Unit	1990	1995	2000	2005	2007	2008	2009	2010
End users [1]	1,000	**54,261**	**58,728**	**61,262**	**64,395**	**65,389**	**65,487**	**65,147**	**64,960**
Residential	1,000	49,802	53,955	56,494	59,569	60,534	60,654	60,344	60,246
Commercial	1,000	4,246	4,530	4,610	4,678	4,718	4,703	4,659	4,582
Industrial and other	1,000	214	242	159	147	137	130	144	132
	Tril.								
Sales [2]	Btu [3]	**9,842**	**9,221**	**9,232**	**8,848**	**8,565**	**8,594**	**8,050**	**7,980**
Residential	Tril. Btu	4,468	4,803	4,741	4,516	4,418	4,541	4,387	4,371
Percent of total	Percent	45	52	51	51	52	53	54	55
Commercial	Tril. Btu	2,192	2,281	2,077	2,056	1,943	2,009	1,901	1,842
Industrial	Tril. Btu	3,010	1,919	1,698	1,654	1,522	1,410	1,193	1,209
Other	Tril. Btu	171	218	715	622	682	635	570	558
Revenues [2]	Mil. dol.	**45,153**	**46,436**	**59,243**	**96,909**	**92,131**	**102,641**	**77,675**	**72,886**
Residential	Mil. dol.	25,000	28,742	35,828	55,680	55,028	60,195	50,500	47,231
Percent of total	Percent	55	62	60	57	60	59	65	65
Commercial	Mil. dol.	10,604	11,573	13,339	22,653	21,248	23,592	18,451	16,578
Industrial	Mil. dol.	8,996	5,571	7,432	13,751	11,323	13,205	6,171	6,437
Other	Mil. dol.	553	549	2,645	4,825	4,533	5,649	2,553	2,640
Prices per mil. Btu [3]	Dollars	**4.59**	**5.05**	**6.42**	**10.95**	**10.76**	**11.94**	**9.65**	**9.13**
Residential	Dollars	5.60	6.00	7.56	12.33	12.46	13.26	11.51	10.81
Commercial	Dollars	4.84	5.07	6.42	11.02	10.93	11.75	9.71	9.00
Industrial	Dollars	2.99	2.98	4.38	8.31	7.44	9.37	5.17	5.32
Gas mains mileage	1,000	**1,189**	**1,278**	**1,369**	**1,438**	**1,520**	**1,525**	**1,526**	**1,531**
Field and gathering	1,000	32	31	27	23	19	20	20	19
Transmission	1,000	292	297	297	297	300	299	297	308
Distribution	1,000	865	950	1,046	1,118	1,201	1,206	1,210	1,204
Construction expenditures [4]	Mil. dol.	**7,899**	**10,760**	**8,624**	**10,089**	**10,987**	**14,090**	**12,146**	**11,042**
Transmission	Mil. dol.	2,886	3,380	1,590	3,368	4,327	6,388	5,377	3,524
Distribution	Mil. dol.	3,714	5,394	5,437	5,129	4,851	5,427	4,948	5,674
Production and storage	Mil. dol.	309	367	138	179	107	174	128	151
General	Mil. dol.	770	1,441	1,273	1,070	1,146	1,228	1,135	1,185
Underground storage	Mil. dol.	219	177	185	343	556	873	559	509

[1] Annual average. [2] Excludes sales for resale. [3] For definition of Btu, see text, this section. [4] Includes general.

Source: American Gas Association, Washington, DC, *Gas Facts*, annual (copyright).

Table 970. Gas Utility Industry—Customers, Sales, and Revenues by State: 2010

[64,960 represents 64,960,000. See headnote, Table 969. For definition of Btu, see text, this section]

State	Customers [1] (1,000) Total	Resi-dential	Sales [2] (tril. Btu) Total	Resi-dential	Revenues [2] (mil. dol.) Total	Resi-dential	State	Customers [1] (1,000) Total	Resi-dential	Sales [2] (tril. Btu) Total	Resi-dential	Revenues [2] (mil. dol.) Total	Resi-dential
U.S.	**64,960**	**60,246**	**7,980**	**4,371**	**72,886**	**47,231**	MO	1,489	1,349	171	111	1,821	1,252
AL	838	769	100	43	1,166	659	MT	291	257	33	22	278	180
AK	134	121	57	19	388	166	NE	483	442	65	36	498	314
AZ	1,195	1,138	77	39	961	600	NV	805	764	93	41	894	482
AR	618	550	63	37	634	418	NH	110	95	13	7	168	97
CA	10,904	10,470	696	503	6,284	4,837	NJ	2,764	2,557	315	218	3,548	2,703
CO	1,781	1,635	198	135	1,521	1,067	NM	606	560	55	36	469	340
CT	542	489	82	43	965	621	NY	3,871	3,604	421	301	5,197	4,040
DE	163	150	17	10	238	153	NC	1,231	1,116	138	77	1,511	932
DC	136	130	14	11	179	139	ND	142	124	28	11	189	85
FL	704	662	47	19	623	328	OH	1,514	1,419	167	128	1,617	1,274
GA	355	321	59	20	526	242	OK	1,004	915	106	68	1,008	728
HI	28	25	3	1	96	23	OR	761	683	79	42	845	510
ID	385	347	38	25	319	215	PA	2,646	2,444	291	211	3,477	2,615
IL	3,824	3,568	485	378	4,312	3,440	RI	247	225	25	17	378	279
IN	1,715	1,574	207	134	1,621	1,121	SC	625	568	92	33	862	420
IA	978	880	121	71	1,016	654	SD	192	170	27	13	201	112
KS	936	854	106	76	1,025	771	TN	1,216	1,085	163	77	1,473	777
KY	811	729	104	54	884	521	TX	4,603	4,286	1,372	234	8,006	2,447
LA	951	892	232	47	1,486	533	UT	884	822	107	68	797	544
ME	29	21	4	1	50	17	VT	43	38	8	3	93	50
MD	980	924	92	71	1,052	836	VA	1,162	1,076	132	83	1,458	1,012
MA	1,524	1,388	158	111	2,110	1,559	WA	1,170	1,068	131	78	1,455	925
MI	3,178	2,953	389	289	4,134	3,167	WV	377	344	45	28	459	308
MN	1,564	1,430	254	127	1,932	1,077	WI	1,832	1,664	223	128	2,015	1,279
MS	488	437	59	28	510	277	WY	132	118	18	10	138	84

[1] Averages for the year. [2] Excludes sales for resale.

Source: American Gas Association, Washington, DC, *Gas Facts*, annual (copyright).

Table 971. Privately Owned Gas Utility Industry—Balance Sheet and Income Account: 1990 to 2010

[In millions of dollars (121,686 represents $121,686,000,000). The gas utility industry consists of pipeline and distribution companies. Excludes operations of companies distributing gas in bottles or tanks]

Item	1990	1995	2000	2005	2006	2007	2008	2009	2010
COMPOSITE BALANCE SHEET									
Assets, total	**121,686**	**141,965**	**165,709**	**196,215**	**203,135**	**205,345**	**230,002**	**219,467**	**220,860**
Total utility plant	112,863	143,636	162,206	207,976	212,500	213,516	237,140	235,426	239,718
Depreciation and amortization	49,483	62,723	69,366	91,794	91,804	86,244	95,211	91,958	92,012
Utility plant (net)	63,380	80,912	92,839	116,183	120,696	127,272	141,929	143,468	147,707
Investment and fund accounts	23,872	26,489	10,846	16,331	17,309	13,677	11,725	9,649	7,132
Current and accrued assets	23,268	18,564	35,691	32,325	26,955	28,871	31,960	27,703	27,288
Deferred debits [1]	9,576	13,923	24,279	29,574	36,278	34,608	42,922	37,037	37,307
Liabilities, total	**121,686**	**141,965**	**165,709**	**196,215**	**203,135**	**205,345**	**230,002**	**219,467**	**220,860**
Capitalization, total	74,958	90,581	96,079	120,949	126,842	127,609	136,108	135,797	133,414
Capital stock	43,810	54,402	47,051	62,470	66,153	71,038	74,610	74,517	74,157
Long-term debts	31,148	35,548	48,267	58,264	60,632	56,538	61,498	61,280	59,223
Current and accrued liabilities	29,550	28,272	42,312	34,936	32,417	34,017	37,450	28,711	28,564
Deferred income taxes [2]	11,360	14,393	17,157	24,937	27,454	27,009	27,637	30,236	34,401
Other liabilities and credits	5,818	8,715	10,161	15,393	16,422	16,709	28,807	24,723	24,515
COMPOSITE INCOME ACCOUNT									
Operating revenues, total	**66,027**	**58,390**	**72,042**	**102,018**	**97,156**	**97,195**	**109,547**	**87,419**	**82,315**
Minus: Operating expenses [3]	60,137	50,760	64,988	89,385	87,013	85,050	97,665	76,240	71,761
Operation and maintenance	51,627	37,966	54,602	77,673	73,459	71,011	82,386	61,865	57,758
Federal, state , and local taxes	4,957	6,182	6,163	7,513	7,350	7,803	8,477	7,889	7,569
Equals: Operating income	5,890	7,630	7,053	12,632	10,144	12,146	11,882	11,179	10,554
Utility operating income	6,077	7,848	7,166	12,812	10,185	12,472	12,293	11,428	11,045
Income before interest charges	8,081	9,484	7,589	13,972	11,586	14,329	13,313	12,232	12,368
Net income	4,410	5,139	4,245	9,777	6,931	9,758	9,067	8,458	8,619
Dividends	3,191	4,037	3,239	2,419	2,304	2,253	2,427	2,162	2,080

[1] Includes capital stock discount and expense and reacquired securities. [2] Includes reserves for deferred income taxes. [3] Includes expenses not shown separately.

Source: American Gas Association, Washington, DC, *Gas Facts*, annual (copyright).

Table 972. Sewage Treatment Facilities: 2009

[Based on the North American Industry Classification System (NAICS), 2007; see text, Section 15]

State	Sewage treatment facilities (NAICS 22132)		State	Sewage treatment facilities (NAICS 22132)	
	Number of establishments	Paid employees		Number of establishments	Paid employees
U.S.	**719**	**7,709**	MO	18	(³)
AL	13	149	MT	3	27
AK	1	(¹)	NE	(NA)	(³)
AZ	15	(³)	NV	(NA)	(NA)
AR	2	(¹)	NH	10	(³)
CA	52	(⁵)	NJ	18	(²)
CO	7	53	NM	3	(³)
CT	14	197	NY	33	349
DE	3	(³)	NC	28	(⁴)
DC	(NA)	(NA)	ND	1	(¹)
FL	70	760	OH	8	(⁴)
GA	9	(⁴)	OK	14	(⁴)
HI	14	(³)	OR	5	(³)
ID	7	41	PA	45	345
IL	32	301	RI	5	(³)
IN	37	453	SC	8	60
IA	4	(³)	SD	1	(¹)
KS	2	(³)	TN	9	104
KY	9	(⁴)	TX	69	(⁶)
LA	32	360	UT	1	(¹)
ME	1	(¹)	VT	3	6
MD	8	(³)	VA	7	(³)
MA	21	(²)	WA	6	(³)
MI	22	(⁴)	WV	13	95
MN	7	(¹)	WI	4	(¹)
MS	22	534	WY	3	(¹)

NA Not available. [1] 0–19 employees. [2] 250–499 employees. [3] 20–99 employees. [4] 100-249 employees. [5] 500-999 employees. [6] 1,000-2,499 employees.

Source: U.S. Census Bureau, "County Business Patterns," June 2011, <http://www.census.gov/econ/cbp/>.

Table 973. Public Drinking Water Systems by Size of Community Served and Source of Water: 2010

[As of September. Covers systems that provide water for human consumption through pipes and other constructed conveyances to at least 15 service connections or serve an average of at least 25 persons for at least 60 days a year. Based on reported data in the Safe Drinking Water Information System maintained by the Environmental Protection Agency]

Type of system	Total [1]	Size of community served					Water source	
		500 or fewer persons	501 to 3,300 persons	3,301 to 10,000 persons	10,001 to 100,000 persons	100,001 persons or more	Ground water	Surface water
Total systems	**152,979**	**124,523**	**19,124**	**5,103**	**3,814**	**415**	**138,527**	**14,371**
COMMUNITY WATER SYSTEMS [2]								
Number of systems	51,460	28,524	13,857	4,882	3,784	413	39,809	11,632
Percent of systems	100	55	27	9	7	1	77	23
Population served (1,000)	297,624	4,796	19,863	28,455	108,132	136,379	88,371	209,243
Percent of population	100	2	7	10	36	46	30	70
NONTRANSIENT NONCOMMUNITY WATER SYSTEM [3]								
Number of systems	18,295	15,559	2,584	132	19	1	17,565	719
Percent of systems	100	85	14	1	–	–	96	4
Population served (1,000)	6,212	2,183	2,680	697	448	203	5,354	855
Percent of population	100	35	43	11	7	3	86	14
TRANSIENT NONCOMMUNITY WATER SYSTEM [4]								
Number of systems	87,672	84,785	2,780	94	12	1	81,153	2,020
Percent of systems	100	97	3	–	–	–	98	2
Population served (1,000)	13,079	7,472	2,704	518	385	2,000	10,068	2,549
Percent of population	100	57	21	4	3	16	80	20

– Represents zero. [1] Includes a small number of systems for which the water source (ground vs. surface) is unknown. [2] A public water system that supplies water to the same population year-round. [3] A public water system that regularly supplies water to at least 25 of the same people at least 6 months per year, but not year-round. Some examples are schools, factories, and office buildings which have their own water systems. [4] A public water system that provides water in a place such as a gas station or campground where people do not remain for long periods of time and is open at least 60 day per year.

Source: U.S. Environmental Protection Agency, *Fiscal Year 2010 Drinking Water and Ground Water Statistics*, February 2012. See also <http://water.epa.gov/drink/>.

Table 974. Public Drinking Water Systems—Number and Population Served by State: 2010

[309,494 represents 309,494,000. See headnote, Table 973]

State	Number of systems	Population served (1,000)				State	Number of systems	Population served (1,000)			
		Total	Commu-nity [1]	Non-tran-sient, non-com-munity [2]	Tran-sient, non-com-munity [3]			Total	Commu-nity [1]	Non-tran-sient, non-com-munity [2]	Tran-sient, non-com-munity [3]
U.S.	**151,093**	**309,494**	**291,059**	**5,843**	**12,592**	MO	2,796	5,385	5,190	77	117
AL	613	5,553	5,532	14	7	MT	2,100	966	717	77	172
AK	1,569	755	588	62	105	NE	1,329	1,579	1,480	47	52
AZ	1,576	6,385	6,156	127	103	NV	551	2,602	2,540	42	21
AR	1,103	2,724	2,695	8	21	NH	2,425	1,265	854	92	319
CA	7,666	41,622	40,450	379	793	NJ	3,940	9,788	8,998	368	422
CO	2,050	5,643	5,324	72	248	NM	1,218	1,922	1,792	49	81
CT	2,624	2,833	2,662	113	58	NY	9,128	21,040	17,903	307	2,830
DE	485	972	895	24	54	NC	6,207	7,955	7,520	119	317
DC	6	607	607	(Z)	–	ND	501	585	566	4	15
FL	5,600	19,573	19,076	246	250	OH	4,938	11,210	10,584	213	413
GA	2,454	8,510	8,368	64	77	OK	1,578	3,590	3,537	22	32
HI	127	1,440	1,429	11	(Z)	OR	2,624	3,517	3,237	71	209
ID	1,959	1,256	1,099	52	105	PA	9,335	12,046	10,759	520	767
IL	5,662	12,589	12,102	133	355	RI	487	1,079	995	23	61
IN	4,231	5,324	4,744	195	384	SC	1,471	3,928	3,842	38	48
IA	1,918	2,792	2,668	49	76	SD	655	746	714	9	23
KS	1,025	2,665	2,639	21	4	TN	864	6,286	6,206	25	54
KY	469	4,446	4,429	12	6	TX	6,824	25,848	25,089	499	260
LA	1,419	5,022	4,906	62	54	UT	1,018	2,815	2,706	29	80
ME	1,893	913	664	68	181	VT	1,359	591	449	44	98
MD	3,487	5,555	5,153	160	242	VA	2,838	7,048	6,558	318	171
MA	1,745	9,534	9,318	75	141	WA	4,128	6,907	6,372	149	387
MI	11,358	8,958	7,616	328	1,014	WV	1,060	1,577	1,504	41	33
MN	7,181	4,861	4,249	77	534	WI	11,452	4,918	3,991	210	716
MS	1,271	3,223	3,137	76	10	WY	776	546	450	22	74

– Represents zero. Z Less than 500. [1] A public water system that supplies water to the same population year-round. [2] A public water system that regularly supplies water to at least 25 of the same people at least 6 months per year, but not year-round. Some examples are schools, factories, and office buildings which have their own water systems. [3] A public water system that provides water in a place such as a gas station or campground where people do not remain for long periods of time and is open at least 60 days per year.

Source: U.S. Environmental Protection Agency, *Fiscal Year 2010 Drinking Water and Ground Water Statistics*, February 2012. See also <http://water.epa.gov/drink/>.

Section 20
Construction and Housing

This section presents data on the construction industry and on various indicators of its activity and costs; on housing units and their characteristics and occupants; and on the characteristics and vacancy rates for commercial buildings. This edition contains data from the *2009 American Housing Survey*.

The principal source of these data is the U.S. Census Bureau, which issues a variety of current publications, as well as data from the decennial census. Current construction statistics compiled by the Census Bureau appear in its *New Residential Construction* and *New Residential Sales* press releases and Web sites at <www.census.gov/construction/nrc/> and <www.census.gov/construction/nrs/>. *Construction Spending* presents data on all types of construction. Reports of the censuses of construction industries (see below) are also issued on various topics.

Other Census Bureau publications include the quarterly *Housing Vacancies*, the quarterly *Market Absorption of Apartments*, the biennial *American Housing Survey* (formerly *Annual Housing Survey*), and reports of the censuses of housing and of construction industries.

The *American Housing Survey* for 2011 was delayed due to budget issues. Consequently, 2011 data was not available at the time of publication.

Other sources include McGraw-Hill Construction, New York, NY, which presents national and state data on construction contracts; the National Association of Home Builders with data on housing starts; the NATIONAL ASSOCIATION OF REALTORS®, which presents data on existing home sales; the Bureau of Economic Analysis, which presents data on residential capital and gross housing product; and the U.S. Energy Information Administration, which provides data on commercial buildings through its periodic sample surveys.

Censuses and surveys—Censuses of the construction industry were first conducted by the Census Bureau for 1929, 1935, and 1939; beginning in 1967, a census has been taken every 5 years (through 2012, for years ending in "2" and "7"). The latest reports are part of the 2007 Economic Census. See text, Section 15, Business Enterprise.

The construction sector of the economic census, covers all employer establishments primarily engaged in (1) building construction by general contractors or operative builders; (2) heavy (nonbuilding) construction by general contractors; and (3) construction by special trade contractors. This sector includes construction management and land subdividers and developers. The 2007 census was conducted in accordance with the 2007 North American Industrial Classification System (NAICS). See text, Section 15, Business Enterprise.

From 1850 through 1930, the Census Bureau collected some housing data as part of its censuses of population and agriculture. Beginning in 1940, separate censuses of housing have been taken at 10-year intervals. For the 1970 and 1980 censuses, data on year-round housing units were collected and issued on occupancy and structural characteristics,

plumbing facilities, value, and rent; for 1990, such characteristics were presented for all housing units.

The *American Housing Survey* (*Current Housing Reports* Series H-150 and H-170), which began in 1973, provided an annual and ongoing series of data on selected housing and demographic characteristics until 1983. In 1984, the name of the survey was changed from the *Annual Housing Survey*. Currently, national data are collected every other year, and data for selected metropolitan areas are collected on a rotating basis. All samples represent a cross section of the housing stock in their respective areas. Estimates are subject to both sampling and nonsampling errors; caution should therefore be used in making comparisons between years.

Data on residential mortgages were collected continuously from 1890 to 1970, except 1930, as part of the decennial census by the Census Bureau. Since 1973, mortgage status data, limited to single family homes on less than 10 acres with no business on the property, have been presented in the American Housing Survey. Data on mortgage activity are covered in Section 25, Banking and Finance.

Housing units—In general, a housing unit is a house, an apartment, a group of rooms or a single room occupied or intended for occupancy as separate living quarters; that is, the occupants live separately from any other individual in the building, and there is direct access from the outside or through a common hall. Transient accommodations, barracks for workers, and institutional-type quarters are not counted as housing units.

Statistical reliability—For a discussion of statistical collection and estimation, sampling procedures, and measures of statistical reliability applicable to Census Bureau data, see Appendix III.

Table 975. Construction—Establishments, Employees, and Payroll by Kind of Business (NAICS Basis): 2009 and 2010

[5,967 represents 5,967,000. Covers establishments with payroll. Excludes most government employees, railroad employees, and self-employed persons. Kind-of-business classification based on North American Industry Classification System (NAICS), 2007. For statement on methodology, see Appendix III]

Industry	2007 NAICS code [1]	Establishments		Paid employees [2] (1,000)		Annual payroll (mil.dol.)	
		2009	2010	2009	2010	2009	2010
Construction...............................	**23**	**712,977**	**682,684**	**5,967**	**5,389**	**280,943**	**260,959**
Construction of buildings............................	236	211,825	201,877	1,291	1,163	63,422	57,525
Residential building construction................	2361	168,894	158,241	639	568	25,487	22,564
New single-family housing construction (except operative builders).................	236115	61,966	50,138	218	169	8,089	6,252
New multifamily housing construction (except operative builders).................	236116	3,659	3,158	40	32	2,361	1,950
New housing operative builders................	236117	18,415	17,014	115	101	6,057	5,374
Residential remodelers............................	236118	84,854	87,931	266	266	8,980	8,987
Nonresidential building construction...........	2362	42,931	43,636	652	595	37,935	34,961
Industrial building construction................	23621	3,353	3,496	73	76	4,113	4,307
Commercial and institutional building construction................................	23622	39,578	40,140	579	519	33,821	30,654
Heavy and civil engineering construction........	237	44,894	43,405	895	842	52,245	50,759
Utility system construction.......................	2371	20,104	19,705	498	463	28,109	27,120
Water and sewer line and related structures........	23711	12,554	12,158	160	148	8,331	7,853
Oil and gas pipeline and related structures........	23712	1,921	1,926	143	127	9,071	8,371
Power and communication line and related structures............................	23713	5,629	5,621	195	188	10,706	10,896
Land subdivision.................................	2372	8,954	7,966	51	41	2,396	2,051
Highway, street, and bridge construction........	2373	11,219	11,106	280	274	17,871	17,587
Other heavy and civil engineering construction.....	2379	4,617	4,628	66	64	3,870	4,000
Specialty trade contractors.........................	238	456,258	437,402	3,781	3,384	165,276	152,676
Foundation, structure, and building exterior contractors............................	2381	97,606	92,555	808	695	31,374	27,730
Poured concrete foundation and structures contractors............................	23811	22,178	20,912	211	176	8,396	7,390
Structural steel and precast concrete contractors............................	23812	3,584	3,449	69	54	3,073	2,528
Framing contractors..............................	23813	12,793	11,675	72	62	2,201	1,858
Masonry contractors.............................	23814	22,087	20,446	167	136	5,991	5,080
Glass and glazing contractors..................	23815	5,286	5,140	55	47	2,539	2,103
Roofing contractors..............................	23816	17,901	17,730	156	151	6,124	5,949
Siding contractors................................	23817	8,490	8,031	36	33	1,257	1,173
Other foundation, structure, and building exterior contractors....................	23819	5,287	5,172	42	37	1,792	1,649
Building equipment contractors....................	2382	175,822	171,333	1,781	1,623	86,906	81,716
Electrical contractors............................	23821	73,817	70,824	749	669	36,202	33,613
Plumbing, heating, and air-conditioning contractors............................	23822	95,212	93,761	895	828	42,701	40,696
Other building equipment contractors..........	23829	6,793	6,748	137	126	8,003	7,407
Building finishing contractors......................	2383	114,233	108,594	716	626	26,127	23,082
Drywall and insulation contractors.............	23831	19,506	18,388	235	195	9,200	7,627
Painting and wall covering contractors........	23832	34,952	33,435	175	158	6,039	5,598
Flooring contractors.............................	23833	14,778	14,320	68	62	2,458	2,266
Tile and terrazzo contractors...................	23834	9,745	9,040	54	44	1,854	1,520
Finish carpentry contractors....................	23835	28,662	26,925	121	106	4,204	3,802
Other building finishing contractors............	23839	6,590	6,486	63	61	2,372	2,268
Other specialty trade contractors.................	2389	68,597	64,920	476	439	20,869	20,148
Site preparation contractors....................	23891	36,965	35,182	283	259	12,666	12,271
All other specialty trade contractors...........	23899	31,632	29,738	193	180	8,202	7,877

[1] North American Industry Classification System code, 2007. See text, Section 15. [2] Employees on the payroll for the pay period including March 12.

Source: U.S. Census Bureau, "County Business Patterns," June 2012, <http://www.census.gov/econ/cbp>.

Table 976. Value of New Construction Put in Place: 1980 to 2011

[In millions of dollars (273,936 represents $273,936,000,000). Represents value of construction put in place during year; differs from building permit and construction contract data in timing and coverage. Includes installed cost of normal building service equipment and selected types of industrial production equipment (largely site fabricated). Excludes cost of shipbuilding, land, and most types of machinery and equipment. For methodology, see Appendix III. For details, see Tables 981 and 978]

Year		Private			Public		
	Total	Total	Residential buildings	Non-residential	Total	Federal	State and local
1980........	273,936	210,290	100,381	109,909	63,646	9,642	54,004
1990........	476,778	369,300	191,103	178,197	107,478	12,099	95,379
1994........	549,420	418,999	258,561	160,438	130,421	14,440	115,981
1995........	567,896	427,885	247,351	180,534	140,011	15,751	124,260
1996........	623,313	476,638	281,115	195,523	146,675	15,325	131,350
1997........	656,171	502,734	289,014	213,720	153,437	14,087	139,350
1998........	706,779	552,001	314,607	237,394	154,778	14,318	140,460
1999........	768,811	599,729	350,562	249,167	169,082	14,025	155,057
2000........	831,075	649,750	374,457	275,293	181,325	14,166	167,157
2001........	864,159	662,247	388,324	273,922	201,912	15,081	186,830
2002........	847,873	634,435	396,696	237,739	213,438	16,578	196,860
2003........	891,497	675,370	446,035	229,335	216,127	17,913	198,214
2004........	991,356	771,173	532,900	238,273	220,183	18,342	201,841
2005........	1,104,136	869,976	611,899	258,077	234,160	17,300	216,860
2006........	1,167,222	911,837	613,731	298,105	255,385	17,555	237,831
2007........	1,152,351	863,278	493,246	370,032	289,073	20,580	268,494
2008........	1,067,564	758,827	350,257	408,569	308,738	23,731	285,007
2009........	903,201	588,306	245,912	342,394	314,895	28,439	286,456
2010........	803,621	500,597	238,801	261,796	303,024	30,819	272,205
2011........	789,791	506,128	237,407	268,721	283,468	29,019	254,449

Source: U.S. Census Bureau, "Construction Spending," <http://www.census.gov/construction/c30/c30index.html>.

Table 977. New Privately Owned Housing Units Authorized by State: 2010 and 2011

[604.6 represents 604,600. Based on about 20,000 places in United States having building permit systems in 2010 and 2011]

State	Housing units (1,000)			Valuation (mil. dol.)			State	Housing units (1,000)			Valuation (mil. dol.)		
	2010	2011 Total	2011 1 unit	2010	2011 Total	2011 1 unit		2010	2011 Total	2011 1 unit	2010	2011 Total	2011 1 unit
U.S.....	604.6	624.1	418.5	101,943	105,269	86,327	MO.......	9.7	9.2	6.1	1,430	2,205	1,704
AL.......	11.3	11.7	8.9	1,547	679	596	MT........	2.0	1.9	1.2	304	5,053	4,491
AK.......	.9	.9	.7	205	436	408	NE........	5.4	5.2	3.6	745	2,760	2,575
AZ.......	12.4	13.0	10.3	2,424	1,761	1,373	NV........	6.4	6.2	4.7	760	3,391	2,870
AR.......	7.2	6.8	4.1	880	432	368	NH........	2.7	2.3	1.6	462	306	268
CA.......	43.7	45.5	21.7	9,121	129	117	NJ........	13.5	13.0	6.5	2,037	1,704	1,508
CO.......	11.6	13.5	8.7	2,608	221	177	NM........	4.5	4.1	3.4	780	915	760
CT.......	3.9	3.2	2.2	861	2,043	1,412	NY........	19.6	22.6	8.4	3,165	724	649
DE.......	3.1	3.0	2.4	364	3,356	2,012	NC........	33.9	32.8	24.9	5,107	2,353	2,068
DC.......	.7	4.6	.2	105	2,546	2,250	ND........	3.8	6.2	2.9	481	861	699
FL........	38.7	42.4	31.9	7,824	2,118	1,570	OH........	13.7	13.8	9.3	2,297	1,919	1,729
GA........	17.3	18.5	13.8	2,659	1,976	1,739	OK........	8.1	8.8	6.4	1,226	1,286	1,134
HI........	3.4	2.7	1.6	773	1,688	1,572	OR........	6.9	7.7	4.9	1,377	14,736	12,542
ID........	4.2	3.8	3.2	732	2,260	1,949	PA........	19.7	15.0	11.8	3,293	2,580	2,301
IL........	12.3	11.8	6.8	2,412	1,606	1,341	RI........	.9	.7	.6	155	2,860	2,418
IN........	13.1	12.6	9.3	1,961	1,246	1,111	SC........	14.0	15.5	12.9	2,489	733	682
IA........	7.6	7.5	5.9	1,222	861	707	SD........	2.9	2.8	2.0	403	286	240
KS.......	5.1	5.4	3.5	812	1,764	1,540	TN........	16.5	15.0	11.5	2,345	789	703
KY.......	8.0	7.8	4.8	1,087	1,426	1,181	TX........	88.5	97.5	65.5	13,740	678	622
LA.......	11.3	12.2	10.0	1,765	726	628	UT........	9.2	10.0	6.9	1,672	1,760	1,519
ME.......	3.0	2.7	2.3	525	784	510	VT........	1.3	1.3	.8	228	425	377
MD......	11.9	13.5	8.4	1,952	392	321	VA........	21.0	23.3	15.6	3,246	204	179
MA.......	9.1	7.7	4.9	1,817	370	322	WA........	20.7	20.9	13.2	3,891	9,639	6,053
MI.......	9.1	9.3	7.9	1,553	609	45	WV........	2.4	2.2	1.6	346	654	513
MN......	9.8	8.9	6.7	1,811	8,815	7,787	WI........	10.9	9.9	6.5	1,794	1,407	1,126
MS.......	5.3	5.3	4.3	715	2,761	2,398	WY........	2.3	2.1	1.5	435	4,036	3,164

Source: U.S. Census Bureau, Construction Reports, "Building Permits Survey," <http://www.census.gov/construction/bps/stateannual.html>.

Table 978. Value of State and Local Government Construction Put in Place: 2000 to 2011

[In millions of dollars (167,157 represents $167,157,000,000). See Tables 976 and 981]

Type of construction	2000	2004	2005	2006	2007	2008	2009	2010	2011
Total construction [1]	167,157	201,841	216,860	237,831	268,494	285,007	286,456	272,205	254,555
Residential	2,962	4,110	4,047	4,349	5,094	4,894	5,772	7,496	6,052
Multifamily	2,945	3,956	3,740	3,990	4,476	4,072	4,849	6,401	5,323
Nonresidential	164,196	197,731	212,813	233,482	263,399	280,113	280,684	264,710	248,503
Office	4,494	6,024	5,211	5,588	7,249	8,515	9,170	8,327	7,655
Commercial [1]	1,820	1,979	1,882	1,567	1,777	1,965	2,003	1,450	1,707
Automotive	1,233	1,501	1,490	1,152	1,012	1,425	1,141	748	904
Parking	1,143	1,356	1,357	1,011	941	1,252	1,031	652	732
Warehouse	330	276	218	230	558	312	440	278	280
Health care	2,829	5,025	5,059	5,615	7,028	7,010	6,837	6,078	6,832
Hospital	1,949	3,324	3,429	4,085	5,304	5,320	5,352	4,656	5,189
Medical building	490	1,211	1,168	919	981	909	876	757	858
Special care	390	490	463	611	743	782	609	665	786
Educational [1]	46,818	59,741	65,750	69,790	78,376	84,489	83,703	71,615	68,083
Primary/secondary [1]	33,764	40,990	44,184	47,846	55,054	57,770	54,650	44,301	40,782
Elementary	12,272	14,308	14,251	13,870	16,786	18,305	17,241	13,128	10,644
Middle/junior high	5,820	8,132	9,069	10,764	11,719	10,937	10,278	6,975	7,978
High	13,326	17,950	19,892	22,631	25,887	27,985	26,729	23,890	21,722
Higher education [1]	10,749	15,864	18,033	18,961	20,556	23,542	25,081	24,292	24,269
Instructional	6,317	8,699	9,275	9,434	11,300	13,251	14,734	14,153	13,532
Parking	514	765	1,013	909	839	732	596	581	710
Administration	294	303	387	657	503	290	382	357	442
Dormitory	1,078	2,673	2,918	3,409	2,657	3,043	3,183	3,325	3,919
Library	308	524	588	493	700	791	871	666	584
Student union/cafeteria	322	632	880	1,028	1,547	1,398	1,440	1,134	1,191
Sports/recreation	966	1,370	1,769	1,748	1,726	2,559	2,357	2,424	2,354
Infrastructure	835	867	1,138	1,227	1,218	1,241	1,291	1,314	1,313
Other educational [1]	1,645	2,357	2,735	2,312	1,890	2,485	3,077	2,240	1,985
Library/archive	976	1,501	2,098	1,857	1,287	1,557	1,865	1,400	1,300
Public safety [1]	5,854	5,477	6,013	6,608	8,423	9,666	9,432	7,551	7,117
Correctional	4,754	3,771	3,958	4,611	5,384	6,375	5,780	4,600	4,784
Detention	3,907	2,787	2,936	3,305	4,026	4,524	3,409	2,780	3,073
Police/sheriff	848	985	1,022	1,307	1,358	1,851	2,371	1,820	1,711
Other public safety	1,100	1,705	2,055	1,997	3,039	3,291	3,652	2,950	2,333
Fire/rescue	994	1,441	1,675	1,615	2,392	2,367	2,470	1,745	1,474
Amusement and recreation [1]	7,583	7,794	7,340	9,444	10,670	10,872	10,585	9,611	8,350
Sports	2,289	1,746	1,587	1,853	2,040	2,548	2,389	1,825	1,173
Performance/meeting center	2,075	2,061	1,921	2,292	1,706	1,631	1,704	1,792	1,788
Convention center	1,397	1,350	1,350	1,422	1,035	1,040	1,013	1,091	1,114
Social center	1,152	1,476	1,006	1,285	1,373	1,587	1,646	1,572	1,033
Neighborhood center	886	1,312	866	1,098	1,053	1,231	1,480	1,407	865
Park/camp	1,930	2,303	2,728	3,887	5,255	4,975	4,733	4,215	4,131
Transportation	13,000	16,440	16,256	17,695	21,144	23,230	25,461	26,299	22,904
Air [1]	6,700	8,715	8,993	9,676	11,390	11,579	12,562	11,888	9,803
Passenger terminal	2,930	3,972	3,310	3,766	5,224	6,164	6,916	6,508	5,623
Runway	3,196	4,049	4,861	4,898	5,164	4,551	4,839	4,699	3,727
Land [1]	5,165	6,415	5,936	6,629	7,593	9,969	11,327	12,784	11,396
Passenger terminal	1,253	1,368	907	969	1,301	2,053	2,789	3,412	3,354
Mass transit	1,484	3,067	3,208	3,228	3,587	4,371	5,223	6,298	5,324
Railroad	1,471	349	552	320	508	585	747	759	660
Water [1]	1,136	1,309	1,327	1,391	2,161	1,682	1,572	1,628	1,706
Dock/marina	863	1,028	930	971	1,465	1,287	1,309	1,101	1,284
Dry dock/marine terminal	236	281	397	420	697	395	263	526	422
Power	5,501	7,044	8,320	7,766	11,449	10,992	11,775	10,899	10,323
Electrical	5,257	5,851	7,091	7,195	10,176	10,192	9,387	10,151	8,577
Distribution	2,087	1,856	1,786	2,187	2,818	3,487	3,276	3,441	1,930
Highway and street [1]	51,574	57,351	63,157	71,032	75,455	80,424	81,254	81,362	77,921
Pavement	37,929	40,274	45,177	45,933	47,679	52,837	55,186	51,474	47,384
Lighting	856	1,146	1,232	1,057	1,709	1,532	1,300	1,998	1,696
Retaining wall	1,099	552	675	1,546	1,073	888	959	1,216	1,028
Tunnel	894	521	373	224	221	264	302	813	887
Bridge	9,302	13,150	14,244	20,057	22,827	23,690	22,075	24,249	25,722
Toll/weigh	325	233	320	657	421	196	268	220	255
Maintenance building	293	170	96	213	102	102	128	276	236
Rest facility/streetscape	878	1,306	1,042	1,347	1,424	916	1,036	1,117	714
Sewage and waste disposal [1]	14,000	17,084	18,336	21,524	23,323	24,102	23,455	24,671	21,430
Sewage/dry waste [1]	9,338	10,836	11,717	13,401	13,891	14,044	13,261	13,243	12,109
Plant	2,765	3,095	3,369	3,410	3,802	3,957	3,453	3,801	3,251
Line/pump station	6,326	7,574	8,243	9,820	9,784	9,823	9,494	9,323	8,784
Waste water	4,663	6,248	6,620	8,124	9,432	10,058	10,194	11,427	9,321
Plant	3,229	4,658	5,231	6,039	7,496	8,688	8,497	9,515	7,879
Line/drain	1,434	1,591	1,389	2,085	1,935	1,370	1,697	1,912	1,442
Water supply [1]	9,528	11,977	13,483	14,299	15,029	16,017	14,838	14,348	13,225
Plant	3,067	4,418	4,943	5,005	5,661	6,500	6,327	5,639	5,350
Well	378	318	360	623	661	460	480	378	363
Line	4,644	5,307	6,234	5,922	6,131	6,191	5,398	6,226	5,831
Pump station	625	705	776	1,285	1,124	1,293	1,372	974	735
Reservoir	266	503	502	700	586	633	335	389	426
Tank/tower	548	727	668	764	867	940	926	741	520
Conservation and development [1]	933	1,466	1,752	2,000	2,198	2,251	2,016	2,009	2,287
Dam/levee	303	297	405	591	640	772	761	740	897
Breakwater/jetty	270	654	726	809	627	645	702	693	627
Dredging	140	138	211	192	204	179	248	178	207

[1] Includes other types of construction, not shown separately.

Source: U.S. Census Bureau, *Construction Spending*, <http://www.census.gov/construction/c30/c30index.html>.

Table 979. Construction Contracts Started - Value of Construction and Floor Space of Buildings by Class of Construction: 1990 to 2011

[246.0 represents $246,000,000,000. Dollar value data includes new construction, additions and alterations. Square footage data includes new construction and additions; alterations which create no net new square footage are not included]

Year	Total	Residential buildings	Nonresidential buildings									Nonbuilding construction
			Total	Commercial [1]	Manufacturing	Education [2]	Health	Public	Religious	Social and recreational	Miscellaneous	
VALUE (bil. dol.)												
1990	246.0	100.9	95.4	44.8	8.4	16.6	9.2	5.7	2.2	5.3	3.1	49.7
1995	306.5	127.9	114.2	46.6	13.8	22.9	10.8	6.3	2.8	7.1	3.8	64.4
2000	472.9	208.3	173.3	80.9	8.9	40.9	12.4	7.5	4.6	13.8	4.4	91.3
2001	496.5	219.7	169.1	70.2	8.0	47.0	14.4	7.8	4.8	12.0	4.8	107.7
2002	504.0	248.7	155.1	59.6	5.5	45.3	16.1	7.3	5.1	11.5	4.7	100.2
2003	531.7	283.4	156.1	58.8	6.9	47.7	15.8	7.1	4.5	11.0	4.3	92.3
2004	593.2	333.1	164.4	67.3	8.0	44.0	17.6	7.2	4.5	11.6	4.4	95.6
2005	670.2	384.0	182.4	72.2	10.1	49.1	22.3	7.9	4.1	11.7	5.0	103.8
2006	689.5	342.1	217.3	92.9	13.7	53.8	24.3	8.2	4.1	14.3	5.9	130.1
2007	640.8	261.5	239.1	100.7	20.7	58.1	24.4	12.4	3.8	13.4	5.5	140.2
2008	556.6	160.5	243.0	81.4	31.0	63.7	30.0	13.4	3.6	13.5	6.5	153.1
2009	426.4	112.3	169.4	47.3	9.8	54.0	20.4	15.5	3.3	11.6	7.6	144.7
2010	432.7	121.6	162.8	41.8	9.5	53.2	24.5	10.5	2.3	11.1	9.8	148.3
2011	435.4	125.3	163.0	47.2	16.6	47.4	23.1	9.3	2.1	10.2	7.0	147.1
FLOOR SPACE (mil. Sq. ft.)												
1990	3,020	1,817	1,203	694	128	152	69	47	29	51	32	(X)
1995	3,454	2,172	1,281	700	163	186	70	40	33	56	33	(X)
1999	5,091	3,253	1,838	1,115	141	261	98	49	48	87	39	(X)
2000	4,982	3,113	1,869	1,180	111	273	88	44	49	94	29	(X)
2001	4,828	3,159	1,669	988	93	295	92	44	50	81	27	(X)
2002	4,792	3,356	1,436	810	68	277	97	37	52	71	26	(X)
2003	5,093	3,689	1,404	794	75	270	92	35	45	67	26	(X)
2004	5,518	4,061	1,457	875	86	231	94	34	43	68	27	(X)
2005	5,872	4,345	1,528	927	79	246	108	33	37	67	29	(X)
2006	5,282	3,647	1,635	1,015	83	254	110	33	35	73	33	(X)
2007	4,312	2,645	1,667	1,051	91	247	104	51	31	66	27	(X)
2008	2,952	1,573	1,379	773	80	253	109	49	28	59	28	(X)
2009	1,890	1,113	776	332	37	199	68	48	25	42	26	(X)
2010	1,840	1,162	678	278	46	175	72	34	15	35	22	(X)
2011	1,840	1,147	692	319	52	156	75	27	14	33	18	(X)

X Not applicable. [1] Includes nonindustrial warehouses. [2] Includes science facilities.

Source: McGraw-Hill Construction, a Division of the McGraw-Hill Companies, New York, NY (copyright) 1-800-591-4462.

Table 980. Construction Contracts Started - Value by Region: 2007 to 2011

[In millions of dollars (640,782 represents 640,782,000,000). Includes new construction, additions and alterations]

Region	2007	2008	2009	2010	2011		
					Total [1]	Residential	Nonresidential
U.S.	**640,782**	**556,602**	**426,441**	**432,698**	**435,380**	**125,314**	**162,961**
New England	24,602	20,550	16,877	19,891	19,739	5,194	8,763
Middle Atlantic	65,464	64,498	51,366	53,661	47,788	10,541	23,730
East North Central	72,382	75,378	50,941	51,784	48,097	11,939	19,492
West North Central	43,283	33,428	30,957	32,083	30,779	8,196	11,140
South Atlantic	150,923	114,955	86,589	80,073	86,433	31,015	31,382
East South Central	36,709	37,928	25,791	25,668	27,860	7,698	9,290
West South Central	85,925	85,806	69,297	67,589	64,760	23,409	22,376
Mountain	68,078	51,088	37,849	38,722	38,691	11,237	14,257
Pacific	93,417	72,971	56,773	63,227	71,233	16,085	22,531

[1] Includes nonbuilding construction, not shown separately.

Source: McGraw-Hill Construction, a Division of the McGraw-Hill Companies, New York, NY (copyright) 1-800-591-4462.

Table 981. Value of Private Construction Put in Place: 2000 to 2011

[In millions of dollars (621,431 represents $621,431,000,000). Represents value of construction put in place during year; differs from building permit and construction contract data in timing and coverage. See Appendix III and Tables 976 and 978]

Type of construction	2000	2004	2005	2006	2007	2008	2009	2010	2011
Total construction [1]	**621,431**	**771,173**	**869,976**	**911,837**	**863,278**	**758,827**	**588,306**	**500,597**	**506,128**
Residential	346,138	532,900	611,899	613,731	493,246	350,257	245,912	238,801	237,407
New single family	236,788	377,557	433,510	415,997	305,184	185,776	105,336	112,569	106,757
New multifamily	28,259	39,944	47,297	52,803	48,959	44,338	28,538	14,668	14,726
Improvements [2]	81,091	115,399	131,092	144,931	139,103	120,144	112,038	111,564	115,922
Nonresidential	275,293	238,273	258,077	298,105	370,032	408,569	342,394	261,796	268,721
Lodging	16,304	11,982	12,666	17,624	27,481	35,364	25,388	10,904	7,966
Office [1]	52,407	32,879	37,276	45,680	53,815	55,502	37,282	24,231	22,590
General	49,637	28,679	32,962	41,085	48,945	50,137	33,346	22,086	20,203
Financial	2,689	4,186	4,285	4,542	4,785	5,054	3,720	2,101	2,137
Commercial [1]	64,055	63,195	66,584	73,368	85,858	82,654	50,460	37,647	40,118
Automotive [1]	5,967	5,235	5,614	5,528	6,281	5,640	4,535	3,567	4,106
Sales	1,629	2,443	2,834	2,285	2,571	2,430	1,564	1,336	1,764
Service/parts	3,009	1,978	1,805	2,184	2,356	1,843	2,056	1,709	1,891
Parking	1,330	814	975	1,059	1,354	1,367	916	522	452
Food/beverage	8,786	8,232	7,795	7,442	8,046	8,029	4,868	4,526	4,899
Food	4,792	3,590	3,128	2,752	2,779	3,124	1,978	2,032	2,582
Dining/drinking	2,935	3,937	4,078	3,780	3,957	3,976	2,237	1,823	1,587
Fast food	1,058	705	590	910	1,310	930	653	671	730
Multiretail [1]	14,911	18,828	22,750	29,218	34,751	31,963	18,390	12,544	13,264
General merchandise	5,100	6,416	6,740	5,699	7,572	4,373	3,976	3,855	3,802
Shopping center	6,803	9,256	12,462	18,417	22,197	22,780	11,447	6,674	6,272
Shopping mall	2,523	2,138	2,631	3,616	4,000	4,045	2,171	1,350	2,273
Other commercial [1]	13,537	13,341	11,744	10,874	13,580	12,087	6,300	4,233	3,818
Drug store	1,682	1,427	1,315	1,238	1,500	1,967	1,882	1,069	754
Building supply store	2,592	2,521	2,416	2,594	3,507	2,539	1,118	784	655
Other stores	8,136	8,229	7,075	6,135	7,744	6,552	2,528	1,729	1,731
Warehouse [1]	14,822	12,074	12,827	14,491	16,909	16,707	9,730	5,584	6,133
General commercial	13,511	10,830	11,468	13,493	15,641	15,482	8,781	5,148	5,819
Ministorage	1,263	1,141	1,311	979	1,218	1,125	873	409	234
Farm	5,988	5,485	5,854	5,817	6,292	8,227	6,637	7,194	7,898
Health care	19,455	26,272	28,495	32,016	35,588	38,437	35,309	30,316	29,283
Hospital	10,183	16,147	18,250	21,914	24,532	25,571	24,723	22,343	20,855
Medical building	5,066	7,615	8,031	7,165	7,981	9,242	7,531	5,273	5,453
Special care	4,206	2,510	2,213	2,937	3,074	3,625	3,055	2,701	2,975
Educational [1]	11,683	12,701	12,788	13,839	16,691	18,624	16,851	13,356	13,780
Preschool	770	674	516	487	704	746	716	500	368
Primary/secondary	2,948	3,202	2,718	3,240	3,968	3,919	3,362	2,535	2,879
Higher education [1]	6,333	6,496	6,946	7,611	9,424	11,587	10,812	8,176	8,118
Instructional	3,058	3,200	3,556	3,501	4,219	5,463	6,211	4,841	4,305
Dormitory	1,356	1,669	1,537	2,065	2,900	3,791	2,496	1,635	2,116
Sports/recreation	645	739	821	858	771	841	832	798	660
Other educational	1,318	1,998	2,294	2,090	2,167	1,965	1,643	1,814	2,030
Gallery/museum	920	1,335	1,745	1,697	1,939	1,708	1,395	1,643	1,609
Religious	8,030	8,153	7,715	7,740	7,522	7,197	6,177	5,156	4,105
House of worship	5,656	6,015	5,992	6,262	6,270	5,884	5,001	4,155	3,154
Other religious	2,347	2,138	1,723	1,478	1,252	1,313	1,176	1,001	952
Auxiliary building	1,280	1,258	1,251	1,219	1,099	1,122	1,031	772	667
Public safety [1]	423	289	408	419	595	623	471	207	191
Amusement and recreation [1]	8,768	8,432	7,507	9,326	10,193	10,508	8,402	6,541	6,553
Theme/amusement park	747	198	200	417	522	324	280	294	279
Sports	1,068	900	807	959	1,902	2,280	2,023	1,694	1,197
Fitness	1,152	1,141	1,425	2,028	1,945	2,051	1,763	1,184	1,056
Performance/meeting center	732	1,054	1,072	737	823	1,102	796	565	482
Social center	2,368	2,594	1,626	1,538	1,602	1,552	1,134	844	536
Movie theater/studio	1,461	1,218	1,248	1,309	1,159	601	338	425	469
Transportation [1]	6,879	6,841	7,124	8,654	9,009	9,934	9,056	9,912	10,784
Air	1,804	869	748	719	732	776	512	276	582
Land	4,907	5,800	6,214	7,764	8,008	9,020	8,484	9,509	10,134
Railroad	4,263	5,392	5,816	7,313	7,423	8,378	8,042	8,972	9,545
Communication	18,799	15,468	18,846	22,187	27,488	26,343	19,712	18,226	17,710
Power [1]	29,344	27,603	29,210	33,654	54,115	69,242	76,064	66,601	78,045
Electricity	23,374	20,928	22,678	26,295	41,460	52,799	60,394	48,438	63,094
Gas	4,891	5,096	5,239	5,528	7,876	10,560	10,849	9,191	7,902
Oil	1,003	1,579	1,293	1,831	4,779	5,883	4,821	8,972	7,049
Sewage and waste disposal [1]	508	331	240	305	408	665	468	421	555
Water supply [1]	714	405	326	477	516	466	319	664	611
Manufacturing	37,583	23,219	28,413	32,264	40,215	52,754	56,296	37,478	36,336
Food/beverage/tobacco	3,985	3,094	4,446	4,330	3,794	4,514	3,280	3,823	4,312
Textile/apparel/leather/furniture	413	185	396	133	35	260	269	518	269
Wood	483	475	933	1,350	702	352	390	441	360
Paper	479	540	442	515	450	577	516	577	536
Print/publishing	848	642	739	670	236	243	169	55	95
Petroleum/coal	1,255	1,181	734	1,650	5,061	14,724	23,453	9,440	4,648
Chemical	3,798	5,406	6,263	8,484	13,279	12,576	10,119	7,593	7,299
Plastic/rubber	1,645	919	834	812	974	1,035	573	600	656
Nonmetallic mineral	1,898	880	1,105	2,388	3,417	2,838	1,782	758	706
Primary metal	1,976	305	793	1,327	1,558	3,329	4,682	4,763	3,276
Fabricated metal	2,148	584	664	517	931	1,474	1,479	1,133	1,517
Machinery	864	633	872	862	489	917	1,055	931	1,010
Computer/electronic/electrical	6,392	2,779	4,039	4,001	2,556	2,129	3,641	4,594	8,092
Transportation equipment	6,318	2,562	3,518	2,422	3,218	4,537	3,524	1,834	2,934

[1] Includes other types of construction, not shown separately. [2] Private residential improvement does not include expenditures on rental, vacant, or seasonal properties.

Source: U.S. Census Bureau, *Construction Spending*, <http://www.census.gov/construction/c30/c30index.html>.

Table 982. New Privately Owned Housing Units Started—Selected Characteristics: 1970 to 2011

[In thousands (1,434 represents 1,434,000). For composition of regions, see map, inside front cover]

Year	Total units	Structures with— 1 unit	Structures with— 2 to 4 units	Structures with— 5 or more units	Region North-east	Region Midwest	Region South	Region West	Units for sale Total	Units for sale Single-family	Units for sale Multi-family
1970	1,434	813	85	536	218	294	612	311	(NA)	(NA)	(NA)
1980	1,292	852	110	331	125	218	643	306	689	526	163
1984	1,750	1,084	121	544	204	243	866	436	934	728	206
1985	1,742	1,072	93	576	252	240	782	468	867	713	154
1986	1,805	1,179	84	542	294	296	733	483	925	782	143
1987	1,621	1,146	65	409	269	298	634	420	862	732	130
1988	1,488	1,081	59	348	235	274	575	404	808	709	99
1989	1,376	1,003	55	318	179	266	536	396	735	648	87
1990	1,193	895	38	260	131	253	479	329	585	529	56
1991	1,014	840	36	138	113	233	414	254	531	490	41
1992	1,200	1,030	31	139	127	288	497	288	659	618	41
1993	1,288	1,126	29	133	127	298	562	302	760	716	44
1994	1,457	1,198	35	224	138	329	639	351	815	763	52
1995	1,354	1,076	34	244	118	290	615	331	763	712	51
1996	1,477	1,161	45	271	132	322	662	361	833	774	59
1997	1,474	1,134	45	296	137	304	670	363	843	784	59
1998	1,617	1,271	43	303	149	331	743	395	941	882	59
1999	1,641	1,302	32	307	156	347	746	392	981	912	69
2000	1,569	1,231	39	299	155	318	714	383	946	871	75
2001	1,603	1,273	37	293	149	330	732	391	990	919	71
2002	1,705	1,359	39	308	158	350	782	416	1,070	999	71
2003	1,848	1,499	34	315	163	374	839	472	1,207	1,120	87
2004	1,956	1,611	42	303	175	356	909	516	1,360	1,240	120
2005	2,068	1,716	41	311	190	357	996	525	1,508	1,358	150
2006	1,801	1,465	43	293	167	280	910	444	1,272	1,121	151
2007	1,355	1,046	32	277	143	210	681	321	875	760	115
2008	906	622	18	266	121	135	453	196	472	408	64
2009	554	445	12	97	62	97	278	117	314	297	17
2010	587	471	11	104	72	98	298	120	(NA)	(NA)	(NA)
2011	609	431	11	167	68	101	308	133	(NA)	(NA)	(NA)

NA Not available.

Source: U.S. Census Bureau, Construction Reports, "New Residential Construction," <http://www.census.gov/construction/nrc/historical_data/>.

Table 983. New Privately Owned Housing Units Started: 1991 to 2011

[In thousands of units (1,014 represents 1,014,000). For composition of regions, see map inside front cover.]

Year	Total	1 unit	Northeast	Midwest	South	West
1991	1,014	840	113	233	414	254
1992	1,200	1,030	127	288	497	288
1993	1,288	1,126	126	298	562	302
1994	1,457	1,198	138	329	639	351
1995	1,354	1,076	118	290	615	331
1996	1,477	1,161	132	321	662	361
1997	1,474	1,134	137	304	670	363
1998	1,617	1,271	148	330	743	395
1999	1,641	1,303	156	347	746	392
2000	1,569	1,231	154	318	713	383
2001	1,603	1,273	149	330	732	391
2002	1,705	1,359	158	350	781	415
2003	1,848	1,499	163	374	839	472
2004	1,956	1,610	175	356	909	516
2005	2,068	1,716	190	357	996	525
2006	1,801	1,465	167	280	910	444
2007	1,355	1,046	143	210	681	321
2008	905	622	121	135	453	196
2009	554	445	62	97	278	117
2010	586	471	71	98	297	120
2011	608	431	67	101	307	133

Source: U.S. Bureau of the Census, *Quarterly Starts and Completions by Purpose and Design*, <http://www.census.gov/construction/nrc/>.

Table 984. Characteristics of New Privately Owned One-Family Houses Completed: 1990 to 2011

[Percent distribution, except total houses. 966 represents 966,000. Data are percent distribution of characteristics for all houses completed (includes new houses completed, houses built for sale completed, contractor-built and owner-built houses completed, and houses completed for rent). Percents exclude houses for which characteristics specified were not reported]

Characteristic	1990	2000	2010	2011	Characteristic	1990	2000	2010	2011
Total houses (1,000)	**966**	**1,242**	**496**	**447**					
					Bedrooms	**100**	**100**	**100**	**100**
Construction type	**100**	**100**	**100**	**100**	2 or less	15	11	13	13
Site built	(NA)	94	95	96	3	57	54	52	48
Modular	(NA)	3	2	2	4 or more	29	35	35	39
Other	(NA)	3	2	2	**Bathrooms**	**100**	**100**	**100**	**100**
Exterior wall material	**100**	**100**	**100**	**100**	1-1/2 or less	13	7	8	8
Brick	18	20	23	24	2	42	39	36	34
Wood	39	14	8	8	2-1/2 or more	27	34	32	31
Stucco	18	17	17	17	3 baths or more	18	20	25	28
Vinyl siding [1]	(NA)	39	36	34	**Heating fuel**	**100**	**100**	**100**	**100**
Aluminum siding	5	1	(NA)	(NA)	Gas	59	70	54	55
Fiber cement	(NA)	(NA)	13	15	Electricity	33	27	43	43
Other [1]	20	8	2	2	Oil	5	3	1	1
Floor area	**(NA)**	**100**	**100**	**100**	Other	3	1	2	2
Under 1,400 sq. ft	(NA)	14	13	13	**Heating system**	**100**	**100**	**100**	**100**
1,400 to 1,799 sq. ft	(NA)	22	19	19	Warm air furnace	65	71	56	56
1,800 to 2,399 sq. ft	(NA)	29	27	25	Electric heat pump	23	23	38	38
2,400 to 2,999 sq. ft	(NA)	17	18	18	Other	12	6	5	6
3,000 tp 3,999 sq. ft	(NA)	13	15	17	**Central air-conditioning**	**100**	**100**	**100**	**100**
4,000 or more	(NA)	5	7	9	With	76	85	88	88
Average (sq. ft.)	2,080	2,266	2,392	2,480	Without	24	15	12	12
Median (sq. ft.)	1,905	2,057	2,169	2,233					
Number of stories	**100**	**100**	**100**	**100**	**Fireplaces**	**100**	**100**	**100**	**100**
1	46	47	47	52	No fireplace	34	40	51	50
2 or more	49	52	46	54	1 or more	66	59	49	50
Split level	4	1	1	(Z)					
Foundation	**100**	**100**	**100**	**100**	**Parking facilities**	**100**	**100**	**100**	**100**
Full or partial basement	38	37	30	30	Garage	82	89	85	86
Slab	40	46	52	53	Carport	2	1	1	1
Crawl space	21	17	18	17	No garage or carport	16	11	13	13

NA Not available. Z Less than 0.5 percent. [1] Prior to 2000, "other" includes vinyl siding.

Source: U.S. Census Bureau and U.S. Department of Housing and Urban Development "Characteristics of New Single Family Houses," <http://www.census.gov/construction/chars/completed.html>.

Table 985. Housing Starts and Average Length of Time From Start to Completion of New Privately Owned One-Unit Residential Buildings: 1980 to 2011

[852 represents 852,000. For buildings started in permit issue places]

Year	Total [1]	Purpose of construction			Region [2]			
		Built for sale	Contractor built	Owner built	North-east	Mid-west	South	West
STARTS (1,000)								
1980	852	526	149	164	87	142	428	196
1990	895	529	196	147	104	193	371	226
1995	1,076	712	199	133	102	234	485	256
1999	1,302	912	208	142	126	289	580	308
2000	1,231	871	195	128	118	260	556	297
2001	1,273	919	186	129	111	269	590	303
2002	1,359	999	198	125	118	277	628	336
2003	1,499	1,120	205	127	116	309	686	388
2004	1,611	1,240	198	130	128	306	743	433
2005	1,716	1,358	197	129	138	306	831	441
2006	1,465	1,121	189	119	118	235	757	356
2007	1,046	760	151	104	93	171	540	242
2008	622	408	107	74	63	102	324	133
2009	445	297	83	51	44	76	232	93
2010	471	306	83	55	52	79	247	93
2011	431	287	74	47	44	74	229	86
COMPLETION (months)								
1980	6.9	6.2	5.5	10.1	7.7	8.0	6.1	7.4
1990	6.4	5.9	5.3	10.3	9.3	5.6	5.7	6.9
1995	5.9	5.2	5.8	9.5	7.4	6.0	5.4	6.0
1999	6.1	5.5	6.4	9.2	7.0	6.4	5.7	6.3
2000	6.2	5.6	6.5	9.2	7.5	6.4	5.9	6.0
2001	6.2	5.6	7.0	9.2	7.6	6.5	5.8	6.3
2002	6.1	5.5	6.6	9.6	7.3	6.4	5.6	6.2
2003	6.2	5.5	6.8	9.9	7.5	6.7	5.7	6.2
2004	6.2	5.7	7.0	9.1	7.3	6.7	5.8	6.3
2005	6.4	5.9	7.6	9.8	7.7	6.6	6.0	6.8
2006	6.9	6.3	7.8	10.7	8.3	7.1	6.3	7.4
2007	7.1	6.5	7.9	10.2	8.5	7.4	6.5	8.0
2008	7.7	6.8	8.5	11.1	8.9	8.2	6.7	9.0
2009	7.9	6.6	8.7	11.9	10.7	8.2	6.7	9.0
2010	6.9	5.8	7.6	11.0	10.1	7.3	5.9	7.3
2011	6.6	5.4	7.7	10.8	8.9	6.9	5.9	6.8

NA Not available. [1] Includes units built for rent not shown separately. [2] For composition of regions, see map, inside front cover.

Source: U.S. Census Bureau, *New Residential Construction*, <http://www.census.gov/construction/nrc/lengthoftime.html>.

Table 986. Price Indexes of New One-Family Houses Sold by Region: 1980 to 2011

[2005 = 100. Based on kinds of homes sold in 2005. Includes value of the lot. For composition of regions, see map, inside front cover]

Year	Total	Northeast	Midwest	South	West
1980	38.9	30.2	41.2	44.4	31.9
1984	45.7	39.2	49.0	52.8	36.2
1985	46.2	43.1	48.2	53.9	36.4
1986	48.0	49.5	51.0	55.5	37.3
1987	50.6	56.2	54.4	57.6	39.3
1988	52.5	57.6	56.8	58.8	41.4
1989	54.6	59.2	58.1	60.5	44.0
1990	55.7	58.0	58.6	60.6	46.2
1991	56.4	56.2	60.1	61.8	46.4
1992	57.2	60.5	61.2	62.4	46.7
1993	59.4	57.4	65.2	65.5	47.8
1994	62.9	62.1	69.4	68.1	51.9
1995	64.3	62.3	70.9	70.1	52.7
1996	66.0	63.2	72.5	71.2	55.3
1997	67.5	65.9	74.3	72.7	56.5
1998	69.2	66.1	76.0	74.4	58.4
1999	72.8	69.1	79.5	78.1	62.0
2000	75.6	73.0	83.5	80.7	64.4
2001	77.9	76.7	84.4	82.8	67.1
2002	81.4	80.2	86.1	86.3	71.5
2003	86.0	84.3	90.6	89.4	78.2
2004	92.8	91.6	96.7	94.4	88.2
2005	100.0	100.0	100.0	100.0	100.0
2006	104.8	102.6	102.9	105.4	105.2
2007	104.9	101.5	102.8	107.5	102.6
2008	99.5	100.8	98.9	103.7	92.7
2009	95.1	97.1	96.0	101.1	84.8
2010	95.0	101.1	96.9	99.5	85.4
2011	94.3	100.0	97.8	99.6	83.1

Source: U.S. Census Bureau, *Construction Price Indexes*, <http://www.census.gov/construction/cpi/>.

Table 987. New Privately Owned One-Family Houses Sold by Region and Type of Financing, 1980 to 2011, and by Sales-Price Group, 2011

[In thousands (545 represents 545,000). Based on a national probability sample of monthly interviews with builders or owners of one-family houses for which building permits have been issued or, for nonpermit areas, on which construction has started. For details, see source and Appendix III. For composition of regions, see map inside front cover. Minus sign (–) indicates decrease]

Year and sales-price group	Total sales	Region				Financing type			
		Northeast	Midwest	South	West	Conven-tional [1]	FHA and VA	Rural-Housing Service [2]	Cash
1980..........................	545	50	81	267	145	302	196	14	32
1985..........................	688	112	82	323	171	403	208	11	64
1990..........................	534	71	89	225	149	337	138	10	50
1995..........................	667	55	125	300	187	490	129	9	39
2000..........................	877	71	155	406	244	695	138	4	40
2003..........................	1,086	79	189	511	307	911	130	4	41
2004..........................	1,203	83	210	562	348	1,047	105	6	46
2005..........................	1,283	81	205	638	358	1,150	79	1	52
2006..........................	1,051	63	161	559	267	948	63	1	38
2007..........................	776	65	118	411	181	693	52	2	30
2008..........................	485	35	70	266	114	-948	-63	(NA)	23
2009..........................	375	31	54	202	87	234	124	(NA)	17
2010..........................	323	31	45	173	74	189	116	(NA)	18
2011..........................	306	21	45	168	72	190	96	(NA)	20
Under $200,000............	118	2	22	76	17	(NA)	(NA)	(NA)	(NA)
$200,000 to $299,999......	99	7	13	50	29	(NA)	(NA)	(NA)	(NA)
$300,000 to $499,999......	66	7	8	32	20	(NA)	(NA)	(NA)	(NA)
$500,000 and over.........	23	4	2	10	6	(NA)	(NA)	(NA)	(NA)

NA Not available. [1] Includes houses reporting other types of financing. [2] Prior to 2000, the Farmers Home Administration.

Source: U.S. Census Bureau and U.S. Department of Housing and Urban Development "New Residential Sales," <http://www.census.gov/construction/nrs/>.

Table 988. Median Sales Price of New Privately Owned One-Family Houses Sold by Region: 1980 to 2011

[In dollars. For definition of median, see Guide to Tabular Presentation. For composition of regions, see map inside front cover. See Appendix III. See also headnote, Table 987]

Year	U.S.	North-east	Mid-west	South	West	Year	U.S.	North-east	Mid-west	South	West
1980.............	64,600	69,500	63,400	59,600	72,300	2005....	240,900	343,800	216,900	197,300	332,600
1985.............	84,300	103,300	80,300	75,000	92,600	2006....	246,500	346,000	213,500	208,200	337,700
1990.............	122,900	159,000	107,900	99,000	147,500	2007....	247,900	320,200	208,600	217,700	330,900
1995.............	133,900	180,000	134,000	124,500	141,400	2008....	232,100	343,600	198,900	203,700	294,800
2000.............	169,000	227,400	169,700	148,000	196,400	2009....	216,700	302,500	189,200	194,800	263,700
2003.............	195,000	264,500	184,300	168,100	260,900	2010....	221,800	329,900	197,700	196,800	259,300
2004.............	221,000	315,800	205,000	181,100	283,100	2011....	227,200	322,800	203,300	211,400	256,000

Source: U.S. Census Bureau and U.S. Department of Housing and Urban Development "New Residential Sales," <http://www.census.gov/construction/nrs/>.

Table 989. New Manufactured (Mobile) Homes Placed for Residential Use and Average Sales Price by Region: 1985 to 2011

[283.4 represents 283,400. A mobile home is a moveable dwelling, 8 feet or more wide and 40 feet or more long, designed to be towed on its own chassis, with transportation gear integral to the unit when it leaves the factory, and without need of permanent foundation. Excluded are travel trailers, motor homes, and modular housing. Data are based on a probability sample and subject to sampling variability; see source. For composition of regions, see map, inside front cover]

Year	Units placed (1,000)					Average sales price (dollars)				
	Total	Northeast	Midwest	South	West	U.S.	Northeast	Midwest	South	West
1985................	283.4	20.2	38.6	187.6	36.9	21,800	22,700	21,500	20,400	28,700
1990................	195.4	18.8	37.7	108.4	30.6	27,800	30,000	27,000	24,500	39,300
1995................	319.4	15.0	57.5	203.2	43.7	35,300	35,800	35,700	33,300	44,100
1998................	373.7	14.7	58.3	250.3	50.4	41,600	42,200	42,400	40,100	48,400
1999................	338.3	14.1	53.6	227.2	43.5	43,300	44,000	44,400	41,900	49,600
2000................	280.9	14.9	48.7	178.7	38.6	46,400	47,000	47,900	44,300	54,100
2001................	196.2	12.2	37.6	116.4	30.0	48,900	50,000	49,100	46,500	58,000
2002................	174.3	11.8	34.2	101.0	27.2	51,300	53,200	51,700	48,000	62,600
2003................	139.8	11.2	25.2	77.2	26.1	54,900	57,300	55,100	50,500	67,700
2004................	124.4	11.0	20.6	67.4	25.5	58,200	60,200	58,800	52,300	73,200
2005................	122.9	9.2	17.1	68.1	28.5	62,600	67,000	60,600	55,700	79,900
2006................	112.4	7.9	14.5	66.1	23.9	64,300	65,300	59,100	58,900	83,400
2007................	94.8	7.0	10.8	59.4	17.7	65,400	66,100	64,900	59,900	85,500
2008................	80.5	5.0	8.2	54.0	13.3	64,700	68,400	65,700	59,600	84,900
2009................	54.5	3.6	5.5	38.0	7.5	63,100	61,400	66,200	59,400	82,100
2010................	49.9	3.8	5.6	34.2	6.4	62,800	65,900	60,900	59,900	79,100
2011................	46.2	3.3	6.2	30.6	6.3	60,800	63,300	60,500	58,900	69,700

Source: U.S. Census Bureau, *Manufactured Housing at a Glance*, <http://www.census.gov/const/www/mhsindex.html>.

Table 990. Existing One-Family Homes Sold and Price by Region: 1990 to 2011

[2,914 represents 2,914,000. Includes existing detached single-family homes and townhomes; excludes condos and co-ops. Based on data (adjusted and aggregated to regional and national totals) reported by participating real estate multiple listing services. For definition of median, see Guide to Tabular Presentation. See Table 993 for data on condos and co-ops. For composition of regions, see map, inside front cover]

Year	Homes sold (1,000)					Median sales price (dollars)				
	U.S.	North-east	Mid-west	South	West	U.S.	North-east	Mid-west	South	West
1990	2,914	513	804	1,008	589	97,300	146,200	76,700	86,300	141,200
1993	3,427	614	961	1,167	685	109,100	149,300	87,600	95,800	144,400
1994	3,544	618	961	1,213	752	113,500	149,300	90,900	97,200	151,900
1995	3,519	615	940	1,212	752	117,000	146,500	96,500	99,200	153,600
1996	3,797	656	986	1,283	872	122,600	147,800	102,800	105,000	160,200
1997	3,964	683	1,004	1,356	921	129,000	152,400	108,900	111,300	169,000
1998	4,495	745	1,129	1,592	1,029	136,000	157,100	116,300	118,000	179,500
1999	4,649	728	1,145	1,704	1,072	141,200	160,700	121,600	122,100	189,400
2000	4,603	715	1,116	1,707	1,065	147,300	161,200	125,600	130,300	199,200
2001	4,735	710	1,154	1,795	1,076	156,600	169,400	132,300	139,600	211,700
2002	4,974	730	1,217	1,872	1,155	167,600	190,100	138,300	149,700	234,300
2003	5,446	770	1,323	2,073	1,280	180,200	220,300	143,700	159,700	254,700
2004	5,958	821	1,389	2,310	1,438	195,200	254,400	151,500	171,800	289,100
2005	6,180	838	1,411	2,457	1,474	219,000	281,600	168,300	181,100	340,300
2006	5,677	787	1,314	2,352	1,224	221,900	280,300	164,800	183,700	350,500
2007	4,398	587	1,091	1,819	901	217,900	288,100	161,400	178,800	342,500
2008	3,665	471	882	1,439	873	196,600	271,500	150,500	169,400	276,100
2009	3,870	480	918	1,460	1,012	172,100	243,200	142,900	155,000	215,400
2010	3,708	465	859	1,426	958	173,100	243,900	140,800	153,700	220,700
2011	3,787	449	863	1,471	1,004	166,200	237,500	135,800	149,300	204,500

Source: National Association of Realtors "Housing Statistics" (copyright). See also <http://www.realtor.org/research-and-statistics>.

Table 991. Median Sales Price of Existing One-Family Homes by Selected Metropolitan Area: 2005 and 2011

[In thousands of dollars (219.0 represents $219,000). Includes existing detached single-family homes and townhouses. Areas are metropolitan statistical areas defined by Office of Management and Budget as of 2004, except as noted]

Metropolitan area	2005	2011	Metropolitan area	2005	2011
United States, total	**219.0**	**166.2**	NY: Nassau-Suffolk, NY	465.2	375.9
Allentown-Bethlehem-Easton, PA-NJ	243.4	185.4	NY: Newark-Union, NJ-PA	416.8	370.5
Anaheim-Santa Ana-Irvine, CA [1]	691.9	512.5	Norwich-New London, CT	255.9	184.1
Atlantic City, NJ	256.1	223.2	Orlando, FL	243.6	124.9
Baltimore-Towson, MD	265.3	230.0	Palm Bay-Melbourne-Titusville, FL	209.7	108.5
Barnstable Town, MA	398.3	311.5	Philadelphia-Camden-Wilmington,		
Boston-Cambridge-Quincy, MA-NH [2]	413.2	346.2	PA-NJ-DE-MD	215.3	210.1
Boulder, CO	348.4	353.1	Phoenix-Mesa-Scottsdale, AZ	247.4	115.5
Bridgeport-Stamford-Norwalk, CT	482.4	390.6	Pittsfield, MA	207.3	188.3
Cape Coral-Fort Myers, FL	269.2	102.9	Portland-South Portland-Biddeford, ME	246.6	213.7
Charleston-North Charleston, SC	197.0	197.0	Portland-Vancouver-Beaverton, OR-WA	244.9	219.5
Chicago-Naperville-Joliet, IL	264.2	176.5	Providence-New Bedford-Fall River, RI-MA	293.4	217.2
Colorado Springs, CO	205.9	187.2	Raleigh-Cary, NC	194.9	(NA)
Deltona-Daytona Beach-Ormond Beach, FL	192.5	104.8	Reno-Sparks, NV	349.9	158.0
Denver-Aurora, CO	247.1	231.4	Richmond, VA	201.9	(NA)
Dover, DE	180.4	170.8	Riverside-San Bernardino-Ontario, CA [1]	374.2	172.3
Eugene-Springfield, OR	197.6	(NA)	Sacramento-Arden-Arcade-Roseville, CA [1]	375.9	167.1
Gainesville, FL	184.0	148.6	Salem, OR	177.7	146.2
Hagerstown-Martinsburg, MD-WV	208.7	131.3	San Diego-Carlsbad-San Marcos, CA [1]	604.3	370.3
Hartford-West Hartford-East Hartford, CT	253.3	227.6	San Francisco-Oakland-Fremont, CA [1]	715.7	483.4
Honolulu, HI	590.0	597.0	San Jose-Sunnyvale-Santa Clara, CA [1]	744.5	570.0
Kingston, NY	251.0	201.2	Sarasota-Bradenton-Venice, FL	354.2	156.2
Las Vegas-Paradise, NV	304.7	124.7	Seattle-Tacoma-Bellevue, WA	316.8	285.0
Los Angeles-Long Beach-Santa Ana, CA [1]	529.0	307.7	Springfield, MA	201.8	181.4
Madison, WI	218.3	213.2	Tampa-St.Petersburg-Clearwater, FL	205.3	127.8
Miami-Fort Lauderdale-Miami Beach, FL	363.9	181.1	Trenton-Ewing, NJ	261.1	240.1
Milwaukee-Waukesha-West Allis, WI	215.7	185.2	Tucson, AZ	231.6	134.5
Minneapolis-St. Paul-Bloomington, MN-WI	234.8	154.7	Virginia Beach-Norfolk-Newport News,		
New Haven-Milford, CT	279.1	223.1	VA-NC	197.2	182.9
New York-Northern New Jersey-Long Island,			Washington-Arlington-Alexandria,		
NY-NJ-PA	445.2	378.7	DC-VA-MD-WV	425.8	325.4
New York-Wayne-White Plains, NY-NJ	495.2	442.6	Worcester, MA	290.7	209.6
NY: Edison, NJ	375.5	313.9			

NA Not available. [1] California data supplied by the California Association of REALTORS. [2] Excludes areas in New Hampshire.

Source: National Association of Realtors (copyright). See also <http://www.realtor.org/research-and-statistics>.

Table 992. Existing Home Sales by State: 2000 to 2010

[In thousands (5,174 represents 5,174,000). Includes condos and co-ops as well as single-family homes. Data shown here reflect revisions from prior estimates]

State	2000	2005	2009	2010	State	2000	2005	2009	2010
United States	**5,174**	**7,076**	**5,156**	**4,908**	Missouri	110.2	142.9	105.9	94.6
Alabama	67.0	128.0	75.0	71.6	Montana	17.4	25.4	21.7	20.4
Alaska	14.3	24.6	22.4	22.4	Nebraska	32.3	41.2	34.7	31.9
Arizona	104.8	199.2	150.8	147.5	Nevada	44.6	98.0	104.9	97.7
Arkansas	45.0	75.3	61.8	59.9	New Hampshire	26.7	(NA)	19.6	18.9
California	573.5	601.1	510.4	468.4	New Jersey	161.1	184.4	115.3	110.0
Colorado	111.5	130.4	96.2	90.5	New Mexico	29.9	57.5	32.2	30.8
Connecticut	61.5	78.0	46.6	46.2	New York	273.3	319.8	253.8	242.0
Delaware	12.9	19.3	12.6	10.9	North Carolina	134.2	215.7	136.4	135.3
District of Columbia	10.6	12.1	8.4	8.7	North Dakota	10.8	15.8	13.1	12.5
Florida	393.6	547.1	357.8	396.5	Ohio	216.4	286.9	248.7	231.9
Georgia	143.6	242.1	176.6	162.7	Oklahoma	67.3	104.6	83.5	72.6
Hawaii	22.1	36.8	18.4	20.9	Oregon	62.6	100.5	55.0	55.2
Idaho	24.1	49.8	33.8	38.8	Pennsylvania	195.9	255.2	176.5	160.2
Illinois	246.8	315.3	184.4	176.7	Rhode Island	17.0	19.8	15.4	13.6
Indiana	111.0	138.3	104.7	97.7	South Carolina	64.3	114.6	71.1	70.7
Iowa	53.3	74.9	58.0	55.7	South Dakota	12.6	18.3	17.4	14.3
Kansas	52.6	77.9	56.5	51.8	Tennessee	100.4	170.9	107.9	101.3
Kentucky	66.0	96.2	73.8	70.3	Texas	381.8	532.5	443.3	420.5
Louisiana	66.8	87.7	54.8	51.6	Utah	35.5	51.7	31.1	28.5
Maine	27.6	33.3	23.1	22.8	Vermont	12.1	15.3	11.3	11.3
Maryland	100.5	135.5	72.5	74.5	Virginia	130.0	182.5	117.0	107.9
Massachusetts	112.3	148.6	107.9	105.3	Washington	112.4	167.8	82.3	83.7
Michigan	185.0	208.6	167.1	150.8	West Virginia	22.9	38.6	27.6	26.5
Minnesota	96.3	134.9	107.4	89.7	Wisconsin	91.6	122.8	84.5	77.7
Mississippi	38.7	61.2	41.9	42.1	Wyoming	9.6	14.3	9.1	8.5

NA Not available.

Source: National Association of Realtors (copyright). The National Association of Realtors state sales series was discontinued in 2011. See also <http://www.realtor.org/research-and-statistics>.

Table 993. Existing Apartment Condos and Co-Ops—Units Sold and Median Sales Price by Region: 1990 to 2011

[272 represents 272,000. Data shown here reflect revisions from prior estimates. For definition of median, see Guide to Tabular Presentation. For composition of regions, see map inside front cover]

Year	Units sold (1,000)					Median sales price (dollars)				
	U.S.	Northeast	Midwest	South	West	U.S.	Northeast	Midwest	South	West
1990	272	73	55	80	64	86,900	107,500	70,200	64,200	114,600
1995	333	108	66	96	63	89,000	92,500	90,700	67,800	114,800
2000	571	197	106	160	108	114,000	108,500	121,700	84,200	149,100
2004	820	292	161	230	137	197,100	214,100	181,000	156,600	258,000
2005	896	331	177	245	143	223,900	245,100	189,100	187,300	283,800
2006	801	299	169	211	122	221,900	249,700	190,900	184,000	264,700
2007	624	126	100	236	162	226,300	256,100	195,200	185,100	263,300
2008	459	103	71	164	121	209,800	252,500	188,200	166,800	218,500
2009	464	105	58	180	121	175,600	232,800	157,100	132,700	162,100
2010	474	95	53	202	124	171,700	242,200	150,500	118,500	154,700
2011	477	89	52	210	126	165,100	237,700	129,000	107,800	176,000

Source: National Association of Realtors (copyright). See <http://www.realtor.org/research-and-statistics>.

Table 994. New Unfurnished Apartments Completed and Rented in 3 Months by Region: 2000 to 2010

[226.2 represents 226,200. Structures with five or more units, privately financed, nonsubsidized, unfurnished rental apartments. Based on sample and subject to sampling variability; see source for details. For composition of regions, see map, inside front cover]

Year and rent	Number (1,000)					Percent rented in 3 months				
	U.S.	North-east	Mid-west	South	West	U.S.	North-east	Mid-west	South	West
2000	226.2	14.8	39.5	125.9	45.9	72	85	76	67	77
2005	113.0	4.7	20.5	57.8	30.0	64	75	64	62	64
2008	146.4	8.9	17.2	88.2	32.1	50	52	58	48	51
2009	163.0	10.0	17.2	93.3	42.4	51	56	74	49	44
2010	**89.1**	**5.9**	**16.2**	**42.8**	**24.1**	**61**	**79**	**68**	**60**	**55**
Less than $850	18.6	2.3	5.4	9.2	1.7	74	94	76	70	62
$850 to $949	12.8	0.2	1.8	8.7	2.0	73	87	92	73	54
$950 to $1,049	11.2	0.1	2.9	6.3	1.8	55	70	58	53	58
$1,050 to $1,149	7.6	0.2	1.3	3.9	2.1	59	69	63	55	63
$1,150 to $1,249	7.6	0.3	0.9	4.0	2.5	60	70	59	59	61
$1,250 or more	31.4	2.8	4.0	10.7	13.9	52	68	57	47	52
Median asking rent	1,077	1,193	983	1,005	1,250	(X)	(X)	(X)	(X)	(X)

X Not applicable.

Source: U.S. Census Bureau, *Survey of Market Absorption*. See also <http://www.census.gov/hhes/www/housing/soma/annual11/ann11-det-tab.html>.

ProQuest Statistical Abstract of the United States: 2013

Table 995. Total Housing Inventory for the United States: 1990 to 2011

[In thousands (106,283 represents 106,283,000), except percent. Based on the Current Population Survey and the Housing Vacancy Survey and subject to sampling error; see source and Appendix III for details]

Item	1990	1995	2000	2005	2006	2007	2008	2009	2010 [2]	2011
All housing units..................	**106,283**	**112,655**	**119,628**	**124,600**	**126,383**	**128,017**	**129,211**	**129,944**	**131,781**	**132,292**
Vacant..........................	12,059	12,669	13,908	15,786	16,487	17,666	18,574	18,785	18,904	18,758
Year-round vacant..................	9,128	9,570	10,439	11,990	12,497	13,288	13,838	14,121	14,419	14,239
For rent........................	2,662	2,946	3,024	3,742	3,747	3,851	4,027	4,386	4,321	4,087
For sale only....................	1,064	1,022	1,148	1,460	1,841	2,118	2,210	2,016	2,000	1,902
Rented or sold....................	660	810	856	1,067	1,110	1,133	1,068	992	916	984
Held off market..................	4,742	4,793	5,411	5,720	5,798	6,186	6,533	6,726	7,182	7,266
Occasional use................	1,485	1,667	1,892	1,896	1,866	1,995	2,056	2,064	2,263	2,268
Usual residence elsewhere.....	1,068	801	1,037	1,136	1,201	1,140	1,162	1,185	1,265	1,197
Other........................	2,189	2,325	2,482	2,688	2,731	3,051	3,315	3,478	3,654	3,801
Seasonal [1].....................	2,931	3,099	3,469	3,796	3,990	4,378	4,736	4,665	4,484	4,519
Total occupied..................	94,224	99,985	105,720	108,814	109,896	110,351	110,637	111,159	112,877	113,534
Owner..........................	60,248	64,739	71,250	74,962	75,596	75,192	75,043	74,892	75,445	75,091
Renter.........................	33,976	35,246	34,470	33,852	34,300	35,159	35,594	36,267	37,432	38,443
PERCENT DISTRIBUTION										
All housing units..................	100.0	100.0	100.0	100.0	100.0	100.0	100.0	100.0	100.0	100
Vacant..........................	11.3	11.2	11.6	12.7	13.0	13.8	14.4	14.4	14.3	14.2
Total occupied..................	88.7	88.8	88.4	87.3	87.0	86.2	85.6	85.6	85.7	85.8
Owner..........................	56.7	57.5	59.6	60.2	60.3	58.7	58.1	0.6	57.3	56.8
Renter.........................	32.0	31.3	28.8	27.2	27.5	27.5	27.5	0.3	28.4	29.1

[1] Includes vacant seasonal mobile homes. [2] Revised based on 2010 housing unit controls.

Source: U.S. Census Bureau, "Housing Vacancies and Home Ownership," <http://www.census.gov/housing/hvs/>.

Table 996. Occupied Housing Inventory by Age of Householder: 1990 to 2011

[In thousands (94,224 represents 94,224,000). Based on the Current Population Survey and Housing Vacancy Survey; see source for details]

Age of householder	1990	1995	2000	2005	2006	2007	2008	2009	2010	2011
Total.....................	**94,224**	**99,986**	**102,560**	**108,231**	**109,576**	**110,306**	**111,409**	**111,344**	**111,860**	**113,534**
Under 25 years old.......	5,143	5,502	5,964	6,536	6,578	6,494	6,272	6,106	6,060	6,079
25 to 29 years old........	9,508	8,662	8,197	8,790	8,975	9,170	9,094	9,076	9,041	9,062
30 to 34 years old........	11,213	11,206	9,939	9,583	9,423	9,349	9,343	9,331	9,477	9,957
35 to 39 years old........	10,914	11,993	11,573	10,526	10,520	10,499	10,550	10,185	9,794	9,667
40 to 44 years old........	9,893	11,151	12,013	11,722	11,484	11,125	10,974	10,705	10,525	10,515
45 to 49 years old........	8,038	10,080	10,835	11,780	11,988	12,007	11,968	11,861	11,690	11,449
50 to 54 years old........	6,532	7,882	9,414	10,595	10,896	11,082	11,415	11,605	11,721	11,784
55 to 59 years old........	6,182	6,355	7,455	9,504	9,919	10,013	10,217	10,226	10,437	10,848
60 to 64 years old........	6,446	5,860	6,011	7,336	7,604	8,108	8,601	8,920	9,345	9,841
65 to 69 years old........	6,407	6,088	5,679	5,900	6,074	6,330	6,642	6,822	7,038	7,306
70 to 74 years old........	5,397	5,693	5,420	5,016	5,057	5,063	5,114	5,288	5,449	5,556
75 years old and over....	8,546	9,514	10,059	10,943	11,058	11,065	11,219	11,220	11,285	11,468

Source: U.S. Census Bureau, "Housing Vacancies and Home Ownership," <http://www.census.gov/housing/hvs/>.

Table 997. Vacancy Rates for Housing Units—Characteristics: 2000 to 2011

[In percent. Rate is relationship between vacant housing for rent or for sale and the total rental and homeowner supply, which comprises occupied units, units rented or sold and awaiting occupancy, and vacant units available for rent or sale. Based on the Current Population/Housing Vacancy Survey; see source for details. For composition of regions, see map, inside front cover]

Characteristic	Rental Units				Homeowner units			
	2000	2005	2010	2011	2000	2005	2010	2011
Total units......................	**8.0**	**9.8**	**10.2**	**9.5**	**1.6**	**1.9**	**2.6**	**2.5**
Northeast......................	5.6	6.5	7.6	7.3	1.2	1.5	1.7	2.2
Midwest.......................	8.8	12.6	10.8	10.2	1.3	2.2	2.6	2.6
South.........................	10.5	11.8	12.7	12.0	1.9	2.1	2.8	2.6
West..........................	5.8	7.3	8.2	7.0	1.5	1.4	2.7	2.3
Units in structure:								
1 unit........................	7.0	9.9	9.2	8.9	1.5	1.7	2.2	2.2
2 units or more..............	8.7	10.0	11.1	10.0	4.7	6.2	9.2	8.3
5 units or more..............	9.2	10.4	11.7	10.3	5.8	6.6	9.2	8.5
Units with—								
3 rooms or less..............	10.3	12.1	13.8	12.8	10.4	12.0	14.8	15.1
4 rooms......................	8.2	9.6	10.5	9.7	2.9	3.3	5.7	5.3
5 rooms......................	6.9	9.3	8.9	8.2	2.0	2.2	3.0	2.8
6 rooms or more..............	5.2	8.1	7.1	6.7	1.1	1.4	1.7	1.7

Source: U.S. Census Bureau, "Housing Vacancies and Home Ownership," <http://www.census.gov/housing/hvs/>.

Table 998. Housing Units and Tenure—States: 2010

[131,791 represents 131,791,000. The American Community Survey universe includes the household population and the population living in institutions, college dormitories, and other group quarters. Based on a sample and subject to sampling variability; see Appendix III]

| State | Housing units | | | | | | Housing tenure | | | |
| | | | Vacant (1,000) | | | | Owner-occupied units | | Renter-occupied units | |
	Total (1,000)	Occu-pied (1,000)	Total	For sea-sonal use [1]	For Rent	For Sale	Total (1,000)	Average house-hold size	Total (1,000)	Average house-hold size
United States...........	131,791	114,567	17,224	5,153	3,587	1,929	74,873	2.70	39,694	2.50
Alabama.................	2,174	1,815	359	83	60	35	1,273	2.60	542	2.50
Alaska..................	307	255	52	30	4	3	163	2.81	92	2.50
Arizona.................	2,847	2,334	513	192	103	70	1,523	2.68	811	2.70
Arkansas...............	1,318	1,115	203	50	43	21	752	2.57	363	2.51
California..............	13,683	12,406	1,277	339	346	157	6,903	2.99	5,503	2.89
Colorado...............	2,214	1,961	254	106	49	33	1,293	2.59	668	2.38
Connecticut............	1,488	1,359	129	30	34	16	924	2.67	435	2.28
Delaware...............	406	329	78	42	14	8	240	2.69	89	2.58
District of Columbia.......	297	252	44	3	16	4	107	2.31	145	2.18
Florida.................	8,994	7,035	1,959	877	318	209	4,794	2.61	2,241	2.64
Georgia................	4,091	3,482	609	98	159	91	2,304	2.73	1,178	2.69
Hawaii.................	520	446	74	32	18	6	259	3.14	187	2.72
Idaho..................	669	577	92	38	15	13	402	2.75	175	2.51
Illinois.................	5,297	4,753	544	46	129	78	3,219	2.73	1,534	2.44
Indiana................	2,797	2,471	326	43	72	46	1,737	2.63	734	2.37
Iowa...................	1,338	1,223	114	21	23	19	885	2.51	338	2.15
Kansas................	1,234	1,102	132	14	29	18	750	2.63	352	2.29
Kentucky...............	1,929	1,684	244	43	44	30	1,156	2.56	528	2.40
Louisiana..............	1,968	1,690	278	54	55	26	1,142	2.66	548	2.52
Maine..................	722	545	177	121	15	12	396	2.47	149	2.09
Maryland...............	2,381	2,127	253	56	58	33	1,426	2.75	701	2.47
Massachusetts..........	2,809	2,520	288	119	59	25	1,568	2.69	952	2.20
Michigan...............	4,531	3,807	725	278	112	71	2,769	2.61	1,037	2.34
Minnesota..............	2,348	2,092	257	120	36	30	1,527	2.59	564	2.17
Mississippi.............	1,276	1,080	196	38	48	19	753	2.67	327	2.65
Missouri...............	2,714	2,351	363	88	66	45	1,621	2.56	729	2.29
Montana...............	483	403	80	38	9	5	281	2.46	122	2.23
Nebraska...............	798	719	78	15	17	8	485	2.60	235	2.21
Nevada................	1,175	990	185	46	52	26	566	2.70	424	2.69
New Hampshire.........	615	515	100	64	8	7	369	2.58	146	2.22
New Jersey.............	3,555	3,172	382	135	87	43	2,107	2.83	1,066	2.49
New Mexico............	902	765	137	50	20	12	520	2.70	245	2.53
New York...............	8,108	7,196	912	298	176	72	3,904	2.76	3,292	2.44
North Carolina..........	4,333	3,671	663	202	135	78	2,466	2.58	1,205	2.45
North Dakota...........	318	280	38	13	6	3	188	2.48	93	1.98
Ohio...................	5,128	4,525	603	59	151	75	3,095	2.56	1,430	2.32
Oklahoma..............	1,666	1,433	233	41	44	24	971	2.59	462	2.45
Oregon................	1,676	1,507	169	61	34	25	943	2.57	564	2.36
Pennsylvania...........	5,569	4,936	633	179	103	64	3,462	2.61	1,474	2.20
Rhode Island...........	463	402	61	17	17	6	245	2.68	158	2.25
South Carolina..........	2,140	1,761	379	126	89	38	1,210	2.56	551	2.53
South Dakota...........	364	319	45	16	8	4	217	2.59	102	2.16
Tennessee..............	2,815	2,441	374	68	92	45	1,663	2.58	778	2.46
Texas..................	9,996	8,739	1,258	242	383	126	5,556	2.93	3,183	2.63
Utah...................	982	880	102	46	19	13	615	3.22	265	2.84
Vermont................	323	257	66	47	6	3	181	2.48	76	1.99
Virginia................	3,369	2,993	376	98	75	45	2,025	2.65	967	2.49
Washington.............	2,889	2,607	282	88	60	43	1,645	2.63	962	2.37
West Virginia...........	882	742	140	45	19	13	553	2.50	189	2.22
Wisconsin..............	2,625	2,280	346	179	47	31	1,566	2.56	713	2.15
Wyoming...............	262	223	39	17	5	2	155	2.49	68	2.44

[1] For seasonal, recreational, or occasional use.

Source: U.S. Census Bureau, 2009 American Community Survey, B25002, "Occupancy Status;" B25003, "Tenure;" B25004, "Vacancy Status;" and B25010, "Average Household Size of Units by Tenure;" using American FactFinder, see <http://factfinder.census.gov>, accessed August 2012.

Table 999. Homeownership and Rental Vacancy Rates by State: 2011

[The American Community Survey universe is limited to the household population and excludes the population living in institutions, college dormitories, and other group quarters. Based on a sample and subject to sampling variability, see Appendix III]

State	Homeowner vacancy rate	Rental vacancy rate	State	Homeowner vacancy rate	Rental vacancy rate	State	Homeowner vacancy rate	Rental vacancy rate
U.S.	2.5	9.5	KS	2.1	8.7			
			KY	2.2	10.5	ND	1.5	9.8
AL	2.8	14.2	LA	1.7	11.7	OH	2.8	10.5
AK	1.3	5.8	ME	2.2	6.1	OK	2.6	10.1
AZ	3.2	12.4	MD	2.7	10.1	OR	2.1	4.0
AR	3.0	12.6	MA	1.6	5.8	PA	2.0	8.6
CA	2.1	6.1	MI	2.4	13.2	RI	2.3	7.9
CO	2.4	7.4	MN	2.0	7.3	SC	3.3	11.6
CT	2.2	9.5	MS	1.7	14.5	SD	1.8	9.2
DE	2.7	11.2	MO	2.2	10.8	TN	2.8	12.0
DC	1.4	8.4	MT	1.6	4.9	TX	1.8	12.3
FL	3.3	14.9	NE	2.1	8.1	UT	1.9	6.4
GA	3.6	10.0	NV	3.6	11.0	VT	1.7	4.2
HI	2.2	9.4	NH	1.9	7.5	VA	2.2	9.9
ID	3.8	8.9	NJ	2.1	8.8	WA	2.3	6.0
IL	3.4	10.2	NM	1.4	7.4	WV	2.4	7.9
IN	2.6	13.0	NY	2.7	6.5	WI	2.1	6.6
IA	2.4	7.2	NC	2.5	11.3	WY	1.3	6.5

Source: U.S. Census Bureau, "Housing Vacancies and Home Ownership," <http://www.census.gov/housing/hvs/>.

Table 1000. Homeownership and Rental Vacancy Rates by Metropolitan Area: 2011

[Based on the Current Population Survey and the Housing Vacancy Survey, subject to sampling error; see source and Appendix III for details]

Metropolitan area	Homeowner vacancy rate	Rental vacancy rate	Metropolitan area	Homeowner vacancy rate	Rental vacancy rate
Inside Metropolitan Areas	**2.5**	**9.5**			
Akron, OH	3.8	11.0			
Albany-Schenectady-Troy, NY	1.8	9.6	Minneapolis-St. Paul-Bloomington, MN-WI	1.8	6.7
Albuquerque, NM	1.4	6.9	Nashville-Davidson-Murfreesboro, TN	2.2	8.2
Allenton-Bethleham-Easton, PA-NJ	1.8	6.2	New Haven-Milford, CT	2.2	10.7
Atlanta-Sandy Springs-Marietta, GA	4.3	11.6	New Orleans-Metairie-Kenner, LA	2.1	13.1
Austin-Round Rock, TX	0.6	6.4	New York-Northern New Jersey-Long Island, NY	2.6	6.4
Bakersfield, CA	1.0	4.0			
Baltimore-Towson, MD	2.8	10.7	Oklahoma City, OK	3.9	9.9
Baton Rouge, LA	2.1	11.0	Omaha-Council Bluffs, NE-IA	1.9	11.1
Birmingham-Hoover, AL	1.6	12.6	Orlando, FL	2.5	19.0
Boston-Cambridge-Quincy, MA-NH	1.4	5.5	Oxnard-Thousand Oaks-Ventura, CA	0.5	3.2
Bridgeport-Stamford-Norwalk, CT	2.0	6.3	Philadelphia-Camden-Wilmington, PA	1.6	12.7
Buffalo-Cheektowaga-Tonawanda, NY	2.0	10.7	Phoenix-Mesa-Scottsdale, AZ	3.1	10.9
Charlotte-Gastonia-Concord, NC-SC	1.9	10.1	Pittsburgh, PA	2.2	6.3
Chicago-Naperville-Joliet, IL	3.6	9.9	Portland-Vancouver-Beaverton, OR-WA	2.0	3.4
Cincinnati-Middletown, OH-KY-IN	3.0	11.1	Poughkeepsie-Newburg-Middletown, NJ	2.1	13.0
Cleveland-Elyria-Mentor, OH	1.9	11.0	Providence-New Bedford-Fall River RI-MA	2.2	8.8
Columbia, SC	5.1	8.7	Raleigh-Cary, NC	2.9	8.9
Columbus, OH	3.2	8.2	Richmond, VA	2.4	13.7
Dallas-Ft. Worth-Arlington, TX	2.0	11.8	Riverside-San Bernardino-Ontario, CA	3.5	8.4
Dayton, OH	5.1	11.1	Rochester, NY	1.0	4.8
Denver-Aurora, CO	1.8	6.8	Sacramento-Arden-Arade-Roseville, CA	2.4	7.1
Detroit-Warren-Livonia, MI	1.8	16.8	St. Louis, MO-IL	2.9	12.6
El Paso, TX	1.3	9.2	Salt Lake City, UT	2.2	7.4
Fresno, CA	1.0	8.0	San Antonio, TX	1.5	9.2
Grand Rapids-Wyoming, MI	2.6	6.1	San Diego-Carlsbad-San Marcos, CA	1.9	6.9
Greensboro-High Point, NC	3.0	11.9	San Francisco-Oakland-Freemont, CA	1.8	6.8
Hartford-West Hartford-East Hartford, CT	1.8	10.0	San Jose-Sunnyvale-Santa Clara, CA	0.9	4.8
Honolulu, HI	0.7	6.9	Seattle-Bellevue-Everett, WA	2.6	6.7
Houston-Baytown-Sugar Land, TX	2.0	16.5	Springfield, MA	2.1	4.0
Indianapolis, IN	3.4	13.1	Syracuse, NY	0.3	5.7
Jacksonville, FL	2.8	13.3	Tampa-St. Petersburg-Clearwater, FL	3.8	11.7
Kansas City, MO-KS	2.7	12.1	Toledo, OH	4.4	12.8
Las Vegas-Paradise, NV	4.1	12.1	Tucson, AZ	4.2	14.8
Los Angeles-Long Beach-Santa Ana, CA	1.8	5.3	Tulsa, OK	2.5	13.0
Louisville, KY-IN	2.4	10.2	Virginia Beach-Norfolk-Newport News, VA	3.2	9.4
Memphis, TN-AR-MS	3.0	15.4	Washington-Arlington-Alexandria, DC-VA-MD-WV	1.8	7.9
Miami-Fort Lauderdale-Miami Beach, FL	1.8	11.8	Worcester, MA	1.3	4.9
Milwaukee-Waukesha-West Allis, WI	2.0	7.6			

Source: U.S. Census Bureau, "Housing Vacancies and Home Ownership," <http://www.census.gov/housing/hvs/>.

Table 1001. Housing Units—Characteristics by Tenure and Region: 2009

[In thousands of units (130,112 represents 130,112,000), except as indicated. As of fall. Based on the American Housing Survey; see Appendix III. For composition of regions, see map, inside front cover]

| Characteristic | Total housing units | Sea-sonal | Year-round units | | | | | | | Vacant |
| | | | Occupied | | | | | | | |
			Total	Owner	Renter	North-east	Mid-west	South	West	
Total units...............	**130,112**	**4,618**	**111,806**	**76,428**	**35,378**	**20,451**	**25,368**	**41,586**	**24,401**	**13,688**
Percent distribution..................	100.0	3.5	85.9	58.7	27.2	15.7	19.5	32.0	18.8	10.5
Units in structure:										
Single family detached.................	82,472	2,795	73,079	63,324	9,755	11,431	17,944	28,063	15,642	6,598
Single family attached.................	7,053	252	5,973	3,952	2,021	1,810	1,055	1,935	1,172	828
2 to 4 units..........	10,160	167	8,350	1,353	6,998	2,571	1,792	2,096	1,892	1,643
5 to 9 units..........	6,347	143	5,269	632	4,637	944	1,043	1,818	1,465	935
10 to 19 units..........	5,722	127	4,661	483	4,178	741	962	1,819	1,139	934
20 or more units..........	9,588	404	7,634	1,266	6,368	2,415	1,429	1,936	1,854	1,550
Manufactured/mobile home [1]..........	8,769	730	6,839	5,418	1,421	540	1,145	3,918	1,236	1,201
Year structure built:										
Median year..........	1974	1975	1974	1975	1971	1958	1970	1979	1976	1973
1980 or later..........	16,283	615	14,028	9,360	4,668	1,758	2,381	6,438	3,451	1,639
1970 to 1979..........	24,799	867	21,248	13,167	8,081	2,864	4,681	8,761	4,941	2,684
1960 to 1969..........	15,261	514	13,326	8,917	4,409	2,451	2,957	4,832	3,086	1,421
1950 to 1959..........	41,406	1,386	35,399	23,076	12,322	10,828	9,780	8,538	6,252	4,622
Stories in structure: [2]										
1 story..........	41,537	1,880	35,364	26,216	9,148	1,109	4,072	19,803	10,381	4,292
2 stories..........	43,447	1,145	37,867	25,210	12,657	6,291	10,192	12,065	9,320	4,435
3 stories..........	27,574	542	24,508	16,721	7,787	8,689	8,530	4,611	2,678	2,524
4 or more stories..........	8,785	320	7,228	2,863	4,365	3,823	1,430	1,190	785	1,237
Foundation: [3]										
Full basement..........	29,104	490	26,713	23,821	2,892	9,022	11,276	4,269	2,145	1,902
Partial building..........	8,991	170	8,208	7,350	858	2,226	3,280	1,565	1,137	613
Crawlspace..........	20,955	965	18,022	14,783	3,240	740	2,523	9,517	5,242	1,968
Concrete slab..........	28,693	1,011	24,917	20,431	4,486	1,146	1,758	13,941	8,071	2,765
Equipment:										
Lacking complete facilities..........	5,586	667	1,751	378	1,374	487	385	406	474	3,168
With complete facilities..........	124,526	3,951	110,054	76,050	34,004	19,964	24,984	41,180	23,927	10,520
Kitchen sink..........	128,769	4,291	111,510	76,329	35,180	20,344	25,308	41,532	24,326	12,968
Refrigerator..........	126,534	4,056	111,530	76,336	35,193	20,372	25,328	41,502	24,328	10,948
Cooking stove or range..........	126,744	4,127	111,038	76,153	34,886	20,329	25,207	41,347	24,155	11,579
Dishwasher..........	82,397	2,111	73,584	57,191	16,393	11,900	15,487	28,691	17,505	6,702
Washing machine..........	101,387	2,482	93,372	73,826	19,545	15,327	21,537	36,611	19,896	5,534
Clothes dryer..........	98,657	2,360	90,905	72,562	18,343	14,512	21,327	35,578	19,489	5,392
Disposal in kitchen sink..........	63,776	1,505	56,531	40,597	15,933	5,332	13,048	20,217	17,934	5,740
Safety Equipment:										
Smoke detector:										
Working..........	116,141	2,989	104,362	71,797	32,565	19,479	24,153	37,942	22,788	8,789
Powered by:										
Electricity..........	9,217	267	8,149	5,620	2,528	1,680	1,534	3,238	1,696	801
Batteries..........	72,868	1,547	66,536	43,210	23,326	12,985	16,379	22,831	14,341	4,785
Both..........	32,128	983	28,421	22,461	5,960	4,654	5,971	11,370	6,426	2,724
Not working..........	9,101	824	6,157	3,686	2,472	739	974	3,045	1,399	2,119
Not reported..........	4,870	804	1,286	945	341	233	241	598	214	2,780
Batteries:										
Replaced in last 6 months..........	77,933	1,626	71,505	50,073	21,432	14,175	17,336	25,312	14,682	4,803
Not replaced in last 6 months.......	23,706	579	21,466	14,678	6,788	3,133	4,557	8,179	5,597	1,661
Not reported..........	3,357	326	1,986	920	1,066	331	457	710	488	1,045
Fire extinguisher purchased or recharged..........	49,902	(X)	49,902	37,922	11,980	9,405	11,183	19,118	10,196	(X)
Sprinkler system inside home.........	6,401	246	5,167	2,086	3,081	938	877	1,845	1,507	988
Working carbon monoxide detector...	43,494	673	40,698	31,691	9,007	12,483	12,688	9,927	5,600	2,123
Main heating equipment: [4]										
Warm-air furnace..........	81,629	2,034	71,141	51,691	19,450	8,925	20,671	25,268	16,277	8,454
Steam or hot water system..........	13,969	259	12,506	7,494	5,012	9,088	2,015	592	811	1,204
Electric heat pump..........	16,059	868	13,264	9,764	3,500	336	706	10,785	1,436	1,927
Built-in electric units..........	5,730	320	4,761	2,120	2,641	1,159	1,134	827	1,641	649
Floor, wall, or pipeless furnace.......	5,525	202	4,802	2,043	2,760	435	388	1,154	2,825	520
Room heaters with flue..........	1,173	73	950	580	370	124	103	478	244	150
Room heaters without flue..........	1,365	99	1,109	694	414	24	52	992	41	157
Portable electric heaters..........	1,405	107	1,167	535	632	29	65	769	304	131
Stoves..........	1,364	203	1,035	845	190	226	158	341	310	125
Fireplaces [5]..........	290	42	215	190	25	27	40	53	94	34
None..........	930	330	386	206	180	3	3	58	321	215
Main cooling equipment:										
Central air conditioning..........	88,668	2,197	78,437	59,357	19,080	6,931	18,340	39,501	13,665	8,034
One or more room units..........	26,850	581	24,582	13,707	10,875	10,499	5,478	4,980	3,625	1,687
Source of water:										
Public system or private company....	113,489	3,238	98,027	64,372	33,655	17,101	21,435	36,594	22,897	12,224
Well serving 1 to 5 units..........	15,846	1,070	13,430	11,769	1,660	3,275	3,878	4,821	1,455	1,346
Means of sewage disposal:										
Public sewer..........	103,155	2,596	89,467	56,736	32,732	16,263	20,432	31,288	21,484	11,092
Septic tank chemical toilet..........	26,662	1,800	22,307	19,667	2,640	4,185	4,930	10,279	2,913	2,555

X Not applicable. [1] Includes trailers. Includes width not reported, not shown separately. [2] Excludes mobile homes; includes basements and finished attics. [3] Limited to single-family units. [4] Includes other items, not shown separately. [5] With and without inserts.

Source: U.S. Census Bureau, Current Housing Reports, Series H150/09, *American Housing Survey for the United States: 2009*. See also <http://www.census.gov/housing/ahs/>.

Table 1002. Housing Units by Units in Structure and State: 2010

[In percent, except as indicated (131,791 represents 131,791,000). The American Community Survey universe includes the household population and the population living in institutions, college dormitories, and other group quarters. Based on a sample and subject to sampling variability; see Appendix III]

Characteristic	Total housing units (1,000)	1-unit detached	1-unit attached	2 units	3 or 4 units	5 or 9 units	10 or 19 units	20 or more units	Mobile homes	Boat, RV, van, etc.
U.S.	131,791	61.4	5.8	3.8	4.4	4.8	4.5	8.5	6.6	0.1
AL	2,174	68.5	1.7	2.2	2.8	4.2	3.1	3.6	13.8	0.1
AK	307	63.2	8.4	4.2	6.2	4.5	3.6	4.7	5.1	0.1
AZ	2,847	63.0	5.2	1.3	3.4	4.3	5.2	6.6	10.8	0.3
AR	1,318	69.5	1.6	3.1	3.3	3.1	3.8	2.4	13.1	0.1
CA	13,683	57.8	7.2	2.7	5.5	6.0	5.3	11.6	3.8	0.1
CO	2,214	62.4	7.1	2.0	3.4	4.6	6.0	10.1	4.3	0.1
CT	1,488	59.0	5.1	8.1	9.2	5.1	3.8	8.8	0.8	(Z)
DE	406	58.6	14.2	1.4	2.5	4.0	5.6	4.3	9.3	(Z)
DC	297	12.2	25.0	3.0	7.3	6.7	10.5	35.1	0.1	(Z)
FL	8,994	54.0	6.3	2.1	3.9	5.0	5.8	13.5	9.3	0.1
GA	4,091	66.4	3.8	2.3	3.1	5.0	4.7	5.4	9.3	0.1
HI	520	54.2	7.4	3.2	4.7	6.2	4.8	19.4	0.2	(Z)
ID	669	71.1	3.1	2.6	4.7	2.9	2.0	3.8	9.6	0.2
IL	5,297	58.3	5.9	5.9	6.7	6.4	3.9	10.1	2.7	(Z)
IN	2,797	72.9	3.3	2.6	3.5	4.6	3.8	4.1	5.2	(Z)
IA	1,338	73.8	3.6	2.5	3.4	3.8	3.6	5.1	4.2	(Z)
KS	1,234	72.1	4.5	2.3	3.7	4.1	3.3	4.6	5.2	(Z)
KY	1,929	67.1	2.4	3.0	4.0	4.5	3.3	3.1	12.6	0.1
LA	1,968	65.1	3.1	3.9	4.4	3.7	2.7	3.8	13.2	0.1
ME	722	69.8	2.4	5.3	5.1	3.8	1.6	3.0	8.9	0.1
MD	2,381	51.4	21.1	1.7	2.3	4.9	8.8	8.1	1.7	(Z)
MA	2,809	51.7	5.2	9.9	11.5	6.2	4.3	10.4	0.8	(Z)
MI	4,531	71.6	4.5	2.8	2.6	4.2	3.7	5.0	5.5	(Z)
MN	2,348	66.9	7.4	2.5	2.0	2.3	3.4	11.8	3.7	(Z)
MS	1,276	69.1	1.2	2.5	3.0	4.6	1.9	2.0	15.6	0.2
MO	2,714	69.7	3.6	3.5	4.5	3.7	3.5	4.5	6.9	0.1
MT	483	69.3	3.0	3.5	4.5	2.8	2.4	3.2	11.1	0.1
NE	798	72.9	3.9	2.0	2.9	3.9	4.4	6.1	3.8	(Z)
NV	1,175	58.6	5.0	1.4	6.1	9.1	6.2	7.2	6.3	0.1
NH	615	63.3	5.1	6.1	5.8	4.9	2.9	5.8	6.0	(Z)
NJ	3,555	53.7	9.4	9.7	6.2	4.8	5.0	10.2	0.9	(Z)
NM	902	64.6	3.5	2.1	4.1	2.7	2.5	3.9	16.5	0.1
NY	8,108	41.9	4.8	10.7	7.6	5.5	4.2	22.8	2.4	(Z)
NC	4,333	65.0	3.8	2.2	2.6	4.4	4.1	3.8	14.0	(Z)
ND	318	60.7	5.8	2.3	3.6	4.4	5.4	9.9	7.9	(Z)
OH	5,128	68.3	4.6	4.4	4.5	4.7	4.2	5.1	4.0	(Z)
OK	1,666	73.3	2.0	2.0	2.7	3.8	3.2	3.4	9.5	0.1
OR	1,676	63.6	4.5	2.9	4.4	4.5	3.7	7.8	8.3	0.3
PA	5,569	56.8	18.2	4.8	4.1	3.4	2.7	5.8	4.2	(Z)
RI	463	54.4	3.0	11.8	13.1	5.7	4.1	7.2	0.8	(Z)
SC	2,140	61.1	2.7	2.3	3.0	4.8	3.6	4.7	17.6	0.1
SD	364	68.3	3.5	2.2	3.5	3.4	3.8	6.4	9.0	(Z)
TN	2,815	68.3	3.2	3.0	3.0	4.5	3.6	4.3	9.9	0.1
TX	9,996	65.1	2.6	2.1	3.1	4.9	6.5	7.9	7.6	0.2
UT	982	68.2	6.1	3.5	4.4	3.8	4.4	5.8	3.8	0.1
VT	323	65.9	3.8	5.9	6.6	5.4	1.7	3.6	6.9	(Z)
VA	3,369	62.4	10.3	1.6	2.6	4.9	5.7	6.8	5.6	(Z)
WA	2,889	63.6	3.6	2.5	3.8	4.9	5.2	9.2	7.1	0.2
WV	882	70.2	1.8	2.2	2.6	3.0	1.7	2.5	16.1	(Z)
WI	2,625	66.3	4.4	6.9	3.7	4.8	3.2	7.0	3.7	(Z)
WY	262	66.3	3.9	2.9	4.3	3.6	2.5	3.1	13.4	0.1

Z Less than .05 percent.

Source: U.S. Census Bureau, 2010 American Community Survey, B25024, "Units in Structure," <http://www.factfinder.census.gov>, accessed August 2012.

Table 1003. Housing Units—Size of Units and Lot: 2009

[In thousands (130,112 represents 130,112,000), except as indicated. As of fall. Based on the American Housing Survey; see Appendix III. For composition of regions, see map, inside front cover]

Item	Total housing units	Sea-sonal	Year-round units								Vacant
			Occupied								
			Total	Owner	Renter	North-east	Mid-west	South	West		
Total units.............	130,112	4,618	111,806	76,428	35,378	20,451	25,368	41,586	24,401		13,688
Rooms:											
1 room..........	579	104	352	26	326	111	60	33	149		123
2 rooms..........	1,423	194	946	68	879	269	130	209	337		283
3 rooms..........	11,290	697	8,711	1,036	7,675	2,235	1,891	2,461	2,124		1,882
4 rooms..........	23,036	1,374	17,828	6,475	11,354	3,277	3,889	6,376	4,287		3,834
5 rooms..........	29,888	1,108	25,444	17,232	8,212	3,854	5,758	10,355	5,476		3,336
6 rooms..........	27,480	632	24,596	20,364	4,232	4,435	5,400	9,918	4,842		2,252
7 rooms..........	17,877	315	16,489	14,754	1,735	3,080	3,904	6,110	3,394		1,073
8 rooms or more..........	18,538	193	17,440	16,474	967	3,189	4,337	6,123	3,791		905
Complete bathrooms:											
No bathrooms..........	1,678	557	403	175	229	98	93	115	97		717
1 bathroom..........	46,977	1,899	38,662	15,767	22,894	9,418	9,760	11,847	7,636		6,416
1 and one-half bathrooms..........	17,233	363	15,656	12,081	3,575	4,066	4,770	4,217	2,603		1,214
2 or more bathrooms..........	64,223	1,798	57,085	48,405	8,680	6,869	10,746	25,406	14,064		5,340
Square footage of unit:											
Single detached and mobile homes..........	91,241	3,524	79,918	68,742	11,176	11,971	19,088	31,981	16,878		7,799
Less than 500..........	988	225	603	383	220	86	104	247	166		161
500 to 749..........	2,765	462	1,771	1,085	686	249	415	810	298		532
750 to 999..........	6,440	593	5,014	3,519	1,495	614	1,340	2,086	973		833
1,000 to 1,499..........	21,224	814	18,419	14,978	3,441	2,047	4,331	7,834	4,207		1,991
1,500 to 1,999..........	20,636	521	18,519	16,284	2,235	2,458	4,039	7,564	4,457		1,596
2,000 to 2,499..........	14,361	284	13,190	12,057	1,134	2,000	3,282	5,165	2,743		886
2,500 to 2,999..........	7,589	141	7,050	6,622	429	1,211	1,594	2,819	1,426		398
3,000 to 3,999..........	7,252	137	6,692	6,391	301	1,119	1,700	2,488	1,385		424
4,000 or more..........	4,456	113	4,030	3,787	243	805	994	1,519	712		313
Other [1]..........	5,529	234	4,630	3,638	992	1,382	1,288	1,449	510		666
Median square footage..........	1,700	1,150	1,800	1,800	1,300	1,900	1,800	1,700	1,700		1,500
Lot size:											
Single detached and attached units and mobile homes..........	95,216	3,512	83,466	70,643	12,823	13,297	19,555	33,222	17,392		8,239
Less than one-eighth acre..........	25,234	946	21,635	16,297	5,338	3,161	4,749	7,268	6,457		2,652
One-eighth to one-quarter acre......	13,706	448	11,981	10,581	1,400	1,610	3,063	3,413	3,896		1,277
One-quarter to one-half acre..........	17,825	518	15,921	13,837	2,084	2,383	4,044	6,523	2,970		1,386
One-half up to one acre..........	11,292	372	10,036	8,874	1,162	1,974	1,964	4,945	1,153		884
1 up to 5 acres..........	19,172	754	17,014	14,895	2,120	3,072	3,669	8,310	1,963		1,404
5 up to 10 acres..........	3,104	120	2,750	2,545	205	464	737	1,106	443		234
10 acres or more..........	4,885	354	4,127	3,614	513	633	1,329	1,656	509		403
Median acreage..........	0.27	0.32	0.27	0.32	0.22	0.34	0.28	0.36	0.18		0.25

[1] Represents units not reported or size unknown.

Source: U.S. Census Bureau, Current Housing Reports, Series H150/09, *American Housing Survey for the United States:2009*, March 2011. See also <http://www.census.gov/housing/ahs/>.

Table 1004. Occupied Housing Units—Tenure by Race of Householder: 1991 to 2009

[In thousands (93,147 represents 93,147,000), except percent. As of fall. Based on the American Housing Survey; see Appendix III]

Race of householder and tenure	1991	1995	1999	2001	2003 [1]	2005	2007	2009
ALL RACES [2]								
Occupied units, total..........	93,147	97,693	102,803	106,261	105,842	108,871	110,692	111,806
Owner-occupied..........	59,796	63,544	68,796	72,265	72,238	74,931	75,647	76,428
Percent of occupied..........	64.2	65.0	66.9	68.0	68.3	68.8	68.3	68.4
Renter-occupied..........	33,351	34,150	34,007	33,996	33,604	33,940	35,045	35,378
WHITE [3]								
Occupied units, total..........	79,140	81,611	83,624	85,292	87,483	89,449	90,413	91,137
Owner-occupied..........	53,749	56,507	60,041	62,465	63,126	65,023	65,554	65,935
Percent of occupied..........	67.9	69.2	71.8	73.2	72.2	72.7	72.5	72.3
Renter-occupied..........	25,391	25,104	23,583	22,826	24,357	24,426	24,859	25,202
BLACK [3]								
Occupied units, total..........	10,832	11,773	12,936	13,292	13,004	13,447	13,856	13,993
Owner-occupied..........	4,635	5,137	6,013	6,318	6,193	6,471	6,464	6,547
Percent of occupied..........	42.8	43.6	46.5	47.5	47.6	48.1	46.7	46.8
Renter-occupied..........	6,197	6,637	6,923	6,974	6,811	6,975	7,392	7,446
HISPANIC ORIGIN [4]								
Occupied units, total..........	6,239	7,757	9,041	9,814	11,038	11,651	12,609	12,739
Owner-occupied..........	2,423	3,245	4,087	4,731	5,106	5,752	6,364	6,439
Percent of occupied..........	38.8	41.8	45.2	48.2	46.3	49.4	50.5	50.5
Renter-occupied..........	3,816	4,512	4,955	5,083	5,931	5,899	6,244	6,300

[1] Based on 2000 census controls. [2] Includes other races not shown separately. [3] The 2003 American Housing Survey (AHS) allowed respondents to choose more than one race. Beginning in 2003, data represent householders who selected this race group only and exclude householders reporting more than one race. The AHS in prior years only allowed respondents to report one race group. See also comments on race in the text for Section 1 and the below cited source. [4] Persons of Hispanic origin may be any race.

Source: U.S. Census Bureau, Current Housing Reports, Series H150/09, *American Housing Survey for the United States: 2009*, March 2011. See also <http://www.census.gov/housing/ahs/>.

Table 1005. Homeownership Rates by Age of Householder and Household Type: 1990 to 2011

[In percent. Represents the proportion of owner households to the total number of occupied households. Based on the Current Population Survey and Housing Vacancy Survey; see source and Appendix III for details]

Age of householder and household type	1990	1995	2000	2005	2006	2007	2008	2009	2010	2011
United States	**63.9**	**64.7**	**67.4**	**68.9**	**68.8**	**68.1**	**67.8**	**67.4**	**66.9**	**66.1**
AGE OF HOUSEHOLDER										
Less than 25 years old	15.7	15.9	21.7	25.7	24.8	24.8	23.6	23.3	22.8	22.6
25 to 29 years old	35.2	34.4	38.1	40.9	41.8	40.6	40.0	37.7	36.8	34.6
30 to 34 years old	51.8	53.1	54.6	56.8	55.9	54.4	53.5	52.5	51.6	49.8
35 to 39 years old	63.0	62.1	65.0	66.6	66.4	65.0	64.6	63.4	61.9	59.8
40 to 44 years old	69.8	68.6	70.6	71.7	71.2	70.4	69.4	68.7	67.9	66.9
45 to 49 years old	73.9	73.7	74.7	75.0	74.9	74.0	73.6	72.3	72.0	71.0
50 to 54 years old	76.8	77.0	78.5	78.3	77.7	76.9	76.4	76.5	75.0	74.4
55 to 59 years old	78.8	78.8	80.4	80.6	80.4	79.9	79.4	78.6	77.7	77.3
60 to 64 years old	79.8	80.3	80.3	81.9	81.5	81.5	80.9	80.6	80.4	79.8
65 to 69 years old	80.0	81.0	83.0	82.8	82.4	81.7	81.6	82.0	81.6	81.7
70 to 74 years old	78.4	80.9	82.6	82.9	83.0	82.4	81.7	81.9	82.4	83.3
75 years old and over	72.3	74.6	77.7	78.4	79.1	78.7	78.6	78.9	78.9	79.3
Less than 35 years old	38.5	38.6	40.8	43.0	42.6	41.7	41.0	39.7	39.1	37.7
35 to 44 years old	66.3	65.2	67.9	69.3	68.9	67.8	67.0	66.2	65.0	63.5
45 to 54 years old	75.2	75.2	76.5	76.6	76.2	75.4	75.0	74.4	73.5	72.7
55 to 64 years old	79.3	79.5	80.3	81.2	80.9	80.6	80.1	79.5	79.0	78.5
65 years and over	76.3	78.1	80.4	80.6	80.9	80.4	80.1	80.5	80.5	80.9
TYPE OF HOUSEHOLD										
Family households:										
Married-couple families	78.1	79.6	82.4	84.2	84.1	83.8	83.4	82.8	82.1	81.5
Male householder, no spouse present	55.2	55.3	57.5	59.1	58.9	57.4	57.6	56.9	56.9	55.6
Female householder, no spouse present	44.0	45.1	49.1	51.0	51.3	49.9	49.5	49.0	48.6	48.1
Nonfamily households:										
One-person	49.0	50.5	53.6	55.6	55.7	55.2	55.0	55.1	55.3	55.0
Male householder	42.4	43.8	47.4	50.3	50.5	50.2	50.6	50.9	51.3	50.6
Female householder	53.6	55.4	58.1	59.6	59.8	59.1	58.6	58.6	58.6	58.5
Other:										
Male householder	31.7	34.2	38.0	41.7	40.8	40.0	41.3	40.2	40.7	39.5
Female householder	32.5	33.0	40.6	44.7	45.5	42.9	42.5	42.5	41.9	43.1

Source: U.S. Census Bureau, "Housing Vacancies and Home Ownership," <http://www.census.gov/housing/hvs/>.

Table 1006. Homeownership Rates by State: 1990 to 2011

[In percent. See headnote, Table 1005]

State	1990	2000	2005	2009	2010	2011	State	1990	2000	2005	2009	2010	2011
United States	**63.9**	**67.4**	**68.9**	**67.4**	**66.9**	**66.1**	Missouri	64.0	74.2	72.3	72.0	71.2	71.1
Alabama	68.4	73.2	76.6	74.1	73.2	72.9	Montana	69.1	70.2	70.4	70.7	68.1	68.4
Alaska	58.4	66.4	66.0	66.8	65.7	64.4	Nebraska	67.3	70.2	70.2	70.2	70.4	68.9
Arizona	64.5	68.0	71.1	68.9	66.6	66.0	Nevada	55.8	64.0	63.4	62.4	59.7	56.2
Arkansas	67.8	68.9	69.2	68.5	67.9	67.6	New Hampshire	65.0	69.2	74.0	76.0	74.9	74.1
California	53.8	57.1	59.7	57.0	56.1	55.3	New Jersey	65.0	66.2	70.1	65.9	66.5	66.4
Colorado	59.0	68.3	71.0	68.4	68.5	65.9	New Mexico	68.6	73.7	71.4	69.1	68.6	69.1
Connecticut	67.9	70.0	70.5	70.5	70.8	70.6	New York	53.3	53.4	55.9	54.4	54.5	53.6
Delaware	67.7	72.0	75.8	76.5	74.7	74.2	North Carolina	69.0	71.1	70.9	70.1	69.5	68.3
Dist. of Columbia	36.4	41.9	45.8	44.9	45.6	44.8	North Dakota	67.2	70.7	68.5	65.7	67.1	68.3
Florida	65.1	68.4	72.4	70.9	69.3	69.0	Ohio	68.7	71.3	73.3	69.7	69.7	68.9
Georgia	64.3	69.8	67.9	67.4	67.1	66.2	Oklahoma	70.3	72.7	72.9	69.6	69.2	69.4
Hawaii	55.5	55.2	59.8	59.5	56.1	55.4	Oregon	64.4	65.3	68.2	68.2	66.3	66.4
Idaho	69.4	70.5	74.2	75.5	72.4	72.0	Pennsylvania	73.8	74.7	73.3	72.2	72.2	71.1
Illinois	63.0	67.9	70.9	69.1	68.8	68.4	Rhode Island	58.5	61.5	63.1	62.9	62.8	63.4
Indiana	67.0	74.9	75.0	72.0	71.2	72.1	South Carolina	71.4	76.5	73.9	74.4	74.8	74.2
Iowa	70.7	75.2	73.9	72.4	71.1	71.2	South Dakota	66.2	71.2	68.4	69.6	70.6	69.3
Kansas	69.0	69.3	69.5	67.4	67.4	65.6	Tennessee	68.3	70.9	72.4	71.1	71.0	69.3
Kentucky	65.8	73.4	71.6	71.2	70.3	69.1	Texas	59.7	63.8	65.9	65.4	65.3	64.3
Louisiana	67.8	68.1	72.5	71.9	70.4	70.1	Utah	70.1	72.7	73.9	74.1	72.5	71.4
Maine	74.2	76.5	73.9	74.0	73.8	73.9	Vermont	72.6	68.7	74.2	74.3	73.6	74.6
Maryland	64.9	69.9	71.2	69.6	68.9	69.7	Virginia	69.8	73.9	71.2	69.7	68.7	67.9
Massachusetts	58.6	59.9	63.4	65.1	65.3	65.3	Washington	61.8	63.6	67.6	65.5	64.4	64.2
Michigan	72.3	77.2	76.4	74.5	74.5	74.1	West Virginia	72.0	75.9	81.3	78.7	79.0	78.7
Minnesota	68.0	76.1	76.5	72.9	72.6	71.3	Wisconsin	68.3	71.8	71.1	70.4	71.0	68.5
Mississippi	69.4	75.2	78.8	75.5	74.8	74.8	Wyoming	68.9	71.0	72.8	73.8	73.4	71.1

Source: U.S. Census Bureau, "Housing Vacancies and Home Ownership," <http://www.census.gov/housing/hvs/>.

Table 1007. Occupied Housing Units—Costs by Region: 2009

[76,428 represents 76,428,000. As of fall. See headnote, Table 1008, for an explanation of housing costs. Based on the American Housing Survey; see Appendix III. For composition of regions, see map, inside front cover]

Category	Number (1,000)					Percent distribution				
	Total units	North-east	Mid-west	South	West	Total units	North-east	Mid-west	South	West
OWNER-OCCUPIED UNITS										
Total........................	**76,428**	**13,378**	**18,249**	**29,193**	**15,607**	**100.0**	**100.0**	**100.0**	**100.0**	**100.0**
Monthly housing costs:										
Less than $200...................	2,635	192	430	1,368	647	3.4	1.4	2.4	4.7	4.1
$200 to $299....................	5,351	366	1,087	3,026	873	7.0	2.7	6.0	10.4	5.6
$300 to $399....................	6,022	653	1,549	2,835	984	7.9	4.9	8.5	9.7	6.3
$400 to $499....................	5,308	738	1,528	2,190	852	6.9	5.5	8.4	7.5	5.5
$500 to $699....................	8,141	1,682	2,093	3,261	1,105	10.7	12.6	11.5	11.2	7.1
$700 to $999....................	10,736	1,938	3,071	4,275	1,452	14.0	14.5	16.8	14.6	9.3
$1,000 to $1,499................	14,984	2,578	4,298	5,563	2,545	19.6	19.3	23.6	19.1	16.3
$1,500 to $2,499................	14,867	3,193	3,211	4,565	3,898	19.5	23.9	17.6	15.6	25.0
$2,500 or more..................	8,383	2,039	982	2,111	3,251	11.0	15.2	5.4	7.2	20.8
Median (dol.) [1]...............	1,000	1,196	937	827	1,389	(X)	(X)	(X)	(X)	(X)
RENTER-OCCUPIED UNITS										
Total........................	**35,378**	**7,073**	**7,119**	**12,392**	**8,794**	**100.0**	**100.0**	**100.0**	**100.0**	**100.0**
Monthly housing costs:										
Less than $200...................	976	190	267	351	168	2.8	2.7	3.7	2.8	1.9
$200 to $299....................	1,381	357	333	408	283	3.9	5.1	4.7	3.3	3.2
$300 to $399....................	1,359	352	371	441	194	3.8	5.0	5.2	3.6	2.2
$400 to $499....................	2,094	335	616	783	360	5.9	4.7	8.7	6.3	4.1
$500 to $699....................	6,793	1,055	1,845	2,712	1,181	19.2	14.9	25.9	21.9	13.4
$700 to $999....................	9,769	1,727	2,082	3,695	2,265	27.6	24.4	29.2	29.8	25.8
$1,000 to $1,499................	7,407	1,819	940	2,271	2,377	20.9	25.7	13.2	18.3	27.0
$1,500 to $2,499................	2,965	727	222	648	1,368	8.4	10.3	3.1	5.2	15.6
$2,500 or more..................	596	169	45	137	245	1.7	2.4	0.6	1.1	2.8
No cash rent....................	2,037	341	398	945	352	5.8	4.8	5.6	7.6	4.0
Median (dol.) [1]...............	808	877	691	764	956	(X)	(X)	(X)	(X)	(X)

X Not applicable. [1] For explanation of median, see Guide to Tabular Presentation.

Source: U.S. Census Bureau, Current Housing Reports, Series H150/09, *American Housing Survey for the United States: 2009*, March 2011. See also <http://www.census.gov/housing/ahs/>.

Table 1008. Occupied Housing Units—Financial Summary by Selected Characteristics of the Householder: 2009

[In thousands of units (111,806 represents 111,806,000), except as indicated. As of fall, housing costs include real estate taxes, property insurance, utilities, fuel, water, garbage collection, homeowner association fees, mobile home fees, and mortgage. Based on the American Housing Survey; see Appendix III]

Characteristic	Total occupied units	Tenure		Black [1]		Hispanic origin [2]		Elderly [3]		Households below poverty level	
		Owner	Renter	Owner	Renter	Owner	Renter	Owner	Renter	Owner	Renter
Total units [4]............	**111,806**	**76,428**	**35,378**	**6,547**	**7,446**	**6,439**	**6,300**	**18,472**	**4,623**	**6,405**	**9,334**
Monthly housing costs:											
$199 or less....................	3,611	2,635	976	322	370	253	132	1,119	261	727	760
$200 to $299....................	6,732	5,351	1,381	467	422	453	200	2,587	461	1,035	895
$300 to $399....................	7,381	6,022	1,359	499	357	445	172	2,897	364	818	599
$400 to $499....................	7,402	5,308	2,094	470	420	371	333	2,395	408	611	823
$500 to $699....................	14,934	8,141	6,793	801	1,569	503	1,165	3,079	827	777	1,929
$700 to $999....................	20,505	10,736	9,769	1,041	2,106	910	1,900	2,502	883	893	2,057
$1,000 to $1,499................	22,391	14,984	7,407	1,313	1,471	1,186	1,508	1,967	533	722	1,166
$1,500 to $2,499................	17,832	14,867	2,965	1,099	348	1,418	593	1,233	277	548	331
$2,500 or more..................	8,980	8,383	596	537	35	900	58	692	129	275	53
Median amount (dol.) [4]........	909	1,000	808	901	746	1,113	854	512	640	502	629
Monthly housing costs as percent of income: [5]											
Less than 5 percent.............	3,065	2,903	162	133	15	171	35	594	23	8	17
5 to 9 percent..................	10,334	9,614	721	617	105	561	83	2,658	79	49	21
10 to 14 percent................	13,111	11,147	1,964	842	295	711	256	2,932	170	109	47
15 to 19 percent................	14,210	10,986	3,224	814	553	719	450	2,410	235	215	87
20 to 24 percent................	13,271	9,589	3,682	754	697	716	603	1,966	329	191	159
25 to 29 percent................	10,775	7,167	3,608	625	708	586	615	1,481	494	262	366
30 to 34 percent................	8,116	5,160	2,956	488	651	579	606	1,024	370	282	360
35 to 39 percent................	6,071	3,753	2,317	429	525	370	388	818	312	242	322
40 percent or more.............	28,695	15,250	13,445	1,743	3,181	1,921	2,808	4,478	2,063	4,245	6,138
Median amount (percent) [6]....	24	21	34	25	38	27	38	21	40	89	82

[1] For persons who selected this race group only. See footnote 3, Table 1004. [2] Persons of Hispanic origin may be of any race. [3] Householders 65 years old and over. [4] Include units with no cash, not shown separately. [5] Money income before taxes. [6] For explanation of median, see Guide to Tabular Presentation.

Source: U.S. Census Bureau, Current Housing Reports, Series H150/09, *American Housing Survey for the United States: 2009*, March 2011. See also <http://www.census.gov/housing/ahs/>.

Table 1009. Owner-Occupied Housing Units—Value and Costs by State: 2010

[In percent, except as indicated (74,873 represents 74,873,000). The American Community Survey universe includes the household population and excludes the population living in institutions, college dormitories, and other group quarters. Based on a sample and subject to sampling variability; see Appendix III. For definition of median, see Guide to Tabular Presentation]

State	Total (1,000)	Percent of units with value of—			Median value (dol.)	Median selected monthly owner costs [1] (dol.)	Selected monthly owner costs as a percent income in the past 12 months			
		$99,999 or less	$100,000 to $199,999	$200,000 or more			Less than 15 percent	15.0 to 24.9 percent	25.0 to 29.9 percent	30.0 percent or more
U.S.	**74,873**	**23.8**	**31.2**	**45.0**	**179,900**	**1,104**	**16.7**	**32.7**	**12.3**	**37.8**
AL.	1,273	40.8	33.8	25.4	123,900	772	21.9	33.7	11.2	32.5
AK.	163	11.1	25.0	63.9	241,400	1,363	20.0	36.2	11.6	32.1
AZ.	1,523	23.1	36.8	40.1	168,800	1,119	15.0	30.9	12.5	40.9
AR.	752	47.2	34.3	18.5	106,300	657	25.2	35.2	11.7	27.4
CA.	6,903	7.9	14.3	77.8	370,900	1,790	10.8	25.3	12.3	50.9
CO.	1,293	10.1	27.9	62.0	236,600	1,327	16.2	32.9	13.0	37.3
CT.	924	3.9	19.3	76.9	288,800	1,704	13.4	31.5	13.4	41.3
DE.	240	10.0	24.0	66.0	243,600	1,242	16.2	34.5	11.9	37.1
DC.	107	3.2	5.9	90.9	426,900	1,869	18.8	31.4	13.5	35.5
FL.	4,794	25.9	35.6	38.5	164,200	1,087	12.3	26.6	11.8	48.3
GA.	2,304	26.2	39.6	34.2	156,200	1,106	16.4	32.7	12.3	37.9
HI.	259	2.5	6.2	91.3	525,400	1,618	11.5	26.0	12.0	50.0
ID.	402	20.1	43.2	36.7	165,100	923	17.1	33.6	12.2	36.6
IL.	3,219	20.7	31.6	47.7	191,800	1,254	15.3	32.4	12.3	39.7
IN.	1,737	36.9	42.1	21.0	123,300	867	23.5	37.6	11.2	27.4
IA.	885	37.6	40.5	22.0	123,400	819	22.8	40.6	11.5	24.7
KS.	750	38.9	37.2	23.8	127,300	882	21.4	40.2	11.6	26.4
KY.	1,156	39.8	38.0	22.2	121,600	741	22.7	36.0	10.8	30.1
LA.	1,142	35.8	36.7	27.5	137,500	705	26.2	33.3	9.9	30.1
ME.	396	21.2	36.0	42.8	179,100	949	17.2	35.7	12.9	33.9
MD.	1,426	6.2	16.2	77.6	301,400	1,672	16.1	32.8	12.8	38.0
MA.	1,568	3.3	12.8	83.9	334,100	1,650	14.7	32.0	13.9	39.0
MI.	2,769	38.3	38.7	23.0	123,300	969	16.7	34.4	12.1	36.2
MN.	1,527	14.9	37.3	47.7	194,300	1,180	17.0	36.1	13.3	33.3
MS.	753	50.0	32.0	18.0	100,100	650	20.8	33.3	10.1	35.2
MO.	1,621	32.7	39.9	27.5	139,000	876	21.1	36.8	11.7	30.1
MT.	281	23.7	32.6	43.7	181,200	794	18.9	33.5	11.2	35.9
NE.	485	34.7	44.1	21.1	127,600	893	22.1	40.7	11.1	25.9
NV.	566	20.1	37.3	42.6	174,800	1,366	12.6	29.4	12.3	44.7
NH.	369	9.3	23.3	67.4	243,000	1,492	12.7	33.1	13.8	40.0
NJ.	2,107	4.5	13.1	82.4	339,200	1,907	11.6	28.6	12.9	46.5
NM.	520	28.9	33.8	37.3	161,200	794	21.0	30.7	12.0	35.9
NY.	3,904	17.3	20.0	62.7	296,500	1,362	16.9	29.7	11.7	41.2
NC.	2,466	27.9	37.7	34.4	154,200	951	18.3	34.8	12.1	34.3
ND.	188	40.0	39.6	20.4	123,000	684	28.2	41.4	11.3	19.0
OH.	3,095	32.1	43.6	24.3	134,400	963	18.4	36.9	12.6	31.8
OK.	971	44.1	37.5	18.4	111,400	747	22.7	37.2	10.9	28.7
OR.	943	11.0	24.1	64.9	244,500	1,228	13.2	30.4	13.3	42.6
PA.	3,462	26.9	33.6	39.5	165,500	968	18.6	35.2	12.6	33.1
RI.	245	3.8	24.1	72.1	254,500	1,555	12.6	29.5	14.0	43.5
SC.	1,210	34.3	35.9	29.8	138,100	838	20.0	34.3	11.3	33.8
SD.	217	36.6	40.1	23.3	129,700	777	21.9	40.1	12.2	25.4
TN.	1,663	32.0	39.7	28.4	139,000	836	18.1	36.1	12.1	33.1
TX.	5,556	36.7	38.1	25.2	128,100	1,016	19.1	36.1	11.7	32.5
UT.	615	7.7	35.7	56.6	217,200	1,208	16.2	34.3	13.9	35.4
VT.	181	11.5	33.2	55.3	216,800	1,155	13.4	33.5	14.0	38.6
VA.	2,025	12.6	24.6	62.8	249,100	1,326	16.8	34.0	13.7	35.0
WA.	1,645	8.3	21.3	70.4	271,800	1,394	13.6	31.4	13.7	40.7
WV.	553	52.4	30.0	17.6	95,100	491	29.1	35.2	9.7	25.5
WI.	1,566	18.7	43.0	38.3	169,400	1,090	15.1	36.7	13.6	34.2
WY.	155	20.1	37.9	42.1	180,100	858	23.2	37.1	11.6	28.0

[1] For homes with a mortgage. Includes all forms of debt where the property is pledged as security for repayment of the debt, including deeds of trust, land contracts, home equity loans. Also includes cost of property insurance, utilities, real estate taxes, etc.

Source: U.S. Census Bureau, 2010 American Community Survey, B25075, "Value for Owner-Occupied Housing Units;" B25077, "Median Value for Owner-Occupied Housing Units;" B25088, "Median Selected Monthly Owner Costs by Mortgage Status;" and B25091, "Mortgage Status by Selected Monthly Owner Cost as a Percentage of Household Income;" <http://factfinder.census.gov>, accessed August 2012.

Table 1010. Renter-Occupied Housing Units—Gross Rent by State: 2010

[In percent, except as indicated (39,694 represents 39,694,000). The American Community Survey universe includes the household population, and excludes the population living in institutions, college dormitories, and other group quarters. Based on a sample and subject to sampling variability; see Appendix III]

State	Total [1] (1,000)	Percent of units with gross rent of—					Median gross rent (dol.)	Gross rent as a percent of household income in the past 12 months [2]			
		$299 or less	$300 to $499	$500 to $749	$750 to $999	$1,000 or more		Less than 15.0 percent	15.0 to 24.9 percent	25.0 to 29.0 percent	30.0 percent or more
U.S.........	39,694	5.0	8.6	23.2	23.1	34.6	855	10.4	22.3	10.7	48.9
AL.............	542	6.8	15.2	32.6	20.5	13.7	667	10.2	20.2	9.3	46.7
AK.............	92	2.6	5.2	12.9	25.1	42.1	981	11.4	23.8	10.7	41.5
AZ.............	811	2.4	7.7	27.2	25.2	32.6	844	9.7	22.9	10.6	49.1
AR.............	363	6.3	16.9	37.7	18.6	9.8	638	12.0	21.3	10.6	43.3
CA.............	5,503	2.8	3.5	10.3	19.5	60.8	1,163	8.4	21.3	11.0	54.4
CO.............	668	4.0	6.1	24.8	26.6	34.5	863	10.0	23.5	11.3	49.0
CT.............	435	6.0	5.4	12.5	25.0	47.3	992	9.7	22.4	11.6	50.5
DE.............	89	4.3	5.7	13.3	29.7	42.0	952	7.6	22.7	11.1	50.9
DC.............	145	6.5	4.8	9.7	17.1	58.7	1,198	10.7	25.6	9.9	47.5
FL.............	2,241	3.4	4.1	17.6	28.1	41.5	947	6.6	19.3	10.5	55.6
GA.............	1,178	4.5	8.4	25.5	27.7	27.4	819	9.7	21.4	10.1	49.0
HI.............	187	3.6	3.4	7.9	14.4	63.9	1,291	8.8	21.5	9.7	51.3
ID.............	175	6.0	14.2	35.7	23.2	14.1	683	11.1	23.9	10.2	46.9
IL.............	1,534	5.0	8.4	22.8	28.1	31.4	848	10.7	23.2	9.9	48.8
IN.............	734	5.9	12.7	38.4	24.0	12.4	683	10.9	22.8	10.5	46.7
IA.............	338	6.6	19.3	38.0	18.4	11.0	629	15.6	24.2	10.0	42.3
KS.............	352	6.0	16.1	34.0	20.6	17.2	682	12.8	26.3	11.1	41.8
KY.............	528	9.0	18.5	35.2	17.5	10.3	613	12.3	22.1	10.2	43.7
LA.............	548	6.1	11.8	28.8	23.9	19.3	736	11.3	20.4	9.0	46.4
ME.............	149	10.7	11.8	29.1	23.8	17.2	707	10.8	23.2	12.2	45.1
MD.............	701	5.0	3.9	9.4	18.9	58.9	1,131	9.0	23.9	12.8	48.7
MA.............	952	8.6	7.2	12.6	19.2	48.8	1,009	11.2	22.6	12.6	47.8
MI.............	1,037	6.0	11.0	33.1	24.7	19.6	730	9.9	20.4	10.1	51.2
MN.............	564	7.8	11.2	27.2	24.4	24.9	764	10.9	23.6	12.2	47.5
MS.............	327	8.0	15.2	29.7	22.5	12.1	672	9.3	18.7	9.7	47.0
MO.............	729	6.5	15.3	34.7	21.7	15.2	682	11.4	23.0	11.2	45.8
MT.............	122	7.0	18.0	32.4	18.3	12.8	642	13.7	22.8	10.9	39.9
NE.............	235	5.5	16.6	35.8	21.7	13.5	669	14.5	25.5	10.4	41.0
NV.............	424	1.9	3.7	19.2	28.2	43.7	952	9.4	24.5	10.5	50.3
NH.............	146	4.9	5.3	14.4	29.0	42.1	951	9.8	23.4	13.1	47.7
NJ.............	1,066	4.6	4.2	8.5	20.8	58.7	1,114	10.2	22.6	10.5	51.5
NM.............	245	5.9	14.7	31.2	20.8	18.5	699	11.8	22.7	10.9	42.4
NY.............	3,292	5.7	7.1	15.8	18.4	49.7	1,020	12.2	21.8	10.2	50.2
NC.............	1,205	5.1	11.0	32.8	24.7	19.0	731	10.4	22.6	10.1	47.2
ND.............	93	8.5	21.8	38.4	14.8	7.9	583	19.0	24.2	10.6	36.2
OH.............	1,430	6.3	13.4	36.9	23.9	14.1	685	11.1	22.9	10.3	47.9
OK.............	462	5.7	15.3	36.9	19.6	12.7	659	12.7	23.1	10.6	41.8
OR.............	564	4.0	6.9	28.1	28.8	27.9	816	8.5	23.0	11.5	51.2
PA.............	1,474	6.9	11.3	27.0	24.1	24.2	763	11.5	22.6	10.9	46.3
RI.............	158	10.2	7.8	15.8	29.1	32.8	868	9.0	22.2	13.6	48.1
SC.............	551	5.0	11.0	31.8	24.5	17.4	728	10.7	20.5	9.4	47.2
SD.............	102	10.4	21.4	33.0	16.1	9.8	591	16.1	24.2	11.8	37.2
TN.............	778	6.8	12.8	32.8	23.4	15.3	697	9.6	21.6	10.8	46.7
TX.............	3,183	3.8	7.7	28.8	27.2	26.6	801	11.4	24.0	10.4	46.3
UT.............	265	3.9	9.1	28.6	26.9	26.6	796	12.2	24.8	11.0	45.8
VT.............	76	7.6	7.7	22.2	30.8	25.8	823	8.6	21.4	12.2	49.9
VA.............	967	4.2	6.2	15.2	20.2	48.2	1,019	10.7	23.3	11.8	46.6
WA.............	962	4.2	6.2	20.5	26.3	38.9	908	10.6	24.2	11.5	48.4
WV.............	189	9.8	20.6	35.1	12.4	6.3	571	15.6	17.6	8.1	40.2
WI.............	713	5.0	12.7	35.5	26.0	16.5	715	11.0	25.5	11.1	46.5
WY.............	68	5.4	15.1	29.0	21.0	16.8	693	16.0	26.3	9.2	34.3

[1] Includes units with no cash rent. [2] Does not include units "not computed."

Source: U.S. Census Bureau, 2010 American Community Survey, B25063, "Gross Rent;" B25064, "Median Gross Rent;" and B25070, "Gross Rent as a Percentage of Household Income;" <http://factfinder.census.gov>, accessed August 2012.

Table 1011. Mortgage Characteristics—Owner-Occupied Units: 2009

[In thousands (76,428 represents 76,428,000). As of fall. Based on the American Housing Survey; see Appendix III]

Mortgage characteristic	Total owner occupied units (1,000)	Housing unit characteristics		Household characteristics			
		New construction[1]	Mobile homes	Black[2]	Hispanic[3]	Elderly[4]	Below poverty level
ALL OWNERS							
Total............................	**76,428**	**3,830**	**5,418**	**6,547**	**6,439**	**18,472**	**6,405**
Mortgages currently on property:[5]							
None, owned free and clear..............	24,206	499	3,237	2,073	1,752	12,071	3,466
Regular and home equity mortgages[6]............	50,300	3,251	2,107	4,338	4,525	5,804	2,710
Regular mortgage..................	46,703	3,174	2,002	4,153	4,325	4,604	2,509
Home equity lump sum mortgage........	4,022	154	57	241	300	522	156
Home equity line of credit........	9,184	297	106	426	579	1,527	334
Number of regular and home equity mortgages:							
1 mortgage............................	35,274	2,391	1,830	3,329	3,307	4,322	1,940
2 mortgages..........................	10,896	621	98	646	928	833	321
3 mortgages or more..................	801	20	2	43	67	76	25
Type of mortgage:							
Regular and home equity lump sum..................	2,779	131	20	152	215	189	76
With home equity line of credit............	429	11	2	16	40	52	10
No home equity line of credit............	2,341	120	17	135	173	137	65
Regular no home equity lump sum........	43,923	3,043	1,982	4,001	4,110	4,415	2,433
With home equity line of credit............	6,153	230	36	294	407	527	189
No home equity line of credit............	34,513	2,594	1,773	3,390	3,486	3,330	1,835
Home equity lump sum no regular..................	1,243	22	37	89	85	333	80
With home equity line of credit............	248	2	–	20	17	80	14
No home equity line of credit............	989	20	37	69	68	252	67
No regular or home equity lump sum........	28,483	634	3,379	2,305	2,029	13,535	3,816
With home equity line of credit............	2,355	54	68	96	115	867	121
No home equity line of credit............	24,458	501	3,247	2,089	1,776	12,312	3,502
OWNERS WITH ONE OR MORE REGULAR OR LUMP SUM HOME EQUITY MORTGAGES							
Total..................	**47,945**	**3,197**	**2,039**	**4,242**	**4,410**	**4,936**	**2,589**
Type of primary mortgage:							
FHA...............................	6,272	457	112	1,038	801	443	352
VA................................	3,660	273	207	316	312	356	140
RHS/RD...........................	435	63	36	51	51	49	41
Other types.......................	34,021	2,161	1,490	2,449	3,001	3,463	1,603
Mortgage origination:							
Placed new mortgage(s)....................	47,616	3,188	2,007	4,212	4,344	4,891	2,556
Primary obtained when property acquired.........	35,884	3,005	1,744	3,436	3,570	3,010	2,075
Obtained later........................	11,733	183	263	776	773	1,881	481
Assumed...............................	259	8	28	19	51	40	25
Wrap-around...........................	27	–	4	4	8	–	3
Combination of the above...............	43	–	–	7	8	5	6
Payment plan of primary mortgage:							
Fixed payment, self amortizing.....................	40,055	2,664	1,713	3,472	3,686	3,820	1,861
Adjustable rate mortgage................	1,942	80	58	201	238	187	97
Adjustable term mortgage................	80	14	3	3	5	26	15
Graduated payment mortgage........................	523	48	–	48	62	26	17
Balloon...............................	220	10	14	5	16	21	13
Combination of the above...............	169	9	–	9	14	21	5
Payment plan of secondary mortgage:							
Units with two or more mortgages...................	5,520	418	67	404	601	309	159
Fixed payment, self amortizing.....................	4,514	359	58	342	482	221	117
Adjustable rate mortgage................	393	15	–	32	53	32	16
Adjustable term mortgage................	71	1	–	1	3	15	3
Graduated payment mortgage........................	71	10	–	3	16	6	–
Balloon...............................	143	20	4	6	8	12	4
Other...............................	2	–	–	–	–	–	–
Combination of the above...............	101	9	–	–	4	1	6
Reason primary refinanced:							
Units with a refinanced primary mortgage[6].........	12,220	224	269	792	947	1,337	429
To get a lower interest rate......................	9,228	174	172	563	666	832	246
To increase payment period.................	180	4	9	4	16	6	11
To reduce payment period.................	573	5	9	25	40	37	19
To renew or extend a loan that has fallen due.....	123	3	2	7	15	20	8
To receive cash.................................	1,587	16	32	147	153	265	72
Other reason..........................	1,655	32	58	96	170	211	65
Cash received in primary mortgage refinance:							
Units receiving refinance cash....................	1,587	16	32	147	153	265	72
Median amount received (dol.).....................	30,000	(B)	(B)	18,000	40,000	50,000	25,000

– Represents or rounds to zero. B means sample too small. [1] Constructed in the past 4 years. [2] For persons who selected this race group only. See footnote 3, Table 1004. [3] Persons of Hispanic origin may be any race. [4] 65 years old and over. [5] Regular mortgages include all mortgages not classified as home-equity or reverse. [6] Figures may not add to total because more than one category may apply to a unit.

Source: U.S. Census Bureau, Current Housing Reports, Series H150/09, *American Housing Survey for the United States: 2009*, March 2011. See also <http://www.census.gov/housing/ahs/>.

Table 1012. Home Purchase Loans by Race and Sex: 2010

[Amount in millions of dollars (446,031 represents $446,031,000,000). Data is the final 2010 National Aggregates data]

Race and Gender [1,2,3]	Applications received Number	Applications received Amount (million dollars)	Loans originated Number	Loans originated Amount (million dollars)	Applications approved not accepted Number	Applications approved not accepted Amount (million dollars)	Applications denied Number	Applications denied Amount (million dollars)	Applications withdrawn Number	Applications withdrawn Amount (million dollars)	Files closed for incompleteness Number	Files closed for incompleteness Amount (million dollars)
Total	2,144,030	446,031	1,373,480	301,102	151,954	29,209	367,657	58,572	203,527	46,143	47,412	11,005
White	1,602,220	315,933	1,058,849	219,212	110,896	19,881	258,893	39,420	142,734	30,739	30,848	6,682
Male	510,670	95,932	320,238	63,054	37,239	6,332	94,241	14,164	47,689	10,003	11,263	2,379
Female	335,272	49,789	211,486	33,591	23,516	3,039	63,527	7,206	29,863	4,851	6,880	1,102
Joint (male/female)	752,653	169,435	525,255	122,146	49,712	10,422	100,369	17,927	64,758	15,772	12,559	3,167
Black	82,119	10,302	34,153	5,153	7,556	760	31,487	3,025	6,942	1,054	1,981	309
Male	27,017	3,491	11,517	1,727	2,479	259	9,799	1,004	2,525	394	697	108
Female	35,832	3,821	14,393	1,825	3,034	265	14,547	1,230	3,010	383	848	118
Joint (male/female)	18,780	2,928	8,148	1,586	1,979	232	6,860	764	1,367	266	426	81
Asian	163,229	46,595	107,117	30,977	11,991	3,527	22,806	5,921	16,531	4,777	4,784	1,393
Male	63,762	17,003	41,089	11,082	4,949	1,377	9,163	2,224	6,488	1,743	2,073	576
Female	36,383	8,469	23,420	5,535	2,683	635	5,594	1,200	3,546	824	1,140	275
Joint (male/female)	62,583	20,981	42,373	14,293	4,294	1,496	7,972	2,477	6,407	2,184	1,537	531
Native Hawaiian/Other Pacific Islander	5,779	1,203	3,307	738	426	83	1,220	202	660	143	166	37
Male	2,358	460	1,288	278	188	33	527	78	290	55	65	16
Female	1,565	275	887	167	112	17	353	51	164	32	49	8
Joint (male/female)	1,809	460	1,105	288	125	33	328	71	201	55	50	13
American Indian/Alaska Native	11,737	1,516	4,668	707	1,177	118	3,875	378	1,777	271	240	42
Male	4,544	613	1,768	285	448	47	1,496	152	711	108	121	20
Female	3,511	383	1,256	169	381	31	1,351	113	455	62	68	8
Joint (male/female)	2,921	448	1,157	209	317	37	914	104	484	84	49	13
Two or more minority races	894	196	475	117	58	12	242	43	98	21	21	3
Male	324	70	174	37	23	5	79	17	43	10	5	1
Female	318	54	149	32	20	3	105	13	31	4	13	2
Joint (male/female)	242	70	149	47	14	4	54	12	23	7	2	-
Joint [4]	29,742	8,058	19,478	5,639	2,223	528	4,730	927	2,688	773	623	191
Race not available [5]	248,310	62,228	145,433	38,560	17,627	4,301	44,404	8,655	32,097	8,366	8,749	2,347
Male	32,926	7,770	17,132	4,470	2,589	517	7,402	1,364	4,588	1,113	1,215	306
Female	20,465	3,708	10,518	2,141	1,555	256	5,092	684	2,690	508	610	119
Joint (male/female)	41,968	12,126	25,678	7,841	2,938	797	6,745	1,568	5,394	1,578	1,213	340

- Rounds to zero. [1] Applicants are shown in only one race category. [2] Total includes those cases in which gender was reported and that information was not available. [3] Applicants are shown in only one gender category. [4] "Joint" means with two applicants, one reported a single designation of "White" and the other applicant reports one or more minority racial designations. [5] "Not Available" includes situations in which information was reported as not provided or not applicable.

Source: Federal Financial Institutions Examination Council, "HMDA National Aggregate Report," annual, <http://www.ffiec.gov/Hmda/default.htm>.

Table 1013. Occupied Housing Units—Neighborhood Indicators by Selected Characteristics of the Householder: 2009

[In thousands (111,806 represents 111,806,000). As of fall. Based on the American Housing Survey; see Appendix III]

Characteristic	Total occu-pied units	Tenure Owner	Tenure Renter	Black [1] Owner	Black [1] Renter	Hispanic origin [2] Owner	Hispanic origin [2] Renter	Elderly [3] Owner	Elderly [3] Renter	Households below poverty level Owner	Households below poverty level Renter
Total units............................	**111,806**	**76,428**	**35,378**	**6,547**	**7,446**	**6,439**	**6,300**	**18,472**	**4,623**	**6,405**	**9,334**
Street noise or traffic present: Bothersome street noise or heavy traffic present [4]..............	111,806	76,428	35,378	6,547	7,446	6,439	6,300	18,472	4,623	6,405	9,334
Yes..................................	25,381	15,223	10,158	1,639	2,460	1,419	1,725	3,497	1,077	1,549	3,110
No...................................	85,122	60,264	24,858	4,836	4,895	4,972	4,545	14,744	3,498	4,692	6,119
Neighborhood crime present: Serious crime in past 12 months...............................	111,806	76,428	35,378	6,547	7,446	6,439	6,300	18,472	4,623	6,405	9,334
Yes..................................	19,299	11,649	7,650	1,428	2,045	1,223	1,403	2,105	658	951	2,254
No...................................	90,116	63,230	26,886	4,958	5,146	5,129	4,814	15,983	3,853	5,194	6,813
Odors present: Bothersome smoke, gas, or bad smell [4].............................	111,806	76,428	35,378	6,547	7,446	6,439	6,300	18,472	4,623	6,405	9,334
Yes..................................	5,434	3,278	2,156	330	614	367	359	663	164	389	727
No...................................	105,015	72,168	32,847	6,142	6,749	6,024	5,907	17,567	4,408	5,843	8,505
Other problems: Noise................................	2,950	1,733	1,217	176	296	165	217	382	95	156	340
Litter or housing deterioration......	1,691	1,101	590	196	203	85	127	266	43	121	213
Poor city or county services........	694	440	254	80	101	49	37	70	21	72	89
People...............................	4,521	2,706	1,815	298	460	269	297	510	115	249	630
Public transportation: [4] With public transportation..........	60,257	35,616	24,641	3,719	5,856	3,998	4,996	8,283	3,245	2,815	6,562
Household uses public transpor-tation regularly for commuting to school or work....................	10,212	3,817	6,395	720	1,959	569	1,682	582	564	308	2,089
Household does not use public transportation regularly for com-muting to school or work..........	49,681	31,606	18,075	2,963	3,838	3,411	3,285	7,679	2,670	2,473	4,427
No public transportation.............	48,532	38,848	9,684	2,689	1,438	2,309	1,217	9,728	1,236	3,337	2,522
Not reported........................	3,017	1,964	1,053	138	152	132	88	461	142	254	250
Police protection: Satisfactory..........................	101,373	69,633	31,740	5,837	6,325	5,742	5,623	16,929	4,294	5,501	8,025
Unsatisfactory.......................	7,356	4,800	2,556	516	835	568	543	1,051	193	608	990
Secured communities: [5] Community access secured with walls or fences.....................	10,759	5,337	5,422	367	1,371	656	1,336	1,512	827	440	1,392
Community access not secured.......................	100,124	70,410	29,714	6,124	6,028	5,736	4,930	16,783	3,758	5,831	7,865
Secured multiunits: Multiunit access secured...........	7,211	1,357	5,854	106	1,301	135	998	454	1,426	118	1,503
Multiunit access not secured.......	16,741	2,151	14,590	216	3,406	237	2,749	608	1,567	163	4,129
Senior citizen communities: Households with persons 55 years old and over..............	45,684	36,591	9,093	3,132	1,842	2,451	1,255	18,472	4,623	3,763	2,645
Community age restricted [6].......	3,080	1,457	1,624	89	300	71	169	1,079	1,374	194	588
Access to structure: Enter building from outside [4,7].....	25,915	3,734	22,181	351	5,056	401	4,212	1,142	3,314	321	6,136
Use of steps not required.........	9,771	1,532	8,239	91	1,915	186	1,519	565	1,780	149	2,386
Use of steps required.............	16,136	2,201	13,935	260	3,141	216	2,690	577	1,529	172	3,750
Enter home from outside [8]........	85,891	72,694	13,197	6,196	2,391	6,038	2,089	17,330	1,309	6,084	3,198
Use of steps not required.........	38,011	32,654	5,357	2,706	951	3,354	950	8,253	551	2,668	1,231
Use of steps required.............	47,752	39,928	7,824	3,487	1,439	2,681	1,139	9,048	751	3,406	1,956
Community quality: Some or all activities present......	49,962	33,117	16,845	2,570	3,392	2,547	2,647	8,356	2,731	2,468	4,197
Community center or clubhouse........................	24,410	14,707	9,703	1,181	2,078	1,127	1,347	4,306	1,888	1,177	2,346
Golf in the community.............	16,709	12,762	3,947	611	471	694	499	3,410	604	832	880
Trails in the community...........	21,609	15,300	6,309	983	1,017	1,099	876	3,509	826	981	1,369
Shuttle bus.......................	9,933	5,718	4,215	422	702	536	713	2,033	1,258	482	1,161
Daycare...........................	15,883	10,633	5,249	1,157	1,297	795	934	2,392	546	822	1,568
Private or restricted beach, park, or shoreline...............	21,432	15,124	6,308	925	1,053	1,158	1,145	3,327	731	964	1,466
Trash, litter, or junk on street: [9] None..............................	99,010	69,415	29,595	5,639	5,764	5,752	5,211	17,001	4,172	5,507	7,264
Minor accumulation................	7,250	3,491	3,759	505	1,064	342	738	673	283	396	1,366
Major accumulation................	2,519	1,426	1,093	201	351	193	235	318	72	187	437

[1] For persons who selected this race group only. See footnote 3, Table 1004. [2] Persons of Hispanic origin may be of any race. [3] Householders 65 years old and over. [4] Includes those not reporting. [5] Public access is restricted (walls, gates, private security). [6] At least one family member must be 55 years old or older. [7] Restricted to multiunits. [8] Restricted to single units. [9] Or on any properties within 300 feet.

Source: U.S. Census Bureau, Current Housing Reports, Series H150/09, *American Housing Survey for the United States: 2009*, March 2011. See also <http://www.census.gov/housing/ahs/>.

Table 1014. Heating Equipment and Fuels for Occupied Units: 1995 to 2009

[97,693 represents 97,693,000. As of fall. Based on American Housing Survey. See Appendix III]

Type of equipment or fuel	Number (1,000)					Percent distribution	
	1995	2003 [1]	2005	2007	2009	2007	2009
Occupied units, total..	97,693	105,842	108,871	110,692	111,806	100.0	100.0
Heating equipment:							
Warm air furnace..	53,165	65,380	68,275	69,582	71,141	62.9	63.6
Steam or hot water......................................	13,669	13,257	12,880	12,760	12,506	11.5	11.2
Heat pumps..	9,406	11,347	12,484	12,996	13,264	11.7	11.9
Built-in electric units....................................	7,035	4,760	4,699	4,802	4,761	4.3	4.3
Floor, wall, or pipeless furnace.......................	4,963	5,322	5,102	4,994	4,802	4.5	4.3
Room heaters with flue.................................	1,620	1,432	1,294	1,135	950	1.0	0.8
Room heaters without flue..............................	1,642	1,509	1,327	1,188	1,109	1.1	1.0
Fireplaces, stoves, portable heaters or other...........	5,150	2,396	2,411	2,756	2,887	2.5	2.6
None...	1,044	439	399	478	386	0.4	0.3
House main heating fuel:							
Electricity..	26,771	32,341	34,263	36,079	37,851	32.6	33.9
Utility gas...	49,203	54,928	56,317	56,681	56,806	51.2	50.8
Bottled, tank, or LP gas................................	4,251	6,134	6,228	6,095	5,817	5.5	5.2
Fuel oil, kerosene, etc..................................	12,029	10,136	9,929	9,317	8,813	8.4	7.9
Coal or coke...	210	126	95	91	98	(Z)	0.1
Wood and other fuel.....................................	4,186	1,735	1,640	1,487	2,035	1.3	1.8
None...	1,042	441	398	464	386	0.4	0.3
Cooking fuel:							
Electricity..	57,621	62,859	65,297	66,276	67,078	59.9	60.0
Gas [2]...	39,218	42,612	43,316	44,194	44,477	39.9	39.8
Other fuel...	566	62	51	26	68	(Z)	0.1
None...	287	309	206	17	183	(Z)	0.2

Z Less than 0.05 percent. [1] Based on 2000 census controls. [2] Includes utility, bottled, tank, and LP gas.

Source: U.S. Census Bureau, Current Housing Reports, Series H150/09, *American Housing Survey for the United States: 2009*, March 2011. See also <http://www.census.gov/housing/ahs/>.

Table 1015. Occupied Housing Units—Housing Indicators by Selected Characteristics of the Householder: 2009

[In thousands of units (111,806 represents 111,806,000) As of fall. Based on the American Housing Survey; see Appendix III]

Characteristic	Total occu-pied units (1,000)	Tenure		Black [1]		Hispanic origin [2]		Elderly [3]		Households below poverty level	
		Owner	Renter	Owner	Renter	Owner	Renter	Owner	Renter	Owner	Renter
Total units...........................	111,806	76,428	35,378	6,547	7,446	6,439	6,300	18,472	4,623	6,405	9,334
Amenities:											
Porch, deck, balcony or patio..........	95,406	70,421	24,984	5,668	5,049	5,732	4,066	16,876	2,836	5,690	6,164
Telephone available....................	109,325	75,129	34,196	6,388	7,114	6,329	6,123	18,286	4,498	6,245	8,933
Usable fireplace........................	38,998	34,458	4,540	2,207	659	2,222	625	7,563	314	1,799	626
Separate dining room...................	53,676	43,717	9,959	3,975	2,298	3,372	1,780	10,171	1,012	2,982	2,163
rooms or rec. rooms....................	33,912	30,978	2,934	2,156	421	1,773	298	6,842	250	1,444	350
Garage or carport with home...........	74,236	60,979	13,258	4,257	1,937	5,030	2,382	14,988	1,563	4,275	2,592
Cars and trucks available:											
No cars, trucks, or vans...............	8,738	2,069	6,669	400	2,141	159	1,238	1,251	1,834	743	3,203
Other households without cars........	13,421	9,006	4,415	609	674	934	974	1,789	340	999	1,082
1 car with or without trucks or vans...	52,458	35,040	17,418	3,111	3,523	2,663	2,824	10,616	2,095	3,352	4,121
2 cars..................................	28,103	22,384	5,719	1,842	951	1,843	1,027	3,935	320	1,081	791
3 or more cars.........................	9,085	7,929	1,157	584	156	839	236	882	35	231	136
Selected deficiencies:											
Signs of rats in last 3 months.........	613	354	258	36	87	58	82	96	15	59	90
Signs of mice in last 3 months........	6,122	3,984	2,138	356	549	239	464	915	225	445	689
Holes in floors.........................	1,141	581	560	78	177	61	116	115	42	119	223
Open cracks or holes..................	5,517	3,101	2,416	383	617	288	402	496	149	433	862
Paint (interior of unit).................	2,378	1,246	1,132	189	306	101	210	269	74	183	423
No electrical wiring....................	84	57	26	–	2	10	7	2	2	11	4
Exposed wiring........................	355	221	134	37	31	23	27	52	27	34	46
Rooms without electric outlet........	1,274	650	624	88	187	58	121	151	56	86	232
Water leakage from inside structure [4].....................	9,007	5,170	3,836	480	958	443	620	861	262	424	1,059
Water leakage from outside structure [4]...................	10,963	7,842	3,121	808	667	562	434	1,548	230	746	874

– Represents or rounds to zero. [1] For persons who selected this race group only. See footnote 3, Table 1004. [2] Persons of Hispanic origin may be any race. [3] Householders 65 years old and over. [4] During the 12 months prior to the survey.

Source: U.S. Census Bureau, Current Housing Reports, Series H150/09, *American Housing Survey for the United States: 2009*, March 2011. See also <http://www.census.gov/housing/ahs/>.

Table 1016. Home Remodeling—Number of Households With Work Done by Amount Spent: 2011

[In thousands, except percent (2,678 represents 2,678,000). As of fall 2011. For work done in the prior 12 months. Based on household survey and subject to sampling error; see source]

Remodeling project	Total households with work done [1]		Households with work done by outside contractor	Number of households by amount spent (dol.)		
	Number	Percent of households		Under $1,000	$1,000 to $2,999	Over $3,000
Conversion of garage/attic/basement into living space	2,678	1.16	782	591	624	722
Remodel bathroom	13,643	5.92	4,127	5,920	2,934	2,451
Remodel kitchen	8,646	3.75	2,755	2,626	1,735	2,653
Remodel bedroom	6,745	2.93	988	4,024	909	517
Convert room to home office	2,417	1.05	300	1,263	319	141
Convert room to home theater	652	0.28	91	138	108	111
Remodel other rooms	6,000	2.60	1,142	2,586	1,060	973
Add bathroom	1,481	0.64	389	305	331	336
Add/extend garage	789	0.34	284	72	134	262
Add other rooms—exterior addition	1,035	0.45	375	102	223	302
Add deck/porch/patio	5,852	2.54	2,384	1,723	1,602	1,511
Roofing	8,593	3.73	5,749	1,661	1,361	4,178
Siding—vinyl/metal	2,575	1.12	1,378	566	509	991
Aluminum windows	1,086	0.47	569	164	246	197
Clad-wood/wood windows	823	0.36	406	81	185	261
Vinyl windows	4,445	1.93	2,548	926	1,240	1,498
Ceramic tile floors	4,845	2.10	1,692	2,510	823	490
Hardwood floors	5,474	2.38	2,157	1,794	1,231	1,302
Laminate flooring	4,581	1.99	1,216	2,010	952	374
Vinyl flooring	3,008	1.31	707	1,748	234	111
Carpeting	7,452	3.23	4,432	2,885	2,096	1,078
Kitchen cabinets	3,763	1.63	1,078	1,069	709	989
Kitchen counter tops	4,276	1.86	2,105	1,285	1,017	1,054
Skylights	797	0.35	379	446	79	24
Exterior doors	5,286	2.29	1,914	3,175	654	218
Interior doors	3,826	1.66	935	2,376	338	118
Garage doors	2,933	1.27	1,674	1,011	826	228
Concrete or masonry work	3,906	1.70	2,036	1,205	943	900
Swimming pool—inground	681	0.30	268	25	24	330
Wall paneling	1,053	0.46	199	362	117	38
Ceramic wall tile	2,191	0.95	831	1,094	435	155

[1] Includes no response and amount unknown.

Source: GfK Mediamark Research & Intelligence, LLC, New York, NY, Top-Line Reports, (copyright), <http://www.gfkmri.com/>.

Table 1017. Home Improvement Loans by Race: 2010

[Applications in thousands (668.9 represents 668,903), amounts in millions of dollars (44,694.5 represents $44,694,515,000). Data is the final 2010 National Aggregates data]

Item	Unit	Total	White, total	Black, total	Asian, total	Joint, total [1]	Race not available, total [2]
Applications received							
Number	1,000	668.9	503.1	59.4	14.0	7.2	75.7
Amount	Mil. dol.	44,694.5	33,631.6	1,891.0	2,139.5	650.3	5,941.5
Loans originated							
Number	1,000	340.6	280.2	19.4	6.4	3.6	28.0
Amount	Mil. dol.	25,719.8	20,329.9	686.2	1,248.7	384.1	2,891.9
Applications approved but not accepted							
Number	1,000	26.9	20.8	1.8	0.7	0.3	29.7
Amount	Mil. dol.	20,673.9	1,544.3	80.7	119.4	35.8	263.7
Applications denied							
Number	1,000	244.2	161.7	34.5	5.2	2.5	34.7
Amount	Mil. dol.	10,722.8	7,506.2	862.9	441.9	142.2	1,598.7
Applications withdrawn							
Number	1,000	45.4	32.6	2.9	1.2	0.6	7.5
Amount	Mil. dol.	4,626.6	3,224.3	204.6	225.7	68.8	846.6
Files closed for incompleteness							
Number	1,000	11.8	7.8	0.7	0.4	0.2	2.5
Amount	Mil. dol.	1,557.9	1,026.9	57.2	103.7	19.5	340.5

[1] Joint means with two applicants, one applicant reports a single designation of "White" and the other applicant reports one or more minority racial designations. [2] "Not available" includes situation in which information was not provided or not applicable.

Source: Federal Financial Institutions Examination Council, "HMDA National Aggregate Report," annual. See also <http://www.ffiec.gov/Hmda/default.htm>.

Table 1018. Net Stock of Residential Fixed Assets: 1990 to 2010

[In billions of dollars (6,256 represents $6,256,000,000,000). End of year estimates]

Item	1990	1995	2000	2005	2006	2007	2008	2009	2010
Total residential fixed assets	**6,256**	**8,009**	**10,899**	**16,862**	**18,028**	**18,299**	**18,017**	**17,671**	**17,726**
By type of owner and legal form of organization:									
Private	6,107	7,821	10,668	16,530	17,682	17,956	17,685	17,346	17,397
Corporate	66	77	105	156	168	174	176	175	175
Noncorporate	6,041	7,743	10,563	16,374	17,514	17,782	17,508	17,171	17,222
Government	149	188	232	332	346	343	333	325	329
Federal	52	62	75	103	107	105	102	98	98
State and local	97	127	156	229	239	237	231	227	231
By tenure group: [1]									
Owner-occupied	4,512	5,975	8,327	13,276	14,229	14,445	14,195	13,918	13,984
Tenant-occupied	1,719	2,005	2,537	3,533	3,743	3,798	3,766	3,697	3,686

[1] Excludes stocks of other nonfarm residential assets, which consists primarily of dormitories, and of fraternity and sorority houses.

Source: U.S. Bureau of Economic Analysis, "Table 5.1 Current-Cost Net Stock of Residential Fixed Assets by Type of Owner, Legal Form of Organization, Industry, and Tenure Group," <http://www.bea.gov/iTable/index_FA.cfm>.

Table 1019. Commercial Buildings—Summary: 2003

[4,645 represents 4,645,000. Excludes mall buildings. Building type based on predominant activity in which the occupants were engaged. Based on a sample survey of building representatives conducted in 2003, therefore subject to sampling variability]

Characteristic	All buildings (1,000)	Total floor-space (mil. sq. ft)	Total workers in all buildings (1,000)	Mean square foot per building [1] (1,000)	Mean square foot per worker [1]	Mean operating hours per week [1]
All buildings	**4,645**	**64,783**	**72,807**	**13.9**	**890**	**61**
Building floorspace (sq. ft.):						
1,001 to 5,000	2,552	6,789	9,936	2.7	683	57
5,001 to 10,000	889	6,585	7,512	7.4	877	61
10,001 to 25,000	738	11,535	10,787	15.6	1,069	67
25,001 to 50,000	241	8,668	8,881	35.9	976	72
50,001 to 100,000	129	9,057	8,432	70.4	1,074	80
100,001 to 200,000	65	9,064	11,632	138.8	779	89
200,001 to 500,000	25	7,176	6,883	289.0	1,043	100
Over 500,000	7	5,908	8,744	896.1	676	115
Principal activity within building:						
Education	386	9,874	12,489	25.6	791	50
Food sales	226	1,255	1,430	5.6	877	107
Food service	297	1,654	3,129	5.6	528	86
Health care	129	3,163	6,317	24.6	501	59
Inpatient	8	1,905	3,716	241.4	513	168
Outpatient	121	1,258	2,600	10.4	484	52
Lodging	142	5,096	2,457	35.8	2,074	167
Retail (other than mall)	443	4,317	3,463	9.7	1,246	59
Office	824	12,208	28,154	14.8	434	55
Public assembly	277	3,939	2,395	14.2	1,645	50
Public order and safety	71	1,090	1,347	15.5	809	103
Religious worship	370	3,754	1,706	10.1	2,200	32
Service	622	4,050	3,667	6.5	1,105	55
Warehouse and storage	597	10,078	4,369	16.9	2,306	66
Other	79	1,738	1,819	21.9	956	63
Vacant	182	2,567	(NA)	14.1	(NA)	(NA)
Energy sources: [2]						
Electricity	4,404	63,307	72,708	14.4	871	62
Natural gas	2,391	43,468	51,956	18.2	837	65
Fuel oil	451	15,157	19,625	33.6	772	68
District heat	67	5,443	10,190	81.4	534	79
District chilled water	33	2,853	7,189	86.7	397	79
Propane	502	7,076	5,858	14.1	1,208	60
Wood	62	289	262	4.6	1,105	46

NA Not available. [1] For explanation of mean, see Guide to Tabular Presentation. [2] More than one type may apply.

Source: U.S. Energy Information Administration, *2003 Commercial Buildings Energy Consumption (CBECS)*, Detailed Tables, Table B1, <http://www.eia.gov/emeu/cbecs/cbecs2003/detailed_tables_2003/detailed_tables_2003.html>.

This section presents summary data for manufacturing as a whole and more detailed information for major industry groups and selected products. The types of measures shown at the different levels include data for establishments, employment and payroll, value and quantity of production and shipments, value added by manufacture, inventories, and various indicators of financial status.

The principal sources of these data are U.S. Census Bureau reports of the censuses of manufactures conducted every 5 years, the *Annual Survey of Manufactures*, and *Current Industrial Reports*. Reports on current activities of industries or current movements of individual commodities are compiled by such government agencies as the Bureau of Economic Analysis; Bureau of Labor Statistics; the Department of Commerce, International Trade Administration; and by private research or trade associations.

The Quarterly Financial Report publishes up-to-date aggregate statistics on the financial results and position of U.S. corporations. Based upon a sample survey, the QFR presents estimated statements of income and retained earnings, balance sheets, and related financial and operating ratios for manufacturing corporations with assets of $250,000 or over, and mining, wholesale trade and retail trade corporations with assets of $50 million and over or above industry-specific receipt cut-off values. These statistical data are classified by industry and by asset size.

Several private trade associations provide industry coverage for certain sections of the economy.

Censuses and annual surveys—The first census of manufactures covered the year 1809. Between 1809 and 1963, a census was conducted at periodic intervals. Since 1967, it has been taken every 5 years (for years ending in "2" and "7"). Results from the 2007 census are presented in this section utilizing the North American Industry Classification System (NAICS). For additional information see text, Section 15, Business Enterprise, and the Census Bureau Web site at <http://www.census.gov/econ/census07/>. Census data, either directly reported or estimated from administrative records, are obtained for every manufacturing plant with one or more paid employees.

The *Annual Survey of Manufactures* (ASM), conducted for the first time in 1949, collects data for the years between censuses for the more general measure of manufacturing activity covered in detail by the censuses. The annual survey data are estimates derived from a scientifically selected sample of establishments. The *Annual Survey of Manufactures* is a sample survey of approximately 50,000 establishments. A new sample is selected at 5-year intervals beginning the second survey year subsequent to the Economic Census—Manufacturing. Since 2009 is the second survey year following the 2007 Economic Census, a new sample was selected based on the 2007 Economic Census—Manufacturing. The sample was supplemented by new establishments entering business in 2007 and 2008.

In 2007, there were approximately 328,500 active manufacturing establishments. For sample efficiency and cost considerations, the 2007 manufacturing population is partitioned into two groups: (1) establishments eligible to be mailed a questionnaire and (2) establishments not eligible to be mailed a questionnaire.

Establishments and classification—Each of the establishments covered in the 2007 Economic Census—Manufacturing was classified in 1 of 480 industries (473 manufacturing industries and 7 former manufacturing industries) in accordance with the industry definitions in the 2007 NAICS manual. In the NAICS system, an industry is generally defined as a group of establishments that have similar production processes. To the extent practical, the system uses supply-based or production-oriented concepts in defining industries. The resulting group of establishments must be significant in terms of number, value added by manufacture, value of shipments, and number of employees. Establishments frequently make products classified both in their industry (primary products) and other industries (secondary products). Industry statistics (employment, payroll, value added by manufacture, value of shipments, etc.) reflect the activities of the establishments, which may make both primary and secondary products. Product statistics, however, represent the output of all establishments without regard for the classification of the producing establishment. For this reason, when relating the industry statistics, especially the value of shipments, to the product statistics, the composition of the industry's output should be considered.

Establishment—An establishment is a single physical location where business is conducted or where services or industrial operations are performed. Data in this sector includes those establishments where manufacturing is performed. A separate report is required for each manufacturing establishment (plant) with one employee or more that is in operation at any time during the year. An establishment not in operation for any portion of the year is requested to return the report form with the proper notation in the "Operational Status" section of the form. In addition, the establishment is requested to report data on any employees, capital expenditures, inventories, or shipment from inventories during the year.

Durable goods—Items with a normal life expectancy of 3 years or more. Automobiles, furniture, household appliances, and mobile homes are common examples.

Nondurable goods—Items which generally last for only a short time (3 years or less). Food, beverages, clothing, shoes, and gasoline are common examples.

Statistical reliability—For a discussion of statistical collection and estimation, sampling procedures, and measures of statistical reliability applicable to Census Bureau data, see Appendix III.

Table 1020. Gross Domestic Product in Current and Real (2005) Dollars by Industry: 2000 to 2011

[In billions of dollars (9,951.5 represents $9,951,500,000,000). Data include nonfactor charges (capital consumption allowances, indirect business taxes, etc.) as well as factor charges against gross product; corporate profits and capital consumption allowances have been shifted from a company to an establishment basis]

Industry	2002 NAICS code [1]	2000	2005	2008	2009	2010	2011
CURRENT DOLLARS							
Gross domestic product, total [2]	(X)	**9,951.5**	**12,623.0**	**14,291.5**	**13,939.0**	**14,526.5**	**15,094.0**
Private industries	(X)	8,736.1	11,037.1	12,437.1	12,018.1	12,558.0	13,097.4
Manufacturing	31–33	1,415.6	1,569.3	1,628.5	1,540.2	1,701.9	1,837.0
Durable goods	33, 321, 327	839.1	878.3	904.1	800.4	914.5	989.3
Wood products	321	28.3	33.0	24.5	20.4	22.3	(NA)
Nonmetallic mineral products	327	41.9	45.3	37.9	33.7	35.1	(NA)
Primary metals	331	46.3	53.8	59.8	37.4	43.2	(NA)
Fabricated metal products	332	120.7	120.5	131.3	113.8	120.6	(NA)
Machinery	333	110.5	109.5	125.0	111.4	139.7	(NA)
Computer and electronic products	334	172.1	183.5	208.4	209.5	264.9	(NA)
Electrical equipment, appliances, and components	335	44.1	39.9	49.6	51.2	44.2	(NA)
Motor vehicles, bodies and trailers, and parts	3361–63	117.4	112.5	68.1	28.8	54.8	(NA)
Other transportation equipment	3364–66, 69	65.8	76.3	91.1	89.6	71.7	(NA)
Furniture and related products	337	33.8	34.3	29.3	23.7	29.5	(NA)
Miscellaneous manufacturing	339	58.3	69.7	79.2	81.0	88.6	(NA)
Nondurable goods	31, 32 (except 321 and 327)	576.5	691.0	724.4	739.8	787.4	847.8
Food and beverage and tobacco products	311, 312	164.8	172.0	186.4	216.6	207.4	(NA)
Textile mills and textile product mills	313, 314	27.9	23.5	22.3	17.9	15.6	(NA)
Apparel and leather and allied products	315, 316	21.4	16.0	13.3	13.3	11.8	(NA)
Paper products	322	61.7	53.9	51.6	59.5	56.6	(NA)
Printing and related support activities	323	40.3	37.5	36.9	32.7	31.7	(NA)
Petroleum and coal products	324	43.6	139.3	150.0	102.1	171.8	(NA)
Chemical products	325	152.2	183.2	204.5	230.8	226.1	(NA)
Plastics and rubber products	326	64.6	65.7	59.4	66.8	66.5	(NA)
CHAINED (2005) DOLLARS							
Gross domestic product, total [2]	(X)	**11,216.4**	**12,623.0**	**13,161.9**	**12,703.1**	**13,088.0**	**13,315.1**
Private industries	(X)	9,786.2	11,037.1	11,468.5	10,964.5	11,354.6	11,554.6
Manufacturing	31–33	1,390.2	1,569.3	1,593.6	1,443.8	1,605.9	1,674.5
Durable goods	33, 321, 327	741.7	878.3	956.8	814.6	953.2	1,028.1
Wood products	321	32.8	33.0	32.7	27.7	29.6	(NA)
Nonmetallic mineral products	327	44.6	45.3	35.3	28.5	31.1	(NA)
Primary metals	331	62.1	53.8	41.7	44.3	39.5	(NA)
Fabricated metal products	332	129.5	120.5	120.3	91.4	103.4	(NA)
Machinery	333	111.4	109.5	121.3	95.9	125.3	(NA)
Computer and electronic products	334	78.0	183.5	294.8	306.4	403.3	(NA)
Electrical equipment, appliances, and components	335	42.6	39.9	45.2	42.1	37.5	(NA)
Motor vehicles, bodies and trailers, and parts	3361–63	93.6	112.5	86.7	23.8	51.5	(NA)
Other transportation equipment	3364–66, 69	78.5	76.3	88.2	82.0	66.1	(NA)
Furniture and related products	337	35.1	34.3	27.8	20.1	25.9	(NA)
Miscellaneous manufacturing	339	60.3	69.7	77.8	75.9	83.5	(NA)
Nondurable goods	31, 32 (except 321 and 327)	649.3	691.0	642.9	625.6	657.4	659.1
Food and beverage and tobacco products	311, 312	175.5	172.0	175.8	172.6	184.7	(NA)
Textile mills and textile product mills	313, 314	27.4	23.5	21.6	16.4	14.6	(NA)
Apparel and leather and allied products	315, 316	19.6	16.0	13.4	13.2	11.7	(NA)
Paper products	322	58.2	53.9	44.6	46.1	42.6	(NA)
Printing and related support activities	323	37.4	37.5	37.3	32.4	32.2	(NA)
Petroleum and coal products	324	74.1	139.3	121.7	106.7	139.3	(NA)
Chemical products	325	170.0	183.2	175.9	182.1	177.9	(NA)
Plastics and rubber products	326	65.7	65.7	54.0	55.3	56.3	(NA)

NA Not available. X Not applicable. [1] North American Industry Classification System, 2002; see text, Section 15. [2] Includes industries, not shown separately. For additional industries, see Table 682.

Source: U.S. Bureau of Economic Analysis, *Survey of Current Business*, May 2012. See also <http://www.bea.gov/industry/gdpbyind_data.htm>.

Table 1021. Manufacturing—Selected Industry Statistics by State: 2007

[13,333 represents 13,333,000. Based on the 2007 Economic Census and the 2007 Nonemployer Statistics. See Appendix III]

State	Employers				Nonemployers	
	Number of establishments	Number of employees (1,000)	Annual payroll (mil. dol.)	Sales, shipments, receipts or revenue (mil. dol.)	Number of establishments	Sales, shipments, receipts or revenue (mil. dol.)
U.S............	293,919	13,333	612,474	5,339,345	328,060	16,333
AL..............	4,928	272	11,352	112,859	4,369	204
AK..............	544	13	490	8,204	1,087	33
AZ..............	5,074	172	8,774	57,978	6,524	318
AR..............	3,088	185	6,518	60,736	2,683	128
CA..............	44,296	1,448	71,247	491,372	43,798	2,817
CO..............	5,288	138	6,790	46,332	6,882	284
CT..............	4,924	191	10,345	58,405	3,776	250
DE..............	673	35	1,760	25,680	596	36
DC..............	137	2	81	333	185	8
FL..............	14,324	355	15,227	104,833	19,505	1,203
GA..............	8,699	411	16,128	144,281	8,891	425
HI..............	984	14	511	8,799	2,075	95
ID..............	1,942	65	2,829	18,011	2,499	91
IL..............	15,704	664	31,716	257,761	10,347	531
IN..............	9,015	537	24,475	221,878	6,650	295
IA..............	3,802	223	9,526	97,592	3,031	117
KS..............	3,170	178	7,983	76,752	2,739	106
KY..............	4,165	247	10,773	119,105	3,874	181
LA..............	3,442	148	7,565	205,055	4,001	190
ME..............	1,825	59	2,524	16,363	2,652	95
MD..............	3,680	128	6,454	41,456	4,031	197
MA..............	7,737	289	15,712	86,429	6,215	315
MI..............	13,675	582	29,910	234,456	11,725	547
MN..............	7,951	341	15,999	107,563	7,516	291
MS..............	2,598	159	5,757	59,869	2,347	103
MO..............	6,886	295	12,997	110,908	5,987	259
MT..............	1,324	20	808	10,638	1,959	67
NE..............	1,984	100	3,789	40,158	1,499	55
NV..............	2,035	52	2,291	15,736	2,217	138
NH..............	2,104	82	4,196	18,592	2,287	101
NJ..............	9,250	311	16,399	116,608	6,503	433
NM..............	1,574	35	1,560	17,123	3,581	103
NY..............	18,629	534	24,268	162,720	18,163	933
NC..............	10,150	506	19,590	205,867	9,828	398
NC..............	767	26	991	11,350	626	21
OH..............	16,237	760	35,485	295,891	12,782	640
OK..............	3,964	142	5,971	60,681	4,099	210
OR..............	5,717	184	8,139	66,881	6,680	258
PA..............	15,406	651	29,433	234,840	14,146	767
RI..............	1,831	54	2,375	12,062	1,290	58
SC..............	4,335	242	10,061	93,977	3,821	174
SD..............	1,052	41	1,539	13,051	877	26
TN..............	6,752	369	15,166	140,448	6,427	306
TX..............	21,115	894	42,836	593,542	28,790	1,369
UT..............	3,368	123	5,508	42,432	3,856	171
VT..............	1,108	36	1,650	10,751	1,738	54
VA..............	5,777	277	12,170	92,418	5,084	201
WA..............	7,650	270	13,275	112,053	8,599	343
WV..............	1,413	60	2,646	25,081	1,363	44
WI..............	9,659	488	21,850	163,563	6,976	312
WY..............	596	12	574	8,835	884	32

Source: U.S. Census Bureau, "2007 Economic Census, Geographic Area Series, Detailed Statistics for the State: 2007," April 2010, <http://www.census.gov/econ/census07/>, and "Nonemployer Statistics," August 2009, <http://www.census.gov/econ/nonemployer/index.html>.

Table 1022. Manufacturing—Establishments, Employees, and Annual Payroll by Industry: 2009 and 2010

[(114,510 represents 114,510,000). Excludes most government employees, railroad employees, and self-employed persons. See Appendix III]

Industry	2007 NAICS code [1]	Establishments		Employees (1,000) [2]		Payroll (mil. dol.)	
		2009	2010	2009	2010	2009	2010
All industries, total...................	(X)	**7,433,465**	**7,396,628**	**114,510**	**111,970**	**4,855,545**	**4,940,983**
Manufacturing, total...............	**31–33**	**308,934**	**299,982**	**11,633**	**10,863**	**549,636**	**550,386**
Percent of all industries............	(X)	4.2	4.1	10.2	9.7	11.3	11.1
Food..........................	311	24,731	24,773	1,435	1,433	52,898	53,823
Beverage and tobacco products.......	312	4,222	4,646	146	140	7,279	7,141
Textile mills........................	313	2,679	2,514	122	109	4,142	4,034
Textile product mills................	314	6,557	6,262	118	111	3,534	3,483
Apparel manufacturing...............	315	7,688	7,206	133	121	3,221	3,059
Leather and allied products...........	316	1,246	1,191	29	27	890	915
Wood products.....................	321	15,142	14,387	386	350	12,381	11,985
Paper.............................	322	4,706	4,602	381	365	19,389	19,619
Printing and related support activities............................	323	30,526	29,118	550	500	21,259	20,244
Petroleum and coal products..........	324	2,281	2,246	100	100	8,283	8,444
Chemical...........................	325	13,138	12,923	759	722	49,740	49,760
Plastics and rubber products..........	326	13,351	12,969	693	668	27,687	28,728
Nonmetallic mineral products..........	327	16,319	15,864	380	344	16,273	15,731
Primary metal......................	331	4,753	4,667	378	352	18,511	20,069
Fabricated metal products.............	332	57,762	55,946	1,401	1,276	59,644	59,653
Machinery.........................	333	24,926	24,255	1,034	929	50,484	50,861
Computer and electronic products.....	334	13,544	13,270	965	878	65,073	63,158
Electrical equipment, appliance and components...........................	335	5,960	5,880	363	329	16,690	16,584
Transportation equipment..............	336	12,091	11,715	1,273	1,202	71,353	73,062
Furniture and related products........	337	18,572	17,468	388	349	12,965	12,234
Miscellaneous......................	339	28,740	28,080	597	558	27,941	27,799

X Not applicable. [1] North American Industry Classification System, 2007; see text, Section 15. [2] Covers full- and part-time employees who are on the payroll in the pay period including March 12.

Source: U.S. Census Bureau, "County Business Patterns," <http://www.census.gov/econ/cbp/>.

Table 1023. Manufacturing—Establishments, Employees, and Annual Payroll by State: 2010

[(10,863 represents 10,863,000). Excludes most government employees, railroad employees, and self-employed persons. Data are for North American Industry Classification System (NAICS), 2007, codes 31–33. See Appendix III]

State	Establishments	Employees (1,000) [1]	Payroll (mil. dol.)	State	Establishments	Employees (1,000) [1]	Payroll (mil. dol.)
United States.....	**299,982**	**10,863**	**550,386**	Missouri..............	6,222	239	10,957
Alabama...............	4,402	229	10,275	Montana..............	1,210	16	644
Alaska................	525	13	512	Nebraska..............	1,845	89	3,660
Arizona...............	4,356	137	7,883	Nevada...............	1,704	39	1,960
Arkansas..............	2,774	155	6,015	New Hampshire.....	1,894	68	3,962
California.............	38,937	1,144	66,259	New Jersey..........	8,088	235	13,985
Colorado..............	4,809	113	5,974	New Mexico..........	1,400	28	1,285
Connecticut...........	4,473	153	9,442	New York............	16,933	434	21,796
Delaware..............	601	28	1,613	North Carolina.......	8,963	400	17,172
District of Columbia...	89	1	62	North Dakota.......	738	22	919
Florida...............	12,616	272	12,961	Ohio................	14,729	599	30,299
Georgia..............	7,683	327	14,263	Oklahoma...........	3,625	119	5,464
Hawaii...............	844	12	449	Oregon.............	5,281	144	6,876
Idaho................	1,757	52	2,419	Pennsylvania........	14,167	543	26,931
Illinois...............	14,210	531	28,019	Rhode Island........	1,554	41	2,025
Indiana..............	8,222	420	20,570	South Carolina......	3,966	204	9,219
Iowa................	3,596	196	9,279	South Dakota........	1,007	39	1,529
Kansas..............	2,955	158	7,557	Tennessee..........	5,961	287	12,894
Kentucky............	3,778	203	9,113	Texas...............	19,593	731	38,849
Louisiana............	3,257	125	7,095	Utah................	3,150	107	5,246
Maine...............	1,630	50	2,280	Vermont.............	986	31	1,535
Maryland............	3,191	105	6,027	Virginia.............	5,313	235	11,433
Massachusetts.......	6,907	227	13,898	Washington.........	7,050	220	12,394
Michigan.............	12,378	445	24,135	West Virginia.......	1,299	52	2,480
Minnesota...........	7,377	287	14,839	Wisconsin...........	9,033	409	19,845
Mississippi...........	2,356	139	5,570	Wyoming............	548	10	516

[1] Covers full- and part-time employees who are on the payroll in the pay period including March 12.

Source: U.S. Census Bureau, "County Business Patterns," June 2012, <http://www.census.gov/econ/cbp/index.html\>.

Table 1024. Manufactures—Summary by Selected Industry: 2010

[10,567.4 represents 10,567,400. Based on the Annual Survey of Manufactures; see Appendix III]

Industry based on shipments	2007 NAICS code [1]	All employees			Production workers [2] (1,000)	Value added by manufactures [3] (mil. dol.)	Value of shipments [4] (mil. dol.)
		Number [2] (1,000)	Payroll				
			Total (mil. dol.)	Per employee (dol.)			
Manufacturing, total............................	31–33	**10,567.4**	**540,001**	**51,101**	**7,318.6**	**2,185,326**	**4,916,647**
Food [5]..	311	1,364.2	52,416	38,424	1,075.5	265,919	646,451
Grain and oil seed milling.........................	3112	50.0	2,837	56,716	37.1	28,675	82,999
Sugar and confectionery products..............	3113	61.7	2,718	44,077	46.7	14,321	28,963
Fruit and vegetable preserving and specialty food..........	3114	165.3	6,391	38,671	137.4	29,332	64,331
Dairy products....................................	3115	132.1	6,253	47,339	96.9	30,772	94,102
Animal slaughtering and processing............	3116	479.6	15,126	31,542	419.3	57,558	175,589
Bakeries and tortilla..............................	3118	247.6	9,142	36,926	169.0	36,015	58,888
Beverage and tobacco products..................	312	132.4	6,983	52,737	78.2	79,995	131,845
Beverage..	3121	118.7	6,049	50,950	67.8	47,083	92,860
Textile mills.......................................	313	107.7	3,909	36,310	88.6	12,742	29,109
Textile product mills..............................	314	108.9	3,510	32,217	84.4	9,931	21,818
Apparel..	315	104.5	2,844	27,226	84.1	6,836	13,643
Cut and sew apparel..............................	3152	81.2	2,198	27,064	65.3	5,062	10,359
Leather and allied products.......................	316	27.6	860	31,156	20.4	2,385	5,049
Wood products [5]..................................	321	329.6	11,767	35,703	264.5	29,013	69,957
Sawmills and wood preservation................	3211	73.2	2,908	39,727	60.8	8,357	22,209
Paper..	322	351.9	19,159	54,439	274.8	79,111	169,954
Pulp, paper, and paperboard mills...............	3221	110.1	7,509	68,226	87.7	40,706	79,324
Converted paper products........................	3222	241.9	11,650	48,166	187.1	38,405	90,630
Printing and related support activities...........	323	468.0	20,064	42,870	333.2	49,527	82,488
Petroleum and coal products.....................	324	99.2	8,422	84,876	65.1	95,099	627,572
Chemical [5].......................................	325	703.3	48,547	69,030	413.4	352,730	701,230
Basic chemical....................................	3251	139.5	10,409	74,614	86.6	89,127	225,898
Pharmaceutical and medicine....................	3254	229.8	18,543	80,682	112.4	132,036	185,759
Soap, cleaning compound, and toilet preparation..........	3256	90.6	4,959	54,738	57.2	45,979	86,707
Plastics and rubber products.....................	326	664.6	28,375	42,692	514.6	89,550	188,583
Plastics products.................................	3261	544.3	22,586	41,495	420.3	72,967	151,312
Rubber product...................................	3262	120.3	5,788	48,108	94.3	16,582	37,270
Nonmetallic mineral products.....................	327	336.2	15,483	46,050	258.8	49,500	90,781
Glass and glass product..........................	3272	75.5	3,730	49,380	59.2	11,510	20,713
Cement and concrete products...................	3273	155.7	6,892	44,279	120.2	20,156	39,430
Primary metal [5]..................................	331	353.7	19,826	56,056	278.8	83,479	231,185
Iron and steel mills and ferroalloy...............	3311	96.9	6,621	68,317	78.3	31,950	94,043
Foundries..	3315	114.6	5,413	47,245	93.5	14,853	27,100
Fabricated metal products [5].....................	332	1,242.9	58,590	47,140	907.5	157,786	295,187
Forging and stamping.............................	3321	99.5	4,845	48,712	73.5	13,189	29,235
Architectural and structural metals..............	3323	301.9	13,425	44,466	212.4	32,447	66,237
Machine shops, turned product and screw, nut, and bolt............	3327	318.7	15,334	48,117	241.5	34,363	54,534
Coating, engraving, heat treating, and allied activities........	3328	107.2	4,603	42,939	82.0	13,597	23,876
Machinery [5]......................................	333	930.3	50,469	54,251	590.4	155,977	317,694
Agriculture, construction, and mining machinery..........	3331	172.8	8,930	51,679	115.6	40,050	87,601
Industrial machinery..............................	3332	103.6	6,566	63,373	54.0	17,274	31,111
HVAC and commercial refrigeration equipment..........	3334	121.0	5,510	45,531	86.1	17,803	36,604
Metalworking machinery..........................	3335	127.9	6,836	53,432	91.0	14,068	23,353
Computer and electronic products [5]............	334	836.5	58,773	70,263	385.4	206,978	340,683
Computer and peripheral equipment............	3341	55.1	3,740	67,887	17.5	19,057	36,644
Communications equipment......................	3342	106.6	7,938	74,466	43.4	24,182	47,262
Semiconductor and other electronic component......	3344	278.2	16,501	59,302	170.6	78,205	117,071
Navigational, measuring, medical, and control instruments.....	3345	370.0	29,204	78,919	137.3	82,322	132,023
Electrical equipment, appliance, and component........	335	327.4	16,513	50,431	222.4	54,898	110,993
Electrical equipment..............................	3353	113.9	5,918	51,980	72.5	18,209	35,219
Other electrical equipment and component......	3359	125.7	6,669	53,065	82.2	23,070	46,503
Transportation equipment [5].....................	336	1,181.4	72,884	61,695	785.4	274,382	633,275
Motor vehicle.....................................	3361	135.9	9,206	67,747	113.9	67,484	207,543
Motor vehicle parts...............................	3363	388.7	19,541	50,278	293.0	67,019	168,297
Aerospace product and parts.....................	3364	383.8	30,352	79,074	192.3	101,628	171,618
Ship and boat building............................	3366	120.8	6,414	53,082	77.2	16,976	27,690
Furniture and related products [5]................	337	332.3	11,951	35,963	247.0	30,665	58,795
Miscellaneous [5]..................................	339	564.8	28,656	50,740	346.3	98,822	150,353
Medical equipment and supplies.................	3391	289.9	16,629	57,366	171.7	63,468	88,189

[1] North American Industrial Classification System, 2007; see text, Section 15. [2] Includes employment and payroll at administrative offices and auxiliary units. "All employees" represents the average of production workers plus all other employees for the payroll period ended nearest the 12th of March. "Production workers" represent the average of the employment for the payroll periods ended nearest the 12th of March, May, August, and November. [3] Adjusted value added; takes into account (a) value added by merchandising operations (that is, difference between the sales value and cost of merchandise sold without further manufacture, processing, or assembly), plus (b) net change in finished goods and work-in-process inventories between beginning and end of year. [4] Includes extensive and unmeasurable duplication from shipments between establishments in the same industry classification. [5] Includes industries not shown separately.

Source: U.S. Census Bureau, Annual Survey of Manufactures, "Statistics for Industry Groups and Industries: 2010 and 2009," <http://www.census.gov/manufacturing/asm/index.html>.

Table 1025. Manufactures—Summary by State: 2010

[10,567.4 represents 10,567,400. Data are for North American Industry Classification System (NAICS) 2007 codes 31–33. Sum of state totals may not add to U.S. total because U.S. and state figures were independently derived. See Appendix III]

State	All employees [1]			Production workers [1]		Value added by manufactures [2]		Value of shipments [3] (mil. dol.)
	Number (1,000)	Payroll		Number (1,000)	Wages (mil. dol.)	Total (mil. dol.)	Per production worker (dol.)	
		Total (mil. dol.)	Per employee (dol.)					
United States.............	**10,567.4**	**540,001**	**51,101**	**7,318.6**	**299,823**	**2,185,326**	**298,597**	**4,916,647**
Alabama......................	217.6	9,982	45,872	162.8	6,480	39,246	241,051	104,183
Alaska.......................	10.6	437	41,113	8.4	293	2,447	290,492	7,274
Arizona......................	128.8	7,755	60,235	72.6	3,112	26,231	361,461	48,257
Arkansas.....................	145.5	5,782	39,738	116.8	4,070	21,758	186,213	54,532
California....................	1,128.2	65,387	57,956	694.8	28,674	230,198	331,326	457,716
Colorado.....................	107.6	5,777	53,711	72.5	3,009	21,868	301,733	44,573
Connecticut..................	155.7	9,309	59,777	94.7	4,506	29,814	314,931	51,410
Delaware.....................	28.6	1,480	51,714	19.1	781	7,045	369,046	21,055
District of Columbia.........	1.3	56	41,895	0.8	35	136	162,118	216
Florida.......................	254.3	12,838	50,490	164.4	6,294	44,877	272,965	88,149
Georgia......................	314.8	13,896	44,142	240.1	8,697	60,441	251,732	131,815
Hawaii.......................	10.7	430	40,093	6.8	239	1,403	207,155	6,424
Idaho........................	50.2	2,220	44,183	38.0	1,416	12,069	317,328	21,740
Illinois.......................	539.2	28,107	52,124	367.2	15,148	103,657	282,296	240,920
Indiana.......................	415.3	20,534	49,442	309.7	13,283	95,336	307,786	207,530
Iowa.........................	183.3	8,737	47,657	132.6	5,175	39,932	301,143	89,232
Kansas.......................	148.0	7,362	49,744	104.3	4,407	27,997	268,448	77,479
Kentucky.....................	197.1	8,900	45,159	151.0	6,035	37,792	250,291	105,553
Louisiana....................	121.7	7,129	58,574	88.1	4,468	57,121	648,195	202,307
Maine........................	48.1	2,249	46,779	34.0	1,407	8,232	242,134	15,158
Maryland.....................	106.8	6,060	56,734	65.2	2,739	22,860	350,807	39,932
Massachusetts...............	226.2	13,329	58,922	138.6	6,113	44,047	317,811	78,157
Michigan.....................	438.3	23,316	53,200	313.8	14,319	85,629	272,890	195,079
Minnesota....................	288.0	14,708	51,063	189.6	7,520	49,208	259,505	107,280
Mississippi...................	129.0	5,340	41,412	99.9	3,493	20,256	202,817	54,168
Missouri......................	226.3	10,821	47,822	166.6	6,972	45,616	273,749	101,134
Montana......................	12.8	597	46,689	8.7	368	2,522	289,724	9,587
Nebraska.....................	88.1	3,662	41,569	67.1	2,470	16,851	251,122	44,806
Nevada.......................	39.3	2,049	52,181	25.5	968	7,575	297,128	13,742
New Hampshire...............	70.0	3,947	56,371	42.9	1,709	10,342	241,013	18,606
New Jersey...................	240.5	14,497	60,277	151.8	6,365	46,609	306,947	98,261
New Mexico..................	25.5	1,251	49,013	17.3	699	11,479	662,394	21,197
New York....................	421.6	21,770	51,640	277.9	11,009	81,642	293,814	150,027
North Carolina...............	388.5	16,760	43,146	291.3	10,395	92,942	319,081	177,658
North Dakota.................	20.4	889	43,638	15.4	577	3,794	247,087	10,308
Ohio.........................	586.7	29,718	50,653	422.9	18,069	110,783	261,960	263,667
Oklahoma....................	118.0	5,478	46,413	87.9	3,486	22,881	260,247	60,004
Oregon.......................	125.3	6,042	48,207	88.9	3,429	34,425	387,067	55,061
Pennsylvania.................	525.4	26,504	50,447	365.7	15,277	98,179	268,464	219,949
Rhode Island.................	37.4	1,985	53,080	24.4	978	5,422	222,118	10,813
South Carolina...............	190.6	8,866	46,523	143.3	5,736	34,567	241,172	81,894
South Dakota.................	37.3	1,560	41,770	27.5	967	5,261	191,262	13,180
Tennessee....................	277.3	12,622	45,519	202.2	7,666	56,774	280,741	124,090
Texas........................	693.6	36,877	53,170	475.6	20,747	188,200	395,713	560,696
Utah.........................	98.8	5,123	51,866	62.8	2,601	25,022	398,150	45,720
Vermont......................	27.9	1,494	53,530	17.3	692	4,663	268,954	10,203
Virginia......................	226.1	11,167	49,396	160.2	6,497	54,674	341,349	92,512
Washington..................	223.4	12,506	55,976	145.8	6,905	56,331	386,387	103,983
West Virginia.................	49.2	2,429	49,403	37.0	1,556	9,461	255,898	21,873
Wisconsin....................	414.3	19,767	47,709	301.1	11,664	67,251	223,334	149,622
Wyoming.....................	8.3	502	60,819	5.6	314	2,465	443,417	7,913

[1] Includes all full-time and part-time employees on the payrolls of operating manufacturing establishments during any part of the pay period that included the 12th of the month. Included are employees on paid sick leave, paid holidays, and paid vacations; not included are proprietors and partners of unincorporated businesses. [2] Value added is derived by subtracting the cost of materials, supplies, containers, fuel, purchased electricity, and contract work from the value of shipments (products manufactured plus receipts for services rendered). The result of this calculation is adjusted by the addition of value added by merchandising operations (i.e., the difference between the sales value and the cost of merchandise sold without further manufacture, processing, or assembly) plus the net change in finished goods and work-in-process between the beginning and end of year inventories. [3] Includes extensive and unmeasurable duplication from shipments between establishments in the same industry classification.

Source: U.S. Census Bureau, Annual Survey of Manufactures, "Geographic Area Statistics: 2009 and 2010," November 2011, <http://www.census.gov/manufacturing/asm/index.html>.

Table 1026. Manufacturing Industries—Employees by Industry: 1990 to 2011

[Annual averages of monthly figures (109,487 represents 109,487,000). Covers all full- and part-time employees who worked during, or received pay for, any part of the pay period including the 12th of the month. Minus sign (–) indicates decrease. See also head note, Table 644]

Industry	2007 NAICS code [1]	All employees (1,000)						Percent change	
		1990	2000	2005	2009	2010	2011	1990–2000	2000–2011
All industries...............................	(X)	**109,487**	**131,785**	**133,703**	**130,807**	**129,874**	**131,359**	**20.4**	**-0.3**
Manufacturing..............................	31–33	17,695	17,263	14,226	11,847	11,528	11,733	-2.4	-32.0
Percent of all industries.....................	(X)	16	13	11	9	9	9	(X)	(X)
Durable goods...........................	(X)	10,737	10,877	8,956	7,284	7,064	7,274	1.3	-33.1
Wood products [2].......................	321	541	613	561	360	342	335	13.4	-45.3
Sawmills & wood preservation.............	3211	148	134	119	83	82	84	-9.6	-37.2
Nonmetallic mineral products [2]............	327	528	554	505	394	371	367	4.9	-33.8
Cement & concrete products...............	3273	195	234	240	185	170	164	20.1	-29.7
Primary metals [2]........................	331	689	622	466	362	362	390	-9.7	-37.4
Iron & steel mills & ferroalloy production...	3311	187	135	96	85	87	94	-27.7	-30.7
Steel products from purchased steel.......	3312	70	73	61	50	52	57	4.0	-21.6
Alumina & aluminum production...........	3313	108	101	73	56	54	56	-7.3	-44.2
Foundries............................	3315	214	217	164	113	112	121	1.4	-44.2
Fabricated metal products [2]...............	332	1,610	1,753	1,522	1,312	1,282	1,344	8.9	-23.3
Architectural & structural metals............	3323	357	428	398	345	321	328	20.0	-23.4
Machine shops & threaded products.......	3327	309	365	345	309	313	341	18.4	-6.7
Coating, engraving, & heat treating metals.................................	3328	143	175	145	121	122	130	22.7	-25.9
Machinery [2].............................	333	1,410	1,457	1,166	1,029	996	1,057	3.3	-27.5
Agricultural, construction, & mining machinery.....................	3331	229	222	208	214	208	226	-2.8	1.7
HVAC & commercial refrigeration equipment............................	3334	165	194	154	129	125	131	17.9	-32.7
Metalworking machinery..................	3335	267	274	202	158	155	167	2.5	-39.2
Turbine & power transmission equipment..	3336	114	111	98	95	92	100	-2.4	-10.4
Other general purpose machinery.........	3339	336	344	269	237	226	240	2.4	-30.3
Computer & electronic products [2]...........	334	1,903	1,820	1,316	1,137	1,095	1,107	-4.3	-39.2
Computer & peripheral equipment.........	3341	367	302	205	166	158	159	-17.8	-47.3
Communications equipment..............	3342	223	239	141	121	117	115	7.0	-51.8
Semiconductors & electronic components...........................	3344	574	676	452	378	369	384	17.8	-43.2
Electronic instruments..................	3345	635	488	441	422	406	404	-23.2	-17.2
Electrical equipment & appliances [2].........	335	633	591	434	374	360	367	-6.7	-37.9
Electrical equipment....................	3353	244	210	152	145	136	139	-13.9	-33.7
Other electrical equipment & components........................	3359	195	191	136	121	119	125	-2.3	-34.8
Transportation equipment [2]...............	336	2,135	2,057	1,772	1,348	1,333	1,382	-3.6	-32.8
Motor vehicles.........................	3361	271	291	248	146	153	160	7.4	-45.2
Motor vehicle bodies & trailers..........	3362	130	183	171	104	107	114	40.8	-37.7
Motor vehicle parts.....................	3363	653	840	678	414	419	443	28.6	-47.2
Aerospace products & parts.............	3364	841	517	455	492	478	488	-38.5	-5.7
Ship & boat building....................	3366	174	154	154	131	125	121	-11.3	-21.7
Furniture & related products [2].............	337	604	683	566	384	357	353	13.0	-48.3
Household & institutional furniture.........	3371	401	443	381	243	223	220	10.6	-50.4
Miscellaneous manufacturing...............	339	686	728	647	584	567	573	6.2	-21.2
Medical equipment & supplies............	3391	283	305	300	307	303	309	7.7	1.2
Other miscellaneous manufacturing........	3399	403	423	347	278	264	265	5.1	-37.4
Nondurable goods.......................	(X)	6,958	6,386	5,271	4,564	4,464	4,460	-8.2	-30.2
Food manufacturing [2]...................	311	1,507	1,553	1,478	1,456	1,451	1,456	3.0	-6.2
Fruit & vegetable preserving & specialty...	3114	218	197	174	172	173	172	-9.5	-12.9
Dairy products.........................	3115	145	136	132	131	130	134	-5.9	-1.8
Animal slaughtering & processing..........	3116	427	507	504	497	489	488	18.6	-3.8
Bakeries & tortilla manufacturing..........	3118	292	306	280	273	277	281	4.9	-8.1
Beverages & tobacco products [2]............	312	218	207	192	187	183	188	-4.9	-9.1
Beverages............................	3121	173	175	167	169	167	172	1.2	-1.6
Textile mills [2].........................	313	492	378	218	124	119	121	-23.1	-68.1
Fabric mills...........................	3132	270	192	104	55	53	56	-29.0	-70.9
Textile product mills [2]....................	314	236	230	176	126	119	117	-2.5	-49.2
Textile furnishings mills.................	3141	127	129	96	62	57	55	1.3	-57.6
Apparel [2].............................	315	903	484	251	168	157	152	-46.4	-68.6
Cut & sew apparel......................	3152	750	380	193	132	124	124	-49.3	-67.5
Leather & allied products.................	316	133	69	40	29	28	29	-48.3	-57.5
Paper & paper products..................	322	647	605	484	407	395	391	-6.6	-35.3
Pulp, paper, & paperboard mills..........	3221	238	191	142	117	112	109	-19.7	-42.7
Converted paper products................	3222	409	413	343	290	282	282	1.1	-31.8
Printing & related support activities........	323	809	807	646	522	488	469	-0.2	-41.8
Petroleum & coal products...............	324	153	123	112	115	114	112	-19.4	-8.8
Chemicals [2]...........................	325	1,036	980	872	804	787	788	-5.3	-19.6
Basic chemicals.......................	3251	249	188	150	145	142	142	-24.4	-24.4
Pharmaceuticals & medicines.............	3254	207	274	288	284	277	273	32.4	-0.5
Soaps, cleaning compounds, and toiletries............................	3256	132	129	114	103	102	103	-2.4	-20.3
Plastics & rubber products [2]...............	326	825	951	802	625	625	636	15.3	-33.2
Plastics products......................	3261	618	737	634	502	502	509	19.2	-30.9
Rubber products.......................	3262	207	214	168	123	123	127	3.3	-40.8

X Not applicable. [1] Based on the North American Industry Classification System, 2007 (NAICS); see text, this section and Section 15. [2] Includes other industries, not shown separately.

Source: U.S. Bureau of Labor Statistics, Current Employment Statistics Program, "Employment, Hours, and Earnings—National," <http://www.bls.gov/ces/home.htm/>.

Table 1027. Manufacturing Industries—Average Weekly Hours and Average Weekly Overtime Hours of Production Workers: 1990 to 2011

[Covers all full- and part-time employees who worked during, or received pay for, any part of the pay period including the 12th of the month]

Industry	2007 NAICS code [1]	Average weekly hours of production workers					Average weekly overtime hours for production workers				
		1990	1995	2000	2010	2011	1990	1995	2000	2010	2011
Total	31–33	40.5	41.3	41.3	41.1	41.4	3.9	4.7	4.7	3.8	4.1
Durable goods	(X)	41.1	42.1	41.8	41.4	41.9	3.9	5.0	4.8	3.8	4.2
Wood products	321	40.4	41.0	41.0	39.1	39.7	3.3	3.9	4.1	3.0	3.1
Nonmetallic mineral products	327	40.9	41.8	41.6	41.7	42.3	5.0	5.7	6.1	4.7	5.0
Primary metals	331	42.1	43.4	44.2	43.7	44.6	4.6	5.7	6.5	5.7	6.3
Fabricated metal products	332	41.0	41.9	41.9	41.4	42.0	3.9	4.8	4.9	3.8	4.4
Machinery	333	42.1	43.5	42.3	42.1	43.1	4.0	5.3	5.1	3.9	4.8
Computer and electronic products	334	41.3	42.2	41.4	40.9	40.5	3.8	4.9	4.6	2.9	2.8
Electrical equipment and appliances	335	41.2	41.9	41.6	41.1	40.8	3.0	3.5	3.7	3.6	4.1
Transportation equipment [2]	336	42.0	43.7	43.3	42.9	43.2	4.5	6.5	5.5	4.7	5.1
Furniture and related products	337	38.0	38.5	39.2	38.5	39.9	2.3	2.8	3.5	2.3	2.9
Miscellaneous manufacturing	339	39.0	39.2	39.0	38.7	38.9	3.0	3.4	3.1	2.7	2.6
Nondurable goods	(X)	39.6	40.1	40.3	40.8	40.8	3.9	4.3	4.5	3.8	4.0
Food manufacturing	311	39.3	39.6	40.1	40.7	40.2	4.4	4.6	5.0	4.5	4.5
Beverages and tobacco products	312	38.9	39.3	42.0	37.5	39.2	3.8	4.8	5.8	2.2	(NA)
Textile mills	313	40.2	40.9	41.4	41.2	41.7	4.2	5.0	4.8	3.3	3.8
Textile product mills	314	38.5	38.6	38.7	39.0	39.1	2.9	3.3	3.4	2.4	2.3
Apparel	315	34.7	35.3	35.7	36.6	38.2	2.0	2.2	2.1	1.1	2.7
Leather and allied products	316	37.4	37.7	37.5	39.1	39.8	4.0	4.0	4.6	2.9	(NA)
Paper and paper products	322	43.6	43.4	42.8	42.9	42.9	4.9	5.5	5.7	4.9	4.7
Printing and related support activities	323	38.7	39.1	39.2	38.2	38.0	3.6	3.8	3.7	2.2	2.2
Petroleum and coal products	324	44.4	43.7	42.7	43.0	43.8	6.2	6.3	6.5	6.4	6.6
Chemicals	325	42.8	43.3	42.2	42.2	42.5	4.9	5.6	5.0	3.6	4.0
Plastics and rubber products	326	40.6	41.1	40.8	41.9	42.0	3.4	3.9	4.0	4.0	3.9

X Not applicable. NA Not available [1] Based on the North American Industry Classification System (NAICS), 2007; see text, this section and Section 15. [2] Includes railroad rolling stock manufacturing, not shown separately.

Source: U.S. Bureau of Labor Statistics, Current Employment Statistics, <http://www.bls.gov/ces/>.

Table 1028. Indexes of Employment and Hours of All Persons in Manufacturing: 1990 to 2011

[2002 = 100. Based on Current Employment Statistics and supplemented with Current Population Survey. Employment and hours of all persons include those of paid employees, the self employed (partners and proprietors), and unpaid family workers. See text, Section 12]

Industry	2007 NAICS code [1]	Employment					Hours				
		1990	2000	2005	2010	2011	1990	2000	2005	2010	2011
Food manufacturing	311	99.0	101.6	97.0	94.9	95.8	98.5	103.0	95.6	97.7	97.2
Beverage and tobacco products	312	104.3	99.1	92.2	88.8	92.0	106.0	107.6	93.9	86.1	93.8
Textile mills	313	166.1	128.0	74.2	42.5	42.8	164.4	130.3	74.0	42.7	42.8
Textile product mills	314	113.9	109.5	87.0	58.9	57.2	113.6	109.6	85.8	60.4	56.9
Apparel manufacturing	315	250.7	135.2	72.6	48.1	45.5	239.7	133.1	71.4	48.0	46.3
Leather and allied products	316	228.7	124.2	74.8	52.7	49.9	231.1	127.9	78.7	54.5	53.9
Wood product manufacturing	321	99.5	111.8	101.7	63.3	62.0	100.3	114.7	101.6	61.2	61.3
Paper manufacturing	322	118.0	110.3	88.4	72.1	71.3	122.3	112.6	89.7	73.9	72.8
Printing and related support activities	323	116.7	114.4	91.8	70.7	66.5	117.1	115.8	91.5	69.2	65.0
Petroleum and coal products	324	128.8	103.7	94.0	95.6	94.5	132.6	103.0	98.3	96.0	95.8
Chemical manufacturing	325	111.8	106.2	94.9	85.5	85.4	111.3	104.6	94.1	84.9	85.2
Plastics and rubber products	326	97.8	112.4	95.0	73.8	75.0	97.5	112.9	93.4	75.5	77.6
Nonmetallic mineral products	327	102.8	107.3	97.7	72.7	72.1	100.3	105.8	97.3	72.7	72.0
Primary metal products	331	135.7	122.0	91.8	71.4	76.6	134.7	127.2	93.8	73.5	80.9
Fabricated metal products	332	104.8	112.7	98.7	83.4	86.8	105.6	116.3	99.3	84.3	89.1
Machinery manufacturing	333	115.5	118.4	94.8	81.0	86.0	118.0	122.9	97.4	84.2	90.7
Computer and electronic products	334	127.6	121.6	87.5	73.0	73.7	132.1	126.1	88.5	75.1	75.0
Electrical equipment and appliances	335	127.7	119.0	87.9	72.6	74.0	130.9	123.4	89.1	74.4	75.2
Transportation equipment	336	116.4	112.3	96.5	73.0	75.7	115.3	114.1	96.3	73.7	76.9
Furniture and related products	337	100.3	111.1	94.9	59.7	58.2	97.3	111.0	95.3	57.9	59.7
Miscellaneous manufacturing	339	101.8	107.2	96.8	82.9	83.6	101.0	106.9	95.7	82.5	84.4

[1] North American Industry Classification System, 2007; see text, Section 15.

Source: Bureau of Labor Statistics, Labor Productivity and Costs, "Industry Employment and Hours,"<http://www.bls.gov/Lpc/iprhours11.htm>.

Table 1029. Average Hourly Earnings of Production Workers in Manufacturing Industries by State: 2008 to 2011

[In dollars. Data are based on the North American Industry Classification System (NAICS), 2007. Based on the Current Employment Statistics Program; see headnote, Table 644, and Appendix III]

State	2008	2009	2010	2011	State	2008	2009	2010	2011
United States........	17.75	18.24	18.61	18.94	Missouri...............	17.70	18.47	18.45	18.66
Alabama..............	15.68	15.43	15.71	16.93	Montana..............	16.66	16.85	17.10	18.34
Alaska................	16.38	17.38	20.43	19.58	Nebraska.............	15.26	16.06	16.13	16.58
Arizona...............	16.44	17.14	17.00	17.60	Nevada...............	15.53	15.61	15.51	16.28
Arkansas.............	14.16	14.07	13.87	14.52	New Hampshire.......	17.30	17.37	17.81	18.24
California.............	16.79	17.80	18.95	19.49	New Jersey...........	17.89	18.31	18.80	19.03
Colorado.............	19.79	21.23	22.07	23.64	New Mexico...........	14.72	14.59	15.76	16.22
Connecticut...........	21.42	23.03	23.68	24.76	New York.............	18.58	18.54	18.39	18.46
Delaware.............	17.42	17.69	16.53	15.94	North Carolina........	15.49	15.88	15.85	16.04
Florida...............	18.29	19.60	19.42	18.82	North Dakota.........	15.15	15.56	15.93	17.02
Georgia..............	14.83	15.43	16.63	17.69	Ohio..................	19.35	18.63	18.66	19.25
Hawaii...............	18.93	19.06	18.58	18.20	Oklahoma............	14.74	14.76	14.33	15.65
Idaho................	19.95	20.30	20.70	20.97	Oregon...............	16.92	17.69	17.60	17.96
Illinois...............	16.44	16.61	16.92	18.01	Pennsylvania.........	15.61	16.28	16.88	17.49
Indiana..............	18.47	18.96	18.52	18.04	Rhode Island.........	13.94	14.12	14.71	16.30
Iowa.................	16.63	16.73	16.73	16.50	South Carolina........	15.92	16.29	16.52	16.73
Kansas...............	18.73	19.09	18.87	19.52	South Dakota.........	14.64	14.82	15.28	16.34
Kentucky.............	17.38	18.11	18.94	18.90	Tennessee............	14.71	14.73	15.33	16.63
Louisiana............	19.98	20.49	21.31	21.15	Texas................	13.78	14.39	14.50	16.41
Maine................	19.71	19.97	20.18	20.21	Utah.................	17.87	18.20	18.46	18.03
Maryland.............	18.04	18.77	20.06	18.60	Vermont..............	16.51	16.41	16.63	17.24
Massachusetts........	20.33	20.66	20.50	20.47	Virginia..............	18.33	18.69	19.11	18.53
Michigan..............	22.11	21.56	21.77	21.08	Washington...........	21.06	23.39	23.48	23.98
Minnesota............	17.74	18.60	18.87	19.04	West Virginia.........	19.02	18.69	18.11	18.03
Mississippi...........	14.43	14.64	14.83	15.12	Wisconsin............	17.94	18.14	18.10	17.71
					Wyoming.............	20.36	20.71	20.49	22.19

Source: U.S. Bureau of Labor Statistics, Current Employment Statistics, "State and Metro Area Employment, Hours, and Earnings," <http://www.bls.gov/ces/home.htm>.

Table 1030. Manufacturing Full-Time Equivalent (FTE) Employees and Wages by Industry: 2004 to 2011

[122,546 represents 122,546,000. Based on National Income and Product Account tables. Full-time equivalent employees equals the number of employees on full-time schedules plus the number of employees for part-time schedules converted to full-time basis]

Industry	2002 NAICS code [1]	Full-time equivalent (FTE) employees (1,000)				Wage and salary accruals per (FTE) worker (dol.)			
		2004	2009	2010	2011	2004	2009	2010	2011
Domestic industries, total...........	(X)	122,546	121,078	120,303	121,757	43,977	51,552	52,974	54,413
Manufacturing.............................	31–33	14,024	11,528	11,238	11,456	49,423	57,383	59,987	61,680
Percent of all industries..................	(X)	11.4	9.5	9.3	9.4	112.4	111.3	113.2	113.4
Durable goods.........................	(X)	8,768	7,106	6,910	7,132	51,828	60,183	63,314	65,448
Wood products.........................	321	542	348	335	328	34,570	37,729	38,139	39,214
Nonmetallic mineral products...........	327	492	377	357	357	43,710	49,000	50,608	51,274
Primary metals.........................	331	459	353	353	378	52,302	57,205	61,044	63,006
Fabricated metal products..............	332	1,465	1,275	1,250	1,313	42,633	49,229	51,418	52,571
Machinery..............................	333	1,121	1,000	976	1,038	52,247	59,577	62,635	65,486
Computer and electronic products......	334	1,299	1,117	1,079	1,091	75,204	87,669	95,959	99,599
Electrical equipment, appliances, and components.............................	335	438	364	351	358	47,611	56,267	59,393	62,284
Motor vehicles, bodies and trailers, and parts...............................	3361–3363	1,108	665	670	719	54,606	57,401	58,405	60,017
Other transportation equipment.........	3364–3365	650	671	645	654	64,276	76,957	79,358	83,538
Furniture and related products..........	337	560	372	346	344	33,862	38,921	39,945	40,412
Miscellaneous manufacturing...........	339	634	562	549	553	46,320	54,615	56,862	58,223
Nondurable goods.......................	(X)	5,255	4,422	4,328	4,324	45,411	52,885	54,676	55,466
Food and beverage and tobacco products.............................	311–312	1,637	1,578	1,562	1,575	38,188	43,199	44,701	45,006
Textile mills and textile product mills. ..	313–314	403	241	230	230	33,463	37,194	39,091	39,511
Apparel and leather and allied products.............................	315	319	189	179	174	30,153	36,913	38,227	38,389
Paper products.........................	322	485	393	382	378	52,209	59,012	61,578	62,591
Printing and related support activities..	323	646	507	476	461	41,315	44,914	45,769	46,481
Petroleum and coal products...........	324	109	113	109	110	76,378	93,317	97,137	102,514
Chemical products......................	325	868	785	774	774	69,885	82,823	84,801	85,956
Plastics and rubber products...........	326	789	615	615	623	40,639	45,772	47,766	48,734

X Not applicable. [1] North American Industry Classification System, 2002; see text, Section 15.

Source: U.S. Bureau of Economic Analysis, National Income and Product Accounts Tables, revised August 2012. See also <http://www.bea.gov/iTable/iTable.cfm?ReqID=9&step=1>.

Table 1031. Manufacturers' Shipments, Inventories, and New Orders: 1996 to 2011

[In billions of dollars (3,597 represents $3,597,000,000,000), except ratio. Based on the Manufacturers' Shipments, Inventories, and Orders (M3) survey. See source for details]

Year	Shipments	Inventories (December 31)[1]	Ratio of inventories to shipments[2]	New orders	Unfilled orders (December 31)
1996	3,597	421	1.40	3,567	485
1997	3,835	433	1.36	3,780	508
1998	3,900	439	1.37	3,808	492
1999	4,032	453	1.34	3,957	501
2000	4,209	470	1.37	4,161	545
2001	3,970	417	1.33	3,865	502
2002	3,915	412	1.30	3,819	468
2003	4,015	398	1.20	3,971	490
2004	4,309	429	1.17	4,283	537
2005	4,742	461	1.14	4,756	626
2006	5,016	509	1.22	5,078	759
2007	5,319	547	1.22	5,390	902
2008	5,468	528	1.42	5,447	995
2009	4,420	491	1.29	4,167	801
2010	4,917	534	1.26	4,919	876
2011	5,491	583	1.28	5,501	966

[1] Inventories are stated at current cost. [2] Ratio based on December seasonally adjusted inventory data.

Source: Census Bureau, Manufacturers' Shipments, Inventories, and Orders, "Historical Data," <http://www.census.gov/manufacturing/m3/historical_data/index.html>.

Table 1032. Ratios of Manufacturers' Inventories to Shipments and Unfilled Orders to Shipments by Industry Group: 2000 to 2011

[Based on the Manufacturers' Shipments, Inventories, and Orders (M3) survey. See source for details]

Industry	2007 NAICS code[1]	2000	2005	2007	2008	2009	2010	2011
INVENTORIES-TO-SHIPMENTS RATIO[2]								
All manufacturing industries	(X)	**1.37**	**1.14**	**1.22**	**1.42**	**1.29**	**1.26**	**1.28**
Durable goods	(X)	1.56	1.33	1.48	1.73	1.63	1.61	1.63
Wood products	321	1.41	1.16	1.39	1.69	1.44	1.42	1.52
Nonmetallic mineral products	327	1.26	1.03	1.25	1.50	1.43	1.43	1.38
Primary metals	331	1.77	1.45	1.52	2.08	1.59	1.47	1.15
Fabricated metals	332	1.56	1.44	1.53	1.76	1.67	1.65	1.65
Machinery	333	2.05	1.66	1.79	1.99	2.00	1.85	1.95
Computers and electronic products	334	1.46	1.38	1.35	1.42	1.56	1.53	1.60
Electrical equipment, appliances, and components	335	1.42	1.33	1.47	1.63	1.51	1.48	1.52
Transportation equipment	336	1.43	1.10	1.43	1.75	1.58	1.64	1.78
Furniture and related products	337	1.37	1.14	1.13	1.20	1.18	1.19	1.16
Miscellaneous products	339	1.83	1.66	1.64	1.76	1.65	1.78	1.75
Nondurable goods	(X)	1.13	0.95	0.96	1.11	1.00	0.96	0.97
Food products	311	0.86	0.74	0.79	0.77	0.77	0.78	0.74
Beverages and tobacco products	312	1.50	1.37	1.53	1.48	1.62	1.56	1.47
Textile mills	313	1.55	1.22	1.39	1.66	1.25	1.28	1.43
Textile product mills	314	1.88	1.19	1.40	1.77	1.45	1.65	1.70
Apparel	315	1.93	1.48	1.79	1.72	1.68	1.62	1.78
Leather and allied products	316	2.01	1.80	2.37	2.38	2.15	1.63	1.82
Paper products	322	1.11	1.07	1.02	1.12	0.98	0.98	1.01
Printing	323	0.79	0.80	0.79	0.86	0.78	0.81	0.80
Petroleum and coal products	324	0.68	0.67	0.71	0.97	0.79	0.74	0.79
Basic chemicals	325	1.37	1.13	1.14	1.37	1.21	1.15	1.16
Plastics and rubber products	326	1.25	1.10	1.22	1.34	1.17	1.20	1.22
UNFILLED ORDERS-TO-SHIPMENTS RATIO								
Durable goods	(X)	4.02	4.52	5.92	7.20	6.15	6.17	6.16
Primary metals	331	1.52	1.86	1.80	1.85	1.49	1.60	1.20
Fabricated metals	332	2.14	2.52	2.67	2.93	2.68	3.00	2.98
Machinery	333	2.65	3.07	4.14	4.96	4.00	4.02	4.76
Computers and electronic products	334	4.25	5.15	5.28	5.71	5.96	6.59	6.69
Electrical equipment, appliances, and components	335	1.86	2.04	2.37	2.43	2.05	2.00	2.42
Transportation equipment	336	8.10	8.84	13.87	18.27	13.58	13.94	14.93
Furniture and related products	337	1.29	1.30	1.33	1.44	1.49	1.42	1.38

X Not applicable. [1] Based on the North American Industry Classification System, 2007; see text, this section and Section 15. [2] Ratio based on December seasonally adjusted inventory data.

Source: Census Bureau, Manufacturers' Shipments, Inventories, and Orders, "Historical Data," <http://www.census.gov/manufacturing/m3/historical_data/index.html>.

Table 1033. Value of Manufacturers' Shipments, Inventories, and New Orders by Industry: 2000 to 2011

[In billions of dollars (4,209 represents $4,209,000,000,000). Based on the Manufacturers' Shipments, Inventories, and Orders (M3) survey. See source for details]

Industry	2007 NAICS code [1]	2000	2005	2008	2009	2010	2011
SHIPMENTS							
All manufacturing industries	(X)	**4,209**	**4,742**	**5,468**	**4,420**	**4,917**	**5,491**
Durable goods	(X)	2,374	2,425	2,620	2,063	2,299	2,515
Wood products	321	94	112	88	65	70	69
Nonmetallic mineral products	327	97	115	115	90	91	94
Primary metals	331	157	203	283	169	231	305
Fabricated metals	332	268	289	358	281	295	317
Machinery	333	292	303	356	288	318	357
Computers and electronic products	334	511	373	384	321	341	341
Electrical equipment, appliances, and components	335	125	112	130	105	111	116
Transportation equipment	336	640	691	673	540	633	694
Furniture and related products	337	75	84	80	60	59	62
Miscellaneous products	339	115	143	153	144	150	160
Nondurable goods	(X)	1,835	2,317	2,848	2,357	2,618	2,976
Food products	311	435	532	650	627	646	711
Beverages and tobacco products	312	112	124	125	128	132	141
Textile mills	313	52	42	32	26	29	30
Textile product mills	314	34	35	27	21	22	23
Apparel	315	60	31	19	14	14	15
Leather and allied products	316	10	6	5	4	5	5
Paper products	322	165	162	179	162	170	170
Printing	323	104	97	99	83	82	82
Petroleum and coal products	324	235	476	770	496	628	831
Basic chemicals	325	449	611	739	624	701	765
Plastics and rubber products	326	178	200	204	171	189	202
INVENTORIES (December 31)							
All manufacturing industries	(X)	**470**	**461**	**528**	**491**	**534**	**584**
Durable goods	(X)	298	276	322	289	316	348
Wood products	321	10	12	10	8	8	9
Nonmetallic mineral products	327	10	10	12	10	10	11
Primary metals	331	22	26	35	26	31	34
Fabricated metals	332	34	36	46	38	41	45
Machinery	333	49	43	55	49	52	60
Computers and electronic products	334	63	44	43	41	43	44
Electrical equipment, appliances, and components	335	15	12	15	13	14	14
Transportation equipment	336	69	65	80	78	89	102
Furniture and related products	337	8	8	7	6	6	6
Miscellaneous products	339	18	20	21	20	22	23
Nondurable goods	(X)	172	185	206	202	218	236
Food products	311	32	33	41	40	43	45
Beverages and tobacco products	312	14	14	16	17	17	18
Textile mills	313	6	4	4	3	3	3
Textile product mills	314	5	3	3	3	3	3
Apparel	315	9	4	2	2	2	2
Leather and allied products	316	2	1	1	1	1	1
Paper products	322	15	14	15	13	14	14
Printing	323	6	6	6	5	5	5
Petroleum and coal products	324	13	27	29	36	42	51
Basic chemicals	325	52	59	70	65	69	72
Plastics and rubber products	326	18	19	20	17	19	21
NEW ORDERS							
All manufacturing industries	(X)	**4,161**	**4,756**	**5,447**	**4,167**	**4,919**	**5,501**
Durable goods	(X)	2,327	2,439	2,599	1,810	2,302	2,525
Wood products	321	94	112	88	65	66	(NA)
Nonmetallic mineral products	327	97	115	115	90	92	(NA)
Primary metals	331	154	209	274	163	240	308
Fabricated metals	332	270	298	357	267	308	323
Machinery	333	295	312	369	252	332	388
Computers and electronic products	334	436	302	313	254	283	260
Electrical equipment, appliances, and components	335	126	115	129	100	112	120
Transportation equipment	336	663	750	722	417	657	740
Furniture and related products	337	75	85	79	59	59	62
Miscellaneous products	339	117	142	153	144	151	(NA)
Nondurable goods	(X)	1,835	2,317	2,848	2,359	2,614	(NA)

NA Not available. X Not applicable. [1] Based on the North American Industry Classification System, 2007; see text, this section and Section 15.

Source: Census Bureau, Manufacturers' Shipments, Inventories, and Orders, "Historical Data," <http://www.census.gov/manufacturing/m3/historical_data/index.html>.

Table 1034. Value of Manufacturers' Shipments, Inventories, and New Orders by Market Grouping: 2000 to 2011

[In millions of dollars (4,209 represents $4,209,000,000,000). Based on the Manufacturers' Shipments, Inventories, and Orders (M3) survey. See source for details]

Market grouping	2000	2005	2007	2008	2009	2010	2011
SHIPMENTS							
All manufacturing industries	**4,209**	**4,742**	**5,319**	**5,468**	**4,420**	**4,917**	**5,491**
Consumer goods	1,501	1,895	2,106	2,253	1,846	2,059	2,372
Consumer durable goods	391	423	422	359	272	330	375
Consumer nondurable goods	1,109	1,473	1,684	1,893	1,575	1,729	1,997
Aircraft and parts	112	114	157	162	151	148	150
Defense aircraft and parts	25	38	44	58	62	64	54
Nondefense aircraft and parts	87	76	113	104	89	85	96
Construction materials and supplies	445	510	560	544	426	446	470
Motor vehicles and parts	471	501	501	413	302	400	466
Computers and related products	110	65	65	66	50	37	37
Information technology industries	400	295	323	315	264	267	266
Nondefense capital goods	808	730	836	838	692	723	787
Excluding aircraft	758	687	769	772	637	672	729
Defense capital goods	67	92	100	115	123	127	106
INVENTORIES (December 31)							
All manufacturing industries	**470**	**461**	**547**	**528**	**491**	**534**	**584**
Consumer goods	128	140	166	150	154	164	176
Consumer durable goods	26	27	27	24	21	23	24
Consumer nondurable goods	102	113	139	126	132	141	152
Aircraft and parts	36	33	48	46	47	55	66
Defense aircraft and parts	9	12	14	11	12	12	13
Nondefense aircraft and parts	27	22	33	34	35	43	53
Construction materials and supplies	49	53	61	60	50	53	57
Motor vehicles and parts	22	23	25	22	19	21	24
Computers and related products	8	4	5	5	4	3	4
Information technology industries	51	38	38	37	36	36	37
Nondefense capital goods	127	107	127	130	122	135	155
Excluding aircraft	107	90	102	104	95	101	111
Defense capital goods	17	16	19	16	19	20	21
NEW ORDERS							
All manufacturing industries	**4,161**	**4,766**	**5,399**	**5,447**	**4,167**	**4,919**	**5,501**
Consumer goods	1,502	1,894	2,106	2,251	1,846	2,059	2,372
Consumer durable goods	393	421	422	358	271	330	375
Consumer nondurable goods	1,109	1,473	1,684	1,893	1,572	1,755	(NA)
Aircraft and parts	131	178	272	209	49	166	197
Defense aircraft and parts	31	35	46	65	51	65	57
Nondefense aircraft and parts	99	143	226	143	-2	100	140
Construction materials and supplies	447	517	565	544	414	453	473
Motor vehicles and parts	468	503	499	410	300	403	467
Computers and related products	108	64	65	66	51	35	37
Information technology industries	410	301	324	315	256	282	267
Nondefense capital goods	831	818	963	883	554	758	858
Excluding aircraft	768	706	790	783	590	691	761
Defense capital goods	80	82	103	127	104	143	110

NA Not available.

Source: Census Bureau, Manufacturers' Shipments, Inventories, and Orders, "Historical Data," <http://www.census.gov/manufacturing/m3/historical_data/index.html>.

Table 1035. Finances and Profits of Manufacturing Corporations: 2000 to 2011

[In billions of dollars (4,548 represents $4,548,000,000,000). Data exclude estimates for corporations with less than $250,000 in assets at time of sample selection. Minus sign (-) indicates loss]

Item	2000 [1]	2001 [1]	2001 [2]	2005 [2]	2006 [2]	2007 [2]	2008 [3]	2009 [3]	2010 [3]	2011 [3]
Net sales	4,548	4,308	4,295	5,411	5,783	6,060	6,374	5,110	5,756	6,489
Net operating profit	348	185	186	359	405	416	358	289	420	484
Net profit:										
Before taxes	381	82	83	524	605	603	388	361	584	725
After taxes	275	36	36	401	470	443	266	286	478	598
Cash dividends	132	102	103	179	178	178	182	172	180	187
Net income retained in business	143	-67	-66	222	292	265	84	115	298	411

[1] Based on the Standard Industrial Classification system. [2] Based on the North American Industry Classification System, 2002; see text, Section 15. [3] Based on the North American Industry Classification System, 2007; see text, Section 15.

Source: U.S. Census Bureau, *Quarterly Financial Report for Manufacturing, Mining, Trade, and Selected Service Industries*. See also *2011 4th Quarter Press Release*, March 2012, <http://www.census.gov/econ/qfr>.

Table 1036. Manufacturing Corporations—Assets and Profits by Asset Size: 1990 to 2011

[In millions of dollars (2,629,458 represents $2,629,458,000,000). Corporations and assets as of end of 4th quarter; profits for entire year. Through 2000, based on Standard Industrial Classification code (SIC); beginning 2001, based on the North American Industry Classification System; see text, Section 15. For corporations above a certain asset value based on complete canvass. The asset value for complete canvass was raised in 1988 to $50 million and in 1995 to $250 million. Asset sizes less than these values are sampled, except as noted. For details regarding survey description, data analysis, and methodology, see source, 4th quarter report. Minus sign (–) indicates loss]

Year	Total	Asset–size class						
		Under $10 million [1]	$10 to $25 million	$25 to $50 million	$50 to $100 million	$100 to $250 million	$250 million to $1 billion	$1 billion and over
Assets:								
1990	2,629,458	142,498	74,477	55,914	72,554	123,967	287,512	1,872,536
1995	3,345,229	155,618	87,011	68,538	87,262	159,133	370,263	2,417,403
1998	3,967,309	170,068	87,937	69,627	86,816	148,060	419,153	2,985,647
1999	4,382,814	170,058	85,200	67,352	97,810	138,143	398,881	3,425,370
2000	4,852,106	171,666	85,482	72,122	90,866	149,714	389,537	3,892,720
2001 [2]	4,747,789	169,701	84,664	67,493	88,088	131,617	393,752	3,812,474
2002	4,823,219	166,191	82,369	62,654	81,667	134,821	407,423	3,888,095
2003	5,162,852	161,462	80,681	62,592	77,205	126,826	392,192	4,261,894
2004	5,538,113	163,072	80,085	71,674	81,741	126,950	414,144	4,600,447
2005	5,828,716	165,195	85,785	68,731	87,818	142,900	423,917	4,854,370
2006	6,179,142	168,537	93,786	72,494	91,877	146,651	418,501	5,187,295
2007	6,891,131	180,319	98,348	80,400	93,017	144,254	433,634	5,861,160
2008	6,819,681	180,025	99,430	80,757	98,478	137,907	420,104	5,802,981
2009	6,942,972	166,590	106,773	71,642	76,308	126,202	413,856	5,981,600
2010	7,432,384	165,598	105,661	74,081	82,713	130,428	405,113	6,468,791
2011	7,905,346	171,469	118,255	78,199	87,875	130,209	428,463	6,890,877
Net profit: [3]								
1990	110,128	8,527	5,160	2,769	2,661	3,525	7,110	80,377
1995	198,151	13,224	5,668	3,767	5,771	7,000	16,549	146,172
1998	234,386	18,350	6,421	3,790	4,681	5,610	14,364	181,170
1999	257,805	17,398	7,618	3,504	4,798	4,795	12,756	206,934
2000	275,313	16,578	6,820	3,403	2,742	3,510	15,121	227,136
2001 [2]	36,168	8,387	3,366	-408	403	-543	-6,782	31,746
2002	134,686	10,003	2,784	807	1,699	3,356	-1,227	117,262
2003	237,041	9,821	3,374	2,005	2,256	2,973	4,115	212,497
2004	348,151	14,970	5,745	3,858	3,080	5,140	12,787	302,571
2005	401,344	17,357	6,057	4,066	3,781	7,678	15,967	346,438
2006	470,282	22,301	8,685	5,260	4,601	8,901	21,405	399,131
2007	442,734	22,930	9,006	4,402	6,518	8,400	17,565	373,915
2008	266,346	18,182	7,472	5,820	3,739	3,403	2,239	225,492
2009	286,491	9,692	5,979	4,617	2,500	2,723	2,653	258,310
2010	477,884	16,637	7,670	4,181	5,880	5,390	19,494	417,121
2011	597,792	20,563	9,506	5,327	5,681	7,236	17,855	531,627

[1] Excludes estimates for corporations with less than $250,000 in assets at time of sample selection. [2] Beginning 2001, data reported based on the North American Industry Classification System. [3] After taxes.

Source: U.S. Census Bureau, *Quarterly Financial Report for Manufacturing, Mining, Trade, and Selected Service Industries*. See also *2011 Fourth Quarter Press Release*, March 2012, <http://www.census.gov/econ/qfr>.

Table 1037. Manufacturing Corporations—Selected Finances: 1990 to 2011

[In billions of dollars (2,811 represents $2,811,000,000,000). Data are not necessarily comparable from year to year due to changes in accounting procedures, industry classifications, sampling procedures, etc.; for detail, see source. See headnote, Table 1035. Minus sign (–) indicates loss]

Year	All manufacturing corporations			Durable goods			Nondurable goods		
	Sales	Profits [1]		Sales	Profits [1]		Sales	Profits [1]	
		Before taxes	After taxes		Before taxes	After taxes		Before taxes	After taxes
1990	2,811	158	110	1,357	57	41	1,454	101	69
1995	3,528	275	198	1,808	131	94	1,721	144	104
1997	3,922	331	244	2,076	167	121	1,847	164	123
1998	3,949	315	234	2,169	175	128	1,781	140	107
1999	4,149	355	258	2,314	199	140	1,835	157	117
2000	4,548	381	275	2,457	191	132	2,091	190	144
2001 [2]	4,295	83	36	2,321	-69	-76	1,974	152	112
2002	4,217	196	135	2,261	45	21	1,955	149	113
2003	4,397	306	237	2,283	118	88	2,114	188	149
2004	4,934	447	348	2,537	200	157	2,397	248	192
2005	5,411	524	401	2,731	211	161	2,681	313	240
2006	5,783	605	470	2,910	249	193	2,873	356	278
2007	6,060	603	443	3,016	247	159	3,044	356	283
2008	6,374	388	266	2,970	98	43	3,405	290	223
2009	5,110	361	286	2,427	84	55	2,683	276	232
2010	5,756	584	478	2,708	287	232	3,048	297	245
2011	6,489	725	598	2,929	337	286	3,560	388	312

[1] Beginning 1998, profits before and after income taxes reflect inclusion of minority stockholders' interest in net income before and after income taxes. [2] Beginning 2001, data reported based on the North American Industry Classification System.

Source: U.S. Census Bureau, *Quarterly Financial Report for Manufacturing, Mining, Trade, and Selected Service Industries*. See also *2011 Fourth Quarter Press Release*, March 2012, <http://www.census.gov/econ/qfr>.

Table 1038. Textiles—Production and Foreign Trade: 2010

[595,198 represents 595,198,000. Fabric blends as shown in the report are reported based on the chief weight of the fiber; whereas, fabrics blends as shown for imports and exports are based on the chief value of the fiber]

Product description	Unit	Quantity (1,000)			Value ($1,000)	
		Manufacturers' production	Exports of domestic merchandise [1]	Imports for consumption [2]	Exports of domestic merchandise [1]	Imports for consumption [2,3]
YARN						
Spun cotton yarns, carded, 85 percent or more cotton	Kilograms	595,198	309,578	19,631	808,737	91,863
Textured, crimped, twisted, or bulked filament yarns, nylon	Kilograms	641,728	28,929	60,281	147,086	253,367
Textured, crimped, twisted, or bulked filament yarns, polyester	Kilograms	287,168	28,888	40,463	98,180	97,217
BROADWOVEN FABRICS [4]						
Yarn dyed fabrics, blue denim	Sq. meters	124,273	119,894	30,057	248,802	86,954
85 percent or more spun yarn fabrics and blends (except yarn dyed), chiefly man made fiber, twills and sateens [5]	Sq. meters	168,042	(NA)	22,530	(NA)	31,204
85 percent or more filament yarn fabrics, man made, high tenacity yarn fabrics of nylon, polyester, or rayon	Sq. meters	141,686	18,163	14,426	75,034	58,408
85 percent or more filament yarn fabrics, man made, glass fiber fabrics	Sq. meters	161,877	44,480	56,564	152,206	76,699
85 percent or more filament yarn fabrics, all other man made filament fiber fabrics, including saran, olefin, and carpet backing	Sq. meters	530,281	31,519	675,795	68,777	203,430
KNIT FABRICS						
Pile fabrics	Kilograms	5,498	(S)	149,404	(S)	162,053
Elastic fabrics (over 12 inches in width) (weight 5 percent or more elastomeric yarn or rubber thread)	Kilograms	8,940	(S)	17,506	(S)	168,153
Elastic fabrics (12 inches or less in width), (weight 5 percent or more elastomeric yarn or rubber thread)	Kilograms	19,797	3,414	1,032	38,860	6,805
TOWELS						
Finished towels [6]	Dozens	1,929	341	155,616	25,845	1,823,394

NA Not available. S Withheld because estimate did not meet publication standards. [1] Source: U.S. Census Bureau report EM 545, *U.S. Exports*. [2] Source: U.S. Census Bureau report IM 145, *U.S. Imports for Consumption*. [3] Dollar value represents the c.i.f. (cost, insurance, and freight) at the first port of entry in the United States plus calculated import duty. [4] Represents production of gray broadwoven fabrics; import and export data represent gray as well as finished broadwoven fabrics. [5] Total for manmade fiber fabrics does not include chiefly manmade/wool blends. [6] "Manufacturers' production" of "finished towels" does not include washcloths, whereas the quantity and value for imports and exports does include washcloths.

Source: U.S. Census Bureau, Current Industrial Reports, "Textiles," Series MQ313A, June 2011 <http://www.census.gov/manufacturing/cir/historical_data/mq313a/index.html>.

Table 1039. Pharmaceutical Preparations—Value of Shipments: 1990 to 2010

[In millions of dollars (33,954 represents $33,954,000,000)]

Product description	Product code	1990	2000	2005	2007	2008	2009	2010
Pharmaceutical preparations, except biologicals	(X)	33,954	79,262	118,647	(NA)	(NA)	(NA)	(NA)
Affecting neoplasms, endocrine systems, and metabolic disease	3254121	2,743	9,784	23,779	28,497	33,260	33,340	29,557
Acting on the central nervous system and sense organs	3254124	7,219	18,508	25,627	28,714	26,430	29,158	27,998
Acting on the cardiovascular system	3254127	4,815	8,993	10,232	11,969	11,543	12,739	11,427
Acting on the respiratory system	325412A	3,724	10,179	16,367	16,177	16,573	16,357	17,980
Acting on the digestive system	325412D	4,840	10,046	16,829	9,822	9,949	10,980	10,355
Acting on the skin	325412G	1,558	2,941	3,657	3,498	3,635	3,790	4,166
Vitamin, nutrient, and hematitic preparations	325412L	2,588	5,676	7,556	8,062	8,749	8,933	9,070
Affecting parasitic and infective disease	325412P	5,411	11,037	11,228	11,014	9,403	9,636	8,727
Pharmaceutical preparations for veterinary use	325412T	1,057	2,096	3,371	3,206	3,280	2,971	2,618

NA Not available. X Not applicable.

Source: U.S. Census Bureau, Current Industrial Reports, "Pharmaceutical Preparations, Except Biologicals," Series MA325G, <http://www.census.gov/manufacturing/cir/historical_data/ma325g/index.html>.

Table 1040. Inorganic Chemicals and Fertilizers—Production: 2000 to 2010

[In 1,000 short tons (15,809 represents 15,809,000.) 1,000 short tons = 2,000 lb.]

Product description	Product code	2000	2005	2007	2008	2009	2010
FERTILIZERS (MQ325B)							
Ammonia, synthetic anhydrous.	3253111120	15,809	11,181	11,448	10,549	10,330	11,115
Ammonium nitrate (original melt liquor).	3253111201	7,979	7,212	8,236	7,841	6,943	7,484
Ammonium sulfate.	3253111240	2,808	2,906	3,145	2,783	2,499	2,740
Urea (original melt liquor) (100%).	3253114101	7,682	5,807	6,156	5,776	5,604	5,646
Nitric acid (100%).	3253111111	8,708	7,398	8,623	7,370	6,531	7,640
Phosphoric acid (100% P2O5).	3253121111	12,492	12,621	12,081	10,158	9,542	10,378
Sulfuric acid (100%).	3251881100	43,643	40,996	39,745	34,855	32,126	35,877
Superphosphates and other fertilizer materials (100% P2O5).	3253124102	8,899	8,141	7,241	6,014	6,142	6,897
INORGANIC CHEMICALS (MQ325A)							
Chlorine gas (100 percent) [1].	3251811111	14,000	10,272	11,895	10,673	9,391	10,715
Sodium hydroxide, liquid (caustic soda) (100 percent) all process: liquid [2].	3251814111	11,523	8,517	8,869	8,111	7,242	8,245
Potassium hydroxide (caustic potash) (88-92 percent) liquid [2].	3251817111	539	527	621	582	404	481
Finished sodium bicarbonate (58 percent) NaHCO3.	3251817131	536	581	663	682	641	686
Hydrochloric acids (100 percent) byproduct and other [3].	3251884131	4,717	4,619	4,331	3,902	3,584	3,907
Aluminum oxide, except natural alumina (100 percent A12O3).	3313110100	(D)	(D)	(D)	(D)	2,918	(D)
Aluminum sulfate (commercial) (17 percent aluminum oxide) [4].	3251887151	1,076	967	967	(S)	831	(S)
Sodium chlorite (100 percent).	325188A141	940	523	617	607	420	544
Sodium silicates (soluble silicate glass, liquid and solid) (anhydrous) [5].	325188A181	1,136	1,309	1,182	1,106	981	1,308
Metasilicate anhydrous (100 percent).	325188A187	72	59	(D)	(D)	(D)	(D)
Sodium sulfate (100 percent).	325188A1A7	509	93	93	87	47	81
Granular carbons, activated (dry weight) [6,7].	325998H1E4	95	(D)	27	(S)	(S)	(S)
Pulverized carbons, activated, (dry weight) [6].	325998H1E7	71	(D)	98	(S)	(S)	(S)
Hydrogen peroxide (100 percent by weight).	325188G181	1,083	365	429	437	377	425

D Withheld to avoid disclosing data for individual companies. S Does not meet publication standards. [1] Production includes amounts liquefied. [2] Liquid production figures represent total production, including quantities later evaporated to solid caustic. [3] Includes production from salt and acid. [4] Excludes quantities produced and consumed in municipalities. [5] Excludes amounts produced and consumed in making meta, ortho, and sesquisilicates. [6] Excludes reactivated carbon. [7] Includes pelleted carbon.

Source: U.S. Census Bureau, Current Industrial Reports, "Inorganic Chemicals," Series MQ325A, July 2010, and "Fertilizers and Related Chemicals," Series MQ325B, June 2010, <http://www.census.gov/manufacturing/cir/historical_data/mq325a/index.html> and <http://www.census.gov/manufacturing/cir/historical_data/mq325b/index.html>.

Table 1041. Metalworking Machinery—Value of Shipments: 2005 to 2010

[In thousands of dollars (2,800,272 represents $2,800,272,000)]

Product description	Product code	2005	2007	2008 [1]	2009 [1]	2010 [1]
Metalworking machinery.	**(X)**	**2,800,272**	**3,318,208**	**3,435,540**	**1,936,986**	**2,055,877**
Metal cutting type machine tools.	333512 (pt)	2,079,874	2,533,389	2,650,662	1,424,012	1,519,966
Boring and drilling machines.	333512A1	110,971	130,220	161,393	92,715	87,615
Grinding and polishing machines.	33351221	265,035	237,928	270,339	165,445	152,430
Lathes [2].	33351231	248,240	375,871	396,793	204,478	207,404
Milling machines [3].	33351241	53,582	81,294	(D)	(D)	(D)
Machining centers.	33351271	619,563	807,425	(D)	(D)	(D)
Station type machines [4].	33351281	104,481	(D)	(D)	117,891	43,831
Other metal cutting machine tools.	33351291	431,962	585,522	543,791	282,570	330,441
Remanufactured metal cutting machine tools.	3335126111	93,404	81,004	(D)	(D)	(D)
Metal forming type machine tools.	333513 (pt)	720,398	784,819	784,878	512,974	535,911
Punching, shearing, bending, and forming machines.	33351311	344,273	409,791	391,607	256,996	263,422
Presses (excluding forging) [5].	33351331	139,924	135,292	142,282	75,299	93,217
All other metal forming type machines [5].	33351351	206,547	209,309	231,257	167,733	163,427
Remanufactured metal forming machine tools.	3335137121	(D)	10,382	19,732	12,946	15,845

D Withheld to avoid disclosing data for individual companies. S Figure does not meet publication standards. X Not applicable. [1] Data shown for years 2008-2010 do not include metal cutting and forming type machine tools valued under $3,025 each. [2] Data for product code 3335123126, "Vertical NC turning machines" are included in total "Metal cutting type," but excluded from product code 33351231. [3] Data for product code 3335124101, "All milling machines valued under $3,025 each" are included in total "Metal cutting type," but excluded from product code 33351241. [4] Data for "Station type machines" are included in total "Metal cutting type." [5] Data for product codes 3335133101 "All presses valued under $3,025 each" and 3335135101 "All other metal forming type machine tools valued under $3,025 each" are included in total "Metal forming type," but excluded from product codes 33351331 and 33351351, respectively.

Source: U.S. Census Bureau, Current Industrial Reports, "Metalworking Machinery," Series MQ333W, August 2011, <http://www.census.gov/manufacturing/cir/historical_data/mq333w/index.html>.

Table 1042. Semiconductors, Electronic Components, and Semiconductor Manufacturing Equipment—Value of Shipments: 2005 to 2010

[In millions of dollars (9,728 represents $9,728,000,000)]

Product description	Product code	2005	2007	2008	2009	2010
Semiconductor machinery	3332950	9,728	13,190	9,357	4,996	9,747
Transmitting, industrial, and special purpose electron tubes [1]	3344111	652	734	806	770	788
Receiving type electron tubes [2]	3344114	621	(D)	(D)	(D)	(D)
Electron tubes and parts	3344117	72	36	31	30	32
Bare printed circuit boards	3344120	4,856	4,443	5,269	4,113	4,335
Integrated microcircuits [3]	3344131	61,631	49,781	51,104	40,235	49,704
Transistors	3344134	603	599	409	(S)	(S)
Diodes and rectifiers	3344137	372	457	458	350	545
Other semiconductor devices [4]	334413A	8,330	10,176	11,363	10,995	13,520
Capacitors for electronic circuitry	3344140	1,113	945	937	736	891
Resistors for electronic circuitry	3344150	653	645	622	488	563
Electronic coils, transformers, and other inductors	3344160	1,216	1,393	1,380	1,076	1,099
Connectors for electronic circuitry	3344170	3,589	4,189	4,065	3,088	3,720
Printed circuit assemblies, loaded boards and modules [5]	334418B	20,106	20,382	20,257	14,370	16,724
Crystals, filters, piezoelectric, and other related electronic devices [6]	3344191	779	689	656	570	544
All other miscellaneous transducers [7]	3344194	1,401	1,466	1,352	1,058	1,175
Switches, mechanical types for electronic circuitry	3344197	794	662	581	396	360
Microwave components and devices [8]	334419A	1,306	1,541	1,286	1,191	1,304
All other miscellaneous electronic components	334419E	4,040	4,831	4,772	3,947	4,371

D Figure withheld to avoid disclosure. S Estimates did not meet publication standards. [1] Except X-ray. [2] Including cathode ray (new and rebuilt). [3] Includes semiconductor networks, microprocessors, and MOS memories. [4] Includes semiconductor parts such as chips, wafers, and heat sinks. [5] Printed circuit boards with inserted electronic components. [6] Except microwave filters. [7] Includes electrical-electronic input/output transducers. [8] Except antennae, tubes, and semiconductors.

Source: U.S. Census Bureau, Current Industrial Reports, "Semiconductors, Electronic Components, and Semiconductor Manufacturing Equipment," Series MA334Q, September 2010, <http://www.census.gov/manufacturing/cir/historical_data/ma334q/index.html>.

Table 1043. Computers and Peripheral Equipment—Value of Shipments: 2004 to 2010

[In millions of dollars (37,895 represents $37,895,000,000)]

Product description	Product code	2004	2006	2007	2008	2009	2010
Electronic computers	334111	37,895	37,657	36,859	37,542	31,513	(D)
Host computers, multiusers	3341111	10,993	(D)	(D)	(D)	(D)	(D)
Single user computers, microprocessor-based, capable of supporting attached peripherals	3341117	26,309	(D)	(D)	(D)	(D)	(D)
Personal computers	3341117107	15,690	(D)	(D)	(D)	(D)	(D)
Workstations	3341117109	1,848	(D)	2,442	(D)	2,338	(D)
Mobile computers, including notebooks, subnotebooks, laptop, and tablet PCs	3341117127	8,456	(D)	(D)	(D)	(D)	(D)
Smart handheld devices	3341117129	(D)	(D)	(D)	(D)	(D)	(D)
All other single user computers	3341117130	(D)	(D)	25	(D)	(D)	(D)
Other computers (array, analog, hybrid, and special-use computers)	334111D	593	(D)	299	(S)	186	(S)
Computer storage devices (except parts, attachments, and accessories)	3341121	5,034	6,956	7,872	6,367	6,019	7,800
Disk subsystem and disk arrays for multiuser computer systems	3341121109	1,362	(D)	2,531	(D)	(D)	(D)
Disk drives (all sizes)	3341121112	69	(D)	150	201	297	(S)
Storage Area Networks (SANs)	3341121123	(D)	(D)	2,892	(D)	2,677	(S)
Tape drives (all sizes)	3341121138	278	285	239	264	(D)	133
Other computer storage devices	3341121150	(D)	3,795	2,061	1,321	1,090	(D)
Parts, attachments, and accessories for computer storage devices	3341124	1,039	1,929	1,426	1,327	853	854
Computer terminals (except point-of-sale and funds-transfer devices, parts, attachments, and accessories)	3341131	274	268	331	245	267	(S)
Parts, attachments, and accessories for computer terminals (except point-of-sale and funds-transfer devices)	3341134	2	(D)	(D)	(D)	(D)	(D)
All other miscellaneous computer peripheral (input/output) equipment (except parts, attachments and accessories)	3341191	4,705	4,517	4,427	4,245	3,530	4,026
Parts, subassemblies, and accessories for computer peripheral equipment	3341194	2,257	2,720	3,171	2,600	2,229	(S)
Point-of-sale terminals and funds-transfer devices	3341197	513	621	1,034	958	343	198
Parts and attachments for point-of-sale terminals and funds-transfer devices	334119D	(D)	35	12	9	(S)	(S)
Magnetic and optical recording media	3346130	1,586	1,364	1,381	(S)	839	(S)

D Withheld to avoid disclosing data for individual companies. S Withheld because estimates did not meet publication standards.

Source: U.S. Census Bureau, Current Industrial Reports, Computers and Peripheral Equipment, Series MA334R (beginning with 2006, MQ334R), June 2011, <http://www.census.gov/manufacturing/cir/historical_data/mq334r/index.html>.

Table 1044. Telecommunication Equipment—Value of Shipments: 2000 to 2010

[In millions of dollars (15,174 represents $15,174,000,000)]

Product description	Product code	2000	2005	2007	2008	2009	2010
Telephone switching and switchboard equipment.........	3342101	15,174	1,576	1,959	1,674	1,068	847
Carrier line equipment and modems........................	3342104	13,112	2,824	3,512	3,137	2,851	3,035
Wire line voice and data network equipment..............	3342107	28,971	12,289	11,181	4,574	3,187	3,384
Broadcast, studio, and related electronic equipment......	3342202	4,029	3,289	3,350	4,110	4,574	4,554
Wireless networking equipment.............................	3342203	(NA)	(NA)	6,159	4,845	3,633	3,885
Radio station equipment....................................	3342205	(NA)	(NA)	17,824	16,456	16,437	15,255
Other communications systems equipment...............	3342209	(NA)	(NA)	6,355	10,882	8,970	8,301
Alarm systems [1]...	3342901	2,755	1,910	2,044	2,090	1,663	1,733
Vehicular and pedestrian traffic control equipment [2]......	3342902	838	1,020	1,239	1,231	(S)	(S)
Intercommunications systems [3]...........................	3342903	447	416	438	458	389	399
Modems, consumer type...................................	3344184	95	98	82	87	(D)	(D)

D Withheld to avoid disclosing data of individual companies. NA Not available. S Estimates did not meet publication standards. [1] Includes electric sirens and horns. [2] Includes electrical railway signals and attachments. [3] Includes inductive paging systems (selective calling), except telephone and telegraph.

Source: U.S. Census Bureau, Current Industrial Reports, "Telecommunications," Series MQ334P, <http://www.census.gov/manufacturing/cir/historical_data/mq334p/index.html>.

Table 1045. Motor Vehicle Manufactures—Summary by Selected Industry: 2010

[32,578 represents $32,578,000,000. Based on the Annual Survey of Manufactures; see Appendix III]

Industry	2007 NAICS code [1]	All employees [2]			Produc-tion workers [2]	Value of ship-ments [3] (mil. dol.)
		Number	Payroll			
			Total (mil. dol.)	Payroll per employee (dol.)		
Motor vehicle manufacturing, total.....................	**3361–3363**	**615,153**	**32,578**	**52,959**	**476,360**	**390,597**
Motor vehicle, total...	3361	135,881	9,206	67,747	113,863	205,776
Automobile and light duty motor vehicle....................	33611	113,693	8,046	70,771	97,296	185,258
Automobile..	336111	60,200	4,008	66,575	49,854	73,055
Light truck and utility vehicle..............................	336112	53,493	4,038	75,494	47,442	112,203
Heavy duty truck...	33612	22,188	1,159	52,252	16,567	20,518
Motor vehicle body and trailer..............................	3362	90,615	3,832	42,283	69,520	23,222
Motor vehicle body and trailer manufacturing..............	33621	90,615	3,832	42,283	69,520	23,222
Motor vehicle body......................................	336211	36,040	1,576	43,717	26,542	9,045
Truck trailer...	336212	18,418	746	40,488	14,631	4,978
Motor home...	336213	6,431	284	44,180	4,691	2,037
Travel trailer and camper...............................	336214	29,726	1,226	41,248	23,657	7,162
Motor vehicle parts...	3363	388,657	19,541	50,278	292,977	161,599
Motor vehicle gasoline engine and engine parts..........	33631	45,261	2,476	54,702	34,814	20,747
Motor vehicle electrical and electronic equipment........	33632	41,596	2,256	54,232	28,323	14,602
Motor vehicle steering and suspension....................	33633	26,295	1,268	48,238	19,377	8,968
Motor vehicle brake system...............................	33634	19,478	824	42,315	14,628	7,692
Motor vehicle transmission and power train parts.........	33635	47,146	3,055	64,795	36,153	29,477
Motor vehicle seating and interior trim....................	33636	38,016	1,675	44,068	28,083	15,334
Motor vehicle metal stamping.............................	33637	67,960	3,552	52,269	54,308	24,127
Other motor vehicle parts.................................	33639	102,905	4,434	43,091	77,291	40,652

[1] North American Industry Classification System, 2007; see text, Section 15. [2] Includes all full-time and part-time employees on the payrolls of operating manufacturing establishments during any part of the pay period that included the 12th of the month specified on the report form. Included are employees on paid sick leave, paid holidays, and paid vacations; not included are proprietors and partners of unincorporated businesses. [3] Includes extensive and unmeasurable duplication from shipments between establishments in the same industry classification.

Source: U.S. Census Bureau, Annual Survey of Manufactures, "Statistics for Industry Groups and Industries: 2010 and 2009," November 2011, <http://www.census.gov/manufacturing/asm/index.html>.

Table 1046. Motor Vehicle Manufactures—Employees, Payroll, and Shipments by Major State: 2010

[9,205,573 represents $9,205,573,000. Industry based on the 2007 North American Industry Classification System (NAICS); see text, Section 15. See footnote 3, Table 1045 for information regarding shipments. Based on the Annual Survey of Manufactures; see Apppendix III]

State	Motor vehicle manufacturing (NAICS 3361)			Motor vehicle parts manufacturing (NAICS 3363)		
	Employees	Payroll (1,000 dol.)	Value of shipments (1,000 dol.)	Employees	Payroll (1,000 dol.)	Value of shipments (1,000 dol.)
United States [1]	**135,881**	**9,205,573**	**207,542,991**	**388,657**	**19,540,845**	**168,296,739**
Alabama	10,380	731,860	17,990,632	13,950	665,311	7,319,560
Arizona	–	–	–	2,276	108,874	605,006
Arkansas	–	–	–	4,287	168,707	1,035,887
California	6,586	429,723	1,902,327	16,584	724,780	6,333,417
Connecticut	–	–	–	([2])	(D)	(D)
Florida	–	–	–	3,108	135,107	840,360
Georgia	([3])	(D)	(D)	7,244	341,003	4,066,524
Illinois	5,613	340,874	5,301,491	16,852	813,139	5,863,037
Indiana	12,558	863,880	24,970,755	41,276	2,248,478	18,408,795
Iowa	–	–	–	3,138	138,623	1,016,268
Kansas	([3])	(D)	(D)	([2])	(D)	(D)
Kentucky	12,618	808,195	18,550,261	21,948	996,668	11,385,757
Louisiana	–	–	–	1,276	49,149	273,220
Massachusetts	–	–	–	1,745	147,051	891,552
Michigan	24,289	1,769,061	43,613,613	76,476	4,336,016	36,559,950
Minnesota	1,704	88,997	2,003,776	2,084	88,989	549,219
Missouri	([4])	(D)	(D)	8,178	346,641	3,236,574
Nebraska	–	–	–	3,460	135,350	985,006
New Hampshire	–	–	–	10,886	637,053	3,489,749
New York	([2])	(D)	(D)	12,803	623,142	7,257,095
North Carolina	18038	1,285,543	21,983,234	53,225	2,828,226	20,108,178
Ohio	([2])	48,853	(D)	2,130	99,109	892,587
Oklahoma	([2])	(D)	(D)	1,251	64,124	337,712
Oregon	–	–	–	7,247	315,654	2,163,213
Pennsylvania	([3])	(D)	(D)	12,206	595,748	6,404,289
South Carolina	–	–	–	1,200	50,449	325,328
Tennessee	4785	364,812	(D)	24,046	1,054,685	12,291,281
Texas	5,100	397,099	17,769,753	10,091	469,399	4,241,513
Utah	–	–	–	2,943	152,638	(D)
Virginia	([2])	(D)	(D)	4,582	202,983	1,166,715
Washington	–	–	–	1,963	82,900	519,866
West Virginia	–	–	–	1,578	90,340	(D)
Wisconsin	([3])	(D)	(D)	9,211	378,152	3,162,855

– Represents zero. D Withheld to avoid disclosing data on individual companies. [1] Includes states not shown separately. [2] Employee class size of 1,000 to 2,499. [3] Employee class size of 2,500 to 4,999. [4] Employee class size of 5,000 to 9,999.

Source: U.S. Census Bureau, Annual Survey of Manufactures, "Geographic Area Statistics: Statistics for all Manufacturing by State: 2010 and 2009," November 2011, <http://www.census.gov/manufacturing/asm/index.html>.

Table 1047. Aerospace—Sales, New Orders, and Backlog: 2000 to 2010

[In billions of dollars (109.3 represents $109,300,000,000), except as indicated. Reported by establishments in which the principal business is the development and/or production of aerospace products]

Item	2000	2005	2006	2007	2008	2009	2010
Net sales	**109.3**	**124.2**	**155.9**	**126.8**	**135.2**	**148.0**	**134.1**
U.S. Government net sales	41.0	62.8	69.7	48.4	59.5	59.7	58.6
Percent U.S. Government	37.5	50.6	44.7	38.2	44.0	40.3	43.7
Complete aircraft and parts	57.2	49.9	(D)	(D)	(D)	(D)	(D)
Aircraft engines and parts	12.5	18.5	28.6	15.5	(D)	(D)	(D)
Net, new orders	**140.1**	**186.4**	**202.8**	**231.6**	**189.3**	**106.6**	**145.6**
Backlog, December 31	215.0	290.0	334.5	437.1	482.1	433.0	430.1

D Withheld to avoid disclosing data of individual companies.

Source: U.S. Census Bureau, Current Industrial Reports, "Civil Aircraft and Aircraft Engines; and Aerospace Industry," Series MA336G, June 2011. See also <http://www.census.gov/manufacturing/cir/historical_data/ma336g/index.html>.

Table 1048. Net Orders for U.S. Civil Jet Transport Aircraft: 1990 to 2011

[1990 data are net new firm orders; beginning 2000, net announced orders. Minus sign (–) indicates net cancellations. In 1997, Boeing acquired McDonnell Douglas]

Type of aircraft and customer	1990	2000	2005	2007	2008	2009	2010	2011
Total number [1]	**670**	**585**	**1,004**	**1,417**	**662**	**142**	**530**	**805**
U.S. customers	259	412	220	281	112	24	232	596
Foreign customers	411	193	811	1,136	550	118	298	209
Boeing 737, total	189	378	571	846	484	178	486	551
U.S. customers	38	302	152	164	107	34	206	525
Foreign customers	151	86	439	682	377	144	280	26
Boeing 747, total	153	24	43	25	3	2	-1	-1
U.S. customers	24	1	13	–	–	-2	-2	-1
Foreign customers	129	18	30	25	3	4	1	–
Boeing 757, total	66	43	–	–	–	–	–	–
U.S. customers	33	38	–	–	–	–	–	–
Foreign customers	33	14	–	–	–	–	–	–
Boeing 767, total	60	6	15	36	28	2	3	42
U.S. customers	23	-2	–	27	–	-1	–	31
Foreign customers	37	14	20	9	28	3	3	11
Boeing 777, total	34	113	154	141	54	19	46	200
U.S. customers	34	60	10	23	11	-7	3	37
Foreign customers	–	53	146	118	43	26	43	163
Boeing 787, total	–	–	235	369	93	-59	-4	13
U.S. customers	–	–	45	67	-6	–	25	4
Foreign customers	–	–	190	302	99	-59	-29	9
McDonnell Douglas MD-11, total	52	–	–	–	–	–	–	–
U.S. customers	16	–	–	–	–	–	–	–
Foreign customers	36	–	–	–	–	–	–	–
McDonnell Douglas MD-80/90, total	116	–	–	–	–	–	–	–
U.S. customers	91	–	–	–	–	–	–	–
Foreign customers	25	–	–	–	–	–	–	–
McDonnell Douglas MD-95, total	–	21	–	–	–	–	–	–
U.S. customers	–	13	–	–	–	–	–	–
Foreign customers	–	8	–	–	–	–	–	–

– Represents zero. [1] Beginning 2000, includes unidentified customers.

Source: Aerospace Industries Association of America, Washington, DC, "Orders: U.S. Civil Jet Transport Aircraft," Statistical Series 22, <http://www.aia-aerospace.org/economics/aerospace_statistics/> (copyright).

Table 1049. U.S. Aircraft Shipments: 1990 to 2010

[Value in millions of dollars (38,585 represents $38,585,000,000)]

Year	Total		Civil						Military	
			Large transports		General aviation [1]		Rotocraft			
	Units	Value	Units	Value	Units	Value	Units	Value	Units	Value
1990	3,321	38,585	521	22,215	1,144	2,007	603	254	1,053	14,109
1995	2,441	33,658	256	15,263	1,077	2,842	292	194	816	15,359
1996	2,220	37,518	269	18,915	1,115	3,048	278	193	558	15,363
1997	2,780	43,652	374	26,929	1,549	4,593	346	231	511	11,899
1998	3,534	53,728	559	35,663	2,193	5,534	363	252	419	12,280
1999	3,797	56,692	620	38,171	2,475	6,803	345	200	357	11,518
2000	4,113	50,289	485	30,327	2,802	8,040	493	270	333	11,652
2001	3,904	56,221	526	34,155	2,616	7,991	415	247	347	13,828
2002	3,252	49,361	379	27,547	2,196	7,261	318	157	359	14,396
2003	3,261	42,431	281	21,033	2,080	6,205	517	366	383	14,827
2004	3,802	43,555	283	20,484	2,296	6,918	805	515	418	15,639
2005	4,677	51,190	290	22,116	2,853	8,632	947	816	587	19,626
2006	5,426	55,472	398	25,875	3,134	9,550	898	843	996	19,204
2007	5,350	68,823	441	29,160	3,279	11,941	1,009	1,330	1,062	26,392
2008	5,263	72,892	375	24,076	3,079	13,348	1,084	1,486	725	33,982
2009	3,399	71,272	381	27,350	1,585	9,082	564	972	869	33,868
2010	2,842	71,831	459	29,265	1,334	7,875	249	791	800	33,900

[1] Excludes off-the-shelf military aircraft.

Source: U.S. Department of Commerce, International Trade Administration, "Shipments of Complete U.S. Aircraft, 1971–2010," <http://trade.gov/static/doc_aero_stats.asp>.

Table 1050. Aerospace Industry Sales by Product Group and Customer: 2000 to 2011

[In billions of dollars (144.7 represents $144,700,000,000). Due to reporting practices and tabulatimg methods, figures may differ from those in Table 1048]

Group	2000	2005	2006	2007	2008	2009	2010	2011
CURRENT DOLLARS								
Total sales...........	**144.7**	**167.1**	**182.6**	**196.5**	**199.5**	**208.9**	**208.9**	**215.8**
Product group:								
Aircraft, total..........................	81.6	86.7	98.3	105.6	102.9	110.2	109.3	116.6
Civil [1].......................	47.6	37.2	45.8	52.6	48.2	51.3	48.2	53.1
Military..........................	34.0	49.5	52.4	53.0	54.7	58.9	61.2	63.5
Missiles............................	9.3	18.4	20.3	22.0	23.2	24.2	24.5	24.6
Space............................	29.7	36.7	37.6	39.9	43.2	45.0	45.4	44.6
Related products and services [2]..............	24.1	25.4	26.5	29.1	30.2	29.4	29.7	30.0
Customer group:								
Aerospace products and services, total.............	120.6	141.8	156.1	167.5	169.3	179.4	179.3	185.8
DOD [3]............................	47.5	77.8	79.8	84.3	89.2	96.7	99.9	102.5
NASA [4] and other agencies.....................	13.4	17.3	17.2	17.8	19.5	20.8	20.6	19.5
Other customers [5]........................	59.7	46.7	59.1	65.3	60.6	61.9	58.8	63.9
Related products and services [2]..............	24.1	25.4	26.5	29.1	30.2	29.4	29.7	30.0
CONSTANT (2005) DOLLARS [6]								
Total sales.........................	**152.2**	**167.1**	**177.3**	**192.0**	**194.7**	**203.0**	**203.6**	**210.0**
Product group:								
Aircraft, total..........................	85.8	86.7	95.4	103.2	100.4	107.1	106.5	113.5
Civil [1].......................	50.0	37.2	44.5	51.4	47.0	49.9	46.9	51.7
Military..........................	35.8	49.5	50.9	51.8	53.4	57.2	59.6	61.8
Missiles............................	9.8	18.4	19.7	21.5	22.6	23.5	23.9	23.9
Space............................	31.2	36.7	36.5	39.0	42.2	43.8	44.2	43.4
Related products and services [3]..............	25.4	25.4	25.7	28.4	29.5	28.6	28.9	29.2
Customer group:								
Aerospace products and services, total.............	126.8	141.8	151.6	163.6	165.3	174.4	174.6	180.8
DOD [3]............................	49.9	77.8	77.5	82.4	87.1	94.0	97.3	99.7
NASA [4] and other agencies.....................	14.1	17.3	16.7	17.4	19.0	20.2	20.1	19.0
Other customers [5]........................	62.8	46.7	57.4	63.8	59.1	60.2	57.3	62.1
Related products and services [3]..............	25.4	25.4	25.7	28.4	29.5	28.6	28.9	29.2

[1] All civil sales of aircraft (domestic and export sales of jet transports, commuters, business, and personal aircraft and helicopters). [2] Electronics, software, and ground support equipment, plus sales of non-aerospace products which are produced by aerospace-manufacturing use technology, processes, and materials derived from aerospace products. [3] Department of Defense. [4] National Aeronautics and Space Administration. [5] Includes civil aircraft sales (see footnote 1), commercial space sales, all exports of military aircraft and missiles and related propulsion and parts. [6] Based on Aerospace Industry Association's aerospace composite price deflator (2005=100).

Source: Aerospace Industries Association (AIA) (copyright), based on company reports and data from the National Aeronautics and Space Administration (NASA), U.S. Census Bureau, the Office of Management and Budget, and the Department of Defense. See also <http://www.aia-aerospace.org/economics/year_end_review_and_forecast>.

Table 1051. Major Household Appliances—Value of Shipments: 2000 to 2010

[In millions of dollars (2,170 represents $2,170,000,000)]

Product description	Product code	2000	2005	2007	2008	2009	2010
Electric household ranges, ovens and surface cooking units, equipment and parts......................	3352211	2,170	2,577	2,736	2,506	2,041	2,217
Gas household ranges, ovens, and surface cooking units, equipment and parts................................	3352213	779	1,392	1,541	1,473	1,117	1,254
Other household ranges, cooking equipment and outdoor cooking equipment [1]...........................	3352215	1,251	965	491	510	517	580
Household refrigerators, including combination refrigerator-freezers...	3352221	5,396	5,405	5,440	5,891	5,188	5,466
Parts and attachments for household refrigerators and freezers..	3352223	(D)	(D)	159	107	92	96
Household laundry machines and parts...................	3352240	4,047	5,236	5,232	5,835	4,820	4,657
Water heaters, electric.....................................	3352281	573	638	950	953	869	852
Water heaters, except electric............................	3352283	844	970	1,572	1,547	1,452	1,525
Household appliances, n.e.c and parts [2]..................	3352285	2,066	2,433	2,717	2,602	2,159	2,176

D Withheld to avoid disclosing data of individual companies. [1] Includes parts and accessories. [2] n.e.c. means not elsewhere classified.

Source: U.S. Census Bureau, Current Industrial Reports, "Major Household Appliances," Series MA335F, <http://www.census.gov/manufacturing/cir/historical_data/mq335f/index.html>.

Section 22
Wholesale and Retail Trade

This section presents statistics relating to the distributive trades, specifically wholesale trade and retail trade. Data shown for the trades are classified by kind of business and cover sales, establishments, employees, payrolls, and other items. The principal sources of these data are from the U.S. Census Bureau and include the *2007 Economic Census*, annual and monthly surveys, and the *County Business Patterns* program. These data are supplemented by several tables from trade associations, such as the National Automobile Dealers Association (Table 1067).

Data on wholesale and retail trade also appear in several other sections. For instance, labor force employment and earnings data appear in Section 12, Labor Force, Employment, and Earnings; gross domestic product of the industry (Table 682) appears in Section 13, Income, Expenditures, Poverty, and Wealth; and financial data (several tables) from the quarterly *Statistics of Income Bulletin*, published by the Internal Revenue Service, appear in Section 15, Business Enterprise.

Censuses—Censuses of wholesale trade and retail trade have been taken at various intervals since 1929. Beginning with the 1967 census, legislation provides for a census of each area to be conducted every 5 years (for years ending in "2" and "7"). For more information on the most recent census, see the *Guide to the 2007 Economic Census* found at <http://www.census.gov/econ/census07/www/user_guide.html>. The industries covered in the censuses and surveys of business are defined in the *North American Industry Classification System*, (NAICS). Retail trade refers to places of business primarily engaged in retailing merchandise to the general public; and wholesale trade, to establishments primarily engaged in selling goods to other businesses and normally operating from a warehouse or office that have little or no display of merchandise. Many Census Bureau tables in this section utilize the 2007 NAICS codes, updating the 2002 codes, which replaced the Standard Industrial Classification (SIC) system. NAICS made substantial structural improvements and identifies over 250 new industries. At the same time, it causes breaks in time series far more profound than any prior revision of the previously used SIC system. For information on this system and how it affects the comparability of wholesale and retail statistics historically, see text, Section 15, Business Enterprise, and especially the Census Bureau Web site at <http://www.census.gov/eos/www/naics>. In general, the *2007 Economic Census* has three series of publications for these two sectors: 1) subject series with reports such as product lines and establishment and firm sizes, 2) geographic reports with individual reports for each state, and 3) industry series with individual reports for industry groups. For information on these series, see the Census Bureau Web site at <http://www.census.gov/econ/census07/>.

Current surveys—Current sample surveys conducted by the Census Bureau cover various aspects of wholesale and retail trade. Its *Monthly Retail Trade and Food Services* release at <http://www.census.gov/retail> contains monthly estimates of sales, inventories, and inventory/sales ratios for the United States, by kind of business. Annual figures on retail sales, year-end inventories, purchases, accounts receivable, and gross margins by kind of business are located on the Census Bureau Web site at <http://www.census.gov/econ/retail.html>. Additionally, annual data for accommodation and food services are located at the same site.

Statistics from the Census Bureau's monthly wholesale trade survey include national estimates of sales, inventories, and inventory/sales ratios for merchant wholesalers excluding manufacturers' sales branches and offices. Data are presented by major summary groups "durable and nondurable," and 4-digit NAICS industry groups. Merchant wholesalers excluding manufacturers' sales branches and offices are those wholesalers who take title to the goods they sell (e.g., jobbers, exporters, importers, industrial distributors). These data, based on reports submitted by a sample of firms, appear in the *Monthly Wholesale Trade Report* at <http://www.census.gov/wholesale>. This report, along with monthly sales, inventories, and inventories/sales ratios, also provides data on annual sales, inventories, and year-end inventories/sales ratios. The *Annual Wholesale Trade Survey* provides data on merchant wholesalers excluding manufacturer sales branches and offices as well as summary data for all merchant wholesalers. This report also provides separate data for manufacturer sales branches and offices, and electronic markets, agents, brokers, and commission merchants. Also included in the *Monthly Wholesale Trade Report are* data on annual sales, year-end inventories, inventories/sales ratios, operating expenses, purchases, and gross margins. Data are presented by major summary groups "durable and nondurable" and 4-digit NAICS industry groups for sales, end-of-year inventories, and operating expenses. The reports are available as documents on the Census Bureau Web site at <http://www.census.gov/econ/wholesale.html>.

E-commerce—Electronic commerce (or e-commerce) is the sale of goods and services over the Internet and extranet, electronic data interchange (EDI), or other online systems. Payment may or may not be made online. E-commerce data were collected in four separate Census Bureau surveys. These surveys used different measures of economic activity such as shipments for manufacturing, sales for wholesale and retail trade, and revenues for service industries. Consequently, measures of total economic and e-commerce activity vary by economic sector, are conceptually and definitionally different, and therefore, are not additive. This edition has several tables on e-commerce sales, such as Tables 1055, 1065, and 1066 in this section; and Table 1293 in Section 27, Accommodation, Food Services, and Other Services.

Statistical reliability—For a discussion of statistical collection and estimation, sampling procedures, and measures of statistical reliability applicable to Census Bureau data, see Appendix III.

Table 1052. Wholesale and Retail Trade—Establishments, Sales, Payroll, and Employees: 2002 and 2007

[435.5 represents $435,500. Covers establishments with payroll. For statement on methodology, see Appendix III]

Kind of business	2002 NAICS code [1]	Establishments (1,000)		Sales (bil. dol.)		Annual payroll (bil. dol.)		Paid employees (1,000)	
		2002	2007	2002	2007	2002	2007	2002	2007
Wholesale trade........................	**42**	**435.5**	**435.0**	**4,635**	**6,516**	**260**	**336**	**5,878**	**6,227**
Wholesale trade, durable goods....................	423	260.4	255.0	2,171	2,898	157	207	3,357	3,619
Wholesale trade, nondurable goods................	424	142.7	134.6	1,980	2,991	93	116	2,273	2,320
Wholesale electronic markets and agents and brokers....................	425	32.4	45.4	483	627	10	13	249	289
Retail trade............................	**44–45**	**1,114.6**	**11,281.0**	**3,056**	**3,918**	**302**	**363**	**14,648**	**15,515**
Motor vehicle and parts dealers....................	441	125.1	126.8	802	891	65	73	1,845	1,914
Furniture and home furnishings stores..............	442	65.2	65.1	92	108	13	15	535	557
Electronics and appliance stores....................	443	46.8	50.8	82	109	9	11	391	486
Building material and garden equipment and supplies dealers....................	444	(NA)	91.1	(NA)	318	(NA)	38	(NA)	1,331
Food and beverage stores..........................	445	148.8	146.1	457	539	49	55	2,839	2,827
Health and personal care stores....................	446	81.8	88.5	178	234	20	28	1,024	1,068
Gasoline stations..................................	447	121.4	118.8	249	450	14	15	927	891
Clothing and clothing accessories stores..............	448	149.8	156.5	168	216	21	27	1,427	1,644
Sporting goods, hobby, book, and music stores.......	451	62.2	57.4	73	81	9	9	611	619
General merchandise stores........................	452	40.7	45.9	445	577	43	54	2,525	2,763
Miscellaneous store retailers......................	453	129.5	121.9	91	104	13	14	792	792
Nonstore retailers................................	454	54.9	59.4	173	290	17	23	571	621

NA Not available. [1] North American Industrial Classification System; see text, Section 15.

Source: U.S. Census Bureau, "2007 Economic Census, Comparative Statistics for the United States, (2002 NAICS Basis): 2007 and 2002," July 2010, <http://www.census.gov/econ/census07/>.

Table 1053. Wholesale Trade—Nonemployer Firms and Receipts by Industry Type: 2009

[32,825,333 represents $32,825,333,000. Includes only firms subject to federal income tax. Nonemployers are businesses with no paid employees. A firm is a single physical location where business is conducted or services or industrial operations are performed. Each distinct business income tax return filed by a nonemployer business is counted as a firm. Based on NAICS 2007, see text, Section 15]

Industry type	2007 NAICS code [1]	Firms				Receipts ($1,000)
		Total	Corporations [2]	Individual proprietorships [3]	Partnerships [4]	
Wholesale trade, total........................	**42**	**390,126**	**69,245**	**297,303**	**23,578**	**32,825,333**
Durable goods merchant wholesalers....................	**423**	**194,201**	**38,706**	**142,794**	**12,701**	**17,135,675**
Motor vehicle and motor vehicle parts and supplies merchant wholesalers....................	4231	16,416	3,698	11,681	1,037	2,214,969
Furniture and home furnishing merchant wholesalers............	4232	13,363	2,290	10,331	742	971,390
Lumber and other construction materials merchant wholesalers....................	4233	8,402	1,861	5,769	772	806,689
Professional and commercial equipment and supplies merchant wholesalers....................	4234	10,739	2,150	7,824	765	985,361
Metal and mineral (except petroleum) merchant wholesalers....................	4235	3,265	770	2,247	248	389,672
Electrical and electronic goods merchant wholesalers..............	4236	10,765	3,093	6,784	888	1,155,418
Hardware and plumbing and heating equipment and supplies merchant wholesalers....................	4237	4,953	1,164	3,423	366	458,320
Machinery, equipment, and supplies merchant wholesalers....................	4238	18,969	5,340	12,176	1,453	2,164,078
Miscellaneous durable goods merchant wholesalers............	4239	107,329	18,340	82,559	6,430	7,989,778
Nondurable goods merchant wholesalers....................	**424**	**145,944**	**25,009**	**112,003**	**8,932**	**12,645,174**
Paper and paper product merchant wholesalers..............	4241	6,691	1,132	5,210	349	493,896
Drugs and druggists' sundries merchant wholesalers.............	4242	2,716	649	1,856	211	233,230
Apparel, piece goods, and notions merchant wholesalers....................	4243	23,194	4,313	17,306	1,575	1,587,199
Grocery and related products merchant wholesalers.............	4244	27,224	4,811	20,767	1,646	3,814,162
Farm product raw material merchant wholesalers..............	4245	4,705	605	3,861	239	523,169
Chemical and allied products merchant wholesalers.............	4246	3,668	1,105	2,219	344	411,766
Petroleum and petroleum products merchant wholesalers....................	4247	2,301	445	1,668	188	304,926
Beer, wine, and distilled alcoholic beverage merchant wholesalers....................	4248	4,521	847	3,115	559	393,193
Miscellaneous nondurable goods merchant wholesalers....................	4249	70,924	11,102	56,001	3,821	4,883,633
Wholesale electronic markets and agents and brokers........................	**425**	**49,981**	**5,530**	**42,506**	**1,945**	**3,044,484**
Business to business electronics markets....................	42511	7,433	852	6,226	355	447,195

[1] North American Industry Classification System, 2007. See text, Section 15. [2] A legally incorporated business under state laws. [3] Also referred to as "sole proprietorship," an unincorporated business with a sole owner. Includes self-employed persons. [4] An unincorporated business where two or more persons join to carry on a trade or business with each having a shared financial interest in the business.

Source: U.S. Census Bureau, "Nonemployer Statistics," revised August 2012, <http://www.census.gov/econ/nonemployer/index.html>.

Table 1054. Wholesale Trade—Establishments, Employees, and Payroll: 2008 and 2009

[429.5 represents 429,500. Covers establishments with payroll. Excludes self-employed individuals, employees of private households, railroad employees, agricultural production employees, and most government employees. For statement on methodology, see Appendix III]

Kind of business	2007 NAICS code [1]	Establishments (1,000)		Employees [2] (1,000)		Payroll (bil. dol.)	
		2008	2009	2008	2009	2008	2009
Wholesale trade, total..........................	**42**	**429.5**	**419.8**	**6,165**	**5,828**	**353.1**	**334.2**
Merchant wholesalers, durable goods...........................	423	248.5	241.3	3,553	3,335	215.8	200.6
Motor vehicle/motor vehicle parts and supply merchant wholesalers..	4231	26.0	24.9	395	362	17.9	16.6
Furniture and home furnishing merchant wholesalers..........	4232	13.6	12.6	169	145	8.2	7.0
Lumber and other construction materials merchant wholesalers..	4233	19.4	18.8	256	214	12.1	10.0
Professional and commercial equipment and supplies merchant wholesalers....................................	4234	35.0	34.4	724	696	55.8	53.2
Metal and mineral (except petroleum) merchant wholesalers..	4235	11.1	10.8	169	154	10.0	8.3
Electrical goods merchant wholesalers...................	4236	30.0	29.1	510	519	41.2	41.6
Hardware, plumbing and heating equipment and supplies merchant wholesalers.........................	4237	20.2	19.9	244	224	12.7	11.5
Machinery, equipment, and supplies merchant wholesalers..	4238	59.5	58.3	738	705	41.4	37.7
Miscellaneous durable goods merchant wholesalers..........	4239	33.6	32.6	349	316	16.6	14.6
Merchant wholesalers, nondurable goods........................	424	129.8	127.2	2,313	2,196	122.3	119.1
Paper and paper product merchant wholesalers...............	4241	11.5	11.0	171	155	8.6	7.8
Drugs and druggists' sundries merchant wholesalers..........	4242	8.6	8.8	274	267	22.6	23.2
Apparel, piece goods and notions merchant wholesalers......	4243	16.5	15.8	211	187	10.9	9.7
Grocery and related product merchant wholesalers..........	4244	33.0	33.0	796	764	36.2	35.7
Farm product raw material merchant wholesalers.............	4245	6.3	6.1	61	61	2.9	2.9
Chemical and allied products merchant wholesalers..........	4246	12.8	12.4	150	146	9.8	9.6
Petroleum and petroleum products merchant wholesalers.....	4247	7.3	7.2	105	102	6.3	6.3
Beer, wine, and distilled alcoholic beverages...............	4248	4.2	4.1	184	178	9.7	9.6
Miscellaneous nondurable goods merchant wholesalers......	4249	29.6	28.7	362	336	15.3	14.3
Wholesale electronic markets and agents and brokers..........	425	51.2	51.2	299	297	15.0	14.5

[1] North American Industry Classification System, 2007. See text, Section 15. [2] Covers full- and part-time employees who are on the payroll in the pay period including March 12.

Source: U.S. Census Bureau, "County Business Patterns," June 2012, <http://www.census.gov/econ/cbp/index.html>.

Table 1055. Merchant Wholesale Trade Sales—Total and E-Commerce: 2010

[4,132,327 represents $4,132,327,000,000. Covers only businesses with paid employees. Excludes manufacturers' sales branches and offices. Based on the Annual Wholesale Trade Survey, see Appendix III]

Kind of business	2002 NAICS code [1]	2010			
		Value of sales (mil. dol.)		E-commerce as percent of total sales	Percent distribution of E-commerce sales
		Total	E-commerce		
Total merchant wholesale trade.......................	**42**	**4,132,327**	**833,019**	**20.2**	**100.0**
Durable goods..	**423**	**1,875,793**	**328,180**	**17.5**	**39.4**
Motor vehicles, parts and supplies................	4231	294,687	113,751	38.6	13.7
Furniture and home furnishings....................	4232	52,499	6,892	13.1	0.8
Lumber and other construction materials.............	4233	92,038	5,196	5.6	0.6
Professional and commercial equipment and supplies..............	4234	361,382	106,681	29.5	12.8
Computer, peripheral equipment, and software........	42343	187,865	67,680	36.0	8.1
Metals and minerals (except petroleum)................	4235	124,694	3,941	3.2	0.5
Electrical goods.................................	4236	346,362	44,832	12.9	5.4
Hardware, and plumbing and heating equipment and supplies...	4237	94,875	11,143	11.7	1.3
Machinery, equipment and supplies....................	4238	296,518	13,145	4.4	1.6
Miscellaneous durable goods.......................	4239	212,738	22,599	10.6	2.7
Nondurable goods...	**424**	**2,256,534**	**504,839**	**22.4**	**60.6**
Paper and paper products..........................	4241	83,458	18,619	22.3	2.2
Drugs and druggists' sundries.......................	4242	391,482	293,192	74.9	35.2
Apparel, piece goods and notions....................	4243	132,514	39,141	29.5	4.7
Groceries and related products......................	4244	499,533	96,966	19.4	11.6
Farm product raw materials.........................	4245	182,756	9,631	5.3	1.2
Chemical and allied products........................	4246	102,247	5,528	5.4	0.7
Petroleum and petroleum products...................	4247	541,307	(S)	(S)	(S)
Beer, wine, and distilled alcoholic beverages..........	4248	111,218	3,491	3.1	0.4
Miscellaneous nondurable goods.......................	4249	212,019	27,938	13.2	3.4

S Figure does not meet publication standards. [1] North American Industry Classification System, 2002. See text, Section 15.

Source: U.S. Census Bureau, "E-Stats, 2010 E-commerce Multi-sector Report," May 2012, <http://www.census.gov/econ/estats/>.

Table 1056. Merchant Wholesalers—Summary: 2000 to 2010

[In billions of dollars (2,814.6 represents $2,814,600,000,000), except ratios. Inventories and inventories/sales ratios, as of December, not seasonally adjusted. Excludes manufacturers' sales branches and offices. Data adjusted using final results of the 2007 Economic Census. Based on data from the Annual Wholesale Trade Survey and the Monthly Wholesale Trade Survey; see Appendix III]

Kind of business	2002 NAICS code [1]	2000	2005	2006	2007	2008	2009	2010
SALES								
Merchant wholesalers............................	42	**2,814.6**	**3,613.4**	**3,904.2**	**4,174.3**	**4,431.8**	**3,699.2**	**4,132.3**
Durable goods.................................	423	**1,486.7**	**1,814.4**	**1,982.8**	**2,074.5**	**2,076.3**	**1,669.7**	**1,875.8**
Motor vehicles, parts, and supplies...........................	4231	222.2	303.8	335.8	341.2	308.1	251.3	294.7
Furniture and home furnishings....................	4232	52.7	63.0	69.1	69.1	64.2	51.0	52.5
Lumber and other construction materials....................	4233	87.2	139.0	141.7	126.5	116.4	90.4	92.0
Professional, commercial equipment and supplies........	4234	282.2	316.9	330.9	354.3	357.8	334.9	361.4
Computer, peripheral equipment and software...........	42343	174.8	163.1	161.4	171.3	175.4	165.8	187.9
Metal and mineral (except petroleum).................	4235	93.8	136.1	158.2	165.9	177.5	103.6	124.7
Electrical and electronic goods.....................	4236	260.0	284.4	319.6	349.0	354.4	310.1	346.4
Hardware, plumbing, heating equipment and supplies. . . .	4237	72.1	95.0	109.1	112.2	108.4	89.6	94.9
Machinery, equipment, and supplies........................	4238	256.1	287.7	311.9	328.8	349.7	270.5	296.5
Miscellaneous durable goods......................	4239	160.3	188.5	206.6	227.4	239.9	168.4	212.7
Nondurable goods...........................	424	**1,327.9**	**1,799.0**	**1,921.4**	**2,099.8**	**2,355.5**	**2,029.5**	**2,256.5**
Paper and paper products.....................	4241	77.8	87.2	90.4	91.3	90.5	81.3	83.5
Drugs and druggists' sundries......................	4242	176.0	322.4	340.8	351.8	369.0	376.6	391.5
Apparel, piece goods, and notions.................	4243	96.5	121.2	128.5	139.7	136.6	123.4	132.5
Grocery and related products....................	4244	374.7	422.2	436.7	475.8	489.9	480.0	499.5
Farm product raw materials....................	4245	102.7	106.0	111.9	145.8	196.4	164.6	182.8
Chemical and allied products....................	4246	62.3	90.9	94.7	102.3	115.5	88.9	102.2
Petroleum and petroleum products..................	4247	195.8	369.9	428.5	486.9	628.8	402.0	541.3
Beer, wine, and distilled alcoholic beverages..............	4248	71.3	92.2	98.4	103.8	109.3	108.7	111.2
Miscellaneous nondurable goods..........................	4249	170.9	187.1	191.5	202.5	219.6	204.2	212.0
INVENTORIES								
Merchant wholesalers................................	42	**309.8**	**368.8**	**399.9**	**426.7**	**442.9**	**391.5**	**432.1**
Durable goods................................	423	**198.6**	**232.4**	**255.4**	**261.9**	**276.2**	**225.8**	**245.1**
Motor vehicles, parts, and supplies...........................	4231	28.8	37.8	40.5	42.1	46.3	35.2	38.3
Furniture and home furnishings....................	4232	6.4	7.9	8.5	8.6	8.2	6.5	7.0
Lumber and other construction materials....................	4233	8.3	13.9	14.1	13.3	12.8	10.3	11.0
Professional, commercial equipment and supplies........	4234	27.3	26.7	29.2	29.8	30.2	27.7	29.6
Computer, peripheral equipment and software...........	42343	12.1	10.3	10.8	10.6	10.7	10.4	11.3
Metal and mineral (except petroleum).................	4235	13.6	21.1	26.5	25.1	29.1	18.7	21.8
Electrical and electronic goods.....................	4236	31.3	31.0	34.9	37.6	39.7	33.4	37.4
Hardware, plumbing, heating equipment and supplies. . . .	4237	11.5	15.3	17.2	18.1	17.3	15.0	15.9
Machinery, equipment, and supplies........................	4238	51.1	55.7	60.8	63.9	68.4	58.2	61.8
Miscellaneous durable goods......................	4239	20.2	23.0	23.6	23.3	24.2	20.7	22.3
Nondurable goods...........................	424	**111.2**	**136.5**	**144.5**	**164.8**	**166.7**	**165.7**	**186.9**
Paper and paper products.....................	4241	6.7	7.2	7.3	7.5	7.8	6.9	7.4
Drugs and druggists' sundries......................	4242	23.9	30.2	30.9	32.1	32.5	33.0	34.8
Apparel, piece goods, and notions.................	4243	14.2	17.4	17.8	18.2	19.4	15.6	18.4
Grocery and related products....................	4244	20.5	22.6	23.9	26.8	28.8	27.5	30.2
Farm product raw materials....................	4245	11.5	11.3	14.6	21.0	18.0	20.4	28.3
Chemical and allied products....................	4246	6.0	8.3	8.4	9.5	10.4	8.7	9.9
Petroleum and petroleum products..................	4247	5.2	12.6	13.9	18.5	15.0	21.8	24.0
Beer, wine, and distilled alcoholic beverages..............	4248	6.5	8.4	9.1	10.3	11.5	10.8	11.2
Miscellaneous nondurable goods..........................	4249	16.6	18.6	18.5	20.9	23.4	21.0	22.6
INVENTORIES/SALES RATIO								
Merchant wholesalers................................	42	**1.10**	**1.02**	**1.02**	**1.02**	**1.00**	**1.06**	**1.05**
Durable goods................................	423	**1.34**	**1.28**	**1.29**	**1.26**	**1.33**	**1.35**	**1.31**
Motor vehicles, parts, and supplies...........................	4231	1.30	1.24	1.21	1.23	1.50	1.40	1.30
Furniture and home furnishings....................	4232	1.22	1.26	1.24	1.25	1.28	1.27	1.34
Lumber and other construction materials....................	4233	0.96	1.00	1.00	1.05	1.10	1.14	1.19
Professional, commercial equipment and supplies........	4234	0.97	0.84	0.88	0.84	0.84	0.83	0.82
Computer, peripheral equipment and software...........	42343	0.69	0.63	0.67	0.62	0.61	0.63	0.60
Metal and mineral (except petroleum).................	4235	1.45	1.55	1.67	1.52	1.64	1.80	1.75
Electrical and electronic goods.....................	4236	1.20	1.09	1.09	1.08	1.12	1.08	1.08
Hardware, plumbing, heating equipment and supplies. . . .	4237	1.60	1.61	1.58	1.61	1.60	1.68	1.68
Machinery, equipment, and supplies........................	4238	1.99	1.94	1.95	1.94	1.96	2.15	2.09
Miscellaneous durable goods......................	4239	1.26	1.22	1.14	1.02	1.01	1.23	1.05
Nondurable goods...........................	424	**0.84**	**0.76**	**0.75**	**0.78**	**0.71**	**0.82**	**0.83**
Paper and paper products.....................	4241	0.87	0.82	0.81	0.82	0.86	0.85	0.89
Drugs and druggists' sundries......................	4242	1.36	0.94	0.91	0.91	0.88	0.88	0.89
Apparel, piece goods, and notions.................	4243	1.47	1.43	1.39	1.30	1.42	1.26	1.39
Grocery and related products....................	4244	0.55	0.54	0.55	0.56	0.59	0.57	0.61
Farm product raw materials....................	4245	1.12	1.06	1.31	1.44	0.92	1.24	1.55
Chemical and allied products....................	4246	0.97	0.91	0.89	0.93	0.90	0.98	0.97
Petroleum and petroleum products..................	4247	0.27	0.34	0.33	0.38	0.24	0.54	0.44
Beer, wine, and distilled alcoholic beverages..............	4248	0.91	0.91	0.93	0.99	1.05	0.99	1.01
Miscellaneous nondurable goods..........................	4249	0.97	0.99	0.97	1.03	1.06	1.03	1.06

[1] North American Industry Classification System, 2002. See text, Section 15.

Source: U.S. Census Bureau, "2010 Annual Wholesale Trade Report," February 2012, <http://www.census.gov/wholesale/>.

Table 1057. Wholesale and Retail Trade—Establishments, Employees, and Payroll by State: 2008 and 2009

[6,165 represents 6,165,000. Covers establishments with payroll. Excludes most government employees, railroad employees, and self-employed persons. Based on North American Industry Classification System (NAICS) 2007. See text, Section 15. For statement on methodology, see Appendix III]

State	Wholesale trade (NAICS 42)						Retail trade (NAICS 44, 45)					
	Establishments		Employees [1] (1,000)		Annual payroll (mil. dol.)		Establishments		Employees [1] (1,000)		Annual payroll (mil.dol.)	
	2008	2009	2008	2009	2008	2009	2008	2009	2008	2009	2008	2009
U.S.........	429,463	419,758	6,165	5,828	353,061	334,158	1,100,943	1,076,645	15,615	14,803	369,289	355,493
AL...........	5,621	5,456	80	75	3,722	3,430	19,131	18,649	244	229	5,246	5,055
AK...........	761	758	9	9	469	471	2,578	2,547	35	34	971	961
AZ...........	6,933	6,699	101	94	5,295	5,222	19,112	18,441	343	316	7,891	7,304
AR...........	3,459	3,387	47	43	2,040	1,960	11,467	11,146	142	137	3,024	3,026
CA...........	60,768	59,169	888	827	58,314	54,299	111,200	107,971	1,669	1,544	43,881	41,302
CO...........	7,410	7,215	105	98	6,429	5,924	18,990	18,734	262	247	6,641	6,276
CT...........	4,579	4,499	78	76	5,563	5,190	13,485	13,062	193	180	5,176	4,983
DE...........	1,021	1,004	19	18	1,444	1,393	3,804	3,682	55	51	1,321	1,237
DC...........	414	416	5	5	360	359	1,821	1,764	20	19	521	515
FL...........	31,713	30,517	318	288	15,215	14,070	72,118	70,628	996	922	23,662	22,485
GA...........	13,888	13,323	205	191	11,614	11,048	35,371	34,136	476	440	10,641	10,109
HI...........	1,829	1,788	21	19	875	823	4,891	4,737	71	67	1,786	1,704
ID...........	2,094	2,041	26	24	1,116	1,041	6,225	5,979	82	74	1,892	1,761
IL...........	19,756	19,407	318	305	19,575	18,705	41,743	40,856	653	600	15,722	14,613
IN...........	8,034	7,925	117	109	5,415	5,048	22,936	22,262	331	314	7,122	6,865
IA...........	4,929	4,860	66	66	2,927	2,870	12,780	12,486	180	178	3,753	3,732
KS...........	4,501	4,437	61	61	3,079	2,941	10,978	10,760	151	147	3,261	3,232
KY...........	4,428	4,328	75	72	3,674	3,622	16,024	15,653	230	222	5,204	5,137
LA...........	5,579	5,503	77	77	3,797	3,758	16,866	16,762	234	230	5,239	5,180
ME...........	1,606	1,582	19	18	838	816	6,775	6,565	85	80	1,931	1,884
MD...........	5,905	5,844	98	91	5,640	5,397	19,088	18,540	294	277	6,999	6,991
MA...........	8,647	8,352	143	135	10,289	9,522	25,121	24,597	361	343	9,176	8,834
MI...........	11,806	11,617	171	159	9,723	8,758	36,381	35,465	466	448	10,359	10,083
MN...........	8,462	8,297	138	132	8,721	8,320	20,206	19,751	304	291	6,787	6,773
MS...........	2,890	2,851	37	35	1,504	1,474	12,148	11,836	145	138	2,965	2,879
MO...........	8,268	8,067	131	124	6,118	5,678	22,577	22,170	319	308	7,127	7,032
MT...........	1,451	1,448	15	14	600	560	5,137	5,026	60	57	1,380	1,310
NE...........	3,014	2,988	42	39	2,052	1,904	7,623	7,446	109	107	2,323	2,312
NV...........	3,009	2,901	40	35	2,038	1,779	8,387	8,234	142	131	3,681	3,387
NH...........	1,860	1,840	26	25	1,692	1,591	6,473	6,278	102	98	2,437	2,363
NJ...........	15,724	15,181	270	257	19,783	19,129	33,564	32,701	465	445	12,386	12,041
NM...........	2,028	1,994	23	22	1,012	971	7,107	6,948	101	97	2,306	2,210
NY...........	34,112	33,391	394	370	23,764	21,904	75,853	75,778	892	859	23,090	22,302
NC...........	12,070	11,787	181	168	9,920	9,266	35,676	34,702	477	447	10,549	9,985
ND...........	1,513	1,488	19	19	851	865	3,294	3,232	45	45	966	991
OH...........	15,026	14,624	232	219	12,060	11,264	38,650	37,590	585	561	13,062	12,627
OK...........	4,602	4,591	62	60	3,002	2,780	13,218	13,069	178	174	3,844	3,807
OR...........	5,730	5,610	77	83	4,106	5,146	14,486	14,085	206	186	4,951	4,581
PA...........	15,559	15,252	248	239	14,049	13,610	45,583	44,735	677	655	15,249	15,048
RI...........	1,464	1,447	21	21	1,062	1,057	4,017	3,849	50	47	1,229	1,188
SC...........	5,033	4,955	67	62	3,256	2,908	18,461	17,918	237	224	5,019	4,792
SD...........	1,403	1,398	16	16	689	682	4,069	4,020	51	50	1,063	1,075
TN...........	7,291	7,080	127	114	6,289	5,888	23,568	22,940	327	308	7,310	7,005
TX...........	31,815	31,555	491	479	28,811	28,035	77,669	76,795	1,171	1,149	27,484	26,967
UT...........	3,631	3,562	56	54	2,715	2,557	8,955	8,846	148	140	3,471	3,281
VT...........	851	848	11	11	509	485	3,734	3,713	41	39	964	938
VA...........	7,659	7,504	114	106	6,200	5,924	28,872	28,087	434	413	9,894	9,705
WA...........	9,717	9,475	138	127	7,698	7,071	22,481	22,044	332	310	8,701	8,319
WV...........	1,576	1,565	21	19	907	869	6,846	6,745	93	90	1,847	1,854
WI...........	7,194	7,110	115	109	5,796	5,343	20,542	19,897	319	302	6,984	6,680
WY...........	830	822	8	8	445	430	2,862	2,788	33	32	800	769

[1] Covers full- and part-time employees who are on the payroll in the pay period including March 12.

Source: U.S. Census Bureau, "County Business Patterns," June 2011, <http://www.census.gov/econ/cbp/index.html>.

Table 1058. Retail Trade—Establishments, Employees, and Payroll: 2008 and 2009

[1,100.9 represents 1,100,900. Covers establishments with payroll. Excludes most government employees, railroad employees, and self-employed persons. For statement on methodology, see Appendix III]

Kind of business	2007 NAICS code [1]	Establishments (1,000) 2008	Establishments (1,000) 2009	Employees (1,000) [2] 2008	Employees (1,000) [2] 2009	Payroll (bil. dol.) 2008	Payroll (bil. dol.) 2009
Retail trade, total..........	**44–45**	**1,100.9**	**1,076.6**	**15,615**	**14,803**	**369.3**	**355.5**
Motor vehicle and parts dealers..........	441	122.4	119.8	1,884	1,656	69.1	61.2
Automobile dealers..........	4411	49.5	46.9	1,254	1,052	51.1	43.8
New car dealers..........	44111	24.2	22.9	1,125	941	47.2	40.2
Used car dealers..........	44112	25.3	24.0	129	111	4.0	3.6
Other motor vehicle dealers..........	4412	16.7	15.9	165	138	5.6	4.6
Recreational vehicle dealers..........	44121	3.0	2.8	40	31	1.4	1.1
Motorcycle and boat and other motor vehicle dealers..........	44122	13.8	13.1	124	107	4.2	3.5
Motorcycle dealers..........	441221	6.0	5.7	70	61	2.3	1.9
Automotive parts, accessories, and tire stores..........	4413	56.1	57.0	466	467	12.3	12.7
Automotive parts, accessories and tire stores..........	44131	37.6	36.9	303	297	7.2	7.1
Tire dealers..........	44132	18.5	20.1	163	170	5.1	5.7
Furniture and home furnishing stores..........	442	61.7	57.5	533	450	13.9	11.9
Furniture stores..........	4421	27.3	26.0	253	219	7.4	6.5
Home furnishings stores..........	4422	34.4	31.5	281	230	6.5	5.4
Floor covering stores..........	44221	13.9	12.9	84	72	3.0	2.4
Other home furnishings stores..........	44229	20.5	18.6	196	159	3.5	3.0
Window treatment stores..........	442291	2.5	2.2	8	7	0.2	0.2
Electronics and appliance stores..........	443	49.2	48.5	465	449	11.2	10.8
Appliance, TV, and all other electronics stores..........	44311	37.1	36.8	364	353	8.5	8.2
Household appliance stores..........	443111	8.9	8.6	69	65	2.1	1.9
Radio, television, and other electronics stores..........	443112	28.2	28.2	295	288	6.4	6.3
Computer and software stores..........	44312	10.2	10.0	88	86	2.3	2.4
Bldg. material & garden equip. & supp. dealers..........	444	89.2	85.9	1,335	1,221	38.4	35.4
Building material & supplies dealers [3]..........	4441	69.4	66.7	1,171	1,069	34.1	31.3
Home centers..........	44411	7.0	6.9	(NA)	(NA)	(D)	(D)
Hardware stores..........	44413	16.0	15.7	143	137	3.3	3.1
Lawn & garden equip. & supplies stores [3]..........	4442	19.8	19.2	164	152	4.3	4.1
Nursery and garden centers..........	44422	15.6	15.1	137	127	3.6	3.3
Food & beverage stores..........	445	143.7	145.2	2,862	2,855	56.7	58.3
Grocery stores..........	4451	89.1	90.3	2,571	2,562	51.5	53.0
Supermarkets & grocery (except convenience) stores..........	44511	63.4	63.6	2,450	2,440	49.5	51.0
Convenience stores..........	44512	25.7	26.6	121	121	1.9	2.0
Specialty food stores..........	4452	23.9	23.9	145	146	2.4	2.5
Beer, wine, & liquor stores [4]..........	4453	30.7	31.0	146	148	2.8	2.8
Health & personal care stores [3]..........	446	88.4	89.2	1,025	995	31.3	32.0
Pharmacies & drug stores..........	44611	42.0	42.4	756	730	24.7	25.1
Cosmetics, beauty supplies, & perfume stores..........	44612	14.0	14.3	95	95	1.6	1.7
Optical goods stores..........	44613	13.2	12.9	74	71	2.0	1.9
Gasoline stations..........	447	114.1	112.1	897	856	15.3	15.1
Gasoline stations with convenience stores..........	44711	95.1	94.0	725	693	11.8	11.7
Other gasoline stations..........	44719	19.1	18.2	171	163	3.5	3.4
Clothing & clothing accessories stores..........	448	155.6	150.2	1,648	1,536	26.7	25.9
Clothing stores [3]..........	4481	99.5	97.4	1,287	1,203	19.2	18.8
Men's clothing stores..........	44811	8.1	7.7	58	52	1.4	1.2
Women's clothing stores..........	44812	36.0	34.6	343	325	5.2	5.0
Children's & infants' clothing stores..........	44813	7.3	7.1	91	84	1.1	1.0
Family clothing stores..........	44814	28.4	28.5	662	607	9.3	9.3
Shoe stores..........	4482	28.2	26.7	208	195	3.3	3.3
Jewelry, luggage, & leather goods stores..........	4483	27.9	26.1	153	138	4.2	3.8
Jewelry stores..........	44831	26.7	25.0	146	131	4.0	3.6
Sporting goods, hobby, book, & music stores..........	451	55.8	53.5	618	577	10.0	9.5
Sporting goods/hobby/musical instrument stores [3]..........	4511	40.9	39.3	432	403	7.4	7.0
Sporting goods stores..........	45111	22.1	21.6	228	226	4.2	4.1
Hobby, toy, and game stores..........	45112	9.2	8.4	124	102	1.8	1.7
Book, periodical, & music stores [3]..........	4512	14.9	14.1	186	174	2.6	2.4
Book stores..........	451211	9.7	9.4	152	143	2.0	1.9
Prerecorded tape, CD, & record stores..........	45122	3.7	3.4	27	24	0.4	0.4
General merchandise stores..........	452	45.7	45.6	2,977	2,917	59.2	59.5
Department stores..........	4521	8.8	8.7	1,292	1,197	24.0	23.4
Other general merchandise stores..........	4529	36.9	37.0	1,685	1,720	35.2	36.1
Warehouse clubs & superstores..........	45291	4.4	4.5	1,374	1,410	30.7	31.5
All other general merchandise stores..........	45299	32.5	32.5	311	309	4.4	4.6
Miscellaneous store retailers [3]..........	453	117.2	112.8	779	733	14.7	13.7
Florists..........	4531	18.5	17.1	90	76	1.3	1.1
Office supplies, stationery, and gift stores..........	4532	38.8	36.7	305	278	5.0	4.6
Office supplies and stationery stores..........	45321	9.4	8.9	114	104	2.4	2.2
Gift, novelty, and souvenir stores..........	45322	29.4	27.7	191	174	2.6	2.4
Used merchandise stores..........	4533	17.7	17.4	135	139	2.3	2.4
Other miscellaneous store retailers [3]..........	4539	42.2	41.6	250	240	6.0	5.5
Nonstore retailers [3]..........	454	57.9	56.3	592	557	22.9	22.4
Electronic shopping & mail-order houses..........	4541	21.9	21.9	332	321	14.2	14.1
Direct selling establishments..........	4543	31.1	29.8	212	198	7.4	7.2
Fuel dealers..........	45431	10.0	9.8	84	81	3.2	3.3

D Figure withheld to avoid disclosure. NA Not available. [1] Based on North American Industry Classification System, 2007. See text, Section 15. [2] See footnote 2, Table 1054. [3] Includes other kinds of business, not shown separately. [4] Includes government employees.

Source: U.S. Census Bureau, "County Business Patterns," June 2011, <http://www.census.gov/econ/cbp/index.html>.

Table 1059. Retail Trade—Nonemployer Firms and Receipts by Industry Type: 2009

[74,432,867 represents $74,432,867,000. See headnote, Table 1053]

| Industry type | 2007 NAICS code [1] | Firms | | | | Receipts ($1,000) |
		Total	Corpora-tions [2]	Individual proprietor-ships [3]	Partner-ships [4]	
Retail trade, total..........	**44–45**	**1,826,224**	**116,547**	**1,643,918**	**65,759**	**74,432,867**
Motor vehicle & parts dealers......................	441	160,824	16,409	137,527	6,888	16,885,824
Furniture & home furnishings stores....................	442	42,536	6,161	33,522	2,853	2,420,001
Electronics and appliance stores....................	443	30,205	4,021	24,770	1,414	1,498,224
Bldg material & garden equip. & supplies dealers........	444	37,283	4,068	31,313	1,902	2,244,406
Building material & supplies dealers.....................	4441	26,444	3,241	21,790	1,413	1,723,581
Food & beverage stores....................	445	103,131	12,355	83,897	6,879	8,323,597
Grocery stores......................	4451	44,080	5,163	36,444	2,473	4,072,990
Specialty food stores......................	4452	47,190	5,116	38,882	3,192	2,464,371
Health & personal care stores....................	446	137,922	5,946	129,416	2,560	3,099,701
Gasoline stations......................	447	9,274	1,751	6,821	702	1,339,618
Clothing & clothing accessories stores....................	448	138,498	9,513	122,698	6,287	5,034,308
Clothing stores......................	4481	89,049	6,502	77,738	4,809	3,245,906
Jewelry, luggage, and leather goods stores..............	4483	44,583	2,481	40,882	1220	1,530,599
Sporting goods, hobby, book, & music stores....................	451	81,460	5,893	71,182	4,385	3,334,265
Book, periodical, and music stores....................	4512	24,333	1,365	21,976	992	740,888
General merchandise stores....................	452	33,103	2,855	28,593	1,655	1,423,627
Miscellaneous store retailers....................	453	267,812	21,968	231,491	14,353	10,994,214
Office supplies, stationery, and gift stores....................	4532	55,928	4,489	48,190	3,249	1,866,342
Nonstore retailers....................	454	784,176	25,607	742,688	15,881	17,835,082
Electronic shopping & mail-order houses....................	4541	82,069	6,112	71,871	4,086	3,126,440
Direct selling establishments....................	4543	675,525	17,338	647,915	10,272	13,922,686

[1] North American Industry Classification System, 2007. See text, Section 15. [2] A legally incorporated business under state laws. [3] Also referred to as "sole proprietorship," an unincorporated business with a sole owner. Includes self-employed persons. [4] An unincorporated business where two or more persons join to carry on a trade or business with each having a shared financial interest in the business.

Source: U.S. Census Bureau, "Nonemployer Statistics," August 2012, <http://www.census.gov/econ/nonemployer/index.html>.

Table 1060. Retail Industries—Employees, Average Weekly Hours, and Average Hourly Earnings: 2000 to 2010

[Annual averages of monthly figures (15,280 represents 15,280,000). Covers all full- and part-time employees who worked during, or received pay for, any part of the pay period including the 12th of the month]

| Industry | 2007 NAICS code [1] | Employees (1,000) | | | Average weekly hours | | | Average hourly earnings (dol.) | |
		2000	2005	2010	2000	2005	2010	2000	2010
Retail trade, total............	**44,45**	**15,280**	**15,280**	**14,414**	**30.7**	**30.6**	**30.2**	**10.86**	**13.24**
Motor vehicle and parts dealers [2]............	441	1,847	1,919	1,625	35.9	35.8	36.5	14.94	17.06
Automobile dealers............	4411	1,217	1,261	1,006	35.1	35.8	36.7	16.95	18.23
Other motor vehicle dealers............	4412	132	166	128	35.1	34.7	33.6	12.35	17.22
Auto parts, accessories, and tire stores............	4413	499	491	490	38.2	36.0	36.9	11.04	14.54
Automotive parts and accessories............	44131	339	329	323	38.6	34.8	36.6	10.67	14.03
Furniture and home furnishings stores [2]............	442	544	576	436	31.2	30.7	29.2	12.33	15.25
Furniture stores............	4421	289	298	217	31.7	31.7	33.8	13.37	16.17
Home furnishings stores............	4422	254	278	220	30.7	29.5	24.7	11.06	14.04
Electronics and appliance stores [2]............	443	564	536	498	31.4	32.8	32.0	13.67	16.99
Building material and garden supply stores [2]............	444	1,142	1,276	1,126	35.7	36.8	33.9	11.25	14.11
Building material and supplies dealers............	4441	982	1,134	1,001	36.2	37.3	34.2	11.30	14.12
Home centers............	44411	479	637	621	36.5	37.8	32.7	10.97	12.85
Lawn and garden equipment and supplies stores............	4442	160	142	125	32.5	32.6	31.7	10.89	13.99
Food and beverage stores [2]............	445	2,993	2,818	2,811	31.7	30.1	29.0	9.76	12.04
Grocery stores............	4451	2,582	2,446	2,464	31.9	30.0	29.0	9.71	12.12
Supermarkets and other grocery stores............	44511	2,438	2,301	2,327	31.9	30.0	28.9	9.84	12.27
Specialty food stores............	4452	270	236	211	31.6	33.0	29.7	9.97	11.13
Health and personal care stores [2]............	446	928	954	979	29.8	29.3	29.4	11.68	16.99
Pharmacies and drug stores............	44611	677	695	714	29.7	28.9	29.3	11.89	17.59
Gasoline stations [2]............	447	936	871	816	31.6	31.6	30.7	8.05	10.24
Gasoline stations with convenience stores............	44711	787	751	719	31.3	31.3	30.4	7.87	9.99
Clothing and clothing accessories stores [2]............	448	1,322	1,415	1,377	24.9	24.4	21.2	9.96	11.57
Clothing stores............	4481	954	1,066	1,063	24.4	23.1	20.1	9.88	10.90
Jewelry, luggage, and leather goods stores............	4483	175	169	131	27.7	31.9	28.1	11.48	15.57
Sporting goods, hobby, book, and music stores [2]............	451	686	647	601	26.4	23.3	23.4	9.33	11.67
Sporting goods and musical instrument stores............	4511	437	447	460	27.0	23.5	23.8	9.55	11.82
Book, periodical, and music stores............	4512	249	200	140	25.4	23.0	22.0	8.91	11.11
General merchandise stores............	452	2,820	2,934	2,971	27.8	29.4	31.7	9.22	10.98
Miscellaneous store retailers [2]............	453	1,007	900	760	29.2	28.5	28.0	10.20	12.50
Office supplies, stationary, and gift stores............	4532	471	391	305	29.7	27.8	27.1	10.46	13.06
Gift, novelty, and souvenir stores............	45322	266	213	159	26.0	24.3	23.2	8.28	10.86
Used merchandise stores............	4533	107	113	124	26.7	27.8	29.5	8.07	10.72
Pet and pet supplies stores............	45391	72	88	99	27.0	28.9	27.4	9.78	12.83
Nonstore retailers [2]............	454	492	435	416	35.4	34.5	36.3	13.22	17.71
Electronic shopping and mail-order houses............	4541	257	240	244	36.2	33.0	35.9	13.38	18.19
Direct selling establishments............	4543	169	145	132	34.1	36.0	37.1	13.70	17.16
Fuel dealers............	45431	106	94	81	37.6	38.2	38.6	13.79	17.13

[1] Based on the North American Industry Classification System (NAICS), 2007; see text, this section and Section 15. [2] Includes other kind of businesses, not shown separately.

Source: U.S. Bureau of Labor Statistics, Current Employment Statistics, "Employment, Hours, and Earnings—National," <http://www.bls.gov/ces/data.htm>.

Table 1061. Retail Trade and Food Services—Sales by Kind of Business: 2000 to 2010

[In billions of dollars (3,287.5 represents $3,287,500,000,000)]

Kind of Business	2007 NAICS code [1]	2000	2005	2006	2007	2008	2009	2010
Retail sales and food services, total	**44, 45, 722**	**3,287.5**	**4,086.6**	**4,296.9**	**4,443.8**	**4,402.5**	**4,078.7**	**4,307.5**
Retail sales, total	**44, 45**	**2,983.3**	**3,690.2**	**3,874.1**	**3,999.3**	**3,946.4**	**3,627.6**	**3,841.5**
GAFO, total [2]	(X)	862.7	1,060.5	1,112.7	1,147.5	1,143.0	1,096.6	1,125.5
Motor vehicle and parts dealers	441	796.2	888.3	900.0	910.1	787.1	673.5	746.9
Automobile and other motor vehicle dealers	4411, 4412	732.8	818.2	827.7	835.4	710.8	599.5	669.1
Automobile dealers	4411	687.8	753.1	760.8	767.4	650.9	554.2	625.7
New car dealers	44111	630.1	681.9	685.6	687.7	576.6	488.3	551.9
Auto parts, accessories, and tire stores	4413	63.4	70.1	72.3	74.7	76.3	74.0	77.8
Furniture, home furnishings, electronics and appliance stores	442, 443	173.4	210.5	220.8	221.8	208.2	184.1	186.4
Furniture and home furnishings stores	442	91.2	109.1	112.8	111.1	99.6	86.1	87.2
Furniture stores	4421	50.6	58.7	60.1	59.3	52.9	46.1	47.2
Home furnishings stores	4422	40.6	50.4	52.7	51.9	46.6	40.0	40.0
Electronics and appliance stores [3]	443	82.2	101.3	108.0	110.7	108.7	98.0	99.2
Appliances, televisions, and other electronics stores	44311	58.2	78.3	84.4	86.2	84.4	75.7	73.5
Building materials, garden equipment, and supply stores [3]	444	229.0	320.8	334.1	320.9	304.6	266.9	267.9
Hardware stores	44413	16.2	18.9	20.0	20.5	20.2	19.0	19.2
Food and beverage stores [3]	445	444.8	508.5	525.2	547.8	569.7	568.8	582.0
Grocery stores	4451	402.5	457.7	471.7	491.4	511.4	510.1	521.4
Supermarkets and other grocery (except convenience) stores	44511	381.4	435.5	448.7	468.4	487.7	487.1	495.2
Beer, wine and liquor stores	4453	28.5	33.6	36.0	38.1	39.5	40.1	41.4
Health and personal care stores	446	155.2	210.1	223.3	237.2	246.8	253.2	261.2
Pharmacies and drug stores	44611	130.9	179.2	191.0	202.3	211.0	217.6	222.8
Gasoline stations	447	249.8	378.9	422.0	451.8	503.0	389.7	446.2
Clothing and clothing access. stores [3]	448	167.7	201.0	213.2	221.2	215.8	204.6	213.7
Clothing stores [3]	4481	118.1	145.6	154.5	161.6	157.9	151.7	158.8
Women's clothing stores	44812	31.4	37.1	38.8	40.3	38.3	35.9	37.4
Shoe stores [3]	4482	22.9	25.3	26.7	26.8	26.7	25.1	26.4
Jewelry stores	44831	24.8	28.4	30.1	30.8	29.2	26.0	26.4
Sporting goods, hobby, book & music stores [3]	451	75.8	80.9	83.1	84.7	84.0	80.9	81.6
Sporting goods stores	45111	25.3	30.7	33.9	35.8	37.1	37.1	38.3
Hobby, toy, and game stores	45112	16.9	16.3	16.0	16.3	16.2	15.6	16.0
General merchandise stores	452	404.2	528.4	554.3	578.6	596.4	591.6	608.0
Department stores (excluding L.D.) [4]	4521	232.5	215.3	213.2	209.4	198.7	187.6	186.2
Discount department stores	452112	136.2	130.5	132.9	132.5	127.9	124.8	122.1
Department stores (including L.D.) [4]	4521	239.9	220.7	218.1	213.9	202.9	190.8	189.3
Discount department stores	452112	139.6	133.2	135.5	134.9	130.1	126.4	123.7
Warehouse clubs and superstores	45291	139.6	271.9	298.0	325.0	352.1	356.5	371.0
Miscellaneous store retailers	453	106.7	107.3	113.7	116.4	111.6	102.9	106.5
Office supplies, stationery, and gift stores	4532	41.7	39.8	41.3	41.2	38.6	35.4	35.8
Office supplies and stationery stores	45321	22.7	22.2	22.8	23.2	21.7	20.2	19.9
Used merchandise stores	4533	9.8	9.3	10.4	10.9	11.0	10.4	11.1
Nonstore retailers [3]	454	180.5	255.6	284.3	308.8	319.3	311.4	341.2
Electronic shopping and mail-order houses	4541	113.8	175.9	202.3	223.7	228.2	233.5	260.6
fuel dealers	45431	26.7	34.3	35.5	37.4	44.2	35.1	37.9
Food services and drinking places [5]	**722**	**304.3**	**396.5**	**422.8**	**444.6**	**456.1**	**451.1**	**466.0**

X Not applicable. [1] North American Industry Classification System, 2007; see text, Section 15. [2] GAFO (General Merchandise, Apparel, Furniture, and Office Supplies) represents stores classified in the following NAICS codes: 442, 443, 448, 451, 452, and 4532. [3] Includes other kinds of businesses, not shown separately. [4] L.D. represents leased departments. [5] See also Table 1296.

Source: U.S. Census Bureau, "Annual Revision of Monthly Retail and Food Services: Sales and Inventories—January 1992 Through March 2010," March 2011, <http://www.census.gov/retail/index.html>.

Table 1062. Retail Trade Corporations—Sales, Net Profit, and Profit Per Dollar of Sales: 2010 and 2011

[Represents North American Industry Classification System, 2007 (NAICS) groups 44 and 45. Profit rates are averages of quarterly figures at annual rates. Covers corporations with assets of $50,000,000 or more]

Item	Unit	Total retail trade		Food and beverage stores (NAICS 445)		Clothing and general merchandise stores (NAICS 448, 452)		All other retail stores	
		2010	2011	2010	2011	2010	2011	2010	2011
Sales	Bil. dol	2,158	2,314	396	425	773	802	989	1,087
Net profit:									
Before income taxes	Bil. dol	99.9	104.7	7.0	8.4	48.6	48.7	44.3	47.5
After income taxes	Bil. dol	67.8	68.1	4.1	5.4	33.1	30.9	30.7	31.8
Profits per dollar of sales:									
Before income taxes	Cents	4.6	4.5	1.8	2.0	6.2	6.8	4.5	4.4
After income taxes	Cents	3.1	2.9	1.0	1.3	4.2	3.8	3.1	2.9
Profits on stockholders' equity:									
Before income taxes	Percent	22.5	23.3	15.7	17.9	26.0	26.3	20.9	21.9
After income taxes	Percent	15.3	15.2	9.0	11.5	17.7	16.6	11.9	14.7

Source: U.S. Census Bureau, *Quarterly Financial Report for Manufacturing, Mining and Trade Corporations*, annual, <http://www.census.gov/econ/qfr/>.

Table 1063. Retail Trade and Food Services—Estimated Per Capita Sales by Selected Kind of Business: 2000 to 2010

[Estimates are shown in dollars and are based on data from the Annual Retail Trade Survey and the Census Bureau's Population Estimates Program. Based on estimated resident population estimates as of July 1. For additional information, see <http://www.census.gov/popest/>. For statement on methodology, see Appendix III]

Kind of business	2007 NAICS code [1]	2000	2005	2006	2007	2008	2009	2010
Retail and food service sales	**44–45,722**	**11,651**	**13,829**	**14,401**	**14,752**	**14,478**	**13,296**	**13,924**
Retail sales, total	**44–45**	**10,573**	**12,487**	**12,984**	**13,276**	**12,978**	**11,825**	**12,418**
Total (excluding motor vehicle and parts dealers)	*44–45 ex 441*	7,751	9,481	9,967	10,255	10,389	9,630	10,004
Motor vehicle and parts dealers	441	2,822	3,006	3,016	3,021	2,588	2,196	2,414
Furniture and home furnishings stores	442	323	369	378	369	327	281	282
Electronics and appliance stores	443	291	343	362	367	358	320	321
Building material and garden equipment and supplies dealers	444	812	1,086	1,120	1,065	1,002	870	865
Food and beverage stores	445	1,576	1,721	1,760	1,819	1,874	1,854	1,881
Health and personal care stores	446	550	711	748	787	812	825	844
Gasoline stations	447	885	1,282	1,414	1,500	1,654	1,270	1,442
Clothing and clothing accessories stores	448	594	680	714	734	710	667	691
Sporting goods, hobby, book, and music stores	451	269	274	279	281	276	264	264
General merchandise stores	452	1,433	1,788	1,858	1,921	1,961	1,929	1,965
Miscellaneous store retailers	453	378	363	381	386	367	336	344
Nonstore retailers	454	640	865	953	1,025	1,050	1,015	1,104
Food services and drinking places, total	**722**	**1,078**	**1,342**	**1,417**	**1,476**	**1,500**	**1,471**	**1,506**

[1] North American Industry Classification System, 2007; see text, Section 15.

Source: U.S. Census Bureau, "2010 Annual Retail Trade Survey," March 2012 <http://www.census.gov/retail/>.

Table 1064. Retail Trade—Merchandise Inventories and Inventory/Sales Ratios by Kind of Business: 2000 to 2011

[Inventories in billions of dollars (405.9 represents $405,900,000,000). As of Dec. 31, seasonally adjusted. Estimates exclude food services. Includes warehouses. Adjusted for seasonal variations. Sales data also adjusted for holiday and trading-day differences. Based on data from the Monthly Retail Trade Survey, Annual Retail Trade Survey, and administrative records; see Appendix III. Data have been adjusted using results of the 2007 Economic Census]

Kind of business	2007 NAICS code [1]	Inventories				Inventory/sales ratio			
		2000	2005	2010	2011	2000	2005	2010	2011
Retail Inventories, total [2]	**44–45**	**405.9**	**471.5**	**455.3**	**471.7**	**1.62**	**1.50**	**1.37**	**1.33**
Total excluding motor vehicle and parts dealers	*44–45 ex 441*	277.8	318.6	327.4	339.4	1.49	1.33	1.23	1.20
Motor vehicle and parts dealers	441	128.1	152.9	127.9	132.3	2.02	2.08	1.93	1.81
Furniture, home furnishings, electronics, and appliance stores	442, 443	25.6	30.8	28.1	27.3	1.85	1.73	1.82	1.71
Building material and garden equipment and supplies dealers	444	34.3	45.0	43.6	44.0	1.77	1.64	1.90	1.79
Food and beverage stores	445	32.1	33.8	38.4	40.6	0.84	0.79	0.78	0.79
Clothing and clothing accessories stores	448	36.8	43.1	42.9	46.2	2.61	2.50	2.37	2.39
General merchandise stores	452	64.9	74.2	73.6	76.7	1.87	1.65	1.44	1.45
Department stores	4521	42.7	38.0	30.9	31.0	2.17	2.14	2.00	2.02

[1] North American Industry Classification System, 2007; see text, Section 15. [2] Includes other kind of businesses, not shown separately.

Source: U.S. Census Bureau, "Annual Revision of Monthly Retail and Food Services: Sales and Inventories—January 1992 Through March 2012," March 2012, <http://www.census.gov/retail/index.html>.

Table 1065. Retail Trade Sales—Total and E-Commerce by Kind of Business: 2010

[3,841,530 represents $3,841,530,000,000. Covers retailers with and without payroll. Based on the Annual Retail Trade Survey; see Appendix III]

Kind of business	2007 NAICS code [1]	Value of sales (mil. dol.)		E-commerce as percent of total sales	Percent distribution of E-commerce sales
		Total	E-commerce		
Retail trade, total [2]	**44–45**	**3,841,530**	**168,965**	**4.4**	**100.0**
Motor vehicle and parts dealers	441	746,924	20,561	2.8	12.2
Electronics and appliance stores	443	99,152	1,049	1.1	0.6
Building material and garden equipment and supplies stores	444	267,900	555	0.2	0.3
Food and beverage stores	445	581,972	862	0.1	0.5
Health and personal care stores	446	261,190	229	0.1	0.1
Clothing and clothing accessories stores	448	213,735	3,469	1.6	2.1
Sporting goods, hobby, book, and music stores	451	81,620	2,192	2.7	1.3
General merchandise stores	452	607,968	281	(Z)	0.2
Miscellaneous store retailers	453	106,514	2,504	2.4	1.5
Nonstore retailers	454	341,189	135,572	39.7	80.2
Electronic shopping and mail-order houses	45411	260,557	131,786	50.6	78.0

Z Less than 0.05 percent. [1] North American Industry Classification System, 2007; see text, Section 15. [2] Includes other kinds of businesses, not shown separately.

Source: U.S. Census Bureau, "E-Stats, 2010 E-commerce Multi-sector Report," May 2012, <http://www.census.gov/econ/estats/>.

Table 1066. Electronic Shopping and Mail-Order Houses—Total and E-Commerce Sales by Merchandise Line: 2009 and 2010

[233,530 represents $233,530,000,000. Represents North American Industry Classification System code 4541 which comprises establishments primarily engaged in retailing all types of merchandise using nonstore means, including catalogs, toll-free telephone numbers, or electronic media, such as interactive television or computer. Covers businesses with and without paid employees. Based on the Annual Retail Survey; see Appendix III]

Merchandise lines	Value of sales, 2009 (mil. dol.)	2010				
		Value of sales (million dollars)		E-commerce as percent of total sales	Percent distribution	
		Total	E-commerce		Total	E-commerce
Total...........................	233,530	260,557	131,786	50.6	100.0	100.0
Books and magazines......................	6,595	7,536	6,231	82.7	2.9	4.7
Clothing and clothing accessories (includes footwear)...................	25,931	29,510	23,157	78.5	11.3	17.6
Computer hardware.......................	21,519	24,187	11,421	47.2	9.3	8.7
Computer software........................	5,621	6,078	3,315	54.5	2.3	2.5
Drugs, health aids, beauty aids.................	71,512	78,341	7,220	9.2	30.1	5.5
Electronics and appliances.................	18,463	21,259	17,462	82.1	8.2	13.3
Food, beer, and wine......................	3,698	3,819	2,391	62.6	1.5	1.8
Furniture and home furnishings.................	13,262	15,182	11,882	78.3	5.8	9.0
Music and videos.........................	5,944	6,872	6,042	87.9	2.6	4.6
Office equipment and supplies.................	7,217	7,190	5,343	74.3	2.8	4.1
Sporting goods...........................	7,087	7,785	5,741	73.7	3.0	4.4
Toys, hobby goods, and games.................	5,866	6,656	4,395	66.0	2.6	3.3
Other merchandise [1].....................	28,586	32,094	17,048	53.1	12.3	12.9
Nonmerchandise receipts [2].................	12,229	14,048	10,138	72.2	5.4	7.7

[1] Includes jewelry, collectibles, souvenirs, auto parts and accessories, hardware, and lawn and garden equipment and supplies. [2] Includes auction commissions, shipping and handling, customer training, customer support, and advertising.

Source: U.S. Census Bureau, "E-Stats, 2010 E-Commerce Multi-sector Report," May 2012, <http://www.census.gov/econ/estats/>.

Table 1067. Franchised New Car Dealerships—Summary: 1990 to 2011

[316 represents $316,000,000,000]

Item	Unit	1990	2000	2004	2005	2006	2007	2008	2009	2010	2011
Dealerships [1]....................	Number	24,825	22,250	21,650	21,640	21,495	21,200	20,770	20,010	18,460	17,700
Sales............................	Bil. dol.	316	650	699	714	699	675	693	571	492	553
New cars sold [2].................	Millions	9.3	8.8	7.6	7.5	7.7	7.8	7.6	6.8	5.5	5.7
Used vehicles sold.............	Millions	14.2	20.5	19.5	19.7	19.7	19.2	18.5	15.0	14.9	15.3
Employment....................	1,000	924	1,114	1,130	1,130	1,138	1,120	1,115	1,057	913	892
Dealer pretax profits as a percentage of sales..........	Percent	1.0	1.6	1.7	1.7	1.6	1.5	1.5	1.0	1.5	2.1
Inventory: [3]											
Domestic: [4]											
Total.........................	1,000	2,537	3,183	3,085	3,267	2,991	2,943	2,712	2,478	1,697	1,687
Days' supply.................	Days	73	68	63	75	70	71	67	80	72	60
Imported: [4]											
Total.........................	1,000	707	468	618	646	566	605	619	687	519	494
Days' supply.................	Days	72	50	49	59	52	51	51	65	61	55

[1] At end of year. [2] Data provided by Ward's Automotive Reports. [3] Annual average. Includes light trucks. [4] Classification based on where automobiles are produced (i.e., automobiles manufactured by foreign companies but produced in the U.S., Canada, and Mexico are classified as domestic).

Source: National Automobile Dealers Association, McLean, VA, *NADA Data*, annual (copyright). See also <http://www.nada.org/Publications/NADADATA>.

Table 1068. Retail Sales and Leases of New and Used Vehicles: 1990 to 2010

[In thousands, except as noted (52,484 represents 52,484,000)]

Item	1990	2000	2004	2005	2006	2007	2008	2009	2010
Vehicle sales and leases, total (number of vehicles).................	52,484	64,320	62,839	64,626	62,744	61,562	52,845	48,545	51,434
New vehicle sales and leases..............................	14,954	22,700	20,294	20,488	20,178	20,143	16,315	13,053	14,550
New vehicle sales...	13,890	17,410	16,850	16,990	16,460	16,230	13,300	10,550	11,580
New vehicle leases..	1,064	5,290	3,444	3,498	3,718	3,913	3,015	2,503	2,970
Used vehicle sales [1].....................................	37,530	41,620	42,545	44,138	42,566	41,419	36,530	35,492	36,884
Vehicle sales, total value (bil. dol.) [2]..................	447	736	765	776	786	774	643	575	635
New vehicle sales (bil. dol.)..............................	227	380	407	421	445	435	351	274	311
Used vehicle sales (bil. dol.)..............................	220	356	358	355	341	339	292	301	324
Average price (current dol.): [2]									
New vehicle sales...	16,350	21,850	24,082	24,796	26,854	26,950	26,477	26,245	26,850
Used vehicle sales..	5,857	8,547	8,410	8,036	8,009	8,186	7,986	8,483	8,786

[1] Used car sales include sales from franchised dealers, independent dealers, and casual sales. [2] Includes leased vehicles.

Source: U.S. Bureau of Transportation Statistics, "National Transportation Statistics," <http://www.bts.gov/publications/national_transportation_statistics/>.

Table 1069. New Motor Vehicle Sales and Car Production: 1990 to 2011

[In thousands (14,137 represents 14,137,000). Includes leases]

Type of vehicle	1990	2000	2006	2007	2008	2009	2010	2011
New motor vehicle sales	**14,137**	**17,806**	**17,049**	**16,460**	**13,494**	**10,601**	**11,772**	**13,041**
New-car sales and leases	9,300	8,852	7,821	7,618	6,814	5,456	5,729	6,194
Domestic	6,897	6,833	5,476	5,253	4,535	3,613	3,884	4,247
Import	2,403	2,019	2,345	2,365	2,278	1,843	1,844	1,947
New-truck sales and leases	4,837	8,954	9,228	8,842	6,680	5,145	6,044	6,847
Light	4,560	8,492	8,683	8,471	6,382	4,945	5,826	6,541
Domestic	3,957	7,651	7,337	7,083	5,285	4,061	4,927	5,558
Import	603	841	1,347	1,388	1,097	884	899	983
Other	278	462	544	371	299	200	218	306
Domestic-car production	6,231	5,542	4,367	3,924	3,777	2,247	2,840	3,085
Average expenditure per new car [1] (dol.)	14,371	21,041	23,634	23,892	23,441	23,276	24,296	(NA)
Domestic (dol.)	13,936	19,586	22,166	22,284	22,204	22,148	23,095	(NA)
Import (dol.)	15,510	25,965	27,062	27,465	25,903	25,499	26,808	(NA)

NA Not available. [1] Estimate based on the manufacturer's suggested retail price.

Source: U.S. Bureau of Economic Analysis, "Auto and Truck Seasonal Adjustment," April 2012, <http://www.bea.gov/national/xls/gap_hist.xls>. Data are mainly from "Ward's Automotive Reports," published by Ward's Communications, Southfield, MI.

Table 1070. Food and Alcoholic Beverage Sales by Sales Outlet: 1990 to 2010

[In billions of dollars (569.8 represents $569,800,000,000)]

Sales outlet	1990	2000	2004	2005	2006	2007	2008	2009	2010
Food sales, total [1]	**569.8**	**833.3**	**997.4**	**1,053.4**	**1,102.0**	**1,159.9**	**1,204.8**	**1,199.8**	**1,241.0**
Food at home	324.6	444.6	523.8	550.2	568.8	598.7	627.8	625.2	646.8
Food stores [2]	256.4	303.5	327.5	339.2	349.8	364.3	379.2	378.1	386.5
Other stores [3]	25.6	74.9	124.3	133.9	142.2	149.2	160.0	160.4	170.0
Home-delivered, mail order	5.3	19.4	19.6	20.4	21.7	22.9	22.7	21.5	24.2
Farmers, manufacturers, wholesalers	25.6	32.4	36.0	38.9	37.9	42.8	45.3	44.5	44.9
Home production and donations	11.7	14.4	16.5	17.8	17.2	19.5	20.7	20.6	21.2
Food away from home [4]	245.2	388.7	473.6	503.2	533.2	561.2	576.9	574.6	594.3
Alcoholic beverage sales, total	**69.4**	**107.3**	**124.7**	**129.3**	**137.0**	**139.4**	**149.3**	**147.7**	**155.9**
Packaged alcoholic beverages	34.9	48.4	60.8	63.7	67.3	70.0	79.5	78.4	83.9
Liquor stores	18.6	24.5	30.8	32.3	34.8	37.0	38.5	39.4	40.1
Food stores	10.8	15.9	18.1	18.6	19.0	19.6	20.4	20.3	20.9
All other	5.4	8.0	11.9	12.8	13.5	13.4	20.6	18.8	22.9
Alcoholic drinks away from home	34.5	58.9	63.9	65.6	69.7	69.5	69.8	69.3	72.0
Eating and drinking places [5]	26.5	41.7	50.2	51.5	53.8	54.4	54.6	54.2	56.6
Hotels and motels [5]	3.4	6.8	4.9	5.1	5.1	5.2	5.2	5.1	5.1
All other	4.6	10.4	8.8	9.1	10.7	10.0	10.1	9.9	10.3

[1] Includes taxes and tips. [2] Excludes sales to restaurants and institutions. [3] Includes eating and drinking establishments, trailer parks, commissary stores, and military exchanges. [4] Includes food furnished and donations. [5] Includes tips.

Source: U.S. Department of Agriculture, Economic Research Service, "Food CPI and Expenditures: Food Expenditure Tables," June 2012, <http://www.ers.usda.gov/Briefing/CPIFoodAndExpenditures/Data/Expenditures_tables/>.

Section 23
Transportation

This section presents data on civil air transportation, both passenger and cargo, and on water transportation, including inland waterways, oceanborne commerce, the merchant marine, cargo, and vessel tonnages.

This section also presents statistics on revenues, passenger and freight traffic volume, and employment in various revenue-producing modes of the transportation industry, including motor vehicles, trains, and pipelines. Data are also presented on highway mileage and finances, motor vehicle travel, accidents, and registrations; and characteristics of public transit, railroads, and pipelines.

Principal source of transportation data is the annual *National Transportation Statistics* publication of the U.S. Bureau of Transportation Statistics. Principal sources of air and water transportation data are the *Annual Report* issued by Airlines for America, Washington, DC and the annual *Waterborne Commerce of the United States* issued by the Corps of Engineers of the Department of Army. In addition, the U.S. Census Bureau in its Commodity Flow Survey (part of the Census of Transportation, taken every 5 years through 2007, for years ending in "2" and "7") provides data on the type, weight, and value of commodities shipped by manufacturing establishments in the United States, by means of transportation, origin, and destination. The advance reports for 2007 are part of the 2007 Economic Census. This census was conducted in accordance with the 2002 North American Industry Classification System (NAICS). See text, Section 15, Business Enterprise, for a discussion of the Economic Census and NAICS.

The Bureau of Transportation Statistics (BTS) was established within the U.S. Department of Transportation (USDOT) in 1992 to collect, report, and analyze transportation data. Today, BTS is a component of the USDOT Research and Innovative Technology Administration (RITA). BTS products include reports to Congress, the Secretary of Transportation, and stakeholders in the nation's transportation community. These stakeholders include: federal agencies, state and local governments, metropolitan planning organizations, universities, the private sector and general public. Congress requires the BTS to report (congressional mandate, laid out in 49 U.S.C. 111 (1)) on transportation statistics to the President and Congress. *The Transportation Statistics Annual Report* (TSAR), provides a data overview of U.S. transportation issues. As required by Congress, each TSAR has two essential components: a review of the state of transportation statistics with recommendations for improvements and a presentation of the data. The BTS publication *National Transportation Statistics (NTS)*, a companion report to the TSAR, has more comprehensive and longer time-series data. NTS presents information on the U.S. transportation system, including its physical components, safety record, economic performance, energy use, and environmental impacts. The BTS publication *State Transportation Statistics* presents a statistical profile of transportation in the 50 states and the District of Columbia. This profile includes infrastructure, freight movement and passenger travel, system safety, vehicles, transportation-related economy and finance, energy usage and the environment.

The principal compiler of data on public roads and on operation of motor vehicles is the U.S. Department of Transportation's (DOT) Federal Highway Administration (FHWA). These data appear in FHWA's annual *Highway Statistics* and other publications.

The U.S. National Highway Traffic Safety Administration (NHTSA), through its *Traffic Safety Facts FARS/GES Annual Report*, presents descriptive statistics about traffic crashes of all severities, from those that result in property damage to those that result in the loss of human life. The data for this report is a compilation of motor vehicle crash data from the *Fatality Analysis Reporting System (FARS) and the General Estimates System (GES)*. For other publications and reports, go to the National Center for Statistics and Analysis (NCSA), Publications and Data Request. The Web site is located at <http://www-nrd.nhtsa.dot.gov/CATS/Index.aspx>. DOT's Federal Railroad Administration (FRA), Office of Safety Analysis presents railroad safety information including accidents and incidents, inspections and highway-rail crossing data in its annual report *Railroad Safety Statistics*. The Web site is located at <http://safetydata.fra.dot.gov/officeofsafety>.

Data are also presented in many nongovernment publications. Among them are the weekly and annual *Freight Commodity Statistics* and the annual *Industry Information, Industry Statistics, Railroad Statistics*, both published by the Association of American Railroads, Washington, DC; *Public Transportation Fact Book*, containing electric railway and motorbus statistics, published annually by the American Public Transportation Association, Washington, DC.

Civil aviation—Federal promotion and regulation of civil aviation have been carried out by the Federal Aviation Administration (FAA) and the Civil Aeronautics Board (CAB). The CAB promoted and regulated the civil air transportation industry within the United States and between the United States and foreign countries. The Board granted licenses to provide air transportation service, approved or disapproved proposed rates and fares, and approved or disapproved proposed agreements and corporate relationships involving air carriers. In December 1984, the CAB ceased to exist as an agency. Some of its functions were transferred to the DOT, as outlined below. The responsibility for investigation of aviation accidents resides with the National Transportation Safety Board.

The Office of the Secretary, DOT aviation activities include: negotiation of international air transportation rights, selection of U.S. air carriers to serve capacity controlled international markets, oversight of international rates and fares, maintenance of essential air service to small communities, and consumer affairs. DOT's Bureau of Transportation Statistics (BTS) handles aviation information functions formerly assigned to CAB. Prior to BTS, the Research and Special Programs Administration handled these functions.

The principal activities of the FAA include: the promotion of air safety; controlling the use of navigable airspace; prescribing regulations dealing with the competency of airmen, airworthiness of aircraft and air traffic control; operation of air route traffic control centers, airport traffic control towers, and flight service stations; the design, construction, maintenance, and inspection of navigation, traffic control, and communications equipment; and the development of general aviation.

The CAB published monthly and quarterly financial and traffic statistical data for the certificated route air carriers. BTS continues these publications, including both certificated and noncertificated (commuter) air carriers. The FAA annually publishes data on the use of airway facilities; data related to the location of airmen, aircraft, and airports; the volume of activity in the field of nonair carrier (general aviation) flying; and aircraft production and registration.

General aviation comprises all civil flying (including such commercial operations as small demand air taxis, agriculture application, powerline patrol, etc.) but excludes certificated route air carriers, supplemental operators, large-aircraft commercial operators, and commuter airlines.

Air carriers and service—The CAB previously issued "certificates of public convenience and necessity" under Section 401 of the Federal Aviation Act of 1958 for scheduled and nonscheduled (charter) passenger services and cargo services. It also issued certificates under Section 418 of the Act to cargo air carriers for domestic all-cargo service only. The DOT Office of the Secretary now issues the certificates under a "fit, willing, and able" test of air carrier operations. Carriers operating only a 60-seat-or-less aircraft are given exemption authority to carry passengers, cargo, and mail in scheduled and nonscheduled service under Part 298 of the DOT (formerly CAB) regulations. Exemption authority carriers who offer scheduled passenger service to an essential air service point must meet the "fit, willing, and able" test.

Vessel shipments, entrances, and clearances—Shipments by dry cargo vessels comprise shipments on all types of watercraft, except tanker vessels; shipments by tanker vessels comprise all types of cargo, liquid and dry, carried by tanker vessels. A vessel is reported as entered only at the first port which it enters in the United States, whether or not cargo is unloaded at that port.

A vessel is reported as cleared only at the last port at which clearance is made to a foreign port, whether or not it takes on cargo. Army and Navy vessels entering or clearing without commercial cargo are not included in the figures.

Units of measurement—Cargo (or freight) tonnage and shipping weight both represent the gross weight of the cargo including the weight of containers, wrappings, crates, etc. However, shipping weight excludes lift and cargo vans and similar substantial outer containers. Other tonnage figures generally refer to stowing capacity of vessels, 100 cubic feet being called 1 ton. Gross tonnage comprises the space within the frames and the ceiling of the hull, together with those closed-in spaces above deck available for cargo, stores, passengers, or crew, with certain minor exceptions. Net or registered tonnage is the gross tonnage less the spaces occupied by the propelling machinery, fuel, crew quarters, master's cabin, and navigation spaces. Substantially, it represents space

available for cargo and passengers. The net tonnage capacity of a ship may bear little relation to weight of cargo. Deadweight tonnage is the weight in long tons required to depress a vessel from light water line (that is, with only the machinery and equipment on board) to load line. It is, therefore, the weight of the cargo, fuel, etc., which a vessel is designed to carry with safety.

Federal-aid highway systems—The Intermodal Surface Transportation Efficiency Act (ISTEA) of 1991 eliminated the historical Federal-Aid Highway Systems and created the National Highway System (NHS) and other federal-aid highway categories. The final NHS was approved by Congress in December of 1995 under the National Highway System Designation Act.

Functional systems—Roads and streets are assigned to groups according to the character of service intended. The functional systems are (1) arterial highways that generally handle the long trips, (2) collector facilities that collect and disperse traffic between the arterials and the lower systems, and (3) local roads and streets that primarily serve direct access to residential areas, farms, and other local areas.

Regulatory bodies— The Federal Energy Regulatory Commission (FERC) is an independent agency that regulates the interstate transmission of electricity, natural gas, and oil. FERC also reviews proposals to build liquefied natural gas (LNG) terminals and interstate natural gas pipelines as well as licensing hydropower projects. The Energy Policy Act of 2005 gave FERC additional responsibilities such as regulating the transmission and wholesale sales of electricity in interstate commerce. See source for more details.

Railroads—The Surface Transportation Board (STB) was created in the Interstate Commerce Commission Termination Act of 1995, Pub. L. No.104-88, 109 Stat. 803 (1995) (ICCTA), and is the successor agency to the Interstate Commerce Commission. The STB is an economic regulatory agency that Congress charged with the fundamental missions of resolving railroad rate and service disputes and reviewing proposed railroad mergers. The STB is decisionally independent, although it is administratively affiliated with the Department of Transportation.

The STB serves as both an adjudicatory and a regulatory body. The agency has jurisdiction over railroad rate and service issues and rail restructuring transactions (mergers, line sales, line construction, and line abandonment); certain trucking company, moving van, and noncontiguous ocean shipping company rate matters; certain intercity passenger bus company structure, financial, and operational matters; and rates and services of certain pipelines not regulated by the Federal Energy Regulatory Commission. Other ICC regulatory functions were either eliminated or transferred to the Federal Highway Administration or the Bureau of Transportation Statistics within DOT.

Class I Railroads are regulated by the STB and subject to the Uniform System of Accounts and required to file annual and periodic reports. Railroads are classified based on their annual operating revenues. The class to which a carrier belongs is determined by comparing its adjusted operating revenues for 3 consecutive years to the following scale: Class I, $250 million or more; Class II, $20 million to $250 million; and Class III, $0 to $20 million. Operating revenue dollar ranges are indexed for inflation.

Postal Service—The U.S. Postal Service provides mail processing and delivery services within the United States. The Postal Accountability and Enhancement Act of 2006 was the first major legislative change to the Postal Service since 1971 when the Postal Reorganization Act of 1970 created the Postal Service as an independent establishment of the Federal Executive Branch. The Act of 2006 changed the way the U.S. Postal Service operates and conducts business. Now annual rate increases for market dominant products are linked to the Consumer Price Index and the Postal Service has more flexibility for pricing competitive products, enabling it to respond to dynamic market conditions and changing customer needs.

Revenue and cost analysis describes the Postal Service's system of attributing revenues and costs to classes of mail and service. This system draws primarily upon probability sampling techniques to develop estimates of revenues, volumes, and weights, as well as costs by class of mail and special service. The costs attributed to classes of mail and special services are primarily incremental costs which vary in response to changes in volume; they account for roughly 60 percent of the total costs of the Postal Service. The balance represents "institutional costs." Statistics on revenues, volume of mail, and distribution of expenditures are presented in the Postal Service's annual report, *Cost and Revenue Analysis*, and its *Annual Report of the Postmaster General* and its annual *Comprehensive Statement on Postal Operations*.

Statistical reliability—For a discussion of statistical collection and estimation, sampling procedures, and measures of statistical reliability applicable to Census Bureau data, see Appendix III.

Table 1071. Transportation-Related Components of U.S. Gross Domestic Product: 2000 to 2010

[In billions of dollars (1,045.3 represents $1,045,300,000,000), except percent. For explanation of chained dollars, see Section 13 text. Minus sign (–) indicates a decrease]

Item	2000	2005	2007	2008	2009	2010
CURRENT DOLLARS						
Total transportation-related final demand [1]	**1,045.3**	**1,264.8**	**1,403.9**	**1,386.1**	**1,221.6**	**1,319.4**
Total gross domestic product (GDP)	9,951.5	12,623.0	14,028.7	14,291.5	13,939.0	14,526.5
Transportation as a percent of GDP	10.5	10.0	10.0	9.7	8.8	9.1
Personal consumption of transportation	798.4	978.0	1,049.9	1,029.7	882.7	967.0
Motor vehicles and parts	363.2	408.2	399.9	339.3	316.5	340.1
Motor vehicle fuels, lubricants, and fluids	172.9	283.8	343.0	384.5	279.1	331.4
Transportation services	262.3	286.0	307.0	305.9	287.1	295.5
Gross private domestic investment	177.6	188.8	199.2	156.8	86.9	132.6
Transportation structures	6.8	7.1	9.0	9.9	9.1	9.9
Transportation equipment	170.8	181.7	190.2	146.9	77.8	122.7
Net exports of transportation-related goods and service [2]	-109.0	-136.6	-112.8	-86.7	-39.5	-80.5
Exports (+)	179.0	216.6	260	270.5	218.1	254.8
Civilian aircraft, engines, and parts	48.1	55.9	73.0	74.0	74.8	72.0
Automotive vehicles, engines, and parts	80.4	98.4	121.3	121.5	81.7	112.0
Passenger fares	20.7	21.0	25.6	31.0	26.1	30.9
Other transportation	29.8	41.3	40.3	44.0	35.5	39.9
Imports (–)	288.0	353.2	373.0	357	257.6	335.3
Civilian aircraft, engines, and parts	26.4	25.8	34.4	35.5	30.7	31.2
Automotive vehicles, engines, and parts	195.9	239.4	256.7	233.2	159.2	225.6
Passenger fares	24.3	26.1	28.4	31.8	25.1	27.3
Other transportation	41.4	61.9	53.5	56.7	42.6	51.2
Government transportation-related purchases	178.3	234.6	267.6	286.3	291.5	300.3
Federal purchases [3]	19.3	30.1	32.0	34.7	35.9	38.7
State and local purchases [3]	150.0	188.6	215.9	230.9	233.1	237.1
Defense-related purchases [4]	9.0	15.9	19.7	20.7	22.5	24.5
CHAINED (2005) DOLLARS						
Total transportation-related final demand [1]	**1,211.9**	**1,264.8**	**1,270.8**	**1,176.3**	**1,102.2**	**1,125.9**
Total gross domestic product (GDP)	11,216.4	12,623.0	13,206.4	13,161.9	12,703.1	13,088.0
Transportation as a percent of GDP	10.8	10.0	9.6	8.9	8.7	8.6
Personal consumption of transportation	903.7	978.0	966.1	884.1	833.7	844.5
Motor vehicles and parts	356.1	408.2	401.4	346.8	322.5	330.1
Motor vehicle fuels, lubricants, and fluids	261.3	283.8	276.8	265.3	263.1	264.2
Transportation services	286.3	286.0	287.9	272.0	248.1	250.2
Gross private domestic investment	194.1	188.8	194.3	151.8	78.9	128.2
Transportation structures	7.9	7.1	8.5	9.1	8.2	8.9
Transportation equipment	186.2	181.7	185.8	142.7	70.7	119.3
Net exports of transportation-related goods and service [2]	-109.3	-136.6	-118.5	-87.6	-43.8	-82.1
Exports (+)	204.5	216.6	246.8	246.1	198.3	226.1
Civilian aircraft, engines, and parts	58.4	55.9	67.1	64.9	62.5	58.6
Automotive vehicles, engines, and parts	83.2	98.4	118.4	117.2	78.4	106.9
Passenger fares	28.6	21.0	23.4	25.8	24.8	25.3
Other transportation	34.3	41.3	37.9	38.2	32.6	35.3
Imports (–)	313.8	353.2	365.3	333.7	242.1	308.2
Civilian aircraft, engines, and parts	30.7	25.8	31.5	30.6	25.1	24.9
Automotive vehicles, engines, and parts	202.9	239.4	253.1	224.3	151.9	213.9
Passenger fares	29.1	26.1	25.1	24.5	20.9	20.0
Other transportation	51.1	61.9	55.6	54.3	44.2	49.4
Government transportation-related purchases	223.4	234.6	228.9	228.0	233.4	235.3
Federal purchases [3]	23.1	30.1	29.6	31.3	32.0	33.6
State and local purchases [3]	189.1	188.6	180.5	179.0	180.5	180.2
Defense-related purchases [4]	11.2	15.9	18.8	17.7	20.9	21.5

[1] Sum of total personal consumption of transportation, total gross private domestic investment, net exports of transportation-related goods and services, and total government transportation-related purchases. [2] Exports minus imports. [3] Federal purchases and state and local purchases are the sum of consumption expenditures and gross investment. [4] Defense-related purchases are the sum of transportation of material and travel.

Source: U.S. Bureau of Transportation Statistics, *National Transportation Statistics*, <http://www.bts.gov/publications/national_transportation_statistics/>.

Table 1072. Employment in Transportation and Warehousing: 1990 to 2011

[In thousands (3,476 represents 3,476,000). Annual average of monthly figures. Based on Current Employment Statistics program; see Appendix III]

Industry	NAICS code [1]	1990	1995	2000	2005	2009	2010	2011
Transportation and warehousing	**48–49**	**3,476**	**3,838**	**4,410**	**4,361**	**4,236**	**4,191**	**4,292**
Air transportation	481	529	511	614	501	463	458	456
Rail transportation	482	272	233	232	228	218	216	229
Water transportation	483	57	51	56	61	63	62	63
Truck transportation	484	1,122	1,249	1,406	1,398	1,268	1,250	1,299
Transit and ground	485	274	328	372	389	422	430	436
Pipeline transportation	486	60	54	46	38	43	42	43
Scenic and sightseeing	487	16	22	28	29	28	27	29
Support activities	488	364	430	537	552	549	543	564
Couriers and messengers	492	375	517	605	571	546	528	529
Warehousing and storage	493	407	444	514	595	637	633	646

[1] North American Industry Classification System 2007, see text, Sections 12 and 15.

Source: U.S. Bureau of Labor Statistics, Current Employment Statistics, National, "Employment, Hours, and Earnings," <http://www.bls.gov/ces/data.htm/>, accessed April 2012.

Table 1073. Transportation and Warehousing—Establishments, Employees, and Payroll by Kind of Business (NAICS Basis): 2008 and 2009

[4,438.9 represents 4,438,900. Covers establishments with payroll. Excludes self-employed individuals, railroad employees, and most government employees. For statement on methodology, see Appendix III. County Business Patterns excludes rail transportation (NAICS 482) and the National Postal Service (NAICS 491)]

Industry	NAICS code [1]	Establishments		Paid employees (1,000)		Annual payroll (mil. dol.)	
		2008	2009	2008	2009	2008	2009
Transportation & warehousing............	**48–49**	**217,083**	**210,088**	**4,438.9**	**4,159.6**	**176,164.6**	**164,542.8**
Air transportation................	481	5,558	5,355	485.7	438.3	24,863.5	23,149.2
Scheduled air transportation............	4811	3,036	2,897	445.3	403.2	22,168.5	20,778.1
Scheduled passenger air transportation...........	481111	2,556	2,425	423.1	383.7	21,266.3	19,964.2
Scheduled freight air transportation.............	481112	480	472	22.2	(NA)	902.2	813.9
Nonscheduled air transportation...............	4812	2,522	2,458	40.4	35.1	2,694.9	2,371.1
Water transportation................	483	1,748	1,775	69.0	68.5	4,763.1	4,480.7
Deep sea, coastal, & Great Lakes water transportation................	4831	1,126	1,150	49.4	48.4	3,549.2	3,237.4
Inland water transportation............	4832	622	625	19.6	20.1	1,213.8	1,243.3
Inland water freight transportation...........	483211	364	368	16.9	17.2	1,098.8	1,121.6
Inland water passenger transportation...........	483212	258	257	2.8	2.9	115.1	121.6
Truck transportation................	484	115,321	109,911	1,426.9	1,327.0	56,703.2	50,735.5
General freight trucking............	4841	65,196	62,719	947.2	882.9	38,417.1	34,320.7
General freight trucking, local............	48411	27,113	25,913	176.8	163.8	6,276.6	5,718.6
General freight trucking, long distance...........	48412	38,083	36,806	770.4	719.1	32,140.5	28,602.1
Specialized freight trucking............	4842	50,125	47,192	479.6	444.1	18,286.1	16,414.9
Used household & office goods moving...........	48421	8,059	7,653	97.8	86.6	3,117.1	2,765.0
Specialized freight (except used goods) trucking, local............	48422	31,483	29,269	207.0	190.5	7,952.8	7,079.4
Specialized freight (except used goods) trucking, long-distance............	48423	10,583	10,270	174.9	167.0	7,216.2	6,570.5
Transit & ground passenger transportation............	485	18,011	18,030	449.4	437.0	10,057.9	10,118.5
Urban transit systems............	4851	871	874	47.8	48.0	1,792.7	1,862.9
Mixed mode systems............	485111	36	53	(NA)	(NA)	(D)	(D)
Commuter rail............	485112	22	27	(NA)	3.5	175.5	220.3
Bus and other motor vehicle mode systems.........	485113	806	784	41.8	41.1	1,499.8	1,526.0
Other............	485119	7	10	(NA)	(NA)	(D)	(D)
Interurban & rural bus transportation............	4852	487	422	15.0	13.4	421.9	349.3
Taxi & limousine service............	4853	7,413	7,243	71.0	64.7	1,626.6	1,465.1
Taxi service............	48531	2,897	2,947	29.7	29.2	625.5	611.6
Limousine service............	48532	4,516	4,296	41.4	35.5	1,001.1	853.5
School & employee bus transportation............	4854	4,501	4,557	219.6	213.9	3,886.8	4,073.5
Charter bus industry............	4855	1,335	1,327	30.7	29.2	757.0	727.6
Other transit & ground passenger transportation......	4859	3,404	3,607	65.3	67.9	1,572.7	1,640.2
Special needs transportation............	485991	2,396	2,499	52.2	54.5	1,278.5	1,351.2
Pipeline transportation............	486	2,871	2,904	40.2	41.6	3,568.8	3,794.7
Pipeline transportation of crude oil............	4861	370	387	6.1	7.1	661.0	710.5
Pipeline transportation of natural gas............	4862	1,638	1,640	24.0	24.3	2,125.6	2,261.2
Other pipeline transportation............	4869	863	877	10.0	10.2	782.3	823.1
Scenic & sightseeing transportation............	487	2,589	2,557	23.0	21.7	678.8	651.6
Scenic & sightseeing transportation, land............	4871	643	647	9.6	8.8	242.6	232.0
Scenic & sightseeing transportation, water............	4872	1,747	1,715	11.4	10.6	354.0	340.6
Scenic & sightseeing transportation, other............	4879	199	195	2.1	2.3	82.2	78.9
Support activities for transportation............	488	42,296	41,358	645.7	603.2	28,169.7	25,917.3
Support activities for air transportation............	4881	5,785	5,757	174.4	163.6	6,770.8	6,423.1
Airport operations............	48811	2,048	2,009	89.5	80.0	2,528.1	2,297.9
Air traffic control............	488111	202	166	2.0	1.3	122.6	80.2
Other support activities for air transportation.........	48819	3,737	3,748	84.9	83.6	4,242.7	4,125.2
Support activities for rail transportation............	4882	1,023	1,109	25.8	25.0	990.7	1,016.8
Support activities for water transportation............	4883	2,462	2,412	93.7	85.7	4,907.9	4,362.4
Port and harbor operations............	48831	268	258	5.6	5.1	282.7	250.4
Marine cargo handling............	48832	532	541	63.7	56.4	3,272.7	2,776.8
Navigational services to shipping............	48833	868	846	13.4	12.7	847.9	826.4
Other............	48839	794	767	10.9	11.5	504.5	508.9
Support activities for road transportation............	4884	10,112	9,978	78.0	75.0	2,311.1	2,189.4
Motor vehicle towing............	48841	8,400	8,263	55.3	52.3	1,629.5	1,551.9
Freight transportation arrangement............	4885	21,418	20,583	246.1	228.9	11,970.4	10,729.5
Other support activities for transportation............	4889	1,496	1,519	27.6	25.0	1,218.9	1,196.1
Couriers & messengers............	492	14,339	13,774	596.3	548.6	21,568.3	20,784.5
Couriers............	4921	9,717	9,296	559.1	517.4	20,624.0	20,000.3
Local messengers & local delivery............	4922	4,622	4,478	37.1	31.2	944.3	784.2
Warehousing & storage............	493	14,350	14,424	702.8	673.7	25,791.3	24,910.7

NA Not available. D Data withheld to avoid disclosure. [1] Based on the North American Industry Classification System (NAICS), 2007. See text, Section 15.

Source: U.S. Census Bureau, "County Business Patterns," June 2011, <http://www.census.gov/econ/cbp/index.html>.

Table 1074. Transportation and Warehousing—Establishments, Revenue, Payroll, and Employees by Industry: 2002 and 2007

[382,152 represents $382,152,000,000. For establishments with payroll. Based on the 2002 and 2007 Economic Censuses. Paid employees for pay period including March 12. See Appendix III]

Kind of business	NAICS code [1]	Number of establish- ments	Revenue (mil. dol.)	Annual payroll (mil. dol.)	Paid employees (1,000)
Transportation and warehousing total, 2002	**48–49**	**199,618**	**382,152**	**115,989**	**3,650.9**
Air transportation [2]	481	3,847	19,735	3,805	99.1
Water transportation	483	1,890	23,331	3,194	66.2
Truck transportation	484	112,642	164,219	47,750	1,435.2
Transit and ground passenger transportation	485	17,260	18,850	7,675	398.4
Pipeline transportation	486	2,188	22,031	2,477	36.8
Scenic and sightseeing transportation	487	2,523	1,859	526	22.5
Support activities for transportation	488	33,942	57,414	16,202	465.6
Couriers and messengers	492	12,655	58,165	17,175	561.5
Warehousing and storage	493	12,671	16,548	17,183	565.5
Transportation and warehousing total, 2007	**48–49**	**219,706**	**639,916**	**173,183**	**4,454.4**
Air transportation	481	5,661	146,612	26,120	478.2
Water transportation	483	1,721	34,447	4,544	76.0
Truck transportation	484	120,390	217,833	58,266	1,507.9
Transit and ground passenger transportation	485	17,791	26,465	9,844	444.9
Pipeline transportation	486	2,529	25,718	3,219	37.0
Scenic and sightseeing transportation	487	2,542	2,448	653	24.4
Support activities for transportation	488	42,130	86,596	24,579	608.4
Couriers and messengers	492	13,004	77,877	20,431	557.2
Warehousing and storage	493	13,938	21,921	25,526	720.5

[1] 2002 data based on the 1997 North American Industry Classification System (NAICS), 2007 data are based on the 2002 NAICS; see text, Section 15. [2] Excludes large certificated passenger carriers that do not report to the Office of Airline Information, U.S. Department of Transportation.

Source: U.S. Census Bureau, 2007 Economic Census, EC0748A2, "Transportation and Warehousing: Geographic Area Series: Comparative Statistics for the United States, (2002 NAICS Basis): 2007 and 2002," <http://factfinder.census.gov/>, accessed March 2011.

Table 1075. Transportation and Warehousing—Nonemployer Establishments and Receipts by Kind of Business: 2007 to 2009

[1,083.1 represents 1,083,100. Includes only firms subject to federal income tax. Nonemployers are businesses with no paid employees. Data originate chiefly from administrative records of the Internal Revenue Service; see Appendix III]

Kind of Business	NAICS code [1]	Establishments (1,000)			Receipts (mil. dol.)		
		2007	2008	2009	2007	2008	2009
Transportation and warehousing	**48–49**	**1,083.1**	**1,039.5**	**1,002.1**	**66,633**	**67,026**	**54,453**
Air transportation	481	21.0	20.5	19.8	1,347	1,349	1,192
Water transportation	483	6.5	6.4	6.3	516	538	429
Truck transportation	484	542.5	508.0	483.5	47,927	47,880	37,244
General freight trucking	4841	489.2	459.5	438.4	43,816	43,936	34,248
General freight trucking, local	48411	193.1	180.2	168.8	14,263	13,873	10,984
General freight trucking, long-distance	48412	296.1	279.3	269.6	29,553	30,063	23,263
Specialized freight trucking	4842	53.3	48.6	45.1	4,111	3,944	2,997
Transit and ground passenger transportation	485	202.1	207.1	210.8	6,759	7,256	6,987
Urban transit system	4851	1.2	1.2	1.1	43	48	39
Interurban and rural bus transportation	4852	1.7	1.6	1.6	77	78	67
Taxi and limousine service	4853	161.4	166.8	170.5	5,270	5,726	5,684
School and employee bus transportation	4854	7.2	6.9	6.8	202	214	191
Charter bus industry	4855	3.8	3.8	3.7	194	182	174
Other transit and ground passenger transportation	4859	26.8	26.8	27.0	973	1,009	832
Pipeline transportation	486	0.8	0.8	0.8	75	81	62
Scenic and sightseeing transportation	487	5.1	4.7	4.5	197	185	142
Support activities for transportation	488	106.3	102.2	99.6	4,759	4,821	4,203
Couriers and messengers	492	190.5	180.9	168.0	4,513	4,362	3,743
Warehousing and storage	493	8.3	8.7	8.8	542	553	450

[1] Based on the 2007 North American Industry Classification System (NAICS); see text, Section 15.

Source: U.S. Census Bureau, "Nonemployer Statistics," revised August 2012, <http://www.census.gov/econ/nonemployer/index.html>.

Table 1076. Transportation System Mileage Within the United States: 1980 to 2009

[3,860 represents 3,860,000. Numbers, except where indicated]

System	Unit	1980	1985	1990	1995	2000	2005	2007	2008	2009
Highway [1]	1,000	3,860	3,864	3,867	3,912	3,936	3,996	4,032	4,043	4,051
Class 1 rail [2]	Number	164,822	145,764	119,758	108,264	99,250	95,664	94,313	94,082	93,921
Amtrak	Number	24,000	24,000	24,000	24,000	23,000	22,007	21,708	21,178	21,178
Transit: [3]										
Commuter rail [4]	Number	(NA)	3,574	4,132	4,160	5,209	7,118	7,135	7,261	7,561
Heavy rail [5]	Number	(NA)	1,293	1,351	1,458	1,558	1,622	1,623	1,623	1,623
Light rail [6]	Number	(NA)	384	483	568	834	1,188	1,341	1,397	1,477
Navigable channels	Number	26,000	26,000	26,000	26,000	26,000	26,000	25,320	25,320	25,320
Oil pipeline [7]	Number	218,393	213,605	208,752	181,912	176,996	162,919	166,256	169,586	172,048
Gas pipeline [8]	1,000	1,052	1,111	1,270	1,332	1,377	1,484	1,523	1,533	1,540

NA Not available. [1] All public road and street mileage in the 50 states and the District of Columbia. [2] Data represent miles of road owned (aggregate length of road, excluding yard tracks, sidings, and parallel lines). [3] Transit system length is measured in directional route-miles; see source. [4] Also called metropolitan rail or regional rail. [5] Also called metro, subway, rapid transit, or rapid rail. [6] Also called streetcar, tramway, or trolley. [7] Includes trunk and gathering lines for crude-oil pipeline. [8] Excludes service pipelines.

Source: U.S. Bureau of Transportation Statistics, *National Transportation Statistics*, <http://www.bts.gov/publications/national_transportation_statistics>.

Table 1077. U.S. Aircraft, Vehicles, and Other Conveyances: 2000 to 2010

[133,621 represents 133,621,000]

System	2000	2003	2004	2005	2006	2007	2008	2009	2010
Air:									
Air carrier [1]	8,055	8,176	8,186	8,225	8,089	8,044	7,856	7,771	7,431
General aviation [2] (active fleet)	217,533	209,708	219,426	224,352	221,943	231,607	228,663	223,877	223,370
Highway, registered vehicles (1,000):									
Light duty vehicle, short wheel base [3]	133,621	135,670	136,431	136,568	135,400	196,491	196,763	193,980	190,203
Motorcycle	4,346	5,370	5,768	6,227	6,679	7,138	7,753	7,930	8,212
Light duty vehicle, long wheel base [4]	79,085	87,187	91,845	95,337	99,125	39,187	39,685	40,488	40,242
Trucks [5]	8,023	7,757	8,171	8,482	8,819	10,752	10,873	10,973	10,770
Bus	746	777	795	807	822	834	843	842	846
Transit:									
Motor bus	58,578	61,659	61,318	62,284	64,025	63,359	63,151	63,343	63,108
Light rail cars [6]	1,306	1,482	1,622	1,645	1,801	1,802	1,948	2,059	2,096
Heavy rail cars [7]	10,311	10,754	10,858	11,110	11,052	11,222	11,377	11,461	11,510
Trolley bus	652	672	597	615	609	559	590	531	571
Commuter rail cars and locomotives	5,497	5,866	6,130	6,290	6,300	6,279	6,494	6,722	6,768
Demand response	22,087	25,873	26,333	28,346	29,406	29,433	30,773	34,235	33,555
Other [8]	7,705	8,626	10,544	11,622	12,454	12,953	14,953	17,766	18,066
Rail:									
Class I, freight cars (1,000)	560	467	474	475	475	460	450	416	398
Class I, locomotive	20,028	20,774	22,015	22,779	23,732	24,143	24,003	24,045	23,893
Nonclass I freight cars	132,448	124,580	120,169	120,195	120,688	120,463	109,487	108,233	101,755
Car companies' and shippers' freight cars	688,194	687,337	693,978	717,211	750,404	805,074	833,188	839,020	809,544
Amtrak, passenger train car	1,894	1,623	1,211	1,186	1,191	1,164	1,177	1,214	1,274
Amtrak, locomotive	378	442	276	258	319	270	278	274	282
Water:									
Non-self-propelled vessels [9]	31,360	31,335	31,296	33,152	32,211	31,654	31,238	31,008	31,412
Self-propelled vessels [10]	8,202	8,648	8,994	8,976	8,898	9,041	9,063	9,101	9,100
Ocean-going self-propelled vessels (1,000 gross tons and over)	454	418	423	366	344	275	272	196	(NA)
Recreational boats (1,000)	12,782	12,795	12,781	12,942	12,746	12,873	12,693	12,722	12,439

NA Not available. [1] Air carrier aircraft are those carrying passengers or cargo for hire under 14 CFR 121 and 14 CFR 135. [2] Includes air taxi aircraft. [3] Data for 2000-06 are for passenger cars. Data for 2007-10 are for Light Duty Vehicles Short Wheel Base - passenger cars, light trucks, vans and sport utility vehicles with a wheelbase of 121 inches or less. [4] Data for 2000-06 are for 2-axle, 4-tire vehicles other than passenger cars, motorcycles, and buses. Data for 2007-10 are for Light Duty Vehicles Long Wheel Base - large passenger cars, vans, pickup trucks, and sport/utility vehicles with wheelbases larger than 121 inches. [5] Includes trucks on a single frame with at least 2 axles and 6 tires, and combinations. [6] Fixed rail streetcar or trolley, for example. [7] Metro, subway, or rapid transit, for example. [8] Includes aerial tramway, automated guideway transit, cablecar, ferry boat, inclined plane, monorail, and vanpool. [9] Includes dry-cargo barges, tank barges, and railroad-car floats. [10] Includes dry-cargo and/or passenger, offshore supply vessels, railroad-car ferries, tankers, and towboats.

Source: U.S. Bureau of Transportation Statistics, *National Transportation Statistics*, <http://www.bts.gov/publications/national_transportation_statistics/>.

Table 1078. Shipment Characteristics by Mode of Transportation: 2002 and 2007

[8,397,210 represents $8,397,210,000,000 (except as indicated otherwise). For business establishments in mining, manufacturing, wholesale trade, and selected retail industries. 2007 industries classified by the 2002 North American Industry Classification System (NAICS). 2002 industries classified by the 1997 NAICS. Selected auxiliary establishments are also included. Based on the 2007 Economic Census; see Appendix III]

Mode of transportation	Value (mil. dol.)		Tons (1,000)		Ton-miles (mil.)		Average miles per shipment	
	2002	2007	2002	2007	2002	2007	2002	2007
All modes	**8,397,210**	**11,684,872**	**11,667,919**	**12,543,425**	**3,137,898**	**3,344,658**	**546**	**619**
Single modes	**7,049,383**	**9,539,037**	**11,086,660**	**11,698,128**	**2,867,938**	**2,894,251**	**240**	**234**
Truck [1]	6,235,001	8,335,789	7,842,836	8,778,713	1,255,908	1,342,104	173	206
For-hire truck	3,757,114	4,955,700	3,657,333	4,075,136	959,610	1,055,646	523	599
Private truck	2,445,288	3,380,090	4,149,658	4,703,576	291,114	286,457	64	57
Rail	310,884	436,420	1,873,884	1,861,307	1,261,612	1,344,040	807	728
Water	89,344	114,905	681,227	403,639	282,659	157,314	568	520
Shallow draft	57,467	91,004	458,577	343,307	211,501	117,473	450	144
Great Lakes	843	(S)	38,041	17,792	13,808	6,887	339	657
Deep draft	31,034	23,058	184,610	42,540	57,350	32,954	664	923
Air (includes truck and air)	264,959	252,276	3,760	3,611	5,835	4,510	1,919	1,304
Pipeline [2]	149,195	399,646	684,953	650,859	(S)	(S)	(S)	(S)
Multiple modes	**1,079,185**	**1,866,723**	**216,686**	**573,729**	**225,715**	**416,642**	**895**	**975**
Parcel, U.S. Postal Service or courier	987,746	1,561,874	25,513	33,900	19,004	27,961	894	975
Truck and rail	69,929	187,248	42,984	225,589	45,525	196,772	1,413	1,007
Truck and water	14,359	58,389	23,299	145,521	32,413	98,396	1,950	1,429
Rail and water	3,329	13,892	105,107	54,878	114,986	47,111	957	1,928
Other multiple modes	3,822	45,320	19,782	113,841	13,788	46,402	(S)	1,182
Other and unknown modes	**268,642**	**279,113**	**364,573**	**271,567**	**44,245**	**33,764**	**130**	**116**

S Data do not meet publication standards due to high sampling variability or other reasons. [1] Truck as a single mode includes shipments that went by private truck only, for-hire truck only, or a combination of private truck and for-hire truck. [2] Commodity Flow Survey data exclude shipments of crude oil.

Source: U.S. Department of Transportation, Research and Innovative Technology Administration, Bureau of Transportation Statistics, and U.S. Department of Commerce, U.S. Census Bureau, 2007 Commodity Flow Survey, <http://www.census.gov/econ/cfs/>, accessed October 2012.

Table 1079. Hazardous Shipments—Value, Tons, and Ton-Miles: 2002 and 2007

[660,181 represents $660,181,000,000. For business establishments in mining, manufacturing, wholesale trade, and selected retail industries. 2007 industries classified by the 2002 North American Industry Classification System (NAICS). 2002 industries classified by the 1997 NAICS. Selected auxiliary establishments are also included. Based on the 2007 Economic Census; see Appendix III]

Mode of transportation	Value (mil. dol.)		Tons (1,000)		Ton-miles (mil.)		Average miles per shipment	
	2002	2007	2002	2007	2002	2007	2002	2007
All modes	**660,181**	**1,448,218**	**2,191,519**	**2,231,133**	**326,727**	**323,457**	**136**	**96**
Single modes	**644,489**	**1,370,615**	**2,158,533**	**2,111,622**	**311,897**	**279,105**	**105**	**65**
Truck [1]	419,630	837,074	1,159,514	1,202,825	110,163	103,997	86	59
For-hire truck	189,803	358,792	449,503	495,077	65,112	63,288	285	214
Private truck	226,660	478,282	702,186	707,748	44,087	40,709	38	32
Rail	31,339	69,213	109,369	129,743	72,087	92,169	695	578
Water	46,856	69,186	228,197	149,794	70,649	37,064	(S)	383
Air (includes truck and air)	1,643	1,735	64	(S)	85	(S)	2,080	1,095
Pipeline [2]	145,021	393,408	661,390	628,905	(S)	(S)	(S)	(S)
Multiple modes [3]	**9,631**	**71,069**	**18,745**	**111,022**	**12,488**	**42,886**	**849**	**834**
Parcel, U.S. Postal Service or courier	4,268	7,675	245	236	119	151	837	836
Other and unknown modes	**6,061**	**6,534**	**14,241**	**8,489**	**2,342**	**1,466**	**57**	**58**
Class of material	660,181	1,448,218	2,191,519	2,231,133	326,727	323,457	136	96
Class 1, Explosives	7,901	11,754	5,000	3,047	1,568	911	651	738
Class 2, Gasses	73,932	131,810	213,358	250,506	37,262	55,260	95	51
Class 3, Flammable and combustible liquid	490,238	1,170,455	1,788,986	1,752,814	218,574	181,615	106	91
Class 4, Flammable solid; spontaneously combustible material; dangerous when wet material	6,566	4,067	11,300	20,408	4,391	5,547	158	309
Class 5, Oxidizers and organic peroxides	5,471	6,695	12,670	14,959	4,221	7,024	407	361
Class 6, Toxic materials and infectious substances	8,275	21,198	8,459	11,270	4,254	5,667	626	467
Class 7, Radioactive materials	5,850	20,633	57	515	44	37	(S)	(S)
Class 8, Corrosive materials	38,324	51,475	90,671	114,441	36,260	44,395	301	208
Class 9, Miscellaneous hazardous material	23,625	30,131	61,018	63,173	20,153	23,002	368	484

S Data do not meet publication standards due to high sampling variability or other reasons. [1] Truck as a single mode includes shipments that went by private truck only, for-hire truck only, or a combination of private truck and for-hire truck. [2] Commodity Flow Survey Data exclude shipments of crude oil. [3] Includes other modes not shown. Multimode data for 2007 and 2002 are not comparable due to methodological changes; see source.

Source: U.S. Department of Transportation, Research and Innovative Technology Administration, Bureau of Transportation Statistics, and U.S. Department of Commerce, U.S. Census Bureau, 2007 Commodity Flow Survey, <http://www.census.gov/econ/cfs/>, accessed October 2012.

Table 1080. Transportation Accidents, Deaths, and Injuries: 1990 to 2010

[6,471 represents 6,471,000. Number, except as indicated]

Mode	Accidents 1990	Accidents 1995	Accidents 2000	Accidents 2005	Accidents 2010	Deaths 1990	Deaths 1995	Deaths 2000	Deaths 2005	Deaths 2010	Injuries 1990	Injuries 1995	Injuries 2000	Injuries 2005	Injuries 2010
Transit type:															
Air:															
Air carrier [1]	24	36	56	40	28	39	168	92	22	2	29	25	29	14	15
Commuter [2]	15	12	12	6	6	6	9	5	–	–	11	17	7	–	2
On-demand [3]	107	75	80	65	31	51	52	71	18	17	36	14	12	23	6
General aviation	2,242	2,055	1,837	1,670	1,436	770	734	596	563	450	409	396	309	267	256
Land:															
Highway crashes (1,000) [4]	6,471	6,699	6,394	6,159	5,419	44.6	41.8	41.9	43.5	(NA)	3,231	3,465	3,189	2,699	(NA)
Passenger car occupants	5,561	5,594	4,926	4,499	(NA)	24.1	22.4	20.7	18.5	(NA)	2,376	2,469	2,052	1,573	(NA)
Motorcyclists	103	66	69	101	(NA)	3.2	2.2	2.9	4.6	(NA)	84	57	58	87	(NA)
Light truck occupants	2,152	2,750	3,208	3,382	(NA)	8.6	9.6	11.5	13.0	(NA)	505	722	887	872	(NA)
Large truck occupants	372	363	438	423	(NA)	0.7	0.6	0.8	0.8	(NA)	42	30	31	27	(NA)
Bus occupants	60	59	56	50	(NA)	(Z)	(Z)	(Z)	0.1	(NA)	33	19	18	11	(NA)
Pedestrians	(NA)	(NA)	(NA)	(NA)	(NA)	6.5	5.6	4.8	4.9	(NA)	105	86	78	64	(NA)
Pedacyclists	(NA)	(NA)	(NA)	(NA)	(NA)	0.9	0.8	0.7	0.8	(NA)	75	67	51	45	(NA)
Other	(NA)	(NA)	(NA)	(NA)	(NA)	0.6	0.5	0.6	0.8	(NA)	11	14	15	18	(NA)
Railroad [5]	8,594	7,092	6,485	6,332	3,911	1,297	1,146	937	884	725.0	25,143	14,440	11,643	9,550	8,268
Highway-rail grade crossing	5,715	4,633	3,502	3,066	2,017	698	579	425	359	256	2,407	1,894	1,219	1,053	849
Railroad	2,879	2,459	2,983	3,266	1,894	599	567	512	525	469	22,736	12,546	10,424	8,497	7,419
Transit [6]	58,002	25,683	24,261	8,151	3,492	339	274	295	236	279	54,556	57,196	56,697	18,131	23,414
Waterborne:															
Waterborne (vessel related) [7]	3,613	5,349	5,403	4,977	4,295	85	53	53	78	32	175	154	150	140	139
Recreational boating [8]	6,411	8,019	7,740	4,969	4,604	865	829	701	697	672	3,822	4,141	4,355	3,451	3,153
Pipeline: [9]	379	349	380	721	587	9	21	38	14	22	76	64	81	48	109
Hazard liquid	180	188	146	369	347	3	3	2	2	1	7	11	4	2	4
Gas	199	161	234	352	240	6	18	37	12	21	69	53	77	46	105
Hazardous materials [10, 11]	8,879	14,853	17,557	15,929	14,795	8	7	16	34	8	423	400	251	915	170

– Represents or rounds to zero. Z Less than 50. NA Not available. [1] See footnote 1, Table 1086. Injuries classified as serious. [2] See footnote 2, Table 1086. Injuries classified as serious. [3] See footnote 3, Table 1086. Injuries classified as serious. [4] Data on deaths are from U.S. National Highway Traffic Safety Administration and are based on deaths within 30 days of the accident. Includes only police reported crashes. For more details, see Table 1119. [5] Accidents which result in damages to railroad property. Grade crossing accidents are also included when classified as a train accident. Deaths exclude fatalities in railroad-highway grade crossing accidents. [6] Includes motor bus, commuter rail, heavy rail, light rail, demand response, van pool, and automated guideway. Starting with 2002, only injuries requiring immediate medical treatment away from the scene now qualify as reportable. [7] Accidents resulting in death, injury, or requiring medical treatment beyond first aid; damages exceeding $500; or a person's disappearance. [8] Covers accidents involving commercial vessels which must be reported to U.S. Coast Guard if there is property damage exceeding $25,000; material damage affecting the seaworthiness or efficiency of a vessel; stranding or grounding; loss of life; or injury causing a person's incapacity for more than 3 days. [9] Beginning 1990, pipeline accidents/incidents are credited to year of occurrence; prior data are credited to the year filed. [10] Incidents, deaths, and injuries involving hazardous materials cover all types of transport. Excludes pipelines and bulk, nonpackaged water incidents. [11] The data reported under accidents are incident numbers.

Source: U.S. Bureau of Transportation Statistics, National Transportation Statistics, <http://www.bts.gov/publications/national_transportation_statistics/>.

Table 1081. U.S. Scheduled Airline Industry—Summary: 1995 to 2011

[For calendar years or December 31, (547.8 represents 547,800,000). For domestic and international operations. Covers carriers certificated under Section 401 of the Federal Aviation Act. Table data have been revised for 2000 through 2009. Minus sign (–) indicates loss]

Item	Unit	1995	2000	2006	2007	2008	2009	2010	2011
SCHEDULED SERVICE									
Revenue passengers enplaned....	Mil.	547.8	666.1	744.7	769.6	743.3	703.9	720.5	730.8
Revenue passenger miles..........	Bil.	540.7	692.8	797.4	829.4	812.4	769.5	798.0	814.4
Available seat miles................	Bil.	807.1	957.0	1,006.3	1,037.7	1,021.3	957.2	972.6	992.7
Revenue passenger load factor....	Percent	67.0	72.4	79.2	79.9	79.5	80.4	82.1	82.0
Mean passenger trip length [1].......	Miles	987	1,040	1,071	1,078	1,093	1,093	1,108	1,114
Cargo ton miles.....................	Mil.	16,921	23,888	29,340	29,571	28,119	24,970	27,885	28,123
Aircraft departures..................	1,000	8,062	9,035	11,268	11,399	10,897	10,145	10,095	10,057
FINANCES [2]									
Total operating revenue [3]......	**Mil. dol.**	**95,117**	**130,248**	**165,532**	**174,696**	**186,087**	**155,051**	**174,677**	**192,362**
Passenger revenue.................	Mil. dol.	69,470	93,639	101,968	107,678	111,511	91,443	103,978	113,948
Cargo revenue......................	Mil. dol.	8,619	12,667	21,914	24,002	29,192	23,014	17,622	(NA)
Charter revenue....................	Mil. dol.	3,350	4,366	6,095	5,544	4,338	3,841	3,254	(NA)
Total operating expense............	Mil. dol.	89,266	123,234	157,892	165,353	189,437	152,716	164,160	185,261
Operating profit (or loss)...........	Mil. dol.	5,852	7,014	7,640	9,344	-3,350	2,335	10,517	7,101
Interest income (or expense).......	Mil. dol.	-2,446	-2,414	-4,182	-3,915	-3,743	-4,214	-4,215	-3,982
Net profit (or loss)...................	Mil. dol.	2,314	2,533	18,186	7,691	-23,750	-2,610	3,666	1,481
Revenue per passenger mile.......	Cents	12.8	13.5	12.8	13.0	13.7	11.9	13.0	14.0
Operating profit margin.............	Percent	6.2	5.4	4.6	5.3	-1.8	1.5	6.0	3.7
Net profit margin....................	Percent	2.4	1.9	11.0	4.4	-12.8	-1.7	2.1	0.8
Adjusted net profit (or loss) [4].......	Percent	2.4	1.9	11.0	4.4	-12.8	-1.6	(NA)	(NA)
EMPLOYEES [5]									
Total................................	1,000	546.6	679.7	565.0	576.0	559.6	526.9	531.2	538.3
Pilots and copilots..................	1,000	55.3	72.2	75.7	74.8	75.6	72.0	73.7	71.4

NA Not available. [1] For definition of mean, see Guide to Tabular Presentation. [2] 2011 data are preliminary. [3] Includes other types of revenues, not shown separately. [4] Excludes special items: bankruptcy-related reorganization charges and fresh-start accounting gains, and special goodwill charges. [5] Average full-time equivalents.

Source: Airlines for America, Washington, DC, *Economic Report*, annual (copyright); and Bureau of Transportation Statistics, <http://www.transtats.bts.gov/>, accessed October 2012.

Table 1082. Passenger Airline Cost Indexes: 1980 to 2011

[2000 = 100. To be included in the cost index, carriers must have met the following criteria on an annual basis: 1) must report both passenger revenue and revenue passenger miles (RPMs) and 2) passenger revenue must be greater than or equal to 25 percent of total operating revenue]

Index	1980	1990	1995	2000	2003	2004	2005	2006	2007	2008	2009	2010	2011
Composite index [1]..............	**77.4**	**101.1**	**99.0**	**100.0**	**122.8**	**149.1**	**177.9**	**195.8**	**199.8**	**262.0**	**147.4**	**160.6**	**195.0**
Labor costs...........................	52.0	73.1	91.3	100.0	122.7	122.3	117.3	119.0	119.1	119.8	127.4	135.3	136.7
Fuel...................................	113.7	98.1	69.7	100.0	107.9	144.1	206.6	242.8	258.0	374.2	233.9	269.3	350.4
Aircraft ownership [2].................	33.5	71.1	83.0	100.0	101.8	103.4	99.1	98.9	94.3	91.0	92.8	92.9	91.9
Nonaircraft ownership...............	40.4	88.1	103.3	100.0	111.4	104.1	106.1	104.2	106.6	118.8	115.2	111.4	111.4
Professional services...............	27.0	67.5	85.4	100.0	98.4	103.4	105.5	111.2	115.8	125.4	118.5	118.5	121.4
Food and beverage.................	88.5	125.5	106.9	100.0	74.6	67.1	61.3	57.9	57.8	60.0	59.7	59.5	61.7
Landing fees........................	49.2	81.0	95.8	100.0	130.8	131.2	130.7	135.6	136.7	148.6	158.9	169.8	166.3
Maintenance material...............	73.3	119.2	94.0	100.0	67.3	64.8	59.1	62.2	69.9	77.0	83.5	82.9	92.0
Aircraft insurance...................	246.1	161.0	341.5	100.0	180.9	174.3	157.1	181.0	152.3	124.0	150.7	164.9	163.9
Nonaircraft insurance...............	73.3	68.2	223.8	100.0	450.9	373.7	319.9	259.3	222.1	195.4	184.4	188.2	167.6
Passenger commissions............	121.5	227.0	184.8	100.0	41.9	37.2	31.6	29.2	28.2	27.0	26.7	26.4	25.7
Communication......................	50.3	85.7	86.5	100.0	82.0	76.1	73.3	68.5	71.2	79.2	77.2	75.3	80.0
Advertising and promotion..........	112.9	165.0	107.8	100.0	69.1	77.8	75.5	80.9	67.3	59.0	61.7	61.0	65.2
Utilities and office supplies.........	67.9	97.7	87.0	100.0	81.0	81.3	87.6	94.3	102.2	108.8	99.8	118.4	119.2
Transportation-related expenses...	46.0	55.0	57.5	100.0	256.4	397.4	475.0	508.4	506.7	604.5	158.9	157.9	185.1
Other operating expenses...........	56.0	87.4	74.1	100.0	94.9	94.3	108.6	108.1	116.1	156.8	123.7	121.5	137.0
Interest [3]............................	160.7	182.0	174.6	100.0	93.3	96.3	120.6	133.5	120.3	105.6	116.2	125.3	113.4

[1] Weighted average of all components, including interest. [2] Includes lease, aircraft and engine rentals, depreciation, and amortization. [3] Interest on long-term debt and capital and other interest expense.

Source: Airlines for America, Washington, DC, *U.S. Passenger Airline Cost Index*, Major and National Carriers (copyright). See also <http://www.airlines.org/>.

Table 1083. Top 40 Airports in 2010—Passengers Enplaned: 2000 and 2010

[In thousands (679,525 represents 679,525,000), except rank. For calendar year. Airports ranked by total passengers enplaned by large certificated air carriers on scheduled and nonscheduled operations, 2010]

Airport	2000 Rank	2000 Total	2010 Rank	2010 Total	Airport	2000 Rank	2000 Total	2010 Rank	2010 Total
All airports............	(X)	679,525	(X)	677,217	Baltimore, MD (BWI Intl).............	23	8,982	21	10,754
Total, top 40.................	(X)	483,221	(X)	518,486	Fort Lauderdale-Hollywood Intl, FL...	29	7,142	22	10,036
Atlanta, GA (Hartsfield Intl).......	1	38,262	1	42,655	Salt Lake City Intl, UT................	25	8,703	23	9,910
Chicago, IL (O'Hare Intl)...........	2	30,891	2	30,033	Washington, DC (Dulles Intl).........	32	6,657	24	9,817
Dallas/Fort Worth Intl, TX)........	3	27,877	3	26,786	Washington, DC (Ronald				
Denver Intl, CO....................	5	17,671	4	24,944	Reagan Washington Natl.)...........	30	6,987	25	8,617
Los Angeles Intl, CA..............	4	25,131	5	22,861	Chicago, IL (Midway).................	31	6,972	26	8,470
Houston, Intercontinental, TX.....	11	15,817	6	18,726	San Diego Intl, CA...................	27	7,636	27	8,347
Phoenix Sky Harbor Intl, AZ......	6	17,246	7	18,658	Tampa Intl, FL.......................	28	7,436	28	7,949
Charlotte-Douglas Intl, NC........	21	10,378	8	18,536	Honolulu Intl, HI.....................	24	8,717	29	7,484
Las Vegas, NV (McCarran Intl). ..	9	16,861	9	17,852	Portland Intl, OR....................	33	6,562	30	6,517
					St. Louis, MO (Lambert-St Louis				
San Francisco Intl, CA.............	10	16,704	10	16,752	Intl)....................	13	15,110	31	6,014
New York, NY (JFK Intl)...........	20	10,653	11	16,389	Kansas City Intl, MO................	36	5,751	32	4,937
Orlando Intl, FL....................	14	13,520	12	15,727	Memphis Intl, TN....................	38	4,993	33	4,924
Minneapolis-St. Paul Intl, MN.....	8	16,874	13	15,471	Milwaukee, WI (Mitchell Field).......	56	2,838	34	4,753
Detroit, MI (Wayne County).......	7	16,947	14	15,442	Cleveland, OH				
Newark, NJ (Liberty Intl).........	12	15,218	15	14,927	(Hopkins Intl).....................	34	6,155	35	4,573
Seattle-Tacoma Intl, WA..........	15	13,319	16	14,839	Oakland Intl, CA.....................	37	5,128	36	4,567
Philadelphia Intl, PA...............	19	10,977	17	14,703	Raleigh, NC (Raleigh-Durham Intl). ..	39	4,840	37	4,435
Miami Intl, FL.....................	16	12,669	18	14,004	Nashville Intl, TN....................	42	4,366	38	4,411
Boston, MA (Logan Intl)..........	17	11,593	19	12,282	Sacramento Intl, CA.................	45	3,873	39	4,392
New York, NY (La Guardia).......	18	11,445	20	11,634	Houston, TX (William P. Hobby)......	43	4,322	40	4,357

X Not applicable.

Source: U.S. Bureau of Transportation Statisics, "National Transportation Statistics," quarterly, <http://www.bts.gov/publications/national_transportation_statistics/>.

Table 1084. Domestic Airline Markets--Average Daily Passengers: 2011

[For calendar year. Data are for the 25 top markets and include all commercial airports in each metro area. Data represent traffic each way between origin and final destinations]

Market	Passengers	Market	Passengers
Los Angeles - New York............................	4,541	Honolulu - Maui........................	1,794
Chicago - New York................................	4,480	Dallas - New York......................	1,788
Ft. Lauderdale - New York........................	4,390	New York - Tampa......................	1,775
New York - Orlando...............................	4,062	Boston - New York......................	1,758
New York - San Francisco........................	3,417	Chicago - Orlando......................	1,713
Atlanta - New York................................	2,800	Chicago - Las Vegas...................	1,699
Los Angeles - San Francisco.....................	2,649	Chicago - Washington..................	1,695
Miami - New York.................................	2,559	Las Vegas - San Francisco............	1,644
Las Vegas - New York.............................	2,146	Las Vegas - Los Angeles..............	1,634
Chicago - Los Angeles............................	2,111	Orlando - Philadelphia.................	1,611
Boston - Washington..............................	1,971	Boston - Chicago......................	1,578
New York - West Palm Beach.....................	1,943	Dallas - Houston......................	1,575
		Chicago - San Francisco..............	1,574

Source: Airlines for America, Washington, DC, *Annual Report*, (copyright).

Table 1085. U.S. Carrier Delays, Cancellations, and Diversions: 1995 to 2010

[In thousands (5,327.4 represents 5,327,400). For calendar year. See headnote, Table 1088]

Item	1995	2000	2003	2004	2005	2006	2007	2008	2009	2010
Total operations........	5,327.4	5,683.0	6,488.5	7,129.3	7,140.6	7,141.9	7,455.5	7,009.7	6,450.3	6,450.1
Delays:										
Late departures [1]........	827.9	1,131.7	834.4	1,187.6	1,279.4	1,424.8	1,573.0	1,327.2	1,084.3	1,111.9
Late arrivals [2]............	1,039.3	1,356.0	1,057.8	1,421.4	1,466.1	1,615.5	1,804.0	1,524.7	1,218.3	1,174.9
Cancellations [3]............	91.9	187.5	101.5	127.8	133.7	121.9	160.8	137.4	89.4	113.3
Diversions [4]...............	10.5	14.3	11.4	13.8	14.0	16.2	17.2	17.3	15.5	15.5

[1] Late departures comprise flights departing 15 minutes or more after the scheduled departure time. [2] Late arrivals comprise flights arriving 15 minutes or more after the scheduled arrival time. [3] A cancelled flight is one that was not operated, but was listed in a carrier's computer reservation system within seven days of the scheduled departure. [4] A diverted flight is one that left from the scheduled departure airport but flew to a destination point other than the scheduled destination point.

Source: U.S. Bureau of Transportation Statistics, *National Transportation Statistics*, <http://www.bts.gov/publications/national_transportation_statistics/>.

Table 1086. Aircraft Accidents: 1990 to 2011

[For years ending December 31]

Item	Unit	1990	1995	2000	2005	2009	2010	2011, prel.
Air carrier accidents, all services [1]	Number	24	36	56	40	30	29	31
Fatal accidents	Number	6	3	3	3	2	1	–
Fatalities	Number	39	168	92	22	52	2	–
Aboard	Number	12	162	92	20	51	2	–
Rates per 100,000 flight hours:								
Accidents	Rate	0.198	0.267	0.306	0.206	0.170	0.163	0.175
Fatal accidents	Rate	0.049	0.022	0.016	0.015	0.011	0.006	–
Commuter air carrier accidents [2]	Number	15	12	12	6	2	6	4
Fatal accidents	Number	3	2	1	–	–	–	–
Fatalities	Number	6	9	5	–	–	–	–
Aboard	Number	4	9	5	–	–	–	–
Rates per 100,000 flight hours:								
Accidents	Rate	0.641	0.457	3.247	2.002	0.648	1.947	1.303
Fatal accidents	Rate	0.128	0.076	0.271	–	–	–	–
On-demand air taxi accidents [3]	Number	107	75	80	65	47	31	50
Fatal accidents	Number	29	24	22	11	2	6	16
Fatalities	Number	51	52	71	18	17	17	41
Aboard	Number	49	52	68	16	14	17	41
Rates per 100,000 flight hours:								
Accidents	Rate	4.76	3.02	2.04	1.70	1.62	1.00	1.50
Fatal accidents	Rate	1.29	0.97	0.56	0.29	0.07	0.19	0.48
General aviation accidents [4]	Number	2,242	2,056	1,837	1,670	1,480	1,439	1,466
Fatal accidents	Number	444	413	345	321	275	268	263
Fatalities	Number	770	735	596	563	479	454	444
Aboard	Number	765	728	585	558	470	451	433
Rates per 100,000 flight hours:								
Accidents	Rate	7.85	8.21	6.57	7.20	7.08	6.63	6.51
Fatal accidents	Rate	1.55	1.63	1.21	1.38	1.32	1.23	1.17

– Represents zero. [1] U.S. air carriers operating under 14 CFR 121. Beginning 2000, includes aircraft with 10 or more seats, previously operating under 14 CFR 135. [2] All scheduled service of U.S. air carriers operating under 14 CFR 135. Beginning 2000, only aircraft with fewer than 10 seats. [3] All nonscheduled service of U.S. air carriers operating under 14 CFR 135. [4] U.S. civil registered aircraft not operated under 14 CFR 121 or 135.

Source: U.S. National Transportation Safety Board, "Aviation Accident Statistics," <http://www.ntsb.gov/data/aviation_stats.html>, accessed August 2012.

Table 1087. Consumer Complaints Against U.S. Airlines: 1990 to 2011

[Calendar year data. Represents complaints filed by consumers to the U.S. Department of Transportation, Aviation Consumer Protection Division, regarding service problems with air carrier personnel. See source for data on individual airlines]

Complaint category	1990	2000	2005	2006	2007	2008	2009	2010	2011
Total	7,703	20,564	6,900	6,452	10,960	10,643	8,821	10,988	11,545
Flight problems [1]	3,034	8,698	1,942	1,845	4,097	3,247	2,041	3,337	3,656
Baggage	1,329	2,753	1,586	1,400	2,154	2,081	1,607	1,938	1,850
Ticketing/boarding [2]	624	1,405	679	708	1,136	1,404	1,583	1,510	1,447
Customer service [3]	758	4,074	800	870	1,214	1,333	1,103	1,345	1,287
Refunds	701	803	530	485	745	803	669	730	986
Fares [4]	312	708	219	173	315	389	436	465	634
Disability [5]	(NA)	612	430	368	428	474	519	572	630
Oversales [6]	399	759	284	275	420	432	370	544	509
Discrimination [7]	(NA)	(NA)	100	90	82	115	131	143	127
Advertising	96	42	45	30	34	39	53	77	81
Tours	29	25	([8])	([8])	([8])	([8])	([8])	([8])	([8])
Animals	(NA)	1	3	3	7	5	5	8	9
Smoking	74	([9])	([9])	([9])	([9])	([9])	([9])	([9])	([9])
Credit	5	([9])	([9])	([9])	([9])	([9])	([9])	([9])	([9])
Other	342	684	282	205	328	321	304	319	329

NA Not available. [1] Cancellations, delays, etc., from schedule. [2] Errors in reservations and ticketing; problems in making reservations and obtaining tickets. Includes disability complaints prior to 1998. [3] Unhelpful employees, inadequate meals or cabin service, treatment of delayed passengers. [4] Incorrect or incomplete information about fares, discount fare conditions, and availability, etc. [5] Prior to 2000, included in ticketing/boarding. [6] All bumping problems, whether or not airline complied with DOT regulations. [7] Allegations of discrimination by airlines due to factors other than disability, such as race, religion, national origin or sex. [8] Included in "Other" beginning 2002. [9] Included in "Other" beginning 2000.

Source: U.S. Department of Transportation, Aviation Consumer Protection Division, *Air Travel Consumer Report*, monthly. See also <http://www.dot.gov/airconsumer>.

Table 1088. On-Time Flight Arrivals and Departures at Major U.S. Airports: 2011

[In percent. Quarterly, based on gate arrival and departure times for domestic scheduled operations of U.S. major airlines. All U.S. airlines with 1 percent or more of total U.S. domestic scheduled airline passenger revenues are required to report on-time data. A flight is considered on time if it operated less than 15 minutes after the scheduled time shown in the carrier's computerized reservation system. See source for data on individual airlines]

Airport	On-time arrivals				On-time departures			
	1st quarter	2nd quarter	3rd quarter	4th quarter	1st quarter	2nd quarter	3rd quarter	4th quarter
Total, all airports................................	**76.8**	**76.5**	**80.2**	**85.1**	**78.4**	**78.3**	**81.3**	**85.9**
Atlanta, Hartsfield....................................	76.6	77.3	80.6	86.8	80.5	79.8	83.3	89.3
Boston, Logan International.....................	72.6	67.4	71.6	84.0	73.3	72.8	75.6	84.7
Baltimore/Washington International...........	80.4	79.2	78.4	89.1	79.4	79.1	79.6	88.3
Charlotte, Douglas..................................	80.0	74.2	75.7	87.7	84.4	81.0	82.5	90.4
Washington, Reagan National..................	78.2	73.9	73.5	85.8	81.0	79.2	78.5	88.2
Denver International................................	80.0	80.9	82.5	85.2	81.0	81.0	83.3	85.9
Dallas-Fort Worth International.................	81.1	77.5	85.6	85.9	82.7	79.1	85.2	87.9
Detroit, Metro Wayne County...................	77.6	78.3	81.1	88.6	78.2	79.5	82.8	88.7
Newark International................................	70.0	60.4	63.8	72.9	71.0	64.8	69.9	74.3
Fort Lauderdale-Hollywood International......	75.9	77.3	78.0	84.7	77.4	79.7	81.2	86.7
Washington/Dulles.................................	80.1	75.0	75.0	84.9	80.6	79.2	78.9	85.6
Houston, George Bush...........................	80.0	78.8	81.7	83.6	85.1	83.4	84.6	86.7
New York, JFK International.....................	74.7	71.8	71.3	84.3	75.1	75.8	75.5	85.4
Las Vegas, McCarran International...........	78.8	79.6	85.3	86.8	79.1	79.8	83.7	86.7
Los Angeles International.......................	76.6	77.4	82.2	81.9	80.7	81.4	82.6	84.7
New York, La Guardia............................	71.3	67.1	71.5	79.2	72.5	70.4	74.2	81.4
Orlando International...............................	78.0	79.8	79.3	85.9	79.8	81.3	81.7	87.8
Chicago, Midway...................................	78.4	78.2	84.2	89.9	75.2	75.8	82.8	86.4
Miami International.................................	77.2	79.7	76.6	85.5	78.9	80.6	79.4	86.7
Minneapolis-St. Paul International.............	74.1	80.1	85.0	90.7	77.2	81.7	85.0	89.6
Chicago, O'Hare....................................	72.4	69.4	77.2	83.2	75.3	71.9	78.5	84.0
Portland International..............................	77.8	81.0	87.0	85.4	80.2	81.9	85.0	87.0
Philadelphia International.........................	77.0	73.1	73.0	81.8	77.9	76.8	77.5	84.0
Phoenix, Sky Harbor International.............	81.4	83.0	87.3	88.0	82.8	83.7	85.8	88.4
San Diego, Lindbergh Field....................	76.1	77.5	84.0	84.4	77.7	78.5	82.2	85.0
Seattle-Tacoma International...................	77.5	83.3	88.4	86.0	81.9	84.0	86.3	88.0
San Francisco International.....................	68.5	71.1	70.6	75.1	71.4	74.4	70.7	76.9
Salt Lake City International......................	80.9	85.5	89.2	90.1	82.7	86.3	88.1	89.9
Tampa, Tampa International....................	78.6	80.6	80.1	87.4	79.2	80.0	81.3	87.1

Source: U.S. Department of Transportation, Aviation Consumer Protection Division, *Air Travel Consumer Report*, monthly. See also <http://www.dot.gov/airconsumer>.

Table 1089. Worldwide Airline Accidents and Fatalities by World Region: 2005 to 2011

[In thousands (27,278 represents 27,278,000)]

Year	Departures	Accidents	Accident rate [1]	Fatalities	Fatal accidents
2005...	27,278	119	4.4	824	23
2006...	27,482	112	4.1	806	15
2007...	28,911	122	4.2	645	15
2008...	28,859	138	4.8	524	17
2009...	27,870	113	4.1	670	13
2010...	29,023	121	4.2	707	19
2011..	**30,053**	**126**	**4.2**	**414**	**16**
Oceania..	855	4	4.7	55	2
North America................................	10,979	38	3.5	0	0
Latin America and Caribbean.............	2,625	15	5.7	60	4
Europe...	7,143	39	5.5	60	4
Asia...	7,561	22	2.9	98	3
Africa...	891	7	7.9	141	3

[1] Number of accidents per million departures of scheduled commercial operations that involve the transportation of passengers, cargo and mail for remuneration or hire.

Source: International Civil Aviation Organization, Montreal, Canada, "Integrated Safety Trend Analysis and Reporting System,"<http://www2.icao.int/en/ism/istars/pages2/homepage.aspx>, accessed September 2012 (Copyright).

Table 1090. Airports, Aircraft, and Airmen: 1980 to 2010

[As of December 31 or for years ending December 31]

Item	1980	1990	1995	2000	2005	2008	2009	2010
Airports, total [1]	**15,161**	**17,490**	**18,224**	**19,281**	**19,854**	**19,930**	**19,750**	**19,802**
Public [1]	4,814	5,589	5,415	5,317	5,270	5,202	5,178	5,175
Percent—with lighted runways	66.2	71.4	74.3	75.9	76.8	(NA)	(NA)	(NA)
With paved runways	72.3	70.7	73.3	74.3	74.8	(NA)	(NA)	(NA)
Private	10,347	11,901	12,809	13,964	14,584	14,451	14,298	14,353
Percent—with lighted runways	15.2	7.0	6.4	7.2	9.2	(NA)	(NA)	(NA)
With paved runways	13.3	31.5	33.0	32.0	33.2	(NA)	(NA)	(NA)
Certificated [2]	730	680	667	651	575	560	559	551
Civil	(X)	(X)	572	563	(X)	(X)	(X)	(X)
Civil military	(X)	(X)	95	88	(X)	(X)	(X)	(X)
General aviation	14,431	16,810	17,557	18,630	19,279	19,370	19,191	19,251
Active air carrier fleet [3]	3,805	6,083	7,411	8,049	8,225	7,856	(NA)	(NA)
Fixed wing	3,803	6,072	7,293	8,010	8,182	7,808	(NA)	(NA)
Helicopter	2	11	118	39	43	48	(NA)	(NA)
General aviation fleet [4]	211,043	198,000	188,089	217,533	224,352	228,663	223,877	(NA)
Fixed-wing	200,094	184,500	162,342	183,276	185,373	182,961	177,446	(NA)
Turbojet	2,992	4,100	4,559	7,001	9,823	11,042	11,268	(NA)
Turboprop	4,089	5,300	4,995	5,763	7,942	8,906	9,054	(NA)
Piston	193,013	175,200	152,788	170,513	167,608	163,012	157,123	(NA)
Rotorcraft	6,001	6,900	5,830	7,150	8,728	9,876	9,984	(NA)
Other	4,945	6,600	4,741	6,701	6,454	5,652	5,480	(NA)
Gliders	(X)	(X)	2,182	2,041	2,074	1,914	1,808	(NA)
Lighter than air	(X)	(X)	2,559	4,660	4,380	3,738	3,672	(NA)
Experimental	(X)	(X)	15,176	20,407	23,627	23,364	24,419	(NA)
Airman certificates held: [5]								
Pilot, total	827,071	702,659	639,184	625,581	609,737	613,746	594,285	627,588
Women	52,902	40,515	38,032	35,607	36,584	37,981	36,808	42,218
Student	199,833	128,663	101,279	93,064	87,213	80,989	72,280	119,119
Recreational	(X)	87	232	340	278	252	234	212
Airplane:								
Private	357,479	299,111	261,399	251,561	228,619	222,596	211,619	202,020
Commercial	183,442	149,666	133,980	121,858	120,614	124,746	125,738	123,705
Air transport	69,569	107,732	123,877	141,596	141,992	146,838	144,600	142,198
Rotorcraft only [6]	6,030	9,567	7,183	7,775	9,518	14,647	15,298	15,377
Glider only	7,039	7,833	11,234	9,387	21,369	21,055	21,268	21,275
Flight instructor certificates	60,440	63,775	77,613	80,931	90,555	93,202	94,863	96,473
Instrument ratings	260,462	297,073	298,798	311,944	311,828	325,247	323,495	318,001
Nonpilot [7]	368,356	492,237	651,341	547,453	644,016	678,181	682,315	686,717
Mechanic	250,157	344,282	405,294	344,434	320,293	326,276	329,027	331,989
Repairmen	(X)	(X)	61,233	38,208	40,030	41,056	41,389	41,267
Parachute rigger	9,547	10,094	11,824	10,477	8,150	8,248	8,362	8,407
Ground instructor	61,550	66,882	96,165	72,326	74,378	74,983	75,461	75,205
Dispatcher	6,799	11,002	15,642	16,340	18,079	19,590	20,132	20,691
Flight navigator	1,936	1,290	916	570	298	222	181	174
Flight attendant	(X)	(X)	(X)	(X)	125,032	154,671	156,741	159,946
Flight engineer	38,367	58,687	60,267	65,098	57,756	53,135	51,022	49,038

NA Not available. X Not applicable. [1] Existing airports, heliports, seaplane bases, etc., recorded with Federal Aviation Administration (FAA). Includes civil and joint-use civil-military airports, heliports, STOL (short takeoff and landing) ports, and seaplane bases in the United States and its territories. Sole-use military airports are included beginning in 2007. Includes U.S. Island Areas. Airport-type definitions: Public—publicly owned and under control of a public agency; private—owned by a private individual or corporation. May or may not be open for public use. [2] Certificated airports serve air-carriers with aircraft seating more than 9 passengers. As of 2005, the Federal Aviation Administration (FAA) no longer certificates military airports. [3] Air-carrier aircraft are aircraft carrying passengers or cargo for hire under 14 CFR 121 (large aircraft—more than 30 seats) and 14 CFR 135 (small aircraft--30 seats or fewer). Beginning in 1990, the number of aircraft is the monthly average reported in use for the last three months of the year. Prior to 1990, it was the number of aircraft reported in use during December of a given year. [4] 2000 dip in helicopters due to estimating methods. [5] Beginning 1995 excludes commuters. [6] Data for 1980 are for helicopters only. [7] All certificates on record. No medical examination required.

Source: U.S. Bureau of Transportation Statistics, *National Transportation Statistics*, annual. See also <http://www.bts.gov/publications/national_transportation_statistics/>. Airmen certificates held: U.S. Federal Aviation Administration, <http://www.faa.gov/data_research/aviation_data_statistics/civil_airmen_statistics/>. Prior to 2000: *FAA Statistical Handbook of Aviation*, annual.

Table 1091. Commuter/Regional Airline Operations Summary: 2005 to 2010

[152.6 represents 152,600,000. Calendar year data. Commuter/regional airlines operate primarily aircraft of predominately 75 passengers or less and 18,000 pounds of payload capacity serving short haul and small community markets. Represents operations within all North America by U.S. Regional Carriers. Averages are means. For definition of mean, see Guide to Tabular Presentation]

Item	Unit	2005	2007	2008	2009	2010
Passenger carriers operating	Number	75	72	(NA)	62	61
Passengers enplaned	Millions	152.6	159.0	(NA)	159.5	163.5
Average passengers enplaned per carrier	1,000	2,034.0	2,208.5	(NA)	2,572.6	2,680.3
Revenue passenger miles (RPM)	Billions	67.4	73.8	(NA)	72.9	75.8
Average RPMs per carrier	Millions	898.8	1,024.7	(NA)	1,176.0	1,243.0
Available seat miles	Billions	95.6	99.0	(NA)	97.6	99.2
Average load factor	Percent	70.5	74.6	(NA)	74.7	76.5
Departures completed	Millions	4.6	5.0	(NA)	4.8	4.8
Airports served	Number	666	666	(NA)	644	673
Average trip length	Miles	442.0	464.0	(NA)	457.0	464.0
Average seating capacity (seats)	Number	50.0	52.4	(NA)	55.0	56.0
Fleet flying hours	1,000	5,714.0	7,306.7	(NA)	5,162.0	5,211.0

NA Not available.

Source: Regional Airline Association, *Annual Report* (copyright). See also <http://www.raa.org/>.

Table 1092. Freight Carried on Major U.S. Waterways: 1990 to 2010

[In millions of short tons (4.2 represents 4,200,000). One short ton equals 2,000 pounds]

Item	1990	1995	2000	2005	2007	2008	2009	2010
Atlantic Intracoastal Waterway.........	4.2	3.5	3.1	2.7	2.5	2.9	2.5	2.9
Great Lakes.............................	167.1	177.8	187.5	169.4	161.0	152.4	108.7	129.5
Gulf Intracoastal Waterway............	115.4	118.0	113.8	116.1	125.1	115.9	108.1	116.2
Mississippi River system [1]............	659.1	707.2	715.5	678.0	699.0	681.6	622.1	663.2
Mississippi River main stem...........	475.3	520.3	515.6	464.6	500.5	486.8	447.1	483.2
Ohio River system [2]..................	260.0	267.6	274.4	280.1	260.2	259.2	229.5	245.2
Columbia River........................	51.4	57.1	55.2	51.5	58.1	54.8	46.0	54.7
Snake River...........................	4.8	6.8	6.7	5.3	5.4	3.7	4.4	3.4

[1] Main channels and all tributaries of the Mississippi, Illinois, Missouri, and Ohio Rivers. [2] Main channels and all navigable tributaries and embayments of the Ohio, Tennessee, and Cumberland Rivers.

Source: U.S. Army Corps of Engineers, *Waterborne Commerce of the United States*, annual. See also <http://www.ndc.iwr.usace.army.mil//wcsc/wcsc.htm>.

Table 1093. Waterborne Commerce by Type of Commodity: 1995 to 2010

[In millions of short tons (2,240.4 represents 2,240,400,000). One short ton equals 2,000 pounds. Domestic trade includes all commercial movements between United States ports and on inland rivers, Great Lakes, canals, and connecting channels of the United States, Puerto Rico, and Virgin Islands]

Commodity	1995	2000	2005	2010 Total	2010 Domestic	2010 Foreign imports	2010 Foreign exports
Total...............................	2,240.4	2,424.6	2,527.6	2,334.4	893.5	883.1	557.8
Coal.................................	324.5	297.0	316.6	309.6	215.1	19.3	75.3
Petroleum and petroleum products....	907.1	1,044.0	1,111.4	1,018.8	315.7	578.3	124.8
Crude petroleum.....................	504.6	571.4	602.7	508.5	60.3	448.2	–
Petroleum products [1]...............	402.5	472.4	508.8	510.4	255.5	130.1	124.8
Gasoline........................	114.4	125.2	156.1	137.8	68.8	43.1	26.0
Distillate fuel oil................	76.7	91.7	141.1	185.4	73.6	64.2	47.6
Residual fuel oil.................	111.9	131.6	96.1	81.1	67.8	4.7	8.5
Chemicals and related products.......	153.7	172.4	174.9	180.1	71.6	45.7	62.8
Fertilizers..........................	35.7	35.1	34.5	35.8	13.9	11.5	10.4
Other chemicals and related products...	118.0	137.3	140.4	144.3	57.7	34.1	52.4
Crude material, inedible...............	381.7	380.3	386.0	307.0	162.0	78.5	66.5
Forest products, wood and chips......	47.2	33.1	29.4	20.8	5.8	4.3	10.8
Pulp and waste paper...............	14.9	13.6	18.7	21.4	–	2.1	19.3
Soil, sand, gravel, rock, and stone [1]....	152.5	165.0	177.9	120.3	90.0	26.8	3.5
Limestone.......................	54.0	67.4	73.5	61.3	44.7	13.9	2.7
Phosphate rock..................	10.7	3.4	6.0	4.6	2.5	2.2	–
Sand & gravel...................	77.0	79.0	80.2	46.3	39.7	5.9	0.7
Iron ore and scrap..................	104.9	97.9	85.7	82.0	48.3	9.7	24.0
Marine shells.......................	0.5	0.3	–	0.1	0.1	–	–
Nonferrous ores and scrap..........	27.9	29.2	29.2	23.9	5.7	14.7	3.5
Sulphur, clay, and salt..............	23.4	11.3	8.7	6.3	0.5	1.4	4.4
Slag...............................	1.9	4.0	6.0	4.3	2.0	2.1	0.3
Other nonmetal minerals............	8.4	25.9	30.4	27.8	9.7	17.4	0.7
Primary manufactured goods..........	106.3	153.0	166.4	103.7	28.4	53.3	22.0
Papers products....................	13.1	12.1	13.7	13.7	0.1	5.2	8.3
Lime, cement, and glass............	33.9	55.9	62.4	27.6	13.9	12.0	1.7
Primary iron and steel products.....	44.1	57.1	52.1	33.5	9.4	21.4	2.7
Primary nonferrous metal products..	12.3	25.5	33.5	26.7	4.9	12.8	9.1
Primary wood products.............	2.9	2.5	4.8	2.2	0.1	1.8	0.3
Food and farm products..............	303.2	283.3	251.3	300.1	84.8	37.2	178.1
Fish...............................	3.6	2.4	3.0	3.1	0.1	2.0	1.1
Grain [1]...........................	167.9	145.2	124.0	131.8	45.4	1.7	84.7
Wheat...........................	48.5	43.4	36.4	38.4	8.8	0.7	29.0
Corn............................	105.0	88.2	75.2	81.8	33.5	0.1	48.1
Oilseeds [1]........................	46.1	57.6	47.2	76.9	26.8	0.3	49.8
Soybeans........................	42.0	47.3	40.8	67.4	23.6	0.1	43.7
Vegetables products................	9.0	8.9	8.3	12.9	1.2	5.1	6.5
Processed grain and animal feed.....	33.0	23.1	18.4	20.6	5.8	0.8	13.9
Other agricultural products..........	43.5	46.1	50.5	54.9	5.4	27.4	22.1
All manufactured equip, machinery and products.....	57.0	83.6	110.3	104.1	14.3	67.0	22.8
Waste and scrap, n.e.c. [2].............	5.4	4.3	2.0	1.3	1.3	–	–
Unknown or n.e.c. [2].................	1.6	6.8	8.7	9.6	0.2	3.9	5.6

– Represents or rounds to zero. [1] Includes commodities not shown separately. [2] Not elsewhere classified.

Source: U.S. Army Corps of Engineers, *Waterborne Commerce of the United States*, annual. See also <http://www.ndc.iwr.usace.army.mil//wcsc/wcsc.htm>.

Table 1094. Top U.S. Ports by Tons of Traffic: 2010

[In thousands of short tons (39,629 represents 39,629,000), except rank. One short ton equals 2,000 lbs. For calendar year. For the top 30 ports. Represents tons of cargo shipped from or received by the specified port. Excludes cargo carried on general ferries; coal and petroleum products loaded from shore facilities directly onto bunkers of vessels for fuel; and amounts of less than 100 tons of government-owned equipment in support of Corps of Engineers projects]

Port name	Rank	Total	Foreign Total	Inbound	Outbound	Domestic
Baltimore, MD............................	16	39,629	30,167	13,516	16,651	9,462
Baton Rouge, LA.........................	13	55,537	20,768	14,126	6,642	34,769
Beaumont, TX............................	4	76,959	51,782	44,310	7,472	25,177
Corpus Christi, TX.......................	6	73,663	54,823	41,655	13,168	18,841
Duluth-Superior, MN and WI............	18	36,598	9,662	331	9,331	26,936
Freeport, TX.............................	27	26,676	22,328	20,084	2,245	4,347
Houston, TX.............................	2	227,133	159,561	88,508	71,053	67,573
Huntington - Tristate [1].................	9	61,522	–	–	–	61,522
Lake Charles, LA........................	14	54,615	33,001	26,928	6,072	21,614
Long Beach, CA.........................	5	75,435	62,565	38,816	23,748	12,870
Los Angeles, CA........................	8	62,387	55,944	34,649	21,295	6,443
Mobile, AL..............................	12	55,713	29,357	15,061	14,296	26,357
New Orleans, LA........................	7	72,411	34,079	15,721	18,358	38,331
New York, NY and NJ...................	3	139,198	83,714	63,884	19,830	55,484
Norfolk Harbor, VA......................	15	41,569	35,389	8,795	26,594	6,180
Pascagoula, MS.........................	17	37,276	26,598	20,026	6,572	10,678
Philadelphia, PA.........................	21	34,036	21,471	20,987	484	12,565
Pittsburgh, PA...........................	22	33,843	–	–	–	33,843
Plaquemines, LA, Port of...............	11	55,837	18,909	1,357	17,552	36,928
Port Arthur, TX..........................	25	30,232	19,465	10,783	8,682	10,767
Portland, OR............................	28	25,949	17,771	3,473	14,298	8,179
Richmond, CA...........................	29	24,178	12,765	10,668	2,098	11,412
Savannah, GA...........................	19	34,682	32,893	17,505	15,388	1,789
Seattle, WA.............................	26	27,192	22,097	8,607	13,491	5,094
South Louisiana, LA, Port of...........	1	236,262	115,151	41,167	73,984	121,111
St. Louis, MO and IL....................	24	30,773	–	–	–	30,773
Tacoma, WA............................	30	22,399	17,045	4,861	12,183	5,354
Tampa, FL...............................	20	34,202	11,196	5,757	5,439	23,006
Texas City, TX..........................	10	56,591	40,076	32,553	7,522	16,515
Valdez, AK..............................	23	31,902	–	–	–	31,902

– Represents zero. [1] The Port of Huntington is the largest inland shipping port in the United States.

Source: U.S. Army Corps of Engineers, *Waterborne Commerce of the United States*, 2010. See also <http://www.ndc.iwr.usace.army.mil//wcsc/wcsc.htm>.

Table 1095. Top U.S. Ports/Waterways by Container Traffic: 2010

[In thousands of twenty-foot equivalent units (TEUs) (31,507.4 represents 31,507,400). For calendar year. For the 30 leading ports/waterways in total TEUs. A TEUs is a measure of containerized cargo capacity equal to one standard 20-foot length by 8-foot width by 8-foot, 6 inch height container]

Port/waterway name	Rank	Total loaded	Domestic loaded Total [1]	Inbound	Outbound	Foreign loaded Total	Inbound
Total [2]...........................	(X)	31,507.4	4,684.6	1,962.7	1,962.7	27,582.0	16,448.4
Anchorage, AK.........................	18	267.6	273.9	219.0	48.4	0.3	–
Apra Harbor, GU........................	29	67.3	76.1	57.3	10.1	–	–
Baltimore, MD...........................	16	495.2	72.4	26.8	24.3	444.0	277.7
Boston, MA..............................	24	130.2	12.2	3.7	3.2	123.3	79.6
Camden-Gloucester, NJ................	26	85.5	52.6	19.1	33.5	33.0	25.5
Charleston, SC..........................	10	1,061.3	–	–	–	1,061.3	543.3
Chester, SC.............................	28	80.6	–	–	–	80.6	46.8
Gulfport, MS.............................	20	177.2	–	–	–	177.2	101.1
Honolulu, HI.............................	12	749.4	954.4	495.1	225.4	28.9	17.8
Houston, TX.............................	8	1,341.9	15.2	11.4	1.6	1,328.8	510.6
Jacksonville, FL.........................	13	725.5	489.5	69.8	419.6	236.0	91.5
Kahului, Maui, HI........................	30	59.0	92.4	45.6	13.4	–	–
Long Beach, CA.........................	2	4,736.9	374.1	50.6	276.1	4,410.2	3,036.1
Los Angeles, CA........................	1	5,479.4	–	–	–	5,479.4	3,817.2
Miami, FL................................	14	678.9	–	–	–	678.9	305.4
Mobile, AL...............................	27	81.0	0.1	–	–	81.0	34.3
New Orleans, LA........................	17	274.7	–	–	–	274.7	76.8
New York (NY and NJ).................	3	4,216.1	231.1	91.5	119.0	4,005.7	2,605.7
Norfolk Harbor, VA......................	7	1,472.9	76.0	27.0	26.8	1,419.0	710.2
Oakland, CA.............................	5	1,673.9	242.2	29.5	150.1	1,494.2	733.9
Palm Beach, FL.........................	25	109.0	–	–	–	109.0	24.8
Philadelphia, PA.........................	21	166.3	3.6	–	2.7	163.7	119.9
Port Everglades, FL.....................	15	579.0	6.5	–	6.5	572.5	244.2
Portland, OR............................	23	135.9	10.9	6.9	0.0	129.0	67.3
San Juan, PR............................	11	825.0	609.2	498.6	110.5	215.8	151.2
Savannah, GA...........................	4	2,147.8	–	0.0	0.0	2,147.8	1,042.1
Seattle, WA.............................	6	1,601.8	294.6	44.1	145.0	1,412.8	865.3
Tacoma, WA............................	9	1,086.3	276.2	54.2	221.9	810.3	493.5
Wilmington, NC.........................	19	199.7	–	–	–	199.7	113.8
Wilmington, DE.........................	22	154.7	–	–	–	154.7	132.0

– Represents zero. X Not applicable. [1] Includes empty TEUs. [2] Includes other ports/waterways not shown separately.

Source: U.S. Army Corps of Engineers, *U.S. Waterborne Container Traffic for U.S. Port/Waterway in 2010*, <http://www.ndc.iwr.usace.army.mil//wcsc/wcsc.htm>, accessed April 2012.

Table 1096. Highway Mileage—Urban and Rural by Ownership: 1990 to 2008

[In thousands (3,880 represents 3,880,000). As of December 31. Includes Puerto Rico beginning 2000]

Type and Control	1990	1995	2000	2004	2005	2006	2007	2008	2009
Total mileage [1].	**3,880**	**3,912**	**3,951**	**3,997**	**4,012**	**4,033**	**4,049**	**4,059**	**4,063**
Urban mileage [2].	757	819	859	994	1,023	1,043	1,058	1,079	1,086
Under state control.	96	112	112	130	144	148	149	152	152
Under local control [1].	661	706	746	861	874	890	904	920	926
Rural mileage.	3,123	3,093	3,092	3,003	2,989	2,990	2,991	2,980	2,977
Under state control.	703	691	664	650	637	636	635	633	632
Under local control [1].	2,242	2,231	2,311	2,236	2,228	2,231	2,230	2,223	2,221
Under federal control [2].	178	170	117	118	123	123	126	124	124

[1] Includes state park, state toll, other state agency, other local agency and other roadways not identified by ownership. [2] Includes roadways in federal parks, forest, and reservations that are not part of the state and local highway system.

Source: U.S. Federal Highway Administration, *Highway Statistics*, annual. See also <http://www.fhwa.dot.gov/policy/ohpi/hss/index.cfm>.

Table 1097. Highway Mileage by State—Functional Systems and Urban/Rural: 2010

[As of December 31. Excludes Puerto Rico. For definition of functional systems, see text, this section]

State	Total	Functional systems					Urban	Rural
		Interstate	Other freeways and expressways	Arterial	Collector	Local		
U.S.	**4,067,077**	**46,900**	**14,619**	**400,009**	**799,226**	**2,806,322**	**1,089,701**	**2,977,376**
AL.	101,575	906	35	9,423	22,065	69,145	25,190	76,384
AK.	16,303	1,084	–	1,559	2,763	10,896	2,585	13,718
AZ.	64,308	1,168	176	5,825	8,113	49,027	23,066	41,242
AR.	100,068	655	220	7,051	20,947	71,196	12,956	87,112
CA.	172,139	2,453	1,526	27,456	32,416	108,288	90,092	82,046
CO.	88,353	953	314	8,925	16,270	61,891	19,430	68,923
CT.	21,391	346	279	2,724	3,202	14,840	15,175	6,216
DE.	6,337	41	30	645	1,044	4,577	2,991	3,346
DC.	1,503	14	17	268	157	1,047	1,503	–
FL.	121,702	1,496	746	12,797	14,496	92,167	81,513	40,189
GA.	122,917	1,248	141	14,127	23,028	84,373	39,824	83,093
HI.	4,395	55	34	755	829	2,722	2,345	2,050
ID.	48,771	612	–	4,252	10,490	33,418	5,822	42,949
IL.	139,519	2,182	99	14,667	21,816	100,755	41,320	98,199
IN.	96,988	1,171	171	8,485	22,299	64,861	26,877	70,111
IA.	114,383	782	–	9,736	31,614	72,251	11,391	102,992
KS.	140,653	874	187	9,520	33,587	96,485	12,978	127,675
KY.	79,184	762	690	5,492	16,537	55,702	12,556	66,628
LA.	61,327	905	51	5,522	10,035	44,815	16,335	44,992
ME.	22,864	369	19	2,180	5,930	14,365	3,005	19,859
MD.	31,526	481	300	3,798	5,052	21,895	17,437	14,089
MA.	36,248	573	345	6,132	4,829	24,370	28,265	7,983
MI.	121,969	1,244	705	14,302	24,473	81,244	35,983	85,985
MN.	138,164	914	187	13,411	30,440	93,212	20,632	117,532
MS.	75,080	699	69	7,559	15,543	51,211	11,031	64,050
MO [1].	130,360	1,181	408	10,276	24,895	93,599	23,592	106,767
MT.	74,793	1,192	–	6,037	16,192	51,372	3,174	71,619
NE.	93,653	482	406	7,727	20,774	64,264	6,428	87,225
NV.	35,061	571	69	3,448	5,428	25,546	8,033	27,028
NH.	16,085	225	74	1,522	2,743	11,520	4,935	11,150
NJ.	39,242	431	407	5,764	4,145	28,496	31,868	7,373
NM.	68,378	1,000	5	5,138	8,471	53,763	7,909	60,469
NY.	114,574	1,704	1,111	13,494	20,772	77,493	48,427	66,146
NC.	105,653	1,172	481	9,532	17,327	77,141	35,567	70,086
ND.	86,842	571	–	5,932	11,898	68,442	1,919	84,923
OH.	123,192	1,574	484	10,965	22,643	87,526	45,007	78,185
OK.	112,873	933	186	8,233	25,305	78,217	16,089	96,784
OR.	59,151	730	59	7,083	17,691	33,588	12,899	46,252
PA.	119,685	1,856	855	12,913	19,837	84,224	46,180	73,506
RI.	6,490	71	90	839	881	4,608	5,267	1,223
SC.	66,024	851	82	7,151	15,088	42,852	16,372	49,651
SD.	82,447	679	11	6,401	19,013	56,343	2,961	79,486
TN.	94,207	1,104	152	9,125	17,951	65,874	24,236	69,971
TX.	311,249	3,231	1,512	31,729	64,901	209,876	97,936	213,313
UT.	45,124	937	20	3,728	8,193	32,246	11,239	33,885
VT.	14,437	320	18	1,304	3,108	9,687	1,466	12,970
VA.	74,378	1,124	262	8,507	14,342	50,143	23,852	50,526
WA.	83,822	764	1,019	7,271	17,322	57,446	23,510	60,312
WV.	38,625	555	9	3,488	8,604	25,970	5,367	33,258
WI.	114,963	743	557	12,182	22,553	78,928	22,451	92,512
WY [1].	28,105	913	3	3,610	11,173	12,406	2,713	25,392

– Represents zero. [1] 2009 data.

Source: U.S. Federal Highway Administration, *Highway Statistics*, annual. See also <http://www.fhwa.dot.gov/policy/ohpi/hss/index.cfm>.

Table 1098. Bridge Inventory—Total Deficient and Obsolete: 1997 to 2011, and by State, 2010

[As of December 2011. Based on the National Bridge Inventory program; for details, see source]

State and year	Number of bridges	Deficient and obsolete		Structurally deficient [1]		Functionally obsolete [2]	
		Total number	Percent	Number	Percent	Number	Percent
1997.............	582,751	175,885	30.2	98,475	16.9	77,410	13.3
1998.............	582,984	172,582	29.6	93,076	16.0	79,506	13.6
1999.............	585,542	170,050	29.0	88,150	15.1	81,900	14.0
2000.............	587,458	167,581	28.5	86,692	14.8	80,889	13.8
2001.............	590,066	165,099	28.0	83,630	14.2	81,469	13.8
2002.............	591,220	163,010	27.6	81,437	13.8	81,573	13.8
2003.............	592,246	160,819	27.2	79,811	13.5	81,008	13.7
2004.............	593,885	158,318	26.7	77,758	13.1	80,560	13.6
2005.............	594,616	156,177	26.3	75,871	12.8	80,306	13.5
2006.............	596,842	153,990	25.8	73,764	12.4	80,226	13.4
2007.............	599,766	152,316	25.4	72,524	12.1	79,792	13.3
2008.............	601,411	151,391	25.2	71,469	11.9	79,922	13.3
2009.............	603,245	149,647	24.8	71,179	11.8	78,468	13.0
2010.............	604,474	146,633	24.3	69,223	11.5	77,410	12.8
U.S. total, 2011........	**605,086**	**143,889**	**23.8**	**67,526**	**11.2**	**76,363**	**12.6**
Alabama.................	16,061	3,574	22.3	1,518	9.5	2,056	12.8
Alaska..................	1,156	250	21.6	131	11.3	119	10.3
Arizona.................	7,738	928	12.0	259	3.3	669	8.6
Arkansas...............	12,641	2,742	21.7	886	7.0	1,856	14.7
California..............	24,609	6,895	28.0	2,927	11.9	3,968	16.1
Colorado...............	8,551	1,380	16.1	582	6.8	798	9.3
Connecticut............	4,200	1,413	33.6	390	9.3	1,023	24.4
Delaware...............	857	161	18.8	50	5.8	111	13.0
District of Columbia......	245	159	64.9	32	13.1	127	51.8
Florida.................	11,986	1,830	15.3	273	2.3	1,557	13.0
Georgia................	14,694	2,661	18.1	901	6.1	1,760	12.0
Hawaii.................	1,132	506	44.7	144	12.7	362	32.0
Idaho..................	4,164	782	18.8	371	8.9	411	9.9
Illinois.................	26,436	4,061	15.4	2,319	8.8	1,742	6.6
Indiana.................	18,640	3,939	21.1	2,043	11.0	1,896	10.2
Iowa...................	24,537	6,619	27.0	5,408	22.0	1,211	4.9
Kansas.................	25,233	4,594	18.2	2,742	10.9	1,852	7.3
Kentucky...............	13,948	4,257	30.5	1,282	9.2	2,975	21.3
Louisiana..............	13,153	3,635	27.6	1,637	12.4	1,998	15.2
Maine..................	2,402	721	30.0	342	14.2	379	15.8
Maryland...............	5,214	1,308	25.1	354	6.8	954	18.3
Massachusetts..........	5,099	2,487	48.8	517	10.1	1,970	38.6
Michigan...............	10,957	2,666	24.3	1,288	11.8	1,378	12.6
Minnesota..............	13,117	1,461	11.1	1,082	8.2	379	2.9
Mississippi.............	17,032	3,829	22.5	2,480	14.6	1,349	7.9
Missouri................	24,286	6,720	27.7	3,783	15.6	2,937	12.1
Montana................	5,097	866	17.0	386	7.6	480	9.4
Nebraska...............	15,395	3,731	24.2	2,757	17.9	974	6.3
Nevada.................	1,783	216	12.1	40	2.2	176	9.9
New Hampshire..........	2,423	746	30.8	364	15.0	382	15.8
New Jersey.............	6,514	2,288	35.1	656	10.1	1,632	25.1
New Mexico.............	3,932	636	16.2	322	8.2	314	8.0
New York...............	17,384	6,429	37.0	2,092	12.0	4,337	24.9
North Carolina..........	18,214	4,937	27.1	2,334	12.8	2,603	14.3
North Dakota...........	4,410	941	21.3	719	16.3	222	5.0
Ohio...................	27,403	6,381	23.3	2,654	9.7	3,727	13.6
Oklahoma..............	23,730	6,784	28.6	5,244	22.1	1,540	6.5
Oregon.................	7,353	1,623	22.1	448	6.1	1,175	16.0
Pennsylvania...........	22,320	9,312	41.7	5,563	24.9	3,749	16.8
Rhode Island...........	751	381	50.7	158	21.0	223	29.7
South Carolina.........	9,270	1,943	21.0	1,155	12.5	788	8.5
South Dakota...........	5,877	1,435	24.4	1,217	20.7	218	3.7
Tennessee..............	19,937	3,855	19.3	1,260	6.3	2,595	13.0
Texas..................	51,862	9,060	17.5	1,533	3.0	7,527	14.5
Utah...................	2,946	414	14.1	121	4.1	293	9.9
Vermont................	2,717	811	29.8	254	9.3	557	20.5
Virginia................	13,524	3,402	25.2	1,261	9.3	2,141	15.8
Washington.............	7,743	1,939	25.0	391	5.0	1,548	20.0
West Virginia...........	7,099	2,501	35.2	990	13.9	1,511	21.3
Wisconsin..............	14,024	1,898	13.5	1,204	8.6	694	4.9
Wyoming...............	3,068	672	21.9	411	13.4	261	8.5
Puerto Rico.............	2,222	1,110	50.0	251	11.3	859	38.7

[1] Bridges are structurally deficient if they have been restricted to light vehicles, require immediate rehabilitation to remain open, or are closed. [2] Bridges are functionally obsolete if they have deck geometry, load carrying capacity, clearance or approach roadway alignment that no longer meet the criteria for the system of which the bridge is carrying a part.

Source: U.S. Federal Highway Administration, Office of Bridge Technology, "Deficient Bridges by State and Highway System," <http://www.fhwa.dot.gov/bridge/nbi.htm>.

Table 1099. Funding for Highways and Disposition of Highway–User Revenue: 1990 to 2010

[In millions of dollars (75,444 represents $75,444,000,000). Data compiled from reports of state and local authorities]

Type	1990	1995	2000	2004	2005	2006	2007	2008	2010 [3]
Total receipts	75,444	96,269	131,115	145,315	154,690	165,443	193,876	192,718	220,977
Current income	69,880	87,620	119,815	129,521	137,668	147,615	168,219	172,785	187,960
Highway-user revenues	44,346	59,331	81,335	83,006	90,343	93,648	98,210	94,152	93,830
Other taxes and fees	19,827	21,732	31,137	38,956	39,214	44,455	54,189	61,163	80,220
Investment income, other receipts	5,707	6,557	7,342	7,560	8,111	9,512	15,820	17,471	13,910
Bond issue proceeds [1]	5,564	8,649	11,301	15,794	17,022	17,828	25,657	19,933	33,017
Funds drawn from or placed in reserves [2]	-36	-2,791	-8,418	2,174	-1,990	-4,382	-12,815	-10,660	-15,664
Total funds available	75,408	93,478	122,697	147,489	152,700	161,061	181,061	182,058	205,313
Total disbursements	75,408	93,478	122,697	147,489	152,700	161,061	181,061	182,058	205,313
Current disbursements	72,457	88,994	117,592	139,478	144,629	153,413	173,095	173,869	193,034
Capital outlay	35,151	44,228	61,323	70,274	75,162	78,676	90,911	91,144	100,175
Maintenance and traffic services	20,365	24,319	30,636	36,327	37,882	40,426	44,715	44,972	48,773
Administration and research	6,501	8,419	10,020	12,737	11,126	13,189	14,428	14,711	16,165
Highway law enforcement and safety	7,235	8,218	11,031	14,322	14,066	14,482	14,723	14,565	18,080
Interest on debt	3,205	3,810	4,583	5,819	6,392	6,639	8,318	8,477	9,842
Bond retirement [1]	2,951	4,484	5,105	8,011	8,071	7,648	7,966	8,189	12,279

[1] Proceeds and redemptions of short-term notes and refunding issues are excluded. [2] Negative numbers indicate that funds were placed in reserves. [3] No 2009 data available. Some 2010 data are preliminary.

Source: U.S. Federal Highway Administration, *Highway Statistics*, annual. See also <http://www.fhwa.dot.gov/policy/ohpi/hss/index.cfm>.

Table 1100. Federal Aid to State and Local Governments for Highway Trust Fund by State: 2010

[30,117 represents $30,117,000,000. Year ending Sept. 30]

State	Total (mil. dol.)	Per capita (dol.) [1]	State	Total (mil. dol.)	Per capita (dol.) [1]	State	Total (mil. dol.)	Per capita (dol.) [1]	State	Total (mil. dol.)	Per capita (dol.) [1]
U.S. [2]	30,117	97	ID	286	182	MO	939	157	PA	1,235	97
AL	675	141	IL	859	67	MT	342	345	RI	175	166
AK	352	492	IN	722	111	NE	131	71	SC	456	98
AZ	512	80	IA	349	114	NV	290	107	SD	214	262
AR	341	117	KS	398	139	NH	161	123	TN	660	104
CA	1,881	50	KY	497	114	NJ	622	71	TX	1,611	64
CO	416	83	LA	604	133	NM	305	148	UT	248	89
CT	584	163	ME	151	114	NY	1,632	84	VT	163	261
DE	1,547	1,719	MD	418	72	NC	376	39	VA	854	106
DC	154	255	MA	623	95	ND	192	284	WA	479	71
FL	1,269	67	MI	809	82	OH	968	84	WV	396	213
GA	1,135	117	MN	511	96	OK	653	174	WI	660	116
HI	138	102	MS	377	127	OR	513	134	WY	239	423

[1] Based on estimated population as of July 1. [2] For the 50 states and the District of Columbia.

Source: U.S. Census Bureau, *Federal Aid to States for Fiscal Year 2010*, September 2011. See also <http://www.census.gov/prod/www/abs/fas.html>.

Table 1101. State Motor Fuel Tax Receipts, 2009 and 2010, and Gasoline Tax Rates, 2010

[635 represents $635,000,000. Federal tax rate is 18.4 cents a gallon]

State	Net receipts (mil. dol.) 2009	Net receipts (mil. dol.) 2010	Tax rate [1] 2010	State	Net receipts (mil. dol.) 2009	Net receipts (mil. dol.) 2010	Tax rate [1] 2010	State	Net receipts (mil. dol.) 2009	Net receipts (mil. dol.) 2010	Tax rate [1] 2010
AL	635	648	18.00	KY	621	655	25.60	ND	143	146	23.00
AK	7	25	8.00	LA	598	593	20.00	OH	1,707	1,771	28.00
AZ	633	629	18.00	ME	229	247	29.50	OK	438	431	17.00
AR	446	482	21.50	MD	734	721	23.50	OR	421	610	24.00
CA	3,025	3,014	18.00	MA	653	654	21.00	PA	2,040	3,341	31.20
CO	542	557	22.00	MI	947	945	19.00	RI	0	139	32.00
CT	614	632	25.00	MN	751	831	27.50	SC	502	509	16.00
DE	115	113	23.00	MS	407	378	18.40	SD	128	134	22.00
DC	24	21	23.50	MO	681	684	17.00	TN	818	825	20.00
FL	2,149	2,184	16.00	MT	177	187	27.75	TX	3,001	3,061	20.00
GA	467	474	7.50	NE	314	319	27.10	UT	334	338	24.50
HI	73	78	17.00	NV	453	457	24.00	VT	80	96	20.00
ID	216	227	25.00	NH	145	144	19.60	VA	897	871	17.50
IL	1,260	1,248	19.00	NJ	559	556	10.50	WA	1,165	1,180	37.50
IN	918	817	18.00	NM	321	270	18.88	WV	339	349	32.20
IA	428	429	21.00	NY	1,625	1,589	24.35	WI	949	952	30.90
KS	414	436	24.00	NC	1,505	1,541	32.15	WY	87	94	14.00

[1] State gasoline tax rates in cents per gallon. In effect December 31.

Source: U.S. Federal Highway Administration, *Highway Statistics*, annual. See also <http://www.fhwa.dot.gov/policy/ohpi/hss/index.cfm>.

Table 1102. Public Obligations for Highways—Changes in Indebtedness During the Year: 1995 to 2010

[In millions of dollars (37,449 represents $37,449,000,000). Table summarizes state indebtedness from all state bond issues, including the toll facility issues and the state issues for local roads. This table is compiled from reports of state authorities. Table also summarizes the change in status of the highway obligations of local governments including toll authorities]

Item	1995	2000	2005	2006	2007	2008	2009	2010
STATE GOVERNMENT								
Obligations outstanding, beginning of year.........	37,449	56,264	82,476	89,642	89,899	102,039	111,600	138,798
Obligations issued..................................	4,718	9,067	19,784	15,651	20,924	20,769	22,372	26,895
Obligations retired.................................	2,940	3,897	14,072	8,780	7,108	12,183	8,326	11,143
Obligations outstanding, end of year...............	39,228	61,434	88,187	96,513	103,715	110,625	125,646	154,550
LOCAL GOVERNMENT [1,2]								
Obligations outstanding, beginning of year.........	26,393	34,904	44,406	47,346	50,092	52,478	55,514	(NA)
Bonds outstanding, beginning of year............	25,613	34,229	43,403	46,344	48,854	51,103	53,894	(NA)
Bonds outstanding, end of year..................	29,505	34,949	46,168	49,130	51,049	53,895	56,334	(NA)
Obligations outstanding, end of year..............	30,295	35,557	47,170	50,366	52,336	55,414	58,123	(NA)

NA Not available. [1] Short-term notes data not shown. The data are included in beginning and ending year obligations. [2] The number of local government data estimated varied year to year.

Source: U.S. Federal Highway Administration, *Highway Statistics*, annual. See also <http://www.fhwa.dot.gov/policy/ohpi/hss/index.cfm>.

Table 1103. State Disbursements for Highways by State: 1995 to 2010

[In millions of dollars (67,615 represents $67,615,000,000). Comprise disbursements from current revenues or loans for construction, maintenance, interest and principal payments on highway bonds, transfers to local units, and miscellaneous. Includes transactions by state toll authorities. Data exclude amounts allocated for collection expenses and nonhighway purposes, and mass transit]

State	1995	2000	2005	2006	2007	2008	2009	2010
United States...............	**67,615**	**89,832**	**116,517**	**117,048**	**130,306**	**139,584**	**143,767**	**145,944**
Alabama.........................	1,002	1,246	1,519	1,684	1,752	1,916	1,969	1,781
Alaska..........................	438	501	643	654	710	730	935	756
Arizona.........................	1,199	2,040	2,458	2,662	2,335	2,806	2,988	2,663
Arkansas........................	666	817	1,078	1,134	1,036	1,051	1,072	1,376
California.......................	5,966	6,750	8,308	10,571	13,288	14,697	21,808	19,961
Colorado........................	922	1,392	1,652	1,490	1,601	1,695	1,906	2,249
Connecticut.....................	1,153	1,304	1,434	1,223	1,265	1,370	2,175	1,761
Delaware........................	441	595	1,104	804	676	683	711	1,353
District of Columbia............	140	244	327	287	334	335	469	582
Florida..........................	3,421	4,208	7,369	7,725	8,069	8,698	7,194	7,867
Georgia.........................	1,437	1,567	2,070	2,655	2,878	3,817	3,506	2,926
Hawaii..........................	360	272	506	323	352	444	504	460
Idaho...........................	350	492	608	622	758	802	890	959
Illinois..........................	3,006	3,447	4,201	4,974	5,424	6,299	5,385	5,385
Indiana.........................	1,433	1,932	2,235	2,416	3,251	3,280	3,280	2,839
Iowa............................	1,078	1,494	1,392	1,515	1,564	1,505	1,721	1,888
Kansas.........................	1,019	1,206	1,394	1,521	1,414	1,487	1,464	1,571
Kentucky........................	1,397	1,651	1,723	1,635	2,194	2,404	2,522	2,528
Louisiana.......................	1,198	1,301	1,387	1,866	1,923	2,488	3,480	2,457
Maine...........................	379	488	616	628	584	739	652	684
Maryland........................	1,289	1,599	2,049	2,304	2,689	2,747	2,800	2,255
Massachusetts..................	2,501	3,524	3,196	2,723	2,815	2,898	2,810	2,923
Michigan........................	1,974	2,748	3,561	3,263	3,240	3,269	3,178	3,484
Minnesota.......................	1,210	1,692	2,131	2,143	2,168	2,352	2,365	2,625
Mississippi......................	662	1,039	1,081	1,272	1,647	1,346	1,301	1,345
Missouri.........................	1,313	1,818	2,069	2,430	3,955	2,545	2,846	2,814
Montana.........................	388	474	664	696	622	651	708	778
Nebraska........................	578	745	876	882	1,436	1,352	1,398	1,409
Nevada..........................	484	651	865	1,144	1,063	906	1,221	1,007
New Hampshire..................	328	387	389	524	693	681	641	793
New Jersey......................	2,102	4,503	7,119	5,561	4,018	3,921	4,222	5,201
New Mexico......................	535	1,162	911	942	942	860	1,272	1,163
New York........................	4,584	5,307	9,638	5,659	7,459	7,537	6,977	7,711
North Carolina..................	1,871	2,621	3,698	3,330	3,385	3,584	3,659	3,646
North Dakota....................	270	385	456	506	441	471	478	559
Ohio............................	2,637	3,351	4,040	4,251	4,418	4,631	4,852	4,520
Oklahoma.......................	828	1,417	1,163	2,001	1,282	1,634	1,765	2,040
Oregon..........................	888	1,010	1,628	1,254	1,736	1,364	1,395	1,522
Pennsylvania....................	3,153	4,517	4,567	5,537	5,999	5,956	6,979	8,835
Rhode Island....................	290	256	407	488	494	419	389	540
South Carolina..................	668	970	1,360	1,476	1,472	1,470	1,353	1,899
South Dakota...................	286	466	466	491	402	451	500	532
Tennessee......................	1,230	1,440	1,718	1,658	1,657	1,771	1,936	2,076
Texas...........................	3,593	5,665	8,918	9,101	13,136	15,948	9,883	9,365
Utah............................	431	1,072	986	1,128	1,335	1,229	1,855	2,303
Vermont.........................	194	287	310	335	368	395	400	436
Virginia.........................	2,107	2,678	3,384	3,195	3,228	3,875	3,572	3,334
Washington.....................	1,909	1,871	2,625	2,656	3,057	3,901	3,807	4,149
West Virginia...................	781	1,170	1,425	1,117	1,057	1,208	1,410	1,327
Wisconsin.......................	1,252	1,663	2,363	2,161	2,279	2,392	2,549	2,702
Wyoming........................	272	396	429	434	484	574	611	605

Source: U.S. Federal Highway Administration, *Highway Statistics*, annual. See also <http://www.fhwa.dot.gov/policy/ohpi/hss/index.cfm>.

Table 1104. State Motor Vehicle Registrations: 1990 to 2010

[In thousands (188,798 represents 188,798,000). Compiled principally from information obtained from state authorities, but it was necessary to draw on other sources and to make numerous estimates in order to complete series. Excludes motorcycles; see Table 1106]

Type	1990	1995	2000	2005	2008	2009	2010
All motor vehicles.............	**188,798**	**201,530**	**221,475**	**241,194**	**248,165**	**246,283**	**242,061**
Private and commercial.............	185,541	197,941	217,567	237,140	243,953	242,058	237,784
Publicly owned......................	3,257	3,589	3,908	4,054	4,212	4,225	4,277
Automobiles [1].........................	133,700	128,387	133,621	136,568	137,080	134,880	130,892
Private and commercial.............	132,164	126,900	132,247	135,192	135,638	133,438	129,434
Publicly owned......................	1,536	1,487	1,374	1,376	1,442	1,442	1,458
Buses...................................	627	686	746	807	843	842	846
Private and commercial.............	275	288	314	331	350	351	347
Publicly owned......................	351	398	432	476	493	491	499
Trucks [1]................................	54,470	72,458	87,108	103,819	110,242	110,561	110,322
Private and commercial.............	53,101	70,754	85,005	101,616	107,965	108,269	108,003
Publicly owned......................	1,369	1,704	2,103	2,203	2,277	2,292	2,319

[1] Trucks include pickups, panels, and delivery vans. Beginning 1995 personal passenger vans, passenger minivans, and utility-type vehicles are no longer included in automobiles but are included in trucks.

Source: U.S. Federal Highway Administration, *Highway Statistics*, annual. See also <http://www.fhwa.dot.gov/policy/ohpi/hss/index.cfm>.

Table 1105. Alternative Fueled Vehicles and Estimated Consumption of Vehicle Fuels by Fuel Type: 2005 to 2010

[In thousands, (420,778 represents 420,778,000). Vehicles in use do not include concept and demonstration vehicles that are not ready for delivery to end users. Vehicles in use represent accumulated acquisitions, less retirements, as of the end of each calendar year]

Vehicles and fuel consumption	Unit	2005	2008	2009	2010
ALTERNATIVE FUELED VEHICLES IN USE					
Total....................................	Number	592,125	775,667	826,318	938,643
Compressed Natural Gas (CNG).......................	Number	117,699	113,973	114,270	115,863
Electric [1]............................	Number	51,398	56,901	57,185	57,462
Ethanol, 85 percent (E85) [2, 3]...........................	Number	246,363	450,327	504,297	618,506
Hydrogen.............................	Number	119	313	357	421
Liquefied Natural Gas (LNG).........................	Number	2,748	3,101	3,176	3,354
Liquefied Petroleum Gas (LPG).......................	Number	173,795	151,049	147,030	143,037
Other fuels [4]........................	Number	3	3	3	–
FUEL CONSUMPTION					
Alternative fuels:......................	1,000 gal.(g-e-g) [5]	420,778	430,329	431,107	457,755
Compressed Natural Gas (CNG).......................	1,000 gal.(g-e-g) [5]	166,878	189,358	199,513	210,007
Electric [1]............................	1,000 gal.(g-e-g) [5]	5,219	5,050	4,956	4,847
Ethanol, 85 percent (E85) [2]...........................	1,000 gal.(g-e-g) [5]	38,074	62,464	71,213	90,323
Hydrogen.............................	1,000 gal.(g-e-g) [5]	25	117	140	152
Liquefied Natural Gas (LNG).........................	1,000 gal.(g-e-g) [5]	22,409	25,554	25,652	26,072
Liquefied Petroleum Gas (LPG).......................	1,000 gal.(g-e-g) [5]	188,171	147,784	129,631	126,354
Other fuels [4]........................	1,000 gal.(g-e-g) [5]	2	2	2	–
Biodiesel..............................	1,000 gal.(g-e-g) [5]	93,281	324,329	325,102	235,188
Oxygenates:					
Methyl Tertiary Butyl Ether (MTBE)....................	1,000 gal.(g-e-g) [5]	1,654,500	–	–	–
Ethanol in Gasohol...................	1,000 gal.(g-e-g) [5]	2,756,663	6,442,781	7,343,133	8,527,431
Total alternative and replacement fuels........	1,000 gal.(g-e-g) [5]	4,925,222	7,197,439	8,099,342	9,220,374
FUEL CONSUMPTION IN NATIVE UNITS					
Alternative fuels:					
Compressed Natural Gas (CNG).......................	million cubic feet	20,106	22,814	24,038	25,302
Electric [1]............................	1,000 kwh	173,967	168,333	165,200	161,567
Ethanol, 85 percent (E85) [2]...........................	1,000 gallons	52,881	86,756	98,907	125,449
Hydrogen.............................	1,000 kilograms	23	107	128	138
Liquefied Natural Gas (LNG).........................	1,000 gallons	33,953	38,718	38,867	39,503
Liquefied Petroleum Gas (LPG).......................	1,000 gallons	254,285	199,708	175,177	170,749
Biodiesel..............................	1,000 gallons	90,827	315,796	316,549	229,000
Oxygenates:					
Methyl Tertiary Butyl Ether (MTBE)....................	1,000 gallons	2,035,320	–	–	–
Ethanol in Gasohol...................	1,000 gallons	4,013,679	9,435,428	10,753,990	12,495,404

– Represents zero. X Not applicable. [1] Excludes gasoline-electric and diesel-electric hybrids because the input fuel is gasoline or diesel rather than an alternative transportation fuel. [2] The remaining portion of E85 percent ethanol is gasoline. Consumption data include the gasoline portion of the fuel. [3] For 2010, the EIA estimates that the number of E85 vehicles that are capable of operating on E85, gasoline, or both, is about 8.6 million. Many of these alternative-fueled vehicles (AFVs) are sold and used as traditional gasoline-powered vehicles. In this table, AFVs in use include only those E85 vehicles believed to be used as AFVs. These are primarily fleet-operated vehicles. [4] May include P-Series fuel or any other fuel designated by the Secretary of Energy as an alternative fuel in accordance with the Energy Policy Act of 1995. [5] Gasoline equivalent gallons.

Source: U.S. Energy Information Administration, "Alternatives to Traditional Transportation Fuels," <http://www.eia.gov/renewable/data.cfm>.

Table 1106. State Motor Vehicle Registrations, 1990 to 2010, Motorcycle Registrations and Licensed Drivers by State: 2010

[In thousands (188,798 represents 188,798,000). Motor vehicle registrations cover publicly, privately, and commercially owned vehicles. For uniformity, data have been adjusted to a calendar-year basis as registration years in states differ; figures represent net numbers where possible, excluding reregistrations and nonresident registrations. See also Table 1104]

State	Motor vehicle registrations [1]						2010		Motor cycle registra-tions, [2] 2010	Licensed drivers, 2010
	1990	1995	2000	2005	2008	2009	Total	Auto mobiles (incl. taxis)		
U.S.........	188,798	201,530	221,475	241,194	248,165	246,283	242,061	130,892	8,166	210,115
AL............	3,744	3,553	3,960	4,545	4,730	4,611	4,654	2,212	123	3,806
AK............	477	542	594	673	691	695	710	228	30	515
AZ............	2,825	2,873	3,795	3,972	4,373	4,358	4,320	2,201	136	4,444
AR............	1,448	1,613	1,840	1,940	2,041	2,037	2,073	945	278	2,078
CA [3]........	21,926	22,432	27,698	32,487	33,483	34,433	31,014	17,978	743	23,753
CO............	3,155	2,812	3,626	1,808	1,618	1,429	4,180	1,891	110	3,779
CT [4]........	2,623	2,622	2,853	3,059	3,094	3,072	3,082	1,986	65	2,935
DE............	526	592	630	737	868	843	799	434	27	695
DC............	262	243	242	237	224	218	212	160	1	385
FL............	10,950	10,369	11,781	15,691	16,462	15,315	14,373	7,295	594	13,950
GA [3]........	5,489	6,120	7,155	8,063	8,570	8,507	7,702	3,739	196	6,508
HI............	771	802	738	948	945	895	904	450	54	909
ID............	1,054	1,043	1,178	1,374	1,318	1,375	1,325	541	53	1,070
IL............	7,873	8,973	8,973	9,458	9,794	9,891	10,079	5,773	350	8,374
IN............	4,366	5,072	5,571	4,955	5,848	5,848	5,698	2,986	204	5,550 [5]
IA............	2,632	2,814	3,106	3,398	3,431	3,363	3,313	1,691	187	2,167
KS............	2,012	2,085	2,296	2,368	2,449	2,425	2,436	880	87	2,033
KY............	2,909	2,631	2,826	3,428	3,604	3,585	3,589	1,890	72	2,950
LA............	2,995	3,286	3,557	3,819	3,979	4,033	4,086	1,917	68	3,134
ME............	977	967	1,024	1,075	1,074	1,056	1,054	519	56	1,020
MD............	3,607	3,654	3,848	4,322	4,525	4,484	4,557	2,591	80	3,918
MA [3]........	3,726	4,502	5,265	5,420	5,328	5,262	5,334	3,145	159	4,593
MI [3]........	7,209	7,674	8,436	8,247	7,945	7,913	9,286	5,136	279	7,083
MN............	3,508	3,882	4,630	4,647	4,783	4,796	4,848	2,459	255	3,281
MS............	1,875	2,144	2,289	1,978	2,035	2,026	2,016	1,144	28	1,928
MO............	3,905	4,255	4,580	4,589	4,866	4,904	5,153	2,579	109	4,246
MT............	783	968	1,026	1,009	927	925	926	352	126	744
NE............	1,384	1,467	1,619	1,703	1,757	1,793	1,802	773	51	1,352
NV............	853	1,047	1,220	1,349	1,417	1,397	1,362	690	66	1,691
NH [4]........	946	1,122	1,052	1,174	1,214	1,212	1,203	619	80	1,037
NJ............	5,652	5,906	6,390	6,262	6,247	6,114	6,628	3,972	327	5,953
NM............	1,301	1,484	1,529	1,548	1,570	1,621	1,612	703	53	1,406
NY............	10,196	10,274	10,235	11,863	11,089	11,245	10,255	7,950	348	11,286
NC............	5,162	5,682	6,223	6,148	6,249	6,047	5,743	3,282	134	6,537
ND............	630	695	694	695	717	722	736	341	34	483
OH............	8,410	9,810	10,467	10,634	10,933	11,022	9,801	5,615	382	7,963
OK............	2,649	2,856	3,014	3,725	3,292	3,396	3,357	1,582	125	2,349
OR............	2,445	2,785	3,022	2,897	3,106	3,046	3,050	1,489	107	2,770
PA [4]........	7,971	8,481	9,260	9,864	10,366	9,857	9,991	5,682	411	8,737
RI [4]........	672	699	760	812	794	789	782	479	33	748
SC............	2,521	2,833	3,095	3,339	3,604	3,614	3,661	2,031	107	3,337
SD............	704	709	793	854	907	926	926	407	66	602
TN............	4,444	5,400	4,820	4,980	5,098	5,140	5,114	2,734	163	4,418
TX [3]........	12,800	13,682	14,070	17,470	18,208	18,208	17,194	8,331	428	15,158
UT............	1,206	1,447	1,628	2,210	2,439	2,454	2,655	1,317	59	1,660
VT............	462	492	515	508	581	557	567	293	29	513
VA............	4,938	5,613	6,046	6,591	6,526	6,302	6,149	3,510	74	5,402
WA [3]........	4,257	4,503	5,116	5,598	5,980	5,581	4,683	2,600	216	5,106
WV............	1,225	1,425	1,442	1,352	1,402	1,412	1,436	703	48	1,206
WI............	3,815	3,993	4,366	4,725	4,999	4,874	4,968	2,461	322	4,133
WY............	528	601	586	646	664	652	663	210	31	419

[1] Automobiles, trucks, and buses (excludes motorcycles). Excludes vehicles owned by military services. [2] Private and commercial. [3] State did not provide complete current data. Table displays estimates by FHWA. [4] The following farm trucks, registered at a nominal fee and restricted to use in the vicinity of the owner's farm, are not included in 2010 data in this table: Connecticut, 6,823; New Hampshire, 13,001; Pennsylvania, 11,038; and Rhode Island, 1,491.

Source: U.S. Federal Highway Administration, *Highway Statistics*, annual. See also <http://www.fhwa.dot.gov/policy/ohpi/hss/index.cfm>.

Table 1107. Motor Vehicle Distance Traveled by Type of Vehicle: 1970 to 2010

[1,110 represents 1,110,000,000,000. The travel data by vehicle type and stratification of trucks are estimated by the Federal Highway Administration (FHWA)]

Year	Vehicle—miles of travel (bil.) [1]					Average miles traveled per vehicle (1,000) [1]				
	Total [2]	Light duty vehicle short WB [2,3]	Buses [4]	Light duty vehicle long WB [3]	Trucks [5,6]	Total [2]	Light duty vehicle short WB [2,3]	Buses [4]	Light duty vehicle long WB [3]	Trucks [5,6]
1970.........	1,110	920	4.5	123	62	10.0	10.0	12.0	8.7	13.6
1980.........	1,527	1,122	6.1	291	108	9.5	8.8	11.5	10.4	18.7
1985.........	1,775	1,256	4.5	391	124	10.0	9.4	7.5	10.5	20.6
1990.........	2,144	1,418	5.7	575	146	11.1	10.3	9.1	11.9	23.6
1992.........	2,247	1,381	5.8	707	153	11.6	10.6	9.0	12.4	25.4
1993.........	2,296	1,385	6.1	746	160	11.6	10.5	9.4	12.4	26.3
1994.........	2,358	1,416	6.4	765	170	11.7	10.8	9.6	12.2	25.8
1995.........	2,423	1,438	6.4	790	178	11.8	11.2	9.4	12.0	26.5
1996.........	2,486	1,470	6.6	817	183	11.8	11.3	9.4	11.8	26.1
1997.........	2,562	1,503	6.8	851	191	12.1	11.6	9.8	12.1	27.0
1998.........	2,632	1,550	7.0	868	196	12.2	11.8	9.8	12.2	25.4
1999.........	2,691	1,569	7.7	901	203	12.2	11.9	10.5	12.0	26.0
2000.........	2,747	1,967	14.8	491	262	12.2	11.0	19.8	14.6	29.1
2001.........	2,796	1,987	13.0	512	272	11.9	10.7	17.3	14.7	28.9
2002.........	2,856	2,036	13.3	520	276	12.2	11.1	17.5	14.3	29.4
2003.........	2,890	2,051	13.4	528	286	12.2	11.1	17.2	14.8	30.3
2004.........	2,965	2,083	13.5	569	284	12.2	11.0	17.0	15.2	29.7
2005.........	2,989	2,096	13.2	581	285	12.1	11.0	16.3	14.8	28.8
2006.........	3,014	2,048	14.0	633	301	12.0	10.5	17.1	16.3	29.1
2007.........	3,031	2,104	14.5	587	304	11.9	10.7	17.4	15.0	28.3
2008.........	2,977	2,025	14.8	605	311	11.6	10.3	17.6	15.3	28.6
2009.........	2,957	2,016	14.4	617	288	11.6	10.4	17.1	15.2	26.3
2010.........	2,966	2,025	13.8	622	287	11.9	10.6	16.3	15.5	26.6

[1] FHWA updated VM-1 from 2000 to 2010 using an enhanced methodology implemented in March 2011. Prior to 2000, "Light Duty Vehicles Short WB" were categorized as "Cars;" and "Light Duty Vehicles Long WB" were categorized as "Vans, pickups, sport utility vehicles." [2] Motorcycles included with "Cars" through 1994; thereafter in total, shown separately. [3] Light Duty Vehicles Short WB—passenger cars, light trucks, vans and sport utility vehicles with a wheelbase (WB) equal to or less than 121 inches. Light Duty Vehicles Long WB—large passenger cars, vans, pickup trucks, and sport/utility vehicles with wheelbases (WB) larger than 121 inches. [4] Includes school buses. [5] Includes combinations. [6] 2000 to 2010: Single-Unit—single frame trucks that have 2-axles and at least 6 tires or a gross vehicle weight rating exceeding 10,000 lbs.

Source: U.S. Federal Highway Administration, *Highway Statistics*, annual. See also <http://www.fhwa.dot.gov/policyinformation/statistics.cfm>.

Table 1108. Domestic Motor Fuel Consumption by Type of Vehicle: 1970 to 2010

[Consumption in billions (92.3 represents 92,300,000,000 gallons). Comprises all fuel types used for propulsion of vehicles under state motor fuels laws. Excludes federal purchases for military use. Minus sign (–) indicates decrease]

Year	Annual fuel consumption (bil. gal.) [1]						Average miles per gallon [1]				
	All vehicles [2]	Annual percent change [3]	Light duty vehicle short WB [2,4]	Buses [5]	Light duty vehicle long WB [4]	Trucks [6,7]	All vehicles [2]	Light duty vehicle short WB [2,4]	Buses [5]	Light duty vehicle long WB [4]	Trucks [6,7]
1970......	92.3	4.8	67.8	0.8	12.3	11.3	12.0	13.5	5.5	10.0	5.5
1980......	115.0	-5.9	70.2	1.0	23.8	20.0	13.3	16.0	6.0	12.2	5.4
1985......	121.3	2.2	71.7	0.8	27.4	21.4	14.6	17.5	5.4	14.3	5.8
1990......	130.8	-0.8	69.8	0.9	35.6	24.5	16.4	20.3	6.4	16.1	6.0
1992......	132.9	3.3	65.6	0.9	40.9	25.5	16.9	21.0	6.6	17.3	6.0
1993......	137.3	3.3	67.2	0.9	42.9	26.2	16.7	20.6	6.6	17.4	6.1
1994......	140.8	2.5	68.1	1.0	44.1	27.7	16.7	20.8	6.6	17.3	6.1
1995......	143.8	2.1	68.1	1.0	45.6	29.0	16.8	21.1	6.6	17.3	6.1
1996......	147.4	2.5	69.2	1.0	47.4	29.6	16.9	21.2	6.6	17.2	6.2
1997......	150.4	2.0	69.9	1.0	49.4	29.9	17.0	21.5	6.7	17.2	6.4
1998......	155.4	3.3	71.7	1.1	50.5	32.0	16.9	21.6	6.7	17.2	6.1
1999......	161.4	3.9	73.2	1.1	52.8	33.9	16.7	21.4	6.7	17.0	6.0
2000......	162.5	0.7	88.9	2.2	28.9	42.0	16.9	22.1	6.7	17.0	6.2
2001......	163.5	0.6	87.8	1.9	30.1	43.0	17.1	22.6	6.8	17.0	6.3
2002......	168.7	3.2	91.5	1.9	30.8	43.3	17.0	22.3	6.9	16.9	6.4
2003......	170.0	0.8	91.6	1.9	31.3	44.8	17.0	22.4	7.1	16.9	6.4
2004......	173.5	2.1	93.4	1.9	33.8	44.4	17.1	22.3	7.1	16.9	6.4
2005......	174.8	0.7	93.2	1.9	34.4	44.5	17.2	22.5	7.1	16.9	6.4
2006......	175.0	0.1	88.6	2.0	37.0	46.4	17.2	23.1	7.1	17.1	6.5
2007......	176.2	0.7	89.6	2.0	36.9	47.2	17.2	22.9	7.2	17.1	6.4
2008......	170.8	-3.1	85.6	2.1	34.9	47.7	17.4	23.7	7.2	17.3	6.5
2009......	168.1	-1.6	85.7	2.0	35.7	44.3	17.6	23.5	7.2	17.3	6.5
2010......	169.7	0.9	86.2	1.9	36.1	45.0	17.5	23.5	7.2	17.2	6.4

[1] See footnote 1, Table 1107. [2] Motorcycles included with "Cars" through 1994; thereafter in total, not shown separately. [3] Change from immediate prior year. [4] Light Duty Vehicles Short WB—passenger cars, light trucks, vans and sport utility vehicles with a wheelbase (WB) equal to or less than 121 inches. Light Duty Vehicles Long WB—large passenger cars, vans, pickup trucks, and sport/utility vehicles with wheelbases (WB) larger than 121 inches. [5] Includes school buses. [6] Includes combinations. [7] 2000 to 2010: Single-Unit—single frame trucks that have 2-axles and at least 6 tires or a gross vehicle weight rating exceeding 10,000 lbs.

Source: U.S. Federal Highway Administration, *Highway Statistics*, annual. See also <http://www.fhwa.dot.gov/policy/ohpi/hss/index.cfm>.

Table 1109. Fatal Motor Vehicle Accidents—National Summary: 1990 to 2010

[Based on data from the Fatality Analysis Reporting System (FARS). FARS gathers data on accidents that result in loss of human life. FARS is operated and maintained by National Highway Traffic Safety Administration's (NHTSA), National Center for Statistics and Analysis (NCSA). FARS data are gathered on motor vehicle accidents that occurred on a roadway customarily open to the public, resulting in the death of a person within 30 days of the accident. Collection of these data depend on the use of police, hospital, medical examiner/coroner, and Emergency Medical Services reports; state vehicle registration, driver licensing, and highway department files; and vital statistics documents and death certificates. See source for further detail]

Item	1990	1995	2000	2005	2007	2008	2009	2010
Fatal crashes, total	**39,836**	**37,241**	**37,526**	**39,252**	**37,435**	**34,172**	**30,862**	**30,196**
One vehicle involved	23,445	21,250	21,117	22,678	22,167	20,644	18,745	18,156
Two or more vehicles involved	16,391	15,991	16,409	16,574	15,268	13,528	12,052	12,040
Persons killed in fatal crashes [1]	**44,599**	**41,817**	**41,945**	**43,510**	**41,259**	**37,423**	**33,883**	**32,885**
Occupants	33,890	33,064	36,348	33,070	30,527	26,791	24,526	23,303
Drivers	22,854	22,370	25,567	23,237	21,717	19,279	17,640	16,824
Passengers	10,931	10,576	10,695	9,750	8,716	7,441	6,793	6,414
Other	105	118	86	83	94	71	63	65
Motorcyclists	3,244	2,227	2,897	4,576	5,174	5,312	4,469	4,502
Nonoccupants	7,465	6,526	5,597	5,864	5,558	5,320	4,888	5,080
Pedestrians	6,482	5,584	4,763	4,892	4,699	4,414	4,109	4,280
Pedalcyclists	859	833	693	786	701	718	628	618
Other	124	109	141	186	158	188	151	182
Occupants killed by vehicle type:								
Passenger cars	24,092	22,423	20,699	18,512	16,614	14,646	13,095	12,435
Mini-compact (95 inches)	3,556	2,207	1,113	452	347	270	212	171
Subcompact (95 to 99 inches)	4,753	4,584	3,660	2,536	1,931	1,667	1,333	1,252
Compact (100 to 104 inches)	5,310	6,899	7,022	6,288	5,538	4,780	4,128	3,954
Intermediate (105 to 109) inches	4,849	4,666	5,204	5,571	5,243	4,763	4,393	4,227
Full-size (110 to 114) inches	2,386	2,116	2,287	2,491	2,410	2,210	2,175	1,982
Largest (115 inches and over)	2,249	1,297	897	796	780	755	674	681
Unknown	989	654	516	378	365	201	180	168
Motorcycles and other motorized cycles	3,129	2,114	2,897	4,576	5,174	5,312	4,462	4,502
Motorcycles	3,014	2,001	2,783	4,418	4,986	5,060	4,222	4,266
Other motorized cycles	115	113	114	158	188	252	240	236
Light trucks [2]	8,601	9,568	11,526	13,037	12,458	10,816	10,287	9,752
Pickup	5,979	5,938	6,003	6,067	5,847	5,097	4,792	4,473
Utility	1,214	1,935	3,358	4,831	4,834	4,214	4,091	3,930
Van	1,154	1,639	2,129	2,112	1,764	1,492	1,394	1,342
Other	254	56	36	27	13	13	10	7
Large trucks [3]	705	648	754	804	805	682	503	529
Medium trucks	134	96	106	118	112	91	81	79
Heavy trucks	571	552	648	686	693	592	422	447
Buses	32	33	22	58	36	67	26	44
Other vehicles	296	307	401	492	540	523	481	451
Unknown	164	85	49	167	74	57	82	92
Persons involved in fatal crashes	**107,777**	**102,102**	**100,716**	**101,262**	**94,338**	**84,510**	**76,309**	**(NA)**
Occupants	99,297	94,621	94,325	94,614	88,136	78,500	70,845	68,927
Drivers	58,893	56,164	57,280	59,220	56,019	50,416	45,230	44,440
Passengers	40,229	38,252	36,889	35,231	31,919	27,924	25,470	(NA)
Other	175	205	156	163	198	160	145	(NA)
Nonoccupants	8,480	7,481	6,391	6,648	6,202	6,010	5,464	(NA)
Vehicle miles traveled (VMT) [4] (bil.)	2,144	2,423	2,747	2,989	3,031	2,977	2,957	2,967
Licensed drivers (1,000)	167,015	176,628	190,625	200,549	205,742	208,321	209,618	210,115
Registered vehicles (1,000)	184,275	197,065	217,028	247,031	257,472	259,360	258,958	257,515
Percent distribution of fatal accidents by the highest driver (BAC) in accident: [5]								
0.00 percent	54.0	62.1	62.7	63.3	62.4	63.1	62.3	63.0
0.01 to 0.07 percent	6.3	5.5	5.6	5.4	5.9	5.6	5.6	5.0
0.08 percent and over	39.4	32.1	31.4	31.1	31.5	31.1	31.9	31.0
Percent distribution of fatal accidents by the highest (BAC) in accident: [5]								
0.00 percent	49.5	57.7	58.7	59.5	58.4	58.6	58.0	(NA)
0.01 to 0.07 percent	6.5	5.7	5.9	5.6	6.1	5.8	5.7	(NA)
0.08 percent and over	44.0	36.7	35.4	34.9	35.6	35.5	36.3	(NA)
Fatalities per 100,000 resident population								
Under 5 years old	4.90	4.30	3.70	2.94	2.44	1.95	2.02	1.99
5 to 9 years old	5.14	4.48	3.55	3.00	2.36	1.95	1.84	1.73
10 to 15 years old	7.60	7.23	5.65	4.67	4.27	3.41	3.02	2.70
16 to 20 years old	36.66	31.59	29.38	27.48	24.97	20.78	18.08	15.45
21 to 24 years old	33.47	29.68	27.02	27.73	26.74	23.25	19.11	19.43
25 to 34 years old	22.78	19.44	17.29	17.82	16.92	15.66	13.69	13.43
35 to 44 years old	16.11	15.10	15.08	15.08	14.27	12.88	11.62	11.07
45 to 54 years old	14.83	13.39	13.79	14.59	14.06	13.07	12.10	11.28
55 to 64 years old	15.00	13.92	13.61	13.88	12.61	12.03	10.87	10.90
65 to 74 years old	17.03	16.64	15.29	15.16	13.46	12.26	11.42	10.89
75 years old and over	25.45	26.09	23.29	20.47	18.17	16.56	15.52	16.70
Fatalities per 100 million VMT [4]	2.08	1.73	1.53	1.46	1.36	1.26	1.15	1.11
Fatalities per 100,000 licensed drivers	26.70	23.68	22.00	21.70	20.05	17.96	16.16	15.65
VMT [4] per registered vehicle	11,635	12,295	12,601	12,100	11,772	11,478	11,419	11,522
Fatalities per 100,000 registered vehicles	24.20	21.22	19.33	17.61	16.02	14.43	13.08	12.77
Fatal crashes per 100 million VMT [4]	1.86	1.54	1.37	1.31	1.24	1.15	1.04	1.02
Fatalities per 100,000 resident population	17.88	15.91	14.87	14.72	13.70	12.31	11.05	10.63

NA Not available. [1] Deaths within 30 days of the accident. Starting with 1995, total does not include motorcyclist data. [2] Trucks with a gross vehicle weight rating of 10,000 pounds or less, including pickups, vans, truck-based station wagons, and utility vehicles. [3] Trucks with a gross vehicle weight rating of over 10,000 pounds. [4] VMT = vehicle miles of travel. [5] BAC = blood alcohol concentration.

Source: U.S. National Highway Traffic Safety Administration, Fatality Analysis Reporting System, annual. See also <http://www-nrd.nhtsa.dot.gov/CATS/index.aspx>.

Table 1110. Traffic Fatalities by State: 1990 to 2010

[For deaths within 30 days of the accident]

State	1990	2000	2005	2010	Fatality rate [1] 1990	Fatality rate [1] 2010	State	1990	2000	2005	2010	Fatality rate [1] 1990	Fatality rate [1] 2010
U.S.....	44,599	41,945	43,510	32,885	2.1	1.1	MO......	1,097	1,157	1,257	819	2.2	1.2
AL.......	1,121	996	1,148	862	2.6	1.3	MT......	212	237	251	189	2.5	1.7
AK.......	98	106	73	56	2.5	1.2	NE......	262	276	276	190	1.9	1.0
AZ.......	869	1,036	1,179	762	2.5	1.3	NV......	343	323	427	257	3.4	1.2
AR.......	604	652	654	563	2.9	1.7	NH......	158	126	166	128	1.6	1.0
CA.......	5,192	3,753	4,333	2,715	2.0	0.8	NJ.......	886	731	747	556	1.5	0.8
CO......	544	681	606	448	2.0	1.0	NM......	499	432	488	346	3.1	1.4
CT.......	385	341	278	319	1.5	1.0	NY......	2,217	1,460	1,434	1,200	2.1	0.9
DE.......	138	123	133	101	2.1	1.1	NC......	1,385	1,557	1,547	1,319	2.2	1.3
DC.......	48	48	48	24	1.4	0.7	ND......	112	86	123	105	1.9	1.3
FL.......	2,891	2,999	3,518	2,445	2.6	1.3	OH......	1,638	1,366	1,321	1,080	1.8	1.0
GA.......	1,562	1,541	1,729	1,244	2.2	1.1	OK......	641	650	803	668	1.9	1.4
HI........	177	132	140	113	2.2	1.1	OR......	579	451	487	317	2.2	0.9
ID.......	244	276	275	209	2.5	1.3	PA......	1,646	1,520	1,616	1,324	1.9	1.3
IL.......	1,589	1,418	1,363	927	1.9	0.9	RI.......	84	80	87	66	1.1	0.8
IN.......	1,049	886	938	754	2.0	1.0	SC......	979	1,065	1,094	810	2.8	1.7
IA.......	465	445	450	390	2.0	1.2	SD......	153	173	186	140	2.2	1.6
KS.......	444	461	428	431	1.9	1.4	TN......	1,177	1,307	1,270	1,031	2.5	1.5
KY.......	849	820	985	760	2.5	1.6	TX.......	3,250	3,779	3,536	2,998	2.1	1.3
LA.......	959	938	963	710	2.5	1.6	UT.......	272	373	282	236	1.9	0.9
ME......	213	169	169	161	1.8	1.1	VT.......	90	76	73	71	1.5	1.0
MD......	707	588	614	493	1.7	0.9	VA......	1,079	929	947	740	1.8	0.9
MA......	605	433	441	314	1.3	0.6	WA.....	825	631	649	458	1.8	0.8
MI......	1,571	1,382	1,129	942	1.9	1.0	WV.....	481	411	374	315	3.1	1.6
MN......	566	625	559	411	1.5	0.7	WI......	769	799	815	572	1.7	1.0
MS......	750	949	931	641	3.1	1.6	WY......	125	152	170	155	2.1	1.6

[1] Deaths per 100 million vehicle miles traveled.

Source: U.S. National Highway Traffic Safety Administration, *Traffic Safety Facts*, annual. See also <http://www-nrd.nhtsa.dot.gov/CATS/index.aspx>.

Table 1111. Motor Vehicle Occupants and Nonoccupants Killed and Injured: 1980 to 2010

[3,231 represents 3,231,000. For deaths within 30 days of the accident]

Year	Total	Occupants Total	Occupants Passenger cars	Occupants Light trucks [1]	Occupants Large trucks [1]	Occupants Buses	Occupants Other/un-known [2]	Motor-cycle riders [3]	Nonoccupants Total	Nonoccupants Pedes-trian	Nonoccupants Pedal-cyclist	Nonoccupants Other/un-known [2]
KILLED												
1980.............	51,091	36,783	27,449	7,486	1,262	46	540	5,144	9,164	8,070	965	129
1985.............	43,825	31,479	23,212	6,689	977	57	544	4,564	7,782	6,808	890	84
1990.............	44,599	33,890	24,092	8,601	705	32	460	3,244	7,465	6,482	859	124
1995.............	41,817	33,064	22,423	9,568	648	33	392	2,227	6,526	5,584	833	109
1999.............	41,717	33,392	20,862	11,265	759	59	447	2,483	5,842	4,939	754	149
2000.............	41,945	33,451	20,699	11,526	754	22	450	2,897	5,597	4,763	693	141
2001.............	42,196	33,243	20,320	11,723	708	34	458	3,197	5,756	4,901	732	123
2002.............	43,005	34,105	20,569	12,274	689	45	528	3,270	5,630	4,851	665	114
2003.............	42,884	33,627	19,725	12,546	726	41	589	3,714	5,543	4,774	629	140
2004.............	42,836	33,276	19,192	12,674	766	42	602	4,028	5,532	4,675	727	130
2005.............	43,510	33,070	18,512	13,037	804	58	659	4,576	5,864	4,892	786	186
2006.............	42,708	32,119	17,925	12,761	805	27	601	4,837	5,752	4,795	772	185
2007.............	41,259	30,527	16,614	12,458	805	36	614	5,174	5,558	4,699	701	158
2008.............	37,423	26,791	14,646	10,816	682	67	580	5,312	5,320	4,414	718	188
2009.............	33,883	24,526	13,135	10,312	499	26	554	4,469	4,888	4,109	628	151
2010.............	32,885	23,303	12,435	9,752	529	44	543	4,502	5,080	4,280	618	182
INJURED (1,000)												
1990.............	3,231	2,960	2,376	505	42	33	4	84	187	105	75	7
1995.............	3,465	3,246	2,469	722	30	19	4	57	162	86	67	10
1999.............	3,236	3,047	2,138	847	33	22	7	50	140	85	51	3
2000.............	3,189	2,997	2,052	887	31	18	10	58	134	78	51	5
2001.............	3,033	2,841	1,927	861	29	15	9	60	131	78	45	8
2002.............	2,926	2,735	1,805	879	26	19	6	65	126	71	48	7
2003.............	2,889	2,697	1,756	889	27	18	7	67	124	70	46	8
2004.............	2,788	2,594	1,643	900	27	16	7	76	118	68	41	9
2005.............	2,699	2,494	1,573	872	27	11	10	87	118	64	45	8
2006.............	2,575	2,375	1,475	857	23	10	11	88	112	61	44	7
2007.............	2,491	2,264	1,379	841	23	12	8	103	124	70	43	10
2008.............	2,346	2,120	1,304	768	23	15	9	96	130	69	52	9
2009.............	2,217	2,011	1,216	759	17	12	7	90	116	59	51	7
2010.............	2,239	2,027	1,253	733	20	17	5	82	130	70	52	8

[1] See footnotes 2 and 3, Table 1112. [2] Includes combination trucks. [3] Includes motorized cycles.

Source: U.S. National Highway Traffic Safety Administration, *Traffic Safety Facts*, annual. See also <http://www-nrd.nhtsa.dot.gov/CATS/index.aspx>.

Table 1112. Vehicles Involved in Crashes by Vehicle Type, Rollover Occurrence, and Crash Severity: 2010

[9,470.0 represents 9,470,000. Excludes motorcycles]

Crash severity by vehicle type	Total		Rollover occurrence			
			Yes		No	
	Number (1,000)	Percent	Number (1,000)	Percent	Number (1,000)	Percent
Vehicles involved in all crashes [1]........	**9,470.0**	**100.0**	**204.0**	**2.2**	**9,266.0**	**97.8**
Passenger cars..................................	5,350.0	100.0	75.0	1.4	5,275.0	98.6
Light trucks: [2]						
Pickup..	1,369.0	100.0	46.0	3.4	1,323.0	96.6
Utility..	1,659.0	100.0	58.0	3.5	1,601.0	96.5
Van...	632.0	100.0	11.0	1.7	621.0	98.3
Other...	115.0	100.0	3.0	2.6	112.0	97.4
Large truck [3]..................................	276.0	100.0	10.0	3.6	266.0	96.4
Bus...	54.0	100.0	(Z)	(Z)	54.0	100.0
Other/unknown................................	15.0	100.0	2.0	13.3	13.0	86.7
Fatal crashes................................	40.1	100.0	8.2	20.6	31.8	79.4
Passenger cars..................................	17.7	100.0	2.7	15.5	15.0	84.5
Light trucks: [2]						
Pickup..	8.2	100.0	2.2	27.0	6.0	73.0
Utility..	6.8	100.0	2.2	32.4	4.6	67.6
Van...	2.4	100.0	0.4	16.4	2.0	83.6
Other...	(Z)	100.0	(Z)	9.1	(Z)	90.9
Large truck [3]..................................	3.5	100.0	0.4	12.7	3.0	87.3
Bus...	0.2	100.0	(Z)	4.0	0.2	96.0
Other/unknown................................	1.2	100.0	0.2	18.9	1.0	81.1

Z less than 50 or 0.05. [1] Includes injury and property-only crashes, not shown separately. [2] Trucks of 10,000 pounds gross vehicle weight rating or less, including pickups, vans, truck-based station wagons and utility vehicles. [3] Trucks over 10,000 pounds gross vehicle weight rating.

Source: U.S. National Highway Traffic Safety Administration, *Traffic Safety Facts*, annual. See also <http://www-nrd.nhtsa.dot.gov/CATS/index.aspx>.

Table 1113. Distracted Drivers—Crashes/Road Fatalities and Injuries: 2005 to 2010

["Distraction" is defined as a specific type of inattention that occurs when drivers divert their attention from the driving task to focus on some other activity instead. It is worth noting that "distraction" is a subset of "inattention" (which also includes fatigue, physical conditions of the driver, and emotional conditions of the driver). For more information, see the appendices of the report at <http://www-nrd.nhtsa.dot.gov/Pubs/811379.pdf>]

Description	2005	2009	2010	Description	2005	2009	2010
Fatal crashes [1]				Drivers.....................	4,217	5,084	2,912
				Percentage...............	7	11	7
Overall:				Fatalities..................	4,472	5,474	3,092
Crashes......................	39,252	30,797	30,196	Percentage...............	10	16	9
Drivers	59,220	45,230	44,440	People injured in crashes: [3]			
Fatalities.....................	43,510	33,808	32,885	Overall......................	2,699,000	2,217,000	2,239,000
Involving driver distraction: [2]				Involving distraction:			
Crashes......................	4,026	4,898	2,843	Estimate....................	604,000	448,000	416,000
Percentage...................	10	16	9	Percentage of total..........	22	20	19

[1] Source: NHTSA's Fatality Analysis Reporting System (FARS). [2] For multi-vehicle crashes, the crash was reported as a distracted-driving crash if at least one driver was reported as distracted. In some of these multi-vehicle crashes, multiple drivers were reported as distracted. [3] Source: National Automotive Sampling System (NASS) General Estimates System (GES).

Source: U.S. National Highway Traffic Safety Administration, *Traffic Safety Facts*, Research Note, "An Examination of Driver Distraction as Recorded in the NHTSA Databases" and "Distracted Driving 2010." See also <http://www-nrd.nhtsa.dot.gov/CATS/index.aspx> and <www.distraction.gov>.

Table 1114. Speeding-Related Traffic Fatalities by Road Type, Speed Limit, and State: 2009

[Speeding consists of exceeding the posted speed limit or driving too fast for the road conditions or any speed-related violation charged (racing, driving above speed limit, speed greater than reasonable, exceeding special speed limit)]

State	Traffic fatalities, total	Speeding-related fatalities by road type and speed limit								
		Total [1]	Interstate		Non-Interstate					
			Over 55 mph	At or under 55 mph	55 mph	50 mph	45 mph	40 mph	35 mph	Under 35 mph
United States........	33,808	10,591	964	287	2,701	465	1,508	724	1,279	1,277
Alabama..................	848	327	21	2	75	10	100	24	27	27
Alaska....................	64	26	5	5	8	1	6	–	1	–
Arizona...................	807	283	54	6	23	20	61	13	25	33
Arkansas.................	585	105	19	2	39	3	11	4	12	11
California.................	3,081	1,087	145	18	266	39	100	100	161	119
Colorado.................	465	171	17	8	21	14	11	21	21	23
Connecticut..............	223	103	10	6	6	4	13	15	7	40
Delaware.................	116	44	5	1	8	14	6	3	2	3
District of Columbia......	29	10	–	1	–	–	1	–	–	8
Florida...................	2,558	535	56	17	78	19	127	36	73	85
Georgia..................	1,284	238	17	13	54	10	42	12	47	30
Hawaii...................	109	59	–	5	2	1	10	1	20	20
Idaho....................	226	81	8	–	15	8	8	–	4	7
Illinois...................	911	325	41	10	113	5	23	15	27	64
Indiana..................	693	174	20	3	53	8	27	16	19	25
Iowa.....................	372	62	5	3	28	4	3	1	8	8
Kansas...................	386	103	9	–	43	3	6	5	5	15
Kentucky.................	791	154	7	3	85	4	18	–	24	11
Louisiana................	821	288	30	1	115	8	49	5	35	19
Maine....................	159	61	2	2	10	7	18	4	7	5
Maryland.................	547	184	10	21	15	39	11	37	18	28
Massachusetts...........	334	76	13	4	4	3	4	4	9	30
Michigan.................	871	205	16	2	95	7	16	7	17	34
Minnesota................	421	95	5	5	48	4	2	2	1	20
Mississippi...............	700	106	9	1	24	4	25	4	18	10
Missouri.................	878	379	26	12	124	23	29	19	54	38
Montana.................	221	86	15	1	5	1	5	–	6	8
Nebraska.................	223	30	7	–	1	7	1	2	1	2
Nevada..................	243	91	12	2	11	–	23	–	20	8
New Hampshire...........	110	39	3	1	2	6	1	1	14	11
New Jersey...............	583	95	2	3	5	24	8	4	13	29
New Mexico..............	361	69	5	5	9	1	4	5	6	11
New York................	1,156	368	6	8	142	11	32	22	20	57
North Carolina...........	1,314	517	32	2	270	9	125	8	49	13
North Dakota.............	140	32	4	1	10	–	3	–	1	2
Ohio.....................	1,021	287	22	4	129	11	21	12	55	25
Oklahoma................	738	234	26	2	25	7	83	18	8	14
Oregon..................	377	125	7	1	55	3	16	6	8	8
Pennsylvania.............	1,256	634	19	37	152	12	131	94	116	54
Rhode Island.............	83	28	–	5	–	2	–	–	4	9
South Carolina...........	894	337	37	1	99	9	84	29	43	22
South Dakota.............	131	41	12	–	19	2	2	–	2	–
Tennessee...............	989	209	10	10	35	10	48	30	29	30
Texas....................	3,071	1,228	106	37	149	40	116	104	132	140
Utah.....................	244	104	23	5	9	9	5	12	10	10
Vermont.................	74	22	1	–	2	8	–	2	5	3
Virginia..................	757	147	8	8	45	3	20	8	27	18
Washington..............	492	208	16	–	15	22	15	10	41	44
West Virginia.............	356	120	20	1	44	2	13	5	11	8
Wisconsin................	561	203	8	2	105	–	21	3	14	36
Wyoming.................	134	56	13	–	11	4	4	1	2	2

– Represents zero. [1] Includes fatalities that occurred on roads for which the speed limit was unknown.

Source: U.S. National Highway Traffic Safety Administration, *Traffic Safety Facts, Speeding*, annual. See also <http://www-nrd.nhtsa.dot.gov/CATS/index.aspx>.

Table 1115. Crashes by Crash Severity: 1990 to 2009

[6,471 represents 6,471,000. A crash is a police-reported event that produces injury and/or property damage, involves a vehicle in transport and occurs on a trafficway or while the vehicle is in motion after running off the trafficway]

Item	1990	1995	2000	2005	2006	2007	2008	2009	2010
Crashes (1,000)...............	**6,471**	**6,699**	**6,394**	**6,159**	**5,973**	**6,024**	**5,811**	**5,505**	**5,419**
Fatal.................	39.8	37.2	37.5	39.3	38.6	37.4	34.2	30.8	30.2
Nonfatal injury....................	2,122	2,217	2,070	1,816	1,746	1,711	1,630	1,517	1,542
Property damage only..........	4,309	4,446	4,286	4,304	4,189	4,275	4,146	3,957	3,847
Percent of total crashes:									
Fatal.................	0.6	0.6	0.6	0.6	0.6	0.6	0.6	0.6	0.6
Nonfatal injury...................	32.8	33.1	32.4	29.5	29.2	28.4	28.1	27.6	28.5
Property damage only..........	66.6	66.4	67.0	69.9	70.1	71.0	71.4	71.9	71.0

Source: U.S. National Highway Safety Traffic Administration, *Traffic Safety Facts*, annual. See also <http://www-nrd.nhtsa.dot.gov/CATS/index.aspx>.

Table 1116. Traffic Fatalities by State and Highest Driver Blood Alcohol Concentration (BAC) in the Crash: 2010

[See headnote, Table 1117]

State	Traffic fatalities, total [1]	(BAC=.00)		(BAC=.01–.07)		Alcohol impaired driving fatalities (BAC=.08 or more)		(BAC=.01 or more)	
		Number	Percent	Number	Percent	Number	Percent	Number	Percent
United States......	**32,885**	**20,838**	**63**	**1,720**	**5**	**10,228**	**31**	**11,948**	**36**
Alabama...............	862	548	64	35	4	279	32	314	36
Alaska.................	56	39	69	1	3	16	28	17	31
Arizona...............	762	505	66	38	5	194	25	231	30
Arkansas.............	563	365	65	23	4	173	31	196	35
California.............	2,715	1,787	66	133	5	791	29	924	34
Colorado.............	448	306	68	15	3	127	28	142	32
Connecticut..........	319	180	56	16	5	121	38	138	43
Delaware.............	101	58	58	7	7	36	36	43	42
District of Columbia...	24	16	65	4	15	5	20	9	35
Florida................	2,445	1,686	69	91	4	660	27	751	31
Georgia...............	1,244	894	72	48	4	298	24	346	28
Hawaii................	113	64	57	6	5	42	37	48	42
Idaho.................	209	127	61	11	5	71	34	82	39
Illinois................	927	559	60	69	7	298	32	366	40
Indiana...............	754	533	71	25	3	195	26	220	29
Iowa..................	390	286	73	13	3	90	23	103	26
Kansas...............	431	239	55	25	6	168	39	192	45
Kentucky.............	760	549	72	39	5	171	23	210	28
Louisiana.............	710	429	60	55	8	225	32	280	39
Maine.................	161	113	70	10	6	38	23	48	30
Maryland.............	493	303	62	34	7	154	31	188	38
Massachusetts.......	314	172	55	26	8	115	36	141	45
Michigan.............	942	653	69	55	6	230	24	285	30
Minnesota............	411	276	67	8	2	127	31	135	33
Mississippi...........	641	383	60	23	4	236	37	259	40
Missouri..............	819	503	61	55	7	258	32	313	38
Montana..............	189	104	55	11	6	73	39	84	44
Nebraska.............	190	131	69	7	4	51	27	59	31
Nevada...............	257	172	67	17	7	69	27	85	33
New Hampshire.......	128	75	58	9	7	44	35	53	42
New Jersey...........	556	369	66	35	6	153	27	187	34
New Mexico..........	346	225	65	10	3	111	32	121	35
New York.............	1,200	768	64	64	5	364	30	428	36
North Carolina.......	1,319	859	65	65	5	388	29	453	34
North Dakota.........	105	54	52	4	4	47	44	51	48
Ohio..................	1,080	666	62	71	7	341	32	413	38
Oklahoma............	668	420	63	29	4	220	33	248	37
Oregon...............	317	223	70	20	6	71	22	91	29
Pennsylvania.........	1,324	817	62	69	5	433	33	502	38
Rhode Island.........	66	36	55	4	6	25	38	30	45
South Carolina.......	810	400	49	53	7	357	44	410	51
South Dakota........	140	93	66	9	7	37	26	46	33
Tennessee............	1,031	689	67	57	6	283	27	340	33
Texas.................	2,998	1,540	51	190	6	1,259	42	1,450	48
Utah..................	236	187	79	5	2	44	19	49	21
Vermont..............	71	46	65	7	10	18	25	25	35
Virginia...............	740	487	66	41	6	211	29	253	34
Washington...........	458	263	57	25	5	170	37	194	42
West Virginia.........	315	214	68	13	4	88	28	101	32
Wisconsin.............	572	332	58	34	6	205	36	240	42
Wyoming..............	155	97	62	5	3	54	35	59	38

[1] Total fatalities include those in which there was no driver or motorcycle rider present.

Source: U.S. National Highway Traffic Safety Administration, *Traffic Safety Facts*, annual. See also <http://www-nrd.nhtsa.dot.gov/CATS/index.aspx>.

Table 1117. Fatalities by Highest Driver Blood Alcohol Concentration (BAC) in the Crash: 1990 to 2010

[g/dl means grams per deciliter. A motor vehicle crash is considered to be alcohol-impaired if at least one driver involved in the crash is determined to have had a BAC of .08 g/dl or higher. Thus, any fatality that occurs in an alcohol-impaired crash is considered an alcohol-impaired-driving fatality. The term "alcohol-impaired" does not indicate that a crash or fatality was caused by the presence of alcohol. A person is considered to be legally impaired with a BAC of .08 g/dl or more]

Item	1990	1995	2000	2005	2007	2008	2009	2010
Total Fatalities [1].................	**44,599**	**41,817**	**41,945**	**43,510**	**41,259**	**37,423**	**33,883**	**32,885**
BAC=.00								
Number...........................	23,823	25,768	26,082	27,423	25,611	23,499	21,051	20,838
Percent............................	53.4	61.6	62.2	63.0	62.1	62.8	62.1	63.4
BAC=.01–.07								
Number...........................	2,901	2,416	2,422	2,404	2,494	2,115	1,972	1,720
Percent............................	6.5	5.8	5.8	5.5	6.0	5.7	5.8	5.2
Alcohol-Impaired-Driving Fatalities BAC=.08+								
Number...........................	17,705	13,478	13,324	13,582	13,041	11,711	10,759	10,228
Percent............................	39.7	32.2	31.8	31.2	31.6	31.3	31.8	31.1

[1] Total fatalities include those in which there was no driver or motorcycle rider present.

Source: U.S. National Highway Traffic Safety Administration, *Traffic Safety Facts*, annual. See also <http://www-nrd.nhtsa.dot.gov/CATS/index.aspx>.

Table 1118. Alcohol Involvement for Drivers in Fatal Crashes: 1999 and 2010

[BAC = blood alcohol concentration]

Age, sex, and vehicle type	1999		2010	
	Number of drivers	Percentage with BAC of .08% or greater	Number of drivers	Percentage with BAC of .08% or greater
Total drivers involved in fatal crashes [1]......................	**56,502**	**20.3**	**44,440**	**21.8**
Drivers by age group:				
Under 16 years old............................	333	9.6	160	8.0
16 to 20 years old.............................	7,985	16.9	4,487	18.0
21 to 24 years old.............................	5,639	31.4	4,585	34.0
25 to 34 years old.............................	11,763	27.6	8,540	30.0
35 to 44 years old.............................	11,059	24.8	7,313	25.0
45 to 54 years old.............................	7,708	17.1	7,490	21.0
55 to 64 years old.............................	4,608	10.8	5,554	14.0
65 to 74 years old.............................	3,251	6.9	2,894	8.0
75 years old and over........................	3,346	3.7	2,666	5.0
Drivers by sex:				
Male..	41,012	23.4	31,965	24.0
Female...	14,835	11.6	11,811	15.0
Drivers by vehicle type:				
Passenger cars.................................	27,878	21.3	17,623	23.0
Light trucks [2]................................	19,865	22.3	17,322	22.0
Large trucks [2]...............................	4,868	1.5	3,446	2.0
Motorcycles....................................	2,528	32.8	4,629	28.0
Buses..	318	0.9	(NA)	(NA)

NA Not available. [1] Includes age and sex unknown, and other and unknown types of vehicles. [2] See footnotes 2 and 3, Table 1112.

Source: U.S. National Highway Traffic Safety Administration, *Traffic Safety Facts*, annual. See also <http://www-nrd.nhtsa.dot.gov/CATS/index.aspx>.

Table 1119. Motor Vehicle Crashes—Number and Deaths: 1995 to 2010

[6,699 represents 6,699,000. This table replaces Table 1103 in the 2012 Edition of the Statistical Abstract. That table, prepared by the National Safety Council, included data on the number of deaths within one year of the crash as well as a broader definition of motor vehicle accidents than that used by the National Highway Traffic Safety Administration]

Item	Unit	1995	2000	2005	2006	2007	2008	2009	2010
CRASHES									
Total [1]	1,000	6,699	6,394	6,159	5,973	6,024	5,811	5,505	5,419
Fatal	1,000	37	38	39	39	37	34	31	30
Injury	1,000	2,217	2,070	1,816	1,746	1,711	1,630	1,517	1,542
Property Damage Only	1,000	4,446	4,286	4,304	4,189	4,275	4,146	3,957	3,847
DEATHS									
Deaths within 30 days of crash	1,000	41.8	41.9	43.5	42.7	41.3	37.4	33.9	32.9
Occupants	1,000	33.1	33.5	33.1	32.1	30.5	26.8	24.5	23.3
Passenger cars	1,000	22.4	20.7	18.5	17.9	16.6	14.6	13.1	12.4
Light trucks [2]	1,000	9.6	11.5	13.0	12.8	12.5	10.8	10.3	9.8
Large trucks [2]	1,000	0.6	0.8	0.8	0.8	0.8	0.7	0.5	0.5
Buses	1,000	0.0	0.0	0.1	0.0	0.0	0.1	0.0	0.0
Other/unknown	1,000	0.4	0.5	0.7	0.6	0.6	0.6	0.6	0.5
Motorcycle riders [3]	1,000	2.2	2.9	4.6	4.8	5.2	5.3	4.5	4.5
Nonoccupants	1,000	6.5	5.6	5.9	5.8	5.6	5.3	4.9	5.1
Pedestrians	1,000	5.6	4.8	4.9	4.8	4.7	4.4	4.1	4.3
Pedalcyclist	1,000	0.8	0.7	0.8	0.8	0.7	0.7	0.6	0.6
Other/unknown	1,000	0.1	0.1	0.2	0.2	0.2	0.2	0.2	0.2
Traffic death rates: [4]									
Per 100 million vehicle miles	Rate	1.7	1.5	1.5	1.4	1.4	1.3	1.2	1.1
Per 100,000 licensed drivers	Rate	23.7	22.0	21.7	21.1	20.1	18.0	16.2	15.7
Per 100,000 registered vehicles	Rate	21.2	19.3	17.7	17.0	16.0	14.4	13.1	12.8
Per 100,000 resident population	Rate	15.9	14.9	14.7	14.3	13.7	12.3	11.1	10.6

[1] Covers police-reported accidents in which at least one person dies within 30 days of the crash; or no one dies but at least one person is injured; or no one is injured but property damage has occurred. [2] See footnotes 2 and 3 in Table 1112. [3] Includes motor scooters, minibikes, and mopeds. [4] Based on 30-day definition of traffic deaths.

Source: National Highway Traffic Safety Administration, Fatality Analysis Reporting System (FARS) and *Traffic Safety Facts, 2010*. See also <http://www.nhtsa.gov/NCSA>.

Table 1120. Licensed Drivers and Number in Fatal Accidents by Age and Sex: 2010

[104,374 represents 104,374,000]

Age group	Licensed drivers (1,000)			Drivers in fatal accidents			Accident rates per number of drivers [2]	
	Male	Female	Both sexes	Male	Female	Both sexes [1]	Male	Female
Total	104,374	105,740	210,215	31,892	11,794	44,440	31	11
19 years old and under	4,880	4,676	9,556	2,446	1,119	3,565	50	24
Under 16 years old	199	198	398	113	47	160	57	24
16 years old	608	605	1,213	302	167	469	50	28
17 years old	1,025	1,004	2,028	501	239	740	49	24
18 years old	1,408	1,323	2,731	748	325	1,073	53	25
19 years old	1,641	1,546	3,187	782	341	1,123	48	22
20 to 24 years old	8,817	8,651	17,468	4,147	1,519	5,666	47	18
20 years old	1,744	1,682	3,426	785	296	1,081	45	18
21 years old	1,756	1,717	3,473	894	345	1,239	51	20
22 years old	1,757	1,725	3,482	823	304	1,127	47	18
23 years old	1,767	1,748	3,515	818	290	1,108	46	17
24 years old	1,792	1,779	3,571	827	284	1,111	46	16
25 to 29 years old	9,179	9,253	18,431	3,423	1,216	4,639	37	13
30 to 34 years old	8,934	8,915	17,849	2,830	1,070	3,900	32	12
35 to 39 years old	9,079	9,082	18,161	2,633	1,005	3,638	29	11
40 to 49 years old	19,994	19,998	39,992	5,657	1,882	7,539	28	9
50 to 59 years old	19,367	19,701	39,068	5,070	1,697	6,767	26	9
60 to 69 years old	13,499	13,827	27,326	3,084	1,024	4,108	23	7
70 to 79 years old	6,995	7,393	14,389	1,562	681	2,243	22	9
80 to 84 years old	2,090	2,373	4,463	547	305	852	26	13
85 and over	1,541	1,870	3,411	493	276	769	32	15

[1] Total includes 754 unknown/unreported instances. [2] Per 100,000 male/female licensed drivers. Rates for drivers 19 years old and under are likely overstated because of a higher proportion of unlicensed drivers.

Source: Federal Highway Administration, Highway Statistics Series, September 2011; and National Highway Traffic Safety Administration, Fatality Analysis Reporting System (FARS). See also <http://www.nhtsa.gov/FARS> and <http://www.fhwa.dot.gov/policyinformation/statistics/2010/dl20.cfm>.

Table 1121. Roadway Congestion by Urbanized Area: 2010

[14,933 represents 14,933,000. Various federal, state, and local information sources were used to develop the database with the primary source being the Federal Highway Administration's Highway Performance Monitoring System]

Urbanized area	Freeway daily vehicle miles of travel		Annual person hours of delay		Annual congestion cost [1]		
	Total miles (1,000)	Per lane-mile of freeway	Total hours (1,000)	Per person [2]	Per person (dol.) [2]	Delay and fuel cost (mil. dol.)	Fuel wasted (gal. per person) [2]
Total, average...................	**14,933**	**15,614**	**42,461**	**25**	**523**	**890**	**11**
Akron, OH.................	5,259	12,090	6,198	10	194	120	2
Albany-Schenectady, NY.................	6,829	11,103	7,467	12	252	155	4
Albuquerque, NM.................	4,935	14,585	10,477	17	365	228	3
Allentown-Bethlehem, PA-NJ.................	4,730	11,340	9,777	15	311	197	3
Atlanta, GA.................	46,779	18,379	115,958	27	578	2,489	12
Austin, TX.................	12,080	14,442	31,038	24	473	617	6
Baltimore, MD.................	26,026	16,684	87,199	35	738	1,853	14
Birmingham, AL.................	9,402	13,758	15,832	18	380	326	7
Boston, MA-NH-RI.................	40,402	15,765	117,234	27	557	2,393	12
Bridgeport-Stamford, CT-NY.................	10,226	16,818	21,233	23	474	441	7
Buffalo, NY.................	6,461	9,940	11,450	11	223	234	3
Charleston-North, Charleston, SC...........	3,631	13,249	9,160	17	372	195	5
Charlotte, NC-SC.................	11,654	13,866	17,730	17	359	378	5
Chicago, IL-IN.................	54,959	18,108	367,122	43	956	8,206	21
Cincinnati, OH-KY-IN.................	18,121	14,600	23,297	14	284	486	3
Cleveland, OH.................	16,961	12,029	21,380	13	245	418	3
Colorado Springs, CO.................	3,949	11,673	11,897	22	421	231	6
Columbus, OH.................	14,599	15,057	14,651	11	226	289	3
Dallas-Fort, Worth-Arlington, TX...........	63,405	17,114	163,585	32	652	3,365	16
Dayton, OH.................	7,047	12,046	7,096	10	189	140	2
Denver-Aurora, CO.................	20,091	15,541	80,837	35	719	1,659	17
Detroit, MI.................	29,553	15,510	87,572	23	472	1,828	11
El Paso, TX-NM.................	5,577	12,409	10,452	14	296	214	3
Fresno, CA.................	3,876	12,793	5,999	9	180	123	2
Grand Rapids, MI.................	4,874	10,832	7,861	13	257	156	3
Hartford, CT.................	10,666	13,434	15,072	17	326	295	4
Honolulu, HI.................	5,902	14,152	15,035	21	403	287	4
Houston, TX.................	54,833	16,571	153,391	38	790	3,203	19
Indianapolis, IN.................	13,191	14,119	20,800	17	362	443	4
Jackson, MS.................	4,764	12,988	5,488	13	303	128	3
Jacksonville, FL.................	11,760	14,811	18,005	17	346	371	5
Kansas City, MO-KS.................	20,899	10,777	24,185	15	318	501	5
Las Vegas, NV.................	10,533	18,623	27,386	19	370	530	5
Los Angeles-Long Beach-Santa Ana, CA...	132,195	23,447	521,449	40	838	10,999	21
Louisville, KY-IN.................	11,985	14,368	17,033	16	328	353	4
Memphis, TN-MS-AR.................	8,274	12,666	17,197	16	340	358	5
Miami, FL.................	39,439	18,001	139,764	26	539	2,906	12
Milwaukee, WI.................	10,296	13,820	26,699	18	368	549	5
Minneapolis-St Paul, MN.................	28,250	16,343	78,483	29	584	1,595	13
Nashville-Davidson, TN.................	14,574	13,420	26,475	23	492	556	6
New Haven, CT.................	7,421	14,134	11,643	19	381	235	5
New Orleans, LA.................	4,824	12,611	20,565	20	431	453	6
New York-Newark, NY-NJ-CT.................	114,743	15,892	465,564	25	520	9,794	10
Oklahoma City, OK.................	9,519	12,240	16,848	17	342	331	3
Omaha, NE-IA.................	4,059	12,964	9,299	15	270	173	3
Orlando, FL.................	13,265	14,433	38,260	26	558	811	8
Oxnard-Ventura, CA.................	6,993	17,615	9,009	13	261	184	4
Philadelphia, PA-NJ-DE-MD.................	35,655	14,721	134,899	25	530	2,842	10
Phoenix, AZ.................	30,171	18,933	81,829	23	525	1,905	13
Pittsburgh, PA.................	11,754	9,183	41,081	23	483	850	6
Portland, OR-WA.................	13,121	16,549	41,743	22	447	850	6
Providence, RI-MA.................	10,879	11,761	15,539	13	244	302	4
Raleigh-Durham, NC.................	11,522	13,113	19,247	17	372	417	6
Richmond, VA.................	11,512	10,858	13,800	14	271	262	3
Riverside-San Bernardino, CA.................	23,328	20,903	40,875	20	452	902	11
Sacramento, CA.................	15,242	18,383	29,602	16	321	603	5
Salt Lake City, UT.................	7,614	13,225	18,366	18	353	357	5
San Antonio, TX.................	19,758	15,806	30,207	20	388	593	6
San Diego, CA.................	37,382	18,645	72,995	24	499	1,541	12
San Francisco-Oakland, CA.................	48,207	19,110	120,149	30	611	2,479	13
San Jose, CA.................	16,251	17,779	42,846	24	464	842	8
Seattle, WA.................	29,941	15,981	87,919	27	591	1,913	14
St Louis, MO-IL.................	28,773	12,270	47,042	20	442	1,034	10
Tampa-St Petersburg, FL.................	13,600	15,290	53,047	22	464	1,097	12
Toledo, OH-MI.................	3,769	11,250	4,223	8	164	85	2
Tucson, AZ.................	3,668	14,528	11,412	16	368	262	3
Tulsa, OK.................	7,032	9,283	9,086	13	257	183	3
Virginia Beach, VA.................	13,036	13,795	36,538	24	447	693	6
Washington, DC-VA-MD.................	37,637	17,959	188,650	42	849	3,849	21
Worcester, MA.................	5,743	11,782	5,639	13	249	111	4

[1] Value of extra time (delay) and the extra fuel consumed by vehicles traveling at slower speeds. Fuel cost per gallon is the average price for each state. [2] Per person data are based on total population.

Source: Texas A&M Transportation Institute, College Station, Texas, *2011 Urban Mobility Report*, September 2011 (copyright). See also <http://mobility.tamu.edu/ums/>.

Table 1122. Commuting to Work by State: 2010

[In percent, except as indicated. Workers in thousands (136,941 represents 136,941,000). For workers 16 years old and over. The American Community Survey universe includes the household population and the population living in institutions, college dormitories, and other group quarters. Based on a sample and subject to sampling variability; see Appendix III]

| State | Total workers (1,000) | Commuted by car, truck, or van | | Percent of workers who— | | | | Mean travel time to work (min.) |
		Drove alone	Car-pooled	Used public transpor-tation [1]	Walked	Used other means [2]	Worked at home	
U.S............	136,941	76.6	9.7	4.9	2.8	1.7	4.3	25.3
AL................	1,952	84.5	10.0	0.4	1.3	0.9	2.9	24.1
AK................	343	67.0	13.2	1.2	7.9	5.2	5.5	18.8
AZ................	2,622	76.5	11.6	1.8	2.0	2.3	5.8	24.5
AR................	1,226	82.0	11.3	0.5	1.8	1.5	3.0	21.2
CA................	15,921	73.2	11.5	5.2	2.7	2.3	5.2	26.9
CO................	2,428	75.5	10.0	3.0	3.0	2.2	6.4	24.1
CT................	1,708	79.7	8.0	4.5	2.8	1.1	3.9	24.7
DE................	404	80.4	9.5	3.0	2.2	1.3	3.7	24.3
DC................	297	34.8	5.9	38.3	11.8	4.2	5.0	29.4
FL................	7,866	79.9	9.6	2.0	1.7	2.1	4.6	25.5
GA................	4,118	79.3	10.3	2.3	1.5	1.8	4.8	27.0
HI................	657	66.6	13.8	6.6	4.5	3.4	5.1	25.5
ID................	670	77.8	9.9	0.8	3.2	2.3	6.0	20.4
IL................	5,793	73.8	8.7	8.5	3.1	1.6	4.3	27.9
IN................	2,845	83.8	8.5	1.0	2.2	1.2	3.3	23.2
IA................	1,514	79.3	9.7	1.1	3.6	1.4	4.8	19.1
KS................	1,359	82.1	9.1	0.5	2.6	1.2	4.4	19.1
KY................	1,803	82.2	10.3	1.1	1.7	1.0	3.7	22.6
LA................	1,932	81.7	10.7	1.4	2.0	2.0	2.2	24.8
ME................	628	80.5	8.9	0.5	3.5	1.5	5.2	23.3
MD................	2,848	73.0	10.7	8.6	2.3	1.1	4.3	31.8
MA................	3,152	72.8	7.8	9.1	4.7	1.4	4.2	27.6
MI................	4,045	83.3	8.6	1.3	2.2	1.1	3.6	23.9
MN................	2,650	78.2	8.5	3.5	2.8	1.6	5.4	22.9
MS................	1,159	84.1	10.0	0.4	1.7	1.2	2.4	23.8
MO................	2,706	81.7	9.3	1.6	2.1	1.2	4.2	23.0
MT................	460	75.6	9.7	0.8	5.2	2.1	6.5	18.6
NE................	921	81.4	9.8	0.6	2.8	1.2	4.3	18.4
NV................	1,184	78.3	11.0	3.3	1.8	2.0	3.7	23.3
NH................	668	81.6	7.7	0.9	2.8	1.1	5.9	25.9
NJ................	4,054	72.3	8.4	10.8	2.9	1.9	3.6	30.3
NM................	858	79.8	10.4	1.2	2.2	1.6	4.9	22.2
NY................	8,724	54.4	6.9	26.7	6.2	1.9	4.0	31.3
NC................	4,120	81.9	10.1	1.0	1.8	1.2	4.0	23.4
ND................	360	80.0	8.6	0.7	3.8	1.7	5.2	16.1
OH................	5,071	83.8	7.8	1.7	2.3	1.0	3.5	22.8
OK................	1,654	81.0	11.2	0.5	1.8	1.4	4.1	20.8
OR................	1,666	72.2	10.0	4.2	3.9	3.2	6.5	22.3
PA................	5,723	77.0	8.8	5.4	3.8	1.2	3.7	25.9
RI................	480	80.3	8.2	2.8	3.8	1.5	3.3	22.9
SC................	1,948	82.9	9.3	0.5	1.9	1.7	3.7	23.5
SD................	404	78.2	10.0	0.5	4.4	1.7	5.2	16.8
TN................	2,676	83.6	10.0	0.7	1.2	1.0	3.4	24.0
TX................	11,145	79.8	11.1	1.5	1.7	1.8	4.1	24.6
UT................	1,210	77.6	11.2	2.1	2.9	1.8	4.4	21.2
VT................	314	74.9	9.5	1.3	5.5	1.4	7.4	21.7
VA................	3,846	77.1	10.0	4.4	2.7	1.4	4.3	27.5
WA................	3,047	73.0	10.5	5.5	3.5	2.2	5.3	25.1
WV................	728	82.9	9.4	0.7	3.1	1.0	2.8	25.6
WI................	2,758	80.5	8.8	1.7	3.1	1.7	4.2	21.6
WY................	279	75.9	11.1	1.7	4.4	2.0	4.9	18.3

[1] Excluding taxicabs. [2] Includes taxicabs, motorcycles, bicycles, and other means.

Source: U.S. Census Bureau, 2010 American Community Survey, B08006, "Sex of Worker by Means of Transportation to Work" and R0801, "Mean Travel Time to Work of Workers 16 Years Old and Over Who Did Not Work At Home (minutes)," <http://factfinder.census.gov/>, accessed April 2012.

Table 1123. Passenger Transit Industry—Summary: 1990 to 2010

[16,053 represents $16,053,000,000. Includes Puerto Rico. Includes aggregate information for all transit systems in the United States. Excludes nontransit services such as taxicab, school bus, unregulated jitney (a small bus or automobile that transports passengers on a route for a small fare), sightseeing bus, intercity bus, and special application mass transportation systems (e.g., amusement parks, airports, island, and urban park ferries). Includes active vehicles only]

Item	Unit	1990	1995	2000	2005	2008	2009	2010
Operating systems..................	Number	5,078	5,973	6,000	6,429	7,700	7,200	7,300
Motor bus systems.................	Number	2,688	2,250	2,262	1,500	1,100	1,088	1,206
Revenue vehicles, active...........	Number	93,553	116,473	131,918	150,827	169,436	172,893	174,425
Motor bus.........................	Number	58,714	67,107	75,013	82,027	66,506	64,832	66,239
Commuter rail.....................	Number	5,007	5,164	5,498	6,392	6,617	6,941	6,927
Demand response [1]................	Number	16,471	29,352	33,080	41,958	65,799	68,957	68,621
Heavy rail.........................	Number	10,419	10,157	10,591	11,110	11,377	11,461	11,510
Light rail..........................	Number	913	999	1,577	1,645	1,969	2,068	2,104
Trolley bus........................	Number	832	885	951	615	590	531	571
Other..............................	Number	1,197	2,809	5,208	7,080	16,578	18,103	18,453
Operating funding, total............	Mil. dol.	16,053	18,241	24,243	31,708	37,975	38,918	39,117
Agency funds.....................	Mil. dol.	6,786	8,069	11,004	12,559	14,304	14,549	14,675
Passenger funding................	Mil. dol.	5,891	6,801	8,746	10,269	11,860	12,273	12,556
Other............................	Mil. dol.	895	1,268	2,258	2,290	2,444	2,276	2,119
Government funds [2]...............	Mil. dol.	9,267	10,172	13,239	19,149	23,671	24,369	24,442
Directly generated [3].............	Mil. dol.	([4])	1,544	1,959	2,694	2,448	2,543	2,549
Local............................	Mil. dol.	5,327	3,981	5,319	6,658	8,754	8,763	8,458
State............................	Mil. dol.	2,970	3,830	4,967	7,495	9,795	9,857	9,761
Federal.........................	Mil. dol.	970	817	994	2,303	2,674	3,207	3,675
Operating expense.................	Mil. dol.	15,742	17,849	22,646	30,295	36,398	37,245	37,755
Vehicle operations.................	Mil. dol.	6,654	8,282	10,111	13,793	16,780	16,997	17,009
Maintenance......................	Mil. dol.	4,631	5,047	6,445	8,259	9,651	9,693	9,797
General administration.............	Mil. dol.	3,450	2,590	3,329	4,075	4,983	5,330	5,731
Purchased transportation..........	Mil. dol.	1,008	1,930	2,761	4,168	4,983	5,225	5,218
Capital expenditures...............	Mil. dol.	(NA)	7,230	9,587	12,383	17,765	17,919	17,824
Vehicle-miles operated.............	Million	3,242	3,550	4,081	4,601	5,204	5,219	5,455
Motor bus........................	Million	2,130	2,184	2,315	2,485	2,377	2,332	2,413
Trolley bus.......................	Million	14	14	14	13	12	13	12
Heavy rail........................	Million	537	537	595	646	674	685	666
Light rail.........................	Million	24	35	53	69	88	91	94
Commuter rail....................	Million	213	238	271	303	339	344	345
Demand response [1]...............	Million	306	507	759	978	1,495	1,529	1,694
Other............................	Million	18	37	74	107	219	227	232
Trips taken.........................	Million	8,799	7,763	9,363	9,815	10,521	10,381	10,218
Motor bus........................	Million	5,677	4,848	5,678	5,855	5,573	5,452	5,256
Trolley bus.......................	Million	126	119	122	107	101	104	99
Heavy rail........................	Million	2,346	2,033	2,632	2,808	3,547	3,490	3,550
Light rail.........................	Million	175	251	320	381	454	465	457
Commuter rail....................	Million	328	344	413	423	472	468	464
Demand response [1]...............	Million	68	88	105	125	191	190	190
Other............................	Million	79	80	93	117	183	212	203
Avg. fare per trip...................	Cents	67	88	93	102	113	118	(NA)
Employees, number (avg.) [5]........	1,000	273	311	360	367	400	403	394
Payroll, employee..................	Mil. dol.	7,226	8,213	10,400	12,177	13,914	14,212	14,286
Fringe benefits, employee..........	Mil. dol.	3,986	4,484	5,413	8,093	9,366	9,927	10,342

NA Not available. [1] This operation (also called paratransit or dial-a-ride) is comprised of passenger cars, vans or small buses operating in response to calls from passengers or their agents to the transit operator, who then dispatches a vehicle to pick up the passengers and transport them to their destinations. [2] Represents the sum of federal, state, and local assistance, and that portion of directly generated funds that accrue from tax collections, toll transfers from other sectors of operations, and bond proceeds. [3] These are any funds generated from taxes controlled by the transit agency. [4] Funds data are included in local government data through 1993. [5] Through 1990, represents employee equivalents of 2,080 hours = one employee; beginning 1995, equals actual employees.

Source: American Public Transportation Association, Washington, DC, *Public Transportation Fact Book*, annual (copyright). See also <http://www.apta.com/resources/statistics/Pages/default.aspx>.

Table 1124. Top Twenty Cities—Transit Savings: 2012

[Individuals who ride public transportation can save on average $9,743 annually based on the June 11, 2012 national average gas price and the national unreserved monthly parking rate. On a per month basis, transit riders can save on average $812 per month. See the monthly press release dated June 11 at http://www.apta.com/mediacenter/pressreleases/2012/Pages/120906_TSR_June.aspx. This release and other monthly "Transit Savings" releases contain information and methodology on how savings are calculated. The cities with the highest transit ridership are ranked in order of their transit savings based on the purchase of a monthly public transit pass and factoring in local gas prices and the local monthly unreserved parking rate]

City	Savings (dollars)		City	Savings (dollars)	
	Monthly	Annual		Monthly	Annual
New York...............	1,195	14,340	Minneapolis...........	866	10,389
Boston..................	1,089	13,071	Denver.................	843	10,118
San Francisco..........	1,082	12,980	Baltimore..............	830	9,959
Seattle..................	991	11,887	Washington, D.C.......	800	9,604
Chicago.................	975	11,700	Cleveland..............	798	9,576
Philadelphia............	962	11,538	Pittsburgh.............	791	9,492
Honolulu................	940	11,281	Miami..................	763	9,159
Los Angeles............	910	10,916	Atlanta................	757	9,082
Portland................	879	10,546	Las Vegas..............	752	9,026
San Diego..............	869	10,425	Dallas.................	748	8,977

Source: American Public Transportation Association, Media Center, Press Releases (copyright). See also <http://www.apta.com/mediacenter/pressreleases/2012/Pages/120906_TSR_June.aspx>.

Table 1125. Characteristics of Rail Transit by Transit Authority: 2010

Mode and transit agency	Primary city served	States served	Direc- tional route– miles [1,2]	Number of high- way- rail cross- ings [1]	Number of stations	Number of ADA acces sible stations [3]
Total [4]	**37**	**33**	**11,683.8**	**6,557**	**3,109**	**2,049**
Heavy rail	**11**	**17**	**1,596.6**	**27**	**1,025**	**506**
Chicago Transit Authority	Chicago	IL, IN	207.8	25	143	90
Greater Cleveland Regional Transit Authority	Cleveland	OH	38.1	–	18	13
L.A. County Metropolitan Transportation Authority	Los Angeles	CA	31.9	–	16	16
Maryland Transit Administration	Baltimore	MD	29.4	–	14	14
Massachusetts Bay Transportation Authority	Boston	MA, NH, RI	76.3	–	53	49
Metropolitan Atlanta Rapid Transit Authority	Atlanta	GA	96.1	–	38	38
Miami-Dade Transit Agency	Miami	FL	45.0	–	22	22
MTA New York City Transit	New York	NY, NJ, CT	487.5	–	468	88
Port Authority Trans-Hudson Corporation	New York	NY, NJ, CT	28.6	2	13	7
Port Authority Transit Corporation	Philadelphia	PA, NJ, DE	31.5	–	13	5
San Francisco Bay Area Rapid Transit District	San Francisco	CA	209.0	–	43	43
Southeastern Pennsylvania Transportation Authority	Philadelphia	PA	74.9	–	75	30
Staten Island Rapid Transit Operating Authority	New York	NY, CT	28.6	–	23	5
Washington Metropolitan Area Transit Authority	Washington	DC, MD, VA	211.8	–	86	86
Commuter rail [5]	**21**	**25**	**8,590.3**	**3,405**	**1,235**	**808**
Alaska Railroad Corporation	Anchorage	AK	959.9	133	10	10
Altamont Commuter Express	San Jose	CA	172.0	127	10	10
Capital Metropolitan Transportation	Austin	TX	64.24	–	9	9
Central Puget Sound Regional Transit Authority	Seattle	WA	146.9	101	10	10
Connecticut Department of Transportation	Hartford	CT	101.2	3	9	8
Dallas Area Rapid Transit	Dallas	TX	72.3	43	10	10
Maryland Transit Administration	Baltimore	MD	400.4	40	42	24
Massachusetts Bay Transportation Authority	Boston	MA, NH, RI	737.5	257	133	96
Metro Transit	Minneapolis	MN	77.9	36	6	6
MTA Long Island Rail Road	New York	NY, NJ, CT	638.2	343	124	103
MTA Metro-North Commuter Railroad Co	New York	NY, NJ, CT	545.7	156	110	43
New Jersey Transit Corporation	New York	NY, NJ, CT	1,001.8	330	164	72
North County Transit District	San Diego	CA	82.2	34	8	8
NE Illinois Regional Commuter Rail Corporation	Chicago	IL, WI	980.4	579	240	169
Northern Indiana Commuter Transportation District	Chicago	IL, IN	179.8	117	20	13
Northern New England Passenger Rail Authority	Boston	MA, ME, NH	230.4	65	10	10
Peninsula Corridor Joint Powers Board	San Francisco	CA	153.7	47	32	26
Pennsylvania Department of Transportation	Philadelphia	PA	144.4	7	12	4
Regional Transportation Authority	Nashville	TN	62.8	35	6	6
Rio Metro Regional Transit District	Albuquerque	NM	193.1	86	12	12
South Florida Regional Transportation Authority	Miami	FL	142.2	73	18	18
Southeastern Pennsylvania Transportation Authority	Philadelphia	PA	446.9	283	154	55
Southern California Regional Rail Authority	Los Angeles	CA	777.8	434	55	55
Tri-County Metropolitan Transportation District of Oregon	Portland	OR	29.2	27	5	5
Utah Transit Authority	Salt Lake City	UT	87.7	29	8	8
Virginia Railway Express	Washington	DC, VA, MD	161.5	20	18	18

– Represents zero. [1] Vehicles operated in maximum services (VOMS) include directly operated (DO) and Purchase Transportation (PT) by mode. [2] The mileage in each direction over which public transportation vehicles travel while in revenue service. The mileage is computed without regard to the number of traffic lanes or rail tracks existing in the right-of-way. [3] Number of stations that comply with the Americans with Disabilities Act of 1992 (ADA). Additional stations may be wheelchair accessible but not comply with other provisions of the ADA. [4] Includes light rail, not shown separately. [5] Excludes commuter-type services operated independently by Amtrak.

Source: U.S. Department of Transportation, Federal Transit Administration, National Transit Database, <http://www.ntdprogram.gov/ntdprogram/data.htm>, accessed April 2012.

Table 1126. Transit Ridership in Selected Urbanized Areas: 2009

Urbanized areas	Annual unlinked passenger trips [1] (1,000)	Area rank based on trips per capita [2]	Unlinked passenger trips per capita	Percent distribution				
				Motor bus	Heavy rail [3]	Light rail [4]	Commuter rail [5]	Other [6]
U.S. urbanized areas....................	10,063,138	(X)	51.9	53.0	34.6	4.6	4.6	3.1
Atlanta, GA.................................	168,714	26	48.2	49.5	49.4	–	–	1.1
Austin, TX..................................	39,439	27	43.7	97.4	–	–	–	2.6
Baltimore, MD............................	125,162	17	60.3	74.5	10.8	7.1	6.5	1.2
Boston, MA-NH-RI......................	375,540	8	93.1	28.8	39.6	18.8	10.9	1.8
Chicago, IL-IN............................	633,465	11	76.2	55.1	32.0	–	11.9	0.9
Cincinnati, OH-KY-IN..................	27,106	95	18.0	98.3	–	–	–	1.7
Cleveland, OH............................	46,457	63	26.0	83.5	9.7	5.1	–	1.8
Dallas-Fort Worth-Arlington, TX..........	73,616	99	17.8	66.4	–	25.8	3.7	4.1
Denver-Aurora, CO.....................	98,356	25	49.6	78.5	–	20.1	–	1.4
Detroit, MI.................................	54,590	127	14.0	94.1	–	–	–	5.9
Houston, TX...............................	88,734	73	23.2	82.2	–	13.1	–	4.7
Indianapolis, IN..........................	8,450	231	6.9	97.0	–	–	–	3.0
Kansas City, MO-KS....................	16,093	154	11.8	96.2	–	–	–	3.8
Las Vegas, NV............................	67,126	24	51.1	98.5	–	–	–	1.5
Los Angeles-Long Beach-Santa Ana, CA.............	704,768	18	59.8	83.6	6.7	6.5	1.7	1.5
Miami, FL...................................	159,650	48	32.5	78.4	11.4	–	2.6	7.6
Milwaukee, WI............................	49,597	36	37.9	97.2	–	–	–	2.8
Minneapolis-St. Paul, MN............	89,624	38	37.5	86.6	–	11.0	0.1	2.3
New York-Newark, NY-NJ-CT........	4,019,430	1	225.8	31.1	60.8	0.6	6.5	1.0
Philadelphia, PA-NJ-DE-MD..............	368,902	13	71.6	51.5	28.5	8.0	9.8	2.2
Phoenix-Mesa, AZ.......................	78,135	60	26.9	90.0	–	7.1	–	2.9
Pittsburgh, PA............................	70,309	32	40.1	85.0	–	10.4	–	4.5
Portland, OR-WA........................	115,380	12	72.9	64.6	–	34.1	0.1	1.2
Providence, RI-MA......................	21,487	93	18.3	96.2	–	–	–	3.8
Riverside-San Bernardino, CA...........	24,159	107	16.0	95.8	–	–	–	4.2
Sacramento, CA..........................	39,933	55	28.7	55.5	–	43.4	–	1.1
San Antonio, TX.........................	44,500	44	33.5	97.3	–	–	–	2.7
San Diego, CA............................	106,735	33	39.9	59.3	–	36.7	1.4	2.7
San Francisco-Oakland, CA..............	443,459	2	137.4	41.0	25.9	11.4	2.6	19.1
San Jose, CA.............................	46,600	51	30.3	74.6	–	23.1	–	2.3
Seattle, WA...............................	189,536	15	69.9	69.7	–	2.0	1.3	26.9
St. Louis, MO-IL..........................	55,500	61	26.7	62.9	–	35.0	–	2.1
Tampa-St. Petersburg, FL............	27,001	141	13.1	96.3	–	1.9	–	1.8
Virginia Beach, VA......................	18,907	135	13.6	96.0	–	–	–	4.0
Washington, DC-VA-MD................	495,268	3	125.9	38.7	59.9	–	0.8	0.5

– Represents zero. X Not applicable. [1] The number of times passengers board public transportation vehicles. A passenger is counted each time he or she boards a vehicle even if the boarding is part of the same journey from origin to destination. [2] As of April 1. Based on the decennial census. [3] Also called metro, subway, rapid transit, or rapid rail. [4] Also called streetcar, tramway, or trolley. [5] Also called metropolitan rail or regional rail. [6] Includes such modes as trolley bus, ferry, cable car, vanpool, automated guideway, monorail, publico, inclined plane, and demand response (see footnote 1, Table 1123).

Source: U.S. Department of Transportation, Federal Transit Administration, National Transit Database; Access NTD data, Historical Data Files, <http://www.ntdprogram.gov/ntdprogram/data.htm>.

Table 1127. Federal Aid to State and Local Governments for Federal Transit Administration (FTA) by State: 2010

[13,041 represents $13,041,000,000. Year ending September 30]

State	Total (mil. dol.)	Per capita [1] (dol.)	State	Total (mil. dol.)	Per capita [1] (dol.)	State	Total (mil. dol.)	Per capita [1] (dol.)	State	Total (mil. dol.)	Per capita [1] (dol.)
Total [2]......	13,041	42	ID...........	23	14	MT...........	26	26	RI.........	44	42
U.S. [3].......	12,710	41	IL...........	618	48	NE...........	31	17	SC.........	50	11
AL...........	57	12	IN...........	150	23	NV...........	106	39	SD........	17	21
AK...........	80	112	IA...........	70	23	NH...........	18	14	TN........	118	19
AZ...........	184	29	KS...........	36	13	NJ...........	713	81	TX........	661	26
AR...........	43	15	KY...........	86	20	NM...........	42	20	UT........	267	96
CA...........	1,553	42	LA...........	89	20	NY...........	2,684	138	VT........	24	39
CO...........	240	48	ME...........	21	16	NC...........	128	13	VA........	249	31
CT...........	157	44	MD...........	257	44	ND...........	17	25	WA........	427	63
DE...........	26	28	MA...........	302	46	OH...........	276	24	WV........	41	22
DC...........	480	793	MI...........	205	21	OK...........	57	15	WI........	108	19
FL...........	357	19	MN.........	247	47	OR...........	256	67	WY........	11	20
GA...........	200	21	MS...........	27	9	PA	599	47			
HI...........	35	26	MO	193	32						

[1] Based on estimated population as of July 1. [2] Includes Island Areas and undistributed funds, not shown separately. [3] For the 50 states and the District of Columbia.

Source: U.S. Census Bureau, Federal, State, and Local Governments, *Federal Aid to States for Fiscal Year, 2010*, published September 2011. See <http://www.census.gov/prod/www/abs/fas.html>.

Table 1128. Commuting Time to Work for Top Metropolitan Statistical Areas: 2011

[132,276 represents 132,276,000, except percent. For workers 16 years and over who did not work at home. Based on a sample, subject to sampling variability]

State	Total Commuters	Percent over 35 minutes	Less than 10 minutes	10 to 14 minutes	15 to 19 minutes	20 to 24 minutes	25 to 29 minutes	30 to 34 minutes	35 to 44 minutes	45 to 59 minutes	60 or more minutes
United States	132,276	22	17,788	18,929	20,508	19,619	8,022	18,177	8,489	9,963	10,779
Atlanta-Sandy Springs-Marietta, GA	2,265	33	180	242	281	308	137	374	204	264	275
Baltimore-Towson, MD	1,262	31	100	128	170	184	84	205	105	135	151
Boston-Cambridge-Quincy, MA-NH	2,194	31	238	256	272	284	122	342	182	240	258
Chicago-Joliet-Naperville, IL-IN-WI	4,143	34	370	443	488	533	241	641	389	480	557
Cincinnati-Middletown, OH-KY-IN	945	19	107	127	149	161	75	148	67	70	41
Dallas-Fort Worth-Arlington, TX	2,918	24	297	353	422	451	177	508	217	277	216
Denver-Aurora-Broomfield, CO	1,223	23	113	144	185	198	88	211	99	100	85
Detroit-Warren-Livonia, MI	1,708	24	169	215	249	272	124	264	153	150	113
Houston-Sugar Land-Baytown, TX	2,683	26	234	299	377	415	169	484	204	267	234
Los Angeles-Long Beach-Santa Ana, CA	5,429	27	463	663	765	811	289	959	390	489	598
Miami-Fort Lauderdale-Pompano Beach, FL	2,396	25	186	269	328	401	173	451	196	208	184
Minneapolis-St. Paul-Bloomington, MN-WI	1,619	21	173	210	251	271	132	248	128	121	84
New York-Northern New Jersey-Long Island, NY-NJ-PA	8,296	40	655	795	858	983	413	1,285	691	955	1,661
Orlando-Kissimmee-Sanford, FL	950	24	71	116	152	158	69	155	77	96	58
Philadelphia-Camden-Wilmington, PA-NJ-DE-MD	2,600	29	270	311	358	377	154	377	215	266	271
Phoenix-Mesa-Glendale, AZ	1,713	23	172	212	254	272	125	290	143	140	105
Pittsburgh, PA	1,046	24	134	136	154	158	70	139	82	94	79
Portland-Vancouver-Hillsboro, OR-WA	985	21	115	134	158	157	70	146	70	74	61
Riverside-San Bernardino-Ontario, CA	1,542	30	162	207	228	194	76	208	88	129	251
St. Louis, MO-IL	1,260	21	146	161	190	220	92	182	98	102	68
San Diego-Carlsbad-San Marcos, CA	1,327	17	128	187	240	247	103	191	80	77	74
San Francisco-Oakland-Fremont, CA	1,921	31	159	223	280	256	109	308	160	210	217
Seattle-Tacoma-Bellevue, WA	1,609	26	155	180	231	243	112	262	135	154	137
Tampa-St. Petersburg-Clearwater, FL	1,128	22	119	141	181	179	75	183	84	96	70
Washington-Arlington-Alexandria, DC-VA-MD-WV	2,832	41	183	227	323	337	155	440	275	404	488

Source: U.S. Census Bureau, 2011 American Community Survey, B08134: "Means of Transportation to Work by Travel Time to Work," <http://www.census.gov/acs/www/>, accessed September 2012.

Table 1129. Commuters Who Ride Bicycles or Walk to Work by Sex—Selected Cities: 2009

[Covers cities with the highest percent of commuters who walk or bike to work, based on the National Household Travel Survey and the American Community Survey. Data are weighted 3-year averages for 2007-2009]

Leading Cities	Walking — Percent of commuters who walk to work	Percent male	Percent female	Leading Cities	Biking — Percent of commuters who bike to work	Percent male	Percent female
Boston, MA	13.9	48	52	Portland, OR	5.5	62	38
Washington, DC	11.4	50	50	Minneapolis, MN	4.1	63	37
New York, NY	10.3	49	51	Seattle, WA	2.9	68	32
San Francisco, CA	10.0	54	46	San Francisco, CA	2.8	70	30
Seattle, WA	8.6	53	47	Sacramento, CA	2.2	67	33
Philadelphia, PA	8.4	45	55	Oakland, CA	2.1	66	34
Honolulu, HI	8.0	53	47	Washington, DC	2.0	67	33
Baltimore, MD	6.7	46	54	Tucson, AZ	1.9	71	29
Minneapolis, MN	6.4	58	42	Denver, CO	1.8	70	30
Chicago, IL	5.8	48	52	Honolulu, HI	1.7	72	28
New Orleans, LA	5.8	60	40	New Orleans, LA	1.7	76	24
Portland, OR	5.2	53	47	Philadelphia, PA	1.6	70	30
Milwaukee, WI	4.6	50	50	Boston, MA	1.5	67	33
Cleveland, OH	4.4	47	53	Albuquerque, NM	1.3	69	31
Oakland, CA	4.4	53	47	Austin, TX	1.2	72	28
Atlanta, GA	4.2	62	38	Chicago, IL	1.1	76	24
Denver, CA	4.1	55	45	Mesa, AZ	1.1	84	16
Miami, FL	3.8	57	43	Long Beach, CA	1.0	85	15
Tucson, AZ	3.6	54	46	Los Angeles, CA	0.9	80	20
Los Angeles, CA	3.5	52	48	San Diego, CA	0.9	72	28
Detroit, MI	3.3	59	41	San Jose, CA	0.9	79	21
Sacramento, CA	3.3	51	49	Atlanta, GA	0.8	71	29
Long Beach, CA	3.0	55	45	Columbus, OH	0.8	76	24
San Diego, CA	2.9	53	47	Milwaukee, WI	0.8	73	27
Omaha, NE	2.7	59	41	Baltimore, MD	0.7	77	23

Source: Alliance for Biking and Walking, *Biking and Walking in the United States: 2012 Benchmarking Report* (copyright). See also <http://www.peoplepoweredmovement.org/>.

Table 1130. Truck Transportation, Couriers and Messengers, and Warehousing and Storage—Estimated Revenue: 2005 to 2010

[In millions of dollars (285,655 represents $285,655,000,000). For taxable employer firms. Estimates have been adjusted to the results of the 2007 Economic Census]

Kind of business	NAICS code [1]	2005	2006	2007	2008	2009	2010
Selected transportation and warehousing industries	**48, 49**	**285,655**	**306,771**	**317,631**	**324,138**	**272,847**	**290,483**
Truck transportation	484	200,512	213,316	217,833	222,109	180,460	194,616
General freight trucking	4841	133,731	141,023	142,508	146,091	117,821	128,881
General freight trucking, local	48411	20,029	21,769	21,174	21,609	17,750	19,336
General freight trucking, long-distance	48412	113,702	119,254	121,334	124,482	100,071	109,545
General freight trucking, long-distance, truckload	484121	79,548	82,481	83,386	86,557	70,587	77,526
General freight trucking, long-distance, less than truckload	484122	34,154	36,773	37,948	37,925	29,484	32,019
Specialized freight trucking	4842	66,781	72,293	75,325	76,018	62,639	65,735
Used household and office goods moving	48421	14,836	15,079	14,549	14,226	11,891	11,940
Specialized freight (except used goods) trucking, local	48422	27,208	29,954	31,549	31,746	26,046	27,643
Specialized freight (except used goods) trucking, long-distance	48423	24,737	27,260	29,227	30,046	24,702	26,152
Couriers and messengers	492	66,484	72,895	77,877	78,836	69,849	71,622
Couriers	4921	63,313	69,650	74,392	75,594	67,145	68,799
Local messengers and local delivery	4922	3,171	3,245	3,485	3,242	2,704	2,823
Warehousing and storage	493	18,659	20,560	21,921	23,193	22,538	24,245
General warehousing and storage	49311	12,346	14,046	15,187	16,130	15,704	16,770
Refrigerated warehousing and storage	49312	3,011	3,156	3,391	3,487	3,467	4,034
Farm product warehousing and storage	49313	747	775	864	899	801	743
Other warehousing and storage	49319	2,555	2,583	2,479	2,677	2,566	2,698

[1] Data are based on 2002 North American Industry Classification System (NAICS); see text, this section and Section 15.

Source: U.S. Census Bureau, "Service Annual Survey: 2010, Truck Transportation, Messenger Services and Warehousing," January 2012, <http://www.census.gov/services/index.html>.

Table 1131. Truck Transportation—Summary: 2005 to 2010

[In millions of dollars (200,512 represents $200,512,000,000), except where noted. For taxable and tax-exempt employer firms. Covers NAICS 484. Estimates have been adjusted to the results of the 2007 Economic Census. Data are based on the 2002 North American Industry Classification System (NAICS); see text, this section and Section 15]

Item	2005	2007	2008	2009	2010
Total operating revenue	**200,512**	**217,833**	**222,109**	**180,460**	**194,616**
Total motor carrier revenue	187,989	204,212	208,484	169,532	183,496
Local trucking [1]	61,806	69,368	70,476	61,201	64,632
Long-distance trucking [1]	126,183	134,844	138,008	108,331	118,864
Size of shipments:					
Less-than-truckload	43,100	53,411	53,896	43,364	46,201
Truckload	144,889	150,801	154,588	126,168	137,295
Commodities handled:					
Agricultural and fish products	16,853	17,853	18,558	18,597	21,868
Grains, alcohol, and tobacco products	6,803	9,510	9,987	8,947	8,715
Stone, nonmetallic minerals, and metallic ores	13,070	16,137	15,376	12,628	13,226
Coal and petroleum products	6,821	7,991	8,998	7,734	8,153
Pharmaceutical and chemical products	10,251	11,751	11,677	9,807	10,402
Wood products, textiles, and leathers	16,704	17,685	18,613	14,341	15,234
Base metal and machinery	15,908	17,934	18,168	13,746	15,781
Electronic, motorized vehicles, and precision instruments	14,856	14,744	15,067	11,677	11,238
Used household and office goods	11,573	12,457	11,936	9,710	10,168
New furniture and miscellaneous manufactured products	21,508	19,955	20,945	16,319	16,787
Other goods	53,642	58,195	59,159	46,026	51,924
Hazardous materials	15,837	14,543	14,109	12,593	12,549
Origin and destination of shipments:					
U.S. to U.S.	180,797	195,667	199,811	162,556	175,366
U.S. to Canada	1,546	1,954	2,213	1,654	1,985
U.S. to Mexico	1,587	1,563	1,526	1,079	1,352
Canada to U.S.	1,284	1,177	1,312	1,052	1,180
Mexico to U.S.	1,321	(S)	1,740	1,522	1,644
All other destinations	1,454	1,909	1,882	1,669	1,969
Inventory of revenue-generating equipment (1,000):					
Trucks	216	243	246	235	229
Owned and/or leased with drivers	190	215	223	212	201
Leased without drivers	26	28	23	23	28
Truck-tractors	854	884	857	795	804
Owned and/or leased with drivers	722	739	723	678	685
Leased without drivers	132	145	134	117	119
Trailers	1,902	1,927	1,940	1,829	1,821
Owned and/or leased with drivers	1,560	1,593	1,629	1,530	1,552
Leased without drivers	342	334	311	299	269
Highway miles traveled (mil.):					
Total	88,064	88,054	85,838	75,179	76,740
By loaded or partially loaded vehicles	71,093	71,210	69,024	60,214	62,145
By empty vehicles	16,971	16,844	16,814	14,965	14,595

S Estimate does not meet publication standards. [1] Local trucking is the carrying of goods within a single metro area and its adjacent nonurban areas; long-distance trucking is the carrying of goods between metro areas.

Source: U.S. Census Bureau, "Service Annual Survey, 2010: Truck Transportation, Messenger Services and Warehousing," January 2012, <http://www.census.gov/services/index.html>.

Table 1132. Railroads, Class I—Summary: 1990 to 2010

[216 represents 216,000. As of December 31, or calendar year data, except as noted. Compiled from annual reports of Class I railroads only, except where noted. Minus sign (−) indicates deficit]

Item	Unit	1990	2000	2005	2006	2007	2008	2009	2010
Class I line-hauling companies [1]	Number	14	8	7	7	7	7	7	7
Employees [2]	1,000	216	168	162	168	167	164	152	152
Compensation	Mil. dol.	8,654	9,623	10,879	11,419	11,599	11,977	10,960	11,213
Average per hour	Dollars	15.8	21.5	25.7	26.0	27.3	28.9	29.7	29.8
Average per year	Dollars	39,987	57,157	66,975	68,141	69,367	72,836	72,153	73,843
Mileage:									
Railroad line owned [3]	1,000	146	121	121	120	120	119	119	118
Railroad track owned [4]	1,000	244	205	208	207	207	206	206	214
Equipment:									
Locomotives in service	Number	18,835	20,028	22,779	23,730	24,143	24,003	24,045	23,893
Average horsepower	1,000 lb.	2,665	3,261	3,467	3,485	3,518	3,601	3,598	3,614
Cars in service:									
Freight train [5]	1,000	1,212	1,381	1,312	1,347	1,386	1,393	1,363	1,309
Freight cars [6]	1,000	659	560	475	475	460	450	416	398
Average capacity	Tons	87.5	92.3	95.1	96.0	96.7	97.7	98.0	98.6
Income and expenses:									
Operating revenues	Mil. dol.	28,370	34,102	46,118	52,152	54,600	61,243	47,849	58,406
Operating expenses	Mil. dol.	24,652	29,040	37,843	40,980	42,747	47,348	37,225	42,708
Net revenue from operations	Mil. dol.	3,718	5,062	8,275	11,172	11,852	13,895	10,624	15,698
Income before fixed charges	Mil. dol.	4,627	5,361	8,361	11,276	12,084	13,863	11,167	16,255
Provision for taxes [7]	Mil. dol.	1,088	1,430	2,224	3,643	4,108	4,645	3,576	5,731
Ordinary income	Mil. dol.	1,961	2,501	4,917	6,482	6,797	8,102	6,429	9,262
Net income	Mil. dol.	1,977	2,500	4,917	6,482	6,797	8,102	6,423	9,247
Net railway operating income	Mil. dol.	2,648	3,924	6,075	7,560	7,765	9,248	7,045	9,959
Total taxes [8]	Mil. dol.	3,780	4,379	5,176	6,830	7,272	8,069	6,519	8,924
Indus. return on net investment	Percent	8.1	6.5	8.5	10.2	9.9	10.7	8.0	10.4
Gross capital expenditures	Mil. dol.	3,591	5,290	7,068	8,159	9,853	10,189	9,701	9,618
Equipment	Mil. dol.	996	1,508	1,026	1,470	2,213	2,315	2,597	1,914
Roadway and structures	Mil. dol.	2,644	4,549	5,364	6,982	6,944	7,907	7,352	7,854
Other	Mil. dol.	−49	−767	678	−293	696	−32	−248	−150
Balance sheet:									
Total property investment	Mil. dol.	70,348	106,136	141,400	148,320	156,666	164,286	171,769	182,894
Accrued depreciation and amortization	Mil. dol.	22,222	23,989	32,508	35,763	38,702	41,187	44,195	36,140
Net investment	Mil. dol.	48,126	82,147	108,892	112,556	117,963	123,099	127,574	146,754
Shareholder's equity	Mil. dol.	23,662	32,401	55,828	58,901	59,300	62,787	67,826	96,934
Net working capital	Mil. dol.	−3,505	−5,783	−4,729	−4,461	−5,482	−3,592	−1,033	1,143
Cash dividends	Mil. dol.	2,074	819	1,267	1,089	6,427	3,345	1,377	1,989
Amtrak passenger traffic:									
Passenger revenue	Mil. dol.	941.9	1,201.6	1,461.7	1,606.0	1,774.7	1,964.7	1,819.6	1,990.3
Revenue passengers carried	1,000	22,382	22,985	25,076	24,549	26,550	28,705	27,279	29,141
Revenue passenger miles	Million	6,125	5,574	5,381	5,410	5,784	6,179	5,914	6,420
Averages:									
Revenue per passenger	Dollars	42.1	52.3	58.3	65.4	66.8	68.4	66.7	68.3
Revenue per passenger mile	Cents	15.4	21.6	27.2	27.2	30.7	31.8	30.8	31.0
Freight service:									
Freight revenue	Mil. dol.	24,471	33,083	44,457	50,315	52,932	59,409	46,127	56,310
Per ton-mile	Cents	2.7	2.3	2.6	2.8	3.0	3.3	3.0	3.3
Per ton originated	Dollar	19.3	19.0	23.4	25.7	27.3	30.7	27.7	30.4
Revenue-tons originated	Million	1,425	1,738	1,899	1,957	1,940	1,934	1,668	1,851
Revenue-tons carried	Million	2,024	2,179	2,448	2,517	2,431	2,420	2,058	2,280
Tons carried one mile	Billion	1,034	1,466	1,696	1,772	1,771	1,777	1,532	1,691
Average miles of road operated	1,000	133	121	121	120	120	119	119	121
Revenue ton-miles per mile of road	1,000	7,763	12,156	14,071	14,805	14,801	14,887	12,857	13,996
Revenue per ton-mile	Cents	3	2	3	3	3	3	3	3
Train miles	Million	380	504	548	563	543	524	436	476
Net ton-miles per train-mile [9]	Number	2,755	2,923	3,115	3,163	3,274	3,414.0	3,546.0	3,585
Net ton-miles per loaded car-mile [9]	Number	69.1	73.1	79	82	84	87	88	86
Train-miles per train-hour	Miles	24	21	19	18	19	19	21	20
Haul per ton, U.S. as a system	Miles	726	843	893	906	913	919	918	914
Accidents/incidents: [10]									
Casualties—all railroads:									
Persons killed	Number	1,297	937	884	903	851	803	696	726
Persons injured	Number	25,143	11,643	9,550	8,795	9,639	9,058	8,002	8,316
Class I railroads: [11]									
Persons killed	Number	1,166	778	745	788	714	660	587	603
Persons injured	Number	19,284	7,655	6,414	5,817	6,254	5,864	5,033	5,251

[1] See text, this section, for definition of Class I. [2] Average midmonth count. [3] Represents the aggregate length of roadway of all line-haul railroads. Excludes yard tracks, sidings, and parallel lines. (Includes estimate for Class II and III railroads). [4] Includes multiple main tracks, yard tracks, and sidings owned by both line-haul and switching and terminal. (Includes estimate for Class II and III railroads). [5] Includes cars owned by all railroads, private car companies, and shippers. [6] Class I railroads only. Excludes Canadian-owned Class I railroads Grand Trunk Corporation and Soo Line Corporation. [7] Includes state income taxes. [8] Includes payroll, income, and other taxes. [9] Revenue and nonrevenue freight. [10] Includes grade crossings and trespassers. Source for selected data prior to 2008: Federal Railroad Administration, *Railroad Safety Statistics*, <http://www.fra.dot.gov/>. [11] Includes Amtrak data. Includes highway grade crossing casualties.

Source: Except as noted, Association of American Railroads, Washington, DC, *Industry Information, Industry Statistics, Railroad Statistics*, (copyright). See also <http://www.aar.org/StatisticsandPublications.aspx>.

Table 1133. Railroads, Class-I Line-Haul-Revenue Freight Originated by Commodity Group: 1990 to 2011

[21,401 represents 21,401,000]

Commodity group	1990	1995	2000	2005	2007	2008	2009	2010	2011
Carloads (1,000) [1]	**21,401**	**23,726**	**27,763**	**31,142**	**31,459**	**30,625**	**26,005**	**29,209**	**29,997**
Farm products	1,690	1,692	1,437	1,510	1,681	1,726	1,531	1,758	1,719
Metallic ores	508	463	322	662	662	671	527	841	889
Coal	5,912	6,095	6,954	7,202	7,480	7,713	6,842	7,065	7,055
Nonmetallic minerals	1,202	1,159	1,309	1,488	1,398	1,325	1,054	1,217	1,263
Food and kindred products	1,307	1,377	1,377	1,448	1,493	1,501	1,462	1,619	1,585
Lumber and wood products	780	719	648	611	456	392	285	317	325
Pulp, paper, allied products	611	628	633	679	652	666	546	629	659
Chemicals, allied products	1,531	1,642	1,820	1,937	2,050	2,040	1,895	2,215	2,260
Petroleum and coal products	573	596	565	689	691	578	494	553	576
Stone, clay, and glass products	539	516	541	603	513	467	372	420	439
Primary metal products	477	575	723	680	666	634	354	521	579
Fabricated metal products	31	32	30	36	55	58	62	85	93
Machinery, exc. electrical	39	41	35	42	40	44	38	47	58
Transportation equipment	1,091	1,473	1,984	1,923	1,810	1,521	1,105	1,332	1,452
Waste and scrap materials	439	623	619	706	726	729	568	635	640
Misc. mixed shipments	3,436	4,715	6,796	8,153	8,465	8,078	6,897	7,464	7,858
Tons (mil.) [1]	**1,425**	**1,550**	**1,738**	**1,899**	**1,940**	**1,934**	**1,668**	**1,851**	**1,885**
Farm products	147	154	136	140	152	156	137	159	157
Metallic ores	47	44	32	60	59	60	44	71	76
Coal	579	627	758	804	850	879	787	814	816
Nonmetallic minerals	109	110	126	146	138	132	105	123	128
Food and kindred products	81	91	94	102	105	105	101	109	107
Lumber and wood products	53	51	49	48	36	31	22	25	25
Pulp, paper, allied products	33	36	36	38	35	34	28	31	32
Chemicals, allied products	126	138	155	165	176	175	162	186	192
Petroleum and coal products	40	43	42	57	57	46	39	43	45
Stone, clay, and glass products	44	43	48	55	48	45	35	40	42
Primary metal products	38	47	60	57	56	54	30	44	49
Fabricated metal products	1	1	1	1	1	1	1	1	1
Machinery, exc. electrical	1	1	1	1	1	1	1	1	1
Transportation equipment	23	30	42	38	34	27	19	25	27
Waste and scrap materials	28	38	40	47	48	49	37	43	43
Misc. mixed shipments	58	77	101	120	125	120	103	110	117
Gross revenue (mil. dol.) [1]	**29,775**	**33,782**	**36,331**	**46,743**	**54,637**	**60,513**	**48,041**	**57,438**	**65,258**
Farm products	2,422	3,020	2,673	3,628	4,529	5,403	4,413	5,281	5,556
Metallic ores	408	394	338	485	542	637	404	605	699
Coal	6,954	7,356	7,794	9,393	11,471	14,200	12,052	13,914	16,138
Nonmetallic minerals	885	875	969	1,293	1,527	1,749	1,320	1,817	2,340
Food and kindred products	2,188	2,464	2,424	3,253	4,041	4,610	4,261	4,794	5,133
Lumber and wood products	1,390	1,385	1,524	2,278	1,987	1,684	1,095	1,252	1,370
Pulp, paper, allied products	1,486	1,543	1,526	1,953	2,100	2,228	1,656	1,883	2,090
Chemicals, allied products	3,933	4,553	4,636	5,432	6,830	7,655	6,781	8,122	8,904
Petroleum and coal products	918	997	1,010	1,500	1,853	1,930	1,590	1,828	2,105
Stone, clay, and glass products	931	1,044	1,113	1,505	1,607	1,636	1,215	1,424	1,599
Primary metal products	979	1,199	1,371	1,734	2,267	2,572	1,312	1,966	2,381
Fabricated metal products	42	44	48	55	86	92	77	115	136
Machinery, exc. electrical	67	69	61	91	126	166	116	132	187
Transportation equipment	3,100	3,269	3,843	3,960	4,292	3,964	2,677	3,695	4,418
Waste and scrap materials	504	685	706	1,070	1,276	1,415	1,022	1,206	1,294
Misc. mixed shipments	2,728	3,768	4,927	6,998	7,863	8,184	6,240	7,121	8,245

[1] Includes commodity groups and small packaged freight shipments, not shown separately.

Source: Association of American Railroads, Washington, DC, *Freight Commodity Statistics*, annual, (copyright). See also <http://www.aar.org/>.

Table 1134. Railroads, Class-I Cars of Revenue Freight Loaded, 1990 to 2011, and by Commodity Group, 2010 and 2011

[In thousands (16,177 represents 16,177,000). Figures are 52-week totals. Intermodal traffic is excluded]

Year	Car-loads [1]	Commodity group	Carloads		Commodity group	Carloads	
			2010 [1]	2011 [1,2]		2010 [1]	2011 [1,2]
1990	16,177	Coal	6,675	6,700	Metals and products	457	515
2000 [1]	16,354	Metallic ores	230	265	Stone, clay, and glass products	352	370
2005 [1]	16,691	Chemicals, allied products	1,483	1,533	Crushed stone, gravel, sand	809	860
2006 [1]	16,936	Grain	1,151	1,123	Nonmetallic minerals	253	256
2007 [1]	16,564	Motor vehicles and equipment	627	688	Waste and scrap materials	410	405
2008 [1]	16,208	Pulp, paper, allied products	299	312	Lumber, wood products	132	143
2009 [1]	13,563	Primary forest products	83	77	Coke	170	171
2010 [1]	14,567	Food and kindred products	327	327	Petroleum products	333	370
2011 [1,2]	14,875	Grain mill products	515	495	All other carloads	260	268

[1] Excludes 3 Class I railroads. See text this section for definition of Class I railroads. [2] 2011 data are preliminary.

Source: Association of American Railroads, Washington, DC, *Weekly Railroad Traffic*, annual (copyright). See also <http://www.aar.org/>.

Table 1135. Petroleum Pipeline Companies—Characteristics: 1980 to 2011

[173 represents 173,000. Covers pipeline companies operating in interstate commerce and subject to the jurisdiction of the Federal Energy Regulatory Commission]

Item	Unit	1980	1985	1990	1995	2000	2005	2009	2010	2011
Miles of pipeline, total..........	1,000	173	171	168	177	152	131	149	148	150
Gathering lines................	1,000	36	35	32	35	18	14	11	10	13
Trunk lines....................	1,000	136	136	136	142	134	118	137	138	137
Total deliveries.................	Mil. Bbl.	10,600	10,745	11,378	12,862	14,450	12,732	12,791	13,518	13,568
Crude oil.......................	Mil. Bbl.	6,405	6,239	6,563	6,952	6,923	6,675	6,431	7,204	7,032
Products.......................	Mil. Bbl.	4,195	4,506	4,816	5,910	7,527	6,057	6,360	6,314	6,537
Total trunk line traffic...........	Bil. Bbl. miles	3,405	3,342	3,500	3,619	3,508	3,485	3,337	3,565	3,608
Crude oil......................	Bil. Bbl. miles	1,948	1,842	1,891	1,899	1,602	1,571	1,462	1,634	1,653
Products.......................	Bil. Bbl. miles	1,458	1,500	1,609	1,720	1,906	1,914	1,875	1,931	1,955
Carrier property value..........	Mil. dol.	19,752	21,605	25,828	27,460	29,648	29,526	41,565	45,380	49,157
Operating revenues............	Mil. dol.	6,356	7,461	7,149	7,711	7,483	7,917	9,987	11,219	12,562
Net income.....................	Mil. dol.	1,912	2,431	2,340	2,670	2,705	3,076	4,131	4,582	6,109

Source: PennWell Publishing Co., Houston, Texas, *Oil & Gas Journal*, annual (copyright). See also <http://www.ogj.com/>.

Table 1136. U.S. Postal Service Rates for Letters and Postcards: 1991 to 2012

[In dollars. International rates exclude Canada and Mexico]

Domestic mail date of rate change	Letters First ounce	Letters Each added ounce	Post-cards	Express mail— first 1/2 pound	International air mail date of rate change	Letters— first ounce [1]	Post-cards	Aero grammes
1991 (Feb. 3)..........	0.29	0.23	0.19	9.95	**First 1/2 ounce.....**			
1995 (Jan. 1)..........	0.32	0.23	0.20	10.75	1991 (Feb. 3)......	0.50	0.40	0.45
1999 (Jan. 10).........	0.33	0.22	0.20	11.75	1995 (July 9)......	0.60	0.40	0.45
2001 (Jan. 7)..........	0.34	0.21	0.20	12.25	1999 (Jan. 10).....	0.60	0.50	0.50
2001 (July 1)	0.34	0.23	0.21	12.45	**First ounce [1].......**			
2002 (June 30).........	0.37	0.23	0.23	13.65	2001 (Jan. 7)......	0.80	0.70	0.70
2006 (Jan. 8).........	0.39	0.24	0.24	14.40	2006 (Jan. 8)......	0.84	0.75	0.75
2007 (May 14).........	0.41	0.17	0.26	16.25	2007 (May 14).....	0.90	0.90	([2])
2008 (May 12).........	0.42	0.17	0.27	[3] 12.60	2008 (May 12).....	0.94	0.94	([2])
2009 (May 11).........	0.44	0.17	0.28	[4] 13.05	2009 (May 11).....	0.98	0.98	([2])
					2010 (no			
2010 (January 4)......	0.44	0.17	0.28	[5] 13.65	change).............	0.98	0.98	([2])
					2011 (no			
2011 (April 17).........	0.44	0.20	0.29	[6] 13.25	change).............	0.98	0.98	([2])
2012 (January 22).....	0.45	0.20	0.32	[7] 12.95	2012 (Jan. 22).....	1.05	1.05	([2])

[1] International letter prices after the first ounce vary according to the price group that is applicable to each destination country.
[2] Aerogrammes were discontinued on May 14, 2007. [3] On May 12, 2008, the Postal Service initiated a zoned pricing structure for Express Mail. Prices for a mail piece weighing up to a half-pound range from $12.60 to zones 1 and 2 to $19.50 to zone 8. [4] Express Mail prices increased on January 18, 2009. Prices for a mail piece weighing up to a half-pound range from $13.05 to zones 1 and 2 to $21.20 to zone 8. [5] Express Mail prices increased on January 4, 2010. Prices for a mail piece weighing up to a half-pound range from $13.65 to zones 1 and 2 to $22.20 to zone 8. [6] Express Mail prices changed on January 2, 2011. Prices for a mail piece weighing up to a half-pound range from $13.25 to zones 1 and 2 to $26.65 to zone 8. [7] Express Mail prices changed on January 22, 2012. Prices for a mail piece weighing up to a half-pound range from $12.95 to zones 1 and 2 to $28.00 to zone 8.

Source: U.S. Postal Service, *Domestic Rate History* and Price List Notice 123. See also <https://www.usps.com/ship/service-chart.htm>.

Table 1137. U.S. Postal Service—Summary: 1990 to 2011

[166,301 represents 166,301,000,000 except as indicated. For years ending September 30. Includes Puerto Rico and all Island Areas. See text, this section]

Item	1990	1995	2000	2005	2009	2010	2011
Offices, stations, and branches........	**40,067**	**39,149**	**38,060**	**37,142**	**36,496**	**36,222**	**35,756**
Number of post offices....................	28,959	28,392	27,876	27,385	27,161	27,077	26,927
Number of stations and branches..........	11,108	10,757	10,184	9,757	9,335	9,145	8,829
Delivery Points (mil.)..................	(NA)	(NA)	135.9	144.3	150.1	150.9	151.5
Residential............................	(NA)	(NA)	123.9	131.3	136.6	137.5	138.4
City.................................	(NA)	(NA)	76.1	78.5	80.2	80.5	80.8
P.O. Box............................	(NA)	(NA)	15.9	15.6	15.6	15.7	15.9
Rural/highway contract...............	(NA)	(NA)	31.9	37.2	40.8	41.2	41.7
Business.............................	(NA)	(NA)	12.1	13.0	13.5	13.3	13.1
Pieces of mail handled (mil.)...........	**166,301**	**180,734**	**207,882**	**211,743**	**176,744**	**170,860**	**167,934**
Domestic..............................	165,503	179,933	206,782	210,891	175,363	169,471	166,461
First class mail [1].....................	89,270	96,296	103,526	98,071	83,776	78,514	73,521
Priority mail [2, 3]..................	518	869	1,223	888	([2])	([2])	([2])
Express mail [2, 4]..................	59	57	71	56	([2])	([2])	([2])
Periodicals (formerly 2nd class)......	10,680	10,194	10,365	9,070	7,901	7,269	7,077
Standard Mail (formerly Standard A)......	63,725	71,112	90,057	100,942	82,448	82,525	84,692
Package Services (formerly Standard B)...	663	936	1,128	1,166	731	657	675
U.S. Postal Service....................	538	412	363	621	455	438	434
Free for the blind....................	35	52	47	76	62	68	62
Shipping Services Volume [2]...........	(X)	(X)	(X)	(X)	1,381	1,389	1,473
International economy mail (surface) [2]......	166	106	79	23	([2])	([2])	([2])
International airmail [2]................	632	696	1,021	829	([2])	([2])	([2])
Employees, total (1,000)..............	**843**	**875**	**901**	**803**	**712**	**672**	**646**
Career................................	761	753	788	705	623	584	557
Headquarters.........................	2	2	2	3	3	3	3
Headquarters support.................	6	4	6	4	4	5	4
Inspection Service...................	4	4	4	3	3	2	2
Inspector General...................	(X)	(X)	1	1	1	1	1
Field Career..........................	749	743	775	693	612	573	547
Postmasters.........................	27	27	26	25	24	23	22
Supervisors/managers.................	43	35	39	33	29	28	25
Professional, administrative, and technical..........................	10	11	10	9	6	6	5
Clerks...............................	290	274	282	222	178	157	150
Mail handlers........................	51	57	61	56	53	49	47
City carriers........................	236	240	241	228	201	192	184
Motor vehicle operators..............	7	8	9	9	8	7	7
Rural carriers.......................	42	46	57	64	68	67	66
Special delivery messengers..........	2	2	(X)	(X)	(X)	(X)	(X)
Building and equipment maintenance.....	33	38	42	40	40	37	36
Vehicle maintenance..................	5	5	6	5	5	5	5
Other [5]............................	1	2	2	2	(X)	(X)	(X)
Noncareer.............................	83	122	114	98	89	88	89
Casuals..............................	27	26	30	19	4	7	3
Transitional.........................	(X)	32	13	8	17	16	14
Rural substitutes....................	43	50	58	57	55	52	50
Relief/Leave replacements............	12	13	12	12	11	11	9
Nonbargaining temporary..............	(Z)	1	1	1	2	2	2
Compensation and employee benefits (mil. dol.)............................	34,214	41,931	49,532	53,932	50,883	48,909	48,310
Avg. salary per employee (dol.) [6]......	37,570	45,001	50,103	62,635	70,140	72,099	(NA)
Pieces of mail per employee (1,000).......	197	207	231	264	248	254	260
Total revenue (mil. dol.) [7]............	**40,074**	**54,509**	**64,540**	**69,993**	**68,116**	**67,077**	**(NA)**
Operating postal revenue...............	39,201	54,176	64,476	69,798	68,090	67,052	65,711
Mail revenue.........................	37,892	52,490	62,284	66,649	56,950	54,907	53,432
First class mail.....................	24,023	31,955	35,516	36,062	35,883	34,153	32,179
Priority mail [2, 3].................	1,555	3,075	4,837	4,634	([2])	([2])	([2])
Express mail [2, 4].................	630	711	996	872	([2])	([2])	([2])
Periodicals (formerly 2nd class)......	1,509	1,972	2,171	2,161	2,038	1,879	1,821
Standard Mail (formerly Standard A).....	8,082	11,792	15,193	18,954	17,345	17,331	17,826
Package Services (formerly Standard B)........................	919	1,525	1,912	2,201	1,684	1,544	1,606
Shipping Services [2]................	(X)	(X)	(X)	(X)	8,254	8,464	8,994
International economy mail (surface) [2]....	222	205	180	134	([2])	([2])	([2])
International Airmail [2].............	941	1,254	1,477	1,631	([2])	([2])	([2])
Service revenue......................	1,310	1,687	2,191	3,150	2,886	3,681	3,285
Registry [8].........................	174	118	98	77	50	48	45
Certified [8]........................	310	560	385	601	731	791	709
Insurance [8]........................	47	52	109	132	129	128	117
Collect-on-delivery..................	26	21	22	9	(NA)	(NA)	(NA)
Money orders........................	155	196	235	208	190	182	172
Other [8]............................	592	737	1,342	2,122	1,786	2,532	2,242
Operating expenses (million dollars) [9].......	40,490	50,730	62,992	68,283	71,830	75,426	70,634

NA Not available. X Not applicable. Z Fewer than 500. [1] Items mailed at 1st class rates and weighing 11 ounces or less. [2] "Volume" and "Mailing & Shipping Revenue" restructured for the "Postal Accountability and Enhancement Act (PAEA) of 2006." [3] Provides 2 to 3 day delivery service. [4] Overnight delivery of packages weighing up to 70 pounds. [5] Includes discontinued operations, area offices, and nurses. Beginning 2009, nurses are included with clerks, and no "other" employment is reported. [6] For career bargaining unit employees. Includes fringe benefits. [7] Net revenues after refunds of postage. Includes operating reimbursements, stamped envelope purchases, indemnity claims, and miscellaneous revenue and expenditure offsets. Shown in year which gave rise to the earnings. [8] Beginning 2000, return receipt revenue broken out from registry, certified, and insurance and included in "other." [9] Shown in year in which obligation was incurred.

Source: U.S. Postal Service, *Annual Report of the Postmaster General and Comprehensive Statement on Postal Operations*, annual, and unpublished data. See also <http://about.usps.com/strategic-planning/future-postal-service/publications.htm>.

Information and Communications

This section presents statistics on the various information and communications media: publishing, including newspapers, periodicals, books, and software; motion pictures, sound recordings, broadcasting, and telecommunications; and information services, such as libraries. Statistics on computer use and Internet access are also included.

Information industry—The U.S. Census Bureau's *Service Annual Survey, Information Services Sector*, provides estimates of operating revenue of taxable firms and revenues and expenses of firms exempt from federal taxes for industries in the information sector of the economy. Similar estimates were previously issued in the *Annual Survey of Communications Services*. Data are based on the North American Industry Classification System (NAICS). The information sector is a newly created economic sector. It comprises establishments engaged in the following processes: (a) producing and distributing information and cultural products, (b) providing the means to transmit or distribute these products as well as data or communications, and (c) processing data. It includes establishments previously classified in the Standard Industrial Classification (SIC) in manufacturing (publishing); transportation, communications, and utilities (telecommunications and broadcasting); and services (software publishing, motion picture production, data processing, online information services, and libraries).

This new sector is comprised of industries which existed previously, were revised from previous industry definitions, or are completely new industries. Among those which existed previously are newspaper publishers, motion picture and video production, and online information services. Revised industries include book publishers, libraries, and archives.

Newly created industries include database and directory publishers, record production, music publishers, sound recording studios, cable networks, wired telecommunications carriers, paging, and satellite telecommunications.

Data from 1998 to 2003 are based on the 1997 NAICS; beginning 2004, data are variously based on 2002 and 2007 NAICS. Major revisions in many communications industries affect the comparability of these data. The following URL contains detailed information about NAICS, see <http://www.census.gov/eos/www/naics/>. See also the text in Section 15, Business Enterprise.

Several industries in the information sectors have been consolidated: paging is now included in Wireless Telecommunications Carriers (except Satellite). Cable and other program distribution and most Internet service providers are now included in Wired Telecommunications Carriers.

The 1997 Economic Census was the first economic census to cover the new information sector of the economy. The census, conducted every 5 years, for the years ending "2" and "7," provides information on the number of establishments, receipts, payroll, and paid employees for the United States and various geographic levels. The most recent reports are from the 2007 Economic Census. This census was conducted in accordance with the 2007 NAICS.

The Federal Communications Commission (FCC), established in 1934, regulates wire and radio communications. Only the largest carriers and holding companies file annual financial reports which are publically available. The FCC has jurisdiction over interstate and foreign communication services but not over intrastate or local services. Also, the gross operating revenues of the telephone carriers reporting publically available data annually to the FCC are estimated to cover about 90 percent of the revenues of all U.S. telephone companies. Data are not service comparable with Census Bureau's *Annual Survey* because of coverage and different accounting practices for those telephone companies which report to the FCC.

Reports filed by the broadcasting industry cover all radio and television stations operating in the United States. The private radio services represent the largest and most diverse group of licensees regulated by the FCC. These services provide voice, data communications, point-to-point, and point-to-multipoint radio communications for fixed and mobile communicators. Major users of these services are small businesses, the aviation industry, the maritime trades, the land transportation industry, the manufacturing industry, state and local public safety and governmental authorities, emergency medical service providers, amateur radio operators, and personal radio operations (CB and the General Mobile Radio Service). The FCC also licenses entities as private and common carriers. Private and common carriers provide fixed and land mobile communications service on a for-profit basis. Principal sources of wire, radio, and television data are the FCC's Annual Report and its annual *Statistics of Communications Common Carriers* at <http://fcc.gov/wcb/iatd/stats.html/>.

Statistics on publishing are available from the Census Bureau, as well as from various private agencies. Editor & Publisher Co., New York, NY, presents annual data on the number and circulation of daily and Sunday newspapers in its *International Year Book*. The Book Industry Study Group, New York, NY, collects data on books sold and domestic consumer expenditures. Data on academic and public libraries are collected by the Institute of Museums and Library Services. Data on Internet use by adults are collected by the Pew Internet and American Life Project, Washington, DC, and Gfk Mediamark Research and Intelligence, LLC., New York, NY.

Statistical reliability—For a discussion of statistical collection and estimation, sampling procedures, and measures of statistical reliability applicable to Census Bureau data, see Appendix III.

Table 1138. Information Industries—Type of Establishment, Employees, and Payroll: 2009

[(3,288.1 represents 3,288,100). Excludes self-employed individuals, employees of private households, railroad employees, agricultural production employees, and most government employees. For more information see source and Appendix III]

Industry	2007 NAICS code [1]	Establishments				Employ-ees [6] (1,000)	Annual payroll (mil. dol.)
		Total [2]	Corpora-tions [3]	Sole proprietor-ships [4]	Non profits [5]		
Information industries............................	**51**	**135,726**	**71,740**	**7,486**	**5,081**	**3,288.1**	**225,101**
Publishing industries......................................	511	29,126	13,563	1,613	853	963.3	74,899
Newspaper, periodical, book, and database publishers...	5111	21,479	8,706	1,487	835	593.3	30,621
Newspaper publishers................................	51111	8,041	3,837	737	183	299.1	12,045
Periodical publishers................................	51112	7,600	2,629	412	364	143.8	9,440
Book publishers......................................	51113	3,038	1,029	196	256	83.7	5,349
Database and directory publishers.................	51114	1,731	923	62	10	45.7	2,736
Other publishers......................................	51119	1,069	288	80	22	20.9	1,052
Greeting card publishers.......................	511191	99	28	6	(X)	11.0	564
All other publishers..............................	511199	970	260	74	22	9.8	487
Software publishers.....................................	5112	7,647	4,857	126	18	370.0	44,278
Motion picture and sound recording industries.......	512	23,921	7,511	1,324	535	340.1	15,998
Motion picture and video industries................	5121	20,250	6,509	1,032	444	316.4	13,931
Motion picture and video production..............	51211	12,384	3,477	549	246	146.5	9,929
Motion picture and video distribution.............	51212	509	199	13	15	8.4	699
Motion picture and video exhibition..............	51213	4,947	2,101	349	174	136.8	1,432
Motion picture theaters (except drive-ins)........	512131	4,687	2,037	288	173	135.7	1,410
Drive-in motion picture theaters.................	512132	260	64	61	1	1.1	22
Post production and other motion picture and video industries.................................	51219	2,410	732	121	9	24.6	1,871
Teleproduction and other postproduction services...........................	512191	2,147	645	95	6	21.5	1,632
Other motion picture and video industries........	512199	263	87	26	3	3.1	239
Sound recording industries...........................	5122	3,671	1,002	292	91	23.6	2,067
Record production....................................	51221	349	100	27	6	1.1	100
Integrated record production/distribution..........	51222	430	157	25	7	7.8	1,117
Music publishers.....................................	51223	749	237	62	6	5.9	429
Sound recording studios.............................	51224	1,674	385	157	9	5.6	265
Other sound recording industries.................	51229	469	123	21	63	3.2	155
Broadcasting (except Internet)........................	515	9,782	4,608	384	1,173	272.8	17,793
Radio and television broadcasting...................	5151	9,111	4,358	355	1,021	232.7	13,828
Radio broadcasting..................................	51511	6,890	3,142	283	718	109.8	5,501
Radio networks....................................	515111	1,051	280	75	192	14.0	919
Radio stations.....................................	515112	5,839	2,862	208	526	95.8	4,582
Television broadcasting.............................	51512	2,221	1,216	72	303	122.9	8,327
Cable and other subscription programming.........	5152	671	250	29	152	40.1	3,964
Telecommunications...................................	517	52,092	36,564	3,372	310	1,185.3	77,367
Wired telecommunications carriers...................	5171	33,975	30,464	263	258	840.5	55,669
Wireless telecommunications carriers (except satellite).....................................	5172	11,795	3,753	2,809	10	277.6	17,055
Satellite telecommunications........................	5174	574	260	23	5	8.5	771
Other telecommunications...........................	5179	5,748	2,087	277	37	58.7	3,872
Telecommunications resellers.....................	517911	2,263	823	89	2	22.4	1,275
Data processing, hosting, and related services...	518	12,410	6,667	436	97	387.2	26,992
Other information services............................	519	8,395	2,827	357	2,113	139.6	12,053
News syndicates......................................	51911	514	352	17	10	8.9	852
Libraries and archives................................	51912	2,257	97	92	1,989	29.0	804
Internet publishing and broadcasting and Web search portals..................................	51913	4,924	2,175	205	104	91.1	9,891
All other information services........................	51919	700	203	43	10	10.5	506

X Not applicable. [1] 2007 North American Industry Classification System; see text, this section and Section 15. [2] Includes other types of establishments, not shown separately. [3] An incorporated business that is granted a charter recognizing it as a separate legal entity having its own privileges, and liabilities distinct from those of its members. [4] An unincorporated business with a sole owner. [5] An organization that does not distribute surplus funds to its owners or shareholders, but instead uses surplus funds to help pursue its goals. Most non-profit organizations are exempt from income taxes. [6] For employees on the payroll for the pay period including March 12.

Source: U.S. Census Bureau, "County Business Patterns," June 2011, <http://www.census.gov/econ/cbp/index.html>.

Table 1139. Information Sector Services—Estimated Revenue and Expenses: 2008 to 2010

[In millions of dollars (1,108,349 represents $1,108,349,000). For taxable and tax-exempt employer firms. Estimates have been adjusted to the results of the 2007 Economic Census. Based on the Service Annual Survey and administrative data; see Appendix III]

Industry	2002 NAICS [1] code	Operating revenue			Operating expenses		
		2008	2009	2010	2008	2009	2010
Information industries..............................	**51**	**1,108,349**	**1,074,959**	**1,110,225**	**866,043**	**845,267**	**862,505**
Publishing industries (except Internet)................	511	284,613	264,194	265,718	204,389	187,951	188,787
Newspaper, periodical, book, and directory publishers..................................	5111	141,896	125,213	120,293	109,948	98,185	94,110
Newspaper publishers.............................	51111	43,919	36,358	34,695	40,380	34,558	31,731
Periodical publishers...............................	51112	44,985	39,099	38,395	33,931	30,390	29,344
Book publishers...................................	51113	28,032	27,404	28,121	17,459	16,268	16,403
Directory and mailing list publishers..............	51114	18,371	16,670	13,475	13,633	12,755	12,617
Other publishers..................................	51119	6,589	5,682	5,607	4,545	4,214	4,015
Greeting card publishers........................	511191	4,443	3,862	3,852	2,878	2,769	2,655
All other publishers.............................	511199	2,146	1,820	1,755	1,667	1,445	1,360
Software publishers..................................	5112	142,717	138,981	145,425	94,441	89,766	94,677
Motion picture and sound recording industries.......	512	95,271	90,398	95,118	82,097	79,134	83,125
Motion picture and video industries.................	5121	80,004	75,979	81,331	70,343	68,366	72,591
Motion picture and video production and distribution...	51211,12	62,161	57,910	62,567	55,124	53,113	56,834
Motion picture and video exhibition................	51213	12,782	13,293	13,454	10,739	10,855	11,171
Motion picture theaters (except drive-ins)........	512131	12,687	13,198	13,363	10,687	10,784	11,096
Drive-in motion picture theaters.................	512132	(S)	(S)	(S)	(S)	(S)	(S)
Postproduction services and other motion picture and video industries.......................	51219	5,061	4,776	5,310	4,480	4,398	4,586
Teleproduction and other post-production services..............................	512191	4,361	4,127	4,715	3,889	3,818	4,028
Other motion picture and video industries........	512199	700	649	595	591	580	558
Sound recording industries...........................	5122	15,267	14,419	13,787	11,754	10,768	10,534
Record production...................................	51221	351	425	453	284	372	407
Integrated record production/distribution..........	51222	8,953	8,665	8,258	8,014	7,358	7,309
Music publishers...................................	51223	4,713	4,155	3,793	2,352	2,009	1,752
Sound recording studios............................	51224	810	749	839	743	668	737
Other sound recording industries...................	51229	(S)	425	444	(S)	361	(S)
Broadcasting (except Internet)........................	515	104,584	98,934	107,520	76,408	71,782	75,789
Radio and television broadcasting....................	5151	55,015	47,503	52,352	44,997	40,443	42,599
Radio broadcasting.................................	51511	18,253	15,950	17,018	15,393	13,590	13,589
Radio networks...................................	515111	4,341	4,307	4,883	4,714	4,099	4,298
Radio stations...................................	515112	13,912	11,643	12,135	10,679	9,491	9,291
Television broadcasting.............................	51512	36,762	31,553	35,334	29,604	26,853	29,010
Cable and other subscription programming.........	5152	49,569	51,431	55,168	31,411	31,339	33,190
Internet publishing and broadcasting..................	516	17,763	19,111	21,273	15,457	16,731	18,770
Telecommunications...................................	517	498,058	495,062	507,533	397,783	402,093	405,380
Wired telecommunications carriers...................	5171	184,197	172,675	168,759	153,890	153,093	149,482
Wireless telecommunications carriers (except satellite)...................................	5172	181,475	185,684	195,525	136,943	138,687	142,473
Paging...	517211	846	742	710	654	561	530
Cellular and other wireless telecommunications................................	517212	180,629	184,942	194,815	136,289	138,126	141,943
Telecommunications resellers........................	5173	11,105	10,044	9,817	6,787	6,550	6,520
Satellite telecommunications........................	5174	4,767	5,203	5,296	3,779	4,148	4,096
Cable and other program distribution................	5175	109,351	114,327	121,300	90,568	94,035	97,354
Other telecommunications...........................	5179	(S)	7,129	6,836	(S)	5,580	5,455
Internet service providers, Web search portals, and data processing services.......................	518	101,411	100,719	106,582	84,732	82,435	85,514
Internet service providers and Web search portals...	5181	29,713	29,105	30,426	18,274	19,782	20,932
Internet service providers........................	518111	10,614	10,441	9,974	8,169	9,152	9,259
Web search portals..............................	518112	19,099	18,664	20,452	10,105	10,630	11,673
Data processing, hosting, and related services..	5182	71,698	71,614	76,156	66,458	62,653	64,582
Other information services............................	519	6,649	6,541	6,481	5,177	5,141	5,140
News syndicates.....................................	51911	2,092	1,953	1,960	1,719	1,589	1,530
Libraries and archives...............................	51912	2,034	2,016	1,897	1,725	1,760	1,760
Other information services...........................	51919	2,523	2,572	2,624	1,733	1,792	1,850

S Data do not meet publication standards. [1] North American Industry Classification System (NAICS), 2002; see text, Section 15.

Source: U.S. Census Bureau, "Service Annual Survey 2010: Information Sector Services," February 2012, <http://www.census.gov/econ/www/servmenu.html>.

Table 1140. Information Industries—Establishments, Revenue, Payroll, and Employees by Kind of Business: 2007

[For establishments with payroll (1,072,343, represents $1,072,343,000,000). Based on the 2007 Economic Census; see Appendix III]

Kind of business	2007 NAICS code [1]	Establish-ments	Receipts (mil. dol.)	Annual payroll (mil. dol.)	Paid employees (1,000)
Information industries...............................	**51**	**141,566**	**1,072,343**	**228,837**	**3,497**
Publishing industries (except Internet)................................	511	30,958	282,224	80,867	1,093
Newspaper, periodical, book, & directory publishers...............	5111	22,683	146,823	34,504	706
Software publishers..	5112	8,275	135,401	46,363	387
Motion picture & sound recording industries.........................	512	23,891	94,986	17,635	336
Motion picture & video industries................................	5121	20,164	79,797	15,494	309
Sound recording industries.....................................	5122	3,727	15,189	2,142	27
Broadcasting (except Internet)...................................	515	10,188	99,919	18,076	295
Cable & other subscription programming...........................	5152	717	44,926	3,751	46
Telecommunications..	517	51,999	491,124	75,401	1,251
Wired telecommunications carriers...............................	5171	33,548	290,781	54,192	885
Wireless telecommunications carriers (except satellite)...........	5172	11,973	170,584	16,201	289
Satellite telecommunications....................................	5174	823	4,450	793	10
Other telecommunications.......................................	5179	5,655	25,309	4,216	67
Data processing, hosting, and related services.....................	518	17,129	66,652	26,428	394
Other information services.......................................	519	7,401	37,438	10,428	128

[1] North American Industry Classification System, 2007; see text, this section and Section 15.

Source: U.S. Census Bureau, "2007 Economic Census; Geographic Area Series: Summary Statistics for the United States, EC0751A1, (2007 NAICS Basis)," June 2010, <http://www.census.gov/econ/census07/>.

Table 1141. Information Industries—Establishments, Employees, and Payroll by State: 2007

[(228,837 represents 228,837,000,000, for payroll data). Based on 2007 Economic Census and the 2007 Nonemployer Statistics. Data are for North American Industry Classification System (NAICS) 2007 code 51]

State	Establish-ments	Annual payroll (mil. dol)	Paid employ ees [1]	Non-employer establish-ments	State	Establish-ments	Annual payroll (mil. dol)	Paid employ ees [1]	Non-employer establish-ments
U.S..........	**141,566**	**228,837**	**3,496,773**	**307,143**	MO.........	2,627	3,880	73,040	4,563
AL.............	1,700	1,875	40,054	2,760	MT.........	638	343	9,500	940
AK.............	407	374	6,754	527	NE.........	957	984	20,217	1,299
AZ.............	2,275	3,006	52,573	5,325	NV.........	1,109	973	17,914	3,121
AR.............	1,034	1,343	26,074	1,618	NH.........	790	1,149	15,482	1,542
CA.............	21,068	48,147	556,535	54,910	NJ.........	4,092	8,950	134,356	9,712
CO.............	3,183	5,663	84,564	7,036	NM.........	828	495	13,987	1,606
CT.............	1,834	2,556	40,345	4,036	NY.........	11,326	22,538	301,340	27,846
DE.............	383	457	8,565	683	NC.........	3,481	4,263	76,413	7,368
DC.............	749	2,129	24,499	1,359	NC.........	367	332	7,124	411
FL.............	8,296	9,663	175,382	20,284	OH.........	4,199	5,178	97,360	9,042
GA.............	4,328	8,156	122,496	9,370	OK.........	1,585	1,463	32,481	2,740
HI.............	622	510	10,083	1,234	OR.........	1,992	2,055	39,258	4,139
ID.............	717	528	15,163	1,318	PA.........	5,302	7,774	137,115	10,094
IL.............	5,696	8,630	136,589	11,757	RI.........	394	416	8,059	964
IN.............	2,282	2,089	45,786	4,510	SC.........	1,410	1,581	33,052	2,945
IA.............	1,590	1,426	34,397	2,168	SD.........	437	313	7,296	588
KS.............	1,502	3,064	52,737	2,047	TN.........	2,491	2,370	50,778	6,142
KY.............	1,594	1,252	33,996	2,648	TX.........	9,541	15,460	250,410	21,144
LA.............	1,455	1,361	30,537	2,695	UT.........	1,412	1,762	33,310	3,409
ME.............	777	523	13,520	1,260	VT.........	514	255	6,048	839
MD.............	2,571	3,764	63,081	6,993	VA.........	4,064	7,533	104,147	7,545
MA.............	3,772	8,623	110,038	7,997	WA.........	3,301	11,277	111,840	6,557
MI.............	3,791	4,314	77,639	7,800	WV.........	679	387	10,285	897
MN.............	2,772	4,232	70,314	5,642	WI.........	2,286	2,625	54,179	3,889
MS.............	1,017	646	15,902	1,367	WY.........	329	151	4,159	457

[1] Number of paid employees for pay period including March 12.

Source: U.S. Census Bureau, "2007 Economic Census, Geographic Area Series," April 2010, <http://www.census.gov/econ/census07/>, and "Nonemployer Statistics," August 2009, <http://www.census.gov/econ/nonemployer/index.html>.

Table 1142. Utilization and Number of Selected Media: 2000 to 2010

[100.2 represents 100,200,000]

Media	Unit	2000	2002	2003	2004	2005	2006	2007	2008	2009	2010
Households with—											
Telephones [1]	Millions	100.2	104.0	107.1	106.4	107.0	108.8	112.2	112.7	114.0	(NA)
Telephone service [1]	Percent	94.1	95.3	94.7	93.5	92.9	93.4	94.9	95.0	95.7	96.0
Land line households with											
wireless telephone [2]	Percent	(X)	(X)	(X)	(X)	42.4	45.6	58.9	58.5	59.4	58.1
Wireless-only [2]	Percent	(X)	(X)	(X)	(X)	7.3	10.5	13.6	17.5	22.7	26.6
Radio [3]	Millions	100.5	105.1	106.7	108.3	109.9	110.5	110.5	115.6	114.0	115.0
Percent of total households	Percent	99.0	99.0	99.0	99.0	99.0	99.0	99.0	99.0	99.0	99.0
Average number of sets	Number	5.6	5.6	8.0	8.0	8.0	8.0	8.0	8.0	8.0	8.0
Total broadcast stations [4,5]	Number	(NA)	26,319	26,613	26,254	27,354	27,807	29,593	29,832	30,503	30,630
Radio stations	Number	(NA)	13,331	13,563	13,525	13,660	13,837	13,977	14,253	14,420	14,619
AM stations	Number	4,685	4,804	4,794	4,774	4,757	4,754	4,776	4,786	4,790	4,782
FM commercial	Number	5,892	6,173	6,217	6,218	6,231	6,266	6,309	6,427	6,479	6,526
FM educational	Number	(NA)	2,354	2,552	2,533	2,672	2,817	2,892	3,040	3,151	3,311
Television stations [4]	Number	1,663	1,719	1,733	1,748	1,750	1,756	1,759	1,759	1,782	1,781
Commercial	Number	1,288	1,338	1,352	1,366	1,370	1,376	1,379	1,378	1,392	1,390
VHF TV band	Number	567	583	585	589	588	587	583	582	373	368
UHF TV band	Number	721	755	767	777	782	789	796	796	1,019	1,022
Educational	Number	(NA)	381	381	382	380	380	380	381	390	391
VHF TV band	Number	(NA)	127	127	125	126	128	128	129	107	107
UHF TV band	Number	(NA)	254	254	257	254	252	252	252	283	284
Broadband subscribers: [6]											
Total fixed broadband [7]	Millions	6.8	19.4	27.7	37.4	47.8	60.2	70.2	75.7	80.0	84.5
Mobile broadband	Millions	(NA)	(NA)	(NA)	(NA)	(NA)	(NA)	(NA)	26.5	51.6	84.4

NA Not available. [1] As of November. Based on Current Population Survey. For occupied housing units. Source: Federal Communications Commission, *Telephone Subscribership in the United States*, May 2011. [2] From January to June. Based on National Health Interview Survey for families living in the same housing unit. Source: National Center for Health Statistics, *Wireless Substitution: Early Release of Estimates From the National Health Interview Survey*, July–December 2011. See also <http://www.cdc.gov/nchs/nhis/releases.htm>. A "family" can be an individual or a group of two or more related persons living together in the same housing unit (a "household"). [3] Source: Radio Advertising Bureau, New York, NY, *Radio Marketing Guide*, annual (copyright). [4] As of December, 31. Source: Federal Communications Commission, *Broadcast Station Totals Index*, <http://transition.fcc.gov/mb/audio/BroadcastStationTotals.html>. [5] Includes Class A, Low Power TV, UHF and VHF Translators; FM Translators and Boosters; and Low Power FM stations. [6] As of December. Connections over 200/kbps in at least one direction. Source: Federal Communications Commission, Wireline Competition Bureau, "Internet Access Services," June 2011. FCC Form 477 gathers standardized information about subscribership to high-speed Internet access services from telephone companies, cable system operators, terrestrial wireless service providers, satellite service providers, and any other facilities-based providers of advanced telecommunications capability. Includes wireline, cable modem, and satellite and fixed wireless. [7] Includes aDSI, sDSL, cable modem, FTTP, satellite, fixed wireless, power line, and other.

Source: Compiled from sources mentioned in footnotes.

Table 1143. Multimedia Audiences—Summary: 2011

[In percent, except total (230,416 represents 230,416,000). As of fall 2011. For persons 18 years old and over. Represents the percent of persons participating during the prior week, except as indicated. Based on sample and subject to sampling error; see source for details]

Item	Total population (1,000)	Television viewing	Television prime time viewing	Cable viewing [1]	Radio listening	Newspaper reading	Accessed Internet [2]
Total	**230,416**	**92.56**	**82.47**	**82.13**	**81.80**	**63.01**	**78.72**
18 to 24 years old	29,441	88.22	70.95	79.04	84.72	53.17	93.64
25 to 34 years old	41,294	89.30	78.68	78.05	87.22	55.10	91.06
35 to 44 years old	40,658	90.89	81.52	80.60	87.57	61.54	86.26
45 to 54 years old	44,642	93.56	84.63	83.47	86.62	65.31	81.50
55 to 64 years old	35,570	95.58	87.59	86.52	81.35	68.39	76.23
65 years old and over	38,811	97.15	89.08	84.86	62.62	72.85	45.44
Male	111,472	92.35	81.48	81.65	82.87	62.59	78.32
Female	118,944	92.76	83.40	82.58	80.79	63.40	79.10
Not high school graduate	31,650	94.17	82.22	70.72	73.21	48.23	40.93
High school graduate	71,520	93.29	83.29	82.79	79.91	62.06	69.98
Attended college	64,372	92.25	82.09	84.40	84.91	64.89	90.15
College graduate	62,874	91.24	82.07	84.79	85.08	69.61	95.99
Household income:							
Less than $10,000	11,678	89.41	80.73	63.38	70.22	51.16	53.25
$10,000 to $19,999	20,163	90.23	79.89	65.67	72.23	54.42	47.89
$20,000 to $29,999	23,130	92.45	81.71	75.05	73.04	58.53	58.89
$30,000 to $34,999	11,515	92.64	83.93	77.56	77.25	56.90	67.80
$35,000 to $39,999	11,164	92.47	82.48	78.14	80.57	64.77	72.80
$40,000 to $49,999	20,210	92.66	80.89	82.35	79.82	62.35	77.83
$50,000 to $74,999	44,241	93.37	84.08	84.85	84.06	65.22	83.86
$75,000 to $99,999	30,891	92.92	82.47	88.60	88.42	65.57	91.55
$100,000 or more	57,423	93.21	83.07	90.62	87.57	68.27	95.50

[1] In the past 7 days. [2] In the last 30 days.

Source: GfK Mediamark Research & Intelligence, LLC, New York, NY, Multimedia Audiences, fall 2011 (copyright). See <http://www.gfkmri.com>.

Table 1144. Publishing Industries—Estimated Revenue by Source and Media Type: 2006 to 2010

[In millions of dollars (269,907 represents $269,907,000,000). For taxable and tax-exempt employer firms. Covers NAICS 5111. Estimates have been adjusted to the results of the 2007 Economic Census. Based on the North American Industry Classification System (NAICS), 2007. See text, this section and Section 15, and Appendix III]

Source of revenue and media type	2006	2007	2008	2009	2010
Publishing industries (except Internet) [1]	**269,907**	**282,223**	**284,613**	**264,194**	**265,718**
Newspaper publishers	**48,949**	**47,563**	**43,919**	**36,358**	**34,695**
General newspapers	41,963	39,947	36,808	29,792	28,653
Subscription and sales	8,674	8,288	8,323	7,962	8,285
Advertising space	33,289	31,659	28,485	21,830	20,368
Specialized newspapers	1,877	2,091	2,029	1,815	1,675
Subscription and sales	(S)	(S)	(S)	(S)	(S)
Advertising space	1,538	1,724	1,678	1,475	(S)
Other operating revenue	5,109	5,525	5,082	4,751	4,367
Printing services	1,401	1,371	1,271	1,249	1,158
Distribution services	2,009	1,956	1,681	1,419	1,526
All other	1,699	2,198	2,130	2,083	1,683
Print newspapers	41,756	39,874	36,473	30,043	28,399
Online newspapers	1,449	1,655	2,045	1,277	1,699
Other media newspapers	635	509	319	287	230
Periodical publishers	**44,757**	**46,003**	**44,985**	**39,099**	**38,395**
General interest periodicals	22,501	22,425	20,714	17,023	15,505
Subscription and sales	7,356	7,281	6,707	6,111	5,817
Advertising space	15,145	15,144	14,007	10,912	9,688
Professional and academic periodicals	7,955	8,156	7,510	6,440	6,985
Subscription and sales	4,830	4,781	4,166	4,097	4,464
Advertising space	3,125	3,375	3,344	2,343	2,521
Other periodicals	2,653	3,029	2,853	2,413	2,020
Subscription and sales	1,345	1,175	985	863	746
Advertising space	1,308	1,854	1,868	1,550	1,274
Other operating revenue	11,648	12,393	13,908	13,223	13,885
Printing services for others	1,269	1,271	1,264	1,094	1,125
Licensing of rights to content	430	454	445	412	331
All other	9,949	10,668	12,199	11,717	12,429
Print	29,614	29,961	26,891	21,988	20,326
Online	2,889	2,776	3,233	2,903	3,153
Other media	606	873	953	985	(S)
Book publishers	**26,722**	**27,807**	**28,032**	**27,404**	**28,121**
Books, print	23,012	23,578	23,825	22,916	23,445
Textbooks	10,100	10,652	11,117	9,838	10,192
Children's books	2,397	2,636	2,524	2,565	2,607
General reference books	862	794	754	693	704
Professional, technical, and scholarly books	3,007	2,926	3,138	3,887	4,269
Adult trade books	6,646	6,570	6,292	5,933	5,673
All other operating revenue	3,710	4,229	4,207	4,488	4,676
Print books	21,268	21,515	21,587	20,709	20,432
Online books	864	1,009	1,143	1,295	2,055
Other media books	880	1,054	1,095	912	958
Directory and mailing list publishers	**17,617**	**18,515**	**18,371**	**16,670**	**13,475**
Directories	12,594	12,632	11,730	10,139	7,113
Subscription and sales	318	315	330	281	218
Advertising space	12,276	12,317	11,400	9,858	6,895
Database and other collections	3,068	3,779	4,121	4,280	4,132
Subscription and sales	2,416	2,884	2,946	2,949	2,905
Advertising space	652	895	1,175	1,331	1,227
Other operating revenue	1,955	2,104	2,520	2,251	(S)
Rental or sale of mailing lists	542	693	705	624	(S)
All other	1,413	(S)	1,815	(S)	(S)
Print directories, databases, and other collections of information	12,126	12,153	11,349	9,844	6,712
Online directories, databases, and other collections of information	2,767	3,390	3,805	4,199	4,204
Other media directories, databases, and other collections of information	769	868	697	376	(S)

S Figure does not meet publication standards. [1] Includes other industries not shown separately.

Source: U.S. Census Bureau, "Service Annual Survey 2010: Information Sector Services," February 2012, <http://www.census.gov/econ/www/servmenu.html>.

Table 1145. Daily and Sunday Newspapers—Number and Circulation: 1970 to 2009

[Number of newspapers as of February 1 the following year. Circulation figures as of September 30 of year shown (62.1 represents 62,100,000). For English language newspapers only]

Type	1970	1980	1990	2000	2002	2003	2004	2005	2006	2007	2008	2009
NUMBER												
Daily: Total [1]	1,748	1,745	1,611	1,480	1,457	1,456	1,457	1,452	1,437	1,422	1,408	1,397
Morning	334	387	559	766	777	787	814	817	833	867	872	869
Evening	1,429	1,388	1,084	727	692	680	653	645	614	565	546	528
Sunday	586	736	863	917	913	917	915	914	907	907	902	919
NET PAID CIRCULATION (mil.)												
Daily: Total [1]	62.1	62.2	62.3	55.8	55.2	55.2	54.6	53.3	52.3	50.7	48.6	46.3
Morning	25.9	29.4	41.3	46.8	46.6	46.9	46.9	46.1	45.4	44.5	42.8	40.8
Evening	36.2	32.8	21.0	9.0	8.6	8.3	7.7	7.2	6.9	6.2	5.8	5.5
Sunday	49.2	54.7	62.6	59.4	58.8	58.5	57.8	55.3	53.2	51.2	49.1	46.8
PER CAPITA CIRCULATION [2]												
Daily: Total [1]	0.30	0.27	0.25	0.20	0.19	0.19	0.19	0.18	0.18	0.17	0.16	0.15
Morning	0.13	0.13	0.17	0.17	0.16	0.16	0.16	0.16	0.15	0.15	0.14	0.13
Evening	0.18	0.14	0.08	0.03	0.03	0.03	0.03	0.02	0.02	0.02	0.02	0.02
Sunday	0.24	0.24	0.25	0.21	0.20	0.20	0.20	0.19	0.18	0.17	0.16	0.15

[1] All-day newspapers are counted in both morning and evening columns but only once in total. Circulation is divided equally between morning and evening. [2] Based on U.S. Census Bureau estimated resident population as of July 1.

Source: Editor & Publisher Co., New York, NY, *Editor & Publisher International Year Book*, annual (copyright). See also <http://www.editorandpublisher.com/>.

Table 1146. Daily and Sunday Newspapers—Number and Circulation, 1991 to 2009, and by State, 2009

[Number of newspapers as of February 1 the following year. Circulation as of September 30 (60,687 represents 60,687,000). For English language newspapers only. California, New York, Massachusetts, and Virginia Sunday newspapers include national circulation]

State	Daily Number	Daily Circulation [1] Net paid (1,000)	Daily Circulation [1] Per capita [2]	Sunday Number	Sunday Net paid circulation [1] (1,000s)	State	Daily Number	Daily Circulation [1] Net paid (1,000)	Daily Circulation [1] Per capita [2]	Sunday Number	Sunday Net paid circulation [1] (1,000s)
Total, 1991	1,586	60,687	0.24	875	62,068	IA	37	518	0.17	13	553
Total, 1992	1,570	60,164	0.23	891	62,160	KS	35	331	0.12	13	297
Total, 1993	1,556	59,812	0.23	884	62,566	KY	22	486	0.11	14	528
Total, 1994	1,548	59,305	0.23	886	62,294	LA	24	530	0.12	18	579
Total, 1995	1,533	58,193	0.22	888	61,529	ME	7	186	0.14	4	151
Total, 1996	1,520	56,983	0.21	890	60,798	MD	10	390	0.07	8	527
Total, 1997	1,509	56,728	0.21	903	60,484	MA	32	1,073	0.16	16	1,026
Total, 1998	1,489	56,182	0.20	898	60,066	MI	48	1,372	0.14	28	1,660
Total, 1999	1,483	55,979	0.20	905	59,894	MN	25	754	0.14	15	926
Total, 2000	1,480	55,773	0.20	917	59,421	MS	22	293	0.10	19	305
Total, 2001	1,468	55,578	0.19	913	59,090	MO	42	747	0.12	22	1,000
Total, 2002	1,457	55,186	0.19	913	58,780	MT	11	172	0.18	7	172
Total, 2003	1,456	55,185	0.19	917	58,495	NE	15	348	0.19	6	322
Total, 2004	1,457	54,626	0.19	915	57,753	NV	6	248	0.09	5	281
Total, 2005	1,452	53,345	0.18	914	55,270	NH	9	163	0.12	8	184
Total, 2006	1,437	52,329	0.18	907	53,175	NJ	17	906	0.10	14	1,103
Total, 2007	1,422	50,742	0.17	907	51,246	NM	17	244	0.12	12	243
Total, 2008	1,408	48,598	0.16	902	49,115	NY	60	5,981	0.31	44	4,374
						NC	46	1,042	0.11	38	1,193
Total, 2009	**1,397**	**46,278**	**0.15**	**919**	**46,895**	ND	10	146	0.23	7	147
AL	24	537	0.11	20	605	OH	82	1,836	0.16	42	2,106
AK	7	87	0.12	4	89	OK	37	485	0.13	30	580
AZ	16	579	0.09	12	733	OR	18	541	0.14	12	560
AR	25	421	0.15	15	485	PA	80	2,349	0.19	43	2,600
CA	83	6,041	0.16	59	4,737	RI	6	142	0.14	3	173
CO	29	779	0.16	15	840	SC	16	499	0.11	14	585
CT	17	526	0.15	13	614	SD	11	132	0.16	4	110
DE	1	105	0.12	2	130	TN	26	731	0.12	19	851
DC	2	650	1.08	2	868	TX	81	2,105	0.08	78	2,714
FL	37	2,660	0.14	36	3,347	UT	6	307	0.11	6	355
GA	34	753	0.08	29	1,022	VT	9	104	0.17	4	82
HI	4	235	0.18	6	252	VA	26	2,937	0.37	20	861
ID	11	187	0.12	9	261	WA	22	645	0.10	17	1,303
IL	63	1,753	0.14	30	1,980	WV	20	334	0.18	15	424
IN	67	1,082	0.17	27	1,118	WI	33	724	0.13	17	870
						WY	9	82	0.15	5	67

[1] Circulation figures based on the principal community served by a newspaper which is not necessarily the same location as the publisher's office. [2] Per capita based on estimated resident population as of July 1.

Source: Editor & Publisher Co., New York, NY, *Editor & Publisher International Year Book*, annual (copyright). See also <http://www.editorandpublisher.com>.

Table 1147. Book Publishers' Net Shipments: 2008 to 2010

[Represents net publishers' shipments after returns. Includes all titles released by publishers in the United States and imports which appear under the imprints of American publishers. Multivolume sets, such as encyclopedias, are counted as one unit. Due to changes in methodology and scope, these data are not comparable to those previously published]

Type of publication	2008, estimated	2009, estimated	2010, estimated
Total..................................	**2,468,992,795**	**2,509,774,182**	**2,570,791,667**
Trade [1]..................................	2,164,090,241	2,211,100,456	2,261,275,477
Higher education.........................	45,927,021	50,250,083	50,254,242
Elementary and high school.............	92,291,245	79,396,646	82,580,465
Professional..............................	160,834,053	163,476,620	171,032,837
Scholarly..................................	5,850,235	5,550,377	5,648,646

[1] Includes adult, juvenile, and religious.

Source: Book Industry Study Group, Inc. and Association of American Publishers, New York, NY, *BookStats,* annual (copyright 2011). See also <http://www.bisg.org/>.

Table 1148. Software Publishers—Estimated Revenue by Source of Revenue and Software Type: 2006 to 2010

[In millions of dollars (125,203 represents $125,203,000,000). For taxable and tax-exempt employer firms. Covers NAICS 5112. Estimates have been adjusted to the results of the 2007 Economic Census. Based on the North American Industry Classification System (NAICS), 2002. See text, this section, and Section 15, See also Appendix III]

Item	2006	2007	2008	2009	2010
Operating revenue..	**125,203**	**135,401**	**142,717**	**138,981**	**145,425**
Source of revenue:					
System software publishing [1]...........................	44,166	49,038	52,552	48,948	50,808
Operating system software............................	15,434	17,759	18,680	17,975	17,393
Network software..	12,869	13,857	14,701	12,483	14,827
Database management software.....................	8,275	9,337	10,226	9,480	10,225
Development tools and programming languages software..................	3,059	2,987	3,047	3,019	3,221
Application software publishing [1]......................	43,301	45,445	45,573	47,193	49,129
General business productivity and home use applications...............	18,956	19,311	19,868	23,111	23,172
Cross-industry application software..................	12,751	12,949	12,264	11,383	13,434
Vertical market application software.................	6,787	7,378	7,304	6,412	6,198
Utilities application software...........................	1,372	1,459	1,568	1,688	1,765
Other services [1]...	37,736	40,918	44,592	42,840	45,488
Customization and integration of packaged software........................	4,705	4,077	5,259	4,656	4,213
Information technology technical consulting services.......................	5,421	6,064	5,829	5,614	5,344
Application service provisioning......................	(S)	(S)	(S)	(S)	(S)
Resale of computer hardware and software.......	3,115	3,993	4,776	4,152	3,513
Information technology-related training services..............	1,662	1,712	1,844	1,385	1,888
Breakdown of revenue by software sales type:					
System software..	44,166	49,038	52,552	48,948	50,808
Personal computer software...........................	14,441	17,348	18,269	17,428	17,406
Enterprise or network software.......................	17,407	17,644	18,329	16,575	19,309
Mainframe computer software.........................	9,246	9,679	10,533	9,615	9,890
Other system software..................................	3,072	4,367	5,421	5,330	(S)
Application software..	43,301	45,445	45,573	47,193	49,129
Personal computer software...........................	(S)	19,348	19,759	21,238	21,794
Enterprise or network software.......................	16,236	18,357	18,015	17,880	18,811
Mainframe computer software.........................	2,548	2,525	2,152	2,145	3,134
Other application software..............................	5,118	5,215	(S)	5,930	5,390

S Data do not meet publication standards. [1] Includes other sources of revenue and other expenses, not shown separately.

Source: U.S. Census Bureau, "Service Annual Survey 2010: Information Sector Services," February 2012, <http://www.census.gov/econ/www/servmenu.html>.

Table 1149. Internet Publishing and Broadcasting—Estimated Revenue and Expenses: 2006 to 2010

[In millions of dollars (11,510 represents $11,510,000,000). For taxable and tax-exempt employer firms. Covers NAICS 516. Establishments engaged in publishing and/or broadcasting on the Internet exclusively. Estimates have been adjusted to the results of the 2007 Economic Census. Based on the North American Industry Classification System (NAICS), 2002. See text, Section 15, and Appendix III]

Item	2006	2007	2008	2009	2010
Operating revenue	**11,510**	**15,035**	**17,763**	**19,111**	**21,273**
Source of revenue:					
Publishing and broadcasting of content on the Internet	6,344	7,669	8,998	10,014	10,696
Online advertising space	2,579	3,469	4,298	4,957	5,623
Licensing of rights to use intellectual property	442	486	498	561	690
All other operating revenue	(S)	(S)	3,969	3,579	4,264
Breakdown of revenue by type of customer:					
Government	(S)	(S)	(S)	(S)	(S)
Business firms and not-for-profit organizations	7,866	9,691	11,960	12,918	14,694
Household consumers and individual users	3,019	4,437	4,631	4,968	5,177
Operating expenses	**10,102**	**13,211**	**15,457**	**16,731**	**18,770**
Personnel	4,398	5,648	6,793	6,845	8,144
Gross annual payroll	3,513	4,189	5,095	5,142	6,054
Employer's cost for fringe benefits	636	892	(S)	(S)	1,118
Temporary staff and leased employee expense	249	(S)	(S)	(S)	(S)
Expensed materials, parts and supplies (not for resale)	322	(S)	(S)	(S)	638
Expensed equipment	123	(S)	(S)	(S)	(S)
Expensed purchase of other materials, parts and supplies	199	(S)	235	372	395
Expensed purchased services	1,789	(S)	2,775	3,328	3,258
Expensed purchases of software	245	(S)	307	(S)	279
Purchased electricity and fuels (except motor fuel)	22	(S)	(S)	(S)	(S)
Lease and rental payments	343	(S)	537	(S)	(S)
Purchased repair and maintenance	96	(S)	(S)	(S)	(S)
Purchased advertising and promotional services	1,083	1,366	1,756	(S)	2,184
Other operating expenses	3,593	(S)	5,448	5,944	6,730
Depreciation and amortization charges	811	(S)	1,272	(S)	1,600
Government taxes and license fees	66	(S)	83	107	93

S Data do not meet publication standards.

Source: U.S. Census Bureau, "Service Annual Survey 2010: Information Sector Services," February 2012, <http://www.census.gov/econ/www/servmenu.html>.

Table 1150. Motion Picture and Sound Recording Industries—Estimated Revenue and Sources of Revenue: 2006 to 2010

[In millions of dollars (93,265 represents $93,265,000,000). For taxable and tax-exempt employer firms. Covers NAICS 512. Estimates have been adjusted to the results of the 2007 Economic Census. Based on the North American Industry Classification System (NAICS), 2002. See text Section 15 and Appendix III]

Kind of business	2006	2007	2008	2009	2010
Operating revenue	**93,265**	**94,986**	**95,271**	**90,398**	**95,118**
Motion picture and video industries	**76,444**	**79,797**	**80,004**	**75,979**	**81,331**
Motion picture and video production and distribution [1]	59,170	61,911	62,161	57,910	62,567
Domestic licensing of rights to motion picture films	13,665	13,067	10,976	10,633	11,045
Domestic licensing of rights to television programs	8,964	10,142	9,327	9,968	10,101
International licensing of rights to motion picture films	6,378	6,808	7,282	6,710	8,233
International licensing of rights to television programs	3,022	2,954	3,466	3,317	3,295
Sale of audiovisual works for wholesale, retail, and rental markets	12,621	14,829	14,548	12,511	12,305
Motion picture and video exhibition [1]	12,326	12,705	12,782	13,293	13,454
Feature film exhibition revenue	8,108	8,483	8,545	8,959	9,137
Admissions to domestic films	8,059	8,421	8,476	8,888	9,064
Admissions to foreign films	(S)	62	69	71	73
Food and beverage sales	3,543	3,711	3,722	3,825	3,807
Postproduction services and other motion picture and video industries [1]	4,948	5,181	5,061	4,776	5,310
Audiovisual postproduction services	2,573	2,733	2,618	2,601	2,829
Motion picture film laboratory services	(S)	491	446	366	387
Duplication and copying services	1,038	(S)	1,053	1,124	1,244
Sound recording industries	**16,821**	**15,189**	**15,267**	**14,419**	**13,787**
Integrated record production and distribution [1]	10,642	9,082	8,953	8,665	8,258
Licensing revenue	1,512	1,299	1,441	1,392	1,190
Sales of recordings	(S)	7,454	6,914	6,493	6,294
Music publishers [1]	4,646	4,466	4,713	4,155	3,793
Licensing of rights to use musical compositions	2,323	(S)	2,886	2,861	2,901
Print music	1,928	1,667	1,252	(S)	300
Sound recording studios [1]	831	854	810	749	839
Studio recording	502	506	497	441	480

S Data do not meet publication standards. [1] Includes other sources of revenue not shown separately.

Source: U.S. Census Bureau, "Service Annual Survey 2010: Information Sector Services," February 2012, <http://www.census.gov/econ/www/servmenu.html>.

Table 1151. Recording Media—Manufacturers' Shipments and Value: 2000 to 2011

[1,079.2 represents 1,079,200,000. Based on reports of Recording Industry Association of America member companies who distributed about 85 percent of the prerecorded music in 2011. These data are supplemented by other sources]

Medium	2000	2004	2005	2006	2007	2008	2009	2010	2011
UNIT SHIPMENTS (mil.)									
Total [1]	**1,079.2**	**958.0**	**1,301.8**	**1,588.5**	**1,774.3**	**1,919.2**	**1,851.8**	**1,739.6**	**1,800.2**
Physical:									
Compact disks [2]	942.5	767.0	705.4	619.7	511.1	368.4	292.9	253.0	240.8
Music video [3]	18.2	32.8	33.8	23.2	27.5	25.1	23.0	17.6	14.9
Other albums [4]	78.2	2.5	2.0	1.3	1.7	3.0	3.2	4.2	5.5
Other singles [5]	40.3	6.6	5.1	3.2	3.2	1.1	1.2	1.3	1.7
Digital:									
Download single	(X)	139.4	366.9	586.4	809.9	1,042.7	1,138.3	1,177.4	1,306.2
Download album	(X)	4.6	13.6	27.6	42.5	63.6	76.4	85.8	104.8
Kiosk [6]	(X)	(X)	0.7	1.4	1.8	1.6	1.7	1.7	1.4
Music video	(X)	(X)	1.9	9.9	14.2	20.8	20.4	18.4	16.3
Mobile [7]	(X)	(X)	170.0	315.3	361.0	405.1	305.8	188.5	115.9
Subscription [8]	(X)	(X)	1.3	1.7	1.8	1.6	1.2	1.5	1.8
VALUE (mil. dol.)									
Total [1]	**14,323.7**	**12,345.0**	**12,296.9**	**11,758.2**	**10,372.1**	**8,768.4**	**7,683.9**	**6,995.0**	**7,007.7**
Physical:									
Compact disks [2]	13,214.5	11,446.5	10,520.2	9,372.6	7,452.3	5,471.3	4,274.1	3,389.4	3,100.7
Music video [3]	281.9	607.2	602.2	451.1	484.9	434.6	418.9	347.3	295.5
Other albums [4]	653.7	66.1	48.5	22.1	29.3	57.6	60.2	88.9	119.4
Other singles [5]	173.6	34.9	24.1	17.6	16.2	6.4	5.6	5.2	8.1
Digital:									
Download single	(X)	138.0	363.3	580.6	801.8	1,032.2	1,220.3	1,317.4	1,492.7
Download album	(X)	45.5	135.7	275.9	424.9	635.3	763.4	872.4	1,091.4
Kiosk [6]	(X)	(X)	1.0	1.9	2.6	2.6	6.3	6.4	3.3
Music video	(X)	(X)	3.7	19.7	28.2	41.3	40.6	36.6	32.4
Mobile [7]	(X)	(X)	421.6	774.5	878.9	977.1	728.8	448.0	277.4
Subscription [8]	(X)	(X)	149.2	206.2	200.9	221.4	213.1	212.4	241.0

X Not applicable [1] Net, after returns. [2] Includes DualDisc. [3] Includes DVD video. [4] Includes cassette, LP/EP, DVD audio, and super audio CD (SACD). [5] Includes CD single and vinyl single. [6] Includes singles and albums. [7] Includes master ringtones, ringbacks, music videos, full length downloads and other mobile. [8] Weighted annual average. Number of units not included in total.

Source: Recording Industry Association of America, Washington, DC, *2011 Year-End Shipment Statistics* (copyright). See also <http://www.riaa.com/keystatistics.php>.

Table 1152. Radio and Television Broadcasting—Estimated Revenue and Expenses: 2009 and 2010

[In millions of dollars (4,307 represents $4,307,000,000). For taxable and tax-exempt employer firms. Estimates have been adjusted to the results of the 2007 Economic Census. Based on the North American Industry Classification System (NAICS), 2002. See text, Section 15 and Appendix III]

Item	Radio networks (NAICS 515111)		Radio stations (NAICS 515112)		TV broadcasting (NAICS 51512)	
	2009	2010	2009	2010	2009	2010
Operating revenue	**4,307**	**4,883**	**11,643**	**12,135**	**31,553**	**35,334**
Air time	876	1,020	9,780	10,228	23,973	27,033
National/regional air time	432	472	2,477	2,846	15,346	17,317
Local air time	444	548	7,303	7,382	8,627	9,716
Other operating revenue	3,431	3,863	1,863	1,907	7,580	8,301
Network compensation	186	215	347	345	1,313	1,410
Public and noncommercial programming services	365	381	(S)	(S)	1,892	1,964
All other operating revenue	2,880	3,267	885	929	4,375	4,927
Operating expenses	**4,099**	**4,298**	**9,491**	**9,291**	**26,853**	**29,010**
Personnel costs	866	905	4,911	4,852	7,959	8,241
Gross annual payroll	757	781	4,133	4,084	6,722	6,815
Employer's cost for fringe benefits	97	113	637	620	1,088	1,254
Temporary staff and leased employee expense	12	11	141	148	149	172
Expensed materials, parts and supplies (not for resale)	29	35	98	87	271	296
Expensed equipment	12	16	39	34	120	138
Expensed purchase of other materials, parts and supplies	17	19	59	53	151	158
Expensed purchased services	377	367	970	998	1,692	1,731
Expensed purchases of software	21	32	44	43	124	134
Purchased electricity and fuels (except motor fuel)	24	27	192	189	254	219
Lease and rental payments	138	122	412	395	445	413
Purchased repair and maintenance	25	26	76	98	191	208
Purchased advertising and promotional services	169	160	246	273	678	757
Other operating expenses	2,827	2,991	3,512	3,354	16,931	18,742
Depreciation and amortization charges	461	440	661	667	1,629	1,516
Governmental taxes and license fees	23	16	82	91	160	171
Broadcast rights and music license fees	596	631	747	683	10,090	11,092
Network compensation fees (networks only)	145	161	75	(S)	279	281
All other operating expenses	1,602	1,743	1,947	1,833	4,773	5,682

S Data do not meet publication standards.

Source: U.S. Census Bureau, "Service Annual Survey 2010: Information Sector Services," February 2012, <http://www.census.gov/econ/www/servmenu.html>.

Table 1153. Cable and Premium TV—Summary: 1980 to 2010

[17,500 represents 17,500,000. Cable TV for calendar year. Premium TV as of December 31 of year shown]

| | Cable TV | | | | Premium TV | | | | | |
| | | | Revenue [1] | | Units [2] | | | Monthly rate [4] | | |
Year	Average basic sub-scribers (1,000)	Average monthly basic rate (dol.)	Total (mil. dol.)	Basic (mil. dol.)	Total premium [3] (1,000)	Premium cable (1,000)	Non-cable delivered premium (1,000)	All premium weighted average [5] (dollars)	Premium cable (dollars)	Non-cable delivered premium (dollars)
1980......	17,500	7.69	2,609	1,615	8,581	7,336	(NA)	8.91	8.62	(NA)
1985......	35,440	9.73	8,831	4,138	29,885	29,418	(NA)	10.29	10.25	(NA)
1990......	50,520	16.78	17,582	10,174	39,902	39,751	(NA)	10.35	10.30	(NA)
1995......	60,550	23.07	24,137	16,763	60,098	46,600	8,725	8.32	8.54	6.99
1997......	63,600	26.48	28,931	20,213	72,910	51,450	17,500	8.33	8.43	8.00
1998......	64,650	27.81	31,191	21,574	79,483	54,410	21,355	8.60	8.74	8.22
1999......	65,500	28.92	34,095	22,732	84,234	56,985	25,532	8.75	8.85	8.50
2000......	66,250	30.37	36,427	24,142	94,100	62,618	30,158	8.72	8.81	8.48
2001......	66,732	32.87	41,847	26,324	101,676	68,353	32,780	8.97	9.10	8.66
2002......	66,472	34.71	47,989	27,690	109,046	71,637	37,024	9.19	9.29	9.00
2003......	66,050	36.59	53,242	29,000	108,522	71,740	36,364	9.38	9.45	9.23
2004......	65,727	38.14	58,586	30,080	118,151	76,844	40,892	9.91	9.92	9.88
2005......	65,337	39.63	64,891	31,075	126,067	81,790	43,780	9.95	9.97	9.93
2006......	65,319	41.17	71,887	32,274	132,951	85,055	47,514	10.01	10.02	9.98
2007......	65,141	42.72	78,937	33,393	143,009	90,878	51,595	10.05	10.06	10.02
2008......	64,274	44.28	85,232	34,151	149,749	92,364	56,825	10.08	10.10	10.06
2009......	62,874	46.13	89,479	34,804	150,111	85,818	64,293	10.12	10.13	10.09
2010......	60,958	47.89	93,368	35,031	166,241	88,359	77,882	10.15	10.17	10.13

NA Not available. [1] Includes installation revenue, subscriber revenue, and nonsubscriber revenue; excludes telephony and high-speed access. [2] Individual program services sold to subscribers. [3] Includes multipoint distribution service (MDS), satellite TV (STV), multipoint multichannel distribution service (MMDS), satellite master antenna TV (SMATV), C-band satellite, DBS satellite and Telco Video for full- and mini-premium services. [4] Weighted average representing 8 months of unregulated basic rate and 4 months of FCC rolled-back rate. [5] Includes average premium unit price based on data for major premium movie services.

Source: SNL Kagan, a division of SNL Financial, LC. From the *Broadband Cable Financial Databook*, annual (copyright); the *Cable Program Investor* and *Cable TV Investor: Deals & Finance* newsletters (monthly); and various other SNL Kagan publications.

Table 1154. Cable and Other Subscription Programming—Estimated Revenue and Expenses: 2006 to 2010

[In millions of dollars (40,907 represents $40,907,000,000). For taxable and tax-exempt employer firms. Covers NAICS 51521. Estimates have been adjusted to the results of the 2007 Economic Census. Based on the North American Industry Classification System (NAICS), 2002. See text, Section 15 and Appendix III]

Item	2006	2007	2008	2009	2010
Operating revenue........	**40,907**	**44,926**	**49,569**	**51,431**	**55,168**
Source of revenue:					
Licensing of rights to broadcast specialty programming [1]......................	21,196	23,563	26,183	28,698	31,184
Air time...............	17,107	18,605	19,958	19,911	21,082
All other operating services revenue............	2,604	2,758	3,428	2,822	2,902
Operating expenses............	**26,463**	**29,073**	**31,411**	**31,339**	**33,190**
Personnel costs........	4,754	5,592	5,894	6,066	6,463
Gross annual payroll............	3,726	4,192	4,496	4,606	4,991
Employer's cost for fringe benefits............	610	874	868	970	998
Temporary staff and leased employee expense............	418	526	530	490	474
Expensed materials, parts and supplies (not for resale)............	138	137	171	133	143
Expensed equipment............	50	67	80	69	73
Expensed purchase of other materials, parts and supplies............	88	70	91	64	70
Expensed purchased services............	2,789	2,460	3,282	3,218	3,598
Expensed purchases of software............	40	49	157	60	57
Purchased electricity and fuels (except motor fuel)............	39	40	69	70	77
Lease and rental payments............	494	473	550	568	591
Purchased repair and maintenance............	81	64	118	121	130
Purchased advertising and promotional services............	2,135	1,834	2,388	2,399	2,743
Other operating expenses............	18,782	20,884	22,064	21,922	22,986
Depreciation and amortization charges............	2,662	2,885	3,307	3,309	3,181
Government taxes and license fees............	79	65	66	64	53
Program and production costs............	12,202	13,804	14,263	14,409	14,973
All other operating expenses............	3,839	4,130	4,428	4,140	4,779

[1] Protected by copyright.

Source: U.S. Census Bureau, "Service Annual Survey 2010: Information Sector Services," February 2012, <http://www.census.gov/econ/www/servmenu.html>.

Table 1155. Telecommunications Industry—Carriers and Revenue: 2000 to 2009

[Revenue in millions of dollars (292,762 represents $292,762,000,000). Based on annual Telecommunications Reporting Worksheets (FCC Form 499-A) filed by telecommunications providers. Revenues are categorized as those billed to universal service contributors for resale (carrier's carrier revenues); and, those billed to telecommunication providers with annual contributions less than $10,000 and end user revenues (end user revenues). Does not include any revenues, such as from Internet access or other information services, customer premises equipment, inside wiring, or published directories, that are not assessable for contributions to universal service support and cost recovery mechanisms]

Category	Carriers (number)				Telecommunications revenue (mil. dol.)			
	2000	2005	2008	2009	2000	2005	2008	2009
Total [1]	4,879	5,005	5,354	(NA)	292,762	297,921	297,365	281,052
Local service providers (fixed local & pay phone)	2,641	2,922	3,168	(NA)	128,075	122,609	116,447	111,949
Incumbent local exchange carriers (ILECs)	1,335	1,303	1,297	(NA)	116,158	103,561	89,732	83,451
Competitors of incumbent local exchange carriers	607	1,043	1,462	(NA)	10,945	18,568	26,440	28,289
CAPs and CLECs [2]	479	734	813	(NA)	9,814	16,930	20,980	16,880
Interconnected VoIP providers [3]	(NA)	(NA)	334	(NA)	(NA)	(NA)	3,541	9,379
Private carriers	([4])	([4])	([4])	(NA)	39	770	1,051	1,190
Wireless service providers [5]	1,430	905	870	(NA)	63,280	108,809	128,314	120,597
Telephony [6]	783	402	412	(NA)	59,823	107,834	127,730	120,007
Paging service providers	425	300	229	(NA)	3,102	579	426	361
Toll service providers	808	1,178	1,316	(NA)	101,407	66,503	52,604	48,507
Interexchange carriers	212	262	237	(NA)	87,311	46,856	37,358	32,780
Operator service providers	20	23	31	(NA)	635	548	1,063	940
Prepaid service providers	23	69	121	(NA)	727	1,828	1,999	1,869
Satellite service carriers	25	40	45	(NA)	336	714	860	910
Toll resellers	493	721	654	(NA)	10,641	13,362	8,256	8,021
Other toll carriers, including VoIP [3]	35	63	228	(NA)	1,758	3,195	3,068	3,987

NA Not available. [1] Revenue data include adjustments, not shown separately [2] Competitive access providers (CAPs) and competitive local exchange carriers (CLECs). [3] Voice Over Internet Protocol. [4] Data not available separately. [5] Includes specialized mobile radio services and other services, not shown separately. [6] Cellular service, personal communications service, and specialized mobile radio.

Source: U.S. Federal Communications Commission, Wireline Competition Bureau, *Telecommunications Industry Revenues* and *Trends in Telephone Service*. See also <http://www.fcc.gov/wcb/iatd/stats.html\>.

Table 1156. Wired and Wireless Telecommunications Carriers— Estimated Revenue: 2006 to 2010

[In millions of dollars (193,434 represents $193,434,000,000). For taxable and tax-exempt employer firms. Covers NAICS 5171 Wired Telecommunications and NAICS 517211 Paging and NAICS 517212 Cellular and Other Wireless. Estimates have been adjusted to the results of the 2007 Economic Census. Based on the North American Industry Classification System (NAICS), 2002. See text Section 15 and Appendix III]

Item	2006	2007	2008	2009	2010
Wired telecommunications carriers operating revenue	**193,434**	**186,060**	**184,197**	**172,675**	**168,759**
Fixed services	89,791	87,307	84,109	73,099	66,675
Fixed local	57,429	56,088	53,473	46,436	43,303
Fixed long-distance	30,917	29,717	29,430	25,658	22,517
Fixed all distance [1]	1,445	1,502	1,206	1,005	855
Other telecommunication services	88,182	86,057	87,299	85,207	88,402
Carrier services	30,131	25,163	23,221	21,002	19,796
Private network services	23,238	22,460	22,641	21,747	23,976
Subscriber line charges	7,587	5,856	5,109	4,072	3,885
Internet access services	15,272	20,045	22,468	25,020	28,640
Internet telephony	1,826	2,049	2,333	2,314	2,966
Telecommunications network installation services	5,876	6,142	7,062	7,262	5,174
Reselling services for telecommunications equipment, retail	3,320	3,256	3,307	2,533	2,353
Rental of telecommunications equipment	(S)	323	271	343	484
Repair and maintenance services for telecommunications equipment	729	763	887	914	1,128
All other operating revenue	15,461	12,696	12,789	14,369	13,682
Wireless telecommunications carriers operating revenue [2]	**156,013**	**170,583**	**181,475**	**185,684**	**195,525**
Paging	1,294	889	846	742	710
Messaging (paging) services	1,031	708	688	587	559
Mobile services	122,125	128,025	131,601	130,791	136,772
Mobile telephony	55,441	55,435	59,478	56,134	59,403
Mobile long distance	4,950	5,436	4,865	4,672	2,890
Mobile all-distance	(S)	59,217	57,458	58,344	62,185
Other mobile services	5,500	(S)	9,800	11,641	12,294
Other telecommunications services	17,363	23,123	30,621	34,300	40,064
Internet access services	7,650	12,731	20,069	24,598	28,604
Installation services for telecommunications networks	153	189	327	222	161
Reselling services for telecommunications equipment, retail	8,557	9,008	8,994	8,276	10,054
Rental of telecommunications equipment	(S)	72	(D)	(D)	(D)
Repair and maintenance services for telecommunications equipment	(S)	(S)	(D)	(D)	(D)
All other operating revenue	(S)	(S)	18,407	19,851	17,979

D Data withheld to avoid disclosure. S Estimate does not meet publication standard. [1] No distinction between local or long distance. [2] Excludes satellite.

Source: U.S. Census Bureau, "Service Annual Survey 2010: Information Sector Services," February 2012, <http://www.census.gov/econ/www/servmenu.html>.

Table 1157. Telephone Systems—Summary: 1990 to 2008

[130 represents 130,000,000. Covers principal carriers filing annual reports with Federal Communications Commission]

Item	Unit	1990	1995	2000	2002 [1]	2003 [1]	2004 [1]	2005 [1]	2006 [1]	2007 [1]	2008 [1]
LOCAL EXCHANGE CARRIERS											
Carriers [2]	Number	51	53	52	53	54	56	56	56	55	55
Access lines [3]	Millions	130	166	245	264	275	286	349	379	424	(NA)
Operating revenues [4]	Bil. dol.	84	96	117	111	109	107	106	105	103	(NA)
Average monthly residential local telephone rate [4]	Dollars	19.24	20.01	20.78	24.07	24.52	24.52	24.64	25.26	25.62	(NA)
Average monthly single-line business telephone rate [4]	Dollars	41.21	41.80	41.80	41.95	41.96	43.49	43.75	45.32	48.17	(NA)
INTERNATIONAL TELEPHONE SERVICE [5]											
Number of U.S. billed minutes	Millions	8,030	15,889	30,135	35,988	45,904	63,653	70,064	72,440	69,975	74,934
Revenue from private-line service	Mil. dol.	201	514	1,502	988	899	711	738	792	717	817
Revenue from resale service	Mil. dol.	167	1,756	7,367	5,101	5,760	5,226	5,750	6,077	6,959	8,459

NA Not available. [1] Beginning 2001, detailed financial data are only filed by Regional Bell Operating Companies (RBOCs). Access lines and calls reported by all subject reporting companies. [2] Beginning 1985, the number of carriers dropped due to a change in the reporting threshold for carriers from $1 million to $100 million in annual operating revenue. [3] Beginning 2008, carriers no longer report this data to the Federal Communications Commission. [4] Gross operating revenues, gross plant, and total assets of reporting carriers estimated at more than 90 percent of total industry. New accounting rules became effective in 1988; prior years may not be directly comparable on a one-to-one basis. Includes Virgin Islands, and prior to 1991, Puerto Rico. Beginning 2008, carriers no longer report this data to the Federal Communications Commission. [5] Beginning 1991, data are for all U.S. points, and include calls to and from Alaska, Hawaii, Puerto Rico, Guam, the U.S. Virgin Islands, and offshore U.S. points. Beginning 1991, carriers first started reporting traffic to and from Canada and Mexico. Data for Canada and Mexico in prior years are staff estimates. Beginning 2004, revenue from private-line service includes non-confidential private line service revenue and the total of private line and miscellaneous service revenue for carriers requesting confidential treatment for international telephone service.

Source: U.S. Federal Communications Commission, *Statistics of Communications Common Carriers*, *Trends in Telephone Service*, and *Trends in the International Telecommunications Industry*. See also <http://www.fcc.gov/wcb/iatd/stats.html>.

Table 1158. Average Annual Telephone Service Expenditures by All Consumer Units: 2001 to 2010

[In dollars except percent distribution. Based on Consumer Expenditure Survey. A consumer unit is defined as members of a household related by blood, marriage, adoption, or some other legal arrangement; a single person living alone or sharing a household with others, but who is financially independent; or two or more persons living together who share responsibility for at least two out of the three major types of expenses: food, housing, and other expenses]

Year	Average annual telephone service (dol.)				Percent distribution			
	Total telephone services	Residential telephone/ pay phone	Cellular phone service	Other services [1]	Total telephone services	Residential telephone/ pay phone	Cellular phone service	Other services [1]
2001	914	686	210	19	100.0	75.0	23.0	2.0
2002	957	641	294	22	100.0	67.0	30.7	2.3
2003	956	620	316	20	100.0	64.8	33.1	2.1
2004	990	592	378	20	100.0	59.8	38.2	2.0
2005	1,048	570	455	23	100.0	54.4	43.4	2.2
2006	1,087	542	524	21	100.0	49.9	48.2	2.0
2007	1,110	482	608	20	100.0	43.4	54.8	1.8
2008	1,127	467	643	17	100.0	41.4	57.1	1.5
2009	1,162	434	712	17	100.0	37.3	61.3	1.4
2010	1,178	401	760	17	100.0	34.1	64.5	1.4

[1] Phone cards, pager services, and beginning in 2007, Voice over Internet Protocol, known as VoIP.

Source: Bureau of Labor Statistics, "Consumer Expenditures--2010," News Release, USDL-11-1395, September 2011, and unpublished data. See also <http://www.bls.gov/news.release/cesan.htm>.

Table 1159. Cellular Telecommunications Industry: 1990 to 2011

[Calendar year data, except as noted (5,283 represents 5,283,000). Based on a survey sent to facilities-based commercial mobile radio service providers, including cellular, personal communications services, advanced wireless service, mobile WiMAX, and enhanced special mobile radio (ESMR) systems. The number of operational systems beginning 2000 differs from that reported for previous periods as a result of the consolidated operation of ESMR systems in a broader service area instead of by a city-to-city basis]

Item	Unit	1990	2000	2005	2007	2008	2009	2010	2011
Subscribers	1,000	5,283	109,478	207,896	255,396	270,334	290,941	310,997	331,595
Cell sites [1]	Number	5,616	104,288	183,689	213,299	242,130	247,081	253,086	283,385
Employees	Number	21,382	184,449	233,067	266,782	268,528	249,247	250,393	238,071
Service revenue	Mil. dol.	4,548	52,466	113,538	138,869	148,084	152,552	159,930	169,767
Roamer revenue [2]	Mil. dol.	456	3,883	3,786	3,742	3,739	3,061	3,026	3,315
Capital investment [3]	Mil. dol.	6,282	89,624	199,025	244,591	264,761	285,122	310,015	335,332
Average monthly bill [4]	Dollars	80.90	45.27	49.98	49.79	50.07	48.16	47.21	47.00
Average length of call [4]	Minutes	2.20	2.56	3.00	(NA)	2.27	1.81	1.79	1.78
Number of text messages [5]	Billions	(NA)	(Z)	9.8	48.1	110.4	152.7	187.7	193.1
Number of MMS [5, 6]	Billions	(NA)	(NA)	0.2	0.8	1.6	4.3	4.3	5.0

NA Not available. Z Entry less than half the unit of measurement shown. [1] The basic geographic unit of a wireless PCS or cellular system. [2] Service revenue generated by subscribers' calls outside of their system areas. [3] Beginning 2005, cumulative capital investment figure reached by summing the incremental capital investment in year shown with cumulative capital investment of prior year. [4] As of December 31. [5] Number of messages in final month of survey (December). [6] Multimedia Messaging Service.

Source: CTIA-The Wireless Association, Washington, DC, *Semi-annual Wireless Survey*, (copyright).

Table 1160. Cable and Other Programming Distribution—Estimated Revenue: 2006 to 2010

[In millions of dollars (88,474 represents $88,474,000,000). For taxable and tax-exempt employer firms. Covers NAICS 5175. Estimates have been adjusted to the results of the 2007 Economic Census. Based on the North American Industry Classification System (NAICS), 2002. See text, Section 15 and Appendix III]

Item	2006	2007	2008	2009	2010
Operating revenue	**88,474**	**100,416**	**109,351**	**114,327**	**121,300**
Sources of revenue:					
Multichannel programming distribution services	55,564	60,529	64,556	66,908	69,198
Basic programming package	42,294	45,468	47,913	49,864	50,921
Premium programming package	10,159	11,441	12,837	13,318	14,447
Pay-per-view	3,111	3,620	3,806	3,726	3,830
Other revenue	32,910	39,887	44,795	47,419	52,102
Air time	3,878	3,936	4,076	3,617	4,444
Rental and reselling services for program distribution equipment	3,152	3,910	4,381	5,078	6,253
Installation services for connections to program distribution networks	723	931	963	946	846
Internet access services	13,736	16,281	18,070	19,332	20,944
Internet telephony	1,577	3,433	5,167	6,309	6,601
Fixed local telephony	2,134	2,614	2,818	3,072	3,215
Fixed long-distance telephony	414	194	177	206	202
All other operating revenue	7,296	8,588	9,143	8,859	9,597
Type of customer:					
Government	522	581	660	711	335
Business firms and not for profit organizations	6,971	8,682	8,598	9,604	10,984
Household customers and individual customers	80,981	91,153	100,093	104,012	109,981

Source: U.S. Census Bureau, "Service Annual Survey 2010: Information Sector Services," February 2012, <http://www.census.gov/econ/www/servmenu.html>.

Table 1161. Internet Service Providers and Data Processing, Hosting, and Related Services—Estimated Revenue: 2005 to 2010

[In millions of dollars (13,784 represents $13,784,000,000). For taxable and tax-exempt employer firms. Estimates have been adjusted to the results of the 2007 Economic Census. Based on the North American Industry Classification System (NAICS), 2002. See text, Section 15, and Appendix III]

Item	Internet service providers (NAICS 518111)			Data processing, hosting, and related services (NAICS 5182)		
	2005	2009	2010	2005	2009	2010
Operating revenue	**13,784**	**10,441**	**9,974**	**(X)**	**(X)**	**(X)**
Internet access service	10,281	5,431	5,082	(X)	(X)	(X)
Online advertising space	1311	2158	1873	(X)	(X)	(X)
Internet backbone services	(S)	271	(S)	(X)	(X)	(X)
Internet telephony	(S)	(S)	96	(X)	(X)	(X)
Web site hosting services	668	568	573	(X)	(X)	(X)
Information technology design and development services	(S)	(S)	(S)	(X)	(X)	(X)
All other operating revenue	1137	(S)	(S)	(X)	(X)	(X)
Operating revenue	**(X)**	**(X)**	**(X)**	**59,369**	**71,614**	**76,156**
Data processing IT infrastructure provisioning, and hosting services	(X)	(X)	(X)	30,181	40,912	43,525
Business processing management services	(X)	(X)	(X)	15,523	19,895	21,256
Data management services	(X)	(X)	(X)	6,086	7,053	6,742
Application service provisioning	(X)	(X)	(X)	5,315	9,091	9,733
Web site hosting services	(X)	(X)	(X)	(S)	1,868	2,188
Collocation services	(X)	(X)	(X)	(S)	(S)	(S)
Other operating revenue	(X)	(X)	(X)	29,188	30,702	32,631
IT design and development services	(X)	(X)	(X)	6,491	(S)	(S)
IT technical support services	(X)	(X)	(X)	1,448	1,942	1,823
IT technical consulting services	(X)	(X)	(X)	2,243	2,607	2,888
Information and document transformation services	(X)	(X)	(X)	3,109	3,296	3,298
Software publishing	(X)	(X)	(X)	1,699	2,421	2,636
Reselling services for computer hardware and software, retail	(X)	(X)	(X)	1,225	(S)	(S)
All other operating revenue	(X)	(X)	(X)	12,973	13,200	14,581

S Data do not meet publication standards. X Not applicable.

Source: U.S. Census Bureau, "Service Annual Survey 2010: Information Sector Services," February 2012, <http://www.census.gov/econ/www/servmenu.html>.

Table 1162. Household Internet Usage In and Outside of the Home by Selected Characteristics: 2010

[In thousands except percent. (119,545 represents 119,545,000). As of October. Internet Use Supplement 2010. Excludes GPS devices, digital music players, and devices with only limited computing capabilities, for example: household appliances. Based on the Current Population Survey. See text, Section 1 and Appendix III]

Characteristics	Total house-holds	In the home — All house-holds (Percent)	In the home — Dial-up (Percent)	In the home — Broad-band (Percent)	Anywhere — Total house-holds	Anywhere — Percent of house-holds	No internet use — Total house-holds	No internet use — Percent of house-holds
All households	**119,545**	**71.06**	**2.82**	**68.24**	**95,907**	**80.23**	**23,638**	**19.77**
Age of householder:								
Under 25 years old	6,575	70.35	1.80	68.54	5,722	87.03	853	12.97
25 to 34 years old	19,838	77.45	1.23	76.22	17,815	89.81	2,022	10.19
35 to 44 years old	21,595	81.53	1.95	79.58	19,771	91.55	1,825	8.45
45 to 54 years old	24,704	77.27	2.92	74.35	21,353	86.43	3,352	13.57
55 years and older	46,833	60.36	3.98	56.38	31,246	66.72	15,586	33.28
Sex of householder:								
Male	60,064	73.96	2.78	71.18	49,215	81.94	10,849	18.06
Female	59,481	68.13	2.85	65.28	46,691	78.50	12,789	21.50
Race and ethnicity of householder: [1]								
White	83,613	74.86	3.02	71.83	68,766	82.24	14,847	17.76
Black	14,863	57.83	2.38	55.45	10,797	72.64	4,067	27.36
American Indian/Alaskan Native	731	56.82	4.55	52.28	531	72.64	200	27.36
Asian	4,667	82.77	1.86	80.91	4,084	87.51	583	12.49
Hispanic	14,142	59.11	2.21	56.90	10,437	73.80	3,705	26.20
Educational attainment of householder:								
Elementary	5,309	29.41	2.25	27.16	2,197	41.38	3,112	58.62
Some high school	8,870	39.49	2.70	36.79	4,864	54.84	4,006	45.16
High school diploma/GED	34,947	60.33	3.43	56.89	25,049	71.68	9,898	28.32
Some college	34,168	77.42	3.10	74.32	29,783	87.17	4,385	12.83
Bachelor's degree or more	36,251	89.24	2.07	87.17	34,014	93.83	2,238	6.17
Family income of householder: [1]								
Less than $15,000	15,369	39.58	2.87	36.71	8,797	57.24	6,572	42.76
15,000 to 24,999	11,116	52.61	3.40	49.21	7,380	66.39	3,736	33.61
25,000 to 34,999	11,971	63.27	3.38	59.89	9,097	75.99	2,874	24.01
35,000 to 49,999	13,333	77.88	3.37	74.51	11,615	87.11	1,718	12.89
50,000 to 74,999	16,391	87.14	2.83	84.31	15,327	93.51	1,064	6.49
75,000 to 99,999	9,785	93.84	2.13	91.71	9,513	97.22	272	2.78
100,000 to 149,000	8,685	96.38	1.57	94.81	8,531	98.22	154	1.78
150,000 and over	5,961	97.99	0.68	97.31	5,899	98.97	61	1.03

[1] Includes other groups, not shown separately.

Source: U.S. Department of Commerce, National Telecommunications and Information Administration, "Digital Nation: Expanding Internet Usage," February 2011. See also <http://www.ntia.doc.gov/reports.html>.

Table 1163. Household Internet Usage In and Outside of the Home by State: 2010

[In percent. As of October. See headnote, Table 1162]

State	Any-where	In the home — Total	In the home — Dial-up	In the home — Broad-band	No Internet use	State	Any-where	In the home — Total	In the home — Dial-up	In the home — Broad-band	No Internet use
U.S.	**80.23**	**71.06**	**2.82**	**68.24**	**19.77**	MO	78.21	67.82	3.47	64.35	21.79
AL	74.18	60.03	4.51	55.52	25.82	MT	75.74	65.33	3.96	61.37	24.26
AK	88.64	78.67	5.30	73.37	11.36	NE	82.54	71.25	2.33	68.92	17.46
AZ	83.46	75.50	1.30	74.20	16.54	NV	84.33	76.58	2.37	74.20	15.67
AR	70.87	58.76	6.38	52.38	29.13	NH	86.35	80.98	3.15	77.82	13.65
CA	84.19	75.86	2.75	73.11	15.81	NJ	82.86	74.76	1.49	73.28	17.14
CO	82.68	74.78	3.14	71.63	17.32	NM	76.77	62.60	4.90	57.70	23.23
CT	81.95	76.49	1.65	74.84	18.05	NY	79.30	71.06	2.05	69.01	20.70
DE	79.08	71.72	3.37	68.35	20.92	NC	76.53	68.42	3.29	65.14	23.47
DC	80.95	73.40	1.71	71.69	19.05	ND	79.87	73.13	2.25	70.88	20.13
FL	79.93	72.02	1.83	70.19	20.07	OH	78.44	67.47	3.58	63.89	21.56
GA	79.89	70.43	1.82	68.60	20.11	OK	77.30	66.20	3.74	62.46	22.70
HI	78.57	71.09	1.93	69.15	21.43	OR	86.18	78.31	3.59	74.72	13.82
ID	84.12	75.54	3.55	71.98	15.88	PA	78.13	70.21	2.85	67.36	21.87
IL	79.85	70.71	2.04	68.67	20.15	RI	79.84	72.08	1.33	70.75	20.16
IN	74.73	61.29	2.44	58.85	25.27	SC	74.38	63.77	4.25	59.52	25.62
IA	79.45	70.70	3.24	67.46	20.55	SD	80.97	69.04	3.50	65.54	19.03
KS	84.78	76.38	1.75	74.63	15.22	TN	72.20	63.29	3.80	59.49	27.80
KY	72.02	61.27	3.52	57.75	27.98	TX	80.23	69.51	2.67	66.84	19.77
LA	74.94	62.81	2.35	60.47	25.06	UT	90.10	82.31	2.64	79.67	9.90
ME	81.72	73.36	5.99	67.36	18.28	VT	83.52	74.69	5.47	69.21	16.48
MD	83.25	76.34	2.23	74.11	16.75	VA	79.84	72.99	3.47	69.51	20.16
MA	83.82	77.53	1.64	75.89	16.18	WA	88.37	79.70	3.00	76.70	11.63
MI	80.81	69.76	3.43	66.34	19.19	WV	72.87	65.12	5.98	59.13	27.13
MN	83.44	73.65	3.08	70.56	16.56	WI	83.15	73.69	3.17	70.52	16.85
MS	71.43	57.66	5.98	51.68	28.57	WY	84.35	74.40	1.46	72.94	15.65

Source: U.S. Department of Commerce, National Telecommunications and Information Administration, "Digital Nation: Expanding Internet Usage," February 2011. See also <http://www.ntia.doc.gov/reports.html>.

Table 1164. Internet Access by Selected Characteristics: 2011

[For persons 18 years old and over (230,416 represents 230,416,000). As of fall 2011. Based on sample and subject to sampling error; see source for details]

Characteristic	Total adults	Accessed the Internet					
		At home	At work	At school or a library	At another place	Using a cellphone or mobile device	Using WIFI or wireless connection outside of home
Total adults (1,000) [1]	**230,416**	**165,295**	**82,369**	**23,703**	**44,535**	**87,278**	**53,061**
PERCENT DISTRIBUTION							
Total	100.00	100.00	100.00	100.00	100.00	100.00	100.00
Age:							
18 to 34 years old	30.70	34.70	32.63	61.89	50.48	50.49	45.68
35 to 54 years old	37.02	39.79	49.67	28.05	35.09	38.24	39.28
55 years old and over	32.28	25.51	17.69	10.06	14.43	11.27	15.04
Sex:							
Male	48.38	48.19	49.72	43.92	51.05	50.02	51.90
Female	51.62	51.81	50.28	56.08	48.95	49.98	48.10
Census region: [2]							
Northeast	18.26	19.46	19.26	20.00	17.74	18.01	20.17
Midwest	37.03	34.34	34.71	32.56	33.44	36.64	34.49
South	21.80	21.97	22.30	22.80	20.25	20.36	19.28
West	22.91	24.22	23.74	24.63	28.57	24.99	26.07
Household size:							
1 to 2 persons	45.77	41.60	40.18	31.58	37.17	34.35	38.16
3 to 4 persons	37.35	41.10	44.83	46.72	44.72	45.64	44.51
5 or more persons	16.88	17.30	14.99	21.70	18.12	20.01	17.33
Any child in household	40.45	44.07	47.37	46.42	46.34	51.25	46.67
Marital status:							
Single	26.85	27.56	23.86	53.95	40.75	38.13	35.47
Married	54.15	58.26	63.25	35.09	46.13	50.24	53.70
Other	19.00	14.18	12.89	10.96	13.12	11.63	10.83
Educational attainment:							
Graduated college plus	27.29	35.15	48.41	32.29	37.71	37.71	44.74
Attended college	27.94	32.12	31.77	43.46	33.64	33.08	34.13
Did not attend college	44.78	32.72	19.81	24.24	28.65	29.22	21.12
Employed full-time	47.83	54.49	85.80	39.03	54.18	62.42	61.88
Employed part-time	11.92	12.96	13.65	20.90	15.00	13.11	13.84
Household income:							
Less than $50,000	42.47	30.74	16.76	41.86	33.58	27.70	22.36
$50,000 to $74,999	19.20	20.79	19.94	15.87	17.78	19.18	19.07
$75,000 to $149,999	28.26	35.29	44.36	31.46	32.04	36.31	38.63
$150,000 or more	10.06	13.18	18.94	10.81	16.60	16.81	19.93

[1] Includes other labor force status not shown separately. [2] For composition of regions, see map inside front cover.

Source: GfK Mediamark Research & Intelligence, LLC, New York, NY, CyberStats, fall 2011 (copyright). See <http://www.gfkmri.com>.

Table 1165. Percent of Adults Who Own Electronic Devices by Age: 2010

[In percent. Based on a telephone survey of 3,001 adults 18 and older conducted August 9-September 13, 2010, including 1,000 reached via cell phone. Interviews were conducted in English and Spanish]

Device	All Adults (18 years old and over)	18 to 34 years	35 to 46 years	47 to 56 years	57 to 65 years	66 to 74 years	75 years and over
Cell phone	85	95	92	86	84	68	48
Desktop computer	59	57	69	65	64	48	28
Laptop computer	52	70	61	49	43	30	10
iPod/MP3 music player	47	74	56	42	26	16	3
Game console	42	63	63	38	19	8	3
e-Book reader, such as Kindle or Nook	5	5	5	7	3	6	2
Tablet, like iPad	4	5	5	4	3	1	1
None of these	9	1	3	8	8	20	43

Source: Pew Research Center, Pew Internet & American Life Project, *Generations and Their Gadgets*, <http://pewinternet.org/Reports/2011/Generations-and-gadgets.aspx>, (copyright).

Table 1166. Internet Activities of Adults by Geographic Community Type: 2010 to 2012

[In percent. For Internet users 18 years old and over. Represents persons who have ever performed the activity. Based on telephone surveys of persons with land-line telephones and cell phones. In August 2012, 2,253 persons were interviewed including 900 cell phone users. The response rate for the landline sample was 12 percent. The response rate for the cellular sample was 11 percent. This survey includes interviews conducted in English and Spanish. For earlier survey information, see headnote, Table 1168]

| Activity | Survey date (month, year) | Total adults | Internet users performing activity | | | |
			Total	Urban	Suburban	Rural
Buy a product online........................	May 2011	55	71	73	72	70
Buy or make a reservation for travel..........	May 2011	51	65	66	66	60
Categorize or tag online content like a photo, news story or blog post....	Sept. 2010	24	33	37	32	25
Create or work on your own online journal or blog....	May 2011	11	14	16	13	11
Do any banking online........................	May 2011	47	61	68	60	50
Get news online.............................	Aug. 2012	67	78	77	81	70
Look for health or medical information online....	May 2011	55	71	72	69	81
Look for news or information about politics....	May 2011	47	61	64	61	48
Look online for info about a job..............	May 2011	44	56	63	56	45
Look for information on Wikipedia..........	Feb. 2012	47	58	65	57	50
Make a donation to a charity online...........	May 2011	19	25	31	26	15
Make a phone call online, using a service such as Skype or Vonage....	May 2011	18	24	25	27	13
Pay bills online.............................	Sept. 2010	42	57	55	62	45
Pay to access or download digital content online, such as music video, or newspaper articles....	Sept. 2010	32	43	47	43	35
Play online games..........................	Sept. 2010	27	36	36	38	34
Post a comment or review online about a product you bought or a service you received....	Sept. 2010	24	32	34	35	24
Rate a product, service, or person..........	May 2011	29	37	40	38	26
Research a product or service online..........	Sept. 2010	58	78	79	79	77
Search online for a map or driving directions....	Sept. 2010	60	82	84	83	79
Send instant messages......................	Nov. 2010	34	46	49	47	42
Send or read e-mail........................	Nov. 2010	68	92	93	93	90
Take part in chat rooms or online discussions....	Sept. 2010	17	22	25	21	20
Use a search engine to find information..........	Feb. 2012	73	91	90	93	90
Use a social networking site like Facebook, LinkedIn or Google Plus....	Feb. 2012	53	66	69	65	64
Use Twitter...............................	Feb. 2012	12	15	19	14	8
Visit a local, state, or federal government Web site....	May 2011	52	67	68	69	61
Watch a video on a video-sharing site..........	May 2011	55	71	72	71	68

Source: Pew Internet & American Life Project Surveys, <http://www.pewinternet.org>, (copyright).

Table 1167. Online News Consumption by Selected Characteristics: 2000 to 2012

[Percent of Internet users 18 years old and over. Represents persons who report getting news online "ever" or "yesterday." Based on telephone surveys of persons with land-line telephones, unless otherwise noted. In May 2010, 2,252 persons were interviewed including 744 cell phone users. The response rate for the landline sample was 21.8 percent. The response rate for the cellular sample was 19.3 percent. In May 2011, 2,277 persons were interviewed including 755 cell phone users. The response rate for the landline sample was 13.6 percent. The response rate for the cellular sample was 11.5 percent. This survey includes interviews conducted in English and Spanish. In August 2012, 2,253 persons were interviewed including 900 cell phone users. The response rate for the landline sample was 12 percent. The response rate for the cellular sample was 11 percent. This survey includes interviews conducted in English and Spanish.]

| Characteristic | "Ever" get news online | | | | Got news online "yesterday" | | | |
	2000	2010	2011 [1]	2012 [1]	2000	2010	2011 [1]	2012 [1]
Total adult Internet users..........	**60**	**75**	**76**	**78**	**22**	**43**	**45**	**(NA)**
Age:								
18 to 29 years old....................	56	75	72	84	16	44	43	(NA)
30 to 49 years old....................	63	78	83	83	25	45	51	(NA)
50 to 64 years old....................	57	76	77	71	25	42	44	(NA)
65 years old and over.................	53	62	60	66	28	34	32	(NA)
Sex:								
Male................................	66	77	77	76	29	48	52	(NA)
Female..............................	53	74	76	80	16	38	39	(NA)
Race/ethnicity:								
White, non-Hispanic..................	60	75	76	79	23	43	46	(NA)
Black, non-Hispanic..................	63	72	77	74	13	42	34	(NA)
English-speaking Hispanic..........	57	73	72	73	23	35	40	(NA)
Annual household income:								
Less than $30,000....................	55	64	65	69	21	28	31	(NA)
$30,000 to $49,999..................	57	74	79	80	20	35	44	(NA)
$50,000 to $74,999..................	63	78	82	81	22	47	52	(NA)
$75,000 or more......................	69	84	88	89	31	60	62	(NA)
Frequency of Internet use:								
Daily................................	66	82	(NA)	(NA)	33	54	(NA)	(NA)
Several times per week..............	59	64	(NA)	(NA)	17	14	(NA)	(NA)
Less often...........................	51	38	(NA)	(NA)	12	5	(NA)	(NA)

NA Not available. [1] Includes interviews conducted in English and Spanish.

Source: Pew Internet & American Life Project Surveys from March 2000; May 2010; May 2011; and August 2012. See <http://www.pewinternet.org>, (copyright).

Table 1168. Typical Daily Internet Activities of Adult Internet Users: 2010 to 2012

[In percent. For Internet users 18 years old and over. Represents persons who have ever performed the activity. Based on telephone surveys of persons with land-line telephones and cell phones. In September 2010, 3,001 persons were interviewed including 1,000 cell phone users. The response rate for the landline sample was 13.6 percent. The response rate for the cellular sample was 17 percent. In November 2010, 2,257 persons were interviewed including 755 cell phone users. The response rate for the landline sample was 13.7 percent. The response rate for the cellular sample was 15 percent. In May 2011, 2,277 persons were interviewed including 755 cell phone users. The response rate for the landline sample was 13.6 percent. The response rate for the cellular sample was 11.5 percent. In February 2012, 2,253 persons were interviewed including 901 cell phone users. The response rate for the landline sample was 11 percent. The response rate for the cellular sample was 11 percent. This survey includes interviews conducted in English and Spanish]

Activity	Survey date (month, year)	Total Internet users	Age 18 to 29 years old	Age 30 to 49 years old	Age 50 to 64 years old	Age 65 years old and over	Sex Male	Sex Female
Buy a product online	May 2011	6	7	5	7	7	7	5
Buy or make a reservation for travel	May 2011	4	4	4	3	1	4	3
Categorize or tag online content like a photo, news story or blog post	Sept. 2010	11	18	12	5	4	12	10
Create or work on your own online journal or blog	May 2011	4	4	6	3	2	6	3
Do any banking online	May 2011	24	19	28	27	15	24	23
Get news online	May 2011	45	43	51	44	32	52	39
Look for health or medical information online	May 2011	10	8	9	11	10	8	11
Look for news or information about politics	May 2011	30	27	34	34	19	36	26
Look online for info about a job	May 2011	11	15	12	9	1	11	11
Look for information on Wikipedia	Feb. 2012	16	19	15	15	11	18	13
Make a donation to a charity online	May 2011	1	1	1	2	1	1	1
Make a phone call online, using a service, such as Skype or Vonage	May 2011	5	6	5	5	2	6	4
Pay bills online	Sept. 2010	15	14	19	11	11	15	15
Pay to access or download digital content online, such as music video, or newspaper articles	Sept. 2010	10	13	9	12	3	13	8
Play online games	Sept. 2010	13	16	15	10	9	13	13
Post a comment or review online about a product you bought or a service you received	Sept. 2010	4	6	5	2	3	5	4
Rate a product, service, or person	May 2011	4	4	4	6	2	5	4
Research a product or service online	Sept. 2010	28	27	32	26	16	31	24
Search online for a map or driving directions	Sept. 2010	14	15	17	12	7	16	12
Send instant messages	Nov. 2010	18	29	17	13	4	18	18
Send or read e-mail	Nov. 2010	61	64	63	61	46	59	64
Take part in chat rooms or online discussions	Sept. 2010	7	9	9	5	2	8	6
Use a search engine to find information	Feb. 2012	59	66	65	52	38	59	60
Use a social networking site, like Facebook, LinkedIn or Google Plus	Feb. 2012	48	70	52	31	18	42	54
Use Twitter	Feb. 2012	8	17	7	4	1	8	8
Visit a local, state, or federal government Web site	May 2011	13	11	15	13	6	14	12
Watch a video on a video-sharing site	May 2011	28	47	27	20	11	32	25

Source: Pew Internet & American Life Project Surveys, <http://www.pewinternet.org>, (copyright).

Table 1169. Public Libraries, Selected Characteristics: 2009

[11,594 represents $11,594,000,000. Based on survey of public libraries. Data are for public libraries in the 50 states and the District of Columbia. The response rates for these items are between 97 and 100 percent. See source for details]

Population of service area	Number of— Public libraries	Number of— Stationary outlets [1]	Operating income Total [2] (mil. dol.)	Operating income Source State government (percent)	Operating income Source Local government (percent)	Paid staff [3] Total	Paid staff [3] Librarians with ALA-MLS [4]	Average number of public use Internet computers per stationary outlet [5]
Total	9,225	16,698	11,594	7.5	84.2	144,261	32,977	13.9
1,000,000 or more	28	1,153	1,897	5.1	83.6	18,357	5,087	26.2
500,000 to 999,000	56	1,139	1,716	7.7	85.4	19,544	4,774	22.5
250,000 to 499,999	104	1,129	1,323	8.7	84.2	16,008	3,961	19.3
100,000 to 249,999	351	2,061	1,890	8.1	84.8	23,857	5,211	18.0
50,000 to 99,999	556	1,624	1,423	9.4	84.1	18,586	4,296	16.9
25,000 to 49,999	974	1,719	1,432	7.4	84.8	18,519	4,458	15.5
10,000 to 24,999	1,772	2,286	1,177	6.9	84.5	16,595	3,634	12.4
5,000 to 9,999	1,498	1,648	432	8.0	80.7	6,898	1,103	9.1
2,500 to 4,999	1,321	1,353	175	6.5	79.0	3,152	310	6.6
1,000 to 2,499	1,508	1,527	100	5.9	76.4	2,029	125	4.9
Fewer than 1,000	1,057	1,059	30	8.1	73.7	716	21	3.6

[1] The sum of central and branch libraries. The total number of central libraries was 9,046; the total of branch libraries was 7,652. [2] Includes income from the federal government (0.4%) and other sources (7.9%), not shown separately. [3] Full-time equivalents. [4] Librarians with master's degrees from a graduate library education program accredited by the American Library Association (ALA). Total librarians, including those without ALA-MLS, were 48,014. [5] The average per stationary outlet was calculated by dividing the total number of public use Internet computers in central and branch outlets by the total number of such outlets.

Source: Institute of Museum and Library Services, *Public Libraries Survey: Fiscal Year 2009*, (IMLS-2011–PLS-02), October 2011. See also <http://harvester.census.gov/imls/pubs/pls/index.asp>.

Table 1170. Number of Public Libraries and Library Services by State: 2009

[For Fiscal Year. 1,591,293 represents 1,591,293,000. Based on survey of public libraries. Public libraries can have one or more outlets that provide direct service to the public. The three types of outlets include central libraries, branch libraries, and bookmobiles]

State	Number of public libraries [1]	Library visits (1,000s)	Per capita visits [2]	Per capita circulation of materials [2]	Average number of public use Internet computers per stationary outlet [3]
U.S.....	9,225	1,591,293	5.4	8.1	13.9
AL......	210	16,945	3.7	4.6	15.9
AK......	87	3,532	5.1	6.4	6.1
AZ......	89	29,624	4.4	7.4	18.6
AR......	52	10,660	4.0	5.3	9.3
CA......	181	182,181	4.8	6.2	15.9
CO.....	114	32,812	6.7	13.0	16.6
CT......	195	24,659	7.0	9.7	15.5
DE......	21	4,357	5.6	10.5	15.2
DC......	1	2,945	4.9	3.9	23.8
FL......	80	89,381	4.8	6.8	27.4
GA.......	61	40,923	4.3	5.1	16.6
HI.......	1	6,020	4.7	5.6	10.5
ID........	104	9,149	6.8	10.3	8.5
IL........	634	82,482	7.0	9.7	14.6
IN........	238	42,205	7.4	14.1	16.7
IA........	541	19,467	6.5	9.7	6.9
KS......	328	15,674	6.6	11.8	8.7
KY......	117	19,113	4.5	6.9	17.8
LA......	68	15,592	3.5	4.2	13.0
ME.....	269	7,194	5.9	7.9	5.3
MD.....	24	34,474	6.1	10.7	21.6
MA.....	370	42,238	6.5	8.9	11.3
MI......	384	59,126	6.0	8.6	15.5
MN.....	138	29,544	5.6	11.2	13.3
MS.....	50	9,456	3.2	3.0	9.5
MO......	150	30,347	5.9	10.1	12.3
MT........	80	4,387	4.9	6.9	8.1
NE......	269	9,182	6.8	10.4	6.8
NV......	22	11,585	4.3	7.2	14.5
NH......	230	7,678	5.9	8.9	5.4
NJ........	301	51,019	6.1	7.8	15.5
NM......	91	7,800	5.0	6.5	12.0
NY........	756	119,811	6.3	8.4	14.9
NC......	77	44,409	4.8	6.0	16.2
ND......	85	2,514	4.4	7.8	6.3
OH......	251	92,402	8.0	17.0	15.8
OK......	115	21,171	7.0	7.1	11.3
OR......	127	24,681	6.8	15.4	12.0
PA........	458	49,246	4.1	6.0	11.4
RI........	48	6,814	6.4	7.3	15.2
SC........	42	18,106	4.2	6.1	16.0
SD........	112	3,976	5.4	8.4	6.1
TN........	186	21,545	3.5	4.0	14.2
TX........	559	79,152	3.5	5.1	18.5
UT........	71	19,038	7.0	13.4	14.2
VT........	184	3,932	6.5	7.8	5.1
VA........	91	42,301	5.5	9.8	16.3
WA......	63	44,124	6.7	12.9	15.7
WV......	97	6,082	3.4	4.3	7.4
WI........	380	36,481	6.4	11.5	10.7
WY.......	23	3,756	7.1	9.5	9.9

[1] Of the 9,225 public libraries, 7,466 were single outlet libraries and 1,759 were multiple outlet libraries. Single outlet libraries are a central library, bookmobile, or books by mail only outlet. Multiple outlet libraries have two or more direct service outlets including some combination of single outlet libraries. [2] Per capita rate and per 1,000 population based on total unduplicated population of legal service area given by the state library agency of each state. [3] The average per stationary outlet was calculated by dividing the total number of public use Internet computers in central and branch outlets by the total number of such outlets.

Source: Institute of Museum and Library Services, *Public Libraries Survey: Fiscal Year 2009*, (IMLS-2011–PLS-02), October 2011. See also <http://harvester.census.gov/imls/pubs/pls/index.asp>.

Table 1171. Public Library Use of the Internet: 2009 and 2010

[In percent, except number of outlets. As of spring. Based on sample survey; see source for details]

Item	2009				2010			
		Metropolitan status [1]				Metropolitan status [1]		
	Total	Urban	Suburban	Rural	Total	Urban	Suburban	Rural
Total libraries [2]............................	16,620	2,940	5,421	8,259	16,802	2,898	5,841	8,063
Connected with public access.............	99.0	99.0	99.4	98.7	99.3	99.5	99.4	99.3
Average number of workstations........	14.2	25.4	15.8	9.2	16.0	28.0	19.6	9.6
Speed of access:								
Less than 256 kbps.....................	3.4	(3)	1.0	3.6	1.4	(3)	(3)	2.3
257 kbps to 768 kbps..................	9.2	1.9	5.0	8.5	5.0	(3)	4.2	6.9
769 kbps to 1.4 mbps..................	9.3	2.1	5.8	8.3	5.6	1.4	4.2	5.8
1.5 mbps...............................	25.5	15.8	25.8	32.6	22.7	9.8	21.1	28.0
1.6 mbps to 3 mbps....................	10.0	11.0	8.4	12.9	12.0	11.1	9.9	13.7
3.1 mbps to 6 mbps....................	11.2	10.1	9.9	10.2	11.3	12.2	10.7	11.5
6.1 mbps to 10 mbps...................	11.0	19.0	15.9	7.4	12.1	16.3	14.6	9.0
10.1mbps to 20mbps...................	(X)	16.4	9.2	3.7	10.8	22.2	12.3	6.1
20.1mbps to 30mbps...................	(X)	2.3	1.2	(3)	2.0	2.7	2.4	1.4
30.1mbps to 40mbps...................	(X)	3.6	1.3	(3)	1.4	1.0	2.1	1.1
Greater than 40mbps...................	(X)	14.8	9.5	4.5	10.7	20.8	13.1	5.8
Don't know.............................	8.1	2.2	6.9	6.8	5.0	1.4	4.7	6.3
Public library availability of wireless Internet access:								
Currently available......................	82.2	87.5	87.3	76.5	85.7	91.5	89.3	81.2
Plan to make available within the next year.............................	6.8	6.0	6.9	15.0	5.9	4.9	4.4	7.2

[1] Urban = inside central city; Suburban = In metro area, outside of a central city; Rural = outside a metro area. [2] Central libraries and branches; excludes bookmobiles. [3] Less than 1 percent.

Source: Information Policy and Access Center, College of Information Studies, University of Maryland, College Park, MD, 2010–2011 Public Library Funding and Technology Access Survey: Survey Findings and Results by John Carlo Bertot, et al., University of Maryland, College Park, MD (copyright). Study funded by the American Library Association.

Table 1172. Adult Computer and Internet Users by Selected Characteristics: 2000 to 2012

[Percent of persons 18 years old and over. Represents persons who use a computer or the Internet at a workplace, school, home, or anywhere else, on at least an occasional basis. Based on telephone surveys of persons with land-line telephones unless otherwise noted. May 2011 and April 2012 surveys include interviews conducted in English and Spanish. In April 2012, 2,254 persons were interviewed including 903 cell phone users. The response rate for the landline sample was 11 percent. The response rate for the cellular sample was 11 percent. In May 2011, 2,277 persons were interviewed including 755 cell phone users. The response rate for the landline sample was 13.6 percent. The response rate for the cellular sample was 11.5 percent. For 2000, Internet users include persons who ever go online to access the Internet or World Wide Web or to send and receive e-mail. For 2005 and 2011, Internet users include those who at least occasionally use the Internet or send and receive e-mail]

Characteristic	Adult computer users				Adult Internet users				All adults, by type of home connection, 2012 [1]	
	2000	2005	2011 [1]	2012 [1]	2000	2005	2011 [1]	2012 [1]	Broad-band	Dial-up
Total adults	**65**	**71**	**(NA)**	**(NA)**	**53**	**69**	**78**	**82**	**66**	**3**
Age:										
18 to 29 years old	82	83	(NA)	(NA)	72	82	95	97	75	4
30 to 49 years old	76	81	(NA)	(NA)	62	80	87	91	76	2
50 to 64 years old	61	72	(NA)	(NA)	48	68	74	77	62	3
65 years old and over	21	31	(NA)	(NA)	15	28	42	53	39	4
Sex:										
Male	66	72	(NA)	(NA)	56	70	78	83	66	3
Female	64	70	(NA)	(NA)	51	67	78	82	66	3
Race/ethnicity:										
White, non-Hispanic	66	72	(NA)	(NA)	55	70	79	84	70	3
Black, non-Hispanic	59	60	(NA)	(NA)	42	54	67	77	54	3
English-speaking Hispanic	64	75	(NA)	(NA)	48	73	78	75	51	5
Educational attainment:										
Less than high school	28	36	(NA)	(NA)	19	35	42	58	34	5
High school graduate [2]	56	63	(NA)	(NA)	41	59	69	75	55	4
Some college	80	81	(NA)	(NA)	69	80	89	90	74	3
College graduate or higher	88	90	(NA)	(NA)	79	88	94	95	87	2
Annual household income:										
Less than $30,000	48	52	(NA)	(NA)	35	50	63	71	46	3
$30,000 to $49,999	74	76	(NA)	(NA)	61	74	85	87	68	5
$50,000 to $74,999	85	88	(NA)	(NA)	74	86	89	93	85	3
$75,000 or more	90	92	(NA)	(NA)	81	91	96	97	87	2

NA Not available. [1] 2011 and 2012 surveys include interviews conducted in English and Spanish. [2] Includes those with a GED certificate.

Source: Pew Internet & American Life Project Surveys from September-December 2000; September and December of 2005; May 2011; and April 2012. See <http://www.pewinternet.org>.

Table 1173. Public Library Systems Operating Budget Change by Metropolitan Status: 2009 to 2012

[In percent. For fiscal year ending in year shown. Data from 2011-2012 Public Library Funding & Technology Survey, conducted by The American Library Association Office for Research & Statistics and the Information Policy & Access Center at the University of Maryland. Based upon responses from 7,260 public libraries. See footnote 1 Table 1171 for description of metropolitan status]

Change in Budget	Urban				Suburban				Rural				All			
	2009	2010	2011	2012	2009	2010	2011	2012	2009	2010	2011	2012	2009	2010	2011	2012
Increased up to 6%	47.3	28.2	25.2	26.1	51.1	35.1	35.3	32.0	50.6	38.8	35.8	39.0	50.5	37.0	35.0	38.4
Increased 6% or more	10.6	5.2	4.2	1.9	9.0	5.2	5.2	4.9	9.4	7.2	5.4	4.8	9.4	6.7	5.3	4.8
Decreased less than 6%	14.7	24.2	31.9	30.9	13.0	24.2	22.0	21.9	8.9	15.5	17.3	15.9	10.6	17.1	19.7	18.7
Decreased more than 6%	7.4	30.4	22.6	14.7	3.6	17.4	14.2	10.2	3.3	11.0	9.6	6.7	3.7	14.3	11.9	8.3
Stayed same	19.9	11.4	16.2	25.6	23.3	22.7	23.2	23.3	27.8	27.5	32.0	33.7	25.9	25.0	28.2	29.7

Source: American Library Association (ALA) *Public Library Funding & Technology Access Study 2011-2012,* published as a supplement to *American Libraries,* Summer 2012. See also <http://www.ala.org/research/plftas/2011_2012>, (copyright).

Banking, Finance, and Insurance

This section presents data on the nation's finances, various types of financial institutions, money and credit, securities, insurance, and real estate. The primary sources of these data are publications of several departments of the federal government, especially the U.S. Treasury Department, and independent agencies such as the Federal Deposit Insurance Corporation, the Board of Governors of the Federal Reserve System, and the Securities and Exchange Commission. National data on insurance are available primarily from private organizations, such as the American Council of Life Insurers and the National Association of Insurance Commissioners.

Flow of funds—The flow of funds accounts of the Federal Reserve Board bring together statistics on all of the major forms of financial instruments to present an economy-wide view of asset and liability relationships. In flow form, the accounts relate borrowing and lending to one another and to the nonfinancial activities that generate income and production. Each claim outstanding is included simultaneously as an asset of the lender and as a liability of the debtor. The accounts also indicate the balance between asset totals and liability totals over the economy as a whole. Several publications of the Federal Reserve Board contain information on the flow of funds accounts: Summary data on flows and outstandings, in the statistical release *Flow of Funds Accounts of the United States* (quarterly); and concepts and organization of the accounts in *Guide to the Flow of Funds Accounts* (2012). Data are also available on the Federal Reserve Board's Web site at <http://www.federalreserve.gov/>.

Survey of Consumer Finances (SCF)—The Federal Reserve Board, in cooperation with the Treasury Department, sponsors this survey, which is conducted every 3 years to provide detailed information on the finances of U.S. families. Among the topics covered are the balance sheet, pension, income, and other demographic characteristics of U.S. families. The survey also gathers information on the use of financial institutions. Since 1992, data for the SCF have been collected by the National Organization for Research at the University of Chicago. Data and information on the survey are available on the Federal Reserve Board's Web site at <http://www.federalreserve.gov/econresdata/scf/scfindex.htm>.

Banking system—Banks in this country are organized under the laws of both the states and the federal government and are regulated by several bank supervisory agencies. National banks are supervised by the Comptroller of the Currency. *Reports of Condition and Income*, commonly known as call reports, have been collected from national banks since 1863. Summaries of these reports are published in the Comptroller's *Annual Report*, which also presents data on the structure of the national banking system.

The Federal Reserve System was established in 1913 to exercise central banking functions, some of which are shared with the U.S. Treasury. It includes national banks and such state banks that voluntarily join the system. Statements of state bank members are consolidated by the Federal Reserve Board with data for national banks collected by the Comptroller of the

Currency into totals for all member banks of the system. Balance sheet data for member banks and other commercial banks are available on the Federal Reserve Board's Web site at <http://www.federalreserve.gov/econresdata/statisticsdata.htm>.

The Federal Deposit Insurance Corporation (FDIC), established in 1933, insures each depositor up to $250,000. Major item balance sheet and income data for all insured financial institutions are published in the *FDIC Quarterly Banking Profile*. This publication is also available on the Internet at the following address: <http://www2.fdic.gov/qbp/>. Quarterly financial information for individual institutions is available through the FDIC and Federal Financial Institutions Examination Council Web sites at <http://www.fdic.gov> and <http://www.ffiec.gov>.

Credit unions—Federally chartered credit unions are under the supervision of the National Credit Union Administration. State-chartered credit unions are supervised by the respective state supervisory authorities. The administration publishes comprehensive program and statistical information on all federal and federally insured state credit unions in the *Annual Report of the National Credit Union Administration*.

Other credit agencies—Insurance companies, finance companies dealing primarily in installment sales financing, and personal loan companies represent important sources of funds for the credit market. Statistics on loans, investments, cash, etc., of life insurance companies are published principally by the American Council of Life Insurers in its *Life Insurers Fact Book*. Consumer credit data are available on the Federal Reserve Board's Web site at <http://www.federalreserve.gov/econresdata/statisticsdata.htm>. Government corporations and credit agencies make available credit of specified types or to specified groups of private borrowers, either by lending directly or by insuring or guaranteeing loans made by private lending institutions. Data on operations of government credit agencies, along with other government corporations, are available in reports of individual agencies.

Securities—The Securities and Exchange Commission (SEC) was established in 1934 to protect the interests of the public and investors against malpractices in the securities and financial markets and to provide the fullest possible disclosure of information regarding securities to the investing public.

Data on the securities industry and securities transactions are also available from a number of private sources. The Securities Industry and Financial Markets Association, New York, NY, <http://www.sifma.org/>, publishes the *Securities Industry Fact Book* and *Securities Industry Yearbook*. The Investment Company Institute, Washington, DC, <http://www.ici.org/>, publishes a reference book, research newsletters, and a variety of research reports that examine the industry, its shareholders, or industry issues. The annual *Investment Company Fact Book* is a guide to trends and statistics observed in the investment company industry. *Fundamentals* is a newsletter summarizing the findings of major Institute research projects. Institute research reports provide a detailed examination of shareholder demographics and other aspects of fund ownership.

Among the many sources of data on stock and bond prices and sales are the New York Stock Exchange, New York, NY, <http://www.nyse.com/>; NASDAQ, Washington, DC, <http://www.nasdaq.com/>; Global Financial Data, Los Angeles, CA, <http://www.globalfinancialdata.com/>; and Dow-Jones & Company, Inc., New York, NY, <http://www.djindexes.com>.

Insurance—Insuring companies, which are regulated by the various states or the District of Columbia, are classified as either life or property. Both life and property insurance companies may underwrite health insurance. Insuring companies, other than those classified as life, are permitted to underwrite one or more property lines provided they are so licensed and have the necessary capital or surplus. There are a number of published sources for statistics on the various classes of insurance—life, health, fire, marine, and casualty. Organizations representing certain classes of insurers publish reports for these classes. The American Council of Life Insurers publishes statistics on life insurance purchases, ownership, benefit payments, and assets in its *Life Insurers Fact Book*.

Statistical reliability—For a discussion of statistical collection, estimation, and sampling procedures and measures of reliability applicable to data from the Census Bureau and the Federal Reserve Board's Survey of Consumer Finances, see Appendix III.

Table 1174. Gross Domestic Product in Finance, Insurance, Real Estate, Rental and Leasing in Current and Chained (2005) Dollars: 2000 to 2011

[In billions of dollars, except percent (762 represents $762,000,000,000.) Represents value added by industry. Data for 2000 based on the 1997 North American Classification System (NAICS); beginning 2009 based on 2002 NAICS. See text, Section 15. For definition of gross domestic product and explanation of chained dollars, see text, Section 13, Income]

Industry	NAICS code	Current Dollars				Chained (2005) dollars			
		2000	2009	2010	2011	2000	2009	2010	2011
Finance & insurance, total.............	**52**	**762**	**1,099**	**1,242**	**1,256**	**841**	**1,044**	**1,112**	**1,132**
Percent of gross domestic product......		7.7	7.9	8.5	8.3	7.5	8.5	8.5	8.5
Monetary authorities–central bank, credit intermediation, and related activities.....	521,522	338	525.2	587.8	(NA)	371	503	507	(NA)
Security, commodity contracts, & investment activities......................	523	126	169.7	201.4	(NA)	124	159	189	(NA)
Insurance carriers & related activities.....	524	274	369.9	404.6	(NA)	339	353	376	(NA)
Funds, trusts, & other financial vehicles (part).............................	525	24	34	48	(NA)	20	33	47	(NA)
Real estate & rental & leasing, total. ..	**53**	**1,236**	**1,866**	**1,765**	**1,752**	**1,422**	**1,699**	**1,625**	**1,583**
Percent of gross domestic product		12.4	13.3	12.2	11.6	12.7	12.4	11.9	11.9
Real estate..............................	531	1,098	1679	1564	(NA)	1,266	**1,528**	**1,440**	(NA)
Rental & leasing services and lessors of other nonfinancial intangible assets [1]....	532533	138	186	201	(NA)	156	171	185	(NA)

NA Not available. [1] Includes lessors of other nonfinancial intangible assets.

Source: U.S. Bureau of Economic Analysis, <http://www.bea.gov/Industry/Index.htm>.

Table 1175. Finance and Insurance/Real Estate and Rental and Leasing—Establishments, Revenue, Payroll, and Employees by Kind of Business (2002 NAICS Basis): 2002 and 2007

[2,804 represents $2,804,000,000,000. For establishments with payroll. Based on the 2002 and 2007 Economic Censuses; see Appendix III]

Kind of business	2002 NAICS code [1]	Number of establishments		Revenue (bil. dol.)		Annual payrol (bil. dol.)		Paid employees (1,000)	
		2002	2007	2002	2007	2002	2007	2002	2007
Finance & insurance [2]........................	**52**	**440,268**	**506,507**	**2,804**	**3,711**	**377.8**	**505.2**	**6,579**	**6,649**
Monetary authorities—central bank............	521	47	47	29	45	1.2	1.3	22	19
Credit intermediation & related activities........	522	196,451	231,439	1,056	1,343	151.2	180.9	3,300	3,280
Security, commodity contracts, & like activity...	523	72,338	85,475	316	612	103.4	166.3	832	885
Insurance carriers & related activities...........	524	169,520	184,752	1,380	1,669	120.6	153.9	2,406	2,423
Real estate & rental & leasing...............	**53**	**322,815**	**379,503**	**336**	**452**	**60.2**	**85.2**	**1,949**	**2,249**
Real estate.............................	531	256,086	308,004	224	289	41.7	58.6	1,305	1,487
Rental & leasing services.........................	532	64,344	65,120	95	122	16.9	21.1	617	630
Lessors of other nonfinancial intangible assets.............................	533	2,385	2,447	17	33	1.7	2.3	27	29

[1] Based on the North American Industry Classification System (NAICS); see text, Section 15. [2] Total does not include NAICS 525, Funds, trusts, and other financial vehicles, not published in the 2007 Economic Census.

Source: U.S. Census Bureau, "2007 Economic Census; Core Business Statistics Series: Advance Comparative Statistics for the United States (2002 NAICS Basis): 2007 and 2002," June 2010, see <http://www.census.gov/econ/census07/>.

Table 1176. Finance and Insurance—Nonemployer Establishments and Receipts by Kind of Business: 2007 to 2009

[763.5 represents 763,527. Includes only firms subject to federal income tax. Nonemployers are businesses with no paid employees. Data originate chiefly from administrative records of the Internal Revenue Service; see Appendix III]

Kind of business	NAICS code [1]	Establishments (1,000)			Receipts (mil. dol.)		
		2007	2008	2009	2007	2008	2009
Finance and insurance........................	**52**	**763.5**	**733.5**	**733.7**	**54,351**	**56,434**	**51,579**
Credit intermediation & related activities.......................	522	92.7	72.8	63.0	4,591	3,394	3,034
Depository credit intermediation..................	5221	7.6	7.4	6.7	228	202	180
Nondepository credit intermediation...............	5222	31.7	27.0	25.1	2,376	1,900	1,711
Activities related to credit intermediation..................	5223	53.4	38.4	31.2	1,986	1,292	1,143
Security, commodity contracts, & like activity....	523	281.7	270.9	279.3	29,618	32,752	30,249
Securities & commodity contracts interm & brokerage.......	5231	32.6	30.8	30.5	5,496	6,631	5,345
Investment banking and securities dealing..................	52311	8.1	7.4	7.6	1,596	2,175	1,663
Securities brokerage..................	52312	19.8	19.0	18.7	2,977	3,360	3,025
Commodity contracts dealing..................	52313	1.4	1.3	1.2	412	582	284
Commodity contracts brokerage..................	52314	3.4	3.1	3.0	511	514	373
Securities & commodity exchanges..................	5232	1.9	1.9	1.9	578	846	885
Other financial investment activities..................	5239	247.1	238.2	247.0	23,544	25,276	24,019
Insurance carriers & related activities...........................	524	389.2	389.8	391.3	20,143	20,288	18,295
Insurance carriers..................	5241	2.9	3.1	3.2	189	191	191
Agencies & other insurance-related activities.................	5242	386.2	386.7	388.2	19,954	20,097	18,105
Insurance agencies & brokerages..................	52421	268.5	267.1	269.7	15,016	14,977	13,572
Other insurance related activities..................	52429	117.7	119.6	118.4	4,938	5,119	4,533

[1] Data for 2007-2009 is based on 2007 North American Industry Classification System (NAICS). For more information, see text, Section 15.

Source: U.S. Census Bureau, "Nonemployer Statistics," accessed October 2012, <http://www.census.gov/econ/nonemployer/index.html>.

Table 1177. Finance and Insurance—Establishments, Employees, and Payroll: 2008 and 2009

[501.9 represents 501,900. Covers establishments with payroll. Employees are for the week including March 12. Excludes most government employees, railroad employees, and self-employed persons. For statement on methodology, see Appendix III]

Kind of business	NAICS code [1]	Establishments (1,000)		Employees(1,000)		Payroll (bil.dol.)	
		2008	2009	2008	2009	2008	2009
Finance & insurance, total [2]...........	52	501.9	488.9	6,512	6,171	522.3	460.7
Monetary authorities—central bank..............	521	0.1	0.0	19	18	1.4	1.5
Credit intermediation & related activities..............	522	225.0	209.6	3,077	2,859	175.3	160.2
Depository credit intermediation [2]..................	5221	129.8	129.0	2,135	2,032	119.4	111.4
Commercial banking........................	52211	95.6	95.3	1,644	1,560	97.1	90.5
Savings institutions.......................	52212	16.1	15.7	235	215	12.3	10.5
Credit unions.............................	52213	18.0	17.9	253	254	9.8	10.2
Nondepository credit intermediation [2]............	5222	51.0	43.6	645	558	41.9	35.7
Real estate credit..........................	522292	20.4	15.5	276	226	18.0	14.2
Activities related to credit intermediation..............	5223	44.3	37.0	297	269	13.9	13.1
Security, commodity contracts & like activity..........	523	92.7	98.3	974	928	184.3	143.2
Security & commodity contracts intermediation & brokerage [2]	5231	42.3	47.7	534	489	104.5	72.9
Investment banking & securities dealing............	52311	4.5	4.9	137	115	46.9	28.9
Securities brokerage........................	52312	35.4	40.5	375	353	53.8	40.6
Securities & commodity exchanges.................	5232	0.1	0.1	(NA)	5	(NA)	0.8
Other financial investment activities...............	5239	50.2	50.5	432	433	78.8	69.5
Insurance carriers & related activities................	524	183.2	180.0	2,432	2,359	159.9	154.7
Insurance carriers [2].......................	5241	35.7	35.2	1,518	1,484	108.8	105.8
Direct life insurance carriers....................	524113	8.6	9.2	399	367	31.3	28.0
Direct health & medical insurance carriers.........	524114	4.7	5.0	469	474	30.7	31.5
Direct property & casualty insurance carriers.......	524126	15.3	14.6	549	558	39.2	40.3
Agencies & other insurance-related activities [2]......	5242	147.5	144.8	914	874	51.1	48.8
Insurance agencies & brokerages..................	52421	134.6	132.3	696	662	38.8	36.8

NA Not available. [1] 2008 and 2009 data use 2007 North American Industry Classification System (NAICS). 2007 data use NAICS 2002 For more information, see text, Section 15. [2] Includes industries not shown separately.

Source: U.S. Census Bureau, "County Business Patterns," May 2012, <http://www.census.gov/econ/cbp/index.html>.

Table 1178. Flow of Funds Accounts—Financial Assets of Financial and Nonfinancial Institutions by Holder Sector: 1990 to 2011

[In billions of dollars (35,926 represents $35,926,000,000,000). As of Dec. 31]

Sector	1990	1995	2000	2005	2006	2007	2008	2009	2010	2011
All sectors.................	35,926	53,793	90,615	125,802	140,191	152,482	140,747	146,404	153,333	156,862
Households [1].....................	14,695	21,780	33,767	44,889	49,418	52,157	42,861	45,727	49,404	50,229
Nonfinancial business........................	3,981	5,568	11,235	14,505	15,784	17,358	16,631	16,934	17,647	18,544
Nonfinancial noncorporate................	391	592	1,473	2,597	3,116	3,596	3,693	3,592	3,456	3,470
Nonfinancial corporations...................	3,589	4,975	9,762	11,909	12,668	13,762	12,938	13,341	14,191	15,074
State and local government.................	1,020	1,122	1,662	2,194	2,296	2,517	2,423	2,503	2,632	2,525
U.S. Government...........................	442	432	570	644	637	681	1,262	1,344	1,571	1,349
Monetary authority.........................	342	472	636	879	908	951	2,271	2,267	2,453	2,947
Private depository institutions...............	4,510	5,332	7,351	10,643	11,368	12,362	14,115	13,425	13,543	14,635
U.S.-chartered depository institutions.....	3,941	4,344	6,089	9,100	9,785	10,513	11,639	11,257	11,291	11,706
Foreign banking offices in U.S...........	367	671	805	818	828	1,048	1,625	1,267	1,337	1,999
Banks in U.S.-affiliated areas..............	26	37	62	106	105	105	102	95	80	76
Credit unions.............................	176	280	395	619	650	696	749	806	836	854
Life insurance companies....................	1,351	2,064	3,136	4,351	4,685	4,950	4,515	4,824	5,176	5,340
Property-casualty insurance companies.......	533	740	858	1,246	1,336	1,386	1,306	1,384	1,404	1,434
Private pension funds.......................	1,629	2,899	4,468	5,389	6,083	6,411	4,553	5,471	6,100	6,070
Defined benefit plans.....................	900	1,466	1,979	2,281	2,530	2,596	1,853	2,105	2,264	2,206
Defined contribution plans.................	729	1,433	2,489	3,107	3,553	3,815	2,699	3,366	3,836	3,864
State and local government employee retirement funds.................	730	1,327	2,293	2,721	3,090	3,199	2,325	2,674	2,931	2,849
Federal government retirement funds................................	340	541	797	1,072	1,141	1,197	1,221	1,324	1,425	1,509
Money market mutual funds.................	493	741	1,812	2,007	2,312	3,033	3,757	3,258	2,755	2,643
Mutual funds..............................	608	1,853	4,433	6,049	7,068	7,829	5,435	6,962	7,935	8,000
Closed-end funds..........................	53	136	142	271	293	316	201	225	240	237
Exchange-traded funds.....................	-	1	66	301	423	608	531	773	986	1,035
Government-sponsored enterprises (GSE).....	478	897	1,965	2,819	2,873	3,174	3,408	3,047	6,721	6,480
Agency- and GSE-backed mortgage pools.....	1,020	1,571	2,493	3,548	3,841	4,464	4,961	5,377	1,139	1,305
Asset-backed securities issuers..............	268	663	1,497	3,389	4,176	4,531	4,120	3,306	2,276	2,018
Finance companies.........................	596	705	1,213	1,857	1,891	1,911	1,852	1,662	1,590	1,546
Real estate investment trusts................	28	33	65	306	345	318	251	241	283	401
Security brokers and dealers................	262	568	1,221	2,127	2,742	3,092	2,217	2,084	2,075	1,954
Holding companies........................	325	494	899	1,651	1,938	2,141	2,430	3,317	3,313	3,357
Funding corporations.......................	236	366	1,165	1,344	1,476	1,858	2,862	2,420	2,311	2,207
Rest of the world..........................	1,984	3,487	6,873	11,599	14,068	16,038	15,240	15,854	17,419	18,245

– Represents zero. [1] Includes nonprofit organizations.

Source: Board of Governors of the Federal Reserve System, "Federal Reserve Statistical Release, Z.1, Flow of Funds Accounts of the United States," June 2012, <http://www.federalreserve.gov/releases/z1/>.

Table 1179. Flow of Funds Accounts—Credit Market Debt Outstanding: 1990 to 2011

[In billions of dollars (13,757 represents $13,757,000,000,000). As of December 31. Excludes corporate equities and mutual fund shares. Represents credit market debt owed by sectors shown]

Item	1990	1995	2000	2005	2006	2007	2008	2009	2010	2011
Credit market debt............................	**13,757**	**18,604**	**27,208**	**42,136**	**46,174**	**50,898**	**53,285**	**53,189**	**53,397**	**54,243**
Domestic nonfinancial................................	10,825	13,810	18,225	27,665	30,013	32,548	34,453	35,390	36,862	38,195
Households [1].........................	3,572	4,846	6,964	11,701	12,835	13,681	13,666	13,394	13,116	12,930
Nonfinancial corporate business................	2,577	3,106	4,766	5,742	6,259	7,102	7,445	7,232	7,533	8,032
Nonfinancial noncorporate business............	1,191	1,175	1,912	2,898	3,313	3,775	4,093	3,959	3,762	3,773
State and local governments....................	987	1,047	1,198	2,623	2,721	2,868	2,888	2,999	3,065	3,007
Federal government................................	2,498	3,637	3,385	4,702	4,885	5,122	6,362	7,805	9,386	10,454
Rest of the world....................................	318	568	815	1,514	1,883	2,126	1,709	2,090	2,273	2,254
Financial sectors....................................	2,614	4,226	8,168	12,957	14,279	16,224	17,123	15,708	14,262	13,794
U.S.-chartered depository institutions............	179	193	531	728	768	991	990	717	942	869
Foreign banking offices in U.S..................	35	10	2	1	–	1	–	–	–	–
Credit unions..	–	–	3	15	19	32	41	27	26	24
Life insurance companies.........................	–	1	2	11	14	29	55	48	45	47
Government-sponsored enterprises (GSE).....	399	807	1,826	2,592	2,628	2,910	3,182	2,707	6,435	6,247
Agency- and GSE-backed mortgage pools.....	1,020	1,571	2,493	3,548	3,841	4,464	4,961	5,377	1,139	1,305
Asset-backed securities issuers.................	269	666	1,504	3,394	4,180	4,534	4,123	3,308	2,278	2,019
Finance companies.................................	398	500	807	1,109	1,144	1,280	1,200	1,044	962	915
Real estate investment trusts....................	28	45	168	395	411	421	367	317	315	343
Brokers and dealers...............................	15	29	41	62	69	65	143	93	130	92
Holding companies.................................	125	155	288	482	559	711	808	1,254	1,237	1,221
Funding corporations..............................	147	249	503	620	645	786	1,253	817	751	711

– Represents or rounds to zero. [1] Includes nonprofit organizations.

Source: Board of Governors of the Federal Reserve System, "Federal Reserve Statistical Release, Z.1, Flow of Funds Accounts of the United States," June 2012, <http://www.federalreserve.gov/releases/z1/>.

Table 1180. Flow of Funds Accounts—Financial Assets and Liabilities of Foreign Sector: 1990 to 2011

[In billions of dollars (1,984 represents $1,984,000,000,000). As of December 31. Minus sign (–) indicates loss]

Type of instrument	1990	1995	2000	2005	2006	2007	2008	2009	2010	2011
Total financial assets [1].....................	**1,984**	**3,487**	**6,873**	**11,599**	**14,068**	**16,038**	**15,240**	**15,854**	**17,419**	**18,245**
Net interbank assets..............................	61	248	154	133	165	54	464	194	146	367
U.S. checkable deposits and currency...........	86	158	236	300	312	306	370	361	390	466
U.S. time deposits.................................	40	40	102	156	167	208	273	230	247	273
Credit market instruments........................	882	1,465	2,451	5,191	6,200	7,273	7,505	7,724	8,374	8,576
Open market paper..............................	11	43	114	240	286	278	233	192	191	191
Treasury securities..............................	438	817	1,021	1,984	2,126	2,376	3,253	3,671	4,385	4,651
Official...	286	490	640	1,341	1,558	1,737	2,401	2,880	3,321	3,444
Private..	152	327	382	644	568	640	852	792	1,065	1,206
Agency- and GSE-backed securities [2]........	49	123	348	1,013	1,264	1,582	1,407	1,155	1,077	1,033
Official...	5	18	116	487	695	954	941	749	669	660
Private..	44	106	232	526	568	628	466	406	408	373
Municipal securities.............................	2	4	8	29	34	45	50	59	72	83
U.S. corporate bonds [3].........................	209	355	842	1,763	2,321	2,719	2,354	2,465	2,489	2,416
Loans to U.S. corporate business.............	172	122	117	163	169	271	207	182	160	203
U.S. corporate equities............................	243	485	1,483	2,039	2,448	2,812	1,807	2,477	2,926	2,948
Mutual fund shares................................	0	60	149	242	317	373	256	364	514	560
Trade receivables..................................	46	49	49	57	63	84	90	97	116	133
Miscellaneous assets..............................	599	903	2,140	3,220	3,997	4,536	4,282	4,244	4,678	4,850
Foreign direct investment in U.S. [4]...........	505	680	1,421	1,906	2,154	2,346	2,397	2,442	2,659	2,887
Other...	94	223	719	1,314	1,843	2,190	1,885	1,802	2,019	1,963
Total liabilities...................................	**1,454**	**2,165**	**3,611**	**6,158**	**7,322**	**8,704**	**8,844**	**9,043**	**9,985**	**11,039**
U.S. official reserve assets.......................	72	75	57	54	55	60	67	120	121	130
U.S. private deposits...............................	298	419	803	998	1,085	1,341	947	841	912	848
Credit market instruments [1].....................	318	568	815	1,514	1,883	2,126	1,709	2,090	2,273	2,254
Commercial paper...............................	75	56	121	384	482	413	342	401	399	345
Bonds...	145	413	573	1,012	1,276	1,587	1,237	1,570	1,737	1,742
Depository institution loans n.e.c. [5]........	19	35	71	84	98	103	108	97	115	144
Trade payables....................................	29	47	51	54	61	73	63	69	96	69
Miscellaneous liabilities [1].......................	737	1,058	1,886	3,537	4,239	5,105	6,059	5,923	6,582	7,739
U.S. equity in IBRD, [6] etc.....................	20	27	35	43	45	47	48	50	52	55
Nonofficial foreign currencies.................	1	2	3	1	1	24	554	11	1	101
U.S. direct investment abroad [3, 4]...........	630	886	1,532	2,652	2,948	3,553	3,749	4,068	4,429	4,836
Investment by holding companies.............	8	18	-7	27	68	111	102	125	136	162

[1] Includes other items not shown separately. [2] GSE = Government-sponsored enterprises. [3] Through 1992, corporate bonds include net issues by Netherlands Antillean financial subsidiaries; U.S. direct investment abroad excludes net inflows from those bond issues. [4] Direct investment is valued on a current-cost basis. [5] Not elsewhere classified. [6] International Bank for Reconstruction and Development.

Source: Board of Governors of the Federal Reserve System, "Federal Reserve Statistical Release, Z.1, Flow of Funds Accounts of the United States," June 2012, <http://www.federalreserve.gov/releases/z1/>.

Table 1181. Flow of Funds Accounts—Assets of Households and Nonprofit Organizations: 1990 to 2011

[As of December 31 (14,695 represents $14,695,000,000,000). See also Table 734]

Type of instrument	Total (billion dollars)						Percent distribution			
	1990	2000	2005	2009	2010	2011	1990	2000	2010	2011
Total financial assets...................	**14,695**	**33,767**	**44,889**	**45,727**	**49,404**	**50,229**	**100.0**	**100.0**	**100.0**	**100.0**
Deposits..	3,366	4,440	6,232	7,969	7,966	8,651	22.9	13.1	16.1	17.2
Foreign deposits.............................	13	48	60	51	55	51	0.1	0.1	0.1	0.1
Checkable deposits and currency........	451	405	286	374	348	660	3.1	1.2	0.7	1.3
Time and savings deposits...............	2,512	3,049	4,937	6,232	6,434	6,833	17.1	9.0	13.0	13.6
Money market fund shares...............	389	937	949	1,313	1,130	1,107	2.6	2.8	2.3	2.2
Credit market instruments.................	1,741	2,564	4,298	5,244	5,423	5,148	11.8	7.6	11.0	10.2
Open-market paper.........................	94	97	98	35	63	58	0.6	0.3	0.1	0.1
Treasury securities.........................	504	579	471	816	1,207	1,115	3.4	1.7	2.4	2.2
Agency and GSE-backed securities [1]....	117	594	513	142	126	93	0.8	1.8	0.3	0.2
Municipal securities.........................	648	531	1,639	1,897	1,955	1,892	4.4	1.6	4.0	3.8
Corporate and foreign bonds............	238	657	1,429	2,227	1,956	1,887	1.6	1.9	4.0	3.8
Other loans and advances [2]............	0	2	9	27	26	23	0.0	0.0	0.1	0.0
Mortgages....................................	141	103	139	101	90	79	1.0	0.3	0.2	0.2
Corporate equities [3]........................	1,961	8,140	8,084	7,398	8,579	8,357	13.3	24.1	17.4	16.6
Mutual fund shares...........................	512	2,708	3,676	4,165	4,613	4,652	3.5	8.0	9.3	9.3
Security credit.................................	62	412	575	669	694	752	0.4	1.2	1.4	1.5
Life insurance reserves....................	392	819	1,083	1,109	1,137	1,201	2.7	2.4	2.3	2.4
Pension fund reserves [4]...................	3,310	9,171	11,460	11,915	13,091	13,147	22.5	27.2	26.5	26.2
Equity in noncorporate business..........	3,097	5,133	8,873	6,472	7,070	7,444	21.1	15.2	14.3	14.8
Miscellaneous assets......................	254	379	609	787	831	877	1.7	1.1	1.7	1.7

[1] GSE = government-sponsored enterprises. [2] Syndicated loans to nonfinancial corporate business by nonprofits and domestic hedge funds. [3] Only those directly held and those in closed-end and exchange-traded funds. Other equities are included in mutual funds and life insurance and pension reserves. [4] See also Table 1230.

Source: Board of Governors of the Federal Reserve System, "Federal Reserve Statistical Release, Z.1, Flow of Funds Accounts of the United States," June 2012, <http://www.federalreserve.gov/releases/z1/>.

Table 1182. Financial Assets Held by Families by Type of Asset: 2007 and 2010

Median value in thousands of constant 2010 dollars (21.5 represents $21,500). All dollar figures are adjusted to 2010 dollars using the "current methods" version of the consumer price index for all urban consumers published by U.S. Bureau of Labor Statistics. Families include one-person units; for definition of family, see text, Section 1. Based on Survey of Consumer Finances; see Appendix III]

Age of family head and family income	Any financial asset [1]	Trans-action accounts [2]	Certifi-cates of deposit	Savings bonds	Stocks [3]	Pooled invest-ment funds [4]	Retire-ment accounts [5]	Life insur-ance [6]	Other man-aged [7]
PERCENT OF FAMILIES OWNING ASSET									
2007, total...........................	93.9	92.1	16.1	14.9	17.9	11.4	53.0	23.0	5.8
2010, total..........................	**94.0**	**92.5**	**12.2**	**12.0**	**15.1**	**8.7**	**50.4**	**19.7**	**5.7**
Under 35 years old..................	91.3	89.0	5.7	10.0	10.1	3.6	41.1	9.6	0.9
35 to 44 years old...................	92.7	90.6	5.7	11.6	12.1	7.7	52.2	12.3	2.0
45 to 54 years old...................	94.2	92.5	10.0	15.0	16.0	9.6	60.0	19.8	4.5
55 to 64 years old...................	95.8	94.2	14.6	14.3	19.5	11.3	59.8	25.7	7.7
65 to 74 years old...................	96.2	95.8	20.6	9.1	16.1	11.1	49.0	28.4	11.4
75 years old and over..............	96.4	96.4	27.2	10.1	20.1	11.9	32.8	32.4	14.1
Percentiles of income: [8]									
Less than 20..........................	79.2	76.2	5.7	3.6	3.8	2.1	11.2	10.7	1.7
20 to 39.9..............................	93.6	91.1	11.1	6.0	6.0	3.5	30.5	17.2	4.2
40 to 59.9..............................	97.8	96.4	11.7	10.8	11.7	5.8	52.8	19.5	5.5
60 to 79.9..............................	99.6	98.9	15.8	16.0	17.3	8.8	69.7	22.8	6.9
80 to 89.9..............................	100.0	99.8	12.1	23.0	25.7	14.6	85.7	25.8	7.8
90 to 100..............................	100.0	99.9	21.5	24.4	47.8	32.1	90.1	30.9	12.3
MEDIAN VALUE [9]									
2007, total...........................	30.2	4.2	21.0	1.0	17.8	58.7	47.1	8.4	73.3
2010, total..........................	**21.5**	**3.5**	**20.0**	**1.0**	**20.0**	**80.0**	**44.0**	**7.3**	**70.0**
Under 35 years old..................	5.5	2.1	5.2	0.5	5.4	8.5	10.5	2.1	9.0
35 to 44 years old...................	14.5	2.5	7.0	0.9	10.0	41.0	31.2	5.0	10.0
45 to 54 years old...................	33.7	3.5	16.0	0.8	30.0	110.0	60.0	10.0	50.0
55 to 64 years old...................	55.8	5.0	20.0	1.2	35.0	110.0	100.0	9.3	65.0
65 to 74 years old...................	45.2	5.7	25.0	4.0	48.0	115.0	100.0	10.0	95.0
75 years old and over..............	43.8	7.2	32.2	1.0	45.0	120.0	54.0	7.0	82.0

[1] Includes other types of financial assets, not shown separately. [2] Checking, savings, and money market deposit accounts, money market mutual funds, and call accounts at brokerages. [3] Covers only those stocks and bonds that are directly held by families outside mutual funds, retirement accounts, and other managed assets. [4] Excludes money market mutual funds and indirectly held mutual funds and includes all other types of directly held pooled investment funds, such as traditional open-ended and closed-end mutual funds, real estate investment trusts, and hedge funds. [5] The tax-deferred retirement accounts consist of IRAs, Keogh accounts, and certain employer-sponsored accounts. Employer-sponsored accounts include 401(k), 403(b), and thrift saving accounts from current or past jobs; other current job plans from which loans or withdrawals can be made; and accounts from past jobs from which the family expects to receive the account balance in the future. [6] The value of such policies according to their current cash value, not their death benefit. [7] Includes personal annuities and trusts with an equity interest and managed investment accounts. [8] Percentiles of income distribution in 2010 dollars: 20th: $20,400; 40th: $35,600; 60th: $57,800; 80th: $94,600; 90th: $142,300. Percentiles of distribution of net worth in 2007 dollars: 25th: $8,300; 50th: $77,300; 75th: $301,700; 90th: $952,500. Percentile: A value on a scale of zero to 100 that indicates the percent of a distribution that is equal to or below it. [9] Median value of financial asset for families holding such assets.

Source: Board of Governors of the Federal Reserve System, "2010 Survey of Consumer Finances," June 2012; and previous edition. See <http://www.federalreserve.gov/pubs/bulletin/default.htm>.

Table 1183. Flow of Funds Accounts—Liabilities of Households and Nonprofit Organizations: 1990 to 2011

[As of December 31 (3,694 represents $3,694,000,000,000). See also Table 734]

Type of instrument	Total (bil. dol.)						Percent distribution			
	1990	2000	2005	2009	2010	2011	1990	2000	2010	2011
Total liabilities	**3,694**	**7,353**	**12,142**	**13,872**	**13,693**	**13,481**	**100.0**	**100.0**	**100.0**	**100.0**
Credit market instruments	3,572	6,964	11,701	13,394	13,116	12,930	96.7	94.7	95.8	95.9
Home mortgages [1]	2,489	4,814	8,891	10,353	10,051	9,819	67.4	65.5	73.4	72.8
Consumer credit	824	1,741	2,321	2,439	2,412	2,508	22.3	23.7	17.6	18.6
Municipal securities	86	138	214	265	262	254	2.3	1.9	1.9	1.9
Depository institution loans, not elsewhere classified	14	19	-16	10	73	36	0.4	0.3	0.5	0.3
Other loans and advances	82	119	119	134	136	138	2.2	1.6	1.0	1.0
Commercial mortgages	77	133	173	194	181	175	2.1	1.8	1.3	1.3
Security credit	39	235	232	203	278	239	1.1	3.2	2.0	1.8
Trade payables	67	135	186	253	274	288	1.8	1.8	2.0	2.1
Unpaid life insurance premiums [2]	16	20	22	22	25	24	0.4	0.3	0.2	0.2

[1] Includes loans made under home equity lines of credit and home equity loans secured by junior liens. [2] Includes deferred premiums.

Source: Board of Governors of the Federal Reserve System, "Federal Reserve Statistical Release, Z.1, Flow of Funds Accounts of the United States," June 2012, <http://www.federalreserve.gov/releases/z1/>.

Table 1184. Financial Debt Held by Families by Type of Debt: 2007 and 2010

[Median debt in thousands of constant 2010 dollars (70.7 represents $70,700). See headnote, Table 1182]

Age of family head and family income	Any debt	Secured by residential property		Lines of credit not secured by residential property	Installment loans	Credit card balances [2]	Other [3]
		Primary residence [1]	Other				
PERCENT OF FAMILIES HOLDING DEBT							
2007, total	77.0	48.7	5.5	1.7	46.9	46.1	6.8
2010, total	**74.9**	**47.0**	**5.3**	**2.1**	**46.3**	**39.4**	**6.4**
Under 35 years old	77.8	34.0	2.9	1.8	61.9	38.7	5.5
35 to 44 years old	86.0	57.6	5.1	2.2	60.0	45.6	8.6
45 to 54 years old	84.1	60.4	7.6	2.7	49.8	46.2	9.7
55 to 64 years old	77.7	53.6	7.6	3.0	40.7	41.3	6.7
65 to 74 years old	65.2	40.5	5.0	1.2	30.4	31.9	2.3
75 years old and over	38.5	24.2	2.9	(B)	12.3	21.7	2.0
Percentiles of income: [4]							
Less than 20	52.5	14.8	1.3	1.2	34.1	23.2	4.2
20 to 39.9	66.8	29.6	1.7	2.2	40.8	33.4	4.2
40 to 59.9	81.8	51.6	3.5	2.1	49.9	45.0	6.8
60 to 79.9	86.9	65.4	6.0	1.9	56.6	53.1	7.8
80 to 89.9	88.9	74.5	9.1	2.0	58.8	51.0	11.8
90 to 100	84.5	72.8	19.4	3.7	41.8	33.6	6.6
MEDIAN DEBT [5]							
2007, total	67.3	107.0	100.0	3.8	13.0	3.0	5.0
2010, total	**70.7**	**109.6**	**98.0**	**6.0**	**12.6**	**2.6**	**4.5**
Under 35 years old	39.6	120.0	89.0	2.0	14.0	1.6	2.0
35 to 44 years old	108.0	139.9	85.0	2.5	14.7	3.5	4.4
45 to 54 years old	91.8	114.0	115.0	6.0	12.0	3.5	5.0
55 to 64 years old	76.9	97.0	98.0	11.0	11.3	2.8	6.0
65 to 74 years old	45.0	70.0	125.0	8.1	10.0	2.2	6.0
75 years old and over	30.0	52.0	74.8	(B)	7.8	1.8	13.0

B Base figure too small. [1] First and second mortgages and home equity loans and lines of credit secured. [2] Families that had an outstanding balance on any of their credit cards after paying their most recent bills. [3] Includes loans on insurance policies, loans against pension accounts, borrowing on margin accounts and unclassified loans. [4] See footnote 8, Table 1182. [5] Median amount of financial debt for families holding such debts.

Source: Board of Governors of the Federal Reserve System, "2010 Survey of Consumer Finances," June 2012, <http://www.federalreserve.gov/pubs/bulletin/default.htm>.

Table 1185. Amount of Debt Held by Families—Percent Distribution: 2007 and 2010

[See headnote, Table 1182]

Type of debt	2007	2010	Purpose of debt	2007	2010	Type of lending institution	2007	2010
Total..........................	**100.0**	**100.0**	**Total**...................	**100.0**	**100.0**	**Total**................	**100.0**	**100.0**
Secured by residential property:			Primary residence:			Commercial bank.....	37.3	45.1
Primary residence...........	74.7	74.1	Purchase...............	69.5	69.5	Thrift institution........	4.2	4.1
Other........................	10.1	9.8	Improvement...........	2.3	1.9	Credit union...........	4.2	5.1
Lines of credit not secured by residential property......................	0.4	1.0	Other residential property................	10.8	10.5	Finance or loan company............... Brokerage.............	3.4 41.6	4.0 6.9
Installment loans..............	10.2	11.1	Investments, excluding real estate.............	1.6	2.0	Real estate lender [1]...	1.4	26.9
Credit card balances..........	3.5	2.9	Vehicles................	5.5	4.7	Individual lender.......	2.0	1.0
Other........................	1.1	1.1	Goods and services....	6.2	5.7	Other nonfinancial....	0.4	2.4
			Education..............	3.6	5.2	Government...........		.8
			Other loans.............	0.5	0.4	Credit card issuer.....	3.6	2.9
						Other type of lender...	0.4	.5

[1] Includes mortgage lender.

Source: Board of Governors of the Federal Reserve System, "2007 Survey of Consumer Finances," February 2009, <http://www.federalreserve.gov/pubs/oss/oss2/2007/scf2007home.html> and "2010 Survey of Consumer Finances," June 2012, <http://www.federalreserve.gov/econresdata/scf/scf_2010.htm#bullart>.

Table 1186. Ratios of Debt Payments to Family Income: 2004 to 2010

[In percent. All dollar figures are adjusted to 2010 dollars using the "current methods" version of the consumer price index for all urban consumers published by U.S. Bureau of Labor Statistics. Families include one-person units; for definition of family, see text, Section 1. Based on Survey of Consumer Finance; see Appendix III. For definition of median, see Guide to Tabular Presentation]

Age of family head and family income (constant [2010] dollars)	Ratio of debt payments to family income						Percent of debtors with—					
	Aggregate			Median for debtors			Ratios above 40 percent			Any payment 60 days or more past due		
	2004	2007	2010	2004	2007	2010	2004	2007	2010	2004	2007	2010
All families..........	**14.4**	**14.6**	**14.7**	**18.1**	**18.7**	**18.1**	**12.3**	**14.8**	**13.8**	**8.9**	**7.1**	**10.8**
Under 35 years old....	17.8	19.7	17.0	18.0	17.6	16.4	12.8	15.1	11.6	13.7	9.4	10.4
35 to 44 years old.....	18.3	18.6	18.4	20.6	20.3	20.9	12.4	12.8	16.4	11.7	8.6	15.7
45 to 54 years old.....	15.4	15.0	16.2	18.5	19.6	19.2	13.3	16.3	15.5	7.6	7.3	12.6
55 to 64 years old.....	11.6	12.6	12.5	15.9	17.5	17.6	10.3	14.5	13.0	4.2	4.9	8.4
65 to 74 years old.....	8.7	9.6	11.3	15.6	17.9	17.0	11.6	15.6	12.1	3.4	4.4	6.1
75 years old and over..................	7.1	4.4	6.8	12.8	13.0	14.1	10.7	13.9	11.9	3.9	1.0	3.2
Percentiles of income: [1]												
Less than 20..........	18.2	17.7	23.5	19.7	19.1	16.3	26.8	26.9	26.1	15.9	15.1	21.2
20 to 39.9.............	16.7	17.2	16.9	17.4	17.1	17.5	18.6	19.5	18.6	13.8	11.5	15.2
40 to 59.9.............	19.4	19.8	19.5	19.5	20.3	20.0	13.8	14.5	15.4	10.4	8.3	10.2
60 to 79.9.............	18.6	21.8	19.3	20.7	21.9	20.4	7.3	12.9	11.0	7.1	4.1	8.8
80 to 89.9.............	17.4	19.8	18.0	18.3	19.3	19.3	2.6	8.2	5.3	2.3	2.1	5.4
90 to 100.............	9.3	8.4	9.4	12.7	12.5	13.1	1.5	3.8	2.9	0.3	0.2	2.1

[1] See footnote 8, Table 1182.

Source: Board of Governors of the Federal Reserve System, "2010 Survey of Consumer Finances," June 2012, <http://www.federalreserve.gov/pubs/bulletin/default.htm>.

Table 1187. Household Debt-Service Payments and Financial Obligations as a Percentage of Disposable Personal Income: 1990 to 2011

[As of end of year, seasonally adjusted. Household debt service ratio is an estimate of the ratio of debt payments to disposable personal income. Debt payments consist of the estimated required payments on outstanding mortgage and consumer debt. The financial obligations ratio adds automobile lease payments, rental payments on tenant-occupied property, homeowners' insurance, and property tax payments to the debt service ratio]

Year	Household debt service ratio	Financial obligations ratio			Year	Household debt service ratio	Financial obligations ratio		
		Total	Renter	Home-owner			Total	Renter	Home-owner
1990...............	12.03	17.46	24.85	15.57	2007.......	13.89	18.76	25.02	17.48
1995...............	11.67	17.10	26.67	14.80	2008......	13.51	18.43	25.24	17.05
2000...............	12.59	17.66	30.44	15.13	2009......	12.67	17.63	24.76	16.16
2005...............	13.77	18.46	25.19	17.12	2010......	11.75	16.64	23.88	15.13
2006...............	13.87	18.65	25.38	17.33	2011......	10.88	15.93	24.38	14.17

Source: Board of Governors of the Federal Reserve System, "Household Debt Service and Financial Obligations Ratios," <http://www.federalreserve.gov/releases/housedebt/default.htm>.

Table 1188. FDIC-Insured Financial Institutions—Deposit Insurance Fund (DIF): 1990 to 2011

[In billions of dollars, except as indicated (4,735 represents $4,735,000,000,000). As of December 31. Includes Island Areas. Includes insured branches of foreign banks. Minus sign (–) indicates decrease]

Item	1990	2000	2005	2006	2007	2008	2009	2010	2011
Number of institutions..........................	15,369	9,920	8,845	8,691	8,544	8,314	8,021	7,666	7,357
Assets, total [1]................................	4,735	7,472	10,895	11,882	13,051	13,894	13,112	13,352	13,883
Domestic deposits, total [2]...................	3,415	4,212	6,230	6,640	6,922	7,505	7,705	7,888	8,755
Estimated insured deposits [3]..............	2,697	3,055	3,891	4,154	4,292	4,751	5,408	6,221	6,956
DIF balance (BIF/SAIF prior to 2006)......	4	42	49	50	52	17	-21	-7	8
Reserve ratio [4]................................	0.15	1.36	1.25	1.21	1.22	0.36	-0.39	-0.12	0.13
Number of problem institutions..............	1,496	94	52	50	76	252	702	884	813
Assets of problem institutions...............	646.8	23.8	6.6	8.3	22.2	159.4	402.8	390.0	319.4
Number of assisted institutions.............	1	–	–	–	–	5	8	–	–
Assets of assisted institutions...............	(Z)	–	–	–	–	1,306.0	1,917.5	–	–
Number of failed institutions.................	381	7	–	–	3	25	140	157	92
Assets of assisted institutions...............	146.6	0.4	–	–	2.6	371.9	169.7	92.1	34.9

– Represents zero. Z Less than $50 million. [1] Does not include foreign branch assets. [2] Excludes foreign office deposits, which are uninsured. [3] In general, insured deposits are total domestic deposits minus estimated uninsured deposits. Prior to September 30, 2009 insured deposits included deposits in accounts of $100,000 or less, beginning September 30, 2009, insured deposits include deposits in accounts of $250,000 or less. The Dodd-Frank Wall Street Reform and Consumer Protection Act temporarily provides unlimited coverage for noninterest bearing transaction accounts for two years begining December 31, 2010. Begining in the fourth quarter of 2010, estimates of insured deposits include the entire balance of noninterest bearing transaction accounts. [4] DIF balance as percent of DIF-insured deposits.

Source: U.S. Federal Deposit Insurance Corporation, *The FDIC Quarterly Banking Profile*, <http://www2.fdic.gov/qbp/index.asp>.

Table 1189. FDIC-Insured Financial Institutions—Number, Assets, and Liabilities: 1990 to 2011

[In billions of dollars, except as indicated (4,649 represents $4,649,000,000,000). As of December 31. Includes Island Areas. Excludes insured branches of foreign banks. Except as noted, includes foreign branches of U.S. banks]

Item	1990	2000	2005	2006	2007	2008	2009	2010	2011
Commercial bank offices, total [1]........	**63,205**	**73,174**	**80,967**	**83,860**	**86,398**	**89,975**	**95,056**	**94,552**	**94,289**
Number of main offices...................	12,347	8,315	7,526	7,401	7,283	7,086	6,995	6,676	6,413
Number of branches......................	50,858	64,859	73,441	76,459	79,115	82,889	88,061	87,876	87,876
Savings institutions offices, total [2].....	**2,815**	**1,589**	**1,307**	**1,279**	**1,251**	**1,219**	**1,180**	**1,135**	**1,100**
Number of financial institutions reporting..	15,162	9,905	8,833	8,680	8,534	8,305	8,012	7,658	7,357
Assets, total [3]............................	**4,649**	**7,462**	**10,878**	**11,862**	**13,034**	**13,841**	**13,087**	**13,319**	**13,885**
Net loans and leases.......................	2,867	4,576	6,640	7,156	7,804	7,700	7,053	7,144	7,276
Real estate loans.........................	1,612	2,396	4,141	4,508	4,782	4,705	4,462	4,267	4,129
1–4 family residential mortgages........	859	1,340	2,042	2,735	2,853	2,713	2,577	2,537	2,481
Commercial real estate...................	(NA)	873	1,509	1,712	1,867	1,934	1,813	1,071	1,060
Construction and development..........	171	197	450	590	629	591	451	321	240
Home equity loans [4]..................	86	151	534	559	611	668	662	637	603
Commercial and industrial loans..........	646	1,086	1,086	1,215	1,439	1,494	1,222	1,185	1,347
Loans to individuals........................	451	672	949	955	1,058	1,089	1,058	1,318	1,308
Credit cards and related plans...........	142	266	396	385	422	445	421	702	745
Farm loans................................	33	49	52	54	57	60	60	59	61
Other loans and leases....................	218	448	494	504	573	529	483	549	625
Less: Reserve for losses..................	65	71	77	78	103	174	228	231	191
Less: Unearned income...................	29	3	3	2	2	2	3	4	2
Securities.................................	890	1,361	1,893	1,981	1,954	2,035	2,500	2,668	2,850
Domestic office assets.....................	4,259	6,702	9,824	10,557	11,475	12,321	11,651	11,693	12,091
Foreign office assets.......................	390	760	1,054	1,304	1,559	1,520	1,437	1,626	1,794
Liabilities and capital, total.............	**4,649**	**7,462**	**10,878**	**11,862**	**13,034**	**13,841**	**13,087**	**13,319**	**13,885**
Noninterest-bearing deposits..............	511	802	1,267	1,270	1,260	1,481	1,618	5,669	2,362
Interest-bearing deposits...................	3,127	4,113	5,874	6,555	7,156	7,554	7,609	7,650	7,825
Other borrowed funds.......................	569	1,467	2,063	2,121	2,517	2,570	1,782	1,051	857
Subordinated debt..........................	28	90	131	161	185	185	157	147	133
Other liabilities............................	128	356	424	507	569	759	476	318	352
Equity capital..............................	286	634	1,119	1,248	1,347	1,291	1,424	1,511	1,569
Domestic office deposits....................	3,344	4,208	6,221	6,631	6,913	7,496	7,697	7,873	8,758
Foreign office deposits.....................	293	707	921	1,194	1,503	1,539	1,530	1,550	1,428

NA Not available. [1] Includes insured branches of foreign banks that file a Call Report. [2] Main offices. [3] Includes other items not shown separately. [4] For one- to four-family residential properties.

Source: U.S. Federal Deposit Insurance Corporation, *The FDIC Quarterly Banking Profile*, <www2.fdic.gov/qbp/>; and *Historical Statistics on Banking*, <http://www2.fdic.gov/hsob/index.asp> annual; and *Statistics on Banking*, annual <http://www2.fdic.gov/sdi/sob/>.

Table 1190. FDIC-Insured Financial Institutions—Income and Selected Measures of Financial Condition: 1990 to 2011

[In billions of dollars, except as indicated (437.7 represents $437,700,000,000). Includes Island Areas. Includes foreign branches of U.S. banks. Minus sign (–) indicates decrease]

Item	1990	2000	2005	2006	2007	2008	2009	2010	2011
Interest income	437.7	511.9	522.0	643.5	724.8	603.2	541.1	536.9	507.3
Interest expense	295.9	276.6	205.0	313.4	372.1	245.6	145.5	106.9	84.8
Net interest income	141.8	235.3	317.0	330.1	352.7	357.7	395.8	422.5	430.0
Provisions for loan losses	41.4	32.1	29.8	29.6	69.3	176.2	249.5	158.0	76.9
Noninterest income	62.2	165.6	223.4	240.4	233.1	207.7	260.4	235.7	230.4
Net operating revenue	204.0	401.0	130.3	141.4	102.4	9.5	-6.1	7.7	6.5
Percent of net operating revenue [1]	23.3	33.7	58.3	59.7	53.9	4.9	-1.5	34.4	35.3
Noninterest expense	144.2	242.3	317.4	332.3	367.0	368.3	405.3	391.8	411.6
Income taxes	9.1	43.6	64.6	68.1	46.4	6.3	5.7	50.6	50.6
Net income	11.3	81.5	133.8	145.2	100.0	4.5	-10.6	86.2	120.3
PERFORMANCE RATIOS									
Return on assets [2] (percent)	0.24	1.14	1.28	1.28	0.81	0.03	-0.08	0.65	0.88
Return on equity [3] (percent)	3.95	13.53	12.43	12.3	7.75	0.35	-0.77	5.85	7.86
Net interest margin [4] (percent)	3.47	3.77	3.47	3.31	3.29	3.16	3.47	3.76	3.60
Net charge-offs [5]	34.80	26.30	31.59	27.02	44.11	100.36	188.80	187.15	112.96
Net charge-offs to loans and leases, total (percent)	1.19	0.59	0.49	0.39	0.59	1.29	2.52	2.55	1.55
Net charge-off rate, credit card loans (percent)	3.39	4.36	4.74	3.44	4.06	5.44	9.26	10.08	5.45
CONDITION RATIOS									
Equity capital to assets (percent)	6.16	8.49	10.28	10.52	10.34	9.33	10.88	11.16	11.18
Noncurrent assets plus other real estate owned to assets [6] (percent)	3.16	0.71	0.50	0.54	0.95	1.91	3.36	3.11	2.55

[1] Net operating revenue equals net interest income plus noninterest income. Net operating revenue equals income excluding discretionary transactions such as gains or losses on the sale of investment securities and extraordinary items. Income taxes subtracted from operating income have been adjusted to exclude the portion applicable to securities gains or losses. [2] Net income (including securities transactions and nonrecurring items) as a percentage of average total assets. [3] Net income as a percentage of average total equity capital. [4] Interest income less interest expense as a percentage of average earning assets (i.e. the profit margin a bank earns on its loans and investments). [5] Total loans and leases charged off (removed from balance sheet because of uncollectibility), less amounts recovered on loans and leases previously charged off. [6] Noncurrent assets: the sum of loans, leases, debt securities and other assets that are 90 days or more past due, or in nonaccrual status. Other real estate owned, primarily foreclosed property.

Source: U.S. Federal Deposit Insurance Corporation, *FDIC Quarterly Banking Profile*, <http://www2.fdic.gov/qbp/>.

Table 1191. FDIC-Insured Financial Institutions by Asset Size: 2011

[12,639.7 represents $12,639,700,000,000. Preliminary. Minus sign (–) indicates loss. See headnote, Table 1190]

Item	Unit	Total	Less than $100 mil.	$100 mil. to $1 bil.	$1 bil. to $10 bil.	Greater than $10 bil.
COMMERCIAL BANKS						
Institutions reporting	Number	6,292	2,143	3,633	429	85
Assets, total	Bil. dol.	12,639.7	123.3	1,056.1	1,100.7	10,359.6
Deposits	Bil. dol.	9,253.9	105.1	884.3	853.9	7,410.6
Net income	Bil. dol.	110,880.0	712.0	6,368.0	9,414.0	94,386.0
Return on assets	Percent	0.90	0.59	0.61	0.88	0.94
Return on equity	Percent	8.06	5.03	5.91	7.52	8.36
Equity capital to assets	Percent	11.42	11.59	10.58	11.84	11.09
Noncurrent assets plus other real estate owned to assets	Percent	2.54	2.32	3.07	3.14	2.42
Net charge-offs to loans and leases	Percent	1.61	0.06	0.92	1.26	1.75
Percentage of banks losing money	Percent	14.70	15.40	14.80	12.10	4.70
SAVINGS INSTITUTIONS						
Institutions reporting	Number	1,067	273	651	121	22
Assets, total	Bil. dol.	1,243.3	15.5	225.0	307.1	695.7
Deposits	Bil. dol.	929.5	12.5	179.6	235.4	502.0
Net income	Bil. dol.	8.3	(Z)	1.0	1.9	5.4
Return on assets	Percent	0.68	0.00	0.00	0.01	0.01
Return on equity	Percent	5.75	1.47	4.06	5.37	6.53
Equity capital to assets	Percent	11.85	14.02	11.49	11.51	12.06
Noncurrent assets plus other real estate owned to assets	Percent	2.64	2.45	2.70	3.00	2.46
Net charge-offs to loans and leases	Percent	1.05	0.56	0.72	0.81	1.29
Percentage of banks losing money	Percent	20.90	30.40	18.74	13.22	9.09

Z Less than $500 million.

Source: U.S. Federal Deposit Insurance Corporation, *Quarterly Banking Profile*, <http://www2.fdic.gov/qbp/>.

Table 1192. FDIC-Insured Financial Institutions—Number and Assets by State and Island Areas: 2011

[In billions of dollars, except as indicated (13,812.7 represents $13,812,700,000,000). As of December 31. Information is obtained primarily from the Federal Financial Institutions Examination Council (FFIEC) Call Reports and the Office of Thrift Supervision's Thrift Financial Reports. Data are based on the location of each reporting institution's main office. Reported data may include assets located outside of the reporting institution's home state]

State or Island Area	Number of institutions	Assets by asset size of bank				State or Island Area	Number of institutions	Assets by asset size of bank			
		Total	Less than $100 mil.	$100 mil. to $1 bil.	Greater than $1 bil.			Total	Less than $100 mil.	$100 mil. to $1 bil.	Greater than $1 bil.
Total........	7,224	13,812.7	137.4	1,253.7	12,448.6	NV..........	26	103.8	.6	3.0	100.3
AL............	141	223.7	3.3	23.2	200.2	NH..........	23	10.2	.2	8.0	4.2
AK [1]........	4	4.7	.1	.7	3.9	NJ............	111	171.2	.6	29.9	140.8
AZ [1]........	30	12.0	.8	4.4	6.7	NM..........	49	14.6	.8	10.0	5.1
AR............	127	58.5	2.2	23.3	34.7	NY..........	178	769.5	1.2	44.6	723.7
CA............	253	491.7	1.7	55.9	434.2	NC..........	96	1,715.4	.9	23.4	1,691.1
CO............	108	43.6	2.5	16.2	24.9	ND..........	91	25.5	2.7	11.2	13.4
CT............	53	79.2	.4	15.9	62.8	OH..........	236	2,499.7	4.6	38.0	2,457.0
DE............	27	1,029.4	.0	3.1	1,026.3	OK..........	240	88.6	5.6	28.9	54.2
DC [1]........	6	1.5	.1	1.5	2.2	OR..........	35	34.8	.5	5.4	30.4
FL............	227	138.1	2.9	49.7	85.5	PA..........	208	208.8	1.8	56.8	150.2
GA............	242	269.2	4.6	38.3	226.3	RI............	14	133.2	.2	3.6	130.5
HI [1]........	7	35.2	.1	1.2	33.8	SC..........	76	37.5	1.1	18.2	18.2
ID............	20	7.8	.4	5.3	3.5	SD..........	82	2,494.8	2.1	9.7	2,482.9
IL............	577	400.7	13.7	85.1	301.8	TN..........	188	84.9	1.9	42.1	40.9
IN............	41	10.8	.7	7.5	2.6	TX..........	596	397.4	11.2	102.4	283.7
IA............	345	68.6	9.4	40.6	18.5	UT..........	56	375.8	.8	10.8	364.2
KS............	318	61.9	9.2	31.7	21.0	VT..........	14	6.0	.1	4.4	5.4
KY............	194	55.3	3.3	32.0	20.0	VA..........	112	525.1	.8	27.8	496.6
LA [1]........	124	62.3	1.8	26.5	34.0	WA..........	72	63.5	.9	14.1	48.5
ME............	29	31.9	.5	10.6	20.8	WV [1]......	58	25.6	.8	10.1	14.7
MD............	84	32.9	.9	20.9	13.4	WI..........	271	97.4	5.8	49.0	42.5
MA............	160	317.2	1.5	41.4	274.3	WY [1]......	34	7.4	.5	6.9	1.5
MI............	132	65.9	2.4	25.4	38.1						
MN............	390	66.8	11.4	38.4	17.1	AS..........	(NA)	(NA)	(NA)	(NA)	(NA)
MS............	88	57.3	1.5	19.2	38.0	GU [1]......	3	1.4	.1	.3	1.1
MO............	331	141.1	8.1	47.4	85.6	FM..........	(NA)	(NA)	(NA)	(NA)	(NA)
MT............	73	22.4	1.9	8.6	12.9	PR [1]......	7	73.3	.1	.6	73.3
NE............	217	57.7	6.0	20.6	31.0	VI............	(NA)	(NA)	(NA)	(NA)	(NA)

NA Not available. AS—American Samoa, GU—Guam, FM—Federated States of Micronesia, PR—Puerto Rico, VI—Virgin Islands. [1] Data include commercial banks only.

Source: U.S. Federal Deposit Insurance Corporation, *Statistics on Banking*, <http://www2.fdic.gov/sdi/sob/>, accessed August 2012.

Table 1193. U.S. Banking Offices of Foreign Banks—Summary: 1990 to 2011

[In billions of dollars, except as indicated (1,358 represents $1,358,000,000,000). As of December. Covers the U.S. offices of foreign banking organizations that are located in the 50 states and the District of Columbia. Offices located in Puerto Rico, American Samoa, Guam, the Virgin Islands and other U.S.-affiliated insular areas are excluded. Foreign-owned institutions are those owned by a bank located outside of the United States and its affiliated insular areas. The U.S. offices of foreign banking organizations consist of U.S. branches and agencies of foreign banks and bank subsidiaries of foreign banking organizations. The latter are U.S. commercial banks of which more than 25 percent are owned by a foreign banking organization or where the relationship is reported as being a controlling relationship by the filer of the FR Y-10 (Report of Changes in Organizational Structure) report form]

Item	1990	2000	2005	2007	2008	2009	2010	2011	Share [1]			
									1990	2000	2005	2011
Assets........	834	1,358	2,123	2,871	3,032	2,872	2,839	3,161	20.9	18.9	20.6	21.5
Loans, total...	412	557	802	1,055	1,167	1,022	961	1,065	17.2	13.5	14.1	14.8
Business....	199	309	276	412	483	384	327	372	27.7	25.0	24.5	25.2
Deposits......	425	770	1,162	1,629	1,606	1,795	1,752	1,717	14.6	16.5	17.3	16.9

[1] Foreign owned banks plus U.S. branches and offices of foreign banks as percent of all banks in the United States.

Source: Board of Governors of the Federal Reserve System, "Share Data for U.S. Offices of Foreign Banks," May 2012, <http://www.federalreserve.gov/econresdata/statisticsdata.htm>.

Table 1194. FDIC-Insured Financial Institutions—Number of Offices and Deposits by State: 2010

[As of June 30, 2010 (7,663.0 represents $7,663,000,000,000). Includes insured U.S. branches of foreign banks. The term "offices" includes both main offices and branches. "Banking office" is defined to include all offices and facilities that actually hold deposits, and does not include loan production offices, computer centers, and other nondeposit installations, such as automated teller machines (ATMs). Several institutions have designated home offices that do not accept deposits; these have been included to provide a more complete listing of all offices. The figures for each geographical area only include deposits of offices located within that area. Based on the Summary of Deposits survey]

State	Number of offices	Total deposits (bil. dol.)	State	Number of offices	Total deposits (bil. dol.)	State	Number of offices	Total deposits (bil. dol.)
Total.........	98,913	7,663.00	IA..............	1,621	66.49	NC..........	2,779	207.41
U.S..........	97,952	7,676.88	KS.............	1,561	60.03	ND..........	444	17.58
AL...........	1,578	82.06	KY.............	1,827	68.87	OH..........	4,015	226.37
AK...........	133	8.91	LA.............	1,650	82.82	OK..........	1,411	69.04
AZ...........	1,381	86.15	ME............	511	27.60	OR..........	1,124	53.66
AR...........	1,483	50.88	MD............	1,804	112.80	PA..........	4,720	285.77
CA...........	7,176	845.69	MA............	2,217	205.20	RI..........	259	39.83
CO...........	1,662	91.23	MI.............	3,008	155.70	SC..........	1,458	70.25
CT...........	1,296	95.83	MN............	1,842	129.66	SD..........	487	107.44
DE...........	274	290.31	MS............	1,209	45.12	TN..........	2,298	114.69
DC...........	244	27.36	MO............	2,436	128.96	TX..........	6,965	499.21
FL............	5,666	409.89	MT............	392	17.55	UT..........	602	271.95
GA...........	2,758	180.86	NE............	1,092	43.03	VT..........	266	10.63
HI............	284	28.35	NV............	550	183.50	VA..........	2,684	214.27
ID............	541	18.66	NH............	433	26.37	WA..........	1,891	109.22
IL............	4,942	361.77	NJ.............	3,338	246.49	WV..........	664	28.78
IN............	2,400	98.45	NM............	514	25.79	WI..........	2,351	126.66
			NY.............	5,479	854.83	WY..........	235	12.03

Source: U.S. Federal Deposit Insurance Corporation, Summary of Deposits <http://www2.fdic.gov/sod/>.

Table 1195. Federal and State-Chartered Credit Unions—Summary: 1990 to 2011

[Except as noted, as of December 31 (36,241 represents 36,241,000). Federal data include District of Columbia, Puerto Rico, Guam, and Virgin Islands. Excludes state-insured, privately insured, and noninsured state-chartered credit unions and corporate central credit unions, which have mainly other credit unions as members]

Year	Operating credit unions		Number of failed institutions [1]	Members (1,000)		Assets (mil. dol.)		Loans outstanding (mil. dol.)		Savings (mil. dol.)	
	Federal	State		Federal	State	Federal	State	Federal	State	Federal	State
1990.......	8,511	4,349	164	36,241	19,454	130,073	68,133	83,029	44,102	117,892	62,082
2000.......	6,336	3,980	29	43,883	33,705	242,881	195,363	163,851	137,485	210,188	169,053
2004.......	5,572	3,442	21	46,858	36,710	358,701	288,294	223,878	190,376	308,317	247,804
2005.......	5,393	3,302	27	47,612	36,895	377,804	300,868	249,515	208,728	321,820	255,804
2006.......	5,189	3,173	22	48,262	37,487	394,125	315,817	270,420	223,917	333,914	267,275
2007.......	5,036	3,065	12	48,474	38,363	417,578	335,885	289,169	237,755	349,100	283,298
2008.......	4,847	2,959	19	49,129	39,437	447,024	364,043	309,276	256,719	373,369	307,762
2009.......	4,714	2,840	31	49,599	40,333	482,612	401,993	311,146	261,367	408,832	343,836
2010.......	4,589	2,750	29	50,081	40,447	500,075	414,395	306,276	258,555	427,603	358,877
2011.......	4,447	2,647	16	50,743	41,093	525,633	436,121	308,845	262,640	449,316	378,093

[1] 1990 for year ending September 30; beginning 2000, reflects calendar year. A failed institution is defined as a credit union which has ceased operation because it was involuntarily liquidated or merged with assistance from the National Credit Union Share Insurance Fund.

Source: National Credit Union Administration, <http://www.ncua.gov/>.

Table 1196. Noncash Payments by Method of Payment and ATM Cash Withdrawals: 2006 and 2009

[95.2 represents 95,200,000,000. Based on two data collection efforts to estimate the annual number and value of significant types of noncash. Estimates of check payments and ATM withdrawals were based on findings from the payments. Depository Institutions Based on two data collection efforts to estimate the annual number and value of significant types of noncash payments. Estimates of check payments and ATM withdrawals were based on findings from the Depository Institutions Payments Study (2010 DI study). Electronic payments volume estimates were based on findings from the Electronic Payments Study and supplemented by the 2010 DI study. The Depository Institutions Payments Study collected the number and value of different types of payments from deposit accounts at a representative, random sample of depository institutions. A total of 1,311 depository institutions (commercial banks, savings institutions, and credit unions) from a stratified random sample of 2,700 institutions provided data for the survey. The Electronic Payments Study estimated the number and value of electronic payments in the United States. Data were collected by surveying payment networks and card issuers. Of the 116 organizations asked to participate, 94 of the largest organizations provided data. Respondents to this study collectively accounted for an estimated 95.5 percent of the electronic transactions and 99.6 percent of the electronic payments value in the United States]

Method of payment	Transactions (billions)		Value (trillion dollars)		Average value per transaction (dollars)	
	2006	2009	2006	2009	2006	2009
Noncash payments, total.............	**95.2**	**109.0**	**75.7**	**72.2**	**796**	**663**
Checks (paid)..............................	30.5	24.5	41.6	31.6	1,363	1,292
Commercial checks......................	30.1	24.1	41.4	31.2	1,371	1,295
Commercial banks......................	25.1	20.7	39.0	29.2	1,550	1,414
Credit unions...........................	2.7	2.1	0.8	0.7	288	352
Savings institutions.....................	2.3	1.3	1.6	1.3	696	973
U.S. Treasury checks...................	0.2	0.2	0.2	0.3	1,203	1,545
Postal money orders.....................	0.2	0.1	(Z)	(Z)	164	183
Electronic payments.....................	64.7	84.5	34.1	40.6	544	480
Automated Clearing House (ACH)......	14.6	19.1	31.0	37.2	2,122	1,946
Debit cards..............................	25.0	37.9	1.0	1.4	39	38
Signature [1].............................	15.7	23.4	0.6	0.9	40	37
PIN [2]...................................	9.4	14.5	0.3	0.6	37	39
Credit cards [3].........................	21.7	21.6	2.1	1.9	98	89
Prepaid and EBT [4].....................	3.3	6.0	0.1	0.1	23	24
Memo:						
ATM cash withdrawals.................	**5.8**	**6.0**	**0.6**	**0.6**	**100**	**108**
Checks (written) [5]......................	33.1	27.8	42.3	32.4	1,277	1,165
Checks converted to ACH..............	2.6	3.3	0.7	0.8	267	227

Z Less than $50 billion. [1] Signature debit card payments are made like credit card payments, but use funds from transaction deposit accounts. [2] PIN debit card payments also use funds from transaction deposit accounts and typically require the entry of the same personal identification number (PIN) used to access automated teller machines (ATMs). Excludes a portion estimated to have been returned to the customer as cash. [3] Credit cards include both general purpose and private-label cards. [4] Includes general purpose and private label prepaid cards, which use funds from a nontraditional prefunded transaction account, as well as electronic benefit transfers. [5] Includes the use of checks as source documents to initiate electronic payments.

Source: Board of Governors of the Federal Reserve System "The 2010 Federal Reserve Payments Study, Noncash Payment Trends in the United States: 2006–2009;" April 2011; <http://www.frbservices.org/files/communications/pdf/research/2010_payments_study.pdf>.

Table 1197. Percentage of Households Using Selected Electronic Banking Technologies: 1995 to 2007

[Covers only those households that access services (other than by check or credit card) at a bank, thrift institution, or credit union. Based on sample surveys. For details on the Survey of Consumer Finances, see Appendix III and the Federal Reserve Board, <http://www.federalreserve.gov/econresdata/scf/scfindex.htm>. The Reuters/University of Michigan Surveys of Consumers is based on data from approximately 1,000 respondents. For details, see the University of Michigan Survey Research Center, <http://www.sca.isr.umich.edu/>]

Technology	Survey of Consumer Finances					Reuters/University of Michigan Surveys of Consumers		
	1995	1998	2001	2004	2007	1999	2003	2006
ELECTRONIC								
Direct deposit of any type..........	53	67	71	75	80	65	70	77
ATM card.............................	35	55	57	65	76	59	65	69
Debit card [1].........................	20	37	50	62	71	(NA)	54	62
Preauthorized debts..................	25	40	43	50	49	31	46	57
Automated phone system.........	(NA)	26	22	20	25	40	44	46
Computer banking..................	4	7	19	34	53	10	32	51
Smart card [2].......................	1	2	3	(NA)	(NA)	(NA)	6	12
Prepaid card [3]......................	(NA)	(NA)	(NA)	(NA)	(NA)	(NA)	73	73
NONELECTRONIC								
In person............................	87	81	78	78	85	(NA)	(NA)	(NA)
Mail..................................	59	55	51	51	59	(NA)	(NA)	(NA)
Phone (talk in person)..............	(NA)	43	42	42	57	(NA)	(NA)	(NA)

NA Not available. [1] A debit card is a card that automatically deducts the amount of a purchase from the money in an account. [2] A smart card is a type of payment card containing a computer chip which is set to hold a sum of money. As the card is used, purchases are subtracted from that sum. [3] Prepaid cards are cards that contain a stored value, or a value that has been paid up-front, allowing you to use the card much like cash. As you use the card, the prepaid value is drawn down. Examples are phone cards and gift cards. Smart cards are different from prepaid cards in that you can add money to the card at special machines designed for smart cards or sometimes at ATMs.

Source: Board of Governors of the Federal Reserve System, *Federal Reserve Bulletin*, July 2009, <http://www.federalreserve.gov/pubs/bulletin/2009/default.htm>; and unpublished data.

Table 1198. Percent of U.S. Households That Use Selected Payment Instruments: 2001 and 2007

[In percent. Based on Survey of Consumer Finances conducted by the Board of Governors of the Federal Reserve System; see Appendix III]

Characteristic of head of household	Any of these instruments		ATM [1]		Debit card		Direct deposit		Automatic bill paying		Software [2]	
	2001	2007	2001	2007	2001	2007	2001	2007	2001	2007	2001	2007
All households............	**88.9**	**91.8**	**69.8**	**79.7**	**47.0**	**67.0**	**67.3**	**74.9**	**40.3**	**45.5**	**18.0**	**19.1**
Under 30 years old.........	83.8	88.6	78.1	84.8	60.6	78.3	48.8	61.3	32.1	35.7	17.0	21.4
30 to 60 years old..........	89.9	92.4	76.8	85.9	53.4	74.9	64.8	72.6	44.1	48.8	22.0	21.6
61 years old and over......	89.4	92.1	48.9	63.5	24.6	43.9	83.2	86.4	35.9	42.9	9.0	12.3
Household income: [3]												
Low income.................	74.3	79.7	46.8	58.8	29.2	48.1	51.9	60.5	18.2	23.8	6.1	7.7
Moderate income.........	88.6	91.1	67.4	78.5	46.3	68.0	63.1	68.5	35.1	37.8	10.7	10.7
Middle income.............	92.5	96.4	75.2	87.5	50.0	75.0	65.7	76.8	45.1	50.2	16.3	18.8
Upper income.............	97.1	98.4	83.7	91.0	57.8	75.8	80.2	86.6	55.2	61.6	29.9	30.5
No college degree.........	85.1	88.4	63.7	74.0	42.3	63.7	61.8	68.9	33.7	38.0	10.9	11.9
College degree.............	96.4	98.2	81.6	90.3	56.2	72.9	78.0	85.9	53.2	59.3	31.8	32.2

[1] The question on ATM cards asked whether any member of the household had an ATM card, not whether the member used it. The other questions asked about usage of other instruments. [2] The question on software asked whether the respondent or spouse/ partner uses any type of computer software to help in managing their money. [3] Low income is defined as less than 50 percent of the median household income; moderate income is 50 to 80 income is 80 to 120 percent of the median; and upper income is greater than 120 percent of the median. Each survey refers to income in the previous year. Median income was $41,990 in 2000 and $48,201 in 2006.

Source: Mester, Loretta J., "Changes in the Use of Electronic Means of Payment: 1995-2007," Business Review, Third Quarter 2009, published by Federal Reserve Bank of Philadelphia. See also <http://www.philadelphiafed.org/research-and-data/publications/business-review /2009/q3/brq309_changes-in-electronic-payment.pdf>.

Table 1199. Debit Cards: Holders, Number, Transactions, and Volume, 2000 and 2010, and Projections, 2013

[160 represents 160,000,000]

Type of debit card	Cardholders (mil.)			Number of cards (mil.)			Number of point-of-sale transactions (mil.)			Purchase volume (bil. Dol.)		
	2000	2010	2013, proj.	2000	2010	2013, proj.	2000	2010	2013, proj.	2000	2010	2013, proj.
Total [1].....................	**160**	**185**	**194**	**235**	**549**	**580**	**8,291**	**44,156**	**53,968**	**311**	**1,652**	**2,036**
Bank [2].........................	137	164	171	137	516	550	5,290	36,879	42,753	210	1,387	1,632
EFT Systems [3].............	159	184	192	223	281	296	2,979	7,239	11,092	100	262	395
Other [4].......................	11	13	20	11	13	20	22	39	124	1	3	8

[1] Cardholders may hold more than one type of card. Bank cards and EFT cards are the same pieces of plastic that carry multiple brands. The total card figure shown does not include any duplication. [2] Visa and MasterCard debit cards, including prepaid cards. For 2006 and later, includes Interlink & MasterCard PIN debit. [3] Cards issued by financial institution members of regional and national switches such as Star, Interlink (before 2006), Pulse, Nyce, etc. EFT = Electronic funds transfer. [4] Retail cards such as those issued by Target, Nordstrom, etc.

Source: The Nilson Report, Carpinteria, CA, Twice-monthly. (Copyright used by permission.)

Table 1200. Credit Cards: Holders, Number, Transactions, and Volume, 2000 and 2010, and Projections, 2013

[160 represents 160,000,000]

Type of credit card	Cardholders (mil.)			Number of cards (mil.)			Credit card purchase volume (bil. dol.)			Credit card debt outstanding (bil. dol.)		
	2000	2010	2013, proj.	2000	2010	2013, proj.	2000	2010	2013, proj.	2000	2010	2013, proj.
Total [1].....................	**159**	**152**	**166**	**1,425**	**1,014**	**1,049**	**1,242**	**2,061**	**2,745**	**680**	**814**	**844**
Visa........................	93	100	104	255	240	247	487	809	1,104	268	332	344
Master Card...................	86	75	79	200	171	181	281	479	587	212	240	234
Store.........................	114	95	100	597	318	343	120	138	171	92	92	98
Oil company.................	76	56	56	98	57	56	45	47	62	5	8	11
Discover.....................	36	41	47	50	55	65	69	106	132	48	50	57
American Express............	23	34	37	33	49	55	221	476	684	50	90	98
The Rest.....................	133	95	81	192	124	102	18	5	6	5	2	2

[1] Cardholders may hold more than one type of card. [2] Includes Universal Air Travel Plan (UATP), phone cards, automobile rental, and miscellaneous cards; credit card purchase volume and cardholders excludes phone cards.

Source: The Nilson Report, Carpinteria, CA, Twice-monthly. (Copyright used by permission.)

Table 1201. Usage of General Purpose Credit Cards by Families: 1995 to 2010

[General purpose credit cards include Master Card, Visa, Optima, and Discover cards. Excludes cards used only for business purposes. All dollar figures are given in constant 2010 dollars based on consumer price index data as published by U.S. Bureau of Labor Statistics. Families include one-person units; for definition of family, see text, Section 1. Based on Survey of Consumer Finances; see Appendix III. For definition of median, see Guide to Tabular Presentation]

Age of family head, family income, and housing tenure	Percent having a general purpose credit card	Median number of cards	Median new charges on last month's bill (dollars)	Percent having a balance after last month's bill	Median balance [1] (dollars)	Percent of card holding families who—		
						Almost always pay off the balance	Sometimes pay off the balance	Hardly ever pay off the balance
1995, total....................	66.4	2	200	56.0	2,000	52.4	20.1	27.5
2001, total....................	72.7	2	200	53.6	2,100	55.3	19.1	25.6
2007, total....................	70.2	2	300	58.3	3,000	55.3	19.4	25.4
2010, total....................	**65.1**	**2**	**300**	**52.4**	**2,900**	**56.4**	**18.6**	**25.0**
Under 35 years old.............	54.1	2	200	61.1	1,700	49.5	21.6	28.9
35 to 44 years old.............	59.7	2	300	66.3	4,000	42.6	23.6	33.8
45 to 54 years old.............	67.9	2	300	60.8	3,500	47.6	22.3	30.1
55 to 64 years old.............	72.1	3	400	49.4	3,100	60.6	16.3	23.2
65 to 74 years old.............	72.9	2	400	35.5	2,200	72.4	12.2	15.4
75 years old and over..........	70.5	2	300	27.1	1,700	78.3	11.3	10.4
Less than $10,000.............	25.9	2	200	48.7	1,800	56.5	21.1	22.4
$10,000 to $24,999.............	38.6	2	100	57.2	1,100	51.2	16.9	31.8
$25,000 to $49,999.............	58.2	2	200	54.0	2,000	52.5	18.9	28.6
$50,000 to $99,999.............	80.6	2	300	59.0	3,000	51.7	21.4	26.8
$100,000 and more.............	94.8	3	1,300	40.0	6,500	68.7	15.3	15.9
Owner occupied................	77.2	2	400	48.9	3,600	59.6	17.2	23.2
Renter occupied or other.......	40.3	2	100	66.2	1,300	43.6	24.3	32.1

[1] Among families having a balance.

Source: Board of Governors of the Federal Reserve System, unpublished data.

Table 1202. Consumer Credit Outstanding and Finance Rates: 1990 to 2011

[In billions of dollars (808 represents $808,000,000,000), except percent. Covers most short- and intermediate-term credit extended to individuals, excluding loans secured by real estate. Estimated amounts of seasonally adjusted credit outstanding as of end of year; finance rates, annual averages]

Type of credit	1990	2000	2004	2005	2006	2007	2008	2009	2010	2011
Total.......................	**808**	**1,717**	**2,192**	**2,291**	**2,385**	**2,522**	**2,561**	**2,449**	**2,408**	**2,495**
Revolving........................	239	683	800	830	871	942	958	866	801	804
Nonrevolving [1]	570	1,034	1,393	1,461	1,514	1,580	1,604	1,584	1,607	1,691
FINANCE RATES (percent)										
Commercial banks:										
New automobiles (48 months)..........	11.78	9.34	6.60	7.07	7.72	7.77	7.02	6.72	6.21	5.75
Other consumer goods (24 months)....	15.46	13.90	11.89	12.06	12.41	12.38	11.37	11.10	10.87	10.92
Credit card plans........................	18.17	15.78	12.72	12.51	13.21	13.30	12.08	13.40	13.78	12.74
Finance companies:										
New automobiles....................	12.54	6.85	4.92	6.02	4.99	4.87	5.52	3.82	4.26	4.73
Used automobiles....................	15.99	13.47	8.81	8.81	9.61	9.24	8.74	9.41	8.16	7.73

[1] Comprises automobile loans and all other loans not included in revolving credit, such as loans for mobile homes, education, boats, trailers, or vacations. These loans may be secured or unsecured.

Source: Board of Governors of the Federal Reserve System, "Consumer Credit-G.19," March 2012, <http://www.federalreserve.gov/econresdata/statisticsdata.htm> and "Finance Companies-G.20," April 2012, <http://www.federalreserve.gov/econresdata/statisticsdata.htm>.

Table 1203. Consumer Credit by Type of Holder: 1990 to 2011

[In billions of dollars (824 represents $824,000,000,000). As of December 31. Not seasonally adjusted]

Type of holder	1990	2000	2004	2005	2006	2007	2008	2009	2010	2011
Total........................	**824**	**1,741**	**2,220**	**2,321**	**2,385**	**2,529**	**2,549**	**2,439**	**2,412**	**2,508**
Nonfinancial corporate business........	67	81	59	60	57	59	56	52	53	53
Federal government [1]	–	60	86	90	87	93	104	179	309	417
U.S.-chartered depository institutions. ..	432	616	796	816	836	895	965	906	1,185	1,192
Credit unions........................	92	184	215	229	236	237	236	237	226	223
Government-sponsored enterprises.....	19	37	–	–	–	–	–	–	–	–
Asset-backed securities issuers..........	77	528	572	610	636	673	633	593	63	55
Finance companies......................	138	234	492	517	532	572	554	472	575	567

– Represents or rounds to zero. [1]Includes loans originated by the Department of Education under the Federal Direct Loan Program, as well as Federal Family Education Loan Program loans that the government purchased from depository institutions and finance companies.

Source: Board of Governors of the Federal Reserve System, "Federal Reserve Statistical Release, Z.1, Flow of Funds Accounts of the United States," June 2012, <http://www.federalreserve.gov/releases/z1>.

Table 1204. Mortgage Debt Outstanding by Type of Property and Holder: 1990 to 2011

[In billions of dollars (3,781 represents $3,781,000,000,000). As of December 31]

Type of property and holder	1990	2000	2004	2005	2006	2007	2008	2009	2010	2011
Total mortgages [1]	**3,781**	**6,769**	**10,654**	**12,085**	**13,461**	**14,521**	**14,610**	**14,329**	**13,815**	**13,477**
Home [2]	2,606	5,122	8,285	9,399	10,465	11,176	11,071	10,873	10,527	10,268
Multifamily residential	287	402	605	665	702	785	838	847	838	844
Commercial	820	1,160	1,668	1,916	2,186	2,448	2,566	2,478	2,314	2,232
Farm	68	85	96	105	108	113	135	131	136	132
Household sector	141	103	131	139	122	110	111	101	90	79
State and local governments	110	131	141	148	154	167	163	172	176	172
Federal government	83	76	74	77	80	82	96	108	107	111
U.S.-chartered depository institutions	1,601	2,350	3,605	4,055	4,416	4,659	4,615	4,372	4,195	4,050
Credit unions	33	120	199	226	253	280	312	317	317	321
Life insurance companies	268	236	273	285	304	326	342	326	317	333
Government-sponsored enterprises (GSE)	156	264	629	589	607	643	705	708	5,021	4,924
Agency- and GSE-backed mortgage pools	1,020	2,493	3,384	3,548	3,841	4,464	4,961	5,377	1,139	1,305
Asset-backed securities issuers	66	604	1,450	2,140	2,767	2,946	2,594	2,228	1,901	1,679
Finance companies	114	238	476	541	594	532	448	397	344	303
Real estate investment trusts	8	18	118	147	136	123	76	48	42	42
HOME MORTGAGES [2]										
Total [1]	**2,606**	**5,122**	**8,285**	**9,399**	**10,465**	**11,176**	**11,071**	**10,873**	**10,527**	**10,268**
Household sector	129	87	113	118	103	91	91	83	75	67
State and local governments	61	67	72	75	79	86	84	88	90	88
U.S.-chartered depository institutions	1,031	1,555	2,440	2,730	2,933	3,068	2,884	2,687	2,614	2,540
Credit unions	33	120	199	226	253	280	312	317	317	321
Government-sponsored enterprises (GSE)	119	210	509	454	458	448	457	445	4,702	4,603
Agency- and GSE-backed mortgage pools	991	2,426	3,277	3,446	3,749	4,372	4,864	5,267	1,069	1,217
Asset-backed securities issuers	55	385	1,055	1,634	2,153	2,189	1,876	1,557	1,284	1,092
Finance companies	80	187	422	490	538	473	375	328	281	247
Memo:										
Home equity loans included above [1,3]	215	408	776	917	1,067	1,132	1,115	1,033	950	873
U.S.-chartered depository institutions	175	308	605	701	791	873	895	841	783	723
Credit unions	20	41	64	76	87	94	99	95	88	82
Finance companies	19	49	84	98	108	95	75	66	56	49

[1] Includes other holders not shown separately. [2] Mortgages on one- to four-family properties including mortgages on farm houses. [3] Loans made under home equity lines of credit and home equity loans secured by junior liens. Excludes home equity loans held by individuals.

Source: Board of Governors of the Federal Reserve System, "Federal Reserve Statistical Release, Z.1, Flow of Funds Accounts of the United States," June 2012, <http://www.federalreserve.gov/releases/z1/>.

Table 1205. Characteristics of Conventional First Mortgage Loans for Purchase of Single-Family Homes: 2000 to 2010

[In percent, except as indicated (for purchase price, 234.9 represents $234,900). Annual averages. Covers fully amortized conventional mortgage loans used to purchase single-family nonfarm homes. Excludes refinancing loans, nonamortized and balloon loans, loans insured by the Federal Housing Administration, and loans guaranteed by the Veterans Administration. Based on a sample of mortgage lenders, including savings and loans associations, savings banks, commercial banks, and mortgage companies]

Loan characteristics	New homes						Previously occupied homes					
	2000	2005	2007	2008	2009	2010	2000	2005	2007	2008	2009	2010
Contract interest rate, all loans [1]	7.4	5.9	6.3	5.9	5.0	4.7	7.9	5.8	6.5	6.1	5.1	4.8
Fixed-rate loans	8.0	6.1	6.3	5.9	5.0	4.7	8.2	6.0	6.5	6.1	5.1	4.9
Adjustable-rate loans [2]	6.5	5.3	6.2	5.7	([5])	4.3	7.2	5.6	6.3	5.7	([5])	4.2
Initial fees, charges [3]	0.69	0.54	0.81	0.84	1.00	0.82	0.66	0.33	0.40	0.46	0.55	0.71
Effective interest rate, all loans [4]	7.5	5.9	6.4	6.1	5.1	4.8	8.1	5.9	6.5	6.2	5.1	4.9
Fixed-rate loans	8.2	6.2	6.4	6.1	5.2	4.8	8.3	6.0	6.5	6.2	5.2	5.0
Adjustable-rate loans [2]	6.5	5.3	6.3	5.8	([5])	4.4	7.2	5.6	6.4	5.8	([5])	4.3
Term to maturity (years)	29.2	29.2	29.4	29.1	28.8	28.5	28.6	28.3	29.3	28.3	28.1	27.5
Purchase price ($1,000)	234.9	328.5	360.4	350.6	332.3	335.3	191.8	291.3	286.2	296.4	303.6	297.7
Loan-to-price ratio	77.4	75.2	77.1	76.2	73.9	73.4	77.9	74.6	79.9	77.0	74.6	74.2
Percent of number of loans with adjustable rates	40	29	11	4	([5])	3	21	30	11	8	([5])	5

[1] Initial interest rate paid by the borrower as specified in the loan contract. [2] Loans with a contractual provision for periodic adjustments in the contract interest rate. [3] Includes all fees, commissions, discounts, and "points" paid by the borrower, or seller, in order to obtain the loan. Excludes those charges for mortgage, credit, life, or property insurance; for property transfer; and for title search and insurance. [4] Contract interest rate plus fees and charges amortized over a ten year period. [5] Insufficient data to report meaningful numbers.

Source: U.S. Federal Housing Finance Agency, *Monthly Interest Rate Survey*, Historical Summary Table, <http://www.fhfa.gov/Default.aspx?Page=252>.

Table 1206. Mortgage Originations and Delinquency and Foreclosure Rates: 1990 to 2011

[In percent, except as indicated (459 represents $459,000,000,000). Covers one- to four-family residential nonfarm mortgage loans. Mortgage origination is the making of a new mortgage, including all steps taken by a lender to attract and qualify a borrower, process the mortgage loan, and place it on the lender's books. Based on the National Delinquency Survey which covers 45 million loans on one- to four-unit properties, representing between 80 to 85 percent of all 'first-lien' residential mortgage loans outstanding. Loans surveyed were reported by approximately 120 lenders, including mortgage bankers, commercial banks, and thrifts]

Item	1990	2000	2005	2006	2007	2008	2009	2010	2011
MORTGAGE ORIGINATIONS									
Total (bil. dol.)	**459**	**1,139**	**2,908**	**2,726**	**2,306**	**1,509**	**1,995**	**1,572**	**1,262**
Purchase (bil. dol.)	389	905	1,512	1,399	1,140	731	664	473	404
Refinance (bil. dol.)	70	234	1,397	1,326	1,166	777	1,331	1,099	858
DELINQUENCY RATES [1]									
Total	**4.7**	**4.4**	**4.5**	**4.6**	**5.4**	**6.9**	**9.4**	**9.3**	**8.0**
Prime conventional loans	(NA)	2.3	2.3	2.4	2.9	4.3	6.5	6.5	5.3
Subprime conventional loans	(NA)	11.9	10.8	12.3	15.6	19.9	25.5	25.9	23.0
Federal Housing Administration loans	6.7	9.1	12.5	12.7	12.7	13.0	14.0	12.8	12.3
Veterans Administration loans	6.3	6.8	7.0	6.7	6.4	7.2	7.9	7.5	6.8
FORECLOSURE RATES									
Total loans in foreclosure process [2]	**0.9**	**1.2**	**1.0**	**1.2**	**2.0**	**3.3**	**4.3**	**4.6**	**4.4**
Prime conventional loans	(NA)	0.4	0.4	0.5	1.0	1.9	3.0	3.5	3.4
Subprime conventional loans	(NA)	9.4	3.3	4.5	8.7	13.7	15.1	14.5	14.7
Federal Housing Administration loans	1.3	1.7	2.3	1.9	2.3	2.4	3.2	3.5	3.4
Veterans Administration loans	1.2	1.2	1.1	1.0	1.1	1.7	2.2	2.4	2.3
Loans entering foreclosure process [3]	1.2	1.5	1.6	1.9	2.8	4.2	5.4	5.0	4.1
Prime conventional loans	(NA)	0.6	0.7	0.8	1.3	2.4	4.0	4.0	3.3
Subprime conventional loans	(NA)	9.2	5.6	7.3	11.7	16.5	16.2	12.9	12.1
Federal Housing Administration loans	1.7	2.3	3.4	3.3	3.6	3.8	4.8	4.7	3.3
Veterans Administration loans	1.6	1.5	1.5	1.4	1.6	2.3	3.1	3.3	2.4

NA Not available. [1] Number of loans delinquent 30 days or more as percentage of mortgage loans serviced in survey. Annual average of quarterly figures. Delinquency rate does not include loans in the process of foreclosure. [2] Percentage of loans in the foreclosure process at year-end, not seasonally adjusted. [3] Percentage of loans entering foreclosure process at year-end, not seasonally adjusted.

Source: Mortgage Bankers Association of America, Washington, DC, "MBA Mortgage Originations Estimates," National Delinquency Survey, quarterly, <http://www.mortgagebankers.org/>; and unpublished data (copyright).

Table 1207. Delinquency Rates and Charge-Off Rates on Loans at Insured Commercial Banks: 1990 to 2011

[In percent. Annual averages of quarterly figures, not seasonally adjusted. Delinquent loans are those past due 30 days or more and still accruing interest as well as those in nonaccrual status. They are measured as a percentage of end-of-period loans. Charge-offs, which are the value of loans removed from the books and charged against loss reserves, are measured net of recoveries as a percentage of average loans and annualized. Includes only U.S.-chartered commercial banks]

Type of loan	1990	2000	2005	2006	2007	2008	2009	2010	2011
DELINQUENCY RATES									
Total loans	**5.33**	**2.18**	**1.57**	**1.57**	**2.06**	**3.67**	**6.56**	**6.97**	**5.78**
Real estate	6.10	1.89	1.37	1.49	2.27	4.67	8.46	9.70	8.72
Residential [1]	(NA)	2.11	1.55	1.73	2.55	5.01	9.14	10.84	10.25
Commercial [2]	(NA)	1.49	1.07	1.12	1.94	4.44	7.90	8.52	6.87
Consumer	3.83	3.55	2.81	2.90	3.13	3.76	4.70	4.15	3.35
Credit cards	(NA)	4.50	3.70	4.01	4.25	5.02	6.52	4.90	3.55
Other	(NA)	2.98	2.24	2.21	2.46	3.00	3.57	3.33	2.88
Leases	1.97	1.59	1.28	1.26	1.20	1.58	2.30	1.89	1.04
Commercial and industrial	5.34	2.22	1.51	1.27	1.22	1.88	3.90	3.44	2.00
Agricultural	3.84	2.54	1.30	1.11	1.21	1.19	2.37	3.05	2.11
CHARGE-OFF RATES									
Total loans	**1.44**	**0.66**	**0.54**	**0.42**	**0.61**	**1.43**	**2.66**	**2.65**	**1.63**
Real estate	0.85	0.10	0.06	0.09	0.23	1.21	2.29	2.15	1.46
Residential [1]	(NA)	0.12	0.08	0.11	0.26	1.28	2.36	2.12	1.50
Commercial [2]	(NA)	0.05	0.05	0.06	0.20	1.20	2.36	2.32	1.39
Consumer	1.82	2.36	2.75	2.05	2.49	3.53	5.49	5.87	3.62
Credit cards	3.46	4.46	4.84	3.64	4.00	5.52	9.40	9.34	5.68
Other	1.03	1.14	1.38	1.06	1.58	2.34	3.05	2.05	1.40
Leases	0.66	0.31	0.58	0.17	0.24	0.54	1.29	0.72	0.20
Commercial and industrial	1.29	0.76	0.26	0.29	0.49	0.98	2.30	1.69	0.85
Agricultural	0.21	0.25	0.07	0.10	0.10	0.17	0.51	0.80	0.25

NA Not available. [1] Residential real estate loans include loans secured by one- to four-family properties, including home equity lines of credit, booked in domestic offices, only. [2] Commercial real estate loans include construction and land development loans, loans secured by multifamily residences, and loans secured by nonfarm, nonresidential real estate, booked in domestic offices, only.

Source: <http://www.federalreserve.gov/releases/chargeoff/>.

Table 1208. Mortgaged Residential Properties in Negative Equity by State: 2012

[(48,057 represents 48,057,000), except percent. As of March. Covers 85% of all mortgages in the U.S. "Negative equity" properties, often said to be "under water" or "upside-down," have mortgages with outstanding balances exceeding the property's current value. Outstanding balances include first and second liens as well as home equity utilizations. Estimates are based on a valuation model applied to public records data]

State	Properties with a mortgage outstanding, number (1,000)			Percent in or near negative equity	State	Properties with a mortgage outstanding, number (1,000)			Percent in or near negative equity
	Total	In negative equity	Near negative equity [1]			Total	In negative equity	Near negative equity [1]	
U.S. total...	48,057	11,374	2,345	29	MO............	777	119	43	21
AL.............	352	49	21	20	MT............	117	9	4	11
AK.............	87	5	4	10	NE............	226	27	15	19
AZ.............	1,292	561	64	48	NV............	555	340	27	66
AR.............	249	31	16	19	NH............	218	47	12	27
CA.............	6,787	2,072	301	35	NJ.............	1,883	355	79	23
CO.............	1,145	237	79	28	NM............	245	34	12	19
CT.............	822	121	30	18	NY............	1,897	148	50	10
DE.............	182	32	9	23	NC............	1,558	229	106	22
DC.............	100	13	4	17	ND............	61	4	2	10
FL.............	4,220	1,902	169	49	OH............	2,158	530	126	30
GA.............	1,601	595	101	43	OK............	417	34	24	14
HI.............	229	24	7	14	OR............	699	142	40	26
ID.............	245	64	13	31	PA............	1,847	174	71	13
IL.............	2,232	625	110	33	RI............	228	53	9	27
IN.............	638	67	27	15	SC............	621	118	42	26
IA.............	373	39	17	15	SD............	(NA)	(NA)	(NA)	(NA)
KS.............	302	29	14	14	TN............	959	155	67	23
KY.............	293	30	14	15	TX............	3,361	330	163	15
LA.............	(NA)	(NA)	(NA)	(NA)	UT............	478	101	31	28
ME.............	(NA)	(NA)	(NA)	(NA)	VT............	(NA)	(NA)	(NA)	(NA)
MD.............	1,354	335	66	30	VA............	1,317	294	76	28
MA.............	1,486	250	52	20	WA............	1,416	292	77	26
MI.............	1,351	481	67	41	WV............	(NA)	(NA)	(NA)	(NA)
MN.............	597	108	31	23	WI............	664	110	35	22
MS.............	(NA)	(NA)	(NA)	(NA)	WY............	(NA)	(NA)	(NA)	(NA)

NA Not available, often because of insufficient public records data. [1] Mortgage holders with 0 to 5 percent positive equity in their homes.

Source: CoreLogic, Negative Equity Report (copyright), July 2012. See also <http://www.corelogic.com/about-us/research.aspx>.

Table 1209. Mortgage Loan Applications and Lender Denials by State: 2005 and 2010

[(35,041 represents 35,041,000). Includes loans for home purchase, home improvement, and refinancing. Covers loan processing by all lending institutions except nondepository institutions with assets of $10 million or less and depository institutions with assets of $39 million or less]

State	Applications, number (1,000)		Percent Denied [1]		State	Applications, number (1,000)		Percent Denied [1]	
	2005	2010	2005	2010		2005	2010	2005	2010
U.S. total [2]...	35,041.0	23,264.5	19	22	MO............	657.9	505.0	20	19
AL.............	395.3	310.6	24	30	MT............	72.1	78.5	19	19
AK.............	48.3	49.9	19	20	NE............	129.8	145.2	19	17
AZ.............	1,244.4	429.2	15	23	NV............	593.3	127.5	16	29
AR.............	187.4	183.1	21	26	NH............	168.3	131.4	17	21
CA.............	5,488.1	3,102.5	16	18	NJ.............	1,037.0	765.1	17	22
CO.............	745.5	580.0	18	18	NM............	183.5	131.6	22	28
CT.............	414.3	317.2	17	19	NY............	1,304.7	794.9	22	27
DE.............	123.1	80.7	20	24	NC............	829.9	708.6	22	24
DC.............	68.2	59.5	14	16	ND............	33.7	45.8	16	16
FL.............	2,934.9	863.7	18	32	OH............	1,100.3	782.3	25	27
GA.............	1,081.2	574.6	21	27	OK............	287.4	217.1	25	27
HI.............	128.4	91.3	13	17	OR............	487.0	367.7	16	20
ID.............	187.9	124.3	19	23	PA............	1,223.5	978.4	23	23
IL.............	1,415.2	1,135.5	19	18	RI............	144.5	82.1	16	22
IN.............	600.2	483.4	26	25	SC............	428.6	313.6	21	28
IA.............	237.8	261.3	19	16	SD............	52.4	65.0	19	18
KS.............	238.1	204.5	22	19	TN............	595.0	425.9	23	25
KY.............	323.5	313.2	25	26	TX............	1,939.3	1,421.3	24	24
LA.............	338.4	284.6	26	28	UT............	337.2	262.6	17	19
ME.............	136.2	116.2	19	23	VT............	52.1	64.0	17	17
MD.............	927.5	525.0	15	20	VA............	1,038.3	699.3	16	18
MA.............	728.3	775.9	16	14	WA............	858.2	691.5	16	18
MI.............	1,214.6	604.3	23	24	WV............	122.1	98.5	27	30
MN.............	599.9	502.2	16	17	WI............	570.1	651.4	17	16
MS.............	192.2	161.5	25	30	WY............	49.0	41.5	21	23

[1] Loan applications may be denied for failing to meet lender requirements for debt/income ratio, employment and credit history, collateral, cash, and application completeness. [2] Total includes unreported states as well as data for Puerto Rico.

Source: Federal Financial Institutions Examination Council, Home Mortgage Disclosure Act data. See also <http://www.ffiec.gov/hmda/>.

Table 1210. Money Stock: 1990 to 2011

[In billions of dollars (825 represents $825,000,000,000). As of December. Seasonally adjusted averages of daily figures]

Item	1990	2000	2004	2005	2006	2007	2008	2009	2010	2011
M1, total.................	**825**	**1,088**	**1,377**	**1,375**	**1,367**	**1,375**	**1,607**	**1,698**	**1,840**	**2,169**
Currency [1]..................	247	531	698	724	750	760	816	863	918	1,000
Travelers' checks [2]...........	8	8	8	7	7	6	6	5	5	4
Demand deposits [3]...........	277	310	344	325	306	304	475	447	519	755
Other checkable deposits [4]......	294	238	328	319	305	305	310	382	398	410
M2, total.................	**3,273**	**4,898**	**6,385**	**6,647**	**7,032**	**7,438**	**8,169**	**8,472**	**8,766**	**9,617**
M1..........................	825	1,088	1,377	1,375	1,367	1,375	1,607	1,698	1,840	2,169
Non-M1 components of M2.........	2,448	3,810	5,009	5,273	5,665	6,063	6,562	6,774	6,926	7,448
Retail money funds............	352	885	674	678	771	926	1,019	778	673	661
Savings deposits (including MMDAs)......................	922	1,883	3,509	3,605	3,697	3,872	4,090	4,822	5,348	6,022
Commercial banks.............	581	1,428	2,633	2,776	2,913	3,044	3,321	3,985	4,429	5,024
Thrift institutions.............	341	455	876	829	784	828	769	837	919	998
Small time deposits [5]...........	1,171	1,047	828	994	1,208	1,279	1,461	1,185	928	765
Commercial banks.............	610	702	552	647	782	861	1,081	864	657	536
Thrift institutions.............	562	346	276	347	426	418	380	320	271	229

[1] Currency outside U.S. Treasury, Federal Reserve Banks and the vaults of depository institutions. [2] Outstanding amount of U.S. dollar-denominated travelers' checks of nonbank issuers. Travelers' checks issued by depository institutions are included in demand deposits. [3] Demand deposits at domestically chartered commercial banks, U.S. branches and agencies of foreign banks, and Edge Act corporations (excluding those amounts held by depository institutions, the U.S. government, and foreign banks and official institutions) less cash items in the process of collection and Federal Reserve float. [4] Negotiable order of withdrawal (NOW) and automatic transfer service (ATS) balances at domestically chartered commercial banks, U.S. branches and agencies of foreign banks, Edge Act corporations, and thrift institutions, credit union share draft balances, and demand deposits at thrift institutions. [5] Small-denomination time deposits are those issued in amounts of less than $100,000. All Individual Retirement Account (IRA) and Keogh account balances at commercial banks and thrift institutions are subtracted from small time deposits.

Source: Board of Governors of the Federal Reserve System, Federal Reserve Statistical Release H.6, weekly <http://www.federalreserve.gov/econresdata/statisticsdata.htm>.

Table 1211. Bond Yields: 1990 to 2010

[Percent per year. Annual averages of daily figures, except as indicated]

Type	1990	2000	2003	2004	2005	2006	2007	2008	2009	2010
U.S. Treasury, constant maturities: [1, 2]										
1-year.....................	7.89	6.11	1.24	1.89	3.62	4.94	4.53	1.83	0.47	0.32
2-year.....................	8.16	6.26	1.65	2.38	3.85	4.82	4.36	2.01	0.96	0.70
3-year.....................	8.26	6.22	2.10	2.78	3.93	4.77	4.35	2.24	1.43	1.11
5-year.....................	8.37	6.16	2.97	3.43	4.05	4.75	4.43	2.80	2.20	1.93
7-year.....................	8.52	6.20	3.52	3.87	4.15	4.76	4.51	3.17	2.82	2.62
10-year....................	8.55	6.89	4.41	4.69	4.73	5.33	5.24	4.25	3.44	3.26
20-year....................	(NA)	6.23	4.96	5.04	4.64	5.00	4.91	4.36	4.11	4.03
Municipal (Bond Buyer, 20 bonds).......	7.27	5.71	4.75	4.68	4.40	4.40	4.40	4.85	4.62	4.30
High-grade municipal bonds (Standard & Poor's) [3]..................	7.25	5.77	4.73	4.63	4.29	4.42	4.42	4.80	4.64	4.16

NA Not available. [1] Yields on actively traded non-inflation-indexed issues adjusted to constant maturities. Data from U.S. Treasury. [2] Through 1995, yields are based on closing bid prices quoted by at least five dealers. Beginning 2000, yields are based on closing indicative prices quoted by secondary market participants. [3] Source: U.S. Council of Economic Advisors, Economic Indicators, monthly.

Source: Except as noted, Board of Governors of the Federal Reserve System, "H15, Selected Interest Rates," <http://www.federalreserve.gov/releases/h15/data.htm>.

Table 1212. Volume of Debt Markets by Type of Security: 1990 to 2011

[In billions of dollars (1,081 represents $1,081,000,000,000). Covers debt markets as represented by the source]

Type of Security	1990	2000	2006	2007	2008	2009	2010	2011
NEW ISSUE VOLUME [1]								
Total	**1,081**	**2,489**	**5,884**	**5,989**	**4,662**	**6,696**	**6,575**	**5,892**
U.S. Treasury securities [2]	398	312	789	752	1,037	2,075	2,304	2,103
Federal agency debt [3]	55	447	747	942	985	1,117	1,033	704
Municipal	128	201	387	429	390	410	433	295
Mortgage-backed securities [4]	380	660	2,149	2,231	1,404	2,041	1,976	1,660
Asset-backed securities [5]	44	282	754	507	139	151	107	125
Corporate debt [6]	77	588	1,059	1,128	707	902	1,063	1,006
DAILY TRADING VOLUME								
Total	**111.2**	**357.6**	**893.1**	**1,014.9**	**1,036.1**	**817.8**	**954.0**	**908.7**
U.S. Treasury securities [2, 7]	111.2	206.5	524.7	570.2	553.1	407.9	528.2	567.8
Federal agency debt [7]	(NA)	72.8	74.4	83.0	104.5	77.7	71.5	53.0
Municipal [8]	(NA)	8.8	22.5	25.1	19.4	12.5	13.3	11.3
Mortgage-backed securities [4, 7]	(NA)	69.5	254.6	320.1	344.9	299.9	320.6	250.0
Corporate [6]	(NA)	(NA)	16.9	16.4	14.3	19.9	20.5	20.6
VOLUME OF SECURITIES OUTSTANDING								
Total	**7,657**	**16,925**	**29,427**	**32,220**	**33,646**	**34,636**	**36,258**	**36,756**
U.S. Treasury securities [2]	2,196	2,952	4,323	4,517	5,774	7,250	8,853	9,928
Federal agency debt	422	1,854	2,634	2,906	3,211	2,727	2,539	2,327
Municipal	1,179	1,481	3,212	3,448	3,543	3,698	3,796	3,743
Mortgage-backed securities [4]	1,278	3,566	7,085	8,161	8,396	8,508	8,517	8,440
Asset-backed securities [5]	76	1,052	2,702	2,952	2,614	2,334	2,044	1,825
Money market instruments [9]	1,157	2,663	4,009	4,171	3,791	3,127	2,867	2,572
Corporate debt [6]	1,350	3,358	5,462	6,065	6,317	6,992	7,643	7,921

NA Not available. [1] Covers only long-term issuance. [2] Marketable public debt. [3] Includes overnight discount notes. Beginning 2004 excludes Sallie Mae. [4] Includes only Government National Mortgage Association (GNMA), Federal National Mortgage Association (FNMA), Federal Home Loan Mortgage Corporation (FHLMC) mortgage-backed securities (MBS), and collateralized mortgage obligations (CMOs), and CMBS, and private-label MBS/CMOs. Beginning with 2004, Sallie Mae has been excluded from "Issuance in the U.S. Bond Market" data. [5] Excludes mortgage-backed assets. Includes auto, credit card, home equity loans, manufacturing, student loan and other. (Collaterized debt obligations are included) [6] Includes nonconvertible corporate debt, Yankee bonds, and MTNs (Medium-Term Notes), but excludes all issues with maturities of one year or less, agency debt, and all certificates of deposit. [7] Primary dealer transactions. [8] Beginning September 1998, includes customer-to-dealer and dealer-to-dealer transactions. [9] Commercial paper, bankers acceptances, and large time deposits.

Source: The Securities Industry and Financial Markets Association, New York, NY. Copyright. Based on data supplied by Board of Governors of the Federal Reserve System, U.S. Dept. of Treasury, Thomson Reuters, FHLMC, FNMA, GNMA, Federal Home Loan Banks, Student Loan Marketing Association, Federal Farm Credit Banks, Tennessee Valley Authority, Bloomberg, Loan Performance, Dealogic and Municipal Securities Rulemaking Board. For more information: <http://www.sifma.org/>.

Table 1213. Total Returns of Stocks, Bonds, and Treasury Bills: 1980 to 2011

[In percent. Average annual percent change. Stock return data are based on the Standard & Poor's 500 index. Minus sign (–) indicates loss]

Period	Stocks				Treasury bills, total return	Bonds (10-year), total return
	Total return before inflation	Capital gains	Dividends and reinvestment	Total return after inflation		
1980 to 1989	17.55	12.59	4.40	11.85	9.13	13.01
1990 to 1999	18.21	15.31	2.51	14.85	4.95	8.02
2000 to 2009	-0.45	-2.73	2.27	-3.39	2.74	6.63
2002	-22.10	-23.37	1.65	-23.91	1.61	15.37
2003	28.68	26.38	1.82	26.31	1.03	0.46
2004	10.88	8.99	1.73	7.38	1.43	4.61
2005	4.91	3.00	1.85	1.45	3.30	3.09
2006	15.80	13.62	1.91	11.97	4.97	2.21
2007	5.49	3.53	1.89	1.35	4.52	10.54
2008	-37.00	-38.49	1.88	-37.10	1.24	20.23
2009	26.25	23.45	2.44	23.11	0.15	-9.50
2010	15.06	12.78	2.02	13.36	0.03	7.26
2011	2.96	0.00	2.96	0.83	0.06	16.89

Source: Global Financial Data, Los Angeles, CA, "GFD Guide to Total Returns," <http://www.globalfinancialdata.com>, and unpublished data (copyright).

Table 1214. Equities, Corporate Bonds, and Treasury Securities— Holdings and Net Purchases by Type of Investor: 2000 to 2011

[In billions of dollars (17,575 represents $17,575,000,000,000). Holdings as of December 31. Minus sign (–) indicates net sales]

Type of investor	Holdings					Net purchases				
	2000	2005	2009	2010	2011	2000	2005	2009	2010	2011
EQUITIES [1]										
Total [2]	17,575	20,636	20,123	23,250	22,522	5.6	-76.7	313.4	-8.0	-227.7
Household sector [3]	8,140	8,084	7,398	8,579	8,357	-637.5	-368.3	88.0	-132.6	-174.8
Rest of the world [4]	1,483	2,039	2,477	2,926	2,948	199.7	56.9	157.2	67.3	-43.1
Life insurance companies	892	1,162	1,208	1,403	1,443	111.3	65.9	33.4	45.6	32.7
Private pension funds	1,971	2,442	1,836	2,081	2,005	62.8	-42.0	-175.6	-50.5	-24.5
State and local government retirement funds	1,299	1,716	1,550	1,782	1,691	11.6	-5.6	-17.3	-25.8	-65.7
Mutual funds	3,227	4,176	4,136	4,763	4,427	193.1	129.6	86.3	42.8	1.5
Exchange-traded funds	66	286	670	854	864	42.4	50.0	70.5	88.2	71.5
CORPORATE & FOREIGN BONDS										
Total [2]	4,932	8,820	11,577	11,539	11,587	362.8	863.4	-36.8	-86.9	48.5
Household sector [3]	657	1,429	2,227	1,956	1,887	88.6	122.1	-127.7	-281.5	-69.0
Rest of the world [4]	842	1,763	2,465	2,489	2,416	168.2	328.5	-127.4	-36.5	-72.2
U.S.-chartered depository institutions	311	492	667	549	552	47.6	68.1	25.9	-98.8	3.0
Property-casualty insurance companies	188	263	298	323	361	6.4	17.5	30.8	24.3	38.4
Life insurance companies	1,215	1,825	1,927	2,030	2,129	47.9	74.7	97.6	102.9	98.5
Private pension funds	266	290	443	440	441	-76.3	22.2	42.8	-2.8	0.8
Mutual funds	338	663	1,127	1,275	1,466	-10.6	65.9	146.2	148.7	190.3
Funding corporations	25	67	710	760	742	-8.9	-29.4	43.6	51.9	-17.4
TREASURY SECURITIES										
Total [2]	3,358	4,678	7,782	9,361	10,428	-294.9	307.3	1,443.7	1,579.6	1,066.8
Household sector [3]	579	471	816	1,207	1,115	-210.5	-96.2	422.5	451.2	-91.7
State and local governments	310	475	494	504	445	5.5	85.9	18.8	9.7	-59.0
Rest of the world [4]	1,021	1,984	3,671	4,385	4,651	-75.2	245.1	555.0	654.2	265.4
Monetary authority	512	744	777	1,021	1,663	33.7	26.4	300.7	244.9	642.0
Private pension funds	112	117	311	391	436	-9.9	3.5	125.8	80.3	45.2
Money market mutual funds	92	89	406	335	443	-12.9	-9.6	-171.3	-71.0	107.9
Mutual funds	127	156	255	297	353	10.2	6.6	67.6	41.9	55.3

– Represents zero. [1] Excludes mutual fund shares; see Table 1228. [2] Includes other types, not shown separately. [3] Includes nonprofit organizations. [4] Holdings and net purchases of U.S. issues by foreign residents.

Source: Board of Governors of the Federal Reserve System, "Federal Reserve Statistical Release, Z.1, Flow of Funds Accounts of the United States," June 2012, <http://www.federalreserve.gov/releases/z1/>.

Table 1215. New Security Issues of Corporations by Type of Offering: 2000 to 2011

[In billions of dollars (1,075 represents $1,075,000,000,000). Represents gross proceed of issues maturing in more than one year. Figures are the principal amount or the number of units multiplied by the offering price. Excludes secondary offerings, employee stock plans, investment companies other than closed-end, intracorporate transactions, Yankee bonds, and private placements listed. Stock data include ownership securities issued by limited partnerships]

Type of Offering	2000	2005	2010	2011	Type of Offering	2000	2005	2010	2011
Total	1,075	2,362	1,114	1,228	Nonfinancial	360	211	574	617
					Financial	679	2,036	409	483
Bonds, total	940	2,247	983	1,100	Stocks, total	135	115	131	128
Sold in the U.S.	827	2,115	701	868	Nonfinancial	118	55	61	58
Sold abroad	112	131	282	232	Financial	17	61	70	71

Source: Source: Board of Governors of the Federal Reserve System, "New Security Issues, U.S. Corporations," <http://www.federalreserve.gov/econresdata/statisticsdata.htm>.

Table 1216. U.S. Purchases and Sales of Foreign Bonds and Stocks, 1990 to 2011, and by Selected Country, 2011

[In billions of dollars (31.2 represents $31,200,000,000). Covers transactions in all types of long-term foreign securities by foreigners as reported to the Treasury International Capital Reporting System by banks, brokers, and other entities in the United States. Data cover new issues of securities, transactions in outstanding issues, and redemptions of securities. Includes transactions executed in the United States for the account of foreigners, and transactions executed abroad for the account of reporting institutions and their domestic customers. Data by country show the country of location of the foreign buyers and sellers who deal directly with reporting institutions in the United States. The data do not necessarily indicate the country of beneficial owner or issuer. The term "foreigner" covers all institutions and individuals domiciled outside the United States, including U.S. citizens domiciled abroad, and the foreign branches, subsidiaries, and other affiliates abroad of U.S. banks and businesses; the central governments, central banks, and other official institutions of foreign countries; and international and regional organizations. "Foreigner" also includes persons in the United States to the extent that they are known by reporting institutions to be acting on behalf of foreigners. Excludes acquisitions of foreign stocks through mergers that involve stock swaps. Including stock swaps, net sales of foreign securities was $135 billion in 2011. Minus sign (–) indicates net sales by U.S. investors or a net inflow of capital into the United States]

Year and country	Net Purchases			Total transactions [1]			Bonds		Stocks	
	Total	Bonds	Stocks	Total	Bonds	Stocks	Pur-chases	Sales	Pur-chases	Sales
1990.................	31.2	21.9	9.2	907	652	255	337	315	132	123
2000.................	17.1	4.1	13.1	5,539	1,922	3,617	963	959	1,815	1,802
2004.................	152.8	67.9	85.0	6,399	2,986	3,413	1,527	1,459	1,749	1,664
2005.................	172.4	45.1	127.3	7,572	2,965	4,608	1,505	1,460	2,367	2,240
2006.................	250.9	144.5	106.5	11,283	3,904	7,379	2,024	1,880	3,743	3,636
2007.................	229.2	133.9	95.3	16,607	6,081	10,527	3,107	2,973	5,311	5,216
2008.................	-74.2	-53.9	-20.2	15,356	4,489	10,866	2,218	2,272	5,423	5,443
2009.................	186.8	127.5	59.4	10,430	4,031	6,398	2,079	1,952	3,229	3,170
2010.................	115.3	54.6	60.6	14,763	7,355	7,408	3,705	3,650	3,734	3,674
2011, [2] total......	-123.9	-52.7	-71.2	15,120	7,114	8,006	3,530	3,583	3,968	4,039
United Kingdom......	50.7	47.9	2.8	4,531.5	1,980.0	2,551.5	1,014.0	966.0	1,277.1	1,274.4
Cayman Islands......	14.8	-14.3	29.1	3,430.0	2,026.7	1,403.3	1,006.2	1,020.5	716.2	687.1
Canada..............	-294.6	-131.3	-163.3	1,457.2	711.2	746.1	289.9	421.2	291.4	454.7
Hong Kong...........	-8.3	-8.4	.2	698.9	60.8	638.1	26.2	34.6	319.1	319.0
Japan...............	-2.8	1.5	-4.3	504.1	113.7	390.4	57.6	56.1	193.1	197.3
Bermuda.............	-1.8	-1.8	.0	717.5	513.9	203.6	256.1	257.9	101.8	101.8
France..............	-4.5	-8.7	4.2	313.5	121.9	191.6	56.6	65.3	97.9	93.7
Australia............	1.0	1.3	-.2	218.0	82.9	135.1	42.1	40.8	67.4	67.7
Germany.............	20.1	-38.3	58.4	288.8	151.5	137.4	56.6	94.9	97.9	39.5
British Virgin Islands..............	-3.1	-3.9	.8	287.4	88.4	199.0	42.2	46.2	99.9	99.1
Netherlands..........	-10.0	-12.7	2.6	134.9	62.2	72.8	24.8	37.4	37.7	35.1
Bahamas, The........	1.4	.4	1.0	123.9	44.4	79.5	22.4	22.0	40.2	39.3
Switzerland..........	-3.9	-.3	-3.6	136.7	33.8	103.0	16.7	17.0	49.7	53.3
Brazil...............	2.8	-5.5	8.4	184.0	79.7	104.3	37.1	42.6	56.3	48.0

[1] Total purchases plus total sales. [2] Includes other countries not shown separately.

Source: U.S. Department of Treasury, *Treasury Bulletin*, quarterly, Capital Movements Tables (Section IV). See <http://www.fms.treas.gov/bulletin/index.html>.

Table 1217. U.S. Holdings of Foreign Stocks and Bonds by Country: 2009 to 2011

[In billions of dollars (3995.3 represents $3,995,300,000,000). See also Table 1303.]

Country	Stocks			Country	Bonds		
	2009	2010	2011		2009	2010	2011
Total holdings..............	3,995.3	4,646.9	4158.2	Total holdings...................	1,570.3	1,689.5	1763.8
Europe [1]...................	1,961.9	2,113.4	1914.6	Europe [1]......................	741.4	767.6	822.3
United Kingdom............	592.4	659.1	650.1	United Kingdom................	254.4	265.0	327.4
Switzerland...............	298.3	319.4	264.5	Belgium & Luxembourg...........	64.6	69.0	147.4
France...................	250.7	244.2	213.5	Germany......................	76.0	70.6	29.2
Germany.................	192.7	206.8	174.8	Netherlands...................	106.2	103.2	95.5
Netherlands..............	108.8	120.5	110.6	France.......................	76.1	76.6	71.9
Spain....................	87.4	65.5	56.7	Ireland.......................	25.8	27.4	53.8
Ireland...................	79.2	101.4	114.4	Sweden.......................	25.5	29.8	23.7
Sweden..................	44.0	63.2	55.1	Canada.........................	219.5	252.8	288.8
Belgium and Luxembourg........	59.8	61.5	56.2	Caribbean financial centers [1]......	251.0	230.7	213.9
Canada....................	295.1	408.6	375	Cayman Islands................	217.5	196.5	184.0
Caribbean financial centers [1].....	334.7	395.8	381.8	Bermuda......................	26.8	25.4	23.8
Bermuda.................	121.1	134.1	117.1	Latin America, excluding			
Cayman Islands...........	147.5	166.4	175.2	Caribbean financial centers [1]....	94.2	117.7	133.0
Latin America, excluding				Mexico.......................	22.6	32.1	50.3
Caribbean financial centers [1].....	276.6	314.8	275.3	Asia [1].......................	101.0	134.1	117.4
Brazil....................	180.3	193.9	181.3	Japan........................	26.6	30.5	32.5
Mexico...................	65.1	76.6	56.2	Africa........................	9.3	12.7	13.2
Asia [1]....................	929.3	1,167.6	979.7	Other countries [1]..............	153.9	173.8	175.1
Japan...................	370.8	450.1	374.7	Australia.....................	107.3	123.0	125.8
Hong Kong...............	91.4	132.5	108.1				
China [2].................	101.6	100.6	91.3				
Korea, South.............	87.9	122.4	113.0				
Taiwan [2]................	76.6	94.3	71.9				
Africa [1]..................	58.0	82.7	69.7				
South Africa.............	49.5	70.3	59.5				
Other countries [1]...........	139.8	163.9	162.2				
Australia.................	127.9	149.7	149.4				

[1] Includes other countries, not shown separately. [2] See footnote 3, Table 1219.

Source: U.S. Bureau of Economic Analysis, *Survey of Current Business*, July 2012, <http://www.bea.gov/scb/date_guide.asp>.

Table 1218. Foreign Purchases and Sales of U.S. Securities by Type of Security, 1990 to 2011, and by Selected Country, 2011

[In billions of dollars (18.7 represents $18,700,000,000). Covers transactions in all types of long-term domestic securities by foreigners as reported as reported to the Treasury International Capital Reporting System by banks, brokers, and other entities in the United States (except nonmarketable U.S. Treasury notes, foreign series; and nonmarketable U.S. Treasury bonds and notes, foreign currency series). Data by country show the country of domicile of the foreign buyers and sellers of the securities; in the case of outstanding issues, this may differ from the country of the original issuer. Excludes U.S. equities acquired through mergers and reincorporations that involve stock swaps and principal repayment flows on foreign holdings of U.S. government agency and corporate asset-backed securities (ABS). Including stock swaps and accounting for ABS repayment flows, net purchases of U.S. securities was $276 billion in 2011. Minus sign (–) indicates net sales by foreigners or a net outflow of capital from the United States]

Year and country	Net purchases					Total transactions [1]				
	Total	Treasury bonds and notes [2]	U.S. government corporations [3] bonds	Corporate bonds [4]	Corporate stocks	Total	Treasury bonds and notes [2]	U.S. government corporations [3] bonds	Corporate bonds [4]	Corporate stocks
1990..........................	18.7	17.9	6.3	9.7	-15.1	4,204	3,620	104	117	362
2000..........................	457.8	-54.0	152.8	184.1	174.9	16,910	7,795	1,305	775	7,036
2002..........................	547.6	119.9	195.1	182.3	50.2	25,498	14,409	3,261	1,459	6,369
2003..........................	719.9	263.6	155.8	265.7	34.7	26,332	15,739	2,725	1,694	6,174
2004..........................	916.5	352.1	226.4	309.5	28.5	29,441	17,520	2,192	2,033	7,696
2005..........................	1,011.5	338.1	219.3	372.2	82.0	33,303	19,764	1,976	2,182	9,382
2006..........................	1,143.2	195.5	286.5	510.8	150.4	41,011	21,720	2,858	2,846	13,587
2007..........................	1,005.8	198.0	219.0	393.4	195.5	58,455	30,057	3,882	3,433	21,083
2008..........................	414.9	314.9	-38.7	93.9	44.8	61,035	28,944	5,219	2,841	24,031
2009..........................	638.9	538.4	-11.5	-40.8	152.7	40,321	22,648	2,098	2,420	13,155
2010..........................	908.2	703.7	108.0	-13.2	109.7	49,125	31,676	2,109	1,956	13,385
2011, total [5]...............	**439.2**	**378.3**	**80.9**	**-45.2**	**25.2**	**70,160**	**35,403**	**2,184**	**2,037**	**15,415**
United Kingdom...............	133.3	156.9	-3.0	-23.7	3.0	23,130	7,462	239	367	1,298
Cayman Islands...............	27.7	-21.2	10.4	9.5	28.9	13,909	2,248	235	218	2,553
France..........................	4.9	32.3	8.3	-9.1	-26.6	9,444	3,736	43	16	772
Canada..........................	33.9	17.7	3.5	-1.4	14.1	4,254	838	31	52	494
Japan............................	197.9	148.5	36.5	9.5	3.4	2,518	786	183	51	85
Bermuda........................	10.4	5.1	2.0	1.9	1.5	1,942	106	34	31	446
Bahamas, The.................	12.5	11.8	0.2	1.0	-0.4	772	167	4	28	131
British Virgin Islands........	9.7	5.1	-0.2	1.6	3.2	1,154	145	2	17	275
Anguilla........................	-1.4	0.5	0.0	-0.1	-1.8	1,395	19	0	0	562
China [6]........................	-25.7	-47.0	17.8	3.1	0.4	784	287	45	11	17
Israel............................	335.5	336.3	-0.4	0.1	-0.4	790	360	2	2	15
Ireland..........................	-17.8	-11.6	-4.7	-1.6	0.1	728	157	53	17	37

[1] Total purchases plus total sales. [2] Marketable bonds and notes. [3] Includes federally sponsored agencies. [4] Includes transactions in directly placed issues abroad by U.S. corporations and issues of states and municipalities. [5] Includes other countries, not shown separately. [6] See footnote 3, Table 1219.

Source: U.S. Department of Treasury, *Treasury Bulletin*, Capital Movements Tables (Section IV). <http://www.fms.treas.gov/index.html>.

Table 1219. Foreign Holdings of U.S. Securities by Country: 2009 to 2011

[In billions of dollars (3,670.6 represents $3,670,600,000,000). Covers only private holdings of U.S. securities, except as noted. See also Table 1304]

Country	2009	2010	2011	Country	2009	2010	2011
U.S. Treasury securities [1, 2].........	**3,670.6**	**4,466.6**	**5,071.1**	Japan........................	261.2	274.7	304.3
China [3]........................	1,036.4	1,277.4	1283.7	Taiwan [3].....................	43.5	56.1	62.1
Japan............................	750.2	860.9	1050.1	Hong Kong..................	24.6	30.9	15.8
OPEC Asia [4]..................	169.5	181.7	222.7	Africa........................	2.7	2.5	2.5
Brazil............................	156.3	169.1	152.2	Other countries [2].........	48.9	44.0	40.9
Russia..........................	166.1	173.2	201.5	Australia.....................	25.7	24.4	23.9
Hong Kong.....................	125.8	150.8	147.1	**Corporate stocks**............	**2,494.3**	**3,018.3**	**3,058.2**
Taiwan [3].......................	145.9	133.5	(NA)	Europe [2].....................	1,281.1	1,561.6	1533.0
Belgium and Luxembourg......	111.3	167.7	239.7	United Kingdom...........	372.0	441.2	430.2
Switzerland....................	91.0	109.0	132.2	Belgium and Luxembourg..........	197.6	263.8	293.1
United Kingdom...............	29.7	101.8	180.7	Switzerland................	166.0	207.8	208.4
Corporate and agency bonds.......	**2,825.6**	**2,915.7**	**2910.0**	Netherlands................	159.5	169.0	155.0
Europe [2]........................	1,782.6	1,814.9	1763.6	France......................	116.1	152.3	111.7
Belgium and Luxembourg......	705.7	686.8	665.5	Ireland......................	78.3	97.7	100.3
United Kingdom..............	546.4	575.0	543.7	Germany...................	57.2	71.2	77.2
Ireland........................	154.5	154.9	150.2	Sweden.....................	46.0	58.8	55.9
Switzerland....................	113.4	127.6	134.9	Canada.....................	306.0	371.7	392.6
Germany........................	85.5	86.8	89.1	Caribbean financial centers [2]........	424.2	507.5	532.9
Netherlands..................	73.7	67.9	66.2	Cayman Islands..........	299.2	355.9	380.8
France........................	49.0	59.7	62.1	Latin America, excluding			
Canada..........................	70.1	86.0	88.7	Caribbean financial centers.........	54.5	66.7	68.7
Caribbean financial centers [2]...........	516.8	534.6	556.5	Mexico......................	14.5	21.5	23.4
Cayman Islands..............	354.1	360.5	377.3	Asia [2]......................	336.4	400.6	416.8
Bermuda......................	124.1	135.4	136.9	Japan.......................	231.2	281.5	292.3
Latin America, excluding Caribbean				Africa.......................	5.9	6.9	8.0
financial centers [2]......................	26.7	27.9	34.0	Other countries [2].........	86.2	103.3	106.2
Asia [2]........................	377.9	405.8	423.8	Australia....................	77.5	95.3	99.5

NA Not available. [1] Includes foreign official holdings. [2] Includes other countries not shown separately. [3] With the establishment of diplomatic relations with China on January 1, 1979, the U.S. government recognized the People's Republic of China as the sole legal government of China and acknowledged the Chinese position that there is only one China and that Taiwan is part of China. [4] Comprises Indonesia, Iran, Iraq, Kuwait, Qatar, Saudi Arabia, and the United Arab Emirates.

Source: U.S. Bureau of Economic Analysis, *Survey of Current Business*, July 2012, <http://www.bea.gov/scb/index.htm>.

Table 1220. Stock Prices and Yields: 2000 to 2011

[Closing values as of end of December, except as noted]

Index	2000	2005	2007	2008	2009	2010	2011
STOCK PRICES							
Standard & Poor's indices: [1]							
S&P 500 composite (1941–43 = 10)	1,320	1,248	1,468	903	1,115	1,257	1,258
S&P 400 MidCap Index (1982 = 100)	517	738	858	538	727	907	879
S&P 600 SmallCap Index (Dec. 31, 1993 = 100)	220	351	395	269	333	416	415
S&P 500 Citigroup Value Index (Dec. 31, 1974 = 35)	636	648	761	447	525	590	573
S&P 500 Citigroup Growth Index (Dec. 31, 1974 = 35)	688	597	703	451	582	659	678
Russell indices: [2]							
Russell 1000 (Dec. 31, 1986 = 130)	700	679	800	488	612	697	693
Russell 2000 (Dec. 31, 1986 = 135)	484	673	766	499	625	784	741
Russell 3000 (Dec. 31, 1986 = 140)	726	723	849	521	653	749	743
N.Y. Stock Exchange common stock index:							
Composite (Dec. 31, 2002 = 5000)	6,946	7,754	9,740	5,757	7,185	7,964	7,477
Yearly high	7,165	7,868	10,387	9,713	7,288	7,983	8,718
Yearly low	6,095	6,903	8,344	4,607	4,182	6,356	6,415
American Stock Exchange Composite Index (Dec. 29, 1995 = 550)	898	1,759	2,410	1,398	1,825	2,208	2,278
NASDAQ Composite Index (Feb. 5, 1971 = 100)	2,471	2,205	2,653	1,577	2,269	2,653	2,605
Nasdaq-100 (Jan. 31, 1985 = 125)	2,342	1,645	2,085	1,212	1,860	2,218	2,278
Industrial (Feb. 5, 1971 = 100)	1,483	1,860	2,179	1,191	1,748	2,184	2,168
Banks (Feb. 5, 1971 = 100)	1,939	3,078	2,663	2,026	1,651	1,847	1,618
Computers (Oct. 29, 1993 = 200)	1,295	992	1,283	684	1,168	1,372	1,379
Transportation (Feb. 5, 1971 = 100)	1,160	2,438	2,673	1,885	1,951	2,562	2,173
Telecommunications (Oct. 29, 1993 = 200)	463	184	257	146	217	226	197
Biotech (Oct. 29, 1993 = 200)	1,085	790	835	730	844	970	1,085
Dow-Jones and Co., Inc.:							
Composite (65 stocks)	3,317	3,638	4,394	3,086	3,567	4,033	4,232
Industrial (30 stocks)	10,787	10,718	13,265	8,776	10,428	11,578	12,218
Transportation (20 stocks)	2,947	4,196	4,571	3,537	4,100	5,107	5,020
Utility (15 stocks)	412	405	533	371	398	405	465
Dow-Jones Wilshire 5000 Composite Index [3] (December 31, 1980 = 1,405) [3]	12,176	12,518	14,820	9,087	11,497	13,290	13,110
COMMON STOCK YIELDS (percent)							
Standard & Poor's Composite Index (500 stocks): [4]							
Dividend-price ratio [5]	1.15	1.83	1.86	2.37	2.01	1.81	2.07
Earnings-price ratio [6]	3.63	5.36	5.29	3.54	4.55	5.93	6.8

[1] Standard & Poor's Indices are market-value weighted and are chosen for market size, liquidity, and industry group representation. The S&P 500 index represents 500 large publicly-traded companies. The S&P MidCap Index tracks mid-cap companies. The S&P SmallCap Index consists of 600 domestic small-cap stocks. [2] The Russell 1000 and 3000 indices show respectively the 1000 and 3000 largest capitalization stocks in the United States. The Russell 2000 index shows the 2000 largest capitalization stocks in the United States after the first 1000. [3] Dow-Jones Wilshire 5000 Composite Index (full-cap) measures the performance of all U.S. headquartered equity securities with readily available prices. Source: Dow-Jones & Company, Inc., New York, NY, Dow-Jones Indexes, (copyright). [4] Source: U.S. Council of Economic Advisors, Economic Indicators, monthly. [5] Aggregate cash dividends (based on latest known annual rate) divided by aggregate market value based on Wednesday closing prices. Averages of monthly figures. [6] Averages of quarterly ratios which are ratio of earnings (after taxes) for 4 quarters ending with particular quarter- to-price index for last day of that quarter.

Source: Except as noted, Global Financial Data, Los Angeles, CA, (copyright), <http://www.globalfinancialdata.com/>.

Table 1221. Stock Ownership by Age of Head of Family and Family Income: 2004 to 2010

[Median value in thousands of constant 2007 dollars (37.7 represents $37,700). Constant dollar figures are based on consumer price index data published by U.S. Bureau of Labor Statistics. Families include one-person units; for definition of family, see text, Section 1. Based on Survey of Consumer Finance; see Appendix III. For definition of median, see Guide to Tabular Presentation]

Age of family head and family income (constant (2007) dollars)	Families having direct or indirect stock holdings [1] (percent)			Median value among families with holdings			Stock holdings share of total financial assets (percent)		
	2004	2007	2010	2004	2007	2010	2004	2007	2010
All families	**50.2**	**53.2**	**49.9**	**37.7**	**35.5**	**29.0**	**51.4**	**54.0**	**47.0**
Under 35 years old	40.8	41.6	39.8	9.2	6.8	7.0	40.4	45.6	39.3
35 to 44 years old	54.5	55.9	50.1	23.0	25.7	19.8	53.7	54.7	50.5
45 to 54 years old	56.6	63.1	58.0	57.5	47.1	37.8	53.8	54.5	48.6
55 to 64 years old	63.2	60.8	59.7	80.5	81.7	56.0	55.2	55.6	48.3
65 to 74 years old	46.9	53.1	45.6	80.5	58.1	78.1	51.5	55.6	44.2
75 years old and over	34.8	40.2	42.0	98.8	47.1	55.0	39.3	48.2	44.6
Percentiles of income: [2]									
Less than 20	11.7	14.3	12.5	8.6	6.3	5.3	32.0	39.2	40.5
20 to 39.9	29.8	36.5	30.5	11.5	8.7	7.1	30.9	34.6	31.3
40 to 59.9	51.9	52.9	51.7	16.9	18.3	12.0	43.4	39.5	37.5
60 to 79.9	69.9	73.3	68.1	30.6	35.2	22.3	41.9	53.1	41.6
80 to 89.9	83.9	86.3	82.6	65.0	66.1	57.9	48.8	50.5	44.4
90 to 100	92.7	91.5	90.6	235.8	234.7	267.5	57.5	58.3	50.9

[1] Indirect holdings are those in retirement accounts and other managed assets. [2] See footnote 8, Table 1182.

Source: Board of Governors of the Federal Reserve System, "2010 Survey of Consumer Finances"; (published June 2012); <http://www.federalreserve.gov/pubs/bulletin/default.htm>.

Table 1222. Dow Jones U.S. Total Market Index by Industry: 2000 to 2011

[As of end of year]

Industry	2000	2005	2007	2008	2009	2010	2011
U.S. Total Market Index, total............	**306.88**	**302.37**	**357.48**	**219.66**	**276.57**	**316.56**	**314.50**
Basic materials.............................	154.49	205.79	307.92	147.91	239.44	309.95	259.10
Consumer goods...........................	219.82	265.88	320.39	231.71	278.07	323.20	342.44
Consumer services........................	279.11	298.62	310.76	211.93	278.96	340.32	359.04
Oil and gas.................................	272.96	422.12	679.31	429.60	494.01	580.28	593.75
Financial...................................	440.91	510.02	474.23	226.52	258.79	287.09	245.11
Health care................................	360.18	315.50	354.89	268.73	320.51	328.59	359.62
Industrials.................................	276.11	280.72	351.44	207.77	255.47	315.97	307.42
Technology.................................	749.01	513.48	645.98	365.85	595.55	664.45	658.94
Telecommunications......................	210.38	126.90	179.65	115.34	119.63	133.50	132.47
Utilities....................................	177.80	152.41	204.52	137.79	148.29	153.14	175.04

Source: Dow-Jones & Company, Inc., New York, NY, *Dow-Jones Indexes* (copyright).

Table 1223. Volume of Trading on New York Stock Exchange: 1990 to 2011

[39,946 represents 39,946,000,000. Round lot: A unit of trading or a multiple thereof. On the NYSE the unit of trading is generally 100 shares in stocks. For some inactive stocks, the unit of trading is 10 shares. Odd lot: An amount of stock less than the established 100-share unit or 10-share unit of trading]

Item	Unit	1990	2000	2005 [1]	2006	2007	2008	2009	2010	2011
Shares traded......	**Million**	**39,946**	**265,499**	**523,811**	**597,720**	**671,402**	**806,883**	**738,193**	**601,275**	**534,269**
Round lots..............	Million	39,665	262,478	516,743	588,127	664,020	802,170	738,193	601,275	534,269
Average daily										
shares................	Million	157	1,042	2,051	2,343	2,645	3,171	2,929	2,386	2,120
High day..............	Million	292	1,561	3,628	3,853	5,505	7,342	5,043	5,557	5,209
Low day...............	Million	57	403	694	797	917	849	585	849	885
Odd lots...............	Million	282	3,021	7,068	9,593	7,383	4,713	([2])	([3])	([3])
Value of shares										
traded..............	**Bil. dol.**	**1,336**	**11,205**	**18,174**	**22,247**	**28,805**	**28,272**	**17,562**	**17,852**	**18,090**
Round lots..............	Bil. dol.	1,325	11,060	17,858	21,790	28,428	28,080	17,562	17,852	18,090
Odd lots................	Bil. dol.	11	145	316	458	378	192	([2])	([3])	([3])

[1] Beginning 2005, reflects trades of NYSE Group. [2] This is a discontinued data series and is no longer collected due to the rescinding of the rules 440F & 440G. [3] Excludes odd lot statistics.

Source: New York Stock Exchange, Inc., New York, NY, "Facts & Figures." All rights in the Facts & Figures are owned exclusively by NYSE Group, Inc., © 2012 NYSE Group, Inc., All Rights Reserved. More up-to-date information may be available at <http://www.nyxdata.com/factbook>.

Table 1224. Transaction Activity in Equities, Options, and Security Futures, 1990 to 2010, and by Exchange, 2010

[In billions of dollars (2,229 represents $2,229,000,000,000). Market value of all sales of equities and options listed on an exchange or subject to last-sale reporting. Also reported are the value of such options that were exercised and the value of single-stock futures that were delivered. Excludes options and futures on indexes]

Year and exchange	Market value of sales (billion dollars)			
	Total	Equity trading	Option trading	Option exercises and futures deliveries
1990..	2,229	2,154	27	48
2000..	36,275	35,557	485	233
2003..	22,737	22,292	164	282
2004..	27,876	27,158	223	495
2005..	34,568	33,223	350	995
2006..	43,941	41,798	531	1,611
2007..	66,136	63,064	861	2,211
2008..	82,012	78,653	1,096	2,264
2009..	59,850	57,556	710	1,574
2010, total [1]...................................	**64,008**	**61,146**	**725**	**2,137**
BATS (Better Alternative Trading System)				
Exchange, Inc..................................	6,779	6,764	3	11
Chicago Board Options Exchange, Inc....................	687	112	144	432
EDGX Exchange, Inc..............................	1,101	1,101	–	–
FINRA, Inc. [2].....................................	18,120	18,120	–	–
International Securities Exchange, LLC..........	883	410	120	352
NASDAQ OMX BX................................	1,625	1,565	16	45
The Nasdaq Stock Market LLC.....................	13,433	13,317	27	89
National Stock Exchange.........................	331	331	–	–
New York Stock Exchange, Inc....................	8,403	8,403	–	–
NYSE Arca, Inc. [3]..................................	10,024	9,670	91	263

– Represents zero. [1] Includes other exchanes not shown separately. [2] Financial Industry Regulatory Authority. [3] NYSE Euronext completed its acquisition of the American Stock Exchange (Amex) on October 1, 2008. Post merger, the Amex equities business was branded NYSE Alternext US.

Source: U.S. Securities and Exchange Commission, "Select SEC and Market Data." For more information, see <http://www.sec.gov>.

Table 1225. Households Owning Mutual Funds by Age and Income: 2001 and 2011

[In percent. Ownership includes money market, stock, bond, and hybrid mutual funds, variable annuities, and mutual funds owned through Individual Retirement Accounts (IRAs), Keoghs, and employer-sponsored retirement plans. In 2011, an estimated 52,300,000 households own mutual funds. A mutual fund is an open-end investment company that continuously issues and redeems shares that represent an interest in a pool of financial assets]

Age of household head and household income [1,2]	Percent distribution, 2011	As a percent of all households		Age of household head and household income [1,2]	Percent distribution, 2011	As a percent of all households	
		2001	2011			2001	2011
Total.........................	**100**	**49**	**44**	Less than $25,000..............	7	14	12
Less than 35 years old.........	16	45	32	$25,000 to $34,999.............	7	32	29
35 to 44 years old...............	21	59	52	$35,000 to $49,999.............	10	52	32
45 to 54 years old...............	24	59	52	$50,000 to $74,999.............	21	71	52
55 to 64 years old...............	21	49	50	$75,000 to $99,999.............	17	85	67
65 years old and over..........	18	33	37	$100,000 to $199,999.........	31	88	80
				$200,000 and over.............	7	56	87

[1] Age is based on the sole or co-decision maker for household saving and investing. [2] Total reported is household income before taxes in prior year.

Source: Investment Company Institute, Washington, DC, *ICI Research Perspective*, Vol. 17, No. 5, October 2011 (copyright).

Table 1226. Characteristics of Mutual Fund Owners: 2011

[In percent, except as indicated. Mutual fund ownership includes holdings of money market, stock, bond, and hybrid mutual funds; and funds owned through variable annuities, Individual Retirement Accounts (IRAs), Keoghs, and employer-sponsored retirement plans. Based on a national probability sample of 1,859 primary financial decision-makers in households with mutual fund investments. For definition of mutual fund, see headnote, Table 1227. For definition of median, see Guide to Tabular Presentation]

Characteristic	Total	Age [1]			Household income [2]			
		Under 40 years old	40 to 64 years old	65 years old and over	Less than $50,000	$50,000 to $99,000	$100,000 to $149,000	$150,000 or more
Median age [1] (years).........................	50	33	52	72	53	50	48	48
Median household income [2] (dol.)...........	80,000	80,000	87,500	55,000	32,000	70,800	114,900	188,000
Median household financial assets [3] (dollars).....................................	200,000	75,000	200,000	375,000	50,000	150,000	300,000	450,000
Own an IRA.....................................	65	50	68	73	53	64	72	73
Household with defined contribution retirement plan(s) [4]........................	78	85	84	51	57	80	90	89
401(k) plan....................................	62	72	68	31	39	65	72	78
403(b), state, local, or federal government plan...........................	34	34	36	28	26	32	44	36
Median mutual fund assets (dol.)...........	120,000	40,000	150,000	200,000	30,000	80,000	200,000	250,000
Own:								
Equity funds..................................	81	83	83	73	69	81	84	91
Bond funds....................................	44	41	46	41	38	41	47	54

[1] See Table 1225, footnote 1. [2] See Table 1225, footnote 2. [3] Includes assets in employer-sponsored retirement plans but excludes value of primary residence. [4] For definition of defined contribution plan, see headnote, Table 562.

Source: Investment Company Institute, Washington, DC, *Profile of Mutual Fund Shareholders, 2011*, February 2012 (copyright).

Table 1227. Mutual Funds—Summary: 1990 to 2011

[Number of funds and assets as of December 31 (1,065 represents $1,065,000,000,000). A mutual fund is an open-end investment company that continuously issues and redeems shares that represent an interest in a pool of financial assets. Excludes data for funds that invest in other mutual funds. Minus sign (−) indicates net redemptions]

Type of fund	Unit	1990	2000	2005	2006	2007	2008	2009	2010	2011
Number of funds, total.................	**Number**	**3,079**	**8,155**	**7,974**	**8,118**	**8,026**	**8,022**	**7,684**	**7,580**	**7,637**
Equity funds..............................	Number	1,099	4,372	4,571	4,750	4,742	4,802	4,616	4,547	4,581
Hybrid funds.............................	Number	193	519	482	495	476	483	471	475	495
Bond funds...............................	Number	1,046	2,225	2,051	2,026	2,003	1,954	1,893	1,906	1,929
Money market funds, taxable [1].........	Number	505	704	593	573	545	534	476	442	431
Money market funds, tax-exempt [2]......	Number	236	335	277	274	260	249	228	210	201
Assets, total.........................	**Bil. dol.**	**1,065**	**6,965**	**8,891**	**10,398**	**12,001**	**9,604**	**11,120**	**11,821**	**11,622**
Equity funds..............................	Bil. dol.	239	3,939	4,887	5,833	6,417	3,641	4,880	5,585	5,205
Hybrid funds.............................	Bil. dol.	36	364	610	721	807	552	695	799	839
Bond funds...............................	Bil. dol.	291	817	1,368	1,505	1,692	1,578	2,229	2,633	2,886
Money market funds, taxable [1].........	Bil. dol.	415	1,611	1,690	1,969	2,618	3,339	2,917	2,474	2,400
Money market funds, tax-exempt [2]......	Bil. dol.	84	234	336	369	468	494	399	330	292
Net new cash flow:										
Equity funds..............................	Bil. dol.	13	315	124	148	74	-228	0	-37	-130
Hybrid funds.............................	Bil. dol.	1	-36	37	18	42	-26	10	24	30
Bond funds...............................	Bil. dol.	7	-50	31	60	108	30	380	241	124
Money market funds.....................	Bil. dol.	23	159	62	245	654	637	-539	-525	-124

[1] Funds invest in short-term, high-grade securities sold in the money market. [2] Funds invest in municipal securities with relatively short maturities.

Source: Investment Company Institute, Washington, DC, *Investment Company Fact Book*, annual (copyright). For more information, see <http://www.ici.org/>.

Table 1228. Mutual Fund Shares—Holdings and Net Purchases by Type of Investor: 2000 to 2011

[In billions of dollars (4,433 represents $4,433,000,000,000). Holdings as of Dec. 31. For definition of mutual fund, see headnote, Table 1227. Excludes money market mutual funds. Minus sign (−) indicates net sales]

Type of investor	Holdings					Net purchases				
	2000	2005	2009	2010	2011	2000	2005	2009	2010	2011
Total	**4,433**	**6,049**	**6,962**	**7,935**	**8,000**	**237.6**	**260.2**	**490.5**	**389.3**	**402.9**
Households, nonprofit organizations	2,708	3,676	4,165	4,613	4,652	79.5	175.6	304.8	202.0	297.9
Nonfinancial corporate business	118	134	162	187	167	0.3	0.7	35.5	11.2	-11.2
State and local governments	31	29	34	31	30	1.2	-0.5	-7.7	-8.5	-1.2
Rest of the world	149	242	364	514	560	-9.2	32.2	56.5	112.2	70.5
U.S.-chartered depository institutions	15	17	46	45	42	2.5	-1.8	14.8	-5.8	-0.8
Credit unions	2	2	1	2	2	-0.3	-1.0	-0.7	0.2	0.3
Property-casualty insurance companies	3	6	5	6	5	0.4	0.3	0.1	-0.1	-0.1
Life insurance companies	97	109	141	156	150	5.6	-9.9	0.0	1.0	1.1
Private pension funds	1,132	1,585	1,817	2,121	2,145	107.7	70.0	89.8	80.9	56.1

State and local government retirement funds

Source: Board of Governors of the Federal Reserve System, "Federal Reserve Statistical Release, Z.1, Flow of Funds Accounts of the United States," June 2012, <http://www.federalreserve.gov/releases/z1/>.

Table 1229. Retirement Assets by Type of Asset: 1990 to 2011

[In billions of dollars, except as indicated (3,923 represents $3,923,000,000,000). As of December 31]

Institution	1990	2000	2006	2007	2008	2009	2010	2011
Retirement assets, total	**3,923**	**11,604**	**16,603**	**17,843**	**14,050**	**16,165**	**17,729**	**17,811**
IRA assets	636	2,629	4,207	4,748	3,681	[1] 4,363	[1] 4,839	[1] 4,872
Bank and thrift deposits [2]	266	250	313	340	391	431	461	482
Life insurance companies [3]	40	204	322	331	318	[1] 323	[1] 345	358
Mutual funds	142	1,262	2,033	2,306	1,605	1,972	2,219	2,196
Securities held in brokerage accounts [4]	188	913	1,540	1,771	1,366	[1] 1,637	[1] 1,814	[1] 1,835
Traditional	(NA)	2,407	3,722	4,187	3,257	[1] 3,855	[1] 4,250	[1] 4,280
Roth	(X)	134	236	266	201	[1] 235	[1] 260	[1] 261
SEP and SAR-SEP [5]	(NA)	78	196	232	177	[1] 215	[1] 265	[1] 266
SIMPLE [6]	(X)	10	52	62	46	[1] 58	[1] 64	[1] 65
Defined contribution plans	892	2,867	4,084	4,354	3,378	4,018	4,452	4,496
401(k) plans	(NA)	1,739	2,782	2,983	2,208	2,746	3,070	3,120
403(b) plans	(NA)	518	692	736	620	701	759	748
457 plans	(NA)	110	158	173	140	169	189	193
Other defined contribution plans [7]	(NA)	500	453	461	411	402	435	435
State and local government pension plans	742	2,340	3,157	3,298	2,415	2,760	3,024	2,968
Private defined benefit plans	922	2,020	2,493	2,646	1,979	2,228	2,395	2,335
Federal pension plans [8]	340	797	1,141	1,197	1,221	1,324	1,425	1,509
Annuities [9]	391	951	1,521	1,600	1,376	1,471	1,593	1,630
Memo:								
Mutual fund retirement assets	208	2,568	4,274	4,822	3,326	4,184	4,745	4,698
Percent of total retirement assets	5	22	26	27	24	26	27	26
Percent of all mutual funds	20	37	41	40	35	38	40	40

NA Not available. X Not applicable. [1] Data are estimated. [2] Includes Keogh deposits. [3] Annuities held by IRAs, excluding variable annuity mutual fund IRA assets. [4] Excludes mutual fund assets held through brokerage accounts, which are included in mutual funds. [5] Simplified Employee Pension IRAs and salary reduction (SAR) SEP IRAs. [6] Savings Incentive Match Plan for Employees (SIMPLE) IRAs. [7] Includes Keoghs and other defined contribution plans (profit-sharing, thrift-savings, stock bonus, and money purchase) without 401(k) features. [8] Federal pension plans include U.S. Treasury security holdings of the civil service retirement and disability fund, the military retirement fund, the judicial retirement funds, the Railroad Retirement Board, and the foreign service retirement and disability fund. These plans also include securities held in the National Railroad Retirement Investment Trust and Federal Employees Retirement System (FERS) Thrift Savings Plan (TSP). [9] Annuities include all fixed and variable annuity reserves at life insurance companies less annuities held by IRAs, 403(b) plans, 457 plans, and private pension funds. Some of these annuity reserves represent assets of individuals held outside retirement plan arrangements and IRAs; however, information to separate out such reserves is not available.

Source: Investment Company Institute, "The U.S. Retirement Market, Fourth Quarter 2011," April, 2011, <www.ici.org/info/ret_11_q4_data.xls>.

Table 1230. Assets of Private and Public Pension Funds by Type of Fund: 1990 to 2011

[In billions of dollars (3,269 represents $3,269,000,000,000). As of end of year. Except for corporate equities, represents book value. Excludes social security trust funds; see Table 557]

Type of pension fund	1990	2000	2005	2006	2007	2008	2009	2010	2011
Total, all types.................	**3,269**	**9,084**	**11,379**	**12,646**	**13,257**	**10,283**	**11,792**	**12,962**	**12,992**
Private funds.........................	2,199	5,994	7,586	8,415	8,861	6,737	7,794	8,605	8,633
Insured [1]..........................	570	1,526	2,197	2,332	2,451	2,185	2,323	2,505	2,563
Noninsured [2,3]....................	1,629	4,468	5,389	6,083	6,411	4,553	5,471	6,100	6,070
Credit market instruments [3].....	464	622	700	758	861	951	1,063	1,122	1,161
Treasury securities............	122	112	117	131	170	185	311	391	436
Corporate and foreign bonds..	158	266	290	318	357	400	443	440	441
Corporate equities...............	606	1,971	2,442	2,725	2,673	1,600	1,836	2,081	2,005
Mutual fund shares.............	40	1,132	1,585	1,880	2,111	1,366	1,817	2,121	2,145
Unallocated insurance contracts [4]............	215	308	338	388	431	318	413	457	451
State and local government employee retirement funds [3]........	730	2,293	2,721	3,090	3,199	2,325	2,674	2,931	2,849
Credit market instruments [3].....	402	743	693	808	820	834	825	816	835
Agency- and GSE-backed securities [5].......	63	179	258	308	331	337	307	285	290
Corporate and foreign bonds..	142	314	228	283	297	313	309	312	321
Corporate equities................	285	1,299	1,716	1,926	2,014	1,238	1,550	1,782	1,691
Federal government retirement funds [6]..........	340	797	1,072	1,141	1,197	1,221	1,324	1,425	1,509

[1] Annuity reserves held by life insurance companies, excluding unallocated contracts held by private pension funds. [2] Private defined benefit plans and defined contribution plans (including 401(k) type plans). [3] Includes other types of assets not shown separately. [4] Assets held at life insurance companies (e.g., guaranteed investment contracts (GICs), variable annuities). [5] GSE = Government-sponsored enterprises. [6] Includes the Federal Employees Retirement System Thrift Savings Plan, the National Railroad Retirement Investment Trust, and nonmarketable government securities held by federal government retirement funds.

Source: Board of Governors of the Federal Reserve System, "Federal Reserve Statistical Release, Z.1, Flow of Funds Accounts of the United States," June 2012, <http://www.federalreserve.gov/releases/z1/>.

Table 1231. Annual Revenues of Selected Securities Industries: 2005 to 2010

[In millions of dollars (428,365 represents $428,365,000,000). Covers taxable and tax-exempt employer firms only. Based on Service Annual Survey. Estimates have been adjusted to the results of the 2007 Economic Census. See Appendix III]

Kind of business	NAICS code [1]	2005	2006	2007	2008	2009	2010
Total.........................	**523x**	**428,365**	**533,132**	**572,358**	**395,136**	**472,659**	**474,570**
Securities and commodity contracts intermediation and brokerage.....................	5231	295,806	366,977	371,500	199,367	295,424	284,557
Investment banking and securities dealing......	52311	155,507	201,501	203,139	118,246	167,559	155,868
Securities brokerage.................	52312	131,833	154,984	155,797	68,118	115,635	114,544
Commodity contracts dealing....................	52313	4,941	5,884	6,981	6,114	7,025	8,748
Commodity contracts brokerage............	52314	3,525	(S)	5,583	6,889	5,205	5,397
Other financial investment activities [2]..............	5239x	132,559	166,155	200,858	195,769	177,235	190,013
Portfolio management...................	52392	113,562	144,322	177,941	173,590	154,688	167,061
Investment advice.....................	52393	18,997	21,833	22,917	22,179	22,547	22,952

S Estimate does not meet publication standards. [1] Data is based on 2002 NAICS; see text, this section and Section 15. [2] Excludes NAICS 52391 (miscellaneous intermediation) and NAICS 52399 (all other financial investment activities).

Source: U.S. Census Bureau, "Service Annual Survey: 2010," February 2012, <http://www.census.gov/services/index.html>.

Table 1232. Securities Industry—Financial Summary: 1990 to 2010

[In billions of dollars, except as indicated. (71.4 represents $71,400,000,000). Minus sign (–) indicates negative loss]

Type	1990	2000	2004	2005	2006	2007	2008	2009	2010
Number of firms........................	8,437	7,258	6,284	6,016	5,808	5,562	5,178	5,063	4,577
Revenues, total........................	**71.4**	**349.5**	**242.9**	**332.5**	**440.4**	**475.8**	**281.5**	**279.1**	**247.8**
Commissions............................	12.0	54.1	47.6	46.8	49.2	53.9	54.7	48.5	45.6
Trading/investment gains..............	15.7	70.8	30.7	30.7	48.2	-3.0	-61.9	39.3	24.3
Underwriting profits......................	3.7	18.7	19.1	19.9	23.6	26.5	16.3	22.6	24.0
Margin interest........................	3.2	24.5	7.0	13.3	23.7	32.3	18.1	4.5	4.9
Mutual fund sales......................	3.2	19.4	18.5	20.7	23.3	26.2	22.1	17.2	18.8
Other.................................	33.4	161.9	120.1	201.2	272.3	339.8	232.2	147.0	130.2
Expenses, total........................	**70.6**	**310.4**	**219.7**	**311.3**	**407.0**	**475.6**	**313.7**	**207.3**	**213.3**
Interest expense.......................	28.1	131.9	59.7	140.2	217.9	271.9	121.3	21.4	21.9
Compensation.........................	22.9	95.2	83.5	88.8	102.2	105.1	93.4	94.6	97.8
Commissions/clearance paid.............	3.0	15.5	17.4	18.6	21.5	25.3	25.7	22.2	22.6
Other.................................	16.6	67.8	59.2	63.6	63.8	71.5	71.5	67.3	69.1
Net income, pretax....................	**0.8**	**39.1**	**23.2**	**21.2**	**33.3**	**.2**	**-32.2**	**71.8**	**34.5**
Pre-tax profit margin (percent)..........	1.1	11.2	9.5	6.4	7.6	0	-11.4	25.7	13.9
Pre-tax return on equity (percent).......	2.2	31.1	15.0	13.1	21.3	0.1	19.2	38.9	16.5
Assets................................	657	2,866	4,831	5,215	5,908	6,414	4,281	4,213	4,617
Liabilities..............................	623	2,728	4,671	5,051	5,743	6,245	4,114	4,012	4,400
Ownership equity......................	34	138	160	164	165	169	167	202	217

Source: U.S. Securities and Exchange Commission, "Select SEC and Market Data Fiscal 2011," <http://www.sec.gov/about.shtml>.

Table 1233. Life Insurance in Force and Purchases in the United States— Summary: 1990 to 2011

[As of December 31 or calendar year, as applicable (389 represents 389,000,000). Covers life insurance with life insurance companies only. Data represents all life insurance in force on lives of U.S. residents whether issued by U.S. or foreign companies]

Year	Number of policies, total (millions)	Life insurance in force			Life insurance purchases [1]					
		Value (bil. dol.)			Number (1,000)			Amount (bil. dol.)		
		Total [2]	Individual	Group	Total	Individual	Group	Total	Individual	Group
1990........	389	9,393	5,391	3,754	28,791	14,199	14,592	1,529	1,070	459
2000........	369	15,953	9,376	6,376	34,882	13,345	21,537	2,515	1,594	921
2005........	373	18,399	9,970	8,263	34,519	11,407	23,112	2,836	1,796	1,040
2006........	375	19,112	10,057	8,906	29,287	10,908	18,378	2,835	1,813	1,022
2007........	374	19,539	10,232	9,158	30,788	10,826	19,962	2,994	1,891	1,103
2008........	335	19,120	10,254	8,717	28,599	10,207	18,392	2,943	1,870	1,073
2009........	291	18,138	10,324	7,688	29,190	10,139	19,051	2,900	1,744	1,156
2010........	284	18,426	10,484	7,831	28,621	10,123	18,498	2,809	1,673	1,135
2011........	286	19,219	10,994	8,120	27,177	10,309	16,867	2,832	1,673	1,160

[1] Excludes revivals, increases, dividend additions, and reinsurance acquired. Includes long-term credit insurance (life insurance on loans of more than 10 years' duration). [2] Includes other types of policies not shown separately.

Source: American Council of Life Insurers, Washington, DC, *Life Insurers Fact Book*, annual (copyright).

Table 1234. U.S. Life Insurance Companies—Summary: 1990 to 2011

[As of December 31 or calendar year, as applicable (402.2 represents $402,200,000,000). Covers domestic and foreign business of U.S. companies. Beginning in 2000, includes annual statement data for companies that primarily are health insurance companies. Beginning in 2005, includes fraternal benefit societies]

Item	Unit	1990	2000	2005	2006	2007	2008	2009	2010	2011
U.S. companies [1].....................	Number	2,195	1,269	1,119	1,072	1,009	976	946	917	895
Income...............................	**Bil. dol.**	402.2	811.5	779.0	883.6	950.4	940.6	781.4	862.6	915.3
Life insurance premiums...........	Bil. dol.	76.7	130.6	142.3	149.2	142.7	147.2	124.6	104.6	127.5
Annuity considerations [2]...........	Bil. dol.	129.1	306.7	277.1	302.7	314.2	328.1	231.6	293.6	334.9
Health insurance premiums........	Bil. dol.	58.3	105.6	118.3	141.2	151.5	165.0	166.2	172.7	171.6
Investment and other..............	Bil. dol.	138.2	268.5	241.4	290.4	342.0	300.3	259.1	291.6	281.3
Payments under life insurance and annuity contracts.............	Bil. dol.	88.4	375.2	365.7	422.7	461.0	445.1	374.9	365.6	393.2
Payments to life insurance beneficiaries........................	Bil. dol.	24.6	44.1	53.0	55.7	58.0	59.9	59.5	58.4	62.1
Surrender values under life insurance [3]........................	Bil. dol.	18.0	27.2	39.2	38.5	47.7	58.6	48.1	35.8	33.5
Surrender values under. annuity contracts [3,4]........................	Bil. dol.	(NA)	214.0	190.3	237.8	262.3	236.7	182.7	184.1	206.2
Policyholder dividends.............	Bil. dol.	12.0	20.0	17.9	18.4	19.5	19.1	16.2	15.9	15.5
Annuity payments [4]...............	Bil. dol.	32.6	68.7	63.9	71.1	72.3	69.6	67.1	70.1	74.5
Matured endowments..............	Bil. dol.	0.7	0.6	0.6	0.6	0.6	0.6	0.6	0.6	0.6
Other payments....................	Bil. dol.	0.6	0.6	0.7	0.6	0.6	0.6	0.8	0.7	0.7
Health insurance benefit payments.........................	Bil. dol.	40.0	78.8	79.6	97.0	106.1	118.9	122.0	122.5	120.6
BALANCE SHEET										
Assets..............................	**Bil. dol.**	1,408	3,182	4,482	4,823	5,092	4,648	4,959	5,311	5,493
MBS		(NA)	(NA)	(NA)	(NA)	(NA)	633	658	631	607
Government bonds.................	Bil. dol.	211	364	590	579	580	261	331	413	463
Corporate securities...............	Bil. dol.	711	2,238	3,136	3,413	3,662	2,671	2,979	3,271	3,353
Percent of total assets..........	Percent	50	70	70	71	71	77	80	81	81
Bonds...........................	Bil. dol.	583	1,241	1,850	1,882	1,991	1,535	1,593	1,700	1,807
Stocks..........................	Bil. dol.	128	997	1,285	1,531	1,670	1,136	1,386	1,570	1,546
Mortgages.......................	Bil. dol.	270	237	295	314	336	353	336	327	343
Real estate......................	Bil. dol.	43	36	33	33	35	32	28	28	29
Policy loans.....................	Bil. dol.	63	102	110	113	117	122	123	127	129
Other...........................	Bil. dol.	110	204	319	371	362	576	504	515	568
Interest earned on assets [5]........	Percent	8.89	7.05	4.90	5.35	5.71	5.70	4.60	4.33	4.35
Obligations and surplus funds [6].....	Bil. dol.	1,408	3,182	4,482	4,823	5,092	4,648	4,959	5,311	5,493
Policy reserves....................	**Bil. dol.**	1,197	2,712	3,360	3,608	3,791	3,471	3,812	4,098	4,244
Annuities [7].......................	Bil. dol.	798	1,841	2,174	2,328	2,458	2,137	2,422	2,660	2,729
Group..........................	Bil. dol.	516	960	758	807	843	716	798	863	871
Individual........................	Bil. dol.	282	881	1,415	1,521	1,615	1,422	1,624	1,780	1,840
Supplementary contracts [8].......	Bil. dol.	17	34	16	17	18	13	16	17	18
Life insurance...................	Bil. dol.	349	742	1,029	1,110	1,148	1,134	1,178	1,224	1,286
Health insurance..................	Bil. dol.	33	96	141	153	166	186	196	214	229
Liabilities for deposit-type contracts [9]......................	Bil. dol.	18	21	456	487	517	454	416	420	413
Capital and surplus................	Bil. dol.	91	188	256	266	282	263	301	319	321

NA Not available. [1] Beginning 2000, includes life insurance companies that sell accident and health insurance. [2] Beginning 2003, excludes certain deposit-type funds from income due to codification. [3] Beginning with 2000, "surrender values" include annuity withdrawals of funds, which were not included in 1990. [4] Beginning 2003, excludes payments under deposit-type contracts. [5] Net rate. [6] Includes other obligations not shown separately. [7] Beginning 2003, excludes reserves for guaranteed interest contracts (GICs). [8] Through 2000, includes reserves for contracts with and without life contingencies; beginning 2003, includes only reserves for contracts with life contingencies. [9] Policyholder dividend accumulations for all years. Beginning 2003, also includes liabilities for guaranteed interest contracts, supplementary contracts without life contingencies, and premium and other deposits.

Source: American Council of Life Insurers, Washington, DC, *Life Insurers Fact Book*, annual (copyright).

Table 1235. Property and Casualty Insurance—Summary: 2000 to 2009

[In billions of dollars (305.1 represents $305,100,000,000). Minus sign (–) indicates loss]

Item	2000	2005	2006	2007	2008	2009	2010
Premiums, net written [1]	305.1	427.6	447.8	446.7	439.9	422.9	426.1
Automobile, private [2]	120.0	159.6	160.5	159.7	158.6	157.4	160.26
Automobile, commercial [2]	19.8	26.8	26.7	25.6	23.8	21.9	21.12
Homeowners' multiple peril	32.7	53.0	55.8	55.6	56.4	57.7	61.3
Commercial multiple peril	(NA)	29.7	31.9	31.2	30.2	28.9	28.85
Marine, inland and ocean	8.3	11.2	12.3	13.0	12.5	11.6	90.15
Workers' compensation	26.2	39.7	41.8	40.6	36.5	32.0	31.48
Medical malpractice	(NA)	9.7	10.4	10.0	9.5	9.2	9.09
Other liability [3]	(NA)	39.4	42.2	41.2	38.5	36.0	35.68
Reinsurance	(NA)	6.6	12.9	13.1	13.8	12.6	12.28
Losses and expenses	321.3	421.4	401.0	417.1	457.6	423.3	57.05
Underwriting gain/loss	-27.3	-3.8	34.7	21.6	-19.6	1.5	-8.3
Net investment income	42.0	50.1	53.1	56.4	53.1	48.4	48.5
Operating earnings after taxes	4.4	46.7	66.4	63.6	3.7	32.2	37.4

NA Not available. [1] Excludes state funds. Includes other lines of insurance not shown separately. [2] Includes premiums for automobile liability and physical damage. [3] Coverages protecting against legal liability resulting from negligence, carelessness, or failure to act.

Source: Insurance Information Institute, New York, NY, *The III Insurance Fact Book*, annual; and *Financial Services Fact Book*, annual (copyright). Data from ISO and SNL Financial LC. See also <http://www.iii.org>.

Table 1236. Automobile Insurance—Average Expenditures Per Insured Vehicle by State: 2000 and 2009

[In dollars. Average expenditure equals total premiums written divided by liability car-years. A car-year is equal to 365 days of insured coverage for a single vehicle. The average expenditures for automobile insurance in a state are affected by a number of factors, including the underlying rate structure, the coverages purchased, the deductibles and limits selected, the types of vehicles insured, and the distribution of driver characteristics. The NAIC does not rank state average expenditures and does not endorse any conclusions drawn from this data]

State	2000	2009	State	2000	2009	State	2000	2009	State	2000	2009
U.S.	690	785	ID	505	555	MO	612	668	PA	699	811
AL	594	652	IL	652	728	MT	530	655	RI	825	969
AK	770	897	IN	570	620	NE	533	559	SC	620	738
AZ	792	837	IA	479	532	NV	829	944	SD	482	521
AR	606	656	KS	540	578	NH	665	718	TN	592	634
CA	672	754	KY	616	699	NJ	977	1,101	TX	678	860
CO	755	741	LA	806	1,099	NM	674	713	UT	620	716
CT	871	952	ME	528	598	NY	939	1,057	VT	568	646
DE	849	1,021	MD	757	929	NC	564	610	VA	576	667
DC	996	1,128	MA	946	860	ND	477	510	WA	722	826
FL	781	1,006	MI	702	913	OH	579	616	WV	680	815
GA	674	754	MN	696	694	OK	603	680	WI	545	591
HI	702	786	MS	654	738	OR	625	723	WY	496	623

Source: National Association of Insurance Commissioners (NAIC), Kansas City, MO, Auto Insurance Database Report, annual (copyright). Reprinted with permission of the NAIC. Further reprint or distribution strictly prohibited without prior written permission of the NAIC.

Table 1237. Renters and Homeowners Insurance—Average Premiums by State: 2009

[In dollars. Average premium equals premiums divided by exposure per house-years. A house-year is equal to 365 days of insured coverage for a single dwelling and is the standard measurement for homeowners insurance. The NAIC does not rank state average expenditures and does not endorse any conclusions drawn from these data]

State	2009		State	2009		State	2009	
	Renters [1]	Home-owners [2]		Renters [1]	Home-owners [2]		Renters [1]	Home-owners [2]
U.S.	184	880	KS	172	991	NC	127	725
AL	216	987	KY	165	711	ND	114	853
AK	181	892	LA	245	1,430	OH	173	613
AZ	201	642	ME	144	651	OK	220	1,123
AR	226	919	MD	152	779	OR	174	544
CA	218	922	MA	219	1,035	PA	143	694
CO	176	893	MI	182	740	RI	182	1,069
CT	193	1,016	MN	144	919	SC	198	970
DE	154	610	MS	251	1,185	SD	116	645
DC	169	1,069	MO	178	881	TN	211	794
FL	208	1,460	MT	149	751	TX [3]	222	1,511
GA	214	787	NE	143	849	UT	155	544
HI	193	879	NV	202	703	VT	157	717
ID	158	485	NH	151	757	VA	150	734
IL	171	789	NJ	169	848	WA	173	552
IN	172	717	NM	188	751	WV	175	671
IA	135	645	NY	213	1,021	WI	125	542
						WY	159	727

[1] Based on the HO-4 renters insurance policy for tenants. Includes broad named-peril coverage for the personal property of tenants. [2] Based on the HO-3 homeowner package policy for owner-occupied dwellings, 1–4 family units. Provides "all risks" coverage (except those specifically excluded in the policy) on buildings, broad named-peril coverage on personal property, and is the most common package written. [3] The Texas Insurance Commissioner promulgates residential policy forms which are similar but not identical to the standard forms.

Source: National Association of Insurance Commissioners (NAIC), Kansas City, MO, Dwelling Fire, Homeowners Owner-Occupied, and Homeowners Tenant and Condominium/Cooperative Unit Owners Insurance (copyright). Reprinted with permission of the NAIC. Further reprint or distribution strictly prohibited without prior written permission of the NAIC.

Table 1238. Real Estate and Rental and Leasing—Nonemployer Establishments and Receipts by Kind of Business: 2007 to 2009

[2,327.1 represents 2,327,100. Includes only firms subject to federal income tax. Nonemployers are businesses with no paid employees. Data originate chiefly from administrative records of the Internal Revenue Service; see Appendix III]

Kind of business	NAICS code [1]	Establishments (1,000)			Receipts (mil. dol.)		
		2007	2008	2009	2007	2008	2009
Real estate & rental & leasing, total....................	**53**	**2,327.1**	**2,130.4**	**2,372.9**	**183,264**	**163,461**	**208,306**
Real estate..	531	2,243.5	2,049.7	2,290.8	176,526	156,793	201,787
Lessors of real estate............................	5311	780.0	731.1	987.3	102,825	94,785	134,896
Offices of real estate agents & brokers...........	5312	790.7	700.3	658.8	31,460	24,935	24,721
Activities related to real estate..................	5313	672.8	618.4	644.7	42,242	37,073	42,169
Rental & leasing services.......................	532	81.8	79.1	80.1	6,583	6,516	6,328
Automotive equipment rental & leasing...........	5321	20.3	19.7	19.0	1,057	1,059	997
Consumer goods rental...........................	5322	18.5	17.9	18.0	898	881	765
General rental centers............................	5323	3.9	4.0	4.6	348	347	392
Commercial/industrial equipment rental & leasing........	5324	39.1	37.4	38.6	4,280	4,230	4,175
Lessors of other nonfinancial intangible assets...........	533	1.7	1.6	1.9	154	152	191

[1] Data use 2007 North American Industry Classification System (NAICS). For more information, see text, Section 15.

Source: U.S. Census Bureau, "Nonemployer Statistics," accessed October 2012, <http://www.census.gov/econ/nonemployer/index.html>.

Table 1239. Real Estate and Rental and Leasing—Establishments, Employees, and Payroll: 2008 and 2009

[(365.7 represents 365,700). Covers establishments with payroll. Employees are for the week including March 12. Most government employees are excluded. For statement on methodology, see Appendix III]

Kind of business	NAICS code [1]	Establishments (1,000)		Employees (1,000)		Payroll (bil. dol.)	
		2008	2009	2008	2009	2008	2009
Real estate & rental & leasing, total..............	**53**	**365.7**	**351.0**	**2,196.3**	**2,036.6**	**88.8**	**81.1**
Real estate..	531	298.8	287.0	1,528.3	1,445.4	63.9	58.7
Lessors of real estate............................	5311	115.7	113.6	539.9	521.2	19.8	18.5
Offices of real estate agents & brokers...........	5312	99.9	91.2	342.3	297.8	15.8	13.1
Activities related to real estate..................	5313	83.2	82.1	646.0	626.5	28.3	27.1
Rental & leasing services.......................	532	64.4	61.7	636.1	557.0	22.5	20.0
Automotive equipment rental & leasing.............	5321	13.9	13.5	191.2	168.5	6.5	5.9
Passenger car rental & leasing.................	53211	7.5	7.7	([3])	([3])	4.3	3.9
Truck, utility trailer & RV rental & leasing...........	53212	6.3	5.8	54.8	48.6	2.2	2.0
Consumer goods rental [2].......................	5322	31.6	29.8	236.6	208.4	5.6	5.1
Video tape & disc rental.........................	53223	14.3	12.9	113.7	93.2	1.6	1.3
General rental centers............................	5323	4.6	4.3	43.5	26.1	1.5	0.9
Commercial/industrial equipment rental & leasing. ...	5324	14.4	14.1	164.7	154.0	8.9	8.1
Lessors of other nonfinancial intangible assets........	533	2.4	2.4	32.0	34.2	2.4	2.5

[1] 2008 and 2009 data use 2007 North American Industry Classification System (NAICS). For more information, see text, Section 15. [2] Includes industries not shown separately. [3] Over 100,000 employees.

Source: U.S. Census Bureau, "County Business Patterns," June 2011, <http://www.census.gov/econ/cbp/>.

Table 1240. Rental and Leasing Services—Revenue by Kind of Business: 2005 to 2010

[In millions of dollars (107,559 represents $107,559,000). Covers taxable and tax-exempt employer firms. Estimates have been adjusted using the results of the 2002 Economic Census. Based on Service Annual Survey; see Appendix III]

Kind of business	NAICS code [1]	2005	2006	2007	2008	2009	2010
Rental & leasing services............................	**532**	**107,559**	**117,349**	**121,685**	**123,566**	**110,223**	**111,250**
Automotive equipment rental & leasing..................	5321	42,324	44,598	44,982	46,094	41,987	42,385
Passenger car rental & leasing.........................	53211	26,305	28,179	29,222	30,299	28,537	28,922
Truck, utility trailer, & RV rental & leasing...............	53212	16,019	16,419	15,760	15,795	13,450	13,463
Consumer goods rental [2].................................	5322	22,840	23,702	24,750	24,143	22,100	21,914
Video tape & disc rental.................................	53223	9,023	9,194	9,262	8,474	7,384	6,579
General rental centers....................................	5323	3,553	3,934	4,249	4,188	3,727	3,897
Commercial/industrial equip. rental & leasing............	5324	38,842	45,115	47,704	49,141	42,409	43,054

[1] Data are based on 2002 NAICS; see text, this section and Section 15. [2] Includes other kinds of business, not shown separately.

Source: U.S. Census Bureau, "Service Annual Survey: 2010," February 2012, <http://www.census.gov/services/index.html>.

Arts, Recreation, and Travel

This section presents data on the arts, entertainment, and recreation economic sector of the economy, and personal recreational activities, the arts and humanities, and domestic and foreign travel.

Arts, Entertainment, and Recreation Industry—The U.S. Census Bureau surveys—*County Business Patterns, Economic Census, Nonemployer Statistics* and *Service Annual Survey*, provide data on the *Arts, Entertainment, and Recreation Sector.* The County Business Patterns annual data includes number of establishments, number of employees, first quarter and annual payrolls, and number of establishments by employment size class. The Economic Census, conducted every five years for the years ending '2' and '7,' provides information on the number of establishments, receipts, payroll, and paid employees for the United States and various geographic levels. Nonemployer statistics are an annual tabulation of economic data by industry for active businesses without paid employees that are subject to federal income tax. The Service Annual Survey provides estimates of operation revenue of taxable firms and revenues and expenses of firms exempt from federal taxes for industries in this sector of the economy. See Appendix III for more details.

Recreation and leisure activities—Data on the participation in various recreation and leisure time activities are based on several sample surveys. Data on the public's involvement with arts events and activities are published by the National Endowment for Arts (NEA). The NEA's Survey of Public Participation in the Arts remains the largest periodic study of arts participation in the United States. The most recent data are from the 2008 survey. Data on participation in fishing, hunting, and other forms of wildlife associated recreation are published periodically by the U.S. Department of Interior, Fish and Wildlife Service. The most recent data are from the 2006 survey. Data on participation in various sports recreation activities are published by the National Sporting Goods Association. GfK Mediamark Research and Intelligence, LLC. also conducts periodic surveys on sports and leisure activities, as well as other topics.

Parks and recreation—The Department of the Interior has responsibility for administering the national parks. The National Park Service publishes information on visits to national park areas in its annual report, *National Park Statistical Abstract. The National Parks*: Index (year) is an annual report which contains brief descriptions, with acreage and visits for each area administered by the service, plus certain "related" areas. This information can be found at: <https://irma.nps.gov/Stats/>. Statistics for state parks are compiled by the National Association of State Park Directors.

Travel—Statistics on arrivals and departures to the United States, cities and states visited by overseas travelers, and tourism sales and employment are reported by the International Trade Administration (ITA), Office of Travel & Tourism Industries (OTTI). Data on domestic travel and travel expenditures are published by the research department of the U.S. Travel Association. Other data on household transportation characteristics are in Section 23, Transportation.

Statistical reliability—For a discussion of statistical collection and estimation, sampling procedures, and measures of statistical reliability applicable to Census Bureau data, see Appendix III.

Table 1241. Arts, Entertainment, and Recreation Services—Estimated Revenue: 2005 to 2010

[In millions of dollars (166,912 represents $166,912,000,000). For taxable and tax-exempt employer firms. Selected estimates have been adjusted using the results of the 2007 Economic Census. Based on the Service Annual Survey, see Appendix III]

Industry	2002 NAICS Code [1]	2005	2006	2007	2008	2009	2010
Arts, entertainment, and recreation	**71**	**166,912**	**178,879**	**189,418**	**192,584**	**188,158**	**191,982**
Performing arts, spectator sports, and related industries	711	65,405	72,647	77,772	80,075	79,940	81,581
Performing arts companies	7111	13,144	13,493	13,573	13,753	14,321	14,822
Spectator sports	7112	24,842	27,500	30,403	31,767	31,590	32,379
Sports teams and clubs	711211	14,564	16,401	18,794	20,393	20,691	21,504
Racetracks	711212	7,358	7,975	8,197	7,545	7,069	7,216
Other spectator sports	711219	2,920	3,124	3,412	3,829	3,830	3,659
Promoters of performing arts, sports, and similar events	7113	12,374	14,933	16,122	16,299	16,167	16,327
Agents and managers for artists, athletes, entertainers and other public figures	7114	4,176	4,521	4,919	5,224	5,025	4,968
Independent artists, writers, and performers	7115	10,869	12,200	12,755	13,032	12,837	13,085
Museums, historical sites, and similar institutions	712	12,471	11,982	13,286	12,382	11,588	11,736
Amusement, gambling, and recreation industries	713	89,036	94,250	98,360	100,127	96,630	98,665
Amusement parks and arcades	7131	11,926	12,417	13,544	14,071	13,330	13,991
Amusement and theme parks	71311	10,491	10,816	11,890	12,268	11,589	12,197
Amusement arcades	71312	1,435	1,601	1,654	1,803	1,741	1,794
Gambling industries	7132	24,040	25,175	25,135	25,624	25,100	25,729
Casinos (except casino hotels)	71321	15,753	16,505	16,557	16,874	16,410	16,619
Other gambling industries	71329	8,287	8,670	8,578	8,750	8,690	9,110
Other amusement and recreation industries	7139	53,070	56,658	59,681	60,432	58,200	58,945
Golf courses and country clubs	71391	19,356	20,523	21,195	21,077	20,342	19,980
Skiing facilities	71392	1,989	2,178	2,257	2,476	2,440	2,514
Marinas	71393	3,561	3,853	4,042	3,774	3,303	3,461
Fitness and recreational sports centers	71394	18,286	19,447	21,416	22,394	21,966	22,503
Bowling centers	71395	3,232	3,094	3,403	3,338	3,123	3,103
All other amusement and recreation industries	71399	6,646	7,563	7,368	7,373	7,026	7,384

[1] Based on 2002 North American Industry Classification System (NAICS); see text, this section and Section 15.

Source: U.S. Census Bureau, Service Annual Survey: 2010, February 2012, <http://www.census.gov/services/index.html>.

Table 1242. Arts, Entertainment, and Recreation—Establishments, Revenue, Payroll, and Employees by Kind of Business: 2002 and 2007

[141,904 represents $141,904,000,000. For establishments with payroll only. Definition of paid employees varies among NAICS sectors. Data are based on the 2002 and 2007 economic censuses which are subject to nonsampling error. For details on survey methodology, sampling and nonsampling errors, see Appendix III]

Kind of business	2002 NAICS code [1]	Number of establishments		Revenue (mil. dol.)		Annual payroll (mil. dol.)		Paid employees (1,000)	
		2002	2007	2002	2007	2002	2007	2002	2007
Arts, entertainment, and recreation, total	**71**	**110,313**	**124,620**	**141,904**	**189,417**	**45,169**	**58,359**	**1,849**	**2,061**
Performing arts, spectator sports, and related industries [2]	711	37,735	43,868	58,286	77,773	21,231	27,839	423	438
Performing arts companies	7111	9,303	8,838	10,864	13,574	3,267	3,980	138	128
Spectator sports	7112	4,072	4,237	22,313	30,403	10,206	14,136	108	121
Promoters of performing arts, sports and similar events	7113	5,236	6,647	12,169	16,122	2,184	2,957	102	121
Agents and managers for artists, athletes, entertainers and others	7114	3,262	3,534	3,602	4,919	1,251	1,694	17	19
Museums, historical sites, and similar institutions [2]	712	6,663	7,125	8,608	13,285	2,935	3,662	123	130
Amusement, gambling, and recreation industries [2]	713	65,915	73,627	75,010	98,359	21,002	26,859	1,303	1,494
Amusement parks and arcades	7131	3,015	3,145	9,443	13,544	2,069	2,802	122	134
Gambling industries	7132	2,072	2,327	18,893	25,135	3,596	4,566	158	170
Other amusement and recreation services	7139	60,828	68,155	46,674	59,680	15,337	19,490	1,023	1,190

[1] Based on 2002 North American Industry Classification System (NAICS); see text, this section and section 15. [2] Includes other industries not shown separately.

Source: U.S. Census Bureau, 2007 Economic Census, Core Business Statistics, *Comparative Statistics 2007 and 2002, Arts, Entertainment and Recreation*, accessed July 2012, <http://www.census.gov/econ/census07/>.

Table 1243. Arts, Entertainment, and Recreation—Nonemployer Establishments and Receipts by Kind of Business (NAICS Basis): 2007 to 2009

[1,119.6 represents 1,119,600. Includes only firms subject to federal income tax. Nonemployers are businesses with no paid employees but with annual receipts of $1,000 or more.]

Kind of business	2007 NAICS code [1]	Firms (1,000)			Receipts (mil.dol.)		
		2007	2008	2009	2007	2008	2009
Arts, entertainment, and recreation...............	**71**	**1,119.6**	**1,121.4**	**1,124.0**	**27,357**	**27,837**	**25,623**
Performing arts, spectator sports, and related industries.......	711	967.4	970.8	974.4	20,841	21,226	20,093
Performing arts companies.............	7111	53.4	55.6	58.7	1,132	1,163	1,157
Spectator sports.............	7112	141.6	143.7	147.1	2,532	2,552	2,466
Promoters of performing arts, sports, and similar events.......	7113	39.8	40.8	42.5	1,584	1,631	1,581
Agents/managers for artists, athletes, and other public figures.......	7114	33.8	34.2	35.2	1,294	1,326	1,231
Independent artists, writers, and performers..............	7115	698.9	696.5	691.0	14,299	14,555	13,658
Museums, historical sites, and similar institutions...........	712	6.2	6.3	6.0	103	102	95
Amusement, gambling, and recreation industries.......	713	145.9	144.3	143.6	6,413	6,509	5,435
Amusement parks and arcades.............	7131	5.5	5.2	4.9	330	322	250
Gambling industries.............	7132	10.4	10.3	10.2	1,278	1,334	1,166
Other amusement and recreation services.........	7139	130.0	128.8	128.5	4,805	4,852	4,019

[1] Data for 2007 based on the 2002 North American Industry Classification System (NAICS), 2008 and 2009 data is based on 2007 NAICS; see text, Section 15.

Source: U.S. Census Bureau, "Nonemployer Statistics," released July 2011, <http://www.census.gov/econ/nonemployer>.

Table 1244. Arts, Entertainment, and Recreation—Establishments, Employees, and Payroll by Kind of Business (NAICS Basis): 2008 to 2009

[2,069.3 represents 2,069,300. Covers establishments with paid employees. Excludes self-employed individuals, employees of private households, railroad employees, agricultural production employees, and most government employees. For statement on methodology, see Appendix III. "County Business Patterns" excludes rail transportation (NAICS 482), National Postal Service (NAICS 491), and other NAICS industries]

Kind of business	2007 NAICS code [1]	Establishments		Employees [2] (1,000)		Payroll (mil. dol.)	
		2008	2009	2008	2009	2008	2009
Arts, entertainment, & recreation..................	**71**	**124,279**	**122,857**	**2,069.3**	**2,010.3**	**62,343**	**61,179**
Performing arts, spectator sports.......................	711	44,477	43,985	452.2	429.0	30,495	30,067
Performing arts companies...........................	7111	8,911	8,730	131.3	120.0	4,269	3,983
Theater companies & dinner theaters..............	71111	3,418	3,298	71.7	65.2	2,142	1,954
Dance companies.............................	71112	647	643	8.9	8.8	237	221
Musical groups & artists......................	71113	4,438	4,389	41.1	36.8	1,607	1,507
Other performing arts companies..................	71119	408	400	9.5	9.3	283	301
Spectator sports.................................	7112	4,416	4,384	127.3	122.6	15,438	15,252
Sports teams & clubs.........................	711211	850	803	56.4	55.8	12,981	12,900
Racetracks...................................	711212	718	698	50.7	47.7	1,397	1,323
Other spectator sports......................	711219	2,848	2,883	20.2	19.1	1,060	1,028
Promoters of performing arts, sports, and similar events.....................	7113	6,649	6,603	129.8	124.6	3,090	3,336
Promoters of performing arts, sports, & similar events with facilities........................	71131	2,665	2,677	103.1	100.0	2,039	2,354
Promoters of performing arts, sports, & similar events without facilities.....................	71132	3,984	3,926	26.7	24.7	1,051	982
Agents/managers for artists, athletes, and other public figures.....................	7114	3,558	3,557	18.9	18.6	1,944	1,894
Independent artists, writers, & performers...........	7115	20,943	20,711	45.0	43.1	5,756	5,603
Museums, historical sites, & similar institutions.......	712	7,272	7,310	133.5	128.6	3,845	3,792
Museums.............................	71211	4,723	4,794	85.3	82.4	2,527	2,464
Historical sites........................	71212	1,222	1,211	10.4	9.8	250	227
Zoos & botanical gardens....................	71213	600	586	31.4	30.1	882	915
Nature parks & other similar institutions..............	71219	727	719	6.4	6.2	186	186
Amusement, gambling, & recreation industries.......	713	72,530	71,562	1,483.7	1,452.7	28,002	27,320
Amusement parks & arcades.....................	7131	3,144	3,070	142.4	137.0	2,864	2,660
Amusement & theme parks..................	71311	524	536	110.3	106.8	2,450	2,271
Amusement arcades.....................	71312	2,620	2,534	32.1	30.2	414	389
Gambling industries.......................	7132	2,481	2,521	174.3	173.8	4,960	5,015
Casinos (except casino hotels)................	71321	349	351	114.4	117.7	3,417	3,548
Other gambling industries...................	71329	2,132	2,170	59.8	56.1	1,544	1,467
Other amusement & recreation services.............	7139	66,905	65,971	1,166.9	1,142.0	20,178	19,645
Golf courses & country clubs.....................	71391	12,059	11,853	322.6	302.5	8,378	8,043
Skiing facilities.............................	71392	373	371	78.4	77.3	681	663
Marinas.................................	71393	3,972	3,891	28.7	26.6	954	905
Fitness & recreational sports centers..............	71394	30,961	30,338	563.1	564.7	7,232	7,148
Bowling centers............................	71395	4,492	4,349	81.3	78.1	1,021	985
All other amusement & recreation industries.......	71399	15,048	15,169	92.8	92.8	1,912	1,900

[1] 2008 and 2009 data based on 2007 NAICS; see text, this section and Section 15. [2] For employees on the payroll for the period including March 12.

Source: U.S. Census Bureau, "County Business Patterns," released June 2011, <http://www.census.gov/econ/cbp/index.html>.

Table 1245. Expenditures Per Consumer Unit for Entertainment and Reading: 1985 to 2010

[Data are annual averages. In dollars, except as indicated. Based on Consumer Expenditure Survey (CE). For description of survey, see text, Section 13; also see headnote, Table 700. For composition of regions, see map, inside front cover]

Year and characteristic	Entertainment and reading		Entertainment				Reading
	Total	Percent of total expenditures	Total	Fees and admissions	Audio and visual equipment and services	Other entertainment, supplies, and equipment services [1]	
1985.........	1,311	5.6	1,170	320	371	479	141
1990.........	1,575	5.6	1,422	371	454	597	153
1994.........	1,732	5.5	1,567	439	533	595	165
1995.........	1,775	5.5	1,612	433	542	637	163
1996.........	1,993	5.9	1,834	459	561	814	159
1997.........	1,977	5.7	1,813	471	577	766	164
1998.........	1,907	5.4	1,746	449	535	762	161
1999.........	2,050	5.5	1,891	459	608	824	159
2000.........	2,009	5.3	1,863	515	622	727	146
2001.........	2,094	5.3	1,953	526	660	767	141
2002.........	2,218	5.5	2,079	542	692	845	139
2003.........	2,187	5.4	2,060	494	730	835	127
2004.........	2,348	5.4	2,218	528	788	903	130
2005.........	2,514	5.4	2,388	588	888	912	126
2006.........	2,493	5.2	2,376	606	906	863	117
2007.........	2,816	5.7	2,698	658	987	1,053	118
2008.........	2,951	5.8	2,835	616	1,036	1,183	116
2009.........	2,803	5.7	2,693	628	975	1,090	110
2010, total.......	**2,604**	**5.4**	**2,504**	**581**	**954**	**970**	**100**
Age of reference person:							
Under 25 years old.........	1,260	4.6	1,221	235	595	390	39
25 to 34 years old.........	2,312	5.0	2,251	460	965	826	61
35 to 44 years old.........	3,138	5.6	3,058	849	1,078	1,130	80
45 to 54 years old.........	3,192	5.5	3,088	780	1,025	1,284	104
55 to 64 years old.........	2,809	5.5	2,683	545	1,061	1,077	126
65 to 74 years old.........	2,488	6.0	2,341	473	864	1,004	147
75 years old and over.........	1,509	4.8	1,374	283	700	390	135
Hispanic or Latino origin of reference person:							
Hispanic.........	1,681	4.1	1,644	332	802	510	37
Non-Hispanic.........	2,731	5.6	2,623	616	975	1,032	108
Race of reference person:							
White, and all other races [2].........	2,796	5.7	2,687	627	975	1,086	109
Asian.........	2,281	3.9	2,192	785	886	521	89
Black.........	1,393	3.9	1,352	195	841	317	41
Region of residence:							
Northeast.........	2,812	5.3	2,688	666	997	1,026	124
Midwest.........	2,649	5.9	2,548	574	911	1,064	101
South.........	2,427	5.5	2,347	477	964	906	80
West.........	2,679	5.0	2,568	690	946	933	111
Size of consumer unit:							
One person.........	1,522	5.2	1,441	264	661	516	81
Two or more persons.........	3,051	5.5	2,943	712	1,075	1,155	108
Two persons.........	2,835	5.6	2,707	576	1,055	1,076	128
Three persons.........	2,910	5.2	2,810	624	1,056	1,131	100
Four persons.........	3,494	5.5	3,396	1,056	1,172	1,168	98
Five persons or more.........	3,344	5.5	3,276	808	1,041	1,427	68
Income before taxes:							
Quintiles of income:							
Lowest 20 percent.........	1,063	5.1	1,018	131	538	349	45
Second 20 percent.........	1,516	5.0	1,450	193	698	558	66
Third 20 percent.........	2,068	5.0	1,984	373	919	692	84
Fourth 20 percent.........	2,899	5.3	2,792	599	1,129	1,065	107
Highest 20 percent.........	5,474	5.9	5,277	1,610	1,487	2,180	197
Education:							
Less than a high school graduate.........	1,209	4.1	1,174	113	620	441	35
High school graduate.........	1,931	5.1	1,864	296	878	691	67
High school graduate with some college.........	2,515	5.8	2,425	442	943	1,041	90
Associate's degree.........	2,800	5.5	2,710	487	1,050	1,173	90
Bachelor's degree.........	3,509	5.5	3,366	1,002	1,144	1,220	143
Master's, professional, doctoral degree.........	4,439	5.9	4,226	1,492	1,179	1,555	213

[1] Other equipment and services include pets, toys, hobbies, and playground equipment; and other entertainment supplies, equipment, and services. [2] All other races includes Native Hawaiian or other Pacific Islander, American Indian or Alaska Native, and approximately 1 percent reporting more than one race.

Source: U.S. Bureau of Labor Statistics, Consumer Expenditure Survey, "Consumer Expenditures in 2010," September 2011. See also <http://www.bls.gov/cex/home.htm#tables>.

Table 1246. Personal Consumption Expenditures for Recreation: 1990 to 2010

[In billions of dollars (314.7 represents $314,700,000,000), except percent. Represents market value of purchases of goods and services by individuals and nonprofit institutions. In August 2011 BEA revised NIPA data for 2003-2010 to reflect newly available source data. For more on these changes and revisions, see <http://www.bea.gov/scb/pdf/2011/08%20August/0811_nipa_annual_article.pdf>]

Type of product or service	1990	2000	2005	2007	2008	2009	2010
Total recreation expenditures	**314.7**	**639.9**	**817.7**	**918.7**	**923.5**	**881.0**	**907.0**
Percent of total personal consumption [1]	8.2	9.4	9.3	9.4	9.2	8.9	9.0
Video and audio equipment, computers, and related services	81.1	184.4	252.5	291.1	294.6	284.7	295.6
Video and audio equipment	43.7	83.1	111.0	118.9	119.7	111.2	111.2
Information processing equipment	9.6	44.1	67.0	86.1	84.9	82.4	91.7
Services related to video and audio goods and computers	27.8	57.2	74.6	86.1	89.9	91.0	92.7
Sports and recreational goods and related services	74.2	147.9	186.4	202.7	197.6	178.8	180.9
Sports and recreational vehicles	16.6	34.9	45.7	47.3	42.7	33.5	32.2
Other sporting and recreational goods	55.4	108.7	135.4	149.4	149.3	140.4	143.6
Maintenance and repair of recreational vehicles and sports equipment	2.1	4.2	5.3	5.9	5.6	4.9	5
Membership clubs, sports centers, parks, theaters, and museums	49.7	91.9	115.2	131.8	135.0	131.6	135.1
Membership clubs and participant sports centers	14.3	26.4	31.1	35.0	35.5	33.7	34.1
Amusements parks, campgrounds, and related recreational services	19.2	31.1	36.4	42.4	44.7	43.2	45.1
Admissions to specified spectator amusements	14.4	30.6	41.6	48.4	49.0	48.9	50.1
Motion picture theaters	5.1	8.6	9.9	11.0	11.0	11.6	11.8
Live entertainment, excluding sports	4.5	10.4	15.3	17.4	17.5	17.4	18.0
Spectator sports	4.8	11.6	16.4	20.0	20.5	19.9	20.4
Museums and libraries	1.9	3.8	6.1	5.9	5.9	5.8	5.8
Magazines, newspapers, books, and stationery	47.3	81.0	85.6	87.6	88.5	87.2	92.5
Gambling	23.7	67.6	92.9	105.7	103.8	97.8	98.1
Pets, pet products, and related services	18.8	39.7	55.6	66.5	70.6	70.7	73.3
Photographic goods and services	16.7	19.7	19.8	21.3	20.8	19.1	19.1
Package tours [2]	3.2	7.8	9.6	12.1	12.6	11.2	12.3

[1] See Table 689. [2] Consists of tour operators' and travel agents' margins. Purchases of travel and accommodations included in tours are accounted for separately in other personal consumption expenditures categories.

Source: U.S. Bureau of Economic Analysis, National Economic Accounts, *National Income and Product Account Tables, Table 2.5.5*, August 2011. See also <http://www.bea.gov/iTable/iTable.cfm?ReqID=9&step=1>.

Table 1247. Performing Arts—Selected Data: 1990 to 2010

[Sales, receipts, and expenditures in millions of dollars (282 represents $282,000,000). For season ending in year shown, except as indicated]

Item	1990	1995	2000	2004	2005	2006	2007	2008	2009	2010
Legitimate theater: [1]										
Broadway shows:										
New productions	40	33	37	39	39	39	35	36	43	39
Attendance (mil.)	8.0	9.0	11.4	11.6	11.5	12.0	12.3	12.3	12.1	11.9
Playing weeks [2,3]	1,070	1,120	1,464	1,451	1,494	1,501	1,509	1,560	1,548	1,464
Gross ticket sales	282	406	603	771	769	862	939	938	943	1,020
Broadway road tours: [4]										
Attendance (mil.)	11.1	15.6	11.7	12.9	18.2	17.1	16.7	15.3	14.3	15.9
Playing weeks	944	1,242	888	1,060	1,389	1,377	1,400	1,138	1,112	1,242
Gross ticket sales	367	548	572	700	707	831	833	955	881	947
Nonprofit professional theatres: [5]										
Companies reporting [6]	185	215	262	1,477	1,490	1,893	1,910	1,919	1,825	1,807
Gross income	308	444	791	1,571	1,647	1,791	1,881	1,884	1,779	1,913
Earned income	188	281	466	856	845	923	962	955	811	964
Contributed income	119	163	325	715	802	868	919	929	968	948
Gross expenses	306	445	708	1,464	1,530	1,667	1,742	1,860	1,892	1,870
Productions	2,265	2,646	3,241	11,000	12,000	14,000	17,000	15,000	17,000	16,000
Performances	46,131	56,608	66,123	169,000	169,000	172,000	197,000	202,000	187,000	163,000
Total attendance (mil.)	15.2	18.6	22.0	32.1	32.5	30.5	31.0	32.0	30.0	31.0
OPERA America professional member companies: [7]										
Number of companies reporting [8]	98	88	98	95	93	94	97	85	84	97
Expenses [8]	321	435	637	678	742	752	872	826	816	883
Performances [8]	2,336	2,120	1,768	1,946	1,893	1,851	1,961	1,753	1744	1,677
Total attendance (mil.) [8,9]	7.5	4.1	6.2	5.1	5	5.3	5.3	5.1	4.3	6.8
Main season attendance (mil.) [8,10]	4.1	3.9	3.8	3.4	3.3	3.4	3.6	3.1	2.9	2.2
Symphony orchestras: [11]										
Concerts	18,931	29,328	33,154	37,263	37,196	36,731	37,169	33,029	32,813	34,446
Attendance (mil.)	24.7	30.9	31.7	27.7	26.5	29.1	28.8	28.7	25.4	25.8
Gross revenue	378	536	734	827	812	945	1,052	992	969	1,030
Operating expenses	622	859	1,126	1,483	1,513	1,603	1,808	1,862	1,864	1,849
Support	258	351	521	639	626	713	721	785	726	695

[1] Source: The Broadway League, New York, NY. For season ending in year shown. [2] All shows (new productions and holdovers from previous seasons). [3] Eight performances constitute one playing week. [4] North American Tours include U.S. and Canadian companies. [5] Source: Theatre Communications Group, New York, NY. For years ending on or prior to August 31. [6] Beginning in 2002, nonprofit theatre data is based on survey responses and extrapolated data from IRS Form 990. [7] Source: OPERA America, New York, NY. For years ending on or prior to August 31. [8] U.S. and Canadian companies for 1999 and 2009-10; U.S. companies only for all other years. [9] Includes educational performances, outreach, etc. [10] For paid performances. Data for the Metropolitan Opera are not included. [11] Source: League of American Orchestras, New York, NY. For years ending August 31. Prior to 1995, represents 254 U.S. orchestras; beginning 1995, represents all U.S. orchestras, excluding college/university and youth orchestras. Beginning 1995, data based on 1,200 orchestras.

Source: Compiled from sources listed in footnotes. See also <http://www.livebroadway.com/>; <http://www.tcg.org/>; <http://www.operaamerica.org/>; and <http://www.americanorchestras.org/>.

Table 1248. Arts and Humanities—Selected Federal Aid Programs: 1990 to 2010

[In millions of dollars (170.8 represents $170,800,000), except as indicated. For fiscal year ending September 30. FY 2009 and FY 2010 include funds from the American Recovery and Reinvestment Act]

Type of fund and program	1990	1995	2000	2005	2006	2007	2008	2009	2010
National Endowment for the Arts:									
Funds available [1]	170.8	152.1	85.2	108.8	112.8	111.7	129.3	186.8	153.1
Program appropriation [2]	152.3	138.1	79.6	99.5	100.7	100.3	119.6	178.1	138.7
Grants awarded (number) [3]	4,252	3,534	1,906	2,161	2,293	2,158	2,219	3,075	2,731
Funds obligated [4,5]	157.6	147.9	83.5	104.4	107.0	106.5	125.5	176.2	141.1
National Endowment for the Humanities:									
Funds available [1]	140.6	152.3	102.6	119.8	121.5	122.3	128.6	134.5	146.6
Program appropriation	114.2	125.7	82.7	99.9	102.2	102.2	105.7	114.7	125.7
Matching funds [6]	26.3	25.7	15.1	15.9	15.2	15.2	14.3	14.3	14.3

[1] Includes other program funds not shown separately. Excludes administrative funds. [2] FY 1990–FY 1996 include Regular Program Funds, Treasury Funds, Challenge Grant Funds, and Policy, Planning, and Research Funds. FY 1997 includes Regular Program Funds, Matching Grant Funds, and Policy, Research and Technology Funds. FY 1998–FY 2000 includes Regular Program Funds and Matching Grant Funds. [3] Excludes cooperative agreements and interagency agreements. [4] Includes obligations for new grants, supplemental awards on previous years' grants, cooperative agreements, and interagency agreements. Excludes obligations funded with administrative funds. [5] Beginning with 1997 data, the grantmaking structure changed from discipline-based categories to thematic ones. [6] Represents federal funds obligated only upon receipt or certification by endowment of matching nonfederal gifts. Funds for matching grants are not allocated by program area because they are awarded on a grant-by-grant basis.

Source: U.S. National Endowment for the Arts unpublished data; and U.S. National Endowment for the Humanities, *Annual Report*. See also <http://arts.endow.gov/> and <http://www.neh.gov/>.

Table 1249. Total State Arts Agency Legislative Appropriations: 2011 to 2012

[In thousands of dollars (273,958 represents 273,958,000). For fiscal year ending June 30 in most states. The National Assembly of State Arts Agencies (NASAA) is the membership organization of the nations' state and jurisdictional arts agencies. Legislative appropriations include funds designated to the state arts agency by state legislatures. These include line items, which are not controlled by the agency but passed through to designated entities. State arts agencies also receive monies from other sources including other state funds, the federal government (primarily the National Endowment for the Arts), private funds, and legislative earmarks. Minus sign (–) indicates decrease in spending]

State	Legislative appropriations including line items 2011	Legislative appropriations including line items 2012	Percent change, 2011 to 2012	State	Legislative appropriations including line items 2011	Legislative appropriations including line items 2012	Percent change, 2011 to 2012	State	Legislative appropriations including line items 2011	Legislative appropriations including line items 2012	Percent change, 2011 to 2012
U.S. [1]	273,958	263,032	-4.0	KS [2]	811	0	-100.0	NC	8,710	7,321	-15.9
AL	4,626	3,485	-24.7	KY	3,070	3,056	-0.5	ND	684	682	-0.4
AK	693	790	14.0	LA	3,925	3,277	-16.5	OH	6,594	7,606	15.3
AZ [2]	666	0	-100.0	ME	654	689	5.2	OK	4,407	4,010	-9.0
AR	2,098	2,943	40.3	MD	13,267	13,163	-0.8	OR	1,917	1,995	4.1
CA	4,158	3,893	-6.4	MA	9,099	9,200	1.1	PA	8,422	9,065	7.6
CO	2,433	2,022	-16.9	MI	1,417	1,317	-7.1	RI	2,500	2,114	-15.4
CT	6,112	7,526	23.1	MN	29,990	29,673	-1.1	SC	2,051	1,938	-5.5
DE	1,683	1,682	-0.1	MS	1,682	1,663	-1.1	SD	669	669	0.0
DC	5,126	4,798	-6.4	MO	7,612	7,000	-8.0	TN	8,106	8,192	1.1
FL	6,357	6,023	-5.2	MT	440	478	8.6	TX	6,075	2,543	-58.1
GA	791	574	-27.4	NE	1,433	1,368	-4.5	UT	2,815	5,149	82.9
HI	5,080	5,152	1.4	NV	1,106	962	-13.1	VT	508	508	0.0
ID	716	675	-5.7	NH	462	355	-23.2	VA	3,795	3,795	0.0
IL	9,472	8,998	-5.0	NJ	20,699	16,397	-20.8	WA	1,228	1,107	-9.9
IN	3,202	2,722	-15.0	NM	1,779	1,478	-16.9	WV	1,204	1,215	0.9
IA	1,024	934	-8.8	NY	43,135	36,209	-16.1	WI	2,418	840	-65.3
								WY	1,295	1,397	7.9

[1] Includes U.S. territories. [2] These states eliminated state arts agency funding from their FY 2012 budgets.

Source: National Assembly of State Arts Agencies, "Legislative Appropriations Annual Survey," February 2012, <http://www.nasaa-arts.org/> (copyright).

Table 1250. Personal Participation in Various Arts or Creative Activities: 2008

[In percent, except as indicated (224.8 represents 224,800,000). For persons 18 years old and over. Represents participation at least once in the prior 12 months]

Item	Adult population (millions)	Classical music [1]	Paint-ing [2]	Pottery/ Jewelry	Sewing [3]	Photo-graphy	Creative writing	Pur-chased art [4]	Choir/ chorale
Total	**224.8**	**3.1**	**9.0**	**6.0**	**13.1**	**14.7**	**6.9**	**5.9**	**5.2**
Sex: Male	108.5	3.0	7.1	4.5	2.3	13.3	6.2	5.8	3.9
Female	116.3	3.2	10.7	7.4	23.2	16.1	7.5	5.9	6.3
Race and ethnicity:									
White alone	154.5	3.5	9.4	6.9	15.5	16.1	7.0	7.4	4.9
African American alone	25.6	2.0	6.8	3.5	7.6	10.0	7.5	1.8	10.3
Other alone	14.3	4.7	11.9	6.1	10.2	16.2	8.2	2.3	5.5
Hispanic	30.4	1.1	7.4	3.6	7.1	10.9	5.3	2.8	2.2
Age: 18 to 24 years old	28.9	5.9	14.7	6.4	9.0	17.8	11.3	4.3	6.1
25 to 34 years old	39.9	3.7	11.3	6.1	10.0	16.1	9.7	6.8	3.8
35 to 44 years old	41.8	3.0	9.9	7.5	11.4	18.6	6.2	5.6	4.3
45 to 54 years old	43.9	2.5	7.4	7.0	15.4	14.6	6.4	6.6	6.8
55 to 64 years old	33.3	2.4	6.8	5.4	15.7	13.0	4.4	6.8	5.3
65 to 74 years old	19.9	1.8	5.0	4.1	17.7	10.4	5.2	6.0	6.2
75 years old and older	17.1	1.4	4.4	2.1	15.4	5.5	3.1	2.9	3.6

[1] Of those who reported playing a musical instrument in the last 12 months. [2] Includes painting, drawing, sculpture, and printmaking. [3] Includes weaving, crocheting, quilting, needlepoint, and sewing. [4] Of those who reported owning original art.

Source: U.S. National Endowment for the Arts, "2008 Survey of Public Participation in the Arts," <http://www.nea.gov/pub/>.

Table 1251. Attendance/Participation Rates for Various Arts Activities: 2008

[In percent, except as indicated (224.8 represents 224,800,000). For persons 18 years old and over. Represents attending, visiting, or reading at least once in the prior twelve months. Excludes elementary and high school performances]

Item	Adult popu-lation (million)	Jazz concert	Classical music concert	Musicals	Non-musical plays	Art muse-ums/ galleries	Craft/ visual art festivals	Parks/ historic build-ings [1]	Read litera-ture [2]
Total	**224.8**	**7.8**	**9.3**	**16.7**	**9.4**	**22.7**	**24.5**	**24.9**	**50.2**
Sex:									
Male	108.5	7.7	8.5	14.4	8.2	21.4	20.5	24.4	41.9
Female	116.3	7.9	10.0	18.9	10.6	24.0	28.3	25.4	58.0
Race and ethnicity:									
White alone	154.5	8.8	11.3	20.0	11.4	26.0	29.3	29.5	55.7
African American alone	25.6	8.6	4.3	8.6	5.5	12.0	12.2	12.6	42.6
Other alone	14.3	4.0	8.8	13.4	6.1	23.4	17.0	20.0	43.9
Hispanic	30.4	3.9	3.8	8.1	4.3	14.5	13.7	14.0	31.9
Age:									
18 to 24 years old	28.9	7.3	6.9	14.5	8.2	22.9	17.8	21.9	51.7
25 to 34 years old	39.9	7.7	7.0	16.0	9.2	24.3	22.7	25.7	50.1
35 to 44 years old	41.8	7.2	8.9	18.2	8.9	25.7	27.2	26.8	50.8
45 to 54 years old	43.9	9.8	10.2	17.4	8.7	23.3	29.1	28.0	50.3
55 to 64 years old	33.3	9.7	11.6	19.5	12.3	24.3	28.9	27.6	53.1
65 to 74 years old	19.9	6.1	12.2	18.0	11.0	19.9	24.8	24.1	49.1
75 years old and older	17.1	4.0	9.7	10.0	7.4	10.5	12.7	11.2	42.3
Education:									
Grade school	11.2	1.5	1.8	1.7	0.7	3.8	4.9	3.8	18.5
Some high school	22.1	2.4	2.3	5.2	2.8	9.2	11.2	9.1	34.3
High school graduate	68.3	3.9	3.1	8.1	4.0	9.6	17.3	14.6	39.1
Some college	61.4	8.1	9.1	17.1	9.0	23.8	27.5	28.4	56.2
College graduate	41.3	13.7	16.7	30.1	17.5	40.6	35.8	39.4	66.6
Graduate school	20.5	17.4	27.1	37.9	24.3	52.2	41.6	48.1	71.2
Income: [3]									
Less than $10,000	11.6	4.3	4.0	6.6	4.2	9.4	10.7	10.3	38.6
$10,000 to $19,999	19.3	3.6	3.9	6.3	3.7	10.3	13.0	11.4	38.3
$20,000 to $29,999	23.4	4.1	4.4	7.7	4.1	11.9	15.5	13.9	41.7
$30,000 to $39,999	22.6	7.1	6.8	11.0	6.7	16.3	21.8	19.9	43.2
$40,000 to $49,999	18.8	8.9	8.7	15.4	7.4	20.2	24.7	23.2	51.9
$50,000 to $74,999	40.7	7.6	9.5	15.4	8.6	23.9	26.2	26.8	50.1
$75,000 to $99,999	27.2	8.7	11.7	21.8	13.4	31.3	33.8	32.6	59.1
$100,000 to $149,999	21.4	13.4	14.8	32.0	14.1	34.4	34.5	41.2	62.1
$150,000 and over	16.0	15.4	22.8	40.1	24.2	51.9	37.5	47.3	71.2

[1] Visiting historic parks or monuments or touring buildings or neighborhoods for the historic or design value. [2] Literature is defined as poetry, novels, short stories, or plays. [3] Excludes results for respondents who did not report income.

Source: U.S. National Endowment for the Arts, "2008 Survey of Public Participation in the Arts," <http://www.nea.gov/pub/>.

Table 1252. Attendance/Participation in Various Leisure Activities: 2008

[In percent, except as indicated (224.8 represents 224,800,000). See headnote, Table 1250]

Item	Adult population (mil.)	Attendance at—		Participation in—					
		Movies	Sports events	Exercise	Playing sports	Outdoor activities	Garden-ing	Volun-teering/ charity work	Com-munity activities
Total.................	**224.8**	**53.3**	**30.6**	**52.9**	**26.3**	**28.2**	**41.6**	**32.0**	**27.8**
Sex:									
Male................	108.5	52.7	34.9	52.1	33.2	31.1	33.6	28.9	26.2
Female...............	116.3	54.0	26.6	53.6	20.0	25.4	48.9	34.9	29.3
Race and Ethnicity:									
White alone................	154.5	55.7	34.0	57.4	29.2	16.9	47.2	35.8	31.8
African American alone......	25.6	47.4	24.5	42.6	21.0	7.2	24.4	27.0	21.9
Other alone.................	14.3	49.3	21.8	48.6	23.5	26.1	40.1	25.7	22.7
Hispanic.................	30.4	48.1	22.1	40.7	17.9	17.3	28.0	20.1	14.7
Age:									
18 to 24 years old...........	28.9	74.2	37.4	57.4	42.0	34.8	15.1	27.2	19.4
25 to 34 years old...........	39.9	64.5	37.3	57.5	34.9	35.7	34.8	29.4	23.5
35 to 44 years old...........	41.8	59.5	36.7	59.5	32.0	34.3	43.9	37.6	33.2
45 to 54 years old...........	43.9	52.6	31.3	51.8	23.9	29.0	49.1	35.7	31.8
55 to 64 years old...........	33.3	46.2	25.9	51.8	17.1	22.4	52.4	33.4	29.7
65 to 74 years old...........	19.9	31.7	18.2	47.6	13.3	17.9	54.5	30.2	30.9
75 years old and over.......	17.1	18.9	10.3	30.0	6.4	6.3	41.0	23.2	21.5
Education:									
Grade school................	11.2	15.9	6.6	21.1	6.7	8.2	30.3	11.4	8.4
Some high school...........	22.1	37.9	17.8	35.7	19.0	17.8	29.5	17.7	14.8
High school graduate.......	68.3	42.5	22.8	40.0	17.4	20.8	37.7	20.9	18.3
Some college...............	61.4	60.8	33.7	58.5	29.1	30.9	43.2	35.6	29.5
College graduate...........	41.3	68.8	44.9	70.8	38.9	39.8	49.0	48.1	42.6
Graduate school............	20.5	71.6	44.2	77.1	40.0	42.3	53.3	51.5	48.0
Income: [1]									
Less than $10,000..........	11.6	32.3	14.9	35.6	15.9	14.6	25.3	16.0	15.0
$10,000 to $19,999.........	19.3	32.4	13.4	35.3	14.5	15.3	30.4	18.8	14.8
$20,000 to $29,999.........	23.4	38.2	21.1	40.4	14.9	18.3	35.4	19.6	18.1
$30,000 to $39,999.........	22.6	48.6	22.3	46.8	23.3	24.2	37.7	29.2	22.9
$40,000 to $49,999.........	18.8	54.0	28.7	54.9	26.5	28.7	44.9	31.5	25.9
$50,000 to $74,999.........	40.7	58.5	33.3	55.6	26.0	31.6	42.8	32.2	27.5
$75,000 or more............	27.2	67.5	42.2	66.2	37.0	40.9	50.2	42.0	35.0
$100,000 to $149,999......	21.4	71.4	46.8	73.3	39.1	39.7	54.0	49.6	47.2
$150,000 or more...........	16.0	76.7	53.1	73.2	46.0	43.9	50.9	49.0	43.9

[1] Excludes results for respondents who did not report income.

Source: U.S. National Endowment for the Arts, "2008 Survey of Public Participation in the Arts," <http://www.nea.gov/pub/>.

Table 1253. Household Pet Ownership: 2006

[In percent, except as indicated (72.1 represents 72,100,000). Based on a sample survey of 47,000 households in 2006]

Item	Dogs	Cats	Birds	Horses
Total companion pet population (millions) [1]......................	72.1	81.7	11.2	7.3
Number of households owning pets (millions)......................	43.0	37.5	4.5	2.1
Percent of households owning companion pets [1]......................	37.2	32.4	3.9	1.8
Average number owned per household......................	1.7	2.2	2.5	3.5
PERCENT OF HOUSEHOLDS OWNING PETS				
Annual household income:				
Under $20,000......................	30.7	30.1	4.4	1.5
$20,000 to $34,999......................	37.3	33.6	4.2	1.7
$35,000 to $54,999......................	39.8	34.1	4.4	2.1
$55,000 to $84,999......................	42.8	35.5	3.7	1.9
$85,000 and over......................	42.1	33.3	3.7	2.3
Household size: [1]				
One person......................	21.9	24.7	2.1	0.8
Two persons......................	37.6	33.4	3.9	1.7
Three persons......................	47.5	39.1	5.1	2.3
Four persons......................	51.9	38.5	5.4	2.7
Five or more persons......................	54.3	40.0	6.6	3.6

[1] As of December 31, 2006.

Source: American Veterinary Medical Association, Schaumburg, IL, *U.S. Pet Ownership and DemographicsSourcebook, 2007*, (copyright). See also <http://www.avma.org/reference/marketstats/sourcebook.asp>.

Table 1254. Adult Participation in Selected Leisure Activities by Frequency: 2011

[In thousands (17,172 represents 17,172,000), except percent. For Fall 2011. Percent is based on total projected population of 230,416,000. Based on sample and subject to sampling error; see source]

Activity	Participated in the last 12 months [1]		Freqency of participation							
			Two or more times a week		Once a week		Two to three times a month		Once a month	
	Number	Percent	Number	Percent	Number	Percent	Number	Percent	Number	Percent
Adult education courses.....................	17,172	7.5	3,374	1.5	1,939	0.8	889	0.4	1,162	0.5
Attend auto shows............................	18,178	7.9	236	0.1	215	0.1	416	0.2	836	0.4
Attend art galleries or shows................	18,321	8.0	67	(Z)	106	0.1	735	0.3	1,774	0.8
Attend classical music/opera performances...............................	8,693	3.8	57	(Z)	75	(Z)	346	0.2	891	0.4
Attend country music performances........	11,988	5.2	122	0.1	147	0.1	338	0.2	427	0.2
Attend dance performances.................	9,046	3.9	36	(Z)	73	(Z)	297	0.1	680	0.3
Attend horse races..........................	6,324	2.7	174	0.1	88	(Z)	356	0.2	288	0.1
Attend other music performances [2].........	24,181	10.5	245	0.1	389	0.2	921	0.4	2,209	1.0
Attend rock music performances...........	22,037	9.6	206	0.1	160	0.1	382	0.2	1,451	0.6
Backgammon...............................	4,334	1.9	271	0.1	145	0.1	459	0.2	413	0.2
Baking.....................................	57,742	25.1	10,475	4.6	7,913	3.4	12,288	5.3	9,782	4.3
Barbecuing.................................	78,057	33.9	11,574	5.0	13,337	5.8	18,219	7.9	11,363	4.9
Billiards/pool...............................	18,917	8.2	1,389	0.6	1,615	0.7	2,092	0.9	2,011	0.9
Bird watching...............................	12,586	5.5	5,805	2.5	877	0.4	847	0.4	836	0.4
Board games...............................	35,597	15.5	2,423	1.1	3,501	1.5	6,143	2.7	7,367	3.2
Book clubs.................................	5,739	2.5	85	(Z)	465	0.2	522	0.2	1,902	0.8
Chess......................................	7,427	3.2	911	0.4	323	0.1	804	0.4	658	0.3
Concerts on radio...........................	7,173	3.1	995	0.4	670	0.3	677	0.3	631	0.3
Cooking for fun.............................	49,998	21.7	18,159	7.9	7,677	3.3	7,474	3.2	4,415	1.9
Crossword puzzles..........................	26,425	11.5	11,311	4.9	2,343	1.0	2,997	1.3	1,618	0.7
Dance/go dancing...........................	20,823	9.0	1,723	0.8	1,972	0.9	2,694	1.2	2,873	1.3
Dining out..................................	107,744	46.8	17,581	7.6	24,341	10.6	27,842	12.1	13,547	5.9
Entertain friends or relatives at home.......	85,434	37.1	7,447	3.2	9,362	4.1	18,021	7.8	18,619	8.1
Fantasy sports league......................	10,616	4.6	3,125	1.4	2,210	1.0	641	0.3	345	0.2
Furniture refinishing.........................	6,358	2.8	148	0.1	111	0.1	333	0.1	475	0.2
Go to bars/night clubs......................	41,987	18.2	3,059	1.3	4,447	1.9	7,090	3.1	6,443	2.8
Go to beach................................	56,080	24.3	2,827	1.2	1,841	0.8	4,871	2.1	4,626	2.0
Go to live theater..........................	28,096	12.2	284	0.1	336	0.2	919	0.4	2,822	1.2
Go to museums.............................	32,346	14.0	204	0.1	208	0.1	947	0.4	2,928	1.3
Home decoration and furnishing.............	20,567	8.9	1,114	0.5	640	0.3	2,239	1.0	2,930	1.3
Karaoke....................................	8,695	3.8	191	0.1	363	0.2	699	0.3	1,272	0.6
Painting, drawing...........................	14,280	6.2	2,254	1.0	1,027	0.5	1,727	0.8	1,632	0.7
PC/computer games (play online with software)................................	16,259	7.1	8,091	3.5	1,419	0.6	1,334	0.6	533	0.2
PC/computer games (play online without software)................................	23,265	10.1	12,268	5.3	2,399	1.0	1,922	0.8	997	0.4
PC/computer games (play offline with software)................................	17,940	7.8	8,450	3.7	1,803	0.8	1,619	0.7	1,175	0.5
Photo album/scrap book....................	14,127	6.1	866	0.4	890	0.4	1,471	0.6	2,403	1.0
Photography................................	23,886	10.4	4,087	1.8	2,454	1.1	4,289	1.9	3,404	1.5
Picnic......................................	25,795	11.2	324	0.1	587	0.3	1,542	0.7	3,359	1.5
Play bingo..................................	9,562	4.2	640	0.3	945	0.4	752	0.3	1,059	0.5
Play cards..................................	42,735	18.6	4,725	2.1	4,548	2.0	6,815	3.0	6,519	2.8
Play musical instrument.....................	15,199	6.6	5,478	2.4	1,531	0.7	1,887	0.8	1,158	0.5
Reading books..............................	85,711	37.2	47,602	20.7	7,705	3.3	7,132	3.1	5,659	2.5
Reading comic books........................	5,109	2.2	1,074	0.5	344	0.2	514	0.2	619	0.3
Sudoku puzzles.............................	25,465	11.1	9,069	3.9	2,947	1.3	3,041	1.3	2,670	1.2
Trivia games................................	11,763	5.1	2,320	1.0	1,066	0.5	1,249	0.5	1,633	0.7
Woodworking...............................	9,999	4.3	1,665	0.7	791	0.3	1,172	0.5	1,263	0.6
Word games................................	23,058	10.0	9,298	4.0	2,891	1.3	2,750	1.2	1,347	0.6
Zoo attendance.............................	28,379	12.3	102	(Z)	131	0.1	513	0.2	1,598	0.7

Z represents less than 0.05. [1] Includes those participating less than once a month not shown separately. [2] Excluding country and rock.

Source: GfK Mediamark Research & Intelligence, LLC, New York, NY, *Top-line Reports* (copyright). See also <http://www.gfkmri.com/>.

Table 1255. Retail Sales and Household Participation in Lawn and Garden Activities: 2005 to 2011

[(35,208 represents $35,208,000,000). For calendar year. Subject to sampling variability; see source]

Activity	Retail sales (mil. dol.)					Percent households engaged in activity				
	2005	2008	2009	2010	2011	2005	2008	2009	2010	2011
Total........................	**35,208**	**36,060**	**30,121**	**28,409**	**29,097**	**83**	**70**	**72**	**68**	**70**
Lawn care.........................	9,657	9,638	8,075	7,765	8,330	54	46	46	45	45
Indoor houseplants..............	1,464	1,177	1,081	920	991	42	31	30	29	29
Flower gardening................	3,003	2,679	2,299	1,933	2,109	41	32	31	28	29
Insect control....................	1,869	1,734	1,567	1,350	1,693	30	25	22	22	23
Shrub care.......................	1,109	746	623	930	1,099	31	22	21	20	23
Vegetable gardening............	1,154	1,402	1,762	1,701	1,630	25	23	27	26	25
Tree care.........................	2,820	2,473	1,743	2,086	2,558	26	20	19	16	19
Landscaping.....................	9,078	11,712	8,418	7,232	6,250	31	28	27	24	26
Flower bulbs.....................	945	796	748	660	627	29	20	19	18	18
Fruit trees........................	507	538	575	702	509	13	10	11	10	10
Container gardening............	1,295	1,003	994	836	937	26	19	19	17	18
Raising transplants [1]...........	237	220	241	286	296	11	8	9	8	8
Herb gardening..................	371	391	423	428	442	17	12	14	15	15
Growing berries..................	151	138	229	159	168	8	6	8	8	7
Ornamental gardening..........	678	424	445	504	378	12	6	6	6	6
Water gardening.................	870	989	898	917	1,080	11	10	11	12	13

[1] Starting plants in advance of planting in ground.

Source: The National Gardening Association, Burlington, VT, *National Gardening Survey*, annual (copyright). See also <http://www.garden.org/>.

Table 1256. Selected Recreational Activities: 1990 to 2011

[21,000 represents 21,000,000]

Activity	Unit	1990	1995	2000	2005	2007	2008	2009	2010	2011
Golf facilities [1].................	Number	12,846	14,074	15,489	16,052	15,970	15,979	15,979	15,890	15,753
Tennis players: [2]...............	1,000	21,000	17,820	22,900	24,720	25,130	26,880	30,130	27,810	27,050
Skiing: [3]										
Skier visits [4]....................	Million	50.0	52.7	52.2	56.9	55.1	60.5	57.4	59.8	60.5
Operating resorts...............	Number	591	520	503	492	481	473	471	471	486.0
Boating: [5]										
People participating in recreational boating [6]..........................	Million	67.4	70.0	67.5	57.9	66.4	70.1	65.9	75.0	82.7
Retail expenditures on boating [7]....	Mil. dol.	13,731	17,226	27,065	37,317	37,416	33,809	30,821	30,434	32,271
Recreational boats in use by boat type [8]............................	Million	16.0	15.4	16.8	17.7	16.9	16.8	16.8	16.5	16.4
Outboard..........................	Million	(NA)	(NA)	8.3	8.5	8.3	8.3	8.3	8.1	8.1
Inboard............................	Million	(NA)	(NA)	1.0	1.1	1.1	1.1	1.1	1.1	1.2
Sterndrive.........................	Million	(NA)	(NA)	1.6	1.7	1.7	1.6	1.6	1.5	1.5
Personal Watercraft.............	Million	(NA)	(NA)	1.2	1.2	1.2	1.2	1.3	1.3	1.2
Sailboat...........................	Million	(NA)	(NA)	1.6	1.6	1.6	1.5	1.5	1.6	1.6
Other..............................	Million	(NA)	(NA)	3.1	3.6	3.1	3.1	3.0	3.0	2.9

NA Not available. [1] Source: National Golf Foundation, Jupiter, FL. [2] Source: Tennis Industry Association, Hilton Head, SC. Based on a nationwide telephone survey of households, in which all household members ages 6 and up are enumerated with data on tennis participation collected for each person. [3] Source: National Ski Areas Association, Kottke National End of Season Survey Report (copyright). [4] Represents one person visiting a ski area for all or any part of a day or night, and includes full-and half-day, night, complimentary, adult, child, season, and other types of tickets. Data are estimated and are for the season ending in the year shown. [5] Source: National Marine Manufacturers Association, Chicago, IL. (copyright). [6] People participating is now measured as adults 18 years and older. [7] Represents estimated expenditures for new and used boats, motors and engines, accessories, safety equipment, fuel, insurance, docking, maintenance, launching, storage, repairs, and other expenses. [8] 2011 data are estimated.

Source: Compiled from sources listed in footnotes.

Table 1257. Leisure Time Use on Weekends and Holidays by Type of Activity and Selected Demographic Characteristics: 2011

[Data are based on interviews of approximately 12,500 individuals 15 years and over who reported their activities for one 24-hour period. Respondents engaging in more than one activity at a time reported only their primary activity; except for child care, secondary activities were not reported]

Selected Characteristics	Average hours per day spent on all leisure and sports activities			Percent distribution of leisure time on weekends and holidays						
	All Days (hours)	Week-days (hours)[1]	Weekends and Holidays (hours)	Sports, exercise, recreation	Socializing, Communicating	Watching TV	Reading	Relaxing, thinking	Playing games, using computers for leisure	Other[1]
Men	5.6	5.0	6.8	7	13	53	4	5	8	10
Women	4.9	4.5	5.9	4	20	48	6	6	6	10
Age:										
Total, 15 years and over	5.2	4.7	6.3	6	17	50	5	5	7	10
15 to 19 years	6.0	5.5	7.1	11	19	38	2	3	16	11
20 to 24 years	5.1	4.8	5.7	10	20	42	1	(S)	10	13
25 to 34 years	4.2	3.6	5.7	7	22	45	3	4	7	11
35 to 44 years	4.2	3.6	5.7	7	19	51	4	4	5	10
45 to 54 years	4.7	4.1	6.1	5	14	54	5	6	6	10
55 to 64 years	5.6	5.1	6.5	4	14	54	7	6	5	10
65 to 74 years	6.9	6.6	7.6	2	12	59	9	7	5	7
75 years and over	7.4	7.1	8.2	2	12	56	12	8	4	6
Race/ethnicity:										
White	5.1	4.6	6.4	6	17	49	6	5	7	10
Black	5.8	5.5	6.5	3	15	57	2	9	6	8
Hispanic origin	4.8	4.3	5.9	5	21	52	2	6	5	10
Employment status:										
Employed	4.2	3.6	5.6	7	18	49	4	5	6	11
Full-time workers	4.0	3.2	5.7	7	18	49	4	5	5	11
Part-time workers	5.0	4.7	5.6	5	19	45	5	6	8	13
Not employed	6.9	6.6	7.4	5	15	52	6	6	8	8
Weekly earnings:[2]										
$0 - $520	4.2	3.5	5.6	6	17	54	2	5	5	10
$521 - $810	4.1	3.3	6.1	6	22	51	4	4	4	10
$811 - $1,240	4.0	3.3	6.0	9	17	49	5	4	6	10
$1,241 and higher	3.8	2.9	5.7	8	18	43	7	6	7	12
Presence and age of children:[2]										
No household children under 18	5.7	5.3	6.8	5	15	51	6	5	7	10
Household children under 18	4.4	3.9	5.5	6	19	49	3	5	7	10
Children 13 to 17 years, none younger	4.9	4.5	5.8	8	14	51	4	5	8	10
Children 6 to 12 years, none younger	4.4	3.8	5.8	7	18	47	4	6	8	10
Youngest child under 6 years	4.1	3.6	5.2	6	23	50	2	4	5	10
Educational attainment, 25 years and over:										
Less than a high school diploma	6.1	5.7	7.0	4	13	62	2	9	4	6
High school graduates, no college	5.7	5.3	6.8	4	14	56	5	6	5	8
Some college or associate degree	4.9	4.5	6.0	5	17	52	7	4	6	10
Bachelor's degree and higher	4.4	3.8	5.9	7	18	44	9	4	6	11

S Figure does not meet publication standards. [1] Includes other leisure and sports activities,, not elsewhere classified, and travel related to leisure and sports activities. [2] These values are based on usual weekly earnings. The earnings data are limited to wage and salary workers (both incorporated and unincorporated self-employed workers are excluded). Each earnings range represents approximately 25 percent of full-time wage and salary workers who held only one job.

Source: Bureau of Labor Statistics, "American Time Use Survey, 2011," <http://www.bls.gov/tus/home.htm>.

Table 1258. Amusement Park Attendance at Top 15 U.S. Facilities: 2007 to 2011

[In thousands (108,130 represents 108,130,000). Covers gated commercial theme parks, amusement parks, and water parks with annual attendance of one million of more]

Park Name	Location	Attendance					Percent change 2010-2011
		2007	2008	2009	2010	2011	
Total Top 15		**108,130**	**107,300**	**107,348**	**109,321**	**112,509**	**2.9**
Magic Kingdom, Walt Disney World.......	Orlando, FL	17,060	17,063	17,233	16,972	17,142	1.0
Disneyland.................................	Anaheim, CA	14,870	14,741	15,900	15,980	16,140	1.0
EPCOT, Walt Disney World.................	Lake Buena Vista, FL	10,930	10,395	10,990	10,825	10,825	0.0
Disney's Animal Kingdom..................	Lake Buena Vista, FL	9,490	9,540	9,590	9,886	9,783	-1.0
Disney's Hollywood Studios...............	Lake Buena Vista, FL	9,510	9,608	9,700	9,603	9,699	1.0
Islands of Adventure......................	Orlando, FL	5,430	5,207	4,627	5,949	7,674	29.0
Disney's California Adventure.............	Anaheim, CA	5,680	5,566	6,095	6,278	6,341	1.0
Universal Studios..........................	Orlando, FL	6,200	6,231	5,530	5,925	6,044	2.0
Seaworld Florida..........................	Orlando, FL	5,800	5,920	5,800	5,100	5,202	2.0
Universal Studios Hollywood..............	Universal City, CA	4,700	4,583	4,308	5,040	5,141	2.0
Seaworld California........................	San Diego, CA	4,260	4,147	4,200	3,800	4,294	13.0
Busch Gardens............................	Tampa, FL	4,400	4,410	4,100	4,200	4,284	2.0
Knotts Berry Farm.........................	Buena Park, CA	3,630	3,565	3,333	3,600	3,654	1.5
Kings Island...............................	Kings Island, OH	3,050	3,126	3,000	3,112	3,143	1.0
Cedar Point...............................	Sandusky, OH	3,120	3,198	2,942	3,051	3,143	3.0

Source: Themed Entertainment Association and AECOM, Theme Index: Global Attractions Attendance Report (copyright). See also <http://www.teaconnect.org/> and <http://www.aecom.com/What+We+Do/Economics>.

Table 1259. College and Professional Football Summary: 1990 to 2011

[35,330 represents 35,330,000. For definition of median, see Guide to Tabular Presentation]

Sport	Unit	1990	1995	2000	2005	2008	2009	2010	2011
NCAA college: [1]									
Teams.................................	Number	534	600	624	618	633	633	644	638
Attendance..........................	1,000	35,330	35,638	39,059	43,487	48,839	48,285	49,671	49,699
National Football League: [2]									
Teams.................................	Number	28	30	31	32	32	32	32	32
Attendance, total [3]..................	1,000	17,666	19,203	20,954	21,792	21,859	21,285	21,107	20,959
Regular season.....................	1,000	13,960	15,044	16,387	17,012	17,057	16,651	16,570	16,563
Average per game...............	Number	62,321	62,682	66,078	66,455	66,629	65,043	64,978	64,699
Postseason games [4]..............	1,000	848	(NA)	809	802	807	824	800	906
Players' salaries: [5]									
Average............................	$1,000	354	584	787	1,400	1,824	1,896	2,000	2,250
Median base salary................	$1,000	275	301	441	569	788	790	906	826

NA Not available. [1] Source: National Collegiate Athletic Association, Indianapolis, IN, <http://www.ncaa.org/wps/wcm/connect/public/NCAA/Resources/Stats/> (copyright). [2] Source: National Football League, New York, NY, <http://www.nfl.com/>. [3] Preseason attendance data are included in totals but not shown separately. [4] Includes Pro Bowl (a nonchampionship game) and Super Bowl. [5] Source: National Football League Players Association, Washington, DC., <http://www.nflpa.org/>.

Source: Compiled from sources listed in footnotes.

Table 1260. Selected Spectator Sports: 1990 to 2011

[55,512 represents 55,512,000]

Sport	Unit	1990	1995	2000	2005	2007	2008	2009	2010	2011
Baseball, major leagues: [1]										
Attendance...................	1,000	55,512	51,289	74,340	76,286	80,759	79,975	74,823	74,508	75,504
Regular season.............	1,000	54,824	50,469	72,749	74,926	79,503	76,043	73,368	73,054	73,416
National League..........	1,000	24,492	25,110	39,851	41,644	44,114	41,579	41,128	40,890	40,741
American League..........	1,000	30,332	25,359	32,898	33,282	35,390	34,464	32,239	32,164	32,675
Playoffs [2].................	1,000	479	533	1,314	1,191	1,083	1,167	1,166	1,210	1,745
World Series...............	1,000	209	286	277	168	173	219	289	244	343
Players' salaries: [3]										
Average...................	1,000	598	1,111	1,896	2,476	2,825	2,926	2,996	3,015	3,095
Basketball: [4,5]										
NCAA—Men's college:										
Teams......................	Number	768	866	937	984	1,017	1,017	1,033	1,027	1,030
Attendance................	1,000	28,741	28,225	28,949	30,940	33,396	33,111	32,821	32,632	32,781
NCAA—Women's college:										
Teams......................	Number	782	864	958	1,018	1,013	1,032	1,037	1,048	1,055
Attendance [6].............	1000	2,777	4,962	8,825	9,903	11,121	11,160	11,135	11,160	11,211
National Hockey League: [7]										
Regular season										
attendance.................	1,000	12,580	9,234	18,800	(NA)	20,862	21,236	21,475	20,996	20,928
Playoffs attendance.........	1,000	1,356	1,329	1,525	(NA)	1,497	1,587	1,640	1,702	(NA)
Professional rodeo: [8]										
Rodeos.....................	Number	754	739	688	662	592	609	560	570	572
Performances................	Number	2,159	2,217	2,081	1,940	1,733	1,861	1,656	1,671	1,669
Members....................	Number	5,693	6,894	6,255	6,127	5,528	5,825	5,653	5,323	5,137
Permit-holders (rookies).....	Number	3,290	3,835	3,249	2,701	2,186	2,233	2,042	1,881	1,883
Total prize money............	Mil. dol.	18.2	24.5	32.3	36.6	40.5	39.1	38.0	39.9	38.8

NA Not Available. [1] Source: Major League Baseball (previously, The National League of Professional Baseball Clubs), New York, NY, National League Green Book, and The American League of Professional Baseball Clubs, New York, NY, American League Red Book. [2] Beginning 1995, two rounds of playoffs were played. Prior years had one round. [3] Source: Major League Baseball Players Association, New York, NY. [4] Season beginning in year shown. [5] Source: National Collegiate Athletic Association, Indianapolis, IN (copyright). [6] Attendance for women's basketball includes doubleheaders with men's teams beginning with the 1997 season, if attendance was taken by halftime of the women's game. [7] For season ending in year shown. Source: National Hockey League, Montreal, Quebec. In September 2004, franchise owners locked out their players upon the expiration of the collective bargaining agreement. The entire season was cancelled in February 2005. [8] Source: Professional Rodeo Cowboys Association, Colorado Springs, CO, Official Professional Rodeo Media Guide, annual (copyright).

Source: Compiled from sources listed in footnotes.

Table 1261. Adult Attendance at Sports Events by Frequency: 2011

[In thousands (74 represents 74,000), except percent. For fall 2011. Percent is based on total projected population of 230,416,000. Data not comparable to previous years. Based on survey and subject to sampling error; see source]

Event	Attend regularly		Attend on occasion		Event	Attend regularly		Attend on occasion	
	Number	Percent	Number	Percent		Number	Percent	Number	Percent
Alpine skiing and ski jumping.....................	74	0.03	994	0.43	Professional (NFL) Monday or Thursday night games.....	859	0.37	5,574	2.42
Auto racing - NASCAR........	576	0.25	4,961	2.15	NFL weekend games........	1,454	0.63	10,630	4.61
Auto racing - Other............	651	0.28	2,522	1.09	NFL playoffs/Super Bowl....	623	0.27	3,191	1.39
Baseball:					Golf - Professional (PGA, LPGA) and other..............	549	0.24	2,784	1.21
College......................	428	0.19	2,588	1.12	Gymnastics..................	340	0.15	1,159	0.50
Professional (MLB).........	2,177	0.94	20,878	9.06	High school sports...........	4,810	2.09	7,255	3.15
Basketball:					Horse racing.................	586	0.25	2,507	1.09
					Ice hockey - Professional			6,733	2.92
College......................	953	0.41	6,213	2.70	(NHL)........................	841	0.36		
Professional (NBA, WNBA)......................	1,210	0.53	7,201	3.31	Lacrosse - MLL................	173	0.08	885	0.38
Beach volleyball - Professional..............	111	0.05	1,056	0.46	Marathon/Road Running,Triathlon & Other Endurance Events............	238	0.10	1,187	0.52
Bicycle racing.................	192	0.08	952	0.41	Mixed martial arts (MMA). ...	263	0.11	1,089	0.47
Bowling......................	352	0.15	1,461	0.63	Motorcycle racing.............	213	0.09	1,457	0.63
Boxing.......................	219	0.09	1,177	0.51	Olympics - Summer...........	124	0.05	1,060	0.46
Bull riding - Professional......	162	0.07	1,470	0.64	Olympics - Winter.............	176	0.08	1,224	0.53
Equestrian events............	463	0.20	1,466	0.64	Poker........................	182	0.08	1,079	0.47
Extreme Sports - Summer....	139	0.06	796	0.35	Rodeo........................	499	0.22	2,630	1.14
Extreme Sports - Winter......	179	0.08	837	0.36	Soccer - Professional (MLS) and World Cup.................	864	0.38	1,904	0.83
Figure skating.................	110	0.05	1,038	0.45	Tennis - Men's and women's......................	287	0.12	181	0.66
Fishing.......................	569	0.25	1,801	0.78	Truck and tractor pull/ mud racing.......................	256	0.11	1,864	0.81
Football: College	2,857	1.24	10,878	4.72	Weightlifting...................	160	0.07	875	0.38

Source: GfK Mediamark Research & Intelligence. LLC, New York, NY, Top-line Reports (copyright). See <http://www.gfkmri.com>.

Table 1262. Participation in NCAA Sports by Sex: 2010/11

[For the academic year]

Sport	Males			Females		
	Teams	Athletes	Average squad	Teams	Athletes	Average squad
Total	**8,690**	**256,344**	**(X)**	**9,827**	**193,232**	**(X)**
Archery [1]	(X)	(X)	(X)	(X)	(X)	(X)
Badminton [1]	(X)	(X)	(X)	(X)	(X)	(X)
Baseball	922	31,264	33.9	(X)	(X)	(X)
Basketball	1,051	17,500	16.7	1,072	15,708	14.7
Bowling	1	39	39	62	565	9.1
Cross country [2]	952	13,976	14.7	1,026	15,319	14.9
Equestrian [1,2]	7	11	1.6	46	1,490	32.4
Fencing [2]	34	605	17.8	41	655	16.0
Field hockey	(X)	(X)	(X)	264	5,729	21.7
Football	644	67,887	105.4	(X)	(X)	(X)
Golf [2]	811	8,436	10.4	575	4,565	7.9
Gymnastics	17	318	18.7	83	1,463	17.6
Ice hockey	135	3,944	29.2	87	2,049	23.6
Lacrosse	280	10,424	37.2	357	8,068	22.6
Rifle [2]	28	208	7.4	34	181	5.3
Rowing	60	2,269	37.8	142	6,974	49.1
Rugby [1]	1	64	64.0	5	197	39.4
Sailing [1]	23	520	22.6	(X)	(X)	(X)
Skiing [2]	32	470	14.7	35	485	13.9
Soccer	794	22,573	28.4	984	24,671	25.1
Softball	(X)	(X)	(X)	969	18,188	18.8
Squash [1]	30	495	16.5	29	401	13.8
Swimming/diving [2]	410	9,213	22.5	523	12,105	23.1
Synchronized swimming [1]	(X)	(X)	(X)	1	13	13.0
Tennis	758	8,050	10.6	921	8,908	9.7
Track, indoor [2]	616	22,750	36.9	694	23,413	33.7
Track, outdoor [2]	722	26,118	36.2	778	25,295	32.5
Volleyball	95	1,456	15.3	1,039	15,597	15.0
Water polo	43	1,018	23.7	60	1,193	19.9
Wrestling	224	6,736	30.1	(X)	(X)	(X)

X Not applicable. [1] Sport recognized by the NCAA but does not have an NCAA championship. [2] Co-ed championship sport.

Source: The National Collegiate Athletic Association (NCAA), Indianapolis, IN, *NCAA Sports Sponsorship and Participation Rates Report* (copyright), <http://www.ncaa.publications.com>.

Table 1263. Participation in High School Athletic Programs by Sex: 1980 to 2011

[For academic years. Data based on number of state associations reporting and may underrepresent the number of schools with and participants in athletic programs]

Year	Participants [1]		Sex and sport	Most popular sports, 2010–2011 [2]	
	Males	Females		Schools	Participants
1980–81	3,503,124	1,853,789	MALE		
1985–86	3,344,275	1,807,121	Football (11-player)	14,279	1,108,441
1988–89	3,416,844	1,839,352	Track & field (outdoor)	15,954	579,302
1989–90	3,398,192	1,858,659	Basketball	18,150	545,844
1990–91	3,406,355	1,892,316	Baseball	15,863	471,025
1991–92	3,429,853	1,940,801	Soccer	11,503	398,351
1992–93	3,416,389	1,997,489	Wrestling	10,407	273,732
1993–94	3,472,967	2,130,315	Cross country	14,097	246,948
1994–95	3,536,359	2,240,461	Tennis	9,839	161,367
1995–96	3,634,052	2,367,936	Golf	13,681	156,866
1996–97	3,706,225	2,474,043	Swimming & diving	6,899	133,900
1997–98	3,763,120	2,570,333			
1998–99	3,832,352	2,652,726			
1999–00	3,861,749	2,675,874			
2000–01	3,921,069	2,784,154	FEMALE		
2001–02	3,960,517	2,806,998	Track & field (outdoor)	16,030	475,265
2002–03	3,988,738	2,856,358	Basketball	17,767	438,933
2003–04	4,038,253	2,865,299	Volleyball	15,479	409,332
2004–05	4,110,319	2,908,390	Softball (fast pitch)	15,338	373,535
2005–06	4,206,549	2,953,355	Soccer	11,047	361,556
2006–07	4,321,103	3,021,807	Cross country	13,839	204,653
2007–08	4,372,115	3,057,266	Tennis	10,181	182,074
2008–09	4,422,662	3,114,091	Swimming & diving	7,164	160,881
2009–10	4,455,740	3,172,637	Competitive spirit squads	4,266	96,718
2010–11	4,494,406	3,173,549	Lacrosse	1,999	74,927

[1] A participant is counted in the number of sports participated in. [2] Ten most popular sports for each sex in terms of number of participants.

Source: National Federation of State High School Associations, Indianapolis, IN, *The 2010–2011 High School Athletics Participation Survey* (copyright), <http://www.nfhs.org/>.

Table 1264. Sporting Goods Sales by Product Category: 1990 to 2010, and Projection, 2011

[In millions of dollars (50,725 represents $50,725,000,000), except percent. Data are based on an online survey of 41,000 households. Prior to 2010, Alaska and Hawaii were not included in sample. Minus sign (-) indicates decrease]

Selected product category	1990	2000	2005	2006	2007	2008	2009	2010	2011, proj.
Sales, all products..................	**50,725**	**74,442**	**88,434**	**90,472**	**91,423**	**80,431**	**71,832**	**77,493**	**79,710**
Annual percent change [1]................	(NA)	4.6	3.1	2.3	1.1	-12.0	-12.0	7.3	2.8
Percent of retail sales..................	(NA)	2.5	2.4	2.3	2.3	2.0	2.0	2.0	(NA)
Athletic and sport clothing...............	10,130	11,030	10,898	10,580	10,834	10,113	9,246	10,172	10,665
Athletic and sport footwear [2]..............	11,654	13,026	15,719	16,910	17,524	17,190	17,069	17,476	17,639
Aerobic shoes........................	611	292	261	262	280	260	223	249	252
Basketball shoes.....................	918	786	878	964	892	718	741	721	729
Cross training shoes..................	679	1,528	1,437	1,516	1,584	1,626	2,071	2,121	2,143
Golf shoes...........................	226	226	259	232	244	239	202	208	210
Gym shoes, sneakers.................	2,536	1,871	2,314	2,434	2,699	2,639	3,377	3,577	3,612
Jogging and running shoes............	1,110	1,638	2,157	2,260	2,193	2,301	2,363	2,316	2,328
Tennis shoes........................	740	533	528	505	452	467	396	404	408
Walking shoes.......................	2,950	3,317	3,673	4,091	4,197	4,204	4,416	4,256	4,299
Athletic and sport equipment [2].............	14,439	21,608	23,735	24,497	25,061	24,862	24,666	26,009	26,431
Archery.............................	265	259	372	396	396	394	411	444	451
Baseball and softball.................	217	319	372	388	401	396	381	447	452
Billiards and indoor games............	192	516	572	574	531	396	318	345	350
Camping.............................	1,072	1,354	1,447	1,526	1,453	1,461	1,496	1,700	1,751
Exercise.............................	1,824	3,610	5,177	5,239	5,500	5,328	5,319	5,387	5,467
Fishing tackle.......................	1,910	2,030	2,139	2,218	2,247	2,067	1,859	2,052	2,093
Golf.................................	2,514	3,805	3,466	3,669	3,722	3,495	2,927	3,197	3,293
Hunting and firearms.................	2,202	2,274	3,563	3,732	3,942	4,548	5,187	5,345	5,372
Optics...............................	438	729	887	1,014	1,019	1,024	1,135	1,259	1,296
Skin diving and scuba................	294	355	358	369	376	373	343	345	348
Snow skiing [3]........................	475	495	643	501	531	482	502	600	619
Tennis...............................	333	383	397	418	440	387	368	417	425
Recreational transport.................	14,502	28,779	38,082	38,485	38,003	28,266	20,851	23,836	24,975
Bicycles and supplies................	2,423	5,131	5,343	5,161	5,393	5,285	4,471	5,943	5,960
Pleasure boats, motors, accessories........	7,644	13,224	17,634	17,907	17,473	13,679	10,815	10,358	10,550
Recreational vehicles................	4,113	9,529	14,366	14,732	14,505	8,758	5,152	7,100	8,000
Snowmobiles........................	322	894	739	685	632	544	414	435	465

NA Not available. [1] Represents change from immediate prior year. [2] Includes other products not shown separately. [3] Data through 2004 categorized as "Skiing Downhill."

Source: National Sporting Goods Association, Mt. Prospect, IL, *The Sporting Goods Market in 2011* and prior issues, (copyright). See <http://www.nsga.org/i4a/pages/index.cfm?pageid=3345>.

Table 1265. Consumer Purchases of Sporting Goods by Consumer Characteristics: 2010

[Shown as percent of dollar purchases. Data are based on an online survey of 41,000 households. Because surveys prior to 2010 were conducted by mail, current data may not be fully comparable to past years]

Characteristic	Total	Footwear					Equipment				
		Aerobic shoes	Fitness shoes	Gym shoes/ sneakers	Jog-ging/ running shoes	Walking shoes	Multi pur-pose home gyms	Rod/ reel combi-nation	Golf club sets	Rifles	Soccer balls
Total......................	**100**	**100**	**100**	**100**	**100**	**100**	**100**	**100**	**100**	**100**	**100**
Age of user:											
Under 14 years old............	18.8	3.4	4.8	20.8	5.7	3.2	1.4	8.4	5.7	2.3	45.1
14 to 17 years old.............	5.5	5.2	4.4	11.2	5.9	1.8	0.0	1.4	3.8	1.1	10.5
18 to 24 years old.............	9.9	3.2	5.6	8.7	9.5	3.6	14.5	3.8	0.6	2.2	7.3
25 to 34 years old.............	13.5	22.8	18.1	15.9	26.6	9.0	23.0	22.0	17.6	11.8	19.0
35 to 44 years old.............	13.5	22.9	20.4	12.7	23.5	11.8	26.7	11.7	13.7	22.6	9.6
45 to 64 years old.............	25.9	32.9	38.4	23.4	25.1	48.9	23.1	45.8	46.4	47.1	7.8
65 years old and over...........	12.9	9.6	8.3	7.3	3.7	21.7	11.3	6.9	12.2	12.9	0.7
Multiple ages..................	–	–	–	–	–	–	–	–	–	–	–
Sex of user:											
Male...........................	49.3	17.8	38.0	40.7	43.8	34.0	56.6	84.0	81.9	80.9	65.0
Female.........................	50.7	82.2	62.0	59.3	56.2	66.0	43.4	16.0	18.1	19.1	35.0
Household use.................	–	–	–	–	–	–	–	–	–	–	–
Annual household income:											
Under $15,000.................	13.0	6.1	6.2	9.0	6.9	7.5	9.6	7.0	1.2	5.5	6.3
$15,000 to $24,999............	11.9	6.8	5.3	7.9	5.3	10.2	2.0	12.5	2.0	4.9	5.6
$25,000 to $34,999............	11.1	7.9	6.7	8.5	5.9	9.8	2.9	11.4	7.0	12.0	3.6
$35,000 to $49,999............	14.1	10.6	12.4	11.8	10.7	13.7	12.7	9.1	14.7	6.3	6.7
$50,000 to $74,999............	18.0	17.9	18.5	18.8	18.2	19.0	18.8	22.8	17.1	16.1	19.8
$75,000 to $99,999............	11.6	12.0	16.7	14.8	16.0	14.2	12.8	17.7	20.1	13.9	16.1
$100,000 to $149,999...........	12.0	22.0	18.9	16.6	19.0	14.7	23.9	13.2	18.9	25.9	20.3
$150,000 and over.............	8.3	16.7	15.3	12.6	18.0	10.9	17.3	6.3	19.0	15.4	21.6
Education of household head:											
Less than high school...........	11.8	2.4	3.4	3.7	5.1	2.3	0.2	3.6	1.2	1.8	6.3
High school....................	30.3	4.8	10.2	14.1	8.1	16.7	9.7	17.1	5.0	15.8	9.3
Some college..................	28.3	32.1	36.0	36.5	27.0	39.3	35.3	42.6	28.4	44.3	28.6
College graduate................	29.6	60.7	50.4	45.7	59.8	41.7	54.8	36.7	65.4	38.1	55.8

– Represents or rounds to zero.

Source: National Sporting Goods Association, Mt. Prospect, IL, *The Sporting Goods Market in 2010*, (copyright). See <http://www.nsga.org/i4a/pages/index.cfm?pageid=1>.

Table 1266. Participation in Selected Sports Activities: 2010

[In thousands (280,215 represents 280,215,000). Data are based on an online survey of 41,000 households; survey response rate was 35%. The questionnaire asked the male and female heads of households and up to two other household members who were at least seven years of age to indicate their age, the sports in which they participated in 2010, and the number of days of participation in 2010. A participant is defined as an individual seven years of age or older who participates in a sport more than once a year. See source for methodology]

Activity	All persons Number	Sex		Age								Household income (dollars)						
		Male	Female	7-17 years	18-24 years	25-34 years	35-44 years	45-54 years	55-64 years	65-74 years	75 and over	Under 25,000	25,000- 34,999	35,000- 49,999	50,000- 74,999	75,000- 99,999	100,000- 149,999	150,000 and over
Total Participants	280,215	137,479	142,736	45,199	30,712	41,819	41,278	44,703	36,274	21,464	18,766	69,591	30,471	38,596	50,420	33,208	34,122	23,808
SERIES I SPORTS																		
Number participated in—																		
Aerobic exercising [1]	38,541	11,665	26,876	4,437	4,555	8,761	6,960	5,808	4,235	2,387	1,398	5,746	2,858	4,237	7,263	6,049	6,898	5,490
Backpacking [2]	11,136	7,189	3,947	2,597	1,268	2,758	2,006	1,626	655	181	45	2,372	688	919	1,762	1,757	2,116	1,524
Baseball	12,533	10,018	2,514	6,265	1,507	1,876	1,588	962	273	62	-	1,916	858	1,209	2,228	1,778	2,667	1,877
Basketball	26,875	19,761	7,114	11,957	4,689	4,547	3,053	1,976	537	115	-	4,494	1,865	3,302	5,156	3,928	4,606	3,523
Bicycle riding [1]	39,789	22,112	17,677	14,587	3,867	4,803	6,096	4,926	3,417	1,313	778	6,706	2,784	4,441	7,401	6,265	6,706	5,443
Billiards/Pool [1]	24,014	14,925	9,089	3,425	3,682	5,827	4,612	3,593	1,747	626	501	5,342	2,049	3,442	3,670	3,085	3,484	2,942
Bowling [3]	38,980	20,640	18,340	10,193	6,091	8,248	6,518	4,523	2,141	837	429	6,507	3,311	4,631	7,788	6,274	6,296	4,173
Camping [3]	44,738	23,151	21,588	9,596	4,987	7,541	6,690	7,379	4,921	2,884	741	8,352	5,043	5,481	9,402	6,080	6,506	3,874
Dart throwing	10,521	6,490	4,030	1,661	1,377	3,025	2,212	1,419	655	140	31	2,115	808	1,427	1,595	1,635	1,559	1,381
Exercise walking [1]	95,803	37,087	58,716	8,172	7,434	14,311	15,245	18,178	15,837	9,337	7,288	19,188	9,840	13,258	18,115	12,709	13,415	9,279
Exercising with equipment [1]	55,286	25,885	29,401	4,863	7,936	10,917	9,271	9,432	6,615	3,751	2,501	8,397	4,498	6,128	10,546	7,963	9,451	8,302
Fishing (net)	33,810	23,228	10,582	7,571	2,905	5,095	5,357	5,655	4,214	2,135	878	6,736	3,434	4,234	6,687	4,716	4,696	3,309
Fishing--fresh water	29,927	20,528	9,399	6,860	2,497	4,501	4,752	5,008	3,639	1,915	754	6,173	3,109	3,803	5,960	4,066	4,132	2,686
Fishing--salt water	9,757	7,017	2,740	2,106	834	1,583	1,528	1,579	1,219	581	328	1,372	813	1,043	1,636	1,549	1,622	1,722
Football--tackle	9,318	8,184	1,134	4,792	2,079	1,397	680	316	49	5	-	2,088	818	887	1,525	1,454	1,483	1,063
Golf	21,872	16,465	5,407	2,685	1,935	4,387	3,184	3,433	3,184	1,687	1,073	1,889	1,249	2,701	4,480	3,249	4,602	3,702
Gymnastics	4,756	1,181	3,575	2,961	352	637	305	206	97	72	126	761	194	496	823	911	778	793
Hiking	37,704	19,243	18,462	6,180	4,091	7,704	6,826	6,444	4,195	1,791	474	5,722	2,856	4,044	7,758	5,604	5,968	5,752
Lacrosse	2,625	1,713	912	720	1,168	373	241	79	9	4	30	994	64	97	136	307	486	542
Running/jogging [1]	35,524	18,664	16,860	8,438	6,601	9,057	5,971	3,515	1,291	472	179	5,477	2,526	3,835	6,399	5,717	6,341	5,228
Soccer	13,534	8,630	4,905	7,801	1,794	1,999	1,337	452	118	18	16	2,143	740	1,055	2,409	2,524	2,863	1,800
Softball	10,841	6,086	4,755	3,637	1,495	2,542	1,710	921	390	145	-	1,615	940	1,182	2,013	1,567	1,982	1,542
Swimming [1]	51,943	24,641	27,302	17,666	5,557	7,535	7,443	6,027	4,314	2,198	1,203	8,722	3,926	6,228	9,349	7,933	9,301	6,482
Tennis	12,250	6,378	5,872	3,333	1,831	2,633	1,915	1,446	680	262	149	1,529	891	958	1,894	2,015	2,308	2,657
Volleyball [1]	10,621	4,765	5,855	4,486	1,790	1,866	1,217	840	294	84	44	2,015	929	998	1,702	1,515	1,788	1,674
Weightlifting [1]	31,480	20,628	10,852	4,035	5,987	7,339	5,667	4,324	2,697	1,095	336	4,975	2,254	3,022	5,939	4,711	5,820	4,760
Wrestling	2,940	2,534	407	1,182	549	631	440	64	18	4	52	661	183	355	316	549	421	454
Yoga	20,166	4,116	16,050	1,877	2,813	6,011	4,084	2,777	1,716	600	289	3,394	1,628	2,387	3,639	2,879	3,228	3,011
SERIES II SPORTS																		
Archery (target)	6,516	4,833	1,683	2,520	636	1,166	886	843	294	143	28	1,143	550	594	1,152	872	1098	1,106
Boating-motor/power	20,081	11,662	8,420	3,518	2,065	3,614	3,168	3,201	2,485	1,386	644	2,992	1,324	2,244	3,715	3,021	3,710	3,076
Hockey (ice)	3,299	2,610	690	1,120	485	839	524	292	39	-	-	336	102	104	406	523	924	904
Hunting with bow & arrow	5,157	4,228	929	789	441	1,403	971	856	438	176	82	1,111	497	573	915	635	784	643
Hunting with firearms	16,273	13,945	2,328	2,027	920	2,639	2,998	3,589	2,594	1,279	227	3,504	2,000	2,609	2,755	2,279	2,160	968
In-line roller skating	7,448	3,771	3,676	3,458	997	1,332	1,000	460	183	18	-	1,261	441	678	1,272	1,229	1,261	1,306
Kayaking	5,570	3,028	2,542	590	654	1,294	1,013	1,053	612	244	109	514	209	700	1,453	1,122	1,037	1,165
Mountain biking-off road	7,242	4,428	2,814	1,700	879	1,431	1,369	1,348	373	60	83	1,042	335	724	1,458	1,162	1,262	1,260
Muzzleloading	3,051	2,520	532	481	261	798	402	570	309	192	38	746	264	207	467	470	469	430
Paintball games	6,100	4,697	1,403	2,211	1,500	1,395	594	296	94	11	-	1,125	296	823	621	946	1,267	1,022
Scooter riding	7,354	4,252	3,102	4,976	581	851	408	249	178	46	66	1,150	442	890	1,084	1,331	1,340	1,118
Skateboarding	7,706	5,863	1,842	4,989	1,211	765	450	209	77	6	-	1,675	695	728	1,036	1,241	1,240	1,091
Skiing-alpine	7,383	4,570	2,813	2,312	773	1,334	1,275	1,099	401	130	58	306	213	297	800	1,086	2,090	2,591
Skiing-cross country	2,026	1,060	967	238	359	333	316	368	235	124	53	175	110	188	385	408	358	404

See footnotes at end of table.

Table 1266. Participation in Selected Sports Activities: 2010-Continued.

See headnote on page 798.

Activity	All persons Number	Sex		Age								Household income (dollars)						
		Male	Female	7–17 years	18–24 years	25–34 years	35–44 years	45–54 years	55–64 years	65–74 years	75 and over	Under 25,000	25,000–34,999	35,000–49,999	50,000–74,999	75,000–99,999	100,000–149,999	150,000 and over
Snowboarding............	6,112	4,109	2,003	1,985	1,457	1,615	646	324	54	-	30	759	265	558	919	889	1,245	1,476
Table tennis/ping pong.......	12,810	7,383	5,426	3,186	2,143	2,824	1,831	1,517	924	235	149	1,916	843	966	1,871	2,084	2,948	2,182
Target shooting (All gun types)...	19,826	14,932	4,894	3,427	2,407	3,694	2,924	3,272	2,352	1,114	637	3,391	1,644	3,030	4,190	2,829	2,996	1,747
Target shooting-handgun..	11,993	8,838	3,155	881	1,397	2,702	2,034	1,831	1,768	859	520	1,663	932	1,409	2,856	1,943	2,086	1,103
Water skiing..........	5,220	3,206	2,013	1,502	1,014	1,186	720	515	220	40	23	624	264	397	752	845	1,316	1,021
Work-out at club [1]	36,278	17,492	18,787	2,322	5,764	7,972	6,323	5,791	4,077	2,459	1,570	4,182	2,607	3,730	6,471	5,994	6,953	6,340

– Represents zero. [1] Participant engaged in activity at least six times in the year. [2] Includes wilderness camping. [3] Vacation/overnight.

Source: National Sporting Goods Association, Mt. Prospect, IL, *Sports Participation in 2010: Series 1 and Series II*, (copyright). See <http://www.nsga.org/i4a/pages/index.cfm?pageid=3346>.

Table 1267. National Park System—Summary: 1990 to 2010

Table 1267. National Park System—Summary: 1990 to 2010

[986 represents $986,000,000. For year ending September 30, except as noted. Includes data for five areas in Puerto Rico and Virgin Islands, one area in American Samoa, and one area in Guam]

Item	1990	1995	2000	2005	2007	2008	2009	2010
Finances (mil. dol.): [1]								
Expenditures reported	986	1,445	1,833	2,451	2,412	2,614	2,888	3,239
Salaries and wages	459	633	799	984	1,005	1,066	1,143	1,237
Improvements, maintenance	160	234	299	361	381	428	466	531
Construction	109	192	215	381	280	303	354	443
Other	259	386	520	725	746	817	925	1,028
Funds available	1,506	2,225	3,316	4,218	4,266	4,537	5,416	5,402
Appropriations	1,053	1,325	1,881	2,425	2,484	2,636	3,467	2,848
Other [2]	453	900	1,435	1,793	1,782	1,901	1,949	2,554
Revenue from operations	79	106	234	286	346	404	352	387
Recreation visits (millions): [3]								
All areas	258.7	269.6	285.9	273.5	275.6	274.9	285.6	281.3
National parks [4]	57.7	64.8	66.1	63.5	62.3	61.2	63.0	64.6
National monuments	23.9	23.5	23.8	20.9	19.7	20.2	22.6	23.0
National historical, commemorative, archaeological [5]	57.5	56.9	72.2	74.9	75.1	76.2	82.6	80.0
National parkways	29.1	31.3	34.0	31.7	31.1	30.2	29.9	28.6
National recreation areas [4]	47.2	53.7	50.0	46.8	48.9	49.6	50.9	49.0
National seashores and lakeshores	23.3	22.5	22.5	21.7	19.9	19.3	20.6	22.2
National Capital Parks	7.5	5.5	5.4	4.3	4.9	5.1	4.8	3.0
Recreation overnight stays (millions)	17.6	16.8	15.4	13.5	13.8	13.7	14.6	14.4
In commercial lodgings	3.9	3.8	3.7	3.4	3.6	3.6	3.5	3.5
In Park Service campgrounds	7.9	7.1	5.9	5.2	5.1	5.0	5.4	5.5
In backcountry	1.7	2.2	1.9	1.7	1.7	1.8	1.9	1.8
Other	4.2	3.7	3.8	3.2	3.4	3.3	3.8	3.8
Land (1,000 acres): [6, 7]								
Total	76,362	77,355	78,153	79,048	78,845	78,859	80,442	80,527
Parks	46,089	49,307	49,785	49,910	49,911	49,916	50,592	50,662
Recreation areas	3,344	3,353	3,388	3,391	3,413	3,413	3,414	3,418
Other	26,929	24,695	24,980	25,747	25,521	25,530	26,436	26,447
Acquisition, net	21	27	186	17	23	9	18	23

[1] Financial data are those associated with the National Park System. Certain other functions of the National Park Service (principally the activities absorbed from the former Heritage Conservation and Recreation Service in 1981) are excluded. [2] Includes funds carried over from prior years. [3] For calendar year. Includes other areas, not shown separately. [4] For 1990, combined data for North Cascades National Park and two adjacent National Recreation Areas are included in National Parks total. [5] Includes military areas. [6] Federal land only, as of December 31. Federal land acreages, in addition to National Park Service administered lands, also include lands within national park system area boundaries but under the administration of other agencies. Year-to-year changes in the federal lands figures includes changes in the acreages of these other lands and hence often differ from "net acquisition." [7] The decrease in land totals after 2005 reflects corrected acreage by the Bureau of Land Management, and not by the National Park Service lands.

Source: U.S. National Park Service, *National Park Statistical Abstract*, annual, and unpublished data. See also <http://www2.nature.nps.gov/stats/>.

Table 1268. State Parks and Recreation Areas by State: 2011

[13,998 represents 13,998,000. For year ending June 30. Data are shown as reported by state park directors. In some states, park agency has forests, fish and wildlife areas, and/or other areas under its control. In other states, park agency is responsible for state parks only]

State	Acreage (1,000)	Visitors (1,000) [1]	Revenue Total ($1,000)	Revenue Percent of operating expenditures	State	Acreage (1,000)	Visitors (1,000) [1]	Revenue Total ($1,000)	Revenue Percent of operating expenditures
United States	**13,998**	**720,604**	**1,004,947**	**44.3**	Missouri	204	16,706	10,868	38.5
					Montana	46	1,798	1,619	23.6
Alabama	48	4,410	26,833	77.5	Nebraska	135	12,194	19,289	88.9
Alaska	3,387	5,405	2,317	27.0	Nevada	146	2,932	3,587	36.4
Arizona	64	2,051	10,629	61.2	New Hampshire	233	958	17,592	119.1
Arkansas	54	8,242	22,684	44.1	New Jersey	439	17,170	11,019	29.0
California	1,575	63,964	98,864	27.1	New Mexico	197	4,572	5,925	29.1
Colorado	225	12,339	25,655	37.7	New York	1,354	56,277	90,596	41.9
Connecticut	207	7,757	6,507	37.9	North Carolina	214	14,574	6,938	20.7
Delaware	26	4,653	13,349	55.2	North Dakota	20	1,053	1,807	33.2
Florida	708	20,442	54,977	65.4	Ohio	174	51,815	26,852	41.9
Georgia	93	8,859	32,222	67.3	Oklahoma	70	9,907	29,598	102.0
Hawaii	40	10,278	2,921	30.0	Oregon	106	42,304	19,161	33.4
Idaho	59	4,382	6,791	45.6	Pennsylvania	295	37,630	20,122	25.9
Illinois	480	42,001	7,488	12.5	Rhode Island	9	6,079	5,601	58.9
Indiana	171	15,834	44,300	87.6	South Carolina	85	7,291	19,993	82.9
Iowa	71	13,908	3,883	27.7	South Dakota	103	7,469	16,055	98.6
Kansas	33	6,208	6,583	58.3	Tennessee	184	31,719	36,117	46.6
Kentucky	46	6,922	49,889	63.3	Texas	615	7,699	37,667	47.6
Louisiana	44	2,242	10,506	33.2	Utah	151	4,821	12,280	40.0
Maine	98	2,554	3,463	42.8	Vermont	69	815	7,841	91.2
Maryland	135	10,776	11,491	34.8	Virginia	72	8,062	16,041	46.0
Massachusetts	352	30,180	10,257	16.6	Washington	121	38,896	20,291	31.4
Michigan	286	19,583	47,463	96.4	West Virginia	177	7,508	21,479	56.7
Minnesota	284	8,868	17,597	22.8	Wisconsin	151	14,261	18,992	82.9
Mississippi	25	1,257	8,928	61.8	Wyoming	119	2,979	2,021	25.4

[1] Includes overnight visitors.

Source: National Association of State Park Directors, Tucson, AZ, *2010-2011 Annual Information Exchange*, February 2012 (copyright). See <http://www.naspd.org/>.

Table 1269. National Park Service (NPS) Visits and Acreage by State: 2011

State	Recreation visits [1]	Gross area acres	Federal land — NPS fee acres [2]	Federal land — NPS/OTFED less than fee acres [3]	Federal land — Other federal fee acres [4]	Nonfederal land — Other public acres	Nonfederal land — Private acres
Total...................	276,626,130	84,335,659	79,597,345	355,633	423,139	1,291,427	2,668,116
Alabama...............	755,264	22,737	17,379	202	–	3,296	1,860
Alaska..................	2,333,919	54,654,040	52,469,328	105,671	8	331,750	1,747,284
Arizona................	10,134,892	2,962,866	2,619,005	115	76,800	57,067	209,879
Arkansas..............	2,879,494	104,977	98,287	3,428	20	2,761	481
California.............	35,448,424	8,113,069	7,578,949	22,446	11,268	318,607	181,799
Colorado..............	5,819,069	674,720	611,040	6,859	42,451	862	13,508
Connecticut..........	22,415	7,782	5,719	1,055	–	874	133
District of Columbia.....	30,579,692	7,124	6,975	12	6	127	4
Florida.................	10,580,858	2,638,393	2,468,044	1,330	45,839	98,648	24,533
Georgia...............	7,167,680	63,325	39,781	167	1,461	16,857	5,060
Hawaii.................	4,784,285	369,166	357,814	1	22	11,228	100
Idaho..................	601,668	518,042	511,510	1,138	173	901	4,320
Illinois.................	296,214	115	12	–	–	17	86
Indiana................	2,094,529	15,427	10,630	500	–	3,281	1,015
Iowa...................	216,830	2,713	2,708	–	–	5	1
Kansas................	90,383	11,636	461	269	–	39	10,866
Kentucky..............	1,666,505	95,699	94,678	137	–	832	52
Louisiana.............	577,755	24,788	16,815	1	892	2,670	4,411
Maine..................	2,374,645	90,283	66,966	11,181	22	10,648	1,466
Maryland..............	6,064,410	73,388	40,543	5,938	480	23,806	2,621
Massachusetts.........	10,231,394	57,962	32,957	1,029	44	21,919	2,013
Michigan..............	1,961,506	718,148	631,843	731	42	58,515	27,017
Minnesota.............	572,795	301,333	139,573	3,193	142	98,790	59,634
Mississippi............	6,990,401	118,744	104,015	5,232	–	71	9,427
Missouri...............	3,913,220	83,475	54,382	9,262	–	14,070	5,760
Montana...............	4,061,967	1,274,364	1,214,184	1,826	6,137	1,464	50,753
Nebraska..............	276,058	45,735	5,650	494	981	386	38,223
Nevada................	4,888,963	778,512	774,751	–	2,508	81	1,172
New Hampshire........	32,695	21,932	13,211	1,556	5,772	162	1,232
New Jersey............	5,357,781	99,243	35,362	140	3,208	59,036	1,497
New Mexico...........	1,491,144	391,364	376,880	39	2,715	3,362	8,368
New York..............	16,206,130	72,921	33,635	3,903	164	19,938	15,282
North Carolina........	17,191,874	406,304	363,284	12,272	20,782	3,289	6,677
North Dakota..........	591,668	72,569	71,250	256	151	55	857
Ohio...................	2,417,080	34,126	19,999	1,329	84	8,205	4,508
Oklahoma.............	1,223,134	10,241	10,008	9	189	8	27
Oregon................	839,614	199,318	192,127	1,404	4,975	295	517
Pennsylvania..........	8,526,173	137,770	50,965	2,597	387	19,627	64,194
Rhode Island..........	50,909	5	5	–	–	–	–
South Carolina........	1,589,650	32,618	31,972	61	5	51	530
South Dakota..........	3,807,375	302,969	147,028	122,326	–	78	33,537
Tennessee.............	7,767,864	386,427	358,407	1,679	9,629	3,616	13,095
Texas..................	4,211,655	1,245,085	1,202,155	85	1,013	5,079	36,753
Utah...................	9,281,567	2,117,043	2,097,106	833	1,142	12,803	5,160
Vermont...............	29,049	23,184	9,461	3,874	8,809	544	495
Virginia................	23,459,706	363,702	304,351	7,032	25,049	7,001	20,268
Washington............	7,419,258	1,967,449	1,834,486	2,147	100,194	12,806	17,817
West Virginia..........	1,477,886	92,682	65,054	369	314	6,894	20,050
Wisconsin..............	312,905	133,755	61,744	11,484	802	47,628	12,097
Wyoming..............	5,955,778	2,396,390	2,344,852	21	48,462	1,380	1,675

– Represents or rounds to zero. [1] See footnote 1, Table 1270. [2] See footnote 2, Table 1270. [3] See footnote 3, Table 1270.

Source: U.S. National Park Service, Land Resource Division, and unpublished data. See also <https://irma.nps.gov/Stats/>.

Table 1270. National Park Service (NPS) Visits and Acreage by Type of Area: 2011

[Includes data for five areas in Puerto Rico and Virgin Islands, one area in American Samoa, and one area in Guam]

Type of area	Recreation visits [1]	Gross area acres	Federal land — NPS fee acres [2]	Federal land — NPS/OTFED less than fee acres [3]	Federal land — Other federal fee acres [4]	Non-federal land — Other public acres	Non-federal land — Private acres
Total [5].........................	278,939,216	84,394,246	79,612,289	355,636	453,983	1,297,615	2,674,722
National historic sites..........	9,600,827	34,344	21,594	765	58	951	10,976
National historical parks.......	27,685,059	185,649	132,492	4,174	1,255	28,950	18,777
National memorials.............	30,644,202	10,736	9,550	9	25	81	1,072
National monuments...........	23,048,300	2,027,661	1,845,538	14,830	40,167	5,999	121,128
National parks..................	62,614,260	52,100,512	50,358,656	226,592	47,595	533,678	933,992
National recreation areas.......	47,365,896	3,701,961	3,152,675	23,812	243,101	110,144	172,229
National seashores.............	18,801,331	596,589	404,446	14,947	61,226	106,668	9,301
National parkways..............	29,713,173	178,196	158,570	9,108	213	303	10,002

[1] Recreation visit represents the entry of a person onto lands or waters administered by the National Park Service (NPS) for recreational purposes excluding government personnel, through traffic (commuters), trades-persons, and persons residing within park boundaries. [2] Fee represents complete Federal ownership of all rights in the land. [3] Represents Federal ownership of some rights in the land. [4] NPS acreage lies under the jurisdiction of another federal agency (such as Bureau of Land Management). [5] Includes other "type of areas," not shown separately.

Source: U.S. National Park Service, Land Resource Division, and unpublished data. See also <https://irma.nps.gov/Stats/>.

Table 1271. Participants in Wildlife-Related Recreation Activities: 2006

[In thousands (33,916 represents 33,916,000). For persons 16 years old and over engaging in activity at least once in 2006. Based on survey and subject to sampling error; see source for details]

Participant	Number	Days of participation	Trips	Participant	Number	Days of participation
Total sportspersons [1]	**33,916**	**736,707**	**588,891**	Wildlife watchers [1]	71,132	(X)
Total anglers	29,952	516,781	403,492	Away from home [2]	22,977	352,070
Freshwater	25,431	433,337	336,528	Observe wildlife	21,546	291,027
Excluding Great Lakes	25,035	419,942	323,265	Photograph wildlife	11,708	103,872
Great Lakes	1,420	18,016	13,264	Feed wildlife	7,084	77,329
Saltwater	7,717	85,663	66,963			
				Around the home [3]	67,756	(X)
Total hunters	12,510	219,925	185,399	Observe wildlife	44,467	(X)
Big game	10,682	164,061	115,255	Photograph wildlife	18,763	(X)
Small game	4,797	52,395	40,856	Feed wildlife	55,512	(X)
Migratory birds	2,293	19,770	16,390	Visit public parks	13,271	(X)
Other animals	1,128	15,205	12,898	Maintain plantings or natural areas	14,508	(X)

X Not applicable. [1] Detail does not add to total due to multiple responses and nonresponse. [2] Persons taking a trip of at least 1 mile from home for activity. [3] Activity within 1 mile of home.

Source: U.S. Fish and Wildlife Service, *2006 National Survey of Fishing, Hunting, and Wildlife Associated Recreation*, October 2007. See also <http://wsfrprograms.fws.gov/Subpages/NationalSurvey/nat_survey2006_final.pdf>.

Table 1272. Expenditures for Wildlife-Related Recreation Activities: 2006

[42,156 represents $42,156,000,000. For persons 16 years old and over. Based on survey and subject to sampling error; see source for details]

Expenditure item	Fishing			Hunting			Wildlife watching		
	Expenditures (mil. dol.)	Spenders		Expenditures (mil. dol.)	Spenders		Expenditures [1] (mil. dol.)	Spenders	
		Number (1,000)	Percent of anglers		Number (1,000)	Percent of hunters		Number (1,000)	Percent of watchers [2]
Total, all items [3]	**42,156**	**28,401**	**95**	**22,893**	**12,153**	**97**	**45,655**	**55,979**	**79**
Total trip-related	17,879	26,318	88	6,679	10,828	87	12,875	19,443	85
Food and lodging	6,303	22,572	75	2,791	9,567	76	7,516	16,415	71
Food	4,327	22,415	75	2,177	9,533	76	4,298	16,261	71
Lodging	1,975	5,304	18	614	1,599	13	3,218	6,624	29
Transportation	4,962	22,361	75	2,697	10,064	80	4,456	18,329	80
Public	524	1,163	4	214	401	3	1,567	2,902	13
Private	4,438	21,979	73	2,483	9,982	80	2,889	17,447	76
Other trip costs	6,614	22,275	74	1,190	3,416	27	903	7,681	33
Total equipment and other expenditures	24,133	25,355	85	16,215	11,745	94	32,780	52,178	73
Equipment [4]	5,332	19,082	64	5,366	9,287	74	9,870	49,040	69
Auxiliary equipment	779	3,837	13	1,330	4,196	34	1,033	4,848	7
Special equipment [5]	12,646	1,818	6	4,035	505	4	12,271	1,914	3
Other expenditures [6]	5,375	20,638	69	5,483	10,632	85	9,606	19,070	27
Magazines, books	115	2,944	10	84	1,767	14	360	9,490	13
Licenses, stamps, tags, and permits	648	17,995	60	743	9,862	79	(X)	(X)	(X)

X Not applicable. [1] Information on trip-related expenditures for wildlife watching was collected for away-from-home participants only. Equipment and other expenditures for wildlife watching are based on information collected from both away-from-home and around-the-home participants. [2] Percent of wildlife-watching participants column is based on away-from-home participants for trip-related expenditures. For equipment and other expenditures the percent of wildlife-watching participants is based on total participants. [3] Total not adjusted for multiple responses or nonresponse. [4] Includes fishing, hunting, and wildlife-watching. [5] Special equipment includes boats, campers, cabins, trail bikes, etc. [6] Other expenditures not shown.

Source: U.S. Fish and Wildlife Service, *2006 National Survey of Fishing, Hunting, and Wildlife Associated Recreation*, October 2007. See <http://wsfrprograms.fws.gov/Subpages/NationalSurvey/nat_survey2006_final.pdf>.

Table 1273. Tribal Gaming Revenues: 2004 to 2010

[In millions (22,579 represents $22,579,000,000). For year ending September 30]

Region	2005		2006		2007		2008		2009		2010	
	Number of operations	Revenue	Number of operations	Revenue	Number of operations	Revenue	Number of operations	Revenue	Number of operations	Revenue	Number of operations	Revenue
Total [1]	**392**	**22,579**	**394**	**24,889**	**391**	**26,143**	**405**	**26,739**	**419**	**26,482**	**422**	**26,503**
Region I	49	1,829	46	2,080	46	2,264	47	2,376	49	2,521	50	2,655
Region II	57	6,993	56	7,675	58	7,796	59	7,363	62	6,970	62	6,794
Region III	48	2,529	45	2,719	46	2,874	46	2,774	47	2,600	48	2,539
Region IV	118	3,984	122	4,070	111	4,225	115	4,402	120	4,384	119	4,452
Region V	92	1,730	98	2,126	102	2,584	110	3,047	113	3,225	116	3,352
Region VI	28	5,514	27	6,219	28	6,400	28	6,776	28	6,783	27	6,711

[1] Portland (Region I): Alaska, Idaho, Oregon, and Washington. Sacramento (Region II): California, and Northern Nevada. Phoenix (Region III): Arizona, Colorado, New Mexico, and Southern Nevada. St. Paul (Region IV): Iowa, Michigan, Minnesota, Montana, North Dakota, Nebraska, South Dakota, Wisconsin, and Wyoming. Data for Montana not included for 2004. Oklahoma City/Tulsa (Region V): Oklahoma, Texas, Kansas. Washington (Region VI): Alabama, Connecticut, Florida, Louisiana, Mississippi, North Carolina, and New York.

Source: National Indian Gaming Commission, *Gaming Revenue reports*. See also <http://www.nigc.gov>.

Table 1274. Gaming Revenue by Industry: 2000 to 2009

[In millions of dollars (62,154 represents \$62,154,000,000). Data shown are for gross revenue. Gross gambling revenue (GGR) is the amount wagered minus the winnings returned to players, a true measure of the economic value of gambling. GGR is the figure used to determine what an operation earns before taxes, salaries, and other expenses are paid]

Industry	2000	2003	2004	2005	2006	2007	2008	2009
Total [1]	**62,154**	**73,036**	**78,589**	**84,433**	**90,931**	**[2] 92,272**	**[2,3] 92,157**	**[2,3] 89,262**
Card rooms	949	979	989	1,025	1,104	[3] 1,180	[3] 1,282	[3] 1,232
Commercial casinos	26,455	[2] 28,669	[2] 30,595	[2] 31,775	[2] 34,113	[3] 34,407	[2,3] 33,031	[2,3] 31,379
Charitable games and bingo	2,466	2,331	2,336	[3] 2,338	[3] 2,237	[3] 2,220	[3] 2,131	[3] 2,067
Legal bookmaking	131	128	116	130	192	168	136	136
Lotteries	17,277	20,283	21,405	22,898	24,631	24,780	25,698	25,139
Parimutuel wagering	3,935	3,821	3,750	3,683	3,677	[3] 3,529	[3] 3,141	[3] 2,827

[1] Includes industry not shown separately. [2] Amount includes deepwater cruise ships, cruises-to-nowhere and noncasino devices. [3] Data are estimated.

Source: Christiansen Capital Advisors, LLC. Prepared for the American Gaming Association (AGA). Industry Information, Fact Sheets, *Gaming Revenue: Current-Year Data* (copyright), <http://www.americangaming.org/industry-resources/research/fact-sheets> and <www.cca-i.com>.

Table 1275. North America Cruise Industry in the United States: 2008 to 2011

[Passenger data are in thousands (9,942 represents 9,942,000). Covers 20 major cruise lines that offer North American cruises with a U.S. port of call. These statistics are not directly comparable to data from the Cruise Lines International Association as published in previous editions of the Statistical Abstract. The Association defined the industry as "those cruise lines that primarily market their cruises in North America"]

Item	2008	2009	2010	2011	Item	2008	2009	2010	2011
Vessels and traffic:					**Passengers by destination:**				
Number of ships	120	113	114	115	Alaska	1,015	1,011	872	884
Cruises	4,239	4,126	4,216	4,222	Bahamas	1,449	1,741	1,972	2,318
Passengers	9,942	9,866	10,627	10,887	Bermuda	224	264	269	338
Passenger nights	64,344	63,874	69,827	71,821	Canada/New England	237	232	276	269
Passenger departures by port:					Caribbean, Western [1]	2,821	2,830	3,264	3,355
Miami, FL	2,114	2,044	2,151	1,970	Caribbean, Eastern [2]	1,403	1,244	1,656	1,409
Fort Lauderdale, FL	1,187	1,277	1,759	1,826	Caribbean, Southern [3]	869	807	820	958
Port Canaveral, FL	1,226	1,189	1,299	1,496	Hawaii	250	193	188	215
New York, NY	480	406	562	612	Mexico (Pacific)	1,265	1,095	878	697
San Juan, PR	521	507	522	522	Transatlantic	173	158	158	197
Galveston, TX	413	386	440	462	Other	235	291	273	247
					Passengers for top 5 cruise				
Tampa, FL	393	401	425	458	**lines:**				
Seattle, WA	435	430	469	439	Carnival Cruise Line	3,551	3,832	3,977	4,133
Long Beach, CA	365	415	414	405	Royal Caribbean International	2,619	2,222	2,507	2,369
New Orleans, LA	185	243	261	373	Norwegian Cruise Line	1,039	1,096	1,171	1,295
Other U.S. ports	1,906	1,840	1,721	1,625	Princess Cruises	1,009	973	1,023	928
Rest of the world	310	302	334	374	Holland America Line	627	649	654	679

[1] Area west of Haiti; includes ports in Mexico, Central America, and Colombia. [2] Area as far south as St. Martin, as far west as Haiti. [3] Area south of St. Martin to northern coast of South America as far as Aruba.

Source: Maritime Administration (MARAD), Cruise Statistics, June 2012, <http://www.marad.dot.gov/library_landing_page/data_and_statistics/Data_and_Statistics.htm>.

Table 1276. Top States and Cities Visited by Overseas Travelers: 2000 to 2011

[25,975 represents 25,975,000. Includes travelers for business and pleasure, international travelers in transit through the United States, and students. Excludes travel by international personnel and international businessmen employed in the United States. Starting with the 2006 data, the statistical policy for visitation estimates of international visitation requires a minimum sample of 400 respondents. States and cities are ranked by the latest overseas visitors data]

State and other area	Overseas visitors [1] (1,000)				City	Overseas visitors [1] (1,000)			
	2000	2005	2010	2011		2000	2005	2010	2011
Total overseas travelers [2,3]	**25,975**	**21,679**	**26,363**	**27,883**	New York, NY [4]	5,714	5,810	8,462	9,285
New York	5,922	6,092	8,647	9,508	Los Angeles, CA	3,533	2,580	3,348	3,653
Florida	6,364	4,791	5,615	6,134	Miami, FL	2,935	2,081	3,111	2,956
California	6,026	4,379	5,826	5,688	San Francisco, CA	2,831	2,124	2,636	2,872
Nevada	2,364	1,821	2,504	2,872	Las Vegas, NV	2,260	1,778	2,425	2,788
Hawaiian Islands	2,727	2,255	2,135	2,286	Orlando, FL	3,013	2,016	2,715	2,788
Guam	1,429	867	1,292	1,422	Washington, DC	1,481	1,106	1,740	1,812
Massachusetts	1,169	954	1,028	1,283	Oahu/Honolulu, HI	2,234	1,821	1,634	1,785
Illinois	1,377	1,149	1,186	1,255	Boston, MA	1,325	802	1,186	1,311
Texas	1,325	1,127	1,318	1,227	Chicago, IL	1,351	1,084	1,134	1,199
New Jersey	909	997	975	976	San Diego, CA	701	499	765	753
Pennsylvania	649	629	923	920	Philadelphia, PA	390	434	633	613
Georgia	883	564	765	864	Houston, TX	442	(B)	448	586
Arizona	805	650	817	669	Atlanta, GA	701	564	712	586
Washington	468	369	501	502	Flagstaff, AZ [5]	(B)	(B)	501	586
Utah	(B)	(B)	475	502	Seattle, WA	416	347	475	474
Virginia	519	(B)	343	446	Dallas-Plano-Irving, TX	494	(B)	343	418
Colorado	364	(B)	369	362	San Jose, CA	494	347	290	362
North Carolina	416	(B)	343	335	Anaheim-Santa Ana, CA	494	390	369	362

B Figure too small to meet statistical standards for reliability of a derived figure. [1] Excludes Canada and Mexico. [2] A person is counted in each area visited, but only once in the total. [3] Includes other states and cities, not shown separately. [4] Data include New York City-White Plains-Wayne, NY-NJ grouped together. [5] Data include Flagstaff, Grand Canyon and Sedona grouped together.

Source: U.S. Department of Commerce, International Trade Administration, Office of Travel and Tourism, *Overseas Visitation Estimates for U.S.: States, Cities, and Census Regions*, May 2012, <http://www.tinet.ita.doc.gov/outreachpages/inbound.general_information.inbound_overview.html>.

Table 1277. Real Tourism Output: 2000 to 2010

[In millions of dollars (574,304 represents 574,304,000,000)]

Commodity	Direct output (current dollars)			Real output (chained 2005 dollars)		
	2000	2005	2010	2000	2005	2010
Total	**574,304**	**701,516**	**750,327**	**640,882**	**701,516**	**654,881**
Traveler accommodations	103,122	128,397	150,616	116,936	128,397	141,936
Food services and drinking places	86,964	115,058	119,253	100,240	115,058	101,529
Domestic passenger air transportation services	71,255	68,841	68,959	64,556	68,841	57,619
International passenger air transportation services	29,142	39,013	55,536	36,997	39,013	45,924
Passenger rail transportation services	1,045	1,208	1,413	1,034	1,208	1,187
Passenger water transportation services	6,348	8,171	8,056	5,056	8,171	9,008
Interurban bus transportation	1,362	1,738	1,747	1,619	1,738	1,398
Interurban charter bus transportation	1,614	1,782	1,751	1,888	1,782	1,574
Urban transit systems and other transportation services	3,147	3,629	3,362	3,785	3,629	2,869
Taxi service	3,710	3,876	4,016	4,637	3,876	3,363
Scenic and sightseeing transportation services	2,549	2,876	3,619	2,980	2,876	3,254
Automotive rental	25,759	28,213	31,528	28,454	28,213	24,613
Other vehicle rental	622	715	776	660	715	678
Automotive repair services	11,516	11,574	9,049	13,440	11,574	7,555
Parking lots and garages	1,262	2,094	2,039	1,579	2,094	1,616
Highway tolls	506	673	684	618	673	525
Travel arrangement and reservation services	29,579	32,223	38,516	28,742	32,223	35,816
Motion pictures and performing arts	10,332	14,049	12,720	12,233	14,049	11,253
Spectator sports	5,515	7,371	6,482	6,924	7,371	5,394
Participant sports	9,177	11,294	8,376	9,895	11,294	7,968
Gambling	25,620	34,559	36,845	29,055	34,559	32,953
All other recreation and entertainment	13,988	17,627	16,517	16,548	17,627	14,491
Gasoline	37,495	57,801	72,015	56,869	57,801	57,794
Nondurable PCE [1] commodities other than gasoline	92,675	108,731	96,450	98,346	108,731	86,889

[1] Personal consumption expenditures.

Source: U.S. Bureau of Economic Analysis, "Industry Economic Accounts, U.S. Travel and Tourism Satellite Accounts for 1998-2011," <http://www.bea.gov/industry/tourism_data.htm>.

Table 1278. Domestic and International Travel Expenditures by State: 2010

[In millions of dollars (747,427 represents $747,427,000,000). Shows aggregate spending by foreign visitors and by U.S. residents on domestic overnight trips and day trips of 50 miles or more, one way, away from home]

State	Total (mil. dol.)	Percent distribu-tion	Rank	State	Total (mil. dol.)	Percent distribu-tion	Rank	State	Total (mil. dol.)	Percent distribu-tion	Rank
U.S. total	**747,427**	**100.0**	**(X)**	KS	5,582	0.7	38	ND	2,169	0.3	47
				KY	7,549	1.0	31	OH	15,468	2.1	13
AL	7,740	1.0	30	LA	9,329	1.2	25	OK	6,307	0.8	33
AK	2,028	0.3	48	ME	2,881	0.4	43	OR	8,028	1.1	29
AZ	14,464	1.9	16	MD	12,944	1.7	19	PA	20,784	2.8	8
AR	5,605	0.7	37	MA	15,530	2.1	12	RI	1,732	0.2	50
CA	95,585	12.8	1	MI	15,323	2.1	15	SC	10,477	1.4	23
CO	13,854	1.9	18	MN	11,043	1.5	22	SD	2,344	0.3	46
CT	9,060	1.2	27	MS	6,153	0.8	34	TN	14,133	1.9	17
DE	1,518	0.2	51	MO	11,674	1.6	21	TX	50,022	6.7	4
DC	8,439	1.1	28	MT	3,158	0.4	42	UT	6,057	0.8	35
FL	66,706	8.9	2	NE	3,844	0.5	39	VT	1,904	0.3	49
GA	21,046	2.8	7	NV	26,858	3.6	6	VA	19,347	2.6	9
HI	15,404	2.1	14	NH	3,266	0.4	41	WA	12,080	1.6	20
ID	3,359	0.4	40	NJ	18,500	2.5	10	WV	2,582	0.3	45
IL	29,287	3.9	5	NM	5,767	0.8	36	WI	9,514	1.3	24
IN	9,073	1.2	26	NY	51,734	6.9	3	WY	2,657	0.4	44
IA	6,727	0.9	32	NC	17,606	2.4	11	Other [1]	23,193	3.1	(X)

X Not applicable. [1] This category includes foreign visitor spending in U.S. territories, and Canadian and Mexican visitor spending in the U.S. Those dollars are not represented in state totals.

Source: U.S. Travel Association, Washington, DC, *Impact of Travel on State Economies*, 2012 Research Report (copyright). See also <http://www.ustravel.org/research>.

Table 1279. Travel Forecast Summary: 2009 to 2016

[In billions of dollars (12,703 represents $12,703,000,000,000)]

Measurement	Unit	2009	2010	2011	2012 [1]	2013 [2]	2014 [2]	2015 [2]	2016 [2]
Real GDP	Billions	12,703	13,088	13,315	13,634	13,990	14,438	14,897.9	15,338.3
Unemployment rate	Percent	9.3	9.6	9.0	8.3	7.8	6.8	6.0	5.4
Consumer price index (CPI) [3]	Percent	214.6	218.1	219.2	230.9	234.8	240.4	245.5	250.9
Travel price index (TPI) [3]	Percent	241.5	249.5	253.1	276.4	285.5	297.3	307.1	315.8
Total travel expenditures in U.S.	Billions	699.8	747.4	812.9	855.1	889.2	937.1	981.8	1,025.6
U.S. residents	Billions	605.6	643.9	696.7	730.2	755.7	792.9	827.5	861.0
International visitors [4]	Billions	94.2	103.5	116.3	124.9	133.5	144.3	154.3	164.7
Total international visitors to the United States	Millions	55.0	59.8	62.3	65.4	68.3	71.1	73.8	76.6
Total domestic person trips [5]	Millions	1,900.1	1,963.7	1,997.6	2,035.5	2,062.5	2,098.5	2,131.2	2,161.0

[1] Projected. [2] Forecast. [3] 1982 through 1984 = 100. [4] Excludes international visitors' spending on traveling to the U.S. on U.S. flag carriers, and other misc. transportation. [5] One person on one trip 50 miles or more, one way, away from home or including one or more nights away from home.

Source: U.S.Travel Association's Travel Forecast Model, Bureau of Labor Statistics, Department of Commerce, Bureau of Economic Analysis, Office of Travel and Tourism Industries. See <http://www.ustravel.org/research/travel-industry-forecasts>.

Table 1280. Chain-Type Price Indexes for Direct Tourism Output: 2000 to 2011

[Index numbers, 2005=100. See headnote, Table 1281. For explanation of chain-type price indexes, see text, Section 13]

Tourism goods and services group	2000	2003	2004	2005	2006	2007	2008	2009	2010	2011
Traveler accommodations	88.2	92.7	95.1	100.0	103.6	108.1	110.2	106.7	107.9	111.0
Transportation	90.3	89.6	92.8	100.0	107.0	111.5	122.1	111.0	119.3	128.3
Passenger air transportation	99.7	92.9	93.6	100.0	106.7	109.7	121.0	110.7	120.8	128.8
All other transportation-related commodities	83.9	87.1	92.2	100.0	107.3	112.8	122.9	111.0	118.1	127.8
Food services and drinking places	86.8	94.0	96.9	100.0	103.2	107.0	111.9	116.0	117.6	120.4
Recreation, entertainment, and shopping	90.8	95.8	97.8	100.0	102.4	105.0	108.8	110.2	111.2	113.6
Recreation and entertainment	86.6	94.5	96.9	100.0	103.2	106.5	110.1	110.6	111.5	112.7
Shopping	94.2	96.8	98.5	100.0	101.7	103.9	107.8	109.9	111.1	114.5
All tourism goods and services	89.6	92.6	95.3	100.0	104.5	108.3	114.5	110.7	114.8	120.0

Source: U.S. Department of Commerce, Bureau of Economic Analysis, Office of Travel and Tourism Industries, *United States Travel and Tourism Satellite Accounts (TTSAs)*, <http://bea.gov/industry/tourism_data.htm>.

Table 1281. Tourism Sales by Commodity Group and Tourism Employment by Industry Group: 2005 to 2011

[Sales in billions of dollars (693 represents $693,000,000,000). Employment in thousands (5,876 represents 5,876,000). Direct tourism-related sales comprise all output consumed directly by visitors (e.g., traveler accommodations, passenger air transportation, souvenirs). Direct tourism-related employment comprises all jobs where the workers are engaged in the production of direct tourism-related output (e.g., hotel staff, airline pilots, and souvenir sellers)]

Tourism commodity group	Direct tourism sales (bil. dol.)				Tourism industry group	Direct tourism employment (bil. dol.)			
	2005	2009	2010	2011		2005	2009	2010	2011
All commodities [1]	**693**	**699**	**746**	**807**	**All industries**	**5,876**	**5,406**	**5,331**	**5,410**
Traveler accommodations	124	131	140	154	Traveler accommodations	1,334	1,250	1,241	1,266
Transportation	264	274	310	342	Transportation	1,158	1,087	1,071	1,087
Passenger air transportation	108	113	134	147	Air transportation services	487	453	444	451
All other transportation-related commodities	156	162	176	196	All other transportation-related industries	672	635	628	636
Food services and drinking places	113	112	114	120	Food and beverage services	1,878	1,716	1,691	1,734
					Recreation, entertainment, and shopping	1,254	1,120	1,099	1,089
Recreation, entertainment, and shopping	192	182	182	191	Recreation and entertainment	651	586	569	571
Recreation and entertainment	84	87	86	89	Shopping	604	534	530	518
Shopping	107	96	96	102	All other industries	251	233	229	234

[1] Commodities that are typically purchased by visitors from the producer: such as airline passenger fares, meals, or hotel services.

Source: U.S. Bureau of Economic Analysis, "Industry Economic Accounts, Satellite Industry Accounts, Travel and Tourism." See <http://www.bea.gov/industry/index.htm#satellite#>.

Table 1282. International Travelers and Payments: 1990 to 2011

[47,880 represents $47,880,000,000. For coverage, see Table 1283. Some traveler data revised since originally issued]

Year	Travel and passenger fare (mil. dol.)				U.S. net travel and passenger receipts (mil. dol.)	U.S. travelers to international countries (1,000)	International travelers to the U.S. (1,000)
	Payments by U.S. travelers		Receipts from international visitors				
	Total [1]	Travel payments	Total [1]	Travel receipts			
1990............	47,880	37,349	58,305	43,007	10,425	44,624	39,363
1995............	59,579	44,916	82,304	63,395	22,725	51,285	43,318
2000............	88,979	65,366	103,088	82,891	14,109	61,327	51,238
2004............	90,468	66,738	93,397	75,465	2,929	61,809	46,086
2005............	95,119	69,930	102,769	82,160	7,650	63,502	49,206
2006............	99,605	72,959	107,825	86,187	8,220	63,663	50,977
2007............	104,808	77,127	122,542	97,355	17,734	64,029	55,978
2008............	112,335	80,494	141,380	110,423	29,045	63,563	57,942
2009............	99,249	74,132	120,290	94,187	21,041	61,419	54,962
2010............	102,766	75,510	134,464	103,481	31,698	60,271	59,796
2011............	109,760	78,651	152,746	116,115	42,986	58,702	62,711

[1] Includes passenger fares, not shown separately.

Source: U.S. Department of Commerce, International Trade Administration, Office of Travel and Tourism Industries, and the Bureau of Economic Analysis (BEA), June and July 2012, <http://www.tinet.ita.doc.gov>.

Table 1283. International Travel: 1990 to 2011

[In thousands (44,619 represents 44,619,000). U.S. travelers cover residents of the United States, its territories and possessions. International travelers to the U.S. include travelers for business and pleasure, excludes travel by international personnel and international businessmen employed in the United States. Some traveler data revised since originally issued]

Item and area	1990	1995	2000	2005	2007	2008	2009	2010	2011
U.S. travelers to international countries [1]........	**44,619**	**51,285**	**61,327**	**63,503**	**64,028**	**63,564**	**61,419**	**60,271**	**58,702**
Canada..........	12,252	13,005	15,189	14,391	13,375	12,504	11,667	11,749	11,595
Mexico..........	16,377	18,771	19,285	20,325	19,425	20,271	19,452	20,015	20,084
Total overseas....	15,990	19,059	26,853	28,787	31,228	30,789	30,300	28,507	27,023
Europe..........	8,043	8,596	13,373	11,976	12,304	11,238	10,635	9,806	9,674
International travelers to the U.S....................	**39,363**	**43,318**	**51,238**	**49,206**	**55,978**	**57,942**	**54,962**	**59,796**	**62,711**
Canada..........	17,263	14,663	14,667	14,862	17,759	18,915	17,977	19,964	21,337
Mexico..........	7,041	8,016	10,596	12,665	14,327	13,686	13,229	13,469	13,491
Total overseas....	15,059	20,639	25,975	21,679	23,892	25,341	23,756	26,363	27,883
Europe..........	6,659	8,793	11,597	10,313	11,406	12,783	11,550	11,985	12,660
Asia.............	4,360	6,616	7,554	6,198	6,377	6,179	5,669	7,020	7,247
South America......	1,328	2,449	2,941	1,820	2,274	2,556	2,742	3,250	3,757
Caribbean........	1,137	1,044	1,331	1,135	1,317	1,201	1,206	1,201	1,091
Oceania..........	662	588	731	737	834	852	872	1,095	1,243
Central America....	412	509	822	696	786	776	758	760	747
Middle East.......	365	454	702	527	620	681	666	736	811
Africa............	137	186	295	252	278	315	294	316	327

[1] A person is counted in each area visited but only once in the total.

Source: U.S. Department of Commerce, International Trade Administration, Office of Travel and Tourism, *United States Resident Travel Abroad*, July 2012; and *Profile of Overseas Travelers to the United States*, July 2012, <http://www.tinet.ita.doc.gov>.

Table 1284. Top 20 U.S. Gateways for Nonstop International Air Travel: 2009 and 2010

[151,324 represents 151,324,000. International passengers are residents of any country traveling nonstop to and from the United States on U.S. and foreign carriers. The data cover all passengers arriving and departing from U.S. airports on nonstop commercial international flights with 60 seats or more]

Gateway airport	2009 [1]	2010	Percent change 2009–2010	Gateway airport	2009 [1]	2010	Percent change 2009–2010
Total.............................	**151,324**	**160,018**	**5.7**	Washington (Dulles), DC.......	5,986	6,170	3.1
Total, top 20......................	**136,317**	**144,724**	**6.2**	Dallas-Ft. Worth, TX............	4,667	5,050	8.2
Top 20, percentage of total...	**90.1**	**90.4**	**0.4**	Philadelphia, PA.................	3,738	3,799	1.6
				Boston, MA.....................	3,472	3,647	5.0
New York (JFK), NY..............	21,487	22,783	6.0	Honolulu, HI.....................	3,276	3,609	10.2
Miami, FL......................	15,836	16,734	5.7	Fort Lauderdale, FL.............	2,932	3,328	13.5
Los Angeles, CA.................	14,833	15,518	4.6	Orlando, FL.....................	2,815	3,078	9.3
Newark, NJ......................	10,676	11,376	6.6	Detroit, MI......................	2,738	2,884	5.3
Chicago (O'Hare), IL............	10,184	10,444	2.5	Guam Island, GU................	2,333	2,732	17.1
Atlanta, GA.....................	8,764	9,124	4.1	Charlotte, NC...................	2,344	2,690	14.8
San Francisco, CA...............	7,889	8,479	7.5	Seattle-Tacoma, WA...........	2,528	2,672	5.7
Houston (G. Bush), TX...........	7,605	8,323	9.4	Minneapolis-St. Paul, MN......	2,213	2,283	3.1

[1] Data have been revised.

Source: U.S. Department of Transportation, Research and Innovative Technology Administration, Bureau of Transportation Statistics, Office of Airline Information, T-100 International Segment data, September 2011, <http://www.transtats.bts.gov/>.

Table 1285. Selected U.S.-Canadian and U.S.-Mexican Border Land— Passenger Gateways: 2011

[31,596 represents 31,596,000]

Item and gateway	Entering the U.S. (1,000)	Item and gateway	Entering the U.S. (1,000)
All U.S.-Canadian land gateways [1]		**All U.S.-Mexican land gateways** [1]	
Personal vehicles...........................	31,596	Personal vehicles..............	61,180
Personal vehicle passengers........................	59,192	Personal vehicle passengers..............	110,962
Buses..	114	Buses..................................	208
Bus passengers................................	2,452	Bus passengers.........................	2,720
Train passengers..............................	277	Train passengers.......................	4
Pedestrians....................................	407	Pedestrians.............................	40,021
Selected top five gateways:		**Selected top five gateways:**	
Personal vehicles		Personal vehicles	
Buffalo-Niagara Falls, NY............................	5,912	San Ysidro, CA..................	12,373
Blaine, WA..........................	4,289	El Paso, TX.....................	9,148
Detroit, MI.........................	4,174	Hidalgo, TX.....................	4,878
Port Huron, MI......................	1,843	Laredo, TX......................	4,746
Point Roberts, WA...................	1,094	Otay Mesa, CA...................	4,214
Personal vehicle passengers		Personal vehicle passengers	
Buffalo-Niagara Falls, NY............	12,687	San Ysidro, CA..................	21,523
Blaine, WA..........................	8,313	El Paso, TX.....................	14,941
Detroit, MI.........................	7,203	Hidalgo, TX.....................	9,040
Port Huron, MI......................	3,768	Laredo, TX......................	8,458
Champlain-Rouses Pt., NY.............	2,402	Brownsville, TX.................	7,972
Pedestrians		Pedestrians	
Buffalo-Niagara Falls, NY............	283	San Ysidro, CA..................	8,454
Sumas, WA...........................	27	El Paso, TX.....................	6,172
Detroit, MI.........................	21	Calexico, CA....................	4,451
International Falls, MN..............	19	Nogales, AZ.....................	3,526
Point Roberts, WA...................	17	Laredo, TX......................	3,090

[1] Data reflect all personal vehicles and buses, passengers, and pedestrians entering the U.S.-Canadian border and U.S.-Mexican border, regardless of nationality.

Source: U.S. Department of Transportation, Bureau of Transportation Statistics, based on data from the Department of Homeland Security, U.S. Customs and Border Protection, Office of Field Operations, Operations Management Reporting system. See also <http://www.bts.gov/programs/international/>.

Table 1286. Foreign Visitors for Pleasure Admitted by Country of Citizenship: 2000 to 2009

[In thousands (30,511 represents 30,511,000). For years ending September 30. Represents non-U.S. citizens (also known as nonimmigrants) admitted to the country for a temporary period of time]

Country	2000 [1]	2005	2008	2009	Country	2000 [1]	2005	2008	2009
All countries [2]	**30,511**	**23,815**	**29,442**	**27,800**	Thailand....................	76	37	48	42
					Turkey......................	93	57	71	65
Europe [3]	11,806	10,016	12,558	11,785	United Arab Emirates......	36	3	5	6
Austria.................	182	116	154	160	Africa [3]	327	212	253	252
Belgium.................	254	154	231	220	Egypt.......................	44	19	27	29
Czech Republic..........	44	26	36	58	Nigeria.....................	27	40	54	55
Denmark.................	150	153	236	235	South Africa................	114	64	65	59
Finland.................	95	76	100	113	Oceania [3]	748	723	878	857
France..................	1,113	1,007	1,345	1,375	Australia...................	535	527	672	671
Germany.................	1,925	1,248	1,579	1,587	New Zealand.................	170	184	195	176
Greece..................	60	40	52	48	North America [3, 5]	6,501	5,546	7,867	5,629
Hungary.................	58	30	34	45	Canada......................	277	23	43	38
Iceland.................	27	34	49	30	Mexico......................	3,972	4,070	6,112	5,591
Ireland.................	325	398	585	488	Caribbean...................	1,404	876	1,049	968
Italy...................	626	636	884	861	Bahamas, The................	24	257	302	253
Netherlands.............	559	483	638	598	Dominican Republic......	195	189	207	196
Norway..................	144	117	184	176	Haiti.......................	72	65	93	86
Poland..................	116	119	125	108	Jamaica.....................	240	152	200	187
Portugal................	86	81	114	102	Trinidad and Tobago......	133	106	128	132
Russia..................	74	53	94	110	Central America.............	792	578	663	640
Spain...................	370	402	699	647	Costa Rica..................	172	109	138	131
Sweden..................	321	249	356	322	El Salvador.................	175	147	129	113
Switzerland.............	400	207	267	281	Guatemala...................	177	135	161	151
United Kingdom..........	4,671	4,232	4,568	3,979	Honduras....................	87	75	101	105
Asia [3]	7,853	5,688	5,693	5,188	Nicaragua...................	47	33	40	38
China [4]	656	221	319	317	Panama......................	106	64	77	84
India...................	253	247	421	410	South America [3]	2,867	1,498	2,114	2,304
Indonesia...............	62	42	45	38	Argentina...................	515	145	261	297
Israel..................	319	220	254	256	Bolivia.....................	48	18	25	27
Japan...................	4,946	3,758	3,266	2,878	Brazil......................	706	385	600	718
Korea, South............	606	528	600	565	Chile.......................	194	82	106	100
Malaysia................	64	32	37	31	Colombia....................	411	282	379	381
Pakistan................	47	34	35	35	Ecuador.....................	122	119	132	143
Philippines.............	163	144	170	166	Peru........................	190	142	148	153
Saudi Arabia............	67	10	19	24	Uruguay.....................	66	24	28	30
Singapore...............	131	57	77	62	Venezuela...................	570	270	404	421

[1] Due to the temporary expiration of the Visa Waiver Program from May through October 2000, data for business and pleasure not available separately for 2000 and 2001. [2] Total includes visitors of unknown country of citizenship. [3] Total includes other countries, not shown separately. [4] See footnote 4, Table 1348. [5] The majority of short-term admissions from Canada and Mexico are excluded.

Source: U.S. Dept. of Homeland Security, Office of Immigration Statistics, *2009 Yearbook of Immigration Statistics*: Supplemental Tables. See also <http://www.dhs.gov/files/statistics/publications/yearbook.shtm>.

Section 27
Accommodation, Food Services, and Other Services

This section presents statistics relating to services other than those covered in the previous few sections (22 to 26) on wholesale and retail trade, transportation, communications, financial services, and recreation services. Data shown for services are classified by kind of business and cover sales or receipts, establishments, employees, payrolls, and other items.

The principal sources of these data are from the U.S. Census Bureau and include the *2007 Economic Census*, annual surveys, and the *County Business Patterns* program. These data are supplemented by data from several sources such as the National Restaurant Association on food and drink sales (Table 1298), the American Hotel & Lodging Association on lodging (Table 1297), and Magna Global on advertising (Table 1294).

Data on these services also appear in several other sections. For instance, labor force employment and earnings data appear in Section 12, Labor Force, Employment, and Earnings; gross domestic product of the industry (Table 682) appears in Section 13, Income, Expenditures, Poverty, and Wealth; and financial data (several tables) from the quarterly *Statistics of Income Bulletin*, published by the Internal Revenue Service, appear in Section 15, Business Enterprise.

Censuses—Limited coverage of the service industries started in 1933. Beginning with the 1967 census, legislation provides for a census of each area to be conducted every 5 years (for years ending in "2" and "7"). For more information on the most current census, see the Economic Census, *Guide to Economic Census*, found at <http://www.census.gov/econ/census07/www/user_guide.html>. The industries covered in the censuses and surveys of business are defined in the

North American Industry Classification System (NAICS). For information on NAICS, see the Census Web site at <http://www.census.gov/eos/www/naics/>.

In general, the 2007 Economic Census has two final series of publications for these sectors: 1) subject series with reports such as product lines, and establishment and firm sizes and 2) geographic reports with individual reports for each state. For information on these series, see the Census Bureau Web site at <http://www.census.gov/econ/census07>.

Current surveys—The *Service Annual Survey* provides annual estimates of nationwide receipts for selected personal, business, leasing and repair, amusement and entertainment, social and health, and other professional service industries in the United States. For selected social, health, and other professional service industries, separate estimates are developed for receipts of taxable firms and revenue and expenses for firms and organizations exempt from federal income taxes. Several service sectors from this survey are covered in other sections of this publication. The estimates for tax exempt firms in these industries are derived from a sample of employer firms only. Estimates obtained from annual and monthly surveys are based on sample data and are not expected to agree exactly with results that would be obtained from a complete census of all establishments. Data include estimates for sampling units not reporting.

Statistical reliability—For a discussion of statistical collection and estimation, sampling procedures, and measures of statistical reliability applicable to Census Bureau data, see Appendix III.

Table 1287. Selected Service-Related Industries—Establishments, Sales, Payroll, and Employees by Kind of Business: 2007

[1,251,004 represents $1,251,004,000,000. Covers only establishments with payroll. For statement on methodology, see Appendix III]

Kind of business	2007 NAICS code [1]	Establishments, (number)	Sales or receipts (mil. dol.)	Annual payroll (mil. dol.)	Paid employees [2] (1,000)
Professional, scientific, and technical services..........................	**54**	**847,492**	**1,251,004**	**502,074**	**7,870**
Professional, scientific, and technical services............................	541	847,492	1,251,004	502,074	7,870
Management of companies and enterprises............................	**55**	**51,451**	**104,443**	**249,511**	**2,664**
Administrative and support and waste management and remediation services...........................	**56**	**395,292**	**630,771**	**301,450**	**10,251**
Administrative and support services............................	561	373,505	555,583	284,603	9,865
Waste management and remediation services.........................	562	21,787	75,188	16,848	386
Accommodation and food services..........................	**72**	**634,361**	**613,796**	**170,827**	**11,601**
Accommodation...........................	721	62,740	180,391	46,393	1,971
Food services and drinking places..........................	722	571,621	433,405	124,434	9,630
Other services (except public administration)..........................	**81**	**540,148**	**405,284**	**99,123**	**3,479**
Repair and maintenance...........................	811	222,151	137,733	40,070	1,261
Personal and laundry services...........................	812	210,151	82,105	26,759	1,338
Religious, grantmaking, civic, professional, and similar organizations...........................	813	107,846	185,447	32,294	880

[1] North American Industrial Classification System, 2007; see text, Section 15. [2] For employees on the payroll during the pay period including March 12.

Source: U.S. Census Bureau, 2007 Economic Census, "Economy-Wide Key Statistics," <http://factfinder2.census.gov>, accessed Aug. 2012.

Table 1288. Selected Service-Related Industries—Nonemployer Establishments and Receipts by Kind of Business: 2007 to 2009

[For number of firms 3,029 represents 3,029,000. Includes only firms subject to federal income tax. Nonemployers are businesses with no paid employees. Data originate chiefly from administrative records of the Internal Revenue Service; see Appendix III]

Kind of business	2007 NAICS code [1]	Firms (1,000)			Receipts (mil. dol.)		
		2007	2008	2009	2007	2008	2009
Professional, scientific, and technical services............	**54**	**3,029**	**3,029**	**3,067**	**130,386**	**131,521**	**123,437**
Professional, scientific, and technical services [2].............	541	3,029	3,029	3,067	130,386	131,521	123,437
Legal services...............	5411	256	255	266	15,744	15,923	16,669
Accounting, tax preparation, bookkeeping, and payroll services...............	5412	355	350	355	8,103	8,233	8,545
Architectural, engineering [3]...............	5413	232	226	222	11,420	11,197	9,580
Management, scientific and technical consulting............	5416	642	641	654	29,011	29,722	27,869
Scientific research and development services...............	5417	35	35	35	1,196	1,263	1,111
Administrative and support and waste management and remediation services............	**56**	**1,793**	**1,826**	**1,865**	**39,811**	**40,415**	**37,429**
Administrative and support services [2]...............	561	1,771	1,806	1,845	38,280	38,737	36,130
Office administrative services...............	5611	198	204	202	3,191	3,250	3,048
Business support services...............	5614	224	219	214	5,969	5,927	5,448
Services to buildings and dwellings...............	5617	1,047	1,083	1,142	20,625	21,110	20,431
Waste management and remediation services...............	562	21	21	20	1,531	1,678	1,299
Accommodation and food services.........................	**72**	**303**	**308**	**314**	**16,071**	**16,100**	**14,015**
Accommodation...............	721	55	54	53	3,592	3,484	2,827
Food services and drinking places.........................	722	249	254	260	12,479	12,616	11,188
Full-service restaurants...............	7221	40	42	42	4,005	4,075	3,038
Limited-service eating places...............	7222	49	48	48	3,456	3,425	2,934
Special food services...............	7223	133	137	142	3,352	3,438	3,585
Drinking places (alcoholic beverages)...............	7224	26	27	28	1,666	1,679	1,632
Other services (except public administration)............	**81**	**2,965**	**3,029**	**3,149**	**80,653**	**81,042**	**76,290**
Repair and maintenance [2]...............	811	704	699	711	28,183	27,567	24,210
Automotive repair and maintenance...............	8111	305	302	308	14,634	14,334	12,534
Personal and household goods repair [4]...............	8114	297	297	303	8,853	8,616	7,884
Personal and laundry services...............	812	2,054	2,124	2,233	49,282	50,257	48,955
Personal care services...............	8121	911	967	1,042	20,661	21,680	22,033
Death care services...............	8122	16	16	16	856	886	777
Drycleaning and laundry services...............	8123	35	34	34	2,004	1,978	1,836
Other personal services...............	8129	1,093	1,108	1,141	25,760	25,713	24,309
Religious, grantmaking, civic, professional, and similar organizations...............	813	206	206	205	3,189	3,218	3,125

[1] North American Industry Classification System, see text, Section 15. Data for 2002-2007 based on NAICS 2002; beginning 2008 nonemployer data is based on NAICS 2007. [2] Includes other kinds of business not shown separately. [3] Includes related services. [4] Includes maintenance.

Source: U.S. Census Bureau, "Nonemployer Statistics," July 2011, <http://www.census.gov/econ/nonemployer/index.html>.

Table 1289. Selected Service-Related Industries—Establishments, Employees, and Payroll by Industry: 2008 and 2009

[848 represents 848,000, except payroll. Covers establishments with paid employees. Excludes most government employees, railroad employees, and self-employed persons. For statement on methodology, see Appendix III]

Kind of business	2007 NAICS code [1]	Establishments (1,000)		Employees [2] (1,000)		Annual payroll (bil. dol.)	
		2008	2009	2008	2009	2008	2009
Professional, scientific, & technical services.............	**54**	**848**	**843**	**8,033**	**7,840**	**539.1**	**527.0**
Professional, scientific, & technical services..................	541	848	843	8,033	7,840	539.1	527.0
Legal services..................................	5411	188	186	1,199	1,173	91.8	89.5
Offices of lawyers..........................	54111	173	173	1,110	1,097	88.3	86.0
Accounting, tax preparation, bookkeeping, and payroll services.........	5412	123	124	1,319	1,289	56.8	56.3
Tax preparation services..................	541213	25	26	213	215	2.1	2.0
Architectural, engineering, & related services [3].............	5413	115	111	1,458	1,366	103.1	95.7
Architectural services......................	54131	25	23	210	180	14.2	11.2
Engineering services.......................	54133	59	58	998	962	76.4	73.5
Specialized design services [3].............	5414	33	31	130	114	6.7	5.9
Graphic design services...................	54143	16	16	60	55	2.9	2.6
Computer systems design & related services [3]..........	5415	119	120	1,325	1,352	107.7	108.8
Custom computer programming services..........	541511	55	54	586	580	48.0	46.1
Computer systems design services.............	541512	48	49	499	483	40.6	39.3
Management, scientific, technical consulting services [3]....	5416	142	144	870	863	63.0	62.2
Management consulting services............	54161	108	110	703	690	51.9	50.8
Environmental consulting services..........	54162	10	9	72	71	4.3	4.3
Scientific research & development services..........	5417	16	16	634	643	59.8	60.9
Research & development in the physical engineering & life sciences..........	54171	14	14	594	604	57.1	58.4
Advertising & related services [3]...........	5418	41	39	479	433	27.5	25.0
Advertising agencies......................	54181	14	14	165	157	12.4	11.5
Direct mail advertising....................	54186	3	3	73	61	3.1	2.5
Other professional, scientific, & tech services..............	5419	72	71	620	608	22.6	22.7
Veterinary services.........................	54194	29	29	302	300	9.2	9.4
Management of companies and enterprises...............	**55**	**52**	**52**	**2,887**	**2,853**	**273.3**	**264.7**
Administrative and support and waste management and remediation services........	**56**	**394**	**384**	**10,225**	**9,061**	**313.9**	**289.8**
Administrative & support services [3]...............	561	372	362	9,857	8,713	297.0	273.8
Employment services.......................	5613	54	50	5,231	4,290	153.0	136.2
Temporary help services..................	56132	34	32	2,875	2,157	68.5	57.0
Business support services [3]................	5614	36	36	828	821	24.2	23.7
Telephone call centers....................	56142	5	5	429	432	9.2	9.3
Collection agencies.......................	56144	5	5	151	150	4.9	5.0
Credit bureaus............................	56145	1	1	21	19	1.8	1.7
Travel arrangement & reservation services........	5615	22	22	259	234	12.7	11.6
Travel agencies...........................	56151	16	15	123	107	6.8	5.7
Investigation & security services.............	5616	26	26	832	793	21.3	20.6
Investigation, guard, & armored car services..............	56161	15	15	710	677	16.3	15.7
Security systems services.................	56162	10	10	122	116	5.0	4.9
Services to buildings & dwellings.............	5617	177	175	1,702	1,626	40.7	39.1
Waste management & remediation services..........	562	22	21	367	348	16.9	16.0
Waste collection...........................	5621	10	10	195	187	8.7	8.3
Waste treatment & disposal.................	5622	3	3	50	46	2.6	2.4
Remediation & other waste mgmt services.............	5629	9	9	122	115	5.6	5.3
Accommodation & food services.............	**72**	**637**	**635**	**11,926**	**11,443**	**183.2**	**179.5**
Accommodation..............................	721	63	63	1,976	1,839	48.0	44.8
Traveler accommodation....................	7211	54	54	1,926	1,790	46.8	43.5
Hotels (except casino hotels) & motels...........	72111	49	49	1,489	1,392	33.3	31.1
RV (recreational vehicle) parks & recreational camps......	7212	7	7	40	38	1.1	1.1
Rooming & boarding houses.................	7213	2	2	11	10	0.2	0.2
Food services & drinking places.............	722	574	572	9,950	9,605	135.2	134.6
Full-service restaurants....................	7221	221	222	4,708	4,505	68.9	68.5
Limited-service eating places..............	7222	269	268	4,225	4,111	49.6	49.8
Special food services.....................	7223	38	38	661	641	12.1	11.8
Drinking places (alcoholic beverages).......	7224	45	44	356	348	4.6	4.6
Other services (except public administration).............	**81**	**731**	**723**	**5,453**	**5,264**	**143.1**	**139.3**
Repair & maintenance [3].....................	811	217	212	1,272	1,189	41.8	39.9
Automotive repair & maintenance............	8111	161	157	866	806	25.1	23.8
Personal & household goods repair & maintenance........	8114	21	20	82	74	2.3	2.1
Personal & laundry services [3]...............	812	209	206	1,368	1,318	28.2	27.2
Personal care services....................	8121	113	112	637	620	11.4	11.1
Death care services.......................	8122	21	21	136	135	4.2	4.3
Drycleaning & laundry services.............	8123	39	37	331	316	7.6	7.2
Religious/grantmaking/civic/professional [4]...........	813	304	304	2,813	2,757	73.1	72.2
Religious organizations...................	8131	180	181	1,699	1,693	31.7	31.9
Grantmaking & giving services.............	8132	17	17	192	170	9.6	8.3
Social advocacy organizations.............	8133	16	16	140	140	5.3	5.5
Civic & social organizations...............	8134	29	28	263	247	4.5	4.4
Business/professional/labor/political [4].........	8139	62	62	519	507	22.0	22.1
Labor unions [4]............................	81393	15	15	173	165	5.2	5.2

[1] North American Industry Classification System, 2007. See text, section 15. [2] Includes employees on the payroll for the pay period including March 12. [3] Includes other kinds of business, not shown separately. [4] And similar organizations.

Source: U.S. Census Bureau, "County Business Patterns," June 2011, <http://www.census.gov/econ/cbp/index.html>.

Table 1290. Employed Persons—Sex, Race, and Hispanic or Latino Origin by Industry: 2011

[15,819 represents 15,819,000. Civilian noninstitutionalized population 16 years and older. Based on the Current Population Survey (CPS); see text, Section 1, and Appendix III. For information on employees in other sectors, see Tables 626 and 644.]

Industry	2007 NAICS code [1]	Total employed (1,000)	Percent of total			
			Female	Black [2]	Asian [2]	Hispanic or Latino [3]
Professional and business services...................	(X)	**15,819**	**41.0**	**8.7**	**6.1**	**14.7**
Professional and technical services....................	**54**	**9,461**	**42.5**	**5.9**	**8.3**	**6.9**
Legal services................................	5411	1,665	54.4	6.7	3.9	6.6
Accounting, tax preparation, bookkeeping, & payroll services........................	5412	1,012	62.6	7.4	6.1	8.6
Architectural, engineering, and related services..............	5413	1,496	23.0	5.2	4.7	6.6
Specialized design services....................	5414	379	53.2	3.4	4.2	9.6
Computer systems design & related services..........	5415	1,935	25.0	5.6	19.4	5.8
Management, scientific, and technical consulting services...............	5416	1,309	41.1	5.9	7.5	5.6
Scientific research & development services...............	5417	541	45.4	6.0	10.5	8.0
Advertising and related services................	5418	518	51.8	5.9	3.7	5.3
Other professional, scientific, and technical services [4]........	5419	270	79.5	3.0	2.5	8.8
Veterinary services...............	54194	335	56.0	6.8	5.5	11.7
Management, administrative, and waste services..........	**55–56**	**6,358**	**38.6**	**12.8**	**2.9**	**26.3**
Management of companies and enterprises..............	55	195	47.1	7.6	3.9	10.7
Employment services................	5613	895	51.6	20.5	3.7	21.1
Business support services..................	5614	830	62.9	14.5	3.1	12.1
Travel arrangement & reservation services..........	5615	262	57.6	10.1	7.8	10.7
Investigations & security services...............	5616	800	22.0	22.6	4.1	15.3
Services to buildings and dwellings [5]..........	5617	1,373	52.4	11.2	2.1	37.2
Landscaping services.............	56173	1,258	9.7	5.1	1.2	43.7
Other administrative and support services..........	5611,2,9	275	44.9	10.0	4.6	16.8
Waste management and remediation services..........	562	469	18.8	9.7	1.4	21.7
Accommodation and food services................	**72**	**9,775**	**51.9**	**12.0**	**6.8**	**22.1**
Accommodation...............	721	1,407	53.5	14.4	8.6	23.6
Traveler accommodation..............	7211	1,301	53.7	15.1	9.0	25.0
Recreational vehicle parks and camps, and rooming and board houses....	7212,3	106	52.2	5.1	3.8	5.6
Food services and drinking places..........	722	8,368	51.6	11.6	6.5	21.9
Restaurants and other food services [6].........	722	8,148	51.5	11.8	6.6	22.1
Drinking places, alcoholic beverages..........	7224	220	56.2	5.9	2.2	12.8
Other services..............	**81**	**6,724**	**52.0**	**9.1**	**6.6**	**16.6**
Other services (except private households)............	81	6,002	47.5	9.2	6.9	14.3
Repair and maintenance...............	811	1,984	10.7	6.4	4.0	20.3
Automotive repair and maintenance [7]............	8111	1,132	8.4	6.1	3.2	20.4
Car washes...............	811192	165	11.8	10.3	4.8	38.4
Electronic & precision equipment repair and maintenance..............	8112	182	11.0	11.3	7.7	15.4
Commercial and industrial machinery & equipment repair and maintenance..........	8113	308	8.5	3.7	2.6	15.7
Personal and household goods repair and maintenance [8].........	8114	192	26.7	5.0	6.8	16.8
Footwear and leather goods repair............	81143	4	(Z)	(Z)	(Z)	(Z)
Personal and laundry services...............	812	2,218	74.6	11.1	12.7	14.4
Barber shops................	812111	97	23.4	22.5	3.1	18.0
Beauty salons................	812112	961	91.5	11.8	5.7	13.1
Nail salons and other personal care services..............	812113, 81219	377	78.1	3.8	40.3	4.2
Drycleaning & laundry services..............	8123	327	58.5	15.1	18.6	29.2
Funeral homes, cemeteries, and crematories..........	8122	106	38.6	10.7	2.8	9.7
Other personal services..............	8129	350	64.6	10.2	1.8	15.7
Membership associations and organizations............	813	1,800	54.6	10.1	3.0	7.6
Religious organizations..............	8131	1,025	48.4	9.9	3.1	6.8
Civic, social, advocacy organizations, grantmaking & giving services........	8132,3,4	579	67.0	11.1	3.0	9.2
Business, professional, political, and similar organizations [9]........	8139	76	37.3	9.9	3.1	11.1
Labor unions.............	81393	121	58.8	6.6	2.2	4.5
Private households............	814	722	89.3	8.4	3.7	35.2

X Not applicable. Z Base less than 50,000. [1] Based on the North American Industry Classification System, 2007; see Section 15. [2] The Current Population Survey (CPS) allows respondents to choose more than one race. Data represent persons who selected this race group only and exclude persons reporting more than one race. See also comments on race in text for Section 1. [3] Persons of Hispanic or Latino ethnicity may be of any race. [4] Excludes NAICS 54194 (veterinary services). [5] Excludes NAICS 56173 (landscaping services). [6] Excludes NAICS 7224 (drinking places, alcoholic beverages). [7] Excludes NAICS 811192 (car washes). [8] Excludes NAICS 81143 (footwear and leather goods repair). [9] Excludes NAICS 81393 (labor unions).

Source: U.S. Bureau of Labor Statistics, "Employment and Earnings Online," <http://www.bls.gov/opub/ee/home.htm> and <http://www.bls.gov/cps/home.htm>.

Table 1291. Selected Service-Related Industries—Establishments, Employees, and Annual Payroll by State: 2010

[For employees, 7,822 represents 7,822,000. Covers establishments with paid employees. Excludes most government employees, railroad employees, and self-employed persons. For statement on methodology, see Appendix III]

State	Professional, scientific, and technical services (NAICS 54) [1]			Administrative and support and waste management and remediation services (NAICS 56) [1]			Accommodation and food services (NAICS 72) [1]		
	Establish-ments	Employ-ees [2] (1,000)	Annual payroll (mil. dol.)	Establish-ments	Employ-ees [2] (1,000)	Annual payroll (mil. dol.)	Establish-ments	Employ-ees [2] (1,000)	Annual payroll (mil. dol.)
United States........	851,506	7,822	543,074	381,774	8,977	304,091	643,960	11,312	185,591
Alabama...............	9,386	94	5,820	4,117	118	3,015	8,123	147	1,972
Alaska.................	1,966	17	1,068	1,067	20	937	1,993	26	592
Arizona................	16,263	127	7,632	8,219	206	7,393	11,438	236	3,793
Arkansas..............	5,759	33	1,522	2,526	50	1,260	5,290	90	1,135
California..............	113,033	1,168	88,649	41,160	1,072	40,807	75,463	1,303	23,656
Colorado...............	23,712	174	12,826	8,247	203	8,557	12,207	220	3,690
Connecticut............	9,477	99	7,653	5,241	81	3,362	8,004	129	2,548
Delaware..............	2,519	24	1,912	1,352	26	1,008	1,910	31	539
District of Columbia.....	4,955	89	10,113	1,147	34	1,335	2,264	55	1,443
Florida................	69,056	418	24,367	32,062	1,168	40,887	35,543	730	12,406
Georgia...............	27,903	229	14,625	11,767	306	9,176	18,567	343	5,100
Hawaii................	3,342	25	1,295	1,852	44	1,237	3,483	90	2,180
Idaho.................	4,232	32	1,601	2,146	34	792	3,512	51	677
Illinois................	38,655	349	26,770	16,535	444	13,306	26,879	454	7,490
Indiana...............	12,912	100	5,241	7,141	150	4,459	12,718	245	3,332
Iowa..................	6,243	46	2,344	3,581	65	1,802	6,918	111	1,400
Kansas................	7,172	58	3,037	3,494	71	2,117	5,898	102	1,297
Kentucky..............	8,132	66	2,944	4,011	82	2,051	7,517	151	2,031
Louisiana..............	11,555	88	4,734	4,537	101	3,033	8,657	178	2,861
Maine.................	3,516	23	1,221	1,954	22	598	3,960	46	829
Maryland..............	19,613	233	17,575	7,973	170	6,191	10,986	191	3,284
Massachusetts.........	21,334	247	22,752	9,730	191	7,431	16,437	252	4,813
Michigan..............	21,847	234	15,518	11,378	268	8,112	19,449	324	4,489
Minnesota.............	16,439	135	8,239	6,975	130	4,521	11,165	210	3,152
Mississippi............	4,751	32	1,393	2,248	45	1,109	4,956	113	1,804
Missouri..............	13,366	139	8,210	7,275	144	4,216	12,313	231	3,332
Montana..............	3,545	17	743	1,672	19	504	3,391	45	623
Nebraska..............	4,409	50	2,604	2,620	46	1,379	4,243	67	827
Nevada................	8,147	52	3,038	4,051	84	2,672	5,733	289	7,873
New Hampshire.........	3,921	29	1,710	2,182	48	1,925	3,538	52	884
New Jersey.............	29,890	317	24,266	13,230	257	9,184	19,543	275	5,430
New Mexico............	4,769	47	3,052	1,892	41	1,092	4,089	79	1,180
New York..............	58,887	566	46,116	25,009	465	20,468	47,433	616	12,799
North Carolina..........	22,693	180	11,387	11,510	224	6,619	19,120	338	4,858
North Dakota...........	1,553	11	520	928	11	291	1,833	32	408
Ohio..................	24,294	228	13,394	13,361	304	9,070	23,143	422	5,511
Oklahoma.............	9,326	63	3,346	4,395	89	2,693	7,131	131	1,720
Oregon................	11,638	95	4,448	5,249	76	2,260	10,319	144	2,295
Pennsylvania...........	29,692	309	20,826	14,809	273	8,509	27,683	422	6,321
Rhode Island...........	3,027	23	1,520	1,686	21	641	2,945	41	684
South Carolina.........	9,701	78	4,177	5,407	122	3,412	9,532	175	2,485
South Dakota..........	1,809	11	432	1,073	11	289	2,359	38	513
Tennessee.............	11,039	101	5,420	6,477	185	5,577	11,689	229	3,291
Texas.................	59,757	566	40,436	25,295	830	27,249	46,045	909	13,645
Utah..................	8,726	67	3,479	3,908	102	3,057	4,851	91	1,265
Vermont...............	2,176	21	1,053	1,081	8	214	1,896	30	467
Virginia...............	28,959	415	33,973	10,262	232	8,969	16,219	301	4,735
Washington............	20,062	161	11,233	8,812	125	4,878	16,039	224	3,947
West Virginia..........	2,994	24	1,037	1,467	30	816	3,682	61	821
Wisconsin.............	11,316	102	5,380	6,716	123	3,444	14,130	218	2,715
Wyoming..............	2,038	9	420	947	6	169	1,724	26	446

[1] North American Industry Classification System, 2007. See text, section 15. [2] For employees on the payroll for the pay period including March 12.

Source: U.S. Census Bureau, "County Business Patterns," June 2012, <http://www.census.gov/econ/cbp/index.html>.

Table 1292. Professional, Scientific, and Technical Services—Estimated Revenue: 2005 to 2010

[In millions of dollars (1,069,684 represents $1,069,684,000,000). For taxable employer firms. Estimates have been adjusted to the results of the 2007 Economic Census. Based on the Service Annual Survey and administrative data; see Appendix III]

Kind of business	2002 NAICS code [1]	2005	2006	2007	2008	2009	2010
Professional, scientific, and technical services (except notaries)	**54**	**1,069,684**	**1,150,967**	**1,258,014**	**1,323,897**	**1,258,045**	**1,304,872**
Legal services (except notaries)	5411	216,352	227,575	239,397	244,511	237,200	240,313
Offices of lawyers	54111	204,121	215,254	227,768	232,770	226,033	229,082
Other legal services	54119	12,231	12,321	11,629	11,741	11,167	11,231
Accounting, tax preparation, bookkeeping and payroll services	5412	97,088	103,482	114,110	120,060	118,031	116,142
Offices of certified public accountants	541211	56,285	60,244	66,588	69,233	68,915	66,509
Tax preparation services	541213	4,617	4,832	5,251	5,526	5,665	5,664
Payroll services	541214	23,835	25,646	28,916	31,050	28,932	29,073
Other accounting services	541219	12,351	12,760	13,355	14,251	14,519	14,896
Architectural, engineering, & related services	5413	213,247	232,296	254,201	267,915	234,960	226,199
Architectural services	54131	30,186	32,587	37,150	37,759	29,802	26,050
Landscape architectural services	54132	3,711	4,085	4,365	4,365	3,385	3,058
Engineering services	54133	159,245	173,861	187,532	199,943	178,375	172,403
Testing laboratories	54138	9,605	10,093	12,387	13,469	12,701	13,631
Other related services	54134,5,6,7	10,500	11,670	12,767	12,379	10,697	11,057
Specialized design services	5414	18,761	19,548	20,554	19,963	16,180	16,109
Interior design services	54141	8,040	8,899	9,799	9,290	6,814	6,394
Graphic design services	54143	8,328	8,342	8,281	8,286	7,133	7,478
All other design services	54142,9	2,393	2,307	2,474	2,387	2,233	2,237
Computer systems design and services	5415	196,050	213,359	244,389	265,719	260,466	283,790
Custom computer programming services	541511	67,163	72,232	84,896	92,246	89,766	102,625
Computer systems design services	541512	89,144	98,047	110,159	116,817	110,227	116,441
Computer facilities management services	541513	24,473	26,368	30,133	35,778	39,245	42,759
Other computer-related services	541519	15,270	16,712	19,201	20,878	21,228	21,965
Management, scientific, and technical consulting services	5416	129,231	135,965	146,814	154,160	141,972	152,632
Management consulting services	54161	109,196	114,531	122,380	128,165	115,901	124,389
Environmental consulting services	54162	8,322	9,225	10,423	11,125	10,856	11,095
Other scientific and technical consulting services	54169	11,713	12,209	14,011	14,870	15,215	17,148
Scientific research and development services	5417	78,312	87,457	94,518	101,903	105,756	117,373
Research and development in physical, engineering and life sciences	54171	73,839	82,874	89,413	96,460	100,275	111,375
Research and development in social sciences and humanities	54172	4,473	4,583	5,105	5,443	5,481	5,998
Advertising and related services	5418	71,194	79,107	87,434	89,200	82,518	88,844
Advertising agencies	54181	25,425	27,879	30,666	32,058	30,887	33,476
Public relations agencies	54182	7,542	8,630	9,279	9,247	8,855	10,004
Media buying agencies	54183	2,689	3,696	4,606	4,955	4,321	4,375
Media representatives	54184	2,892	3,231	3,577	3,691	3,407	3,559
Display advertising	54185	7,015	7,842	9,111	9,142	7,595	7,799
Direct mail advertising	54186	12,342	12,464	12,360	11,486	10,048	10,745
All other advertising	54187,9	13,289	15,365	17,835	18,621	17,405	18,886
Other professional, scientific, and technical services	5419	49,449	52,178	56,597	60,466	60,962	63,470
Marketing research and public opinion polling	54191	12,806	14,170	15,493	16,322	15,501	16,738
Photographic services	54192	6,738	6,693	6,767	7,017	6,516	6,347
Photography studios, portrait	541921	4,904	4,856	5,055	5,139	4,956	4,808
Commercial photography	541922	1,834	1,837	1,712	1,878	1,560	1,539
Translation and interpretation services	54193	1,345	1,502	1,895	2,122	(S)	(S)
Veterinary services	54194	20,703	22,372	24,568	25,794	25,658	26,634
All other professional, scientific, and technical services	54199	7,857	7,441	7,874	9,211	10,218	10,475

S Data did not meet publication standards. [1] Based on the North American Industry Classification System, 2002; see Section 15.

Source: U.S. Census Bureau, "Service Annual Survey 2009: Professional, Scientific, and Technical Sector Services," February 2012, <http://www.census.gov/services/index.html>.

Table 1293. Selected Service Industries—E-Commerce Revenue: 2009 and 2010

[153,531 represents $153,531,000,000. Includes data only for businesses with paid employees, except for accommodation and food services, which also includes businesses with and without paid employees. Except as noted, based on the Service Annual Survey]

Kind of business	2002 NAICS code [1]	E-commerce revenue (mil. dol.) 2009	E-commerce revenue (mil. dol.) 2010	E-commerce as percent of total revenue, 2010	E-commerce revenue, percent distribution, 2010
Selected service industries, total	(X)	**153,531**	**164,567**	**2.3**	**100.0**
Selected transportation and warehousing [2]	(X)	6,774	7,021	2.4	2.8
Truck transportation	484	6,579	6,772	3.5	2.7
Couriers and messengers	492	(S)	(S)	(S)	(S)
Warehousing and storage	493	(S)	(S)	(S)	(S)
Information	51	53,872	55,335	5.0	21.7
Publishing industries	511	20,908	22,174	8.3	8.7
Online information services	51811	7,061	6,486	21.3	2.5
Selected finance [3]	(X)	12,583	12,892	2.7	5.1
Securities and commodity contracts intermediation and brokerage	5231	11,987	11,687	4.1	4.6
Rental and leasing services	532	9,576	9,503	8.5	3.7
Selected professional, scientific, and technical services [4]	54	23,532	25,406	1.9	10.0
Computer systems design and related services	5415	5,147	5,682	2.0	2.2
Administrative and support and waste management and remediation services	56	17,395	19,176	3.0	7.5
Travel arrangements and reservation services	5615	7,656	8,307	22.5	3.3
Health care and social assistance services	62	1,350	3,229	0.2	1.3
Arts, entertainment, and recreation services	71	4,158	4,618	2.4	1.8
Accommodation and food services [5]	72	16,655	18,620	3.0	7.3
Selected other services [6]	81	7,636	8,767	2.3	3.4
Repair and maintenance	811	920	974	0.7	0.4
Religious, grantmaking, civic, professional, and similar organizations	813	4,826	5,448	3.2	2.1

X Not applicable. S Data do not meet publication standards. [1] North American Industry Classification System (NAICS), 2002; see text Section 15. [2] Excludes NAICS 481 (air transportation), 482 (rail transportation), 483 (water transportation), 485 (transit and ground passenger transportation), 486 (pipeline transportation), 487 (scenic and sightseeing transportation), 488 (support activities for transportation), and 491 (postal service). [3] Excludes NAICS 521 (monetary authorities-central bank), 522 (credit intermediation and related activities), 5232 (securities and commodity exchanges), NAICS 52391 (miscellaneous intermediation), 52399 (all other financial investment activities), 524 (insurance carriers and related activities), and 525 (funds and trusts). [4] Excludes NAICS 54112 (offices of notaries). [5] Based on 2010 Annual Retail Trade Survey. [6] Excludes NAICS 81311 (religious organizations), 81393 (labor and similar organizations), 81394 (political organizations), and 814 (private households).

Source: U.S. Census Bureau, "E-Stats," <http://www.census.gov/econ/estats/>.

Table 1294. Forecast Summary—Media Supplier Advertising Revenues: 2000 to 2010

[In millions of dollars (177,500 represents $177,500,000,000). See source for definitions of types of advertising]

Media supplier	2000	2004	2005	2006	2007	2008	2009	2010
Total supplier ad revenue	**177,500**	**188,942**	**196,668**	**204,889**	**205,847**	**194,328**	**163,184**	**170,456**
Total [1]	175,535	186,979	196,398	202,701	205,523	191,951	162,744	167,936
Direct	31,108	39,688	42,477	45,882	48,680	48,190	42,444	42,484
Direct mail	18,250	22,559	23,085	24,478	24,890	23,459	19,853	20,604
Direct online [2]	560	4,440	6,371	8,785	11,355	13,554	13,656	15,022
Directories [3]	12,299	12,689	13,021	12,619	12,435	11,177	8,934	6,858
National	53,494	55,699	59,200	61,858	64,498	63,132	56,797	61,009
National television [3, 4]	25,574	31,452	33,231	33,712	34,820	35,141	33,723	36,210
Magazines [3]	19,025	17,961	19,351	20,373	20,975	19,533	15,554	15,623
National digital/online [5]	5,665	3,541	3,931	5,067	6,098	6,057	5,549	7,144
Network and satellite radio	1,065	1,175	1,161	1,178	1,226	1,220	1,100	1,145
National newspapers [3]	2,165	1,570	1,527	1,527	1,379	1,180	873	887
Local	90,933	91,591	94,721	94,961	92,345	80,630	63,504	64,443
Local newspapers [3]	46,506	45,133	45,880	45,074	40,830	33,559	23,949	21,909
Local TV [3, 6]	18,530	20,047	21,281	21,023	22,001	19,706	16,995	18,670
Local radio [3]	18,819	18,932	19,018	19,031	18,476	16,536	13,203	13,847
Emerging outdoor	195	377	425	545	741	914	920	1,146
Other outdoor	5,040	5,457	5,876	6,260	6,542	6,077	4,980	4,997
Local digital/online [5]	1,843	1,645	2,241	3,028	3,755	3,837	3,456	3,874
Political [7]	1,180	1,259	270	1,538	324	1,777	439	2,033
Olympics [8]	785	704	–	650	–	600	–	488

– Represents zero. [1] Excludes political and Olympic revenue. [2] Includes paid search, lead generation, and Internet yellow pages. [3] Excludes Internet-based advertising revenues. [4] Includes English and Spanish-language network TV, national cable, and national syndication. Excludes incremental olympic revenues. [5] Includes rich/online video, Internet classifieds, e-mail, digital display, and mobile. [6] Includes local broadcast and local cable TV. Excludes local political advertising revenues. [7] Total political advertising revenue on local broadcast and local cable TV. [8] Incremental advertising revenue from Olympics on network TV.

Source: MAGNAGLOBAL, New York, NY, (copyright), <http://www.magnaglobal.com>.

Table 1295. Administrative and Support and Waste Management and Remediation Services—Estimated Revenue: 2005 to 2010

[In millions of dollars (542,407 represents $542,407,000,000). For taxable and tax-exempt employer firms. Estimates have been adjusted to results of the 2007 Economic Census. Based on the Service Annual Survey and administrative data; see Appendix III]

Kind of business	2002 NAICS code [1]	2005	2006	2007	2008	2009	2010
Administrative and support and waste management and remediation services.................	**56**	**542,407**	**585,387**	**623,761**	**640,809**	**595,620**	**636,388**
Administrative and support services.............................	561	477,169	513,554	548,574	561,957	522,818	554,454
Office administrative services....................................	56111	38,143	38,654	39,295	40,970	42,558	45,520
Facilities support services......................................	56121	18,246	21,746	25,735	28,994	29,280	29,946
Employment services...	5613	171,183	188,935	202,682	204,867	184,183	206,574
Employment placement agencies.............................	56131	8,788	10,115	11,786	12,418	10,463	10,786
Temporary help services..	56132	90,654	98,710	105,691	103,792	86,111	100,689
Professional employer organizations.........................	56133	71,741	80,110	85,205	88,657	87,609	95,099
Business support services.......................................	5614	54,820	59,733	62,297	62,797	59,626	59,244
Document preparation services................................	56141	2,881	3,193	3,404	3,286	2,891	2,825
Telephone call centers..	56142	15,138	16,370	16,955	17,156	16,761	15,635
Telephone answering services.............................	561421	1,988	1,962	2,289	2,327	2,260	2,287
Telemarketing bureaus......................................	561422	13,150	14,408	14,666	14,829	14,501	13,348
Business service centers..	56143	9,962	9,663	10,368	10,323	9,167	9,024
Private mail centers...	561431	2,022	2,107	2,149	2,146	1,947	1,953
Other business service centers (including copy shops)............................	561439	7,940	7,556	8,219	8,177	7,220	7,071
Collection agencies..	56144	11,557	11,704	12,245	11,986	11,120	11,742
Credit bureaus..	56145	6,246	8,063	8,191	7,860	7,760	7,794
Other business support services..............................	56149	9,036	10,740	11,134	12,186	11,927	12,224
Repossession services.......................................	561491	609	645	717	810	862	764
Court reporting and stenotype services..................	561492	1,953	2,175	2,248	2,207	2,205	2,233
All other business support services.......................	561499	6,474	7,920	8,169	9,169	8,860	9,227
Travel arrangement and reservation services..............	5615	30,978	33,339	37,112	38,006	33,863	36,997
Travel agencies...	56151	12,986	14,820	17,289	17,093	14,792	16,449
Tour operators..	56152	3,818	3,856	4,397	5,279	4,887	5,283
Other travel arrangement and reservation services..........	56159	14,174	14,663	15,426	15,634	14,184	15,265
Convention and visitors bureaus............................	561591	1,239	1,302	1,503	1,559	1,437	1,414
All other travel arrangement and reservation services..	561599	12,935	13,361	13,923	14,075	12,747	13,851
Investigation and security services............................	5616	37,299	38,274	40,904	43,065	42,179	41,871
Investigation, guard, and armored car services...............	56161	23,348	23,816	24,911	25,804	25,403	24,561
Investigation services..	561611	3,294	3,611	3,887	3,820	3,889	4,085
Security guards and patrol services.......................	561612	17,887	17,964	18,799	19,619	19,129	18,082
Armored car services...	561613	2,167	2,241	2,225	2,365	2,385	2,394
Security systems services......................................	56162	13,951	14,458	15,993	17,261	16,776	17,310
Security systems services (except locksmiths).............	561621	12,474	12,853	14,360	15,624	15,312	15,822
Locksmiths..	561622	1,477	1,605	1,633	1,637	1,464	1,488
Services to buildings and dwellings...........................	5617	90,841	96,422	103,364	105,353	97,616	99,920
Exterminating and pest control services.....................	56171	8,118	8,483	8,693	8,936	9,135	9,543
Janitorial services..	56172	29,779	30,116	33,021	34,887	32,591	33,565
Landscaping services...	56173	45,856	50,398	53,910	53,200	47,929	49,307
Carpet and upholstery cleaning services....................	56174	2,877	2,900	2,962	3,097	2,870	2,629
Other services to buildings and dwellings..................	56179	4,211	4,525	4,778	5,233	5,091	4,876
Other support services..	5619	35,659	36,451	37,185	37,905	33,513	34,382
Packaging and labeling services..............................	56191	5,097	5,050	5,050	5,188	4,874	5,309
Convention and trade show organizers......................	56192	10,625	11,264	11,238	11,998	9,618	10,128
All other support services......................................	56199	19,937	20,137	20,897	20,719	19,021	18,945
Waste management and remediation services..............	562	65,238	71,833	75,187	78,852	72,802	81,934
Waste collection..	5621	34,936	38,857	40,462	43,276	40,049	41,373
Solid waste collection...	562111	32,534	35,910	36,999	39,495	36,797	37,962
Hazardous waste collection....................................	562112	1,547	1,728	1,857	1,986	1,824	1,994
Other waste collection..	562119	855	1,219	1,606	1,795	1,428	1,417
Waste treatment and disposal..................................	5622	13,104	14,096	14,264	14,496	13,211	14,097
Hazardous waste treatment and disposal...................	562211	4,532	5,138	5,864	5,972	5,945	6,605
Solid waste landfill...	562212	5,858	5,902	5,648	5,695	4,983	5,091
Solid waste combustors and incinerators...................	562213	2,051	2,348	2,081	2,123	1,729	1,897
Other nonhazardous waste treatment and disposal..........	562219	663	708	671	706	554	504
Remediation and other waste management services.........	5629	17,198	18,880	20,461	21,080	19,542	26,464
Remediation services..	56291	10,776	11,950	12,424	12,544	12,256	17,860
Materials recovery facility......................................	56292	2,984	3,264	4,072	4,636	3,679	4,854
All other waste management services........................	56299	3,438	3,666	3,965	3,900	3,607	3,750
Septic tank and related services............................	562991	2,277	2,428	2,553	2,573	2,403	2,504
All other miscellaneous waste management services..	562998	1,161	1,238	1,412	1,327	1,204	1,246

[1] North American Industry Classification System, 2002; see text, Section 15.

Source: U.S. Census Bureau, "Service Annual Survey 2010: Administrative and Support and Waste Management and Remediation Sector Services," February 2012, <http://www.census.gov/services/index.html>.

Table 1296. Estimated Accommodation and Food Service Sales by Kind of Business: 2000 to 2010

[In millions of dollars (441,944 represents $441,944,000,000). Estimates are based on data from the Annual Retail Trade Survey and administrative records and have been adjusted to the final results of the 2007 Economic Census]

Kind of business	2007 NAICS code [1]	2000	2005	2006	2007	2008	2009	2010
Accommodation and food services, total	72	**441,944**	**558,465**	**596,497**	**628,055**	**639,596**	**613,086**	**629,268**
Accommodation	721	137,683	162,002	173,711	183,504	183,494	162,016	163,267
Traveler accommodation	7211	133,118	156,856	168,089	177,599	177,444	156,076	157,263
RV parks and recreational camps	7212	3,588	4,108	4,507	4,740	4,867	4,748	4,797
Rooming and boarding houses	7213	977	1,038	1,115	1,165	1,183	1,192	1,207
Food services and drinking places [2]	722	304,261	396,463	422,786	444,551	456,102	451,070	466,001
Full service restaurants	7221	133,579	174,119	186,091	195,505	196,641	192,766	197,193
Limited service eating places	7222	127,519	169,034	178,189	186,001	194,260	195,233	203,997
Drinking places	7224	15,330	18,053	19,333	19,888	20,232	19,900	20,129

[1] North American Industry Classification System, 2007; see text, Section 15. [2] Includes other kinds of business not shown separately.

Source: U.S. Census Bureau, "Annual Accommodation and Food Services 2010," March 2012, <http://www.census.gov/retail/>.

Table 1297. Lodging Industry Summary: 1990 to 2011

Year	Average occupancy rate (percent)	Average room rate (dollars)	Room size of property	2011 Establish-ments	2011 Rooms (millions)	Item	2011 Business traveler	2011 Leisure traveler
1990	63.3	57.96	Total	51,015	4.8	Typical night:		
1995	65.5	66.65				Made reservations		
2000	63.7	85.89	Percent:			(percent)	94	91
2005	63.1	91.04	Under 75 rooms	56.6	25.4	Amount paid (dol.)	$129.00	$109.00
2008	60.4	107.40	75--149 rooms	33.5	36.9	Length of stay:		
2009	54.7	98.07	150--299 rooms	8.6	18.1	One night	40	47
2010	57.6	98.06	300--500 rooms	2.2	8.7	Two nights	22	27
2011	60.0	101.70	Over 500 rooms	1.0	10.8	Three or more	38	26

Source: American Hotel & Lodging Association, Washington, DC Lodging Industry Profile, annual (copyright). See also <http://www.ahla.com>.

Table 1298. Commercial and Noncommercial Services—Food and Drink Establishments and Sales: 1990 to 2012

[In millions of dollars (238,149 represents $238,149,000,000). Excludes military. Data refer to sales to consumers of food and alcoholic beverages. Sales are estimated. For details, see source]

Type of establishment	Establish-ments, 2008	Sales (mil. dol.) 1990	1995	2000	2005	2010	2011 [1]	2012 [1]
Total	957,354	238,149	294,631	377,652	486,494	581,065	608,066	629,330
Commercial restaurant services [2,3]	753,197	211,606	265,910	345,345	445,078	531,732	555,778	575,103
Eating and drinking places [2]	507,507	155,552	198,293	259,743	329,598	391,423	424,942	438,126
Full-service restaurants	222,070	77,811	96,396	133,834	165,170	188,706	195,711	201,387
Limited-service restaurants [4]	213,835	[5] 69,798	[5] 92,901	107,147	136,903	162,350	168,527	173,751
Snack and nonalcoholic beverage bars [5]	53,678	([5])	([5])	12,867	17,150	25,309	26,580	27,670
Bars and taverns [6]	46,624	9,533	9,948	12,412	15,002	17,722	18,359	18,910
Managed services [2]	23,250	14,149	18,186	24,841	32,030	40,331	42,595	44,417
Manufacturing and industrial plants	(NA)	3,856	4,814	6,223	6,570	6,696	7,007	7,340
Colleges and universities	(NA)	2,788	3,989	5,879	9,283	13,097	13,889	14,418
Recreation and sports	24,942	2,871	3,866	4,772	11,397	12,679	12,923	13,497
Lodging places	11,620	13,568	15,561	19,438	23,854	27,167	30,000	31,414
Retail hosts [2,7]	132,792	9,513	12,589	14,869	22,502	30,774	33,153	35,112
Department store restaurants	2,222	876	1,038	903	490	(NA)	(NA)	(NA)
Grocery store restaurants [7]	54,397	5,432	6,624	7,116	12,032	(NA)	(NA)	(NA)
Gasoline service stations	59,087	1,718	2,520	4,693	6,137	(NA)	(NA)	(NA)
Noncommercial restaurant services [2]	204,157	26,543	28,722	32,307	41,416	49,333	52,288	54,227
Employee restaurant services	3,003	1,864	1,364	986	548	406	424	441
Industrial, commercial organizations	765	1,603	1,129	717	260	(NA)	(NA)	(NA)
Educational restaurant services	106,224	7,671	9,059	9,977	11,007	12,787	13,824	14,324
Elementary and secondary schools	101,957	3,700	4,533	5,039	5,320	6,243	6,618	6,845
Hospitals	5,799	8,968	9,219	9,982	12,332	15,611	15,755	16,376
Miscellaneous	52,448	2,892	3,673	4,898	9,703	11,167	(NA)	(NA)
Clubs	29,246	1,993	2,278	3,164	7,555	9,000	9,404	9,712

NA Not available. [1] Projection. [2] Includes other groupings, not shown separately. [3] Data for establishments with payroll. [4] Fast-food restaurants. [5] Snack and nonalcoholic beverage bars included in limited service restaurants prior to 1997. [6] For establishments serving food. [7] Includes a portion of delicatessen sales in grocery stores.

Source: National Restaurant Association, *Restaurant Numbers: 25 Year History, 1970–1995,* Washington, DC, 1998; *Restaurant Industry in Review,* annual; and *Restaurant Industry Forecast, 2012* (copyright).

Table 1299. Other Services—Estimated Revenue for Employer Firms by Kind of Business: 2007 to 2010

[In millions of dollars (405,282 represents $405,282,000,000). For employer firms. Estimates have been adjusted to the results of the 2007 Economic Census. Based on the Service Annual Survey; see Appendix III]

Kind of business	2002 NAICS code [1]	2007	2008	2009	2010
Other services [2]	**81**	**405,282**	**384,778**	**363,920**	**384,313**
Repair and maintenance [3]	811	137,732	137,127	128,212	131,468
Automotive repair and maintenance	8111	85,887	84,055	79,682	82,485
Automotive mechanical and electrical repair and maintenance	81111	43,555	42,253	40,243	41,825
General automotive repair	811111	37,722	36,763	34,864	36,559
Automotive body, paint, interior, and glass repair	81112	30,006	29,662	27,655	28,531
Automotive body, paint, and interior repair and maintenance	811121	26,413	25,983	24,390	25,500
Other automotive repair and maintenance	81119	12,326	12,140	11,784	12,129
Electronic and precision equipment repair and maintenance	8112	19,327	18,837	18,976	19,150
Commercial and industrial machinery and equipment (except automotive and electronic) repair and maintenance	8113	25,962	27,581	23,510	24,030
Personal and household goods repair and maintenance	8114	6,556	6,654	6,044	5,803
Home and garden equipment and appliance repair and maintenance	81141	2,595	2,599	2,464	2,388
Personal and laundry services [3]	812	82,105	83,430	81,391	82,776
Personal care services	8121	26,304	27,236	26,783	27,532
Hair, nail, and skin care services	81211	20,903	21,378	21,159	21,971
Barber shops	812111	568	580	582	599
Beauty salons	812112	19,010	19,231	18,913	19,507
Nail salons	812113	1,325	1,567	1,664	1,865
Other personal care services	81219	5,401	5,858	5,624	5,561
Death care services	8122	15,293	15,451	15,180	15,537
Funeral homes and funeral services	81221	11,943	12,354	12,181	12,566
Cemeteries and crematories	81222	3,350	3,097	2,999	2,971
Drycleaning and laundry services	8123	23,234	22,790	21,968	21,967
Coin-operated laundries and drycleaners	81231	3,354	3,340	3,299	3,546
Drycleaning and laundry services (except coin-operated)	81232	8,086	7,919	7,664	7,538
Linen and uniform supply	81233	11,794	11,531	11,005	10,883
Pet care (except veterinary) services	81291	2,346	2,499	2,544	2,772
Photofinishing	81292	2,025	1,964	1,913	1,907
Parking lots and garages	81293	8,276	8,310	8,330	8,388
All other personal services	81299	4,627	5,180	4,673	4,673
Religious, grantmaking, civic, professional, and similar organizations (except religious, labor, and political organizations) [4]	813	185,445	164,221	154,317	170,069
Grantmaking and giving services	8132	93,275	70,433	59,944	71,998
Social advocacy organizations	8133	19,729	21,095	21,221	22,676
Civic and social organizations	8134	15,444	15,164	14,750	15,042
Business, professional, and other organizations (except labor and political organizations)	8139	56,997	57,529	58,402	60,353

[1] Based on the North American Industry Classification System, 2002; see Section 15. [2] Except public administration, religious, labor, and political organizations, and private households. [3] For taxable firms only. [4] For tax-exempt firms only.

Source: U.S. Census Bureau, "Service Annual Survey 2010: Other Sector Services," February 2012, <http://www.census.gov/services/index.html>.

Table 1300. National Nonprofit Associations—Number by Type: 1980 to 2012

[Data compiled during last few months of year previous to year shown and the beginning months of year shown]

Type	1980	1990	2000	2005	2007 [1]	2008	2009	2010	2011	2012
Total	**14,726**	**22,289**	**21,840**	**22,720**	**25,048**	**25,176**	**24,100**	**23,983**	**24,168**	**23,809**
Trade, business, commercial	3,118	3,918	3,880	3,789	4,072	4,003	3,840	3,761	3,792	3,715
Agriculture and environment	677	940	1,103	1,170	1,353	1,439	1,365	1,442	1,449	1,463
Legal, governmental, public admin., military	529	792	790	868	938	951	927	913	915	893
Scientific, engineering, technical	1,039	1,417	1,302	1,354	1,505	1,588	1,549	1,563	1,569	1,561
Educational	[2] 2,376	1,291	1,297	1,318	1,471	1,530	1,462	1,444	1,446	1,444
Cultural	([2])	1,886	1,786	1,733	1,881	1,896	1,761	1,717	1,721	1,677
Social welfare	994	1,705	1,829	2,072	2,307	2,582	2,531	2,673	2,727	2,805
Health, medical	1,413	2,227	2,495	2,982	3,383	3,552	3,460	3,481	3,511	3,569
Public affairs	1,068	2,249	1,776	1,854	1,951	1,842	1,769	1,734	1,749	1,697
Fraternal, nationality, ethnic	435	573	525	550	580	523	482	461	465	347
Religious	797	1,172	1,123	1,147	1,204	1,146	1,101	1,056	1,058	1,023
Veteran, hereditary, patriotic	208	462	835	774	774	645	602	585	587	565
Hobby, avocational	910	1,475	1,330	1,433	1,615	1,511	1,421	1,374	1,385	1,330
Athletic sports	504	840	717	762	960	1,008	972	946	955	931
Labor unions	235	253	232	208	227	212	195	188	190	182
Chambers of Commerce [3]	105	168	143	135	169	162	147	142	144	135
Greek and non-Greek letter societies	318	340	296	349	335	325	309	305	305	299
Fan clubs	(NA)	581	381	314	323	261	207	198	200	173

NA Not available. [1] The increase in the number of associations comes from the increase in newly discovered and established associations. [2] Data for cultural associations included with educational associations. [3] National and binational. Includes trade and tourism organizations.

Source: Gale, Cengage Learning, Farmington Hills, MI, compiled from *Encyclopedia of Associations,* annual (copyright).

Section 28
Foreign Commerce and Aid

This section presents data on the flow of goods, services, and capital between the United States and other countries; changes in official reserve assets of the United States; international investments; and foreign assistance programs.

The Bureau of Economic Analysis publishes current figures on U.S. international transactions and the U.S. international investment position in its monthly Survey of *Current Business*. *Statistics* for the foreign aid programs are presented by the Agency for International Development (AID) in its annual U.S. *Overseas Loans and Grants and Assistance from International Organizations.*

The principal source of merchandise import and export data is the U.S. Census Bureau. Current data are presented monthly in *U.S. International Trade in Goods and Services report Series* FT 900. The *Guide to Foreign Trade Statistics*, found on the Census Bureau Web site at <http://www.census.gov/foreign-trade/guide/index.html>, lists the Census Bureau's monthly and annual products and services in this field. In addition, the International Trade Administration and the Bureau of Economic Analysis present summary as well as selected commodity and country data for U.S. foreign trade on their Web sites: <http://www.trade.gov/mas/ian/tradestatistics/index.asp> and <http://www.bea.gov/international/index.htm>, respectively. The merchandise trade data published by the Bureau of Economic Analysis in the *Survey of Current Business* and on the Web include balance of payments adjustments to the Census Bureau data. The U.S. Treasury Department's *Monthly Treasury Statement of Receipts and Outlays of the United States Government* contains information on import duties. The International Trade Commission, U.S. Department of Agriculture (agricultural products), U.S. Department of Energy (mineral fuels, like petroleum and coal), and the U.S. Geological Survey (minerals) release various reports and specialized products on U.S. trade.

International accounts—The international transactions tables (Tables 1286 to 1288) show, for given time periods, the transfer of goods, services, grants, and financial assets and liabilities between the United States and the rest of the world. The international investment position table (Table 1289) presents, for specific dates, the value of U.S. investments abroad and of foreign investments in the United States. The movement of foreign and U.S. capital as presented in the balance of payments is not the only factor affecting the total value of foreign investments. Among the other factors are changes in the valuation of assets or liabilities, including changes in prices of securities, defaults, expropriations, and write-offs.

Direct investment abroad means the ownership or control, directly or indirectly, by one person of 10 percent or more of the voting securities of an incorporated business enterprise or an equivalent interest in an unincorporated business enterprise. Direct investment position is the value of U.S. parents' claims on the equity of and receivables due from foreign affiliates, less foreign affiliates' receivables due from their U.S. parents. Income consists of parents' shares in the earnings of their affiliates plus net interest received by parents on intercompany accounts, less withholding taxes on dividends and interest.

Foreign aid—Foreign assistance is divided into three major categories—grants (military supplies and services and other grants), credits, and other assistance (through net accumulation of foreign currency claims from the sale of agricultural commodities). *Grants* are transfers for which no payment is expected (other than a limited percentage of the foreign currency "counterpart" funds generated by the grant), or which at most involve an obligation on the part of the receiver to extend aid to the United States or other countries to achieve a common objective. *Credits* are loan disbursements or transfers under other agreements which give rise to specific obligations to repay, over a period of years, usually with interest. All known returns to the U.S. government stemming from grants and credits (reverse grants, returns of grants, and payments of principal) are taken into account in net grants and net credits, but no allowance is made for interest or commissions. *Other assistance* represents the transfer of U.S. farm products in exchange for foreign currencies (plus, since enactment of Public Law 87-128, currency claims from principal and interest collected on credits extended under the farm products program), less the government's disbursements of the currencies as grants, credits, or for purchases. The net acquisition of currencies represents net transfers of resources to foreign countries under the agricultural programs, in addition to those classified as grants or credits.

In 1952, economic, technical, and military aid programs were combined under the Mutual Security Act, which in turn was followed by the Foreign Assistance Act passed in 1961. Appropriations to provide military assistance were also made in the Department of Defense Appropriation Act (rather than the Foreign Assistance Appropriation Act) beginning in 1966 for certain countries in Southeast Asia and in other legislation concerning programs for specific countries (such as Israel). Figures on activity under the Foreign Assistance Act as reported in the *Foreign Grants and Credits* series differ from data published by AID or its immediate predecessors, due largely to differences in reporting, timing, and treatment of particular items.

Exports—Export statistics consist of goods valued at more than $2,500 per commodity shipped by individuals and organizations (including exporters, freight forwarders, and carriers) from the U.S. to other countries. The Census Bureau compiles export data primarily from three sources: Shipper's Export Declaration documents filed with Customs and Border Protection and sent to the U.S. Census Bureau (3 percent of all transactions), comparable data in electronic form submitted directly by exporters and their agents (63 percent), and special computer tapes from Canada for U.S. exports to Canada (34 percent). Estimates are made for low-value exports by country of destination, and based on bilateral trade patterns. They include U.S. exports under mutual security programs and exclude shipments to U.S. Armed Forces for their own use.

The value reported in the export statistics is generally equivalent to a free alongside ship (f.a.s.) value at the U.S. port of export, based on the transaction price, including inland freight, insurance, and other charges incurred in placing the merchandise alongside the carrier at the U.S. port of exportation. This value, as defined, excludes the cost of loading merchandise aboard the exporting carrier and also excludes freight, insurance, and any other charges or transportation and other costs beyond the U.S. port of exportation. The country of destination is defined as the country of ultimate destination or country where the merchandise is to be consumed, further processed, or manufactured, as known to the shipper at the time of exportation. When ultimate destination is not known, the shipment is statistically credited to the last country to which the shipper knows the merchandise will be shipped in the same form as exported.

Statistics for U.S. exports to Canada are based on import documents filed with Canadian agencies and forwarded to the U.S. Census Bureau under a 1987 data exchange agreement. Under this agreement, each country eliminated most cross-border export documents; maintains detailed statistics on cross-border imports; exchanges monthly files of cross-border import statistics; and publishes exchanged statistics in place of previously compiled export statistics.

Prior to 1989, exports were based on Schedule B, Statistical Classification of Domestic and Foreign Commodities Exported from the United States. Beginning in 1989, Schedule B classifications are based on the Harmonized System and coincide with the Standard International Trade Classification, Revision 3. This revision will affect the comparability of most export series beginning with the 1989 data for commodities.

Imports—Import statistics consist of goods valued at more than $2,000 per commodity shipped by individuals and organizations (including importers and customs brokers) into the U.S. from other countries. The Census Bureau compiles import data from records filed with Customs and Border Protection, usually within 10 days after the merchandise enters the United States. Estimates are made for low-value shipments by country of origin, based on previous bilateral trade patterns and periodically updated. Statistics for over 95 percent of all commodity transactions are compiled from records filed electronically with Customs and forwarded as

computer tape files to the U.S. Census Bureau. Statistics for other transactions are compiled from hard-copy documents filed with Customs and forwarded on a flow basis for U.S. Census Bureau processing.

Data on import values are presented on two valuations bases in this section: The c.i.f. (cost, insurance, and freight) and the customs import value (as appraised by the U.S. Customs Service in accordance with legal requirements of the Tariff Act of 1930, as amended). This latter valuation, primarily used for collection of import duties, frequently does not reflect the actual transaction value. Country of origin is defined as country where the merchandise was grown, mined, or manufactured. If country of origin is unknown, country of shipment is reported.

Imports are classified either as "General imports" or "Imports for consumption." *General imports* are a combination of entries for immediate consumption, entries into customs bonded warehouses, and entries into U.S. Foreign Trade Zones, thus generally reflecting total arrivals of merchandise. *Imports for consumption* are a combination of entries for immediate consumption, withdrawals from warehouses for consumption, and entries of merchandise into U.S. customs territory from U.S. Foreign Trade Zones, thus generally reflecting the total of the commodities entered into U.S. consumption channels.

Beginning in 1989, import statistics are based on the Harmonized Tariff Schedule of the United States, which coincides with import Standard International Trade Classification, Revision 3. This revision will affect the comparability of most import series beginning with the 1989 data.

Area coverage—Except as noted, the geographic area covered by the export and import trade statistics is the United States Customs area (includes the 50 states, the District of Columbia, and Puerto Rico), the U.S. Virgin Islands (effective January 1981), and U.S. Foreign Trade Zones (effective July 1982). Data for selected tables and total values for 1980 have been revised to reflect the U.S. Virgin Islands' trade with foreign countries, where possible.

Statistical reliability—For a discussion of statistical collection and estimation, sampling procedures, and measures of statistical reliability applicable to Census Bureau data, see Appendix III.

Table 1301. U.S. International Transactions by Type of Transaction: 1990 to 2011

[In millions of dollars (706,975 represents $706,975,000,000). Minus sign (−) indicates debits]

Type of transaction [1]	1990	1995	2000	2005	2006	2007	2008	2009	2010	2011
Exports of goods and services and income receipts [1]	706,975	1,004,631	1,425,260	1,824,780	2,144,443	2,488,394	2,656,585	2,180,553	2,518,767	2,847,988
Exports of goods and services	535,233	794,387	1,072,782	1,287,441	1,459,823	1,654,561	1,842,682	1,578,945	1,842,485	2,103,367
Goods, balance of payments basis [2]	387,401	575,204	784,781	911,686	1,039,406	1,163,957	1,307,499	1,069,733	1,288,882	1,497,406
Services [2]	147,832	219,183	288,002	375,755	420,417	490,604	535,183	509,212	553,603	605,961
Transfers under U.S. military agency sales contracts [3][4]	9,932	14,643	6,210	12,082	15,587	17,091	14,711	16,013	14,752	17,946
Travel	43,007	63,395	82,891	82,160	86,187	97,355	110,423	94,187	103,481	116,115
Passenger fares	15,298	18,909	20,197	20,609	21,638	25,187	30,957	26,103	30,983	36,631
Other transportation	22,042	26,081	25,562	32,013	35,824	40,638	44,016	36,087	40,817	43,064
Royalties and license fees [5]	16,634	30,289	51,808	74,448	83,549	97,803	102,125	98,406	107,165	120,836
Other private services [5]	40,251	65,048	100,792	153,665	176,798	211,641	232,019	237,348	255,293	270,193
U.S. government miscellaneous services	668	818	542	778	834	890	933	1,069	1,112	1,176
Income receipts	171,742	210,244	352,478	537,339	684,620	833,834	813,903	601,609	676,282	744,621
Income receipts on U.S.-owned assets abroad	170,570	208,065	348,083	532,542	679,608	828,732	808,721	596,131	670,641	738,810
Direct investment receipts	65,973	95,260	151,839	294,538	324,816	370,758	413,739	357,793	444,044	480,238
Other private receipts	94,072	108,092	192,398	235,120	352,122	455,436	389,881	233,546	225,103	256,649
U.S. government receipts	10,525	4,713	3,846	2,884	2,670	2,538	5,101	4,792	1,494	1,923
Compensation of employees	1,172	2,179	4,395	4,796	5,012	5,102	5,182	5,478	5,641	5,811
Imports of goods and services and income payments	-759,290	-1,080,124	-1,782,832	-2,464,813	-2,853,549	-3,083,637	-3,207,834	-2,439,990	-2,829,645	-3,180,861
Imports of goods and services	-616,097	-890,771	-1,449,532	-1,996,065	-2,213,111	-2,351,288	-2,541,020	-1,958,099	-2,337,222	-2,663,247
Goods, balance of payments basis [2]	-498,438	-749,374	-1,230,568	-1,692,416	-1,875,095	-1,982,843	-2,137,608	-1,575,491	-1,934,006	-2,235,819
Services [2]	-117,659	-141,397	-218,964	-303,649	-338,016	-368,446	-403,413	-382,608	-403,216	-427,428
Direct defense expenditures [6]	-17,531	-10,043	-12,698	-27,676	-27,330	-27,917	-28,311	-30,474	-30,391	-29,510
Travel	-37,349	-44,916	-65,366	-69,930	-72,959	-77,127	-80,494	-74,132	-75,510	-78,651
Passenger fares	-10,531	-14,663	-23,613	-25,189	-26,646	-27,681	-31,841	-25,117	-27,256	-31,109
Other transportation	-24,966	-27,034	-37,209	-54,212	-55,320	-55,773	-56,696	-42,601	-51,258	-54,711
Royalties and license fees [5]	-3,135	-6,919	-16,606	-25,577	-25,038	-26,479	-29,623	-31,297	-33,434	-36,620
Other private services [5]	-22,229	-35,199	-61,085	-97,720	-127,308	-149,848	-172,543	-174,573	-180,586	-191,973
U.S. government miscellaneous services	-1,919	-2,623	-2,386	-3,345	-3,415	-3,621	-3,905	-4,415	-4,781	-4,854
Income payments	-143,192	-189,353	-333,300	-468,748	-640,438	-732,349	-666,814	-481,891	-492,423	-517,614
Income payments on foreign-owned assets in the United States	-139,728	-183,090	-322,345	-453,800	-624,912	-717,623	-650,880	-468,579	-479,624	-503,796
Direct investment payments	-3,450	-30,318	-56,910	-121,333	-150,770	-126,174	-129,447	-104,828	-146,149	-158,559
Other private payments	-95,508	-97,149	-180,918	-228,408	-338,897	-426,796	-354,609	-219,396	-196,354	-212,506
U.S. government payments	-40,770	-55,623	-84,517	-104,059	-135,245	-164,653	-166,824	-144,355	-137,121	-132,731
Compensation of employees	-3,464	-6,263	-10,955	-14,948	-15,526	-14,725	-15,934	-13,312	-12,799	-13,817
Unilateral current transfers, net [4]	-26,654	-38,074	-58,767	-105,741	-91,515	-115,061	-125,885	-122,459	-131,074	-133,053
U.S. government grants [4]	-10,359	-11,190	-16,836	-33,615	-27,767	-34,567	-36,461	-42,699	-42,736	-47,350
U.S. government pensions and other transfers	-3,224	-3,451	-4,705	-6,303	-6,508	-7,323	-8,390	-8,874	-9,581	-8,947
Private remittances and other transfers [7]	-13,070	-23,433	-37,226	-65,822	-57,240	-73,170	-81,034	-70,886	-78,757	-76,756
Capital account transactions, net	-7,220	-222	-1	13,116	-1,788	384	6,010	-140	-157	-1,212
U.S.-owned assets abroad, excl. financial derivatives (increase/financial outflow (−))	-81,234	-352,264	-560,523	-546,631	-1,285,729	-1,453,604	332,109	-119,535	-939,484	-483,653
U.S. official reserve assets	-2,158	-9,742	-290	14,096	2,374	-122	-4,848	-52,256	-1,834	-15,877
Special drawing rights	-192	-808	-722	4,511	-223	-154	-106	-48,230	-31	1,752
Reserve position in the International Monetary Fund	731	-2,466	2,308	10,200	3,331	1,021	-3,473	-3,357	-1,293	-18,079
Foreign currencies	-2,697	-6,468	-1,876	-615	-734	-989	-1,269	-669	-510	450
U.S. government assets, other than official reserve assets	2,317	-984	-941	5,539	5,346	-22,273	-529,615	541,342	7,540	-103,666
U.S. credits and other long-term assets	-8,410	-4,859	-5,182	-2,255	-2,992	-2,475	-2,202	-4,069	-4,976	-7,307
Repayments on U.S. credits and other long-term assets [8]	10,856	4,125	4,265	5,603	8,329	4,104	2,354	2,133	2,408	3,333
U.S. foreign currency holdings and U.S. short-term assets	-130	-250	-24	2,191	9	-23,902	-529,766	543,278	10,108	-99,692
U.S. private assets	-81,393	-341,538	-559,292	-566,266	-1,293,449	-1,431,209	866,571	-608,622	-945,189	-364,110
Direct investment	-37,183	-98,750	-159,212	-36,235	-244,922	-414,039	-329,081	-289,451	-327,877	-419,332
Foreign securities	-28,765	-122,394	-127,908	-251,199	-365,129	-366,512	197,347	-227,024	-138,984	-146,797
U.S. claims on unaffiliated foreigners reported by U.S. nonbanking concerns [9]	-27,824	-45,286	-138,790	-71,207	-181,299	-928	456,177	153,695	32,969	-11,608
U.S. claims reported by U.S. banks and securities brokers [9]	12,379	-75,108	-133,382	-207,625	-502,099	-649,730	542,128	-245,842	-511,297	213,627

See footnotes at end of table.

Table 1301. U.S. International Transactions by Type of Transaction: 1990 to 2011-Continued.

See headnote on page 821.

Type of transaction [1]	1990	1995	2000	2005	2006	2007	2008	2009	2010	2011
Foreign-owned assets in the United States, excluding financial derivatives (increase/financial inflow (+))	139,357	435,102	1,038,224	1,247,347	2,065,169	2,064,642	431,406	314,390	1,308,279	1,000,990
Foreign official assets in the United States	33,910	109,880	42,758	259,268	487,939	481,043	554,634	480,286	398,188	211,826
U.S. government securities	**30,243**	**72,712**	**35,710**	**213,334**	**428,401**	**269,897**	**591,381**	**437,324**	**353,294**	**158,735**
U.S. Treasury securities	29,576	68,977	-5,199	112,841	208,564	98,432	548,653	569,893	442,012	171,179
Other	667	3,735	40,909	100,493	219,837	171,465	42,728	-132,569	-88,718	-12,444
Other U.S. government liabilities	1,868	-105	-1,825	-421	2,816	5,436	9,029	58,206	12,321	9,063
U.S. liabilities reported by U.S. banks and securities brokers	3,385	34,008	5,746	26,260	22,365	109,019	-149,676	-68,848	-7,967	30,010
Other foreign official assets	-1,586	3,265	3,127	20,095	34,357	96,691	103,900	53,604	40,540	14,018
Other foreign assets in the United States	105,447	325,222	995,466	988,079	1,577,230	1,583,599	-123,228	-165,896	910,091	789,164
Direct investment	48,494	57,776	321,274	112,638	243,151	221,166	310,092	150,442	205,831	233,988
U.S. Treasury securities	-2,534	91,544	-69,983	132,300	-58,229	66,845	162,944	-15,451	297,797	240,878
U.S. securities other than U.S. Treasury securities	1,592	77,249	459,889	450,386	683,245	605,414	-165,639	1,855	139,316	-56,442
U.S. currency	16,586	8,840	-3,357	8,447	2,227	-10,675	29,187	12,635	28,319	54,996
U.S. liabilities to unaffiliated foreigners reported by U.S. nonbanking concerns	45,133	59,637	170,672	69,572	244,793	183,221	-31,475	8,956	62,957	6,567
U.S. liabilities reported by U.S. banks and securities brokers [9]	-3,824	30,176	116,971	214,736	462,043	517,628	-428,337	-324,330	175,871	309,177
Financial derivatives, net	(NA)	(NA)	(NA)	(NA)	-6,742	6,222	-32,947	44,816	14,076	39,010
Statistical discrepancy	28,066	30,951	-61,361	31,942	29,710	92,660	-59,443	142,365	59,237	-89,208
Balance on goods	-111,037	-174,170	-445,787	-780,730	-835,689	-818,886	-830,109	-505,758	-645,124	-738,413
Balance on services	30,173	77,786	69,038	72,106	82,402	122,158	131,770	126,603	150,387	178,533
Balance on goods and services	**-80,864**	**-96,384**	**-376,749**	**-708,624**	**-753,288**	**-696,728**	**-698,338**	**-379,154**	**-494,737**	**-559,880**
Balance on income	28,550	20,891	19,178	68,591	44,182	101,485	147,089	119,717	183,859	227,007
Unilateral current transfers, net	-26,654	-38,074	-58,767	-105,741	-91,515	-115,061	-125,885	-122,459	-131,074	-133,053
Balance on current account	-78,968	-113,567	-416,338	-745,774	-800,621	-710,303	-677,135	-381,896	-441,951	-465,926

NA Not available. [1] Credits, +: Exports of goods and services and income receipts; unilateral current transfers to the United States; capital account transactions receipts; financial inflows—increase in foreign-owned assets (U.S. liabilities) or decrease in U.S.-owned assets (U.S. claims). Debits, −: Imports of goods and services and income payments; unilateral current transfers to foreigners; capital account transactions payments; financial outflows—decrease in foreign-owned assets (U.S. liabilities) or increase in U.S.-owned assets (U.S. claims). [2] Includes some goods: Mainly military equipment and supplies that are commingled in the source data and cannot be separately identified. [3] Includes transfers of goods and services under U.S. military grant programs. [4] Beginning in 1999, excludes equipment and supplies exported under the U.S. Foreign Military Sales program that can be separately identified. [5] Gross basis. The definition of exports excludes U.S. parents' payments to foreign affiliates and includes U.S. affiliates' receipts from foreign parents. The definition of imports includes U.S. parents' payments to foreign affiliates and to exclude U.S. affiliates' receipts from foreign parents. [6] Beginning in 1999, excludes petroleum purchases abroad by U.S. military agencies that can be separately identified. [7] "Other transfers" component includes taxes paid by U.S. private residents to foreign governments and taxes paid by private nonresidents to the U.S. Government. [8] Includes sales of foreign obligations to foreigners. [9] Beginning in 2003, includes securities brokers' claims/liabilities on their foreign affiliates. Prior to 2003, they are included in the claims/liabilities of nonbanking concerns.

Source: U.S. Bureau of Economic Analysis, *Survey of Current Business*, July 2012; <http://www.bea.gov/scb/>.

Table 1302. U.S. Balances on International Transactions by Area and Selected Country: 2010 and 2011

[In millions of dollars (–645,124 represents –$645,124,000,000). Country data are based on information available from U.S. reporting sources. In some instances, the statistics may not necessarily reflect the ultimate foreign transactor. Minus sign (–) indicates debits]

Area or Country	2010, balance on—				2011, balance on—			
	Goods [1]	Services	Income	Current account	Goods [1]	Services	Income	Current account
All areas	-645,124	150,387	183,859	-441,951	-738,413	178,533	227,007	-465,926
Europe	-95,844	41,271	70,653	8,193	-118,212	49,440	65,376	-13,448
European Union	-79,750	36,512	53,674	7,239	-100,146	40,383	55,226	-7,068
Euro Area [2]	-66,269	23,264	56,119	10,433	-90,860	29,034	52,565	-10,377
Germany	-34,340	-4,978	-7,053	-45,740	-49,799	-5,104	-10,607	-63,607
Italy	-14,375	425	608	-14,016	-18,081	836	539	-17,279
Netherlands	15,735	4,914	44,984	65,209	18,588	6,047	39,295	63,797
United Kingdom	-1,668	9,510	-1,640	6,387	5,158	7,301	2,675	14,452
Canada	-30,902	24,350	26,526	18,088	-38,261	27,807	39,682	27,068
Latin America, other Western Hemisphere	-62,144	21,458	71,522	2,602	-74,486	29,584	78,514	16,009
Brazil	11,150	11,305	11,984	34,104	11,272	14,751	13,808	39,398
Mexico	-69,195	10,400	302	-72,623	-68,634	11,334	2,626	-69,307
Asia and Pacific	-371,987	54,855	-32,119	-383,909	-400,805	60,280	-13,915	-395,296
Australia	12,981	7,772	11,127	31,532	17,025	9,821	14,540	39,784
China [3]	-273,096	11,497	-35,963	-300,356	-295,378	15,335	-32,016	-315,033
Hong Kong	22,830	-973	1,273	22,727	32,796	-862	3,222	34,672
India	-10,347	-3,806	3,150	-19,797	-14,722	-5,814	4,057	-25,056
Japan	-61,442	19,563	-33,737	-76,530	-64,632	17,479	-32,400	-81,697
Korea, South	-9,741	4,809	1,574	-4,504	-12,304	5,742	2,904	-4,844
Singapore	10,652	6,478	12,549	29,608	11,292	6,139	16,706	34,017
Taiwan [3]	-9,211	3,547	-3,614	-9,663	-14,413	3,764	-2,895	-13,816
Middle East	-27,393	3,112	2,756	-33,254	-47,134	5,062	8,617	-45,001
Africa	-56,855	4,002	7,796	-60,030	-59,514	4,145	9,313	-63,033
International organizations and unallocated	(X)	1,340	36,725	6,359	(X)	2,215	39,420	7,775

X Not applicable. [1] Adjusted to balance of payments basis. [2] See footnote 3, table 1369. [3] See footnote 4, table 1348.

Source: U.S. Bureau of Economic Analysis, *Survey of Current Business*, July 2012. See also <http://www.bea.gov/iTable/index_ita.cfm>.

Table 1303. Private International Service Transactions by Selected Type of Service and Selected Country: 2000 to 2011

[In millions of dollars (281,249 represents $281,249,000,000). Country data are based on information available from U.S. reporting sources. In some instances, the statistics may not necessarily reflect the ultimate foreign transactor. For all transactions, see Table 1301]

Type of Service and country	Exports				Imports			
	2000	2005	2010	2011	2000	2005	2010	2011
Private services, total	281,249	362,895	537,740	586,839	203,880	272,627	368,044	393,065
TYPE OF SERVICE								
Travel	82,891	82,160	103,481	116,115	65,366	69,930	75,510	78,651
Passenger fares	20,197	20,609	30,983	36,631	23,613	25,189	27,256	31,109
Other transportation	25,562	32,013	40,817	43,064	37,209	54,212	51,258	54,711
Freight	12,791	16,261	20,601	21,730	27,885	44,193	38,001	40,337
Port services	12,771	15,752	20,216	21,334	9,324	10,019	13,257	14,374
Royalties and license fees	51,808	74,448	107,165	120,836	16,606	25,577	33,434	36,620
Other private services	100,792	153,665	255,293	270,193	61,085	97,720	180,586	191,973
By type:								
Financial services	(NA)	(NA)	70,346	74,055	(NA)	(NA)	14,763	16,207
Insurance services	3,631	7,566	14,530	15,477	11,284	28,710	61,013	56,619
Business, professional, and technical services	(NA)	(NA)	127,834	134,416	(NA)	(NA)	90,526	104,773
AREA AND COUNTRY								
Europe	106,296	150,571	206,149	225,179	88,741	120,254	151,554	163,334
European Union	93,103	131,216	174,175	188,802	76,840	103,436	125,549	136,807
Euro Area [1]	56,036	76,089	108,942	120,858	45,039	59,599	74,628	81,112
France	10,474	12,646	16,749	17,792	10,498	11,931	14,708	15,775
Germany	15,595	20,449	24,216	25,520	12,240	18,512	21,306	22,928
Italy	5,403	7,031	8,524	9,275	5,059	5,973	6,718	7,005
Netherlands	6,975	8,481	13,016	14,668	5,559	7,450	8,033	8,532
United Kingdom	31,706	44,793	50,694	52,720	27,869	34,736	40,219	44,447
Canada	24,613	32,719	50,806	56,076	17,875	21,977	26,180	28,028
Latin America, other Western Hemisphere	55,633	63,355	105,827	115,208	37,607	51,062	84,685	85,448
Brazil	6,236	5,761	16,853	21,702	1,946	1,975	5,525	6,929
Mexico	15,532	22,192	24,097	25,207	10,780	14,177	13,543	13,745
Asia and Pacific	77,560	95,946	144,308	157,434	49,620	65,091	87,680	97,266
Australia	5,541	7,558	13,360	16,088	3,412	4,583	5,714	6,315
China [2]	5,020	8,403	21,483	26,702	3,171	6,146	9,947	11,329
Hong Kong	3,794	3,778	5,666	6,087	4,129	4,995	6,570	6,886
India	2,563	5,081	10,317	11,019	1,887	4,964	14,155	16,877
Japan	32,843	40,517	44,985	44,393	16,387	20,483	23,401	24,772
Korea, South	6,924	9,565	15,085	16,561	4,587	5,875	7,656	8,377
Singapore	6,031	5,608	9,989	10,451	2,312	3,541	3,627	4,442
Taiwan [2]	4,616	5,795	9,351	10,445	4,154	6,415	5,993	6,762
Middle East	6,753	8,939	16,956	18,377	3,380	5,239	9,581	11,007
Africa	4,997	6,247	11,264	12,181	2,708	3,919	7,120	7,695
International organizations and unallocated	5,396	5,117	2,431	2,381	3,949	5,085	1,243	288

NA Not available. [1] See footnote 3, table 1369. [2] See footnote 4, table 1348.

Source: U.S. Bureau of Economic Analysis, *Survey of Current Business*, July 2012. See also <http://www.bea.gov/iTable/index_ita.cfm>.

Table 1304. International Investment Position by Type of Investment: 2000 to 2011

[In billions of dollars (–1,337 represents –$1,337,000,000,000). Estimates for end of year; subject to considerable error due to nature of basic data. Unless otherwise specified, types below refer to current-cost method. For information on current-cost method and market value, see article cited in source]

Type of investment	2000	2005	2007	2008	2009	2010	2011, prel.
Net international investment position.....	**-1,337**	**-1,932**	**-1,796**	**-3,260**	**-2,322**	**-2,474**	**-4,030**
Financial derivatives, net [1].....	(X)	58	71	160	126	110	126
Net international investment position, excluding financial derivatives.....	-1,337	-1,990	-1,867	-3,420	-2,448	-2,584	-4,157
U.S.-owned assets abroad.....	**6,239**	**11,962**	**18,400**	**19,465**	**18,512**	**20,298**	**21,132**
Financial derivatives (gross positive fair value) [1].....	(X)	1,190	2,559	6,127	3,490	3,652	4,705
U.S.-owned assets abroad, excluding financial derivatives.....	6,239	10,772	15,840	13,337	15,022	16,646	16,428
U.S. official reserve assets.....	128	188	277	294	404	489	536
Gold [2].....	72	134	218	227	284	368	400
Special drawing rights.....	11	8	9	9	58	57	55
Reserve position in the International Monetary Fund.....	15	8	4	8	11	12	30
Foreign currencies.....	31	38	45	49	50	52	51
U.S. government assets, other than official reserve assets.....	85	78	94	624	83	75	179
U.S. credits and other long-term assets [3].....	83	77	70	70	72	74	78
U.S. foreign currency holdings and U.S. short-term assets [4].....	3	1	24	554	11	1	101
U.S. private assets.....	6,025	10,506	15,469	12,419	14,535	16,082	15,713
Direct investment at current cost.....	1,532	2,652	3,553	3,749	4,029	4,307	4,682
Foreign securities.....	2,426	4,329	6,835	3,986	5,566	6,336	5,922
Bonds.....	573	1,012	1,587	1,237	1,570	1,689	1,764
Corporate stocks.....	1,853	3,318	5,248	2,748	3,995	4,647	4,158
U.S. claims on unaffiliated foreigners reported by U.S. nonbanking concerns.....	837	1,018	1,233	931	930	875	797
U.S. claims reported by U.S. banks and securities brokers, not included elsewhere.....	1,232	2,507	3,847	3,754	4,010	4,564	4,312
Foreign-owned assets in the United States.....	**7,576**	**13,894**	**20,196**	**22,725**	**20,833**	**22,772**	**25,163**
Financial derivatives (gross negative fair value) [1].....	(X)	1,132	2,488	5,968	3,363	3,542	4,578
Foreign-owned assets in the Unites States, excluding financial derivatives.....	7,576	12,762	17,708	16,757	17,470	19,230	20,584
Foreign official assets in the United States.....	1,037	2,313	3,412	3,944	4,403	4,913	5,251
U.S. government securities.....	756	1,725	2,540	3,264	3,589	3,993	4,277
U.S. Treasury securities.....	640	1,341	1,737	2,401	2,880	3,365	3,653
Other.....	116	385	803	864	709	629	624
Other U.S. government liabilities.....	26	23	32	41	99	110	119
U.S. liabilities reported by U.S. banks and securities brokers, not included elsewhere.....	153	297	406	256	188	180	210
Other foreign official assets.....	102	269	434	383	528	629	645
Other foreign assets.....	6,539	10,448	14,296	12,813	13,067	14,317	15,333
Direct investment at current cost.....	1,421	1,906	2,346	2,397	2,398	2,598	2,909
U.S. Treasury securities.....	382	644	640	852	791	1,102	1,418
U.S. securities other than U.S. Treasury securities.....	2,623	4,353	6,190	4,621	5,320	5,934	5,968
Corporate and other bonds.....	1,069	2,243	3,289	2,771	2,826	2,916	2,910
Corporate stocks.....	1,554	2,110	2,901	1,850	2,494	3,018	3,058
U.S. currency.....	205	280	272	301	314	342	397
U.S. liabilities to unaffiliated foreigners reported by U.S. nonbanking concerns.....	739	658	863	741	706	644	630
U.S. liabilities reported by U.S. banks and securities brokers, not included elsewhere.....	1,169	2,607	3,985	3,901	3,538	3,698	4,012
Memoranda:							
Direct investment abroad at market value.....	2,694	3,638	5,275	3,102	4,287	4,767	4,500
Direct investment in the United States at market value.....	2,783	2,818	3,551	2,486	2,995	3,397	3,509

X Not applicable. [1] A break in series in 2005 reflects the introduction of U.S. Department of the Treasury data on financial derivatives. [2] U.S. official gold stock is valued at market price. [3] Also includes paid-in capital subscriptions to international financial institutions and resources provided to foreigners under foreign assistance programs requiring repayment over several years. Excludes World War I debts that are not being serviced. [4] Beginning in 2007, includes foreign-currency-denominated assets obtained through temporary reciprocal currency arrangements between the Federal Reserve System and foreign central banks.

Source: U.S. Bureau of Economic Analysis, *Survey of Current Business*, July 2012. See also <http://www.bea.gov/international/index.htm#iip>.

Table 1305. U.S. Reserve Assets: 1990 to 2011

[In billions of dollars (83.3 represents $83,300,000,000). As of end of year]

Type	1990	2000	2005	2006	2007	2008	2009	2010	2011
Total.....	**83.3**	**67.6**	**65.1**	**65.9**	**70.6**	**77.6**	**130.8**	**132.4**	**148.0**
Gold stock.....	11.1	11.0	11.0	11.0	11.0	11.0	11.0	11.0	11.0
Special drawing rights.....	11.0	10.5	8.2	8.9	9.5	9.3	57.8	56.8	55.0
Foreign currencies.....	52.2	31.2	37.8	40.9	45.8	49.6	50.5	52.1	51.9
Reserve position in IMF [1].....	9.1	14.8	8.0	5.0	4.2	7.7	11.4	12.5	30.1

[1] International Monetary Fund.

Source: U.S. Department of the Treasury, *Treasury Bulletin*, quarterly. See also <http://www.fms.treas.gov/bulletin/index.html>.

Table 1306. Foreign Direct Investment Position in the United States on a Historical-Cost Basis by Selected Country, 2000 to 2011, and by Industry, 2011

[In millions of dollars (1,256,867 represents $1,256,867,000,000). Foreign direct investment is defined as the ownership or control, directly or indirectly, by one foreign entity (as used here, "entity" is synonymous with "person" as the term is used in a broad legal sense including any individual, branch, partnership, association, trust, corporation, or government) of 10 percent or more of the voting interest of a U.S. business enterprise. Data are based on surveys of U.S. affiliates of foreign companies]

Country	2000	2005	2009	2010	2011 Total [1]	2011 Manufac-turing	2011 Wholesale trade	2011 Finance [2] and insur-ance
All countries.................	1,256,867	1,634,121	2,069,438	2,264,385	2,547,828	838,340	309,959	376,770
Canada.........................	114,309	165,667	188,943	188,350	210,864	32,259	6,763	62,920
Europe [3].....................	887,014	1,154,048	1,504,727	1,652,599	1,811,875	676,127	163,117	298,233
Austria.........................	3,007	2,425	4,622	4,532	4,781	2,262	381	1
Belgium.......................	14,787	10,024	36,292	74,888	86,021	50,273	19,587	(D)
Denmark.......................	4,025	6,117	6,806	6,895	7,854	2,183	3,451	1
Finland.........................	8,875	5,938	5,415	4,949	5,511	2,169	1,629	(Z)
France.........................	125,740	114,260	158,924	174,698	198,741	60,201	31,295	(D)
Germany.......................	122,412	177,176	183,966	200,565	215,938	64,042	23,986	42,744
Ireland.........................	25,523	17,465	21,044	25,975	24,974	11,762	866	4,242
Italy.............................	6,576	7,725	18,567	19,881	23,021	7,517	1,362	(D)
Luxembourg..................	58,930	79,680	138,667	168,426	190,380	69,203	5,287	45,883
Netherlands..................	138,894	156,602	206,622	244,524	240,306	100,894	27,376	37,426
Norway.........................	2,665	9,810	9,866	10,538	18,056	1,867	4,944	(D)
Spain...........................	5,068	7,472	38,984	42,023	44,750	5,865	60	2,937
Sweden.........................	21,991	22,269	28,941	39,940	42,313	29,557	6,558	138
Switzerland...................	64,719	133,387	140,819	187,170	211,700	106,038	9,422	44,774
United Kingdom.............	277,613	371,350	414,590	387,163	442,179	139,862	25,786	87,198
Latin America and other Western Hemisphere [3]........	53,691	57,175	32,961	59,638	85,695	(D)	7,266	-14,114
South and Central America [3].....	13,384	22,507	14,583	17,940	25,010	(D)	6,029	515
Brazil.........................	882	2,051	-1,430	1,378	5,038	-130	4,100	(D)
Mexico........................	7,462	3,595	11,111	11,267	13,763	3,424	1,608	173
Venezuela....................	792	5,292	2,612	2,890	3,784	(D)	7	3
Other Western Hemisphere [3]....	40,307	34,668	18,377	41,698	60,686	503	1,238	-14,630
Curacao.......................	(X)	(X)	(X)	(X)	3,736	475	44	33
Netherlands Antilles...........	3,807	5,531	6,513	2,405	(X)	(X)	(X)	(X)
U.K. Islands, Caribbean.........	15,191	23,063	21,227	36,437	53,493	2,568	1,889	4,568
Africa [3]......................	2,700	2,341	1,225	2,265	4,281	(D)	582	(D)
Middle East [3]................	6,506	8,306	18,177	16,452	25,363	(D)	6,931	(D)
Israel..........................	3,012	4,231	8,122	8,538	15,007	(D)	451	(D)
Asia and Pacific [3]...........	192,647	246,585	323,404	345,080	409,749	111,889	125,300	29,478
Australia.......................	18,775	36,392	36,760	38,770	55,862	5,242	241	4,067
China [4].......................	(NA)	574	1,624	3,245	3,815	-266	998	42
Hong Kong.....................	1,493	3,467	4,236	4,378	4,854	2,242	1,650	-11
India...........................	(NA)	1,497	2,555	4,110	4,888	512	(D)	(Z)
Japan...........................	159,690	189,851	238,140	252,077	289,490	82,667	103,216	22,104
Korea, South..................	3,110	6,077	12,969	14,821	18,421	3,060	14,039	173
Singapore.....................	5,087	3,338	20,757	20,946	23,528	16,105	1,973	(D)
Taiwan [4].....................	3,174	3,731	3,885	4,541	5,180	2,059	1,436	(D)

D Suppressed to avoid disclosure of data of individual companies. NA Not available. X Not applicable. Z Less than $500,000. [1] Includes other industries, not shown separately. [2] Excludes depository institutions. [3] Includes other countries, not shown separately. [4] See footnote 4, Table 1348.

Source: U.S. Bureau of Economic Analysis, *Survey of Current Business*, September 2012, and previous issues. See also <http://www.bea.gov/scb/index.htm>.

Table 1307. U.S. Majority-Owned Affiliates of Foreign Companies—Selected Financial and Operating Data by Industry of Affiliate: 2010

[In billions of dollars (11,830 represents $11,830,000,000,000), except as indicated. Data are preliminary. A majority-owned U.S. affiliate is a U.S. business enterprise in which a foreign entity (as used here, "entity" is synonymous with "person" as the term is used in a broad legal sense including any individual, branch, partnership, association, trust, corporation, or government) has a direct or indirect voting interest greater than 50 percent]

Industry	2007 NAICS Code	Total assets	Sales	Employ-ment (1,000)	Employee compen-sation	Gross property, plant, and equipment	Mer-chandise exports	Mer-chandise imports
All industries..................................	(X)	11,830	3,086	5,270	408	1,520	229	518
Manufacturing [1]............................	31–33	1,600	1,257	1,986	169	684	136	221
Petroleum and coal products..................	324	242	246	56	10	197	13	70
Chemicals.....................................	325	390	276	300	38	129	35	45
Machinery.....................................	333	135	89	213	20	26	15	12
Transportation equipment.....................	336	225	203	410	28	88	23	46
Wholesale trade...............................	42	598	816	552	45	190	81	272
Retail trade...................................	44–45	80	136	478	16	49	1	9
Information....................................	51	273	122	245	25	61	1	(D)
Finance and insurance.........................	52	8,190	355	399	64	83	0	(Z)
Real estate and rental and leasing.............	53	133	24	39	3	103	(D)	(D)
Professional, scientific, and technical services....................................	54	134	82	255	24.3	13	1	(Z)
Other industries...............................	(X)	822	296	1,318	62.6	336	(D)	(D)

D Suppressed to avoid disclosure of data of individual companies. X Not applicable. Z Less than $500,000. [1] Includes industries not shown separately.

Source: U.S. Bureau of Economic Analysis, *Survey of Current Business*, August 2012. See also <http://www.bea.gov/international/di1fdiop.htm>.

Table 1308. Foreign Direct Investment in the United States—Property, Plant, and Equipment and Employment of Majority-Owned U.S. Affiliates of Foreign Companies by State: 2002 to 2010

[Gross book value of property, plant, and equipment in millions of dollars (1,035,916 represents $1,035,916,000,000); employment in thousands (5,570.4 represents 5,570,400). A U.S. majority-owned affiliate is a U.S. business enterprise in which a foreign entity (as used here, "entity" is synonymous with "person" as the term is used in a broad legal sense including any individual, branch, partnership, association, trust, corporation, or government) has a direct or indirect voting interest greater than 50 percent]

State and other area	Gross book value of property, plant, and equipment (mil. dol.)		Employment			
					2010	
	2002	2007	2002 (1,000)	2007 (1,000)	Total (1,000)	Percentage of total employment in the state or area [1]
Total	1,035,916	1,293,735	5,570.4	5,588.2	5,270.4	4.7
Alabama	15,520	22,885	75.1	81.1	81.2	5.3
Alaska	30,052	34,473	12.6	11.4	13.6	5.6
Arizona	(D)	13,016	57.6	73.2	73.1	3.7
Arkansas	4,872	4,914	35.7	36.6	34.8	3.6
California	89,193	108,572	635.3	602.9	567.0	4.7
Colorado	13,026	(D)	77.7	83.5	77.3	4.1
Connecticut	(D)	13,356	(D)	103.3	101.2	7.3
Delaware	6,252	4,480	23.6	28.7	25.2	7.2
District of Columbia	5,135	5,567	17.5	16.3	19.6	4.2
Florida	28,993	35,052	258.3	248.2	223.6	3.6
Georgia	(D)	(D)	191.4	180.6	183.4	5.7
Hawaii	(D)	6,184	(D)	31.0	26.2	5.5
Idaho	2,131	2,028	12.5	14.4	13.7	2.7
Illinois	41,862	48,626	281.5	280.5	245.9	5.1
Indiana	27,991	(D)	133.3	149.1	133.6	5.6
Iowa	5,776	9,476	36.6	45.5	43.9	3.5
Kansas	5,238	7,863	34.9	58.9	54.8	5.0
Kentucky	24,091	28,188	88.4	92.9	89.5	6.1
Louisiana	26,993	31,226	50.5	49.1	51.7	3.3
Maine	5,511	6,279	31.7	29.6	30.4	6.2
Maryland	(D)	13,016	(D)	103.6	99.2	4.9
Massachusetts	(D)	26,939	(D)	183.7	177.5	6.3
Michigan	(D)	24,052	(D)	152.6	141.7	4.3
Minnesota	9,805	16,237	88.1	98.2	89.3	3.9
Mississippi	5,097	8,250	25.8	26.5	25.9	3.0
Missouri	14,484	(D)	91.5	82.4	79.9	3.6
Montana	1,824	3,366	5.9	8.1	(D)	(D)
Nebraska	1,840	(D)	18.7	23.4	24.2	3.1
Nevada	(D)	9,716	25.9	33.8	37.9	3.9
New Hampshire	(D)	5,246	(D)	38.9	39.7	7.5
New Jersey	30,956	38,425	230.1	227.4	223.4	6.9
New Mexico	(D)	4,813	13.0	17.0	14.9	2.5
New York	68,310	80,474	440.8	429.3	388.5	5.5
North Carolina	(D)	28,918	(D)	211.0	188.2	5.8
North Dakota	1,100	1,438	7.4	7.5	11.6	3.8
Ohio	32,124	43,438	214.2	238.2	206.5	4.8
Oklahoma	7,434	10,578	33.9	35.4	36.0	3.0
Oregon	(D)	9,971	51.3	45.8	41.8	3.1
Pennsylvania	(D)	39,824	(D)	264.4	251.0	5.1
Rhode Island	(D)	5,426	(D)	25.7	26.0	6.5
South Carolina	21,573	(D)	133.1	111.3	104.3	7.0
South Dakota	685	1,277	7.6	6.8	7.2	2.2
Tennessee	16,795	22,688	130.7	139.2	112.5	5.0
Texas	88,116	128,424	353.0	422.6	428.1	4.9
Utah	10,612	6,544	32.3	33.2	29.0	2.9
Vermont	1,286	1,735	11.1	10.1	11.0	4.4
Virginia	(D)	(D)	142.2	158.1	140.8	4.8
Washington	(D)	21,558	84.7	90.5	92.3	4.0
West Virginia	7,388	6,298	22.7	21.1	24.8	4.4
Wisconsin	16,103	14,560	107.1	82.0	76.0	3.3
Wyoming	10,551	11,116	8.5	8.9	7.2	3.4
Puerto Rico	2,583	2,579	19.8	20.9	21.6	(NA)
Other U.S. areas	(D)	73,436	10.2	12.6	14.7	(NA)
Foreign	2,328	2,162	0.3	1.0	(D)	(D)
Unspecified [2]	66,341	93,505	(NA)	(NA)	(NA)	(NA)

D Suppressed to avoid the disclosure of data of individual companies. NA Not available. [1] The data on total employment in the state or area that is used to calculate the shares shown in this table are equal to employment in private industries less employment of private households. For consistency with the coverage of the private-industry employment data, U.S.-affiliate employment in Puerto Rico, in "other U.S. areas," and in "foreign" was excluded from the U.S.-affiliate employment total when the percentage shares were computed. [2] Includes aircraft, railroad rolling stock, satellites, undersea cable, and trucks engaged in interstate transportation.

Source: U.S. Bureau of Economic Analysis, *Survey of Current Business*, August 2012, and *Foreign Direct Investment in the United States: Final Results from the 2007 Benchmark Survey*, September 2011. See also <http://www.bea.gov/international/di1fdiop.htm>.

Table 1309. U.S. Businesses Acquired or Established by Foreign Direct Investors—Investment Outlays by Industry of U.S. Business Enterprise and Country of Ultimate Beneficial Owner: 2000 to 2008

[In millions of dollars (335,629 represents $335,629,000,000). Foreign direct investment is the ownership or control, directly or indirectly, by one foreign individual branch, partnership, association, trust, corporation, or government of 10 percent or more of the voting securities of a U.S. business enterprise or an equivalent interest in an unincorporated one. Data represent number and full cost of acquisitions of existing U.S. business enterprises, including business segments or operating units of existing U.S. business enterprises and establishments of new enterprises. Investments may be made by the foreign direct investor itself, or indirectly by an existing U.S. affiliate of the foreign direct investor. Covers investments in U.S. business enterprises with assets of over $1 million, or with ownership of 200 acres of U.S. land]

Industry and country	2000	2003	2004	2005	2006	2007	2008
Total [1]	**335,629**	**63,591**	**86,219**	**91,390**	**165,603**	**251,917**	**260,362**
By type of investment:							
U.S. businesses acquired	322,703	50,212	72,738	73,997	148,604	223,616	242,799
U.S. businesses established	12,926	13,379	13,481	17,393	16,999	28,301	17,564
By type of investor:							
Foreign direct investors	105,151	27,866	34,184	40,304	44,129	88,337	47,078
U.S. affiliates	230,478	35,725	52,035	51,086	121,474	163,580	213,284
INDUSTRY [2]							
Manufacturing	143,285	10,750	18,251	34,036	56,330	118,370	141,079
Wholesale trade	8,561	1,086	(D)	3,489	8,273	5,631	3,977
Retail trade	1,672	941	3,073	1,262	1,295	6,867	2,775
Information	67,932	9,236	4,315	8,487	10,341	8,585	22,214
Depository institutions	2,636	4,864	(D)	7,973	7,547	12,307	15,996
Finance (except depository institutions) and insurance	44,420	23,511	26,234	5,529	33,776	27,497	29,584
Real estate and rental and leasing	4,526	2,817	6,335	8,756	12,441	17,852	3,796
Professional, scientific, and technical services	32,332	1,955	(D)	6,407	8,923	9,018	15,167
Other industries	30,264	8,429	10,121	15,453	26,677	45,790	25,775
COUNTRY [3]							
Canada	28,346	9,157	31,502	13,640	12,121	38,502	25,181
Europe [1]	249,167	39,024	43,815	56,416	106,732	132,454	157,853
France	26,149	2,955	6,415	5,608	18,140	14,307	16,565
Germany	18,452	8,830	4,788	7,239	20,514	15,831	12,823
Netherlands	47,686	1,077	461	2,609	4,769	8,357	12,545
Switzerland	22,789	649	6,505	2,332	12,401	6,501	9,041
United Kingdom	110,208	20,373	23,288	30,420	26,261	56,051	19,657
Latin America and other Western Hemisphere	15,400	1,607	2,629	5,042	(D)	(D)	18,259
South and Central America	5,334	182	1,382	980	2,273	(D)	3,551
Other Western Hemisphere	10,066	1,425	1,247	4,062	(D)	1,933	14,708
Africa	(D)	(D)	(D)	(D)	(D)	(D)	129
Middle East	947	1,738	1,318	5,068	11,755	21,882	12,263
Asia and Pacific [1]	40,282	11,469	6,015	10,924	15,759	34,408	44,863
Australia	(D)	9,032	3,850	4,713	5,650	12,983	10,522
Japan	26,044	1,544	1,027	4,245	8,350	7,928	28,041

D Suppressed to avoid disclosure of data of individual companies. [1] Includes other countries, not shown separately. [2] Based on 1997 North American Industry Classification System (NAICS). Beginning 2002, based on NAICS 2002; see text, Section 15. [3] For investments in which more than one investor participated, each investor and each investor's outlays are classified by country of each ultimate beneficial owner.

Source: U.S. Bureau of Economic Analysis, *Survey of Current Business*, June 2009. See also <http://www.bea.gov/scb/index.htm>.

Table 1310. U.S. Direct Investment Position Abroad, Capital Outflows, and Income by Industry of Foreign Affiliates: 2000 to 2011

[In millions of dollars (1,316,247 represents $1,316,247,000,000). See headnote, Table 1311]

Industry	Direct investment position on a historical-cost basis			Financial outflows [inflows(−)] [1]			Income [1, 2]		
	2000	2010	2011	2000	2010	2011	2000	2010	2011
All industries, total [3]	1,316,247	3,790,918	4,155,551	142,627	304,399	396,656	133,692	420,566	457,562
Mining	72,111	171,576	188,003	2,174	13,013	24,738	13,164	29,160	38,789
Manufacturing [3]	343,899	533,063	588,736	43,002	46,261	59,177	42,230	62,012	73,806
Food	23,497	48,553	52,873	2,014	5,345	4,269	2,681	4,208	4,901
Chemicals	75,807	116,653	132,123	3,812	14,636	16,310	(D)	14,594	16,532
Primary and fabricated metals	21,644	17,240	19,505	1,233	1,382	2,715	1,536	1,431	1,955
Machinery	22,229	42,560	49,105	2,659	5,092	6,456	2,257	4,704	6,023
Computer and electronic products	59,909	79,599	86,155	17,303	8,900	8,279	8,860	10,857	12,421
Electrical equipment, appliances, and components	10,005	20,403	22,104	2,100	1,897	−5	1,079	1,745	1,743
Transportation equipment	49,887	51,629	60,782	7,814	−68	8,873	4,107	6,765	9,887
Wholesale trade	93,936	168,884	193,767	11,938	11,558	24,274	14,198	25,389	29,989
Information	52,345	119,707	127,170	16,531	8,080	11,773	-964	12,660	14,476
Depository institutions	40,152	119,804	107,913	-1,274	-4,392	-8,910	2,191	2,072	7,132
Finance and insurance	217,086	738,516	777,152	21,659	24,795	36,930	15,210	38,694	36,662
Professional, scientific, and technical services	32,868	83,450	90,109	5,441	7,551	8,047	3,548	8,069	9,176
Holding companies (nonbank)	(NA)	1,615,434	1,809,073	(NA)	175,792	207,586	(NA)	217,456	221,295

D Withheld to avoid disclosure of individual company data. NA Not available. [1] Without current-cost adjustment. [2] For 2000, income is shown net of withholding taxes. Beginning in 2010, income is shown gross of withholding taxes. [3] Includes other industries, not shown separately.

Source: U.S. Bureau of Economic Analysis, *Survey of Current Business*, July 2012, and "U.S. Direct Investment Abroad: Balance of Payments and Direct Investment Position Data, Annual Data." See <http://www.bea.gov/international/di1usdbal.htm>.

Table 1311. U.S. Direct Investment Position Abroad on a Historical-Cost Basis by Selected Country: 2000 to 2011

[In millions of dollars (1,316,247 represents $1,316,247,000,000). U.S. investment abroad is the ownership or control by one U.S. person of 10 percent or more of the voting securities of an incorporated foreign business enterprise or an equivalent interest in an unincorporated foreign business enterprise. Negative position can occur when a U.S. parent company's liabilities to the foreign affiliate are greater than its equity in and loans to the foreign affiliate]

Country	2000	2005	2006	2007	2008	2009	2010	2011
All countries	1,316,247	2,241,656	2,477,268	2,993,980	3,232,493	3,518,655	3,790,918	4,155,551
Canada	132,472	231,836	205,134	250,642	246,483	265,326	289,535	318,964
Europe [1]	687,320	1,210,679	1,397,704	1,682,023	1,844,182	1,987,278	2,102,834	2,307,697
Austria	2,872	11,236	14,897	14,646	13,546	18,522	18,951	20,852
Belgium	17,973	49,306	51,862	62,491	65,279	44,759	48,496	52,888
Czech Republic	1,228	2,729	3,615	4,066	5,053	5,200	4,886	5,261
Denmark	5,270	6,914	5,849	8,950	10,481	10,577	10,381	14,034
Finland	1,342	1,950	2,107	2,202	2,012	1,417	1,379	1,504
France	42,628	60,526	63,008	74,179	84,409	87,077	91,487	89,293
Germany	55,508	100,473	93,620	100,601	107,833	106,103	100,185	106,887
Greece	795	1,884	1,804	2,179	2,092	1,899	1,798	1,252
Hungary	1,920	2,795	2,602	6,457	3,737	3,862	4,540	3,263
Ireland	35,903	55,173	86,372	117,708	150,131	129,253	157,565	188,274
Italy	23,484	24,528	25,435	28,216	27,663	26,482	25,465	25,338
Luxembourg	27,849	79,937	125,146	144,180	172,251	222,025	271,518	335,279
Netherlands	115,429	240,205	279,373	412,122	423,059	507,735	542,656	595,139
Norway	4,379	8,533	9,667	12,188	24,706	24,928	28,773	28,462
Poland	3,884	5,575	6,934	15,614	12,489	13,427	13,502	12,327
Portugal	2,664	2,138	2,832	2,991	3,006	2,828	2,909	2,879
Russia	1,147	9,363	11,371	15,029	19,777	20,070	8,347	9,733
Spain	21,236	50,197	49,356	61,093	54,194	57,513	54,839	58,619
Sweden	25,959	30,153	33,857	36,615	35,876	37,395	24,865	26,953
Switzerland	55,377	100,692	102,022	94,675	133,222	132,943	127,817	124,964
Turkey	1,826	2,563	3,141	5,584	4,542	3,457	4,041	5,203
United Kingdom	230,762	351,513	406,358	426,357	448,412	487,604	514,887	549,399
Latin America and other Western Hemisphere	266,576	379,582	418,429	556,160	588,992	695,754	747,784	831,151
South America [1]	84,220	73,311	80,477	104,732	98,603	115,553	131,355	148,386
Argentina	17,488	10,103	13,174	13,692	12,197	12,310	11,241	13,309
Brazil	36,717	30,882	33,504	48,807	43,953	53,281	64,165	71,101
Chile	10,052	11,127	10,927	16,337	16,286	25,385	30,507	34,187
Colombia	3,693	4,292	3,799	4,552	5,028	6,364	6,424	6,874
Ecuador	832	941	904	1,007	1,098	1,151	1,199	1,201
Peru	3,130	5,542	5,561	5,964	4,448	5,546	6,364	7,753
Venezuela	10,531	8,934	10,922	12,871	13,545	9,711	9,716	12,110
Central America [1]	73,841	82,496	91,811	102,472	101,291	95,223	96,287	103,752
Costa Rica	1,716	1,598	2,105	2,267	2,414	1,818	1,456	1,542
Honduras	399	821	864	626	809	865	999	930
Mexico	39,352	73,687	82,965	91,046	87,443	82,286	84,288	91,402
Panama	30,758	4,826	4,636	6,171	5,963	6,523	5,562	5,692
Other Western Hemisphere [1]	108,515	223,775	246,142	348,956	389,098	484,979	520,142	579,014
Bahamas, The	3,291	13,451	13,703	16,567	23,127	25,038	27,932	31,373
Barbados	2,141	3,881	4,831	2,136	3,154	4,742	6,471	10,889
Bermuda	60,114	113,222	133,480	211,708	207,547	282,662	297,096	327,185
Dominican Republic	1,143	815	789	712	806	1,065	1,289	1,710
Jamaica	2,483	1,018	940	801	940	708	570	567
Trinidad and Tobago	1,550	2,219	2,940	3,916	5,109	4,779	5,520	(D)
U.K. Islands, Caribbean	33,451	83,164	84,817	105,829	134,298	150,903	164,097	180,761
Africa [1]	11,891	22,756	28,158	32,607	36,746	43,018	53,412	56,632
Egypt	1,998	5,475	5,564	7,023	7,804	10,009	12,224	14,581
Nigeria	470	1,105	1,677	1,584	3,254	4,803	4,974	4,994
South Africa	3,562	3,969	3,980	5,240	4,999	5,805	6,465	6,546
Middle East [1]	10,863	21,115	24,206	28,448	31,294	35,004	34,739	35,905
Israel	3,735	7,978	9,168	9,487	9,444	9,007	9,337	9,562
Saudi Arabia	3,661	3,830	4,410	5,012	5,126	8,150	7,861	8,659
United Arab Emirates	683	2,285	2,670	2,967	3,337	4,381	4,663	5,785
Asia and Pacific [1]	207,125	375,689	403,637	444,101	484,796	492,275	562,613	605,202
Australia	34,838	75,669	67,632	84,331	92,668	105,890	123,492	136,249
China [2]	11,140	19,016	26,459	29,710	53,927	50,048	58,509	54,234
Hong Kong	27,447	36,415	39,636	40,720	40,042	49,685	48,219	52,542
India	2,379	7,162	9,746	14,622	18,354	19,166	24,822	24,663
Indonesia	8,904	8,603	9,484	14,978	16,273	9,573	10,604	11,591
Japan	57,091	81,175	84,428	85,224	99,803	93,576	102,597	116,533
Korea, South	8,968	19,760	27,299	23,558	22,426	24,770	26,954	31,751
Malaysia	7,910	11,097	11,185	12,140	12,243	9,061	12,030	13,903
New Zealand	4,271	5,191	5,933	5,527	4,451	5,508	6,203	6,741
Philippines	3,638	6,522	6,948	6,953	5,505	4,453	5,382	5,321
Singapore	24,133	76,390	81,879	93,529	83,169	84,778	104,309	116,616
Taiwan [2]	7,836	14,356	16,999	15,807	18,053	19,403	21,783	15,803
Thailand	5,824	10,252	10,642	10,284	9,162	9,371	10,505	11,308

D Suppressed to avoid disclosure of data of individual companies. [1] Includes other countries, not shown separately. [2] See footnote 4, Table 1348.

Source: U.S. Bureau of Economic Analysis, *Survey of Current Business*, July 2012, and "U.S. Direct Investment Abroad: Balance of Payments and Direct Investment Position Data, Annual Data." See <http://www.bea.gov/scb/index.htm>.

Table 1312. U.S. Government Foreign Grants and Credits by Type and Country: 2000 to 2010

[In millions of dollars (1,500 represents 1,500,000,000). See text, this section. Negative figures (–) occur when the total of grant returns, principal repayments, and/or foreign currencies disbursed by the U.S. Government exceeds new grants and new credits utilized and/or acquisitions of foreign currencies through new sales of farm products]

Country	2000	2004	2005	2006	2007	2008	2009	2010
Investment in financial institutions.............................	1,500	1,994	1,263	2,024	1,651	1,385	1,676	2,337
Western Europe [1]...	**429**	**346**	**327**	**60**	**182**	**225**	**253**	**340**
Ireland...	–	50	–	30	–	34	7	14
Spain...	-19	-19	-19	-205	(Z)	(Z)	(Z)	(Z)
Yugoslavia [2]..	1	13	4	-73	-2	3	-5	-2
Bosnia and Herzegovina.................................	52	66	72	49	45	29	27	41
Macedonia...	50	42	68	31	1	35	21	29
Former Yugoslavia - Regional [2].....................	63	38	66	120	45	53	168	83
Other [3] and unspecified [4].............................	478	47	29	5	5	18	4	5
Eastern Europe [1]...	**2,270**	**1,276**	**-95**	**266**	**1,089**	**2,010**	**1,644**	**1,490**
Albania..	26	43	54	31	43	38	32	29
Romania...	38	35	59	42	41	9	12	24
Newly Independent States of the former Soviet Union:								
Armenia...	20	66	85	62	74	87	71	34
Azerbaijan..	8	47	74	51	44	36	29	34
Belarus..	1	1	2	4	6	8	10	4
Georgia..	36	113	131	85	104	421	232	67
Kazakhstan...	42	57	69	41	42	44	41	158
Kyrgyzstan..	15	39	60	50	26	40	44	41
Moldova..	32	27	39	26	21	53	43	19
Russia..	797	251	-681	-920	-41	403	331	223
Tajikistan..	8	40	61	35	33	24	33	32
Turkmenistan...	4	4	13	3	(Z)	-9	11	9
Ukraine...	138	114	147	120	72	83	112	125
Uzbekistan..	22	53	52	23	13	11	9	5
Former Soviet Union—Regional [4]...................	501	372	456	470	461	508	535	485
Other [3] and unspecified [4].............................	419	105	153	73	73	76	73	100
Near East and South Asia [1]..........................	**3,378**	**3,135**	**5,515**	**4,767**	**9,947**	**9,038**	**11,780**	**14,413**
Afghanistan...	5	1,382	2,304	3,807	7,541	6,125	8,555	10,862
Bangladesh...	43	50	52	44	81	76	53	71
Egypt...	3,139	2,689	2,827	149	1,766	1,797	1,749	1,216
Greece...	-149	-457	-114	-103	-74	-66	-74	-76
India..	-64	-40	-69	63	46	28	28	41
Nepal...	15	37	51	58	64	64	80	57
Pakistan...	366	-341	532	712	527	688	1,254	1,528
Turkey..	-80	-298	-225	-191	-296	-43	-28	46
UNRWA [5]..	97	27	57	137	135	–	–	–
Other and unspecified [3].................................	21	79	54	47	117	310	141	635
Africa [1]...	**1,054**	**2,228**	**2,120**	**1,261**	**3,546**	**4,778**	**6,425**	**7,315**
Algeria...	-53	-145	-173	-1,324	-18	-18	-11	-13
Burundi...	3	27	6	37	18	16	32	27
Cameroon..	1	2	7	10	5	6	7	11
Cape Verde..	1	4	4	9	7	28	38	2
Congo (Kinshasa) [6]...	(Z)	(Z)	17	1	10	11	12	7
Ethiopia..	142	234	308	233	278	447	440	550
Ghana..	40	67	53	57	65	87	157	123
Guinea...	19	33	36	29	15	75	31	20
Kenya..	44	82	96	187	179	284	390	340
Liberia..	19	50	40	61	81	261	142	135
Madagascar...	21	34	42	45	60	82	68	64
Malawi..	45	54	46	68	75	88	95	92
Mali...	50	46	55	57	55	58	114	94
Mozambique...	119	105	65	98	111	152	192	146
Nigeria...	-17	41	67	-178	123	200	211	255
Rwanda...	26	36	49	55	70	93	111	103
Senegal..	27	53	40	39	40	70	73	106
Somalia..	7	16	10	33	40	168	108	35
South Africa..	68	332	103	106	155	242	360	266
Sudan...	17	120	130	390	364	529	513	521
Tanzania...	15	66	65	76	114	129	207	215
Uganda...	92	120	149	154	184	194	228	237
Zambia...	44	56	91	91	119	164	151	121
Zimbabwe..	23	31	27	32	69	141	153	113
Other and unspecified [4].................................	164	407	513	621	1,070	767	1,826	3,102
Far East and Pacific [1].................................	**551**	**-133**	**67**	**-93**	**144**	**696**	**621**	**865**
Cambodia..	23	44	58	56	61	60	66	90
Hong Kong..	-15	-28	-28	-28	-28	-23	-16	-15
Indonesia..	272	-157	-3	-68	-14	-84	-46	66
Korea, South..	-132	-110	-43	-43	-40	182	-68	-67
Laos..	5	5	2	1	1	3	5	6
Malaysia...	134	-45	-40	-41	-185	2	2	4
Philippines..	22	-14	-31	-25	51	143	128	133
Thailand..	-99	8	9	-62	1	19	8	14
Pacific Islands, Trust Territory of the Pacific Island [7].......	145	204	190	174	195	211	348	185
Other and unspecified [4].................................	19	40	47	37	182	200	215	214
Western Hemisphere [1].................................	**1,621**	**1,907**	**2,096**	**1,512**	**1,398**	**2,087**	**4,311**	**2,977**
Bolivia..	136	217	159	142	155	135	139	79
Brazil...	195	-136	-93	-344	-181	-166	-87	-303
Colombia...	33	467	598	620	771	914	1,223	642
Ecuador..	14	37	60	80	73	52	60	47
El Salvador..	27	103	51	28	42	58	100	48
Guatemala...	49	40	21	34	25	55	66	68
Haiti...	63	83	118	154	164	192	232	1,047
Honduras...	100	83	71	63	87	100	133	56

See footnotes at end of table.

Table 1312. U.S. Government Foreign Grants and Credits by Type and Country: 2000 to 2010-Continued.

See headnote on page 829.

Country	2000	2004	2005	2006	2007	2008	2009	2010
Mexico	-123	14	40	30	51	52	1,277	418
Nicaragua	53	28	37	56	75	97	91	37
Panama [8]	-13	14	8	11	6	9	7	9
Peru	87	168	127	71	-258	128	539	188
Other [9] and unspecified [4]	1,100	725	745	471	407	366	426	439
Other international organizations	**2,837**	**3,015**	**4,608**	**4,114**	**4,857**	**5,348**	**7,908**	**8,652**
Middle East	**4,345**	**8,413**	**16,705**	**10,220**	**10,195**	**10,801**	**9,608**	**9,028**
Iraq [10]	(Z)	5,040	10,857	9,157	7,039	6,228	5,269	2,942
Israel	3,932	2,163	4,953	390	2,373	2,955	1,994	2,692
Jordan	317	801	583	463	422	643	687	802
Lebanon	22	29	37	46	147	253	244	119
Yemen	16	31	25	30	40	22	31	48
West Bank-Gaza Regional	64	171	179	128	152	474	812	687

– Represents zero. Z Less than $500,000. [1] Includes other countries, not shown separately. [2] In 1992, some successor countries assumed portions of outstanding credits of the former Yugoslavia (assignment of the remaining portions is pending). Subsequent negative totals reflect payments to the United States on these assumed credits which were greater than the extension of new credits and grants to these countries. [3] Includes European Atomic Energy Community, European Coal and Steel Community, European Payments Union, European Productivity Agency, North Atlantic Treaty Organization, and Organization for European Economic Cooperation. [4] In recent years, significant amounts of foreign assistance have been reported on a regional, inter-regional, and worldwide basis. Country totals in this table may understate actual assistance to many countries. [5] United Nations Relief and Works Agency for Palestine Refugees. [6] See footnote 5, table 1348. [7] Excludes transactions with Commonwealth of the Northern Mariana Islands after October 1986; includes transactions with Federated States of Micronesia, Republic of the Marshall Islands, and Republic of Palau. [8] Includes transfer of Panama Canal to the Republic of Panama in December 1999. [9] Includes Andean Development Corporation, Caribbean Development Bank, Central American Bank for Economic Integration, Eastern Caribbean Central Bank, Inter-American Institute of Agricultural Science, Organization of American States, and Pan American Health Organization. [10] Foreign assistance to Iraq in 1991–96 was direct humanitarian assistance to ethnic minorities of northern Iraq after the conflict in the Persian Gulf. Foreign assistance to Iraq in 2003 thru 2009 includes Iraq Reconstruction and humanitarian assistance.

Source: U.S. Bureau of Economic Analysis, press releases, and unpublished data. See <http://www.bea.gov/scb/index.htm>.

Table 1313. U.S. Foreign Economic and Military Aid Programs: 1980 to 2010

[In millions of dollars (9,682 represents $9,682,000,000). For years ending September 30. Total aid programs are the sum of economic and military assistance. Major components in recent years include U.S. Agency for International Development (USAID), U.S. Department of Agriculture (USDA), State Department, and voluntary contributions to international financial institutions. Annual figures are in obligations]

Year and Region	Total foreign assistance	Military assistance	Economic assistance, by funding agency					
			Total	USAID	USDA	State Department	Other U.S. agencies	Multilateral organizations
1980	9,682	2,110	7,572	4,062	1,437	459	137	1,478
1985	18,107	5,780	12,327	8,132	2,052	431	164	1,548
1990	16,003	4,959	11,044	6,964	1,643	590	378	1,469
1995	16,301	4,090	12,210	7,281	1,401	763	984	1,781
2000	17,833	4,943	12,890	5,907	2,567	2,367	939	1,110
2005	37,254	7,861	29,394	10,128	2,318	5,122	10,167	1,659
2006	39,580	12,664	26,916	9,620	2,033	5,441	8,330	1,492
2007	41,057	13,754	27,303	11,416	1,835	5,746	6,572	1,733
2008	48,981	16,479	32,502	9,428	2,883	9,872	8,434	1,885
2009	48,518	14,898	33,620	11,793	2,701	11,328	5,470	2,328
2010, total	**52,728**	**15,058**	**37,671**	**14,069**	**2,638**	**12,224**	**5,836**	**2,904**
Asia	16,426	7,801	8,625	5,258	449	2,069	849	0
Eurasia	2,610	446	2,164	864	162	267	871	0
Eastern Europe	747	132	614	296	0	68	251	0
Latin America and Caribbean	4,771	431	4,340	1,582	243	1,591	683	242
Middle East and North Africa	8,963	5,518	3,446	1,825	22	1,103	496	0
Oceania	331	2	329	21	0	3	305	0
Sub-Saharan Africa	10,310	574	9,736	2,378	1,588	4,501	1,114	155
Western Europe	93	7	85	19	0	18	49	0
Canada	26	0	26	0	0	0	26	0
World, not specified	8,452	147	8,306	1,826	174	2,605	1,194	2,507

Source: U.S. Agency for International Development (USAID), *U.S. Overseas Loans and Grants: Obligations and Loan Authorizations*, annual. See also <http://gbk.eads.usaidallnet.gov/data/detailed.html>.

Table 1314. U.S. Foreign Economic and Military Aid by Major Recipient Country: 2000 to 2010

[In millions of dollars (17,833 represents $17,833,000,000). For years ending September 30. Annual figures are in obligations]

Region/Country	2000	2005	2008	2009	2010 Total	2010 Economic aid	2010 Military aid
Total [1]	17,833	37,254	48,981	48,518	52,728	37,671	15,058
Middle East & North Africa [1]	6,799	15,123	13,860	12,062	8,963	3,446	5,518
Egypt	2,076	1,567	1,493	1,782	1,699	397	1,302
Iraq	1	9,482	7,496	4,852	2,088	1,082	1,006
Israel	3,863	2,713	2,425	2,423	2,836	36	2,800
Jordan	448	683	875	815	767	463	304
Lebanon	35	25	198	215	159	156	3
Morocco	51	55	532	249	69	56	12
West Bank/Gaza [2]	122	350	524	1,039	693	693	0
Yemen	57	30	37	174	139	125	14
Sub-Saharan Africa [1]	2,037	5,156	10,620	10,709	10,310	9,736	574
Angola	105	67	59	55	100	99	0
Botswana	1	42	211	104	62	61	1
Burkina Faso	18	33	45	506	38	38	0
Chad	4	63	127	222	172	172	1
Congo (Kinshasa) [3]	33	121	260	401	389	359	30
Ethiopia	278	694	1,007	953	982	982	0
Ghana	67	72	210	174	252	249	4
Kenya	94	263	717	917	819	816	3
Lesotho	2	4	357	34	56	56	0
Liberia	22	149	312	274	297	269	28
Madagascar	27	84	110	60	81	81	0
Malawi	44	84	104	137	207	207	0
Mali	44	55	138	225	167	166	1
Mozambique	88	127	794	325	404	404	1
Namibia	16	50	131	388	114	114	0
Nigeria	113	151	485	501	459	456	3
Rwanda	39	83	172	170	222	221	1
Senegal	38	48	79	135	702	698	4
Somalia	14	45	351	695	265	61	204
South Africa	57	187	570	568	568	566	2
Sudan	51	1,047	1,416	1,267	976	871	105
Tanzania	45	137	990	379	555	554	1
Uganda	76	291	456	476	487	451	36
Zambia	35	144	263	292	332	331	0
Zimbabwe	21	61	234	286	219	219	0
Latin America & Caribbean [1]	2,344	2,636	2,660	3,033	4,771	4,340	431
Bolivia	241	162	128	101	98	97	1
Colombia	1,169	824	888	897	864	678	186
El Salvador	45	59	208	152	131	125	6
Guatemala	87	96	111	141	169	160	9
Haiti	85	224	310	369	1,408	1,406	2
Honduras	42	262	75	38	117	113	5
Mexico	44	103	95	499	718	622	96
Peru	204	191	162	151	213	189	24
Asia [1]	1,262	4,839	11,842	12,335	16,426	8,625	7,801
Afghanistan	54	2,252	8,892	8,817	11,447	4,647	6,800
Bangladesh	78	84	171	172	230	227	3
Cambodia	28	98	76	83	93	91	2
India	188	215	148	133	146	145	1
Indonesia	298	588	209	231	338	313	25
Mongolia	26	19	129	39	241	235	6
Nepal	23	73	106	89	80	78	2
Pakistan	37	758	964	1,782	2,854	1,940	914
Philippines	112	167	161	184	244	208	36
Sri Lanka	11	160	69	83	111	110	2
Oceania [1]	165	163	196	222	331	329	2
Micronesia, Federated States of	81	94	79	108	109	108	1
Eurasia [1]	1,972	2,495	2,571	1,989	2,610	2,164	446
Armenia	114	80	220	66	92	88	4
Georgia	117	109	278	606	438	420	18
Kazakhstan	53	69	117	103	322	305	17
Kyrgyzstan	47	52	81	58	130	115	15
Moldova	49	34	25	32	309	308	2
Russia	1,162	1,603	1,292	508	506	379	127
Ukraine	200	161	132	186	308	288	20
Eastern Europe [1]	1,045	631	611	520	747	614	132
Kosovo	165	41	208	136	172	169	3
Poland	85	96	34	82	221	166	56
Western Europe	24	132	82	97	93	85	7

[1] Includes other countries, not shown separately. [2] See footnote 7, Table 1348. [3] See footnote 5, Table 1348.

Source: U.S. Agency for International Development, *U.S. Overseas Loans and Grants, Obligations and Loan Authorizations*, annual. See also <http://gbk.eads.usaidallnet.gov>.

Table 1315. U.S. International Trade in Goods and Services: 2000 to 2011

[In millions of dollars (–376,749 represents –$376,749,000,000). Data presented on a balance of payments basis and will not agree with the following merchandise trade tables in this section]

Category	2000	2005	2006	2007	2008	2009	2010	2011
TRADE BALANCE								
Total	**-376,749**	**-708,624**	**-753,288**	**-696,728**	**-698,338**	**-379,154**	**-494,737**	**-559,880**
Goods	-445,787	-780,730	-835,689	-818,886	-830,109	-505,758	-645,124	-738,413
Services	69,038	72,106	82,401	122,158	131,770	126,603	150,387	178,533
Travel	17,525	12,230	13,228	20,228	29,929	20,055	27,971	37,464
Passenger fares	-3,416	-4,580	-5,008	-2,494	-884	986	3,727	5,522
Other transportation	-11,647	-22,199	-19,496	-15,135	-12,680	-6,514	-10,441	-11,647
Royalties, license fees	35,202	48,871	58,511	71,324	72,502	67,109	73,731	84,216
Other private services	39,707	55,945	49,490	61,793	59,476	62,775	74,707	78,220
Other [1]	-6,488	-15,594	-11,743	-10,826	-13,600	-14,461	-15,639	-11,564
U.S. govt misc. services	-1,844	-2,567	-2,581	-2,731	-2,972	-3,346	-3,669	-3,678
EXPORTS								
Total	**1,072,783**	**1,287,441**	**1,459,823**	**1,654,561**	**1,842,682**	**1,578,945**	**1,842,485**	**2,103,367**
Goods	784,781	911,686	1,039,406	1,163,957	1,307,499	1,069,733	1,288,882	1,497,406
Services	288,002	375,755	420,417	490,604	535,183	509,212	553,603	605,961
Travel	82,891	82,160	86,187	97,355	110,423	94,187	103,481	116,115
Passenger fares	20,197	20,609	21,638	25,187	30,957	26,103	30,983	36,631
Other transportation	25,562	32,013	35,824	40,638	44,016	36,087	40,817	43,064
Royalties, license fees	51,808	74,448	83,549	97,803	102,125	98,406	107,165	120,836
Other private services	100,792	153,665	176,798	211,641	232,019	237,348	255,293	270,193
Other [1]	6,210	12,082	15,587	17,091	14,711	16,013	14,752	17,946
U.S. govt misc. services	542	778	834	890	933	1,069	1,112	1,176
IMPORTS								
Total	**1,449,532**	**1,996,065**	**2,213,111**	**2,351,289**	**2,541,020**	**1,958,099**	**2,337,222**	**2,663,247**
Goods	1,230,568	1,692,416	1,875,095	1,982,843	2,137,608	1,575,491	1,934,006	2,235,819
Services	218,964	303,649	338,016	368,446	403,413	382,608	403,216	427,428
Travel	65,366	69,930	72,959	77,127	80,494	74,132	75,510	78,651
Passenger fares	23,613	25,189	26,646	27,681	31,841	25,117	27,256	31,109
Other transportation	37,209	54,212	55,320	55,773	56,696	42,601	51,258	54,711
Royalties, license fees	16,606	25,577	25,038	26,479	29,623	31,297	33,434	36,620
Other private services	61,085	97,720	127,308	149,848	172,543	174,573	180,586	191,973
Other [1]	12,698	27,676	27,330	27,917	28,311	30,474	30,391	29,510
U.S. govt misc. services	2,386	3,345	3,415	3,621	3,905	4,415	4,781	4,854

[1] Represents transfers under U.S. military sales contracts for exports and direct defense expenditures for imports.

Source: U.S. Census Bureau, *U.S. International Trade in Goods and Services, Annual Revision for 2011*, Series FT-900(12-04) and previous reports. See also <http://www.census.gov/foreign-trade/Press-Release/2011pr/final_revisions/>.

Table 1316. U.S. International Trade in Goods by Related Parties: 2000 to 2011

[In millions of dollars (1,205,339 represents $1,205,339,000,000). "Related party trade" is trade by U.S. companies with their subsidiaries abroad as well as trade by U.S. subsidiaries of foreign companies with their parent companies. Based on the North American Industry Classification System (NAICS), 2002; see text, Section 15]

Country and commodity	2002 NAICS code	2000	2005	2009	2010	2011
IMPORTS FOR CONSUMPTION						
Total imports	(X)	1,205,339	1,662,380	1,549,163	1,898,610	2,186,951
Related party trade, total [1]	**(X)**	**563,084**	**775,730**	**740,481**	**922,202**	**1,056,215**
Canada	(X)	100,689	127,719	107,315	138,222	162,045
Mexico	(X)	89,068	99,709	100,935	135,984	155,713
China [2]	(X)	18,061	62,716	84,829	107,038	111,599
Japan	(X)	108,290	108,322	73,859	93,892	97,789
Germany	(X)	37,781	51,870	45,000	53,951	65,756
Computer & electronic products	334	166,279	176,719	163,662	203,900	208,047
Transportation equipment	336	161,150	188,445	132,812	179,516	200,525
Chemicals	325	45,452	84,459	118,149	134,065	152,928
Oil & gas	211	13,241	48,725	61,700	80,071	97,024
Petroleum & coal products	324	12,655	42,572	40,601	54,618	77,258
EXPORTS						
Total exports	(X)	780,418	803,992	1,056,932	1,277,504	1,480,552
Related party trade, domestic exports, total [1]	**(X)**	**196,596**	**245,712**	**261,332**	**314,489**	**365,014**
Canada	(X)	64,133	76,331	71,478	88,689	98,098
Mexico	(X)	34,249	44,570	39,653	49,313	60,515
Japan	(X)	20,313	17,427	15,038	16,718	18,673
Netherlands	(X)	6,845	9,308	15,784	15,070	17,088
China [2]	(X)	1,552	4,909	8,954	13,436	15,325
Chemicals	325	26,376	48,121	54,655	64,548	73,517
Transportation equipment	336	46,288	52,513	43,758	55,400	65,533
Computer & electronic products	334	51,210	41,882	36,405	42,689	40,614
Petroleum & coal products	324	1,253	4,974	18,654	23,101	40,237
Machinery, except electrical	333	19,831	25,473	26,418	32,301	36,841

X Not applicable. [1] Includes other countries and other commodities, not shown separately. [2] See footnote 4, Table 1348.

Source: U.S. Census Bureau, *Related Party Trade - 2011*. See <http://www.census.gov/foreign-trade/Press-Release/2011pr/aip/related_party/>.

Table 1317. U.S. Freight Gateways—Value of Shipments: 2010

[In billions of dollars (3,688.3 represents $3,688,300,000,000), except as indicated. For the top 50 gateways ranked by value of shipments]

Port	Mode	Rank	Total trade	Exports	Imports	Exports as a percent of total
Total U.S. merchandise trade.........................	(X)	(X)	**3,688.3**	**1,480.4**	**2,207.8**	**40.1**
Top 50 gateways..................................	(X)	(X)	2,943.9	1,157.5	1,786.4	39.3
As a percent of total.................................	(X)	(X)	79.8	78.2	80.9	(X)
Los Angeles, CA..................................	Water	1	273.1	43.8	229.3	16.0
JFK International Airport, NY.........................	Air	2	189.9	96.1	93.8	50.6
Houston, TX......................................	Water	3	168.7	88.5	80.3	52.4
Laredo, TX.......................................	Land	4	149.7	68.3	81.5	45.6
Newark, NJ.......................................	Water	5	139.3	13.3	126.0	9.5
Detroit, MI.......................................	Land	6	134.3	72.0	62.2	53.6
Chicago, IL.......................................	Air	7	115.5	35.9	79.6	31.1
Long Beach, CA..................................	Water	8	94.7	34.8	59.8	36.8
Port Huron, MI...................................	Land	9	90.3	43.1	47.2	47.7
Buffalo-Niagara Falls, NY...........................	Land	10	85.7	45.1	40.6	52.6
Los Angeles International Airport, CA.................	Air	11	83.2	40.5	42.7	48.7
Savannah, GA....................................	Water	12	71.7	30.9	40.7	43.2
New York, NY.....................................	Water	13	62.0	42.9	19.2	69.1
Miami International Airport, FL.......................	Air	14	61.0	40.9	20.1	67.1
El Paso, TX......................................	Land	15	60.9	26.8	34.1	44.0
New Orleans, LA..................................	Air	16	59.1	24.0	35.1	40.7
Charleston, SC...................................	Water	17	58.9	22.2	36.7	37.7
New Orleans, LA..................................	Water	18	58.5	32.5	25.9	55.7
Norfolk, VA......................................	Water	19	53.9	23.9	30.0	44.4
Baltimore, MD....................................	Water	20	51.2	20.5	30.8	40.0
San Francisco International Airport, CA...............	Air	21	50.3	26.5	23.8	52.7
Dallas-Fort Worth, TX..............................	Air	22	45.6	17.0	28.6	37.3
Oakland, CA.....................................	Water	23	45.5	18.0	27.5	39.6
Anchorage, AK...................................	Air	24	44.5	9.9	34.5	22.3
Seattle, WA......................................	Water	25	43.3	12.9	30.4	29.8
Cleveland, OH....................................	Air	26	37.9	22.7	15.2	60.0
Atlanta, GA......................................	Air	27	37.2	13.4	23.8	36.0
Philadelphia, PA..................................	Water	28	35.0	3.4	31.6	9.6
Tacoma, WA.....................................	Water	29	34.4	7.6	26.9	21.9
Otay Mesa Station, CA.............................	Land	30	34.2	11.5	22.8	33.5
Morgan City, LA..................................	Water	31	34.0	0.3	33.8	0.8
Corpus Christi, TX................................	Water	32	30.8	10.0	20.8	32.5
Champlain-Rouses Point, NY........................	Land	33	28.9	10.3	18.6	35.6
Chicago, IL.......................................	Land	34	28.2	0.4	27.8	1.3
Port Arthur, TX...................................	Water	35	26.6	3.3	23.4	12.2
Hildago, TX......................................	Land	36	25.4	9.7	15.8	38.0
Gramercy, LA....................................	Water	37	25.4	13.5	11.8	53.4
Miami, FL..	Water	38	24.9	11.9	13.0	47.7
Texas City, TX...................................	Water	39	23.3	5.5	17.9	23.4
Port Everglades, FL...............................	Water	40	23.3	13.3	10.0	57.1
Pembina, ND.....................................	Land	41	22.5	13.1	9.5	58.0
Nogales, AZ......................................	Land	42	22.5	8.1	14.4	36.1
Blaine, WA.......................................	Land	43	21.5	13.7	7.8	63.6
Jacksonville, FL..................................	Water	44	20.9	10.8	10.1	51.8
Houston Intercontinental Airport, TX..................	Air	45	20.2	10.3	9.9	50.9
San Juan International Airport, PR....................	Air	46	20.1	10.4	9.6	52.0
Lake Charles, LA.................................	Water	47	19.7	4.2	15.5	21.4
Eagle Pass, TX...................................	Land	48	19.7	7.6	12.0	38.7
Santa Teresa, NM................................	Land	49	18.3	7.5	10.8	41.0
Washington, DC..................................	Air	50	18.2	4.8	13.4	26.6
Beaumont, TX....................................	Water	50	12.2	2.5	9.7	20.4

X Not applicable.

Source: U.S. Census Bureau, Foreign Trade Division, USA Trade Online, special tabulation, available at <http://data.usatradeonline.gov/> as of December 2010. Land: U.S. Department of Transportation, Research and Innovative Technology Administration, Bureau of Transportation Statistics, TransBorder Freight Data, special tabulation, available at <http://www.bts.gov/programs/international/transborder/> as of March 2011.

Table 1318. U.S. Exports and General Imports of Merchandise by Customs District: 2005 to 2011

[In billions of dollars (901.1 represents $901,100,000,000). Exports are f.a.s. (free alongside ship) value all years; imports are on customs-value basis. These data may differ from those in Tables 1316, 1321, and 1322. For methodology, see Foreign Trade Statistics in Appendix III]

Customs district	Exports					General imports				
	2005	2008	2009	2010	2011	2005	2008	2009	2010	2011
Total [1]	901.1	1,287.4	1,056.0	1,278.3	1,480.7	1,673.5	2,103.6	1,559.6	1,913.2	2,207.0
Anchorage, AK	12.1	13.5	11.9	14.5	15.4	10.4	10.7	12.4	16.2	15.2
Baltimore, MD	9.0	16.5	11.2	14.7	21.0	29.6	31.3	21.0	28.8	32.3
Boston, MA	10.4	11.9	8.3	8.2	8.1	21.7	24.4	17.4	19.2	20.9
Buffalo, NY	35.0	43.5	35.7	40.4	46.5	42.6	46.0	31.6	39.2	41.9
Charleston, SC [2]	16.2	22.3	16.4	19.5	22.5	31.9	36.5	26.3	29.4	36.2
Chicago, IL	29.9	36.6	31.5	35.8	36.6	78.7	116.9	96.7	125.6	139.9
Cleveland, OH	20.8	23.8	21.4	25.3	29.9	49.0	70.4	55.8	69.2	79.4
Columbia-Snake, OR	6.3	14.3	10.3	12.3	14.4	14.2	16.9	11.0	12.2	12.5
Dallas/Fort Worth, TX	17.8	19.8	17.4	18.1	18.4	31.8	37.1	30.8	38.4	45.5
Detroit, MI	106.9	119.1	89.6	113.3	122.9	123.1	117.4	81.3	106.1	120.8
Duluth, MN	1.9	3.2	2.3	2.6	3.6	9.3	8.5	5.8	6.8	8.3
El Paso, TX	19.9	21.1	19.8	29.3	34.7	28.0	32.4	30.4	44.1	47.5
Great Falls, MT	9.8	18.0	15.3	17.4	22.9	27.1	34.9	21.7	26.3	29.1
Honolulu, HI	2.4	5.6	5.8	7.4	7.5	3.7	6.0	3.8	4.6	5.7
Houston/Galveston, TX	47.0	89.9	75.1	94.6	119.4	89.4	151.0	92.4	116.8	148.6
Laredo, TX	60.5	79.6	66.8	81.3	95.7	78.7	95.1	80.0	104.2	120.2
Los Angeles, CA	78.4	110.0	86.1	105.2	121.1	215.5	247.1	196.4	242.7	266.1
Miami, FL	34.1	54.9	49.5	58.8	69.3	31.8	35.4	29.6	36.6	43.6
Milwaukee, WI	0.1	0.2	0.1	0.1	0.3	1.3	1.1	0.7	0.9	1.3
Minneapolis, MN	2.3	2.3	2.0	2.6	2.6	6.9	16.6	11.4	13.6	16.4
Mobile, AL [2]	5.0	8.5	7.3	8.8	11.6	14.3	24.7	17.3	20.8	26.8
New Orleans, LA	32.6	65.6	57.0	68.1	83.9	97.8	151.3	94.2	125.3	150.6
New York, NY	90.9	143.7	110.9	136.3	161.1	176.7	209.5	155.6	190.5	227.1
Nogales, AZ	6.9	9.2	7.6	8.8	10.5	13.0	16.8	14.0	17.4	18.4
Norfolk, VA [2]	16.8	25.8	19.8	21.1	24.3	23.5	29.6	21.6	23.9	25.5
Ogdensburg, NY	13.3	16.5	13.5	16.2	18.6	28.2	33.0	23.9	27.8	30.1
Pembina, ND	13.6	22.0	16.9	21.3	25.5	12.8	17.4	12.5	14.7	16.3
Philadelphia, PA	10.2	19.4	13.1	14.3	17.3	47.8	73.3	49.2	56.9	67.1
Port Arthur, TX	2.1	5.3	4.9	6.5	10.8	20.9	32.4	20.1	26.4	33.5
Portland, ME	2.8	4.8	4.2	4.4	4.7	11.2	11.6	10.0	9.8	12.2
Providence, RI	0.1	0.3	0.2	0.3	0.4	4.4	5.7	4.0	5.8	7.0
San Diego, CA	15.0	16.6	14.0	16.2	18.6	28.4	37.4	30.4	32.4	34.2
San Francisco, CA	36.6	43.7	37.0	47.1	49.8	62.4	71.6	49.7	60.6	69.7
San Juan, PR	9.7	17.2	18.8	20.7	16.5	19.5	21.6	18.9	19.4	24.5
Savannah, GA	24.7	38.3	33.8	41.1	49.5	47.9	62.7	53.4	68.0	76.6
Seattle, WA	44.1	59.9	53.9	58.6	69.5	51.7	60.7	47.7	52.6	58.9
St. Albans, VT	4.3	3.8	2.9	3.3	3.2	12.6	10.2	7.6	6.9	8.6
St. Louis, MO	1.3	2.8	1.6	1.0	0.8	9.7	12.7	10.1	11.5	19.2
Tampa, FL	10.1	18.1	10.4	14.4	17.5	19.3	22.2	13.6	16.4	18.9
Virgin Islands, U.S.	0.5	2.7	1.2	1.9	2.3	9.1	16.6	9.2	10.5	12.2
Washington, DC	3.7	5.7	6.0	6.0	5.2	3.7	8.8	10.2	8.2	9.0
Wilmington, NC	2.2	3.2	4.0	5.3	5.5	15.4	15.3	12.9	12.8	15.2

[1] Totals shown for exports reflect the value of estimated parcel post and Special Category shipments, and adjustments for undocumented exports to Canada, which are not distributed by customs district. The value of bituminous coal exported through Norfolk, VA; Charleston, SC; and Mobile, AL is reflected in the total but not distributed by district. [2] Excludes exports of bituminous coal, which are included in "Total."

Source: U.S. Census Bureau, U.S. *Merchandise Trade: Selected Highlights*, December issues, series FT920, and unpublished data. See also <http://www.census.gov/foreign-trade/Press-Release/ft920_index.html>.

Table 1319. U.S. Exports of Goods by State of Origin: 2000 to 2011

[In millions of dollars (782,429 represents $782,429,000,000), except as indicated. Exports are on a f.a.s. (free along ship) value basis. Exports are based on origin of movement]

State and other areas	Exports 2000	Exports 2010	2011 Total	2011 Rank	State and other areas	Exports 2000	Exports 2010	2011 Total	2011 Rank
Total	**782,429**	**1,278,263**	**1,480,665**	(X)	Nebraska	2,511	5,820	7,578	34
					Nevada	1,482	5,912	7,978	33
United States	**712,055**	**1,207,883**	**1,410,410**	(X)	New Hampshire	2,373	4,367	4,294	42
Alabama	7,317	15,502	17,893	24	New Jersey	18,638	32,154	38,241	11
Alaska	2,464	4,155	5,238	40	New Mexico	2,391	1,541	2,090	46
Arizona	14,334	15,636	17,501	25	New York	42,846	69,696	82,894	3
Arkansas	2,599	5,219	5,559	38	North Carolina	17,946	24,905	26,964	16
California	119,640	143,192	159,354	2	North Dakota	626	2,536	3,379	44
Colorado	6,593	6,727	7,334	35	Ohio	26,322	41,494	46,408	9
Connecticut	8,047	16,056	16,198	26	Oklahoma	3,072	5,353	6,218	36
Delaware	2,197	4,966	5,509	39	Oregon	11,441	17,671	18,292	22
District of Columbia	1,003	1,501	1,055	(X)	Pennsylvania	18,792	34,928	41,030	10
Florida	26,543	55,365	64,756	4	Rhode Island	1,186	1,949	2,300	45
Georgia	14,925	28,950	34,713	12	South Carolina	8,565	20,329	24,680	17
Hawaii	387	684	909	50	South Dakota	679	1,259	1,455	48
Idaho	3,559	5,157	5,899	37	Tennessee	11,592	25,943	29,973	14
Illinois	31,438	50,058	64,565	6	Texas	103,866	206,961	249,860	1
Indiana	15,386	28,745	32,200	13	Utah	3,221	13,809	18,929	21
Iowa	4,466	10,880	13,283	28	Vermont	4,097	4,277	4,328	41
Kansas	5,145	9,905	11,572	29	Virginia	11,698	17,163	18,105	23
Kentucky	9,612	19,343	20,066	20	Washington	32,215	53,353	64,632	5
Louisiana	16,814	41,356	55,124	7	West Virginia	2,219	6,449	9,002	32
Maine	1,779	3,164	3,461	43	Wisconsin	10,508	19,790	22,049	18
Maryland	4,593	10,163	10,879	31	Wyoming	503	983	1,222	49
Massachusetts	20,514	26,304	27,711	15					
Michigan	33,845	44,768	50,802	8	Puerto Rico	9,735	22,784	18,653	(X)
Minnesota	10,303	18,904	20,276	19	Virgin Islands	174	1,899	2,293	(X)
Mississippi	2,726	8,229	10,926	30	Other [1]	60,810	45,698	49,321	(X)
Missouri	6,497	12,926	14,145	27	Timing adjustments	-346	(NA)	-12	(X)
Montana	541	1,389	1,581	47					

NA Not available. X Not applicable. [1] Includes unreported, not specified, special category, estimated shipments, and re-exports.

Source: U.S. Census Bureau, *U.S. International Trade in Goods and Services*, December issues, series FT-900. See <http://www.census.gov/foreign-trade/Press-Release/2011pr/12/>.

Table 1320. U.S. Agricultural Exports by State: 2000 to 2010

[In millions of dollars (51,265 represents $51,265,000,000). Calendar year. Export estimates based on U.S. farm cash receipts]

State	2000	2005	2008	2009	2010	State	2000	2005	2008	2009	2010
U.S.	**51,265**	**63,182**	**114,760**	**98,453**	**115,815**						
AL	489	695	989	907	985	MT	483	604	1,055	813	1,058
AK	22	11	11	11	12	NE	2,531	2,914	6,178	5,674	6,584
AZ	682	909	1,278	1,030	1,247	NV	95	106	169	137	146
AR	1,181	1,779	3,199	2,610	2,904	NH	31	34	57	49	54
CA	6,445	9,117	13,045	12,399	14,061	NJ	216	255	397	362	416
CO	1,049	1,038	1,751	1,475	1,728	NM	435	495	653	579	776
CT	246	196	211	200	202	NY	484	580	1,127	880	1,115
DE	129	141	227	214	231	NC	1,630	1,838	3,024	2,767	3,065
FL	1,661	1,799	2,476	2,219	2,554	ND	1,081	1,438	3,548	2,751	3,317
GA	1,187	1,342	2,301	1,893	2,297	OH	1,468	1,629	3,269	2,816	3,456
HI	150	213	295	327	381	OK	848	1,016	1,706	1,182	1,630
ID	774	975	1,655	1,288	1,525	OR	999	1,162	1,606	1,343	1,441
IL	3,196	3,884	8,005	7,010	7,785	PA	666	829	1,413	1,122	1,381
IN	1,757	1,973	4,428	3,834	4,501	RI	9	15	20	18	21
IA	3,621	4,458	9,853	8,456	9,508	SC	351	418	717	635	756
KS	2,105	2,372	4,305	4,035	4,818	SD	1,232	1,433	3,321	2,920	3,210
KY	1,353	1,390	2,112	1,820	1,999	TN	567	793	1,147	1,194	1,327
LA	556	711	1,245	1,062	1,291	TX	2,791	3,807	6,446	5,078	6,934
ME	121	129	175	152	180	UT	193	247	396	270	355
MD	323	301	511	452	502	VT	50	65	113	89	116
MA	119	116	207	172	185	VA	499	538	865	749	828
MI	867	1,082	2,265	1,837	2,331	WA	1,284	1,554	2,574	2,016	2,497
MN	2,180	2,651	6,434	5,079	6,078	WV	58	65	101	100	103
MS	582	962	1,634	1,357	1,519	WI	914	1,262	2,482	1,943	2,586
MO	1,364	1,686	3,489	2,869	3,520	WY	193	157	274	258	304

Source: U.S. Department of Agriculture, Economic Research Service, "State Export Data," <http://www.ers.usda.gov/data-products/state-export-data.aspx#25535>.

Table 1321. U.S. Exports, Imports, and Merchandise Trade Balance by Country: 2005 to 2011

[In millions of dollars (901,082 represents $901,082,000,000). Includes silver ore and bullion. Country totals include exports of special category commodities, if any. Data include nonmonetary gold and include trade of Virgin Islands with foreign countries. For methodology, see Foreign Trade Statistics in Appendix III. Minus sign (–) denotes an excess of imports over exports]

Country	Exports, domestic and foreign					General imports					Merchandise trade balance				
	2005	2008	2009	2010	2011	2005	2008	2009	2010	2011	2005	2008	2009	2010	2011
Total [1]	901,082	1,287,442	1,056,043	1,278,263	1,480,432	1,673,455	2,103,641	1,559,625	1,913,160	2,207,824	-772,373	-816,199	-503,582	-634,897	-727,392
Afghanistan	262	482	1,509	2,156	2,924	67	85	116	85	26	195	397	1,392	2,071	2,898
Albania	19	40	48	46	48	37	12	15	30	26	-19	28	33	16	21
Algeria	1,106	1,243	1,108	1,195	1,595	10,446	19,355	10,718	14,518	14,609	-9,340	-18,112	-9,610	-13,323	-13,014
Angola	929	2,019	1,423	1,294	1,502	8,484	18,911	9,339	11,940	13,598	-7,555	-16,892	-7,916	-10,646	-12,095
Antigua and Barbuda	190	183	157	158	155	4	5	9	5	7	186	178	148	153	148
Argentina	4,122	7,536	5,569	7,395	9,917	4,584	5,822	3,890	3,803	4,502	-462	1,714	1,679	3,592	5,415
Armenia	65	151	77	113	94	46	43	78	75	93	19	109	0	38	2
Aruba	559	680	446	541	713	2,920	3,179	1,278	19	3,262	-2,361	-2,499	-833	522	-2,549
Australia	15,589	22,219	19,599	21,798	27,542	7,342	10,589	8,012	8,583	10,241	8,246	11,630	11,588	13,215	17,301
Austria	2,544	2,649	2,537	2,428	2,888	6,103	8,457	6,379	6,835	9,482	-3,558	-5,808	-3,842	-4,407	-6,593
Azerbaijan	132	239	185	253	337	45	4,361	1,973	1,989	2,425	87	-4,122	-1,787	-1,736	-2,088
Bahamas, The	1,787	2,760	2,504	3,178	3,442	700	604	819	807	765	1,087	2,155	1,685	2,371	2,677
Bahrain	351	830	667	1,250	1,213	432	539	463	420	518	-81	291	204	830	695
Bangladesh	320	468	435	578	1,144	2,693	3,748	3,699	4,294	4,877	-2,373	-3,280	-3,264	-3,716	-3,733
Barbados	395	497	405	397	439	32	40	33	43	47	363	457	372	354	393
Belarus	35	134	137	133	156	345	1,070	574	175	363	-310	-935	-437	-42	-206
Belgium	18,691	28,903	21,608	25,456	29,899	13,023	17,308	13,826	15,552	17,431	5,668	11,595	7,782	9,904	12,468
Belize	218	353	253	289	356	98	154	100	120	191	119	199	153	169	165
Benin	72	846	397	463	618	1	31	0	0	2	72	815	397	463	616
Bermuda	490	822	807	637	611	87	140	13	22	60	403	682	794	615	551
Bolivia	219	389	431	507	667	293	511	504	680	902	-74	-122	-73	-173	-235
Botswana	67	62	93	48	44	178	219	132	170	293	-111	-157	-39	-122	-249
Brazil	15,372	32,299	26,095	35,425	42,944	24,436	30,453	20,070	23,958	31,736	-9,064	1,846	6,026	11,467	11,208
Brunei	50	112	100	124	184	563	114	42	12	23	-513	-3	59	112	161
Bulgaria	268	509	224	171	259	454	391	228	260	416	-186	119	-4	-89	-157
Cambodia	70	154	127	154	186	1,767	2,412	1,924	2,301	2,712	-1,697	-2,257	-1,797	-2,147	-2,527
Cameroon	117	125	154	132	221	158	614	250	297	330	-41	-489	-96	-165	-110
Canada	211,899	261,150	204,658	249,105	280,890	290,384	339,491	226,248	277,647	315,347	-78,486	-78,342	-21,590	-28,542	-34,457
Cayman Islands	681	746	643	582	617	53	14	14	11	18	627	732	630	571	598
Chad	54	63	63	88	35	1,498	3,334	1,984	2,044	3,174	-1,444	-3,272	-1,921	-1,956	-3,139
Chile	5,134	11,857	9,346	10,905	15,986	6,664	8,196	5,949	7,009	9,074	-1,531	3,661	3,396	3,896	6,913
China [2]	41,192	69,733	69,497	91,881	103,939	243,470	337,773	296,374	364,944	399,362	-202,278	-268,040	-226,877	-273,063	-295,423
Colombia	5,462	11,437	9,451	12,069	14,321	8,849	13,093	11,323	15,659	23,113	-3,387	-1,656	-1,872	-3,590	-8,793
Congo (Brazzaville) [3]	104	185	277	254	327	1,623	5,074	3,105	3,316	2,420	-1,519	-4,889	-2,828	-3,062	-2,193
Congo (Kinshasa) [3]	65	130	79	93	166	264	266	331	528	606	-199	-136	-251	-435	-440
Costa Rica	3,599	5,680	4,700	5,180	6,062	3,415	3,938	5,612	8,697	10,119	183	1,742	-912	-3,517	-4,057
Cote d'Ivoire	124	254	206	163	130	1,198	1,092	745	1,177	1,271	-1,074	-838	-539	-1,014	-1,140
Croatia	159	467	202	312	511	364	271	251	333	438	-206	196	-49	-21	73
Cuba	369	712	533	368	363	0	0	0	0	0	369	711	533	368	363
Curacao [4]	(X)	(X)	(X)	(X)	483	(X)	(X)	(X)	(X)	555	(X)	(X)	(X)	(X)	-72
Cyprus	84	217	179	134	97	31	14	53	11	21	54	204	126	123	77
Czech Republic	1,054	1,378	970	1,411	1,680	2,193	2,569	1,933	2,450	3,344	-1,139	-1,190	-964	-1,039	-1,664
Denmark	1,918	2,711	2,056	2,133	2,243	5,144	6,446	5,511	6,011	6,760	-3,226	-3,735	-3,454	-3,878	-4,517
Djibouti	48	141	196	123	128	2	7	62	3	4	46	134	134	120	124
Dominica	62	105	77	73	74	4	2	3	2	2	58	103	74	71	72
Dominican Republic	4,719	6,594	5,269	6,579	7,318	4,604	3,978	3,329	3,672	4,191	115	2,617	1,939	2,907	3,127
Ecuador	1,964	3,450	3,938	5,410	6,065	5,759	9,048	5,273	7,451	9,622	-3,795	-5,598	-1,335	-2,041	-3,557
Egypt	3,159	6,002	5,253	6,835	6,222	2,091	2,370	2,058	2,238	2,059	1,068	3,632	3,195	4,597	4,164
El Salvador	1,854	2,462	2,019	2,433	3,370	1,989	2,228	1,822	2,206	2,484	-134	234	197	227	886
Equatorial Guinea	281	185	306	272	285	1,561	3,367	2,489	2,214	1,191	-1,280	-3,183	-2,184	-1,942	-906
Estonia	145	226	189	188	310	511	392	162	698	962	-366	-167	27	-510	-653
Ethiopia	456	302	267	773	691	62	152	113	128	144	394	149	154	645	546
Faroe Islands	3	14	10	2	4	4	16	62	72	106	-2	-2	-52	-70	-102
Fiji	28	55	31	44	43	169	162	144	179	132	-141	-107	-113	-135	-89

See footnotes at end of table.

Table 1321. U.S. Exports, Imports, and Merchandise Trade Balance by Country: 2005 to 2011-Continued.

See headnote on page 836.

Country	Exports, domestic and foreign					General imports					Merchandise trade balance				
	2005	2008	2009	2010	2011	2005	2008	2009	2010	2011	2005	2008	2009	2010	2011
Finland	2,254	3,761	1,662	2,181	3,156	4,342	5,903	3,985	3,884	4,417	-2,088	-2,142	-2,323	-1,703	-1,262
France	22,259	28,840	26,493	26,969	27,803	33,842	44,049	34,236	38,355	40,040	-11,583	-15,209	-7,743	-11,386	-12,237
French Polynesia	112	130	113	122	126	60	72	29	53	54	52	58	83	69	72
Gabon	99	284	171	243	204	2,816	2,279	1,231	2,212	4,567	-2,716	-1,995	-1,060	-1,969	-4,363
Georgia	214	586	364	301	579	194	208	70	198	176	20	379	294	103	403
Germany	34,184	54,505	43,306	48,161	49,156	84,751	97,497	71,498	82,429	98,663	-50,567	-42,991	-28,192	-34,268	-49,507
Ghana	337	608	716	989	1,197	158	222	135	273	779	179	386	581	716	418
Gibraltar	163	2,641	1,087	1,494	3,149	5	2	1	1	1	159	2,639	1,086	1,493	3,148
Greece	1,192	1,932	2,487	1,108	1,121	884	999	841	798	865	309	933	1,647	310	256
Grenada	82	84	59	71	82	6	7	6	8	7	77	77	53	63	75
Guadeloupe	55	384	206	365	431	2	7	2	2	2	52	377	204	363	429
Guatemala	2,835	4,718	3,875	4,478	6,145	3,137	3,463	3,148	3,193	4,714	-302	1,256	727	1,285	1,432
Guinea	94	102	95	85	256	75	106	67	69	81	19	-5	28	16	175
Guyana	177	289	260	290	364	120	146	173	299	425	57	143	87	-9	-61
Haiti	710	944	790	1,209	1,059	447	450	552	551	742	262	494	238	658	317
Honduras	3,254	4,846	3,368	4,606	6,144	3,749	4,041	3,319	3,932	4,501	-495	805	48	674	1,643
Hong Kong	16,351	21,499	21,051	26,570	36,449	8,892	6,483	3,571	4,296	4,401	7,459	15,015	17,480	22,274	32,048
Hungary	1,023	1,431	1,233	1,290	1,474	2,561	3,103	2,223	2,489	2,949	-1,538	-1,672	-991	-1,199	-1,475
Iceland	512	470	350	325	628	269	241	179	201	216	243	229	170	124	412
India	7,919	17,682	16,441	19,250	21,501	18,804	25,704	21,166	29,533	36,153	-10,886	-8,022	-4,725	-10,283	-14,652
Indonesia	3,054	5,644	5,107	6,946	7,414	12,014	15,799	12,939	16,478	19,111	-8,960	-10,155	-7,832	-9,532	-11,697
Iran	96	683	280	208	229	174	104	65	95	1	-79	579	216	113	228
Iraq	1,374	2,070	1,772	1,642	2,411	9,054	22,080	9,263	12,143	16,960	-7,680	-20,010	-7,491	-10,501	-14,549
Ireland	8,447	7,611	7,465	7,276	7,644	28,733	31,346	28,101	33,848	39,370	-20,286	-23,736	-20,636	-26,572	-31,725
Israel	9,737	14,487	9,559	11,294	13,936	16,830	22,336	18,744	20,982	23,039	-7,093	-7,849	-9,185	-9,688	-9,103
Italy	11,524	15,461	12,268	14,219	16,007	31,009	36,135	26,430	28,505	33,951	-19,485	-20,674	-14,162	-14,286	-17,944
Jamaica	1,701	2,643	1,441	1,662	1,931	376	729	468	328	566	1,325	1,915	973	1,334	1,365
Japan	54,681	65,142	51,134	60,486	65,706	138,004	139,262	95,804	120,545	128,925	-83,323	-74,120	-44,669	-60,059	-63,219
Jordan	644	940	1,192	1,174	1,454	1,267	1,137	924	974	1,061	-623	-197	268	200	393
Kazakhstan	538	986	603	730	826	1,101	1,603	1,544	1,872	1,679	-563	-618	-940	-1,142	-854
Kenya	573	442	654	375	463	348	344	281	311	382	225	99	373	64	81
Korea, South	27,572	34,669	28,612	38,846	43,415	43,781	48,069	39,216	48,875	56,661	-16,210	-13,400	-10,604	-10,029	-13,247
Kuwait	1,975	2,719	1,951	2,774	2,726	4,335	7,093	3,783	5,382	7,809	-2,360	-4,374	-1,831	-2,608	-5,082
Kyrgyzstan	31	44	57	79	104	5	2	6	4	3	27	42	51	75	101
Laos	10	18	20	12	26	4	42	43	59	59	6	-24	-23	-47	-33
Latvia	178	394	289	345	585	362	228	142	193	363	-185	166	147	152	222
Lebanon	466	1,464	1,852	2,009	1,806	86	99	77	84	79	379	1,365	1,775	1,925	1,727
Lesotho	4	1	17	11	13	404	374	304	299	384	-400	-373	-288	-288	-371
Liberia	69	157	95	191	195	91	143	80	180	158	-22	13	14	11	37
Libya	84	721	666	666	307	1,590	4,179	1,919	2,117	645	-1,506	-3,458	-1,253	-1,451	-338
Liechtenstein	20	29	23	29	62	296	245	180	213	251	-276	-216	-156	-184	-188
Lithuania	390	831	399	628	1,141	634	750	590	637	1,044	-244	81	-191	-9	97
Luxembourg	711	988	1,292	1,439	1,585	389	536	443	451	495	323	452	849	988	1,090
Macau	102	307	209	225	291	1,249	915	237	141	113	-1,147	-609	-28	84	178
Macedonia	32	36	35	34	29	48	78	44	37	53	-17	-42	-9	-3	-23
Madagascar	28	71	106	116	56	324	324	253	108	87	-295	-254	-148	8	-31
Malawi	28	45	40	37	57	116	65	63	72	65	-87	-20	-23	-35	-8
Malaysia	10,461	12,949	10,403	14,080	14,247	33,685	30,736	23,283	25,900	25,777	-23,224	-17,787	-12,879	-11,820	-11,530
Malta	194	253	208	457	752	283	279	219	262	244	-89	-26	-10	195	508
Marshall Islands	75	25	78	91	144	17	19	14	12	15	58	6	64	79	129
Martinique	35	289	263	297	340	22	8	5	23	8	13	281	258	274	332
Mauritania	86	107	56	83	243	1	46	35	53	1	85	60	22	30	242
Mauritius	31	51	70	40	46	222	176	169	196	252	-191	-125	-99	-156	-206
Mexico	120,248	151,220	128,892	163,473	198,378	170,109	215,942	176,654	229,908	262,864	-49,861	-64,722	-47,762	-66,435	-64,487
Mongolia	22	57	41	115	314	144	53	15	12	11	-122	4	26	103	303
Morocco	481	1,436	1,630	1,947	2,822	446	879	468	685	996	35	557	1,162	1,262	1,827
Mozambique	63	213	190	224	459	12	17	39	65	35	51	197	151	159	424

See footnotes at end of table.

Table 1321. U.S. Exports, Imports, and Merchandise Trade Balance by Country: 2005 to 2011—Continued.

See headnote on page 836.

Country	Exports, domestic and foreign					General imports					Merchandise trade balance				
	2005	2008	2009	2010	2011	2005	2008	2009	2010	2011	2005	2008	2009	2010	2011
Namibia	112	280	202	111	137	130	301	329	195	436	-17	-21	-126	-84	-300
Nepal	25	29	31	28	40	111	85	55	61	77	-87	-56	-24	-33	-37
Netherlands	26,468	39,719	32,242	34,939	42,351	14,862	21,123	16,098	19,055	23,451	11,606	18,597	16,143	15,884	18,899
Netherlands Antilles [4]	1,138	2,952	2,056	2,943	1,187	922	809	476	1,026	865	215	2,142	1,580	1,917	322
New Caledonia	38	89	78	108	115	27	50	27	71	91	11	39	51	37	24
New Zealand	2,592	2,534	2,159	2,819	3,571	3,155	3,171	2,558	2,762	3,163	-563	-637	-399	57	408
Nicaragua	625	1,094	715	981	1,058	1,181	1,704	1,612	2,007	2,603	-555	-609	-897	-1,026	-1,545
Niger	79	50	58	48	48	66	44	106	27	289	13	6	-48	22	-241
Nigeria	1,620	4,102	3,687	4,068	4,912	24,239	38,068	19,128	30,516	33,854	-22,620	-33,966	-15,441	-26,448	-28,942
Norway	1,942	3,292	2,790	3,099	3,634	6,776	7,315	5,688	6,950	8,305	-4,834	-4,023	-2,898	-3,851	-4,671
Oman	571	1,382	1,126	1,105	1,434	555	852	907	773	2,208	16	530	219	332	-775
Pakistan	1,252	1,898	1,618	1,901	1,987	3,253	3,591	3,163	3,509	3,830	-2,002	-1,693	-1,545	-1,608	-1,843
Panama	2,162	4,887	4,293	6,063	8,248	327	379	302	381	389	1,835	4,508	3,991	5,682	7,859
Papua New Guinea	55	70	218	186	304	58	106	103	97	142	-3	-36	-115	89	162
Paraguay	896	1,610	1,355	1,810	1,975	52	78	56	62	110	844	1,532	1,299	1,748	1,865
Peru	2,309	6,183	4,919	6,754	8,336	5,119	5,812	4,223	5,057	6,605	-2,810	371	696	1,697	1,731
Philippines	6,895	8,295	5,766	7,376	7,705	9,250	8,713	6,794	7,982	9,145	-2,355	-418	-1,028	-606	-1,440
Poland	1,268	4,131	2,302	2,982	3,137	1,949	2,587	2,038	2,964	4,378	-681	1,544	263	18	-1,241
Portugal	1,132	2,646	1,085	1,058	1,316	2,329	2,451	1,577	2,141	2,582	-1,197	195	-492	-1,083	-1,266
Qatar	987	2,716	2,713	3,160	2,799	448	484	506	466	1,234	539	2,232	2,207	2,694	1,565
Reunion	4	8	9	8	155	6	3	9	-1	12	-2	5	-1	-1	143
Romania	609	1,048	672	730	912	1,208	1,107	752	1,008	1,435	-599	-58	-80	-278	-523
Russia	3,962	9,335	5,332	6,006	8,286	15,307	26,783	18,200	25,691	34,619	-11,344	-17,448	-12,868	-19,685	-26,333
Rwanda	11	20	34	31	120	6	14	21	21	7	4	7	10	10	89
Saudi Arabia	6,805	12,484	10,792	11,556	13,830	27,193	54,747	22,053	31,413	47,476	-20,387	-42,263	-11,261	-19,857	-33,647
Senegal	141	137	176	218	264	4	18	7	5	7	138	119	169	213	257
Serbia	(X)	207	113	104	126	9	72	62	164	134	(X)	136	51	-60	-7
Sierra Leone	38	59	43	61	103	9	48	24	29	27	29	12	18	32	76
Singapore	20,466	27,854	22,232	29,017	31,223	15,110	15,885	15,705	17,427	19,113	5,356	11,969	6,527	11,590	12,110
Sint Maarten [4]	(X)	(X)	(X)	(X)	399	(X)	(X)	(X)	(X)	24	(X)	(X)	(X)	(X)	375
Slovakia	150	548	210	256	302	961	1,301	628	1,073	1,408	-811	-754	-418	-817	-1,105
Slovenia	234	310	244	328	668	413	467	388	465	545	-179	-157	-144	-137	123
South Africa	3,907	6,490	4,453	5,631	7,257	5,886	9,948	5,879	8,220	9,487	-1,979	-3,458	-1,426	-2,589	-2,230
Spain [2]	6,839	12,190	8,717	10,178	10,849	8,615	11,094	7,857	8,553	11,017	-1,776	1,096	860	1,625	-168
Sri Lanka	198	283	230	179	303	2,083	1,962	1,593	1,748	2,086	-1,885	-1,679	-1,363	-1,569	-1,783
St. Kitts and Nevis	94	124	108	131	116	50	54	48	51	55	44	70	60	80	61
St. Lucia	135	241	136	401	316	32	26	18	18	18	103	215	119	383	298
St. Vincent and the Grenadines	45	83	75	86	81	16	1	1	2	2	30	82	74	84	79
Suriname	246	406	380	362	433	165	127	139	191	302	80	280	241	171	131
Swaziland	12	12	15	24	20	199	134	110	121	89	-187	-122	-95	-97	-69
Sweden	3,715	5,018	4,561	4,706	5,259	13,821	12,498	8,186	10,495	11,488	-10,106	-7,480	-3,625	-5,789	-6,229
Switzerland	10,718	22,024	17,504	20,687	24,425	13,000	17,782	16,053	19,136	24,358	-2,282	4,242	1,451	1,551	68
Syria [2]	155	409	304	503	230	324	352	303	429	393	-169	57	74	74	-163
Taiwan	21,614	24,926	18,486	26,043	25,889	34,826	36,326	28,362	35,846	41,405	-13,211	-11,400	-9,877	-9,803	-15,516
Tajikistan	29	51	41	57	178	241	8	49	2	12	-212	43	33	55	166
Tanzania	96	169	158	164	258	34	56	49	43	59	63	114	109	121	199
Thailand	7,257	9,067	6,918	8,977	10,900	19,890	23,538	19,082	22,693	24,830	-12,633	-14,472	-12,164	-13,716	-13,931
Togo	28	117	125	158	210	6	11	9	9	31	21	106	118	149	179
Trinidad and Tobago	1,417	2,250	1,988	1,926	2,183	7,891	9,030	5,180	6,613	8,113	-6,474	-6,780	-3,192	-4,687	-5,930
Tunisia	261	502	501	571	588	264	644	326	405	352	-3	-142	176	166	236
Turkey	4,239	9,959	7,095	10,546	14,657	5,182	4,642	3,662	4,207	5,220	-943	5,317	3,433	6,339	9,438
Turkmenistan	215	60	294	40	71	135	140	93	48	43	80	-80	201	-8	28
Turks and Caicos Islands	238	434	248	190	205	9	10	11	12	9	228	424	237	178	196
Uganda	63	89	119	94	94	26	53	31	58	46	37	36	88	36	48
Ukraine	533	1,868	887	1,359	2,137	1,098	2,340	495	1,078	1,457	-565	-472	392	281	680
United Arab Emirates	8,120	14,417	12,211	11,673	15,900	1,468	1,286	1,498	1,145	2,440	6,651	13,131	10,713	10,528	13,461

See footnotes at end of table.

Table 1321. U.S. Exports, Imports, and Merchandise Trade Balance by Country: 2005 to 2011-Continued

See headnote on page 836.

Country	Exports, domestic and foreign					General imports					Merchandise trade balance				
	2005	2008	2009	2010	2011	2005	2008	2009	2010	2011	2005	2008	2009	2010	2011
United Kingdom.........	38,568	53,599	45,704	48,414	55,881	51,033	58,587	47,480	49,775	51,236	-12,465	-4,988	-1,776	-1,361	4,645
Uruguay...............	357	893	745	975	1,257	732	244	239	235	292	-376	649	506	740	965
Uzbekistan...........	74	301	98	101	100	96	292	89	68	51	-22	8	8	33	49
Venezuela.............	6,421	12,610	9,315	10,649	12,343	33,978	51,424	28,059	32,707	43,256	-27,557	-38,814	-18,744	-22,058	-30,913
Vietnam...............	1,193	2,789	3,097	3,709	4,309	6,631	12,901	12,288	14,868	17,487	-5,438	-10,112	-9,191	-11,159	-13,178
Virgin Islands, British..	125	310	233	146	151	34	11	6	19	6	91	299	227	127	145
Yemen.................	219	401	381	391	390	279	8	7	181	562	-60	393	374	210	-172
Zambia................	29	79	57	56	130	32	51	9	30	47	7	27	49	26	82
Zimbabwe..............	46	93	85	68	62	94	112	22	59	51	-15	-19	63	9	10

X Not applicable. [1] Includes timing adjustment and unidentified countries, not shown separately. [2] See footnote 4, Table 1348. [3] See footnote 5, Table 1348. [4] See footnote 8, Table 1348.

Source: U.S. Census Bureau, *U.S. International Trade in Goods and Services, Annual Revision for 2011*, Series FT-900, released June 8, 2012, and earlier releases. See also <http://www.census.gov/foreign-trade/Press-Release/2011pr/final_revisions/>.

Table 1322. U.S. Exports and General Imports by Selected SITC Commodity Groups: 2000 to 2011

[In millions of dollars (781,918 represents $781,918,000,000). SITC = Standard International Trade Classification. For methodology, see Foreign Trade Statistics in Appendix III. N.e.s. = not elsewhere specified]

Selected commodity	Exports [1]				General imports [2]			
	2000	2009	2010	2011	2000	2009	2010	2011
Total..........................	781,918	1,056,043	1,278,263	1,480,432	1,218,022	1,559,625	1,913,160	2,207,824
Agricultural commodities [3].........	51,296	98,423	115,786	136,351	39,186	71,849	82,015	99,124
Animal feeds...........................	3,780	7,763	8,996	9,288	597	1,162	1,349	1,929
Cereal flour............................	1,310	2,957	3,037	3,379	1,753	4,161	4,519	5,055
Coffee..................................	9	7	6	4	2,350	3,375	4,055	6,906
Corn.....................................	4,695	9,146	10,181	14,064	160	283	300	399
Cotton, raw and linters..............	1,893	3,365	5,896	8,468	28	1	8	17
Meat and preparations..............	7,004	11,618	13,216	16,627	3,841	4,598	5,071	5,734
Oils/fats, vegetable..................	814	1,997	2,650	2,532	1,188	3,424	3,940	6,099
Soybeans..............................	5,284	16,443	18,589	17,581	31	210	220	219
Manufactured goods [3]............	625,894	743,321	873,246	971,671	1,012,855	1,185,889	1,438,617	1,611,456
ADP equipment, office machinery.................	46,595	21,282	22,238	21,906	92,133	91,098	113,476	116,490
Airplanes, engines, and parts.......	(NA)	78,273	74,741	82,550	(NA)	22,073	22,417	25,393
Alcoholic beverage, distilled........	424	1,007	1,126	1,285	2,946	5,011	5,608	6,248
Aluminum..............................	3,780	4,291	5,171	6,433	6,949	8,679	10,815	11,896
Artwork/antiques.....................	1,387	4,605	3,034	3,112	5,864	5,031	6,268	6,903
Basketware, etc.......................	3,309	8,068	8,360	8,699	4,840	11,530	13,316	14,458
Chemicals - cosmetics..............	5,292	11,120	12,488	13,244	3,539	8,396	9,564	10,613
Chemicals - dyeing..................	4,089	5,546	7,407	8,542	2,667	2,424	3,105	3,458
Chemicals - fertilizers...............	2,249	3,475	3,731	5,133	1,684	4,156	6,647	9,165
Chemicals - inorganic...............	5,359	10,203	11,806	13,345	6,108	10,790	13,833	17,019
Chemicals - medicinal...............	12,893	41,809	41,960	40,011	14,685	60,002	65,170	69,678
Chemicals - n.e.s.....................	12,264	20,428	24,136	27,127	5,725	9,582	11,379	13,294
Chemicals - organic..................	17,990	27,779	37,494	43,571	28,578	42,183	45,792	54,367
Chemicals - plastics.................	19,519	33,078	42,019	46,195	10,647	13,694	17,825	20,744
Clothing................................	8,191	2,919	3,197	3,339	64,296	69,326	78,518	85,559
Copper.................................	1,425	2,375	3,496	3,644	4,471	5,596	7,821	10,154
Cork, wood, lumber..................	4,320	3,495	4,732	5,498	8,227	3,574	4,479	4,452
Crude fertilizers......................	1,724	1,765	2,367	2,619	1,401	1,682	2,257	2,848
Electrical machinery.................	89,917	63,964	77,019	77,799	108,747	91,683	119,634	137,937
Fish and preparations...............	2,806	3,763	4,223	5,279	9,907	12,982	14,576	16,519
Footwear..............................	663	620	728	832	14,842	17,523	20,902	22,652
Furniture and bedding...............	4,744	4,023	4,821	5,259	18,923	24,588	31,124	32,365
Gem diamonds........................	1,289	2,156	2,862	3,092	12,068	12,736	18,599	22,299
General industrial machinery.......	33,094	45,034	51,793	60,082	34,667	50,181	60,426	74,175
Glass...................................	2,502	2,828	3,380	3,657	2,248	2,117	2,588	2,665
Gold, nonmonetary...................	5,898	13,898	17,458	33,675	2,657	8,810	12,491	16,394
Iron and steel mill products.........	5,715	12,022	15,720	18,467	15,807	18,230	24,440	32,894
Jewelry.................................	1,574	4,322	4,848	5,222	6,459	8,676	10,085	11,091
Lighting, plumbing....................	1,384	2,141	2,509	2,848	5,104	6,120	7,397	8,018
Metal manufactures, n.e.s..........	13,453	14,669	17,491	20,256	16,204	21,414	25,913	29,614
Metal ores; scrap....................	4,234	20,058	28,366	32,838	3,817	5,460	7,293	9,423
Metalworking machinery............	6,191	4,294	5,330	6,246	7,726	4,961	5,565	8,619
Nickel..................................	401	931	1,130	1,582	1,425	1,665	2,976	3,718
Optical goods.........................	3,246	2,773	3,278	3,262	4,019	4,513	5,507	5,896
Paper and paperboard...............	10,640	12,891	14,920	15,988	15,185	14,443	15,285	15,795
Photographic equipment............	4,236	3,211	3,345	3,259	6,896	1,776	2,048	2,183
Plastic articles, n.e.s................	7,607	8,224	9,710	10,439	8,034	13,743	16,042	17,402
Platinum...............................	888	844	1,370	1,036	5,566	2,982	4,146	5,555
Power generating machinery.......	32,743	28,056	33,013	36,341	33,773	36,181	42,465	52,074
Printed materials.....................	4,776	5,601	5,879	5,859	3,680	4,231	4,585	4,512
Pulp and waste paper...............	4,576	6,694	8,640	9,709	3,381	2,441	3,887	4,020
Records/magnetic media...........	5,395	4,413	4,424	4,368	5,172	5,183	5,296	5,716
Rubber articles, n.e.s................	1,673	1,625	2,049	2,332	1,962	2,481	3,310	3,763
Rubber tires and tubes..............	2,379	3,641	4,159	5,155	4,785	8,136	10,673	13,377
Scientific instruments...............	30,984	38,105	44,276	48,247	22,007	31,975	37,795	43,527
Silver and bullion.....................	227	888	1,672	3,094	775	2,139	4,383	8,577
Specialized industrial machinery...............	30,959	36,956	46,754	51,655	22,711	24,235	30,912	41,407
Television, VCR, etc..................	27,921	19,992	21,511	23,397	70,468	119,392	137,305	137,952
Textile yarn, fabric...................	10,534	9,288	11,384	12,880	15,171	18,232	22,120	24,135
Toys/games/sporting goods........	3,609	4,170	4,245	4,334	20,011	27,918	30,630	28,650
Travel goods..........................	351	449	463	526	4,430	6,444	8,012	9,033
Vehicles................................	57,421	65,288	88,119	106,196	161,544	127,863	178,946	198,707
Wood manufactures..................	1,842	1,725	2,053	2,092	7,228	6,230	6,920	6,783
Mineral fuel [3]......................	13,179	54,536	80,460	128,564	135,367	271,739	354,968	453,872
Coal....................................	2,162	6,162	10,100	16,204	805	1,766	2,018	2,133
Crude oil..............................	463	1,618	1,368	1,463	89,876	194,603	260,105	336,687
Petroleum preparations.............	5,746	36,351	53,528	90,458	25,673	52,584	67,409	92,281
Liquified propane/butane............	663	1,409	2,448	3,459	1,508	2,202	2,541	2,629
Natural gas...........................	411	3,271	4,921	6,432	12,594	16,056	17,402	13,567
Mineral fuels, other mineral........	3,734	5,131	7,434	10,119	4,911	2,444	3,410	4,548
Reexports.............................	68,203	120,345	155,847	182,017	(X)	(X)	(X)	(X)

NA Not available. X Not applicable. [1] Free alongside ship (f.a.s) basis. Exports by commodity are only for domestic exports. [2] Customs value basis. [3] Includes other commodities, not shown separately.

Source: U.S. Census Bureau, *U.S. International Trade in Goods and Services*, series FT 900 (12-04), and other final reports. See also <http://www.census.gov/foreign-trade/Press-Release/2011pr/final_revisions/>.

Table 1323. U.S. Total and Aerospace Foreign Trade: 1990 to 2011

[In millions of dollars (–101,718 represents –$101,718,000,000), except percent. Data are reported as exports of domestic merchandise, including Department of Defense shipments and undocumented exports to Canada, f.a.s. (free alongside ship) basis, and imports for consumption, customs value basis. Minus sign (–) indicates deficit]

Year	U.S. Merchandise Trade			Aerospace Trade						
						Exports				
								Civil		
	Trade balance [1]	Imports	Exports	Trade balance	Imports	Total	Percent of U.S. exports	Total	Transports	Military
1990......	-101,718	495,311	393,592	27,282	11,801	39,083	9.9	31,517	16,691	7,566
1995......	-158,801	743,543	584,742	21,562	11,509	33,071	5.7	25,079	10,606	7,991
1996......	-170,214	795,289	625,075	26,602	13,668	40,270	6.4	29,477	13,624	10,792
1997......	-180,522	869,704	689,182	32,240	18,134	50,374	7.3	40,075	21,028	10,299
1998......	-229,758	911,896	682,138	40,961	23,110	64,071	9.4	51,999	29,168	12,072
1999......	-328,821	1,024,618	695,797	37,381	25,063	62,444	9.0	50,624	25,672	11,820
2000......	-436,104	1,218,022	781,918	26,735	27,944	54,679	7.0	45,566	19,615	9,113
2001......	-411,899	1,140,999	729,100	26,035	32,473	58,508	8.0	49,371	22,151	9,137
2002......	-468,263	1,161,366	693,103	29,553	27,242	56,775	8.2	47,348	21,626	9,427
2003......	-532,350	1,257,121	724,771	27,111	25,393	52,504	7.2	44,366	19,149	8,138
2004......	-654,830	1,469,704	814,875	31,002	25,815	56,817	7.0	47,772	18,577	9,045
2005......	-772,373	1,673,455	901,082	39,783	27,649	67,433	7.5	57,587	21,888	9,845
2006......	-827,971	1,853,938	1,025,967	54,809	30,453	85,262	8.3	71,857	32,897	13,404
2007......	-808,763	1,956,962	1,148,199	60,614	36,610	97,224	8.5	83,977	40,297	13,247
2008......	-816,199	2,103,641	1,287,442	57,389	37,694	95,082	7.4	82,264	33,326	12,819
2009......	-503,582	1,559,625	1,056,043	56,034	25,132	81,166	7.7	70,500	(NA)	10,666
2010......	-634,897	1,913,160	1,278,263	51,152	26,351	77,503	6.1	67,128	(NA)	10,375
2011.......	-727,392	2,207,824	1,480,432	55,753	29,573	85,326	5.8	75,275	(NA)	10,051

NA Not available. [1] Exports minus imports.

Source: Aerospace Industries Association of America, Washington, DC, *Aerospace Industry Report 2011*, (previously issued as *Aerospace Facts and Figures*), annual, (copyright). See <http://www.aia-aerospace.org/economics/aerospace_facts_and_figures/>.

Table 1324. U.S. High Technology Exports by Industry and Selected Major Country: 2000 to 2011

[In billions of dollars (222.5 represents $222,500,000,000)]

Selected industry	2000	2010	2011	Selected country	2000	2010	2011
Total exports...........	**222.5**	**228.4**	**238.5**	**Total exports**..........	**222.5**	**228.4**	**238.5**
Computers and office equipment.....	57.8	44.0	48.3	Canada...................	34.4	29.5	32.3
Consumer electronics.................	10.0	9.6	10.2	China [1]...................	4.6	16.8	15.2
Communications equipment..........	26.9	34.1	38.8	Japan....................	19.9	9.4	10.3
Electronic components................	22.1	20.0	21.2	Korea, South............	12.1	7.4	8.1
Semiconductors.....................	60.0	60.4	54.9	Malaysia.................	7.8	8.2	7.6
Industrial electronics.................	30.5	34.6	38.1	Mexico..................	30.0	36.4	40.3
Electromedical equipment............	8.1	21.6	22.7	Singapore...............	(NA)	8.1	7.7
Photonics............................	7.1	4.2	4.4	European Union 27 [2]....	51.5	40.7	41.5

NA Not available. [1] See footnote 4, Table 1348. [2] See footnote 4, Table 1391.

Source: TechAmerica Foundation, Washington, DC, unpublished data (copyright). <http://www.techamericafoundation.org/>.

Table 1325. U.S. Exporting Companies Profile by Employment-Size Class: 2000 and 2010

[668,310 represents $668,310,000,000. Based on data from export trade information and the Business Register. For information on data limitations, see Technical Documentation in source]

Employment-size class	Number of exporters		Known export value [1] (mil. dol.)		Percent of—			
					Number of exporters		Known export value	
	2000	2010	2000	2010	2000	2010	2000	2010
All companies, total..........	**246,452**	**293,131**	**668,310**	**1,137,635**	**100.0**	**100.0**	**100.0**	**100.0**
Number of employees unknown [2]......................	74,772	112,166	47,024	106,751	30.3	38.3	7.0	9.4
1 to 19 employees................	96,268	112,479	45,272	82,662	39.1	38.4	6.8	7.3
20 to 49 employees..............	31,362	30,963	21,262	44,974	12.7	10.6	3.2	4.0
50 to 99 employees..............	16,988	15,165	19,711	43,650	6.9	5.2	2.9	3.8
100 to 249 employees...........	13,685	11,568	32,192	59,217	5.6	3.9	4.8	5.2
250 to 499 employees...........	5,454	4,320	27,397	46,159	2.2	1.5	4.1	4.1
500 or more employees..........	7,923	6,470	475,453	754,222	3.2	2.2	71.1	66.3

[1] Known value is defined as the portion of U.S. total exports that could be matched to specific companies. Export values are on f.a.s. or "free alongside ship basis." [2] Includes missing employment data, nonemployers, and companies that reported annual payroll but did not report any employees on their payroll.

Source: U.S. Census Bureau, *Profile of U.S. Importing and Exporting Companies 2009-2010*, and earlier reports. See also <http://www.census.gov/foreign-trade/Press-Release/edb/2010/index.html>.

Table 1326. Domestic Exports and Imports for Consumption of Merchandise by Selected NAICS Product Category: 2000 to 2011

[In millions of dollars (712,285 represents $712,285,000,000). Includes nonmonetary gold. For methodology, see Foreign Trade Statistics in Appendix III. NAICS = North American Industry Classification System; see text, Section 15]

Product category	2000	2005	2008	2009	2010	2011
Domestic exports, total	**712,285**	**798,997**	**1,156,376**	**935,698**	**1,122,416**	**1,299,301**
Agricultural, forestry, and fishery products	29,153	37,109	68,233	55,552	65,737	79,081
Agricultural products, total	23,596	30,683	61,073	49,069	58,000	69,538
Livestock and livestock products	1,255	1,118	1,520	1,409	1,540	1,918
Forestry products, not elsewhere specified	1,644	1,686	1,894	1,622	2,178	2,560
Fish, fresh or chilled, and other marine products	2,658	3,622	3,746	3,452	4,010	5,065
Mining, total	6,187	12,629	24,751	17,332	26,234	36,931
Oil and gas	1,706	4,547	8,706	6,570	9,090	11,484
Minerals and ores	4,481	8,082	16,045	10,762	17,144	25,447
Manufacturing, total	644,440	708,205	987,582	802,183	952,409	1,095,096
Food and kindred products	24,966	28,937	48,476	43,843	50,910	58,668
Beverages and tobacco products	5,568	3,423	4,793	4,373	5,341	6,202
Textiles and fabrics	7,010	8,483	8,213	6,434	7,832	9,063
Textile mill products	2,236	2,344	2,611	2,276	2,582	2,742
Apparel and accessories	8,104	4,075	3,055	2,812	3,071	3,203
Leather and allied products	2,322	2,300	2,266	1,876	2,420	2,838
Wood products	4,854	4,463	5,041	3,976	5,073	5,567
Paper products	15,539	16,640	21,713	19,175	22,962	24,745
Printed, publishing, & similar products	4,869	5,526	6,504	5,747	6,020	6,036
Petroleum and coal products	8,862	17,979	58,440	41,494	61,003	100,319
Chemicals	77,649	114,821	166,249	145,896	171,443	187,657
Plastics and rubber products [1]	16,970	18,784	23,403	20,340	24,255	27,133
Nonmetallic mineral products [1]	7,830	6,663	8,927	7,482	9,223	10,051
Primary metal products	20,126	27,455	54,713	38,173	49,708	65,266
Fabricated metal products	21,737	23,370	32,483	27,737	32,667	36,744
Machinery, except electrical	85,038	97,001	134,117	104,139	126,040	142,994
Computers and electronic products [1]	161,449	122,744	134,757	106,782	121,111	123,463
Electrical equipment, appliances and components [1]	25,401	26,457	34,548	26,498	30,998	34,142
Transportation equipment [1]	121,701	144,985	192,296	154,120	176,397	200,735
Furniture and fixtures	2,882	2,844	3,999	3,525	3,980	4,348
Miscellaneous manufactured commodities	19,327	28,909	40,978	35,486	39,373	43,055
Special classification provisions	32,505	41,055	75,010	59,866	77,186	88,193
Waste & scrap	4,948	10,389	28,943	21,784	29,411	39,118
Used or second-hand merchandise	1,950	2,570	7,326	6,005	4,712	5,194
Goods returned or reimported	333	65	47	31	29	23
Special classification provision, not elsewhere specified	25,274	28,030	38,693	32,046	43,034	43,858
Imports for consumption, total	**1,205,339**	**1,664,497**	**2,093,578**	**1,551,063**	**1,899,886**	**2,186,951**
Agricultural, forestry, and fishery products	24,378	30,761	41,068	36,802	42,683	51,373
Agricultural products, total	11,771	15,818	22,477	21,508	24,014	28,825
Livestock and livestock products	3,085	3,277	4,435	3,600	4,115	4,249
Forestry products, not elsewhere specified	1,409	2,250	3,417	1,773	3,356	5,402
Fish, fresh or chilled, and other marine products	8,113	9,416	10,739	9,920	11,198	12,897
Mining, total	79,841	192,115	341,123	184,585	235,394	289,077
Oil and gas	76,166	185,621	329,397	177,929	228,066	279,779
Minerals and ores	3,675	6,494	11,726	6,655	7,328	9,298
Manufacturing, total	1,040,329	1,372,004	1,627,042	1,260,343	1,549,521	1,767,633
Food and kindred products	18,944	29,779	39,987	36,131	41,037	50,118
Beverages and tobacco products	8,350	12,849	15,877	14,454	15,514	17,017
Textiles and fabrics	7,042	7,450	6,943	5,283	6,524	7,314
Textile mill products	7,347	13,508	14,984	13,227	15,824	16,943
Apparel and accessories	62,928	74,478	76,182	66,818	75,407	82,118
Leather and allied products	21,463	26,559	29,479	25,548	30,857	33,912
Wood products	15,388	23,654	14,142	9,746	11,363	11,321
Paper products	19,080	22,094	24,014	18,514	21,029	21,896
Printed, publishing, & similar products	4,197	5,599	6,170	4,890	5,323	5,242
Petroleum and coal products	40,156	81,359	130,639	75,139	102,161	141,244
Chemicals	76,606	131,936	195,731	162,366	187,631	216,035
Plastics and rubber products	17,362	28,072	33,006	27,749	34,363	39,736
Nonmetallic mineral products	14,740	18,445	18,070	13,081	16,078	17,753
Primary metal products	43,833	64,666	99,327	55,412	79,025	102,992
Fabricated metal products	27,974	41,026	51,934	39,780	46,691	53,528
Machinery, except electrical	79,366	109,619	123,669	86,832	104,797	133,770
Computers and electronic products	250,694	269,921	300,391	265,557	324,372	342,594
Electrical equipment, appliances and components	39,567	55,179	67,758	55,519	68,462	75,761
Transportation equipment	213,110	251,386	254,296	180,256	239,809	267,865
Furniture and fixtures	15,607	25,096	26,321	21,566	25,702	26,259
Miscellaneous manufactured commodities	56,577	79,329	98,121	82,475	97,552	104,216
Special classification provisions	60,791	69,617	84,308	69,301	72,253	78,869
Waste & scrap	1,875	3,207	5,669	3,459	5,260	6,659
Used or second-hand merchandise	6,345	6,026	7,757	5,205	6,403	7,082
Goods returned or reimported	33,851	37,024	40,134	38,101	40,985	44,542
Special classification provision, not elsewhere specified	18,720	23,359	30,747	22,535	19,605	20,586

[1] Due to non-disclosure requirements, certain 10-digit Schedule B commodity classifications for 2011 are subject to supression and require a change in aggregation.

Source: U.S. Census Bureau, *U.S. International Trade in Goods and Services*, series FT-900, December 2011, and previous reports, <http://www.census.gov/foreign-trade/Press-Release/2011pr/12/>.

Table 1327. Export and Import Unit Value Indexes—Selected Countries: 2006 to 2010

[Indexes in U.S. dollars, 2000 = 100. A unit value is an implicit price derived from value and quantity data. This table replaces Table 1304 in the 2012 edition of the Statistical Abstract. That table, prepared by the International Monetary Fund, used 2005 as its base year]

Country	Export unit value					Import unit value				
	2006	2007	2008	2009	2010	2006	2007	2008	2009	2010
United States	**132.8**	**148.7**	**166.4**	**135.1**	**163.4**	**152.3**	**160.4**	**172.3**	**127.5**	**156.3**
Australia	193.0	220.9	292.7	240.9	332.5	194.7	231.1	280.0	231.3	281.9
Belgium	195.0	229.0	250.1	196.0	219.2	198.4	232.1	262.3	198.0	220.3
Canada	140.8	150.6	163.5	114.3	139.6	146.1	159.0	170.5	134.8	159.8
France	151.6	171.0	187.8	147.7	159.4	160.1	186.3	211.1	165.2	179.4
Germany	201.1	239.7	261.7	202.7	230.3	182.6	212.4	238.0	186.0	214.9
Greece	176.9	200.9	224.2	173.9	183.8	190.3	234.8	276.1	207.1	189.9
Ireland	140.7	157.2	162.1	149.5	151.0	143.5	164.4	164.2	122.7	118.0
Italy	173.6	208.1	225.3	168.9	186.3	185.7	214.5	235.0	173.6	203.5
Japan	135.6	149.0	163.2	121.2	160.6	152.7	163.3	201.0	145.1	182.5
Korea, South	188.9	215.6	245.0	209.9	270.7	192.8	222.4	271.2	201.2	265.0
Netherlands	199.2	236.5	273.2	213.2	246.3	191.3	226.0	265.7	202.7	237.2
Norway	203.3	227.1	287.4	201.3	218.8	186.9	233.7	262.5	201.5	224.6
Spain	185.7	220.0	243.9	196.9	213.5	210.8	249.6	269.1	187.5	201.6
Sweden	169.9	194.0	210.1	150.1	182.0	175.3	210.5	230.8	164.5	204.4
Switzerland	197.2	205.8	188.5	160.9	169.8	183.9	175.6	163.9	154.3	161.9
United Kingdom	157.4	154.0	160.8	123.4	142.3	173.1	179.2	181.6	138.5	161.4

Source: World Bank, World Development Indicators (copyright). See also <http://data.worldbank.org/>.

Table 1328. U.S. Trade with China, Leading Commodity Imports and Exports: 2007 to 2011

[In billions of dollars (321.5 represents $321,500,000,000), except as noted. Data compiled by the Congressional Research Service from U.S. International Trade Commission (USTIC) DataWeb]

Commodity	2007 NAICS code [1]	2007	2008	2009	2010	2011	2010-2011 percent change
IMPORTS FROM CHINA							
Total imports	(X)	**321.5**	**337.8**	**296.4**	**364.9**	**399.3**	**9.4**
Computer equipment	3341	44.5	45.8	44.8	59.8	68.3	14.2
Communications equipment	3342	23.2	26.6	26.4	33.5	39.8	19.0
Misc. manufactured commodities	3399	34.8	35.8	30.7	34.2	32.7	-4.4
Apparel	3152	23.0	22.6	22.7	22.6	27.6	3.6
Semiconductors and other electronic components	3344	15.6	13.6	12.4	18.3	19.8	8.6
Footwear	3162	13.9	14.2	13.1	15.7	16.5	5.2
Audio and video equipment	3343	19.1	19.7	18.3	19.5	15.9	-18.7
Furniture and kitchen cabinets	3371	11.9	11.1	9.1	11.1	11.4	2.5
Household appliances and misc. machines	3352	8.3	8.5	7.7	9.1	9.6	5.3
Other fabricated metal products	3329	6.8	7.2	5.7	7.2	8.6	19.5
EXPORTS TO CHINA							
Total exports	(X)	**65.2**	**71.5**	**69.6**	**91.9**	**103.9**	**13.1**
Waste and scrap	9100	7.3	7.6	7.1	8.6	11.5	34.8
Oilseeds and grains	1111	4.1	7.3	9.4	11.2	11.5	2.6
Aerospace products and parts	3364	7.4	5.5	5.3	5.8	6.4	10.9
Semiconductors and other electronic components	3344	7.4	7.5	6.0	7.6	5.7	-25.0
Motor vehicles	3361	0.9	1.2	1.1	3.5	5.4	52.7
Basic chemicals	3251	2.9	3.1	3.4	4.2	4.7	10.8
Resin, synthetic rubber, artificial and synthetic fibers and filaments	3252	3.3	3.5	4.0	4.3	4.5	3.2
Navigational, measuring, electromedical, and control instruments	3345	2.4	2.9	2.9	3.8	4.3	13.0
Other general purpose machinery	3339	1.9	2.3	1.9	2.4	3.1	27.3
Other agricultural products	1119	1.6	1.8	1.0	2.3	2.8	21.4

X Not applicable. [1] Based on the 2007 North American Industry Classification System (NAICS).

Source: Congressional Research Service, *China-U.S. Trade Issues*, May 2012.

Section 29
Puerto Rico and the Island Areas

This section presents summary economic and social statistics for Puerto Rico, the U.S. Virgin Islands, Guam, American Samoa, and the Northern Mariana Islands. Primary sources include the decennial censuses of population and housing and the annual Puerto Rico Community Survey conducted by the U.S. Census Bureau; "County Business Patterns" and other Census Bureau publications and databases; other U.S. government publications, such as the National Vital Statistics Reports (NSVR) series, issued by the National Center for Health Statistics; and the annual *Economic Report for the Governor and Legislative Assembly* of the Puerto Rico Planning Board.

Jurisdiction—The United States gained jurisdiction over these areas as follows: the islands of Puerto Rico and Guam, surrendered by Spain in December 1898, were ceded to the United States by the Treaty of Paris, ratified in 1899. Puerto Rico became a commonwealth on July 25, 1952, thereby achieving a high degree of local autonomy under its own constitution. The U.S. Virgin Islands, comprising approximately 50 islands and cays, was purchased by the United States from Denmark in 1917. American Samoa, a group of seven islands, was acquired in accordance with a convention among the United States, Great Britain, and Germany, ratified in 1900 (Swains Island was annexed in 1925). By an agreement approved by the United Nations Security Council and the United States, the Northern Mariana Islands, previously under Japanese mandate, was administered by the United States between 1947 and 1986 under the United Nations trusteeship system. The Northern Mariana Islands became a U.S. commonwealth in 1986.

Censuses—Because characteristics of Puerto Rico and the island areas differ, the presentation of census data for them is not uniform. The 1960 Census of Population covered all the territories listed above except the Northern Mariana Islands (their census was conducted in April 1958 by the Office of the High Commissioner of the Trust Territory of the Pacific Islands), while the 1960 Census of Housing excluded American Samoa. The 1970, 1980, 1990, 2000, and 2010 censuses of population and housing covered all five areas. Beginning in 1967, Congress authorized the economic censuses, to be taken at 5-year intervals, for years ending in "2" and "7." Prior economic censuses were conducted in Puerto Rico for 1949, 1954, 1958, and 1963 and in Guam and the U.S. Virgin Islands for 1958 and 1963. In 1967, the census of construction industries was added for the first time in Puerto Rico; in 1972, the U.S. Virgin Islands and Guam were covered; and in 1982, the economic census was taken for the first time for the Northern Mariana Islands. Agricultural censuses have been conducted with increasing regularity in Puerto Rico since 1910, in the U.S. Virgin Islands since 1917, and in Guam and American Samoa since 1920; the first agricultural census in the Northern Mariana Islands was conducted in 1970.

Puerto Rico Community Survey—The Puerto Rico Community Survey (PRCS) began in 2005 and was an important element in the Census Bureau's re-engineered 2010 census plan. The American Community Survey (ACS) is the equivalent of the PRCS for the United States (50 states and District of Columbia). The PRCS collects and produces population and housing information every year instead of every 10 years. About 36,000 households are surveyed each year from across every municipio in Puerto Rico.

Information in other sections—In addition to the statistics presented in this section, other data on Puerto Rico and the island areas are included in many tables showing distribution by states in various sections of the *Abstract*. See "Puerto Rico" and "Island Areas of the U.S." in the Index. For definitions and explanations of terms used, see Sections 1, 2, 4, 5, 8, 12, 13, 15, 17, 20, 28, and 30.

Selected Island Areas of the United States

Caribbean Region

United States

ATLANTIC OCEAN

The Bahamas

Turks and Caicos Islands (U.K.)

Cuba

Cayman Islands (U.K.)

Haiti Dominican Republic

PUERTO RICO (U.S.)

B.V.I. (U.K.)

Jamaica

VIRGIN ISLANDS (U.S.)

Caribbean Sea

Pacific Region

NORTHERN MARIANA ISLANDS (U.S.)

· Wake Island (U.S.)

Johnston Atoll (U.S.) ·

GUAM (U.S.)

PACIFIC OCEAN

Kingman Reef (U.S.)

Marshall Islands

Palmyra Atoll (U.S.) ·

Federated States of Micronesia

Kiribati

Nauru

Howland Island (U.S.)

Baker Island (U.S.)

Papua New Guinea

Solomon Islands

Tuvalu

Vanuatu

Coral Sea

Samoa

Australia

Fiji

AMERICAN SAMOA (U.S.)

Table 1329. Estimated Resident Population With Projections: 1990 to 2025

[In thousands (47 represents 47,000). Population as of July 1. Population data generally are de facto figures for the present territory. Data are adjusted to the 2010 Census of Population. See text, Section 30, for general comments regarding the data. For details of methodology, coverage, and reliability, see source]

Area	1990	2000	2005	2009	2010	2011	2012	Projected		
								2015	2020	2025
American Samoa..............	47	58	57	56	55	55	55	54	54	53
Guam.........................	134	155	158	159	159	160	160	162	168	177
Northern Mariana Islands......	44	70	71	55	54	52	51	52	58	62
Puerto Rico....................	3,537	3,811	3,821	3,740	3,722	3,707	3,691	3,638	3,528	3,388
Virgin Islands.................	104	109	108	107	106	106	105	104	100	96

Source: U.S. Census Bureau, "International Data Base," <http://www.census.gov/ipc/www/idb/>, accessed June 2012.

Table 1330. Vital Statistics, by Specified Area: 1990 to 2009

[Births, deaths, and infant deaths by place of residence. Rates for 1990 and 2000 based on population enumerated as of April 1; for other years, on population estimated as of July 1]

Area and year	Births		Deaths		Infant deaths	
	Number	Rate [1]	Number	Rate [1]	Number	Rate [2]
Puerto Rico:						
1990..............	66,417	18.8	25,957	7.3	888	13.4
2000..............	59,333	15.2	28,365	7.2	574	9.7
2005..............	50,564	12.9	29,531	7.5	466	9.2
2006..............	48,597	12.4	28,206	7.2	426	8.8
2007..............	46,642	11.8	29,169	7.4	394	8.5
2008..............	45,620	11.5	29,050	7.3	388	8.5
2009..............	44,773	11.3	29,005	7.3	353	7.9
Guam:						
1990..............	3,839	28.6	520	3.9	31	8.1
2000..............	3,766	24.4	648	4.2	22	5.8
2005..............	3,187	18.9	677	4.0	34	10.7
2006..............	3,391	19.8	679	4.0	45	13.3
2007..............	3,483	20.1	778	4.5	36	10.3
2008..............	3,457	19.6	783	4.4	30	8.7
2009..............	3,417	19.2	835	4.7	36	10.5
Virgin Islands:						
1990..............	2,267	21.8	480	4.6	33	14.6
2000..............	1,564	12.9	641	5.3	21	13.4
2005..............	1,605	14.8	663	6.1	11	(B)
2006..............	1,687	15.5	624	5.7	9	(B)
2007..............	1,697	15.5	703	6.4	12	(B)
2008..............	1,784	16.2	749	6.8	9	(B)
2009..............	1,687	15.4	675	6.1	11	(B)
American Samoa:						
2000..............	1,731	26.4	219	3.3	11	(B)
2005..............	1,720	27.6	272	4.4	12	(B)
2008..............	1,332	20.5	241	3.7	13	(B)
2009..............	1,340	20.4	310	4.7	15	(B)
Northern Marianas:						
2000..............	1,431	19.9	136	1.9	11	(B)
2005..............	1,335	16.6	186	2.3	6	(B)
2008..............	1,265	22.9	178	3.2	5	(B)
2009..............	1,109	21.5	203	3.9	2	(B)

B Base figure too small to meet statistical standards of reliability. [1] Per 1,000 population. [2] Rates are infant deaths (under 1 year) per 1,000 live births.

Source: U.S. National Center for Health Statistics, National Vital Statistics Reports (NVSR), *Births: Final Data for 2009*, Vol. 60, No. 1, November 2010, and *Deaths: Final Data for 2009*, Vol. 60, No. 3, December 2011. See also <http://www.cdc.gov/nchs/nvss.htm>.

Table 1331. Public Elementary and Secondary Schools by Area: 2009

[Enrollment and staff are for Fall of year shown. Revenues and expenditures are for school year ending in year shown]

Item	Puerto Rico	Guam	U.S. Virgin Islands	American Samoa	Northern Marianas	Item	Puerto Rico	Guam	U.S. Virgin Islands	American Samoa	Northern Marianas
Enrollment (fall).......	493,393	[1] 30,986	15,493	[2] 16,400	10,961	Teachers..........	39,102	[1] 1,434	1,425	[2] 971	552
						Student support staff...............	3,435	[1] 174	330	[2] 218	45
Elementary (pre-kindergarten–grade 8)...........	347,638	[1] 21,946	10,409	[2] 11,763	7,743	Other support services staff......	13,218	[1] 299	339	[2] 101	99
Secondary (grades 9–12)......	145,755	[1] 9,040	5,084	[2] 4,637	3,218 3,097	Revenues, total [3] ($1,000)...........	3,542,658	262,823	243,079	79,922	65,538
Total staff (fall)........	63,198	[1] 3,455	2,854	[2] 1,869	1,155	Current expenditures [4] ($1,000)...........	3,502,757	235,711	201,326	65,436	62,787
School district staff................	1,406	[1] 285	119	[2] 186	89	Per pupil [4] (dol.)..........	7,790	[1] 6,781	13,062	[2] 3,481	5,882
School staff.........	45,139	[1] 2,890	2,066	[2] 1,364	922						

[1] 2005 data. [2] 2006 data. [3] Includes federal, territorial, local, and private revenues. [4] Includes current expenditures only, and excludes capital expenditures, interest on school debt, community services, private school programs, adult education, and other expenditures not directly allocable to public school operations.

Source: U.S. National Center for Education Statistics, *Digest of Education Statistics*, 2011, annual. See also <http://nces.ed.gov/annuals>.

Table 1332. Occupational Employment and Average Annual Wages in Guam, Puerto Rico, and Virgin Islands: 2011

[The Occupational Employment Survey (OES) program conducts a semiannual mail survey designed to produce estimates of employment and wages for specific occupations. For more details on the survey, see <http://www.bls.gov/oes/oes_emp.htm#scope>]

Selected occupation	SOC code [1]	Guam		Puerto Rico		Virgin Islands	
		Employment	Average annual wages [2]	Employment	Average annual wages [2]	Employment	Average annual wages [2]
Total, all occupations [3, 4]	(X)	**59,560**	**31,840**	**930,940**	**27,190**	**43,310**	**37,690**
Management occupations	11	5,080	59,280	34,160	69,790	2,480	75,460
Business and financial operations	13	2,270	48,160	40,410	37,720	1,370	51,630
Computer and mathematical	15	670	42,830	9,240	41,990	390	61,400
Architecture and engineering	17	970	55,510	12,740	49,300	320	69,590
Life, physical, and social science	19	360	45,400	6,430	42,750	370	49,510
Community and social services	21	550	36,380	18,330	27,530	620	45,720
Legal occupations	23	240	64,660	4,710	60,160	460	92,690
Education, training, and library	25	(NA)	(NA)	93,360	31,470	3,040	40,640
Arts, design, entertainment sports	27	530	29,310	6,210	29,850	300	40,630
Healthcare practitioner and technical	29	1,520	59,770	45,220	35,420	1,150	60,500
Healthcare support	31	770	24,740	12,020	20,220	450	28,510
Protective service	33	2,380	30,640	62,790	23,260	2,790	32,290
Food preparation and serving related	35	6,090	18,250	66,530	18,510	3,940	22,420
Buildings and grounds cleaning and maintenance	37	2,990	19,770	42,010	18,520	2,480	23,250
Personal care and service	39	1,620	21,950	13,820	19,430	990	22,230
Sales and related occupations	41	3,890	22,020	106,920	22,660	4,910	26,560
Office and administrative support	43	10,630	26,810	169,640	23,420	8,670	32,380
Farming, fishing, and forestry	45	(NA)	(NA)	1,310	24,870	(NA)	(NA)
Construction and extraction	47	5,650	27,330	34,800	20,990	2,230	43,390
Installation, maintenance, and repair	49	3,700	29,190	30,780	28,160	2,530	43,730
Production occupations	51	1,710	26,540	67,090	22,270	1,840	46,520
Transportation and material moving	53	3,740	29,270	52,410	20,970	1,970	29,800

NA Not available. X Not applicable. [1] Office of Management and Budget's Standard Occupational Classification (SOC) is used to define occupations. SOC categorizes workers into 1 of 801 detailed occupations and aggregates; the detailed occupations into 23 major occupational groups. [2] Annual wages have been calculated by multiplying the hourly mean wage by a "year-round, full-time" hours figure of 2,080 hours; for those occupations where there is not an hourly mean wage published, the annual wage has been directly calculated from the reported survey data. [3] Estimates for detailed occupations do not sum to the totals because the totals include occupations not shown separately. 4 Estimates do not include self-employed workers.

Source: U.S. Bureau of Labor Statistics, "Occupational Employment Statistics," <http://www.bls.gov/oes/data.htm>, accessed April 2012.

Table 1333. Prisoners in Custody of Correctional Authorities in U.S. Territories and Commonwealths: 2007 and 2008

[As of December 31. Minus sign (–) indicates decrease]

Jurisdiction	Total inmates			Sentenced to more than 1 year			
	2007	2008	Percent change 2007–2008	2007	2008	Percent change 2007–2008	Incarceration rate, 2008 [1]
Total [2]	**14,678**	**13,576**	**-7.5**	**11,465**	**10,346**	**-9.8**	**237**
American Samoa	236	132	-44.1	122	48	-60.7	74
Guam [2]	535	578	8.1	320	304	-5.0	173
Northern Mariana Islands	137	124	-9.5	78	78	0.0	141
Puerto Rico	13,215	12,130	-8.2	10,553	9,642	-8.6	244
U.S. Virgin Islands	555	612	10.3	392	274	-30.1	249

[1] The number of prisoners with a sentence of more than 1 year per 100,000 persons in the resident population. [2] Data for Guam 2008 are estimates.

Source: U.S. Bureau of Justice Statistics, *Prisoners in 2008*, NCJ 228417, December 2009. See also <http://bjs.ojp.usdoj.gov/index.cfm?ty=pbdetail&iid=1763>.

Table 1334. Federal Direct Payments: 2010

[In thousands of dollars (7,951,300 represents $7,951,300,000). For fiscal years ending September 30]

Selected program payment	Puerto Rico	Guam	Virgin Islands	American Samoa	Northern Mariana Islands
Direct payments to individuals for retirement and disability [1]	7,951,300	294,106	239,101	60,683	32,971
Social security:					
Retirement insurance	3,439,821	110,217	149,834	16,732	8,840
Survivors' insurance	1,501,662	51,479	37,149	17,319	6,469
Disability insurance	2,208,140	26,131	26,871	15,258	2,208
Federal retirement and disability:					
Civilian [2]	299,200	57,295	19,140	1,882	7,841
Military	22,873	23,861	2,004	1,603	853
Veterans benefits:					
Service-connected disability	314,132	21,393	2,604	6,909	1,066
Other benefit payments	131,627	2,591	504	838	65
Other	33,846	1,138	995	142	324

[1] Includes other payments, not shown separately. [2] Includes retirement and disability payments to former U.S. Postal Service employees.

Source: U.S. Census Bureau, *Consolidated Federal Funds Report for Fiscal Year 2010*, CFFR/10, annual. See also <http://www.census.gov/govs/cffr/>.

Table 1335. Selected Social, Demographic, and Housing Characteristics in Puerto Rico: 2010

[The Puerto Rico Community Survey universe includes the household population and the population living in institutions, college dormitories, and other group quarters. Based on a sample and subject to sampling variability; see text, this section and Appendix III]

Characteristic	Estimate	Percent	Characteristic	Estimate	Percent
Total Population............	**3,722,133**	**100.0**	**Females 15 years and over**................	**1,583,954**	**100.0**
			Never married........................	523,558	33.1
SEX AND AGE			Now married, except separated...............	601,632	38.0
Male...........................	1,785,266	48.0	Separated............................	50,458	3.2
Female.........................	1,936,867	52.0	Widowed.............................	171,416	10.8
			Divorced............................	236,890	15.0
Under 5 years..................	223,247	6.0			
5 to 9 years...................	236,531	6.4	HOUSEHOLDS		
10 to 14 years.................	268,378	7.2	**Total households**...................	**1,319,448**	**100.0**
15 to 19 years.................	284,254	7.6	Family households (families).............	966,123	73.2
20 to 24 years.................	264,790	0.1	With own children under 18 years.........	405,933	30.8
25 to 34 years.................	482,756	13.0	Married-couple families.................	557,851	42.3
35 to 44 years.................	487,539	13.1	With own children under 18 years.........	200,406	15.2
45 to 54 years.................	486,273	13.1	Male householder, no wife present...........	82,129	6.2
55 to 59 years.................	219,460	5.9	With own children under 18 years.........	39,285	3.0
60 to 64 years.................	223,184	6.0	Female householder, no husband present...	326,143	24.7
65 to 74 years.................	313,604	8.4	With own children under 18 years.........	166,242	12.6
75 to 84 years.................	170,712	4.6	Nonfamily households.....................	353,325	26.8
85 years and over..............	61,405	1.6	Householder living alone.................	306,036	23.2
			65 years and over....................	125,754	9.5
MARITAL STATUS					
Males 15 years and over....	**1,410,023**	**100.0**	Average household size.......................	2.79	(X)
Never married..................	566,489	40.2	Average family size.......................	3.28	(X)
Now married, except					
separated.....................	610,584	43.3	DISABILITY STATUS		
Separated......................	39,169	2.8	Total civilian		
Widowed........................	39,752	2.8	noninstitutionalized population................	3,695,636	100.0
Divorced.......................	154,029	10.9	With a disability..............................	726,334	19.7

X Not applicable.

Source: U.S. Census Bureau, 2010 Puerto Rico Community Survey, DP-02-PR, "Selected Social Characteristics in Puerto Rico," and DP-05, "Demographic and Housing Estimates," <http://factfinder.census.gov/>, accessed August 2012.

Table 1336. Tenure by Household Type in Puerto Rico: 2010

[The Puerto Rico Community Survey universe includes the household population and the population living in institutions, college dormitories, and other group quarters. Based on a sample and subject to sampling variability; see text, this section and Appendix III]

Household Type	Owner occupied	Renter occupied	Household Type	Owner occupied	Renter occupied
Total households...................	**929,831**	**389,617**	Householder 15 to 34 years.........	20,298	59,970
Family households......................	704,899	261,224	Householder 35 to 64 years.........	114,189	69,118
Married-couple family..................	465,523	92,328	Householder 65 years and over....	53,256	9,312
Householder 15 to 34 years..........	39,413	31,583	Nonfamily households...................	224,932	128,393
Householder 35 to 64 years..........	298,582	49,677	Householder living alone...............	197,255	108,781
Householder 65 years and over.....	127,528	11,068	Householder 15 to 34 years.........	10,141	17,781
Other family..........................	239,376	168,896	Householder 35 to 64 years.........	93,715	58,645
Male householder, no wife present..	51,633	30,496	Householder 65 years and over....	93,399	32,355
Householder 15 to 34 years........	7,857	14,029	Householder not living alone...........	27,677	19,612
Householder 35 to 64 years........	30,323	13,849	Householder 15 to 34 years.........	3,571	8,702
Householder 65 years and over....	13,453	2,618	Householder 35 to 64 years.........	17,536	9,376
Female householder, no husband					
present.................................	187,743	138,400	Householder 65 years and over....	6,570	1,534

Source: U.S. Census Bureau, 2010 Puerto Rico Community Survey, B25011, "Tenure by Household Type and Age of Householder," <http://factfinder.census.gov/>, accessed August 2012.

Table 1337. Puerto Rico— Socioeconomic Summary: 1990 to 2010

[3,512.4 represents 3,512,400, except as indicated]

Item	Unit	1990	2000	2005	2006	2007	2008	2009	2010
POPULATION									
Total [1]	1,000	3,512.4	3,808.0	3,903.5	3,919.9	3,934.6	3,947.7	3,960.7	3,973.0
Persons per family	Number	3.7	3.4	3.3	3.2	3.2	3.2	3.2	3.1
EDUCATION [2]									
Enrollment, total	1,000	953.0	971.5	958.7	1,017.7	1,000.5	964.1	951.3	952.4
Public (except public colleges or universities)	1,000	651.2	612.3	575.6	564.3	540.5	526.5	503.7	493.3
College and university	1,000	156.0	175.5	208.0	209.5	224.0	227.5	235.6	249.4
Expenses	Mil. dol.	1,686.4	4,254.1	5,902.4	6,353.4	6,588.5	6,852.6	7,331.7	7,371.7
As percent of GNP	Percent	7.8	10.3	11.0	11.2	11.1	11.1	11.2	11.6
Public	Mil. dol.	1,054.2	3,160.4	4,274.6	4,533.9	4,811.9	5,026.3	5,403.1	5,416.1
Private	Mil. dol.	644.2	1,093.7	1,627.8	1,819.5	1,776.6	1,826.3	1,928.6	1,955.6
LABOR FORCE [3]									
Total [4]	1,000	1,124	1,303	1,385	1,422	1,409	1,368	1,349	1,313
Employed [5]	1,000	963	1,159	1,238	1,256	1,263	1,218	1,168	1,103
Agriculture [6]	1,000	36	24	26	22	16	15	19	17
Manufacturing	1,000	168	159	138	136	135	129	112	102
Trade	1,000	185	239	261	271	260	257	244	240
Government	1,000	222	249	274	280	296	279	271	261
Unemployed	1,000	161	143	147	166	147	151	181	210
Unemployment rate [7]	Rate	14.0	11.0	10.6	11.7	10.4	11.0	13.4	16.0
Compensation of employees	Mil. dol.	13,639	23,504	29,372	30,027	30,234	30,869	30,743	29,894
Average compensation	Dollar	14,854	20,280	23,725	23,907	23,938	25,344	26,321	27,102
Salary and wages	Mil. dol.	13,639	23,504	25,393	25,844	26,102	26,700	26,510	25,807
INCOME [8]									
Personal income:									
Current dollars	Mil. dol.	21,105	38,856	48,820	50,842	52,110	56,124	58,562	60,401
Constant (1954) dollars	Mil. dol.	5,551	8,491	9,611	9,555	9,542	9,761	9,791	9,850
Disposable personal income:									
Current dollars	Mil. dol.	19,914	36,239	45,488	47,333	48,752	53,075	55,639	57,547
Constant (1954) dollars	Mil. dol.	5,238	7,919	8,955	8,896	8,927	9,230	9,303	9,385
Average family income:									
Current dollars	Dollar	22,232	34,693	41,273	41,505	42,381	45,494	47,315	47,129
Constant (1954) dollars	Dollar	5,847	7,581	8,125	7,800	7,761	7,926	7,911	7,700
BANKING [9]									
Assets	Mil. dol.	27,902	58,813	109,292	112,658	109,320	110,558	106,960	82,851
TOURISM [8]									
Number of visitors	1,000	3,426	4,566	5,073	5,022	5,062	5,213	4,783	4,872
Visitor expenditures	Mil. dol.	1,366	2,388	3,239	3,369	3,414	3,535	3,473	3,598
Average per visitor	Dollar	399	523	638	671	674	678	726	738
Net income from tourism	Mil. dol.	383	615	771	806	(NA)	(NA)	(NA)	(NA)

NA Not available. [1] 1990 and 2000 enumerated as of April 1; all other years estimated as of July 1. [2] Enrollment for the first school month. Expenses for school year ending in year shown. "Public" includes: public preschool, public elementary, public intermediate, public high school, public post-high school, public technological, public adult education, public vocational education, and public special education. "College and university" includes both public and private colleges and universities. [3] Annual average of monthly figures. For fiscal years. [4] For population 16 years old and over. [5] Includes other employment not shown separately. [6] Includes forestry and fisheries. [7] Percent unemployed of the labor force. [8] For fiscal years. [9] As of June 30. Does not include federal savings banks and international banking entities.

Source: Puerto Rico Planning Board, San Juan, PR, *Economic Report for the Governor and Legislative Assembly*, annual, accessed August 2012. See also <http://www.gdb-pur.com/economy/statistical-appendix.html>.

Table 1338. Puerto Rico—Business Summary by Industry: 2010

[Payroll in thousands of dollars (16,243,239 represents $16,243,239,000). Covers establishments with payroll. Excludes self-employed individuals, employees of private households, railroad employees, agricultural production employees, and most government employees. For statement on methodology, see Appendix III]

Industry	2007 NAICS code [1]	Establishments	Employees [2]	Annual payroll (1,000)
Total, all industries [3]	(X)	**44,693**	**678,376**	**16,243,239**
Construction	23	2,277	33,151	633,493
Manufacturing	31–33	1,912	88,191	3,027,120
Wholesale trade	42	2,187	32,921	1,141,477
Retail trade	44–45	10,479	128,024	2,230,752
Transportation and warehousing	48–49	1,048	15,353	410,976
Information	51	564	18,169	731,650
Finance and insurance	52	1,979	34,906	1,430,413
Real estate and rental and leasing	53	1,635	11,695	257,850
Professional, scientific, and technical services	54	4,232	27,250	871,502
Management of companies and enterprises	55	84	3,923	208,894
Admin/support waste mgt/remediation services	56	1,798	72,271	1,328,393
Educational services	61	799	37,548	773,181
Health care and social assistance	62	7,272	78,678	1,765,297
Arts, entertainment, and recreation	71	415	3,465	61,270
Accommodation and food services	72	4,280	71,408	974,255

X Not applicable. [1] 2007 North American Industry Classification System. See text, section 15. [2] Covers full- and part-time employees who are on the payroll in the pay period including March 12. [3] Includes other industries, not shown separately.

Source: U.S. Census Bureau, "County Business Patterns, 2010" <http://www.census.gov/econ/cbp/index.html>.

Table 1339. Puerto Rico—Gross Product and Net Income: 1990 to 2010

[In millions of dollars (21,619 represents $21,619,000,000). For fiscal years ending June 30. Data for 2010 are preliminary. Minus sign (−) indicates decrease]

Item	1990	1995	2000	2005	2008	2009	2010
Gross product	**21,619**	**28,452**	**41,419**	**53,752**	**61,665**	**62,678**	**63,292**
Agriculture	434	318	407	499	519	506	553
Manufacturing	12,126	17,867	24,489	35,581	40,234	44,019	44,641
Contract construction and mining [1]	720	1,006	2,157	2,155	2,032	1,818	1,658
Transportation, warehousing, and utilities	2,468	3,276	2,579	2,841	3,097	2,881	2,835
Trade (wholesale and retail)	4,728	5,989	6,093	7,368	7,520	7,549	7,708
Finance, insurance, and real estate	3,896	5,730	10,511	14,694	19,185	18,206	18,862
Services [2]	3,015	4,724	9,987	11,520	11,258	11,186	11,728
Government	3,337	4,440	5,478	8,151	8,762	9,047	8,276
Commonwealth	2,884	3,793	4,601	7,032	7,350	7,567	6,740
Municipalities	453	647	877	1,118	1,412	1,480	1,536
Rest of the world	-8,985	-14,195	-20,283	-29,056	-30,941	-32,534	-32,969
Statistical discrepancy	-121	-703	585	141	-312	-512	-340
Net income	**17,941**	**23,653**	**32,610**	**43,484**	**48,993**	**49,989**	**49,547**
Agriculture	486	442	385	479	519	506	554
Manufacturing	11,277	16,685	22,627	33,427	37,299	40,974	41,356
Mining [1]	26	30	34	42	36	28	27
Contract construction	679	903	1,764	1,718	1,661	1,473	1,305
Transportation, warehousing, and utilities	1,778	2,360	1,961	2,075	2,382	2,134	2,044
Trade (wholesale and retail)	3,420	4,108	4,995	6,043	6,162	6,180	6,232
Finance, insurance, and real estate	3,280	4,735	8,175	11,634	13,909	12,803	13,051
Services [2]	2,643	4,146	7,475	8,972	9,202	9,377	9,671
Government	3,337	4,440	5,478	8,151	8,762	9,047	8,276
Rest of the world	-8,985	-14,195	-20,283	-29,056	-30,941	-32,534	-32,969

[1] Mining includes only quarries. [2] Includes all other services not elsewhere classified.

Source: Puerto Rico Planning Board, San Juan, PR, *Economic Report for the Governor and Legislative Assembly*, annual. Accessed August 2012. See also <http://www.gdb-pur.com/economy/statistical-appendix.html>.

Table 1340. Puerto Rico—Transfer Payments: 1990 to 2010

[In millions of dollars (4,871 represents $4,871,000,000). Data represent transfer payments between federal and state governments and other nonresidents. Data for 2010 are preliminary]

Item	1990	1995	2000	2005	2008	2009	2010
Total receipts	**4,871**	**6,236**	**8,659**	**10,551**	**13,985**	**15,445**	**17,259**
Federal government	4,649	5,912	7,966	9,673	12,858	14,192	16,325
Transfers to individuals [1]	4,577	5,838	7,868	9,547	12,672	13,978	16,082
Veterans benefits	349	440	491	491	609	518	778
Medicare	368	661	1,196	1,825	2,306	2,461	2,510
Old age, disability, survivors (social security)	2,055	2,912	3,863	5,118	6,134	6,620	6,829
Nutritional assistance	880	1,063	1,193	1,306	1,513	1,547	1,605
Industry subsidies	72	74	98	127	185	213	243
U.S. state governments	18	18	15	15	24	36	45
Other nonresidents	205	307	679	863	1,103	1,217	890
Total payments	**1,801**	**2,301**	**2,763**	**3,583**	**3,655**	**4,050**	**4,349**
Federal government	1,756	2,132	2,693	3,516	3,588	3,883	4,132
Transfers from individuals	817	1,052	1,326	1,792	1,834	1,866	1,871
Contribution to Medicare	97	162	191	303	393	441	449
Employee contribution for social security	720	888	1,133	1,483	1,436	1,421	1,419
Transfers from industries	16	49	51	74	104	101	98
Unemployment insurance	247	184	234	221	252	534	782
Employer contribution for social security	675	847	1,081	1,429	1,398	1,382	1,381
Other nonresidents [2]	45	164	70	67	67	167	217
Net balance	**3,070**	**3,935**	**5,897**	**6,968**	**10,330**	**11,394**	**12,911**
Federal government	2,893	3,780	5,273	6,157	9,270	10,308	12,193
U.S. state governments	16	13	10	10	21	32	40
Other nonresidents	162	143	614	801	1,040	1,055	677

[1] Includes other receipts and payments not shown separately. [2] Includes U.S. state governments.

Source: Puerto Rico Planning Board, San Juan, PR, *Economic Report for the Governor and Legislative Assembly*, annual. Accessed August 2012. See also <http://www.gdb-pur.com/economy/statistical-appendix.html>.

Table 1341. Puerto Rico—Merchandise Imports and Exports: 1980 to 2011

[In millions of dollars (9,018 represents $9,018,000,000). Imports are imports for consumption; see text, Section 28]

Item	1980	1985	1990	1995	2000	2005	2006	2007	2008	2009	2010	2011
Imports	9,018	10,162	16,200	18,969	27,006	40,418	42,462	43,496	41,559	38,775	39,778	44,597
From U.S.	5,345	6,130	10,792	12,213	15,172	20,994	21,982	22,402	19,777	20,038	20,641	20,346
From other	3,673	4,032	5,408	6,756	11,834	19,424	20,480	21,094	21,783	18,737	19,137	24,251
Exports	6,576	11,087	20,402	23,573	43,191	56,843	59,218	62,398	63,663	59,601	68,392	57,444
To U.S.	5,643	9,873	17,915	20,986	38,335	47,121	47,452	47,507	46,439	40,779	47,630	40,942
To other	933	1,214	2,487	2,587	4,856	9,722	11,766	14,891	17,224	18,822	20,762	16,503

Source: U.S. Census Bureau, *Foreign Commerce and Navigation: U.S. Trade with Puerto Rico and U.S. Possessions* (FT 895) and *U.S. Merchandise Trade: Selected Highlights* (FT920). See <http://www.census.gov/foreign-trade/statistics/index.html>. See also USATradeOnLine, <http://www.usatradeonline.gov/>.

Table 1342. Puerto Rico—Agricultural Summary: 2002 and 2007

[1 cuerda = 0.97 acre]

All farms	Unit	2002	2007	All farms	Unit	2002	2007
Farms..................	Number	17,659	15,745	Tenants.................	Number	1,636	2,425
Farm land..................	Cuerdas	690,687	557,530	Farms by type:			
Average size of farm.....	Cuerdas	39.1	35.4	organization:			
Approximate land area....	Cuerdas	2,254,365	2,254,365	Individual or family......	Number	15,843	13,958
Proportion in farms.......	Percent	30.6	24.7	Partnership..............	Number	162	49
Farms by size:				Corporation..............	Number	595	575
Less than 10 cuerdas....	Number	7,943	7,502	Other...................	Number	1,059	1,163
10 to 19 cuerdas.........	Number	3,847	3,545	Farms by value of sales:			
20 to 49 cuerdas..........	Number	3,228	2,680	Less than $1,000.........	Number	3,977	4,442
50 to 99 cuerdas..........	Number	1,282	865	$1,000 to $2,499..........	Number	3,471	2,771
100 to 174 cuerdas.......	Number	590	524	$2,500 to $4,499..........	Number	3,044	2,428
175 to 259 cuerdas.......	Number	281	207	$5,000 to $7,499..........	Number	1,575	1,206
260 cuerdas or more.....	Number	488	422	$7,500 to $9,999..........	Number	1,087	882
Tenure of operator:				$10,000 to $19,999.......	Number	1,781	1,497
Operators................	Number	17,659	15,745	$20,000 to $39,999.......	Number	1,062	1,030
Full owners..............	Number	13,693	11,402	$40,000 to $59,999.......	Number	375	281
Part owners.............	Number	2,330	1,918	$60,000 or more..........	Number	1,287	1,208

Source: U.S. Department of Agriculture, National Agricultural Statistics Service (NASS), *2007 Census of Agriculture: Puerto Rico, Island and Municipio Data*, Geographic Area Series, Volume 1: Part 52, 2009. See also <http://www.agcensus.usda.gov/Publications/2007/Full_Report/index.asp>.

Table 1343. Puerto Rico—Farms and Market Value of Agricultural Products Sold: 2007

[For total market value, 515,686 represents $515,686,000]

Type of product	Number of farms	Market value ($1,000)	Average value per farm (dol.)	Type of product	Number of farms	Market value ($1,000)	Average value per farm (dol.)
Total.........................	**15,745**	**515,686**	**32,752**	Horticultural specialties.........	524	44,576	85,068
Crops, including horticultural				Grasses and other crops.......	256	13,372	52,236
specialties........................	10,206	218,835	(NA)				
Coffee............................	5,678	41,824	7,366	Livestock, poultry, and their			
Pineapples.......................	53	527	9,942	products........................	5,662	296,850	52,428
Plantains.........................	3,756	44,875	11,947	Cattle and calves................	3,568	33,005	9,250
Bananas..........................	1,980	10,082	5,092	Poultry and poultry products....	1,079	63,574	58,919
Grains............................	969	1,553	1,603	Dairy products...................	354	184,543	521,307
Root crops or tubers.............	1,691	6,683	3,952	Hogs and pigs...................	1,075	6,239	5,803
Fruits and coconuts..............	2,350	19,904	8,470	Aquaculture.....................	40	833	20,818
Vegetables and melons [1]........	1,007	35,440	35,194	Other............................	787	8,657	11,000

NA Not available. [1] Includes hydroponic crops.

Source: U.S. Department of Agriculture, National Agricultural Statistics Service (NASS), *2007 Census of Agriculture: Puerto Rico, Island and Municipio Data*, Geographic Area Series, Volume 1: Part 52, 2009. See also <http://www.agcensus.usda.gov/Publications/2007/Full_Report/index.asp>.

Table 1344. Guam, Virgin Islands, and Northern Mariana Islands— Economic Summary by Sector: 2007

[Sales and payroll in millions of dollars (6,244 represents $6,244,000,000). Based on the 2007 Economic Census; see Appendix III]

Selected kinds of business	Guam	Virgin Islands	Northern Mariana Islands	Selected kinds of business	Guam	Virgin Islands	Northern Mariana Islands
Total:				Paid employees [2].............	2,394	797	872
Establishments [1].............	3,143	2,583	1,191	Retail trade:			
Sales...........................	6,244	19,479	1,284	Establishments.................	660	641	255
Annual payroll.................	1,101	1,085	246	Sales...........................	1,618	1,397	272
Paid employees [2].............	52,394	35,300	22,622	Annual payroll.................	150	146	29
Construction:				Paid employees [2].............	8,219	6,773	2,770
Establishments.................	317	195	50	Professional, scientific, and			
Sales...........................	579	352	31	technical services:			
Annual payroll.................	121	115	7	Establishments.................	227	257	87
Paid employees [2].............	6,011	3,388	528	Sales...........................	231	284	25
Manufacturing:				Annual payroll.................	77	60	9
Establishments.................	63	70	59	Paid employees [2].............	2,217	1,370	404
Sales...........................	167	(D)	190	Accommodation & food			
Annual payroll.................	39	(D)	57	services:			
Paid employees [2].............	1,495	([3])	7,094	Establishments.................	429	255	140
Wholesale trade:				Sales...........................	635	461	173
Establishments.................	191	58	72	Annual payroll.................	155	130	45
Sales...........................	800	288	143	Paid employees [2].............	11,477	6,146	4,772
Annual payroll.................	56	25	10				

D Withheld to avoid disclosing data for individual companies; data are included in higher level totals. [1] Includes other industries, not shown separately. [2] For pay period including March 12. [3] 1,000 to 2,499 employees.

Source: U.S. Census Bureau, "General Statistics by Kind of Business," *2007 Economic Census of the Island Areas*, Geographic Area Series, accessed August 2010. See also <http://www.census.gov/econ/islandareas/>.

International Statistics

This section presents statistics for the world as a whole and for many countries on a comparative basis with the United States. Data are shown for population, births and deaths, social and economic indicators, finances, agriculture, energy, communication, and military affairs.

Statistics for individual countries may be found primarily in official national publications, generally in the form of yearbooks, issued by most countries at various intervals in their own national languages and expressed in their own customary units of measure. (For a listing of selected publications, see Appendix I, Guide to Sources.)

For international comparisons, the United Nations Statistics Division compiles data as submitted by member countries and issues a number of summary publications, generally in English and French. Among these are the annual *Statistical Yearbook; Demographic Yearbook; Population and Vital Statistics Report; International Trade Statistics Yearbook; Energy Statistics Yearbook; Industrial Commodity Statistics Yearbook; National Accounts Statistics: Main Aggregates and Detailed Tables;* and the *Monthly Bulletin of Statistics.* Specialized agencies of the United Nations also issue international summary publications on various topics, including agricultural, labor, health, and trade statistics. Among these are *Food Outlook: Global Market Analysis* and the Statistical Yearbook issued by the Food and Agriculture Organization (FAO); the *Yearbook of Labour Statistics* issued by the International Labor Organization (ILO); *World Health Statistics* issued by the World Health Organization (WHO); and the *Handbook of Statistics* issued by the Conference on Trade and Development (UNCTAD).

The U.S. Census Bureau publishes estimates and projections of key demographic measures for countries and regions of the world in its International Data Base at <http://www.census.gov/ipc/www/idb/>.

The International Monetary Fund (IMF), the World Bank, and the Organisation for Economic Co-operation and Development (OECD) also compile data on international statistics. The IMF publishes a series of reports related to financial data. These include *International Financial Statistics, Direction of Trade Statistics,* and *Balance of Payments Statistics Yearbook.* The World Bank publishes many reports on a wide range of topics related to international development. Three of their flagship statistical publications are World Development Report, World Development Indicators, and Global Economic Prospects. The OECD also produces numerous statistical publications in fields including economics, health, and education. Among these are the *OECD Factbook; Economic Outlook; National Accounts of OECD Countries; Science, Technology and Industry Outlook; International Migration Outlook; Employment Outlook; Health at a Glance;* and *Education at a Glance.*

Statistical coverage, country names, and classifications—Problems of space and availability of data limit the number of countries and the extent of statistical coverage shown. The list of countries included and the spelling of country names are based almost entirely on the list of independent nations, dependencies, and areas of special sovereignty provided by the U.S. Department of State.

In the last quarter-century, several important changes took place in the status of the world's nations. In 1991, the Soviet Union broke up into 15 independent countries: Armenia, Azerbaijan, Belarus, Estonia, Georgia, Kazakhstan, Kyrgyzstan, Latvia, Lithuania, Moldova, Russia, Tajikistan, Turkmenistan, Ukraine, and Uzbekistan.

Germany was reunified in 1990, when the German Democratic Republic (former East Germany) joined the Federal Republic of Germany (former West Germany) to form a single country. On January 1, 1993, Czechoslovakia was succeeded by two independent countries: the Czech Republic and Slovakia.

Following the breakup of the Socialist Federal Republic of Yugoslavia in 1992, the United States recognized Bosnia and Herzegovina, Croatia, Slovenia, and Macedonia as independent countries. Serbia and Montenegro, both former republics of Yugoslavia, became independent of one another on May 31, 2006. This separation is seen in the population estimates of Table 1348, but some tables may still show both countries as combined. On February 17, 2008, Kosovo declared its independence from Serbia.

The Treaty of Maastricht created the European Union (EU) in 1992 with 12 member countries. The EU is not a state intended to replace existing states, but it is more than just an international organization. Its member states have set up common institutions to which they delegate some of their sovereignty so that decisions on specific matters of joint interest can be made democratically at a European level. This pooling of sovereignty is also called "European integration." The EU has grown in size with successive waves of accessions in 1995, 2004, and 2007. The 27 current members of the EU are: Austria, Belgium, Bulgaria, Cyprus, Czech Republic, Denmark, Estonia, Finland, France, Germany, Greece, Hungary, Ireland, Italy, Latvia, Lithuania, Luxembourg, Malta, the Netherlands, Poland, Portugal, Romania, Slovakia, Slovenia, Spain, Sweden, and the United Kingdom.

In 1992, the EU decided to establish an economic and monetary union (EMU), with the introduction of a single European currency managed by a European Central Bank. The single currency—the euro—became a reality on January 1, 2002, when euro notes and coins replaced national currencies in 12 of the then 15 countries of the European Union (Belgium, Germany, Greece, Spain, France, Ireland, Italy, Luxembourg, the Netherlands, Austria, Portugal, and Finland). Since then, 12 additional countries have acceded to EU membership, but Slovakia, Slovenia, Malta, Cyprus, and Estonia have been the only new members of the EU to adopt the euro as the national currency.

Elsewhere in the world, Eritrea announced its independence from Ethiopia in April 1993 and was subsequently recognized as an independent nation by the United States. In the South Pacific, the Marshall Islands, Micronesia, and Palau gained independence from the United States in 1991. In May of 2002,

Timor-Leste won independence from Indonesia. The Netherlands Antilles dissolved on October 10, 2010. As a result, Curaçao and Sint Maarten became autonomous territories of the Netherlands.

The population estimates and projections used in Tables 1348 through 1351, 1353, and 1357 were prepared by the Census Bureau. For each country, available data on population, by age and sex, fertility, mortality, and international migration were evaluated and, where necessary, adjusted for inconsistencies and errors in the data. In most instances, comprehensive projections were made by the cohort-component method, resulting in distributions of the population by age and sex and requiring an assessment of probable future trends of fertility, mortality, and international migration.

Economic associations—The Organisation for European Economic Co-operation (OEEC), a regional grouping of Western European countries established in 1948 for the purpose of harmonizing national economic policies and conditions, was succeeded on September 30, 1961, by the Organisation for Economic Co-operation and Development (OECD). The member nations of the OECD are Australia, Austria, Belgium, Canada, Chile, Czech Republic, Denmark, Estonia, Finland, France, Germany, Greece, Hungary, Iceland, Ireland, Israel, Italy, Japan, Luxembourg, Mexico, the Netherlands, New Zealand, Norway, Poland, Portugal, Slovakia, Slovenia, South Korea, Spain, Sweden, Switzerland, Turkey, the United Kingdom, and the United States.

Quality and comparability of the data—The quality and comparability of the data presented here are affected by a number of factors:

1 The year for which data are presented may not be the same for all subjects for a particular country or for a given subject for different countries, though the data shown are the most recent available. All such variations have been noted. The data shown are for calendar years except as otherwise specified.

2 The bases, methods of estimating, methods of data collection, extent of coverage, precision of definition, scope of territory, and margins of error may vary for different items within a particular country, and for like items for different countries. Footnotes and headnotes to the tables describe some of the major coverage qualifications attached to the figures; considerably more detail is presented in the source publications. Many of the measures shown are merely rough indicators of magnitude.

3 Figures shown in this section for the United States may not always agree with figures shown in the preceding sections. Disagreements may be attributable to the use of differing original sources, differences in the definition of geographic limits (the 50 states, continental U.S. only, or the U.S. including certain outlying areas and possessions), or to possible adjustments made to the U.S. figures

in order to make them more comparable with figures from other countries.

International comparisons of national accounts data—To compare national accounts data for different countries, it is necessary to convert each country's data into a common unit of currency, usually the U.S. dollar. The market exchange rates, which often are used in converting national currencies, do not necessarily reflect the relative purchasing power in the various countries. It is necessary that the goods and services produced in different countries be valued consistently if the differences observed are meant to reflect real differences in the volumes of goods and services produced. The use of purchasing power parities (see Tables 1363, 1364, and 1371) instead of exchange rates is intended to achieve this objective.

The method used to present the data shown in Table 1364 is to construct volume measures directly by revaluing the goods and services sold in different countries at a common set of international prices. By dividing the ratio of the gross domestic products of two countries expressed in their own national currencies by the corresponding ratio calculated at constant international prices, it is possible to derive the implied purchasing power parity (PPP) between the two currencies concerned. PPPs show how many units of currency are needed in one country to buy the same amount of goods and services that one unit of currency will buy in the other country. For further information, see *National Accounts, Main Aggregates, Volume I*, issued annually by the Organisation for Economic Co-operation and Development (OECD), Paris, France.

International Standard Industrial Classification—The original version of the International Standard Industrial Classification of All Economic Activities (ISIC) was adopted in 1948. A number of countries have utilized ISIC as the basis for devising their industrial classification schemes. Substantial comparability has been attained among the industrial classification schemes of many countries, including the United States, by ensuring that national classification categories correspond to ISIC categories. The United Nations, the International Labour Organization, the Food and Agriculture Organization, and other international bodies use ISIC in publishing and analyzing statistical data. Revisions of ISIC were issued in 1958, 1968, 1989, 2002, and 2008.

International Maps—A series of regional world maps is provided within this section. References are included in Table 1348 for easy location of individual countries on the maps. Map projection will be distorted due to being portrayed on a flat surface. For additional information and maps see the Central Intelligence Agency's *The World Factbook*, at <https://www.cia.gov/library/publications/the-world-factbook/>.

50

Political Map of the World, June 2012

CENTRAL AMERICA AND THE CARIBBEAN

Scale 1:35,000,000
Azimuthal Equal-Area Projection

0 — 500 Kilometers
0 — 500 Miles

Boundary representation is
not necessarily authoritative.

803543AI (G00186) 6-12

803539AI (G00772) 6-12

Scale 1:51,400,000

Azimuthal Equal-Area Projection

Boundary representation is
not necessarily authoritative.

803535AI (G00392) 6-12

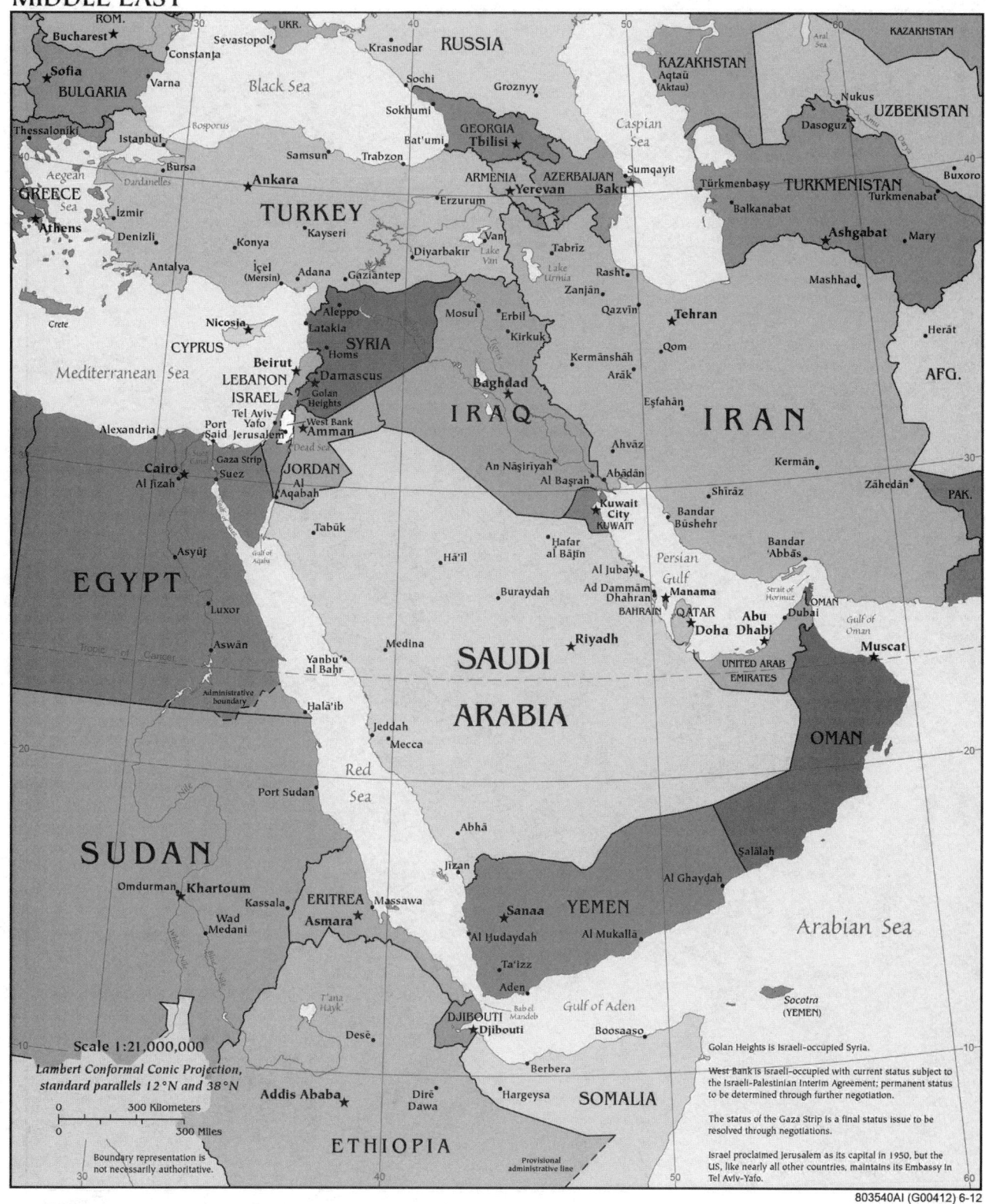

Scale 1:21,000,000

Lambert Conformal Conic Projection, standard parallels 12°N and 38°N

0   300 Kilometers

0   300 Miles

Boundary representation is
not necessarily authoritative.

Golan Heights is Israeli-occupied Syria.

West Bank is Israeli-occupied with current status subject to the Israeli-Palestinian Interim Agreement; permanent status to be determined through further negotiation.

The status of the Gaza Strip is a final status issue to be resolved through negotiations.

Israel proclaimed Jerusalem as its capital in 1950, but the US, like nearly all other countries, maintains its Embassy in Tel Aviv-Yafo.

803540AI (G00412) 6-12

Scale 1:48,000,000

Azimuthal Equal-Area Projection

Boundary representation is
not necessarily authoritative.

803537AI (G00543) 6-12

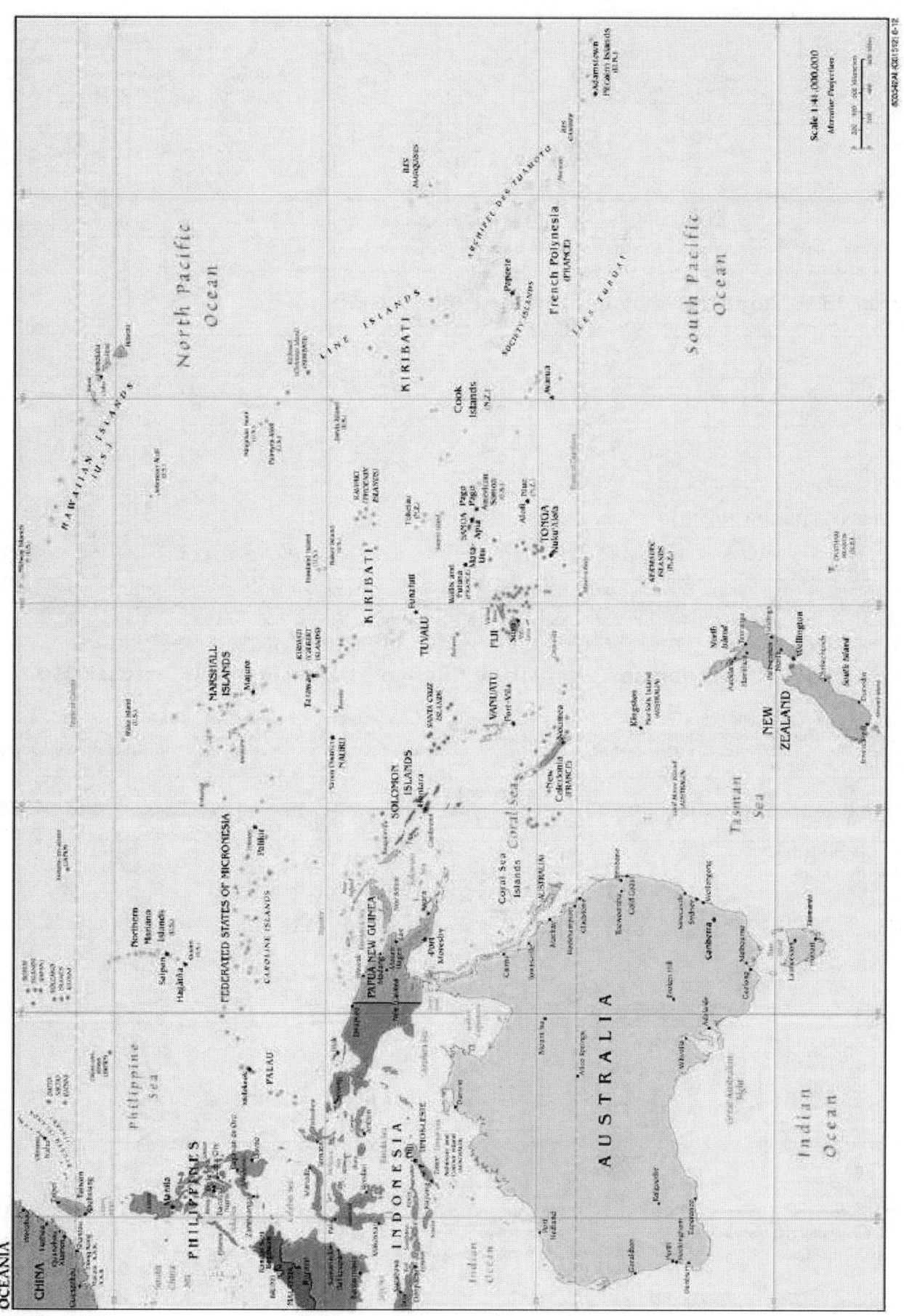

Table 1345. Total World Population: 1980 to 2050

[4,453 represents 4,453,000,000. As of midyear]

Year	Population (mil.)	Average annual [1] Growth rate (percent)	Average annual [1] Population change (mil.)	Year	Population (mil.)	Average annual [1] Growth rate (percent)	Average annual [1] Population change (mil.)
1980............	4,453	1.9	82.9	2015............	7,255	1.1	76.7
1985............	4,860	1.7	83.9	2020............	7,632	1.0	73.3
1990............	5,291	1.6	83.0	2025............	7,990	0.9	68.6
1995............	5,703	1.4	80.4	2030............	8,323	0.8	63.9
2000............	6,095	1.3	77.2	2035............	8,634	0.7	59.6
2005............	6,480	1.2	78.1	2040............	8,925	0.6	55.5
2010............	6,869	1.1	77.5	2045............	9,194	0.6	51.2
2011............	6,946	1.1	77.3	2050............	9,441	(NA)	(NA)

NA Not available. [1] Represents change from year shown to immediate succeeding year.

Source: U.S. Census Bureau, International Data Base, <http://www.census.gov/ipc/www/idb/>, accessed June 2011.

Table 1346. Population by Continent: 1980 to 2050

[In millions, except percent (4,453 represents 4,453,000,000). As of midyear]

Year	World	Africa [1]	North America [1]	South America [1]	Asia	Europe [1]	Oceania
1980..........................	4,453	479	371	242	2,644	695	23
1990..........................	5,291	632	424	297	3,190	723	26
2000..........................	6,095	807	486	348	3,694	730	30
2010..........................	6,869	1,028	536	395	4,138	736	35
2020..........................	7,632	1,289	588	439	4,543	734	39
2030..........................	8,323	1,583	638	475	4,861	723	43
2040..........................	8,925	1,913	681	502	5,078	705	46
2050..........................	9,441	2,270	719	518	5,206	679	48
PERCENT DISTRIBUTION							
1980..........................	100.0	10.8	8.3	5.4	59.4	15.6	0.5
2000..........................	100.0	13.2	8.0	5.7	60.6	12.0	0.5
2050..........................	100.0	24.0	7.6	5.5	55.1	7.2	0.5

[1] Estimates and projections for France include the four overseas departments of French Guiana, Guadeloupe, Martinique, and Reunion in the national total. These areas are included in the same regions as France (Europe). Saint Barthelemy and Saint Martin recently voted to become French overseas collectivities apart from Guadeloupe and are included in the totals for North America.

Source: U.S. Census Bureau, International Data Base, <http://www.census.gov/ipc/www/idb/>, accessed June 2011.

Table 1347. Population and Population Change by Development Status: 1950 to 2050

[2,557 represents 2,557,000,000. As of midyear. Minus sign (–) indicates decrease. The "less developed" countries include all of Africa, all of Asia except Japan, the Transcaucasian and Central Asian republics of the New Independent States, all of Latin America and the Caribbean, and all of Oceania except Australia, New Zealand, and Hawaii. This category matches the "less developed country" classification employed by the United Nations]

Year	Number (mil.) World	Number (mil.) Less developed countries [1]	Number (mil.) More developed countries [1]	Percent of world Less developed countries [1]	Percent of world More developed countries [1]
POPULATION					
1950.........................	2,557	1,749	807	68.4	31.6
1960.........................	3,042	2,132	911	70.1	29.9
1970.........................	3,713	2,709	1,004	73.0	27.0
1980.........................	4,453	3,372	1,082	75.7	24.3
1990.........................	5,291	4,147	1,144	78.4	21.6
2000.........................	6,095	4,901	1,193	80.4	19.6
2010.........................	6,869	5,637	1,231	82.1	17.9
2020.........................	7,632	6,371	1,262	83.5	16.5
2030.........................	8,323	7,044	1,279	84.6	15.4
2040.........................	8,925	7,639	1,286	85.6	14.4
2050.........................	9,441	8,157	1,285	86.4	13.6
POPULATION CHANGE					
1950–1960....................	486	382	104	78.7	21.3
1960–1970....................	671	578	93	86.2	13.8
1970–1980....................	741	662	78	89.5	10.5
1980–1990....................	838	775	62	92.6	7.4
1990–2000....................	804	754	49	93.9	6.1
2000–2010....................	774	736	38	95.1	4.9
2010–2020....................	764	733	30	96.0	4.0
2020–2030....................	691	674	18	97.4	2.6
2030–2040....................	601	594	7	98.9	1.1
2040–2050....................	517	518	-1	100.3	-0.3

[1] See footnote 1, Table 1346.

Source: U.S. Census Bureau, International Data Base, <http://www.census.gov/ipc/www/idb/>, accessed June 2011.

Table 1348. Population by Country or Area: 1990 to 2020

[5,291,102 represents 5,291,102,000. Covers countries or areas with populations of 5,000 or more in 2010. Population data generally are de facto figures for the present territory. Population estimates were derived from information available as of June 2011. See text of this section for general comments concerning the data. For details of methodology, coverage, and reliability, see source. Minus sign (–) indicates decrease]

Country or area	Map refer- ence [1]	Mid-year population (1,000)				Popula- tion rank, 2010	Annual rate of growth, [2] 2010 to 2020	Popula- tion per sq. mile, 2010	Area [3] (sq. mile)
		1990	2000	2010	2020, proj.				
World.............................	S0	5,291,102	6,094,670	6,868,528	7,632,247	(X)	1.1	135	50,939,127
Afghanistan......................	S7	13,568	22,461	29,121	36,644	40	2.3	116	251,827
Albania...........................	S4	3,245	3,158	2,987	3,075	135	0.3	282	10,578
Algeria...........................	S5	25,089	30,429	34,586	38,594	35	1.1	38	919,595
Andorra..........................	S4	53	65	85	86	199	0.1	468	181
Angola...........................	S5	9,485	12,683	17,043	22,484	60	2.8	35	481,354
Antigua and Barbuda............	S2	64	75	87	98	198	1.2	508	171
Argentina........................	S3	33,036	37,336	41,343	45,379	32	0.9	39	1,056,642
Armenia..........................	S6	3,377	3,043	2,967	3,017	137	0.2	272	10,889
Australia.........................	S8	16,956	19,053	21,516	23,939	54	1.1	7	2,966,153
Austria...........................	S4	7,723	8,113	8,214	8,220	92	(Z)	258	31,832
Azerbaijan.......................	S6	7,497	8,463	9,302	10,206	89	0.9	292	31,903
Bahamas, The...................	S2	245	283	310	338	177	0.8	80	3,865
Bahrain..........................	S6	506	655	1,180	1,505	157	2.4	4,021	293
Bangladesh......................	S7	112,213	132,151	156,118	183,109	8	1.6	3,106	50,258
Barbados........................	S2	262	274	286	295	179	0.3	1,721	166
Belarus..........................	S4	10,201	10,034	9,613	9,249	88	-0.4	123	78,340
Belgium..........................	S4	9,969	10,264	10,423	10,465	79	(Z)	892	11,690
Belize...........................	S2	191	248	315	380	176	1.9	36	8,805
Benin............................	S5	4,705	6,619	9,056	11,956	91	2.8	212	42,711
Bhutan...........................	S7	615	606	700	782	164	1.1	47	14,824
Bolivia...........................	S3	6,574	8,195	9,947	11,640	83	1.6	24	418,265
Bosnia and Herzegovina.........	S4	4,424	4,035	4,622	4,592	120	-0.1	234	19,763
Botswana........................	S5	1,265	1,680	2,029	2,312	144	1.3	9	218,816
Brazil............................	S3	151,170	176,320	201,103	222,608	5	1.0	62	3,266,199
Brunei...........................	S8	253	325	395	464	175	1.6	194	2,033
Bulgaria.........................	S4	8,894	7,818	7,149	6,569	98	-0.9	171	41,888
Burkina Faso....................	S5	8,361	11,588	16,242	21,978	63	3.0	154	105,715
Burma...........................	S7	40,464	47,439	53,414	59,126	24	1.0	212	252,321
Burundi..........................	S5	5,536	6,823	9,863	13,429	84	3.1	995	9,915
Cambodia........................	S7	9,368	12,351	14,454	16,927	67	1.6	212	68,153
Cameroon.......................	S5	11,884	15,343	19,294	23,471	58	2.0	106	182,514
Canada..........................	S1	27,791	31,100	33,760	36,387	36	0.8	10	3,511,023
Cape Verde......................	S5	340	430	509	583	170	1.4	327	1,557
Central African Republic........	S5	3,085	3,980	4,845	5,991	117	2.1	20	240,535
Chad............................	S5	5,841	7,943	10,543	12,756	77	1.9	22	486,180
Chile............................	S3	13,129	15,156	16,746	18,058	61	0.8	58	287,187
China [4].........................	S7	1,148,364	1,263,638	1,330,141	1,384,545	1	0.4	360	3,694,959
Colombia........................	S3	33,147	38,910	44,205	49,085	29	1.1	110	401,044
Comoros.........................	S5	430	545	706	846	163	1.8	818	863
Congo (Brazzaville) [5]..........	S5	2,266	3,104	4,126	5,444	125	2.8	31	131,854
Congo (Kinshasa) [5]............	S5	39,151	52,445	69,851	89,250	19	2.5	80	875,312
Costa Rica.......................	S2	3,023	3,883	4,516	5,098	122	1.2	229	19,714
Cote d'Ivoire.....................	S5	12,491	16,885	21,059	25,504	57	1.9	171	122,782
Croatia...........................	S4	4,508	4,411	4,487	4,427	123	-0.1	208	21,612
Cuba............................	S2	10,507	11,072	11,098	10,932	73	-0.2	262	42,402
Cyprus...........................	S6	745	920	1,103	1,267	159	1.4	309	3,568
Czech Republic..................	S4	10,310	10,270	10,202	10,013	81	-0.2	342	29,825
Denmark.........................	S4	5,141	5,337	5,516	5,642	109	0.2	337	16,384
Djibouti..........................	S5	499	669	741	922	162	2.2	83	8,950
Dominica.........................	S2	70	71	73	74	201	0.2	251	290
Dominican Republic..............	S2	7,084	8,469	9,824	11,109	85	1.2	527	18,656
Ecuador..........................	S3	10,318	12,446	14,791	16,905	66	1.3	138	106,889
Egypt............................	S5	54,907	65,159	80,472	96,260	16	1.8	209	384,345
El Salvador.......................	S2	5,110	5,850	6,052	6,217	106	0.3	757	8,000
Equatorial Guinea...............	S5	371	491	651	836	166	2.5	60	10,831
Eritrea...........................	S5	3,138	4,197	5,793	7,260	107	2.3	149	38,996
Estonia..........................	S4	1,569	1,380	1,291	1,203	155	-0.7	79	16,366
Ethiopia..........................	S5	48,397	64,165	88,013	120,420	14	3.1	228	386,102
Fiji..............................	S8	740	805	876	936	160	0.7	124	7,056
Finland..........................	S4	4,986	5,169	5,255	5,272	112	(Z)	45	117,304
France...........................	S4	58,168	61,137	64,768	67,518	21	0.4	262	247,126
Gabon............................	S5	938	1,236	1,545	1,877	152	1.9	16	99,486
Gambia, The.....................	S5	951	1,357	1,755	2,174	148	2.1	455	3,861
Georgia..........................	S6	5,426	4,777	4,601	4,440	121	-0.4	171	26,911
Germany [6]......................	S4	79,380	82,184	81,644	80,160	15	-0.2	607	134,623
Ghana...........................	S5	15,408	19,752	24,340	28,784	47	1.7	277	87,851
Greece...........................	S4	10,130	10,559	10,750	10,742	75	(-Z)	213	50,443
Grenada.........................	S2	94	102	108		190	0.5	812	133
Guatemala.......................	S2	8,966	11,085	13,550	16,264	69	1.8	328	41,374
Guinea...........................	S5	6,118	8,350	10,324	13,420	80	2.6	109	94,872
Guinea-Bissau...................	S5	996	1,279	1,565	1,893	151	1.9	144	10,857
Guyana..........................	S3	772	786	748	754	161	0.1	10	76,004
Haiti.............................	S2	6,798	8,413	9,649	10,693	87	1.0	907	10,641
Honduras.........................	S2	4,794	6,359	7,989	9,465	93	1.7	185	43,201
Hungary..........................	S4	10,372	10,147	9,992	9,772	82	-0.2	289	34,598
Iceland...........................	S1	255	281	309	329	178	0.6	8	38,707
India.............................	S7	838,159	1,006,300	1,173,108	1,326,093	2	1.2	1,022	1,147,956
Indonesia........................	S8	181,770	213,829	242,968	267,532	4	1.0	347	699,451
Iran..............................	S6	58,100	68,632	76,923	86,543	18	1.2	130	591,352
Iraq..............................	S6	18,140	22,679	29,672	36,889	39	2.2	176	168,868
Ireland...........................	S4	3,508	3,822	4,623	5,177	119	1.1	174	26,596

See footnotes at end of table.

Table 1348. Population by Country or Area: 1990 to 2020-Continued.

See headnote on page 865.

Country or area	Map reference [1]	Mid-year population (1,000)				Population rank, 2010	Annual rate of growth, [2] 2010 to 2020	Population per sq. mile, 2010	Area [3] (sq. mile)
		1990	2000	2010	2020, proj.				
Israel	S6	4,478	6,115	7,354	8,479	96	1.4	937	7,849
Italy	S4	56,713	57,784	60,749	62,403	23	0.3	535	113,568
Jamaica	S2	2,347	2,616	2,847	3,051	138	0.7	681	4,182
Japan	S7	123,537	126,776	127,579	125,507	10	-0.2	906	140,728
Jordan	S6	3,267	4,688	6,407	7,278	102	1.3	187	34,287
Kazakhstan	S7	16,775	15,687	17,085	19,092	59	1.1	16	1,042,360
Kenya	S5	23,361	30,606	40,843	49,858	33	2.0	186	219,746
Kiribati	S8	71	85	99	112	195	1.2	318	313
Korea, North	S7	20,451	22,785	24,326	25,643	48	0.5	523	46,490
Korea, South	S7	42,869	46,839	48,636	49,362	26	0.2	1,300	37,421
Kosovo	S4	1,862	1,700	1,815	1,933	147	0.6	432	4,203
Kuwait	S6	2,131	1,972	2,543	2,994	139	1.6	370	6,880
Kyrgyzstan	S7	4,382	4,851	5,509	6,314	110	1.4	74	74,055
Laos	S7	4,210	5,397	6,368	7,447	104	1.6	71	89,112
Latvia	S4	2,664	2,376	2,218	2,077	141	-0.7	92	24,034
Lebanon	S6	3,440	3,791	4,125	4,243	126	0.3	1,044	3,950
Lesotho	S5	1,703	1,916	1,920	1,969	146	0.3	164	11,720
Liberia	S5	2,139	2,601	3,685	4,727	129	2.5	99	37,189
Libya	S5	4,146	5,125	6,461	7,759	101	1.8	10	679,362
Liechtenstein	S4	29	33	36	39	213	0.8	585	62
Lithuania	S4	3,695	3,654	3,545	3,435	130	-0.3	147	24,201
Luxembourg	S4	383	439	498	556	171	1.1	498	998
Macedonia	S4	1,861	2,015	2,072	2,113	143	0.2	211	9,820
Madagascar	S5	11,633	15,742	21,282	28,374	55	2.9	95	224,534
Malawi	S5	9,546	11,802	15,448	20,204	65	2.7	425	36,324
Malaysia	S8	17,882	23,151	28,275	32,652	43	1.4	223	126,895
Maldives	S7	217	300	396	392	174	-0.1	3,439	115
Mali	S5	8,327	10,621	13,796	17,890	68	2.6	29	471,118
Malta	S4	359	390	407	419	173	0.3	3,334	122
Marshall Islands	S8	46	53	66	78	204	1.7	942	70
Mauritania	S5	1,925	2,501	3,205	4,005	133	2.2	8	397,955
Mauritius	S5	1,062	1,186	1,294	1,379	154	0.6	1,651	784
Mexico	S1	84,914	99,927	112,469	124,654	11	1.0	150	750,561
Micronesia, Federated States of	S8	109	108	107	102	191	-0.5	395	271
Moldova	S4	4,374	4,180	3,732	3,364	128	-1.0	294	12,699
Monaco	S4	30	32	31	31	215	0.1	39,609	1
Mongolia	S7	2,218	2,664	3,087	3,535	134	1.4	5	599,831
Montenegro	S4	583	732	667	639	165	-0.4	128	5,194
Morocco	S5	24,000	28,113	31,627	34,956	38	1.0	184	172,317
Mozambique	S5	12,989	17,997	22,417	28,603	51	2.4	74	303,623
Namibia	S5	1,471	1,893	2,128	2,263	142	0.6	7	317,874
Nauru	S8	9	10	9	10	224	0.5	1,143	8
Nepal	S7	18,918	24,818	28,952	34,209	41	1.7	523	55,348
Netherlands	S4	14,966	15,930	16,574	17,280	62	0.4	1,267	13,086
New Zealand	S8	3,414	3,802	4,252	4,615	124	0.8	41	103,363
Nicaragua	S2	3,644	4,866	5,604	6,203	108	1.0	121	46,328
Niger	S5	7,842	10,951	15,878	22,749	64	3.6	32	489,076
Nigeria	S5	96,690	124,207	161,605	207,699	7	2.5	459	351,649
Norway	S4	4,242	4,492	4,676	4,836	118	0.3	40	117,484
Oman	S6	1,794	2,432	2,968	3,635	136	2.0	25	119,499
Pakistan	S7	118,816	152,429	184,405	213,719	6	1.5	620	297,637
Palau	S8	15	19	21	22	219	0.4	118	177
Panama	S2	2,393	2,900	3,411	3,894	131	1.3	119	28,703
Papua New Guinea	S8	3,683	4,813	6,065	7,259	105	1.8	35	174,850
Paraguay	S3	4,200	5,418	6,376	7,192	103	1.2	41	153,399
Peru	S3	21,565	25,797	28,948	31,915	42	1.0	59	494,209
Philippines	S7	65,088	81,222	99,900	119,329	12	1.8	868	115,124
Poland	S4	38,119	38,654	38,464	37,949	34	-0.1	327	117,474
Portugal	S4	9,923	10,336	10,736	10,842	76	0.1	304	35,317
Qatar	S6	433	640	1,719	2,444	149	3.5	384	4,473
Romania	S4	22,866	22,447	21,959	21,303	53	-0.3	247	88,761
Russia	S7	147,973	146,710	139,390	132,242	9	-0.5	22	6,323,482
Rwanda	S5	6,999	8,398	11,056	14,327	74	2.6	1,161	9,524
Saint Kitts and Nevis	S2	42	46	50	54	208	0.8	495	101
Saint Lucia	S2	138	153	161	166	187	0.3	688	234
Saint Vincent and the Grenadines	S2	107	108	104	101	194	-0.3	694	150
Samoa	S8	163	176	192	204	184	0.6	176	1,089
San Marino	S4	23	27	31	34	214	0.8	1,336	24
Sao Tome and Principe	S5	116	141	176	211	186	1.8	472	372
Saudi Arabia	S6	16,061	21,312	25,732	29,819	46	1.5	31	830,000
Senegal	S5	7,348	9,469	12,323	15,736	71	2.4	166	74,336
Serbia	S4	7,786	7,604	7,345	7,012	97	-0.5	246	29,913
Seychelles	S5	71	79	88	96	197	0.8	503	176
Sierra Leone	S5	4,228	3,809	5,246	6,625	113	2.3	190	27,653
Singapore	S8	3,047	4,063	5,140	6,210	114	1.9	19,378	265
Slovakia	S4	5,263	5,400	5,470	5,494	111	(Z)	294	18,573
Slovenia	S4	1,991	2,011	2,003	1,951	145	-0.3	257	7,780
Solomon Islands	S8	321	434	559	685	168	2.0	52	10,805
Somalia	S5	6,692	7,501	9,768	11,757	86	1.9	40	242,216
South Africa	S5	38,476	45,064	49,109	48,530	25	-0.1	105	468,909
Spain	S4	39,351	40,588	46,506	50,016	27	0.7	241	192,657
Sri Lanka	S7	16,862	19,041	21,084	22,889	56	0.8	845	24,954
Sudan	S5	25,888	34,109	43,940	56,292	30	2.5	48	917,379
Suriname	S3	416	464	546	610	169	1.1	9	60,232

See footnotes at end of table.

Table 1348. Population by Country or Area: 1990 to 2020-Continued.

See headnote on page 865.

Country or area	Map refer-ence [1]	Mid-year population (1,000)				Popula-tion rank, 2010	Annual rate of growth, [2] 2010 to 2020	Popula-tion per sq. mile, 2010	Area [3] (sq. mile)
		1990	2000	2010	2020, proj.				
Swaziland........................	S5	882	1,144	1,354	1,513	153	1.1	204	6,643
Sweden..........................	S4	8,601	8,924	9,074	9,245	90	0.2	57	158,431
Switzerland......................	S4	6,837	7,267	7,623	7,751	94	0.2	494	15,443
Syria............................	S6	12,500	16,471	22,198	24,744	52	1.1	313	70,900
Tajikistan.......................	S7	5,272	6,230	7,487	8,874	95	1.7	137	54,637
Tanzania........................	S5	25,214	33,712	41,893	49,989	31	1.8	123	342,009
Thailand........................	S7	55,197	61,904	66,336	69,558	20	0.5	336	197,256
Timor-Leste.....................	S8	746	847	1,155	1,389	158	1.8	201	5,743
Togo............................	S5	3,721	4,992	6,587	8,608	100	2.7	314	20,998
Tonga...........................	S8	96	100	106	106	192	(Z)	382	277
Trinidad and Tobago.............	S2	1,255	1,252	1,229	1,209	156	-0.2	621	1,980
Tunisia..........................	S5	8,207	9,508	10,525	11,494	78	0.9	175	59,985
Turkey..........................	S6	56,561	67,329	77,804	86,757	17	1.1	262	297,157
Turkmenistan....................	S6	3,658	4,385	4,941	5,529	116	1.1	27	181,441
Tuvalu..........................	S8	9	10	10	11	223	0.8	1,043	10
Uganda.........................	S5	17,456	23,956	33,399	47,691	37	3.6	439	76,101
Ukraine.........................	S4	51,622	49,005	45,416	42,561	28	-0.7	203	223,681
United Arab Emirates............	S6	1,826	3,219	4,976	6,495	115	2.7	154	32,278
United Kingdom.................	S4	57,411	59,140	62,348	65,761	22	0.5	667	93,410
United States...................	**S1**	**249,623**	**282,172**	**308,282**	**336,836**	**3**	**0.9**	**87**	**3,531,905**
Uruguay........................	S3	3,085	3,220	3,301	3,388	132	0.3	49	67,574
Uzbekistan......................	S7	20,530	25,042	27,866	30,565	44	0.9	170	164,248
Vanuatu.........................	S8	154	190	222	251	182	1.2	47	4,706
Venezuela.......................	S3	19,325	23,493	27,223	31,276	45	1.4	80	340,561
Vietnam.........................	S7	67,258	79,178	89,571	98,721	13	1.0	748	119,719
Yemen..........................	S6	12,416	17,407	23,495	29,727	49	2.4	115	203,850
Zambia..........................	S5	7,858	10,345	13,460	18,065	70	2.9	47	287,028
Zimbabwe.......................	S5	10,156	11,820	11,652	15,832	72	3.1	78	149,362
OTHER									
Taiwan [4].......................	S7	20,278	22,183	23,025	23,278	50	0.1	1,848	12,456
AREAS OF SPECIAL SOVEREIGNTY AND DEPENDENCIES									
American Samoa.................	S8	47	58	66	75	203	1.2	865	77
Anguilla.........................	S1	8	11	15	18	221	2.0	420	35
Aruba...........................	S1	63	90	105	119	193	1.3	1,505	69
Bermuda........................	S1	58	63	68	72	202	0.5	3,274	21
Cayman Islands.................	S1	26	38	50	62	207	2.1	493	102
Cook Islands....................	S8	18	16	11	9	222	-2.9	126	91
Curacao [7]......................	S2	145	134	143	151	188	0.5	837	171
Faroe Islands...................	S4	47	46	49	52	209	0.5	91	538
French Polynesia................	S8	200	236	269	295	180	0.9	182	1,478
Gaza Strip [8]....................	S6	646	1,130	1,604	2,121	150	2.8	11,542	139
Gibraltar........................	S4	29	27	29	30	218	0.2	11,506	3
Greenland.......................	S1	56	57	58	58	206	(-Z)	0	836,330
Guam...........................	S8	134	155	181	204	185	1.2	861	210
Guernsey........................	S4	63	62	65	67	205	0.4	2,151	30
Hong Kong......................	S7	5,688	6,659	7,090	7,328	99	0.3	17,422	407
Isle of Man......................	S4	69	76	84	90	200	0.8	380	221
Jersey...........................	S4	84	87	93	101	196	0.8	2,085	45
Macau..........................	S7	352	432	568	614	167	0.8	52,163	11
Mayotte.........................	S5	87	157	206	229	183	1.0	1,428	144
Montserrat......................	S2	11	4	5	5	228	0.5	130	39
New Caledonia..................	S8	169	211	252	290	181	1.4	36	7,056
Northern Mariana Islands.........	S8	44	70	48	49	210	0.1	270	179
Puerto Rico.....................	S2	3,537	3,814	3,979	4,051	127	0.2	1,162	3,424
Saint Barthelemy................	S2	5	7	7	7	226	-0.4	913	8
Saint Helena....................	S5	7	7	8	8	225	0.3	64	119
Saint Martin.....................	S2	30	28	30	33	216	0.7	1,440	21
Saint Pierre and Miquelon........	S1	6	6	6	5	227	-1.1	64	93
Sint Maarten [7].................	S2	29	31	38	44	212	1.5	2,886	13
Turks and Caicos Islands.........	S2	12	19	43	56	211	2.6	118	366
Virgin Islands, British............	S2	16	23	30	37	217	2.3	508	58
Virgin Islands, U.S..............	S2	104	109	110	108	189	-0.1	822	134
Wallis and Futuna...............	S8	13	15	15	16	220	0.3	280	55
West Bank [8]...................	S6	1,253	1,980	2,515	3,058	140	2.0	1,155	2,178
Western Sahara.................	S5	217	336	492	652	172	2.8	5	102,703

X Not applicable. Z Less than 0.05 percent or less than one person per square mile. [1] See maps for geographic locations, as indicated. [2] Computed by the exponential method. For explanation of average annual percent change, see Guide to Tabular Presentation. [3] Data converted from square kilometers to square miles. [4] With the establishment of diplomatic relations with China on January 1, 1979, the U.S. government recognized the People's Republic of China as the sole legal government of China and acknowledged the Chinese position that there is only one China and that Taiwan is part of China. [5] "Congo" is the official short-form name for both the Republic of Congo and the Democratic Republic of the Congo. To distinguish one from the other the U.S. Department of State adds the capital in parentheses. This practice is unofficial and provisional. [6] Data for 1990 are for former West Germany and East Germany combined. [7] The Netherlands Antilles dissolved on October 10, 2010. Curacao and Sint Maarten became autonomous territories of the Kingdom of the Netherlands. [8] The Gaza Strip and West Bank are Israeli occupied with interim status subject to Israeli/Palestinian negotiations. The final status is yet to be determined.

Source: U.S. Census Bureau, International Data Base, <http://www.census.gov/ipc/www/idb/>, accessed June 2011.

Table 1349. Foreign or Foreign-Born Population, Labor Force, and Net Migration in Selected OECD Countries: 2000 to 2009

[30,273 represents 30,273,000. In Australia and the United States, the data refer to residents who are foreign born. In the European countries and Japan, they represent the legal nationality or citizenship status of residents. Data are based on censuses, population registers, residence permits, and/or labor force surveys. For details about data methodology for individual countries, see source. Minus sign (-) indicates net loss]

Country	Foreign population Number (1,000) 2000	Number (1,000) 2009	Percent of total population 2000	Percent of total population 2009	Foreign labor force Number (1,000) 2000	2005	2008	2009	Average net migration 1990-2009 (per 1,000 population)
United States........	30,273	38,453	11.0	12.7	18,029	22,422	25,086	24,815	3.9
Australia..............	4,412	5,804	23.0	26.5	2,373	2,618	3,000	3,144	6.0
Austria................	702	895	8.8	10.7	320	374	474	479	3.8
Belgium..............	862	1,058	8.4	9.8	388	440	469	498	3.2
Denmark.............	259	330	4.8	6.0	101	115	145	(NA)	2.4
France................	(NA)	(NA)	(NA)	(NA)	1,578	1,406	1,558	1,540	1.3
Germany.............	7,297	6,695	8.9	8.2	3,546	3,823	3,893	(NA)	3.8
Italy...................	1,380	4,235	2.4	7.1	838	1,419	1,387	(NA)	3.7
Japan.................	1,686	2,185	1.3	1.7	155	180	212	213	-0.1
Luxembourg.........	165	216	37.3	43.8	153	196	233	231	10.3
Netherlands.........	668	735	4.2	4.4	300	287	(NA)	(NA)	1.8
Spain.................	1,371	5,748	(NA)	12.4	455	1,689	1,882	(NA)	7.0
Sweden..............	472	595	5.4	6.4	222	177	(NA)	(NA)	3.4
Switzerland..........	1,384	1,680	19.3	21.7	717	830	927	974	5.0
United Kingdom......	2,342	4,348	4.0	7.1	1,107	1,504	2,278	2,280	1.4

NA Not available.

Source: Organisation for Economic Co-operation and Development (OECD), 2012, "International migration database," OECD International Migration Statistics (database); and *International Migration Outlook 2011*, OECD Publishing (2011); accessed August 2012 (copyright). See also <http://dx.doi.org/10.1787/data-00342-en> and <http://dx.doi.org/10.1787/migr_outlook-2011-55-en>.

Table 1350. Age Distribution by Country or Area: 2011 and 2020

[In percent. Covers countries with 13 million or more population in 2010]

Country or area	2011 Under 15 years old	2011 65 years old and over	2020, proj. Under 15 years old	2020, proj. 65 years old and over	Country or area	2011 Under 15 years old	2011 65 years old and over	2020, proj. Under 15 years old	2020, proj. 65 years old and over
World.............	26.4	7.9	24.8	9.5	Madagascar........	43.1	3.0	41.4	3.3
					Malawi.............	45.1	2.7	43.1	2.8
Afghanistan...........	43.7	2.5	40.6	2.7	Malaysia.............	29.6	5.0	26.8	6.9
Algeria................	24.2	5.2	21.9	6.9	Mali.................	47.3	3.0	44.9	2.9
Angola................	44.3	2.9	42.1	3.1	Mexico.............	28.2	6.6	25.0	8.3
Argentina.............	25.4	11.0	23.7	12.4	Morocco.............	27.8	6.1	24.9	7.5
Australia..............	18.3	14.0	17.6	17.0	Mozambique........	45.9	3.0	44.1	2.9
Bangladesh...........	34.3	4.7	28.3	5.8	Nepal................	34.6	4.4	27.6	5.1
Brazil.................	26.2	6.7	23.6	8.8	Netherlands.........	17.4	16.0	16.1	19.8
Burkina Faso........	45.8	2.5	44.3	2.4	Niger.................	49.6	2.3	48.4	2.3
Burma................	27.5	5.0	24.7	6.2	Nigeria.............	44.0	3.0	42.2	3.1
Cambodia.............	32.2	3.8	30.2	4.6	Pakistan.............	35.4	4.2	29.7	4.8
Cameroon.............	40.5	3.3	37.4	3.7	Peru.................	28.5	6.4	25.4	8.0
Canada................	15.7	15.9	15.4	20.1	Philippines..........	34.6	4.3	31.6	5.4
Chile..................	22.3	9.6	19.9	12.4	Poland..............	14.7	13.7	14.6	18.6
China [1].............	17.6	8.9	17.0	12.4	Romania.............	14.8	14.8	14.1	17.6
Colombia [2]........	26.7	6.1	23.3	8.4	Russia..............	15.2	13.0	16.3	16.0
Congo (Kinshasa) [2]..	44.4	2.6	40.3	2.7	Saudi Arabia........	29.4	3.0	25.0	3.8
Cote d'Ivoire.........	39.8	3.0	35.6	3.7	South Africa.........	28.5	5.7	26.9	7.4
Ecuador...............	30.1	6.4	25.8	8.1	Spain................	15.1	17.1	15.0	18.5
Egypt.................	32.7	4.5	30.3	6.0	Sri Lanka............	24.9	7.9	23.1	10.6
Ethiopia..............	46.3	2.7	45.4	2.7	Sudan..............	42.1	2.7	39.6	3.1
France................	18.5	16.8	17.8	20.0	Syria.................	35.2	3.8	30.0	4.6
Germany..............	13.3	20.6	12.9	23.0	Taiwan [1]...........	15.6	10.9	12.9	15.5
Ghana................	36.5	3.6	32.4	4.0	Tanzania............	42.0	2.9	36.4	3.3
Guatemala............	38.1	3.9	33.0	4.9	Thailand............	19.9	9.2	18.1	12.4
India.................	29.7	5.5	26.3	6.7	Turkey..............	26.6	6.3	23.4	8.1
Indonesia.............	27.3	6.1	23.8	7.7	Uganda.............	49.9	2.1	49.5	1.9
Iran...................	24.1	5.0	23.3	6.1	Ukraine.............	13.7	15.5	14.5	17.8
Iraq...................	38.0	3.1	33.7	3.9	United Kingdom....	17.3	16.5	17.6	18.5
Italy..................	13.8	20.3	13.4	22.1	United States......	20.0	13.2	19.8	16.2
Japan.................	13.6	23.1	12.5	29.2	Uzbekistan..........	26.5	4.7	23.2	5.9
Kazakhstan...........	24.2	6.8	26.1	8.4	Venezuela..........	29.5	5.4	26.1	7.4
Kenya................	42.6	2.7	36.8	3.3	Vietnam.............	25.2	5.5	22.6	6.9
Korea, North.........	22.4	9.1	20.5	9.7	Yemen..............	43.0	2.6	37.3	3.0
Korea, South.........	15.7	11.4	12.6	15.6	Zambia.............	46.7	2.5	46.2	2.5

[1] See footnote 4, Table 1348. [2] See footnote 5, Table 1348.

Source: U.S. Census Bureau, International Data Base, <http://www.census.gov/ipc/www/idb/>, accessed June 2011.

Table 1351. Births to Unmarried Women by Country: 1980 to 2008

[Percent of all live births]

Country	1980	1990	2000	2005	2006	2007	2008
United States...............	**18.4**	**28.0**	**33.2**	**36.9**	**38.5**	**39.7**	**40.6**
Canada...............................	12.8	24.4	28.3	25.6	27.1	27.3	(NA)
Japan................................	0.8	1.1	1.6	2.0	2.1	(NA)	(NA)
Denmark............................	33.2	46.4	44.6	45.7	46.4	46.1	46.2
France...............................	11.4	30.1	43.6	48.4	50.5	51.7	52.6
Germany [1].......................	(X)	15.1	23.4	29.2	30.0	30.8	32.1
Ireland..............................	5.9	14.6	31.5	31.8	32.7	(NA)	(NA)
Italy..................................	4.3	6.5	9.7	15.2	16.2	17.7	(NA)
Netherlands.......................	4.1	11.4	24.9	34.9	37.1	39.5	41.2
Spain................................	3.9	9.6	17.7	26.6	28.4	30.2	31.7
Sweden.............................	39.7	47.0	55.3	55.4	55.5	54.8	54.7
United Kingdom..................	11.5	27.9	39.5	42.9	43.7	(NA)	(NA)

NA Not available. X Not applicable. [1] Data are for 1991 instead of 1990.

Source: U.S. Bureau of Labor Statistics, updated and revised from "Families and Work Transition in 12 Countries, 1980–2001," *Monthly Labor Review*, September 2003, with national sources, some of which may be unpublished.

Table 1352. Marriage and Divorce Rates by Country: 1980 to 2008

[Per 1,000 population aged 15–64 years]

Country	Marriage rate				Divorce rate			
	1980	1990	2000	2008	1980	1990	2000	2008
United States [1]................	**15.9**	**14.9**	**12.5**	**10.6**	**7.9**	**7.2**	**6.2**	**5.2**
Canada...........................	11.5	10.0	7.5	6.4	3.7	4.2	3.4	(NA)
Japan.............................	9.8	8.4	9.2	(NA)	1.8	1.8	3.1	(NA)
Denmark..........................	8.0	9.1	10.8	10.3	4.1	4.0	4.0	4.1
France............................	9.7	7.7	7.9	6.6	2.4	2.8	3.0	(NA)
Germany [2]......................	(X)	8.2	7.6	6.9	(X)	2.5	3.5	3.5
Ireland [3]........................	10.9	8.3	7.6	(NA)	(NA)	(NA)	1.0	(NA)
Italy...............................	8.7	8.2	7.3	6.3	0.3	0.7	1.0	1.3
Netherlands......................	9.6	9.4	8.2	6.7	2.7	2.8	3.2	2.9
Spain..............................	9.4	8.5	7.9	6.2	(NA)	0.9	1.4	3.5
Sweden...........................	7.1	7.4	7.0	8.3	3.7	3.5	3.8	3.5
United Kingdom.................	11.6	10.0	8.0	(NA)	4.1	4.1	4.0	(NA)

NA Not available. X Not applicable. [1] Divorce rates exclude data for California, Georgia, Hawaii, Indiana, Louisiana, and Minnesota in 2008. [2] Data are for 1991 instead of 1990. [3] Divorce not allowed by law prior to 1997.

Source: U.S. Bureau of Labor Statistics, updated and revised from "Families and Work in Transition in 12 Countries, 1980–2001," *Monthly Labor Review*, September 2003, with national sources, some of which may be unpublished.

Table 1353. Single-Parent Households: 1980 to 2009

[In thousands (6,061 represents 6,061,000), except for percent. Data are generally from population censuses, household surveys, and national government agencies. Definitions of children vary by age classification, residence, marital status, and school enrollment. For details on statistical methodology of individual countries, see source article.

Country and year	Number (1,000)	Percent of all households with children	Country and year	Number (1,000)	Percent of all households with children
United States:			Germany:		
1980.............................	6,061	19.5	1991..............................	1,429	15.2
1990.............................	7,752	24.0	1995 [1]...........................	2,496	18.8
2000.............................	9,357	27.0	2000 [1]...........................	2,274	17.6
2008.............................	10,536	29.5	2008..............................	2,616	21.7
Canada:			Ireland: [2]......................		
1981.............................	437	12.7	1981..............................	30	7.2
1991.............................	572	16.2	1991..............................	44	10.7
2001 [1]..........................	1,184	23.5	2002..............................	50	17.4
2006.............................	1,276	24.6	2006..............................	78	22.6
Japan:			Netherlands:		
1980.............................	796	4.9	1985..............................	179	9.6
1990.............................	934	6.5	2000..............................	240	13.0
2000.............................	996	8.3	2009 [1]...........................	310	16.0
2005.............................	1,163	10.2	Sweden:		
Denmark: [2]			1985..............................	117	11.2
1980.............................	99	13.4	1995 [1]...........................	189	17.4
1990.............................	117	17.8	2000..............................	233	21.4
2001.............................	120	18.4	2008..............................	200	18.7
2009 [1]..........................	165	21.7	United Kingdom: [3]		
France:			1981..............................	1,010	13.9
1982.............................	887	10.2	1991..............................	1,344	19.4
1990.............................	1,175	13.2	2000..............................	1,434	20.7
1999.............................	1,494	17.4	2008..............................	1,750	25.0
2005 [1]..........................	1,725	19.8			

[1] Break in series. [2] Data are from family-based, rather than household-based, statistics. [3] Great Britain only (excludes Northern Ireland).

Source: U.S. Bureau of Labor Statistics, updated and revised from "Families and Work in Transition in 12 Countries, 1980–2001," *Monthly Labor Review*, September 2003, with national sources, some of which may be unpublished.

Table 1354. Percent Distribution of Households by Type and Country: 1980 to 2009

[Data are generally from population censuses, household surveys, and national government agencies. Definitions of children vary by age classification, residence, marital status, and school enrollment. Married-couple households may include unmarried, cohabiting couples. For details on statistical methodology of individual countries, see source article]

| Year | Total | Married-couple households | | | Single parent | One person | Other [1] |
		Total	With children	Without children			
United States:							
1980	100.0	60.8	30.9	29.9	7.5	22.7	9.0
1990	100.0	56.0	26.3	29.8	8.3	24.6	11.0
1995	100.0	54.4	25.5	28.9	9.1	25.0	11.5
2000	100.0	52.8	24.1	28.7	8.9	25.5	12.7
2008	100.0	50.0	21.6	28.4	9.0	27.5	13.5
Canada:							
1981	100.0	66.8	36.3	30.5	5.3	20.3	7.6
1991	100.0	62.8	29.6	33.2	5.7	22.9	8.6
2001 [2]	100.0	58.5	33.4	25.2	10.2	25.7	5.5
2006	100.0	57.4	31.4	26.1	10.3	26.8	5.5
Japan:							
1980	100.0	68.4	42.9	25.6	2.2	19.8	9.5
1990	100.0	65.2	33.1	32.1	2.3	23.1	9.4
1995	100.0	62.8	27.4	35.4	2.0	25.6	9.6
2000	100.0	60.3	23.6	36.7	2.1	27.6	10.0
2005	100.0	57.6	20.8	36.8	2.4	29.5	10.5
Denmark: [3]							
1980	100.0	50.3	25.0	25.3	3.9	44.9	1.0
1990	100.0	45.6	19.5	26.1	4.2	49.6	0.6
1995	100.0	44.9	18.2	26.6	4.2	50.4	0.5
2001	100.0	45.7	18.5	27.2	4.2	49.6	0.6
2009 [2]	100.0	47.4	21.2	26.1	5.9	46.2	0.6
France:							
1982	100.0	67.5	39.8	27.7	4.5	24.6	3.4
1990	100.0	64.0	35.9	28.1	5.5	27.1	3.4
1999	100.0	59.3	29.9	29.4	6.3	31.0	3.4
2005 [2]	100.0	56.4	27.2	29.2	6.7	32.8	4.1
Germany:							
1991	100.0	55.3	31.6	23.7	7.1	33.6	4.0
1995	100.0	53.3	29.2	24.0	6.8	34.9	5.1
2000 [2]	100.0	56.8	28.0	28.8	6.0	36.1	1.2
2005	100.0	54.7	25.5	29.1	6.4	37.5	1.4
2008	100.0	52.6	23.6	29.0	6.5	39.4	1.5
Ireland:							
1981	100.0	(NA)	(NA)	(NA)	(NA)	16.9	(NA)
1991	100.0	61.6	47.9	13.7	10.6	20.2	7.6
1996	100.0	59.6	44.5	15.1	11.2	21.5	7.7
2002	100.0	59.2	41.4	17.7	11.7	21.6	7.6
2006	100.0	57.3	37.4	20.0	11.6	22.4	8.7
Netherlands:							
1988	100.0	64.7	37.3	27.4	5.4	28.7	1.2
1993	100.0	63.1	33.3	29.9	5.0	30.9	1.0
2000 [2]	100.0	60.2	30.6	29.6	5.6	33.4	0.7
2005	100.0	58.5	29.4	29.1	6.3	34.5	0.7
2007	100.0	57.7	28.7	28.9	6.4	35.3	0.7
2009	100.0	57.0	28.1	28.9	6.5	35.8	0.7
Sweden:							
1985	100.0	54.8	23.8	31.0	3.2	36.1	5.9
1990	100.0	52.1	21.9	30.2	3.9	39.6	4.4
1995 [2]	100.0	50.7	21.2	29.4	4.6	42.3	2.4
2000	100.0	45.8	19.1	26.7	5.3	46.5	2.3
2008	100.0	44.5	18.6	25.9	4.4	48.1	3.0
United Kingdom: [4]							
1981	100.0	65.0	31.0	34.0	5.0	22.0	8.0
1991	100.0	61.0	25.0	36.0	6.0	27.0	6.0
1994–95	100.0	58.0	25.0	33.0	7.0	27.0	8.0
2000	100.0	58.0	23.0	35.0	6.0	29.0	7.0
2008	100.0	56.0	21.0	35.0	7.0	30.0	7.0

NA Not available. [1] Includes both family and nonfamily households not elsewhere classified. These households comprise, for example, siblings residing together, other households composed of relatives, and households made up of roommates. Some unmarried cohabiting couples may also be included in the "other" group; see source for details. [2] Break in series. [3] From family-based statistics. However, one person living alone constitutes a family in Denmark. In this respect, the Danish data are closer to household statistics. [4] Great Britain only (excludes Northern Ireland).

Source: U.S. Bureau of Labor Statistics, updated and revised from "Families and Work in Transition in 12 Countries, 1980–2001," *Monthly Labor Review*, September 2003, with national sources, some of which may be unpublished.

Table 1355. Births, Deaths, and Life Expectancy by Country or Area: 2011 and 2020

[Covers countries with 13 million or more population in 2011]

Country or area	Crude birth rate [1]		Crude death rate [2]		Expectation of life at birth (years)		Infant mortality rate [3]		Total fertility rate per woman [4]	
	2011	2020, proj.	2011	2020, proj.	2011	2020, proj.	2011	2020, proj.	2011	2020, proj.
United States	**13.7**	**13.3**	**8.4**	**8.5**	**78.4**	**79.5**	**6.1**	**5.4**	**2.06**	**2.06**
Afghanistan	39.5	36.7	14.8	12.7	49.3	52.8	123.9	104.3	5.75	4.82
Algeria	16.7	14.9	4.7	5.0	74.5	76.5	25.8	18.7	1.75	1.70
Angola	39.6	37.5	12.3	10.5	54.1	57.5	85.3	69.9	5.60	5.07
Argentina	17.5	15.6	7.4	7.3	77.0	78.5	10.8	8.5	2.31	2.15
Australia	12.3	11.9	6.9	7.5	81.8	82.5	4.6	4.1	1.78	1.76
Bangladesh	23.0	19.5	5.8	5.6	69.8	72.4	50.7	36.8	2.60	2.24
Brazil	17.8	15.5	6.4	6.6	72.5	74.8	21.2	15.9	2.18	2.06
Burkina Faso	43.6	39.9	12.7	10.6	53.7	56.9	81.4	67.8	6.14	5.49
Burma	19.3	17.3	8.2	7.9	64.9	68.0	49.2	37.2	2.26	2.09
Cambodia	25.4	21.3	8.1	7.3	62.7	65.9	55.5	43.7	2.84	2.39
Cameroon	33.0	28.3	11.8	10.7	54.4	57.0	60.9	50.4	4.17	3.47
Canada	10.3	10.1	8.0	9.0	81.4	82.2	4.9	4.4	1.58	1.61
Chile	14.3	13.2	6.0	6.7	77.7	79.2	7.3	6.0	1.88	1.77
China [5]	12.3	11.0	7.0	8.3	74.7	76.0	16.1	12.6	1.54	1.58
Colombia	17.5	15.4	5.3	5.6	74.6	76.6	16.4	12.3	2.15	1.94
Congo (Kinshasa) [6]	37.7	31.3	11.1	9.1	55.3	58.8	78.4	63.6	5.24	3.99
Cote d'Ivoire	31.0	26.1	10.2	9.1	56.8	59.9	64.8	51.6	3.92	3.15
Ecuador	20.0	17.0	5.0	5.2	75.7	77.5	19.7	15.0	2.42	2.09
Egypt	24.6	20.8	4.8	4.8	72.7	74.9	25.2	17.9	2.97	2.67
Ethiopia	43.0	39.8	11.0	9.1	56.2	59.4	77.1	61.7	6.02	5.53
France	12.3	11.3	8.8	9.6	81.2	82.0	3.3	3.1	1.96	1.90
Germany	8.3	8.6	10.9	12.1	80.1	81.1	3.5	3.3	1.41	1.47
Ghana	27.6	22.7	8.8	7.3	61.0	65.3	48.6	38.1	3.48	2.75
Guatemala	27.0	22.7	5.0	4.6	70.9	73.4	26.0	19.2	3.27	2.57
India	21.0	18.2	7.5	7.3	66.8	69.7	47.6	35.4	2.62	2.35
Indonesia	18.1	15.6	6.3	6.6	71.3	73.7	28.0	20.4	2.25	2.04
Iran	18.6	16.2	5.9	6.0	70.1	72.4	42.3	33.6	1.88	1.81
Iraq	28.8	23.4	4.8	4.3	70.6	73.1	41.7	30.3	3.67	2.96
Italy	9.2	8.4	9.8	10.7	81.8	82.5	3.4	3.2	1.39	1.47
Japan	8.5	7.3	9.1	10.2	83.6	86.0	2.3	1.9	1.38	1.43
Kazakhstan	20.8	16.4	8.6	8.2	69.3	72.0	23.8	17.9	2.44	2.16
Kenya	33.7	20.8	7.4	6.6	62.7	65.1	45.2	34.0	4.19	2.57
Korea, North	14.5	14.5	9.1	9.4	68.9	71.6	27.1	20.0	2.02	1.92
Korea, South	8.6	8.2	6.3	7.6	79.1	81.1	4.2	3.6	1.23	1.29
Madagascar	37.5	33.8	7.8	6.4	63.6	66.8	51.5	40.2	5.02	4.44
Malawi	40.9	36.5	13.2	10.9	51.7	55.3	81.0	63.1	5.43	4.68
Malaysia	21.1	18.3	4.9	5.3	73.8	75.9	15.0	11.4	2.67	2.43
Mali	45.6	41.0	14.3	11.4	52.6	56.6	111.4	91.9	6.44	5.51
Mexico	19.1	17.0	4.9	5.3	76.5	78.1	17.3	13.2	2.29	2.14
Morocco	19.2	16.9	4.8	5.0	75.9	77.7	27.5	19.5	2.21	2.07
Mozambique	39.6	37.2	13.0	10.9	51.8	54.8	79.0	60.5	5.46	4.90
Nepal	22.2	19.7	6.8	6.4	66.2	69.2	44.5	33.2	2.47	2.11
Netherlands	11.0	11.0	8.3	9.2	80.8	81.7	3.8	3.5	1.78	1.77
Niger	50.5	46.7	14.1	11.3	53.4	57.0	112.2	92.9	7.60	6.79
Nigeria	39.7	36.2	13.8	11.5	51.6	55.2	75.8	63.5	5.44	4.88
Pakistan	24.8	20.7	6.9	6.2	66.0	69.0	63.3	47.2	3.17	2.42
Peru	19.4	17.0	5.9	6.2	72.5	74.7	22.2	16.7	2.32	2.04
Philippines	25.3	22.2	5.0	4.9	71.7	74.0	19.3	14.7	3.19	2.83
Poland	10.0	8.8	10.2	10.8	76.1	77.8	6.5	5.6	1.30	1.39
Romania	9.6	8.5	11.8	12.0	74.0	76.0	11.0	8.7	1.29	1.38
Russia	11.1	9.3	16.0	15.6	66.3	68.6	10.1	8.6	1.42	1.48
Saudi Arabia	19.3	17.8	3.3	3.4	74.1	76.1	16.2	12.0	2.31	2.04
South Africa	19.5	18.1	17.1	17.3	49.3	51.4	43.2	36.8	2.30	2.12
Spain	10.7	8.7	8.8	9.3	81.2	82.0	3.4	3.2	1.47	1.51
Sri Lanka	17.4	14.2	5.9	6.5	75.7	77.5	9.7	7.8	2.20	2.01
Sudan	36.1	31.2	11.0	6.9	55.4	64.4	68.1	38.9	4.84	4.04
Syria	24.0	19.7	3.7	3.7	74.7	76.6	15.6	11.7	2.94	2.34
Taiwan [5]	8.9	8.2	7.0	8.2	78.3	79.7	5.2	4.6	1.15	1.23
Tanzania	32.6	25.6	12.1	11.2	52.9	54.9	66.9	56.4	4.16	3.00
Thailand	13.0	11.8	7.3	8.2	73.6	75.6	16.4	12.4	1.66	1.66
Turkey	17.9	15.1	6.1	6.3	72.5	74.8	23.9	17.3	2.15	1.96
Uganda	47.5	45.4	11.7	10.3	53.2	55.2	62.5	51.7	6.69	6.31
Ukraine	9.6	8.5	15.7	15.4	68.6	70.7	8.5	7.3	1.28	1.35
United Kingdom	12.3	11.9	9.3	9.5	80.1	81.1	4.6	4.1	1.91	1.86
Uzbekistan	17.4	16.1	5.3	5.4	72.5	74.8	21.9	16.3	1.89	1.74
Venezuela	20.1	18.1	5.2	5.6	73.9	75.3	20.6	17.0	2.42	2.22
Vietnam	17.1	14.5	6.0	6.0	72.2	74.4	20.9	15.7	1.91	1.77
Yemen	33.5	25.6	7.0	5.7	63.7	66.9	55.1	41.9	4.63	3.20
Zambia	44.1	38.9	12.6	11.0	52.4	54.1	66.6	50.6	5.98	5.26

[1] Number of births during 1 year per 1,000 persons (based on midyear population). [2] Number of deaths during 1 year per 1,000 persons (based on midyear population). [3] Number of deaths of children under 1 year of age per 1,000 live births in a calendar year. [4] Average number of children that would be born if all women lived to the end of their childbearing years and, at each year of childbearing age, they experienced the birth rates occurring in the specified year. [5] See footnote 4, Table 1348. [6] See footnote 5, Table 1348.

Source: U.S. Census Bureau, International Data Base, <http://www.census.gov/ipc/www/idb/>, accessed June 2011.

Table 1356. Life Expectancy at Birth and at Age 65 by Sex— Selected Countries: 2000 and 2010

Country	Life expectancy at birth (years)				Life expectancy at age 65 (years)			
	Females		Males		Females		Males	
	2000	2010	2000	2010	2000	2010	2000	2010
United States...........	79.3	[1] 81.1	74.1	[1] 76.2	19.0	[1] 20.3	16.0	[1] 17.7
Australia...................	82.0	84.0	76.6	79.5	20.4	21.8	16.9	18.9
Austria...................	81.2	83.5	75.2	77.9	19.6	21.4	16.0	17.9
Belgium....................	81.0	83.0	74.6	77.6	19.7	21.3	15.6	17.6
Brazil........................	74.1	76.7	66.4	69.7	18.1	19.2	15.7	16.4
Canada.....................	81.7	[2] 83.1	76.3	[2] 78.5	20.2	[2] 21.5	16.5	[2] 18.3
Czech Republic..........	78.5	80.9	71.7	74.5	17.3	19.0	13.8	15.5
Denmark....................	79.2	81.4	74.5	77.2	18.3	19.7	15.2	17.0
France.......................	82.8	[1] 84.7	75.3	[1] 78.0	21.2	[3] 22.6	16.7	[3] 18.4
Germany...................	81.2	83.0	75.1	78.0	19.6	20.9	15.8	17.8
Greece......................	80.6	82.8	75.5	78.4	18.4	20.4	16.1	18.5
Hungary....................	75.9	78.1	67.4	70.5	16.5	17.6	12.7	13.8
Ireland......................	79.2	83.2	74.0	78.7	18.0	21.1	14.6	18.1
Italy..........................	82.8	[4] 84.6	76.9	[4] 79.4	20.7	[4] 22.1	16.7	[4] 18.3
Japan........................	84.6	86.4	77.7	79.6	22.4	23.9	17.5	18.9
Korea, South..............	79.6	84.1	72.3	77.2	18.2	21.6	14.3	17.2
Mexico......................	76.5	77.8	71.3	73.1	18.1	18.3	16.5	16.8
Netherlands...............	80.5	82.7	75.5	78.8	19.2	21.2	15.3	17.9
New Zealand..............	80.8	82.8	75.9	79.1	19.8	21.2	16.5	18.8
Norway.....................	81.5	83.3	76.0	79.0	19.9	21.2	16.1	18.0
Poland.......................	78.0	80.6	69.7	72.1	17.5	19.4	13.6	15.1
Portugal....................	80.2	82.8	73.2	76.7	18.9	20.6	15.4	17.1
Russia.......................	72.3	74.9	59.1	63.0	15.2	[4] 16.5	11.1	[4] 11.9
Spain........................	82.9	85.3	75.8	79.1	20.8	22.7	16.7	18.6
South Africa..............	57.3	52.8	52.3	51.4	15.4	[4] 15.8	11.8	[4] 11.9
Sweden.....................	82.0	83.5	77.4	79.5	20.0	21.1	16.7	18.2
Switzerland...............	82.8	84.9	77.0	80.3	20.9	22.5	17.0	19.0
Turkey......................	73.1	76.8	69.0	71.8	15.1	16.1	13.4	14.1
United Kingdom..........	80.3	82.6	75.5	78.6	19.0	20.9	15.8	18.3

[1] 2010 estimate. [2] 2008 data. [3] 2009 estimate. [4] 2009 data.

Source: Organisation for Economic Co-operation and Development (OECD), 2012, "OECD Health Data," OECD Health Statistics (database), <http://www.oecd.org/health/healthpoliciesanddata/oecdhealthdata2012.htm>, accessed on 08 August 2012 (copyright).

Table 1357. Percentage of the Adult Population Considered to Be Obese: 2010

[Obesity rates are defined as the percentage of the population with a Body Mass Index (BMI) over 30 kg/m^2. The BMI is a single number that evaluates an individual's weight status in relation to height (weight/height^2). For the United States, Australia, Canada, Czech Republic, Hungary, Ireland, Japan, South Korea, Luxembourg, Mexico, New Zealand, Slovakia, and the United Kingdom, figures are based on health examinations, rather than self-reported information. Obesity estimates derived from health examinations are generally higher and more reliable than those coming from self-reports because they preclude any misreporting of people's height and weight. However, health examinations are only conducted regularly in a few countries. For more information on methods, see source]

Country	2010	Country	2010	Country	2010
United States..........	35.9	France.................	12.9	Luxembourg............	22.5
Australia.................	[3] 24.6	Germany...............	[1] 14.7	Mexico....................	[4] 30.0
Belgium..................	[2] 13.8	Greece.................	[1] 17.3	New Zealand...........	[1] 27.8
Brazil......................	15.0	Hungary...............	[1] 28.5	Norway...................	[2] 10.0
Canada...................	[2] 24.2	Ireland.................	[3] 23.0	Spain.....................	[1] 16.0
Czech Republic.........	21.0	Italy.....................	10.3	Sweden..................	12.9
Denmark.................	13.4	Japan...................	3.5	Switzerland.............	[3] 8.1
Finland...................	15.6	Korea, South.........	4.1	United Kingdom........	26.1

[1] 2009 data. [2] 2008 data. [3] 2007 data. [4] 2006 data.

Source: Organisation for Economic Co-operation and Development (OECD) 2012, "OECD Health Data," OECD Health Statistics (database), <http://www.oecd.org/health/healthpoliciesanddata/oecdhealthdata2012.htm>, accessed 08 August 2012 (copyright).

Table 1358. Daily Tobacco Consumption by Country and Sex: 2000 and 2010

[Daily smokers as percent of adult population. Includes tobacco forms consumed by smoking only]

Country	Total		Females		Males	
	2000	2010	2000	2010	2000	2010
United States...............	**19.1**	**15.1**	**17.3**	**13.6**	**21.2**	**16.7**
Australia.......................	[2] 19.8	15.1	[2] 18.2	13.9	[2] 21.4	16.4
Canada.........................	[2] 22.4	16.3	[2] 20.2	13.7	[2] 24.7	19.0
Chile............................	[4] 33.0	[3] 29.8	[4] 28.5	[3] 26.0	[4] 38.8	[3] 33.0
China...........................	28.9	24.1	[5] 4.0	2.0	[5] 53.4	45.4
France..........................	27.0	23.3	21.0	20.7	33.0	26.4
Germany.......................	[1] 24.7	[3] 21.9	[1] 18.9	[3] 17.6	[1] 30.9	[3] 26.4
Greece.........................	35.0	[3] 31.9	27.0	[3] 26.1	44.0	[3] 38.0
India............................	[5] 16.2	10.7	[5] 2.4	2.4	[5] 29.3	18.3
Italy............................	24.4	23.1	17.4	17.1	31.9	29.6
Japan..........................	27.0	19.5	11.5	8.4	47.4	32.2
Korea, South.................	[2] 26.1	[3] 22.9	[2] 4.2	[1] 5.2	[2] 52.9	[1] 40.8
Netherlands...................	32.0	20.9	29.0	18.8	35.0	23.1
Norway.........................	32.0	[3] 19.0	32.0	[3] 19.0	31.0	[3] 19.0
Russia..........................	34.9	33.8	12.6	[3] 16.3	62.2	[3] 55.0
Spain...........................	[2] 31.7	[3] 26.2	[2] 24.6	[3] 21.3	[2] 39.2	[3] 31.2
Sweden........................	18.9	14.0	21.0	15.1	16.8	12.8
Turkey..........................	[4] 32.1	25.4	[4] 17.8	12.3	[4] 51.1	39.0
United Kingdom..............	27.0	[3] 21.5	26.0	[3] 20.7	28.0	[3] 22.3

NA Not available. [1] 1999 data. [2] 2001 data. [3] 2009 data. [4] 2003 data. [5] 1998 data.

Source: Organisation for Economic Co-operation and Development (OECD), 2012, "OECD Health Data," OECD Health Statistics (database), <http://www.oecd.org/health/healthpoliciesanddata/oecdhealthdata2012.htm>, accessed on 08 August 2012 (copyright).

Table 1359. Road Fatalities by Country: 1990 to 2010

[Fatalities include any person killed immediately or dying within 30 days as a result of an injury accident. For countries that do not apply the threshold of 30 days, conversion coefficients are estimated so that comparisons on the basis of the 30 day-definition can be made]

Country	1990	2000	2005	2009	2010	Country	1990	2000	2005	2009	2010
United States.....	44,599	41,945	43,443	33,808	32,788	Japan..............	14,595	10,403	7,931	5,772	5,745
Australia...........	2,331	1,817	1,627	1,489	1,367	Korea, South......	14,174	10,236	6,376	5,835	5,505
Austria.............	1,391	976	768	633	552	Mexico.............	5,469	5,224	4,710	4,870	(NA)
Belgium............	1,976	1,470	1,089	943	812	Netherlands.......	1,376	1,166	817	720	600
Canada............	3,963	2,903	2,898	2,217	(NA)	New Zealand......	729	462	405	385	375
China..............	(NA)	(NA)	98,738	67,759	(NA)	Norway............	332	341	224	212	208
Czech Republic. ..	(NA)	1,486	1,286	901	802	Poland.............	7,333	6,294	5,444	4,572	3,907
Denmark..........	634	498	331	303	255	Portugal...........	2,646	1,857	1,247	840	845
Estonia............	436	204	170	100	78	Russia.............	35,366	29,594	33,957	27,659	26,567
Finland............	649	396	379	279	272	Slovakia...........	(NA)	648	600	384	353
France.............	11,215	8,079	5,318	4,273	3,992	Slovenia...........	517	313	258	171	138
Germany..........	7,906	7,503	5,361	4,152	3,648	Spain..............	6,948	5,776	3,857	2,714	2,478
Greece............	1,737	2,037	1,658	1,453	1,265	Sweden............	772	591	440	358	266
Hungary...........	2,432	1,200	1,278	822	740	Switzerland........	954	592	409	349	327
India...............	(NA)	78,911	94,968	125,660	(NA)	Turkey.............	6,317	5,510	4,505	4,324	4,045
Ireland.............	478	415	396	238	212	Ukraine............	9,616	5,185	7,229	5,348	(NA)
Italy................	7,151	7,061	5,818	4,237	4,090	United Kingdom. ..	5,402	3,580	3,336	2,337	1,905

NA Not available.

Source: International Transport Forum (ITF) / Organisation for Economic Co-operation and Development (OECD), 2012, "Road injury accidents," *Transport Statistics*, <http://www.internationaltransportforum.org/> (copyright).

Table 1360. Suicide Rates by Sex and Country: 2009

[Per 100,000 persons]

Country	Total	Men	Women	Country	Total	Men	Women
OECD total [1]..........	**11.3**	**18.1**	**5.1**	Italy.....................	4.9	8.0	2.1
United States...........	**10.5**	**17.1**	**4.3**	Japan...................	19.7	29.2	10.5
Australia..................	7.5	11.9	3.3	Korea, South...........	28.4	39.3	19.7
Austria....................	12.0	19.7	5.2	Mexico..................	4.4	7.5	1.5
Belgium...................	16.2	24.6	8.4	Netherlands.............	7.8	11.2	4.6
Canada...................	10.2	15.7	4.9	New Zealand...........	11.2	17.8	5.0
Czech Republic.........	11.4	20.1	3.4	Norway..................	10.9	15.7	6.2
Denmark..................	9.9	15.0	5.3	Poland...................	12.9	23.2	3.5
Finland...................	17.3	26.0	8.9	Portugal.................	7.3	12.5	2.9
France....................	13.8	21.6	6.8	Russia [2]................	26.5	49.4	7.9
Germany..................	9.1	14.5	4.3	Slovakia.................	9.3	17.9	1.7
Greece....................	2.8	4.8	0.8	Spain....................	6.0	9.7	2.6
Hungary..................	19.8	33.8	8.0	Sweden..................	11.0	16.1	6.0
Iceland...................	10.3	16.6	3.9	Switzerland.............	14.3	20.6	8.7
Ireland....................	11.3	18.0	4.6	United Kingdom........	6.2	9.8	2.6

[1] For OECD membership listing, see Section 30 introduction. [2] Russia, which is not an OECD member country, is included for comparison.

Source: Organisation for Economic Co-operation and Development (OECD), 2012, "OECD Health Data," OECD Health Statistics (database), <http://www.oecd.org/health/healthpoliciesanddata/oecdhealthdata2012.htm>, accessed on 08 August 2012 (copyright).

Table 1361. Health Expenditures by Country: 1980 to 2010

[In percent. GDP = gross domestic product]

Country	Total expenditures on health (percent of GDP)					Public expenditures on health (percent of total)				
	1980	1990	2000	2005	2010	1980	1990	2000	2005	2010
United States	**9.0**	**12.4**	**13.7**	**15.8**	**17.6**	**41.0**	**39.4**	**43.0**	**44.2**	**48.2**
Australia	6.1	6.7	8.0	8.4	(NA)	62.6	66.2	66.8	66.9	(NA)
Austria	7.4	8.4	10.0	10.4	11.0	68.8	72.9	75.6	75.3	76.2
Belgium	6.3	7.2	8.1	10.1	10.5	(NA)	(NA)	74.6	75.8	75.6
Canada	7.0	8.9	8.8	9.8	11.4	75.6	74.5	70.4	70.2	71.1
Czech Republic	(NA)	4.5	6.3	6.9	7.5	96.8	97.4	90.3	87.3	83.8
Denmark	8.9	8.3	8.7	9.8	11.1	87.8	82.7	83.9	84.5	85.1
Finland	6.3	7.7	7.2	8.4	8.9	79.0	80.9	71.3	75.4	74.5
France	7.0	8.4	10.1	11.2	11.6	80.1	76.6	79.4	78.8	77.0
Germany [1]	8.4	8.3	10.4	10.8	11.6	78.7	76.2	79.5	76.6	76.8
Greece	5.9	6.7	8.0	9.7	10.2	55.6	53.7	60.0	60.1	59.4
Hungary	(NA)	(NA)	7.2	8.4	7.8	(NA)	(NA)	70.7	70.0	64.8
Iceland	6.3	7.8	9.5	9.4	9.3	88.2	86.6	81.1	81.4	80.4
Ireland	8.2	6.0	6.1	7.6	9.2	82.0	71.7	75.1	75.9	69.5
Italy	(NA)	7.7	8.0	8.9	9.3	(NA)	79.5	72.5	76.2	79.6
Japan	6.4	5.8	7.6	8.2	(NA)	71.3	77.6	80.8	81.6	(NA)
Korea, South	3.7	4.0	4.5	5.7	7.1	21.6	38.4	48.6	52.9	58.2
Luxembourg	5.2	5.4	7.5	7.9	(NA)	92.8	93.1	85.1	84.9	(NA)
Mexico	(NA)	4.4	5.1	5.9	6.2	(NA)	40.4	46.6	45.0	47.3
Netherlands	7.4	8.0	8.0	9.8	12.0	69.4	67.1	63.1	(NA)	(NA)
New Zealand	5.8	6.8	7.6	8.4	10.1	88.0	82.4	78.0	79.7	83.2
Norway	7.0	7.6	8.4	9.0	9.4	85.1	82.8	82.5	83.5	85.5
Poland	(NA)	4.8	5.5	6.2	7.0	(NA)	91.7	70.0	69.3	71.7
Portugal	5.1	5.7	9.3	10.4	10.7	64.3	65.5	66.6	68.0	65.8
Slovakia	(NA)	(NA)	5.5	7.0	9.0	(NA)	(NA)	89.4	74.4	64.5
Spain	5.3	6.5	7.2	8.3	9.6	79.9	78.7	71.6	71.0	74.2
Sweden	8.9	8.2	8.2	9.1	9.6	92.5	89.9	84.9	81.2	81.0
Switzerland	7.4	8.2	10.2	11.2	11.4	(NA)	52.4	55.4	59.5	65.2
Turkey	2.4	2.7	4.9	5.4	(NA)	29.4	61.0	62.9	67.8	(NA)
United Kingdom	5.6	5.9	7.0	8.2	9.6	89.4	83.6	78.8	81.7	83.2

NA Not available. [1] Data prior to 1991 are for former West Germany.

Source: Organisation for Economic Co-operation and Development (OECD), 2012, "OECD Health Data," OECD Health Statistics (database), <http://www.oecd.org/health/healthpoliciesanddata/oecdhealthdata2012.htm>, accessed on 08 August 2012 (copyright).

Table 1362. Physicians and Inpatient Hospital Care—Selected Countries: 2000 to 2010

Country	Practicing physicians per 1,000 population			Acute inpatient hospital care					
				Beds per 1,000 population			Average length of stay (days)		
	2000	2005	2010	2000	2005	2010	2000	2005	2010
United States	**2.3**	**2.4**	**2.4**	**3.0**	**2.7**	**(NA)**	**5.8**	**5.6**	**5.4**
Australia	2.5	2.8	(NA)	3.6	3.5	(NA)	6.1	6.0	(NA)
Austria	3.9	4.3	4.8	6.2	5.8	5.5	7.6	6.9	6.6
Belgium	2.8	2.9	2.9	4.7	4.4	4.1	7.7	7.7	(NA)
Canada [1]	2.1	2.2	2.4	3.2	2.8	(NA)	7.2	7.2	(NA)
Czech Republic	3.4	3.6	3.6	5.7	5.3	4.9	7.9	7.1	7.0
Denmark	2.9	3.3	(NA)	3.5	3.2	2.9	3.8	(NA)	(NA)
Finland	2.5	2.6	(NA)	2.4	2.2	1.8	5.7	5.5	5.4
France [1]	3.3	3.3	3.3	4.1	3.7	3.5	5.6	5.4	5.2
Germany	3.3	3.4	3.7	6.4	5.9	5.7	9.2	8.1	7.3
Greece [1]	4.3	5.0	6.1	3.7	3.9	(NA)	6.2	5.6	(NA)
Hungary	2.7	2.8	2.9	5.6	5.5	4.1	7.1	6.5	5.8
Ireland [2]	2.2	3.5	4.2	2.8	2.8	2.3	6.4	6.5	6.1
Israel	3.4	3.3	3.5	2.3	2.1	1.9	4.3	4.2	4.0
Italy [1]	4.2	3.8	3.9	4.1	3.3	2.8	7.0	6.7	(NA)
Japan	1.9	(NA)	2.2	9.6	8.2	8.1	24.8	19.8	18.2
Korea, South	1.3	1.6	2.0	3.9	4.6	5.5	11.0	(NA)	(NA)
Mexico	1.6	1.8	2.0	1.8	1.7	1.6	4.0	4.0	3.9
Netherlands [1]	2.4	2.7	(NA)	3.1	2.9	3.0	9.0	7.2	5.6
New Zealand	2.2	2.1	2.6	(NA)	(NA)	(NA)	4.3	5.6	5.5
Norway	3.4	3.6	4.1	3.1	2.9	2.4	6.0	5.2	4.5
Poland	2.2	2.1	2.2	5.1	4.7	4.4	8.9	6.5	5.0
Portugal [2]	3.1	3.4	3.8	3.0	2.9	2.8	7.7	7.1	(NA)
Russia	4.2	4.2	(NA)	(NA)	(NA)	(NA)	13.5	11.9	(NA)
Slovakia [1]	3.4	3.0	3.3	5.7	5.0	4.7	8.5	7.3	6.6
Spain	3.3	3.8	3.8	2.8	2.6	2.5	7.1	6.7	6.3
Sweden	3.1	3.5	(NA)	2.5	2.2	2.0	5.3	4.9	4.6
Switzerland [1]	3.5	3.8	3.9	4.1	3.7	3.1	9.3	8.5	6.9
Turkey [1]	1.3	1.3	1.7	1.9	2.1	2.4	5.6	5.1	3.9
United Kingdom	2.0	2.4	2.7	3.1	2.9	2.4	8.0	7.5	6.6

NA Not available. [1] Data refer to all professionally active physicians, including those who do not work directly with patients. [2] Data refer to all physicians licensed to practice, including those not currently working in the medical professions.

Source: Organisation for Economic Co-operation and Development (OECD), 2012, "OECD Health Data," OECD Health Statistics (database), <http://www.oecd.org/health/healthpoliciesanddata/oecdhealthdata2012.htm>, accessed on 08 August 2012 (copyright).

Table 1363. Gross National Income (GNI) by Country: 2000 and 2011

[For total GNI, 32,292,622 represents $32,292,622,000,000. GNI measures the total domestic and foreign value added claimed by residents. GNI comprises GDP plus net receipts of primary income (compensation of employees and property income) from nonresident sources]

Country	Gross national income [1]				GNI on purchasing power parity basis [2]			
	Total (mil. dol.)		Per capita (dol.)		Total (mil. dol.)		Per capita (dol.)	
	2000	2011	2000	2011	2000	2011	2000	2011
World	**32,292,622**	**66,164,277**	**5,278**	**9,488**	**42,096,286**	**80,714,952**	**6,881**	**11,574**
Algeria	48,963	160,814	1,600	4,470	156,584	301,065	5,130	8,370
Angola	5,904	79,720	420	4,060	24,963	103,737	1,790	5,290
Argentina	275,544	397,190	7,460	9,740	327,933	703,278	8,880	17,250
Australia	407,125	(NA)	21,260	(NA)	492,189	(NA)	25,700	(NA)
Bangladesh	49,769	116,429	380	770	115,591	291,453	890	1,940
Belarus	13,773	55,264	1,380	5,830	51,380	137,941	5,140	14,560
Belgium	260,723	508,092	25,430	46,160	289,968	432,566	28,290	39,300
Brazil	673,693	2,107,628	3,860	10,720	1,189,809	2,261,060	6,820	11,500
Burkina Faso	2,885	9,696	230	570	9,290	22,221	760	1,310
Cambodia	3,622	11,816	290	830	11,058	32,401	890	2,260
Canada	680,920	1,570,886	22,130	45,560	851,327	1,373,419	27,670	39,830
Chile	74,596	212,003	4,840	12,280	137,391	279,061	8,910	16,160
China	1,168,776	6,628,086	930	4,930	2,951,385	11,325,385	2,340	8,430
Colombia	93,540	286,546	2,350	6,110	228,101	452,399	5,740	9,640
Congo, (Kinshasa) [3]	1,767	9,417	560	2,270	6,133	13,581	1,960	3,280
Costa Rica	14,557	36,191	3,710	7,660	26,075	56,494	6,650	11,950
Cote d'Ivoire	10,783	22,071	650	1,100	24,841	34,772	1,500	1,730
Czech Republic	(NA)	195,335	(NA)	18,520	156,976	255,087	15,280	24,190
Denmark	169,966	336,626	31,830	60,390	150,646	235,962	28,210	42,330
Dominican Republic	22,495	52,647	2,620	5,240	42,182	95,392	4,910	9,490
Ecuador	16,462	60,657	1,330	4,140	53,716	121,881	4,350	8,310
Egypt	97,275	214,684	1,440	2,600	250,856	508,214	3,710	6,160
Ethiopia	8,391	33,825	130	400	30,451	94,253	460	1,110
France	1,478,256	2,775,664	24,270	42,420	1,555,029	2,346,351	25,530	35,860
Germany	2,079,948	3,594,303	25,300	43,980	2,095,454	3,283,320	25,490	40,170
Ghana	6,459	35,110	340	1,410	17,603	45,528	920	1,820
Greece	136,073	282,976	12,460	25,030	200,013	294,312	18,320	26,040
Hong Kong	177,103	248,671	26,570	35,160	177,283	364,103	26,600	51,490
Hungary	46,722	126,921	4,580	12,730	115,324	203,230	11,290	20,380
India	473,698	1,746,481	450	1,410	1,593,207	4,488,038	1,510	3,620
Indonesia	119,462	712,737	560	2,940	452,327	1,098,925	2,120	4,530
Iran	106,662	(NA)	1,630	(NA)	435,124	(NA)	6,660	(NA)
Israel	112,152	224,684	17,830	28,930	135,061	211,900	21,480	27,290
Italy	1,196,353	2,146,998	21,010	35,330	1,455,575	1,966,087	25,560	32,350
Japan	4,445,186	5,774,376	35,040	45,180	3,343,128	4,538,987	26,350	35,510
Kazakhstan	18,740	136,120	1,260	8,220	66,484	187,329	4,470	11,310
Kenya	13,168	34,211	420	820	35,217	71,728	1,130	1,720
Korea, South	465,914	1,038,981	9,910	20,870	804,280	1,507,707	17,110	30,290
Lithuania	11,188	39,322	3,200	12,280	29,639	63,074	8,470	19,690
Malaysia	80,182	243,108	3,420	8,420	194,857	438,252	8,320	15,190
Mexico	500,874	1,060,221	5,010	9,240	878,098	1,736,215	8,780	15,120
Morocco	38,194	97,619	1,310	2,970	73,299	161,176	2,520	4,910
Mozambique	4,198	11,240	230	470	7,644	23,442	420	980
Netherlands, The	423,282	830,219	26,580	49,730	478,443	730,846	30,040	43,770
Nigeria	33,449	195,333	270	1,200	141,138	374,124	1,140	2,300
Norway	161,062	440,185	35,860	88,890	160,100	287,677	35,650	58,090
Pakistan	67,667	197,604	470	1,120	233,618	509,615	1,620	2,880
Peru	53,340	161,701	2,060	5,500	123,803	298,599	4,790	10,160
Philippines	81,319	209,450	1,050	2,210	184,935	394,938	2,390	4,160
Poland	176,720	477,009	4,600	12,480	402,910	781,573	10,480	20,450
Qatar	(NA)	150,427	(NA)	80,440	(NA)	162,745	(NA)	87,030
Romania	38,029	169,192	1,690	7,910	126,108	323,882	5,620	15,140
Russia	250,286	1,476,086	1,710	10,400	973,728	2,845,251	6,660	20,050
Saudi Arabia	168,133	500,543	8,390	17,820	362,295	698,484	18,070	24,870
Serbia [4]	10,529	41,237	1,400	5,680	43,344	84,524	5,770	11,640
Singapore	98,680	222,550	24,500	42,930	135,088	309,920	33,540	59,790
South Africa	134,396	352,038	3,050	6,960	291,137	545,680	6,620	10,790
Spain	620,843	1,432,813	15,420	30,990	850,977	1,476,382	21,140	31,930
Sri Lanka	16,407	53,832	860	2,580	49,948	115,991	2,610	5,560
Sudan	11,075	(NA)	320	(NA)	38,724	(NA)	1,130	(NA)
Sweden	261,623	503,188	29,490	53,230	245,948	400,373	27,720	42,350
Switzerland	289,326	603,917	40,270	76,380	244,762	402,449	34,070	50,900
Syria	15,898	(NA)	990	(NA)	50,847	(NA)	3,180	(NA)
Tanzania	10,109	24,291	310	540	25,289	67,815	760	1,510
Thailand	122,102	307,129	1,930	4,420	303,165	583,285	4,800	8,390
Turkey	265,345	766,441	4,170	10,410	580,565	1,231,767	9,120	16,730
Uganda	6,398	17,458	260	510	16,327	45,650	670	1,320
Ukraine	34,350	142,812	700	3,120	156,401	323,780	3,180	7,080
United Kingdom	1,531,984	2,366,544	26,010	37,780	1,532,471	2,315,736	26,020	36,970
United States	**9,845,288**	**15,097,083**	**34,890**	**48,450**	**10,070,500**	**15,232,385**	**35,690**	**48,890**
Uzbekistan	15,431	44,232	630	1,510	35,128	100,949	1,430	3,440
Venezuela	99,740	349,054	4,100	11,920	203,835	369,504	8,380	12,620
Vietnam	30,204	110,907	390	1,260	108,423	286,641	1,400	3,260
Yemen	7,418	26,419	420	1,070	30,657	54,066	1,730	2,180
Zimbabwe	6,117	8,110	490	640	(NA)	(NA)	(NA)	(NA)

NA Not available. [1] Gross national income calculated using the World Bank Atlas method; for details, see source. [2] For explanation of Purchasing Power Parity, see headnote, Table 1364. [3] See footnote 5, Table 1348. [4] In June 2006, Serbia and Montenegro became separate countries (formerly Yugoslavia). Data for 2000 are for Serbia and Montenegro. Starting in 2006, data excludes Montenegro.

Source: The World Bank, Washington, DC, *World Development Indicators*, annual (copyright). See also <http://data.worldbank.org\>, accessed August 2012.

Table 1364. Real Gross Domestic Product (GDP) Per Capita and Per Employed Persons by Country: 1990 to 2010

[U.S. figures based on the System of National Income and Product Accounts (NIPA) from the Bureau of Economic Analysis. All other countries, based on the 1993 United Nations System of National Accounts. Per capita data based on total resident population. Real GDP is a macroeconomic measure of the size of an economy adjusted for price changes and inflation. Employment data include people serving in the armed forces for some countries. Real dollars are calculated based on 2010 Purchasing Power Parities (PPPs). PPPs are currency conversion rates used to convert GDP expressed in different currencies to a common value (U.S. dollars in this case). A PPP for a given country is the number of national currency units needed to buy the specific basket of goods and services that one dollar will buy in the United States. See text, this section]

Country	Real GDP per capita (2010 U.S. dollars)				Real GDP per employed person (2010 U.S. dollars)			
	1990	2000	2009	2010	1990	2000	2009	2010
United States............	35,612	44,081	45,854	46,844	73,655	90,001	99,624	103,229
Canada....................	30,040	36,153	38,323	39,104	63,395	75,075	76,545	77,948
Australia..................	27,150	34,101	39,137	39,497	58,449	72,254	78,061	78,047
Japan.....................	28,848	31,586	32,424	33,612	55,437	61,405	65,364	68,233
Korea, South............	11,781	20,225	27,562	29,184	27,926	44,940	57,158	59,858
Austria....................	29,153	35,851	39,222	39,928	62,590	75,816	80,393	82,064
Belgium..................	28,526	34,521	36,792	37,411	73,949	86,123	89,505	90,839
Denmark..................	30,374	37,791	38,284	38,778	59,846	74,378	74,858	77,821
France....................	28,004	32,596	33,853	34,168	69,062	77,971	81,974	83,050
Germany [1]............	29,444	34,698	36,635	38,021	61,246	72,852	74,482	76,769
Italy.......................	29,315	34,176	32,723	32,997	73,542	84,869	79,299	80,917
Netherlands..............	29,491	37,810	41,033	41,512	69,351	76,492	78,904	82,403
Norway....................	38,474	52,279	56,443	55,938	79,260	101,221	104,581	105,202
Spain......................	23,933	30,432	32,774	32,625	61,907	71,320	74,976	76,670
Sweden...................	28,668	34,038	37,594	39,407	53,350	70,219	78,141	81,678
United Kingdom..........	26,204	32,716	35,389	35,621	55,816	70,096	75,509	76,334

[1] Prior to 1991, data are for the former West Germany.

Source: U.S. Bureau of Labor Statistics, "International Comparisons of GDP per Capita and per Hour, 1960–2010," August 2011, <http://www.bls.gov/fls/intl_gdp_capita_gdp_hour.htm>.

Table 1365. Average Annual Percent Changes in International Economic Composite Indexes by Country: 1990 to 2011

[Change from previous year; derived from indexes with base 2000 = 100. The coincident index changes are for calendar years and the leading index changes are for years ending June 30 because they lead the coincident indexes by about 6 months, on average. The G-7 countries are United States, Canada, France, Germany, Italy, United Kingdom, and Japan. Minus sign (–) indicates decrease]

Country	Leading index						Coincident index					
	1990	2000	2005	2009	2010	2011	1990	2000	2005	2009	2010	2011
Total, 13 countries.........	2.2	7.1	5.1	-10.8	8.1	5.0	5.6	5.2	1.9	-13.5	3.1	1.0
12 countries, excluding U.S...............	3.9	8.5	5.5	-6.9	4.4	5.2	8.4	5.7	1.5	-12.0	4.6	0.2
G-7 countries..............	2.1	6.7	5.0	-11.4	8.0	4.8	5.6	5.1	1.7	-14.0	2.7	0.7
North America..............	-0.8	4.9	4.3	-16.3	13.8	4.4	-0.3	5.0	2.7	-16.1	0.6	2.5
United States.............	-0.9	4.7	4.4	-17.4	15.0	4.4	-0.3	4.5	2.6	-16.6	0.1	2.3
Canada...................	-0.4	7.3	3.2	-4.7	3.0	4.4	-2.0	10.5	4.6	-11.8	5.4	3.5
Four European countries...	1.7	5.2	4.0	-7.4	6.0	5.6	6.7	10.3	1.8	-10.3	3.2	3.7
France....................	0.3	2.0	6.5	-8.0	11.9	2.6	6.5	13.2	1.8	-15.1	0.4	1.9
Germany..................	4.9	8.0	4.5	-7.4	4.1	8.4	8.5	8.8	-0.5	-7.5	7.1	7.6
Italy......................	0.6	6.2	2.2	-7.0	4.3	4.3	11.9	16.8	4.8	-15.1	-0.3	1.6
United Kingdom...........	-0.6	3.4	1.4	-7.1	4.1	5.8	0.4	4.4	3.3	-4.1	3.2	0.9
Seven Pacific region countries..................	6.1	12.1	7.1	-6.6	3.0	4.9	10.3	1.2	0.9	-12.5	5.8	-3.3
Australia..................	-2.2	8.4	5.2	-7.7	4.5	4.9	-0.4	4.7	3.5	-1.8	3.4	1.6
Taiwan [1].................	5.0	9.7	6.5	-0.8	10.6	6.8	5.2	4.8	5.2	-6.4	13.6	6.8
Thailand...................	12.7	10.7	5.3	-0.6	9.7	10.5	12.3	7.7	6.6	-2.2	10.7	3.8
Japan.....................	6.5	11.9	7.3	-7.5	1.4	4.3	11.0	-0.5	-0.1	-14.9	5.4	-5.2
Korea, South.............	6.0	20.7	7.6	-0.2	12.3	9.9	9.6	14.8	4.6	0.1	7.5	5.2
Malaysia..................	4.6	20.6	9.1	-3.8	17.1	12.5	9.2	11.1	3.1	-6.4	6.5	3.9
New Zealand..............	3.5	5.0	1.5	-1.9	7.1	-2.1	-1.3	3.0	6.1	-7.2	2.3	2.5

[1] See footnote 4, Table 1348.

Source: Foundation for International Business and Economic Research, New York, NY, *International Economic Indicators*, monthly (copyright).

Table 1366. Sectoral Contributions to Gross Value Added: 2000 and 2011

[In percent. According to the 1993 System of National Accounts (SNA) and the International Standard Industrial Classification (ISIC), Revision 3 (1990). Value added is estimated at basic prices and includes financial intermediation services indirectly measured (FISIM). Value added represents an industry's contribution to national GDP and is calculated as the difference between production and intermediate inputs. Value added comprises labor costs, consumption of fixed capital, indirect taxes less subsidies, and net operating surplus and mixed income]

| Country | Agriculture [1] | | Industry | | | | Services | |
| | | | Total [2] | | Manufacturing | | | |
	2000	2011	2000	2011	2000	2011	2000	2011
United States [3]	**1.2**	[4] **1.2**	**23.4**	[4] **20.0**	**15.9**	[4] **13.2**	**75.4**	[4] **78.8**
Australia	3.8	[4] 2.8	26.2	[4] 27.8	12.3	[4] 8.3	70.0	[4] 69.4
Austria	1.9	1.6	31.4	29.3	20.1	18.7	66.7	69.0
Belgium	1.3	0.7	27.2	22.7	18.7	13.8	71.5	76.6
China	15.1	10.1	45.9	46.8	(NA)	(NA)	39.0	43.1
Czech Republic	3.6	2.1	37.5	37.7	25.9	24.3	58.9	60.2
Denmark	2.5	1.4	26.6	22.3	15.4	10.9	70.9	76.3
Finland	3.5	2.9	34.4	27.8	25.6	17.3	62.1	69.4
France	2.5	1.8	22.8	18.7	15.2	10.1	74.7	79.5
Germany	1.1	0.9	30.5	30.8	22.3	22.6	68.4	68.3
Greece	(NA)	3.1	(NA)	18.0	(NA)	9.9	(NA)	78.9
Hungary	5.9	5.4	32.5	32.6	22.9	24.3	61.7	62.0
Indonesia	15.6	[4] 15.3	45.9	[4] 47.0	27.7	[4] 24.8	38.5	[4] 37.6
Ireland	3.4	[4] 1.7	40.8	[4] 30.9	32.3	[4] 25.8	55.8	[4] 67.4
Italy	2.8	2.0	27.7	24.6	20.1	15.9	69.5	73.4
Japan [5]	[6] 1.5	[4] 1.2	[6] 31.3	[4] 27.5	[6] 21.5	[4] 19.5	[6] 67.3	[4] 71.4
Korea	4.6	2.7	38.6	39.7	28.3	31.2	56.8	57.6
Mexico	[6] 4.2	[4] 3.5	[6] 35.8	[4] 34.3	[6] 21.6	[4] 18.1	[6] 61.5	[4] 62.2
Netherlands	2.5	1.7	24.8	24.2	14.6	12.7	72.7	74.1
Norway	2.1	1.5	41.7	42.3	9.8	7.7	56.2	56.3
Poland	4.9	3.6	31.1	33.3	17.2	18.0	64.0	63.0
Portugal	3.6	2.1	28.5	23.3	17.1	13.0	67.9	74.6
Russia	[6] 6.4	4.3	[6] 37.7	37.0	(NA)	16.0	[6] 56.0	58.7
Slovakia	4.5	3.2	36.1	41.9	23.9	25.9	59.4	54.9
South Africa	3.3	2.4	31.8	30.6	19.0	13.4	64.9	67.0
Spain	4.2	2.6	31.1	28.3	17.9	13.4	64.7	69.0
Sweden	2.0	1.7	28.5	26.3	21.3	16.0	69.5	72.0
Switzerland	1.3	[4] 0.8	26.5	[4] 26.2	17.9	[4] 18.4	72.2	[4] 73.0
Turkey	10.8	9.2	30.0	27.7	21.4	18.4	59.2	63.2
United Kingdom	1.0	0.7	27.0	23.2	15.6	10.8	71.9	76.2

NA Not available [1] Includes forestry, fishing, and hunting sectors. [2] Includes construction, energy, and manufacturing sectors. [3] Value added is estimated at factor cost for U.S. [4] 2010 data. [5] Value added is estimated approximately at market prices for Japan. [6] Estimate.

Source: Organisation for Economic Co-operation and Development (OECD), 2012, "National accounts at a glance," OECD National Accounts Statistics (database), <http://dx.doi.org/10.1787/data-00369-en>, accessed on 08 August 2012 (copyright).

Table 1367. Index of Industrial Production by Country: 1990 to 2011

[Annual averages of monthly data. Industrial production indexes generally measure output in the manufacturing, mining, electric, gas, and water utilities sectors. Minus sign (–) indicates decrease]

| Country | Index (2005 = 100) | | | | | | | | Annual percent change | | | | |
	1990	1995	2000	2005	2008	2009	2010	2011	2005 to 2006	2007 to 2008	2008 to 2009	2009 to 2010	2010 to 2011
United States	65.2	75.2	96.7	100.0	101.0	89.5	94.3	98.2	2.5	-3.5	-11.4	5.4	4.1
Australia	74.3	81.9	94.0	100.0	107.6	105.8	110.4	109.2	2.9	2.4	-1.7	4.4	-1.1
Austria	59.6	64.4	85.3	100.0	116.0	103.1	110.2	118.3	5.6	1.9	-11.1	7.0	7.3
Belgium	76.7	77.1	85.5	100.0	108.4	95.5	103.5	107.8	5.0	1.4	-11.9	8.4	4.2
Brazil	70.8	78.2	85.8	100.0	112.4	104.1	115.0	115.4	6.0	3.1	-7.4	10.5	0.4
Canada	68.3	77.7	98.9	100.0	94.1	83.3	88.4	91.6	-0.8	-4.5	-11.5	6.1	3.6
Chile	(NA)	74.0	80.0	100.0	107.7	100.5	101.0	106.5	4.1	0.2	-6.7	0.5	5.4
Czech Republic	89.9	67.9	74.9	100.0	117.7	101.6	112.1	119.3	10.6	-1.8	-13.6	10.3	6.5
Denmark	72.1	82.3	96.5	100.0	101.0	85.8	87.3	88.9	-1.9	-1.1	-15.0	1.8	1.8
Finland	58.9	66.6	91.2	100.0	115.5	94.6	100.0	100.8	4.6	0.8	-18.1	5.7	0.8
France	88.2	88.3	99.8	100.0	99.2	86.5	90.8	92.5	1.3	-2.5	-12.8	5.0	1.9
Germany [1]	85.7	82.5	93.9	100.0	113.7	94.1	105.0	114.3	6.9	0.2	-17.3	11.6	8.8
Greece	83.7	82.1	100.6	100.0	102.4	92.4	87.0	79.8	2.0	-0.3	-9.7	-5.8	-8.3
Hungary	51.9	45.6	76.0	100.0	118.5	97.6	107.8	113.7	7.9	-0.1	-17.6	10.5	5.4
India	(NA)	53.4	72.2	100.0	127.8	136.3	150.7	(NA)	10.4	4.8	6.6	10.6	(NA)
Ireland	23.6	37.5	74.9	100.0	106.1	101.4	109.0	109.0	5.2	-2.2	-4.5	7.5	0.0
Italy	90.2	96.9	104.3	100.0	101.8	82.7	88.3	88.4	1.8	-3.4	-18.8	6.7	0.1
Japan	96.9	94.0	98.4	100.0	103.8	81.7	94.8	92.4	2.8	-3.2	-21.3	16.0	-2.5
Korea, South	31.7	47.9	74.3	100.0	119.8	119.7	139.2	148.8	6.9	3.4	-0.1	16.3	6.9
Mexico [2]	67.1	70.2	99.7	100.0	107.7	99.5	105.6	109.8	2.0	-0.1	-7.7	6.2	4.0
Netherlands	78.4	84.9	95.7	100.0	107.0	99.2	106.7	106.2	4.0	0.8	-7.3	7.6	-0.5
New Zealand	73.6	83.9	89.2	100.0	100.8	94.1	96.1	95.5	3.0	-1.1	-6.7	2.1	-0.6
Norway	74.2	93.7	104.5	100.0	97.1	93.3	88.1	83.7	-1.2	0.5	-3.9	-5.6	-5.0
Poland	47.3	53.6	76.8	100.0	125.8	121.0	134.4	143.6	9.3	2.7	-3.8	11.1	6.9
Russia	(NA)	76.6	75.6	100.0	114.5	103.8	112.4	117.7	6.9	0.6	-9.3	8.3	4.8
Spain	79.1	82.0	97.8	100.0	98.4	82.8	83.5	82.3	2.1	-7.3	-15.8	0.8	-1.4
Sweden	64.3	77.0	92.4	100.0	104.5	85.9	93.3	98.7	4.0	-3.0	-17.8	8.7	5.8
Switzerland	78.3	81.3	99.0	100.0	119.6	110.1	117.1	118.2	9.5	1.3	-7.9	6.3	0.9
Turkey	57.0	66.6	80.8	100.0	114.2	102.9	116.4	126.8	7.0	-0.6	-9.9	13.1	8.9
United Kingdom	81.3	86.3	103.4	100.0	97.9	89.0	90.9	90.3	0.5	-2.7	-9.1	2.1	-0.7

NA Not available [1] Data prior to 1991 are for former West Germany. [2] Including construction.

Source: Organisation for Economic Co-operation and Development (OECD), 2012, "Production and Sales," Main Economic Indicators (database), <http://dx.doi.org/10.1787/data-00048-en>, accessed on 08 August 2012 (copyright).

Table 1368. Selected Indexes of Manufacturing Activity by Country: 1990 to 2010

[2002 = 100. Data relate to employees (wage and salary earners) in Belgium, and to all employed persons (employees, self-employed workers, and unpaid family workers) in the other countries. Minus sign (−) indicates decrease]

Index	United States	Can-ada	Japan	Bel-gium	France	Ger-many [1]	Italy	Nether-lands	Nor-way	Swe-den	United King-dom
Output per hour:											
1990	58.1	70.7	70.9	74.8	64.8	69.8	78.1	69.4	87.8	49.4	70.3
1995	68.5	83.4	83.4	87.1	77.7	80.6	94.2	82.0	88.1	64.9	81.2
2000	88.8	100.7	98.5	98.2	95.0	96.5	100.9	96.8	94.6	91.6	93.3
2005	122.8	104.8	121.7	106.7	112.1	112.1	100.8	114.6	119.1	128.0	116.3
2009	139.1	105.4	119.5	113.6	113.1	108.2	93.8	117.0	118.1	124.4	120.6
2010	147.1	110.0	136.2	117.3	122.1	115.6	100.4	127.6	123.7	141.1	125.6
Average annual percent change:											
2000-2010	5.5	1.4	3.6	2.0	2.9	2.4	0.5	3.3	2.8	4.9	3.4
2008-2009	5.0	0.9	-9.0	1.9	-2.0	-9.2	-6.1	-4.7	0.8	-7.3	-3.7
2009-2010	5.8	4.3	13.9	3.3	7.9	6.9	7.0	9.1	4.7	13.4	4.2
Compensation per hour: [2,3]											
1990	62.1	68.3	77.4	70.1	64.1	59.7	61.3	63.1	58.5	61.0	59.3
1995	73.4	81.6	92.4	84.5	79.4	81.2	82.5	77.0	69.2	71.8	71.6
2000	91.3	94.2	98.0	93.5	91.9	94.7	94.1	90.7	89.0	90.7	90.2
2005	112.5	112.8	99.6	104.8	109.7	104.1	110.8	109.9	112.6	110.8	116.7
2009	129.1	121.0	99.5	123.0	122.9	118.1	125.4	124.4	139.4	129.4	135.0
2010	131.2	120.9	98.2	123.0	125.4	116.0	128.1	125.3	144.9	126.3	139.3
Average annual percent change:											
2000-2010	4.1	2.6	0.0	2.7	3.4	2.4	3.1	3.4	5.0	3.4	4.6
2008-2009	4.5	-1.5	1.1	6.2	3.0	5.1	3.5	3.3	5.5	4.0	3.6
2009-2010	1.6	-0.1	-1.3	0.0	2.1	-1.8	2.1	0.7	3.9	-2.4	3.1
Real hourly compensation: [4]											
1990	82.9	87.4	82.7	89.4	79.3	78.2	93.4	86.9	76.9	80.8	82.8
1995	86.0	93.5	92.3	95.6	87.5	89.4	98.0	92.2	80.9	78.4	84.6
2000	95.4	98.7	96.5	97.3	95.2	97.9	99.1	97.6	92.9	95.1	93.3
2005	103.7	105.4	100.2	98.3	103.1	99.8	103.6	104.5	107.7	107.7	107.1
2009	108.3	105.2	99.8	106.6	108.4	105.9	108.2	111.0	122.1	114.9	111.3
2010	108.2	103.1	99.2	104.3	108.9	102.9	108.8	110.4	123.8	111.8	109.7
Average annual percent change:											
2000-2010	1.6	0.5	0.3	0.6	1.5	0.8	0.9	1.3	2.9	2.1	1.8
2008-2009	4.9	-2.1	2.6	6.2	2.7	4.7	2.7	2.1	3.3	4.5	4.1
2009-2010	0.0	-2.0	-0.6	-2.1	0.4	-2.9	0.6	-0.6	1.4	-2.7	-1.4
Unit labor costs, national currency: [2,3]											
1990	107.0	96.6	109.2	93.6	99.1	85.5	78.6	91.0	66.6	123.3	84.3
1995	107.1	97.9	110.8	97.0	102.2	100.8	87.7	93.9	78.5	110.6	88.2
2000	102.8	93.5	99.5	95.1	96.7	98.1	93.2	93.8	94.1	99.0	96.7
2005	91.6	107.7	81.8	98.1	97.8	92.9	110.0	95.9	94.5	86.6	100.3
2009	92.8	114.8	83.2	108.3	108.6	109.2	133.7	106.4	118.0	104.0	112.0
2010	89.2	109.9	72.1	104.8	102.7	100.4	127.6	98.2	117.2	89.5	110.9
Average annual percent change:											
2000-2010	-1.2	1.3	-3.2	0.7	0.5	0.2	2.7	0.3	2.3	-0.9	1.2
2008-2009	-0.5	-2.4	11.1	4.2	5.0	15.7	10.3	8.4	4.7	12.3	7.5
2009-2010	-4.0	-4.3	-13.3	-3.2	-5.4	-8.1	-4.6	-7.7	-0.7	-13.9	-1.0
Unit labor costs, U.S. dollar basis: [2]											
1990	107.0	130.1	94.3	119.5	126.2	109.4	134.3	116.5	85.0	202.4	100.1
1995	107.1	112.1	147.7	140.5	142.2	145.6	110.2	136.4	98.9	150.7	92.7
2000	102.8	98.8	115.6	92.9	94.5	95.8	91.1	91.6	85.2	105.0	97.5
2005	91.6	139.6	93.0	129.2	128.8	122.3	144.8	126.3	117.2	112.7	121.6
2009	92.8	158.0	111.2	159.6	160.1	161.0	197.1	156.8	149.8	132.2	116.7
2010	89.2	167.6	102.9	147.0	144.1	140.8	179.0	137.8	154.7	120.8	114.1
Average annual percent change:											
2000-2010	-1.2	4.9	-0.7	3.1	2.9	2.6	5.3	2.7	4.9	0.4	1.0
2008-2009	-0.5	-8.8	22.6	-1.4	-0.6	9.5	4.4	2.6	-6.2	-3.4	-9.2
2009-2010	-4.0	6.1	-7.5	-7.9	-10.0	-12.6	-9.2	-12.2	3.3	-8.6	-2.3
Employment:											
1990	116.1	98.7	128.7	118.3	116.7	131.2	110.8	109.1	102.2	119.9	137.0
1995	113.3	91.7	120.1	106.0	103.3	106.1	100.6	101.6	104.1	100.3	118.0
2000	113.0	102.2	108.0	102.8	101.4	101.9	99.4	102.5	105.0	101.3	110.3
2005	93.5	98.3	94.9	94.1	92.6	94.4	99.1	92.2	92.6	91.7	86.3
2009	78.2	80.8	89.3	87.8	85.2	93.5	95.4	90.5	98.1	83.9	75.1
2010	76.0	80.4	87.2	85.0	82.0	91.8	91.8	88.2	94.7	83.0	72.9
Average annual percent change:											
2000-2010	-3.5	-1.8	-2.1	-1.6	-1.9	-0.8	-0.8	-1.3	-1.1	-1.7	-4.0
2008-2009	-11.3	-10.1	-6.1	-4.5	-4.0	-2.9	-4.5	-2.8	-4.2	-9.9	-5.5
2009-2010	-2.8	-0.4	-2.3	-3.2	-3.8	-1.8	-3.8	-2.5	-3.5	-1.0	-2.9
Aggregate hours:											
1990	116.5	97.2	139.6	116.0	127.8	135.4	113.0	110.9	104.1	110.2	135.0
1995	115.9	91.8	122.0	102.8	111.3	111.7	101.6	103.8	107.3	101.3	119.6
2000	115.1	102.7	109.0	102.4	105.4	104.0	100.5	103.3	107.1	103.8	111.1
2005	93.5	97.9	96.3	95.9	93.7	95.0	97.0	91.7	95.8	94.3	87.5
2009	77.4	78.2	84.3	84.6	84.6	86.1	88.1	88.6	99.3	83.4	74.7
2010	77.4	79.2	86.3	85.1	81.2	89.6	86.0	87.2	96.7	85.0	74.3
Average annual percent change:											
2000-2010	-3.6	-1.9	-2.0	-1.6	-2.5	-1.3	-1.4	-1.6	-1.2	-1.6	-4.0
2008-2009	-13.0	-12.1	-11.8	-10.0	-6.3	-9.8	-10.6	-4.1	-6.5	-11.5	-7.2
2009-2010	0.0	1.3	2.4	0.6	-4.0	4.1	-2.3	-1.7	-2.6	2.0	-0.6

[1] Data prior to 1991 are for the former West Germany. [2] In Canada, France, Sweden, and the United Kingdom, compensation adjusted for employment taxes and government subsidies to estimate the actual cost to employers.. [3] Indexes in national currency adjusted for changes in prevailing exchange rates. [4] Index of hourly compensation divided by the index of consumer prices to adjust for changes in purchasing power

Source: U.S. Bureau of Labor Statistics, *International Comparisons of Manufacturing Productivity and Unit Labor Cost Trends 2010, Supplementary Tables 1950–2010*, December 2011. See also <http://www.bls.gov/ilc>.

Table 1369. Indexes of Hourly Compensation Costs for All Employees in Manufacturing by Country: 2000 to 2010

[United States = 100. Compensation costs include pay for time worked, other direct pay (including holiday and vacation pay, bonuses, other direct payments, and the cost of pay in kind), employer expenditures for legally required insurance programs and contractual and private benefit plans, and for some countries, other labor taxes. Data adjusted for exchange rates. Area averages are trade-weighted to account for difference in countries' relative importance to U.S. trade in manufactured goods. The trade weights used to compute the average compensation cost measures for selected economic groups are based on the relative dollar value of U.S. trade in manufactured commodities (exports plus imports) with each country or area in 2010; see source for detail]

Area or country	2000	2005	2008	2009	2010	Area or country	2000	2005	2008	2009	2010
United States.........	**100**	**100**	**100**	**100**	**100**	Ireland...............	64	94	117	112	104
Total [1]..............	**63**	**73**	**82**	**76**	**79**	Israel...............	52	47	60	54	58
OECD [2]................	67	78	87	81	84	Italy..................	66	92	107	100	96
Europe.............	85	110	127	118	113	Japan................	101	85	85	89	92
Euro Area [3]............	86	112	132	123	116	Korea, South.........	39	50	50	43	48
Eastern Europe [4].....	13	21	32	27	27	Mexico...............	19	19	20	17	18
East Asia [5]............	35	38	42	36	39	Netherlands..........	84	115	133	125	118
Argentina.............	32	18	30	30	36	New Zealand.........	37	55	59	52	59
Australia..............	67	96	113	100	117	Norway...............	98	139	174	155	166
Austria...............	89	111	135	129	118	Philippines...........	4	4	5	5	5
Belgium..............	105	137	165	154	146	Poland...............	13	18	29	22	23
Brazil................	17	17	26	24	29	Portugal.............	23	31	38	36	34
Canada..............	75	89	99	89	103	Singapore............	47	44	58	51	55
Czech Republic......	14	24	37	33	33	Slovakia.............	10	19	33	33	31
Denmark.............	90	119	143	136	131	Spain................	50	69	84	82	77
Finland..............	80	112	134	129	122	Sweden..............	94	117	135	119	126
France...............	86	110	132	123	117	Switzerland..........	106	133	151	153	153
Germany.............	102	126	145	135	126	Taiwan [6]............	29	26	26	23	24
Hungary.............	12	22	30	25	24	United Kingdom.......	83	99	104	86	85

[1] Trade-weighted measure includes all 31 foreign economies as well as Estonia and Greece. [2] Organization for Economic Cooperation and Development; see text, this section. [3] Euro area refers to European Union member countries that have adopted the Euro as the common currency as of January 1, 2011 (Austria, Belgium, Cyprus, Estonia, Finland, France, Germany, Greece, Ireland, Italy, Luxembourg, Malta, Netherlands, Portugal, Slovakia, Slovenia, and Spain). [4] Czech Republic, Hungary, Poland, and Slovakia. [5] Excludes Japan. [6] See footnote 4, Table 1348.

Source: U.S. Bureau of Labor Statistics, *International Comparisons of Hourly Compensation Costs in Manufacturing, 2010*, Dec. 2011. See also <http://www.bls.gov/ilc/>.

Table 1370. Annual Percent Change in Labor Productivity and Hours Worked by Country: 1995 to 2010

[Change for period shown. For all advanced economies and Eastern European countries, labor productivity growth refers to the growth in gross domestic product (GDP) per hour worked. Data are derived from The Conference Board Total Economy Database, in association with the Groningen Growth and Development Centre at the University of Groningen, Netherlands. Growth for regional aggregates is based on the weighted sum of country labor productivity growth, with the weight calculated as the two-period average of country share in nominal GDP, adjusted for purchasing power parity (PPP), plus a reallocation term. GDP for each country is measured in constant 2010 U.S. dollars, using GDP deflator changes. Minus sign (–) indicates decrease]

Country	Labor productivity		Total hours worked		Country	Labor productivity		Total hours worked	
	1995 to 2000	2000 to 2010	1995 to 2000	2000 to 2010		1995 to 2000	2000 to 2010	1995 to 2000	2000 to 2010
Advanced economies [1].....	2.3	1.6	0.9	0.2	Estonia...............	8.7	5.3	-2.2	-1.0
United States......	**2.3**	**1.8**	**1.7**	**(Z)**	Hungary..............	1.6	3.0	1.0	-0.8
Japan..............	1.9	1.8	-0.9	-0.9	Latvia...............	5.2	4.8	-0.9	-1.0
					Lithuania............	7.6	4.9	-1.8	0.0
European Union (EU-15, old) [2]....	1.8	1.1	1.0	0.3	Malta................	2.5	0.6	1.1	0.8
Austria.............	3.2	1.6	-0.1	0.1	Poland...............	5.4	2.2	0.1	1.6
Belgium...........	1.6	0.8	1.2	0.8	Romania.............	1.7	5.3	-1.5	-1.5
Denmark..........	1.2	0.8	1.6	0.1	Slovakia.............	4.9	4.3	-1.2	0.1
Finland............	2.6	1.8	1.9	0.3	Slovenia.............	4.5	2.5	0.2	0.3
France............	2.1	1.2	0.5	0.2	European Union (EU-27, enlarged) [4]...	2.2	1.3	0.6	0.3
Germany.........	1.9	1.2	-0.1	-0.1					
Greece...........	3.6	1.8	-0.4	0.5	Addenda:				
Ireland............	4.7	2.5	4.1	0.5	Other Advanced Economies..........	3.2	2.4	1.0	0.9
Italy...............	1.2	0.2	0.8	0.3	Australia.............	2.3	1.5	1.7	1.6
Luxembourg......	1.9	0.8	3.3	2.3	Canada.............	1.8	1.0	2.0	1.2
Netherlands.......	1.6	1.2	2.2	0.4	Hong Kong..........	0.6	3.3	2.0	1.0
Portugal..........	1.3	0.3	2.9	0.6	Iceland.............	1.2	2.4	2.8	-0.1
Spain.............	0.7	0.9	3.5	1.4	Israel...............	1.2	1.4	3.7	2.2
Sweden...........	2.5	1.8	1.0	0.5	New Zealand........	1.5	1.1	1.6	1.5
United Kingdom...	2.3	1.4	1.0	0.2	Norway.............	2.4	0.9	1.3	0.8
European Union (EU-12, new) [3]...	4.1	3.4	-0.5	0.2	Singapore...........	3.3	2.6	2.6	3.1
Bulgaria..........	2.0	3.7	-1.8	0.4	South Korea........	5.4	4.1	0.2	0.3
Cyprus...........	1.5	1.2	1.6	1.8	Switzerland..........	1.6	1.0	0.2	0.8
Czech Republic...	2.7	3.6	-0.2	-0.2	Taiwan [5]............	4.8	3.4	0.4	0.6

Z Less than 0.05 percent. [1] "Advanced" includes the U.S., EU-15, Japan, and "other advanced" economies. [2] Referring to membership of the European Union until 30 April 2004. [3] Referring to new membership of the European Union as of 1 January 2007. [4] Referring to all 27 current members of the European Union. [5] See footnote 4, Table 1348.

Source: The Conference Board, New York, NY, The Conference Board, "Total Economy Database," January 2012, <https://www.conferenceboard.org/data/economydatabase/> (copyright). Reproduced with permission from The Conference Board, Inc., 2012, The Conference Board, Inc.

Table 1371. Comparative Price Levels—Selected OECD Countries: June 2012

[Purchasing power parities (PPPs) are rates of currency conversion that eliminate the differences in price levels between countries. Comparative price levels are defined as the ratios of PPPs to exchange rates. The PPPs are given in national currency units per U.S. dollar. This table should be read vertically. Each column shows the number of specified monetary units needed in each of the countries listed to buy the same representative basket of consumer goods and services. In each case the representative basket costs a hundred units in the country whose currency is specified. For example, in June 2012, an item that costs $1.00 in the United States would cost $1.49 (U.S. dollars) in Japan]

Country	United States (U.S. dollar)	Canada (Canadian dollar)	Mexico (Mexican peso)	Japan (Yen)	France (Euro)	Germany (Euro)	Italy (Euro)	United Kingdom (Pound)
United States	**100**	**79**	**155**	**67**	**87**	**94**	**101**	**76**
Australia [1]	157	124	243	105	137	147	159	119
Austria	111	88	173	75	97	104	112	85
Belgium	117	92	181	78	102	109	118	89
Canada	127	100	197	85	110	119	128	96
Chile	73	57	113	49	63	68	74	55
Czech Republic	80	63	124	53	69	75	80	61
Denmark	149	118	232	100	130	140	151	114
Estonia	84	67	131	57	74	79	85	64
Finland	127	100	197	85	111	119	128	97
France	115	91	178	77	100	107	116	87
Germany	107	84	166	72	93	100	108	81
Greece	100	79	155	67	87	94	101	76
Hungary	70	55	109	47	61	66	71	53
Iceland	118	93	184	80	103	111	120	90
Ireland	125	99	194	84	109	117	127	95
Israel	117	92	181	78	102	109	118	89
Italy	99	78	153	66	86	93	100	75
Japan	149	118	231	100	130	139	151	113
Korea, South	80	63	124	54	70	75	81	61
Luxembourg	124	98	193	83	108	116	126	94
Mexico	64	51	100	43	56	60	65	49
Netherlands	111	87	172	74	97	104	112	84
New Zealand [1]	126	100	196	85	110	118	128	96
Norway	160	126	249	108	140	150	162	122
Poland	59	47	92	40	51	55	60	45
Portugal	99	78	154	67	87	93	100	75
Slovakia	76	60	118	51	66	71	77	58
Spain	103	81	159	69	89	96	104	78
Sweden	128	101	199	86	112	120	129	97
Switzerland	174	137	270	117	152	163	176	132
Turkey	56	44	87	37	49	52	56	42
United Kingdom	132	104	204	88	115	123	133	100

[1] Estimates based on quarterly consumer prices.

Source: Organisation for Economic Co-operation and Development (OECD), 2012, "Prices: Comparative Price Levels," Main Economic Indicators (database), <http://dx.doi.org/10.1787/data-00536-en>, accessed on 08 August 2012 (copyright).

Table 1372. Indexes of Living Costs Abroad: 2012

[As of April 2012. Washington, DC=100. Indexes compare the costs in dollars of representative goods and services (excluding housing and education) purchased at the foreign location and the cost of comparable goods and services in the Washington, D.C. area. The indexes are computed for private American employees and exclude special advantages that may be available only to U.S. Government employees. The indexes are place-to-place comparisons at specific times and currency exchange rates. They cannot be used for measuring cost changes over time at a foreign location. Since the indexes reflect only the expenditure pattern and living costs of American families, they should not be used to compare living costs of Americans in the United States with the living costs of foreign nationals living in their own country]

Country/Territory	City	Survey date	Local index [1]	Country/Territory	City	Survey date	Local index [1]
Algeria	Algiers	2/16/2009	127	Kenya	Nairobi	8/15/2011	155
Angola	Luanda	2/17/2011	176	Korea	Seoul	2/16/2010	140
Argentina	Buenos Aires	12/16/2010	135	Kuwait	Kuwait City	11/21/2009	136
Armenia	Yerevan	3/14/2010	113	Laos	Vientiane	9/21/2010	125
Australia	Canberra	7/29/2010	135	Latvia	Riga	9/22/2010	138
Austria	Vienna	3/23/2011	177	Lebanon	Beirut	4/18/2010	121
Azerbaijan	Baku	2/1/2009	156	Liberia	Monrovia	8/14/2009	149
Bahamas	Nassau	6/24/2009	143	Lithuania	Vilnius	5/22/2010	122
Bahrain	Bahrain	11/3/2009	123	Luxembourg	Luxembourg	1/24/2011	164
Bangladesh	Dhaka	2/15/2011	98	Macedonia	Skopje	4/11/2010	125
Belarus	Minsk	3/29/2011	131	Madagascar	Antananarivo	1/30/2011	139
Belgium	Brussels	3/18/2011	173	Malaysia	Kuala Lumpur	11/21/2010	133
Belize	Belmopan	10/25/2011	131	Mexico	Mexico City	3/6/2009	99
Bolivia	La Paz	7/21/2011	120	Moldova	Chisinau	2/23/2010	115
Bosnia-Herzegovina	Sarajevo	8/6/2009	126	Mongolia	Ulaanbaatar	6/2/2011	139
Botswana	Gaborone	6/16/2009	119	Morocco	Rabat	9/15/2010	142
Brazil	Rio de Janeiro	12/29/2009	156	Mozambique	Maputo	8/16/2009	141
Bulgaria	Sofia	5/11/2010	135	Namibia	Windhoek	11/23/2009	138
Burma	Rangoon	3/7/2011	153	Nepal	Kathmandu	9/22/2009	103
Burundi	Bujumbura	3/14/2011	144	Netherlands	The Hague	11/28/2011	155
Cambodia	Phnom Penh	2/27/2011	121	New Zealand	Wellington	9/27/2010	159
Cameroon	Yaounde	4/25/2010	158	Nicaragua	Managua	11/9/2010	111
Canada	Toronto	1/18/2011	157	Niger	Niamey	6/7/2010	124
Central African Republic	Bangui	8/13/2008	189	Nigeria	Abuja	9/30/2010	156
Chad	Ndjamena	8/26/2009	176	Norway	Oslo	1/26/2009	176
Chile	Santiago	10/22/2010	135	Oman	Muscat	5/17/2010	131
China [2]	Beijing	5/17/2010	138	Pakistan	Islamabad	12/10/2004	102
Colombia	Bogota	1/4/2008	109	Panama	Panama City	7/31/2008	119
Congo [3]	Kinshasa	3/25/2011	171	Paraguay	Asuncion	5/5/2010	115
Costa Rica	San Jose	12/10/2009	123	Peru	Lima	1/14/2010	142
Cote d'Ivoire	Abidjan	1/21/2011	136	Philippines	Manila	5/4/2010	108
Croatia	Zagreb	5/31/2010	132	Poland	Warsaw	9/17/2009	130
Cuba	Havana	4/30/2010	146	Portugal	Lisbon	2/13/2011	154
Cyprus	Nicosia	5/17/2010	156	Qatar	Doha	5/12/2010	149
Czech Republic	Prague	9/15/2005	130	Romania	Bucharest	10/25/2010	130
Denmark	Copenhagen	3/30/2009	190	Russia	Moscow	5/8/2011	206
Djibouti	Djibouti City	2/20/2011	145	Rwanda	Kigali	5/2/2010	149
Ecuador	Quito	8/10/2009	120	Saudi Arabia	Riyadh	4/9/2010	122
Egypt	Cairo	3/13/2006	96	Serbia	Belgrade	4/19/2011	109
El Salvador	San Salvador	3/7/2011	127	Sierra Leone	Freetown	6/15/2009	131
Estonia	Tallinn	7/6/2010	116	Singapore	Singapore	3/16/2011	152
Ethiopia	Addis Ababa	4/17/2010	115	Slovakia	Bratislava	12/7/2009	172
Finland	Helsinki	4/14/2009	171	South Africa	Johannesburg	9/30/2010	143
France	Paris	10/11/2009	201	Spain	Madrid	4/11/2010	160
Gabon	Libreville	8/7/2011	165	Sri Lanka	Colombo	3/17/2010	105
Georgia	Tbilisi	4/14/2009	140	Sudan	Khartoum	10/26/2011	160
Germany	Berlin	6/23/2010	168	Sweden	Stockholm	5/13/2010	185
Ghana	Accra	1/20/2010	138	Switzerland	Geneva	11/15/2010	217
Greece	Athens	12/14/2010	158	Syria	Damascus	10/13/2010	116
Guatemala	Guatemala City	5/17/2011	119	Taiwan [2, 4]	Taipei	3/26/2011	143
Guinea	Conakry	10/29/2008	162	Tajikistan	Dushanbe	4/18/2010	105
Guyana	Georgetown	7/28/2009	150	Tanzania	Dar es Salaam	11/16/2009	117
Haiti	Port-au-Prince	12/13/2010	150	Thailand	Bangkok	2/26/2008	126
Honduras	Tegucigalpa	8/11/2010	99	Timor-Leste	Timor Leste	3/15/2011	134
Hong Kong	Hong Kong	4/26/2011	151	Turkey	Istanbul	4/11/2011	135
Hungary	Budapest	10/13/2010	139	Turkmenistan	Ashgabat	11/17/2009	130
Iceland	Reykjavik	5/17/2010	148	Uganda	Kampala	6/7/2010	124
India	New Delhi	12/1/2010	129	Ukraine	Kyiv	12/21/2010	127
Indonesia	Jakarta	11/22/2011	123	United Arab Emirates	Dubai	8/24/2011	128
Ireland	Dublin	7/7/2010	164	United Kingdom	London	3/19/2012	208
Israel	Tel Aviv	6/8/2010	146	Uruguay	Montevideo	10/31/2011	148
Italy	Rome	3/31/2009	183	Uzbekistan	Tashkent	11/30/2010	128
Jamaica	Kingston	1/21/2011	123	Venezuela	Caracas	9/23/2010	180
Japan	Tokyo City	5/12/2011	213	Vietnam	Hanoi	3/19/2012	112
Jordan	Amman	12/20/2010	138	Yemen	Sanaa	4/25/2009	92
Kazakhstan	Almaty	9/1/2011	125	Zambia	Lusaka	7/1/2009	130
				Zimbabwe	Harare	6/2/2010	156

[1] Living cost index is also called the "local index" which measures living costs for private American citizens. The local index is a comparison of prices at the foreign post and in Washington, D.C., with the price ratios weighted by the expenditure pattern of American employees living at the foreign post. It is, thereby, a measure of the cost of living for Americans at the foreign post compared with the cost of living in Washington, DC. This is the index most appropriate for use by business firms and other private organizations to establish cost-of-living allowances for their American employees stationed abroad. [2] See footnote 4, Table 1348. [3] See footnote 5, Table 1348. [4] There are no U.S. Government employees in Taiwan. The figures listed in this column represent a living cost comparison for American employees of the American Institute in Taiwan, who have some duty-free and other special benefits that may not be available to other Americans in Taiwan.

Source: U.S. Department of State, Bureau of Administration, "Indexes of Living Costs Abroad, Quarters Allowances, and Hardship Differentials," January-April 2012, <http://aoprals.state.gov/content.asp?content_id=186&menu_id=81>.

Table 1373. Percent of Household Final Consumption Expenditures Spent on Food, Alcohol, and Tobacco Consumed at Home by Selected Countries: 2010

Country/Territory	Food [1]	Alcoholic beverages and tobacco	Country/Territory	Food [1]	Alcoholic beverages and tobacco	Country/Territory	Food [1]	Alcoholic beverages and tobacco
United States	**6.4**	**2.1**	Hong Kong	12.1	0.8	Philippines	36.4	1.5
Algeria	43.7	2.0	Hungary	17.9	10.0	Poland	20.2	6.5
Australia	10.7	3.7	Indonesia	32.2	5.8	Portugal	15.6	2.8
Austria	11.1	2.9	Ireland	10.2	5.1	Romania	29.7	3.9
Azerbaijan	45.3	2.1	Israel	17.6	1.7	Russia	29.0	2.2
Belarus	42.1	5.6	Italy	14.8	2.7	Saudi Arabia	23.7	1.3
Belgium	12.7	3.5	Japan	14.8	2.8	Singapore	7.5	2.2
Bolivia	28.0	2.1	Jordan	40.6	5.0	Slovakia	17.9	4.2
Brazil	24.8	1.9	Kazakhstan	35.9	2.6	Slovenia	14.9	4.6
Bulgaria	21.3	3.8	Korea, South	15.0	2.6	South Africa	19.6	4.5
Canada	9.8	3.6	Kuwait	14.5	1.8	Spain	13.1	3.1
Chile	23.2	0.8	Latvia	17.5	6.5	Sweden	12.6	3.2
China [2]	22.3	2.3	Lithuania	21.7	5.6	Switzerland	10.3	3.3
Colombia	18.8	3.2	Malaysia	13.9	1.1	Taiwan [2]	23.9	2.0
Croatia	23.2	4.4	Mexico	22.7	2.3	Thailand	25.0	5.1
Czech Republic	16.0	7.6	Morocco	40.5	1.3	Tunisia	35.6	1.0
Ecuador	17.8	1.5	Netherlands	11.6	2.9	Turkey	21.4	4.1
Egypt	38.0	2.2	New Zealand	15.0	2.8	Turkmenistan	25.8	2.2
Estonia	20.3	8.1	Nigeria	39.8	2.5	Ukraine	41.7	6.4
Finland	12.5	4.8	Norway	13.4	4.2	United Arab Emirates	14.5	0.2
France	13.2	2.8	Pakistan	41.9	1.1	United Kingdom	9.7	3.6
Germany	11.0	3.1	Peru	28.9	2.0	Venezuela	28.9	3.0
						Vietnam	38.0	2.5

[1] Includes nonalcoholic beverages. [2] See footnote 4, Table 1348.

Source: U.S. Department of Agriculture, Economic Research Service, Food Expenditure Series, <http://www.ers.usda.gov/data-products/food-expenditures.aspx#26654>, June 2011.

Table 1374. Gross Public Debt, Expenditures, and Receipts by Country: 1990 to 2011

[Percent of nominal gross domestic product. Gross debt includes one-off revenues from the sale of the mobile telephone licenses. Expenditures and receipts refer to the general government sector, which is a consolidation of accounts for the central, state, and local governments plus social security. Expenditures, or total outlays, are defined as current outlays plus capital outlays. Receipts cover current receipts, but exclude capital receipts. Nontax receipts consist of property income (including dividends and other transfers from public enterprises), fees, charges, sales, fines, capital transfers received by the general government, etc. Minus sign (-) indicates deficit]

Country	Gross debt 1990	Gross debt 2000	Gross debt 2011	Expenditures 1990	Expenditures 2000	Expenditures 2011	Receipts 1990	Receipts 2000	Receipts 2011
United States [1]	**-4.3**	**1.5**	**-9.4**	**37.2**	**33.9**	**40.9**	**32.9**	**35.4**	**31.5**
Australia	-2.0	0.9	-2.6	35.8	35.2	36.1	33.7	36.1	33.5
Austria	-2.5	-1.9	-5.8	51.5	52.2	52.8	49.0	50.3	47.1
Belgium	-6.8	-0.1	-5.2	52.3	49.2	54.0	45.5	49.1	48.8
Canada	-5.8	2.9	-4.5	48.8	41.1	42.9	43.0	44.1	38.4
Czech Republic	(X)	-3.7	-5.0	(X)	41.6	45.4	(X)	37.9	40.3
Denmark	-1.3	2.3	-4.0	55.9	53.3	58.4	54.6	55.5	54.4
Finland	5.4	6.9	-5.2	47.9	48.3	58.1	53.3	55.2	52.9
France	-2.4	-1.5	-8.0	49.4	51.6	54.8	47.0	50.1	46.8
Germany	(X)	1.3	-4.6	(X)	45.1	47.6	(X)	46.4	42.9
Greece	-14.0	-3.7	-10.0	44.9	46.7	50.1	30.8	43.0	40.1
Hungary	(NA)	-3.0	-3.6	(NA)	46.9	48.8	(NA)	43.9	45.2
Iceland	-3.3	1.7	-5.8	38.9	41.9	49.2	35.6	43.6	43.4
Ireland	-2.8	4.8	-11.6	42.8	31.3	45.8	40.0	36.1	34.3
Italy	-11.4	-0.9	-5.1	52.9	46.1	50.6	41.5	45.3	45.5
Japan [2]	2.0	-7.6	-9.4	31.6	39.0	42.2	33.6	31.4	32.7
Korea, South	3.1	5.4	1.1	19.0	22.4	30.9	22.1	27.9	32.0
Netherlands	-5.3	2.0	-5.3	54.9	44.2	51.1	49.6	46.1	45.7
New Zealand	-4.5	1.9	-3.9	53.2	39.2	43.7	48.7	41.1	39.8
Norway	2.2	15.4	10.8	53.3	42.3	44.1	55.5	57.7	54.9
Portugal	-6.1	-3.0	-7.8	40.5	43.1	51.3	34.5	40.2	43.5
Spain	-4.1	-1.0	-7.7	42.8	39.1	46.6	38.7	38.1	38.9
Sweden	3.4	3.7	-2.0	60.1	57.0	55.2	63.4	60.7	53.2
United Kingdom	-2.0	3.7	-12.5	41.5	36.6	53.2	39.4	40.3	40.7

NA Not available. X Not applicable. [1] Receipts exclude the operating surpluses of public enterprises, while expenditures include them. [2] The 2000 expenditures include capital transfers to the Deposit Insurance Company. Receipts include deferred tax payments on postal savings accounts in 2000.

Source: Organisation for Economic Cooperation and Development (OECD), 2011, *OECD Economic Outlook*, Vol. 2010/2 (copyright), OECD Publishing. See also <http://dx.doi.org/10.1787/eco_outlook-v2010-2-en>.

Table 1375. Percent Distribution of Tax Receipts by Country: 1990 to 2008

Country	Total [1]	Income and profits taxes [2]			Social security contributions			Taxes on goods and services [5]		
		Total [3]	Individual	Corporate	Total [4]	Employees	Employers	Total [3]	General consumption taxes [6]	Taxes on specific goods, services [7]
United States:										
1990	100.0	46.0	37.1	8.9	25.1	11.0	12.9	17.4	8.0	7.0
2000	100.0	50.7	41.9	8.7	23.2	10.4	11.6	16.1	7.6	6.3
2008	100.0	46.8	37.9	8.9	24.5	10.8	12.4	17.0	7.8	6.2
Canada:										
1990	100.0	48.6	40.8	7.0	12.1	4.4	7.6	25.8	14.1	10.3
2000	100.0	50.1	36.8	12.2	13.6	5.5	7.8	24.2	14.2	8.6
2008	100.0	49.5	37.3	10.7	14.5	5.8	8.3	23.4	13.2	8.5
France:										
1990	100.0	16.1	10.7	5.3	44.1	13.2	27.2	28.4	18.8	8.7
2000	100.0	24.9	18.0	6.9	36.0	8.9	24.8	25.7	16.9	8.2
2008	100.0	24.1	17.4	6.8	37.2	9.2	25.3	24.5	16.8	6.9
Germany:										
1990	100.0	32.4	27.6	4.8	37.5	16.2	19.1	26.7	16.6	9.2
2000	100.0	30.1	25.3	4.8	39.0	17.2	19.2	28.1	18.4	8.8
2008	100.0	31.9	26.8	5.2	36.4	15.9	17.2	28.9	19.4	8.5
Italy:										
1990	100.0	36.5	26.3	10.0	32.9	6.3	23.6	28.0	14.7	10.6
2000	100.0	33.1	24.8	6.9	28.6	5.4	19.9	27.9	15.4	9.6
2008	100.0	34.6	26.8	8.6	31.1	5.5	21.2	24.4	13.7	8.3
Japan:										
1990	100.0	50.2	27.8	22.4	26.4	10.6	12.7	13.7	4.4	7.5
2000	100.0	34.8	21.1	13.8	35.2	14.7	16.4	19.3	9.1	8.0
2008	100.0	55.4	32.6	22.8	(NA)	(NA)	(NA)	29.1	14.5	11.2
United Kingdom:										
1990	100.0	39.3	29.4	9.9	17.0	6.6	9.9	31.1	16.9	12.6
2000	100.0	39.1	29.3	9.8	17.0	6.8	9.6	31.9	18.1	12.4
2008	100.0	39.9	29.9	9.9	19.2	7.9	10.8	28.8	17.8	9.8

NA Not available. [1] Includes property taxes, employer payroll taxes other than social security contributions, and miscellaneous taxes, not shown separately. [2] Includes taxes on capital gains. [3] Includes other taxes, not shown separately. [4] Includes contributions of self-employed, not shown separately. [5] Taxes on the production, sales, transfer, leasing, and delivery of goods and services and rendering of services. [6] Primary value-added and sales taxes. [7] For example, excise taxes on alcohol, tobacco, and gasoline.

Source: Organisation for Economic Cooperation and Development (OECD), 2010, "Comparative Tables," Taxing Wages database (copyright), <http://dx.doi.org/10.1787/data-00265-en>, accessed May 2010.

Table 1376. Household Tax Burden by Country: 2008

[Percent of gross wage earnings of the average production worker. The tax burden reflects income tax plus employee social security contributions less cash benefits. Minus sign (–) indicates tax credit]

Country	Single person without children	One earner family with two children	Country	Single person without children	One earner family with two children
United States	**22.4**	**5.2**	Japan	20.1	13.8
Australia	22.0	8.6	Korea, South	11.8	9.1
Austria	32.7	18.1	Luxembourg	26.4	0.9
Belgium	41.5	20.2	Mexico	5.3	5.3
Canada	22.8	8.8	Netherlands	31.8	22.6
Czech Republic	22.2	-6.5	New Zealand	18.4	0.6
Denmark	39.4	28.8	Norway	29.3	21.8
Finland	29.2	22.6	Poland	24.3	17.8
France	27.7	17.1	Portugal	22.3	8.7
Germany	41.3	20.8	Slovakia	21.3	2.4
Greece	25.1	25.4	Spain	19.7	12.0
Hungary	38.2	25.3	Sweden	25.3	17.9
Iceland	23.9	3.0	Switzerland	21.5	8.1
Ireland	20.9	2.2	Turkey	27.2	25.7
Italy	29.3	15.1	United Kingdom	25.3	18.5

Source: Organisation for Economic Cooperation and Development (OECD), 2010, "Comparative Tables," Taxing Wages database (copyright), <http://dx.doi.org/10.1787/data-00265-en>, accessed May 2010.

Table 1377. Household Net Saving Rates by Country: 1995 to 2009

[As a percentage of household disposable income. Household savings are estimated by subtracting household consumption expenditure from household disposable income, plus the change in net equity of households in pension funds. Households include households plus nonprofit institutions serving households. Net saving rates are measured after deducting consumption of fixed capital (depreciation), with respect to assets used in enterprises operated by households, as well as owner-occupied dwellings. The household saving rate is calculated as the ratio of household savings to household disposable income (plus the change in net equity of households in pension funds). Minus sign (–) indicates an excess of expenditures over income]

Country	1995	2000	2003	2004	2005	2006	2007	2008	2009
United States	**5.7**	**3.0**	**3.8**	**3.4**	**1.5**	**2.5**	**2.1**	**4.2**	**6.2**
EU-27 [1]	(NA)	6.4	6.9	6.3	6.0	5.6	5.3	5.4	7.8
Australia [2]	6.4	2.6	-0.9	-1.5	0.4	1.3	0.5	4.5	(NA)
Austria	11.8	9.2	9.1	9.3	9.7	10.4	11.6	11.8	11.1
Belgium	16.4	12.3	12.2	10.8	10.2	11.0	11.4	11.9	13.5
Canada	9.4	4.8	2.7	3.2	2.2	3.6	2.9	3.7	4.7
Chile	(NA)	6.1	6.1	6.8	6.7	7.3	7.3	7.4	7.2
Czech Republic	10.0	3.3	2.4	0.5	3.2	4.8	6.3	5.7	4.5
Denmark	1.3	-4.0	2.4	-1.3	-4.2	-2.3	-4.0	-3.3	-0.5
Finland	3.9	0.5	1.4	2.7	0.9	-1.1	-0.9	-0.2	3.9
France	12.7	11.8	12.5	12.4	11.4	11.4	11.9	11.6	12.5
Germany	11.0	9.2	10.3	10.4	10.5	10.6	10.8	11.7	11.1
Greece	(NA)	-4.5	-6.2	-6.9	-9.7	-9.5	-3.0	-8.3	-3.2
Ireland	(NA)	(NA)	2.4	5.5	3.6	2.2	(NA)	3.8	12.1
Italy	17.0	8.4	10.3	10.2	9.9	9.1	8.4	8.2	7.1
Japan	(NA)	8.8	3.9	3.6	3.9	3.7	2.5	2.3	(NA)
Korea, South	(NA)	9.3	5.2	9.2	7.2	5.2	2.9	2.9	3.6
Netherlands	14.0	6.9	7.6	7.4	6.4	6.1	6.9	5.7	6.8
Norway	4.8	4.3	8.9	7.2	10.1	0.1	1.5	3.7	7.3
Poland	14.6	10.0	7.7	7.0	7.3	7.5	6.1	0.8	7.8
Russia	(NA)	(NA)	(NA)	(NA)	11.0	12.4	12.1	10.9	(NA)
Slovakia	5.2	6.0	1.1	0.3	1.1	0.4	2.4	1.5	(NA)
Slovenia	(NA)	7.0	7.6	9.2	11.5	11.9	9.9	9.8	10.2
Spain	(NA)	5.9	6.0	4.9	4.7	4.2	3.6	6.6	11.9
Sweden	9.5	4.3	7.2	6.1	5.5	6.6	8.8	11.2	12.9
Switzerland	12.7	11.7	9.4	9.0	10.1	11.4	12.6	11.8	(NA)
United Kingdom	6.9	0.1	0.4	-1.6	-1.2	-2.2	-3.2	-2.8	1.2

NA Not available. [1] See footnote 4, Table 1391 for list of EU-27 countries. [2] Data refer to fiscal year.

Source: Organisation for Economic Cooperation and Development (OECD), 2011, *OECD Factbook 2011-2012: Economic, Environmental and Social Statistics*, OECD Publishing (copyright), accessed October 2012, <http://www.oecd-ilibrary.org/economics/oecd-factbook-2011-2012_factbook-2011-en>.

Table 1378. Insurance and Pensions by Country: 1999 and 2009

| Country | Insurance | | | | | | Pension, [1] 2009 | | |
| | Direct gross premiums (percent of GDP) | | 2009 premiums (mil. U.S. dol.) | | Financial assets [2] (mil. U.S. dol.) | | Financial to assets (mil. U.S. dol.) | Contributions to pension funds (percent of GDP) | Benefits paid by pension funds (percent of GDP) |
	1999	2009	Life	Non-life	1999	2009			
United States	**10.5**	**11.4**	**802,310**	**1,222,375**	**3,334,437**	**628,045**	**9,603,619**	**[3] 3.4**	**[3] 4.5**
Australia	8.8	[4] 5.6	31,995	25,435	133,167	[4] 209,523	808,224	8.9	4.9
Austria	5.4	6.0	[4] 10,576	[4] 15,705	[5] 45,066	101,436	18,987	[4] 0.4	[4] 0.2
Belgium	6.9	8.2	25,650	13,927	(NA)	(NA)	19,165	0.4	0.3
Canada	6.4	7.3	38,478	74,215	190,851	388,908	806,350	3.2	2.7
Czech Republic	3.0	3.9	3,162	4,405	3,620	15,915	11,332	0.9	0.4
Denmark	6.4	[4] 9.5	[4] 21,948	[4] 10,551	[6] 60,856	(NA)	133,980	0.6	0.7
Finland	4.4	3.9	4,654	4,816	25,186	63,633	182,286	9.8	10.5
France	8.3	10.4	50,763	95,777	115,468	2,094,590	[4] 21,931	(NA)	(NA)
Germany	6.6	[4] 6.6	114,003	132,765	777,311	258,647	173,810	0.3	0.2
Greece	2.0	[4] 2.2	3,316	3,900	[7] 3,351	11,032	63	(Z)	(Z)
Iceland	2.6	2.3	26	251	577	(NA)	14,351	6.6	5.0
Ireland	14.0	20.3	37,759	8,902	[5] 23,251	58,922	100,278	(NA)	(NA)
Italy	5.5	7.7	115,096	51,748	[7] 156,926	517,175	86,818	0.6	0.2
Japan	7.4	[4] 8.3	376,297	96,709	1,923,772	[4] 3,045,193	[8] 301,994	[8] 0.4	[8] 0.2
Korea, South	11.6	11.1	61,514	37,629	98,057	2,586	29,632	0.2	0.3
Luxembourg	27.5	44.1	21,502	1,562	22,130	[9] 67,921	1,171	0.9	0.1
Mexico	1.7	[4] 1.7	7,719	9,821	(NA)	33,888	107,135	0.6	0.2
Netherlands	9.3	7.9	34,142	33,027	257,354	323,717	997,922	5.3	3.9
Norway	4.5	5.6	[4] 14,186	9,287	[7] 51,063	14,053 [4]	27,852	0.5	0.3
Poland	2.7	3.8	9,708	6,772	6,097	30,185	58,143	1.6	(Z)
Portugal	5.6	8.2	13,957	5,770	20,515	73,573	30,441	0.6	0.7
Slovakia	2.8	3.3	1,487	1,401	878	6,295	5,508	6.2	(NA)
Spain	5.5	5.7	40,563	44,605	(NA)	225,037	118,159	0.6	0.4
Sweden	6.8	5.8	12,933	12,536	211,523	328,973	33,435	(NA)	(NA)
Switzerland	12.5	10.0	27,341	29,958	(NA)	371,870	551,450	8.4	5.5
Turkey	1.4	[3] 1.3	1,439	7,032	1,984	7,299	14,017	[9] 0.3	0.1
United Kingdom	13.9	[4] 14.5	[4] 282,776	[4] 116,853	1,473,777	[4] 2,385,748	1,753,016	2.7	3.2

NA Not available or not applicable. Z Less than 0.05 percent. [1] All types of plans are included (occupational and personal, mandatory and voluntary) covering both public and private sector workers. Further details can be found at <www.oecd.org/daf/pensions/gps>. [2] Investments by direct insurance companies. [3] 2007 data. [4] 2008 data. [5] 1996 data. [6] 1993 data. [7] 1997 data. [8] 2005 data. [9] 2006 data.

Source: Organization for Economic Cooperation and Development (OECD), 2011, *OECD Insurance Statistics* database (copyright), <http://dx.doi.org/10.1787/ins-data-en>, accessed April 2011.

Table 1379. Annual Percent Changes in Consumer Prices by Country: 2005 to 2011

[Change from previous year. These statistics are generally comparable to those prepared by the International Monetary Fund and published in previous editions of the Statistical Abstract. For general comments concerning the data, see text, this section. For additional qualifications of the data for individual countries, see source. Minus sign (-) indicates decrease]

Country	2005	2008	2009	2010	2011	Country	2005	2008	2009	2010	2011
United States	**3.4**	**3.8**	**-0.4**	**1.6**	**2.6**	Malaysia	3.0	5.4	0.6	1.6	2.7
						Mexico	4.0	5.1	5.3	4.2	2.5
Argentina	9.6	8.6	6.3	10.5	6.7	New Zealand	3.0	4.0	2.1	2.3	3.4
Australia	2.7	4.4	1.8	2.8	2.5	Niger	7.8	11.3	4.4	0.8	3.2
Bangladesh	7.0	8.9	5.4	8.1	6.3	Nigeria	17.8	11.6	11.6	13.7	8.3
Bolivia	5.4	14.0	3.3	2.5	7.6	Norway	1.5	3.8	2.2	2.4	1.2
Brazil	6.9	5.7	4.9	5.0	4.8	Pakistan	9.1	20.3	13.7	13.9	9.1
Cambodia	6.4	24.9	-0.6	4.0	4.2	Paraguay	6.8	10.2	2.6	4.7	7.2
Canada	2.2	2.4	0.3	1.8	2.3	Peru	1.6	5.8	2.9	1.5	2.0
Chile	3.1	8.7	0.4	1.4	2.6	Philippines	7.7	9.3	3.3	3.8	3.7
China	1.8	5.9	-0.7	3.3	3.8	Poland	2.1	4.4	3.8	2.7	3.3
Colombia	5.1	7.0	4.2	2.3	2.3	Romania	9.1	7.9	5.6	6.1	4.9
Denmark	1.8	3.4	1.3	2.3	2.1	Russia	12.7	14.1	11.7	6.9	6.8
Ecuador	2.4	8.4	5.2	3.6	2.6	Saudi Arabia	0.5	9.9	5.1	5.3	2.8
Hungary	3.6	6.1	4.2	4.9	3.2	Singapore	0.5	6.6	0.6	2.8	3.8
Iceland	4.0	12.7	12.0	5.4	2.2	South Africa	3.4	11.5	7.1	4.3	2.9
India	4.2	8.4	10.8	12.0	6.6	Sri Lanka	11.0	22.6	3.4	5.9	6.7
Indonesia	10.5	9.5	4.8	5.1	4.4	Sweden	0.5	3.5	-0.3	1.3	2.2
Iran	13.4	25.6	13.5	10.2	9.6	Switzerland	1.2	2.4	-0.5	0.7	0.7
Israel	1.3	4.6	3.3	2.7	3.3	Thailand	4.5	5.5	-0.8	3.3	2.8
Japan	-0.3	1.4	-1.4	-0.7	0.2	Turkey	8.2	10.5	6.2	8.6	3.5
Kenya	10.2	26.3	9.2	4.0	6.5	United Kingdom	2.1	3.6	2.2	3.3	3.5
Korea, South	2.7	4.7	2.8	3.0	3.3	Venezuela	16.0	31.5	28.6	29.1	16.8

Source: World Bank, Global Economic Monitor, (Copyright), <http://data.worldbank.org/data-catalog/global-economic-monitor>, accessed September 2012.

Table 1380. Unemployment Rates by Country: 2000 to 2011

[Annual averages. The standardized unemployment rates shown here are calculated as the number of unemployed persons as a percentage of the civilian labor force. The unemployed are persons of working age who, in the reference period, are without work, available for work, and have taken specific steps to find work]

Country	2000	2005	2010	2011	Country	2000	2005	2010	2011
OECD, total [1]	6.1	6.6	8.3	(NA)	Ireland	4.5	4.7	13.7	14.4
EU-27 [2]	9.2	8.9	9.6	9.6	Italy	10.7	7.8	8.5	8.4
United States	**4.0**	**5.1**	**9.6**	**8.9**	Japan	4.7	4.4	5.1	4.5
Australia	6.3	5.0	5.2	5.1	Korea, South	4.4	3.7	3.7	3.4
Austria	3.6	5.2	4.4	4.2	Mexico	2.6	3.5	5.2	5.2
Belgium	7.0	8.4	8.3	7.1	Netherlands	2.7	4.7	4.5	4.4
Canada	6.8	6.8	8.0	7.4	New Zealand	6.2	3.8	6.5	6.5
Chile	9.2	8.0	8.1	7.2	Norway	3.5	4.6	3.6	3.3
Czech Republic	8.9	8.0	7.3	6.7	Poland	16.1	17.7	9.6	9.6
Denmark	4.6	5.0	7.6	7.8	Portugal	4.0	7.7	10.8	12.8
Finland	9.8	8.4	8.4	7.8	Spain	13.9	9.2	20.1	21.7
France	8.4	8.7	9.3	(NA)	Sweden	5.9	7.8	8.4	7.5
Germany	7.8	11.2	7.1	5.9	Switzerland	2.5	4.2	4.2	3.8
Greece	11.2	9.6	11.8	16.3	Turkey	6.5	10.6	11.9	9.8
Hungary	6.5	7.3	11.2	11.0	United Kingdom	5.5	4.7	7.8	7.9

NA Not available. [1] For complete OECD membership listing, see Section 30 introduction. [2] See footnote 4, Table 1391.

Source: Organisation for Economic Co-operation and Development (OECD), 2012, "Labour: Labour force statistics," Main Economic Indicators (database), <http://dx.doi.org/10.1787/data-00046-en>, accessed 08 August 2012 (copyright).

Table 1381. Civilian Labor Force, Employment, and Unemployment by Country: 1990 to 2011

[125,840 represents 125,840,000. Data based on U.S. labor force definitions (see source) except that minimum age for population base varies as follows: United States, Canada, France, Sweden, and United Kingdom, 16 years; Australia, Japan, Netherlands, Germany, and Italy (beginning 1993), 15 years; and Italy (prior to 1993), 14 years]

Year	United States	Canada	Aus-tralia	Japan	France	Ger-many [1]	Italy	Nether-lands	Swe-den	United King-dom
Civilian labor force (1,000):										
1990	[2] 125,840	14,047	8,444	62,986	24,605	29,412	22,670	6,767	4,597	28,766
2000	[2] 142,583	15,632	9,591	66,710	25,970	39,301	23,766	[2] 8,008	4,490	28,962
2005	149,320	17,056	10,529	65,384	27,033	[2] 40,696	24,179	8,400	[2] 4,695	30,148
2010	153,889	18,263	11,868	65,111	28,053	41,495	24,699	[2] 8,568	4,945	31,424
2011	153,617	18,434	12,049	65,040	28,102	42,046	24,820	8,572	5,004	31,646
Labor force participation rate: [3]										
1990	[2] 66.5	67.4	64.7	62.6	56.8	55.0	47.2	57.0	67.4	64.3
2000	67.1	66.0	64.4	61.7	56.3	56.7	49.5	[2] 63.0	63.8	62.8
2005	66.0	67.3	65.4	59.5	56.2	[2] 57.5	48.7	64.2	[2] 64.8	63.1
2010	64.7	67.0	66.5	59.1	56.5	58.6	48.1	[2] 63.7	64.9	63.2
2011	64.1	66.8	66.5	58.7	56.3	59.2	48.1	63.3	65.1	63.2
Civilian employment (1,000):										
1990	[2] 118,793	12,964	7,859	61,706	22,629	27,952	21,080	6,251	4,513	26,713
2000	[2] 136,891	14,677	8,989	63,790	23,731	36,236	21,358	[2] 7,762	4,230	27,375
2005	141,730	16,032	9,998	62,908	24,601	[2] 36,123	22,290	7,959	[2] 4,334	28,681
2010	139,064	16,969	11,247	62,011	25,400	38,549	22,597	[2] 8,178	4,534	28,945
2011	139,869	17,238	11,435	62,307	25,474	39,544	22,712	8,183	4,631	29,086
Employment-population ratio: [4]										
1990	[2] 62.8	62.2	60.2	61.3	52.2	52.3	43.9	52.7	66.1	59.8
2000	64.4	62.0	60.3	59.0	51.5	52.2	44.5	[2] 61.1	60.1	59.4
2005	62.7	63.3	62.1	57.3	51.1	[2] 51.1	44.9	60.9	[2] 59.8	60.0
2010	58.5	62.3	63.0	56.2	51.2	54.4	44.0	[2] 60.8	59.5	58.2
2011	58.4	62.5	63.1	56.2	51.0	55.7	44.0	60.5	60.3	58.0
Unemployment rate:										
1990	[2] 5.6	7.7	6.9	2.0	8.0	5.0	7.0	7.6	1.8	7.1
2000	4.0	6.1	6.3	4.4	8.6	7.8	10.1	[2] 3.1	5.8	5.5
2005	5.1	6.0	5.0	3.8	9.0	[2] 11.2	7.8	5.3	[2] 7.7	4.9
2010	9.6	7.1	5.2	4.8	9.5	7.1	8.5	[2] 4.6	8.3	7.9
2011	8.9	6.5	5.1	4.2	9.4	6.0	8.5	4.5	7.5	8.1
Under 25 years old	17.3	12.8	11.3	8.1	22.3	8.5	29.4	7.8	22.7	21.2
Teenagers [5]	24.4	17.7	16.1	9.7	29.6	9.9	47.4	10.7	34.1	31.2
20 to 24 years old	14.6	10.1	8.4	7.7	20.6	8.1	26.5	5.7	18.3	16.5
25 years old and over	7.6	5.4	3.7	3.9	7.9	5.6	7.0	3.9	5.2	5.8

[1] Unified Germany for 1991 onward. Prior to 1991, data relate to the former West Germany. [2] Break in series. Data not comparable with prior years. [3] Civilian labor force as a percent of the civilian working-age population. Germany and Japan include the institutionalized population as part of the working-age population. [4] Civilian employment as a percent of the civilian working-age population. Germany and Japan include the institutionalized population as part of the working-age population. [5] 16 to 19-year-olds in the United States, Canada, France, Sweden, and the United Kingdom; 15 to 19-year-olds in Australia, Japan, Germany, Italy, and the Netherlands.

Source: U.S. Bureau of Labor Statistics, *International Comparisons of Annual Labor Force Statistics, Adjusted to U.S. Concepts, 16 Countries, 1970–2011*, June 2012. See also <http://www.bls.gov/fls/flscomparelf.htm>.

Table 1382. Percent of Persons Not in Education or at Work: 2008

[Represents those persons not in education and either unemployed or not in the labor force]

Country	15 to 19 years old			20 to 24 years old		
	Total	Unemployed	Not in the labor force	Total	Unemployed	Not in the labor force
Australia............................	6.3	3.0	3.3	10.5	3.7	6.8
Belgium.............................	5.5	1.9	3.6	14.2	7.8	6.4
Brazil................................	13.8	3.7	10.1	22.5	7.6	14.9
Canada..............................	7.3	2.9	4.4	13.0	5.6	7.4
Czech Republic...................	2.7	1.6	1.1	10.6	4.1	6.5
Denmark............................	2.8	1.1	1.7	7.7	2.8	4.9
Finland..............................	5.1	1.9	3.2	12.0	5.5	6.5
France...............................	5.3	2.6	2.7	13.8	8.3	5.5
Germany............................	3.7	2.0	1.7	14.0	7.0	7.0
Greece..............................	8.4	2.3	6.1	17.1	9.9	7.2
Hungary............................	5.7	1.6	4.1	18.4	7.5	10.9
Israel................................	22.3	1.2	21.1	37.5	5.3	32.2
Italy..................................	9.6	2.7	6.9	22.0	8.3	13.7
Mexico..............................	23.2	2.8	20.4	(NA)	(NA)	(NA)
Poland...............................	2.3	0.7	1.6	15.6	7.1	8.5
Portugal............................	7.1	3.7	3.4	13.4	8.2	5.2
Spain................................	10.6	5.4	5.2	19.5	10.4	9.1
Sweden.............................	4.4	1.8	2.6	12.9	6.5	6.4
Switzerland........................	9.4	2.4	7.0	9.1	3.7	5.4
United States..................	**7.3**	**2.4**	**4.9**	**17.2**	**6.4**	**10.8**

NA Not available.

Source: Organization for Economic Cooperation and Development (OECD), 2010, "How successful are students in moving from education to work?," Education at a Glance 2010: OECD Indicators, OECD Publishing (copyright). See also <http://dx.doi.org/10.1787/eag-2010-24-en>, accessed April 2011.

Table 1383. Female Labor Force Participation Rates by Country: 1980 to 2011

[In percent. Female labor force of all ages divided by female population 15-64 years old]

Country	1980	1990	2000	2010	2011	Country	1980	1990	2000	2010	2011
OECD, total [1].........	**(NA)**	**(NA)**	**60.4**	**4 62.8**	**(NA)**	Ireland...............	36.3	43.8	56.9	63.4	63.4
						Italy..................	39.6	45.9	46.8	51.5	52.0
EU–27 [2]..............	(NA)	(NA)	61.0	65.4	65.8	Korea, South........	54.8	60.3	64.0	68.6	65.2
United States........	**59.5**	**68.6**	**70.8**	**68.9**	**68.3**	Japan.................	46.1	51.2	54.9	58.3	58.6
Australia..............	52.5	62.2	66.1	71.7	72.3	Luxembourg.........	39.9	50.3	69.4	5 95.7	(NA)
Austria................	48.7	55.4	62.2	70.0	70.2	Mexico...............	34.0	23.4	43.3	49.1	(NA)
Belgium...............	46.9	52.4	56.6	62.2	(NA)	Netherlands.........	35.5	52.4	65.5	72.8	(NA)
Canada...............	57.3	67.5	69.8	74.4	74.5	New Zealand........	44.5	65.4	68.0	74.1	74.9
Chile..................	(NA)	(NA)	38.5	52.1	54.7	Norway..............	62.3	71.2	76.2	77.1	77.5
Czech Republic.......	(NA)	69.1	64.2	62.3	(NA)	Poland...............	(NA)	(NA)	60.5	58.4	59.0
Denmark..............	71.1	78.2	75.6	76.1	75.7	Portugal.............	54.6	62.4	67.3	73.8	(NA)
Finland................	70.1	73.8	72.2	73.3	73.6	Slovakia.............	(NA)	(NA)	63.0	61.5	(NA)
France.......... [3]...	54.0	59.5	64.9	67.3	(NA)	Spain.................	32.4	41.5	52.0	66.1	67.2
Germany [3]...........	52.8	56.7	63.6	71.5	72.5	Sweden..............	74.3	80.9	75.0	77.8	79.0
Greece................	33.0	43.6	49.5	5 55.0	(NA)	Switzerland.........	54.3	65.7	76.8	82.2	(NA)
Hungary..............	(NA)	(NA)	52.1	56.4	56.7	Turkey...............	(NA)	36.8	30.3	30.4	31.8
Iceland...............	(NA)	(NA)	82.8	82.1	81.6	United Kingdom.....	58.2	66.4	67.8	70.5	70.8

NA Not available. [1] For complete OECD membership listing, see Section 30 introduction. [2] See footnote 4, Table 1391. [3] Prior to 1991, data are for former West Germany. [4] 2009 data. [5] 2009 estimate.

Source: Organisation for Economic Co-operation and Development (OECD), 2012, "Labour Market Statistics: Labour force statistics by sex and age: indicators," OECD Employment and Labour Market Statistics (database), <http://dx.doi.org/10.1787/data-00310-en>, accessed 08 August, 2012 (copyright).

Table 1384. Civilian Employment-Population Ratio: 1990 to 2011

[Civilian employment as a percent of the civilian working-age population. See headnote, Table 1381]

Country	Women					Men				
	1990	2000	2005	2010	2011	1990	2000	2005	2010	2011
United States [1]..................	**54.3**	**57.5**	**56.2**	**53.6**	**53.2**	**72.0**	**71.9**	**69.6**	**63.7**	**63.9**
Canada...........................	54.1	56.0	58.1	58.5	58.5	70.6	68.2	68.6	66.2	66.6
Australia..........................	49.4	52.5	55.0	56.6	56.8	71.3	68.4	69.4	69.5	69.5
Japan..............................	48.0	46.4	45.7	45.7	45.6	75.4	72.5	69.7	67.5	67.6
France............................	42.7	44.6	45.6	46.5	46.4	62.8	59.1	57.3	56.3	56.1
Germany [1, 2, 3, 4].................	40.5	44.4	44.9	48.9	50.2	65.6	60.6	57.7	60.2	61.5
Italy [1]............................	29.2	32.7	34.1	34.5	34.7	60.0	57.4	56.8	54.4	54.2
Netherlands [1, 3, 4]...............	39.5	51.7	53.9	55.3	55.4	66.5	70.8	68.1	66.4	65.7
Sweden [4]........................	61.8	56.0	56.0	55.6	56.6	70.6	64.2	63.8	63.5	64.0
United Kingdom..................	50.3	52.5	53.7	52.9	52.8	70.0	66.9	66.8	63.8	63.6

[1] Break in series between 1990 and 1995. [2] Unified Germany for 1991 onward. Prior to 1991, data relate to the former West Germany. [3] Break in series between 1995 and 2000. [4] Break in series between 2000 and 2009.

Source: U.S. Bureau of Labor Statistics, International Comparisons of Annual Labor Force, Adjusted to U.S. Concepts, 16 Countries, 1970–2011, June 2012. See also <http://www.bls.gov/fls/flscomparelf.htm>.

Table 1385. Civilian Employment by Industry and Country: 2000 and 2011

[136,891 represents 136,891,000. Civilian employment approximating U.S. concepts. See headnote, Table 1381]

Industry	United States [1,2]	Canada [1]	Australia	Japan	France [2]	Germany [2]	Italy	Sweden [2]	United Kingdom
TOTAL EMPLOYMENT (1,000)									
2000, total	**136,891**	**14,677**	**8,989**	**63,790**	**23,731**	**36,236**	**21,358**	**4,230**	**27,375**
Agriculture, forestry, fishing [3]	2,464	479	442	3,070	1,097	959	1,006	122	330
Industry [4]	30,050	3,204	1,856	19,710	5,836	11,898	6,541	1,000	6,205
Manufacturing	19,644	2,240	1,083	13,180	4,241	8,647	4,891	762	4,057
Services [5]	104,377	10,994	6,691	41,010	16,798	23,379	13,811	3,108	20,840
2011, total	**139,869**	**17,238**	**11,435**	**62,307**	**25,474**	**39,544**	**22,712**	**4,631**	**29,086**
Agriculture, forestry, fishing [3]	2,254	367	329	2,341	753	648	848	93	354
Industry [4]	24,192	3,290	2,235	15,486	5,328	10,666	6,194	884	5,142
Manufacturing	14,336	1,758	971	10,469	3,410	7,923	4,309	563	2,840
Services [5]	113,423	13,581	8,871	44,480	19,393	28,230	15,670	3,654	23,590
PERCENT DISTRIBUTION [6]									
2000, total	**100.0**	**100.0**	**100.0**	**100.0**	**100.0**	**100.0**	**100.0**	**100.0**	**100.0**
Agriculture, forestry, fishing [3]	1.8	3.3	4.9	4.8	4.6	2.6	4.7	2.9	1.2
Industry [4]	22.0	21.8	20.6	30.9	24.6	32.8	30.6	23.6	22.7
Manufacturing	14.4	15.3	12.0	20.7	17.9	23.9	22.9	18.0	14.8
Services [5]	76.2	74.9	74.5	64.3	70.8	64.6	64.7	73.5	76.1
2011, total	**100.0**	**100.0**	**100.0**	**100.0**	**100.0**	**100.0**	**100.0**	**100.0**	**100.0**
Agriculture, forestry, fishing [3]	1.6	2.1	2.9	3.8	3.0	1.6	3.7	2.0	1.2
Industry [4]	17.3	19.1	19.5	24.9	20.9	27.0	27.3	19.1	17.7
Manufacturing	10.2	10.2	8.5	16.8	13.4	20.0	19.0	12.2	9.8
Services [5]	81.1	78.8	77.6	71.3	76.1	71.4	69.0	78.9	81.1

[1] Data for the United States and Canada are based on the 2002 North American Industry Classification System (NAICS). [2] Break in series between 2000 and 2011. [3] Includes hunting. [4] Includes manufacturing, mining, and construction. [5] Transportation, communication, public utilities, trade, finance, public administration, private household services, and miscellaneous services. [6] Percent of total civilian employment.

Source: U.S. Bureau of Labor Statistics, *International Comparisons of Annual Labor Force Statistics, Adjusted to U.S. Concepts, 16 Countries, 1960–2011*, June 2012. See also <http://www.bls.gov/fls/flscomparelf.htm>.

Table 1386. Educational Performance: 2008 and 2009

[Tertiary-type A includes education leading to a BA, Master's, or equivalent degree, and advanced research programs. Performance figures were gathered from the Program for International Student Assessment (PISA), an internationally standardized assessment jointly developed by participating countries, which takes place in 3-year cycles. To implement PISA, each of the participating countries selects a nationally representative sample of 15-year-olds, regardless of grade level. Tests are typically administered to between 4,500 and 10,000 students in each country]

Country	Student performance on the combined reading, scientific, and mathematical literacy scales, 2009			Educational attainment of adult population and current graduation rates, 2008 (percent)	
	Mean score on the combined reading literacy scale [1]	Mean score on the mathematical literacy scale [2]	Mean score on the scientific literacy scale [3]	Upper secondary or higher attainment (25 to 64 years old) [4]	Tertiary-type A attainment (25 t o 64 years old) [5]
Australia	515	514	527	70	26
Austria	470	496	494	81	11
Canada	524	527	529	87	25
Czech Republic	478	493	500	91	14
Finland	536	541	554	81	22
France	496	497	498	70	16
Germany	497	513	520	85	16
Greece	483	466	470	61	17
Italy	486	483	489	53	14
Japan	520	529	539	(NA)	24
Korea	539	546	538	79	26
Luxembourg	472	489	484	68	20
Mexico	425	419	416	34	15
Poland	500	495	508	87	20
Spain	481	483	488	51	20
Sweden	497	494	495	85	23
Switzerland	501	534	517	87	23
United Kingdom	494	492	514	70	24
United States	**500**	**487**	**502**	**89**	**32**
OECD mean	493	496	501	71	21

NA Not available. [1] Reading literacy is understanding, using, and reflecting on written texts in order to achieve one's goals, to develop one's knowledge and potential, and to participate in society. [2] Mathematical literacy is an individual's capacity to identify and understand the role that mathematics plays in the world, to make well-founded judgements, and to use and engage with mathematics in ways that meet the needs of that individual's life. [3] Scientific literacy is the capacity to use scientific knowledge to identify questions and to draw evidence-based conclusions in order to understand and help make decisions about the natural world and the changes made to it through human activity. [4] Excluding ISCED 3C short programs. [5] Includes advanced research programs.

Source: Organisation for Economic Cooperation and Development (OECD), 2010, *Education at a Glance 2010: OECD Indicators*, OECD Publishing (copyright). See also <http://www.pisa.oecd.org>.

Table 1387. World Supply and Utilization of Major Crops, Livestock, and Products: 2004 to 2011

[In millions of units (210.0 represents 210,000,000). For major crops, data ending in year shown. For meat and dairy, calendar year data, selected countries]

Commodity	2004	2005	2006	2007	2008	2009	2010	2011
Wheat:								
Area (hectares)	210.0	217.2	219.7	213.0	218.2	225.3	227.2	222.6
Production (metric tons)	555.4	626.7	619.1	596.3	612.1	682.8	684.3	648.7
Exports (metric tons) [1]	108.7	111.8	117.0	111.8	117.2	143.5	135.8	131.4
Consumption (metric tons) [2]	589.6	607.1	622.2	616.1	617.7	642.7	650.5	653.5
Ending stocks (metric tons) [3]	135.9	155.5	152.5	132.6	127.0	167.1	200.9	196.1
Coarse grains:								
Area (hectares)	306.0	300.5	301.3	305.4	318.7	313.5	310.7	310.3
Production (metric tons)	916.1	1,015.6	980.3	988.6	1,080.8	1,111.3	1,116.3	1,100.4
Exports (metric tons) [1]	103.2	101.0	107.3	117.8	127.2	113.1	122.9	115.3
Consumption (metric tons) [2]	944.8	978.8	994.3	1,013.5	1,057.9	1,081.6	1,114.7	1,127.7
Ending stocks (metric tons) [3]	143.3	180.2	166.2	141.2	164.1	193.9	195.5	168.1
Rice, milled:								
Area (hectares)	149.3	151.8	153.8	154.5	155.2	157.8	156.0	157.3
Production (metric tons)	392.5	401.2	418.2	420.0	432.3	447.5	440.5	451.2
Exports (metric tons) [1]	27.4	28.3	29.7	31.4	31.7	28.9	31.2	33.7
Consumption (metric tons) [2]	413.9	408.7	415.6	421.5	427.4	435.9	437.9	447.5
Ending stocks (metric tons) [3]	81.5	74.0	76.6	75.1	80.0	91.5	94.2	97.9
Total grains: [4]								
Area (hectares)	665.3	669.6	674.8	673.0	692.1	696.5	693.9	690.2
Production (metric tons)	1,864.1	2,043.6	2,017.7	2,004.8	2,125.2	2,241.6	2,241.1	2,200.3
Exports (metric tons) [1]	239.4	241.0	254.0	261.0	276.1	285.5	289.9	280.3
Consumption (metric tons) [2]	1,948.3	1,994.7	2,032.1	2,051.2	2,103.0	2,160.2	2,203.0	2,228.7
Ending stocks (metric tons) [3]	360.8	409.7	395.3	348.9	371.1	452.5	490.6	462.2
Oilseeds:								
Crush (metric tons)	279.7	302.2	319.5	328.6	339.8	338.9	357.5	375.3
Production (metric tons)	335.8	381.3	391.3	403.6	391.3	396.5	442.7	453.1
Exports (metric tons)	66.8	74.4	75.4	82.8	91.8	94.2	108.1	107.8
Ending stocks (metric tons)	45.0	57.8	64.5	72.4	60.4	55.0	71.2	78.9
Meals: [5]								
Production (metric tons)	190.9	206.5	217.1	224.5	231.8	229.0	243.7	256.4
Exports (metric tons)	59.1	61.3	66.4	69.6	72.3	69.3	72.0	76.9
Oils: [6]								
Production (metric tons)	102.9	111.7	118.9	121.8	128.6	133.7	140.2	146.6
Exports (metric tons)	39.3	42.9	47.8	49.2	53.9	56.0	58.1	59.8
Cotton:								
Area (hectares)	32.3	35.7	34.7	34.5	32.8	30.6	30.1	33.5
Production (bales) [7]	96.7	121.6	116.4	122.2	119.7	107.3	101.6	115.3
Exports (bales) [7]	33.2	35.0	44.9	37.6	39.1	30.2	35.6	35.6
Consumption (bales) [7]	97.2	107.9	115.0	122.1	121.5	107.7	118.9	114.4
Ending stocks (bales) [7]	48.1	60.6	61.8	62.4	60.9	60.8	44.2	45.2
Beef and Pork:								
Production (metric tons)	146.7	149.7	152.9	152.4	156.0	157.6	159.8	158.0
Consumption (metric tons)	146.2	148.8	151.8	151.7	155.5	156.7	158.8	156.7
Exports (metric tons) [1]	11.4	12.4	12.8	12.8	13.8	13.1	13.8	14.4
Broilers and Turkeys:								
Production (metric tons)	66.5	69.8	71.1	75.3	78.9	79.3	83.6	86.3
Consumption (metric tons)	65.7	69.1	70.9	75.0	78.0	78.7	82.5	85.0
Exports (metric tons) [1]	6.6	7.5	7.2	8.0	9.1	8.8	9.5	9.8
Dairy:								
Milk production (metric tons)	415.3	421.6	427.9	437.1	435.4	435.1	441.6	449.1

[1] Excludes intra-EU (European Union) trade but includes intra-FSU (Former Soviet Union) trade. [2] Where stocks data are not available, consumption includes stock changes. [3] Stocks data are based on differing marketing years and do not represent levels at a given date. Data not available for all countries. [4] Wheat, coarse grains, and rice. [5] Includes the following types of meals: copra, cottonseed, fishmeal, palm kernel, rapeseed, sunflower, soybean, and peanut. [6] Includes the following types of oils: coconut, cottonseed, olive, palm, palm kernel, peanut, sunflower, rapeseed, and soybean. [7] 480-pound bales.

Source: U.S. Department of Agriculture, Economic Research Service, "Agricultural Outlook: Statistical Indicators," January 2012, <http://www.ers.usda.gov/publications/agoutlook/aotables/>.

Table 1388. World Crop Production Summary: 2010 to 2012

[In millions of metric tons, (651.1 represents 651,100,000)]

Country	Wheat 2010–2011	Wheat 2011–2012 prel.	Coarse grains 2010–2011	Coarse grains 2011–2012 prel.	Rice (milled) 2010–2011	Rice (milled) 2011–2012 prel.	Oilseeds [1] 2010–2011	Oilseeds [1] 2011–2012 prel.	Cotton 2010–2011	Cotton 2011–2012 prel.
World............	651.1	694.2	1,096.6	1,145.0	449.4	464.0	456.5	437.0	116.4	123.1
United States......	60.1	54.4	330.2	323.7	7.6	5.9	100.4	91.3	18.1	15.6
Canada............	23.2	25.3	22.3	21.9	(2)	(2)	17.2	18.4	(2)	(2)
Mexico............	3.7	3.7	29.3	25.8	0.1	0.1	0.7	0.9	0.7	1.2
EU-27 [3]............	135.7	137.4	140.6	146.0	2.0	2.0	29.1	29.0	1.2	1.6
Russia.............	41.5	56.2	16.4	32.8	0.7	0.7	7.2	12.4	(2)	(2)
Ukraine............	16.8	22.1	21.4	33.3	0.1	0.1	11.6	13.2	(2)	(2)
China.............	115.2	117.4	183.4	199.7	137.0	140.7	58.1	57.8	30.5	33.5
India..............	80.8	86.9	43.4	41.9	96.0	103.4	34.8	35.5	26.4	26.5
Indonesia.........	(2)	(2)	6.8	8.7	35.5	36.3	9.6	10.1	—	—
Pakistan..........	23.9	24.2	3.6	3.6	5.0	6.5	4.8	5.8	8.6	10.6
Thailand..........	(2)	(2)	4.3	4.4	20.3	20.5	0.6	0.7	—	—
Argentina.........	16.1	14.5	31.7	29.4	1.1	1.0	54.1	46.2	1.4	1.1
Brazil.............	5.9	5.8	60.4	71.8	9.3	7.9	79.2	69.4	9.0	9.1
Australia..........	27.9	29.5	11.8	13.2	0.5	0.7	3.8	4.8	4.2	4.7
South Africa.......	1.4	1.9	11.3	12.0	(2)	(2)	1.7	1.3	0.1	0.1
Turkey............	17.0	18.8	10.2	11.3	0.5	0.5	1.9	2.1	2.1	3.3
All others.........	82.0	96.1	169.6	165.5	133.6	137.8	41.8	38.0	14.1	15.8

— Represents zero. [1] Includes soybean, cottonseed, peanut (in shell), sunflower seed, rapeseed for individual countries. Copra and palm kernel are added to world totals. [2] Indicates no reported or insignificant production. [3] See footnote 4, Table 1391.

Source: U.S. Department of Agriculture, Foreign Agricultural Service, *World Agricultural Production*, June 2012. See also <http://www.fas.usda.gov/wap_arc.asp>.

Table 1389. Wheat, Rice, and Corn—Exports and Imports of Leading Countries: 2005 to 2012

[In thousands of metric tons (29,009 represents 29,009,000). All data represent January-December trade years. Countries listed are the ten leading exporters or importers in 2012]

Leading exporters	Exports 2005	Exports 2010	Exports 2012 [1]	Leading importers	Imports 2005	Imports 2010	Imports 2012 [1]
WHEAT				**WHEAT**			
United States.........	29,009	23,930	28,712	Egypt............	8,150	10,500	11,000
Australia.............	14,722	14,827	22,500	EU-27 [2]................	7,061	5,519	7,500
Russia..............	7,951	18,556	21,000	Brazil.............	5,238	7,161	7,300
Canada.............	14,872	19,042	17,300	Japan.............	5,744	5,502	6,400
EU-27 [2]............	14,745	22,115	16,200	Indonesia.........	4,720	5,364	6,400
Kazakhstan..........	3,079	8,254	11,000	Algeria...........	5,358	5,167	6,100
Argentina...........	11,898	5,099	10,100	Korea, South.......	3,591	4,470	5,400
Ukraine.............	4,403	9,337	5,000	Mexico...........	3,717	3,196	5,100
Turkey..............	2,017	4,266	3,600	Nigeria............	3,014	4,020	3,900
Brazil...............	15	1,162	2,000	Philippines........	2,593	3,188	3,800
RICE				**RICE**			
India................	4,569	2,082	8,000	Nigeria............	1,369	1,750	2,500
Vietnam.............	5,174	6,734	7,000	Indonesia.........	500	1,150	1,950
Thailand............	7,274	9,047	6,500	Iran..............	1,200	1,300	1,900
Pakistan............	2,801	4,000	3,750	EU-27 [2]............	1,095	1,317	1,550
United States.........	3,496	3,514	3,207	Philippines........	1,500	2,200	1,500
Uruguay.............	775	711	900	Iraq..............	786	1,060	1,200
Brazil...............	282	502	850	Saudi Arabia.......	1,500	1,069	1,150
Cambodia...........	200	750	800	Malaysia..........	700	907	1,085
Argentina...........	325	488	650	China [3]............	609	388	1,000
Egypt...............	1,095	705	600	Cote d'Ivoire.......	800	900	950
CORN				**CORN**			
United States.........	46,181	50,295	41,912	Japan............	16,485	15,979	15,500
Ukraine.............	2,334	5,072	14,000	Mexico...........	5,945	8,298	10,500
Argentina...........	14,574	16,504	13,000	Korea, South.......	8,633	8,461	7,500
Brazil..............	682	11,599	12,000	EU-27 [2]............	2,469	2,931	5,500
EU-27 [2]............	678	1,519	2,700	Egypt............	5,398	5,832	5,000
India................	448	1,939	2,400	China [3]............	2	1,296	5,000
Russia..............	44	427	2,000	Taiwan [3]...........	4,562	4,521	4,200
Serbia..............	(X)	1,343	1,700	Colombia..........	2,256	3,651	3,700
South Africa..........	2,143	2,064	1,500	Iran..............	2,558	4,300	3,600
Paraguay............	476	1,418	1,500	Malaysia..........	2,406	3,107	3,100

X Not available. [1] Estimates. [2] See footnote 4, Table 1391. [3] See footnote 4, Table 1348.

Source: U.S. Department of Agriculture, Economic Research Service, unpublished data from the PS&D (Production, Supply, and Distribution) database. See <http://www.fas.usda.gov/psdonline/psdhome.aspx>.

Table 1390. Meat Production by Type and Country: 2010 and 2011

[In thousands of metric tons (57,117 represents 57,117,000). Carcass weight basis for beef, veal, and pork. Chicken (16-week-old broiler) weight based on ready-to-cook equivalent]

Country	Beef and veal [1]		Country	Pork		Country	Chicken [2]	
	2010	2011		2010	2011		2010	2011
World	**57,117**	**56,888**	**World**	**102,902**	**101,662**	**World**	**77,729**	**80,420**
United States	**12,047**	**11,997**	China	51,070	49,500	**United States**	**16,563**	**16,694**
Brazil	9,115	9,000	EU-27 [3]	22,571	22,750	China	12,550	13,200
EU-27 [3]	8,048	8,030	**United States**	**10,186**	**10,332**	Brazil	12,312	12,863
China	5,600	5,550	Brazil	3,195	3,227	EU-27 [3]	9,202	9,420
India	2,842	3,170	Russia	1,920	1,995	India	2,650	2,900
Argentina	2,620	2,530	Vietnam	1,930	1,960	Mexico	2,822	2,900
Australia	2,087	2,150	Canada	1,772	1,770	Russia	2,310	2,575
Mexico	1,751	1,825	Japan	1,292	1,267	Argentina	1,680	1,770
Pakistan	1,470	1,435	Philippines	1,255	1,260	Turkey	1,430	1,614
Russia	1,435	1,360	Mexico	1,165	1,182	Indonesia	1,465	1,515
Canada	1,272	1,170	Korea, South	1,110	837	Thailand	1,280	1,350
Other countries	8,830	8,641	Other countries	5,436	5,582	Other countries	13,465	13,619

[1] May include meat of other bovines. [2] Excludes chicken paws. [3] See footnote 4, Table 1391.

Source: U.S. Department of Agriculture, Foreign Agricultural Service, *Livestock and Poultry: World Markets and Trade*, semiannual, April 2012. See also <http://www.fas.usda.gov/currwmt.asp>.

Table 1391. Meat Consumption by Type and Country: 2010 and 2011

[In thousands of metric tons (56,217 represents 56,217,000). Carcass weight basis for beef, veal, and pork. Chicken (16-week-old broiler) weight based on ready-to-cook equivalent]

Country	Beef and veal [1]		Country	Pork		Country	Chicken [2]	
	2010	2011		2010	2011		2010	2011
World	**56,217**	**55,698**	**World**	**102,684**	**101,286**	**World**	**76,829**	**79,591**
United States	**12,039**	**11,658**	China [3]	51,157	50,004	**United States**	**13,470**	**13,655**
EU–27 [4]	8,147	7,948	EU-27 [4]	20,841	20,564	China [3]	12,457	13,015
Brazil	7,592	7,730	**United States**	**8,653**	**8,339**	Brazil	9,132	9,645
China	5,589	5,523	Russia	2,835	2,940	EU-27 [4]	8,954	9,102
Russia	2,505	2,486	Brazil	2,577	2,644	Mexico	3,364	3,470
Argentina	2,325	2,279	Japan	2,488	2,522	Russia	2,961	3,040
India	1,925	1,950	Vietnam	1,940	1,995	India	2,648	2,890
Mexico	1,944	1,942	Mexico	1,774	1,690	Japan	2,075	2,087
Pakistan	1,436	1,397	Korea, South	1,539	1,487	South Africa	1,524	1,633
Japan	1,225	1,238	Philippines	1,358	1,358	Argentina	1,475	1,570
Canada	999	1,021	Taiwan [3]	901	894	Indonesia	1,465	1,515
Other countries	10,491	10,526	Other countries	6,621	6,849	Other countries	17,304	17,969

[1] May include meat of other bovines. [2] Excludes chicken paws. [3] See footnote 4, Table 1348. [4] European Union-27: Austria, Belgium, Bulgaria, Cyprus, Czech Republic, Denmark, Estonia, Finland, France, Germany, Greece, Hungary, Ireland, Italy, Latvia, Lithuania, Luxembourg, Malta, Netherlands, Poland, Portugal, Romania, Slovakia, Slovenia, Spain, Sweden, and United Kingdom.

Source: U.S. Department of Agriculture, Foreign Agricultural Service, *Livestock and Poultry: World Markets and Trade*, semiannual, April 2012. See also <http://www.fas.usda.gov/currwmt.asp>.

Table 1392. EU and U.S. Organic Land and Farm Sector: 2007 and 2008

[EU numbers for land and farms include those certified organic and in-conversion; U.S. numbers include only certified organic farms and land. "Certified organic" means that agricultural products have been grown and processed according to USDA's national organic standards and certified by USDA-accredited state and private certification organizations. 1 hectare = 2.47 acres]

Country	2007			2008		
	Total organic land (hectares)	Organic farms (number)	Farmland under organic production (percent)	Total organic land (hectares)	Organic farms (number)	Farmland under organic production (percent)
United States	**1,736,825**	**11,352**	**(NA)**	**1,949,781**	**12,941**	**0.6**
Austria	372,026	19,997	13.4	491,825	19,961	17.4
Belgium	32,628	821	2.4	35,721	901	2.6
Denmark	145,393	2,835	5.5	150,104	2,753	4.6
Finland	148,760	4,406	6.5	150,374	3,991	6.6
France	557,133	11,978	1.9	580,956	13,298	2.1
Germany	865,336	18,703	5.1	907,786	19,813	5.4
Greece	278,397	23,769	3.3	317,824	24,057	3.8
Ireland	41,122	1,134	1.0	44,751	1,220	1.1
Italy	1,150,253	45,231	9.1	1,002,414	44,371	7.9
Luxembourg	3,380	81	2.6	3,535	85	2.7
Netherlands	47,019	1,374	2.5	50,434	1,402	2.6
Portugal	233,475	1,949	6.4	229,717	1,949	6.6
Spain	988,323	18,226	3.9	1,129,844	21,291	4.5
Sweden	248,104	3,028	8.0	336,439	3,686	10.8
United Kingdom	660,200	5,506	4.2	737,631	5,383	4.6
EU-15 [1]	5,771,549	159,038	(NA)	6,169,355	164,161	(NA)

NA Not available. [1] European Union-15: Austria, Belgium, Denmark, Finland, France, Germany, Greece, Ireland, Italy, Luxembourg, Netherlands, Portugal, Spain, Sweden, and United Kingdom.

Source: U.S. Department of Agriculture, Economic Research Service, "Market-Led Versus Government-Facilitated Growth: Development of the U.S. and EU Organic Agricultural Sectors," August 2005, and unpublished data.

Table 1393. World Production of Major Mineral Commodities: 1990 to 2011

[Units are as noted]

Commodity	Unit	1990	2000	2010	2011, prel.	Leading producers, 2010
MINERAL FUELS						
Coal............................	million short tons	5,347	4,894	7,985	(NA)	China, United States, India
Dry natural gas......................	billion cubic feet	73,788	87,100	111,845	(NA)	United States, Russia, Canada
Natural gas plant liquids............	million barrels [1]	1,696	2,327	3,088	3,131	United States, Saudi Arabia, Canada
Petroleum, crude....................	million barrels [1]	22,081	25,011	26,992	27,028	Russia, Saudi Arabia, United States
NONMETALLIC MINERALS						
Cement, hydraulic...................	million metric tons	1,160	1,660	3,310	3,400	China, India, United States
Diamond, gem and industrial........	million carats	111	122	144	144	Russia, Botswana, Congo (Kinshasa)
Nitrogen in ammonia................	million metric tons	97.5	108	131	136	China, India, Russia
Phosphate rock, marketable........	million metric tons	162	132	181	191	China, United States, Morocco/W. Sahara
Potash, marketable..................	million metric tons	27.5	27.0	33.7	37.0	Canada, Russia, Belarus
Salt................................	million metric tons	183	195	280	290	China, United States, Germany
Sulfur, elemental basis..............	million metric tons	57.8	59.3	68.1	69.0	China, United States, Canada
METALS						
Aluminum [2].........................	million metric tons	19.3	24.3	40.8	44.1	China, Russia, Canada
Bauxite, gross weight...............	million metric tons	113	136	209	220	Australia, China, Brazil
Chromite, gross weight.............	thousand metric tons	13,200	14,700	23,700	24,000	South Africa, Kazakhstan, India
Copper, metal content [3].............	thousand metric tons	8,950	13,300	16,000	16,100	Chile, Peru, China
Gold, metal content.................	metric tons	2,180	2,570	2,560	2,700	China, Australia, United States
Iron ore, gross weight [4].............	million metric tons	983	1,079	2,590	2,800	China, Australia, Brazil
Lead, metal content [3]...............	thousand metric tons	3,370	3,170	4,140	4,500	China, Australia, United States
Nickel, metal content [3].............	thousand metric tons	974	1,290	1,590	1,800	Russia, Indonesia, Philippines
Steel, crude........................	million metric tons	771	850	1,410	1,500	China, Japan, United States
Tin, metal content [3]..................	thousand metric tons	221	278	265	253	China, Indonesia, Peru
Zinc, metal content..................	thousand metric tons	7,180	8,770	12,000	12,400	China, Australia, Peru

NA Not available. [1] 42-gallon barrels. [2] Unalloyed ingot metal. [3] Mine output. [4] Includes iron ore concentrates and iron ore agglomerates.

Source: Mineral fuels, U.S. Energy Information Administration, "International Energy Statistics" database, <http://www.eia.gov/cfapps/ipdbproject/IEDIndex3.cfm>, accessed July 2012; nonmetallic minerals and metals, U.S. Geological Survey, *Minerals Yearbook, 2010*, annual; and *Mineral Commodity Summaries, 2012*, annual, <http://minerals.er.usgs.gov/minerals/pubs/>.

Table 1394. World Primary Energy Production by Region and Type: 1980 to 2009

[In quadrillion Btu (287.3 represents 287,300,000,000,000,000). Btu = British thermal unit. For Btu conversion factors, see source]

Region and type	1980	1990	1995	2000	2004	2005	2006	2007	2008	2009
World total.................	**287.3**	**349.5**	**363.1**	**392.4**	**442.3**	**456.4**	**465.8**	**472.8**	**488.6**	**484.1**
North America..................	83.2	91.8	96.1	98.8	98.9	98.3	100.3	100.7	101.3	99.5
United States [1].............	**67.2**	**70.7**	**71.2**	**71.3**	**70.2**	**69.4**	**70.8**	**71.4**	**73.1**	**72.6**
Central and South America. ..	12.1	16.7	21.1	26.0	27.0	28.0	29.0	29.0	29.5	29.5
Europe........................	40.2	46.8	49.0	50.5	50.3	48.5	47.3	46.2	46.4	44.7
Eurasia [2]......................	56.5	72.1	51.9	54.1	64.3	66.0	67.8	69.3	70.0	66.1
Middle East....................	42.3	41.0	48.3	57.5	62.2	65.3	65.3	64.5	68.2	66.2
Africa.........................	17.4	21.6	24.0	27.7	31.8	34.4	35.1	36.1	37.0	36.1
Asia and Oceania..............	35.8	59.5	72.7	77.8	108.0	115.7	121.0	126.9	136.0	142.1
Petroleum [3]....................	133.1	136.2	136.7	151.6	162.3	165.3	165.2	164.2	166.6	163.7
Dry natural gas................	54.8	76.1	80.4	89.7	98.5	101.5	105.2	107.4	111.2	108.5
Coal..........................	71.2	90.9	88.0	89.1	116.6	123.3	127.7	133.4	141.3	142.3
Hydroelectric power...........	17.9	22.3	25.3	26.7	27.9	28.9	29.8	29.6	30.7	30.7
Nuclear electric power.........	7.6	20.4	23.3	25.7	27.3	27.5	27.8	27.1	27.2	26.8
Geothermal, solar, wind, tidal, biomass, and waste.........	0.3	1.5	2.0	2.7	3.5	3.9	4.2	4.8	5.4	6.1

[1] Includes biomass, geothermal, and solar energy produced in the United States and not used for generating electricity. [2] Prior to 1992, data were for the former U.S.S.R. [3] Includes only crude oil, lease condensate, and natural gas plant liquids.

Source: U.S. Energy Information Administration, International Energy Statistics database, <http://www.eia.gov/cfapps/ipdbproject/IEDIndex3.cfm>, accessed July 2012.

Table 1395. World Primary Energy Consumption by Region and Type: 1980 to 2009

[In quadrillion Btu (283.0 represents 283,000,000,000,000,000). Btu = British thermal unit. For Btu conversion factors, see source]

Region and type	1980	1990	1995	2000	2004	2005	2006	2007	2008	2009
World total [1]	**283.0**	**346.9**	**364.4**	**395.0**	**446.3**	**458.7**	**468.3**	**478.5**	**490.8**	**483.0**
North America	91.5	100.1	108.5	118.2	120.4	121.2	120.8	122.6	120.5	114.6
United States [2]	**78.1**	**84.5**	**91.0**	**98.8**	**100.2**	**100.3**	**99.6**	**101.3**	**99.3**	**94.5**
Central and South America	11.5	14.5	17.6	20.8	22.5	23.2	24.3	24.6	25.6	25.2
Europe	71.7	76.3	76.7	81.2	85.3	85.8	86.4	85.7	85.6	81.1
Eurasia [3]	46.7	61.0	42.2	39.2	42.7	42.8	42.4	43.9	44.9	40.2
Middle East	5.8	11.2	13.8	17.4	21.0	22.9	24.0	23.9	26.1	27.8
Africa	6.8	9.5	10.6	12.0	14.0	14.5	14.6	15.2	16.2	16.1
Asia and Oceania	48.9	74.4	94.9	106.2	140.5	148.3	155.9	162.5	171.9	178.0
Petroleum [4]	131.0	136.2	142.5	155.6	167.0	170.1	170.8	171.8	172.3	169.9
Dry natural gas	53.9	75.4	81.1	89.9	100.2	103.2	106.0	109.5	113.2	108.8
Coal	69.9	89.1	87.9	92.3	118.0	122.5	127.0	132.8	138.8	137.3

[1] Includes hydroelectric power, nuclear electric power, and geothermal, solar, wind, tidal, biomass, and waste, not shown separately. [2] See footnote 1, Table 1394. [3] Prior to 1992, data were for the former U.S.S.R. [4] Includes all refined petroleum products.

Source: U.S. Energy Information Administration, International Energy Statistics database, <http://www.eia.gov/cfapps/ipdbproject/IEDIndex3.cfm>, accessed July 2012.

Table 1396. World Daily Crude Oil Production by Major Producing Country: 1980 to 2011

[In thousands of barrels per day (59,558 barrels represents 59,558,000 barrels). Ranked for top 30 countries]

Country	1980	1990	1995	2000	2005	2008	2009	2010	2011
World, total [1]	**59,558**	**60,497**	**62,434**	**68,522**	**73,637**	**73,575**	**72,230**	**73,950**	**74,051**
Russia	(X)	(X)	5,995	6,479	9,043	9,357	9,495	9,694	9,774
Saudi Arabia	9,900	6,410	8,231	8,404	9,550	9,261	8,250	8,900	9,458
United States	**8,597**	**7,355**	**6,560**	**5,822**	**5,178**	**4,950**	**5,361**	**5,483**	**5,675**
China	2,114	2,774	2,990	3,249	3,609	3,790	3,799	4,076	4,073
Iran	1,662	3,088	3,643	3,696	4,139	4,050	4,037	4,080	4,054
Canada	1,435	1,553	1,805	1,977	2,369	2,579	2,579	2,734	2,904
United Arab Emirates	1,709	2,117	2,233	2,368	2,535	2,681	2,413	2,415	2,688
Iraq	2,514	2,040	560	2,571	1,878	2,375	2,391	2,399	2,626
Mexico	1,936	2,553	2,711	3,104	3,423	2,839	2,646	2,621	2,596
Kuwait	1,656	1,175	2,057	2,079	2,529	2,586	2,350	2,300	2,530
Nigeria	2,055	1,810	1,993	2,165	2,627	2,165	2,208	2,455	2,525
Venezuela	2,168	2,137	2,750	3,155	2,565	2,394	2,239	2,146	2,240
Brazil	182	631	695	1,269	1,634	1,812	1,950	2,055	2,105
Angola	150	475	646	746	1,250	1,981	1,907	1,939	1,786
Norway	486	1,630	2,766	3,222	2,698	2,182	2,067	1,869	1,752
Kazakhstan	(X)	(X)	414	718	1,288	1,345	1,455	1,525	1,553
Algeria	1,106	1,180	1,162	1,214	1,692	1,705	1,585	1,540	1,540
Qatar	472	406	442	737	835	924	927	1,127	1,296
Azerbaijan	(X)	(X)	175	280	433	870	1,006	1,035	983
Indonesia	1,577	1,462	1,503	1,428	1,067	986	969	953	918
Colombia	126	440	585	691	526	588	671	786	914
Oman	282	685	851	970	774	757	813	865	886
India	182	660	703	646	665	694	680	751	782
Argentina	491	483	715	761	704	661	654	632	588
Egypt	595	873	920	768	623	566	587	575	564
Malaysia	283	619	682	690	631	609	578	554	512
Ecuador	204	285	392	395	532	505	486	486	500
Libya	1,787	1,375	1,390	1,410	1,633	1,736	1,650	1,650	465
Sudan	—	—	—	186	350	478	483	511	450
Australia	380	575	562	722	446	477	475	435	356

— Represents zero. X Not applicable. [1] Includes countries not shown separately.

Source: U.S. Energy Information Administration, International Energy Statistics database, <http://www.eia.gov/cfapps/ipdbproject/IEDIndex3.cfm>, accessed July 2012.

Table 1397. Energy Consumption by Country: 2000 and 2009

[For total consumption, 395.0 represents 395,000,000,000,000,000. For per capita consumption, 64.9 represents 64,900,000. See text of this section for general comments about the data. For data qualifications for countries and Btu conversion factors, see source]

Country	Total (quad. Btu) 2000	2009	Per capita (mil. Btu) 2000	2009	Country	Total (quad. Btu) 2000	2009	Per capita (mil. Btu) 2000	2009
World, total........	395.0	483.0	64.9	71.3	Japan...........	22.4	20.6	176.8	162.1
United States........	98.8	94.5	350.2	308.0	Korea, North.........	0.9	0.8	40.4	37.1
Algeria.............	1.2	1.8	40.7	53.8	Korea, South.........	7.8	10.0	167.3	205.3
Argentina...........	2.7	3.3	71.5	80.8	Kuwait.............	0.9	1.2	460.8	462.3
Australia...........	4.8	5.6	253.7	262.9	Libya..............	0.6	0.8	122.9	123.4
Austria............	1.4	1.5	171.6	178.0	Malaysia...........	2.0	2.7	85.4	96.8
Bahrain............	0.4	0.6	574.7	764.7	Mexico.............	6.3	7.0	63.4	62.9
Bangladesh..........	0.5	0.9	3.8	6.2	Morocco............	0.4	0.6	15.9	19.5
Belarus............	1.1	1.0	104.9	108.6	Netherlands.........	3.8	4.0	238.5	242.3
Belgium............	2.7	2.6	266.3	250.2	New Zealand........	0.8	0.8	218.4	201.7
Brazil.............	8.5	10.3	48.4	51.8	Nigeria............	0.8	0.8	6.6	5.2
Bulgaria...........	0.9	0.7	111.0	103.5	Norway............	2.0	1.9	436.1	407.9
Burma.............	0.2	0.3	3.3	4.8	Pakistan...........	1.9	2.5	12.2	13.9
Canada............	13.1	13.0	420.0	389.5	Peru..............	0.5	0.8	20.3	26.3
Chile.[1]...........	1.0	1.2	66.8	72.9	Philippines.........	1.1	1.2	14.0	12.2
China [1]...........	36.4	90.3	28.8	68.2	Poland............	3.6	4.0	93.8	103.5
Colombia...........	1.2	1.3	30.1	30.6	Portugal...........	1.1	1.1	103.5	98.1
Congo (Kinshasa) [2]......	0.1	0.1	1.8	1.6	Romania...........	1.6	1.5	70.7	66.1
Cuba.............	0.5	0.4	41.4	33.6	Russia............	26.1	26.8	178.2	191.5
Czech Republic.......	1.4	1.5	135.9	149.9	Saudi Arabia........	4.9	7.8	227.7	309.3
Denmark...........	0.9	0.8	163.6	143.4	Serbia............	(X)	0.7	(X)	77.0
Ecuador...........	0.3	0.5	27.7	35.4	South Africa........	4.6	5.5	101.7	111.5
Egypt.............	2.0	3.4	30.8	42.9	Spain.............	5.5	6.1	136.3	131.2
Finland............	1.2	1.2	234.9	227.6	Sweden............	2.3	2.1	254.2	230.0
France............	10.9	10.7	181.7	169.2	Switzerland.........	1.3	1.3	177.6	171.9
Germany...........	14.2	13.5	173.3	163.5	Syria.............	0.8	0.9	47.5	39.4
Greece............	1.3	1.4	126.7	131.6	Taiwan [1]...........	3.8	4.5	171.7	195.5
Hong Kong..........	0.8	1.1	121.0	155.7	Thailand...........	2.6	4.0	41.6	60.0
Hungary...........	1.0	1.0	100.8	103.2	Trinidad and Tobago....	0.4	0.9	336.0	697.8
India.............	13.5	21.7	13.4	18.7	Tunisia............	0.3	0.3	31.5	29.3
Indonesia..........	3.9	6.1	18.0	25.2	Turkey............	3.2	4.0	47.0	52.6
Iran..............	5.0	9.0	73.2	118.7	Ukraine...........	5.8	4.7	117.4	102.9
Iraq..............	1.1	1.4	47.8	48.8	United Arab Emirates....	1.9	3.3	579.7	679.4
Ireland............	0.6	0.6	157.0	137.9	United Kingdom........	9.7	8.9	163.8	143.0
Israel.............	0.8	0.9	132.7	125.8	Venezuela..........	2.8	3.2	117.9	118.7
Italy.............	7.6	7.3	131.4	125.9	Vietnam...........	0.7	1.7	9.3	19.2

X Not applicable. [1] See footnote 4, Table 1348. [2] See footnote 5, Table 1348.

Source: U.S. Energy Information Administration, International Energy Statistics database, <http://www.eia.gov/cfapps/ipdbproject/IEDIndex3.cfm>, accessed July 2012.

Table 1398. World Energy Consumption by Region and Energy Source, 2006 to 2008, and Projections, 2020 to 2035

[In quadrillion Btu (481.3 represents 481,300,000,000,000,000). Btu = British thermal units. For Btu conversion factors, see source. Energy totals include net imports of coal coke and electricity generated from biomass in the United States. The electricity portion of the national consumption values consists of generation for domestic use plus an adjustment for electricity trade based on a fuel's share of total generation in the exporting country. OECD = Organization for Economic Cooperation and Development; see text, this section]

Region and energy source	2006	2007	2008	Projections 2020	2025	2030	2035
World, total..............	481.3	492.6	504.7	619.5	671.5	721.5	769.8
OECD Americas.............	122.3	124.3	122.9	131.0	135.9	141.6	147.7
United States.............	99.8	101.7	100.1	104.9	108.0	111.0	114.2
OECD Europe..............	82.8	82.3	82.2	86.9	89.7	91.8	93.8
OECD Asia...............	39.2	39.4	39.2	42.7	44.2	45.4	46.7
Non-OECD Europe and Eurasia............	48.9	49.6	50.5	52.3	54.0	56.0	58.4
Non-OECD Asia............	121.0	128.6	137.9	215.0	246.4	274.3	298.8
Middle East..............	24.0	24.0	25.6	33.9	37.3	41.3	45.3
Africa..................	17.2	17.8	18.8	23.6	25.9	28.5	31.4
Central and South America............	25.9	26.5	27.7	34.2	38.0	42.6	47.8
Liquids.................	171.7	172.7	173.0	195.8	207.0	216.6	225.2
Natural gas..............	107.5	110.9	114.3	138.0	149.4	162.3	174.7
Coal...................	127.2	133.3	139.0	164.6	179.7	194.7	209.1
Nuclear.................	27.8	27.1	27.2	38.9	43.7	47.4	51.2
Other..................	47.1	48.5	51.3	82.2	91.7	100.6	109.5

Source: U.S. Energy Information Administration, International Energy Outlook 2011, annual. See also <http://www.eia.gov/oiaf/ieo/ieorefcase.html>.

Table 1399. World Dry Natural Gas Production by Major Producing Country: 1980 to 2010

[In billion cubic feet (53,375 represents 53,375,000,000,000)]

Country	Natural gas production								
	1980	1990	2000	2005	2006	2007	2008	2009	2010
World, total [1]	**53,375**	**73,788**	**87,100**	**98,393**	**101,993**	**104,162**	**107,923**	**104,831**	**111,845**
United States	**19,403**	**17,810**	**19,182**	**18,051**	**18,504**	**19,266**	**20,159**	**20,624**	**21,332**
Russia	(X)	(X)	19,335	21,224	21,736	21,595	21,515	18,890	20,915
Canada	2,759	3,849	6,470	6,561	6,548	6,416	6,046	5,634	5,390
Iran	250	837	2,127	3,655	3,836	3,952	4,107	4,986	5,161
Qatar	184	276	1,028	1,617	1,790	2,232	2,719	3,154	4,121
Norway	917	976	1,867	3,072	3,094	3,168	3,503	3,664	3,756
China	505	508	962	1,763	2,067	2,446	2,685	2,975	3,334
Netherlands	3,398	2,693	2,559	2,773	2,730	2,687	2,957	2,786	3,131
Saudi Arabia	334	1,077	1,759	2,516	2,594	2,628	2,841	2,770	3,096
Algeria	411	1,787	2,940	3,151	3,079	2,996	3,055	2,876	2,988
Indonesia	654	1,602	2,237	2,001	2,199	2,422	2,472	2,557	2,917
Malaysia	56	654	1,600	1,967	1,973	1,962	2,161	2,133	2,171
Egypt	30	286	646	1,501	1,596	1,642	2,083	2,214	2,166
Uzbekistan	(X)	(X)	1,992	2,108	2,216	2,302	2,387	2,169	2,123
United Kingdom	1,323	1,754	3,826	3,118	2,819	2,553	2,469	2,087	1,988
India	51	399	795	1,056	1,088	1,108	1,137	1,437	1,848
United Arab Emirates	200	780	1,355	1,659	1,723	1,778	1,774	1,724	1,811
Australia	313	723	1,159	1,440	1,509	1,545	1,580	1,653	1,730
Mexico	900	903	1,314	1,349	1,741	1,678	1,694	1,722	1,722
Turkmenistan	(X)	(X)	1,642	2,225	2,232	2,432	2,490	1,347	1,600
Trinidad and Tobago	81	177	493	1,069	1,287	1,378	1,388	1,437	1,499
Argentina	280	630	1,321	1,611	1,628	1,583	1,556	1,461	1,416
Pakistan	286	482	856	1,088	1,276	1,300	1,342	1,367	1,400
Thailand	0	208	658	837	859	918	1,016	1,091	1,281
Nigeria	38	131	440	791	1,006	1,148	1,159	912	1,024
Oman	28	99	322	699	837	849	850	875	957
Bangladesh	50	162	343	494	541	575	632	692	711
Venezuela	517	761	961	828	918	732	733	651	697
Ukraine	(X)	(X)	636	685	689	689	699	715	684
Libya	180	219	212	399	466	540	562	562	594

X Not applicable. [1] Includes countries not shown separately.

Source: U.S. Energy Information Administration, International Energy Statistics database, <http://www.eia.gov/cfapps/ipdbproject/IEDIndex3.cfm>, accessed July 2012.

Table 1400. World Coal Production by Major Producing Country: 1980 to 2010

[In millions of short tons (4,181.9 represents 4,181,900,000)]

Country	Coal production								
	1980	1990	2000	2005	2006	2007	2008	2009	2010
World, total [1]	**4,181.9**	**5,346.7**	**4,893.7**	**6,553.9**	**6,773.6**	**7,052.9**	**7,459.6**	**7,545.7**	**7,984.9**
China	683.6	1,190.4	1,271.5	2,500.9	2,573.9	2,746.3	3,048.5	3,226.1	3,523.0
United States	**829.7**	**1,029.1**	**1,073.6**	**1,131.5**	**1,162.7**	**1,146.6**	**1,171.8**	**1,074.9**	**1,085.3**
India	125.8	247.6	370.0	473.3	500.2	531.5	568.4	613.4	622.8
Australia	115.2	225.5	338.1	404.9	405.0	430.1	431.5	444.1	463.3
Indonesia	0.6	11.6	84.5	188.2	249.7	287.2	301.6	332.4	370.4
Russia	(X)	(X)	264.9	311.8	313.7	318.6	336.2	304.2	357.0
South Africa	131.9	193.2	248.9	270.1	269.8	273.0	278.0	276.2	280.8
Germany	(X)	(X)	226.0	227.0	220.6	225.5	214.3	202.4	201.0
Poland	253.5	237.1	179.2	175.0	171.1	159.8	158.0	148.4	146.2
Kazakhstan	(X)	(X)	85.4	96.1	106.6	107.8	122.4	111.2	122.1
Colombia	4.5	22.6	42.0	65.1	72.3	77.1	81.0	80.3	82.0
Turkey	20.8	52.3	69.7	64.3	70.8	83.1	87.5	87.6	79.1
Canada	40.4	75.3	76.2	72.0	72.8	76.5	74.7	69.4	74.8
Greece	25.6	57.2	70.4	76.5	71.4	73.1	72.4	71.5	62.3
Czech Republic	(X)	(X)	71.8	68.4	69.3	69.0	66.4	62.2	60.9
Ukraine	(X)	(X)	68.8	66.5	68.0	65.0	65.7	60.6	60.1
Vietnam	5.7	5.1	12.8	35.7	42.9	46.9	44.8	48.4	49.2
Serbia	(X)	(X)	(X)	(X)	40.5	40.9	42.7	42.4	41.2
Korea, North	48.6	51.0	32.8	38.2	38.7	33.4	35.6	34.8	34.8
Romania	38.8	42.1	32.3	34.3	38.5	39.4	39.5	37.4	34.0
Bulgaria	33.3	34.9	29.2	27.2	28.3	31.4	31.7	30.0	32.3
Mongolia	5.3	7.9	5.7	8.3	8.9	10.2	11.1	15.9	27.8
Thailand	1.6	13.7	19.6	23.0	21.0	20.1	20.2	19.6	20.3
Estonia	(X)	(X)	12.9	16.1	15.5	18.2	17.8	16.5	19.8
United Kingdom	143.8	104.1	33.7	22.1	19.9	18.2	19.4	19.2	19.6
Bosnia and Herzegovina	(X)	(X)	8.2	10.1	11.2	11.7	12.9	12.6	12.1
Mexico	4.0	8.6	12.5	11.9	12.7	13.8	12.6	11.6	11.0
Hungary	28.7	19.7	15.5	10.5	11.0	10.8	10.4	9.9	10.0
Venezuela	(Z)	2.4	8.7	7.9	8.7	8.4	8.4	9.7	9.7
Spain	30.9	39.2	25.9	21.5	20.3	18.9	11.2	10.4	9.3

X Not applicable. Z Less than 50,000 tons. [1] Includes countries not shown separately.

Source: U.S. Energy Information Administration, International Energy Statistics database,<http://www.eia.gov/cfapps/ipdbproject/IEDIndex3.cfm>, accessed July 2012.

Table 1401. Net Electricity Generation by Type and Country: 2009

[18,979.9 represents 18,979,900,000,000. kWh = kilowatt hours]

Country	Total [1] (bil. kWh)	Percent distribution			Country	Total [1] (bil. kWh)	Percent distribution		
		Thermal [2]	Hydro	Nuclear			Thermal [2]	Hydro	Nuclear
World, total [3]	**18,979.9**	**66.8**	**16.6**	**13.5**	Sweden	132.3	2.8	49.3	37.5
					Egypt	131.3	89.5	9.7	—
United States	**3,950.3**	**69.0**	**6.9**	**20.2**	Norway	129.9	3.2	96.2	—
China [4]	3,445.7	81.3	15.9	1.9	Venezuela	117.4	26.9	73.1	—
Japan	984.8	62.6	7.6	27.0	Argentina	116.0	63.3	28.9	6.7
Russia	929.6	65.6	17.5	16.7	Netherlands	106.9	85.1	0.1	3.8
India	847.4	83.6	12.5	1.7	Malaysia	99.1	93.3	6.7	—
Canada	586.0	22.0	61.5	14.7	Pakistan	90.9	66.6	30.6	2.8
					United Arab				
Germany	546.8	59.4	3.4	23.4	Emirates	85.1	100.0	—	—
France	510.2	10.3	11.1	76.3	Belgium	84.4	39.8	0.4	53.1
Brazil	458.1	7.8	84.5	2.7	Vietnam	79.7	62.8	37.2	—
Korea, South	425.2	66.1	0.7	33.0	Czech Republic	77.0	60.8	3.1	33.6
United Kingdom	349.7	74.2	1.5	18.8	Kazakhstan	74.3	90.8	9.2	—
Spain	274.7	56.0	9.5	18.2	Finland	68.3	36.1	18.4	32.7
Italy	272.2	74.8	17.9	—	Austria	64.0	27.2	62.3	—
Mexico	246.9	81.4	10.7	4.0	Switzerland	64.0	1.2	55.2	41.1
Australia	245.9	92.5	4.9	—	Philippines	58.8	66.7	16.5	—
South Africa	232.1	94.1	0.6	5.6	Chile	58.3	49.9	43.0	—
Taiwan [4]	213.2	78.0	1.7	18.8	Greece	57.6	86.4	9.2	—
Iran	212.8	96.5	3.4	—	Colombia	55.9	26.1	72.8	—
Saudi Arabia	204.1	100.0	—	—	Romania	54.9	51.3	28.3	20.3
Turkey	184.9	79.6	19.3	—	Paraguay	54.4	—	100.0	—
Ukraine	164.5	45.0	7.1	47.9	Israel	51.5	99.8	—	—
Indonesia	146.9	86.3	7.7	—	Kuwait	50.0	100.0	—	—
Poland	142.0	94.2	1.7	—	Uzbekistan	47.4	80.5	19.5	—
Thailand	139.8	90.9	5.1	—	Portugal	46.8	62.0	17.5	—

— Represents zero. [1] Includes thermal, hydro, nuclear, geothermal, solar, wind, tidal, biomass, and waste. [2] Electricity generated from coal, oil, and gas. [3] Includes countries not shown separately. [4] See footnote 4, Table 1348.

Source: U.S. Energy Information Administration, International Energy Statistics database, <http://www.eia.gov/cfapps/ipdbproject/IEDIndex3.cfm>, accessed July 2012.

Table 1402. Commercial Nuclear Power Generation by Country: 1990 to 2010

[For gross generation, 1,743.9 represents 1,743,900,000,000 kWh. Generation for calendar years; other data as of December. For gross capacity, 301,745 represents 301,745,000 kW). kWh = kilowatt-hours. kW = kilowatts]

Country	Reactors				Gross electricity generated (bil. kWh)				Gross capacity (1,000 kW)			
	1990	2000	2009	2010	1990	2000	2009	2010	1990	2000	2009	2010
Total	**368**	**433**	**441**	**441**	**1,743.9**	**2,540.5**	**2,546.6**	**2,591.9**	**301,745**	**373,804**	**397,295**	**396,693**
United States	**112**	**104**	**104**	**104**	**606.4**	**789.1**	**833.6**	**864.1**	**105,998**	**103,129**	**107,023**	**107,642**
Argentina	2	2	2	2	7.0	6.2	8.2	7.1	1,005	1,005	1,005	1,005
Armenia	(NA)	1	1	1	(NA)	(NA)	2.5	2.4	(NA)	408	408	408
Belgium	7	7	7	7	42.7	48.2	47.2	47.9	5,740	5,995	6,207	6,211
Brazil	1	2	2	2	2.0	6.1	12.9	14.5	657	1,966	2,007	2,007
Bulgaria	(NA)	6	2	2	(NA)	(NA)	15.3	15.2	(NA)	3,760	2,000	2,000
Canada	19	21	21	19	74.0	73.8	90.9	52.2	13,855	15,795	15,367	14,331
China [1]	(NA)	2	11	13	(NA)	14.7	(NA)	(NA)	(NA)	1,968	9,014	10,744
Czech Republic	(NA)	4	6	6	(NA)	13.6	27.1	27.8	(NA)	1,760	3,876	3,892
Finland	4	4	4	4	18.9	22.5	23.5	22.8	2,400	2,760	2,800	2,820
France	58	57	58	58	314.1	395.7	410.0	428.2	58,862	62,920	65,880	65,880
Germany	22	19	17	17	147.2	169.7	134.9	140.5	23,973	22,234	21,497	21,517
Great Britain	42	33	19	19	68.8	83.6	(NA)	(NA)	15,274	15,272	12,540	11,709
Hungary	4	4	4	4	13.6	14.1	15.4	15.7	1,760	1,851	2,000	2,000
India	6	13	17	19	6.0	15.5	17.0	23.3	1,330	2,960	4,120	4,560
Italy	2	(NA)	(NA)	(NA)	(NA)	(NA)	(NA)	(NA)	1,132	(NA)	(NA)	(NA)
Japan	40	52	56	54	191.9	319.8	272.3	292.3	31,645	45,082	50,492	48,847
Korea, South	9	16	20	20	52.8	108.9	147.8	149.7	7,616	13,768	18,393	18,509
Lithuania	(NA)	2	1	—	(NA)	7.8	11.6	—	(NA)	3,000	1,300	—
Mexico	1	2	2	2	2.1	8.2	10.5	5.8	675	1,350	1,364	1,502
Netherlands	2	1	1	1	3.4	3.9	4.2	3.9	540	480	515	515
Pakistan	1	1	2	2	0.4	0.4	2.9	2.7	137	137	462	462
Romania	(NA)	1	2	2	(NA)	5.5	11.7	11.6	(NA)	706	1,412	1,412
Russia	(NA)	29	31	32	(NA)	128.9	163.3	167.8	(NA)	21,266	23,242	24,242
Slovakia	(NA)	6	4	4	(NA)	16.5	(NA)	(NA)	(NA)	2,640	1,894	1,894
Slovenia	1	1	1	1	4.6	4.8	5.7	5.6	664	664	727	727
South Africa	2	2	2	2	8.9	13.6	12.1	13.5	1,930	1,930	1,930	1,930
Spain	10	9	8	8	54.3	62.2	52.9	61.9	7,984	7,808	7,735	7,800
Sweden	12	11	10	10	68.2	57.3	52.3	58.2	10,344	9,844	9,685	9,743
Switzerland	5	5	5	5	23.6	26.3	27.5	26.5	3,079	3,322	3,370	3,405
Taiwan [1]	6	6	6	6	32.9	38.5	41.6	41.6	5,146	5,144	5,144	5,144
Ukraine	(NA)	14	15	15	(NA)	77.3	82.2	89.1	(NA)	12,880	13,880	13,835

– Represents zero. NA Not available. [1] See footnote 4, Table 1348.

Source: Platts/The McGraw-Hill Companies, Inc., New York, NY, *Nucleonics Week*, February issue (copyright).

Table 1403. Carbon Dioxide Emissions From Consumption of Fossil Fuels by Country: 1980 to 2010

[In million metric tons of carbon dioxide (18,434.2 represents 18,434,200,000). Ranked for top 25 countries. Includes carbon dioxide emissions from the consumption of petroleum, natural gas, coal, and the flaring of natural gas]

Region/Country	1980	1990	2000	2005	2007	2008	2009	2010
World, total [1]	**18,434.2**	**21,615.5**	**23,738.4**	**28,291.5**	**29,590.4**	**30,318.0**	**29,777.7**	**31,780.4**
China [2]	1,448.5	2,269.7	2,849.7	5,512.7	6,184.1	6,721.4	7,204.9	8,321.0
United States	**4,776.8**	**5,040.6**	**5,861.3**	**5,991.8**	**6,015.8**	**5,835.4**	**5,427.1**	**5,610.1**
India	291.2	578.6	1,003.0	1,183.3	1,368.4	1,474.2	1,622.7	1,695.6
Russia	(X)	(X)	1,498.8	1,574.2	1,566.4	1,631.0	1,448.5	1,633.8
Japan	947.0	1,047.0	1,201.4	1,241.3	1,254.4	1,215.5	1,104.6	1,164.5
Germany	(X)	(X)	854.7	847.4	827.2	823.1	763.0	793.7
Korea, South	131.7	242.1	438.8	493.8	503.1	521.8	531.1	579.0
Iran	116.8	202.1	321.7	451.0	489.3	512.1	548.9	560.3
Canada	457.4	470.6	573.3	623.8	609.9	600.0	551.2	548.8
United Kingdom	613.6	601.8	560.3	583.1	569.9	563.9	519.0	532.4
Saudi Arabia	176.9	208.0	290.5	405.5	396.5	425.7	438.2	478.4
South Africa	235.0	298.0	386.0	432.5	463.8	486.5	458.9	465.1
Brazil	185.7	237.3	344.4	369.7	400.4	426.5	414.7	453.9
Mexico	240.3	302.2	383.0	397.8	444.3	452.8	432.4	445.3
Italy	371.8	415.4	447.7	471.9	459.5	449.7	408.5	416.4
Australia	198.8	267.6	356.3	397.2	408.5	412.9	411.6	405.3
France	488.9	367.7	401.7	414.0	423.1	428.5	395.5	395.2
Indonesia	85.8	156.0	266.3	330.6	390.2	405.4	417.6	389.4
Spain	195.0	224.1	317.5	382.9	387.9	360.1	326.7	316.4
Taiwan [2]	70.6	118.3	256.1	288.8	293.7	290.4	279.0	305.4
Poland	428.9	333.8	292.6	287.6	295.9	294.8	304.5	303.7
Thailand	33.6	83.9	161.8	241.8	247.4	255.0	258.9	278.5
Ukraine	(X)	(X)	324.9	353.6	354.1	352.8	260.3	275.5
Turkey	68.6	129.5	201.9	230.9	280.2	272.9	257.0	263.5
Netherlands	201.1	211.1	246.3	268.5	258.1	249.5	248.8	263.4

X Not applicable. [1] Includes other countries not shown separately. [2] See footnote 4, Table 1348.

Source: U.S. Energy Information Administration, International Energy Statistics database, <http://www.eia.gov/cfapps/ipdbproject/IEDIndex3.cfm>, accessed July 2012.

Table 1404. Average Temperatures and Precipitation—Selected International Cities

[In degrees Fahrenheit, except as noted. Data are generally based on a standard 30-year period; for details, see source. For data on U.S. cities, see Tables 397 through 402. Minus sign (−) indicates degrees below zero]

City	January Average high	January Average low	January Warm-est	January Coldest	January Average pre-cipitation (inches)	July Average high	July Average low	July Warm-est	July Coldest	July Average pre-cipitation (inches)
Amsterdam, Netherlands	41	34	57	3	3.1	69	55	90	39	2.9
Athens, Greece	55	44	70	28	1.9	89	73	108	61	0.2
Baghdad, Iraq	58	38	75	25	1.1	110	78	122	61	−
Bangkok, Thailand	89	71	95	54	0.4	90	78	99	72	6.2
Beijing, China	34	17	54	1	0.2	86	72	104	63	8.8
Berlin, Germany	35	26	58	-11	(NA)	73	56	95	41	(NA)
Bogota, Colombia	66	43	84	27	1.9	64	47	82	32	1.8
Brasilia, Brazil	81	64	95	54	(NA)	79	52	97	37	(NA)
Buenos Aires, Argentina	85	64	104	44	4.2	58	41	88	23	2.3
Cairo, Egypt	65	49	86	32	0.2	93	72	108	63	−
Frankfurt, Germany	38	30	56	-4	1.8	75	57	97	38	2.4
Geneva, Switzerland	39	29	57	-2	2.2	77	56	96	41	2.8
Hong Kong, China	67	58	79	43	1.1	89	81	97	70	14.3
Istanbul, Turkey	46	37	64	16	3.7	82	66	100	50	0.7
Jakarta, Indonesia	83	75	92	72	(NA)	88	74	92	67	(NA)
Karachi, Pakistan	76	55	93	39	0.3	89	83	109	68	3.5
Lagos, Nigeria	82	79	93	64	(NA)	79	76	88	70	(NA)
London, England	45	36	61	15	2.4	72	56	93	45	1.8
Madrid, Spain	51	32	68	14	1.8	90	61	104	46	0.4
Manila, Philippines	86	71	95	61	0.8	88	76	99	70	15.9
Mexico City, Mexico	70	45	86	26	0.3	74	56	86	37	5.1
Montreal, Canada	21	7	52	-31	2.8	79	61	93	43	3.4
Moscow, Russia	21	11	46	-33	1.4	71	55	95	41	3.2
Nairobi, Kenya	77	58	88	45	1.8	71	54	85	43	0.5
New Delhi, India	68	48	85	32	0.9	93	81	111	70	7.9
Paris, France	43	34	59	1	(NA)	75	58	95	41	(NA)
Rio De Janeiro, Brazil	91	74	109	64	5.3	81	64	102	52	1.8
Rome, Italy	55	39	64	19	3.2	83	66	100	55	0.6
Seoul, Korea	33	21	55	-1	(NA)	82	71	97	55	(NA)
Singapore, Singapore	85	73	100	66	9.4	86	76	99	70	5.9
Sydney, Australia	79	65	109	49	4.0	62	44	80	32	2.5
Tel Aviv, Israel	62	46	84	32	(NA)	87	69	100	50	(NA)
Tokyo, Japan	48	35	66	25	2.0	82	71	95	55	5.3
Toronto, Canada	28	15	59	-24	1.9	79	60	99	45	2.8

− Represents zero. NA Not available.

Source: U.S. National Oceanic and Atmospheric Administration, *Climates of the World*. See also <http://www.ncdc.noaa.gov/oa/oldpubs/>.

Table 1405. Telephones, Cellular Phones, and Internet Use by Country: 2011

[Rates per 100 persons, except as indicated. For data qualifications for countries, see source]

Country	Telephone main lines [1]	Cellular phone sub- scribers	Internet users (percent of population)	Country	Telephone main lines [1]	Cellular phone sub- scribers	Internet users (percent of population)
Afghanistan...............	0.04	54.26	4.58	Iran...........................	37.12	74.93	21.00
Australia....................	46.63	108.34	78.95	Italy..........................	34.64	151.84	56.82
Azerbaijan.................	18.09	108.75	50.75	Japan........................	51.06	102.67	78.71
Belize........................	9.07	63.87	(NA)	Korea, South.............	60.90	108.50	81.46
Brazil........................	21.88	123.18	45.00	Mali..........................	0.66	68.32	2.00
Bulgaria.....................	31.03	140.68	50.80	Mexico......................	17.15	82.38	36.15
Cambodia...................	3.70	69.90	3.10	Morocco....................	11.05	113.26	51.00
Canada......................	47.86	75.28	82.68	Namibia.....................	6.02	104.96	12.00
China [2]....................	21.16	73.19	38.40	Nicaragua..................	4.90	82.15	10.60
Colombia....................	15.19	98.45	40.40	Pakistan....................	3.24	61.61	9.00
Cuba.........................	10.60	11.69	23.23	Portugal....................	42.33	114.92	55.57
Denmark....................	45.13	126.46	89.98	Romania....................	21.93	109.16	44.12
Dominican Republic......	10.38	87.22	35.50	Russia......................	30.93	179.31	49.31
Egypt........................	10.56	101.08	35.62	Saudi Arabia..............	16.50	191.24	47.50
Estonia......................	35.10	138.98	76.53	Serbia.......................	37.32	125.39	47.19
Ethiopia.....................	0.98	16.67	1.10	Singapore..................	38.88	149.49	75.06
France.......................	55.92	105.03	76.77	Slovakia....................	19.30	109.35	74.87
Gambia......................	2.76	89.02	10.87	Slovenia....................	42.89	106.56	71.40
Georgia......................	31.01	102.35	35.28	Spain........................	42.34	114.23	67.92
Germany.....................	63.05	132.30	83.44	Sweden.....................	48.72	118.57	90.88
Greece.......................	49.91	106.48	53.40	Switzerland................	60.82	130.06	82.99
Haiti..........................	(NA)	41.49	(NA)	Syria.........................	20.92	63.17	22.44
Honduras....................	7.86	103.97	15.90	Timor-Leste...............	0.26	53.23	0.88
Hong Kong, China........	61.06	209.64	75.03	Turkey.......................	20.66	88.70	42.10
Hungary.....................	29.43	117.30	58.97	United Kingdom...........	53.24	130.75	81.71
India.........................	2.63	72.00	10.07	**United States.............**	**47.91**	**105.91**	**78.24**
Indonesia...................	15.94	97.72	18.00	Venezuela..................	24.91	97.78	40.44

NA Not applicable. [1] A fixed telephone line (previously called main telephone line in operation) is an active line (those that have registered an activity in the past three months) connecting the subscriber's terminal equipment to the public switched telephone network (PSTN) and which has a dedicated port in the telephone exchange equipment. This term is synonymous with the terms main station or Direct Exchange Line (DEL) that are commonly used in telecommunication documents. It may not be the same as an access line or a subscriber. This should include the active number of analog fixed telephone lines, ISDN channels, fixed wireless (WLL), public payphones and VoIP subscriptions. Fixed telephone lines per 100 inhabitants is calculated by dividing the number of fixed telephone lines by the population and multiplying by 100. [2] See footnote 4, Table 1348.

Source: International Telecommunication Union, *World Telecommunication/ICT Development Report*, and database; and World Bank estimates. See also <http://data.worldbank.org/>.

Table 1406. Patents by Country: 2011

[Includes only U.S. patents granted to residents of areas outside of the United States and its territories. See also Tables 789 and 790]

Country	Total [1]	Inventions	Designs	Country	Total [1]	Inventions	Designs
Total......................	**126,466**	**115,879**	**9,600**	Australia...................	2,213	1,919	265
Japan........................	48,256	46,139	1,869	Israel.......................	2,108	1,981	93
Korea, South..............	13,239	12,262	902	Netherlands..............	2,049	1,743	148
Germany....................	12,968	11,920	909	Switzerland..............	1,865	1,663	199
Taiwan [2]..................	9,907	8,781	1,086	Sweden....................	1,864	1,711	142
Canada.....................	5,753	5,012	704	India.......................	1,259	1,234	24
France......................	5,022	4,531	458	Finland....................	1,023	951	65
United Kingdom...........	4,924	4,307	575	Belgium...................	958	802	128
China [2]....................	3,786	3,174	603	Austria....................	927	753	171
Italy.........................	2,333	1,885	437	Other countries.........	6,012	5,111	822

[1] Includes patents for botanical plants and reissues, not shown separately. [2] See footnote 4, Table 1348.

Source: U.S. Patent and Trademark Office, "Patent Counts, 2011, Single Year Report," Technology Assessment and Forecast Database, <http://www.uspto.gov/web/offices/ac/ido/oeip/taf/reports_stco.htm>.

Table 1407. Key Global Telecom Indicators for the World Telecommunication Service Sector: 2005 to 2011

[In millions (1,243 represents 1,243,000,000), except as indicated]

Indicators	2005	2008	2009	2010	2011
NUMBER (mil.)					
Fixed telephone lines [1]...............................	1,243	1,249	1,214	1,188	(NA)
Mobile cellular subscribers............................	2,207	4,031	4,647	5,309	5,960
Internet users..	1,022	1,556	1,743	2,012	2,264
Fixed broadband subscriptions........................	219	408	465	528	588
PER 100 INHABITANTS					
Fixed telephone lines [1]...............................	19.4	18.5	18.3	17.8	17.3
Mobile cellular subscriptions..........................	34.0	59.9	68.2	77.1	85.6
Internet users..	15.8	23.2	25.7	29.5	32.8
Fixed broadband subscriptions........................	3.4	6.2	7.0	7.7	8.6

NA Not available. [1] See footnote 1, Table 1405.

Source: International Telecommunication Union, *World Telecommunication/ICT Development Report*, and database; and World Bank estimates; <http://www.data.worldbank.org>.

ProQuest Statistical Abstract of the United States: 2013

Table 1408. Dow Jones Global Index by Country and Industry: 2000 to 2011

[Index figures shown are as of December 31. 1991 = 100. Based on share prices denominated in U.S. dollars. Stocks in countries that impose significant restrictions on foreign ownership are included in the world index in the same proportion that shares are available to foreign investors]

Country and industry	2000	2005	2010	2011	Country and industry	2000	2005	2010	2011
World, total	**210.9**	**234.1**	**253.9**	**228.8**	Asia/Pacific	93.0	132.0	142.5	117.7
Americas	299.1	307.3	340.9	329.3	Australia	156.0	312.5	436.9	369.3
United States	**306.9**	**302.4**	**316.6**	**314.5**	Hong Kong	245.6	273.6	479.6	367.9
Canada	225.3	365.4	526.6	452.3	Indonesia	31.2	79.0	210.4	215.6
Mexico	132.2	360.1	626.8	535.2	Japan	88.3	113.5	91.8	78.4
Europe	241.2	264.8	270.2	232.0	Malaysia	88.5	119.5	254.0	248.6
Austria	86.2	335.5	277.4	176.5	New Zealand	96.7	227.3	181.9	180.1
Belgium	196.9	321.2	337.0	293.2	Singapore	135.2	176.3	327.6	263.4
Denmark	220.1	375.1	556.0	458.0	Thailand	27.2	76.7	152.1	144.1
Finland	1,537.8	948.5	936.0	624.5					
France	252.9	273.3	269.0	217.0	Basic materials	117.6	213.8	373.9	284.2
Germany	219.1	224.3	282.7	226.3	Consumer goods	183.8	241.9	318.4	308.9
Ireland	312.3	470.4	189.9	188.7	Consumer services	192.8	214.4	238.5	233.2
Italy	192.2	213.8	135.1	98.6	Oil and Gas	230.7	383.3	485.9	459.8
Netherlands	335.7	309.6	279.8	232.4	Financial	207.1	259.8	182.0	145.4
Norway	151.8	276.1	388.7	326.2	Healthcare	329.9	310.6	328.1	348.1
Spain	193.5	288.6	282.2	234.6	Industrial	167.1	192.4	228.8	200.1
Sweden	339.0	378.3	544.6	450.8	Technology	552.7	375.1	450.3	421.4
Switzerland	388.8	452.5	572.9	526.3	Telecommunications	273.3	201.6	234.5	224.5
United Kingdom	199.8	217.6	211.7	197.8	Utilities	156.0	176.9	195.1	180.0

Source: CME Group Index Services, LLC, New York, NY, Dow Jones Indexes (copyright), <http://www.djindexes.com/>.

Table 1409. Foreign Stock Market Activity—MSCI Indexes: 2000 to 2011

[Index figures shown are as of December 31. January 1, 1970 = 100, except as noted. Minus sign (–) indicates decrease. Based on share prices denominated in U.S. dollars. EM = Emerging Markets]

Index and country	Index			Percent change [1]		Index and country	Index			Percent change [1]	
	2000	2010	2011	2010	2011		2000	2010	2011	2010	2011
ALL COUNTRY (AC) INDEXES						Hong Kong	5,475	8,724	7,119	19.7	-18.4
ACWI [2]	290	331	300	10.4	-9.4	Israel	196	282	(NA)	2.2	(NA)
ACWI						Japan	2,552	2,496	2,091	13.4	-16.2
except USA [2]	194	263	221	8.4	-16.1	Singapore	2,081	4,212	3,329	18.4	-21.0
AC Asia Pacific [2]	90	138	114	14.3	-17.3						
AC Europe [2]	377	407	348	1.6	-14.5	**EMERGING MARKETS**					
European Union [2]	362	365	311	-0.2	-14.8	EM Far East index [2]	128	405	340	16.1	-16.1
						China [5, 6]	23	66	53	2.3	-20.3
DEVELOPED MARKETS						India [5]	115	559	347	19.4	-38.0
World index	1,221	1,280	1,183	9.6	-7.6	Indonesia	78	833	866	31.2	4.0
EAFE index [3]	1,492	1,658	1,413	4.9	-14.8	Korea, South	79	410	357	25.3	-12.8
Europe index	1,378	1,457	1,256	1.0	-13.8	Malaysia	161	453	440	32.5	-2.9
Pacific index	1,832	2,269	1,901	13.1	-16.2	Pakistan [5]	45	98	81	19.5	-17.1
Far East index	2,583	2,710	2,255	14.2	-16.8	Philippines	147	351	339	30.3	-3.2
						Sri Lanka [5]	36	288	205	71.9	-28.9
United States	**1,250**	**1,201**	**1,200**	**13.2**	**-0.1**	Taiwan [6]	192	313	240	18.3	-23.3
Canada	833	1,861	1,593	18.2	-14.4	Thailand	59	340	322	50.8	-5.6
Australia	318	884	753	10.0	-14.8	EM Latin America index	916	4,614	3,602	12.1	-21.9
New Zealand [2]	56	99	100	3.2	1.1	Argentina	1,233	3,573	2,050	70.1	-42.6
						Brazil	763	3,761	2,827	3.8	-24.9
Austria	708	1,509	939	7.3	-37.8	Chile	605	2,910	2,268	41.8	-22.1
Belgium	1,222	1,051	919	-2.2	-12.6	Colombia [5]	42	1,113	1,034	40.8	-7.1
Denmark	2,201	5,494	4,570	29.8	-16.8	Mexico	1,465	6,473	5,602	26.0	-13.5
Finland [2]	922	493	324	7.1	-34.2	Peru [5]	125	1,817	1,383	49.2	-23.9
France	1,509	1,492	1,204	-6.7	-19.3	Venezuela [5]	106	(NA)	(NA)	(NA)	(NA)
Germany	1,436	1,711	1,368	6.0	-20.1						
Greece [2]	476	224	82	-46.4	-63.6	EM Europe, Middle East, and Africa index [7]	100	392	(NA)	20.9	(NA)
Ireland [2]	308	106	118	-19.7	11.4	Czech Republic [8]	80	504	447	-7.4	-11.3
Italy	447	316	235	-17.6	-25.8	Egypt [8]	136	860	(NA)	9.5	(NA)
Luxembourg [4]	492	(NA)	(NA)	(NA)	(NA)	Hungary [8]	234	663	433	-10.7	-34.7
Netherlands	2,177	1,998	1,711	-0.6	-14.4	Jordan	55	132	109	-12.0	-17.1
Norway	1,181	2,965	2,584	7.4	-12.8	Morocco [8]	168	461	(NA)	10.8	(NA)
Portugal [2]	128	125	93	-14.6	-25.7	Poland [5]	499	1,016	685	12.6	-32.6
Spain	347	502	417	-25.4	-16.9	Russia [8]	155	932	737	17.2	-20.9
Sweden	4,240	6,888	5,662	31.3	-17.8	South Africa [5]	158	612	506	30.7	-17.3
Switzerland	2,695	3,915	3,561	9.8	-9.1	Turkey	248	625	395	18.4	-36.8
United Kingdom	1,146	1,138	1,068	5.2	-6.1						

NA Not available. [1] Percent change during calendar year (e.g., December 31, 2009 through December 31, 2010). Adjusted for foreign exchange fluctuations relative to U.S. dollar. [2] January 1, 1988 = 100. [3] Europe, Australasia, Far East Index. Comprised of all European and Far East countries classified as developed markets plus Australia, New Zealand, and Israel (reclassified May 2010). [4] MSCI Luxembourg Index discontinued as of March 29, 2002. [5] January 1, 1993 = 100. [6] See footnote 4, Table 1348. [7] January 1, 2001 = 100 [8] January 1, 1995 = 100.

Source: MSCI <http://www.msci.com/products/indices/> (copyright). The MSCI data contained herein is the property of MSCI Inc. (MSCI). MSCI, its affiliates and information providers make no warranties with respect to any such data. The MSCI data contained herein is used under license and may not be further used, distributed, or disseminated without the express written consent of MSCI.

Table 1410. Foreign Stock Market Indices: 1980 to 2011

[As of year end. The DAX-30 index is a total return index which includes dividends, whereas the other foreign indices are price indices which exclude dividends]

Year	London FTSE 100	Tokyo Nikkei 225	Hong Kong Hang Seng	Germany DAX-30	Paris CAC-40	Dow Jones Europe STOXX 50
1980	647	7,116	1,477	481	(X)	(X)
1985	1,413	13,113	1,752	1,366	(X)	(X)
1990	2,144	23,849	3,025	1,398	1,518	835
1995	3,689	19,868	10,073	2,254	1,872	1,538
1998	5,883	13,842	9,507	5,002	3,943	3,320
1999	6,930	18,934	16,962	6,958	5,958	4,742
2000	6,223	13,786	15,096	6,434	5,926	4,557
2001	5,217	10,543	11,397	5,160	4,625	3,707
2002	3,940	8,579	9,321	2,893	3,064	2,408
2003	4,477	10,677	12,576	3,965	3,558	2,660
2004	4,814	11,489	14,230	4,256	3,821	2,775
2005	5,619	16,111	14,876	5,408	4,715	3,349
2006	6,221	17,226	19,965	6,597	5,542	3,697
2007	6,457	15,308	27,813	8,067	5,614	3,684
2008	4,434	8,860	14,388	4,810	3,218	2,065
2009	5,413	10,546	21,873	5,957	3,936	2,579
2010	5,900	10,229	23,035	6,914	3,805	2,586
2011	5,572	8,455	18,434	5,898	3,160	2,370

X Not applicable.

Source: Global Financial Data, Los Angeles, CA, <http://www.globalfinancialdata.com>, unpublished data (copyright).

Table 1411. U.S. and Foreign Stock Markets—Market Capitalization and Value of Shares Traded: 2000 to 2011

[In billions of U.S. dollars (15,104.0 represents $15,104,000,000,000). Market capitalization is the market value of all domestic listed companies at the end of the year. The market value of a company is the share price times the number of shares outstanding. Value of shares traded is the annual total turnover of listed company shares]

Country	Market capitalization				Value of shares traded			
	2000	2005	2010	2011	2000	2005	2010	2011
United States	**15,104.0**	**16,970.9**	**17,139.0**	**15,640.7**	**31,862.5**	**21,510.0**	**30,454.8**	**30,750.6**
Australia	372.8	804.1	1,454.5	1,198.2	226.3	616.1	1,221.9	1,246.4
Austria	29.9	124.4	67.7	82.4	9.4	45.9	48.1	38.7
Belgium	182.5	288.5	269.3	229.9	38.0	125.7	111.5	107.2
Brazil	226.2	474.6	1,545.6	1,229.0	101.3	154.2	901.1	961.3
Canada	841.4	1,480.9	2,160.2	1,906.6	634.7	845.0	1,365.7	1,520.0
Chile	60.4	136.4	341.6	270.3	6.1	18.9	54.3	56.9
China [1]	581.0	780.8	4,762.8	3,389.1	721.5	586.3	8,030.0	7,671.4
Colombia	9.6	46.0	208.5	201.3	0.4	6.4	23.0	27.2
Denmark	107.7	178.0	231.7	179.5	91.6	152.0	144.6	150.5
Egypt	28.7	79.7	82.5	48.7	11.1	25.4	37.1	22.0
Finland	293.6	209.5	118.2	143.1	206.6	273.5	101.9	174.3
France	1,446.6	1,758.7	1,926.5	1,568.7	1,083.3	1,526.1	1,467.1	1,474.2
Germany	1,270.2	1,221.3	1,429.7	1,184.5	1,069.1	1,763.2	1,405.0	1,758.2
Greece	110.8	145.0	72.6	33.6	95.1	65.3	43.1	24.7
Hong Kong	623.4	693.5	1,079.6	889.6	377.9	294.1	1,597.5	1,551.6
India	148.1	553.1	1,615.9	1,015.4	509.8	433.9	1,056.8	740.2
Indonesia	26.8	81.4	360.4	390.1	14.3	41.9	129.5	139.6
Iran	34.0	38.7	86.6	107.2	5.0	8.2	17.1	20.1
Israel	64.1	120.1	218.1	145.0	23.4	59.9	133.4	117.4
Italy	768.4	798.2	318.1	431.5	778.4	1,115.2	539.3	887.5
Japan	3,157.2	4,736.5	4,099.6	3,540.7	2,693.9	4,997.4	4,280.4	4,160.5
Korea, South	171.6	718.2	1,089.2	994.3	1,067.7	1,203.0	1,626.6	2,032.9
Kuwait	20.8	130.1	119.6	100.9	4.2	94.0	41.8	21.4
Malaysia	116.9	181.2	410.5	395.1	58.5	50.0	90.2	128.9
Mexico	125.2	239.1	454.3	408.7	45.3	52.7	108.5	112.0
Netherlands	640.5	592.9	661.2	594.7	677.2	835.8	592.1	554.3
New Zealand	18.6	43.4	36.3	71.7	10.8	17.4	17.9	21.4
Norway	65.0	191.0	250.9	219.2	60.1	194.8	217.1	208.4
Philippines	51.6	40.2	157.3	165.4	8.2	7.0	26.8	32.9
Poland	31.3	93.9	190.2	138.2	14.6	30.0	77.5	95.9
Qatar	(NA)	87.3	123.6	125.4	(NA)	28.1	18.3	23.1
Russia	38.9	548.6	1,004.5	796.4	20.3	159.3	799.7	1,146.4
Saudi Arabia	67.2	646.1	353.4	338.9	17.3	1,103.5	203.2	293.0
Singapore	152.8	316.7	370.1	308.3	91.5	119.8	282.1	253.8
South Africa	205.0	565.4	1,012.5	855.7	77.5	200.7	340.0	372.2
Spain	504.2	960.0	1,171.6	1,031.0	985.9	1,557.2	1,360.9	1,419.2
Sweden	328.3	403.9	581.2	470.1	390.0	464.0	439.6	505.6
Switzerland	792.3	938.6	1,229.4	932.2	609.1	883.3	869.4	928.1
Taiwan [1]	247.6	516.0	804.1	623.4	983.5	716.5	892.6	866.6
Thailand	29.5	124.9	277.7	268.5	23.3	89.3	217.9	232.4
Turkey	69.7	161.5	306.7	201.8	179.2	201.3	421.6	413.7
United Arab Emirates	23.3	225.6	104.7	93.8	(NA)	143.1	27.4	15.8
United Kingdom	2,580.0	3,058.2	3,107.0	2,903.2	1,835.3	4,167.0	3,006.7	2,971.8

NA Not available [1] See footnote 4, Table 1348.

Source: Standard and Poor's, New York, NY, *Standard & Poor's Global Stock Markets Factbook 2012* (copyright), <http://www.standardandpoors.com>.

Table 1412. Foreign Exchange Rates: 2011

[Foreign currency units per U.S. dollar. Rates shown are annual averages, including market and official exchange rates]

Country	Currency	2011 [1]	Country	Currency	2011 [1]
Afghanistan	Afghani	45.37	Kuwait	Kuwaiti dinar	0.29
Albania	Lek	99.50	Kyrgyzstan	Som	46.05
Algeria	Algerian dinar	72.51	Laos	Kip	8,043.70
Angola	Kwanza	93.21	Latvia	Lat	0.50
Argentina	Argentine peso	4.13	Lebanon	Lebanese pound	1,507.50
Armenia	Dram	371.00	Lesotho	Loti	7.30
Australia	Australian dollar	0.97	Liberia	Liberian dollar	74.20
Austria	Euro	0.71	Libya	Libyan dinar	1.60
Azerbaijan	Manat	0.79	Lithuania	Lita	2.45
Bahrain	Bahrain dinar	0.38	Macedonia	Denar	43.64
Bangladesh	Taka	73.70	Madagascar	Malagasy ariary	1,950.00
Belarus	Belarusian ruble	4,351.10	Malawi	Kwacha	159.00
Belgium	Euro	0.71	Malaysia	Ringgit	3.01
Benin	CFA franc	473.70	Mali	CFA franc	473.70
Bolivia	Boliviano	6.98	Mauritania	Ouguiya	273.30
Bosnia and Herzegovina	Konvertibilna marka	1.39	Mauritius	Mauritian rupee	28.67
Botswana	Pula	6.70	Mexico	Peso	12.39
Brazil	Real	1.60	Moldova	Leu	11.67
Bulgaria	Leva	1.39	Mongolia	Togrog	1,228.00
Burkina Faso	CFA franc	473.70	Morocco	Dirham	8.08
Burma	Kyat	815.00	Mozambique	Metical	28.50
Cambodia	Riel	4,085.90	Namibia	Namibia dollar	7.08
Cameroon	CFA franc	473.70	Nepal	Nepalese rupee	83.31
Canada	Canadian dollar	0.98	Netherlands	Euro	0.71
Central African Republic	CFA franc	473.70	New Zealand	New Zealand dollar	1.27
Chad	CFA franc	473.70	Nicaragua	Cordoba	22.45
Chile	Chilean peso	470.90	Niger	CFA franc	473.70
China [2]	Yuan	6.46	Nigeria	Naira	152.70
Colombia	Colombian peso	1,812.80	Norway	Krone	5.43
Congo (Kinshasa) [3]	Congolese franc	1,000.00	Oman	Omani rial	0.38
Congo (Brazzaville) [3]	CFA franc	473.70	Pakistan	Pakistan rupee	85.99
Costa Rica	Colon	503.50	Panama	Balboa	1.00
Cote d'Ivoire	CFA franc	465.20	Papua New Guinea	Kina	2.21
Croatia	Kuna	5.25	Paraguay	Guarani	4,188.10
Cuba	Peso	0.98	Peru	Nuevo sol	2.75
Curacao [4]	Guilder	1.79	Philippines	Philippine peso	43.44
Czech Republic	Koruna	17.25	Poland	Zloty	2.83
Denmark	Krone	5.29	Portugal	Euro	0.71
Djibouti	Djibouti franc	177.70	Qatar	Riyal	3.64
Dominican Republic	Dominican peso	38.19	Romania	Leu	3.02
Ecuador	U.S. dollar	1.00	Russia	Ruble	28.35
Egypt	Egyptian pound	5.94	Rwanda	Rwandan franc	607.20
El Salvador	U.S. dollar	1.00	Saint Lucia	East Caribbean dollar	2.70
Eritrea	Nakfa	15.38	Saudi Arabia	Riyal	3.75
Estonia	Euro	0.71	Senegal	CFA franc	473.70
Ethiopia	Birr	17.20	Serbia	Serbian dinar	72.46
Fiji	Fijian dollar	1.86	Sierra Leone	Leone	4,400.00
Finland	Euro	0.71	Singapore	Singapore dollar	1.23
France	Euro	0.71	Slovakia	Euro	0.71
Gabon	CFA franc	465.20	Slovenia	Euro	0.71
Gambia, The	Dalasi	30.29	South Africa	Rand	7.16
Georgia	Lari	1.70	Spain	Euro	7.11
Germany	Euro	0.71	Sri Lanka	Sri Lankan rupee	112.00
Ghana	Cedi	1.50	Sudan	Sudanese dinar	2.80
Greece	Euro	0.71	Swaziland	Emalangeni	7.30
Guatemala	Quetzal	7.80	Sweden	Krona	6.35
Guinea	Guinean franc	6,600.00	Switzerland	Swiss franc	0.87
Guinea-Bissau	CFA franc	473.70	Syria	Syrian pound	47.20
Haiti	Gourde	39.80	Tajikistan	Tajik somoni	4.54
Honduras	Lempira	18.90	Tanzania	Tanzania shilling	1,571.10
Hong Kong	Hong Kong dollar	7.76	Taiwan [2]	New Taiwan dollar	29.05
Hungary	Forint	195.90	Thailand	Baht	30.18
Iceland	Krona	117.70	Togo	CFA franc	473.70
India	Rupee	44.64	Trinidad and Tobago	Tr. and Tob. Dollar	6.41
Indonesia	Rupiah	8,696.10	Tunisia	Tunisian dinar	1.40
Iran	Rial	10,800.00	Turkey	Lira	1.67
Iraq	Dinar	1,170.00	Turkmenistan	Manat	2.85
Ireland	Euro	0.71	Uganda	Uganda shilling	2,567.10
Israel	Shekel	3.53	Ukraine	Hryvnia	7.96
Italy	Euro	0.71	United Arab Emirates	Dirham	3.67
Jamaica	Jamaican dollar	86.36	United Kingdom	Pound sterling	0.62
Japan	Yen	79.67	Uruguay	Uruguayan peso	19.04
Jordan	Jordanian dinar	0.71	Uzbekistan	Soum	1,714.10
Kazakhstan	Tenge	145.60	Venezuela	Bolivar	4.43
Kenya	Kenyan shilling	86.23	Vietnam	Dong	20,585.60
Korea, North	North Korean won	145.00	Yemen	Yemeni rial	229.80
Korea, South	Won	1,107.30	Zambia	Zambian kwacha	4,869.90

[1] End-of-year values were used if annual averages were unavailable. Some values were estimated using partial year data. [2] See footnote 4, Table 1348. [3] See footnote 5, Table 1348. [4] The Netherlands Antilles dissolved on October 10, 2010. Curaçao and Sint Maarten became autonomous territories of the Kingdom of the Netherlands.

Source: U.S. Central Intelligence Agency, *The World Factbook, 2011,* annual, accessed July 2012, <https://www.cia.gov/library/publications/the-world-factbook/index.html/>.

Table 1413. Research and Development (R&D) Expenditures by Country

[Figures are for 2007, except as noted, or latest year available. GDP = gross domestic product; for explanation, see text, Section 13]

| Country | Gross domestic expenditure on R&D (GERD) | | | Per capita at current U.S. dollars, PPPs [1] | Higher education expenditure on R&D (HERD) | |
| | Percent of GDP | Percent financed by— | | | Percent of GERD | Percent of GDP |
		Government	Industry			
OECD total................	**2.29**	**28.56**	**63.79**	**748**	**16.8**	**0.38**
EU-15 [2]........................	1.90	33.36	55.60	635	21.6	0.41
EU-27 [3]........................	1.77	34.11	54.98	530	21.8	0.39
Australia [4].....................	2.01	38.37	57.23	716	25.7	0.52
Austria [4].......................	2.56	35.60	47.68	952	24.1	0.62
Belgium........................	1.87	24.65	59.68	662	21.8	0.41
Brazil...........................	1.02	57.88	39.38	92	(NA)	(NA)
Canada [4]......................	1.88	31.42	49.40	724	33.7	0.63
China [5, 6].....................	1.49	24.62	70.37	77	8.5	0.13
Czech Republic..............	1.54	41.19	53.96	369	16.9	0.26
Denmark.......................	2.55	27.58	59.53	917	27.5	0.70
Finland.........................	3.47	24.05	68.20	1,206	18.7	0.65
France..........................	2.08	38.42	52.44	680	19.2	0.40
Germany.......................	2.54	27.76	68.07	874	16.3	0.41
Greece.........................	0.57	46.82	31.06	163	50.4	0.29
Hungary........................	0.97	44.41	43.86	181	23.4	0.23
Iceland.........................	2.75	38.80	50.35	980	25.1	0.69
India............................	0.71	80.81	16.11	13	4.9	0.03
Ireland.........................	1.31	30.13	59.26	591	26.4	0.35
Italy............................	1.13	48.32	40.42	334	30.3	0.34
Japan [4].......................	3.44	15.63	77.71	1,157	12.6	0.43
Korea..........................	3.47	24.80	73.65	861	10.7	0.37
Luxembourg...................	1.63	16.61	79.72	1,300	3.0	0.05
Mexico.........................	0.46	45.34	46.49	57	27.4	0.13
Netherlands...................	1.70	36.23	51.06	669	26.6	0.45
New Zealand..................	1.21	42.66	40.14	325	30.1	0.36
Norway.........................	1.64	44.87	45.25	878	31.4	0.51
Poland..........................	0.57	58.61	34.26	91	33.9	0.19
Portugal........................	1.18	55.20	36.27	269	29.9	0.35
Russia..........................	1.12	62.62	29.45	165	6.3	0.07
Slovakia........................	0.46	53.92	35.60	92	25.0	0.11
South Africa...................	0.92	38.19	43.87	76	19.3	0.18
Spain...........................	1.27	42.49	47.07	401	26.4	0.33
Sweden........................	3.60	24.43	63.86	1,320	21.3	0.77
Switzerland....................	2.90	22.71	69.73	1,003	22.9	0.66
Turkey..........................	0.71	47.07	48.45	92	48.2	0.34
United Kingdom..............	1.79	29.33	47.19	640	24.5	0.44
United States [4, 7, 8].........	**2.68**	**27.73**	**66.44**	**1,221**	**13.3**	**0.36**

NA Not available or not applicable. [1] Purchasing power parities. See headnote, Table 1364. [2] European Union-15: Austria, Belgium, Denmark, Finland, France, Germany, Greece, Ireland, Italy, Luxembourg, Netherlands, Portugal, Spain, Sweden, and United Kingdom. [3] See footnote 4, Table 1391. [4] Government budget appropriations for R&D: federal government only. [5] See footnote 4, Table 1348. [6] Percent of GERD/BERD financed by government or industry: the sum of the breakdown does not add to the total. BERD is Business Enterprise Research and Development. [7] GERD, BERD: Excluding most or all capital expenditures. [8] HERD: Excluding most or all capital expenditures.

Source: Organisation for Economic Cooperation and Development (OECD), 2010, "Main Science and Technology Indicators," *OECD Science, Technology and R&D Statistics* database (copyright), <http://dx.doi.org/10.1787/data-00182-en>, accessed May 2010.

Table 1414. Development Assistance by Country: 2009

[119,782 represents $119,782,000,000]

Country	Official development aid (ODA)			Multilateral ODA (mil. U.S. dol.)	Net private grants (mil. U.S. dol.)
	Mil. U.S. dollars	Percent of GNI [1]	Percent of total DAC [2] ODA		
DAC [2] total........................	119,782	0.31	100.0	36,278	22,047
EU-15 [3].............................	67,211	0.44	56.1	26,226	3,328
United States....................	**28,831**	**0.21**	**24.1**	**3,658**	**16,288**
Australia............................	2,762	0.29	2.3	450	(NA)
Austria..............................	1,142	0.30	1.0	635	140
Belgium.............................	2,610	0.55	2.2	1,025	377
Canada..............................	4,000	0.30	3.3	859	1,338
Denmark............................	2,810	0.88	2.3	904	116
Finland..............................	1,290	0.54	1.1	499	17
France..............................	12,602	0.47	10.5	5,581	(NA)
Germany............................	12,079	0.35	10.1	4,983	1,369
Greece..............................	607	0.19	0.5	310	2
Ireland..............................	1,006	0.54	0.8	313	182
Italy.................................	3,297	0.16	2.8	2,423	162
Japan...............................	9,457	0.18	7.9	3,290	533
Korea...............................	816	0.10	0.7	235	156
Luxembourg.........................	415	1.04	0.3	149	13
Netherlands.........................	6,426	0.82	5.4	1,628	542
New Zealand........................	309	0.28	0.3	83	46
Norway..............................	4,086	1.06	3.4	918	(NA)
Portugal............................	513	0.23	0.4	236	4
Spain................................	6,584	0.46	5.5	2,111	(NA)
Sweden.............................	4,548	1.12	3.8	1,539	74
Switzerland.........................	2,310	0.45	1.9	559	357
United Kingdom.....................	11,283	0.51	9.4	3,891	329

NA Not available. [1] Gross national income. See headnote, Table 1363. [2] DAC: OECD Development Assistance Committee. [3] European Union-15: Austria, Belgium, Denmark, Finland, France, Germany, Greece, Ireland, Italy, Luxembourg, Netherlands, Portugal, Spain, Sweden, and United Kingdom.

Source: Organisation for Economic Cooperation and Development (OECD), 2011, "Aggregate Aid Statistics: ODA by donor," *OECD International Development Statistics* database (copyright); <http://dx.doi.org/10.1787/data-00063-en>, accessed April 2011.

Table 1415. Net Flow of Financial Resources to Developing Countries and Multilateral Organizations, by Donor Country: 1995 to 2010

[167,206 represents $167,206,000,000. Net flow covers offical and private loans, grants, development assistance, and technical assistance, minus amortization on loans. Military flows are excluded. GNI = gross national income. For explanation of GNI, see headnote, Table 1363. Minus sign (–) indicates net inflow]

Country	Amount (million dollars)				Percent of GNI			
	1995	2000	2005	2010	1995	2000	2005	2010
DAC countries total [1].............	**167,206**	**134,168**	**307,531**	**494,416**	**0.73**	**0.54**	**0.93**	**1.23**
G-7 countries total [2]................	144,858	82,122	231,936	386,726	0.75	0.39	0.86	1.21
United States........................	**46,984**	**25,252**	**113,526**	**214,378**	**0.65**	**0.25**	**0.92**	**1.46**
Australia.............................	2,536	1,891	5,201	14,531	0.73	0.51	0.77	1.23
Austria..............................	958	1,135	4,837	4,830	0.41	0.61	1.60	1.29
Belgium.............................	-234	2,281	3,142	7,896	-0.09	1.00	0.84	1.68
Canada..............................	5,724	6,483	13,373	22,636	1.04	0.95	1.20	1.46
Denmark............................	1,799	2,176	2,215	4,794	1.07	1.39	0.85	1.52
Finland..............................	604	1,087	1,642	4,312	0.48	0.91	0.84	1.78
France..............................	12,477	5,557	15,744	35,198	0.81	0.41	0.74	1.35
Germany............................	21,197	12,331	30,683	31,197	0.87	0.66	1.10	0.93
Greece..............................	(NA)	229	709	761	(NA)	0.20	0.32	0.26
Ireland..............................	247	740	5,298	2,695	0.46	0.93	3.09	1.57
Italy.................................	2,800	10,846	4,103	9,608	0.26	1.01	0.23	0.47
Japan...............................	42,295	11,423	23,238	48,076	0.79	0.24	0.50	0.86
Korea...............................	1,973	44	4,910	11,834	0.38	0.01	0.62	1.17
Luxembourg.........................	72	129	265	411	0.40	0.73	0.82	1.07
Netherlands.........................	6,795	6,947	22,781	13,013	1.71	1.85	3.65	1.67
New Zealand........................	166	142	401	426	0.31	0.32	0.40	0.32
Norway..............................	1,670	1,437	4,637	4,589	1.15	0.87	1.56	1.10
Portugal............................	395	4,622	1,109	162	0.38	4.45	0.62	0.07
Spain................................	2,025	23,471	6,801	10,340	0.37	4.25	0.61	0.74
Sweden.............................	2,224	3,952	3,545	5,127	1.00	1.76	0.99	1.10
Switzerland.........................	1,118	1,765	8,103	21,968	0.35	0.68	1.99	3.86
United Kingdom.....................	13,382	10,230	31,269	25,632	1.19	0.72	1.37	1.12

NA Not available. [1] The OECD Development Assistance Committee (DAC) is comprised of the above-listed 23 member countries plus the European Union. [2] Group of seven (G7) major industrialized countries: United States, Canada, France, Germany, Italy, United Kingdom, and Japan.

Source: Organisation for Economic Co-operation and Development (OECD), 2012, "Official and private flows," OECD International Development Statistics (database), <http://dx.doi.org/10.1787/data-00072-en>, accessed on 08 August, 2012 (copyright).

Table 1416. External Debt by Developing Country: 1990 to 2010

[In millions of dollars (28,147 represents $28,147,000,000). Total external debt is debt owed to nonresidents repayable in foreign currency, goods, or services. Total external debt is the sum of public, publicly guaranteed, and private nonguaranteed long-term debt, use of IMF credit, and short-term debt. Short-term debt includes all debt having an original maturity of one year or less and interest in arrears on long-term debt]

Country	1990	2000	2009	2010	Country	1990	2000	2009	2010
Algeria	28,147	25,388	5,424	5,276	Malaysia	15,328	41,765	66,272	81,497
Angola	8,592	9,408	16,616	18,562	Mexico	104,442	150,901	171,485	200,081
Argentina	62,233	140,914	120,283	127,849	Morocco	25,004	20,674	23,751	25,403
Bangladesh	12,285	15,535	23,802	24,963	Nepal	1,627	2,867	3,683	3,702
Brazil	119,732	241,550	276,910	346,978	Nigeria	33,439	31,355	7,713	7,883
Bulgaria	10,890	11,212	53,499	48,077	Pakistan	20,589	32,732	54,588	56,773
Burma	4,695	5,975	8,186	6,352	Panama	6,492	6,567	11,267	11,412
Cameroon	6,563	10,323	2,946	2,964	Papua New Guinea	2,594	2,292	1,573	5,822
Chile	19,226	37,239	73,145	86,349	Peru	20,054	28,632	36,393	36,271
China	55,301	145,339	432,197	548,551	Philippines	30,580	58,304	63,116	72,337
Colombia	17,222	33,937	52,120	63,064	Romania	1,140	11,160	118,008	121,505
Congo (Kinshasa) [1]	10,259	11,692	12,276	5,774	Russia [2]	(NA)	159,993	373,419	384,740
Cote d'Ivoire	17,251	12,138	11,702	11,430	Serbia [3]	17,792	11,499	33,111	32,222
Dominican Republic	4,372	4,541	11,046	13,045	South Africa	(NA)	24,861	42,466	45,165
Ecuador	12,107	13,254	14,130	14,815	Sri Lanka	5,863	9,087	17,213	20,452
Egypt	32,992	29,010	33,308	34,844	Sudan	14,762	15,983	20,746	21,846
Ethiopia	8,645	5,495	5,030	7,147	Syria	17,353	22,156	5,112	4,729
Ghana	3,734	6,116	6,331	8,368	Tanzania	6,446	7,142	7,324	8,664
Guatemala	2,845	3,853	13,764	14,340	Thailand	28,094	79,720	57,886	71,263
India	85,661	100,243	249,993	290,282	Tunisia	7,688	11,307	21,711	21,584
Indonesia	69,848	143,344	162,850	179,064	Turkey	49,424	116,646	271,225	293,872
Iran	9,020	7,717	13,464	12,570	Ukraine	(NA)	12,185	103,435	116,808
Jamaica	4,761	4,724	10,987	13,865	Uruguay	4,415	8,408	11,131	11,347
Kazakhstan	(NA)	12,433	111,115	118,723	Venezuela	33,171	42,338	55,235	55,572
Latvia	(NA)	4,855	41,822	39,555	Vietnam	23,270	12,822	28,718	35,139
Lebanon	1,787	10,244	24,500	24,293	Zimbabwe	3,279	3,807	4,801	5,016

NA Not available. [1] See footnote 5, Table 1348. [2] The debt of the former Soviet Union is included in Russia's data after 1990 on the assumption that 100 percent of all outstanding external debt as of December 1991 has become a liability of Russia. Beginning in 2000, the data for Russia has also been revised to include obligations to members of the former Council for Mutual Economic Assistance and other countries in the form of trade-related credits amounting to $15.4 billion as of the end of 1996. [3] In June 2006, Serbia and Montenegro became separate countries (formerly Yugoslavia). Data for 2000 are for Serbia and Montenegro. Starting 2006, data excludes Montenegro. External debt obligations—excluding IBRD, IMF, and short-term—of Bosnia and Herzegovina before 2000 are included under Serbia and Montenegro. Data from 2000 onwards are estimates and also reflect borrowing by the former Yugoslavia that are not yet allocated to the successor republics.

Source: The World Bank, Washington, DC, *World Development Indicators*, annual (copyright). Accessed August 2012. See also <http://data.worldbank.org/>.

Table 1417. Foreign Direct Investment Flows in Selected Countries: 2005 to 2011

[In billions of dollars (112.6 represents $112,600,000,000). Data are converted to U.S. dollars using the yearly average exchange rate]

Country	Inflows				Outflows			
	2005	2010	2011 [1]	Cumulative 2005-2010	2005	2010	2011 [1]	Cumulative 2005-2010
United States	112.6	205.8	234.0	1,243.3	36.2	327.9	419.3	1,641.6
Australia	-24.2	34.0	67.5	159.9	-31.1	27.3	16.2	88.6
Austria	10.8	4.3	14.1	70.3	11.1	7.7	30.5	111.0
Belgium	34.4	81.2	89.2	523.2	32.6	55.7	70.8	449.0
Brazil	15.1	48.5	66.7	188.0	2.5	11.6	-1.0	59.7
Canada	25.7	23.4	40.9	302.1	27.5	38.6	49.6	289.7
China	117.2	185.0	228.6	875.7	11.3	60.1	43.0	207.0
Czech Republic	11.7	6.1	5.4	43.1	(Z)	1.2	1.2	9.5
Denmark	12.9	-7.4	14.8	25.8	16.2	3.5	23.7	68.3
France	84.9	30.6	41.0	371.9	114.9	76.9	90.2	728.8
Germany	47.4	46.9	40.4	262.4	75.8	109.3	54.4	622.6
Greece	0.6	0.4	1.8	15.4	1.5	1.0	1.8	16.2
Hungary	7.7	2.3	4.7	30.8	2.2	1.3	4.5	15.2
India	7.6	25.9	34.2	158.3	3.0	14.8	12.4	84.6
Ireland	-31.7	42.8	11.5	39.6	14.3	22.3	-4.3	118.7
Italy	20.0	9.2	29.1	117.9	41.8	32.7	47.3	295.5
Japan	2.8	-1.3	-1.8	53.9	45.8	56.3	114.3	428.6
Korea, South	6.3	1.1	4.7	18.3	6.4	23.3	20.4	98.0
Mexico	24.4	20.7	19.6	140.0	6.5	13.6	8.9	42.2
Netherlands	39.0	-9.0	17.1	204.0	123.0	55.2	31.9	401.4
New Zealand	1.5	0.6	3.6	14.0	-1.5	0.6	2.8	2.4
Norway	5.4	17.5	3.6	62.0	22.0	23.1	20.0	128.0
Poland	10.3	8.9	15.2	90.1	3.4	5.5	5.9	32.3
Russia	12.9	43.3	52.9	252.5	12.8	52.5	67.3	233.6
South Africa	6.6	1.2	5.8	27.7	0.9	-0.1	-0.6	7.9
Spain	25.0	40.8	29.5	248.1	41.8	38.3	37.3	409.2
Sweden	11.9	-1.3	12.1	114.3	27.7	18.0	26.9	168.3
Switzerland	-0.9	20.4	-0.2	139.5	51.0	64.8	69.5	315.8
Turkey	10.0	9.0	15.9	89.2	1.1	1.5	2.5	9.7
United Kingdom	177.9	50.6	53.9	749.8	80.0	39.5	107.1	749.5

Z Less than $50 million. [1] Preliminary.

Source: Organisation for Economic Co-operation and Development (OECD), 2012, "Foreign direct investment: flows by partner country," OECD International Direct Investment Statistics (database), <http://dx.doi.org/10.1787/data-00335-en>, accessed on 08 August 2012 (copyright).

Table 1418. International Tourism Arrivals, Expenditures, and Receipts--Leading Countries: 2002 to 2010

[Arrivals in thousands of non-resident tourists at national borders except as noted (77,012 represents 77,012,000). Expenditures and receipts in millions of current U.S. dollars (23,769 represents 23,769,000,000). Receipts are dollars spent by foreign tourists on travel inside the country shown and include other prepayment for goods or services in destination country. Expenditures are dollars visitors (same-day visitors and tourists) from a given country of origin spend on travel outside their country of residence. Some countries do not include receipts and expenditures for passenger transport items. Excludes international transport receipts. Sources and collection methods differ, thus caution should be used in comparing data across countries]

Country	Arrivals (1,000)					Expenditures (mil. dol.)					Receipts (mil. dol.)				
	2002	2005	2008	2009	2010	2002	2005	2008	2009	2010	2002	2005	2008	2009	2010
France	77,012	74,988	79,218	76,764	77,148	23,769	31,727	41,067	38,327	38,562	35,011	43,954	56,565	49,473	46,597
United States	43,581	49,206	57,937	54,884	59,791	62,671	74,790	86,904	80,829	82,696	88,136	106,162	139,123	123,855	134,847
China	36,803	46,809	53,049	50,875	55,664	15,398	21,759	36,157	43,702	54,880	20,385	29,296	40,843	39,675	45,814
Spain	50,331	55,914	57,192	52,178	52,677	7,295	15,046	20,363	16,911	16,764	31,880	47,789	61,978	53,337	52,187
Italy	39,799	36,513	42,734	43,239	43,626	16,924	22,370	30,931	27,950	26,907	26,873	35,319	46,193	40,378	38,438
United Kingdom	22,307	28,039	30,142	28,199	28,295	41,744	59,532	69,792	50,559	48,618	20,549	30,573	36,424	30,498	30,580
Turkey	12,790	20,273	24,994	25,506	27,000	1,880	2,872	3,506	4,147	4,826	11,901	18,152	21,951	21,250	20,807
Germany	17,969	21,500	24,884	24,220	26,875	53,006	74,189	91,598	81,400	77,580	19,278	29,121	39,915	34,725	34,560
Malaysia	13,292	16,431	22,052	23,646	24,577	2,618	3,711	6,709	6,508	7,943	7,118	8,846	15,293	15,798	18,315
Russia	23,309	22,201	23,676	21,339	22,281	10,918	17,314	23,778	20,905	26,516	4,040	5,870	11,842	9,366	8,970
Mexico	19,667	21,915	22,637	21,454	22,260	6,060	7,600	8,526	7,132	7,284	8,858	11,803	13,289	11,275	11,760
Austria	18,611	19,952	21,935	21,355	22,004	6,901	9,316	11,432	10,813	10,125	10,803	16,243	21,630	15,159	18,758
Ukraine	10,517	17,631	25,449	20,798	21,203	657	2,805	4,023	3,330	3,742	788	3,125	5,768	3,576	3,788
Hong Kong	10,689	14,773	17,319	16,926	20,085	12,418	13,305	16,095	15,669	17,461	7,410	10,179	15,043	16,078	21,775
Canada	20,057	18,771	17,142	15,737	16,097	11,722	18,017	27,210	24,169	29,477	10,687	13,768	15,668	13,707	15,775
Thailand	10,873	11,567	14,584	14,150	15,936	3,303	3,039	5,003	4,343	5,054	7,901	9,577	18,163	15,665	19,714
Greece	14,180	14,765	15,939	14,915	15,007	2,436	3,039	3,930	3,381	2,854	9,909	13,334	17,416	14,681	12,479
Egypt	4,906	8,244	12,296	11,914	14,051	1,266	1,629	2,915	2,538	2,240	3,764	6,851	10,985	10,755	12,528
Poland	13,980	15,200	12,960	11,890	12,470	3,278	5,548	9,903	7,372	8,570	4,314	6,274	11,768	9,011	9,526
Macao	6,565	9,014	10,610	10,402	11,926	492	552	834	901	1,035	4,205	7,618	16,948	18,142	27,790
Netherlands	9,595	10,012	10,104	9,921	10,883	12,976	16,140	21,828	20,758	19,489	7,710	10,450	13,343	12,401	12,861
Saudi Arabia	7,511	8,037	14,757	10,897	10,850	(NA)	9,087	15,129	20,419	21,135	(NA)	4,626	5,909	5,995	6,712
Hungary	(NA)	9,979	8,814	9,058	9,510	2,133	2,277	3,225	2,750	2,404	3,728	4,120	6,033	5,712	5,339
Morocco	4,453	5,843	7,879	8,341	9,288	444	612	1,090	1,106	1,203	2,646	4,610	7,221	6,626	6,702
Singapore	5,855	7,079	7,778	7,489	9,161	8,212	10,070	15,197	15,010	16,770	4,458	6,205	10,711	9,383	14,181
Croatia	6,944	7,743	8,665	8,694	9,111	781	754	1,113	1,013	833	3,811	7,463	11,280	9,000	8,050
South Korea	5,347	6,023	6,891	7,818	8,798	10,465	15,406	19,065	15,040	17,669	5,936	5,806	9,774	9,819	9,765
Denmark	3,436	9,178	9,016	8,547	8,744	5,838	6,850	9,698	8,968	9,082	4,791	5,293	6,281	5,617	5,704
Switzerland	6,868	7,229	8,608	8,294	8,628	5,537	8,782	10,913	10,951	11,159	7,260	10,041	14,457	14,148	14,978
Japan	5,239	6,728	8,351	6,790	8,611	26,656	37,565	27,901	25,199	27,950	3,497	12,430	10,820	10,329	13,224
Syria	2,661	3,571	5,430	6,092	8,546	760	550	800	882	1,510	970	1,944	3,150	3,757	6,190
Czech Republic	(NA)	6,336	9,373	8,390	8,185	1,597	2,405	4,652	4,077	4,064	2,964	4,813	7,857	7,013	7,121
South Africa	6,430	7,369	9,592	7,012	8,074	1,811	3,374	4,404	4,151	5,595	2,923	7,516	7,956	7,624	9,085
Belgium	6,720	6,747	7,165	6,815	7,186	10,185	14,948	19,859	20,432	18,679	6,935	9,845	11,788	10,202	10,235
Indonesia	5,033	5,002	6,234	6,324	7,003	3,289	3,584	5,554	5,316	6,395	5,285	4,522	7,377	5,598	6,958
Tunisia	5,064	6,378	7,050	6,901	6,903	260	374	458	415	547	1,523	2,143	2,953	2,773	2,645
Portugal	5,560	5,769	6,962	6,439	6,756	2,125	3,050	4,328	3,776	3,905	5,798	7,676	10,980	9,693	10,007
Ireland	6,476	7,333	8,026	7,189	(NA)	3,755	6,074	10,413	8,773	7,691	3,097	4,782	6,356	4,894	4,040
Romania	4,794	5,839	8,862	7,575	(NA)	396	925	2,176	1,472	1,636	335	1,052	1,991	1,229	1,125
United Arab Emirates	5,445	7,126	(NA)	(NA)	(NA)	(NA)	(NA)	(NA)	(NA)	(NA)	(NA)	(NA)	(NA)	(NA)	(NA)

NA Not available.

Source: The World Bank, Washington DC, <http://search.worldbank.org/data> (copyright), accessed August 2012. See also: World Tourism Organization, Madrid, Spain, *World Tourism Barometer*.

Table 1419. International Transaction Balances and Trade in Relation to Gross Domestic Product (GDP) by Country: 2000 to 2010

[In millions of U.S. dollars (-416,343 represents -$416,343,000,000), except as noted. Minus sign (-) indicates debits. This table replaces Table 1399 in the 2012 edition of the Statistical Abstract. That table, prepared by the International Monetary Fund, included data on reserve assets and currency holdings. It did not include data on trade as a percent of GDP]

Country	Current account balance			Merchandise trade balance			Exports as percent of GDP (%)		Imports as percent of GDP (%)	
	2000	2005	2010	2000	2005	2010	2005	2010	2005	2010
United States	**-416,343**	**-745,780**	**-470,902**	**-382,100**	**-722,700**	**-516,900**	**10.4**	**12.7**	**16.1**	**16.3**
Algeria	(NA)	21,180	12,146	10,860	23,923	15,119	47.6	30.8	24.3	21.5
Argentina	-8,981	5,274	2,932	-1,801	10,770	12,191	25.1	21.7	19.2	18.4
Australia	-14,763	-41,033	-31,990	-8,531	-17,509	-3,503	18.0	19.8	20.6	20.1
Austria	-1,339	6,245	11,671	3,356	12,151	16,225	53.8	54.0	49.9	49.7
Bangladesh	-306	-176	2,109	-2,473	-3,897	-6,634	16.6	18.4	23.0	25.0
Belgium	(NA)	7,703	6,132	6,811	14,842	12,595	78.7	79.9	74.7	77.2
Brazil	-24,225	13,985	-47,323	-11,369	31,832	-22,102	15.1	10.9	11.5	11.9
Cameroon	-218	-493	-856	362	-169	-699	20.5	28.9	21.5	32.0
Chile	-898	1,449	3,802	1,402	8,456	13,308	38.8	38.1	31.9	31.9
China	20,518	134,082	305,374	28,873	124,798	232,074	37.1	29.5	31.6	25.6
Colombia	795	-1,886	-8,760	-367	-2,599	-6,389	17.0	15.7	18.8	17.9
Cote d'Ivoire	-241	40	(NA)	740	1,221	1,046	51.1	40.6	43.6	36.1
Czech Republic	-2,690	-1,210	-7,602	-1,259	3,553	6,310	64.4	67.9	61.7	64.7
Denmark	2,262	11,104	17,134	9,662	12,640	16,439	49.0	50.3	44.1	45.1
Ecuador	926	347	-1,785	967	-405	-3,287	30.9	32.9	32.0	38.6
Egypt, Arab Rep	-971	2,103	-4,504	-6,605	-2,032	-10,468	30.3	21.3	32.6	26.1
Finland	10,526	6,469	3,495	11,131	8,012	2,070	41.8	40.1	37.7	39.2
France	19,674	-10,260	-44,499	13,202	-13,529	-55,458	26.4	25.6	27.0	27.7
Georgia	-177	-710	-1,197	-510	-1,142	-2,041	33.7	34.9	51.6	52.4
Germany	-32,484	140,216	200,708	5,804	144,245	178,224	41.3	46.8	36.1	41.4
Ghana	-386	-1,105	-2,700	-918	-2,709	-3,804	36.4	29.4	61.7	41.2
Greece	-9,820	-18,233	-30,897	-17,266	-22,303	-26,552	23.2	21.5	32.5	30.4
Hungary	-4,004	-8,238	1,515	-1,600	-2,324	8,363	65.9	86.5	68.1	80.0
Iceland	-847	-2,648	-1,009	-633	-1,997	1,262	31.7	56.1	44.0	46.1
India	-4,601	-10,284	-51,781	-4,246	-22,898	-69,904	19.3	22.8	22.0	26.9
Indonesia	7,992	278	5,144	17,356	11,854	11,549	34.1	24.6	29.9	22.9
Ireland	-356	-7,150	954	13,001	23,714	39,174	81.1	101.1	69.4	82.0
Israel	-2,056	4,101	6,336	-209	-463	4,227	42.7	36.9	43.1	34.9
Italy	-5,781	-29,744	-72,015	10,526	-1,078	-39,721	25.9	26.6	25.9	28.5
Japan	119,660	165,783	203,916	68,541	64,360	65,656	14.3	15.2	12.9	14.0
Jordan	27	-2,272	-1,312	-2,257	-5,224	-5,613	52.7	47.8	94.2	69.0
Kenya	-199	-252	-2,512	-1,286	-1,398	-3,331	28.5	27.5	36.0	37.9
Korea, Rep	14,803	18,607	28,214	15,239	22,829	28,299	39.3	52.4	36.6	49.6
Kuwait	14,672	30,071	36,822	9,930	28,853	42,015	64.0	60.1	28.3	26.3
Libya	6,270	14,945	16,801	6,826	16,778	(NA)	66.4	(NA)	28.3	(NA)
Malaysia	8,488	19,980	27,290	18,019	31,496	42,354	117.5	97.3	94.6	79.5
Mexico	-18,743	-5,861	-3,094	-11,595	-12,324	-14,999	27.1	30.3	28.6	31.7
Morocco	-475	1,041	-3,925	-1,988	-3,334	-9,004	32.3	33.0	37.9	42.9
Nepal	-131	153	-128	-502	-1,211	-4,292	14.6	9.6	29.5	36.4
Netherlands	7,264	46,618	55,393	21,360	54,426	57,803	69.6	78.0	61.1	70.6
New Zealand	-2,407	-8,777	-4,994	861	-2,509	2,132	27.4	28.2	29.6	26.7
Nigeria	7,427	36,529	2,476	10,093	17,388	13,123	46.5	37.9	31.0	31.2
Norway	25,079	49,003	51,444	28,792	49,395	51,753	44.1	41.1	27.8	28.8
Oman	3,129	5,178	5,871	5,529	8,460	(NA)	58.6	(NA)	31.2	(NA)
Pakistan	-85	-3,606	-1,354	-922	-4,246	-9,217	15.7	13.6	19.6	18.8
Panama	-673	-1,022	-2,862	320	995	-1,426	75.5	68.9	69.1	74.2
Peru	-1,546	1,148	-2,315	-1,148	4,702	4,500	25.1	25.7	19.2	22.7
Philippines	-2,228	1,980	8,922	-1,613	-5,776	-3,618	46.1	34.8	51.7	36.6
Poland	-10,343	-7,242	-21,873	-10,999	-2,253	-5,671	37.1	42.2	37.8	43.5
Portugal	-12,189	-19,821	-22,813	-12,892	-18,059	-16,285	27.7	31.0	37.1	38.2
Romania	-1,355	-8,504	-7,284	-1,930	-10,247	-10,135	32.9	23.5	43.3	29.8
Russian Federation	46,839	84,602	71,080	52,012	104,614	123,426	35.2	29.9	21.5	21.6
Saudi Arabia	14,317	90,061	66,751	35,333	104,406	87,656	60.9	58.1	27.8	38.6
Singapore	10,244	26,429	49,558	12,327	36,313	60,582	229.7	207.2	200.3	178.7
South Africa	-191	-8,518	-10,117	3,927	-1,162	-720	27.4	27.3	27.9	27.5
Spain	-23,185	-83,388	-63,129	-18,163	-59,571	-29,304	25.7	27.0	30.9	29.1
Sri Lanka	-1,044	-650	-1,418	-1,732	-2,179	-4,527	32.3	21.7	41.3	30.8
Sudan	-518	-2,768	157	-297	-2,710	577	18.2	19.8	28.1	18.9
Sweden	10,074	25,057	30,513	15,711	28,994	28,919	48.4	49.7	40.6	43.5
Switzerland	32,830	53,149	74,015	14,535	25,064	60,050	49.0	53.6	42.3	42.2
Syrian Arab Republic	1,061	299	-367	1,316	-357	-254	40.4	35.3	41.6	35.8
Thailand	9,313	-7,647	13,099	10,595	-1,974	23,479	73.6	71.3	74.7	63.9
Ukraine	1,481	2,531	-3,018	1,573	721	-3,844	51.5	50.7	50.6	53.6
United Kingdom	-38,800	-59,406	-75,229	-27,261	-77,644	-56,520	26.4	30.1	29.8	32.6
Venezuela	11,853	41,021	12,071	13,626	27,924	45,124	39.7	28.5	20.5	17.1
Vietnam	1,106	-560	-4,287	-768	-2,213	-10,936	69.4	77.5	73.5	87.8

NA Not available.

Source: The World Bank, Washington, DC, Economic Policy and External Debt data, (copyright). Accessed September 2012. See also <http://data.worldbank.org/topic/economic-policy-and-external-debt>.

Table 1420. Military Expenditures, 2009, and Manpower, 2010, by Country

[For manpower, 120,022 represents 120,022,000. Manpower covers males and females deemed fit for military service, ages 16–49, and who are not otherwise disqualified for health reasons]

Country	Expenditures (percent of GDP [1])	Manpower (1,000)	Country	Expenditures (percent of GDP [1])	Manpower (1,000)
United States	[2] **4.1**	**120,022**	Ireland	[2] 0.9	1,944
Afghanistan	1.9	7,847	Israel	[3] 7.3	2,964
Algeria	[3] 3.3	17,249	Italy	[2] 1.8	22,596
Argentina	0.8	16,873	Japan	[3] 0.8	43,931
Australia	3.0	8,652	Kazakhstan	[7] 1.1	6,438
Austria	0.8	3,134	Korea, North	(NA)	10,067
Belgium	[2] 1.3	3,812	Korea, South	[3] 2.7	21,033
Bolivia	1.3	3,776	Lebanon	[2] 3.1	1,863
Brazil	1.7	83,836	Libya	[2] 3.9	2,970
Bulgaria	[2] 2.6	2,659	Malaysia	[2] 2.0	12,423
Burma	[2] 2.1	21,633	Mexico	[3] 0.5	48,882
Cambodia	[2] 3.0	5,603	Morocco	[8] 5.0	14,403
Canada	[2] 1.1	13,023	Netherlands	[2] 1.6	6,324
Chile [4]	[3] 2.7	7,183	Nicaragua	[3] 0.6	2,563
China [4]	[3] 4.3	618,589	Nigeria	[3] 1.5	40,708
Colombia	[2] 3.4	19,012	Norway	[2] 1.9	1,754
Congo (Kinshasa) [5]	[3] 2.5	20,500	Pakistan	[6] 3.0	75,327
Cote d'Ivoire	1.5	6,556	Peru	[3] 1.5	12,354
Cuba	[3] 3.8	4,822	Philippines	0.9	41,571
Czech Republic	[6] 1.5	4,061	Poland	[2] 1.7	15,584
Denmark	[6] 1.3	2,018	Russia	[2] 3.9	46,813
Ecuador	0.9	6,104	Saudi Arabia	[2] 10.0	13,043
Egypt	[2] 3.4	35,305	South Africa	[3] 1.7	14,093
El Salvador	0.6	2,452	Spain	[2] 1.2	18,721
Ethiopia	1.2	24,757	Sudan	[2] 3.0	13,316
France	[2] 2.6	23,747	Sweden	[2] 1.5	3,359
Germany	[2] 1.5	29,538	Syria	[2] 5.9	9,940
Greece	[2] 4.3	4,049	Thailand	[2] 1.8	27,491
Hungary	[2] 1.8	3,800	Turkey	[2] 5.3	35,005
India	[3] 2.5	489,571	Ukraine	[2] 1.4	15,686
Indonesia	[2] 3.0	107,539	United Kingdom	[2] 2.4	24,035
Iran	[3] 2.5	39,566	Venezuela	[2] 1.2	11,690
Iraq	[3] 8.6	13,013	Vietnam	[2] 2.5	41,504

NA Not available. [1] GDP calculated on an exchange rate basis. [2] 2005 data. [3] 2006 data. [4] See footnote 4, Table 1348. [5] See footnote 5, Table 1348. [6] 2007 data. [7] 2010 data. [8] 2003 data.

Source: Central Intelligence Agency, *The World Factbook*, annual, <https://www.cia.gov/library/publications/the-world-factbook/index.html>, accessed August 2012.

Guide to Sources of Statistics, State Statistical Abstracts, and Foreign Statistical Abstracts

Alphabetically arranged, this guide contains references to important primary sources of statistical information for the United States and other countries. Secondary sources have been included if the information contained in them is presented in a particularly convenient form or if primary sources are not readily available. Nonrecurrent publications presenting compilations or estimates for years later than 2000, or types of data not available in regular series, are also included. Data are also available in press releases.

Valuable information may also be found in state reports, foreign statistical abstracts, which are included at the end of this appendix, and in reports for particular commodities, industries, or similar segments of our economic and social structures, many of which are not included here.

Publications listed under each subject are divided into two main groups: "U.S. Government" and "Nongovernment." The location of the publisher of each report is given except for federal agencies located in Washington, DC. Most federal publications may be purchased from the Superintendent of Documents, U.S. Government Printing Office, Washington, DC, tel. 202-512-1800, (Web site<http://bookstore.gpo.gov>). In some cases, federal publications may be obtained from the issuing agency.

Appendix I Table: Sources of Statistics, State Statistical Abstracts, and Foreign Statistical Abstracts

Title	Frequency	Paper	Internet PDF	Internet Other Formats
U.S. GOVERNMENT				
Administrative Office of the United States Courts				
http://www.uscourts.gov				
Calendar Year Reports on Authorized Wiretaps (state and federal)	Annual		X	
Federal Court Management Statistics	Semiannual		X	X
Federal Judicial Caseload Statistics	Annual		X	
Judicial Business of the United States Courts	Annual		X	
Statistical Tables for the Federal Judiciary	Semiannual	X	X	
Agency for International Development				
http://www.usaid.gov				
U.S. Overseas Loans and Grants: Obligations and Loan Authorizations	Annual		X	X
Army Corps of Engineers				
http://www.usace.army.mil				
Waterborne Commerce of the United States (in five parts)	Annual		X	X
Board of Governors of the Federal Reserve System				
http://www.federalreserve.gov				
Assets and Liabilities of Commercial Banks in the United States H.8	Weekly	X	X	X
Consumer Credit G.19	Monthly	X	X	X
Federal Reserve Bulletin	Monthly		X	X
Flow of Funds Accounts of the United States Z.1	Quarterly	X	X	X
Foreign Exchange Rates H.10	Weekly			X
Industrial Production and Capacity Utilization G.17	Monthly	X	X	X
Money Stock Measures H.6	Weekly		X	X
Bureau of Economic Analysis				
http://www.bea.gov				
Survey of Current Business	Monthly	X	X	X
Bureau of Justice Statistics				
http://bjs.ojp.usdoj.gov				
American Indians and Crime: A BJS Statistical Profile, December 2004	Periodic	X	X	X
Background Checks for Firearm Transfers	Annual		X	X
Capital Punishment	Annual		X	X
Carjacking, 1993-2002, July 2004	Periodic		X	X
Census of Publicly Funded Forensic Crime Laboratories, 2009, August 2012	Periodic		X	X
Census of State and Federal Correctional Facilities, 2005, October 2008	Periodic		X	X
Civil Rights Complaints in U.S. District Courts, 1990-2006, August 2008	Periodic	X	X	X
Civil Trial Cases and Verdicts in Large Counties, 2001, April 2004	Periodic	X	X	X
Compendium of Federal Justice Statistics, 2004, December 2006	Periodic	X	X	X
Contacts Between Police and Public: Findings from the 2008 National Survey, October 2011	Periodic		X	X
Contract Trials and Verdicts in Large Counties, 2001, February 2005	Periodic	X	X	X
Crime and the Nation's Households, 2005, April 2007	Periodic		X	X
Crimes Against Persons Age 65 or Older, 1993-2002, January 2005	Periodic	X	X	X
Criminal Victimization in the United States, 2010, September 2011	Annual		X	X
Cross-National Studies in Crime and Justice, September 2004	Periodic	X	X	X
Defense Counsel in Criminal Cases, November 2000	Periodic	X	X	X
Education and Correctional Populations, January 2003	Periodic	X	X	X
Family Violence Statistics	Periodic	X	X	X
Federal Criminal Case Processing, 2002, January 2005	Periodic	X	X	X
Federal Law Enforcement Officers, 2008, June 2012	Periodic		X	X
Felony Defendants in Large Urban Counties, 2006, May 2010	Biennial		X	X
Felony Sentences in State Courts, 2006, December 2009	Biennial		X	X

See footnotes at end of table.

Appendix I Table: Sources of Statistics, State Statistical Abstracts, and Foreign Statistical Abstracts-Continued.

See headnote on page 909.

Title	Frequency	Paper	Internet	
			PDF	Other Formats
Firearm Use by Offenders, November 2001	Periodic	X	X	X
Hepatitis Testing and Treatment in State Prisons, April 2004	Periodic	X	X	X
Hispanic Victims of Violent Crime, 1993-2000, April 2002	Periodic	X	X	X
HIV in Prisons 2007-2008	Periodic		X	X
Homicide Trends in the United States, 1980-2008	Periodic		X	X
Identity Theft, 2007, June 2010	Periodic		X	X
Immigration Offenders in the Federal Criminal Justice System, 2010, July 2012	Periodic		X	X
Incarcerated Parents and Their Children, August 2000	Periodic	X	X	X
Indicators of School Crime and Safety	Annual		X	X
Intimate Partner Violence, 1993-2001, February 2003	Periodic	X	X	X
Jail Inmates at Midyear, 2011, April 2012	Annual		X	X
Jails in Indian Country, 2010, December 2011	Annual		X	X
Justice Expenditure and Employment Extract Series, 2008, May 2012	Annual		X	X
Juvenile Offenders and Victims	Periodic	X	X	X
Juvenile Victimization and Offending, 1993-2003	Periodic	X	X	X
Law Enforcement Management and Administrative Statistics 2000: Data for Individual State and Local Agencies with 100 or More Officers	Periodic	X	X	X
Local Police Departments, 2007, December 2010	Periodic		X	X
Medical Malpractice Trials and Verdicts in Large Counties, April 2004	Periodic	X	X	X
Money Laundering Offenders, 1994-2001, July 2003	Periodic	X	X	X
Prevalence of Imprisonment in the U.S. Population, 1974-2001, August 2003	Periodic	X	X	X
Prisoners in 2010, December 2011	Annual		X	X
Probation and Parole in the United States	Annual		X	X
Profile of Jail Inmates, 2002, July 2004	Periodic	X	X	X
Prosecutors in State Courts, 2007, December 2011	Biennial		X	X
Rape and Sexual Assault: Reporting to Police and Medical Attention, August 2002	Periodic	X	X	X
Reentry Trends in the United States Current Data Electronic	Periodic		X	X
Sheriffs' Offices, 2003, April 2006	Periodic	X	X	X
Sourcebook of Criminal Justice Statistics	Periodic		X	X
State Court Prosecutors in Large Districts, 2001, December 2001	Periodic	X	X	X
State Court Prosecutors in Small Districts, 2001, January 2003	Periodic	X	X	X
State Court Sentencing of Convicted Felons, 2004, July 2007	Periodic		X	X
State Prison Expenditures, 2001, June 2004	Periodic	X	X	X
Summary of State Sex Offender Registries, 2001, March 2002	Periodic	X	X	X
Survey of DNA Crime Laboratories, 2001, January 2002	Periodic	X	X	X
Survey of State Criminal History Information Systems, 2010, November 2011	Biennial	X	X	X
Survey of State Procedures Related to Firearm Sales, 2005, November 2006	Periodic	X	X	X
Tort Trials and Verdicts in Large Counties, November 2004	Periodic	X	X	X
Traffic Stop Data Collection Policies for State Police, 2004, June 2005	Periodic	X	X	X
Violent Victimization of College Students, 1995-2002, January 2005	Periodic	X	X	X
Weapon Use and Violent Crime, 1993-2001, September 2003	Periodic	X	X	X

Bureau of Labor Statistics
http://www.bls.gov

Title	Frequency	Paper	Internet	
100 Years of U.S. Consumer Spending: Data for the Nation, New York City, and Boston, Report 991	Periodic	X	X	
College Enrollment and Work Activity of High School Graduates	Annual		X	
Compensation and Working Conditions	Periodic		X	X
Consumer Expenditure Survey, Integrated Diary and Interview Survey data	Annual		X	X
Consumer Prices	Monthly		X	X
Consumer Price Index (CPI) Detailed Report	Monthly		X	X
Employer Costs for Employee Compensation	Quarterly		X	X
Employment and Earnings	Monthly		X	X
Employment and Wages	Annual		X	X
Employment Characteristics of Families	Annual		X	X
Employment Cost Index	Quarterly		X	X
Employment Cost Indexes and Levels	Annual		X	X
The Employment Situation	Monthly		X	X
Geographic Profile of Employment and Unemployment	Annual		X	X
International Comparisons of Annual Labor Force Statistics, 16 Countries	Annual		X	X
International Comparisons of Hourly Compensation Costs for Production Workers in Manufacturing	Annual		X	X
International Comparisons of Manufacturing Productivity and Unit Labor Cost Trends	Annual		X	X
Metropolitan Area Employment and Unemployment	Monthly		X	X
Monthly Labor Review	Monthly		X	X
National Compensation Survey	Annual		X	X
Occupational Injuries and Illnesses in the United States by Industry	Annual		X	X
Occupational Projections and Training Data	Biennial		X	X
Producer Price Index (PPI) Detailed Report	Monthly		X	X
Productivity and Costs by Industry	Periodic		X	X
Real Earnings	Monthly		X	X
Regional and State Employment and Unemployment	Monthly		X	X
Relative Importance of Components in the Consumer Price Indexes	Annual		X	X
U.S. Import and Export Price Indexes	Monthly		X	X
Union Members	Annual		X	X
Usual Weekly Earnings of Wage and Salary Workers	Quarterly		X	X
Work Experience of the Population	Annual		X	X

Bureau of Land Management
http://www.blm.gov

Title	Frequency	Paper	Internet	
Public Land Statistics	Annual		X	

See footnotes at end of table.

Appendix I Table: Sources of Statistics, State Statistical Abstracts, and Foreign Statistical Abstracts-Continued.

See headnote on page 909.

Title	Frequency	Paper	Internet PDF	Internet Other Formats
Census Bureau				
http://www.census.gov				
2002 Economic Census, Bridge Between North American Industry Classification System (NAICS) and Standard Industrial Classification (SIC)	Quinquennial			X
2007 Economic Census, Company Statistics Series, Survey of Business Owners	Quinquennial			X
2007 Economic Census, Company Statistics Series, Survey of Business Owners: American Indian- and Alaska Native-Owned Firms	Quinquennial			X
2007 Economic Census, Company Statistics Series, Survey of Business Owners: Asian-Owned Firms	Quinquennial			X
2007 Economic Census, Company Statistics Series, Survey of Business Owners: Black-Owned Firms	Quinquennial			X
2007 Economic Census, Company Statistics Series, Survey of Business Owners: Hispanic-Owned Firms	Quinquennial			X
2007 Economic Census, Company Statistics Series, Survey of Business Owners: Native Hawaiian- and other Pacific Islander-Owned Firms	Quinquennial			X
2007 Economic Census, Comparative Statistics	Quinquennial			X
2007 Economic Census, Industry/Geography	Quinquennial			X
American Community Survey Annual Earnings and Poverty Report, 2007	Annual		X	
Annual Revision of Monthly Retail and Food Services: Sales and Inventories	Annual		X	
Annual Revision of Monthly Wholesale Distributors: Sales and Inventories	Annual		X	X
Annual Survey of Manufactures	Annual		X	
Census of Governments	Quinquennial		X	
Census of Governments, Volume 3, No. 2, Compendium of Public Employment	Quinquennial		X	X
Census of Housing Decennial (2010, most recent)	Decennial	X	X	X
Census of Population Decennial (2010, most recent)	Decennial	X	X	X
Consolidated Federal Funds Report (CFFR) (discontinued)	Annual	X	X	X
Consumer Income and Poverty, Alternative Poverty Estimates in the United States: 2003	Periodic	X	X	
Consumer Income and Poverty, Income, Poverty, and Health Insurance Coverage in the United States, 2010	Annual	X	X	X
Consumer Income and Poverty, P60, and Household Economic Studies, P70	Periodic	X	X	
County Business Patterns	Annual		X	X
CRRF: State and County Areas (discontinued)	Annual	X	X	X
Current Construction Reports, Residential Improvements and Repairs, C50 (discontinued)	Monthly		X	
Current Construction Reports: New Residential Construction and New Residential Sales	Annual		X	
Current Construction Reports: Value of Construction Put in Place, C30	Monthly		X	
Current Housing Reports, American Housing Survey for Selected Metropolitan Areas, H170	Biennial	X	X	X
Current Housing Reports, American Housing Survey for the United States, H150	Biennial	X	X	X
Current Housing Reports, Characteristics of Apartments Completed, H131	Annual		X	X
Current Housing Reports, Housing Vacancies, H111	Quarterly		X	X
Current Housing Reports, Survey of Market Absorption of Apartments (SOMA)	Quarterly		X	X
Current Housing Reports, Who Can Afford to Buy a Home in 2002, H121	Occasional	X	X	X
Current Industrial Reports (discontinued)	Annual		X	
Current Population Reports (Series P20 and P23)	Periodic		X	X
Economic Census of Island Areas	Quinquennial			X
Federal Aid to States for Fiscal Year	Annual	X	X	
Global Population Profile: 2002 (Series WP)	Periodic	X	X	X
International Briefs (Series IB) (discontinued)		X	X	
International Data Base	Annual			X
International Population Reports (Series P95)	Periodic		X	
Manufacturer's Shipments, Inventories, and Orders	Monthly		X	
Manufacturer's Shipments, Inventories, and Orders: 1992-2011	Annual			X
New York City Housing and Vacancy Survey, 2011	Every 3 years			X
Nonemployer Statistics	Annual			X
Population Estimates and Projections	Annual			X
Quarterly Financial Report for Manufacturing, Mining, and Trade Corporations	Quarterly		X	
Residential Finance Survey, 2001	Every 10 years	X	X	X
Service Annual Survey Report	Annual		X	
Survey of Plant Capacity Utilization	Quarterly			X
U.S. International Trade in Goods and Services: includes cumulative data	Annual		X	X
U.S. Trade with Puerto Rico and U.S. Possessions (FT 895)	Monthly		X	
Vehicle Inventory and Use Survey (discontinued)	Quinquennial	X	X	X
Centers for Disease Control and Prevention, Atlanta, Georgia				
http://www.cdc.gov				
CDC Injury Fact Book	Periodic	X	X	X
Morbidity and Mortality Weekly Report	Annual		X	X
Centers for Medicare and Medicaid Services (CMS)				
http://www.cms.gov				
CMS Statistics	Annual		X	X
Data Compendium	Annual		X	X
Health Care Financing Review (discontinued)	Quarterly	X	X	
Health Care Financing Review. Medicare and Medicaid Statistical Supplement	Annual	X	X	
Medicare and Medicaid Research Review	Irregular		X	
Trustees Report	Annual	X	X	
Wallet Card	Annual	X	X	X
Central Intelligence Agency				
http://www.cia.gov				
World Factbook	Annual	X	X	X

See footnotes at end of table.

Title	Frequency	Paper	Internet PDF	Internet Other Formats
Coast Guard (See Department of Homeland Security)				
Comptroller of the Currency				
http://www.occ.treas.gov				
Quarterly Journal	Quarterly	X	X	
Office of the Clerk, U.S. House of Representatives				
http://clerk.house.gov				
Statistics of the Presidential and Congressional Election	Biennial		X	
Council of Economic Advisers				
http://www.whitehouse.gov/administration/eop/cea				
Economic Indicators	Monthly	X	X	X
Economic Report of the President	Annual	X	X	X
Department of Agriculture, Economic Research Service				
http://www.ers.usda.gov				
Agricultural Income and Finance	Annual	X	X	X
Amber Waves	Periodic	X	X	X
America's Diverse Family Farms: Structure and Finances	Annual	X	X	
Cotton and Wool Yearbook	Annual			X
Dairy Yearbook	Periodic			X
Feed Grains Yearbook	Annual		X	X
Food Spending in American Households	Periodic		X	
Fruit and Tree Nut Yearbook	Annual		X	X
Oil Crops Yearbook	Annual			X
Poultry Yearbook	Annual			X
Red Meat Yearbook	Periodic			X
Rice Yearbook	Annual		X	X
Sugar and Sweeteners Yearbook	Annual			X
Situation and Outlook Reports. Issued for agricultural exports, feed, fruit and tree nuts, livestock and poultry, oil crops, rice, sugar and sweeteners, vegetables, wheat, and world agriculture	Periodic	X	X	
Structure and Finances of U.S. Farms: Family Farm Report	Annual	X	X	
Vegetable and Melons Yearbook	Annual			X
World Agricultural Supply and Demand Estimates	Monthly	X	X	X
Department of Agriculture, Food and Nutrition Service				
http://www.fns.usda.gov/fns/				
Characteristics of Supplemental Nutrition Assistance Program Households	Annual	X	X	
WIC Participant and Program Characteristics	Biennial	X	X	
Department of Agriculture, Foreign Agricultural Service				
http://www.fas.usda.gov				
Livestock and Poultry World Markets and Trade	Semiannual	X	X	
Department of Agriculture, National Agricultural Statistics Service				
http://www.nass.usda.gov				
Agricultural Chemical Usage	Periodic			X
Agricultural Statistics	Annual	X	X	
Catfish Production	Semiannual	X	X	X
Cattle	Semiannual	X	X	X
Census of Agriculture	Quinquennial	X	X	X
Cherry Production	Annual	X	X	X
Chickens and Eggs	Monthly/Annual	X	X	X
Citrus Fruits	Annual	X	X	X
Cranberries	Annual	X	X	X
Crop Production	Monthly	X	X	X
Crop Progress	Weekly	X	X	X
Crop Values	Annual	X	X	X
Dairy Products	Monthly/Annual	X	X	X
Farm Labor	Semiannual	X	X	X
Farms, Land in Farms, and Livestock Operations	Annual	X	X	X
Floriculture Crops	Annual	X	X	X
Land Value and Cash Rents	Annual	X	X	X
Livestock Slaughter	Monthly	X	X	X
Meat Animals Production, Disposition, and Income	Annual	X	X	X
Milk Production	Monthly	X	X	X
Milk Production, Disposition, and Income	Annual	X	X	X
Noncitrus Fruits and Nuts	Semiannual	X	X	X
Poultry: Production and Value Summary	Annual	X	X	X
Stock Reports. Stocks of grain, peanuts, potatoes, and rice	Periodic	X	X	X
Trout Production	Annual	X	X	X
Turkeys: Hatchery and Raised	Annual	X	X	X
Usual Planting and Harvesting Dates	Periodic	X	X	X
Vegetables	Periodic	X	X	X
Weekly Weather and Crop Bulletin	Weekly	X	X	
Winter Wheat Seedlings	Monthly	X	X	X
Department of Agriculture, Natural Resources and Conservation Service				
http://www.nrcs.usda.gov				
National Resources Inventory	Periodic	X	X	
Department of Defense				
http://www.defenselink.mil/pubs				
Foreign Military Sales, Foreign Military Construction Sales, and Other Security Cooperation Historical Facts	Annual	X	X	
Personnel Statistics	Periodic		X	

See footnotes at end of table.

Title	Frequency	Paper	Internet PDF	Internet Other Formats
Department of Education http://www.ed.gov				
Annual Report for Federal Student Aid	Annual		X	
Annual Report on Teacher Quality	Annual		X	
Federal Campus-Based Programs Data Book	Annual			X
Federal Pell Grant Program, End of Year Report	Annual		X	X
Department of Health and Human Services http://www.hhs.gov				
Health Care Fraud and Abuse Control Program Annual Report	Annual	X	X	
Profile of Older Americans	Annual	X	X	
Department of Homeland Security http://www.dhs.gov/index.shtm				
Budget in Brief	Annual	X	X	
Department of Homeland Security, Coast Guard http://www.uscg.mil/default.asp				
Fact File	Periodic	X	X	X
Department of Homeland Security, Office of Immigration Statistics http://www.dhs.gov/immigration-statistics				
Yearbook of Immigration Statistics	Annual	X	X	X
Department of Housing and Urban Development http://www.hud.gov				
U.S. Housing Market Conditions	Quarterly	X	X	
Department of Justice, Bureau of Alcohol, Tobacco, Firearms and Explosives http://www.atf.gov/				
Annual Firearms Manufacturing and Export Report	Annual		X	
Firearms Trace Data (by State)	Annual		X	
Department of Labor http://www.dol.gov				
Agency Financial Report	Annual	X	X	
Annual Performance Report	Annual	X	X	
Department of State http://www.state.gov				
United States Contributions to International Organizations	Annual			X
Department of Transportation http://www.dot.gov				
Air Travel Consumer Report	Monthly	X	X	X
Airport Activity Statistics of Certified Route Air Carriers	Annual	X	X	X
U.S. International Air Travel Statistics	Monthly, Quarterly, Annual	X	X	X
Wage Statistics of Class I Railroads in the United States	Annual	X	X	
Department of the Treasury, Alcohol and Tobacco Tax and Trade Bureau http://www.ttb.gov				
Tobacco Products Monthly Statistical Releases	Monthly	X	X	
Department of the Treasury, Bureau of Public Debt http://www.publicdebt.treas.gov				
Monthly Statement of the Public Debt of the United States	Monthly	X	X	X
Department of the Treasury, Financial Management Services http://www.fms.treas.gov				
Active Foreign Credits of the United States Government	Quarterly	X		
Combined Statement of Receipts, Outlays, and Balances	Annual	X	X	X
Financial Report of the United States Government	Annual	X	X	X
Monthly Treasury Statement of Receipts and Outlays of the United States Government	Monthly	X	X	X
Treasury Bulletin	Quarterly	X	X	X
Department of Veterans Affairs http://www.va.gov				
Compensation and Pension Data by County	Annual			X
Disability Compensation, Pension, and Death Pension Data	Annual			X
Performance and Accountability Report	Annual	X	X	
Servicemembers' and Veterans' Group Life Insurance Programs Annual Report	Annual	X	X	
Drug Enforcement Administration http://www.justice.gov/dea				
Drug Abuse and Law Enforcement Statistics	Irregular	X	X	X
Employment and Training Administration http://www.doleta.gov				
Unemployment Insurance Claims	Weekly			X
Energy Information Administration http://www.eia.gov				
Annual Energy Outlook	Annual	X	X	X
Annual Energy Review	Annual	X	X	X
Annual Coal Report	Annual		X	X
Electric Power Annual	Annual		X	X
Electric Power Monthly	Monthly		X	X
Electric Sales, Revenue and Retail Price	Annual		X	X
Emissions of Greenhouse Gases in the U.S.	Annual		X	X
International Energy Statistics portal	Ongoing			X
International Energy Outlook	Annual	X	X	X

See footnotes at end of table.

Appendix I Table: Sources of Statistics, State Statistical Abstracts, and Foreign Statistical Abstracts-Continued.

See headnote on page 909.

Title	Frequency	Paper	Internet PDF	Internet Other Formats
Monthly Energy Review	Monthly		X	X
Performance Profiles of Major Energy Producers	Annual		X	X
Petroleum Marketing Annual	Monthly		X	X
Petroleum Marketing Monthly	Monthly		X	
Petroleum Supply Annual Volume 1	Annual		X	X
Petroleum Supply Annual Volume 2	Annual		X	X
Petroleum Supply Monthly	Monthly		X	X
Quarterly Coal Report	Quarterly		X	X
Renewable Energy Annual	Annual		X	X
Residential Energy Consumption Survey	Quadrennial		X	X
State Electricity Profiles	Annual		X	X
State Energy Data Report	Annual		X	X
State Energy Price and Expenditure Report	Annual		X	X
U.S. Crude Oil, Natural Gas, and Natural Gas Liquids Reserves	Annual		X	X
Weekly Coal Production	Weekly			X
Environmental Protection Agency http://www.epa.gov				
Air Quality Data	Annual		X	X
Clean Watersheds Needs Survey	Quadrennial		X	
Drinking Water Infrastructure Needs Survey	Periodic		X	
National Water Quality Inventory	Biennial		X	X
Toxics Release Inventory	Annual		X	X
Export-Import Bank of the United States http://www.exim.gov				
Annual Report	Annual	X	X	
Report to the U.S. Congress on Export Credit Competition and the Export-Import Bank of the United States	Annual	X	X	
Farm Credit Administration http://www.fca.gov/index.html				
Annual Report on the Farm Credit System	Annual	X	X	
Federal Bureau of Investigation http://www.fbi.gov/ucr/ucr.htm				
Crime in the United States	Annual		X	X
Hate Crime Statistics	Annual		X	X
Law Enforcement Officers Killed and Assaulted	Annual		X	X
Federal Communications Commission http://www.fcc.gov				
Annual Assessment of the Status of Competition in the Market for the Delivery of Video Programming	Annual		X	X
Annual Report	Annual	X	X	
High-Speed Services for Internet Access	Semi-Annual	X	X	X
International Telecommunications Data	Annual		X	X
Statistics of Communications Common Carriers	Annual	X	X	X
Telecommunications Industry Revenues	Annual	X	X	X
Trends in Telephone Service	Annual	X	X	
Federal Deposit Insurance Corporation http://www.fdic.gov				
Annual Report	Annual	X	X	X
FDIC Quarterly	Quarterly	X	X	X
Historical Statistics on Banking	Annual			X
Quarterly Banking Profile	Quarterly		X	X
Statistics on Banking	Quarterly			X
Summary of Deposits	Annual			X
Federal Highway Administration http://www.fhwa.dot.gov				
Highway Statistics	Annual	X	X	X
Federal Railroad Administration http://safetydata.fra.dot.gov/OfficeofSafety/default.aspx				
Railroad Safety Statistics	Annual	X	X	
Fish and Wildlife Service http://www.fws.gov				
Federal Aid in Fish and Wildlife Restoration	Annual		X	
National Survey of Fishing, Hunting, and Wildlife Associated Recreation	Quinquennial	X	X	
Forest Service http://www.fs.fed.us				
An Analysis of the Timber Situation in the United States 1952-2050	Periodic	X	X	
Land Areas of the National Forest System	Annual	X	X	
RPA Assessment Tables	Periodic	X	X	X
U.S. Timber Production, Trade, Consumption, and Price Statistics 1965-2005	Biennial	X	X	
General Services Administration http://www.gsa.gov				
Federal Real Property Profile	Annual		X	X
Geological Survey http://www.usgs.gov/				
Estimated Use of Water in the United States	Quinquennial	X	X	X
Mineral Commodity Summaries	Annual	X	X	
Mineral Industry Surveys	Monthly & Quarterly		X	X
Minerals Yearbook	Annual	X	X	X

See footnotes at end of table.

Appendix I Table: Sources of Statistics, State Statistical Abstracts, and Foreign Statistical Abstracts-Continued.

See headnote on page 909.

Title	Frequency	Paper	Internet PDF	Internet Other Formats
Internal Revenue Service				
http://www.irs.gov/taxstats/				
Corporation Income Tax Returns	Annual	X	X	X
Individual Income Tax Returns	Annual	X	X	X
IRS Data Book	Annual	X	X	X
Statistics of Income Bulletin	Quarterly	X	X	X
International Trade Administration, Office of Travel and Tourism Industries				
http://www.tinet.ita.doc.gov				
U.S. Travel and Tourism Statistics	Annual	X		X
International Trade Commission				
http://www.usitc.gov				
Recent Trends in U.S. Services Trade	Annual	X	X	
Library of Congress				
http://www.loc.gov				
Annual Report	Annual	X	X	
Maritime Administration				
http://www.marad.dot.gov				
Annual Report	Annual	X	X	
Cruise Statistics	Quarterly		X	X
Fleet Statistics 10,000 Deadweight Tons or Greater	Annual			X
U.S. Waterborne Foreign Trade	Annual			X
Vessel Calls	Annual		X	X
Mine Safety and Health Administration				
http://www.msha.gov				
Informational Reports by Mining Industry: Coal, Metallic Minerals, Nonmetallic Minerals (except stone and coal), Sand and Gravel, and Stone	Annual		X	X
Mine Injuries and Worktime	Quarterly	X	X	X
National Aeronautics and Space Administration				
http://www.nasa.gov				
Annual Procurement Report	Annual	X	X	
National Center for Education Statistics				
http://nces.ed.gov				
Academic Libraries	Biennial		X	X
Characteristics of the 100 Largest Public Elementary and Secondary School Districts in the United States	Annual	X	X	X
Characteristics of Private Schools in the United States	Annual	X	X	X
Characteristics of Schools, Districts, Teachers, Principals, and School Libraries in the United States	Annual	X	X	
Computer and Internet Use by Students	Periodic	X	X	
The Condition of Education	Annual	X	X	X
Digest of Education Statistics	Annual	X	X	X
Enrollment in Postsecondary Institutions, Graduation Rates, and Financial Statistics	Annual		X	
Indicators of School Crime and Safety	Annual	X	X	X
The Nation's Report Card: History 2010	Periodic	X	X	
The Nation's Report Card: Mathematics 2011	Periodic	X	X	
The Nation's Report Card: Reading 2011	Periodic	X	X	
The Nation's Report Card: Science 2011	Periodic	X	X	
The Nation's Report Card: Writing 2007	Periodic	X	X	
Projections of Education Statistics	Annual	X	X	X
School and Staffing Survey	Quadrennial			X
Status and Trends in the Education of Racial and Ethnic Minorities	Irregular	X	X	X
Trends in High School Dropout and Completion Rates in the United States	Annual		X	X
National Center for Health Statistics				
http://www.cdc.gov/nchs/				
Health: United States	Annual	X	X	X
National Health Statistics Reports	Periodic	X	X	
National Hospital Discharge Survey: Annual Summary	Annual		X	
National Vital Statistics Reports	Periodic	X	X	
Vital and Health Statistics:				
Series 10: Data from the National Health Interview Survey	Annual	X	X	
Series 11: Health and Nutrition Examination Survey Statistics	Irregular	X	X	
Series 13: Data on Health Resources Utilization	Irregular	X	X	
Series 20: Data on Mortality	Irregular	X	X	
Series 21: Data on Natality, Marriage, and Divorce	Irregular	X	X	
Series 23: Data from the National Survey of Family Growth	Irregular	X	X	
National Credit Union Administration				
http://www.ncua.gov				
Annual Report	Annual	X	X	
Yearend Statistics for Federally Insured Credit Unions	Annual	X	X	
National Endowment for the Arts				
http://www.nea.gov				
Annual Report	Annual		X	X
Research Notes	Periodic	X	X	
Research Reports	Periodic	X	X	
National Endowment for the Humanities				
http://www.neh.gov				
Budget Request	Annual	X	X	

See footnotes at end of table.

Appendix I Table: Sources of Statistics, State Statistical Abstracts, and Foreign Statistical Abstracts-Continued.

See headnote on page 909.

Title	Frequency	Paper	Internet PDF	Internet Other Formats
National Guard Bureau				
http://www.nationalguard.mil/				
Annual Review of the Chief	Annual	X	X	
National Highway Traffic Safety Administration				
http://www.nhtsa.gov				
Traffic Safety Facts	Annual	X	X	
National Oceanic and Atmospheric Administration				
http://www.noaa.gov				
Climatic Data for the World	Monthly		X	
Comparative Climatic Data	Annual	X	X	X
Daily Normals of Temperature, Precipitation, Heating Degree Days (HDD), and Cooling Degree Days (CDD)	Periodic			X
Fisheries of the United States	Annual	X	X	X
Hourly Precipitation Data. Monthly with annual summary; for each state	Monthly		X	X
Local Climatological Data. Monthly with annual summary; for major cities	Monthly		X	X
Monthly Normals of Temperature, Precipitation, Heating Degree Days (HDD), and Cooling Degree Days (CDD)	Periodic			X
Our Living Oceans	Periodic	X	X	
Storm Data	Monthly		X	
Tornado Summaries	Monthly/Annual			X
U.S. Climate Normals	Annual	X	X	X
National Park Service				
http://www.nps.gov				
Federal Recreation Fee Report	Annual	X		
National Park Statistical Abstract	Annual	X	X	
National Science Foundation				
http://www.nsf.gov/statistics				
Academic Institutional Profiles	Annual			X
Academic Research and Development Expenditures	Annual		X	X
Characteristics of Doctoral Scientists and Engineers in the United States	Biennial		X	X
Characteristics of Recent Science/Engineering Graduates	Biennial		X	X
Doctorate Recipients from U.S. Universities	Annual		X	X
Federal Funds for Research and Development	Annual		X	X
Federal Research and Development Funding by Budget Function	Annual		X	X
Federal Science and Engineering Support to Universities, Colleges, and Nonprofit Institutions	Annual		X	X
Graduate Students and Postdoctorates in Science and Engineering	Annual		X	X
National Patterns of Research and Development Resources	Annual		X	X
Research and Development in Industry	Annual		X	X
Science and Engineering Degrees	Biennial		X	X
Science and Engineering Degrees, by Race/Ethnicity of Recipients	Biennial		X	X
Science and Engineering Doctorate Awards	Annual		X	X
Science and Engineering Indicators	Biennial	X	X	X
Science and Engineering State Profiles	Annual			X
Science Resources Statistics Info Briefs (various topics)	Frequent	X	X	X
Scientific and Engineering Research Facilities at Universities and Colleges	Biennial		X	X
Women, Minorities, and Persons with Disabilities in Science and Engineering	Biennial		X	X
National Transportation Safety Board				
http://www.ntsb.gov				
Annual Review of Aircraft Accident Data: U.S. Air Carrier Operations	Annual		X	
Annual Review of Aircraft Accident Data: U.S. General Aviation	Annual		X	
Office of Juvenile Justice and Delinquency Prevention				
http://ojjdp.gov				
Highlights of the National Youth Gang Survey	Annual	X	X	X
Juvenile Arrests	Annual	X	X	X
Victims of Violent Juvenile Crime	Periodic	X	X	X
Office of Management and Budget				
http://www.whitehouse.gov/omb				
The Budget of the United States Government	Annual	X	X	
Office of Personnel Management				
http://www.opm.gov				
Demographic Profile of the Federal Workforce	Biennial		X	
Employment and Trends	Bimonthly		X	X
The Fact Book	Annual		X	X
Statistical Abstract for the Federal Employee Benefit Programs	Annual			X
Work Years and Personnel Costs	Annual		X	
Patent and Trademark Office				
http://www.uspto.gov				
Technology Assessment and Forecast Reports	Periodic	X	X	X
All Technologies (Utility Patents)	Annual	X	X	X
Patent Counts by Country/State and Year	Annual	X	X	X
Patenting Trends in the United States	Annual	X		X
Railroad Retirement Board, Chicago, Illinois				
http://www.rrb.gov/default.asp				
Annual Report	Annual	X	X	
Quarterly Benefit Statistics	Quarterly	X	X	
Securities and Exchange Commission				
http://www.sec.gov/about.shtml				
Select SEC and Market Data	Annual		X	

See footnotes at end of table.

Title	Frequency	Paper	Internet	
			PDF	Other Formats
Small Business Administration				
http://www.sba.gov				
Annual Report	Annual	X		X
Quarterly Indicators	Quarterly		X	X
Small Business and Micro Business Lending	Annual		X	X
The Small Business Economy	Annual		X	X
State and Territory Small Business Profiles	Annual		X	X
Social Security Administration				
http://www.ssa.gov				
Annual Statistical Report on the Social Security Disability Insurance Program	Annual	X	X	X
Annual Statistical Supplement to the Social Security Bulletin	Annual	X	X	X
Children Receiving Social Security Income (SSI) (discontinued)	Annual	X	X	X
Congressional Statistics	Annual	X	X	X
Fast Facts & Figures about Social Security	Annual	X	X	X
Income of the Population 55 and over	Biennially	X	X	X
OASDI Beneficiaries by State and County	Annual	X	X	X
Social Security Bulletin	Quarterly	X	X	X
SSI Annual Statistical Report	Annual	X	X	X
SSI Disabled Recipients Who Work (discontinued)	Annual	X	X	X
SSI Recipients by State and County	Annual	X	X	X
State Assistance Programs for Social Security Income (SSI) Recipients	Annual	X	X	X
Substance Abuse and Mental Health Services Administration				
http://www.samhsa.gov				
National Survey on Drug Use and Health	Annual	X	X	X
National Survey on Substance Abuse Treatment Services (N-SSATS)	Annual	X	X	X
U.S. Copyright Office				
http://www.copyright.gov/				
Annual Report	Annual		X	
NONGOVERNMENT				
Aerospace Industries Association, Arlington, VA				
http://www.aia-aerospace.org				
Aerospace Foreign Trade: Export Activity	Annual		X	
Aerospace Foreign Trade: Import Activity	Annual		X	
Aerospace Industries Report: Facts, Figures & Outlook for the Aviation and Aerospace Manufacturing Industry	Annual	X	X	X
Aerospace Industry Year-End Review and Forecast	Annual		X	
Manufacturing Production, Capacity, and Utilization in Aerospace and Aircraft and Parts	Quarterly		X	
Orders, Shipments, and Backlog for Large Civil Jet Transport Aircraft	Periodic		X	
Total and Production Workers Employment in the Aerospace Industry	Annual		X	
Airlines for America, Washington, DC				
http://www.airlines.org				
Airlines for America Economic Report	Annual	X	X	
American Bureau of Metal Statistics, Inc., Chatham, NJ				
http://www.abms.com				
Non-Ferrous Metal Yearbook	Annual	X		X
American Council of Life Insurers, Washington, DC				
http://www.acli.com				
Life Insurers Fact Book	Annual		X	
American Dental Association, Chicago, IL				
http://www.ada.org				
Distribution of Dentists in the United States by Region and State	Annual	X	X	
Survey of Dental Practice	Annual	X	X	
American Forest and Paper Association, Washington, DC				
http://www.afandpa.org				
Annual Statistical Summary of Recovered Paper Utilization	Annual		X	
Statistics of Paper, Paperboard, and Wood Pulp	Monthly		X	X
American Gas Association, Washington, DC				
http://www.aga.org				
Gas Facts	Annual	X	X	
American Iron and Steel Institute, Washington, DC				
http://www.steel.org				
Annual Statistical Report	Annual	X		
American Medical Association, Chicago, IL				
http://www.ama-assn.org				
Physician Characteristics and Distribution in the U.S.	Annual	X		X
State Medical Licensure Statistics, and License Requirements	Annual	X		X
American Osteopathic Association, Chicago, IL				
http://www.osteopathic.org/index.cfm				
Osteopathic Medical Profession Report	Annual		X	
American Petroleum Institute, Washington, DC				
http://www.api.org				
The Basic Petroleum Data Book (online subscription)	Semiannual	X	X	
Joint Association Survey on Drilling Costs (JA5)	Annual	X	X	
Quarterly Well Completion Report (online subscription)	Quarterly	X	X	

See footnotes at end of table.

Title	Frequency	Paper	Internet	
			PDF	Other Formats
American Public Transportation Association, Washington, DC				
http://www.apta.com				
Public Transportation Fact Book	Annual		X	X
Association for Manufacturing Technology, McLean, VA				
http://www.amtonline.org				
Economic Handbook of the Machine Tool Industry	Annual		X	X
Association of American Railroads, Washington, DC				
http://www.aar.org				
Analysis of Class I Railroads	Annual	X	X	X
Freight Commodity Statistics	Annual	X	X	X
Railroad Facts	Annual	X	X	
Association of Racing Commissioners International, Inc., Lexington, KY				
http://www.arci.com				
Pari-Mutuel Racing	Annual	X		
Bloomberg BNA, Washington, DC				
http://www.bna.com				
Basic Patterns in Union Contracts	Annual	X		
BNA's Employment Outlook Report	Quarterly	X		
BNA's Job Absence and Turnover Report	Quarterly	X		
Directory of U.S. Labor Organizations	Annual	X		
National Labor Relations Board Election Statistics	Semiannual	X		
Source Book on Collective Bargaining	Annual	X		
Union Membership and Earnings Data Book	Annual	X		
Book Industry Study Group, and Association of American Publishers, New York, NY				
http://www.bisg.org				
BookStats	Annual	X	X	X
Used-Book Sales	Periodic	X		
Boy Scouts of America, Irving, TX				
http://www.scouting.org				
Annual Report	Annual	X	X	X
Chronicle of Higher Education, Inc., Washington, DC				
http://chronicle.com				
Almanac of Higher Education	Annual	X		X
College Board, New York, NY				
http://www.collegeboard.com				
College-Bound Seniors Total Group Profile Report	Annual	X	X	X
Commodity Research Bureau, Chicago, IL				
http://www.crbtrader.com				
CRB Commodity Index Report	Weekly		X	X
CRB Commodity Yearbook	Annual	X		X
CRB Futures Perspective	Daily in digital only/Bi-Weekly	X		X
CRB Infotech CD	Monthly			X
Final Markets End-of-Day Data	Daily			X
Futures Market Service	Daily in digital only/Weekly		X	X
Trends In Futures	Daily			X
The Conference Board, New York, NY				
http://www.conference-board.org				
Business Cycle Indicators	Monthly		X	X
Corporate Contributions Report	Annual		X	
Performance: Productivity, Employment, and Growth in the World's Economies	Annual		X	
Congressional Quarterly (CQ) Press, Washington, DC				
http://www.cqpress.com				
America Votes	Biennial	X		
Consumer Electronics Association, Arlington, VA				
http://www.ce.org				
U.S. Consumer Electronics Sales and Forecasts	Semiannual	X	X	X
Council of State Governments, Lexington, KY				
http://www.csg.org				
The Book of the States	Annual	X	X	
Directory I: Elected Officials	Annual	X		X
Directory II: Legislative Leadership, Committees, and Staff	Annual	X		X
Directory III: Administrative Officials	Annual	X		X
Credit Union National Association, Madison, WI				
http://www.cuna.org				
Credit Union Ranking Report	Periodic	X		
Credit Union Services Profile	Periodic	X	X	
Operating Ratios and Spreads	Quarterly		X	
Dow Jones and Company, New York, NY				
http://www.dj.com				
Wall Street Journal	Daily	X		X
Duncan McIntosh Company, Inc., Irvine, CA				
http://www.editorandpublisher.com				
Editor and Publisher	Monthly	X		X

See footnotes at end of table.

Title	Frequency	Paper	Internet	
			PDF	**Other Formats**
International Year Book	Annual	X		X
Market Guide	Periodic	X		
Edison Electric Institute, Washington, DC				
http://www.eei.org				
Statistical Yearbook of the Electric Power Industry	Annual	X	X	X
Euromonitor International, London, England				
http://www.euromonitor.com				
Consumer Asia Pacific and Australasia	Annual	X	X	
Consumer China	Annual	X		
Consumer Eastern Europe	Annual	X		
Consumer Europe	Annual	X	X	
Consumer International	Periodic	X		
Consumer Latin America	Periodic	X		
European Marketing Data and Statistics	Annual	X	X	
International Marketing Data and Statistics	Annual	X	X	
Latin America Marketing Data and Statistics	Annual	X	X	
World Consumer Expenditure Patterns	Periodic	X		
World Consumer Income Patterns	Periodic	X		
World Economic Factbook	Annual	X	X	
World Retail Data and Statistics	Annual	X	X	
Federal National Mortgage Association, Washington, DC				
http://www.fanniemae.com				
Annual Report on Form 10-K	Annual	X	X	
Food and Agriculture Organization of the United Nations, Rome, Italy				
http://www.fao.org				
Fertilizer Yearbook	Periodic	X		
Production Yearbook	Periodic	X		
Trade Yearbook	Periodic	X		
Yearbook of Fishery Statistics	Periodic	X		
Yearbook of Forest Products	Annual	X	X	
The Foundation Center, New York, NY				
http://www.foundationcenter.org				
Foundation Yearbook	Annual	X		
FC Stats	Annual			X
General Aviation Manufacturers Association, Washington, DC				
http://www.gama.aero/home.php				
General Aviation Airplane Shipment Report	Quarterly	X	X	X
General Aviation Statistical Databook & Industry Outlook	Annual		X	
Girl Scouts of the USA, New York, NY				
http://www.girlscouts.org				
Annual Report	Annual		X	
Giving USA Foundation, Chicago, IL				
http://www.givingusareports.org				
Giving USA	Annual			X
Guttmacher Institute, New York, NY				
http://www.guttmacher.org				
Perspectives on Sexual and Reproductive Health				
Health Forum, an American Hospital Association Company, Chicago, IL				
http://www.ahadata.com				
AHA Annual Survey Data Base	Annual			X
AHA Hospital Statistics	Annual	X		X
IHS Global, Inc., Englewood, CO				
http://www.janes.com				
IHS Jane's All the World's Aircraft: Development & Production	Annual	X		X
IHS Jane's Defence: C4ISR & Mission Systems	Annual	X		X
IHS Jane's Fighting Ships	Annual	X		X
IHS Jane's Flight Avionics	Annual	X		X
IHS Jane's Land Warfare Platforms: Armoured Fighting Vehicles	Annual	X		X
IHS Jane's Land Warfare Platforms: Logistics, Support & Unmanned	Annual	X		X
IHS Jane's Merchant Ships	Annual	X		X
IHS Jane's Simulation & Training Systems	Annual	X		X
IHS Jane's Space Systems & Industry	Annual	X		X
IHS Jane's Weapons: Air-Launched	Annual	X		X
IHS Jane's Weapons: Infantry	Annual	X		X
Independent Petroleum Association of America, Washington, DC				
http://www.ipaa.org				
IPAA Oil & Gas Producing Industry in Your State	Annual	X	X	
U.S. Petroleum Statistics	Annual	X	X	
Infobase Publishing, New York, NY				
http://www.worldalmanac.com				
The World Almanac and Book of Facts	Annual	X		X
Information Today, Inc., Medford, NJ				
http://www.infotoday.com				
American Library Directory	Annual	X		X
Library and Book Trade Almanac (formerly The Bowker Annual)	Annual	X		
Institute for Criminal Justice Ethics, New York, NY				
http://www.lib.jjay.cuny.edu/cje				

See footnotes at end of table.

Appendix I Table: Sources of Statistics, State Statistical Abstracts, and Foreign Statistical Abstracts-Continued.

See headnote on page 909.

Title	Frequency	Paper	Internet PDF	Internet Other Formats
Criminal Justice Ethics	Semiannual	X		
Insurance Information Institute, New York, NY http://www.iii.org				
The Financial Services Fact Book (published jointly with the Financial Services Roundtable)	Annual	X		X
The I.I.I. Insurance Fact Book	Annual	X	X	X
Inter-American Development Bank, Washington, DC http://www.iadb.org				
Annual Report	Annual	X	X	
Economic and Social Progress in Latin America	Periodic	X	X	
International Air Transport Association, Montreal, Canada and Geneva, Switzerland http://www.iata.org				
World Air Transport Statistics	Annual	X	X	X
International City Management Association, Washington, DC http://www.icma.org				
ICMA Chief Administrative Officers Salary & Compensation Survey	Annual		X	
Municipal Year Book	Annual	X		
International Labour Organization, Geneva, Switzerland http://www.ilo.org				
Yearbook of Labour Statistics	Annual	X		X
International Monetary Fund, Washington, DC http://www.imf.org				
Annual Report	Annual	X	X	X
Balance of Payments Statistics	Monthly	X	X	X
Direction of Trade Statistics	Monthly	X	X	X
Government Finance Statistics Yearbook	Annual	X	X	X
International Financial Statistics	Monthly	X	X	X
International Telecommunication Union, Geneva, Switzerland http://www.itu.int/home/index.html				
ITU Yearbook of Statistics	Annual	X	X	
World Telecommunication Indicators	Annual	X	X	X
Investment Company Institute, Washington, DC http://www.ici.org				
Investment Company Fact Book	Annual	X	X	X
Joint Center for Housing Studies of Harvard University, Cambridge, MA http://www.jchs.harvard.edu/				
The State of the Nation's Housing	Annual	X	X	
Joint Center for Political and Economic Studies, Washington, DC http://www.jointcenter.org				
Black Elected Officials: A Statistical Summary	Ongoing	X	X	
McGraw-Hill Construction Dodge, a Division of the McGraw-Hill Companies, New York, NY http://construction.com/dodge/dodge-reports-print.asp				
Dodge Construction Potential Bulletin	Monthly		X	X
Media Source, Inc., New York, NY http://www.mediasourceinc.com				
Library Journal	Semimonthly	X		X
School Library Journal	Monthly	X		X
National Academy of Social Insurance, Washington, DC http://www.nasi.org/				
Workers Compensation: Benefits, Coverage, and Costs	Annual	X	X	
National Association of Home Builders, Washington, DC http://www.nahb.org				
HousingEconomics.com (online subscription)	Ongoing			X
National Association of Latino Elected and Appointed Officials, Los Angeles, CA http://www.naleo.org				
National Directory of Latino Elected Officials	Annual		X	X
National Association of Realtors, Washington, DC http://www.realtor.org				
Economist's Commentary	Daily			X
Investment and Vacation Home Buyers Survey	Annual		X	
NAR Member Profile	Annual	X	X	
NAR Profile of Home Buyer and Sellers	Annual	X	X	
National Association of State Budget Officers, Washington, DC http://www.nasbo.org				
State Expenditure Report	Annual	X	X	
Fiscal Survey of the States	Semiannual	X	X	
National Association of State Park Directors, Raleigh, NC http://www.naspd.org				
Annual Information Exchange: Statistical Report of State Park Operations	Annual	X	X	
National Catholic Educational Association, Arlington, VA http://www.ncea.org				
Catholic Schools in America	Annual	X	X	X

See footnotes at end of table.

Appendix I Table: Sources of Statistics, State Statistical Abstracts, and Foreign Statistical Abstracts-Continued.

See headnote on page 909.

Title	Frequency	Paper	Internet	
			PDF	Other Formats
Dollars & Sense: A Report for the National Catholic Educational Association Secondary Schools Department	Biennial	X	X	
Financing the Mission: A Profile of Catholic Elementary Schools in the U.S.	Biennial	X	X	
U.S. Catholic Elementary and Secondary Schools: The Annual Statistical Report on Schools, Enrollment and Staffing	Annual	X	X	
National Council of Churches USA, New York, NY http://www.ncccusa.org				
Yearbook of American and Canadian Churches	Annual	X		X
National Education Association, Washington, DC http://www.nea.org				
Rankings & Estimates: Rankings of the States and Estimates of School Statistics	Annual	X	X	
Status of the American Public School Teacher, 2005-2006	Quinquennial	X	X	
National Fire Protection Association, Quincy, MA http://www.nfpa.org				
National Fire Protection Association (NFPA) Journal	Bimonthly	X		X
National Golf Foundation, Jupiter, FL http://www.ngf.org				
Golf Consumer Profile	Periodic	X	X	
Golf Facilities in the U.S.	Annual	X	X	
National Marine Manufacturers Association, Chicago, IL http://www.nmma.org				
Recreational Boating Statistical Abstract	Annual		X	
U.S. Recreational Boat Registration Statistics	Annual		X	
National Restaurant Association, Washington, DC http://www.restaurant.org				
Hourly Wages for Food Service Occupations	Periodic		X	
Restaurant Industry Forecast	Annual	X	X	
Restaurant Industry in Review	Periodic	X	X	
Restaurant Industry Operations Report	Biennial	X	X	
Restaurant Industry Pocket Factbook	Annual	X		
Restaurant Industry 2010	Decennially	X		
Restaurant Performance Index	Monthly	X		
Restaurant Spending	Periodic	X	X	
Restaurant Trendmapper (online subscription)	Ongoing			X
State of the Restaurant Industry Work Force	Periodic	X		
National Safety Council, Itasca, IL http://www.nsc.org				
Injury Facts	Annual	X	X	X
National Sporting Goods Association, Mount Prospect, IL http://www.nsga.org				
Sporting Goods Market	Annual	X	X	
Sports Participation	Annual	X	X	
North American Jewish Data Bank, Storrs, CT http://www.jewishdatabank.org/				
Jewish Population in the United States	Annual		X	X
NYSE Euronext, New York, NY http://www.nyse.com				
NYSE Facts & Figures (formerly the online NYSE Fact Book)	Ongoing			X
Organization for Economic Cooperation and Development, Paris, France http://www.sourceoecd.org http://www.oecdbookshop.org/ http://www.oecd-ilibrary.org/				
OECD-FAO Agricultural Outlook	Annual	X		X
Bank Profitability: Financial Statements of Banks	Biennial	X		X
Central Government Debt: Statistical Yearbook	Annual	X		X
Coal Information	Annual	X		X
CO2 Emissions From Fuel Combustion	Annual	X		X
OECD Communications Outlook	Biennial	X		X
Education at a Glance: OECD Indicators	Annual	X		X
Electricity Information	Annual	X		X
Energy Balances of Non-OECD Countries	Annual	X		X
Energy Balances of OECD Countries	Annual	X		X
Energy Prices and Taxes	Quarterly	X	X	
Energy Statistics of Non-OECD Countries	Annual	X		X
Energy Statistics of OECD Countries	Annual	X		X
Environmental Data Compendium	Annual	X		X
Environmental Outlook	Periodic	X	X	
Financial Market Trends	Triennial	X	X	
Geographical Distribution of Financial Flows to Aid Recipients	Annual	X		
Historical Statistics, 1970-2000. 2001 Edition	Discontinued	X	X	X
Information Technology Outlook	Biennial	X	X	X
Insurance Statistics Yearbook	Annual	X	X	X
International Development Statistics	Annual			X
Internal Migration Outlook	Annual	X	X	
International Trade by Commodity Statistics	Annual	X	X	
Iron and Steel Industry	Periodic			
Labor Force Statistics	Annual	X	X	
Main Economic Indicators	Monthly	X	X	
Main Science and Technology Indicators	Semiannual	X	X	

See footnotes at end of table.

Title	Frequency	Paper	Internet PDF	Internet Other Formats
Measuring Globalisation: OECD Economic Globalisation Indicators 2010	Periodic	X	X	
Monthly Statistics of International Trade	Monthly	X	X	
National Accounts of OECD Countries	Annual	X	X	X
Volume I: Main Aggregates	Annual	X	X	X
Volume II: Detailed Tables	Annual	X	X	X
Volume IIIa: Financial Accounts	Annual	X	X	X
Volume IIIb: Financial Balance Sheets	Annual	X	X	X
Volume IV: Summary of General Aggregates and Balances	Annual	X	X	X
Natural Gas Information	Annual	X	X	
Nuclear Energy Data	Annual	X	X	
OECD Economic Outlook	Semiannual	X	X	
OECD Economic Studies	Periodic	X	X	
OECD Economic Surveys	Periodic	X	X	
OECD Employment Outlook	Annual	X	X	
OECD Factbook	Annual	X	X	
OECD Health Data	Annual			X
OECD in Figures	Periodic	X	X	
OECD Science, Technology, and Industry Outlook	Biennial	X	X	
OECD Territorial Reviews	Periodic	X	X	
Oil Information	Annual	X	X	
Oil, Gas, Coal, and Electricity Quarterly Statistics	Quarterly	X	X	
Quarterly National Accounts	Quarterly	X	X	
Research and Development Statistics	Periodic	X		X
Revenue Statistics	Annual	X	X	
Review of Fisheries in Organisation for Economic Cooperation and Development (OECD) Countries-Policies and Summary Statistics	Annual	X	X	
Structural Statistics for Industry and Services	Periodic	X	X	
Taxing Wages	Annual	X	X	
Uranium Resources Production and Demand	Biennial	X	X	
World Energy Outlook	Annual	X	X	
Penguin Group (USA), Inc., New York, NY http://us.penguingroup.com				
The New York Times Almanac	Annual	X		
PennWell Corporation, Tulsa, OK http://www.pennwell.com				
Offshore	Monthly	X	X	X
Oil and Gas Journal	Weekly	X	X	X
Puerto Rico Planning Board, San Juan, PR http://www.jp.gobierno.pr				
Economic Report to the Governor	Annual	X		
External Trade Statistics, 2007	Periodic	X		X
Income and Product	Periodic	x		
Projections	Annual	X		
Selected Statistics on Construction Industry	Periodic	X		
Statistical Appendix-Economic Report to the Governor	Periodic	X		x
PWxyz, LLC, New York, NY http://www.publishersweekly.com				
Publishers Weekly	Weekly	X		X
Radio Advertising Bureau, New York, NY http://www.rab.com				
Media Facts	Ongoing		X	X
Radio Marketing Guide and Fact Book	Ongoing		X	X
Regional Airline Association, Washington, DC http://www.raa.org				
Statistical Report	Annual	X	X	
Securities Industry and Financial Markets Association, New York, NY http://www.sifma.org				
Foreign Activity Report	Quarterly		X	X
SIFMA Fact Book	Annual	X	X	
Standard and Poor's Financial Services LLC, New York, NY http://www.standardandpoors.com				
Analyst's Handbook	Monthly	X		X
Corporation Records: Corporate Description	Monthly	X		
Corporation Records: Daily News	Daily		X	
Daily Stock Price Records	Quarterly			X
Standard and Poor's Global Stock Markets Factbook	Annual	X		
United Nations Statistics Division, New York, NY <http://unstats.un.org/unsd/default.htm>. <https://unp.un.org/Default.aspx>				
Compendium of Human Settlements Statistics (Series N)	Periodic	X	X	
Compendium of Social Statistics and Indicators				
Demographic Yearbook (Series R)	Annual	X	X	
Energy Balances and Electricity Profiles (Series W)	Annual	X	X	
Energy Statistics Yearbook (Series J)	Annual	X	X	
Industrial Commodity Statistics Yearbook: Production Statistics	Annual	X	X	
International Trade Statistics Yearbook (Series G)	Annual	X	X	
Main Aggregates and Detailed Tables	Annual	X	X	X
Monthly Bulletin of Statistics (Series Q)	Monthly	X	X	
National Accounts Statistics: Analysis of Main Aggregates	Annual	X		
National Accounts Statistics (Series X)	Annual	X	X	
Population and Vital Statistics Report (Series A)	Quarterly	X	X	

See footnotes at end of table.

Appendix I Table: Sources of Statistics, State Statistical Abstracts, and Foreign Statistical Abstracts-Continued.

See headnote on page 909.

Title	Frequency	Paper	Internet	
			PDF	Other Formats
Statistical Yearbook	Annual	X	X	
World Statistics Pocketbook (Series V)	Annual	X	X	
The World's Women: Progress in Statistics	Quinquennial	X	X	
United Nations Conference on Trade and Development, Geneva, Switzerland http://www.unctad.org				
Development and Globalization: Facts and Figures	Periodic	X	X	X
Handbook of Statistics	Annual	X	X	X
University of Michigan, Inter-University Consortium for Political and Social Research, Institute for Social Research, Ann Arbor, MI http://www.icpsr.umich.edu/icpsrweb/ICPSR/studies/8475				
American National Election Studies Cumulative Datafile	Biennial		X	X
Warren Communications News, Washington, DC http://www.warren-news.com				
Cable and TV Station Coverage Atlas	Annual			X
Television and Cable Factbook	Annual	X		X
The World Bank Group, Washington, DC http://www.worldbank.org				
Atlas of Global Development	Annual	X	X	
Global Development Finance	Annual	X	X	
The Little Data Book	Annual	X	X	
World Development Indicators	Annual	X		X
World Health Organization, Geneva, Switzerland http://www.who.int/en/				
Aids Epidemic Update	Annual	X	X	
World Health Statistics Report	Annual	X	X	
World Trade Organization, Geneva, Switzerland http://www.wto.org				
International Trade Statistics	Annual	X	X	X
STATE STATISTICAL ABSTRACTS FROM UNIVERSITIES				
Pennsylvania State University, Pennsylvania State Data Center, Middletown, PA http://pasdc.hbg.psu.edu/				
Pennsylvania Abstract: A Statistical Fact Book	Annual	X	X	X
State University of New York: Nelson A. Rockefeller Institute of Government, Albany, NY <http://www.rockinst.org/>				
New York State Statistical Yearbook	Annual	X	X	X
University of Florida: Bureau of Economic and Business Research, Gainesville, FL http://www.bebr.ufl.edu/				
Florida Statistical Abstract	Annual	X	X	X
University of Georgia: Selig Center for Economic Growth, Athens, GA http://www.terry.uga.edu/selig/				
Georgia Statistical Abstract	Biennial	X	X	X
University of Kansas: Institute for Policy and Social Research, Lawrence, KS http://www.ipsr.ku.edu/				
Kansas Statistical Abstract	Annual		X	X
University of Missouri-Columbia: Economic and Policy Analysis Research Center, Columbia, MO http://eparc.missouri.edu/				
Missouri Statistical Data Archive (online)	Ongoing		X	
University of Oklahoma: Center for Economic and Management Research, Norman, OK http://www.ou.edu/content/price/cemr/				
Oklahoma Statistical Abstract	Annual	X		
STATE STATISTICAL ABSTRACT FROM ONE ASSOCIATION				
Texas State Historical Society, Denton, TX http://www.texasalmanac.com/				
Texas Almanac	Annual	X		X
STATE STATISTICAL ABSTRACTS FROM STATE AGENCIES				
California Department of Finance, Economic Research Unit, Sacramento, CA http://www.dof.ca.gov/HTML/FS_DATA/STAT-ABS/Statistical_Abstract.php				
California Statistical Abstract	Ongoing		X	
Hawaii State Department of Business, Economic Development & Tourism, Honolulu, HI http://hawaii.gov/dbedt/info/economic/databook				
State of Hawaii Data Book: A Statistical Abstract	Annual		X	
Maryland State Data Center, Maryland Department of Planning, Baltimore, MD http://www.mdp.state.md.us/msdc/				
Maryland Statistical Handbook	Annual		X	

See footnotes at end of table.

Appendix I Table: Sources of Statistics, State Statistical Abstracts, and Foreign Statistical Abstracts-Continued.

See headnote on page 909.

Title	Frequency	Paper	Internet	
			PDF	Other Formats
South Carolina, Budget and Control Board, Office of Research and Statistics, Columbia, SC http://abstract.sc.gov/ South Carolina Statistical Abstract	Ongoing			X

Source: ProQuest research.

Guide to State Statistical Abstracts

This bibliography includes the most recent statistical abstracts for states published since 2000. For some states, a near equivalent has been listed in substitution for, or in addition to, a statistical abstract. All sources contain statistical tables on a variety of subjects for the state as a whole, its component parts, or both. Internet sites also contain statistical data.

Alabama

University of Alabama, Center for Business and Economic Research, Box 870221, Tuscaloosa, AL 35487-0221. 205-348-6191. Fax: 205-348-2951. Internet site <http://cber.cba.ua.edu/publications.html>.
Alabama Economic Outlook, 2011. Revised annually.

Alaska

Department of Commerce, Community and Economic Development, 550 West 7 th Avenue, Suite 1770, Anchorage, AK 99501. 907-269-8100. Fax 907-269-8125. Internet site <http://www.dced.state.ak.us/dca/misc_resources.htm>.
The Alaska Economic Performance Report, 2006. Online.

Arizona

University of Arizona, Economic and Business Research Center, Eller College of Management, 1130 East Helen Street, McClelland Hall, Rm. 103, P.O. Box 210108, Tucson, AZ 85721-0108. 520-621-2155. Fax: 520-621-2150. Internet site <http://www.ebr.eller.arizona.edu/>.
Arizona Statistical Abstract, 2003.
Arizona's Economy. Quarterly Online. Online.
Arizona Economic Indicators. Quarterly.

Arkansas

University of Arkansas at Little Rock, Institute for Economic Advancement, Economic Research, 2801 South University Avenue, Little Rock, AR 72204-1099. 501-569-8519. Fax: 501-569-8538. Internet site <http://www.iea.ualr.edu>.
Arkansas State and Country Economic Data, 2011. Annual.
Arkansas Personal Income Handbook, 2011. Annual.
Arkansas Statistical Abstract, 2008. Discontinued.

California

Department of Finance, 915 L Street, Sacramento, CA 95814. 916-445-3878. Internet site <http://www.dof.ca.gov/>.
California Statistical Abstract, 2009. Annual. Online only.

Colorado

University of Colorado at Boulder, Government Publications Library, University Libraries, 184 UCB, 1720 Pleasant Street, Boulder, CO 80309-0184. 303-492-8705. Internet site <http:/ucblibraries.colorado.edu/libraries/govpubs/online.htm>.
Colorado by the Numbers. Online only.

Colorado Office of Economic Development and International Trade, 1625 Broadway, Suite 2700, Denver, CO 80202. 303-892-3840. Fax: 303-892-3848. Internet site <http://www.colorado.gov/>.
Colorado Data Book, 2010-11. Online only.

Connecticut

Connecticut Department of Economic and Community Development, 505 Hudson Street, Hartford, CT 06106-7106. 860-270-8000. Internet site <http://www.ct.gov/ecd/site/default.asp>.
Connecticut Town Profiles, 2012. Recurring.

Delaware

Delaware Economic Development Office, 99 Kings Highway, Dover, DE 19901-7305. 302-739-4271. Fax: 302-739-5749. Internet site <http://dedo.delaware.gov>.
Delaware Data Book, 2012.

District of Columbia

Business Resource Center, John A. Wilson Building, 1350 Pennsylvania Avenue, NW, Washington, DC 20004. 202-727-1000. Internet site <http://brc.dc.gov/resources/facts.asp>.
Market Facts and Statistics. Online only.

Florida

University of Florida, Bureau of Economic and Business Research, P.O. Box 117145, 221 Matherly Hall, Gainesville, FL 32611-7145. 352-392-0171, ext. 219. Fax: 352-392-4739. Internet site <http://www.bebr.ufl.edu>.
Florida Statistical Abstract, 2011. Annual. Also available on CD-ROM.
Florida County Perspective, 2011. One profile for each country. Annual. Also available on CD-ROM.
Florida County Rankings, 2011. Annual. Also available on CD-ROM.

Georgia

University of Georgia, Terry College of Business, Selig Center for Economic Growth, Athens, GA 30602-6254. 706-542-8100. Fax: 706-542-3835. Internet site <http://www.selig.uga.edu/>.
Georgia Statistical Abstract, 2010-11. Biennial.

University of Georgia, Center for Agribusiness and Economic Development, 301 Lumpkin House, Athens, GA 30602-7509. 706-542-2434. Fax: 706-542-0770. Internet site <http://www.georgiastats.uga.edu/>.
The Georgia County Guide, 2012. Annual.

Hawaii

Hawaii State Department of Business, Economic Development & Tourism, Research and Economic Analysis Division, Statistics and Data Support Branch, P.O. Box 2359, Honolulu, HI 96804. 808-586-2423. Fax: 808-587-2790. Internet site <http://www.hawaii.gov/dbedt/>.
The State of Hawaii Data Book 2011. Annual.

Idaho

State of Idaho Department of Labor, 317 West Main St., Boise, ID 83735. 208-332-3570. Fax: 208-334-6430. Internet site <http://labor.idaho.gov/dnn/default.aspx?alias=labor.idaho.gov/dnn/idl/>.

Idaho Department of Commerce, 700 W. State St. P.O. Box 83720, Boise, ID 83720. 208-334-2470. Internet site <http://commerce.idaho.gov>.
Idaho Community Profiles. Online.
Idaho at a Glance. Online.

Illinois

The Institute of Government and Public Affairs, University of Illinois, 1007 W. Nevada Street, Urbana, IL 61801, MC-037. 217-333-3340. Fax: 217-244-4817. Internet site <http://www.igpa.uiuc.edu/>.
2002-03 Illinois Statistical Abstract. Online.

Indiana

Indiana University, Kelley School of Business, Indiana Business Research Center, 100 South Avenue, Suite 240, Bloomington, IN 47404. 812-855-5507. Internet site <http://www.ibrc.indiana.edu/>.
STATS Indiana. Online only.

Iowa

Iowa State University of Science and Technology: Community Indicators Program, 17 East Hall, Ames, IA 50010. 515-294-9903. Internet site <http://www.seta.iastate.edu/>.
Community Indicators. Online only.

State Library of Iowa, State Data Center, Ola Babcock Miller Building, 1112 East Grand, Des Moines, IA 50319-0233. 800-248-4483. Fax: 515-242-6543. Internet site <http://www.iowadatacenter.org>.

Kansas

University of Kansas, Policy Research Institute, 1541 Lilac Lane, 607 Blake Hall, Lawrence, KS 66045-3129. 785-864-3701. Fax: 785-864-3683. Internet site <http://www.ipsr.ku.edu/>.
Kansas Statistical Abstract, 2011. Annual. Online only.

Kentucky

Kentucky Cabinet for Economic Development, Old Capitol Annex, 300 West Broadway, Frankfort, KY 40601. 800-626-2930. Fax: 502-564-3256. Internet site <http://www.thinkkentucky.com/>.

Louisiana

Louisiana State Census Data Center, Office of Electronic Services, 1201 N. Third Street, Suite. 7-210, Baton Rouge, LA, 70802. Fax: 225-219-4027. Internet site <http://www.louisiana.gov/Explore/Demographics_and_Geography/>.

Maine

Maine State Planning Office, 38 State House Station, 19 Union Street, Augusta, ME 04333-0038. 800-662-4545. Fax: 207-287-6077. Internet site <http://www.maine.gov/spo/>.

Maryland

Maryland Department of Planning, 301 W. Preston St. #1101, Baltimore, MD 21201. 410-676-4500. Internet site <http://wwwnew.towson.edu/>.
Maryland Statistical Abstract, 2006. Discontinued.

Massachusetts

MassCHIP, Massachusetts Department of Public Health, 250 Washington Street, Boston, MA 02108-4619. 617-624-6000. Internet site <http://masschip.state.ma.us/>.
Instant Topics. Online only.

Michigan

Michigan Economic Development Corporation, 300 North Washington Square, Lansing, MI 48913. 1-888-522-0103. Internet site <http://www.michigan.org/medc/miinfo>.

Minnesota

Minnesota Department of Employment and Economic Development, 1st National Bank Building, 332 Minnesota Street Suite E200, Saint Paul, MN 55101-1351. 800-657-3858. Internet site <http://www.positivelyminnesota.com/mwa/deed/comparemn.aspx>.
Compare Minnesota: Profiles of Minnesota's Economy & Population. Online only.

Minnesota State Demographic Center, 658 Cedar Street Room 300, Saint Paul, MN 55155, 651-296-2557. Internet site <http://www.demography.state.mn.us/>.

Mississippi

Mississippi State University, College of Business, Office of Business Research and Services, P.O. Box 5288, Mississippi State, MS 39762. 662-325-2850. Fax: 662-325-2410. Internet site <http://business.msstate.edu/>.
Mississippi Statistical Abstract, 2007. Discontinued.

Missouri

University of Missouri-Columbia, Economic and Policy Analysis Research Center, 10 Professional Building, Columbia, MO 65211. 573-882-4805. Fax: 573-882-5563. Internet site <http://eparc.missouri.edu/>.
Missouri Statistical Data Archive. Online only.

Montana

Montana Department of Commerce, Census and Economic Information Center, 301 S. Park Ave., P.O. Box 200505, Helena, MT 59620-0505, 406-841-2740. Fax: 406-841-2731. Internet site <http://ceic.mt.gov/>.

Nebraska

Nebraska Department of Economic Development, P.O. Box 94666, 301 Centenial Mall South, Lincoln, NE 68509-4666. 800-426-6505. Fax: 402-471-3778. Internet site <http://info.neded.org/>.

Nevada

Nevada Department of Administration, Budget and Planning Division, 209 East Musser Street, Room 200, Carson City, NV 89701-4298. 775-684-0222. Fax: 775-684-0260. Internet site <http://www.budget.state.nv.us/>.

New Hampshire

New Hampshire Office of Energy and Planning, 4 Chenell Drive, Concord, NH 03301-8501. 603-271-2155. Fax: 603-271-2615. Internet site <http://www.nh.gov/oep/index.htm>.

New Jersey

New Jersey State Data Center, NJ Department of Labor and Workforce Development, 1 John Fitch Plaza, P.O. Box 110 Trenton, NJ 08625-0110. 609-984-2595. Fax: 609-984-6833. Internet site <http://lwd.dol.state.nj.us/labor/lpa/content/njdc-index.html>.
Labor Market Information. Online only.

New Mexico

University of New Mexico, Bureau of Business and Economic Research, MSC06 3510, 1 University of New Mexico, Albuquerque, NM 87131-0001. 505-277-6626. Fax: 505-277-2773. Internet site <http://bber.unm.edu/>.
New Mexico Business, Current Economic Report Monthly. FOR-UNM Bulletin. Quarterly.

New York

Nelson A. Rockefeller Institute of Government, 411 State Street, Albany, NY 12203-1003. 518-443-5522. Fax: 518-443-5788. Internet site <http://www.rockinst.org/>.
New York State Statistical Yearbook, 2010.

North Carolina

Office of State Budget and Management, 116 west Jones Street, Raleigh, NC 27603-8005. 919-807-4700. Fax: 919-733-0640. Internet site <http://www.osbm.state.nc.us/osbm/>.
State Comparisons. Online only.

North Dakota

University of North Dakota, Bureau of Business and Public Administration, P.O. Box 8098, Grand Forks, ND 58202-8098. 800-225-5863. Fax: 701-777-2019. Internet site <http://business.und.edu/>.

Ohio

Office of Strategic Research, Ohio Department of Development, 77 South High Street, P.O. Box 1001, Columbus, OH 43216-1001. 614-466-2116. Fax: 614-466-9697. Internet site <http://www.odod.state.oh.us/research>.
Research products and services. Updated continuously.
Ohio County Trends. Online only.

Oklahoma

University of Oklahoma, Center for Economic and Management Research, Michael F. Price College of Business, 307 West Brooks, Suite 4, Norman OK 73019-4004. 405-325-2931. Fax: 405-325-7688. Internet site <http://www.ou.edu/price/cemr.html/>.
Statistical Abstract of Oklahoma, 2010. Paper only.

Oregon

Secretary of State, Archives Division, Archives Bldg., 800 Summer Street, NE, Salem, OR 97310. 503-373-0701 ext.1. Fax: 503-378-4188. Internet site <http://www.sos.state.or.us/bbook>.
Oregon Blue Book. 2011 Centennial. Biennial.

Pennsylvania

Pennsylvania State Data Center, Institute of State and Regional Affairs, Penn State Harrisburg, 777 West Harrisburg Pike, Middletown, PA 17057-4898. 717-948-6336. Fax: 717-948-6754. Internet site <http://pasdc.hbg.psu.edu>.
Pennsylvania Statistical Abstract, 2012. Annual. Also Available on CD-Rom.

Rhode Island

Rhode Island Economic Development Corporation, 315 Iron Horse Way, Suite 101, Providence, RI 02908. 401-278-9100. Fax: 401-273-8270. Internet site <http://www.riedc.com/>.
State and Community Profiles. Online only.

South Carolina

Budget and Control Board, Office of Research and Statistics, 1919 Blanding Street, Columbia 29201. 803-898-9960. Internet site <http://ors.sc.gov/>.
South Carolina Statistical Abstract Ongoing online. Also available on CD-Rom.

South Dakota

University of South Dakota, State Data Center, Business Research Bureau, The University of South Dakota, 414 E. Clark Street, Vermillion, SD 57069. 605-677-5708. Fax: 605-677-5427. Internet site <http://www.usd.edu/>.
2008 South Dakota Community Abstracts. Discontinued.

Tennessee

College of Business Administration, The University of Tennessee, 916 Volunteer Blvd., 716 Stokely Management Center, Knoxville, Tennessee 37996-0570. 865-974-5441. Fax: 865-974-3100. Internet site <http://cber.bus.utk.edu/Default.htm>.
Tennessee Statistical Abstract, 2003. Last printed edition.

Texas

Texas State Historical Association, 1155 Union Circle #311580, Denton, TX 76203. 940-369-5243. Internet site <http://www.texasalmanac.com/>.
Texas Almanac, 2012-2013.

Texas State Data Center and Office of the State Demographer, Institute for Demographic and Socioeconomic Research (IDSER), 501 West Durango Blvd., San Antonio, TX 78207-4415. 210-458-6543. Fax: 210-458-6541. Internet site <http://txsdc.utsa.edu/>.

Utah

Governor's Office of Planning and Budget, Demographic & Economic Analysis, Suite 150, P.O. Box 132210, Salt Lake City, UT 84114-2210. 801-538-1027. Fax: 801-538-1547. Internet site <http://www.governor.utah.gov/dea>.
2011 Economic Report to the Governor. Annual.
Utah Data Guide Newsletter, 2012. Quarterly. Also available online.

Vermont

Department of Labor, Labor Market Information, 3 Green Mountain Drive, P.O. Box 488, Montpelier, VT 05601-0488. 802-828-4202. Fax: 802-828-4050. Internet site <http://www.vtlmi.info/>.
Vermont Economic-Demographic Profile, 2012. Annual.

Virginia

University of Virginia, Weldon Cooper Center for Public Service, 2400 Old ivy Road P.O. Box 400206, Charlottesville, VA 22904-4206. 434-982-5522. Fax: 434-982-5524. Internet site <http://www.coopercenter.org/>.
Stat Chat. Online only.

Washington

Washington State Office of Financial Management, Forecasting Division, P.O. Box 43113, Olympia, WA 98504-3113. 360-902-0555. Internet site <http://www.ofm.wa.gov/>.
Washington State Data Book, 2011. Online only.

West Virginia

West Virginia University, College of Business and Economics, Bureau of Business and Economic Research, 1601 University Ave, P.O. Box 6025, Morgantown, WV 26506-6025. 304-293-4092. Fax: 304-293-5652. Internet site <http://www.be.wvu.edu/bber/index.htm>.
West Virginia Data Profile.
West Virginia Economic Outlook, 2013. Annual. Online.

Wisconsin

Wisconsin Legislative Reference Bureau, One East Main Street, Suite 200, Madison, WI 53701-2037. 608-266-0341. Internet site <http://www.legis.state.wi.us/lrb/pubs/bluebook.htm/>.
2011-12 Wisconsin Blue Book. Biennial. Online.

Wyoming

Department of Administration and Information, Economic Analysis Division, 2800 Central Avenue, Suite 206, Cheyenne, WY 82002-0060. 307-777-7504. Fax: 307-632-1819. Internet site <http://eadiv.state.wy.us/index.asp>.
The Equality State Almanac, 2010. Online.

Guide to Foreign Statistical Abstracts

This bibliography presents recent statistical abstracts for member nations of the Organization for Economic Cooperation and Development and Russia. All sources contain statistical tables on a variety of subjects for the individual countries. Many of the following publications provide text in English as well as in the national language(s) For further information on these publications, contact the named statistical agency which is responsible for editing the publication.

Australia

Australian Bureau of Statistics, Canberra. <http://www.abs.gov.au>.
Year Book Australia. Annual. 2012. (In English.)

Austria

Statistik Austria, 1110 Wien. <http://www.statistik.at/web_en/>.
Statistisches Jahrbuch Osterreichs. Annual. 2012. With CD-ROM. (In German.) With English translations of table headings.

Belgium

L'Institut National de Statistique, Rue de Louvain; 44-1000 Bruxelles. <http://statbel.fgov.be/info/links_en.asp>.
Annuaire statistique de la Belgique. annual. 1995. (In French.)

Canada

Statistics Canada, Ottawa, Ontario, KIA OT6. <http://www.statcan.gc.ca/start-debut-eng.html>.
Canada Year book. 2011. (In English.)

Czech Republic

Czech Statistical Office, Na padesatem 81, Praha 10. <http://www.czso.cz/>.
Statisticka Rocenka Ceske Republiky. 2011. With CD-ROM. (In English and Czech.)

Denmark

Danmarks Statistik, Sejrogade 11, 2100 Kobenhavn O. <http://www.dst.dk>.
Statistisk Arbog. 2012. Annual. English version available only on internet and is free of charge at: <www.dst.dk/yearbook>. (Printed version- In Danish only.)

Finland

Statistics Finland, Helsinki. <http://www.stat.fi/index_en.html>.
Statistical Yearbook of Finland, Annual. 2011. With CD-ROM. (In English, Finnish, and Swedish.)

France

Institut National de la Statistique et des Etudes Economiques, Paris 18, Bld. Adolphe Pinard, 75675 Paris (Cedex 14). <http://www.insee.fr/fr/home/home_page.asp>.
Annuaire Statistique de la France. Annual. (In French.) Ongoing. Online only.

Germany

Statistiches Bundesamt, Wiesbaden. <http://www.destatis.de/contact>.
Statistisches Jahrbuch fur die Bundesrepublik Deutschland. Annual. 2012. (In German.)
Statistisches Jahrbuch fur das Ausland. 2006.

Greece

Hellenic Statistica Authority. <http://www.statistics.gr/>.
Concise Statistical Yearbook 2009. (In English and Greek.)
Statistical Yearbook of Greece. Annual. 2009/2010. (In English and Greek.)

Hungary

Hungarian Central Statistical Office, 1024 Budapest. <http://www.ksh.hu>.
Statistical Yearbook of Hungary, 2011. With CD-ROM. (In English and Hungarian.)

Iceland

Reykjavik/Statistics Iceland. <http://www.staticd.is>.
Statistical Yearbook of Iceland. 2011. (In English and Icelandic.)

Ireland

Central Statistics Office, Skehard Road, Cork. <http://www.cso.ie>.
Statistical Yearbook of Ireland. Annual. 2012. (In English.)

Italy

Istituto Nazionale di Statistica. Via Cesare Balbo 16 Roma. <http://www.istat.it>.
Annuario Statistico Italiano. Annual. 2011. With CD-ROM. (In Italian.)

Japan

Statistics Bureau, Ministry of Internal Affairs and Communications, Tokyo, Japan. <http://www.stat.go.jp/english/data/index.htm>.
Japan Statistical Yearbook. Annual. 2012. (In English and Japanese.)

Korea, South

Statistics Korea, Daejeon Government, #920 Dunsan-dong Seo-gu, Daejeon, Korea 302 701. <http://korstat.go.kr/>.
Korea Statistical Yearbook. Annual. 2011. (In Korean and English.)

Luxembourg

Service Central de la Statistique et des Etudes Economiques, Luxembourg. <www.statec.lu/>.
Annuaire Statisque du Luxembourg. 2011. (In French.) (Alphabetical numbering system).

Mexico

Instituto Nacional de Estadistica Y Geografia e Informatica, Av. Heroe Nacozari Num. 2301 Sur Fracc. Jardines del Parque, CP 20270 Aguascalientes, Ags. <http://www.inegi.org.mx>.
Anuario estadistico de los Estados Unidos Mexicanos. Annual. 2011. (In Spanish.) Agenda Estadistica 1999.

Netherlands

Statistics Netherlands, Henri Faasdreef 312, 2492 JP The Hague. <http://www.cbs.nl/en/>.
Statistical Yearbook 2012 of the Netherlands. (In English.)

New Zealand

Statistics New Zealand, Wellington. <http://www.stats.govt.nz/>.
New Zealand Official Yearbook. Annual. 2012. (In English.)

Norway

Statistics Norway, Oslo/Kongsvinger. <http://www.ssb.no/en/>.
Statistical Yearbook of Norway. Annual. 2012. (In English.)

Poland

Central Statistical Office al. Niepodleglosci 208, 00-925 Warsaw. <http://www.stat.gov.pl/english/index.htm>.
Concise Statistical Yearbook of Poland. 2012 (In Polish and English.)
Statistical Yearbook of the Republic of Poland. 2011. (In Polish and English.)

Portugal

INE (Instituto Nacional de Estatistica.) Av. Antonio Jose de Almeida P-1000-043 Lisboa. <http://www.ine.pt/index_eng.htm>.
Anuario Estatistico de Portugal. 2010. (In Portuguese and English.)

Russia

Federal State Statistics Service, Moscow. <http://www.gks.ru/>.
Russia in Figures. 2011. (In Russian.)

Slovakia

Statistical Office of the Slovak Republic, Postovy Priecinok 2, 845 02 Bratislava 45. <http://portal.statistics.sk>.
Statisticka Rocenka Slovenskej Republiky. 2011. (In English and Slovak.) With CD-ROM.

Spain

INE (Instituto Nacional de Estadistica); Paseo de la Castellana, 183, Madrid 16. <http://www.ine.es/welcoing.htm>.
Anuario Estadistico de Espana. 2012. (In Spanish.)

Sweden

Statistics Sweden, SE-104 51 Stockholm. <http://www.scb.se/indexeng.asp>.
Statistik Arsbok for Sverige. Annual. 2012. (In English and Swedish.)

Switzerland

Neve Zurcher Zeitung, Zurich.
Statisches Jahrbuch der Schweiz. Annual. 2012. With CD-ROM. (In French and German.) Available for purchase only.

Turkey

Turkish Statistical Institute, Ankara. <http://www.turkstat.gov.tr>.
Turkey's Statistical Yearbook. 2011. (In English and Turkish.)
Turkey in Statistics. 2011. (In English only.)

United Kingdom

Office for National Statistics, London, <http://www.statistics.gov.uk/>.
Annual Abstract of Statistics. Annual. 2010. (In English.)

Metropolitan and Micropolitan Statistical Areas: Concepts, Components, and Population

The United States Office of Management and Budget (OMB) defines metropolitan and micropolitan statistical areas according to published standards that are applied to U.S. Census Bureau data. The general concept of a metropolitan or micropolitan statistical area is that of a core area containing a substantial population nucleus, together with adjacent communities having a high degree of economic and social integration with that core. Currently defined metropolitan and micropolitan statistical areas are based on application of 2000 standards (which appeared in the Federal Register on December 27, 2000) to 2000 decennial census data. Current metropolitan and micropolitan statistical area definitions were announced by OMB effective June 6, 2003, and subsequently updated as of December 2003, November 2004, December 2005, December 2006, November 2007, November 2008, and December 2009.

Standard definitions of metropolitan areas were first issued in 1949 by the then Bureau of the Budget (predecessor of OMB), under the designation "standard metropolitan area" (SMA). The term was changed to "standard metropolitan statistical area" (SMSA) in 1959 and to "metropolitan statistical area" (MSA) in 1983. The term "metropolitan area" (MA) was adopted in 1990 and referred collectively to metropolitan statistical areas (MSAs), consolidated metropolitan statistical areas (cMSAs), and primary metropolitan statistical areas (PMSAs). The term "core-based statistical area" (CBSA) became effective in 2000 and refers collectively to metropolitan and micropolitan statistical areas.

OMB has been responsible for the official metropolitan areas since they were first defined, except for the period 1977 to 1981, when they were the responsibility of the Office of Federal Statistical Policy and Standards, U.S. Department of Commerce. The standards for defining metropolitan areas were modified in 1958, 1971, 1975, 1980, 1990, and 2000.

Defining Metropolitan and Micropolitan Statistical Areas—The 2000 standards provide that each CBSA must contain at least one urban area of 10,000 or more population. Each metropolitan statistical area must have at least one urbanized area of 50,000 or more inhabitants. Each micropolitan statistical area must have at least one urban cluster of at least 10,000 but less than 50,000 population.

Under the standards, the county (or counties) in which at least 50 percent of the population resides within urban areas of 10,000 or more population, or that contain at least 5,000 people residing within a single urban area of 10,000 or more population, is identified as a "central county"(counties). Additional "outlying counties" are included in the CBSA if they meet specified requirements of commuting to or from the central counties. Counties or equivalent entities form the geographic "building blocks" for metropolitan and micropolitan statistical areas throughout the United States and Puerto Rico.

If specified criteria are met, a metropolitan statistical area containing a single core with a population of 2.5 million or more may be subdivided to form smaller groupings of counties referred to as "metropolitan divisions."

As of December 2009, there are 366 metropolitan statistical areas and 576 micropolitan statistical areas in the United States. In addition, there are eight metropolitan statistical areas and five micropolitan statistical areas in Puerto Rico.

Principal Cities and Metropolitan and Micropolitan Statistical Area Titles—The largest city in each metropolitan or micropolitan statistical area is designated a "principal city." Additional cities qualify if specified requirements are met concerning population size and employment. The title of each metropolitan or micropolitan statistical area consists of the names of up to three of its principal cities and the name of each state into which the metropolitan or micropolitan statistical area extends. Titles of metropolitan divisions also typically are based on principal city names, but in certain cases consist of county names.

Defining New England City and Town Areas—In view of the importance of cities and towns in New England, the 2000 standards also provide for a set of geographic areas that are defined using cities and towns in the six New England states. The New England city and town areas (NECTAs) are defined using the same criteria as metropolitan and micropolitan statistical areas and are identified as either metropolitan or micropolitan, based, respectively, on the presence of either an urbanized area of 50,000 or more population or an urban cluster of at least 10,000 but less than 50,000 population. If the specified criteria are met, a NECTA containing a single core with a population of at least 2.5 million may be subdivided to form smaller groupings of cities and towns referred to as New England city and town area divisions.

Changes in Definitions Over Time—Changes in the definitions of these statistical areas since the 1950 census have consisted chiefly of (1) the recognition of new areas as they reached the minimum required city or urbanized area population and (2) the addition of counties (or cities and towns in New England) to existing areas as new decennial census data showed them to qualify.

In some instances, formerly separate areas have been merged, components of an area have been transferred from one area to another, or components have been dropped from an area. The large majority of changes have taken place on the basis of decennial census data. However, Census Bureau data serve as the basis for intercensal updates in specified circumstances.

Because of these historical changes in geographic definitions, users must be cautious in comparing data for these statistical areas from different dates. For some purposes, comparisons of data for areas as defined at given dates may be appropriate; for other purposes, it may be preferable to maintain consistent area definitions. Historical metropolitan area definitions are available for 1999, 1993, 1990, 1983, 1981, 1973, 1970, 1963, 1960, and 1950.

Excluding Tables 20 and 25 through 22 in the Population section; Table 605 in the Labor Force section; Table 695 in the Income section, and the tables that follow in this appendix, the tables presenting data for metropolitan areas in this edition of the Statistical Abstract are based on the 1999 or earlier metropolitan area definitions. For a list of component counties according to the 1999 definition, see Appendix II in the 2002 edition of the Statistical Abstract or <http://www.census.gov/population/www/ estimates/pastmetro.html>.

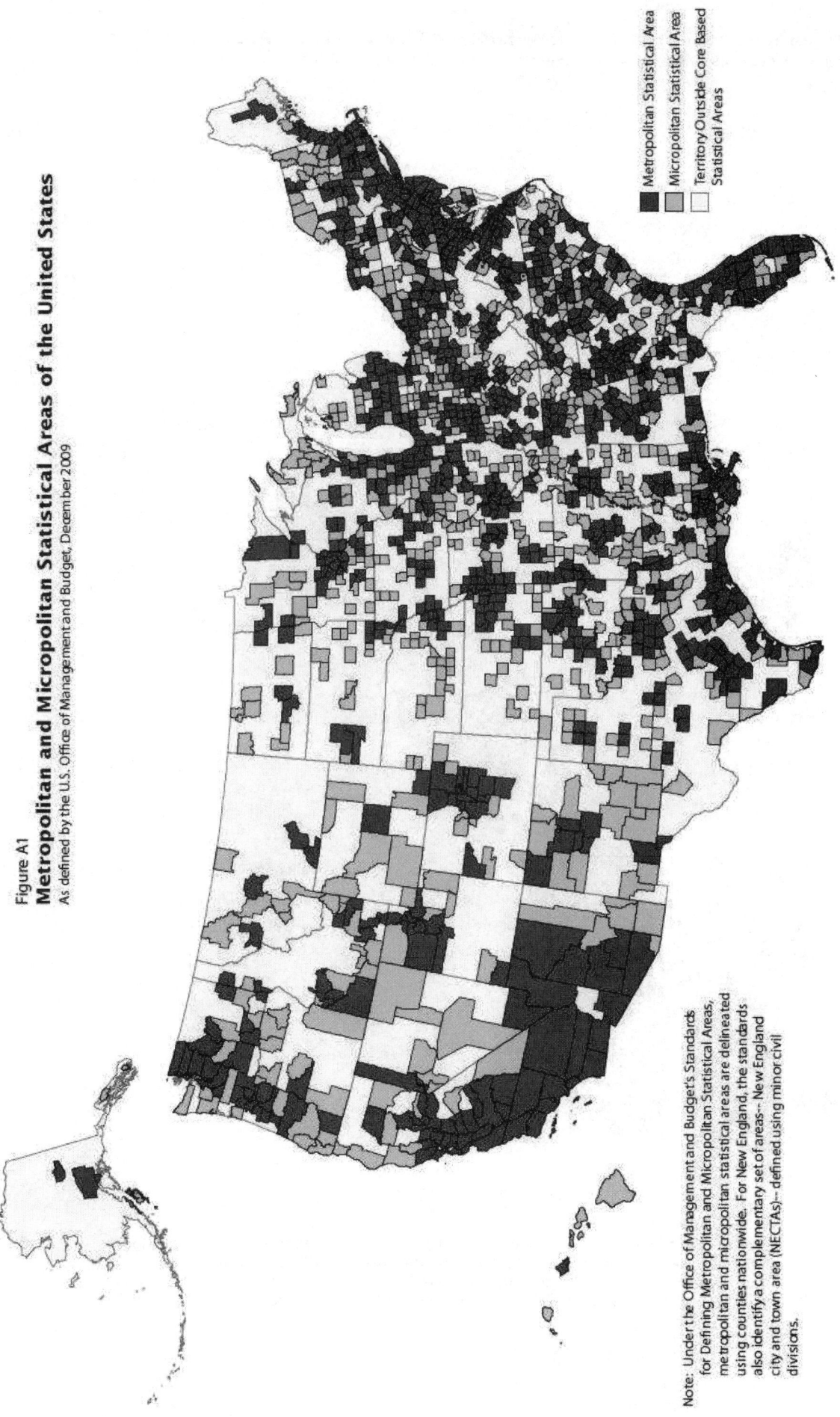

Figure A1
Metropolitan and Micropolitan Statistical Areas of the United States
As defined by the U.S. Office of Management and Budget, December 2009

Metropolitan Statistical Area
Micropolitan Statistical Area
Territory Outside Core Based
Statistical Areas

Note: Under the Office of Management and Budget's Standards for Defining Metropolitan and Micropolitan Statistical Areas, metropolitan and micropolitan statistical areas are delineated using counties nationwide. For New England, the standards also identify a complementary set of areas-- New England city and town area (NECTAs)-- defined using minor civil divisions.

Metropolitan and Micropolitan New England City and Town Areas (NECTAs)
As defined by the U.S. Office of Management and Budget, December 2009

Metropolitan NECTA

Micropolitan NECTA

Territory Outside NECTAs

Note: Under the Office of Management and Budget's Standards for Defining Metropolitan and Micropolitan
Statistical Areas, metropolitan and micropolitan statistical areas are delineated using counties
nationwide. For New England, the standards also identify a complementary set of areas--
New England city and town area (NECTAs)-- defined using minor civil divisions.

Table A. Metropolitan Statistical Areas and Components—Population: 2010

[Population as of April 2010. (165 represents 165,000). Metropolitan statistical areas defined by the U.S. Office of Management and Budget as of December 2009. All metropolitan statistical areas are arranged alphabetically]

Metropolitan Statistical Area / Metropolitan Division / Component county	Population, 2010 (1,000)
Abilene, TX	**165**
Callahan County, TX	14
Jones County, TX	20
Taylor County, TX	132
Akron, OH	**703**
Portage County, OH	161
Summit County, OH	542
Albany, GA	**157**
Baker County, GA	3
Dougherty County, GA	95
Lee County, GA	28
Terrell County, GA	9
Worth County, GA	22
Albany-Schenectady-Troy, NY	**871**
Albany County, NY	304
Rensselaer County, NY	159
Saratoga County, NY	220
Schenectady County, NY	155
Schoharie County, NY	33
Albuquerque, NM	**887**
Bernalillo County, NM	663
Sandoval County, NM	132
Torrance County, NM	16
Valencia County, NM	77
Alexandria, LA	**154**
Grant Parish, LA	22
Rapides Parish, LA	132
Allentown-Bethlehem-Easton, PA-NJ	**821**
Warren County, NJ	109
Carbon County, PA	65
Lehigh County, PA	349
Northampton County, PA	298
Altoona, PA	**127**
Blair County, PA	127
Amarillo, TX	**250**
Armstrong County, TX	2
Carson County, TX	6
Potter County, TX	121
Randall County, TX	121
Ames, IA	**90**
Story County, IA	90
Anchorage, AK	**381**
Anchorage Municipality, AK	292
Matanuska-Susitna Borough, AK	89
Anderson, IN	**132**
Madison County, IN	132
Anderson, SC	**187**
Anderson County, SC	187
Ann Arbor, MI	**345**
Washtenaw County, MI	345
Anniston-Oxford, AL	**119**
Calhoun County, AL	119
Appleton, WI	**226**
Calumet County, WI	49
Outagamie County, WI	177
Asheville, NC	**425**
Buncombe County, NC	238
Haywood County, NC	59
Henderson County, NC	107
Madison County, NC	21
Athens-Clarke County, GA	**193**
Clarke County, GA	117
Madison County, GA	28
Oconee County, GA	33
Oglethorpe County, GA	15
Atlanta-Sandy Springs-Marietta, GA	**5,269**
Barrow County, GA	69
Bartow County, GA	100
Butts County, GA	24
Carroll County, GA	111
Cherokee County, GA	214
Clayton County, GA	259
Cobb County, GA	688
Coweta County, GA	127

Metropolitan Statistical Area / Metropolitan Division / Component county	Population, 2010 (1,000)
Dawson County, GA	22
DeKalb County, GA	692
Douglas County, GA	132
Fayette County, GA	107
Forsyth County, GA	176
Fulton County, GA	921
Gwinnett County, GA	805
Haralson County, GA	29
Heard County, GA	12
Henry County, GA	204
Jasper County, GA	14
Lamar County, GA	18
Meriwether County, GA	22
Newton County, GA	100
Paulding County, GA	142
Pickens County, GA	29
Pike County, GA	18
Rockdale County, GA	85
Spalding County, GA	64
Walton County, GA	84
Atlantic City-Hammonton, NJ	**275**
Atlantic County, NJ	275
Auburn-Opelika, AL	**140**
Lee County, AL	140
Augusta-Richmond County, GA-SC	**557**
Burke County, GA	23
Columbia County, GA	124
McDuffie County, GA	22
Richmond County, GA	201
Aiken County, SC	160
Edgefield County, SC	27
Austin-Round Rock-San Marcos, TX	**1,716**
Bastrop County, TX	74
Caldwell County, TX	38
Hays County, TX	157
Travis County, TX	1,024
Williamson County, TX	423
Bakersfield-Delano, CA	**840**
Kern County, CA	840
Baltimore-Towson, MD	**2,710**
Anne Arundel County, MD	538
Baltimore County, MD	805
Carroll County, MD	167
Harford County, MD	245
Howard County, MD	287
Queen Anne's County, MD	48
Baltimore city, MD	621
Bangor, ME	**154**
Penobscot County, ME	154
Barnstable Town, MA	**216**
Barnstable County, MA	216
Baton Rouge, LA	**802**
Ascension Parish, LA	107
East Baton Rouge Parish, LA	440
East Feliciana Parish, LA	20
Iberville Parish, LA	33
Livingston Parish, LA	128
Pointe Coupee Parish, LA	23
St. Helena Parish, LA	11
West Baton Rouge Parish, LA	24
West Feliciana Parish, LA	16
Battle Creek, MI	**136**
Calhoun County, MI	136
Bay City, MI	**108**
Bay County, MI	108
Beaumont-Port Arthur, TX	**389**
Hardin County, TX	55
Jefferson County, TX	252
Orange County, TX	82
Bellingham, WA	**201**
Whatcom County, WA	201
Bend, OR	**158**
Deschutes County, OR	158
Billings, MT	**158**

Metropolitan Statistical Area / Metropolitan Division / Component county	Population, 2010 (1,000)
Carbon County, MT	10
Yellowstone County, MT	148
Binghamton, NY	**252**
Broome County, NY	201
Tioga County, NY	51
Birmingham-Hoover, AL	**1,128**
Bibb County, AL	23
Blount County, AL	57
Chilton County, AL	44
Jefferson County, AL	658
St. Clair County, AL	84
Shelby County, AL	195
Walker County, AL	67
Bismarck, ND	**109**
Burleigh County, ND	81
Morton County, ND	27
Blacksburg-Christiansburg-Radford, VA	**163**
Giles County, VA	17
Montgomery County, VA	94
Pulaski County, VA	35
Radford city, VA	16
Bloomington, IN	**193**
Greene County, IN	33
Monroe County, IN	138
Owen County, IN	22
Bloomington-Normal, IL	**170**
McLean County, IL	170
Boise City-Nampa, ID	**617**
Ada County, ID	392
Boise County, ID	7
Canyon County, ID	189
Gem County, ID	17
Owyhee County, ID	12
Boston-Cambridge-Quincy, MA-NH	**4,552**
Boston-Quincy, MA	**1,888**
Norfolk County, MA	671
Plymouth County, MA	495
Suffolk County, MA	722
Cambridge-Newton-Framingham, MA	**1,503**
Middlesex County, MA	1,503
Peabody, MA	**743**
Essex County, MA	743
Rockingham County-Strafford County, NH	**418**
Rockingham County, NH	295
Strafford County, NH	123
Boulder, CO	**295**
Boulder County, CO	295
Bowling Green, KY	**126**
Edmonson County, KY	12
Warren County, KY	114
Bremerton-Silverdale, WA	**251**
Kitsap County, WA	251
Bridgeport-Stamford-Norwalk, CT	**917**
Fairfield County, CT	917
Brownsville-Harlingen, TX	**406**
Cameron County, TX	406
Brunswick, GA	**112**
Brantley County, GA	18
Glynn County, GA	80
McIntosh County, GA	14
Buffalo-Niagara Falls, NY	**1,136**
Erie County, NY	919
Niagara County, NY	216
Burlington, NC	**151**
Alamance County, NC	151
Burlington-South Burlington, VT	**211**
Chittenden County, VT	157
Franklin County, VT	48
Grand Isle County, VT	7
Canton-Massillon, OH	**404**
Carroll County, OH	29

See footnotes at end of table.

Table A. Metropolitan Statistical Areas and Components—Population: 2010-Continued.

See headnote on page 935.

Metropolitan Statistical Area Metropolitan Division Component county	Population, 2010 (1,000)
Stark County, OH................	376
Cape Coral-Fort Myers, FL.....	**619**
Lee County, FL.................	619
Cape Girardeau-Jackson, MO-IL	**96**
Alexander County, IL...........	8
Bollinger County, MO...........	12
Cape Girardeau County, MO. ..	76
Carson City, NV.................	**55**
Carson City, NV.................	55
Casper, WY.....................	**75**
Natrona County, WY.............	75
Cedar Rapids, IA...............	**258**
Benton County, IA..............	26
Jones County, IA...............	21
Linn County, IA................	211
Champaign-Urbana, IL..........	**232**
Champaign County, IL...........	201
Ford County, IL................	14
Piatt County, IL...............	17
Charleston, WV.................	**304**
Boone County, WV...............	25
Clay County, WV................	9
Kanawha County, WV.............	193
Lincoln County, WV.............	22
Putnam County, WV.............	55
Charleston-North Charleston-Summerville, SC.	**665**
Berkeley County, SC............	178
Charleston County, SC..........	350
Dorchester County, SC..........	137
Charlotte-Gastonia-Rock Hill, NC-SC....................	**1,758**
Anson County, NC...............	27
Cabarrus County, NC............	178
Gaston County, NC..............	206
Mecklenburg County, NC........	920
Union County, NC...............	201
York County, SC................	226
Charlottesville, VA.............	**202**
Albemarle County, VA...........	99
Fluvanna County, VA............	26
Greene County, VA..............	18
Nelson County, VA..............	15
Charlottesville city, VA........	43
Chattanooga, TN-GA............	**528**
Catoosa County, GA.............	64
Dade County, GA................	17
Walker County, GA..............	69
Hamilton County, TN............	336
Marion County, TN..............	28
Sequatchie County, TN.........	14
Cheyenne, WY..................	**92**
Laramie County, WY.............	92
Chicago-Joliet-Naperville, IL-IN-WI....................	**9,461**
Chicago-Joliet-Naperville, IL..	**7,883**
Cook County, IL................	5,195
DeKalb County, IL..............	105
DuPage County, IL..............	917
Grundy County, IL..............	50
Kane County, IL................	515
Kendall County, IL.............	115
McHenry County, IL.............	309
Will County, IL................	678
Gary, IN......................	**708**
Jasper County, IN..............	33
Lake County, IN................	496
Newton County, IN.............	14
Porter County, IN..............	164
Lake County-Kenosha County, IL-WI..............	**870**
Lake County, IL................	703
Kenosha County, WI.............	166
Chico, CA.....................	**220**
Butte County, CA...............	220
Cincinnati-Middletown, OH-KY-IN................	**2,130**
Dearborn County, IN............	50
Franklin County, IN............	23

Metropolitan Statistical Area Metropolitan Division Component county	Population, 2010 (1,000)
Ohio County, IN................	6
Boone County, KY...............	119
Bracken County, KY............	8
Campbell County, KY............	90
Gallatin County, KY............	9
Grant County, KY...............	25
Kenton County, KY..............	160
Pendleton County, KY...........	15
Brown County, OH...............	45
Butler County, OH..............	368
Clermont County, OH............	197
Hamilton County, OH............	802
Warren County, OH..............	213
Clarksville, TN-KY............	**274**
Christian County, KY...........	74
Trigg County, KY...............	14
Montgomery County, TN.........	172
Stewart County, TN.............	13
Cleveland, TN.................	**116**
Bradley County, TN.............	99
Polk County, TN................	17
Cleveland-Elyria-Mentor, OH...	**2,077**
Cuyahoga County, OH...........	1,280
Geauga County, OH.............	93
Lake County, OH................	230
Lorain County, OH..............	301
Medina County, OH.............	172
Coeur d'Alene, ID.............	**138**
Kootenai County, ID............	138
College Station-Bryan, TX.....	**229**
Brazos County, TX..............	195
Burleson County, TX............	17
Robertson County, TX...........	17
Colorado Springs, CO..........	**646**
El Paso County, CO.............	622
Teller County, CO..............	23
Columbia, MO...................	**173**
Boone County, MO...............	163
Howard County, MO.............	10
Columbia, SC...................	**768**
Calhoun County, SC.............	15
Fairfield County, SC...........	24
Kershaw County, SC.............	62
Lexington County, SC...........	262
Richland County, SC............	385
Saluda County, SC..............	20
Columbus, GA-AL...............	**295**
Russell County, AL.............	53
Chattahoochee County, GA. ...	11
Harris County, GA..............	32
Marion County, GA..............	9
Muscogee County, GA..........	190
Columbus, IN..................	**77**
Bartholomew County, IN........	77
Columbus, OH..................	**1,837**
Delaware County, OH...........	174
Fairfield County, OH...........	146
Franklin County, OH............	1,163
Licking County, OH.............	166
Madison County, OH............	43
Morrow County, OH.............	35
Pickaway County, OH...........	56
Union County, OH..............	52
Corpus Christi, TX.............	**428**
Aransas County, TX.............	23
Nueces County, TX.............	340
San Patricio County, TX........	65
Corvallis, OR..................	**86**
Benton County, OR.............	86
Crestview-Fort Walton Beach-Destin, FL..........	**181**
Okaloosa County, FL...........	181
Cumberland, MD-WV............	**103**
Allegany County, MD...........	75
Mineral County, WV............	28
Dallas-Fort Worth-Arlington, TX.........................	**6,372**
Dallas-Plano-Irving, TX........	**4,236**
Collin County, TX..............	782

Metropolitan Statistical Area Metropolitan Division Component county	Population, 2010 (1,000)
Dallas County, TX..............	2,368
Delta County, TX...............	5
Denton County, TX.............	663
Ellis County, TX...............	150
Hunt County, TX...............	86
Kaufman County, TX............	103
Rockwall County, TX...........	78
Fort Worth-Arlington, TX.....	**2,136**
Johnson County, TX............	151
Parker County, TX.............	117
Tarrant County, TX.............	1,809
Wise County, TX...............	59
Dalton, GA....................	**142**
Murray County, GA.............	40
Whitfield County, GA...........	103
Danville, IL...................	**82**
Vermilion County, IL...........	82
Danville, VA...................	**107**
Pittsylvania County, VA........	64
Danville city, VA..............	43
Davenport-Moline-Rock Island, IA-IL.............	**380**
Henry County, IL...............	50
Mercer County, IL..............	16
Rock Island County, IL.........	148
Scott County, IA...............	165
Dayton, OH....................	**842**
Greene County, OH.............	162
Miami County, OH..............	103
Montgomery County, OH........	535
Preble County, OH.............	42
Decatur, AL....................	**154**
Lawrence County, AL...........	34
Morgan County, AL.............	119
Decatur, IL....................	**111**
Macon County, IL..............	111
Deltona-Daytona Beach-Ormond Beach, FL...	**495**
Volusia County, FL.............	495
Denver-Aurora-Broomfield, CO.........................	**2,543**
Adams County, CO..............	442
Arapahoe County, CO...........	572
Broomfield County, CO.........	56
Clear Creek County, CO........	9
Denver County, CO.............	600
Douglas County, CO............	285
Elbert County, CO.............	23
Gilpin County, CO.............	5
Jefferson County, CO...........	535
Park County, CO...............	16
Des Moines-West Des Moines, IA.........................	**570**
Dallas County, IA..............	66
Guthrie County, IA.............	11
Madison County, IA............	16
Polk County, IA................	431
Warren County, IA.............	46
Detroit-Warren-Livonia, MI.....	**4,296**
Detroit-Livonia-Dearborn, MI.........................	**1,821**
Wayne County, MI..............	1,821
Warren-Troy-Farmington Hills, MI...................	**2,476**
Lapeer County, MI.............	88
Livingston County, MI..........	181
Macomb County, MI............	841
Oakland County, MI............	1,202
St. Clair County, MI...........	163
Dothan, AL....................	**146**
Geneva County, AL.............	27
Henry County, AL..............	17
Houston County, AL............	102
Dover, DE.....................	**162**
Kent County, DE...............	162
Dubuque, IA...................	**94**
Dubuque County, IA............	94
Duluth, MN-WI.................	**280**

See footnotes at end of table.

Table A. Metropolitan Statistical Areas and Components—Population: 2010-Continued.

See headnote on page 935.

Metropolitan Statistical Area / Metropolitan Division / Component county	Population, 2010 (1,000)
Carlton County, MN..............	35
St. Louis County, MN...........	200
Douglas County, WI.............	44
Durham-Chapel Hill, NC.............	**504**
Chatham County, NC...........	64
Durham County, NC...........	268
Orange County, NC...........	134
Person County, NC............	39
Eau Claire, WI................	**161**
Chippewa County, WI...........	62
Eau Claire County, WI..........	99
El Centro, CA..................	**175**
Imperial County, CA............	175
Elizabethtown, KY..............	**120**
Hardin County, KY.............	106
Larue County, KY.............	14
Elkhart-Goshen, IN.............	**198**
Elkhart County, IN.............	198
Elmira, NY......................	**89**
Chemung County, NY...........	89
El Paso, TX.....................	**801**
El Paso County, TX.............	801
Erie, PA........................	**281**
Erie County, PA...............	281
Eugene-Springfield, OR........	**352**
Lane County, OR.............	352
Evansville, IN-KY................	**359**
Gibson County, IN.............	34
Posey County, IN..............	26
Vanderburgh County, IN........	180
Warrick County, IN.............	60
Henderson County, KY..........	46
Webster County, KY............	14
Fairbanks, AK..................	**98**
Fairbanks North Star Borough, AK............	98
Fargo, ND-MN..................	**209**
Clay County, MN..............	59
Cass County, ND..............	150
Farmington, NM................	**130**
San Juan County, NM...........	130
Fayetteville, NC................	**366**
Cumberland County, NC........	319
Hoke County, NC.............	47
Fayetteville-Springdale-Rogers, AR-MO............	**463**
Benton County, AR.............	221
Madison County, AR............	16
Washington County, AR.........	203
McDonald County, MO..........	23
Flagstaff, AZ....................	**134**
Coconino County, AZ...........	134
Flint, MI........................	**426**
Genesee County, MI............	426
Florence, SC....................	**206**
Darlington County, SC..........	69
Florence County, SC...........	137
Florence-Muscle Shoals, AL...	**147**
Colbert County, AL.............	54
Lauderdale County, AL..........	93
Fond du Lac, WI................	**102**
Fond du Lac County, WI.........	102
Fort Collins-Loveland, CO.....	**300**
Larimer County, CO............	300
Fort Smith, AR-OK.............	**299**
Crawford County, AR...........	62
Franklin County, AR............	18
Sebastian County, AR..........	126
Le Flore County, OK............	50
Sequoyah County, OK..........	42
Fort Wayne, IN..................	**416**
Allen County, IN.............	355
Wells County, IN.............	28
Whitley County, IN.............	33
Fresno, CA.....................	**930**
Fresno County, CA.............	930
Gadsden, AL....................	**104**
Etowah County, AL.............	104
Gainesville, FL..................	**264**

Metropolitan Statistical Area / Metropolitan Division / Component county	Population, 2010 (1,000)
Alachua County, FL.............	247
Gilchrist County, FL............	17
Gainesville, GA..................	**180**
Hall County, GA..............	180
Glens Falls, NY..................	**129**
Warren County, NY.............	66
Washington County, NY.........	63
Goldsboro, NC..................	**123**
Wayne County, NC.............	123
Grand Forks, ND-MN...........	**98**
Polk County, MN..............	32
Grand Forks County, ND........	67
Grand Junction, CO............	**147**
Mesa County, CO..............	147
Grand Rapids-Wyoming, MI. .	**774**
Barry County, MI..............	59
Ionia County, MI..............	64
Kent County, MI..............	603
Newaygo County, MI...........	48
Great Falls, MT..................	**81**
Cascade County, MT...........	81
Greeley, CO.....................	**253**
Weld County, CO..............	253
Green Bay, WI...................	**306**
Brown County, WI.............	248
Kewaunee County, WI..........	21
Oconto County, WI.............	38
Greensboro-High Point, NC....	**724**
Guilford County, NC...........	488
Randolph County, NC..........	142
Rockingham County, NC.......	94
Greenville, NC...................	**190**
Greene County, NC............	21
Pitt County, NC..............	168
Greenville-Mauldin-Easley, SC............	**637**
Greenville County, SC..........	451
Laurens County, SC...........	67
Pickens County, SC...........	119
Gulfport-Biloxi, MS..............	**249**
Hancock County, MS...........	44
Harrison County, MS...........	187
Stone County, MS.............	18
Hagerstown-Martinsburg, MD-WV......................	**269**
Washington County, MD........	147
Berkeley County, WV...........	104
Morgan County, WV...........	18
Hanford-Corcoran, CA...........	**153**
Kings County, CA..............	153
Harrisburg-Carlisle, PA..........	**549**
Cumberland County, PA........	235
Dauphin County, PA...........	268
Perry County, PA..............	46
Harrisonburg, VA................	**125**
Rockingham County, VA........	76
Harrisonburg city, VA...........	49
Hartford-West Hartford-East Hartford, CT............	**1,212**
Hartford County, CT............	894
Middlesex County, CT..........	166
Tolland County, CT.............	153
Hattiesburg, MS.................	**143**
Forrest County, MS............	75
Lamar County, MS.............	56
Perry County, MS.............	12
Hickory-Lenoir-Morganton, NC......................	**365**
Alexander County, NC..........	37
Burke County, NC.............	91
Caldwell County, NC...........	83
Catawba County, NC..........	154
Hinesville-Fort Stewart, GA....	**78**
Liberty County, GA.............	63
Long County, GA.............	14
Holland-Grand Haven, MI.......	**264**
Ottawa County, MI..............	264
Honolulu, HI.....................	**953**

Metropolitan Statistical Area / Metropolitan Division / Component county	Population, 2010 (1,000)
Honolulu County, HI.............	953
Hot Springs, AR.................	**96**
Garland County, AR............	96
Houma-Bayou Cane-Thibodaux, LA........	**208**
Lafourche Parish, LA...........	96
Terrebonne Parish, LA..........	112
Houston-Sugar Land-Baytown, TX..........	**5,947**
Austin County, TX.............	28
Brazoria County, TX............	313
Chambers County, TX..........	35
Fort Bend County, TX...........	585
Galveston County, TX..........	291
Harris County, TX..............	4,092
Liberty County, TX.............	76
Montgomery County, TX........	456
San Jacinto County, TX.........	26
Waller County, TX..............	43
Huntington-Ashland, WV-KY-OH..................	**288**
Boyd County, KY.............	50
Greenup County, KY...........	37
Lawrence County, OH..........	62
Cabell County, WV............	96
Wayne County, WV............	42
Huntsville, AL....................	**418**
Limestone County, AL..........	83
Madison County, AL............	335
Idaho Falls, ID..................	**130**
Bonneville County, ID..........	104
Jefferson County, ID...........	26
Indianapolis-Carmel, IN.........	**1,756**
Boone County, IN.............	57
Brown County, IN.............	15
Hamilton County, IN...........	275
Hancock County, IN...........	70
Hendricks County, IN..........	145
Johnson County, IN...........	140
Marion County, IN.............	903
Morgan County, IN............	69
Putnam County, IN............	38
Shelby County, IN.............	44
Iowa City, IA.....................	**153**
Johnson County, IA............	131
Washington County, IA.........	22
Ithaca, NY.......................	**102**
Tompkins County, NY...........	102
Jackson, MI......................	**160**
Jackson County, MI............	160
Jackson, MS.....................	**539**
Copiah County, MS............	29
Hinds County, MS.............	245
Madison County, MS...........	95
Rankin County, MS............	142
Simpson County, MS...........	28
Jackson, TN......................	**115**
Chester County, TN............	17
Madison County, TN...........	98
Jacksonville, FL..................	**1,346**
Baker County, FL..............	27
Clay County, FL..............	191
Duval County, FL..............	864
Nassau County, FL.............	73
St. Johns County, FL...........	190
Jacksonville, NC..................	**178**
Onslow County, NC............	178
Janesville, WI....................	**160**
Rock County, WI..............	160
Jefferson City, MO...............	**150**
Callaway County, MO..........	44
Cole County, MO.............	76
Moniteau County, MO..........	16
Osage County, MO............	14
Johnson City, TN................	**199**
Carter County, TN.............	57
Unicoi County, TN.............	18
Washington County, TN.........	123
Johnstown, PA...................	**144**

See footnotes at end of table.

Metropolitan Statistical Area Metropolitan Division Component county	Population, 2010 (1,000)
Cambria County, PA............	144
Jonesboro, AR..................	**121**
Craighead County, AR............	96
Poinsett County, AR............	25
Joplin, MO......................	**176**
Jasper County, MO..............	117
Newton County, MO..............	58
Kalamazoo-Portage, MI........	**327**
Kalamazoo County, MI............	250
Van Buren County, MI...........	76
Kankakee-Bradley, IL..........	**113**
Kankakee County, IL............	113
Kansas City, MO-KS............	**2,035**
Franklin County, KS.............	26
Johnson County, KS.............	544
Leavenworth County, KS.......	76
Linn County, KS................	10
Miami County, KS...............	33
Wyandotte County, KS..........	158
Bates County, MO..............	17
Caldwell County, MO............	9
Cass County, MO...............	99
Clay County, MO................	222
Clinton County, MO..............	21
Jackson County, MO.............	674
Lafayette County, MO............	33
Platte County, MO..............	89
Ray County, MO................	23
Kennewick-Pasco-Richland, WA......................	**253**
Benton County, WA.............	175
Franklin County, WA............	78
Killeen-Temple-Fort Hood, TX.......................	**405**
Bell County, TX................	310
Coryell County, TX.............	75
Lampasas County, TX...........	20
Kingsport-Bristol-Bristol, TN-VA...................	**310**
Hawkins County, TN............	57
Sullivan County, TN.............	157
Scott County, VA...............	23
Washington County, VA.........	55
Bristol city, VA................	18
Kingston, NY...................	**182**
Ulster County, NY..............	182
Knoxville, TN...................	**698**
Anderson County, TN...........	75
Blount County, TN..............	123
Knox County, TN...............	432
Loudon County, TN.............	49
Union County, TN..............	19
Kokomo, IN.....................	**99**
Howard County, IN.............	83
Tipton County, IN..............	16
La Crosse, WI-MN..............	**134**
Houston County, MN............	19
La Crosse County, WI...........	115
Lafayette, IN...................	**202**
Benton County, IN..............	9
Carroll County, IN..............	20
Tippecanoe County, IN..........	173
Lafayette, LA...................	**274**
Lafayette Parish, LA............	222
St. Martin Parish, LA...........	52
Lake Charles, LA...............	**200**
Calcasieu Parish, LA............	193
Cameron Parish, LA............	7
Lake Havasu City-Kingman, AZ.......................	**200**
Mohave County, AZ.............	200
Lakeland-Winter Haven, FL....	**602**
Polk County, FL................	602
Lancaster, PA..................	**519**
Lancaster County, PA...........	519
Lansing-East Lansing, MI......	**464**
Clinton County, MI.............	75
Eaton County, MI..............	108
Ingham County, MI.............	281
Laredo, TX.....................	**250**
Webb County, TX...............	250

Metropolitan Statistical Area Metropolitan Division Component county	Population, 2010 (1,000)
Las Cruces, NM.................	**209**
Doña Ana County, NM.........	209
Las Vegas-Paradise, NV.......	**1,951**
Clark County, NV...............	1,951
Lawrence, KS...................	**111**
Douglas County, KS............	111
Lawton, OK.....................	**124**
Comanche County, OK..........	124
Lebanon, PA....................	**134**
Lebanon County, PA............	134
Lewiston, ID-WA...............	**61**
Nez Perce County, ID...........	39
Asotin County, WA.............	22
Lewiston-Auburn, ME..........	**108**
Androscoggin County, ME......	108
Lexington-Fayette, KY..........	**472**
Bourbon County, KY............	20
Clark County, KY...............	36
Fayette County, KY.............	296
Jessamine County, KY..........	49
Scott County, KY...............	47
Woodford County, KY..........	25
Lima, OH.......................	**106**
Allen County, OH...............	106
Lincoln, NE.....................	**302**
Lancaster County, NE...........	285
Seward County, NE.............	17
Little Rock-North Little Rock-Conway, AR...........	**700**
Faulkner County, AR............	113
Grant County, AR..............	18
Lonoke County, AR.............	68
Perry County, AR..............	10
Pulaski County, AR.............	383
Saline County, AR..............	107
Logan, UT-ID...................	**125**
Franklin County, ID.............	13
Cache County, UT..............	113
Longview, TX...................	**214**
Gregg County, TX..............	122
Rusk County, TX...............	53
Upshur County, TX.............	39
Longview, WA..................	**102**
Cowlitz County, WA............	102
Los Angeles-Long Beach-Santa Ana, CA........	**12,829**
Los Angeles-Long Beach-Glendale, CA..........	**9,819**
Los Angeles County, CA.........	9,819
Santa Ana-Anaheim-Irvine, CA.......................	**3,010**
Orange County, CA..............	3,010
Louisville/Jefferson County, KY-IN...................	**1,284**
Clark County, IN...............	110
Floyd County, IN...............	75
Harrison County, IN............	39
Washington County, IN.........	28
Bullitt County, KY..............	74
Henry County, KY..............	15
Jefferson County, KY...........	741
Meade County, KY.............	29
Nelson County, KY.............	43
Oldham County, KY............	60
Shelby County, KY.............	42
Spencer County, KY............	17
Trimble County, KY............	9
Lubbock, TX....................	**285**
Crosby County, TX.............	6
Lubbock County, TX............	279
Lynchburg, VA..................	**253**
Amherst County, VA............	32
Appomattox County, VA........	15
Bedford County, VA............	69
Campbell County, VA...........	55
Bedford city, VA...............	6
Lynchburg city, VA.............	76
Macon, GA.....................	**232**
Bibb County, GA...............	156

Metropolitan Statistical Area Metropolitan Division Component county	Population, 2010 (1,000)
Crawford County, GA...........	13
Jones County, GA..............	29
Monroe County, GA............	26
Twiggs County, GA.............	9
Madera-Chowchilla, CA.......	**151**
Madera County, CA.............	151
Madison, WI....................	**569**
Columbia County, WI...........	57
Dane County, WI...............	488
Iowa County, WI...............	24
Manchester-Nashua, NH.......	**401**
Hillsborough County, NH........	401
Manhattan, KS.................	**127**
Geary County, KS..............	34
Pottawatomie County, KS.......	22
Riley County, KS...............	71
Mankato-North Mankato, MN...	**97**
Blue Earth County, MN..........	64
Nicollet County, MN............	33
Mansfield, OH..................	**124**
Richland County, OH............	124
McAllen-Edinburg-Mission, TX.......................	**775**
Hidalgo County, TX.............	775
Medford, OR....................	**203**
Jackson County, OR.............	203
Memphis, TN-MS-AR...........	**1,316**
Crittenden County, AR..........	51
DeSoto County, MS.............	161
Marshall County, MS...........	37
Tate County, MS...............	29
Tunica County, MS.............	11
Fayette County, TN.............	38
Shelby County, TN.............	928
Tipton County, TN..............	61
Merced, CA.....................	**256**
Merced County, CA.............	256
Miami-Fort Lauderdale-Pompano Beach, FL..................	**5,565**
Fort Lauderdale-Pompano Beach-Deerfield Beach, FL..	**1,748**
Broward County, FL............	1,748
Miami-Miami Beach-Kendall, FL.......................	**2,496**
Miami-Dade County, FL.........	2,496
West Palm Beach-Boca Raton-Boynton Beach, FL...	**1,320**
Palm Beach County, FL.........	1,320
Michigan City-La Porte, IN.....	**111**
LaPorte County, IN.............	111
Midland, TX....................	**137**
Midland County, TX.............	137
Milwaukee-Waukesha-West Allis, WI...................	**1,556**
Milwaukee County, WI..........	948
Ozaukee County, WI...........	86
Washington County, WI.........	132
Waukesha County, WI..........	390
Minneapolis-St. Paul-Bloomington, MN-WI...	**3,280**
Anoka County, MN.............	331
Carver County, MN.............	91
Chisago County, MN............	54
Dakota County, MN.............	399
Hennepin County, MN..........	1,152
Isanti County, MN..............	38
Ramsey County, MN............	509
Scott County, MN..............	130
Sherburne County, MN.........	88
Washington County, MN........	238
Wright County, MN.............	125
Pierce County, WI..............	41
St. Croix County, WI...........	84
Missoula, MT...................	**109**
Missoula County, MT...........	109
Mobile, AL.....................	**413**
Mobile County, AL..............	413

See footnotes at end of table.

Table A. Metropolitan Statistical Areas and Components—Population: 2010-Continued.

See headnote on page 935.

Metropolitan Statistical Area Metropolitan Division Component county	Population, 2010 (1,000)
Modesto, CA	**514**
Stanislaus County, CA	514
Monroe, LA	**176**
Ouachita Parish, LA	154
Union Parish, LA	23
Monroe, MI	**152**
Monroe County, MI	152
Montgomery, AL	**375**
Autauga County, AL	55
Elmore County, AL	79
Lowndes County, AL	11
Montgomery County, AL	229
Morgantown, WV	**130**
Monongalia County, WV	96
Preston County, WV	34
Morristown, TN	**137**
Grainger County, TN	23
Hamblen County, TN	63
Jefferson County, TN	51
Mount Vernon-Anacortes, WA	**117**
Skagit County, WA	117
Muncie, IN	**118**
Delaware County, IN	118
Muskegon-Norton Shores, MI	**172**
Muskegon County, MI	172
Myrtle Beach-North Myrtle Beach-Conway, SC	**269**
Horry County, SC	269
Napa, CA	**136**
Napa County, CA	136
Naples-Marco Island, FL	**322**
Collier County, FL	322
Nashville-Davidson--Murfreesboro--Franklin, TN	**1,590**
Cannon County, TN	14
Cheatham County, TN	39
Davidson County, TN	627
Dickson County, TN	50
Hickman County, TN	25
Macon County, TN	22
Robertson County, TN	66
Rutherford County, TN	263
Smith County, TN	19
Sumner County, TN	161
Trousdale County, TN	8
Williamson County, TN	183
Wilson County, TN	114
New Haven-Milford, CT	**862**
New Haven County, CT	862
New Orleans-Metairie-Kenner, LA	**1,168**
Jefferson Parish, LA	433
Orleans Parish, LA	344
Plaquemines Parish, LA	23
St. Bernard Parish, LA	36
St. Charles Parish, LA	53
St. John the Baptist Parish, LA	46
St. Tammany Parish, LA	234
New York-Northern New Jersey-Long Island, NY-NJ-PA	**18,897**
Edison-New Brunswick, NJ	**2,340**
Middlesex County, NJ	810
Monmouth County, NJ	630
Ocean County, NJ	577
Somerset County, NJ	323
Nassau-Suffolk, NY	**2,833**
Nassau County, NY	1,340
Suffolk County, NY	1,493
Newark-Union, NJ-PA	**2,148**
Essex County, NJ	784
Hunterdon County, NJ	128
Morris County, NJ	492
Sussex County, NJ	149

Metropolitan Statistical Area Metropolitan Division Component county	Population, 2010 (1,000)
Union County, NJ	536
Pike County, PA	57
New York-White Plains-Wayne, NY-NJ	**11,576**
Bergen County, NJ	905
Hudson County, NJ	634
Passaic County, NJ	501
Bronx County, NY	1,385
Kings County, NY	2,505
New York County, NY	1,586
Putnam County, NY	100
Queens County, NY	2,231
Richmond County, NY	469
Rockland County, NY	312
Westchester County, NY	949
Niles-Benton Harbor, MI	**157**
Berrien County, MI	157
North Port-Bradenton-Sarasota, FL	**702**
Manatee County, FL	323
Sarasota County, FL	379
Norwich-New London, CT	**274**
New London County, CT	274
Ocala, FL	**331**
Marion County, FL	331
Ocean City, NJ	**97**
Cape May County, NJ	97
Odessa, TX	**137**
Ector County, TX	137
Ogden-Clearfield, UT	**547**
Davis County, UT	306
Morgan County, UT	9
Weber County, UT	231
Oklahoma City, OK	**1,253**
Canadian County, OK	116
Cleveland County, OK	256
Grady County, OK	52
Lincoln County, OK	34
Logan County, OK	42
McClain County, OK	35
Oklahoma County, OK	719
Olympia, WA	**252**
Thurston County, WA	252
Omaha-Council Bluffs, NE-IA	**865**
Harrison County, IA	15
Mills County, IA	15
Pottawattamie County, IA	93
Cass County, NE	25
Douglas County, NE	517
Sarpy County, NE	159
Saunders County, NE	21
Washington County, NE	20
Orlando-Kissimmee-Sanford, FL	**2,134**
Lake County, FL	297
Orange County, FL	1,146
Osceola County, FL	269
Seminole County, FL	423
Oshkosh-Neenah, WI	**167**
Winnebago County, WI	167
Owensboro, KY	**115**
Daviess County, KY	97
Hancock County, KY	9
McLean County, KY	10
Oxnard-Thousand Oaks-Ventura, CA	**823**
Ventura County, CA	823
Palm Bay-Melbourne-Titusville, FL	**543**
Brevard County, FL	543
Palm Coast, FL	**96**
Flagler County, FL	96
Panama City-Lynn Haven-Panama City Beach, FL	**169**
Bay County, FL	169

Metropolitan Statistical Area Metropolitan Division Component county	Population, 2010 (1,000)
Parkersburg-Marietta-Vienna, WV-OH	**162**
Washington County, OH	62
Pleasants County, WV	8
Wirt County, WV	6
Wood County, WV	87
Pascagoula, MS	**162**
George County, MS	23
Jackson County, MS	140
Pensacola-Ferry Pass-Brent, FL	**449**
Escambia County, FL	298
Santa Rosa County, FL	151
Peoria, IL	**379**
Marshall County, IL	13
Peoria County, IL	186
Stark County, IL	6
Tazewell County, IL	135
Woodford County, IL	39
Philadelphia-Camden-Wilmington, PA-NJ-DE-MD	**5,965**
Camden, NJ	**1,251**
Burlington County, NJ	449
Camden County, NJ	514
Gloucester County, NJ	288
Philadelphia, PA	**4,009**
Bucks County, PA	625
Chester County, PA	499
Delaware County, PA	559
Montgomery County, PA	800
Philadelphia County, PA	1,526
Wilmington, DE-MD-NJ	**706**
New Castle County, DE	538
Cecil County, MD	101
Salem County, NJ	66
Phoenix-Mesa-Glendale, AZ	**4,193**
Maricopa County, AZ	3,817
Pinal County, AZ	376
Pine Bluff, AR	**100**
Cleveland County, AR	9
Jefferson County, AR	77
Lincoln County, AR	14
Pittsburgh, PA	**2,356**
Allegheny County, PA	1,223
Armstrong County, PA	69
Beaver County, PA	171
Butler County, PA	184
Fayette County, PA	137
Washington County, PA	208
Westmoreland County, PA	365
Pittsfield, MA	**131**
Berkshire County, MA	131
Pocatello, ID	**91**
Bannock County, ID	83
Power County, ID	8
Portland-South Portland-Biddeford, ME	**514**
Cumberland County, ME	282
Sagadahoc County, ME	35
York County, ME	197
Portland-Vancouver-Hillsboro, OR-WA	**2,226**
Clackamas County, OR	376
Columbia County, OR	49
Multnomah County, OR	735
Washington County, OR	530
Yamhill County, OR	99
Clark County, WA	425
Skamania County, WA	11
Port St. Lucie, FL	**424**
Martin County, FL	146
St. Lucie County, FL	278
Poughkeepsie-Newburgh-Middletown, NY	**670**
Dutchess County, NY	297
Orange County, NY	373
Prescott, AZ	**211**
Yavapai County, AZ	211

See footnotes at end of table.

Table A. Metropolitan Statistical Areas and Components—Population: 2010-Continued.

See headnote on page 935.

Metropolitan Statistical Area / Metropolitan Division / Component county	Population, 2010 (1,000)
Providence-New Bedford-Fall River, RI-MA	**1,601**
Bristol County, MA	548
Bristol County, RI	50
Kent County, RI	166
Newport County, RI	83
Providence County, RI	627
Washington County, RI	127
Provo-Orem, UT	**527**
Juab County, UT	10
Utah County, UT	517
Pueblo, CO	**159**
Pueblo County, CO	159
Punta Gorda, FL	**160**
Charlotte County, FL	160
Racine, WI	**195**
Racine County, WI	195
Raleigh-Cary, NC	**1,130**
Franklin County, NC	61
Johnston County, NC	169
Wake County, NC	901
Rapid City, SD	**126**
Meade County, SD	25
Pennington County, SD	101
Reading, PA	**411**
Berks County, PA	411
Redding, CA	**177**
Shasta County, CA	177
Reno-Sparks, NV	**425**
Storey County, NV	4
Washoe County, NV	421
Richmond, VA	**1,258**
Amelia County, VA	13
Caroline County, VA	29
Charles City County, VA	7
Chesterfield County, VA	316
Cumberland County, VA	10
Dinwiddie County, VA	28
Goochland County, VA	22
Hanover County, VA	100
Henrico County, VA	307
King and Queen County, VA	7
King William County, VA	16
Louisa County, VA	33
New Kent County, VA	18
Powhatan County, VA	28
Prince George County, VA	36
Sussex County, VA	12
Colonial Heights city, VA	17
Hopewell city, VA	23
Petersburg city, VA	32
Richmond city, VA	204
Riverside-San Bernardino-Ontario, CA	**4,225**
Riverside County, CA	2,190
San Bernardino County, CA	2,035
Roanoke, VA	**309**
Botetourt County, VA	33
Craig County, VA	5
Franklin County, VA	56
Roanoke County, VA	92
Roanoke city, VA	97
Salem city, VA	25
Rochester, MN	**186**
Dodge County, MN	20
Olmsted County, MN	144
Wabasha County, MN	22
Rochester, NY	**1,054**
Livingston County, NY	65
Monroe County, NY	744
Ontario County, NY	108
Orleans County, NY	43
Wayne County, NY	94
Rockford, IL	**349**
Boone County, IL	54
Winnebago County, IL	295
Rocky Mount, NC	**152**
Edgecombe County, NC	57
Nash County, NC	96
Rome, GA	**96**
Floyd County, GA	96
Sacramento--Arden-Arcade--Roseville, CA	**2,149**
El Dorado County, CA	181
Placer County, CA	348
Sacramento County, CA	1,419
Yolo County, CA	201
Saginaw-Saginaw Township North, MI	**200**
Saginaw County, MI	200
St. Cloud, MN	**189**
Benton County, MN	38
Stearns County, MN	151
St. George, UT	**138**
Washington County, UT	138
St. Joseph, MO-KS	**127**
Doniphan County, KS	8
Andrew County, MO	17
Buchanan County, MO	89
DeKalb County, MO	13
St. Louis, MO-IL [1]	**2,813**
Bond County, IL	18
Calhoun County, IL	5
Clinton County, IL	38
Jersey County, IL	23
Macoupin County, IL	48
Madison County, IL	269
Monroe County, IL	33
St. Clair County, IL	270
Franklin County, MO	101
Jefferson County, MO	219
Lincoln County, MO	53
St. Charles County, MO	360
St. Louis County, MO	999
Warren County, MO	33
Washington County, MO	25
St. Louis city, MO	319
Salem, OR	**391**
Marion County, OR	315
Polk County, OR	75
Salinas, CA	**415**
Monterey County, CA	415
Salisbury, MD	**125**
Somerset County, MD	26
Wicomico County, MD	99
Salt Lake City, UT	**1,124**
Salt Lake County, UT	1,030
Summit County, UT	36
Tooele County, UT	58
San Angelo, TX	**112**
Irion County, TX	2
Tom Green County, TX	110
San Antonio-New Braunfels, TX	**2,143**
Atascosa County, TX	45
Bandera County, TX	20
Bexar County, TX	1,715
Comal County, TX	108
Guadalupe County, TX	132
Kendall County, TX	33
Medina County, TX	46
Wilson County, TX	43
San Diego-Carlsbad-San Marcos, CA	**3,095**
San Diego County, CA	3,095
Sandusky, OH	**77**
Erie County, OH	77
San Francisco-Oakland-Fremont, CA	**4,335**
Oakland-Fremont-Hayward, CA	**2,559**
Alameda County, CA	1,510
Contra Costa County, CA	1,049
San Francisco-San Mateo-Redwood City, CA	**1,776**
Marin County, CA	252
San Francisco County, CA	805
San Mateo County, CA	718
San Jose-Sunnyvale-Santa Clara, CA	**1,837**
San Benito County, CA	55
Santa Clara County, CA	1,782
San Luis Obispo-Paso Robles, CA	**270**
San Luis Obispo County, CA	270
Santa Barbara-Santa Maria-Goleta, CA	**424**
Santa Barbara County, CA	424
Santa Cruz-Watsonville, CA	**262**
Santa Cruz County, CA	262
Santa Fe, NM	**144**
Santa Fe County, NM	144
Santa Rosa-Petaluma, CA	**484**
Sonoma County, CA	484
Savannah, GA	**348**
Bryan County, GA	30
Chatham County, GA	265
Effingham County, GA	52
Scranton--Wilkes-Barre, PA	**564**
Lackawanna County, PA	214
Luzerne County, PA	321
Wyoming County, PA	28
Seattle-Tacoma-Bellevue, WA	**3,440**
Seattle-Bellevue-Everett, WA	**2,645**
King County, WA	1,931
Snohomish County, WA	713
Tacoma, WA	**795**
Pierce County, WA	795
Sebastian-Vero Beach, FL	**138**
Indian River County, FL	138
Sheboygan, WI	**116**
Sheboygan County, WI	116
Sherman-Denison, TX	**121**
Grayson County, TX	121
Shreveport-Bossier City, LA	**399**
Bossier Parish, LA	117
Caddo Parish, LA	255
De Soto Parish, LA	27
Sioux City, IA-NE-SD	**144**
Woodbury County, IA	102
Dakota County, NE	21
Dixon County, NE	6
Union County, SD	14
Sioux Falls, SD	**228**
Lincoln County, SD	45
McCook County, SD	6
Minnehaha County, SD	169
Turner County, SD	8
South Bend-Mishawaka, IN-MI	**319**
St. Joseph County, IN	267
Cass County, MI	52
Spartanburg, SC	**284**
Spartanburg County, SC	284
Spokane, WA	**471**
Spokane County, WA	471
Springfield, IL	**210**
Menard County, IL	13
Sangamon County, IL	197
Springfield, MA	**693**
Franklin County, MA	71
Hampden County, MA	463
Hampshire County, MA	158
Springfield, MO	**437**
Christian County, MO	77
Dallas County, MO	17
Greene County, MO	275
Polk County, MO	31
Webster County, MO	36
Springfield, OH	**138**
Clark County, OH	138
State College, PA	**154**
Centre County, PA	154
Steubenville-Weirton, OH-WV	**124**
Jefferson County, OH	70
Brooke County, WV	24

See footnotes at end of table.

Table A. Metropolitan Statistical Areas and Components—Population: 2010-Continued.

See headnote on page 935.

Metropolitan Statistical Area / Metropolitan Division / Component county	Population, 2010 (1,000)
Hancock County, WV	31
Stockton, CA	**685**
San Joaquin County, CA	685
Sumter, SC	**107**
Sumter County, SC	107
Syracuse, NY	**663**
Madison County, NY	73
Onondaga County, NY	467
Oswego County, NY	122
Tallahassee, FL	**367**
Gadsden County, FL	46
Jefferson County, FL	15
Leon County, FL	275
Wakulla County, FL	31
Tampa-St. Petersburg-Clearwater, FL	**2,783**
Hernando County, FL	173
Hillsborough County, FL	1,229
Pasco County, FL	465
Pinellas County, FL	917
Terre Haute, IN	**172**
Clay County, IN	27
Sullivan County, IN	21
Vermillion County, IN	16
Vigo County, IN	108
Texarkana, TX-Texarkana, AR	**136**
Miller County, AR	43
Bowie County, TX	93
Toledo, OH	**651**
Fulton County, OH	43
Lucas County, OH	442
Ottawa County, OH	41
Wood County, OH	125
Topeka, KS	**234**
Jackson County, KS	13
Jefferson County, KS	19
Osage County, KS	16
Shawnee County, KS	178
Wabaunsee County, KS	7
Trenton-Ewing, NJ	**367**
Mercer County, NJ	367
Tucson, AZ	**980**
Pima County, AZ	980
Tulsa, OK	**937**
Creek County, OK	70
Okmulgee County, OK	40
Osage County, OK	47
Pawnee County, OK	17
Rogers County, OK	87
Tulsa County, OK	603
Wagoner County, OK	73
Tuscaloosa, AL	**219**
Greene County, AL	9
Hale County, AL	16
Tuscaloosa County, AL	195
Tyler, TX	**210**
Smith County, TX	210
Utica-Rome, NY	**299**
Herkimer County, NY	65
Oneida County, NY	235

Metropolitan Statistical Area / Metropolitan Division / Component county	Population, 2010 (1,000)
Valdosta, GA	**140**
Brooks County, GA	16
Echols County, GA	4
Lanier County, GA	10
Lowndes County, GA	109
Vallejo-Fairfield, CA	**413**
Solano County, CA	413
Victoria, TX	**115**
Calhoun County, TX	21
Goliad County, TX	7
Victoria County, TX	87
Vineland-Millville-Bridgeton, NJ	**157**
Cumberland County, NJ	157
Virginia Beach-Norfolk-Newport News, VA-NC	**1,672**
Currituck County, NC	24
Gloucester County, VA	37
Isle of Wight County, VA	35
James City County, VA	67
Mathews County, VA	9
Surry County, VA	7
York County, VA	65
Chesapeake city, VA	222
Hampton city, VA	137
Newport News city, VA	181
Norfolk city, VA	243
Poquoson city, VA	12
Portsmouth city, VA	96
Suffolk city, VA	85
Virginia Beach city, VA	438
Williamsburg city, VA	14
Visalia-Porterville, CA	**442**
Tulare County, CA	442
Waco, TX	**235**
McLennan County, TX	235
Warner Robins, GA	**140**
Houston County, GA	140
Washington-Arlington-Alexandria, DC-VA-MD-WV	**5,582**
Bethesda-Rockville-Frederick, MD	**1,205**
Frederick County, MD	233
Montgomery County, MD	972
Washington-Arlington-Alexandria, DC-VA-MD-WV	**4,377**
District of Columbia, DC	602
Calvert County, MD	89
Charles County, MD	147
Prince George's County, MD	863
Arlington County, VA	208
Clarke County, VA	14
Fairfax County, VA	1,082
Fauquier County, VA	65
Loudoun County, VA	312
Prince William County, VA	402
Spotsylvania County, VA	122
Stafford County, VA	129
Warren County, VA	38
Alexandria city, VA	140
Fairfax city, VA	23

Metropolitan Statistical Area / Metropolitan Division / Component county	Population, 2010 (1,000)
Falls Church city, VA	12
Fredericksburg city, VA	24
Manassas city, VA	38
Manassas Park city, VA	14
Jefferson County, WV	53
Waterloo-Cedar Falls, IA	**168**
Black Hawk County, IA	131
Bremer County, IA	24
Grundy County, IA	12
Wausau, WI	**134**
Marathon County, WI	134
Wenatchee-East Wenatchee, WA	**111**
Chelan County, WA	72
Douglas County, WA	38
Wheeling, WV-OH	**148**
Belmont County, OH	70
Marshall County, WV	33
Ohio County, WV	44
Wichita, KS	**623**
Butler County, KS	66
Harvey County, KS	35
Sedgwick County, KS	498
Sumner County, KS	24
Wichita Falls, TX	**151**
Archer County, TX	9
Clay County, TX	11
Wichita County, TX	132
Williamsport, PA	**116**
Lycoming County, PA	116
Wilmington, NC	**362**
Brunswick County, NC	107
New Hanover County, NC	203
Pender County, NC	52
Winchester, VA-WV	**128**
Frederick County, VA	78
Winchester city, VA	26
Hampshire County, WV	24
Winston-Salem, NC	**478**
Davie County, NC	41
Forsyth County, NC	351
Stokes County, NC	47
Yadkin County, NC	38
Worcester, MA	**799**
Worcester County, MA	799
Yakima, WA	**243**
Yakima County, WA	243
York-Hanover, PA	**435**
York County, PA	435
Youngstown-Warren-Boardman, OH-PA	**566**
Mahoning County, OH	239
Trumbull County, OH	210
Mercer County, PA	117
Yuba City, CA	**167**
Sutter County, CA	95
Yuba County, CA	72
Yuma, AZ	**196**
Yuma County, AZ	196

[1] The portion of Sullivan city in Crawford County, Missouri, is legally part of the St. Louis, MO-IL Metropolitan Statistical Area. The estimate shown here for the St. Louis, MO-IL Metropolitan Statistical Area does not include this area.

Source: U.S. Census Bureau, 2011 Population Estimates, <http://www.census.gov/popest/data/metro/totals/2011/>.

Table B. Micropolitan Statistical Areas and Components—Population: 2010

[Population as of April 2010. (58 represents 58,000). Micropolitan statistical areas defined by the U.S. Office of Management and Budget as of December 2009. All micropolitan statistical areas are arranged alphabetically]

Micropolitan Statistical Area Component county	Population, 2010 (1,000)
Abbeville, LA.	**58**
Vermilion Parish, LA.	58
Aberdeen, SD.	**41**
Brown County, SD.	37
Edmunds County, SD.	4
Aberdeen, WA.	**73**
Grays Harbor County, WA.	73
Ada, OK.	**37**
Pontotoc County, OK.	37
Adrian, MI.	**100**
Lenawee County, MI.	100
Alamogordo, NM.	**64**
Otero County, NM.	64
Albany-Lebanon, OR.	**117**
Linn County, OR.	117
Albemarle, NC.	**61**
Stanly County, NC.	61
Albert Lea, MN.	**31**
Freeborn County, MN.	31
Albertville, AL.	**93**
Marshall County, AL.	93
Alexander City, AL.	**53**
Coosa County, AL.	12
Tallapoosa County, AL.	42
Alexandria, MN.	**36**
Douglas County, MN.	36
Alice, TX.	**41**
Jim Wells County, TX.	41
Allegan, MI.	**111**
Allegan County, MI.	111
Alma, MI.	**42**
Gratiot County, MI.	42
Alpena, MI.	**30**
Alpena County, MI.	30
Altus, OK.	**26**
Jackson County, OK.	26
Americus, GA.	**38**
Schley County, GA.	5
Sumter County, GA.	33
Amsterdam, NY.	**50**
Montgomery County, NY.	50
Andrews, TX.	**15**
Andrews County, TX.	15
Angola, IN.	**34**
Steuben County, IN.	34
Arcadia, FL.	**35**
DeSoto County, FL.	35
Ardmore, OK.	**57**
Carter County, OK.	48
Love County, OK.	9
Arkadelphia, AR.	**23**
Clark County, AR.	23
Ashland, OH.	**53**
Ashland County, OH.	53
Ashtabula, OH.	**101**
Ashtabula County, OH.	101
Astoria, OR.	**37**
Clatsop County, OR.	37
Atchison, KS.	**17**
Atchison County, KS.	17
Athens, OH.	**65**
Athens County, OH.	65
Athens, TN.	**52**
McMinn County, TN.	52
Athens, TX.	**79**
Henderson County, TX.	79
Auburn, IN.	**42**
DeKalb County, IN.	42
Auburn, NY.	**80**
Cayuga County, NY.	80
Augusta-Waterville, ME.	**122**
Kennebec County, ME.	122
Austin, MN.	**39**
Mower County, MN.	39
Bainbridge, GA.	**28**
Decatur County, GA.	28
Baraboo, WI.	**62**
Sauk County, WI.	62

Micropolitan Statistical Area Component county	Population, 2010 (1,000)
Barre, VT.	**60**
Washington County, VT.	60
Bartlesville, OK.	**51**
Washington County, OK.	51
Bastrop, LA.	**28**
Morehouse Parish, LA.	28
Batavia, NY.	**60**
Genesee County, NY.	60
Batesville, AR.	**37**
Independence County, AR.	37
Bay City, TX.	**37**
Matagorda County, TX.	37
Beatrice, NE.	**22**
Gage County, NE.	22
Beaver Dam, WI.	**89**
Dodge County, WI.	89
Beckley, WV.	**79**
Raleigh County, WV.	79
Bedford, IN.	**46**
Lawrence County, IN.	46
Beeville, TX.	**32**
Bee County, TX.	32
Bellefontaine, OH.	**46**
Logan County, OH.	46
Bemidji, MN.	**44**
Beltrami County, MN.	44
Bennettsville, SC.	**29**
Marlboro County, SC.	29
Bennington, VT.	**37**
Bennington County, VT.	37
Berlin, NH-VT.	**39**
Coos County, NH.	33
Essex County, VT.	6
Big Rapids, MI.	**43**
Mecosta County, MI.	43
Big Spring, TX.	**35**
Howard County, TX.	35
Bishop, CA.	**19**
Inyo County, CA.	19
Blackfoot, ID.	**46**
Bingham County, ID.	46
Bloomsburg-Berwick, PA.	**86**
Columbia County, PA.	67
Montour County, PA.	18
Bluefield, WV-VA.	**107**
Tazewell County, VA.	45
Mercer County, WV.	62
Blytheville, AR.	**46**
Mississippi County, AR.	46
Bogalusa, LA.	**47**
Washington Parish, LA.	47
Bonham, TX.	**34**
Fannin County, TX.	34
Boone, IA.	**26**
Boone County, IA.	26
Boone, NC.	**51**
Watauga County, NC.	51
Borger, TX.	**22**
Hutchinson County, TX.	22
Bozeman, MT.	**90**
Gallatin County, MT.	90
Bradford, PA.	**43**
McKean County, PA.	43
Brainerd, MN.	**91**
Cass County, MN.	29
Crow Wing County, MN.	63
Branson, MO.	**84**
Stone County, MO.	32
Taney County, MO.	52
Brenham, TX.	**34**
Washington County, TX.	34
Brevard, NC.	**33**
Transylvania County, NC.	33
Brigham City, UT.	**50**
Box Elder County, UT.	50
Brookhaven, MS.	**35**
Lincoln County, MS.	35
Brookings, OR.	**22**
Curry County, OR.	22

Micropolitan Statistical Area Component county	Population, 2010 (1,000)
Brookings, SD.	**32**
Brookings County, SD.	32
Brownsville, TN.	**19**
Haywood County, TN.	19
Brownwood, TX.	**38**
Brown County, TX.	38
Bucyrus, OH.	**44**
Crawford County, OH.	44
Burley, ID.	**43**
Cassia County, ID.	23
Minidoka County, ID.	20
Burlington, IA-IL.	**48**
Henderson County, IL.	7
Des Moines County, IA.	40
Butte-Silver Bow, MT.	**34**
Silver Bow County, MT.	34
Cadillac, MI.	**48**
Missaukee County, MI.	15
Wexford County, MI.	33
Calhoun, GA.	**55**
Gordon County, GA.	55
Cambridge, MD.	**33**
Dorchester County, MD.	33
Cambridge, OH.	**40**
Guernsey County, OH.	40
Camden, AR.	**31**
Calhoun County, AR.	5
Ouachita County, AR.	26
Campbellsville, KY.	**25**
Taylor County, KY.	25
Cañon City, CO.	**47**
Fremont County, CO.	47
Canton, IL.	**37**
Fulton County, IL.	37
Carbondale, IL.	**60**
Jackson County, IL.	60
Carlsbad-Artesia, NM.	**54**
Eddy County, NM.	54
Cedar City, UT.	**46**
Iron County, UT.	46
Cedartown, GA.	**41**
Polk County, GA.	41
Celina, OH.	**41**
Mercer County, OH.	41
Central City, KY.	**31**
Muhlenberg County, KY.	31
Centralia, IL.	**39**
Marion County, IL.	39
Centralia, WA.	**75**
Lewis County, WA.	75
Chambersburg, PA.	**150**
Franklin County, PA.	150
Charleston-Mattoon, IL.	**65**
Coles County, IL.	54
Cumberland County, IL.	11
Chester, SC.	**33**
Chester County, SC.	33
Chillicothe, OH.	**78**
Ross County, OH.	78
Claremont, NH.	**44**
Sullivan County, NH.	44
Clarksburg, WV.	**94**
Doddridge County, WV.	8
Harrison County, WV.	69
Taylor County, WV.	17
Clarksdale, MS.	**26**
Coahoma County, MS.	26
Clearlake, CA.	**65**
Lake County, CA.	65
Cleveland, MS.	**34**
Bolivar County, MS.	34
Clewiston, FL.	**39**
Hendry County, FL.	39
Clinton, IA.	**49**
Clinton County, IA.	49
Clovis, NM.	**48**
Curry County, NM.	48
Coffeyville, KS.	**35**
Montgomery County, KS.	35

See footnotes at end of table.

Table B. Micropolitan Statistical Areas and Components—Population: 2010-Continued.

See headnote on page 942.

Micropolitan Statistical Area Component county	Population, 2010 (1,000)
Coldwater, MI	**45**
Branch County, MI	45
Columbia, TN	**81**
Maury County, TN	81
Columbus, MS	**60**
Lowndes County, MS	60
Columbus, NE	**32**
Platte County, NE	32
Concord, NH	**146**
Merrimack County, NH	146
Connersville, IN	**24**
Fayette County, IN	24
Cookeville, TN	**106**
Jackson County, TN	12
Overton County, TN	22
Putnam County, TN	72
Coos Bay, OR	**63**
Coos County, OR	63
Corbin, KY	**36**
Whitley County, KY	36
Cordele, GA	**23**
Crisp County, GA	23
Corinth, MS	**37**
Alcorn County, MS	37
Cornelia, GA	**43**
Habersham County, GA	43
Corning, NY	**99**
Steuben County, NY	99
Corsicana, TX	**48**
Navarro County, TX	48
Cortland, NY	**49**
Cortland County, NY	49
Coshocton, OH	**37**
Coshocton County, OH	37
Crawfordsville, IN	**38**
Montgomery County, IN	38
Crescent City, CA	**29**
Del Norte County, CA	29
Crossville, TN	**56**
Cumberland County, TN	56
Crowley, LA	**62**
Acadia Parish, LA	62
Cullman, AL	**80**
Cullman County, AL	80
Culpeper, VA	**47**
Culpeper County, VA	47
Danville, KY	**53**
Boyle County, KY	28
Lincoln County, KY	25
Daphne-Fairhope-Foley, AL	**182**
Baldwin County, AL	182
Decatur, IN	**34**
Adams County, IN	34
Defiance, OH	**39**
Defiance County, OH	39
Del Rio, TX	**49**
Val Verde County, TX	49
Deming, NM	**25**
Luna County, NM	25
DeRidder, LA	**36**
Beauregard Parish, LA	36
Dickinson, ND	**25**
Billings County, ND	1
Stark County, ND	24
Dillon, SC	**32**
Dillon County, SC	32
Dixon, IL	**36**
Lee County, IL	36
Dodge City, KS	**34**
Ford County, KS	34
Douglas, GA	**51**
Atkinson County, GA	8
Coffee County, GA	42
Dublin, GA	**58**
Johnson County, GA	10
Laurens County, GA	48
DuBois, PA	**82**
Clearfield County, PA	82
Dumas, TX	**22**

Micropolitan Statistical Area Component county	Population, 2010 (1,000)
Moore County, TX	22
Duncan, OK	**45**
Stephens County, OK	45
Dunn, NC	**115**
Harnett County, NC	115
Durango, CO	**51**
La Plata County, CO	51
Durant, OK	**42**
Bryan County, OK	42
Dyersburg, TN	**38**
Dyer County, TN	38
Eagle Pass, TX	**54**
Maverick County, TX	54
East Liverpool-Salem, OH	**108**
Columbiana County, OH	108
Easton, MD	**38**
Talbot County, MD	38
East Stroudsburg, PA	**170**
Monroe County, PA	170
Edwards, CO	**60**
Eagle County, CO	52
Lake County, CO	7
Effingham, IL	**34**
Effingham County, IL	34
El Campo, TX	**41**
Wharton County, TX	41
El Dorado, AR	**42**
Union County, AR	42
Elizabeth City, NC	**64**
Camden County, NC	10
Pasquotank County, NC	41
Perquimans County, NC	13
Elk City, OK	**22**
Beckham County, OK	22
Elko, NV	**51**
Elko County, NV	49
Eureka County, NV	2
Ellensburg, WA	**41**
Kittitas County, WA	41
Emporia, KS	**36**
Chase County, KS	3
Lyon County, KS	34
Enid, OK	**61**
Garfield County, OK	61
Enterprise-Ozark, AL	**100**
Coffee County, AL	50
Dale County, AL	50
Escanaba, MI	**37**
Delta County, MI	37
Espanola, NM	**40**
Rio Arriba County, NM	40
Eufaula, AL-GA	**30**
Barbour County, AL	27
Quitman County, GA	3
Eureka-Arcata-Fortuna, CA	**135**
Humboldt County, CA	135
Evanston, WY	**21**
Uinta County, WY	21
Fairmont, MN	**21**
Martin County, MN	21
Fairmont, WV	**56**
Marion County, WV	56
Fallon, NV	**25**
Churchill County, NV	25
Faribault-Northfield, MN	**64**
Rice County, MN	64
Farmington, MO	**65**
St. Francois County, MO	65
Fergus Falls, MN	**57**
Otter Tail County, MN	57
Fernley, NV	**52**
Lyon County, NV	52
Findlay, OH	**75**
Hancock County, OH	75
Fitzgerald, GA	**27**
Ben Hill County, GA	18
Irwin County, GA	10
Forest City, NC	**68**
Rutherford County, NC	68

Micropolitan Statistical Area Component county	Population, 2010 (1,000)
Forrest City, AR	**28**
St. Francis County, AR	28
Fort Dodge, IA	**38**
Webster County, IA	38
Fort Leonard Wood, MO	**52**
Pulaski County, MO	52
Fort Madison-Keokuk, IA-MO	**43**
Lee County, IA	36
Clark County, MO	7
Fort Morgan, CO	**28**
Morgan County, CO	28
Fort Payne, AL	**71**
DeKalb County, AL	71
Fort Polk South, LA	**52**
Vernon Parish, LA	52
Fort Valley, GA	**28**
Peach County, GA	28
Frankfort, IN	**33**
Clinton County, IN	33
Frankfort, KY	**71**
Anderson County, KY	21
Franklin County, KY	49
Fredericksburg, TX	**25**
Gillespie County, TX	25
Freeport, IL	**48**
Stephenson County, IL	48
Fremont, NE	**37**
Dodge County, NE	37
Fremont, OH	**61**
Sandusky County, OH	61
Gaffney, SC	**55**
Cherokee County, SC	55
Gainesville, TX	**38**
Cooke County, TX	38
Galesburg, IL	**71**
Knox County, IL	53
Warren County, IL	18
Gallup, NM	**71**
McKinley County, NM	71
Garden City, KS	**37**
Finney County, KS	37
Gardnerville Ranchos, NV	**47**
Douglas County, NV	47
Georgetown, SC	**60**
Georgetown County, SC	60
Gettysburg, PA	**101**
Adams County, PA	101
Gillette, WY	**46**
Campbell County, WY	46
Glasgow, KY	**52**
Barren County, KY	42
Metcalfe County, KY	10
Gloversville, NY	**56**
Fulton County, NY	56
Granbury, TX	**60**
Hood County, TX	51
Somervell County, TX	8
Grand Island, NE	**73**
Hall County, NE	59
Howard County, NE	6
Merrick County, NE	8
Grants, NM	**27**
Cibola County, NM	27
Grants Pass, OR	**83**
Josephine County, OR	83
Great Bend, KS	**28**
Barton County, KS	28
Greeneville, TN	**69**
Greene County, TN	69
Greensburg, IN	**26**
Decatur County, IN	26
Greenville, MS	**51**
Washington County, MS	51
Greenville, OH	**53**
Darke County, OH	53
Greenwood, MS	**43**
Carroll County, MS	11
Leflore County, MS	32
Greenwood, SC	**70**

See footnotes at end of table.

Table B. Micropolitan Statistical Areas and Components—Population: 2010-Continued.

See headnote on page 942.

Micropolitan Statistical Area Component county	Population, 2010 (1,000)
Greenwood County, SC	70
Grenada, MS	**22**
Grenada County, MS	22
Guymon, OK	**21**
Texas County, OK	21
Hammond, LA	**121**
Tangipahoa Parish, LA	121
Hannibal, MO	**39**
Marion County, MO	29
Ralls County, MO	10
Harriman, TN	**54**
Roane County, TN	54
Harrisburg, IL	**25**
Saline County, IL	25
Harrison, AR	**45**
Boone County, AR	37
Newton County, AR	8
Hastings, NE	**38**
Adams County, NE	31
Clay County, NE	7
Havre, MT	**16**
Hill County, MT	16
Hays, KS	**28**
Ellis County, KS	28
Heber, UT	**24**
Wasatch County, UT	24
Helena, MT	**75**
Jefferson County, MT	11
Lewis and Clark County, MT	63
Helena-West Helena, AR	**22**
Phillips County, AR	22
Henderson, NC	**45**
Vance County, NC	45
Hereford, TX	**19**
Deaf Smith County, TX	19
Hilo, HI	**185**
Hawaii County, HI	185
Hilton Head Island-Beaufort, SC	**187**
Beaufort County, SC	162
Jasper County, SC	25
Hobbs, NM	**65**
Lea County, NM	65
Homosassa Springs, FL	**141**
Citrus County, FL	141
Hood River, OR	**22**
Hood River County, OR	22
Hope, AR	**32**
Hempstead County, AR	23
Nevada County, AR	9
Houghton, MI	**39**
Houghton County, MI	37
Keweenaw County, MI	2
Hudson, NY	**63**
Columbia County, NY	63
Humboldt, TN	**50**
Gibson County, TN	50
Huntingdon, PA	**46**
Huntingdon County, PA	46
Huntington, IN	**37**
Huntington County, IN	37
Huntsville, TX	**68**
Walker County, TX	68
Huron, SD	**17**
Beadle County, SD	17
Hutchinson, KS	**65**
Reno County, KS	65
Hutchinson, MN	**37**
McLeod County, MN	37
Indiana, PA	**89**
Indiana County, PA	89
Indianola, MS	**29**
Sunflower County, MS	29
Iron Mountain, MI-WI	**31**
Dickinson County, MI	26
Florence County, WI	4
Jackson, WY-ID	**31**
Teton County, ID	10
Teton County, WY	21
Jacksonville, IL	**41**
Morgan County, IL	36

Micropolitan Statistical Area Component county	Population, 2010 (1,000)
Scott County, IL	5
Jacksonville, TX	**51**
Cherokee County, TX	51
Jamestown, ND	**21**
Stutsman County, ND	21
Jamestown-Dunkirk-Fredonia, NY	**135**
Chautauqua County, NY	135
Jasper, IN	**55**
Dubois County, IN	42
Pike County, IN	13
Jennings, LA	**32**
Jefferson Davis Parish, LA	32
Jesup, GA	**30**
Wayne County, GA	30
Juneau, AK	**31**
Juneau City and Borough, AK	31
Kahului-Wailuku, HI	**155**
Maui County, HI	155
Kalispell, MT	**91**
Flathead County, MT	91
Kapaa, HI	**67**
Kauai County, HI	67
Kearney, NE	**53**
Buffalo County, NE	46
Kearney County, NE	6
Keene, NH	**77**
Cheshire County, NH	77
Kendallville, IN	**48**
Noble County, IN	48
Kennett, MO	**32**
Dunklin County, MO	32
Kerrville, TX	**50**
Kerr County, TX	50
Ketchikan, AK	**13**
Ketchikan Gateway Borough, AK	13
Key West, FL	**73**
Monroe County, FL	73
Kill Devil Hills, NC	**34**
Dare County, NC	34
Kingsville, TX	**32**
Kenedy County, TX	(Z)
Kleberg County, TX	32
Kinston, NC	**59**
Lenoir County, NC	59
Kirksville, MO	**30**
Adair County, MO	26
Schuyler County, MO	4
Klamath Falls, OR	**66**
Klamath County, OR	66
Kodiak, AK	**14**
Kodiak Island Borough, AK	14
Laconia, NH	**60**
Belknap County, NH	60
La Follette, TN	**41**
Campbell County, TN	41
La Grande, OR	**26**
Union County, OR	26
LaGrange, GA	**67**
Troup County, GA	67
Lake City, FL	**68**
Columbia County, FL	68
Lamesa, TX	**14**
Dawson County, TX	14
Lancaster, SC	**77**
Lancaster County, SC	77
Laramie, WY	**36**
Albany County, WY	36
Las Vegas, NM	**29**
San Miguel County, NM	29
Laurel, MS	**85**
Jasper County, MS	17
Jones County, MS	68
Laurinburg, NC	**36**
Scotland County, NC	36
Lawrenceburg, TN	**42**
Lawrence County, TN	42
Lebanon, MO	**36**

Micropolitan Statistical Area Component county	Population, 2010 (1,000)
Laclede County, MO	36
Lebanon, NH-VT	**175**
Grafton County, NH	89
Orange County, VT	29
Windsor County, VT	57
Levelland, TX	**23**
Hockley County, TX	23
Lewisburg, PA	**45**
Union County, PA	45
Lewisburg, TN	**31**
Marshall County, TN	31
Lewistown, PA	**47**
Mifflin County, PA	47
Lexington, NE	**26**
Dawson County, NE	24
Gosper County, NE	2
Lexington Park, MD	**105**
St. Mary's County, MD	105
Liberal, KS	**23**
Seward County, KS	23
Lincoln, IL	**30**
Logan County, IL	30
Lincolnton, NC	**78**
Lincoln County, NC	78
Lock Haven, PA	**39**
Clinton County, PA	39
Logansport, IN	**39**
Cass County, IN	39
London, KY	**59**
Laurel County, KY	59
Los Alamos, NM	**18**
Los Alamos County, NM	18
Lufkin, TX	**87**
Angelina County, TX	87
Lumberton, NC	**134**
Robeson County, NC	134
Macomb, IL	**33**
McDonough County, IL	33
Madison, IN	**32**
Jefferson County, IN	32
Madisonville, KY	**47**
Hopkins County, KY	47
Magnolia, AR	**25**
Columbia County, AR	25
Malone, NY	**52**
Franklin County, NY	52
Manitowoc, WI	**81**
Manitowoc County, WI	81
Marble Falls, TX	**43**
Burnet County, TX	43
Marinette, WI-MI	**66**
Menominee County, MI	24
Marinette County, WI	42
Marion, IN	**70**
Grant County, IN	70
Marion, OH	**67**
Marion County, OH	67
Marion-Herrin, IL	**66**
Williamson County, IL	66
Marquette, MI	**67**
Marquette County, MI	67
Marshall, MN	**26**
Lyon County, MN	26
Marshall, MO	**23**
Saline County, MO	23
Marshall, TX	**66**
Harrison County, TX	66
Marshalltown, IA	**41**
Marshall County, IA	41
Marshfield-Wisconsin Rapids, WI	**75**
Wood County, WI	75
Martin, TN	**35**
Weakley County, TN	35
Martinsville, VA	**68**
Henry County, VA	54
Martinsville city, VA	14
Maryville, MO	**23**
Nodaway County, MO	23

See footnotes at end of table.

Table B. Micropolitan Statistical Areas and Components—Population: 2010-Continued.

See headnote on page 942.

Micropolitan Statistical Area Component county	Population, 2010 (1,000)
Mason City, IA	**52**
Cerro Gordo County, IA	44
Worth County, IA	8
Mayfield, KY	**37**
Graves County, KY	37
Maysville, KY	**31**
Lewis County, KY	14
Mason County, KY	17
McAlester, OK	**46**
Pittsburg County, OK	46
McComb, MS	**54**
Amite County, MS	13
Pike County, MS	40
McMinnville, TN	**40**
Warren County, TN	40
McPherson, KS	**29**
McPherson County, KS	29
Meadville, PA	**89**
Crawford County, PA	89
Menomonie, WI	**44**
Dunn County, WI	44
Meridian, MS	**107**
Clarke County, MS	17
Kemper County, MS	10
Lauderdale County, MS	80
Merrill, WI	**29**
Lincoln County, WI	29
Mexico, MO	**26**
Audrain County, MO	26
Miami, OK	**32**
Ottawa County, OK	32
Middlesborough, KY	**29**
Bell County, KY	29
Midland, MI	**84**
Midland County, MI	84
Milledgeville, GA	**55**
Baldwin County, GA	46
Hancock County, GA	9
Minden, LA	**41**
Webster Parish, LA	41
Mineral Wells, TX	**28**
Palo Pinto County, TX	28
Minot, ND	**70**
McHenry County, ND	5
Renville County, ND	2
Ward County, ND	62
Mitchell, SD	**23**
Davison County, SD	20
Hanson County, SD	3
Moberly, MO	**25**
Randolph County, MO	25
Monroe, WI	**37**
Green County, WI	37
Montrose, CO	**41**
Montrose County, CO	41
Morehead City, NC	**66**
Carteret County, NC	66
Morgan City, LA	**55**
St. Mary Parish, LA	55
Moscow, ID	**37**
Latah County, ID	37
Moses Lake, WA	**89**
Grant County, WA	89
Moultrie, GA	**45**
Colquitt County, GA	45
Mountain Home, AR	**42**
Baxter County, AR	42
Mountain Home, ID	**27**
Elmore County, ID	27
Mount Airy, NC	**74**
Surry County, NC	74
Mount Pleasant, MI	**70**
Isabella County, MI	70
Mount Pleasant, TX	**32**
Titus County, TX	32
Mount Sterling, KY	**44**
Bath County, KY	12
Menifee County, KY	6
Montgomery County, KY	26

Micropolitan Statistical Area Component county	Population, 2010 (1,000)
Mount Vernon, IL	**47**
Hamilton County, IL	8
Jefferson County, IL	39
Mount Vernon, OH	**61**
Knox County, OH	61
Murray, KY	**37**
Calloway County, KY	37
Muscatine, IA	**54**
Louisa County, IA	11
Muscatine County, IA	43
Muskogee, OK	**71**
Muskogee County, OK	71
Nacogdoches, TX	**65**
Nacogdoches County, TX	65
Natchez, MS-LA	**53**
Concordia Parish, LA	21
Adams County, MS	32
Natchitoches, LA	**40**
Natchitoches Parish, LA	40
New Bern, NC	**127**
Craven County, NC	104
Jones County, NC	10
Pamlico County, NC	13
Newberry, SC	**38**
Newberry County, SC	38
New Castle, IN	**49**
Henry County, IN	49
New Castle, PA	**91**
Lawrence County, PA	91
New Iberia, LA	**73**
Iberia Parish, LA	73
New Philadelphia-Dover, OH	**93**
Tuscarawas County, OH	93
Newport, TN	**36**
Cocke County, TN	36
Newton, IA	**37**
Jasper County, IA	37
New Ulm, MN	**26**
Brown County, MN	26
Nogales, AZ	**47**
Santa Cruz County, AZ	47
Norfolk, NE	**48**
Madison County, NE	35
Pierce County, NE	7
Stanton County, NE	6
North Platte, NE	**38**
Lincoln County, NE	36
Logan County, NE	1
McPherson County, NE	1
North Vernon, IN	**29**
Jennings County, IN	29
North Wilkesboro, NC	**69**
Wilkes County, NC	69
Norwalk, OH	**60**
Huron County, OH	60
Oak Harbor, WA	**79**
Island County, WA	79
Oak Hill, WV	**46**
Fayette County, WV	46
Ocean Pines, MD	**51**
Worcester County, MD	51
Ogdensburg-Massena, NY	**112**
St. Lawrence County, NY	112
Oil City, PA	**55**
Venango County, PA	55
Okeechobee, FL	**40**
Okeechobee County, FL	40
Olean, NY	**80**
Cattaraugus County, NY	80
Oneonta, NY	**62**
Otsego County, NY	62
Ontario, OR-ID	**54**
Payette County, ID	23
Malheur County, OR	31
Opelousas-Eunice, LA	**83**
St. Landry Parish, LA	83
Orangeburg, SC	**93**
Orangeburg County, SC	93
Oskaloosa, IA	**22**

Micropolitan Statistical Area Component county	Population, 2010 (1,000)
Mahaska County, IA	22
Ottawa-Streator, IL	**155**
Bureau County, IL	35
LaSalle County, IL	114
Putnam County, IL	6
Ottumwa, IA	**36**
Wapello County, IA	36
Owatonna, MN	**37**
Steele County, MN	37
Owosso, MI	**71**
Shiawassee County, MI	71
Oxford, MS	**47**
Lafayette County, MS	47
Paducah, KY-IL	**99**
Massac County, IL	15
Ballard County, KY	8
Livingston County, KY	10
McCracken County, KY	66
Pahrump, NV	**44**
Nye County, NV	44
Palatka, FL	**74**
Putnam County, FL	74
Palestine, TX	**58**
Anderson County, TX	58
Pampa, TX	**23**
Gray County, TX	23
Roberts County, TX	1
Paragould, AR	**42**
Greene County, AR	42
Paris, TN	**32**
Henry County, TN	32
Paris, TX	**50**
Lamar County, TX	50
Parsons, KS	**22**
Labette County, KS	22
Payson, AZ	**54**
Gila County, AZ	54
Pecos, TX	**14**
Reeves County, TX	14
Pella, IA	**33**
Marion County, IA	33
Pendleton-Hermiston, OR	**87**
Morrow County, OR	11
Umatilla County, OR	76
Peru, IN	**37**
Miami County, IN	37
Phoenix Lake-Cedar Ridge, CA	**55**
Tuolumne County, CA	55
Picayune, MS	**56**
Pearl River County, MS	56
Pierre, SD	**20**
Hughes County, SD	17
Stanley County, SD	3
Pierre Part, LA	**23**
Assumption Parish, LA	23
Pittsburg, KS	**39**
Crawford County, KS	39
Plainview, TX	**36**
Hale County, TX	36
Platteville, WI	**51**
Grant County, WI	51
Plattsburgh, NY	**82**
Clinton County, NY	82
Plymouth, IN	**47**
Marshall County, IN	47
Point Pleasant, WV-OH	**58**
Gallia County, OH	31
Mason County, WV	27
Ponca City, OK	**47**
Kay County, OK	47
Pontiac, IL	**39**
Livingston County, IL	39
Poplar Bluff, MO	**43**
Butler County, MO	43
Portales, NM	**20**
Roosevelt County, NM	20
Port Angeles, WA	**71**

See footnotes at end of table.

Table B. Microplitan Statistical Areas and Components—Population: 2010-Continued.

See headnote on page 942.

Micropolitan Statistical Area Component county	Population, 2010 (1,000)	Micropolitan Statistical Area Component county	Population, 2010 (1,000)	Micropolitan Statistical Area Component county	Population, 2010 (1,000)
Clallam County, WA	71	Jackson County, AL	53	**Storm Lake, IA**	**20**
Portsmouth, OH	**79**	**Scottsburg, IN**	**24**	Buena Vista County, IA	20
Scioto County, OH	79	Scott County, IN	24	**Sturgis, MI**	**61**
Pottsville, PA	**148**	**Seaford, DE**	**197**	St. Joseph County, MI	61
Schuylkill County, PA	148	Sussex County, DE	197	**Sulphur Springs, TX**	**35**
Price, UT	**21**	**Searcy, AR**	**77**	Hopkins County, TX	35
Carbon County, UT	21	White County, AR	77	**Summerville, GA**	**26**
Prineville, OR	**21**	**Sebring, FL**	**99**	Chattooga County, GA	26
Crook County, OR	21	Highlands County, FL	99	**Sunbury, PA**	**95**
Pullman, WA	**45**	**Sedalia, MO**	**42**	Northumberland County, PA	95
Whitman County, WA	45	Pettis County, MO	42	**Susanville, CA**	**35**
Quincy, IL-MO	**77**	**Selinsgrove, PA**	**40**	Lassen County, CA	35
Adams County, IL	67	Snyder County, PA	40	**Sweetwater, TX**	**15**
Lewis County, MO	10	**Selma, AL**	**44**	Nolan County, TX	15
Raymondville, TX	**22**	Dallas County, AL	44	**Tahlequah, OK**	**47**
Willacy County, TX	22	**Seneca, SC**	**74**	Cherokee County, OK	47
Red Bluff, CA	**63**	Oconee County, SC	74	**Talladega-Sylacauga, AL**	**82**
Tehama County, CA	63	**Seneca Falls, NY**	**35**	Talladega County, AL	82
Red Wing, MN	**46**	Seneca County, NY	35	**Tallulah, LA**	**12**
Goodhue County, MN	46	**Sevierville, TN**	**90**	Madison Parish, LA	12
Rexburg, ID	**51**	Sevier County, TN	90	**Taos, NM**	**33**
Fremont County, ID	13	**Seymour, IN**	**42**	Taos County, NM	33
Madison County, ID	38	Jackson County, IN	42	**Taylorville, IL**	**35**
Richmond, IN	**69**	**Shawnee, OK**	**69**	Christian County, IL	35
Wayne County, IN	69	Pottawatomie County, OK	69	**The Dalles, OR**	**25**
Richmond-Berea, KY	**100**	**Shelby, NC**	**98**	Wasco County, OR	25
Madison County, KY	83	Cleveland County, NC	98	**The Villages, FL**	**93**
Rockcastle County, KY	17	**Shelbyville, TN**	**45**	Sumter County, FL	93
Rio Grande City-Roma, TX	**61**	Bedford County, TN	45	**Thomaston, GA**	**27**
Starr County, TX	61	**Shelton, WA**	**61**	Upson County, GA	27
Riverton, WY	**40**	Mason County, WA	61	**Thomasville, GA**	**45**
Fremont County, WY	40	**Sheridan, WY**	**29**	Thomas County, GA	45
Roanoke Rapids, NC	**77**	Sheridan County, WY	29	**Thomasville-Lexington, NC**	**163**
Halifax County, NC	55	**Show Low, AZ**	**107**	Davidson County, NC	163
Northampton County, NC	22	Navajo County, AZ	107	**Tiffin, OH**	**57**
Rochelle, IL	**53**	**Sidney, OH**	**49**	Seneca County, OH	57
Ogle County, IL	53	Shelby County, OH	49	**Tifton, GA**	**40**
Rockingham, NC	**47**	**Sierra Vista-Douglas, AZ**	**131**	Tift County, GA	40
Richmond County, NC	47	Cochise County, AZ	131	**Toccoa, GA**	**26**
Rockland, ME	**40**	**Sikeston, MO**	**39**	Stephens County, GA	26
Knox County, ME	40	Scott County, MO	39	**Torrington, CT**	**190**
Rock Springs, WY	**44**	**Silver City, NM**	**30**	Litchfield County, CT	190
Sweetwater County, WY	44	Grant County, NM	30	**Traverse City, MI**	**143**
Rolla, MO	**45**	**Silverthorne, CO**	**28**	Benzie County, MI	18
Phelps County, MO	45	Summit County, CO	28	Grand Traverse County, MI	87
Roseburg, OR	**108**	**Snyder, TX**	**17**	Kalkaska County, MI	17
Douglas County, OR	108	Scurry County, TX	17	Leelanau County, MI	22
Roswell, NM	**66**	**Somerset, KY**	**63**	**Troy, AL**	**33**
Chaves County, NM	66	Pulaski County, KY	63	Pike County, AL	33
Ruidoso, NM	**20**	**Somerset, PA**	**78**	**Truckee-Grass Valley, CA**	**99**
Lincoln County, NM	20	Somerset County, PA	78	Nevada County, CA	99
Russellville, AR	**84**	**Southern Pines-Pinehurst, NC**	**88**	**Tullahoma, TN**	**100**
Pope County, AR	62	Moore County, NC	88	Coffee County, TN	53
Yell County, AR	22	**Spearfish, SD**	**24**	Franklin County, TN	41
Ruston, LA	**63**	Lawrence County, SD	24	Moore County, TN	6
Jackson Parish, LA	16	**Spencer, IA**	**17**	**Tupelo, MS**	**136**
Lincoln Parish, LA	47	Clay County, IA	17	Itawamba County, MS	23
Rutland, VT	**62**	**Spirit Lake, IA**	**17**	Lee County, MS	83
Rutland County, VT	62	Dickinson County, IA	17	Pontotoc County, MS	30
Safford, AZ	**46**	**Starkville, MS**	**48**	**Tuskegee, AL**	**21**
Graham County, AZ	37	Oktibbeha County, MS	48	Macon County, AL	21
Greenlee County, AZ	8	**Statesboro, GA**	**70**	**Twin Falls, ID**	**100**
St. Marys, GA	**51**	Bulloch County, GA	70	Jerome County, ID	22
Camden County, GA	51	**Statesville-Mooresville, NC**	**159**	Twin Falls County, ID	77
St. Marys, PA	**32**	Iredell County, NC	159	**Ukiah, CA**	**88**
Elk County, PA	32	**Staunton-Waynesboro, VA**	**119**	Mendocino County, CA	88
Salina, KS	**62**	Augusta County, VA	74	**Union, SC**	**29**
Ottawa County, KS	6	Staunton city, VA	24	Union County, SC	29
Saline County, KS	56	Waynesboro city, VA	21	**Union City, TN-KY**	**39**
Salisbury, NC	**138**	**Stephenville, TX**	**38**	Fulton County, KY	7
Rowan County, NC	138	Erath County, TX	38	Obion County, TN	32
Sanford, NC	**58**	**Sterling, CO**	**23**	**Urbana, OH**	**40**
Lee County, NC	58	Logan County, CO	23	Champaign County, OH	40
Sault Ste. Marie, MI	**39**	**Sterling, IL**	**58**	**Uvalde, TX**	**26**
Chippewa County, MI	39	Whiteside County, IL	58	Uvalde County, TX	26
Sayre, PA	**63**	**Stevens Point, WI**	**70**	**Valley, AL**	**34**
Bradford County, PA	63	Portage County, WI	70	Chambers County, AL	34
Scottsbluff, NE	**38**	**Stillwater, OK**	**77**	**Van Wert, OH**	**29**
Banner County, NE	1	Payne County, OK	77	Van Wert County, OH	29
Scotts Bluff County, NE	37				
Scottsboro, AL	**53**				

See footnotes at end of table.

Table B. Micropolitan Statistical Areas and Components—Population: 2010-Continued.

See headnote on page 942.

Micropolitan Statistical Area Component county	Popu-lation, 2010 (1,000)	Micropolitan Statistical Area Component county	Popu-lation, 2010 (1,000)	Micropolitan Statistical Area Component county	Popu-lation, 2010 (1,000)
Vermillion, SD	14	**Warsaw, IN**	77	**Willimantic, CT**	118
Clay County, SD	14	Kosciusko County, IN	77	Windham County, CT	118
Vernal, UT	33	**Washington, IN**	32	**Williston, ND**	22
Uintah County, UT	33	Daviess County, IN	32	Williams County, ND	22
Vernon, TX	14	**Washington, NC**	48	**Willmar, MN**	42
Wilbarger County, TX	14	Beaufort County, NC	48	Kandiyohi County, MN	42
Vicksburg, MS	49	**Washington Court House, OH**	29	**Wilmington, OH**	42
Warren County, MS	49	Fayette County, OH	29	Clinton County, OH	42
Vidalia, GA	36	**Watertown, SD**	33	**Wilson, NC**	81
Montgomery County, GA	9	Codington County, SD	27	Wilson County, NC	81
Toombs County, GA	27	Hamlin County, SD	6	**Winfield, KS**	36
Vincennes, IN	38	**Watertown-Fort Atkinson, WI**	84	Cowley County, KS	36
Knox County, IN	38	Jefferson County, WI	84	**Winona, MN**	51
Wabash, IN	33	**Watertown-Fort Drum, NY**	116	Winona County, MN	51
Wabash County, IN	33	Jefferson County, NY	116	**Woodward, OK**	20
Wahpeton, ND-MN	23	**Wauchula, FL**	28	Woodward County, OK	20
Wilkin County, MN	7	Hardee County, FL	28	**Wooster, OH**	115
Richland County, ND	16	**Waycross, GA**	55	Wayne County, OH	115
Walla Walla, WA	59	Pierce County, GA	19	**Worthington, MN**	21
Walla Walla County, WA	59	Ware County, GA	36	Nobles County, MN	21
Walterboro, SC	39	**Weatherford, OK**	27	**Yankton, SD**	22
Colleton County, SC	39	Custer County, OK	27	Yankton County, SD	22
Wapakoneta, OH	46	**West Plains, MO**	40	**Yazoo City, MS**	28
Auglaize County, OH	46	Howell County, MO	40	Yazoo County, MS	28
Warren, PA	42	**West Point, MS**	21	**Zanesville, OH**	86
Warren County, PA	42	Clay County, MS	21	Muskingum County, OH	86
Warrensburg, MO	53	**Whitewater, WI**	102		
Johnson County, MO	53	Walworth County, WI	102		

Z Less than 500

Source: U.S. Census Bureau, 2011 Population Estimates, <http://www.census.gov/popest/data/metro/totals/2011/>.

Appendix III
Limitations of the Data

Appendix III

Introduction-The data presented in this *Statistical Abstract* came from many sources. The sources include not only federal statistical bureaus and other organizations that collect and issue statistics as their principal activity, but also governmental administrative and regulatory agencies, private research bodies, trade associations, insurance companies, health associations, and private organizations such as the National Education Association and philanthropic foundations. Consequently, the data vary considerably as to reference periods, definitions of terms and, for ongoing series, the number and frequency of time periods for which data are available.

The statistics presented were obtained and tabulated by various means. Some statistics are based on complete enumerations or censuses while others are based on samples. Some information is extracted from records kept for administrative or regulatory purposes (school enrollment, hospital records, securities registration, financial accounts, social security records, income tax returns, etc.), while other information is obtained explicitly for statistical purposes through interviews or by mail. The estimation procedures used vary from highly sophisticated scientific techniques to crude "informed guesses."

Each set of data relates to a group of individuals or units of interest referred to as the *target universe* or *target population*, or simply as the *universe* or *population*.

Prior to data collection the target universe should be clearly defined. For example, if data are to be collected for the universe of households in the United States, it is necessary to define a "household." The target universe may not be completely tractable. Cost and other considerations may restrict data collection to a *survey universe* based on some available list, such list may be inaccurate or out of date. This list is called a *survey frame or sampling frame*.

The data in many tables are based on data obtained for all population units, a *census*, or on data obtained for only a portion, or *sample*, of the population units. When the data presented are based on a sample, the sample is usually a scientifically selected *probability sample*. This is a sample selected from a list or sampling frame in such a way that every possible sample has a known chance of selection and usually each unit selected can be assigned a number, greater than zero and less than or equal to one, representing its likelihood or probability of selection.

For large-scale sample surveys, the probability sample of units is often selected as a multistage sample. The first stage of a multistage sample is the selection of a probability sample of large groups of population members, referred to as primary sampling units (PSUs). For example, in a national multistage household sample, PSUs are often counties or groups of counties. The second stage of a multistage sample is the selection, within each PSU selected at the first stage, of smaller groups of population units, referred to as secondary sampling units. In subsequent stages of selection, smaller and smaller nested groups are chosen until the ultimate sample of population units is obtained. To qualify a multistage sample as a probability sample all stages of sampling must be carried out using probability sampling methods.

Prior to selection at each stage of a multistage (or a single stage) sample, a list of the sampling units or sampling frame for that stage must be obtained. For example, for the first stage of selection of a national household sample, a list of the counties and county groups that form the PSUs must be obtained. For the final stage of selection, lists of households, and sometimes persons within the households, have to be compiled in the field. For surveys of economic entities and for the economic censuses the U.S. Census Bureau generally uses a frame constructed from the Bureau's Business Register. The Business Register contains all establishments with payroll in the United States, including small single establishment firms as well as large multi-establishment firms.

Wherever the quantities in a table refer to an entire universe, but are constructed from data collected in a sample survey, the table quantities are referred to as *sample estimates*. In constructing a sample estimate, an attempt is made to come as close as is feasible to the corresponding universe quantity that would be obtained from a complete census of the universe. Estimates based on a sample will, however, generally differ from the hypothetical census figures. Two classifications of errors are associated with estimates based on sample surveys:

1 *sampling error*—the error arising from the use of a sample, rather than a census, to estimate population quantities and

2 *nonsampling error*—those errors arising from nonsampling sources. As discussed below, the magnitude of the sampling error for an estimate can usually be estimated from the sample data. However, the magnitude of the nonsampling error for an estimate can rarely be estimated. Consequently, actual error in an estimate exceeds the error that can be estimated.

The particular sample used in a survey is only one of a large number of possible samples of the same size which could have been selected using the same sampling procedure. Estimates derived from the different samples would, in general, differ from each other. The *standard error* (SE) is a measure of the variation among the estimates derived from all possible samples. The standard error is the most commonly used measure of the sampling error of an estimate. Valid estimates of the standard errors of survey estimates can usually be calculated from the data collected in a probability sample. For convenience, the standard error is sometimes expressed as a percent of the estimate and is called the relative standard error or *coefficient of variation* (CV). For example, an estimate of 200 units with an estimated standard error of 10 units has an estimated CV of 5 percent.

A sample estimate and an estimate of its standard error or CV can be used to construct interval estimates that have a prescribed confidence that the interval includes the average of the estimates derived from all possible samples with a known probability. To illustrate, if all possible samples were selected under essentially the same general conditions and using the same sample design, and if an estimate and its estimated standard error were calculated from each sample, then: 1) approximately 68 percent of the intervals from one standard error below the estimate to one standard error above the estimate would include the average estimate derived from all possible samples; 2) approximately 90 percent of the intervals from 1.6 standard errors below the estimate to 1.6 standard errors above the estimate would include the average estimate derived from all possible samples; and 3) approximately 95 percent of the intervals from two standard errors below the estimate to two standard errors above the estimate would include the average estimate derived from all possible samples.

Thus, for a particular sample one can say with the appropriate level of confidence (e.g., 90 percent or 95 percent) that the average of all possible samples is included in the constructed interval. Example of a confidence interval: An estimate is 200 units with a standard error of 10 units; an approximately 90 percent confidence interval (plus or minus 1.6 standard errors) is from 184 to 216.

All surveys and censuses are subject to nonsampling errors. Nonsampling errors are of two kinds: *random* and *nonrandom*. Random nonsampling errors arise because of the varying interpretation of questions (by respondents or interviewers) and varying actions of coders, keyers, and other processors. Some randomness is also introduced when respondents must estimate. Nonrandom nonsampling errors result from total nonresponse (no usable data obtained for a sampled unit), partial or item nonresponse (only a portion of a response may be usable), inability or unwillingness on the part of respondents to provide correct information, difficulty interpreting questions, mistakes in recording or keying data, errors of collection or processing, and coverage problems (overcoverage and undercoverage of the target universe). Random nonresponse errors usually, but not always, result in an understatement of sampling errors and thus an overstatement of the precision of survey estimates. Estimating the magnitude of nonsampling errors would require special experiments or access to independent data; consequently, the magnitudes are seldom available.

Nearly all types of nonsampling errors that affect surveys also occur in complete censuses. Since surveys can be conducted on a smaller scale than censuses, nonsampling errors can presumably be controlled more tightly. Relatively more funds and effort can perhaps be expended toward eliciting responses, detecting and correcting response error, and reducing processing errors. As a result, survey results can sometimes be more accurate than census results.

To compensate for suspected nonrandom errors adjustments of the sample estimates are often made. For example, adjustments are frequently made for nonresponse, both total and partial. Adjustments made for either type of nonresponse are often referred to as *imputations*. Imputation for total nonresponse is usually made by substituting for the questionnaire responses of the nonrespondents the "average" questionnaire responses of the respondents. These imputations usually are made separately within various groups of sample members, formed by attempting to place respondents and nonrespondents together that have "similar" design or ancillary characteristics. Imputation for item nonresponse is usually made by substituting for a missing item the response to that item of a respondent having characteristics that are "similar" to those of the nonrespondent.

For an estimate calculated from a sample survey, the *total error* in the estimate is composed of the sampling error, which can usually be estimated from the sample, and the nonsampling error, which usually cannot be estimated from the sample. The total error present in a population quantity obtained from a complete census is composed of only nonsampling errors. Ideally, estimates of the total error associated with data in the *Statistical Abstract* tables should be given. However, due to the unavailability of estimates of nonsampling errors, only estimates of the levels of sampling errors, in terms of estimated standard errors or coefficients of variation, are available. To obtain estimates of the estimated standard errors from the sample of interest, obtain a copy of the referenced report which appears at the end of each table.

Source of Additional Material: The Federal Committee on Statistical Methodology (FCSM) is an interagency committee dedicated to improving the quality of federal statistics, <http://www.fcsm.gov>.

Principal data bases-Beginning below are brief descriptions of 35 of the sample surveys and censuses that provide a substantial portion of the data contained in this *Abstract*.

U.S. DEPARTMENT OF AGRICULTURE, National Agriculture Statistics Service

Census of Agriculture

Universes, Frequency, and Types of Data: Complete count of U.S. farms and ranches conducted once every 5 years with data at the national, state, and county level. Data published on farm numbers and related items/characteristics.

Type of Data Collection Operation: Complete census for number of farms; land in farms; farm income; agriculture products sold; farms by type of organization; total cropland; irrigated land; farm operator characteristics; livestock and poultry inventory and sales; and selected crops harvested. Market value of land, buildings, and products sold, total farm production expenses, machinery and equipment, and fertilizer and chemicals.

Data Collection and Imputation Procedures: Data collection is by mailing questionnaires to all farmers and ranchers. Producers can return their forms by mail or online. Nonrespondents are contacted by telephone and correspondence follow-ups. Imputations were made for all nonresponse items/characteristics and coverage adjustments were made to account for missed farms and ranches. The response rate for the 2007 Census was 85.2 percent.

Estimates of Sampling Error: Weight adjustments were made to account for the undercoverage and whole-unit nonresponse of farms on the Census Mail List (CML). These were treated as sampling errors.

Other (nonsampling) Errors: Nonsampling errors are due to incompleteness of the census mailing list, duplications on the list, respondent reporting errors, errors in editing reported data, and errors in imputation for missing data. Evaluation studies are conducted to measure certain nonsampling errors such as list coverage and classification error. It is a reasonable assumption that the net effect of non-measurable errors is zero (the positive errors cancel the negative errors).

Sources of Additional Material: U.S. Department of Agriculture (NASS), 2007 Census of Agriculture, Appendix A-1 Census of Agriculture Methodology, Appendix B-1 General Explanation and Census of Agriculture Report Form.

Basic Area Frame Sample

Universe, Frequency, and Types of Data: The June Agricultural Survey collects data on planted acreage and livestock inventories on all land in the 48 contiguous states and Hawaii. The survey also serves to measure list incompleteness and is subsampled for multiple frame surveys.

Type of Data Collection Operation: Stratified probability sample of about 11,000 land area units of about 1 sq. mile (range from 0.1 sq. mile in cities to several sq. miles in open grazing areas). Sample represents 42,000 operating arrangements. About 20 percent of the sample replaced annually.

Data Collection and Imputation Procedures: Data collection is by personal enumeration. Imputation is based on enumerator observation or data reported by respondents having similar agricultural characteristics.

Estimates of Sampling Error: Estimated CVs range from 1 percent to 2 percent for regional estimates to 3 percent to 6 percent for state estimates of major crop acres and livestock inventories.

Other (nonsampling) Errors: Minimized through rigid quality controls on the collection process and careful review of all reported data.

Sources of Additional Material: U.S. Department of Agriculture, National Agricultural Statistics Service, USDA's National Agricultural Statistics Service: *The Fact Finders for Agriculture*, March 2007.

Multiple Frame Surveys

Universe, Frequency, and Types of Data: Surveys of U.S. farm operators to obtain data on major livestock inventories, selected crop acreage and production, grain stocks, and farm labor characteristics, farm economic data, and chemical use data. Estimates are made quarterly, semi-annually, or annually depending on the data series.

Type of Data Collection Operation: Primary frame is obtained from general or special purpose lists, supplemented by a probability sample of land areas used to estimate for list incompleteness.

Data Collection and Imputation Procedures: Mail, telephone, or personal interviews used for initial data collection. Mail nonrespondent follow-up by phone and personal interviews. Imputation based on average of respondents.

Estimates of Sampling Error: Estimated CVs range from 1 percent to 2 percent at the U.S. level for crop and livestock data series and 3 to 5 percent for economic data. Regional CVs range from 3 to 6 percent, while state estimate CVs run 5 to 10 percent.

Other (nonsampling) Errors: In addition to above, replicated sampling procedures used to monitor effects of changes in survey procedures.

Sources of Additional Material: U.S. Department of Agriculture, National Agricultural Statistics Service), USDA's National Agricultural Statistics Service: *The Fact Finders for Agriculture*, March 2007.

Objective Yield Surveys

Universe, Frequency, and Types of Data: Monthly surveys during the growing season of corn, cotton, potatoes, soybeans, and winter wheat fields in top producing states for forecasting and estimating yield per acre.

Type of Data Collection Operation: Random location of plots in probability sample. Corn, cotton, and soybeans, are selected in June from Basic Area Frame Sample (see above). Winter wheat and potatoes are selected from March and June multiple frame surveys, respectively.

Data Collection and Imputation Procedures: Enumerators count and measure plant characteristics in sample fields. Production is measured from plots at harvest. Harvest loss is measured from post harvest gleanings.

Estimates of Sampling Error: CVs for national estimates of production are about 2 to 3 percent.

Other (nonsampling) Errors: In addition to above, replicated sampling procedures are used to monitor effects of changes in survey procedures.

Sources of Additional Material: U.S. Department of Agriculture, National Agricultural Statistics Service), USDA's National Agricultural Statistics Service: *The Fact Finders for Agriculture*, March 2007.

U.S. BUREAU OF JUSTICE STATISTICS (BJS)

National Crime Victimization Survey

Universe, Frequency, and Types of Data: Monthly survey of individuals and households in the United States to obtain data on criminal victimization of those units for compilation of annual estimates.

Type of Data Collection Operation: National probability sample survey of about 40,000 interviewed households in 203 PSUs every 6 months selected from a list of addresses from the 2000 census, supplemented by new construction permits and an area sample where permits are not required.

Data Collection and Imputation Procedures: Interviews are conducted every 6 months for 3 years for each household in the sample; roughly 7,000 households are interviewed monthly. Personal interviews are used in the first interview; the intervening interviews are conducted by telephone whenever possible.

Estimates of Sampling Error: CVs for 2009 are 4 percent for crimes of violence; 19.1 percent for estimate of rape/sexual assault counts; 10.2 percent for robbery counts; 4.7 percent for assault counts; 18.6 percent for purse snatching/pocket picking; 2.2 percent for property crimes; 4.2 percent for burglary counts; 2.5 percent for theft (of property); and 7.3 percent for motor vehicle theft counts.

Other (nonsampling) Errors: Respondent recall errors which may include reporting incidents for other than the reference period; interviewer coding and processing errors; and possible mistaken reporting or classifying of events. Adjustment is made for a household noninterview rate of about 8 percent and for a within-household noninterview rate of 13 percent.

Sources of Additional Material: U.S. Bureau of Justice Statistics, *Criminal Victimization in the United States*, annual.

U.S. BUREAU OF LABOR STATISTICS

Consumer Expenditure Survey (CE)

Universe, Frequency and Types of Data: Consists of two continuous components: a quarterly interview survey and a weekly diary or recordkeeping survey. They are nationwide surveys that collect data on consumer expenditures, income, characteristics, and assets and liabilities. Samples are national probability samples of households that are representative of the civilian noninstitutional population. The surveys have been ongoing since 1980.

Type of Data Collection Operation: The Interview Survey is a panel rotation survey. Each panel is interviewed for five quarters and then dropped from the survey. About 7,000 consumer units are interviewed each quarter. The Diary Survey sample is new each year and consists of about 7,000 consumer units. Data are collected on an ongoing basis in 105 PSUs.

Data Collection and Imputation Procedures: For the Interview Survey, data are collected by personal interview with each consumer unit once per quarter for five consecutive quarters. Designed to collect information that respondents can recall for 3 months or longer, such as large or recurring expenditures. For the Diary Survey, respondents record all their expenditures in a self-reporting diary for two consecutive one-week periods. Designed to pick up items difficult to recall over a long period, such as detailed food expenditures. Missing or invalid attributes, expenditures, or incomes are imputed. Assets and liabilities are not imputed. The U.S. Census Bureau collects the data for the Bureau of Labor Statistics.

Estimates of Sampling Error: Standard error tables are available since 2000.

Other (nonsampling) Errors: Includes incorrect information given by respondents, data processing errors, interviewer errors, and so on. They occur regardless of whether data are collected from a sample or from the entire population.

Sources of Additional Material: Bureau of Labor Statistics, see <http://www.bls.gov/cex>.

Consumer Price Index (CPI)

Universe, Frequency, and Types of Data: A monthly survey of price changes of all types of consumer goods and services purchased by urban wage earners and clerical workers prior to 1978, and urban consumers thereafter. Both indexes continue to be published.

Type of Data Collection Operation: Prior to 1978, and since 1998, sample of various consumer items in 87 urban areas; from 1978-1997, in 85 PSUs, except from January 1987 through March 1988, when 91 areas were sampled.

Data Collection and Imputation Procedures: Prices of consumer items are obtained each month from about 25,500 retail outlets and from about 4,000 housing units in 87 areas. Prices of food, fuel, and a few other items are obtained monthly; prices of most other commodities and services are collected every month in the three largest geographic areas and every other month in others.

Estimates of Sampling Error: Estimates of standard errors are available.

Other (nonsampling) Errors: Errors result from inaccurate reporting, difficulties in defining concepts and their operational implementation, and introduction of product quality changes and new products.

Sources of Additional Material: U.S. Bureau of Labor Statistics, <http://www.bls.gov/cpi/home.htm> and BLS Handbook of Methods, Chapter 17, see <http://www.bls.gov/opub/hom/pdf/homch17.pdf>.

Current Employment Statistics (CES) Program

Universe, Frequency, and Types of Data: Monthly survey drawn from a sampling frame of roughly 8.9 million unemployment insurance tax accounts in order to obtain data by industry on employment, hours, and earnings.

Type of Data Collection Operation: In 2009, the CES sample included about 140,000 businesses and government agencies, which represent approximately 410,000 individual worksites.

Data Collection and Imputation Procedures: Each month the state agencies cooperating with BLS, as well as BLS Data Collection Centers, collect data through various automated collection modes and mail. BLS Washington staff prepares national estimates of employment, hours, and earnings while states use the data to develop state and area estimates.

Estimates of Sampling Errors: The relative standard error for total nonfarm employment is 0.1 percent. From April 2008 to March 2009, the cumulative net birth/death model added 779,000.

Other (nonsampling) Errors: Estimates of employment adjusted annually to reflect complete universe. Average adjustment is 0.3 percent over the last decade, with an absolute range from 0.1 percent to 0.7 percent.

Sources of Additional Material: U.S. Bureau of Labor Statistics, *Employment and Earnings Online*, monthly. See <http://www.bls.gov/epubs/ees>.

National Compensation Survey (NCS)

Universe, Frequency, and Types of Data: NCS collects data from establishments of all employment-size classes in private industries as well as state and local governments. The survey stratifies its data by geographic area and industry. NCS collects data on work schedules, wages, salaries, and employer costs for employee benefits. For approximately 80 metropolitan areas and the nation, NCS produces information on workers' earnings and benefits in a variety of occupations at different work levels. NCS is also responsible for two quarterly releases: the Employment Cost Index (ECI), which measures percent changes in the cost of employment, and the Employer Costs for Employee Compensation (ECEC), which measures costs per hour worked for individual benefits. The survey provides data by industry sector, industry division, occupational group, bargaining status, metropolitan area status, census region, and census division. ECEC also provides data by establishment-size class.

Type of Data Collection Operation: Establishments are selected for the survey based on a probability-proportionate-to-employment technique. NCS replaces its sample on a continual basis. Private industry establishments are in the survey for approximately 5 years.

Data Collection and Imputation Procedures: A personal visit to the establishment is the initial source for collecting data. Communication via mail, fax, and telephone provide quarterly updates. Imputation is done for individual benefits.

Estimates of Sampling Error: NCS uses standard errors to evaluate published series. These standard errors are available at <http://www.bls.gov/ncs/ect/>.

Other (nonsampling) Errors: Nonsampling errors have a number of potential sources. The primary sources are (1) survey nonresponse and (2) data collection and processing errors. Nonsampling errors are not measured. The use of quality assurance programs reduces the potential for nonsampling errors. These programs include the use of reinterviews, interview observations, and the systematic professional review of reports. The programs also serve as a training device that provides feedback on errors for field economists (or data collectors). Quality assurance programs also provide information on sources of error. This information is used to improve procedures that result in fewer errors. NCS also conducts extensive training of field economists to maintain high standards in data collection.

Sources of Additional Material: Bureau of Labor Statistics, BLS Handbook of methods, Chapter 8 see <http://www.bls.gov/opub/hom//pdf/homch8.pdf>.

Producer Price Index (PPI)

Universe, Frequency, and Types of Data: Monthly survey of producing companies to determine price changes of all commodities and services produced in the United States for sale in commercial transactions. Data on agriculture, forestry, fishing, manufacturing, mining, gas, electricity, construction, public utilities, wholesale trade, retail trade, transportation, healthcare, and other services.

Type of Data Collection Operation: Probability sample of approximately 30,000 establishments that result in about 100,000 price quotations per month.

Data Collection and Imputation Procedures: Data are collected by mail and facsimile. Missing prices are estimated by those received for similar products or services. Some prices are obtained from trade publications, organized exchanges, and government agencies. To calculate index, price

changes are multiplied by their relative weights taken from the Census Bureau's 2002 shipment values from its Census of Industries.

Estimates of Sampling Error: Not applicable.

Other (nonsampling) Errors: Not available at present.

Sources of Additional Material: U.S. Bureau of Labor Statistics, *BLS Handbook of Methods*, Chapter 14, Bulletin 2490. U.S. Bureau of Labor Statistics, see <http://www.bls.gov/opub/hom/>.

BOARD OF GOVERNORS OF THE FEDERAL RESERVE SYSTEM

Survey of Consumer Finances

Universe, Frequency, and Types of Data: Periodic sample survey of families. In this survey a given household is divided into a primary economic unit and other economic units. The primary economic unit, which may be a single individual, is generally chosen as the person or couple who either holds the title to the home or is listed on the lease, along with all other people in the household who are financially interdependent with that person or couple. The primary economic unit is used as the reference family. The survey collects detailed data on the composition of family balance sheets, the terms of loans, and relationships with financial institutions. It also gathers information on the employment history and pension rights of the survey respondent and the spouse or partner of the respondent.

Type of Data Collection Operation: The survey employs a two-part strategy for sampling families. Some families are selected by standard multistage area probability sampling methods applied to all 50 states. The remaining families in the survey are selected using statistical records derived from tax returns, under the strict rules governing confidentiality and the rights of potential respondents to refuse participation.

Data Collection and Imputation Procedures: National Opinion Research Center (NORC) at the University of Chicago has collected data for the survey since 1992. Since 1995, the survey has used computer-assisted personal interviewing. Adjustments for nonresponse are made through multiple imputation of unanswered questions and through weighting adjustments based on data used in the sample design for families that refused participation.

Estimates of Sampling Error: Because of the complex design of the survey, the estimation of potential sampling errors is not straightforward. A replicate-based procedure is available.

Other (nonsampling) Errors: The survey aims to complete 4,500 interviews, with about two thirds of that number deriving from the area-probability sample. The response rate is typically about 70 percent for the area-probability sample and about 35 percent over all strata in the tax-data sample. Proper training and monitoring of interviewers, careful design of questionnaires, and systematic editing of the resulting data were used to control inaccurate survey responses.

Sources of Additional Material: Board of Governors of the Federal Reserve System, "Changes in U.S. Family Finances from 2007 to 2010: Evidence from the

Survey of Consumer Finances," *Federal Reserve Bulletin*, 2012, <http://www.federalreserve.gov/Pubs/Bulletin>.

U.S. CENSUS BUREAU

2007 Economic Census

(Industry Series, Geographic Area Series and Subject Series Reports) (for NAICS sectors 21 to 81).

Universe, Frequency, and Types of Data: Conducted every 5 years to obtain data on number of establishments, number of employees, payroll, total sales/receipts/revenue, and other industry-specific statistics. The universe is all establishments with paid employees excluding agriculture, forestry, fishing and hunting, and government. (Non-employer Statistics, discussed separately, covers those establishments without paid employees.)

Changes for 2007 included tabulations to include Census designated places (unincorporated places), expanded Survey of Business Owners data, data on franchising for more industries, and complete implementation of the North American Product Classification System (NAPCS).

Type of Data Collection Operation: All large employer firms were surveyed (i.e., all employer firms above payroll-size cutoffs established to separate large from small employers) plus, in most sectors, a sample of the small employer firms.

Data Collection and Imputation Procedures: Mail questionnaires were used with both mail and telephone follow-ups for nonrespondents. Businesses also had the option to respond electronically. Data for nonrespondents and for small employer firms not mailed a questionnaire were obtained from administrative records of other federal agencies or imputed.

Estimates of Sampling Error: Not applicable for basic data such as sales, revenue, receipts, payroll, etc. for sectors other than Construction (NAICS 23). Estimates of sampling error for construction industries are included with the data as published on the Census Bureau web site. Other (nonsampling) errors: establishment response rates by NAICS sector in 2002 ranged from 80 percent to 89 percent. Nonsampling errors may occur during the collection, reporting, keying, and classification of the data.

Sources of Additional Material: U.S. Census Bureau, see <http://www.census.gov/econ/census07/www/methodology/>.

American Community Survey (ACS)

Universe, Frequency, and Types of Data: Nationwide survey to obtain annual data about demographic, social, economic, and housing characteristics of housing units and the people residing in them. It covers the household population and, beginning in 2006, also includes the group quarter population living in correctional facilities, skilled-nursing homes, military barracks, college residence halls, and other group quarters.

Type of Data Collection Operation: Housing unit address sampling is performed twice a year in both August and January. First-phase of sampling defines the universe for the second stage of sampling

through two steps. First, all addresses that were eligible for the second-phase sampling within the past four years are excluded from eligibility.

This ensures that no address is in sample more than once in any 5-year period. The second step is to select a 20 percent systematic sample of "new" units, i.e. those units that have never appeared on a previous Master Address File (MAF) extract. All new addresses are systematically assigned to either the current year or to one of four back-samples. This procedure maintains five equal partitions of the universe. The second-phase sampling is done on the current year's partition and results in approximately 3,000,000 housing unit addresses in the U.S. and 36,000 in Puerto Rico (PR). Group quarter sampling is performed separately from the housing unit sampling. The sampling begins with separating the small (15 persons or fewer) and the large (more than 15 persons) group quarters. The target sampling rate for both groups is a 2.5% sample of the group quarters population. It results in approximately 200,000 group quarter residents being selected in the U.S., and an additional 1,000 in Puerto Rico.

Data Collection and Imputation Procedures: The American Community Survey is conducted every month on independent samples. The data collection operation for housing units (HUs) consists of three modes or phases: mail, telephone, and personal visit. For the first phase, each housing unit in the independent monthly samples is mailed a pre-notice letter announcing the selection of the address to participate, a survey questionnaire package, and a reminder postcard. These sample units addresses receive a second (replacement) questionnaire package if the initial questionnaire has not been returned by mid-month. The second phase is for sample addresses for which a questionnaire is not returned in the mail and a telephone number is available, is forwarded to telephone centers is available, is forwarded to telephone centers for follow-up. Interviewers attempt to contact and interview these mail nonresponse cases by telephone. The third phase is for sample addresses that are still unresponsive after two months of attempts are forwarded for a possible personal visit. Mailable addresses with neither a response to the mailout nor a telephone interview are sampled at a rate of 1 in 2, 2 in 5, or 1 in 3 based on the expected rate of completed interviews at the tract level. Unmailable addresses are sampled at a rate of 2 in 3. Those addresses selected through this process are assigned to Field Representatives (FRs), who visit the addresses, verify their existence, determine their occupancy status, and conduct interviews. Collection of group quarters data is conducted by FR's only. Their methods include completing the questionnaire while speaking to the resident in person or over the telephone, or leaving paper questionnaires for residents to complete for themselves and then pick them up later. This last option is used for data collection in federal prisons. If needed, a personal interview can be conducted with a proxy, such as a relative or guardian. After data collection is completed, any remaining incomplete or inconsistent information on the questionnaire are imputed during the final automated edit of the collected data.

Estimates of Sampling Error: The data in the ACS products are estimates and can vary from the actual values that would have been obtained by conducting a census of the entire population. The estimates from the chosen sample addresses can also vary from those that would have been obtained from a different set of addresses. This variation causes uncertainty, which can be measured using statistics such as standard error, margin of error, and confidence interval. All ACS estimates are accompanied by margins of error to assist users.

*Other (nonsampling) Errors:*In addition to sampling error, data users should realize that other types of errors may be introduced during any of the various complex operations used to select, collect and process survey data. An important goal of the ACS is to minimize the amount of nonsampling error introduced through coverage issues in the sample list, nonresponse from sample housing units, and transcribing or editing data. One way of accomplishing this is by finding additional sources of addresses, following up on nonrespondents and maintaining quality control systems.

Sources of Additional Material: U.S. Census Bureau, American Community Survey see <http://www.census.gov/acs/www/index.html> U.S. Census Bureau, American Community Survey Accuracy of the Data documents available on the Internet, <http://www.census.gov/acs/www/ data_documentation/documentation_main/>.

American Housing Survey

Universe, Frequency, and Types of Data: Conducted nationally in odd numbered years to obtain data on the approximately 124 million occupied or vacant housing units in the United States (group quarters are excluded). Data include characteristics of occupied housing units, vacant units, new housing and mobile home units, financial characteristics, recent mover households, housing and neighborhood quality indicators, and energy characteristics.

Type of Data Collection Operation: The national sample was a multistage probability sample with about 54,000 units eligible for interview in 2009. Sample units, selected within 394 PSUs, were surveyed over a 4-month period.

Data Collection and Imputation Procedures: For 2009, the survey was conducted by personal interviews. The interviewers obtained the information from the occupants or, if the unit was vacant, from informed persons such as landlords, rental agents, or knowledgeable neighbors.

Estimates of Sampling Error: For the national sample, illustrations of the Standard Error (SE) of the estimates are provided in Appendix D of the 2009 report.

Other (nonsampling) Errors: Response rate was about 90 percent. Nonsampling errors may result from incorrect or incomplete responses, errors in coding and recording, and processing errors. Appendix D of the 2005 report has a complete discussion of the errors.

Sources of Additional Material: U.S. Census Bureau, *Current Housing Reports*, Series H-150 and H-170, *American Housing Survey* see <http://www.census. gov/hhes/www/ahs.html>.

Annual Survey of Public Employment and Payroll

Universe, Frequency, and Types of Data: The survey measures the number of state, local and federal civilian government employees and their gross payrolls for the pay period including March 12. The survey is conducted annually except in years ending in '2' and '7', when a census of all state and local governments is done. The survey provides data on full-time and part-time employment, part-time hours worked, full-time equivalent employment, and payroll statistics by governmental function (elementary and secondary education, higher education, police protection, fire protection, financial administration, central staff services, judicial and legal, highways, public welfare, solid waste management, sewerage, parks and recreation, health, hospitals, water supply, electric power, gas supply, transit, natural resources, correction, libraries, air transportation, water transport and terminals, other education, state liquor stores, social insurance administration, and housing and community development).

Type of Data Collection Operations: The survey sample was taken from the 2007 Census of Governments and contains approximately 11,000 local government units. These units were sampled from a sampling frame that contained 90,690 local governments (county, city, township, special district, and school districts) in addition to 50 state governments and the District of Columbia. This frame was slightly different from the Annual Finance Survey sampling frame. Forty-five of the state governments provided data from central payroll records for all or most of their agencies/institutions. Data for agencies and institutions for the remaining state governments were obtained by mail canvass questionnaires. Local governments were also canvassed using a mail questionnaire. However, elementary and secondary school system data in Florida, North Dakota, and Washington were supplied by special arrangements with the state education agency in each of these states. All respondents receiving the mail questionnaire had the option of responding using the Employment Web site developed for reporting data. Approximately 21% of the state agencies and 55% of local government respondents chose to respond on the Web.

Editing and Imputation Procedures: Editing is a process that ensures survey data are accurate, complete, and consistent. Efforts are made at all phases of collection, processing, and tabulation to minimize errors. Although some edits are built into the Internet data collection instrument and the data entry programs, the majority of the edits are performed after the case has been loaded into the Census Bureau's database. Edits consist primarily of two types: consistency and a ratio of the current years reported value to the prior year's value. The consistency edits check the logical relationships of data items reported on the form. For example, if a value exists for employees for a function then a value must exist for payroll also. If part-time employees and payroll are reported then part-time hours must be reported and vice versa. The current year/prior year edits compare data for the number of employees, the function reported for the employees, and the average salary between reporting years. If data fall outside of acceptable tolerance levels, the item is flagged for review. Some additional checks are made comparing data from the Annual Finance Survey to data reported on the Annual Survey of Public Employment and Payroll to verify that employees reported on the Annual Survey of Public Employment and Payroll at a particular function have a corresponding expenditure on the Finance Survey. For both types of edits, the edit results are reviewed by analysts and adjusted when needed. When the analyst is unable to resolve or accept the edit failure, contact is made with the respondent to verify or correct the reported data.

Imputation: Not all respondents answer every item on the questionnaire. There are also questionnaires that are not returned despite efforts to gain a response. Imputation is the process of filling in missing or invalid data with reasonable values in order to have a complete data set. For general purpose governments and for schools, the imputations were based on recent historical data from either a prior year annual survey or the most recent Census of Governments, if it was available. These data were adjusted by a growth rate that was determined by the growth of units that were similar (in size, geography, and type of government) to the nonrespondent. If there was no recent historical data available, the imputations were based on the data from a randomly selected donor that was similar to the nonrespondent. This donor's data were adjusted by dividing each data item by the population (or enrollment) of the donor and multiplying the result by the nonrespondent's population (or enrollment). For special districts, if prior year data are available, the data are brought forward with a national level growth rate applied. Otherwise, the data are imputed to be zero. In cases where good secondary data sources exist, the data from those sources were used.

Estimates of Sampling Error: For intercensal surveys, estimated coefficients of variation for all variables are given in tabulations on the Web site. For U.S. and state-and-local government-level estimates of total full-time equivalents and total payroll, most relative standard errors are generally less than one percent, but vary considerably for detailed characteristics.

Other (nonsampling) Errors: Although every effort is made in all phases of collection, processing, and tabulation to minimize errors, the sample data are subject to nonsampling errors such as inability to obtain data for every variable from all units in the sample, inaccuracies in classification, response errors, misinterpretation of questions, mistakes in keying and coding, and coverage errors. These same errors may be evident in census collections and may affect the Census of Governments data used to adjust the sample during the estimation phase and used in the imputation process.

Sources of Additional material: <http://www.census. gov/govs/www/apes/>

Annual Survey of Government Finances

Universe, Frequency, and Types of Data: The U.S. Census Bureau conducts an Annual Survey of Government Finances, as authorized by law under Title 13, United States Code, Section 182. Alternatively, every 5 years, in years ending in a '2' or '7', a Census of Governments, including a Finance portion, is conducted under Title 13, Section 161. The survey coverage includes all state and local governments in the U.S. For both the Census and annual survey, the finance detail data is equivalent, encompassing the entire range of government finance activities-revenue, expenditure, debt, and assets.

Type of Data Collection Operations: The data collection phase for the annual survey made use of three methods to obtain data: mail canvass, internet collection, and central collection from State sources. In 28 states, all or part of the general purpose finance data for local governments was obtained from cooperative arrangements between the Census Bureau and a state government agency. These usually involved a data collection effort carried out to meet the needs of both agencies-the state agency for purposes of audit, oversight, or information, and the Census Bureau for statistical purposes. Data for the balance of local governments in this annual survey were obtained via mail questionnaires sent directly to county, municipal, township, special district, and school district governments. School district data were collected via cooperative arrangements with state education agencies. Data for state governments were compiled by analysts of the Census Bureau, usually with the cooperation and assistance of state officials. The data were compiled from state government audits, budgets, and other financial reports, either in printed or electronic format. The compilation generally involved recasting the state financial records into the classification categories used for reporting by the Census Bureau.

Data Collection and Imputation Procedures: Survey is conducted by mail with mail follow-ups of nonrespondents. Imputation for all nonresponse items is based on previous year reports or, for new governments, on data from similar donors.

Estimates of Sampling Error: The local government statistics in the intercensal survey years are developed from a sample survey. Therefore, the local totals, as well as aggregates of state and local government data, are considered estimated amounts subject to sampling error. State government finance data are not subject to sampling. Consequently, State-local aggregates shown here have a relative standard error less than or equal to the local government estimates they include. Estimates of major U.S. totals for local governments are subject to a computed sampling variability of less than one-half of 1 percent. State and local government totals are generally subject to sampling variability of less than 3 percent.

Other (nonsampling) Errors: The estimates are also subject to inaccuracies in classification, response, and processing. Efforts were made at all phases of collection, processing, and tabulation to minimize errors. However, the data are still subject to errors from imputations for missing data, errors from misreported data, errors from miscoding, and difficulties in identifying every unit that should be included in the report. Every effort was made to keep such errors to a minimum through care in examining, editing, and tabulating the data reported by government officials.

Sources of Additional Material: <http://www.census. gov/govs/index.html> and <http://www.census.gov /govs/estimate/>.

Annual Survey of Manufactures (ASM)

Universe, Frequency, and Types of Data: The Annual Survey of Manufactures is conducted annually, except for years ending in '2' and '7' for all manufacturing establishments having one or more paid employees. The purpose of the ASM is to provide key intercensal measures of manufacturing activity, products, and location for the public and private sectors. The ASM provides statistics on employment, payroll, worker hours, payroll supplements, cost of materials, value added by manufacturing, capital expenditures, inventories, and energy consumption. It also provides estimates of value of shipments for 1,800 classes of manufactured products.

Type of Data Collection Operation: The ASM includes approximately 50,000 establishments selected from the census universe of 329,000 manufacturing establishments. Approximately 20,000 large establishments are selected with certainty, and the remaining 30,000 other establishments are selected with probability proportional to a composite measure of establishment size. The survey is updated from two sources: Internal Revenue Service administrative records are used to include new single-unit manufacturers and the Company Organization Survey identifies new establishments of multiunit forms.

Data Collection and Imputation Procedures: Survey is conducted by mail with phone and mail follow-ups of nonrespondents. Imputation (for all nonresponse items) is based on previous year reports, or for new establishments in survey, on industry averages.

Estimates of Sampling Error: Estimated relative standard errors for number of employees, new expenditures, and for value added totals are given in annual publications. For U.S. level industry statistics, most estimated relative standard errors are 2 percent or less, but vary considerably for detailed characteristics.

Other (nonsampling) Errors: The unit response rate is about 85 percent. Nonsampling errors include those due to collection, reporting, and transcription errors, many of which are corrected through computer and clerical checks.

Sources of Additional Material: <http://www.census.gov/manufacturing/asm/index.html>.

Census of Population

Universe, Frequency, and Types of Data: Complete count of U.S. population conducted every 10 years since 1790. Data obtained on number and characteristics of people in the United States.

Type of Data Collection Operation: In the 1990, 2000, and 2010 censuses the 100 percent items included: age, date of birth, sex, race, Hispanic origin, and relationship to householder. In 1980, approximately 19 percent of the housing units were included in the sample; in 1990 and 2000, approximately 17 percent.

Data Collection and Imputation Procedures: In 1980, 1990, 2000, and 2010 mail questionnaires were used extensively with personal interviews in the remainder. Extensive telephone and personal follow-up for nonrespondents was done in the censuses. Imputations were made for missing characteristics.

Estimates of Sampling Error: Sampling errors for data are estimated for all items collected by sample and vary by characteristic and geographic area. The coefficients of variation (CVs) for national and state estimates are generally very small.

Other (nonsampling) Errors: Since 1950, evaluation programs have been conducted to provide information on the magnitude of some sources of nonsampling errors such as response bias and undercoverage in each census. Results from the evaluation program for the 1990 census indicated that the estimated net undercoverage amounted to about 1.5 percent of the total resident population. For the 2010 Census, the post enumeration survey found a net overcount of 0.01 percent of the resident population.

Sources of Additional Material: U.S. Census Bureau, *The Coverage of Population in the 1980 Census,* PHC80-E4; *Content Reinterview Study: Accuracy of Data for Selected Population and Housing Characteristics as Measured by Reinterview,* PHC80-E2; *1980 Census of Population,* Vol. 1, (PC80-1), Appendixes B, C, and D. *Content Reinterview Survey: Accuracy of Data for Selected Population and Housing Characteristics as Measured by Reinterview,* 1990, CPH-E-1; *Effectiveness of Quality Assurance,* CPH-E-2; *Programs to Improve Coverage in the 1990 Census,* 1990, CPH-E-3. For the 2010 Census evaluations, see <http://www.2010.census.gov/2010census/about/cpex.php>.

County Business Patterns

Universe, Frequency, and Types of Data: County Business Patterns is an annual tabulation of basic data items extracted from the Business Register, a file of all known single- and multilocation employer companies maintained and updated by the U.S. Census Bureau. Data include number of establishments, number of employees, first quarter and annual payrolls, and number of establishments by employment size class. Data are excluded for self-employed individuals, private households, railroad employees, agricultural production workers, and most government employees.

Type of Data Collection Operation: The annual Company Organization Survey and the Economic Census provide individual establishment data for multilocation companies. Data for single establishment companies are obtained from various Census Bureau programs, such as the Annual Survey of Manufactures and Current Business Surveys, as well as from administrative records of the Internal Revenue Service, the Social Security Administration, and the Bureau of Labor Statistics.

Estimates of Sampling Error: Not applicable.

Other (nonsampling) Errors: The data are subject to nonsampling errors, such as inability to identify all cases in the universe; definition and classification difficulties; differences in interpretation of questions; errors in recording or coding the data obtained; and estimation of employers who reported too late to be included in the tabulations and for records with missing or misreported data.

Sources of Additional Material: U. S. Census Bureau,County Business Patterns <http://www.census.gov/econ/cbp/index.html>

Current Population Survey (CPS)

Universe, Frequency, and Types of Data: Nationwide monthly sample designed primarily to produce national and state estimates of labor force characteristics of the civilian noninstitutionalized population 16 years of age and older.

Type of Data Collection Operation: Multistage probability sample that currently includes 60,000 households from 824 sample areas. Sample size increased in some states to improve data reliability for those areas on an annual average basis. A continual sample rotation system is used. Households are in sample 4 months, out for 8 months, and in for 4 more. Month-to-month overlap is 75 percent; year-to-year overlap is 50 percent.

Data Collection and Imputation Procedures: For first and fifth months that a household is in sample, personal interviews; other months, approximately 85 percent of the data collected by phone. Imputation is done for item nonresponse. Adjustment for total nonresponse is done by a predefined cluster of units, by state, metropolitan status and CBSA size; for item nonresponse imputation varies by subject matter.

Estimates of Sampling Error: The national total estimates of the civilian labor force and of employment have monthly CVs of about 0.2 percent and annual average CVs of about 0.1 percent. Unemployment is a much smaller characteristic and consequently has substantially larger CVs than the civilian labor force or employment. The national unemployment rate, the most important CPS statistic, has a monthly CV of about 2 percent and an annual average CV of about 1 percent. Assuming a 6 percent unemployment rate, states have annual average CVs of about 8 percent. CVs for subnational areas, such as states, tend to be larger and vary by area.

Other (nonsampling) Errors: Estimates of response bias on unemployment are available. Estimates of unemployment rate from reinterviews range from -2.4 percent to 1.0 percent of the basic CPS unemployment rate (over a 30-month span from January 2004 through June 2006). Eligible CPS households are approximately 82 percent of the assigned households, with a corresponding response rate of 92 percent.

Sources of Additional Material: U.S. Census Bureau and Bureau of Labor Statistics, Current Population Survey: Design and Methodology, (Technical Paper 66), available on the Internet <http://www.census.gov/prod/2006pubs/tp-66.pdf> and the Bureau of Labor Statistics, <http://www.bls.gov/cps/> and the *BLS Handbook of Methods*, Chapter 1, available on the Internet at <http://www.bls.gov/opub/hom/homch1_a.htm>.

Foreign Trade—Export Statistics

Universe, Frequency, and Types of Data: As of October 1, 2008, the Shipper's Export Declaration (SED) Form 7525-V became obsolete. Electronic Export Information (EEI) replaced the SED and all export information must be filed through the Automated Export System (AES) by either a United States Principal Party in Interest (USPPI) or an Authorized U.S. agent. The EEI filings are processed each month to obtain data on the movement of U.S. merchandise exports to foreign countries. Data obtained include value, quantity, and shipping weight of exports by commodity, country of destination, district of exportation, and mode of transportation and port.

Type of Data Collection Operation: USPPIs or Authorized U.S. Agents are required to submit EEI for exportation of merchandise valued over $2,500. Data for shipments valued under $2,501 are estimated, based on established percentages of individual country totals.

Data Collection and Imputation Procedures: The EEI filings are received on a daily basis from ports throughout the country and subjected to a monthly processing cycle. They are fully processed to the extent they reflect items valued over $2,500. Estimates for shipments valued at $2,500 or less are made, based on established percentages of individual country totals.

Estimates of Sampling Error: Not applicable.

Other (nonsampling) Errors: The goods data are a complete enumeration of EEI reported in AES and are not subject to sampling errors; but they are subject to several types of nonsampling errors. Quality assurance procedures are performed at every stage of collection, processing and tabulation; however the data are still subject to several types of nonsampling errors. The most significant of these include reporting errors, undocumented shipments, timeliness, data capture errors, and errors in the estimation of low-valued transactions.

Sources of additional material: Foreign Trade Statistics Overview <http://www.census.gove/foreign-trade/index.html>.

Foreign Trade—Import Statistics

Universe, Frequency, and Types of Data: The import entry documents collected by U.S. Customs and Border Protection are processed each month to obtain data on the movement of merchandise imported into the United States. Data obtained include value, quantity, and shipping weight by commodity, country of origin, district of entry, and mode of transportation.

Type of Data Collection Operation: Import entry documents, either paper or electronic, are required to be filed for the importation of goods into the United States valued over $2,000 or for articles which must be reported on formal entries. U.S. Bureau of Customs and Border Protection officials collect and transmit statistical copies of the documents to the Census Bureau on a flow basis for data compilation. Estimates for shipments valued under $2,001 and not reported on formal entries are based on estimated established percentages for individual country totals.

Data Collection and Imputation Procedures: Statistical copies of import entry documents, received on a daily basis from ports of entry throughout the country, are subjected to a monthly processing cycle. They are fully processed to the extent they reflect items valued at $2,001 and over or items which must be reported on formal entries.

Estimates of Sampling Error: Not applicable.

Other (nonsampling) Errors: The goods data are a complete enumeration of documents collected by the U.S. Customs and Border Protection and are not subject to sampling errors; but they are subject to several types of nonsampling errors. Quality assurance procedures are performed at every stage of collection, processing, and tabulation; however the data are still subject to several types of nonsampling errors. The most significant of these include reporting errors, undocumented shipments, timeliness, data capture errors, and errors in the estimation of low-valued transactions.

Sources of Additional Material: Foreign Trade Statistics Overview <http://www.census.gov/foreign-trade/index.html>.

Monthly Retail Trade and Food Service Survey

Universe, Frequency, and Types of Data: Provides monthly estimates of retail and food service sales by kind of business and end of month inventories of retail stores.

Type of Data Collection Operation: Probability sample of all firms from a list frame. The list frame is the Bureau's Business Register updated quarterly for recent birth Employer Identification (EI) Numbers issued by the Internal Revenue Service and assigned a kind of business code by the Social Security Administration. The largest firms are included monthly; a sample of others is included every month also.

Data Collection and Imputation Procedures: Data are collected by mail questionnaire with telephone follow-ups and fax reminders for nonrespondents. Imputation is made for each nonresponse item and each item failing edit checks.

Estimates of Sampling Error: For the 2006 monthly surveys, CVs are about 0.4 percent for estimated total retail sales and 0.7 percent for estimated total retail inventories. Sampling errors are shown in monthly publications.

Other (nonsampling) Errors: Imputation rates are about 22 percent for monthly retail and food service sales, and 29 percent for monthly retail inventories.

Sources of Additional Material: U.S. Census Bureau, Current Business Reports, Annual Revision of Monthly Retail and Food Services: Sales and Inventories, see <http://www.census.gov/retail/index.html>.

Monthly Survey of Construction

Universe, Frequency, and Types of Data: Survey conducted monthly of newly constructed housing units (excluding mobile homes). Data are collected on the start, completion, and sale of housing. (Annual figures are aggregates of monthly estimates.)

Type of Data Collection Operation: A multistage probability sample of approximately 900 of the 20,000 permit-issuing jurisdictions in the U.S. was selected. Each month in each of these permit offices, field representatives list and select a sample of permits for which to collect data. To obtain data in areas where building permits are not required, a multistage probability sample of 80 land areas (census tracts or subsections of census tracts) was selected. All roads in these areas are canvassed and data are collected on all new residential construction found. Sampled buildings are followed up until they are completed (and sold, if for sale).

Data Collection and Imputation Procedures: Data are obtained by telephone inquiry and/or field visit. Nonresponse/undercoverage adjustment factors are used to account for late reported data.

Estimates of Sampling Error: Estimated CV of 5 percent to 6 percent for estimates of national totals of units started, but may be higher than 20 percent for estimated totals of more detailed characteristics, such as housing units in multiunit structures.

Other (nonsampling) Errors: Response rate is over 90 percent for most items. Nonsampling errors are attributed to definitional problems, differences in interpretation of questions, incorrect reporting, inability to obtain information about all cases in the sample, and processing errors.

Sources of Additional Material: All data are available on the Internet at <http://www.census.gov/construction/nrc/> and <http://www.census.gov/construction/nrs/> Further documentation of the survey is also available at those sites.

Nonemployer Statistics

Universe, Frequency, and Types of Data: Nonemployer statistics are an annual tabulation of economic data by industry for active businesses without paid employees that are subject to federal income tax. Data showing the number of firms and receipts by industry are available for the U.S., states, counties, and metropolitan areas. Most types of businesses covered by the Census Bureau's economic statistics programs are included in the nonemployer statistics. Tax-exempt and agricultural-production businesses are excluded from nonemployer statistics.

Type of Data Collection Operation: The universe of nonemployer firms is created annually as a byproduct of the Census Bureau's Business Register processing for employer establishments. If a business is active but without paid employees, it becomes part of the potential nonemployer universe. Industry classification and receipts are available for each potential nonemployer business. These data are obtained primarily from the annual business income tax returns of the Internal Revenue Service (IRS). The potential nonemployer universe undergoes a series of complex processing, editing, and analytical review procedures at the Census Bureau to distinguish nonemployers from employers, and to correct and complete data items used in creating the data tables.

Estimates of Sampling Error: Not applicable.

Other (nonsampling) Errors: The data are subject to nonsampling errors, such as industry misclassification as well as errors of response, keying, nonreporting, and coverage.

Sources of Additional Material: U. S. Census Bureau, <http://www.census.gov/econ/nonemployer/index.html>.

Service Annual Survey

Universe, Frequency, and Types of Data: The U.S. Census Bureau conducts the Service Annual Survey (SAS) to provide nationwide estimates of revenues and expenses for selected service industries. Estimates are summarized by industry classification based on the 2007 North American Industry Classification System (NAICS). The SAS was expanded in 2009. Selected service industries covered by the Service Annual Survey include all or part of the following NAICS sectors: Utilities (NAICS 22), Transportation and Warehousing (NAICS 48-49); Information (NAICS 51); Finance and Insurance (NAICS 52); Real Estate and Rental and Leasing (NAICS 53); Professional, Scientific, and Technical Services (NAICS 54); Administrative and

Support and Waste Management and Remediation Services (NAICS 56); Educational Services (NAICS 61); Health Care and Social Assistance (NAICS 62); Arts, Entertainment, and Recreation (NAICS 71); and Other Services, except Public Administration (NAICS 81). Data collected include total revenue, total expenses, detailed expenses, revenue from e-commerce transactions; and for selected industries, revenue from detailed service products, revenue from exported services, and inventories. For industries with a significant nonprofit component, separate estimates are developed for taxable firms and firms and organizations exempt from federal income taxes. Questionnaires are mailed in January and request annual data for the prior year. Estimates are published approximately 12 months after the initial survey mailing.

Type of Data Collection Operation: The Service Annual Survey estimates are developed from a probability sample of employer firms and administrative records for nonemployers. Service Annual Survey questionnaires are mailed to a probability sample that is periodically reselected from a universe of firms located in the United States and having paid employees. The sample includes firms of all sizes and covers both taxable firms and firms exempt from federal income taxes. Updates to the sample are made on a quarterly basis to account for new businesses. Firms without paid employees, or nonemployers, are included in the estimates through imputation and/or administrative records data provided by other federal agencies. Links to additional information about confidentiality protection, sampling error, nonsampling error, sample design, definitions, and copies of the questionnaires may be found at <http://www.census.gov/services/index.html>.

Estimates of Sampling Error: The most recent Service Annual Survey results, including coefficients of variations (CVs), can be found at <http://www.census.gov/services/index.html>. Links to additional information regarding sampling error may be found at <http://www.census.gov/services/sas/cv.html>.

Other (Nonsampling) Errors: Data are imputed for unit nonresponse, item nonresponse, and for reported data that fails edits. The percent of imputed data for total revenue for the 2009 Service Annual Survey estimates range from 6.5 percent to 19.3 percent for total revenue estimates computed at the NAICS sector (2-digit NAICS code) level.

Sources of Additional Material: U.S. Census Bureau, Current Business Reports, *Service Annual Survey*, <http://www.census.gov/services/index.html>.

Survey of Business Owners (SBO)

Universe, Frequency, and Types of Data: The Survey of Business Owners (SBO), formerly known as the Surveys of Minority- and Women-Owned Business Enterprises (SMOBE/SWOBE), provides statistics that describe the composition of U.S. businesses by gender, ethnicity, race, and veteran status. Data are presented for businesses owned by American Indians and Alaska Natives, Asians, Blacks, Hispanics, Native Hawaiians and Other Pacific Islanders, Veterans, and Women. All U.S. firms operating during 2007 with receipts of $1,000 or more, which are classified by the North American Industry Classification System (NAICS) codes 11 through 99, are represented, except for the

following: NAICS 111, 112, 4811 (part), 481111, 482, 491, 525, 813, 814, and 92. The lists of all firms (or sample frames) are compiled from a combination of business tax returns and data collected on other economic census reports. The published data include the number of firms, sales and receipts, number of paid employees, and annual payroll. Data are presented by industry classifications, geographic area (states, metropolitan and micropolitan statistical areas, counties, and corporate municipalities [places] including cities, towns, townships, villages, and boroughs), and size of firm (employment and receipts).

Type of Data Collection Operation: The survey is based on a stratified probability sample of approximately 2.3 million firms from a universe of approximately 27.1 million firms. There were 5.7 million firms with paid employees and 21.4 million firms with no paid employees.

Data Collection and Imputation Procedures: Data were collected through a mailout/mailback operation. Compensation for missing data is addressed through reweighting, edit correction, and standard statistical imputation methods.

Estimates of Sampling Error: Sampling error is present in these estimates because they are based on the results of a sample survey and not on an enumeration of the entire universe. Since these estimates are based on a probability sample, it is possible to estimate the sampling variability of the survey estimates. The standard error (SE) provides a measure of the variation. The relative standard error (RSE) or coefficient of variation (CV) provides a measure of the magnitude of the variation relative to the estimate and is calculated as 100 multiplied by the ratio of the estimate to the SE. The CVs for number of firms and receipts at the national level typically range from 0 to 4 percent.

Other (Nonsampling) Error: Nonsampling errors are attributed to many sources: inability to obtain information for all cases in the universe, adjustments to the weights of respondents to compensate for nonrespondents, imputation for missing data, data errors and biases, mistakes in recording or keying data, errors in collection or processing, and coverage problems. Explicit measures of the effects of these nonsampling errors are not available. However, it is believed that most of the important operational and data errors were detected and corrected through an automated data edit designed to review the data for reasonableness and consistency. Quality control techniques were used to verify that operating procedures were carried out as specified.

Sources of Additional Materials: U.S. Census Bureau, Survey of Business Owners, <http://www.census.gov/econ/sbo/> *2007 Economic Census User Guide:* <http://www.census.gov/econ/census07/www/user_guide.html>.

U.S. DEPARTMENT OF EDUCATION National Center for Education Statistics

Integrated Postsecondary Education Data Survey (IPEDS), Completions

Universe, Frequency, and Types of Data: Annual survey of all Title IV (federal financial aid) eligible postsecondary institutions to obtain data on enrollments; faculty and staff finances; institutional prices; financial aid; and earned degrees and other formal awards, conferred by field of study, level of degree, sex, and by racial/ ethnic characteristics (every other year prior to 1989, then annually).

Type of Data Collection Operation: Complete census.

Data Collection and Imputation Procedures: Data are collected through a Web-based survey in the fall of every year. Missing data are imputed by using data of similar institutions.

Estimates of Sampling Error: Not applicable.

Other (nonsampling Errors): For 2009-10, the response rate for degree-granting institutions was 100.0 percent.

Sources of Additional Material: U.S. Department of Education, National Center for Education Statistics, *Post-secondary Institutions and Price of Attendance in the United States: 2010-2011 and Degrees and Other Awards Conferred: 2009-10 and 12-month enrollment, 2009-10.* See <http://www.nces.ed.gov/ipeds/>.

National Household Education Surveys (NHES) Program

Universe, Frequency, and Types of Data: The National Household Education Surveys Program is a system of telephone surveys of the noninstitutionalized civilian population of the United States. Surveys in NHES have varying universes of interest depending on the particular survey. Specific topics covered by each survey are at the NHES Web site <http://nces.ed.gov/nhes>. A list of the surveys fielded as part of NHES, each universe, and the years they were fielded is provided below.

1 Adult Education—Interviews were conducted with a representative sample of civilian, noninstitutionalized persons aged 16 and older who were not enrolled in grade 12 or below (1991, 1995, 1999, 2001, 2003, 2005).

2 Before- and After-School Programs and Activities—Interviews were conducted with parents of a representative sample of students in grades K through 8 (1999, 2001, 2005).

3 Civic Involvement—Interviews were conducted with representative samples of parents, youth, and adults (1996, 1999).

4 Early Childhood Program Participation—Interviews were conducted with parents of a representative sample of children from birth through grade 3, with the specific age groups varying by survey year (1991, 1995, 1999, 2001, 2005).

5 Household and Library Use—Interviews were conducted with a representative sample of U.S. households (1996).

6 Parent and Family Involvement in Education—Interviews were conducted with parents of a representative sample of children age three through grade 12 or in grades K through 12 depending on the survey year (1996, 1999, 2003, and 2007).

7 School Readiness—Interviews were conducted with parents of a representative sample of 3-7 year-old children (1993 and 1999) and of 3-5 year old children, not yet in kindergarten, 2007).

8 School Safety and Discipline—Interviews were conducted with a representative sample of students in grades 6-12, their parents, and the parents of a representative sample of students in grades 3-12 (1993).

Type of Data Collection Operation: NHES uses telephone interviews to collect data.

Data Collection and Imputation Procedures: Telephone numbers are selected using random digit dialing (RDD) techniques. Approximately 45,000 to 64,000 households are contacted in order to identify persons eligible for the surveys. Data are collected using computer-assisted telephone interviewing (CATI) procedures. Missing data are imputed using hot-deck imputation procedures.

Estimates of Sampling Error: Unweighted sample sizes range between 2,250 and 55,708. The average root design effects of the surveys in NHES range from 1.1 to 1.5, except for the Adult Education survey of 1991. In 1991, average root design effects for the Adult Education survey ranged from 2.3 to 4.5.

Other (nonsampling) Errors: Because of unit nonresponse and because the samples are drawn from households with telephone instead of all households, nonresponse and/or coverage bias may exist for some estimates. However, both sources of potential bias are adjusted for in the weighting process. Analyses of both potential sources of bias in the NHES collections have been studied and no significant bias has been detected.

Sources of Additional Material: Please see the NHES Web site at <http://nces.ed.gov/nhes>.

Schools and Staffing Survey (SASS)

Universe, Frequency and Types of Data: NCES designed the SASS survey system to emphasize teacher demand and shortage, teacher and administrator characteristics, school programs, and general conditions in schools. SASS also collects data on many other topics, including principals' and teachers' perceptions of school climate and problems in their schools; teacher compensation; district hiring practices; basic characteristics of the student population; and for the first time, instructional time and teacher and school performance. The SASS has had four core components: the School Questionnaire, the Teacher Questionnaire, the Principal Questionnaire, and the School District Questionnaire. For the 2007-08 SASS, a sample of public charter schools is included in the sample as part of the public school questionnaire. Since 1987-88, the SASS is the largest, most extensive survey of K through 12 school districts, schools, teachers, and administrators in the U.S. Surveys have been conducted every 3 to 4 years depending on budgetary constraints. The SASS includes data from public, private, and Bureau of Indian Education (BIE) school sectors. Therefore, the SASS provides a multitude of opportunities for analysis and reporting on elementary and secondary educational issues.

Type of Data Collection Operation: The U.S. Census Bureau performs the data collection and begins by sending advance letters to the sampled Local Education Agencies (LEAs) and schools in August and September of collection years. Beginning in October, questionnaires are delivered by U.S. Census Bureau field representatives. The sampling frame for the public school sample is the most recent Common Core of Data (CCD) school file. CCD is a universe file that includes all elementary and secondary schools in the United States. Schools operated by the Department of Defense or those that offered only kindergarten or pre-kindergarten or adult education were excluded from the SASS sample. The list frame used for the private school sample is the most recent Private School Universe Survey (PSS) list, updated with association lists. An area frame supplement is based on the canvassing of private schools within specific geographical areas. A separate universe of schools funded by the Bureau of Indian Education (BIE) is drawn from the Program Education Directory maintained by the BIE. To avoid duplicates in the BIE files, BIE schools in the CCD school file are treated as public schools.

Estimates of Sampling Error: Sample errors can be calculated using replicate weights and Balanced Repeated Replication complex survey design methodology. Errors depend on cell sizes and range from less than 1 percent to over 5 percent (for reasonable cell sizes).

Other (nonsampling) Errors: Because of unit nonresponse, bias may exist in some sample cells. However, bias has been adjusted for in the weighting process. Analysis of bias has been studied and no significant bias has been detected.

Sources of Additional Material: Please see the SASS Web site at <http://nces.ed.gov/surveys/sass/>.

U.S. DEPARTMENT OF JUSTICE, FEDERAL BUREAU OF INVESTIGATION

Uniform Crime Reporting (UCR) Program

Universe, Frequency, and Types of Data: Monthly reports on the number of criminal offenses that become known to law enforcement agencies. Data are also collected on crimes cleared by arrest or exceptional means; age, sex, and race of arrestees and for victims and offenders for homicides, number of law enforcement employees, on fatal and nonfatal assaults against law enforcement officers, and on hate crimes reported.

Type of Data Collection Operation: Crime statistics are based on reports of crime data submitted either directly to the FBI by contributing law enforcement agencies or through cooperating state UCR Programs.

Data Collection and Imputation Procedures: States with UCR programs collect data directly from individual law enforcement agencies and forward reports, prepared in accordance with UCR standards, to the FBI. Accuracy and consistency edits are performed by the FBI.

Estimates of Sampling Error: Not applicable.

Other (nonsampling) Errors: During 2008, law enforcement agencies active in the UCR Program represented 94.9 percent of the total population. The coverage amounted to 96.0 percent of the United States population in Metropolitan Statistical Areas, 87.6 percent of the population in cities outside metropolitan areas, and 90.0 percent in nonmetropolitan counties.

Sources of Additional Material: U.S. Department of Justice, Federal Bureau of Investigation, *Crime in the United States*, annual, *Hate Crime Statistics*,

annual, *Law Enforcement Officers Killed and Assaulted*, annual, <http://www.fbi.gov/about-us/cjis/ucr/ucr>.

U.S. INTERNAL REVENUE SERVICE

Corporation Income Tax Returns

Universe, Frequency, and Types of Data: Annual study of unaudited corporation income tax returns, Forms 1120, 1120-A, 1120-F, 1120-L, 1120-PC, 1120-REIT, 1120-RIC, and 1120S, filed by corporations or businesses legally defined as corporations. Data provided on various financial characteristics by industry and size of total assets, and business receipts.

Type of Data Collection Operation: Stratified probability sample of approximately 112,000 returns for Tax Year 2008, allocated to sample classes which are based on type of return, size of total assets, size of net income or deficit, and selected business activity. Sampling rates for sample classes varied from 0.25 percent to 100 percent.

Data Collection and Imputation Procedures: Computer selection of sample of tax return records. Data adjusted during editing for incorrect, missing, or inconsistent entries to ensure consistency with other entries on return and to comply with statistical definitions.

Estimates of Sampling Error: Estimated CVs for Tax Year 2008: Coefficients of variation are published in the *2008 Statistics of Income Corporation Income Tax Returns*, Table 1, by industry group. Sampling rates are contained in Section 3 of the same report.

Other (nonsampling) Errors: Nonsampling errors include coverage errors, processing errors, and response errors.

Sources of Additional Material: U.S. Internal Revenue Service, *Statistics of Income, Corporation Income Tax Returns*, annual.

Individual Income Tax Returns

Universe, Frequency, and Types of Data: Annual study of unaudited individual income tax returns, Forms 1040, 1040A, and 1040EZ, filed by U.S. citizens and residents. Data provided on various financial characteristics by size of adjusted gross income, marital status, and by taxable and nontaxable returns. Data by state, based on the population of returns filed, also include returns from 1040NR, filed by nonresident aliens plus certain self-employment tax returns.

Type of Data Collection Operation: Stratified probability sample of 328,630 returns for tax year 2008. The sample is classified into sample strata based on the larger of total income or total loss amounts, the size of business plus farm receipts, and other criteria such as the potential usefulness of the return for tax policy modeling. Sampling rates for sample strata varied from 0.10 percent to 100 percent.

Data Collection and Imputation Procedures: Computer selection of sample of tax return records. Data adjusted during editing for incorrect, missing, or inconsistent entries to ensure consistency with other entries on return.

Estimates of Sampling Error: Estimated CVs for tax year 2008: Adjusted gross income less deficit 0.08

percent; salaries and wages 0.16 percent; and tax exempt interest received 1.07 percent. (State data not subject to sampling error.)

Other (nonsampling) Errors: Processing errors and errors arising from the use of tolerance checks for the data.

Sources of Additional Material: U.S. Internal Revenue Service, *Statistics of Income, Individual Income Tax Returns*, annual, (Publication 1304).

Partnership Income Tax Returns

Universe, Frequency, and Types of Data: Annual study of preaudited income tax returns of partnerships related to financial and tax-related activity during calendar year 2008 and reported on Forms 1065 and 1065B to the IRS in calendar year 2009. Data are provided by industry, based on the NAICS industry coding used by IRS.

Type of Data Collection Operation: Stratified probability sample of approximately 34,496 partnership returns from a population of 3.3 million filed during calendar year 2009. The sample is classified based on combinations of industry code, gross receipts, net income or loss, and total assets. Sampling rates vary from 0.04 percent to 100 percent.

Data Collection and Imputation Procedures: The sample of tax return records are selected via computer after data are transcribed by IRS and placed on an administrative file. Data are manually adjusted during editing for incorrect, missing, or inconsistent entries to ensure consistency with other entries on return. Data not available due to regulations are handled with weighting adjustments.

Estimates of Sampling Error: Some of the estimated Coefficients of Variation (the estimated standard error of the total divided by the estimated total) for tax year 2008: For number of partnerships, 0.36 percent; business receipts, 2.63 percent; net income, 2.83 percent; and ordinary business income, 2.23 percent.

Other (nonsampling) Errors: The potential exists for coverage error due to unavailable returns; processing errors; and taxpayer reporting errors, since data are preaudit.

Sources of Additional Material: U.S. Internal Revenue Service, *Statistics of Income, Partnership Returns* and *Statistics of Income Bulletin*, Vol. 31, No. 2 (Fall 2011).

Sole Proprietorship Income Tax Returns

Universe, Frequency, and Types of Data: Annual study of unaudited income tax returns of nonfarm sole proprietorships, Form 1040 with business schedules. Data provided on various financial characteristics by industry.

Type of Data Collection Operation: Stratified probability sample of roughly 90,000 sole proprietorships for tax year 2008. The sample is classified based on presence or absence of certain business schedules; the larger of total income or loss; size of business plus farm receipts, and other criteria such as the potential usefulness of the return for tax policy modeling. Sampling rates vary from 0.1 percent to 100 percent.

Data Collection and Imputation Procedures: Computer selection of sample of tax return records. Data

adjusted during editing for incorrect, missing, or inconsistent entries to ensure consistency with other entries on return.

Estimates of Sampling Error: Estimated CVs for tax year 2008 are available. For sole proprietorships, total business receipts, 0.53 percent; depreciation 1.21 percent.

Other (nonsampling) Errors: Processing errors and errors arising from the use of tolerance checks for the data.

Sources of Additional Material: U.S. Internal Revenue Service, *Statistics of Income, Sole Proprietorship Returns* (for years 1980 through 1983) and *Statistics of Income Bulletin*, Vol. 31, No. 1 (Summer 2011, as well as bulletins for earlier years).

U.S. NATIONAL CENTER FOR HEALTH STATISTICS (NCHS)

National Health Interview Survey (NHIS)

Universe, Frequency, and Types of Data: Continuous data collection covering the civilian noninstitutional population to obtain information on demographic characteristics, conditions, injuries, impairments, use of health services, health behaviors, and other health topics.

Type of Data Collection Operation: Multistage probability sample of 49,000 households (in 198 PSUs) from 1985 to 1994; 36-40,000 households (358 design PSUs, or 449 effective PSUs when divided by state boundaries) from 1995 to 2005; an estimated 35,000 households (428 effective PSUs) beginning in 2006.

Data Collection and Imputation Procedures: Some missing data items (e.g., race, ethnicity) are imputed using a hot deck imputation value. Sequential regression models are used to create multiple imputation files for family income. Unit nonresponse is compensated for by an adjustment to the survey weights.

Estimates of Sampling Error: For 2008, medically attended injury episodes rates (crude) in the past 12 months by falling for: females 50.43 (4.30) and males 34.87 (3.73) per 1,000 population; for 2008, injury episodes rates (crude) during the past 12 months inside the home—27.90 (2.28) per 1,000 population.

Other (nonsampling) Errors: The response rate was 93.8 percent in 1996; in 2008, the total household response rate was 84.9 percent, with the final family response rate of 84.5 percent, and the final sample adult response rate of 62.6 percent. (Note: the NHIS questionnaire was redesigned in 1997, and a new sample design was instituted in 2006).

Sources of Additional Material: National Center for Health Statistics, Summary Health Statistics for the U.S. Population: National Health Interview Survey, 2009, Vital and Health Statistics, Series 10, No. 248; National Center for Health Statistics, Summary Health Statistics for U.S. Children: National Health Interview Survey, 2009, Vital and Health Statistics, Series 10, No. 247; National Center for Health Statistics, Summary Health Statistics for U.S. Adults: National Health Interview Survey, 2009, Vital and Health Statistics, Series 10, No. 249; U.S. National Center for Health Statistics, Design and Estimation for the National Health Interview Survey, 1995-2004, Vital and Health Statistics, Series 2, No. 130.

National Survey of Family Growth (NSFG)

Universe, Frequency, and Types of Data: Periodic survey of men and women 15-44 years of age in the household population of the United States. Interviews were conducted in 2002 in person by trained female interviewers. Interview topics covered include births and pregnancies, marriage, divorce, and cohabitation, sexual activity, contraceptive use, and medical care. For men, data on father involvement with children were collected. The most sensitive data—on sexual behavior related to HIV and Sexually Transmitted Disease risk—were collected in a self-administered form in which the data are entered into a computer.

Type of Data Collection Operation: In the 2002 (Cycle 6) NSFG, the sample was a multistage area probability sample of men and women 15-44 years of age in the household population of the United States. Only one person 15-44 was selected from households with one or more persons 15-44. Data were collected and entered into laptop (notebook) computers. In the self-administered portion, the respondent entered his or her own answers into the computer. Sample included 12,571 interviews. The response rate was 79 percent. Hispanic and Black persons, as well as those 15-19 years of age, were sampled at higher rates than White adults. All percentages and other statistics shown for the NSFG are weighted to make national estimates. The weights adjust for the different rates of sampling for each group, and for nonresponse.

Data Collection and Imputation Procedures: When interviews are received, they are reviewed for consistency and quality, and analysis variables (recodes) are created. Missing data on these recodes were imputed using multiple regression techniques and checked again for consistency. Variables indicating whether a value has been imputed ("imputation flags") are included on the data file.

Estimates of Sampling Error: Sampling error codes are included on the data file so that users can estimate sampling errors for their own analyses. Sampling error estimates for nine illustrative analyses are shown on the NSFG Web site at <http://www.cdc. gov/nchs/nsfg.htm>. Sampling error estimates are also shown in most NCHS reports.

Other (nonsampling) Errors: In any survey, errors can occur because the respondent (the person being interviewed) does not recall the specific fact or event being asked about. The NSFG questionnaire in 2002 was programmed to check the consistency of many variables during the interview, so that the interviewer and respondent had a chance to correct any inconsistent information. Further checking occurred after the interview and during recoding and imputation. Typically, less than 1 percent of cases need imputation because of missing data.

Sources of Additional Material: The following references can be found at <http://www.cdc.gov/ nchs/nsfg.htm>. "National Survey of Family Growth, Cycle 6: Sample Design, Weighting, and Variance Estimation." *Vital and Health Statistics*, Series 2, Number 142, July 2006. "Plan and Operation of Cycle 6 of the National Survey of Family Growth."

Vital and Health Statistics, Series 1, No. 42. August 2005. "Sexual Behavior and Selected Health Measures: Men and Women 15-44 Years of Age, United States, 2002." *Advance Data from Vital and Health Statistics*, No. 362, Sept 15, 2005.

National Vital Statistics System

Universe, Frequency, and Types of Data: Annual data on births and deaths in the United States.

Type of Data Collection Operation: Mortality data based on complete file of death records, except 1972, based on 50 percent sample. Natality statistics 1951-1971, based on 50 percent sample of birth certificates, except a 20 percent to 50 percent sample in 1967, received by NCHS.

Data Collection and Imputation Procedures: Reports based on records from registration offices of all states, District of Columbia, New York City, Puerto Rico, Virgin Islands, Guam, American Samoa, and Northern Marianas.

Estimates of Sampling Error: For recent years, there is no sampling for these files; the files are based on 100 percent of events registered.

Other (nonsampling) Errors: It is believed that more than 99 percent of the births and deaths occurring in this country are registered.

Sources of Additional Material: U.S. National Center for Health Statistics, *Vital Statistics of the United States*, Vol. I and Vol. II, annual, and the *National Vital Statistics Reports*. See the NCHS Web site at <http://www.cdc.gov/nchs/nvss.htm>.

National Highway Traffic Safety Administration (NHTSA)

Fatality Analysis Reporting System (FARS)

Universe, Frequency, and Types of Data: FARS is a census of all fatal motor vehicle traffic crashes that occur throughout the United States including the District of Columbia and Puerto Rico on roadways customarily open to the public. The crash must be reported to the state/jurisdiction and at least one directly related fatality must occur within thirty days of the crash.

Type of Data Collection Operation: One or more analysts, in each state, extract data from the official documents and enter the data into a standardized electronic database.

Data Collection and Imputation Procedures: Detailed data describing the characteristics of the fatal crash, the vehicles and persons involved are obtained from police crash reports, driver and vehicle registration records, autopsy reports, highway department, etc. Computerized edit checks monitor the accuracy and completeness of the data. The FARS incorporates a sophisticated mathematical multiple imputation procedure to develop a probability distribution of missing blood alcohol concentration (BAC) levels in the database for drivers, pedestrians, and cyclists.

Estimates of Sampling Error: Since this is census data, there are no sampling errors.

Other (nonsampling) Errors: FARS represents a census of all police-reported crashes and captures all data reported at the state level. FARS data undergo a rigorous quality control process to prevent inaccurate reporting. However, these data are highly dependent on the accuracy of the police accident reports. Errors or omissions within police accident reports may not be detected.

Sources of Additional Material: The FARS Coding and Validation Manual, ANSI D16.1 Manual on Classification of Motor Vehicle Traffic Accidents (Sixth Edition).

Weights and Measures

U.S. Customary/Metric Conversion Table

[Conversions provided in the table are approximate]

Symbol	When you know U.S. customary	Multiply by	To find metric	Symbol
in	inches	2.54	centimeters	cm
ft	feet	30.48	centimeters	cm
yd	yards	0.091	meters	m
mi	miles	1.61	kilometers	km
in ^{2}	square inches	6.45	square centimeters	cm ^{2}
ft ^{2}	square feet	0.09	square centimeters	cm ^{2}
yd ^{2}	square yards	0.84	square meters	m ^{2}
mi ^{2}	square miles	2.59	square kilometers	km ^{2}
	acre	0.41	hectare	ha
oz	ounces	28.35	grams	g
lb	pounds	0.45	kilograms	kg
oz (troy)	troy ounces	31.1	grams	g
	short tons (2,000 lb)	0.91	metric tons	t
	long tons (2,240 lb)	1.02	metric tons	t
fl oz	fluid ounces	29.57	mililiters	mL
c	cups	0.24	liters	L
pt	pints	0.47	liters	L
qt	quarts	0.95	liters	L
gal	gallons	3.78	liters	L
ft ^{3}	cubic feet	0.03	cubic meters	m ^{3}
yd ^{3}	cubic yards	0.76	cubic meters	m ^{3}
°F	degrees Fahrenheit (subtract 32)	0.55	degrees Celsius	°C

Symbol	When you know metric	Multiply by	To find U.S. customary	Symbol
cm	centimeters	0.39	inches	in
cm	centimeters	0.03	feet	ft
m	meters	1.09	yards	yd
km	kilometers	0.62	miles	mi
cm ^{2}	square centimeters	0.015	square inches	in ^{2}
cm ^{2}	square centimeters	10.76	square feet	ft ^{2}
m ^{2}	square meters	1.2	square yards	yd ^{2}
km ^{2}	square kilometers	0.39	square miles	mi ^{2}
ha	hectare	2.47	acre	
g	grams	0.04	ounces	oz
kg	kilograms	2.21	pounds	lb
g	grams	0.04	troy ounces	oz (troy)
t	metric tons	1.1	short tons (2,000 lb)	
t	metric tons	0.98	long tons (2,240 lb)	
mL	mililiters	0.03	fluid ounces	fl oz
L	liters	4.23	cups	c
L	liters	2.13	pints	pt
L	liters	1.05	quarts	qt
L	liters	0.026	gallons	gal
m ^{3}	cubic meters	35.32	cubic feet	ft ^{3}
m ^{3}	cubic meters	1.32	cubic yards	yd ^{3}
°C	degrees Celsius (after multiplying, add 32)	1.8	degrees Fahrenheit	°F

[1] For weighing ordinary commodities. [2] For weighing previous metals, jewels, etc.

Source: National Institute of Standards and Technology (NIST), Weights and Measures Division. See <http://www.nist.gov/pml/wmd/metric/unit-conversion.cfm>

Index

Agriculture, construction, and mining machinery manufacturing (see also Machine tools, and Machinery manufacturing), 644, 651, 1024

Agriculture, forestry, and fishing industry:
Capital, 792, 796
Earnings, 655, 770, 780, 781, 782, 783, 784, 785, 786, 891, 892
Employees, 630, 770, 780, 781, 782, 783, 784, 785, 786, 891, 892
Establishments, 770, 888, 891, 892
Finances, 757, 760
Gross domestic product, 682, 893
Occupational safety, 670, 673
Profits, 804
Sales, 757, 760, 765, 766, 786, 804, 891

Aid to families with dependent children (See Temporary Assistance for Needy Families.)

AIDS (Acquired Immuno-Deficiency Syndrome), 125, 131, 188, 189, 190, 191

Air conditioning, homes with, 1001

Air Force, personnel, 516, 518

Air pollution:
Air pollution control equipment, 387
Emissions, 379, 380, 381, 382, 383, 388, 389, 390, 1403
Greenhouse gases, 382, 383
Toxic chemicals, 388, 389, 390

Air transportation:
Accidents and deaths, 1080, 1086, 1089
Airports, 1083, 1084, 1088, 1284
Carrier delays, cancellations, 1085
Civil aviation, 1090
Consumer complaints, 1087
Cost indexes, 1082
Employees, 1081
Federal outlays, 481
Finances, 1081
Fleet size, 1077, 1090
Freight, 1081, 1317
Fuel consumption, 940
Jet transport aircraft, orders, 1048
Passenger screening, 546
Price indexes, 739, 750
Regional airlines, 1091
Traffic carried, 546, 1081, 1091, 1284

Air transportation industry:
Capital, 792
Earnings, 644, 1073, 1074, 1289
Employees, 644, 1073, 1074, 1281, 1289
Establishments, 1073, 1074, 1289
Finances, 1081, 1082
Gross domestic product, 682
Productivity, 651
Profits, 1081
Revenues, 1074, 1081

Aircraft manufacturing. (See Aerospace industry.)

Airline operations (see also Air transportation), 1081, 1084

Airplanes, 1322

Airports or airfields, 1090
Federal aid to state and local government, 440
Serving regional airlines, 1091
Traffic, 1083, 1088, 1284

Alaska Native. (See American Indian, Alaska Native population.)

Alcoholic beverages (see also individual types; and Beer, wine, and liquor stores):
Alcoholism treatment, 182, 207
Consumer expenditures, 689, 698, 700, 701, 1070
Consumption, 209, 210
Foreign trade, 1322
Government revenues, 445, 446, 452, 459, 462, 468
Price indexes, 739, 749
Sales, 1066, 1070

Alcohol-induced deaths, 123

Alcohol involvement in fatal crashes, 1116, 1117, 1118

Alcoholism treatment, 182, 207

Aleut population. (See American Indian, Alaska Native population.)

Algeria (See Foreign countries.)

Aliens, illegal, 45, 341, 540, 542

Alimony, 498, 552

Almonds, 855, 876, 877

Alternative fueled vehicles, 1105

Alternative medicine, 170

Alternative minimum tax, 494

Altitudes, geographical, 373

Aluminum:
Consumption, 916
Employment, 916
Foreign trade, 753, 754, 916, 923, 1322
Prices, 749, 753, 754, 916
Recycling, 385, 386
World production, 920

Alzheimer's disease, deaths, 120, 121, 122, 123, 124, 125, 126

Ambulatory health care services industry:
Capital, 792
Earnings, 163, 644, 767
Employees, 644, 767
Establishments, 767
Finances, 757
Gross domestic product, 682
Sales, receipts, 757, 767

American College Testing Program (ACT), 267

American Indian, Alaska Native population, 5, 6, 10, 11, 12, 19
Age and/or sex, 6, 10, 11, 12
Arrests, 333
Births, birth rates, 5, 83, 85, 86, 87, 88, 89
Business owners, 779, 786
Cancer deaths, 129
Charter schools, 244
Children, 10, 11, 12
College enrollment, 279
Deaths, death rates, 5, 112, 113, 114, 127, 129, 130, 131
Degrees conferred, 300, 825
Educational attainment, 36
Elderly, 10, 11, 12
Food stamp participants, 581
Gaming revenue, 1273
Grandparents living with grandchildren, 70
Health care visits to professionals, 169, 171
Heart disease, deaths, 127

Note: Index citations refer to **table** numbers, not **page** numbers

American Indian, Alaska Native population:—Con.
 HIV disease, 131
 Hospital visits, 171, 181
 Housing tenure, 36
 Immunization of children, 196
 Internet usage, 118
 Metropolitan area population, 23
 Migration, 5
 Occupation, 36
 Poverty, 36
 States, 19
 Suicides, death, 130
 Teachers, 257
 Veterans, 531
 Weapons in school, 308
American Samoa. (See Island areas of the U.S.)
American Sign Language, 284
American Stock Exchange, 1220, 1224
AMTRAK, 1132
Amusement and recreation services. (See Arts,
  recreation and travel.)
Amusement, gambling, and recreation industry:
 Capital, 792
 Earnings, 644, 767, 1243, 1244
 Employees, 644, 767,
 Establishments, 767, 1243, 1244
 Gaming revenue, 1273, 1274
 Gross domestic product, 682
 Nonemployer establishments, 1243
 Productivity, 651
 Receipts, revenue, 767, 1243
Amusement parks, 981, 1241, 1243, 1244, 1258
Analgesics, 209
Ancestry, 52
Andorra. (See Foreign countries.)
Anemia, deaths, 123
Anesthesiologists, 167
Angiocardiography, 174
Angola. (See Foreign countries.)
Animal oils and fats. (See Oils, animal.)
Animal slaughtering and processing industry, 644,
  651
Animals, domestic (see also individual classes):
 Charitable contributions, 593
 Livestock, 835, 845, 882
 Pets, 644, 1253, 1299
Annuities. (See Pensions and retirement benefits.)
Antigua and Barbuda. (See Foreign countries.)
Antimony, 916
Apparel goods (see also Clothing and accessory
  stores):
 Consumer expenditures, 689, 698, 700, 701
 Foreign trade, 1322
 Prices, 737, 738, 739, 749, 750
 Sales, 1066
Apparel manufacturing:
 Capital, 792
 Earnings, 644, 1022, 1024, 1030
 Employees, 644, 1022, 1024, 1026, 1030
 Establishments, 1022, 1024
 Finances, 805
 Foreign trade, 1326
 Gross domestic product, 682, 1020
 Industrial production index, 800
 Productivity, 651

Profits, 805
Shipments, 1024
Toxic chemical releases, 389
Appeals Courts, U.S., 343, 345
Apples, 221, 745, 855, 876
Appliances, household:
 Consumer expenditures, 689, 700, 701
 Homes with, 1001
 Injuries associated, 219,
 Price indexes, 739, 749
 Sales and shipments, 1051
Appliances (household) manufacturing:
 Inventories, 1033
 Shipments, 1033
Apricots, 876
Aquaculture, 855, 910
Archery, 1264, 1266
Architects, 626
Architectural services. (See Engineering and
  architectural services.)
Area of:
 Developed land, 374, 375
 Foreign countries, 1348
 Forest land, 374, 375, 376, 896
 Horticultural crops, 880
 Island areas of the U.S., 365
 Lakes, 366, 367, 368
 Parks, 1267, 1268, 1269, 1270
 States, 365
 Timberland, 896
 United States, 1, 365, 1348
 Water, 1, 365, 377
 Wetlands, 375
 World, 1348
Argentina. (See Foreign countries.)
Arizona. (See State data.)
Arkansas. (See State data.)
Armed Forces, 516, 517, 518, 519, 520, 521, 523,
  525, 1420
Armenia. (See Foreign countries.)
Army, personnel, 516, 518
Arrests (see Law enforcement)
Arson, 364
Arthritis, 200
Artists, employed, 626
Arts and humanities:
 Aid to, 1248
 Appropriations by state, 1249
 Attendance, 1247, 1251
 Charitable contributions, 590, 593
 Federal aid, 1248
 Grants, foundations, 593
 Participation, 1250
 Philanthropy, 590, 593
 States, 1249
Arts, recreation, and travel:
 Capital, 792, 794, 796
 Earnings, 642, 644, 655, 767, 770, 771, 780, 781,
  782, 783, 784, 785, 786, 1243
 Employees, 642, 644, 767, 770, 771, 780, 781,
  782, 783, 784, 785, 786, 1242, 1243, 1244
 Equipment and software expenditures, 794

Note: Index citations refer to **table** numbers, not **page** numbers

Note: Index citations refer to **table** numbers, not **page** numbers

---

Note: Index citations refer to **table** numbers, not **page** numbers

Bonds:—Con.
   Prices, yields, sales, and issues, 487, 1211, 1213, 1216, 1218
   U.S. savings, 487, 1182
Book, periodical, and music stores, 644, 651, 1058, 1059, 1061
Book publishing industry, 749, 1138, 1139, 1144, 1147
Bookkeeping. (See Accounting, tax preparation, bookkeeping, and payroll services.)
Books (see also Book publishing industry, Libraries, and Reading), 1066, 1144, 1147
Boots. (See Footwear.)
Borders, Canada and Mexico, 370
Border Patrol activities, 540, 541
Boron, 917, 918
Bosnia and Herzegovina. (See Foreign countries.)
Botox, 185
Botswana. (See Foreign countries.)
Bowling, 1261, 1264, 1266
Bowling center industry, 651, 1241, 1243, 1244
Boxing, 1261
Brazil. (See Foreign countries.)
Bread, 739, 745
Breastfeeding, 95
Bridges, 1098
Broadband, 1142, 1161, 1164, 1171, 1172, 1407
Broadcasting industry:
   Capital, 792
   Earnings, 644, 767, 1138, 1140
   Employees, 644, 767, 1138, 1140
   Establishments, 767, 1138, 1140
   Finances, 757, 1139
   Gross domestic product, 682
   Multinational companies, 807, 808
   Number of stations, 1142
   Productivity, 651
   Receipts, revenue, 757, 767, 1139, 1140
Broadway and off-Broadway shows, 1247
Broccoli, 221, 855, 874
Broilers (see also Poultry), 749, 855, 856, 881, 889, 890
Bromine, 916, 917
Bronchitis, 123, 124, 125, 126, 173, 202
Brunei. (See Foreign countries.)
Buddhist population. (See Religion.)
Budget, federal:
   Debt, 478
   Defense, 512
   Outlays, 477, 479, 480, 481
   Receipts, 477, 483
   Tax expenditures, 485
   Taxes, 483
Building construction:
   Earnings, 644, 975,
   Employees, 644, 975,
   Establishments, 975,
Building materials, and garden supplies stores:
   Earnings, 644, 767, 1058
   Electronic commerce, 1065
   Employees, 644, 767, 1058
   Establishments, 767, 1058, 1059
   Nonemployers, 1059
   Productivity, 651
   Sales, 767, 1059, 1061, 1063

Building permits. (See Construction industry, and Housing and housing units.)
Buildings (see also Construction industry, and Housing and housing units):
   Characteristics of, 1019
   Construction value, 976, 978, 979, 981
   Federal, 510
   Fires and property loss, 363, 364
   Floorspace, 510, 1019
Bulgaria. (See Foreign countries.)
Bullying, 307, 310
Burglaries, 312, 313, 314, 315, 326, 327
Burkina Faso. (See Foreign countries.)
Burma. (See Foreign countries.)
Burundi. (See Foreign countries.)
Buses and bus transportation. (See Passenger transit industry and Motor vehicles.)
Business cycles, 797
Business enterprises (see also individual types of business and industry):
   Ages of firms, 774, 775
   American Indian- and Alaska Native-owned businesses, 779, 786
   Asian-owned businesses, 779, 784
   Bankruptcies filed, 787, 788
   Births and deaths of, 775, 776, 777
   Black-owned businesses, 779, 783
   Capital, 792
   Corporations, partnerships, and proprietorships, 590, 755, 757, 758, 759, 760, 765, 766
   Employees, 769, 770, 772, 773, 774, 775, 777, 806, 1290
   Establishments, 767, 769, 770, 773, 774, 775, 777
   Expansions and contractions, 775, 777
   Finances, 755, 758, 759, 761, 762, 803, 805, 807, 808, 1036, 1037
   Firms, 772, 773, 774, 775, 777
   Flow of funds, 1178
   Foreign investment in the U.S., 1306, 1307, 1308, 1309
   Hispanic-owned businesses, 779, 782
   Leading indicators, 798
   Loans to minority-operated small businesses, 778
   Minority-owned, 779, 781
   Multinational companies, 806, 807, 808, 809
   Native Hawaiian and Other Pacific Islander- owned business, 779, 785
   Patents, 789, 790, 1406
   Payroll, 769, 772, 773
   Profits, 802, 803, 804, 805, 1036, 1037
   Sales, shipments, receipts, 1031, 1033, 1034, 1037
   Small business, 772, 773, 776, 778
   Startups, 774
   Veteran-owned, 779
   White-owned, 779
   Women-owned businesses, 779, 780
Business management, degrees conferred, 298, 301, 302, 303
Butane, 888
Butter, 222, 745, 887

Note: Index citations refer to **table** numbers, not **page** numbers

C

Note: Index citations refer to **table** numbers, not **page** numbers

Note: Index citations refer to **table** numbers, not **page** numbers

Coal (see also Petroleum and coal product manufacturing and Coal mining):
Car loadings, 1133, 1134
Consumption, 931, 937, 938, 942, 946, 958, 1395, 1398
Emissions, 382, 383
Expenditures, 944
Foreign trade, 931, 932, 938, 947, 948, 1322
Net generation, 958
Net summer capacity, 959
Prices, 749, 918, 931, 932
Production, 932, 937, 938
World production, 920, 932, 1393, 1394, 1400
Reserves, 933, 934
Coal bed methane, 930
Coal mining:
Earnings, 892, 913
Employment, 892, 913, 914, 932
Establishments, 892
Fatalities, 914
Gross domestic product, 682
Injuries, 914
Inspections, 914
Mines, 914, 932
Output, 915, 937
Productivity, 915, 932
Safety, 914
Shipments, 913
Supply, 931
Coast Guard, 544
Coastal population, 21, 26, 369
Coastlines, 365, 369, 371
Cobalt, 917
Cocaine (see also Drugs, illegal), 209, 334, 335
Cocoa, 222, 862
Cod, 909, 912
Coffee:
Consumption, 220, 222
Foreign trade, 860, 862
Price indexes, 739
Prices, 739, 745, 749
Cogeneration of electricity (combined-heat-and-power), 941, 958
Cohabitation, unmarried, 63, 93, 98
Coke. (See Coal.)
College:
Costs, 288, 289
Enrollment, 224, 230, 231, 232, 277, 278, 279, 280, 281, 282, 283, 284, 287
Freshmen, 286
Price index, 290, 739
Research & development, 819, 820
Science & engineering, 821, 823, 824
State appropriations, 293
Tuition, 292
Colleges and universities. (See Education, and Higher education institutions.)
Colombia. (See Foreign countries.)
Colorado. (See State data.)
Commerce:
Domestic, by rail, 1133, 1134
Domestic, by water, 1092, 1093
Foreign. (See Foreign trade.)
Commercial buildings:
Characteristics, 1019

Construction value, 979
Crime incidents, 323
Floorspace, 979
Commercial energy, 941, 942, 943, 944, 946, 960, 963, 964, 965, 969
Commodities. (See individual types of commodities.)
Commodity flow, 1078, 1079
Communicable diseases, 188
Communications:
Degrees conferred, 301, 302, 303
Price indexes, 737
Communications equipment manufacturing:
Earnings, 644, 1022, 1024
Employees, 644, 1022, 1024
Establishments, 1022
Foreign trade, 1324
Inventories, 1033
Productivity, 651
Shipments, 1024, 1033, 1044
Communications industry. (See Information industry, and Telecommunications industry)
Community development, 461, 481
Community food, housing services, 587
Community service, 595
Commuting to work, 668, 1122, 1128, 1129
Complementary and alternative medicine, 170
Comoros. (See Foreign countries.)
Compact disks, 1151
Computers:
Broadband, 1142, 1161, 1163, 1164, 1171, 1172
Consumer expenditures, 750
Consumer ownership, 1165
Foreign trade, 1316, 1324, 1326
Injuries associated with, 219
Sales, 794, 1066
Use of, 215, 1142, 1143, 1164, 1166, 1167, 1168, 1172, 1254, 1257, 1405
Cyberbullying, 310
Schools, 263,
Computer programming and data processing services, 644
Computer specialists:
Degrees conferred, 301, 302, 303, 821, 825, 826
Labor force, 626, 628, 828, 831, 832
Research & development, 813, 816, 819, 830
Salary, 298, 832
Computer systems design:
Capital, 792
Earnings, 1289
Employees, 1289
Establishments, 1289
Gross domestic product, 682
Receipts, 1292
Research and development, 816, 817
Computerized axial tomography (CAT scans), 174
Computers and electronic product manufacturing:
Capital, 792
Earnings, 644, 1022, 1024
Employees, 644, 1022, 1024, 1026
Establishments, 1022
Finances, 805
Foreign trade, 1326

Note: Index citations refer to **table** numbers, not **page** numbers

Note: Index citations refer to **table** numbers, not **page** numbers

Note: Index citations refer to **table** numbers, not **page** numbers

Death care services, 644, 739, 1287, 1288, 1289, 1299

Death penalty, 358, 359, 360

Deaths, and death rates (see also Accidents and fatalities):
  Age and sex, 109, 110, 112, 113, 114, 115, 124, 125, 127, 128, 129, 130, 131, 132, 133
  AIDS, 121, 122, 191
  American Indian, Alaska Native population, 5
  Asian population, 5
  Black, African American population, 5, 109, 110, 112, 113, 114, 118, 119, 127, 129, 130, 131
  Causes of death, 120, 121, 122, 123, 124, 125, 126, 127, 128, 129, 130, 131, 132, 1080, 1132
  Fetal and neonatal, 117, 118, 119
  Foreign countries, 1355, 1359, 1360
  Heart disease, 120, 124, 125, 126, 127, 132
  Hispanic or Latino origin, 5, 112, 114, 115, 122, 129, 130, 131
  Industrial, 673
  Infant, 117, 118, 119
  Injuries, 123
  Island areas of the U.S., 116, 119, 126, 1330
  Maternal, 118
  Military deaths, 524
  Native Hawaiian, Other Pacific Islander population, 5
  Race, 5, 109, 110, 112, 114, 118, 119, 127, 129, 130, 131
  States, 15, 116, 119, 126
  Suicide, 120, 124, 125, 130, 133, 524, 1360
  Traffic fatalities, 1080, 1109, 1110, 1111, 1114, 1116, 1117, 1119, 1120, 1359
  Weather related, 394, 398
  Workers' deaths, 671, 673, 914

Deaths, of businesses, 775, 776, 777

Debit cards, 1196, 1197, 1198, 1199

Debt (see also Loans and mortgages):
  City, 465
  Consumer, 1187, 1202
  County governments, 467
  Farm, 851
  Federal government, 478
  Foreign countries, 1416
  Households, 305, 1179, 1184
  Individual, 729
  Local government, 448, 463
  State and local government, 448, 453, 459, 461, 1102
  Student loan debt, household, 305

Deductions, taxes, 497, 498, 499
  Business, 758, 759, 760, 764

Defense, Department of (see also Army, Air Force, Marine Corps, and Navy):
  Budget authority, outlays, 479, 481, 511, 512
  Contract and grant awards, 513, 514
  Employees, civilian, 515, 516
  Expenditures, 138, 141, 513, 514, 515
  Military bases, 515, 516
  Military personnel, 515, 516, 517, 518, 519, 525
  Military reserve and National Guard, 521, 522, 523
  Military retirees, 514, 520, 552, 561

Defined contribution plans, 1178, 1229

Degrees conferred (see also individual fields), 299, 300, 301, 302, 303, 304, 822, 823, 824, 825, 826
  Salary offers, 298

Delaware. (See State data.)

Delinquency. (See Juvenile delinquency.)

Denmark. (See Foreign countries.)

Dentists, 165, 626
  Charges and expenditures for, 137, 139, 140, 143, 145, 750
  Dental schools, students, and graduates, 304
  Medicaid payments, recipients, 154
  Revenue, 163, 164

Department stores:
  Earnings, 644, 1058, 1063
  Employees, 644, 1058, 1063
  Establishments, 1058, 1063
  Inventories, 1064
  Productivity, 651
  Sales, 1061, 1063, 1064, 1298

Deportations, illegal immigrants, 540, 542

Deposit Insurance Fund, 1188

Deposits. (See Banks.)

Dermatologists, 167

Development aid, 1414

Diabetes, 120, 121, 122, 124, 125, 126, 172, 200

Diamonds, 917, 1393

Diatomite, 916, 917

Diesel, fuel, 940, 945

Dietitians and nutritionists, 626

Direct deposit, banking, 1197, 1198

Direct mail advertising industry, 1289, 1292, 1294

Directory and mailing list publications industry, 1138, 1139, 1144

Disabilities:
  Beneficiaries, 552, 555
  Benefits paid, 555, 557
  Elderly, 35
  Food stamp participants, 580, 581
  Government transfer payments, 549, 550, 551
  Hate crimes, 328, 329
  Labor force status, 601
  Learning, 192
  Medicaid payments and or recipients, 154
  Military retirement system, 520
  Payments, 557
  Persons with disability, 570
  Public assistance recipients and/or payments, 572
  Social security recipients, 555, 556
  State data, 195
  Students with disabilities, 193, 194, 285
  Supplemental security income recipients and payments, 572
  Veterans receiving compensation, 530

Disability Insurance Trust Fund (Social Security), 557

Disasters, natural, 394, 395, 398, 403

Diseases (see also specific Diseases, and Deaths and Death rates), 182, 188, 200, 674
  Deaths from, 120, 121, 122, 123, 124, 125, 126

Dishwashers, homes with, 1001

Disposable personal income (see also Income, and National income), 690, 691, 694, 1187

Note: Index citations refer to **table** numbers, not **page** numbers

Note: Index citations refer to **table** numbers, not **page** numbers

Note: Index citations refer to **table** numbers, not **page** numbers

Note: Index citations refer to **table** numbers, not **page** numbers

Note: Index citations refer to **table** numbers, not **page** numbers

---

Note: Index citations refer to **table** numbers, not **page** numbers

Note: Index citations refer to **table** numbers, not **page** numbers

Fishing, commercial, 907, 908, 909, 912
Fishing and hunting industry, 780, 781, 782, 783,
    784, 785, 786, 892, 893, 1264, 1266, 1271
Floods, 394, 398, 403
Floriculture, 855, 880
Florida. (See State data.)
Florists, 644, 651, 1058
Flounder, 909, 912
Flour, 222, 745, 749
Flowers, 1255
Flu (influenza), 120, 124
Fluorspar, 916, 917, 920
Food (see also individual commodities):
    Car loadings, 1133
    Commercial vegetables, 874
    Consumption, 221, 222, 223
    Expenditures, 698, 700, 701, 702, 703, 859,
        1070, 1373
    Fish products, 739, 749, 907, 908, 909, 910, 911,
        912
    Food costs, 740, 744, 745
    Hunger, insecurity, 216
    Prices (see also individual commodities), 737, 738,
        739, 744, 745, 746, 748, 749, 750, 753, 754
    World production, 1387, 1388, 1390
Food and beverage stores:
    Earnings, 644, 767, 1058, 1060
    Employees, 644, 767, 1052, 1058, 1060
    Establishments, 767, 1052, 1058, 1059
    Finances, 757
    Inventories, 1064
    Nonemployers, 1059
    Productivity, 651
    Profits, 805
    Sales, 757, 767, 1059, 1061, 1062, 1063, 1064,
        1070
Food insecurity, 216
Food manufacturing:
    Capital, 792
    Earnings, 644, 1022, 1024, 1030
    Employees, 644, 1022, 1024, 1026, 1030, 1281
    Establishments, 1022
    Finances, 805
    Foreign trade, 1326
    Gross domestic product, 682, 1020
    Industrial production index, 800
    Profits, 805
    Research and development, 816
    Sales or shipments, 1024, 1032, 1033
    Toxic chemical releases, 389
Food services and drinking places:
    Capital, 792
    Earnings, 644, 767, 1060, 1287, 1289
    Employees, 644, 767, 1052, 1060, 1287, 1288,
        1289, 1290
    Establishments, 767, 1052, 1287, 1288, 1289,
        1298
    Finances, 757
    Nonemployers, 1288
    Productivity, 651, 1287, 1288
    Sales, 757, 767, 1061, 1063, 1070, 1281, 1296,
        1298
Food stamps, programs, 553, 578, 579, 580, 581
Football, 1259, 1261, 1262, 1263

Footwear:
    Consumer expenditures, 689, 700, 701
    Foreign trade, 1322
    Prices, 739, 749, 754
    Sport footwear, 1264
Foreign aid or assistance, 1312, 1313, 1314, 1414,
    1415
Foreign-born population, 38, 40, 41, 42
    Age, 40, 41
    Cities, 39
    Doctorates, 822
    Earnings, 40
    Educational attainment, 40, 41
    Employment, 599, 615, 1349
    Foreign countries, 1349
    Households, 40
    Income, 40, 41
    Marital status, 40
    Poverty status, 40, 41
    States, 38
    Students, 233, 279, 280, 282
    Tenure, 40
Foreign companies, U.S. affiliates, 1307, 1308, 1309
Foreign countries:
    Age distribution, 1350
    Agriculture, 1366, 1387, 1388, 1389, 1392
    Agricultural trade, 863, 868, 1320
    Aid to developing countries, 1312, 1313, 1314,
        1414, 1415
    Alcohol, consumption, 1373
    Area, 1348
    Armed Forces personnel, 1420
    Balance of payments, 1419
    Births and birth rates, 1351, 1355
    Border crossings, 1285
    Border lengths, 370
    Carbon dioxide emissions, 1403
    Cellular phones, 1405, 1407
    Cigarettes, 1358, 1373
    Coal production, 932, 1394, 1400
    College students enrolled in U.S., 282
    Communications, 1405
    Consumer prices, 1371, 1379
    Consumption expenditures, 1373
    Corn, 1389
    Cost of living, 1372
    Cotton, 864, 1387, 1388
    Crude oil, 948, 949, 1396, 1398
    Dairy, 1387
    Death and death rates, 1355, 1359, 1360
    Debt, 1374, 1416
    Developing countries, 528, 1347, 1415
    Development aid, 1414
    Doctorates, 822
    Doctors, 1362
    Economic indicators, 1365, 1366, 1367
    Economic sectoral contributions, 1366
    Education, 1386
    Electricity generation, 1401
    Emissions, 1403
    Employment and labor force, 1365, 1368, 1369,
        1380, 1381, 1382, 1383, 1384, 1385
    Energy production and consumption, 1394, 1395,
        1397, 1398

Note: Index citations refer to **table** numbers, not **page** numbers

Foreign countries:—Con.
Exchange rates, 1412
Exports and imports, 1319, 1389
Fertility, 1355
Financial assets, liabilities (flow of funds), 1180
Food consumption, 1373, 1387, 1391
Food production, 1387, 1392
Foreign born, 1349
Foreign direct investment, 1417
Foreign population, 1349
Gas, 1393, 1394, 1395, 1398, 1399
Geothermal energy, 956, 1394, 1395
Government finances, 1364, 1374, 1375
Grain, 864, 1387, 1388
Gross domestic product, 1366
Gross national income, 1363
Health care expenditures, 1361
Hours worked, 1370
Households and families, 1353, 1354, 1373
Hydroelectric power, 1394, 1395, 1401
Immigrant population, 1349
Immigration to U.S., 45, 50, 51
Insurance, 1378
Income taxes, 1375, 1376
Infant mortality, 1355
Inpatient care, 1362
Insurance premiums, 1378
International transactions, balances, 1302, 1303, 1419
Investment in U.S., 1180, 1218, 1219, 1304, 1306, 1307, 1308, 1309
Labor costs, 1368, 1369
Labor force, 1349, 1381, 1383, 1384
Labor productivity, 1370
Life expectancy, 1355, 1356
Living costs, 1372
Manufacturing, 1366, 1368, 1369, 1385
Marriage and divorce, 1352, 1354
Meat, 1387, 1390, 1391
Migration, 1349
Military manpower, 1420
Military personnel, U.S. on active duty, 517, 525
Military sales, 526, 527, 528
Minerals, 1393
Multilateral grants, 1416
Multinational companies, 809
Natural gas, 1394, 1395, 1397, 1398, 1399
Net savings, households, 1377
Nongovernmental organizations, 1414
Nuclear power generation, 1394, 1395, 1398, 1401, 1402
Obesity, 1357
Oil, 948, 949, 1396, 1398
Oil seeds, 864, 1387, 1388
Organic farms, 1392
Patents, 1406
Pensions, 1378
Petroleum production, 1394, 1396
Physicians, 1362
Population, 1348, 1349, 1350
Poultry, 1387, 1390, 1391
Precipitation, in cities, 1404
Prices, 1371, 1379.

Production:
Crops, 864, 1387, 1388
Industrial, 1367
Meat, 1390
Minerals, 920, 1393
Productivity, labor, 1370
Purchasing power parity, 1363, 1364
Rainfall in cities, 1404
Refugees, admitted to U.S., 44, 51
Research and development expenditures, 811, 1413
Rice, 864, 1387, 1388, 1389
Savings rates, households, 1377
Single-parent households, 1353, 1354
Social security contributions, 1375
Stocks and bonds, 1216, 1217, 1218, 1219, 1408, 1409, 1410, 1411
Suicide, 1360
Tax burden, 1375, 1376
Tax revenues, 1374, 1375
Telephones, 1405
Temperature (cities), 1404
Tobacco, 1358, 1373
Tourism, 1418
Trade with United States, 866, 868, 1303, 1321, 1499
Traffic fatalities, 1359
Travelers and expenditures, 1276, 1282, 1283
Unemployment, 1380, 1381, 1382
Unmarried women, births to, 1351
U.S. investment abroad, 1216, 1217, 1311
Visitors from, 1286
Vital statistics, 1355
Weather, 1404
Wheat, 864, 1387, 1388, 1389
Women, 1351, 1383
Foreign exchange rates, 1412
Foreign grants and credits, U.S. government, 1312
Foreign investments, 1180, 1218, 1306, 1307, 1308, 1310
Foreign languages:
Degrees conferred, 301, 302, 303
Persons speaking, 53, 54, 55, 241
Students enrolled, 284
Foreign sales and assistance by U.S. government, 526, 527, 1313, 1314
Foreign students, college, 233, 279, 280, 282
Foreign trade (see also Foreign aid, Foreign countries, and individual commodities), 1316, 1318, 1319, 1320, 1321, 1326, 1327
Aerospace products, 1322, 1323
Agricultural products, 860, 861, 862, 863, 864, 865, 867, 868, 875, 877, 1320
Aircraft and aircraft parts, 1048, 1322
Automobiles, 1322
Balance of trade, 1301, 1302, 1321, 1419
Chemicals, 1316, 1322, 1326
China-U.S. trade, 1328
Coal, 932, 947, 948
Companies exporting, 1325
Computer and electronic products, 1316, 1326
Countries, 1321
Crude oil, 921, 948, 949, 950

Note: Index citations refer to **table** numbers, not **page** numbers

Note: Index citations refer to **table** numbers, not **page** numbers

---

Note: Index citations refer to **table** numbers, not **page** numbers

Grain (see also individual classes):
  Car loadings, 1134
  Consumption, 222, 1387
  Farm marketings, sales, 855
  Foreign trade, 860, 862, 864, 865, 867
  Organic, 845
  Prices, 747, 858
  Production, 853, 864, 870, 1387, 1388
Grandparents, living with grandchildren, 70
Grants, by foundations, 590, 591, 592, 593
Grapefruit, 221, 745, 876
Grapes, 221, 745, 855, 876
Graphite, 917
Great Britain. (See Foreign countries.)
Great Lakes, 366, 367, 368, 1092
Greece. (See Foreign countries.)
Greenhouse and nursery crops, 855
Greenhouse gases, 382, 383
Grocery stores (See also Food and beverage stores),
    644, 651, 1058, 1061
Gross domestic product (GDP):
  Components, annual growth rates, 679, 680, 681
  Federal debt, relation to, 478
  Foreign countries, 1364
  Foreign trade, 1419
  Implicit price deflators for, 679
  Industry, 682
  National defense outlays, 511
  Per capita, 691, 1364
  Per employed person, 1364
  Price indexes, 751
  Relation to national and personal income, 685
  Research and development spending, 811
  Sectoral contributions, 1366
  State, 683, 684
Gross national product, 691, 1363
Gross private domestic investment, 679, 680, 751
Gross value added, 1366
Ground water used, 378
Group quarters population, 72, 74
Guam. (See Island areas of the U.S.)
Guamanian population, 1329
Guatemala. (See Foreign countries.)
Guinea. (See Foreign countries.)
Guinea-Bissau. (See Foreign countries.)
Guns. (See Firearms.)
Guyana. (See Foreign countries.)
Gypsum and gypsum products, 749, 916, 917, 920

H

Haddock, 912
Haiti. (See Foreign countries.)
Halibut, 909
Hallucinogenic drugs, 209
Handguns, 316, 336, 341
Handicapped. (See Disability.)
Harassment victimization, 307, 310, 325
Hate crimes, 328, 329
Hawaii. (See State data.)
Hawaiian population. (See Native Hawaiian and Other
    Pacific Islander population.)
Hay, 855, 870
Hazardous waste/materials, 391, 392, 1079
Hazelnuts (filberts), 876, 877
Head Start program, 584

Health and education service industries, 643, 677
Health and personal care stores:
  Earnings, 644, 767, 1058
  Employees, 644, 767, 1058
  Establishments, 767, 1058, 1059
  Nonemployers, 1059
  Productivity, 651
  Sales, 767, 1059, 1061, 1063
Health care and social assistance industry:
  Capital, 792, 794
  Earnings, 642, 655, 767, 770, 771, 780, 781, 782,
      783, 784, 785, 786, 1289
  Electronic commerce, 1293
  Employees, 163, 642, 767, 780, 781, 782, 783,
      784, 785, 786, 1289
  Equipment and software expenditures, 794
  Establishments, 767, 768
  Finances, 757, 760
  Gross domestic product, 682
  Hires and separations, 649
  Nonemployers, 768
  Profits, 804
  Receipts, 757, 760, 765, 766, 767, 768, 780, 781,
      782, 783, 784, 785, 786
Health insurance (see also Health services,
    Insurance carriers, Medicaid, and Medicare):
  Contributions, 161
  Coverage, 148, 151, 158, 159, 160, 161, 171
  Enrollment, public programs, 148, 149, 150, 154,
      155, 156
  Expenditures, 137, 138, 139, 140, 141, 142, 143,
      144, 146, 148, 161, 548, 700, 701, 702, 750
  Premiums and policy reserves, life insurance
      companies, 1234
  State Children's Health Insurance program, 148
  Uninsured, 159, 160
Health maintenance organizations (HMO), 157
Health sciences, degrees conferred, 301, 302, 303,
    304
Health services:
  Buildings and floor space, 1019
  Charitable contributions, 590, 593
  Construction, value, 978, 981
  Coverage, 149, 150, 151, 155, 158
  Expenditures, 137, 138, 139, 140, 142, 143, 144,
      146, 445, 446, 453, 459, 461, 465, 467, 700,
      701, 702, 703, 1361
  Government employment and payrolls, 470
  Government, federal expenditures, 144, 440, 442,
      482
  Hospitals, 175, 176, 177, 178, 179, 180, 181, 182
  Industry, 165, 644, 670, 792
  Medicaid, 144, 151, 154, 155, 156, 158, 440, 482
  Medicare, 138, 141, 144, 147, 149, 150, 152, 153,
      158, 482, 557
  Nursing homes, 139, 140, 143, 198
  Occupations, 167, 168, 626
  Philanthropy, 590
  Price indexes, 145, 739
  Utilization, 169, 170, 171, 172, 173
  Veterans' health care, 138, 141, 534
  Volunteers, 595
Heart disease, 127, 172, 182, 201
  Deaths, 120, 121, 122, 124, 125, 126
Heating and plumbing equipment, 957, 984, 1001

Note: Index citations refer to **table** numbers, not **page** numbers

Note: Index citations refer to **table** numbers, not **page** numbers

Note: Index citations refer to **table** numbers, not **page** numbers

Note: Index citations refer to **table** numbers, not **page** numbers

Note: Index citations refer to **table** numbers, not **page** numbers

Note: Index citations refer to **table** numbers, not **page** numbers

Note: Index citations refer to **table** numbers, not **page** numbers

Note: Index citations refer to **table** numbers, not **page** numbers

Note: Index citations refer to **table** numbers, not **page** numbers

---

Note: Index citations refer to **table** numbers, not **page** numbers

Note: Index citations refer to **table** numbers, not **page** numbers

Note: Index citations refer to **table** numbers, not **page** numbers

Natural gas:—Con.
  Foreign trade, 938, 947, 948, 1322
  Prices, 739, 917, 929, 939
  Production, 921, 924, 928, 929, 930, 937, 938
    World, 920, 929, 1393, 1394, 1397, 1399
  Reserves, 925, 929
  Shale gas, 930
  Unconventional dry, 930
Natural gas distribution industry, 644, 651
Natural gas plant liquids, 921, 922, 924, 925, 928,
  930
Natural resources (see also Forest products, Minerals
    and mineral products, Timber, and individual
    resources and minerals):
  Federal outlays, 481
  Fisheries and fish products, 907, 908, 909, 910,
    911, 912
  Forests and timberland, 896, 897, 898, 899
  Governmental finances, 446
    Aid to state and local governments, 440
    Government employment and payrolls, 470
    Governmental revenue, 446
    State and local governments, 445, 453
    State governments, 459
  Minerals, 913, 918
    Coal, 931, 932, 933
    Consumption, 882
    Employment, 917
    Mining, 670, 914, 915
    Natural gas, 924, 925, 926, 927, 928, 929, 930
    Petroleum, 922, 924, 925, 926, 927
    Price, 917
    Production, 916, 917, 919, 920, 1393
    Products, 918
    Trade, 917, 923
    Uranium, 934
  Paper products, 901, 904, 905, 906
  Wood products, 900, 901, 902, 904, 905
Natural resource-related industry (see also Mining
    industry, Oil and gas extraction, and individual
    industries):
  Employment, 644, 649, 891, 892
  Establishments, 891, 892
  Gross Domestic Product, 893
  Mineral industry, 913
  Oil and gas extraction, 927
  Payroll and earnings, 644, 891, 892
  Petroleum industry, 922
  Sales and revenue, 891
  Timber-related industry, 894, 895
Naturalized citizens, 42, 47, 409
Nauru. (See Foreign countries.)
Navy, personnel, 516, 518
Nebraska. (See State data.)
Nectarines, 876
Neonatal deaths (see also Deaths and death rates),
  118
Nepal. (See Foreign countries.)
Nephritis, nephrotic syndrome, and nephrosis(See
    Kidney disease), 120, 121, 122, 123, 124, 125,
    126
Netherlands. (See Foreign countries.)
Net worth, personal, 729, 730, 731, 732
Neurologists, 167

Nevada. (See State data.)
New Hampshire. (See State data.)
New Jersey. (See State data.)
New Mexico. (See State data.)
New York. (See State data.)
New York Stock Exchange, 1220, 1224
New Zealand. (See Foreign countries.)
Newspaper, book, and directory publishers:
  Earnings, 644, 1138
  Employees, 644, 1138, 1140
  Establishments, 1138, 1140
  Finances, 1139, 1144
  Productivity, 651
  Revenue, 1139, 1140, 1144
Newspapers (See also Publishing industry):
  Advertising expenditures, 1294
  Expenditures, consumer, 1245
  Number and circulation, 1142, 1145
  Online-news, 1167
  Reading, 1142, 1143
  Recycling, 386
Newsprint, 904, 906
Nicaragua. (See Foreign countries.)
Nickel:
  Consumption, 917
  Employment, 917
  Foreign trade, 917, 923
  Prices, 917
  Production and value, 916, 917, 920
  World production, 920, 1393
Niger. (See Foreign countries.)
Nigeria. (See Foreign countries.)
Nitrogen in ammonia, world production, 916, 1393
Nonalcoholic beverages, 700, 701
Nonemployer establishments, 588, 768, 894, 1021,
    1053, 1059, 1067, 1075, 1238, 1243, 1288
Nonmetallic mineral mining and quarrying, except
    fuels, 792, 805, 893, 913, 914
Nonmetallic mineral product manufacturing (see also
    Metals and metal products):
  Earnings, 644, 1022, 1024, 1030
  Employees, 644, 1022, 1024, 1026, 1030
  Establishments, 1022
  Foreign trade, 1326
  Gross domestic product, 682, 1020
  Productivity, 651
  Profits, 805
  Sales, shipments, receipts, 1024, 1032, 1033
  Stone, clay, and glass, 1133, 1134
  Toxic chemical releases, 389
Nonprofit organizations, 590, 591, 592, 593, 644,
    1299, 1300
Nongovernmental organizations, 1414
North Carolina. (See State data.)
North Dakota. (See State data.)
North Korea. (See Foreign countries.)
Northern Mariana Islands. (See Island areas of the
    U.S.)
Norway. (See Foreign countries.)
Notifiable diseases, 188
Nuclear power, 953, 954, 955
  Capacity, 953, 954, 1402
  Commercial generation, by country, 1402
  Consumption, 937, 938, 1395, 1398

Note: Index citations refer to **table** numbers, not **page** numbers

Note: Index citations refer to **table** numbers, not **page** numbers

Parent Teacher Association (PTA), 252
Parent Teacher Conferences, 252
Parent Teacher Organization (PTO), 252
Paris CAC-40 stock market index, 1410
Parkinson's disease, deaths, 123, 124
Parks, 470, 1267, 1268, 1269, 1270
Parolees (see also Correctional institutions, and
    Prisoners), 355
Parties, political. (See Political parties.)
Partnerships, establishments and finances, 755, 756,
    757, 759, 760
Passenger transit industry (see also Passengers),
    644, 750, 940, 1124
Passengers (see also Passenger transit industry, and
    various transportation modes):
    Arriving from overseas, 1276, 1282, 1283, 1284
    Border crossings, 545, 1285
    Carrier operation, summary, 1081, 1091, 1123,
        1132
    Passenger traffic, volume, 545
    Railroads, 1132
Patents and trademarks, 789, 790, 1406
Pathologists, 167
Payrolls. (See Earnings, and individual industries.)
Peaches, 221, 855, 876
Peanuts, 222, 855, 856
Pears, 221, 745, 876
Peas, green, 874
Peat, 916, 917
Pecans, 876, 877
Pediatricians (see also Physicians), 167
Pennsylvania. (See State data.)
Pensions and retirement benefits (see also Social
    insurance):
    Annuities, 1229, 1234
    Expenditures, 548, 561, 698
    Families receiving, 552
    Foreign countries, 1378
    Funds (flow of funds), 1178, 1181, 1230
    Government employees, 552, 559, 560, 561
    Plans, 563, 1229
    Retirement and pension plans, 558, 561, 562,
        1214, 1228, 1229
    Veterans, 529, 552
Pentanes plus, 921
Peppers, 855, 874
Perch, 912
Performing arts, 1244, 1247, 1251
Performing arts, spectator sports industry:
    Capital, 792
    Earnings, 644, 767, 1243
    Employees, 644, 767, 1244
    Establishments, 767, 1243, 1244
    Nonemployers, 1243
    Receipts, revenue, 767, 1204, 1240
Periodical publishing, 1138, 1139, 1144
Perlite, 916, 917
Personal and laundry services:
    Earnings, 644, 767, 1289
    Employees, 644, 767, 1289, 1290
    Establishments, 767, 1288, 1289
    Finances, 757
    Productivity, 651
    Receipts, 757, 767, 1288, 1299

Personal care, 219, 626, 739
Personal computers (PC's). (See Computers.)
Personal consumption expenditures, 679, 680, 691,
    750, 751, 1245
Personal health care expenditures, 139, 140, 142,
    143
Personal income, 690, 692, 693, 694, 695
Personal savings, 686, 687
Peru. (See Foreign countries.)
Pesticides, 853
Pets, 739, 1253
Petroleum and coal product manufacturing:
    Capital, 792
    Earnings, 644, 891, 1022, 1030
    Employees, 644, 891, 1022, 1026, 1030
    Establishments, 891, 1022
    Finances, 805, 952
    Foreign investments in U.S., 1306, 1307, 1309
    Foreign trade, 1326
    Gross domestic product, 682, 1020
    Industrial production index, 800
    Multinational companies, 807, 808
    Productivity, 651
    Profits, 805, 951, 952
    Research and development, 816, 817
    Sales, shipments, 891, 913, 1032, 1033
    Toxic chemical releases, 389
Petroleum and natural gas extraction, 927
Petroleum and products:
    Consumption, 923, 937, 938, 942, 958, 1395,
        1398
    Disposition, 921
    Electricity generation, 961
    Emissions, 382, 383
    Expenditures, 946
    Foreign trade, 921, 923, 938, 947, 948, 949, 950,
        951, 971, 1316, 1326
    Net summer capacity, 959
    Oilspills, 393
    Prices, 742, 749, 752, 918, 939
    Production, 916, 920, 921, 926, 937, 938
        World, 920, 1393, 1394, 1396
    Railroad car loadings of, 1133, 1134
    Refineries, 921
    Reserves, 925, 926
    Stocks, 921, 950
    Strategic reserve, 921, 950
    Value, 922, 924
    Wells, 922, 926
Pharmaceutical and medicine manufacturing, 644,
    651, 1024, 1039
Pharmacies and drug stores, 162, 1058, 1061, 1063
Pharmacists, 626
Philanthropy, 590, 591, 592, 593, 594
Philippines. (See Foreign countries.)
Phosphate rock, 916, 917, 920, 1393
Photographic equipment and supplies, 1322
Physical activity, 214, 215
Physical sciences:
    Degrees conferred, 301, 302, 303, 821, 825, 826
    Employees, 626, 829, 832,
    Research & development expenditures, 813, 821

Note: Index citations refer to **table** numbers, not **page** numbers

Note: Index citations refer to **table** numbers, not **page** numbers

Population:—Con.
  Immigrants, 38, 39, 40, 41, 42, 43, 44, 45, 48, 50, 51
  Island areas of the U.S., 1329, 1337
  Labor force. (See Labor force.)
  Less developed countries, 1347
  Life expectancy, 1355, 1356
  Marital status. (See Marital status of population.)
  Metropolitan areas, 20, 22, 23, 25
  Migration, 4, 5, 25, 30, 31, 32, 33, 1349
  Mobility, 25, 30, 31, 32, 33
  Native Hawaiian, Other Pacific Islander population. (See Native Hawaiian, Other Pacific Islander population.)
  Nativity, 38, 39, 40
  Obesity, 213, 217, 1357
  Place of birth, 38, 39
  Projections, 3, 4, 9, 12
  Race, 5, 6, 10, 11, 12, 19
  Resident, 1, 2, 3, 4, 7, 13, 21
  Rural, 29
  Sex, 7, 9, 40
  States, 13, 14, 15, 16, 18, 19
    American Indian, Alaska Native population, 19
    Asian population, 19
    Black, African American population, 19
    Density, 14
    Hispanic origin population, 18
    Native Hawaiian, Other Pacific Islander population, 19
    Race, 19
    Voting age, 406, 407
  Total, including Armed Forces overseas, 2
  Urban, 29
  Veterans, 531
  World, 1345, 1347, 1348, 1350
Pork (see also Meat and meat products):
  Consumption, 222, 881, 1391
  Foreign trade, 862, 881
  Prices, 739, 749
  Production, 881, 882, 1387, 1390
  Supply, 881
Portland cement, 916
Portugal. (See Foreign countries.)
Postal rates, 1136
Postal Service, 651, 1137
Potash (potassium salts), 916, 920, 923
Potatoes:
  Acreage, 870, 874
  Consumption, 221, 875
  Farm marketings, sales, 855
  Foreign trade, 875
  Prices, 858, 870
  Production, 870, 874, 875
Poultry (see also Eggs):
  Consumer expenditures, 700, 701
  Consumption, 222, 881, 1387, 1391
  Farm marketings, sales, 855, 856
  Foreign trade, 865, 866, 867, 881
  Number on farms, 889
  Organic, 845
  Prices, 739, 745, 749, 858, 889
  Production and sales, 881, 889, 890, 1387, 1390
  Value, 889

Poverty:
  Asian and Pacific Islander population, 553, 723, 724, 727
  Asian population, 36, 553, 725
  Black, African American population:
    Families, 36, 728
    Households, 553
    Persons, 36, 723, 724, 725, 727
  Children, 724, 725
  Families, 36, 720, 721, 727, 728
    American Indian, Alaska Native population, 36
    Asian and Pacific Islander population, 727
    Asian population, 36, 728
    Black, African American population, 36, 727, 728
    Elderly, 712
    Hispanic origin population, 36, 37, 728
    Housing, 553
    Native Hawaiian, Other Pacific Islander population, 36
  Foreign born, 40
  Hispanic origin population:
    Families, 36, 37, 728
    Households, 553
    Persons, 36, 37, 723, 724, 725
  Native Hawaiian, Other Pacific Islander population, 36
  Persons, 720, 721
    Age, 725, 726
    American Indian, Alaska Native population, 36
    Asian population, 36, 723
    Black, African American population, 36, 723, 724, 725
    Children, 724, 725
    Cities, 720
    Depression, 218
    Elderly, 34, 725
    Hispanic origin population, 36, 37, 723, 724, 725
    Labor force, 726
    Native Hawaiian and Other Pacific Islander population, 36
    State, 721
    Threshold, 722
Power (see also Electric light and power industry):
  Electric, 958, 961, 962, 963, 965, 966
  Nuclear, 953, 1402
  Outages, 968,
  Prices, 742, 749, 944
  Water (see hydroelectric power)
Power generation and supply industry, 644, 651
Power plants. (See Electric light and power industry.)
Precipitation, selected cities, 401, 1404
Pregnancies, (see also Births and birth rates), 101, 172
  Teen pregnancies, 83, 87, 88, 89, 92
Prescription drugs, 137, 139, 140, 141, 144, 145, 162, 739
Presidents, U.S.:
  Campaign finances, 432, 433
  Elections for, 405, 406, 410, 411, 412, 413, 414
  Vetoes, 423

Note: Index citations refer to **table** numbers, not **page** numbers

Prices (see also individual commodities):
  Bonds, 1220
  Electricity, 742, 944, 960, 964
  Energy, 939
  Fish, 908
  Food, 744, 745
  Foreign countries, 1371, 1372, 1379
  Fuel, 742
  Gasoline, 743
  Housing, 741, 988, 989, 990, 991, 993
  Indexes:
    Airline cost, 1082
    Consumer price, 737, 739, 1379
      Foreign countries, 1372, 1379
      Medical care, 145
      Metropolitan areas, 738, 740
    Exports, 751, 752, 753
    Futures price index, 747
    Gross domestic product, 751
    Higher education expenditures, 290
    Housing price index, 741
    Imports, 751, 752, 754
    Producer prices, 736, 748, 749
      Stage-of-processing, 748
      Timber, 904
    Purchasing power of the dollar, 736
    Received by farmers, 858
    Spot market price, 746
    Tourism commodities, 1280
  Lumber and stumpage, 903
  Mineral products (see also individual minerals),
    917
  Received by farmers:
    Crops, 870
    Indexes, 858
    Livestock and products, poultry, 882, 889
  Stocks, 1220
Primary metal manufacturing:
  Capital, 792
  Earnings, 644, 1022, 1024, 1030
  Employees, 644, 1022, 1024, 1026, 1030
  Establishments, 1022
  Finance, 805, 1041
  Foreign trade, 1041, 1326
  Gross domestic product, 682, 1020
  Industrial production index, 800
  Productivity, 651
  Profits, 803, 805
  Research and development, 816
  Shipments, 1024, 1032, 1033
  Toxic chemical releases, 389
Printing and related support activities. (See
  Publishing industry.)
Prisoners (see also Correctional institutions), 72,
  354, 355, 357, 358, 359, 360, 1333
  Death sentences, 358, 359, 360
  Executions, 359, 360
  Jail inmates, 355, 356
Probation, 355
Producer price indexes, 748, 749
  Stage-of-processing, 748
  Timber, 904

Productivity (see also individual industries):
  Capacity utilization, 801
  Farm output, 869
  Labor, 651, 652, 1368, 1369, 1370
  Mining industries, 932
Professional and business services:
  Earnings, 644, 656
  Employees, 643, 644, 1290
  Hires and separations, 649
Professional, scientific and technical services:
  Capital, 792, 794, 796
  Earnings, 642, 644, 767, 770, 771, 780, 781, 782,
    783, 784, 785, 786, 1287, 1292
  E-commerce, 1293
  Employees, 642, 644, 767, 770, 771, 780, 781,
    782, 783, 784, 785, 786, 1287, 1288, 1289,
    1290, 1291
  Equipment and software expenditures, 794
  Establishments, 767, 768, 770, 1287, 1288, 1291
  Finances, 757, 760
  Gross domestic product, 682
  Hours, 642
  Multinational companies, 807, 808, 809
  Nonemployers, 768, 1288
  Occupational safety, 670
  Profits, 804
  Sales, receipts, 757, 760, 765, 766, 767, 768,
    780, 781, 782, 783, 784, 785, 786, 1287,
    1288, 1292
Profits, 764, 1067, 1190, 1191, 1232, 1235
  Corporations, 686, 755, 802, 803, 804, 805, 1035
  Partnerships and proprietorships, 755, 758, 759
Projections:
  Births, 1355
  College enrollment, 224, 226
  Deaths, 1355
  Degrees conferred, 226
  Employment, 628, 631
  Energy, 938, 956
  High school graduates, 226
  Island areas, 1329
  Labor force, 597, 628, 631
  Life expectancy, 108, 1355
  Population, 3, 9, 12, 1329, 1345, 1346, 1347,
    1348
  School enrollment, 224, 226
  Teachers, 226
Propane, 888
Property and casualty insurance, 1214, 1228, 1235
  Fire losses, 361, 363, 364
  National Flood Insurance, 403
Property crime, 312, 313, 314, 315, 326, 327
Property tax, 446, 459
  Rates, selected cities, 456
  State and local government, 445, 446
Proprietors' income, 690
Proprietorships, 755, 757, 758
Propylene, 921
Protective service workers. (See Public safety.)
Protein, available for consumption, 223
Protestants. (See Religions.)
Psychiatric care and institutions. (See Mental
  hospitals.)

Note: Index citations refer to **table** numbers, not **page** numbers

Note: Index citations refer to **table** numbers, not **page** numbers

Note: Index citations refer to **table** numbers, not **page** numbers

Research and development:—Con.
  Nonprofit, 810, 812
  Space related, 810, 814
  State, 818
Residential buildings. (See Construction industry,
    and Housing and housing units.)
Residential capital, 1018
Residential energy, 749, 941, 942, 943, 944, 946,
    960, 963, 964, 965, 969
Respiratory conditions (see also Pulmonary
    diseases), 121, 122, 197, 202
Restaurants. (See Food services and drinking places.)
Retail trade:
  Capital expenditures, 792, 794, 796
  Earnings, 642, 644, 655, 767, 770, 771, 780, 781,
    782, 783, 784, 785, 786, 1057, 1060, 1344
  Employees, 630, 642, 644, 767, 770, 771, 780,
    781, 782, 783, 784, 785, 786, 1052, 1057,
    1060, 1281, 1338, 1344
  Equipment and software expenditures, 794
  Establishments, 767, 768, 770, 1052, 1057, 1059,
    1338, 1344
  Farmers market, 879
  Finances, 757, 760, 805, 1202
  Foreign investments in the U.S., 1307
  Gross domestic product, 682, 684
  Hires and separations, 649
  Hours, 642, 1060
  Inventories, 799, 1064
  Multinational companies, 807, 808
  Nonemployers, 768, 1059
  Occupational safety, 670
  Productivity, 651
  Profits, 803, 805
  Sales, 757, 760, 765, 766, 767, 768, 780, 781,
    782, 783, 784, 785, 786, 799, 1052, 1057,
    1059, 1061, 1062, 1064, 1281, 1344
Retirement systems:
  Benefits paid, 548, 561
  Civil service, 559, 561, 1230
  Defined benefit retirement plans, 558, 562, 563,
    1229
  Defined contribution plans, 558, 1178, 1229
  Federal government, 559, 561, 1178, 1229, 1230
  401(k) plans, 567, 1229
  Government transfer payments, 549, 550, 551
  Military retirement system, 520
  Old-age, survivors, disability, and health insurance.
    (See Social insurance.)
  Pension plans, 548, 561, 562, 1229, 1230
  Public employees, 548, 561
  Railroad, 1230
  Social security trust funds, 557
  State and local government, 459, 1229, 1230
Reunion. (See Foreign countries.)
Revolvers. (See Firearms.)
Rhode Island. (See State data.)
Rice:
  Acreage, 1387
  Consumption, 222, 1387
  Farm marketings, sales, 855
  Foreign trade, 860, 864
  Prices, 745, 749
  Production, 864, 1387, 1388

Rifles (NCAA), 1262
Rivers, 372, 1092
Roads, public. (See Highways.)
Roadway congestion, 1121
Robbery, 312, 313, 314, 315, 321, 322, 323, 327
Rodeos, 1261
Roller skating, 1266
Romania. (See Foreign countries.)
Roth IRAs, 564, 565, 566, 1229
Rowing, 1262
Rubber, crude natural, 860, 862
Rubber products, 749, 1322
Rubella, 188, 196
Rugs, 749
Running/jogging, 1266
Rural population, 29
Russell, stock index, 1220
Russia. (See Foreign countries.)
Rwanda. (See Foreign countries)

S

Safety and security measures, 309, 672, 914
Sailing, 1266
Saint Kitts and Nevis. (See Foreign countries.)
Saint Lucia. (See Foreign countries.)
Saint Vincent and the Grenadines. (See Foreign
    countries.)
Salad and cooking oils, consumption, 222
Salaries and wages. (See Earnings.)
Sales. (See individual commodities and industries.)
Salesworkers, 626, 638, 657
Salmon, 909, 911, 912
Salmonellosis, 188
Salt (common), production/value, 916, 917, 1393
Samoa. (See Foreign countries.)
Samoa, American. (See Island areas of the U.S.)
Samoan population, 1329
San Marino. (See Foreign countries.)
Sand and gravel industry (see also Mining industry),
    749, 916
Sanitation. (See Refuse collection, and Sewage
    treatment.)
Sao Tome and Principe. (See Foreign countries.)
Sardines, 912
Saudi Arabia. (See Foreign countries.)
Savings:
  Credit unions, 1195
  Deposits, 687, 1181
  Gross savings, sources and uses, 686
  Personal, 686, 690
  Rates, 1377
Savings banks. (See Savings institutions.)
Savings bonds, 487, 1182
Savings institutions:
  Consumer credit, 1203
  Debt held by families, 1185
  Earnings, 1177
  Employees, 1177
  Establishments, 1177, 1189
  Finances, 1178, 1179, 1188, 1191, 1204, 1210
  Individual Retirement Accounts (IRAs), 1229
Saw logs, 900, 904
Saw mills, 892, 894, 895
Scallops, 909, 911

Note: Index citations refer to **table** numbers, not **page** numbers

Note: Index citations refer to **table** numbers, not **page** numbers

Note: Index citations refer to **table** numbers, not **page** numbers

State and regional data:—Con.
  Earnings, 659, 1023, 1029, 1057
  Education, (see also Education), 238, 249, 251,
    256, 268, 269, 275,280, 293
  Elections, 406, 408, 413, 414, 415, 418, 419, 425,
    427
  Electrical power, 961, 963, 964, 968
  Elevations, 373
  Employees, 473, 474, 506, 643, 772, 1023, 1025,
    1046, 1057, 1291
  Energy consumption, 942
  Energy expenditures, 946
  Energy, renewable, 967
  Establishments, 772, 1023, 1057, 1291
  Exports, 1319, 1320
  Farms, 837, 850
    Government payments, 854
    Income, 850, 854, 857
  Federal employees, 506
  Federal funds, 486
  Financial institutions, 1194
  Food stamp program, 579
  Foreign born, 38
  Foreign investment in the U.S., 1308
  Foreign trade, 1319, 1320
  Foreign travel to, 1276
  Forest land, 896, 897
  Fraud, 331
  Fuel production, 924
  Gas utility industry, 970
  Gasoline tax rates, 1101
  Government finances:
    Agricultural payments, 854
    Federal aid to state and local governments,
    441, 442, 443, 444
    Federal (income tax returns), 501
    Homeland security grants, 537
    Local government, 462
    State and local governments, 451, 452, 453
    State governments, 454, 459, 461, 468
    Tax collections, 457, 460
    Transfer payments, 551
  Governors, vote cast, 425
  Gross domestic product, 683, 684
  Hazardous waste, 390, 391, 392
  Health insurance coverage, 159
  Health maintenance organizations (HMO), 157
  Highway funds, 1103
  Highway mileage, 1097
  Highway trust fund, 1100
  Hispanic elected officials, 429
  Hispanic origin population, 18
  Hospitals, 177, 453, 473
  HIV diagnoses, 189
  Homeowners insurance, 1237
  Housing, 741, 977, 983, 992, 998, 1002, 1006,
    1009, 1010
  Identity theft, 331
  Immigrants, unauthorized, 45
  Income, 854
    Disposable personal, 694
    Family, 697
    Household, 696
    Personal, 692, 693

Income tax returns, 501
Internet usage/connection, 1163
Job gains/losses, 648
Lakes, 368
Land cover/use, 376
Language spoken at home, 54
Legislatures, composition, 427
Libraries, 1170
Livestock, 845, 885, 886
Local government units, 437
Lotteries, revenue from, 457
Lyme disease, 189
Manufactures, summary statistics, 1021, 1029
Marriages and divorces, 134, 135
Medicaid, 155, 156
Medicare, 150
Metropolitan area population, 24
Migration, 15, 33
Military personnel, 516, 520
Milk production, 886
Millionaires, 731
Minimum wage, 664
Mining, mineral production value, 919
Mortgages, 1208, 1209
Motor fuel tax, 1101
Motor vehicle manufacturing, 1046
Motor vehicle registrations, 1106
Motorcycles, 1106
Native Hawaiian, Other Pacific Islander population,
  19
Natural gas, 924, 925, 927, 930
Newspapers, number and circulation, 1146
Nurses, 168
Nursing homes, 198
Occupations, 627
Parks, 1268, 1269, 1270
Patents, 790
Philanthropy, 594
Physicians, 168
Police protection, 461, 473
Population, 13, 14, 15, 16, 19, 74
  Age distribution, 16
  American Indian, Alaska Native population, 19
  Asian population, 19
  Black African American population, 19
  Components of change, 15
  Density, 14
  Dependency ratio, 17
  Hispanic origin population, 19
  Metropolitan area population, 24
  Native Hawaiian, Other Pacific Islander
    population, 19
Poultry, 890
Poverty, 721
Power outages, 968
President, vote cast, 413, 414
Prisoners, 354
Public aid, 574
Public road and street mileage, 1097
Public water systems, 974
Recreational areas, 1268
Renters insurance, 1237
Representatives, U.S. vote cast for, 417

Note: Index citations refer to **table** numbers, not **page** numbers

Note: Index citations refer to **table** numbers, not **page** numbers

Tariff. (See Customs receipts.)

Taxes:
  Corporate, 481, 483, 488, 756, 764, 802
  Deductions, 497, 498, 499, 758, 759
  Employment taxes, 483, 488
  Estate and gift taxes, 483, 488
  Excise taxes, 452, 459, 460, 468, 483, 488
  Individual income, 446, 452, 459, 460, 468, 483,
      488, 489, 490, 491, 492, 493, 494, 495, 496,
      497, 498, 499, 500, 501

Tax receipts:
  Foreign countries, 1374, 1375
  Governmental revenue, by type of tax, 446
  Motor-fuel taxes and motor-vehicle fees, 1101
  Federal budget receipts, 483
  Marginal tax rates, 502, 503
  Property taxes:
    City government, 464
    County government, 466
    Rates, selected cities, 456
    State and local government, 445, 446, 452, 460
  State and local government:
    City government, 456, 464
    County government, 466
    Household tax burden, 455
    Local government, 462
    State government, 459, 461, 468
    Type of tax, 445, 446, 452
  Tax expenditures (revenue foregone), 485

Tea, 220, 739

Teachers:
  Catholic schools, 264
  Conferences, 252
  Degrees conferred, 300, 301, 302, 303
  Employment, 247, 254, 260, 278, 296, 297, 626
    Projections, 226, 628
  Higher education institutions, 278, 295, 296, 297
  Mobility, turnover, 257, 258
  Private schools, 264, 265
  Public schools, 226, 247, 256
    Experience, and degrees held, 255
    Number, 226, 247, 250, 254, 255, 256
    Salaries, 247, 256
  States, 256

Technicians, 828, 829, 832

Teenagers:
  Abortions, 105
  Abuse victims, 352
  AIDS, 191
  Alcohol use, 209
  American Indian, Alaska Native population, 10, 11,
    12
  Births/birth rates, 83, 87, 88, 89, 92, 94
  Black, African American population, 10, 11, 12
  Bullying, in school, 310
  Cigarette smoking, 209
  College freshmen, 286, 287
  Contraception use, 100, 103
  Cost of raising, 703
  Crimes, arrests, 332
  Depression, 218
  Disabled, 192, 194
  Drug use, 209, 332
  Education:
    College costs, 288, 289

College freshmen, characteristics, 286
  Enrollment, 224, 226, 228, 229, 230, 231, 247,
    251, 253, 264, 276, 277, 283
  High school dropouts, 270, 271
  High school graduates, 247, 269, 276
  Test scores, 266, 267, 1386
Health insurance coverage, 158
Hispanic or Latino origin population, 10, 11, 12
Juvenile delinquency and crime, 338, 346, 350,
    351
Labor force (16 to 19 years old), 597
  Employed, 612, 615, 618, 620, 622
  Employment status, 606
  Minimum wage workers, 665
  Multiple job holders, 620
  Participation rates, 607
  School enrollment status, 606, 1382
  Sex, 597, 602
  Unemployed, 635, 636, 640
Life expectancy, 110
Marital status, 57
Mobility status, 30
Native Hawaiian, Other Pacific Islander
    population, 10, 11, 12
Physical activity, 215
Population, 7, 9, 10, 11, 12
Sexual activity, 98, 99
Sports activity participation, 1263, 1266
Sporting goods purchasers, 1265
Suicides, 124
Victimization, 308, 317, 322
Telecommunications, 1044, 1155
Telecommunications industry (See also
    Broadcasting):
  Broadcast stations, 1142
  Earnings, 644, 1138, 1140
  Employees, 644, 1138, 1140
  Establishments, 1138, 1140
  Finances, 757, 1139, 1140, 1155, 1156
  Productivity, 651
  Receipts, 757, 1139, 1156
Telemarketers, 626
Telephone carriers, 1155
  Cellular, 1158, 1159, 1405
Telephone communication:
  Earnings, 644, 1155, 1157
  Employees, 644, 1157, 1159
  Finances, 1157, 1159
  Price indexes, 739
  Productivity, 651
  Receipts, 1157
Telephones:
  Access lines, 1157, 1407
  Calls, 1157
  Consumer expenditures, 689, 700, 701, 1158
  Households with service, 1142, 1157, 1158
  Number, 1157, 1405
  Sales or shipments, 1044
  Text messages, 1159
Television broadcasting (see also Cable and other
    pay TV services):
  Advertising expenditures, 1294
  Broadcasting stations, 1142

Note: Index citations refer to **table** numbers, not **page** numbers

---

Note: Index citations refer to **table** numbers, not **page** numbers

Transportation:—Con.
  Carriers of passengers, 1081, 1123, 1132, 1284
  Carriers of property, 1133, 1134
  Commodity shipments, 1078, 1079
  Commuting to work, 1122
  Construction, value, 978, 981
  Consumer complaints, 1087
  Consumer expenditures, 689, 698, 699, 700, 701, 702
  Consumer price indexes, 737, 738, 739, 750
        Motor fuel, 739
    New cars and new trucks, 739
  Cost indexes, 740
          Airlines, 1082
          Tourism commodities, 1280
  Energy, 940, 941, 942, 943, 944, 960
  Federal government:
      Aid to state and local governments, 440
          Outlays, 481, 814
  Freight, 1317
  Government employees and payrolls, 470
  Government finances, 445, 446, 447, 449, 459, 461, 468, 481
  Gross domestic product, 1071
  Hazardous shipments, 1079
  Metropolitan areas, 1084
  Occupations, 626, 638
  Port traffic, 1094
  Stock and bond prices and yields, 1220
  System mileage, 1076
  Transit subsidies, 1124
  Travel trends, 1279
  Travel volume, 1081, 1091
  Waterborne commerce, 1092, 1093, 1094, 1095
Transportation and warehousing:
  Capital, 792, 794, 796
  Earnings, 642, 644, 656, 767, 770, 771, 1074
  Employees, 642, 644, 767, 770, 771, 1072, 1073, 1074
  Equipment and software expenditures, 794
  Establishments, 767, 768, 770, 1074
  Finances, 757, 760
  Hires and separations, 649
  Hours, 642
  Nonemployers, 768
  Occupational safety, 670
  Productivity, 651
  Revenue, 1074, 1130, 1131
  Sales, 757, 760, 765, 766, 767, 768
Transportation equipment manufacturing (see also Aerospace, Motor vehicles):
  Earnings, 644, 1022, 1024, 1030
  Employees, 644, 1022, 1024, 1026, 1030
  Establishments, 1022
  Finances, 805
  Gross domestic product, 682
  Inventories, 1033
  Multinational companies, 807, 808, 809
  Productivity, 651
  Profits, 805
  Research and development, 816
  Shipments, 1024, 1032, 1033, 1078
  Toxic chemical releases, 389

Transportation, communications, and utilities industry (see also Energy, Information industry, Transportation and warehousing, and Utilities):
  Earnings, 780, 781, 782, 783, 784, 785, 786, 935, 936
  Employees, 780, 781, 782, 783, 784, 785, 786, 935, 936, 972
  Profits, 935, 942, 964, 966, 969
Transportation support services industry, 1071, 1073, 1074
Travel (see also Arts, recreation, and travel):
  Accidents, 1080, 1086, 1089, 1282
  Border crossings, 545, 1285
  Business, pleasure travelers, 1286
  Cruise ships, 1275
  Domestic, 1278, 1279, 1285
  Forecast, 1279
  Foreign, 1276, 1282, 1283, 1418
  Highway mileage, 1096, 1097
  International expenditures, 1279, 1282
  Passengers, 1081, 1091, 1282, 1283, 1284
  Person trips, 1268, 1279
  Price indices, 1280
  Services, 1315
  Tourism output, 1277
  Tourists, 1276, 1282, 1283, 1284, 1418
  Volume, 1081, 1091
Travel accommodations industry, 644, 651, 1280, 1281
Travel arrangement industry, 644, 1289, 1295
Travelers' checks, 1210
Treasury bonds, 762, 1211, 1212, 1214, 1218, 1219
Trichinosis, 188
Trinidad and Tobago. (See Foreign countries.)
Trout, 910
Truck and tractor pull, 1261
Truck transportation industry:
  Capital, 792
  Commodities handled, 1131
  Earnings, 644, 1073, 1074
  Employees, 644, 1073, 1074
  Establishments, 1073, 1074
  Finances, 1130
  Gross domestic product, 682
  Productivity, 651
  Revenue, 1074, 1130, 1131
  Shipping, 1079, 1080
  Trucks, 940, 1069, 1108
Tuberculosis, 175, 188
Tuition and fees, 292, 739
Tuna, 909, 911, 912
Tungsten, 916, 917, 920, 923
Tunisia. (See Foreign countries.)
Turbines. (See Steam engines.)
Turkey. (See Foreign countries.)
Turkeys, 745, 749, 855, 881, 890
Turkmenistan. (See Foreign countries.)
Turks and Caicos Islands. (See Foreign countries.)
Tuvalu. (See Foreign countries.)
Typhoid fever, 188

Note: Index citations refer to **table** numbers, not **page** numbers

U

Uganda (See Foreign countries.)
Ukraine (See Foreign countries.)
Ulcers, 200
Ultrasound, diagnostic, 174
Unemployment. (See Labor force, unemployed workers.)
Unemployment insurance:
  Beneficiaries, 552, 568, 569, 641
  Governmental finances, 445, 459, 483
  Mass layoffs, 646
  Payments, 548, 549, 550, 551, 568, 569
Union membership, 676, 677, 678
United Arab Emirates. (See Foreign countries.)
United Kingdom. (See Foreign countries.)
United States securities (see also Debt), 1181, 1189, 1211, 1212, 1214, 1218, 1219
Universities. (See Education, higher education institutions.)
Unpaid work, 654
Uranium (see also Nuclear power), 916, 934, 955
Urban population, 29, 80
Urban transit systems industry, 1074
Uruguay. (See Foreign countries.)
Utah. (See State data.)
Utilities (see also Electric light power industry, and Gas utility industry.):
  Capital, 792, 794, 796, 936, 969, 970, 972, 973, 974
  Cost of living, 740
  Customers and bills, 965
  Earnings, 642, 644, 655, 656, 767, 770, 771, 780, 781, 782, 783, 784, 785, 786, 935, 936
  Electric, 962
  Employees, 642, 644, 767, 770, 780, 781, 782, 783, 784, 785, 786, 935, 936
  Equipment and software expenditures, 794
  Establishments, 767, 768, 770, 936
  Expense, 966
  Finances, 757, 760
  Gross domestic product, 682
  Gas, 969, 970, 971
  Hours, 642
  Income, 966
  Industrial production index, 800
  Industry, 767, 935, 936, 962
  Investor owned, 966
  Multinational companies, 807, 808
  Net generation, 962, 965
  Net summer capacity, 962
  Nonemployers, 768
  Occupational safety, 670
  Price indexes, 738
  Productivity, 651
  Profits, 803
  Revenue, 965, 966
  Sales, 757, 760, 765, 766, 767, 768, 780, 781, 782, 783, 784, 785, 786
  Sewage treatment, 936, 972
  States, 964
  Water, 936, 973, 974
Uzbekistan. (See Foreign countries.)

V

Vacancy rates, housing, 995, 997, 998, 999 1000
Vaccination, 196
Vanadium, 920, 923
Vanuatu. (See Foreign countries.)
Veal (see also Beef, Meat, and meat products), 222, 749, 881, 1391
Vegetable oils. (See Oils.)
Vegetables (see also individual commodities):
  Acreage, 874
  Consumer expenditures, 700, 701
  Consumption, 221, 875
  Farm marketings, sales, 853, 855
  Foreign trade, 860, 862, 865, 867, 875, 1322
  Gardens, 1255
  Organic, 845
  Prices, 739, 749, 753, 858
  Production, 874, 875
Vehicles. (See Motor vehicles.)
Veneer, wood products, 892, 894, 895
Venereal diseases (see also AIDS), 188
Venezuela. (See Foreign countries.)
Vermiculite, 916, 917
Vermont. (See State data.)
Vessels. (See Ships.)
Veterans:
  Business owners, 779
  Characteristics, 531, 532
  Employment, 600
  Homeless programs, 534
  Number, 529, 532
  Pensions and other benefits:
    Service-connected compensation, 530, 533
    Disbursements, 511, 533, 548, 549, 550, 551
    Federal aid to state and local governments, 440
    Federal payments, 482
    Health expenditures, 138, 141
    Veterans or dependents receiving, 530, 552
Veterans Affairs, Dept. of:
  Expenditures, 138, 141, 530, 533, 534, 549, 550, 551
  Home loans, 1206
Vetoed bills, Congressional, 423
Victimizations, criminal, 317, 319, 321, 322, 323, 324, 325, 326, 327, 328, 329
Vietnam. (See Foreign countries.)
Violent crime, (see also Crime), 306, 312, 313, 314, 315, 316, 318, 672
Virgin Islands. (See Island areas of the U.S.)
Virginia. (See State data.)
Visa holders, doctorates, 822
Vital statistics. (See Births and birth rates, Deaths and death rates, Divorces, and Marriages.):
Vitamins, 223
Vocational rehabilitation, 138, 587
Volleyball, 1262, 1263, 1266
Volunteer activities, 252, 595, 1252
Votes:
  Congressional, 405, 406, 415, 417, 418
  Gubernatorial, 425
  Presidential, 405, 406, 410, 411, 412, 413, 414
  Votes cast, 405, 407, 408, 409
Voting-age population, 405, 406, 407, 408

Note: Index citations refer to **table** numbers, not **page** numbers

W

Wage earners. (See Labor force and individual industries.)
Wages and wage rates. (See Earnings.)
Walnuts, 855, 876, 877
Warehouse clubs and superstores, 1058, 1061
Warehousing and storage industry:
    Capital, 792
    Earnings, 644, 1074
    Employees, 644, 1019, 1073, 1074
    Establishments, 1019, 1074
    Gross domestic product, 682
    Revenue, 1074, 1130
Washing machines, homes with, 1001
Washington. (See State data.)
Waste management & remediation services, 767, 792
Wastepaper, 749, 904
Wastewater treatment, 935, 936, 972
Watches. (See Clocks and watches.)
Water (see also Wastewater treatment, and Water transportation industry):
    Area, 1, 365
    Consumption, 378
    Freight, 1092, 1093
    Lakes, 366, 367, 368
    Pollution, 388, 393
    Power, 967
    Public supply, 378, 973, 974, 1001
    Vessels, 1077, 1256
Water polo, 1262
Water transportation industry:
    Capital, 792
    Earnings, 644, 1073, 1074
    Employees, 644, 1073, 1074
    Establishments, 1073, 1074
    Foreign trade, 1093
    Freight, 1092, 1093, 1317
    Fuel consumption, 940
    Gross domestic product, 682, 1317
    Occupational safety, 1080
    Outlays, 481
Water utility, 700, 701, 739, 935, 936, 973, 974
Water, sewage and other systems, 644, 935, 936, 972, 973, 974
Waterborne commerce, 1092, 1093, 1094, 1095
Watermelons, 855, 874
Waterways, 1092
Wealth:
    Business, 735
    Families, 732, 733
    Family farms, 842
    Government, 735
    Households, 735
    Millionaires, 731
    Persons, 729, 730, 731
Weather, 394, 397, 398, 399, 400, 401, 402, 614, 968, 1404
Weight, 212
Welfare services. (See Public aid, assistance, Social welfare, and individual programs.)
West Bank. (See Foreign countries.)
West Nile virus, 188
West Virginia. (See State data.)
Western Sahara. (See Foreign countries.)

Wetlands, 375, 377
Wheat:
    Acreage, 870, 873, 1387
    Farm marketings, sales, 855
    Farm prices, 870, 873
    Foreign trade, 857, 860, 866, 867, 870, 1322, 1389
    Price indexes, 749, 753
    Production, 864, 870, 873, 1387, 1388
    Supply and disappearance, 870
Wheat flour, 222
Whiting, 909
Wholesale trade:
    Capital expenditures, 792, 794, 796
    Earnings, 642, 644, 655, 767, 770, 771, 780, 781, 782, 783, 784, 785, 786, 1052, 1054, 1344
    Electronic commerce, 1055
    Employees, 630, 642, 644, 767, 770, 771, 780, 781, 782, 783, 784, 785, 786, 1052, 1054, 1338, 1344
    Equipment and software expenditures, 794
    Establishments, 767, 768, 770, 1052, 1053, 1054, 1338, 1344
    Finances, 757, 760, 805
    Foreign investments in U.S., 1307, 1309
    Gross domestic product, 682, 684
    Hires and separations, 649
    Hours, 642
    Inventories, 1056
    Multinational companies, 807, 808, 809
    Nonemployers, 768
    Occupational safety, 670
    Productivity, 651
    Profits, 803, 805
    Sales, 757, 760, 765, 766, 767, 768, 780, 781, 782, 783, 784, 785, 786, 1052, 1053, 1056, 1344
Whooping cough (pertussis), 188
Wildfires, 396
Wildlife, 404, 1271, 1272
Wilshire equity index, 1220
Wind:
    Energy sources, 937, 943, 956, 958, 959, 967
    Average speed, 402
Wines (see also Alcoholic beverages), 739, 860, 862
Wisconsin. (See State data.)
Women:
    Abortions, 104, 105
    Age, 7, 9
    AIDS, 190, 191
    American Indian, Alaska Native population, 6
    Apparel, 700, 701
    Asian population, 6
    Births and birth rates, 81, 82, 83, 88, 90, 94, 97, 1355
        Births to unmarried women, 88, 89, 92, 94, 1351
        Breastfeeding, 95
        Cesarean section deliveries, 90, 174
        Induction of labor, 91
    Black, African American population, 6
    Body Mass Index (BMI), 213
    Business owners, 779, 780
    Cancer, 129, 186, 187

Note: Index citations refer to **table** numbers, not **page** numbers

Note: Index citations refer to **table** numbers, not **page** numbers

Work flexibility, 617, 618, 619
Work stoppages, 675
Workplace deaths/injuries, 669, 670, 671, 673, 674
Workplace violence/security measures, 672
Workers. (See Employment, and Labor force.)
Workers' compensation program, 138, 164, 548, 550, 552, 571, 573
Workstations. (See Computers.)
World. (See Foreign countries, International Affairs, and World summary statistics.)
World summary statistics:
  Age distribution, 1350
  Agriculture, 1387, 1388
  Comparative data (area, population, etc.), 1348, 1350
  Emissions, 1403
  Energy, 1394, 1395, 1397, 1398, 1401, 1402
  Farm commodities, 864, 1388
  Labor, 1369
  Mineral production, 929, 932
  Minerals, 1393
  Natural resources (oil, gas, coal), 1396, 1399, 1400
  Patents, 1406
  Population, 1345, 1346, 1348, 1350
  Stock market, 1408, 1409
  Telecommunications, 1407
Wrestling, 1261, 1262, 1263
Wyoming. (See State data.)

Note: Index citations refer to **table** numbers, not **page** numbers